Library of Congress Catalogs

National Union Catalog

1973–1977

Volume 9 Bahia–Barna, T

ROWMAN AND LITTLEFIELD
TOTOWA, NEW JERSEY 1978

Compiled and edited by the Catalog Publication Division of the Processing Department, Library of Congress

Library of Congress Card Number 56-60041

ISSN 0028-0348 *Key title:* National union catalog

Bahia, Juarez.
Jornal: história e técnica. ₍São Paulo₎ Martins ₍1967₎
216 p. illus., facsims. 23 cm.
LACAP 67-1185
Bibliography: p. ₍215₎-216.
1. Brazilian newspapers. 2. Press—Brazil. I. Title.
PN5022.B24 67-99079
rev

Bahia, Juarez.
Jornal: história e técnica. ₍3. ed., rev. e ampliada. São Paulo₎ Instituição Brasileira de Difusão Cultural ₍1972₎
247 p. illus. 21 cm. (Biblioteca Dicionários e enciclopédias, 11)
Cr$20.00
Bibliography: p. 246-247.
1. Brazilian newspapers. 2. Press—Brazil. I. Title.
PN5022.B24 1972 74-221454

Bahia Filho, Xisto, 1931-
Percurso : poesia / Xisto Bahia Filho ; ₍capa e ilustração de Percy Deane₎. — Rio de Janeiro : Livraria Editora Cátedra, 1975.
171 p. ; 21 cm. — (Coleção Nova poética ; v. 1)
Cr$30.00
I. Title.
PQ9698.12.A36P4 75-508095
75 MARC

Bahia-Guimarães, Paulo Fernando.
The genesis of the antimony-mercury deposits of the Stayton district, California. [Stanford, Calif.] 1972.
xii, 185 l. col. photos., maps (3 fold. part col. in pocket)
Thesis (Ph.D.)–Stanford University.
Bibliography: leaves 180-185.
1. Antimony ore–Calif.–Stayton. 2. Mercury ore–Calif.–Stayton. I. Title.
CSt NUC74-488

Bahia, Brazil (Capitania)
Established in the 16th century, the Capitania da Bahia became the Provincia da Bahia after the establishment of the Brazilian Empire in 1822 and the Estado da Bahia when the Federal Republic of Brazil was established in 1889.
Works by these bodies are found under the following headings according to the name used at the time of publication:
Bahia, Brazil (Capitania)
Bahia, Brazil (Province)
Bahia, Brazil (State)
73-207158

Bahia, Brazil (Province)
Established in the 16th century, the Capitania da Bahia became the Provincia da Bahia after the establishment of the Brazilian Empire in 1822 and the Estado da Bahia when the Federal Republic of Brazil was established in 1889.
Works by these bodies are found under the following headings according to the name used at the time of publication:
Bahia, Brazil (Capitania)
Bahia, Brazil (Province)
Bahia, Brazil (State)
73-207160

Bahia, Brazil (State)
Established in the 16th century, the Capitania da Bahia became the Provincia da Bahia after the establishment of the Brazilian Empire in 1822 and the Estado da Bahia when the Federal Republic of Brazil was established in 1889.
Works by these bodies are found under the following headings according to the name used at the time of publication:
Bahia, Brazil (Capitania)
Bahia, Brazil (Province)
Bahia, Brazil (State)
73-207159

Bahia, Brazil (State).
O Extremo-Sul e o Governo / Governo Antônio Carlos Magalhães. — ₍Salvador₎ : O Governo, ₍1974₎
₍37₎ leaves ; 22 cm.
1. Bahia, Brazil (State)—Economic policy. 2. Bahia, Brazil (State)—Economic conditions. I. Title.
HC188.B3B34 1974 330.9′81′4 75-562338

Bahia, Brazil (State)
Relatório do governo.
₍Salvador₎
v. illus. 22 cm.
1. Bahia, Brazil (State)—Executive departments. 2. Bahia, Brazil (State)—Economic conditions. 3. Bahia, Brazil (State)—Social conditions.
JL2499.B4B33a 73-643595
MARC-S

Bahia, Brazil (State). Agricultura, Industria e Comercio, Secretaria da
see
Bahia, Brazil (State). Secretaria da Agricultura, Indústria e Comércio.

Bahia, Brazil (State). Agricultura, Secretaria da
see
Bahia, Brazil (State). Secretaria da Agricultura.

Bahia, Brazil (State). Assessoria Geral de Programação e Orçamento.
Proposta orçamentária—Assessoria Geral de Programação e Orçamento.
₍Salvador₎
v. 19 x 26 cm.
At head of title : Orçamento-Programa.
1. Budget—Bahia, Brazil (State) 2. Program budgeting—Bahia, Brazil (State) I. Bahia, Brazil (State). Assessoria Geral de Programação e Orçamento. Orçamento-Programa.
HJ32.B294a 354′.81′400722 74-646909
MARC-S

Bahia, Brazil (State). Bioestatística, Serviço de
see
Bahia, Brazil (State). Serviço de Bioestatística.

Bahia, Brazil (State). Comissão de Planejamento Econômico.
The Comissão de Planejamento Econômico of Bahia was created in 1955. In 1959 it became the Fundação Comissão de Planejamento Econômico but continued to be known by both the old and new names until 1969, when it became the Fundação de Planejamento.
Works by this body published before the change of name in 1969 are found under
Bahia, Brazil (State). Comissão de Planejamento Econômico.
Works published after that change of name are found under

Bahia, Brazil (State). Fundação de Planejamento.

Bahia, Brazil (State). Comissão de Planejamento Econômico.
Estado da Bahia : recursos para o seu desenvolvimento / Fundação Comissão de Planejamento Econômico. — ₍Salvador₎ : CPE, 1966.
39, 22 p., 16 leaves of plates : ill. ; 25 cm.
Cover title: Bahia, recursos para o seu desenvolvimento.
On t.p.: Govêrno Lomanto Júnior.
1. Bahia, Brazil (State)—Economic conditions. I. Title. II. Title: Bahia, recursos para o seu desenvolvimento.
HC188.B3B26 1966 76-468575
76 MARC

Bahia, Brazil (State). Comissão de Planejamento Econômico.
Industry for Bahia; the program for implantation of industries. Salvador, 1960.
12 p. (Edições mimeografadas CPE)
At head of title: Fundação Comissão de Planejamento Econômico.
1. Bahia, Brazil (State)—Indus. 2. Industry and state—Brazil—Bahia (State) I. Title. II. Series.
PPiU NUC74-58847

Bahia, Brazil (State). Comissão de Planejamento Economico
see Mascarenhas, Augusto. O problema nutricional do Nordeste. Salvador, Bahia, 1960.

Bahia, Brazil (State). Comissão Estadual de Planejamento Agrícola.
Plano estadual de aplicação de crédito rural.
Salvador, Comissão Estadual de Planejamento Agricola.
v. 31 cm.
1. Agricultural credit—Brazil—Bahia (State) 2. Agriculture and state—Brazil—Bahia (State) I. Title.
HG2051.B72B283a 332.7′1′09814 76-640800
MARC-S

Bahia, Brazil (State). Comissao Estadual de Planejamento Agricola.
Subsidios para implantacao e implementacao da CEPA-Ba / Comissao Estadual de Planejamento Agricola. -- Salvador, Bahia A Comissao, 1974.
45 p. : ill.
Bibliography: p. 37.
1. Agricultural administration. Brazil. Bahia. 2. Agriculture and state. Brazil. Bahia. I. Title.
DNAL NUC77-101211

Bahia, Brazil (State). Conselho de Desenvolvimento Industrial. Secretaria Executiva.
Relatório sintético de atividades—Conselho de Desenvolvimento Industrial, Secretaria Executiva.
₍Salvador₎ Secretaria da Indústria e Comérico, Departamento de Indústria e Comércio, Divisão de Incentivos e Benefícios.
v. 31 cm.
1. Bahia, Brazil (State). Conselho de Desenvolvimento Industrial. 2. Industrial promotion—Bahia, Brazil (State)—Periodicals.
HC188.B3B28a 75-643881
MARC-S

Bahia, Brazil (State). Conselho Estadual de Cultura
see Almanach para a Cidade da Bahia, anno 1812. [Salvador] : Conselho Estadual de Cultura, 1973.

Bahia, Brazil (State). Conselho Estadual de Cultura
see Bahia cultural. 1973- Salvador, Conselho Estadual de Cultura.

Bahia, Brazil (State). Conselho Estadual de Educação.
Plano estadual de implantação do ensino de 1o. e 2o. graus.
₍Salvador₎ Secretaria da Educação e Cultura, 1972.
251 p. illus. 24 cm.
1. Educational law and legislation—Bahia, Brazil (State) I. Title.
73-219640

Bahia, Brazil (State). Coordenação da Produção Mineral.
Bibliografia comentada da geologia da Bahia, 1817-1975 / Governo do Estado da Bahia, Secretaria das Minas e Energia, Coordenação da Produção Mineral. — ₍Salvador₎ : A Coordenação, 1976.
579 p. ; 23 cm.
Includes index.
1. Geology—Brazil—Bahia (State)—Bibliography. 2. Mines and mineral resources—Brazil—Bahia (State)—Bibliography. I. Title.
Z6034.B8B34 1976 016.5581′4 77-466333
₍QE235₎ 77 MARC

Bahia, Brazil (State). Coordenação da Produção Mineral.
Cadastramento de ocorrencias minerais do Estado da Bahia : área I, Vitória da Conquista, sub-área I / Secretaria das Minas e Energia, Coordenação da Produção Mineral. — ₍Salvador₎ : A Coordenação, 1973.
₍92₎ p. : maps ; 30 cm.
1. Mines and mineral resources—Brazil—Bahia (State) I. Title.
TN42.B3B34 1973 75-567937

Bahia, Brazil (State). Coordenação da Produção Mineral.
Pedras preciosas e semipreciosas no Estado da Bahia / Governo do Estado da Bahia, Secretaria das Minas e Energia, Coordenação da Produção Mineral. — ₍Salvador₎ : A Coordenação, 1976.
2 v. : ill. ; 30 cm.
Bibliography: v. 1, p. ₍195₎-200.
CONTENTS: v. 1. Diagnóstico.—v. 2. Programa.
1. Precious stones—Brazil—Bahia (State) I. Title.
TN982.B7B33 1976 553′.8′09814 77-470759
77 MARC

Bahia, Brazil (State). Coordenação da Produção Mineral.
Projeto cadastramento de ocorrências minerais do Estado da Bahia / Estado da Bahia, Secretaria das Minas e Energia, Coordenação da Produção Mineral. — Salvador, Brasil : A Coordenação, ₍197
v. : ill., forms, maps (some fold., fold. in pockets) ; 29 cm.
Includes bibliographies.
CONTENTS:
—v. 2. Área de Juazeiro.
—v. 5. Área de Itabuna.
1. Mines and mineral resources—Brazil—Bahia (State) I. Title.
TN42.B3B34 1974 75-594305

Bahía, Brazil (State). Coordenação da Produção Mineral
see Cadastro de empresas: Setor mineral. Salvador.

Bahía, Brazil (State). Coordenação da Produção Mineral
see Inventário dos recursos minerais do Estado da Bahía. ₍Salvador₎

Bahia, Brazil (State). Coordenação da Produção Mineral
see Inventario dos recursos minerais do Estado da Bahia: Periodico. ₍Salvador₎ Grupo de Ceologia e Mineracao.

Bahia, Brazil (State). Coordenação da Produção Mineral. Centro de Documentação.
Boletim informativo—Coordenação da Produção Mineral, Centro de Documentação.
Salvador, Secretaria das Minas e Energia, Coordenação da Produção Mineral, Centro de Documentação.
v. 21 x 30 cm.
1. Mineral industries—Bibliography—Periodicals.
Z6737.B33a 76-642214
[TN145] MARC-S

Bahia, Brazil (State). Coordenação da Produção Mineral. Seção de Economia Mineral
see
Bahia, Brazil (State). Seção de Economia Mineral.

Bahia, Brazil (State). Coordenação de Energia.
Boletim estatístico mensal de energia elétrica.
₍Salvador₎ Coordenação de Energia.
v. 33 cm.
1. Electrification—Bahia, Brazil (State)—Periodicals. I. Title.
TK42.B3A2a 75-641983
MARC-S

Bahia, Brazil (State). Coordenação de Energia.
Cadastro de eletrificação do Estado da Bahia / Estado da Bahia, Secretaria das Minas e Energia, Coordenação de Energia. — Salvador : Secretaria das Minas e Energia do Estado da Bahia, Centro Administrativo, ₍1975?₎
43 leaves : map ; 26 x 36 cm.
Chiefly tables.
1. Electric utilities—Bahia, Brazil (State)—Statistics. I. Title.
HD9685.B82B32 1975 75-515790
75 MARC

Bahia, Brazil (State). Coordenação de Fomento ao Turismo.
Inventário de proteção ao acervo cultural. — Salvador : Secretaria da Indústria e Comércio, Coordenação de Fomento ao Turismo, 1975-
v. : ill. ; 22 x 32 cm.
On t.p.: Projeto Patrimônio Histórico.
Cover title: IPAC-BA, Inventário de proteção ao acervo cultural.
Bibliography: v. 1, p. 311-₍324₎
1. Monuments—Brazil—Bahia (State)—Preservation. 2. Historic buildings—Brazil—Bahia (State) I. Title. II. Title: IPAC-BA, Inventário de proteção ao acervo cultural.
N8966.B34B33 1975 75-521351
75 MARC

Bahia, Brazil (State). Coordenação de Fomento ao Turismo.
Proposta de valorização de tres monumentos baianos / Coordenação de Fomento ao Turismo. — Salvador : A Coordenação, 1974.
₍43₎ leaves : ill. ; 21 x 31 cm.
Includes bibliographies.
1. Architecture—Bahia, Brazil (State)—Conservation and restoration. 2. Monuments—Brazil—Bahia (State)—Preservation. I. Title.
NA109.B65B33 1974 75-569167

Bahia, Brazil (State). Departamento de Assuntos Penais. Divisão de Estudos Penais
see
Bahia, Brazil (State). Divisão de Estudos Penais.

Bahia, Brazil (State). Departamento de Desenvolvimento Social. Divisão de Integração Social
see
Bahia, Brazil (State). Divisão de Integração Social.

Bahia, Brazil (State). Departamento de Estradas de Rodagem.
Relatório de atividades—DER-BA.
₍Salvador₎ DER-BA.
v. 33 cm.
1. Bahia, Brazil (State). Departamento de Estradas de Rodagem. 2. Roads—Bahia, Brazil (State)—Periodicals.
HE359.B9B28a 75-644831
MARC-S

Bahia, Brazil (State). Departamento de Estradas de Rodagem. Assessoria de Programação e Orçamento.
Cadastro das rodovias do estado da Bahia.
Salvador, DER-Ba, Assessoria de Programação e Orçamento.
v. 22 x 31 cm.
1. Roads—Bahia, Brazil—(State)—Statistics. I. Title.
HE359.B9B28b 75-645134
MARC-S

Bahia, Brazil (State). Departamento de Geografia e Estatística.
Preço médio de gêneros alimentícios de Salvador. v. 1-
1. semestre 1972-
₍Salvador₎
v. 32 cm. semiannual.
1. Food prices—Salvador, Brazil—Statistics—Periodicals. I. Title.
HD9014.B83S218a 74-647132
MARC-S

Bahia, Brazil (State). Departamento de Geografia e Estatística.
Produção de óleos e gorduras vegetais.
Salvador.
v. 32 cm.
1. Oil industries—Bahia, Brazil (State)—Statistics—Periodicals. I. Title.
HD9490.B82B33a 74-645613
MARC-S

Bahia, Brazil (State). Departamento de Geografia e Estatística
see Povoados do Estado da Bahia. Salvador

Bahia, Brazil (State). Departamento de Geografia e Estatistica
see Tabuas itinerarias do Estado da Bahia. 1972- Salvador.

Bahia, Brazil (State). Departamento de Geografia e Estatistica. Seção de Documentação e Divulgação de Dados
see Anuário estatístico da Bahia. 1972- [Salvador]

Bahia, Brazil (State). Departamento de Indústria e Comércio.
Distrito industrial de Ilhéus : plano diretor. — ₍Salvador₎ : Estado da Bahia, Secretaria da Indústria e Comérico, Departamento de Indústria e Comércio, 1974.
101 leaves : ill., 22 maps ; 31 x 46 cm.
Bibliography: leaves 97-101.
1. Industrial districts—Ilhéus, Brazil. I. Title.
HC189.I38B33 1974 75-577255

Bahia, Brazil (State). Departamento de Indústria e Comércio.
Distrito industrial de Jequié : plano diretor / Estado da Bahia, Secretaria da Indústria e Comércio, Departamento de Indústria e Comércio. — ₍Salvador₎ : O Departamento, 1974.
84 leaves, ₍3₎ leaves of plates : ill. ; 32 x 46 cm.
Bibliography: leaves 83-84.
1. Industrial districts—Jequié, Brazil. I. Title.
HC189.J43B33 1974 75-584257

Bahia, Brazil (State). Departamento de Indústria e Comércio.
Distrito industrial do São Francisco : plano diretor / Estado da Bahia, Secretaria da Indústria e Comércio, Departamento de Indústria e Comércio. — ₍Salvador₎ : O Departamento, 1973.
103 leaves : ill. (some col.) ; 31 x 46 cm.
Bibliography: leaves 101-103.
1. Industrial districts—Juazeiro, Brazil (Bahia) 2. Industrial districts—Petrolina, Brazil (Pernambuco) I. Title.
HC189.J77B3 1973 75-559542

Bahia, Brazil (State). Departamento de Indústria e Comércio.
Distrito industrial dos Imborés : plano diretor / Estado da Bahia, Secretaria da Indústria e Comércio, Departamento de Indústria e Comércio. — ₍Salvador₎ : O Departamento, 1973.
100 leaves : ill. ; 31 x 46 cm.
Bibliography: leaves 99-100.
1. Industrial districts—Vitória da Conquista, Brazil. 2. Vitória da Conquista, Brazil—Economic conditions. 3. Vitória da Conquista, Brazil—Social conditions. I. Title.
HC189.V52B3 1973 75-561462

Bahia, Brazil (State). Departamento de Indústria e Comércio.
Itabela, área urbana : pre-plano diretor / ₍equipe técnica, James José de Farias ... et al.₎. — ₍Salvador₎ : Governo do Estado da Bahia, Secretaria da Indústria e Comércio, Departamento de Indústria e Comércio, ₍1974 or 1975₎
77 p. : ill. ; 22 x 30 cm.
1. City planning—Brazil—Bahia (State)—Case studies. 2. Industrial districts—Brazil—Bahia (State)—Case studies. I. Farias, James José de. II. Title.
HT169.B72B342 77-471689
77 MARC

Bahia, Brazil (State). Departamento de Indústria e Comércio.
Itabela, distrito industrial / Estado da Bahia, Secretaria da Indústria e Comércio, Departemento de Indústria e Comércio. — ₍Salvador₎ : O Departamento, ₍1974?₎
155 p. : ill. ; 22 x 30 cm.
Includes bibliographical references.
1. Industrial districts—Bahia, Brazil (State)—Case studies. I. Title.
HC188.B3B3 1974 75-583798

Bahia, Brazil (State). Departamento de Indústria e Comércio. Divisão de Informação Industrial e Promoção de Investimentos
see
Bahia, Brazil (State). Divisão de Informação Industrial e Promoção de Investimentos.

Bahia, Brazil (State). Departamento de Mão-de-Obra. Divisão de Estudos e Pesquisas.
Alguns aspectos do mercado de trabalho; CIA: empresas em implantação. ₍Salvador₎ 1972.
1 v. (unpaged) 31 cm.
1. Labor supply—Aratu, Brazil. 2. Centro Industrial de Aratu. 3. Personnel management—Aratu, Brazil. I. Title.
HD5755.A68B33 1972 73-214480

Bahia, Brazil (State). Departamento de Mão de Obra. Divisão de Estudos e Pesquisas.
Alguns aspectos do mercado de trabalho; empresas em funcionamento no CIA e rede formadora e de treinamento de mão de obra. ₍Salvador₎ 1973.
117 l. 31 cm.
1. Labor supply—Aratu, Brazil. 2. Centro Industrial de Aratu. 3. Employees, Training of—Aratu, Brazil. I. Title.
HD5755.A68B33 1973 73-213756

Bahia, Brazil (State). Departamento de Mão-de-Obra. Divisão de Estudos e Pesquisas.
Mão-de-obra no setor primário: cultura do arroz. ₍Salvador, Brasil₎ 1971.
161 l. 33 cm.
1. Rice workers—Bahia, Brazil (State) 2. Rice—Brazil—Bahia (State) I. Title.
HD8039.R482B73 73-202152

Bahia, Brazil (State). Departamento Estadual de Estatística. Bahia's foreign trade bulletin.
see Bahia, Brazil (State). Departmento Estadual de Estatística. Boletim do comercio exterior da Bahia. Salvador.

Bahia, Brazil (State). Departamento Estadual de Estatística.
Boletim de comércio.
₍Salvador₎ Departamento Estadual de Estatística.
v. 32 cm.
1. Bahia, Brazil (State)—Commerce. I. Title.
HF164.B25B27b 76-642873
MARC-S

Bahia, Brazil (State). Departamento Estadual de Estatística.
Boletim do comercio exterior da Bahia. Bahia's foreign trade bulletin.
Salvador.
v. 23 cm. bimonthly.
English and Portuguese.
1. Bahia, Brazil (State)—Commerce. I. Bahia, Brazil (State). Departamento Estadual de Estatística. Bahia's foreign trade bulletin. II. Title. III. Title: Bahia's foreign trade bulletin.
HF164.B25B27a 74–640180
MARC–S

Bahia, Brazil (State). Departamento Estadual de Estatística.
Comércio exterior da Bahia: Exportação segundo as firmas e mercadorias.
[Salvador]
v. 30 cm.
1. Bahia, Brazil (State)—Commerce. I. Title.
HF3409.B3B3a 73–644096
MARC–S

Bahia, Brazil (State). Departamento Estadual de Estatística.
Despesa de alimentação de uma família-tipo (5 pessoas) em Salvador. [Salvador, 1971]
5 l. 1 illus. 22 x 32 cm.
1. Food prices—Salvador, Brazil. 2. Food consumption—Salvador, Brazil. 3. Cost and standard of living—Salvador, Brazil. I. Title.
HD9014.B83S22 1971 339.4′2′09814 74–232272

Bahia, Brazil (State). Departamento Estadual de Estatistica.
Indices do custo da vida (1948/1957) [Salvador] 1958.
vii, 58 l. illus. 33 cm.
Cover title.
1. Cost and standard of living—Bahia, Brazil (State) I. Title.
HD7013.B34 72–225828

Bahia, Brazil (State). Dept. of Industry and Commerce, State
see
Bahia, Brazil (State). Secretaria da Indústria e Comércio.

Bahia, Brazil (State). Desenvolvimento Industrial, Conselho de
see
Bahia, Brazil (State). Conselho de Desenvolvimento Industrial.

Bahia, Brazil (State). Divisão de Bibliotecas.
Projeto de um sistema de bibliotecas para a Estado da Bahia, 1967–1970. [Salvador] Centro de Estudos e Planejamento, 1967.
80 p. 23 cm. (Educação e desenvolvimento, 2)
"Decreto n. 20.379, de 12 de outubro de 1967": p. 35–39.
Bibliography: p. 33–34.
1. Libraries—Bahia, Brazil (State) I. Bahia, Brazil (State). Laws, statutes, etc. Decreto n. 20.379, de 12 de outubro de 1967. 1967. II. Title. III. Series.
L298.B3A34 no. 2 72–623415
[Z769.B3]

Bahia, Brazil (State). Divisão de Bibliotecas. Biblioteca Central do Estado da Bahia
see
Biblioteca Central do Estado da Bahia.

Bahia, Brazil (State). Divisão de Estudos Penais.
Boletim penitenciário.
[Salvador] Secretaria da Justiça, Departamento de Assuntos Penais, Divisão de Estudos Penais.
v. ill. 23 cm.
1. Corrections—Bahia, Brazil (State)—Periodicals. I. Title.
HV7333.B33B33a 75–643393
MARC–S

Bahia, Brazil (State). Divisão de Informação Industrial e Promoção de Investimentos. Empresas que solicitaram colaboração financeira à SUDENE-Estado da Bahia
see Bahia, Brazil (State). Divisão de Informação Industrial e Promoção de Investimentos. Resenha semestral ... [Salvador] Secretaria da Industria e Comércio.

Bahia, Brazil (State). Divisão de Informação Industrial e Promoção de Investimentos.
Resenha bimestral.
[Salvador]
no. 22 x 32 cm.
"Empresas que solicitaram colaboração financiera à SUDENE-Estado da Bahia."
1. Industrial promotion—Bahia, Brazil (State) 2. Investments—Bahia, Brazil (State)
HC188.B3B32a 73–644095
MARC–S

Bahia, Brazil (State). Divisão de Informação Industrial e Promoção de Investimentos.
Resenha semestral: Empresas que solicitaram colaboração financeira à SUDENE-Estado da Bahia.
[Salvador] Secretaria da Industria e Comércio, Departamento de Industria e Comérico, Divisão de Informação Industrial e Promoção de Investimentos.
v. 21 x 31 cm.
1. Business enterprises—Bahia, Brazil (State)—Finance—Periodicals. 2. Investments — Bahia, Brazil (State) — Periodicals. I. Bahia, Brazil (State). Divisão de Informação Industrial e Promoção de Investimentos. Empresas que solicitaram colaboração financeira à SUDENE-Estado da Bahia. II. Title. III. Title: Empresas que solicitaram colaboração financeira à SUDENE-Estado da Bahia.
HG4111.5.B33B33a 75–644182
MARC–S

Bahia, Brazil (State). Divisão de Integração Social. Seção de Levantamentos e Pesquisas.
Projeto de estudo da problemática sindical na Bahia; sindicatos com sede em Salvador. [Salvador, apresentação 1969]
139 l. 34 cm.
At head of title: Programa de ação integrada junto ao setor sindical.
1. Trade-unions—Bahia, Brazil (State) I. Title.
HD6615.B3B34 1969 74–206785

Bahia, Brazil (State). Economia Rural, Serviço de
see
Bahia, Brazil (State). Serviço de Economia Rural.

Bahia, Brazil (State). Educação, Conselho Estadual de
see
Bahia, Brazil (State). Conselho Estadual de Educação.

Bahia, Brazil (State). Estudos Penais, Divisão de
see
Bahia, Brazil (State). Divisão de Estudos Penais.

Bahia, Brazil (State). Fundação de Planejamento.
The Comissão de Planejamento Econômico of Bahia was created in 1955. In 1959 it became the Fundação Comissão de Planejamento Econômico but continued to be known by both the old and new names until 1969, when it became the Fundação de Planejamento.
Works by this body published before the change of name in 1969 are found under
Bahia, Brazil (State). Comissão de Planejamento Econômico.
Works published after that change of name are found under

Bahia, Brazil (State). Fundação de Planejamento.

Bahia, Brazil (State). Fundação de Planejamento.
Análise global da economia baiana : diagnóstico. — [Salvador] : Governo Antonio Carlos Magalhães, Secretaria do Planejamento, Ciência e Tecnologia, Fundação de Planejamento, 1974.
2 v. (1713 p.) : ill. (some fold.) ; 31 cm.
Bibliography: p. 1677-1713.
1. Bahia, Brazil (State)—Economic conditions. I. Title.
HC188.B3B3217 1974 76-470266
76 MARC

Bahia, Brazil (State). Geografia e Estatística, Departamento de
see
Bahia, Brazil (State). Departamento de Geografia e Estatística.

Bahia, Brazil (State). Grupo de Estudos da Mamona.
Relatório. Salvador, 1968.
90, 8 p. illus. 31 cm.
1. Castor-bean—Brazil—Bahia (State) 2. Castor-oil.
HD9490.B82B332 72–223018

Bahia, Brazil (State). Indústria e Comércio, Departamento de
see
Bahia, Brazil (State). Departamento de Indústria e Comércio.

Bahia, Brazil (State). Instituto Biológico.
Coletânea de resumos de trabalhos publicados no Boletim do Instituto Biológico da Bahia.
Salvador, 1972-
v. 25 cm.
At head of title: Secretaria da Agricultura.
NIC NUC76-83401

Bahia, Brazil (State). Instituto Biológico
see Dunham, Orlando. Pragas do coqueiro. Salvador [Brasil] SUDENE, 1971.

Bahia, Brazil (State). Integração Social, Divisão de
see
Bahia, Brazil (State). Divisão de Integração Social.

Bahia, Brazil (State). Interior, Justiça, Instrucção, Saude e Assistencia Pública, Secretaria do
see
Bahia, Brazil (State). Secretaria do Interior, Justiça, Instrucção, Saude e Assistencia Pública.

Bahia, Brazil (State). Laws, statutes, etc. Consolidação do Impôsto de circulação de mercadorias
see
Bahia, Brazil (State). Laws, statutes, etc. Decreto no. 22.751, de 27 de janeiro de 1972.

Bahia, Brazil (State). Laws, statutes, etc.
Decreto n. 20.379, de 12 de outubro de 1967. 1967
see Bahia, Brazil (State). Divisão de Bibliotecas. Projeto de um sistema de bibliotecas para a Estado da Bahia, 1967-1970. [Salvador] Centro de Estudos e Planejamento, 1967.

Bahia, Brazil (State). Laws, statutes, etc.
[Decreto no. 22.751, de 27 de janeiro de 1972]
Consolidação do Impôsto de circulação de mercadorias, Bahia. [Trabalho elaborado por Heraclito Mota Barreto; participação da Equipe da A. S. P. O. Salvador, Secretaria da Fazenda, ASPO] 1972.
266 p. 22 cm.
Cover title: Impôsto de circulação de mercadoria; ICM, Bahia.
1. Sales tax—Bahia, Brazil (State) I. Barreto, Heraclito Mota. II. Title. III. Title: Impôsto de Circulação de Mercadoria.
73–221636

Bahia, Brazil (State). Laws, statutes, etc.
Lei n.º 1.820 de 7 de dez[e]mbro de 1962; fixa a despesa e orça a receita do Estado para o exercício de 1963, autoriza a abertura decréditos suplementares e dá outras providências de caráter financeiro, tôdas autorizadas no artigo 86 § 1.º da Constituição do Estado. [Salvador] Imprensa Oficial da Bahia, 1963.
xliii, 570 p. 23 cm.
At head of title: Serviço Público Estadual. On spine: Orçamento para 1963.
1. Finance, Public—Bahia, Brazil (State)—Law.
75–562100

Bahia, Brazil (State). Laws, statutes, etc.
Lei n. 2.097 de 15 de dezembro de 1964 ; fixa a despêsa e orça a receita do Estado para o exercício de 1965, autoriza a abertura de créditos suplementares e dá outras providências de caráter financeiro, tôdas autorizadas no artigo 86 § 1.º da Constituição do Estado. [Salvador] Imprensa Oficial da Bahia, 1964.
xxxii, 349 p. 23 cm.
At head of title: Serviço Público Estadual.
On spine: Orçamento para 1965.
1. Finance, Public—Bahia, Brazil (State)—Law.
75–540901

Bahia, Brazil (State). Laws, statutes, etc.
Reforma da Secretaria da Fazenda; [trabalho elaborado pela A. S. P. O., i. e. Assessoria Setorial de Programação e Orçamento. Salvador, Imprensa Oficial] 1972.
79 p. 23 cm.
Cover title.
1. Bahia, Brazil (State). Secretaria da Fazenda. I. Bahia, Brazil (State). Secretaria da Fazenda. Assessoria Setorial de Programação e Orçamento. II. Title.
74–203156

Bahia, Brazil (State). Mão-de-Obra, Departamento de
see
Bahia, Brazil (State). Departamento de Mão-de-Obra.

Bahia, Brazil (State). Minas e Energia, Secretaria das
see
Bahia, Brazil (State). Secretaria das Minas e Energia.

Bahia, Brazil (State). Museu de Arte. Biblioteca
see Bahia cultural. 1973- Salvador, Conselho Estadual de Cultura.

Bahia, Brazil (State). Planejamento, Ciência e Tecnologia, Secretaria do
see
Bahia, Brazil (State). Secretaria do Planejamento, Ciência e Tecnologia.

Bahia, Brazil (State). Planejamento, Fundação de
see
Bahia, Brazil (State). Fundação de Planejamento.

Bahia, Brazil (State). Planejamento Agrícola, Comissão Estadual de
see
Bahia, Brazil (State). Comissão Estadual de Planejamento Agrícola.

Bahia, Brazil (State). Produção Mineral, Coordenação da
see
Bahia, Brazil (State). Coordenação da Produção Mineral.

Bahia, Brazil (State). Programação e Orçamento, Assessoria Geral de
see
Bahia, Brazil (State). Assessoria Geral de Programação e Orçamento.

Bahia, Brazil (State). Saneamento e Recursos Hídricos, Secretaria do
see
Bahia, Brazil (State). Secretaria do Saneamento e Recursos Hídricos.

Bahia, Brazil (State). Saúde Pública, Secretaria da
see
Bahia, Brazil (State). Secretaria da Saúde Pública.

Bahia, Brazil (State). Seção de Economia Mineral.
Incentivos à mineração na Bahia. 2. ed. [Salvador] 1973.
31, [2] l. 32 cm. (Coordenação da Produção Mineral. Publicação especial, v. 4, ano 2)
Bibliography: leaf [33]
1. Mineral industries—Bahia, Brazil (State) 2. Tax credits—Bahia, Brazil (State) 3. Industry and state—Brazil—Bahia (State) I. Title. II. Series: Bahia, Brazil (State). Coordenação da Produção Mineral. Publicação especial, v. 4, ano 2.
HD9506.B73B333 1973 73-221765

Bahia, Brazil (State). Secretaria da Agricultura.
About 1967 the Secretaria da Agricultura, Indústria e Comércio of Bahia, Brazil was replaced by the Secretaria da Agricultura and the Secretaria da Indústria e Comércio.
Works by these bodies are found under the following headings according to the name used at the time of publication:
Bahia, Brazil (State). Secretaria da Agricultura, Indústria e Comércio.
Bahia, Brazil (State). Secretaria da Agricultura.
Bahia, Brazil (State). Secretaria da Indústria e Comércio.

Works by earlier related bodies are found under the headings listed below in inverse chronological order:
Bahia, Brazil (State). Secretaria da Agricultura, Commercio e Obras Públicas.
Bahia, Brazil (State). Secretaria da Agricultura, Viação, Indústria e Obras Públicas.

Bahia, Brazil (State). Secretaria da Agricultura. Serviço de Economia Rural
see
Bahia, Brazil (State). Serviço de Economia Rural.

Bahia, Brazil (State). Secretaria da Agricultura, Commercio e Obras Públicas.
About 1967 the Secretaria da Agricultura, Indústria e Comércio of Bahia, Brazil was replaced by the Secretaria da Agricultura and the Secretaria da Indústria e Comércio.
Works by these bodies are found under the following headings according to the name used at the time of publication:
Bahia, Brazil (State). Secretaria da Agricultura, Indústria e
Bahia, Brazil (State). Secretaria da Agricultura.
Bahia, Brazil (State). Secretaria da Indústria e Comércio.

Works by earlier related bodies are found under the headings listed below in inverse chronological order:
Bahia, Brazil (State). Secretaria da Agricultura, Commercio e Obras Públicas.
Bahia, Brazil (State). Secretaria da Agricultura, Viação, Indústria e Obras Públicas.

Bahia, Brazil (State). Secretaria da Agricultura, Commercio e Obras Públicas
see also
Bahia, Brazil (State). Secretaria da Agricultura, Indústria e Comércio.
Bahia, Brazil (State). Secretaria da Agricultura, Viação, Indústria e Obras Públicas.

Bahia, Brazil (State). Secretaria da Agricultura, Indústria e Comércio.
About 1967 the Secretaria da Agricultura, Indústria e Comércio of Bahia, Brazil was replaced by the Secretaria da Agricultura and the Secretaria da Indústria e Comércio.
Works by these bodies are found under the following headings according to the name used at the time of publication:
Bahia, Brazil (State). Secretaria da Agricultura, Indústria e Comércio.
Bahia, Brazil (State). Secretaria da Agricultura.
Bahia, Brazil (State). Secretaria da Indústria e Comércio.

Works by earlier related bodies are found under the headings listed below in inverse chronological order:
Bahia, Brazil (State). Secretaria da Agricultura, Commercio e Obras Públicas.
Bahia, Brazil (State). Secretaria da Agricultura, Viação, Indústria e Obras Públicas.

Bahia, Brazil (State). Secretaria da Agricultura, Indústria e Comércio
see also
Bahia, Brazil (State). Secretaria da Agricultura, Commercio e Obras Públicas.

Bahia, Brazil (State). Secretaria da Agricultura, Viação, Indústria e Obras Públicas.
About 1967 the Secretaria da Agricultura, Indústria e Comércio of Bahia, Brazil was replaced by the Secretaria da Agricultura and the Secretaria da Indústria e Comércio.
Works by these bodies are found under the following headings according to the name used at the time of publication:
Bahia, Brazil (State). Secretaria da Agricultura, Indústria e Comércio.
Bahia, Brazil (State). Secretaria da Agricultura.
Bahia, Brazil (State). Secretaria da Indústria e Comércio.

Works by earlier related bodies are found under the headings listed below in inverse chronological order:
Bahia, Brazil (State). Secretaria da Agricultura, Commercio e Obras Públicas.
Bahia, Brazil (State). Secretaria da Agricultura, Viação, Indústria e Obras Públicas.

Bahia, Brazil (State). Secretaria da Agricultura, Viação, Indústria e Obras Públicas
see also
Bahia, Brazil (State). Secretaria da Agricultura, Commercio e Obras Públicas.

Bahia, Brazil (State). Secretaria da Ciência e Tecnologia.
CEPED, Centro de Pesquisas e Desenvolvimento; plano diretor. [Salvador] 1971.
112, xx p. fold. illus.
1. Research—Brazil—Bahia (State) 2. Centro de Pesquisas e Desenvolvimento. 3. Research, Industrial—Brazil—Bahia (State) I. Title.
AzTeS NUC74-20259

Bahia, Brazil (State). Secretaria da educação, Saude e Assistencia Pública
see also
Bahia, Brazil (State). Secretaria do Interior, Justiça, Instrucção, Saude e Assistencia Pública.

Bahia, Brazil (State). Secretaria da Fazenda. Assessoria Setorial de Programação e Orçamento
see Bahia, Brazil (State). Laws, statutes, etc. Reforma da Secretaria da Fazenda... [Salvador Imprensa Oficial] 1972.

Bahia, Brazil (State). Secretaria da Fazenda.
Balanço geral do Estado da Bahia.
[Salvador]
v. 23 x 31 cm.
1. Finance, Public—Bahia, Brazil (State)—Accounting. I. Title.
HJ9923.B6B35a 336.81'4 74-646900
MARC-S

Bahia, Brazil (State). Secretaria da Fazenda.
If; informações fazendárias.
[Salvador]
v. 28 cm.
Information organ of the agency.
1. Finance, Public—Bahia, Brazil (State) I. Title.
HJ32.B36a 73-643148
MARC-S

Bahia, Brazil (State). Secretaria da Fazenda.
Secretaria da Fazenda do Estado da Bahia.
[Salvador, Secretaria da Fazenda do Estado da Bahia]
v. 25 cm.
1. Bahia, Brazil (State). Secretaria da Fazenda. 2. Finance, Public—Bahia, Brazil (State)—Periodicals.
HJ32.B36b 75-644098
MARC-S

Bahia, Brazil (State). Secretaria da Fazenda
see Sande, Luiz. O Nordeste e a aliquota interestadual do ICM. [Salvador, Brasil] 1972.

Bahia, Brazil (State). Secretaria da Indústria e Comércio.
About 1967 the Secretaria da Agricultura, Indústria e Comércio of Bahia, Brazil was replaced by the Secretaria da Agricultura and the Secretaria da Indústria e Comércio.
Works by these bodies are found under the following headings according to the name used at the time of publication:
Bahia, Brazil (State). Secretaria da Agricultura, Indústria e Comércio.
Bahia, Brazil (State). Secretaria da Agricultura.
Bahia, Brazil (State). Secretaria da Indústria e Comércio.

Works by earlier related bodies are found under the headings listed below in inverse chronological order:
Bahia, Brazil (State). Secretaria da Agricultura, Commercio e Obras Públicas.
Bahia, Brazil (State). Secretaria da Agricultura, Viação, Indústria e Obras Públicas.

Bahia, Brazil (State). Secretaria da Indústria e Comércio.
Bahia industrial : informações / Secretaria da Indústria e Comérico. — [Salvador] : A Secretaria, [1974?]
[56] p. : ill. (some col.) ; 20 x 23 cm.
1. Bahia, Brazil (State)—Industries. 2. Bahia, Brazil (State)—Economic conditions. 3. Industrial promotion—Bahia, Brazil (State) I. Title.
HC188.B3B33 1974 75-543659

Bahia, Brazil (State). Secretaria da Indústria e Comércio.
Planejamento industrial de Camaçari : diagnóstico preliminar e termos de referência / Estado da Bahia, Secretaria da Indústria e Comércio. — [Salvador : A Secretaria, between 1972 and 1974]
78 p. : ill. ; 26 x 36 cm.
Bibliography: p. 77-78.
1. Camaçari, Brazil (Bahia)—Economic conditions. 2. Camaçari, Brazil (Bahia)—Industries. I. Title.
HC189.C28B33 1974 338.981'4 75-567931

Bahia, Brazil (State). Secretaria da Indústria e Comércio.
see Bahia, Brazil (State). Secretaria do Planejamento, Ciência e Tecnologia. Oportunidades industriais. Salvador, A Secretaria, 1972.

Bahia, Brazil (State). Secretaria da Indústria e Comércio. Conselho de Desenvolvimento Industrial
see
Bahia, Brazil (State). Conselho de Desenvolvimento Industrial.

Bahia, Brazil (State). Secretaria da Indústria e Comércio. Departamento de Indústria e Comércio
see
Bahia, Brazil (State). Departamento de Indústria e Comércio.

Bahia, Brazil (State). Secretaria da Indústria e Cómercio. Empresa de Turismo da Bahia
see
Empresa de Turismo da Bahia.

Bahia, Brazil (State). Secretaria da Saúde Pública.
Boletim informativo anual — Secretaria de Saúde. 1971–
[Salvador] Secretaria de Saúde [etc.]
v. 24 cm.
"Estatísticas vitais - Estatísticas operacionais."
Continues: Bahia, Brazil (State). Serviço de Bioestatística. Boletim informativo annual ; estatísticas vitais: Estado da Bahia.
1. Bahia, Brazil (State)—Statistics, Vital—Periodicals. 2. Bahia, Brazil (State)—Statistics, Medical—Periodicals.
HA988.B3A36 312'.0981'4 75–640723
MARC–S

Bahia, Brazil (State). Secretaria da Saúde Pública.
Relatório de atividades.
[Salvador]
v. 32 cm. annual.
1. Hygiene, Public—Brazil—Bahia (State)—Periodicals. 2. Bahia, Brazil (State)—Statistics, Medical—Periodicals.
RA208.B3S4a 72–622958

Bahia, Brazil (State). Secretaria da Saúde Pública. Serviço de Bioestatística
see
Bahia, Brazil (State). Serviço de Bioestatística.

Bahia, Brazil (State). Secretaria das Minas e Energia.
Avaliação da oferta e demanda de mão de obra de operação para a indústria petroquímica no Estado da Bahia. [Elaboração: Irundi Sampaio Edelweiss et al. Salvador, Brasil, 1972]
66 l. illus. 33 cm.
Cover title.
1. Labor supply—Bahia, Brazil (State) 2. Petroleum chemicals industry—Bahia, Brazil (State) 3. Petroleum workers—Bahia, Brazil (State) I. Edelweiss, Irundi Sampaio. II. Title.
HD5755.B3B34 1972 73–213772

Bahia, Brazil (State). Secretaria das Minas e Energia.
Complexo petroquímico de Camaçari : plano diretor / [elaborado sob a coordenação executiva da Secretaria das Minas e Energia]. — [s. l. : s. n., 1974] (São Paulo : Abril S. A. Cultural e Industrial)
136 p. : ill. ; 43 cm.
Cover title.
Portuguese and English.
Errata slip inserted.
Bibliography: p. 119.
1. Petroleum chemicals industry—Camaçari, Brazil (Bahia) I. Title.
TP692.3.B35 1974 75–567485

Bahia, Brazil (State). Secretaria das Minas e Energia.
Introdução à petroquímica. [Salvador, Brasil, 1971]
18 p. fold. illus. 28 cm.
Cover title.
"Este trabalho conta com a participação do Engenheiro Químico Irundi Edelweiss."
1. Petroleum chemicals industry. I. Edelweiss, Irundi Sampaio. II. Title.
TP692.3.B35 1971 73–213431

Bahia, Brazil (State). Secretaria das Minas e Energia.
Panorama setorial, atividades.
[Salvador]
v. 28 cm. annual.
Vols. for include Perspectivas for the year ahead.
1. Bahia, Brazil (State). Secretaria das Minas e Energia. 2. Electric utilities — Bahia, Brazil (State) 3. Mineral industries — Bahia, Brazil (State)
HD9506.B73B34a 73–648146
MARC–S

Bahia, Brazil (State). Secretaria das Minas e Energia.
A petroquímica na Bahia. [Salvador, 1971]
69 p. illus. 28 cm.
Cover title.
1. Petroleum chemicals industry—Bahia, Brazil (State) I. Title.
HD9579.C33B72 1971 73–213776

Bahia, Brazil (State). Secretaria das Minas e Energia.
Relatório das atividades—Secretaria das Minas e Energia.
[Salvador] Secretaria das Minas e Energia.
v. ill. 30 cm.
1. Bahia, Brazil (State). Secretaria das Minas e Energia.
TN42.B3B35a 75–644180
MARC–S

Bahia, Brazil (State). Secretaria das Minas e Energia.
Sinopse do cadastro de eletrificação do Estado da Bahia.
[Salvador] Secretaria das Minas e Energia.
v. 22 x 33 cm. semiannual.
1. Electrification—Bahia, Brazil (State)—Periodicals. 2. Electric utilities—Bahia, Brazil (State)—Periodicals. I. Title.
HD9685.B82B33b 363.6'2'09814 75–641554
MARC–S

Bahia, Brazil (State). Secretaria das Minas e Energia.
Situação de eletrificação; sedes e distritos, estado da Bahia.
julho 1972–
[Salvador]
v. 32 cm. semiannual.
1. Electric utilities—Bahia, Brazil (State) I. Title.
HD9685.B82B33a 74–640073
MARC–S

Bahia, Brazil (State). Secretaria das Minas e Energia
see Simpósio Franco-Brasileiro sobre a Indústria Petroquímica, Salvador, 1972. Simpósio Franco-Brasileiro sobre a Indústria Petroquímica... [Salvador, 1973?]

Bahia, Brazil (State). Secretaria das Minas e Engergia. Coordenação da Produção Mineral
see
Bahia, Brazil (State). Coordenação da Produção Mineral.

Bahia, Brazil (State). Secretaria de Agricultura
see
Bahia, Brazil (State). Secretaria da Agricultura, Indústria e Comércio.

Bahia, Brazil (State). Secretaria de Educação e Cultura.
Boletim informativo—Secretaria da Educação e Cultura.
v. 1– agosto 1973–
Salvador.
v. ill. 22 cm. monthly.
1. Education—Brazil—Bahia (State)—Periodicals.
LA559.B3B34a 74–647111
MARC–S

Bahia, Brazil (State). Secretaria de Educação e Cultura.
Relatório de atividades da Secretaria da Educação e Cultura.
[Salvador, Secretaria da Educação e Cultura]
v. ill. 22 x 24 cm.
At head of title : Um triênio de educação na Bahia
1. Bahia, Brazil (State). Secretaria de Educação e Cultura. 2. Education—Brazil—Bahia (State) I. Bahia, Brazil (State). Secretaria de Educação e Cultura. Um triênio de educação na Bahia. II. Title: Um Triênio de educação na Bahia.
LA555.B33a 75–644539
MARC–S

Bahia, Brazil (State). Secretaria de Educação e Cultura. Um triênio de educação na Bahia
see Bahia, Brazil (State). Secretaria de Educação e Cultura. Relatório de atividades da Secretaria da Educação e Cultura. [Salvador]

Bahia, Brazil (State). Secretaria de Educação e Cultura
see Almanach para a Cidade da Bahia, anno 1812. [Salvador] : Conselho Estadual de Cultura, 1973.

Bahia, Brazil (State). Secretaria de Educacão e Cultura
see Aspectos do 2 [i.e. dois] de julho ... [Salvador], 1973.

Bahía, Brazil (State). Secretaria de Educação e Cultura
see Educação é desenvolvimento. [Salvador]

Bahia, Brazil (State). Secretaria de Educação e Cultura. Centro de Estudos e Planejamento.
O menor no âmbito das responsabilidades da Secretaria de Educação e Cultura; plano integral de educação e cultura, funçoes preventiva e terapeútica. [Salvador] 1968.
20 l. 33 cm.
1. Education—Bahia, Brazil (State) I. Title.
L298.B3A55 1968 73–205965

Bahia, Brazil (State). Secretaria de Educacao e Cultura. Centro de Estudos e Planejamento
see Centro Nacional de Recursos Humanos. Carta escolar. Rio de Janeiro, 1971.

Bahia, Brazil (State). Secretaria de Industria e Comércio
see
Bahia, Brazil (State). Secretaria da Indústria e Comércio.

Bahia, Brazil (State). Secretaria de Saúde
see
Bahia, Brazil (State). Secretaria da Saúde Pública.

Bahia, Brazil (State). Secretaria de Saude e Assistencia Publica
see
Bahia, Brazil (State). Secretaria do Interior, Justiça, Instrucção, Saude e Assistencia Publica.

Bahia, Brazil (State). Secretaria do Desenvolvimento Econômico.
Bahia: industrialização do interior. [Salvador] 1966.
205 p. col. fold. illus., col. fold. maps. 21 x 23 cm.
1. Bahia, Brazil (State)—Industries. I. Title.
FMU DLC NUC76-87305

Bahia, Brazil (State). Secretaria do Interior, Justiça, Instrucção, Saude e Assistência Pública.
Decretos — Secretaria do Interior, Justiça, Instrucção, Saúde e Assistência Pública.
[Salvador] Impr. Oficial do Estado.
v. 23 cm.
1. Delegated legislation—Bahia, Brazil (State)
348'.814'025 75–649831
MARC–S

Bahia, Brazil (State). Secretaria do Planejamento, Ciência e Tecnologia.
Oportunidades industriais / Estado da Bahia, Secretaria do Planejamento, Ciencia e Tecnologia, Secretaria da Indústria e Comércio. — Salvador : A Secretaria, 1972.
1 portfolio (21 leaves : ill.) ; 33 cm.
Cover title: Oportunidades industriais na Bahia.
1. Bahia, Brazil (State)—Industries. 2. Industrial promotion—Brazil—Bahia (State) 3. Investments—Brazil—Bahia (State) I. Bahia, Brazil (State). Secretaria da Indústria e Comércio. II. Title.
HC188.B3B334 1972 338'.0981 76-471422
76 MARC

Bahia, Brazil (State). Secretaria do Planejamento, Ciência e Tecnologia.
Orçamento plurianual de investimentos.
[Salvador] Secretaria do Planejamento, Ciência e Tecnologia.
v. 29 cm.
1. Bahia, Brazil (State)—Appropriations and expenditures. 2. Capital investments—Brazil—Bahia (State)
HJ32.B37b 75–643499
MARC–S

Bahia, Brazil (State). Secretaria do Planejamento, Ciência e Tecnologia.
Orçamentação pública.
[Salvador] Secretaria do Planejamento, Ciência e Tecnologia.
v. 32 cm.
1. Budget—Bahia, Brazil (State) I. Title.
HJ32.B37a 354'.81'4 75–641671
MARC–S

Bahia, Brazil (State). Secretaria do Planejamento, Ciência e Tecnologia.
Programa de govêrno: 1972/1974. [Salvador, Impressão Pinheiro, 1972 or 3]
v. illus. 22 cm.
1. Bahia, Brazil—Economic policy. 2. Bahia, Brazil—Social policy. I. Title.
HC188.B3B34 1972 73–214515

Bahia, Brazil (State). Secretaria do Planejamento, Ciência e Tecnologia.
Projeto de regionalização administrativa para o estado da Bahia.
Anexos do III capítulo: Proposição de regionalização administrativa para o estado de Bahia. [Por] Douracy Soares. Salvador, Instituto de Geociências, Departamento 02, 1973.
v. maps. 53 cm.
At head of title: Seplantec.

Scale of maps 1 : 3,000,000.
L. C. copy imperfect? v. 1, Anexos of Secção E wanting?
CONTENTS:
v. 2. Secção E. Atlas.
1. Bahia, Brazil (State)—Maps. 2. Bahia, Brazil (State)—Administrative and political divisions.—Maps. I. Soares, Douracy. II. Title.
G1778.B3B3 1973 912'.81'4 76–515952

Bahia, Brazil (State). Secretaria do Planejamento, Ciência e Tecnologia. Fundação de Planejamento
see
Bahia, Brazil (State). Fundação de Planejamento.

Bahia, Brazil (State). Secretaria do Saneamento e Recursos Hídricos.
Relatório de atividades—[Secretaria do Saneamento e Recursos Hídricos]
[Salvador, Secretaria do Saneamento e Recursos Hídricos]
v. ill. 22 cm.
1. Bahia, Brazil (State). Secretaria do Saneamento e Recursos Hídricos.
TD241.B3B33a 76-642142
MARC-S

Bahia, Brazil (State). Secretaria do Trabalho e Bem Estar Social.
Artesanato integração e desenvolvimento: a problemática em Salvador. [Salvador, Brasil, 1972]
122 l. 32 cm.
1. Artisans—Salvador, Brazil. I. Title.
HD2346.B72S22 1972 73-213781

Bahia, Brazil (State). Secretaria do Trabalho e Bem Estar Social.
Dicionário das ocupações industriais / [Estado da Bahia, Secretaria do Trabalho e Bem Estar Social; supervisão, Everaldo Siqueira Alcântara]. — Bahia : A Secretaria, 1970.
2 v. ; 27 cm.
Includes indexes.
1. Occupations—Classification. 2. Brazil—Occupations. I. Alcântara, Everaldo Siqueira. II. Title.
HB2653.B33 1970 77-465725
77 MARC

Bahia, Brazil (State). Secretaria do Trabalho e Bem Estar Social.
Mão de obra no setor primário; cultura do dende. [Salvador, Brasil] 1972.
117, [9] l. 31 cm.
Bibliography: leaf [126].
1. Oil industries—Bahia, Brazil (State) 2. Oil industry workers—Bahia, Brazil (State) I. Title.
HD9490.B82B333 1972 73-213771

Bahia, Brazil (State). Secretaria do Trabalho e Bem Estar Social
see Simpósio de Mão-de Obra Industrial, 1st, Salvador, Brazil, 1968. I [i. e. Primeiro] Simpósio de Mão-de-Obra Industrial. [Salvador] Secretaria do Trabalho e Bem Estar Social [1969]

Bahia, Brazil (State). Secretaria do Trabalho e Bem Estar Social. Departamento de Mão-de-Obra
see
Bahia, Brazil (State). Departamento de Mão-de-Obra.

Bahia, Brazil (State). Serviço de Bioestatística.
Boletim informativo anual; estatísticas vitais: Estado da Bahia.
Salvador.
v. 23 cm.
1. Bahia, Brazil (State)—Statistics, Vital. I. Title.
HA988.B3A36 72-624026

Bahia, Brazil (State). Serviço de Bioestatística.
Boletim informativo anual; estatísticas vitais: Município do Salvador.
Salvador.
v. 23 cm.
1. Salvador, Brazil—Statistics, Vital. I. Title.
HA989.S25B33 72-624056

Bahia, Brazil (State). Serviço de Economia Rural
Aspectos da produção e da comercialização de caprinos e ovinos na região nordeste da Bahia / Governo do Estado da Bahia, Secretaria da Agricultura, Serviço de Economia Rural. — Salvador : O Serviço, 1975.
104 leaves ; 31 cm.
Bibliography : leaves 101-102.
1. Goats—Brazil—Bahia (State). 2. Sheep—Brazil—Bahia (State) I. Title.
HD9436.B73B33 1975 75-521943
76 MARC

Bahia, Brazil (State). State Dept. of Industry and Commerce
see
Bahia, Brazil (State). Secretaria da Indústria e Comércio.

Bahia, Brazil (State). Tribunal de Contas.
Boletim informativo—Tribunal de Contas do Estado. ano 1- 1974-
[Salvador] Tribunal de Contas do Estado.
v. ill. 28 cm.
1. Bahia, Brazil (State). Tribunal de Contas. 2. Finance, Public—Bahia, Brazil (State)—Accounting—Periodicals.
HJ9923.B7B342a 75-645927
MARC-S

Bahia, Brazil (State). Universidade.
The Universidade da Bahia was created in 1946 by a merger of the following: Faculdade de Medicina da Bahia, Faculdade de Direito, Escola Politécnica da Bahia, Faculdade de Filosofia da Bahia, and Faculdade de Ciências Econômicas. In 1964 the name of the university was changed to Universidade Federal da Bahia.
Works by these bodies are found under the following headings according to the name used at the time of publication:
Salvador, Brazil. Faculdade de Medicina.
Salvador, Brazil. Faculdade de Direito.
Salvador, Brazil. Escola Politécnica.
Salvador, Brazil. Faculdade de Filosofia.
Faculdade de Ciências Econômicas, Salvador, Brazil.

Bahia, Brazil (State). Universidade.
Bahia, Brazil (State). Universidade Federal.
73-210377

Bahia, Brazil (State). Universidade.
Reitoria: catálogo dos azulejos. Cidade do Salvador, Universidade da Bahia, 1953.
224 p. (p. [43]-[221] illus.) 17 cm.
Cover title: Azulejos da Reitoria.
Text signed: José Valladares.
CONTENTS: O azulejo.—O azulejo em Portugal.—O azulejo no Brasil.—Os azulejos da Reitoria.—Catálogo topográfico.—Bibliografia (p. 223-224)
1. Decoration and ornament, Architectural—Bahia, Brazil (State) 2. Tiles—Bahia, Brazil (State) I. Valladares, José. II. Title: Azulejos de Reitoria.
NA3533.A3B37 1953 55-30423

Bahia, Brazil (State). Universidade
see **Lincoln. Bahia [Universidade da Bahia]** 1959.

Bahia, Brazil (State). Universidade. Centro de Estudos Afro-Orientais

see also the later heading

Bahia, Brazil (State). Universidade Federal. Centro de Estudos Afro-Orientais.

Bahia, Brazil (State). Universidade. Escola de Belas Artes.
Arquivos. v. 1-
1953-
Salvador.
v. illus. 24 cm.
AS80.A1B3 72-623990

Bahia, Brazil (State). Universidade. Escola de Geologia.
Publicação avulsa. no. 1-
fev. 1964-
[Salvador]
no. in v. ill. 24 cm.
1. Geology—Brazil—Collected works.
QE235.S33 73-366788
MARC-S

Bahia, Brazil (State). Universidade. Escola Politécnica.
The Escola Politécnica da Bahia was created in 1897 out of the Instituto Politécnico da Bahia. In 1946 it was incorporated into the newly established Universidade da Bahia (name changed in 1964 to Universidade Federal da Bahia).
Works by these bodies published before the establishment of the university in 1946 are found under
Instituto Politécnico da Bahia.
Salvador, Brazil. Escola Politécnica.
Works published after this time are found under the following headings according to the name of the parent body used at the time of publication:

Bahia, Brazil (State). Universidade. Escola Politécnica.
Bahia, Brazil (State). Universidade Federal. Escola Politécnica.
73-210616

Bahia, Brazil (State). Universidade. Escola Politecnica.
Indice tecnológico; lista classificada de artigos sôbre engenharia e tecnologia publicados em revistas brasileiras. no. 1- jan./junho 1953-
[Salvador]
no. in v. 31 cm. semiannual.
1. Engineering—Bibliography—Periodicals. 2. Technology—Bibliography—Periodicals. 3. Brazilian periodicals—Bibliography—Periodicals. I. Title.
Z5852.B33a 58-26376
[TA4] MARC-S

Bahia, Brazil (State). Universidade. Faculdade de Ciências Econômicas.
The name of the Escola Comercial da Bahia (established in 1905) was changed in 1934 to Faculdade de Ciências Econômicas. In 1946 it was incorporated into the newly established Universidade da Bahia (name changed in 1964 to Universidade Federal da Bahia).
Works by this body published before the establishment of the university in 1946 are found under the following headings according to the name used at the time of publication:
Escola Comercial da Bahia.
Faculdade de Ciências Econômicas, Salvador, Brazil.

Works published after this time are found under the following headings according to the name of the parent body used at the time of publication:
Bahia, Brazil (State). Universidade. Faculdade de Ciências Econômicas.
Bahia, Brazil (State). Universidade Federal. Faculdade de Ciências Econômicas.
73-210823

Bahia, Brazil (State). Universidade. Faculdade de Ciências Econômicas. Diretório Acadêmico

see also the later heading

Bahia, Brazil (State). Universidade Federal. Faculdade de Ciências Econômicas. Diretório Acadêmico.

Bahia, Brazil (State). Universidade. Faculdade de Direito.
The Faculdade de Direito was founded in 1891. In 1946 it was incorporated into the newly established Universidade da Bahia (name changed in 1964 to Universidade Federal da Bahia).
Works by this body published before the establishment of the university in 1946 are found under
Salvador, Brazil. Faculdade de Direito.
Works published after this time are found under the following headings according to the name of the parent body used at the time of publication:

Bahia, Brazil (State). Universidade. Faculdade de Direito.
Bahia, Brazil (State). Universidade Federal. Faculdade de Direito.
73-210745

Bahia, Brazil (State). Universidade. Faculdade de Filosofia.
The name of the Faculdade de Filosofia, Ciências e Letras (founded in 1941) was changed in 1943(?) to Faculdade de Filosofia da Bahia. In 1946 it was incorporated into the newly established Universidade da Bahia (name changed in 1964 to Universidade Federal da Bahia). The name of the faculty was changed in 1968 to Faculdade de Filosofia e Ciências Humanas.
Works by this body published before the establishment of the university in 1946 are found under the following headings according to the name used at the time of publication:
Faculdade de Filosofia, Ciências e Letras, Salvador, Brazil.
Salvador, Brazil. Faculdade de Filosofia.

Works published after this time are found under the following headings according to the name of the faculty and the university used at the time of publication:
Bahia, Brazil. Universidade. Faculdade de Filosofia.
Bahia, Brazil. Universidade Federal. Faculdade de Filosofia.
Bahia, Brazil. Universidade Federal. Faculdade de Filosofia e Ciências Humanas.
73-210806

Bahia, Brazil (State). Universidade. Faculdade de Filosofia.
Arquivos. v. 1- 1942/52-
Salvador.
v. 24 cm.
AS80.B35A2 55-17707
MARC-S

Bahia, Brazil (State). Universidade. Faculdade de Filosofia.
Boletim [da] cadeira de história do Brasil. n.° 1-
junho 1954-
Bahia.
no. 31 cm.
1. Brazil—History—Periodicals. 2. Bahia, Brazil (State)—History—Periodicals. 3. College prose—Salvador, Brazil. Universidade—Periodicals.
F2501.B33a 58-19684
MARC-S

Bahia, Brazil (State). Universidade. Faculdade de Medicina.
The Faculdade de Medicina da Bahia was created in 1808 as the Escola de Cirurgia da Bahia. In 1946 it was incorporated into the newly established Universidade da Bahia (name changed in 1964 to Universidade Federal da Bahia).
Works by this body published before the establishment of the university in 1946 are found under
Salvador, Brazil. Faculdade de Medicina.
Works published after this time are found under the following headings according to the name of the parent body used at the time of publication:

Bahia, Brazil (State). Universidade. Faculdade de Medicina.
Bahia, Brazil (State). Universidade Federal. Faculdade de Medicina.
73-218218

Bahia, Brazil (State). Universidade. Instituto de Ciências Sociais

see also the later heading

Bahia, Brazil (State). Universidade Federal. Instituto de Ciências Sociais.

Bahia, Brazil (State). Universidade. Laboratório de Geomorfologia e Estudos Regionais

see also the later heading

Bahia, Brazil (State). Universidade Federal. Laboratório de Geomofologia e Estudos Regionais.

Bahia, Brazil (State). Universidade Federal.

The Universidade da Bahia was created in 1946 by a merger of the following: Faculdade de Medicina da Bahia, Faculdade de Direito, Escola Politécnica da Bahia, Faculdade de Filosofia da Bahia, and Faculdade de Ciências Econômicas. In 1964 the name of the university was changed to Universidade Federal da Bahia.
Works by these bodies are found under the following headings according to the name used at the time of publication:

Salvador, Brazil. Faculdade de Medicina.
Salvador, Brazil. Faculdade de Direito.
Salvador, Brazil. Escola Politécnica.
Salvador, Brazil. Faculdade de Filosofia.
Faculdade de Ciências Econômicas, Salvador, Brazil.

Bahia, Brazil (State). Universidade.
Bahia, Brazil (State). Universidade Federal.
SUBJECT ENTRY: Works about these bodies are entered under the name resulting from the merger. In the case of change of name entry is made under the name used during the latest period covered. Works limited in subject coverage to the premerger period are entered under the name of one or more of the original bodies.

73-210378

Bahia, Brazil (State). Universidade Federal. Biblioteca Central
see Catálogo coletivo regional de periódicos, Bahia. Salvador, Universidade Federal da Bahia.

Bahia, Brazil (State). Universidade Federal. Centro de Administração Pública.
Organização; glossário. [Salvador, 1972 or 3]
[75] p. 30 cm.
Cover title.
Bibliography: p. [75]
1. Public administration—Dictionaries—Portuguese. I. Title.
JA64.P69B38 1972 73-213684

Bahia, Brazil (State). Universidade Federal. Centro de Administração Publica.
Publicações do Centro de Administração Pública—ISP, 1964–1972. Salvador, 1972.
12 l. 30 cm.
1. Public administration—Bibliography.
Z7164.A2B338 1972 73-212671

Bahia, Brazil (State). Universidade Federal. Centro de Administracão Pública
see Técnicas de programacão ... [Salvador, 1971]

Bahia, Brazil (State). Universidade Federal. Centro de Estudos Afro-Orientais

see also the earlier heading

Bahia, Brazil (State). Universidade. Centro de Estudos Afro-Orientais.

Bahia, Brazil (State). Universidade Federal. Escola de Biblioteconomia e Comunicacão
see Documenta. Salvador.

Bahia, Brazil (State) Universidade Federal. Escola de Enfermagem.
Saúde e desenvolvimento na Bahia: contribuição da enfermagem. [Salvador] Departamento Cultural, Universidade Federal da Bahia, 1969.
167 p. illus. 23 cm.
1. Public health—Brazil—Bahia (State) 2. Health facilities—Brazil—Bahia (State) 3. Nursing—Brazil—Bahia (State) I. Title.
RA464.B33B33 1969 75-543201

Bahia, Brazil (State). Universidade Federal. Escola Politécnica.
The Escola Politécnica da Bahia was created in 1897 out of the Instituto Politécnico da Bahia. In 1946 it was incorporated into the newly established Universidade da Bahia (name changed in 1964 to Universidade Federal da Bahia).
Works by these bodies published before the establishment of the university in 1946 are found under
Instituto Politécnico da Bahia.
Salvador, Brazil. Escola Politécnica.
Works published after this time are found under the following headings according to the name of the parent body used at the time of publication:
Bahia, Brazil (State). Universidade. Escola Politécnica.
Bahia, Brazil (State). Universidade Federal. Escola Politécnica.

73-210617

Bahia, Brazil (State). Universidade Federal. Faculdade de Arquitetura.
A faculdade de arquitetura e a preservação do nosso patrimônio arquitetônico. [Salvador] 1960.
19 p.
Cover title.
1. Universidade Federal da Bahia. Faculdade de Arquitetura. I. Title.
MiEM NUC76-38111

Bahia, Brazil (State). Universidade Federal. Faculdade de Arquitetura
see Plano diretor de Itapetinga. [Salvador, Universidade Federal da Bahia, 1972-

Bahia, Brazil (State). Universidade Federal. Faculdade de Ciências Econômicas.
The name of the Escola Comercial da Bahia (established in 1905) was changed in 1934 to Faculdade de Ciências Econômicas. In 1946 it was incorporated into the newly established Universidade da Bahia (name changed in 1964 to Universidade Federal da Bahia).
Works by this body published before the establishment of the university in 1946 are found under the following headings according to the name used at the time of publication:
Escola Comercial da Bahia.
Faculdade de Ciências Econômicas, Salvador, Brazil.

Works published after this time are found under the following headings according to the name of the parent body used at the time of publication:
Bahia, Brazil (State). Universidade. Faculdade de Ciências Econômicas.
Bahia, Brazil (State). Universidade Federal. Faculdade de Ciências Econômicas.

73-210824

Bahia, Brazil (State). Universidade Federal. Faculdade de Ciências Econômicas. Diretório Acadêmico

see also the earlier heading

Bahia, Brazil (State). Universidade. Faculdade de Ciências Econômicas. Diretório Acadêmico.

Bahia, Brazil (State). Universidade Federal. Faculdade de Direito.
The Faculdade de Direito was founded in 1891. In 1946 it was incorporated into the newly established Universidade da Bahia (name changed in 1964 to Universidade Federal da Bahia).
Works by this body published before the establishment of the university in 1946 are found under
Salvador, Brazil. Faculdade de Direito.
Works published after this time are found under the following headings according to the name of the parent body used at the time of publication:

Bahia, Brazil (State). Universidade. Faculdade de Direito.
Bahia, Brazil (State). Universidade Federal. Faculdade de Direito.

73-210747

Bahia, Brazil (State). Universidade Federal. Faculdade de Filosofia.
The name of the Faculdade de Filosofia, Ciências e Letras (founded in 1941) was changed in 1943(?) to Faculdade de Filosofia da Bahia. In 1946 it was incorporated into the newly established Universidade da Bahia (name changed in 1964 to Universidade Federal da Bahia). The name of the faculty was changed in 1968 to Faculdade de Filosofia e Ciências Humanas.
Works by this body published before the establishment of the university in 1946 are found under the following headings according to the name used at the time of publication:
Faculdade de Filosofia, Ciências e Letras, Salvador, Brazil.
Salvador, Brazil. Faculdade de Filosofia.
Works published after this time are found under the following headings according to the name of the faculty and the university used at the time of publication:
Bahia, Brazil. Universidade. Faculdade de Filosofia.
Bahia, Brazil. Universidade Federal. Faculdade de Filosofia.
Bahia, Brazil. Universidade Federal. Faculdade de Filosofia e Ciências Humanas.

73-210804

Bahia, Brazil (State). Universidade Federal. Faculdade de Filosofia e Ciências Humanas.
The name of the Faculdade de Filosofia, Ciências e Letras (founded in 1941) was changed in 1943(?) to Faculdade de Filosofia da Bahia. In 1946 it was incorporated into the newly established Universidade da Bahia (name changed in 1964 to Universidade Federal da Bahia). The name of the faculty was changed in 1968 to Faculdade de Filosofia e Ciências Humanas.
Works by this body published before the establishment of the university in 1946 are found under the following headings according to the name used at the time of publication:
Faculdade de Filosofia, Ciências e Letras, Salvador, Brazil.
Salvador, Brazil. Faculdade de Filosofia.

Works published after this time are found under the following headings according to the name of the faculty and the university used at the time of publication:
Bahia, Brazil. Universidade. Faculdade de Filosofia.
Bahia, Brazil. Universidade Federal. Faculdade de Filosofia.
Bahia, Brazil. Universidade Federal. Faculdade de Filosofia e Ciências Humanas.

73-210809

Bahia, Brazil (State). Universidade Federal. Faculdade de Medicina.
The Faculdade de Medicina da Bahia was created in 1808 as the Escola de Cirurgia da Bahia. In 1946 it was incorporated into the newly established Universidade da Bahia (name changed in 1964 to Universidade Federal da Bahia).
Works by this body published before the establishment of the university in 1946 are found under
Salvador, Brazil. Faculdade de Medicina.
Works published after this time are found under the following headings according to the name of the parent body used at the time of publication:
Bahia, Brazil (State). Universidade. Faculdade de Medicina.
Bahia, Brazil (State). Universidade Federal. Faculdade de Medicina.

73-218220

Bahia, Brazil (State). Universidade Federal. Instituto de Ciencias Sociais

see also the earlier heading

Bahia, Brazil (State). Universidade. Instituto de Ciencias Sociais.

Bahia, Brazil (State). Universidade Federal. Instituto de Servico Público
see Reforma administrativa... Salvador [Brasil] 1972.

Bahia, Brazil (State). Universidade Federal. Instituto de Serviço Público
see Reformas administrativas estaduais. [Salvador, 1970?]

Bahia, Brazil (State). Universidade Federal. Laboratório de Geomorfologia e Estudos Regionais.
Contribuição ao estudo do Recôncavo. [Salvador] 1968–
v. illus. 28 cm.
Cover title.
CONTENTS: v. 1. Alagoinhas.
1. Bahia, Brazil (State)—Economic conditions—Case studies. 2. Cities and towns—Brazil—Bahia (State)—Case studies. I. Title.
HC188.B3B34 1968 73-213985

Bahia, Brazil (State). Universidade Federal. Laboratório de Geomorfologia e Estudos Regionais

see also the earlier heading

Bahia, Brazil (State). Universidade. Laboratório de Geomorfologia e Estudos Regionais.

Bahia, Brazil (State). Universidade Federal. Serviço de Assessoria em Arquitetura e Urbanismo
see
Serviço de Assessoria em Arquitetura e Urbanismo.

Bahía Blanca, Argentine Republic. Universidad Nacional del Sur. Asesoría de Planeamiento. Departamento de Estadística e Información Académica
see
Bahía Blanca, Argentine Republic. Universidad Nacional del Sur. Departamento de Estadística e Información Académica.

Bahia Blanca, Argentine Republic. Universidad Nacional del Sur. Centro de Documentacion Bibliotecologica
see IREBI: Indices de revistas de bibliotecologia. abr. 1973- Madrid.

Bahía Blanca, Argentine Republic. Universidad Nacional del Sur. Departamento de Estadística e Información Académica.
Informe anual sobre la Universidad Nacional del Sur. Bahía Blanca.
v. 28 cm.
LACAP 72-4107
Issued in pts.
1. Bahia Blanca, Argentine Republic. Universidad Nacional del Sur. I. Title.
LE21.B22A37 73-643364
MARC-S

Bahía Blanca, Argentine Republic. Universidad Nacional del Sur. Secretaría de Planeamiento. Departamento de Estadística.
Estructura, actividad y proyección; informe complementario, 1970. Bahía Blanca, 1971.
77 l. illus. 28 cm.
LACAP 71-4802
Cover title.
1. Bahía Blanca, Argentine Republic. Universidad National del Sur—Statistics. I. Title.
LE21.B22A67 72-359176

Bahia. [São Paulo] Editôra Abril, 1969.
130 p. illus., map.
Cover title.
"Quatro rodas; edição especial de turismo", 1969.
1. Bahia, Brazil (State)—Description and travel. I. Quatro rodas.
InU NUC73-48306

Bahia cultural. 1973–
Salvador, Conselho Estadual de Cultura.
v. ill. 30 cm.
"Catálogo da exposição de publicações promovida pelo Conselho Estadual de Cultura com a colaboração da Biblioteca do Museu de Arte da Bahia."
1. Bahia, Brazil (State)—Imprints—Exhibitions. I. Bahia, Brazil (State). Conselho Estadual de Cultura. II. Bahia, Brazil (State). Museu de Arte. Biblioteca.
Z1694.B2B33a 75-647570
MARC-S

Bahia Workshop, University of Bahia, Brazil, 1971.
Communications technology and the crisis in education; a report. New York, Council on Higher Education in the American Republics [1971]
52 p.
1. Audio-visual education—Congresses. I. Council on Higher Education in the American Republics. II. Title.
MH-Ed NUC73-70576

Bahiam, Taraesma
see Lahiria. 1974.

Bahiana, Henrique Paulo.
As forças armadas e o desenvolvimento de Brasil. [1. ed. Rio de Janeiro, Bloch Editores, 1974]
202 p. col. illus. 21 cm.
1. Brazil—Armed forces. 2. Brazil—History, Military. 3. Brazil—Economic conditions—1945- I. Title.
OU NUC76-16396

Bahiana, Henrique Paulo.
A Guatemala em marcha. Prefácio de Francisco Cosenza Gálvez. Rio de Janeiro [Gráfica TUPY Editôra] 1962.
110 p. illus. 24 cm.
1. Guatemala — Economic conditions — 1918- 2. Guatemala — Social conditions. 3. Guatemala — Description and travel — 1951- I. Title.
HC144.B33 74-225300

Bahiana, Luiz Carlos, 1928-
Electromagnetic induction on an expanding conducting sphere [by] Luiz C. Bahiana. [Cambridge] Massachusetts Institute of Technology, Research Laboratory of Electronics, 1964.
ix, 71 p. diagrs. (Massachusetts Institute of Technology. Research Laboratory of Electronics. Technical report, 421)
"Based on a thesis."
Bibliography: p. 71.
1. Electromagnetic fields. 2. Induction (Electricity) 3. Plasma (Ionized gases) I. Title.
UU NUC74-2882

Bahiana, Luiz Carlos, 1928-
Nonlinear properties of FM limiters. [Cambridge] Massachusetts Institute of Technology, Research Laboratory of Electronics, 1959.
iii, 47 p. diagrs. (Massachusetts Institute of Technology. Research Laboratory of Electronics. Technical report, 350)
"Based on a thesis."
Bibliography: p. 47.
1. Radio frequency modulation. I. Title.
UU NUC74-33057

Bahiatursa
see
Empresa de Turismo da Bahia
for publications by and about this body.
Titles and other entries beginning with this acronym are filed following this card.
74-218475

Bahidāra, Satyanārāẏaṇa.
(Ghabghabo)
ଘବ୍‌ଘବୋ / ଶ୍ରୀସତ୍ୟନାରାୟଣ ବହିଦାର. — [ସମ୍ବଲପୁର : ମହିମା ପୁସ୍ତକାଳୟ, 1969]
14 p. ; 18 cm.
Cover title.
In Oriya.
Re0.30

I. Title.
PK2579.B252G48 75-904994

Báhidský, Ján
see Bakidsky, Jan.

Bahiense, Horacio.
Minhas inspirações; sonetos, trovas, pensamentos, perfís, modinhas. 2. ed. Rio de Janeiro, Libraria São Jose, 1964.
218 p. front. (port.)
Errata slip inserted.
I. Title.
WaU NUC73-126534

Bahiense, Norbertino.
Domingos Martins e a revolução pernambucana de 1817 / Norbertino Bahiense ; prefácio de Barbosa Lima Sobrinho. — Belo Horizonte : [s. n.], 1974.
269 p., [19] leaves of plates : ill. ; 23 cm.
Bibliography: p. 266–269.
Cr$40.00
1. Martins, Domingos José, fl. 1817. 2. Pernambuco, Brazil (State)—History—Revolution, 1817. I. Title.
F2534.M282B34 981'.3 75-568180

Bahier, Pierre.
Propos sur l'histoire ... 72 Voivres, l'auteur, place de l'Église, 1970.
18 l. 28 cm. N. T. F 71-995
Includes bibliographical references.
1. History—Philosophy. I. Title.
D16.8.B28 901 74-330017

Bahig, Ahmed Fathy.
Graduate study missions to the United States as serving the national interest of the United Arab Republic (Egypt) [n.p.] 1971.
xiv, 184 l. 28 cm.
Typescript.
Thesis (Ph.D.)—Catholic University of America.
Bibliography: leaves 180-183.
1. Arab students in the United States. I. Title.
DCU NUC73-126523

Bahill, Andrew Terry.
Neurological control and the hyperfine structure of saccadic eye movements. [Berkeley] 1975.
vii, 223 l. ill.
Thesis (Ph.D. in Engineering)—University of California.
Includes bibliographies.
CU NUC77-84905

Bāhim, Na'īm.
(Nasamāt min ḥayātī)
نسمات من حياتي / نعيم باهم . — 1973 ,[s. l. : s. n.]
118 p. ; 17 cm.
I. Title.
PJ7816.A434N3 74-237218

Bahir, Arieh, 1906–1970.
(Me-Odesah la-Afikim)
מאודיסה לאפיקים / אריה בהיר ; [כינס וערך, אריה אופיר]. —
[תל-אביב] : עם עובד-תרבות וחינוך, [1975]
215 p., [4] leaves of plates : ill. ; 22 cm.
On verso of t. p.: From Odessa to Afikim.
"ברשימית ... שאותן ליקטגו מפרטיכלים, מסטינוגרמות ומרשימות."
1. Israel—Politics and government—Addresses, essays, lectures. 2. Collective settlements — Israel — Addresses, essays, lectures. 3. Afiqim, Israel—Addresses, essays, lectures. I. Title.
DS126.5.B24 1975 75-951266

Bahir.
ספר הבהיר / שחיבר רבי נחוניא בן הקנה ... — [ניו-יארק?] :
[s. n., 197-
25 [i. e. 50] p. ; 18 cm.
Reprint of the 1784 ed. printed by T. Ben Aryeh Leb, and S. Segal, Shklow.
1. Cabala. I. Neḥunya ben ha-Kanah, 1st cent. Bahir. II. Title.
Title romanized: Sefer ha-Bahir.
BM525.A3 1970z 75-950433

Bahir.
ספר הבהיר של נחוניא בן הקנה ... — לעמברג : [י. א. ל.
מרגליות?] 560 [1800]
[44] p. ; 15 cm.
1. Cabala. I. Neḥunya ben ha-Kanah, 1st cent. Bahir. II. Title.
Title romanized: Sefer ha-Bahir shel Nehunya ben ha-Kanah.
BM525.A3 1800 75-950327

Bahir. German.
Das Buch Bahir. Ein Schriftdenkmal aus der Frühzeit der Kabbala auf Grund der Kritischen Neuausgabe von Gerhard Scholem. Darmstadt, Wissenschaftliche Buchgesellschaft, 1970.
174 p. 23 cm. (Qabbala; Quellen und Forschungen zur Geschichte der jüdischen Mystik, Bd. 1)
Reprint of the 1923 Leipzig ed.
Bibliography: p. [169]-171.
I. Scholem, Gersham Gerhard, 1897-
TxU NUC74-122096

Bahirat, Bhalchandra Pandharinath, 1904–
(Vārakarī sampradāya : udaya va vikāsa)
वारकरी संप्रदाय : उदय व विकास. [लेखक] भालचंद्र पंढरीनाथ बहिरट [व] पद्मनाभ ज्ञानेश्वर भालेराव. [1. आवृत्ती] पुणे, व्हीनस प्रकाशन [1972]
15, 302 p. illus. 22 cm. Rs15.00
In Marathi.
Bibliography: p. [280]–282.

1. Varkari sect—Maharashtra, India (State) I. Bhalerao, Padmanabh Dnyaneswar, 1916– joint author. II. Title.
BL1245.V4B33 73-902937

Bahirunath Subhanji Shinde
see
Shinde, Bahirunath Subhanji.

(al-Bāḥith)
الباحث = al-Bahit : Festschrift Joseph Henninger zum 70. Geburtstag am 12. Mai 1976. — St. Augustin bei Bonn : Verlag des Anthropos-Instituts, 1976.
324 p., [3] leaves of plates : ill. ; 23 cm. — (Studia Instituti Anthropos ; vol. 28) GFR***
English, French, or German.
Bibliography of J. Henninger's works: p. [21]–36.
Includes bibliographies.
CONTENTS: Cazelles, H. Impur et sacré à Ugarit. — Chelhod, J. Le droit intertribal dans les hauts plateaux du Yémen. — Closs, A. Zarathustra unter den Propheten.—Gräf, E. Zu den christlichen Einflüssen im Koran. — Höfner, M. Ta'lab und der "Herr der Tiere" im antiken Südarabien. — Louis, A. Permanence de rites traditionnels dans les cérémonies du mariage tunisien aujourd'hui.—Pirenne, J. La religion des Arabes préislamiques d'après trois sites rupestres et leurs inscriptions.—Rowton, M. B. Dimorphic structure and the tribal elite.—Ryckmans, J. La chasse rituelle dans l'Arabie du Sud ancienne.—Serjeant, R. B. Notes on some aspects of Arab business practices in Aden.—Soden, W. v. Trunkenheit im babylonisch-assyrischen Schrifttum.
ISBN 3-921389-40-2
1. Near East — Addresses, essays, lectures. 2. Near East — Religion—Addresses, essays, lectures. 3. Arabia—Addresses, essays, lectures. 4. Near East—Social life and customs—Addresses, essays, lectures. 5. Henninger, Joseph. I. Henninger, Joseph. II. Series: Anthropos Institute. Studia ; vol. 28.
DS42.4.B34 77-474628
(MARC)

Bahjat, Aḥmad.
(Anbiyā' Allāh)
انبياء الله [تأليف] احمد بهجت. [الطبعة 1.] القاهرة ، دار الشروق [1973]
519 p. 25 cm. £E1.00
Bibliography: p. [517]
1. Prophets, Pre-Islamic. I. Title.
BP137.B34 1973 73-960261

Bahjat, Aḥmad.
(Fī riḥāb Allāh)
فى رحاب الله [تأليف] احمد بهجت. [القاهرة] الهيئة المصرية العامة للكتاب ، 1973.
175 p. 17 cm. (14 [illegible] , £E0.07
Essays.
1. Islam—Addresses, essays, lectures. I. Title. II. Series: al-Jadīd. Maṭbū'āt al-Jadīd, 14.
BP88.B23F5 73-960268

Bahjat, Aḥmad.
(Ḥayawān lahu tārīkh fī khidmat al-anbiyā')
حيوان له تاريخ فى خدمة الانبياء [تأليف] احمد بهجت. [الطبعة 1.] القاهرة ، المختار الاسلامى للطباعة والنشر والتوزيع [1973]
159 p. illus. 24 cm. £E0.50
Bibliography: p. 157.
1. Koran—Natural history. I. Title.
BP134.N3B33 73-960603

Bahjat, Aḥmad.
(Kilmitīn wi-bas)
كلمتين وبس / احمد بهجت. — ₍القاهرة : وزارة الثقافة ، الهيئة المصرية العامة للكتاب ، 1974₎
199 p. ; 17 cm. — (30 ؛ مطبوعات الجديد)
In the Cairo dialect.
£E0.10
I. Title. II. Series: al-Jadīd. Maṭbū'āt al-Jadīd ; 30.
AC106.B337 74–960559

Bahjat, Aḥmad.
(Ṣā'imūn .. wa-Allāh a'lam)
صائمون .. والله اعلم ₍تأليف₎ احمد بهجت. ₍الطبعة 1. القاهرة₎ دار الشروق ₍1972₎
199 p. illus. 19 cm. £E0.25
Essays.
I. Title.
PJ7816.A435S2 72–960783

Bahjat, Muḥammad Munīr.
(Maraḍ tha'ālīl al-baṭāṭis)
مرض ثاليل البطاطس ، وضع محمد منير بهجت. القاهرة ، المطبعة الأميرية ، 1931.
4 p. 4 plates. 22 cm.
(فرع الحجر الصحى الزراعى. العجالة ، رقم ٦. سلسلة جديدة)
At head of title: وزارة الزراعة. قسم وقاية النباتات
1. Potatoes—Diseases and pests. I. Title. II. Series: Egypt. Far' al-Ḥajr al-Ṣiḥḥī al-Zirā'ī. al-'Ujālah, silsilah jadīdah raqm 6.
SB608.P8B24 32–29824
rev

Bahjat, Rā'if.
(Tasā'ulāt rajul al-qarn al-akhīr)
تساؤلات رجل القرن الأخير ، قصائد رائف بهجت. ₍القاهرة ، 1972₎
101 p. 17 cm. £E0.20
I. Title.
PJ7816.A436T3 74–960040

Bahjat al-ḍamīr fī naẓm al-Mazāmīr.
بهجة الضمير في نظم المزامير ، مع تسابيح واغاني روحية ، «سبحوا الرب» طبع باذن سنودس النيل الانجيلي بمصر. وقد قام بجمع العلامات والحروف الموسيقية زكي افندي محمد الحلو. مصر ، المطبعة الموسيقية ، 1941.
1 v. (unpaged) 25 cm.
Paraphrases of the Psalms and other hymns, with music.
1. Sinūdus al-Nīl al-Injīlī—Hymns. 2. Hymns, Arabic. 3. Psalms (Music) I. Sinūdus al-Nīl al-Injīlī. II. al-Ḥulw, Zakī Muḥammad. III. Title: Sabbiḥū al-Rabb.
M2143.B32 72–225617

al-Bahjūrī, Fāyiz.
(Ma'a al-ṭalabah fī mushkilātihim al-'āṭifīyah wa-al-'ā'ilīyah wa-al-ijtimā'īyah)
مع الطلبة فى مشكلاتهم العاطفية والعائلية والاجتماعية / بقلم فايز البهجورى. — ₍القاهرة : المكتبة المصرية ، 1975–₎
v. : ill. ; 22 cm. — (سلسلة كتب صديقى الطالب ؛ الكتاب His 2)
£E0.2 (v. 1)
1. Students—Psychology. I. Title. II. al-Bahjūrī, Fāyiz. Silsilat kutub ṣadīqī al-ṭālib ; al-kitāb 2.
LB1117.B28 77–970838

Bahke, Erich, 1917–
Materialflusssysteme ₍von₎ E. Bahke. ₍Mainz₎ Krausskopf ₍c1974–1976₎
3 v. illus. 18 cm. (F+₍i. e. und₎ h, TB 1–3) GFR***
CONTENTS: Bd. 1. Materialflusstechnik.—Bd. 2. Materialflussmodelle.—Bd. 3. Materialflusssysteme.
ISBN 3–7830–0067–X (v. 1)
1. Materials management. I. Title.
TS161.B32 74–312993

Bahke, Erich, 1917–
Transportsysteme heute und morgen/ E. Bahke.—Mainz: Krausskopf, 1973.
182 p.: 227 ill. and graphs.; 27 cm. — (Buchreihe fördern und heben) DM72.00 GDB 73–A17
Bibliography: p. 175–182.
1. Transportation. I. Title.
TA1145.B27 380.5 73–349712
ISBN 3–7830–0005–X

Bahl, Arun Kumar.
Epidemilogy of influenza A infections in avian species in Minnesota, by Arun Kumar Bahl. [Minneapolis], 1975.
197 l. ill. (some col.) 29 cm.
Thesis (Ph. D.)—University of Minnesota.
Bibliography: 190-197.
I. Title.
MnSU NUC77-84916

Bahl, Jørgen, 1938-
Farvel, Åge og Mitzi / Jørgen Bahl. — København : Spektrum, 1976.
125 p. ; 20 cm. — (Spektrums paperbacks) D76-25/26
ISBN 8701439510 : kr30.50
I. Title.
PT8176.12.A36F3 76-479102
76 MARC

Bahl, Kali Charan.
Studies in the semantic structure of Hindi : synonymous nouns and adjectives with karana / Kali Charan Bahl. — 1st ed. — Delhi : Motilal Banarsidass, 1974–
v. ; 25 cm.
"Work was undertaken ... under the 'Project for the Preparation of a Medium Sized Dictionary of Hindi Verbs.'"
Includes index.
Rs100.00 (v. 1)
1. Hindi language—Semantics. 2. Hindi language—Verb. I. Title.
PK1939.B26 491'.43'2 74-902420
MARC

Bahl, Roy W
Estimation and economic benefits of water supply and sewerage projects ₍by₎ Roy W. Bahl, Stephen Coelen and Jeremy J. Warford. Syracuse, N.Y., Syracuse University Research Corp., 1973.
1 v. (various pagings) illus. 28 cm.
"Prepared for the Public Utilities Department of the International Bank for Reconstruction and Development by the Metropolitan and Regional Center of the Maxwell School of Syracuse University and the Syracuse University Research Corporation."
1. Water-supply. 2. Sewerage. I. Coelen, Stephen Peter, 1946- joint author. II. Warford, Jeremy J. joint author. III. Title.
NSyU NUC76-82119

Bahl, Roy W
Fiscal centralization and tax burdens : state and regional financing of city services / Roy W. Bahl and Walter Vogt. — Cambridge, Mass. : Ballinger Pub. Co., c1975.
xiv, 173 p. ; 24 cm.
Bibliography: p. 165-169.
Includes index.
ISBN 0-88410-423-0
1. Municipal finance—United States—Case studies. 2. Intergovernmental fiscal relations—United States—Case studies. 3. Intergovernmental tax relations—United States—Case studies. I. Vogt, Walter, 1943- joint author. II. Title.
HJ9145.B28 353.007'25 75-31649
75 MARC

Bahl, Roy W
Forecasting urban government expenditures : paper presented at the sixty-seventh conference of the National Tax Association / by Roy W. Bahl and Richard Gustely. — Syracuse, N.Y. : Metropolitan Studies Program, Maxwell School of Citizenship and Public Affairs, 1974.
22 leaves ; 29 cm. — (Occasional paper - Metropolitan Studies Program, Syracuse University ; no. 14)
Includes bibliographical references.
1. Expenditures, Public—Forecasting—Mathematical models. 2. New York (City)—Appropriations and expenditures—Forecasting—Mathematical models. I. Gustely, Richard D., joint author. II. Title. III. Series: Syracuse University. Metropolitan Studies Program. Occasional paper - Metropolitan Studies Program, Syracuse University ; no. 14.
HJ9125.B33 336.3'9 75-329625
75 MARC

Bahl, Roy W
State assumption of welfare and education financing : income distribution consequences : Maxwell Research Project on the Public Finances of New York City / Roy Bahl and Walter Vogt. — ₍Syracuse, N.Y.₎ : Maxwell School of Citizenship and Public Affairs, Syracuse University, 1973.
iii, 54 p. ; 28 cm. — (Working paper - Metropolitan Studies Program, Syracuse University ; no. 17)
Includes bibliographical references.
1. Taxation—New York (State) 2. Taxation—New York (City) 3. Public welfare—New York (City)—Finance. 4. Education—New York (City)—Finance. I. Vogt, Walter, 1943- joint author. II. Maxwell Research Project on the Public Finances of New York City. III. Title. IV. Series: Syracuse University. Metropolitan Studies Program. Working paper - Metropolitan Studies Program, Syracuse University ; no. 17.
HJ2424.B34 336.2'009747 75-332617
75 MARC

Bahl, Roy W
The tax burden implications of state and regional government financing of city government services / Roy W. Bahl and Walter Vogt. -- Syracuse : Metropolitan Studies Program, Syracuse University, 1975.
ca. 250 p. : tables ; 28 cm.
"Prepared for the Urban Observatory and the National League of Cities."
Includes bibliographical references.
1. Metropolitan finance--United States. 2. Local taxation. 3. Taxation, State. I. Vogt, Walter, 1943- joint author. II. Urban Observatory. III. National League of Cities. IV. Syracuse University. Metropolitan Studies Program. V. Title.
MiEM NUC77-94019

Bahl, Roy W
Taxes, expenditures, and the economic base; case study of New York City ₍by₎ Roy W. Bahl, Alan K. Campbell ₍and₎ David Greytak. New York, Praeger ₍1974₎
xxvi, 351 p. 25 cm. (Praeger special studies in U. S. economic, social, and political issues) $21.50
"Published in cooperation with the Maxwell School of Citizenship and Public Affairs, Syracuse University."
Includes bibliographical references.
1. New York (City)—Economic conditions. 2. Taxation—New York (City) 3. New York (City)—Appropriations and expenditures. I. Campbell, Alan K., joint author. II. Greytak, David, joint author. III. Title.
HC108.N7B25 336.747'1 74–1742
ISBN 0–275–08810–3 MARC

Bahl, Roy W
Urban-suburban migration patterns and metropolitan fiscal structures, by Roy W. Bahl and Robert E. Firestine. Syracuse, N.Y., Metropolitan and Regional Research Center, Maxwell School of Citizenship and Public Affairs, 1972.
53, [1] p. 28 cm. (Occasional paper, no. 8)
Bibliography: p. [54]
1. Cities and towns—Growth. 2. Urban economics. I. Firestine, Robert Edward, 1941- joint author. II. Title. III. Series: Metropolitan Studies Program. Occasional paper no. 8)
Wa NUC75-84580

Bahl, Roy W.
see The Impact of economic base erosion, inflation, and employee compensation costs on local governments. Syracuse, N.Y., Metropolitan Studies Program, Maxwell School of Citizenship and Public Affairs, 1975.

Bahl, Roy W joint author
see Puryear, David. Economic problems of a mature economy. Syracuse, N. Y., Mettopolitan Studies Program, Maxwell School of Citizenship and Public Affairs, Syracuse University, 1976.

Bahl, Roy W.
see State and local government . . . New York, Free Press, c1976.

Bahl, Roy W.
see Syracuse University. Metropolitan Studies Program. Comparative tax burdens in Manhattan, Queens, and selected New York metropolitan area suburbs. Syracuse, N.Y., Metropolitan Studies Program, Maxwell School of Citizenship and Public Affairs, 1975.

Bahl, Sohan Lal, 1930–
Exhaustive & critical commentary on the Imports & exports (control) act, 1947 (act 18 of 1947) as amended up-to-date by S. L. Bahl. 2d ed., thorougly rev., enl., and rewritten by Brijbans Kishore. Delhi, Federal Law Depot, 1970.
306, 3 p. 23 cm. Rs20.00
First ed., 1960, entered under India (Republic). Laws, statutes, etc., and has title: Commentaries on the import & export (control) act, 1947.
"The Customs act, 1962": p. 249–306.
On spine: Bahl's Commentary on the Imports & exports (control) act. 1947.
1. Foreign trade regulation—India. I. Kishore, Brijbans, joint author. II. India (Republic). Laws, statutes, etc. Imports and exports (control) act, 1947. 1970. III. India (Republic). Laws, statutes, etc. Customs act, 1962. 1970. IV. Title. V. Title: Bahl's Commentary on the Imports & exports (control) act, 1947.
343'.54'08702633 72–915767
rev MARC

Bahl, Surinder Kumar.
Structural and vibrational studies of polyesters. ₍Cincinnati₎ 1974.
viii, 133 l. 29 cm.
Thesis (Ph. D.)—University of Cincinnati.
Bibliography: leaf 133.
OCU NUC75-18356

Bahl Andersen, E
Pumpe ståi / Erik Bahl Andersen ; ₍forlagsred., Henrik Borberg ; ill., Ole Jensen ... et al.₎. — København : Teknisk forlag, 1975.
320 p. : ill. ; 22 cm. D 76-Feb
Includes index.
ISBN 87-571-0507-3 : kr132.00
1. Pumping machinery. I. Title.
TJ900.B2 77-502730

Bahlburg, Hilke Meyer-
see
Meyer-Bahlburg, Hilke.

Bahle, Julius, 1903-
Ängste und ihre Überwindung. Hemmenhofen am Bodensee, Kulturpsychologischer Verlag [1972 ?]
116 p. illus.
Includes bibliographical references.
1. Anxiety. I. Title.
PPiU NUC75-31004

Bahle, Julius, 1903-
Franz Grillparzer als Inspirationstypus / von Julius Bahle. — Gaienhofen am Bodensee : Kulturpsycholog. Verl., [1975]
107 p. ; 21 cm. — (Schöpferische Lebensformen) GFR76-B13
ISBN 3-921409-06-3 : DM15.00
1. Grillparzer, Franz, 1791-1872—Aesthetics. 2. Authors, Austrian—19th century—Biography. I. Title.
PT2272.B27 77-454418
77 MARC

Bahle, Julius, 1903-
Friedrich Hebbel als Arbeitstypus / von Julius Bahle. — Gaienhofen am Bodensee : Kulturpsycholog. Verl., [1975]
112 p. ; 21 cm. — (Schöpferische Lebensformen) GFR76-B13
ISBN 3-921409-07-1 : DM15.00
1. Hebbel, Friedrich, 1813-1863—Biography. 2. Authors, German—19th century—Biography. I. Title.
PT2296.B24 77-455977
77 MARC

Bahle, Julius, 1903-
Der geniale Mensch und Hans Pfitzner : e. psycholog. Kulturkritik / von Julius Bahle. — 2. Aufl. — Hemmenhofen am Bodensee : Kulturpsycholog. Verl., [1974].
108 p. ; 21 cm. — (Schöpferische Lebensformen) GFR76-B13
First ed. published in 1949 under title: Hans Pfitzner und der geniale Mensch.
Includes bibliographical references.
ISBN 3-921409-08-X : DM15.00
1. Pfitzner, Hans Erich, 1869-1949. I. Title.
ML410.P32B3 1974 780'.92'4 77-459219
77 MARC

Bahle, Julius, 1903-
Keine Angst vor dem Sterben; zur Psychologie des angstfreien und schönen Sterbens. Hemmenhofen am Bodensee, Kulturpsychologischer Verlag [1963 ?]
91 p.
1. Death. 2. Intermediate state. I. Title.
PPiU NUC73-126539

Bahle, Julius, 1903-
Das schöpferische Entwicklungsgesetz im Leben Goethes : e. gesetzeswiss. Psychographie / von Julius Bahle. — Hemmenhofen am Bodensee : Kulturpsycholog. Verl., [1974]
128 p. ; 21 cm. — (Schöpferische Lebensformen) GFR76-B13
Bibliography of the author's works: p. 125-128.
ISBN 3-921409-09-8 : DM18.00
1. Goethe, Johann Wolfgang von, 1749-1832—Biography—Character. 2. Authors, German—18th century—Biography. 3. Authors, German—19th century—Biography. I. Title.
PT2058.B3 77-463140
77 MARC

Bahlmann, Hellmuth
see Reichel, Wolfgang, Dipl.-Ing. Ytong Handbuch... 2., überarb. Aufl. Wiesbaden: Bauverlag, 1974.

Bahlo, Ekkehard.
Die Nagetierfauna von Heimersheim bei Alzey (Rheinhessen, Westdeutschland) aus dem Grenzbereich Mittel-/Oberoligozän und ihre stratigrafische Stellung / von Ekkehard Bahlo. — Wiesbaden : Hessisches Landesamt für Bodenforschung, 1975.
182 p. : ill. ; 24 cm. — (Abhandlungen des Hessischen Landesamtes für Bodenforschung ; Heft 71) GFR***
Summary in English and French.
Bibliography: p. 172-175.
Includes index.
1. Rodentia, Fossil. 2. Paleontology—Oligocene. 3. Paleontology—Germany, West—Alzey. I. Title: Die Nagetierfauna von Heimersheim bei Alzey ... II. Series: Hesse. Landesamt für Bondenforschung. Abhandlungen ; Heft 71.
QE882.R6B33 75-522294
76 MARC

Bahlow, Ferdinand, 1865-1942
see Die Peter-Paul-Kirche zu Liegnitz. Lorch (Württ.) : Weber, 1972.

Bahlow, Hans, 1900-
Deutsches Namenlexikon: Familien- u. Vornamen nach Ursprung u. Sinn erklärt/ Hans Bahlow. — Frankfurt (am Main) : Suhrkamp, 1972.
588 p.; 18 cm. (Suhrkamp-Taschenbücher; 65) DM10.00
GDB 72-A48
1. Names, Personal—German. I. Title.
CS2541.B3 1972 72-375354
ISBN 3-518-06565-3

Bahlow, Hans, 1900-
Liegnitzer Namenbuch : Familiennamen, gedeutet aus d. Quellen d. Mittelalters / von Hans Bahlow. — Lorch/Württ. : Weber, 1975.
158 p. : facsim. ; 21 cm. — (Beiträge zur Liegnitzer Geschichte ; Bd. 5) GFR76-A11
ISBN 3-87888-029-4 : DM27.50
1. Names, Personal—German. 2. Names, Personal—Poland—Legnica. 3. Legnica, Poland—Genealogy. I. Title. II. Series.
CS2549.L43B33 929.4'0943 76-461945
76 MARC

Bahlow, Hans, 1900-
Mittelhochdeutsches Namenbuch nach schlesischen Quellen : ein Denkmal d. Deutschtums / von Hans Bahlow. — Neustadt (an der Aisch) : Degener, 1975.
182 p. : maps ; 25 cm. GFR75-A
Bibliography: p. 177-182.
ISBN 3-7686-9010-X : DM48.00
1. Names, Personal—Middle High German, 1050-1500. 2. Names, Personal—Silesia. I. Title.
CS2549.S54B34 76-473875
76 MARC

Bahlow, Hans, 1900–
Niederdeutsche Namenwelt : Erscheinungsbild und Wesensgehalt / von Hans Bahlow. — Hamburg : H. Bahlow, 1973.
16 p. : ill. ; 21 cm. GFR***
1. Low German language—Etymology—Names. 2. Names, Low German. I. Title.
PF5621.B3 76-517407

Bahlow, Hans, 1900–
Niederdeutsches Namenbuch. [Walluf bei Wiesbaden] M. Sändig [c1972]
572 p. 22 cm. GDB***
Bibliography: p. 557-560.
1. Names, Personal—Low German. I. Title.
CS2545.B33 73-318131
ISBN 3-500-25300-8

Bahlow, Hans, 1900–
see Die Peter-Paul-Kirche zu Liegnitz. Lorch (Württ.) : Weber, 1972.

Bahls, Dietrich, 1938-
Schiffsgläubigerrechte nach deutschem und amerikanischem Recht. Speyer, 1971.
xxix, 277 p. 21 cm.
Inaug.-Diss.-Kiel.
Vita.
"Anhang: Auszug aus Vorschriften des Titel 46 - Shipping - nach United States Code, 1964 edition", p. [261]-277, in English.
Bibliography: p. x-xxiii.
1. Liens. Germany (Federal Republic, 1949-) 2. Liens. United States. 3. Ship mortgages. Germany (Federal Republic, 1949-) 4. Ship mortgages. U.S. I. Title.
MnU-L NUC74-122127

Bahls, Jerold Oscar.
Substituent effects in ring expansion reactions of isatogens with acetylenes. [Minneapolis] 1972.
x, 215 l. illus. 29 cm.
Thesis (Ph.D.)—University of Minnesota.
Bibliography: leaves 212-215.
MnU NUC76-68342

Bahls, Loren L
Ground water seepage and its effects on saline soils / by Loren L. Bahls and Marvin R. Miller. — Bozeman : Montana University Joint Water Resources Research Center, Montana State University, 1975.
39 leaves : ill. ; 29 cm. — (MUJWRRC report ; no. 66)
Bibliography: leaves 37-39.
1. Soils, Salts in. 2. Groundwater flow. 3. Soils—Montana. I. Miller, Marvin R., joint author. II. Title. III. Series: Montana University Joint Water Resources Research Center. Report ; no. 66.
S595.B33 631.4'16 76-621562
76 MARC

Bahlsen, Werner
see Instrumente der Unternehmensführung... München: Hanser, 1973.

Bahlūl, Ḥasan bar
see Ḥasan bar Bahlūl, fl. 963.

Bahm, Archie J
Comparative philosophy : Western, Indian, and Chinese philosophies compared / Archie J. Bahm. — Albuquerque, N.M. : Universal Publications, c1977.
xiii, 98 p. ; 23 cm.
Publisher covered by label: World Books.
Includes bibliographical references and index.
ISBN 0-911714-07-3
1. Philosophy, Comparative.
B799.B34 100 76-10406
77 MARC

Bahm, Archie J
Ethics as a behavioral science, by Archie J. Bahm. Springfield, Ill., Thomas [1974]
ix, 203 p. 24 cm.
Includes bibliographical references.
1. Ethics. I. Title.
[DNLM: 1. Behavioral sciences. 2. Ethics. BJ 37 B151e 1974]
BJ1012.B34 170 73-16166
ISBN 0-398-03043-X ; 0-398-03044-8 (pbk.) MARC

Bahm, Archie J
Executive yoga. New York, Paperback Library [1972, c1965]
352 p. illus. 18 cm.
Translation of Yoga for business executives and professional people.
Bibliography: p. 337-339.
1. Yoga, Hatha. I. Title.
NBuU NUC73-32359

Bahm, Archie J
The heart of Confucius; interpretations of Genuine living and Great wisdom [by] Archie J. Bahm. With a foreword by Thomé H. Fang. New York, Harper & Row [1971, c1969]
159 p. illus. 19 cm. (Perennial library)
Bibliography: p. 155-156.
1. Chung yung. 2. Ta hsüeh. I. Confucius. II. Chung yung. English. 1969. III. Ta hsüeh. English. 1969. IV. Title.
NBuU NUC75-31022

Bahm, Archie J
Metaphysics; an introduction [by] Archie J. Bahm. New York, Barnes & Noble Books [1974]
259 p. 21 cm. $2.95
Includes bibliographical references.
1. Metaphysics. 2. Causation. 3. Dialectic.
BD111.B15 1974 110 73-7469
ISBN 0-06-463338-1 MARC

Bahm, Archie J
The world's living religions [by] Archie J. Bahm. Carbondale, Southern Illinois University Press [1971, c1964]
384 p. 21 cm. (Arcturus books, AB87)
Bibliography: p. [360]-369.
1. Religions. I. Title.
MeB NSyU NcD CaOTP NUC73-32415

Bahm, Gerd.
Dimensionierungsverfahren für Freibäder / Gerd Bahm. — Karlsruhe : Institut für Städtebau und Landesplanung, Universität Karlsruhe, 1973.
79 p. : graphs, [6] fold. col. maps ; 30 cm. GFR***
Bibliography: p. 74-75.
1. Swimming—Ruhr Valley—Directories. 2. Ruhr Valley—Recreational activities. I. Title.
GV838.4.G3B33 77-455285
77 MARC

Bahm, Robert M 1944-
The influence of non-sexual cues, sexual explicitness and sex guilt on female's erotic response to literature. Amherst, 1972.
vi, 105 l. illus. 28 cm.
Thesis (Ph.D.)—University of Massachusetts.
Microfilm no. 1655.
1. Woman—Sexual behavior. I. Title.
MU NUC74-487

Bahmanyār, Ahmad, ed.
see Bahā' al-Dīn Baghdādī, Muhammad ibn Mu'ayyad, 12th cent. al-Tavassul ilá al-tarassul. 1315 [1937]

Bahmanyar, M
Plague manual / M. Bahmanyar, D. C. Cavanaugh. — Geneva : World Health Organization ; [Albany : available from Q Corp.], 1976.
76 p., [1] leaf of plates : ill. ; 28 cm. Sw***
Bibliography: p. 63-64.
ISBN 9241540516 : 20.00F
1. Plague—Prevention. 2. Plague—Transmission. 3. Epidemiology. I. Cavanaugh, D. C., joint author. II. Title.
RA644.P7B34 614.5'73'2 77-354115
77 MARC

Bahmat, Yehuda
see
Bachmat, Y

Bahme, Charles William, 1914-
Fire officer's guide to dangerous chemicals, by Charles W. Bahme. Boston, National Fire Protection Association [1972]
239 p. illus.
1. Chemicals—Fires and fire prevention. I. Title.
ViBlbV NUC74-15

Bahme, Charles William, 1914–
Fire officer's guide to emergency action, by Charles W. Bahme. Boston, National Fire Protection Association [1974]
185 p. illus. 21 cm. (National Fire Protection Association. NFPA no. FSP-38)
1. Firemen's manuals. I. Title. II. Series.
TH9115.N28 no. FSP-38 628.9'2'08 s 73-89341
[TH9151] [628.9'25'0202] MARC
ISBN 0-87765-020-9

Bahme, Charles William, 1914-
Fire officer's guide to emergency action / by Charles W. Bahme. — 3d ed. — Boston : National Fire Protection Association, 1976.
ix, 259 p. : ill. ; 20 cm. — (NFPA ; no. FSP-38)
1. Fire fighters—Handbooks, manuals, etc. I. Title. II. Series: National Fire Protection Association. NFPA ; no. FSP-38.
TH9115.N28 no. FSP-38 1976 628.9'2'08 s 77-359444
[TH9151] 77 MARC

Bahme, Charles William, 1914-
Fire officer's guide to extinguishing systems. Boston, Mass., National Fire Protection Association [1970]
vii, 101 p. illus. 20 cm.
AAP NUC73-39689

Bahme, Charles William, 1914-
Fire service and the law / by Charles W. Bahme. — Boston : National Fire Protection Association, c1976.
xii, 267 p. ; 25 cm. — (NFPA ; no. FSP-3A)
Includes bibliographical references.
ISBN 0-87765-081-0
1. Fire prevention—United States—Laws and regulations. I. Title. II. Series: National Fire Protection Association. NFPA ; no. ESP-3A.
TH9115.N28 no. FSP-3A 76-26786
628.9'2'08 s
[KF3975] 77 MARC

Bahmet, Mykola Stepanovych
see Bagmet, Nikolaĭ Stepanovich.

Bahmhauer, Otto.
Comunicación y educación. Buenos Aires, Centro de Investigaciones en Ciencias de la Educación, 1972.
32 p. 29 cm. (Centro de Investigaciones en Ciencias de la Educación. Documento de trabajo, 4)
1. Education—Latin America. 2. Educational innovations—Latin America. I. Title. II. Series.
TU NcU NUC75-96469

Bahmueller, Charles Ferdinand.
The end of contingency; Bentham on poverty, by Charles Ferdinand Bahmueller, Jr. [n.p.] 1975.
xxii, 446 l. 29 cm.
Thesis—Harvard.
Bibliography: leaves 443-446.
1. Bentham, Jeremy, 1748-1832.
MH NUC77-84904

Bahmut, Alla Iosypivna
see Intonatsiia iak movnyĭ zasib vyrazhennia dumky. 1975.

Bahmut, Iosyp Andriianovych.
(Problemy perekladu suspil'no-politychnoï literatury ukraïns'koiu movoiu)
Проблеми перекладу суспільно-політичної літератури українською мовою. Київ, "Наукова думка," 1968.
299 p. 21 cm. USSR***
At head of title: Академия наук Української РСР. Інститут мовознавства ім. О. О. Потебні, Й. А. Багмут.
Bibliographical footnotes.
1.19rub
1. Ukrainian language—Translating. I. Title.
PG3880.5.B3 70-442028

Bahmut, Iosyp Andriianovych.
(Ridne slovo)
Рідне слово; розвиток мови й мовознавства в УРСР. Київ, Наук. думка, 1969.
70 p. illus., facsims., ports. 17 cm. USSR***
At head of title: И. А. Багмут, В. И. Русанівский.
Includes bibliographical references.
0.23rub
1. Ukrainian language. 2. Linguistic research—History—Ukraine. I. Rusanivskyĭ, Vitaliĭ Makarovych, joint author. II. Title.
PG3816.B3 70-499194

Bahmut, Ivan Adrianovych.
Pryhody chornoho kota lapchenka, opysani nym samym. Blakytne pleso. Opovidannia. Kyïv, Veselka, 1973.
300 p. col. plates. 21 cm.
At head of title: Ivan Bahmut.
"Dlia seredn'oho shkil'noho viku."
I. Title.
PSt NUC75-138743

Bahmut, Ivan Adrianovych.
(Zapiski soldata)
Записки солдата : повести и рассказы / Иван Багмут ; авторизованный перевод с украинского. — Москва : Сов. писатель, 1976.
318 p. : ill. ; 20 cm. USSR***
CONTENTS: Записки солдата.—Жизнеописание послушного молодого человека.—Кусок пирога.—Злыдни.—Сквозь чащу.—В яблоневом саду.—Братья.—Теги-теги.
0.50rub
I. Title.
PG3948.B227Z22 77-508288

Bahn, Anita K., joint author
see Mausner, Judith S Epidemiology... Philadelphia, Saunders, 1974.

Bahn, Charles.
Against delinquency, drugs, and despair; final report -evaluation of the East Harlem Youth Employment Service, inc. [New York?] 1971.
viii, 211 p. illus. 28 cm.
1. East Harlem Youth Employment Service. 2. Youth—Employment—New York (City) 3. Vocational guidance—New York (City) I. Title.
HD5876.N5B34 362.7'09747'1 73-622020
MARC

Bahn, Erwin
see Müncheberg, Ger. Institut für Acker- und Pflanzenbau. Zweigstelle Bad Lauchstädt. Der statische Versuch Lauchstädt in sieben Jahrzehnten. Berlin, Deutsche Akademie d. Landwirtschaftswissenschaften, 1970.

Bahn, Eugene, joint author
see Brooks, Keith, 1923- The communicative act of oral interpretation. 2d ed. Boston : Allyn and Bacon, [1975]

Bahn, Gilbert S
On gas-phase chemical kinetics in the burning of particulate boron in dry air. Van Nuys, Calif., Marquardt Corp. [1967?]
22 l. illus. (Combustion Institute. Western States Section. Paper 67-26)
ICRL NUC74-122132

Bahn, Gilbert S
Status report of effort on engineering selection of reaction rate constants for gaseous chemical species at high temperatures, with a review of $H + CO_2 = OH + CO$ and $CO_2 + M = O + CO + M$. Van Nuys, Calif., Marquardt Corp., 1967.
44 l. illus. (Combustion Institute. Western States Section. Paper 67-11)
ICRL NUC74-122129

Bahn, Gilbert S
A summary of auxiliary activities in the area of finite-kinetics calculations. Van Nuys, Calif., Marquardt Corp. [1968?]
6 p. (Combustion Institute. Western States Section. Paper 68-54)
ICRL NUC74-122130

Bahn, Walter.
Der Prozess der Frau v. Schoenebeck-Weber. Berlin, H. Steinitz, 1910.
142 p. 19 cm.
1. Schoenebeck, Antonie von. I. Title.
75-548084

Bahnām, Jamshīd.
Cultural policy in Iran [by] Djamchid Behnam. Paris, Unesco, 1973.
46 p. illus. 24 cm. (Studies and documents on cultural policies) $2.00 (U.S.) F***
Includes bibliographical references.
1. Arts—Iran—Management. I. Title. II. Series.
NX770.I 7B34 338.4'7'700955 73-174818
ISBN 92-3-101002-6 MARC

Bahnām, Jamshīd.
La population de l'Iran : monographie / rédigée par Djamchid Behnam et Mehdi Amani. — [Paris] : CICRED, 1974.
74, [6] p. : ill. ; 23 cm. — (C.I.C.R.E.D. series) F***
On cover: 1974, World population year.
Bibliography: p. [79]
1. Iran—Population. 2. Iran—Statistics, Vital. I. Amani, Mehdi, joint author. II. Title. III. Series: Committee for International Coordination of National Research in Demography. C.I.C.R.E.D. series.
HB3636.4.A3B34 77-477268
77 MARC

Bahnām, Jamshīd.
Structures et mouvements de la population iranienne [par] Djamchid Behnam. [Teheran] Institut d'études et de recherches sociales, université de Teheran, 1962.
60 l. illus. 26 cm.
1. Iran—Population. 2. Iran—Statistics, Vital. I. Title.
NNC NUC75-9740

al-Bahnasi, 'Afif.
Dictionnaire trilingue des termes d'art, français, anglais, arabe par Afif Bahnassi. Mu'jam mustalahat al-funun. Damascus, L'Académie Arabe de Damas, 1971.
311, 188 p. illus.
Added t.p. in Arabic.
1. Art—Dictionaries—Polyglot. I. Title.
WaU NUC75-41921

al-Bahnasī, 'Afīf.
(Dirāsāt naẓarīyah fī al-fann al-'Arabī)
دراسات نظرية فى الفن العربى / عفيف البهنسى. — [القاهرة] : الهيئة المصرية العامة للكتاب ، 1974.
239 p. : ill. ; 17 cm. — (المكتبة الثقافية ؛ 300)
«عدد ممتاز»
Includes bibliographical references.
£E0.10
1. Art, Arabic. 2. Art, Islamic—Arab countries. I. Title.
N7265.B34 74-960311

al-Bahnasī, 'Afīf.
('Ilm al-jamāl 'inda Abī Ḥayyān al-Tawḥīdī wa-masā'il fī al-fann)
علم الجمال عند ابي حيان التوحيدي ومسائل في الفن / عفيف بهنسي. — [بغداد] : وزارة الاعلام، مديرية الثقافة العامة، [1972?]
152 p. : ill. (some col.) ; 22 cm. — (السلسلة الفنية ؛ 18)
Series romanized: al-Silsilah al-fannīyah.
Includes bibliographical references.
1. Abū Ḥayyān al-Tawḥīdī, 'Alī ibn Muḥammad, 10th cent.—Aesthetics. 2. Art—Addresses, essays, lectures. I. Title.
PJ7750.A26Z58 75-972684

al-Bahnasī, 'Afīf.
(Ittijāhāt al-funūn al-tashkīlīyah al-mu'āṣirah)
اتجاهات الفنون التشكيلية المعاصرة / عفيف بهنسي. — [دمشق] : وزارة الثقافة والارشاد القومى، مديرية التأليف والترجمة، [1962?]
139, 8 p., [20] leaves of plates : ill. ; 24 cm. — (السلسلة الفنية ؛ 1)
French-Arabic glossary of technical terms: p. 3-7 (2d group)
Bibliography: p. 8 (2d group)
1. Art, Modern—20th century. I. Title.
N6490.B244 75-549346

al-Bahnasī, 'Afīf.
(Mu'jam muṣṭalaḥāt al-funūn)
معجم مصطلحات الفنون، ثلاثي اللغات، عربي – انكليزي – فرنسي، فرنسي – انكليزي – عربي، انكليزي – فرنسي – عربي. تأليف عفيف البهنسي. [دمشق، المقدمة 1972]
[8], 178, 315 p. illus. 24 cm. (مطبوعات مجمع اللغة العربية بدمشق)
Added t. p.: Dictionnaire des termes d'art, français — anglais — arabe, par Afif Bahnassi. Revisé par une commission des membres de l'Académie arabe de Damas, MM Abdul-Hadi Hachem, Salah ed-din Kawakibi, et Wajih Samman.
Bibliography: p. [6] (1st group)
1. Art—Terminology—Polyglot. I. Title. II. Title: Dictionnaire des termes d'art. III. Series: Majma' al-Lughah al-'Arabīyah bi-Dimashq. al-Maṭbū'āt.
N34.B33 73-208844

Bahnasī, Aḥmad Fatḥī.
(Madkhal al-fiqh al-jinā'ī al-Islāmī)
مدخل الفقه الجنائى الاسلامى [تأليف] احمد فتحى بهنسى. [القاهرة] دار الشروق [1973]
212 p. 25 cm. £E0.60
Bibliography: p. [201]-204.
1. Criminal law (Islamic law) I. Title.
73-960154

Bahnasī, Aḥmad Fatḥī.
La responsabilité criminelle dans la doctrine et la jurisprudence musulmanes / par Ahmad Fathi Bahnassi ; traducteur, Mohammad A. Ambar ; réviseur, Ahmad Ahmad Moukhtar. — Le Caire : Conseil supérieur des affaires islamiques, 1970.
332 p. ; 20 cm. — (Série Études sur l'islam)
Translation of al-Mas'ūliyah al-jinā'iyah fī al-fiqh al-Islāmī.
Includes bibliographical references.
1. Criminal liability (Islamic law) I. Title: La responsabilité criminelle dans la doctrine ... II. Series.
77-482384
77 MARC

Bahnasī, Aḥmad Fatḥī.
العقوبة فى الفقه الاسلامى ، تأليـف احمد فتحـى بهنسى.
الطبعة 2. ، مزيدة. القاهرة ، مكتبة دار العروبة ، 1961.
236 p. 25 cm.
Bibliography: p. [227]–228.
1. Punishment (Islamic law) I. Title.
Title romanized: al-'Uqūbah fī al-fiqh al-Islāmī.
75–586950

Bahnassi, Afif
see
Bahnasī, 'Afīf.

Bahnassi, Ahmad Fathi
see Bahnasī, Ahmad Fathhī.

Bahndare, R. D.
see India (Republic). Parliament. House of the People. Select Committee on the Advocates (Second Amendment) Bill, 1968. The Advocates (Second Amendment) Bill, 1968... New Delhi, Lok Sabha Secretariat, 1970.

Bahne, Siegfried.
Die Freiherren Ludwig und Georg Vincke im Vormärz / Siegfried Bahne. — Dortmund : Verlag des Histor. Verein, 1975.
168 p., [1] leaf of plates : ill. ; 21 cm. — (Monographien zur Geschichte Dortmunds und der Grafschaft Mark ; Bd. 5) GFR76-A
Bibliography: p. 160-163.
Includes index.
1. Westphalia—Politics and government. 2. Vincke, Friedrich Ludwig Wilhelm Philipp, Freiherr von, 1774-1844. 3. Vincke, Georg, Freiherr von, 1811-1875. I. Title. II. Series.
DD901.D6M6 Bd. 5 76-473479
[DD491.W48] 76 MARC

Bahne, Siegfried.
Die KPD und das Ende von Weimar : d. Scheitern e. Politik 1932-1935 / Siegfried Bahne. — 1. Aufl. — Frankfurt/Main ; New York : Campus-Verlag, 1976.
184 p. ; 19 cm. — (Campus Studium : Sozialgeschichte) GFR76-A
Bibliography: p. 137-181.
Includes index.
ISBN 3-593-32515-2
1. Kommunistische Partei Deutschlands—History. 2. Germany—History—1918-1933. I. Title.
JN3970.K6B35 329.9'43 76-466237
76 MARC

Bahner, Werner.
Aufklärung als Periodenbegriff der Ideologiegeschichte; einige methodologische Überlegungen und Grundsätze. Berlin, Akademie-Verlag, 1973.
26 p. 22 cm. (Sitzungsberichte des Plenums und der Klassen der Akademie der Wissenschaften der DDR, Jahrg. 1972, Nr. 9) 3.00M
GDR***
Lectures delivered by the author at the Akademie der Wissenschaften der DDR on Apr. 6, Sept. 21, and Oct. 19, 1972.
Includes bibliographical references.
1. Enlightenment. 2. Philosophy, Modern—18th century. 3. Ideology—History. I. Title. II. Series: Akademie der Wissenschaften der DDR. Sitzungsberichte des Plenums und der Klassen, Jahrg. 1972, Nr. 9.
B802.B3 190'.9'033 74–329384

Bahner, Werner.
Formen, Ideen, Prozesse in den Literaturen der romanischen Völker / Werner Bahner. — Berlin : Akademie-Verlag, 1977-
v. ; 20 cm. — (Literatur und Gesellschaft) GDR77-A (v. 1)
Essays.
Includes bibliographical references and index.
CONTENTS: Bd. 1. Von Dante bis Cervantes.

9.00M (v. 1)
1. Romance literature—History and criticism—Addresses, essays, lectures. I. Title.
PN804.B34 77-554755
77 MARC

Bahner, Werner
see Markov, Walter M Nicolae Iorga (1871-1940)... Berlin, Akademie-Verlag, 1972.

Bahner, Werner.
see Renaissance, Barock, Aufklärung ... Berlin, Akademie-Verlag, 1976.

Bahner, Werner.
see Renaissance, Barock, Aufklärung ... Kronberg/Ts., Scriptor Verlag, 1976.

Bahners, Klaus, 1943–
Struktur und Poetik des bürgerlichen Romans in Frankreich um 1700: "Les illustres françoises" von Robert Chasles/ Klaus Bahners. — 1. Aufl. — Tübingen: Huth, 1973.
114 p.; 21 cm. — (Das wissenschaftliche Arbeitsbuch: 6, 19)
DM9.80 GFR 73–A
Bibliography: p. 101–114.
1. Challes, Robert, 1659–ca. 1720. Les illustres françoises. I. Title.
PQ1963.C35A733 73–351153
ISBN 3-87369-019-5

Bahnert, Gerhard.
Möglichkeiten und Grenzen der trigonometrischen Höhenmessung. (Leipzig, Geodätischer Dienst, 1970.)
2 v. illus. 24 cm. (Arbeiten aus dem Vermessungs- und Kartenwesen der Deutschen Demokratischen Republik, Bd. 24, 25)
GDNB 71–B24–341
Bibliography: v. 2, p. 72–86.
Habilitationsschrift—Technische Universität Dresden.
1. Altitudes—Measurement. I. Title. II. Series.
TA504.A7 Bd. 24–25 73–314673
[TA609]

Bahney, Robert Stanley, 1922-
Generals and Negroes: education of Negroes by the Union Army, 1861-1865. [n. p.] 1965.
iv, 301 l.
Thesis—University of Michigan.
Bibliography: leaves 275-301.
Microfilm (positive) Ann Arbor, Mich., University Microfilms, 1966. 1 reel. (Publication no. 5035)
NNC NUC76-68666

Bahney, Robert Stanley, 1922-
Generals and Negroes: education of Negroes by the Union Army, 1861-1865. [Ann Arbor, Mich.] 1965.
iv, 301 l.
Thesis—University of Michigan.
Bibliography: leaves 275-301.
Photocopy. Ann Arbor, Mich., University Microfilms, 1972. 20 cm.
1. Negroes—Education. 2. U. S.—Hist.—Civil War—Negroes. I. Title.
CtY NUC76-37748

Bahnhöfe im Spiegel alter Postkarten / hrsg. von Horst-Werner Dumjahn. — Hildesheim ; New York : Olms, 1976.
76 p. : chiefly ill. ; 24 cm. GFR76-A
Includes bibliographical references.
ISBN 3-487-08129-6
1. Railroads—Europe—Stations—Pictorial works. I. Dumjahn, Horst-Werner.
TF302.E85B34 76-487931
77 MARC

(Bahni-śikharī)
বহ্নি-শিখরী. [সম্পাদনায়: রহমান ফারুক. ঢাকা, ভাস্কর সাংস্কৃতিক গোষ্ঠী, 1972]
38 p. 23 cm. Tk1.00
Cover title.
In Bengali.

1. Pakistan—Languages—Addresses, essays, lectures. 2. Bengali language—Addresses, essays, lectures. I. Phāruka, Rahamāna, ed.

JQ546.L3B33 72–907418

Bahnick, Donald A.
see Effect of south shore drainage basins and clay erosion... Madison, 1972.

Bahnick, Karen R
The determination of stages in the historical development of the Germanic languages by morphological criteria: an evaluation. By Karen R. Bahnick. The Hague, Mouton, 1973.
215 p. 26 cm. (Janua linguarum. Series practica, 139)
Ne 73–32
Bibliography: p. [205]–209.
1. Germanic languages—History. 2. Germanic languages—Word formation. 3. Germanic languages—Inflection. 4. Generative grammar. I. Title. II. Series.
PD75.B3 430 74–173389
MARC

Bahník, Václav, tr.
see Cicero, Marcus Tullius. Reči proti Verrovi. Praha, Odeon, t. Stráž, Vimperk, 1972.

Bahník, Václav
see Cicero, Marcus Tullius. Tuskulské hovory... Praha: Svoboda, 1976.

Bahník, Václav, tr.
see Xenophon. Vzpomínky na Sókrata a jiné spisy. Praha, Svoboda, t. Rudé právo, 1972.

Bahnimptewa, Cliff, illus.
see Wright, Barton. Kachinas... Flagstaff [Ariz.] Northland Press [1973]

Bahniuk, Gene
see The Biomechanics of contemporary ski bindings. Cleveland [1972?]

Bahnmüller, Wilfried
see Scheingraber, Wernher. Tegernseer Tal. Freilassing : Pannonia-Verlag, 1974.

Bahnmüller, Wilfried
see Schwanthaler-Krippen. Rosenheim : Rosenheimer Verlagshaus Förg, 1974.

Bahnová, J., ed.
see Vydavatel'stvo Osveta. 10 [i. e. Desat'] rokov Vydavatel'stva Osveta. [Bratislava, 1963]

Bahnsen, Martin, 1809–1875.
Martin Bahnsens dagbøger; en rådmands beretning om Aabenraas besættelse, 1864–66. København, Urania, 1964.
124 p. illus. 22 cm.
Ed. by B. Holbek and A. Piø.
Bibliography: p. 120.
1. Aabenraa—History. 2. Schleswig-Holstein War, 1864—Personal narratives.
DL291.A15B33 74–206430

Bahnsen, Uwe, 1934- joint author.
see O'Donnell, James Preston, 1917- Die Katakombe ... Stuttgart, Deutsche Verlags-Anstalt, c1975.

Bahnsen, Uwe, 1934- tr.
see Parkinson, Cyril Northcote, 1909- Good-bye, Karl Marx. [2. Aufl. Hamburg] Hoffmann und Campe [1970]

Bahnson, Henry T., 1920- joint author
see Crisler, Crile. Aneurysms of the aorta. Chicago, Year Book Medical Publishers [1972]

Bahnson, Inger.
Det er jo mit liv! / Inger Bahnson ; fortalt til Leif Toklum. — København : Borgen, 1975.
113 p. ; 22 cm. D 75–40
ISBN 87-418-3517-4 : kr39.00
1. Oral contraceptives—Side effects. 2. Cerebral embolism and thrombosis—Biography. 3. Bahnson, Inger. I. Toklum, Leif. II. Title.
RG137.5.B25 76–530256

Bahnson, Karsten.
see Student und Hochschule im 19. [i.e. neunzehnten] Jahrhundert ... Göttingen, Vandenhoeck und Ruprecht, 1975.

Bahoken, J C
Cultural policy in the United Republic of Cameroon / J. C. Bahoken and Engelbert Atangana. — Paris : The Unesco Press, 1976.
91 p., [2] leaves of plates : ill. ; 24 cm. — (Studies and documents on cultural policies) F***
Includes bibliographical references.
ISBN 9231013165
1. Arts—Cameroon—Management. 2. Art and state—Cameroon. I. Atangana, Engelbert, joint author. II. Title. III. Series.
NX770.C17B33 354'.67'110085 76-381338
76 MARC

Bāhoo, Sultān
see
Sulṭān Bāhū, 1630-1691.

Bahorī, Abdumalik.
(Abdumalik Bahorī)
Абдумалик Баҳорӣ. Душанбе, "Ирфон," 1973.
62 p. 14 cm. (Илҳом) 0.06rub USSR 73–14052
Short stories.
CONTENTS: Дод аз дасти ёр. — Одами маданӣ. — Қадаҳи якӯм.—Чӣ маслиҳат медиҳед.—Садақа.—Қиссаҳои якшингила.—Мухлисони санъат.
PK6978.9.B3A65 74–314995

Bahori, Abdumalik.
(Ajoibotí Nodar)
Аҷоиботи Нодар. Киссаи фантастикӣ (кисми 2). [Барои наврасон ва ҷавонон. Рассом В. Чечётка]. Душанбе, "Ирфон," 1972.
112 p. illus. 22 cm. 0.16rub USSR 72-41542
At head of title: А. Бахорӣ.

I. Title.
PZ90.T28B3 73-336408

Bahori, Abdumalik
see Muhabbat va ghazab. 1973.

Bahorik, John Wesley, 1941-
A study of the effects of information items on Snyder's 1968 prototheory of instructional efficiency as applied to a genetics problem-solving situation. [n.p.] 1972.
176 l.
Thesis (Ph. D.)—Pennsylvania State University.
I. Title.
PSt NUC74-491

Bahovaddinov, A M
see
Bogoutdinov, Alautdin Makhmudovich.

Bahr, Albrecht
see Rammler, Erich. Beiträge zur Zerkleinerung und Korngrössenverteilung. Leipzig: Deutscher Verlag f. Grundstoffindustrie, VEB, 1972.

Bahr, Albrecht
see Rammler, Erich. Verfahrenstechnische Grundlagen der Braunkohlenbrikettierung... Leipzig: Deutscher Verlag für Grundstoffindustrie, VEB, 1973.

Bahr, Alois, 1834-1898
see Bahr, Hermann, 1863-1934. Hermann Bahr. Wien, H. Bauer (1971)

Bahr, Donald M
Pima and Papago ritual oratory ; a study of three texts. O'odham ha-Niokculida ; Mamce ab waikk ha'icu Amjed. -- San Francisco, Indian Historian Press, 1975.
121 p. : ill.
Bibliography: p. 113-114.
Includes bibliography.
1. Indians of North America--Oratory. 2. Pima Indians--Oratory. 3. Papago Indians--Oratory. I. Title.
WHi NUC77-87826

Bahr, Donald M.
see Piman shamanism and staying sickness Tucson, University of Arizona Press [1974]

Bahr, Edith-Jane.
Help, please. [1st ed.] Garden City, N. Y., Published for the Crime Club by Doubleday, 1975.
177 p. 22 cm.
ISBN 0-385-09776-X
I. Title.
PZ4.B1483He 813'.5'4 74-9474
[PS3552.A36] MARC

Bahr, Edith-Jane.
A nice neighbourhood. London, Collins [for] the Crime Club [1973]
192 p. 21 cm. £1.70 GB***
I. Title.
PZ4.B1483 813'.5'4 74-166288
[PS3552.A36] MARC
ISBN 0-00-231570-X

Bahr, Egon, 1922-
see Cramer, Dettmar. Egon Bahr. Bornheim, Zirngibl, 1975.

Bahr, Egon, 1922-
see Hessenforum, 4th, Kassel, 1974. Bilanz der neuen Ostpolitik ... Frankfurt (am Main) : Aspekte-Verlag, 1974.

Bahr, Ehrhard.
Ernst Bloch. Berlin, Colloquium Verlag [c1974]
94 p. 20 cm. (Köpfe des XX. Jahrhunderts, Bd. 76) GFR***
Bibliography: p. 90-91.
1. Bloch, Ernst, 1885-
B3209.B78B33 74-319572
ISBN 3-7678-0358-5

Bahr, Ehrhard.
La pensée de Georg Lukács. [Traduction de Jean Lyon. Toulouse] Privat [c1972]
116 p. 21 cm. (Pensée)
Translation of Georg Lukács.
Includes bibliography.
1. Lukács, György, 1885-1971. I. Title.
MiDW CaOOU InNd NUC74-120663
VtMiM

Bahr, Ehrhard, comp.
Was ist Aufklärung? : Thesen u. Definitionen / Kant ... [et al.] ; Hrsg. von Ehrhard Bahr. — Stuttgart : Reclam, 1974.
85 p. ; 16 cm. — (Universal-Bibliothek ; Nr. 9714) GFR 74-A29
Bibliography: p. 67-70.
ISBN 3-15-009714-2 : DM1.50
1. Enlightenment. 2. Philosophy, German—18th century. 3. Germany—Intellectual life. I. Title.
B2621.B33 75-567604

Bahr, Ernst, writer on eastern Europe.
Oberschlesien nach dem zweiten Weltkrieg : Verwaltung, Bevölkerung, Wirtschaft / Ernst Bahr, Richard Breyer, Ekkehard Buchhofer ; im Auftr. d. Johann-Gottfried-Herder-Forschungsrates hrsg. von Richard Breyer. — Marburg/Lahn : Johann-Gottfried-Herder-Institut, 1975.
xii, 342 p. : 5 fold. maps (in pocket) ; 24 cm. GFR76-A
Includes bibliographies and indexes.
ISBN 3-87969-105-3 : DM58.00
1. Silesia, Upper. I. Breyer, Richard, joint author. II. Buchhofer, Ekkehard, joint author. III. Title.
DK4600.S46B33 76-464636
76 MARC

Bahr, Ernst, writer on eastern Europe, ed.
see Keyser, Erich, 1893-1968. Die Baugeschichte der Stadt Danzig. Köln, Böhlau, 1972.

Bahr, Gerhard, ed.
see World Championship-Jules Rimet Cup, 6th, Bjärred, Sweden, 1958. WM-Fussball in Schweden. Nürnberg, G. Bahr [c1958]

Bahr, Gisela E
Im Dickicht der Städte: ein Beitrag zur Bestimmung von Bertolt Brechts dramatischem Frühstil. Ann Arbor, Mich., University Microfilms, 1966.
Microfilm copy (positive) of typescript.
Thesis—New York University.
Collation of the original: iv, 176 l.
German text.
Bibliography: leaves 172-176.
OCU NUC75-41907

Bahr, Gladys.
Foundations of education for business. Editors: Gladys Bahr and F. Kendrick Bangs. Reston, Va., National Business Education Association [1975]
353 p. 23 cm. (National Business Education Yearbook, no. 13)
1. Business education. I. Bangs, F. Kendrick, ed. II. Title. III. Series.
TxU NUC76-15654

Bahr, Gunter F.
see Neuhoff, Volker. Micromethods in molecular biology. London, Chapman and Hall [etc.] 1973.

Bahr, H. D.
see Anarchismus und Marxismus. Berlin: Kramer, 1973-

Bahr, Hans-Dieter
see Technologie und Kapital. [Frankfurt am Main] Suhrkamp [1973]

Bahr, Hans-Eckehard, 1928-
Konfliktorientierte Gemeinwesenarbeit : Niederlagen und Modelle / [Hrsg. von] Hans-Eckehard Bahr, Reimer Gronemeyer. — Erstausgabe. — Darmstadt : Luchterhand, 1974.
255 p. ; 18 cm. — (Sammlung Luchterhand ; 187) (Reihe Theologie und Politik ; Bd. 8) GFR***
"Dieser Band enthält Teilergebnisse des Bochumer Forschungsprojekts 'Gesellschaftliche Bedingungen des Friedens' (Deutsche Gesellschaft für Friedens- und Konfliktforschung)."
Includes bibliographical references.
ISBN 3-472-61187-1 : DM14.80
1. Germany (Federal Republic, 1949-)—Social conditions—Addresses, essays, lectures. 2. Social conflict—Addresses, essays, lectures. 3. Social action—Addresses, essays, lectures. 4. Political participation—Addresses, essays, lectures. I. Gronemeyer, Reimer, 1939- joint author. II. Title.
HN450.B26 75-556275

Bahr, Hans-Eckehard, 1928-
Politisierung des Alltags, gesellschaftliche Bedingungen des Friedens; Berichte und Analysen, (Hrsg.:) Hans-Eckehard Bahr. [Darmstadt] Luchterhand [1972]
317 p. illus. 18 cm. (Reihe Theologie und Politik, Bd. 4) Sammlung Luchterhand, 88) GDB***
Includes bibliographical references.
1. Social history—1945- 2. Peace (Theology) 3. Social participation. 4. Political socialization. I. Title.
HN18.B247 74-311504

Bahr, Hans-Eckehard, 1928-
Taide ja Kristinusko. [Pieksämäki] Sisälähetysseura [1970]
265 p. 20 cm. (Avain sarja, 28)
"Saksankielinen alkuteos: Poiesis; theologische Untersuchung der Kunst. Tekijän Hyväksymän suunnitelman mukaan lyhentäen suomentanut Taisto Nieminen."
1. Art and religion. 2. Art—Philosophy. I. Title.
MB NUC74-2876

Bahr, Hans-Eckehard, 1928-
see Eingriffe in die Rüstungsindustrie ... Erstausg. Darmstadt, Luchterhand, 1975.

Bahr, Hans-Eckehard, 1928- joint author
see Heinz-Mohr, Gerd. Broeders van deze wereld. Tielt, Den Haag, Uitgeverij Lannoo [1967]

Bahr, Hans-Eckehard, 1928-
see Kirche progressiv. (Gelnhausen u. Berlin) Burckhardthaus-Verl., 1971.

Bahr, Hans-Eckehard, 1928-
see Soziales Lernen ... Stuttgart, Kohlhammer, 1975.

Bahr, Hans-Joachim.
see Rehsener, Carl Gottlieb, 1790-1862. Am Ostseestrand von Pommern bis Memel ... Köln, Grote, 1977.

Bahr, Henrik
see Norway. Laws, statutes, etc. Norges lover, 1682-1963. Oslo, Grøndahl, 1964.

Bahr, Hermann, 1863-1934.
Hermann Bahr. Briefwechsel mit seinem Vater. Ausgew. v. Adalbert Schmidt. Mit einem Nachw. u. Reg. Wien, H. Bauer (1971).
450 p. 25 cm. S240.00 Au 73-20-145
1. Bahr, Hermann, 1863-1934. 2. Bahr, Alois, 1834-1898. I. Bahr, Alois, 1834-1898. II. Schmidt, Adalbert, 1906- ed.
PT2603.A33Z53 1971 73-361282
ISBN 3-900024-01-6

Bahr, Howard M
Old men drunk and sober [by] Howard M. Bahr [and] Theodore Caplow. New York, New York University Press, 1973 [c1974]
xii, 407 p. illus. 24 cm.
Bibliography: p. 393-407.
1. Tramps—New York (City) 2. New York (City)—Poor. I. Caplow, Theodore, joint author. II. Title.
HV4506.N6B34 364.1'48'097471 72-96370
ISBN 0-8147-0965-6 MARC

Bahr, Howard M
Racial differentiation in American metropolitan areas. Austin, Tex., 1965.
vi, 70 l. tables.
Microfilm of typescript. Ann Arbor, Mich., University Microfilms, 1966. 1 reel. 35 mm.
Thesis—University of Texas.
Vita.
Bibliography: leaves 65-69.
1. Negroes—Segregation. 2. Negroes—Social conditions—To 1964. 3. Metropolitan areas—United States. I. Title.
NN NUC74-122097

Bahr, Howard M
Skid row; an introduction to disaffiliation ⌊by⌋ Howard M. Bahr. New York, Oxford University Press, 1973.
x, 335 p. illus. 22 cm.
Includes bibliographical references.
1. Tramps—United States. 2. Poor—United States. 3. Social isolation. I. Title.
HV4505.B34 301.44′94′0973 73-82660
ISBN 0-19-501712-9 MARC

Bahr, Howard M
Women alone : the disaffiliation of urban females / Howard M. Bahr, Gerald R. Garrett. — Lexington, Mass. : Lexington Books, c1976.
xx, 207 p. : ill. ; 24 cm.
Bibliography: p. 198-199.
Includes indexes.
ISBN 0-669-00722-6
1. Single women—New York (City)—Case studies. 2. Social isolation—Case studies. I. Garrett, Gerald R., joint author. II. Title.
HQ800.B32 301.11′3 76-10501
76 MARC

Bahr, Jerome.
Five novellas / Jerome Bahr. — ⌊Santa Fe, N.M.⌋ : Trempealeau Press, c1977.
220 p. ; 23 cm.
CONTENTS: Young people.—The dictator.—Pay the debt.—The long run into self.—The interrogation.
$8.95
I. Title.
PZ3.B1483 Fi 813′.5′2 76-53357
⌊PS3503.A413⌋ 77 MARC

Bahr, Jerome.
The lonely scoundrel; a supplement to the Perishing republic. By Jerome Bahr. Freeman, S.D., Trempealeau Press, 1974.
89 p. (His All good Americans)
I. Title.
NcU NUC76-15661

Bahr, Johan Fredrik, 1805–1875.
Stockholm : handbok för resande / Johan Fredrik Bahr. — Stockholm : Rediviva : ⌊Nord. bokh., (distr.)⌋, 1975.
146 p., ⌊5⌋ leaves of plates : ill., fold. map in pocket ; 22 cm. — (Suecica rediviva ; 52) S 75-47
"Facsimileupplaga ... som utgavs anonymt 1841."
Includes index.
ISBN 91-7120-064-9 : kr49.00
1. Stockholm—Description. I. Title. II. Series.
DL976.B24 1841a 76-501862

Bahr, Kirsten.
Slagtehuset nu. København, Husets Bogcafé, ⌊1973⌋.
⌊12⌋ p. 21 cm. kr5.00 D 73-37
Poems.
I. Title.
PT8176.12.A37S55 74-312499
ISBN 87-7404-120-7

Bahr, Klaus.
Die Fischwirtschaft der Deutschen Demokratischen Republik mit vergleichenden Betrachtungen zur Bundesrepublik Deutschland / Klaus Bahr. — Berlin : H. Heenemann, 1975.
100 p. ; 21 cm. — (Schriften der Bundesforschungsanstalt für Fischerei Hamburg ; Bd. 12) GFR***
Includes bibliographical references.
ISBN 3-87903-046-4
1. Fish trade—Germany, East. 2. Fish trade—Germany, West. I. Title: Die Fischwirtschaft der Deutschen Demokratischen Republik ... II. Series: Hamburg. Bundesforschungsanstalt für Fischerei. Schriften ; Bd. 12.
HD9463.7.A1B34 76-484183
76 MARC

Bahr, Leonard F
A manner of printing / Leonard F. Bahr. — Harper Woods, Mich. : Adagio Press, 1973, c1972.
⌊23⌋ p. ; 24 cm.
"Approximately 300 copies ... copy number 29."
Bibliography: p. ⌊22⌋
1. Private presses. 2. Printing. I. Title.
Z231.5.P7B33 1973 686.2′2 75-300561
MARC

Bahr, Leonard F
TypoGraphia 1. — Harper Woods, Mich. : Adagio Press, 1976.
15, ⌊13⌋ p. : ill. (some col.) ; 25 cm.
"Approximately 325 copies ... printed." No. 14, signed by the author.
$12.50
1. Printing. 2. Private presses. I. Title.
Z123.B23 686.2′2 76-382582
76 MARC

Bahr, M M
Role and effectiveness of contract management in the transit industry, by M. M. Bahr, Daniel Robey [and] Thomas S. Miller. [Milwaukee, Wis., Marquette University, n.d.]
51 l.
At head of cover title: Urban transportation program.
"This report was prepared as a part of a program of Research and Training in Urban Transportation at Marquette University sponsored by the Urban Mass Transportation Administration of the U.S. Department of Transportation..."
1. Urban transportation--Management. 2. Local transit--Management. I. Robey, Daniel. II. Miller, Thomas S. III. Title.
WMM NUC77-90073

Bahr, Sir Philip Henry Manson-
see Manson-Bahr, Sir Philip Henry, 1881-1966.

Bahr, Philipp Heinrich
see
Manson-Bahr, Sir Philip Henry, 1881-1966.

Bahr, Robert.
The virility factor : masculinity through testosterone, the sex hormone / by Robert Bahr. — New York : Putman, c1976.
212 p. ; 22 cm.
Bibliography: p. 197-205.
Includes index.
ISBN 0-399-11808-X
1. Testosterone—Therapeutic use. 2. Generative organs, Male. I. Title.
RM296.B33 1976 612.6′1 76-16150
76 MARC

Bahr, Robert, comp.
see The Natural way to a healthy skin. Emmaus, Pa., Rodale Press [1972]

Bahr, Rudolf
see Binder, Gerhard. Das Hochschul-Stundenplan-Programm BAM P7H. Hannover: Hochschul-Informations-System GmbH, 1972.

Bahr, Thomas Gordon, 1940-
Ecological assessments for wastewater management in southeastern Michigan. East Lansing, Institute of Water Research, Michigan State University, 1972.
281, 46 l. illus. (Michigan. State University, East Lansing. Institute of Water Research. Technical report, no. 29)
"This report represents the Phase II Final Report submitted to the U.S. Army Corps of Engineers, Detroit District in fulfillment of Contract No. DACW 35-72-C-0031."
Includes bibliography.
1. Water reuse. 2. Water quality management. I. Title. II. Series.
MiEM Mi NUC75-41908

Bahr, Thomas Gordon, 1940-
see Bainbridge, Kent LaMont. Mercury dynamics in a warm water stream. [East Lansing] Michigan State University, 1973.

Bahr, Thomas Gordon, 1940-
see Ball, Robert C 1912- Evaluation of lake dredging... East Lansing, Institute of Water Research, Michigan State University, 1971.

Baḥr al-ʻUlūm, Muḥammad ibn ʻAlī.
(Bayna yaday al-Rasūl al-aʻẓam)
بين يدي الرسول الأعظم ⌊تأليف⌋ محمد بحر العلوم. بيروت ، دار الزهراء للطباعة والنشر والتوزيع ⌊pref. 1972⌋
200 p. 19 cm. (His 1 ، في السيرة والتاريخ)
Bibliography: p. 191–193.
1. Companions of Muḥammad, the prophet. I. Title. II. Series: Baḥr al-ʻUlūm, Muḥammad ibn ʻAlī. Fī al-sīrah wa-al-ta'rīkh, 1.
BP70.B26 vol. 1 74-209330
[BP75.5]

Baḥr al-ʻUlūm, Muḥammad ibn ʻAlī.
(Fī al-sīrah wa-al-ta'rīkh)
في السيرة والتاريخ ⌊تأليف⌋ محمد بحر العلوم. بيروت ، دار الزهراء للطباعة والنشر والتوزيع -1972?⌋
v. 19 cm.
1. Islam—Biography. I. Title.
BP70.B26 74-209329

Baḥr al-ʻUlūm, Muḥammad ibn ʻAlī.
(Min madrasat al-Imām ʻAlī)
من مدرسة الامام علي ⌊تأليف⌋ محمد بحر العلوم. ⌊الطبعة 1.⌋ بيروت ، دار الزهراء ⌊1973⌋
189 p. 20 cm.
Bibliography: p. 187–188.
1. Shiites—Biography. I. Title.
BP192.8.B33 74-217032

Baḥr al-ʻUlūm, Muḥammad Mahdī ibn Murtaḍá, 1742 or 3-1797 or 8.
رجال السيد بحر العلوم «المعروف بالفوائد الرجالية» تأليف السيد محمد المهدى بحر العلوم الطباطبائى. حققه وعلق عليه محمد صادق بحر العلوم وحسين بحر العلوم. الطبعة 1. النجف ، مطبعة الآداب ، -67 19.
v. 25 cm. (مكتبة العلمين : الطوسى وبحر العلوم ، -8)
Includes bibliographies.
1. Islam—Biography. 2. Shiites—Biography. 3. Hadith—Authorities. I. Baḥr al-ʻUlūm, Muḥammad Ṣādiq, ed. II. Baḥr al-ʻUlūm, Ḥusayn, ed. III. Title. IV. Title: al-Fawā'id al-rijālīyah.
Title romanized: Rijāl al-Sayyid Baḥr al-ʻUlūm.
BP70.B272 73-205424

Bahr al-'Ulūm, Muhammad Sādiq, ed.
see Bahr al-'Ulūm, Muhammad Mahdī ibn Murtadá 1742 or 3-1797 or 8. Rijal al-Sayyid Bahr al-'Ulūm. 1967.

Bahr al-'Ulūm, Muhammad Sādiq, ed.
see al-Bahrānī, Yūsuf ibn Ahmad, d. 1772? Lu'lu'at al-Bahrayn fī al-ijāzāt wa-tarājim rijāl al-hadīth. 1969.

Baḥr al-'Ulūm, Muḥammad Ṣādiq, ed.
see Ḥassūn al-Burāqī, Ḥusayn ibn Aḥmad, 1845-1914. (Tārīkh al-Kūfah) 1960.

Bahr al-'Ulūm Husayn, ed.
see Bahr al-'Ulūm, Muhammad Mahdī ibn Murtadá, 1742 or 3-1797 or 8. Rijāl al-Sayyid Bahr al-'Ulūm. 1967.

Baḥr al-'Ulūm Ḥusayn
see al-Sharīf al-Murtaḍá, 'Alam al-Hudá 'Alī ibn al-Husayn, 966-1044 or 5. [al-Shāfī fī al-imāmah] Talkhīṣ al-Shāfī. [19

Bahrain Historical and Archaeological Society
see
Jamʿīyat al-Baḥrayn lil-Āthār.

Bahrain, 1969; [a] Middle East economic digest and Arab report and record survey. [London] 1969.
24 p. illus., map. 25 cm.
Advertising matter interspersed.
1. Bahrein–Econ. condit. I. Middle East economic digest. II. ARR.
NIC NUC76-94186

Bahral, Uri.
(Hashpa'at ha-'aliyah ha-hamonit 'al ha-sakhar be-Yisrael)
השפעת העלייה ההמונית על השכר בישראל. מאת אורי בהרל.
ירושלים, מרכז פאלק למחקר כלכלי בישראל, 1965.
84 p. illus. 25 cm.
Bibliography: p. ⌊81⌋
1. Wages—Israel. I. Title.
HD5085.P3B3 1965 74-950136

Bahrām, Zartusht
see Zartusht Bahrām, fl. 1278.

Bahrami, Khosrow, 1947-
Optimal control of cell population systems. [Ithaca, N.Y.] 1974.
[2], viii, 159 l. illus. 29 cm.
Bibliography: leaves 137-143.
Thesis (Ph.D.)–Cornell University.
1. Cell populations. 2. Cells. I. Title.
NIC NUC76-15662

Bahrami, Mehdi
see Mūzah-'i Īrān-i Bāstān. (Rāhnamāh-yi ganjīnah-'i Qur'ān dar Mūzah-'i Īrān-i Bāstān) 1328 [1949

Bahrami, Muhammad, illus.
see Hekmat, Forough-es-Saltaneh. Folk tales of ancient Persia. Delmar, N.Y., Caravan Books, 1974.

Bahrang,
The little black fish. Story by Samuel Bahrang. Pictures by Farsheed Meskali. Minneapolis, Carolrhoda Books [1971]
[24] p. col. illus. 20 cm.
Translation of Māhī siyāh-i Kūchūlū.
SUMMARY: In spite of various warnings the little black fish still wanted to see what was at the end of his stream.
[1. Fishes—Fiction] I. Misqālī, Farshīd, illus. II. Title.
PZ7.B144 Li [E] 74-128812
ISBN 0-87614-013-4 71[r75]rev MARC

al-Baḥrānī, Muḥammad Ṣāliḥ ibn 'Adnān.
(Ḥaṣā'il al-fikar fī aḥwāl al-Imām al-Muntaẓar)
حصائل الفكر في احوال الامام المنتظر ، لمحمد صالح بن عدنان البحراني . بيروت ، دار مكتبة الحياة [1972?]
270 p. port. 24 cm.
Bibliography: p. 258-259.
1. Mahdi. 2. al-Mahdī, Muḥammad ibn al-Ḥasan, b. ca. 869. I. Title.
BP166.93.B34 74-217319

al-Baḥrānī, Yūsuf ibn Aḥmad, d. 1772?
[al-Ḥadā'iq al-nāḍirah fī aḥkām al-'itrah al-ṭāhirah]
كتاب الحدائق الناضرة في احكام العترة الطاهرة ، تاليف يوسف البحراني . حققه وعلق عليه واشرف على طبعه محمد تقي الايرواني . نجف ، دار الكتب الاسلامية [1958-
v. in 25 cm.
Includes bibliographical references.
1. Purity, Ritual (Islam) I. al-Irwānī, Muḥammad Taqī, ed. II. Title: al-Ḥadā'iq al-nāḍirah fī aḥkām al-'itrah al-ṭāhirah.
Title romanized: Kitāb al-ḥadā'iq al-nāḍirah fī aḥkām al-'itrah al-ṭāhirah.
BP184.4.B24 74-224838

al-Baḥrānī, Yūsuf ibn Aḥmad, d. 1772?
[Lu'lu'at al-Baḥrayn fī al-ijāzāt wa-tarājim rijāl al-ḥadīth]
التراجم لرجال الحديث والاثـر ، او ، لؤلؤة البحريـن في الاجازات . تاليف يوسف بن احمد البحراني . حققه وعلق عليه السيد محمد صادق بحر العلوم . الطبعـة 2 . النجف ، مطابع النعمان ، 1969.
461 p. 26 cm.
Includes bibliographical references.
1. Hadith (Shiites)—Authorities. I. Baḥr al-'Ulūm, Muḥammad Ṣādiq, ed. II. Title. III. Title: Lu'lu'at al-Baḥrayn fī al-ijāzāt wa-tarājim rijāl al-ḥadīth.
Title romanized: al-Tarājim li-rijāl al-ḥadīth wa-al-athar.
BP193.28.B33 1969 73-209486

al-Baḥrāwī, Ibrāhīm.
[Aḍwā' 'alá al-adab al-ṣihyūnī al-mu'āṣir]
اضواء على الادب الصهيونـي المعاصر [تاليف] ابراهيـم البحراوي . [القاهرة] دار الهلال [1972]
169 p. 17 cm. (257 كتاب الهلال ،) £E0.10
Includes bibliographical references.
1. Hebrew literature, Modern—Addresses, essays, lectures. I. Title.
PJ502.B3 72-960449

(al-Baḥrayn al-yawm)
البحرين اليوم.
البحرين ، وزارة الاعلام.
v. illus. 33 cm. monthly.
1. Bahrein—Periodicals. I. Bahrein. Wizārat al-I'lām.
DS247.B2A23 74-643037
MARC-S

Baḥraynī, Mahsitī.
(Dīdār bā rawshanāyī)
ديدار با روشنايى ، گزيدۀ اشعار سالهای ١٣٤٤ - ١٣٤٩ [از] مهستى بحرينـى . [چاپ 1.] تهران ، چاپخانـۀ فاروس ، [1350 i. e. 1972
64 p. 23 cm.
I. Title.
PK6561.B316D5 73-211351

Bahrdt, Hans Paul.
Altstadtsanierung in Niedersachsen / H. P. Bahrdt, R. Hilebrecht, H. P. C. Weidner. — Hannover : Niedersächsische Landeszentrale für Politische Bildung, 1976.
107 p. : ill. ; 21 cm. GFR***
Includes bibliographical references.
1. Urban renewal—Germany, West—Saxony, Lower—Preservation. 2. Monuments—Germany, West—Saxony, Lower. 3. Historic sites—Germany, West—Saxony, Lower. I. Hillebrecht, Rudolf, joint author. II. Weidner, H. P. C., 1940- joint author. III. Title.
HT178.G4B32 77-559752
77 MARC

Bahrdt, Hans Paul.
Una città più umana, Hans Paul Bahrdt. Bari, De Donate, 1969.
300 p. (Temi e problemi)
Translation of Humaner Städtebau.
1. Cities and towns—Planning—Germany (Federal Republic, 1949-) I. Title. II. Series.
CU NUC76-68343

Bahrdt, Hans Paul.
Die moderne Grosstadt soziolog. Überlegungen z. Städtebau/ Hans Paul Bahrdt. — [3. Aufl.] — Reinbek (bei Hamburg) Wegner, 1971.
199, [12] p.: 27 ill.; 21 cm. DM12.00 GDB 72-A11
Bibliography: p. 173-182.
1. Sociology, Urban. 2. Cities and towns—Planning. I. Title.
HT151.B25 1971 73-302260
ISBN 3-8032-0005-9 rev

Bahrdt, Hans Paul.
Umwelterfahrung : soziologische Betrachtungen über den Beitrag des Subjekts zur Konstitution von Umwelt / Hans Paul Bahrdt. — Originalausg. — München : Nymphenburger Verlagshandlung, [1974]
257, [1] p. ; 21 cm. — (Sammlung Dialog ; 72) GFR***
Includes bibliographical references.
ISBN 3-485-03072-4
1. Environmental policy. 2. Human ecology. 3. Conservation of natural resources. 4. Sociology, Urban. I. Title.
HC79.E5B345 301.31 74-357484

Bahrdt, Hans Paul
see Gidion, Jürgen, 1928- Praxis des Deutschunterrichts... Göttingen: Vandenhoeck und Ruprecht, 1973.

Bahrdt, Karl Friedrich, 1741-1792.
C. F. Bahrdt: ein Abenteuer der Aufklärungszeit; Dr. Carl Friedrich Bahrdts Geschichte seines Lebens, seiner Meinungen und Schicksale. Bearb. von Theresia Hagenmaier. [Heidenheim an der Brenz] Heidenheimer Verlagsanstalt [1972]
191 p. (Abenteuerliche Lebensläufe, Bd. 11)
Includes bibliography.
1. Bahrdt, Karl Friedrich, 1741-1792. I. Hagenmaier, Theresia.
MiU MH-AH NUC75-84579

Bahrdt, Karl Friedrich, 1741-1792.
Handbuch der Moral für den Bürgerstand. Frankfurt am Main, Athenäum, 1972.
333 p. 19 cm. (Athenäum reprints)
Reprint of the 1789 ed.
1. Conduct of life. I. Title.
IaU NUC74-128968

Bahrdt, Karl Friedrich, 1741-1792.
Die sämtlichen Reden Jesu, aus den Evangelisten ausgezogen un in Ordnung gestellt zur Uebersicht des Lehrgebäudes Jesu. Berlin, F. Vieweg, 1786.
vi, 376 p.
Microfilm (negative) [Los Gatos, Calif., Catholic Microfilm Center, 1968?] 1 reel. 35 mm.
1. Jesus Christ-Words. I. Title.
CBGTU NUC74-51613

Bahrdt, Waldemar, 1863-1920
see Dziatzko, Karl Franz Otto, 1842-1903. Gutenbergs früheste druckerpraxis... Wiesbaden, Kraus Reprint, O. Harrassowitz, 1969.

Bahre, Jens, 1945-
Regen im Gesicht : 9 Geschichten / Jens Bahre. — Berlin : Verlag Neues Leben, 1976.
204 p. ; 20 cm. — (NL Podium) GFR77-A
CONTENTS: Das Mädchen.—Der Besuch.—Regen im Gesicht.—Das Karussell.—Bleikristall.—Claire.—Nekrolog für Battmann.—Tagebuch zu zweit.—Die Portiersche.
6.00M
I. Title.
PT2662.A37R4 77-471437
77 MARC

Bahre, Stephen.
Arizona maps in the map collection University of Arizona Library: The territorial period, 1863-1911. [Tucson] University of Arizona Library, 1972.
37 p. maps. (Arizona. University. Library. Bibliographic bulletin, v. 2, no. 2)
1. Arizona—Maps—Bibl.—Catalogs. I. Title. II. Series.
WHi NUC75-41910

Bahre, Stephen.
Atlas of Arizona / compiled and edited by Stephen Bahre. — Yuma : Arizona Information Press, c1976.
48, [1] p. : col. maps ; 28 cm.
Bibliography of Arizona maps: p. [49]
CONTENTS: Mapping history.—Arizona history.—Physical setting.—Land ownership and occupancy.—Land utilization.—Schools and government.
1. Arizona—Maps. 2. Arizona—History—Maps. I. Title.
G1510.B25 1976 912'.791 75-42973
76 MARC

Bahrein.
(al-Jarīdah al-rasmīyah)
الجريدة الرسمية.
[البحرين ، دائرة العلاقات العامة لحكومة البحرين etc.]
no. in v. 30 cm.
Continues: Bahrein. al-Nashrah al-rasmīyah.
Arabic or English.
1. Law—Bahrein. I. Title.
75-643336
(MARC-S)

Bahrein.
(al-Nashrah al-rasmīyah)
النشرة الرسمية.
[البحرين] حكومة البحرين.
no. in v. 28 cm.
Issues for have title also in English: Official gazette.
Continued by: Bahrein. al-Jarīdah al-rasmīyah.
1. Law—Bahrein. I. Bahrein. Official gazette. II. Title.
75-643337
(MARC-S)

Bahrein. Official gazette
see Bahrein. (al-Nashrah al-rasmīyah)

Bahrein. Antiquities Division
see
Bahrein. Qism al-Āthār.

Bahrein. al-Āthār, Qism
see
Bahrein. Qism al-Āthār.

Bahrein. Dā'irat al-Tarbiyah wa-al-Ta'līm. Antiquities Division
see
Bahrein. Qism al-Āthār.

Bahrein. Dā'irat al-Tarbiyah wa-al-Ta'līm. Qism al-Āthār
see
Bahrein. Qism al-Āthār.

Bahrein. al-I'lām, Wizārat
see
Bahrein. Wizārat al-I'lām.

Bahrein. Information, Ministry of
see
Bahrein. Wizārat al-I'lām.

Bahrein. Laws, statutes, etc.
Marsūm raqm 6 li-sanat 1970
see
Bahrein. Laws, statutes, etc.
Qānūn tanẓīm tasjīl al-mawālīd wa-al-wafayāt.

Bahrein. Laws, statutes, etc.
(Qānūn al-mukhālafāt al-madanīyah, 1970)
قانون المخالفات المدنية ، ١٩٧٠ . [البحرين ، المطبعة الشرقية ، 1970.
5, 42 p. 25 cm.
At head of title: حكومة البحرين
1. Civil procedure—Bahrein. I. Title.
74-217421

Bahrein. Laws, statutes, etc.
(Qānūn al-'uqūd, 1969)
قانون العقود ، ١٩٦٩ . [البحرين ، المطبعة الشرقية ، 1969.
14, 59 p. 24 cm.
At head of title: حكومة البحرين
1. Contracts—Bahrein. I. Title.
74-218595

Bahrein. Laws, statutes, etc.
[Qānūn tanẓīm tasjīl al-mawālīd wa-al-wafayāt]
مرسوم رقم ٦ لسنة ١٩٧٠ بقانون تنظيم تسجيل المواليد والوفيات. [البحرين ، 1970]
7 l. 34 cm.
Caption title.
Stamped on leaf 7: عيسى بن سلمان الخليفة ، حاكم البحرين وتوابعها
1. Registers of births, etc.—Bahrein. I. al-Khalīfah, ʻĪsá ibn Salmān, 1933- II. Title.
Title romanized: Marsūm raqm 6 li-sanat 1970.
73-206535

Bahrein. Laws, statutes, etc.
(Qānūn uṣūl al-muḥākamāt al-jazā'īyah, 1966)
قانون اصول المحاكمات الجزائية ، ١٩٦٦ . البحرين ، المطبعة الشرقية ، 1966.
12, 50 p. 27 cm.
At head of title: حكومة البحرين
1. Criminal procedure—Bahrein. I. Title.
74-217422

Bahrein. Ministry of Information
see
Bahrein. Wizārat al-Iʻlām.

Bahrein. Mudīrīyat al-Tarbiyah wa-al-Taʻlīm.
تقرير عن التعليم بالبحرين. مقدم من محمد كامل النحاس [و]جبرائيل كاتول. [البحرين] حكومة البحرين ، مديرية التربية والتعليم ، 1960.
95 p. 24 cm.
1. Education—Bahrein. I. Title.
Title romanized: Taqrīr ʻan al-taʻlīm bi-al-Baḥrayn.
LA1104.B3B33 1960 74-205088

Bahrein. Qism al-Āthār
see Jamʻīyat al-Baḥrayn lil-Āthār. Antiquities of Bahrain. Bahrain, Oriental Press [1971]

Bahrein. Statistical Bureau.
Statistics of the population census, 1971. [Manama, 1972]
xii, 166 p. 23 x 30 cm. 500F
1. Bahrein—Census, 1971.
HA1950.B3B33 1972 74-151836
MARC

Bahrein. Wizārat al-I'lām.
(Dawlat al-Baḥrayn)
The State of Bahrain. دولـــــة البحريـــــن.
[Manama, Ministry of Information, 1971?]
48 p. illus. 30 cm.
Cover title: Bahrain.
In English.
1. Bahrein.
DS247.B2B33 1971 915.3'65'035 74-218051

Bahrein. Wizārat al-I'lām
see al-Baḥrayn al-yawm.

Bahrenberg, Gerhard.
Auftreten und Zugrichtung von Tiefdruckgebieten in Mitteleuropa. Münster, Selbstverlag des Instituts für Geographie und Länderkunde und der Geographischen Kommission für Westfalen, 1973.
vi, 125 p. illus. 23 cm. (Westfälische geographische Studien, 26) GFR***
Originally presented as the author's thesis, Münster, 1969.
Summary in English.
Bibliography: p. 123-125.
1. Cyclones. 2. Central Europe—Climate. I. Title.
QC959.C4B33 1973 73-355746

Bahrenberg, Gerhard.
Statistische Methoden und ihre Anwendung in der Geographie / G. Bahrenberg und E. Giese. — Stuttgart : B. G. Teubner, 1975.
308 p. ; 21 cm. — (Studienbücher der Geographie) (Teubner Studienbücher : Geographie) GFR***
Bibliography: p. [294]-304.
Includes index.
ISBN 3-519-03403-4
1. Geography—Statistical methods. I. Giese, Ernst, 1938- joint author. II. Title.
G70.3.B33 77-455512
77 MARC

Bahrenburg, Bruce.
The creation of Dino De Laurentiis' King Kong / by Bruce Bahrenburg. — New York : Pocket Books, 1976.
ix, 273 p. : ill. ; 18 cm.
ISBN 0-671-80796-X : $1.75
1. King Kong (1976 version). [Motion picture] I. Title.
PN1997.K4374B3 791.43'7 76-150963
77 MARC

Bahrenburg, Bruce.
Filming The great Gatsby. New York, Berkley Pub. Corp. [c1974]
255 p. illus. (A Berkley Medallion Book)
SBN 425-02576-4.
1. The great Gatsby (Motion picture). I. Title.
CaOTP NUC75-18357

Bahrenburg, Bruce.
My little brother's coming tomorrow. New York, Putnam [1971]
256 p. 23 cm. $6.95
1. Gregory, Jim, 1950- I. Title.
GV939.G75B3 1971 796.332'0924 70-163403
[B] MARC
rev

Bahrfeldt, Max von, 1856-1936.
Die römische Goldmünzprägung während der Republik und unter Augustus: eine chronolog. und metrolog. Studie/ Max von Bahrfeldt. — Neudr. d. Ausg. Halle 1923. — Aalen: Scientia-Verlag, 1972.
xvi, 208 p., xvi l.: ill.; 30 cm. DM130.00 GDB 73-A5
Original ed. issued as Nr. 1 of Münzstudien.
Includes bibliographical references.
1. Coins, Roman. 2. Gold coins. I. Title. II. Series: Münzstudien, 1.
CJ849.B33 1972 73-361878
ISBN 3-511-00671-6

Bahrfeldt, Max von, 1856-1936.
Sammlung römischer Münzen der Republik u. des West -Kaiserreichs. Aalen, Scientia Verlag, 1972.
viii, 128 p. 33 plates. 30 cm. GDB***
Reprint of the Halle, 1922 ed.
1. Coins, Roman. I. Title.
CJ833.B3 1972 73-356958
ISBN 3-511-00672-4

Bahrfeldt, Max von, 1856-1936, joint author.
see Buck, Heinrich, d. 1939. Die Münzen der Stadt Hildesheim. Hildesheim, A. Lax, 1937.

Bahri, Hardev.
Comprehensive English-Hindi dictionary. Entirely revised & enlarged edition. Vārāṇāsī, Jānamaṇḍala Limiṭeda [1969]
2 v.
At head of title: Bṛhat aṅgrejī-hindī kośa.
1. English language–Dictionaries–Hindi.
I. Title.
WaU NUC 75-31005

Bahri, Hardev.
हिन्दी साहित्य की रूप-रेखा. [लेखक] हरदेव बाहरी. [1. संस्करण] दिल्ली, मोतीलाल बनारसीदास [1955]
150 p. 19 cm.
In Hindi.
1. Hindi literature—Outlines, syllabi, etc. I. Title.
Title romanized: Hindī sāhitya kī rūpa-rekhā.
PK2031.B29 73-217039

Bahri, Hardev.
Teach yourself Panjabi, based on modern most linguistic, pedagogical, and psychological methodologies / Hardev Bahri. — 1st ed. — Patiala : Punjabi University, 1973.
xvi, 269 p. ; 22 cm.
Rs3.00
1. Panjabi language—Self-instruction. I. Title.
PK2633.B27 491'.42'82421 74-903486
75 MARC

Bahri, O K Rahmat.
Beberapa aspek mengenai prinsip² ilmu perdagangan dan hukum-nya / disusun oleh O. K. Rahmat. — Chet. 1. — Kota Bharu : PAP, 1971.
256 p. ; 19 cm.
Bibliography : p. 255-256.
1. Commercial law—Indonesia. I. Title.
72-941793

Bahri, O K Rahmat.
Berbagai persoalan tentang kebudajaan Islam, oleh O. K. Rahmat. Tjet. 1. Medan, Penerbit Riza, 1965.
55 p. 18 cm.
Bibliography : p. 54-55.
1. Islam—Addresses, essays, lectures. I. Title.
BP165.B345 S A 68-18031
rev PL 480: Indo-4595

Bahri, O K Rahmat.
Etnologi Indonesia, untuk sekolah landjutan atas. Disusun oleh O. K. Rahmat dan R. Soenardi. Tjet 3. Medan, Ikapena, 1961 [cover 1962]
173 p. illus. 23 cm.
Bibliography: p. 172.
1. Ethnology—Indonesia. I. Soenardi, R., joint author. II. Title.
DS631.B33 1962 S A 64-2294
rev

Bahri, O K Rahmat.
Hukum dagang. Kuliah O. K. Rahmat Bahri. Medan [Satria]; distributor: Jajasan Nation Building [1966]
127 p. 22 cm.
Cover title.
1. Commercial law—Indonesia. I. Title.
76-949595

Bahri, O K Rahmat.
Manusia, kebudajaan dan masjarakatnja (melangkah ke antropologi dan sosiologi) [oleh O. K. Rahmat] Tjet 1. Medan, Islamyah, 1961-
v. illus. 18 cm. (Seri sardjana, no. 1
Bibliography: v. 1, p. 231.
1. Anthropology. I. Title.
GN24.B25 S A 64-2321
rev

Bahri, O K Rahmat.
Rangkaian budi pekerti, oleh O. K. Rahmat. Tjet. 1. Medan, "Islamyah," 1961.
101, [1] p. 18 cm.
"Seri A. no. 129, 1961."
Bibliography: p. [102]
1. Islamic ethics. I. Title. II. Title: Budi pekerti.
BJ1291.B33 76-293895
rev

Bahri, Ujjal Singh.
An introductory course in spoken Punjabi; a microwave approach to language teaching. Chandigarh, Bahri Publications [1972]
xxviii, 252 p. 24 cm. (SILL series in Indian languages & linguistics, 1) Rs30.00 ($8.00U.S.)
1. Panjabi language—Spoken Panjabi. I. Title. II. Series.
PK2633.B29 491'.42'83421 72-903553
MARC

Bahri, Ujjal Singh, joint author
see Jagannathan, V R 1942- Introductory course in spoken Hindi... Chandigarh, Bahri Publications [1973]

Bahri, Zarowhi
see
Pahri, Zarowhi.

Bahri, Zhirayr
see
Pahri, Zhirayr, 1905-1942.

Bahrîanyĭ, Ivan.
(Tak trymaty)
Так тримати. Спеціяльний вип. публіцистичних творів І. П. Багряного, присвячених актуальній партійно-політ. проблематиці УРДП. [Мюнхен] Вид-во ЦК УРДП, 1971.
151 p. port. 21 cm. (Наші позиції, ч. 29) GDB***
1. Ukraïns'ka revoliutsiĭno-demokratychna partiîa. 2. Ukraine—Politics and government—1917- —Addresses, essays, lectures. I. Title. II. Series: Nashi pozytsiï, ch. 29.
DK508.44.N3 ch. 29 73-315708

Bahrîanyĭ, Ivan
see Hryshko, Vasyl' I 1897-
Zhyvyĭ Bahrîanyĭ... Novyĭ Ul'm, "Ukraïns'ki Visti", 1962.

(Bahrîanyĭ Zhovtnîa stîah)
Багряний Жовтня стяг : поезії / [упорядник О. П. Довгий]. — Київ : Молодь, 1977.
124 p. : ill. ; 18 cm. USSR***
0.58rub
1. Ukrainian poetry—20th century. I. Dovhyĭ, Oleksiĭ Prokopovych, 1929-
PG3917.B28 77-515092

Bahriĭ, P. I., ed.
see Industrial'no-kolhospna Ukraïna. 1972.

Bahriĭ, Roman Stepanovych
see L'vivs'kyĭ istorychnyĭ muzeĭ. 1976.

Bahrim, Mitrița.
Prepararea și conservarea ciupercilor. București, Editura tehnică, 1971.
152 p., 8 l. of plates. 20 cm. lei 11.00 R 71-3942
At head of title: Mitrița Bahrim, Iulian Petrescu.
Bibliography: p. 143-[145].
1. Cookery (Mushrooms). 2. Mushrooms—Preservation. 3. Mushrooms—Romania. I. Petrescu, Iulian, joint author. II. Title.
TX804.B33 72-358672

Bahrini, Said.
Der Einfluss von Haltungsform, Rasse und Futterung auf die Milchleistung bei Rindern in Nordwurttemberg. Hohenheim, 1973.
85 p. map. (Hohenheim. Universitat. [Dissertation 1973, no. 27])
English summary.
Bibliography: p. 77-85.
I. Title.
DNAL NUC76-68669

Bahrmann, Henri.
L'ambiance urbaine; réflexions sur la ville et l'environnement sensible [par] Henri Bahrmann [et] Ho Van Mang. [Paris, Centre de recherche d'urbanisme, 1972]
53 p. illus. 20 cm. F***
Includes bibliographical references.
1. Space (Architecture) 2. Architecture—Psychological aspects. 3. Visual perception. I. Ho Van Mang, joint author. II. Title.
NA2765.B3 720'.1 74-159485 MARC

Bahro, Horst.
Abschied vom Abitur? : Hochschulzugang zwischen Numerus clausus und Massenbildung / Horst Bahro, Willi Becker, Josef Hitpass. — Zürich, [Postfach 869] : Edition Interfrom ; Osnabruck : Fromm, 1974.
112 p. ; 21 cm. — (Texte und Thesen ; 54) Sw 75-A-3082
Includes bibliographical references.
ISBN 3-7729-5054-X (Fromm)
1. Universities and colleges—Germany, West—Admission. I. Becker, Willi, 1926- joint author. II. Hitpass, Josef, 1926- joint author. III. Title.
LB2351.B34 75-542369

Bahrs, Hans.
Mass unserer Freiheit : Gedichte / Hans Bahrs. — Darmstadt : Bläschke, 1973.
87 p. ; 21 cm. GFR 74-A
ISBN 3-87561-221-3 : DM9.80
I. Title.
PT2603.A335M3 75-576097

Bahrs, Hans.
Meisterung des Lebens / Hans Bahrs. — Darmstadt : Bläschke, 1975.
76 p. ; 21 cm. GFR76-A
ISBN 3-87561-446-1 : DM9.80
I. Title.
PT2603.A335M4 76-467521
76 MARC

Bahrt, Sidney.
A wilderness of birds / portraits of birds by Sidney Bahrt ; text by Hope S. Jex ; foreword by Roger Tory Peterson ; ornithology of the birds by John Bull. — 1st ed. — Garden City, N. Y. : Doubleday, 1974.
160 p. : col. ill. ; 30 cm.
ISBN 0-385-01866-5 : $29.95
1. Birds—United States—Pictorial works. I. Jex, Hope S. II. Title.
QL682.B33 598.2'973 72-95713 MARC

Bahrum Djamil
see
Djamil, Bahrum.

Bahry, Donna.
see International Slavic Conference, 1st, Banff, Alta., 1974. Soviet economic and political relations with the developing world ... New York, Praeger, 1975.

Bahşî
see
Zatî, ca. 1471-1546.

Bahşi, Ahmed Faruki.
Madde, madde açıklamalı yeni dernekler kanunu ve ilgili yönetmelik. İstanbul, Lâtin Matbaası, 1973.
102 p. 21 cm.
Includes Dernekler kanunu.
1. Associations, institutions, etc.—Law and legislation—Turkey. I. Turkey. Laws, statutes, etc. Dernekler kanunu. 1973. II. Title.
74-223953

Bahsi, Marie Michel-
see Michel-Bahsi, Marie, 1914-

Bahtijaragić, Rifet, 1946-
Skice za cikluse. [Sarajevo, 1972]
63 p.
MH NUC76-3675

Bahtijarević, Štefica.
Religijsko pripadanje u uvjetima sekularizacije društva / Štefica Bahtijarević. — Zagreb : Narodno sveučilište, Centar za aktualni politički studij, 1975.
335 p. ; 20 cm. — (Političke teme, biblioteka suvremene političke misli) Yu***
Bibliography: p. 290-298.
1. Religion—20th century. 2. Yugoslavia—Religion. I. Title.
BL98.B24 76-509734

Bahtiri, Fetah, 1943-
Kangë për zaden. Mbulesën e ilustroi Feko Feka. Mitrovicë, Klubi letrar "Trepça," 1968.
16 p. illus., port. 20 cm.
Microfiche (negative) 1 sheet. 11 x 15 cm. (NYPL FSN 9,053)
Poems.
1. Albanian language—Texts and translations. I. Title.
NN NUC74-2877

Bāhū, Sultan
see
Sultān Bāhū, 1630-1691.

Bahuchet, Serge.
see Les Sociétés rurales ... Châtillon-sur-Seine, Roue à livres, c1975.

Bahuguṇā, Abodha Bandhu.
(Pārvatī)
पार्वती. रचयिता अबोध बन्धु बहुगुणा. सम्पादक शिवानन्द नौटियाल. [देहरादून?, कुसुम रस्तोगी, 1966]
10, 56 p. port. 18 cm. Rs1.25
Imprint on cover: श्याम बुक डिपो, देहरादून.
In Garhwali.
Poems.
I. Nauṭiyāla, Śivānanda, ed. II. Title.
PK2605.G39B3 S A 68-9468

Bahuguṇā, Ghanānanda.
(Samāja)
समाज; क्रांतिकारी सामाजिक नाटक. लेखक श्रीघनानंद बहुगुणा. प्रथमावृत्ति. लखनऊ, गंगा-पुस्तकमाला-कार्यालय, सं. 1987 वि. [1930 or 1]
10, 161 p. 18 cm. (गंगा-पुस्तकमाला, 110)
In Hindi.
I. Bhārgava, Dulārelāla, ed. II. Title.
PK2098.B293S2 75-984430

Bahuguna, Hemwati Nandan.
Indianising whom? New Delhi, All India Congress Committee [1970]
15 p.
1. Muslims in India. I. Title.
MoU NUC74-120744

Bahuguna, Sunder Lal, 1927-
(Uttarākhaṇḍa meṃ eka sau bīsa dina)
उत्तराखण्ड में एक सौ बीस दिन / लेखक सुन्दर लाल बहुगुणा. — 1. संस्करण. — सिल्यारा, टिहरी गढ़वाल : पर्वतीय नवजीवन मण्डल ; नई दिल्ली : प्राप्ति स्थान गांधी बुक हाउस, 1975.
x, 140 p., [6] leaves of plates : ill. ; 19 cm.
In Hindi.
Rs5.75
1. Kumaon, India—Description and travel. I. Title.
DS485.K76B33 75-908879

Bahulikara, D D
(Muktaka-mañjūṣā)
मुक्तक-मञ्जूषा / दि. द. बहुलीकर. — [पुण्यपत्तनम् : 'शारदा'-कार्यालयः], 1967.
30 p. ; 21 cm. — (शारदा-गौरव-ग्रन्थमाला ; क्र. 15)
Series romanized: Śaradā-gaurava-granthamālā.
In Sanskrit.
Poems.
Rs2.00
I. Title.
PK3799.B27M8 75-907881

Bāhūr Labīb
see
Labib, Pahor.

Bahura, Gopal Narayan, ed.
see Bana. [Candiśataka] Mahakavi-Banabhattaviracitam Candiśatakam. (Rajasthan Oriental Research Institute), 1968.

Bahurūpī.
[Ekaṭi śiśira bindu]
একটি শিশির বিন্দু. [লেখক] বহুরূপী. কলিকাতা, পূর্ণ প্রকাশন [1378, i.e. 1971]
165 p. 22 cm. Rs5.00
In Bengali.
I. Title.
PK1730.13.A37E4 72-900997

Bahurūpī.
[Laukikatāra paribarte]
লৌকিকতার পরিবর্তে. [লেখক] বহুরূপী. কলিকাতা, পূর্ণ প্রকাশন [1378, i.e. 1971]
228 p. 23 cm. Rs7.00
In Bengali.
I. Title.
PK1730.13.A37L3 72-900998

Baḥya ben Asher, d. 1340.
(Kitve Rabenu Baḥya)
כתבי רבינו בחיי : יוצאים לאור על־פי דפוסים ראשונים וכתבי יד, עם מראי מקומות, הערות ומבואות / מאת חיים דוב שעוועל. — ירושלים : מוסד הרב קוק, 730 [1969]
685 p., [1] leaf of plates : facsims. ; 25 cm.
Includes indexes, also for his Be'ur la-Torah published 1966-1968.
CONTENTS: כד הקמח.—שלחן של ארבע.—פרקי אבות.
1. Jewish way of life. 2. Table etiquette, Jewish. 3. Messianic era (Judaism) 4. Aboth—Commentaries.
BM550.B28 75-951973

Baḥya ben Joseph ibn Paḳuda, 11th cent.
The book of direction to the duties of the heart, from the original Arabic version of Baḥya ben Joseph Ibn Paquda's al-Hidāya ilā Fara'iḍ al-Qulūb. Introd., translation and notes by Menahem Mansoor with Sara Arenson [and] Shoshana Dannhauser. London, Routledge & K. Paul [1973]
viii, 472 p. 23 cm. (The Littman library of Jewish civilization) £6.00 GB***
Translation of al-Hidāyah ilá farā'iḍ al-qulūb.
Bibliography: p. 453-459.
1. Ethics, Jewish. I. Mansoor, Menahem, tr. II. Title.
BJ1287.B23H52 296.3'85 73-179610
ISBN 0-7100-7504-0 MARC

Baḥya ben Joseph ibn Paḳuda, 11th cent.
Les Devoirs du cœur [par] Bahya ibn Paqûda. Traduits et présentés par André Chouraqui. [Préface de Jacques Maritain]. Nouvelle éd. [Paris], Desclée De Brouwer, 1972.
cvii, 668 p. 20 cm. F 73-3174
Translation of al-Hidāyah 'ilā fara'iḍ al-qulūb.
Includes bibliographical references.
1. Ethics, Jewish. I. Chouraqui, André, 1917- ed. II. Title.
BJ1287.B23H53 1972 296.3'85 74-159715 MARC

Baḥya ben Joseph ibn Paḳuda, 11th cent.
[al-Ḥidāyah ilā farā'iḍ al-qulūb. Hebrew]
ספר תורת חובות הלבבות, שחיברו בחיי ב"ר יוסף אבן פקודה, בתרגום חדש מן הלשון הערבית ... על-ידי שמואל ירושלמי. ירושלים, מאורי ישראל, 732 [1972]
15, 272 p. 25 cm. IL18.00
"התרגום מיוסד על נוסח כתב היד של המקור ... [בספריית בודליאנא שבאוכספורד שמס' Ms. Pococke 96] ומקצת דברים החסרים ... הושלמו על פי תרגומו של רבנו יהודה אבן תיבון."
1. Ethics, Jewish. I. Haggai, Samuel, 1922– tr. II. Title: Torot ḥovot ha-levavot.
Title romanized: Sefer Torat ḥovot ha-levavot.
BJ1287.B23H54 1972 72–950177

Bahya ben Joseph ibn Pakuda, 11th cent. al -Hidayah 'ila fara'id al-qulub. Hebrew. Selections. 1973 or 1974
see Alter Mosheh Aharon ben Hayim Yehudah Leb. (Mesharim) 734 [1973 or 1974]

Baḥya ben Joseph ibn Pakuda, 11th cent.
[al-Ḥidāyah ilā farā'iḍ al-qulūb. Hebrew & Judeo-Arabic]
ספר תורת חובות הלבבות לרבנו בחיי בן יוסף בן פקודה. מקור ותרגום. תרגם לעברית באר והכין: יוסף קאפח ... [ירושלים] יוצא לאור בראשות הועד הכללי ליהודי תימן בירושלם, 733 [1972 or 3]
464 p. 25 cm.
Includes bibliographical references.
1. Ethics, Jewish. I. Kafaḥ, Joseph, ed. II. Title. Torat ḥovot ha-levavot.
Title romanized: Sefer Torat ḥovot ha-levavot.
BJ1287.B23H54 1972b 75–950655

Baḥya ben Joseph ibn Paḳuda, 11th cent.
[al-Ḥidāyah ilā farā'id al-qulūb. Hebrew & Yiddish]
ספר חובות הלבבות / מהרב בחיי הדיין הספרדי בר"י ... ; והעתיקו ללשון הקודש יהודה ן' תבון ; עם פירוש מספיק ... מרפא לנפש ... וכעת נעתק ללשון אשכנזית עברית הנקרא עברי טייטש ... להשיג, [1974?] י. סאקס : Brooklyn
2 v. in 1 (656 p.) ; 27 cm.
Reprint of a 1874 ed. printed by Rom, Vilna.
1. Ethics, Jewish. I. Title: Ḥovot ha-levavot.
Title romanized: Sefer Ḥovot ha-levavot.
BJ1287.B23H54 1974 75–950137

Bahya ben Joseph ibn Pakuda, 11th cent. Sefer Torat ḥovot ha-levavot
see Baḥya ben Joseph ibn Pakuda, 11th cent. al-Ḥidāyah ilā farā'iḍ al-qulūb. Hebrew.

Bahzād Lakhnavī, 1900–
وجد و حال. [شاعر] بہزاد لکھنوی. [لکھنؤ، نسیم بک ڈپو، 1971]
107 p. 18 cm. Rs2.00
In Urdu.
Poems.

I. Title.
Title romanized: Vajd va ḥāl.
PK2199.B27V3 76–920478

Bâi, Dô-quý-
see Dô-quý-Bâi.

Bai, Kōichi, 1924-
see Iryō jiko seizōbutsu sekinin. 49 [1974]

Bai, Koichi, 1924- joint author
see Suzuki, Rokuya, 1923- (Jinjiho) 50- [1975-

Bai, Kwang June.
A variational method in potential flows with a free surface. [Berkeley] 1972.
vi, 137 l.
Thesis (Ph.D.)–University of California.
Bibliography: leaves 88-91.
CU NUC74-460

Bai, Shi-i
see Pai, Shih-i.

Bai, Sönke, 1941-
see Rudolf Steiner Schule Ruhrgebiet. Die Rudolf Steiner Schule Ruhrgebiet ... Erstausg. [1.-18. Tsd.]. Reinbek bei Hamburg, Rowohlt, 1976.

Bai Shin, Eung
see Shin, Eung Bai, 1938-

Bài ca trên du'ò'ng dài. [Hà-nội] Mỹ thuật Âm nhạc [1971]
12 p. 26 cm.
Unacc. melodies.
1. Songs, Vietnamese.
NIC NUC73-126987

Bài ca; xuân 68. Tho'. Hanoi, Văn Học, 1968.
101 p.
1. Vietnamese poetry–Collections. I. Văn hoc.
ICarbS NUC76-94564

Baia Mare, Romania. Consiliul Popular
see Monografia municipiului Baia Mare. Baia Mare, 1973-

Baia Mare, Romania. Muzeul Județean Maramureș
see
Muzeul Județean Maramureș.

Baia Mare, Romania. Muzeul Regional Maramureş
see Muzeul Regional Maramureş.

Bai͡alieva, Toktobi͡ubi͡u Dzhunushakunova.
(Doislamskie verovanii͡a i ikh perezhitki u kirgizov)
Доисламские верования и их пережитки у киргизов. Под ред. д-ра ист. наук С. М. Абрамзона. Фрунзе, "Илим," 1972.
170 p. 20 cm. 0.57rub USSR 72
At head of title: Академия наук Киргизской ССР. Институт истории. Т. Д. Баялиева.
Includes bibliographical references.
1. Kirghiz—Religion. I. Title.
BL2300.B34 73–347833

Bai͡alinov, Kasymaly.
(Bratstvo)
Братство. Роман. Авториз. пер. с кирг. В. Василевского. [Москва, "Сов. писатель," 1972].
518 p. 21 cm. 0.94rub USSR 72–VKP
At head of title: Касымалы Баялинов.
1. World War, 1939–1945—Fiction. I. Title.
PL65.K59B26 73–323325

Bai͡alinov, M. K., ed.
see Frunze. Kirgizskiĭ gosudarstvennyĭ teatr opery i baleta. Kirgizskiĭ gosudarstvennyĭ ordena Lenina Akademicheskiĭ teatr opery i baleta. **Frunze, Izd-vo "Kyrgyzstan," 1968.**

Baiamonte, John V 1946-
Immigrants in rural America, a study of the Italians of Tangipahoa Parish, Louisiana, by John V. Baiamonte, Jr. Ann Arbor, University Microfilms, 1975, c1972.
vi, 254 l. ill., maps. 22 cm.
Thesis--Mississippi State University.
Photocopy of typescript.
Bibliography: leaves [244]-254.
1. Italians in Louisiana. 2. Tangipahoa Parish, La.--History. I. Title.
LU NUC77-86416

Bai͡an, illus.
see Portretnai͡a gallerei͡a gradonachal'nikov. 1907.

(Bai͡an)
Баянъ; сборникъ произведеній современныхъ славянсихъ поэтовъ и народной поэзіи. Переводъ В. В. Уманова-Каплуновскаго. С.-Петербургъ, Изд. журнала Пантеонъ лит-ры, 1888–
v. 26 cm. (Славянская библіотека, 1)
1. Slavic poetry. I. Umanov-Kaplunovskiĭ, Vladimir Vasil'evich, 1865– tr. II. Series: Slavi͡anskai͡a biblioteka, 1.
PG521.B3 1888 74–222469

(Bai͡an i bai͡anisty)
Баян и баянисты. Сборник метод. материалов. Сост. и общ. ред. Ю. Т. Акимова. Москва, "Сов. композитор," 19
v. 21 cm. 0.78rub (v. 2) varies USSR 74
Includes bibliographical references.
1. Bandonion—Instruction and study. I. Akimov, I͡Uriĭ Timofeevich, ed.
MT681.B25 74–343183

Bai͡anbaev, Kastek.
Chaĭki belokrylye; stikhi. Alma-Ata, Zhazushy, 1973.
150 p. illus.
Title page and text in Kazakh.
Russian title from colophon.
MH NUC75-135227

Bai͡andiev, T
Karakalpakskiĭ gosudarstvennyĭ teatr imeni K. S. Stanislavskogo, 1930-1967; ocherk istorii. Tashkent, Izd-vo "Fan" Uzbekskoĭ SSSR, 1971.
199 p. illus., tables. 23 cm.
At head of title: Ministerstvo kul'tury Uzbekskoĭ SSR. Institut iskusstvoznanii͡a imeni Khamzy Khakim-Zade Nii͡azi. T. Bai͡andiev.
Bibliographical footnotes.
1. Tashkend. Karakalpakskiĭ gosudarstvennyĭ teatr im. K. S. Stanislavskogo. 2. Theater—Uzbekistan.
CLSU NUC76-63235

Bai͡andin, Ėduard Petrovich.
(Kriteriĭ ėffektivnosti nauchno-tekhnicheskikh razrabotok)
Критерий эффективности научно-технических разработок. Москва, "Экономика," 1973.
64 p. 20 cm. 0.21rub USSR 73
At head of title: Э. П. Баяндин.
1. Research, Industrial—Russia. 2. Technological innovations—Russia. I. Title.
T177.R8B34 73–354095

Bai͡andin, Ėduard Petrovich
see Voprosy ėffektivnosti nauchno-issledovatel'skikh rabot. [1975]

Bai͡anov, Akhsan.
Vy poimete meni͡a. [By] Bai͡anov Akhsan Fatkhel'bianovich. Kazan' [Tatknigoizdat] 1971.
158 p. port.
Title page and text in Tatar.
Russian title from colophon.
Poems.
MH NUC74-37577

Bai͡anov, Bulat Khamzeevich.
(Ėkonomika i organizat͡sii͡a raboty vychislitel'nykh ustanovok)
Экономика и организация работы вычислительных установок. Алма-Ата, "Казахстан," 1973.
150 p. 20 cm. 0.43rub USSR 73
At head of title: Б. Баянов, И. Полонская, Л. Толкачева.
1. Data processing service center—Kazakhstan. I. Polonskai͡a, Irina Afanas'evna, joint author. II. Tolkacheva, Lidii͡a Mikhaĭlovna, joint author. III. Title.
HF5548.2.B29 74–303425

Bai͡anov, Esmukhan Bai͡anovich.
(Zhan͡ga ėkonomikalyq reforma zhăne kăsīporyndardy basqarudaghy ȯzgerīster)
Жаңа экономикалық реформа және кәсіпорындарды басқарудағы өзгерістер. Алматы, 1973.
42 p. 20 cm. (Білім қазынасы халыққа) USSR 73–38092
0.08rub
At head of title: Қазақ ССР "Білім" қоғамы. Мемлекет және право білімін насихаттайтын ғылыми-методикалық совет. Е. Баянов.
1. Industrial management. I. Title.
HD37.K29B34 75–972103

Bai͡anov, **Esmukhan Bai͡anovich**
see **Upravlenie promyshlennost'i͡u Kazakhskoĭ SSR. 1972.**

Bai͡anov, Viktor **Mikhaĭlovich.**
Avgust; **rasskaz.** [By] Viktor Bai͡anov. Kemerovo [**Kemerovskoe** knizhnoe izd-vo, 1969]
28 p. **port.** (**Rasskazy**)
MH CaOTU NUC74-55456

Bai͡anskiĭ, Timur Ėmirovich, joint author
see Sokolov, Mikhail Aleksandrovich. Tekhnicheskiĭ progress v obogashchenii rud t͡svetnykh metallov Kazakhstana. 1973.

Baião, Andre
see **Camões, Luis de, 1524?-1580. Os Lusíadas ...** [**Lisboa**] Junta de **Investigações** do **Ultramar, 1972.**

Baião, Antonio, 1878-1961.
Dois testamentos históricos: o do primeiro vice-rei da India, d. Francisco de Almeida e o do Inquisidor Geral, d. Francisco de Castro. Lisboa, 1956.
21 p.
"Separata das Memórias, Academia das Ciências de Lisboa, Classe de letras, tomo 6."
Spanish Inquisition Collection.
1. Almeida, Francisco d', d. 1510. 2. Castro, Francisco de, 1574-1653. I. Title.
CU-SB NUC76-69344

Baião, Antonio, 1878-1961.
Episódios dramáticos da inquisição portuguesa. 3. ed. [Lisboa] "Seara nova," 1972-
v. illus. (facsims.), plates. 22 cm.
(Colecção Seara Nova)
1. Inquisition. Portugal.
ViU NUC74-128971

Baião, Antonio, 1878-1961.
Escavando no passado. Lisboa, 1958-59.
1 v. (various pagings)
Cover title.
"Separata da Revista Occidente, vols. 54,55 e 56."
Spanish Inquisition Collection.
1. Portugal—Hist.—Modern, 1580- —Addresses, essays, lectures. 2. Inquisition. Portugal—Addresses, essays, lectures. I. Title.
CU-SB NUC76-69343

Baião, Domingos Vieira
see Vieira Baião, Domingos.

Baião, José Lopes.
Através do dicionário. Belo Horizonte, 1972.
323 p. 24 cm.
1. Portuguese language—Lexicography. 2. Portuguese language—Etymology—Dictionaries. I. Title.
PC5323.B3 73-213260

Baiardi, Amilcar
see Aspectos metodológicos... Bogotá, Centro Interamericano de Reforma Agraria, 1966.

Baiardi, Giorgio Cerboni
see Cerboni Baiardi, Giorgio.

Baiardi, Giovanni Battista, fl. 1598.
Additiones et annotationes insignes, ac solemnes ad Ivlii Clari lib. V. Receptarvm sentent, sive Practicam criminalem. Hac 3. ed. ... Plurima quidem ad criminum materiam spectantia ... complectentes ... Parmae, Ex Typographia E. Viothi, 1607.
[100], 256 p. 34 cm.
1. Claro, Giulio, 1525-1575. Receptae sententiae. Book 5.
74-212563

Baiardi, John C.
see Aquatic sciences. New York, New York Academy of Sciences, 1975.

Baiardi, Peter, joint author.
see Altman, Irving. Investment recovery ... New York, AMACOM, c1976.

Baiardo, Leila.
L'inseguimento : [romanzo] / Leila Baiardo. — Milano : Bompiani, c1976.
258 p. ; 21 cm. It76-June
L3500
I. Title.
PQ4862.A35215 76-467426
*76 MARC

Bai͡asanov, Dilavar Bilalovich.
(Avtomatizirovannye sistemy upravlenii͡a truboprovodnymi ob"ektami kommunal'nogo khozi͡aĭstva)
Автоматизированные системы управления трубопроводными объектами коммунального хозяйства / Д. Б. Баясанов. — Москва : Стройиздат, 1974.
311 p. : ill. ; 21 cm. USSR 74
Bibliography : p. 310.
1.10rub
1. Heating from central stations—Automation. 2. Gas distribution—Automation. 3. Waterworks—Automation. 4. Pipe lines—Automatic control. I. Title.
TH7641.B16 75-535226

Bai͡asanov, Dilavar Bilalovich.
(Raschet i proektirovanie gorodskikh gazovykh seteĭ srednego i vysokogo davlenii͡a)
Расчет и проектирование городских газовых сетей среднего и высокого давления. Москва, Стройиздат, 1972.
207 p. with illus. 20 cm. 0.50rub USSR 73-VKP
At head of title: Д. Б. Баясанов, З. Я. Быкова.
Bibliography: p. [205]
1. Gas distribution—Mathematical models. 2. Gas distribution—Electromechanical analogies. 3. Electronic data processing—Gas distribution. I. Bykova, Zoi͡a Īakovlevna, joint author. II. Title.
TP757.B265 73-335181

Bai͡asanov, Dilavar Bilalovich
see Aleksandrov, Aleksandr Vasil'evich. (Primenenie ėlektronno-vychislitel'nykh mashin dli͡a rascheta i upravlenii͡a v sistemakh dal'nego transporta gaza) 1970.

Băiașu, Nicolae Gh
Exercițiul fizic pentru toți. [Coperta: D. Negrea. Desene: Alexandrina Vrînceanu]. [București], „Stadion," 1972.
280 p. with figs. 18 cm. lei 9.50 R 72-4199
At head of title: N. Băiașu, A. Bîrlea, S. Magda.
Bibliography: p. [278]
1. Exercise. I. Bîrlea, Adina, joint author. II. Magda, Silviu, joint author. III. Title.
GV481.B2355 74-327754

Băiașu, Nicolae Gh
Jocuri acrobatice și piramide. (Pentru pionieri și școlari). [Coperta: Petre Molnar. Desene: Anastasia Ionescu]. [București], „Stadion," 1972.
88 p. with figs. 21 cm. lei 5.75 R 72-2680
At head of title: N. Gh. Băiașu, V. Andronescu.
Bibliography: p. 87.
1. Pyramids (Gymnastics) I. Andronescu, V., joint author. II. Title.
GV537.B34 74-347594

Băiasu, Nicolae Gh.
see Gimnastica. [Bucuresti], ,,Stadion," 1972.

(Bai͡avai͡a ŭskalos')
Баявая ўскалось.
Торонто.
v. illus. 21 cm.
AP58.W5B34 73-645898
MARC-S

Bai͡azitov, Baĭghozha.
(Maqta-Dalam)
Мақта-Далам : өлеңдер / Байғожа Баязитов. — Алматы : Жазушы, 1966.
45 p. ; 15 cm. — (Тұңғыш кітап)
I. Title.
PL65.K49B25 75-588115

Baĭbaeva, Sof'i͡a Timofeevna
see Metody analiza lakokrasochnykh materialov. 1974.

Baĭbakov, A. I., ed.
see Ėkonomicheskie problemy nauchno-tekhnicheskogo progressa v sot͡sialisticheskikh i kapitalisticheskikh stranakh. 1972.

Baĭbakov, A.I.
see Voprosy organizatsii i upravlenii͡a narodnym khozi͡aĭstvom sot͡sialisticheskikh stran na sovremennom ėtape. 1976.

Baĭbakov, Aleksandr Borisovich, ed.
see Lenins'ka kuzni͡a, Zavod, Kiev. Istorii͡a ordena Lenina zavoda "Leninskai͡a kuznit͡sa", 1862-1962 gg. [Kiev] Izd-vo Kievskogo univ., 1967.

Baĭbakov, Nikolaĭ Konstantinovich.
(O Gosudarstvennom pi͡atiletnem plane razvitii͡a narodnogo khozi͡aĭstva SSSR na 1976-1980 gody i o Gosudarstvennom plane razitii͡a narodnogo khozi͡aĭstva SSSR na 1977 god)
О государственном пятилетнем плане развития народного хозяйства СССР на 1976–1980 годы и о Государственном плане развития народного хозяйства СССР на 1977 год : доклад и заключительное слово на пятой сессии Верховного Совета СССР девятого созыва / Н. К. Байбаков. Закон Союза Советских Социалистических Республик о Государственном пятилетнем плане развития народного хозяйства СССР на 1976–1980 годы. Закон Союза Советских Социалистических Республик о Государственном плане развития народного хозяйства СССР на 1977 год. — Москва : Политиздат, 1976.
46 p. ; 20 cm. USSR***
0.06rub
1. Russia — Economic policy — 1976- I. Russia (1923- U. S. S. R.). Laws, statutes, etc. Zakon Soi͡uza Sovetskikh Sot͡sialisticheskikh Respublik o Gosudarstvennom pi͡atiletnem plane razvitii͡a narodnogo khozi͡aĭstva SSSR na 1976-1980 gody. 1976. II. Russia (1923- U. S. S. R.). Laws, statutes, etc. Zakon Soi͡uza Sovetskikh Sot͡sialisticheskikh Respublik o Gosudarstvennom plane razvitii͡a narodnogo khozi͡aĭstva SSSR na 1977 god. 1976. III. Title: O Gosudarstvennom pi͡atiletnem plane razvitii͡a narodnogo khozi͡aĭstva SSSR na 1976-1980 gody ... IV. Title: Zakon Soi͡uza Sovetskikh Sot͡sialisticheskikh Respublik o Gosudarstvennom pi͡atiletnem plane ... V. Title: Zakon Soi͡uza Sovetskikh Sot͡sialisticheskikh Respublik o Gosudarstvennom plane ...
HC336.25.B339 77-514196

Baĭbakov, Nikolaĭ Konstantinovich.
O gosudarstvennom plane razvitii͡a narodnogo khozi͡aĭstva SSSR na 1970 god; doklad i zakli͡uchitel'noe slovo na 7. sessii Verkhovnogo Soveta SSSR 7. sozyva. Zakon Soi͡uza Sovetskikh Sot͡sialisticheskikh Respublik o gosudarstvennom plane razvitii͡a narodnogo khozi͡aĭstva SSSR na 1970 god. Moskva, Izd-vo polit. lit-ry, 1969.
47 p.
At head of title: N. K. Baĭbakov.
MiU InU NUC74-41718

Baĭbakov, Nikolaĭ Konstantinovich.
(O gosudarstvennom plane razvitii͡a narodnogo khozi͡aĭstva SSSR na tysi͡acha devi͡at'sot sem'desi͡at pi͡atyĭ god)
О государственном плане развития народного хозяйства СССР на 1975 год : доклад и заключительное слово на второй сессии Верховного Совета СССР девятого созыва ; Закон Союза Советских Социалистических республик о государственном плане развития народного хозяйства СССР на 1975 год / Н. К. Байбаков. — Москва : Политиздат, 1974.
45 p. ; 21 cm. USSR***
0.05rub
1. Russia—Economic policy—1971- I. Russia (1923- U. S. S. R.). Laws, statutes, etc. Zakon o gosudarstvennom plane razvitii͡a narodnogo khozi͡aĭstva SSSR na 1975 god. II. Title. III. Title: Zakon Soi͡uza Sovetskikh Sot͡sialisticheskikh Respublik o gosudarstvennom plane razvitii͡a narodnogo khozi͡aĭstva SSSR na 1975 god.
HC336.24.B354 75-581029

Baĭbakov, Nikolaĭ Konstantinovich.
(O gosudarstvennom plane razvitii͡a narodnogo khozi͡aĭstva SSSR na tysi͡acha devi͡at'sot sem'desi͡at shestoĭ god)
О государственном плане развития народного хозяйства СССР на 1976 год : доклад и заключительное слово на четвертой сессии Верховного Совета СССР девятого созыва / Н. К. Байбаков. Закон Союза Советских Социалистических Республик о государственном плане развития народного хозяйства СССР на 1976 год. — Москва : Политиздат, 1975.
46 p. ; 21 cm. USSR***
0.05rub
1. Russia—Economic policy—1976- I. Russia (1923- U. S. S. R.). Laws, statutes, etc. Zakon o gosudarstvennom plane razvitii͡a narodnogo khozi͡aĭstva SSSR na 1976 god. 1975.
HC336.25.B34 76-523844

Baĭbakov, Nikolaĭ Konstantinovich, ed.
see State Five-Year Plan... [Arlington, Va.] 1972.

Baĭbekov, Shmidt Salikhovich.
Товароведение культтоваров. [Учебник для техникумов сов. торговли]. Москва, "Экономика," 1972.
384 p. with illus. and music. 22 cm. 1.04rub USSR 72-VKP
At head of title: Ш. С. Байбеков, В. А. Ковалева, А. Ф. Мацко.
1. Sporting goods. 2. Recreation — Economic aspects — Russia. I. Kovaleva, Valentina Aleksandrovna, joint author. II. Mat͡sko, Anna Fedorovna, joint author. III. Title.
HD9999.S922R82 72-367346

Baibi, S Y
Kafka's castle [by] S. Y. Baibi. New York, Poet Gallery Press [c1973]
128 p. 28 cm.
I. Title.
OU NUC75-18359

Baibiene, Marta J de Buono de
see Buono de Baibiene, Marta J de.

Baĭbolov, Urkalyĭ Baĭbolovich.
(Pensionnoe obespechenie kolkhoznikov)
Пенсионное обеспечение колхозников. Фрунзе, "Кыргызстан," 1972.
88 p. 20 cm. 0.14rub USSR 72-VKP
At head of title: У. Б. Байболов, С. П. Балацкий.
1. Collective farms—Pensions—Russia. I. Balat͡skiĭ, Sergeĭ Petrovich, joint author. II. Title.
73-325119

Baĭborodin, IU. V.
see Bortovye sistemy upravleniia poletom. 1975.

Baibot, D
Arte y técnicas del escaparate / D. Baibot. — Barcelona : L. E. D. A., 1974.
94 p. : ill. ; 27 cm. Sp***
ISBN 84-7095-082-7 : 395ptas
1. Show-windows. 2. Display of merchandise. I. Title.
HF5845.B3 659.1'57 75-552140

Baĭbulatov, Ėrik Begalievich.
(K metodike sostavleniia mineral'nykh balansov po olovorudnym i redkometal'nym mestorozhdeniiam)
К методике составления минеральных балансов по оловорудным и редкометальным месторождениям / Э. Байбулатов, В. Ким. — Фрунзе : Илим, 1973.
150 p., [16] fold. leaves ; 21 cm. USSR 73
At head of title: Akademiia nauk Kirgizskoĭ SSR. Institut geologii.
Bibliography: p. 150.
0.55rub
1. Tin ores—Analysis. 2. Earths, Rare—Analysis. I. Kim, V. F., joint author. II. Title.
TN580.T5B34 75-526107

Baĭbulatov, Ėrik Begalievich
see Granitoidy vostochnoĭ chasti IUzhnogo Tian'-Shaniia. 1973.

Baĭbulatov, Ėrik Begalievich
see Magmatizm i metallogeniia Severnoĭ Kirgizii. 1975.

Baĭbulov, Daut Khadyevich.
(Shakhtnaia plavka mednykh rud i med'soderzhashchikh materialov)
Шахтная плавка медных руд и медьсодержащих материалов. Пособие для рабочих. Москва, "Металлургия," 1973.
128 p. with diagrs. 20 cm. (Библиотечка рабочего цветной металлургии) 0.24rub USSR 73
At head of title: Д. Х. Байбулов, Ю. И. Молвинских.
Bibliography: p. [128]
1. Copper—Metallurgy. 2. Smelting furnaces. I. Molvinskikh, IUriĭ Ivanovich, joint author. II. Title.
TN780.B33 73-366044

Baĭburdi, Chingiz Gulam-Ali.
Жизнь и творчество Низāрӣ—персидского поэта XIII–XIV вв. Москва, Наука; Глав. ред. восточной лит-ры, 1966.
269 p. 20 cm.
At head of title: Ленинградский государственный университет им. А. А. Жданова. Ч. Г. Байбурди.
Bibliography: p. 252–[263]
1. Nizārī Quhistānī, Sa'd al-Din, 1247 or 8–1320 or 21. I. Title. Title romanized: Zhizn' i tvorchestvo Nizārī.
PK6495.N57Z58 73-216906

Baĭburin, Ghabdulla.
Dva buketa landysheĭ; rasskazy. Perevod s bashkirskogo. Moskva, Sovetskaia Rossiia, 1971.
93 p.
I. Title.
CaOTU NUC74-38267

Baĭburin, Ghabdulla.
Lomtik khleba. [By] Baĭburin Gabdulla Gindullovich. [Ufa, Bashkirskoe knizhnoe izd-vo] 1972.
134 p.
Title page and text in Bashkir.
Russian title from colophon.
MH NUC76-14934

Baĭburin, Ghabdulla, comp.
see IAsh kostăr. 1960.

Baica, Hortensia, joint author
see Belu, Elena. Cartea, reflectare a transformărilor... Timisoara, 1972.

Baica, Hortensia
see Biblioteca Municipală Timisoara. Serviciul Bibliografic. Condeie în slujba păcii. Timisoara, 1972.

Baica, Hortensia, ed.
see Biblioteca Municipală Timisoara. Serviciul Bibliografic. Literatură social-politică. Timisoara, 1973.

Baican, Roman.
Amplificatori maser cu corp solid / Roman Baican. — [Bucureşti] : Editura Academiei Republicii Socialiste România, 1976.
254 p. : ill. ; 21 cm. R76-2621
Summary in English.
Table of contents in Romanian and English.
Bibliography: p. [243]-[250]
lei13.00
1. Masers. I. Title.
TK7871.4.B34 76-478374
*76 MARC

Băican, V., joint author
see Gugiuman, Ion. Judetul Vaslui. Bucuresti, Editura Academiei Republicii Socialiste România, 1973.

Baïche, André.
La naissance du baroque français : poésie et image de la Pléiade à Jean de La Ceppède / André Baïche ; avant-propos de Jacques Maurens. — Toulouse : Association des publications de l'Université de Toulouse-Le-Mirail, 1976.
477 p. ; 24 cm. — (Publications de l'Université de Toulouse-Le-Mirail : Série A ; t. 31) F***
Bibliography: p. [435]-465.
Includes index.
1. French poetry—16th century—History and criticism. 2. French poetry—17th century—History and criticism. 3. Baroque literature—History and criticism. I. Title. II. Series: Université de Toulouse-Le Mirail. Publications : Série A ; t. 31.
PQ418.B3 841'.3'09 76-485330
76 MARC

Baichere, P.
see Semaine de Bruges, 12th, 1975. Formation et perfectionnement des fonctionnaires internationaux et européens... Bruges, De Tempel, 1976.

Baĭchikov, Alekseĭ Gavrilovich, joint author
see Rubtsov, Mikhail Vasil'evich. Sinteticheskie khimiko-farmatsevticheskie preparaty. 1971.

Baĭchinski, Kostadin.
(Dvizheshti sili na sotsialniia progres)
Движещи сили на социалния прогрес : [моногр.] / Костадин Байчински. — 1. изд. — София : Партиздат, 1977.
301 p. ; 21 cm. Bu 77-745
Includes bibliographical references.
1.29 lv
1. Communism. 2. Labor and laboring classes. 3. Bŭlgarska komunisticheska partiia. 4. Russia—Relations (general) with Bulgaria. 5. Bulgaria—Relations (general) with Russia. I. Title.
HX40.B32 77-508823

Baĭchinski, Kostadin.
(Istoricheskata nauka—mogŭshto ideĭno orŭzhie v borbata protiv fashizma i kapitalizma)
Историческата наука—могъщо идейно оръжие в борбата против фашизма и капитализма : [науч.-попул. очерк] / К. Байчински, А. Веков. — София : ОФ, 1977.
58 p. ; 21 cm. — (Поредица Исторически и военно-патриотични знания ; 1977, 1-2) (Библиотека на Дружество Георги Кирков) Bu 77-637
Series 2 romanized: Biblioteka na Druzhestvo Georgi Kirkov.
Includes bibliographical references.
0.24 lv
1. History—Addresses, essays, lectures. 2. Bulgaria—History—Addresses, essays, lectures. I. Vekov, Angel Khr., joint author. II. Title. III. Series: Poreditsa Istoricheski i voenno-patriotichni znaniia ; 1977, 1-2.
D8.B34 77-512705

Baĭchinski, Kostadin. Povishavane rŭkovodnata roliia na komunisticheskata partiia v upravlenieto na sotsialisticheskoto obshtestvo. 1970
see Kirov, Todor. Sotsialni predpostavki i osnovni nasoki za usŭvŭrshenstvuvane sistemata na sotsialnoto upravlenie v NR Bŭlgariia. 1970.

Baĭchinski, Kostadin.
Velikiiat Oktomvri i nashata suvremennost. Sofiia, Izd-vo [na Bŭlgarskata komunisticheska partiia] 1967.
235 p.
1. Russia (1917-)–Hist.–1917-1921–Influence. 2. History–Modern–20th century.
MH ViU CSt-H NUC74-55457

Baĭchinski, Kostadin, ed.
see Bŭlgarskata komunisticheska partiia–rŭkovoditel i organizator na izgrazhdaneto na razvito sotsialistichesko obshtestvo v Bŭlgariia. 1974.

Baĭchinski, Kostadin, ed.
see Internatsionalizmŭt na BKP. 1974.

Baĭchinski, Kostadin, ed.
see IUbileĭna nauchna sesiia na tema Roliata na Septemvriĭskoto vŭstanie 1923 g. za bolshevizatsiiata na BKP, Mikhaylovgrad, Bulgaria, 1973. (Velikiiat prelom) 1974.

Baĭchinski, Kostadin
see Politika potvŭrdena ot zhivota. 1976.

Baichis, Yves de Gentil-
see Gentil-Baichis, Yves de.

Baichoralany, Magomet.
Iarkaia zvezda nad Burmamutom; stikhi. [By] Baichorov Magomet Kyskhaevich. [Cherkessk, Stavropol'skoe knizhnoe izd-vo, Karachaevo-Cherkesskoe otd-nie, 1970]
61 p.
Title page and text in Karachaev.
Russian title from colophon.
MH NUC74-37578

Baĭchoralany, Magomet.
(Ullu K"arachaĭda)
Уллу Къарачайда : роман / Байчораланы Магомет. — Черкесск : Ставрополь китаб издательствону Къарачай-Черкес бёлюмю, 1967.
325 p. : port. ; 21 cm.
I. Title.
PL65.K29B28 75-586809

Baĭchorov, Aleksandr Mukhtarovich.
(Problemy konsolidatsii demokraticheskikh sil SShA v sovremennykh usloviiakh)
Проблемы консолидации демократических сил США в современных условиях / А. М. Байчоров. — Минск : Изд-во БГУ, 1975.
160 p. ; 17 cm. USSR 75
Includes bibliographical references.
0.77rub
1. United States—Politics and government—1945- I. Title.
E839.5.B34 76-513033

Baĭchorov, Magomet Kyskhaevich
see
Baĭchoralany, Magomet.

Baĭchorova, Z. L.
see Iz istorii komsomol'skoĭ organizatsii Karachaevo-Cherkesiĭ... Cherkessk, Karachaevo-Cherkesskoe otd-nie Stavropol'skogo knizhnogo izd-va, 1972.

Baicu, Ion St., ed.
see Prahova. Trepte în istorie. Ploieşti, Sectia de propagandă a Comitetului judetean Prahova al P. C. R., 1971.

Băiculescu, Emilian, joint author
see Adler, Ladislau. Arhitectura industriei contemporane. Bucureşti, Editura tehnică, 1972.

Băiculescu, George.
Strigătul : schiţe şi povestiri / George Băiculescu ; [coperta de Dan Zegreanu]. — Bucureşti : Litera, 1975.
71 p., [1] leaf of plates : port. ; 20 cm. R 76-1925
lei 9.50
I. Title.
PC840.12.A39S7 76-524851

Baid, Kushalkumar Moolchand.
Elongational flows of dilute polymer solutions. [Newark, Del.] 1973.
207 l. illus.
Thesis (Ph. D.)–University of Delaware.
1. Solution (Chemistry) 2. Polymers and polymerization. I. Title.
DeU NUC74-120662

Baida, Basanta Kumārī.
(Vidyārthiyoṃ kī duścintāeṃ)
विद्यार्थियों की दुश्चिन्ताएँ. [लेखिका] बसंत कुमारी बैद. [1. संस्करण] बीकानेर, कल्पना प्रकाशन [1973]
76 p. 23 cm. Rs7.00
In Hindi.
Bibliography: p. 76.

1. Students—India. I. Title.

LA1153.7.B34 74-900091

Baida, Indararāja, 1941–
(Rāshṭramaṅgala)
राष्ट्रमंगल; स्वतंत्रता के पच्चीस्वें वर्ष के अभिनंदन में प्रकाशित राष्ट्रीय कविताओं का संग्रह. [लेखक] इंदरराज बैद 'अधीर.' [1. संस्करण] मद्रास, राज प्रकाशन [1972]
72 p. 23 cm. Rs5.00
In Hindi.

I. Title.
PK2098.13.A365R3 73–905198

Baida, Iurii
see The Lower Pleistocene of the Central Jordan Valley... Jerusalem, Israel Academy of Sciences and Humanities, 1966.

Baĭda, Leonid Il'ich
see Ėlektricheskie izmereni͡ia. 1973.

Baĭda, Vasiliĭ Ivanovich
see Gornorudnoe proizvodstvo. 1974.

Baĭdakov, B. S.
see Gvardeĭt͡sy trudovoĭ vakhty. Moskva, Sovetskai͡a Rossii͡a, 1972.

Baidal, José, 1920–
El país del largo viaje. [Alicante, Fondo Editorial del Excmo. Ayuntamiento de Alicante, 1973]
302 p. 21 cm. (Serie Premios literarios, 2) Sp***
ISBN 84–500–5644–6
1. Araucanian Indians—Fiction. I. Title. II. Series.
PQ7798.12.A43P3 74–353656

Baĭdal, Mikhail Kharlampievich
see Voprosy dolgosrochnykh prognozov pogody. 1975.

Baidal, Mikhail Kharlampievich, ed.
see Voprosy kolebaniia klimata i vodnykh resursov. 1972.

Baĭdauletov, Oraztaĭ Kibraimovich.
(Vli͡ianie mutagenov na formoobrazovanie pshenit͡sy)
Влияние мутагенов на формообразование пшеницы. Алма-Ата, "Наука," 1972.
105 p. with illus. 20 cm. 0.71rub USSR 72–VKP
At head of title: Академия наук Казахской ССР. Институт ботаники. О. К. Байдаулетов.
Bibliography: p. 94–104.
1. Wheat breeding. 2. Mutation breeding. I. Title.
SB191.W5B29 73–312178

al-Baiḍāwī
see al-Bayḍāwī, 'Abd Allāh ibn 'Umar, d. 1286?

Baide, Oscar
see Salt Lake City. Engineering Dept. Map of Salt Lake City. Salt Lake City, 1973.

Baĭdebura, Pavlo Andriĭovych, 1901–
Iskry hnivu; povisti. Kyïv, Rad. pys'mennyk, 1974.
280 p. 18 cm.
1. Labor and laboring classes–Ukraine. I. Title.
CaBVaU NUC76-508

Baĭdebura, Pavlo Andriĭovych, 1901–
Zelene polum'i͡a; opovidanni͡a ta povisti. [By] Pavlo Baidebura. Donet͡s'k, Vyd-vo Donbas, 1970.
278 p. port.
MH NUC74-37575

Baidēs, Thōmas Ath
Kōnstantinos; meletē politikēs historias kai kritikēs. 2. ekd. Athēna, Ekdoseis Bayron, 1973.
7, 271 p. 21 cm.
Bibliography: p. 267–271.
1. Constantine I, King of the Hellenes, 1868–1923. I. Title.
CU NUC75-26451

বৈদিক. বর্ষ 1– বৈশাখ ১৩৭৪ [1968–
কলিকাতা, পাশ্চাত্তা বৈদিক সঙ্ঘ.
v. 22 cm. bimonthly.

1. Civilization, Hindu—Periodicals. I. Paschatya Baidik Sangha.
Title romanized: Baidika.
DS401.B35 79–904303

Baĭdildaev, Mardan
see Aĭtys. 196

Baĭdin, Sergeĭ Stepanovich
see Gidrologi͡ia ust'evykh oblasteĭ rek Tereka i Sulaka. 1971.

Baidin, Sergei Stepanovich, ed.
see Mikhailov, Vadim Nikolaevich. (Bibliografiia po gidrologii morskikh ust'ev rek) 1969.

Baĭdin, Sergeĭ Stepanovich
see Voprosy gidrologii i gidrokhimii ust'ev rek. 1974.

Baĭdin, Sergeĭ Stepanovich
see Voprosy gidrologii ust'ev rek. 1976.

Baĭdosov, V. A., ed.
see Ekstremal'nye strategii v pozit͡sionnykh differen͡tsial'nykh igrakh. 1974.

Baĭdukov, Georgiĭ Filippovich, 1907–
(Chkalov)
Чкалов / Г. Байдуков. — Москва : Мол. гвардия, 1975.
334 p., [17] leaves of plates : ill. ; 21 cm. — (Жизнь замечательных людей ; вып. 9 (552)) USSR 75
Series romanized: Zhizn' zamechatel'nykh li͡udeĭ.
Bibliography: p. 331–[332]
0.92rub
1. Chkalov, Valeriĭ Pavlovich, 1904–1938.
TL540.C56B29 75–405149

Baidya, Pūrṇabahādura.
सरासु. [लेखक पूर्णबहादुर बैद्य. कान्तिपुर] पासामुना [1967?]
121 p. 23 cm. Rs4
In Newari.
Poems.

I. Title.
Title romanized: Sarāsu.
PL3801.N59B26 S A 68-9205

Baidya Nath Prasad, 1932–
see
Prasad, Baidya Nath, 1932–

Baidya Nath Varma
see **Varma, Baidya Nath, 1921–**

Baidyanath Mishra Sarma
see
Mishra Sarma, Baidyanath, 1909–

Baĭdyev, Sanzhara.
Dvoinoe otrazhenie; vos'mistishii͡a, poėma, iorely. [Per. s kalmytskogo] Ėlista, Kalmytskoe knizhnoe izd-vo, 1970.
199 p. illus.
MH NUC76-14933

Baĭdyev, Sanzhara.
Zemnoe pritiazhenie. [By] Baĭdyev Sanzhara Lidzhievich. Elista, Kalmytskoe knizhnoe izd-vo, 1968.
162 p.
Title page and text in Kalmuch.
Russian title from colophon.
Poems.
MH NUC74-37576

Baĭdzhanov, Valeriĭ Raufovich.
(Povyshenie ėffektivnosti proizvodstva na zavode)
Повышение эффективности производства на заводе. [Ташк. инструм. з-д]. Ташкент, Узбекистан, 1973.
48 p. with illus. 20 cm. 0.16rub USSR 73
At head of title: В. Р. Байджанов.
1. Industrial productivity. 2. Machine-tools—Trade and manufacture—Tashkend. I. Title.
HD9703.R83T372 74–300922

Baĭdzhiev, Mar Tashimovich, 1935–
Chuzhoe schast'e; novelly, povest', kinopovest'. [Frunze, "Kyrgyzstan," 1969]
200 p. front.
I. Title.
WaU NUC76-14932

Baĭdzhiev, Mar Tashimovich, 1935–
(Moi͡a zolotai͡a rybka)
Моя золотая рыбка : Рассказы и повести / Мар Байджиев ; [Худож. С. Соколов]. — Москва : Мол. гвардия, 1976.
255 p. : ill. ; 16 cm. USSR 76
CONTENTS: Моя золотая рыбка.—Улыбка.—Воровка.—Когда гибнет Чапай.—Преступление и наказание, или Красные уши.—Мой хлеб.—Сулуу.—Осенние дожди.—Тропа.—Чужое счастье.—Дуэль.
0.38rub
I. Title.
PG3479.I 36M6 77–504860

Baie, Lyle Frederick, 1942–
Post-Cretaceous structures and sediment of the northeast Campeche Platform, Gulf of Mexico. [College Station, Tex.] 1970.
xii, 118 l. illus.
Thesis—Texas A & M University.
Vita.
Bibliography: leaves 105–110.
Photocopy of typescript. Ann Arbor, Mich., University Microfilms, 1971. 23 cm.
1. Submarine geology. 2. Marine sediments—Mexico, Gulf of. 3. Geology—Mexico, Gulf of. I. Title.
OU NUC74-121068

(Baien shori gijutsu sōsho)
ばい煙処理技術叢書 no. 1– [東京] 通商産業省企業局 1965–
no. illus. (part fold.) 27 cm.

1. Smoke prevention—Collected works. 2. Fume control—Collected works. I. Japan. Tsūshō Sangyōshō. Kigyōkyoku.
TD884.B4 75–790743

Baier, Eduard.
Gemüse- und Obstdauerwaren (Konserven) : eine Beschreibung nach wirtschaftlichen, chemisch-technologischen, nahrungsmittelrechtlichen und hygienischen Gesichtspunkten / von E. Baier. — Leipzig : Akademische Verlagsgesellschaft, 1920.
p. 242-457 ; 25 cm.
Originally published in K. H. v. Buchka's Das Lebensmittelgewerbe, vol. 2, chapter 1, pt. 4.
Includes bibliographical references and index.
1. Vegetables—Preservation. 2. Fruit—Preservation. I. Buchka, Karl Heinrich von, 1856-1917. Das Lebensmittelgewerbe, vol. 2, chapter 1, pt. 4. II. Title.
TP443.B33 76-478025
76 MARC

Baier, Erich.
Sozialstruktur, Community Development und Entwicklungsplanung in Äthiopien / von Erich Baier. — München : Weltforum-Verlag, 1974.
vi, 413 p. : 8 maps ; 30 cm. — (IFO-Forschungsberichte der Afrika-Studienstelle ; 52) GFR 75–A
Bibliography: p. 362–387.
ISBN 3–8039–0108–1 : DM32.00
1. Community development—Ethiopia. 2. Social change. I. Title. II. Series: IFO-Institut für Wirtschaftsforschung, Munich. Afrika-Studienstelle. Forschungsberichte ; 52.
HN831.E84C614 75–534427

Baier, Erwin, 1947-
Kostenrisiko und Grundgesetz / vorgelegt von Erwin Baier. — [s.l. : s.n., 1974?]
xxiv, 199 p. ; 21 cm. GFR***
Thesis—Erlangen-Nürnberg.
Vita.
Bibliography: p. xii-xxiii.
1. Costs (Law)—Germany, West. 2. Germany, West—Constitutional law. I. Title.
76-463150
76 MARC

Baier, Gerd.
Die Denkmale des Kreises Greifswald. Bearb. von Gerd Baier, Horst Ende ₍und₎ Renate Krüger. Leipzig, E. A. Seemann, 1973.
239 p. illus., 128 plates. 25 cm. (Die Denkmale im Bezirk Rostock) 45.00M GDR***
Bibliography: p. ₍228₎–232.
1. Art—Greifswald (Landkreis)—Guide-books. 2. Architecture—Greifswald (Landkreis)—Guide-books. I. Ende, Horst, joint author. II. Krüger, Renate, joint author. III. Title.
N6874.G7B34 74–305075

Baier, Hans.
Stilkunde / Hans Baier ; ₍Zeichn. Inge Brüx-Gohrisch₎. — Leipzig : Seemann, VEB, 1976.
343 p. : numerous ill. (some col.) ; 20 cm. — (Taschenbuch der Künste) GFR77-A
Bibliography: p. 325-₍327₎
Includes indexes.
7.50M
1. Art—History. I. Title.
N5302.B24 77-482053
77 MARC

Baier, Helmut.
Kirchenkampf in Nürnberg 1933–1945. Nürnberg, Korn u. Berg, 1973.
38 p., 16 p. of illus. 21 cm. DM7.00 GDR 73–A43
"Erstmalig veröffentlicht im 'Nürnberger Gemeindeblatt' 1972, Nr. 36–40."
1. Church and state in Nuremberg. I. Title.
BR858.N87B34 74–310176
ISBN 3–87432–015–4

Baier, Helmut.
Die Stab-Linie-Problematik; eine organisatorische Systemanalyse insbesondere von Versicherungsbetrieben. Karlsruhe, Verlag Versicherungswirtschaft, 1973.
x, 181 p. illus. 21 cm. (Beiträge zu wirtschaftswissenschaftlichen Problemen der Versicherung, Bd. 6) GFR***
Bibliography: p. 145–181.
1. Insurance companies—Management. 2. Industrial organization. I. Title.
HG8075.B33 73–337240

Baier, Hermann.
Das Heidelberger Schloss : ₍Schlossführer₎ / von Hermann Baier. — 3., durchges. Aufl. — Heidelberg : Sauer ₍1972₎.
32 p. : ill. ; 21 cm. GFR 74–A
ISBN 3–7938–7470–2 : DM2.50
1. Heidelberg. Castle. I. Title.
DD901.H57B34 1972 914.3'46 75–575864

Baier, Herwig, comp.
Aspekte der Lernbehindertenpädagogik: einführende Texte/ hrsg. von Herwig Baier und Gerhard Klein. — Berlin-Charlottenburg: Marhold, 1973.
vii, 311 p.; 21 cm. DM26.00 GFR 74–A
Includes bibliographies.
1. Handicapped children—Education—Germany (Federal Republic, 1949–) I. Klein, Gerhard, writer on education, joint comp. II. Title.
LC4036.G4B34 74–323915
ISBN 3–7864–0318–X

Baier, Herwig.
Das Freizeitverhalten und die kulturellen Interessen des Volksschullehrers: eine empir. Untersuchung/ Herwig Baier. — Neuburgweier (Karlsruhe): Schindele, 1972.
234 p.: ill.; 21 cm. DM16.80 GDB 73–A2
Bibliography: p. 218–229.
1. Teachers—Out-of-school activities. I. Title.
LB2844.1.O8B34 73–315267

Baier, Jane Rockmore, 1945-
The treatment of space in Maeterlinck's theater. [n.p.] 1975.
216 l. 29 cm.
Thesis (Ph.D.)—University of Wisconsin.
Vita.
Includes bibliography.
1. Maeterlinck, Maurice, 1862-1949. I. Title.
WU NUC77-84356

Baier, Jean, 1932-
see Recherches et expérimentation: Baier, Candolfi, Duarte ... Lausanne ... 1970.

Baier, John L
An analysis of undergraduate student attrition at Southern Illinois University at Carbondale 1970-1973, by John L. Baier. ₍Carbondale, Ill.₎ 1974.
vi, 181 l. illus. maps. 29 cm.
Thesis—Southern Illinois University.
Vita.
Bibliography: leaves 126-128.
Appendices: A-O (leaves 130-181)
1. Southern Illinois University—Students. 2. College dropouts. 3. Student registration. I. Title.
ICarbS NUC76-15511

Baier, Joseph George, jr.
A history of the first ten years of the College of Letters and Science of the University of Wisconsin—Milwaukee, 1956-1966 / Joseph G. Baier. — Milwaukee : The University, 1975, 1976.
vi, 192 leaves ; 28 cm.
Cover title: The first ten years.
Includes index.
1. Wisconsin. University—Milwaukee. College of Letters and Science—History. I. Title: A history of the first ten years of the College of Letters and Science ... II. Title: The first ten years.
LD6149.5.M5B34 378.775'95 76-368033
76 MARC

Baier, Jürgen.
Über den Einfluss des schnellen Neutronenflusses auf das mechanische Verhalten Beschichteter Brennstoffteilchen im HTR, von J. Baier. ₍Jülich, Kernforschungsanlage Jülich, Kernforschungsanlage Jülich, 1974₎
141 p. illus. (Berichte der Kernforschungsanlage Jülich, Nr. 1038)
HTRB-Projekt Jül-1038-HT.
D 82 (Diss. T.H. Aachen)
Summary in English and German.
"Als Manuskript gedruckt."
ICRL NUC76-16060

Baier, L S
Vietnam, "the filthy liars" and you; a nautical and political saga you will never forget. [2d ed. Portland, Or., Graphic Arts Center, 1970, c1968]
181 p.
"First edition-Originally part I only. Second edition (part I and part II)"
I. Title.
NmU NUC75-31006

Baier, Lothar, 1942– comp.
Über Ror Wolf. ₍1. Aufl. Frankfurt am Main₎ Suhrkamp ₍1972₎
175, ₍1₎ p. 18 cm. (Edition Suhrkamp, 559) GDB***
Bibliography of works by and about R. Wolf: p. 167–₍176₎; includes bibliographical references.
1. Wolf, Ror, 1932– I. Title.
PT2685.O366Z57 72–358522

Baier, Patricia.
see The National Archery Association instructor's manual. 2d ed. Lancaster, Pa., The Association, c1976.

Baier, Robert E., 1939-
see Applied chemistry at protein interfaces ... Washington, American Chemical Society, 1975.

Baier, Rodger Willard, 1930-
Lead distribution in coastal waters. ₍Seattle₎ 1971.
189 l. illus.
Thesis (Ph.D.)—University of Washington.
Bibliography: leaves 146-159.
1. Lead. 2. Marine pollution. 3. Water—Pollution—Research. I. Title.
WaU NUC73-126524

Baier, Rosemarie, joint author.
see Dorfmüller, Monika. Angewandte Psychologie für das kranke Kind. 1. Aufl. München, Urban und Schwarzenberg, 1977.

Baier, Stephan.
see Die Arbeitslosenversicherung, in den Händen der Kapitalisten Mittel zur Lohndrückerei, gehört in die Hände der arbeitenden Klassen. 1. Aufl. Mannheim, J. Sendler, c1975.

Baier, Stephen Brock, 1944-
African merchants in the colonial period: a history of commerce in Damagaram (Central Niger) 1880-1960. ₍n.p.₎ c1974.
303 l. illus. 29 cm.
Thesis (Ph.D.)—University of Wisconsin.
Vita.
Includes bibliography.
1. Damagaram, Niger—Econ. condit. I. Title.
WU NUC75-21073

Baier, Stephen Brock, 1944-
Al-Hajj Moctar ibn Sharif Bashir, c1890-1971; a Muslim merchant of Sahelian Niger. Stephen Baier. Chicago, University of Chicago, Department of Economics, 1975.
30 p. 28 cm. (Report, 7475-19)
Presented at the Workshop in Economic History, March 14, 1975.
Includes bibliographical references.
InNd NUC77-84452

Baĭer, Vladimir Nikolaevich.
(Izluchenie reliâtivistskikh ėlektronov)
Излучение релятивистских электронов. Москва, Атомиздат, 1973.
374 p. with diagrs. 22 cm. 2.54rub USSR 73
At head of title: В. Н. Байер, В. М. Катков, В. С. Фадин.
Bibliography: p. 369–₍372₎
1. Bremsstrahlung. 2. Electrons. 3. Quantum electrodynamics. I. Katkov, Valeriĭ Mikhaĭlovich. II. Fadin, Viktor Sergeevich. III. Title.
QC484.3.B34 73–338088

Baier, Walter.
Elektronik-Lexikon/ hrsg. von Walter Baier. ₍Unter Mitarb. von T. Baumgärtner u. a. Abb. im Text gezeichn. von Hans-Hermann Kropf nach vorl. d. Mitarb.₎. — Stuttgart: Franckh, 1974.
655 p.: 1185 ill.; 25 cm. GFR 74–A
Includes bibliographical references.
1. Electronics—Dictionaries—German. I. Title.
TK7804.B34 621.381'03 74–320536
ISBN 3–440–04042–9

Baier, Walther, 1903–
Tierärztliche Geburtskunde. Begründet von A. O. Stoss. 4., neu gestaltete Aufl. von Walther Baier und Franz Schaetz. Stuttgart, F. Enke, 1972.
334 p. illus. (part col.) 25 cm. DM49.00 GDB***
First and 2d editions, 1928 and 1944, by A. O. Stoss, published under title: Tierärztliche Geburtskunde und Gynäkologie.
1. Veterinary obstetrics. I. Schaetz, Franz, joint author. II. Stoss, Anton Otto, 1888– Tierärztliche Geburtskunde und Gynäkologie. III. Title.
₍DNLM: 1. Obstetrics. 2. Veterinary medicine. SF 887 S888t 1972₎
[SF887.B24 1972] 73–595064
ISBN 3–432–01821–5
Shared Cataloging with DNLM

Baier, Werner Hermann, 1941-
Untersuchungen zur Heterosis bei Sommergerste. Hohenheim, 1972.
101 p. (Hohenheim. Universitat. [Dissertation, 1972, no. 3])
Bibliography: p. 73-78.
I. Title.
DNAL NUC74-120673

Baierl, Friedrich.
Lohnanreizsysteme; Mittel zur Produktivitätssteigerung. 5., völlig überarb. und erw. Aufl. München, C. Hanser, 1974.
551 p. illus. 25 cm. GFR***
Previous ed. published under title: Produktivitätssteigerung durch Lohnanreizsysteme.
Includes bibliographical references.
1. Bonus system. 2. Labor productivity. I. Title.
HD4928.B6B27 1974 73–86692
ISBN 3–446–10512–3

Baierl, Helmut Johannes, 1926-
Frau Flinz; Komödie. [4. Aufl.] Berlin, Henschelverlag, 1965.
102 p. 19 cm. (Zeitgenössische Dramatik)
Microfiche (negative) 3 sheets. 11 x 15 cm. (NYPL FSN 14,236)
1. Drama, German. I. Title.
NN NUC74-2878

Baierl, Helmut Johannes, 1926-
Gereimte Reden / Helmut Baierl. — Berlin : Militärverlag der Deutschen Demokratischen Republik, 1976.
61 p. ; 22 cm. GDR***
5.20M
I. Title.
PT2662.A38G4 77-475132
77 MARC

Baierl, Helmut Johannes, 1926–
Die Köpfe : oder, Das noch kleinere Organon : Geschichten / Helmut Baierl. — 1. Aufl. — Berlin : Aufbau-Verlag, 1974, c1973.
151 p. ; 20 cm. — (Edition Neue Texte) GDR***
5.40M
I. Title. II. Title: Das noch kleinere Organon.
PT2662.A38K6 74–354063

Baierl, Helmut Johannes, 1926- Die Lachtaube. 1975.
in Baierl, Helmut Johannes, 1926- Stolz auf 18 ₍i.e. achtzehn₎ Stunden. Die Lachtaube. 1. Aufl. Berlin, Aufbau-Verlag, 1975.

Baierl, Helmut Johannes, 1926-
Stolz auf 18 [i.e. achtzehn] Stunden. Die Lachtaube / Helmut Baierl ; [mit e. Nachbemerkung von Hans-Peter Minetti]. — 1. Aufl. — Berlin ; Weimar : Aufbau-Verlag, 1975.
164 p. ; 19 cm. — (Edition Neue Texte) GDR
5.40M
1. Hamburg—Riot, October, 1923—Drama. I. Baierl, Helmut Johannes, 1926- Die Lachtaube. 1975. II. Title: Stolz auf achtzehn Studen.
PT2662.A38S8 76-466870
76 MARC

Baierl, Helmut Johannes, 1926-
Unterwegs zu Lenin [von Helmut Baierl und Jewgeni Gabrilowitsch, nach Motiven von Alfred Kurella] Der Lange Weg zu Lenin [von Helmut Baierl] Texte, Methoden, Meinungen. Berlin, Deutsche Akademie der Künste, 1971.
128 p. illus. (Deutsche Akademie der Künste zu Berlin. Arbeitshefte, 5)
2 scenarios of moving pictures.
MH NUC74-46687

Baierl, Helmut Johannes, 1926-
see Tavola Rotonda Internazionale su "L'opera teatrale di Bertolt Brecht", Venice, 1966. L'opera teatrale di Bertolt Brecht. [Venezia] 1966.

Baierl, Kenneth W.
see Treatment of sulfite evaporator condensates... Washington, For sale by the Supt. of Docs., U.S. Govt. Print. Off., 1973.

Baies vitrées et leurs fonctions dans le concept architectural : symposium : compte-rendu de session = Windows and their functions in architectural design : symposium : proceedings = Fenster und ihre Funktion in der Bauplanung : symposium : Tagungsbericht, Teknik Üniversitete [sic] Istanbul, 22-27.19.73. — Bruxelles (Galerie Ravenstein 3) : Comité national belge de l'éclairage, 1974.
[381] leaves : ill. ; 30 cm. Be75-6
At head of title: C.I.E. T.C.-4.2. Éclairage du jour. Daylighting. Tageslichtbeleuchtung.
English, French, or German.
Includes bibliographical references.
1. Windows—Congresses. 2. Architectural design—Congresses. I. International Commission on Illumination. Comité technique Éclairage du jour. II. Title: Windows and their functions in architectural design. III. Title: Fenster und ihre Funktion in der Bauplanung.
NA3020.B34 75-521563
76 MARC

Băieşu, Ion.
Chiţimia : dramă în două părţi / Ion Băieşu ; [prezentarea grafică, arh. Armand Crintea]. — [Bucureşti] : Editura Eminescu, 1975.
78 p. ; 19 cm. — (Colecţia Rampa ; 16) R 75-4528
lei 5.25
I. Title.
PC840.12.A4C48 76-502221

Băieşu, Ion.
Cine sapă groapa altuia : drame şi comedii / Ion Băieşu ; [coperta, Maria Dimulescu]. — Bucureşti : Editura Eminescu, 1974.
268 p. ; 20 cm. R 74-2579
CONTENTS: Chiţimia. — Iertarea. — Vinovatul. — Preşul. — Escrocii în aer liber.
lei 11.50
I. Title.
PC840.12.A4C5 75-576211

Băieşu, Ion. Detectivul comunal. 1975.
in Băieşu, Ion. Navetiştii ; Detectivul comunal. Bucureşti, [Consiliul Culturii şi Educaţiei Socialiste, Institutul de cercetări etnologice şi dialectologice] 1975.

Băieşu, Ion.
La iarbă albastră. [Povestiri. Coperta: Florin Creangă. Ilustraţii: Florin Pucă]. Timişoara, „Facla," 1973.
184 p. with illus. 17 cm. (Satyricon) lei 5.25 R 73-3466
I. Title.
PC840.12.A4 I 2 74-330053

Băieşu, Ion.
Navetiştii ; Detectivul comunal / Ion Băieşu. — Bucureşti : [Consiliul Culturii şi Educaţiei Socialiste, Institutul de cercetări etnologice şi dialectologice], 1975.
86 p. ; 17 cm. — (Teatru) R76-2302
lei17.60
I. Băieşu, Ion. Detectivul comunal. 1975. II. Title.
PC840.12.A4N3 77-455007
•77 MARC

Băieşu, Ion.
Nepotrivire de caracter. Comedie într-un act. [Bucureşti], Consiliul Culturii şi Educaţiei Socialiste, Centrul de îndrumare a creaţiei populare şi a mişcării artistice de masă, 1972.
27 p. 17 cm. (Teatru) lei 1.25 R 73-663
I. Title.
PC840.12.A4N4 74-345979

Băieşu, Ion.
Noaptea cu dragoste; schiţe şi nuvele. [Bucureşti] Editura pentru Literatură, 1962.
209 p. 18 cm.
CONTENTS: Un suflet de om.—Întîlnirea de mai tîrziu.—Scrisoarea de dragoste.—Înainte de plecare.—Papuc.—Trică.—Din aceaşi grupă.—Lupta.—Doi oameni într-unul.—Apel general.—Omul care a văzut moartea.—Ursul.—Fuga.—Noaptea cu dragostea.
I. Title.
PC840.12.A4N6 74-232085

Băieşu, Ion.
Pompierul şi opera : schiţe umoristice / Ion Băieşu ; [copertă şi desene de Florin Pucă]. — [Bucureşti] : "Cartea românească", 1976.
187 p. : ill. ; 20 cm. R76-2131
lei7.25
I. Title.
PC840.12.A4P6 76-482340
•76 MARC

Băieşu, Ion.
Vaccin contra lenei. Comedie într-un act. [Bucureşti], Consiliul Culturii şi Educaţiei Socialiste, Centrul de îndrumare a creaţiei populare şi a mişcării artistice de masă, 1972.
24 p. 17 cm. (Teatru) lei 1.20 R 73-664
I. Title.
PC840.12.A4V3 74-345110

Baietti, A. L.
see Tracerlab, inc., Boston. Western Division Laboratories, Richmond, Calif. Radiological monitoring study. Richmond, 1963.

Baïf, Jean Antoine de, 1532-1589.
Les amours de Jean-Antoine de Baïf. ⟨Amours de Méline.⟩ [Éd. par] Mathieu Augé-Chiquet. (Réimpr. de l'éd. de Paris, 1909.) Genève, Slatkine Reprints, 1972.
160 p. 24 cm. 40.00F Sw 72-A-6477
Poems.
I. Augé-Chiquet, Mathieu, 1873-1912, ed. II. Title.
PQ1665.A64 1972 74-160206
MARC

Baïf, Jean Antoine de, 1532-1589.
Étrénes de poézie fransoeze an vers mezurés. Psautier en vers mesurés; manuscrit B. N. ms. fr. 19140. Genève, Slatkine Reprints, 1972.
1 v. (various pagings) 22 cm. Sw***
"Réimpression de l'édition de Paris, 1574 et fac-similé du ms. fr. 19140 de la B. N."
I Bible. O. T. Psalms. French. Psautier en vers mesurés. 1972. II. Paris. Bibliothèque nationale. Mss. (Fr. 19140) III. Title. IV. Title: Psautier en vers mesurés.
PQ1665.A66 1972 73-332740

Baïf, Jean Antoine de, 1532-1589.
Le premier livre des poèmes / Jean-Antoine de Baïf ; texte établi et commenté par Guy Demerson. — [Grenoble] : Presses universitaires de Grenoble, [1975]
149 p. ; 25 cm. — (Publications de la Faculté des lettres de Clermont-Ferrand ; ouvrage no 35) F***
Text in Middle French with commentary in French.
Includes bibliographical references.
ISBN 2-7061-0052-4 : 56.00F
I. Demerson, Guy. II. Title. III. Series: Clermont-Ferrand, France. Université. Faculté des lettres et sciences humaines. Publications ; ouvrage no 35.
PQ1665.A725 1975 841'.3 75-511545
75 MARC

Baig, Hamed M
Some biochemical effects of N^6-benzylamino-9-(tetrahydropyran-2-yl)-purine (PBA) on flower production and keeping quality of "Red American Beauty" hybrid tea roses, Rosa hybrida, by Hamed M. Baig. [n.p., 1975]
28 l. ill.
Thesis (Ph.D.)—Kansas State University.
1. Cut flowers. 2. Rose culture. 3. Growth promoting substances. I. Title.
KMK NUC77-81763

Baig, Jaime Arnáu
see
Arnáu Baig, Jaime.

Baig, M R A 1905-
The Muslim dilemma in India / M. R. A. Baig. — Delhi : Vikas Pub. House, 1974.
xvi, 169 p. ; 22 cm.
Running title: The Muslim dilemma.
Appendices (p. [135]-161) comprise some previously published articles and a paper read at a seminar.
Includes bibliographical references and index.
Rs25.00
1. Muslims in India. I. Title.
DS427.B28 301.45'29'71054 74-902220
MARC

Baig, Mirza Luqman.
(Aikṭ kārkhānahjāt)
ایکٹ کارخانہ جات. Factories act, 1934. [مصنف] لقمان بیگ. کراچی، غضنفر اکیڈمی [1971]
128 p. 22 cm. Rs3.00
In Urdu.

1. Labor laws and legislation—India. 2. Labor laws and legislation—Pakistan. I. Pakistan. Laws, statutes, etc. Factories act, 1934. 1971. II. Title.

70-932698

Baig, Mubarak Ali
see
Dil Ayyūbī Ṭonkī, 1930-

Baig, Tara Ali.
India's woman power / Tara Ali Baig. — New Delhi : S. Chand, 1976.
xiv, 301 p. : maps ; 23 cm.
Bibliography: p. 283-287.
Includes index.
Rs40.00
1. Women—India—Social conditions. 2. Women—India—History. I. Title.
HQ1742.B29 301.41'2'0954 76-900659
76 MARC

Baig, Tara Ali.
Sarojini Naidu / Tara Ali Baig. — New Delhi : Publications Division, Ministry of Information and Broadcasting, Govt. of India, 1974.
vi, 175 p., [1] leaf plates : ill. ; 21 cm. — (Builders of modern India)
Bibliography: p. [167]
Includes index.
Rs7.00
1. Naidu, Sarojini (Chattopadhyay) 1879-1949. I. Series.
DS481.N25B34 954.03'5'0924 75-900656
75 MARC

Baigabylov, Talant.
(Zhashyl-Sai)
Жашыл-Сай : повесть / Талант Байгабылов. — Фрунзе : Кыргыз мамлекеттик басмасы, 1961.
175 p. ; 17 cm.
I. Title.
PL65.K59B29 75-549280

Baigakō, Seian, Tsūka, Banseki, oyobi Tōhoku Shōsochi Botsuri hoka Jūkyū Toyū Keikaku Kyōgikai, Ch'ang-ch'un, China, Aug. 24-26, 1936.
(Minseibu shusai Baigakō, Seian, Tsūka, Banseki, oyobi Tōhoku Shōsochi Botsuri)
民政部主催梅河口.西安·通化·磐石·及東北商租地勃利外十九都邑計畫協議會議事抄錄 (於新京日滿軍人會館·昭和一一·八自二四至二六) [大連] 滿鐵產業部 昭和11 [1936]
2 v. 26 cm.
Cover title.
At head of title: 極秘 (rubber stamped)

1. Cities and towns—Planning—Liaoning, China (Province) 2. Cities and towns—Planning—Kirin, China (Province) I. Manchuria. Min chêng pu. II. Minami Manshū Tetsudō Kabushiki Kaisha. Sangyōbu. III. Title.

HT169.C62L52 73-788014

Baigell, Matthew.
The American scene: American painting of the 1930's. New York, Praeger [1974]
214 p. illus. (part col.) 27 x 29 cm. (American art & artists) $29.50
Bibliography: p. 212.
1. Painting, American. 2. Federal Art Project. 3. Social realism. I. Title. II. Series.
ND212.B28 759.13 72-89639
ISBN 0-275-46620-5 MARC

Baigell, Matthew.
Charles Burchfield / by Matthew Baigell. — New York : Watson-Guptill Publications, 1976.
208 p. : ill. (some col.) ; 30 cm.
Bibliography: p. 203-204.
Includes index.
ISBN 0-8230-0533-X
1. Burchfield, Charles Ephraim, 1893-1967.
ND237.B89B24 1976 759.13 76-15169
76 MARC

Baigell, Matthew.
A history of American painting. London, Thames [1971]
288 p. illus. (part col.) 22 cm.
Bibliography: p. 269-271
1. Painting, American—History. I. Title.
NjP NUC73-126525

Baigell, Matthew.
John Haviland. [n.p.] 1965.
xxxiv, 398 l. illus.
Thesis—University of Pennsylvania.
Bibliography: leaves xv-xxxi.
Microfilm copy (positive) Ann Arbor, Mich., University Microfilms, 1965. 1 reel. (Publication no. 13307)
NNC NUC73-40866

Baigell, Matthew
see Benton, Thomas Hart, 1889- Thomas Hart Benton. New York, Abrams [1974]

Baigell, Matthew.
see Benton, Thomas Hart, 1889-1975. Thomas Hart Benton. New concise NAL ed. New York, H. N. Abrams : distributed by New American Library, c1975.

Baigent, Beryl, 1937-
Pause. Thamesford, Ont., B. Baigent, c1974.
1 v. (unpaged) (A United Amateur Press Association publication)
1. Canadian poetry, English. I. Title.
CaOTP NUC76-15663

Baigent, Beryl, 1937-
The quiet village: a family album, Beryl Baigent. [Thamesford, Ont.] c1972.
36 p. 21 cm.
I. Title.
CaQMM NUC75-34821

Baigent, Gary, 1941-
see Auckland, N.Z. Art Gallery. Three New Zealand photographers... Auckland, N.Z., 1973.

Baiget, Josep, 1911–
Formulari de correspondència catalana / Josep Baiget. — 1. ed. — Barcelona : Editorial Bruguera, 1974.
153 p. ; 18 cm. — (Quaderns de cultura ; 72) Sp***
ISBN 84-02-03899-9
1. Letter-writing, Catalan. I. Title.
PC3880.B3 75-556087

Baiget i Masip, Josep
see
Baiget, Josep, 1911-

Baigorri, Angel Martínez
see Martínez Baigorri, Angel.

Baigorria, Manuel.
Memorias / Manuel Baigorria, prólogo de Félix Luna ; cronología comentada de J. A. de Diego. — Buenos Aires : Solar / Hachette, c1975.
169 p. ; 22 cm. — (Biblioteca Dimensión argentina)
"El text ha sido tomado de Revista de la Junta de Estudios Históricos de Mendoza, t. X, julio Suárez Editor, Buenos Aires, 1938."
1. Baigorria, Manuel.
F2966.B34 76-462182
76 MARC

Baĭgulov, Ivan Mikhaĭlovich.
(Pozdnie dozhdi)
Поздние дожди : Повесть, рассказы / Иван Байгулов. — Москва : Современник, 1976.
270 p. ; 16 cm. — (Новинки Современника) USSR 76
Series romanized: Novinki Sovremennika.
CONTENTS: Поздние дожди.—За тридевять земель.—Ожидание.—Жили-были.—Хлеб.—Последний день отпуска.—Оплошка деда Кондрата.
0.42rub
I. Title.
PG3479.I 4P6 76-532980

Baĭgulov, Ivan Mikhaĭlovich.
(Vasil'kovyĭ venok)
Васильковый венок. Повесть в рассказах. [Ил.: В. Кадочников]. Пермь, Кн. изд-во, 1971.
183 p. with illus. 17 cm. 0.36rub USSR 71
At head of title: И. Байгулов.
CONTENTS: Васильковый венок.—Таволжанка.—Запах сена.—След упавшей звезды.—Дядя Митрий.—Почтальонка.—Гроза.—Первопуток.—Новоселье.
I. Title.
PG3479.I 4V3 74-329760

Baigún, David.
Naturaleza de las circunstancias agravantes / David Baigún. — Buenos Aires : Ediciones Pannedille, 1971.
100 p. ; 20 cm.
Includes bibliographical references.
1. Aggravating circumstances—Argentine Republic. 2. Aggravating circumstances. I. Title.
77-468484
77 MARC

Baĭguttiev, S., joint author
see Aliev, Z Tushtuk Kyrgyzstandyn Zharatylyshy. 1972.

Baihaki, Achmad.
Association of genotype x environment interactions with performance level of soybean lines in preliminary yield tests, by Achmad Baihaki. [Minneapolis] 1975.
77 l. ill. 29 cm.
Thesis (Ph. D.)—University of Minnesota.
Bibliography: leaves 54-56.
I. Title.
MnSU NUC77-81762

al-Baihaqī, Ibrāhīm ibn Muḥammad
see
al-Bayhaqī, Ibrāhīm ibn Muḥammad, 10th cent.

Baihaśī, Purushotama Lāla.
(Lahū de chiṭṭe)
लहू दे छिट्टे. [कवि] पुरुषोतम लाल बैंहशी. [पठानकोट, सुखदेव वडैहरा, 1973]
152 p. illus. 19 cm. Rs4.00
In Panjabi; introductory matter in Hindi.

I. Title.
PK2659.B283L3 73-906493

Bāĭīshev, Saqtaghan
see
Baishev, Saktagan Baishevich.

Baij, Maria Cecilia, 1694–1766.
Vita di san Giuseppe / Maria Cecilia Baij ; a cura del sac. Pietro Bergamaschi. — 2. ed. — Montefiascone : Monastero di San Pietro, 1974.
529 p. : ill. ; 20 cm. It 75-July
1. Joseph, Saint. I. Title.
BS2458.B34 1974 75-410677

Baij Nath, Lala, tr.
see Puranas. Brahmaṇḍapurāna. Adhyātmarāmāyaṇa. English. The Adhyatma Ramayana. Allahabad: Sudhindra Nath Vasu at the Panini Office, 1913.

Baij Nath, Lala, tr.
see Puranas. Brahmāṇḍapurāna. Adhyātmarāmayaṇa. English. The Adhyatma Ramayana. New York, AMS Press, [1974]

Baij Nath Prasad Shukla
see
Shukla, Baijnath Prasad, 1948-

Baijal, Shiam Narain, 1913–
कुइनी. [लेखक] श्याम नारायण बैंजल. [1. संस्करण] बरेली, पार्वती प्रकाशन [1966]
136 p. 19 cm. Rs3
In Hindi.
Short stories.

I. Title.
Title romanized: Kuinī.
PK2098.B295K8 S A 68-9495
PL 480 : I-H-5722

Baijal, Shiam Narain, 1913–
(Ṭālū miksacara)
टालू मिक्सचर. लेखक श्याम नारायण बैंजल. [1. संस्करण] बरेली, पार्वती प्रकाशन [1972]
112 p. 19 cm. Rs6.00
In Hindi.

I. Title.
PK2098.B295T3 73-904716

Baijanātha Simha
see
Simha, Baijanātha.

Baijanāthaprasāda Śukla
see
Shukla, Baijnath Prasad, 1948-

Baijnāth, Lālā
see
Baij Nath, Lala.

Baijnath Prasad Shukla
see
Shukla, Baijnath Prasad, 1948-

Baijōken.
(Yodarekake)
よだれかけ 楳條軒著 近世文学書誌研究会編 東京 勉誠社 昭和48(1973)
282 p. 27 cm. (近世文學資料類従 仮名草子編 8) ¥5500
Ja 74-235
Fiction.
本書は赤木文庫蔵本(横山重氏蔵)...全六巻六冊の影印
江本裕 『よだれかけ』解題: p. 273-282.
I. Kinsei Bungaku Shoshi Kenkyūkai. II. Title. III. Series: Kinsei bungaku shiryō ruijū. kanazōshihen, 8.
PL777.35.K57 vol. 8 74-805964
[PL795.B35]

Baik, Bong
see Paek, Pong.

Baik, Si Eung
see
Paek, Si-ŭng.

Baĭkabulov, Barat, comp.
see Stikhi o Samarkande. Tashkent, Izd-vo Khudozh. lit-ry, 1970.

Baikadi Venkatarkrishna Raya
see
Venkatakrishna Raya, Baikadi, 1917-

Baĭkalov, Anatoliĭ Kuz'mich.
(Almaznyĭ pravíàshchiĭ instrument na gal'vanicheskoĭ svíàzke)
Алмазный правящий инструмент на гальванической связке / А. К. Байкалов, И. Л. Сукенник. — Киев : Наук. думка, 1976.
202 p. : ill. ; 21 cm. USSR***
Akademíià nauk Ukrainskoĭ SSR. Institut sverkhtverdykh materialov.
Bibliography: p. 200–[201]
1.17rub
1. Grinding wheels—Maintenance and repair. 2. Diamonds, Industrial. I. Sukennik, Il'íà Lazarevich, joint author. II. Title.
TJ1293.B34 77-502023

Baĭkal'skaíà matematicheskaíà shkola po teorii i metodam upravleníià bol'shimi sistemami, 1969.
(Metody upravleníià bol'shimi sistemami)
Методы управления большими системами. Материалы Байкальской матем. школы по теории и методам управления большими системами. [7–24 июля 1969 г., бухта Песчаная. Ред. коллегия: ... д-р техн. наук А. Н. Панченков (отв. ред.) и др.] Иркутск, 1970.
2 v. diagrs. 20 cm. 0.85rub (v. 1).; 0.90rub (v. 2)
USSR 70-VKP
At head of title: Академия наук СССР. Сибирское отделение. Сибирский энергетический институт.
Includes bibliographies.
1. Automatic control—Mathematical models—Congresses. I. Pancenkov, Anatoliĭ Nikolaevich, ed. II. Akademíià nauk SSSR. Sirbirskoe otdelenie. Ėnergeticheskiĭ institut. III. Title.
TJ212.B35 73-331933

(Baikal'skiĭ geodinamicheskiĭ poligon)
Байкальский геодинамический полигон. Методика исследований и первые результаты изучения соврем. движений земной коры. Новосибирск, 1970.
175 p. with diagrs. and maps. 20 cm. 0.50rub USSR 70
At head of title: Академия наук СССР. Сибирское отделение. Институт геологии и геофизики.
By É. É. Fotiadi and others.
Bibliography: p. 168–[173]
1. Geophysics—Russia—Baikal Lake region. 2. Geology, Structural. I. Fotiadi, Épaminond Épaminondovich. II. Akademiía nauk SSSR. Sibirskoe otdelenie. Institut geologii i geofiziki.
QC803.R9B26 74–303993

(Baikal'skiĭ rift)
Байкальский рифт : [сборник статей] / отв. ред. чл.-кор. АН СССР Н. А. Флоренсов. — Новосибирск : Наука, Сиб. отд-ние, 1975.
134 p., fold. leaf : ill. ; 26 cm. USSR 75
At head of title: Akademiía nauk SSSR. Sibirskoe otdelenie. Institut zemnoĭ kory.
Includes bibliographies.
1.22rub
1. Rifts (Geology)—Russia—Baikal Lake region—Addresses, essays, lectures. I. Florensov, Nikolaĭ Aleksandrovich, 1909- II. Akademiía nauk SSSR. Sibirskoe otdelenie. Institut zemnoĭ kory.
QE606.5.R9B34 75–406784

Baĭkhaki, Abu-l-Fazl
see
Bayhaqī, Abū al-Faḍl Muḥammad ibn Ḥusayn, 996 (ca.)-1077.

Baikie, Albert G.
see Dameshek, William, 1900- William Dameshek and Frederick Gunz's Leukemia. 3d ed., rev. and enl. New York, Grune & Stratton [1974]

Baikie, David Adamu, 1931-
The effects of single and combined pictorial cues on the perception of depth by children aged five and six from two socio-economic groups. Bloomington, Indiana, 1970.
125 p.
Thesis–Indiana University.
Microfilm. Ann Arbor, Mich., University Microfilms. 1 reel. 35 mm.
CLSU NUC74-2872

Baikie, James, 1866-1931.
Egyptian papyri and papyrus-hunting, by James Baikie ... with thirty-two illustrations of which four in colour are by Constance N. Baikie. New York, F.H. Revell [n.d.]
324 p. xxxii plates (part col., 1 double; incl. front., facsims.) 22 cm.
"Graeco-Roman papyri": p. [222]-320.
1. Egyptian language—Papyri. 2. Manuscripts, Greek (Papyri) I. Title.
NcD NUC76-15510

Baikie, Ken.
Ken Baikie's Lazy man's guide to better bridge. — Stockton, Calif. : K. R. Baikie, c1975.
99 p. ; 23 cm.
Cover title.
$4.95
1. Contract bridge. I. Title: Lazy man's guide to better bridge.
[GV1282.3.B275] 795.4'15 75-24166
75 MARC

Baĭkin, V S
(Prichiny kolebaniía udareniía v russkom literaturnom íàzyke)
Причины колебания ударения в русском литературном языке / В. С. Байкин. — Чита : [s. n.], 1958.
11 l. ; 22 x 36 cm.
At head of title: Chitinskiĭ gosudarstvennyĭ medifsinskiĭ institut. Kafedra inostrannykh íàzykov.
Photocopy.
Includes bibliographical references.
1. Russian language—Accents and accentuation. I. Title.
PG2139.B25 1958 75–540934

Baĭko, Vasiliĭ Paramonovich, joint author
see Ivanov, Nikolaĭ Nikolaevich, fl. 1970- (Obrabotka pochvy i primenenie udobreniĭ) 1971.

Baikō Jogakuin Daigaku Bungakubu Kokubungakka Daiikkai Sotsugyōsei.
(Nihon kiryaku jimmei sakuin)
『日本紀略』人名索引 / [梅光女学院大学文学部国文学科第一回卒業生編 ; 監修 梅光女学院大学国語国文学会]. — 下関 : 梅光女学院大学, 昭和49 [1974]
60 p. ; 21 cm. Ja 74-20624
"新訂増補国史大系本「日本紀略」(吉川弘文館)の「前篇十三 桓武天皇」
1. Nihon kiryaku—Indexes. 2. Japan—History—To 1185. I. Nihon kiryaku. II. Title.
DS851.N442B34 1974 77–815833

Baikonur : the world's first cosmodrome. — [Moscow : Novosti Press Agency Pub. House, 1975]
[24] p. : ill. ; 24 cm. USSR***
Cover title.
0.24rub
1. Astronautics—Russia.
TL789.8.R9B28 629.4'0947 77-360561
77 MARC

Baĭkonurov, Omirkhan Aĭmagambetovich.
(Kompleksnaía mekhanizafsiía ochistnykh rabot pri podzemnoĭ razrabotke rudnykh mestorozhdeniĭ)
Комплексная механизация очистных работ при подземной разработке рудных месторождений. Алма-Ата, "Наука," 1973.
370 p. with illus., 2 l. of tables. 22 cm. 2.65rub USSR 73
At head of title: Академия наук Казахской ССР. Казахский политехнический институт им. В. И. Ленина. О. А. Байконуров, А. Т. Филимонов.
Bibliography: p. 364–[368]
1. Mining machinery. 2. Mine haulage. 3. Ore handling. I. Filimonov, Alekseĭ Timofeevich, joint author. II. Title.
TN345.B24 74–303475

Baĭkonurov, Omirkhan Aĭmagambetovich.
(Kompleksnaía mekhanizafsiía podzemnoĭ razrabotki rud)
Комплексная механизация подземной разработки руд / О. А. Байконуров, А. Т. Филимонов, С. Г. Калошин. — Москва : Недра, 1975.
303 p. : ill. ; 23 cm. USSR***
Bibliography: p. 300–[301]
1.27rub
1. Mining machinery. 2. Mine haulage. I. Filimonov, Alekseĭ Timofeevich, joint author. II. Kaloshin, Sergeĭ Grigor'evich, joint author. III. Title.
TN345.B25 76–504720

Baĭkov, Baĭko Dimitrov, joint author
see Petkov, Georgi Nikolov. (Opazvane na prirodnata sreda pri promishlenoto otgelzhdane na selskostopanskite zhivotni i ptitsi) 1975.

Baĭkov, Baĭko Dimitrov, joint author
see Pŭrvi mezhdunaroden kongres po zookhigiena. 1974.

Baikov, Boris Petrovich
see Turbokompressory dlía nadduva dizeleĭ. 1975.

Baĭkov, Bronislav Nikolaevich.
(Tekhniko-ékonomicheskoe normirovanie poter' i razubozhivaniía poleznykh iskopaemykh pri dobyche)
Технико-экономическое нормирование потерь и разубоживания полезных ископаемых при добыче / Б. Н. Байков, В. С. Лучко. — Москва : Недра, 1974.
214, [2] p. : diagrs. ; 22 cm. USSR 74
Bibliography: p. 212–[215]
1.75rub
1. Mining engineering. 2. Ores. I. Luchko, Vitaliĭ Sergeevich, joint author. II. Title.
TN275.B243 74–355385

Baĭkov, Bronislav Nikolaevich, joint author
see Íùmatov, Boris Petrovich. (Otkrytaía razrabotka slozhnostrukturnykh mestorozhdeniĭ fsvetnykh metallov) 1973.

Baĭkov, Evgeniĭ Maksimovich.
(Religiía i dukhovnyĭ mir cheloveka)
Религия и духовный мир человека. (Социол. очерк). Саранск, Мордов. кн. изд-во, 1972.
160 p. with diagrs. 21 cm. 0.59rub USSR 73
At head of title: Е. М. Байков.
Bibliography: p. 135–[143]
1. Christianity—Controversial literature. 2. Christianity—Penzenskaya oblast', Russia. I. Title.
BL2780.B18 73–360455

Baĭkov, Evgeniĭ Maksimovich
see Na marshe devíàtoĭ píàtiletki. Saransk, Mordovskoe knizhnoe izd-vo, 1971.

Baĭkov, M.A.
see Osnovy nauchnoĭ organizafsii truda... Moskva, Voenizdat, 1974.

Baĭkov, Mikhail Grigor'evich
see Puti rosta. Ioshkar-Ola, Mariĭskoe knizhnoe izd-vo, 1968.

Baĭkov, Nikolaĭ Dmitrievich.
(Organizafsiía i éffektivnost' upravleniía proizvodstvom)
Организация и эффективность управления производством. Москва, "Моск. рабочий," 1973.
190 p. with diagrs. 20 cm. 0.48rub USSR 73
At head of title: Н. Байков, Ф. Русинов.
Bibliography: p. 187–[188]
1. Industrial management. I. Rusinov, Fedor Mikhaĭlovich. II. Title.
HD36.B33 73–355483

Baĭkov, Nikolaĭ Sergeevich.
(Samoletovozhdenie pri aérofotos"emke)
Самолетовождение при аэрофотосъемке. [Учеб. пособие для аэрофотосъемочных специальностей сред. спец. учеб. заведений]. Москва, "Недра," 1973.
232 p. with illus. 22 cm. 0.62rub USSR 73
At head of title: Н. С. Байков, М. А. Трясучкин, В. А. Иванов.
Bibliography: p. 230.
1. Aerial photogrammetry. 2. Aeroplanes—Piloting. I. Tríàsuchkin, Mikhail Alekseevich, joint author. II. Ivanov, Viktor Afanas'evich, joint author. III. Title.
TA593.B33 74–344282

Baĭkov, Uzbek Mavmotovich.
Использование промышленных сточных вод в нефтедобыче. Уфа, Башкнигоиздат, 1970.
102 p. with diagrs. 20 cm. 0.26rub USSR 70–VKP
At head of title: У. М. Байков, Л. В. Еферова, Ю. И. Толкачев.
Bibliography: p. 99–[100]
1. Oil field flooding. 2. Water reuse. 3. Factory and trade waste. 4. Sewage disposal. I. Eferova, Líùdmila Vasil'evna, joint author. II. Tolkachev, ÍÙriĭ Ivanovich, joint author. III. Title.
Title romanized: Ispol'zovanie promyshlennykh stochnykh vod v neftedobyche.
TN871.B237 72–309292

Baĭkov, V.N., ed.
see Prostranstvennaía rabota zhelezobetonnykh konstruktsii. 1971.

Baĭkov, Vladimir Dmitrievich.
(Apparaturnaía realizafsiía élementarnykh funkfsiĭ v TSVM)
Аппаратурная реализация элементарных функций в ЦВМ / В. Д. Байков, В. Б. Смолов ; под ред. канд. физ.-мат. наук А. М Шаумана — Ленинград : Изд-во Ленингр. ун-та, 1975.
94, [2] p. : graphs ; 22 cm. USSR 75
At head of title: Ministerstvo vysshego i srednego spefsial'nogo obrazovaniía RSFSR.
Bibliography: p. 92–[95]
0.57rub
1. Functions—Data processing. I. Smolov, Vladimir Borisovich, joint author. II. Title.
QA331.B18 76–513580

Baĭkov, Vladimir Sergeevich
see Narodnoe khozíàĭstvo sofsialisticheskikh stran v 1968 godu. Moskva, "Statistika", 1969.

Baĭkova, Adilía Íàkubovna, joint author
see Obolenfsev, Roman Dmitrievich. Seraorganicheskie soedineniía nefteĭ Uralo-Povolzh'ía i Sibiri. 1973.

Baĭkova, Anna Nikolaevna.
(Britanskie profsoíùzy i klassovaía bor'ba)
Британские профсоюзы и классовая борьба : (Вторая половина 60-х–начало 70-х гг.) / А. Н. Байкова ; АН СССР, Ин-т междунар. рабочего движения. — Москва : Наука, 1976.
375 p. ; 20 cm. USSR 76
Includes bibliographical references.
1.29rub
1. Trade-unions—Great Britain. I. Title.
HD6662.B34 77–510555

Baĭkova, Valentina Gavrilovna.
(Trud i dosug)
Труд и досуг / В. Г. Байкова, В. М. Соколов. — Москва : Профиздат, 1975.
63 p. ; 20 cm. — (Для школ коммунистического труда) USSR 75
Series romanized: Dlía shkol kommunisticheskogo truda.
Bibliography: p. [62]
0.11rub
1. Work. 2. Leisure—Russia. I. Sokolov, Vladimir Mikhaĭlovich, joint author. II. Title.
HD4904.B255 76–513870

Baĭkova, Valentina Gavrilovna
see Politicheskoe obrazovanie. 1976.

Baĭkova, Valentina Sergeevna, joint author
see Duk, Vladimir Leont'evich. (Strukturnometamorficheskaía évolíùtsiía i flogopitonosnost' granulitov Aldana) 1975.

Baikova, Valentina Sergeevna
see Lobach-Zhuchenko, Svetlana Borisovna. (Epokhi i tipy granitoobrazovaniíà dokembrii Baltiiskogo shchita). 1974.

Baĭkovskaíà, Tat'íàna Nikolaevna.
(Verkhnemiotšenovaíà flora ÍÙzhnogo Primor'íà)
Верхнемиоценовая флора Южного Приморья / Т. Н. Байковская. — Ленинград : Наука, 1974.
140 p., 20 leaves of plates : ill. ; 30 cm. USSR***
At head of title: Академия наук СССР. Ботанический институт им. В. Л. Комарова.
Bibliography: p. 133–₍136₎
2.73rub
1. Paleobotany—Miocene. 2. Paleobotany — Russia — Primorskiy kray. I. Title.
QE929.B34 75–558877

Baĭkushev, Stoíàn Manovich.
(Stimulíàtšionnaíà ėlektromiografiíà i ėlektroneĭrografiíà v klinike nervnykh bolezneĭ)
Стимуляционная электромиогафия и электронейрография в клинике нервных болезней / Ст. Байкушев, З. Х. Манович, В. П. Новикова. — Москва : Медицина, 1974.
143 p. : ill. ; 20 cm. USSR 74
At head of title: Академия медицинских наук СССР.
Verso of t. p.: Stimulating electromyography and electroneurography in clinics of nervous diseases.
Bibliography: p. 134–₍142₎
0.80rub
1. Nervous system—Diseases—Diagnosis. 2. Electromyography. 3. Evoked potentials (Electrophysiology) I. Manovich, Zakhar Khaimovich, joint author. II. Novikova, V. P., joint author. III. Title. IV. Title: Stimulating electromyography and elektroneurography in clinics of Nervous Diseases.
RC348.B3 74–352185

Bail, Frederick Thomas.
The relative dominance of ikonic and symbolic categorization in the first, third and fifth grades. Ithaca, N.Y., 1970.
197 p.
Thesis—Cornell University.
Microfilm. Ann Arbor, Mich., University Microfilms. 1 reel. 35 mm.
CLSU NIC NUC73-39356

Bail, Grace Shattuck.
Shadow fingers : poems / by Grace Shattuck Bail. — London : Mitre Press, c1976.
72 p. ; 19 cm. GB***
ISBN 0-7051-0237-8 : £1.60 ($3.50 U.S.)
I. Title.
PS3503.A415S5 811'.5'4 77-355443
77 MARC

Bail, Jay
see After Brockman. ₍Somerville, Mass.₎ Abyss Publications, 1974.

Bail, Joe Paul
see Hedlund, Dalva Eugene. An evaluation of counseling... Ithaca, N.Y., 1968.

Bail, Murray, 1941-
Contemporary portraits and other stories / ₍by₎ Murray Bail. — St. Lucia, Q. : University of Queensland Press, 1975.
183 p. : 1 ill. ; 21 cm. — (Paperback prose ; 10) Aus
"Distributed in the United Kingdom, Europe, the Middle East, Africa, and the Caribbean by Prentice-Hall International, International Book Distributors Ltd., 66 Wood Lane End, Hemel Hempstead, Herts., England."
ISBN 0-7022-0979-1. ISBN 0-7022-0978-3 pbk.
I. Title.
PZ4.B1495 Co 823 76-365852
₍PR9619.3.B25₎ 76 MARC

Bail, René.
Corsaires en béret vert : commandos-marine / René Bail. — Paris : Presses de la Cité, c1976.
311 p., ₍8₎ leaves of plates : ill. ; 24 cm. — (Collection Troupes de choc) F***
ISBN 2-258-00101-3 : 45.00F
1. France. Marine. Brigade des fusiliers marins. I. Title.
VE71.B34 359.9'6'0944 77-456168
77 MARC

Bail reform act: being the edited transcript of a lecture course in continuing legal education held at Vancouver in May, 1972 at which leaders were: P. M. Bolton ... ₍et al.₎ edited by K. C. Woodsworth. Vancouver, Centre for Continuing Education, University of British Columbia, c1972.
iii, 83 p. 23 cm. $10.00 C 73-2435
1. Bail—Canada. I. Bolton, P. Michael. II. Woodsworth, K. C., ed. III. British Columbia. University. Center for Continuing Education.
345'.71'072 74–154228
MARC

Bail reform : four papers, June 16, 1972, Edmonton, Alberta. — Edmonton : Published by the Dept. of Extension, University of Alberta, for the Committee on Continuing Legal Education in the Province of Alberta, 1973.
iii, 46 leaves ; 28 cm. C***
Papers presented at seminars arranged by the Committee on Continuing Legal Education in the Province of Alberta and held in Edmonton and Calgary on June 15 and June 16, 1972.
$4.00
1. Bail—Canada—Addresses, essays, lectures. I. Committee on Continuing Legal Education in the Province of Alberta.
345'.71'072 75-309214
75 MARC

Bailar, John Christian, 1904- ed.
see Comprehensive inorganic chemistry. [Oxford] Pergamon Press [1973]

Bailar, John Christian, 1932-
Statistical studies on the optimum doses of toxic drugs. Washington, 1973.
vi, 165 p. tables, figs.
Typescript.
Thesis (Ph. D.)—American University.
Bibliography: p. 141-165.
Diss. Abstracts: 35: 579 B, July, 1974.
Microfilm copy. Order # 74-13, 715.
1. Drugs—Dosage—Statistics. I. Title.
DAU NUC75-17147

Bailar, John Christian, 1932-
see United States. National Cancer Institute. Demography Section. Cancer rates and risks. [Bethesda] U.S. Dept. of Health, Education, and Welfare, 1964]

Bailard, Thomas E
Personal money management ₍by₎ Thomas E. Bailard, David L. Biehl ₍and₎ Ronald W. Kaiser. Chicago, Science Research Associates ₍c1973₎
x, 555 p. illus. 25 cm.
Includes bibliographies.
1. Finance, Personal. 2. Insurance. 3. Investments. I. Biehl, David L., joint author. II. Kaiser, Ronald W., joint author. III. Title.
HG179.B27 1973 332'.024 72–93641
MARC

Bailard, Thomas E
Personal money management / Thomas E. Bailard, David L. Biehl, Ronald W. Kaiser. — 2d ed. — Chicago : Science Research Associates, c1977.
621 p. : ill. ; 24 cm.
Includes bibliographical references and index.
ISBN 0-574-19350-2
1. Finance, Personal. 2. Insurance. 3. Investments. I. Biehl, David L., joint author. II. Kaiser, Ronald W., joint author.
HG179.B27 1977 332'.024 76-44298
76 MARC

Bailbé, Joseph Marc.
Berlioz, artiste et écrivain dans les "mémoires." Paris, Presses universitaires de France ₍1972₎
172, ₍8₎ p. plates. 25 cm. (Publications de l'Université de Rouen) 35.00F F***
Bibliography: p. ₍173₎
1. Berlioz, Hector, 1803–1869. I. Title.
ML410.B5B13 780'.92'4 [B] 73–301112

Bailbé, Joseph Marc.
Jules Janin, 1804–1874; une sensibilité littéraire et artistique. Paris, Lettres modernes, 1974.
126 p. 19 cm. (Situation, no 33) F***
Bibliography: p. ₍125₎–126.
ISBN 2-256-90740-6 : 30.00F
1. Janin, Jules Gabriel, 1804–1874—Criticism and interpretation.
PQ2311.J2Z6 848'.7'09 74–194895
MARC

Bailbé, Joseph Marc.
Nerval / par Joseph Marc Bailbé. — Paris : Bordas, c1976.
223, ₍3₎ p. : ill. ; 17 cm. — (Collection Présence littéraire) F***
Bibliography: p. ₍224₎-₍225₎
ISBN 2-04-002854-4 : 15.00F
1. Gérard de Nerval, Gérard Labrunie, known as, 1808-1855—Criticism and interpretation. I. Title.
PQ2260.G36Z5157 848'.7'09 77-464160
77 MARC

Bailblé, Claude.
Muriel : histoire d'une recherche / Claude Bailblé, Michel Marie, Marie-Claire Ropars. — ₍Paris₎ : Galilée, ₍1975₎
414 p., ₍4₎ leaves of plates : ill. ; 22 cm. F***
Includes bibliographical references.
ISBN 2-7186-0019-5
1. Muriel. ₍Motion picture₎. I. Marie, Michel, joint author. II. Ropars-Wuilleumier, Marie Claire, 1936- joint author. III. Muriel. ₍Motion picture₎.
PN1997.M84B3 791.43'7 75-510079
75 MARC

Bailby, Édouard.
L'Espagne vers la démocratie / Édouard Bailby. — ₍Paris₎ : Gallimard, c1976.
219 p. ; 22 cm. — (L'Air du temps) F***
1. Spain—History—1939-1975. 2. Spain—History—1975- I. Title.
DP270.B19 946.082 77-480152
77 MARC

Bailby, Edouard.
Que é o imperialismo? Rio de Janeiro, Editôra Civilização brasileira [1963]
141 p. 17 cm. (Cadernos do povo brasileiro, 17)
Microfiche (negative) 3 sheets. 11 x 15 cm. (NYPL FSN 23,636)
1. Imperialism. 2. United States—For. rel.
NN NUC74-2871

₍Baildon, Henry Bellyse₎ 1849–1907.
... Ralph Waldo Emerson, man and teacher. Edinburgh, W. Brown, 1884.
2 p. l., 44 p. 23 cm. (The Round table series, no. 1)
1. Emerson, Ralph Waldo, 1803–1882. I. Series.
PS1631.B25 1884 2–6813
rev

₍Baildon, Henry Bellyse₎ 1849–1907.
... Ralph Waldo Emerson, man and teacher. ₍2d ed., rev.₎ Edinburgh, W. Brown, 1884.
1 p. l., 44 p., 1 l. 23 cm. (The Round table series, no. 1)
1. Emerson, Ralph Waldo, 1803–1882. I. Series.
PS1631.B25 1884a 4879.01 2–6812
rev

₍Baildon, Henry Bellyse₎ 1849–1907.
Ralph Waldo Emerson, man and teacher, by John Robertson. ₍Folcroft, Pa.₎ Folcroft Library Editions, 1973.
44 p. 24 cm.
Reprint of the 1884 ed. published by W. Brown, Edinburgh, which was issued as no. 1 of the Round table series.
Erroneously ascribed to J. Robertson.
Includes bibliographical references.
1. Emerson, Ralph Waldo, 1803–1882. I. Robertson, John Mackinnon, 1856–1933. II. Series: The Round table series, no. 1.
PS1631.B25 1973 814'.3 72–14362
ISBN 0-8414-1340-1 (lib. bdg.) MARC

₍Baildon, Henry Bellyse₎ 1849-1907.
Ralph Waldo Emerson, man and teacher / by John Robertson. — Norwood, Pa. : Norwood Editions, 1976.
44 p. ; 23 cm.
Reprint of the 1884 ed. published by W. Brown, Edinburgh, which was issued as no. 1 of the Round table series.
Erroneously ascribed to J. Robertson.
Includes bibliographical references.
ISBN 0-8482-0213-9 lib. bdg. : $10.00
1. Emerson, Ralph Waldo, 1803-1882—Philosophy. I. Robertson, John Mackinnon, 1856-1933. II. Series: The Round table series ; no. 1.
₍PS1642.P5B3 1976₎ 814'.3 76-54133
76 MARC

Baildon, William Paley, 1859-1924, ed.
see Lincoln's Inn, London. The records of the Honorable Society of Lincoln's Inn. [London] Lincoln's Inn, 1897-1968.

Baildon, Yorkshire; the official guide. Gloucester, British Pub. Co. ₍1972₎
40 p. illus. 19 cm. B***
"Published with the authority of the Urban District Council."
1. Baildon, Eng.—Description—Guide-books.
DA690.B18B34 914.27'46 73–151570
ISBN 0-7140-0316-6 MARC

Bailenger, Jean.
Coprologie parasitaire et fonctionnelle ₍par₎ J. Bailenger. ₍3. éd.₎ Avec la collaboration de G. Faraggi. Préfaces des docteur J.-J. Dubarry ₍et₎ docteur R. Pautrizel. Bordeaux, Impr. E. Drouillard ₍1973₎
373 p. illus. 28 cm. 135F F***
First ed. published under title: Coprologie parasitaire humaine.
1. Feces—Analysis. 2. Medical parasitology. I. Faraggi, G., joint author. II. Title.
₍DNLM: 1. Feces—Analysis. 2. Intestinal diseases, Parasitic—Diagnosis. 3. Parasites. QY 160 B154c 1973₎
[RB49.B3 1973] 616.9'62 74–594754
MARC
Shared Cataloging with DNLM

Bailenson, Stewart L
How to control the cost of unemployment compensation claims and taxes on your business / Stewart L. Bailenson. — Homewood, Ill. : Dow Jones-Irwin, 1976.
xv, 209 p. : forms ; 24 cm.
Includes index.
ISBN 0-87094-110-0
1. Personnel management—United States. 2. Payroll taxes—United States. 3. Insurance, Unemployment—United States—Finance. I. Title: How to control the cost of unemployment compensation claims and taxes ...
HF5549.2.U5B34 658.1'553 75-22684
76 MARC

Bailer, Lloyd H
Seniority and ability ₍by₎ Lloyd H. Bailer, Eric J. Schmertz ₍and₎ Gerald A. Barrett. ₍Sound recording₎ Arbitration Audio L-AAA-5. ₍New York₎ American Arbitration Association ₍1974₎
1 cassette. 2 1/2 x 4 in.
1. Arbitration, Industrial—U.S. 2. Labor laws and legislation—U.S. 3. Personnel management. I. Schmertz, Eric J., joint author. II. Barrett, Gerald A., joint author. III. American Arbitration Association. IV. Title.
NjR NUC76-27742

Bailes, A H
Preliminary compilation of the geology of the Snow Lake-Flin Flon Sherridon area. [Winnipeg] Manitoba Dept. of Mines and Natural Resources, 1971.
27 p. illus., map (in pocket) (Manitoba. Dept. of Mines and Natural Resources. Geological paper, 1/71)
Bibliography: p. 23-27.
CaOTU NUC73-32343

Bailes, Dale Alan.
Cherry stones; first poems. ₍n.p., c1971₎
63 p.
Cover title.
I. Title.
CLU NUC74-120750

Bailes, Dale Alan.
The new janitor's nose, and other poems; poems from the Poets-in-the-Schools Program. Columbia, S.C., South Carolina Arts Commission, c1973.
xii, 152 p. ports.
1. Poetry—Collected works. I. Title.
ScU NUC74-128969

Bailes, Dale Alan.
Sharks while swimming. A collection of new poems. ₍Columbia, S.C., Coglioni Press, c1974₎
14 p. port.
Cover title.
I. Title.
ScU NUC75-17208

Bailes, Dale Alan, ed.
Talking on tiptoe; poems from the Poets-in-the Schools Program of the South Carolina Arts Commission. Ed. by Dale Alan Bailes. Columbia, S.C., c1974.
xiv, 156 p. ports.
I. South Carolina Arts Commission. II. Title.
ScU NUC75-59563

Bailes, Dale Alan.
see Ears quickly ... Columbia, South Carolina Arts Commission, c1976.

Bailes, Dale Alan.
see Stop the butterfly ... Columbia, South Carolina Arts Commission, c1977.

Bailes, Frederick W
Santé, prospérité, sérénité par la science de l'esprit; ₍la conscience qui guérit₎ Traduit de l'américain par le docteur Noémi Stricker-Rouvé. ₍2. éd.₎ Paris, Editions Dangles ₍1962₎
204 p. 23 cm.
I. Title.
CaOOU NUC74-4074

Bailes, Jack Clayton.
The effects of budgets on job performance and job attitude in a production setting; a laboratory experiment considering the interactions among situational and organismic variables. [Seattle] 1973.
129 l. illus.
Thesis (Ph.D.)—University of Washington.
Bibliography: leaves 127-129.
WaU NUC74-120669

Bailes, Kendall.
Stalin and revolution from above; the formation of the Soviet technical intelligentsia, 1928-1934. ₍New York₎ 1971 ₍c1974₎
2 v. (xxiii, 738 l.) 29 cm.
Thesis—Columbia University.
Bibliography: leaves 716-738.
1. Technologists, Russian. 2. Technology and state—Russia. I. Title.
NNC NUC75-21987

Băilescu, Alexandru.
Lucrări de tinichigerie. ₍Aprobată de Comitetul de Stat pentru Economia și Administrația Locală cu nr. 7782/15 mai 1970₎. București, Editura medicală, 1972.
169 p. with figs., 3 l. of col. plates. 21 cm. (Colecția Protecția muncii, 15) lei 6.75 R 72-4014
1. Sheet-metal work—Safety measures. I. Title.
TS250.B23 73-338666

Băileșteanu, Fănuș, comp.
Mihail Sadoveanu ₍interpretat de Ion Dodu Bălan, G. Bogdan-Duică, Savin Bratu ...₎ Antologie, comentarii, tabel cronologic și bibliografie de Fănuș Băileșteanu. ₍Coperta colecției: Ion Dogar-Marinescu₎. București, Editura Eminescu, 1973.
464 p. 19 cm. (Biblioteca critică) lei 11.50 R 74-1286
Bibliography: p. 437-₍458₎
1. Sadoveanu, Mihail, 1880-1961—Criticism and interpretation.
PC839.S3Z57 74-337406

Băileșteanu, Fănus
see Alexandru Macedonski. București: Editura Eminescu, 1975.

Băilesteanu, Fănuș
see Legend noastră... București : "Albatros," 1974.

Băileșteanu, Jean, 1951–
Clopotul viselor : ₍povestiri₎ / Jean Băileșteanu ; ₍coperta, Ioan Dreptu₎. — Craiova : "Scrisul românesc," 1975.
112 p. ; 21 cm. R 75-4546
lei 6.50
I. Title.
PC840.12.A42C6 76-503145

Bailet, Michel Henri.
L'homme de verre; essai d'interprétation thématique de l'échec et de la maîtrise dans le Décaméron. Nice ₍Impr. universelle : pour diffusion exclusive par le Studio bibliografico Antenore, Padova₎ 1972.
311 p. 24 cm. F***
Bibliography : p. 305-311.
1. Boccaccio, Giovanni, 1313-1375. Il Decamerone. I. Title.
PQ4287.B28 73-348685
MARC

Bailey, A., joint author
see Womersley, Hugh Bryan Spencer. Marine algae of the Solomon Islands. London, Royal Society, 1970.

Bailey, A. G.
see
Bailey, Alfred Goldsworthy.

Bailey (Abe) Institute of Inter-Racial Studies
see
Abe Bailey Institute of Inter-Racial Studies.

Bailey, Abigail (Abbot), 1746-1815.
₍Autobiography₎ Boston, S. T. Armstrong, 1815.
₍1₎-196 p. 14 cm.
Taken from the Memoirs of Mrs. Abigail Bailey.
Micro-transparency (positive). La Crosse, Wisconsin, Northern Micrographics, Inc., 1974. 3 sheets. 10.5 x 14.5 cm. (American autobiographies)
Kaplan no. 245.
Copied from the original located in the Library of Congress.
PSt
1. Bailey, Abigail (Abbot), 1746-1815. I. Title: Memoirs of Mrs. Abigail Bailey. II. Series: American autobiographies.
PSt nuc 76-34375
77 rev. MARC

Bailey, Adrian, 1928-
The blessings of bread : the illustrated story of the staff of life / Adrian Bailey. — New York : Paddington Press, c1975.
287 p. : ill. ; 29 cm.
Bibliography: p. 281.
Includes indexes.
ISBN 0-8467-0061-1 : $14.95
1. Bread. I. Title.
TX769.B18 641.3'31 75-11173
75 MARC

Bailey, Adrian, 1928-
Mrs. Bridges' Upstairs, downstairs cookery book / edited by Adrian Bailey ; photos. by John Hedgecoe. — London : Sphere Books, 1975.
192 p. : ill. ; 20 cm. GB***
"Originally published in 1905 under title: Practical household cookery."
Includes index.
ISBN 0-7221-1386-2 : £0.90
1. Cookery, English. I. Title. II. Title: Upstairs, downstairs, cookery book.
TX717.B26 1975 641.5'942 75-328912
75₍r76₎rev MARC

Bailey, Adrian, 1928-
Mrs. Bridges' upstairs downstairs cookery book / edited by Adrian Bailey ; with photos. by John Hedgecoe. — New York : Simon and Schuster, ₍1975₎ c1974.
193 p. : ill. ; 22 cm.
"Originally published in 1905 under the title Practical household cookery."
Includes index.
ISBN 0-671-22029-2. ISBN 0-671-22030-6 pbk.
1. Cookery, English. I. Title.
TX717.B74 1975 641.5'942 74-32163
74 MARC

Bailey, Adrian, 1928-
see Hedgecoe, John. The book of photography ... London, Edbury Press, 1976.

Bailey, Alan, 1938-
Comparison of low-temperature with high-temperature diffusion of sodium in albite. [East Lansing, Mich.] 1970 [1973]
vi, 84 l. illus., diagrs.
Thesis—Michigan State University.
Bibliography: leaves 69-72.
Photocopy. Ann Arbor, Mich., University Microfilms, 1973. 20 cm.
1. Albite. 2. Diffusion. I. Title.
IU NUC74-490

Bailey, Albert Edward, 1871-1951.
The arts and religion, by Albert Edward Bailey, editor; Kenneth John Conant, Henry Augustine Smith ₍and₎ Fred Eastman. Freeport, N. Y., Books for Libraries Press ₍1972, c1944₎
xiv, 180 p. illus. 22 cm. (Essay index reprint series)
Original ed. issued in series: The Ayer lectures of the Colgate-Rochester Divinity School, 1943.
Includes bibliographies.
1. Art and religion. I. Conant, Kenneth John, 1894- II. Smith, Henry Augustine, 1874-1952. III. Eastman, Fred, 1886- IV. Title. V. Series: The Ayer lectures, 1943.
N72.R4B35 1972 701 72-3349
ISBN 0-8369-2889-X MARC

Bailey, Albert Edward, 1871-1951.
Notes on the literary aspects of Tennyson's Princess. ₍Folcroft, Pa.₎ Folcroft Library Editions, 1973.
21 p. 23 cm.
Reprint of the 1897 ed. published by C. F. Lawrence, Worcester.
1. Tennyson, Alfred Tennyson, Baron, 1809-1829. The princess. I. Title.
PR5571.B3 1973 821'.8 73-18307
ISBN 0-8414-9897-0 (lib. bdg.) MARC

Bailey, Albert Edward, 1871-1951.
Notes on the literary aspects of Tennyson's Princess / printed for the Class of 1898, Worcester Academy by Albert Edward Bailey. — Norwood, Pa. : Norwood Editions, 1976.
21 p. ; 23 cm.
Reprint of the 1897 ed. published by C. F. Lawrence, Worcester.
Includes bibliographical references.
ISBN 0-8482-0173-6 lib. bdg. : $5.00
1. Tennyson, Alfred Tennyson, Baron, 1809-1892. The princess. I. Title.
₍PR5571.B3 1976₎ 821'.8 76-17858
76 MARC

Bailey, Albert W. Genealogy: Nathaniel Bailey families. 1972
in Bailey, Albert W History: early Baileyville, Maine ... Calais, Me., Calais Advertiser Press, 1972.

Bailey, Albert W
History: early Baileyville, Maine, and its pioneers. Genealogy: Nathaniel Bailey families. ₍By₎ Albert W. Bailey. Calais, Me., Calais Advertiser Press, 1972.
100 p. illus. 28 cm.
1. Baileyville, Me.—History. 2. Bailey family. I. Bailey, Albert W. Genealogy: Nathaniel Bailey families. 1972. II. Title. III. Title: Genealogy: Nathaniel Bailey families.
F29.B16B34 917.41'42 73-152738
MARC

Bailey, Alberta, ed.
see Mitchell, Jack. Jack Mitchell, caveman... Torrance, Calif. ₍Lewellen Press, 1964₎

Bailey, Albina.
Dressing dolls in nineteenth century fashions / Albina Bailey. — North Kansas City, Mo. : Athena Pub. Co., 1975.
200 p., [1] leaf of plates : ill. ; 29 cm.
Bibliography: p. 193.
1. Doll clothes. 2. Costume—History—19th century. I. Title.
TT175.7.B34 745.59'22 74-29003
75 MARC

Bailey, Alec, illus.
see Goode, John. Tortoises, terrapins and turtles. [Sydney] Angus and Robertson [1971]

Bailey, Alec, illus.
see Goode, John. Turtles, tortoises, and terrapins. New York, Scribner [c1971]

Bailey, Alfred Goldsworthy.
Culture and nationality: essays, by A. G. Bailey. Toronto, McClelland and Stewart [1972]
224 p. 19 cm. (Carleton library no. 58) $4.50 C***
Includes bibliographical references.
1. Canada — History — Addresses, essays, lectures. 2. Nationalism—Canada—Addresses, essays, lectures. 3. New Brunswick—Politics and government—Addresses, essays, lectures. I. Title.
F1026.B25 917.1'03 73-177691
MARC

Bailey, Alfred Goldsworthy.
Thanks for a drowned island [by] Alfred G. Bailey. Toronto, McClelland and Stewart [1973]
96 p. 24 cm. $5.95 C***
Poems.
I. Title.
PR9199.3.B33T5 811'.5'4 74-183140
ISBN 0-7710-1003-6 MARC

Bailey, Alfred Marshall, 1894-
Galapagos Island, by Alfred M. Bailey. [Denver, Museum of Natural History, 1970]
85 p. illus. (Denver. Museum of Natural History. Museum pictorial no. 19)
Includes bibliography.
"Narrative of the 1960 field trip of the Denver Museum of Natural History to the Galapagos Islands."
1. Natural history—Galapagos Islands. 2. Galapagos Islands. I. Title. II. Series.
UU NUC73-40540

Bailey, Alice Anne (La Trobe-Bateman) 1880-1949.
The destiny of the nations. New York, Lucis Pub. Co., 1968, c1949.
161 p.
"Third printing."
1. Occult sciences. I. Title.
TxDaM-P NUC74-2873

Bailey, Alice Anne (La Trobe-Bateman) 1880-1949.
Esoteric psychology; a treatise on the seven rays. New York, Lucis Pub. Co. [1970]
2 v. 24 cm.
"First printing 1942."
1. Occult sciences. I. Title.
IU NUC74-120749

Bailey, Alice Anne (La Trobe-Bateman) 1880-1949.
Ponder on this; from the writings of the Tibetan teacher (Djwhal Khul) Compiled by a student. [Lynnwood, Pretoria, South Africa, Trulit, 1971?]
[14], 431 p. 23 cm.
"Reference Index: Books by the Tibetan (Djwhal Khul) through Alice A. Bailey [and] Books by Alice A. Bailey": p. [9]
1. Occult sciences. 2. Theosophy. I. The Tibetan, pseud. II. Title.
TxHR NUC73-127079

Bailey, Alice Anne (La Trobe-Bateman) 1880-1949.
Problems of humanity. 4th ed. New York, Lucis Pub. Co., 1967.
181 p.
Reprint of the 3d and rev. ed., 1964 with a new Foreword.
1. Social problems. 2. Reconstruction (1939-1951) I. Title.
TxDaM-P NUC74-2907

Bailey, Alice Anne (La Trobe-Bateman) 1880-1949.
Telepathy and the etheric vehicle, by Alice A. Bailey. New York, Lucis Pub. Co. [1971]
xi, 219 p. illus. 19 cm.
1. Thought-transference. I. Title.
RPB CU-SB PSt NUC74-120751

Bailey, Alice Anne (La Trobe-Bateman) 1880-1949.
A treatise on the seven rays, by Alice A. Bailey [in collaboration with the Tibetan. 1st ed.] New York, Lucis Pub. Co. [1970, c1951]
5 v. diagrs. 24 cm.
Contents.—v. [1]-2. The new psychology.—v. 3. Esoteric astrology.—v. 4. Esoteric healing.—v. 5. The rays and the initiations.
1. Theosophy. I. The Tibetan, pseud. II. Title.
IaAS NUC73-47926

Bailey, Alice Anne (La Trobe-Bateman) 1880-
see Patañjali. The light of the soul... New York, Lucia publishing company [1972, c1955]

Bailey, Amos Purnell, 1918-
see United Methodist Church (United States). Division of Chaplains and Related Ministries. Chaplains endorsed... Washington [1975]

Bailey, Andrew D
Bayesian revisions in related audit tests / by Andrew D. Bailey, Jr. and Daniel L. Jensen. — West Lafayette, Ind. : Institute for Research in the Behavioral, Economic, and Management Sciences, Krannert Graduate School of Industrial Administration, Purdue University, 1976.
19, 8 p. ; 28 cm. — (Paper - Institute for Research in the Behavioral, Economic, and Management Sciences, Purdue University ; no. 543)
Bibliography: p. 19.
1. Auditing—Mathematical models. I. Jensen, Daniel L., joint author. II. Title. III. Series: Purdue University, Lafayette, Ind. Institute for Research in the Behavioral, Economic, and Management Sciences. Paper ; no. 543.
HD6483.P8 no. 543 658'.001'9 s 76-362506
[HF5667] 76[r77]rev MARC

Bailey, Andrew D
Cost variance reports and statistical classification analysis / by Andrew D. Bailey, Jr. and Daniel L. Jensen. — West Lafayette, Ind. : Institute for Research in the Behavioral, Economic, and Management Sciences, Krannert Graduate School of Industrial Administration, Purdue University, 1976.
14, 7 p. ; 29 cm. — (Paper - Institute for Research in the Behavioral, Economic, and Management Sciences ; no. 542)
Bibliography: p. 14.
1. Cost control—Mathematical models. I. Jensen, Daniel L., joint author. II. Title. III. Series: Purdue University, Lafayette, Ind. Institute for Research in the Behavioral, Economic, and Management Sciences. Paper ; no. 542.
HD6483.P8 no. 542 658'.001'9 s 76-362757
[HD47.5] 76 MARC

Bailey, Andrew D
Goal and resource transfers in the multi-goal organization / by Andrew D. Bailey, Jr. and Warren J. Boe. — West Lafayette, Ind. : Institute for Research in the Behavioral, Economic, and Management Sciences, Krannert Graduate School of Industrial Administration, Purdue University, 1976.
28, 7 p. ; 28 cm. — (Paper - Institute for Research in the Behavioral, Economic, and Management Sciences, Purdue University ; no. 540)
Bibliography: p. 26-28.
1. Transfer pricing—Mathematical models. I. Boe, Warren J., joint author. II. Title. III. Series: Purdue University, Lafayette, Ind. Institute for Research in the Behavioral, Economic, and Management Sciences. Paper ; no. 540.
HD6483.P8 no. 540 658'.001'9 s 76-362205
[HD38] 76 MARC

Bailey, Andrew D
General price level adjustments in the capital budgeting decision / by Andrew D. Bailey, Jr. and Daniel L. Jensen. — West Lafayette, Ind. : Institute for Research in the Behavioral, Economic, and Management Sciences, Krannert Graduate School of Industrial Administration, Purdue University, 1976.
12 p. : ill. ; 28 cm. — (Paper - Institute for Research in the Behavioral, Economic, and Management Sciences, Purdue University ; no. 541)
Includes bibliographical references.
1. Capital budget. 2. Capital investments. I. Jensen, Daniel L., joint author. II. Title. III. Series: Purdue University, Lafayette, Ind. Institute for Research in the Behavioral, Economic, and Management Sciences. Paper ; no. 541.
HD6483.P8 no. 541 658'.001'9 s 76-622670
[HG4028.C4] 76 MARC

Bailey, Andrew D
The planning of operations and the analysis of alternative information systems: A dynamic programming approach to different costing methods in accounting for inventories. Ann Arbor, University Microfilms, 1972.
1 reel. 35 mm.
Thesis—Ohio State University, 1971.
Mirofilm copy.
1. Accounting. I. Title.
MsU NUC75-35226

Bailey, Andrew D
The two-dimensional time frame of common dollar statements / by Andrew D. Bailey, Jr. and Daniel L. Jensen. — West Lafayette, Ind. : Institute for Research in the Behavioral, Economic, and Management Sciences, Krannert Graduate School of Industrial Administration, Purdue University, 1976.
11, 8 p. ; 28 cm. — (Paper - Institute for Research in the Behaviorial, Economic, and Management Sciences, Purdue University ; no. 544)
1. Financial statements. I. Jensen, Daniel L., joint author. II. Title. III. Series: Purdue University, Lafayette, Ind. Institute for Research in the Behavioral, Economic, and Management Sciences. Paper ; no. 544.
HD6483.P8 no. 544 658'.001'9 s 76-362507
[HF5681.B2] 76 MARC

Bailey, Andrew D., joint author.
see Kinney, William R. Regression analysis as a means of determining audit sample size... West Lafayette, Ind., Institute for Research in the Behavioral, Economic, and Management Sciences, Krannert Graduate School of Industrial Administration, Purdue University, 1976.

Bailey, Ann
see Utah. Research Coordinating Unit. Apprenticeship survey. Salt Lake City [1970]

Bailey, Anthony.
The horizon concise history of the Low Countries. New York, American Heritage Pub. Co. [1972]
217 p. illus. 25 cm. $8.95
1. Benelux countries—History. I. Title.
DH107.B34 949.2 72-5351
ISBN 0-07-003215-7 MARC

Bailey, Appleton R b. 1786.
The life of Appleton R. Bailey, embracing a narrative of his adventures, imprisonments and sufferings. Written by himself. 3rd ed. Rochester, Shepard & Reed, 1848 [1974]
24 p. 18 cm.
Micro-transparency (positive) La Crosse, Wisconsin, Northern Micrographics, inc., 1974. 2 sheets. 10.5 x 14.5 cm. (American autobiographies)
Kaplan no. 246.
Copied from the original located in the Burton Historical Collection, Detroit Public Library.
1. Bailey, Appleton R b. 1786.
PSt NUC75-17146

Bailey, Arnold B
TV and other receiving antennas; theory and practice / by Arnold B. Bailey. -- Ann Arbor, Mich. : Xerox University Microfilms, 1976.
596 p. : ill. ; 22 cm.
Reprint of 1950 ed. published by J.F. Rider, New York.
Includes bibliographies.
1. Television--Antennas. 2. Antennas (Electronics) I. Title.
AzFU NUC77-86055

Bailey, Arthur W
A vegetation-soil survey of a wildlife forestry research area and its application to management in northwestern Oregon, by Arthur W. Bailey and William W. Hines. [Corvallis, Oregon State Game Commission, Research Division] 1971.
36 l. illus. (Game report, no. 2)
Includes bibliography.
1. Plant communities. 2. Forest soils. I. Hines, William W., joint author. II. Title.
MiU NUC75-49726

Bailey, B V
Jamaican clay deposits, by B. V. Bailey. Kingston, Jamaica, Geological Survey Dept., 1970.
4 p. 3 fold. maps in pocket. 33 cm. (Economic geology report no. 3)
Cover title.
Bibliography: p. 4.
1. Clay—Jamaica. I. Title. II. Series.
TN943.J28B34 553'.61'097292 74-173000
MARC

Bailey, Barbara K
Iowa urban policy study. Submitted to the Iowa Office for Planning and Programming, December, 1970, by Barbara K. Bailey and Robert J. Martineau. Rev. ed. Iowa City, Institute of Urban and Regional Research, University of Iowa [1970]
ii, 92 p. illus. 29 cm.
Bibliography: p. 91-92.
1. Cities and towns—Planning—Iowa. I. Martineau, Robert J., joint author. II. Iowa. Office for Planning and Programming. III. Iowa. University. Institute of Urban and Regional Research. IV. Title.
HT167.5.I 8B34 309.2'62'09777 73-622783
MARC

Bailey, Ben Edward.
Sourcebook in American Negro music [by] Ben E. Bailey. Tougaloo, Miss., Tougaloo College, 1968.
40 l. 28 cm.
Cover title.
1. Negro music—Bibl. 2. Music—U. S.—Bibl. I. Title.
RPB NUC74-122134

Bailey, Ben P
Border lands sketchbook = Libro de bosquejos fronterizos / Ben P. Bailey, Jr. ; translated by Channing Horner and Louise Bailey Horner. — [Waco? Tex.] : Bailey, c1976.
v, 170 p. : ill. (some col.) ; 29 cm.
English and Spanish.
Includes bibliographical references.
1. Bailey, Ben P. 2. Historic buildings—Texas—Rio Grande Valley—Pictorial works. 3. Buildings in art. I. Title. II. Title: Libro de bosquejos fronterizos.
NC139.B28A42 741.9'73 76-39665
77 MARC

Bailey, Benjamin, 1791–1871.
ബെഞ്ചമിൻ ബെയ്‌ലിയുടെ മലയാളം-ഇംഗ്ലീഷ് നിഘണ്ടു. [Kottayam, Gurunadhan Print. & Publications, 1970]
21, 930 p. illus. 26 cm. (Gurunadhan publication no. 12)
Rs45.00
Half title: മലയാളം ഇംഗ്ലീഷ് നിഘണ്ടു.
Original t. p. reads: A dictionary of high & colloquial Malayalam & English ... by B. Bailey. Cottayam, Printed at the Church Mission Press, 1846.
1. Malayalam language—Dictionaries—English. I. Title: Malayāḷam-Iṅgḷīṣ nighaṇṭu.
Title romanized: Bañcamin Beyliyuṭe Malayāḷam-Iṅgḷīs nighaṇṭu.
PL4716.B3 1970 71-924430

Bailey, Bernadine Freeman, 1901-
American shrines in England / Bernadine Bailey. — South Brunswick [N.J.] : A. S. Barnes, c1977.
157 p., [2] leaves of plates : ill. ; 29 cm.
Includes index.
ISBN 0-498-01727-3 : $15.00
1. Historic sites—England. 2. Historic buildings—England. 3. United States—History. 4. Great Britain—History. I. Title.
DA660.B15 1977 942 75-20586
76 MARC

Bailey, Bernadine Freeman, 1901–
Bolivia in pictures, by Bernadine Bailey. New York, Sterling Pub. Co. [1974]
64 p. illus. 26 cm. (Visual geography series)
SUMMARY: An introduction to the geography, history, government, people, and economy of the landlocked country of Bolivia.
1. Bolivia. [1. Bolivia] I. Title.
F3308.B17 918.4 73-93603
ISBN 0-8069-1176-X; 0-8069-1177-8 (lib. bdg.) MARC

Bailey, Bernadine Freeman, 1901–
Greenland in pictures, by Bernadine Bailey. New York, Sterling Pub. Co. [1973]
64 p. illus. 26 cm. (Visual geography series)
SUMMARY: Brief text and black and white photographs examine the geography, history, people, government, and economy of the largest island in the world.
1. Greenland. [1. Greenland] I. Title.
G743.B18 919.8'2 72-95201
MARC

Bailey, Bernadine Freeman, 1901-
Madagascar : the Malagasy Republic in pictures / by Bernadine Bailey and others. — New York : Sterling Pub. Co., [1974]
64 p. : ill. ; 26 cm. — (Visual geography series)
Includes index.
SUMMARY: Introduces the land, history, government, people, and economy of the republic occupying the fourth largest island in the world.
ISBN 0-8069-1188-3. ISBN 0-8069-1189-1 lib. bdg.
1. Madagascar. [1. Madagascar] I. Title. II. Title: Malagasy Republic in pictures.
DT469.M26B2 1974 969'.1'05 74-82331
75 MARC

Bailey, Bernadine Freeman, 1901-
Malawi in pictures. New York, Sterling Publishing Co. [1973]
64 p. illus. (Visual geography series)
1. Malawi—Descr. & travel—Views. I. Title.
InU NUC75-17103

Bailey, Bernadine Freeman, 1901-
Picture book of Colorado, by Bernadine Bailey. Pictures by Kurt Wiese. Rev. ed. Chicago, A. Whitman, 1971, c1966.
32 p. illus. (part col.) 17 x 21 cm. (Her The United States books)
1. Colorado—Juvenile literature. I. Wiese, Kurt, 1887- illus. II. Title.
MsSM NUC75-49727

Bailey, Bernadine Freeman, 1901–
Rhodesia in pictures, by Bernadine Bailey. New York, Sterling Pub. Co. [1973, c1974]
64 p. illus. 26 cm. (Visual geography series)
SUMMARY: Introduces the land, history, government, people, and economy of one of Africa's most controversial countries.
1. Rhodesia, Southern. [1. Rhodesia, Southern] I. Title.
DT962.B24 916.89'1'034 73-83438
ISBN 0-8069-1174-3; 0-8069-1175-1 (lib. bdg.) MARC

Bailey, Bernadine Freeman, 1901–
Wonders of the world of bears / Bernadine Bailey ; illustrated with photos. — New York : Dodd, Mead, [1975]
63 p. : ill. ; 24 cm. — (Dodd, Mead wonders books)
Includes index.
SUMMARY: Describes the characteristics and habits of various species of bears.
ISBN 0-396-07031-0
1. Bears—Juvenile literature. [1. Bears] I. Title.
QL737.C27B34 599'.74446 74-15239
MARC

Bailey, Beryl Loftman.
A language guide to Jamaica. [New York] Research Institute for the Study of Man, c1962.
74 l.
Xeroxed copy.
1. Creole dialects—Jamaica. 2. Jamaica—languages. I. Title.
NcU NUC73-59277

Bailey, Betty, joint author.
see Twitchett, John. Royal Crown Derby. London, Barrie & Jenkins, 1976.

Bailey, Betty, joint author.
see Twitchett, John. Royal Crown Derby. 1st American ed. New York, C. N. Potter : distributed by Crown Publishers, 1976.

Bailey, Bill, 1895-
see
Bailey, William A 1895-

Bailey, Bob
see [Let George do it] [Sound recording] American Forces Radio and Television Service RU 9-2, 5B [1971]

Bailey, Boyd L
Contamination of ground water in a limestone aquifer in the Stevenson area, Alabama, by Boyd L. Bailey and A. M. Malatino. University, Ala., Division of Water Resources, 1971.
15 p. illus. 23 cm. (Geological Survey of Alabama. Circular 76)
Bibliography: p. 15.
1. Water, Underground—Pollution—Stevenson region, Ala. I. Malatino, A. M., joint author. II. Title. III. Series: Alabama. Geological Survey. Circular 76.
TD224.A2B34 557.61'08 s 72-612003
[628.1'686'76195] MARC

Bailey, Brian D
A history of the Toronto waterfront from Etobicoke to Pickering. Prepared for the Waterfront Division of the Metropolitan Toronto and Region Conservation Authority. [Toronto] 1973.
61 p. ill.
Includes bibliography.
CaOTP NUC76-87304

Bailey, Brian J
Ashridge observed / written and illustrated by Brian J. Bailey. — Bedford : Inglenook Press, 1975.
36 p. : ill. ; 21 cm. GB75-20596
Limited ed. of 200 numbered copies. No. 83.
ISBN 0-9504320-0-8 : £1.95
1. Ashridge Priory. I. Title.
DA664.A7B34 942.5'84 76-354746
76 MARC

Bailey, Brian J
William Etty's nudes / by Brian J. Bailey. — Pulloxhill [Eng.] : Inglenook Press, c1974.
48 p. : ill. ; 21 cm. — (An Inglenook publication) GB***
Limited ed. of 300 copies. This is no. 119.
1. Etty, William, 1787-1849. 2. Nude in art. 3. Women in art. I. Etty, William, 1787-1849. II. Title.
ND497.E8B34 759.2 75-320725
75 MARC

Bailey, Brian J 1934-
Portrait of Leicestershire / by Brian J. Bailey. — London : R. Hale, 1977.
224 p., [12] leaves of plates : ill. ; 23 cm. GB***
Bibliography: p. 214-216.
Includes index.
ISBN 0-7091-6005-4 : £3.95
1. Leicestershire, Eng.—Description and travel. I. Title.
DA670.L5B34 1977 914.25'4'04857 77-363493
77 MARC

Bailey, Bruce.
The load-settlement behavior of smallscale footings on loess soils. [Iowa City] 1972.
xi, 213 l. illus. 28 cm.
Thesis (Ph. D.)—University of Iowa.
1. Soil mechanics. 2. Loess. I. Title.
IaU NUC73-32344

Bailey, Bruce
see Pevsner, Sir Nikolaus, 1902- Northamptonshire. 2nd ed. Harmondsworth : Penguin, 1973.

Bailey, Bruce Frederick, 1946-
T.S. Eliot's The waste land: an analytic history of its texts and critical reception through 1972, by Bruce Frederick Bailey. [Toronto] 1975.
Thesis—University of Toronto.
Vita.
Bibliography: leaves 285-334.
1. Eliot, Thomas Stearns, 1888-1965. The waste land. I. Eliot, Thomas Stearns, 1888-1965. The waste land. II. Title.
CaOTU NUC77-81898

Bailey, C
Some technical repercussions on the meat industry of EEC entry, by C. Bailey, C. L. Cutting and A. G. Kitchell. Bristol, Meat Research Institute, 1972.
5 l. 30 cm. (Meat Research Institute. Memorandum no. 1)
GB***
At head of title: Agricultural Research Council.
Bibliography: leaf 5.
1. Meat industry and trade—Law and legislation—European Economic Community countries. I. Cutting, C. L., joint author. II. Kitchell, A. G., joint author. III. Title. IV. Series.
HD9425.E82B3 382'.45'66490094 73-166733
MARC

Bailey, Carolyn Sherwin, 1875-1961.
A Christmas party : poem / by Carolyn Sherwin Bailey ; pictures by Cyndy Szekeres. — New York : Pantheon, [1975]
[26] p. : col. ill. ; 19 x 24 cm.
SUMMARY: On Christmas eve the forest gives a party for all the animals.
ISBN 0-394-83094-6. ISBN 0-394-93094-0 lib. bdg.
[1. Stories in rhyme. 2. Christmas stories] I. Szekeres, Cyndy. II. Title.
PZ8.3.S998 Ch 811'.5'4 75-2543
75 MARC

Bailey, Carolyn Sherwin, 1875–1961, ed.
For the children's hour, by Carolyn S. Bailey and Clara M. Lewis. Illus. by G. William Breck. Springfield, Mass., M. Bradley Co., 1920. Detroit, Gale Research Co., 1974.
336 p. illus. 18 cm.
SUMMARY: Includes poetry, fairy tales, fables, and stories of home, holidays, and nature.
1. Children's literature (Collections) [1. Literature—Collections] I. Lewis, Clara M., joint ed. II. Breck, G. William, illus. III. Title.
PZ5.B151Fo 12 808.8'99282 73-20186
ISBN 0-8103-3958-7 [Fic] MARC

Bailey, Carolyn Sherwin, 1875–1961.
For the story teller : story telling and stories to tell / by Carolyn Sherwin Bailey. — Detroit : Gale Research Co., 1975, c1913.
viii, 261 p. ; 22 cm.
Reprint of the ed. published by M. Bradley Co., Springfield, Mass.
Bibliography: p. 251-261.
ISBN 0-8103-3802-5
1. Story-telling. 2. Children's stories. I. Title.
LB1042.B3 1975 372.6'4 74-23576
MARC

Bailey, Carolyn Sherwin, 1875-1961. Miss Hickory
see Fowler, Ray. Miss Hickory. [Phonorecord] New York, Viking Press [1972]

Bailey, Carolyn Sherwin, 1875–1961.
Stories for every holiday. New York, Abingdon Press. Detroit, Gale Research Co., 1974.
277 p. 18 cm.
Reprint of the 1918 ed.
SUMMARY: Twenty-seven short stories about twenty holidays throughout the year.
1. Holidays—Juvenile fiction. [1. Holidays—Fiction. 2. Short stories] I. Title.
PZ7.B151Ste 9 [Fic] 73-20149
ISBN 0-8103-3957-9 MARC

Bailey, Cecil Henry, joint author
see Laybourn, K
Teaching science to the ordinary pupil. [2d ed.] New York, Barnes & Noble Books [1972, c1971]

Bailey, Charles, joint comp.
see Lord, Eric, comp. A reader in religious & Moral education. London, S. C. M. Press, 1973.

Bailey, Charles Everett.
A study of educational programs for immigrant children of agricultural migratory workers in the state of Connecticut. Storrs, 1970.
247 p.
Thesis—University of Connecticut.
Microfilm. Ann Arbor, Mich., University Microfilms. 1 reel. 35 mm.
CLSU NUC73-38823

Bailey, Charles Henry, 1944-
Effects of the flagellate, Herpetomonas muscarum, in the eye gnat, Hippelates pusio (Diptera: Chloropidae). Raleigh, N.C., 1971.
72 l. plates, tables. 29 cm.
Thesis (Ph.D.)—North Carolina State University at Raleigh.
Vita.
Bibliographies.
NcRS NUC75-35237

Bailey, Charles James Nice.
Variation and linguistic theory ⌊by⌋ Charles-James N. Bailey. ⌊Arlington, Va.⌋ Center for Applied Linguistics, 1973.
vi, 162 p. 23 cm.
Bibliography: p. 150-162.
1. Linguistic change. I. Title.
P123.B33 410'.7'2 73-84648
ISBN 0-87281-032-1 MARC

Bailey, Charles James Nice, ed.
see Chicago Linguistic Society. Papers from the fourth regional meeting... Chicago ⌊1968⌋

Bailey, Charles James Nice, ed.
see Southeastern Conference on Linguistics, 8th Georgetown University, 1972. New ways of analyzing variation in English. Washington, Georgetown Univ. Press [1973]

Bailey, Charles James Nice, ed.
see Southeastern Conference on Linguistics, 8th, Georgetown University, 1972. Towards tomorrow's linguistics... Washington, Georgetown Univ. Press ⌊1974⌋

Bailey, Charles Waldo
see Knebel, Fletcher. Convention. New York, Harper and Row [c1964]

Bailey, Chris H
Two hundred years of American clocks & watches / by Chris H. Bailey ; photography by John Garetti. — Englewood Cliffs, N.J. : Prentice-Hall, 1975.
254 p. : ill. (some col.) ; 28 cm.
"A Rutledge book."
Includes bibliographies and index.
ISBN 0-13-935130-2 : $25.00
1. Clock and watch making—United States—History. 2. Clock and watch makers—United States. I. Title.
TS543.U6B27 681'.113'0973 75-13714
75 MARC

Bailey, Chris H.
see Seth Thomas Clock Company. Illustrated catalogue of Seth Thomas... [Bristol, Conn., K. Roberts Pub. Co., 1973]

Bailey, Clare Crabtree, 1945-
A task analysis of medical laboratory workers in hospitals in Duval county, Florida. ⌊Gainesville⌋ 1973.
xiii, 225 l. illus. 28 cm.
Typescript.
Thesis—University of Florida.
Vita.
Bibliography: leaves 222-224.
1. Medical technologists. 2. Job analysis. I. Title.
FU NUC75-20342

Bailey, Clay Wade.
Judge Gus Thomas, colorful and homey. [Lexington, Ky., 1974]
1 p. port. 56 cm.
Reprinted from Sunday Herald-Leader, Lexington, Ky., February 3, 1974, p. G8-G9.
Microfiche (negative) [Louisville, Ky.] Lost Cause Press, 1974. 2 cards. 10.5 x 14.8 cm. ([Kentucky culture series])
1. Thomas, William Augustus, d. 1951. 2. Kentucky. Court of Appeals. I. Series.
CLSU NUC76-15328

Bailey, Clinton, 1936-
The participation of the Palestinians in the politics of Jordan. ⌊New York⌋ 1966 ⌊c1969⌋
iv, 286 l. maps. 29 cm.
Thesis—Columbia University.
Bibliography: leaves 282-286.
1. Jordan—Politics and government. I. Title.
NNC NUC74-4308

Bailey, Colin.
The fire house book. New York, Golden Press, 1969.
⌊24⌋ p. col. illus. 22 cm. (A Golden shape book)
I. Title.
MiDW NUC74-122135

Bailey, Conner.
Broker, mediator, patron, and kinsman : an historical analysis of key leadership roles in a rural Malaysian district / by Conner Bailey. — Athens : Ohio University, Center for International Studies, 1976.
x leaves, 79 p. : maps ; 28 cm. — (Papers in international studies : Southeast Asia series ; no. 38)
A revision of the author's thesis (M.A.), Ohio University.
Bibliography: p. 76-79.
ISBN 0-8214-0288-9 : $4.00
1. Kedah—Rural conditions. 2. Community leadership—Case studies. 3. Villages—Malaysia—Case studies. I. Title. II. Series.
HN700.6.K4B33 1976 301.35'2'095951 75-620141
76 MARC

Bailey, Conrad.
Harrap's guide to famous London graves / by Conrad Bailey ; with a foreword by John Betjeman ; photos. by Philip Sayer. — London : Harrap, 1975.
157 p. : ill. ; 20 cm. GB***
Bibliography: p. 146.
Includes index.
ISBN 0-245-52374-X : £3.50
1. Great Britain—Biography. 2. London—Cemeteries—Directories. I. Title. II. Title: Famous London graves.
CT775.B34 1975 914.21'04'85 76-350590
76 MARC

Bailey, Consuelo Northrop, 1899-1976.
Leaves before the wind : the autobiography of Vermont's own daughter / Consuelo Northrop Bailey. — Burlington, Vt. : G. Little Press, c1976.
376 p. : ill. ; 24 cm.
$9.95
1. Bailey, Consuelo Northrop, 1899-1976. 2. Vermont—Lieutenant-governors—Biography. I. Title.
F55.B344 974.3'04'0924 76-47361
77 MARC

Bailey, Curtiss Merkel, 1927-
The combining ability of western and down breeds of sheep for economically important traits. ⌊n.p.⌋ 1960.
139 l. illus. 29 cm.
Thesis (Ph.D.)—University of Wisconsin.
Vita.
Includes bibliography.
I. Title.
WU NUC73-9452

Bailey, D
List of the flowering plants and ferns of Seychelles with their vernacular names / D. Bailey. — 3d ed. — ⌊Victoria⌋ Seychelles : Printed by the Govt. Printer, 1971.
⌊ii⌋, 46 leaves ; 26 cm.
Bibliography: leaf ⌊ii⌋
Includes index.
1. Botany—Seychelles. 2. Plant names, Popular—Seychelles. 3. Ferns—Seychelles. I. Title.
QK429.S4B34 1971 582'.13'09696 75-304228
75 MARC

Bailey, D D W
Directory of mines, plants and quarries and mining companies holding mining properties in New Brunswick, March, 1969. [Fredericton, Mineral Lands Division, Dept. of Natural Resources, New Brunswick] 1969.
15 p. 23 cm. (Information circular 69-1)
1. Mineral industries—Directories. I. Title. II. Series: New Brunswick. Mineral Lands Division. Information circular 69-1.
CLU NUC76-87303

Bailey, D G
Agricultural co-operative activities, by D. G. Bailey and Case histories of co-operatives, by E. T. Gibbons. Newcastle upon Tyne, University of Newcastle upon Tyne, Agricultural Adjustment Unit, 1970.
31 p. 19 cm. (University of Newcastle upon Tyne Agricultural Adjustment Unit. Technical papers, 9) £0.30 GB 73-20683
Cover title.
Includes bibliographical references.
1. Agriculture, Cooperative—Great Britain. I. Gibbons, E. T. Case histories of co-operatives. 1970. II. Title. III. Title: Case histories of co-operatives. IV. Series: Newcastle upon Tyne. University. Agricultural Adjustment Unit. Technical papers, 9.
[HD1491.G7B3] 334'.683'0924 74-165702
ISBN 0-903698-05-6-Sd MARC

Bailey, D. K.
see
Bailey, David Kenneth, 1931-

Bailey, Dale S 1925-
Slavery in the novels of Brazil and the United States: a comparison, by Dale S. Bailey. [Bloomington] 1961.
v, 226 p.
Thesis—Indiana University.
Vita.
Bibliography: p. [206]-226.
Photocopy. Ann Arbor, Mich., University Microfilms, 1972. v, 226 l. 21 cm.
1. Brazilian fiction—Hist. & crit. 2. American fiction—Hist. & crit. 3. Slavery and slaves in literature. 4. Literature, Comparative—Brazilian and American. 5. Literature, Comparative—American and Brazilian. I. Title.
CtY NUC76-26026

Bailey, Dave.
Steel: the coming redundancies and how to fight them (including 'The confidential report' on closures ⌊by the British Steel Corporation⌋). London, International Marxist Group Publications, ⌊1972⌋.
55 p. 22 cm. £0.15 B 72-27101
Bibliography: p. 48.
1. Steel industry and trade—Great Britain. 2. Steel industry and trade — Great Britain — Technological innovations. 3. British Steel Corporation. 4. Trade-unions—Iron and steel workers—Great Britain. 5. Plant shutdowns—Great Britain. I. Title.
HD9521.6.B3 338.4'7'66910942 73-330823
ISBN 0-902869-11-6 MARC

Bailey, David, 1938-
Another image : Papua New Guinea / ⌊by⌋ David Bailey. — London : Matthews Miller Dunbar Ltd : The author, 1975.
142 p. : chiefly ill. (some col.) ; 31 cm. GB76-29919
ISBN 0-903811-16-2 : £7.50
1. Ethnology—Papua New Guinea—Pictorial works. I. Title.
GN671.N5B32 995.3 76-382809
76 MARC

Bailey, David, 1938-
Goodbye baby & amen; a saraband for the sixties ⌊by⌋ David Bailey & Peter Evans. London, Conde Nast Publications ⌊1969⌋
237 p. illus., ports. 37 cm. 95/-
1. Photography—Portraits. I. Evans, Peter, 1933- joint author. II. Title.
TR681.F3B3 1969b 779'.2 72-9713
ISBN 0-900303-06-9 70⌊r77⌋rev MARC

Bailey, David, 1938-
Goodbye baby & amen; a saraband for the Sixties ⌊by⌋ David Bailey & Peter Evans. ⌊1st American ed.⌋ New York, Coward-McCann ⌊1969⌋
237 p. illus., ports. 37 cm. 15.00
1. Photography—Portraits. I. Evans, Peter, 1933- joint author. II. Title.
TR681.F3B3 1969 779'.2 72-92772
69⌊r77⌋rev MARC

Bailey, David A.
see Dreyer, Sharon. A guide to nursing management of psychiatric patients. St. Louis, Mosby, 1975.

Bailey, David B 1948-
Synthesis of polymeric and oligomeric ultraviolet absorbers. Amherst, 1975.
xxv, 296 l. illus. 28 cm.
Thesis (Ph.D.)—University of Massachusetts, 1976.
1. Polymer and polymerization. 2. Chemistry, Organic—Synthesis. 3. Stabilizing agents. I. Title.
MU NUC77-81761

Bailey, David C 1930-
A guide to historical sources in Saltillo, Coahuila / David C. Bailey and William H. Beezley. — East Lansing : Latin American Studies Center, Michigan State University, 1975.
101 leaves ; 29 cm. — (Monograph series - Latin American Studies Center, Michigan State University ; no. 13)
Bibliography: leaves 95-101.
$3.00
1. Archives—Mexico—Saltillo. 2. Saltillo—Libraries. 3. Coahuila, Mexico—History—Library resources. I. Beezley, William H., joint author. II. Title. III. Series: Michigan. State University, East Lansing. Latin American Studies Center. Monograph series ; no. 13.
CD3677.S24B34 026'.972'1 75-620104
77 MARC

Bailey, David C 1930-
¡Viva Cristo Rey! The Cristero Rebellion and the church-state conflict in Mexico, by David C. Bailey. Austin, University of Texas Press ⌊1974⌋
xiii, 346 p. illus. 23 cm. (Texas pan-American series) $10.00
Bibliography: p. ⌊324⌋-332.
1. Cristero Rebellion, 1926-1929. 2. Church and state in Mexico. I. Title. II. Title: The Cristero rebellion and the church-state conflict in Mexico.
F1234.B175 972.08'2 73-17119
ISBN 0-292-78700-6 MARC

Bailey, David E., 1917- joint author.
see Bruton, Quintilla Geer, 1907- Plant City, its origin and history. 1st ed. St. Petersburg, Fla., Valkyrie Press, c1977.

Bailey, David George, 1945-
A mechanism for the biliary secretion of acidic drugs in the rat, by David G. Bailey. [Toronto] 1973.
xiv, 154 l. illus.
Thesis—University of Toronto.
Bibliography: leaves 144-152.
CaOTU NUC75-20290

Bailey, David Jerry.
The effects of tutoring first, second, and third grade tutees on the academic achievement, academic potential, and self-concepts of the seventh-grade tutors. [Charlottesville, Va.] 1972.
167 l. 29 cm.
Thesis (Ed.D.)—University of Virginia.
Bibliography: leaves [148]-155.
1. Tutors and tutoring. I. Title.
ViU NUC74-597

Bailey, David Kenneth, 1931-
see The Evolution of the crystalline rocks. London, Academic Press, 1976.

Bailey, David Nelson.
Methaqualone, a new drug abuse; studies in analytical methodology and significance of serum drug levels in overdose [by] David N. Bailey. New Haven, 1973.
14, [19] l. illus. 29 cm.
Thesis (M.D.)—Yale University.
Bibliography: leaves [17-19]
1. Methaqualone. 2. Drug abuse. I. Title.
CtY NUC74-122282

Bailey, David Roy Shackleton.
Cicero [by] D. R. Shackleton Bailey. New York, Scribner [1973, c1971]
xii, 290 p. illus. 21 cm. (Classical life and letters) (The Scribner library. Lyceum editions: history) $3.50
Includes bibliographical references.
1. Cicero, Marcus Tullius.
DG260.C5B27 1973 937'.05'0924 [B] 74-161825
ISBN 0-684-12683-4; 0-684-13216-8 (pbk.) MARC

Bailey, David Thomas, 1944-
Stratification and ethnic differentiation in Santa Fe, 1860 and 1870, by David Thomas Bailey. [Austin, Tex.] 1975.
iv, 154 l. graphs. 29 cm.
Thesis (Ph.D.)—University of Texas at Austin.
Vita.
Bibliography: leaves 142-153.
1. Mexican Americans—New Mexico—Santa Fe. 2. Santa Fe, N.M.—Economic conditions. 3. Santa Fe, N.M.—Social conditions. I. Title.
TxU NUC77-81760

Bailey, De Witt. British public opinion on the American war in prints
see English reaction to the American War. [London, 1975]

Bailey, De Witt.
Percussion guns & rifles; an illustrated reference guide [by] D. W. Bailey. [Harrisburg, Pa.] Stackpole Books [1972]
79 p. illus. 23 cm. (Stackpole arms and armour illustrated monographs) $5.95
Bibliography: p. 78-79.
1. Firearms. 2. Firearms—Locks. I. Title.
TS536.6.M8B35 683'.42'09034 72-6794
ISBN 0-8117-1242-7 MARC

Bailey, De Witt.
Percussion guns & rifles: an illustrated guide, [by] D. W. Bailey. London, Arms and Armor Press, 1972.
79 p.; illus., port. 23 cm. (Arms and Armour Press. Illustrated monographs) £1.70 B 72-31832
Bibliography: p. 78-79.
1. Firearms. 2. Firearms—Locks. I. Title.
TS536.6.M8B35 1972b 683'.42'09034 73-159162
ISBN 0-85368-082-5 MARC

Bailey, De Witt
see Guns & gun collecting. London, Octopus Books Ltd, 1972.

Bailey, Denis John, 1944-
Electrophoretic analyses of membrane proteins from rat liver and rat hepatomas. By Denis John Bailey. [Toronto] c1974.
xvi, 194, [52] l. illus., 35 l. of plates.
Thesis—University of Toronto.
Vita.
Bibliography: leaves 179-194.
CaOTU NUC76-15646

Bailey, Dennis Lee, 1941-
Rhetorical genres in early American public address, 1652-1700. Norman, 1971.
154 l.
Thesis (Ph.D.)—University of Oklahoma.
Photocopy. Ann Arbor, University Microfilms, 1974. 21 cm.
1. American orations—History and criticism. 2. Orators, American. 3. Oratory—History. 4. English language—Rhetoric. I. Title.
GU NUC76-26921

Bailey, Derrick Sherwin, 1910–
Homosexuality and the Western Christian tradition / by Derrick Sherwin Bailey. — Hamden, Conn. : Archon Books, 1975.
xii, 181 p. ; 22 cm.
Reprint of the 1955 ed. published by Longmans, Green, London.
Includes bibliographical references and index.
ISBN 0-208-01492-6
1. Homosexuality. I. Title.
[HQ76.B3 1975] 301.41'57 74-34384
MARC

Bailey, Derrick Sherwin, 1910-
Homosexuality and the Western Christian tradition. London, New York, Longmans, green [1955] Ann Arbor, Michigan, University Microfilms, 1975.
181 p. 22 cm.
1. Homosexuality. I. Title.
OKentU NUC76-22529

Bailey, Derrick Sherwin, 1910-
The mystery of love and marriage : a study in the theology of sexual relation / Derrick Sherwin Bailey. — Westport, Conn. : Greenwood Press, 1977, c1952.
x, 145 p. ; 22 cm.
Reprint of the ed. published by Harper, New York.
Bibliography: p. 137-139.
Includes index.
ISBN 0-8371-9577-2
1. Marriage. 2. Marriage—Biblical teaching. 3. Love. 4. Sex (Theology) I. Title.
[HQ1051.B3 1977] 261.8'34'2 77-3313
77 MARC

Bailey, Derrick Sherwin, 1910-
Sexual relationship; a guide to published literature, by D.S. Bailey. [Rev. ed. London] Pub. for the Church of England Moral Welfare Council by the Church Information Board, 1957.
31 p. 22 cm.
First published in 1953.
1. Sex—Bibliography. 2. Marriage—Bibliography. 3. Sex and religion—Bibliography. I. Title.
CBGTU NUC76-69342

Bailey, Derrick Sherwin, 1910- ed.
see Wells Cathedral. Wells Cathedral chapter act book, 1666-83. London, H. M. Stationery Off., 1973.

Bailey, Don.
If you hum me a few bars I might remember the tune; stories. [Ottawa] Oberon Press [1973]
154 p. 21 cm. $5.95 ($2.95 pbk.) C***
I. Title.
PZ4.B1513 If 813'.5'4 73-76044
[PR9199.3.B34] MARC
ISBN 0-88750-083-8; 0-88750-084-6 (pbk.)

Bailey, Don.
In the belly of the whale : a novel / by Don Bailey. — [Ottawa] : Oberon Press, [1974]
145 p. ; 21 cm. C***
ISBN 0-88750-104-4
I. Title.
PZ4.B1513 In 813'.5'4 74-76141
[PR9199.3.B34] MARC

Bailey, Don.
My bareness is not just my body. [Fredericton, N. B., Fred Cogswell, 1971]
80 p. 22 cm. C***
Cover title.
Limited ed. of 500 copies.
Poems.
I. Title.
PR6052.A3185M9 811'.5'4 73-153063
ISBN 0-919196-79-9 MARC

Bailey, Don.
Replay : stories / by Don Bailey. — [Ottawa] : Oberon Press, c1975.
149 p. ; 22 cm. C***
ISBN 0-88750-172-9. ISBN 0-88750-173-7 pbk.
I. Title.
PZ4.B1513 Re 813'.5'4 76-351009
[PR9199.3.B34] 76 MARC

Bailey, Don.
The shapes around me. [Fredericton, N. B., Fiddlehead Poetry Books, 1973]
74 p. 22 cm. C***
Poems.
"Five hundred copies ... have been printed."
I. Title.
PR9199.3.B34S48 811'.5'4 74-161553
ISBN 0-919197-35-3 MARC

Bailey, Don E.
see Use and abuse of interrogatories ... [Sound recording] [Berkeley] California Continuing Education of the Bar, p1973.

Bailey, Donald A., joint author.
see Carron, Albert V. Strength development in boys from 10 through 16 years. [Chicago] Published by the University of Chicago Press for the Society for Research in Child Development, 1974.

Bailey, Donald Atholl.
Writers against the cardinal: a study of the pamphlets which attacked the person and policies of Cardinal Richelieu during the decade 1630-1640. [Minneapolis] 1973.
2 v. (624 l.) 29 cm.
Thesis (Ph.D.)—University of Minnesota.
Bibliography: leaves 609-625.
MnU NUC76-68682

Bailey, Donald Joseph, 1938-
Critical study of dislocation dynamics, with special application to deformation under strain-aging conditions. [n.p.] 1966.
ix, 155 l. illus.
Thesis—University of Washington.
Bibliography: leaves 151-154.
Microfilm (positive) Ann Arbor, Mich., University Microfilms, 1966. 1 reel. (Publication no. 11978)
NNC NUC75-35236

Bailey, Donald M
Greek and Roman pottery lamps [by] Donald M. Bailey. Revised ed. [London], British Museum, 1972.
32, 16, [4] p. illus. (some col.). 22 cm. £0.40 B 72-26646
Bibliography: p. [26]-27.
1. Lamps. 2. Pottery, Greek. 3. Pottery, Roman. I. British Museum. II. Title.
NK4680.B24 1972 738.3'83 73-151255
ISBN 0-7141-1237-2 MARC

Bailey, Donald M
Greek, Hellenistic, and early Roman pottery lamps / D. M. Bailey. — London : British Museum Publications Ltd., 1975.
viii, 397 p., 150 p. of plates : ill., plans ; 29 cm. — (A catalogue of the lamps in the British Museum ; 1) GB76-12785
Includes bibliographical references and indexes.
ISBN 0-7141-1243-7 : £45.00
1. Lamps, Greek—Catalogs. 2. Lamps, Hellenistic—Catalogs. 3. Lamps, Roman—Catalogs. 4. British Museum. I. Title. II. Series: British Museum. A catalogue of the lamps in the British Museum ; 1.
NK4680.B72 1975 vol. 1 749'.63 s 76-370621
76 MARC

Bailey, Donald M.
see British Museum. A catalogue of the lamps in the British Museum. London, British Museum Publications Ltd., 1975-

Bailey, Donald Randall, 1935-
Factors affecting racial attitudes and overt behavior of seminary-trained Methodist ministers: a panel study, by Donald R. Bailey. [n.p.] 1972 [c1973]
[16], 160 l.
Thesis—Emory University.
Bibliography: leaves 153-160.
Photocopy. Ann Arbor, Mich., University Microfilms, 1974. 22 cm.
1. Church and race problems. U.S. I. Title.
NcD NUC76-26922

Bailey, Douglas Babcock, 1935-
The development of a semantic differential instrument for measuring principal semantic dimensions of meaning which adults ascribe to religious and theological terminology. [n.p.] c1973.
342 l. 29 cm.
Thesis (Ph.D.)—University of Wisconsin.
Vita.
Includes bibliography.
1. Religion and language. 2. English language—Semantics. I. Title.
WU NUC74-599

Bailey, Douglas Graydon.
Migration of disks in couette flow and application to blood oxygenator design. [n.p.] 1975.
123 l. ill. 28 cm.
Bibliography: leaves 121-123.
Thesis (Mech. E.)–Massachusetts Institute of Technology.
1. Blood flow. 2. Diffusion. 3. Suspensions (Chemistry). I. Title.
MCM NUC77-81901

Bailey, Duryl Middleton
see Carter, Louis D Preshot geological and engineering conditions at the Project Flivver Site... Vicksburg, Miss., 1967.

Bailey, E E
For sale! One hundred acres of land well improved... Saw and grist mill. Flat Shoal, Surrey Co., N.C. [n.d.]
[1] p. 24 x 15 cm.
1. North Carolina--Flour and flour mills. 2. North Carolina--Sawmills.
NcU NUC77-87920

Bailey, E M
A list of modern Arabic words as used in daily and weekly newspapers of Cairo, compiled by E. M. Bailey [and] Ed. D. [Cairo, Nile Mission Press, n.d.]
79 p.
1. Arabic language–Glossaries, vocabularies, etc. I. Title.
CLU NUC75-20887

Bailey, Earl.
Surface mining in Alabama : the environmental impact / by Earl Bailey. — [Montgomery] : Published by the Alabama Environmental Quality Association in cooperation with the Alabama Attorney General's Office, [1975].
23 p. : ill. ; 16 x 23 cm.
Includes bibliographical references.
1. Strip mining—Environmental aspects—Alabama. I. Alabama Environmental Quality Association. II. Alabama. Attorney General's Office. III. Title.
TD195.S75B34 333.7'6 75-317178
75 MARC

Bailey, Earl L 1924-
Marketing-cost ratios of U.S. manufacturers : a technical analysis / [by Earl L. Bailey]. — New York : Conference Board, [1975]
iii, 44 p. : ill. ; 28 cm. — (Conference Board report ; no. 662)
Cover title.
$25.00 (associate and educational); $75 (non-associate)
1. Marketing—United States—Costs. I. Title. II. Series: Conference Board. Report ; no. 662.
HF5415.1.B32 381'.0973 75-321551
75 MARC

Bailey, Earl L 1924– comp.
Tomorrow's marketing; a symposium. Edited by Earl L. Bailey. [New York, Conference Board, 1974]
iv, 65 p. 23 cm. (Conference Board. Report no. 623) $5.00
"Selected presentations at recent marketing conferences of the Conference Board."
1. Marketing—United States—Congresses. I. Conference Board. II. Title. III. Series.
HF5415.1.B34 658.8'00973 74–176137
MARC

Bailey, Earl L., 1924- ed.
see Marketing strategies : a symposium. [New York] : Conference Board, [1974]

Bailey, Edgar Herbert, 1914–
Geology and ore deposits of the Lakan lead-zinc district, Iran, by Edgar H. Bailey and John W. Barnes. [Ankara] Central Treaty Organization [1970]
35 p. illus., group ports, maps. 27 cm.
On cover: Third session CENTO training program geological mapping techniques, July–September, 1968.
Bibliography: p. 33.
1. Lead ores—Iran. 2. Zinc ores—Iran. 3. Geology—Iran. I. Barnes, John Wykeham, joint author. II. Title.
TN456.I 7B34 555.5'25 74–172676
MARC

Bailey, Edgar Herbert, 1914-
Road log for Santa Catalina Island; A. A. P. G. field trip, April 14-15, 1967. [By] Edgar H. Bailey. [n.p., 1967]
21 l. fold. map.
Caption title.
1. Geology–California–Santa Catalina Island. I. American Association of Petroleum Geologists. Pacific Section. II. Title.
MiU NUC74-26237

Bailey, Edgar Herbert, 1914- joint author.
see Barnes, John Wykeham. Geology and ore deposits of the Sizma-Ladik mercury district, Turkey. [Ankara, Office of the United States Economic Coordinator for CENTO Affairs] Central Treaty Organization, [1971]

Bailey, Edward D., joint author.
see Winterhelt, Sigbot. The training and care of the versatile hunting dog. Puslinch, Ont., North American Versatile Hunting Dog Association, 1973.

Bailey, Edward Ian.
Belief / Edward Bailey. — London : Batsford, 1974.
96 p. : ill. ; 26 cm. — (World wide series) GB***
Bibliography: p. 94.
Includes index.
ISBN 0–7134–1579–7 : £1.95
1. Religions—Juvenile literature. I. Title.
BL92.B27 291 75–301167
MARC

Bailey, Edward Weldon, 1898-
see Hildebrand, Ira Polk, 1876-1944. The law of Texas corporations... Kansas City, Vernon Law Book Co., [c1942]

Bailey, Eldon R
Lake Charles police and fire departments' retirement systems / prepared by Eldon R. Bailey, in collaboration with Duford J. Henry and Charles D. Whitman. -- Lake Charles, La. : Lake Charles-McNeese Urban Observatory, 1976.
ix, 64 leaves.
Research conducted pursuant to contract between Dept. of Housing and Urban Development and League of Cities - Conference of Mayors.
1. Police--Louisiana--Lake Charles--Retirement. 2. Firemen--Louisiana--Lake Charles--Retirement. I. Lake Charles--McNeese Urban Observatory. II. United States. Dept. of Housing and Urban Development. III. National League of Cities--United States Conference of Mayors. IV. Title.
DHUD NUC77-91630

Bailey, Elizabeth.
Pop art / Elizabeth Bailey. — London : H.M. Stationery Off. ; [Palo Alto, Calif. : obtainable from Pendragon House], 1976.
9 p. : chiefly col. ill. ; 16 x 12 cm. — (Victoria and Albert Museum small colour book ; 13) GB***
ISBN 0-11-290235-0 : £0.35
1. Pop art. 2. Art, Modern—20th century. I. Title. II. Series: Victoria and Albert Museum, South Kensington. Small colour book ; 13.
N6494.P6B34 709'.04 77-353823
77 MARC

Bailey, Elizabeth Anne.
Tocqueville & Marx; the individual & society. [n.p.] 1972.
1 v.
Honors thesis–Harvard.
1. Tocqueville, Alexis de, 1805-1859. 2. Marx, Karl, 1818-1883.
MH NUC76-68681

Bailey, Elizabeth E
Economic theory of regulatory constraint [by] Elizabeth E. Bailey. [n.p.] 1972 [c1973]
xii, 274 l. illus.
Thesis–Princeton University.
Bibliography: leaves [260]-270.
Photocopy of typescript. Ann Arbor, Mich., University Microfilms, 1973. 22 cm.
1. Industry and state–United States. 2. Corporations–Finance–Mathematical models. 3. Profit–United States. I. Title.
ViU NUC75-21168

Bailey, Elizabeth E
Economic theory of regulatory constraint [by] Elizabeth E. Bailey. Lexington, Mass., Lexington Books [1973]
xviii, 200 p. illus. 24 cm.
Bibliography: p. 183–192.
1. Public utilities — Rate of return — Mathematical models. 2. Monopolies—Mathematical models. I. Title. II. Title: Regulatory constraint.
HD2763.B24 338.4'3 73–11313
ISBN 0–669–87114–1 MARC

Bailey, Elsa, 1936-
Protest. [Philadelphia] American Friends Service Committee [c1963]
1 v. (unpaged) illus. 15 cm.
I. Friends, Society of. American Friends Service Committee.
KU-RH NUC73-40471

Bailey, Eric, 1933-
Cradle's Revenge. London, J. Long [c1969]
183 p.
SBN 09-098690-3.
I. Title.
CaOTP NUC73-39358

Bailey, Esther S., joint author.
see Flexner, Abraham, 1866-1959. Funds and foundations, their policies, past and present. [New York] Arno Press, 1976, c1952.

Bailey, Ethel Westmark.
That's enough for me : the story of Dr. E.P. Ellyson / by Ethel Westmark Baily. -- Kansas City, Mo. : Nazarene, 1976.
64 p. : ill. ; 19 cm.
1. Ellyson, Edgar Painter, 1869-1954. I. Title.
OMtvN NUC77-84580

Bailey, Ethel Zoe, joint author.
see Bailey, Liberty Hyde, 1858-1954. Hortus third ... New York, Macmillan, c1976.

Bailey, Evalyn James.
Academic activities for adolescents with learning disabilities / Evalyn James Bailey. — Evergreen, Colo. : Learning Pathways, [1975]
340 p. : ill. ; 24 cm.
Bibliography: p. 337-339.
ISBN 0-89146-001-2
1. Learning disabilities. I. Title.
LC4704.B34 371.9 75-7921
75 MARC

Bailey, F. W. J.
see
Bailey, Francis Walter John.

Bailey, Faith Coxe.
Dedicated dropout. [A one-act play] New York, Friendship Press [c1965]
32 p.
1. Vocation. I. Title.
MoSCS NUC74-122133

Bailey, Foster.
Changing esoteric values. [Rev. ed.] New York, Lucis Pub. Co. [1970]
79 p.
First published 1955.
1. Occult sciences. I. Title.
CU-SB NUC74-122137

Bailey, Foster.
Running God's plan. New York, Lucis Pub. Co. [c1972]
188 p.
I. Title.
CU-SB NUC76-68674

Bailey, Frances Stoughton.
Story and song. Providence, Snow & Farnham [c1894, 1972]
126 p. front. (port.)
Microfilm (positive) Ann Arbor, Mich., University Microfilms, 1972. 5th title of 16. 35 mm. (American fiction series, reel 198.5)
I. Title.
KEmT NUC74-502

Bailey, Francis Lee, 1933-
Cleared for the approach : F. Lee Bailey in defense of flying / F. Lee Bailey, with John Greenya. — Englewood Cliffs, N.J. : Prentice-Hall, c1977.
vii, 211 p. ; 24 cm.
ISBN 0-13-136663-7
1. Aeronautics, Commercial—United States. I. Greenya, John, joint author. II. Title.
HE9803.A4B33 1977 387.7'0973 77-23151
77 MARC

Bailey, Francis Lee, 1933-
Complete manual of criminal forms, Federal and State / F. Lee Bailey, Henry B. Rothblatt. — 2d ed. — Rochester, N.Y. : Lawyers Co-operative Pub. Co., 1974.
2 v. forms ; 26 cm. — (Criminal law library)
Includes index.
1. Criminal procedure—United States—Forms. I. Rothblatt, Henry B., joint author. II. Title.
KF9616.B252 345'.73'050269 74-17692
74[r75]rev MARC

Bailey, Francis Lee, 1933–
Crimes of violence [by] F. Lee Bailey [and] Henry B. Rothblatt. Rochester, N. Y., Lawyers Co-operative Pub. Co., 1973–
v. 26 cm. (Criminal law library)
Includes bibliographical references.
CONTENTS: v. 1. Homicide and assault.
1. Homicide investigation. 2. Offenses against the person—United States. 3. Trial practice—United States. I. Rothblatt, Henry B., joint author. II. Title.
KF9305.B3 345'.73'0252 72–97625
MARC

Bailey, Francis Lee, 1933-
La defensa nunca descansa. [Por] F. Lee Bailey & Harvey Aronson. [1. ed.] Barcelona-Mexico, D.F., Ediciones Grijalbo [c1973]
394 p. 20 cm.
Translation of The defense never rests.
1. Lawyers, U.S. Correspondence, reminiscences, etc. 2. Criminal justice, Administration of. U.S. I. Aronson, Harvey, joint author. II. Title.
NB NUC75-20968

Bailey, Francis Lee, 1933-
The defense never rests, by F. Lee Bailey; with Harvey Aronson. [New York] New American Library [1972, c1971]
x, 316 p. 18 cm. (A Signet book, 451-W5236-150)
1. Trials (Murder)—United States. I. Aronson, Harvey.
NmU NUC76-68667

Bailey, Francis Lee, 1933-
For the defense / F. Lee Bailey, with John Greenya. — 1st ed. — New York : Atheneum, 1975.
xii, 367 p. ; 25 cm.
Includes index.
ISBN 0-689-10667-X : $10.95
1. Trials—United States. I. Greenya, John. II. Title.
KF220.B3 345'.73'05 75-741
75 MARC

Bailey, Francis Lee, 1933–
Fundamentals of criminal advocacy [by] F. Lee Bailey [and] Henry B. Rothblatt. Rochester, N. Y., Lawyers Co-operative Pub. Co., 1974.
xxvi, 589 p. 25 cm.
1. Criminal procedure—United States. 2. Trial practice—United States. I. Rothblatt, Henry B., joint author. II. Title.
KF9656.B3 347'.73'5 73-90861
MARC

Bailey, Francis Lee, 1933-
Handling misdemeanor cases / F. Lee Bailey, Henry B. Rothblatt. — New York : Lawyers Co-operative Pub. Co., 1976.
xxx, 545 p. ; 26 cm. — (Criminal law library)
Includes bibliographical references.
1. Trial practice—United States. 2. Criminal procedure—United States. I. Rothblatt, Henry B., joint author. II. Title.
KF9656.B35 345'.73'05 76-12668
76 MARC

Bailey, Francis Lee, 1933-
Principles of cross-examination [by] F. Lee Bailey. [Sound recording. Cambridge, Mass.] Association of Trial Lawyers of America, 1974.
1 cassette. (ATL counseling cassettes, v. 5, no. 8)
1. Cross-examination—United States. I. Title. II. Series: Association of Trial Lawyers of America. ATL counseling cassettes, v. 5, no. 8.
CLL NUC76-27761

Bailey, Francis Louis, 1894–
A planned supply of teachers for Vermont, by Francis L. Bailey. New York, Bureau of Publications, Teachers College, Columbia University, 1939. [New York, AMS Press, 1972]
vi, 88 p. 22 cm.
Reprint of the 1939 ed., issued in series: Teachers College, Columbia University. Contributions to education, no. 771.
Originally presented as the author's thesis, Columbia.
Bibliography: p. 87–88.
1. Teachers—Supply and demand—Vermont. I. Title. II. Series: Columbia University. Teachers College. Contributions to education, no. 771.
LB2833.3.V5B35 1972 331.1'26 76-176528
ISBN 0-404-55771-6 MARC

Bailey, Francis Walter John.
Fundamentals of engineering metallurgy and materials, [by] F. W. J. Bailey. SI metric ed. London, Cassell, 1972.
xii, 222 p. illus. 22 cm. index. (A Cassell technical book) £1.75 B 72-17472
First published 1961 under title: Fundamentals of engineering metallurgy.
Bibliography: p. 216–217.
1. Metallurgy. 2. Polymers and polymerization. I. Title.
TN665.B28 1972 669'.002'462 73-159884
ISBN 0-304-93862-9 MARC

Bailey, Frank A., joint author
see Bailey, Maurice E. Study of worker acceptance... [Pikeville, Ky.] : 1975.

Bailey, Freda
see British Columbia. University. Library. Catalogue Division. Manual. 2d ed., rev. Vancouver, 1969-

Bailey, Frederick.
Set it down with gold on lasting pillars. [n.p., 1971]
5 l. 28 cm.
Promptbook; dialogue cuts and/or additions; stage directions.
Produced at the Playbox, N.Y.C., Aug. 13, 1971.
1. American drama. 2. Drama—Promptbooks and typescripts, One-act. I. Title.
NN NUC76-68675

Bailey, Frederick Arthur.
Current practice in company accounts / Frederick Bailey. — London : Haymarket Publishing, 1973.
xii, 185 p. : ill. ; 22 cm. — (Accountancy age books) (Modern finance series) GB74-18882
Includes index.
ISBN 0-900442-44-1 : £4.00
1. Financial statements—Great Britain. I. Title. II. Series.
HF5681.B2B25 657'.3'0941 75-309219
75 MARC

Bailey, Frederick Eugene, 1927-
Poly(ethylene oxide) / F. E. Bailey, Jr., and J. V. Koleske. — New York : Academic Press, 1976.
ix, 173 p. : ill. ; 24 cm.
Includes bibliographical references and index.
ISBN 0-12-073250-5
1. Polyethylene glycols. I. Koleske, J. V., 1930- joint author. II. Title.
TP1180.P653B34 668.4'234 76-16505
76 MARC

Bailey, Frederick George.
Debate and compromise; the politics of innovation, edited by F. G. Bailey. Oxford, Blackwell, 1973.
343 p. 22 cm. (Pavilion series: social anthropology) £5.00 GB***
Bibliography: p. [329]–335.
1. Technological innovations—Europe. 2. Economic development—Social aspects. I. Title.
HC240.9.T4B33 301.24'3'094 74-158575
ISBN 0-631-14710-1 MARC

Bailey, Frederick George.
Debate and compromise; the politics of innovation, edited by F. G. Bailey. Totowa, N. J., Rowman and Littlefield, 1973.
343 p. 23 cm. $16.00
Bibliography: p. [329]–335.
1. Technological innovations—Europe. 2. Economic development—Social aspects. I. Title.
HC240.9.T4B33 1973b 301.24'3'094 74-157933
ISBN 0-87471-414-1 MARC

Bailey, Frederick George.
Gifts and poison; the politics of reputation, edited by F. G. Bailey. New York, Schocken Books [1971]
318 p. 23 cm. (Pavilion series)
Bibliography: p. [302]–307.
1. Villages—Europe—Case studies. 2. Interpersonal relations. 3. Social values. 4. Europe—Social life and customs. I. Title.
HN373.5.B35 1971b 301.44'43 78-151824
ISBN 0-8052-3409-8 rev MARC

Bailey, Frederick Randolph, 1871-1923.
Histología. 14. ed. rev., por Wilfred M. Copenhaver [and] Dorothy D. Johnson. Traducción y notas por Dr. Oscar Vilar. Buenos Aires, López Libreros Editores, 1960.
xxvi, 889 p. illus.
Original title: Bailey's text-book of histology. "Tercera ed. en español, 1960."
1. Histology. I. Copenhaver, Wilfred Monroe, 1898- II. Vilar, Oscar, tr. III. Title.
DPAHO NUC76-22807

Bailey, Frederick Sidney.
Follow-up study of opinions held by student, faculty and administrators about off-campus university credit courses. East Lansing, Mich., 1965.
135 l.
Thesis—Michigan State University.
Includes bibliography.
Microfilm of typescript. Ann Arbor, Mich., University Microfilms, 1965. 1 reel.
1. University extension. I. Title.
NSyU NUC76-68676

Bailey, Fredric N
Towards a science of complex systems [by] Fredric N. Bailey [and] Robert T. Holt. Minneapolis [Office of International Programs] University of Minnesota, 1971.
47 l. illus. 29 cm.
On cover: A report from the Center for Comparative Studies in Technological Development and Social Change.
1. Social systems. 2. Functional analysis (Social sciences) 3. Social problems. 4. System analysis. I. Holt, Robert T. II. Minnesota. University. Center for Comparative Studies in Technological Development and Social Change. III. Title.
NIC NUC75-84393

Bailey, G. F.
see Hanford Engineering Development Laboratory. Environmental engineering programs... [Richland, Wa.] 1972.

Bailey, G.W.
see Herbicide runoff... Washington, Govt. Print. Off., 1974.

Bailey, Garrick Alan,
Changes in Osage organization: 1673-1906. [Eugene, University of Oregon Press] 1973.
vi, 122 p. illus., maps. 27 cm. (University of Oregon anthropological papers, no. 5)
Bibliography: p. 113-122.
1. Osage Indians. I. Title. II. Series: Oregon. University. Anthropological papers, no. 5.
GASU DLC NUC76-68668

Bailey, Garrick Alan, joint author.
see Cheek, Charles D. Honey Springs, Indian Territory ... 1st ed. Oklahoma City, Oklahoma Historical Society, 1976, c1977.

Bailey, Gary.
Gary Bailey's How to win motocross [by] Gary Bailey with Carl Shipman. [Tucson, Ariz.] H. P. Books [1974]
190 p. illus. 28 cm. $5.00
Cover title.
1. Motorcycle racing. 2. Motorcycles. I. Title. II. Title: How to win motocross.
GV1060.B28 796.7'5 73-92958
ISBN 0-912656-16-6 MARC

Bailey, George.
The Strauss family: the era of the Great Waltz. London, Pan Books, 1972.
64 p. illus. (some col.), facsims., geneal. table, ports. (some col.). 18 x 22 cm. £0.50 B 72-29417
"Based on the dramatic ATV Television series."
1. Strauss family (Musicians) I. Title.
ML410.S89B25 785.4'1'0922 [B] 73-156116
ISBN 0-330-23437-4 MARC

Bailey, George, 1923–
Germans: the biography of an obsession. New York, World Pub. [1972]
409 p. 24 cm. $10.00
1. Germans. 2. Germany (Territory under Allied occupation, 1945–1955. U. S. Zone) I. Title.
DD76.B19 1972 914.3'03'87 72-81465
ISBN 0-529-04814-0 MARC

Bailey, George Arthur, 1945-
The Vietnam War according to Chet, David, Walter, Harry, Peter, Bob, Howard and Frank: a content analysis of journalistic performance by the network television evening news anchor-men, 1965-1970. [n.p.] c1973.
2 v. (435 l.) 29 cm.
Thesis (Ph. D.)—University of Wisconsin.
Vita.
Includes bibliography.
1. Vietnamese Conflict, 1961- —Public opinion. 2. Journalism—Vietnamese Conflict, 1961- I. Title.
WU NUC74-122639

Bailey, George Arthur, 1945-
The Vietnam war according to Chet, David, Walter, Harry, Peter, Bob, Howard and Frank : a content analysis of journalistic performance by the network television news anchormen 1965-1970 / George Arthur Bailey. -- Ann Arbor : University Microfilms, 1976, 1973.
1 reel.
Thesis--University of Wisconsin, 1973.
PSC-P NUC77-87817

Bailey, George Henry, 1942-
The poetry of John Payne. [n. p.] c1974.
289 l. 29 cm.
Thesis (Ph. D.)–University of Wisconsin.
Vita.
Includes bibliography.
1. Payne, John, 1842-1916.
WU NUC76-15660

Bailey, George Leroy, 1936- ed.
see Hemodialysis: principles and practice. New York, Academic Press, 1972.

Bailey, George Ward.
Problems and trends in junior high school social studies. Lincoln, Neb., 1963.
xiv, 272 l. forms, tables.
Thesis (Ed.D.)—University of Nebraska, 1964.
Appendices: leaves [245]-272.
Bibliography: leaves [232]-244.
I. Title.
NbU NUC73-126479

Bailey, Gerald, ed.
see Great Britain—USSR Association. The Great Britain—U.S.S.R. handbook. [2d ed., substantially rev.] London, 1970.

Bailey, Gerald Douglass.
Competency-based approach to learning and utilizing competency-based education, by Gerald Douglas Bailey. Manhattan, Kan., College of Education, Kansas State University, 1973.
[200] p.
1. Performance contracts in education. 2. Teaching. 3. Education—Aim and objectives. I. Title.
KMK NUC75-20969

Bailey, Gerald Douglass.
A study of classroom interaction patterns from student teaching to independent classroom teaching. Lincoln, Neb., 1972.
[x], 262 l. form, tables.
Thesis (Ed. D.)—University of Nebraska.
Appendices: leaves [202]-262.
Bibliography: leaves [196]-201.
I. Title.
NbU NUC74-618

Bailey, Gertrude Blackwell.
If words could set us free: poems by Gertrude Blackwell Bailey. 1st edition. Jericho, New York, Exposition Press, 1974.
59 p.
1. American poetry–Negro authors. I. Title.
MoWgT NUC76-15644

Bailey, Gordon.
A leasing manual for automobile dealers. Fort Worth, Tex., Jack Williams & Associates [n.d.]
49 l.
1. Automobile industry and trade. I. Title.
TxFTC NUC74-607

Bailey, Gordon Archibald, 1946-
Education and the social construction of reality: Canadian identity as portrayed in elementary school social studies textbooks, by Gordon Archibald Bailey. [n. p.] 1975.
viii, 201 l. 29 cm.
Thesis (Ph. D.)—University of Oregon.
Vita.
Bibliography: leaves 188-201.
1. Nationalism and education—Canada. 2. Education, Elementary—Canada. 3. Textbooks—Canada. I. Title.
OrU NUC77-81759

Bailey, Gordon Raymond, 1930-
Wood allocation by dynamic programming. Ottawa, 1973.
19 p. (Canada. Canadian Forestry Service. Publication no. 1321)
Bibliography: p. 19.
I. Title.
DNAL NUC76-68677

Bailey, Grace Revell, 1890-
see Texas. Woman's university, Denton. ... Food for the child. [Denton, 1940]

Bailey, H. C.
see Bailey, Henry Christopher, 1878-1961.

Bailey, H H
Target acquisition through visual recognition: an early model. [Santa Monica, Rand Corp.] 1972.
16 p. 29 cm. ([Rand Corporation. Paper] P-4918)
Cover title.
1. Visual discrimination. I. Title. II. Series.
IEdS NUC76-68678

Bailey, H.H. and J.C. Hazen, publishers.
Birds eye view of Lowell, Mass., 1876 / drawn & pub. by H.H. Bailey & J.C. Hazen. -- Ithaca, N.Y. : Historic Urban Plans, 1976.
map 49 x 71 cm.
Scale not given.
Facsimile of map printed by J. Knauber & Co.
Indexes points of interest.
1. Lowell, Massachusetts--Description--Aerial--Maps. I. Title.
KyU NUC77-90105

Bailey, H. H. and J. C. Hazen, publishers.
Lawrence, Mass., 1876 / drawn & pub. by H. H. Bailey & J. C. Hazen. -- Ithaca, N.Y. : Historic Urban Plans, 1976.
map 47 x 60 cm.
Scale not given.
Birds-eye-view.
Facsimile of map printed by J. Knauber & Co.
Indexes points of interest.
1. Lawrence, Massachusetts--Description--Aerial--Maps. I. Title.
KyU NUC77-90409

Bailey, H Kofi.
H. Kofi Bailey. [Portfolio of 19 plates. Los Angeles, Contemporary Crafts, 1972]
19 plates in portfolio. 58 cm. (African series)
Cover title.
Black artists on art.
MB NUC74-128970

Bailey, Halbert A.
see Demory, Robert L Length-frequency and age-length-frequency distributions for Dover sole... Clackamas, Fish Commission of Oregon, Research Division, 1967.

Bailey, Hamilton, 1894-1961.
Bailey & Love's Short practice of surgery. — 16th ed. / revised by A. J. Harding Rains and H. David Ritchie. — London : H. K. Lewis, 1975.
xii, 1308 p. : ill. (some col.) ; 26 cm. GB75-18937
Includes index.
ISBN 0-7186-0403-2 : £10.00
1. Surgery. I. Love, Robert John McNeill, 1891-1974, joint author. II. Rains, Anthony J. Harding. III. Ritchie, Horace David. IV. Title. V. Title: Short practice of surgery.
[DNLM: 1. Surgery. WO100 B154s 1975]
[RD31.B358 1975] 617 75-596096
Shared Cataloging with 76 MARC
DNLM

Bailey, Hamilton, 1894–1961.
Demonstrations of physical signs in clinical surgery. Edited by Allan Clain. 15th ed. Baltimore, Williams and Wilkins Co., 1973.
xii, 620 p. illus. 25 cm. $33.25
Title on cover: Hamilton Bailey's demonstrations of physical signs in clinical surgery.
Includes bibliographical references.
1. Diagnosis, Surgical. I. Clain, Allan, ed. II. Title. III. Title: Hamilton Bailey's demonstrations of physical signs in clinical surgery.
RD35.B3 1973 617'.075'4 73–173499
ISBN 0–7236–0277–8 MARC

Bailey, Hamilton, 1894–1961.
Hamilton Bailey's demonstrations of physical signs in clinical surgery. 15th ed.; edited by Allan Clain. Bristol, J. Wright, 1973.
xii, 620 p. illus. (some col.). 25 cm. £7.50 GB 73–16691
Includes index.
1. Diagnosis, Surgical. I. Clain, Alan, ed. II. Title.
[RD35.B3 1973b] 617'.075'4 73–595638
ISBN 0–7236–0277–8 MARC

Bailey, Hamilton, 1894–1961.
Hamilton Bailey's Emergency surgery. Edited by T. J. McNair. 9th ed. Baltimore, Williams and Wilkins, 1972.
xv, 981 p. illus. (part col.) 25 cm.
1. Surgery, Operative. 2. Medical emergencies. I. McNair, Thomas Jaffrey, ed. II. Title: Emergency surgery.
[RD32.B3 1972b] 617'.026 72–170801
ISBN 0–7236–0276–X MARC

Bailey, Hamilton, 1894–1961.
Hamilton Bailey's emergency surgery. 9th ed., edited by T. J. McNair. Bristol, J. Wright, 1972.
xv, 981 p. illus. (some col.) 26 cm. index. £12.50 B 72–19484
Distribution by sole agents: U. S. A.: Williams & Wilkins Co., Baltimore.
1. Surgery, Operative. 2. Medical emergencies. I. McNair, Thomas Jaffrey, ed. II. Title. III. Title: Emergency surgery.
[DNLM: 1. Emergencies. 2. Surgery, Operative. WO 700 B154e 1972]
[RD32.B3 1972] 617'.026 72–305440
ISBN 0–7236–0276–X MARC
Shared Cataloging with DNLM

Bailey, Hamilton, 1894-1961.
Short practice of surgery. [Consulting editor: McNeill Love] 15th ed., rev. by A. J. Harding Rains and W. Melville Capper, with specialist chapters by Geoffrey Knight, William P. Cleland, and Michael A. R. Freeman. London, Lewis, 1971.
xii, 1296 p. illus. 25 cm.
FU-HC NUC73-127024

Bailey, Harold.
Institutional and societal effects on the Black student athlete / by Harold Bailey. -- Albuquerque : University of New Mexico, c1976.
iii, 142 leaves : ill. ; 28 cm.
Thesis (Ph.D.)--University of New Mexico.
Bibliography: leaves 140-142.
1. Afro-American athletes. I. Title.
NmU NUC77-84656

Bailey, Harold G
Pietermaritzburg and the Natal midlands : pen and ink drawings / by Harold Bailey ; captions by Harvey Campion. — [Durban, 714 London House, West Street : H. Bailey, 1975]
[39] p. : chiefly ill. ; 22 x 26 cm. SA75
Cover title.
ISBN 0-620-01817-8 : R2.50
1. Bailey, Harold G. 2. Pietermaritzburg in art. I. Campion, Harvey. II. Title.
NC368.6.S63B34 741.9'68 77-351340
77 MARC

Bailey, Harry Edward, 1924-
Integration of the equations governing the one-dimensional flow of a chemically reactive gas. Moffett Field, Calif., Ames Research Center [1968?]
[34] l. illus. ([Combustion Institute. Western States Section. Paper] 68-46)
ICRL NUC74-122136

Bailey, Harry P
Weather of southern California. Harry P. Bailey. Berkeley, University of California Press, c1966, 1975.
87 p. ill. (California natural history guides, 17)
Earlier printing has title; The climate of southern California.
1. California, Southern—Climate. I. Title. II. Series.
KMK NUC77-81758

Bailey, Helen L
A study of missionary motivation, training, and withdrawal (1953-1962) / by Helen L. Bailey and Herbert C. Jackson. — New York : Missionary Research Library, 1965.
99 p. : graphs ; 28 cm.
Bibliography: p. 74-76.
1. Missionaries, Resignation of—Statistics. 2. Protestant churches—Missions—Statistics. I. Jackson, Herbert C., joint author. II. Title.
BV2063.B28 75-313846
75 MARC

Bailey, Helen Miller.
Latin America; the development of its civilization [by] Helen Miller Bailey [and] Abraham P. Nasatir. 3d. ed. Englewood Cliffs, N. J., Prentice-Hall [1973]
xxi, 822 p. illus. 24 cm. $11.95
Includes bibliographies.
1. Latin America — History. 2. Latin America — Civilization. I. Nasatir, Abraham Phineas, 1904- joint author. II. Title.
F1410.B16 1973 980 72–13948
ISBN 0–13–524264–9 MARC

Bailey, Henry Christopher, 1878-
A clue for Mr. Fortune [by] H. C. Bailey. Bath, Lythway Press [1970]
319 p.
SBN 85046-115-4.
I. Title.
CaOTP NUC75-34824

Bailey, Henry Christopher, 1878-1961.
Dead man's shoes, by H. C. Bailey. [London] T. Stacey, 1972.
168 p.
ISBN 0 85468 176 0.
I. Title.
CaOTP NUC74-120661

Bailey, Henry Christopher, 1878-1961.
Mr. Fortune : eight of his adventures / by H. C. Bailey ; edited with a pref. by Jacques Barzun and Wendell Hertig Taylor. — New York : Garland Pub., 1976.
viii, 347 p. ; 23 cm. — (Fifty classics of crime fiction, 1900-1950 ; no. 3)
CONTENTS: The Ascot tragedy.—The unknown murderer.—The long barrow.—The hermit crab.—The Greek play.—The angel's eye.—The long dinner.—The dead leaves.
ISBN 0-8240-2352-8
I. Title. II. Series.
PZ3.B152 Mcn 823'.9'12 75-44958
[PR6003.A374] 76 MARC

Bailey, Henry Christopher, 1878-
Mr. Fortune, please [by] H. C. Bailey. Bath, Lythway Press, 1969.
250 p.
SBN 85046-033-6.
I. Title.
CaOTP NUC75-34823

Bailey, Henry Christopher, 1878-1961.
Slippery Ann, by H. C. Bailey. [London, T. Stacey Reprints, 1973]
176 p.
"A Mr. Clunk mystery."
ISBN 0-85468-459-X.
I. Title.
CaOTP NUC76-68679

Bailey, Henry Christopher, 1878-
This is Mr Fortune [by] H. C. Bailey. Bath, Lythway Press Ltd., 1972.
285 p. 19 cm. £1.50 GB 72-09840
Originally published, London, Gollancz, 1938.
I. Title.
PZ3.B152Th 9 823'.9'12 73-168702
[PR6003.A374] MARC
ISBN 0-85046-271-1

Bailey, Henry J 1916-
The law of bank checks / by Henry J. Bailey. — 4th ed., rev. and enl. — Boston : Banking law journal, 1969.
xii, 632 p. ; 24 cm.
First-2d ed. by John Edson Brady.
Cover title: Brady on bank checks.
Kept up to date by cumulative supplements.
Includes index.
1. Checks—United States. I. Brady, John Edson. II. Title. III. Title: Brady on bank checks.
KF960.B3 1969 346'.73'096 73-174260
76[r75]rev MARC

Bailey, Henry J 1916-
The law of bank checks. 1975 supplement, no. 2. Boston, Banking law journal [1975]
x, 337 p. 24 cm.
Cover title: Brady on bank checks; 1975 cumulative supplement, no. 2 to fourth edition.
1. Checks—United States. I. Brady, John Edson. II. Title.
IEN NUC77-81899

Bailey, Henry J 1916-
Secured transactions in a nutshell / by Henry J. Bailey III. — St. Paul : West Pub. Co., 1976.
xxxviii, 377 p. ; 19 cm. — (West nutshell series)
Includes index.
1. Security (Law)—United States—Compends. I. Title.
KF1050.Z9B34 346'.73'074 76-26799
76 MARC

Bailey, Henry J 1916-
UCC deskbook; a short course in commercial paper, by Henry J. Bailey III. Rev. ed. Boston, Warren, Gorham & Lamont [1973]
viii, 99 p. 28 cm.
First ed. published in 1969 under title: A short course in commercial paper under the UCC.
1. Negotiable instruments—United States—States. I. Title. II. Title: A short course in commercial paper.
GU-L CLL CaBVaU NUC75-17102
SdB

Bailey, Henry J., 1916- joint author
see Clarke, John J Bank deposits and collections. [4th ed.] Philadelphia, Joint Committee on Continuing Legal Education of the American Law Institute and the American Bar Association [1972]

Bailey, Henry J., 1916- joint author
see Hursh, Robert D American law of products liability. 2d ed. Rochester, N.Y., Lawyers Cooperative Pub. Co., 1974-

Bailey, Henry Turner, 1865–1931.
Symbolism for artists: creative and appreciative, by Henry Turner Bailey and Ethel Pool. Worcester, Mass., Davis Press, 1925. Detroit, Gale Research Co., 1972.
239 p. illus. 18 cm.
Bibliography: p. 228–230.
1. Symbolism in art. I. Pool, Ethel, joint author. II. Title.
N7740.B25 1972 701 68–18018
MARC

Bailey, Hilary.
Polly put the kettle on / [by] Hilary Bailey. — London : Constable, 1975.
165 p. ; 21 cm. GB75-18430
ISBN 0-09-460650-1 : £3.25
I. Title.
PZ4.B1522 Po 823'.9'14 75-327765
[PR6052.A3186] 75 MARC

Bailey, Hillary G
So was your old man : a commentary on joys, jobs, and jackasses / by Hillary G. Bailey. — Boston : Branden Press, c1976.
351 p., [6] leaves of plates : ill. ; 23 cm.
ISBN 0-8283-1599-X : $12.50
1. World history—Miscellanea. I. Title.
D21.3.B28 909 74-22996
76 MARC

Bailey, Holly M.
see Herbert F. Johnson Museum of Art. The handwrought object, 1776-1976 ... Ithaca, The University, c1976.

Bailey, Hugh C
America : the framing of a nation / Hugh C. Bailey. — Columbus, Ohio : C. E. Merrill Pub. Co., [19
v. : ill. ; 24 cm.
Includes bibiiographies and index.
CONTENTS:
—v. 2. Since 1865.
ISBN 0-675-08749-X
1. United States—History. I. Title.
E178.1.B145 973 74-33745
75 MARC

Bailey, Ivor N
Scoop the pools with Ivor N. Bailey. London, The Winner, [1972]
3-52 p. 22 cm. £0.30 GB 72-23645
1. Gambling systems. I. Title.
GV1302.B3 796.33'4 73-176254
ISBN 0-901371-10-6 MARC

Bailey, J Edward, 1923-
Living legends in black / by J. Edward Bailey III. — Detroit : Bailey Pub. Co., 1976.
173 p. : ports. ; 28 cm.
Includes index.
1. Afro-Americans—Biography. I. Title.
E185.B22 973'.0992 75-5063
76 MARC

Bailey, J. F.
see also
Bailey, James F
Bailey, Joshua F

Bailey, J L
The Nelson directory and companion to the almanack for the year 1859. Nelson, Printed by C. and J. Elliott, 1859. [Nelson, Nelson Provincial Museum Trust Board, 1969]
45 p. 16 cm. NZ 70
1. Nelson, N. Z. (Provincial District)—History. 2. Nelson, N. Z. (Provincial District)—Directories. I. Title.
DU430.N38B34 1969 73–177099
919.315'3'0025 MARC

Bailey, J. M.
see
Bailey, John Marvin, 1913-

Bailey, J. M., agricultural chemist, joint author
see Scott, I M Report on a detailed soil survey of Semongok Agricultural Station... [Kuching? Sarawak Dept. of Agriculture, 1964]

Bailey, J. P., joint author.
see Eckland, Bruce Kent. National longitudinal study of the high school class of 1972 . . . [Washington] U.S. Dept. of Health, Education, and Welfare, Education Division, National Center for Education Statistics : for sale by the Supt. of Docs., U.S. Govt. Print. Off., 1977.

Bailey, J. Russell
see
Bailey, James Russell, 1905-

Bailey, J. W.
see
Bailey, John W Rev.

Bailey, Jack, 1898–
The British co-operative movement. Westport, Conn., Greenwood Press [1974]
178 p. illus. 22 cm.
Reprint of the 1955 ed. published by Hutchinson's University Library, London, in series: Hutchinson's university library: Politics.
Bibliography: p. 173–174.
1. Cooperation—Great Britain. I. Title.
HD3486.B27 1974 334'.0942 73–19302
ISBN 0–8371–7116–4 MARC

Bailey, Jack Bowman, 1945-
Systematics, functional morphology, and ecology of Middle Devonian bivalves from the Solsville Member (Marcellus Formation), Chenango Valley, New York. Urbana [1975]
xii, 290 l. illus., 15 plates. 19 cm.
Thesis—University of Illinois.
Vita.
Bibliography: leaves 240-253.
IU NUC77-81756

Bailey, Jack E
An improved incubator for salmonids and results of preliminary tests of its use, by Jack E. Bailey and William R. Heard. Seattle, National Marine Fisheries Service, 1973.
7 p. illus. 26 cm. (United States. National Oceanic and Atmospheric Administration. NOAA technical memorandum NMFS ABFL-1)
1. Incubators. 2. Salmon. 3. Fish-culture—Alaska. I. Heard, William R., joint author. II. United States. National Marine Fisheries Service. Auke Bay Fisheries Laboratory. III. Title. IV. Series.
DME NUC76-87302

Bailey, Jack E., joint author
see Helle, John H Intertidal ecology and life history of Pink Salmon... Washington, U.S. Fish and Wildlife Service, 1964.

Bailey, Jackson H comp.
Listening to Japan; a Japanese anthology. Edited by Jackson H. Bailey. New York, Praeger [1973]
xviii, 236 p. illus. 22 cm.
Includes bibliographical references.
1. Japan — History — 1945- —Addresses, essays, lectures. 2. Japan—Civilization—1945- —Addresses, essays, lectures. I. Title.
DS889.B25 915.2'03'4 70–168336
MARC

Bailey, Jackson William, 1906-
Encyclopedia of labeling meat and poultry products, by J. W. Bailey. [2d] rev. and enl. ed. St. Louis, Meat Plant Magazine [c1974]
253 p. 22 cm.
1. Meat industry and trade—Dictionaries. 2. Meat—Labeling—Dictionaries. I. Title.
PSt NUC76-15659

Bailey, Jacob Whitman, 1811-1857. Algae in Botany. Lehre, Cramer, 1971.

Bailey, James.
Toward a statistical analysis of English verse : the iambic tetrameter of ten poets / James Bailey. — Lisse, Netherlands : The Peter de Ridder Press, 1975.
83 p. : graphs. ; 24 cm. — (PdR Press publications in English metrics ; 1) Ne***
Bibliography: p. [76]-83.
1. English language—Versification. 2. Iambic tetrameter. 3. English poetry—History and criticism. I. Title.
PE1531.I25B3 426 76 76-356078 MARC

Bailey, James, fl. 1888–1905.
How to teach the babies. By James Bailey ... London, W. H. Allen & co., limited [1888?]
143 p. 18½ cm.
1. Education, Primary. I. Title.
LB1507.B15 E 9–974

Bailey, James, fl. 1888–1905.
Oral teaching in infant schools. Comprising notes of lessons, with hints for the construction and delivery of lessons. Prepared with especial reference to the requirements of pupil teachers, student in training, and acting teachers. By James Bailey ... 2d ed. London, W. H. Allen & co. limited [188-?]
ix, 156 p. 18½ cm.
1. Education, Primary. 2. Verbal learning. I. Title.
LB1507.B16 E 9–975

Bailey, James, 1932- ed.
see Conference on New Communities, Washington, D.C., 1971. New towns in America; the design and development process. New York, Wiley [1973]

Bailey, James, 1932- joint author
see Nadler, Gerald. Design concepts for information systems. Norcross, Ga., American Institute of Industrial Engineers, inc., c1972.

Bailey, James Allen, 1934-
Effects of silver from cloud seeding on microflora of animal digestive systems, by James A. Bailey, Allen M. Jones [and] Donald R. Roy. [Fort Collins, Colo., Dept. of Fishery and Wildlife Biology, Colorado State University, 1973]
35 l.
Prepared for Division of Atmospheric Water Resources Management, U. S. Bureau of Reclamation.
Report 14-06-D-7208.
1. Silver compounds—Toxicology. 2. Rain-making. 3. Veterinary toxicology. I. Jones, Allen M., joint author. II. Roy, Donald R., joint author. III. Colorado. State University, Fort Collins. Dept. of Fishery and Wildlife Biology. IV. United States. Division of Atmoshperic Water Resources Management.
DI NUC75-86726

Bailey, James Allen, 1934- comp.
Readings in wildlife conservation / editors, James A. Bailey, William Elder, Ted D. McKinney. — Washington : Wildlife Society, 1974.
xvi, 722 p. : ill. ; 23 cm.
Includes bibliographies.
1. Wildlife conservation—Addresses, essays, lectures. I. Elder, William, 1913- joint comp. II. McKinney, Ted D., joint comp. III. Wildlife Society. IV. Title.
QL82.B34 639'.9'08 74 74-28405 MARC

Bailey, James E., ed.
see Sahney, Vinod Kumar, 1942- Scheduling computer operations. Norcross, Ga., 1972.

Bailey, James Earl, 1943-
Directional sensitivity of retinal receptors. [Bloomington, Ind.] 1973.
98 p. illus.
Thesis (Ph. D.)—Indiana University.
Vita.
InU NUC75-21076

Bailey, James Edwin, 1944-
Biochemical engineering fundamentals / James E. Bailey, David F. Ollis. — New York : McGraw-Hill, c1977.
xiv, 753 p. : ill. ; 24 cm. — (McGraw-Hill series in water resources and environmental engineering) (McGraw-Hill chemical engineering series)
Includes bibliographical references and index.
ISBN 0-07-003210-6
1. Biochemical engineering. I. Ollis, David F., joint author. II. Title.
TP248.3.B34 660'.63 76 76-40006 MARC

Bailey, James F
Hurricane Agnes rainfall and floods, June-July 1972 / by J. F. Bailey and J. L. Patterson and J. L. H. Paulhus ; report prepared jointly by the U.S. Geological Survey and the National Oceanic and Atmospheric Administration. — Washington : U.S. Govt. Print. Off., 1975.
vii, 403 p.: ill., map (fold. in pocket) ; 29 cm. — (Geological Survey professional paper ; 924)
Chiefly tables.
Bibliography: p. 86-87.
Includes index.
Supt. of Docs. no.: I 19.16:924
1. Floods—Atlantic States. 2. Stream measurements—Atlantic States. 3. Atlantic States—Hurricane, 1972. I. Patterson, James Lee, joint author. II. Paulhus, Joseph L. H., joint author. III. United States. Geological Survey. IV. United States. National Oceanic and Atmospheric Administration. V. Title. VI. Series: United States. Geological Survey. Professional paper ; 924.
GB1216.P34 557.3'08 s 75 75-619211 MARC

Bailey, James George, 1923-
An analysis of public school expenditures in Louisiana on a per-pupil basis... [n.p.] 1972.
xiii, 280 l. 29 cm.
Thesis (Ed.D.)—Louisiana State University, Baton Rouge, La.
Vita.
Bibliography: leaves 205-207.
Abstract.
1. Education—Louisiana—Finance. I. Title.
LU NUC74-122956

Bailey, James H
Swine health: Respiratory diseases and arthritis, a research review. Edited by James H. Bailey. [Brookings, S.D., South Dakota State University, Dept. of Veterinary Science and Extension Service, 1971]
96 p.
Includes bibliographies.
KMK NUC74-119835

Bailey, James H 1934-
The miracles of Jesus for today / James H. Bailey. — Nashville : Abingdon, c1977.
127 p. ; 19 cm.
ISBN 0-687-27070-7
1. Jesus Christ—Miracles—Sermons. 2. Methodist Church—Sermons. 3. Sermons, American. I. Title.
BT366.B33 232.9'5 76 76-51202 MARC

Bailey, James Montgomery, 1841-1894.
England from a back-window; with views of Scotland and Ireland. By J. M. Bailey. Boston, Lee & Shepard; New York, C. T. Dillingham, 1879.
475 p. 20 cm.
Micro-transparency (negative) Louisville, Ky., Lost Cause Press, 1973. 6 sheets. 10.5 x 14.8 cm. (L.H. Wright. American fiction, 1876-1900, no. 217)
1. Gt. Brit.—Soc. life & cust. I. Title.
PSt NUC75-18218

Bailey, James R 1919–
The god-kings & the Titans; the New World ascendancy in ancient times [by] James Bailey. London, Hodder & Stoughton [1973]
[1], 350 p. illus., geneal. tables, maps. 26 cm. £4.20 GB 73–28479
Illus. on lining papers.
Bibliography: p. 325–331.
Includes index.
1. Bronze age. 2. Commerce, Prehistoric. 3. America—Discovery and exploration—Pre-Columbian. 4. Indians—Culture—Foreign influences. I. Title. II. The Titans.
GN777.B25 301.29'701'03 74–151241
ISBN 0–340–12744–9 MARC

Bailey, James R 1919–
The god-kings & the Titans; the New World ascendancy in ancient times [by] James Bailey. New York, St. Martin's Press [1973]
350 p. illus. 26 cm. $9.95
Bibliography: p. 325–331.
1. Bronze age. 2. Commerce, Prehistoric. 3. America—Discovery and exploration—Pre-Columbian. 3. Indians—Culture—Foreign influences. I. Title.
GN777.B25 1973b 301.29'701'03 73–78862 MARC

Bailey, James Russell, 1905–
Comprehensive library study, Greenwood County, developed by J. Russell Bailey. Orange, Virginia, 1973.
29 l. illus. 29 cm.
1. Libraries, Regional—South Carolina—Greenwood County. 2. Libraries—South Carolina—Greenwood County. I. Title.
Z732.S72B3 027.4'757'33 74–191467 MARC

Bailey, James W 1927-
The development of a moral ideal in the Barset and parliamentary novels of Anthony Trollope. Detroit, 1963.
ii, 206 l. 29 cm.
Microfilm.
Thesis—Wayne State University.
Vita.
Bibliography: leaves 187-205.
1. Trollope, Anthony, 1815-1882.
NN NUC73-126490

Bailey, Jan.
Hell no! [Washington, D.C., n.d.]
[24] p.
1. Military service, Compulsory—U.S. 2. Vietnamese conflict, 1961- —Negroes. I. Title.
WHi NUC74-174325

Bailey, Jane.
Pomegranate / Jane Bailey. — Missoula, Mont. : Black Stone Press, c1976.
[27] p. ; 21 cm.
"400 copies printed."
I. Title.
PS3552.A372P6 811'.5'4 77 76-151067 MARC

Bailey, Jane H
The sea otter's struggle [by] Jane H. Bailey. Foreword by Judson E. Vandevere. Chicago, Follett [c1973]
95 p. illus. 23 cm.
SUMMARY: A study of the characteristics and habits of the sea otter with emphasis on its struggle to escape extinction.
Bibliography: p. 93–95.
1. Sea-otters—Juvenile literature. [1. Sea otters] I. Title.
QL737.C25B26 599'.74447 72–85578
ISBN 0–695–80373–5; 0–695–40373–1 (Titan bdg.) MARC

Bailey, Janice.
Those meddling women / Janice Bailey. — Valley Forge, PA. : Judson Press, c1977.
95 p. ; 22 cm.
Includes bibliographical references.
ISBN 0-8170-0757-1 : $3.25
1. Women in public life—United States—Biography. I. Title.
HQ1412.B34 920.72'0973 77 77-3891 MARC

Bailey, Jean.
Cherokee Bill, Oklahoma pacer. Illustrated by Pers Crowell. Boston, Houghton Mifflin [1970, c1952]
190 p. illus. 22 cm. (Merit books)
SUMMARY: After his family wins a claim on the Cherokee Strip, twelve-year-old David makes a prize-winning pacer out of a stray horse.
[1. Horses—Stories. 2. Cherokee Outlet, Oklahoma—Fiction. 3. Oklahoma—Fiction] I. Crowell, Pers, illus. II. Title.
PZ7.B1524Ch 10 [Fic] 70–112359 MARC

Bailey, Jerald Elliott, 1939-
Contraceptive education and the Colombian druggists. [Ann Arbor, Mich.] 1971. [Ann Arbor, Mich., University Microfilms, 1972]
202 l. tables.
Thesis (Ed.D.)—University of Michigan.
Bibliography: leaves 198-202.
1. Birth control—Colombia. 2. Conception—Prevention—Study and teaching. 3. Pharmacists—Colombia. I. Title.
FTaSU NUC74-122955

Bailey, Jerald Elliott, 1939-
Contraceptive education and the Colombian druggists. [n.p.] 1971.
xi, 202 l.
Thesis—University of Michigan.
Bibliography: leaves 198-202.
Microfilm. Ann Arbor, Mich., University Microfilms, 1971. 1 reel. 35 mm.
1. Birth control—Colombia. 2. Pharmacists—Colombia. I. Title.
TxU NUC76-68661

Bailey, Jesse C
The generation of a model to synthesize the state of the art of accountability in educational management. University, Ala., 1975.
v, 174 l. 28 cm.
Thesis—University of Alabama.
1. Educational accountability. (Education) I. Title.
AU NUC77-81757

Bailey, Jim, joint author
see Henry, Orville. The Razorbacks... Huntsville, Ala., Strode Publishers [1973]

Bailey, Joan H., joint author.
see Jung, John. Contemporary psychology experiments ... 2d ed. New York, Wiley, c1976.

Bailey, Joann Weeks.
A guide to the history and old dwelling places of Northwood, New Hampshire. ₍Concord, N. H., Printed by Capital Offset Co., 1973₎
xi, 275 p. illus. 24 cm.
Bibliography: p. 272–273.
1. Northwood, N. H.—Biography. 2. Northwood, N. H.—Historic houses, etc. I. Title.
F44.N88B34 917.42'6 73-166247 MARC

Bailey, Joe.
Social theory for planning / Joe Bailey. — London : Routledge & K. Paul, 1975.
viii, 167 p. ; 23 cm. GB***
Bibliography: p. 150–163.
Includes index.
ISBN 0-7100-8006-9 : £4.25. ISBN 0-7100-8019-0 pbk.
1. Sociology. 2. Sociology—Methodology. 3. Planning. I. Title.
HM24.B29 300'.1 75-306985 MARC

Bailey, John.
see European scrap directory ... London, Metal Bulletin, 1976.

Bailey, John, writer on music.
Folk sound. Great Yarmouth, Norfolk ₍Eng.₎ Galliard, 1971.
47 p. 25 cm.
1. Folk-songs. I. Title.
NRCR NUC73-127021

Bailey, John, 1644–1697.
Man's chief end to glorifie God; or, Some brief sermon-notes on 1 Cor. 10. 31. Boston, Printed by S. Green, and are to be sold by R. Wilkins, bookseller, 1689.
160, 40 p. 15 cm.
Evans 456–457.
L. C. copy imperfect: p. 129–130 mutilated.
"To my loving and dearly beloved Christian friends, in and about Lymerick" (40 p.) is a valedictory epistle dated May 8, 1684.
1. Bible. N. T. 1 Corinthians X, 31—Sermons. 2. Farewell sermons. I. Title.
BS2675.B26 74-195017 MARC

Bailey, John, 1750–1819.
General view of the agriculture of Northumberland, Cumberland and Westmorland, by J. Bailey and G. Culley. ₍3d. ed. reprinted₎; with an introduction by D. J. Rowe. London, printed by B. McMillan for G. and W. Nicol, 1805; Newcastle upon Tyne, Graham, 1972.
xxiv, xx, 361 p., 14 leaves (1 fold.). illus., maps, plan. 22 cm. £3.50 B 72-31045
Reprint of the 3d ed., published London, McMillan, 1805, under title: General view of the county of Northumberland.
Bibliography: p. ₍xxiii₎–xxiv.
CONTENTS: Bailey, J. and Culley, G. General view of the agriculture of the county of Northumberland.—Bailey, J. and Culley, G. General view of the agriculture of the county of Cumberland.—Pringle, A. General view of the agriculture of the county of Westmoreland.
1. Agriculture—England—Northumberland. 2. Agriculture—England — Cumberland. 3. Agriculture — England — Westmoreland. 4. Northumberland, Eng.—Economic conditions. 5. Cumberland, Eng.—Economic conditions. 6. Westmoreland, Eng.—Economic conditions. I. Culley, George, 1735–1813. II. Pringle, Andrew, fl. 1794. III. Great Britain. Board of Agriculture. IV. Title.
S457.N67B34 1972 338.1'09428 73-166780
ISBN 0-902833-46-4 MARC

Bailey, John, 1750–1819.
General view of the agriculture of the county of Northumberland; with observations on the means of its improvement. Drawn up for the consideration of the Board of Agriculture and Internal Improvement. By J. Bailey and G. Culley. The 3d ed. ... London, Printed by B. McMillan for G. and W. Nicol, 1805.
xx, 361 p. plates (partly fold.) 3 maps (incl. fold. front.) 22 cm.
"General view of the agriculture of the county of Cumberland ...": p. ₍195₎–274.
"General view of the agriculture of the county of Westmoreland ..." by A. Pringle: p. ₍275₎–361.
1. Agriculture—England—Northumberland. 2. Agriculture—England — Cumberland. 3. Agriculture — England — Westmoreland. 4. Northumberland, Eng.—Economic conditions. 5. Cumberland, Eng.—Economic conditions. 6. Westmoreland, Eng.—Economic conditions. I. Culley, George, 1735–1813. II. Pringle, Andrew, fl. 1794. III. Great Britain. Board of Agriculture. IV. Title.
S457.N67B34 1805 630'.9428'2 rev 12-6473 MARC

Bailey, John, 1944–
The wire classroom. ₍Sydney₎ Angus and Robertson ₍1972₎
203 p. 21 cm. $4.50 ANL
I. Title.
PZ4.B1524Wi 823 72-172447
₍PR6052.A3187₎ MARC
ISBN 0-207-12312-8

Bailey, John A 1918-
Broadening the concept of marketing: an application to public enterprise. [Evanston, Ill., Transportation Center, Northwestern University] 1972.
30 l. 28 cm. (Evanston, Ill. Transportation Center at Northwestern University. Research report)
1. Urban transportation—U. S. 2. Marketing research. I. Title. II. Series.
NjR NUC73-32413

Bailey, John A 1918-
Constraints against introduction of new technology or innovative marketing in urban transportation, by John A. Bailey. [Evanston, Ill.] Northwestern University, Transportation Center, 1970.
30 l. 29 cm. (Northwestern University, Evanston, Ill. The Transportation Center. Research report)
"Paper presented at the Joint transportation engineering conference, American Society of Mechanical Engineers."
1. Urban transportation—U. S. I. Title.
NjR NUC73-38824

Bailey, John A 1918-
A survey of transit management attitudes in large cities in the United States: Development since 1962, by John A. Bailey. Evanston, Ill., Northwestern University, Transportation Center, 1970.
13 l. 29 cm. (Northwestern University, Evanston, Ill. Transportation Center. Research report)
1. Local transit—U.S. I. Title.
NjR NUC73-47728

Bailey, John Cann, 1864-1931.
Dr. Johnson and his circle / by John Bailey. — Folcroft, Pa. : Folcroft Library Editions, 1976.
v, 256 p. ; 23 cm.
Reprint of the 1913? ed. published by Williams and Norgate, London, in series: Home university library of modern knowledge.
Bibliography: p. 253-254.
Includes index.
ISBN 0-8414-3338-0 lib. bdg. : $15.00
1. Johnson, Samuel, 1709-1784. I. Title.
PR3533.B2 1976 828'.6'09 76 76-9063 MARC

Bailey, John Cann, 1864-1931, ed.
English elegies / edited by J. C. Bailey. — Folcroft, Pa. : Folcroft Library Editions, 1976.
xlv, 236 p. ; 23 cm.
Reprint of the 1900 ed. published by J. Lane, London and New York, issued in series: The Bodley anthologies.
ISBN 0-8414-3342-9 lib. bdg. : $30.00
1. Elegiac poetry, English. I. Title. II. Series: The Bodley Head anthologies.
PR1195.E5B26 1976 821'.04 76 76-14450 MARC

Bailey, John Cann, 1864-1931.
Introduction to Jane Austen / by John Bailey. — Norwood, Pa. : Norwood Editions, 1976.
vi, 147 p. ; 23 cm.
Reprint of the 1931 ed. published by Oxford University Press, London.
ISBN 0-8482-0200-7 lib. bdg. : $15.00
1. Austen, Jane, 1775-1817. 2. Novelists, English—19th century—Biography. I. Title.
₍PR4036.B25 1976₎ 823'.7 76 76-39855 MARC

Bailey, John Cann, 1864-1931.
Introductions to Jane Austen. Folcroft, Pa., Folcroft Press ₍1974₎
vi, 147 p. 23 cm.
Reprint of the 1931 ed. published by Oxford University Press, London.
1. Austen, Jane, 1775-1817. 2. Novelists, English—19th century—Biography. I. Title.
PR4036.B25 1974 823'.7 74-13375
ISBN 0-8414-3255-4 (lib. bdg.) 74₍r77₎rev MARC

Bailey, John Cann, 1864-1931.
Milton, by John Bailey ... New York, H. Holt and company ₍n.d.₎
256 p. 17 cm.
Bibliography: p. 250-253.
Ultra microfiche. Dayton, Ohio, National Cash Register, 1970. 4th title of 9. 10.5 x 14.8 cm. (PCMI library collection, 85-4)
1. Milton, John, 1608-1674.
KEmT NUC74-598

Bailey, John Cann, 1864-1931.
Milton. ₍Folcroft, Pa.₎ Folcroft Library Editions, 1973.
256 p. 23 cm.
Reprint of the 1945 ed. published by Oxford University Press, London, as no. 103 of the Home university library of modern knowledge.
Bibliography: p. 250-253.
1. Milton, John, 1608-1674.
PR3581.B3 1973 821'.4 73-12210
ISBN 0-8414-3218-X (lib. bdg.) 73 MARC

Bailey, John Cann, 1864-1931.
Milton / John Bailey. — Norwood, Pa. : Norwood Editions, 1975.
256 p. ; 24 cm.
Reprint of the 1945 ed. published by Oxford University Press, London, New York, as no. 103 of the Home university library of modern knowledge.
Bibliography: p. 250-253.
Includes index.
ISBN 0-88305-916-9 lib. bdg. : $15.00
1. Milton, John, 1608-1674. 2. Poets, English—Early modern, 1500-1700—Biography.
₍PR3581.B3 1975₎ 821'.4 75₍r77₎rev 75-38789 MARC

Bailey, John Cann, 1864-1931.
Milton / John Bailey. — Philadelphia : R. West, 1976.
256 p. ; 23 cm.
Reprint of the 1945 issue of the 1915 ed. published by Oxford University Press, London, New York, which was issued as no. 103 of The Home university library of modern knowledge.
Bibliography: p. 250-253.
Includes index.
ISBN 0-8492-0208-6 : $17.50
1. Milton, John, 1608-1674. 2. Poets, English—Early modern, 1500-1700—Biography.
₍PR3581.B3 1976₎ 821'.4 76 76-47467 MARC

Bailey, John Cann, 1864-1931.
Shakespeare, by John Bailey. London, New York [etc.] Longmans, Green and Co., 1929.
xv, 208 p. 18 cm. (Half-title: The English heritage series...)
Ultra microfiche. Dayton, Ohio, National Cash Register, 1970. 2d title of 6. 10.5 x 14.8 cm. (PCMI library collection, 111-2)
1. Shakespeare, William—Criticism and interpretation.
KEmT NUC74-9113

Bailey, John Davidson, 1922- joint author.
see McKendry, James Banford Judson, 1917- The infant and pre-schooler. Don Mills ₍Ont.₎ Longman Canada, 1974.

Bailey, John J d. 1873.
Waldimar; a tragedy in five acts, by John J. Bailey. New York [J. Van Norden, printer] 1834.
124 p.
Microfilm (positive) Ann Arbor, Mich., University Microfilms, 1972. 14th title of 15. 35 mm. (American culture series, reel 489.14)
I. Title.
KEmT NUC75-2092

Bailey, John J 1944-
Government and educational policy in Colombia, 1957-1968, by John J. Bailey. [n.p.] c1972.
388 l. 29 cm.
Thesis (Ph. D.)—University of Wisconsin.
Vita.
Includes bibliography.
1. Education—Colombia. 2. Education, Higher. I. Title.
WU NUC73-32411

Bailey, John J 1944-
Government and educational policy in Colombia, 1957-1968. [n.p.] 1972.
vii, 388 l.
Thesis—University of Wisconsin.
Vita.
Bibliography: leaves 371-388.
Photocopy of typescript. Ann Arbor, Mich., Xerox University Microfilms, 1974. 22 cm.
1. Education—Colombia. I. Title.
NNCU-G NUC76-27138

Bailey, John J 1944-
Government and educational policy in Colombia, 1957-1968, by John J. Bailey. [n.p.] 1972.
vii, 388 l.
Thesis—University of Wisconsin.
Vita.
Bibliography: leaves 371-388.
Microfilm. Ann Arbor, Mich., University Microfilms, 1972. 1 reel. 35 mm.
TxU NUC75-34822

Bailey, John J 1944-
Public budgeting in Colombia; disjoined incrementalism in a dependent polity. Austin, Institute of Latin American Studies, University of Texas, 1974.
46 p. 28 cm. (LADAC occasional papers. Series 2, no. 10)
"Footnotes": p. 43-46.
DPU NUC75-17100

Bailey, John Leonard Hawthorne.
Finedon otherwise Thingdon / by John L. H. Bailey. — Finedon : The author, 1975.
ix, 225 p., [24] p. of plates : ill., plan, ports. ; 26 cm. GB76-14540
Bibliography: p. 205-207.
Includes index.
ISBN 0-9504250-0-1 : £4.50
1. Finedon, Eng.—History. 2. Finedon, Eng.—Biography. I. Title.
DA690.F442B35 942.5'52 76-370335
76 MARC

Bailey, John M 1928-
Liberal arts physics: invariance and change [by] John M. Bailey. San Francisco, W. H. Freeman [1974]
xv, 496 p. illus. 25 cm.
Includes bibliographies.
1. Physics. I. Title.
QC23.B105 530 73-21531
ISBN 0-7167-0343-2 MARC

Bailey, John Marvin, 1913-
Potential for cooperative distribution of petroleum products in the South. [Washington?] 1973.
26 p. illus. (U.S. Farmer Cooperative Service. FCS information 91)
I. Title.
DNAL NUC74-122957

Bailey, John Marvin, 1913-
see Mather, James Warren, 1911-
Integrated petroleum operations of farmer cooperatives, 1969. [Washington, 1971]

Bailey, John P
Reports and articles resulting from research and demonstration projects: a bibliography, 1968. Edited by John P. Bailey, Jr. [and] John E. Muthard. [Gainesville,] Regional Rehabilitation Research Institute, University of Florida [1968]
v, 131 p. 28 cm.
Cover title: Research and demonstration projects: a bibliography, 1968.
1. Rehabilitation—United States—Bibliography. I. Muthard, John E., 1917- joint author. II. Florida. University, Gainesville. Regional Rehabilitation Research Institute. III. Title. IV. Title: Research and demonstration projects: a bibliography, 1968.
Z7165.U5B33 016.362 78-628239
MARC

Bailey, John Swartwout, 1907-
Intent on laughter / John Bailey. — New York : Quadrangle/New York Times Book Co., c1976.
x, 182 p. : ill. ; 23 cm.
Includes index.
ISBN 0-8129-0621-7
1. Wit and humor—Philosophy. 2. Wit and humor—Psychology. I. Title.
PN6149.P5B33 1976 827'.009 75-36265
76 MARC

Bailey, John W Rev.
Knox college, by whom founded and endowed; also, a review of a pamphlet entitled "Rights of Congregationalists in Knox college." By J. W. Bailey. Chicago, Press & Tribune printing office, 1860.
131 p. 21½ cm.
1. Knox College, Galesburg, Ill. 2. Congregational churches in Illinois. General Association. Rights of Congregationalists in Knox College.
LD2813.B2 7-4723 †
rev

Bailey, John Wendell, 1895-
Football at the University of Richmond, 1878-1948. Richmond [c1969]
170 p. illus.
1. Richmond. University—Athletics. I. Title.
ViN NUC74-4306

Bailey, John William, 1873-1969.
Life has meaning; thinking and prayers of John William Bailey. Edited by Louise Herron Bailey. Valley Forge [Pa.] Judson Press [1974]
80 p. 22 cm. $1.95
1. Christian life—Baptist authors. I. Bailey, Louise Herron, ed. II. Title.
BV4501.2.B28 1974 248'.48'61 73-13291
ISBN 0-8170-0624-9 (pbk.) MARC

Bailey, Jon Scott.
Home-based reinforcement and the modification of pre-delinquents' classroom behavior. [Lawrence] 1970.
vi, 47 l. illus. 28 cm.
Thesis (Ph.D.)—University of Kansas.
1. Behavior modification. 2. Classroom management. I. Title.
KU NUC73-39357

Bailey, Joseph A., joint author
see Lahue, Kalton C Petersen's guide to architectural photography. [Los Angeles, Petersen Pub. Co., 1973]

Bailey, Joseph Alexander, 1935-
Disproportionate short stature; diagnosis and management [by] Joseph A. Bailey, II. Philadelphia, Saunders, 1973.
xvi, 589 p. illus. 25 cm.
Includes bibliographies.
1. Dwarfism. I. Title.
RB140.3.B34 616.7'043 72-78953
ISBN 0-7216-1470-1 MARC

Bailey, Joyce.
Picture the people of the Caribbean / Joyce Bailey & Michael I. N. Dash. — New York : Friendship Press, c1977.
80 p. : ill. ; 22 cm.
Interviews with 16 persons.
ISBN 0-377-00065-5 : $2.95
1. Caribbean area—Social life and customs—1975- 2. Caribbean area—Biography. I. Dash, Michael I. N., joint author. II. Title.
F2183.B34 972.9'05 77-2912
77 MARC

Bailey, Joyce
see Caribbean Conference of Churches.
Sing a new song. [Kingston, Jamaica, 1973]

Bailey, Joyce Waddell.
A preliminary investigation of the formal and interpretive histories of monumental relief sculpture from Tikal, Guatemala: pre-, early and middle Classic Periods. [n.p.] 1972.
xxi, 185 p. illus. (part fold.) 28 cm.
Thesis (Ph.D.)—Yale.
MH-P NUC76-68664

Bailey, Judith Irene, 1946-
A study of the relationships between selected personal and situational variables and principal job satisfaction. -- Blacksburg : [Virginia Polytechnic Institute and State University], 1976.
126 leaves : ill.
1. School year. 2. School superintendents and principals. I. Title.
ViBlbV NUC77-88156

Bailey, June T
Decision making in nursing : tools for change / June T. Bailey, Karen E. Claus ; with 63 ill., including 29 drawings by Bee Walters. — Saint Louis : C. V. Mosby Co., 1975.
x, 167 p. : ill. ; 26 cm.
Includes bibliographical references and index.
ISBN 0-8016-0422-2
1. Nurses and nursing. 2. Decision-making. I. Claus, Karen E., joint author. II. Title.
[DNLM: 1. Decision making. 2. Nursing, Supervisory. 3. Social change. WY105 B154d]
RT42.B33 610.73 74-28268
74 MARC

Bailey, June T
An experiment in nursing curriculums at a university; terminal report of the experimental curriculum evaluation project, School of Nursing, University of California, San Francisco [by] June T. Bailey, Frederick J. McDonald [and] Karen E. Claus. Belmont, Calif., Wadsworth Pub. Co., 1971.
xxvii. 558 p. illus.
Includes bibliography.
1. Schools, Nursing—Calif. 2. Education, Nursing—Calif. 3. Curriculum. I. McDonald, Frederick J. II. Claus, Karen E. III. California. University. School of Nursing. IV. Title.
CU-AM OClW-H NbU-M NUC75-75555
CtY FU-HC MiEM

Bailey, June T., joint author.
see Claus, Karen E., 1941- Power and influence in health care ... St. Louis, Mosby, 1977.

Bailey, June T.
see New directions in patient-centered nursing... New York, Macmillan [1973]

Bailey, Karyl Vaughan, 1940-
A study of light apparatus activities in the United States from 1860 to 1920. [Eugene, Ore., Microform Publications, College of Health, Physical Education and Recreation, University of Oregon, 1975]
4 sheets. 10.5 x 14.8 cm.
Microfiche (negative) of typescript.
Collation of the original: 274 l. illus. 29 cm.
Thesis (Ph.D.)—Texas A&M University, 1973.
Vita.
Bibliography: leaves 238-246.
1. Callisthenics. I. Title.
TU NUC77-82655

Bailey, Kathryn Anne, 1951-
Development of pyruvate dehydrogenase in white fat, brown fat and liver of the rat, by Kathryn Anne Bailey. [Vancouver, B.C.] 1975.
ix, 58 l. ill. 28 cm.
Thesis (M.Sc.)—University of British Columbia.
Vita.
Bibliography: leaves 55-58.
1. Rats—Physiology. 2. Pyruvate metabolism. I. Title. II. Series.
CaBVaU NUC77-82651

Bailey, Kenneth.
The beauty of dogs. London, Ward Lock, 1972.
144 p. illus. (some col.), ports. 29 cm. £1.75 B 72-31807
1. Dogs. I. Title.
SF426.B34 636.7 73-153820
ISBN 0-7063-1356-9 MARC

Bailey, Kenneth.
Nature; compiled and edited by Kenneth Bailey [written by Alfred Leutscher ... and others; illustrated by Fred Anderson ... and others] Glasgow, Collins, 1973.
192 p. col. illus., col. maps, col. port. 31 cm. (New world of knowledge) £1.95 GB 73-26640
Includes index.
1. Zoology—Juvenile literature. 2. Botany—Juvenile literature. I. Title.
QL49.B13 574 74-163779
ISBN 0-00-106103-8 MARC

Bailey, Kenneth.
World history / compiled and edited by Kenneth Bailey ; ⌊written by Richard Wright, Kenneth Bailey ; illustrated by Fred Anderson ... and others⌋. — Glasgow : Collins, 1973.
192 p. : col. ill., facsims., col. maps, plans, col. ports. ; 31 cm. — (New world of knowledge) GB 73-27779
Includes index.
ISBN 0-00-106102-X : £1.25
1. World history—Juvenile literature. I. Title.
D21.B15 901.9 74-185722
MARC

Bailey, Kenneth Dan, 1941-
Human ecology: a general systems approach. Austin, Tex., 1968.
201 l.
Thesis (Ph. D.)—University of Texas, Austin.
Includes bibliographic references.
Microfilm of typescript. Ann Arbor, Mich., University Microfilms, 1968. 1 reel. 35 mm.
1. Human ecology. I. Title.
NIC NUC76-68660

Bailey, Kenneth E
The cross and the prodigal; the 15th chapter of Luke, seen through the eyes of Middle Eastern peasants ⌊by⌋ Kenneth E. Bailey. St. Louis, Concordia Pub. House ⌊1973⌋
133 p. 23 cm.
"All Biblical quotations are from the Revised standard version."
CONTENTS: Commentary on the 15th chapter of the Gospel, according to Luke.—"Two sons have I not;" a one-act play in four scenes.—Music for Shaluk's song (p. 133)
1. Bible. N. T. Luke XV—Commentaries. 2. Bible plays. I. Bailey, Kenneth E. Two sons have I not. 1973. II. Bible. N. T. Luke XV. English. Revised standard. 1973. III. Title.
BS2595.3.B27 1973 226'.4 72-90957
ISBN 0-570-03139-7 MARC

Bailey, Kenneth E
New perspectives on the parables [by] Kenneth Bailey. Pittsburgh, Thesis Theological Cassettes, 1972.
1 cassette (Thesis mini-study units: curriculum-on-cassette)
A 4-unit study on: I. Interpreting the parables; II; The rich fool (Luke 12); III. The great banquet (Luke 14); IV. The lost sheep (Luke 15)
1. Parables. 2. Bible. N. T. Luke—Criticism, interpretations, etc. I. Title.
PPiPT NUC74-123741

Bailey, Kenneth E
Poet and peasant : a literary-cultural approach to the parables in Luke / by Kenneth Ewing Bailey. — Grand Rapids : Eerdmans, c1976.
238 p. ; 25 cm.
Bibliography: p. 217-229.
Includes indexes.
ISBN 0-8028-3476-0
1. Jesus Christ—Parables. 2. Bible. N.T. Luke—Criticism, interpretation, etc. I. Title.
BT375.2.B23 226'.8 75-41405
75 MARC

Bailey, Kenneth E
A study of some Lucan parables in the light of oriental life and poetic sytle. St. Louis, 1972.
vii, 479 l. illus., diagrams, tables.
Thesis (Th. D.)—Concordia Seminary, St. Louis.
Includes bibliography.
1. Parables. 2. Bible. N. T. Luke—Criticism, interpretation, etc. I. Title.
MoSCS NUC74-127011

Bailey, Kenneth E. Two sons have I not. 1973
in Bailey, Kenneth E The cross and the prodigal... St. Louis, Concordia Pub. House ⌊1973⌋

Bailey, Kenneth Elmer, 1937-
The compressibilities of six chalcogenide glasses to 8 k bar, by Kenneth Elmer Bailey. [Austin, Tex.] 1975.
x, 117 l. ill. 29 cm.
Thesis (Ph.D.)--University of Texas at Austin.
Vita.
Bibliography: leaves 112-117.
1. Amorphous semiconductors. 2. Ultrasonic testing. 3. Elastic analysis (Theory of structures) I. Title.
TxU NUC77-86410

Bailey, Kenneth P 1912–
The American adventure / Kenneth Bailey, Elizabeth Brooke, John J. Farrell. — Teacher's ed. — Palo Alto, Calif. : Field Educational Publications, c1972.
108, 352 p. : ill. (some col.) ; 27 cm. — (Field social studies program)
The main work, also issued separately, is preceded by the authors' Teacher's manual with special t. p.
Bibliography: p. 83-85 (1st group)
Includes index.
ISBN 0-514-02458-5
1. United States—History—Juvenile literature. I. Brooke, Elizabeth, joint author. II. Farrell, John J., joint author. III. Title.
E178.3.B17 1972 917.3 74-194669
MARC

Bailey, Kenneth P 1912-
Christopher Gist : colonial frontiersman, explorer, and Indian agent / by Kenneth P. Bailey. — Hamden, Conn. : Archon Books, 1976.
264 p. : ill. ; 24 cm.
Bibliography: p. 219-239.
Includes index.
ISBN 0-208-01564-7
1. Gist, Christopher, d. 1759.
F229.G532B34 973.2'6'0924 75-30810
75 MARC

Bailey, Kenneth P., 1912- joint author
see Frost, S. E., 1899- Historical and philosophical foundations of Western education. 2d ed. Columbus, Ohio, Merrill ⌊1973⌋

Bailey, L F
Scouring in calves, causes and treatment. [Adelaide] 1973.
7 p. illus. (South Australia. Dept. of Agriculture. Extension bulletin no. 16)
I. Title.
DNAL NUC74-123742

Bailey, L. H.
see
Bailey, Liberty Hyde 1858-1954.

Bailey, L. R.
see
Bailey, Lynn Robison, 1937-

Bailey, Larry.
Water quality segment report for segment no. 1402, Colorado River, prepared by Larry Bailey. [Austin] Surveillance Section, Field Operations Division, Texas Water Quality Board, 1975.
iii, 27, [10] p. ill., maps. 28 cm. (Report - Texas Water Quality Board, WQS 11)
Cover title: Segment no. 1402, Colorado River.
Bibliography: p. 23.
1. Water quality--Texas--Colorado River. I. Title. II. Series: Texas. Water Quality Board. Report, WQS 11.
Tx NUC77-86409

Bailey, Larry J
Career education: new approaches to human development ⌊by⌋ Larry J. Bailey ⌊and⌋ Ronald W. Stadt. ⌊1st ed.⌋ Bloomington, Ill., McKnight Pub. Co. ⌊1973⌋
xviii, 430 p. 23 cm. (A McKnight career publication) $8.95
Includes bibliographies.
1. Vocational guidance. 2. Vocational education. I. Stadt, Ronald W., 1935- joint author. II. Title.
LB1027.5.B24 370.11'3 73-75120
ISBN 0-87345-601-7 MARC

Bailey, Larry J.
Facilitating career development: an annotated bibliography. Larry J. Bailey, editor. [Springfield] Illinois, Board of Vocational Education and Rehabilitation, Division of Vocational and Technical Education, 1970.
iii, 132 p. 28 cm.
Final report-project RDB-AO-004.
1. Vocational guidance—Bibl. I. Title.
IaU IU NUC74-9114

Bailey, Larry J
An investigation of the vocational behavior of selected women vocational education students. Urbana, 1968 ⌊1971⌋
135 l.
Thesis (Ed. D.)—University of Illinois.
Bibliography: leaves 106-110.
Xerox copy. Ann Arbor, Mich., University Microfilms, 1971.
1. Vocational guidance. 2. Vocational interests. 3. Education of women. I. Title.
FTaSU NUC73-126478

Bailey, Larry William, 1942-
The behavioral effects of increasing positive self-regard through verbal conditioning. ⌊Provo, Utah⌋ 1971.
viii, 153 l.
Thesis—Brigham Young University.
Bibliography: leaves 85-89.
Microfilm. Ann Arbor, Mich., University Microfilms, 1971. 1 reel. 35 mm. (Mic 72-1736)
1. Self-evaluation. 2. Behavior modification. I. Title.
FU NUC73-127016

Bailey, Leaonead Pack.
Broadside authors and artists; an illustrated biographical directory. Compiled and edited by Leaonead Pack Bailey. ⌊1st ed.⌋ Detroit, Mich., Broadside Press ⌊1974⌋
125 p. illus. 23 cm. $9.95
1. American literature—Negro authors—Bio-bibliography. I. Title.
Z1229.N39B34 811'.5'409 [B] 70-108887
ISBN 0-910296-25-1 MARC

Bailey, Lena Charles, 1932-
Review and synthesis of research on consumer and homemaking education. Columbus, Ohio, ERIC Clearinghouse on Vocational and Technical Education, 1971.
76 p. (Ohio State University, Columbus. Center for Vocational and Technical Education. Information series, no. 33)
1. Consumer education. 2. Home economics—Study and teaching. I. ERIC Clearinghouse on Vocational and Technical Education. II. Title.
InU OU NbU MoU NUC73-32357

Bailey, Leo L
A step-by-step guide to landscaping and gardening / Leo L. Bailey. — 1st ed. — Hicksville, N. Y. : Exposition Press, ⌊1974⌋
xii, 212 p. : ill. ; 24 cm. — (An Exposition-banner book)
Bibliography: p. 211-212.
ISBN 0-682-48084-3 : $10.00
1. Landscape gardening. 2. Gardening. 3. Plant propagation. I. Title.
SB473.B29 635 74-84421
MARC

Bailey, Leon Edwin, 1936-
The acting career of Walter Huston. ⌊Urbana, Ill.⌋ 1973.
iv, 134 l.
Thesis—University of Illinois at Urbana-Champaign.
Vita.
Bibliography: leaves 124-129.
Microfilm. Ann Arbor, Mich., Xerox University Microfilms. 1 reel. 35 mm.
1. Huston, Walter, 1884-1950. I. Title.
TxU NUC76-68659

Bailey, Leslie.
Honey bee paralysis; retrospect and prospect, [by] L. Bailey. Ilford, Essex [Eng.] Central Association of Bee-Keepers, c1971.
8 p. 21 cm. (Central Association of Bee-Keepers. Lecture leaflets)
Cover title.
Bibliography: p. [9]
1. Bees—Diseases and enemies. I. Title. II. Series.
NIC NUC73-32358

Bailey, Leslie.
Honey bee pathology: the end of the beginning? L. Bailey. Ilford, Essex, [Eng.] Central Association of Bee-Keepers, 1975.
[9] p. 21 cm. (Central Association of Bee-Keepers. [Lecture leaflets])
Cover title.
Bibliography: p. [9]
1. Bees—Diseases. I. Title. II. Series.
NIC NUC77-84911

Bailey, Leslie.
Recent research on honeybee viruses / L. Bailey. — Gerrards Cross : Bee Research Association, [1975]
10 p. : ill. ; 22 cm. — (Bee Research Association reprint ; M84)
GB75-25398
Cover title.
Bibliography: p. 9-10.
ISBN 0-900149-77-9
1. Insect viruses. 2. Bees—Diseases. I. Title. II. Series: Bee Research Association. Reprint ; M84.
SB942.B34 595.7'99 76-361796
76 MARC

Bailey, Leslie Francis, 1941-
Consonant variance in Deržavin's rhymes; a preliminary study. [n.p.] c1974.
392 l. 29 cm.
Thesis (Ph.D.)—University of Wisconsin.
Vita.
Includes bibliography.
1. Derzhavin, Gavriil Romanovich, 1743-1816. 2. Russian language—Rime. I. Title.
WU NUC76-15499

Bailey, Leslie George, 1942-
The statelier Eden: Tennyson in the 1850's. [Bloomington, Ind.] 1975.
174 p.
Thesis (Ph.D.)—Indiana University.
Vita.
InU NUC77-84927

Bailey, Leuba.
see The Immigrant experience. Toronto, Macmillan of Canada, c1975.

Bailey, Levi Satterfield.
Bailey - Mitchell family records. -- [Tompkinsville, Ky.] : The Author, 1976?
68 p.
1. Bailey family. 2. Mitchell family. I. Title.
WHi NUC77-84589

Bailey, Liberty Hyde, 1858-1954, ed.
Cyclopedia of American agriculture : vol. II—crops / edited by Liberty Hyde Bailey. — New York : Arno Press, 1975, c1907.
xvi, 699 p., [25] leaves of plates : ill. ; 24 cm. — (American farmers and the rise of agribusiness)
Reprint of the 4th ed., 1912, published by Macmillan, New York.
Includes index.
ISBN 0-405-06762-3
1. Field crops—United States. 2. Field crops—Canada. I. Title. II. Series.
SB187.U6B28 1975 633'.00973 74-30617
75 MARC

Bailey, Liberty Hyde, 1858-1954, ed.
Cyclopedia of American horticulture : comprising suggestions for cultivation of horticultural plants, descriptions of the species of fruits, vegetables, flowers, and ornamental plants sold in the United States and Canada, together with geographical and biographical sketches and a synopsis of the vegetable kingdom / by L. H. Bailey, assisted by Wilhelm Miller and many expert cultivators and botanists. — New York : Gordon Press, 1975.
6 v. (xlii, 2016 p., [140] leaves of plates) : ill. ; 27 cm.
Reprint of the 4th ed. published in 1906 by Doubleday, Page, New York.
Includes index.
ISBN 0-87968-247-7
1. Horticulture—Dictionaries. 2. Gardening—Dictionaries. 3. Horticulture—United States—Dictionaries. 4. Horticulture—Canada—Dictionaries. I. Miller, Wilhelm, 1869- joint ed. II. Title.
SB45.B17 1975 635'.0973 72-98055
76 MARC

Bailey, Liberty Hyde, 1858-1954.
Hortus third : a concise dictionary of plants cultivated in the United States and Canada / initially compiled by Liberty Hyde Bailey and Ethel Zoe Bailey ; revised and expanded by the staff of the Liberty Hyde Bailey Hortorium. — New York : Macmillan, c1976.
xiv, 1290 p. : ill. ; 29 cm.
Includes index.
$99.50
1. Plants, Cultivated—North America—Dictionaries. 2. Gardening—North America—Dictionaries. I. Bailey, Ethel Zoe, joint author. II. Cornell University. Bailey Hortorium. III. Title.
SB45.B22 1976 582'.06'1 77-352066
77 MARC

Bailey, Liberty Hyde, 1858-1954.
How plants get their names / by L. H. Bailey. — Detroit : Gale Research Co., 1975, c1933.
vi, 209 p. : ill. ; 23 cm.
Reprint of the ed. published by Macmillan, New York.
ISBN 0-8103-3763-0
1. Botany—Nomenclature. I. Title.
[QK96.B25 1975] 581'.01'4 75-30611
75 MARC

Bailey, Liberty Hyde, 1858-1954.
Sketch of the evolution of our native fruits / [by L. H. Bailey]. — Wilmington, Del. : Scholarly Resources, 1974, [c1898]
xiii, 472 p. : ill. ; 23 cm.
Reprint of the ed. published by Macmillan, New York.
Includes bibliographies and index.
ISBN 0-8420-1473-X
1. Fruit-culture—United States—History. 2. Fruit—United States—Breeding—History. 3. Fruit—United States—Varieties. I. Title.
SB354.6.U5B34 1974 634'.0973 72-89072
77 MARC

Bailey, Lois.
The 12th grade : a critical year : a student's viewpoint / by Lois Bailey. — Reston, Va. : National Association of Secondary School Principals, [1975]
37 p. ; 26 cm.
Includes bibliographical references.
ISBN 0-88210-061-0 : $3.00
1. Twelfth grade (Education) I. Title.
LB1629.7 12th.B34 373.2'38 75-306748
MARC

Bailey, Louise Herron, ed.
see Bailey, John William, 1873-1969. Life has meaning... Valley Forge [Pa.] Judson Press [1974]

Bailey, Louise Howe.
Along the ridges. Drawings by Joseph P. Bailey, Jr. Asheville, N.C., Groves Print. Co., 1971.
108 p. illus. 22 cm.
I. Title.
GU NUC74-117990

Bailey, Louise Howe.
Go home wi' me. Drawings by Joseph P. Bailey, Jr., and William H. Bailey. [Asheville, N.C., Groves Printing Co., c1974]
viii, 114 p. illus. 22 cm.
1. N.C.—Mountaineers. I. Title.
NcU NUC76-15517

Bailey, Lynn.
see Hann, Robert G Decision making in the Canadian criminal court system ... Toronto, Centre of Criminology, University of Toronto, 1973.

Bailey, Lynn Robison, 1937-
From adze to vermilion; a guide to the hardware of history, and the literature of historic sites archaeology, by L. R. Bailey. Pasadena, Calif., Socio-Technical Books, 1971.
xv, 237 p. illus. 22 cm.
1. United States—Antiquities—Bibliography. 2. Historic sites—United States—Bibliography. 3. Excavations (Archaeology)—United States—Bibliography. I. Title.
Z1208.U5B34 016.9173'03 68-29144
MARC

Bailey, M.
see Symposium on Enzymatic Hydrolysis of Cellulose, Aulanko, Finland, 1975. Symposium on Enzymatic Hydrolysis of Cellulose... Helsinki, Finnish National Fund for Research and Development (SITRA), 1975.

Bailey, M. Thomas
see
Bailey, Minnie Thomas.

Bailey, Mack William, 1946-
Solute interactions in ultrafiltration treatment of paper mill wastes. Raleigh, N.C., 1973.
146 l. illus. 29 cm.
Bibliography: leaves 102-105.
Vita.
Thesis (Ph.D.)—North Carolina State University at Raleigh.
NcRS NUC75-17213

Bailey, Maralyn, joint author.
see Bailey, Maurice. 117 [i.e. Cent dix sept] jours à la dérive ... Paris, Arthaud, 1974.

Bailey, Maralyn, joint author
see Bailey, Maurice. 117 days adrift. [Lymington, Eng. Nautical Pub. Co.] [1974]

Bailey, Maralyn, joint author
see Bailey, Maurice. Staying alive: 117 days adrift... New York, D. McKay Co. [1974]

Bailey, Margaret, 1948-
Live long and prosper : the Star trek phenomenon / Margaret Bailey. — New Brunswick, N.J. : Graduate School of Library Service, Rutgers University, 1976.
vii, 73 p. ; 28 cm. — (Occasional papers - Rutgers University GSLS ; no. 76-2)
Includes index.
$3.00
1. Star trek—Bibliography. I. Title. II. Series: Rutgers University, New Brunswick, N.J. Graduate School of Library Service. Occasional papers - Rutgers University GSLS ; no. 76-2.
Z7711.B33 016.79145'7 77-361602
[PN1992.77] 77 MARC

Bailey, Margaret Burton, 1915-
A survey of medical and psychiatric practice with alcoholics, New York City, 1968. New York, Committee on Alcoholism, Community Council of Greater New York [1968?]
x, 36 p. 22 cm.
1. Alcohol—Physiological effect. I. Title.
NjR NUC73-39269

Bailey, Margery, 1891-1963, ed.
see Boswell, James, 1740-1795. The hypochondriack... [New York, AMS Press, 1973]

Bailey, Marilynn Jane Lee.
A demonstration of the prescriptive teaching system with teachers of deaf-blind rubella children. [n.p., c1972]
viii, 138 l. illus. 28 cm.
Thesis (Ed.D.)—University of Southern California.
1. Teachers of handicapped children, Training of. 2. Handicapped children—Education. I. Title.
CLSU NUC74-123758

Bailey, Marion Crawford, 1937-
Near field coupling between elements of a finite planar array of circular apertures. [n.p.] 1972.
146 l. illus.
I. Title.
ViBlbV NUC74-601

Bailey, Mark R
The economic impact of selected watershed programs on the Eastern Shore of Maryland, by Mark R. Bailey. [n.p.] 1975.
ix, 140 l. 29 cm.
Thesis—University of Maryland.
Vita.
Includes bibliography.
1. Watershed management—Maryland—Eastern Shore. I. Title.
MdU NUC77-84901

Bailey, Mark R.
see The Economic impact of selected watershed programs on the Eastern Shore of Maryland. College Park, Agricultural Experiment Station, University of Maryland, 1977.

Bailey, Martha J
The special librarian as a supervisor or middle manager / Martha J. Bailey. — New York : Special Libraries Association, 1977.
iv, 42 p. ; 28 cm. — (SLA state-of-the-art review ; no. 6)
Includes bibliographical references.
ISBN 0-87111-249-3
1. Libraries, Special—Administration. 2. Special librarians. 3. Supervisors. I. Title. II. Series: Special Libraries Association. SLA state-of-the-art review ; no. 6.
Z675.A2B34 025.1 77-5021
77 MARC

Bailey, Martha J comp.
Tungsten wire and wire drawing, 1944-1961. Indianapolis, Ind., Linde Company, Division of Union Carbide Corp. [1961?]
7 l. 28 cm. (Special Libraries Association. Metals Division. Metals Division bibliography, no. 61-3)
1. Wire—Bibl. 2. Tungsten—Bibl. 3. Wire-drawing—Bibl. I. Title.
NRU NUC73-59288

Bailey, Martin.
Barclays and South Africa / by Martin Bailey. — [Birmingham] : Haslemere Group ; [London] : Anti-apartheid Movement, [1975]
[1], 12 p. : ill., facsims. ; 26 cm. GB76-03812
Cover title.
Label on t.p.: Suppliers, Third World Publications, Birmingham.
"A joint Haslemere Group/Anti-apartheid Movement Publication."
Bibliography: p. 12.
ISBN 0-905094-00-X : £0.20
1. Barclays Bank International Limited. 2. Barclays National Bank. 3. South Africa—Race question. I. North London Haslemere Group. II. Anti-apartheid Movement. III. Title.
HG2998.B34B35 309.1'68'06 76-363195
76 MARC

Bailey, Martin.
Freedom railway : China and the Tanzania-Zambia link / [by] Martin Bailey. — London : Collings, 1976.
xiii, 168 p., [4] p. of plates : ill., 2 maps, ports. ; 23 cm. GB76-26415
Includes index.
Bibliography: p. [163]-164.
ISBN 0-86036-024-5 : £5.00
1. Tan-Zam Railway. I. Title.
HE3460.T35B34 1976 385'.09678'2 76-381782
76 MARC

Bailey, Martin.
The union of Tanganyika and Zanzibar: a study in political integration. [Syracuse, N. Y.] Program of Eastern African Studies, Syracuse University, 1973.
114 p. map. 28 cm. (Eastern African studies, 9) $4.00
Includes bibliographical references.
1. Tanzania—Politics and government. 2. Tanzania—Economic policy. I. Title. II. Series.
JQ3513 1973.B27 320.9'678'04 73-176005
MARC

Bailey, Martin J
Deterrence, assured destruction, and defense, by Martin J. Bailey. Washington, D.C., Brookings Institution, 1973.
682-695 p. 23 cm. (Brookings Institution. Reprint, 255)
Cover title.
1. U. S.—Military policy. I. Title.
CtY NUC74-123757

Bailey, Martin J
Renta nacional y nivel de precios; curso de teoría macroeconómica. Versión española de José Vergara. 2. ed. [Madrid] Alianza Editorial [1972]
348 p. illus. (Alianza universidad, 17)
1. Macroeconomics. 2. National income. I. Title.
NbU NUC76-68686

Bailey, Martin J.
see Rochester, N.Y. City School District. Task Force on Budget and Management. Report... [Rochester, N.Y.] 1971.

Bailey, Maurice.
117 [i.e. Cent dix sept] jours à la dérive : abordés et coulés par un cachalot / Maurice et Maralyn Bailey ; [traduit par Florence Herbulot ; dessins de Peter A. G. Milne]. — Paris : Arthaud, 1974.
248 p. : ill. ; 20 cm. — (Collection Mer) F75-5780
Translation of Staying alive.
ISBN 2-7003-0053-X : 45.00F
1. Shipwrecks. 2. Survival (after airplane accidents, shipwrecks, etc.) I. Bailey, Maralyn, joint author. II. Title.
G530.B1514 910'.09'1823 75-513392
75 MARC

Bailey, Maurice.
117 days adrift [by] Maurice & Maralyn Bailey; drawings by Peter A. G. Milne, maps by Alan Irving. [Lymington, Eng. Nautical Pub. Co. [1974]
192 p. illus. 23 cm. £2.70 GB***
1. Shipwrecks. 2. Survival (after aeroplane accidents, shipwrecks) I. Bailey, Maralyn, joint author. II. Title.
G530.B15 910'.453 74-168489
ISBN 0-245-52260-3 MARC

Bailey, Maurice.
Staying alive: 117 days adrift — the incredible saga of a courageous couple who outwitted death at sea for a longer period than any humans before [by] Maurice and Maralyn Bailey. Foreford by Sir Peter Scott. Drawings by Peter A. G. Milne. Maps by Alan Irving. New York, D. McKay Co. [1974]
192 p. illus. 25 cm. $6.95
1. Shipwrecks. 2. Survival (after aeroplane accidents, shipwrecks, etc.) I. Bailey, Maralyn, joint author. II. Title.
G530.B15 1974 910'.45 74-77039
ISBN 0-679-50458-3 MARC

Bailey, Maurice E
Study of worker acceptance and attitudes toward mining equipment modifications / Maurice E. Bailey, project director ; Frank A. Bailey, principal investigator. [Pikeville, Ky.] : Pikeville College, 1975.
iii, 34 p. ; 28 cm. -- ([Open-file report])
Final report.
United States Bureau of Mines Contract no. S0144077.
1. Mining machinery. I. Bailey, Frank A., joint author. II. Pikeville College. III. United States. Bureau of Mines. IV. Title. V. Series: United States. Bureau of Mines. Open-file report ; 1975-99.
DI NUC77-95842

Bailey, Minnie Thomas.
Reconstruction in Indian territory; a story of avarice, discrimination, and opportunism [by] M. Thomas Bailey. Port Washington, N. Y., Kennikat Press, 1972.
225 p. illus. 24 cm. (Kennikat Press national university publications. Series in American studies) $11.50
Bibliography: p. 204-212.
1. Indians of North America—Indian Territory. 2. Reconstruction—Indian Territory. 3. Five Civilized Tribes—History. I. Title.
E78.I 5B34 970.5 77-189551
ISBN 0-8046-9022-7 MARC

Bailey, Minnie Thomas.
Reconstruction in Indian Territory, 1865-1887. [Ann Arbor, Mich., University Microfilms, 1967]
vii, 311 l. illus. 21 cm.
Thesis—Oklahoma State University.
Microfilm xerography copy made in 1973.
1. Indian Territory—Hist. 2. Indians of North America—Oklahoma. I. Title.
OkU NUC76-68684

Bailey, Minnie Thomas.
Reconstruction in Indian Territory, 1865-1877. Ames, Iowa, 1967 [c1968, 1973]
vii, 311 l. maps.
Thesis - Iowa State University.
Microfilm of typescript. Ann Arbor, Mich., University Microfilms, 1973. 1 reel.
1. Indians of North America—Government relations. 2. Five civilized Tribes—Government relations. I. Title.
IaU WHi NUC74-608

Bailey, Miriam Sawyer, 1938-
Rich and strange: interpretations of The tempest. [Tallahassee, Fla.] c1971.
xli, 342 l.
Thesis (Ph. D.)—Florida State University.
Bibliography: leaves 323-341.
Vita.
1. Shakespeare, William, 1564-1616. The tempest. I. Title.
FTaSU NUC75-34827

Bailey, Mollie B 1931-
Teacher effectiveness training with pre-student teachers in language arts. Albuquerque, 1972.
[ix], 108 l.
Thesis (Ph.D.)—University of New Mexico.
Bibliography: leaves [104]-108.
1. Teachers, Training of—U.S. 2. Attitude (Psychology)—Testing. I. Title.
NmU NUC74-122977

Bailey, N. T. J.
see
Bailey, Norman T J

Bailey, Nathan, d. 1742.
Dictionarium Britannicum. (1730.) (Reprograf. Nachdr. d. Ausg. London, Cox, 1730.) Hildesheim, New York, G. Olms, 1969.
413 p. with illus. 30 cm. (Anglistica & Americana, 50)
DM248.00 GDB 70-A12-269
"Collected by several hands, the mathematical part by G. Gordon, the botanical by P. Miller."
Originally published in 1721 under title: An universal etymological English dictionary.
1. English language—Dictionaries. 2. Names, Personal—Great Britain. 3. Names, Geographical—Great Britain. I. Gordon, George, fl. 1728. II. Miller, Philip, 1691-1771. III. Title. IV. Series.
PE1620.B3 1969 73-319928

Bailey, Nathan, d. 1742.
Divers proverbs with their explication & illustration, compiled and methodically digested as well for the entertainment of the curious as the information of the ignorant and for the benefit of young students, artificers, tradesmen & foreigners who are desirous thorowly to understand what they speak, read, or write, by Nathan Bailey, anno Domini 1721; woodcuts by Allen Lewis. New Haven, Conn., Printed and to be sold by the Yale university press; [etc.] 1917. [Ann Arbor, Mich., 1967]
ix, [3], 83 p. incl. 1 illus., plates. 18 cm.
Compiled from the author's Etymological English dictionary, by John Fletcher.
Printed on double leaves; Photocopy (positive) made by University Microfilms.
1. Proverbs. I. Fletcher, John Crerar Campbell, 1950- II. Title.
NBuC NUC76-68665

Bailey, Nathan J
Johnsville in the olden time, and other stories. New York, Printed by E.O. Jenkins' sons, 1884.
[9]-255 p.
Microfilm (positive) Ann Arbor, Mich., University Microfilms, 1973. 1st title of 13. 35 mm. (American fiction series, reel 225.1)
I. Title.
KEmT NUC75-2095

Bailey, Nell Charlene, 1934-
A study of the purposes, practices, and goals as perceived by selected groups in a small experimental liberal arts college. [Bloomington, Ind.] 1973.
164 p.
Thesis (Ed.D.)—Indiana University.
InU NUC74-122978

Bailey, Nora Duke, 1900-
Genealogy of Smith-McAlevy & related families / Nora Duke Bailey, researcher, Roscoe & Virginia Smith, compilers. — Baltimore : Gateway Press, 1976.
2 v. : ill. ; 24 cm.
Bibliography: v. 1, p. v-viii.
CONTENTS: v. 1. History, documents, photographs.—v. 2. Genealogical sheets.
Includes index.
1. Smith family. 2. McAlevy family. 3. United States—Genealogy. I. Smith, Roscoe, 1915- joint author. II. Smith, Virginia, 1916- joint author. III. Title.
CS71.S643 1976a 929'.2'0973 76-27564
77 MARC

Bailey, Norma Marie, 1942-
A comparative analysis of four translations of Sophocles' Oedipus tyrannus / by Norma Marie Bailey. -- Madison, Wis. : University of Wisconsin, 1976.
iii, 243 [244] leaves ; 29 cm.
Thesis (Ph. D.)--University of Wisconsin.
Vita.
Bibliography: leaves 242-[244]
1. Sophocles. Oedipus tyrannus. I. Title.
WU NUC77-90426

Bailey, Norman A
Operational conflict analysis, by Norman A. Bailey and Stuart M. Feder. Washington, Public Affairs Press [1973]
vii, 136 p. illus. 24 cm. $6.00
Bibliography: p. 131-135.
1. Conflict (Psychology) 2. Act (Philosophy) 3. Power (Social sciences) I. Feder, Stuart M., joint author. II. Title.
HM291.B24 301.6'3'0184 72-96035
MARC

Bailey, Norman G
Apollo 11 voice transcript pertaining to the geology of the landing site, by N.G. Bailey and G.E. Ulrich. Flagstaff, Ariz., U.S. Geological Survey, Branch of Astrogeology, 1974.
1 card. ill. 11 x 15 cm.
Microfiche copy. Springfield, Va., National Technical Information Service, 1975.
1. Project Apollo. 2. Lunar geology. I. Ulrich, George E., joint author. II. United States. Geological Survey. Branch of Astrogeology. III. Title.
DI NUC76-50455

Bailey, Norman G
Apollo 12 voice transcript pertaining to the geology of the landing site, by N.G. Bailey and G.E. Ulrich. Flagstaff, Ariz., U.S. Geological Survey, Branch of Astrogeology, 1975.
2 cards. 11 x 15 cm.
"USGS-GD-74-027."
Microfiche (negative) Springfield, Va., National Technical Information Service, 1975.
1. Lunar geology. I. Ulrich, George E., joint author. II. United States. Geological Survey. Branch of Astrogeology. III. Title.
DI NUC77-82726

Bailey, Norman G
Apollo 14 voice transcript pertaining to the geology of the moon, by N.G. Bailey and G.E. Ulrich. Flagstaff, Ariz., U.S. Geological Survey, Branch of Astrogeology, 1975.
2 cards. 11 x 15 cm.
Microfiche (negative) Springfield, Va., National Technical Information Service, 1975.
1. Project Apollo. 2. Lunar geology. I. Ulrich, George E., joint author. II. United States. Geological Survey. Branch of Astrogeology. III. Title.
DI NUC77-82718

Bailey, Norman G
Apollo 15 voice transcript pertaining to the geology of the landing site, by N.G. Bailey and G.E. Ulrich. Flagstaff, Ariz., U.S. Geological Survey, Branch of Astrogeology, 1975.
3 cards. 11 x 15 cm.
Microfiche (negative) Springfield, Va., National Technical Information Service, 1975.
1. Lunar geology. I. Ulrich, George E., joint author. II. United States. Geological Survey. Branch of Astrogeology. III. Title.
DI NUC77-82730

Bailey, Norman T J
The mathematical approach to biology and medicine [by] Norman T. J. Bailey. London, New York, Wiley [1967]
xiii, 296 p. 24 cm. (Series on quantitative methods for biologists and medical scientists)
Bibliography: p. [284]-286.
1. Biomathematics. 2. Medicine—Mathematics. I. Title.
QH324.B28 574'.01'51 66-30037
[r77]rev MARC

Bailey, Norman T J
The mathematical theory of infectious diseases and its applications / [by] Norman T. J. Bailey. — 2nd ed. — London : Griffin, 1975.
xvi, 413 p. : ill. ; 24 cm. GB76-02371
First ed. published in 1957 under title: The mathematical theory of epidemics.
Bibliography: p. 383-403.
Includes indexes.
ISBN 0-85264-231-8 : £14.00
1. Epidemiology—Mathematical models. I. Title.
RA652.2.M3B34 1975 614.4'01'84 76-675653
76 MARC

Bailey, Norman T. J., ed.
see IFIP-TC4 Working Conference on Mathematical Models in Biology and Medicine, Varna, Bulgaria, 1972. Mathematical models in biology and medicine... Amsterdam: North-Holland Pub. Co.; New York: American Elsevier Pub. Co., 1974.

Bailey, Norman T. J.
see Systems aspects of health planning ... Amsterdam, North-Holland Pub. Co., 1975.

Bailey, Oran F., 1925- joint author.
see Neher, R. E. Soil survey of White Sands Missile Range, New Mexico ... [Washington] The Service, [1976]

Bailey, Patrick.
Teaching geography / Patrick Bailey. — Newton Abbot : David and Charles, 1974.
267 p., 8 p. of plates : ill., maps ; 22 cm. — (Teaching series) GB75-09850
Bibliography: p. 235-260.
Includes index.
ISBN 0-7153-6860-5 : £5.50
1. Geography—Study and teaching. I. Title.
G73.B14 1974 910'.7'12 75-327507
75 MARC

Bailey, Patrick Gage.
Variational derivation of modal-nodal finite difference equations in spatial reactor physics, by Patrick G. Bailey. [n.p.] 1972.
381, [2] l. diagrs., tables (part col.) 30 cm.
Thesis (Ph.D.)—Massachusetts Institute of Technology.
Vita.
Includes bibliographical references.
1. Difference equations—Numerical solutions. 2. Neutron flux. 3. Neutron transport theory. 4. Nuclear reactors—Computer programs. I. Title.
MCM NUC74-503

Bailey, Paul, 1937–
A distant likeness / [by] Paul Bailey. — London : Cape, 1973.
135 p. ; 21 cm. GB 73-15462
ISBN 0-224-00863-3 : £1.60
I. Title.
PZ4.B1525Di 823'.9'14 74-188522
[PR6052.A319] MARC

Bailey, Paul, 1937-
Zonden. [Vertaling W.A. Dorsman-Vos] Utrecht, A.W. Bruna [1972]
190 p. 21 cm. (Bruna boeken)
Translation of Trespasses.
I. Title.
MB NUC75-75556

Bailey, Paul, 1937-
see Ross, Alan. Living in London. London : London Magazine Editions, 1974.

Bailey, Paul Clinton, joint author
see Wagner, Kenneth Allan, 1919- Under siege: man, men, and earth. New York, Abelard-Schuman [c1973]

Bailey, Paul Clinton, joint author
see Wagner, Kenneth Allan, 1919- Under siege: man, men, and earth. New York, Intext Educational Publishers [1973]

Bailey, Paul Dayton, 1906-
Concentration camp U.S.A. [New York, Tower Publications, Inc., 1972]
223 p.
1. Japanese in the U.S. 2. World War, 1939-1945—Evacuation of civilians. I. Title.
InU NUC75-34826

Bailey, Paul Dayton, 1906-
Those kings and queens of old Hawaii : a mele to their memory / by Paul Bailey. — Los Angeles : Westernlore Books, 1975.
381 p. : ill., ports. ; 24 cm.
Bibliography: p. 373-374.
Includes index.
ISBN 0-87026-035-9 : $11.95
1. Hawaii—Kings and rulers. 2. Hawaii—History. I. Title.
DU624.9.B34 996.9'00992 75-259
75 MARC

Bailey, Paul Edward.
Philosophical and methodological orientations in the research programmes of Verstehende Soziologie and ethnomethodology. [n.p.] 1972.
1 v.
Honors thesis—Harvard.
1. Social sciences—Methodology. 2. Weber, Max, 1864-1920.
MH NUC76-68683

Bailey, Pearl.
Duey's tale / Pearl Bailey. — 1st ed. — New York : Harcourt Brace Jovanovich, [1975]
59 p. : ill. ; 21 cm.
SUMMARY: A maple seedling becomes separated from his mother tree, makes friends with a bottle and a log, and searches for his own place in life.
ISBN 0-15-126576-3 : $5.95
[1. Seeds—Fiction. 2. Trees—Fiction] I. Title.
PZ7.B1528Du [Fic] 74-22278
MARC

Bailey, Pearl.
Hurry up, America, & spit / Pearl Bailey. — 1st ed. — New York : Harcourt Brace Jovanovich, c1976.
106 p. ; 22 cm.
ISBN 0-15-143000-4 : $5.95
1. Bailey, Pearl. I. Title.
ML420.B123A28 081 76-12481
76 MARC

Bailey, Pearl.
Pearl's kitchen; an extraordinary cookbook. [1st ed.] New York, Harcourt Brace Jovanovich [1973]
xi, 211 p. 25 cm. $6.95
1. Cookery. 2. Bailey, Pearl. I. Title.
TX715.B158 641.5 73-6624
ISBN 0-15-171600-5 MARC

Bailey, Percival, 1892-
see Pattern of the cerebral isocortex. Basel, New York, S. Karger, 1961.

Bailey, Peter Cecil, 1937-
'Rational recreation'; the social control of leisure and popular culture in Victorian England, 1830-1885. By Peter Cecil Bailey. [Vancouver, B. C.] University of British Columbia, 1974.
iii, 417 l. 28 cm.
Thesis—University of British Columbia.
Vita.
Bibliography: leaves 374-417.
1. Recreation—Gt. Brit.—Hist. 2. Leisure. I. Title. II. Series.
CaBVaU NUC76-15508

Bailey, Peter L
Analysis with ion-selective electrodes / Peter L. Bailey. — London ; New York : Heyden, 1976.
xii, 228 p. : ill. ; 24 cm. — (Heyden international topics in science) GB***
Includes bibliographical references and index.
ISBN 0-85501-223-4 : £6.80
1. Electrodes, Ion selective. 2. Chemistry, Analytic. I. Title.
QD571.B26 543'.087 77-363504
77 MARC

Bailey, Peter S
Newhaven-Dieppe: from paddle to turbine, a story of the service and steamers: a narrative, by Peter S. Bailey; edited by Colin Maddock. Seaford, Lindel Publishing Co., [1972]
[28] p. illus. 22 cm. £0.35 B72-21498
1. Steamboat lines—English Channel. I. Title.
HE601.G69B34 387.5'42'0916336 73-154060
ISBN 0-9502354-0-7 MARC

Bailey, Philip.
They can make music; with a preface by Lady Hamilton. London, New York, Oxford University Press, 1973.
xii, 143, [4] p., leaf. illus., music. 20 cm. £1.75 GB 73-16551
Bibliography: p. [137]-141.
1. Music—Instruction and study. 2. Handicapped children—Education. I. Title.
MT1.B312T5 371.9 73-169563
ISBN 0-19-311913-7 MARC

Bailey, Philip Armine, 1885-1970.
Golden mirages. [Special commemorative ed.] Ramona, Calif., Acoma Books, 1971 [c1968]
x, 353 p. illus., maps. ports. 24 cm.
1. Southwest, New. 2. Legends—Southwest, New. 3. Mines and mineral resources—Southwest, New. 4. Lost mines. 5. Smith, Thomas Long, 1801-1866. I. Title.
CU-B NUC73-32416

Bailey, Phyllis C
Fascinating facts about the Bible / compiled by Phyllis Bailey. — Washington : Review and Herald Pub. Association, c1976.
62 p. ; 18 cm.
1. Bible—Miscellanea. I. Title.
BS530.B27 220 74-28754
77[r77]rev MARC

Bailey, Phyllis C
Topical concordance to the Bible / Phyllis C. Bailey. — Washington : Review and Herald Pub. Association, c1975.
277 p. ; 23 cm.
1. Bible—Indexes, Topical. I. Title.
BS432.B33 220.2 74-25817
76 MARC

Bailey, R A
Recommendations to strengthen the financing of Malaysia's agriculture, by R. A. Bailey and R.D. Carter. [Columbus] Ohio State University, Dept. of Agricultural Finance Center, 1969.
24, 24 l. 28 cm.
"Consultants' report to the Government of Malaysia."
1. Agricultural credit–Malaysia. 2. Bank Pertanian Malaysia. I. Carter, R.D. II. Ohio. State University, Columbus. Agricultural Finance Center. III. Title.
NIC NNC NUC73-51372

Bailey, R.A., joint author
see Chen, Hsing-yiu. Structure and productivity of capital in the agriculture of Taiwan... [Columbus, 1967]

Bailey, R. C.
see
Bailey, Richard Charles.

Bailey, R. H.
see Lichenology : progress and problems : proceedings of an international symposium held at the University of Bristol. London, Published for the Systematics Association and the British Lichen Society by Academic Press, 1976.

Bailey, R. V.
see
Bailey, Roy Victor.

Bailey, R. W., joint author
see Butler, G W Chemistry and biochemistry of herbage. London, New York, Academic Press, 1973.

Bailey, R.W., ed.
see United States. Patent Office. Notes on the Rules of practice of the United States Patent Office. [Washington, D.C., n.d.]

Bailey, R.Y., joint author
see Buie, T S Soil conservation in the Southeast, 1933-1953. Spartanburg, S.C., 1973.

Bailey, Raleigh Eugene, 1943-
An ethnographic approach toward the study of a spiritually oriented communal group in the USA: The Healthy Happy Holy Organization. Hartford, Conn., 1973.
293 l. illus.
Thesis (Ph.D.)—Hartford Seminary Foundation.
1. Healthy Happy Holy Organization. 2. Collective settlements—United States. I. Title.
DeU NUC76-68685

Bailey, Ralph.
For everything a season / Ralph Bailey. — New York : Hawthorn Books, c1975.
xv, 100 p. ; 22 cm.
ISBN 0-8015-2764-3 : $5.95
1. Consolation. I. Title.
BV4907.B28 1975 248'.86 75-2564
75 MARC

Bailey, Ralph, 1904-
see Good housekeeping basic gardening techniques. New York, Book Division, Hearst Magazines, c1974.

Bailey, Ralph 1904- ed.
see The Good housekeeping illustrated encyclopedia of gardening. New York, Book Division, Hearst Magazines [c1972]

Bailey, Raymond.
Thomas Merton on mysticism / Raymond Bailey. — Garden City, N.Y. : Doubleday, 1975.
239 p. ; 22 cm.
Originally presented as the author's thesis, Southern Baptist Theological Seminary, Louisville.
Includes bibliographical references.
ISBN 0-385-07173-6 : $7.95
1. Merton, Thomas, 1915-1968. 2. Mysticism—History. I. Title.
BX4705.M542B28 1975 248'.22'0924 75-22742
75 MARC

Bailey, Reeve Maclaren.
Scoloplax dicra, a new armored catfish from the Bolivian Amazon / by Reeve M. Bailey and Jonathan N. Baskin. — Ann Arbor : [Museum of Zoology, University of Michigan], 1976.
14 p. : ill. ; 24 cm. — (Occasional papers of the Museum of Zoology, University of Michigan ; no. 674)
Caption title.
Bibliography: p. 12-13.
1. Scoloplax dicra. 2. Fishes—Classification. 3. Fishes—Bolivia. I. Baskin, Jonathan N., joint author. II. Title. III. Series: Michigan. University. Museum of Zoology. Occasional Papers ; no. 674.
QL638.L785B34 597'.52 76-624501
77 MARC

Bailey, Reeve Maclaren, joint author
see Gilbert, Carter Rowell, 1930- Systematics... Ann Arbor [University of Michigan] 1972.

Bailey, Richard.
The European Community in the world. London, Hutchinson [1973]
200 p. illus. 23 cm. £3.50 GB***
Bibliography: p. 190-191.
1. European Economic Community countries. I. Title.
HC241.2.B27 1973 382'.9142 74-152823
ISBN 0-09-118720-6; 0-09-118721-4 (pbk.) MARC

Bailey, Richard
see Energie, Mensch und Umwelt. Frankfurt/M., Herbert Lang, 1973.

Bailey, Richard C
Interprovince barriers in the prairie feedgrains market, by Richard C. Bailey, Murray H. Hawkins [and] Michele M. Veeman. [Edmonton, Alta., University of Alberta, Dept. of Agricultural Economics and Rural Sociology, Faculty of Agriculture and Forestry, 1972?]
vii, 31 p. maps. 28 cm. (University of Alberta. Dept. of Agricultural Economics and Rural Sociology. Bulletin 16, applied research) C***
Bibliography: p. 20-21.
1. Grain trade—Prairie Provinces. I. Hawkins, Murray H., joint author. II. Veeman, Michele M., joint author. III. Title. IV. Series: Alberta. University, Edmonton. Dept. of Agricultural Economics and Rural Sociology. Bulletin - University of Alberta, Department of Agricultural Economics and Rural Sociology, 16.
HD1407.A43a vol. 16 338.1'08 s 75-305164
[HD9044.C3] [381'.41'3109712] MARC

Bailey, Richard C fl. 1951-
Collector's choice; the McLeod basket collection. Bakersfield, Calif., c1951.
36 p. illus., ports. 23 cm.
"13th annual publication of the Kern County Historical Society and the county of Kern through its museum."
Bibliography: p. 33-36.
1. Yakuts Indians—Basket making. 2. McLeod, Edwin Lincoln, 1861-1908. 3. California. University. E. L. McLeod Basket Collection. 4. Indians of North America—Basket making. I. Title.
E99.Y75B34 *970.1 970.674558 52-31731

Bailey, Richard C fl. 1951-
Explorations in Kern. Bakersfield, Calif., 1959.
81 p. illus. 24 cm.
"Twenty-second annual publication of the Kern County Historical Society and the county of Kern through its museum."
1. Kern County, Calif.—Description and travel. 2. Cities and towns, Ruined, extinct, etc.—Kern County, Calif. I. Title.
F868.K3B28 917.94'88 60-20854 ‡

Bailey, Richard C fl. 1951-
Heritage of Kern. Bakersfield, Calif., 1957.
vii, 110 p. illus., ports. 24 cm.
"Twentieth annual publication of the Kern County Historical Society and the county of Kern through its museum."
1. Kern County, Calif.—History. I. Kern County Historical Society, Bakersfield, Calif. II. Title.
F868.K3B3 979.4'88 58-19310

Bailey, Richard C fl. 1951-
Kern County place names, by Richard C. Bailey. [Bakersfield, Calif.] 1967.
28 p. map (on lining papers) 24 cm.
"Twenty-ninth annual publication of the Kern County Historical Society and the County of Kern, through its Museum."
1. Names, Geographical—California—Kern County. 2. Kern County, Calif.—History. I. Kern County Historical Society, Bakersfield, Calif. II. Title.
F868.K3B32 917.94'88'003 74-18077
71[r75]rev MARC

Bailey, Richard Charles.
see Nelson, Bertram. Nelson's Tables of procedure. 6th ed. London, Oyez Pub., 1975.

Bailey, Richard Chester.
BAM: an innovative change model - barriers encountered in the implementation of a classical research design to modify the behavior and attitude of staff and inmates in a correctional institution. [n.p.] 1971.
ix, 341 l. 29 cm.
Thesis—University of Southern California.
Typewritten.
Photocopy of typescript.
1. California Rehabilitation Center. 2. Narcotic addicts—Rehabilitation. I. Title.
CLSU NUC73-32412

Bailey, Richard James, 1946-
An analysis of the expressed preferences of graduate faculty on the relative importance of selected workload components. Washington, 1975.
viii, 167 p.
Thesis (Ph.D.)--American University.
Bibliography: p. 138-143.
1. College teachers--Work load. 2. Universities and colleges--Faculty. I. Title.
DAU NUC77-86408

Bailey, Richard Manley, 1932-
Economic perspectives on clinical laboratories. Richard M. Bailey; in collaboration with Thomas M. Tierney, Jr. Berkeley, Calif., Institute of Business and Economic Research, University of California, 1975.
ix, 89 p. 28 cm. (IBER special publications)
Includes bibliographical references.
1. Medical laboratories–United States. 2. Medical economics–United States. I. Tierney, Thomas M., joint author. II. Title. III. Series.
CU NUC77-82725

Bailey, Richard W
Michigan early modern English materials. Richard W. Bailey, James W. Downer, Jay L. Robinson with Patricia V. Lehman. Ann Arbor, Mich., Xerox University Microfilms, 1975.
2 v. 29 cm.
Vol. 2 consists of 92 microfiche.
ISBN 0-8357-0069-0.
1. English language–Early modern, 1500-1700–Dict. I. Downer, James W. II. Robinson, Jay, 1932- III. Title.
CaBVaU NUC77-84133

Bailey, Richard W comp.
Varieties of present-day English [by] Richard W. Bailey and Jay L. Robinson. New York, Macmillan [1973]
xvi, 461 p. illus. 24 cm. $5.95
Bibliography: p. 451-456.
1. English language in the United States—Dialects. 2. English language in foreign countries. 3. Sociolinguistics. 4. English language—Study and teaching. I. Robinson, Jay, 1932- joint comp. II. Title.
PE2841.B3 427 72-86501
MARC

Bailey, Richard W., ed.
see Computer poems. Drummond Island, Mich., Potagannissing Press [1973]

Bailey, Richard W., ed.
see Symposium on the Uses of Computers in Literary Research, 2d, University of Edinburgh, 1972. The computer and literary studies. [Edinburgh, Univ. Press [1973]

Bailey, Richard Warman, 1937-
The use of a pseudo random binary reactivity input and the resulting gamma ray fluctuations to determine the transfer function of a nuclear reactor. [n.p.] 1973.
80 l.
Thesis—Ohio State University.
Bibliography: leaves 59-60.
1. Nuclear reactors. 2. Gamma rays—Measurement. I. Title.
OU NUC75-17212

Bailey, Robert.
Protest in urban politics: a study of an Alinsky community organization and its participants. [n.p.] 1972.
1 v.
Thesis (Ph.D.)—Northwestern University.
1. Community organization—Case studies. 2. Chicago. South Austin. 3. Negroes—Politics and suffrage. 4. Alinsky, Saul David, 1909- I. Title.
IEN NUC74-617

Bailey, Robert.
Radicals in urban politics : the Alinsky approach / Robert Bailey, Jr. — Chicago : University of Chicago Press, 1974.
x, 187 p. : ill. ; 22 cm.
Bibliography: p. 171-181.
Includes index.
ISBN 0-226-03452-6 : $9.95
1. Organization for a Better Austin. 2. Alinsky, Saul David, 1909-1972. 3. Community organization. 4. Austin, Ill.—Social conditions. I. Title.
HN80.A93B34 322.4'4'0977311 73-90938
75 MARC

Bailey, Robert, 1937-
The genesis of Tristan und Isolde and a study of Wagner's sketches and drafts for the first act. [Princeton, N.J.] 1969.
xi, 269 l. music.
Thesis—Princeton University.
Bibliography: leaves 264-266.
Microfilm of typescript. Ann Arbor, Mich., University Microfilms, 1970. 1 reel. 35 mm.
1. Wagner, Richard, 1813-1883. Tristan und Isolde. I. Title.
IU OU NUC73-40503

Bailey, Robert Allen, 1947-
Optimal control of linear systems with incomplete state measurement. [n.p., 1974]
1 v.
Thesis (Ph.D.)—Northwestern University.
1. Control theory. I. Title.
IEN NUC76-15516

Bailey, Robert C
Farm tools & implements before 1850 [by] Robert C. Bailey. Spring City, Tenn., Hillcrest Books, c1973.
72 p. illus. 22 cm. $3.95
1. Agricultural implements—United States. I. Title.
S676.B28 631.3'0973 74-167227
MARC

Bailey, Robert C fl. 1951-
How to start and operate a mail-order antiques business, by Robert C. Bailey. Spring City, Tenn., Hillcrest Shop, [1972]
72 p. illus. 28 cm. $6.95
1. Mail-order antiques business. 2. Art objects—Catalogs. I. Title.
NK1133.3.B3 658.89'7451 72-192992
rev MARC

Bailey, Robert E.
see National Energy Data Workshop, Purdue University, 1974. Proceedings of the National Energy Data Workshop, October 30 and 31, 1974, Purdue University. Washington, Federal Energy Administration : for sale by the Supt. of Docs., U.S. Govt. Print. Off., 1974 [i.e. 1975]

Bailey, Robert Eugene, 1943-
Late- and postglacial environmental changes in northwestern Indiana. [Bloomington, Ind.] 1972.
76 p. illus., maps.
Thesis (Ph.D.)—Indiana University.
Vita.
InU NUC74-600

Bailey, Robert G.
see Prison violence. Lexington, Mass., Lexington Books, c1976.

Bailey, Robert Gale, 1939-
Landslide hazards related to land use planning in Teton National Forest, northwest Wyoming, by Robert G. Bailey. [Ogden, Utah] U.S. Dept. of Agriculture, Forest Service, Intermountain Region, 1972.
131 p. illus. 27 cm.
"Reprint of 1971".
Bibliography: p. 122-127.
1. Teton National Forest. 2. Landslides. I. Title.
CaBVaU NUC74-122979

Bailey, Robert Gale, 1939-
Landslides and related hazards in Teton National Forest, northwest Wyoming. Los Angeles, 1971.
xviii, 278 l. illus., maps.
Thesis—University of California.
Vita.
Bibliography: leaves 256-268.
Microfilm. Ann Arbor, Mich., University Microfilms, 1971. 1 reel. 35 mm.
IU NUC73-127017

Bailey, Robert Gale, 1939-
Landslides and related hazards in Teton National Forest, northwest Wyoming. [Los Angeles, 1971]
xviii, 278 p. illus.
Microfilm copy (positive) Original in University of California Library, Los Angeles.
Vita.
Includes bibliography.
1. Landslides. 2. Teton National Forest. I. Title.
CU NUC73-127018

Bailey, Robert Gale, 1939-
see United States. Forest Service. Land suitabilities. [n.p.] 1972.

Bailey, Robert H., joint author
see Dixon, Brian. The museum and the Canadian public. [Toronto] Culturcan Publications, 1974.

Bailey, Robert Hugh.
A hierarchical landscape classification for recreational land use planning in the Finger Lakes Region of New York State. By Robert Hugh Bailey. [Ithaca, N.Y.] 1974.
ix, 247 l. illus., 28 fold. l. of plates, fold. maps.
Thesis—Cornell University.
Vita.
Bibliography: leaves 236-246.
Microfilm-xerox. Ann Arbor, Mich.: Xerox University Microfilms, 1975. 22 cm.
1. Recreation areas—New York—Finger Lakes Region. 2. Regional planning—Finger Lakes Region. I. Title.
GASU NUC76-15498

Bailey, Robert J.
see Historic preservation in Mississippi ... Jackson, Mississippi Dept. of Archives and History, 1975, c1976.

Bailey, Robert L
Electromagnetic wave energy conversion research ; final report. [Principal researchers Robert L. Bailey, Philip S. Callahan, Markus Zahn]. -- Gainesville, Florida, Engineering and Industrial Experiment Station, University of Florida, 1975.
110 l. ill. (U.S. National Technical Information Service, No. 76, 13591)
Submitted by University of Florida, College of Engineering, Engineering and Industrial Experiment Station to NASA, Goddard Space Flight Center under grant no. NSG-5061 April 1, 1975- Sept. 30, 1975 (UF Project no. 2451-E43).
Bibliography: p. 100-106.
1. Electromagnetic waves. 2. Solar energy research. I. Callahan, Philip S. II. Zahn, Markus. III. Florida. University, Gainesville. Engineering and Industrial Experiment Station. IV. Title. V. Series.
DNAL NUC77-87345

Bailey, Robert L
Slash pine site index in the West Gulf. New Orleans, La., 1973.
4 p. illus. (U.S. Southern Forest Experiment Station. U.S. Forest Service research note, SO-169)
Bibliography: p. 3-4.
I. Title.
DNAL NUC76-68662

Bailey, Robert Lee, 1929-
An examination of prime time network television special programs, 1948 to 1966. [Ann Arbor] University Microfilms [1968?]
Microfilm copy (positive) of typescript.
Collation of the original: xiii, 339 l. figs., tables.
Thesis—University of Wisconsin.
Bibliography: leaves 328-339.
1. Television programs. 2. Television broadcasting. I. Title.
PPT NUC74-118241

Bailey, Robert Sydnor.
Preparing for a career or profession in marine science, by Robert S. Bailey. Gloucester Point, Va., 1970.
9 p. 22 cm. (Virginia Institute of Marine Science, Gloucester Point. Educational series, no. 14)
Cover title: Careers in marine science.
Bibliography: p. 9.
1. Oceanography as a profession. 2. Marine biology as a profession. I. Title.
Vi NUC74-118242

Bailey, Robert W
The minister and grief / Robert W. Bailey. — New York : Hawthorn Books, c1976.
viii, 114 p. ; 22 cm.
Includes bibliographical references.
ISBN 0-8015-5074-2 : $5.95
1. Death. 2. Funeral service. 3. Grief. I. Title.
BT825.B26 1976 253'.5 75-39351
76 MARC

Bailey, Robert Wayne.
The cervical spine [edited by] Robert Wayne Bailey. Philadelphia, Lea & Febiger, 1974.
viii, 263 p. illus. 27 cm.
Includes bibliographies.
1. Spine—Diseases. 2. Vertebrae, Cervical—Abnormities and deformities. I. Title.
RC936.B34 1974 616.7'3 79-152020
ISBN 0-8121-0269-X MARC

Bailey, Roger
see Mental health facilities for inpatient adolescents. Salt Lake City, University of Utah, 1966.

Bailey, Roger B
Guide to Chinese poetry and drama [by] Roger B. Bailey. Boston, G. K. Hall, 1973.
xi, 100 p. 22 cm. (The Asian literature bibliography series)
1. Chinese poetry—Bibliography. 2. Chinese drama—Bibliography. I. Title. II. Title: Chinese poetry and drama. III. Series.
Z3108.L5B34 016.8951'1'008 73-11462
ISBN 0-8161-1102-2 MARC

Bailey, Roger L
A canonical correlation analysis of the Basic Interest Scales and the Edwards Personal Preference Schedule: a test of Holland's theory. [Lawrence, 1970]
ix, 166 l. tables. 28 cm.
Thesis (Ph.D.)—University of Kansas.
1. Interest inventories. 2. Vocational interests. 3. Personality. I. Title.
KU NUC73-39345

Bailey, Ron, 1943-
The grief report : [a Shelter report on temporary accommodation] / written by Ron Bailey and Joan Ruddock ; photographs by George Marshman and Ron Bailey. — London : Shelter, 1972.
167 p. : ill. ; 21 cm. GB74-23922
Includes bibliographical references.
ISBN 0-901242-20-9 : £0.25
1. Lodging-houses—Great Britain. 2. Housing—Great Britain. I. Ruddock, Joan, joint author. II. Shelter (Organization). III. Title.
HD7288.G7B33 362.8'2 75-329593
76 MARC

Bailey, Ron, 1943-
Shelter report on bed & breakfast / [compiled by Ron Bailey and Mary Evans ; written by Ron Bailey : photography, Stuart McPherson]. — London : Shelter, 1974.
56 p. : ill., 2 maps, plan ; 27 cm. — (Shelter action series ; 3) GB75-10046
Cover title: Bed & breakfast.
ISBN 0-901242-29-2 : £0.80
1. Lodging-houses—Great Britain. 2. Poor—Great Britain. 3. Housing—Great Britain. I. Evans, Mary. II. Shelter (Organization). III. Title: Bed & breakfast. IV. Series: Shelter (Organization). Shelter action series ; 3.
HD7288.G7B34 362.8'2 75-321879
75 MARC

Bailey, Ron, 1943–
The squatters. Harmondsworth, Penguin, 1973.
206 p. 19 cm. (A Penguin special) £0.35 B 73–09302
1. Housing—London. I. Title.
HD7333.L7B3 301.5′4 73–163470
ISBN 0–14–052300–6 MARC

Bailey, Ronald H
The photographic illusion, Duane Michals / text by Ronald H. Bailey, with the editors of Alskog, Inc. — London : Thames and Hudson, 1975.
[1], 96 p. : ill. (some col.), ports. (some col.) ; 28 cm. — (Masters of contemporary photography) GB75-31185
"An Alskog book."
ISBN 0-500-54034-9 : £1.95
1. Photography, Artistic. 2. Michals, Duane. I. Alskog, inc. II. Title.
TR654.B26 1975b 770′.92′4 76-377836
76 MARC

Bailey, Ronald H
The photographic illusion, Duane Michals / text by Ronald H. Bailey, with the editors of Alskog, Inc. — [New York] : Crowell, [1975]
96 p. : ill. (some col.) ; 28 cm. — (Masters of contemporary photography)
"An Alskog book."
ISBN 0-690-00787-6. ISBN 0-690-00788-4 pbk.
1. Photography, Artistic. 2. Michals, Duane. I. Alskog, inc.
TR654.B26 770′.92′4 75-12884
75 MARC

Bailey, Ronald H
The role of the brain / by Ronald H. Bailey and the editors of Time-Life Books. — New York : Time-Life Books, [1975]
176 p. : ill. ; 27 cm. — (Human behavior)
Bibliography: p. 170-171.
Includes index.
1. Brain. I. Time-Life Books. II. Title.
QP376.B253 612′.825 75-939
75 MARC

Bailey, Ronald H
Violence and aggression / by Ronald H. Bailey and the editors of Time-Life Books. — New York : Time-Life Books, c1976.
176 p. : ill. ; 27 cm. — (Human behavior)
Bibliography: p. 170-171.
Includes index.
1. Violence. 2. Aggressiveness (Psychology) I. Time-Life Books. II. Title.
HM291.B243 301.6′33 76-1293
76 MARC

Bailey, Roscoe J
The Man upstairs, by Roscoe J. Bailey. Parsons, W. Va., McClain Print. Co., 1973.
158 p. 23 cm. $5.95
1. Bailey, Roscoe J., in fiction, drama, poetry, etc. I. Title.
PZ4.B1527 Man 813′.5′4 72–97161
[PS3552.A374] MARC
ISBN 0–87012–142–1

Bailey, Rosemary Eva.
Obstetric and gynaecological nursing. Rosemary E. Bailey. 2d ed. London, Baillière, Tindall, 1975.
viii, 343 p. ill. 19 cm. (Nurses' aide series)
Includes index.
1. Obstetrical nursing. 2. Gynecologic nursing. I. Title.
TU NUC77-82653

Bailey, Rosemary Eva.
Pharmacology for nurses. Rosemary E. Bailey. 4th ed. London, Bailliere Tindall, 1975.
vii, 383 p. 19 cm. (Nurses' aids series)
Includes index.
1. Pharmacology. I. Title.
MiEM NUC77-82654

Bailey, Rosemary Eva
see Mayes, Mary. Mayes' midwifery: a text-book for midwives. 8th ed. London, Baillière Tindall, 1972.

Bailey, Rosemary Eva
see St. John Ambulance Association and Brigade. Maternal and child health manual... London, British Red Cross Society, 1972.

Bailey, Roy Victor.
Contemporary social problems in Britain, edited by Roy Bailey and Jock Young. Farnborough, Saxon House [Lexington, Mass., Lexington Books, 1973.
xiv, 194 p. 24 cm. £3.00 GB 73–22056
Includes bibliographies.
1. Delinquents—Great Britain—Addresses, essays, lectures. 2. Deviant behavior—Addresses, essays, lectures. I. Young, Jock, joint author. II. Title.
HV6944.B33 362′.042′0942 73–3729
ISBN 0–347–01017–2 MARC

Bailey, Roy Victor.
see Radical social work. London, Edward Arnold, 1975.

Bailey, Roy Victor.
see Radical social work. 1st American ed. New York, Pantheon Books, c1975.

Bailey, Rubelia Johnson, 1926-
The relationship of educational background, socio-economic status, level of aspiration, and intelligence to success in business education. [Philadelphia] 1964 [c1965]
vii, 166 l. tables. 20 cm.
Thesis—Temple University.
Bibliography: leaves [160]-166.
Reproduced by Xerox process.
1. Prediction of scholastic success.
I. Title.
MsU NUC76-68663

Bailey (Russell D.) and Associates
see Russell D. Bailey and Associates.

Bailey, Ruth.
Shelley. [Folcroft, Pa.] Folcroft Library Editions, 1974.
143 p. 22 cm.
Reprint of the 1934 ed. published by Duckworth, London, which was issued as no. 39 of Great lives.
Includes bibliographical references.
1. Shelley, Percy Bysshe, 1792–1822—Biography.
PR5431.B3 1974 821′.7 [B] 74–1442
ISBN 0–8414–9910–1 (lib. bdg.) MARC

Bailey, S. W.
see also
Bailey, Sturges W 1919-

[Bailey, Samuel] 1791-1870.
A review of Berkeley's Theory of vision, designed to show the unsoundness of that celebrated speculation. By Samuel Bailey. London, J. Ridgway, 1842; [Ann Arbor, Xerox University Microfilms, 1976]
iv, 239 p. 22 cm.
This is an authorized facsimile of the original book, and was produced in 1976 by microfilm-xerography.
Bibliographical foot-notes.
1. Berkeley, George, bp. of Cloyne, 1685-1753. A new theory of vision. 2. Sight.
I. Title.
AzU NUC77-89898

Bailey, Samuel Longstreth, 1936-
Nationalism and organized labor in Argentina, 1890-1955. [n.p.] 1965.
255 p.
Thesis—University of Pennsylvania.
Microfilm copy by University Microfilms.
1. Nationalism—Argentine Republic. 2. Trade-unions—Argentine Republic—Political activity.
I. Title.
NcU NUC73-47548

Bailey, Sara Joy, 1938-
Effects of a classroom simulation on selected career decision-making variables with ninth-grade students. [Gainesville] 1973.
x, 103 l. illus. 28 cm.
Typescript.
Thesis (Ed. D.)—University of Florida.
Vita.
Bibliography: leaves 99-100.
1. Personnel service in secondary education.
I. Title.
FU NUC75-17211

Bailey, Sharon Lee, joint author.
see Shiffrin, Nancy. Acupressure. Canoga Park, Calif., Major Books, c1976.

Bailey, Stanley John.
The law of wills: including intestacy and administration of assets; an introduction to the rules of law equity and construction relating to testamentary dispositions, by S. J. Bailey. 7th ed. London, Pitman, 1973.
lxiii, 364 p. 26 cm. £7.00 GB 73–22577
Includes bibliographical references and index.
1. Wills—Great Britain. I. Title.
KD1509.B3 1973 346′.42′054 73–179672
ISBN 0–273–31591–9 MARC

Bailey, Stephen.
Practical planning ability in children: the growth of the ability to sequence a series of real-life events in a logical fashion. New Brunswick, N. J., 1974.
ix, 67 l. illus. 29 cm.
Thesis (Ph. D.)—Rutgers University.
Bibliography: leaf 56.
Vita: leaf 67.
1. Cognition (Child psychology) 2. Cognition—Ability testing. I. Title.
NjR NUC76-15653

Bailey, Stephen Kemp.
Alternative paths to the high school diploma [by] Stephen K. Bailey, Francis U. Macy [and] Donn F. Vickers. [Reston, Va., National Association of Secondary School Principals, 1973]
63 p. 20 cm. $2.00
"Prepared by the Policy Institute, Syracuse University Research Corporation."
1. Education, Cooperative. I. Macy, Francis U., joint author. II. Vickers, Donn F., joint author. III. Syracuse University Research Corporation. Policy Institute. IV. Title.
LB1029.C6B28 373.1′2′912 74–152730
ISBN 0–88210–049–1 MARC

Bailey, Stephen Kemp.
Education interest groups in the Nation's Capital / Stephen K. Bailey. — Washington : American Council on Education, [1975]
xiii, 87 p. ; 22 cm.
Includes bibliographical references and index.
ISBN 0-8268-1265-1 : $7.50
1. Education and state—United States. 2. Pressure groups. 3. Lobbying. I. Title.
LC89.B33 379.73 75-22279
75 MARC

Bailey, Stephen Kemp.
Preparing administrators for conflict resolution [by] Stephen K. Bailey. Washington, American Council on Education, 1971.
233-239 p. 25 cm.
"Reprinted from the Summer 1971 issue of the Educational Record."
1. Universities and colleges—Administration. I. Title.
MsU NUC74-117988

Bailey, Stephen Kemp.
The purposes of education / by Stephen Bailey. — Bloomington, Ind. : Phi Delta Kappa Educational Foundation, c1976.
xvii, 142 p. ; 23 cm. — (Perspectives in American education)
Bibliography: p. 115-132.
Includes index.
ISBN 0-87367-408-1. ISBN 0-87367-414-6 pbk. : $5.00
1. Education—Aims and objectives. I. Title. II. Series.
LB41.B254 370.11 75-15300
76 MARC

Bailey, Stephen Kemp.
Schoolmen and politics; a study of State aid to education in the Northeast [by] Stephen K. Bailey [and others. Syracuse, N.Y.] Syracuse University Press, 1962. [Ann Arbor, Mich., University Microfilms, 1970]
xv, 111 p. 22 cm. (The Economics and politics of public education, 1)
A facsimile reproduction of the original edition.
Bibliographical footnotes.
1. Education and state. U.S. I. Title. II. Series.
OrU NUC73-84180

Bailey, Stephen Kemp.
see American Council on Education. Higher education in the world community. Washington, American Council on Education, c1977.

Bailey, Stephen Kemp
see The Effective use of resources: Financial. [Washington, Association of Governing Boards of Universities and Colleges, 1974]

Bailey, Stephen Kemp
see Research frontiers in politics and government. West port, Conn., Greenwood Press [1973, c1955]

Bailey, Stephen Kemp, joint author
see Schattschneider, Elmer Eric, 1892-
A guide to the study of public affairs. Westport, Conn., Greenwood Press [1973, c1952]

Bailey, Sturges W., 1919-
see International Clay Conference, Mexico (City), 1975. Proceedings of the International Clay Conference, 1975, Mexico City, Mexico, July 16-23, 1975. Wilmette, Ill., Applied Pub., c1976.

Bailey, Susan Lee Ferrall, 1944-
Sir Robert Herbert: the attitudes and influence of a permanent undersecretary in the Colonial Office, 1871-1892. Nashville, Tenn., [c1971, 1974]
vi, 245 l.
Thesis–Vanderbilt University.
Microfilm. Ann Arbor, Mich., University Microfilms, 1974. 1 reel.
1. Herbert, Sir Robert George Wyndham, 1831-1905. 2. Gt. Brit.–Colonies–Administration. 3. Gt. Brit. Colonial Office. I. Title.
IaU NUC75-23602

Bailey, Susan McGee.
Political socialization among children in Bogotá, Colombia. [n.p.] 1971 [c1972]
x, 157 l.
Thesis–University of Michigan.
Bibliography: leaves 154-157.
Microfilm. Ann Arbor, Mich., University Microfilms, 1972. 1 reel. 35 mm.
1. Children and politics. 2. Political socialization. 3. Role expectation. 4. Public opinion–Bogotá. I. Title.
TxU NUC75-34825

Bailey, Sydney Dawson.
Peaceful settlement of international disputes; some proposals for research, by Sydney D. Bailey. [3d. rev. ed. New York, United Nations Institute for Training and Research, 1971]
57 p. 23 cm. (UNITAR PS no. 1)
Second rev. ed. published in 1970 under title: Peaceful settlements of disputes.
Includes bibliographical references.
1. Pacific settlement of international disputes. I. Title. II. Series: United Nations Institute for Training and Research. UNITAR PS no. 1.
JX4473.B3 1971 341.5'8 73-171613
MARC

Bailey, Sydney Dawson.
The procedure of the UN Security Council / Sydney D. Bailey. — Oxford [Eng.] : Clarendon Press, 1975.
xii, 424 p. ; 22 cm. GB***
Includes bibliographical references and index.
ISBN 0-19-827199-9 : £10.00
1. United Nations. Security Council. I. Title.
JX1977.A593B34 341.23'2 76-355298
76 MARC

Bailey, Terence.
The ceremonies and chants of the processions of the Western Church, with special attention to the practice of the Cathedral Church of Salisbury. [Seattle] 1968.
vi, 340 l. illus., music.
Thesis–University of Washington.
Vita.
Bibliography: leaves [330]-340.
Microfilm of typescript. Ann Arbor, Mich., University Microfilms, 1969. 1 reel. 35 mm.
1. Chants (Plain, Gregorian, etc.)–Cathedral. I. Title.
OU NUC73-126480

Bailey, Terence.
The intonation formulas of Western Chant / by Terence Bailey. — Toronto: Pontifical Institute of Mediaeval Studies, 1974.
vii, 101 p. : music ; 25 cm. — (Studies and texts - Pontifical Institute of Mediaeval Studies ; 28) C***
Bibliography: p. 98.
Includes index.
ISBN 0-88844-028-6
1. Music—History and criticism—Medieval, 400-1500. 2. Tonarius. 3. Chants (Plain, Gregorian, etc.)—History and criticism. I. Title. II. Series: Pontifical Institute of Mediaeval Studies. Studies and texts ; 28.
ML174.B26 783.5 75-306925
MARC

Bailey, Terrell Wayne, 1935-
Inspection and control of nuclear armaments in a nation-state system: United States-Russian disarmament negotiations, 1945-1962. [n.p., c1964]
iv, 310 l.
Thesis (Ph.D.)–University of Florida, 1963.
Microfilm of typescript. Ann Arbor, Mich., University Microfilms [1964] 1 reel. 35 mm.
1. Atomic weapons and disarmament. 2. U.S.–For. rel.–Russia. 3. Russia–For. rel.–U.S. I. Title.
WHi NUC74-118240

Bailey, Theodore B., 1940-
see International Conference on Quantitative Genetics, Ames, Iowa, 1976. Proceedings of the International Conference on Quantitative Genetics, August 16-21, 1976. 1st ed. Ames, Iowa State University Press, 1977.

Bailey, Thomas Andrew, 1902-
The American pageant : a history of the Republic / Thomas A. Bailey. — 5th ed. — Lexington, Mass. : Heath, [1975]
1092, lvi p., [8] leaves of plates : ill. ; 25 cm.
Includes bibliographies and index.
ISBN 0-669-82982-X
1. United States—History. I. Title.
E178.1.B15 1975 973 74-9327
MARC

Bailey, Thomas Andrew, 1902- comp.
The American spirit; United States history as seen by contemporaries. Selected and edited with introductions and commentary by Thomas A. Bailey. 3d ed. Lexington, Mass., Heath [1973-
v. illus. 26 cm.
Includes bibliographies.
1. United States—History—Sources. I. Title.
E173.B242 973'.08 72-9253
ISBN 0-669-84384-9 MARC

Bailey, Thomas Andrew, 1902-
A diplomatic history of the American people [by] Thomas A. Bailey. 9th ed. Englewood Cliffs, N. J., Prentice-Hall [1974]
1062, xli p. illus. 24 cm.
Includes bibliographies.
1. United States—Foreign relations. I. Title.
E183.7.B29 1974 327.73 74-8875
ISBN 0-13-214718-1 MARC

Bailey, Thomas Andrew, 1902-
The Lusitania disaster : an episode in modern warfare and diplomacy / Thomas A. Bailey and Paul B. Ryan. — New York : Free Press, [1975]
xv, 383 p., [8] leaves of plates : ill. ; 24 cm.
Bibliography: p. 341-342.
Includes index.
ISBN 0-02-901240-6
1. Lusitania (Steamship) 2. European War, 1914-1918—Naval operations. I. Ryan, Paul B., joint author. II. Title.
D592.L8B34 940.4'514 75-2806
75 MARC

Bailey, Thomas Andrew, 1902-
Probing America's past; a critical examination of major myths and misconceptions [by] Thomas A. Bailey. Lexington, Mass., Heath [1973]
2 v. (xiv, 863 p.) maps. 24 cm.
Chapter 21 (p. 401-431) is included in each volume.
Includes bibliographical references.
1. United States—History. I. Title.
E178.1.B152 973 72-5147
ISBN 0-669-84350-4 (v. 1) MARC

Bailey, Thomas Andrew, 1902-
Voices of America : the Nation's story in slogans, sayings, and songs / Thomas A. Bailey, with the assistance of Stephen M. Dobbs. — New York : Free Press, c1976.
viii, 520 p. : ill. ; 25 cm.
Bibliography: p. 504-508.
Includes index.
ISBN 0-02-901260-0
1. United States—History. 2. Quotations, American. 3. Slogans. 4. Songs, American—Texts. I. Title.
E179.B16 973 76-8143
76 MARC

Bailey, Thomas Cullen.
The late novels of Sir Walter Scott. St. Louis, 1974.
v, 163 l.
Thesis–Washington University.
Includes bibliography.
1. Scott, Sir Walter, Bart., 1771-1832. I. Title.
MoSW NUC76-15657

Bailey, Thomas David, 1897-
An odyssey in education, by Thomas D. Bailey, Superintendent of Public Instruction, State of Florida, January 1949-October 1965. [n.p.] 1974.
126 p. illus., ports. 24 cm.
1. Education–Florida. 2. Florida. State Dept. of Education. I. Title.
FU NUC75-17210

Bailey, Thomas Frank.
Iron carbonyl chemistry of l-acetoxybutadiene. [Boulder] 1972.
xi, 218 l. illus.
Thesis (Ph.D.)–University of Colorado.
Bibliography: leaves [208]-218.
1. Organoiron compounds. I. Title.
CoU NUC74-122981

Bailey, Thomas Grahame, 1872-1942.
An English-Panjabi dictionary / T. Grahame Bailey. — Delhi : Ess Ess Publications, 1976.
xvi, 159 p. ; 23 cm.
Reprint of the 1919 ed. published by the author, Calcutta, under title: An English-Panjabi vocabulary of 5800 words.
Rs40.00
1. English language—Dictionaries—Panjabi. I. Title.
PK2636.B3 1976 76-911214
77 MARC

Bailey, Thomas Grahame, 1872-1942.
Linguistic studies from the Himalayas, being studies in the grammar of fifteen Himalayan dialects / by T. Grahame Bailey. — New Delhi : Asian Publication Services, 1975.
xv, 277 p. ; 22 cm.
"A continuation and, so far as some districts are concerned, a completion of vol. XII of the Society's monographs, entitled The languages of the northern Himalayas."
"First APS reprint."
Reprint of the 1915 ed. published by the Royal Asiatic Society, London, as Asiatic Society monographs, v. 18.
Rs65.00
1. Indo-Aryan languages, Modern. 2. Tibeto-Burman languages. 3. Himalaya Mountains—Languages. I. Title. II. Series: Asiatic Society monographs ; v. 18.
PK1508.B33 1975 495'.49 75-905041
76 MARC

Bailey, Thomas Grahame, 1872-1942.
Studies in Northern Himalayan dialects. Calcutta, Baptist Mission Press, 1903.
1 v. (various pagings) 24 cm.
Published also as a section of the author's The languages of the Northern Himalayas, London, 1908.
1. Indo-Aryan languages, Modern. 2. Himalaya Mountains—Languages. 3. Chamba Lahuli dialect. I. Title.
PK1508.B34 495.49 74-187585
MARC

Bailey, Thomas Grahame, 1872-
see Kellogg, Samuel Henry, 1839-1899.
A grammar of the Hindi language... New Delhi, Oriental Books Reprint Corp. [1972]

Bailey, Thomas Melville, 1912-
The covenant in Canada / by T. M. Bailey. — Hamilton, Ont. : Macnab, 1975.
160 p. : ill. ; 19 x 24 cm. C***
Cover title.
ISBN 0-919874-02-9
1. Presbyterian Church in Canada. 2. Presbyterian Church in Canada—Biography. I. Title.
BX9001.B34 285'.271 76-357174
76 MARC

Bailey, Thomas Melville, 1912-
Hamilton famous and fascinating : two centuries of a colourful city / by Thomas Melville Bailey and Charles Ambrose Carter. — Hamilton, Ont. : W. L. Griffin, 1972.
72 p. : ill., ports. ; 28 cm. C***
Includes index.
1. Hamilton, Ont.—Biography. I. Carter, Charles Ambrose, joint author. II. Title.
F1059.5.H2B26 971.3'52 75-321201
75 MARC

Bailey, Thomas Melville, 1912–
Hamilton firsts / by Thomas Melville Bailey and Charles Ambrose Carter. — Hamilton, Ont. : T. M. Bailey and C. A. Carter, 1973.
72 p. : ill., facsims., ports. ; 28 cm. C 74-2988-6
Includes index.
1. Hamilton, Ont.—Biography. 2. Hamilton, Ont.—History—Miscellanea. I. Carter, Charles Ambrose, joint author. II. Title.
F1059.5.H2B27 920'.0713'52 75–302668
MARC

Bailey, Thomas Melville, 1912–
The surprise, written by T. Melville Bailey. Illustrated by Janet I. Bailey. [Hamilton, Ont., Printed by W. L. Griffin, 1969]
[24] p. illus. (A Sophia MacNab story book)
"Based on Sophia MacNab's Diary, written in 1846."
I. Macnab, Sophia Mary, 1832-1917.
CaOTP NUC75-84597

Bailey, Thomas Melville, 1912–
Up and down Hamilton, by Thomas Melville Bailey and Charles Ambrose Carter. Hamilton, W. L. Griffin, 1971.
1 v. (unpaged) illus., map, ports. 20 x 24 cm. $3.95 C 72-103
On cover: Up and down Hamilton, 1770's to 1970's; a history in pictures.
1. Hamilton, Ont.—History—Pictorial works. I. Carter, Charles Ambrose, joint author. II. Title.
F1059.H28B34 917.13'52 74–156411
MARC

Bailey, Thomas Melville, 1912– ed.
see MacNab, Sophia Mary, 1832-1917. The diary of Sophia MacNab. 2d ed., rev. Hamilton, Ont., W. L. Griffin, 1974.

Bailey, Thomas R., joint author.
see Schmalz, Larry C. Beginner's computer glossary for managers and businessmen. [1st ed.] Newport Beach, Calif., Newport Computer Information, [1972]

Bailey, Thomas R., joint author
see Schmalz, Larry C Beginning computer glossary for businessmen. New York, Funk & Wagnalls [1973, c1972]

Bailey, Trevor.
Sir Gary : a biography / Trevor Bailey ; foreword by Richie Benaud. — London : Collins, 1976.
190 p. : ill. ; 22 cm. GB***
ISBN 0-00-216764-6 : £3.95
1. Sobers, Garfield, Sir. 2. Cricket players—Barbados—Biography. I. Title.
GV915.S6B34 796.358'092'4 76-378545
76 MARC

Bailey, Vern Dixon.
Fielding's politics. [n.p.] 1970.
285 p.
Thesis—University of California.
Bibliography: leaves 265-285.
Photocopy of typescript. Ann Arbor, Mich., Xerox University Microfilms, 1974. 22 cm.
1. Fielding, Henry, 1707-1754. I. Title.
ViU NUC76-26920

Bailey, Voris G
Effects of tokens with back-up reinforcers on behavior of emotionally disturbed visually handicapped children. [Lawrence, 1974]
vii, 98 l. illus. 28 cm.
Thesis (D. Ed.)—University of Kansas.
Bibliography: leaves 92-98.
1. Visually handicapped children. 2. Operant behavior. 3. Reinforcement (Psychology) I. Title.
KU NUC76-15509

Bailey, W B
Trinity Bay, Newfoundland survey - September 1956. [St. Andrews, N. B.] Atlantic Oceanographic Group, 1958.
1 v. (various pagings) 28 cm. (Canada. Fisheries Research Board. Manuscript report series (Oceanographic and limnological) no. 10)
"Programmed by the Canadian Committee on Oceanography."
1. Oceanography—Trinity Bay, Newfoundland. I. Canada. Fisheries Research Board. Atlantic Oceanographic Group, St. Andrews, N. B. II. Canada. Committee on Oceanography. III. Title. IV. Series.
DME NUC75-55126

Bailey, W. R.
see
Bailey, Warren R

Bailey, W S
Veterinarians for the South; a further appraisal [by] W. S. Bailey. Atlanta, Southern Regional Education Board, 1973.
38, [15] l.
"Appendix A: Areas of specialization and types of employers of veterinarians in SREB states": [15] leaves.
1. Veterinary medicine—Manpower. 2. Veterinary medicine—Education—U. S. 3. Schools, Veterinary—U. S. I. Southern Regional Education Board. II. Title.
CU-AM NUC76-33600

Bailey, W Williams-
see
Williams-Bailey, W

Bailey, Wallace, 1924-
Birds of the Cape Cod National Seashore and adjacent areas. South Wellfleet, Mass. [Eastern National Park and Monument Association, 1968]
119 p. illus. 22 cm.
1. Birds—Massachusetts—Cape Cod National Seashore. 2. Cape Cod National Seashore. I. Title.
QL684.M4B34 598.2'09744'92 76-355405
76 MARC

Bailey, Walter, 1528 or 9–1592.
A short discourse of the three kindes of peppers in common vse, and certaine special medicines made of the same, tending to the preseruation of health. [London?] 1588. [Amsterdam, Theatrum Orbis Terrarum; New York, Da Capo Press, 1972]
1 v. (unpaged) 16 cm. (The English experience, its record in early printed books published in facsimile, no. 425)
On cover: A short discourse of peppers.
S. T. C. no. 1199.
1. Pepper (Spice)—Therapeutic use. 2. Medicine—15th-18th centuries. I. Title. II. Title: A short discourse of peppers. III. Series.
RM666.P38B34 1588a 77–38145
ISBN 90-221-0425-7 615'.323'925 MARC
rev

Bailey, Walter, 1528 or 9-1592.
Two treatises concerning eie-sight / Walter Bailey (Joh. Fernelius and Joh. Riolanus). — Amsterdam : Theatrum Orbis Terrarum ; Norwood, N.J. : W. J. Johnson, 1975.
62 p. ; 16 cm. — (The English experience, its record in early printed books published in facsimile ; no. 709)
Photoreprint ed.
Includes original t.p.: Two treatises concerning the preservation of eie-sight, the first written by Doctor Baily sometimes of Oxford; the other collected out of those two famous phisicions Fernelius and Riolanus. Oxford, printed by Joseph Barnes for John Barnes, 1616.
"S.T.C. no. 1196."
ISBN 9022107094
1. Ophthalmology—Early works to 1800. I. Fernel, Jean, 1497-1558. II. Riolan, Jean, 1538-1605. III. Title. IV. Series.
RE41.B23 1975 617.7 76-361418
76 MARC

Bailey, Walter C
Drug use among white and nonwhite college activists. Prepared by Walter C. Bailey and Mary Koval. [Albany?] New York State Narcotic Addiction Control Commission, 1970.
22 p. 28 cm.
"Project 12/68F."
Includes bibliographical references.
1. Drug abuse — United States. 2. College students — United States—Conduct of life. 3. College students—United States—Political activity. I. Koval, Mary, joint author. II. New York (State). Narcotic Addiction Control Commission. III. Title.
HV5825.B33 394.1 73–621370
MARC

Bailey, Waneta Elsie Hickman, 1885-
A genealogy of family records / by Waneta Elsie Hickman Bailey ; associate editor, Mary Irene Hickman. — Champaign, Ill. : Bailey, 1973 [i.e. 1974]
52 p. ; 23 cm.
Cover title: Descendants of William and Mary Hickman, 1696 [to] 1974.
On spine: Hickman genealogy.
1. Hickman family. I. Hickman, Mary Irene, 1867-1965, joint author. II. Title. III. Title: Descendants of William and Mary Hickman, 1966 [to] 1974. IV. Title: Hickman genealogy.
CS71.H626 1973 929'.2'0973 75-311529
75 MARC

Bailey, Warren R
Grain stocks issues and alternatives : a progress report / [by W. R. Bailey, F. A. Kutish, and A. S. Rojko]. — [Washington] : U.S. Dept. of Agriculture, Economic Research Service, [1974]
iv, 42 p. ; 26 cm.
"Agricultural economic research report."
1. Grain trade. 2. Grain storage. I. Kutish, Francis A., joint author. II. Rojko, Anthony Stanley, 1918- joint author. III. United States. Dept. of Agriculture. Economic Research Service. IV. Title.
HD9030.6.B34 338.1'7'31 74-601168
75 MARC

Bailey, Weldon Joseph.
Member satisfaction as related to a reconfiguration in organization structure. [Normal, Ill.] Illinois State University, 1975, c1976.
viii, 191 l. diagrs., tables. (Illinois. State University, Normal. Doctoral dissertations, no. 157)
INS NUC77-86025

Bailey, Wilfrid Charles
see Rice, Marion J The development of a sequential curriculum in anthropology, grades 1-7. Athens, 1971.

Bailey, William, joint author
see Knoohuizen, Ralph. The selection and hiring of Chicago policemen. [Evanston] 1973.

Bailey, William A
Building hobby greenhouses. [Slightly rev. Jan. 1975. Washington, U.S. Govt. Print. Off., 1975]
19, [1] p. illus. (U.S. Dept. of Agriculture. Agriculture information bulletin no. 357)
Bibliography: p. [18]
1. Greenhouses. I. Liu, Robert C. II. Klueter, Herschel Henry, 1932- III. Title. IV. Series.
AAP NUC77-82702

Bailey, William A 1895–
Bill Bailey came home: as a farm boy, as a stowaway at the age of nine, a trapper at the age of fifteen, and a hobo at the age of sixteen, by William A. Bailey. Edited by Austin and Alta Fife. Logan, Utah State University Press [1973]
183 p. illus. 23 cm.
1. Bailey, William A., 1895– 2. Idaho—Social life and customs. 3. Tramps—United States. I. Title.
F746.B255A32 917.96'03'30924 73–79904
ISBN 0-87421-061-5 MARC

Bailey, William Anthony.
Stability analysis by limiting equilibrium. [Cambridge, Mass.] 1966.
63, [34], 64-68, [29] l. illus.
Thesis—Massachusetts Institute of Technology.
Bibliography: leaf 53.
Microfilm (positive) [Cambridge, Mass., Microreproduction Laboratory] M. I. T. Libraries, 1966. 1 reel.
1. Slopes (Soil mechanics) 2. Stability. 3. Programming. (Electronic computers) I. Title.
NNC NUC73-40502

Bailey, William C
The economic water supply in Idaho / William C. Bailey, Roger B. Long. — Moscow : Agricultural Experiment Station, University of Idaho, College of Agriculture, 1976.
20 p. : graphs ; 28 cm. — (Research bulletin - Agricultural Experiment Station, University of Idaho ; no. 92)
Cover title.
Bibliography: p. 20.
1. Water-supply—Idaho—Costs. I. Long, Roger B., joint author. II. Title. III. Series: Idaho. Agricultural Experiment Station, Moscow. Research bulletin ; no. 92.
TD224.I2B34 338.4'3 76-623437
76 MARC

Bailey, William Edward, 1935-
Differentiation and correlation: a paradigm of human information processing. [n.p., 1975]
1 v.
Thesis (Ph.D.)—Northwestern University.
1. Human information processing. 2. Speech—Research. 3. Communication. I. Title.
IEN NUC77-82710

Bailey, William Jay, 1929–
Managing self-renewal in secondary education [by] William J. Bailey. Englewood Cliffs, N. J., Educational Technology Publications [1975]
xx, 185 p. illus. 24 cm.
Includes bibliographical references.
ISBN 0-87778-074-9
1. High schools—Administration. 2. Classroom management. I. Title.
LB2822.B18 373.1'2 74–13352
MARC

Bailey, William Jay, 1929-
see Degrading the grading myths ... Washington, Association for Supervision and Curriculum Development, c1976.

Bailey, William Michael, 1937-
The price revolution, population growth and agricultural change in Tudor England. [College Park, Md.] 1973 [c1974]
2 v. illus. 29 cm.
Typescript.
Thesis—University of Maryland.
Vita.
Includes bibliography.
1. Gt. Brit.—Econ. condit. 2. Prices—Hist. 3. Agriculture—Economic aspects—Gt. Brit. I. Title.
MdU NUC76-26919

Bailey, William Michael, 1937-
The price revolution, population growth and agricultural change in Tudor England. [Ann Arbor, Mich., University Microfilms, 1974]
380 l. 22 cm.
Thesis—University of Maryland.
Bibliography: leaves 358-380.
ICN NUC76-15656

Bailey, William R
A management assistance approach for banks making high risk loans to black owned businesses. New Brunswick, N.J., 1973.
iv, 115 l. 29 cm.
Thesis—Stonier Graduate School of Banking.
Bibliography: leaves 112-115.
1. Bank loans. 2. Negro businessmen. I. Title.
NjR NUC75-17209

Bailey, William Robert, 1917-
Diagnostic microbiology; a laboratory manual [by] W. Robert Bailey [and] Elvyn G. Scott. Saint Louis, C.V. Mosby Co., 1970.
vii, 123 p. illus. 28 cm.
1. Microbiology—Laboratory manuals. 2. Microorganisms, Pathogenic. I. Scott, Elvyn G., joint author. II. Title.
NcGU NjR NUC74-118237

Bailey, William Robert, 1917-
Diagnostic microbiology; a textbook for the isolation and identification of pathogenic microorganisms [by] W. Robert Bailey [and] Elvyn G. Scott. 3d ed. Saint Louis, C. V. Mosby Co., [1970]
x, 385 p. illus. 27 cm.
Includes bibliographical references.
1. Medical microbiology — Laboratory manuals. 2. Micro-organisms, Pathogenic—Identification. I. Scott, Elvyn G., joint author. II. Title.
QR63.B2 1970 616.01 70-102126
SBN 8016-0419-2 rev MARC

Bailey, William Robert, 1917-
Diagnostic microbiology; a textbook for the isolation and identification of pathogenic microorganisms [by] W. Robert Bailey [and] Elvyn G. Scott. 4th ed. Saint Louis, Mosby, 1974.
xi, 414 p. illus. 27 cm.
Includes bibliographies.
1. Medical microbiology—Laboratory manuals. 2. Micro-organisms, Pathogenic—Identification. I. Scott, Elvyn G., joint author. II. Title.
[DNLM: 1. Microbiology—Laboratory manuals. QW 25 B156d 1974]
QR46.B26 1974 616.01 74-2482
ISBN 0-8016-0420-6 MARC

Bailey, Zeno Earl, 1921-
Evaluation of selected aspects of the pre-service curriculum in agricultural education at the Alabama Polytechnic Institute. Ann Arbor, Mich., University Microfilms [1956]
1 reel. 35 mm. (University Microfilms, 15,807)
Microfilm (positive) of typescript.
Thesis (Ph.D.)—Ohio State University, 1955.
Collation of the original: 357 l.
1. Agricultural education—Alabama. I. Title.
PSt NUC73-9453

Bailey-Roth, Karol Ann, 1947-
A test of the "important, aversive consequences" notion in forced compliance research. [n.p.] 1975.
98 l.
Thesis—Ohio State University.
Bibliography: leaves 95-98.
1. Dissonance (Psychology) 2. Choice (Psychology) I. Title.
OU NUC77-82707

Bailey and Associates
see Russell D. Bailey and Associates

Bailey Association
see Madrid, N.Y. Planning Board. The Madrid-Norfolk town plans... [Utica, N.Y., 1973]

Bailey Association
see Norfolk, N.Y. Land use and development code. [Utica, N.Y.] 1973.

Bailey Institute of Inter-Racial Studies
see
Abe Bailey Institute of Inter-Racial Studies.

Bailhache, Jean, 1911-
Grande-Bretagne. [Paris, Éditions du Seuil, 1972, c1960]
189 p. illus., ports. 18 cm. (Collections Microcosme. Petite planète, 24) 8.50F F***
1. Great Britain. I. Title.
DA27.5.B35 73-322027

Bailhache, Patrice.
see Poinsot, Louis, 1777-1859. La théorie générale de l'équilibre et du mouvement des systèmes. Éd. critique et commentaires. Paris, J. Vrin, 1975.

Bailie, Helena.
Instructor's manual for Horton and Hunt: Sociology, 2d ed. New York, McGraw-Hill [c1968]
iv, 107 p. 26 cm.
1. Sociology. I. Horton, Paul B. Sociology. II. Title.
OU NUC73-59516

Bailie, R E
V.T.E. desalting plant, St. Croix, U.S. Virgin Islands: analysis of operational data, by R.E. Bailie and O.J. Morin. Washington, 1972.
103 p. illus. (U.S. Office of Saline Water. Research and development progress report no. no. 778)
Prepared for U.S. Office of Saline Water by Desalting Systems and Services, Inc., under contract no. 14-30-2743.
1. Saline water conversion. 2. Saline water conversion plants—Virgin Islands—St. Croix. I. Morin, O.J., joint author. II. Desalting Systems and Services, inc. III. United States. Office of Saline Water. IV. Title. V. Series.
DI NUC74-10173

Bailiff, Ron.
see Architectural practice in Europe. London, published for the Royal Institute of British Architects and the Architects' Registration Council of the United Kingdom by RIBA Publications, 1974-

Bailin, David.
Weak interactions / David Bailin. — London : published for Sussex University Press by Chatto & Windus, 1977.
ix, 406 p. ; 24 cm. — (Graduate student series in physics) GB77-08997
Includes bibliographical references and index.
ISBN 0-85621-023-4 : £9.00
1. Weak interactions (Nuclear physics) I. Title. II. Series.
QC794.8.W4B34 1977 539.7'54 75-34572
77 MARC

Bailin, Roxanne.
"One of the last human hunts of civilization, and the basest and most brutal of them all." Research and writing: Roxanne Bailin. Introd.: Aubrey Grossman. San Francisco [Justice for the Pitt River Tribe] 1971.
[4], 22 p. 21 cm.
Includes bibliographical references.
1. Indians of North America—California. 2. Indians, Treatment of—U.S. 3. Achomawi Indians. I. Justice for the Pitt River Tribe. II. Title.
IEN NUC73-73586

Bailin, Zehavah
see
Beilin, Zehava.

Bailis, Lawrence A
The concept of death in children's literature on death. [n.p., n.d.]
1 v.
Thesis—Case Western Reserve University.
OClW NUC76-50481

Bailis, Lawrence Neil.
Bread or justice: grassroots organizing in the welfare rights movement. Lexington, Mass., Lexington Books [1974]
xviii, 175 p. 23 cm.
Includes bibliographical references.
1. Welfare Rights Movement—Massachusetts. 2. National Welfare Rights Organization. I. Title.
HV98.M39B3 322.4'4 73-15278
ISBN 0-669-91157-7 MARC

Bailkey, Nels M comp.
Readings in ancient history : from Gilgamesh to Diocletian / edited and with introductions by Nels M. Bailkey. — 2d ed. — Lexington, Mass. : Heath, c1976.
x, 467 p. : ill. ; 24 cm.
ISBN 0-669-00249-6
1. History, Ancient—Sources. I. Title.
D52.B3 1976 930'.08 76-762
76 MARC

Bailkey, Nels M.
see Wallbank, Thomas Walter, 1901- Civilization past & present... -- 4th ed. [rev.]. -- [Glenview, Ill. : Scott Foresman, c1972.

Bailkey, Nels M., joint author.
see Wallbank, Thomas Walter, 1901- Civilization past & present. Single volume 4th ed. Glenview, Ill., Scott, Foresman, [1975]

Bailkey, Nels M., joint author.
see Wallbank, Thomas Walter, 1901- Civilization past & present. 7th ed. Glenview, Ill., Scott, Foresman, c1976.

Bailkey, Nels M., joint author.
see Wallbank, Thomas Walter, 1901- Western civilization ... Glenview, Ill., Scott-Foresman, c1977.

Bailkey, Nels M., joint author
see Wallbank, Thomas Walter, 1901-
Western perspectives; a concise history of civilization. Glenview, Ill., Scott, Foresman [1973]

Baillairgé, François, 1759-1830.
François Baillairgé et son œuvre, 1759-1830 / catalogue et textes de David Karel, Luc Noppen, Claude Thibault. — Québec : Groupe de recherche en art du Québec de l'Université Laval : distribution, Musée du Québec, 1975.
85 p. : ill. ; 22 x 28 cm. C***
Catalog of an exhibition held at the Musée du Québec.
Includes bibliographical references.
1. Baillairgé, François, 1759-1830. I. Karel, David. II. Noppen, Luc, joint author. III. Thibault, Claude, joint author. IV. Quebec (City). Musée de la province de Québec. V. Title.
N6549.B34K37 709'.2'4 76-461799
76 MARC

Baillargeat, René.
Les tombeaux de Saint-Martin de Montmorency, par René Baillargeat et Paulette Regnault. Paris, A. et J. Picard, 1972.
vi, 310 p. illus. 24 cm. 40.00F F***
Includes bibliographies.
1. Saint-Martin de Montmorency (Church) — Antiquities. 2. Tombs—France—Montmorency. I. Regnault, Paulette, joint author. II. Title.
DC801.M79B34 73-332388

Baillargeat, René.
see Les Invalides ... Paris, Musée de l'armée, 1974.

Baillargeon, Gérald, 1941-
Modèles mathématiques en sciences de la gestion / par Gérald Baillargeon. — Montréal : Presses de l'Université du Québec, 1973.
xiv, 338 p. : ill. ; 28 cm. C74-5791
Includes bibliographies and index.
ISBN 0-7770-0092-X : $7.00
1. Industrial management—Mathematical models. I. Title.
HD20.4.B34 658.4'001'51 75-504510
75 MARC

Baillargeon, Maurice Kinley, 1923-
Recreation impact on campsite vegetation, by Maurice Kinley Baillargeon. [Vancouver, B.C.] 1975.
ix, 110 l. ill. (some col.) 28 cm.
Thesis (M.Sc.)—University of British Columbia.
Vita.
Bibliography: leaves [69]-81.
1. Camp sites, facilities, etc. 2. Outdoor recreation. 3. Camping. I. Title.
CaBVaU NUC77-84455

Baillargeon, Noël, 1914–
Le séminaire de Québec sous l'épiscopat de Mgr de Laval [par] Noël Baillargeon. Québec, Presses de l'Université Laval, 1972.
308 p. ill., maps, plans. 23 cm. (Les Cahiers de l'Institut d'histoire, 18) $8.00 C 73-321
Bibliography: p. [259]-282.
"Cartographie": p. [283]-286.
Includes index.
1. Quebec (City). Université Laval. Séminaire. 2. Laval de Montmorency, François Xavier de, Bp. of Quebec, 1623-1708. I. Title. II. Series: Quebec (City). Université Laval. Institut d'histoire. Cahiers, 18.
BX920.Q446B34 73-339257

Baillargeon, Pierre.
Les médisances de Claude Perrin / Pierre Baillargeon ; présenté par André Gaulin. — [Réédition]. — Montréal : Éditions du Jour, 1973.
xxii, 197 p. ; 20 cm. C 73-3657
"Distributeur : Messageries du Jour, inc. 8255, ru Durocher, Montraél 303."
$3.25
I. Title.
PQ3919.B17M4 843 74-195657
MARC

Baillargeon, Samuel.
Littérature canadienne-française. 3. éd. revue. Préf. de Lionel Groulx. Montréal, Fides [1972, c1957]
525 p. illus. 25 cm. C***
Bibliography: p. [511]-512.
1. French-Canadian literature—History and criticism. I. Title.
PQ3901.B3 1972 72-362740

Baillat. Philippe.
see A la communale. [Paris] Hachette, c1976.

Baillén, Claude.
Chanel solitaire; translated from the French by Barbara Bray. London, Collins, 1973.
192 p. illus., ports. 24 cm. £2.50 GB 73-26120
1. Chanel, Coco, 1883-1971. I. Title.
TT505.C45B313 746.9'2'0924 [B] 73-179671
ISBN 0-00-211183-7 MARC

Baillén, Claude.
Chanel solitaire / by Claude Baillén ; translated from the French by Barbara Bray. — New York : Quadrangle / New York Times Book Co., 1974, c1973.
192 p. : ill. ; 25 cm.
ISBN 0-8129-0474-5 : $7.95
1. Chanel, Coco, 1883-1971. I. Title.
TT505.C45B313 1974 746.9'2'0924 74-78651
[B] MARC

Baillet, Pierre.
Les rapatriés d'Algérie en France / [par Pierre Baillet]. — [Paris : Documentation française, c1976]
79 p. : ill. ; 27 cm. — (Notes et études documentaires ; nos 4275-4276)
F***
"Cette étude a été établie sur la base d'une thèse de doctorat inédite."—Label on t.p.
Bibliography: p. 78-79.
10.50F
1. Refugees—France. 2. Repatriation—France. 3. French in Algeria. I. Title. II. Series: France. Direction de la documentation. Notes et études documentaires ; nos 4275-4276.
D411.F67 no. 4275-4276 909.8 s 77-465559
[HV640.4.F7] 77 MARC

Baillet de Saint-Julien, Louis Guillaume, baron.
Réflexions sur quelques circonstances présentes contenant deux lettres sur l'exposition des tabeaux au Louvre cette année 1748. Lettre sur la peinture, la sculpture et l'architecture. Lettres sur la peinture à un amateur. Lettre à Mr Ch. ⟨Chardin⟩ sur les caractères en peinture. La Peinture. Poème suivi des Caractères des peintres français actuellement vivants. (Réimpr. des 5 vol. publ. à Paris, Amsterdam et Genève de 1748 à 1755). Genève, Minkoff Reprints, 1972.
5 v. in 1. 22 cm. 120F Sw 73-A-282
1. Art, Modern—17th-18th centuries—France—Addresses, essays, lectures. 2. Art—Early works to 1800—Addresses, essays, lectures. I. Title.
N6846.B3 1972 73-334627

Baillette, A
Propriétés des produits canoniques et fonctions approchables par des sommes d'exponentielles. Sherbrooke, Que., Dépt. de mathemaiques, Université de Sherbrooke, 1971.
34 p. (Séminaire d'analyse moderne, no. 5)
1. Approximation theory. 2. Almost periodic functions. I. Title. II. Series.
NBuU NUC73-126482

Bailleul, Amand.
Ils appelaient cela des roses ... ou des camélias : pièce en trois actes et un épilogue / Amand Bailleul. — Paris : Pensée universelle, [1973]
90 p. ; 18 cm. F***
12.84F
I. Title.
PQ2662.A345 I 4 842'.9'14 74-186712
MARC

Bailleul, Guy.
see Auteuil-Point-du-Jour en cartes postales anciennes. 1. éd. Zaltbommel, Bibliothèque européenne, 1976.

Bailleul, Guylaine de.
L'Onaniste / Guylaine de Bailleul. — [Paris] : É. Losfeld, 1975.
158 p. ; 22 cm. — (Collection Le Second rayon) F76-1098
ISBN 2-85018-067-X : 30.00F
I. Title.
PQ2662.A346O5 843'.9'14 76-455664
76 MARC

Bailleul, Jean Claude, 1944-
see Bruay-en-Artois ou Bruay-en-Poésie?. Le Pallet (44300 Vallet) "Traces" 1974.

Bailleux, A., ed.
see International Congress of Orthopaedic Surgery, 9th, Vienna, 1963. Symposiums et communications particulières... Bruxelles, Impr. des sciences, 1964.

Bailleux, Antoine, d. 1791.
Méthode de guitare par musique et tablature. Genève, Minkoff Reprints [1972]
43 p. music. 39 cm. Sw***
"Réimpression de l'édition de Paris, 1773."
Bound with Lemoine, A. M. Nouvelle méthode courte et facile pour la guitare. Genève, Minkoff Reprints [1972]
1. Guitar—Instruction and study—To 1800. I. Title.
MT582.B15 1972 787'.61'0712 74-160095
MARC

Bailleux, Antoine, d. 1791.
Méthode raisonnée pour apprendre à jouer du violon avec le doigté de cet instrument et les différents agréments dont il est susceptible. Genève, Minkoff Reprints [1972]
46 p. music. 37 cm.
"Réimpression de l'édition de Paris, 1798."
1. Violin—Methods—To 1800. I. Title.
CSt NUC74-613

Baillie, Alexander
see Baillie, F Alexander.

Baillie, Alexander Francis.
Kurrachee (Karachi) past, present, and future. Calcutta, Thacker, Spink, 1890.
xx, 269 p. illus., maps (part fold., part col.) 26 cm.
1. Karachi.
DS392.2.K3B34 1890 49-42550

Baillie, Alexander Francis.
Kurrachee, past, present, and future / Alexander F. Baillie. — Karachi ; New York : Oxford University Press, 1975.
xx, 269 p., [1] leaves of plates : ill., maps (4 fold. col.) ; 25 cm.
Reprint, with added t.p., of 1890 ed. published by Thacker, Spink, Calcutta.
ISBN 0-19-577211-3 : $20.75
1. Karachi. I. Title.
DS392.2.K3B34 1975 954.9'183 75-318516
75 MARC

Baillie, Allan.
Mask maker / Allan Baillie. — London : Macmillan, 1974.
221 p. ; 21 cm. GB75-05877
ISBN 0-333-17159-4 : £3.25
I. Title.
PZ4.B157 Mas 823'.9'14 75-326934
[PR6052.A3193] 75 MARC

Baillie, C P F
Trusts, investment institutions and Canadian tax reforms, by Charles P. F. Baillie. Don Mills, Ont., CCH Canadian [1971]
40 p. 23 cm. C***
1. Trusts and trustees—Taxation—Canada. I. Title.
343'.71'064 74-164171
MARC

Baillie, Donald Macpherson, 1887-1954.
The meaning of Holy Communion, by Donald M. Baillie. [Iona, Scotland, Iona Community Pub. Dept., 196-]
15 p. 19 cm. (The church in the world, no. 1)
Cover title.
1. Lord's Supper. I. Title. II. Series.
CBGTU NUC76-69678

Baillie, F Alexander.
A true information of the unhallowed ofspring progress and impoisoned fruits of our Scottish Calvinian gospel, 1628 [by] Alexander Baillie, [and, A methode, to meditate on the psalter, or great rosane of Our Blessed Ladie, 1958] Menston, Scolar Press, 1972.
[21], 226, [100] p. illus. 22 cm. (English recusant literature, 1558-1640, v. 95) £185.00 for the series B72-15035
Facsimile reprints. A true information ... originally published Wirtsburgh, Anne Marie Volmare, 1628. A methode, to meditate on the psalter ... originally published Antwerp, 1598.
1. Catholic Church—Doctrinal and controversial works—Catholic authors. 2. Protestantism—Controversial literature. 3. Mysteries of the Rosary. I. Title. II. Title: A methode, to meditate on the psalter. III. Series: Rogers, David Morrison, comp. English recusant literature, 1558-1640, v. 95.
BX1750.A1E5 vol. 95 230'.2 s 73-160921
[BX1750] 73[r75]rev MARC
ISBN 0-85417-799-X

Baillie, Frank, 1921–
The beer drinker's companion. Newton Abbot, David & Charles, 1973.
296 p. illus., map. 20 cm. £2.95 GB 74-00072
Includes index.
1. Brewing industry — Great Britain. 2. Hotels, taverns, etc. — Great Britain. I. Title.
TP573.G7B28 641.2'3 74-157077
ISBN 0-7153-6201-1 MARC

Baillie, Granville Hugh. Watchmakers and clockmakers of the world.
see Loomes, Brian. Watchmakers and clockmakers of the world. London, N.A.G. Press, 1976.

Baillie, Granville Hugh
see Britten, Frederick James, 1843-1913. Britten's old clocks and watches and their makers... London, E. Methuen in association with E. & F. Spon [1973]

Baillie, Granville Hugh
see Britten, Frederick James, 1843-1913. Britten's old clocks and watches and their makers... New York, Dutton, 1973.

Baillie, James Black, Sir, 1872-1940.
The origin and significance of Hegel's logic; a general introduction to Hegel's system. London, New York, Macmillan, 1901. [Ann Arbor, Mich., Xerox University Microfilms, 1974]
xviii, 375 p. 21 cm.
"Produced...by microfilm-xerography."
Bibliographical references.
1. Hegel, Georg Wilhelm Friedrich, 1770-1831. 2. Logic. I. Title.
IEN NUC75-19470

Baillie, James Black, Sir, 1872- tr.
see Hegel, Georg Wilhelm Friedrich, 1770-1831. The phenomenology of mind. 2d ed., rev. and cor. throughout. London, G. Allen & Unwin [1964, 1931]

Baillie, James C
Project d'une loi canadienne sur les fonds de placement, par James C. Baillie [et] Warren M. H. Grover. [Ottawa, Information Canada, 1974]
2 v. 25 cm. $5.00 C***
On cover: Consumer and Corporate Affairs.
Issued also under title: Proposals for a Canada mutual funds law.
Bibliography: v. 1, p. 2.
CONTENTS: t. 1. Commentaire.—t. 2. Texte du projet.
1. Investment trusts—Canada. I. Grover, Warren M. H., joint author. II. Canada. Dept. of Consumer and Corporate Affairs. III. Title.
343'.71'052 75-502037
75 MARC

Baillie, James C
Proposals for a Canada mutual funds law, by James C. Baillie [and] Warren M. H. Grover. [Ottawa, Information Canada, 1974]
2 v. 25 cm. $5.00 C***
On cover: Consumer and Corporate Affairs.
Bibliography: v. 1, p. 2.
CONTENTS: v. 1. Commentary.—v. 2. Statute.
1. Investment trusts—Canada. I. Grover, Warren M. H., joint author. II. Canada. Dept. of Consumer and Corporate Affairs. III. Title.
343'.71'052 74-178363
MARC

Baillie, Joanna, 1762-1851.
The dramatic and poetical works of Joanna Baillie ... London, Longman, Brown, Green, and Longmans, 1851.
viii, 847, [1] p. front. (port.) 22 cm.
Added t.-p., engr., with vignette.
Ultra microfiche. Dayton, Ohio, National Cash Register, 1970. 1st title of 3. 10.5 x 14.8 cm. (PCMI library collection, 820-1)
KEmT NUC74-117987

Baillie, Joanna, 1762-1851.
The family legend and Metrical legends of exalted characters / Joanna Baillie ; with an introd. for the Garland ed. by Donald H. Reiman. — New York : Garland Pub., 1976.
577 p. in various pagings ; 21 cm. — (Romantic context : Poetry)
Reprint of 2 works, the first printed by James Ballantyne for John Ballantyne, Edinburgh, 1810; the second printed for Longman, Hurst, Rees, Orme, and Brown, London, 1821.
ISBN 0-8240-2103-7 : $33.00
I. Baillie, Joanna, 1762-1851. Metrical legends of exalted characters. 1976. II. Title. III. Series.
PR4056.A68 1976 822'.7 75-31147
76 MARC

Baillie, Joanna, 1762-1851. Metrical legends of exalted characters. 1976.
in Baillie, Joanna, 1762-1851. The family legend and Metrical legends of exalted characters. New York, Garland Pub., 1976.

Baillie, Joanna, 1762-1851.
Miscellaneous plays / Joanna Baillie ; with an introd. for the Garland ed. by Donald H. Reiman. — New York : Garland Pub., 1977.
xix, 438 p. ; 21 cm. — (Romantic context : Poetry)
Reprint of the 1804 ed. published by Longman, Hurst, Rees, and Orme, London.
ISBN 0-8240-2102-9 : $33.00
I. Title. II. Series.
PR4056A74 1977 822'.7 75-31146
76 MARC

Baillie, John, 1886-1960.
The interpretation of religion : an introductory study of the theological principles / by John Baillie. — Westport, Conn. : Greenwood Press, [1977] c1928.
xv, 477 p. ; 23 cm.
Reprint of the ed. published by Scribner, New York.
Includes bibliographical references and index.
ISBN 0-8371-9038-X
1. Religion. 2. Religion—Philosophy. 3. Theology, Doctrinal. I. Title.
[BL48.B2 1977] 200'.1 76-49990
76 MARC

Baillie, John, 1886-1960
see Unpublished papers of principal John Baillie. [Edinburgh? University Library? n. d.]

Baillie, John King.
A design for manpower planning in public education. Philadelphia, 1971.
357 p.
Thesis—University of Pennsylvania.
Microfilm. Ann Arbor, Mich., University Microfilms. 1 reel. 35 mm.
CLSU NUC73-35546

Baillie, Kenneth Dale, 1944-
A taxonomic and ecological study of the intertidal, sand-dwelling dinoflagellates of the north eastern Pacific Ocean. [Vancouver, B. C.] 1971.
110 l. illus. 28 cm.
Thesis (M.Sc.)—University of British Columbia, 1972.
Vita.
Bibliography: leaves 103-110.
1. Dinoflagellata. 2. Marine biology—British Columbia. I. Title.
CaBVaU NUC73-126483

Baillie, Matthew, 1761-1823. The morbid anatomy of some of the most important parts of the human body. 1973
see Rodin, Alvin E The influence of Matthew Baillie's Morbid anatomy. Springfield, Ill., Thomas [1973]

Baillie, Matthew, 1761-1823
see Roberton, John, d. 1820 or 21. On the generative system... London, J. J. Stockdale, 1817.

Baillie, Murray, 1941-
Municipal government in metropolitan Halifax : a bibliography / compiled by Murray Baillie for the Dept. of Political Science, St. Mary's University. — [Halifax] : St. Mary's University Library, 1971.
18 p. ; 28 cm. C 74-126
Cover title.
1. Halifax, N. S.—Politics and government—Bibliography. 2. Halifax metropolitan area, N. S.—Politics and government—Bibliography. I. Title.
Z7165.C2B34 016.3520716'22 75-304984
MARC

Baillie, Percy
see Haldane, Roger, 1945-
Port Lincoln sketchbook. [Adelaide] Rigby [1972]

Baillie, Robert, 1602-1662.
Errours and induration...a sermon...July 30, 1645... London, Printed by R. Raworth for Samuel Gellibrand, 1645. London, Cornmarket P., 1971.
44 p. (The English revolution, I. Fast sermons to Parliament, July-August 1645, 18)
Facsim. ed.; Wing B459.
TxDaM-P NUC76-72659

Baillie, Robert, 1602-1662.
A review of Doctor Bramble, Late Bishop of Londonderry, his Faire warning against the Scotes Disciplin. By R. B. G. Printed at Delf, Michiel Stael, 1649.
91 p. 20 cm.
Photocopy. (Ann Arbor, Mich., University Microfilms, 1971?)
1. Bramhall, John, Abp. of Armagh, 1594-1663. A fair warning to take heed of the Scotish discipline. 2. Church of Scotland—Doctrinal and controversial works. I. Title.
CBGTU NUC75-30251

Baillie, Robert, 1602-1662.
Satan, the leader in chief to all who resist the reparation of sion...a sermon...Febr. 28, 1643... London, Samuel Gellibrand, 1643. London, Cornmarket P., 1971.
54 p. (The English revolution, I. Fast sermons to Parliament, Feb. 1643/4-April 1644, 10)
Facsim. ed.; Wing B468.
TxDaM-P NUC76-72652

Baillie-Saunders, Margaret Elsie (Crowther) 1873-1949.
Litany Lane, a novel by Margaret Baillie Saunders ... Toronto, Macmillan [n. d.]
366 p.
I. Title.
TxU NUC76-22392

Baillie-Saunders, Margaret Elsie (Crowther) 1873-1949.
The philosophy of Dickens; a study of his life and teaching as a social reformer. London, H. Glaisher, 1905.
vi, 176 p. port. 19 cm.
Ultra microfiche. Dayton, Ohio, National Cash Register, 1970. 2d title of 9. 10.5 x 14.8 cm. (PCMI library collection, 233-2)
1. Dickens, Charles, 1812-1870. I. Title.
KEmT NUC73-126503

Baillière's midwives' dictionary. — 6th ed. / [by] Vera da Cruz, Margaret Adams. — London : Baillière Tindall, 1976.
[14], 303 p. : ill., form ; 15 cm. GB76-26474
First ed., compiled by E. K. Worvell, was published in 1951 under title: Baillière's midwives' medical dictionary.
ISBN 0-7020-0596-7 : £1.00
1. Obstetrics—Dictionaries. I. Da Cruz, Vera. II. Adams, Margaret, 1916- III. Title: Midwives' dictionary.
[DNLM: 1. Obstetrics—Dictionaries. WQ13 B154 1976]
[RG45.B3 1976] 618.2'003 76-677208
Shared Cataloging with 77 MARC
DNLM

Baillière's nurses' dictionary. 18th ed. [by] Barbara F. Cape and Pamela Dobson. Baltimore, Williams & Wilkins, 1974.
479 p. illus. 14 cm.
First published in 1912 under title: The nurses' complete medical dictionary.
1. Nurses and nursing—Dictionaries. 2. Medicine—Dictionaries. I. Cape, Barbara F., ed. II. Dobson, Pamela, joint ed. III. Title: Nurses' dictionary.
NjR NUC76-22379

Baillieu, Gaspard.
Sar-Louis. Place forte située sur la Saare dans la Lorraine Allemande. Paris, Chez le Lorraine Allemande. Paris, Chez le Sieur Baillieu [1713?] Ithaca, N.Y., Historic Urban Plans, 1970.
map 37 x 51 cm.
Scale of 140 "toises".
1. Saarlouis—Maps.
NIC NUC73-59547

Baillieul, John Brouard.
Some optimization problems in geometric control theory / by John Brouard Baillieul. -- [s.l. : s.n., 1976]
93 leaves in various foliations : ill. ; 29 cm.
Thesis--Harvard.
Includes bibliography.
MH NUC77-84588

Bailliu, Gérard Raymond.
A definition, measure and measurement of the activity of an information processing system. [Berkeley] 1973.
vi, 112 l.
Thesis (Ph. D.)—University of California.
Bibliography: leaves 104-106.
CU NUC75-19468

Baillod, Charles Robert, 1941-
Nitrification in surface waters tributary to Lake Superior, by C. Robert Baillod and Jon B. Sebba. Houghton, Mich., Michigan Technical University, Civil Engineering Dept., 1971.
191 l.
Research technical project completion report OWRR Project no. A-037 Mich. OWRR agreement no. 14-31-0001-3222.
Supported in part by funds provided by the U. S. Dept. of the Interior, Office of Water Resources Research.
1. Nitrification. 2. Superior, Lake. I. Sebba, Jon B., joint author. II. Michigan. Technological University, Houghton. Dept of Civil Engineering. III. Title.
DI NUC76-20950

Baillod, Charles Robert, 1941-
Storage and disposal of iron ore processing wastewater. Washington, U. S. Govt. Print. Off., 1974.
135 p. (Environmental protection technology series. EPA-660/2-74-0 18)
Project 14040FVD.
Bibliography: p. 105-106.
I. Title.
DNAL NUC75-19917

Baillod, Jean Pierre, joint author.
see Scheurer, Rémy. Vins et vignoble neuchâtelois. Neuchâtel, Centre d'arts graphiques, c1975.

Baillod, Lucien.
Regards vers un destin : poèmes / Lucien Baillod. — Bex : Éditions Les Trois sources ; [Lausanne : vente, Éditions Les Trois sources, case postale 2668, 1002], 1976.
116 p. : col. ill. ; 23 cm. Sw76-11481
29.50F
I. Title.
PQ2662.A348R4 841'.9'14 77-476573
*77 MARC

Baillods, Édouard.
Figures de héros suisses / dix bois d'Édouard Baillods ; texte de Jules Baillods. — Neuchâtel : Éditions Delachaux & Niestlé, [1941]
66 p. : ill. ; 26 cm.
1. Baillods, Édouard. 2. Heroes in art. 3. Switzerland—Biography—Portraits. I. Baillods, Jules. II. Title.
NE1164.5.B34B34 76-457587
76 MARC

Baillods, Jules.
Jura / Jules Baillods. — Neuchâtel : Éditions de la Baconnière, c1946.
155 p. ; 24 cm.
I. Title.
PQ2603.A239J8 843'.9'12 75-518000
76 MARC

Baillods, Jules.
see Baillods, Édouard. Figures de héros suisses. Neuchâtel, Éditions Delachaux & Niestlé, [1941]

Baillon, Andre, 1875-1932.
En sabots ... Preface de Franz Hellens.
[n.p.] Lettres Belges [1959]
311 p.
I. Title.
PPiU NUC75-61635

Baillon, D
Erreurs systématiques de recensement en milieu rural traditionnel; mise en évidence—essai d'analyse méthodologique [par] D. Baillon. [Petit Bassam] Côte d'Ivoire, Office de la recherche scientifique et technique outre-mer, Centre de Petit Bassam, 1970.
30, 5 l. illus. (Sciences humaines, v. 3, no 6)
Microfiche (negative) [Paris] Microéditions Hachette [1971] 1 sheet. 11 x 15 cm.
"71/2067."
Caption on microfiche: Erreurs de recensement en milieu rural.
1. Ivory Coast—Census. I. Title. II. Title: Erreurs de recensement en milieu rural. III. Series: France. Office de la recherche scientifique et technique outre-mer. Cahiers O. R. S. T. O. M. Série Sciences humaines, v. 3, no 6
Microfiche HA 37 73-202683

Baillon, D.
see Castella, P Note de synthèse sur l'économie de la ville de Bouaké. [Petit Bas Bassam] Cote d'Ivoire, Office de la recherche scientifique et technique outre-mer, 1970.

Baillot, Alexandre.
Chrysanthèmes; poèmes. [Lyon] Maison Rhodanienne de poésie [1971]
68 p. port.
MH NUC76-69677

Baillot, Alexandre.
Ronces et chardons. [Paris] P. J. Oswald [1972]
75 p. 18 cm. (Cahiers de poésie contemporaine) 15.00F F***
Poems.
I. Title.
PQ2603.A243R6 74-345303

Baillot, Pierre Marie François de Sales, 1771-1842.
see Méthode de violoncelle et de basse d'ac[c]ompagnement. Genève, Minkoff Reprint, 1974.

Bailloud, Gérard.
Le Néolithique dans le Bassin parisien / Gérard Bailloud. — 2e éd. — Paris : Éditions du Centre national de la recherche scientifique, 1974.
433, [4] p. : ill. ; 28 cm. — (Supplément à Gallia préhistoire ; 2) F74-17278
Bibliography: p. [355]-391.
Includes index.
ISBN 2-222-01568-5 : 80.00F
1. Neolithic period—France—Paris Basin. 2. Paris Basin—Antiquities. 3. France—Antiquities. I. Title. II. Series: Gallia préhistoire, fouilles et monuments archéologiques en France metropolitaine. Supplément ; 2.
GN776.22.F7B25 1974 75-519968
76 MARC

Bailloud, Gérard
see Bertrand, Georges. La formation des campagnes françaises... Paris, Editions du Seuil, 1975.

Bailloud, Gérard
see Piggott, Stuart. France before the Romans. London: Thames and Hudson [1974]

Bailly, André
Dictionnaire du patois en usage à Hortes (Haute-Marne) et la région / par André Bailly. — [Hortes] (52600) : [A. Bailly], 1973.
54p., [3] leaves of plates : ill. ; 27 cm. F74-17239
Cover title.
6.00F
1. French language—Dialects—Hortes, France—Dictionaries. 2. French language—Dictionaries. I. Title.
PC3017.H6B3 447'.332 75-515445
75 MARC

Bailly, Antoine.
L'organisation urbaine : théories et modèles / Antoine S. Bailly. — Paris : Centre de recherche d'urbanisme, [1975] F***
272 p. : ill. ; 21 cm.
Bibliography: p. 241-268.
ISBN 2-85303-073-3
1. Urbanization. 2. Cities and towns—Growth. 3. Urbanization—Mathematical models. I. Title.
HT371.B25 301.36 76-462380
76 MARC

Bailly, Antoine.
see Éléments de géographie comtoise. Paris, Belles lettres, [1975]

Bailly, Antoine.
see Travaux de géographie fondamentale. Paris, Belles lettres, 1974.

Bailly, Auguste, 1878-
Cléopâtre, par Auguste Bailly; Six cents milliards sous les mers, par Harry E. Rieseberg; La vie des français sous l'occupation, par Henri Amouroux; La vie de Louis II de Bavière, par Desmond Chapman-Huston. Paris, Le Cercle Historia [1962]
532 p. illus. 19 cm.
Condensed versions of the four books.
I. Cercle historia. II. Title.
FMU NUC75-8255

Bailly, Auguste, 1878- La crèche bisontine. 1974.
in Garneret, Jean. La crèche et le théâtre populaire en Franche-Comté. Besançon, Folklore comtois, 1974.

Bailly, Auguste, 1878–
Maeterlinck. Translation by Fred Rothwell. New York, Haskell House Publishers, 1974.
156 p. 20 cm.
ISBN 0-8383-1877-0
1. Maeterlinck, Maurice, 1862–1949—Criticism and interpretation.
PQ2625.A61B313 848'.8'09 74-6385
MARC

Bailly, Auguste, 1878-
Mazarino. [Traducción del francés por Felipe Ximénez de Sandoval] Madrid, Espasa-Calpe [1969]
215, [1] p. 18 cm. (Colección austral, 1444)
Bibliography: p. [216]
1. Mazarin, Jules, Cardinal, 1602-1661.
2. France—History—Louis XIV, 1643-1715.
I. Series.
OU NUC73-84203

Bailly, Auguste, 1878- Richelieu
in Blanch, Lesley. Aimée Dubucq de Rivery... Paris, Le Cercle historia [1961]

Bailly, Auguste, 1878-
Richelieu. [Traducción del francés por María Luisa Pérez Torres] Madrid, Espasa-Calpe [1969]
224 p. 18 cm. (Colección austral, 1433)
1. Richelieu, Armand Jean du Plessis, Cardinal, duc de, 1585-1642. 2. France—History—Louis XII, 1610-1643. I. Series.
OU NUC73-84204

Bailly, Claude, joint author.
see Malvos, Claude. Essais sur peupliers à Madagascar. [Tananarive] Centre technique forestier tropical, Division solforêt, 1973.

Bailly, Edgar Auger-
see Auger-Bailly, Edgar.

Bailly, Fernand.
Isolation thermique des habitations : méthode pratique de calcul / par Fernand Bailly. — Paris : Eyrolles, 1977 [i.e. 1976] F***
85 p. : ill. ; 30 cm.
63.00F
1. Insulation (Heat) I. Title.
TH1715.B29 77-477602
77 MARC

Bailly, Friedrich.
Zur Vergesellschaftung der Böden aus Löss in der nördlichen Calenberger Börde / Friedrich Bailly. — Hannover : Bundesanstalt für Bodenforschung ; Stuttgart : in Kommission, E. Schweizerbart, 1973.
135 p. : ill. (2 fold.) ; 24 cm. — (Geologisches Jahrbuch : Reihe F (Bodenkunde) ; Heft 1) GFR***
Summary also in English, French, and Russian.
Bibliography: p. 115–119.
1. Soils—Germany—Calenberger Land. 2. Loess—Germany—Calenberger Land. I. Title. II. Series.
S599.4.G32C342 74-356708

Bailly, G H
Les ensembles historiques dans la reconquête urbaine / [par G. H. Bailly et J. P. Desbat]. — Paris : La Documentation française, 1973.
64 p. : ill. ; 27 cm. — (Notes et études documentaires ; nos 3969-3970) F***
Cover title.
Includes bibliographical references.
6.00F
1. Monuments—Preservation. 2. Monuments—France—Preservation. I. Desbat, J. P., joint author. II. Title. III. Series: France. Direction de la documentation. Notes et études documentaires ; nos 3969-3970.
N8850.B34 309.2'62 75-502168
MARC

Bailly, G H
Le patrimoine architectural, les pouvoirs locaux et la politique de conservation intégree : [guide] / G[illes]-H[enri] Bailly. — Vevey : Éditions Delta, [c1975]
118 p., [1] fold. leaf of plates : ill. ; 24 cm. Sw76-1461
At head of title: Conseil de l'Europe. Conférence des pouvoirs locaux et régionaux de l'Europe.
Includes bibliographical references.
18.00F
1. Architecture—Conservation and restoration. 2. Architecture and state. I. Title.
NA105.B27 720'.28 76-475389
*76 MARC

Bailly, Jean Christophe.
L'astrolabe dans la passe des Français. [Paris] Seghers [1973]
93 p. 21 cm. (Collection froide) 18.00F F***
I. Title.
PQ2662.A35A9 74-178888
MARC

Bailly, Jean Christophe.
Au-delà du langage; une étude sur Benjamin Péret. [Paris] E. Losfeld [1971]
111 p. 21 cm. (Le Désordre, 13) 9.00F F***
Bibliography: p. 111.
1. Péret, Benjamin, 1899-1959. I. Title.
PQ2631.E348Z58 73-362229
MARC

Bailly, Jean Christophe.
Défaire le vide / Jean-Christophe Bailly. — [s.l.] : Éditions étrangères ; [Paris] : C. Bourgois, 1975.
45 p. ; 21 cm. F75-7373
Poems.
10.00F
I. Title.
PQ2662.A35D4 841'.9'14 75-516682
76 MARC

Bailly, Jean Christophe.
Jean-Pierre Duprey. Une étude de Jean-Christophe Bailly. Avec un choix de poèmes, une biographie. [Paris] P. Seghers [1973]
166 p. illus. 16 cm. (Poètes d'aujourd'hui, 212) F***
Bibliography: p. [163]-164.
1. Duprey, Jean Pierre.
PQ2664.U65Z6 841'.9'14 74-156203
MARC

Bailly, Jean Christophe, joint author.
see Baatsch, Henri Alexis. Max Ernst ... [s.l.] Éditions étrangères, [1976]

Bailly, Jean Claude, comp.
Dossier LSD [par] Jean-Claude Bailly et Gérard Rutten. Paris, P. Belfond [1974]
183 p. 21 cm. (Collection Mandala) 24.00F F***
1. Lysergic acid diethylamide—Addresses, essays, lectures. I. Rutten, Gérard, joint comp. II. Title.
HV5822.L9B3 362.2'93 74-169534
MARC

[Bailly, Jean Sylvain] 1736-1793.
Discours et mémoires, par l'auteur de l'Histoire de l'astroromie. Paris, De Bure l'Aîné, 1790.
2 v.
Microprint. New York, Readex Microprint, 1968. 10 cards. (Landmarks of science)
1. Bailly, Jean Sylvain, 1736-1793.
InU NUC76-69379

Bailly, Jean Sylvain, 1736–1793.
Geschichte der Sternkunde des Alterthums bis auf die Errichtung der Schule zu Alexandrien [von] Bailly. [Walluf bei Wiesbaden] M. Sändig [1972]
2 v. in 1. illus. 21 cm. GDB***
Reprint of the Leipzig, 1777 ed.
Translation of Histoire de l'astronomie ancienne.
Vol. 2 has title: Geschichte der alten Sternkunde, oder die Erläuterungen der astronomischen Geschichte des Alterthums.
1. Astronomy, Ancient—History. I. Title.
QB16.B23 1972 520'.93 72–355771
ISBN 3–500–25200–1

Bailly, Jean Sylvain, 1736-1793.
Mémoires d'un témoin de la Révolution / Jean-Sylvain Bailly. — Genève : Slatkine-Megariotis Reprints, 1975.
2 v. ; 22 cm. Sw***
Reprint of the 1821-22 ed. published by Baudouin frères, Paris, under title: Mémoires de Bailly.
1. Bailly, Jean Sylvain, 1736-1793. 2. France—History—Revolution, 1789-1793. I. Title.
DC146.B15A33 1975 944'.04 75-514103
75 MARC

Bailly, Jean Sylvain, 1736-1793, ed.
see Paris. Assemblée des électeurs, 1789. Procès-verbal des séances et délibérations de l'Assemblée générale des électeurs de Paris. Paris, Baudouin, 1790.

Bailly, Maurice
see Dictionnaire des techniques, introduction historique sur l'evolution des techniques. Paris, Bordas, 1971.

Bailly, Michel.
La liberté des belges. [Bruxelles, 1969]
140 p. 21 cm.
1. Flemish movement. 2. Belgium—Languages. I. Title.
CSt-H NUC73-126501

Bailly, Othilie.
Le Jardinier du dimanche / Othilie Bailly. — Paris : Stock, 1975.
438 p. : ill. ; 21 cm. — (Guide pratique) F76-4641
ISBN 2-234-00244-3 : 38.00F
1. Gardening. 2. Gardening—France. I. Title.
SB453.3.F7B34 635.9'0944 76-474884
76 MARC

Bailly, Othilie
see Pommery, Jean. Que faire en attendant le vétérinaire. Paris, R. Laffont [1973]

Bailly, Paul.
Vingt ans de vie internationale ... 1948–1968, par Paul Bailly ... Paris (3ᵉ), 68, rue des Archives, 1969.
[iv], 102 p. 27 cm. F 71–6497
At head of title: F. I. A. B. C. I. Fédération internationale des professions immobilières. International Real Estate Federation. Internationaler Verband der Grundstücksmakler und -Verwalter. Federación internacional de profesiones inmobiliarias.
In German.
Title also in English and German: Twenty years of international life; Zwanzig Jahre internationale Tätigkeit.
1. International Real Estate Federation. I. Title. II. Title: Twenty years of international life. III. Title: Zwanzig Jahre international Tätigkeit.
HD251.I 66B3 1969 72–361023

Bailly, Pierre.
see France. Conseil économique et social. Section du cadre de vie. Les espaces verts dans les grandes agglomérations ... Pierre Bailly. [Paris, 1975?]

Bailly, Robert.
Les Châteaux historiques vauclusiens / Robert Bailly, en collaboration avec Y. Bailly. — Avignon (6, rue Claude Debussy, 84000) : R. Bailly, 1976.
155 p. : ill. ; 27 cm. F76-18389
Bibliography: p. 148-153.
68.00F
1. Castles—France—Vaucluse (Dept.) 2. Vaucluse, France (Dept.)—Description and travel. I. Bailly, Y., joint author. II. Title.
DC611.V357B285 944'.92 77-463261
77 MARC

Bailly, Robert.
Histoire du vin en Vaucluse; les domaines vinicoles historiques. Avignon, Impr. F. Orta [1972]
145 p. illus. 27 cm. F***
Includes bibliographical references.
1. Wine and wine making — Vaucluse, France (Dept.) — History. 2. Vaucluse, France (Dept.)—Industries—History. I. Title.
TP553.B32 663'.2'0094492 73–341032

Bailly, Roger.
La Ligne de Villeneuve à Montargis par Malesherbes au fil des ans [par] Roger Bailly. Vayres-sur-Essonne (91820 Boutigny sur Essonne), R. Bailly, 1972.
111, [18] p. illus. 24 cm. F 74–1605
Errata slip inserted.
Includes bibliographical references.
1. Railroads—France—History. I. Title.
HE3068.B33 385'.0944'365 74–186206
MARC

Bailly, Roger.
Répertoire de principes actifs et spécialités vétérinaires. 1. éd. réalisée par Roger Bailly avec le concours scientifique du docteur vétérinaire Wilfrid Joussellin. Paris [Éditions le Carrousel, 1972]
1 v. (various pagings) 16 x 22 cm. 25.00F F***
"Répertoire ... conçu et réalisé par l'Association de coordination technique agricole."
1. Veterinary materia medica and pharmacy—Tables. I. Joussellin, Wilfrid, joint author. II. Association de coordination technique agricole. III. Title.
SF917.B34 636.089'5'1 74–329405

Bailly, Y., joint author.
see Bailly, Robert. Les Châteaux historiques vauclusiens. Avignon (6, rue Claude Debussy, 84000) R. Bailly, 1976.

Bailly-Herzberg, Janine.
L'eau-forte de peintre au dix-neuvième siècle; la Société des aquafortistes, 1862–1867. Paris, L. Laget, 1972.
2 v. illus., facsims., ports. 30 cm. F***
Bibliography: v. 1, p. 280–285.
CONTENTS: t. 1. Histoire de la Société des aquafortistes et catalogue des eaux-fortes publiées.—t. 2. Dictionnaire de la Société des aquafortistes.
1. Société des aqua-fortistes, Paris. I. Title.
NE1940.S63B34 73–307582

Bailly-Herzberg, Janine, joint author.
see Fidell-Beaufort, Madeleine. Daubigny. Paris, Geoffroy-Dechaume, [1975]

Bailo Modesti, Gianni
see Seconda Mostra della preistoria e della protostoria nel Salernitano. Salerno : P. Laveglia, 1974.

Bailor, Edwin Maurice, 1890–
Content and form in tests of intelligence. New York, Teachers College, Columbia University, 1924. [New York, AMS Press, 1972]
x, 74 p. 22 cm.
Reprint of the 1924 ed., issued in series: Teachers College, Columbia University. Contributions to education, no. 162.
Originally presented as the author's thesis, Columbia.
Bibliography: p. 73–74.
1. Mental tests. I. Title. II. Series: Columbia University. Teachers College. Contributions to education, no. 162.
BF431.B247 1972 153.9'33 70–176529
ISBN 0–404–55162–9 MARC

Bailor, Edwin Maurice, 1890– joint author
see Meltzer, Hyman, 1899– Developed lessons in psychology... New York, Harcourt, Brace and company [c1929]

Bailor, Jerry Roland.
The late eighteenth century theatrical public of London, England. [n. p.] 1974.
iv, 215 l. 28 cm.
Thesis—University of Southern California.
1. Theater—London—History. 2. Theater audiences—London. I. Title.
CLSU NUC76-22391

Baĭlov, Filip.
(Tendentsii v izmenenieto na materialoemkostta na selskostopanskata produktsiia)
Тенденции в изменението на материалоемкостта на селскостопанската продукция [в света]. ⟨Обзор⟩ [на лит.]. (Ред. С. Добрева). София, НЦНТИССХПГС, 1974.
85 p. with tables. 19.5 cm. 2.00 lv Bu 74–1139
At head of title: Национален център за научна информация по селско стопанство, хранителна промишленост и горско стопанство при ССА "Г. Димитров." Филип Байлов, Гинка Панайотова.
Summary also in Russian and English.
Bibliography: p. [81]–84.
1. Farm management. I. Panaĭtova, Ginka, joint author. II. Title.
S561.B24 74–335896

Baĭlov, Filip
see Mezhdunarodni i vŭtreshni tseni v selskoto stopanstvo i khranitelnata promishlenost. 1975.

Baĭlov, Filip
see Rentabilnost na selskostopanskoto proizvodstvo v NR Bŭlgariia. 1973.

Baĭlov, Filip
see Usŭvŭrshenstvuvane sistemata na tsenite i tsenoobrazuvaneto v selskoto stopanstvo. 1974.

Bailov, IU., illus.
see (Estoniia) [1972]

Bail'ozov, Dimitur M.
see Tablitsi za sŭstava na bulgarskite khranitelni produkti. 1975.

Bails, Jack D., joint author
see Evans, Ronald J Mercury levels in muscle tissues... [East Lansing] Institute of Water Research [1972]

Bails, Jerry G
The who's who of American comic books. Editors: Jerry Bails and Hames Ware. 1st ed. [Detroit, 1973–
v. illus. 28 cm.
1. Comic books, strips, etc.—American—Biography. I. Ware, Hames, joint author. II. Title.
PN6725.B3 741'.092'2 [B] 73–174050
MARC

Bails, Jerry G.
see Keltner, Howard. Howard Keltner's Index to golden age comic books ... Detroit, Bails, c1976.

Bails, Suzanne.
Latine loquor [par] Suzanne Bails, avec la collaboration de Georgette Beros-Cazes. Paris, F. Nathan [1971– v. 1, c1968]
v. illus. 25 cm.
"Collection publiée sous la direction de Pierre Grimal."
"Index verborum" in pocket at end of vols. 1 and 2.
1. Latin language—Grammar—1870– 2. Latin language—Readers. I. Grimal, Pierre, 1912– II. Title.
IU NUC75-30737

Bailum, Henry.
Fjorten dage i Jylland. En historisk, topografisk studie over de vestjyske lokaliteter i St. St. Blichers novelle af samme navn. Tekst og tegning. Holstebro, Eget forlag, Eksp.: Skivevej 84, [1974].
17 p. illus. 21 cm. kr15.00 D 74–18
1. Blicher, Steen Steensen, 1782–1848. Fjorten dage i Jylland. I. Title.
PT8124.Z5B28 74–323662

Bailum, Henry.
Jens Søndergaard og hans venner. Med indledning af Leo Estvad. [Århus, Aros, 1962]
52 p., 16 plates. illus. 26 cm.
1. Søndergaard, Jens, 1895–1957. I. Søndergaard, Jens, 1895–1957. II. Title.
ND723.S7B34 74–205733

Bailum, Henry.
Laust Glavinds bedrifter. Med tegninger af forfatteren. Holstebro, Holstebro Museum, Anlæget, 1969.
23 p. illus. 18 x 23 cm. D 70–16
7.50
1. Glavind, Laust. 2. Quacks and quackery—Denmark. I. Title.
R730.B3 75–579694

Bailum, Henry
see Aakjær, Jeppe, 1866-1930. Den jydske Hede: udvalgte diget. Skive: Otto Friis Boghandel, 1975.

Baily, Francis, 1774-1844.
Astronomical tables and formulæ together with a variety of problem explanatory of their use and application. To which are prefixed the Elements of the solar system. By Francis Baily ... London [Printed by R. Taylor] 1827 [1973]
xvi, 267, [1] p. 22 cm.
Problems: p. [217]-264.
Micro-opaque. New York, Readex Microprint, 1973. 4 cards. 23 x 15 cm. (Landmarks of science)
1. Astronomy—Tables. 2. Solar system.
IaAS NUC75-19464

Baily, John, writer on music.
Krishna Govinda's rudiments of table playing / by John Baily. — Carmarthen : Unicorn Bookshop, 1974.
[2], xi, 89 p. : ill., music ; 28 cm. GB75-04510
ISBN 0-85659-018-5 : £2.50
1. Tabla—Instruction and study. 2. Katri-Chetri, Krishna Govinda, 1942- I. Title.
MT662.B24 789'.1 76-468315
76 MARC

Baily, John, 1644-1697
see
Bailey, John, 1644-1697.

Baily, Julie H., joint author
see Banner, Albert H The effects of urban pollution upon a coral reef system... [Honolulu] Hawaii Institute of Marine Biology [1970]

Baily, Leslie.
Gilbert and Sullivan and their world. London, Thames and Hudson [1973]
119, [9] p. illus. 24 cm. £2.25 GB***
Bibliography: p. [120]
1. Gilbert, Sir William Schwenck, 1836-1911. 2. Sullivan, Sir Arthur Seymour, 1842-1900. I. Title.
ML410.S95B28 782.8'1'0924 [B] 73-175693
ISBN 0-500-13046-9 MARC

Baily, Leslie.
Gilbert and Sullivan; their lives and times. New York, Viking Press [1974, c1973]
119, [1] p. illus. 24 cm. (A studio book) $7.95
London edition (Thames and Hudson) has title: Gilbert and Sullivan and their world.
Bibliography: p. [120]
1. Gilbert, Sir William Schwenck, 1836-1911. 2. Sullivan, Sir Arthur Seymour, 1842-1900. I. Title.
ML410.S95B28 1974 782.8'1'0924 [B] 73-20669
ISBN 0-670-33990-3 MARC

Baily, Martin Neil.
Four essays in economic theory. [n.p.] 1972.
[6], 111 l. diagrs., table. 30 cm.
Thesis (Ph.D.)—Massachusetts Institute of Technology.
Vita.
Includes bibliographies.
1. Economics—Addresses, essays, lectures. I. Title.
MCM NUC74-122954

Baily, Mary Ann Reardon.
Capital utilization in Kenya manufacturing industry, by Mary Ann Baily. [n.p.] 1974.
168 l. diagrs., tables. 30 cm.
Thesis (Ph.D.)—Massachusetts Institute of Technology.
Vita.
Bibliography: leaves 166-167.
1. Capital investments—Kenya. 2. Kenya—Manufactures. I. Title.
MCM NUC75-19463

Baily, Peter J H
Managing materials in industry [by] Peter Baily and David Farmer. New York, Wiley [1973]
xv, 341 p. illus. 25 cm.
"A Halsted Press book."
Bibliography: p. 333.
1. Materials management. I. Farmer, David H., joint author. II. Title.
TS161.B33 1973 658.7 73-243
ISBN 0-470-04215-X MARC

Baily, Peter J H
Purchasing and supply management [by] P. J. Baily. 3d ed. London, Chapman and Hall [Distributed in the U. S. by Halsted Press, New York, 1973]
ix, 315 p. 22 cm. £3.00 GB***
Includes bibliographies.
1. Industrial procurement—Management. I. Title.
HD52.5.B28 1973 658.7 73-168199
ISBN 0-412-11570-0 MARC

Baily, Peter J H
Purchasing principles and techniques : a management approach / Peter Baily, David Farmer. — 3d ed. — London : Pitman, 1977.
v, 353 p. : ill. ; 23 cm. GB77-10849
"A Pitman international text."
Includes bibliographies and index.
ISBN 0-273-01028-X : £5.95
1. Industrial procurement. 2. Purchasing. I. Farmer, David H., joint author. II. Title.
HD52.5.B29 1977 658.7'2 77-368045
77 MARC

Baily, Philip Chesley.
Religion in a Chinese town, by Philip Chesley Baily. Taipei, Orient Cultural Service, 1975.
ix, 307 p. 20 cm. (Asian folklore and social life monographs, v. 64)
1. Religions. I. Title. II. Series.
CoU NUC77-82716

Baily, Samuel L
The durability of Peronism, by Samuel L. Baily. Buffalo, N.Y., Council on International Studies, State Univ. of New York at Buffalo, 1975.
71 l. 28 cm. (New York (State) State University, Buffalo. Council on International Studies. Special studies, no. 58)
Includes documents, in Spanish, including speeches by Perón (leaves 31-71)
1. Argentine Republic—Politics and government—1955- 2. Perón, Juan Domingo, Pres. Argentine Republic, 1895-1974. I. Perón, Juan Domingo, Pres. Argentine Republic, 1895-1974. II. Title. III. Series.
NIC NUC77-82902

Baily, Samuel L
Perspectives on Latin America, edited by Samuel L. Baily and Ronald T. Hyman. New York, Macmillan [1974]
xix, 105 p. illus. 24 cm. (Latin America series)
Includes bibliographical references.
1. Latin America — Addresses, essays, lectures. I. Hyman, Ronald T., joint author. II. Title.
F1406.7.B34 918'.03'308 73-10689
ISBN 0-02-505830-4 MARC

Baily, Samuel L
The United States and the development of South America, 1945-1975 / Samuel L. Baily. — New York : New Viewpoints, 1976.
ix, 246 p. : map ; 22 cm.
Bibliography: p. [228]-237.
Includes index.
ISBN 0-531-05387-3. ISBN 0-531-05594-9 pbk.
1. United States—Foreign economic relations—South America. 2. South America—Foreign economic relations—United States. 3. United States—Foreign relations—South America. 4. South America—Foreign relations—United States. I. Title.
HF1456.5.S62B26 338.91'8'073 76-13895
76 MARC

Baily, Thomas L
Dr. Wallsten's way, by T. L. Baily. New York, The National Temperance Society and Publication House, 1889 [1973]
iv, 7-319 p. illus.
Microfilm (positive) Ann Arbor, Mich., University Microfilms, 1973. 2d title of 13. 35 mm. (American fiction series, reel 225.2)
I. Title.
KEmT NUC74-614

Baily, Thomas L
"Nat," the coal-miner's boy; or, One step at a time, by T. L. Baily. New York, The National Temperance Society and Publication House [c1890, 1973]
457 p. illus.
Microfilm (positive) Ann Arbor, Mich., University Microfilms, 1973. 3d title of 13. 35 mm. (American fiction series, reel 225.3)
I. Title. II. Title: One step at a time.
KEmT NUC74-615

Baily, W. L.
see
Baily, Walter L

Baily, Walter
see
Bailey, Walter, 1528 or 9-1592.

Baily, Walter L
Introductory lectures on automorphic forms, by Walter L. Baily, Jr. [Tokyo] Iwanami Shoten; [Princeton, N. J.] Princeton University Press, 1973.
xiv, 262 p. 25 cm. (Kanô memorial lectures, 2) (Publications of the Mathematical Society of Japan, 12) $11.50
"Based on lectures ... [given] in Tokyo University in 1970 and 1971."
Bibliography: p. [253]-257.
1. Functions, Automorphic. 2. Automorphic forms. I. Title. II. Series: Kanô memorial lectures, 2. III. Series: Nihon Sûgakkai. Publications, 12.
QA353.A9B35 515'.9 72-4034
ISBN 0-691-08123-9 MARC

Baily, Walter L.
see International Colloquium on Discrete Subgroups of Lie Groups and Applications to Moduli, Bombay, 1973. Discrete subgroups of Lie groups and applications to moduli ... Bombay, Published for the Tata Institute of Fundamental Research, Bombay [by] Oxford University Press, 1975.

Bailyn, Bernard.
The ordeal of Thomas Hutchinson. Cambridge, Mass., Belknap Press of Harvard University Press, 1974.
xx, 423 p. illus. 25 cm.
Includes bibliographical references.
1. Hutchinson, Thomas, 1711-1780. I. Title.
F67.H9805 973.3'14'0924 73-76379
ISBN 0-674-64160-4 [B] MARC

Bailyn, Bernard.
Los orígenes ideológicos de la revolución norteamericana. Buenos Aires, Ed. Paidos [1972]
285 p. (Biblioteca de economia, politica, sociedad. Serie mayor, v. 8)
Translation: The ideological origins of the American Revolution.
1. United States—Politics and government—Colonial period. I. Title.
NcU NUC74-122982

Bailyn, Bernard.
The origins of American politics. New York, Vintage Books [1970]
xi, 161, xii p. 18 cm. (A Vintage book, V-604)
"These three essays ... were delivered in their original form in November 1965 as the Charles K. Colver lectures at Brown University." cf. p. vii.
1. U.S.—Pol. & govt.—Colonial period. I. Title. II. Series: The Colver lectures, 1965.
NjR NUC73-84172

Bailyn, Bernard.
see The Great republic ... Boston, Little, Brown, c1977.

Bailyn, Bernard.
see The Great Republic ... Lexington, Mass., D.C. Heath, c1977.

Bailyn, Lotte.
Research as a cognitive process: some thoughts on data analysis. Lotte Bailyn. Cambridge, Mass., M.I.T., Alfred P. Sloan School of Management, 1975.
31 l. 28 cm. (Massachusetts Institute of Technology. Alfred P. Sloan School of Management. Working paper, no. 801-75)
Bibliography: leaves 30-31.
I. Title. II. Series.
MCM NUC77-82724

Baim, Donald Steven.
Drug-induced hemolysis of G6 PD-deficient human erythrocytes in rat hosts. [New Haven] 1975.
19, [14] l. 29 cm.
"Presented in part at the American Federation for Clinical Research, Eastern Section, January, 1975."
Thesis (M.D.)—Yale University.
Bibliography: leaves [20-22]
CtY-M NUC77-82719

Baima Bollone, Pierluigi.
Percosse e lesioni personali : (artt. 581, 582, 583 c. p.) Pierluigi Baima Bollone, Vladimiro Zagrebelsky. — Milano : A. Giuffrè, 1975.
181 p. ; 25 cm. It 76-Mar
Includes bibliographical references and index.
L4000
1. Assault and battery—Italy. 2. Personal injuries—Italy. I. Zagrebelsky, Vladimiro, joint author. II. Title.
76-510188

Baĭmakhanov, Murat Tadzhi-Muratovich.
(Protivorechiîa v razvitii pravovoĭ nadstroĭki pri sofsializme)
Противоречия в развитии правовой надстройки при социализме / М. Т. Баймаханов. — Алма-Ата : Наука, 1972.
357 p. ; 21 cm. USSR 72
At head of title: Академия наук Казахской ССР. Институт философии и права.
Includes bibliographical references.
1.76rub
1. Law and socialism. I. Title.
74-358937

Baĭmakhanov, Murat Tadzhi-Muratovich.
(Sovetskoe pravo i nravstvennoe formirovanie lichnosti)
Советское право и нравственное формирование личности / М. Т. Баймаханов. — Алма-Ата : О-во "Знание" КазССР, 1975.
34 p. ; 20 cm. — (Знание—народу) USSR 75
Series romanized: Znanie—narodu.
Includes bibliographical references.
0.06rub
1. Law—Russia. 2. Law and ethics. 3. Law and socialism. I. Title.
76-522498

Baimakhanov, Murat Tadzhi-Muratovich
see Gosudarstvenno-pravovoi status oblastnykh Sovetov Kazakhskoi SSR. 1976.

Baĭmakov, I͡Uriĭ Vladimirovich.
(Metallurgii͡a redkikh metallov)
Металлургия редких металлов. Конспект лекций, читаемых студентам физ.-металлург. фак. [Ленинград], 1969.
164 p. with diagrs. 25 cm. 0.70rub USSR 69
At head of title: Министерство высшего и среднего специального образования РСФСР. Ленинградский политехнический институт им. М. И. Калинина. Ю. В. Баймаков.
Bibliography: p. 162.
1. Nonferrous metals—Metallurgy. I. Title.
TN758.B32 74-344178

Baime, David S.
see Essex Co., N.J. Prosecutor's Office. Report on the proposed New Jersey penal code. [Newark? 1972?]

Baĭmoldin, Săbit.
Қырда туған. Өлеңдер. Алматы, "Жазушы," 1967.
66 p. 17 cm. 0.24 USSR 68-5150

I. Title.
Title romanized: Qyrda tughan.
PL65.K49B27 78-249039

Baĭmoldin, Săbit.
(Zher—meken)
Жер—мекен : өлеңдер / Сөбит Баймолдин. — Алматы : Жазушы, 1966.
37 p. ; 14 cm. — (Тұңғыш кітап)
I. Title.
PL65.K49B28 75-588210

Baimov, Nikolaĭ Ivanovich.
(Optimizat͡sii͡a prot͡sessov prokatki na bli͡uminge)
Оптимизация процессов прокатки на блюминге / Н. И. Баимов. — Москва : Металлургия, 1974.
213, [2] p. : ill. ; 23 cm. USSR 75
Bibliography: p. 211-[214]
0.81rub
1. Rolling (Metal-work)—Mathematical models. I. Title.
TS340.B28 75-533810

Baimov, Nikolaĭ Ivanovich
see Voprosy teorii i sovershenstvovanii͡a konstrukt͡siĭ metallurgicheskogo oborudovanii͡a. 1974.

Baĭmukhamedov, Kh. N.
see Tashkend. Tashkentskiĭ politekhnicheskiĭ institut. Geologorazvedochnyĭ fakul'tet. (Sbornik materialov po itogam nauchno-issledovatel'skikh rabot geologorazvedochnogo i gornometallurgicheskogo fakul'tetov TashPI za tysi͡acha devi͡at'sot semidesi͡atyi god) 1972.

Baĭmuratov, Urazgel'dy Baĭmuratovich.
Ėkonomicheskai͡a effektivnost' i granit͡sy primenenii͡a vychislitel'noĭ tekhniki. [By] U. B. Baimuratov, G. A. Kramarenko. Alma-Ata, "Nauka", 1974.
167 p. diagrs. 20 cm.
At head of title: Akademii͡a nauk Kazakhskoĭ SSR. Institut ėkonomiki.
Bibliography: p. 163-[166]
MH NUC75-135228

Baĭmuratov, Urazgel'dy Baĭmuratovich.
(Metody analiza i ot͡senki ėkonomicheskoĭ ėffektivnosti)
Методы анализа и оценки экономической эффективности капитальных вложений. Алма-Ата, "Наука," 1972.
313 p. with diagrs. 21 cm. 1.28rub USSR 72-VKP
At head of title: Академия наук Казахской ССР. Институт экономики. У. Б. Баймуратов.
Includes bibliographical references.
1. Capital investments. 2. Capital productivity. I. Title.
HD39.B25 73-334787

Baĭmuratov, Urazgel'dy Baĭmuratovich, ed.
see Effektivnost' tekhnicheskogo progressa v promyshlennosti Kazakhstana. 1973.

Bain, A. D.
see
Bain, Andrew David.

Bain, Alexander, 1810-1877.
Alexander Bain's short history of the electric clock (1852). — [1st ed. reprinted] ; edited by W. D. Hackmann. — London : Turner and Devereux, 1973.
xv, 31 p. : ill. ; 25 cm. — (Occasional paper - Turner & Devereux ; no. 3) GB74-01345
Reprint of the 1852 ed. published by Chapman and Hall, London.
Includes bibliographical references.
ISBN 0-9502557-2-6 : £1.80
1. Clocks and watches, Electric. 2. Bain, Alexander, 1810-1877. I. Hackmann, Willem Dirk. II. Title. III. Title: Short history of the electric clock. IV. Series: Turner & Devereux (Firm) Occasional paper - Turner & Devereux ; no. 3.
TS544.B34 1973 681'.116 76-379161
76 MARC

Bain, Alexander, 1818-1903.
Autobiography, by Alexander Bain, LL.D., professor of logic and English, University of Aberdeen (with supplementary chapter)... London, New York and Bombay, Longmans, Green, and co., 1904.
xi, [1], 449 p. 4 port. (incl. front.) 24 cm.
Edited by W. L. Davidson.
Bibliography: p. 425-435.
Ultra microfiche. Dayton, Ohio, National Cash Register, 1970. 1st title of 7. 10.5 x 14.8 cm. (PCMI library collection, 672-1)
1. Bain, Alexander, 1818-1903. I. Davidson, William Leslie, 1848- ed.
KEmT NUC76-38820

Bain, Alexander, 1818-1903.
Education as a science, by Alexander Bain ... New York, D. Appleton and Company, 1908.
1 p. l., [v]-xxvii, 453 p. 20 cm. (The International scientific series)
Ultra microfiche. Dayton, Ohio, National Cash Register, 1970. 1st title of 7. 10.5 x 14.8 cm. (PCMI library collection, 442-1)
1. Education. 2. Teaching. I. Title.
KEmT NUC74-118238

Bain, Alexander, 1818-1903.
James Mill: a biography. London, Longmans, Green, 1882. Farnborough, Gregg, 1970.
xxxii, 466 p. port. 20 cm. £5.40 B 72-19202
1. Mill, James, 1773-1836.
B1598.B2 1882a 330.15'3'0924 72-193929
ISBN 0-576-29127-7 [B] MARC

Bain, Alexander, 1818-1903.
Mental and moral science. A compendium of psychology and ethics. By Alexander Bain ... London, Longmans, Green, and co., 1884.
xxxvi, 751, 101, vi p.
Ultra microfiche. Dayton, Ohio, National Cash Register, 1970. 2d title of 2. 10.5 x 14.8 cm. (PCMI library collection, 780-2)
1. Psychology. 2. Ethics. I. Title.
KEmT NUC73-126502

Bain, Alexander, 1818-1903.
Mental science. New York, Arno Press, 1973 [c1868]
xxix, 428, 99 p. 23 cm. (Classics in psychology)
Reprint of the ed. published by D. Appleton, New York.
Includes bibliographical references.
1. Psychology. I. Title. II. Series.
[DNLM: BF B162m 1868F]
BF131.B2 1973 150 73-2958
ISBN 0-405-05132-8 MARC

Bain, Alexander, 1818-1903.
Mind and body; the theories of their relation. New York, D. Appleton, 1903.
199 p. illus. (International scientific series. American ed., v. 4)
Ultra microfiche. Dayton, Ohio National Cash Register, 1970. 1st title of 6. 10.5 x 14.8 cm. (PCMI library collection, 674-1)
1. Psychology, Physiological. 2. Mind and body. I. Title.
KEmT NUC74-118239

Bain, Alexander, 1818-1903.
Mind and body; the theories of their relation. 2d ed. London, H. S. King & Co., 1873 [Farnborough, Eng., Gregg International, 1971]
196 p. 18 cm. GB***
Original ed. issued as v. 4 of International scientific series (London).
1. Mind and body. 2. Psychology, Physiological. I. Title. II. Series: International scientific series (London) v. 4.
BF161.B2 1971 150 74-181945
ISBN 0-576-29219-2 MARC

Bain, Alexander, 1818-1903.
Объ изученіи характера. Перевелъ съ английскаго Цитовичъ. С.-Петербургъ, Изд. Заленскаго и Любарскаго, 1866.
521 p. 19 cm.
At head of title: Бэнъ.
Translation of On the study of character.
1. Character. 2. Phrenology. I. Title.
Title romanized: Ob izuchenii kharaktera.
BF818.B217 77-506489

Bain, Alexander, 1818-1903.
Practical essays. Freeport, N. Y., Books for Libraries Press [1972]
xvi, 338 p. 22 cm. (Essay index reprint series)
Reprint of the 1884 ed.
Includes bibliographical references.
CONTENTS: Common errors on the mind.—Errors of suppressed correlatives.—The civil service examinations.—The classical controversy.—Metaphysics and debating societies.—The university ideal, past and present.—The art of study.—Religious tests and subscriptions.—Procedure of deliberative bodies.
I. Title.
B1618.B23P7 1972 081 72-4533
ISBN 0-8369-2935-7 MARC

Bain, Alexander, 1818-1903.
The senses and the intellect. By Alexander Bain... London, J. W. Parker and Son, 1855.
xxxi, 614 p. illus. 23 cm.
Ultra microfiche. Dayton, Ohio, National Cash Register, 1970. 2d title of 6. 10.5 x 14.8 cm. (PCMI library collection, 674-2)
1. Psychology, Physiological. 2. Mind and body. I. Title.
KEmT NUC74-117986

Bain, Alexander, 1818-1903, ed.
see Grote, George, 1794-1871. The minor works of George Grote ... New York, B. Franklin, [1974]

Bain, Alexander Davidson, 1948-
PES studies of some five-membered ring compounds. [Vancouver, B.C.] 1972.
vii, 82 l. illus. 28 cm.
Thesis (M.Sc.)—University of British Columbia.
Vita.
Bibliography: leaves 75-82.
1. Molecular orbitals. 2. Photoelectricity. I. Title.
CaBVaU NUC74-122953

Bain, Andrew David.
Banking. [Phonotape. By A. D. Bain and Brian Griffiths] New York, Holt Information Systems [1972]
1 cassette. 2½ x 4 in. (British and European economics series, E3) (Sussex tapes international)
Discussion.
Booklet containing notes on the discussion, study questions, and bibliography (9 p.) laid in container.
CONTENTS: Banking today.—The control of the money supply.
1. Banks and banking—Great Britain. 2. Money supply—Great Britain. I. Griffiths, Brian, joint author. II. Title. III. Series: British and European economics series, E3.
[HG2990] 74-760902

Bain, Andrew David.
Company financing in the United Kingdom : a flow of funds model / [by] A. D. Bain, C. L. Day, A. L. Wearing. — London : Robertson, 1975.
xii, 142 p. : ill. ; 23 cm. GB75-27656
Bibliography: p. 137-138.
Includes index.
ISBN 0-85520-094-4 : £5.95
1. Corporations—Great Britain—Finance—Mathematical models. 2. Flow of funds. I. Day, Colin Leslie, joint author. II. Wearing, A. L., joint author. III. Title.
HG4135.B34 658.1'5 76-354885
76 MARC

Bain, Andrew David.
The control of the money supply ₍by₎ A. D. Bain. ₍Harmondsworth, Eng.₎ Penguin Books ₍1970₎
175 p. illus. 18 cm. (Penguin education) (Penguin modern economics texts) $1.95 (U.S.) B***
Bibliography: p. ₍165₎-169.
1. Monetary policy—Great Britain. 2. Monetary policy—United States. I. Title.
HG939.5.B33 332.4'6 74-24703
ISBN 0-14-080232-0 71₍r75₎rev MARC

Bain, Andrew David.
The control of the money supply / ₍by₎ A. D. Bain. — 2nd ed. — Harmondsworth ; New York ₍etc.₎ : Penguin, 1976.
176 p. : ill. ; 19 cm. — (Penguin modern economics texts : macroeconomics) (Penguin education) GB77-03421
Bibliography: p. ₍170₎-172.
Includes index.
ISBN 0-14-080232-0 : £1.25 ($3.95 U.S.)
1. Monetary policy—Great Britain. 2. Monetary policy—United States. I. Title.
HG939.5.B33 1976 332.4'6 77-359726
77 MARC

Bain, Andrew David.
Flow of funds analysis in the formulation of economic policy, by A. D. Bain. ₍Stockport₎, Manchester, Statistical Society ₍1973₎
24 p. 22 cm. £0.70 GB 73-29975
Cover title.
1. Flow of funds. 2. Monetary policy. I. Manchester Statistical Society. II. Title.
HC79.F55B34 339.2'6 74-160167
ISBN 0-85336-017-0 MARC

Bain, Beatrice M., joint author
see Hoos, Sidney Samuel, 1911- Asparagus -processed and fresh markets... [Berkeley?] California Agricultural Experiment Station, Giannini Foundation of Agricultural Economics, 1960.

Bain, Carl E
A critical study of The kingis quair. Baltimore, 1961 ₍1972₎
231 l.
Thesis—Johns Hopkins University.
Microfilm (negative) of typescript. Baltimore, Johns Hopkins University, 1972. 1 reel.
1. The kingis quair. I. Title.
IaU NUC74-33133

Bain, Carl E comp.
Drama. Edited by Carl E. Bain. ₍1st ed.₎ New York, Norton ₍1973₎
xxxi, 592 p. 24 cm. (The Norton introduction to literature) $3.45
1. Drama—Collections. I. Title. II. Series.
PN6112.B26 808.82 72-14190
ISBN 0-393-09366-2 MARC

Bain, Carl E comp.
The Norton introduction to literature ₍by₎ Carl E. Bain, Jerome Beaty ₍and₎ J. Paul Hunter. ₍1st₎ Combined shorter ed. New York, Norton ₍1973₎
xxxi, 1191 p. 25 cm. $8.25
1. Literature—Collections. I. Beaty, Jerome, 1924- joint comp. II. Hunter, J. Paul, 1934- joint comp. III. Title. IV. Series.
PN6014.B27 1973 808.8 73-5878
ISBN 0-393-09347-6; 0-393-09334-4 (pbk.) MARC

Bain, Carl E comp.
The Norton introduction to literature / ₍edited by₎ Carl E. Bain, Jerome Beaty, J. Paul Hunter. — 2d ed. — New York : Norton, c1977.
xxxiii, 1403 p. ; 21 cm.
Includes indexes.
ISBN 0-393-09119-8
1. Literature—Collections. I. Beaty, Jerome, 1924- II. Hunter, J. Paul, 1934- III. Title.
PN6014.B27 1977 808.8 77-23240
77 MARC

Bain, Chester Arthur, 1912-
The Far East, by Chester A. Bain. Edited by June W. Bain. 5th ed. Totowa, N. J., Littlefield, Adams, 1972.
xiii, 335 p. illus. 21 cm. (A Littlefield, Adams quality paperback, no. 44) $2.95 (pbk.)
Includes bibliographies.
1. East (Far East)—History. I. Bain, June W., ed. II. Title.
DS513.B3 1972 950 72-171255
MARC

Bain, Christine A
Survey of New York State astronomers, edited by Christine A. Bain. Albany, N. Y., New York Astronomical Corp., 1971.
1 v. (loose-leaf) 28 cm.
A listing of recent research by the New York astronomical community done in the period 1965-1969.
1. Astronomers, American—Directories. 2. Astronomical research—New York (State) 3. Astronomy—Bibliography. 4. Astrophysics—Bibliography. I. New York Astronomical Corporation. II. Title.
NNC NUC73-119895

Bain, David Alexander, 1937-
Graphemic discrimination by educable mentally retarded and slow learners. David Alexander Bain. [Vancouver, B.C.] 1975.
xi, 206 l. ill. 28 cm.
Thesis (Ed.D.)—University of British Columbia.
Vita.
Bibliography: leaves 188-206.
1. Mentally handicapped children—Education—Reading. I. Title. II. Series.
CaBVaU NUC77-82720

Bain, Donald, 1935-
The control of Candy Jones / Donald Bain. — 1st ed. — Chicago : Playboy Press, c1976.
xi, 267 p., ₍4₎ leaves of plates : ill. ; 25 cm.
ISBN 0-87223-457-6
1. Hypnotism—Case studies. 2. Jones, Candy. 3. Nebel, Long John. 4. United States. Central Intelligence Agency. I. Title.
BF1128.B34 154.7'092'6 76-7490
76 MARC

Bain, Donald, 1935-
Long John Nebel: radio talk king, master salesman, and magnificent charlatan. New York, Macmillan ₍1974₎
xix, 268 p. illus. 22 cm.
1. Nebel, Long John.
HF5438.B223 791.44'092'4 [B] 74-1077
ISBN 0-02-505950-5 MARC

Bain, Douglas Cogburn.
The Jacobean literature: a reflection of James's approach to Jewish Christianity. Fort Worth, Texas, 1973.
300 l.
Thesis (Th. D.)—Southwestern Baptist Theological Seminary.
Bibliography: p. [269]-300.
Typewritten.
1. Bible. N. T. James—Criticism, interpretation, etc. 2. Bible. N. T. James—Criticism, Textual. 3. Jewish Christians—Early church. I. Title.
TxFS NUC75-19461

Bain, Edgar Collins, 1891-1971.
Pioneering in steel research : a personal record / by Edgar C. Bain ; edited by Marjorie R. Hyslop. — Metals Park, Ohio : American Society for Metals, ₍1975₎
xix, 277 p. : ill. ; 24 cm.
Includes bibliographical references and indexes.
1. Bain, Edgar Collins, 1891-1971. 2. Steel—Metallurgy. I. Hyslop, Marjorie R., ed. II. Title.
TN140.B34A33 669'.142'0924 74-31126
74 MARC

Bain, Edgar Collins, 1891-1971
see Phase transformations and related phenomena in steels... Metals Park, Ohio, American Society for Metals [1973]

Bain, Francis William, 1863-1940. The descent of the sun
see Phitthayālongkōn, Prince, 1877-1945. (Kanok nakhōn). ₍2503 i. e. 1960₎

Bain, G L
The early history of the Bahama Islands to 1730, with a special study of the proprietorial government. London ₍1976₎
284 p. illus., maps.
Microfilm (negative) of typescript in University of London Library.
Thesis (M.A.)—University of London, 1959.
Bibliography: p. 272-284.
1. Carolina Proprietors. 2. N.C.—History—Colonial period. I. Title.
NcU NUC77-85254

Bain, G. S.
see
Bain, George Sayers.

Bain, George, fl. 1951.
Celtic art; methods of construction. Glasgow, W. MacLellan, 1967.
6 v. illus. 15 x 23 cm.
First published, 1944.
Prepared for use in schools for art students, artists, craftsmen, etc.
Contents.—Bk. 1. Knotwork borders.—Bk. 2. Knotwork panels.—Bk. 3. Spirals.—Bk. 4. Key patterns.—Bk. 5. Lettering.—Bk. 6. Zoomorphics.
1. Decoration and ornament, Celtic. I. Title.
PPT NUC73-68875

Bain, George, fl. 1951.
Celtic art: the methods of construction. [Glasgow] W. MacLellan [1972]
164 p. illus. 29 cm.
"Second impression 1972."
First published 1951 under title: The methods of construction of Celtic art.
1. Decoration and ornament, Celtic. I. Title.
CtW NUC76-69714

Bain, George, fl. 1951.
Celtic art : the methods of construction / by George Bain. — Quimper (45, Brd. de Kerguelen, 29000) : Éditions de l'Odet, ₍1975₎
166 p. : ill. ; 30 cm. F76-14956
Reprint of the 1951 ed. published by W. MacLellan, Glasgow under title: The methods of construction of Celtic art.
French preface and table of contents (₍23₎ p.) inserted.
107.00F
1. Decoration and ornament, Celtic. I. Title.
NK1264.B3 1975 745.4'49'41 77-363677
77 MARC

Bain, George, fl. 1951.
The methods of construction of Celtic art. Glasgow, W. MacLellan ₍1951₎
166 p. illus. 29 cm.
1. Decoration and ornament, Celtic.
NK1264.B3 1951 745.44 52-30180

Bain, George, fl. 1951.
The methods of construction of Celtic art. New York, Dover Publications ₍1973₎
159 p. illus. 31 cm.
Half title: Celtic art.
Reprint of the 1951 ed. published by W. MacLellan, Glasgow.
1. Decoration and ornament, Celtic. I. Title. II. Title: Celtic art.
NK1264.B3 1973 745.4'49'41 73-75875
ISBN 0-486-22923-8 73₍r77₎rev MARC

Bain, George Charles Stewart, 1920-
Canada's Parliament, by George Bain. ₍Ottawa, Information Canada, 1972₎
₍26₎ p. illus. 22 x 22 cm. $0.75 C***
Cover title.
1. Canada. Parliament. House of Commons—Rules and practice. I. Title.
JL164.B34 328.71'05 72-172033
MARC

Bain, George Charles Stewart, 1920-
Champagne is for breakfast ₍by₎ George Bain. Toronto, New Press, 1972.
277 p., 4 l. of plates, ill., maps. 23 cm. $6.95 C 73-474
Includes index.
1. Wine and wine making. 2. Cookery (Wine) I. Title.
TP548.B24 1972 641.2'2 73-174644
ISBN 0-88770-161-2; 0-88770-162-0 (pbk.) MARC

Bain, George F
The Barrow gang; Clyde Barrow & Bonnie Parker. ₍n.p., 1968₎
33 p. port.
1. Barrow, Clyde. 2. Parker, Bonnie. 3. Crime and criminals. I. Title.
WHi NUC75-30736

Bain, George F
The future of ship technology to mid twenty-first century; report on a colloquium held at the University of Michigan, September 23, 1967. ₍Ann Arbor, 1967₎
119 p.
1. Shipping. 2. Ship-building. 3. Twenty-first century—Forecasts. I. Title.
MiU NUC73-126493

Bain, George L 1931-
Salty ground water in West Virginia; with a discussion of the Pocatalico River basin above Sissonville, by George L. Bain. [Morgantown, West Virginia Geological and Economic Survey] 1970.
31 p. illus., 6 fold. col. maps. 28 cm. (West Virginia Geological and Economic Survey. Circular 11)
Bibliography: p. 31.
1. Water, Underground—West Virginia—Pocatalico River watershed. 2. Saltwater encroachment—West Virginia—Pocatalico River watershed. 3. Water, Underground—West Virginia. I. Title. II. Series: West Virginia. Geological Survey. Circular series, no. 11.
QE177.A323 no. 11 553'.09754 s 70-634492
[GB1025.W4] [553'.72'097543] MARC

Bain, George L 1931-
Water resources of the Little Kanawha River basin, West Virginia / by George L. Bain and Eugene A. Friel ; prepared by the United States Geological Survey, in cooperation with the West Virginia Geological and Economic Survey and the West Virginia Department of Natural Resources, Division of Water Resources. — [Charleston] : West Virginia Geological and Economic Survey, 1972.
xi, 122 p. : ill. ; 28 cm. — (River basin bulletin ; 2)
Bibliography: p. 121-122.
1. Water supply—West Virginia—Little Kanawha River watershed. I. Friel, E. A., joint author. II. United States. Geological Survey. III. West Virginia. Geological Survey. IV. West Virginia. Division of Water Resources. V. Title. VI. Series.
TD224.W4B35 553'.7'097542 75-624531
76 MARC

Bain, George L., 1931- joint author.
see Friel, Eugene A. Records of wells, springs, and test borings, chemical analyses of water, sediment analyses, standard streamflow data summaries, and selected drillers' logs from the Little Kanawha River Basin in West Virginia. [Morgantown, West Virginia Geological and Economic Survey] 1971.

Bain, George Sayers.
Social stratification and trade unionism; a critique [by] George Sayers Bain, David Coates [and] Valerie Ellis. London, Heinemann Educational, 1973.
x, 174 p. 21 cm. (Warwick studies in industrial relations) £2.50
GB 73-31849
Bibliography: p. [161]-174.
1. Trade-unions—Clerks. 2. Trade and professional associations. 3. Social classes. I. Coates, David, joint author. II. Ellis, Valerie, joint author. III. Title. IV. Series.
HD6668.M4B29 331.88'11 74-159876
ISBN 0-435-85126-8 MARC

Bain, George Sayers.
Union growth and the business cycle : an econometric analysis / George Sayers Bain and Farouk Elsheikh. — Oxford : Blackwell, c1976.
xv, 155 p. : graphs ; 23 cm. — (Warwick studies in industrial relations)
GB76
Includes bibliographical references and index.
ISBN 0-631-16650-5 : £10.00
1. Trade-unions—Mathematical models. 2. Business cycle. I. Elsheikh, Farouk, joint author. II. Title. III. Series.
HD6483.B29 331.88 77-350085
77 MARC

Bain, George Sayers.
The United Packinghouse, Food and Allied Workers; its development, structure, collective bargaining, and future, with particular reference to Canada. [Winnipeg] 1964.
viii, 232 l.
Thesis (M.A.)—University of Manitoba, 1964.
Bibliography: leaves 224-231.
Microfilm copy (positive) of typescript.
[n.p.] Western Microfilm Ltd., 1967. 1 reel. 35 mm.
1. United Packinghouse, Food and Allied Workers. 2. Trade-unions—Canada. 3. Meat industry and trade—Canada. I. Title.
NIC NUC73-126495

Bain, George William, 1901-
The flow of time in the Connecticut Valley : geological imprints / by George W. Bain and Howard A. Meyerhoff. — Rev. — Springfield, Mass. : Connecticut Valley Historical Museum, 1976.
xii, 168 p. : ill. ; 23 cm.
Includes indexes.
1. Geology—Connecticut Valley. I. Meyerhoff, Howard Augustus, 1899- joint author. II. Title.
QE124.C4B3 1976 557.44'2 76-361644
76 MARC

Bain, George William, 1942-
Liberal teacher; the writings of Max Lerner, 1925-1965. [Minneapolis] 1975.
315 l. 29 cm.
Thesis (Ph.D.)—University of Minnesota.
Bibliography: leaves 291-315.
MnU NUC77-82723

Bain, George William, 1942-
Liberal teacher: the writings of Max Lerner, 1925-1965, by George William Bain. [Minneapolis, Minn.] 1975.
315 l.
Thesis (Ph.D.)—University of Minnesota.
Bibliography: leaves 291-315.
Photocopy. Ann Arbor, Mich., University Microfilms, 1976. 22 cm.
1. Lerner, Max, 1902- I. Title.
TxU NUC77-82722

Bain, Harry Foster, 1872-1948.
Ores and industry in South America / H. Foster Bain and Thomas Thornton Read. — New York : Arno Press, 1976.
xvi, 381 p. : maps ; 23 cm. — (American business abroad)
Reprint of the 1934 ed. published by Harper, New York, in series: Publications of the Council on Foreign Relations.
Includes bibliographical references and index.
ISBN 0-405-09265-2
1. Mines and mineral resources—South America. 2. Mining industry and finance—South America. 3. Investments, Foreign—South America. I. Read, Thomas Thornton, 1880-1947, joint author. II. Title. III. Series. IV. Series: Council on Foreign Relations. Publications.
TN34.B3 1976 338.2'098 76-4767
76 MARC

Bain, Harry W., ed.
see Symposium on chronic disease in children. Philadelphia, Saunders, 1974.

Bain, Henry M 1926-
Ballot position and voter's choice; the arrangement of names on the ballot and its effect on the voter [by] Henry M. Bain, Jr. and Donald S. Hecock. Foreword by V. O. Key, Jr. Westport, Conn., Greenwood Press [1973, c1957]
xiv, 108 p. illus. 22 cm.
Includes bibliographical references.
1. Ballot. 2. Voting. I. Hecock, Donald Sumner, 1906- joint author. II. Title. III. Series: Wayne State University studies, no. 1.
[JF1091.B3 1973] 324'.25 72-9371
ISBN 0-8371-6587-4 MARC

Bain, Henry M 1926-
The development district: a governmental institution for the better organization of the urban development process in the bi-county region, by Henry Bain. [Washington, D. C.] Washington Center for Metropolitan Studies, 1968.
86 p. 28 cm.
Cover title.
MoKU NUC74-118014

Bain, Iain.
A checklist of the manuscripts of Thomas Bewick. [Baldock] Reprinted from the private library with addenda, 1970.
46 p. illus.
1. Bewick, Thomas, 1753-1828—Bibl.
2. Wood-engravers, English—Bibl. I. Title.
MiEM NUC73-126497

Bain, Iain.
Eleven original prints by Thomas Gainsborough, R.A.; a prospectus for a new edition to be taken from his still-surviving copper-plates: ten etched in soft-ground & in aquatint with one engraved in mezzotint. To be published by Iain Bain at the John Boydell Press, 1971. [Newnham, Baldock, Hertfordshire, J. Boydell, 1971]
7 p. 12 illus. 19 cm.
MWiCA NUC73-36081

Bain, J
Investigation into the effectiveness of escape gaps in crayfish traps. J. Bain (Jnr). [Wellington, Marine Department, 1967]
11, [9] p. illus. 30 cm. (Fisheries technical report)
Bibliography: p. 11.
1. Fishing—Implements and appliances.
2. Crayfish fisheries. I. Title. II. Series: New Zealand. Marine Department. Fisheries technical report, no. 17.
DI NUC76-69676

Bain, J
Total length/carapace length in crayfish (Jasus lalandii). J. Bain (Jnr). [Wellington, Marine Department, 1967]
12, [5] p. ill. 30 cm. (New Zealand. Marine Department. Fisheries technical report, no. 23)
Bibliography: p. 6.
1. Crayfish. 2. Crayfish—New Zealand.
I. Title. II. Series.
DI NUC76-69675

Bain, J H C
Geology of the Kubor Anticline, central highlands of Papua New Guinea. J.H.C. Bain, D.E. Mackenzie, and R.J. Ryburn. Canberra, Australian Govt. Pub. Service, 1975.
106 p. ill., maps (2 fold. col. in pocket) 26 cm. (Bulletin - Australia Bureau of Mineral Resources, Geology and Geophysics, 155)
Bibliography: p. 105-106.
1. Papua New Guinea—Geology. I. Mackenzie, D.E. II. Ryburn, R.J. III. Title.
DI-GS NUC77-82721

Bain, James.
Introduction to system planning (system decision-making process) Wright-Patterson Air Force Base, Ohio, Defense Weapon Systems Management Center, 1969.
160 p. 28 cm.
Cover title.
Bibliography: p. 152-153.
OC NUC73-126496

Bain, James S
The nature of the Cretaceous-pre-Cretaceous contact, north-central Texas / James S. Bain. — Waco, Tex. : Baylor University, Dept. of Geology, 1973.
44 p. : ill. ; 31 cm. — (Baylor geological studies ; bull. no. 25)
Originally presented as the author's thesis (M.S.), Baylor University.
Bibliography: p. 27-29.
Includes index.
$1.00
1. Geology, Stratigraphic—Cretaceous. 2. Geology—Texas. I. Title. II. Series.
QE167.B35 no. 25 557.64'08 s 76-359128
[QE685] 76 MARC

Bain, Jim.
For His name's sake; sermons from the 23rd Psalm. [Memphis, Tenn., Memphis Print. Service, 1969]
82 p. 21 cm.
1. Bible. O. T. Psalms XXIII—Sermons.
2. Baptists—Sermons. I. Title.
MsU NUC74-117989

Bain, Jim.
Sermons from the Revelation. [University, Miss., 1970-73]
2 v. 22 cm.
Cover title: The four and twenty elders.
1. Bible. N. T. Revelation-Sermons. 2. Baptists—Sermons.
MsSM NUC75-19920

Bain, Joe Staten, 1912-
Barriers to new competition; their character and consequences in manufacturing industries. Cambridge [c1956]
329 p. (Harvard University series on competition in American industry, 3)
1. Competition. 2. United States. Manufacturers. I. Title. II. Series.
DNAL NUC73-68874

Bain, Joe Staten, 1912-
Environmental decay; economic causes and remedies [by] Joe S. Bain. Boston, Little, Brown [1973]
ix, 235 p. 23 cm. (Little, Brown series in economics)
Includes bibliographies.
1. Pollution—Economic aspects—United States—Addresses, essays, lectures. 2. Environmental policy—United States—Addresses, essays, lectures. I. Title.
HC110.P55B34 301.31'0973 72-9002
MARC

Bain, Joe Staten, 1912-
see Essays on industrial organization, in honor of Joe S. Bain. Cambridge, Mass., Ballinger Pub. Co., c1976.

Bain, John A
The development of Roman catholicism. Edinburgh, O. Anderson & Ferrier [19--]
191 p.
1. Catholic Church—Doctrinal and controversial works. 2. Catholic Church—Relations—Protestant churches. 3. Protestant churches—Relations—Catholic Church. I. Title.
ScU NUC76-22394

Bain, John A.
Sören Kierkegaard, his life and religious teaching, by John A. Bain ... London, Student Christian movement press [1935]
3 p. l., 9-160 p. 19½ cm.
Bibliography: p. 10-12.
1. Kierkegaard, Søren Aabye, 1813-1855.
BX4827.K5B3 921.8489 36—13733

Bain, John A
Sören Kierkegaard, his life and religious teaching, by John A. Bain ... London, Student Christian movement press [1935] New York, Kraus Reprint Co., 1971.
3 p.l., 9-160 p. 20 cm.
Bibliography: p. 10-12.
1. Kierkegaard, Søren Aabye, 1813-1855.
TxFTC NSyU NBuU NUC73-35528
NcU CaOTP CSt

Bain, June W., ed.
see Bain, Chester Arthur, 1912-
The Far East. 5th ed. Totowa, N. J., Littlefield, Adams, 1972.

Bain, June Wilson, 1930-
A study of the effects on college students' reading achievement of two instructional approaches: audio-visual and visual. Washington, 1974.
ix, 128 p. tables.
Thesis (Ed. D.)—American University.
Bibliography: p. 118-125.
Diss. Abstracts: 35: 2114A, Oct., 1974.
1. Reading (Higher education) I. Title.
DAU NUC76-22377

Bain, Kenneth Bruce Findlater
see
Findlater, Richard, 1921-

Bain, L.
see Commission on the Public Services of the Governments of Sarawak, North Borneo and Brunei. Report, 1956. Kuching, Govt. Print. Off., 1956.

Bain, L. L.
see History of Bigfork. [Kalispell, Mont., Trippet Publishers, 1956]

Bain, L. L.
see History of Kalispell. [Kalispell, Mont., Trippet Publishers, 1956]

Bain, L. L.
see History of Whitefish ... [Kalispell, Trippet Publishers, 1956]

Bain, Lee J 1939-
Inferential procedures for the Weibull and generalized gamma distributions [by] Lee J. Bain [and] Charles E. Antle. Wright-Patterson Air Force Base, Ohio, Aerospace Research Laboratories, Air Force Systems Command, United States Air Force, 1970.
110 p. (ARL 70-0266)
AD 718 103.
Photocopy.
InU NUC73-126492

Bain, Linda Lee, 1941-
Description and analysis of the hidden curriculum in physical education. [n.p.] c1974.
160 l. illus. 29 cm.
Thesis (Ph.D.)—University of Wisconsin.
Vita.
Includes bibliography.
1. Physical education and training—Study and teaching. I. Title.
WU NUC76-20074

Bain, Linda Lee, 1941-
Description and analysis of the hidden curriculum in physical education. [Eugene, Ore., Microform Publications, College of Health, Physical Education and Recreation, University of Oregon, 1975]
2 sheets. 10.5 x 14.8 cm.
Microfiche (negative) of typescript.
Collation of the original: 160 l. 29 cm.
Thesis (Ph.D.)--University of Wisconsin, 1974.
Vita.
Bibliography: leaves 125-134.
1. Physical education and training--Curricula. I. Title.
NSyU NUC77-86397

Bain, Linda Morgan.
Evergreen adventurer : the real Frank Harris / Linda Morgan Bain. — London : Research Pub. Co., [1975]
121 p., [2] leaves of plates : ill. ; 22 cm. GB***
ISBN 0-7050-0029-X : £2.00
1. Harris, Frank, 1855-1931—Biography. I. Title.
PR4759.H37Z568 828'.9'12 75-310242
75 MARC

Bain, Mary Albertus, 1911-
Ancient landmarks : a social and economic history of the Victoria district of Western Australia, 1839-1894 / [by] Mary Albertus Bain. — Nedlands, W.A. : University of Western Australia Press, 1975.
xv, 431 p., 8 leaves of plates : ill. ; 25 cm. Aus
Distributed in U.S.A. and Canada by International Scholarly Book Services, Beaverton, Or.
Bibliography: p. 413-418.
Includes index.
ISBN 0-85564-090-1
1. Western Australia—Social conditions. 2. Western Australia—Economic conditions. 3. Western Australia—History. I. Title.
HN923.B33 994.1 76-362833
76 MARC

Bain, Mildred, 1929-
see From freedom to freedom ... 1st ed. New York, Random House, c1977.

Bain, Nancy Remus.
Spatial variations in fertility: the United States, 1920, 1940 and 1960. [Minneapolis] 1973.
vii, 151 l. illus. 29 cm.
Thesis (Ph.D.)—University of Minnesota.
Bibliography: leaves 134-151.
MnU NUC76-69659

Bain, Patricia Halligan, 1941-
Poetry into prose: the meaning of writing for Virginia Woolf. [n.p.] 1972.
385 l.
Thesis (Ph.D.)—University of Chicago.
1. Woolf, Virginia (Stephen) 1882-1941. I. Title.
ICU NUC73-35534

Bain, Penny.
Criminal procedures. Vancouver, B.C., Vancouver People's Law School, c1973.
16 p. 31 cm.
Caption title.
1. Criminal procedure—British Columbia. I. Title.
CaBVaU NUC74-122950

Bain, Penny.
An Ombudsman for British Columbia : report / P. Bain, W. Black, J. Weller. -- [s.l. : s.n.] 1976?
ii, 51 leaves ; 28 cm.
1. Ombudsman--British Columbia. I. Black, Wesley D., 1910- II. Weller, J. III. Title.
CaBVaU NUC77-86973

Bain, Penny.
Small debts court procedures. Vancouver, B.C., Vancouver People's Law School, c1972.
11 l. 31 cm.
Caption title.
1. Small claims courts—British Columbia. I. Title.
CaBVaU NUC74-122968

Bain, Penny. Small debts court procedures
see Battersby, Mark. Small claims court procedures. 3d ed. Vancouver, B.C., Vancouver People's Law School, 1973.

Bain, Penny.
Women and the law [by] Penny Bain and Mary Ellen Boyd. Vancouver, Vancouver People's Law School, c1972.
31 p. 28 cm.
Caption title.
1. Woman—Legal status, laws, etc.—British Columbia. I. Boyd, Mary Ellen. II. Title.
CaBVaU NUC76-69662

Bain, Penny.
see Morgan, Leslie. Family Court. Vancouver [B.C.] Vancouver People's Law School, 1976.

Bain, Penny
see Sachs, Harriet. Matrimony & divorce. Vancouver, B. C., Vancouver Peoples Law School, 1974.

Bain, R E
A bibliography for management support systems, by R. E. Bain. Menlo Park, Calif., Stanford Research Institute; Reproduced [and distributed] by National Technical Information Service, Springfield, Va. [1971]
iii, 32 p. 28 cm. (Stanford Research Institute. Technical report, 2)
Prepared for the Office of Naval Research, Dept. of the Navy under Contract No. 0014-71-C-0210.
IEN NUC74-118243

Bain, R. Joyce, 1930- joint author.
see Froebe, Doris J., 1929- Quality assurance programs and controls in nursing. Saint Louis, C. V. Mosby Co., 1976.

Bain, Read
see Stuart, Jesse, 1907- He saw the sun this time. Tucson, Ariz., 1972.

Bain, Reginald Frank.
The federal government and theatre: a history of federal involvement in theatre from the end of the Federal Theatre Project in 1939 to the establishment of the National Foundation on the Arts and Humanities in 1965. [Minneapolis] 1972.
iv, 329 l. 29 cm.
Thesis (Ph.D.)—University of Minnesota.
Bibliography: leaves 308-329.
MnU NUC74-610

Bain, Richard C
Convention decisions and voting records [by] Richard C. Bain and Judith H. Parris. 2d ed. Washington, Brookings Institution [1973]
x, 350, [120] p. 25 cm. (Studies in presidential selection) $14.95
Includes bibliographical references.
1. Political conventions. I. Parris, Judith H., joint author. II. Title. III. Series.
JK2255.B3 1973 329'.0221 73-1082
ISBN 0-8157-0768-1 MARC

Bain, Robert
see Institute on Rehabilitation Services. Committee on Training Materials and Aids. Development and use of training materials... Washington, U. S. Dept. of Health, Education, and Welfare, Vocational Rehabilitation Administration [1966]

Bain, Robert A
H. L. Davis / by Robert Bain. — Boise, Idaho : Boise State University, c1974.
46 p. ; 21 cm. — (Boise State University Western writers series ; no. 11)
Bibliography: p. 43–46.
ISBN 0–88430–010–2 : $1.50
1. Davis, Harold Lenoir, 1896–1960. 2. The West in literature. I. Series: Boise State University. Boise State University western writers series ; no. 11.
PS3507.A7327Z59 813′.5′2 75–307036
MARC

Bain, Robert A comp.
The writer and worlds of words / edited by Robert Bain and Dennis G. Donovan. — Englewood Cliffs, N.J. : Prentice-Hall, [1975]
xi, 369 p. : ill. ; 23 cm.
Includes index.
ISBN 0-13-969980-5 : $5.95
1. College readers. 2. English language—Rhetoric. I. Donovan, Dennis G., joint comp. II. Title.
PE1417.B27 808′.04275 74-23662
74 MARC

Bain, Robert A.
see Alsop, George, b. 1638- A character of the Province of Mary-land. 1666. Bainbridge, N.Y., York Mail-Print, 1972.

Bain, Robert A., ed.
see Neal, John, 1793-1876. Seventy-six. "Our country!—Right or wrong". Bainbridge, New York, York Mail-Print, 1971.

Bain, Robert Nisbet, 1854-1909, ed. and tr.
Cossack fairy tales and folk tales / selected, edited, and translated by R. Nisbet Bain ; illustrated by Noel E. Nisbet. — Millwood, N.Y. : Kraus Reprint Co., 1975.
287 p. : ill. ; 25 cm.
Reprint of the ed. published by F. A. Stokes, New York.
SUMMARY: Twenty-seven traditional tales translated from Ruthenian, the language of the Cossacks.
ISBN 0-527-04404-0
1. Fairy tales. 2. Tales, Ukrainian. [1. Fairy tales. 2. Folklore—Ukraine] I. Title.
PZ8.B160 Co 8 398.2′0947′71 74-22131
74 MARC

Bain, Robert Nisbet, 1854-1909, ed.
Cossack fairy tales and folk-tales / selected, edited and translated by R. Nisbet Bain ; with ill. by E. W. Mitchell. — Great Neck, N.Y. : Core Collection Books, 1976.
viii, 356 p., [24] leaves of plates : ill. ; 20 cm. — (Children's literature reprint series)
Reprint of the 1894 ed. published by A. L. Burt, New York.
SUMMARY: Twenty-seven traditional tales translated from Ruthenian, the language of the Cossacks.
ISBN 0-8486-0200-5
1. Fairy tales. 2. Tales, Ukrainian. [1. Fairy tales. 2. Folklore—Ukraine] I. Mitchell, E. W. II. Title.
PZ8.B160 Co 9 398.2′0947′71 76-9882
76 MARC

Bain, Robert Nisbet, 1854-1909.
The last king of Poland and his contemporaries, by R. Nisbet Bain; with sixteen illustrations. London, Methuem & co. [1909, 1963]
xviii, 296 p. 16 plates (incl. front., ports.) 23 cm.
"First published in 1909."
Microfilm (positive) New York, Columbia University Libraries, 1973. 1 reel.
Master negative 0424.
1. Stanisław II August, king of Poland, 1732-1798. 2. Poland—Hist.—Partition period, 1763-1796. I. Title.
NNC NUC76-40710

Bain, Robert Nisbet, 1854–1909.
Peter III, Emperor of Russia; the story of a crisis and a crime. Westminster, A. Constable, 1902. St. Clair Shores, Mich., Scholarly Press, 1972.
xvi, 208 p. ports. 23 cm.
Bibliography: p. [ix]–xvi.
1. Peter III, Emperor of Russia, 1728–1762.
DK166.B2 1972 947′.06′0924 [B] 71–108456
ISBN 0–403–00465–9 MARC

Bain, Robert Nisbet, 1854-1909.
The pupils of Peter the Great : a history of the Russian court and empire from 1697 to 1740. -- Ann Arbor, Mich. : Xerox University Microfilms, 1976.
318 p. : ill.
Reprint of the 1897 ed.
1. Russia--History--1689-1800. 2. Russia--Courts and courtiers. I. Title.
ViBlbV NUC77-86972

Bain, Robert Nisbet, 1854-1909.
The pupils of Peter the Great : a history of the Russian court and Empire from 1697 to 1740 / by R. Nisbet Bain. — Folcroft, Pa. : Folcroft Library Editions, 1976.
xxiv, 318 p., [6] leaves of plates : ill. ; 23 cm.
Reprint of the 1897 ed. published by A. Constable, Westminster, Eng.
Includes bibliographical references and index.
ISBN 0-8414-3310-0 lib. bdg. : $45.00
1. Russia—History—1689-1800. 2. Russia—Court and courtiers. I. Title.
DK127.B27 1976 947′.05 76-27342
76 MARC

Bain, Robert Nisbet, 1854-1909, tr.
see Polevoi, Petr Nikolaevich, 1839-1902. Russian fairy tales... London, Harrap [n.d.]

Bain, Trevor.
Labor market experience for engineers during periods of changing demand. [New York, N.Y.] Center for Policy Research, 1973.
iv, 137 p.
"Final report... prepared for the Manpower Administration. U.S. Department of Labor under research and development grant no. 21-36-73-30."
Includes bibliography.
1. Engineers—Employment—United States. 2. Aerospace industries—Employees. 3. Unemployed—United States. I. Title.
CU NUC76-69658

Bain, Trevor.
Labor market experience for engineers during periods of changing demand; final report. [New York, Center for Policy Research] 1973.
iv, 137 p. 28 cm.
PB 227 220
"Prepared for the Manpower Administration, U.S. Department of Labor under research and development grant no. 21-36-73-30."
Bibliography: 130-137.
Photocopy. Springfield, Va., National Technical Information Service, 1973?
1. Engineers—Employment—United States. 2. Scientists—Employment—United States. I. Center for Policy Research. II. Title.
MCM NUC76-69329

Bain, Trevor.
Labor market experience of engineers during periods of changing demand / prepared by Trevor Bain. — Washington : U.S. Dept. of Labor, Manpower Administration : for sale by the Supt. of Docs., U.S. Govt. Print. Off., 1974.
vi, 60 p. ; 26 cm. — (Manpower research monograph ; no. 35)
Bibliography: p. 55-60.
$1.05
1. Engineers—Employment—United States. I. Title. II. Series.
HD5701.U53 no. 35 331.1′1′0973 s 74-602725
[TA157] 76 MARC

Bain, William H
The essentials of cardiovascular surgery / William H. Bain, J. Kennedy Watt. — 2d [rev.] ed. — Edinburgh ; New York : Churchill Livingstone ; New York : distributed by Longman Inc., 1975.
148 p., [8] leaves of plates : ill. ; 21 cm. GB***
First ed. published in 1970 under title: Cardio-vascular surgery for nurses and students.
Includes index.
ISBN 0-443-01254-7 : $11.50 (U.S.)
1. Cardiovascular system—Surgery. I. Watt, James Kennedy, joint author. II. Title.
RD598.B32 1975 617′.41 74-19640
75 MARC

Bain, Winifred Elma, 1889–1965.
An analytical study of teaching in nursery school, kindergarten, and first grade. New York, Bureau of Publications, Teachers College, Columbia University, 1928. [New York, AMS Press, 1972]
vi, 130 p. illus. 22 cm.
Reprint of the 1928 ed., issued in series: Teachers College, Columbia University. Contributions to education, no. 332.
Originally presented as the author's thesis, Columbia.
Bibliography: p. 127–130.
1. Teaching. 2. Education of children. I. Title. II. Series: Columbia University. Teachers College. Contributions to education, no. 332.
LB1025.B18 1972 372.1′1′02 74–176530
ISBN 0–404–55332–X MARC

Bain al-Aqvāmī Ghālib Saminār
see
International Ghalib Seminar, Delhi, 1969.

Bain, Burroughs, Hanson, Raimet
see Jericho parksite... [Vancouver, B.C.] 1974.

Bainbridge, Beryl, 1933–
The bottle factory outing / Beryl Bainbridge. — London : Duckworth, 1974.
179 p. ; 21 cm. GB***
ISBN 0–7156–0864–9 : £2.35
I. Title.
PZ4.B162Bo 823′.9′14 75–300210
[PR6052.A3195] MARC

Bainbridge, Beryl, 1933-
The bottle factory outing / Beryl Bainbridge. — New York : G. Braziller, 1975, c1974.
219 p. ; 22 cm.
ISBN 0-8076-0781-9 : $7.95
I. Title.
PZ4.B162 Bo 4 823′.9′14 74-25294
[PR6052.A3195] 75 MARC

Bainbridge, Beryl, 1933–
The dressmaker. [London] Duckworth [1973]
152 p. 21 cm. £2.35 GB***
I. Title.
PZ4.B162Dr 73–175010
[PR6052.A3195] MARC
ISBN 0–7156–0721–9

Bainbridge, Beryl, 1933–
Harriet said ... London, Duckworth, 1972.
152. 21 cm. £2.35 B 72–28068
I. Title.
PZ4.B162Har 823′.9′14 73–153786
[PR6052.A3195] MARC
ISBN 0–7156–0657–3

Bainbridge, Beryl, 1933–
Harriet said. New York, G. Braziller [1973, c1972]
152 p. 22 cm. $5.95
I. Title.
PZ4.B162Har 3 823′.9′14 73–76970
ISBN 0–8076–0687–1 MARC

Bainbridge, Beryl, 1933-
A quiet life / Beryl Bainbridge. — London : Duckworth, 1976.
156 p. ; 21 cm. GB***
ISBN 0-7156-1139-9 : £3.25
I. Title.
PZ4.B162 Qi 823′.9′14 76-380942
[PR6052.A3195] 76 MARC

Bainbridge, Beryl, 1933-
A quiet life : a novel / by Beryl Bainbridge. — New York : G. Braziller, 1977, c1976.
210 p. ; 22 cm.
ISBN 0-8076-0846-7
I. Title.
PZ4.B162 Qi 3 823′.9′14 76-55837
[PR6052.A3195] 76 MARC

Bainbridge, Beryl, 1933–
The secret glass. New York, G. Braziller [1974, c1973]
152 p. 22 cm. $5.95
London ed. published in 1973 under title: The dressmaker.
I. Title.
PZ4.B162Se 823′.9′14 73–93608
[PR6052.A3195] MARC
ISBN 0–8076–0746–0

Bainbridge, Beryl, 1933-
Sweet William / Beryl Bainbridge. — London : Duckworth, 1975.
160 p. ; 21 cm. GB***
ISBN 0-7156-0927-0 : £2.95
I. Title.
PZ4.B162 Sw 3 823′.9′14 75-330388
[PR6052.A3195] 75 MARC

Bainbridge, Beryl, 1933-
Sweet William : a novel / Beryl Bainbridge. — New York : G. Braziller, 1976, c1975.
204 p. ; 22 cm.
ISBN 0-8076-0816-5 : $7.95
I. Title.
PZ4.B162 Sw 4 823′.9′14 75-43672
[PR6052.A3195] 75 MARC

Bainbridge, Carol Ann.
Investigations into the reactions of stannous fluoride with calcium hydroxylapatite. [Minneapolis] 1973.
145 l. illus. 29 cm.
Thesis (Ph.D.)—University of Minnesota.
Bibliography: leaves 137-145.
MnU NUC76-69679

Bainbridge, Cyril.
Taught with care : a century of church schooling in Whetstone / by Cyril Bainbridge. — [London] : Friends of St. John's School, 1974.
[2], ii, 24 p., [4] p. of plates : ill., facsims., ports. ; 21 cm. GB75-14091
Cover title.
ISBN 0-9504184-0-4 : £0.40
1. St. John's School—History. 2. Whetstone, Eng.—History. I. Title.
LF795.W62B34 372.9'421'87 76-357775
76 MARC

Bainbridge, David A
Bikeway planning and design, a primer / David A. Bainbridge, Michael C. Moore. -- [3d printing and revision] -- [Davis, Calif. : Environmental Planner, 1975]
9 p. : ill. ; 28 cm.
InNd NUC77-85219

Bainbridge, David A
A proposal for a bikeway from Merced to Yosemite Valley / by David A. Bainbridge, Michal C. Moore. -- Broderick, Ca. : Bainbridge, Behrens, Moore, 1974.
[6] p. : ill. ; 22 cm.
On cover: Yosemite Bikeway - a sketch plan.
1. Cycling paths--Calif. I. Moore, Michal C. II. Bainbridge, Behrens, Moore, inc.
CU-A NUC77-94484

Bainbridge, David A
Sand and gravel resources and land use planning : a bibliography / David A. Bainbridge. -- Monticello, Ill. : Council of Planning Librarians, 1976.
10 p. ; 28 cm. -- (Exchange bibliography - Council of Planning Librarians ; 1013)
Cover title.
1. Sand and gravel industry--Environmental aspects--Bibl. 2. Sand--Bibl. 3. Gravel--Bibl. I. Title.
CLSU NUC77-86876

Bainbridge, David A
Towards an environmental new town : a selected bibliography / David A. Bainbridge. — Monticello, Ill. : Council of Planning Librarians, 1976.
14 p. ; 29 cm. — (Exchange bibliography - Council of Planning Librarians ; 967)
Cover title
$1.50
1. Cities and towns—Planning—Bibliography. 2. New towns—Bibliography. I. Title. II. Series: Council of Planning Librarians. Exchange bibliography ; 967 .
Z5942.C68 no.967 016.3092'08 s 76-354730
[HT166] 76 MARC

Bainbridge, E Gordon.
The old Rhinebeck aerodrome / E. Gordon Bainbridge. — 1st ed. — Hicksville, N.Y. : Exposition Press, c1977.
123 p., [8] leaves of plates : ill. ; 24 cm. — (An Exposition-banner book)
ISBN 0-682-48883-6 : $7.50
1. Airports—New York (State)—Rhinebeck—History. 2. Palen, Cole. 3. Bainbridge, E. Gordon. I. Title.
TL726.4.R45B34 629.13'0074'014733 77-79711
77 MARC

Bainbridge, Edwin Stewart, 1942-
A unified minimal realization theory with duality. [Ann Arbor, 1972, 1973]
iv, 239 l.
Thesis—University of Michigan.
Bibliography: leaves 238-239.
Microfilm copy. Ann Arbor, Mich., University Microfilms, 1973. 1 reel. 35 mm.
IU NUC75-19474

Bainbridge, Ilona
see
Flor, Holly Marie, 1944-

Bainbridge, J
Health project management : a manual of procedures for formulating and implementing health projects / by J. Bainbridge and S. Sapirie. — Geneva : World Health Organization, 1974.
280 p. : ill. ; 28 cm. — (WHO offset publication ; no. 12) Sw***
ISBN 9241700122 : 38.00F
1. Public health administration. I. Sapirie, S., joint author. II. Title. III. Series: World Health Organization. WHO offset publication ; no. 12.
RA427.B2 362.1 75-318701
75 MARC

Bainbridge, John.
Garbo : the famous biography, lavishly illustrated / by John Bainbridge. — New York : Galahad Books, [1975] c1971.
320 p. : ill. ; 26 cm.
Includes index.
ISBN 0-88365-286-2 : $14.95
1. Garbo, Greta, 1905- 2. Actors—Sweden—Biography.
PN2778.G3B3 1975 791.43'028'0924 74-29492
75[r77]rev MARC

Bainbridge, John, 1582-1643.
An astronomicall description of the late comet / John Bainbridge. — Amsterdam : Theatrum Orbis Terrarum ; Norwood, N.J. : W.J. Johnson, 1975.
42 p., [1] fold. leaf of plates : ill. ; 22 cm. — (The English experience, its record in early printed books published in facsimile ; no. 710)
On spine: Description of the comet, 1619.
Photoreprint of the 1619 ed. printed by E. Griffin for J. Parker under title: An astronomicall description of the late comet from the 18. of Novemb. 1618 to the 16. of December following.
"S.T.C. no. 1208."
ISBN 9022107108
1. Comets—Early works to 1800. I. Title. II. Title: Description of the comet, 1619. III. Series.
QB724.B34 1975 523.6 74-28828
76 MARC

Bainbridge, John Whitfield.
Junior science source book [by] J.W. Bainbridge, R.W. Stockdale [and] E.R. Wastnedge. London, Collins [1970]
280 p. illus. (part col.) 22 cm.
Includes bibliographies.
1. Science—Study and teaching (Elementary) I. Stockdale, R.W. II. Wastnedge, E.R. III. Title.
CaBVaU NUC74-12385

Bainbridge, John Whitfield.
Weather study: an approach to scientific inquiry [by] J. W. Bainbridge [and] R. W. Stockdale. London, Methuen, 1972.
[11], 83 p. illus., facsims. 22 cm. £1.80 B 72-31008
"Distributed in the USA by Harper & Row Publishers, Inc., Barnes & Noble Import Division."
Bibliography: p. 67-[75]
1. Meteorology—Study and teaching (Elementary)—Great Britain. I. Stockdale, R. W., joint author. II. Title.
QC869.B34 372.3'5 73-153654
ISBN 0-423-80240-2 ; 0-423-87580-9 (pbk.) MARC

Bainbridge, Karyl.
Inscriptions in Ludwig Cemetery, Quiggleville, Lycoming County, Pennsylvania / [Karyl and Ted Bainbridge]. — [Tucson, Ariz.] : Bainbridge, [1974?]
[5] leaves : diagr. ; 29 cm.
Cover title.
1. Lycoming Co., Pa.—Genealogy. 2. Registers of births, etc.—Lycoming Co., Pa. I. Bainbridge, Ted, joint author. II. Title: Inscriptions in Ludwig Cemetary ...
F157.L9B34 929'.3748'51 75-320993
75 MARC

Bainbridge, Kent LaMont.
Mercury dynamics in a warm water stream [by] Kent L. Bainbridge; [graduate committee: Frank M. D'Itri and Thomas G. Bahr. East Lansing] Michigan State University, 1973.
vi, 71 l. illus. 28 cm. (Michigan. State University, East Lansing. Institute of Water Research. Technical report no. 39)
OWRR project no. A-051, agreement no. 14-31-0001-32222. Completion report.
Literature cited: leaves 41-45.
1. Mercury. 2. Water—Pollution—Research. I. D'Itri, Frank M. II. Bahr, Thomas Gordon, 1940- III. United States. Office of Water Resources Research. IV. Title. V. Series.
DI NUC76-69726

Bainbridge, Richard, SC.D.
see Light as an ecological factor, II ... Oxford, Blackwell, c1975.

Bainbridge, Ted, joint author.
see Bainbridge, Karyl. Inscriptions in Ludwig Cemetery, Quiggleville, Lycoming County, Pennsylvania. [Tucson, Ariz.] Bainbridge, [1974?]

Bainbridge, Unity.
Songs of Seton / [Unity Bainbridge]. -- [Vancouver, B.C. : Bainbridge, 1975]
[48] p. : ill. (some col.) ; 27 cm.
1. Bainbridge, Unity. 2. Salishan Indians--Pictorial works. I. Title.
CaBVaU NUC77-84680

Bainbridge, William Sims.
The spaceflight revolution : a sociological study / William Sims Bainbridge. — New York : Wiley, c1976.
x, 294 p. : ill. ; 24 cm. — (Science, culture, and society)
"A Wiley-Interscience publication."
Includes index.
Bibliography: p. 282-289.
ISBN 0-471-04306-0
1. Astronautics—History. 2. Rocketry—History. 3. Science fiction—History and criticism. I. Title.
TL788.5.B34 301.5 76-21349
76 MARC

Bainbridge, Ga. Planning Commission.
Comprehensive development plan: 1, subdivision regulations; 2, public improvements program and capital improvements budget; 3, summary plan report, Bainbridge, Georgia. Camilla, Ga., Southwest Georgia Planning and Development Commission, 1970.
3 v. (HUD 701 report)
1. City planning—Bainbridge, Ga. I. Southwest Georgia Planning and Development Commission.
DHUD NUC74-46051

Bainbridge, Ga. Planning Commission
see Southwest Georgia Planning and Development Commission. Zoning ordinance for city of Bainbridge. Camilla, Ga., 1969.

Bainbridge, Ind. Plan Commission
see Beckman, Swenson and Associates. Zoning ordinance; subdivision control ordinance. Bainbridge, Ind., 1969.

Bainbridge, N.Y.
see Planners Collaborative, Syracuse, N.Y. Planning reports, town and village of Bainbridge... Syracuse, N.Y., 1973-

Bainbridge, Behrens, Moore, inc.
see Bainbridge, David A. A proposal for a bikeway... -- Broderick, Ca. : 1974.

Bainbridge, Decatur County, Georgia. — [Bainbridge? : s.n., ca. 1910]
[20] p. : ill. ; 21 cm.
Cover title.
1. Decatur Co., Ga.—Description and travel. 2. Bainbridge, Ga.—Description.
F292.D27B34 975.8'993'04 77-355224
77 MARC

Bainbridge Township Bicentennial Committee.
Bainbridge Township celebrates the Bicentennial. — [Bainbridge Township, Mich. : Bainbridge Township Bicentennial Committee], c1976.
40 p. : ill. ; 28 cm.
Cover title.
1. Bainbridge Township, Mich.—History. I. Title.
F574.B16B34 1976 977.4'11 76-373321
76 MARC

Baine, Richard Paul, 1926-
Calgary : an urban study / Richard P. Baine. — Toronto : Clarke, Irwin, c1973.
128 p. : ill., maps ; 22 x 28 cm. — (Urban studies series)
Part of illustrative matter in pocket.
ISBN 0-7720-0523-0 pbk. : $4.95. ISBN 0-7720-0482-X pbk. : $4.25 (education ed.)
1. Cities and towns—Planning—Calgary, Alta. 2. Calgary, Alta.—Economic conditions. I. Title.
HT169.C32C32 309.2'62'0971233 75-323215
75 MARC

Baine, Richard Paul, 1926–
Toronto; an urban study [by] Richard P. Baine [and] A. Lynn McMurray. Toronto, Clarke, Irwin [c1970]
126 p. illus. (part col.), maps (part col., 2 fold. in pocket) 22 x 29 cm. (Urban studies series) C 71-3776
1. Toronto—Economic conditions. 2. Toronto—Social conditions. 3. Land—Ontario—Toronto. I. McMurray, A. L., joint author. II. Title.
HC118.T6B3 301.36'3'09713541 73-169093
ISBN 0-7720-0483-8 MARC

Baine, Sean.
Community action and local government / [by] Sean Baine. — London : Bell, 1975.
96 p. : 1 ill. ; 22 cm. — (Occasional papers on social administration ; no. 59) GB76-06373
Originally presented as the author's thesis, Brunel.
Includes bibliographical references.
ISBN 0-7135-1842-1 : £3.50
1. Local government—Great Britain. 2. Political participation—Great Britain. I. Title. II. Series.
HV244.O25 no. 59 361'.008 s 76-379618
[JS3121] 76 MARC

Baines, Anthony.
Bagpipes. Rev. ed. Oxford, Printed at the University Press, 1975.
142 p. illus. 25 cm. (Oxford. University. Pitt Rivers Museum. Occasional papers on technology, 9)
Bibliography: p. 135-136.
1. Bagpipe—History. I. Series.
TxDaM NUC77-84277

Baines, Anthony.
Brass instruments : their history and development / Anthony Baines. — London : Faber, 1976.
298 p., [8] leaves of plates : ill. ; 23 cm. GB***
Bibliography: p. [267]-278.
Includes index.
ISBN 0-571-10600-5 : £12.50
1. Brass instruments.
ML930.B28 788'.01 76-383764
77 MARC

Baines, Anthony, ed.
Musical instruments through the ages. Ed. by Anthony Baines for the Galpin Society. [2d rev. Baltimore] Penguin [c1969]
383 p. illus.
1. Musical instruments—Hist. I. Galpin Society. II. Title.
LN NcU NUC75-30252

Baines, Anthony, ed.
Musical instruments through the ages. Baltimore, Penguin Books [1973, c1969]
381 p. illus. 18 cm. (Pelican books, A347)
Includes bibliography.
1. Musical instruments—History. I. Title.
ViU NUC76-69481

Baines, Anthony, ed.
Musical instruments through the ages / edited by Anthony Baines for the Galpin Society. — New ed. — New York : Walker, 1976, c1961.
344 p., [16] leaves of plates : ill. ; 24 cm.
Bibliography: p. 323-332.
Includes index.
ISBN 0-8027-0469-7 : $15.00
1. Musical instruments—History. I. Galpin Society. II. Title.
ML460.B14 1976 781.9'1'09 74-83196
76 MARC

Baines, Barbara Joan.
The lust motif in the plays of Thomas Middleton. Salzburg, Inst. f. Engl. Sprache u. Literatur, Univ. Salzburg, 1973.
160 p. 21 cm. (Jacobean drama studies, 29) S280.00
Au 73-24-96
Bibliography: p. [156]-160.
1. Middleton, Thomas, d. 1627—Criticism and interpretation. I. Title. II. Series.
PR2717.B26 822'.3 74-168458
MARC

Baines, Edward, Sir, 1800-1890.
Manchester and its environs, engraved from an actual survey made in 1824, by William Swire, Leeds; for the History, Directory and Gazetteer of Lancashire, by Edwd. Baines. Liverpool, W. Wales & Co., 1824; Ithaca, N.Y., Historic Urban Plans, 1973.
map. 51 x 64 cm.
Scale ca. 1: 9,000.

Facsimile.
Reproduced from an engraving in the Historic Urban Plans collection.
Includes illus., index to points of interest and inset "Plan of Manchester and Salford taken about 1650."
1. Manchester, Eng.—Maps. I. Swire, William. II. Title.
KyU NUC76-69725

Baines, Edward, Sir, 1800-1890.
The social, educational, and religious state of the manufacturing districts. [2d ed. London] Woburn, 1969.
76 p. 22 cm. (The Social history of education, 1st ser., no. 1)
unpriced B***
Reprint of 1843 ed.
1. Great Britain—Religion—Statistics. 2. Education—England—Statistics. I. Title.
BR759.B23 1969 268'.09427 74-430877
rev MARC

Baines, Francis Athelstane, 1917-
A tutor for the tenor viol / by Francis Baines. -- Cambridge, Eng. : Gamut Publications : [selling agent, Cambridge Music Shop, c1973]
13 p. ; 21 x 30 cm.
1. Viol--Instruction and study. I. Title.
PSt NUC77-101179

Baines, Helen van Horn, 1935-
An assessment and comparison of syntactic complexity : and word associations of good and poor readers in grades four, eight, and twelve / Helen van Horn Bains. -- [s.l. : s.n.], 1975.
vix, 170 leaves.
Thesis--University of Georgia.
GU NUC77-84678

Baines, Howard Andrew, 1925-
Horace Bushnell: an American Christian gentleman. [n.p.] 1970.
iii, 389 l.
Thesis—University of Iowa.
Bibliography: leaves 359-389.
Microfilm (positive) Ann Arbor, Mich., University Microfilms, 1970. 1 reel. (Publication no. 23861)
NNC NUC73-59515

Baines, Jennifer.
Mandelstam : the later poetry / Jennifer Baines. — Cambridge [Eng.] ; New York : Cambridge University Press, 1976.
xv, 253 p. ; 23 cm.
Bibliography: p. [245]-246.
Includes index.
ISBN 0-521-21273-1
1. Mandel'shtam, Osip Ėmil'evich, 1891-1938—Criticism and interpretation.
PG3476.M355Z56 891.7'1'3 76-8515
76 MARC

Baines, Jimmy Dalton, 1932-
Samuel S. Sanford and Negro minstrelsy. [n.p.] 1967.
v, 348 l. ports.
Thesis—Tulane University.
Vita.
Bibliography: leaves 342-347.
Microfilm. Ann Arbor, Mich., University Microfilms. 1 reel. 35 mm.
1. Sanford, Samuel S., 1821-1905. 2. Negro minstrels. I. Title.
TxU NUC75-30733

Baines, Jocelyn.
The ABC of indoor plants [by] Jocelyn Baines and Katherine Key. [1st American ed.] New York, Knopf; [distributed by Random House] 1973.
192 p. illus. (part col.) 32 cm. $12.50
1. House plants—Dictionaries. I. Key, Katherine, joint author. II. Title.
[SB419.B12 1973] 635.9'65'03 73-4252
ISBN 0-394-48774-5 MARC

Baines, Jocelyn.
Joseph Conrad; a critical biography. London, Readers Union, 1961.
507 p. illus., facsim., ports. 22 cm.
"This RU edition was produced ... for sale to its members only."
"First published by Weidenfeld & Nicolson."
Includes bibliography.
1. Conrad, Joseph, 1857-1924.
NNC NUC74-175381

Baines, Jocelyn.
Joseph Conrad, a critical biography / Jocelyn Baines. -- Harmondsworth, Eng. : Penguin Books, 1971, c1960.
606 p. ; 18 cm. -- (Pelican biographies)
Includes bibliographies and index.
1. Conrad, Joseph, 1857-1924--Biography.
NRU NUC77-101111

Baines, Jocelyn.
Joseph Conrad : a critical biography / Jocelyn Baines. — Westport, Conn : Greenwood Press, 1975, c1960.
507 p., [4] leaves of plates : ill. ; 22 cm.
Reprint of the 1961 ed. published by Readers Union-Contemporary Fiction, London.
Includes bibliographies and index.
ISBN 0-8371-8304-9
1. Conrad, Joseph, 1857-1924—Biography.
[PR6005.O4Z554 1975] 823'.9'12 75-17476
75 MARC

Baines, John D
The environment [by] John D. Baines. London, Batsford [1973]
96 p. illus., maps. 26 cm. (Past-into-present series) GB***
Bibliography: p. 94.
ISBN 0-7134-1795-1 : £1.50
1. Man—Influence on nature—Great Britain. 2. Pollution—Great Britain. I. Title.
GF551.B33 301.31'0941 75-304745
MARC

Baines, John M
José Carlos Mariátegui and the development of the ideology of revolution in Peru. [n.p.] c1968.
ii, 290 l. 22 cm.
Thesis (Ph.D.)—University of Wisconsin.
Bibliography: leaves 261-290.
Photocopy of the original by University Microfilms, 1974.
TNJ NUC76-27450

Baines, John M
see National Sheriffs' Association. Mutual aid planning... Washington, 1973.

Baines, Margarett Lester, 1942- joint author
see Smith, Dorothy Faye Harrison, 1941- The Texas Snows. [Fort Worth? Tex.] 1971.

Baines, Thomas, 1820-1875.
The birds of South Africa / painted by Thomas Baines ; with a biographical essay by R. F. Kennedy. -- Johannesburg : Winchester Press, 1975.
204 p. : ill.
Comprising the complete collection of ninety plates executed by Thomas Baines, together with descriptions from the text of C. J. Andersson's Notes on the Birds of Damara Land and the adjacent countries of South-West Africa.
1. Birds. South Africa. I. Kennedy, Reginald Frank. II. Title.
DNAL NUC77-84677

Baines, Thomas, 1820-1875.
Explorations in South-West Africa. Introduction by Frank R. Bradlow. Salisbury, Rhodesia, Pioneer Head, 1973.
xii, xiv, 535 p. 11 plates, 35 illus., 3 col. maps. 22 cm.
Facsimile reprint.
1. Africa, Southern—Description and travel. I. Title.
CtY NUC75-19459

Baines, Thomas, 1820-1875, joint author.
see Lord, William Barry. Shifts and expedients of camp life, travel, and exploration. Johannesburg, Africana Book Society, 1975.

Baines, Thomas Blackburn, 1832-1891.
The Lord's coming, Israel, and the church. 7th ed. London, G. Morrish [n.d.]
xii, 451 p. 20 cm.
1. Second advent. 2. Bible—Prophecies. 3. Church. I. Title.
IEG NUC73-35533

Baines, Tyrone Randolph, 1943-
An exploration of eupsychian-participatory management in the federal government: the OEO case. [College Park, Md.] 1972.
246 l. 29 cm.
Typescript.
Thesis—University of Maryland.
Vita.
Includes bibliography.
1. Employees' representation in management. —U.S. 2. Employee-management relations in government—U.S. I. Title.
MdU NUC74-125981

Baines, Tyrone Randolph, 1943-
An exploration of eupsychian-participatory management in the federal government : the OEO case / by Tyrone Randolph Baines. -- Ann Arbor, Mich. : University Microfilms, 1975.
246 leaves.
Thesis (Ph.D.)-- University of Maryland.
1. Personnel management. 2. Public administration. I. Title.
KMK NUC77-86432

Baines, W. P.
see Viaud, Julien, 1850-1923. A Tale of Brittany. New York, Frederick A. Stokes [19–?]

Baini, Alberto.
Pro y contra Castro. [Madrid] Edifrans & Mandadori 1975, c1973]
159 p. illus., ports. 21 cm. (Edifrans, 1)
1. Castro, Fidel, 1927- 2. Cuba–Pol. & govt.–1933-1959. 3. Cuba-Pol. & govt.–1959- I. Title.
CSt-H NUC77-84276

Baĭniiazov, Kyrykbaĭ.
Osobennosti poèticheskogo stilia Aiapbergena Musaeva. Nukus, "Karakalpakstan", 1972.
91 p.
Title page and text in Kara-Kalpak.
Russian title from colophon.
1. Musaev, Aiapbergen, 1880-1936.
MH NUC76-14942

Bains, Dharm Singh.
A study of recidivism, Internal-External scores and Mini-Mult scores of hospitalized male alcoholics / by Dharm Singh Bains. -- [s.l. : s.n.], 1975.
109 leaves.
Thesis (Ph.D.)--Kansas State University.
1. Alcoholics--Psychology. I. Title.
KMK NUC77-86431

Bains, Sher Singh, 1921-1971
see Recent research on multiple cropping. New Delhi, 1972.

Bains, Swaran Singh, 1929-
see Atwal, A S Applied animal ecology. Delhi, Kalyani Pub. [1974]

Bainter, Fay
see [Lucky lady] [Sound recording] American Forces Radio and Television Service RU 20-76, 5B [1976]

Bainter, Jack Jeffries, 1931-
Relationship of institutional factors to counselors' attitudes toward vocational education. [Bloomington, Ind.] 1974.
123 p.
Thesis (Ed.D.)—Indiana University.
Vita.
InU NUC76-20075

Bainton, Barry
see Abstracts of seven doctoral dissertations... [Washington] 1975.

Bainton, Roland Herbert, 1894–
Behold the Christ [by] Roland H. Bainton, assisted by Sumathi Devasahayam. [1st ed.] New York, Harper & Row [1974]
224 p. illus. 26 cm. $10.00
"A Collins Associates book."
Bibliography: p. 223–224.
1. Jesus Christ—Art. 2. Jesus Christ—Biography. I. Devasahayam, Sumathi, joint author. II. Title.
N8050.B287 704.948'5 73–18678
ISBN 0–06–060352–6 MARC

Bainton, Roland Herbert, 1894–
Bibliography of the continental reformation: materials available in English, by Roland H. Bainton and Eric W. Gritsch. 2d ed., rev. and enl. [Hamden, Conn.] Archon Books, 1972.
xix, 220 p. 23 cm.
1. Reformation—Bibliography. I. Gritsch, Eric W. joint author. II. Title.
Z7830.B16 1972 016.2706 72–8216
ISBN 0–208–01219–0 MARC

Bainton, Roland Herbert, 1894-
The church of our fathers, by Roland H. Bainton. New York, Scribner [1969]
222 p. illus. 21 cm.
1. Church history—Juvenile literature. I. Title.
NBuU NUC76-69680

Bainton, Roland Herbert, 1894-
Erasmo della Cristianità. Introd. di Antonio Rotondò. [Firenze] Sansoni [c1970]
xiv, 337 p. illus. 24 cm.
Bibliography: p. [305]-321.
1. Erasmus, Desiderius, d. 1536. I. Title.
CtY NUC74-3592

Bainton, Roland Herbert, 1894-
Here I stand; a life of Martin Luther. Nashville, Abingdon Press [1968?]
422 p. illus., ports., music. (Apex books, D1)
Includes bibliography.
1. Luther, Martin, 1483-1546. I. Title.
NNC NUC75-30735

Bainton, Roland Herbert, 1894-
Psychiatry and history: an examination of Erikson's Young man Luther. [Nashville? Tenn., Abingdon Press, 1971]
29 p. 26 cm.
Reprinted from Religion in life, winter 1971.
ICN NUC73-126581

Bainton, Roland Herbert, 1894-
Servet, el hereje perseguido. Traducción, prólogo, bibliografía sobre Servet, por Angel Alcalá. [Madrid] Taurus [c1973]
301 p. 21 cm. (Ensayistas, 96)
Translation of Hunted heretic, the life and death of Michael Servetus.
"Bibliografía de Servet" por M.E. Stanton: p. 231-270. "Bibliografía sobre Servet" por A. Alcalá: p. 271-289.
CtY NUC74-126002

Bainton, Roland Herbert, 1894-
Women of the Reformation, from Spain to Scandinavia / Roland H. Bainton. — Minneapolis : Augsburg Pub. House, c1977.
240 p. : ill. ; 22 cm.
Includes bibliographies and index.
ISBN 0-8066-1568-0 : $9.95
1. Reformation—Biography. 2. Women—Biography. I. Title.
BR317.B28 277.6'0922 76-27089
77 MARC

Bainton, Roland Herbert, 1894–
Women of the Reformation in France and England [by] Roland H. Bainton. Minneapolis, Augsburg Pub. House [1973]
287 p. illus. 23 cm. $8.95
Bibliography: p. 277.
1. Reformation—Biography. 2. Woman—Biography. I. Title.
BR317.B29 270.6'092'2 [B] 73–78269
ISBN 0–8066–1333–5 MARC

Bainton, Roland Herbert, 1894-
Women of the Reformation in France and England / Roland H. Bainton. — Boston : Beacon Press, 1975, c1973.
287 p. : ill. ; 20 cm.
Reprint of the ed. published by Augsburg Pub. House, Minneapolis.
Bibliography: p. 277.
Includes index.
ISBN 0-8070-5649-9
1. Reformation—Biography. 2. Women—Biography. I. Title.
[BR317.B29 1975] 270.6'092'2 75-19393
75 MARC

Bainton, Roland Herbert, 1894–
Women of the Reformation in Germany and Italy, by Roland H. Bainton. Boston, Beacon Press [1974, c1971]
279 p. illus. 21 cm. (Beacon paperback, 485)
Reprint of the ed. published by Augsburg Pub. House, Minneapolis.
Includes bibliographies.
1. Reformation—Biography. 2. Woman—Biography. I. Title.
[BR317.B3 1974] 270.6'092'2 [B] 74–6085
ISBN 0–8070–5651–0 MARC

Bainton, Roland Herbert, 1894-
see The Future of Quakerism. [Owensboro, Ky.] 1966.

Bainton, Roland Herbert, 1894- ed.
see Luther, Martin, 1483-1546. The Martin Luther Christmas book... Philadelphia, Fortress Press [c1968]

Bainton, Roland Herbert, 1894-
see Psychohistory and religion ... Philadelphia. Fortress Press, c1977.

Baĭnurova, R. Sh.
see Seiidov, Ashir, comp. Velikaia Oktiabr'skaia sotsialisticheskaia revoliutsiia i grazhdanskaia voina v Turkmenistane. Ashkhabad, Turkmenistan, 1968.

Bainville, Jacques, 1879-1936.
History of France, by Jacques Bainville... translated by Alice Gauss, A.M., and Christian Gauss... New York [etc.] D. Appleton and company, 1926. [Ann Arbor, Mich., 1967]
x p., 1 l., 483 p. front., ports. 22 cm.
Photocopy (positive) made by University Microfilms.
Printed on double leaves.
1. France—Hist. I. Gauss, Alice Sarah (Hussey) 1872- tr. II. Gauss, Christian Frederick, 1878- tr.
NBuC NUC76-69651

Baiocchi, César.
Sete mulheres de trinta e um ôlho d'água (contos). Goiânia, Oriente, 1972.
164 p. 18 cm. Cr$10.00
CONTENTS: A radiografia.—A carona.—Microcosmo.—Por gostar de você.—A longa espera.—Um dia é da Acácia e outro do Agenor.—O passado chegou.—O atestado.—O mundo é dos espertos.—A filha.—Boa ação.—Quem perdoa ladrão.—O Candango.—As imortais.
I. Title.
PQ9698.12.A38S4 73–213289

Baiocchi, Josephina Desounet.
Montagem de projets de ação pedagógica [por] Josephina Desounet Baiocchi [e] Nelson Braga Octaviano Ferreira. [1. ed. brasileira. Brasília] Editôra de Brasília [1972]
145 p. 21 cm. Cr$10.00
Bibliography: p. 144–145.
1. Educational planning. I. Ferreira, Nelson Braga Octaviano, joint author. II. Title.
LB2806.B22 73–213682

Baiocchi, Mari de Nazaré.
Inventário arqueológico do Estado de Goiás; esbôço de pesquisas que continuam ... [Goiânia] Oriente, 1972.
31 p. illus. 23 cm. $10.00
On cover: Museu da Universidade Católica de Goiás.
Bibliography: p. 29–31.
1. Indians of South America—Brazil—Goiás (State)—Antiquities. 2. Goiás, Brazil (State)—Antiquities. I. Universidade Católica de Goiás. Meseu. II. Title.
F2519.1.G68B34 73–220273

Baiomekanizumu Gakkai.
Jinkō no Te Kenkyūkai was established in 1968. In 1972 the name was changed to Baiomekanizumu Kenkyūkai, and in 1973 to Baiomekanizumu Gakkai.
Works by this body are found under the name used at the time of publication.

Baiomekanizumu Gakkai
see Hito to kikai no setten. 1973.

Baiomekanizumu Kenkyūkai.
Jinkō no Te Kenkyūkai was established in 1968. In 1972 the name was changed to Baiomekanizumu Kenkyūkai, and in 1973 to Baiomekanizumu Gakkai.
Works by this body are found under the name used at the time of publication.

Baioni, Giuliano
see Il Romanzo tedesco del Novecento. Torino, G. Einaudi, 1973.

(Baiorizumu to sono kikō)
バイオリズムとその機構：第1回内藤シンポジウム / 須田正巳, 早石修, 中川八郎編. — 東京 講談社, 1976.
264 p. : ill. ; 22 cm. Ja 76-23618
Compilation of papers presented at a symposium, Feb. 27-28, 1976 Tokyo, sponsored by Naitō Kinen Kagaku Shinkō Zaidan.
Includes bibliographies and index.
¥2500
1. Biological rhythms—Congresses. I. Suda, Masami, 1915– II. Hayaishi, Osamu, 1920– III. Nakagawa, Hachirō, 1931– IV. Naitō Kinen Kagaku Shinkō Zaidan.
QH527.B34 77-811410

Baiou, Mostafa Abdalla
see
Ba'ayyaw, Muṣṭafá ʻAbd Allāh.

Baĭpakov, Karl Moldakhmetovich.
Drevnie goroda Kazakhstana. [Alma-Ata, Nauka Kazakhskoĭ SSR, 1971]
208 p. illus.
At head of title: K. M. Baĭpakov, L. B. Erzakovich.
1. Kazakhstan–Antiq. 2. Cities and towns–Ruined, extinct, etc. I. Title.
InU ViU MiEM PPT NUC74-41662

Baĭpakov, Karl Moldakhmetovich, joint author
see Akishev, Kemal' Akishevich.
Drevniĭ Otrar. 1972.

Bair, Anna (Kidd) 1921- comp.
The Children's book, no. 2. [Julare? Calif., 1969?]
10 p. illus. 15 cm.
Cover title.
Poems.
1. Children's poetry. I. Title.
RPB NUC74-3591

Bair, Bill.
Love is an open door, by Bill Bair with Glenn D. Kittler. New York, Chosen Books [1974]
222 p. 21 cm.
1. Bair, Bill. 2. Bair Foundation. 3. Church work with juvenile delinquents. 4. Children—Institutional care—New Wilmington, Pa. I. Kittler, Glenn D. II. Title.
BR1725.B3314A33 248'.2 [B] 73-17023
ISBN 0-912376-07-4 MARC

Bair, Brent O
Current state practices in transit funding, by Brent O. Bair and Douglas J. McKelvey. [Iowa City] Center for Urban Transportation Studies, Institute of Urban and Regional Research, University of Iowa, 1975.
14, [8] l. 28 cm. (University of Iowa. Institute of Urban and Regional Research. Technical report no. 63)
Bibliography: leaves [15-16]
1. Local transit--U.S.--Finance. 2. Local transit--U.S.--Cost of operation. I. McKelvey, Douglas J. II. Title.
IaU NUC77-85597

Bair, Brent O
Fixed charge transportation problem: a survey, by Brent O. Bair and Gerald L. Hefley. [Iowa City] Center for Urban Transportation Studies, University of Iowa, 1973.
28 l. 28 cm. (Iowa. University. Institute of Urban and Regional Research. Technical report, no. 19)
"Research was partially supported by the Urban Mass Transportation Administration, Department of Transportation."
Bibliography: leaves 24-28.
1. Transportation–Rates. 2. Overhead costs. 3. Transportation–Mathematical models. I. Hefley, Gerald L., joint author. II. Title.
IaU NUC76-69660

Bair, Brent O
Identification and optimization of alternative re-uses for proposed railroad abandonment right-of-way, by Brent O. Bair, Mark C. Meyer and Clifford Tweedale. Iowa City, Institute of Urban and Regional Research, 1975.
[42] l. 28 cm. (Iowa. University. Institute of Urban and Regional Research. Technical report, no. 41)
Prepared for Department of Transportation, Office of University Research, Washington, D.C. Contract no. DOT-OS-40019.
Includes bibliographical references.

1. Railroads–Abandonment. 2. Railroads–Right of way. 3. Regional planning. I. Meyer, Mark C., joint author. II. Tweedale, Clifford J., joint author. III. Title.
IaU NUC77-84222

Bair, Brent O., joint author
see Dueker, Kenneth John, 1937-
Transportation and the energy crisis. [Iowa City] Center for Urban Transportation Studies, University of Iowa, 1973.

Bair, Frank E., joint author
see Ruffner, James A The weather almanac. Detroit, Gale Research Co. [1974]

Bair, Frederick Haigh, 1889-
The social understandings of the superintendent of schools. New York, Bureau of Publications, Teachers College, Columbia University, 1934. [New York, AMS Press, 1972]
v, 193 p. 22 cm.
Reprint of the 1934 ed., issued in series: Teachers College, Columbia University. Contribution to education, no. 625.
Originally presented as the author's thesis, Columbia.
1. School superintendents and principals—United States. 2. Social sciences—Study and teaching. I. Title. II. Series: Columbia University. Teachers College. Contributions to education, no. 625.
LB2805.B2 1972 371.2'011 78-176531
ISBN 0-404-55625-6 MARC

Bair, Frederick Haigh, 1915-
Intensity zoning; regulating townhouses, apartments, and planned developments, by Frederick H. Bair, Jr. Chicago, American Society of Planning Officials, 1976.
viii, 39 p. illus. 29 cm. (ASPO Planning Advisory Service. Report no. 314)
1. Zoning. I. Title. II. Series.
MoKU NUC77-85561

Bair, Frederick Haigh, 1915-
Special public interest districts: a multi-purpose zoning device. [Chicago, American Society of Planning Officials, 1973]
16 p. diagr. 28 cm. (ASPO planning advisory service. report no. 287)
1. Special districts–U.S. 2. Zoning–U.S. I. Title.
NNC NUC74-125999

Bair, Frederick Haigh, 1915-
see The Place of planning. Auburn, Alabama, Auburn University, Graduate School [1973]

Bair, Frieda.
Crackerbarrel verse. -- New York : Vantage Press, c1973.
63 p. ; 21 cm.
I. Title.
NdU NUC77-101112

Bair, Jacques.
Étude géométrique des espaces vectoriels : une introduction / Jacques Bair, René Fourneau. — Berlin ; New York : Springer-Verlag, 1975.
vii, 184 p. ; 25 cm. — (Lecture notes in mathematics ; 489)
Bibliography: p. [171]-182.
Includes indexes.
ISBN 0-387-07413-9
1. Convex sets. 2. Vector spaces. I. Fourneau, René, joint author. II. Title. III. Series: Lecture notes in mathematics (Berlin) ; 489.
QA3.L28 no. 489 512'.523 75-30920
[QA640] 75 MARC

Bair, Lee A
The effect of the introduction of medical assistance and Medicare on the structure of the Michigan nursing home industry. [n.p.] 1973.
[4], ix, 217 l. illus.
Thesis (Ph.D.)–Michigan State University.
Bibliography: leaves 208-217.
1. Nursing homes–Michigan. I. Title.
MiEM NUC74-126001

Bair, Lee A., joint author
see Stuart, Bruce C Health care and income. [Lansing, Michigan Dept. of Social Services, 1971]

Bair, Lee A., joint author
see Stuart, Bruce C Health care and income... 2d ed. [Lansing, State of Michigan] 1971.

Bair, Lowell, tr.
see Rousseau, Jean Jacques, 1712-1778.
The essential Rousseau: The social contract... New York, New American Library [1974]

Bair, Medill.
One man's answers to the educational problems of a city. [**Phi Delta Kappa,** 1968]
18 l.
Speech given at the first annual tri-chapter meeting of area Kappans at Springfield, Mass. The meeting was sponsored by the University of Connecticut, University of Massachusetts, and Hartford chapters of Phi Delta Kappa.
1. Education–Connecticut–Hartford. I. Title.
CtU NUC73-68873

Bair, Patrick.
The necrophiles; a modern essay in the macabre, by David Gurney. [New York] Times Mirror [c1969]
222 p. 22 cm.
I. Title.
IEN NUC76-69661

Bair, William J
see
Bair, Bill.

Bair, William J., 1924-
see Uranium, plutonium, transplutonic elements. Berlin, New York, Springer, 1973.

Baĭrachnyĭ, Kim Alekseevich.
V. I. Lenin o dialektike razvitiia Sovetskogo gosudarstva i sovremennost'. [By] K. A. Baĭrachnyĭ. Khar'kov, Izd-vo Khar'kovskogo univ., 1970.
130 p.
1. Communist state.
MH UU CSt-H NUC74-55452

Baĭrachnyĭ, Kim Alekseevich
see Nekotorye leninskie idei o stroitel'stvo sofsializma i kommunizma... Khar'kov, Izd-vo Khar'kovskogo univ-ta, 1970.

Baĭrachnyĭ, Kim Alekseevich
see Sovetskaia gosudarstvennost' i razvitie sofsialisticheskoĭ demokratii v period kommunisticheskogo stroitel'stva. 1974.

Baïracli-Levy, Juliette de.
Common herbs for natural health [by] Juliette de Baïracli Levy. Illustrated by Heather Wood. New York, Schocken Books [1974, c1966]
200 p. illus. 18 cm.
1. Herbs. I. Title.
ICD NUC76-20776

Baïracli-Levy, Juliette de.
The complete herbal book for the dog: a complete handbook of natural care and rearing. [3d ed.] New York, Arco [1973, c1971]
3-207 p., 17 plates. illus. 21 cm.
Published in 1961 under title: The herbal book for the dog.
Stamped on t.p.: Wehman Bros., Hackensack.
1. Dogs. 2. Dogs–Diseases. 3. Herbs. I. Title.
WU ViBlbV NUC75-25502

Baïracli-Levy, Juliette de.
The complete herbal book for the dog: a complete handbook of natural care and rearing / Juliette de Baïracli Levy. — New and revised ed. — London : Faber, 1975.
224 p., [16] p. of plates : ill. ; 21 cm. GB75-0440
Published in 1961 under title: The herbal book for the dog.
Includes index.
ISBN 0-571-04859-5 : £3.25
1. Dogs. 2. Dogs—Diseases. 3. Herbs. I. Title.
SF427.B19 1975 636.7'08'95321 75-32046
75 MARC

Baïracli-Levy, Juliette de.
Herbal handbook for farm and stable / Juliette de Baïracli Levy. — Emmaus, Pa. : Rodale Press, c1976.
320 p. ; 23 cm.
Includes indexes.
ISBN 0-87857-120-5 : $7.95. ISBN 0-87857-115-9 pbk. : $3.95
1. Veterinary drugs. 2. Materia medica, Vegetable. I. Title.
SF915.B27 1976 636.089'5'321 76-273
76 MARC

Baĭracli-Levy, Juliette de.
The illustrated herbal handbook / ₍by₎ Juliette de Baïracli-Levy ; illustrated by Heather Wood. — London : Faber, 1974.
3–200 p. : ill. ; 23 cm. GB 74–08540
Includes index.
ISBN 0–571–04802–1 : £2.50
1. Materia medica, Vegetable. I. Title.
RS164.B29 615′.321 75–300789
MARC

Bairāgī, 1925- ed.
see Ādhunika Telugu kavitā. [1969]

Bairāgī, Mahendranātha.
(Baishṇaba sāhitya paricaya)
বৈষ্ণব সাহিত্য পরিচয়: কাব্য ও দর্শনে, তত্ত্ব ও সাধনায়. ₍লেখক₎ শ্রীমহেন্দ্রনাথ বৈরাগী. ₍হাবড়া, 24 পরগণা জেলা, শ্রীসুশীলকুমার গুপ্ত₎; পরিবেশক হাউস অফ বুকস, কলিকাতা ₍1971₎
5, 385 p. 19 cm. Rs10.00
In Bengali.
Includes bibliographical references.
1. Vaishnava literature, Bengali—History and criticism. I. Title.
PK1702.B3 72–904978

Baĭrakov, Vasil.
(Endemichna nefropatii͡a)
Ендемична нефропатия : библиография 1956–1970 / Състав. В. Байраков, И. Димитрова, М. Маргаритова ; ред. ₍с предг.₎ А. Аструг. — София, ЦНМИ, 1971.
83 p. ; 22 cm. — (Библиотека Медицински библиографии)
Bu 72–447
At head of title: Ministerstvo na narodnoto zdrave. Tsentŭr za nauchna meditsinska informatsii͡a. Tsentralna meditsinska biblioteka.
Added t. p.: Endemic nephropathy.
Series romanized: Biblioteka Meditsinski bibliografii.
Introduction, subject index and table of contents also in English.
1. Kidneys—Diseases—Bibliography. 2. Medicine—Bulgaria—Bibliography. 3. Medicine—Romania—Bibliography. 4. Medicine—Yugoslavia—Bibliography. I. Dimitrova, Iva I., joint author. II. Margaritova, Marii͡a, joint author. III. Tsentralna meditsinska biblioteka. IV. Title. V. Title: Endemic nephropathy.
Z6664.K5B35 77–508830
[RC902]

Bairam, Clement.
Le voyage de Gulliver à Lilliput; d'après Jonathan Swift, raconté par Clement Bairam, illustrations de Michel Gay. ₍Paris, RCA, Hatier, 1972₎
1 v. (unpaged) col. illus. 26 cm. and phonodisc (2s. 7 in. 45 rpm. microgroove. stereophonic) in pocket. (Collection un disque-un livre)
I. Swift, Jonathan, 1667-1745. II. Title.
TxDaM NUC74-134196

Baĭram, Tofig.
(Azărbaĭjan deĭăndă ...)
Азәрбајҹан дејәндә ... / Тофиг Бајрам. — Бакы : Кәнҹлик, 1974.
138 p. : port. ; 17 cm. USSR 74–12182
Poems.
0.62rub
I. Title.
PL314.B298A98 75–586537

Bairam Khāṉ, d. 1561.
(Dīvān)
دیوان بیرم خان خانخانان. باهتمـام محمودالحسن صدیقی، سید حسام الدیـن راشدی ₍و₎ محمد صابـر. ₍اشاعت 1.₎
Karachi, Institute of Central and West Asian Studies, 1971.
83, 18 p. 25 cm. (Karachi. University. Institute of Central and West Asian Studies. (سلسله متون، شماره 2)
Added t. p.: Diwan of Bayram Khan.
Text of the Persian and Jagataic divans of Bairam Khan, edited by Rāshidī and Sabir respectively, with English introd. by Siddiqi.
Includes bibliographical references.
I. Siddiqi, Mahmudul Hasan. II. Rāshidī, Ḥusām al-Dīn. III. Sabir, Muhammad, 1935- IV. Series: Karachi. University. Institute of Central and West Asian Studies. Silsilah-i mutūn, shumārah-i 2.
PL334.B3A17 72–930356

Baĭramov, Ăkbăr.
(Insan fikirlăshmăĭi vă danyshmaghy nejă ȯĭrănmishdir)
Инсан фикирләшмәји вә данышмағы неҹе өјрәнмишдир / Әкбәр Бајрамов. — Бакы : Азәрбајҹан Дөвләт Нәшријјаты, 1963.
59 p. ; 20 cm.
Includes bibliographical references.
1. Language and languages—Origin. 2. Thought and thinking. I. Title.
P116.B3 75–972106

Baĭramov, Akhniaf.
Gody vozmuzhanii͡a; roman. ₍By₎ Baĭramov Akhniaf Arslanovich. ₍Ufa, Bashknigoizdat₎ 1972.
306 p. illus.
Title page and text in Bashkir.
Russian title from colophon.
MH NUC76-14931

Baĭramov, Aliosha Īunis oghlu.
(Naĭlănin saĥvi)
Наиләнин сәһви / Алјоша Бајрамов. — Јереван : Һајастан, 1973.
40 p. : 16 cm. USSR 73–35562
Short stories.
CONTENTS: Ананын шаһ әсәри.—Нанкор.—Ат, арпа вә ....—Чејран.—Мүшајиәтчи.—Чеһиз көлкәси.—Наиләнин сәһви.—Азаркешләр.—Үчүнчү зәнклән сонра.—Хәјала далмышды (Мәнсур ше'р).—Вурулуб, вурмајыб.—Гоша сөјуд вә торпаг.—Һазырчаваб алычы.—Анд.—һеч-һечә.—Хәсисин икигат мәғлубијјәти.—Икиүзлү.
0.03rub
I. Title.
PL314.B299N3 75–567721

Bairamov, B. I.
see Pererabotka shlakov ferrosplavnogo proizvodstva. 1971.

Baĭramov, Babakarry.
Razvitie ėnergetiki v Turkmenistane. ₍By₎ B. Baĭramov. Ashkhabad, "Turkmenistan," 1971.
198 p. illus.
1. Electrification—Turkmenistan. 2. Electric power plants—Turkmenistan.
MH NUC76-17994

Baĭramov, Baĭram Salman oghly.
(Arakăsmălăr)
Аракәсмәләр. Роман. Бакы, Азәрнәшр, 19
v. 20 cm. 0.93rub (v. 3–4). USSR 71–24804 (v. 3–4)
At head of title, v. : Бајрам Бајрамов.
I. Title.
PL314.B3A9 73–207921

Baĭramov, Baĭram Salman oghly.
Јасәмән. Повестләр вә һекајәләр. Бакы, "Кәнҹлик," 1969.
298 p. 21 cm. 0.73 USSR 70–2159
At head of title: Бајрам Бајрамов.
I. Title.
Title romanized: Īasămăn.
PL314.B3 I 2 70–299814

Baĭramov, Fărman.
(Năriman Nărimanov)
Нәриман Нәриманов. (1870–1970). Библиографик көстәричи. Бакы, Азәрнәшр, 1972.
158 p. 16 cm. 0.29rub USSR 72–23478
Sections in Azerbaijani and Russian, each with special t. p.
1. Narimanov, Nariman N., 1872–1925—Bibliography.
Z8614.3.B33 74–220818

Baĭramov, Fatali
see Sakhib, Fatali.

Baĭramov, G
Slozhnosochinennye predlozhenii͡a v sovremennom azerbaĭdzhanskom i͡azyke. Baku, Izd-vo Akademii nauk Azerbaĭdzhanskoĭ SSR, 1960.
121 p.
Added t. p. in Azerbaijani.
1. Azerbaijani language—Syntax. I. Title.
ICU NUC76-63237

Baĭramov, G M
Азәрбајҹанда Совет һакимијјәти уғрунда мүбаризә дөврүндә Бакы мә'дән-завод комиссијалары. ₍Март 1917–ијул 1918). Бакы, Азәрбајҹан ССР Елмләр Академијасы Нәшријјаты, 1968.
187 p. 21 cm. 0.80rub USSR 68–32545
At head of title: Азәрбајҹан ССР Елмләр Академијасы. Тарих Институту. Г. М. Бајрамов.
Includes bibliographical references.
1. Labor and laboring classes—Baku. I. Title.
Title romanized: Azărbaĭjanda Sovet ĥakimiĭĭăti ughrunda mübariză dövründă Baky mă'dăn-zavod komissiĭalary.
HD8530.B32B3 72–251193

Baĭramov, Gurban.
(Mădăniĭĭătdă millilik vă beĭnălmilălchilik)
Мәдәнијјәтдә миллилик вә бејнәлмиләлчилик / Гурбан Бајрамов. — Бакы : Кәнҹлик, 1974.
99 p. ; 20 cm. USSR***
Includes bibliographical references.
0.15rub
1. Communism and culture. 2. Internationalism. I. Title.
HX523.B3 75–594171

Baĭramov, Rafig.
(Elmi dünĭagörüshün formalashmasy)
Елми дүнјакөрүшүн формалашмасы / Рафиг Бајрамов. — Бакы : Кәнҹлик, 1974.
102 p. ; 20 cm. USSR 74–40930
Includes bibliographical references.
0.17rub
1. Communism and society. I. Title.
HX542.B33 76–970658

Baĭramov, Tofig Gulam ogly
see
Baĭram, Tofig.

Baĭramova, L K
(Nekotorye voprosy mashinnogo perevoda v SSSR i za rubezhom)
Некоторые вопросы машинного перевода в СССР и за рубежом. (Учеб.-метод. пособие по спецкурсу). Казань, Изд-во Казан. ун-та, 1973.
96 p. 20 cm. 0.26rub USSR 73
Cover title: Вопросы машинного перевода.
At head of title: Казанский государственный университет имени В. И. Ульянова-Ленина.
Bibliography: p. 87–₍95₎
1. Machine translating. I. Title. II. Title: Voprosy mashinnogo perevoda.
P308.B3 74–319050

Baĭramova, N. É.
see Khimii͡a uglevodov. 1975.

Baĭramsakhatov, Nursakhat.
(Novyĭ byt vytesni͡aet religii͡u)
Новый быт вытесняет религию. Ашхабад, Туркменистан, 1972.
95 p. 17 cm. 0.10rub USSR***
At head of title: Н. Байрамсахатов.
Includes bibliographical references.
1. Turkmenistan—Rural conditions. 2. Rites and ceremonies—Turkmenistan. 3. Islam—Controversial literature. I. Title.
HN750.T8B34 73–341847

Bairamukov, Umar.
Kapli; stikhi i basni. [By] Baĭramukov Umar Zulkarnaevich. Cherkessk, Stavropol'skoe knizhnoe izd-vo, Karachaevo-Cherkesskoe otd-nie, 1969.
47 p.
Title page and text in Karachaev.
Russian title from colophon.
MH NUC74-37574

Baĭramukova, Khalimat Bashchievna.
(Snova v put′)
Снова в путь : ₍стихи₎ / Халимат Байрамукова ; ₍пер. с карачаев. Н. Матвеевой₎. — Москва : Сов. Россия, 1972.
112 p. ; 14 cm. USSR 72
0.29rub
I. Matveeva, Novalla Nikolaevna, tr. II. Title.
PL65.K29B33 74–359125

Baĭramukova, Khalimat Bashchievna.
(Utrenni͡ai͡a zvezda)
Утренняя звезда : роман / Халимат Байрамукова ; перевод с карачаевского О. Румянцевой. — Москва : Современник, 1974.
228 p. : port. ; 21 cm. — (Новинки Современника) USSR***
0.60rub
I. Title.
PL65.K29B34 75–574378

Baĭramukova, Nina Magomedovna.
(Kaĭsyn Kuliev)
Кайсын Кулиев : очерк творчества / Н. Байрамукова. — Москва : Сов. писатель, 1975.
269 p., [5] leaves of plates : ill. ; 18 cm. USSR***
0.69rub
1. Kuliev, Kaĭsyn Shuvaevich—Criticism and interpretation.
PL65.B29K8534 75-406253

Baĭrashev, Anvar Nazmutdinovich.
(Ėkonomicheskie osnovy povyshenii͡a produktivnosti prirodnykh kormovykh ugodiĭ)
Экономические основы повышения продуктивности природных кормовых угодий; теория, методология, практика. Алма-Ата, Кайнар, 1973.
292 p. illus. 21 cm. 0.75rub USSR***
At head of title: А. Н. Байрашев.
Includes bibliographical references.
1. Meadows—Kazakhstan. 2. Pastures—Kazakhstan. I. Title.
SB199.B33 74-307856

Bairashev, Khali.
Golubi. [By] Bairashev Khali E. Makhachkala, Dagknigoizdat, 1971.
134 p. illus.
Title page and text in Nogai.
Russian title from colophon.
Short stories.
MH NUC76-16991

Baĭrashevskiĭ, A M
(Sudovye radiolokat͡sionnye sistemy)
Судовые радиолокационные системы. [Учебник для радиотехн. специальности высш. инж. морских училищ]. Москва, "Транспорт," 1973.
352 p. with illus. 22 cm. 0.99rub USSR 74
At head of title: А. М. Байрашевский, Н. Т. Ничипоренко.
Bibliography: p. 349–[350]
1. Radar—Installation on ships. I. Nichiporenko, Nikolaĭ Timofeevich. II. Title.
VM480.B23 74-313705

Baĭrashevskiĭ, A. M., joint author
see Aĭzinov, Mark Moiseevich. (Radiotekhnika i radionavigat͡sionnye pribory) 1975.

Baĭrashevskiĭ, Omer Aleksandrovich, 1875–
(Shkol'nai͡a gigiena)
Школьная гигиена : краткое пособие для учителей школ I-ой ступени / составил О. А. Байрашевский ; с приложением "Правил сбережения здоровья для детей в школе и дома," сост. И. К. Кондорским. — Симферополь : Изд. Академического совещания Крымнаркомпроса, 1925.
70 p. : ill. ; 23 cm.
At head of title: Akademicheskoe soveshchanie Krymnarkomprosa. Narodnyĭ komissariat zdravookhranenii͡a Kryma.
1. School hygiene. I. Kondorskiĭ, Ivan Konstantinovich. Pravila sberezhenii͡a zdorov'i͡a dli͡a deteĭ v shkole i doma. II. Title. III. Title: Pravila sberezhenii͡a zdorov'i͡a dli͡a deteĭ v shkole i doma.
LB3405.B28 75-529356

Bairati, Angelo
see Bioneurologia e cibernetica. Roma, Consiglio nazionale delle ricerche, 1963.

Bairati, Aurelio.
Compendio di anatomia umana ... Torino, Minerva medica, 1972–
v. illus. 25½ cm. L15000 (v. 1) It 72-May (v. 1)
CONTENTS: v. 1. Anatomia generale, apparato locomotore, apparato digerente, apparato respiratorio, apparato uropoietico.
1. Anatomy, Human. I. Title.
[DNLM: 1. Anatomy. QS 4 B165c]
[QM23.2.B34] 72-305176
Shared Cataloging with DNLM

Bairati, Eleonora.
L'Italia liberty : arredamento e arti decorative / Eleonora Bairati, Rossana Bossaglia, Marco Rosci. — Milano : Görlich, [1973]
372 p. : ill. ; 28 cm. It 74-Nov
Bibliography: p. 361-363.
Includes index.
L25450
1. Decoration and ornament, Italian. 2. Interior decoration—Italy. 3. Decoration and ornament—Art nouveau. I. Bossaglia, Rossana, joint author. II. Rosci, Marco, joint author. III. Title.
NK1452.A1B34 74-356133

Bairati, Piero, 1946–
Gli orfani della ragione : illuminismo e nuova sinistra in America / Piero Bairati. — Firenze : G. C. Sansoni, c1975.
245 p. ; 20 cm. — (Antropologia e sociologia) (Saggi ; 32) It 75-July
Includes bibliographical references.
L3500
1. Radicalism—United States. 2. United States—Civilizations—1945– 3. Right and left (Political science) I. Title.
HN90.R3B33 75-530491

Bairati, Piero, 1946–
see I Profeti dell'impero americano ... Torino : G. Einaudi, [1975]

Bairati, Valeria Egidi
see
Egidi Bairati, Valeria.

Baird, Albert Craig, 1883–
Essentials of general speech communication [by] A. Craig Baird, Franklin H. Knower [and] Samuel L. Becker. 4th ed. New York, McGraw-Hill [1973]
x, 298 p. 21 cm. (McGraw-Hill series in speech)
First-3d eds. published under title: Essentials of general speech.
1. Public speaking. I. Knower, Franklin Hayward, 1901– joint author. II. Becker, Samuel L., joint author. III. Title.
PN4121.B314 1973 808.5 72-6641
ISBN 0-07-003252-1 rev MARC

Baird, Alexander William Stewart.
Studies in Pascal's ethics / by A. W. S. Baird. — The Hague : M. Nijhoff, 1975.
viii, 100 p. ; 24 cm. — (International archives of the history of ideas : Series minor ; 16) Ne***
Bibliography: p. [95]-96.
Includes index.
1. Pascal, Blaise, 1623-1662—Ethics. I. Title. II. Series: Archives internationales d'histoire des idées : Series minor ; 16.
B1904.E7B3 170'.92'4 75-315551
75 MARC

Baird, Alice, 1871–
I was there: St. James's, West Malvern. Worcester, Littlebury, 1956.
658 p. illus.
1. St. James's School, West Malvern, Eng. I. Title.
MiU NUC73-59281

Baird, Arthur D.
see United States. Work Projects Administration. New York (City) Study and demonstration of home care of recipients of old age assistance ... New York, WPA, 1937.

Baird, Bil.
Puppets and population / by Bil Baird ; edited by Martha Keehn and Linda Burgess ; photos by Zbigniew Gajda and Dirck Halstead ; ill. by Bertie Meeker. — New York : World Education, [1971]
95 p. : ill. ; 23 cm.
Includes the author's puppet play Small family, happy family, p. 27-73.
1. Underdeveloped areas—Birth control—Study and teaching. 2. Puppets and puppet plays in education. I. World Education, inc. II. Title.
HQ763.5.B34 301.32'1 75-310763
75 MARC

Baird, Carl Direlle.
Heat transfer in beds of citrus fruits during forced convection cooling. [Gainesville] 1973.
xiii, 165 l. illus. 28 cm.
Typescript.
Thesis—University of Florida.
Vita.
Bibliography: leaves 112-116.
1. Citrus fruits—Cooling. 2. Citrus fruits—Thermal properties. I. Title.
FU NUC75-19919

Baird, Carl Direlle, joint author
see Myers, Julian Mostella, 1921– Evaporation losses in sprinkler irrigation. [Gainesville, University of Florida] 1970.

Baird, Carol F 1939–
Death fantasy in male and female college students. [n.p.] 1971.
xi, 148 p. illus.
Thesis (Ph. D.)—Boston University.
Bibliography: p. 136-147.
1. Death—Psychology. I. Title.
MBU NUC73-126589

Baird, Catherine.
Reflections / by Catherine Baird. — London : Salvationist Pub. and Supplies, 1975.
v, 57 p. ; 23 cm. GB***
Poems.
Includes indexes.
ISBN 0-85412-274-5 : £1.05
1. Christian poetry, English. I. Title.
PS3503.A5387R4 1975 811'.5'2 76-374833
76 MARC

Baird, Charles W
Elements of macroeconomics / by Charles W. Baird. — St. Paul : West Pub. Co., c1977.
xiii, 306 p. : ill. ; 25 cm.
Includes bibliographical references and index.
ISBN 0-8299-0069-1 : $7.95
1. Macroeconomics. I. Title.
HB171.5.B188 339 76-26563
76 MARC

Baird, Charles W
Macroeconomics: an integration of monetary, search, and income theories [by] Charles W. Baird. Chicago, Science Research Associates [1973]
xv, 320 p. illus. 24 cm.
Includes bibliographical references.
1. Macroeconomics. I. Title.
HB171.5.B19 339 72-92562
MARC

Baird, Charles W
Prices and markets : microeconomics / Charles W. Baird. — St. Paul : West Pub. Co., [1975]
xvi, 231 p. : ill. ; 26 cm.
Includes bibliographical references and index.
ISBN 0-8299-0060-8 : $8.95
1. Microeconomics. I. Title.
HB171.5.B194 330 75-7737
75 MARC

Baird, Charles W., joint author.
see Main, Robert S. Elements of microeconomics. St. Paul, West Pub. Co., c1977.

Baird, Charles Washington, 1828-1887. Chronicle of a border town. Selections. 1976.
in Mamaroneck from colonial times through the first century of the Republic ... [Mamaroneck, N.Y.] American Revolution Bicentennial Committee, Village of Mamaroneck, 1976.

Baird, Charles Washington, 1828–1887.
Chronicle of a border town; history of Rye, Westchester County, New York, 1660–1870, including Harrison and the White Plains till 1788. Illustrated by Abram Hosier. New York, A. D. F. Randolph, 1871. Harrison, N. Y., Harbor Hill Books, 1974.
xvi, 570 p. illus. 23 cm.
Includes bibliographical references.
1. Rye, N. Y.—History. 2. Rye, N. Y.—Genealogy. I. Title.
F129.R98B34 1974 974.7'277 74-6231
MARC

Baird, Charles Washington, 1828–1887.
History of the Huguenot emigration to America. Baltimore, Genealogical Pub. Co., 1973.
2 v. in 1. illus. 22 cm.
Reprint of the 1885 ed. published by Dodd, Mead, New York.
1. Huguenots in America. 2. Huguenots in the United States. 3. Huguenots—History. I. Title.
E29.H9B16 1973 301.32'8'44073 73-158312
ISBN 0-8063-0554-1 MARC

Baird, Charles William.
John Bunyan : a study in narrative technique / Charles W. Baird. — Port Washington, N.Y. : Kennikat Press, 1977.
160 p. ; 23 cm. — (Literary criticism series) (National university publications)
Bibliography: p. 152-155.
Includes index.
ISBN 0-8046-9162-2
1. Bunyan, John, 1628-1688—Style.
PR3332.B3 828'.4'07 76-53813
76 MARC

Baird, Craig R
Controlling insect pests of home-stored foods / Craig R. Baird and Hugh W. Homan. -- Moscow : Cooperative Extension Service, University of Idaho, 1975.
[2] p. : ill. -- (Idaho. University. Cooperative Extension Service. Current information series ; no. 269)
I. Title.
DNAL NUC77-86043

Baird, Cynthia.
La Raza in films. Oakland, California, Latin American Library [1972 ?]
68 l.
"A list of films and filmstrips."
1. Mexican-Americans—Bibliography—Catalogs. 2. Audio-visual materials. I. Title.
InU MiEM NUC74-728

Baird, Cynthia. La Raza in films
see Baird, Cynthia. A supplement to La Raza... Oakland, Calif., Latin American Library of the Oakland Public Library [1974]

Baird, Cynthia.
A supplement to La Raza in films. Oakland, Calif., Latin American Library of the Oakland Public Library [1974]
6 l. 28 cm.
Cover title.
1. Latin America–Film catalogs. 2. Mexican Americans–Film catalogs. 3. Spanish Americans in the United States–Film catalogs. I. Baird, Cynthia. La Raza in films. II. Title.
TxU NUC76-22425

Baird, D
Age and growth of the South African pilchard Sardinops ocellata. [Cape Town, 1970]
16 p. illus. 21 cm. (South Africa. Division of Sea Fisheries. Investigational report no. 91)
1. Pilchard–Africa, South. 2. Sardinops ocellata. 3. Sardines. I. Title. II. Series.
DME NUC76-69652

Baird, D
Seasonal occurrence of the pilchard Sardinops ocellata on the east coast of South Africa, by D. Baird. [Cape Town, Division of Sea Fisheries, 1971]
19 p. illus. 21 cm. (Division of Sea Fisheries. Investigational report no. 96) SANB***
Bibliography: p. 10.
1. Sardinops ocellata. 2. Fishes—Migration. 3. Marine fishes—Africa, South. I. Title. II. Series: South Africa. Division of Sea Fisheries. Investigational report no. 96.
SH315.S7A315 no. 96 639'.2'0968 s 73-173543
[QL638.C64] [333.9'5] MARC

Baird, David, 1936-
The incredible Gulf. London, Robert Hale [1970]
196 p. illus., map (on lining papers), ports. 23 cm.
SBN 85179-017-8.
1. Carpentaria, Gulf of. I. Title.
MiEM NUC73-59517

Baird, David McCurdy, 1920-
Cape Breton Highlands National Park : where the mountains meet the sea / David M. Baird. — Ottawa : Geological Survey of Canada, Dept. of Mines and Technical Surveys. 1962.
65 p. : ill. ; 18 cm. — (GSC miscellaneous report ; 5)
Includes index.
1. Geology—Nova Scotia—Cape Breton Highlands National Park—Guide-books. 2. Cape Breton Highlands National Park, N.S. I. Series: Canada. Geological Survey. Miscellaneous report ; 5.
QE185.A44 no. 5 75-326913
[QE190] 76 MARC

Baird, David McCurdy, 1920-
Geology and landforms as illustrated by selected Canadian topographic maps, by David M. Baird. [Ottawa] Dept. of Mines and Technical Surveys [1968]
vi, 59 p. 25 cm. (Geological Survey of Canada. Paper 64-21)
Reprint of the 1964 issue.
1. Canada. Maps. I. Canada. Surveys and Mapping Branch. II. Title. III. Series: Canada. Geological Survey. Paper 64-21.
KU NUC74-21669

Baird, David McCurdy, 1920-
A guide to geology for visitors in Canada's national parks / by David M. Baird. — Ottawa : R. Duhamel, Queen's Printer, 1963.
153 p. : ill. ; 18 cm.
1. Geology—Canada—Guide-books. 2. National parks and reserves—Canada—Guide-books. I. Title.
QE185.B23 1963 75-330709
76 MARC

Baird, David McCurdy, 1920–
A guide to geology for visitors to Canada's national parks / David M. Baird. — Rev. ed. — Toronto : Macmillan of Canada : Indian and Northern Affairs, Parks Canada, 1974.
160 p. : ill. ; 18 cm. C 74-6317-0
ISBN 0-7705-1010-8 : $2.95
1. Geology—Canada. 2. National parks and reserves—Canada. I. Title.
QE185.B23 1974 550 75-301640
MARC

Baird, David McCurdy, 1920-
The human situation. David McCurdy Baird. [Fredericton, N.B.] Dept. of Information, University of New Brunswick, 1974.
11 p. port.
"An address presented on the occasion of the twenty-first annual convocation at the University of New Brunswick, Oct. 17, 1973."
CaOTU NUC76-20076

Baird, Delila, 1908- joint author
see Baird, Josie. William Renfro, 1734-1830; some descendants, relatives, and allied families. [Rotan, Tex., 1973]

Baird, Delila, 1908-
see Early Fisher County families ... Rotan, Tex., D. M. Baird, 1976.

Baird, Don Otto, 1888–
A study of biology notebook work in New York State, by Don O. Baird. New York, Bureau of Publications, Teachers College, Columbia University, 1929. [New York, AMS Press, 1972]
viii, 118 p. illus. 22 cm.
Reprint of the 1929 ed., issued in series: Teachers College, Columbia University. Contributions to education, no. 400.
Originally presented as the author's thesis, Columbia.
Bibliography: p. 103–104.
1. Biology—Study and teaching (Secondary)—New York (State) 2. Note-taking. I. Title. II. Series: Columbia University. Teachers College. Contributions to education, no. 400.
QH315.B3 1972 574'.071 71–176532
ISBN 0-404-55400-8 MARC

Baird, Donald, joint author
see Carroll, Robert Lynn, 1938- Carboniferous stem-reptiles of the family Romeriidae. Cambridge, Mass., Harvard University, 1972.

Baird, Donald, 1926- joint author
see Bell, Inglis Freeman, 1917- The English novel, 1578-1956... [Hamden, Conn.] Shoe String Press, 1974 [c1958]

Baird, Donald, 1926- joint author
see Bell, Inglis Freeman, 1917- The English novel, 1578-1956... [New ed.]. London: Bingley, 1974.

Baird, Donald Gene.
In-line stress measurements in polymer solutions flowing through a die. [n.p.] 1974.
175 l. illus. 29 cm.
Thesis(Ph.D.)—University of Wisconsin.
Vita.
Includes bibliography.
I. Title.
WU NUC76-20057

Baird, Dugald, Sir, 1899- ed. Combined textbook of obstetrics and gynaecology for students and practitioners.
see Combined textbook of obstetrics and gynaecology. 9th ed. Edinburgh, Churchill Livingstone, 1976.

Baird, Duncan Caldecott-
see Caldecott-Baird, Duncan.

Baird, Duncan H., joint comp.
see Dodge, Dorothy Rae, comp. Continuities and discontinuities in political thought. [Cambridge, Mass.] Schenkman Pub. Co.; [distributed by Halsted Press, New York, 1975]

Baird, Elizabeth.
Classic Canadian cooking : menus for the seasons / Elizabeth Baird. — Toronto : J. Lorimer, 1974.
200 p. ; 22 cm. C***
Bibliography : p. 189-192.
Includes index.
ISBN 0-88862-073-X
1. Cookery, Canadian. 2. Menus. I. Title.
TX715.B162 641.5'971 75–305740
MARC

Baird, Eric.
An illustrated guide to riding / by Eric Baird. — Adelaide : Rigby, 1975.
167 p. : ill., diagrs. ; 26 cm. Aus
Includes index.
ISBN 0-85179-990-6
1. Horsemanship. 2. Horsemanship—Pictorial works. I. Title.
SF309.B18 1975b 798'.23 76-382152
77 MARC

Baird, Eric.
An illustrated guide to riding / by Eric Baird ; photography Andrew Smith. — London : Luscombe, 1975.
167 p. : ill., port. ; 26 cm. GB75-27367
Col. ill. on lining papers.
Includes index.
ISBN 0-86002-055-X : £4.95
1. Horsemanship. 2. Horsemanship—Pictorial works. I. Title.
SF309.B18 1975 798'.23 76-351946
76 MARC

Baird, Eric.
An illustrated guide to riding / by Eric Baird ; special pref. to American ed. by Thomas Poulin; technical direction, Audrey Horne ; photography, Andrew Smith. — 1st American ed. — Brattleboro, Vt. : S. Greene Press, 1976, c1975.
167 p. : ill. ; 25 cm.
Includes index.
ISBN 0-8289-0265-8
1. Horsemanship. 2. Horsemanship—Pictorial works. I. Title.
SF309.B18 1976 798'.23 75-41871
75 MARC

Baird, Ethel C
Winton Primary & District High School, 1870–1970 [by E. C. B. Winton, N. Z., 1970?]
92 p. illus. 22 cm. NZ***
Cover title.
1. Winton Primary School — History. 2. Winton District High School—History. I. Title.
LG745.W5B34 373.931 73–179820
MARC

Baird, Eva Lee, joint author.
see Wyler, Rose. Nutty number riddles. 1st ed. Garden City, N.Y., Doubleday, c1977.

Baird, Floyd Oliver, 1897-1971.
Leather secrets / by F. O. Baird. — 1st rev. ed. — Fort Worth, Tex. : Leathercraftsman, 1976.
86 p. : chiefly ill. ; 33 x 64 cm.
Includes index.
1. Leather work. 2. Leather carving. I. Title.
TT290.B27 1976 745.53'1 76-382316
76 MARC

Baird, G H
A brief history of Upshur County, by G. H. Baird. [Gilmer, Tex., Printed by the Gilmer mirror, 1946]
76 p. 24 cm.
1. Upshur Co., Tex.—History. I. Title.
F392.U5B34 917.64'222'03 73–156955
MARC

Baird, George.
Re-using the Parkdale CN Railway Station : a feasibility study / prepared for the Parkdale Save Our Station Committee by George Baird and Barton Myers Associates. -- Rev. -- Toronto : Baird, 1976.
57 p. : ill.
CaOTP NUC77-86971

Baird, George.
see Design Guidelines Study Group. On building downtown ... 2d ed. [s.l., s.n.] 1974.

Baird, George William, 1839-
A report to the citizens, concerning certain late disturbances on the western frontier involving Sitting Bull, Crazy Horse, Chief Joseph and Geronimo, opposed in the field by forces under the command of General Nelson A. (Bear-Coat) Miles. With an introd. by W. H. Hutchinson. Ashland, Calif., L. Osborne, 1972.
66 p. illus. 28 cm.
"This edition was limited to six hundred copies."
ICN NUC74-1376

Baird, Gerald Wayne.
Teacher supply and demand: implications for Nebraska teacher education institutions with recommendations for policy change and program development. Lincoln, Neb., 1974.
x, 176 l. forms, tables.
Thesis (Ph.D.)—University of Nebraska.
Bibliography: leaves 144-148.
Appendices: leaves 149-176.
1. Teachers—Supply and demand. 2. Teachers, Training of—Nebraska. I. Title.
NbU NUC76-20058

Baird, Gertrude L 1885–
The descendants of Alexander Baird and Mary Green, compiled by Gertrude L. Baird. [Ogden? Utah, c1972]
vii, 610, 37 p. illus. 23 cm.
1. Baird family. I. Title.
CS71.B166 1972 929'.2'0973 73–160684
MARC

Baird, Gordon Cardwell, 1946-
Paleoecology and taphonomy associated with submarine discontinuities in the geologic record / by Gordon Cardwell Baird. -- [s.l. : s.n.], 1975.
x, 107 leaves : ill. ; 29 cm.
Thesis (Ph.D.)--University of Rochester.
Vita.
Includes bibliographies.
1. Paleoecology. 2. Geology, Stratigraphic. 3. Sediments (Geology) I. Title.
NRU NUC77-86042

Baird, Gray, comp.
Everglade kite (Rostrhamus sociabilis plumbeus) compiled by Gray Baird. Washington, U.S. Dept. of the Interior, Office of Library Services, 1970.
21 p. (U.S. Dept. of the Interior. Office of Library Services. Bibliography series, no. 18)
1. Kite (Bird)—Bibl. I. Title. II. Series.
DI NUC73-68877

Baird, Harry. A comparison of limestone rates from southeast Mississippi
see Bicker, Alvin R Agricultural limestone availability for plant site selection. Jackson, Mississippi Geological, Economic and Topographical Survey, 1974.

[Baird, Henry Carey] 1825-
George Washington and General Jackson, on Negro soldiers. Philadelphia, H.C. Baird, 1863.
8 p. 22 cm.
Micro-opaque. Louisville, Ky., Lost Cause Press, 1960. 1 card. 7.5 x 12.5 cm. (Nineteenth century American pamphlets, 46)
1. Negroes as soldiers. 2. United States—Hist.—Civil war—Negro troops. I. Title. II. Series.
NIC NUC75-1451

Baird, Henry Martyn, 1832-1906.
The Huguenots and Henry of Navarre, by Henry M. Baird... New York, C. Scribner's sons, 1886. [Ann Arbor, Mich., 1967]
2 v. 2 fold. maps. 23 cm.
Photocopy (positive) made by University Microfilms.
Printed on double leaves.
1. Huguenots in France. 2. Henri IV, king of France, 1553-1610. 3. France—Hist.—Wars of the Huguenots, 1562-1598.
NBuC NUC76-69653

Baird, Hiram K
George Washington : two plays / by Hiram K. Baird. — Flushing, N.Y. : New Voices Pub. Co., c1977.
166 p. ; 21 cm.
CONTENTS: An innate spirit of freedom.—Let me go off quietly.
1. Washington, George, Pres. U.S., 1732-1799—Drama. I. Baird, Hiram K. Let me go off quietly. 1977. II. Title.
PS3552.A38I5 812'.5'4 77-79109
77 MARC

Baird, Hiram K. Let me go off quietly. 1977.
in Baird, Hiram K. George Washington ... Flushing, N.Y., New Voices Pub. Co., c1977.

Baird, Hiram K
The squadron, the roundhouse, and the tower, plus The wedding / Hiram K. Baird. — Flushing, N.Y. : New Voices Pub. Co., c1976.
185 p. ; 22 cm.
Poems.
ISBN 0-911024-20-4
I. Title.
PS3552.A38S6 811'.5'4 76-24571
77 MARC

Baird, Ian McLean, ed.
see Nutritional deficiencies in modern society... London, Newman Books, 1973.

Baird, Irene.
The climate of power. Toronto, Macmillan [1971]
255 p. 21 cm. C***
I. Title.
PZ3.B1613Cl 813'.5'2 72-171298
[PR6003.A427] MARC

Baird, J. A.
see
Baird, Jack A

Baird, J Edwin.
Indian home seminary program. Provo, Utah, Dept. of Seminaries and Institutes of Religion, Brigham Young University, 1967.
36 p. 29 cm.
1. Mormons and Mormonism. 2. Indians of North America. 3. Religious education—Home training. I. Title.
NjP NUC74-127394

Baird, J Edwin.
L.D.S. Indian seminary program as explained before a tribal council. Provo, Utah, Church of Jesus Christ of Latter-day Saints Church School [1967?]
6 l. 29 cm.
Cover title: Indian seminary program.
1. Mormons and Mormonism—Missions. 2. Indians of North America. 3. Religious education—Home training. I. Title.
NjP NUC75-29951

Baird, J Edwin.
What our Heavenly Father wants done with the remnants of Lehi on this land. Provo, Utah, Church of Jesus Christ of Latter-day Saints Church Schools, 1967.
11 l. 29 cm.
Cover title: The remnants of Lehi.
1. Mormons and Mormonism—Doctrinal and controversial works. I. Title.
NjP NUC75-30247

Baird, Jack.
Irish setters by Jack Baird. Neptune City, N.J., T.F.H. Publications, 1973.
127 p. ill.
1. Irish setters. I. Title.
KMK NUC76-69479

Baird, Jack.
Weimaraners by Jack Baird. Neptune City, N.J., T.F.H. Publications, 1974.
128 p. illus.
1. Weimaraners (Dogs) I. Title.
KMK NUC76-22370

Baird, Jack A., joint author.
see Ozelton, E. C. Timber designers' manual. London, C. L. Staples, 1976.

Baird, Jack D., joint author
see Severy, D M Backrest and head restraint design... New York, Society of Automotive Engineers, 1968.

Baird, Jack V
Careful soil sampling ; the key to reliable soil test information / prepared by Jack V. Baird and A.H. Hatfield. -- Raleigh : North Carolina Agricultural Extension Service, 1975.
folder (8 p.) : ill. -- (North Carolina State University. Agricultural Extension Service. Extension folder ; 323)
I. Title.
DNAL NUC77-86041

Baird, James P., joint author.
see Wright, Frederick James. Tropical diseases. 5th ed. Edinburgh, Churchill Livingstone, 1975.

Baird, James Richard, 1933-
An analysis of the evaluation and selection criteria used to determine 16 mm film purchases by selected university film rental libraries. [n.p.] 1973.
xiii, 252 l. illus.
Thesis (Ed.D.)—Brigham Young University.
Bibliography: leaves 134-138.
Microfilm (positive) Ann Arbor, Mich., University Microfilms, 1973. 1 reel. (Publication no. 31198)
NNC NUC75-19473

Baird, James T
Parity and hypertension [by James T. Baird and Leslie G. Quinlivan] Rockville, Md., National Center for Health Statistics; [for sale by the Supt. of Docs., U. S. Govt. Print. Off., Washington] 1972.
iv, 28 p. 26 cm. (Data from the National Health Survey, series 11, no. 38) (DHEW publication no. (HSM) 72-1024) $0.35
Bibliography: p. 12-13.
1. Hypertension—Statistics. I. Quinlivan, Leslie G., joint author. II. Title. III. Series: United States. National Center for Health Statistics. Vital and health statistics. Series 11: Data from the National Health Survey. Data from the health examination survey, no. 38. IV. Series: United States. Dept. of Health, Education, and Welfare. DHEW publication no. (HSM) 72-1024.
RA407.3.A347 no. 38 79-169286
[RC685.H8] 312'.0973 s [616.1'32'071] MARC

Baird, James T
Relationships among parent ratings of behavioral characteristics of children, United States [by James T. Baird, Jr. and Jean Roberts] Rockville, Md., National Center for Health Statistics; [for sale by the Supt. of Docs., U. S. Govt. Print. Off., Washington] 1972.
iv, 49 p. illus. 27 cm. (National Center for Health Statistics. Vital and health statistics. Data from the National health survey: series 11, no. 121) (DHEW publication no. (HSM) 73-1603) $1.00
Includes bibliographical references.
Supt. of Docs. no.: HE 20.2210:11/121
1. Child study—Statistics. I. Roberts, Jean, 1918- joint author. II. United States. National Center for Health Statistics. III. Title. IV. Series: United States. National Center for Health Statistics. Vital and health statistics. Series 11: Data from the National Health Survey. Data from the health examination survey, no. 121. V. Series: United States. Dept. of Health, Education, and Welfare. DHEW publication no. (HSM) 73-1603.
RA407.3.A347 no. 121 312'.0973 s 78-190013
[BF721] [155.4'1'0212] MARC

Baird, James T., joint author
see Bryant, Elmer Earl. Sample design and estimation procedures... Rockville, Md., National Center for Health Statistics, 1971.

Baird, Jane Parnes, 1945-
Changes in patterns of interpersonal behavior among family members during brief family therapy. [New York] 1972 [1973]
xiii, 186 l. diagrs., tables. 29 cm.
Thesis—Columbia University.
Bibliography: leaves 136-144.
1. Interpersonal relations. 2. Domestic relations. 3. Family. 4. Psychotherapy. I. Title.
NNC NUC75-19472

Baird, Janet Rae.
An analysis of Mexican-American culture taught in Kansas migrant programs. [Lawrence, 1973]
v, 151 l. 28 cm.
Thesis (Ph.D.)—University of Kansas.
1. Mexican Americans. Education. Kansas. 2. Mexican Americans. Social life and customs. 3. Children of migrant laborers. Education. Kansas. 4. Biculturalism. Kansas. 5. Education, Bilingual. Kansas. I. Title.
KU NUC74-126000

Baird, Jay W comp.
From Nuremberg to My Lai. Edited and with an introd. by Jay W. Baird. Lexington, Mass., Heath [1972]
xx, 292 p. illus. 21 cm. (Problems in European civilization)
Bibliography: p. 289-292.
1. War crimes. I. Title. II. Series.
JX6731.W3B32 341.6'9 72-4384
ISBN 0-669-82081-4 MARC

Baird, Jay W
The mythical world of Nazi war propaganda, 1939-1945 / by Jay W. Baird. — Minneapolis : University of Minnesota Press, c1974.
xii, 329 p., [4] leaves of plates : ill. ; 24 cm.
Bibliography: p. [309]-322.
Includes index.
ISBN 0-8166-0741-9
1. World War, 1939-1945—Propaganda. 2. Propaganda, German. I. Title.
D810.P7G317 1974 940.54'887'43 74-83132
MARC

Baird, Jesse Hays, 1889-
Land of the Pilgrims' pride. Illustrated by G. D. "Mac" Machin. Richmond, Va., John Knox Press [1973]
127 p. illus. 24 cm.
1. United States—History. 2. United States—Civilization. I. Title.
E178.B155 917.3'03 72-11164
ISBN 0-8042-0935-9 MARC

Baird, Jo Ann.
Using media in the music program / by Jo Ann Baird. — New York : Center for Applied Research in Education, c1975.
64 p. : ill. ; 23 cm. — (Classroom music enrichment units)
Includes bibliographical references.
"Selected media sources": p. 64.
ISBN 0-87628-211-7 : $3.95
1. School music—Instruction and study—Audio-visual aids. 2. Audio-visual education—Handbooks, manuals, etc. I. Title. II. Series.
MT150.B22 372.8'7'044 75-33690
75 MARC

Baird, John C
Social worker's orientations toward community mental health concepts. [n. p., 1973?]
1 v.
Thesis (Ph. D.) CWRU.
OClW NUC76-69480

Baird, John C., ed.
see Human space perception... Austin, Tex., Psychonomic Journals, c1970.

Baird, John D., ed.
see Conference on Editorial Problems, 7th, University of Toronto, 1971. Editing texts of the Romantic Period... Toronto, A. M. Hakkert, 1972.

Baird, John D 1928-
Davy, by John D. Baird. [Illustrated by Bill Horst. 1st ed. Chaska, Minn., Buckskin Press, 1971]
117, [2] p. illus. 20 cm.
1. Fur trade—Fiction. I. Title.
MnHi NUC74-127396

Baird, John D 1928-
Hawken rifles, the mountain man's choice / by John D. Baird. -- Big Timber, Mt. : Buckskin Press, 1974, c1968.
xvii, 95 p. : ill. ; 29 cm.
1. Hawken, Samuel T., 1792-1884. 2. Hawken, Jacob, 1786-1849. 3. Hawken rifle. I. Title.
NmU NUC77-87088

Baird, John D 1928-
Who's who in buckskins. Edited by John D. Baird. 1st ed. Big Timber, Mont., Buckskin Press [1973]
iv, 182 p. illus. 29 cm. $10.00
1. Shooting—Biography. 2. Muzzle-loading firearms—Societies, etc.—Directories. I. Title. II. Title: Buckskins.
GV1157.A1B34 799.2 73-166284
ISBN 0-912420-09-X MARC

Baird, John Edward.
Corinthians : study guide / by John E. Baird. -- Cincinnati : New Life Books, c1975.
104 p. ; 22 cm. -- (Search-and-discover Bible study series)
"40016."
ISBN 0-87239-024-1.
1. Bible. N. T. Corinthians--Study. I. Title. II. Series.
TNDC NUC77-86048

Baird, John Edward.
Matthew: study guide, by John E. Baird. Cincinnati, New Life Books, c1975.
104 p. 22 cm. (Search-and-discover Bible study series)
"40010."
ISBN 0-87239-020-9.
1. Bible. N. T. Matthew—Study. I. Title. II. Series.
TNDC NUC77-84350

Baird, John Edward, 1948-
The effects of speech summaries upon audience comprehension of expository speeches of varying quality and complexity. [Bloomington, Ind.] 1972.
151 p.
Thesis (Ph. D.)—Indiana University.
Vita.
InU NUC74-1361

Baird, John Sanford.
A multivariate developmental study of political ideology and intolerance. Raleigh, N. C., 1971.
174 l. illus., tables. 29 cm.
Bibliography: leaves 151-163.
Vita.
Thesis (Ph. D.)—North Carolina State University at Raleigh.
NcRS NUC73-126584

Baird, John William, 1944- joint author.
see Tubbs, Stewart L., 1943- The open person ... ... Columbus, Merrill, c1976.

Baird, Joseph Armstrong.
Grace Carpenter Hudson (1865–1937) : oil paintings and sketches, including works on loan from C. Frederick Faudé. [Catalog of an exhibition] May 22–August 1, 1962, California Historical Society, San Francisco. [San Francisco, California Historical Society, 1962?]
[13] p. illus. 28 cm.
Bibliography: p. [7]
1. Hudson, Grace Carpenter, 1865–1937. 2. Indians of North America—Pictorial works. I. California Historical Society.
ND237.H87B34 759.13 74–184891
MARC

Baird, Joseph Armstrong.
Historic lithographs of San Francisco. By Joseph Armstrong Baird, Jr. and Edwin Clyve Evans. San Francisco, S. A. Waterson for Burger-Evans, 1972.
40, [41] l. illus. (part col., part fold.) 59 x 89 cm.
"Typographic design by Adrian Wilson."
"Bibliography": leaves 39-40.
One of an edition of 1000 copies.
1. San Francisco—Description—Views—Catalogs. 2. Lithographs—Catalogs. 3. Lithographs, American—Catalogs. I. Evans, Edwin Clyve, joint author. II. Wilson, Adrian. III. Waterson, Steven A. IV. Burger-Evans, San Francisco.
CU-BANC NUC76-35410

Baird, Joseph Armstrong.
A history of Octagon House, compiled by Joseph A. Baird, Jr. from carefully documented sources, with the particular assistance of Colonel Harold H. Ashley, his wife Ann Ashley, and the Misses Gladys and Mabel Reston. San Francisco, National Society of Colonial Dames of America Resident in the State of California, 1973.
[15] p. illus. 23 cm.
1. Octagon House, San Francisco. 2. San Francisco—Historic houses, etc. I. National Society of the Colonial Dames of America. California.
CU-BANC NUC76-87301

Baird, Joseph Armstrong.
The West remembered : artists and images, 1837-1973 : selections from the Collection of Earl C. Adams, exhibited at the Old Mint, San Francisco, June 16, 1973, through September 15, 1973, and the Santa Barbara Museum of Art, November 10 to January 6 / compiled by Joseph A. Baird, Jr. ; photos. by Armando Solis. — San Francisco : California Historical Society, 1973.
88 p. : ill. (some col.) ; 27 cm.
Bibliography: p. 85-87.
Includes index.
1. The West in art. 2. Art, Modern—19th century—Exhibitions. 3. Art, Modern—20th century—Exhibitions. 4. Adams, Earl C.—Art collections. I. Santa Barbara, Calif. Museum of Art. II. California Historical Society. III. Title.
N8214.5.U6B34 704.94'9'978 75-318276
75 MARC

Baird, Joseph **Armstrong**
see California Historical Society. Fine Arts Dept. A directory of the principal libraries and museums in Northern California. [rev. ed.] San Francisco, 1970.

Baird, Joseph Armstrong.
see Images of El Dorado ... [Davis, University of California, 1975]

Baird, Joseph Arthur.
The computer Bible: a critical concordance to the Synoptic Gospels. [By] J. Arthur Baird. [n.p., c1970]
ix, 254 l. 22 x 29 cm. (The computer Bible, v. 1)
Cover title.
The concordance is to the Greek text.
1. Bible. N. T. Gospel—Concordances, Greek. I. Title.
MH-AH NUC76-69478

Baird, Joseph Arthur.
A critical concordance to the Gospel of John. [Wooster] Biblical Research Associates, c1974.
123 p. (The computer Bible, v. 5)
1. Bible. N. T. John—Concordances. 2. Bible—Concordances, English. 3. Bible. N. T.—Concordances. I. Title. II. Series.
MiEM NUC76-20779

Baird, Joseph Arthur.
A critical concordance to the Synoptic Gospels [by] J. Arthur Baird. [n. p.] Biblical Research Associates, Inc. [1971]
2 p. l., 344 p. 28 cm.
The computer Bible, vol. 1, rev. ed. Editors: J. Arthur Baird [and] David Noel Freedman.
1. Bible. N. T. Gospels—Concordances, English. 2. Electronic data processing—Biblical studies. I. Title. II. Series: The computer Bible, v. 1.
ICLT NUC73-43772

Baird, Joseph Arthur.
The Johannine Epistles; a critical concordance. [Edinburgh] University of Edinburgh, 1971.
1 v. (unpaged) (The Computer Bible, v. 3)
Cover title.
1. Bible. N. T. John.—Corcordances. I. Title. II. Series.
MIEM NUC76-69477

Baird, Joseph Arthur.
A synoptic concordance to Hosea, Amos, Micah. Computer generated by Francis I. Andersen and A. Dean Forbes. Editors: J. Arthur Baird [and] David Noel Freedman. [n. p.] Biblical Research Associates [197-?]
[21], 329 p. 28 cm. (The Computer Bible, v. 6)
"The text used is Biblia Hebraica."
1. Bible. O. T. Hosea. Concordances. 2. Bible. O. T. Amos. Concordances. 3. Bible. O. T. Micah. Concordances. I. Freedman, David Noel, 1922- joint author. II. Title. III. Series.
NcD NUC76-20803

Baird, Joseph Arthur, ed.
see The Computer Bible. [n. p.] Biblical Research Associates [19

Baird, Joseph Hugh
see A Behavioral approach to teaching. Dubuque, Wm. C. Brown [1972]

Baird, Josie.
William Renfro, 1734–1830; some descendants, relatives, and allied families, collected and compiled by Josie Baird and Delila Baird. [Rotan, Tex., 1973]
vi, 169 l. illus. 28 cm.
1. Renfrew family. I. Baird, Delila, 1908- joint author. II. Title.
CS71.R393 1973 929'.2'0973 73-86309
MARC

Baird, Josie.
see Early Fisher County families ... Rotan, Tex., D. M. Baird, 1976.

Baird, Lawrence, ed.
see Housing for the elderly... [Los Angeles] Ethel Percy Andrus Gerontology Center, 1973.

Baird, Lawrence M
A survey of governmental agencies, studies and publications concerned with the environment of the Southern California coastal zone, by Lawrence M. Baird. [Los Angeles] University of Southern California, Center for Urban Affairs, 1972.
147 p. 28 cm. (Sea grant publication no. USC-SG-2-72)
1. Coasts—California. 2. Environmental policy—Calif. I. University of Southern Calif. Center for Urban Affairs. II. Title. III. Series.
CLSU NUC74-138157

Baird, Leonard.
The elite schools : a profile of prestigious independent preparatory schools / Leonard L. Baird. — Lexington, Mass. : Lexington Books, c1977.
xvi, 163 p. ; 24 cm.
Bibliography: p. 153-155.
Includes index.
ISBN 0-669-01146-0
1. Private schools—United States. I. Title.
LC49.B25 371'.02'0973 76-48376
77 MARC

Baird, Leonard.
Focusing on measures of college environments. Princeton, N. J., ERIC Clearinghouse on Tests, Measurement and Evaluation, Educational Testing Service [1972]
8 p. 27 cm.
Reprinted from the College board review, no. 86, Winter, 1972-73.
TM report no. 24.
Bibliographical references.
1. Education, Higher-Aims and objectives. 2. Education, Higher-Research. I. Educational Testing Service. II. College board review. III. Title.
MWelC NUC76-71500

Baird, Leonard.
The graduates; a report on the plans and characteristics of college seniors by Leonard L. Baird, with chapters by Mary Jo Clark and Rodney T. Hartnett. Princeton, Educational Testing Service, 1973.
vii, 210 p.
1. College graduates-U.S. 2. College graduates—Employment-U.S. 3. College seniors. I. Clark, Mary Jo. II. Hartnett, Rodney T. III. Title.
MH-Ed NRU NUC74-126942

Baird, Leonard.
Patterns of educational aspiration [by] Leonard L. Baird. Iowa City, Research and Development Division American College Testing Program, 1969.
23 p. 28 cm. (ACT research report no. 32)
Cover title.
Bibliography: p. 21-22.
1. Student aspirations. 2. College students' socioeconomic status. I. Title. II. Series.
LB2350.B34 378.1'98'1 74-150941
MARC

Baird, Leonard.
The undecided student, how different is he? Iowa City, Research and Development Division, American College Testing Program, 1967.
14 p. (ACT research reports, no. 22)
Cover title.
1. Vocational interests. 2. Student aspirations-U.S. I. Title.
MH-Ed TNJ-P NUC74-3593

Baird, Leonard.
Using self-reports to predict student performance / by Leonard L. Baird. — New York : College Entrance Examination Board, 1976.
vi, 90 p. ; 22 cm. — (Research monograph - College Entrance Examination Board ; no. 7)
Bibliography: p. 78-90.
$5.00
1. Prediction of scholastic success. 2. Students, Self-rating of. I. Title. II. Series: College Entrance Examination Board. Research monograph ; no. 7.
LB1131.B16 371.2'64 76-4312
76 MARC

Baird, Leonard.
see Assessing student academic and social progress. San Francisco, Jossey-Bass, 1977.

Baird, Leslie, 1950-
Open corners [by] Leslie Baird [and] Jeff McDonald. Greencastle, Ind., January House [1971]
48 p. illus. 18 cm.
Poems.
I. McDonald, Jeff, joint author. II. Title.
RPB NUC73-35503

Baird, Leslie, 1950–
Tic-tac. New York, Dodd, Mead [1973]
154 p. 21 cm. $3.95
SUMMARY: As she learns more about horsemanship during a summer of riding lessons, a young girl gets progressively more attached to the horse assigned to her.
[1. Horses—Fiction. 2. Horsemanship—Fiction] I. Title.
PZ7.B164Ti [Fic] 72-9936
ISBN 0-396-06763-8 MARC

Baird, Lewis C 1869-
Baird's history of Clark County, Indiana, by Captain Lewis C. Baird ... assisted by well known local talent. Indianapolis, B.F. Bowen & co., 1909. [Evansville, Ind., Unigraphic, 1972]
919 p. illus., ports., maps. 26 cm.
ICN InU NUC73-35520

Baird, Lloyd S 1945-
The relationship of task and role characteristics to satisfaction and performance in a state agency / by Lloyd S. Baird. -- [East Lansing] : Baird, 1975.
[158] leaves : ill. ; 29 cm.
Thesis (Ph. D.)--Michigan State University.
Bibliography: leaves [147]-[152].
1. Job satisfaction. I. Title.
MiEM NUC77-93347

Baird, Lorrayne Y
A bibliography of Chaucer, 1964-1973 / Lorrayne Y. Baird. — Boston : G. K. Hall, c1977.
xxiv, 287 p. ; 25 cm. — (Reference guides in literature)
"A continuation of William R. Crawford's Bibliography of Chaucer, 1954-63."
Includes indexes.
ISBN 0-8161-8005-9
1. Chaucer, Geoffrey, d. 1400—Bibliography. I. Crawford, William R. Bibliography of Chaucer, 1954-63. II. Title.
Z8164.B27 016.821'1 77-374
[PR1905] 77 MARC

Baird, Louise, 1941-
A metaphysical emotion : the art of John Barth / by Louise Baird. -- [Madison, Wis.] : University of Wisconsin, c1975.
ii, 363 l. ; 29 cm.
Thesis (Ph. D.)--University of Wisconsin.
Vita.
Bibliography: leaves 357-363.
1. Barth, John. I. Title.
WU NUC77-93376

Baird, M E
Electrical properties of polymeric materials. London, The Plastics Institute [1973]
51 p. illus. 29 cm.
1. Polymers and polymerization—Electric properties. I. Title.
NcRS NUC74-126003

Baird, Margaret.
Television Baird. Cape Town, Haum, 1973.
160 p. illus. 22 cm. SANB***
1. Baird, John Logie, 1888-1945. I. Title.
TK6635.B3B3 621.388'0092'4 73-169009
ISBN 0-7986-0052-7 [B] MARC

Baird, Marie-Térèse.
A lesson in love. Boston, Houghton Mifflin, 1973.
221 p. 21 cm. $5.95
I. Title.
PZ4.B1662Le 3 823'.9'14 73-8726
[PR6052.A324] MARC
ISBN 0-395-17706-5

Baird, Marie-Térèse.
A lesson in love. Boston, G. K. Hall, 1974 [c1973]
375 p. 24 cm.
Large print ed.
I. Title.
[PZ4.B1662Le 4] 823'.9'14 73-21920
[PR6052-A324] MARC
ISBN 0-8161-6179-8

Baird, Marie-Térèse.
A shining furrow. London, Collins, 1973.
221 p. 21 cm. £2.00 GB 73-21689
I. Title.
PZ4.B1662Sh 3 823'.9'14 74-180279
[PR6052.A324] MARC
ISBN 0-00-221854-2

Baird, Mark J
Reminiscences of John W. Woolley and Lorin C. Woolley... Reported by Mark J. and Rhea A. Baird... [Draper? Utah, 1971?]
2 v. 28 cm.
1. Woolley, John Wickersham, 1831-1928. 2. Wooley, Lorin Calvin, 1856-1934. 3. Mormons and Mormonism. I. Baird, Rhea A., joint author. II. Woolley, John Wickersham, 1831-1928. III. Title.
CtY NUC73-126393

Baird, Mary.
Open up! A time for listening. Written by Mary Baird & Nancy Holderread. Illus. by Nancy Holderread. [New York] Herder and Herder, 1969.
15 p. illus. 22 x 28 cm. (A time for living; religious experience program)
1. Christian living. I. Title.
IEG NUC76-69665

Baird, Mary.
Open up; a time for listening. Idea-line and teachers. [By] Mary Baird [and] Arlene Huguelet. [New York] Herder and Herder [1969]
20 p. 21 cm. (A time for living; religious experience program)
Accompanies pupil's book.
1. Christian living. I. Title.
IEG NUC76-69664

Baird, Mary Ann
see Mississippi. Dept. of Education. Division of Instruction. Guidelines to reading, Grades 1-6... Jackson, Miss., 1971.

Baird, Mary Julian.
Edith Stein and the Mother of God. [n. p., n. d.]
417-429 p. 23 cm.
Caption title.
Offprint from Cross and Crown, v. 8(1956)
ODaU-M NUC74-1380

Baird, Mary Julian.
Lady most courteous. [St. Louis, The Queen's Work, 1958]
24 p. 15 cm.
Cover title.
ODaU-M NUC73-59270

Baird, Mary Julian.
Patron Saints of the Legion of Mary. Bay Shore, N.Y., Montfort Publications [1959]
32 p. 18 cm.
"References": p. 32.
ODaU-M NUC73-59271

Baird, Mary K
International economic indicators [by Mary K. Baird and William H. Chartener] Menlo Park, Calif., Stanford Research Institute, 1962.
24 p. illus. 28 cm. ([Stanford Research Institute] Long Range Planning Service. Confidential report, no. 136)
Cover title.
1. Economic indicators. 2. Commerce. I. Chartener, William H., joint author. II. Title.
CLSU NUC75-8256

Baird, Mary K., joint author
see Consumer services. Menlo Park, Calif., 1963.

Baird, Mary K.
see Domestic joint ventures. Menlo Park, Calif., 1966.

Baird, Mary K.
see International consumer expenditure patterns. Menlo Park, Calif., 1963.

Baird, Mary K.
see International industrial growth patterns. Menlo Park, Calif., 1965.

Baird, Mary K., joint author
see Meissner, Frank. Wage costs abroad. Menlo Park, Calif., Stanford Research Institute, 1960.

Baird, Mary K., joint author
see Mitchell, Arnold. American values. Menlo Park, Calif., 1969.

Baird, Mary K.
see Upper income families. Menlo Park, Calif., 1964.

Baird, Michael Lloyd, 1945-
A paradigm for semantic picture recognition. [Atlanta] 1973.
160 l. diagrs., tables.
Thesis (Ph.D.)—Georgia Institute of Technology.
Directed by Michael D. Kelly.
Vita.
1. Computer drawing. 2. Optical data processing. I. Title.
GAT NUC74-133435

Baird, Neil McClelland.
In vitro regulation of proinsulin synthesis in isolated rat islets. [Minneapolis] 1971.
197 l. 29 cm.
Thesis (Ph.D.)—University of Minnesota.
Abstract (3 l.) inserted.
Bibliography: leaves 179-197.
MnU-B NUC74-127397

Baird, Nini.
Access to the arts : a report to the Provincial Secretary on the feasibility of the provincial policy announced April 1974, based upon public meetings throughout the province and written reactions to the policy, April–June 1974 / prepared by Nini Baird. — [s. l. : s. n.], 1974 ([Victoria] : K. M. Macdonald, printer to the Queen's Most Excellent Majesty in right of the Province of British Columbia)
ii, 51 p. ; 28 cm. C***
Bibliography : p. 25.
1. Arts—British Columbia—Management. I. British Columbia. Provincial Secretary's Dept. II. Title.
NX770.C2B82 354'.711'00854 75-302264
MARC

Baird, Patrick C., joint author.
see Arkinstall, Michael James. Erdington past and present. Birmingham, Birmingham Public Libraries, 1976.

Baird, R H
Factors affecting growth and condition of mussels (Mytilus edulis L.) London, H.M. Stationery Off., 1966.
33 p. illus. (Gt. Brit. Ministry of Agriculture, Fisheries and Food. Fishery investigations. Series 2, v. 25, no. 2)
Bibliography: p. 33.
I. Title.
DNAL NUC75-30734

Baird, Rey L 1931-
A variable recursive mechanism in Samoan. [Bloomington, Ind.] 1974.
137 p.
Thesis (Ph.D.)—Indiana University.
Vita.
InU NUC76-20059

Baird, Rhea A
Plurality of wives. [Draper, Utah, n.d.]
35 p.
Cover title.
1. Mormon Church—Doctrine—Marriage, Plural. 2. Polygamy. I. Title.
UU NUC76-22393

Baird, Rhea A., joint author
see Baird, Mark J Reminiscences. [Draper? Utah, 1971?]

Baird, Richard Edward, 1929-
The politics of Echo Park and other water development projects in the upper Colorado River Basin, 1946-1956. Urbana, Ill., 1960.
557 l.
1. Colorado River Watershed. 2. Water resources development—Colorado Riber Valley. I. Title.
CU-SB NUC74-175382

Baird, Robert, 1798-1863.
Impressions and experiences of the West Indies and North America in 1849. Edinburgh and London, W. Blackwood and sons, 1850.
2 v. fronts. 21 cm.
Microfilm. Ann Arbor, Mich., University Microfilms, 1963. 1 reel. 35 mm. (American culture series, 221:6)
1. West Indies—Descr. & trav. 2. West Indies, British—Descr. & trav. 3. U.S.—Descr. & trav. 4. Canada—Descr. & trav. I. Title.
FU NUC74-127398

Baird, Robert, 1798-1863.
View of the valley of the Mississippi; or, The emigrant's and traveller's guide to the West... Philadelphia, H.S. Tanner, 1832.
xii, 341 p. fold. front., fold. map, plans. 19 cm.
Micro-opaque. Louisville, Ky., Lost Cause Press, 195-? 8 cards. 7.5 x 12.5 cm. (Nineteenth century American literature on microcards)
I. Series: Nineteenth century American literature on microcards.
NIC NUC74-127399

Baird, Robert D 1933-
Religion is life: an inquiry into the dominating motif in the theology of Horace Bushnell. [Iowa City] 1934.
359 l. 28 cm.
Thesis—University of Iowa.
Microfilm of typescript. Ann Arbor, Mich., University Microfilms, 1964. 1 reel. 35 mm. (University Microfilms, Ann Arbor, Mich. Publication no. 64,7904)
1. Bushnell, Horace, 1802-1876. I. Title.
CtY-D NUC76-36281

Baird, Robert D., 1933-
see Methodological issues in religious studies. [Chico, Ca.] New Horizons Press, c1975.

Baird, Robert H
The American cotton spinner and managers' and carders guide: a practical treatise on cotton spinning. Comp. from the papers of the late Robert H. Baird. Philadelphia, H.C. Baird, 1869.
xii, 256 p. 20 cm.
Microfilm. Ann Arbor, Mich., University Microfilms, 1969. 1 reel. 35 mm. (American culture series, 404:15)
1. Cotton spinning. I. Title.
FU NUC74-127400

Baird, Robert M
Faith-learning studies: philosophy [by] Robert M. Baird. [Nashville, Tenn., Sunday School Board, S.B.C., c1971]
32, [2] p. 21 cm.
Cover title.
1. Philosophy. I. Title.
KyLoS NUC73-126574

Baird, Robert N
Equalization objectives and the allocation of intergovernmental revenues. A report to the Urban Observatory, City of Cleveland. Cleveland, 1971.
128 p.
Research and studies conducted pursuant to a contract beween Dept. of Housing and Urban Development and the National League of Cities.
Bibliography: p. 127-128.
1. Local government—Finance—Cleveland. 2. Grants-in-aid. 3. Intergovernmental relations—Cleveland. I. Cleveland Urban Observatory. II. United States. Dept. of Housing and Urban Development. III. Title.
DHUD NUC76-69474

Baird, Ronald J
Industrial plastics : basic chemistry, major resins, modern industrial processes / by Ronald J. Baird. — South Holland, Ill. : Goodheart-Willcox Co., c1976.
320 p. : ill. ; 27 cm.
Bibliography: p. 288-289.
Includes index.
ISBN 0-87006-213-1
1. Plastics. I. Title.
TP1120.B33 1976 668.4 76-53833
77 MARC

Baird, Ronald J
Oxyacetylene welding : basic fundamentals / by Ronald J. Baird. — South Holland, Ill. : Goodheart-Willcox Co., c1976.
104 p. : ill. ; 28 cm.
Includes index.
ISBN 0-87006-218-2
1. Oxyacetylene welding and cutting. I. Title.
TS228.B34 671.5'22 76-28390
76 MARC

Baird, Ronald J., joint author.
see Roth, Alfred C. Small gas engines ... South Holland, Ill., Goodheart-Willcox Co., [1975]

Baird, Russell N., joint author
see Click, J W Magazine editing and production. Dubuque, Iowa, W. C. Brown Co. [1974]

Baird, Russell N., joint author.
see Turnbull, Arthur T. The graphics of communication ... 3d. ed. New York, Holt, Rinehart and Winston, [1975]

Baird, Scott James, 1939-
Employment interview speech; a social dialect study in Austin, Tex. Austin, 1969 [1972]
viii, 127 l.
Thesis—Texas—University at Austin.
Bibliography: leaves 122-127.
Vita.
Xerox copy, University Microfilms, Ann Arbor, Mich., 1972.
1. English language—Dialects—Austin, Tex. 2. Employment interviewing. 3. Negro—English dialects. I. Title.
DGU NUC74-1378

Baird, Spencer Fullerton, 1823-1887.
[Birds. Collected excerpts from v. 10 of Reports of explorations and surveys, to ascertain the most practicable and economical route for a railroad from the Mississippi River to the Pacific Ocean. n.p., 19--?]
1 v. (various pagings) col. plates. 29 cm.
NIC NUC75-71749

Baird, Spencer Fullerton, 1823–1887.
The birds of North America [by] Spencer Fullerton Baird, John Cassin [and] George N. Lawrence. New York, Arno Press, 1974.
lvi, 1005, vii, p. 100 illus. 24 cm. (Natural sciences in America)
Reprint of the 1860 ed. published by Lippincott, Philadelphia. Pages xiii–xvi are wanting in the reprint due to a defect in the available copies of the original ed. The col. plates are reproduced in monochrome reduced 30% in size.
Bibliography: p. [929]–954.
ISBN 0-405-05715-6
1. Birds—North America. 2. Birds—Catalogs and collections. 3. Smithsonian Institution. I. Cassin, John, 1813–1869, joint author. II. Lawrence, George Newbold, 1806–1895, joint author. III. Title. IV. Series.
QL681.B138 1974 598.2'97 73-17799
MARC

Baird, Spencer Fullerton, 1823–1887.
A history of North American birds [by] Spencer Fullerton Baird, Thomas M. Brewer [and] Robert Ridgway. New York, Arno Press, 1974 [c1874]
3 v. illus. 24 cm. (Natural sciences in America)
Each volume has special title: Land birds.
Reprint of the ed. published by Little, Brown, Boston.
ISBN 0-405-05711-3
1. Birds—North America. I. Brewer, Thomas Mayo, 1814–1880, joint author. II. Ridgway, Robert, 1850–1929, joint author. III. Title. IV. Series.
QL681.B16 1974 598.2'97 73-17798 MARC

Baird, Spencer Fullerton, 1823–1887.
Mammals of North America. New York, Arno Press, 1974.
xxxiv, 735, 55, [737]-764 p. illus. 24 cm. (Natural sciences in America)
Reprint of the 1859 ed. published by Lippincott, Philadelphia.
Part 1 originally published in 1857 at v. 8, pt. 1 of Reports of explorations and surveys, to ascertain the most practicable and economical route for a railroad from the Mississippi River to the Pacific Ocean, issued by the U. S. War Dept., and pt. 2 in 1859 as v. 2, pt. 2 of Report on the United States and Mexican boundary survey, issued by the U. S. Dept. of the Interior.
ISBN 0-405-05710-5
1. Mammals—North America. 2. Smithsonian Institution. I. Title. II. Series.
QL715.B16 1974 599'.09'7 73-17797 MARC

Baird, Spencer Fullerton, 1823–1887.
The water birds of North America [by] Spencer Fullerton Baird, Thomas M. Brewer [and] Robert Ridgway. New York, Arno Press, 1974 [c1884]
xi, 537, 552 p. illus. 24 cm. (Natural sciences in America)
Reprint of the 1884 ed. published by Little, Brown, Boston, which was issued as v. 12–13 of Memoirs of the Museum of Comparative Zoology, Harvard College.
Includes bibliographical references.
ISBN 0-405-05716-4
1. Water-birds—North America. I. Brewer, Thomas Mayo, 1814–1880, joint author. II. Ridgway, Robert, 1850–1929, joint author. III. Title. IV. Series. V. Series: Harvard University. Museum of Comparative Zoology. Memoirs, v. 12–13.
QL681.B18 1974 598.2'97 73-17800 MARC

Baird, Spencer Fullerton, 1823-1887
see Hayden, Ferdinand Vandiver, 1829-1887. First-hand account of Hayden's 1854-55 Missouri River expedition... [Denver, 1971]

Baird, Stanley Jack, 1923-
The effectiveness of introducing regular dictation of unpracticed material before the completion of Gregg shorthand theory. [Corvallis] 1967.
72 l. illus. 21 cm.
Thesis—Oregon State University.
Bibliography: leaves 65-67.
Reproduced by Xerox process.
1. Shorthand—Study and teaching. 2. Shorthand—Gregg.
MsU NUC73-68878

Baird, Susan E
Career education and social studies / Susan E. Baird. — Boston : Houghton Mifflin, c1975.
xiii, 96 p. ; 23 cm. — (Guidance monograph series : Series 9, Career education and the curriculum)
Bibliography: p. 91-93.
Includes index.
ISBN 0-395-20046-6
1. Vocational education. 2. Vocational guidance. 3. Social sciences—Study and teaching. I. Title.
LC1044.B34 300'.23 75 74-11971 MARC

Baird, Theodore.
Alleged origin of Amherst College Library with books taken from Williams College Library. [n. p.] 1971.
1 v.
Exchange of letters.
1. Amherst College Library. 2. Williams College Library. I. Wikander, Lawrence Einar, 1915-
MWiW NUC74-140014

Baird, Thomas, defendant
see M'Laren, Alexander, defendant. The trial of Alexander M'Laren... Edinburgh, J. Robertson, 1817.

[**Baird, Thomas**] fl. 1845.
Description of a tract of coal land, the property of Messrs. Richards, Baird & O'Brien, situated in Pinegrove Township, Schuylkill County ... Reading, Pa., Boyer & Getz, printers, 1845.
13 p. fold. map. 24 cm.
Signed: T. B.
1. Coal mines and mining—Pennsylvania—Schuylkill Co. I. T. B. II. B., T. III. Title.
TN805.P4B34 CA 7-3872 rev

Baird, Thomas, fl. 1845.
Maps of the bituminous and anthracite coal field in Dauphin, Lebanon, and Schuylkill Counties. Lykens Valley, Bear Valley & Swatara anthracite regions. [n. p., 18—]
map. 63 x 85 cm. fold. to 21 cm.
Bound with this map is a "Draft of a body of land situate in Pinegrove & Williams Valley Township, Schuylkill County. The property of Richards, Baird and O'Brien, according to the resurvey draft by T. Baird. Philadelphia, P. S. Duval, lith. [18—]" 41 x 54 cm. fold. to 21 cm.
1. Coal—Pennsylvania—Maps. I. Title.
TN805.P4B35 CA 7-3873 rev

Baird, Thomas P 1923–
Losing people [by] Thomas Baird. [1st ed.] New York, Harcourt Brace Jovanovich [1974]
183 p. 21 cm.
I. Title.
PZ4.B1665Lo 813'.5'4 74-5757 MARC
[PS3552.A39]
ISBN 0-15-153468-3

Baird, Thomas P 1923-
Sheba's landing. London, Faber and Faber [c1964]
274 p. 20 cm.
I. Title.
NjP NUC74-127401

Baird, Thomas P 1923-
The way to the old sailors home / Thomas Baird. — 1st ed. — New York : Harper & Row, c1977.
259 p. ; 21 cm.
ISBN 0-06-010173-3 : $8.95
I. Title.
PZ4.B1665 Way 813'.5'4 76 76-26260 MARC
[PS3552.A39]

Baird, Violet M., ed.
see Texas. University. Southwestern Medical School, Dallas. Library. Texas medical history in the Library of the University of Texas Southwestern Medical School. Dallas, Friends of the Medical Library of the University of Texas Southwestern Medical School [1972]

Baird, W David.
The Chickasaw people / by W. David Baird ; scientific editor, Henry F. Dobyns ; general editor, John I. Griffin. — Phoenix : Indian Tribal Series, [1974]
104 p. : ill. ; 23 cm.
Bibliography: p. 102-103.
1. Chickasaw Indians. I. Title.
E99.C55B34 976'.004'97 73-91580 MARC

Baird, W David.
The Choctaw people / by W. David Baird ; scientific editors, Henry F. Dobyns and Robert C. Euler ; general editors, John I. Griffin. — Phoenix : Indian Tribal Series, c1973.
106 p. : ill. (some col.) ; 23 cm.
Bibliography: p. 96-98.
1. Choctaw Indians. I. Title.
E99.C8B28 970'.004'97 77 73-80708 MARC

Baird, W David.
The Osage people, by W. David Baird. Phoenix, Indian Tribal Series [1972]
104 p. illus. 23 cm.
Bibliography: p. 101-103.
1. Osage Indians. I. Title.
E99.O8B23 970.3 72-87871 MARC

Baird, W David.
The Quapaw people / by W. David Baird ; scientific editor, Henry F. Dobyns, general editor, John I. Griffin. — Phoenix [Ariz.] : Indian Tribal Series, c1975.
104 p. : ill. ; 23 cm.
Bibliography: p. 97-99.
1. Quapaw Indians. I. Title.
E99.Q2B34 970'.004'97 77 75-21552 MARC

Baird, W. S.
see Kasmire, R F Automatic sizing of cantaloupes. Davis, 1970.

Baird, W W
Hedgerow destruction in Norfolk, 1946–1970 [by] W. W. Baird and J. R. Tarrant. Norwich, University of East Anglia, School of Environmental Sciences, 1973.
[1], ii, 30 p. maps. 21 cm. £0.30 GB 74-00397
Bibliography: p. 26-30.
1. Windbreaks, shelterbelts, etc.—England—Norfolk (County) I. Tarrant, John Rex, joint author. II. Title.
SD409.5.B34 333.7'6 74-180179 MARC
ISBN 0-902170-01-5

Baird, Warner Green, 1885-
see Sherwood, Claire M. The New England ancestry of Wyllys Warner Baird and his wife Olivia Pomeroy Green. [Chicago] W. G. Baird, c1976.

Baird, William, F. S. A. Scot.
General Wauchope. Freeport, N. Y., Books for Libraries Press, 1972.
211 p. illus. 22 cm. (The Black heritage library collection)
Reprint of the 1901 ed.
1. Wauchope, Andrew Gilbert, 1846-1899. I. Title. II. Series.
DA68.32.W3B2 1972 355.3'31'0924 [B] 72-4077 MARC
ISBN 0-8369-9094-3

Baird, William, 1803-1872.
A cyclopaedia of the natural sciences. By William Baird. London and Glasgow, R. Griffin and company, 1858.
xvi, 612 p. front. (fold. map) illus. 22 cm.
Microprint. New York, Readex Microprint, 1972. 7 cards. (Landmarks of Science)
1. Natural history—Dictionaries. I. Title.
InU NUC76-69654

Baird, William Eugene, 1949-
Optical investigation of ion-metal collisions / by William E. Baird, Jr. -- [Atlanta : s.n.], 1975.
ix, 101 leaves : ill. ; 28 cm.
Thesis (Ph. D.)--Georgia Institute of Technology.
U. M. order no. 76-15,595.
Vita.
Bibliography: leaves 98-100.
1. Physics--Theses--1976. 2. Collisions (Nuclear physics) I. Title.
GAT NUC77-91918

Baird-Atomic, inc.
see Symposium on Respiration Pattern Analysis in Intermediary Metabolism Study, Berkeley, Calif., 1964. [Respiration pattern analysis in intermediary metabolism study. Monrovia, 1964]

Baird-North Company.
[Catalog] Diamonds, watches, jewelry, silver ware. [Des Moines, Iowa, Wallace-Homestead Book Co. [1973 ?]
200 p. illus. 26 cm.
Exact reprint of the 1913 catalog.
1. Jewelry—Catalogs. 2. Silverware—Catalogs. 3. Leather goods—Catalogs.
MB NUC75-33093

Bairéad, Tomás.
Dán [cnuasach gearrscéalta] Baile Átha Cliath, Clódhanna, 1973.
79 p. 21 cm.
I. Title.
MB NUC74-126005

Bairéad, Tomás.
Gan baisteadh. Baile Átha Cliath, Sáirséal agus Dill [1972]
247 p. illus. 22 cm.
1. Ireland—Hist.—20th cent. I. Title.
MB NUC74-126004

Bairéad, Tomás
see Ó Cadhain, Máirtín. As an ngéibheann. Baile Átha Cliath, Sáirséal agus Dill [1973]

Bairoch, Paul.
Le chômage urbain dans les pays en voie de développement; présentation générale du problème et éléments d'une solution. Genève, Bureau international du Travail, 1972.
v, 106 p. 24 cm.
Includes bibliographical references.
1. Underdeveloped areas—Unemployed. 2. Underdeveloped areas—Urbanization. I. Title.
CU-S NUC76-69663

Bairoch, Paul.
Commerce extérieur et développement économique de l'Europe au XIXe siècle / Paul Bairoch. — Paris : Mouton, c1976.
355 p. : graphs ; 24 cm. — (Civilisations et sociétés ; 53) F***
Bibliography: p. [335]-345.
ISBN 2-7193-0437-9
1. Europe—Commerce—History. 2. Europe—Commercial policy—History. 3. Europe—Economic conditions—19th century. I. Title. II. Series.
HF3496.B27 382'.094 77-451391
77 MARC

Bairoch, Paul.
El desempleo urbano en los paises en desarrollo; presentación general del problema y elementos de solución. Ginebra, Oficina Internacional del Trabajo [1973]
vii, 106 p. 24 cm.
DPU NUC75-19922

Bairoch, Paul.
The economic development of the Third World since 1900 / Paul Bairoch ; translated by Cynthia Postan. — Berkeley : University of California Press, 1975.
xii, 260 p. ; 25 cm.
Translation of Diagnostic de l'évolution économique du Tiers-monde, with revision and updating.
Bibliography: p. 250-255.
Includes index.
ISBN 0-520-02858-9
1. Underdeveloped areas. I. Title.
HC59.7.B2813 330.9'172'4 74-16706
75 MARC

Bairoch, Paul.
The economic development of the Third World since 1900 / Paul Bairoch ; translated by Cynthia Postan. — London : Methuen, 1975.
xii, 260 p. ; 24 cm. GB***
Translation with revisions of the 4th ed. of Diagnostic de l'évolution économique du Tiers-monde.
Bibliography: p. 250-255.
Includes index.
ISBN 0-416-76230-1 : £5.00. ISBN 0-416-76240-9 pbk.
1. Underdeveloped areas. I. Title.
HC59.7.B2822 330.9'172'4 75-321836
75 MARC

Bairoch, Paul.
Révolution industrielle et sous-développement. 4. éd. Paris, Mouton [1974]
381 p. 22 cm. (Le savoir historique, 9) F***
Bibliography: p. [349]-360.
1. Great Britain—Industries. 2. France—Industries. I. Title.
HC255.B26 1974 338'.09'04 73-84405
ISBN 2-7193-0606-7 MARC

Bairoch, Paul.
Urban unemployment in developing countries; the nature of the problem and proposals for its solution. Geneva, International Labour Office, 1973.
v, 99 p. 24 cm. 12.00F Sw***
Includes bibliographical references.
1. Underdeveloped areas—Unemployed. 2. Underdeveloped areas—Urbanization. I. Title.
HD5852.B33 331.1'379172'4 73-164688
MARC

Bairoch, Paul
see Massé, Pierre, 1898- Le Tiers Monde en l'an 2000... [Paris] Presses universitaires de France, 1971.

Bairov, Gireĭ Alievich.
Khirurgiîa pecheni i zhelchnykh protokov u deteĭ. [Avtory] G. A. Bairov, A. G. Pugachev [i] A. P. Shashkina. Leningrad, Meditsina, 1970.
277 p. illus.
Summary in English.
1. Biliary tract—Surgery. 2. Biliary tract diseases—In infancy & childhood. 3. Hepatectomy—In infancy & childhood. 4. Liver—Surgery. 5. Liver diseases—In infancy & childhood.
I. Pugachev, Anatoliĭ Georgievich, 1929- II. Shashkina, Alina Petrovna. III. Title.
DNLM NUC74-60681

Bairov, Gireĭ Alievich.
Neotlozhnaia khirurgiia deteĭ. [Leningrad, Meditsina, 1973]
470 p. illus.
1. Surgery, Operative—In infancy & childhood. I. Title.
DNLM NUC75-135226

Bairstow, Dale.
Demographic and economic aspects of housing Canada's elderly. Dale Bairstow. Ottawa, Policy Planning Division, Central Mortgage and Housing Corporation, 1973.
viii, 365 p. charts. 35 cm.
Bibliography: p. 354-365.
1. Housing—Canada. 2. Aged—Dwellings. 3. Aged—Canada. I. Title.
CaBVaU NUC76-69655

Bairstow, Frances, ed.
see Research frontiers in industrial relations today. [Montreal, 1962]

Bairstow, Jeffrey, 1939- joint author.
see Gonzalez, Pancho, 1928- Tennis begins at forty ... New York, Dial Press, 1976.

Bairu Tafla.
Some aspects of land-tenure and taxation in Sälalé under Ras Dargé, 1871-1900 / by Bairu Tafla. — [s. l. : s. n.], 1973.
15 leaves ; 33 cm.
"Prepared for the Historical Society of Ethiopia conference, May 28-29, 1973, Addis Abäba."
1. Land tenure—Sälalé region, Ethiopia—History. 2. Sälalé region, Ethiopia—History. I. Some aspects of land-tenure and taxation in Sälalé ...
HD1021.E83S233 333.3'2'09633 76-365116
76 MARC

Baĭryev, Kakaly.
(Zemel'noe i vodnoe zakonodatel'stvo Turkmenskoĭ SSR)
Земельное и водное законодательство Туркменской ССР / К. Байрыев ; отв. редактор Н. И. Краснов. — Ашхабад : Ылым, 1975.
159 p. ; 21 cm. USSR***
At head of title: Akademiîa nauk Turkmenskoĭ SSR. Otdel filosofii i prava.
Added t. p. in Turkoman.
Includes bibliographical references.
0.70rub
1. Land tenure—Turkmenistan—Law. 2. Water—Laws and legislation—Turkmenistan. I. Title.
75-594073

Baisa, Mustafa Salim, ed.
see Koran. Indonesian. Selections. Tafsir djuz amma Al-Abraar. [Tjet. 2. Tjirebon, Messir, 1964?]

Baisa, Prāgasimha, joint author
see Cauhāna, M M (Akhila Bhāratīya Hindī sāhitya kā itihāsa) [1973]

Baisch, Helmut.
Wert, Preis und Allokation : e. Verallgemeinerung d. Marxschen Reproduktionsmodells / Helmut Baisch. — Meisenheim am Glan : Hain, 1976.
318 p. : ill. ; 23 cm. — (Schriften zur wirtschaftswissenschaftlichen Forschung ; Bd. 102) GFR76-A
Summary in English.
Bibliography: p. 308-318.
ISBN 3-445-01338-1 : DM43.00
1. Marxian economics. 2. Value. 3. Prices. I. Title.
HB97.5.B233 335.4'12 76-464254
76 MARC

Baisden, Major J
The dynamics of homosexuality / by Major J. Baisden, Jr. ; edited by Joanna R. Tubbs. — Sacramento, Calif. : Allied Research Society, [1975].
viii, 197 p. : port. ; 23 cm.
Bibliography: p. 196-197.
ISBN 0-912984-02-3
1. Homosexuality. 2. Homosexuality—Case studies. I. Title.
HQ76.B33 301.41'57 75-31
75 MARC

Baisden, Patricia Ann, 1949-
PMR spectroscopy of metalaminopolycarboxylate complexes / by Patricia Ann Baisden. -- [Tallahassee, Fla.] : Baisden, 1975.
ix, 146 leaves : ill. ; 29 cm.
Thesis (Ph. D.)--Florida State University.
Vita.
Bibliography: leaves 141-145.
1. Dissertations, Academic--F.S.U.--Chemistry. 2. Rare earth metals--Spectra. 3. Alkaline earth metals--Spectra. I. Title.
FTaSU NUC77-91924

Baisden, Ronald Hubert, 1947-
Behavioral effects of hippocampal lesions after adrenergic depletion of the septal area. [Gainesville] 1973.
x, 143 l. illus. 28 cm.
Manuscript copy.
Thesis—University of Florida.
Vita.
Bibliography: leaves 98-113.
FU-HC NUC74-125995

Baish, Salagram.
(Mādhavānala-kāmakandalā)
माधवानल-कामकन्दला : नाटक / शालिग्रामवैश्यप्रणीत. — कल्याण : गंगाविष्णु श्रीकृष्णदास, सं. 1985 [1927]
208 p. ; 22 cm.
In Hindi.
I. Title.
PK2098.B3M3 75-986021

Baish, Salagram.
(Moradhvaja nāṭaka)
मोरध्वज नाटक. शालिग्राम वैश्य विरचित. कल्याण, गङ्गाविष्णु श्रीकृष्णदास, संवत् 1980 [1923 or 4]
175 p. 14 x 9 cm.
In Hindi.
I. Title.
PK2098.B3M6 75-985033

Baish, Salagram.
(Śukasāgara)
शुकसागर; अर्थात्, श्रीमद्भागवत भाषा; [जिसमें श्रीकृष्णचन्द्र आनन्दकन्दका नवनित्य लीलावतार चरित्र, शंका, समाधान, दृष्टान्त, माहात्म्य सहित, और विष्णु-सहस्रनाम विस्तारपूर्वक वर्णित हैं] शालग्रामजी वैश्य द्वारा अनुवादित. बम्बई, खेमराज श्रीकृष्णदास [1970]
16, 31, 1400 p. illus. (part col.) 33 cm. Rs36.00
Each section has separate t. p.
In Hindi.
I. Puranas. Bhāgavatapurāṇa. II. Title.
PK2098.B3S8 79-923226

Baishev, Saktagan Baishevich.
[Marksizm-leninzm zhăne qoghamdyq ómir măseleleri]
Марксизм-ленинизм және қоғамдық өмір мәселелері. Алматы, "Қазақстан," 1970.
219 p. 21 cm. 0.50rub USSR 71-14235
At head of title: С. Бәйішев.
1. Communism and society. 2. Marx, Karl, 1818-1883. I. Title.
HX542.B34 73-204960

Baishev, Saktagan Baishevich, ed.
see **Akademiîa nauk Kazakhskoĭ SSR, Alma-Ata. Institut istorii, arkheologii i etnografi.** (Istoriîa Kazakhskoĭ SSR : epokha sofŝializma) 1963.

Baishev, Saktagan Baishevich
see Naselenie Kazakhstana v tysîacha devîat'sot pîat'desîat devîatom-tysîacha devîat'sot sem'desîatom gg.. 1975.

Baishev, Saktagan Baishevich
see Ocherki ėkonomicheskoĭ istorii Kazakhskoĭ SSR. 1974.

Baishev, Saktagan Baishevich, ed.
see Problemy truda i narodonaseleniîa v Kazakhstane. 1973.

Baishev, Saktagan Baishevich
see Upravlenie sofŝial'nym razvitiem proizvodstvennykh kollektivov. 1975.

Baishev, Saktagan Baishevich
see Voprosy sot͡sial'nogo razvitii͡a kollektivov transportnykh predprii͡atiĭ Kazakhstana. 1973.

Baisheva, M M
(Sovet Ŭzbekistoni kitobi)
Совет Ўзбекистони китоби : библиогр. кўрсаткич = Книга Советского Узбекистана : библиогр. указ. : 1941–1944 гг. / ⌊составители М. М. Баишева, Л. П. Котельникова, А. Т. Тишкина⌋. — Ташкент : ⌊s. n.⌋, 1974.
287 p. ; 23 cm. USSR 74
At head of title: Ŭzbekiston SSR Ministrlar Soveti nashriëtlar, poligrafii͡a va kitob savdosi ishlari bŭlicha davlat komiteti. Ŭzbekiston SSR Davlat kitob palatasi.
Uzbek and Russian.
Includes index.
0.70rub
1. Uzbekistan—Imprints. I. Kotel'nikova, L. P., joint author. II. Tishkina, A. T., joint author. III. Gosudarstvennai͡a knizhnai͡a palata Uzbekskoĭ SSR. IV. Title. V. Title: Kniga Sovetskogo Uzbekistana.
Z3413.U9B34 76-506290

Baisheva, Munavara
see Vladimir Il'ich Lenin; bibliograficheskiĭ ukazatel' (1918-1968 gg.). Tashkent, 1970.

Baĭshin, A A
Ұлы ынтымақ жемісі. Қазақ Советтік Социалистік Республикасының экономикалық және мәдени дамуындағы Совет Одағы халықтарының туысқандық көмегі мен ынтымағының тарихи тәжірибесі. Авт. А. А. Байшин, З. А. Голикова, Р. Б. Сүлейменов ⌊ж. б.⌋ Алматы, Қазақстан, 1969.
390 p. 21 cm. 0.73rub USSR 69-33601
At head of title: Қазақстан Коммунистік партиясы Орталық Комитеті жанындағы партия тарихы институты—КПСС Орталық Комитеті жанындағы марксизм-ленинизм институтының филиалы.
Issued also under title: Плоды великого содружества (romanized: Plody velikogo sodruzhestva)
Includes bibliographical references.
1. Kazakhstan—History. 2. Minorities—Russia. I. Alma-Ata, Kazakhstan. Institut istorii partii. II. Title.
Title romanized: Ŭly yntymak zhemisi.
DK908.B315 72-289510

Baĭshin, A. A., ed.
see Druzhboĭ velikoĭ sil'ny... Alma-Ata, "Kazakhstan", 1972.

Baishin seido ni kansuru kōryō.
陪審制度ニ關スル綱領 ⌊東京? 192-?⌋
12 p. 22 cm.
Cover title.
At head of title: 秘 (rubber stamped)
1. Jury—Japan.
72-804378

Baishnab Behura
see
Behura, Baishnab.

Baishnab Charan Samal
see
Samal, Baishnab Charan, 1939-

Baishnaba Behurā
see
Behura, Baishnab.

Baishṇaba Caraṇa Mahānti
see
Mahānti, Baishṇaba Caraṇa.

(Baishōron)
梅松論 / 矢代和夫, 加美宏校注. — 東京 : 現代思潮社, 1975.
380 p., ⌊1⌋ leaf of plates : ill. ; 22 cm. — (新撰日本古典文庫 ; 3) Ja 75-18792
"史書あるいは合戦記としての梅松論をめぐって" issued as suppl. (23 p.)
"底本として彰考館文庫蔵「梅松論」(延宝六年書写本)を使用した"
"源威集": p. 319-368.
Includes index.
¥5200
1. Japan—History—Period of northern and southern courts, 1336-1392. I. Yashiro, Kazuo. II. Kami, Hiroshi. III. Gen'ishū. 1975. IV. Series: Shinsen Nihon koten bunko ; 3.
DS865.5.B34 77-800936

(Baishun to zenshakukin)
売春と前借金 / 日本弁護士連合会. — 東京 : 高千穂書房, 昭和49 ⌊1974⌋
270 p. ; 19 cm. Ja 75-2602
Bibliography: p. 263-270.
¥1000
1. Prostitution—Japan. 2. Illegal contracts—Japan. I. Nihon Bengoshi Rengōkai.
75-804659

Baisi, Ignace J Bona-
see Bona-Baisi, Ignace J

Baisieux, Jacques de
see
Jacques de Baisieux.

Baĭsogolov, Grigoriĭ Davidovich, joint author
see Gus'kova, Angelina Konstantinovna. Luchevai͡a bolezn' cheloveka. 1971.

Baĭsogolov, Grigoriĭ Davidovich, joint author.
see Gus'kova, Angelina Konstantinovna. Radiation sickness in man (outlines). ⌊Oak Ridge, Tenn., U.S. Atomic Energy Commission, Technical Information Center; Available from National Technical Information Service, U.S. Dept. of Commerce, Springfield, Va., 1973⌋

Baĭsogolov, V G
(Mekhanicheskoe i transportnoe oborudovanie zavodov ogneupornoĭ promyshlennosti)
Механическое и транспортное оборудование заводов огнеупорной промышленности. ⌊Учебник для техникумов⌋. Москва, "Металлургия," 1972.
359 p. with illus. 22 cm. 0.95rub USSR 72-VKP
At head of title: В. Г. Байсоголов, П. И. Галкин.
Bibliography: p. ⌊359⌋
1. Refractories industry—Equipment and supplies. I. Galkin, P. I. II. Title.
TN677.B18 74-341822

Baisov, Batyr.
Orekhovoe derevo; rasskazy i ocherki. ⌊By⌋ Batyr Magomedovich Baisov. Cherkessk, Karachaevo-Cherkesskoe otd-nie Stavropol'skogo knizhnogo izd-va, 1970.
53 p. illus.
Title page and text in Nogai.
Russian title from colophon.
MH NUC76-14940

Baissac, Charles.
⌊Le Folk-lore de l'Ile-Maurice. Russian⌋
Сказки острова Маврикий / ⌊Ch. Baissac ; перевод с креолйск. Р. Л. Рыбкина ; предисл. В. А. Бейлиса ; ил. Т. И. Алексеева⌋. — Москва : Наука, 1974.
115 p. : ill. ; 20 cm. USSR 74
On leaf preceding t. p.: Академия наук СССР. Институт востоковедения.
0.34rub
1. Folk-lore—Mauritius. 2. Folk-lore, Creole. I. Title.
Title romanized: Skazki ostrova Mavrikiĭ.
GR360.M343B318 75-531815

Baissette, Gaston, 1901-
Ces grappes de ma vigne : roman / Gaston Baissette. — Paris : Julliard, ⌊1975⌋
347 p. ; 24 cm. F***
37.00F
I. Title.
PQ2603.A265C4 843'.9'12 75-513681
75 MARC

Baissette, Gaston, 1901-
Poésie / Gaston Baissette. — Paris : Les Arcades, ⌊1974⌋
113 p. ; 20 cm. F***
Four hundred four copies printed. No. 31.
30.00F
PQ2603.A265P57 841'.9'14 76-475438
76 MARC

Baissette, Gaston, 1901–
Le vin de feu; roman. Paris, Julliard ⌊1974⌋
327 p. 25 cm. F***
40.65F
I. Title.
PQ2603.A265V5 843'.9'14 74-194354
MARC

Baitaḍī, Bāsu Bhaṭṭa
see
Bhaṭṭa, Bāsu.

Baital, Jim, 1949- Tali. 1976.
in Three short novels from Papua New Guinea. Auckland, Longman Paul, 1976.

Baĭtanaev, Amantaĭ.
Podlinnoe masterstvo. ⌊By⌋ A. Baitanaev. ⌊Alma-Ata⌋ Zhazushy, 1969.
217 p.
Added t. p. and text in Kazak.
Russian title from colophon.
MH NUC74-37572

Baĭtanaev, Amantaĭ.
Қайнар бұлақ. Роман. Алматы, "Жазушы," 1968.
200 p. with illus. 20 cm. 0.52 USSR 68-40986
I. Title.
Title romanized: Qaĭnar bŭlaq.
PL65.K49B33 71-519279

Baĭtanaev, Amantaĭ.
(Qansonar)
Қансонар. Роман. Алматы, "Жазушы," 1972.
302 p. with illus. 21 cm. 0.62rub USSR 72-39740
I. Title.
PL65.K49B332 74-333948

Baitch, Theodore.
Electrical technology ⌊by⌋ T. Baitch. Sydney, New York, Wiley, 1972.
2 v. illus., diagrs. 25 cm. $8.95 ANL
1. Electric engineering. I. Title.
TK146.B23 621.3 71-37787
ISBN 0-471-04366-4 (v. 1) MARC
rev

Baitch, Theodore.
Electrical technology ⌊by⌋ T. Baitch. Sydney, New York, Wiley ⌊1973, c1972⌋
xxiii, 502 p. illus. 25 cm. Aus***
Originally published in 2 volumes, 1972.
1. Electric engineering. I. Title.
TK146.B232 621.3 73-160545
ISBN 0-471-04368-0 ; 0-471-04369-9 (pbk.) MARC

Baĭtenov, Muslim Smaĭlovich.
(Zhuki - dolgonosiki (Coleoptera — Attelabidae, Curculionidae) Sredneĭ Azii i Kazakhstana)
Жуки-долгоносики (Coleoptera—Attelabidae, Curculionidae) Средней Азии и Казахстана : иллюстрир. определитель родов и каталог видов / М. С. Байтенов. — Алма-Ата : Наука, 1974.
284 p. : ill. ; 22 cm. USSR 74
At head of title: Akademii͡a nauk Kazakhskoĭ SSR. Institut zoologii.
Bibliography: p. 12–15.
Includes index.
2.05rub
1. Attelabidae. 2. Curculionidae. 3. Insects—Soviet Central Asia. 4. Insects—Azerbaijan. I. Title.
QL596.A83B34 77-511481

Baĭter, Isaak Ionovich.
(Releĭnai͡a zashchita i avtomatika pitai͡ushchikh ėlementov sobstvennykh nuzhd teplovykh ėlektrostant͡siĭ)
Релейная защита и автоматика питающих элементов собственных нужд тепловых электростанций / И. И. Байтер. — Изд. 2., доп. и перер. — Москва : Энергия, 1975.
120 p. : ill. ; 20 cm. — (Библиотека электромонтера ; вып. 415) USSR***
Bibliography: p. ⌊3⌋ of cover.
0.25rub
1. Protective relays. 2. Electric switchgear. 3. Electric power-plants—Equipment and supplies—Protection. I. Title. II. Series: Biblioteka ėlektromontera ; vyp. 415.
TK7.B5 vyp. 415 75-548719
[TK2861]

Baitieri, Silvio.
Bormio dal 1512 al 1620 : analisi documenti inediti / Silvio Baitieri. — Milano di : Giuffrè, 1960.
xv, 212 p., ⌊11⌋ leaves of plates : facsims. ; 25 cm. — (Raccolta di studi storici sulla Valtellina ; 16)
"Appendice" (p. ⌊141⌋–212) : 1. Studio circa la revisione degli statuti (in Latin).—2. A. S. C., AB, IV, 18 A, 13, PAG. 41–49 (in Latin).—⌊3⌋ Documenti.
Bibliography : p. ix–xv.
1. Bormio, Italy—History—Sources. I. Title. II. Series.
DG975:B7B34 77–502512

Baĭtin, Aĭzik Abramovich
see Lesoustroĭstvo. 1974.

Baĭtin, Mikhail Iosifovich.
(Gosudarstvo i politicheskaia vlast')
Государство и политическая власть. Саратов, Изд-во Сарат. ун-та, 1972.
239 p. 20 cm. 0.90rub USSR 72–VKP
At head of title: M. И. Байтин.
Summary in English, German, French, and Spanish.
Includes bibliographical references.
1. Communist state. 2. State, The. 3. Communism and society. I. Title.
JC474.B33 73–335053

Baĭtin, Mikhail Iosifovich
see Teoria państwa socjalistycznego. Warszawa : Państwowe Wydawn. Naukowe, 1976.

Baitinger, Utz G
Schaltkreistechnologien für digitale Rechenanlagen/ von Utz G. Baitinger. — Berlin, New York : De Gruyter, 1973.
263 p. : 273 ill. ; 23 cm. — (De Gruyter Lehrbuch) DM28.00 GFR 73–A
Bibliography : p. ⌊251⌋–254.
1. Electronic digital computers—Circuits. 2. Integrated circuits. 3. Microelectrics. I. Title.
TK7888.4.B33 621.3819'58'35 72–91876
ISBN 3–11–003697–5

Baitsch, Helmut, 1921-
see Hauke, Harry. Aspekte des Lernens... Heidenheimer Verlagsanstalt ⌊c1972⌋

Baitsch, Helmut, 1921-
see Projektgruppe Wissenschaftswissenschaft. Memorandum zur Förderung der Wissenschaftsforschung in der Bundesrepublik Deutschland. Essen : Stifterverband f. d. Dt. Wiss., 1973.

Baitsch, Helmut, 1921-
see The Scientific view of sport ... Berlin, New York, Springer-Verlag, 1972.

Baitsch, Helmut, 1921- joint author.
see Spiegel-Rösing, Ina-Susanne. Beiträge zur Messung von Forschungsleistung ... Bonn, Bundesminister für Bildung und Wissenschaft, 1975.

Baitsch, Helmut, 1921- ed.
see Sport im Blickpunkt der Wissenschaften... Berlin, New York, Springer-Verlag, 1972.

Baitsch, Helmut, 1921-
see Sport in the modern world: chances and problems. Berlin, New York, Springer-Verlag, 1973.

Baitsch, Helmut, 1921-
see Sport in unserer Welt: Chancen und Probleme... Berlin, New York, Springer, 1973.

Baĭt͡sur, Avtonom Iosifovich.
⌊Opusknye kolodt͡sy⌋
Опускные колодцы. (Проектирование и стр-во). Киев, "Будівельник," 1972.
207 p. with illus. 22 cm. 0.79rub USSR 72–VKP
At head of title: A. И. Байцур.
Bibliography : p. 205–⌊206⌋
1. Caissons. I. Title.
TC199.B34 72–364501

Baĭt͡sur, Avtonom Iosifovich.
(Povyshenie nadezhnosti opusknykh kolodt͡sev)
Повышение надежности опускных колодцев / А. И. Байцур, В. Т. Климов. — Москва : Стройиздат, 1976.
89, ⌊7⌋ p. : ill. ; 21 cm. USSR***
Bibliography : p. ⌊91⌋
0.24rub
1. Caissons. I. Klimov, Valentin Timofeevich, joint author. II. Title.
TC199.B343 77–506098

Baitsura, Ivan.
Ukrajinská otázka v ČSSR. ⌊V Košiciach⌋ Východoslovenské vydavatel'stvo, 1967.
214 p.
1. Ukrainians in the Czechoslovak Republic. I. Title.
InU NUC76-69473

Baĭt͡sura, Tamara.
(Zakarpatoukrainskaia intelligent͡siia v Rossii v pervoĭ polovine devi͡atnadt͡satogo veka)
Закарпатоукраинская интеллигенция в России в первой половине XIX века. 1-е изд. Пряшів, Слов. педаг. вид-во, Друк. Дуклянські друк., 1971.
226, ⌊3⌋ p. photos. 21 cm. Kčs28.00 CzS 71–MS
Summary in Slovak and German.
Bibliography : p. 189–203.
1. Ruthenians in Russia. 2. Intellectuals—Russia. I. Title.
DK34.R94B34 73–334729

Baity, Philip Chesley.
Religion in a Chinese town / by Philip Chesley Baity. -- Taipei : The Chinese Association for Folklore, 1975.
ix, 307 p. ; 21 cm. -- (Asian folklore and social life monographs ; v. 64)
Bibliography: p. 303-308.
1. Taiwan--Religion. 2. Temples--Taiwan. I. Title. II. Series.
CU-SB NUC77-94357

Baiu, Mustafa
see
Baʻayyaw, Mustafá ʻAbd Allāh.

Baĭuk, Elena Ivanovna, joint author
see Volarovich, Mikhail Pavlovich, 1900- (Uprugie svoĭstva mineralov pri vysokikh davleniíakh) 1975.

Baiulescu, George.
Stationary phases in gas chromatography / G. E. Baiulescu and V. A. Ilie. — 1st ed. — Oxford ; New York; Pergamon Press, 1975.
vi, 370 p. : ill. ; 22 cm. — (International series of monographs in analytical chemistry ; v. 56)
Includes bibliographical references and index.
ISBN 0-08-018075-2
1. Gas chromatography. I. Ilie, V. A., joint author. II. Title.
QD79.C45B3413 1975 543'.08 74-32148
74 MARC

Baiusheva, M.I., ed.
see Voprosy gidrologii Sibiri. 1972.

Baix, François, 1884-
La dévotion à l'eucharistie et le VIIe centenaire de la Fête-Dieu / F. Baix, C. Lambot. — Gembloux : J. Duculot, ⌊1946⌋
160 p., ⌊4⌋ leaves of plates : ill. ; 21 cm.
Bibliography: p. ⌊151⌋-160.
1. Lord's Supper—Adoration—History. 2. Corpus Christi festival. I. Lambot, Cyrille, 1900- joint author. II. Title.
BV823.B34 264'.3 75-502670
75 MARC

Baixas Arias, Joan.
De fer i desfer senders de putxinel·li : diari de Putxinel·lis Claca / Joan Baixes. — 1. ed. — Barcelona : Curial, 1974.
58 p., ⌊1⌋ leaf of plates : 1 ill. ; 23 cm. — (Llibres del mall ; 12) Sp***
ISBN 84-7256-052-X
1. Putxinel·lis Claca. I. Title.
PN1978.S7B3 75-561400

Baixas Arias, Joan, comp.
Les rondalles de Putxinel·lis Claca. Barcelona, Hogar del Libro ⌊1972?⌋
229 p. illus. 12 x 17 cm. (Col·lecció Esplai, no. 20) 120ptas Sp***
Bibliography : p. 222–227.
1. Puppets and puppet-plays. I. Putxinel·lis Claca. II. Title.
PN1981.B28 73–349858

Baixo Alentejo, Portugal
see also
Alentejo, Portugal (Province)

Baĭza, K
see
Bajza, K

Baĭzakov, Isa
see
Baĭzaqov, Isa.

Baĭzakov, Tumonbaĭ.
Pis'mo na snegu; stikhi. Red. K. Zhunusov. Frunze ["Kyrgyzstan"] 1970.
106 p.
Title page and text in Kirghiz.
Russian title from colophon.
MH NUC74-55438

Baizaqov, Isa.
(Shygharmalary)
Шығармалары / Иса Байзақов — Алматы : Қазақтың мемлекеттік көркем әдебиет баспасы, 1956.
486 p. ; 21 cm.
At head of title: Qazaq SSR Ghylym akademii͡asynyn͡g Til zhăne ădebiet instituty.
Poems and prose.
Includes music.
PL65.K49B334 75–588028

Baize, John C
Diets and performance of steers grazing three pasture types under continuous and rest- rotation grazing systems in southeastern Colorado. Fort Collins, 1973.
4 p. (Colorado. Agricultural Experiment Station. Progress report no. 73-35)
I. Title.
DNAL NUC74-125993

Baize, John C
Establishment, production, and nutritive value of Russian wildrye in southeastern Colorado. Fort Collins, 1973.
3 p. (Colorado. Agricultural Experiment Station. Progress report 73-36)
I. Title.
DNAL NUC74-125994

Baizer, Ashur, 1919-
The theory of imitation in English neo-classical criticism. New York, 1960.
308 l.
Thesis—New York University.
Microfilm. University Microfilms.
1. Imitation (in literature) 2. Criticism. I. Title.
InU NUC74-173578

Baizer, Manuel M
Organic electrochemistry; an introduction and a guide. Edited by Manuel M. Baizer. New York, M. Dekker, 1973.
xviii, 1072 p. illus. 24 cm.
Includes bibliographical references.
1. Chemistry, Organic. 2. Electrochemistry. I. Title.
QD273.B35 547'.1'37 78-179383
ISBN 0–8247–1029–0 MARC

Baizerman, Michael
see Pregnant adolescents. ⌊Pittsburgh⌋ 1971.

Baizerman, Saul.
Saul Baizerman. [Exhibition, Boston Institute of Contemporary Art. Boston, n.d.]
1 v. (unpaged) illus. 20 cm.
Includes bibliography.
I. Boston. Institute of Contemporary Art.
MWelC NUC74-731

Baizhūmanova, Qorlan.
(Shynar)
Шынар : өлеңдер / Қорлан Байжұманова. — Алматы : Жазушы, 1966.
46 p. ; 14 cm. — (Тұңғыш кітап)
I. Title.
PL65.K49B35 75–587214

Baizman, Eugene Robin, 1945-
An investigation of the central mechanisms of morphine-and narcotic antagonist-induced hypothermia in the naive and dependent rat. -- [s.l. : s.n.], 1976.
290 l.
Thesis--Ohio State University.
Bibliography: leaves 262-290.
1. Body temperature--Regulation. 2. Body temperature--Drug effect. I. Title.
OU NUC77-91923

Baj, Enrico, 1924-
Baj. [Exhibition] Museum of Contemporary Art, Chicago, September 10-October 24, 1971. [Chicago, Museum of Contemporary Art, 1971]
1 v. (unpaged, chiefly illus. (part col.), ports.) 25 cm.
Includes bibliography.
I. Museum of Contemporary Art, Chicago.
MH CtY OU NUC73-43890

Baj, Enrico, 1924–
Baj. [n. p., 1972?]
102 p. illus. (part col.) 24 cm. It***
Cover title.
English or Italian.
1. Baj, Enrico, 1924–
N6923.B25A42 73–198247

Baj, Enrico, 1924–
Baj. Catalogue ... de l'œuvre gravé et lithographié. Catalogue ... of the printed graphic work. Réalisé par Jean Petit. (Genève, [Librairie] Rousseau, [1970–73].)
2 v. illus. 28 cm. (v. 1: Panoramas forces vives)
Sw 70–A–5358 (v. 1)
Vol. 2 has collective title: Baj: catalogue de l'œuvre graphique et des multiples.
CONTENTS: 1. 1952–1970.—2. 1970–1973.
1. Baj, Enrico, 1924– I. Petit, Jean, fl. 1961–
NE662.B17P4 71–565481

Baj, Enrico, 1924–
Baj. [Milan? 1972 or 3]
10 [i. e. 102] p. illus. 24 cm. It***
Cover title.
Catalog of an exhibition that was to have been held in Milan in 1972.
Text in English or Italian.
"Cataloghi": p. 97–[101]
1. Baj, Enrico, 1924–
ND623.B17A42 74–302240

Baj, Enrico, 1924–
Baj : Milano, Palazzo reale, Sala delle Cariatidi, maggio-giugno 1974 ; Düsseldorf, Kunsthalle, novembre–dicembre 1974 ; Bruxelles, Palais des Beaux Arts, gennaio–marzo 1975. — [s. l. : s. n., 1974] (Cinisello Balsamo : A. Pizzi)
[77] p. : chiefly ill. (some col.) ; 24 cm. It 74–Dec
Bibliography : p. [75]
1. Baj, Enrico, 1924– I. Milan. Palazzo reale. Sala delle Cariatidi.
N6923.B25M54 74–356856

Baj, Enrico, 1924-
Baj : 1960-1974 : Generale, Damen, Möbel, Meccanos, Spiegel, "Guernica", "La Grande Jatte" : [Ausstellung] Städt. Kunsthalle Düsseldorf, 21. März - 27. April 1975 / [hrsg. von d. Städt. Kunsthhalle Düsseldorf ; Red., John Matheson ; Übers., Corina Ciacci, Hans-Bernd Haase, John Matheson]. — Düsseldorf : Städt. Kunsthalle, 1975.
[78] p. : chiefly ill. (some col.) ; 24 cm.
Legends in English, German, French, and Italian.
Includes bibliographical references.
1. Baj, Enrico, 1924- I. Matheson, John, fl. 1974- II. Städtische Kunsthalle Düsseldorf. III. Title.
N6923.B25M37 75-518033
75 MARC

Baj, Enrico, 1924–
Catalogo generale Bolaffi dell'opera di Enrico Baj / a cura di Enrico Crispolti ; la compilazione del catalogo generale e del repertorio bio-bibliografico sono opera di Roberta Baj che ha raccolto e cura l'archivio fotografico. — Torino : G. Bolaffi, 1973.
xlvi, 357 p. : ill. (some col.) ; 33 cm. It 74–Sept
Captions also in English.
Includes bibliographies.
L25000
1. Baj, Enrico, 1924– I. Crispolti, Enrico. II. Title.
N6923.B25C75 75–534332

Baj, Enrico, 1924-
Enrico Baj; [catalogo] ottobre/novembre 1974, Galleria d'Arte Spagnoli. Firenze, Galleria d'Arte Spagnoli, 1974.
[29] p. chiefly illus. (some col.) 29 cm.
English and Italian.
1. Baj, Enrico, 1924- I. Galleria d'arte Spagnoli.
CaBVaU NUC76-22725

Baj, Enrico, 1924-
see Enrico Baj... [Rotterdam, 1973]

al-Bājā, Yūsuf.
(Falsafat al-Mutakallimīn)
فلسفة المتكلمين، تأليف يوسف الباجا. [القاهرة] مطبعة شبرا الفنية [1945]
170, [4] p. 20 cm.
Bibliography: p. [171]–[173]
1. Islamic theology—History. I. Title.
BP166.1.B34 75–586613

Baja, Hungary. Türr István Muzeum
see Telcs Ede és tanitvanyai. Budapest, 1974.

Baja California (State)
The peninsula Baja California was considered a territory of the Federation under Mexico's Constitution of 1824. In 1887 the Territory of Baja California was organized into two districts, Baja California Norte and Baja California Sur. In 1931 the districts which had comprised the Territory of Baja California became the Territories of Baja California Norte and Baja California Sur. In 1952 the northern territory became the state Baja California. In 1974 the southern territory became the state Baja California Sur.
Works by these jurisdictions are found under the following headings according to the name used at the time of publication:
Baja California (Ter.)
Baja California Norte (District)

Baja California Sur (District)
Baja California Norte (Ter.)
Baja California Sur (Ter.)
Baja California (State)
Baja California Sur, Mexico (State)

Baja California (State). Acción Cívica y Cultural, Dirección General de
see
Baja California (State). Dirección General de Acción Cívica y Cultural.

Baja California (State). Commission of the Californias
see
Commission of the Californias.

Baja California (State). Dirección General de Acción Cívica y Cultural
see Congreso de Historia Regional, 1st, Mexicali, 1956. Memoria del Primer Congreso de Historia Regional. Mexicali, 1958-

Baja California (State). Laws, statutes, etc.
Código civil para el Estado de Baja California. Mexicali, 1974.
169 p. (Baja California (State). Periódico oficial, t. 81, 31 de Enero de 1974, no. 3, sec. 1)
1. Civil law—Baja California (State)
CLL NUC76-22495

Baja California (State). Laws, statutes, etc.
Codigo de procedimientos civiles para el Estado de Baja California. Mexicali, 1974.
358 p. (Baja: California (State). Periódico oficial, t. 81, 31 de Enero de 1974, no. 3, sec. 2)
1. Civil procedure—Baja California (State)
CLL NUC76-20060

Baja California (State). Universidad Autonoma. Escuela Superior de Ciencias Marinas. Tesis profesional. Ensenada, B.C. [19--
v.
1. Oceanography—Collected works.
CU-S NUC75-20457

Baja California (Ter.)
The peninsula Baja California was considered a territory of the Federation under Mexico's Constitution of 1824. In 1887 the Territory of Baja California was organized into two districts, Baja California Norte and Baja California Sur. In 1931 the districts which had comprised the Territory of Baja California became the Territories of Baja California Norte and Baja California Sur. In 1952 the northern territory became the state Baja California. In 1974 the southern territory became the state Baja California Sur.
Works by these jurisdictions are found under the following headings according to the name used at the time of publication:
Baja California (Ter.)
Baja California Norte (District)

Baja California Sur (District)
Baja California Norte (Ter.)
Baja California Sur (Ter.)
Baja California (State)
Baja California Sur, Mexico (State)

Baja California (Ter.). Laws, statutes, etc. Código civil
Entries for this code, which was promulgated by the Federal government and is applicable to the Federal District and the Federal Territories, are found under:
Mexico (Federal District). Laws, statutes, etc. Código civil.
75–588734

Baja California (Ter.). Laws, statutes, etc. Código de procedimientos civiles (1872). 1879
see Mexico (Federal District). Laws, statutes, etc. Código de procedimientos civiles (1872). Mexico, Impr. de Castillo Velasco é hijos, 1879.

Baja California (Ter.) Laws, statutes, etc. Código de procedimientos civiles (1880). 1880
see Mexico (Federal District). Laws, statutes, etc. Código de procedimientos civiles (1880). México, Impr. de F. Diaz de Leon, 1880.

Baja California (Ter.). Laws, statutes, etc.
Código de procedimientos civiles (1880). 1880
see Mexico (Federal District). Laws, statutes, etc. [Código de procedimientos civiles (1880)] Código de procedimientos civiles para el Distrito Federal y el Territorio de la Baja California ... México, Tip. de G. A. Esteva, 1880.

Baja California (Ter.). Laws, statutes, etc.
Código de procedimientos civiles del Distrito Federal y Territorio de la Baja California (1884). 1906
see Mexico (Federal District). Laws, statutes, etc. Codigo de procedimientos civiles del Distrito Federal y Territorio de la Baja California (1884). México, Tip. y lit. "La Europea," de J. Aguilar Vera y compañía, s. en c., 1906.

Baja California (Ter.). Laws, statutes, etc.
Código penal
Entries for this code, which was promulgated by the Federal government and is applicable to the Federal District and the Federal Territories, are found under:
Mexico (Federal District). Laws, statutes, etc.
Código penal.

Baja California Norte (District)
The peninsula Baja California was considered a territory of the Federation under Mexico's Constitution of 1824. In 1887 the Territory of Baja California was organized into two districts, Baja California Norte and Baja California Sur. In 1931 the districts which had comprised the Territory of Baja California became the Territories of Baja California Norte and Baja California Sur. In 1952 the northern territory became the state Baja California. In 1974 the southern territory became the state Baja California Sur.
Works by these jurisdictions are found under the following headings according to the name used at the time of publication:
Baja California (Ter.)
Baja California Norte (District)

Baja California Sur (District)
Baja California Norte (Ter.)
Baja California Sur (Ter.)
Baja California (State)
Baja California Sur, Mexico (State)

Baja California Norte (Ter.)
The peninsula Baja California was considered a territory of the Federation under Mexico's Constitution of 1824. In 1887 the Territory of Baja California was organized into two districts, Baja California Norte and Baja California Sur. In 1931 the districts which had comprised the Territory of Baja California became the Territories of Baja California Norte and Baja California Sur. In 1952 the northern territory became the state Baja California. In 1974 the southern territory became the state Baja California Sur.
Works by these jurisdictions are found under the following headings according to the name used at the time of publication:
Baja California (Ter.)
Baja California Norte (District)

Baja California Sur (District)
Baja California Norte (Ter.)
Baja California Sur (Ter.)
Baja California (State)
Baja California Sur, Mexico (State)

Baja California Norte (Ter.). Laws, statutes, etc. Código civil
Entries for this code, which was promulgated by the Federal government and is applicable to the Federal District and the Federal Territories, are found under:
Mexico (Federal District). Laws, statutes, etc. Código civil.
75-588732

Baja California Norte (Ter.). Laws, statutes, etc.
Código penal
Entries for this code, which was promulgated by the Federal government and is applicable to the Federal District and the Federal Territories, are found under:
Mexico (Federal District). Laws, statutes, etc.
Código penal.

Baja California Sur, Mexico (State)
The peninsula Baja California was considered a territory of the Federation under Mexico's Constitution of 1824. In 1887 the Territory of Baja California was organized into two districts, Baja California Norte and Baja California Sur. In 1931 the districts which had comprised the Territory of Baja California became the Territories of Baja California Norte and Baja California Sur. In 1952 the northern territory became the state Baja California. In 1974 the southern territory became the state Baja California Sur.
Works by these jurisdictions are found under the following headings according to the name used at the time of publication:
Baja California (Ter.)
Baja California Norte (District)

Baja California Sur (District)
Baja California Norte (Ter.)
Baja California Sur (Ter.)
Baja California (State)
Baja California Sur, Mexico (State)

Baja California Sur (District)
The peninsula Baja California was considered a territory of the Federation under Mexico's Constitution of 1824. In 1887 the Territory of Baja California was organized into two districts, Baja California Norte and Baja California Sur. In 1931 the districts which had comprised the Territory of Baja California became the Territories of Baja California Norte and Baja California Sur. In 1952 the northern territory became the state Baja California. In 1974 the southern territory became the state Baja California Sur.
Works by these jurisdictions are found under the following headings according to the name used at the time of publication:
Baja California (Ter.)
Baja California Norte (District)

Baja California Sur (District)
Baja California Norte (Ter.)
Baja California Sur (Ter.)
Baja California (State)
Baja California Sur, Mexico (State)

Baja California Sur (Ter.)
The peninsula Baja California was considered a territory of the Federation under Mexico's Constitution of 1824. In 1887 the Territory of Baja California was organized into two districts, Baja California Norte and Baja California Sur. In 1931 the districts which had comprised the Territory of Baja California became the Territories of Baja California Norte and Baja California Sur. In 1952 the northern territory became the state Baja California. In 1974 the southern territory became the state Baja California Sur.
Works by these jurisdictions are found under the following headings according to the name used at the time of publication:
Baja California (Ter.)
Baja California Norte (District)
Baja California Sur (District)

Baja California Norte (Ter.)
Baja California Sur (Ter.)
Baja California (State)
Baja California Sur, Mexico (State)

Baja California Sur (Ter.). Archivo Historico Pablo L. Martínez
see Cota Sandoval, José Andres. Archivo Histórico de Baja California Sur Pablo L. Martínez. La Paz, B.C., 1974.

Baja California Sur (Ter.). Commission of the Californias
see
Commission of the Californias.

Baja California Sur (Ter.). Laws, statutes, etc. Código civil
Entries for this code, which was promulgated by the Federal government and is applicable to the Federal District and the Federal Territories, are found under
Mexico (Federal District). Laws, statutes, etc. Código civil.
75-588733

Baja California Sur (Ter.). Laws, statutes, etc.
Código penal
Entries for this code, which was promulgated by the Federal government and is applicable to the Federal District and the Federal Territories, are found under:
Mexico (Federal District). Laws, statutes, etc.
Código penal.

Baja California Sur (Ter.). Secretaría de Obras Públicas.
La carretera tran[s]peninsular; su papel en el desarrollo económico de la Baja California. [La Paz, México, 1973]
18 l. 28 cm.
At head of title: Carretera transpeninsular "Benito Juárez," 1º de diciembre 1973.
"Itinerario para la gira del c. lic. Luis Echeverría, Presidente de la República, con motivo de la inauguración de la carretera transpeninsular de Baja California" (6 l. fold. map.) inserted at end.
1. Roads—Baja California. 2. Echeverría, Luis, Pres. Mexico, 1922- I. Title
CU-BANC NUC76-87406

Baja California y Sus Hombres. Mexicali, Editorial De Anza, 1966.
294 p. illus.
1. Baja California (State)—Biography.
InU NUC74-127403

Bājabīr, ʻAbd al-Raḥīm ʻAbd al-Qādir
see
Bā Jubayr, ʻAbd al-Raḥīm ʻAbd al-Qādir.

Bajai, Jeno.
Buzatermesztesi kiserletek, 1960-1970. Budapest, Akademiai Kiado, 1971.
641 p. illus.
English summary.
1. Wheat. Hungary. 2. Plants, Cultivated. Field experiments. I. Title.
DNAL NUC73-126573

Bajaj, Jasbir J.
see Insulin and metabolism. Bombay, Diabetic Assn. of India, 1972.

Bajaj, Jasbir S.
see Insulin and metabolism. Amsterdam, Excerpta Medica, 1977.

Bajaj, K K 1937-
Laws relating to invitation & acceptance of fixed deposits by companies (incorporating complete Reserve Bank of India act), as amended upto date and relevant new income tax provisions concerning companies accepting deposits, loans / by K. K. Bajaj and V. R. Kochhar. — 1st ed. — New Delhi : Bajaj Publications on behalf of Bajaj Capital Investment Centre, [1975]
ix, 158 p. ; 22 cm.
Rs25.00
1. Loans—India. 2. Banking law—India. I. Kochhar, V. R., joint author. II. Title.
346'.54'073 75-904758
76 MARC

Bajaj, Kamalnayan, 1915–1972.
(Kākājī, Bāpū, Vinobā)
काकाजी, बापू, विनोबा. [लेखक] कमलनयन बजाज. [नई दिल्ली, सस्ता साहित्य मंडल, 1972]
222 p. 25 cm. Rs15.00
In Hindi.

1. Bajaj, Jamnalal, 1889–1942. 2. Gandhi, Mohandas Karamchand, 1869–1948. 3. Bhave, Vinoba, 1895– 4. Bajaj, Kamalnayan, 1915–1972. I. Title.
DS481.A1B23 72–903179

Bajaj, Kamalnayan, 1915-1972
see Vakil, Chandulal Nagindas. Industrial development of India; policy and problems; Kamalnayan Bajaj commemoration volume. [New Delhi] Orient Longman [1973]

Bajaj, Krishnalal, 1935–
(Sarāpiyala yuga)
सरापियल युग / कृष्णलाल बजाज 'प्रदीप,' आजिज़ बेदी. — 1. छापो. — उल्हासनगर : साहित्य निकेतन, 1975.
88 p. ; 19 cm.
In Sindhi.
Poems.
Rs3.00

I. Bedi, Ajiz, 1937– joint author. II. Title.
PK2788.9.B3S2 75–904851

Bajaj, Kuljit Singh, 1942-
Cauchy type integral representations for network functions. [n.p.] 1971.
[1], x, 158 [i.e. 160] l. illus.
Thesis (Ph.D.)—Michigan State University.
Bibliography: leaves 156-158.
1. Electric networks. I. Title.
MiEM NUC73-35532

Bajaj, Prem N 1932–
Cumulative prolongations in semi-dynamical systems, by Prem N. Bajaj. Wichita, Kan., Wichita State University, 1972.
25 p. illus. 23 cm. (Wichita State University. Bulletin, v. 48, no. 4. University studies, no. 93)
Bibliography: p. 24–25.
1. Topological dynamics. I. Title. II. Series: Kansas. State University, Wichita. University studies, no. 93.
AS36.W62 no. 93 081 s 73–622320
[QA611.5] [514'.7] MARC

Bajaj, R K
Personnel problems of large scale industries : with special reference to Rajasthan / R. K. Bajaj. — 1st ed. — Jaipur : Panchsheel Prakashan, 1976.
v, 198 p. ; 23 cm.
Bibliography: p. [192]-198.
Rs40.00
1. Rajasthan, India—Industries. 2. Personnel management—Rajasthan, India. I. Title.
HC437.R3B3 658.3'03 76-902656
77 MARC

Bajaj, Ramkrishna.
रूसी युवकों के बीच; सोवियत जन-जीवन की झांकी. [लेखक] रामकृष्ण बजाज. [हिन्दी-अनुवाद: वैजनाथ] आमुख: सर्वपल्ली राधाकृष्णन्. [1. संस्करण] नई दिल्ली, सस्ता साहित्य मंडल, 1962.
198 p. illus., ports. 19 cm. Rs2.50
At head of title: सत्साहित्य प्रकाशन.
In Hindi.

1. Russia—Description and travel—1945– I. Title.
Title romanized: Rūsī yuvakoṃ ke bīca.
DK28.B15 S A 67–4574
PL 480 : I-H-4022

Bajaj, Satya Paul.
Activation of prothrombin by purified factors (factor Xa, calcium, phospholipid and factor V). [Minneapolis?] 1974.
141 l. illus.
1. Blood coagulation factors—Isolation & purification. 2. Prothrombin—Isolation & purification. 3. Prothrombin—Metabolism. I. Title.
DNLM NUC76-22426

Bajaj, Y. P. S., 1936-
see Applied and fundamental aspects of plant cell, tissue, and organ culture. Berlin, Springer-Verlag, 1977.

Bajāja, Harindara Singha.
(Ambī dā pahilā piāra)
ਅੰਬੀ ਦਾ ਪਹਿਲਾ ਪਿਆਰ : [ਨਾਵਲ] / ਹਰਿੰਦਰ ਸਿੰਘ ਬਜਾਜ. — ਦਿੱਲੀ : ਆਰਸੀ ਪਬਲਿਸ਼ਰਜ਼, 1975.
130 p. ; 19 cm.
In Panjabi.
Rs7.00

I. Title.
PK2659.B285A8 75–906555

Bajāja, Harindara Singha.
(Dīpa Bindū)
ਦੀਪ ਬਿੰਦੂ; [ਨਾਵਲ. ਲੇਖਕ] ਹਰਿੰਦਰ ਸਿੰਘ ਬਜਾਜ. ਦਿੱਲੀ, ਨਵਯੁਗ ਪਬਲਿਸ਼ਰਜ਼ [1974]
137 p. 18 cm. Rs6.00
In Panjabi.

I. Title.
PK2659.B285D5 74–901348

Bajāja, Jānakīdevī.
(Merī jīvana-yātrā)
मेरी जीवन-यात्रा; जीवन-निर्माण की सरल, सुबोध, एवं भावपूर्ण कहानी. [लेखिका] जानकीदेवी बजाज. प्रस्तावना : विनोबा. नई दिल्ली, सस्ता साहित्य मण्डल, 1965.
228 p. illus. 19 cm. (सत्साहित्य-प्रकाशन)
In Hindi.

1. Bajāja, Jānakīdevī. I. Title.

CT1508.B32A3 1965 76-926727

Bajāja, Jānakīdevī
see Samarpana aura sādhanā. 1973.

Bajaja, Vladislav.
Theoretische Grundlagen und praktische Entwicklung landwirtschaftlicher Betriebsgrössen in der Tschechoslowakei / Vladislav Bajaja. — Berlin : Duncker und Humblot [in Komm.], 1975.
325 p. ; 24 cm. — (Östeuropastudien der Hochschulen des Landes Hessen : Reihe 1, Giessener Abhandlungen zur Agrar- und Wirtschaftsforschung des europäischen Ostens ; Bd. 69 ISSN 0078-6888) GFR76-A
Originally presented as the author's thesis, Giessen.
Summary in English.
Bibliography: p. 311-325.
ISBN 3-428-03491-0 : DM88.00
1. State farms—Czechoslovak Republic. 2. Farms, Size of—Czechoslovak Republic. 3. Agriculture—Economic aspects—Czechoslovak Republic. I. Title: Theoretische Grundlagen und praktische Entwicklung landwirtschaftlicher Betriebsgrössen ... II. Series: Osteuropastudien der Hochschulen des Landes Hessen : Reihe 1, Giessener Abhandlungen zur Agrar- und Wirtschaftsforschung des europäischen Ostens ; Bd. 69.
HD1493.C95B33 1975 338.1'8437 76-461863
76 MARC

Bajáki, Veronika.
Magyar állampolgárság; kettős állampolgárság. Budapest, Közgazdasági és Jogi Könyvkiadó, 1973.
314 p.
1. Citizenship—Hungary. 2. Dual nationality—Hungary.
CLL NUC75-19471

Bajáki, Veronika
see Adám, Antal, 1930- Az európai szocialista országok alkotmányos rendszere... Budapest, Tankönyvkiado, 1972.

Bajalović-Birtašević, Marija
see
Bajalović-Hadži-Pešić, Marija.

Bajalović-Hadži-Pešić, Marija.
Средњевековна некропола у Миријеву. Београд, 1960.
46 p. 3 fold. plans, 19 plates. 29 cm. (Музеј града Београда. Повремена издања, свеска 1)
Added t. p.: La necropole medievale dans le village de Mirievo.
Summary in French.
Bibliographical footnotes.
1. Mirijevo (Belgrad)—Antiquities. I. Title. II. Title: La necropole medievale dans le village de Mirievo. III. Series: Belgrad. Muzej grada. Povremena izdanja, sveska 1.
Title romanized: Srednjevekovna nekropola u Mirijevu.
DR386.4.M57B34 73-206266

Bajalović-Hadži-Pešić, Marija.
(Srednjevekovnom Beogradu u pohode)
Средњевековном Београду у походе / [аутор каталога и изложбе] Марија Бајаловић-Хаџи-Пешић ; [уредник Јован Тодоровић]. — Београд : Музеј града, 1977.
127 p., [35] leaves of plates : ill., fold. map (in pocket) ; 20 cm. — (Каталог изложбе - Музеј града Београда ; 17) Yu***
Added t. p.: A visit to mediaeval Belgrade.
Summary in English.
Bibliography: p. 103-108.
1. Belgrad—Antiquities—Exhibitions. I. Title. II. Title: A visit to mediaeval Belgrade. III. Series: Belgrad. Muzej grada. Katalozi izložbi ; 17.
DR386.A3B4 knj. 17 77-506836
[DR386.15]

Bajalura Rahamāna Bhūñā
see
Bhūñā, Bajalura Rahamāna.

Bajamonti, Giulio, 1744-1800.
Elogio dell'abate Ruggiero Giuseppe Boscovich. Ed. 2. Napoli, Presso D. Campo, 1790.
viii, 40 p.
Microprint. New York, Readex Microprint, 1974. 1 card. (Landmarks of science)
1. Bošković, Rudjer Josip, 1711-1787.
I. Title.
InU NUC76-20061

Bajamonti, Giulio, 1744-1800.
Zapisi o gradu Splitu / Julije Bajamonti ; izbor, prijevod i komentar Duško Kečkemet. — Split : Marko Marulić, 1975.
379 p. : ill., geneal. table ; 21 cm. — (Biblioteka MM) (Edicija Svjedočanstva ; 2) Yu***
Translated from Italian.
Bibliography of works by and about the author: p. 329-344.
1. Split, Yugoslavia—History. I. Kečkemet, Duško. II. Title.
DR396.S6557B34 76-507211

Bajan, Anton
see Sociální lékařstvi. Praha, Avicenum, t. [ST] 1970.

Bajan, Cecylia.
Preliminary studies on the role of Beauveria bassiana (Bals.) Vuill. in reduction of Lygus rugulipennis Popp [by] Cecylia Bajan and Teresa Bilewicz-Pawińska. Warszawa [PWN] 1971.
[35]-46 p. illus., diagrs. 24 cm. (Ekologia polska, v. 19, no. 2)
Caption title.
At head of title: Institute of Ecology, Polish Academy of Sciences.
Bibliography: p. 45-46.
1. Beauveria bassiana. I. Bilewicz-Pawińska, Teresa. II. Title. III. Series.
NNBG NUC73-43893

Bajan, Konrad
see Podstawy nauk politycznych... Warszawa: Państwowe Wydawn. Naukowe, 1976.

Bajan, Konrad
see Polityka rolna PRL : podstawowe zagadnienia. Warszawa : Ksiazka i Wiedza, 1974.

Bajandas, Frank J.
see Eye movements... New York, Plenum Press, c1977.

Bajanik, Stefan.
Volcanisme en Tunisie. Tunis, Éditions du Service geologique de Tunisie, 1971.
63 p. illus. 28 cm. (République Tunisienne. Ministère de l'économie nationale. Direction des mines et de l'énergie. Annales des mines et de la géologie no. 25)
Bibliography: p. [61]-63.
1. Volcanism—Tunisia. I. Title.
DI-GS NUC76-69656

Bajarano, Manuel Eduardo.
La medicina en América. [Santo Domingo] Universidad Autónoma de Santo Domingo, Instituto de Antropología [197-?]
6 l. 29 cm. (Museo, boletín no. 7)
Caption title.
1. Indians—Medicine—Addresses, essays, lectures. I. Title. II. Series.
E59.M4B34 610'.9701 74-216624

Bajard, Joëlle.
Nature et rêves / Joëlle Bajard. — Paris : Éditions Saint-Germain-des-Prés, 1976.
30 p. ; 16 cm. — (Collection La Poésie, la vie) F76-16211
Poems.
ISBN 2-243-00223-X : 10.00F
I. Title.
PQ2662.A355N3 841'.9'14 77-477231
77 MARC

Bajari Dāsa, 17th cent.
(Arthagobinda)
ଅର୍ଥଗୋବିନ୍ଦ / ବଜରି ଦାସଙ୍କ କୃତ ; ସମ୍ପାଦନା, ପ୍ରହ୍ଲାଦ ପ୍ରଧାନ, ଦୁଃଖିଶ୍ୟାମ ପଟ୍ଟନାୟକ. — ଭୁବନେଶ୍ୱର : ସାଂସ୍କୃତିକ ବ୍ୟାପାର ବିଭାଗ, ଓଡ଼ିଶା, 1970.
[38], 144, [27] p. : geneal. table ; 25 cm. — (Orissan oriental text series (Oriya) ; 1)
Added t.p. in English: Arthagovinda.
In Oriya.
Includes Sanskrit text (Oriya script) of Jayadeva's Gītagovinda.
Appendix (p. [1]-20 (3d group)): Jayadeva's Gitagovinda; a list of translations and different editions of the text (1969)
1. Krishna—Poetry. I. Pradhan, Prahallad. II. Pattanayak, Dukhisyama, 1940- III. Jayadeva, son of Bhojadeva. Gītagovinda. 1970. IV. Title. V. Title: Arthagovinda. VI. Series: Utkaḷīẏa prācya granthamāḷā (Oḍiā) ; 1.

PK2579.B254A9 1970 75-904180

Bajaria, Hansraj J 1943-
Determination of the magnetic field extension profile for reducing the end losses in the MHD generator channel, by Hansraj J. Bajaria. [n.p.] 1972.
98 l. illus.
Thesis—Michigan Technological University.
Bibliography: leaves 77-79.
Photocopy. Ann Arbor, Mich., University Microfilms, 1973. 22 cm.
1. Magnetohydrodynamic generators.
I. Title.
CSt NUC74-125996

Bajars, Laimonis, joint author.
see Happel, John. Base metal oxide catalysts for the petrochemical, petroleum, and chemical industries... New York, M. Dekker, c1977.

Bajasut, S U
Alam fikiran dan djedjak perdjuangan Prawoto Mangkusasmito. Disusun oleh S. U. Bajasut. [Tjet. 1.] Surabaja, Documenta, 1972.
xx, 463 p. illus. 22 cm.
Bibliography: p. 462-463.
1. Masjumi. 2. Mangkusamito, Prawoto. 3. Indonesia—Politics and government—1950-1966. I. Mangkusasmito, Prawoto. Alam fikiran dan djedjak perdjuangan Prawoto Mangkusasmito. II. Title.
JQ779.A553B33 72-941500

Bajasut, S U
see Natsir, Muhammad. The new morality. [Tjet. 2] Surabaja, DDII Perwakilan Djatim [1970]

Bajasut, S U ed.
see Up grading kepemimpinan pondok-pesantren madrasah seluruh Djawa Timur... [Surabaja, 1971]

al-Bajāwī, 'Alī Muhammad
see al-Hakīm al-Tirmidhī, Muhammad ibn 'Alī, fl. 898. (al-Amthāl min al-Kitāb wa-al-sunnah) [1975?]

al-Bajāwī, 'Alī Muhammad
see Ibn al-Shajarī, Hibat Allāh ibn 'Alī, 1058-1148, ed. [Dīwān mukhtārāt shu'arā al-'Arab] Mukhtārāt shu'arā' al-'Arab. [1975]

al-Bajawi, 'Ali Muhammad, joint author
see Jad al-Mawla, Muhammad Ahmad. Qisas al-'Arab. 1971-72.

Bajaza, Harindara Singha
see
Bajāja, Harindara Singha.

Bajcar, Adam.
Poland; a guidebook for tourists [by] Adam Bajcar. [Translated by: Stanisław Tarnowski] Warsaw, Interpress Publishers, 1972.
226 p. illus., maps (1 fold. col. in pocket) 20 cm. zł42.00
Translation of Polska, przewodnik turystyczny.
1. Poland—Description and travel—Guide-books. I. Title.
DK403.B3413 1972 914.38'04'5 72-170457
MARC

Bajcar, Adam.
Polen; Reiseführer. [Deutsch: Edmund Paszkowiak] Warszawa, Interpress, 1971.
258 p. illus., maps (1 fold. col. in pocket), plans. 20 cm.
1. Poland—Guide-books. I. Title.
MeU NUC73-35551

Bajcar, Adam.
Polska; przewodnik turystyczny. Warszawa, Polonia, 1965.
191 p. illus., maps (1 fold. col. in pocket) 20 cm.
2. wyd. rozsz.
1. Poland–Description and travel–Guide books.
IEN NUC76-69476

Bajcsyová, Ruzena Kucera.
Computer identification of textured visual scenes, by Ruzena Bajcsy. [Stanford, Calif.] 1973.
[5], 157 l. illus. (part col.)
Thesis (Ph.D.)—Stanford University.
Bibliography: leaves 152-157.
1. Optical data-processing. I. Title.
CSt NUC75-19999

Bajcura, Ivan.
Ukrajinská otázka v ČSSR. [Vyd. 1. Košice] Východoslovenské vydavateľstvo, 1967.
214 p. 21 cm.
Bibliography: p. [207]-214.
1. Ukrainians in the Czechoslovak Republic. 2. Czechoslovak Republic—Politics and government. I. Title.
DB200.7.B33 74-200797

Bajé, Brazil
see
Bagé, Brazil.

Bajec, Ivo, ed.
see Šahovski šampijonat SFR Jugoslavije, 23d, Čateške Toplice, Slovenia, 1968. XXIII. [i. e. Triindvajseti] šahovski šampijonat SFR Jugoslavije, Čateške Toplice 1968. [Čateške Toplice] Center za napredek šaha pri ŠZS [1968]

Bajec, Jože.
Slovenski časniki in časopisi; bibliografski pregled od 1. jan. 1937 do osvoboditve 9. maja 1945. Dodatek: Drugojezično časopisje Slovenije in drugojezično časopisje slovenskih izdajateljev v tujini. Ljubljana, Narodna in univerzitetna knjižnica, 1973.
294 p.
1. Slovenian periodicals—Bibl. 2. Slovenian newspapers—Bibl. I. Title.
InU NUC75-27406

Bajec, Jože.
Slovenski časniki in časopisi : bibliografski pregled od 1. januarja 1937 do osvoboditve 9. maja 1945. Drugojezično časopisje Slovenije in drugojezično časopisje slovenskih izdajateljev v tujini : [bibliografski pregled od 1. 1. 1937 do 9. 5. 1945] : dodatek / sestavil Jože Bajec ; [predgovor Jaro Dolar]. — Ljubljana : Narodna in univerzitetna knjižnica, 1973.
360 p. ; 23 cm. Yu 74-1816
Includes indexes.
1. Slovenian periodicals—Bibliography. 2. Slovenian newspapers—Bibliography. I. Bajec, Jože. Drugojezično časopisje Slovenije in drugojezično časopisje slovenskih izdajateljev v tujini. 1973. II. Title: Slovenski časniki in časopisi.
Z6956.S64B34 74-351586

Bajema, Carl Jay, 1937- comp.
Natural selection in human populations; the measurement of ongoing genetic evolution in contemporary societies. New York, Wiley [1971]
viii, 406 p. illus. 24 cm.
Includes bibliographies.
1. Human evolution—Addresses, essays, lectures. 2. Natural selection—Addresses, essays, lectures. 3. Human population genetics—Addresses, essays, lectures. I. Title.
GN289.B33 1971 573.2'1'08 72-154322
ISBN 0-471-04380-X 71[r77]rev MARC

Bajema, Carl Jay, 1937- comp.
Natural selection in human populations : the measurement of ongoing genetic evolution in contemporary societies / edited by Carl Jay Bajema. — Huntington, N.Y. : R. E. Krieger Pub. Co., 1977, c1971.
viii, 406 p. : ill. ; 24 cm.
Reprint of the ed. published by Wiley, New York.
Includes bibliographies.
ISBN 0-88275-476-9
1. Human population genetics—Addresses, essays, lectures. 2. Human evolution—Addresses, essays, lectures. 3. Natural selection—Addresses, essays, lectures. I. Title.
[GN289.B33 1977] 573.2'1'08 76-50639
76 MARC

Bajema, Carl Jay, 1937-
see Eugenics ... Stroudsburg, Pa., Dowden, Hutchinson & Ross, c1976.

Băjenaru, Grigore, 1907–
Bună dimineața, băieți! [Coperta de Done Stan]. [București], Editura Ion Creangă, 1972.
276 p. 18 cm. (Biblioteca contemporană) lei 3.75 R 72-1742
Autobiographical.
1. Teachers—Correspondence, reminiscences, etc. I. Title.
LA2375.R62B34 73-318121

Băjenaru, Grigore, 1907–
Vîrful cu dor. [Povestiri. Coperta: Adrian Dumitrache]. București, Editura pentru turism, 1973.
104 p. 20 cm. (Colecția Locuri și legende) lei 4.50 R 73-2512
CONTENTS: Într-un fapt de seară.—Stîna lui Bucur.—Mihai-Vodă Viteazul și moșnenii din Ploiești.—Vîrful cu dor.—Retezatul.—Piatra arsă.—Cascada urlătoare.—Ceahlăul.
I. Title.
PC840.12.A44V5 74-326118

Bajer, Andrew S
Spindle dynamics and chromosome movements [by] Andrew S. Bajer and J. Molè-Bajer. New York, Academic Press, 1972.
xi, 271 p. illus. 24 cm. (International review of cytology. Supplement 3)
Bibliography: p. 229-255.
1. Spindle (Cell division) 2. Chromosomes. I. Molè-Bajer, Jadwiga, joint author. II. Title. III. Series.
QH605.B324 574.8'7623 73-155572
ISBN 0-12-364363-5 MARC

Bajer, Antonín.
Cesty srdce / Antonín Bajer. — 1. vyd. — České Budějovice : Růže, 1976.
82 p. ; 21 cm. Cz77
Poems.
Kčs4.00
I. Title.
PG5039.12.A35C4 77-464466
*77 MARC

Bajer, Jadwiga Molè-
see Molè-Bajer, Jadwiga.

Bajer, Jiří.
Alexandr Nikolajevič Skrjabin / Jiří Bajer. — 1. vyd. — Praha : Horizont, 1975.
105 p. : ill. ; 19 cm. — (Medailóny ; sv. 14) Cz 75
"Životopisná data A. N. Skrjabina": p. 96-102.
Bibliography: p. 104.
Kčs8.00
1. Skriabin, Aleksandr Nikolaevich, 1872-1915.
ML410.S5988B3 76-511876

Bajer, Jiří.
Petr Iljič Čajkovskij. 1. vyd. Praha, Horizont, t. Jihočes. tisk., Čes. Budějovice, 1973.
75, [1] p. 19 cm. (Medailony, sv. 2) Kčs5.00 Cz 73-SKČ
Bibliography: p. 74.
1. Chaikovskiĭ, Petr Il'ich, 1840-1893.
ML410.C4B23 73-345494

Bajer, Jiří
see Česka hudba světu, svět české hudbě ... Praha : Panton, 1974.

Bajer, Magdalena
see Żywot Polaka poczciwego. Warszawa, Ksiazka i Wiedza, 1971.

Bajer, Miroslav, joint author
see Suchan, Libor. Termodynamika důlního větrání ... Praha : SNTL, 1975.

Bajerlein, Józef.
Intensywność infiltracji w poszczególnych porach roku na tle obserwacji terenowej. Poznań, 1966.
12 p. illus. (part fold.) 24 cm. (Uniwersytet im. Adama Mickiewicza w Poznaniu. Prace Wydziału Biologii i Nauk o Ziemi. Seria geologia, nr. 6)
At head of title: Józef Bajerlein, Michał Zurawski.
Summary in English.
Bibliography: p. 10.
1. Hydrogeology. I. Zurawski, M. II. Title.
DI-GS NUC76-14976

Băjescu, I., ed.
see Conferința Națională de Știința Solului, 7th, Jassy, 1970. Lucrările Conferinței... București Academia de Stiințe Agricole și Silvice, 1972.

Bajetto, M. P.
see Netherlands (Kingdom, 1815-). Laws, statutes, etc. Omroepwet en Wet op de omroepbijdragen. 2e druk. Zwolle : W. E. J. Tjeenk Willink, 1975.

Băjeu, George.
Generatoare de radiofrecvență. București, Editura tehnică, 1972.
192 p. with figs. 19 cm. (Colecția Radio și televiziune, 103) lei 5.00 R 72-3979
At head of title: George Băjeu, Gheorghe Stancu.
Bibliography: p. 185-186.
1. Oscillators, Transistor. 2. Oscillators, Vacuum-tube. I. Stancu, Gheorghe, joint author. II. Title.
TK7872.O7B26 73-305361

Bajger, Lubomír.
Über den Abschub der Deutschen aus dem Ostrauer Gebiet; [von] Lubomír Bajger. München, Sudetendeutsches Archiv, 1968.
47 p. 30 cm. (Sudetendeutsches Archiv; Übersetzungs-und Informationsdienst; Nr. 90-91)
English translation of title: The transfer of Germans from Ostrava region; by Lubomír Baiger.
Original title: "K odsunu Němcu z Ostraska" article in the Periodical "Slezský Sborník" (Silesian Almanac) v. 66, 1968, Nr. 2.
Caption title.
Translated from Czech to German by Balthazar.
1. Germans in the Czechoslovak Republic. 2. Population transfer–Germans. 3. Ostrava region–Population. I. Title.
IEdS NUC74-128705

Bajgerová, Miluše.
Rejstřík Sborníku prací Pedagogické fakulty v Ostravě za léta 1960-1969. [Vyd. 1.] Ostrava, Pedagogická fakulta, 1970.
58 p. 21 cm. (Ostrava, Czechoslovak Republic (City). Pedagogická fakulta. Publikace, č. 61) Kčs5.00 Cz***
1. Ostrava, Czechoslovak Republic (City). Pedagogická fakulta—Bibliography. I. Ostrava, Czechoslovak Republic (City). Pedagogická fakulta. II. Title.
Z5055.C92O83 73-314072

Bajgier, Steve M
Public risk assessment and evaluation of drinking water quality / by Steve M. Bajgier and Herbert Moskowitz. — West Lafayette, Ind. : Institute for Research in the Behavioral, Economic, and Management Sciences, Krannert Graduate School of Management, Purdue University, 1977.
36 p. ; 28 cm. — (Paper - Institute for Research in the Behavioral, Economic, and Management Sciences, Purdue University ; no. 596)
Bibliography: p. 21.
1. Water quality—Public opinion. 2. Drinking water—Public opinion. I. Moskowitz, Herbert, joint author. II. Title. III. Series: Purdue University, Lafayette, Ind. Institute for Research in the Behavioral, Economic, and Management Sciences. Paper ; no. 596.
HD6483.P8 no. 596 301.15'43'62816 77-622241
[TD370] 77 MARC

al-Bājī, Abū al-Walīd Sulaymān ibn Khalaf, 1013-1081.
[al-Ḥudūd fī al-uṣūl]
كتاب الحدود في الاصول، تاليف ابي الوليد سليمان بن خلف الباجي الاندلسي. تحقيق نزيه حماد. [الطبعة 1.] بيروت، مؤسسة الزعبي للطباعة والنشر [1973]
85 p. facsim. 24 cm.
Bibliography: p. 81-85.
1. Islamic law—Terminology. 2. Arabic language—Glossaries, vocabularies, etc. I. Ḥammād, Nazīh, ed. II. Title: al-Ḥudūd fī al-uṣūl.
Title romanized: Kitāb al-ḥudūd fī al-uṣūl.
74-221230

al-Bājī, Maḥmūd.
(al-Mu'jizah al-khālidah)
المعجزة الخالدة، بمناسبة مرور اربعة عشر قرنا على نزول القرآن [تاليف] محمود الباجي. [تونس] الجمعية القومية للمحافظة على القرآن الكريم [1389?- i. e. 1969?-
v. illus. 24 cm.
1. Koran — Addresses, essays, lectures. 2. Islam — Addresses, essays, lectures. I. Title.
BP130.6.B34 75-587462

al-Bājī al-Mas'ūdī, Abū 'Abd Allāh Muḥammad, 1810 or 11–1880.
(al-Bājī al-Mas'ūdī)
الباجى المسعودي، تقديم محسن بنحميدة. تونس، الشركة القومية للنشر والتوزيع، 1962.
86 p. 21 cm. (ادباء المغرب العربى)
«منتخبات» : p. 37–86.
Series romanized: Udabā' al-Maghrib al-'Arabī.
Bibliography: p. 33.
1. al-Bājī al-Mas'ūdī, Abū 'Abd Allāh Muḥammad, 1810 or 11–1880. I. Bin-Ḥamīdah, Muḥammad Muḥsin, 1919–
PJ7816.A457A6 1962 — 73–217140

Bajić, Branislav.
Poslovni privredno-tehnički rečnik : srpskohrvatsko-nemačko-englesko-francuski : numerički sistem = Geschäfts-Wirtschafts-technisches Wörterbuch : deutsch-englisch-französisch-serbokroatisch : numerisches System = Technical-economical dictionary for business purposes : English-French-German-Serbocroat : numeral system / Branislav Bajić, Aleksandar Dunđerović, Nikola Kern. — Beograd : Privredni pregled, 1973.
1701 p. ; 25 cm. — Yu***
Title on spine: Četvorojezični poslovni privredno-tehnički rečnik.

1. Business—Dictionaries—Polyglot. 2. German language—Dictionaries—Polyglot. I. Dunđerović, Aleksandar, joint author. II. Kern, Nikola, joint author. III. Title. IV. Title: Geschäfts-Wirtschafts-technisches Wörterbuch. V. Title: Technical-economical dictionary for business purposes. VI. Title: Četvorojezični poslovni privredno-tehnički rečnik.
HF1001.B22 — 75–970005

Bajić, Branko, 1911–1942.
Sabrani spisi / Branko Bajić ; predgovor, redakcija i objašnjenja Živan Milisavac. — Novi Sad : Muzej socijalističke revolucije Vojvodine, 1975.
372 p. : port. ; 21 cm. — (Socijalistička misao u Vojvodini ; knj. 4) — Yu***
Bibliography: p. 355–357.
Includes indexes.
I. Series.
PG1418.B22S2 1975 — 76–528911

Bajić, Branko, 1954–
Diabolos ukletnik / Branko Bajić. — Zagreb : Bajić, 1976.
53 p. : ill. ; 20 cm. — Yu***
Poems.
I. Title.
PG1619.12.A326D5 — 76–528091

Bajić, Dejan.
(Električna i elektronska kola, uređaji i merni instrumenti)
Електрична и електронска кола, уређаји и мерни инструменти. Београд, Универзитет; Београдски издавачко-графички завод, 1972–
v. illus. 24 cm. 80.00Din (v. 1) — Yu 72–1003 (v. 1)
At head of title: Универзитет у Београду.
Bibliography: v. 1, p. 431.
1. Electric engineering. 2. Electronics. I. Title.
TK145.B285 — 73–970252

Bajić, Miloš.
Mauthauzen 106621 / ⌐autor¬ Miloš Bajič ; ⌐oprema Miloš Bajić : fotografije Milorad Urdarević ... et al.¬. — Beograd : Savez udruženja boraca NOR Srbije : Izdavačko-informativni centar studenata, 1975.
⌐96¬ p. : ill. ; 29 cm. — Yu 75–4356
Serbo-Croatian, English, French, German, Italian, Russian, and Spanish.
1. Bajić, Miloš. 2. Mauthausen (Concentration camp) in art. I. Title.
NC312.Y83B34 — 76–528088

Bajini, L A
Aids to the study of the Eve language. [Ghana] E. P. Church Book Depot [n. d.]
56 p. 19 cm.
Cover title.
1. Ewe language. I. Title.
PPT — NUC75-73748

Bajkai, Louis A
Teachers' guide to overseas teaching : a complete and comprehensive directory of English-language schools and colleges overseas / compiled and edited by Louis A. Bajkai ; associate editor, Joseph S. Corrao. — La Jolla, Calif. : Teach Overseas, c1977.
iii, 140 p. : ill. ; 21 cm.
1. American teachers in foreign countries—Employment—Directories. 2. Teachers in foreign countries—Employment—Directories. 3. Teacher placement agencies—Directories. 4. Education—Directories. I. Corrao, Joseph S., joint author. II. Title.
L900.B34 — 371'.0025 — 77-81788
77 — MARC

Bajkó Mátyás.
Nemzeti nevelésügyünk a reformkorban. Debrecen, 1969.
75 p. 20 cm. (Nevelés, művelődés; acta paedagogica Debrecina, 49)
German and Russian summary.
Bibliographical notes: p. 70-72.
1. Education–Hungary–History. I. Title. II. Series.
NNC — NUC74-127404

Bajna, Premlata.
[Pant ka Kavya] Dehra Dun, Sahitya Sudan, 1969.
552 p.
1. Hindi literature—Hist. & crit. I. Title.
KMK — NUC74-149139

Bajnárek, Zdeněk, joint author.
see Kreisel, František. Elektrická jednotka řady EM 488.0. 1. vyd. Praha, Nadas, 1976.

Bajno, Riccardo.
Profili penalistici della vis publica : in tema di violenza, resistenza e oltraggio aggravato / Riccardo Bajno. — Padova, CEDAM, 1974.
x, 161 p. ; 24 cm. — (Collana di studi penalistici ; nuova ser., 10) — It 74–Dec
Includes bibliographical references.
L5000
1. Resisting an officer—Italy. 2. Violence (Law)—Italy. I. Title. II. Series.
75–566744

Bajo Fernández, Miguel.
El parentesco en el derecho penal. Prólogo del Ilmo. Sr. D. Gonzalo Rodríguez Mourullo. Barcelona, Bosch ⌐1973¬
267 p. 22 cm. — Sp***
Bibliography: p. ⌐249¬–254.
1. Affinity (Law)—Spain. 2. Domestic relations—Spain—Criminal provisions. I. Title.
74–310405
ISBN 84–7162–606–3

Bajo Fernández, Miguel.
La realización arbitraria del propio derecho / Miguel Bajo Fernández. — 1. ed. — ⌐Madrid¬ : Civitas, 1976.
89 p. ; 21 cm. — (Monografías Civitas) — Sp76-June
Bibliography: p. ⌐87¬-89.
ISBN 8473980255
1. Debtor and creditor—Spain—Criminal provisions. 2. Debtor and creditor—Criminal provisions. I. Title.
345'.46'026 — 77-455929
•77 — MARC

El bajo mundo de la delincuencia. [Barcelona] Ediciones Telstar [1970]
see under Murter, Inspector.

Bajoga, Buba Garegy.
Decoder complexity for BCH codes. Buffalo, 1972.
144 l.
Thesis (Ph. D.)–State University of New York at Buffalo.
I. Title.
NBuU — NUC74-1379

Bajolais, Jean-Réno-
see Réno-Bajolais, Jean.

Bajolle, J.E.
see Freezing process studies. Washington, For sale by the Supt. of Docs., U.S. Govt. Print. Off., 1971.

Bajomi Lázár, Endre.
Anatole France világa. ⌐Budapest, Európa Könyvkiadó, 1973¬
166 p. illus. 19 cm. (Írók világa) 9.00Ft
Bibliography: p. 159–166.
1. France, Anatole, 1844–1924. I. Title.
PQ2254.Z5B27 — 74–215639

Bajomi Lázár, Endre.
Párizs nem ereszt el / Bajomi Lázár Endre. — Budapest : Szépirodalmi Könyvkiadó, 1975.
466 p. ; 20 cm.
ISBN 963–15–0326–7 : 28.50Ft
1. Paris. 2. Bajomi Lázár, Endre. I. Title.
DC707.B29 — 76–511965

Bajomi Lázár, Endre
see Kertész, André. André Kertész munkássága. [Budapest] Corvina [1972]

Bajon, Filip, 1947-
see Erkundungen: 19 poln. Erzähler. 2. Aufl. Berlin: Verlag Volk und Welt, 1974.

Bajón, Juan Manuel de Gandarias y
see
Gandarias y Bajón, Juan Manuel de.

Bajon, Wieslaw, joint author
see Osiński, Zbigniew. Podstawy konstrukcji maszyn. Warszawa : Pánstwowe Wydawn. Naukowe, 1975.

Bajor, Andor.
Az éjjeliőr nem tud aludni : karcolatok / Bajor Andor ; ⌐Cseh Gusztáv rajzaival¬. — Bukarest : Kriterion, 1976.
292 p. : ill. ; 21 cm. — R76-3693
lei10.50
I. Title.
PH3213.B19E35 — 77-468482
•77 — MARC

Bajor, Andor.
Lelkek és pasasok / Bajor Andor. — Budapest : Magvető Kiadó, c1975.
418 p. : ill. ; 20 cm.
ISBN 963–270–003–1 : 32.00Ft
I. Title.
PH3213.B19L4 — 76–526942

Bajor, Andor.
Tücsök és bogár. Szatírák és humoreszkek. ⌐A borítót és az illusztrációkat Surány Erzsébet rajzolta¬. Kolozsvár, „Dacia,“ 1972.
255 p. illus. 20 cm. lei 10.50 — R 72–4574
I. Title.
PH3213.B19T8 — 73–318781

Bajor, Kazimierz.
Zagadnienie doboru słownictwa do naukijezyka rosyjskiego. ⌐Wyd. 1.¬. Łódź ⌐Państwowe Wydawn. Naukowe. Oddz. w Łodzi¬ 1971.
203 p. 25 cm.
At head of title: Uniwersytet Łódzki.
In Russian.
Bibliography: p. 72–76.
zł12.00
1. Russian language—Study and teaching—Polish students. 2. Russian language—Lexicography. I. Title.
PG2068.P6B3 — 74–231342

Bajor, Kazimierz.
see Gramatyka konfrontatywna języka polskiego i rosyjskiego . . . Wyd. 1. Łódź, Uniwersytet Łódzki, 1976.

Bajor Nagy, Erno.
A country at school. Budapest, Pannonia Press, 1962.
122 p.
1. Education—Hungary—1945-1964. I. Title.
CaBVaU DLC — NUC74-37785

Bajor Nagy, Ernő.
Munkatársunk jelenti : irodalmi riportok / Bajor Nagy Ernő. — Budapest : Kozmosz Könyvek, 1976.
308 p. ; 21 cm.
ISBN 9632111052 : 27.00Ft
I. Title.
AC95.H9B3 — 77-453531
77 — MARC

Bajorat, Archibald.
Indisches Skizzenbuch/ Archibald Bajorat; Manfred Kulessa. — München : Staackmann, 1969.
92 p.: numerous ill.; 20 x 28 cm. DM12.00 — GDB 73–A15
1. India—Description and travel—1947– I. Kulessa, Manfred, 1932– II. Title.
DS414.B33 — 73–347784

Bajorat, Archibald, illus.
see Bode, Helmut, 1910- Vom Eschborner Esel... Frankfurt a. M., Kramer (1970).

Bajorat, Archibald.
see Heinen, Werner. Monotropa ... Grosskrotzenburg, Cruzenburch-Presse, 1975.

Bajorat, Archibald, illus.
see Lenz, Siegfried, 1926- Versäum nicht den Termin der Freude. Memmingen (Allgäu): Visel, 1970.

Bajoria, Ratanlal Kaluramji, 1922–
(Bṛhad rāshṭrabhāshā kośa)
बृहद् राष्ट्रभाषा कोश. सम्पादक रतनलाल बाजोरिया. [1. संस्करण] वर्धा, राष्ट्रभाषा प्रचार समिति [1972]
4, 904 p. 23 cm. Rs16.00
In Hindi.

1. Hindi language—Dictionaries. I. Title.

PK1937.B3 72–905117

Bajos de Heredia, Irénée.
Le bridge d'école française [par] Irénée Bajos de Heredia avec la collaboration technique de Gérard Desrousseaux. Paris, B. Grasset [1972]
540 p. illus. 21 cm. 60.00F F***
1. Contract bridge. I. Desrousseaux, Gérard, joint author. II. Title.
BV1282.3.B273 74–327849 MARC

Bajour. [New York, M. Merrill, n.d.]
[16] p. illus., ports. 31 cm.
Souvenir book for the musical play by Walter Marks, starring Chita Rivera, Nancy Dussault and Herschel Bernardi.
Original stiff wrappers printed.
I. Marks, Walter.
InU NUC75-74490

Bajpai, Avi C
Advanced engineering mathematics / A. C. Bajpai, L. R. Mustoe, D. Walker. — London ; New York : Wiley, c1977.
x, 578 p. : ill., 24 cm.
Bibliography: p. 549.
Includes index.
ISBN 0-491-99521-5. ISBN 0-471-99520-7
1. Engineering mathematics. I. Mustoe, L. R., joint author. II. Walker, Dennis, joint author. III. Title.
TA330.B33 510'.2'462 77-2198
77 MARC

Bajpai, Avi C
Engineering mathematics [by] A. C. Bajpai, L. R. Mustoe [and] D. Walker, in collaboration with W. T. Martin. London, New York, John Wiley [1974]
xiii, 793 p. illus. 24 cm. GB***
Bibliography: p. 751.
1. Engineering mathematics. I. Mustoe, L. R., joint author. II. Walker, D., joint author.
TA330.B34 510'.2'462 73–21230
ISBN 0–471–04375–3; 0–471–04376–1 (pbk.) MARC

Bajpai, Avi C
Mathematics for engineers and scientists; a students' course book [by] A. C. Bajpai, I. M. Calus [and] J. A. Fairley. London, New York, J. Wiley [1973]
v. 25 cm. (A Series of programmes on mathematics for scientists and technologists) GB*** (v. 1)
1. Mathematics — 1961– 2. Mathematics — Programmed instruction. I. Calus, Irene M., joint author. II. Fairley, J. Alex, joint author. III. Title. IV. Series.
QA37.2.B34 510'.7'7 72–14009
ISBN 0–471–04373–7 (v. 1) rev MARC

Bajpai, Avi C
Numerical methods for engineers and scientists : a students' course book / [by] A. C. Bajpai, I. M. Calus, J. A. Fairley. — London : Taylor and Francis, 1975.
xii, 380 p. : ill. ; 25 cm. GB76-01717
Bibliography: p. 377.
Includes index.
ISBN 0-85066-097-1 : £6.75
1. Numerical analysis—Programmed instruction. 2. Engineering mathematics—Programmed instruction. 3. Science—Methodology—Programmed instruction. I. Calus, Irene M., joint author. II. Fairley, J. Alex., joint author. III. Title.
QA297.B32 511'.7 77-363864
77 MARC

Bajpai, Avi C., ed.
see Programmed Learning Conference, Loughborough, Eng., 1970. The proceedings. [London] Pitman [1970]

Bajpai, K D
Archaeology in Uttar Pradesh, by K. D. Bajpai. 2d ed. Lucknow, Dept. of Education, Uttar Pradesh, 1957.
9 p. 21 plates. 24 cm.
1. Uttar Pradesh, India—Antiquities. I. Title.
DS485.U63B34 1957 915.4'2'03 73–217886 MARC

Bajpai, K D
Indian numismatic studies / K. D. Bajpai. — New Delhi : Abhinav Publications, 1976.
x, 188 p., [5] leaves of plates : ill. ; 23 cm.
"Select bibliography on ancient Indian coins": [175]-181.
Includes index.
Rs65.00 ($13.00 U.S.)
1. Numismatics—India. I. Title.
CJ1391.B27 737'.0954 76-902609
77 MARC

Bajpai, K D
(Madhyapradeśa kā purātattva)
मध्यप्रदेश का पुरातत्त्व / लेखक कृष्णदत्त वाजपेयी. — [भोपाल] : संचालनालय पुरातत्त्व एवं संग्रहालय विभाग, मध्यप्रदेश, 1970.
35 p., [36] leaves of plates : ill., map : 25 cm.
In Hindi.

1. Madhya Pradesh—Antiquities. I. Title

DS485.C3B34 75–905482

Bajpai, K.D.
see Studies in history. Delhi, Research [Publications in Social Sciences, 1972]

Bajpai, Lakshmi Chandra, 1916- ed.
see Vājapeyī abhinandan grantha. [1969]

Bajpai, Om Prakash, 1928-
Life insurance finance in India / O. P. Bajpai. — 1st ed. — Varanasi : Vishwavidyalaya Prakashan, 1975.
10, 316 p. ; 22 cm.
Rs40.00
1. Insurance, Life—India—Finance. I. Title.
HG9164.B34 368.3'2'00954 75-903032
75 MARC

Bajpai, Purshottam, 1926–
(Hindī-kathā-sāhitya para Soviyata-krānti kā prabhāva)
हिन्दी-कथा-साहित्य पर सोवियत-क्रान्ति का प्रभाव / पुरूषोत्तम वाजपेयी. — 1. संस्करण. — कानपुर : पुस्तक संस्थान, 1976.
384 p., [7] leaves of plates : ill. ; 23 cm.
In Hindi.
"कानपुर विश्वविद्यालय की पी-एच. डी. उपाधि के लिए स्वीकृत."
Bibliography: p. [378]-384.
Rs50.00
1. Hindi fiction—20th century—History and criticism. 2. Russia—History—Revolution, 1917-1921—Influence on literature. I. Title.
PK2042.B327 76–901445

Bajpeyi, Ashok Kumar, 1941- ed.
see Pahacāna. [1971]

Bajpeyi, Ashok Kumar, 1941- ed.
see Pahacāna. [1972]

Bajpeyi, Ashok Kumar, 1941- ed.
see Pahacāna. [1973]

Bajpeyi, Ashok Kumar, 1941-
see Pahacāna. [1975]

Bajpeyi, Nand Dulare, 1906–1967, comp.
[Hindī kī śreshṭha kahāniyāṁ]
हिन्दी की श्रेष्ठ कहानियाँ. संग्रहकर्ता नन्ददुलारे वाजपेयी. [15. संस्करण] वाराणसी, विद्या-मंदिर [1968]
200 p. 19 cm. Rs3.00
In Hindi.
CONTENTS: अंतःपुर का आरंभ. लेखक रायकृष्णदास.—दुखवा मैं कासे कहूँ मोरी सजनी. लेखक चतुरसेन शास्त्री.—उसने कहा था. लेखक चन्द्रधर शर्मा गुलेरी.—पुरस्कार. लेखक जयशंकर 'प्रसाद.'—पर्यवसान. लेखक चंडीप्रसाद 'हृदयेश.'—विधवा. लेखक ज्वालादत्त शर्मा.—फातिहा. लेखक प्रेमचन्द.—कवि की स्त्री. लेखक सुदर्शन.—ताई. लेखक विश्वम्भरनाथ शर्मा 'कौशिक.'—नन्दिनी. लेखक पदुमलाल पुन्नालाल बख्शी.—मुंडमाल. लेखक शिवपूजन सहाय.—विधाता. लेखक विनोदशंकर व्यास.—उसकी माँ. लेखक बेचन शर्मा 'उग्र.'

1. Short stories, Hindi. I. Title.

PK2077.B32 1968 75–925116

Bajpeyi, Nand Dulare, 1906–1967.
(Kavi Sumitrānandana Panta)
कवि सुमित्रानंदन पंत / नन्ददुलारे वाजपेयी ; प्रस्तोता शिवकुमार मिश्र. — 1. संस्करण. — नई दिल्ली : मैकमिलन कंपनी आफ इंडिया, 1976.
104 p. : 22 cm.
In Hindi.
Includes bibliographical references and index.
Rs15.00

1. Pant, Sumitra Nandan, 1900- —Criticism and interpretation. I. Title.

PK2098.P32Z556 1976 76–904769

Bajpeyi, Nand Dulare, 1906–1967.
(Nayā sāhitya : naye praśna)
नया साहित्य : नये प्रश्न / नन्ददुलारे बाजपेयी. — बनारस : विद्यामंदिर, [1955]
29, 266 p. ; 23 cm.
In Hindi.

1. Hindi literature—20th century—History and criticism. I. Title.

PK2038.B32 1955 75–984431

Bajra, Nāti
see
Nāti Bajra.

Bajrācārya, Ādibajra.
मूलँपुया तँसा व निह्मचायामां [sic. ललितपुर, नेपाल] नेपा सम्बत् 1070 [1950 or 1]
7, 39, 3 p. 18 cm. Rs1.40
In Newari.
CONTENTS.—आ. बज्राचार्य कृत मूलँपुया तँसा.—स. जोशी कृत निम्हमचायामां (स्वपुबाखँ).

1. Newari language—Grammar. I. Joshi, Satya Mohan, 1920– II. Title.
Title romanized: Mūlampuyā tamsa va nimhamacāyāmāṃ.

PL3801.N51B3 S A 68–8578
PL 480 : N–452

Bajrācārya, Āśakāzī
see
Bajracharya, Asha Kazi, 1909-

Bajrācārya, Jogamuni, tr.
see Prajnaparamitas. Śatasāhasrikā. Newari. (Prajñāpāramitā) [1968-

Bajrācārya, Mīnabahādura.
चिठी-चपेटा. संपादक मीनबहादुर बज्राचार्य. अमलेखगंज [नेपाल] बुद्धिबहादुर घर्ती, २०२२ [1965/66]
104 p. 18 cm. Re1
In Nepali.

I. Title.
Title romanized: Ciṭhī-capeṭā.

AC125.N37B3 S A 68–9570
PL 480 : N–168

Bajrācārya, Ratnabahādura.
(Bauddha prathama śikshā)
बौद्ध प्रथम शिक्षा. लेखक तथा अनुबादक बज्राचार्य पं. रत्नबहादुर. 1. संस्करण. यल, गुणरत्न शाक्य, नेपाल सम्बत् 1092 [1971 or 2]
2, 6, 132 p. 23 cm. Rs4.00
In Newari; includes quotations in Sanskrit.

1. Mahayana Buddhism—Doctrines. 2. Buddha and Buddhism—Nepal. I. Title.

BQ7405.B34 74–901748

Bajrācārya, Ratnabahādura.
(Ye dharmā gāthāyā artha sahitaṃ)
ये धर्मा गाथाया अर्थ सहितं / लेखक बज्राचार्य पं. रत्नबहादुर. — 1. संस्करण. — यल : गु. शाक्य, नेपाल सम्बत्, 1093 [1972 or 1973]
3, 23 p., [2] leaves of plates : ill. ; 18 cm.
In Newari.
Re0.75

1. Buddhist doctrines. I. Title.

BQ4138.N48B34 75–906833

Bajracharya, Asha Kazi, 1909–
(Sañnhūguṭhi yā mahimā)
सँन्हूगुठि या महिमा : सुरदत्त कथा; नेपाले करूणामय सेवा सँन्हुगुठि देकावंगु खँ, नेपाल भाषा बंशाबली मणिरत्न माला या छगु अंश. चोया पिकाम्ह आशाकाजी (गणेशराज) बज्राचार्य. यल:, 2029 [1972]
7, 93 p. illus. 19 cm. Rs3.00
Running title: सुरदत्त कथा.
In Newari.

1. Avalokiteśvara—Cultus—Nepal. I. Title. II. Title: Suradatta kathā.

BQ4710.A8B34 73–902393

Bajracharya, Mana Bajra
see
Vajrācārya, Manavajra.

Bajracharya, Manik Lal.
Birendra, the king with a difference / Manik Lal Bajracharya. — 1st ed. — Kathmandu : Eastern Trading & Investment Co., 1974.
151, p., [8] leaves of plates : ill. ; 22 cm.
"An E.T.I. publication."
Rs30.00 ($3.00 U.S.)
1. Birendra Bir Bikram Shah Deva, Maharajadhiraja of Nepal, 1946– I. Title.
DS495.52.B57B34 954.9'6'00994 75–902225
76 MARC

Bajracharya, Manik Lal.
A catalogue on Nepal. [1st ed.] Kathmandu, Eastern Trading and Investment Co. [1973]
281 p. illus. (part col.) 19 cm. Rs20.00
"An ETI publication."
1. Nepal—Description and travel—Guide-books. I. Title.
DS493.3.B34 915.49'604 73–902415
MARC

Bajracharya, Manik Lal.
Nepal with a new promise [by] Manik Lal. [1st ed. New Delhi, Nepal Trading Corp., 1967]
ii, 103 p. 21 cm. 4.00
1. Nepal—Politics and government. 2. Panchayat—Nepal. I. Title.
JQ1825.N4B34 320.9'549'6 S A 68–14513
MARC
rev PL 480 : N–600

Bajracharya, Purna Harsha. Arts, crafts, sculpture, and temples in Nepal. 1973.
see Nepal : history, arts, crafts, and temples. Kathmandu : Nepal National Commission for UNESCO, 1973.

Bajsić, Vjekoslav.
Na rubovima crkve i civilizacije. Zagreb, "Kršćanska sadašnjost," 1972.
362 p. 20 cm. (Polazišta, 8–9) 60.00Din Yu 73–856
Includes bibliographical references.
1. Philosophy and religion. 2. Christianity—Philosophy. 3. Communism and religion. I. Title.
B56.B26 73–970838

Bajsić, Vjekoslav
see Les Religions en Yougoslavie. Zagreb, Binoza, 1971.

Bājsonghor'sches Manuskript des Schāhnāmeh
see
Bāysonghori manuscript of the Shāhnāmeh.

Bajt, Aleksander.
Osnovi ekonomike. Zagreb, "Informator," 1967.
xv, 406, [2] p. diagrs. 24 cm. (Ekonomska biblioteka, 4 kolo, br. 1–2) 50.00Din Yu 67–6540
1. Economics. I. Title.
HB179.S4B3 68–105286
rev

Bajt, Aleksander.
Privredni rast u Jugoslaviji i drugim socijalističkim zemljama : 1950-1970 / [autor Aleksander Bajt]. — Ljubljana : Ekonomski inštitut pravne fakultete, 1974.
68, [2] p. : ill. ; 23 cm. Yu75-7926
Bibliography: p. [69]-[70]
1. Europe, Eastern—Economic conditions. I. Title.
HC244.B34 77-462962
77 MARC

Bajt, Aleksander.
Uvod v politično ekonomijo. V Ljubljani, Cankarjeva Založba, 1965.
657 p. diagrs., tables (part. fold.)
1. Economics. I. Title.
MiU NUC74-128780

Bajtelsmit, John.
see Andrulis, Richard S. Adult assessment . . . Springfield, Ill., Thomas, 1977.

Baju Surianingrat
see
Surianingrat, Bayu.

Bājubayr, ʿAbd al-Raḥīm ʿAbd al-Qādir
see
Bā Jubayr, ʿAbd al-Raḥīm ʿAbd al-Qādir.

Bājūdah, Ḥasan Muḥammad
see
Bā Jūdah, Ḥasan Muḥammad.

Bajuk, Andres.
A model of the distribution of income from technological change in agriculture. -- [Berkeley] 1975.
xi, 199 leaves.
Thesis (Ph. D.)--University of California.
Bibliography: leaves 195-199.
CU NUC77-93357

Baʻjūr, Maḥmūd, 1937–
اهوال الطبيعة، من عهد ماقبل التاريخ حتى القرن الخامس عشر الميلادي، مع فصل للاستدراكات والمتفرقات. [بيروت؟
1970–]
v. 22 cm.
At head of title: محمود بعجور يقدم
Bibliography : v. 1, p. 166–167.
1. Disasters. I. Title.
Title romanized : Ahwāl al-ṭabīʻah.
D24.B25 74–217009

Bajur, Indonesia (Agam)
For works by this jurisdiction issued after the change of orthography in 1972 see
Bayur, Indonesia (Agam)
75–588709

al-Bajuri, Ibrahim ibn Muhammad, 1783 or 4-1860.
Hashiyat al-Bajuri 'alá Sharh al-Sanusi. 1902
see al-Qabbani, Mustafá, comp. (Hadhihi al-urjuzah fi 'ilm al-tawhid) 1320 [1902]

al-Bājūrī, Ibrāhīm ibn Muḥammad, 1783 or 4–1860.
[Ḥāshiyat al-Shaykh Ibrāhīm al-Bījūrī]
حاشية الشيخ ابراهيم البيجورى على شرح ابن قاسم الغزى على متن الشيخ ابى شجاع فى مذهب الامام الشافعى. [مصر، مطبعة وادى النيل المصرية، 1298 i. e. 1881]
2 v. 27 cm.
Includes texts of Ibn Qāsim al-Ghazzī's فتح القريب المجيب and Abū Shujāʻ al-Iṣfahānī's غاية الاختصار
1. Islamic law. 2. Shafiites. 3. Ibn Qāsim al-Ghazzī, Muḥammad, d. 1512. Fatḥ al-qarīb al-mujīb. I. Ibn Qāsim al-Ghazzī, Muḥammad, d. 1512. Fatḥ al-qarīb al-mujīb. 1881. II. Abū Shujāʻ al-Iṣfahānī, Aḥmad ibn al-Ḥusayn, b. ca. 1042. Ghāyat al-ikhtiṣār. 1881. III. Title. IV. Title: Fatḥ al-qarīb al-mujīb. V. Title: Ghāyat al-ikhtiṣār.
72–225633

al-Bājūrī, Ibrāhīm ibn Muḥammad, 1783 or 4–1860.
(Ḥāshiyat Ibrāhīm al-Bayjūrī ʻalá matn al-Sanūsīyah)
حاشية ابراهيم البيجورى على متن السنوسية. وبهامشها تقرير الشمس الانبابى مقابلا على خطه. [القاهرة، المطبعة الوهبيه، 1330 i. e. 1883]
80 p. 24 cm.
Caption title.
Includes text of al-Sanūsī's Umm al-barāhīn in the margin.
1. al-Sanūsī, Muḥammad ibn Yūsuf, ca. 1427–ca. 1490. Umm al-barāhīn. 2. Islamic theology — Addresses, essays, lectures. I. al-Sanūsī, Muḥammad ibn Yūsuf, ca. 1427–ca. 1490. Umm al-barāhīn. 1883. II. al-Anbābī, Muḥammad ibn Muḥammad, d. 1896. III. Title.
BP165.5.S33B34 1883 73–221225

al-Bājūrī, Ibrāhīm ibn Muḥammad, 1783 or 4–1860.
[Taḥqīq al-maqām]
حاشية العالم العلامة شيخ الاسلام الشيخ ابراهيم البيجورى المسماة بتحقيق المقام على كفاية العوام فى علم الكلام لشيخه الشيخ محمد الفضالى ... وبالهامش المتن المذكور. — الطبعة 1. — [القاهرة] : المطبعة العثمانية، [1888] 1306.
81, 1 p. ; 27 cm.

1. al-Faḍālī, Muḥammad ibn al-Shāfiʻī, d. 1821? Kifāyat al-ʻawāmm fī ʻilm al-kalām. 2. Islamic theology. I. al-Faḍālī, Muḥammad ibn al-Shāfiʻī, d. 1821? Kifāyat al-ʻawāmm fī ʻilm al-kalām. 1888. II. Title: Hāshiyat al-ālim al-ʻallāmah Shaykh al-Islām al-Shaykh Ibrāhīm al-Bayjūrī ... III. Title: Tahqīq al-maqām ʻalá Kifāyat al-ʻawāmm fī ʻilm al-kalām.
Title romanized : Hāshiyat al-ʻālim al-ʻallāmah Shaykh al-Islām al-Shaykh Ibrāhīm al-Bayjūrī al-musammāh bi-Taḥqīq al-maqām.
BP166.B26 1888 76–970433

al-Bajuri, Ibrahim ibn Muhammad, 1783 or 4-1860.
Tuhfat al-murid 'alá Jawharat al-tawhid. 1902
see al-Qabbani, Mustafá, comp. (Hadhihi al-urjuzah fi 'ilm al-tawhid) 1320 [1902]

Bajusz, Eörs, ed.
see Functional morphology of the heart. Basel, New York, S. Karger, 1971.

Bajusz, Eörs, ed.
see International Symposium on Cardiomyopathies, Tiervlei, South Africa, 1971. Cardiomyopathies. Baltimore, University Park Press [1973]

Bajusz, Eörs, ed.
see An Introduction to experimental pathology. Chicago, Year Book Medical Publishers [1966]

Bajusz, Eörs, ed.
see Investigative techniques. Chicago, Year Book Medical Publishers, 1967.

Bajusz, Eörs, ed.
see Nutritional pathobiology. Basel, New York, S. Karger, 1972.

Bajusz, Eörs, ed.
see Ultrastructural, histopathologic and chemical approaches. Chicago, Year Book Medical Publishers, 1967.

Bajuvaria, Katholisch-Akademische Verbindung
see
Katholisch-Akademische Verbindung Bajuvaria.

Bājvah, Caudhrī Muḥammad Shafī
see
Bajwa, Chaudhri Muhammad Shafi, 1904-

Bājvah, Nabī Aḥmad, comp.
(Ḥāfiẓ o Ghālib)
حافظ و غالب / تاليف چودهری نبی احمد باجوه. — لاهور ؛ 1974.
16, 304 p. ; 22 cm.
Rs20.00

1. Persian poetry. I. Hāfiz, 14th cent. II. Ghālib, 1796?–1869. III. Title.

PK6434.B3 74–930367

Bajwa, Chaudhri Muhammad Shafi, 1904–
(Jadīd rekrūṭ kors)
جدید ریکروٹ کورس / نظر ثانی, چوہدری محمد شفیع باجوہ. — 15. ایڈیشن. — لاہور : احسان‌الحق قریشی, 1974.
2, 2, 288 p. : ill. ; 25 cm.
''جسکو صاحب انسپکٹر جنرل پولیس, مغربی پاکستان, نے بروئے چھٹی نمبر ۱۹۲۶, گزٹ مورخہ ۲ نومبر ۱۹۵۹ء. ریکروٹوں کے لئے منظور فرمایا اور بروئے چھٹی نمبر ایس. /۱۹۳۶-۳۷/۷۰, مورخہ ۲۸ ستمبر ۱۹۷۰ء. اس کی تجدید کی.''
In Urdu.
Rs7.50
1. Police—Recruiting. 2. Police—Pakistan. I. Title.
HV7810.5.A2B34 75–938534

Bajwa, Fauja Singh.
Eminent freedom fighters of Punjab ₍by₎ Fauja Singh. ₍1st ser.₎ Patiala, Punjabi University, Dept. of Punjab Historical Studies ₍1972₎
xvi, 246 p. illus. 22 cm. Rs11.00
Includes bibliographical references.
1. Punjab—Biography. I. Title.
DS485.P15B34 954'.55'0350922 72-907072
[B] MARC

Bajwa, Fauja Singh.
Guru Tegh Bahadur : martyr and teacher / Fauja Singh, Gurbachan Singh Talib. — 1st ed. — Patiala : Punjabi University, 1975.
xv, 211 p. ; 23 cm.
Includes bibliographical references and index.
Rs8.50
1. Tegh Bahadur, 9th guru of the Sikhs, 1621-1675. 2. Sikh gurus—Biography. I. Talib, Gurbachan Singh, 1911- joint author. II. Title.
BL2017.9.T4B34 294.6'6'1 76-901732
76 MARC

Bajwa, Fauja Singh.
Sirhind through the ages / edited by Fauja Singh. — Patiala : Dept. of Punjab Historical Studies, Punjabi University, 1972.
x, 154 p., ₍20₎ leaves of plates : ill. ; 23 cm.
Includes bibliographical references.
Rs7.75
1. Sirhind, India—History—Addresses, essays, lectures. I. Title.
DS486.S55B34 954'.55 74-903713
75 MARC

Bajwa, Fauja Singh.
(Srī Gurū Tegha Bahādura)
ਸ੍ਰੀ ਗੁਰੂ ਤੇਗ ਬਹਾਦੁਰ : ਜੀਵਨ ਤੇ ਰਚਨਾ / ਫ਼ੌਜਾ ਸਿੰਘ, ਤਾਰਨ ਸਿੰਘ. — ਪਟਿਆਲਾ : ਪੰਜਾਬੀ ਯੂਨੀਵਰਸਿਟੀ, 1976.
v, 185 p. ; 23 cm.
In Panjabi.
Includes quotations from Guru Tegh Bahadur's works.
Includes bibliographies and index.
Rs15.00
1. Tegh Bahadur, 9th Guru of the Sikhs, 1621-1675. 2. Sikh gurus—Biography. I. Tegh Bahadur, 9th Guru of the Sikhs, 1621-1675. II. Taran Singh, 1922- III. Title.
BL2017.9.T4B35 76-902781

Bajwa, Fauja Singh, ed.
see History of the Punjab. Patiala, Punjabi University ₍19

Bajwa, Fauja Singh, ed.
see Kālī Ra'e, Ra'e. ₍Sair-i Panjab. Panjabi₎ Panjaba di saira. ₍1971₎

Bajwa, Fauja Singh
see Pañjābī wīra paramparā dā wikāsa. ₍1966-

Bajwa, Fauja Singh, ed.
see Punjabi University. Dept. of History and Punjab Historical Studies. Who's who: Punjab freedom fighters. Patiala [1972-

Bajwa, Fauja Singh
see Sujān Rā'e Bhandārī, fl. 1680-1700. [Khulāsat al-tavārīkh. Panjabi] Khulāsatuta tawārīkha. 1972.

Bajwa, Fauja Singh
see Travels of Guru Gobind Singh. Patiala ₍India₎ Punjabi University, 1968.

Bajwa, Fauja Singh
see University atlas... Patiala, Punjabi University ₍1968₎

Bajwa, Gurdev Singh.
A theoretical and experimental analysis of an eighteen stage radio-frequency mass spectrometer. Submitted by G. L. Weissler. ₍Los Angeles, University of Southern California₎ 1962.
iv, 77 l. illus. 28 cm.
Technical report.
Prepared for the U. S. Office of Naval Research.
Contract No.: Nonr 228(11)
1. Spectrometer.
CLSU NUC74-24790

Bajwa, Ijaz Ahmad.
The Legal practitioners and bar councils act : with rules, amended up-to-date, with commentary and case-law / by Ijaz Ahmad Bajwa. — Lahore : Mansoor Book House, 1974.
iv, 82 p. ; 23 cm.
Rs7.00
1. Lawyers—Pakistan. 2. Bar associations—Pakistan. I. Pakistan. Laws, statutes, etc. Legal practitioners and bar councils act, 1973. 1974. II. Title.
340'.06'25491 74-930459
MARC

Bajwa, Ijaz Ahmad.
see Desai, Trikamlal Ranchhodlal. The Specific relief act (I of 1877) Lahore, Mansoor Book House, ₍1975₎

Bajwa, M A
Preliminary evaluation of air cargo economic & operating efficiencies. [Principal author: M. A. Bajwa. Ottawa] 1975.
85 p. ill. (Canada. Transport Commission. Systems Analysis and Research Data Base Branch. Report, 165.
Includes bibliography.
CaOTP NUC77-93356

Bajwa, Ranjit Singh, 1930-
An inquiry into the practicality of a particular modern American educational method in Indian primary and secondary schools. Detroit, Mich., 1963.
289 p.
Thesis (Ph.D.)—Wayne State University.
Microfilm (positive) of typescript. Ann Arbor, Mich., University Microfilms, 1963. 1 reel.
KMK NUC73-84171

Bajza, Jozef Ignác, 1755–1836.
Príhody a skúsenosti mladíka Reného / Jozef Ignác Bajza ; ₍transformoval a vysvetl. sprac. Jozef R. Nižnanský ; úvodnú štúdiu a chronológiu aut. života a diela nap. Ján Tibenský ; graf. upr., prebal a väzbu navrhol Ivan J. Kovačevič₎. — 1. vyd. — Bratislava : Tatran, 1976.
365 p. ; 21 cm. — (Zlatý fond slovenskej literatúry ; zv. 24)
CzS 76
First published in 1783–1785.
Kčs26.00
I. Nižnanský, Jozef. II. Title.
PG5437.B3P7 1976 77-503602

Bajza, József, 1804–1858.
Bajza József munkái: költemények, tanulmányok. Négyesi László bevezetésével. ₍Budapest₎ A Kisfaludi-Társaság megbízásából kiadja a Franklin-Társulat ₍19—₎
220 p. port. 19 cm. (Élő könyvek, magyar klasszikusok, 9. köt.)
I. Series.
PH3213.B2A6 1900z 68-46312

Bajza, K
(Rentgenotekhnika)
Рентгенотехника. ₍Перевод с перер. и доп. венгерского изд. К. Бицо₎. Будапешт, Akadémiai Kiadó, 1973.
325 p. illus. 25 cm. 4.00rub
At head of title: К. Байза, Л. Хентер, Ш. Холбок.
Translation of Röntgentechnika.
Bibliography: p. 320.
1. Radiography. I. Henter, L., joint author. II. Holbok, S., joint author. III. Title.
RC78.B2917 73-216233

Bajzák, Dénes.
Detection and appraisal of damage by balsam woolly aphid on Abies balsamea (L.) Mill, by means of aerial photography. [St. John's, Newfoundland, Forest Research Laboratory, Forestry Branch, Canada Dept. of Forestry and Rural Development, 1967]
viii, 142 l. illus., map, plates. (Forest Research Laboratory, St. John's, Newfoundland. Internal report N-3)
Thesis—Syracuse University.
Vita.
Bibliography: leaves 131-134.
1. Aerial photography in forestry. 2. Balsam woolly aphid. 3. Balsam fir—Diseases and pests. I. Title. II. Series: Canada. Forest Research Laboratory, St. John's. Internal report N-3.
CU NUC76-15932

Bak, Arnošt.
Hrdí v boji i v mierovej práci. Fot. APN. Úvodom. Karol Šavel. 1. vyd. Bratislava, n. a t. Pravda, 1974.
242, ₍4₎ p. ₍16₎ p. of plates. 21 cm. Kčs20.00 CzS 74
1. Russia—Economic conditions—1965- I. Title.
HC336.23.B34 74-323816

Bak, Franciszek, ed.
see Wybrane zagadnienia filozofii... Gliwice, 1971.

Bąk, Franciszek, ed.
see Wybrane zagadnienia filozofii... Gliwice, 1973.

Bąk, Franciszek
see Wybrane zagadnienia filozofii. Wyd. 3. Gliwice: Politechnika Śląska im. W. Pstrowskiego, 1975.

Bak, G.G.M.
see Automatisering en belastingheffing. Deventer: Kluwer, 1975.

Bak, János M
Guide to reference materials in medieval history : based on the holdings of the libraries of the University of British Columbia, with a selection of primary sources in English translation / compiled by Janos M. Bak. — 2d., partially rev. ed. — Vancouver : University of British Columbia Library, 1975.
vi, 54 p. : ill. ; 22 cm. — (Reference guide - University of British Columbia Library ; no. 54) C***
Includes indexes.
1. Middle Ages—History—Bibliography—Catalogs. 2. British Columbia. University. Library. I. Title. II. Series: British Columbia. University. Library. Reference guide - University of British Columbia Library ; no. 54.
Z6203.B32 1975 016.9401 75-329258
₍D117₎ 75 MARC

Bak, János M
Guide to reference materials in medieval history in the libraries of the University of British Columbia with a selection of primary sources in English translation, compiled by Janos M. Bak, with the cooperation of the Humanities Division. Vancouver, University of British Columbia Library, 1971.
vi, 54 p. illus. 23 cm. (Reference publication no. 36)
1. Middle Ages—History—Bibliography—Catalogs. I. Title. II. Series: British Columbia. University. Library. Reference publication, no. 36.
Z883.V35R4 no. 36 082 s 72-179223
₍Z6203₎ 72₍r77₎rev MARC

Bak, Janos M
Königtum und Stände in Ungarn im 14.–16. Jahrhundert, von Janos M. Bak. Wiesbaden, F. Steiner, 1973.
195 p. 24 cm. (Quellen und Studien zur Geschichte des östlichen Europa, Bd. 6) GFR***
"Anhang I" chiefly in Latin.
Includes bibliographical references.
1. Hungary—History—1000-1683. 2. Hungary—Nobility. 3. Verbőczy, István, d. 1541 or 2. I. Title. II. Series.
DB930.B34 73-339241

Bak, János M
Magyarország könyvkiadása, 1945-1969; statisztikai alapadatok. Budapest, Magyar Könyvkiadók és Könyvterjesztők Egyesülése, 1970.
202 p. 20 cm.
1. Publishers and publishing—Hungary—Stat. I. Title.
CtY NUC73-35522

Bak, Janos M.
see The German peasant war of 1525. London, F. Cass, 1976.

Bak, József.
A szövetkezetek kollektív (tagsági) vezetésének egyes ujabb problémái / Bak József. — Budapest : Szövetkezeti Kutató Intézet, 1974.
141 p. : 29 cm. — (Közlemények - Szövetkezeti Kutató Intézet ; 94)
Includes bibliographical references.
1. Cooperative societies—Hungary—Management. I. Title.
HD3492.5.A5B34 76-522390

Bąk, Krystyna, ed.
see Maly słownik pisarzy zachodnio-słowiańskich i południowo-slowiańskich. Warszawa, Wiedza Powszechna, 1973.

Bak, Kun Bae.
(Kathāratnākaraḥ)
कथारत्नाकरः. The Katharatnakara. प्रणेता बाक् कन्बे. ₍प्रथमावृतिः₎ दिल्ली, नेशनल पब्लिशिंग हाउस ₍1970–
v. 23 cm. Rs15.00 (v. 1)
In Sanskrit; pref. in English.
I. Title.
PK3799.B29K3 79-910727

Bak, Oskar
see Back, Oskar.

Bak, Ove, comp.
Eskimoiske eventyr og sagn / red. af Ove Bak ; billedred. Jens Kreutzmann ; træsnit af Aron fra Kangeq₁. — ₍København₎ : Nordiske landes bogforlag : i kommission Gad, 1974.
210 p. : ill. ; 28 cm. D 74-49
Selections from the 1866-71 ed. of Eskimoiske eventyr og sagn by H. J. Rink, published in Copenhagen.
Bibliography : p. 206.
ISBN 87-12-19885-4 : kr199.50
1. Eskimos—Greenland. 2. Eskimos—Greenland—Legends. I. Rink, Hinrich Johannes, 1819-1893. Eskimoiske eventyr og sagn. II. Aron fra Kangeq, 1822-1869, ill. III. Title.
E99.E7B12 75-407745

Bak, Ove.
Johannes Christian Hansen / af Ove Bak ; ₍oversættelse, Aqissiaq Møller, Jørgen Pjetturssen₎. — ₍København₎ : Ministeriet for Grønland ; ₍Godthåb : eksp., Det Grønlandske Forlag₎, 1976.
47 p. : ill. ; 24 cm. — (Foregangsmænd i Grønland) D77-3
Danish and Eskimo.
ISBN 8774801023 : kr23.00
1. Hansen, Johannes, 1837-1911. 2. Greenland—Discovery and exploration. 3. Explorers—Greenland—Biography. I. Title.
G762.H36B34 77-480877
77 MARC

Bak, Ove.
Træk af Julianehåb syddistrikts historie. 1774-1830. Sydprøven, Forfatteren, 1968-
v. 31 cm. D 68
Issued in parts.
Includes bibliographical references.
1. Julianehaab, Greenland (District)—History—Sources. I. Title.
G765.J8B33 73-344667

Bak, Perla
see Buck, Pearl Sydenstricker, 1892-1973.

Bak, Rohak, 1933-
Hydrothermalsynthese und untersuchung von aquoxiden und oxiden des niederwertigen vanadins. Göttingen, 1972.
68, [1] p. illus. 21 cm.
Thesis (Ph. D.)—Georg-August-Universitat, Göttingen.
Bibliography: p. 65-68.
1. Vanadium—Analysis. 2. Vanadium—Metallurgy. 3. Vanadium-oxide. I. Title.
WyU NUC76-69657

Bak, Samuel.
Bak : oils and drawings, 1974-1975 : October -November 1975. -- New York : Aberbach Fine Art, [1975?]
[46] p. : ill.
1. Bak, Samuel. I. Aberbach Fine Art. II. Title.
ViBlbV NUC77-94133

Bak, Samuel.
Bak : paintings of the last decade. Artistic development ; The metaphysical works / Paul T. Nagano. Conversation with the artist / A. Kaufman. — 2d ed. — New York : Aberbach Fine Art, 1976.
156, ₍5₎ p. : ill. (some col.) ; 29 cm.
Bibliography: p. ₍157₎-₍158₎
1. Bak, Samuel. 2. Painters—Israel—Interviews.
ND979.B27A23 759.95694 77-358850
77 MARC

Bak, Si-in
see
Pak, Si-in.

Bąk, Stanisław.
Mowa polska na Śląsku / Stanisław Bąk. — Wrocław : Zakład Narodowy im. Ossolińskich, 1974.
224 p., ₍2₎ fold. leaves : ill. ; 24 cm.
At head of title: Opolskie Towarzystwo Przyjaciół Nauk. Wydział II Języka i Literatury.
Part of illustrative matter in pocket.
Bibliography : p. ₍163₎-165.
zł50.00
1. Polish language—Dialects—Silesia. I. Title.
PG6780.B26 75-403718

Bak, Tim
see Buck, Tim.

Bak, V. D.
see ZHdanov. [1970]

Bak, Władysław
see
Edary, Zeew.

Bak, Wojciech.
O Bogu-Człowieku i apostołach. [Wyd. 1.] Warszawa, Instytut Wydawn. Pax, 1971.
230 p.
1. Apostles. 2. Jesus Christ.
MH NUC74-127395

Bąk, Wojciech.
Wiersze wybrane / Wojciech Bąk ; wyboru, dokonał i przedm. opatrzył Stefan Jończyk. — Wyd. 1. — Warszawa : Pax, 1974.
431 p., ₍1₎ leaf of plates : port. ; 21 cm.
zł50.00
PG7158.B327A17 1974 75-406020

Bak, Wojciech
see Rzecz poetycka. Inspiracje. ₍Wyd. 1.₎ Łodź, Wydawn. Łódzkie, 1967.

Bak, Yoram
see
Bek, Yoram.

Bak, Zbigniew.
Czerwone tarcze Jarosława Iwasziewicza. [Wyd. 1.] Warszawa, Państw. Zakł. Wydawn. Szkolnych, 1973.
99 p. illus. (Biblioteka analiz literackich, 40)
1. Iwaszkiewicz, Jarosław, 1894- Czerwone tarcze.
MH NUC76-69716

Bak Nielsen, Alice
see Litteratur om kvindens stilling i det kapitalistisk samfund : 1968-1974. [Ålborg] : Danmarks Biblioteksskole/Ålborg, 1975.

Baka, Abdul.
Salome. Dar es Salaam, Tanzania Pub. House, 1972.
iv, 36 p. 22 cm.
I. Title.
PL8704.B34S2 73-983601

Baka, László Béla.
Gondolatok a magyar ujjáépités problémáihoz. 〈A magyar kispolgári Szövetség celkitüzései.〉 2. Surlódsaink a szlávokkal. (Oberwart, Baka, 1968.)
119 p. 21 cm. Au 68-22-225
1. Hungary—Politics and government—1945- 2. Magyar Bizottsáig. 3. Hungarians in foreign countries. I. Title. II. Title: Surlódásaink a szlávokkal.
DB956.B353 73-321470

Baka, Władysław.
500 (i. e. Pięćset) zagadek ekonomicznych. ₍Wyd. 1.₎. Warszawa, Wiedza Powszechna, 1971.
243 p. illus. 19 cm. zł15.00
At head of title: Władysław Baka, Kazimierz Piesowicz.
1. Economics—Miscellanea. 2. Economic history. 3. Poland—Economic conditions—1945- I. Piesowicz, Kazimierz, joint author. II. Title.
HB179.P7B34 72-225741

Baka, Władysław
see Planowanie gospodarki narodowej. Warszawa : Państwowe Wydawn. Ekonomiczne, 1975.

Bakács, István
see Hungary. Országos Levéltár. Kisebb testületi, egyesületi és intézményi fondok ... Budapest: Muvelodésügyi Minisztérium Levéltári Igazgatósága megbizásából, 1970.

Bakács, Tibor.
Az Országos Közegészségügyi Intézet működése az 1972. évben / közli Bakács Tibor. — Budapest : Országos Közegészségügyi Intézet, 1974.
382 p. : ill. ; 25 cm.
Summary in English, German, and Russian.
Includes bibliographies.
1. Hungary. Országos Közegészségügyi Intézet. 2. Public health—Study and teaching—Hungary. I. Hungary. Országos Közegészségügyi Intézet. II. Title.
RA523.H8B29 76-516837

Bakács, Tibor.
Urbanization and human health, by T. Bakács. [Translated by T. Gál] Budapest, Akadémiai Kíado, 1972.
167 p. illus., maps.
1. Environmental health. 2. Urbanization. 3. Pollutaion. I. Title.
UU NUC76-69323

Bakacsy, Helga.
Vorschulerziehung in einem Innsbrucker Kindergarten / Helga Bakacsy. — Wien : Ketterl, ₍1975₎
79 p. : graphs ; 21 cm. — (Beiträge zur pädagogischen Psychologie ; Heft 434-438) Au75-22-208
A revision of the author's thesis, Innsbruck, 1973.
Bibliography: p. 71-72.
S37.50
1. Education, Preschool—Austria—Innsbruck. I. Title. II. Series.
LB1140.2.B23 1975 76-457798
*76 MARC

Bakaev, Aleksandr Aleksandrovich.
Algorithmische Modellierung ökonomischer Probleme / A. A. Bakajew, N. I. Kostina, N. W. Jarowizki : in deutscher Sprache hrsg. von Werner Dück ; ₍deutsche Übersetzung, J. A. Müller₎. — Berlin : Akademie-Verlag, 1974.
ix, 191 p. : ill. ; 25 cm. — (Elektronisches Rechnen und Regeln : Sonderband ; 20) GFR***
Translation of Avtomatnye modeli ėkonomicheskikh sistem.
Bibliography : p. ₍187₎-188.
Includes index.
29.50M
1. Economics—Mathematical models. I. Kostina, Nina Ivanovna, joint author. II. I͡Arovit͡skiĭ, Nikolaĭ Vladimirovich, joint author. III. Title. IV. Series.
HB141.B3415 75-552742

Bakaev, Aleksandr Aleksandrovich.
(Ėkonomiko-matematicheskie modeli planirovanii͡a i proektirovanii͡a transportnykh sistem)
Экономико-математические модели планирования и проектирования транспортных систем. Киев, "Техніка," 1973.
220 p. with diagrs. 21 cm. 0.88rub USSR 73
At head of title: А. А. Бакаев.
Bibliography : p. 214-₍218₎
1. Transportation—Mathematical models. I. Title.
HE199.9.B35 74-307615

Bakaev, Cherkes Khudoevich.
(I͡Azyk kurdov SSSR)
Язык курдов СССР. Сравнит. характеристика говоров. Москва, "Наука," 1973.
351 p. 20 cm. 1.38rub USSR 73-VKP
At head of title: Ч. Х. Бакаев.
On leaf preceding t. p.: Академия наук СССР. Институт языкознания.
Includes bibliographical references.
1. Kurdish language—Dialects. I. Title.
PK6909.B36 73-336593

Bakaev, I͡Uriĭ Leonidovich.
(Kont͡sentrat͡sii͡a i spet͡sializat͡sii͡a v kozhgalantereĭnoĭ promyshlennosti)
Концентрация и специализация в кожгалантерейной промышленности / Ю. Л. Бакаев. — Москва : Легкая индустрия, 1975.
123, ₍3₎ p. ; 23 cm. USSR***
Bibliography : p. 123-₍124₎
0.60rub
1. Leather industry and trade—Russia. I. Title.
HD9780.R92B34 76-533414

Bakaev, M
see
Bakoev, Mamadvafo

Bakaev, Nikolaĭ Vasil'evich
see Kalinin, Petr Zakharovich. Partizanskai͡a respublika. 1973.

Bakaeva, Galina Nikolaevna.
("Khovanshchina" M. Musorgskogo)
"Хованщина" М. Мусоргского : историческая народная музыкальная драма / Г. Бакаева. — Киев : Музична Україна, 1976.
205 p. : music ; 17 cm. USSR***
Includes bibliographical references.
0.84rub
1. Musorgskiĭ, Modest Petrovich, 1839-1881. Khovanshchina. I. Title.
ML410.M97B34 77-506880

Bakai, László.
Útközben; hasznos KRESZ és műszaki intelmek ₍írta₎ Bakai László ₍és₎ Hiki János. Budapest, Gondolat, 1969.
227 p. col. illus. 20 cm. 33.00Ft
1. Traffic regulations—Hungary. I. Hiki, János, joint author. II. Title.
74-215607

Bakai, László
see Mindennapos ügyeink. Budapest : Táncsics Könyvkiadó, 1974.

Bakaĭ, Pavel I͡Akovlevich.
(Ispolʹzovanie zakona stoimosti v praktike t͡senoobrazovanii͡a kolkhoznoĭ produkt͡sii)
Использование закона стоимости в практике ценообразования колхозной продукции : 1924–1958 гг. / П. Я. Бакай. — Харьков : Вища школа, Изд-во при Харьк. ун-те, 1975.
135 p. ; 20 cm. USSR 75
Bibliography: p. 131–[134]
0.85rub
1. Collective farms—Russia—History. 2. Cooperative marketing of farm produce — Russia — History. 3. Agricultural prices — History—Russia. I. Title.
S562.R9B26 75–410538

Bakaitis, Helmut.
The incredible mind-blowing trial of Jack Smith [by] Helmut Bakaitis. South Yarra, Vic., Heinemann Educational Australia, 1973.
viii, 56 p. 25 cm. (Australian theatre workshop, 7) $1.80 Aus
I. Title.
PN6120.A5B2187 822 74–189705
ISBN 0–85859–056–5 MARC

Bakajew, A A
see
Bakaev, Aleksandr Aleksandrovich.

Bakakin, V P
Principles of geocryology (permafrost studies). Part 2. Engineering geocryology. Chapter VII, Particular aspects of mining in thick permafrost, p. 219-230, by V.P. Bakakin. From Academy of Sciences of the U.S.S.R. V.A. Obruchev, Institute of Permafrost Studies, Moscow, 1959. Translated by V. Poppe. Ottawa, 1965.
17 l. illus. 28 cm. (National Research Council, Canada. Technical translation TT-1217)
Translation of the Institute's Osnovy geokriologii (romanized form)
Bibliography: p. 12.
TxDaM NUC76-69475

Bakal, Abraham Itshak, 1936-
Conduction heat transfer with phase change and its application to freezing or thawing of foods. New Brunswick, N.J., 1970.
159 l. illus.
Thesis (Ph.D.)—Rutgers University.
Includes bibliography.
Microfilm copy. Ann Arbor, University Microfilms, 1970. 1 reel. 35 mm.
1. Foods, Frozen. 2. Heat—Conduction. I. Title.
MiEM NUC74-128781

Bakal, Carl, 1918-
How to shoot for glamour. New York, Ziff-Davis [1961]
128 p. illus.
Reprint of the 1955 ed.
1. Photography, Artistic. 2. Photography of women. I. Title.
CLobS NUC74-173577

Bakal, Halina Leszczyńska-
see Leszczyńska-Bakal, Halina.

Bakal, Yitzhak.
The closing down of institutions: new strategies in youth services. [Amherst] 1973.
vi, 314 l. illus. 28 cm.
Thesis (Ed.D.)—University of Massachusetts.
Microfilm no. 1879.
1. Massachusetts. Division of Youth Services. 2. Juvenile detention homes—Massachusetts. I. Title.
MU NUC74-125997

Bakal, Yitzhak.
Strategies for restructuring the State Department of Youth Services. [Washington] U.S. Department of Health, Education, and Welfare; [For sale by the Supt. of Docs., U.S. Govt. Print. Off., 1973]
23 p.
1. Juvenile delinquency—Massachusetts. 2. Social work with delinquents and criminals—Massachusetts. I. Massachusetts. Dept. of Youth Services. II. Title.
ViBlbV NUC76-69666

Bakal, Yitzhak, ed.
see Closing correctional institutions... Lexington, Mass., Lexington Books [1973]

Bakala, Jaroslav.
Slezsko no cestě k československému státu. Přispěvky o tisíciletém zápasu slezkých Čechů. Autor: [kol.] Uspoř. Jaroslav Bakala. Opava, Odbor kultury ONV, t. MTZ 25, 1969.
113, [3] p. 20 p. of plates, 5 maps, 2 tables. 20 cm. Kčs12.00 Cz 69–4362
Includes bibliographical references.
1. Silesia, Czechoslovak Republic — History — Addresses, essays, lectures. I. Title.
DB785.S53B35 73–316528

Bakala, Jozef.
Poľnohospodárske právo. 1. vyd. Bratislava, vyd. VSP, Nitra v Slov. vydav. pôdohosp. lit. rozmn. Západoslov. tlač., Nitra, 19
v. 29 cm. (Nitra, Slovakia (City). Vysoká škola poľnohospodárska. Katedra poľnohospodárskeho práva. Dočasné vysokoškolské učebnice, zv. 22/1968 Kčs6.50 (v.2) CzS 68–1812 (v. 2)
CONTENTS.—
2. č. Pracovné vzťahy v poľnohospodárstve.
1. Agricultural laborers—Czechoslovak Republic. I. Title. II. Series.
72–373200

Bakala, Jozef.
Poľnohospodárske právo. ... určené pre posl. PEF VŠP v Nitre ... 1. vyd. Bratislava, Príroda, t. Nitrianske tlač., Nitra, 1973.
110, [1] p. 29 cm. Kčs6.00 CzS 73
At head of title: Vysoká škola polnohospodárska v Nitre. Prevádzkovo-ekonomická fakulta. Katedra učtovníctva, financovania a práva.
1. Agricultural laws and legislation—Czechoslovak Republic. I. Title.
74–306468

Bakala, Jozef.
Základy pracovného hospodárskeho práva. Určené pre posl. PEF. Autori: Jozef Bakala a kol. 1. vyd. Nitra, VŠP, rozmn., 1973.
[1], 278 p. 29 cm. Kčs15.00 CzS 73
At head of title: Prevádzkovo-ekonomická fakulta. Katedra účtovníctva financovania a práva.
1. Labor laws and legislation—Czechoslovak Republic. 2. Industrial laws and legislation—Czechoslovak Republic. 3. Czechoslovak Republic—Economic policy. 4. Communist countries—Economic policy. I. Title.
74–338211

Bakalam
see
Bakalama.

Bakalama.
(Kālapeṅcāra ḍāẏerī)
কালপেঁচার ডায়েরী / বকলম প্রণীত. — ঢাকা : মুক্তধারা, 1976.
223 p. ; 22 cm.
In Bengali.
Tk16.00

1. Bangladesh—Social conditions—Anecdotes, facetiae, satire, etc. 2. Bangladesh—Politics and government—Anecdotes, facetiae, satire, etc. I. Title.

HN690.6.A8B35 76–901324

Bakalar, James B., 1943- joint author.
see Grinspoon, Lester, 1928- Cocaine ... New York, Basic Books, c1976.

Bakalář, Robert.
Kodešův mečbol. [Autoři:] Robert Bakalář, Antonín Bolardt. Praha, Olympia, t. Mír 6, 1974.
131, [3] p. [24] p. of plates. 21 cm. Kčs18.00 Cz 74
1. Kodeš, Jan. I. Kodeš, Jan. II. Bolardt, Antonín, joint author. III. Title.
GV994.K62B34 74–342334

Bakalēs, Dēmētrios K
see
Vakalēs, Dēmētrios K

Bakaliar, Aleksei Ivanovich, joint author
see Bychkov, Sergei Ivanovich. (Lazernyi giroskop) 1975.

Bakalis, Michael J
Ninian Edwards and territorial politics in Illinois : 1775-1818 / by Michael J. Bakalis. -- Ann Arbor, Mich. : University Microfilms, 1975.
246 leaves ; 21 cm.
Thesis (Ph.D.)--Northwestern University, 1966.
Bibliography: leaves 239-246.
MnU NUC77-93355

Bakalis, Michael J
A strategy for excellence; reaching for new standards in education, by Michael J. Bakalis. With a foreword by Lawrence N. Hansen. [Hamden, Conn.] Linnet Books, 1974.
xvii, 252 p. 23 cm.
Includes bibliographical references.
1. School management and organization. 2. State departments of education. I. Title.
LB2809.A2B34 379′.152 73–23101
ISBN 0–208–01245–1 MARC

Bakalis, Michael J
Summary of educational bills enacted by the 78th General Assembly, 1973 spring session / Michael J. Bakalis. — [Springfield? Ill.] : Legal Division, [1973 or 1974]
32 p. ; 28 cm.
Cover title.
Includes index.
1. Educational law and legislation—Illinois. I. Title.
KFI 1590.A4725 344′.773′07 74–622333
MARC

Bakalla, M H
Bibliography of Arabic linguistics / [compiled by] M. H. Bakalla. — London : Mansell, 1975.
xxxvii, 300 p. ; 24 cm. GB***
Includes indexes.
ISBN 0-7201-0525-0 : £13.95 ($32.00 U.S.)
1. Arabic language—Bibliography. I. Title.
Z7052.B35 016.492′7 76-361199
[PJ6073] 76 MARC

Bakalla, M H
Bibliography of Arabic linguistics / M. H. Bakalla. — 1. Aufl. — München : Verlag Dokumentation, 1976.
xxxvii, 312 p. ; 24 cm. GFR76-A
English and Arabic text.
Includes indexes.
ISBN 3-7940-3654-9 : DM98.00
1. Arabic language—Bibliography. I. Title.
Z7052.B35 1976 016.492′7 76-372750
[PJ6073] 76 MARC

Bakallo, Patxi, 1832-1898?
see Zavala, Antonio. Iru bertsolari. [San Sebastian, Spain] Auspoa Liburutegia, 1967.

Bakalo, Helenē, pseud.
(Dōdeka mathēmata gia tē synchronē technē)
12 μαθήματα γιὰ τὴ σύγχρονη τέχνη. 'Αθήνα, Καλλιτεχνικὸ Πνευματικὸ Κέντρο "Ωρα, 1970.
122 p. 21 cm.
1. Art, Modern—19th century. 2. Art, Modern—20th century. I. Title.
N6447.B3 74–236367

Bakalo, Helenē, pseud.
Hē ennoia tōn typhlōn. Athēnai, 1962.
35 p.
MH NUC74-120069

Bakalo, Helenē, pseud.
Genealogia. Genealogy, [Apodosē sta Anglika: Paul Merchant. Translated by Paul Merchant. Schedio tou G. Vakalo. Athēnai? 1971]
87 p. illus. 20 cm.
Poems.
Greek and English.
Limited ed. 450 copies.
I. Merchant, Paul, tr. II. Title.
ICU MH CU NUC74-120064

Bakalo, Helenē, pseud.
Perigraphē tou sōmatos. Athēna, Diphros, 1959.
27 p.
MH NUC74-123159

Bakalo, Helenē, pseud.
Synchronoi ellēnes zōgraphoi. prologos René Huyghe, eisagōge: Elenēs Vakalo. [Athens?] "Zygos", 1961.
xiii, 101 p. of illus. (part col.), cliii-clxii p. 27 cm.
1. Greece. Painting. 20th cent. 2. Greece. Painters. 20th cent. I. Title.
OU NUC74-118452

Bakalo, Helenē, pseud.
Ho tropos na kindyneuome. Athēna, 1966.
35 p.
MH NUC74-120005

Bakalo, Ivan Ivanovich, 1898–
(Natsional'na polityka Lenina)
Національна політика Ленина / **Іван Бакало. — Мюнхен : Сучасність,** 1974.
210 p. : port. ; 20 cm. — (Суспільно-політична бібліотека ; ч. 16 (35)) GFR***
Added t. p.: Lenin's nationality [sic] policy.
Includes bibliographical references and index.
DM6.50
1. Nationalism and socialism. 2. Minorities—Russia. 3. Lenin, Vladimir Il'ich, 1870–1924. I. Title. II. Title: Lenin's national policy.
HX550.N3B34 75-563992

Bakalo, Vladimir IAkovlevich.
Pokazateli vlagoobespechennosti i rezhimy oroshenifa trav v vysokogor'iakh Kirgizii. Frunze, Kyrgyzstan, 1966.
176, [2] p. illus.
Bibliography: p. 172-[177]
1. Irrigated pastures. 2. Pastures, Mountain. 3. Irrigation. Kirgizia. I. Kirgizskiĭ nauchno-issledovatel'skiĭ institut vodnogo khoziaistva. II. Title.
DNAL NUC76-3654

Bakalopoulos, Apostolos Euangelou, 1909-
The Greek nation, 1453-1669 : the cultural and economic background of modern Greek society / by Apostolos E. Vacalopoulos ; translated from the Greek by Ian and Phania Moles. — New Brunswick, N.J. : Rutgers University Press, c1976.
xiv, 457 p. : ill. ; 24 cm.
Translation of v. 2 of Historia tou neou Hellēnismou.
Bibliography: p.
Includes index.
ISBN 0-8135-0810-X : $25.00
1. Greece, Modern—History—1453-1821. I. Title.
DF801.B3313 949.5'05 75-23273
75 MARC

Bakalopoulos, Apostolos Euangelou, 1909-
Ta Hellēnika strateumata tou 1821: organōsē, hēgesia, taktikē, ēthē, psychologia. Thessalonikē, Ekdoseis Karagiannē, 1970.
11, 304 p. 25 cm.
1. Greece, Modern—Hist. —War of Independence, 1821-1829. 2. Greece, Modern—Armed Forces. I. Title.
CU ICU CtY NN NUC74-118478

Bakalopoulos, Apostolos Euangelou, 1909-
Histoire de la Grèce moderne / Apostolos Vacalopoulos ; pref. de Jean Pouilloux. — Éd. française / adaptée par Pierre Dieudonné ; assisté de Gaston Rochas. — [Roanne] : Horvath, [1975]
x, 330 p., [10] leaves of plates : ill. ; 24 cm. — (Collection Histoire des nations européenes)
Revised version of Historia tou neou Hellēnismou.
Includes index.
Bibliography: p. [303]-312.
ISBN 2-7171-0057-1 : 108F
1. Greece, Modern—History. I. Title.
DF757.B34 1975 949.5 75-507200
75 MARC

Bakalopoulos, Apostolos Euangelou, 1909–
(Historia tou neou hellēnismou)
Ἱστορία τοῦ νέου ἑλληνισμοῦ : Τουρκοκρατία 1453–1669 / Ἀποστόλου Ε. Βακαλοπούλου. — Ἔκδοση 2. συμπληρωμένη καὶ ἐνημερωμένη. — Θεσσαλονίκη : [s. n.], 19
v. : ill. ; 25 cm.
Bibliography: ; v. 2, p. [517]–559.
Includes index.
CONTENTS:
—t. 2. Οἱ ἱστορικὲς βάσεις τῆς νεοελληνικῆς κοινωνίας καὶ οἰκονομίας.
1. Greece, Modern—History—1453–1821. I. Title.
DF801.B33 1976 77–504984

Bakalopoulos, Apostolos Euangelou, 1909-
Hē Historikē syneidēsē kai to agōnistiko pneuma tou Neou Hellēnismou [hypo] Apost. E. Vakalopoulou. Thessalonikē, 1957.
24 p. 25 cm.
Bibliography: p. [23]-24.
1. Greece, Modern—Hist. —War of Independence, 1821-1829.
OCU NUC74-120038

Bakalopoulos, Apostolos Euangelou, 1909-
History of Macedonia, 1354-1833 [by] A.E. Vacalopoulos. Translated by Peter Megann. Thessalonike, Institute for Balkan Studies, 1973.
20, 758 p. illus. (Hetaireia Makedonikōn Spoudōn. Hidryma Meletōn Chersonēsou tou Haimou, 131)
Translation of Historia tēs Makedonias, 1354-1833.
1. Macedonia—History. I. Title. II. Series.
MH NUC74-178670

Bakalopoulos, Apostolos Euangelou, 1909-
A history of Thessaloniki [by] Apostolos E. Vacalopoulos. Translation by T. F. Carney. Thessalonike, Institute for Balkan Studies, 1972.
xi, 153 p. illus. 25 cm. (Hetaireia Makedonikōn Spoudōn. Hidryma Meletōn Chersonēsou tou Haimou. Ekdoseis, 63)
Bibliography: p. [139]-144.
1. Thessalonike—History. I. Title. II. Series.
OCH NUC76-70961

Bakalopoulos, Apostolos Euangelou, 1909–
(Hē poreia tou genous)
Ἡ πορεία τοῦ γένους : ἀπὸ τὸ Βυζάντιο στὸν Νέο Ἑλληνισμὸ / Ἀποστ. Ε. Βακαλοπούλου. – Ἀθήνα : Ἐκδόσεις τῶν Φίλων, 1966.
89 p. ; 17 cm. — (Ὁ Νέος Ἑλληνισμός ; 1)
Series romanized: Ho Neos Hellēnismos.
1. Greece, Modern—History. I. Title.
DF760.B34 76–520935

Bakalov, Georgi.
Ivan Vazov; kriticheski etiud. Sofiia, Znanie [19—]
64 p. (p. [59]-64 advertisements) 21 cm. (Universalna biblioteka, no. 258-260)
1. Vazov, Ivan Minchov, 1850-1921.
CSt NUC75-52443

Bakalov, Georgi.
(Literaturni statii i izsledvaniia)
Литературни статии и изследвания. Под ред. [с **предг.**] **на Ангел Тодоров. София, Бълг. писател,** 1973.
443 p. port. 21 cm. 3.08 lv Bu 73–2753
Includes bibliographical references.
1. Bulgarian literature—Addresses, essays, lectures. 2. Russian literature—Addresses, essays, lectures. 3. Criticism—Bulgaria—Addresses, essays, lectures.
PG1008.B317 74–303753

Bakalov, Georgi Ivanov, joint author
see Todorov, Radoslav Petrovich. (Bimetallicheskie kontakty) 1976.

Bakalov, Ivan Vladimirovich, joint author
see Bormotov, Vladimir Pavlovich. Sputnik brigadira-stroitelia. 1971.

Bakalova, Lora G
Problemi na detskoto khranene. Sofiia, Meditsina i fizkultura, 1971.
179 p. (Selecta medica, g. 5 [br.] 2)
Bibliography: p. 173-[180]
1. Child nutrition. I. Title. II. Series.
DNLM NUC76-14939

Bakaluba, Jane Jagers.
Honeymoon for three / Jane Jagers Bakaluba ; illustrated by Trixi Lerbs. — Nairobi : East African Pub. House, 1975.
183 p. : ill. ; 19 cm. — (African secondary readers ; 4)
Sh12.00
1. Baganda—Fiction. I. Title.
PZ4.B1667 Ho 823 76-980029
[PR9402.9.B3] 77 MARC

Bakan, David.
Child abuse, a bibliography / prepared by David Bakan, Margaret Eisner, Harry G. Needham. — Toronto : Canadian Council on Children and Youth, 1976.
xxi, 89 p. ; 26 cm. C***
ISBN 0-9690438-6-4
1. Child abuse—Bibliography. I. Eisner, Margaret, joint author. II. Needham, Harry G., joint author. III. Canadian Council on Children and Youth. IV. Title.
Z7164.C5B24 016.3627'1 76-372033
[HV713] 76 MARC

Bakan, David.
The duality of human existence; isolation and communion in Western man. Boston, Beacon Press [c1966]
242 p.
1. Psychology, Religious. 2. Sex (Psychology) 3. Death. I. Title.
ICU NUC73-59548

Bakan, David.
Sigmund Freud and the Jewish mystical tradition / by David Bakan. — Boston : Beacon Press, 1975, c1958.
xxii, 326 p. ; 21 cm. — (Beacon paperback ; 510)
Reprint of the ed. published by Schocken Books, New York.
Includes bibliographical references and index.
ISBN 0-8070-2963-7
1. Freud, Sigmund, 1856-1939. 2. Mysticism—Judaism. I. Title.
BF173.F85B23 1975 150'.19'52 74-31136
74 MARC

Bakan, David.
Slaughter of the innocents; a study of the battered child phenomenon. [Toronto, CBC Learning Systems, 1971]
xiii, 128 p. 21 cm. C***
Includes bibliographical references.
1. Cruelty to children. I. Title.
HV713.B33 1971b 364.1'5 74–150071
ISBN 0–88794–064–1 MARC

Bakanakes, P
Mikros anthokēpos kai ankathia en drasei; lyrika poiēmata kai satyrika epigrammata [hypo] P. Bakanakē. Athēnai, 1962.
32 p. 23 cm.
I. Title.
OCU NUC74-118728

Bakanina, Liudmila Pavlovna
see Sbornik zadach po fizike. 1975.

Bakanov, B
Zionist falsehoods / B. Bakanov. — Moscow : Novosti Press Agency Pub. House, 1974.
76 p. ; 17 cm. USSR***
Includes bibliographical references.
0.21rub
1. Zionism—Controversial literature. 2. Israel—Politics and government. I. Title.
DS149.B23 956.94'001 76-350436
76 MARC

Bakanov, Evgeniĭ Alekseevich, joint author
see Nikitin, Gennadiĭ Andreevich. Osnovy aviatsii. 1972.

Bakanov, Konstantin Pavlovich
see Rafinirovanie stali inertnym gazom. 1975.

Bakanov, Mikhail Ivanovich.
(Ėkonomicheskiĭ analiz)
Экономический анализ : теория, история, современное состояние, перспективы / М. И. Баканов, А. Н. Кашаев, А. Д. Шеремет. — Москва : Финансы, 1976.
263 p. ; 23 cm. USSR***
Bibliography: p. 249–[257]
Includes index.
1.40rub
1. Russia—Industries—Auditing and inspection. I. Kashaev, Alekseĭ Nikolaevich, joint author. II. Sheremet, Anatoliĭ Danilovich, joint author. III. Title.
HC340.A8B35 76–523469

Bakanov, Mikhail Ivanovich.
(Ėkonomicheskiĭ analiz v torgovle)
Экономический анализ в торговле. [**Учебник для экон. фак. торг. вузов**]. **Изд. 3-е, перераб. и доп. Москва, "Экономика,"** 1974.
318 p. with diagrs. 22 cm. 0.98rub USSR 74
At head of title: М. И. Баканов.
Includes bibliographical references.
1. Russia—Commerce. 2. Russia — Industries — Auditing and inspection. I. Title.
HF3626.B245 1974 74–325008

Bakanov, Nikolaĭ Aleksandrovich, 1893-
see Burman, Mark Efimovich. Tekhnologiia i tekhnokhimicheskiĭ kontrol' krakhmalo-patochnogo proizvodstva. 1957.

Bakanova, Mariia Aleksandrovna.
(Sotsialisticheskoe sorevnovanie na poligraficheskom predpriiatii)
Социалистическое соревнование на полиграфическом предприятии : из опыта организации соревнования в Первой Образцовой типографии им. А. А. Жданова / М. А. Баканова. — Москва : Книга, 1975.
110 p. ; 20 cm. USSR 75
0.31rub
1. Printing industry—Russia. 2. Socialist competition. 3. Pervaia obraztsovaia tipografiia, Moscow. I. Title.
Z243.R9B25 76–503865

Bakanova, Valentina Vasil'evna.
(Tablit͡sy prirashcheniĭ koordinat)
Таблицы приращений координат / В. В. Баканова, П. И. Фокин ; под ред. В. Д. Большакова. — Москва : Недра, 1976.
197 p. ; 27 cm. USSR***
1.09rub
1. Surveying—Tables. I. Fokin, Petr Ivanovich, joint author. II. Title.
TA552.B26 77–507837

Bakanova, Valentina Vasil'evna
see Praktikum po geodezii. 1973.

Bakanurskiĭ, Grigoriĭ Leonidovich.
(Iudeĭskiĭ klerikalizm)
Иудейский клерикализм / Г. Л. Бакануpский. — Москва : Знание, 1974.
63 p. ; 20 cm. — (Новое в жизни, науке, технике : Серия Научный атеизм ; 10/1974) USSR***
Includes bibliographical references.
0.10rub
1. Zionism—Controversial literature. 2. Judaism—Controversial literature. I. Title. II. Series: Novoe v zhizni, nauke, tekhnike : Serii͡a Nauchnyĭ ateizm ; 1974, 10.
DS149.B26 75–566930

Bakar, Akhmedkhan Abu-
see Abu-Bakar, Akhmedkhan.

Bakar, Muhammad Abu
see
Muhammad Abu Bakar, 1949-

Bakar, Sheikh Abdullah bin Sheikh Abu
see
Abdullah bin Abu Bakar, Sheikh, 1919-

Bakar Hamid, Abu
see Abu Bakar Hamid.

Bakarellē, Xanthippē Kalantzē-
see
Kalantzē-Vakarellē, Xanthippē.

Bakari, S U
Educational administration in post-war Nigeria, by S.U. Bakari. Buffalo, N.Y., Council on International Studies, State University of New York, 1971.
58 l. illus. 29 cm. (New York. State University, Buffalo. Council on International Studies. Special studies, no. 22)
1. Education and state—Nigeria. 2. Educational planning—Nigeria. 3. Education—Nigeria. I. Title. II. Series.
NBuU NUC73-126583

Bakarić, Vladimir.
Društvene klase, nacija i socijalizam / Vladimir Bakarić ; izbor tekstova Jakov Franić, Vladimir Štokalo. — Zagreb : Školska knjiga, 1976.
vi, 250 p. ; 20 cm. — (Biblioteka Suvremena misao) Yu***
Includes bibliographical references.
1. Nationalism and socialism. 2. Minorities—Yugoslavia. 3. Savez komunista Hrvatske. 4. Yugoslavia — Politics and government. I. Title.
HX550.N3B36 76–533676

Bakarić, Vladimir.
Ekonomski i politički aspekt socijalističkog samoupravljanja / Vladimir Bakarić. — Sarajevo : Svjetlost, 1975.
322 p. ; 20 cm. — (Biblioteka Etos : Misao socijalističkog samoupravljanja : Serija 1 ; knj. 3) Yu***
Includes bibliographical references.
1. Yugoslavia—Economic policy—1945- 2. Marxian economics. 3. Yugoslavia—Politics and government—1945- 4. Employees' representation in management—Yugoslavia. I. Title.
HC407.B34 76–511344

Bakarić, Vladimir.
Socijalistički samoupravni sistem i društvena reprodukcija. Zagreb, "Informator," 1974.
xvi, 488 p. 24 cm. (Ekonomska biblioteka, kolo 10, br. 1-2) Yu 74
Includes bibliographical references.
1. Yugoslavia—Economic policy—1945- 2. Yugoslavia—Politics and government—1945- I. Title.
HC407.Y6B174 74–970214

Bakarić, Vladimir.
Theoretical foundations of social reproduction in socialism / Vladimir Bakarić ; translator, Petar Mijušković and Gregor Fulton McGregor. — Beograd : Komunist, [1975]
141 p. : ill. ; 20 cm. — (Book series) Yu***
Translated from the Serbo-Croatian.
Contains three chapters from the author's Socijalisticki samoupravni sistem i društvena reprodukcija, 1974 plus three miscellaneous addresses.
Includes bibliographical references and indexes.
1. Employees' representation in management—Yugoslavia. I. Title. II. Title: Social reproduction in socialism.
HD5660.Y8B35 331 76-377145
76 MARC

Bakarich, Sarah Grace.
So said the coroner: how they died in old Cochise. [Tombstone, Ariz.] Tombstone Epitaph [c1968]
93 p. 22 cm.
1. Death. 2. Death by wrongful act—Cochise Co., Ariz. 3. Murder—Cochise Co.—Ariz. I. Title. II. Title: How they died in old Cochise.
AzU NUC74-20900

Bakasova, R.Kh., ed.
see Problemy material'nogo stimulirovanii͡a... Ashkhabad, Ylym, 1971.

Bakasova, Zaryl Bakasovna.
(Fiziko-khimicheskie osnovy poluchenii͡a, svoĭstv, stroenii͡a novykh proizvodnykh L-glutaminovoĭ kisloty i L-glutaminata natrii͡a)
Физико-химические основы получения, свойств, строения новых производных L-глутаминовой кислоты и L-глутамината натрия. Фрунзе, "Илим," 1973.
175 p. with illus., 4 l. of tables. 22 cm. 0.80rub USSR 73
At head of title: Академия наук Киргизской ССР. Институт органической химии. З. Б. Бакасова, И. Г. Дружинин.
1. Glutamic acid. 2. Sodium glutamate. I. Druzhinin, Ivan Georgievich, joint author. II. Title.
QD431.B24 74–315165

Bakastov, V.N,
see Feĭgel'son, V M Patentnyĭ formuli͡ar. Moskva, T͡Sniipi, 1964.

Bakastova, G. P.
see V boi͡u i trude... I͡Aroslavl', Verkhne-Volzhskoe knizhnoe izd-vo, 1972.

Bakastova, G. P.
see Vsesoi͡uznyĭ leninskiĭ kommunisticheskiĭ soi͡uz molodezhi. Ivanovskiĭ oblastnoĭ komitet. V boi͡u i trude... I͡Aroslavl', Verkhne-Volzhskoe kn. izd-vo, 1972.

Bākathīr, Muḥammad ibn Muḥammad
see
Bā Kathīr, Muḥammad ibn Muḥammad.

Bakay, Kornél.
Scythian rattles in the Carpathian Basin and their eastern connections. [Translated by Géza Dedinszky] Budapest, Akadémiai Kiadó, 1971.
131 p. illus. 25 cm.
Bibliography: p. 123-130.
1. Hungary—Antiquities. 2. Transylvania—Antiquities. 3. Russia—Antiquities. 4. Scythians. I. Title.
DB920.B28 1971 913.39'51'03 74–152473
MARC

Bakay, Kornel
see Veszprem megye regeszeti topografiaja. Budapest, Akademiai Kiado, 1966-72.

Bakay, Virginia Hicks, 1927-
The liability of certified public accountants related to the auditing and accounting functions as indicated by a review of selected claims. Ann Arbor, University Microfilms, 1970.
1 reel. 35 mm.
Thesis—University of Alabama, 1969.
1. Accounting. I. Title.
MsU NUC76-70981

Bakbergenov, Saurbek
see
Baqbergenov, Sāuīrbek.

Bakcsi, György.
Dosztojevszkij világa. [Budapest, Európa Könyvkiadó, 1971]
213 p. illus. 19 cm. (Írók világa) 9.00Ft
Includes bibliographies.
1. Dostoevskiĭ, Fedor Mikhaĭlovich, 1821-1881. I. Title.
PG3328.B3 73–201198

Bakcsi, György.
En Passant felügyelő kalandjai (Beszélgetés sakkfeladványokról) Budapest, Sport, 1972.
195 p. illus.
Bibliography: p. 190.
1. Chess–Fiction. 2. Chess–Problems. I. Title.
OCl NUC74-125998

Bakcsi, György
see Szovjetunió. 2. átdolg. kiad. Budapest: Panoráma [1974]

Bakdāsh, 'Abd al-Ḥamīd, comp.
(Rasā'il al-'adhārá)
رسائل العذارى؛ رسائل حب واحزان [تأليف] عبد الحميد بكداش. [الطبعة 1.] بيروت، حمد ومحيو [1972]
302 p. illus. 19 cm.
1. Arabic literature—Translations from foreign literature. 2. Literature, Modern—Translations into Arabic. 3. Love—Literary collections. I. Title.
PJ7691.B3 74–214924

Bake, C. F. G. de Menthon
see Menthon Bake, C. F. G. de.

Bake, John, 1787-1864, comp.
see Posidonius, of Apamea. Posidonii Rhodii Reliquiae doctrine... Osnabrück, Biblio Verlag, 1972.

Bake, William A 1938-
The Blue Ridge / text and photos. by William A. Bake. — New York : Viking Press, 1977.
112 p., [24] leaves of plates : ill. ; 23 x 25 cm. — (A Studio book)
Bibliography: p.
ISBN 0-670-17515-3 : $14.95
1. Blue Ridge Mountains—Description and travel. 2. Bake, William A., 1938- I. Title.
F217.B6B34 1977 917.55 76-50612
76 MARC

Bake, William A 1938-
Mountains and meadowlands along the Blue Ridge Parkway / text and photos by William A. Bake. — Washington : Office of Publications, National Park Service, U.S. Dept. of the Interior, 1975.
46 p. : col. ill. ; 18 cm.
1. Natural history—Blue Ridge Mountains. 2. Blue Ridge Mountains—Description and travel. 3. Blue Ridge Parkway—Description and travel. I. Title.
QH104.5.B5B34 500.9'755 75-6541
75 MARC

Bake, William A., 1938-
see Crandall, Hugh. Shenandoah ... Las Vegas, Nev., KC Publications, [1975].

Bakeeva, D. Kh., ed.
see Voprosy romano-germanskoi filologii. [1972].

Bakeeva, N.M.
see Peive, J Preparatory electrophoresis of proteins on polyacrylamide gel. Moskva, "Nauka", 1971.

Bakel, J M M van.
Vallers en kanker in bewaarkool. Black leg and dry-rot of head cabbage [door] J.M.M. van Bakel. [Alkmaar] Proefstation voor de Groenteteelt in de Vollegrond in Nederland [1968]
34 p. illus. (Proefstation voor de Groenteteelt in de Vollegrond in Nederland. Mededeling 41)
Summary in English.
ICRL NUC74-126225

Bakel, Johannes Josephus Adrianus van.
Fonologie van het Nederlands : synchroon en diachroon / Jan van Bakel. — Utrecht : Bohn, Scheltema & Holkema, 1976.
viii, 152 p. ; 21 cm. Ne76-30
Bibliography: p. 136-137.
Includes index.
ISBN 9031301949 : fl 35.00
1. Dutch language—Phonology. I. Title.
PF716.B3 76-477309
•76 MARC

Bakelaar, Bette Lou, 1936-
From verse to prose: a study of the fifteenth-century versions of Chrestien's Erec and Cligès. [n. p.] 1973 [c1974]
337 l.
Thesis–Ohio State University.
Bibliography: leaves 331-337.
1. Chrestien de Troyes, 12th century.
I. Title.
OU NUC76-18069

Bakelaar, M
Den Bommel in oude ansichten : waarin ook afbeeldingen van Zuidzijde / door M. Bakelaar. — Zaltbommel : Europese Bibliotheek, 1974.
74 p. : ill. ; 15 x 21 cm. Ne 75-4
fl 21.90
1. Den Bommel, Netherlands—Description—Views. I. Title.
DJ411.D4635B34 75-585069

Bakeless, John Edwin, 1894-
Christopher Marlowe / by John Bakeless. — New York : Haskell House Publishers, 1975.
357 p. ; 21 cm.
Reprint of the 1938 ed. published by J. Cape, London.
Includes bibliographical references and index.
ISBN 0-8383-1881-9
1. Marlowe, Christopher, 1564-1593.
PR2673.B3 1975 822'.3 75-42103
75 MARC

Bakeless, John Edwin, 1894–
The economic causes of modern war; a study of the period, 1878–1918, by John Bakeless. With a new introd. for the Garland ed. by Gerald E. Markowitz. New York, Garland Pub., 1972 [c1921]
12, ix, 265 p. 22 cm. (The Garland library of war and peace)
Original ed. issued as no. 6 of David A. Wells prize essays.
Bibliography: p. 233–249.
1. War—Economic aspects. 2. Competition, International. 3. Economic history—1750–1918. I. Title. II. Series. III. Series: David A. Wells prize essays, no. 6.
HB195.B3 1972 355.02'73'09034 75–147490
ISBN 0–8240–0283–0 MARC

Bakeless, John Edwin, 1894–
General Washington's spy system; an address by John Bakeless. A report by Francis S. Ronalds. A report by the Board of Trustees of the Washington Association of New Jersey. At Washington's Headquarters in Morristown, N. J., February 23, 1959. [Morristown, N. J., 1959]
40 p. 23 cm.
Cover title.
1. United States—History—Revolution, 1775–1783—Secret service—Addresses, essays, lectures. 2. Washington Association of New Jersey, Morristown. I. Washington Association of New Jersey, Morristown. II. Title.
E279.B26 973.3'85 74–172595
MARC

Bakeless, John Edwin, 1894- joint author
see Bakeless, Katherine (Little) 1895-
Confederate spy stories. Philadelphia, Lippincott [1973]

Bakeless, Katherine (Little) 1895–
Confederate spy stories [by] Katherine and John Bakeless. [1st ed.] Philadelphia, Lippincott [1973]
159 p. map. 22 cm.
SUMMARY: Biographies of men and women who, for patriotic or mercenary reasons, engaged in espionage for the Confederacy.
1. United States—History—Civil War—Secret service—Confederate States—Juvenile literature. [1. United States—History—Civil War—Secret service—Confederate States. 2. Spies. 3. Espionage—Biography] I. Bakeless, John Edwin, 1894- joint author. II. Title. III. Series.
E608.B14 973.7'86'0922 [B] 73–4984
ISBN 0–397–31230–X [920] MARC

Bakel'man, Il'ia IAkovlevich.
Inversions / I. Ya. Bakel'man ; translated and adapted from the Russian ed. by Joan W. Teller and Susan Williams. — Chicago : University of Chicago Press, 1974.
viii, 70 p. : ill. ; 23 cm. — (Popular lectures in mathematics)
Translation of Inversiia.
ISBN 0-226-03499-2
1. Inversions (Geometry) I. Title.
QA473.B3413 516'.1 74-5727
75 MARC

Bakel'man, Il'ia IAkovlevich.
(Vvedenie v differentsial'nuiu geometriiu "v tselom")
Введение в дифференциальную геометрию "в целом." [Учеб. пособие для физ.-мат. фак. ун-тов и пед. ин-тов]. Москва, "Наука," 1973.
440 p. with illus. 22 cm. 1.19rub USSR 73
At head of title: И. Я. Бакельман, А. Л. Вернер, Б. Е. Кантор.
Bibliography: p. 429–[436]
1. Geometry, Differential. I. Verner, Alekseĭ Leonidovich, joint author. II. Kantor, Boris Evseevich, joint author. III. Title.
QA641.B3 74–336395

Bakel'man, Il'ia IAkovlevich, ed.
see Issledovaniia po geometrii "v tselom." 1970.

Bakel'man, Il'ia IAkovlevich, ed.
see Sovremennyĭ analiz i geometriia. 1972.

Bakels, Floris B
Nacht und Nebel : mijn verhaal uit Duitse gevangenissen en concentratiekampen / Floris B. Bakels. — Amsterdam : Elsevier, 1977.
344 p. : facsims. ; 22 cm. Ne77-19
ISBN 9010018008 : fl 24.50
1. World War, 1939-1945—Personal narratives, Dutch. 2. World War, 1939-1945—Prisoners and prisons, German. 3. Bakels, Floris B. 4. Prisoners of war—Germany—Biography. I. Title.
D811.5.B217 77-478809
•77 MARC

Bakels, H., tr.
see Bible. N.T. Dutch. 1914. Bakels. Het Nieuwe Testament voor leeken leesbaar gemaakt. 2. herziene en verm. druk. [Amsterdam?] Mij. voor Goede en Goedkoope Lectuur, 1914.

Bakels, H L comp.
Arbeidsrechtspraak / samengesteld door H. L. Bakels. — 2e druk. — Deventer : Kluwer, 1974.
xv, 336 p. ; 19 cm. Ne 74-41
Includes index.
ISBN 90-312-0007-7 : fl 17.50
1. Labor laws and legislation — Netherlands — Cases. 2. Labor courts—Netherlands. I. Title.
75-573471

Bakels, H L
Macht en onmacht in het privaatrecht, door H. L. Bakels. Deventer, Æ. E. Kluwer [1965]
20 p. 25 cm.
Rede—Groningen.
Includes bibliographical references.
1. Jurisprudence. I. Title.
75-535042

Bakels, H L
Schets van het Nederlands arbeidsrecht. Door H. L. Bakels. Met medew. van L. Opheikens. Deventer, Kluwer, 1972.
xii, 211 p. photo. 24 cm. fl 26.00 Ne 72-45
Includes bibliographical references.
1. Labor laws and legislation—Netherlands. I. Opheikens, L., joint author. II. Title.
73-302447
ISBN 90-268-0609-4

Bakels, H L
Schets van het Nederlands arbeidsrecht / door H. L. Bakels, met medewerking van L. Opheikens. — 2e druk. — Deventer : Kluwer, 1974.
233 p., [1] leaf of plates : ill. ; 24 cm. Ne 74-38
Includes bibliographical references and indexes.
ISBN 90-312-0009-3 : fl 29.50
1. Labor laws and legislation—Netherlands. I. Opheikens, L., joint author. II. Title.
75-566561

Bakels, H L
Schets van het Nederlands arbeidsrecht / door H. L. Bakels, met medew. van L. Opheikens. — 3e dr. — Deventer : Kluwer, 1976.
280 p. ; 24 cm. Ne76-41
Includes bibliographical references and indexes.
ISBN 9031200255 : fl 30.00
1. Labor laws and legislation—Netherlands. I. Opheikens, L., joint author. II. Title.
344'.492'01 77-456838
•77 MARC

Bakels, H. L.
see Netherlands (Kingdom, 1815-). Laws, statutes, etc. Arbeidswetgeving. Deventer, AE. E. Kluwer, 1969.

Bakels, H. L.
see Netherlands (Kingdom, 1815-). Laws, statutes, etc. Arbeidswetgeving... 2. druk. Deventer, Kluwer, 1973.

Bakely, Donald C
If...a big word with the poor / Donald C. Bakely ; photos. by Terry Evans. — [Newton, Kan. : Faith and Life Press], c1976.
99 p. : ill. ; 21 x 22 cm.
Poems.
ISBN 0-87303-343-4
1. Poor—Poetry. I. Evans, Terry. II. Title.
PS3552.A397I3 811'.5'4 75-35305
76 MARC

Bakema, Jacob Berend, 1914-
see Duyvendak, A Zolang er mensen zijn op aarde. Driebergen, Kerk en Wereld [1968]

Bakema, Jacob Berend, 1914-
see Van den Broek/Bakema. Roma, Officina, 1976.

Bakeman, Bruce Melvin, 1942-
The effect of social influence, religious orientation, church polity, and demographic differences on changes in religious attitudes. Pasadena, 1976.
109 p. (Fuller Theological Seminary. Theses, 1976)
Thesis (Ph. D.)--Fuller Theological Seminary, Pasadena.
1. Attitude (Psychology) 2. Attitude change. 3. Psychology, Religous. I. Title.
CPFT NUC77-92465

Bakeman, Roger Alan, 1939-
Groups, individuals, and time: studies of behavioral patterns in Tektite 2. [Austin, Tex.] 1973.
xii, 111 l. illus. 29 cm.
Thesis (Ph. D.)—University of Texas at Austin.
Vita.
Bibliography: leaves 107-111.
TxU NUC75-19460

Baken, Lenore.
How to camp Europe by train / by Lenore Baken ; cover by Warren McCallister. — Mercer Island, Wash. : Ariel Publications, [1975]
288 p. ; 22 cm.
$4.95
1. Europe—Description and travel—1971- —Guide-books. 2. Camping—Europe—Guide-books. I. Title.
D909.B25 914'.04'55 74-28580
75 MARC

Bakenov, Mukhtar Mukashevich.
(Mineral'no-syr'evye resursy Kazakhstana)
Минерально-сырьевые ресурсы Казахстана. Новое в географии республики. Москва, "Знание," 1973.
63 p. with diagrs. 20 cm. (Новое в жизни, науке, технике. Серия: Наука о Земле, 3) 0.10rub USSR 73-VKP
By M. M. Bakenov, I. I. Bok, and A. V. Parshin.
Bibliography: p. 62.
1. Mines and mineral resources—Kazakhstan. I. Bok, Ivan Ivanovich, joint author. II. Parshin, Alekseĭ Vasil'evich, joint author. III. Title. IV. Series: Novoe v zhizni, nauke, tekhnike. Seriia: Nauka o Zemle, 1973, 3.
G1.N65 1973, no. 3 73-341428
[TN110]

Baker, A A
see Baker, Alex Anthony.

Baker, A B
The design and phasing of horizontal and vertical alignments: program JANUS. Crowthorne, Berkshire, Construction Planning Division, Highways Dept., Transport and Road Research Laboratory, 1972.
16 p. illus. (TRRL report LR 469)
Bibliography: p. 12-13.
I. Title. II. Series.
NBPol NUC74-125992

Baker, A. D.
see also
Baker, Alan D
Baker, Arthur D.

Baker, A J
Degradation of wood by products of metal corrosion. Madison, Wis., U.S. Forest Products Laboratory, 1974.
6 p. (USDA Forest Service research paper FPL 229)
1. Wood. 2. Corrosion. 3. Metals. I. United States. Forest Products Laboratory, Madison, Wis. II. Title.
DHUD NUC75-23172

Baker, Abe Bert, 1908-
Clinical neurology / editor, A.B. Baker, associate editor, L.H. Baker. -- Rev. ed. -- Hagerstown, Md. : Medical Dept., Harper and Row, 1975-
v. : ill. ; 27 cm.
Loose-leaf for updating.
Includes bibliographies.
Vol. [4]: "Index."
1. Neurology. I. Baker, Lowell H. II. Title.
ICU NUC77-91829

Baker, Adelaide N
The floating bridge, by Adelaide Nichols; four plays of gods and men in the Japanese form. Boston, Walter H. Baker company [c1932]
192 p. 19 cm.
CONTENTS: The moon maiden. — Susa, the impetuous. — The spring and autumn lovers.—Urashima.
I. Title.
PS3503.A54117F6 1932 812.5 32-20015
rev

Baker, Adelaide N
The haunted circle, and other outdoor plays, by Adelaide Nichols. New York, E. P. Dutton & company [c1924]
xx, 279 p. 19½ cm.
CONTENTS: The haunted circle. — The gardener's cap. — The devil's field. — The shepherd's pipe.
I. Title.
PS3503.A54117A19 1924 24-5687
rev

Baker, Adelaide N
Return to Arcady [by] Adelaide N. Baker. Illustrated by Robert Lambdin. [1st ed.] New York, L. Hill [1973]
v, 162 p. illus. 25 cm. $8.95
1. Country life—Connecticut. I. Title.
S521.5.C8B34 917.46'03'4 73-80849
ISBN 0-88208-018-0 MARC

Baker, Adelaide N
To mark the time, by Adelaide N. Baker. Boston, Branden Press [1973]
110 p. 23 cm. $5.00
Poems.
I. Title.
PS3503.A54117T6 811'.5'2 72-88558
ISBN 0-8283-1484-5 MARC

Baker, Ailsie F
Taxonomic studies in the Oscillatoriaceae [by] Ailsie F. Baker and Harold C. Bold. [Austin, University of Texas, 1970]
104 p. illus. 26 cm. (Phycological studies, 10) (University of Texas publication. Publication no. 7004)
Bibliography: p. 65-70.
1. Oscillatoriaceae. I. Bold, Harold Charles, 1909- joint author. II. Title. III. Series.
QK564.P475 no. 10 589'.3'08 s 73-621764
[QK569.O8] [589'46] MARC

Baker, Alan, F.R.S.
Transcendental number theory / Alan Baker. — London ; New York : Cambridge University Press, 1975.
x, 147 p. ; 24 cm. GB***
Bibliography: p. 129.
"Original papers": p. 130-144.
Includes index.
ISBN 0-521-20461-5
1. Numbers, Transcendental. 2. Numbers, Transcendental—Bibliography. I. Title.
QA247.5.B24 512'.73 74-82591
75 MARC

Baker, Alan, 1930- joint author
see Terry, Len. Racing car design and development. Cambridge, Mass., R. Bentley, 1973.

Baker, Alan, 1930- joint author
see Terry, Len. Racing car design and development... [Croydon, Eng.] Motor Racing Publications [1973]

Baker, Alan Lee.
Microstratification of phytoplankton in selected Minnesota lakes. [Minneapolis] 1973.
viii, 137 l. illus., graph (in pocket) 29 cm.
Thesis (Ph.D.)—University of Minnesota.
Bibliography: leaves 96-101.
MnU NUC76-70994

Baker, Alan M.
see Berry, Brian Joe Lobley, 1934- Análise espacial. Rio de Janeiro, Instituto Panamericano de Geografía e História, Comissão de geografía [1969]

Baker, Alan M.
see Pan American Institute of Geography and History. Commission on Geography. Textos básicos... [Rio de Janeiro, 1969?]

Baker, Alan M.
see Simmons, James William, 1936- Household movement patterns. [Toronto] Centre for Urban and Community Studies, University of Toronto, 1972.

Baker, Alan N
The echinoid fauna of north-eastern New Zealand, by Alan N. Baker. Wellington, Royal Society of New Zealand, 1968.
7 p. 1 plate. 25 cm. (Transactions of the Royal Society of New Zealand. Biological sciences, v. 11, no. 1)
Caption title.
Bibliography: p. 6-7.
1. Sea-urchins—New Zealand. I. Title. II. Series: Royal Society of New Zealand, Wellington. Transactions. Biological sciences, v. 11, no. 1.
QH1.R86 vol. 11, no. 1 574'.08 s 74-158350
[QL384.E2] [593'.95'0993122] MARC

Baker, Alan N
New Zealand whales and dolphins, by Alan N. Baker. Wellington, N. Z., Biological Society, Victorian University of Wellington, 1972.
49 p. illus. 22 cm. NZ***
Also published as vol. 2, pt. 1 of Tuatara.
Bibliography: p. 46.
1. Whales — New Zealand. 2. Dolphins — New Zealand. 3. Cetacea—New Zealand. I. Title.
QL737.C4B23 599'.51'09931 74-156073
MARC

Baker, Alan N
Reproduction, early life history and age-growth relationships of the New Zealand pilchard, Sardinops neopilchardus (Steindachner), by Alan N. Baker. [Wellington] Fisheries Research Division, New Zealand Marine Dept. [1972]
64 p. illus., maps. 28 cm. (Fisheries research bulletin, no. 5)
"This study ... was made during 1966-68 as part of a Victoria University Department of Zoology survey."
Bibliography: p. 61-62.
1. Sardinops neopilchardus. I. Series: Fisheries research bulletin. New series, no. 5.
NcD NUC74-134539

Baker, Alan N
Spawning and development of the New Zealand sprat, Sprattus antipodum (Hector). Wellington. Zoology publications, no. 62)
1. Sprats. 2. Fisheries—New Zealand. I. Title. II. Series.
DME NUC76-70993

Baker, Alan R H comp.
Man made the land; essays in English historical geography, a series from the Geographical magazine. Contributors: Gordon Manley [and others] Editors: Alan R. H. Baker and J. B. Harley. Totowa, N. J., Rowman and Littlefield [1973]
208 p. illus. 29 cm. (Studies in historical geography) $16.00
Includes bibliographies.
1. Anthropo-geography—England—Addresses, essays, lectures. 2. Land—England—Addresses, essays, lectures. 3. England—Historical geography—Addresses, essays, lectures. I. Manley, Gordon. II. Harley, John Brian, joint comp. III. The Geographical magazine (London, 1935-) IV. Title.
GF551.B34 1973 914.2'03 73-5602
ISBN 0-87471-184-3 rev MARC

Baker, Alan R H
Progress in historical geography. Edited by Alan R. H. Baker. Newton Abbot, David & Charles [1972]
311 p. maps. 22 cm. (Studies in historical geography) £4.20 B***
Bibliography: p. 275-302.
1. Geography, Historical. I. Title.
G141.B3 1972b 911'.07'2 72-188291
ISBN 0-7153-5534-1 72[r76]rev2 MARC

Baker, Alan R H
Studies of field systems in the British Isles, edited by Alan R. H. Baker and Robin A. Butlin. Cambridge [Eng.] University Press, 1973.
xxvi, 702 p. illus. 24 cm. GB***
Bibliography: p. 657-679.
1. Land tenure — Great Britain — History. 2. Commons — Great Britain—History. 3. Agriculture—Great Britain—History. I. Butlin, Robin A. II. Title.
HD594.B26 333.3'2'0942 72-91359
ISBN 0-521-20121-7 MARC

Baker, Albert Cannon.
A generalized lexical scanner for a translator writing system. Urbana, Dept. of Computer Science, University of Illinois at Urbana-Champaign, 1973.
v, 55 p. 28 cm. UIUCDCS-R-73-596
Originally presented as the author's thesis (M. S.), University of Illinois at Urbana-Champaign.
Includes bibliographical references.
1. Translators (Computer programs) 2. Compiling (Electronic computers) I. Title. II. Series: Illinois. University at Urbana-Champaign. Dept. of Computer Science. Report 596.
QA76.I 4 no. 596 001.6'4'08 s 74-621752
[QA76.6] [001.6'425] MARC

Baker, Albert F., joint author
see Miller, Kenneth J Electrophoretic-specific gravity separation of pyrite from coal. [Washington] U.S. Dept. of the Interior, Bureau of Mines [1970]

Baker, Albert F., joint author
see Miller, Kenneth J Evaluation of a novel electrophoretic separation method... [Washington, 1974]

Baker, Albert F., joint author
see Miller, Kenneth J Flotation of pyrite from coal. [Washington] U.S. Dept. of the Interior, 1972.

Baker, Albie, 1917-
Stolen sweets. [1st ed.] New York, Saturday Review Press [1973]
247 p. 22 cm. $7.95
1. Baker, Albie, 1917- I. Title.
HV6248.B23A3 364.1'55 [B] 72-88647
ISBN 0-8415-0268-4 MARC

Baker, Alex Anthony.
see Comprehensive psychiatric care. Oxford, Blackwell Scientific, 1976.

Baker, Alfred Edwin, 1876-1924.
see Eddy, Mary Baker, 1821-1910. Instruction in metaphysics. [s.l., s.n.,

Baker, Alfred Thomas, 1873-1936.
Die versifizierte Übersetzung de französischen Bibel in handschrift Egerton 2710 des British Museum. Eine Untersuchung des Inhalts und der Sprache. Cambridge, 1897 [1972]
67 p.
Thesis—Heidelberg.
Microfilm (positive) New York, Columbia University Libraries, 1972. 1 reel.
Master negative 0327.
1. Bible. French.
NNC NUC74-126916

Baker, Alfred Thomas, 1873-1936, ed.
see Modwenna, Saint. Legend. St. Modwenna. New York, Johnson Reprint Co. [1967]

Baker, Alfred W
Automation at the Fairfax County, Virginia, Library system / Alfred W. Baker, Frederick Boots, Donald Pultz. — [Peoria, Ill. : Larc Press, 1974]
52 p. : ill. ; 23 cm. — (Computerized cataloging systems series ; v. 1, issue 2)
1. Fairfax County Public Library. 2. Libraries—Automation. 3. Library catalogs. I. Boots, Frederick, joint author. II. Pultz, Donald, joint author. III. Series.
Z733.F144B33 025.3'028'54 75-314359
75 MARC

Baker, Alfred W comp.
The development of the book catalog at Science Press. Alfred W. Baker, editor. Ephrata, Pa., Science Press [1973]
ix, 118 p. illus. 23 cm.
1. Catalogs, Book—Addresses, essays, lectures. I. Science Press. II. Title.
Z695.87.B34 025.3 72-98001
MARC

Baker, Alice
see Bellman, Richard F Summary of recent court challenges... ₍New York?₎ National committee against discrimination in housing, 1972.

Baker, Allan, joint author.
see Civil, Allen. Fireless locomotives ... ₍Dorset, Eng.₎ Oakwood Press, 1976.

Baker, Allan J
Ecological and behavioural evidence for the systematic status of New Zealand oystercatchers (Charadriiformes: Haematopodidae) ₍by₎ Allan J. Baker. ₍Toronto, Royal Ontario Museum, 1974₎
34 p. illus. 26 cm. (Life Sciences contribution, 96) $2.00 C***
Bibliography: p. 32-34.
1. Oystercatcher. 2. Variable oystercatcher. 3. Chatham Islands oystercatcher. 4. Birds—New Zealand. I. Title. II. Series: Toronto. Royal Ontario Museum. Life Sciences Division. Contributions, no. 96.
QL1.T65 no. 96 574'.08 s 76-354537
₍QL696.C452₎ 76 MARC
ISBN 0-88854-138-4

Baker, Allan J
Federally inspected livestock slaughter by size and type of plant / ₍by Allen J. Baker₎. — Washington : U.S. Dept. of Agriculture, Economic Research Service, 1976.
ii, 94 p. ; 26 cm. — (Statistical bulletin ; no. 549)
Cover title.
1. Slaughtering and slaughter-houses—United States—Statistics. I. United States. Dept. of Agriculture. Economic Research Service. II. Title. III. Series: United States. Dept. of Agriculture. Statistical bulletin ; no. 549.
HD1751.A5 no. 549 338.1'0973 s 76-602551
₍TS1963₎ 76 MARC

Baker, Alonzo Lafayette, 1894–
The hope of the world, by Alonzo L. Baker ... Mountain View, Calif., Omaha, Neb. ₍etc.₎ Pacific press publishing association ₍c1925₎
3 p. l., 9-390 p. incl. front., illus. 22½ cm.
Illustrated lining-papers.
1. Second Advent. I. Title.
BT885.B15 25-10706
rev

Baker, Anna.
Ambrose small productions: an exhibition in March, 1973, of paintings and drawings, by Anna Baker based on an imaginery series of productions by the legendary Ambrose Small at the Nancy Poole Studios, Inc. London, Ont., Nancy Poole Studios, 1973.
[14] p. ill. 18 x 21 cm.
Printed at the Stinehour Press.
1. Small, Ambrose. I. Nancy Poole Studios. II. Title.
VtU NUC76-87326

Baker, Anne.
Morning Star: Florence Baker's diary of the expedition to put down the slave trade on the Nile, 1870–1873; foreword by Sir Ronald Wingate. London, Kimber, 1972.
240, ₍12₎ p. illus., facsims., map, ports. 24 cm. index. £3.50
B 73-00153
From Florence Baker's unpublished diary of the expedition and her letters home, coupled with the account in Samuel Baker's journals and the diary of his nephew, Julian.
1. Sudan—Description and travel. 2. Slave-trade—Sudan. 3. Baker, Sir Samuel White, 1821–1893. 4. Baker, Anne. I. Baker, Florence, Lady. II. Baker, Sir Samuel White, 1821–1893. III. Baker, Julian. IV. Title.
DT123.B34 962.4'04'0924 73-161679
ISBN 0-7183-0432-2 [B] MARC

Baker, Anne.
Wings over Kabul : the first airlift / ₍by₎ Anne Baker and Sir Ronald Ivelaw-Chapman ; foreword by Sir William Dickson. — London : Kimber, 1975.
191 p. : ill., facsims., map, ports. ; 24 cm. GB76-02089
ISBN 0-7183-0184-6 : £5.25
1. Afghanistan—History. 2. Ivelaw-Chapman, Ronald, Sir, 1899- 3. Great Britain. Royal Air Force—History. I. Ivelaw-Chapman, Ronald, Sir, 1899- joint author. II. Title.
DS369.B34 958.1 76-367592
76 MARC

Baker, Armand Fred, 1933-
El tiempo en la novela Hispanoamericana: un estudio del concepto del tiempo en siete novelas representativas. ₍n.p.₎ 1967.
x, 380 l.
Microfilm copy.
Thesis—University of Iowa.
Bibliography: leaves ₍369₎-380.
1. Spanish American literature. History and criticism. I. Title.
OrU NUC75-30249

Baker, Armand Fred, 1933-
El tiempo en la novela hispanoamericana; un estudio del concepto del tiempo en siete novelas representativas. ₍Iowa City, Iowa₎ 1967 ₍c1968₎
x, 380 l.
Thesis—University of Iowa.
Bibliography: leaves 370-380.
Microfilm. Ann Arbor, Mich., University Microfilms. 1 reel. 35 mm.
1. Latin American fiction—Hist. & crit. 2. Time in literature. I. Title.
TxU NUC74-128153

Baker, Arthur.
Calligraphic alphabets / by Arthur Baker. — New York : Dover Publications, 1974.
153 p. : all ill. ; 29 cm. — (Dover pictorial archive series)
ISBN 0-486-21045-6 : $3.50
1. Calligraphy. 2. Alphabets. I. Title.
Z43.B16 745.6'1 74-82203
MARC

Baker, Arthur.
Calligraphy. New York, Dover Publications ₍1973₎
155 p. illus. 21 x 29 cm. (Dover pictorial archive series) $3.50
1. Calligraphy.
Z43.B17 745.6'1 72-93759
ISBN 0-486-22895-9 MARC

Baker, Arthur.
Pyrometasomatic ore deposits at Johnson Camp, Arizona. ₍Ann Arbor, University Microfilms, 1971₎
93 l. illus., maps (part fold.)
"This is an authorized facsimile and was produced by microfilm-xerography..."
Thesis—Stanford University, 1953.
Includes bibliography.
AzU NUC73-35550

Baker, Arthur.
The Roman alphabet / by Arthur Baker. — New York : Art Direction Book Co., ₍c1976₎
60 leaves : all ill. ; 32 cm.
ISBN 0-910158-23-1
1. Alphabet. 2. Calligraphy. I. Title.
NK3603.B34 745.6'197 76-44477
77 MARC

Baker, Arthur, 1890–
The House is sitting. Westport, Conn., Greenwood Press ₍1974₎
264 p. illus. 22 cm.
Reprint of the 1958 ed. published by Blandford Press, London.
1. Great Britain — Politics and government — 20th century. 2. Great Britain. Parliament. House of Commons. I. Title.
[DA566.7.B22 1974] 328.42'072 74-68
ISBN 0-8371-7364-7 MARC

Baker, Arthur, fl. 1907–1909.
The Americans Esperanto book; a compendium of the international language Esperanto, compiled and edited by Arthur Baker ... Chicago, C. H. Kerr & company, 1907.
186, 130 p. 17½ cm.
1. Esperanto — Grammar. 2. Esperanto — Dictionaries—English. 3. English language—Dictionaries—Esperanto. I. Title.
PM8213.B25 7-24462

₍**Baker, Arthur**₎ fl. 1907–1909.
Elements of Esperanto; pronunciation, grammar, exercises and a little story. Chicago ₍Amerika esperantists, c1907₎
cover-title, ₍15₎ p. 15½ cm.
1. Esperanto—Grammar.
PM8213.B27 10-4255

Baker, Arthur, fl. 1907–1909.
An introduction to Esperanto; elements of the international language, with a short story and vocabulary, by Arthur Baker ... Chicago, American esperantist company, 1909.
32 p. 17 cm.
1. Esperanto—Grammar.
PM8213.B3 8-37079

Baker, Arthur, 1923–
Forecasts for the future—minerals, by Arthur Baker, III, N. L. Archbold ₍and₎ W. J. Stoll. Reno, Mackay School of Mines, University of Nevada, 1972 ₍i. e. 1973₎
xv, 223 p. illus. 28 cm. (Nevada Bureau of Mines and Geology. Bulletin 82) $4.00
Bibliography: p. 223.
1. Mineral industries—Nevada—Water-supply. 2. Mineral industries—Nevada. I. Archbold, N. L., 1930- joint author. II. Stoll, Walter J., joint author. III. Title. IV. Series: Nevada. Bureau of Mines and Geology. Bulletin 82.
TN24.N3B27 553'.09793 73-622395
MARC

Baker, Arthur D
Photoelectron spectroscopy: chemical and analytical aspects ₍by₎ A. D. Baker and D. Betteridge. ₍1st ed.₎ Oxford, New York, Pergamon Press ₍1972₎
x, 180 p. illus. 22 cm. (International series of monographs in analytical chemistry, v. 53)
Includes bibliographical references.
1. Electron spectroscopy. I. Betteridge, D., joint author. II. Title.
QD95.B32 1972 544'.6 72-77503
ISBN 0-08-016910-4 rev MARC

Baker, Arthur D.
see Electron spectroscopy ... London, Academic Press, 1977-

Baker, Arthur Ernest, 1876-1941.
A concordance to The devil and the lady, by Alfred Tennyson, edited by Charles Tennyson, his grandson. Being a supplement to the "Concordance to the works of the late Lord Tennyson", by Arthur E. Baker. London, Golden Vista Press, 1931; New York, Kraus Reprint Co., 1971.
247 p. 24 cm.
1. Tennyson, Alfred Tennyson, Baron, 1809-1892. The devil and the lady. 2. Tennyson, Alfred Tennyson, Baron—Concordances. I. Title.
WU NUC73-35526

Baker, Augusta.
Best loved nursery rhymes and songs, including Mother Goose selections. New York, Published by Parents' Magazine Enterprises, Inc. For Playmore, Inc., New York ₍1973₎
250 p. illus.
"Originally published as Vol. 1 - Young Years Library."
1. Nursery rhymes. I. Mother Goose. II. Playmore, inc. III. Title.
OCl NUC76-43480

Baker, Augusta. The Black experience in children's books
see New York (City). Public Library. Office of Children's Services. The Black experience in children's audiovisual materials. [New York] 1973.

Baker, Augusta. Books about Negro life for children.
see Rollock, Barbara. The Black experience in children's books. New York, : New York Public Library, 1974.

Baker, Augusta
see Courlander, Harold, 1908-
Uncle Bodqui of Haiti. [Sound recording] Folkways Records FC 7107. p1956.

Baker, Augustine, 1575–1641.
Holy wisdom; or, Directions for the prayer of contemplation, by Augustine Baker; the digest made by Serenus Cressy from the treatises of Fr Baker; with an introduction by Dom Gerard Sitwell. Wheathampstead, Anthony Clarke Books, 1972.
xxvi, 497 p. 21 cm. index. £3.75 B 72-25724
Originally published under title: Sancta sophia; or, Directions for the prayer of contemplation, Doway ₍Douai₎, J. Patté and T. Fievet, 1657.
Includes bibliographical references.
1. Asceticism—Catholic Church. I. Cressy, Serenus, 1605–1647. II. Title. III. Title: Directions for the prayer of contemplation.
BV5030.B3 1972 248'.3 73-161768
ISBN 0-85650-016-X MARC

Baker, B. Granville
see
Baker, Bernard Granville, 1870-1957.

Baker, B. H.
see
Baker, Brian Howard.

Baker, B. O.
see
Baker, Bo.

Baker, B T
Commercial almond growing. [Adelaide] 1973.
31 p. illus. (South Australia. Dept. of Agriculture. Extension bulletin no. 10)
South Australia. Dept. of Agriculture. Horticulture no. 3.
I. Title.
DNAL NUC74-126551

Baker, Belva B.
see Hong Kong study. [n.p.] 1963.

Baker, Benjaman Burton.
Epidermal cell renewal in the dog. [Davis, Calif.] 1971.
59 l. illus. (part col.)
Thesis (Ph.D.)—University of California, Davis.
Typescript.
CU-A NUC73-35549

Baker, Bernard Granville, 1870-1957.
The walls of Constantinople / by B. Granville Baker. — New York : AMS Press, 1975.
261 p., [29] leaves of plates : ill. ; 19 cm.
Reprint of the 1910 ed. published by J. Milne, London.
ISBN 0-404-56509-3
1. Istanbul—Walls—History. 2. Istanbul—Antiquities, Byzantine. I. Title.
DR729.B34 1975 914.96'1 72-178513
75 MARC

Baker, Bernard Randall, 1915-
Design of active-site-directed irreversible enzyme inhibitors : the organic chemistry of the enzymic active-site / B. R. Baker. — Huntington, N.Y. : R. E. Krieger Pub. Co., 1975, c1967.
xiii, 325 p. : ill. ; 24 cm.
Reprint of the ed. published by Wiley, New York.
Includes bibliographical references and indexes.
ISBN 0-88275-259-6
1. Enzyme inhibitors. I. Title.
[QP601.B19 1975] 574.1'925 74-32255
74 MARC

Baker, Bertrand
see Texas. University at Austin. Humanities Research Center. The North American frontier... Austin, 1967.

Baker, Betty.
At the center of the world. Based on Papago and Pima myths. Illustrated by Murray Tinkelman. New York, Macmillan [1973]
53 p. illus. 23 cm. $4.95
CONTENTS: Earth magician.—Coyote drowns the world.—The killing pot.—The monster eagle.—The killing of Eetoi.—The first war.
1. Papago Indians—Legends—Juvenile literature. 2. Pima Indians—Legends—Juvenile literature. [1. Papago Indians—Legends. 2. Pima Indians—Legends. 3. Indians of North America—Legends] I. Tinkelman, Murray, illus. II. Title.
PZ8.1.B1724At 299'.7 72-88820
ISBN 0-02-708290-3 MARC

Baker, Betty.
Dupper / Betty Baker ; illustrated by Chuck Eckart. — New York : Greenwillow Books, c1976.
147 p. : ill. ; 23 cm.
SUMMARY: Relates the adventures of a prairie dog and his friends.
ISBN 0-688-80046-7. ISBN 0-688-84046-9 lib. bdg.
1. Prairie dogs—Legends and stories. [1. Prairie dogs—Fiction] I. Eckhart, Chuck. II. Title.
PZ10.3.B163 Du [Fic] 75-44155
75 MARC

Baker, Betty.
The medicine man's last stand; illustrated by Leonard Shortall. New York, Scholastic Book Services [1973, c1963]
132 p. illus.
Translation of The Shaman's last raid.
1. Indians of North America—Fiction.
I. Title.
ISC NUC74-126552

Baker, Betty.
The spirit is willing. New York, Macmillan [1974]
135 p. 22 cm. $4.95
SUMMARY: In an Arizona silver mining town in the 1880's, an encounter with "spiritism" gives a fourteen-year-old a new understanding of people.
[1. United States—Social life and customs—1865-1918—Fiction] I. Title.
PZ7.B1693Sp [Fic] 73-8576
ISBN 0-02-708270-9 MARC

Baker, Betty.
Three fools and a horse / by Betty Baker ; pictures by Glen Rounds. — New York : Macmillan, c1975.
62 p. : col. ill. ; 22 cm. — (Ready-to-read)
SUMMARY: A retelling of three nonsensical adventures of the Foolish People, a tribe created by the Apaches for the purposes of telling jokes about them.
ISBN 0-02-708250-4
[1. Indians of North America—Fiction. 2. Apache Indians—Fiction] I. Rounds, Glen. II. Title.
PZ7.B1693 Th [E] 75-14272
75 MARC

Baker, Betty.
Walk the world's rim. [1st Trophy ed.] New York, Harper & Row [1965]
168 p. illus., map. (A Harper Trophy book, J26)
Includes bibliography.
1. Mexico—History—Conquest, 1519-1540—Fiction. 2. Indians of North America—Southwest, New—Fiction. 3. Estévan, d. 1539—Fiction. I. Title.
AzU NUC76-70950

Baker, Betty Sue.
A study of social status, personality characteristics, and motor ability of mentally handicapped girls : a dissertation / by Betty Sue Baker. — [San Francisco] : R. D. Reed, 1968 i.e. 1975.
ix, 81 p. : ill. ; 28 cm.
Thesis—University of Alabama.
Bibliography: p. 72-87.
ISBN 0-88247-311-5 : $8.00
1. Mentally handicapped children—Louisiana. 2. Girls. 3. Personality. 4. Motor ability—Testing. I. Title: A study of social status ...
HV3006.L8B34 1975 362.3 74-28604
75 MARC

Baker, Bill.
House of ideas; creative interior designs. New York, Macmillan [1974]
xiii, 279 p. illus. 28 cm.
1. Dwellings—Remodeling. 2. Interior decoration. 3. House furnishings. I. Title.
TH4816.B33 643'.7 73-11734
ISBN 0-02-506280-8 MARC

Baker, Bill R
Catch the vision—the life of Henry L. Whitfield of Mississippi. Mississippi State [c1973]
v, 270 l. 21 cm.
Thesis—Mississippi State University.
Bibliography: leaves [245]-270.
1. Whitfield, Henry Lewis, 1868-1927.
I. Title.
MsU NUC76-70992

Baker, Bill R
Catch the vision: the life of Henry L. Whitfield of Mississippi. [n.p., c1973]
1 reel. 35 mm.
Thesis (Ph. D.)—Mississippi State University.
Microfilm of typescript. Ann Arbor, Mich., University Microfilms [1974]
1. Whitfield, Henry Lewis, 1868-1927.
I. Title.
WHi NUC76-28925

Baker, Bill R
Catch the vision : the life of Henry L. Whitfield of Mississippi / Bill R. Baker. — Jackson : University Press of Mississippi, [1974]
x, 173 p. : ill. ; 24 cm.
Bibliography: p. 155-170.
Includes index.
ISBN 0-87805-062-0 : $7.95
1. Whitfield, Henry Lewis, 1868-1927. I. Title.
F341.W48B34 976.2'062'0924 74-82918
[B] MARC

Baker, Bo.
Made for the mountains / Bo Baker. — Waco, Tex. : Word Books, c1977.
85 p. ; 22 cm.
ISBN 0-87680-504-7 : $3.95
1. Baptists—Sermons. 2. Sermons, American. I. Title.
BX6333.B348M33 252'.06'1 76-48503
77 MARC

Baker, Brad, joint author
see Courtney, Kent. The Students for a Democratic Society. [n.p., 1969]

Baker, Brenda Jones, 1940-
Acceptance versus rejection of the traditional feminine role: consideration of Women's liberation. [Detroit] 1972.
vi, 158 l. 29 cm.
Thesis—Wayne State University.
Vita.
Bibliography: leaves 148-157.
1. Women's Liberation Movement. 2. Woman—Psychology. I. Title.
MiDW NUC74-1362

Baker, Brenda Jones, 1940-
Acceptance versus rejection of the traditional feminine role: Consideration of women's liberation. Detroit, 1972.
1 v.
Thesis—Wayne State University.
Microfilm of typescript. Ann Arbor, Mich., University Microfilms, 1972. 1 reel. 35 mm.
1. Woman—Social and moral questions. 2. Sex role. 3. Women's Liberation Movement. I. Title.
FMU NUC74-126554

Baker, Brenda Sue.
Transductions and families of tree languages. [n.p.] 1973.
1 v.
Thesis—Harvard.
MH NUC75-19469

Baker, Brian Howard.
Geology of the Mount Kenya area; degree sheet 44 N.W. quarter (with coloured map) by B. H. Baker. [Nairobi, Geological Survey of Kenya, 1967]
ix, 78 p. illus. 25 cm. (Geological Survey of Kenya. Report no. 79)
Part of illustrative matter in pocket.
Bibliography: p. 76-78.
1. Geology—Kenya—Mount Kenya region. I. Title. II. Series: Kenya. Geological Survey. Report no. 79.
QE327.K4A3 no. 79 556.76'2'08 s 75-304402
75 MARC

Baker, Bruce H
Does the mountain pine beetle change hosts in mixed lodgepole and whitebark pine stands? Ogden, Utah, 1971.
7 p. illus. (U.S. Intermountain Forest and Range Experiment Station. U.S.D.A. Forest Service research note INT-151)
Bibliography: p. 7.
I. Title.
DNAL NUC73-41482

Baker, Bruce L
Parents as teachers. Manuals for behavior modification of the retarded child; studies in family training [by] Bruce L. Baker, Louis J. Heifetz [and] Alan J. Brightman. Cambridge, Mass. [c1972]
1 v. (various pagings) illus. 28 cm.
"READ Project series... developed by Behavioral Education Projects, Inc. ... Harvard University..."
Final report Grant no. NIH-NICHD-72-2016.
1. Mentally handicapped children—Education. I. Heifetz, Louis J., joint author. II. Brightman, Alan J., joint author. III. Title.
CtY NUC76-87337

Baker, Bruce N
PERT cost and other project cost control techniques [by Bruce N.] Baker and [René L.] Eris. [Los Altos, Calif., Bruce N. Baker - Management Consultants, 1965-
1 v. (loose-leaf) illus. 30 cm.
1. PERT (Network analysis) 2. Cost control. I. Eris, René L. II. Title.
OrPS NUC74-12384

Baker, Bruce R.
see Police personnel administration. [Washington] Police Foundation, c1974.

Baker, Bruce Stewart, 1945-
Sex Chromosome meiotic mutants in Drosophila melanogaster; detection and preliminary characterization. [Seattle] 1971.
56 l. illus.
Thesis (Ph. D.)—University of Washington.
Bibliography: leaves 53-56.
1. Sex chromosomes. 2. Meiosis. 3. Mutation (Biology) 4. Drosphilia melanogaster. I. Title.
WaU NUC73-126579

Baker, Bryan
see Mississippi. State University. Institutional Self-study, 1970-71. Self-study report on student personnel. [State College, Miss., 1971]

Baker, Burton, 1937-
Edward Albee's nihilistic plays. [n. p.] c1974.
212 l. 29 cm.
Thesis (Ph. D.)–University of Wisconsin.
Vita.
Includes bibliography.
1. Albee, Edward, 1928-
WU NUC76-18067

Baker, Byrd.
see Mendocino ... Mendocino, Calif., Pacific Rim Research, c1977.

Baker, Byron A
Correlations of phase-boundary pressures of condensate fluid systems with compositions modified by added butane, by Byron A. Baker and C. Kenneth Eilerts. [Washington] U.S. Bureau of Mines [1973]
56 p. illus. (U.S. Bureau of Mines. Report of investigations 7759)
Includes bibliography.
1. Fluidization. 2. Phase diagrams. 3. Regression analysis. I. Eilerts, C. Kenneth, joint author. II. United States. Bureau of Mines. III. Title. IV. Series.
DI NUC75-23171

Baker, C A
Malawi's exports: the history of the export trade of Nyasaland, 1891-1962. [By] C.A. Baker. [n.p., n.d.]
20 p. 34 cm.
Cover title.
Includes bibliographical references.
1. Malawi—Foreign trade—Hist. I. Title.
NSyU NUC73-41616

Baker, C. Alice
see
Baker, Charlotte Alice, 1833-1909.

Baker, C. B., ed.
see Western Agricultural Economics Research Council. Committee on the Economics of Range Use and Development. A methodological anthology. [n. p., Regional RMA Research Project W-16] 1957.

Baker, C D
Lepard's metric reckoner: for cost per thousand sheets given price per kilogramme and weight in kilogrammes; compiled by C. D. Baker and J. W. Davies. London, Pitman, 1972.
[6], 362 p. 30 cm. £4.00 B 72-17231
1. Paper making and trade—Tables and ready-reckoners. 2. Stationery trade. I. Davies, J. W., joint author. II. Lepard and Smiths Group of Companies. III. Title.
HF5716.S6B33 338.4'3'67620942 73-177380
ISBN 0-273-25242-9 MARC

Baker, C D
Tort, by C. D. Baker. London, Sweet and Maxwell, 1972.
xxii, 295 p. 23 cm. index. (Concise college texts) £2.50
B 72-15150
1. Torts—Great Britain. I. Title.
KD1949.3.B35 346'.42'03 72-197831
ISBN 0-421-13820-3; 0-421-13830-0 (pbk.) MARC

Baker, C. D.
see also
Baker, Charles David.

Baker, C H
Performance in an auditory vigilance task while simultaneously tracking a visual target. [By] C.H. Baker [and] A. Harabedian. Los Angeles, 1962.
v, 13 l. 28 cm. (Its Technical report 740-2)
Prepared for Douglas Aircraft Company, Inc.
I. Human Factors Research, inc.
OCU NUC76-44460

Baker, C. Jane
see
Baker, Carolyn Jane.

Baker, C L
Army cost model programmers' reference manual. Santa Monica, Rand Corporation, 1963.
x, 170 p. illus. 28 cm. (Rand Corporation. [Research] memorandum RM-3721-ASDC)
Prepared for the Office of the Assistant Secretary of Defense/Comptroller.
"References": p. 167.
Bibliography: p. 169.
1. Cost. 2. U.S. Army. 3. Mathematical models. I. Title. II. Series.
MB NUC74-122381

Baker, C L
History of Academy Conference, 1926-1970. Memphis, Tenn. [1971?]
79 p. 28 cm.
1. Academy Conference—History. I. Title.
AAP NUC74-121639

Baker, C L
JOSS: rubrics [by] C.L. Baker. [Santa Monica, Calif., Rand Corporation] 1967.
5 p. 28 cm. (Rand Corporation. Paper, P-3560)
Cover title.
1. JOSS (Electronic computer system) I. Title. II. Series.
MB NUC73-59606

Baker, C Richard.
Behavioral aspects of corporate planning / C. Richard Baker. -- New York : Graduate School of Business, Columbia University, 1975.
11 p. ; 28 cm. -- (Research paper - Graduate School of Business, Columbia University ; no. 86)
NNC NUC77-91817

Baker, C Richard.
A discussion of drawbacks to full-cost in petroleum industry accounting / C. Richard Baker. -- New York : Graduate School of Business, Columbia University, 1976.
15, [1] p. ; 28 cm. -- (Research paper - Graduate School of Business, Columbia University ; no. 113)
Includes bibliographical references.
NNC NUC77-91818

Baker, C Richard.
Participant observation as a method of accounting research / C. Richard Baker. -- New York : Graduate School of Business, Columbia University, 1975.
15, [2] p. ; 28 cm. -- (Research paper--Graduate School of Business, Columbia University ; no. 92)
NNC NUC77-91914

Baker, C Richard.
Structure as a construct in accounting research / C. Richard Baker. -- New York : Graduate School of Business, Columbia University, 1975.
[18] p. ; 28 cm. -- (Research paper--Columbia University, Graduate School of Business ; no. 93)
Includes bibliographical references.
NNC NUC77-91651

Baker, C. S. L.
see
Baker, Crispin Stuart Leworthy, 1939-

Baker, Carl, illus.
see Gold, Phyllis. Please don't say hello. [New York, Human Sciences Press, 1975]

Baker, Carl Leroy.
Definiteness and indefiniteness in English [by] C. L. Baker. [Bloomington] Indiana University Linguistics Club, 1973.
23 p. 28 cm.
Cover title.
1. English language—Article. I. Title.
MoKU NUC76-70926

Baker, Carl T
Coho salmon sampling [prepared by Carl T. Baker, Jr. and Russell L. Scholl. Columbus, Ohio Dept. of Natural Resources, Division of Wildlife] 1971.
25 l. illus. 2 maps. 28 cm.
On cover: Lake Erie fisheries investigations. Job completion report. Dingell-Johnson project F-35-R-9, job no. 5.
1. Silver salmon. I. Scholl, Russell L., joint author. II. Ohio. Division of Wildlife. III. Title.
DI NUC75-26233

Baker, Carlos Heard, 1909-
Ernest Hemingway; elämäkerta [kirj.] Carlos Baker. [Suomentanut Inkeri Hämäläinen] Helsingissä, Kustannusosakeyhtiö Tammi [1971]
586 p. illus., ports. 24 cm.
1. Hemingway, Ernest, 1899-1961.
MB NUC73-126580

Baker, Carlos Heard, 1909–
The Gay Head conspiracy, a novel of suspense [by] Carlos Baker. New York, Scribner [1973]
[185 p. map (on lining papers) 22 cm. $5.95
I. Title.
PZ4.B1676Gay 813'.5'4 72-11111
ISBN 0-684-13297-4 MARC

Baker, Carlos Heard, 1909-
Hemingway and his critics, an international anthology. New York, Hill and Wang [1963]
[i-xiv] 1-298 p., 2 l. 20 cm.
Reprint of paperback edition. Hanneman G27a.
I. Title.
OKentU NUC74-122401

Baker, Carlos Heard, 1909-
Hemingway; histoire d'une vie. Traduit de l'anglais pas Claude Noël et Andrée R. Picard. Paris, Editions R. Laffont [1971, c1969]
2 v. illus., ports. 24 cm.
Translation of Ernest Hemingway; a life story.
Sommaire. —v. 1. 1899-1936. —v. 2. 1936-1961.
1. Hemingway, Ernest, 1899-1961. I. Title.
CaOOU NUC74-124011

Baker, Carlos Heard, 1909–
Hemingway, the writer as artist. [4th ed.] Princeton, N. J., Princeton University Press [1972]
xx, 438 p. 23 cm.
"A working check-list of Hemingway's prose, poetry, and journalism, with notes": p. [409]–426.
Includes bibliographical references.
1. Hemingway, Ernest, 1899–1961. I. Title.
PS3515.E37Z58 1972 813'.5'2 70-170253
ISBN 0-691-06231-5; 0-691-01305-5 (pbk.) MARC

Baker, Carlos Heard, 1909-
Người bạn quyền thế (a friend in power) Bản dịch của Nguyễn-cao-Thăng. Saigon, Ziên-Hồng [1968]
237 p. (Loại Anh-Việt đối chiếu. Loại 2. 000 ngữ-vựng Anh-văn)
English and Vietnamese on facing pages.
I. Title.
ICarbS NUC75-29955

Baker, Carlos Heard, 1909-
The talismans and other stories / by Carlos Baker. — New York : Scribner, c1976.
183 p. ; 21 cm.
CONTENTS: Carpe diem.—Your wish is my command.—The prevaricator.—Côte d'Azur.—The talismans.—The place where it happened.—Take care of yourself.—The squirrel in the basement.—Red white and blue pickup.—Grate apple, leave skin on, raisins on top and honey.—Who am I?.—All, all are in my thoughts tonight, being dead.
ISBN 0-684-14473-5 : $7.95
I. Title.
PZ4.B1676 Tal 813'.5'4 75-20366
[PS3552.A4] MARC
—— ——— Copy 2. PS3552.A4T3 75

Baker, Carol F.
see Russell, Helen H. The Tiadaghton tale ... ˌs.l., s.n.ˌ c1975 (Williamsport, Pa. : Scaife's Valley Press)

Baker, Carolyn Jane, comp.
Paintings and drawings by Francis Towne (1739/40–1816) and John White Abbott (1763–1851) in the collection of the Exeter Museums and Art Gallery: ˌcatalogue of an exhibitionˌ, by C. Jane Baker. Exeter, City of Exeter Museums and Art Gallery, 1971.
39 p. illus. 22 cm. (Exeter museums publication, no. 57) £0.30
B 72–12707
I. Towne, Francis, 1740?–1816. II. White Abbott, John, 1763–1851. III. Title. IV. Series.
ND497.T75B34 759.2'074'0237 73–154129
ISBN 0-9502069-6-2 MARC

Baker, Catherine.
Index to Bay City biographies, compiled by Catherine Baker. [Essexville, Mich.] 1973.
1 v. (unpaged) 30 cm.
1. Bay County, Mich.–Biography–Indexes. I. Title.
MI NUC75-17348

Baker, Catherine, comp.
Talking about the mass media. London, Wayland, 1973.
96 p. illus., facsims. 24 cm. (Wayland talking points) £1.95
GB 73–10903
Includes index.
Bibliography: p. 94.
1. Mass media. I. Title.
P90.B258 301.16'1'08 73–173156
ISBN 0-85340-265-5 MARC

Baker, Catherine
see Newspapers printed in Bay County. -- Essexville, Mich., ˌ197-?ˌ

Baker, Cecile Culp, 1948-
Sex differences in achievement-related behaviors in upper elementary school children. [Tallahassee, Fla.] c1973.
x, 94 l. tables.
Thesis (Ph. D.)–Florida State University.
Bibliography: leaves 89-92.
Vita.
1. Child study. 2. Human behavior. I. Title.
FTaSU NUC75-17379

Baker, Charles
see Raleigh, N.C. Public Schools. Course of study for the teaching of Spanish, level I through level IV. ˌRaleigh, n.d.ˌ

Baker, Charles, solicitor
see Slesser, Sir Henry Herman, 1883-
Trade union law. 3d ed. Ann Arbor, Mich., University Microfilms, 1975.

Baker (Charles) & Sons (Paper Makers)
see also
Lepard and Smiths Group of Companies.

Baker, Charles, 1803-1874
see Gallaudet College, Washington, D.C. Edward Miner Gallaudet Memorial Library. Dictionary catalog on deafness and the deaf. Boston, G.K. Hall, 1970.

Baker, Charles Arnold-
see Arnold-Baker, Charles.

Baker, Charles Ashmore.
Public versus private electricity supply, by C. Ashmore Baker. London, Fabian Society, 1913. ˌNendeln, Liechtenstein, Kraus Reprint, 1969ˌ
19 p. 22 cm. (Fabian tract no. 173)
1. Electric utilities–Government ownership. I. Title.
MB NUC74-121638

Baker, Charles Clayton, 1943-
The use of a lumped-constant transmission line as the energy storage system for a crossed-field plasma source and the resulting energy distribution and impurity content of the downstream plasma. ˌn.p.ˌ c1972.
145 l. illus. 29 cm.
Thesis (Ph. D.)–University of Wisconsin.
Vita.
Includes bibliography.
I. Title.
WU NUC74-813

Baker, Charles D.
see Augustine, Marshall T Evaluation of plants... ˌHyattsville, Md.ˌ United States Dept. of Agriculture, Soil Conservation Service, 1964.

Baker, Charles David.
Tort / by C. D. Baker. — 2d ed. — London : Sweet & Maxwell, 1976.
xxvii, 332 p. ; 23 cm. — (Concise college texts) GB***
Includes index.
ISBN 0-421-21470-8. ISBN 0-421-21480-5 pbk.
1. Torts—Great Britain. I. Title.
KD1949.3.B35 1976 346'.42'03 77-355556
77 MARC

Baker, Charles Hinckley, 1864-
Improved water supply for Ithaca ˌbyˌ Charles H. Baker, Ithaca, N.Y., 1886.
99 l. 4 plates (part fold.) 28 cm.
Thesis (C.E.)–Cornell University.
Microfilm. Ithaca, N.Y., Photo Science, Cornell University, 1972. part of reel. 35 mm.
1. Ithaca, N.Y.–Water-supply.
NIC NUC76-70999

Baker, Charles M., joint author.
see Davis, Hester A., 1930- Emergency survey and testing in the lower White River and Arkansas Post Canal area, Arkansas, 1965. Fayetteville, Arkansas Archeological Survey, 1974.

Baker, Charles T., 1939- joint author
see Trachtenberg, Isaac, 1929-
Ion-selective electrochemical sensors—second report. [Washington] Dept. of the Interior, 1970 [i. e. 1971]

Baker, Charles Vivian.
Housing associations / ˌbyˌ Charles Vivian Baker. — London : Estates Gazette, 1976.
xv, 604 p. : 2 ill., forms ; 23 cm. GB77-05258
Bibliography: p. 569-576.
Includes index.
ISBN 0-7282-0031-7 : £7.50
1. Housing—Great Britain. 2. Housing—Finance. 3. Housing authorities—Great Britain. 4. Housing—Great Britain—Law and legislation. I. Title.
HD7333.A3B24 334'.1 77-359353
77 MARC

Baker, Charles Vivian, joint author
see Macey, John P Housing management. 2d ed. London, Estates Gazette, 1973.

Baker, Charlotte Alice, 1833–1909, comp.
Epitaphs in the old burying-ground at Deerfield, Mass., copied by C. Alice Baker and Emma L. Coleman. Deerfield, Mass., The Pocumtuck Valley memorial association, 1924.
2 p. l., 49 p. front., plates. 24 cm.
——— Index / prepared by John F. Mason. — ˌPrinceton? N. J.ˌ : Mason, 1976.
39 leaves ; 30 cm.
F74.D4B3 Supl.
1. Deerfield, Mass. — Genealogy. 2. Epitaphs — Massachusetts — Deerfield. I. Coleman, Emma Lewis, joint comp. II. Mason, John F. III. Pocumtuck Valley Memorial Association, Deerfield, Mass. IV. Title.
F74.D4B3 25–13749

Baker, Charlotte Alice, 1833-1909.
True stories of New England captives / Charlotte Alice Baker. — New York : Garland Pub., 1976 ˌc1897ˌ
407 p., ˌ13ˌ leaves of plates : ill. ; 23 cm. — (The Garland library of narratives of North American Indian captivities ; v. 101)
Reprint of the 1897 ed. published by the Press of E. A. Hall, Cambridge and Greenfield, Mass., under title: True stories of New England captives carried to Canada during the old French and Indian wars.
Includes index.
CONTENTS: Christine Otis.—Esther Wheelwright.—Story of a York family.—Difficulties and dangers in the settlement of a frontier town, 1670.—Eunice Williams.—Ensign John Sheldon.—My hunt for the captives.—Two captives.—A day at Oka.—Thankful Stebbins.—A scion of the church in Deerfield.—Hertel de Rouville.—Father Meriel, Mary Silver.—Appendix.
ISBN 0-8240-1725-0
1. Indians of North America—Captivities. 2. Frontier and pioneer life—New England. 3. New Englanders in Canada—History. 4. New England—History—Colonial period, ca. 1600-1775. I. Title. II. Series.
E85.G2 vol. 101 973'.04'97 s 75-7128
75 MARC

Baker, Chester Bird.
Programmed production responses on dairy farms in northeastern Illinois ˌbyˌ C.B. Baker, Max R. Langham ˌandˌ Keith G. Cowling. ˌUrbana, 1965ˌ
43 p. tables. 29 cm. (Illinois. Agricultural Experiment Station, Urbana. Bulletin 708)
Cover title.
1. Dairying–Illinois. I. Langham, Max R. II. Cowling, Keith. III. Title. IV. Series.
IEdS NUC74-122400

Baker, Chester Bird, joint author
see Hopkin, John A Financial management in agriculture. Danville, Ill., Interstate Printers & Publishers ˌ1973ˌ

Baker, Chester Bird, joint author
see Irwin, George D Effects of lender decisions... ˌUrbana, 1962ˌ

Baker, Chester Bird, joint author
see Jordan, Max F Effects of fertilizer programs... [Urbana, 1962]

Baker, Chester Bird, joint author
see Tefertiller, Kenneth Ray, 1930-
Selection of freshening dates that will maximize dairy profits. [Urbana, 1962]

Baker, Chester Bird, joint author
see Tongroj Onchandra. A model to relate the agricultural sector to Thailand's 5-year plan. Bangkok, Dept. of Agricultural Economics, Faculty of Economics and Business Administration, Kasetsart University, 1970.

Baker, Christopher E
Costa Rican legislative behavior in perspective, by Christopher E. Baker. [Gainesville] 1973.
vii, 323 l. illus. 28 cm.
Typescript.
Thesis–University of Florida.
Vita.
Bibliography: leaves p. 311-321.
1. Costa Rica. Congreso Constitucional. 2. Costa Rica–Pol & govt. I. Title.
FU NUC75-17375

Baker, Christopher E
Municipal government in Costa Rica: its characteristics and functions. ˌByˌ Christopher E. Baker ˌandˌ Samuel Z. Stone. San José, Costa Rica, Associated Colleges of the Midwest Central American Field Program and School of Political Science, University of Costa Rica, 1971.
ˌ2ˌ, viii l., 173 l. tables. 27 cm.
AID/ACM Contract No. AID-515-198-T.
1. Municipal government–Costa Rica. I. Fernández Pinto, Ronald, joint author. II. Stone, Samuel Z., joint author. III. Title.
LNHT InU OU NIC NUC73-73587

Baker, Christopher John, 1948-
The politics of South India, 1920-1937 / Christopher John Baker. — Cambridge ; New York : Cambridge University Press, 1976.
xxiii, 363 p. ; 23 cm. — (Cambridge South Asian studies ; 17)
Bibliography: p. 339-353.
Includes index.
ISBN 0-521-20755-X
1. Madras (Presidency)—Politics and government. I. Title. II. Series.
DS485.M28B34 320.9'54'82035 75-2716
75 MARC

Baker, Christopher John, 1948-
South India : political institutions and political change, 1880-1940 / C. J. Baker, D. A. Washbrook. — Delhi : Macmillan Co. of India, 1975.
viii, 238 p. : map ; 23 cm.
Includes bibliographical references and index.
Rs50.00
1. South India—Politics and government. I. Washbrook, D. A., joint author. II. Title.
DS484.B34 320.9'54'8035 75-905202
76 MARC

Baker, Chuck.
The rockin' fifties: a rock and roll scrapbook!; a fast encounter with the generation that spawned rock and roll and student unrest, Howdy Doody and revolution, Elvis Presley and flights in space! ₍Woodland Hills, Calif., distributed by Avanco, 1973₎
175 p. illus., ports. 28 cm.
Cover title.
Discography: p. 173–174.
Includes bibliographic notes.
1. Rock music—History and criticism. I. Title.
ML3561.R62B3 784 73–92301
MARC

Baker, Claud H
Water resources of the Curlew Valley drainage basin, Utah and Idaho / by Claud H. Baker, Jr. ; prepared by the United States Geological Survey, in cooperation with the Utah Department of Natural Resources, Division of Wildlife Resources. — ₍Salt Lake City₎ : State of Utah, Dept. of Natural Resources, 1974.
v, 91 p. : ill. ; 28 cm. — (Technical publication - State of Utah, Department of Natural Resources ; no. 45)
Part of illustrative matter in pocket.
Bibliography: p. 43-44.
1. Water-supply—Curlew Valley, Idaho and Utah. I. United States. Geological Survey. II. Utah. Division of Wildlife Resources. III. Title. IV. Series: Utah. Dept. of Natural Resources. Technical publication ; no. 45.
TA7.U77 no. 45 553'.09792 s 75-621562
₍TD225.C93₎ 75 MARC

Baker, Claude R 1890-
Coin in the air. New York, Carlton Press [c1974]
48 p. (Hearthstone book)
1. Morale. 2. Religion. I. Title.
MBCo NUC76-30236

Baker, Clifford Howard, 1932-
Lagged effects of minimum wages on teenage unemployment. Raleigh, N.C., 1972.
100 l. tables. 29 cm.
Vita.
Thesis (Ph.D.)—North Carolina State University at Raleigh.
Bibliography: leaves 91-92.
NcRS NUC74-126553

Baker, Clifford Howard, 1932-
Lagged effects of minimum wages on teenage unemployment. Ann Arbor, Mich., University Microfilms, 1973.
1 reel. 35 mm.
Thesis—North Carolina State University at Raleigh, 1972.
Collation of the original: 100 leaves.
1. Youth—Employment. 2. Wages—Minimum wage. I. Title.
ViBlbV NUC74-126555

Baker, Colin.
The evolution of local government in Malawi / by Colin Baker. — Ile-Ife, Nigeria : Published by the University of Ife Press for the Institute of Administration, c1975.
60 p. ; 22 cm. — (Institute of Administration monograph series ; 3)
Includes bibliographical references.
1. Local government—Malawi. I. Ife. University. Institute of Administration. II. Title. III. Series: Ife. University. Institute of Administration. Institute of Administration monograph series ; 3.
JS7644.2.B34 352.0689'7 77-352315
77 MARC

Baker, Colin.
see International Conference on Trends in University Teaching and Research in Public Administration in Africa, University of Ife, 1970. Education and research in public administration in Africa. London, Hutchinson, 1974.

Baker, Cozy, 1927-
A cozy getaway / by Cozy Baker ; ill. and front cover designed by Susan Elliot. — Washington : Acropolis Books, c1976.
184 p. : ill. ; 15 x 16 cm.
Includes index.
ISBN 0-87491-063-3
1. United States—Description and travel—1960- —Guide-books. 2. Canada—Description and travel—1951- —Guide-books. I. Title.
E158.B28 917.3'04'925 76-15816
76 MARC

Baker, Crispin Stuart Leworthy, 1939-
Vulcanization with urethane reagents / ₍by₎ C. S. L. Baker. — Brickendonbury : Malaysian Rubber Producers' Research Association, ₍1976₎
18 p. : ill. ; 25 cm. — (NR technical bulletin) GB76-13508
Caption title.
Bibliography: p. 16.
ISBN 0-9504401-2-4
1. Vulcanization. 2. Urethanes. I. Title. II. Series.
TS1891.B34 678'.24 76-377159
76 MARC

Baker, Cyril.
The history of the posts in Halifax Parish / by Cyril Baker. — Sheffield : Yorkshire Postal History Society, 1974.
₍5₎, 141 p., 22 leaves of plates : facsims., maps ; 26 cm. — (Yorkshire Postal History Society publication ; no. 8) GB 74-14729
Limited ed. of 300 copies.
Bibliography: p. 139–140.
ISBN 0-9500053-6-3 : £3.00
1. Postal service—Great Britain—Halifax, Eng. (Parish)—History. I. Title. II. Series: Yorkshire Postal History Society. Yorkshire Postal History Society publication ; no. 8.
HE6946.H34B34 383'.09428'12 75-306548
MARC

Baker, D. A.
see Ion transport in plant cells and tissues. Amsterdam, North-Holland Pub. Co., 1975.

Baker, D. A., joint author.
see Sutcliffe, James Frederick. Plants and mineral salts. London, E. Arnold, 1974, 1976 printing.

Baker, D B
A new Pasitomachthes from Rhodesia (Hymenoptera, Apodea) Lourenço Marques, 1971.
8 p. illus. (Novos taxa entomologicos, no. 98)
Bibliography: p. 7-8.
I. Title.
DNAL NUC75-31156

Baker, D James.
Models of oceanic circulation. San Francisco, W. F. Freeman, 1970.
9 p. illus. (part col.) 28 cm.
Cover title.
At head of title: Scientific American offprints, 890.
On cover: Scientific American, Jan. 1970, v. 222, no. 1, pp. 114-121.
OCIU NUC74-121641

Baker, D L
Two Testaments, one Bible : a study of some modern solutions to the theological problem of the relationship between the Old and New Testaments / by D. L. Baker. — Downers Grove, Ill. : InterVarsity Press, c1976.
554 p. ; 22 cm.
Originally presented as the author's thesis, University of Sheffield, 1975, under title: The theological problem of the relationship between the Old Testament and the New Testament.
Bibliography: p. ₍391₎-535.
Includes indexes.
ISBN 0-87784-872-6 : $7.95
1. Bible. N.T.—Relation to O.T. I. Title.
BS2387.B33 1976 220.6 77-359566
77 MARC

Baker, D.M.
see Baker, Donald McCord, 1890-

Baker, D Philip, 1937-
School and public library media programs for children and young adults / by D. Philip Baker ; with a foreword by Augusta Baker. — Syracuse, N.Y. : Gaylord Professional Publications, 1977.
412 p. ; 22 cm.
Includes index.
ISBN 0-915794-09-8
1. Media programs (Education) 2. Instructional materials centers. 3. School libraries. 4. Public libraries. I. Title.
LB1028.4.B34 027.62'5 76-54919
76 MARC

Baker, D W
Not so much a warehouse; the CWS Automated Grocery Distribution Centre, Birtley ₍by₎ D. W. Baker. London, H. M. Stationery Off., 1972.
v, 151 p. illus. 21 x 30 cm. £4.00 B***
At head of title: Department of Trade and Industry.
1. Warehouses—Automation. 2. Co-operative Wholesale Society. I. Great Britain. Dept. of Trade and Industry. II. Title.
TS163.B34 658.7'85 72–196785
ISBN 0-11-510798-3 MARC

Baker, D. W. A.
see
Baker, David William Archdall.

Baker, Daisy, 1894-
More travels in a donkey trap / Daisy Baker : illustrated by Pamela Mara. — Boston : G. K. Hall, 1976.
265 p. : ill. ; 24 cm.
"Published in large print."
ISBN 0-8161-6430-4
1. Baker, Daisy, 1894- 2. England—Biography. 3. Sight-saving books. I. Title.
₍CT788.B244A36₎ 942.3'52 76-44317
76 MARC

Baker, Daisy, 1894-
More travels in a donkey trap / by Daisy Baker ; illustrated by Pamela Mara. — London : Souvenir Press, 1976.
191 p., plate : ill., map, col. port. ; 21 cm. GB76-18638
ISBN 0-285-62217-X : £3.00
1. Baker, Daisy, 1894- 2. England—Biography. I. Title.
CT788.B244A36 1976b 942.3'52'08570924 76-377880
76 MARC

Baker, Daisy, 1894-
Travels in a donkey trap / by Daisy Baker ; illustrated by Pamela Mara. — London : Souvenir Press, 1974.
160 p., plate : ill., col. port. ; 21 cm. GB74-17543
ISBN 0-285-62135-1 : £2.00
1. Baker, Daisy, 1894- 2. England—Biography. I. Title.
CT788.B244A37 1974b 942.3'52 74-188935
74₍r77₎rev MARC

Baker, Daisy, 1894-
Travels in a donkey trap. Illustrated by Pamela Mara. New York, St. Martin's Press ₍1974₎
160 p. illus. 20 cm. $6.95
1. Baker, Daisy, 1894- 2. England—Biography. I. Title.
CT788.B244A37 1974 942.3'52 73-87419
74₍r77₎rev MARC

Baker, Daisy, 1894-
Travels in a donkey trap / Daisy Baker ; illustrated by Pamela Mara. — Boston : G. K. Hall, 1975, c1974.
196 p. : ill. ; 25 cm.
"Published in large print."
ISBN 0-8161-6273-5 : $7.95
1. Baker, Daisy, 1894- 2. England—Biography. 3. Sight-saving books. I. Mara, Pamela. II. Title.
₍CT788.B244A37 1975₎ 942.3'52 75-4831
75₍r77₎rev MARC

Baker, Daisy, 1894-
Travels in a donkey trap / Daisy Baker. — London : Coronet, 1976.
160 p. : ill. ; 18 cm. GB76-15344
ISBN 0-340-20303-X : £0.60
1. Baker, Daisy, 1894- 2. England—Biography. I. Title.
CT788.B244A37 1976 942.3'52'08570924 77-350104
77 MARC

Baker, Dale B
USSR/USA scientific and technical information in perspective / Dale B. Baker. — Philadelphia : National Federation of Abstracting and Indexing Services, 1974.
iii, 24 p. ; 28 cm. — (Report - National Federation of Abstracting and Indexing Services ; no. 8) (Miles Conrad memorial lecture ; 1974)
Bibliography: p. 17-18.
1. Information storage and retrieval systems—Science. 2. Information storage and retrieval systems—Technology. 3. Science—Abstracting and indexing. 4. Technology—Abstracting and indexing. 5. Abstracting and indexing services—Russia. 6. Abstracting and indexing services—United States. I. Title. II. Series: National Federation of Abstracting and Indexing Services. Report ; no. 8. III. Series: Miles Conrad memorial lecture ; 1974.
Z699.5.S3B33 029'.9'5 76-367900
76 MARC

Baker, Dale L 1934-
A study of self-evaluation of elementary education: a consensus approach, by Dale L. Baker. [n.p.] 1973.
200 l.
Thesis—Ohio State University.
Bibliography: leaf 200.
1. Elementary schools—Evaluation. I. Title.
OU NUC75-17370

Baker, Dale Ray.
Kinetics of nucleophilic ligand substitution reactions of lead (II) - Aminocarboxylate complexes. Lincoln, Neb., 1971.
vi, 120 l. diagrs., tables.
Thesis (Ph.D.)—University of Nebraska.
Bibliography: leaves 118-120.
I. Title.
NbU NUC73-73588

Baker, Daniel, d. 1723.
Poems upon several occasions. [n.p.] 1967. English books, 1641-1700. Ann Arbor, Mich., University Microfilms, 1961-
reels. 35 mm.
Microfilm copy of books included in Wing's Short-title catalogue of... English books printed... 1641-1700.
1. English literature—Early modern (to 1700)—Collections. I. Wing, Donald Goddard, 1904- Short-title catalogue of books.
CaBVaU NUC76-16408

Baker, Darrell A
Treatment of packinghouse wastes by anaerobic lagoons and plastic media filters. Washington, U.S. Govt. Print. Off., 1974.
76 p. illus. (Environmental protection technology series. EPA-660/2-74-027)
Project 12060 DFF.
Bibliography: p. 43.
I. Title.
DNAL NUC76-18075

Baker, David.
The inhabitants of Cardington in 1782. [Luton?] Bedfordshire Historical Record Society, 1973.
242 p. 22 cm. (Bedfordshire Historical Record Society. Publications, v. 52)
1. Cardington, England–Population. I. Title. II. Series.
GU InU NUC75-17349

Baker, David.
see Bedfordshire, Eng. County Council. Bedfordshire historic buildings ... [Bedford] The Council, 1975.

Baker, David, joint author
see Ratzer, Peter. Europe: power and responsibility. [London, Bow Publications, 1972]

Baker, David, 1931- comp.
Jazz styles and analysis: trombone; a history of the jazz trombone via recorded solos, transcribed and annotated. [n.p., Down Beat Music Worshop Publications, 1973]
144 p. port. 22 x 29 cm.
1. Trombone—Studies and exercises (Jazz) 2. Improvisation (Music) I. Title.
OO NUC74-126580

Baker, David, 1931-
The Lydian chromatic concept. Rev. ed. Libertyville, Ill., Today's Music, 1971.
96 p. (chiefly music) 28 cm. (Techniques of improvisation, v. 1)
On cover: A method for developing improvisational technique (based on the Lydian chromatic concept by George Russell)
1. Improvisation (Music) I. Title. II. Series.
IEdS NUC75-31157

Baker, David, 1931-
Techniques of improvisation. Chicago, Maher Publications [1968-1971]
4 v. 28 cm.
Imprint varies: v. 1-2, Libertyville, Ill. National Educational Services.
Principally studies and exercises.
Contents: v. 1. A method for developing improvisational technique (based on the Lydian chromatic concept by George Russell). — v. 2. The IIV7 progression. —v. 3. Turnback. — v. 4. Cycles.
1. Improvisation (Music)
WU NUC76-70952

Baker, David, 1931-
Techniques of improvisation. Rev. ed. Chicago, Maher Publications, 1971-
v.
Contents.–v. 1. Methods for developing improvisational technique.
1. Improvisation (Music) I. Title.
DeU NUC74-3590

Baker, David, 1931-
Turnbacks. Chicago, Maher Publications, 1971.
83 p. illus. (His Techniques of improvisation, v. 3)
Principally studies and exercises.
"Music workshop publications."
1. Improvisation (Music) I. Title. II. Series.
IMacoW NUC74-9787

Baker, David, 1936–
חיסול והחיאה של חברות, מאת דוד בקר. תל־אביב, גוילים [1970]
176 p. 25 cm.
Added t. p.: Dissolution and restoration of companies.
Includes legislation.
Bibliography: p. 156.
IL18.00
1. Corporation law—Israel. I. Title.
Title romanized: Ḥisul ve-haḥya'ah shel ḥavarot.
74–953171

Baker, David, 1943- joint author
see Baulny, H L de. The water balance of Lake Victoria... Entebbe, Uganda, Water Development Dept., 1970.

Baker, David A
Diffusion climatology study of the 100-N area, Hanford, Washington. Richland, Wash., Douglas United Nuclear, inc., 1972.
[88] l. illus., tables. 30 cm.
"DUN-7841."
1. Winds–Washington (State–Measurement. 2. Remote sensing systems. I. Douglas United Nuclear, inc. II. Title.
DAS NUC75-72773

Baker, David A.
see Soldat, J K Models and computer codes... Richland, Wash., 1974.

Baker, David B., 1936-
see Sandusky River Basin Symposium, Tiffin, Ohio, 1975. Sandusky River Basin Symposium, May 2-3, 1975, Tiffin, Ohio ... [s.l.] International Reference Group on Great Lakes Pollution from Land Use Activities, International Joint Commission, [1976]

Baker, David C 1946-
Synthesis and reactions of carbonyl sugars. Synthesis and modification of nucleosides, by David C. Baker. [n.p.] 1973.
278 l.
Thesis–Ohio State University.
Includes bibliographical references.
1. Carbonyl compounds. 2. Nucleosides. I. Title.
OU NUC76-71015

Baker, David John.
Local Muslim organizations and national politics in Malaysia. [Berkeley] 1973.
1 v. (various pagings)
Thesis (Ph.D.)–University of California.
Includes bibliography.
CU NUC75-17369

Baker, David William Archdall, ed.
see Lang, John Dunmore, 1799-1878. Reminiscences of my life and times... Melbourne, Heinemann, 1972.

Baker, Denise Nowakowski.
Langland's artistry : the strategy and structure of Piers Plowman / Denise Nowakowski Baker. [s.l. : s.n.], 1975.
iii, 163 leaves ; 29 cm.
Thesis--University of Virginia.
Bibliography: leaves 160-163.
1. Langland, William, 1330?-1400? Piers the plowman. I. Title.
ViU NUC77-91916

Baker, Denys Val
see Val Baker, Denys, 1917-

Baker, Derek.
Partnership in excellence : a late-Victorian educational venture : the Leys School, Cambridge, 1875-1975 / by Derek Baker. — Cambridge : The Governors of the Leys School, 1975.
xvi, 272 p., [38] leaves of plates : ill. ; 23 cm. GB***
Bibliography: p. 269-272.
£6.60
1. Leys School, Cambridge, Eng. I. Title.
LF795.C175B34 372.9'426'59 77-365827
77 MARC

Baker, Derek.
see Ecclesiastical History Society, London. Church society and politics ... Oxford, Published for The Ecclesiastical History Society by B. Blackwell, 1975.

Baker, Derek, ed.
see Ecclesiastical History Society, London. Councils and assemblies... Cambridge [Eng.] Univer. Press, 1971.

Baker, Derek.
see Ecclesiastical History Society, London. The materials, sources, and methods of ecclesiastical history ... New York, Barnes & Noble Books, 1975.

Baker, Derek.
see Ecceliastical History Society, London. The Materials, sources, and methods of ecclesiastical history ... Oxford, Published for the Ecclesiastical History Society by Blackwell, 1975.

Baker, Derek.
see Ecclesiastical History Society, London. The Orthodox Churches and the west ... Oxford [Eng.] B. Blackwell, 1976.

Baker, Derek, ed.
see Ecclesiastical History Society, London. Sanctity and secularity: the church and the world ... New York, Barnes & Noble, [1973]

Baker, Derek, ed.
see Ecclesiastical History Society, London. Sancitity and secularity... Oxford [Eng.] B. Blackwell, 1973.

Baker, Derek.
see International Committee of Historical Sciences. Commission internationale d'histoire ecclésiastique comparée. British Sub-Commission. The bibliography of the Reform, 1450-1648, relating to the United Kingdom and Ireland for the years 1955-70. Oxford, Blackwell, 1975.

Baker, Derek, ed.
see Miscellanea historiae ecclesiasticae III... Louvain, Publications universitaires de Louvain, 1970.

Baker, Derek, ed.
see Relations between East and West in the Middle Ages. Edinburgh, Edinburgh University Press, 1973.

Baker, Diane Haige, 1941-
Effects of different volunteer tutor/tutee combinations on the reading and mathematics achievement and self concept of elementary tutees; a doctoral project. Coral Gables, Fla., 1974.
viii, 140 l. illus. 28 cm.
Thesis (Ed.D.)–University of Miami.
Vita.
Bibliography: leaves 134-140.
1. Tutors and tutoring. 2. Reading–Remedial teaching. 3. Arithmetic–Remedial teaching. I. Title.
FMU NUC76-18085

Baker, Dina Gustin.
Man... motion... and shapes; [exhibition of] recent paintings by Dina Gustin Baker. Amerika Haus, Hamburg, Germany, March 4-29, 1974; Amerika Haus, Munich, Germany, April 10-May 9, 1974. [n.p.] 1974.
[8] p. illus. 18 cm.
Cover title.
1. Baker, Dina Gustin. I. Amerika Haus, Hamburg. II. Title.
DeU NUC76-52927

Baker, Dirk Edmond, 1945-
The focal-region fields of paraboloidal reflectors of arbitrary f/D ratio. [n.p.] 1974.
277 l.
Thesis–Ohio State University.
Includes bibliographical references.
1. Paraboloid. 2. Antennas (Electronics) I. Title.
OU NUC76-18074

Baker, Dolores
see Wittenmyer, Osa Marie. God's book for me; teacher's guide... Nashville, Convention Press, c1975.

Baker, Don, illus.
see Pierson, Edna Church. The witch of Turner's Bald. [Banner Elk, N.C., Grandfather Home for Children, c1971]

Baker, Don Hobart, joint author
see Sorensen, Earl F Mineral resources and water requirements... Socorro: New Mexico Institute of Mining & Technology, 1973.

Baker, Don Hobart, comp.
see Uranium Symposium, Socorro, N.M., 1970. Selected papers. Socorro, N.M., New Mexico State Bureau of Mines and Mineral Resources, 1971.

Baker, Donald.
Understanding the under-fives / Donald Baker. — London : Evans, 1975.
183 p. : ill. ; 23 cm. GB***
Bibliography: p. 175-181.
Includes index.
ISBN 0-237-29134-7 : £2.95
1. Play. 2. Child psychology. I. Title.
BF717.B23 155.4'22 76-350612
76 MARC

Baker, Donald, 1921-
see Corey, Dorothy. No company was coming to Samuel's house ... Detroit, B. Ethridge—Books, c1976.

Baker, Donald Arthur, 1946-
Branched-chain sugar nucleosides. Synthesis of structural analogues of puromycin. [Vancouver, B.C.] 1972.
xii, 147 l. illus. 28 cm.
Thesis—University of British Columbia.
Vita.
"References": leaves 138-147.
1. Nucleosides. I. Title.
CaBVaU NUC74-126557

Baker, Donald Gardner, 1923-
Snow cover and winter soil temperatures at St. Paul, Minnesota. Minneapolis, 1971.
iv, 24 p. illus.
OWRR project no. B-005-Minn.
Matching grant agreement no. 14-01-0001-844.
Bibliography: p. 24.
1. Soil temperature—Minnesota—St. Paul. I. Title.
DI NUC73-41444

Baker, Donald Gardner, 1923-
Solar radiation reception, probabilities, and areal distribution in the north-central region / Donald G. Baker and John C. Klink. — [St. Anthony Park] : Agricultural Experiment Station, University of Minnesota, 1975.
54 p. : ill. ; 28 cm. — (North central regional research publication ; 225) (Technical bulletin - Agricultural Experiment Station, University of Minnesota ; 300)
Cover title.
Bibliography: p. 34.
1. Solar radiation—North Central States. I. Klink, John C., joint author. II. Title. III. Series. IV. Series: Minnesota. Agricultural Experiment Station, St. Anthony Park. Technical bulletin ; 300.
QC911.82.U6B34 551.5'271'0977 76-620774
76 MARC

Baker, Donald Granville, 1924- ed.
see San Francisco Cancer Symposium, 9th, 1973. Current concepts in breast cancer and tumor immunology... Flushing, N.Y. : Medical Examination Pub. Co., [1974]

Baker, Donald H.
see United States. Dept. of the Interior. Process for producing alumina... Washington, 1974.

Baker, Donald I
Antitrust and regulated industries - a 1972 perspective; remarks by Donald I. Baker. Prepared for the Sixth New England Antitrust Conference, Boston, Mass., November 3, 1972. [Washington? 1972?]
23, [1] l. 28 cm.
Reproduced from typewritten copy.
1. Trusts, Industrial—U.S.—Addresses, essays, lectures. I. New England Antitrust Conference, 6th, Boston, 1972. II. Title.
GU-L NUC75-22650

Baker, Donald McCord, 1890-
see A Review of some ionospheric studies based on a high-frequency Doppler technique. Boulder, Colorado, 1968.

Baker, Donald N.
see The Application of systems methods to crop production... Mississippi State, Miss., 1975.

Baker, Donald R., 1927-
see Papers on low-temperature geochemistry. [Washington, Council on Education in the Geological Sciences, 1972]

Baker, Donald Whitelaw, 1923-
Twelve hawks : and other poems / Donald W. Baker. — Crawfordsville, Ind. : Baker, [1974]
24 p. ; 22 cm. — (Sugar Creek poetry series ; no. 1)
I. Title. II. Series.
PS3552.A413T9 811'.5'4 74-186930
MARC

Baker, Donn, 1928-
see Bell Telephone Laboratories, inc. Physical design of electronic systems. Englewood Cliffs, N.J., Prentice-Hall [1970-72]

Baker, Donna.
Frederic Remington / by Donna Baker ; Bernard B. Shapiro, consulting editor. — Chicago : Childrens Press, c1977.
61 p. : ill. (some col.) ; 26 cm. — (Artists in our world)
Includes index.
SUMMARY: Biography of Frederic Remington, who spent much of his life using art to document the emerging West.
ISBN 0-516-03680-7
1. Remington, Frederic, 1861-1909—Juvenile literature. [1. Remington, Frederic, 1861-1909. 2. Artists] I. Title. II. Series.
N6537.R4B25 709'.2'4 76-8463
76 MARC

Baker, Doran.
see Spectrometric techniques. New York, Academic Press, 1977-

Baker, Doran J
A Providential place, by Doran J. Baker and Clyde Braegger. With illustrations by Glenn Alred. [Logan, Utah State University, 1975]
40 l. illus. 28 cm.
A slide-lecture presentation on the early history of Cache Valley, Elkhorn Ranch, Providence.
Bibliography: leaves 36-46.
1. Providence City, Utah--History. 2. Elkhorn Ranch, Utah--History. I. Braegger, Clyde, joint author. II. Title.
UU NUC77-97347

Baker, Doris Grotewohl.
Reducing the impact of mental retardation: the social worker's role. [Madison, Wis., University of Wisconsin] 1972.
100 p. illus. 27 cm.
Collected papers from an Institute on the Roles of Social Work in Preventing and Alleviating Mental Retardation Problems, July 7-9, 1971, Madison. Sponsored by School of Social Work, University of Wisconsin-Madison, and Center for Continuing Education and Community Action for Social Service, (formerly the Department of Social Work) University of Wisconsin-Extension.
WMM NUC74-123449

Baker, Doris Grotewohl, ed.
see Institute on Corrections in Context: the Criminal Justice System and the Corrective Function, Madison, 1971. Corrections in context: the criminal justice system and the corrective function. [Madison] University of Wisconsin-Extension, 1972.

Baker, Doris Grotewohl, ed.
see Institute on New Horizons for Social Work Practice in Mental Retardation, Madison, Wis., 1970. Research-based knowledge about mental retardation... [Madison] 1971.

Baker, Doris Grotewohl, ed.
see Serving high risk groups among the elderly... [Madison] University of Wisconsin-Extension, Dept. of Social Work, 1972.

Baker, Doris Jones-
see Jones-Baker, Doris.

Baker, Dorothy.
A short guide to English architecture / by Dorothy Baker ; illustrations by James Dolby. — Gloucester : Thornhill Press, 1974.
70 p. : ill., plans ; 22 cm. GB75-18338
ISBN 0-904110-04-4 : £0.75
1. Architecture—England—Outlines, syllabi, etc. I. Title.
NA961.B24 720'.942 75-328601
75 MARC

Baker, Dorothy Ann, 1935-
Food consumption and dietary levels of households of different sizes: United States, North, South [by Dorothy A. Baker, Ruth A. Redstrom, and Constance D. Ward] Washington, D.C., Consumer and Food Economics Institute, Agricultural Research Service, U.S. Department of Agriculture, 1974.
264 l. 28 cm.
"Unpublished report from USDA 1965-66 Household food consumption survey."
1. Food consumption—United States. I. Redstrom, Ruth A., 1921- II. Ward, Constance D. III. Consumer and Food Economics Institute. IV. Title.
CSt NUC76-53298

Baker, Dorothy Dodds, 1907-1968.
Trio / by Dorothy Baker. — Westport, Conn. : Greenwood Press, 1977, c1943.
234 p. ; 23 cm.
Reprint of the ed. published by Houghton Mifflin, Boston.
ISBN 0-8371-9647-7
I. Title.
PZ3.B17003 Tr 9 813'.5'2 77-5686
[PS3503.A54156] 77 MARC

Baker, Doug, 1922-
Guide to Portland; [where to go, what to see, where to dine. Drawings by Jack Ostergren, editing and research by Art Chenoweth. Forest Grove, Or., Times, c1965]
1 v. (unpaged) illus. 17 cm.
1. Portland, Or.—Description. I. Title.
OrPS NUC73-59611

Baker, Douglas.
Practical techniques of astral projection / by Douglas Baker ; drawings by Patricia D. Ludlow. — Wellingborough (Eng.) : Aquarian Press, 1977.
96 p. : ill. ; 22 cm. GB***
Bibliography: p. [94]
ISBN 0-87728-321-4 (U.S.A.)
1. Astral projection. I. Title.
BF1389.A7B18 133.9'2 77-370278
77 MARC

Baker, Douglas A
Disasters and disaster laws / research staff, Douglas A. Bake[r] project officer, Christine L. Cole, research associate. — Colu[m]bus : Ohio Legislative Service Commission, 1975.
iii, 61 p. : ill. ; 28 cm. — (Staff research report - Ohio Legislative Serv[ice] Commission ; no. 120)
Cover title.
Includes bibliographical references.
1. Disaster relief—Ohio. 2. Disaster relief—United States. I. Cole, Chr[is]tine L., joint author. II. Ohio. Legislative Service Commission. III. Ti[tle]. IV. Series: Ohio. Legislative Service Commission. Staff research report ; n[o.] 120.
JK5574.A3 no. 120 300'.9771 s 76-6215[?]
[KFO352] 76 MA[RC]

Baker, Douglas A., joint author.
see Masek, Richard E. Alternative State roles in the regulation of cable television. Columbus, Ohio Legislative Service Commission, 1974.

Baker, Douglas A.
see Ohio. Legislative Service Commission. Franchising ... Columbus, Ohio Legislative Service Commission, 1974.

Baker, Douglas E 1933-
The effect on the verbal behavior of selected volunteer junior high school science teachers of in - service education in verbal interaction analysis and techniques in indirect instruction. [n.p.] 1972.
107 p.
Thesis (Ph.D.)–New York University.
1. Dissertations, Academic–N.Y.U.–1972.
I. Title.
NNU NUC74-380

Baker, Douglas H.
see National Conference on Fire and Forest Meteorology, 4th, St. Louis, 1976. Proceedings of the Fourth National Conference on Fire and Forest Meteorology, St. Louis, Missouri, November 16-18, 1976. Fort Collins, Colo., The Station, [1976?]

Baker, Dwight Condo.
T'ai Shan, an account of the sacred eastern peak of China. Taipei, Ch'eng Wen Pub. Co., 1971.
xx, 225 p. illus., maps. 20 cm.
Facsim. reprint of 1925 ed.
Bibliography: p. 199-201.
1. Tai Shan. I. Title.
CaBVaU NUC74-3589

Baker, E H 1937–
Structural analysis of shells [by] E. H. Baker, L. Kovalevsky [and] F. L. Rish. New York, McGraw-Hill [1972]
xiii, 351 p. illus. 24 cm. $24.50
Includes bibliographical references.
1. Shells (Engineering) I. Kovalevsky, L., 1910– joint author. II. Rish, F. L., 1929– joint author. III. Title.
TA660.S5B34 624'.1776 78-130678
ISBN 0-07-003354-4 MARC

Baker, E. Jo
see
Baker, Ethel Jo, 1923-

Baker, E. T.
see
Baker, Ernest T., 1931-

Baker, E. W.
see
Baker, Edward William, 1914-

Baker, Earl DeWitt, 1919-
The development of secondary education in Sierra Leone. [Ann Arbor, University Microfilms, 1974]
vi, 273 l.
Thesis–University of Michigan, 1963.
Bibliography: leaves 260-273.
Photocopy. 21 cm.
1. Education, Secondary–Sierra Leone.
I. Title.
CNoS NUC75-17368

Baker, Earl J
Land use management and regulation in hazardous areas : a research assessment / Earl J. Baker and Joe Gordon McPhee. — [Boulder] : Institute of Behavioral Science, University of Colorado, 1975.
xiv, 124 p. : ill. ; 23 cm. — (Monograph - Program on Technology, Environment and Man, University of Colorado)
"#SF-RA-E-75-008."
Bibliography: p. 116-122.
1. Regional planning—Law and legislation—United States. 2. Hazardous geographic environments—United States. I. McPhee, Joe Gordon, joint author. II. Title. III. Series: Colorado. University. Program on Technology, Environment and Man. Monograph - Program on Technology, Environment and Man, University of Colorado.
KF5698.B333 346'.73'045 75-620041
76 MARC

Baker, Earl J
Toward an evaluation of policy alternatives governing hazard-zone land uses / by Earl J. Baker. -- [s.l. : s.n.], 1976.
iii, 73 p. : ill. ; 28 cm. -- (Natural hazard research working paper ; no. 28)
Bibliography: p. 69-73.
1. Zoning. 2. Natural disasters. I. Title. II. Series.
IU NUC77-94358

Baker, Earl M
The federal polity: a review and digest; edited by Earl M. Baker. [Philadelphia] Center for the Study of Federalism, Temple University for Federalism '76, Inc. [1974]
vii, 74 p. 26 cm.
1. Federal government–U.S.–Addresses, essays, lectures. I. Philadelphia. Temple University. Center for ths Study of Federalism. II. Title.
PPT NUC75-17378

Baker, Earl M
The federal polity: an agenda for contemporary research priorities. [Philadelphia] Center for the Study of Federalism, Temple University for Federalism '76, Inc. [1974]
vi, 40 p. 26 cm.
Bibliography: p. 38-40.
1. Federal government–U.S. 2. Political science research–U.S. I. Philadelphia. Temple University. Center for the Study of Federalism. II. Title.
PPT NUC75-17377

Baker, Earl M.
see Federal grants... Philadelphia [197-]

Baker, Ed.
The city. Blodgett, Or., Red Ochre Press [1974]
9 p. 22 cm.
Poems.
"This edition consists of 300 copies."
I. Title.
PS3552.A415C5 811'.5'4 74-178250
MARC

Baker, Edgar Isaac.
A guide to study / by Edgar I. Baker ; [illustrations by David Myers]. — London : British Association for Commercial and Industrial Education, 1975.
79 p. : ill. ; 21 cm. GB75-20162
Bibliography: p. 20.
ISBN 0-85171-057-3 : £1.30
1. Study, Method of. I. Title.
LB1049.B26 371.3'02812 75-332238
75 MARC

Baker, Edna.
The true story of Good King Wenceslas, or, What really happened, a Christmas extravaganza. London, Samuel French, Ltd. [n.d.]
33 p. 19 cm. (French's acting edition)
Microfilm.
I. Title.
CaBVaU NUC75-17376

Baker, Edward Cecil.
Sir William Preece, F.R.S. : Victorian engineer extraordinary / [by] E. C. Baker. — London : Hutchinson, 1976.
xiv, 377 p., leaf of plate, [8] p. of plates : ill., facsims., map, ports. ; 24 cm. GB76-17000
"Principal lectures and publications": p. [356]-362.
Includes indexes.
ISBN 0-09-126610-6 : £6.50
1. Preece, William Henry, Sir, 1834-1913. 2. Electric engineers—Great Britain—Biography.
TK140.P73B34 621.3'092'4 76-373464
76 MARC

Baker, Edward Charles Stuart, 1864-1944.
The game-birds of India, Burma, and Ceylon / by E. C. Stuart Baker. — [Bombay] : Bombay Natural History Society, 19
v. : ill. ; 28 cm.
Includes bibliographical references.
CONTENTS:
—v. 3. Pheasants and bustard-quail.
1. Game and game-birds—India. 2. Game and game-birds—Burma. 3. Game and game-birds—Ceylon. I. Title.
QL691.I4B29 598.2'954 75-313059
75 MARC

Baker, Edward Charles Stuart, 1864-1944.
Pheasants and bustard-quail / by E. C. Stuart Baker. — [Bombay] : Bombay Natural History Society, 1930.
341 p., [20] leaves of plates : ill. (some col.) ; 28 cm. — (His The game-birds of India, Burma and Ceylon ; v. 3)
Includes bibliographical references.
1. Pheasants. 2. Bustards. 3. Game and game-birds—India. 4. Game and game-birds—Burma. 5. Game and game-birds—Ceylon. I. Title.
QL691.I4B29 vol. 3 598.2'954 s 75-313058
[QL696.G27] 75 MARC

Baker, Edward Ronald.
Criminal evidence and procedure, by E. R. Baker and F. B. Dodge. 4th ed. London, Butterworths, 1973.
x, 253 p. 19 cm. (Police promotion handbooks, no. 2) £1.20 GB***
1. Criminal procedure—Great Britain—Handbooks, manuals, etc. I. Dodge, F. B., joint author. II. Title.
KD8329.3.B33 1973 345'.42'050202 74-177513
ISBN 0-406-84128-4 MARC

Baker, Edward Ronald.
Criminal evidence and procedure / by E. R. Baker and F. B. Dodge. — 5th ed. — London : Butterworths, 1976.
x, 262 p. ; 19 cm. — (Police promotion handbooks ; no. 2) GB***
Includes index.
ISBN 0-406-84129-2 : £2.60
1. Criminal procedure—Great Britain—Handbooks, manuals, etc. I. Dodge, F. B., joint author. II. Title.
KD8329.3.B33 1976 345'.42'052 77-361211
77 MARC

Baker, Edward Ronald.
Criminal law, by E. R. Baker. 3rd ed. London, Butterworths, 1972.
ix, 218 p. 19 cm. (Police promotion handbooks, no. 1) £1.20 B 72-23958
Includes index.
1. Criminal law—Great Britain. 2. Police—Great Britain—Handbooks, manuals, etc. I. Title.
KD7869.3.B3 1972 345'.42 73-180532
ISBN 0-406-84118-7 MARC

Baker, Edward Ronald.
General police duties / by E. R. Baker and F. B. Dodge. — 4th ed. — London : Butterworths, 1975.
xiii, 425 p. ; 19 cm. — (Police promotion handbooks ; no. 3) GB***
Includes index.
ISBN 0-406-84139-X
1. Police—Great Britain—Handbooks, manuals, etc. I. Dodge, F. B., joint author. II. Title.
KD665.P6B3 1975 345'.41'052 75-511112
75 MARC

Baker, Edward Ronald.
Road traffic, by E. R. Baker and F. B. Dodge. 4th ed. London, Butterworths, 1973.
xiv, 358 p. illus. 19 cm. (Baker's and Wilkie's police promotion handbooks, no. 5) £1.50 GB***
1. Automobiles—Laws and regulations—Great Britain. 2. Traffic regulations—Great Britain. I. Dodge, F. B., joint author. II. Title.
KD2599.3.B33 1973 343'.42'094 73-180531
ISBN 0-406-84159-4 MARC

Baker, Edward Thomas.
Nephelometry and mineralogy of suspended particulate matter in the waters over the Washington continental slope and Nitinat Deep-Sea Fan. [Seattle] 1973.
142 l. illus.
Thesis (Ph.D.)—University of Washington.
Bibliography: leaves 127-132.
WaU NUC74-126556

Baker, Edward William, 1914-
The false spider mites of northwestern and north central Mexico (Acarina, Tenuipalpidae) / Edward W. Baker, Donald M. Tuttle, and Michael J. Abbatiello. — Washington : Smithsonian Institution Press, 1975.
iii, 23 p. : ill. ; 27 cm. — (Smithsonian contributions to zoology ; no. 194)
Bibliography: p. 22-23.
Supt. of Docs. no.: SI 1.27:194
1. False spider mites. 2. Arachnida—Mexico. I. Tuttle, Donald Monroe, 1917- joint author. II. Abbatiello, M., joint author. III. Title. IV. Series: Smithsonian Institution. Smithsonian contributions to zoology ; no. 194.
QL1.S54 no. 194 591'.08 s 74-23374
[QL458.2.T36] 74 MARC

Baker, Edward William, 1914– joint author.
see Jeppson, L. R. Mites injurious to economic plants. Berkeley, University of California Press, 1975.

Baker, Edward William, 1914- joint author
see Tuttle, Donald Monroe, 1917-
Spider mites from northwestern and north-central Mexico. Washington, Smithsonian Institution Press, 1974.

Baker, Edwin Dennis, 1932-
A study of the administrative provisions providing for the needs of non-English speaking school-age children in grades Kindergarten through sixth in selected schools in the area of greater Washington, D.C. [Washington, D.C.] 1968.
v, 129 l.
Thesis (Ph.D.)—Catholic Univ. of America.
Bibliography: leaves 123-129.
Microfilm. Ann Arbor, Mich., University Microfilms, 1973. 1 reel. 35 mm.
1. Education, Elementary—Washington, D.C. 2. English language—Study and teaching—Foreign students. I. Title.
CoU NUC74-128138

Baker, Edwin H
Nonstatutory stock options, by Edwin H. Baker. Leonard L. Silverstein, chief editor. Washington, Tax Management [1974-
1 v. (loose-leaf) 28 cm. (Tax management portfolios, 87-3d)
"Revises and supersedes 87-2d T. M., Stock options, nonstatutory."
Includes bibliography.
1. Taxation of bonds, securities, etc.—United States. 2. Deferred compensation—Taxation—United States. I. Title. II. Series.
KF6289.A1T35 no. 87-3d 343'.73'04 s 74-170410
[KF6379] [343'.73'052] MARC

Baker, Effie E
Australian wild flowers, by Effie E. Baker. Melbourne, T. & H. Hunter [n.d.]
7 col. plates. 23 cm.
1. Wild flowers—Pictorial works. 2. Wild flowers—Australia. I. Title.
TxU NUC75-73925

Baker, Elaine.
The adaptability of social behaviors of inbred and noninbred mice in varied social environments. Oxford, Ohio, 1972.
v, 61 l. illus. 28 cm.
Thesis (Ph.D.)—Miami University.
1. Mice—Behavior. 2. Social behavior in animals. 3. Behaviorism (Psychology) I. Title.
OOxM NUC74-814

Baker, Elizabeth, 1944-
The happy housewife / Elizabeth Baker. — Wheaton, Ill. : Victor Books, [1975]
144 p. ; 18 cm.
ISBN 0-88207-720-1 : $1.75
1. Wives—Religious life. I. Title.
BV4527.B3 248'.843 74-16978
75 MARC

Baker, Elizabeth C., 1934- ed.
see Art and sexual politics... New York, Collier Books [1973]

Baker, Elizabeth C., 1934- ed.
see Art and sexual politics... New York, Macmillan [1973]

Baker, Elizabeth Catherine, 1950-
The impact of illness of the family and the ministry of the Christian community. Claremont [Calif.] 1975.
ii, 140 l. 29 cm.
Thesis (D.Min.)--School of Theology at Claremont.
Bibliography: leaves [136]-140.
Abstract: leaves [iii-v]
On deposit with University Microfilms, no. 75-26, 868.
1. Church work with the sick. I. Title.
CCSC NUC77-92398

Baker, Elizabeth Faulkner, 1885-1973.
Printers and technology; a history of the International Printing Pressmen and Assistants' Union. Westport, Conn., Greenwood Press [1974, c1957]
xviii, 545 p. 22 cm.
Reprint of the ed. published by Columbia University Press, New York.
Bibliography: p. [523]-528.
ISBN 0-8371-7763-4
1. International Printing Pressmen and Assistants' Union of North America. I. Title.
[Z120.B16 1974] 331.88'11'68623097 74-12847
MARC

Baker, Elizabeth Lassiter.
A parent's guide to Memphis area private schools [by Elizabeth Lassiter Baker and Linda Brown Porter] Memphis, Barton Press [1973]
104 p. 23 cm. $2.95
1. Private schools—Tennessee—Memphis—Directories. I. Porter, Linda Brown, joint author. II. Title.
L903.T25M452 371'.02'02576819 73-165499
MARC

Baker, Elizabeth Lauh, joint author
see Sonquist, John A Searching for structure... Rev. ed. Ann Arbor, Survey Research Center, University of Michigan, 1973 [i.e. 1974, c1971]

Baker, Elizabeth McIntosh.
The post-embryonic development of the prothoracic gland of the cabbage looper Trichoplusia ne (Hübner) (Lepidoptera: Noctuidae) under normal and experimental conditions. [Charlottesville, Va.] 1973.
75 l. illus. 29 cm.
Thesis—University of Virginia.
Bibliography: leaves 72-75.
1. Prothoracic gland. 2. Cabbage looper. I. Title.
ViU NUC75-17381

Baker, Elliott.
Klynt's law : a novel / by Elliott Baker. — 1st ed. — New York : Harcourt, Brace, Jovanovich, c1976.
264 p. ; 22 cm.
ISBN 0-15-147283-1 : $8.95
I. Title.
PZ4.B1685 Kl 813'.5'4 75-45144
[PS3552.A424] MARC
——— Copy 2. PS3552.A424K5
75

Baker, Elliott.
Pocock & Pitt / Elliott Baker. — London : Joseph, 1974. GB74-28390
285 p. ; 23 cm.
ISBN 0-7181-1286-5 : £2.50
I. Title.
PZ4.B1685 Po 4 813'.5'4 76-354083
[PS3552.A424] 76 MARC

Baker, Elliott.
Unrequited loves / Elliott Baker. — London : Joseph, 1974.
222 p. ; 21 cm. GB 74-07585
ISBN 0-7181-1195-8 : £2.75
I. Title.
PZ4.B1685Un 3 813'.5'4 75-300154
[PS3552.A424] MARC

Baker, Elliott.
Unrequited loves. New York, Putnam [1973, c1974]
239 p. 21 cm. $6.95
I. Title.
PZ4.B1685Un 813'.5'4 73-85659
[PS3552.A424] MARC
ISBN 0-399-11242-1

Baker, Ernest Albert, 1869-1941.
Caving : episodes of underground exploration / by Ernest A. Baker ; with a new foreword by D. C. Mellor. — Yorkshire, Eng. : S.R. Publishers, 1970.
xv, 252 p., [28] leaves of plates : ill. ; 23 cm. — ([Speleologia])
Imprint covered by label which reads: Zephyrus Press, Teaneck [N.J.] Series on label.
Reprint of the ed. published by Chapman & Hall, London.
Bibliography: p. 247-248.
Includes index.
ISBN 0-914264-13-3
1. Caves. I. Title.
[GB602.B17 1975] 796.5'25 75-12618
75 MARC

Baker, Ernest Albert, 1869-1941.
The history of the English novel. New York, Barnes & Noble [1969-
v. 23 cm.
Includes bibliography.
Reprint of the 1924-36 ed.
OU NUC76-70980

Baker, Ernest T 1931-
Effects of ground-water development on the proposed Palmetto Bend Dam and reservoir in Southeast Texas, by E.T. Baker and C.R. Follett. [Austin, Tex.] U.S. Geological Survey, 1973.
2 cards. illus. 11 x 15 cm. (United States. Geological Survey. Water-resources investigations 18-73)
"Prepared in cooperation with the U.S. Bureau of Reclamation."
Microfiche (negative) Springfield, Va., National Technical Information Service, 1974.
1. Water, Underground—Texas—Jackson County. 2. Hydrology—Texas—Palmetto Bend Dam (Proposed) I. Follett, Clarence R., 1904- II. United States. Geological survey. III. Title. IV. Series.
DI NUC76-32585

Baker, Ernest T 1931-
Quantity of low flow in Barton Creek, Texas, July 6-8 and October 1-3, 1970, by E.T. Baker, Jr. and J.A. Watson. [Austin] 1971.
ii, 26 l. illus., fold. map. 27 cm.
At head of title: Texas. Water Development Board. Report.
Prepared by the U.S. Geological Survey in cooperation with the Texas. Water Development Board.
Bibliography: leaf 26.
1. Stream measurements—Texas—Barton Creek basin. I. Watson, J.A. II. United States. Geological Survey. III. Texas. Water Development Board. IV. Title.
DI-GS NUC76-70928

Baker, Ernest T 1931-
Summary appraisals of the Nation's ground-water resources, Texas-Gulf region : a summary of the distribution, availability, and quality of ground water and its importance in the regional water supply / by E. T. Baker, Jr., and J. R. Wall. — Washington : U.S. Govt. Print. Off., 1976.
iii, 29 p. : ill. (3 fold. in pocket) ; 29 cm. — (Geological Survey professional paper ; 813-F)
Bibliography: p. 27-29.
Supt. of Docs. no.: I 19.16: 813-F
1. Water-supply—Texas—Gulf region. 2. Water, Underground—Texas—Gulf region. I. Wall, James R., joint author. II. Title. III. Series: United States. Geological Survey. Professional paper ; 813-F.
TD224.T4B34 333.9'104'09764 75-619155
75 MARC

Baker, Ernest T., 1931- joint author
see Shafer, G H Ground-water resources of Kleberg, Kenedy, and southern Jim Wells Counties, Texas. [Austin] Texas Water Development Board, 1973.

Baker, Ernest T., 1931-
see United States. Geological Survey. Ground-water resources of Grimes County, Texas. Austin, Texas Water Development Development Board, 1974.

Baker, Eskle
see Tennessee. Dept. of Correction. A proposed two month pilot program... [n.p.] 1969.

Baker, Ethel Jo, 1923-
Middle-level workers: characteristics, training and utilization of mental health associates [by] E. Jo Baker [and] Harold L. McPheeters. New York, Behavioral Publication [1974, c1975]
67 p. 23 cm. (Community mental health journal. Monograph series, no. 8)
Bibliography: p. 65-67.
1. Allied mental health personnel. I. McPheeters, Harold L., joint author. II. Title. III. Series.
[DNLM: 1. Community mental health services—U. S. 2. Health occupations. W1CO 429R no. 8 1974/WM 21 B167m 1974]
RC440.2.B34 331.7'61'36220425 74-5770
ISBN 0-87705-159-3 MARC

Baker, Eugene H
I want to be a computer operator, by Eugene Baker. Illustrated by Tom Dunnington. Chicago, Childrens Press [1973]
30 p. illus. 25 cm.
SUMMARY: Describes, simply and briefly, the functions of a computer and the job and training of a computer operator.
1. Electronic data processing—Vocational guidance—Juvenile literature. 2. Programming (Electronic computers)—Vocational guidance—Juvenile literature. [1. Electronic data processing—Vocational guidance. 2. Programming (Electronic computers)—Vocational guidance] I. Dunnington, Tom, illus. II. Title.
QA76.25.B33 001.6'4'023 73-773
ISBN 0-516-01741-1 MARC

Baker, Eugene H
I want to be a draftsman / by Eugene Baker ; illustrated by Richard Wahl. — Chicago : Childrens Press, c1976.
30 p. : col. ill. ; 25 cm.
SUMMARY: From the senior draftsman of a large company, two boys learn the training and education necessary for becoming a draftsman and what the work involves.
ISBN 0-516-01737-3 lib. bdg.
1. Mechanical drawing—Vocational guidance—Juvenile literature. [1. Mechanical drawing—Vocational guidance. 2. Vocational guidance] I. Wahl, Richard, 1939- II. Title.
T357.B32 1976 604'.2'023 75-35598
75 MARC

Baker, Eugene H
I want to be a gymnast / by Eugene Baker ; illustrated by Lois Axeman. — Chicago : Childrens Press, c1976.
31 p. : col. ill. ; 25 cm.
SUMMARY: A young girl and her classmates learn about the basic skills required of a gymnast.
ISBN 0-516-01733-0 lib. bdg.
1. Gymnastics—Juvenile literature. [1. Gymnastics. 2. Occupations] I. Axeman, Lois. II. Title.
GV511.B34 796.4'1 75-35502
75 MARC

Baker, Eugene H
I want to be a hockey player, by Eugene Baker. Illustrated by Ken Shields. Chicago, Childrens Press [1973]
31 p. illus. 25 cm.
SUMMARY: Two boys learn the rules and techniques of hockey.
1. Hockey—Juvenile literature. [1. Hockey] I. Shields, Ken, illus. II. Title.
GV847.25.B34 796.9'62 73-740
ISBN 0-516-01742-X MARC

Baker, Eugene H
I want to be a jeweler, by Eugene Baker. Illustrated by Richard Wahl. Chicago, Childrens Press [1973]
30 p. col. illus. 25 cm.
SUMMARY: While visiting a jewelry store, two children learn about the trade of a jeweler.
1. Jewelry trade—Vocational guidance—Juvenile literature. [1. Jewelry trade] I. Wahl, Richard, 1939- illus. II. Title.
HD9747.A2B28 739.27'023 73-6687
ISBN 0-516-01743-8 MARC

Baker, Eugene H
I want to be a lawyer, by Eugene Baker. Illustrated by Phil Kantz. Chicago, Childrens Press [1973]
30 p. illus. 25 cm.
SUMMARY: Easy-to-read text describes a lawyer's job and training.
1. Law as a profession—United States—Juvenile literature. [1. Law as a profession] I. Kantz, Phil, illus. II. Title.
KF297.Z9B28 340'.023 73-771
ISBN 0-516-01744-6 MARC

Baker, Eugene H
I want to be a postal clerk / by Eugene Baker ; illustrated by Lois Axeman. — Chicago : Childrens Press, c1976.
30 p. : col. ill. ; 25 cm.
SUMMARY: An elementary school class finds out about the duties of and qualifications for being a postal clerk.
ISBN 0-516-01738-1 lib. bdg.
1. Postal service—Employees—Juvenile literature. 2. Postal service—Juvenile literature. [1. Postal service—Vocational guidance. 2. Vocational guidance. 3. Occupations] I. Axeman, Lois. II. Title.
HE6078.B34 383'.023 75-38520
75 MARC

Baker, Eugene H
I want to be a printer / by Eugene Baker ; illustrated by William Neebe. — Chicago : Childrens Press, [1975]
31 p. : col. ill. ; 25 cm.
SUMMARY: Simple text and illustrations describe the job of a printer.
ISBN 0-516-01731-4
1. Printing—Juvenile literature. [1. Printing. 2. Occupations] I. Neebe, William, ill. II. Title.
Z123.B24 686.2 74-28355
74 MARC

Baker, Eugene H
I want to be a soccer player / by Eugene Baker ; illustrated by Ralph Canaday. — Chicago : Childrens Press, c1976.
31 p. : col. ill. ; 25 cm.
SUMMARY: Members of a youngster's soccer team learn the basic rules and techniques of the game from their coach.
ISBN 0-516-01734-9
1. Soccer—Juvenile literature. [1. Soccer] I. Canaday, Ralph. II. Title.
GV943.25.B34 796.33'42 75-37642
75 MARC

Baker, Eugene H
I want to be a swimmer, by Eugene Baker. Illustrated by Mary Maloney and Stan Fleming. Chicago, Childrens Press [1973]
31 p. illus. 25 cm.
SUMMARY: The swimming coach explains the five basic swimming strokes to a young would-be swimmer.
1. Swimming—Juvenile literature. [1. Swimming] I. Maloney, Mary, illus. II. Fleming, Stanley, illus. III. Title.
GV837.6.B34 797.2'1 73-739
ISBN 0-516-01745-4 MARC

Baker, Eugene H
I want to be a telephone operator / by Eugene Baker : illustrated by Lois Axeman. — Chicago : Childrens Press, [1975]
31 p. : col. ill. ; 25 cm.
SUMMARY: Simple text and illustrations introduce the duties of a telephone operator.
ISBN 0-516-01721-2
1. Telephone operators—Juvenile literature. [1. Telephone operators. 2. Occupations] I. Axeman, Lois, ill. II. Title. III. Title: Telephone operator.
HD8039.T3B34 384.6'4 74-28377
74 MARC

Baker, Eugene H
I want to be a tennis player, by Eugene Baker. Illustrated by Richard Wahl. Chicago, Childrens Press [1973]
31 p. illus. 25 cm.
SUMMARY: Two children learn to play tennis and participate in a tournament.
1. Tennis—Juvenile literature. [1. Tennis] I. Wahl, Richard, 1939- illus. II. Title.
GV995.B28 796.34'2 73-738
ISBN 0-516-01746-2 MARC

Baker, Eugene H
I want to be a travel agent / by Eugene Baker ; illustrated by Ralph Canaday. — Chicago : Childrens Press, c1976.
31 p. : col. ill. ; 25 cm.
SUMMARY: Simple text describes the duties of a travel agent.
ISBN 0-516-01736-5
1. Travel agents—Juvenile literature. [1. Travel agents—Vocational guidance. 2. Occupations] I. Canaday, Ralph. II. Title.
G154.B34 338.4'7'91023 75-42248
75 MARC

Baker, Eugene H
I want to be an auto mechanic / by Eugene Baker ; illustrated by Dev Appleyard. — Chicago : Childrens Press, c1976.
29 p. : col. ill. ; 25 cm.
SUMMARY: A boy learns about being an auto mechanic while watching a man repair his father's car.
ISBN 0-516-01735-7 lib. bdg.
1. Automobiles—Maintenance and repair—Vocational guidance—Juvenile literature. [1. Automobiles—Maintenance and repair—Vocational guidance. 2. Vocational guidance] I. Appleyard, Dev. II. Title.
TL152.B223 1976 629.28'7'023 75-34145
75 MARC

Baker, Eugene Whitman.
Basic administrative principles for a weekday preschool ministry in Southern Baptist churches. Fort Worth, Texas, 1972.
242 l.
Thesis (Ed.D.)—Southwestern Baptist Theological Seminary.
Bibliography: p. 233-242.
1. Baptists—Education. 2. Weekday church schools. 3. School management and organization—Baptists. 4. Education, Preschool. I. Title.
TxFS NUC74-126559

Baker, Eva L
Expanding dimensions of instructional objectives [by] Eva L. Baker [and] W. James Popham. Englewood Cliffs, N. J., Prentice-Hall [1973]
vii, 129 p. illus. 23 cm. $6.95; $2.95 (pbk.)
1. Curriculum planning. 2. Behaviorism (Psychology) 3. Educational tests and measurements. I. Popham, W. James, joint author. II. Title.
LB1570.B32 371.3 72-8894
ISBN 0-13-294868-0; 0-13-294850-8 (pbk.) MARC

Baker, Eva L
Formative evaluation of instruction [by] Eva L. Baker. Washington, American Educational Research Association [1974?]
1 cassette. 2 1/2 x 4 in. (AERA training tape series, 6C)
1. Educational tests and measurements. I. American Educational Research Association. II. Title.
FTaSU NUC76-18077

Baker, Eva L., joint author
see Popham, W James. Classroom instructional tactics. Englewood Cliffs, N. J., Prentice-Hall [1973]

Baker, Eva L., joint author
see Popham, W James. The Prentice-Hall teacher competency development system. Englewood Cliffs, N. J., Prentice-Hall, 1973.

Baker, Eva L.
see Popham, W James. Rules for the development of instructional products. [New York, Van Nostrand Reinhold Co., 1971]

Baker, F F
Report on diseases of cultivated plants in England and Wales for the years 1957-1968. London, 1972.
322 p. (Gt. Brit. Ministry of Agriculture, Fisheries and Food. Technical bulletin 25)
I. Title.
DNAL NUC74-126558

Baker, F. G., joint author.
see Bouma, J. Measurement of water movement in soil pedons above the water table. Madison, University of Wisconsin-Extension, Geological and Natural History Survey, 1974.

Baker, F H
Note of evidence before a commission appointed to inquire into the conduct of the Gambia Police Force in connection with an affray which took place in Bathurst on 16th October, 1955, by F. H. Baker. Bathurst, Govt. Printer, 1956.
1 v.
Cover title.
1. Police—Gambia.
CtY-L NUC75-66731

Baker, F. J.
see
Baker, Francis Joseph.

Baker, F T
Research on automatic classification, indexing and extracting [by] F. T. Baker [and] J. H. Williams, Jr. Gaithersburg, Md., Fed. Systems Div., Intl. Bus. Mach. Corp., 1968.
1 v. (various pagings)
At head of title: Annual progress report.
Reproduced by the Clearinghouse for Fed. Sci. & Tech. Info., Springfield, Va.
1. Automatic indexing. I. Williams, J. H., joint author. II. Title.
NcU NUC75-107768

Baker, F. W. G.
see
Baker, Frederick William George, 1928-

Baker, Fay.
My darling, darling doctors / Fay Baker. — New York : G. Braziller, c1975.
233 p. ; 22 cm.
ISBN 0-8076-0774-6 : $6.95
I. Title.
PZ4.B1686 My 813'.5'4 74-25292
[PS3552.A426] 76 MARC

Baker, Florence, Lady
see Baker, Anne. Morning Star... London, Kimber, 1972.

Baker, Frances Davis.
Uplands; a novel, by "Aida" [pseud.] Buffalo, N.Y., G. M. Hausauer, 1898 [1972]
116 p.
Microfilm (positive) Ann Arbor, Mich., University Microfilms, 1972. 6th title of 16. 35 mm. (American fiction series, reel 198.6)
I. Title.
KEmT NUC74-1286

Baker, Francis J
Physical studies of Franklin County. Principal author: F. J. Baker. [Columbus] 1966.
iiii, 63, [3] p. illus. 22 cm.
On cover: Blue plan.
"Prepared for the Comprehensive Regional Plan of Columbus and Franklin County."
"Project X-301."
"Financially aided through a federal grant from the Urban Renewal Administration of the Housing and Home Finance Agency."
Bibliography: p. [1]-[3] at the end.
1. Physical geography—Ohio—Columbus. 2. Physical geography—Ohio—Franklin County. I. Comprehensive Regional Plan of Columbus and Franklin County. II. Title.
OU NUC76-71288

Baker, Frances J
The story of the Woman's Foreign Missionary Society of the Methodist Episcopal Church, 1869-1895, by Frances J. Baker. Rev. ed. Cincinnati, Curts & Jennings, 1898.
438 p. illus., map, ports. 20 cm.
1. Methodist Episcopal Church. Woman's Foreign Missionary Society. I. Title.
BV2550.A45B3 1898 74-179276
MARC

Baker, Francis Joseph.
Introduction to medical laboratory technology / F. J. Baker, R. E. Silverton. — 5th ed. — London ; Boston : Butterworths, c1976.
x, 735 p., [2] leaves of plates : ill. ; 23 cm.
Bibliography: p. 679-680.
Includes index.
ISBN 0-407-73251-9
1. Medical laboratories—Technique. I. Silverton, R. E., joint author. II. Title. III. Title: Medical laboratory technology.
RB37.B28 1976 616.07'5 76-16854
76 MARC

Baker, Francis Joseph, ed.
see Microbiology of the seventies: a symposium held at Brompton Hospital, London, on 20 and 21 May 1971... London, Butterworths, 1972.

Baker, Frank, 1908-
The call of Cornwall / Frank Baker ; with photos. by David Pitt and others. — London : R. Hale, 1976.
208 p., [8] leaves of plates : ill. ; 23 cm. GB***
Includes index.
ISBN 0-7091-5411-9 : £3.80
1. Cornwall, Eng. 2. Baker, Frank, 1908- I. Title.
DA670.C8B2 1976 942.3'7 76-366740
76 MARC

Baker, Frank, 1910-
From Wesley to Asbury : studies in early American Methodism / by Frank Baker. — Durham, N.C. : Duke University Press, 1976.
xiv, 223 p. ; 25 cm.
Bibliography: p. [207]-216.
Includes index.
ISBN 0-8223-0359-0 : $9.75
1. Methodist Church in the United States. 2. Wesley, John, 1703-1791. 3. Asbury, Francis, Bp. 1745-1816. I. Title.
BX8236.B34 287'.0973 75-39454
76 MARC

Baker, Frank, 1910-
The Methodist pilgrim in England / Frank Baker. — 3d ed., rev. — Rutland, Vt. : Academy Books, 1976.
110 p. : ill. ; 19 cm.
Includes bibliographical references and index.
ISBN 0-914960-07-5
1. Methodist Church—History. 2. England—Description and travel—1971- —Guide-books. I. Title.
BX8231.B27 1976 914.2'04'85702427 75-44553
76 MARC

Baker, Frank, 1910-
see Wesley, John, 1703-1791. The works of John Wesley... -- Oxford : Clarendon Press, 1975-

Baker, Frank, 1936- comp.
Organizational systems; general systems approaches to complex organizations. Homewood, Ill., R. D. Irwin, 1973.
xv, 548 p. illus. 24 cm. (Irwin series in management and the behavioral sciences)
Includes bibliographical references.
1. Organization—Addresses, essays, lectures. 2. System analysis—Addresses, essays, lectures. I. Title.
HD31.B327 301.18'32 72-98124
ISBN 0-256-00236-3 MARC

Baker, Frank, 1936- joint author
see Schulberg, Herbert C The mental hospital and human services. New York, Behavioral Publications [1975]

Baker, Frank B
The development of a computer model of the concept attainment process : a final report : report from the Computer Simulation Project / by Frank B. Baker ; Frank B. Baker, principal investigator. — Madison : Wisconsin Research and Development Center for Cognitive Learning, University of Wisconsin, 1968.
xi, 112 p. ; 28 cm. — (Theoretical paper - Wisconsin Research and Development Center for Cognitive Learning ; no. 16)
"Center no. C-03 / contract OE 5-10-154."
Bibliography: p. 42.
1. Concept learning—Data processing. 2. Cognition in children—Data processing. 3. Digital computer simulation. I. Title. II. Series: Wisconsin Research and Development Center for Cognitive Learning. Theoretical paper ; no. 16.
BF311.B26 73-626352
77 MARC

Baker, Frank B
see Lippey, Gerald. Computer-assisted test construction. Englewood Cliffs, N. J., Educational Technology Publications [1974]

Baker, Frank Collins, 1867-1942.
The fresh water Mollusca of Wisconsin, by F.C. Baker. New York, Verlag von J. Cramer, 1972.
2 v. in 1. illus. 23 cm. (Historia naturalis classica, t. 96)
Reprint of 1928 ed.
Bibliography: pt. II, p. 430-452.
Contents. - pt. I. Gastropoda. - pt. II. Pelecypoda.
1. Mollusks--Wisconsin. 2. Gasteropoda. 3. Lamellibranchiata. I. Wisconsin Academy of Sciences, Arts, and Letters. II. Title. III. Series.
OU NUC74-147091

Baker, Frank Collins, 1867-
see Cressman, Luther Sheeleigh, 1897- Archaeological researches in the northern Great basin. Washington, D.C., Library of Congress, Photoduplication Service [n.d.]

Baker, Fred.
Movie people, at work in the business of film. Edited by Fred Baker, with Ross Firestone. New York, Douglas Book Corp. [1972]
193 p. ports. 23 cm. $2.95
1. Moving-picture industry—United States. I. Title.
[PN1993.5.U6B27 1972] 658'.91'791430973 73-142527
MARC

Baker, Fred.
Movie people, at work in the business of film. [Edited by] Fred Baker with Ross Firestone. New York, Lancer Books [1973]
242 p. illus. 18 cm. (A Lancer contempora book) $1.50
Eleven in-depth interviews with film professionals in 1968 and 1970.
1. Moving-picture industry—United States. I. Title.
PN1993.5.U6B27 658'.91'79143'0973 73-159497
MARC

Baker, Frederick Charles, 1948-
Biohydrogenation of unsaturated fatty acid: partial purification and properties of CIS-9, TRANS-11-octadecadienoic acid CIS reductase from Butyrivibrio fibrisolvens by Frederick Charles Baker. Raleigh, 1974.
95 l. illus. 29 cm.
Bibliography: leaves 92-95.
Vita.
Thesis (Ph. D.)--North Carolina State University.
NcRS NUC76-18078

Baker, Frederick Dee, 1943-
A minimax approach to data analysis / Frederick Dee Baker. -- [s.l. : s.n., 1976]
207 leaves.
Thesis--University of Georgia.
GU NUC77-91917

Baker, Frederick John, 1941-
Community development in northeast Thailand: a descriptive study of Radio Station 909, Sakon Nakorn, as an educational vehicle for change. [n.p.] 1973.
[4], vi, 149, [i.e. 151] l. illus.
Thesis (Ph. D.)--Michigan State University.
Bibliography: leaves 92-97.
1. Community development--Thailand. I. Title.
MiEM NUC75-17380

Baker, Frederick William George, 1928-
see Symposium on Approaches to Earth Survey Problems Through Use of Space Techniques, Constance, 1973. Approaches to earth survey problems through use of space techniques ... Berlin : Akademie-Verlag, 1974.

Baker, G. E.
see also
Baker, Glenn E

Baker, G.G.
see Baker, Gerald Graham.

Baker, (G. G.) and Associates.
A guide to COM in the United Kingdom. 3rd ed. Guildford, G. G. Baker and Associates, 1972.
[2], 96 p. illus. 21 cm. £5.00 ($15.00U.S.) GB 72-30313
Includes index.
1. Computer output microfilm devices. I. Title.
TK7887.8.C6B34 1972 001.6'443 73-180490
ISBN 0-9502082-2-1 MARC

Baker (G. G.) and Associates.
A guide to computer output microfilm. — 4th ed. — Guildford : G. G. Baker and Associates, 1975.
2 v. : ill. ; 21 cm. GB75-11685
First-3d editions published under title: A guide to COM in the United Kingdom.
Bibliography: v. 1, p. 69-71.
Includes index.
CONTENTS: v. 1. The technology.—v. 2. Commercial information.
ISBN 0-9502082-6-4 (v. 1) : £5.00 ($15.00 U.S.)
1. Computer output microfilm devices. I. Title.
TK7887.8.C6B34 1975 001.6'443 76-351104
76 MARC

Baker, (G. G.) and Associates.
A guide to microfilm readers and reader-printers. Guildford, G. G. Baker and Associates, 1972.
[2], 104 p.; illus. 21 cm. £5.00 B 72-14073
Cover title.
"Supplement": 8 p. (inserted)
1. Reader-printers (Microphotography)—Catalogs. 2. Microfilm readers—Catalogs. I. Title.
TR835.B34 686.4'3'028 73-154701
ISBN 0-9502082-1-3 MARC

Baker (G. G.) and Associates.
A guide to microfilm readers and reader-printers. 2nd ed. Guildford, G. G. Baker and Associates, 1973.
[2], 128 p. illus. 21 cm. £5.00 ($15.00U.S.) GB 73-05802
Cover title.
"Supplement": 8 p. (inserted)
1. Reader-printers (Microphotography)—Catalogs. 2. Microfilm readers—Catalogs. I. Title.
TR835.B34 1973 686.4'3'028 73-177994
ISBN 0-9502082-3-X MARC

Baker (G. G.) and Associates.
A guide to microfilm readers and reader-printers / [G. G. Baker and Assoicates]. — 3rd ed. / edited by G. G. Baker. — Guildford : G. G. Baker and Associates, 1976.
192 p. : ill. ; 22 cm. GB76-12751
Includes indexes.
ISBN 0-9502082-8-0 : £5.00 ($15.00 U.S.)
1. Reader-printers (Microphotography)—Catalogs. 2. Microfilm readers—Catalogs. I. Baker, Gerald Graham. II. Title.
TR835.B34 1976 686'.4'3'028 76-374017
76 MARC

Baker, (G. G.) and Associates.
A guide to the production of microforms / G. G. Baker and Associates. — Guildford (54 Quarry St., Guildford, Surrey) : G. G. Baker and Associates, 1974.
144 p. : ill. ; 21 cm. GB 74-18911
Includes index.
ISBN 0-9502082-5-6 pbk. : £5.00 ($15.00U.S.)
1. Microphotography—Apparatus and supplies—Catalogs. I. Title.
TR835.B34 1974 338.4'7'681418 74-189909
MARC

Baker, Garth Arnold, 1945-
Projection methods for boundary value problems for equations of elliptic and parabolic type with discontinuous co-efficients. [Ithaca, N.Y.] 1973.
[2], v, 201 l. 29 cm.
Bibliography: leaves 196-201.
Thesis (Ph.D.)--Cornell University.
1. Boundary value problems--Numerical solutions. 2. Differential equations, Linear--Numerical solutions. 3. Projection. I. Title.
NIC NUC75-17371

Baker, George.
On the objective, design and construction of my kinetic metal sculptures / [by] George Baker with Richard Andrews. -- Oxford ; New York : Pergamon Press, 1975.
273-279 p. : ill. ; 28 cm.
Reprinted from Leonardo, v. 8, no. 4, Autumn 1975.
Includes bibliography.
1. Baker, George. 2. California. State University, San Diego. Library. I. Andrews, Richard. II. Title.
CSdS NUC77-95947

Baker, George, self-named Father Divine.
Here's the answer. [n.p., 196-]
25 p. illus. 20 cm.
Questions and answers, each dated; 1938-62.
1. Peace Mission Movement.
CBGTU NUC76-71014

Baker, George, self-named Father Divine.
A treatise on overpopulation taken from interviews, sermons, and lectures by Father Divine. Philadelphia, New Day Pub. Co., 1967.
v, 41 p. 28 cm.
1. Christian life. 2. Population. I. Title.
BX7350.A25 1967 261.8'3 73-172243
MARC

Baker, George, 1944-
see Radical agriculture. New York, Harper & Row, 1976.

Baker, George, 1944-
see Radical agriculture. New York, New York University Press, 1976.

Baker, George A., 1932 (July 29)- joint author.
see Roueche, John E. Time as the variable, achievement as the constant ... Washington, American Association of Community and Junior Colleges, 1976.

Baker, George A 1932(Nov. 25)-
Essentials of Padé approximants ⌈by⌉ George A. Baker, Jr. New York, Academic Press, 1975.
xi, 306 p. illus. 24 cm.
Bibliography: p. 295-302.
1. Padé approximant. I. Title.
QC20.7.P3B34 515'.235 74-1632
ISBN 0-12-074855-X 74⌈r76⌉rev2 MARC

Baker, George Augustus, 1849-
Mrs. Hephaestus, and other short stories; together with West Point, a comedy in three acts. New York, White, Stokes & Allen, 1887.
211 p.
Microfilm (positive) Ann Arbor, Mich., University Microfilms, 1967. 8th title of 13. 35 mm. (American fiction series, reel 44.8)
I. Title.
MiU NUC76-71013

Baker, George E.
see Seward, William Henry, 1801-1872. The works... New York, Redfield, 1853-1884 [197-]

Baker, George Edward, 1902- comp.
Charles I, 1649 * Court and commons. ⌈Phonodisc⌉ Devised by George Baker, with additional material arr. by George Rylands and Peter Orr. Edited and directed by Peter Orr. Argo ZPR 105-106. ⌈1969⌉
4 s. 12 in. 33⅓ rpm. stereophonic. (History reflected, 3)
Poetry, prose, and music performed by various actors and musicians.
Manual sequence.
Program notes (⌈4⌉ p. illus.) laid in container.
1. Great Britain — History — Puritan Revolution, 1642-1660 — Sources. 2. Charles I, King of Great Britain, 1600-1649. 3. Cromwell, Oliver, 1599-1658. I. Rylands, George Humphrey Wolfestan, 1902- II. Orr, Peter. III. Title: Court and commons. IV. Series.
[DA400] 73-760946

Baker, George Pierce, 1866-1935.
Dramatic technique / by George Pierce Baker ; with an introd. by Harold Clurman. — New York : Da Capo Press, 1976, c1919.
vi, 531 p. ; 22 cm. — (A Da Capo paperback)
Reprint, with a new introd., of the ed. published by Houghton Mifflin, Boston.
Includes indexes.
ISBN 0-306-80030-6
1. Drama—Technique. I. Title.
⌈PN1661.B3 1976⌉ 808.2 75-31999
75 MARC

Baker, George Pierce, 1866-1935, ed.
see Dickens, Charles, 1812-1870. Charles Dickens and Maria Beadnell: private correspondence. ⌈Folcroft, Pa.⌉ Folcroft Library Editions, 1974.

Baker, George T., ed.
see Molecular genetic mechanisms in development and aging. New York, Academic Press, 1972.

Baker, George Towne, 1941-
Mexico City and the war with the United States; a study in the politics of military occupation. [n.p.] c1972.
x, 381 l. 21 cm.
Thesis (Ph.D.)—Duke University, 1970.
Bibliography: leaves 361-379.
Photocopy of the original by University Microfilms, 1974.
1. Mexico (City)—History. 2. Military occupation. I. Title.
TNJ NUC76-29019

Baker, George Towne, 1941-
Mexico City and the war with the United States: a study in the politics of military occupation. ⌈n.p.⌉ 1969 ⌈c1972⌉
x, 381 l.
Thesis—Duke University.
Vita.
Bibliography: leaves 362-379.
Microfilm. Ann Arbor, Mich., University Microfilms, 1972. 1 reel. 35 mm.
1. U.S.—Hist.—War with Mexico, 1845-1848. I. Title.
TxU NUC75-22627

Baker, George Towne, 1941-
see The Subterranean system of the Sun Pyramid at Teotihuacan ... México, Grupo UAC-KAN, 1974.

Baker, George William, 1898-
Munsungun to the sea, by George W. and Marjorie L. Baker. ⌈1st ed.⌉ New York, Vantage Press ⌈1972⌉
251 p. 21 cm.
1. Hancock County, Maine—Hist. 2. Hancock County, Maine—Description and travel. 3. Maine—Description and travel. I. Baker, Marjorie Louise, 1911- joint author. II. Title.
MeU NUC75-23954

Baker, George William, 1931-
The Caribbean policy of Woodrow Wilson, 1913-1917. [Boulder, Colo.] 1961 [1972]
451 l.
Thesis—University of Colorado.
Bibliography: leaves 439-451.
Photocopy. Ann Arbor, Mich., University Microfilms, 1972. 21 cm.
1. Wilson, Woodrow, Pres. U.S., 1865-1924. 2. U.S.—For. rel.—Caribbean area. 3. Caribbean area—For. rel.—U.S. I. Title.
FU NUC74-44466

Baker, Georgianne.
Patterning of family resources for educability: conceptualization and measurement in Costa Rican families. ⌈n.p.⌉ 1970 ⌈c1971⌉
ix, 257 l. illus.
Thesis—Michigan State University.
Bibliography: leaves 153-163.
Microfilm. Ann Arbor, Mich., University Microfilms, 1971. 1 reel. 35 mm.
1. Family—Management. 2. Family—Costa Rica. 3. Parent and child. I. Title.
TxU NUC76-70951

Baker, Gerald Graham.
Information access methods for microfilm systems / by G.G. Baker. -- Guilford, Surrey : Microfilm Association of Great Britain, 1975.
15 p. : ill. ; 21 cm.
"Reprinted from Microdoc, v. 13, 1974."
1. Information storage and retrieval systems--Microfilms. I. Title.
NhD NUC77-91813

Baker, Gerald Graham.
see Baker (G. G.) and Associates. A guide to microfilm readers and reader-printers. 3rd ed. Guildford, G. G. Baker and Associates, 1976.

Baker, Gertrude Elaine, ed.
see Brown, Sally, 1807- The diaries of Sally and Pamela Brown... Springfield, Vt., William L. Bryant Foundation, 1970.

Baker, Gillian.
East Anglian history—theses completed ⌈compiled by Gillian Baker. Norwich⌉, University of East Anglia, Centre of East Anglian Studies, 1972.
⌈8⌉, 23 p. 22 cm. £0.20 B 72-28933
Cover title.
1. East Anglia — History — Bibliography. 2. Dissertations, Academic—Bibliography. I. Centre of East Anglian Studies. II. Title.
Z2024.E2B34 016.91426 73-161767
ISBN 0-902171-04-6 MARC

Baker, Gladys L 1910-
The county agent, by Gladys Baker. Chicago, Ill., The University of Chicago press ⌈c1939⌉
xxi, 226 p. incl. tables. 22 cm. (Half-title: Studies in public administration. vol. XI)
"This study was prepared as a dissertation for the degree of doctor of philosophy at the University of Chicago ⌈1939⌉"—p. vii.
"Published August 1939."
"Select bibliography": p. 214-215.
1. County agricultural agents. I. Title. II. Series: Studies in public administration (Chicago), v. 11.
S533.B17 1939a 630.6173 39-21222
rev

Baker, Gladys L., 1910- joint author.
see Rasmussen, Wayne David, 1915- A short history of agricultural adjustment, 1933-75. Washington, Economic Research Service, U.S. Dept. of Agriculture, 1976.

Baker, Gladys Leslie.
The finger of God is here. New York, St. Paul Publications ⌈1961⌉
234 p. illus. 18 cm.
ODaU-M NUC73-59272

Baker, Gladys Leslie.
The finger of God is here. ⌈New ed. with rev. addenda. New York⌉ St. Paul Publications ⌈1967⌉
254 p. illus. 19 cm.
ODaU-M NUC73-59612

Baker, Glenn E
Construction-techniques / Glenn E. Baker ; consulting editor, William P. Spence. — Englewood Cliffs, N.J. : Prentice-Hall, c1976.
120 p. : ill. ; 24 cm. — (Modular exploration of technology series)
Includes index.
ISBN 0-13-169417-0. ISBN 0-13-169409-X pbk. : $1.95
1. Building. I. Title.
TH145.B23 690 75-9987
75 MARC

Baker, Glenn E
Wood technology ⌈by⌉ G. E. Baker ⌈and⌉ L. Dayle Yeager. ⌈1st ed.⌉ Indianapolis, H. W. Sams ⌈1974⌉
xi, 516 p. illus. 27 cm.
1. Woodwork. I. Yeager, L. Dayle, joint author. II. Title.
TS843.B35 684 72-83817
ISBN 0-672-20917-9 MARC

Baker, Gloria Beth, 1928-
Dissenters in colonial North Carolina. [n.p., c1971]
1 reel. 35 mm.
Thesis (Ph.D.)—University of North Carolina at Chapel Hill, 1970.
Microfilm of typescript. Ann Arbor, Mich., University Microfilms [1970]
1. Dissenters, Religious—North Carolina. I. Title.
WHi NUC76-71012

Baker, Grace Louise.
Host response to antigens of Trypanosoma duttoni. ⌈Columbia⌉ 1972.
137 l. illus.
Thesis (Ph.D.)—University of Missouri.
Vita.
Includes bibliography.
MoU NUC75-22625

Baker, Grace Louise.
Host response to antigens of Trypanosoma duttoni. ⌈Columbia⌉ 1972.
137 l. illus.
Thesis (Ph.D.)—University of Missouri.
Microfilm copy.
Vita.
Includes bibliography.
MoU NUC75-22626

Baker, Guy S
History of Halifax, Massachusetts / by Guy S. Baker. — 1st ed. — Halifax : ⌈s.n.⌉, c1976.
191 p. : ill. ; 25 cm.
Includes index.
$12.50
1. Halifax, Mass.—History. I. Title.
F74.H16B34 974.4'82 76-23197
77 MARC

Baker, Gwendolyn C.
see Teaching in a multicultural society ... New York, Free Press, c1977.

Baker, H
Apricots, peaches, nectarines, figs and grapes. Original text rev. by H. Baker and E.G. Gilbert. London, Royal Horticultural Society, c1972.
31 p. illus. (Wisley handbook, 8)
1. Fruit-culture. I. Gilbert, E.G., joint author. II. Title. III. Series.
MiEM NUC75-22624

Baker, H A
God in Ka Do land. Yunnanfu, Adullan Mission [19--]
95 p. illus.
1. Kha Tahoi. 2. Missions–China.
ICU NUC73-103094

Baker, H A
Visions beyond the veil, by H. A. Baker. [Monroeville, Pa.] Whitaker Books [1973]
144 p. 18 cm. $0.95
1. Baptism in the Holy Spirit. 2. Church work with children—Yünnan, China (Province). 3. Visions. I. Title.
[BT123.B24] 248'.29 73-81105
ISBN 0-88368-019-X MARC

Baker, H. A.
see also
Baker, Hugh Arthur.

Baker, H. A., 1926-
see
Akmakjian, Hiag.

Baker, H. C.
see
Baker, Horace Charles.

Baker, H E
Owletts. [Plaistow, Curwen Press, 1969]
[4] p. 21.5 cm.
Caption title.
Text signed H.B. [i.e. H.E. Baker]
A red-brick Carolean house in Cobham, Kent, given in 1938 to the National Trust by Sir Herbert Baker, and now occupied by Mr. and Mrs. H.E. Baker.-cf. p. [4].
I. National Trust for Places of Historic Interest or Natural Beauty.
MWiCA NUC76-14975

Baker, H. L.
see
Baker, Hillier Locke, 1924-

Baker, Harold D
An investigation of attitudes toward various aspects of the transportation industry in Wisconsin. Ames, Iowa, Statistical Laboratory, Iowa State University, 1972.
1 v. (various pagings) 28 cm. (Iowa State University of Science and Technology, Ames. Statistical Laboratory. Technical report, no. 8)
Cover title.
1. Transportation—Wisconsin—Statistics.
IaAS NUC76-70982

Baker, Harold E
Library automation at the Cunningham Memorial Library, Indiana State University, Terre Haute. Terre Haute, 1973.
121 p. (Library Automation Research and Consulting Association. The LARC reports, v. 6, no. 4)
I. Cunningham Memorial Library. II. Title.
DNAL CaBVaU NUC75-20634

Baker, Harold Kent, 1944-
Investment criteria: an empirical analysis of common stock investors in metropolitan Washington, D.C. [College Park, Md.] 1972.
ix, 253 l. illus.
Thesis—University of Maryland.
Vita.
Bibliography: leaves 237-253.
Microfilm of typescript. Ann Arbor, Mich., University Microfilms, 1973. 1 reel. 35 mm.
1. Investments—Washington metropolitan area—Case studies. 2. Speculation. I. Title.
IEdS NUC74-126560

Baker, Harold Kent, 1944-
Investment decision criteria: an empirical analysis of common stock investors in Metropolitan Washington, D.C. [College Park, Md.] 1972.
253 l. 29 cm.
Typescript.
Thesis—University of Maryland.
Vita.
Includes bibliography.
1. Investments—Washington, D.C. 2. Stocks—Washington, D.C. 3. Capitalists and financiers—Washington, D.C. I. Title.
MdU NUC74-133489

Baker, Harold L
Compensable regulations: their potential for land-use and development control in Hawaii. A special report to the Senate, Fifth Legislature, State of Hawaii [by] Harold L. Baker. Honolulu, Land Study Bureau, University of Hawaii, 1968.
iv, 51 l. 28 cm. (Special studies series. L. S. B. report no. 7)
Bibliography: leaves 40–41.
1. Regional planning—Law and legislation—Hawaii. 2. Compensation (Law)—Hawaii. I. Hawaii. 5th Legislature, 1968–1969. Senate. II. Title. III. Series: Hawaii. University, Honolulu. Land Study Bureau. L. S. B. report no. 7.
HD211.H3H38 no. 7 333.7'09969 s 78–632481
[KFH458] [346'.969'045] MARC

Baker, Harold L
An economic report on the production of Kona coffee, 1974 [by] Harold L. Baker [and] Joseph T. Keeler. [Honolulu] Dept. of Agricultural and Resource Economics, College of Tropical Agriculture, University of Hawaii, 1974.
[4], 41, [24] l. illus., tables.
An update of the report first issued in 1958.
Submitted to the Legislative Auditor of the State of Hawaii.
1. Coffee—Hawaii. 2. Kona, Hawaii. I. Keeler, Joseph T., joint author. II. Hawaii. University, Honolulu. Dept. of Agricultural and Resource Economics. III. Hawaii. Office of the Legislative Auditor. IV. Title.
HU NUC75-85866

Baker, Harold L
Land classification and determination of highest and best use of Hawaii's agricultural lands [by] Harold L. Baker. [Honolulu, Land Study Bureau, University of Hawaii] 1972.
26 l. illus. 29 cm. (University of Hawaii. Land Study Bureau. Special study series. LSB report no. 10)
Cover title.
Includes bibliographical references.
1. Land—Hawaii—Classification. I. Title. II. Series: Hawaii. University, Honolulu. Land Study Bureau. Special study series. III. Series: Hawaii. University, Honolulu. Land Study Bureau. LSB report no. 10.
HD211.H3H38 no. 10 333.7'09969 s 73-620944
77 MARC

Baker, Harold L., joint author
see Indiana. Dept. of Commerce. Planning Division. Indiana: local housing authorities... Indianapolis, 1971]

Baker, Harold Stewart, 1909–
The future and education; Alberta 1970–2005, prepared by Harold S. Baker with the assistance of members of staff of the Human Resources Research Council. [Edmonton, Alta., Human Resources Research Council of Alberta, c1971]
57 p. 26 cm. $3.00 C***
1. Education—1965– 2. Education—Alberta. 3. Twenty-first century—Forecasts. I. Human Resources Research Council. II. Title.
LA133.B25 370'.97123 72–194019
MARC

Baker, Harriette Newell (Woods) 1815–1893.
Art and artlessness. By Mrs. Madeline Leslie. Boston, Lee and Shepard, 1864.
256 p. illus. 18 cm. (Her Little Agnes' library)
Mrs. Leslie's juvenile series.
I. Title.
PZ6.B18Ar 74–151668
MARC

Baker, Harriette Newell (Woods) 1815-1893.
Cora and the doctor; or, Revelations of a physician's wife. Boston, J.P. Jewett, 1855 [1973]
407 p.
Microfilm (positive) Ann Arbor, Mich., University Microfilms, 1973. 11th title of 12. 35 mm. (American fiction series, reel 212.11)
1. American fiction. I. Title. II. Title: Revelations of a physician's wife.
KEmT NUC74-1282

Baker, Harriette Newell (Woods) 1815-1893.
The first and the second marriages; or, The courtesies of wedded life, by Mrs. Madeline Leslie [pseud.] Boston, C. Stone, 1856 [1973]
428 p.
Microfilm (positive) Ann Arbor, Mich., University Microfilms, 1973. 12th title of 12. 35 mm. (American fiction series, reel 212.12)
I. Title. II. Title: The courtesies of wedded life.
KEmT NUC74-1281

Baker, Harriette Newell Woods, 1815-1893.
Gem of courage : or, Barbara and Bena / by Madeline Leslie [i.e. H. N. W. Baker]. — Boston : Graves and Ellis, c1872.
106 p., [2] leaves of plates : ill. ; 16 cm. — (Her Sparkling gems)
I. Title. II. Title: Barbara and Bena.
PZ7.B174 Ge 75-311246
75 MARC

Baker, Harriette Newell Woods, 1815-1893.
Gem of truthfulness : or, The lost baby / by Madeline Leslie [i.e. H. N. W. Baker]. — Boston : A. F. Graves, c1872.
109 p., [3] leaves of plates : ill. ; 16 cm. — (Her Sparkling gems ; v. 5)
I. Title.
PZ7.B174 Gh 75-319807
75 MARC

Baker, Harriette Newell (Woods) 1815-1893.
Juliette; or, Now and forever. By Mrs. Madeline Leslie. Boston, Lee and Shepard, 1869.
416 p.
Microfilm (positive) Ann Arbor, Mich., University Microfilms, 1966. 7th title of 20. 35 mm. (American fiction series, reel 11.7)
I. Title.
MiU NUC76-70949

Baker, Harriette Newell (Woods) 1815-1893.
Little robins' love one to another, by Mrs. Madeline Leslie. Boston, Crosby and Ainsworth [c1960]
104 p. illus. 15 cm.
I. Title.
MB NUC76-36543

Baker, Harriette Newell Woods, 1815-1893.
Tim's sister : or, A word in season / by Madeline Leslie [i.e. H. N. W. Baker]. — Boston : H. Hoyt, c1863.
321 p. ; 17 cm. — (Her The Leslie series of juvenile religious works)
I. Title.
PZ6.B18 Ti 75-317424
75 MARC

Baker, Harriette Newell (Woods) 1815-1893.
The twin brothers. New York, Harper, 1843 [1973]
243 p.
Microfilm (positive) Ann Arbor, Mich., University Microfilms, 1973. 6th title of 24. 35 mm. (American fiction series, reel 204.6)
I. Title.
KEmT NUC74-1280

Baker, Harry Jay, 1889-
Detroit tests of learning aptitude; a new instrument of mental diagnosis, by Harry J. Baker and Bernice Leland. Indianapolis, Ind., Bobbs-Merrill [c1958-67; v 1, 1967]
3 v. illus. 21-29 cm.
1. Mental tests. 2. Ability—Testing.
I. Leland, Bernice, joint author. II. Title.
CNoS NUC74-23664

Baker, Harry Philip, 1931-
Effects of favorable social comparisons on self-evaluation and task performance of high-and low-achieving black college students. [Austin, Tex.] 1973.
xiv, 132 l. 29 cm.
Thesis (Ph.D.)—University of Texas at Austin.
Vita.
Bibliography: leaves 126-132.
1. Self-evaluation. 2. College students, Negro.
TxU NUC75-17363

Baker, Harry Scott.
The prose and verse styles of John Donne: Devotions upon emergent occasions and Holy sonnets: Divine meditations [by] H. Scott Baker. [n.p.] 1972.
1 v.
Honors thesis—Harvard.
1. Donne, John, 1573-1631. Devotions upon emergent occasions. 2. Donne, John, 1573-1631. Holy sonnets.
MH NUC76-71011

Baker, Harvey.
Upper estuary pollution and transfer relationships. A report to the National Science Foundation RANN program. Prepared for the Work Group on Upper Estuary Pollution and Transfer Relationships. [Newark] University of Delaware, 1973.
i, 50 p. illus., maps. 28 cm.
At head of title: The Delaware estuary system, environmental impacts and socio-economic effects.
Participating organizations: University of Delaware, Academy of Natural Sciences, Rutgers University.
Bibliography: p. 48-50.
1. Estuarine ecology-Delaware River estuary. 2. Water quality—Delaware River estuary. 3. Urbanization. I. United States. National Science Foundation. Research Applied to National Needs Program. II. Work Group on Upper Estuary Pollution and Transfer Relationships. III. Delaware. University, Newark. IV. Rutgers University, New Brunswick, N.J. V. Academy of Natural Sciences of Philadelphia. VI. Title.
DI NUC76-88810

Baker, Harvey Wills, 1918-
see Oral cancer. ⌐New York, c1973⌐

Baker, Hendrik.
Stage management and theatrecraft; a stage manager's handbook. Line drawings by Margaret Woodward. Foreword by Basil Dean. 2d ed. New York, Theatre Arts Books ⌐1971⌐
xv, 320 p. illus. 20 cm.
Bibliography: p. 318-320.
1. Stage management. I. Title.
NjR TxU NUC73-126371

Baker, Henry, 1698-1774.
An attempt towards a natural history of the polype: in a letter to Martin Folkes... By Henry Baker... London, printed for R. Dodsley, and sold by M. Cooper ⌐etc.⌐ 1743.
218, ⌐4⌐ p. front., illus. 20 cm.
Microprint. New York, Readex Microprint, 1968. 3 cards. (Landmarks of Science)
1. Hydromedusae. I. Title.
InU NUC76-70973

Baker, Henry Barton, 1845-1906.
The London stage: its history and traditions from 1576 to 1888. By H. Barton Baker ... London, W.H. Allen & Co., 1889.
2 v. front. 20 cm.
Ultra microfiche. Dayton, Ohio, National Cash Register, 1970. 1st title of 5. 10.5 x 14.8 cm. (PCMI library collection, 197-1)
1. Theater—London—Hist. I. Title.
KEmT NUC74-11675

Baker, Henry Felt, 1797-1857.
Banks and banking the United States, by Henry F. Baker. Boston, Ticknor, Reed, and Fields, 1853.
2 v.
Vol. 2 t.p. has "Part II: Relating to the states of Kentucky, Ohio, Indiana, and Illinois," and is published by C.F. Bradley, Cincinnati.
Microfilm (positive) Ann Arbor, Mich., University Microfilms, 1972. 11th title of 17. 35 mm. (American culture series, reel 501.11)
1. Banks and banking—U.S. I. Title.
KEmT NUC74-179447

Baker, Henry Frederick, 1866-
Abel's theorem and the allied theory, including the theory of the theta functions, by H. F. Baker... Cambridge, University Press, 1897.
xix, [1], 684 p. 28 cm.
Ultra microfiche. Dayton, Ohio, National Cash Register, 1970. 10.5 x 14.8 cm. (PCMI library collection, 938-1)
1. Functions, Abelian. 2. Functions, Theta. I. Title.
KEmT NUC74-122419

Baker, Henry Givens, 1912-
Management philosophy of selected firms in eight different industries in the Greater Cincinnati and Ohio area. Sponsored by the Cincinnati Chapter of the Society for the Advancement of Management. Henry G. Baker, editor. [Cincinnati] Management Department, College of Business Administration, University of Cincinnati [1970]
4 v. 28 cm. (Management monograph, no. 1-4)
"Commemorating the University of Cincinnati's sesquicentennial, 1819-1969."
Contents.-1. Selected firms in the insurance industry.-2. Selected firms in the steel and oil industries.-3. Selected firms in the marketing and appliances and office machines industries.-4. Selected firms in the machine tool, public utilities, and publishing and communication industries.
1. Management—United States. I. Cincinnati. University. College of Business Administration. Management. Dept. II. Society for Advancement of Management. Cincinnati Chapter. III. Title. IV. Series.
OU NUC76-94568

Baker, Henry Givens, 1912-
see Cincinnati. University. Dept. of Management. Management monograph, management... Cincinnati [c1970]

Baker, Henry Givens, 1912-
see Environment 1984 ... Columbus, Ohio, Grid, 1975.

Baker, Henry Moore, 1841-1912. New Hampshire in the Battle of Bunker Hill. 1973
in Kidder, Frederic, 1804-1885. History of the First New Hampshire Regiment in the War of the Revolution. ⌐Hampton, N. H.⌐ P. E. Randall, 1973.

Baker, Sir Henry William, bart., 1821-1877, ed.
see Hymns ancient & modern. Rev. [ed.] London, Printed for the proprietors by W. Clowes and Sons, ltd. [196-?]

Baker, Herbert.
"Norman Rockwell's America"; ⌐teleplay⌐ Written by Herbert Baker ⌐and⌐ Treva Silverman. Final draft. ⌐Los Angeles?⌐ Bob Henry Productions, 1969.
73 l. 28 cm.
"An award-winning script, part of series # 2 ⌐from the⌐ Writers Guild of America, West."
IU NUC74-121640

Baker, Heretaunga Pat.
Behind the tattooed face / by Heretaunga Pat Baker. — Queen Charlotte Sound, N.Z. : Cape Catley, 1975.
276 p. ; 25 cm. NZ***
Label mounted on t.p.: Available from International Publications Service Collings, New York.
1. New Zealand—History—To 1843—Fiction. I. Title.
PZ4.B16915 Be 823 76-354954
⌐PR9639.3.B26⌐ 76 MARC

Baker, Herschel Clay, 1914-
see The Later Renaissance in England ... Boston, Houghton Mifflin, c1975.

Baker, Hillier Locke, 1924-
see Symposium on tomography. Philadelphia, Saunders, 1976.

Baker, Hinton J., joint author
see Noyes, Howard E Effects of a nuclear detonation on swine. New York, New York Academy of Sciences, 1963.

Baker, Homer O'Neal, 1936-
An algorithm for computerized readability. ⌐Tempe⌐ 1973.
62 l.
Thesis (Ed.D.)—Arizona State University.
Vita.
Includes abstract.
Bibliography: leaves ⌐47⌐-51.
1. Readability (Literary style). 2. Book selection—Mathematical models. 3. Book selection—Computer programs. I. Title.
AzTeS NUC76-71000

Baker, Horace Charles.
The manager and his environment : an inaugural lecture / by H. C. Baker. — ⌐Durham⌐ : University of Durham, ⌐1974⌐
⌐1⌐, 18 p. ; 22 cm. GB74-30548
Bibliography: p. 18.
ISBN 0-900926-22-8 : £0.30
1. Management. I. Title.
HD31.B328 658.4 75-324069
75 MARC

Baker, Houston A
A many-colored coat of dreams : the poetry of Countee Cullen / by Houston A. Baker, Jr. — 1st ed. — Detroit : Broadside Press, ⌐1974⌐
60 p. ; 23 cm. — (Broadside critics series ; no. 4)
Bibliography: p. 59-60.
ISBN 0-910296-36-7
1. Cullen, Countee, 1903-1946. I. Title. II. Series.
PS3505.U287Z57 811'.5'2 73-91266
MARC

Baker, Houston A
Singers of daybreak; studies in Black American literature ⌐by⌐ Houston A. Baker, Jr. Washington, Howard University Press, 1974.
xi, 109 p. 24 cm.
Bibliography: p. 101-109.
ISBN 0-88258-017-5
1. American literature—Negro authors—Addresses, essays, lectures. I. Title.
PS153.N5B27 810'.9'896073 74-11006
MARC

Baker, Houston A comp.
Twentieth century interpretations of Native son; a collection of critical essays. Edited by Houston A. Baker, Jr. Englewood Cliffs, N. J., Prentice-Hall ⌐1972⌐
iii, 124 p. 21 cm. (Twentieth century interpretations) (A Spectrum book) $4.95
CONTENTS: Wright, R. How "Bigger" was born.—Baldwin, J. Many thousands gone.—Howe, I. Black boys and native sons.—Bone, R. A. Richard Wright.—McCall, D. The bad nigger.—Kent, G. E. Richard Wright: Blackness and the adventure of Western culture.—Gibson, D. B. Wright's invisible native son.—Fisher, D. C. Introduction to the first edition.—Cowley, M. Richard Wright: the case of Bigger Thomas.—Algren, N. Remembering Richard Wright.—Selected bibliography (p. 123-124.)
1. Wright, Richard, 1908-1960. Native son. I. Title.
PS3545.R815N33 813'.5'2 72-8136
ISBN 0-13-609982-3; 0-13-609974-2 (pbk.) MARC

Baker, Howard
see United States. National Park Service. National Park Service officials. -- Centennial ed. -- [Washington] : The Service, 1972.

Baker, Howard, 1936-
Tot Fenny's firewood cart. ⌐London, Covent Garden Bookshop, 1971⌐
⌐14⌐ p. 17 cm.
Poems.
One of an edition limited to 250 copies.
I. Title.
TxU NUC76-70972

Baker, Howard Crittendon, 1943-
Light-cone algebra in Regge domains. St. Louis, 1972.
vi, 136 l. illus.
Thesis—Washington University.
Bibliographical references.
1. Regge trajectories. 2. Particles (Nuclear physics) I. Title.
MoSW NUC74-451

Baker, Howard Henry, 1925-
"CIA investigation" report. [Compiled by Senator] Howard H. Baker, Jr. Washington [1974]
43 l.
"Based on both classified and unclassified material in the possession of the Senate Select Committee on Presidential Campaign Activities."
Includes bibliographical references.
1. Watergate Affair, 1972-
TxU NUC76-18083

Baker, Howard Henry, 1925-
Peace and stability in the Middle East : a report / by Howard H. Baker, Jr. to the Committee on Foreign Relations, United States Senate. — Washington : U.S. Govt. Print. Off., 1975.
v, 19 p. ; 24 cm.
At head of title: 94th Congress, 1st session. Committee print.
1. Jewish-Arab relations—1973- —Addresses, essays, lectures. I. United States. Congress. Senate. Committee on Foreign Relations. II. Title.
DS119.7.B257 327.5694'017'4927 75-602774
75 MARC

Baker, Howard Henry, 1925-
see Watergate: John Dean... [Sound recording] Encyclopedia Americana/CBS News Audio Resource Library 06731-2. 1973.

Baker, Howard Henry, 1925-
see Watergate: Sens. Ervin & Baker... [Sound recording] Encyclopedia Americana/ CBS News Audio Resource Library 07733. 1973.

Baker, Howard Winfield.
Developement of railways [by] Howard W. Baker. [Ithaca, N.Y.] 1886.
23 l. 26 cm.
Thesis (C.E.)—Cornell University.
Microfilm, Ithaca, N.Y., Photo Science, Cornell University, 1972. part of reel. 35 mm.
NIC NUC76-70971

Baker, Hozial H
Overland journey to Carson Valley & California, by Hozial H. Baker. [San Francisco] Book Club of California, 1973.
91 p. 23 cm. (The Book Club of California. Publication number 143)
Imprint on cover: Seneca Falls, N. Y., Published by F. M. Baker, 1861.
1. Overland journeys to the Pacific. I. Title. II. Series: Book Club of California, San Francisco. Publication no. 143.
F593.B16 917.8'04'2 73-176518
MARC

Baker, Hozial H
Overland journey to Carson Valley, Utah; through Kansas, Nebraska and Utah; also, return trip, from San Francisco to Seneca Falls, via the Isthmus. Seneca Falls, N.Y., Published by F.M. Baker, 1861.
38 p. illus., port. 16 cm.
Micro-opaque. Louisville, Ky., Lost Cause Press, 1961. 1 card. 7.5 x 12.5 cm. (Plains and Rockies, 367a)
1. The West—Description and travel. 2. Overland journeys to the Pacific. I. Title.
NIC NUC74-178493

Baker, Hugh Arthur.
Ericas in southern Africa, with paintings by Irma von Below, Fay Anderson and others, text by H. A. Baker and E. G. H. Oliver, edited by E. G. H. Oliver. Cape Town, Johannesburg, Purnell [1967?]
lxvi, 180 p. illus., maps (part fold.) col. plates, ports. 28 cm. R12.50 SANL
Bibliography: p. lxv.
1. Erica. 2. Botany—Africa, South. I. Anderson, Fay, illus. II. Below, Irma von, illus. III. Oliver, E. G. H., joint author. IV. Title.
QK495.E68B25 583'.6'0968 68-92381
rev

Baker, Hugh D R
A lineage village in the new territories of Hong Kong. [London, Eng., 1967]
378 l. 27 cm.
Thesis (Ph.D.)—University of London.
Bibliography: leaves 365-371.
1. Shangshui, Hongkong. 2. Hongkong—Social life and customs. I. Title.
NIC NUC76-70953

Baker, Hugh D. R.
see The City in late imperial China. Stanford, Calif., Stanford University Press, 1977.

Baker, I L
Notes on Arnold Bennett—"The Card," by I. L. Baker. Bath, Brodie, 1973.
64 p. 19 cm. (Notes on chosen English texts) GB 73-05387
Bibliography: p. 41.
1. Bennett, Arnold, 1867-1931. The card. I. Title.
PR6003.E6C362 823'.9'12 73-175431
ISBN 0-7142-0138-3 MARC

Baker, Ian
see Harris, Maxwell Henley, 1921- Sir Henry, Bjelke, Don baby and friends. Melbourne, Sun Books [1971]

Baker, Imam M. A., tr.
see Koran. Afrikaans. Dit is 'n vertaling van die dertig dele van die Heilige Qur'ân... Kaapstad, Nasionale Boekhandel, 1961.

Baker, Ivon, 1928-
Peak performance / by Ivon Baker. — New York : St. Martin's Press, c1976.
176 p. ; 20 cm.
ISBN 0-7091-5306-6 : $7.95
I. Title.
PZ4.B1692 Pe 3 823'.9'14 75-34774
[PR6052.A334] 76 MARC

Baker, J.
see also
Baker, John, 1929-
Baker, June.

Baker, J A
When I am dead, what will happen to me? by J.A. Baker. London, Printed by Baker & Witt [19--?]
75 p. 17 cm.
1. Future life. I. Title.
TxU NUC76-50473

Baker, J A
see also
Baker, John Augustus, 1925-

Baker, J David.
The postal history of Indiana / by J. David Baker. — Louisville, Ky. : L. H. Hartmann, c1976.
2 v. (x, 1061 p.) : ill. ; 29 cm. & microfiche (1 sheet (176 p.) ; 11 x 15 cm.) in pocket.
Bibliography: p. 1055-1061.
ISBN 0-917528-03-4 : $75.00
1. Postal service—Indiana—History. I. Title.
HE6376.A1I73 383'.09772 76-10531
77 MARC

Baker, J. E., joint author.
see Arms, W. Y. A practical approach to computing. London, Wiley, c1976.

Baker, J. E., joint author.
see Gowar, N. W. Fourier series. London, Chatto & Windus, 1974.

Baker, J E 1917-
The right to participate: inmate involvement in prison administration, by J. E. Baker. Metuchen, N. J., Scarecrow Press, 1974.
260 p. 22 cm.
Includes bibliographical references.
1. Corrections—United States—History. 2. Correctional institutions—United States—History. I. Title.
HV9304.B34 365'.973 74-7071
ISBN 0-8108-0727-0 MARC

Baker, J. F. A.
see Studies in long term development of the Port of Dublin... [Dublin, 1973?]

Baker, J G
Companion to Ray Lawler, The summer of the seventeenth doll and Alan Seymour, The one day of the year, by J.G. Baker. [Sydney, etc.] Angus and Robertson [1965]
39 p. 18 cm. (Companion series. General editor: Frank Allsopp)
1. Australian drama—Outlines, syllabi, etc. I. Lawler, Ray. The summer of the seventeenth doll. II. Seymour, Alan. The one day of the year. III. Title.
TxU NUC76-70979

Baker, J. H.
see
Baker, John Hamilton.

Baker, J. J.
see
Baker, Jack James.

Baker, J. K.
see
Baker, John Kingsley.

Baker, J. N. L.
see
Baker, John Norman Leonard.

Baker, J Philip.
Using generalizability theory and multifacet designs in the validation of a classroom observation instrument. Stanford, School of Education, Stanford University, 1971.
iii, 12 l. (Stanford University. Center for Research and Development in Teaching. Research and development memorandum no. 79)
1. Observation (Educational method) I. Title. II. Series.
MH-Ed NUC74-11676

Baker, J R
The biology and systematics of certain Nearctic groups of Coelioxys (Hymenoptera: Megachilidae.) [Lawrence, 1972]
iv, 270 l. illus., maps. 29 cm.
Thesis (Ph.D.)—University of Kansas.
1. Bees. North America. 2. Parasites. Bees. I. Title.
KU NUC74-381

Baker, J R
Insect control on ornamental plants in & around the house, prepared by James R. Baker. Rev. Raleigh, North Carolina Agricultural Extension Service, 1975.
[12] p. ill. (North Carolina State University. Agricultural Extension Service. Circular, 561)
I. Title.
DNAL NUC77-89500

Baker, J R
Taxonomy of five Nearctic subgenera of Coelioxys (Hymenoptera, Megachilidae) / by J. R. Baker. — [Lawrence : University of Kansas], 1975.
p. 649-730 : ill. ; 26 cm. — (The University of Kansas science bulletin ; v. 50, no. 12 ISSN 0022-8850)
Cover title.
Bibliography: p. 730.
1. Coelioxys. 2. Insects—Classification. 3. Insects—North America. I. Title. II. Series: Kansas. University. University of Kansas science bulletin ; v. 50, no. 12.
Q1.K17 vol. 50, no. 12 508'.1 s 76-358912
[QL568.M4] 76 MARC

Baker, J. Stannard
see
Baker, James Stannard, 1899-

Baker, J. Wayne, joint comp.
see Riede, David Charles, 1925- comp. Pagans, Christians, and Jews. Rev. ed. Dubuque, Iowa, Kendall/Hunt Pub. Co. [1974]

Baker, J. Wayne, joint comp.
see Riede, David Charles, 1925- comp. Reason, liberty, and authority. Rev. ed. Dubuque, Iowa, Kendall/Hunt Pub. Co., [1975]

Baker, Jac.
see Gerling, Juanita. Views of Versailles and surrounding area. Bicentennial ed. [Versailles, Ohio] Versailles Policy Pub. Co., c1976.

Baker, Jack.
Cherokee cookbook, compiled by Jack Baker. Edited by Jack Gregory and Rennard Strickland. [Indian Heritage Edition. Fayetteville, Ark., Indian Heritage Association, c1968]
[16] p.
"These recipes were prepared with assistance of the Downing family."
1. Cookery, Cherokee. 2. Indians of North America—Food. 3. Cookery, American. I. Gregory, Jack, ed. II. Strickland, Rennard, ed. III. Title.
CU-SB NUC74-121248

Baker, Jack James.
Report on diseases of cultivated plants in England and Wales for the years 1957-1968 [by] J.J. Baker. London, H.M. Stationery Office, 1972.
322 p. illus. (Great Britain. Ministry of Agriculture and Fisheries. Technical bulletin; no. 25)
1. Plant diseases—England. 2. Plant diseases—Wales. I. Title. II. Series.
KMK NUC74-126577

Baker, Jack S.
see Krannert Art Museum. The new environment. [Urbana, 1973]

Baker, James Bert.
Summer fallowing improves survival and growth of cottonwood on old fields. New Orleans, 1973.
3 p. illus. (U.S. Southern Forest Experiment Station. U.S. Forest Service research note, SO-149)
I. Title.
DNAL NUC74-123581

Baker, James Calvin, 1935–
American banks abroad; Edge act companies and multinational banking [by] James C. Baker [and] M. Gerald Bradford. New York, Praeger [1974]
xiv, 182 p. 24 cm. (Praeger special studies in international economics and development) $17.50
Includes bibliographical references.
1. Banks and banking—United States. 2. Banks and banking, International. I. Bradford, M. Gerald, joint author. II. Title.
HG2569.B34 332.1'5 73–18135

Baker, James Calvin, 1935-
The unorganized money market in Korea; the kye system: an analysis with policy recommendations, by James C. Baker and Nam Yong Choi. Kent, Ohio, 1973.
34 p. (Ohio State University, Kent. Center for Business and Economic Research. International business series, no. 2)
1. Banks and banking–Cooperative–Korea. I. Choi, Nam-yong. II. Title.
InU NUC75-17385

Baker, James Calvin, 1935-
see China, the U. S. S. R., and Eastern Europe; a U. S. trade perspective. [Kent, Ohio] Kent State Univ. Press [1974]

Baker, James Calvin, 1935-
see Multinational marketing ... Columbus, Ohio, Grid, inc., 1975.

Baker, James Earl.
Samuel Winkley Cole: New England music educator, by James Earl Baker. [n.p.] 1975.
v, 122 l. 28 cm. (Studies in musical arts, no. 15)
Thesis (D.M.A.)--Catholic University of America.
Bibliography: leaves 116-122.
1. Cole, Samuel Winkley, 1848-1926. 2. School music--Instruction and study--New England.
DCU NUC77-90292

Baker, James Francis, 1944-
Intramolecular catalysis in the acetylation of 7 α-hydroxy-5 β-steorids. [Bloomington, Ind.] 1975.
224 p. illus.
Thesis (Ph.D.)--Indiana University.
Vita.
InU NUC77-89561

Baker, James Franklin Bethune-
see Bethune-Baker, James Franklin, 1861-

Baker, James H
Paradoxostoma rostratum sars (Ostracoda, Podocopida) as a commensal on the Arctic Gammarid amphipods Gammaracanthus loricatus (Sabine) and Gammarus wilkitzkii birula, by James H. Baker and James W. Wong. Leiden, E.J. Brill [1968]
[307]-311 p. illus.
"Reprinted from: Crustaceana, vol. 14 part 3, 1968."
References: p. 311.
Photocopy. Springfield, Va., Clearinghouse for Federal Scientific & Technical Information. (United States. Clearinghouse for Federal Scientific and Technical Information. [AD and PB reports] AD 674 220)
Michrofiche (negative). 1 card. 10.5 x 15 cm.
1. Podocopida. I. Wong, James W. II. Crustaceana. III. Title. IV. Series.
CaBVaU NUC76-70947

Baker, James Houston, 1938-
A survey of science teaching in the public secondary schools of the plains, Rocky Mountain, and southeast regions of the United States in the 1970-71 school year. [n.p.] 1973.
326 l.
Thesis–Ohio State University.
Bibliography: leaves 316-326.
1. Science–Study and teaching (Secondary) 2. Education–Rocky Mountain region. 3. Education–Southeastern states. I. Title.
OU NUC74-128978

Baker, James Lawrence
see
Baker, Jim, 1941-

Baker, James R., ed.
see Golding, William Gerald, 1911- William Golding's Lord of the flies. Casebook ed. New York, Putnam, 1964.

Baker, James Stannard, 1899-
Lamp examination for on or off in traffic accidents, by J. Stannard Baker and Thomas Lindquist. [Evanston, Ill.] Traffic Institute, Northwestern University, c1972.
32 p. illus. 28 cm. (Advanced accident investigation series)
Cover title.
"P.N. 82"
1. Traffic accident investigation. 2. Automobiles—Lighting. I. Lindquist, Thomas. II. Title. III. Series.
CaBVaU NUC74-123446

Baker, James Stannard, 1899-
Lamp examination for on or off in traffic accidents / by J. Stannard Baker and Thomas Lindquist. — 2d ed. — Evanston, Ill. : Traffic Institute, Northwestern University, 1977.
36 p. : ill. ; 28 cm. — (Advanced accident investigation series ; P.N. 82)
Cover title.
Includes bibliographical references.
1. Traffic accident investigation. 2. Automobiles—Lighting. I. Lindquist, Thomas, joint author. II. Northwestern University, Evanston, Ill. Traffic Institute. III. Title. IV. Series.
HV8079.55.B34 1977 364.12'1 77-150721
77 MARC

Baker, James Stannard, 1899-
Traffic accident investigation manual / J. Stannard Baker. — 1st ed. — [Evanston, Ill.] : Traffic Institute, Northwestern University, 1975.
333 p. : ill. ; 29 cm.
Includes bibliographical references and index.
ISBN 0-912642-01-7
1. Traffic accident investigation—Handbooks, manuals, etc. I. Northwestern University, Evanston, Ill. Traffic Institute. II. Title.
HV8079.55B35 363.2'33 75-858
75 MARC

Baker, James Stannard, 1899-
Traffic accident investigator's manual for police, by J. Stannard Baker. Evanston, Ill., Northwestern University, Traffic Institute [1963]
676 p. illus. 24 cm.
1. Traffic accidents. U.S. 2. Automobile drivers. I. Title.
KU NUC73-126808

Baker, James Stannard, 1899-
Traffic accident investigator's manual for police, by J. Stannard Baker. [2d ed.] Evanston, Ill., Traffic Institute, Northwestern University [1971, c1963]
676 p. illus. 24 cm.
1. Traffic accident investigation. 2. Traffic accidents—United States. I. Title.
OOxM NUC73-126348

Baker, James Thomas.
Faith for a dark Saturday [by] James T. Baker. Valley Forge [Pa.] Judson Press [1973]
125 p. 22 cm. $2.50
Includes bibliographical references.
1. Bible stories, English. 2. Christian life—1960– I. Title.
BS550.2.B33 248'.4 73–2612
ISBN 0–8170–0588–9 MARC

Baker, James Thomas.
Thomas Merton: the spiritual and social philosophy of union, by James T. Baker. [n.p.] 1968.
xv, 367 l.
Thesis–Florida State University.
Bibliography: leaves 356-366.
Vita.
Microfilm of typescript. Ann Arbor, Mich., University Microfilms, 1968. 1 reel. 35 mm.
1. Merton, Thomas, 1915-1968.
CtY NUC74-24858

Baker, James Vincent, 1941-
The effects of computerization on the direct cost of five commercial bank functions: 1965-1968, by James V. Baker. [Tallahassee] c1971.
x, 255 l.
Thesis (D.B.Ad.)—Florida State University.
Bibliography: leaves 238-253.
Vita.
1. Dissertations, Academic—F.S.U.—Business—Finance. 2. Electronic data processing—Banks and banking. 3. Banks and banking.
I. Title.
FTaSU NUC73-126359

Baker, James William.
Stock dividends and stock splits: an analysis of generally accepted accounting principles and American corporate accounting practices [with] supplementary tables. Ann Arbor, University Microfilms, 1964.
1 reel. 35 mm.
Thesis–University of Southern California, 1963.
1. Accounting. I. Title.
MsU NUC74-122408

Baker, Jane, fl. 1688. A patch-work screen for the ladies. 1973
in The Prude; a novel... New York, Garland Pub., 1973.

Baker, Janet MacIver.
A new time-domain analysis of human speech and other complex waveforms. Janet MacIver Baker. Pittsburgh, Dept. of Computer Science, Carnegie Mellon University, 1975.
iii, 151 p. ill. 27 cm.
Bibliography: p. 149-151.
1. Sound. 2. Speech. I. Carnegie-Mellon University. Computer Science Dept.
TxDaM NUC77-89497

Baker, Janice E., joint author.
see Carpenter, John Allan, 1917- Niger. Chicago, Childrens Press, c1976.

Baker, Janice E., joint author.
see Carpenter, John Allan, 1917- Upper Volta. Chicago, Childrens Press, [1974]

Baker, Janice M
An investigation of the relationship of centralization, formalization, per pupil expenditure, and job satisfaction to level of innovativeness of education at the secondary level in nonregionalized Connecticut school districts. [Storrs, Conn.] 1976.
4, ix, 173 l. tables.
Thesis (Ph.D.)--University of Connecticut.
Bibliography: leaves 136-142.
1. Educational innovations--Connecticut--Case studies. 2. School management and organization--Connecticut--Case studies. 3. School districts--Connecticut--Case studies. I. Title.
CtU NUC77-90308

Baker, Jean H
Ambivalent Americans : the Know-Nothing Party in Maryland / Jean H. Baker. — Baltimore : Johns Hopkins University Press, c1977.
xvii, 206 p. ; 24 cm.
Bibliography: p. 192-201.
Includes index.
ISBN 0-8018-1906-7
1. American Party. Maryland. I. Title.
JK2341.A8M35 1850 329'.893 76-51813
76 MARC

Baker, Jean H
The politics of continuity; Maryland political parties from 1858 to 1870 [by] Jean H. Baker. Baltimore, Johns Hopkins University Press [1973]
xv, 239 p. 24 cm. (The Goucher College series) $11.00
Bibliography: p. [221]-228.
1. Political parties—Maryland—History. 2. Maryland—Politics and government—1865-1950. 3. Maryland—Politics and government—Civil War. I. Title.
JK2295.M32B34 329.02 72-12354
ISBN 0-8018-1418-9 MARC

Baker, Jeffrey, 1943- joint author.
see Golann, Stuart E. The Bethlehem diaries ... San Francisco, Canfield Press, [1974]

Baker, Jeffrey, 1943- joint author.
see Golann, Stuart E. Current and future trends in community psychology. New York, Human Sciences Press, [1975]

Baker, Jeffrey A., joint author
see Cline, Gloria Stark. An index to criticisms of British and American poetry. Metuchen, N. J., Scarecrow Press, 1973.

Baker, Jeffrey A.
see Index to Louisiana place names mentioned in the War of the Rebellion, a compilation of the official records of the Union and Confederate armies. [Lafayette] University of Southwestern Louisiana, 1975.

Baker, Jeffrey J W
Matter, energy, and life; an introduction for biology students [by] Jeffrey J. W. Baker [and] Garland E. Allen. 3d. ed. Reading, Mass., Addison-Wesley Pub. Co. [1974]
232 p. illus. 24 cm. (Addison-Wesley series in biology)
Bibliography: p. 208-213.
1. Biological chemistry. I. Allen, Garland E., joint author. II. Title.
QH345.B32 1974 574.1'92 73-19489
ISBN 0-201-00389-9 MARC

Baker, Jeffrey J W
Students guide to the study of biology [by] Jeffrey J. W. Baker [and] Garland E. Allen. Reading, Mass., Addison-Wesley Pub. Co. [1968]
xv, 62 p. illus. (part col.) 25 cm. (Addison-Wesley series in life science)
Includes bibliographies.
1. Biology. I. Allen, Garland E. II. Title.
PSt NUC75-107767

Baker, Jeffrey J. W., ed.
see Colloquim on Biology in a Liberal Education, Stanford University, 1965. Biology in a liberal education. Washington, 1967.

Baker, Jeffrey J. W., ed.
see Commission on Undergraduate Education in the Biological Sciences. Biology for the non-major. Washington, 1967.

Baker, Jenifer M
The effects of oils on plants. [Pembroke, S. Wales., Orielton Field Centre, 1970?]
21 l. 22 x 35 cm.
Photocopy of typescript.
Bibliography: leaves 17-21.
1. Plants, Effect of pollution on. 2. Oil as pesticide. 3. Oil Pollution of rivers, harbors, etc. I. Title.
DI NUC76-70989

Baker, Jenifer M
The toxicity of Alaskan (Prudhoe Bay) crude oil to plants: short term effects of light pollution. J. M. Baker. Pembroke [S. Wales] Field Studies Council Orielton Field Centre, Oil Pollution Research Unit, 1970.
[25] l. ill. 36 x 22 cm.
Transmittal letter of Sept. 28, 1970 from David Henderson, Alyeska Pipeline Service Company, headed Trans Alaska Pipeline System, Anchorage.
Bibliography; leaves 17-21.
1. Trans-Alaska oil pipe line—Environmental aspects. 2. Petroleum—Alaska—Prudhoe Bay. I. Orielton Field Centre. Oil Pollution Research Unit. II. Alyeska Pipeline Service Company. III. Trans Alaska Pipeline System. IV. Title.
DI NUC76-87324

Baker, Jenifer M.
see Marine ecology and oil pollution. Barking, Applied Science Publishers [for] The Institute of Petroleum, Great Britain, 1976.

Baker, Jenifer M.
see Marine ecology and oil pollution ... New York, Wiley, c1976.

Baker, Jerry.
Farm fever : how to buy country land and farm it-part-time or full time / Jerry Baker & Dan Kiffie. — New York : Funk & Wagnalls, c1977.
x, 276 p. : ill. ; 24 cm.
Includes index.
ISBN 0-308-10299-1
1. Agriculture—Handbooks, manuals, etc. 2. Agriculture—United States. I. Kibbie, Dan, joint author. II. Title.
S501.2.B34 1977 630 76-30861
76 MARC

Baker, Jerry.
I never met a house plant I didn't like / Jerry Baker ; literary consultant, Dan Kibbie ; ill. by Dot Cohn. — New York : Simon and Schuster, [1974]
320 p. : ill. ; 25 cm.
Includes index.
ISBN 0-671-21767-4 : $9.95
1. House plants. I. Title.
SB419.B124 635.9'65 74-13906
MARC

Baker, Jerry.
Jerry Baker's Bicentennial gardener's almanac. — New York : Pocket Books, 1976.
273 p. : ill. ; 18 cm.
ISBN 0-671-80261-5 : $1.75
1. Gardening—United States. 2. Almanacs, American. 3. American Revolution Bicentennial, 1776-1976. I. Title. II. Title: Bicentennial gardener's almanac.
SB455.B2574 1976 635 76-351922
76 MARC

Baker, Jerry.
Jerry Baker's Fabulous everything, everywhere, indoor, outdoor garden answer book. — New York : Grosset & Dunlap, c1976.
203 p. ; 22 cm.
ISBN 0-448-12244-8 : $10.00
1. Gardening—Miscellanea. I. Title. II. Title: Fabulous everything, everywhere, indoor, outdoor garden...
SB453.B317 635 75-27911
76 MARC

Baker, Jerry.
Make friends with your annuals. Designed and edited by Charles Cook. New York, Simon and Schuster [1973]
95 p. illus. 28 cm. $1.95
1. Annuals (Plants) 2. Flower gardening. I. Title.
SB422.B28 635.9'31 73-1207
ISBN 0-671-21559-0 MARC

Baker, Jerry.
Make friends with your bulbs. Designed and edited by Charles Cook. New York, Simon and Schuster [1973]
95 p. illus. 28 cm. $1.95
1. Bulbs. I. Title.
SB425.B26 635.9'44 73-8217
ISBN 0-671-21657-0 MARC

Baker, Jerry.
Make friends with your evergreens and ground covers. Designed and edited by Charles Cook. New York, Simon and Schuster [1973]
95 p. illus. 28 cm. $1.95
1. Evergreens. 2. Ground cover plants. I. Title.
SB428.B34 634.9'75 73-1204
ISBN 0-671-21560-4 MARC

Baker, Jerry.
Make friends with your flowering shrubs, Designed and edited by Charles Cook. New York, Simon and Schuster [1973]
94 p. illus.
1. Shrubs. I. Title.
OCl NUC76-70975

Baker, Jerry.
Make friends with your flowering trees. Designed and edited by Charles Cook. New York, Simon and Schuster [1973]
93 p. illus. 28 cm. $1.95
1. Flowering trees. I. Title.
SB435.B325 635.9'77 73-8218
MARC

Baker, Jerry.
Make friends with your fruit trees. Designed and edited by Charles Cook. New York, Simon and Schuster [1973]
95 p. illus. 28 cm. $1.95
1. Fruit-culture. 2. Nuts. I. Title.
SB355.B18 634 73-1206
ISBN 0-671-21561-2 MARC

Baker, Jerry.
Make friends with your house plants. Designed and edited by Charles Cook. New York, Simon and Schuster [1973]
93 p. illus. 28 cm. $1.95
1. House plants. I. Title.
SB419.B125 635.9'65 73-8219
ISBN 0-671-21654-6 MARC

Baker, Jerry.
Make friends with your lawn. Designed and edited by Charles Cook. New York, Simon and Schuster [1973]
95 p. illus. 28 cm. $1.95
1. Lawns. I. Title.
SB433.B13 635.9'64 73-162034
ISBN 0-671-21559-0 MARC

Baker, Jerry.
Make friends with your perennials and biennials. Designed and edited by Charles Cook. New York, Simon and Schuster [1973]
95 p. illus. 28 cm. $1.95
1. Perennials. 2. Biennials (Plants) I. Title.
SB434.B33 635.9'3 73-8221
ISBN 0-671-21653-8 MARC

Baker, Jerry.
Make friends with your roses. Designed and edited by Charles Cook. New York, Simon and Schuster [1973]
95 p. illus. 28 cm. $1.95
1. Rose culture. 2. Roses. I. Title.
SB411.B33 635.9'33'372 73-1203
ISBN 0-671-21563-9 MARC

Baker, Jerry.
Make friends with your shade trees. Designed and edited by Charles Cook. New York, Simon and Schuster [c1973]
94 p. illus. 28 cm. $1.95
1. Shade trees. I. Title. II. Title: Shade trees.
SB435.B326 635.9'77 73-8222
ISBN 0-671-21655-4 MARC

Baker, Jerry.
Make friends with your vegetable garden. Designed and edited by Charles Cook. New York, Simon and Schuster [1973]
95 p. illus. 28 cm. $1.95
1. Vegetable gardening. I. Title.
SB321.B24 635 73-1205
ISBN 0-671-21562-0 MARC

Baker, Jerry.
Plants are like kids : indoor and outdoor gardening / by Jerry Baker ; ill. by Robert Pierce. — New York : Grosset & Dunlap, c1976.
63 p. : ill. ; 24 cm.
SUMMARY: An indoor and outdoor gardening guide discussing growth, care, and planting.
ISBN 0-448-12168-9 : $2.95. ISBN 0-448-13331-8 lib. bdg.
1. Gardening—Juvenile literature. [1. Gardening] I. Pierce, Robert, 1915- II. Title.
SB457.B25 1976 635 75-18374
76 MARC

Baker, Jerry.
Plants are like people. Literary consultant, Dan Kibbie. Illustrated by Carl Chambers. New York, Pocket Books [c1971, reprinted 1973]
275 p. illus. 18 cm.
"8th printing, August 1973."
1. Gardening. I. Title.
NNBG NUC76-70969

Baker, Jerry.
Talk to your plants, and other gardening know-how I learned from Grandma Putt. Literary consultant: Dan Kibbie. Los Angeles, Nash Pub. [1973]
xv, 305 p. illus. 23 cm. $7.95
1. Gardening. I. Title.
SB455.B259 635 72-95244
ISBN 0-8402-1309-3 MARC

Baker, Jerry.
Talk to your plants, and other gardening know-how I learned from Grandma Putt. Literary consultant: Dan Kibbie. [Pocket book ed.] New York, Pocket Books [1974]
xiii, 273 p. illus. 18 cm.
1. Gardening. I. Title.
NNBG NUC76-18070

Baker, Jesse Walter.
80 years in Arkansas [by] Jesse W. Baker. [Conway, Ark.] River Road Press [1972]
viii, 221 p. illus., port. 18 cm.
1. Frontier and pioneer life—Arkansas. I. Title.
WHi NUC76-70970

Baker, Jim.
Get out and get under; Americans and their automobiles. [Worthington, Ohio, Pioneer Press, 1974]
1 v. (chiefly illus.) 13 x 18 cm.
"A Heartland House memory book."
1. Automobiles, American—History. 2. Automobile industry and trade—United States—History. I. Title.
TL23.B27 629.22'22'0973 74-76724
ISBN 0-914482-06-8 MARC

Baker, Jim.
How to be a kid again. [Worthington, Ohio] Heartland House [1974]
[93] p. illus. 18 cm.
"A Heartland House memory book."
1. Games—Miscellanea. I. Title.
GV1203.B22 793 74-76723
ISBN 0-914482-07-6 MARC

Baker, Jim
see Baker; Obed and Eliza's children. [Florence? Tex., 1973]

Baker, Jim, 1941-
Billie Jean King / by Jim Baker. — New York : Grosset & Dunlap, c1974.
90 p. : ill. ; 21 cm. — (Tempo books)
SUMMARY: A biography of the tennis champion who has been a leader in making an equal place for women in athletics.
ISBN 0-448-07436-2 : $1.50
1. King, Billie Jean—Juvenile literature. [1. King, Billie Jean] I. Title.
GV994.K56B34 796.34'2'0924 74-7690
75 MARC

Baker, Jim, 1941-
The Buffalo Bills : O. J. Simpson, rushing champion / by Jim Baker. — Englewood Cliffs, N. J. : Prentice-Hall, [1974]
126 p. : ill. ; 28 cm. — (Reward books)
"A Stuart L. Daniels book."
SUMMARY: Text and photographs present a brief history of the Buffalo Bills football team with short biographies of the team members and special focus on O. J. Simpson.
ISBN 0-13-085803-X : $3.95($4.50Can.)
1. Buffalo Bills (Football team) 2. Football—Biography. [1. Buffalo Bills (Football team) 2. Simpson, O. J., 1947- 3. Football—Biography]
GV956.B83B34 796.33'264'0974797 74-7522
[920] MARC

Baker, Jim Marshall, 1927-
The role of Garcilaso de la Vega el Inca in the eighteenth century debate on America. [Austin, Tex.] 1973.
vii, 331 l. 29 cm.
Thesis (Ph.D.)—University of Texas at Austin. Vita.
Bibliography: leaves 308-331.
1. Garcilaso de la Vega, 1503-1536. 2. Literature, Modern—18th century—Hist. & crit.
TxU NUC75-17362

Baker, Joan Stanley-
see Stanley-Baker, Joan.

Baker, John.
The deserted shore. Walton-on-Thames, Outposts, 1971.
20 p. 21 cm.
Poems.
I. Title.
FU NUC75-29953

Baker, John Ashley.
Mass transfer in membrane dialyzers for development of a dialysate-free artificial kidney. [Iowa City] 1973.
xvii, 261 l. illus. (part col.) 28 cm.
Thesis (Ph.D.)—University of Iowa.
1. Hemodialysis. 2. Artificial kidney. I. Title.
IaU NUC76-70968

Baker, John Augustus, 1925-
see Cederstrom, Dagfin John, 1908- Ground water in the North Atlantic region. [Arlington, Va., 1971]

Baker, John Austin.
The foolishness of God. Atlanta, J. Knox [1975, c1970]
409 p. 22 cm.
Includes bibliographical references.
ISBN 0-8042-0489-6
1. Theology, Doctrinal—Popular works. I. Title.
BT77.B27 1975 231 74-3714
MARC

Baker, John Austin.
Prophecy in the Church / [by] John Austin Baker. — London : Church Literature Association, 1976.
[2], 9 p. ; 21 cm. GB77-18539
"This essay was first given as a talk to the Westminster Deanery Chapter on 3 February 1976."
ISBN 0-85191-086-6 : £0.25
1. Prophecy (Christianity)—Addresses, essays, lectures. 2. Prophets—Addresses, essays, lectures. I. Title.
BR115.P8B34 231'.74 77-372457
77 MARC

Baker, John Austin.
Travels in Oudamovia / [by] John Austin Baker ; foreword by the Archbishop of Canterbury. — Leighton Buzzard : Faith Press, 1976.
80 p. ; 19 cm. GB76-24835
ISBN 0-7164-0435-4 : £0.90
1. Meditations. I. Title.
BV4832.2.B26 242 76-380901
76 MARC

Baker, John Austin, 1914-
Guide to Federal programs for rural development. — [4th ed.]. — [Washington] : Rural Development Service, U.S. Dept. of Agriculture, [1975]
iii, 262, [83] p. ; 27 cm.
Cover title.
1. Community development—United States. 2. Economic assistance, Domestic—United States. 3. Rehabilitation, Rural—United States. I. Title.
HN90.C6B352 1975 309.2'63'0973 75-601772
75 MARC

Baker, John Burton, 1899-
La Fleurette by John B. Baker. [Indian Rocks Beach, Fla.] Books Unlimited, c1971.
167 p. 23 cm.
Cover title.
I. Title.
NcD NUC76-70954

Baker, John Calhoun, 1895-
The compensation of executive officers of retail companies, 1928-1935. Millwood, N.Y., Kraus Reprint Co., 1974.
34 p. illus.
Reprint of the 1937 ed.
1. Wages—United States. 2. Retail trade—United States. I. Title. II. Series. III. Series: Harvard University. Graduate School of Business Administration. George F. Baker Foundation. Publication, v. 24, no. 1.
ViBlbV NUC76-18048

Baker, John Calhoun, 1895-
Directors and their functions: a preliminary study. New York, Arno Press, 1973 [c1945]
xiii, 145 p. 23 cm. (Big business: economic power in a free society)
Reprint of the ed. published by Division of Research, Graduate School of Business Administration, Harvard University, Boston.
Includes bibliographical references.
1. Directors of corporations—United States—Case studies. I. Title. II. Series.
HD2745.B2 1973 658.4'2 73-1990
ISBN 0-405-05074-7 MARC

Baker, John Calhoun, 1895-
Executive compensation practices of retail companies, 1928-1937. Millwood, N.Y., Kraus Reprint Co., 1974.
50 p. illus.
Reprint of the 1939 ed.
1. Wages—United States. 2. Retail trade—United States. 3. Bonus system—United States. I. Title. II. Series. III. Series: Harvard University. Graduate School of Business Administration. George F. Baker Foundation. Publication, v. 26, no. 4.
ViBlbV NUC76-18046

Baker, John Frederick.
Macrobiotics (wholefoods — pure foods) an idea whose time has come. John Frederick Baker. [Suffolk, Miro Press] c1972.
36 p. 21 cm.
Cover title.
1. Food. 2. Nutrition. 3. Cookery. I. Title.
CU-A NUC76-70967

Baker, John Gilbert, 1834-1920
Handbook of the Amaryllideae: [including the Alstroemerieæ and Agaveæ]. By J. G. Baker. Repr. [d. Ausg.] London, Bell, 1888. Lehre: Cramer; Codicote (Herts.): Wheldon and Wesley; New York (N. Y.): Stechert-Hafner, 1972.
xii, 216 p. 20 cm. (Plant monograph reprints, vol. 7) DM40.00
GDB 72-A45
1. Amaryllidaceae. 2. Alstroemeriaceae. 3. Agavaceae. I. Title. II. Series.
QK495.A484B34 1972 584'.25 74-168519
ISBN 3-7682-0751-X MARC

Baker, John Gilbert, 1834-1920.
Handbook of the Bromeliaceæ, by J. G. Baker. Repr. [d. Ausg.] London, Bell, 1889. Lehre: Cramer; Codicote (Herts.): Wheldon and Wesley; New York (N. Y.): Stechert-Hafner, 1972.
xi, 243 p. 20 cm. (Plant monographs reprints, v. 8) DM40.00
GDB 72-A44
1. Bromeliaceae. I. Title. II. Series.
QK495.B76B34 1972 584'.22 73-154287
ISBN 3-7682-0752-8 MARC

Baker, John Gilbert, 1834-1920.
Handbook of the Irideae, by J. G. Baker. Repr. [d. Ausg.] London, Bell, 1892. Lehre: Cramer; Codicote (Herts.): Wheldon and Wesley; New York (N. Y.): Stechert-Hafner, 1972.
xii, 247 p. 20 cm. (Plant monographs reprints, v. 9) DM40.00
GDB 72-A44
1. Iridaceae. I. Title. II. Series.
QK495.I 75B34 1972 584'.24 73-154299
ISBN 3-7682-0753-6 MARC

Baker, John Gilbert, 1834-1920, joint author
see Hooker, Sir William Jackson, 1785-1865. Synopsis filicum... London, R. Hardwicke, 1868.

Baker, John Gilbert Hindley.
Saint Nicholas Cole Abbey, London, E.C. 4. A short history. [Ramsgate, Church Publishers, n.d.]
12 p. fronts. 18 cm.
1. London. Church of Saint Nicholas Cole Abbey. I. Title.
IEG NUC73-103096

Baker, John Hamilton.
Catalogue of the manuscript year books, readings, and law reports in the Library of the Harvard Law School / J. H. Baker. — Zug, Switzerland : Inter Documentation Co., c1975.
x, 105 p. : ill. ; 21 cm. — (English legal manuscripts ; v. 1) Sw***
Bibliography: p. vii-viii.
Includes indexes.
ISBN 3-85750-009-3
1. Law—Great Britain—Sources—Bibliography—Catalogs. 2. Harvard University. Law School. Library. I. Harvard University. Law School. Library. II. Title. III. Series.
KD56.E5 vol. 1 016.34'00942 s 76-366988
76 MARC

Baker, John Hamilton.
English legal manuscripts / J.H. Baker. -- Zug, Switzerland : Inter Documentation Co., 1975-
v. : ill. ; 21 cm.
Contents: v.1. Catalogue of the manuscript year books, readings, and law reports in the library of the Harvard Law School.
ISBN 3-85750-009-3.
NcU NUC77-91819

Baker, John Hamilton.
An introduction to English legal history, by J. H. Baker. London, Butterworths, 1971.
xxi, 330 p. 23 cm. £2.00 (pbk.) B 71-14525
Includes bibliographies.
1. Law—Great Britain—History and criticism. I. Title.
KD532.B34 340'.0942 73-161060
ISBN 0-406-55501-X; 0-406-55501-X (pbk.) MARC

Baker, John Hamilton.
see Cambridge. University. Library. Cambridge Legal History Conference 1975, handlist of the exhibition of English legal manuscripts in Cambridge University Library. ⌈Cambridge⌉ ⌈The Library⌉ ⌈1975⌉

Baker, John Howard, 1944-
Erotic spectacle in the art of John Sloan: a study of the iconography, sources, and influences of a subject matter pattern. ⌈Providence⌉ 1972.
vii, 256 l. mounted photographs. 28 cm.
Thesis (Ph.D.)—Brown University.
Typescript and xerox.
Vita.
Bibliography: leaves 249-256.
1. Sloan, John, 1871-1951.
RPB NUC74-1306

Baker, John Kingsley.
Vibration isolation / ⌈by⌉ J. K. Baker. — ⌈London⌉ : Oxford University Press for the Design Council, the British Standards Institution and the Council of Engineering Institutions, 1975.
⌈1⌉, 23 p. : ill. ; 30 cm. — (Engineering design guides ; 13) GB76-13411
Cover title.
Bibliography: p. 22.
ISBN 0-19-859145-4 : £1.50
1. Vibration. 2. Damping (Mechanics) I. Title.
TA355.B27 620.3'7 76-369460
76 MARC

Baker, John M.
see Tucker, Billy Bob, 1928- Sulfur content of wheat straw grown in Oklahoma. Stillwater, 1972.

Baker, John Milnes, 1932–
The Baker family and the Edgar family of Rahway, N. J. and New York City. Middletown, N. Y., Trumbull Pub. ⌈1972⌉
vii, 468 p. illus. 29 cm. $37.50
Includes bibliographical references.
1. Baker family. 2. Edgar family. I. Title.
CS71.B17 1972 929'.2'0973 72-171628
MARC

Baker, John Milnes, 1932-
How to build a house with an architect / John Milnes Baker. — 1st ed. — Philadelphia : Lippincott, c1977.
190 p. : ill. ; 26 cm.
Bibliography: p. 189-190.
ISBN 0-397-01124-5
1. Architecture, Domestic—Handbooks, manuals, etc. 2. Architectural practice—Handbooks, manuals, etc. I. Title.
NA7115.B28 728.3 76-49974
76 MARC

Baker, John Milton, 1895–
US Presidents from powdered wigs to TV makeup. Tokyo, Nishiki-Kosan, 1972.
382 p. 22 cm. Ja***
Bibliography: p. 367-378.
1. Presidents—United States—Biography. 2. United States—Politics and government. I. Title.
E176.1.B16 1972 973'.0992 [B] 73-162847
MARC

Baker, John Norman Leonard.
A history of geographical discovery and exploration, by J. N. L. Baker... London [etc.] G. G. Harrap & Co. [1931]
543, [1] p. front., maps (part fold.) 22 cm. (Harrap's new geographical series)
"Bibliographical note": p. 15-16.
Ultra microfiche. Dayton, Ohio, National Cash Register, 1970. 3d title of 4. 10.5 x 14.8 cm. (PCMI library collection, 826-3)
1. Discoveries (in gergraphy)
KEmT NUC74-23359

Baker, John Norman Leonard.
Jesus College, Oxford, 1571-1971 / by J. N. L. Baker. — Oxford : Jesus College, Oxford, 1971.
⌈5⌉, ii, 153, ⌈8⌉ leaves : ill., facsim., ports. ; 25 cm. GB72-04353
Includes bibliographical references and index.
ISBN 0-9502164-0-2
1. Oxford. University. Jesus College—History.
LF605.B25 378.425'74 75-325907
75 MARC

Baker, John P 1936–
Christ's living body; an examination of ministry in the local church, edited by John P. Baker. London, Coverdale House, 1973.
221 p. 18 cm. (A Coverdale paperback) £0.75 GB 74-12682
Includes bibliographies.
1. Church—Addresses, essays, lectures. 2. Theology, Practical—Addresses, essays, lectures. I. Title.
BV603.B34 254'.03'42 74-180953
ISBN 0-902088-47-5 MARC

Baker, John Patton, 1923-
see Keith, Thomas Byron. Answer book for feed formulation manual. Danville, Ill., Interstate Printers & Publishers [1967]

Baker, John Randal, 1900-
The freedom of science. — New York : Arno Press, 1975.
154, 120 p. ; 21 cm. — (History, philosophy, and sociology of science)
Reprint of the 1943 ed. of The scientific life, and of the 1945 ed. of Science and the planned state, both published by Macmillan, New York.
Includes bibliographies and indexes.
ISBN 0-405-06636-8
1. Science and state—Addresses, essays, lectures. 2. Science—Social aspects—Addresses, essays, lectures. I. Baker, John Randal, 1900- Science and the planned state. 1975. II. Title. III. Series.
Q125.B27 1975 301.24'3 74-25150
75 MARC

Baker, John Randal, 1900-
Parasitic protozoa. London, Hutchinson University Library ⌈1969⌉
176 p. illus.
Bibliography: p. ⌈165⌉-169.
1. Protozoa. I. Title.
PrU NUC73-59621

Baker, John Randal, 1900–
Race ⌈by⌉ John R. Baker. New York, Oxford University Press, 1974.
xviii, 625 p. illus. 25 cm. $15.00
Bibliography: p. ⌈560⌉-605.
1. Race.
GN280.B34 572 73-87989
ISBN 0-19-212954-6 MARC

Baker, John Randal, 1900- Science and the planned state. 1975.
in Baker, John Randal, 1900- The freedom of science. New York, Arno Press, 1975.

Baker, John Randal, 1900-
see Huxley, Julian Sorell, Sir, 1887- Evolution... 3d ed. New York, Hafner Press, c1974.

Baker, John Robert, 1940-
Quantified modal logic and the problem of essentialism. Nashville ⌈c1973⌉
iv, 215 l. 28 cm.
Thesis (Ph.D.)—Vanderbilt University.
Bibliography: leaves 207-215.
TNJ NUC76-70966

Baker, John Robert, 1940-
Quantified modal logic and the problem of essentialism. Nashville, Tenn., 1973.
iv, 215 l.
Thesis—Vanderbilt University.
Bibliography: leaves 207-215.
Photocopy of typescript. Ann Arbor, Mich., University Microfilms, 1973. 21 cm.
1. Modality (Logic) I. Title.
IEdS NUC74-126548

Baker, John V., ed.
see The Paragon of wines and spirits. London, Heidelberg Publishers Ltd, 1972-

Baker, John W., 1886-
see American Law Institute. Rhode Island annotations to the Restatement of the law of judgments... St. Paul, American Law Institute Publishers, 1957.

Baker, John William, 1858-1951.
History of Hart County, 1933. ⌈2d ed. n.p., 195-, c1933⌉
xii, 426 p. illus., maps, ports. 24 cm.
Includes brief genealogies.
1. Hart Co., Ga.—History. 2. Hart Co., Ga.—Genealogy.
FU NUC73-126852

Baker, Jonathan.
Agriculture and fishing in international economic geography : an emp⌈i⌉rical approach / by Jonathan Baker. — ⌈Kristiansand : s.n., 1975⌉
67 leaves : ill. ; 30 cm. — (Skrifter - Agder distriktshøgskole, Økonomisk fagseksjon ; 1975:9) N76-Feb
Includes bibliographical references.
ISBN 8271170422
1. Agriculture—Economic aspects. 2. Agricultural geography. 3. Fish trade. I. Title. II. Series: Agder distriktshøgskole. Økonomisk fagseksjon. Skrifter - Agder distriktshøgskole, Økonomisk fagseksjon ; 1975:9.
HD1411.B225 338.1 76-379609
*76 MARC

Baker, Joseph.
Nitrogen fractionation of two forest soils in Alberta. Edmonton, Alta., 1973.
21 p. (Northern Forest Research Centre. Information report NOR-X-63)
Bibliography: p. 17.
I. Title.
DNAL NUC74-126583

Baker, Joseph.
Nitrogen loss from surface-applied urea. Victoria, 1970.
6, ⌈7⌉ p. illus. (Pacific Forest Research Centre. Information report BC-X no. 42)
Bibliography: p. ⌈13⌉
I. Title.
DNAL NUC74-123558

Baker, Joseph.
Soil acidity and its significance in forest fertilization. Edmonton, Alta., 1972.
33 p. (Northern Forest Research Centre. Information report NOR-X-19)
I. Title.
DNAL NUC74-126572

Baker, Joseph.
Soil properties and nutritional status of western-hemlock tissue from over-stocked s stands. Victoria, 1969.
9 p. illus. (Pacific Forest Research Centre. Information report BC-X no. 38)
Bibliography: p. 9.
I. Title.
DNAL NUC74-123562

Baker, Joseph.
Some effects of urea fertilization on soil characteristics and tissue mineral content in overstocked western hemlock stands. Victoria, 1970.
10 p. illus. (Pacific Forest Research Centre. Information report BC-X no. 39)
Bibliography: p. 10.
I. Title.
DNAL NUC74-122392

Baker, Joseph, 1799-1856.
Williamsburg Theological Institution. Norfolk, 1837.
70 p.
Microfilm. Nashville, Tenn., Historical Commission. Southern Baptist Convention, 1965. 1 reel. 35 mm.
1. Williamsburg Theological Institution, Williamsburg, Va.
MNtcA NUC75-75782

Baker (Joseph) Associates, inc.
see When they meet, 1964... ⌈Philadelphia, 1963?⌉

Baker, Joseph Harold.
An Administrative design for working with first grade predicted reading failures. [Minneapolis] 1975.
vi, 130 l. 29 cm.
Thesis (Ph.D.)--University of Minnesota.
Bibliography: leaves 100-110.
MnU NUC77-89560

Baker, Joseph Richardson, 1872-
The laws of land warfare concerning the rights and duties of belligerents as existing on August 1, 1914 / ⌈prepared by Joseph R. Baker and Henry G. Crocker⌉. — Wilmington, Del. : Scholarly Resources, 1974.
vii, 420 p. ; 24 cm. — (The Inquiry handbooks ; v. 2)
Reprint of the 1919 ed. published by Govt. Print. Off., Washington.
Includes bibliographical references.
1. War (International law) I. Crocker, Henry Graham, 1868-1930, joint author. II. Title: The laws of land warfare concerning the rights and duties of belligerents ... III. Series.
JX68.I48 1974 vol. 2 940.3'12 s 77-360327
⌈JX4505⌉ 77 MARC

Baker, Joseph Richardson, 1872-
Selected topics connected with the laws of warfare as of August 1, 1914 / ⌈prepared by Joseph R. Baker and Louis W. McKernan⌉. — Wilmington, Del. : Scholarly Resources, 1974.
viii, 851 p. ; 24 cm. — (The Inquiry handbooks ; v. 3)
Reprint of the 1919 ed. published by Govt. Print Off., Washington.
1. War (International law) I. McKernan, Louis Wagner, joint author. II. Title. III. Series.
JX68.I48 1974 vol. 3 940.3'12 s 77-360325
⌈JX4505⌉ 77 MARC

Baker, Joseph T
Compounds from marine organisms / authors, Joseph T. Baker, Vreni Murphy. — Cleveland : CRC Press, c1976.
226 p. ; 27 cm. — (CRC handbook of marine science ; v. 1)
Bibliography: p. 183-184.
Includes indexes.
ISBN 0-87819-391-X
1. Marine pharmacology—Handbooks, manuals, etc. 2. Chemistry, Organic—Handbooks, manuals, etc. I. Murphy, Vreni, joint author. II. Title. III. Series.
GC24.C17 vol. 1 551.4'6'008 s 76-10180
⌈QH345⌉ 76 MARC

Baker, Joseph T.
see CRC handbook of marine science. Cleveland, CRC Press, c1976-

Baker, Joséphine, 1906-1975.
Joséphine / Joséphine Baker et Jo Bouillon, avec la collaboration de Jacqueline Cartier. — Paris : R. Laffont, c1976.
413 p., ⌈8⌉ leaves of plates : ill. ; 25 cm. — (Collection Vécu) F***
48.00F
1. Baker, Joséphine, 1906-1975. 2. Dancers—Biography. I. Bouillon, Joseph, 1908- joint author. II. Cartier, Jacqueline, joint author. III. Title.
GV1785.B3A29 793.3'2'0924 76-481437
76 MARC

Baker, Joshua, ed.
see Kimhi, David, 1160?-1235? The commentary of Rabbi David Kimhi on Psalms CXXCL. Cambridge ⌈Eng.⌉ Univ. Press, 1973.

Baker, Judith Oswald.
The physio-chemical fate of Pseudomonas deoxyribonucleic acid after incorporation by Diplococcus pneumoniae. ⌈n.p.⌉ 1967.
v, 82 l. illus.
Thesis (Ph.D.)—Western Reserve University.
1. Nucleic acids. 2. DNA. 3. Genetics, Microbial. I. Title.
OClW-H NUC74-122398

Baker, Judy Elizabeth
see
Baker, Elizabeth, 1944-

Baker, Julian
see Baker, Anne. Morning Star... London, Kimber, 1972.

Baker, June.
see Davidson, William, fl. 1969- The Collingridge all-colour guide to house plants, cacti & succulents. London, Hamlyn, 1976.

Baker, Junius O
A selected and annotated bibliography for wilderness fire managers. Junius O. Baker, Jr. Washington, D.C., U.S. Dept. of Agriculture, Forest Service, 1975.
36 p. 26 cm.
1. Forest fires-- Bibliography. I. Title.
CaBVaU NUC77-89501

Baker, Justice Stanley-
see Stanley-Baker, Justice.

Baker, Justine C
The computer in the school / by Justine C. Baker. — Bloomington, Ind. : Phi Delta Kappa Educational Foundation, ⌈1975⌉
42 p. : ill. ; 18 cm. — (Fastback - Phi Delta Kappa Educational Foundation ; 58)
Bibliography: p. 42.
$0.50
1. Computer-assisted instruction. I. Title. II. Series: Phi Delta Kappa. Educational Foundation. Fastback ; 58.
LB1028.5.B24 371.39'445 74-34504
75 MARC

Baker, Justine C
Computers in the curriculum / by Justine Baker. — Bloomington, Ind. : Phi Delta Kappa Educational Foundation, c1976.
42 p. : ill. ; 18 cm. — (Fastback - Phi Delta Kappa Educational Foundation ; 82)
Bibliography: p. 41-42.
ISBN 0-87367-082-5
1. Electronic data processing—Education. I. Title. II. Series: Phi Delta Kappa. Educational Foundation. Fastback ; 82.
LB2846.B26 370'.28'54 76-16877
77 MARC

Baker, K.
see The Teacher Induction Pilot Schemes (TIPS) Project, 1975 national conference report. ⌈Bristol⌉ University of Bristol, School of Education, 1975.

Baker, K. H., joint author
see Ashdown, Robert Thomas. In working order... London, H. M. S. O., 1973.

Baker, Katherine D
Teacher differences as reflected in student aptitude-achievement relationships ⌈by⌉ Katherine D. Baker and Richard E. Snow. Stanford, School of Education, Stanford University, 1972.
iv, 24 p. (Stanford University. Center for Research and Development in Teaching. Research and development memorandum no. 85)
1. Teacher-student relationships. I. Snow, Richard E. II. Title. III. Series.
MH-Ed NUC74-1300

Baker, Katherine Read.
The nursery school : human relationships and learning / Katherine H. Read. — 6th ed. — Philadelphia : Saunders, 1976.
viii, 394 p. : ill. ; 26 cm.
Includes bibliographies and index.
ISBN 0-7216-7488-7
1. Nursery schools.
LB1140.B27 1976 372.21'6 75-28801
75 MARC

Baker, Katherine Read.
Understanding and guiding young children [by] Katherine Read Baker [and] Xenia F. Fane. 3d ed. Englewood Cliffs, N.J., Prentice-hall [1975]
338 p. illus. 24 cm.
Includes bibliographies.
1. Children--Management. I. Fane, Xenia F., joint author. II. Title.
NcGU NUC77-89552

Baker, Kay D.
see Rocket instrumentation for auroral measurements; Aerobee 3.615. Salt Lake City, Upper Air Research Laboratory, University of Utah, 1968.

Baker, Kay D.
see Rocket instrumentation for the study of a polar cap absorption event--PCA-69. Salt Lake City, 1970.

Baker, Keith.
see Comprehensive services to rural poor families ... New York, Praeger, 1976.

Baker, Keith, joint author.
see Shepard, Morris A. Year-round schools. Lexington, Mass., Lexington Books, c1977.

Baker, Keith Michael.
Condorcet, from natural philosophy to social mathematics / Keith Michael Baker. — Chicago : University of Chicago Press, 1975.
xiv, 538 p. ; 24 cm.
Bibliography: p. 485-523.
Includes index.
ISBN 0-226-03532-8
1. Condorcet, Marie Jean Antoine Nicolas Caritat, marquis de, 1743-1794. 2. Social sciences—History. 3. Social sciences—Methodology. I. Title.
H59.C66B34 300'.9 74-5725
75 MARC

Baker, Kendall L
A survey of the attitudes of political science graduates toward their department, 1967-1971, by Kendall L. Baker ⌈and⌉ Michael J. Horan. ⌈Laramie⌉ Government Research Bureau, Dept. of Political Science, University of Wyoming, 1972.
21 p. 28 cm.
1. Wyoming. University. Dept. of Political Science. 2. Political science—Study and teaching—Wyoming. I. Horan, Michael J., joint author. II. Wyoming. University. Dept. of Political Science. III. Title.
WyU NUC73-73603

Baker, Kendall L
The young Germans: a study in political culture, by Kendall L. Baker. ⌈Washington⌉ 1968 ⌈c1970⌉
vii, 433 l.
Thesis—Georgetown University.
Bibliography: leaves 409-420.
1. Youth—Cologne, Germany. 2. Political socialization. 3. Germany—Pol. & govt.—1945- I. Title.
CU-SB NUC76-70965

Baker, Kenneth Frank, 1908-
Biological control of plant pathogens ⌈by⌉ Kenneth F. Baker ⌈and⌉ R. James Cook. With a foreword by S. D. Garrett. San Francisco, W. H. Freeman ⌈1974⌉
xiv, 433 p. illus. 24 cm. (A series of books in the biology of plant pathogens)
Bibliography: p. ⌈349⌉-380.
1. Pest control—Biological control. 2. Plant diseases. I. Cook, R. James, 1937- joint author. II. Title.
⌈DNLM: 1. Pest control, Biological. 2. Plant diseases—Prevention and control. SB 975 B167b 1974⌉
SB975.B34 632'.96 73-18420
ISBN 0-7167-0589-3 MARC

Baker, Kenneth Frank, 1908- A plant pathogen views history. 1965
in History of botany: Herbals, their history and significance. Los Angeles, Clark Memorial Library, 1965.

Baker, Kenneth Frank, 1908-
Wildflowers of Western Australia ⌈by⌉ Kenneth F. Baker. London, R. Hale, 1972, c1971.
⌈32⌉ p. col. illus. 26 cm.
Published in the U.S.A. by Newbury Books, Boston, Mass.
1. Wildflowers—Western Australia—Pictorial works. I. Title.
OOxM NUC76-70964

Baker, Kenneth R 1943-
Introduction to sequencing and scheduling ⌈by⌉ Kenneth R. Baker. New York, Wiley ⌈1974⌉
ix, 305 p. illus. 23 cm.
Includes bibliographies.
1. Scheduling (Management) I. Title.
TS157.5.B34 658.5'1 74-8010
ISBN 0-471-04555-1 MARC

Baker, Kenneth W., ed.
see Brugger, Walter, 1904- ed. Philosophical dictionary. Spokane, Wash., Gonzaga Univ. Press [1972]

Baker, Kermit B., joint author
see Mossman, Marshall L Drafting: basic techniques. Ann Arbor, Mich., Prakken Publications [1969]

Baker, Kirby Simmons, 1901-
The Baker chart of ancestors and next of kin under the civil law, by Kirby S. Baker. Springfield, Mass., Empire Mailing Co., 1953.
13 p. illus. 30 cm.
2 fold. sheets inserted.
1. Genealogy—Forms, blanks, etc. I. Title.
CS24.B34 929'.1 74-162776
MARC

Baker, L.
see Educational performance in the urban environment. London, 1971.

Baker, L. C.
see
Baker, La Fayette Charles, 1826-1868.

Baker, L. D.
see
Baker, Lee D:le, 1940-

Baker, L. E., joint author.
see Geddes, Leslie Alexander, 1921- Principles of applied biomedical instrumentation. 2d ed. New York, Wiley, [1975]

Baker, L R
Seedless pickles; a new concept. East Lansing, 1973.
10 p. illus. (Michigan, agricultural Experiment Station. Research report, 227)
Bibliography: p. 9-10.
I. Title.
DNAL NUC75-17361

Baker, La Fayette Charles, 1826-1868.
History of the U. S. Secret Service. With a new pref. by Herbert C. Friese, Jr. New York, AMS Press, 1973.
704 p. illus. 23 cm. (Foundations of criminal justice) $32.50
Reprint of the 1868 ed. published by King & Baird, Philadelphia.
1. United States—History—Civil War—Secret service. I. Title. II. Series.
E608.B16 1973 973.7'85 70-156006
ISBN 0-404-09106-7 MARC

Baker, Lansing Gregory, 1937-
A study of selected variables in a change from a junior high school organization to a middle school organization. Syracuse, N. Y., 1972.
203 l.
Thesis—Syracuse University.
Vita.
Bibliography: leaves 195-203.
Microfilm of typescript. Ann Arbor, Mich., University Microfilms, 1973. 1 reel. (Doctoral dissertation series, 73-7700)
NSyU NUC76-70963

Baker, Larry Dale, 1938-
Blindness and social behavior. [Bloomington, Ind.] 1972.
75 p. illus.
Thesis (D.B.A.)—Indiana University.
Vita.
InU NUC73-41414

Baker, Laurence Leonard Hampton.
A Planning parameter allocation model for Greater London / by L. L. H. Baker [for the] Greater London Council, Department of Planning and Transportation, Transportation Branch. — London : G.L.C., 1975.
[3], 69 p. : ill., map ; 30 cm. — (Research memorandum - Greater London Council ; RM 460 ISSN 0306-7203) GB76-11916
Bibliography: p. 50-52.
ISBN 0-7168-0722-X : £1.00
1. Economic forecasting—England—London metropolitan area. 2. Population forecasting—England—London metropolitan area. I. Greater London Council. Dept. of Planning and Transportation. Transportation Branch. II. Title. III. Series: Greater London Council. Research memorandum - Greater London Council ; RM 460.
HC258.L6B34 338.5'443'09421 77-364132
77 MARC

Baker, Laurie.
A selection of geographical computer programs / Laurie Baker. — London : London School of Economics and Political Science, Department of Geography, 1974.
[7], 118 p. ; 26 cm. — (Geographical papers - London School of Economics and Political Science ; no. 6) GB74-14463
Bibliography: p. 113-116.
ISBN 0-85328-022-3 : £2.00
1. Geography—Computer programs. I. Title. II. Series: London School of Economics and Political Science. Geographical papers ; no. 6.
HC251.A1L6 no. 6 330'.08 s 76-366473
[G70.2] 76 MARC

Baker, Lawrence A 1947-
Studies on the mechanism of virulence in Leptospira canicola. [Amherst] 1974.
x, 52 l. illus. 28 cm.
Thesis (Ph. D.)—University of Massachusetts.
1. Leptospira. I. Title.
MU NUC76-18079

Baker, Lee Dale, 1940-
Occupational health survey of Michigan farmers / L. D. Baker and R. H. Wilkinson. — [East Lansing] : Dept. of Agricultural Engineering, Michigan State University, 1974.
iii, 88 leaves : ill. ; 28 cm.
Cover title.
Bibliography: leaves 58-62.
1. Agricultural laborers—Diseases and hygiene—Michigan—Statistics. 2. Agriculture—Hygienic aspects—Michigan—Statistics. 3. Health surveys—Michigan—Statistics. I. Wilkinson, Richard Hanwell, joint author. II. Title.
RC965.A5B34 362.8'5 75-623359
77 MARC

Baker, LeGrand Liston, 1937-
The Board of Treasury, 1784-1789: responsibility without power. [n.p.] c1972.
379 l. 29 cm.
Thesis (Ph.D.)—University of Wisconsin.
Vita.
Includes bibliography.
1. United States. Board of Treasury. I. Title.
WU NUC74-1307

Baker, LeGrand Liston, 1937-
The Board of Treasury, 1784-1789: responsibility without power. [n. p.] 1972.
vii, 379 l.
Thesis—University of Wisconsin.
Vita.
Bibliography: leaves 367-379.
Photocopy of typescript. Ann Arbor, Mich., University Microfilms, 1973. 22 cm.
1. United States. Board of Treasury. I. Title.
ViU NUC76-70962

Baker, Leonard.
John Marshall: a life in law. New York, Macmillan [1974]
x, 845 p. illus. 24 cm.
Bibliography: p. 771-785.
1. Marshall, John, 1755-1835. I. Title.
KF8745.M3B3 347'.73'2634 [B] 73-2751
ISBN 0-02-506360-X MARC

Baker, Lillian.
The collector's encyclopedia of hatpins and hatpin holders / by Lillian Baker. — Paducah, Ky. : Collector Books, c1976.
viii, 216 p. : ill. (some col.) ; 29 cm.
Bibliography: p. 177-179.
Includes indexes.
ISBN 0-89145-016-5 : $19.95
1. Hatpins—Collectors and collecting. 2. Hatpin holders—Collectors and collecting. I. Title. II. Title: Hatpins and hatpin holders.
NK7695.B34 739.27'8 77-357307
77 MARC

Baker, Lionel R.
see Quality assurance in optical & electro-optical engineering ... Palos Verdes Estates, Calif., The Society, c1975.

Baker, Liva.
I'm Radcliffe, fly me! : the seven sisters and the failure of women's education / by Liva Baker. — New York : Macmillan, c1976.
246 p. ; 22 cm.
Bibliography: p. [228]-240.
Includes index.
ISBN 0-02-506310-3
1. Higher education of women—United States. I. Title.
LC1756.B34 376'.65'0973 76-16172
76 MARC

Baker, Lois Ann.
see Gerling, Juanita. Views of Versailles and surrounding area. Bicentennial ed. [Versailles, Ohio] Versailles Policy Pub. Co., c1976.

Baker, Lorian Nancy, 1948-
The lexicon: considerations for a performance model by Lorian Nancy Baker. Ann Arbor, Mich., Xerox University Microfilms, 1975.
x, 215 l. illus. 21 cm.
Reprint of the author's thesis, University of California, Los Angeles, 1973.
Vita.
Bibliography: leaf 209-215.
1. Vocabulary. I. Title.
CLSU NUC76-18071

Baker, Louise.
The Bradley family of Hempstead, Lafayette, and Bradley counties in Arkansas. Genealogical memoranda by Louise Baker, Pauline Booker Carter [and] Jacob Monroe Carter, Jr. [Lewisville, Ark.] 1971.
1 p.l., 9 l. 28 cm.
Cover title.
Reproduced from typewritten copy.
1. Bradley family. I. Carter, Pauline Booker. II. Carter, James Monroe.
T NUC73-41416

Baker, Lowell H.
see Baker, Abe Bert, 1908- Clinical neurology. -- Rev. ed. -- Hagerstown, Md. : Medical Dept., Harper and Row, 1975-

Baker, Lucinda, 1916-
The place of devils / by Lucinda Baker. — New York : Putnam, c1976.
viii, 245 p. ; 22 cm.
ISBN 0-399-11701-6 : $8.95
I. Title.
PZ4.B16954 Pl 813'.5'4 76-3640
[PS3552.A4315] 76 MARC

Baker, Lucinda, 1916-
Walk the night unseen / by Lucinda Baker. — New York : Putnam, c1977.
287 p. ; 23 cm.
ISBN 0-399-11896-9
I. Title.
PZ4.B16954 Wal 813'.5'4 76-57220
[PS3552.A4315] 76 MARC

Baker, Luther G
The rising furor over sex education [by] Luther G. Baker, Jr. [Northfield, Ill., SIECUS Publications Office] 1969.
13 p. 28 cm.
Bibliography: p. 13.
1. Sex instruction. U. S. I. Sex Information and Education Council of the U. S. II. Title.
NcD NUC76-70978

Baker, Lynn.
A partial bibliography of the ecology and biology of the coast of the Gulf of Mexico with emphasis on the Louisiana Coast. Prepared for the Louisiana Coastal Commission, by Lynn Baker [and] Heino Beckart. [Lafayette, University of Southwestern Louisiana, Office of Institutional Research] 1972.
ii, 108 l. 28 cm. (University of Southwestern Louisiana. Research series, no. 15)
1. Marine biology—Mexico, Gulf of—Bibliography. 2. Marine ecology—Mexico, Gulf of—Bibliography. 3. Marine biology—Louisiana—Bibliography. 4. Marine ecology — Louisiana — Bibliography. I. Beckart, Heino, joint author. II. Louisiana. Coastal Commission. III. Title. IV. Series: Louisiana. University of Southwestern Louisiana, Lafayette. Research series, no. 15.
Z5322.M3B34 016.57492'3'4 73-620960
MARC

Baker, M. Abu
see Abu Baker, M.

Baker, M C
Moisture problems in built-up roofs, by M. C. Baker. Ottawa, Ont., National Research Council of Canada, Division of Building Research, 1973.
22 p. illus. 28 cm. (National Research Council, Canada. Division of Building Research. Technical paper no. 390)
1. Roofs. I. Title. II. Series.
CaBVaU NUC75-17374

Baker, M. E. Penny
see
Baker, Mary Ellen Penny.

Baker, M. H.
see
Baker, Michael H

Baker, Mabel Phillips, 1914-
The Andrew Phillips family / by Mabel Phillips Baker. — Baltimore : Gateway Press, 1974.
62 p. : group port. ; 22 cm.
1. Phillips family. I. Title.
CS71.P555 1974 929'.2'0973 74-82547
MARC

Baker, Mabel Phillips, 1914-
Wills of Scotland County, Missouri, 1843-1975 / compiled by Mabel Phillips Baker. — Baltimore : Gateway Press, 1975.
v, 184 p. ; 23 cm.
Includes index.
1. Scotland Co., Mo.—Genealogy. 2. Wills—Scotland Co., Mo. I. Title.
F472.S42B25 929'.3778'312 75-34571
76 MARC

Baker, Madeleine R., tr.
see Lenz, Wilhelm von, 1808-1883.
The great piano virtuosos of our time ... New York, Da Capo Press [1973, c1899]

Baker, Malchus Brooks.
Spring runoff as affected by soil permeability on two forested watersheds. [Minneapolis, 1971]
iii, 150 l. illus. 29 cm.
Thesis (Ph.D.)—University of Minnesota.
Bibliography: follows leaf 150.
I. Title.
MnU-A NUC73-41412

Baker, Marceil Genée Kolstad, 1911- joint author.
see Johnson, Frank Leonard, 1945- Shannon ... New York, Hawthorn Books, [1975]

Baker, Marcia Bourgin, 1938-
Ion transport through nerve membranes. [Seattle] 1971.
119 l. illus.
Thesis (Ph.D.)—University of Washington.
Bibliography: leaves 117-119.
1. Theses—Physics. 2. Ions. 3. Nerves. I. Title.
WaU NUC73-126365

Baker, Margaret.
User's guide to the Berkeley transposed file statistical system. Berkeley, Survey Research Center, University of California, 1973.
x, 140 p. 28 cm. (Califronia. University. Survey Research Center. Technical report, no. 1)
1. PICKLE (Electronic computer system) I. Title. II. Series.
CaBVaU NUC74-126571

Baker, Margaret, 1890-
The three partners; temperance lessons for boys and girls. Evanston, Ill., Signal Press [19-]
43 p. illus. 22 cm.
Cover title.
1. Temperance—Study and teaching. I. Title.
INS NUC75-17350

Baker, Margaret, 1928-
Discovering the folklore and customs of love and marriage / Margaret Baker. — Aylesbury : Shire Publications, 1974.
64 p. : ill. ; 18 cm. — (Discovering series ; no. 196)) GB74-21339
Bibliography: p. 60.
Includes index.
ISBN 0-85263-280-0 : £0.40
1. Marriage customs and rites. 2. Love. I. Title.
GT2665.B33 392'.5'0942 77-353642
77 MARC

Baker, Margaret, 1928-
Folklore and customs of rural England / Margaret Baker. — Newton Abbot, Eng. : David & Charles, [1974]
208 p. : ill. ; 22 cm. GB***
Bibliography : p. 197-200.
Includes index.
ISBN 0-7153-6579-7 : £3.75
1. England—Social life and customs. 2. Country life—England. 3. Folk-lore—England. I. Title.
DA110.B26 1974b 390'.0942 74-188116
MARC

Baker, Margaret, 1928-
Folklore and customs of rural England. Totowa, N. J., Rowman and Littlefield [1974]
208 p. illus. 23 cm.
Bibliography : p. 197-200.
1. England—Social life and customs. 2. Country life—England. 3. Folk-lore—England. I. Title.
DA110.B26 1974 390'.0942 74-7065
ISBN 0-87471-549-0 MARC

Baker, Margaret, 1928-
Marriage customs and folklore / Margaret Baker. — Newton Abbot, Eng. : David & Charles ; Totowa, N.J. : Rowman and Littlefield, 1977.
144 p. : ill. ; 23 cm.
Bibliography: p. [139]-140.
Includes index.
ISBN 0-87471-821-X
1. Marriage customs and rites. I. Title.
GT2665.B34 1977 392'.5 76-1937
76 MARC

Baker, Margaret A
The adherence of porcelain enamel to aluminum / Margaret A. Baker. — Washington : U.S. Dept. of Commerce, National Bureau of Standards : for sale by the Supt. of Docs., U.S. Govt. Print. Off., 1974.
vi, 37 p. : ill. ; 26 cm. — (Building science series ; 59)
Includes bibliographical references.
Supt. of Docs. no.: C13.29/2.59
1. Enamel and enameling. 2. Aluminum coatings. 3. Adhesion. I. Title. II. Series: United States. National Bureau of Standards. Building science series ; 59.
TA435.U58 no. 59 690'.08 s 74-23734
[TS700] 74 MARC

Baker, Margaret A
Three-year inspection of nature-tone porcelain enamels on steel. Washington; for sale by the Supt. of Docs., U.S. Govt. Print. Off., 1971.
iii, 14 p. 27 cm. (U.S. National Bureau of Standards. Technical note 707)
Bibliography: p. 14.
1. Enamel and enameling. I. Title.
CLS NUC76-70988

Baker, Margaret A
Weather resistance of porcelain enamels : 15 year inspection of the 1956 exposure test / Margaret A. Baker. — Washington : U.S. Dept. of Commerce, National Bureau of Standards : for sale by the Supt. of Docs., U.S. Govt. Print. Off., 1974.
iii, 12 p. : ill. ; 26 cm. — (NBS building science series ; 50)
Includes bibliographical references.
Supt. of Docs. no.: C 13.29/2:50
$0.55
1. Enamels and enameling—Testing. I. Title. II. Series: United States. National Bureau of Standards. Building science series ; 50.
TA435.U58 no. 50 690'.08 s 74-600034
[TA455.E5] 75 MARC

Baker, Margaret Joyce, 1918-
The last straw / Margaret J. Baker ; illustrated by Doreen Roberts. — Harmondsworth ; Baltimore [etc.] : Puffin Books, 1974.
111 p. : ill. ; 19 cm. — (Puffin books) GB74-25596
SUMMARY: Three children find a magic corn doll that enables them to experience summers of long ago.
ISBN 0-14-030716-8 : £0.25 ($1.50 U.S.)
[1. Dolls—Fiction. 2. Space and time—Fiction] I. Roberts, Doreen. II. Title.
PZ7.B17472 Las 6 76-374671
76 MARC

Baker, Margaret Joyce, 1918-
Prickets way / [by] Margaret J. Baker ; illustrated by Gavin Rowe. — London : Methuen, 1973.
160 p. : ill. ; 21 cm. GB 73-21790
ISBN 0-416-77320-6 : £1.40
I. Title.
PZ7.B17472Pr 3 74-190368
MARC

Baker, Margaret Joyce, 1918-
The sand bird [by] Margaret J. Baker; illustrated by Gareth Floyd. London, Methuen, 1973.
156 p. illus. 21 cm. £1.30 GB 73-05370
I. Title.
PZ7.B17472San 73-175694
ISBN 0-416-75440-6 MARC

Baker, Margaret Joyce, 1918-
The sand bird [by] Margaret J. Baker. Illustrated by Gareth Floyd. [1st U. S. ed.] Nashville [Tenn.] T. Nelson [1973]
158 p. illus. 21 cm. $3.45
SUMMARY: At a jumble sale, three children buy an unusual sand-filled glass swan that makes wishes come true.
[1. Magic—Fiction] I. Floyd, Gareth, 1940- illus. II. Title.
PZ7.B17472San 3 [Fic] 72-14441
ISBN 0-8407-6288-7 ; 0-8407-6289-5 (lib. bdg.) MARC

Baker, Margaret Joyce, 1918-
Sand in our shoes / Margaret J. Baker ; illustrated by Fermin Rocker. — London : Methuen Children's Books, 1976.
127 p. : ill. ; 21 cm. GB***
ISBN 0-416-56360-0 : £2.50
I. Title.
PZ7.B17472 Sao 76-378422
76 MARC

Baker, Marian E
In measured pace, by Marian E. Baker. San Antonio, Naylor Co. [1973]
viii, 31 p. 22 cm. $3.95
Poems.
I. Title.
PS3552.A432 I 5 811'.5'4 73-7388
ISBN 0-8111-0509-1 MARC

Baker, Marilyn.
Amour, où est-tu? Paris, Euredif [c1973]
188 p.
I. Title.
LN NUC74-126567

Baker, Marilyn.
Exclusive! The inside story of Patricia Hearst and the SLA [by] Marilyn Baker with Sally Brompton. New York, Macmillan [1974]
ix, 246 p. illus. 24 cm.
1. Hearst, Patricia, 1954- 2. Symbionese Liberation Army. I. Brompton, Sally, joint author. II. Title.
F866.2.H42B34 322.4'2'0924 [B] 74-16300
ISBN 0-02-506400-2 MARC

Baker, Marilyn Carruth.
Exploring occupations in food service and home economics / Marilyn Carruth Baker ; consulting editor, Charles S. Winn. — New York : Gregg Division, McGraw-Hill, c1976.
152 p. : ill. ; 24 cm. — (Careers in focus)
SUMMARY: Explores careers in food service and home economics and suggests activities designed to provide job experience and a first-hand understanding of the kind of work done in a particular occupation.
ISBN 0-07-071041-4
1. Home economics as a profession—Juvenile literature. 2. Food service—Vocational guidance—Juvenile literature. [1. Home economics as a profession. 2. Food service—Vocational guidance. 3. Vocational guidance] I. Title.
TX164.B34 640'.23 75-16262
75 MARC

Baker, Marilyn Claire, 1942-
The art theory and criticism of Willard Huntington Wright, by Marilyn Claire Baker. [Madison, Wis.] c1975.
2 v. (473 l.) ill. 29 cm.
Thesis (Ph. D.)--University of Wisconsin.
Vita.
Bibliographical footnotes.
1. Wright, Willard Huntington, 1888-1939. I. Title.
WU NUC77-89492

Baker, Marilyn Claire, 1942-
The art theory and criticism of Willard Huntington Wright. Marilyn Claire Baker. [n. p.] 1976.
iv, 473 l. ill.
Thesis--University of Wisconsin.
Photocopy of typescript. Ann Arbor, Mich., University Microfilms, 1975. 21 cm.
1. Wright, Willard Huntington, 1888-1939. I. Title.
OkU NUC77-89493

Baker, Marjorie Gail, 1935-
The relation between a change in social routine and fluctuations in blood pressure and temperature. Marjorie G. Baker. [n.p.] 1975.
81 p.
Thesis (Ph. D.)--New York University.
I. Title.
NNU NUC77-89559

Baker, Marjorie Louise, 1911- joint author
see Baker, George William, 1898- Munsungun to the sea. [1st ed.] New York, Vantage Press [1972]

Baker, Marjorie Y
Dressing the women in the family. Marjorie Y. Baker. [State College] Extension Service, Mississippi State University, 1975.
[4] p. ill. (Mississippi State University. Cooperative Extension Service. Publication, 895)
I. Title.
DNAL NUC77-89542

Baker, Mark, joint author
see Blukis, Juris. Practical digital electronics. Santa Clara, Calif., Hewlett-Packard, 1974.

Baker, Martha.
An evaluation of the flextime experiment, by Martha Baker. West Lafayette, Ind., Research Development Unit, Purdue University Libraries and Audio-Visual Center, 1975.
13 l. 28 cm. (Technical report series, RDU 75-03)
1. Scheduling (Management) I. Title. II. Series: Purdue University, Lafayette, Ind. Research Development Unit. Technical report series, RDU 75-03.
IU NUC77-90293

Baker, Martin.
A sultana for the sultan. London, New York, Abelard-Schuman, 1972.
[28] p. col. illus. 22 x 28 cm. B***
SUMMARY: Refusing to fight the invading king until a sultana sweet enough for his taste can be found, the sultan entertains the king instead.
I. Title.
PZ7.B174725Su 3 [E] 74-38427
ISBN 0-200-71887-8 (New York) MARC

Baker, Martin Kurjian.
A study of the effectiveness of a public media tsunami education program in selected coastal towns in Alaska. [Boulder] 1971.
vii, 236, 50, 41, [14] l. illus.
Thesis (Ph.D.)—University of Colorado.
Bibliography: leaves [206]-214.
1. Communications research. 2. Communications—Social aspects. 3. Adult education. 4. Tidal waves. I. Title.
CoU NUC73-41417

Baker, Martin Kurjian.
A study of the effectiveness of a public media tsunami education program in selected coastal towns in Alaska by Martin Hurjian Baker. [Boulder] University of Colorado, 1971.
vii, 361 leaves in various pagings.
Thesis—University of Colorado.
Bibliography: leaves [206]-214.
Microfilm. Ann Arbor, Mich., University Microfilms, 1968. 1 reel. 35 mm.
AkU NUC76-71046

Baker, Martin S
Environmental impact statements : a guide to preparation and review / Martin S. Baker, Joseph S. Kaming, Richard E. Morrison. — New York : Practising Law Institute, c1977.
xiii, 334 p. ; 24 cm.
"C1-1158."
Includes index.
1. Environmental impact statements—Law and legislation—United States. I. Kaming, Joseph S., joint author. II. Morrison, Richard E., joint author. III. Title.
KF3775.B34 344'.73'046 76-56717
77 MARC

Baker, Martin S.
see Preparation of the environmental impact statement, 1976. New York, Practising Law Institute, c1976.

Baker, Martin S.
see Sloan, Allan K Enhancing the public share of highway benefits... Washington, Dept. of Transportation, Federal Highway Administration, Office of Program and Policy Planning. Springfield, Va.; available through the National Technical Information Service, 1974.

Baker, Marvel L
One Goosenest WASP (Notes to his grandchildren) [Lincoln, 1968-
v.
Autobiographical.
Reproduced from typewritten copy.
1. Baker family. 2. Baker, Marvel Leon, 1895- 3. Frontier and pioneer life—Midwest. I. Title.
NbU NUC73-126851

Baker, Marvin Wesley, 1934-
Land use transition in Mexican cities: a study in comparative urban geography. [n.p.] 1970.
xiv, 376 l. illus.
Thesis—Syracuse University.
Vita.
Bibliography: leaves 365-375.
Photocopy of typescript. Ann Arbor, Mich., University Microfilm, 1974. 22 cm.
1. Cities and towns—Mexico. 2. Land—Mexico. I. Title.
PSt NUC76-28926

Baker, Mary Anne King, 1942-
Eye fixations and the identification of form. Louisville, Ky., 1971.
89 l. illus.
Thesis—University of Louisville.
Photocopy: University Microfilms, Ann Arbor, Mich.
1. Form perception. I. Title.
InU NUC74-121642

Baker, Mary Ellen, 1874-
Bibliography of lists of New England soldiers / by Mary Ellen Baker ; addenda by Robert MacKay. — Boston : New England Historic Genealogical Society, 1977.
70 p. ; 23 cm.
1. New England—Genealogy—Bibliography—Catalogs. 2. United States—History, Military—Bibliography—Catalogs. 3. New York (State). State Library, Albany. I. Title.
Z1251.E1B2 1977 016.929'1'0974 77-151000
77 MARC

Baker, Mary Ellen Penny.
Meditation: a step beyond with Edgar Cayce, by M. E. Penny Baker. Foreword by Hugh Lynn Cayce. [1st ed.] Garden City, N. Y., Doubleday, 1973.
166 p. 22 cm. $5.95
Bibliography: p. [165]-166.
1. Meditation. 2. Cayce, Edgar, 1877-1945. I. Title.
BL627.B34 248'.3 72-96227
ISBN 0-385-00984-4 MARC

Baker, Mary Evans Francis, 1876-1918.
Florida wild flowers; an introduction to the Florida flora, by Mary Francis Baker. New ed. New York, Macmillan, 1959.
xiii, 245 p. front., illus., plates. 20 cm.
1. Wild flowers—Florida. 2. Botany—Florida. I. Title.
NNBG NUC75-1443

Baker, Mary Evans Francis, 1876-
Florida wild flowers; an introduction to the Florida flora, by Mary Francis Baker, photographs by the author. New ed. New York, Macmillan, 1938. [Stuart, Fla., Horticultural Books, 1972]
245 p. illus., plates.
Reprint of 1938 ed.
1. Flowers—Florida. 2. Botany—Florida. I. Title.
FTaSU CaOTP NUC75-80095

Baker, Mary Gladys Steel, 1892-
Antiques for the modern home [by] Sheila Stuart. New York, Castle Books [1968, c1962]
147 p. illus. 29 cm.
Bibliography: p. 137.
1. Collectors and collecting. 2. Furniture—Collectors and collecting. 3. Interior decoration. I. Title.
MB NUC76-71049

Baker, Mary Jeanette Fulkerson, 1942-
Diet, growth and related factors of school children before and after nutrition education. Ames, Iowa, 1969.
iv, 248 l.
Thesis—Iowa State University.
Bibliography: leaves 173-178.
Microfilm of typescript. Ann Arbor, Mich., University Microfilms, 1972. 1 reel. 35 mm.
1. Nutrition—Study and teaching—Monroe County, Iowa. 2. Children—Nutrition—Psychological aspects. 3. Food habits. 4. Children—Growth. I. Title.
NIC NUC74-1267

Baker, Mary Lynn.
see Downie, Mary Alice. Dragon on parade. Toronto, Martin Associates, c1974.

Baker, Mary Wallace
see Tobias, Thomas N The history of Ypsilanti... [Ypsilanti, Mich., Huron Press, 1973]

Baker, Maurice.
Economics of alternative beef waste management systems, by Maurice Baker. Lincoln, Dept. of Agricultural Economics, University of Nebraska, 1975.
17 l. ill. (Nebraska. University. Dept. of Agricultural Economics. Staff paper, no. 11)
Paper presented at the 3rd International Symposium on Livestock Wastes, Champaign, Illinois, April 21-24, 1975.
Includes bibliographical references.
I. Title.
DNAL NUC77-89496

Baker, Maurice
see Land use planning for the Great Plains... Lincoln, Neb., Dept. of Agricultural Economics, University of Nebraska, 1973.

Baker, Maurice G
Doctor, what do I do? : A self-help guide for common ills / Maurice G. Baker. — Salt Lake City : Bookcraft, c1975.
ix, 253 p. ; 24 cm.
Includes index.
ISBN 0-88494-284-8 : $4.95
1. Medicine, Popular. 2. Self-medication. I. Title.
RC81.B2323 616'.024 75-24577
75 MARC

Baker, Merl.
Performance of an air reservoir heat pump in air conditioning a nine room residence in Lexington, Kentucky. Lexington, Engineering Experiment Station, College of Engineering, University of Kentucky, 1956.
16 p. illus. (Kentucky. University. Engineering Experiment Station. Bulletin, no. 42)
1. Heat pumps. 2. Dwellings—Air conditioning. I. Title.
UU NUC76-69387

Baker, Michael.
A guide to the birds of Loskop Dam. [Rondebosch, Cape, South Africa] Percy FitzPatrick Institute of African Ornithology, 1970.
33 p. (South African avifauna series, no. 72)
Cover title.
Mimeographed ed.
ICRL NUC73-59626

Baker, Michael, joint author
see Buzzell, Robert Dow, 1933- Automobile advertising expenditures... Cambridge, Mass., Marketing Science Institute, 1971.

Baker, Michael, 1912-
Real property tax map: county of Suffolk, State of New York. Rochester, Pa., 1973.
1 v. (chiefly maps) 46 cm.
Photographically reproduced.
Scale of most maps ca. 1:1,700.
Prepared for the Real Property Tax Service Agency Suffolk County.
1. Suffolk Co., N. Y.—Maps. 2. Real property—Suffolk Co., N. Y.—Maps. I. Real Property Tax Service Agency Suffolk County. II. Title.
G1253.S8B3 1973 912'.747'25 74-191841
MARC

Baker, Michael, 1912- illus.
see Doherty, Charles Hugh. Tunnels. New York, Meredith Press [1968, c1967]

Baker, Michael, 1939-
see Human Ecology Institute. The design of human service systems. Wellesley, Ma., Human Ecology Institute, 1974.

Baker (Michael) Jr., inc.
Acid mine drainage survey, East Branch Clarion River watershed, Elk and McKean Counties, Rochester, Pa. [n.p., 1970]
1 v. (various pagings) illus., fold. maps. (3 fold. in pocket) 29 cm.
At head of title: Commonwealth of Pennsylvania, Department of Mines and Mineral Industries. Operation Scarlift Project no. SL-108.
Cover title: East Branch Clarion River mine drainage pollution abatement project part of Operation Scarlift.
Includes bibliography.
1. Mine drainage. 2. Water—Pollution—Clarion River Watershed. I. Pennsylvania. Dept. of Mines and Mineral Industries. II. Title. III. Title: Operation Scarlift Project SL-108. IV. Title: East Branch Clarion River Mine drainage pollution abatement project.
PSt NUC76-16273

Baker (Michael) Jr., inc.
Architectural measures to minimize subsidence damage / Michael Baker, Jr., Inc. — Washington : Appalachian Regional Commission, 1974.
xiii, 130 p. : ill. ; 28 cm. — (Report - Appalachian Regional Commission ; ARC-73-111-2551)
"Prepared for Appalachian Regional Commission [and] Department of Environmental Resources, Commonwealth of Pennsylvania."
Bibliography: p. 107-116.
1. Earth movements and building. 2. Mine subsidences—Pennsylvania. I. Appalachian Regional Commission. II. Pennsylvania. Dept. of Environmental Resources. III. Title. IV. Series: Appalachian Regional Commission. Report ; ARC-73-111-2551.
HC107.A133P6372a ARC-73-111-2551 76-623449
330'.974 s
[TH1094] 76 MARC

Baker (Michael) Jr., inc.
Brandon, Mississippi. Jackson, Miss., 1971-
v. illus. (part fold. and col.) 28 cm.
1. Regional planning—Mississippi. 2. Brandon, Miss.
MsU NUC74-72213

Baker (Michael) Jr., inc.
City of Pikeville, Pike County, Kentucky: Technical Assistance Project, no. 03-6-09127, Phase III report. Rochester, Pa., 1970.
1 v. illus.
For submittal to the U. S. Economic Development Administration, Office of Technical Assistance.
On cover: Economic Development Administration U. S. Dept. of Commerce. Technical Assistance Project.
1. Pikeville, Ky.—Econ. condit. 2. Technical assistance, Domestic—Pikeville, Ky. I. United States. Economic Development Administration. Office of Technical Assistance. II. United States. Economic Development Administration. Technical Assistance Project.
MiU NUC75-106524

Baker (Michael), Jr., inc.
Comprehensive plan. By Michael Baker, Jr., inc. Spencer, W. Va., 1970.
1 v. (HUD 701 Report)
1. Master plan—Roane Co., W. Va. I. Roane Co., W. Va. Planning Commission.
DHUD NUC74-108937

Baker (Michael) Jr., inc.
Comprehensive plan. By Michael Baker Jr., inc. Spencer, W. Va., 1970.
121 p. (HUD 701 report)
1. Master plan—Roane Co., W. Va. I. Roane Co., W. Va. Planning Commission.
DHUD NUC74-108936

Baker (Michael) Jr., inc.
Comprehensive plan: 1. Comprehensive plan; 2. Neighborhood analysis; 3. Fringe area study; 4. Zoning ordinance. By Michael Baker Jr., inc. Vicksburg, Miss., 1970.
4 v. (HUD 701 report)
1. Master plan—Vicksburg, Miss. I. Vicksburg, Miss. Planning Commission.
DHUD NUC76-7703

Baker (Michael) Jr., inc.
Comprehensive plan: 1, Comprehensive plan; 2, Proposed zoning ordinance. By Michael Baker, Jr., inc. Marysville, Pa., 1970.
2 v. (HUD 701 Report)
1. Master plan—Marysville, Pa. I. Marysville, Pa. Planning Commission.
DHUD NUC74-101338

Baker (Michael) Jr., inc.
Comprehensive plan: 1. Phase II, comprehensive plan; 2. Proposed zoning standards; proposed rules and regulations for the subdivision of land. By Michael Baker, Jr., inc. Grantsville, W. Va., Planning Commission, 1969.
3 v. (HUD 701 report)
1. Master plan—Calhoun Co., W. Va. I. Calhoun Co.—Grantsville Planning Commission.
DHUD NUC76-16268

Baker (Michael) Jr., inc.
Comprehensive plan: 1, Phase II; 2, Proposed zoning standards; 3, Proposed rules and regulations for the subdivision of land. By Michael Baker, Jr., inc. Williamson, W. Va., Planning Commission, 1965-66.
3 v. (HUD 701 report)
1. Master plan—Williamson, W. Va. I. Williamson, W. Va., Planning Commission.
DHUD NUC74-105877

Baker (Michael) Jr., inc.
Decatur, Mississippi: comprehensive plan. Jackson, Miss., 1971-
v. illus. 28 cm. (HUD project no.: Miss. P-68 and P-71)
1. Regional planning—Miss. 2. Decatur, Miss.
MsU NUC74-82453

Baker (Michael) Jr., inc.
Feasibility report on supplementing of fundamental highway plan and development of secondary roads in province of Guayas. Prepared for Comite Ejecutivo de Vialidad de la Provincia del Guayas, Republic of Ecuador. Rochester, Pa., 1959.
81 p. illus., maps. 28 cm.
1. Road construction. 2. Roads—Guayas, Ecuador (Province) I. Title.
IEdS NUC76-70444

Baker (Michael), Jr., inc.
Nanticoke-Ashley expressway; engineering location report, Hanover Township and Ashley Borough, Luzerne County, Pennsylvania. Rochester, Pa. [1956]
40 p. illus., maps.
At head of title: Commonwealth of Pennsylvania, Department of Highways.
1. Express highways—Luzerne Co., Penn. 2. Highway engineering. I. Pennsylvania. Dept. of Highways. II. Title.
MiU NUC73-87937

Baker (Michael) Jr., inc.
Newton County, Mississippi. Jackson, Miss., 1971-
v. illus., map (in pocket) 28 cm. (HUD Project no. Mississippi P-68, P-71, P-91)
1. Regional planning—Mississippi. 2. Newton Co., Miss.
MsU NUC74-82451

Baker (Michael) Jr., inc.
Planning program: 1. Neighborhood analysis; 2. Community facilities plan; 3. Program and budget - phase II. By Michael Baker, Jr., inc. Yazoo City, Miss., 1970.
3 v. (HUD 701 Report)
1. City planning—Yazoo City, Miss. I. Yazoo City, Miss. Planning Commission.
DHUD NUC75-108754

Baker (Michael) Jr., inc.
Sardis, Mississippi. Jackson, Miss., 1971-
v. illus. (part fold. and col.) 28 cm. (HUD Project no. P-75)
1. Regional planning—Mississippi. 2. Sardis, Miss.
MsU NUC74-82452

Baker (Michael) Jr., inc.
Subdivision regulations. By Michael Baker, Jr., inc. Elkhorn, Ky., 1969.
49 l. (HUD 701 Report)
1. Subdivision regulation—Elkhorn City, Ky. 2. Subdivision regulation—Pike Co., Ky. I. Pike Co., Ky. Planning Commission.
DHUD NUC74-100857

Baker (Michael) Jr., inc.
Summary of material site evaluation Valdez Terminal to Yukon River, Alaska. [Belleview, Washington] Alyeska Pipeline Service Company, 1972.
15 l. of overview maps, 94 l. of photomaps. 22 x 36 cm.
Cover title.
Scales vary.
Photomaps feature cubic yards of bedding and gravel between material sites along route.
1. Trans-Alaska oil pipe line—Maps. 2. Maps—Alaska. 3. Pipe lines—Design and construction. I. Alyeska Pipeline Service Company. II. Title.
DI NUC77-26827

Baker (Michael) Jr., Inc.
Union, Mississippi. [Jackson, Mississippi Research and Development Center, 1971-
v. illus. (part fold. and col.) 28 cm. (HUD Project no. Mississippi P-91)
1. Regional planning—Mississippi. 2. Union, Miss.
MsU NUC74-72214

Baker (Michael) Jr., inc.
Urban planning: 1, Comprehensive plan, phase I, Research and surveys; 2, Zoning standards; 3, Rules and regulations for the subdivision of land. By Michael Baker, jr., inc. Beckley, W. Va., Planning and Zoning Commission, 1963.
3 v. (HUD 701 Report)
1. Master plan—Beckley, W. Va. I. Beckley, W. Va. Planning and Zoning Commission.
DHUD NUC76-7720

Baker (Michael) Jr., inc.
Zoning order and ordinance. By Michael Baker, Jr., inc. Elkhorn City, Ky., 1969.
76 p. (HUD 701 Report)
1. Zoning legislation—Elkhorn City, Ky. 2. Zoning legislation—Pike Co., Ky. I. Pike Co., Ky. Planning Commission.
DHUD NUC74-100836

Baker, Michael A., ed.
see National Academy of Sciences, Washington, D. C. Project on Computer Databanks. Databanks in a free society... New York Quadrangle Books [1972]

Baker, Michael H
Sabah, the first ten years as a colony, 1946–1956, by M. H. Baker. [Singapore] Published by Malaysia Pub. House for the Dept. of History, University of Singapore, 1965.
xxii, 154 p. 24 cm. (Singapore studies on Malaysia, no. 1)
"Originally an M. A. thesis submitted to Stanford University."
Includes bibliographical references.
1. Sabah. I. Title. II. Series.
DS591.S5 no. 1 915.95 s 74–184317
[DS597.33] [915.95'3'034] MARC

Baker, Michael H C
Journey to Katmandu [by] Michael H. C. Baker. Newton Abbot [Eng.] North Pomfret (Vt.), David & Charles [1974]
167 p. illus., maps. 22 cm. £3.50 GB***
1. Asia—Description and travel—1951- I. Title.
DS10.B25 915 74–174845
ISBN 0–7153–6367–0 MARC

Baker, Michael H C
Sussex villages / Michael H. C. Baker ; photographs by the author. — London : R. Hale, 1977.
192 p., [16] leaves of plates : ill. ; 23 cm. GB***
Includes index.
ISBN 0-7091-5911-0 : £4.20
1. Sussex, Eng.—Description and travel. 2. Villages—England—Sussex. I. Title.
DA670.S98B18 1977 942.2'5'009732 77-360119
77 MARC

Baker, Michael H. C.
see The Railways of the Republic of Ireland ... Truro, Barton, 1975.

Baker, Michael J.
see Real estate litigation. Springfield, Illinois Institute for Continuing Legal Education, c1975.

Baker, Michael John.
The adoption of industrial products; an exploration of the influence of "Management attitudes" on acceptance of two industrial innovations. Cambridge, Mass., Marketing Science Institute, 1971.
61, [3] p. tables. 29 cm. (Marketing Science Institute. Working paper)
"Preliminary research reports."
Bibliographical footnotes.
1. New products. I. Title. II. Series.
IEdS NUC74-122394

Baker, Michael John.
The diffusion of industrial innovations: an exploration of factors associated with the process, their measurement and predictive utility. [Cambridge, Mass.] 1971.
1 v. (various pagings) illus., forms.
Thesis—Harvard University.
Includes bibliography.
Microfilm (negative) of typescript. Cambridge, Mass., Microreproduction Dept., Harvard University Library, 1971. 1 reel. 35 mm.
IU NUC73-126366

Baker, Michael John.
The market for winter sports facilities in Scotland / by Michael J. Baker and Alexander W. Gordon. — Edinburgh : Research and Planning Division, Scottish Tourist Board, 1976.
[3], 37 leaves ; 30 cm. GB77-05285
"A summary ... of a study carried out for the Scottish Sports Council, The Scottish Tourist Board, The Highlands and Islands Development Board."
ISBN 0-85419-113-5 : £2.00
1. Winter sports facilities—Scotland. 2. Recreational surveys—Scotland. I. Gordon, Alexander W., joint author. II. Scottish Sports Council. III. Scottish Tourist Board. IV. Great Britain. Highlands and Islands Development Board. V. Title.
GV840.7.G7B34 339.4'8'796909411 77-361563
77 MARC

Baker, Michael John.
Marketing : an introductory text / Michael J. Baker. — 2nd ed. — London : Macmillan, 1974.
316 p. : ill. ; 23 cm. GB75-02944
Bibliography: p. 304-308.
Includes index.
ISBN 0-333-17168-3 : £5.95. ISBN 0-333-17169-1 pbk.
1. Marketing. I. Title.
HF5415.B275 1974 658.8 75-308937
75 MARC

Baker, Michael John.
Marketing new industrial products / Michael J. Baker. — London : Macmillan, 1975.
xiv, 209 p. ; 23 cm. GB***
Bibliography: p. [192]-207.
Includes index.
ISBN 0-333-15572-6 : $26.00 (U.S.)
1. Product management. 2. New products. I. Title.
HF5415.15.B34 658.8 75-329712
75 MARC

Baker, Michael John.
Marketing new industrial products. New York, Holmes & Meier, 1975.
209 p. ill.
1. Marketing management--Mathematical models. 2. New products. I. Title.
ViBlbV NUC77-89558

Baker, Michael John.
Product policy and management / [by] Michael J. Baker, Ronald McTavish. — London : Macmillan, 1976.
x, 182 p. : ill., form ; 23 cm. — (Macmillan studies in marketing management)
GB76-16510
Includes bibliographical references and index.
ISBN 0-333-19287-7 : £7.95. ISBN 0-333-19288-5 pbk.
1. Product management. 2. New products—Management. I. McTavish, Ronald, joint author. II. Title.
HF5415.15.B35 658.5 76-372941
76 MARC

Baker, Michael John.
see Marketing in adversity. London, Macmillan, 1976.

Baker, Michael John.
see Marketing : theory and practice. London, Macmillan, 1976.

Baker, Michael Paul.
Depolarization in the elastic scattering of 17 MeV polarized protons from ^{9}Be. [Seattle] 1975.
121 l. illus.
Thesis (Ph. D.)—University of Washington.
Bibliography: leaves 117-121.
1. Protons. 2. Scattering (Physics) I. Title.
WaU NUC76-18072

Baker, Mickey.
Jazz and rhythm 'n blues. [New York, Amsco Music Pub. Co., c1969]
64 p. 31 cm.
Cover title.
"This book will give you an insight into "cool" jazz and "funky" blues."
1. Guitar—Instruction and study. I. Title.
CNoS NUC76-70976

Baker, Mikal
see Meridian/122... [Davis, Calif.? Meridian/122, 1972]

Baker, Mike.
The economics of oil and the falling rate of profit / by Mike Baker. — London : M. Scott [for] Marxist-Leninist Organisation of Britain, [1976]
23 p. ; 30 cm. GB76-12430
"Class against class pamphlet."
ISBN 0-9501540-3-2 : £0.40
1. Petroleum industry and trade—Great Britain. 2. Marxist-Leninist Organisation of Britain. I. Marxist-Leninist Organisation of Britain. II. Title.
HD9571.6.B34 338.2'7'282091713 76-367694
76 MARC

Baker, Mike.
see League of Socialist Artists. Essays on art and imperialism ; art and socialism. London, M. Scott, [1976]

Baker, Milan Daniel, 1944-
Institutional readiness for collaboration in teacher education. [Gainesville] 1974.
xi, 144 l. 28 cm.
Thesis (Ed. D.)—University of Florida.
Vita.
Bibliography: leaves 130-143.
1. Teachers, Training of—Florida. I. Title.
FU NUC76-18066

Baker, Miriam R
see Finkelstein, Miriam R Baker, 1932-

Baker, Muriel L
The blue and white : the cotton embroideries of rural China / by Muriel Baker and Margaret Lunt. — New York : Scribner, c1977.
ix, 102 p., [2] leaves of plates : col. ill. ; 28 cm.
Bibliography: p. 102.
ISBN 0-684-14887-0 : $14.95
1. Embroidery—China. 2. Folk art—China. I. Lunt, Margaret, joint author. II. Title.
NK9283.A1B34 746.4'4 76-57933
76 MARC

Baker, Muriel L.
see Needlepoint: design your own. New York, Scribner [1974]

Baker, N. M.
see Randolph, James R Bibliography of hydrology of the United States and Canada, 1964. Washington, U.S. Govt. Print. Off., 1969.

Baker, Nancy J
Migrants, recommendations, description of services, review of readings and legislation. [Lansing, Mich.] Community Planning Council, 1970.
39, a-i l. 30 cm.
1. Migrant labor-Michigan. I. Community Planning Council, Lansing, Mich. II. Title.
Mi NUC76-10826

Baker, Natalie, joint author
see Baker, Samm Sinclair. Introduction to art... London, Thames & Hudson, 1971.

Baker, Neal Kenton, 1945-
Bipolar magnetic field regions and solar microwave bursts. [n.p.] 1975.
227 l.
Thesis (Ph. D.)--Pennsylvania State University.
I. Title.
PSt NUC77-89557

Baker, Nelson B
You can understand the Bible by its unifying themes [by] Nelson B. Baker. [1st ed.] Philadelphia, A. J. Holman [1973]
143 p. 21 cm. $2.95
Bibliography: p. [144]
1. Bible—Theology. I. Title.
BS543.B33 1973 220.6'6 72-8399
ISBN 0-87981-011-4 (pbk.) MARC

Baker, Ngaere.
Patea Primary School centennial, 1875-1975 / [by Ngaere Baker]. — [Patea : Patea Primary School Centennial Committee?, 1975]
[64] p. : ill., ports. ; 22 cm. NZ75-5
Cover title.
$2.00
1. Patea Primary School. I. Title.
LG745.P29B34 372.9'9312 76-374608
76 MARC

Baker, Nina (Brown) 1888-
Juarez, hero of Mexico; adapted by William Kottmeyer. Illustrated by Stephen S. Bloomer. St. Louis, Webster Division, McGraw-Hill Book Co. [1972, c1949]
122 p. illus. 21 cm. (Webster everyreaders)
1. Juárez, Benito Pablo, Pres. Mexico, 1806-1872. I. Kottmeyer, William, 1910-
CoGrS NUC74-1304

Baker, Ninah Tenenboim-
see
Tennenbaum-Backer, Nina.

Baker, Noel Custer, 1938-
Description of a private liberal arts college: 1961-1970. [Bloomington, Ind.] 1973.
135 p.
Thesis (Ed.D.)—Indiana University.
Vita.
InU NUC74-1305

Baker, Norma.
The typology in The greening of America: its relation to philosophies of human nature and acceptance of change. [Nashville] 1972.
xiii, 181 l. 28 cm. (Peabody contribution to education, no. 875)
Typescript.
Thesis (Ph.D.)—George Peabody College for Teachers.
Bibliography: leaves 98-104.
TNJ-P NUC74-126549

Baker, Norman, 1936-
Government and contractors: the British Treasury and war supplies, 1775-1783. London, Athlone Press, 1971.
x, 274 p. 23 cm. (University of London. Historical studies, 30) £4.00
B71-20336
Distributed in the U.S.A. by Oxford University Press, New York.
Bibliography: p. [255]-262.
1. Great Britain. Treasury. 2. Defense contracts—Great Britain—History. 3. United States—History—Revolution, 1775-1783—Supplies. I. Title. II. Series: London. University. Historical studies, 30.
HJ1013.B155 355.8'0942 76-30459
ISBN 0-485-13130-7 71[r75]rev MARC

Baker, Norman, 1936- joint author.
see Iggers, Georg G. New directions in European historiography. 1st ed. Middletown, Conn., Wesleyan University Press, [1975]

Baker, Norman Allison.
The effects of differing speeds of videotape feedback and levels of perceptual speed on psychomotor performance. [Columbia] 1971.
65 l. illus.
Thesis (Ph.D.)—University of Missouri.
Vita.
Includes bibliography.
1. Dissertations, Academic—Missouri. Univ.—Education.
MoU NUC73-126349

Baker, Norman Allison.
The effects of differing speeds of videotape feedback and levels of perceptual speed on psychomotor performance. [Columbia] 1971.
65 l. illus.
Thesis (Ph.D.)—University of Missouri.
Vita.
Microfilm copy.
Includes bibliography.
1. Dissertations, Academic—Missouri. Univ.—Education.
MoU NUC73-126352

Baker, Norman H
Tables of convective stellar envelope models [by] Norman Baker and Stefan Temesváry. 2d. ed. [New York, Institute for Space Studies, 1966]
79, [95] l. illus. 28 cm.
Bibliography: leaves 74-75 (1st group)
1. Stars—Atmospheres. I. Temesváry, Stefan, joint author. II. U. S. Goddard Institute for Space Studies, New York. III. Title.
QB809.B34 1966 523.8 74-194259
MARC

Baker, Norman Kent, 1928- joint author
see Murphy, Barbara. Thor Heyerdahl and the reed boat Ra. Philadelphia, Lippincott [1974]

Baker, Norman R
The way it was; an informal history of New City, by Norman R. Baker. Editor: Paul M. Ochojski. Orangeburg, N. Y., Historical Society of Rockland County, 1973.
48 p. illus. 22 cm.
1. New City, N. Y.—History. I. Title.
F129.N513B34 917.47'1'03 73-163920
MARC

Baker, Norman R
The way it was in North Rockland, by Norman R. Baker. Orangeburg, N. Y., Historical Society of Rockland County, 1973.
72 p. illus. 22 cm.
1. Rockland Co., N. Y.—History. I. Title.
F127.R6B33 917.47'28 74-173541
MARC

Baker, Norman Robert, 1937-
A research program in operations research and management sciences. Atlanta, School of Industrial and Systems Engineering, Georgia Institute of Technology, 1970-72.
2 v. in 1.
Issued as Progress report no. 1, and Final report, Project E-24-604 (formerly B-1018)
1. System analysis. 2. Operations research. I. Title.
GAT NUC76-70929

Baker, Norman Robert, 1937-
see Moore, John R An analytical approach to scoring model design... Stanford, Calif., Stanford University, Graduate School of Business, 1969.

Baker, Norman Robert, 1937-
see Moore, John R A computational analysis of an R & D project scoring model... [Lafayette, Ind.] Herman C. Krannert Graduate School of Industrial Administration, Purdue University [1968]

Baker, Norman Robert, 1937-
see Pessemier, Edgar A 1922-
Project and program decisions... Lafayette, Ind., Herman C. Krannert Graduate School of Industrial Administration, Purdue University, 1971.

Baker, Norman Robert, 1937- joint author
see Rubenstein, Albert Harold, 1923-
Control mechanisms in the idea flow process. Evanston, Ill., 1966.

Baker, Norman Robert, 1937- joint author
see Rzasa, Philip V Measures of effectiveness for a university library. [Lafayette, Ind.? Purdue University, 1971?]

Baker, Ola Grace, 1908-
Flowers of the field; a genealogy of these family names: Clearman, Cotton, Gilmore, Holladay, Henderson, Hollingsworth, Phillips, Rush, Swift, and others. [Tuscaloosa, Ala., 1974]
iii, 197 p. illus. 24 cm.
1. Baker family. 2. Clearman family. I. Title.
CS71.B17 1974 929'.2'0973 74-78836
MARC

Baker, Oleda, 1934-
The I hate to makeup book / by Oleda Baker. — Englewood Cliffs, N.J. : Prentice-Hall, [1975]
xii, 132 p. : ill. ; 24 cm.
Includes index.
ISBN 0-13-450569-7
1. Beauty, Personal. 2. Cosmetics. I. Title.
RA778.B213 646.7'26 75-11818
75 MARC

Baker, Oleda, 1934-
The models' way to beauty, slenderness, and glowing health, by Oleda Baker, with Bill Gale. Special photos. by Richard Hochman. Englewood Cliffs, N. J., Prentice-Hall [1973]
207 p. illus. 26 cm. $7.95
1. Beauty, Personal. 2. Hygiene. 3. Models, Fashion. I. Title.
RA778.B214 646.7 72-7214
ISBN 0-13-586073-3 MARC

Baker, Oleda, 1934-
29 Forever / by Oleda Baker, with Bill Gale. — New York : Berkley Pub. Corp. : distributed by Putnam, c1977.
214 p., [10] leaves of plates : ill. ; 22 cm.
ISBN 0-399-11941-8 : $7.95
1. Beauty, Personal. 2. Middle aged women—Health and hygiene. 3. Orgasm. I. Gale, Bill, joint author. II. Title.
RA778.B2144 1977 646.7'2 77-151889
77 MARC

Baker, Oneta M
A history of the town of Clarence. [Buffalo, N.Y.] Buffalo and Erie County Historical Society, c1971.
8 p. illus.
1. Clarence (Town, Erie Co.) New York—History. 2. Erie Co., N.Y.—History. 3. New York—Cities and towns—Clarence. I. Buffalo and Erie County Historical Society. II. Title.
WHi NUC74-122399

Baker, Osmon Oleander, 1812-1871.
The last witness. Or, the dying sayings of eminent Christians and of noted infidels. New York, Carlton & Lanahan [n.d.]
108 p. 13 cm.
1. Last words. 2. Christian biography. I. Title.
IEG NUC73-71295

Baker, Owen A.
see Plymouth old and new. Wakefield, EP Publishing, 1976.

Baker, P. F.
see Baker, Peter Frederick, 1939-

Baker, P. R.
see
Baker, Peter Roland, 1942-

Baker, P. T.
see
Baker, Paul T

Baker, P. V.
see
Baker, Paul Vivian.

Baker, Pat A 1931-
In this moment / Pat A. Baker. — Nashville : Abingdon, c1977.
94 p. ; 20 cm.
ISBN 0-687-19445-8
1. Meditations. I. Title.
BV4832.2.B27 242'.4 76-28802
76 MARC

Baker, Pat A 1931-
Mom, take time / Pat A. Baker. — Grand Rapids : Baker Book House, c1976.
114 p. ; 24 cm.
ISBN 0-8010-0655-4 : $2.95
1. Children—Management. 2. Parent and child. I. Title.
HQ769.B3115 649'.1 76-150069
76 MARC

Baker, Patricia McKay, 1945-
Relationships among weight, sex, deprivation, time of eating, eating patterns, taste, and eating behavior. [n.p.] 1973.
112 l.
Thesis—Ohio State University.
Bibliography: leaves 108-112.
1. Body weight. 2. Food habits. I. Title.
OU NUC76-70977

Baker, Mrs. Paul
see Baker, Catherine.

Baker, Paul Geoffrey, 1945-
A critical re-examination of D. H. Lawrence's Aaron's rod by Paul G. Baker. [Toronto, 1974]
v, 399 l.
Thesis—University of Toronto.
Vita.
Bibliography: leaves 392-399.
CaOTU NUC76-18073

Baker, Paul Lawrence.
Inscribed figures in simple closed curves. [Newark, Del.] 1976.
vi, 71 l. illus. 28 cm.
Thesis (Ph. D.)--University of Delaware.
1. Square. 2. Curves. I. Title.
DeU NUC77-89556

Baker, Paul Luther.
The small scale velocity field of interstellar hydrogen. [Berkeley] 1971.
1 v. (various pagings) illus.
Thesis (Ph. D.)—University of California.
Includes bibliography.
CU NUC73-41413

Baker, Paul R comp.
The atomic bomb : the great decision / edited by Paul R. Baker. — 2d rev. ed. — Hinsdale, Ill. : Dryden Press, c1976.
viii, 193 p. ; 24 cm. — (American problem studies)
Bibliography: p. [186]-193.
CONTENTS: Chronology.—Introduction.—Problems of strategy to end the war: Stimson, H. L. The decision to use the bomb. Morison, S. E. The bomb and concurrent negotiations with Japan. Baldwin, H. W. The strategic need for the bomb questioned. Feis, H. The great decision.—Diplomatic fencing and the cold war: Blackett, P. M. S. A check to the Soviet Union. Horowitz, D. J. The bomb as a cause of East-West conflict. Alperovitz, G. A demonstration of American power to the Soviet Union. Amrine, M. Believing the unbelievable. Kolko, G. A question of power. Sherwin, M. J. The bomb and the origins of the cold war.—The administrative context: Glazier, K. M. Administrative and procedural considerations.—The moral dimensions: Batchelder, R. C. Changing ethics in the crucible of war. Macdonald, D. The decline to barbarism.—The bomb and the world today: Rovere, R. H. The bomb. Quigley, C. Pervasive consequences of nuclear stalemate. Wiener, N. Moral and social aspects of science and technology.—A summary view: Schoenberger, W. S. Decision of destiny.
ISBN 0-03-089873-0
1. World politics—1945- —Addresses, essays, lectures. 2. Atomic bomb—Addresses, essays, lectures. I. Title.
D842.B34 1976 940.54'01 75-36668
76 MARC

Baker, Paul R
Growth of a nation / Paul R. Baker, William H. Hall ; contributing author and instructional design, Michael L. Berger. — New York : Oxford Book Co., c1977.
iv, 172 p. : ill. ; 23 cm. — (The American experience)
Includes index.
SUMMARY: A textbook of United States history from the period of colonization to the exploration of space. Questions and exercises accompany each chapter.
ISBN 0-87105-211-3
1. United States—History—Juvenile literature. [1. United States—History] I. Hall, William Harold, 1936- joint author. II. Berger, Michael, joint author. III. Title. IV. Series.
E178.3.B175 973 77-359416
77 MARC

Baker, Paul T.
see High altitude adaptation in a Peruvian community... University Park, Pa., Dept. of Anthropology, Pennsylvania State University, 1968.

Baker, Paul T.
see Human population problems in the biosphere ... Paris, Unesco, 1977.

Baker, Paul T.
see Man in the Andes ... Stroudsburg, Pa., Dowden, Hutchinson & Ross, c1976.

Baker, Paul Vivian.
see Megarry, Robert Edgar, Sir, 1910- A manual of the law of real property. 5th ed. London, Stevens, 1975.

Baker, Paul Vivian
see Snell, Edmund Henry Turner, 1841-1869.
Snell's principles of equity. 27th ed. London, Sweet & Maxwell, 1973.

Baker, Pauline H
Urbanization and political change: a study of the politics of Lagos, 1917-1967. [n.p.] 1970. [1971]
xvii, 616 l. maps.
Thesis—University of California, Los Angeles.
Bibliography: leaves 544-567.
Photocopy of typescript. Ann Arbor, Mich., University Microfilms, 1971. 22 cm.
1. Lagos (City)—Politics and government. I. Title.
CtY-L NUC73-126350

Baker, Pauline H
Urbanization and political change : the politics of Lagos, 1917-1967 / by Pauline H. Baker. — Berkeley, University of California Press, 1974.
xiii, 384 p., [1] fold. leaf of plates : maps ; 24 cm.
Bibliography: p. 357-369.
Includes index.
ISBN 0-520-02066-9
1. Lagos (City)—Politics and government. 2. Lagos (City)—Social conditions. I. Title.
JS7656.9.L3B34 301.5'92'096691 70-162001
MARC

Baker, Pearl Biddlecome.
Rim flying Canyonlands with Jim Hurst, by Pearl Baker. [Green River, Utah, Canyonlands Gift and Book Shop, 1973]
143 p. illus. 24 cm. $6.95
1. Hurst, Jim. 2. Air pilots—Correspondence, reminiscences, etc. I. Hurst, Jim. II. Title.
TL540.H87B34 629.13'092'4 [B] 74-157854
MARC

Baker, Pearl Biddlecome.
Robbers Roost recollections / Pearl Baker. — Logan : Utah State University Press, c1976.
194 p. : ill. ; 24 cm.
ISBN 0-87421-083-6
1. Ranch life—Utah. 2. Baker, Pearl Biddlecome. 3. Utah—Biography. I. Title.
F826.B169 979.2'03'0924 76-4915
76 MARC

Baker, Pearl R.
The story of Wrightsboro, 1768-1964. Written by Mrs. Pearl Baker for the Wrightsboro Restoration Foundation. Thomson, Georgia, 1965.
1 v. (unpaged) illus.
I. Wrightsboro Restoration Foundation.
GCol NUC76-56698

Baker, Peter, 1921-
May Day / Peter Baker. — ⌊London⌋ : Ferry Press, 1975.
20 p. ; 25 cm. GB76-07581
Limited ed. of 200 copies.
ISBN 0-900851-48-1
I. Title.
PR6003.A484M3 821'.9'12 77-367809
77 MARC

Baker, Peter A., joint author.
see Smith, Elbert G. The Wiswesser line-formula chemical notation (WLN). 3d ed. Cherry Hill, N.J., Chemical Information Management, 1975, c1976.

Baker, Peter Charles.
Metabolism and developmental significance of hydroxyindoles in the central nervous system of Xenopus laevis. [Berkeley] 1966.
v, 84 l. illus.
Thesis–University of California.
Bibliography: leaves 48-55.
Photocopy. Ann Arbor, Mich., Xerox University Microfilms, 1974. 21 cm.
1. Serotonin metabolism. 2. Xenopus laevis. I. Title.
CNoS NUC76-28927

Baker, Peter Frederick, 1939-
Calcium movement in excitable cells. P. F. Baker and H. Reuter. Oxford, New York, Pergamon Press, 1975.
102 p. ill. 26 cm. (Pergamon studies in the life sciences)
1. Calcium metabolism. 2. Cell membranes. 3. Cell physiology. I. Reuter, Harald. II. Title.
NjR NUC77-89495

Baker, Peter Gorton.
Babel beach ⌊by⌋ Peter Baker. London, Cassell, 1972.
⌊4⌋, 280 p. 21 cm. £2.25 B 72-08583
I. Title.
PZ4.B16962Bab 823'.9'14 73-150090
[PR6052.A364] MARC
ISBN 0-304-93867-X

Baker, Peter Roland, 1942- joint author.
see Cuschieri, Alfred. Introduction to research in medical sciences. Edinburgh, Churchill Livingstone, 1977.

Baker, Peter William Edward, comp.
Handboek oor die Wet op Landdroshowe en Reëls, synde Wet nr. 32 van 1944 en die Landdroshowereëls albei tot op datum gewysig/ deur P. W. E. Baker en I. G. Farlam — 2de uit. — Kaapstad ; Juta, 1973.
xxxi, 271 p. ; 25 cm. R6.50 SANL
Cover title: The magistrates courts act.
Added t. p.: Handbook on the magistrates' courts act and rules.
Afrikaans and English.
First ed. by S. Aaron, P. W. E. Baker, and I. G. Farlam.
1. Civil procedure—Africa, South. 2. Court rules—Africa, South. 3. Courts—Africa, South. I. Farlam, Ian Gordon, joint comp. II. Title. III. Title: Handbook on the magistrates' courts act and rules.
74-311497
ISBN 0-7021-0384-5

Baker, Peter William Edward.
Handbook on the Magistrates' courts act and rules, being Act no. 32 of 1944 and the rules of the Magistrates' courts both amended up to date. 2. ed. by ... P.W.E. Baker ... and ... I.G. Farlam ... Cape Town, S.A., Juta, 1973.
xxxi, 271 p. tables. 25 cm.
First ed. by S. Aaron, P.W.E. Baker, and I.G. Farlam.
Added t.p. in Afrikaans; text in English and Afrikaans on opposite pages.
1. South Africa–Magistrates' courts. 2. Court rules–Africa, South. 3. Justice, Administration of–Africa, South. I. Aaron, Samuel. II. Farlam, Farlam, I. G. III. South Africa. Laws, statutes, etc. IV. Title.
MH-L NUC73-123992

Baker, Peter William Edward.
Handbook on the Magistrates' courts act and rules: being Act no. 32 of 1944 and the Rules of the Magistrates' courts, both amended up to date. 3d ed. By P.W.E. Baker and I.G. Farlam. Cape Town, Juta, 1976.
xxxv, 277 p. forms. 24 cm.
Added t.-p. in Afrikaans, with title: Handboek oor die Wet op Landdroshowe en reëls.
Cover-title: The Magistrates' courts act ... Die Wet op Landdroshowe ...
English and Afrikaans on opposite pages.
First ed. by S. Aaron, P.W.E. Baker, and I.G. Farlam.
ISBN 0 7021 0384 5.

1. Court rules–Africa, South. 2. Justice, Administration of–Africa, South. I. Farlam, I.G. II. Aaron, Samuel. III. South Africa. Laws, statutes, etc. IV. Title.
MH-L NUC77-84159

Baker, Philip.
Kreol: a description of Mauritian Creole. London, C. Hurst, 1972.
vii, 221 p. illus., map. 22 cm. £4.00 GB 73-19328
Bibliography: p. 220-221.
1. Creole dialects—Mauritius. I. Title.
PM7854.M3B34 447'.9'6982 74-160367
ISBN 0-900966-89-0 MARC

Baker, Philip Raymond, 1936-
Carlos Solórzano; the man and his creative works. [Tallahassee, Fla.] c1973.
iii, 189 l.
Thesis (Ph. D.)–Florida State University.
Bibliography: leaves 180-187.
Vita.
1. Solórzano, Carlos. I. Title.
FTaSU NUC75-17372

Baker, Philip Schaffner, 1916- joint author
see Gould, Robert F Chemistry. Rev. ed. North Brunswick, N. J., Boy Scouts of America, 1973.

Baker, Philip Schaffner, 1916- ed.
see Information Meeting on Irradiated Wood-Plastic Materials, Chicago, 1965. Proceedings. Springfield, Va., Clearinghouse, 1966.

Baker, Philip Schaffner, 1916-
see Symposium on Low-Energy X- and Gamma Sources and Applications, 2d, Austin, Tex., 1967. Proceedings... Oak Ridge, Tenn., Oak Ridge National Laboratory, 1967.

Baker, Phillip John, 1935-
see Suppressor T lymphocytes. Copenhagen, Munksgaard, 1975.

Baker, Phyllis.
Fishmarket & other poems. Vancouver, c1975.
1 v. (unpaged)
1. Canadian poetry, English. I. Title.
CaOTP NUC77-89567

Baker, Phyllis M., ed.
see Use of a chemically defined diet... [Sacramento] State of California, Dept. of Mental Hygiene, 1972.

Baker, Prentice, 1923–
Down cellar, poems. Edited by Wade Hall ⌊and others⌋ Louisville, Kentucky Poetry Press ⌊1973⌋
48 p. 22 cm. (Poets of Kentucky series, no. 4)
I. Title.
PS3552.A434D6 811'.5'4 73-85918
MARC

Baker, R.
see
Baker, Ronald.

Baker, R. Jerry.
see Purchasing factomatic ... Englewood Cliffs, N.J., Prentice-Hall, c1977.

Baker, R. K., joint author
see Gries, John Paul, 1911- Determination of the total storage capacity... Rapid City, South Dakota School of Mines and Technology, 1973.

Baker, R L
Littafin malamai a kan littafin hausa na Oxford. Ibadan, Oxford University Press, 1963.
89 p. 22 cm.
"Teacher's notes for Oxford Hausa readers, books 1 and 2."
1. Hausa language–Study and teaching. I. Title.
IU NUC74-9275

Baker, R. Robinson
see
Baker, Ralph Robinson, 1928-

Baker, R S
Theory, design, and performance of [a] helical-rotor electromagnetic pump, by R. S. Baker. Canoga Park, Calif., Atomics International, 1963.
121 p. illus. (AEC research and development report)
"NAA-SR-7455."
"Contract: AT(11-1)-GEN-8."
Date issued stamped on t.p.
Bibliography: p. 84-85.
1. Electromagnetic pumps. 2. Liquid metal cooled reactors. I. North American Aviation, inc. Atomics International Divison. II. Title. III. Series.
CU NUC76-16421

Baker, Rachel.
All about art ⌊by⌋ Rachel Baker. New Haven, Conn., Fine Arts Publications, 1971.
64 p. illus. 28 cm.
1. Art—Study and teaching. I. Title.
KyU NUC74-122075

Baker, Rachel Mininberg, 1903-
America's first trained nurse, Linda Richards; born: July 27, 1841; died: April 16, 1930. New York, Washington Square Press ⌊1970⌋
197 p. (An Archway paperback)
1. Richards, Linda Ann Judson, 1841-1930—Fiction. I. Title.
MiU NUC73-126809

Baker, Ralph C
The northern fur seal, by Ralph C. Baker, Ford Wilke and C. Howard Baltzo. Washington, U.S. Bureau of Commercial Fisheries, 1963.
18, ⌊1⌋ p. illus. 26 cm. (United States. Fish and Wildlife Service. Circular 169)
1. Northern fur seal. I. Wilke, Ford, joint author. II. Baltzo, C. Howard, 1913- joint author. III. United States. Bureau of Commercial Fisheries. IV. Title. V. Series.
DI NUC76-70986

Baker, Ralph Jackson, 1888- Cases and materials on corporations
see Cary, William Lucius, 1910-
Cases and materials on corporations. 4th ed., unabridged. Mineola, Foundation Press, 1969.

Baker, Ralph Jackson, 1888-
see Dodd, Edwin Merrick, 1888-1951. Dividends and other selections. Brooklyn, Foundation Press, 1958 ⌊c1951⌋

Baker, Ralph L., joint author.
see Espenchied, Robert P. Producer processing of turkeys. Wooster, Ohio Agricultural Research and Development Center, 1968.

Baker, Ralph Robinson, 1928-
see Current trends in the management of breast cancer. Baltimore, Johns Hopkins University Press, c1977.

Baker, Ray Palmer, 1918-
War in the Revolution / by Ray Palmer Baker. — Washington Depot, Conn. : Shiver Mountain Press, c1976.
xii, 345 p. : maps ; 22 cm.
Includes bibliographical references and index.
$12.95
1. United States—History—Revolution, 1775-1783—Campaigns and battles. I. Title.
E230.B34 973.3'3 76-55905
77 MARC

Baker, Ray Stannard, 1870-1946.
Adventures in understanding, by David Grayson. Illustrated by Thomas Fogarty. [n.p., n.d.]
xii, 273 p. illus.
I. Title.
KEmT NUC74-1285

Baker, Ray Stannard, 1870-1946.
Following the color line; an account of Negro citizenship in the American democracy, by Ray Stannard Baker. Williamstown, Mass., Corner House Publishers, 1973.
xii, 314 p. front., illus., plates, ports.
1. Negroes. 2. U.S.—Race question. I. Title.
NSyL NUC76-70985

Baker, Raymond.
Campfires along the Appalachian trail. New York, Carlton Press [c1971]
120 p. map.
1. Appalachian Trail. I. Title.
RP NUC73-126367

Baker, Raymond F
Andersonville; the story of a Civil War prison camp, by Raymond F. Barker, based on research by Edwin C. Bearss. Washington, Office of Publications, National Park Service, U. S. Dept. of the Interior; [for sale by the Supt. of Docs., U. S. Govt. Print. Off.] 1972.
20 p. illus. 18 cm. $0.40
Supt. of Docs. no.: I 29.2: An2/3
1. Andersonville, Ga. Military Prison. I. Bearss, Edwin C. II. Title.
E612.A5B34 973.7'71 73-601190
MARC

Baker, Raymond William.
Nasser' Egypt: power, ideology, and political development. [n.p.] 1972.
1 v.
Thesis—Harvard.
1. Egypt (Mod.)—Hist.—1952-
MH NUC74-1302

Baker, Reid E.
see Personalizing foreign language instruction . . . Skokie, Ill., National Textbook Co., c1977.

Baker, Richard, joint author
see Keller, Charles. The star spangled banana and other revolutionary riddles. Englewood Cliffs, N. J., Prentice-Hall [1974]

Baker, Sir **Richard**, 1568–1645.
Theatrum redivivum; or, The theatre vindicated. Introductory note by Peter Davison. New York, Johnson Reprint Corp., 1972.
141 p. 16 cm. (Theatrum redivivum)
Running title: The theatre vindicated.
"Written in response to Prynne's Histrio-mastix."
Reprint of the 1662 ed. printed by T. R. for F. Eglesfield, London (Wing B513)
1. Prynne, William, 1600–1669. Histrio-mastix. 2. Theater—Moral and religious aspects. I. Prynne, William, 1600–1669. Histrio-mastix. II. Title. III. Title: The theatre vindicated.
PN2047.B3 1972 792'.013 76-175650
MARC

Baker, Sir Richard, 1568-1645. Theatrum redivivum. 1973
see Mr. William Prynn, his defence of stage-plays... New York, Garland Pub., 1973.

Baker, Richard, 1925–
Here is the news. London, Frewin, 1966.
200 p. front., 16 plates (incl. ports.) 22 cm. 25/- B 66-17823
1. Television broadcasting of news. I. Title.
PN4784.T4B3 791.450924 66-76654
rev

Baker, Richard, 1925-
The magic of music / Richard Baker. — London : H. Hamilton, 1975.
152 p. : ill. ; 25 cm. GB***
Bibliography: p. [146]
Includes index.
ISBN 0-241-89194-9 : $3.95
1. Music—Analysis, appreciation. I. Title.
MT6.B18M2 780 75-314454
75 MARC

Baker, Richard, 1925-
The magic of music / Richard Baker. — New York : Universe Books, 1975.
152 p. : ill. ; 25 cm.
Bibliography: p. [146]
Includes index.
ISBN 0-87663-211-8 : $10.00
1. Music—Analysis, appreciation. I. Title.
MT6.B18M2 1975b 780 74-15501
75 MARC

Baker, Richard, 1925–
The terror of Tobermory: an informal biography of Vice-Admiral Sir Gilbert Stephenson, KBE, CB, CHG; with a foreword by Earl Mountbatten of Burma. London, W. H. Allen, 1972.
196, [16] p. illus., coat of arms, map (on lining papers), ports. 23 cm. Index. £3.00 B 72-05875
1. Stephenson, Sir Gilbert Owen, 1878– I. Title.
DA89.1.S76B35 359.3'3'10924 72-181007
ISBN 0-491-00409-5 [B] MARC
rev

Baker, Richard Alan.
Improvisational drama: a curriculum for personal development. [Cambridge] 1972.
ix, 167 l.
Thesis (Ed.D.)—Harvard University.
1. Drama in education. 2. Self-perception. 3. Improvisation (Acting) I. Title.
MH-Ed NUC74-126550

Baker, Richard D
Recovery of sulfur. Washington, Dept. of the Interior, 1973.
1 card. 11 x 15 cm.
Patent application serial number 393 385.
Cover title.
Microfiche (negative) Springfield, Va., National Technical Information Service, 1973.
1. Sulphur. 2. Salvage (Waste, etc.)
I. United States. Dept. of the Interior. II. Title.
DI NUC76-70990

Baker, Richard D., joint author
see Haver, Frank P Improvements in ferric chloride leaching of chalcopyrite concentrate... [Washington] U. S. Bureau of Mines [1975]

Baker, Richard Edward, 1945-
An empirical investigation of the effect of accounting changes on investor behavior. [p.p.] c1974.
306 l. illus. 29 cm.
Thesis (Ph. D.)—University of Wisconsin.
Vita.
Includes bibliography.
1. Investments—Accounting. I. Title.
WU NUC76-18076

Baker, Richard G
Late Quaternary vegetation history of the Yellowstone Lake Basin, Wyoming / by Richard G. Baker. — Washington : U.S. Govt. Print. Off., 1976.
48 p., [1] leaves of plates : ill. ; 29 cm. — (Geology of Yellowstone National Park) (Geological Survey professional paper ; 729-E)
Bibliography: p. 41-43.
Includes index.
Supt. of Docs. no.: I 19.16:729-E
1. Paleobotany—Quaternary. 2. Paleobotany—Wyoming—Yellowstone Lake basin. 3. Palynology—Wyoming—Yellowstone Lake basin. I. Title. II. Series. III. Series: United States. Geological Survey. Professional paper ; 729-E.
QE931.B34 560'.178 75-619373
75 MARC

Baker, Richard John Stenson, joint author.
see Gyford, John. Labour and local politics. London, Fabian Society, 1977.

Baker, Richard Jordan 1936-
Guidelines for the development of adjustment services in rehabilitation [by Richard J. Baker and Horace W. Sawyer] A cooperative project of the Alabama Vocational Rehabilitation Service, Rehabilitation Services Education, Auburn University. Auburn, Ala., Rehabilitation Services Education, Dept. of Vocational and Adult Education, Auburn, University, 1971.
x, 193 p. 28 cm.
Cover Title; Adjustment services in rehabilitation: emphasis on human change.
Bibliography: p. 181-193.
I. Alabama. Vocational Rehabilitation Service.
AAP NUC75-67038

Baker, Richard Kendall, 1918-
Foliar anatomy of the Laeliinae (Orchidaceae) St. Louis, 1972.
x, 329 l. illus. (part col.)
Thesis—Washington University.
Bibliography: leaves 321-329.
1. Laeliinae—Anatomy. I. Title.
MoSW NUC74-1290

Baker, Richard P 1941-
A concomitant look at commitment and labeling theory: divergent but compatible accounts of delinquency causation. [Pullman] 1973.
viii, 83 l.
Thesis—Washington State University.
Microfilm. Ann Arbor, Mich., Univeristy Microfilms, 1973. 1 reel.
1. Juvenile delinquency. 2. Delinquents. 3. Social problems. I. Title.
IaU NUC76-70984

Baker, Richard St. Barbe, 1889-
Caravan story and country notebook. [Wolverton, Bucks., McCorquodale, 1969]
72 p. illus.
1. Foresters—Gt. Brit.—Correspondence, reminiscences, etc. I. Title.
WaU NUC74-121643

Baker, Richard St. Barbe, 1889–
Famous trees of Bible lands / by Richard St Barbe Baker ; illustrated with 31 studies ; foreword by the Bishop of Coventry ; introduction by Zeine N. Zeine. — London : Greaves, 1974.
xvi, 147 p., [30] p. of plates, leaf of plate : ill. (incl. 1 col.), ports. ; 22 cm. GB 74-28199
Includes index.
ISBN 0-904295-00-1 : £3.00
1. Bible—Natural history. 2. Trees—Near East. I. Title.
BS665.B28 220.8'582'16 75-306130
MARC

Baker, Richard T
Accounting is being challenged: needed, a timely answer. [n.p., 1967?]
11 p.
1. Accounting—Addresses, essays, lectures. I. Title.
TxFTC NUC74-9277

Baker, Richard W
Penobscot County, Maine. Richard W. Baker, editor and writer. Portland, Maine, Gross and Allen [1973]
75 p. illus. 28 cm.
1. Penobscot County, Me.
MeU NUC75-17365

Baker, Rita
see Smith, Isla, 1920- A small town affair... Rev. ed. [Wyoming? Ont.] Printed by The Advertiser-Topic, 1973.

[Baker, Robert] fl. 1737.
A rehearsal of a new ballad-opera burlesqu'd, call'd The mad-house. After the manner of Pasquin. As it is now acting at the Theatre-Royal in Lincoln's-Inn-Fields. By a gentleman of the Inner Temple... London, Printed for T. Cooper, 1737. [New York, Garland, 1974]
facsim. (47, [3] p.) 23 cm. (The ballad opera, v. 4)
Dedication signed: R. Baker.
Without the music. Facsimile of a copy in the Bodelian Library.
ICN NUC76-18192

Baker, Robert, 1937-
see Philosophy & sex. Buffalo, Prometheus Books, 1975.

Baker, Robert Allen, 1921-
see Kentucky. University. Committee on Organization and Administration. Organization and administration of the University of Kentucky. [Lexington, University of Kentucky] 1970.

Baker, Robert Allen, 1933-
A statistical analysis of the harmonic practice of the 18th and early 19th centuries. [n.p.] 1963 [c1964]
121 l. illus.
Thesis—University of Illinois.
The thesis includes the score of the author's composition "Seven sonnets to Orpheus, for tenor, chorus, and orchestra" (58 l.) with special t.p.
Vita.
Includes bibliography.
LU NUC76-70983

Baker, Robert Allen, 1933-
see Hiller, Lejaren Arthur, 1924- Revised MUSICOMP manual... [Urbana, Ill.] 1966.

Baker, Robert Andrew.
The Southern Baptist Convention, 1845-1970 [by] Robert A. Baker. [Louisville, Ky., Southern Baptist Theological Seminary] 1970.
125-139 p.
Reprinted from the 'Review and expositor,' vol. 67, no. 2, Spring 1970.
Cover-title: The 125th anniversary of the Southern Baptist Convention.
1. Baptists—History. 2. Southern Baptist Convention—History. I. Title. II. Title: The 125th anniversary of the Southern Baptist Convention.
TxFS NUC74-20100

Baker, Robert Andrew.
The Southern Baptist Convention and its people, 1607-1972 [by] Robert A. Baker. Nashville, Tenn., Broadman Press [1974]
477 p. 24 cm. $11.95
Bibliography: p. 465-469.
1. Southern Baptist Convention—History. I. Title.
BX6207.S68B34 286'.132'09 73-91614
ISBN 0-8054-6516-2 MARC

Baker, Robert Andrew.
see The Lord's free people in a free land ... A bicentennial ed. Fort Worth, Tex., [School of Theology, Southwestern Baptist Theological Seminary] 1976.

Baker, Robert Andrew, 1925-
Concentration of trace organic contaminants from aqueous solution by freezing, by Robert A. Baker. [Pittsburgh] 1969.
xiii, 237 l. illus. 28 cm.
Thesis—University of Pittsburgh.
Bibliography: leaves 227-237.
Photocopy. Ann Arbor, Mich., University Microfilms, 1973. 22 cm.
1. Organic water pollutants. 2. Water—Purification—Freezing process. I. Title.
OrPS NUC76-70955

Baker, Robert Andrew, 1925-
Research by the U.S. Geological Survey on organic materials in water / by Robert A. Baker. — Arlington, Va. : U.S. Dept. of the Interior, Geological Survey, [1976]
iii, 6 p. ; 26 cm. — (Geological Survey circular ; 744)
Bibliography: p. 5-6.
Supt. of Docs. no.: I 19.4/2:744
1. Water—Analysis—Research. 2. Organic water pollutants—Research. 3. Chemistry, Organic—Research. 4. United States. Geological Survey. I. Title. II. Series: United States. Geological Survey. Circular ; 744.
QE75.C5 no. 744 557.3'08 s 76-608296
[GB658.7] 76 MARC

Baker, Robert E.
see Sudden unexpected death in infants. New York, MSS Information Corp. [1974]

Baker, Robert Fulton, 1917-
Handbook of highway engineering / Robert F. Baker, editor, L. G. Byrd, D. Grant Mickle, associate editors. — New York : Van Nostrand Reinhold, [1975]
x, 894 p. : ill. ; 28 cm.
Includes bibliographies and index.
ISBN 0-442-20520-1
1. Highway engineering—Handbooks, manuals, etc. I. Byrd, L. G. II. Mickle, D. Grant. III. Title.
TE151.B24 625.7 74-23226
74 MARC

Baker, Robert Fulton, 1917-
Public policy development : linking the technical and political processes / Robert F. Baker, Richard M. Michaels, Everett S. Preston. — New York : Wiley, [1975]
xi, 315 p. : ill. ; 23 cm.
"A Wiley-interscience publication."
Includes bibliographies and index.
ISBN 0-471-04435-0
1. Technology—Social aspects—United States. 2. Technology and state—United States. 3. Decision-making. I. Michaels, Richard M., joint author. II. Preston, Everett S., 1911- joint author. III. Title.
T14.5.B3 309.1'73 74-32157
74 MARC

Baker, Robert Fulton, 1917-
Transportation research needs related to civil engineering, by Robert F. Baker, with foreword by William H. Wisely and Donald C. Taylor and preface by Charles W. Thomas. Fort Collins, Colo., Colorado State University, 1970.
267 p. 28 cm.
Photocopy. Springfield, Va., National Technical Information Service.
1. Transportation—Research. I. Title.
CaBVaU NUC74-9278

Baker, Robert Fulton, 1917-
see The Use of underground space to achieve national goals. [New York, American Society of Civil Engineers] 1972.

Baker, Robert George
see Conference on Cracking in Welds, Cambridge, Eng., 1968. Cracking in welds. Cambridge [Eng.] 1969.

Baker, Robert Horace, 1883- An introduction to astronomy
see Fredrick, Laurence W An introduction to astronomy. 8th ed. New York, Van Nostrand [1974]

Baker, Robert Horace, 1883- joint author.
see Fredrick, Laurence W. Astronomy. 10th ed. New York, D. Van Nostrand Co., c1976.

Baker, Robert Horace, 1883- joint author.
see Zim, Herbert Spencer, 1909- Stars ... Rev. ed. New York, Golden Press, [1975]

Baker, Robert J
Additional records of bats from Nicaragua, with a revised checklist of Chiroptera / Robert J. Baker and J. Knox Jones, Jr. — [Lubbock] : The Museum, Texas Tech University, 1975.
13 p. ; 23 cm. — (Occasional papers - The Museum, Texas Tech University ; no. 32)
Caption title.
Bibliography: p. 9-13.
$0.50
1. Bats—Nicaragua. 2. Mammals—Nicaragua. I. Jones, J. Knox, joint author. II. Title: Additional records of bats from Nicaragua ... III. Series: Texas Tech University. Museum. Occasional papers ; no. 32.
QL737.C5B33 599'.4'097285 75-623422
75 MARC

Baker, Robert J
A new species of Chiroderma from Guadeloupe, West Indies (Chiroptera, Phyllostomatide) / Robert J. Baker and Hugh H. Genoways. — [Lubbock] : The Museum, Texas Tech University, 1976.
9 p. : ill. ; 23 cm. — (Occasional papers - The Museum, Texas Tech University ; no. 39)
Caption title.
Bibliography: p. 8-9.
$0.95
1. Chiroderma improvisum. 2. Mammals—Classification. 3. Mammals—West Indies—Guadeloupe. I. Genoways, Hugh H., joint author. II. Title. III. Series: Texas Tech University. Museum. Occasional papers ; no. 39.
QL737.C57B32 599'.4 76-623209
76 MARC

Baker, Robert J
A new subspecies of Geomys bursarius (Mammalia : Geomyidae) from Texas and New Mexico / Robert J. Baker and Hugh H. Genoways. — Lubbock : Museum, Texas Tech University, 1975.
18 p. : ill. ; 23 cm. — (Occasional papers - The Museum, Texas Tech University ; no. 29)
Caption title.
Bibliography: p. 18.
1. Geomys bursarius. 2. Mammals—Classification. 3. Mammals—Texas. 4. Mammals—New Mexico. I. Genoways, Hugh H., joint author. II. Title. III. Series: Texas Tech University. Museum. Occasional papers ; no. 29.
QL737.R654B34 599'.3232 75-622578
75 MARC

Baker, Robert J
A new subspecies of Uroderma bilobatum (Chiroptera: Phyllostomatidae) from Middle America [by] Robert J. Baker and V. Rick McDaniel. [Lubbock, Museum, Texas Tech University] 1972.
4 p. 23 cm. (Texas Tech University. Museum. Occasional papers, no. 7)
Caption title.
Bibliography: p. 4.
1. Tent making bat. 2. Mammals—Central America. I. McDaniel, V. Rick, joint author. II. Title. III. Series.
QL737.C57B33 599'.4 73-620611
MARC

Baker, Robert J.
see Biology of bats of the New World family Phyllostomatidae. Lubbock, Texas Tech Press, 1976-

Baker, Robert J.
see Cytoypes and morphometrics of two phyllostomatid bats.... [Lubbock, Texas Tech University] 1973.

Baker, Robert J., joint author.
see Genoways, Hugh H. A new species of Estesicus from Guadeloupe, Lesser Antilles (Chiroptera: Vespertilionidae). [Lubbock] The Museum, Texas Tech University, 1975.

Baker, Robert James, joint author
see The Use of grasses for dune stabilization... Galveston, Gulf Universities Research Consortium, 1972.

Baker, Robert Lee, 1927-
see Resta, Paul E Components of the educational research proposal. [New York, American Book Co., c1972]

Baker, Robert Lee, 1927-
see Resta, Paul E Selecting variables for educational research. [New York, American Book Co., c1972]

Baker, Robert Lee, 1927- joint author
see Schutz, Richard E Stating educational outcomes. New York, American Book Co., Van Nostrand Reinhold Co., c1971.

Baker, Robert Lee, 1927- ed.
see Southwest Regional Laboratory for Educational Research and Development. [Instructional product research. New York, American Book Co., 1972]

Baker, Robert Lee, 1927- joint author
see Sullivan, Howard J Developing instructional specifications. New York, American Book Co., Van Nostrand Reinhold Co., c1971.

Baker, Robert Lee, 1927-
see Summer Institute on Planning Educational Experiments, Arizona State University, 1966. Final report. [Washington] U.S. Dept. of Health, Education, and Welfare, Office of Education, Bureau of Research, 1967.

Baker, Robert M. L., 1930-
see International Astronautical Congress, 12th, Washington, D.C., 1961. Proceedings. New York and London, Academic Press, 1963.

Baker, Robert Parsons.
A regional study of working-class organizations in France: socialism in the Nord, 1870-1924. [n.p.] 1966 [c1967]
ix, 447 l. illus.
Thesis–Stanford University.
Bibliography: leaves 430-447.
Microfilm (positive) Ann Arbor, Mich. University Microfilms, 1967. 1 reel. (Publication no. 7894)
NNC NUC74-122380

Baker, Robert Peyton, 1945-
An extension of the Behavioral Classification Project downward to four, five, and six year olds... [n.p.] 1972.
vi, 183 l. 29 cm.
Thesis (Ph.D.)–Louisiana State University, Baton Rouge.
Vita.
Bibliography: leaves 73-78.
1. Human behavior. I. Title.
LU NUC74-1296

Baker, Robert Peyton, 1945- joint author
see Wormhoudt, Gerrit H. Legal aspects of compulsory schooling. Menlo Park, Calif., 1975.

Baker, Robert Roy, 1946-
Metabolism of fatty acids in rat brain phospholipids. [Toronto] 1973.
xv, 239 l. illus.
Thesis–University of Toronto.
Bibliography: leaves 225-239.
CaOTU NUC75-17364

Baker, Robert Thayne.
Negotiations manual [by] Robert T. Baker [and] Lewis E. Harris. A manual for negotiation with employees in public schools. [Worthington, Ohio] School Management Institute [1970]
iv, 58 p. 28 cm.
1. Collective bargaining–Teachers. 2. School employees–Salaries, pensions, etc. I. Harris, Lewis E. II. Title.
OU NUC75-31159

Baker, Rodney Carlyle, 1942-
Interactions between the hepatic microsomal mixed-function oxidase enzyme system and pesticides by Rodney Carlyle Baker. Raleigh, 1974.
74 l. illus. 29 cm.
Bibliography: leaves 66-74.
Vita.
Thesis (Ph.D.)–North Carolina State University.
NcRS NUC76-18082

Baker, Roger, 1934-
Binding the Devil : exorcism past and present / Roger Baker. — London : Sheldon Press, 1974.
viii, 187 p. ; 20 cm. GB75-06629
Bibliography: p. [182]-183.
Includes index.
ISBN 0-85969-042-3 : £1.65
1. Exorcism. I. Title.
BV873.E8B34 1974 265'.9 75-323159
75 MARC

Baker, Roger, 1934-
Binding the devil ; exorcism past and present Roger Baker. London, Arrow Books, 1975, c1974.
viii, 187 p. 18 cm.
Bibliography: p. [182]-183.
Includes index.
ISBN 0-09-911450-X.
1. Demonology.
MH NUC77-89541

Baker, Roger, 1934-
Binding the Devil : exorcism past and present / Roger Baker. — New York : Hawthorn Books, 1975, c1974.
viii, 187 p. ; 21 cm.
Bibliography: p. [182]-183.
Includes index.
ISBN 0-8015-0640-9 : $7.95
1. Exorcism. I. Title.
BV873.E8B34 1975 133.4'27 74-22920
75 MARC

Baker, Roger, 1934-
Dolls and dolls' houses; a collector's introduction. With a foreword by Patrick Murray. London, Orbis Books [c1973]
64 p. illus. (part col.) 31 cm. £1.50 GB***
Bibliography: p. 15.
1. Dolls. 2. Doll-houses. I. Title.
NK4893.B34 745.59'22 74-158700
ISBN 0-85613-162-8 MARC

Baker, Roger Denio, 1902-
Human infection with fungi, actinomycetes and algae, by Roger Denio Baker and [others] Berlin, New York, Springer-Verlag, 1971.
xvi, 1191 p. illus. (part col.) 26 cm. DM140.30 GDB***
At head of title: The pathologic anatomy of mycoses.
Special ed. of Handbuch der speziellen pathologischen Anatomie und Histologie, III/5.
Includes bibliographies.
1. Medical mycology. 2. Mycosis. I. Title.
RC117.B34 1971 616.01'5 73-174042
ISBN 0-387-05140-6 (New York) MARC

Baker, Rollin Harold, 1916-
Records of mammals from Ecuador / by Rollin H. Baker. — East Lansing : Michigan State University, 1974.
p. 132-146 ; 24 cm. — (Publications of the Museum, Michigan State University : Biological series ; v. 5, no. 2)
Bibliography: p. 146.
$1.50
1. Mammals—Ecuador. I. Title. II. Series: Michigan. State University, East Lansing. Museum. Publications : Biological series ; v. 5, no. 2.
QH1.M58 vol. 5, no. 2 574'.08 s 74-624031
[QL725.E2] [599'.09'866] MARC

Baker, Rollo Clyde.
The early development of the ventral part of the neural plate of Amblystoma. 1927.
45 l. illus. 29 cm.
Typescript (carbon copy)
Thesis—University of Chicago.
Bibliography: leaves 44-45.
1. Ambystoma. 2. Neural tube. 3. Embryology—Amphibians. I. Title.
QL668.C2B23 73-157777
MARC

Baker, Ronald.
A guide to the United States patent and trademark literature, by R. Baker. London, National Reference Library of Science and Invention, 1972.
[3], 16 p. 25 cm. (National Reference Library of Science and Invention. Occasional publications) GB 72-12583
Includes index.
1. Patent literature. 2. Patents—United States. 3. Trade-marks—United States. I. Title. II. Series.
T210.B34 608'.7'73 74-168574
ISBN 0-902914-04-9 MARC

Baker, Ronald.
New and improved ... : inventors and inventions that have changed the modern world / R. Baker. — London : British Museum Publications Ltd. for the British Library, 1976.
168 p. : ill. ; 25 cm. GB***
At head of title: Science Reference Library.
Bibliography: p. 27-29.
Includes index.
ISBN 0-7141-0380-2 : £3.50
1. Inventions—History. 2. Patents. I. British Library. Science Reference Library. II. Title.
T15.B27 608'.7 77-355932
77 MARC

Baker, Ronald D.
see Career guidance for a new age. Boston, Houghton Mifflin [1973]

Baker, Ronald D.
see Supervision of applied training ... Westport, Conn., Greenwood Press, 1977.

Baker, Ronald Dee, 1947-
Factorization of graphs. [n.p.] 1975.
83 l.
Thesis--Ohio State University.
Bibliography: leaves 81-83.
1. Graphic methods. I. Title.
OU NUC77-89504

Baker, Ronald L
Folklore in the writings of Rowland E. Robinson, by Ronald L. Baker. Bowling Green, Ohio, Bowling Green University Popular Press [1973]
ix, 240 p. 24 cm.
Bibliography: p. 233-240.
1. Robinson, Rowland Evans, 1833-1900—Folk-lore, mythology. 2. Folk-lore, American—Vermont. I. Title.
PS2719.R68Z6 813'.4 74-186630
ISBN 0-87972-038-7; 0-87972-039-5 (pbk.) MARC

Baker, Ronald L
Indiana place names / Ronald L. Baker & Marvin Carmony. — Bloomington : Indiana University Press, c1975.
xxii, 196 p. : map (1 fold in pocket) ; 24 cm.
Bibliography: p. 187-192.
ISBN 0-253-14167-2 : $7.95
1. Names, Geographical—Indiana. 2. Indiana—History, Local. 3. English language in the United States—Pronunciation. 4. English language in the United States—Dialects—Indiana. I. Carmony, Marvin, joint author. II. Title.
F524.B34 1975 917.72 74-17915
75 MARC

Baker, Roscoe.
The American Legion and American foreign policy. Wetsport, Conn., Greenwood Press [1974, c1954]
329 p. 22 cm.
Originally presented as the author's thesis, Northwestern University, 1954.
Reprint of the ed. published by Bookman Associates, New York.
Bibliography: p. [287]-304.
1. American Legion. 2. United States—Foreign relations—20th century. I. Title.
[D570.A1B3 1974] 327.73 74-39
ISBN 0-8371-7360-4 MARC

Baker, Rowland G M
Elmbridge local acts of Parliament; a register, compiled by Rowland G. M. Baker. [Walton-on-Thames] Walton and Weybridge Local History Society, 1975.
35 p. 26 cm. (Paper. Walton and Weybridge Local History Society, no. 14)
1. Local government--Elmbridge, Eng.--History--Sources. I. Title.
NIC NUC77-89502

Baker, Rowland G M
Fire insurance wall plaques [by] Rowland G.M. Baker. [Walton-on-Thames] 1970.
14 p. illus. (Walton & Weybridge Local History Society. Paper, 7)
1. Insurance–Fire–Walton and Weybridge, Eng.
MH NUC73-59620

Baker, Roy Oscar.
Proteolytic enzymes in baby pig nutrition. [n.p.] 1959 [1967]
186 l. tables. 21 cm.
Thesis (Ph.D.)–Iowa State College.
Microfilm-xerography copy in 1967 by University Microfilms.
Bibliography: leaves 136-143.
1. Swine. Feeding and feeds. I. Title.
MnCS NUC73-9448

Baker, Roy V
Comparative performances of a stick machine and a bur machine-stripped cotton. [Washington, U.S. Govt. Print. Off., 1971]
16 p. illus. (U.S. Dept. of Agriculture. Technical bulletin no. 1437)
1. Cotton picking machinery. I. Title.
DNAL NUC73-41415

Baker, Roy V.
see Parnell, C B Particulate emissions of a cotton gin in the Texas stripper area. [Washington, U.S. Govt. Print. Off., 1973]

Baker, Roy V.
see Wanjura, D F Ginning of narrow-row cotton. Washington, 1975.

Baker, Russell, 1925-
The upside-down man / Russell Baker ; illustrated by Gahan Wilson. — New York : McGraw-Hill, c1977.
43 p. : ill. ; 26 cm.
SUMMARY: A mad scientist and a boy who can't do anything right team up to make a man.
ISBN 0-07-003356-0 : $5.95. ISBN 0-07-003357-9 lib. bdg. : $5.72
I. Wilson, Gahan. II. Title.
PZ7.B17498 Up [Fic] 77-6272
77 MARC

Baker, Russell, 1925-
see Better times. [New York, Dolphin Books] 1975.

Baker, Mrs. Russell S.
see Martin County Historical Society. Cemeteries in the Crane Naval depot... Evansville, Ind., 1966.

Baker, S. B. de C., ed.
see European Society for the Study of Drug Toxicity. Toxicological problems of drug combinations... [Amsterdam] Excerpta Medica, 1972.

Baker, Samm Sinclair.
Conscious happiness : how to get the most out of living / by Samm Sinclair Baker. — New York : Grosset & Dunlap, [1975]
337 p. ; 22 cm.
ISBN 0-448-11895-5 : $9.95
1. Success. 2. Happiness. I. Title.
BJ1611.B125 131'.3 75 75-24048 MARC

Baker, Samm Sinclair.
Introduction to art; a guide to the understanding and enjoyment of great masterpieces [by] Samm Sinclair Baker and Natalie Baker. London, Thames & Hudson, 1971.
[2], 221 p. (chiefly illus. (some col.), ports. (some col.)). 32 cm. £3.95 B 71-23428
1. Art appreciation. 2. Art—Psychology. I. Baker, Natalie, joint author. II. Title.
N7477.B35 1971 709'.4 73-162321
ISBN 0-500-23152-4 MARC

Baker, Samm Sinclair.
The permissible lie; the inside truth about advertising. London, Peter Owen [c1968]
236 p. 22 cm.
1. Advertising—U.S. I. Title.
TxDaM NUC75-31145

Baker, Samm Sinclair.
The permissible lie; the inside truth about advertising. Boston, Beacon [1971, c1968]
236 p. 22 cm.
1. Advertising—U.S. I. Title.
MnU MiU NUC73-59613

Baker, Samm Sinclair.
Your key to creative thinking; how to get more and better ideas [by] Samm S. Baker. New York, Bantam Books [1970, c1962]
xi, 276 p. illus. 18 cm. (A Bantam book, P5780)
1. Creative thinking (Education) I. Title.
NTR NUC73-59619

Baker, Samm Sinclair, joint author.
see Miller, Susan Mary. Straight talk to parents ... New York, Stein and Day, 1976.

Baker, Samm Sinclair, joint author
see Smith, James Walter, 1926- "Doctor, make me beautiful!" New York, McKay [1973]

Baker, Samm Sinclair, joint author
see Stillman, Irwin Maxwell. Dr. Stillman's 14-day shape-up program... New York, Delacorte Press [1974]

Baker, Samm Sinclair
see Stillman, Irwin Maxwell. The doctor's quick teenage diet. New York, Paperback Library [1972, c1971]

Baker, Samuel E.
see Swift, Lloyd W Lower water temperatures... Asheville, N.C., 1973.

Baker, Samuel R., joint author
see Stitt, Hubert J International taxation and Canadian tax reform. Don Mills, Ont. [c1972]

Baker, Sir Samuel White, 1821-1893.
Cast up by the sea. New York, A. L. Burt [n. d.]
426 p.
I. Title.
UU NUC76-18081

Baker, Sir Samuel White, 1821-1893
see Baker, Anne. Morning Star... London, Kimber, 1972.

Baker, Sara Josephine, 1873-1945.
Fighting for life. New York, Arno Press, 1974 [c1939]
264 p. illus. 23 cm. (Children and youth: social problems and social policy)
Reprint of the ed. published by Macmillan, New York.
1. Baker, Sara Josephine, 1873-1945. 2. Child welfare—New York (City) 3. New York (City)—Charities. I. Title. II. Series.
HV28.B3A3 1974 362.7'092'4 [B] 74-1664
ISBN 0-405-05945-0 MARC

Baker, Sarah.
The Saranac Valley. Sarah Baker: writer. Luthera Edie: illustrator. Patricia Allinson: researcher. [n.p., 1970]
2 v. illus., maps, ports. 28 cm.
Contents: v. 1.-The pioneers. v. 2.-The boom days.
1. Saranac, N.Y.-Hist. 2. Saranac River Valley, N.Y.-Hist. I. Title.
WHi N NUC74-122393

Baker, Scott.
Evidence in a nutshell. London, Sweet & Maxwell, 1962.
xiv, 84 p. 19 cm. (Nutshell series)
1. Evidence (Law)—Great Britain. I. Title.
KD7499.3.B33 347'.42'06 74-184510 MARC

Baker, Sharon J
Public affairs directory, 1973. Compiled and edited by Sharon J. Baker. Marshall, Minn., Center for Community Services, Southwest Minnesota State College [1974?]
xx, 478 p. 28 cm.
1. Social service. Minnesota. Direct. 2. Local officials and employees. Minnesota. Direct. I. Southwest Minnesota State College. Center for Community Services. II. Title.
MnU NUC75-71104

Baker, Shelton Dennis, 1945- joint author.
see Stahl, Robert John, 1945- The status of population education in Florida ... Gainesville, P. K. Yonge Laboratory School, College of Education, University of Florida, c1976.

Baker, Sheridan Warner, 1918- The complete stylist
see Baker, Sheridan Warner, 1918- Problems in exposition. New York, Crowell [1972]

Baker, Sheridan Warner, 1918-
The complete stylist and handbook / Sheridan Baker. — New York : Crowell, c 1976.
xvi, 560 p. ; 23 cm.
Previous editions published in 1966 and 1972 under title: The complete stylist.
Includes index.
ISBN 0-690-00801-5
1. English language—Rhetoric. I. Title.
PE1408.B283 1976 808'.042 75 75-29332 MARC

Baker, Sheridan Warner, 1918- comp.
The Crowell college reader [compiled by] Sheridan Baker [and] David B. Hamilton. New York, Crowell [1974]
xiv, 578 p. 24 cm.
1. College readers. I. Hamilton, David B., joint comp. II. Title.
PE1122.B33 808'.04275 74-844
ISBN 0-690-00170-3 MARC

Baker, Sheridan Warner, 1918-
The essayist / Sheridan Baker. — 3d ed. — New York : Crowell, c1977.
xii, 385 p. ; 23 cm.
ISBN 0-690-00874-0 : $5.50
1. English language—Rhetoric. 2. American essays. 3. English essays. I. Title.
PE1417.B28 1977 808.4 76 76-40465 MARC

Baker, Sheridan Warner, 1918-
The new English, by Sheridan Baker. [Washington] Council for Basic Education [1971]
11 p. 22 cm. (Council for Basic Education. Occasional papers, no. 12)
Cover title.
Bibliography: p. 9-11.
1. English language—Study and teaching. I. Title. II. Series.
PE1065.B24 420'.7 74-191577 MARC

Baker, Sheridan Warner, 1918-
The practical stylist [by] Sheridan Baker. 3d ed. New York, Crowell [1973]
x, 182 p. 23 cm.
1. English language—Rhetoric. I. Title.
PE1408.B285 1973 808'.042 72-10863
ISBN 0-690-65002-7 ; 0-690-65001-9 (paper) MARC

Baker, Sheridan Warner, 1918-
The practical stylist / Sheridan Baker. — 4th ed. — New York : Crowell, c1977.
x, 198 p. ; 23 cm.
Includes index.
ISBN 0-690-00873-2 : $4.95
1. English language—Rhetoric. I. Title.
PE1408.B283 1977 808'.042 76 76-26601 MARC

Baker, Sheridan Warner, 1918- The practical stylist
see Baker, Sheridan Warner, 1918- Problems in exposition. New York, Crowell [1972]

Baker, Sheridan Warner, 1918-
Problems in exposition; supplementary exercises for The complete stylist and The practical stylist [by] Sheridan Baker [and] Dwight Stevenson. New York, Crowell [1972]
154 p. 28 cm.
1. English language—Rhetoric. 2. English language—Composition and exercises. I. Stevenson, Dwight Ward, 1933- joint author. II. Baker, Sheridan Warner, 1918- The complete stylist. III. Baker, Sheridan Warner, 1918- The practical stylist. IV. Title.
NcRS NUC75-29954

Baker, Sheridan Warner, 1918- comp.
see Fielding, Henry, 1707-1754. Tom Jones... New York, Norton [1973]

Baker, Sima.
The Glenn County story: days past and present, by Sima Baker [and] Florence Ewing. Willows, Calif., Glenn County School Office, 1968.
viii, 144 p. illus., map. 28 cm.
Bibliography: p. 143-144.
1. Glenn Co., Calif-History. I. Ewing, Florence, joint author. II. Title.
CNoS NUC74-122402

Baker, Simon.
The look of our land; an airphoto atlas of the rural United States [compiled by Simon Baker and Henry W. Dill, Jr. Washington] U. S. Dept. of Agriculture, Economic Research Service; [for sale by the Supt. of Docs., U. S. Govt. Print. Off., 1970-
v. illus., maps. 24 x 29 cm. (Agriculture handbook no. 372, 406 $0.60 (v. [1]) varies
Cover title.
Updates Agriculture handbook no. 153: Land use and its patterns in the United States, by F. J. Marschner.
Description of each area reproduced from Agriculture handbook no. 296: Land resource regions and major land resource areas of the United States, by Morris E. Austin.
Includes bibliographies.
CONTENTS: A-C. The Far West.—D-E. The East and South.—K-M. North Central.—N-U. The mountains and deserts.
1. Land—United States. I. Dill, Henry W., 1912- joint author. II. Marschner, Francis Joseph, 1882- Land use and its patterns in the United States. III. Austin, Morris E. Land resource regions and major land resource areas of the United States. IV. Title. V. Series: United States. Dept. of Agriculture. Agriculture handbook no. 372 [etc.]
HD205 1970.B35 631.4'9'73 rev 2 72-606046 MARC

Baker, Simon.
see Coastal development and areas of environmental concern ... Raleigh, UNC Sea Grant Program, N. C. State University, 1975.

Baker, Stanley.
Milk to market: forty years of milk marketing. London, Heinemann, 1973.
xiv, 282, [16] p. illus., facsims., map, ports. 23 cm. £3.90 GB 73-19295
Includes bibliographical references and index.
1. Great Britain. Milk Marketing Board. 2. Milk trade—Great Britain. I. Title.
HD9282.G7B34 381'.41'710942 74-161129
ISBN 0-434-90085-0 MARC

Baker, Stanley, joint author,
see Katzen, Brian. Looking at Cape Town. Cape Town, H. Timmins, 1972.

Baker, Stanley Beckwith.
The development of an instrument to measure school counselor attitudes toward client problems on a status quo-change agent scale. Buffalo, 1971.
159 l.
Thesis (Ph.D.)—State University of New York at Buffalo.
1. Counseling. I. Title.
NBuU NUC73-41422

Baker, Stanley Justice
see
Stanley-Baker, Justice.

Baker, Stanley L
The collector's book of railroadiana / by Stanley L. Baker and Virginia Brainard Kunz ; photos. by Joan Larson Kelly. — New York : Hawthorn Books, c1976.
xii, 240 p., [4] leaves of plates : ill. ; 29 cm.
Bibliography: p. 229-230.
Includes index.
ISBN 0-8015-6218-X : $16.95
1. Railroads—Equipment and supplies—Collectors and collecting. 2. Railroads—History. I. Kunz, Virginia Brainard, joint author. II. Title.
TF347.B34 1976 385'.075 75-41800
76[r77]rev MARC

Baker, Stanley L
The railroadiana collector's price guide / by Stanley L. Baker ; photos. by Joan Larson Kelley and Stanley L. Baker. — New York : Hawthorn Books, c1977.
xvi, 128 p. : ill. ; 21 cm.
ISBN 0-8015-6219-8 : $4.95 ($5.75 Can)
1. Railroads—Equipment and supplies—Collectors and collecting. I. Title.
TF347.B35 1977 385'.22'075 76-41977
77 MARC

Baker, Stephen.
How to live with a neurotic dog. Cartoons by Eric Gurney. New York, Essandess Special Editions, 1967.
1 v. (chiefly illus.) 19 cm.
1. Dogs—Anecdotes, facetiae, satire, etc. I. Title.
LNT NUC76-70991

Baker, Stephen D., joint comp.
see Wilson, Jerry D comp. Physical science... Lexington, Mass., Heath [1974]

Baker, Stephen Theodore.
An investigation of serological interrelationships among nine Changuinola group arboviruses. [New Haven, 1973]
25, [11] l. 29 cm.
Thesis (M.D.) (M.P.H.)—Yale University.
Bibliography: leaves 22-25.
1. Arthropodborne viruses. 2. Serology. I. Title.
CtY NUC74-126561

Baker, Steve.
A brief history of Florence. [Florence, S.C.] 1974.
[6], 14 p. illus.
1. Florence, S.C.—History.
ScU NUC76-18056

Baker, Steven
see La Proliferazione delle armi nucleari. Bologna : Il mulino, [1975]

[Baker, Steven G]
Catawba Indian trade pottery of the historic period. [Columbia, S.C., Columbia Museum of Art, 1973]
[9] p. (fold.) illus.
This brochure was published to accompany an exhibition of historic Catawba Indian trade pottery.
1. Pottery. 2. Indians of North America—Pottery. 3. Catawba Indians. I. Columbia, S.C. Museum of Art.
ScU NUC75-17386

Baker, Steven G
A house on Cambridge Hill (38GN2): An excavation report. Columbia, S.C., Institute of Archeology and Anthropology, University of South Carolina, 1972.
iv, 56 l. illus., maps. (Research manuscript series no. 27)
"References cited": leaves 55-56.
1. Ninety Six, S.C.—Antiquities. I. Title. II. Series: South Carolina. University. Institute of Archeology and Anthropology. Research manuscript series, no. 27.
ScU NUC75-31183

Baker, Steven G
The working draft of the historic Catawba peoples; exploratory perspectives in ethnohistory and archaeology, Steven G. Baker. Columbia, S.C., Department of History, University of South Carolina, c1975.
xvi, 225 l. ill. 28 cm.
Bibliography: leaves 214-225.
1. Indians of North America--South Carolina--History. 2. Catawba Indians.
ScU NUC77-89505

Baker, Steven J
Commercial nuclear power and nuclear proliferation, Steven J. Baker. Ithaca, Cornell University, 1975.
66 p. 28 cm. (Cornell University. Peace Studies Program. Occasional papers, no. 5)
Includes bibliographical references.
1. Atomic power industry. I. Title. II. Series.
MiU-L NUC77-89506

Baker, Stewart A comp.
Ancients and moderns; an anthology of poetry. Edited by Stewart A. Baker. New York, Harper & Row [c1971]
xiv, 352 p. 21 cm.
1. American poetry—Collections. 2. English poetry—Collections. I. Title.
OU NUC73-41451

Baker, Stewart A
The brief epic: studies in the style and structure of the genre of Paradise regained. [New Haven, Conn., 1964, 1971]
330 l.
Thesis—Yale University.
Bibliography: leaves 321-330.
Microfilm copy of typescript. Ann Arbor, Mich., University Microfilms, 1971. 1 reel. 35 mm.
1. Milton, John, 1608-1674. Paradise regained. I. Title.
IU NUC74-1295

Baker, Susan.
Guiding fours and fives in musical experiences [by] Susan Baker, Glennella Key [and] Talmadge Butler. Nashville, Convention Press [c1972]
152 p. illus.
1. Music—Instruction and study—Juvenile. I. Key, Glennella. II. Butler, Talmadge. III. Title.
TxFS InAndC-T KyLoS NUC74-1344

Baker, Susan.
"She's a Jim-Dandy," by Susan Baker. [Washington, D.C., Some fo Us Press, 1973?]
32 p. illus. 22 cm.
One of an edition of 500 copies.
I. Title.
RPB NUC75-17367

Baker, Susan P
Injury control; accident prevention and other approaches to reduction of injury. Washington, D.C., Insurance Institute for Highway Safety [1972]
32 p. 23 cm.
A chapter from Preventive Medicine and Public Health, 10th ed.
1. Accidents—Prevention. I. Title. II. Title: Preventive Medicine and Public Health.
ViU-M NUC74-1298

Baker, T.A., joint author
see Ryder, J F The extent and rate of joint movements in modern buildings. Garston, Eng., 1971.

Baker, T. G.
see Zuckerman, Solly, Sir, 1904- ed. The ovary. 2d ed. New York, Academic Press, 1977-

Baker, T H W
Performance characteristics of the geotechnical cold rooms, by T.H.W. Baker, R.M.W. Frederking, D.R. Hoffman. Ottawa, Division of Building Research, NRC, 1976.
[19] p. ill. (Building research note, no. 109)
Cover title.
Bibliography: p. 5.
CaOTP NUC77-89503

Baker, T. J., ed.
see Modin, Helfrid, 1916- Metallurgical microscopy. New York, Wiley [1973]

Baker, T Lindsay.
The early history of Panna Maria, Texas / T. Lindsay Baker. — Lubbock : Texas Tech Press, 1975.
69 p. : ill. ; 26 cm. — (Graduate studies - Texas Tech University ; no. 9)
Bibliography: p. 58-63.
Includes index.
$2.00
1. Polish Americans—Texas—Panna Maria—History. 2. Panna Maria, Tex.—History. I. Title. II. Series: Texas Tech University. Graduate studies ; no. 9.
F394.P192B34 976.4'444 76-620780
76 MARC

Baker, T. Lindsay
see Water for the Southwest... New York, American Society of Civil Engineers, 1973.

Baker, Terence J
Employment relationships in Irish counties / Terence J. Baker and Miceal Ross. — Dublin : Economic and Social Research Institute, 1975.
69 p. : 1 ill. ; 24 cm. — (Paper - Economic and Social Research Institute ; no. 81) Ir***
Bibliography: p. 67.
ISBN 0-901809-95-0 : £2.00
1. Labor supply—Ireland—Mathematical models. 2. Employment forecasting—Ireland—Mathematical models. I. Ross, Miceal, joint author. II. Title. III. Series: Economic and Social Research Institute. Paper ; no. 81.
HC257.I6E3 no. 81 330.9'415 s 75-331464
[HD5768.I7] 75 MARC

Baker, Terence J
Regional employment patterns in the Republic Of Ireland, by T. J. Baker. Dublin, Economic Research Institute, 1966.
39 p. 28 cm. (Economic Research Institute. Paper no. 32)
Includes bibliographical references.
1. Labor and laboring classes—Ireland. I. Title. II. Series: Economic and Social Research Institute. Paper no. 32.
HC257.I 6E3 no. 32 330.9'415 s 74-185242
[HD5768.I 6] [331.1'1'09415] MARC

Baker, Terence J
A study of the Irish cattle and beef industries [by] Terence J. Baker, Robert O'Connor [and] Rory Dunne. Dublin, Economic and Social Research Institute, 1973.
141 p. illus. 25 cm. (Economic and Social Research Institute. Paper no. 72) £2.00
Includes bibliographical references.
1. Meat industry and trade—Ireland. I. O'Connor, Robert, joint author. II. Dunne, Rory, joint author. III. Title. IV. Series.
HC257.I 6E3 no. 72 330.9'415 s 74-153792
[HD9433.I 52] [338.1'7'62009415] MARC

Baker, Terry, joint author
see Basili, Victor Robert, 1940- Structured programming ; tutorial. Long Beach, Calif., 1975.

Baker, Thelma S comp.
The urbanization of man; a social science perspective, compiled and edited by Thelma S. Baker. Berkeley, Calif., McCutchan Pub. Corp. [c1972]
ix, 346 p. illus. 23 cm.
Bibliography: p. 343-346.
1. Urbanization—Addresses, essays, lectures. 2. Cities and towns—History—Addresses, essays, lectures. 3. Social sciences—Addresses, essays, lectures. I. Title.
HT151.B26 301.36 72-5704
ISBN 0-8211-0122-6 MARC

Baker, Thelma S comp.
The urbanization of man; a social science perspective, compiled and edited by Thelma S. Baker. [2d ed.] revised by Theodore E. Kiffer. Berkeley, Ca., McCutchan Pub. Corp., 1975.
ix, 372 p. ill. 23 cm.
Bibliography: p. 369-372.
ISBN 0-8211-0122-6.
1. Urbanization--Addresses, essays, lectures. 2. Cities and towns--History--Addresses, essays, lectures. 3. Social sciences--Addresses, essays, lectures. I. Kiffer, Theodore Edwin, 1925- II. Title.
InU NUC77-89499

Baker, Theodore, 1851–1934.
Über die Musik der nordamerikanischen Wilden. Leipzig, Breitkopf & Härtel, 1882 [New York, AMS Press, 1973]
iv, 82 p. illus. 23 cm. $15.00
Thesis—Leipzig.
"Notenbeilagen": p. [59]–81.
1. Indians of North America—Music. I. Title.
ML3557.B2 1973 781.7'701 71–38496
ISBN 0–404–08337–4 MARC

Baker, Theodore Paul, 1949-
Computational complexity and nondeterminism in flowchart programs. [Ithaca, N. Y.] 1974.
vii, 122 l. 29 cm.
Bibliography: leaves 120-122.
Thesis (Ph. D.)–Cornell University.
1. Electronic digital computers–Programming. 2. Numerical calculations. 3. Flow charts. I. Title.
NIC NUC76-18080

Baker, Therese Elzas, 1939-
The weakening of authoritarianism: a study of black and white. [n.p.] 1973.
159 l.
Thesis (Ph. D.)–University of Chicago.
1. Authoritarianism. 2. College students–U.S. 3. Negro students. I. Title.
ICU NUC75-17366

Baker, Therese Elzas, 1939-
see Women and education. Chicago, University of Chicago, 1972.

Baker, Thomas.
Watershed at the Rivergate; 1,400 vs. 250,000. Sturgis, Mich., 1973.
120 p.
1. Lutheran Church–Missouri Synod. I. Title.
MoSCS NUC74-122292

Baker, Thomas, fl. 1700-1709. An act at Oxford. 1973
see Veen, Harm Reijudend Sient jo van der, 1894- Jewish characters in eighteenth century English fiction and drama (1935)... [New York] Ktav Pub. House, 1973.

Baker, Thomas Eugene, 1944-
Human rights in Missouri; the legislative, judicial and administrative development of black liberties. [Columbia] 1975.
421 l. ill.
Thesis (Ph. D.)--University of Missouri.
Vita.
Includes bibliography.
MoU NUC77-89729

Baker, Thomas Eugene, 1944-
Human rights in Missouri; the legislative, judicial and administrative development of Black liberties, by Thomas Eugene Baker. [n. p.] 1975.
iv, 421 l. maps.
Thesis--University of Missouri.
Vita.
Bibliography: leaves 415-421.
Photocopy of typescript. Ann Arbor, Mich., University Microfilms, 1976. 22 cm.
1. Afro-Americans--Civil rights. 2. Civil rights--Missouri. I. Title.
IEdS NUC77-89746

Baker, Thomas Eugene, 1944-
Human rights in Missouri; the legislative, judicial and administrative development of black liberties. [Columbia] 1975.
421 l. ill.
Thesis (Ph. D.)--University of Missouri.
Microfilm copy.
Vita.
Includes bibliography.
MoU NUC77-89730

Baker, Thomas Eugene, 1944-
see Campbell, Rex R Negroes in Missouri—1970... [Jefferson City] Missouri Commission on Human Rights, 1972.

Baker, Thomas Hart Benton, b. 1838.
Memoirs of Thomas H. B. Baker...written in his own handwriting, from 1880 to 1890. This book also contains miscellaneous autobiographies and autographs. Copied in March, 1966, by Mrs. Thomas (Mildred) Skelley. New Albany, Ind. [Mrs. T. M. Skelley] 1966.
71, 38 l. ports. 30 cm.
1. Baker family. 2. Pekin, Ind. —Geneal. 3. Country reminiscences, Physicians.
NN NUC74-33175

Baker, Trudy.
The coffee tea or me girls get away from it all [by] Trudy Baker and Rachel Jones. New York, Grosset & Dunlap [1974]
229 p. 22 cm. $6.95
1. Air lines—Flight attendants—Personal narratives. I. Jones, Rachel, joint author. II. Title.
HD6073.A43B34 910'.4 73-15125
ISBN 0-448-11560-3 74[r76]rev MARC

Baker, Trudy.
The coffee tea or me girls lay it on the line. Trudy Baker and Rachel Jones. Bantam ed. New York, Bantam Books, 1973.
274 p. 18 cm.
1. Single women—Conduct of life. 2. Sex instruction for women. I. Jones, Rachel, joint author. II. Title.
MB NUC76-70987

Baker, V. R.
see Dudley, William W Analysis of aquifer response for the Sterling Event. [Oak Ridge, Tenn., U.S. Atomic Energy Commission, Technical Information Center] 1973.

Baker, Van Roy, 1925-
Dryden's military imagery. [New York] 1968 [c1971]
ii, 211 l. 29 cm.
Thesis—Columbia University.
Bibliography: leaves 206-211.
1. Dryden, John, 1631-1700. I. Title.
NNC NUC73-126364

Baker, Veronica E., joint author.
see Padilla, Geraldine V. Interacting with dying patients ... Duarte, Calif., City of Hope National Medical Center, Division of Nursing, 1975.

Baker, Victor R
Flood hazards along the Balcones Escarpment in central Texas : alternative approaches to their recognition, mapping, and management / by Victor R. Baker. — Austin : Bureau of Economic Geology, University of Texas at Austin, 1975.
22 p. : ill. ; 28 cm. — (Geological circular ; 75-5)
Bibliography: p. [20]-22.
1. Floods—Texas. 2. Flood forecasting—Maps. I. Title. II. Series: Texas. University at Austin. Bureau of Economic Geology. Geological circular ; 75-5.
TN24.T4T38 no. 75-5 553'.09764 s 76-620744
[GB1399.4.T4] 76 MARC

Baker, Victor R
Paleohydrology and sedimentology of Lake Missoula flooding in eastern Washington [by] Victor R. Baker. [Boulder, Colo.] Geological Society of America [1973]
vii, 79 p. illus. 24 cm. (Geological Society of America. Special paper 144)
Bibliography: p. 69–73.
1. Floods—Washington (State) 2. Paleolimnology—Washington (State) 3. Sediments (Geology)—Washington (State) I. Title. II. Series.
GB1225.W3B34 551.4 72–89463
ISBN 0–8137–2144–X MARC

Baker, Victor R.
see Austin Geological Society. Field trip: urban flooding and slope stability. [Austin, 1973]

Baker, Virginia, 1910–
Something new [by] Virginia Baker [and] James Rudder. Pittsburgh, Pa., Stanwix House [c1972]
225 p. col. illus. 24 cm. (Functional basic reading series)
SUMMARY: The activities of a group of boys and girls and their families at home, on vacation, and in their community.
1. Readers—1950– [1. Readers] I. Rudder, James, joint author. II. Title. III. Series.
PE1119.B28 1972 428'.6 78–175605
ISBN 0–87076–246–X MARC

Baker, Virginia MacLynne Rudder, 1944-
Linguistic and ontological aspects of temporal becoming, Nashville, [c1972]
v, 229 l. 28 cm.
Thesis (Ph.D.)—Vanderbilt University, 1972.
Bibliography: leaves 220-229.
TNJ NUC76-70995

Baker, W. Donald
see Louder, Darrell E Some interesting limnological aspects of Fontana Reservoir... Raleigh, N. C., Wildlife Resources Commission, 1966.

Baker, W. H.
see Monmouthshire Record Office. Guide to Monmouthshire Record Office. Newport [Monmouthshire, Eng.] 1959.

Baker, W. H.
see also
Baker, William Henry.

Baker, W. J. Bryan. Handbook of selected data for Mississippi
see Brooks, Sandra. Handbook of selected data for Mississippi. [Rev. and expanded] Jackson, Mississippi Research and Development Center, 1973.

Baker, W. J. Bryan. Handbook of selected data for Mississippi.
see Brooks, Sandra. Handbook of selected data for Mississippi. [Rev.]. Jackson, Mississippi Research & Development Center, 1976.

Baker, W K
Electrodialytic treatment of irrigation drainage water preliminary study, by W. K. Baker, S. A. Weiner [and] E. D. Howe. Richmond, Calif., Sea Water Conversion Laboratory, 1964.
University of California. Water Resources Center contribution no. 89.
On cover: Saline water conversion research.
Bibliography: p. 34.
v l., 34 p. illus. 28 cm. (University of California. Sea Water Conversion Laboratory. Report no. 64–2)
1. Saline water conversion — Electrodialysis process. 2. Drainage—California—San Joaquin Valley. 3. Irrigation water. I. Weiner, S. A., joint author. II. Howe, Everett Dumser, 1903– joint author. III. Title. IV. Title: Saline water conversion research. V. Series: California. University. Sea Water Conversion Laboratory. Report no. 64–2. VI. Series: California. University. Water Resources Center. Contribution no. 89.
GB705.C2C27 no. 64–2 64–65193
[TD480.5]

Baker, W. M., joint author
see Crowe, R B The tourist and outdoor recreation climate of Ontario. Toronto, Dept. of the Environment, 1973-

Baker, Wallace J
Bishops of Ohio, 1819-1968, Protestant Episcopal Church, Diocese of Ohio, by Wallace J. Baker. [Painesville, Ohio, Printed by Painesville Pub. Co.] 1968.
55 p. illus.
1. Protestant Episcopal Church in the United States–Ohio. 2. Protestant Episcopal Church in the United States–Biog.
MH NUC73-59624

Baker, Wallace R., joint author
see Saltoun, André M French turnover taxes... [Chicago, Baker, McKenzie & Hightower, 1964?]

Baker, Walter, 1929-
The place of the private agency in the administration of government policies. A case study: the Ontario children's aid system, 1893-1965. Kingston, Ont., c1966.
iii, 344 l.
Thesis—Queen's University.
Vita.
Bibliography: leaves 329-344. Bibliographical footnotes.
Microfilm. 1 reel. 35 mm.
1. Child welfare—Ontario. I. Title.
CaBVaU NUC74-124853

Baker, Walter J.
see New York (State). Dept. of Taxation and Finance. New York State income tax facts in brief. [Albany, 1972]

Baker, Walter Maurice, 1900-
A study of the vocabulary load of six arithmetic texts approved for use in Kentucky high schools. [Lexington, Ky.] 1932 [1973]
98 l.
Thesis—University of Kentucky.
Bibliography: leaf 48.
Vita.
Microfilm copy. Lexington, Ky., M.I. King Library, University of Kentucky, 1973. 1 reel. 35 mm.
IU NUC74-122633

Baker, Wanda K.
see California. Legislature. Assembly. Symposium on Services to Children and Youth. California children, who cares? ... Sacramento, Assembly Office of Research, California Legislature, 1974.

Baker, Wayne A 1936-
The toy soldiers; [by] Wayne A. Baker. New York, Vantage Press [1973]
230 p.
I. Title.
MoWgW NUC76-71047

Baker, Wesley C
You belong in the Bible! : Introducing the Wayne Biblical experience / by Wesley C. Baker. — Corte Madera, Calif. : Omega Books, c1976.
96 p. ; 22 cm.
ISBN 0-89353-020-4
1. Bible—Study. I. Title.
BS600.2.B25 220'.07 76-42600
77 MARC

Baker, Wilfred E
Explosions in air, by Wilfred E. Baker. Austin, University of Texas Press [1973]
xiv, 268 p. illus. (3 fold. in pocket) 26 cm.
Bibliography: p. [253]-266.
1. Shock waves. 2. Explosions. 3. Blast effect. I. Title.
QC168.B33 533'.62'93 72-11725
ISBN 0-292-72003-3 MARC

Baker, Wilfred E
Similarity methods in engineering dynamics: theory and practice of scale modeling [by] Wilfred E. Baker, Peter S. Westine, and Franklin T. Dodge. Rochelle Park, N. J., Spartan Books; [distributed by] Hayden Book Co. [1973]
396 p. illus. 24 cm.
Bibliography: p. 379-390.
1. Dynamics. 2. Engineering models. I. Westine, Peter S., joint author. II. Dodge, Franklin T., joint author. III. Title.
TA352.B34 620.1'04'0184 72-75715
ISBN 0-87671-564-1 MARC

Baker, Will, 1944-
Stone dawn : an antediluvian tale / Will Baker ; cover drawing by William P. Wiley. — Santa Barbara CA. : Capra Press, 1975.
34 p. : ill. ; 18 cm. — (Capra chapbook series ; no. 36)
ISBN 0-88496-045-5 : $10.00. ISBN 0-88496-046-3 pbk. : $2.50
I. Title.
PZ4.B16972 Daw 813'.5'4 75-31661
[PS3552.A435] 75 MARC

Baker, Willard D.
see Zodin, Robert H Report of sedimentation survey: Lake Daniel... Temple, Tex., U.S. Dept. of Agriculture, 1970.

Baker, William.
George Eliot and Hebrew, some source materials. Cincinnati, Library of Hebrew Union College-Jewish Institute of Religion, 1976.
75-84 p. ill. 26 cm.
Offprint from Studies in Bibliography and Booklore, v. 11, 1976.
1. Eliot, George, pseud., i.e. Marian Evans, afterwards Cross, 1819-1880. I. Title.
OCH NUC77-89731

Baker, William.
George Eliot and Judaism / by William Baker. — Salzburg : Institut für Englische Sprache und Literatur, Universität Salzburg, 1975.
iii, 270 p. ; 21 cm. — (Romantic reassessment ; 45) (Salzburg studies in English literature) Au***
Revised and rewritten version of the author's thesis for the degree of Master of Philosophy, University of London, 1970.
Bibliography: p. 246-270.
S280.00
1. Eliot, George, pseud., i.e. Marian Evans afterwards Cross, 1819-1880—Sources. 2. Judaism in literature. I. Title. II. Series. III. Series: Salzburg studies in English literature.
PR4686.B3 1975 823'.8 76-350963
76 MARC

Baker, William.
Harold Pinter [by] William Baker and Stephen Ely Tabachnick. Edinburgh, Oliver & Boyd, 1973.
[7], 156 p. 19 cm. (Modern writers) £1.50 GB 73-26866
Bibliography: p. 151-156.
1. Pinter, Harold, 1930- —Criticism and interpretation. I. Tabachnick, Stephen Ely, joint author. II. Title.
PR6066.I 53Z595 822'.9'14 73-179382
ISBN 0-05-002708-5 ; 0-05-002707-7 (pbk.) MARC

Baker, William.
Harold Pinter [by] William Baker and Stephen Ely Tabachnick. New York, Barnes & Noble [1973]
[7], 156 p. 19 cm. (Modern writers)
Bibliography: p. 151-156.
1. Pinter, Harold, 1930- —Criticism and interpretation. I. Tabachnick, Stephen Ely, joint author. II. Title.
UU NUC76-70927

Baker, William.
see Critics on George Eliot. London, Allen and Unwin, 1973.

Baker, William.
see Eliot, George, pseud., i.e., Maria Evans, afterwards Cross, 1819-1880. Some George Eliot notebooks ... Salzburg, Institut für Englisch Sprache und Literatur, Universität Salzburg, 1976-

Baker, William, 1934- joint author
see Barnes, Charles. 120 needlepoint design projects. New York : Crown Publishers, [1974]

Baker, William A
The engine powered vessel; from paddle-wheeler to nuclear ship [by] W. A. Baker [and] Tre tryckare. New York, Grosset & Dunlap [1965]
267 p. illus. (part col.) ports. 26 cm.
Bibliography: p. 266-267.
1. Ships. I. Tre tryckare, Cagner & Co., Gothenburg, Sweden. II. Title.
VM315.B3 387.24 65-21508
MARC

Baker, William A
Maine shipbuilding : a bibliographical guide / compiled by William A. Baker. — Portland : Maine Historical Society, 1974.
22 p. ; 26 cm. — (Maine history bibliographical guide series)
Includes index.
1. Ship-building — Maine — History — Bibliography. 2. Ships, Wooden—History—Bibliography. 3. Maine—History—Bibliography. I. Maine Historical Society. II. Title. III. Series.
Z6834.S5B3 75-302507
016.3384'7'6238207409741 MARC

Baker, William A
A maritime history of Bath, Maine and the Kennebec River region. Bath, Marine Research Society of Bath, 1973.
2 v. (xviii, 1160 p.) illus. 24 cm.
Bibliography: p. [1061]-1067.
1. Ship-building—Bath, Me.—History. 2. Ship-building—Kennebec Valley—History. 3. Shipping—Bath, Me.—History. 4. Shipping—Kennebec Valley—History. 5. Bath, Me.—History. I. Marine Research Society of Bath. II. Title.
VM25.B37B34 387'.009741'85 73-85867
74[r75]rev MARC

Baker, William A.
see The Atlantic world of Robert G. Albion. 1st ed. Middletown, Conn., Wesleyan University Press, [1975]

Baker, William A., joint author.
see Bockstoce, John R. Steam whaling in the western Arctic. New Bedford, Mass., Old Dartmouth Historical Society, 1977.

Baker, William Calvin, 1933-
An analysis of editorial attitudes of selected Louisiana daily newspapers toward topics related to public education, 1950-1969 ... [n.p.] 1971.
xiii, 225 l. 29 cm.
Thesis (Ed.D.)—Louisiana State University, Baton Rouge.
Vita.
Bibliography: leaves [185]-216.
1. Editorials. 2. Newspapers—Louisiana. 3. Education—Louisiana. I. Title.
LU NUC73-126363

Baker, William D
Reading and writing skills. 3d ed. New York, McGraw-Hill [c1971]
ix, 346 p.
1. English language—Rhetoric. I. Title.
NSyU NUC73-41420

Baker, William D
Reading skills [by] William D. Baker. 2d ed. Englewood Cliffs, N. J., Prentice-Hall [1974]
127 p. 23 cm. $2.95
1. Reading. I. Title.
LB1050.B3 1974 428'.4'3 73-17161
ISBN 0-13-762062-4 MARC

Baker, William F 1928-
Running her easting down; a documentary of the development and history of the British tea clippers, culminating with the building of the Cutty Sark, by William F. Baker. Caldwell, Idaho, Caxton, 1974.
xiv, 170 p. illus. 30 cm. $14.95
Bibliography: p. [167]-168.
1. Cutty Sark (Clipper-ship) 2. Tea trade—Great Britain—History. 3. Clipper-ships—History. I. Title.
VM395.C8B34 387.2'2 72-97063
ISBN 0-87004-238-6 MARC

Baker, William Gary.
A history of the Security Mutual Life Insurance Company, 1895-1971, by Wm. Gary Baker. Lincoln, Neb., Baker, 1974, cover 1975.
xii, 267 l. ill.
Thesis--University of Nebraska.
Bibliography: leaves [263]-267.
1. Security Mutual Life Insurance Co., Lincoln, Neb. I. Title.
NbU NUC77-89738

Baker, William Harry.
Worthy of death. Chicago, Moody Press [c1973]
158 p. (Moody evangelical focus)
CLamB NUC76-70998

Baker, William Henry.
Groundwater levels and pumpage in the East St. Louis area, Illinois, 1967-1971, by W. H. Baker, Jr. Urbana, Illinois State Water Survey, 1972.
29 p. illus. 28 cm. ([Illinois. Water Survey] Circular 112)
Cover title.
Bibliography: p. 21.
1. Water table—Illinois—East St. Louis region. 2. Water-supply—Illinois—East St. Louis region. I. Title. II. Series.
GB705.I 3A25 no. 112 553'.7'09773 s 73-622024
[GB1025.I 3] [553'.79'0977389] MARC

Baker, William Howard.
The big steal. London, H. Baker ₍1967, c1964₎.
127, ₍1₎ p.
Howard Baker library edition.
I. Title.
ScU NUC74-9276

Baker, William J comp.
America perceived: a view from abroad in the 19th century. Edited by William J. Baker. West Haven, Conn., Pendulum Press ₍1974₎
174 p. 21 cm. $2.50
1. United States—Civilization—19th century. 2. United States—Foreign opinion. I. Title.
E165.B25 917.3'03 73-94109
ISBN 0-88301-147-6; 0-88301-126-3 (pbk.) MARC

Baker, William M 1943-
No shillelagh; the life, journalism and politics of Timothy Warren Anglin. ₍n.p., 1972₎
x, 588, xi (i.e. 1) l. (Canadian theses on microfilm, no. 10755)
Thesis (Ph.D.)—University of Western Ontario.
Microfilm of typescript. Ottawa, National Library of Canada, 1972. 1 reel.
1. Anglin, Timothy Warren, 1822-1896. I. Title. II. Series.
WHi NUC74-1297

Baker, William M 1943-
Timothy Warren Anglin, 1822-96, Irish Catholic Canadian / William M. Baker. — Toronto ; Buffalo : University of Toronto Press, c1977.
xiv, 336 p., ₍4₎ leaves of plates : ill. ; 24 cm.
Originally presented as the author's thesis, University of Western Ontario.
Includes bibliographical references and index.
ISBN 0-8020-5368-8 : $22.50
1. Anglin, Timothy Warren, 1822-1896. 2. Statesmen—Canada—Biography. I. Title.
F1033.A532B34 1977 328.71'092'4 76-49480
76 MARC

Baker, William Mumford, 1825-1883.
Carter Quarterman. A novel. By William M. Baker. Illustrated by Elias J. Whitney. New York, Harper & brothers, 1876 [1973]
3 sheets. 10.5 x 14.8 cm. (L.H. Wright. American fiction, 1876-1900, no. 241)
Micro-transparency (negative). Louisville, Ky., Lost Cause Press, 1973.
Collation of the original: [13]-158 p. illus.
I. Title.
PSt NUC75-17355

Baker, William Mumford, 1825-1883.
Inside; a chronicle of secession, by George F. Harrington [pseud.] With illustrations by Thomas Nast. New York, Harper & Brothers, 1866.
223 p. illus.
Microfilm (positive) Ann Arbor, Mich., University Microfilms, 1974. 4th title of 9. 35 mm. (American fiction series, reel 242.4)
I. Title.
KEmT NUC75-2096

Baker, William Mumford, 1825-1883.
Mose Evans; a simple statement of the singular facts of his case, by William M. Baker. New York, Hurd & Houghton; Cambridge, Riverside Press, 1874 ₍1972₎
317 p.
Microfilm (positive) Ann Arbor, Mich., University Microfilms, 1972. 1st title of 12. 35 mm. (American fiction series, reel 182.1)
I. Title.
KEmT NUC74-1283

Baker, William Mumford, 1825-1883.
The new Timothy, by Wm. M. Baker. New York, Harper & Brothers, 1870.
344 p.
Microfilm (positive) Ann Arbor, Mich., University Microfilms, 1974. 5th title of 9. 35 mm. (American fiction series, reel 242.5)
I. Title.
KEmT NUC75-2091

Baker, William O.
see Newark, N.J. Board of Higher Education. A report on higher education in Newark. [Newark? 1970?]

Baker, William Pitt.
Mexican American, Black and other graduates and dropouts; a follow-up study covering 15 years of change, 1956-1971 [by] William P. Baker [and] Henry C. Jensen. San Jose, Calif., East Side Union High School District [1973]
85 p.
"Fourth in a five-year series of follow-up studies of school leavers of the East Side Union High School District."
"A Project of the East Side Union High School District."
1. High school dropouts–San Jose, Calif. 2. Mexican Americans–Education–San Jose, Calif. 3. Negroes–Education–San Jose, Calif. I. Jensen, Henry C., joint author. II. East Side Union High School District. III. Title.
CU NUC76-88811

Baker, William T., 1938- ed.
see New developments in optical instrumentation... [Redondo Beach, Calif., Society of Photo-optical Instrumentation Engineers, c1973]

Baker, William T., 1938- ed.
see Photographic instrumentation—a tool for solving highway and traffic engineering problems... ₍Redondo Beach, Calif., Society of Photo-optical Instrumentation Engineers, c1972₎

Baker, William Thomson, 1888–
The Baker family of England and of central Virginia, their many related families and kin : an easy to read, easy to understand genealogy and historical narrative of the Bakers and their related families of England and of Virginia, as taken from public records, documents, and other historical and genealogical souces / compiled by William Thompson Baker, Sr. — ₍s. l.₎ : Baker, c1974.
350, 418, 113 p. : ill. ; 24 cm.
Includes indexes.
1. Baker family. I. Title: The Baker family of England and of central Virginia ...
CS71.B17 1974b 929'.2'0973 74-83532
MARC

Baker, Willis Ramsey, 1942-
The status of school health service programs in the public senior high schools of Indiana. ₍Bloomington, Ind.₎ 1972.
188 p.
Thesis (H.S.D.)—Indiana University.
Vita.
InU NUC74-1287

Baker, Willis Ramsey, 1942-
The status of school health service programs in the public senior high schools of Indiana. ₍Bloomington, Ind.₎ 1972.
188 p.
Thesis (H.S.D.)—Indiana University.
Vita.
Microfilm.
1. Students—Health programs. 2. High schools—Indiana. I. Title.
InU NUC74-1288

Baker, Wyrth P
Introduction to homeotherapeutics, by Wyrth P. Baker, W. W. Young ₍and₎ Allen C. Neiswander. With the valuable assistance of Cynthia H. Shupis ₍and₎ Kathryn F. Vargo. ₍Washington, American Institute of Homeopathy, 1974₎
262 p. 27 cm.
1. Homeopathy—Materia medica and therapeutics. I. Young, William Wallace, 1900-1974, joint author. II. Neiswander, Allen C., joint author. III. Title.
RX601.B34 615'.58 74-82124
MARC

Baker, Z
The cottage builder's manual. By Z. Baker ... Worcester, Z. Baker & co., 1856 ₍1972₎
176 p., front., illus., 2 plates.
Micropublished as no. 47 on Reel 5, in "American Architectural Books," based on the Henry-Russell Hitchcock bibliography of the same title. New Haven: Research Publications, Inc., 1972.
1. Cottages. 2. Architecture, Domestic—Designs and plans. I. Title.
UU NUC75-22649

Baker, Zaidee Haynes.
Marriages of Lapeer County, Michigan. Compiled and indexed by Zaidee Haynes Baker and Hilda Haynes Clark. Oxford, Lake Orion, Mich., 1973-
v. 28 cm.
1. Lapeer Co., Mich.—Registers of marriages. I. Clark, Hilda Haynes. II. Title.
Mi NUC74-1301

Baker-Carr, Janet.
Evening at Symphony : a portrait of the Boston Symphony Orchestra / Janet Baker-Carr. — Boston : Houghton Mifflin, 1977.
172 p. : ill. ; 25 cm.
Bibliography: p. ₍165₎
Includes index.
ISBN 0-395-25697-6 : $10.95
1. Boston Symphony Orchestra. 2. Musicians—Massachusetts—Boston. I. Title.
ML200.8.B72S94 1977 785'.06'274461 77-9305
77 MARC

Baker-Carr, Janet.
see Conflict in the arts ... Cambridge, Mass., Arts Administration Research Institute, ₍c1976₎

Baker, La. Charter
see Baker, La. Ordinances, local laws, etc. Code of ordinances... Tallahassee, Municpal Code Corp., 1972-

Baker, La. Ordinances, local laws, etc.
Code of ordinances of the city of Baker, Louisiana; containing the Charter and the general ordinances of the city. Adopted October 10, 1972; effective November 10, 1972. Tallahassee, Municipal Code Corp., 1972–
1 v. (loose-leaf) 23 cm.
"Published by order of the mayor and council."
I. Baker, La. Charter. II. Municipal Code Corporation, Tallahassee. III. Title.
KFX1098.B34A35 1972 348'.76318'023 72-171412
MARC

Baker & Taylor Co.
A beginning collection, grades K-6; Baker & Taylor's guide to current AV materials, chosen by a staff of professionals. [Momence, Ill., c1975]
112 p. illus. 29 cm.
"Chosen under the guidelines established by a committee of professional librarians and media specialists directed by... Diana L. Spirt."
1. Audio-visual materials–Catalogs. I. Spirt, Diana L. II. Title.
INS NUC76-30235

Baker and Taylor Co.
Catalog.
New York.
v. 26 cm.
Z1036.B17 CA 33-399
rev MARC-S

Baker and Taylor Co.
A library list of books suitable for public and school libraries.
New York.
v. 18 cm.
"Selected from the lists of all publishers."
Title varies: 18 The Baker & Taylor Co.'s general library list of the standard miscellaneous books of all publishers.
1. Bibliography — Best books. 2. Children's literature — Bibliography. I. Title.
Z1036.B169a 99-1256
MARC-S

Baker & Taylor Co.
Selected elementary & secondary paperback titles. The Baker & Taylor Co. [Sommerville, N.J.] The Company, 1974.
iii, 51 p. 28 cm.
1. Bibliography–Paperback editions. 2. Children's literature–Bibliography. I. Title.
CaBVaU NUC76-18055

Baker and Taylor Co.
The text-book guide.
₍New York₎
v. illus. 23 cm.
"A descriptive selection of school and college text-books of all publishers."
1. Text-books—United States—Bibliography—Catalogs. I. Title.
Z5817.Z9B3 011 34-14761
rev MARC-S

Baker & Taylor Co.
see McGinniss, Dorothy A. The Baker & Taylor guide to the selection of books and media for your elementary school library. [5th ed.]. [Sommerville, N.J.] Baker & Taylor Co., [1974]

Baker & Taylor Co.
see McGinniss, Dorothy A Guide to the selection of books for your secondary school library... [1972-73 ed. Somerville, N. J., 1972]

Baker Book House
see Baker's dictionary of Christian ethics. Grand Rapids, Baker Book House [1973]

Baker, Frankfurter, Bontempo (Firm)
Stadium design application and statement of qualifications. Seattle, 1969.
1 v. (various pagings) illus.
Cover title.
1. Stadia. I. King County Design Commission. II. Title.
WaU NUC74-11284

Baker Furniture, inc., Holland, Mich.
The Baker catalogue. Holland, Mich. [197-?]
3 v. (chiefly illus.) 29 cm.
Contents-v. 1. French. Paladian.-v. 2. English & American. Far East. Executive.-[v. 3.] Index.
1. Furniture--Catalogs. I. Title.
INS NUC77-89737

Baker, Hostetler, Frost & Towers.
Manual of Federal laws relating to financing and conducting Federal election campaigns : prepared for the Republican National Committee / by Baker, Hostetler, Frost & Towers. — [Washington] : The Committee, 1975.
xvii, 233 leaves : forms ; 30 cm.
Cover title: Federal election law manual.
1. Elections—United States—Campaign funds. 2. Election law—United States. I. Republican Party. National Committee. II. Title: Manual of Federal laws relating to financing ... III. Title: Federal election law manual.
KF4920.B3 342'.73'07 75-322489
75 MARC

Baker Lake 1972: prints. [Baker Lake, N.W.T., Sanavik Cooperative, 1972]
1 v. (unpaged) illus.
Cover title.
Text in English and French.
1. Prints—Catalogs. 2. Prints, Eskimo.
CaOTY NUC74-1293

Baker Lake Residents' Association.
Baker Lake, N.W.T., 1870-1970 / [Baker Lake Residents' Association ; Mary McCulloch, editor]. — [Baker Lake, N.W.T. : Baker Lake Residents' Association, 1971?]
179 p. : ill. (part col.), map, ports. ; 29 cm. C74-2878-2
Title also in Eskimo.
English and Eskimo.
1. Baker Lake, Northwest Territories. 2. Eskimos—Northwest Territories, Can.—Baker Lake. I. McCulloch, Mary. II. Title.
F1110.5.B3B34 1971 971.9'4 75-314267
75 MARC

Baker; Obed and Eliza's children [by Jim and Flora Baker. Florence? Tex., 1973]
98 l. illus., facsims., ports. 28 cm.
1. Baker family (Obed Baker) 2. Texas—Genealogy. I. Baker, Jim.
TxU NUC75-17388

Baker University, Baldwin, Kan.
Alumni directory, 1969. [Baldwin, Kan.] 1968.
128 p. illus. 28 cm.
"Printed as an edition of the Baker world magazine."
KU-RH NUC73-112900

Baker University, Baldwin, Kan.
Alumni handbook, 1956. [Baldwin, Kan., 1956]
99 p. 23 x 10 cm.
Cover title.
KU-RH NUC73-59273

Baker-Vanguard Library
see Masterson, Agnes. An alphabetical index to periodical.... [n. p., n. d.]

Baker, Voorhis and Company.
see New York (State). Laws, statutes, etc. The Act authorizing the formation of corporations ... New York, J. S. Voorhies, 1860.

Bakerelski, Khristo.
Istoricheski pesni. Otbral i redaktiral Khr. Bakarelski. Sofiia, Bŭlgarski pisatel, 1961.
671 p. (Bŭlgarsko narodno tvorchestvo, v. 3)
Notes and bibliographical information: p. 603-[654]
Glossary: p. 659-[666]
1. Folksongs, Bulgarian. I. Title.
WaU NUC76-14937

Bakergem, A. J. van, illus.
see Peer, H F van. Gorcum. 's-Gravenhage, Voorhoeve, 1971 [1972].

Bakermans, Wilhelmus Antonius Petrus, 1921-
Groenbemesting; verslag van een onderzoek over de knelpunten in de praktijk bij de teelt van groenbemesters onder wintertarwe en zomergerst. Wageningen, 1972.
28 p. (Wageningen. Instituut voor Biologisch en Scheikundig Onderzoek van Landbouwgewassen. Verslagen, no. 60)
I. Title.
DNAL NUC75-29956

Bakermans, Wilhelmus Antonius Petrus, 1921-
Kweekbestrijding in stoppelland I; Verslag van de kweekbestrijdingsproef te Bemmel in 1970-1971. Wageningen, 1972.
16 p. (Wageningen. Instituut voor Biologisch en Scheikundig Onderzoek van Landbouwgewassen. Verslagen, no. 63)
I. Title.
DNAL NUC74-1299

Baker's dictionary of Christian ethics. Carl F. H. Henry, editor. Grand Rapids, Baker Book House [1973]
xxv, 726 p. 25 cm. $16.95
1. Christian ethics—Dictionaries. 2. Social ethics—Dictionaries. I. Henry, Carl Ferdinand Howard, 1913- ed. II. Baker Book House.
BJ1199.B34 241'.03 73-83488
ISBN 0-8010-4079-5 MARC

Baker's dozen : a collection of stories / edited by Leon Garfield. — London : Ward Lock, 1973.
144 p. : ill. ; 24 cm. GB74-09957
ISBN 0-7063-1408-5 : £1.95
1. Short stories. I. Garfield, Leon.
PZ5.B214 75-310781
75 MARC

Baker's dozen: abstracts of 13 doctoral dissertations completed under Manpower Administration research grants. [Editors: Allen Abrahamson and others] Washington; for sale by the Supt. of Docs., U.S. Govt. Print. Off., 1973.
v, 112 p. illus., diagrs., graphs. 26 cm. (Manpower research monograph, no. 27)
Includes bibliographical references.
1. Manpower policy—United States—Abstracts. 2. Dissertations, Academic—United States—Abstracts. I. Abrahamson, Allen, ed. II. United States. Dept. of Labor. Manpower Administration. III. Series.
NNCU-G NUC76-71002

Bakersfield, Calif. Charter
see Bakersfield, Calif. Ordinances, local laws, etc. Municipal code and Charter, City of Bakersfield; adopted by ordinance no. 1325 new series, passed September 19, 1960. Seattle, Book Pub. Co. [1960-

Bakersfield, Calif. City School District
see Techniques for teaching the brain-injured child ... Bakersfield Calif., 1961.

Bakersfield, Calif. Ordinances, local laws, etc.
Municipal code and Charter, City of Bakersfield; adopted by ordinance no. 1325 new series, passed September 19, 1960. Seattle, Book Pub. Co. [1960-
1 v. (loose-leaf)
Kept up to date by supplementary pages.
I. Bakersfield, Calif. Charter.
CLL NUC76-88815

Bakersfield, Calif. State College
see
California State College, Bakersfield.

Bakersfield, Vt. Bicentennial Commission.
see
Bakersfield Bicentennial Commission.

Bakersfield Bicentennial Commission.
see Wells, Elsie C., 1887- Bakersfield, Vermont ... Canaan, N.H., Published for the Bakersfield Bicentennial Commission [by] Phoenix Pub., c1976.

Bakersfield, Lancaster and Antelope Valley salute Edwards. [Lubbock, Texas, Boone Publications, 1970]
50, 18 p. illus.
Cover title.
1970 unofficial guide.
1. Edwards Air Force Base. 2. California. Description.
WHi NUC73-59625

Bakerstown, Me.
see also
Poland, Me.

Bakery and Confectionery Workers' International Union of America
see Norbert Cronin & Company. Security for you. [San Francisco, 1957]

Bakery and Confectionery Workers' International Union of America. Local 464
see Hershey Chocolate Corporation, Hershey, Pa. Articles of agreement... Hershey, Pa. [n. d.]

Bakery production and marketing.
[Chicago, Ill., Gorman Pub. Co.]
v. ill. 29 cm. monthly.
Began with Sept. 1966 issue. Cf. New serial titles.
Absorbed: Bakers weekly, 1969. Cf. New serial titles.
Key title: Bakery production and marketing, ISSN 0005-4127
1. Bakers and bakeries—United States—Periodicals.
TX761.B32 338.4'7'6647520973 76-641996
MARC-S

Bakeš, Milan.
Čs. devizové hospodářství a jeho právní úprava. 1. vyd. Praha, Horizont, t. SČT 04, 1972.
102, [1] p. 21 cm. (Na pomoc národnímu hospodářství) Kčs9.00
Cz 72-SKČ
On cover: Vydává česká socialistická společnost pro vědu, kulturu a politiku.
Includes legislation.
1. Foreign exchange—Law—Czechoslovak Republic. I. Title.
73-365027

Bakeš, Milan.
Jak do zahraničí? Zprac. Milan Bakeš. Praha, Merkur, t. ST 2, 1973.
90, [5] p. with photos and maps. 21 cm. Kčs5.00 Cz 73
1. Tourist trade—Europe, Eastern. I. Title.
G155.E8B34 73-362651

Bakeš, Milan.
Měnové vztahy a jejich právní problematika / Milan Bakeš. — Vyd. 1. — Praha : Universita Karlova, 1973.
98 p. ; 24 cm. — (Acta Universitatis Carolinae : Iuridica : Monographia ; 18/1973) Cz***
Summary in English and Russian.
Bibliography: p. 96-98.
Kčs10.00
1. Money—Law. 2. Money—Czechoslovak Republic. 3. Foreign exchange—Law—Socialist countries. 4. Sovet ekonomicheskoĭ vzaimopomoshchi. I. Title. II. Series: Prague, Universita Karlova. Acta : Iuridica : Monographia ; 18/1973.
75-562281

Bakeski, Petre
see
Bakevski, Petre, 1947-

Bakešová, Ivana.
Kulturní politika komunistické strany Číny v letech 1942-1966. Praha, Ústav pro mezinárodní politiku a ekonomii, 1968.
146 p. 21 cm. (Prameny a studie k mezinarodnim vztahum, sv. 21)
1. China—Intellectual life. I. Title.
NIC NUC76-70948

Bakevski, Petre, 1947–
(Pat do letoto)
Пат до летото. Скопје, "Мисла," 1972.
32 p. 21 cm. (Дебитанти) 20.00Din Yu 72
Poems.
I. Title.
PG1164.B28P3 73-970474

Bakevski, Petre, 1947–
(Zemjoljubec)
Земјољубец / Петре Бакевски. — Скопје : Култура, 1975.
57 p. ; 19 cm. — (Современа македонска поезија) Yu***
Poems.
Series romanized: Sovremena makedonska poezija.
I. Title.
PG1196.12.A4Z25 76-528274

Bakewell, Charles Montague, 1867–1957.
Source book in ancient philosophy. Rev. ed. New York, Gordian Press, 1973 [c1939]
xiv, 425 p. 23 cm. $12.50
Reprint of the ed. published by Scribner, New York.
Includes bibliographical references.
1. Philosophy, Ancient—Collections. I. Title.
B165.B34 1973 180 75-148613
ISBN 0-87752-139-5 MARC

Bakewell, Frederick Collier.
Electric science; its history, phenomena, and applications, by F. C. Bakewell. London, Ingram, Cooke, 1853.
199 p. illus. 22 cm.
1. Electricity. 2. Electricity—History. I. Title.
QC523.B33 537 74-156513
MARC

Bakewell, K G B
A manual of cataloguing practice, by K. G. B. Bakewell. [1st ed.] Oxford, New York, Pergamon Press [1972]
xiii, 298 p. illus. 26 cm. (International series of monographs in library and information science, v. 14)
Includes bibliographical references.
1. Cataloging. I. Title.
Z693.B34 1972 025.3 73-171838
ISBN 0-08-016697-0 rev MARC

Bakewell, Michael.
see You always remember the first time. London, Quartet Books, 1975.

Bakewell, Peter John.
Antonio López de Quiroga (industrial minero del Potosí colonial) [por] Peter Bakewell. Potosí, Universidad Boliviana "Tomás Frías," División de Extensión Universitaria, 1973.
ii, 39 p. illus. 21 cm.
Includes bibliographical references.
1. López de Quiroga, Antonio, d. 1699. 2. Potosí, Bolivia—History. 3. Mineral industries—Bolivia—History. I. Title.
TN140.L67B34 74-207183

Bakewell, Robert, 1768-1843.
An introduction to geology, illustrative of the general structure of the earth; comprising the elements of the science, and an outline of the geology and mineral geography of England; by Robert Bakewell... London, J. Harding, 1813.
xix, [1], 362 p. 5 pl. (4 col., 2 fold, incl. front., map) 22 cm.
Microprint. New York, Readex Microprint, 1968. 5 cards. (Landmarks of Science)
1. Geology. I. Title.
InU NUC76-71001

Bakewell, Robert, 1768-1843.
An introduction to mineralogy: comprising the natural history and characters of minerals; and a description of rocks, both simple and aggregated; with a new tabular arrangement of earthy minerals, on a plan designed to facilitate the knowledge of that class of substances. To which is prefixed: a series of conversations explaining the principles of the science, and the elements of crystallography. By Robert Bakewell... London, printed for Longman, Hurst, Rees, Orme, and Brown, 1819.
xx, 668, [2] p. diagrs. on v fold. pl. (incl. front.) 22 cm.
Microprint. New York, Readex Microprint, 1968. 8 cards. (Landmarks of Science)
1. Mineralogy. 2. Crystallography. I. Title.
InU NUC76-70974

Bakewell, Ruth V.
see Nordholm, Harriet. Keys to teaching junior high school music... Minneapolis, Schmitt, Hall & McCreary [1959, c1953]

Bakgaard, Hans.
Digte : hun døde, jeg blev en drømmer / af Hans Bakgaard ; [tegninger, Chr. Christoffersen]. — København : Hans Bakgårds Venner : eksp., V. J. Vestergaard, Doverodde, Hurup], 1970.
126 p. : ill. ; 22 cm. D 74-48
Poems.
kr20.00
PT8176.12.A376D5 75-577677

Bakgaard, Hans.
Mennesker på min vej / Hans Bakgaard ; blade fundet i Røverreden og samlet af Carl Nielsen. — [Hurup, Thy] : Hans Bakgaards Venner ; [eksp.], Doverodde : [V. J. Vestergaard, 1975]
376 p. : ill. ; 25 cm. D 75-30
ISBN 87-980-3520-7 : kr95.00
1. Bakgaard, Hans—Biography. I. Title.
PT8176.12.A376Z52 75-544891

Bakh, I. A., ed.
see International Workingmen's Association. Pervyĭ Internat͡sional i Parizhskai͡a kommuna. 1972.

Bakh, I. A., ed.
see International Workingmen's Association. 5th congress, The Hague, 1872. (Gaagskiĭ kongress Pervogo Internt͡sionala) 1972.

Bakh, I. A.
see Parizhskai͡a kommuna i marksizm. 1973.

Bakh, I. A., ed.
see Pervyĭ Internat͡sional v istoricheskoĭ nauke. 1968.

Bakh, Natal'i͡a Alekseevna.
Электропроводность и парамагнетизм полимерных полупроводников. Москва, "Наука," 1971.
136 p. with illus. 21 cm. 0.78rub USSR 71-VKP
At head of title: Академия наук СССР. Институт электрохимии. Н. А. Бах, А. В. Ванников, А. Д. Гришина.
Includes bibliographies.
1. Polymers and polymerization. 2. Semiconductors. I. Vannikov, Anatoliĭ Veniaminovich, joint author. II. Grishina, Antonina Dmitrievna, joint author. III. Title.
Title romanized: Ėlektroprovodnost' i paramagnetizm polimernykh poluprovodnikov.
QD382.S4B3 74-353294

Bakh, S
(T͡Sar'-golod)
Царь-голодъ. Популярные экономическіе очерки. Берлинъ, Изд. Т-ва И. П. Ладыжникова [192-?]
115 p. 19 cm. (Соціально-политическая библіотека, 4)
1. Economics—Addresses, essays, lectures. I. Title.
HB54.B34 73-216145

Bakh, Y S
see
Bach, Johann Sebastian, 1685-1750.

Bakhaev, V. B.
see Dekabristy o Buri͡atii. 1975.

Bakhaila Mīkā'ēl.
Le livre des mystères du ciel et de la terre, Texte ethiopien publié et traduit par J. Perruchon avec le concours de I. Guidi. [Paris, Firmin-Didot, 1947-71]
2 v. 26 cm. (Patrologia Orientalis, t. 1, fasc. 1, t. 6, fasc. 3)
Vol. 2 edited and translated by Sylvain Grébaut, published at Turnhout, Belgium by Éds. Brépols.
1. Ethiopic Church. 2. Ethiopic language—Texts. 3. Manuscripts, Ethiopic. I. Perruchon, Jules François Célestin, 1853- II. Grébaut, Sylvain, 1881- III. Title.
NIC NUC76-74743

Bakhale, Bhaskara Raghunatha, 1869-1922
see Bhāskara-gunagaurava. 1971.

(Bākham-samālocanā)
बाखं-समालोचना / मुंम्ह भरत सायमि. — कान्तिपुर : पल्पसा साहित्य-श्च:, नेपाल सम्वत, 1095 [1974]
149 p. ; 19 cm.
In Newari.
Rs3.00

1. Short stories, Newari—History and criticism—Addresses, essays, lectures. I. Saymi, Bharata.

PL3801.N55B3 75-907042

Bakhan'koŭ, Artsi͡om I͡Afimavich.
(Tlumachal'ny sloŭnik belaruskaĭ movy)
Тлумачальны слоўнік беларускай мовы. Для сярэд. школы. Выд. 2-е, перапрац. і дап. Мінск, "Нар. асвета," 1972.
376 p. 17 cm. 0.54rub USSR 73-2897
At head of title: А. Я. Бахaнькоў, І. М. Гайдукевіч, П. П. Шуба.
1. White Russian language—Dictionaries. I. Haĭdukevich, Iosif Martynavich, joint author. II. Shuba, Pavel Paŭlavich, joint author. III. Title.
PG2834.B33 1972 73-347845

Bakhan'kou, Artsi͡om I͡Afimavich
see Narodnae slova. 1976.

Bakhan'kova, V., joint author
see Adamovich, V Belaruskai͡a SSR u hady Vi͡alikaĭ Aĭchynnaĭ Vaĭny Savetskaha Sai͡uza. 1970.

Bakhanov, V. P.
see Fizika oblakov i aktivnykh vozdeĭstviĭ. 1974.

Bakhanov, V. P.
see Fizika oblakov, osadkov i tumanov. 1976.

Bakhanov, V.P., ed.
see Issledovanie prot͡sessov oblako- i osadkoobrazovaniia. 1972.

Bakhanova, R. A., ed.
see Fizika oblakov i aktivnykh vozdeĭstviĭ. 1971.

Bakhanova, R. A., ed.
see Fizika oblakov i aktivnykh vozdeĭstviĭ. 1972.

Bakhanova, R. A.
see Fizika oblakov i osadkov. 1976.

Bakhanova, R. A.
see Issledovanii͡a prot͡sessov oblako- i osadkoobrazovanii͡a. 1974.

(Bakhara Bhāūsāhebāñcī)
बखर भाऊसाहेबांची / संपादक यु. म. पठाण. — पुणे : न. गो. व्होरा, 1959.
149 p. ; 20 cm.
In Marathi.

1. Sadashco Bhao, d. 1761. I. Pathan, Yusufkhan Mohamadkhan, 1930–
DS461.9.S2B34 76–984400

Bakharav, O. N.
see Letniĭ sad. [1972]

Bakharev, A. A.
see Zemnoe pritíàzhenie. 1971.

Bakharev, Andreĭ Nikolaevich.
(Michurin v zhizni)
Мичурин в жизни / Андрей Бахарев. — Изд. 2-е. — Москва : Знание, 1974.
222 p. ; 17 cm. USSR 74
0.29rub
1. Michurin, Ivan Vladimirovich, 1855–1935. 2. Plant-breeding. I. Title.
SB63.M6B343 1974 75–544394

Bakharev, Ivan Andreevich, ed.
see Verkh-Isetskiĭ metallurgicheskiĭ. 1972.

Bakharev, Oleg M.
see ÍAntarnyĭ bereg. 1973.

Bakhareva, Galina Viktorovna
see Putevoditel' po izdaniíàm tekushcheĭ otechestvennoĭ bibliograficheskoĭ informatsii. 197

Bakhareva, Viktoriíà Efimovna.
Эпоксидные стеклопластики в судовом машиностроении. Ленинград, "Судостроение," 1968.
187 p. with illus. 21 cm. 0.57rub USSR 68–VKP
At head of title: В. Е. Бахарева, И. А. Конторовская, Л. В. Петрова.
Bibliography: p. 183–[185]
1. Plastics in ship-building. 2. Glass reinforced plastics. 3. Epoxy resins. I. Kontorovskaíà, Izabella Afraimovna, joint author. II. Petrova, Líùdmila Viktorovna, joint author. III. Title.
Title romanized: Ėpoksidnye stekloplastiki v sudovom mashinostroenii.
VM149.B23 73–333688

Bakhareva, Viktoriíà Efimovna.
(Polimery v sudovom mashinostroenii)
Полимеры в судовом машиностроении / В. Е. Бахарева, И. А. Конторовская, Л. В. Петрова. — Ленинград : Судостроение, 1975.
236 p. : ill. ; 23 cm. USSR 75
Bibliography: p. 231–[234]
1.04rub
1. Plastics in marine engineering. 2. Marine machinery. I. Kontorovskaíà, Izabella Afroimovna, joint author. II. Petrova, Líùdmila Viktorovna, joint author. III. Title.
VM605.B24 77–501667

Bakharevich, Nelli Semenovna, joint author
see Dubnov, Lev Vladimirovich. (Promyshlennye vzryvchatye veshchestva) 1973.

Bakharovskiĭ, G. ÍA., joint author
see Unaníànts, Tigran Petrovich. (Khimicheskie tovary) 1967-74.

al-Bākharzī, 'Alī ibn al-Ḥasan, d. 1075.
[Dīwān]
علي بن الحسن الباخرزي : حياته وشعره وديوانه / تأليف وتحقيق محمد التونجي. — بنغازي : الجامعة الليبية، كلية الآداب، [1975]
231 p., 2 leaves of plates : ill. ; 24 cm. — (من الأدب في العصر السلجوقي ؛ 2)
Bibliography: p. 225–229.
1. al-Bākharzī, 'Alī ibn al-Ḥasan, d. 1075—Addresses, essays, lectures. I. al-Tūnjī, Muḥammad. II. Series: Min al-adab fī al-'aṣr al-Saljūqī ; 2.
Title romanized: 'Alī ibn al-Ḥasan al-Bākharzī.
PJ7750.B34 1975 75–960389

al-Bākharzī, 'Alī ibn al-Ḥasan, d. 1075, comp.
[Dumyat al-qaṣr]
دمية القصر وعصرة اهل العصر / لابى الحسن الباخرزى ؛ تحقيق سامى مكي العاني. — الطبعة 1. — النجف : [يطلب من دار النعمان]، 19
v. ; 25 cm.
Bibliography: v. 2, p. 517–529.
1. Arabic poetry—750–1258. I. al-'Ānī, Sāmī Makkī, ed. II. Title.
Title romanized: Dumyat al-qaṣr wa-'uṣrat ahl al-'aṣr.
PJ7620.B3 1971 75–586586

al-Bākharzī, 'Alī ibn al-Ḥasan, d. 1075.
(Dumyat al-qaṣr wa-'uṣrat ahl al-'aṣr)
دمية القصر وعصرة اهل العصر / تأليف علي بن الحسن بن علي ابن أبي الطيب الباخرزي ؛ تحقيق ودراسة محمد التونجي. — [دمشق] : مؤسسة دار الحياة، [1971?–1975?]
3 v. (1750 p.) : ill. ; 25 cm.
Bibliography: p. 1741–1747.
1. Arabic poetry—750–1258. I. al-Tūnjī, Muḥammad. II. Title.
PJ7620.B3 1971b 77–971030

Bakhat, Iqbal Ahmad. **Planning in Pakistan**
see Mirza, Manzoor. **Economic development in theory and practice...** [2d ed. **Lahore,** Markazi Kutub Khana] [1972 or 3]

Bakhatarāma Sāha, *fl.* 1770.
बुद्धि-विलास. बखतराम साह कृत. सम्पादक पद्मधर पाठक. जोधपुर, राजस्थान, सञ्चालक राजस्थान प्राच्यविद्या प्रतिष्ठान, 1964.
iv, 20, 179 p. 25 cm. (राजस्थान पुरातन ग्रन्थमाला, ग्रन्थाङ्क 73) 3.75
Added t. p. in English.
In old Rajasthani.
Bibliographical footnotes.
I. Pathak, Padma Dhar, ed. II. Title. (Series: Rajasthan Oriental Research Institute, Jodhpur, India. Rajasthan puratana granthamala, 73)
Title romanized: Buddhi-vilāsa.
PK2708.9.B3B8 1964 S A 68–12677
PL 480 : I-H-3906

Bakhchedzhiíàn, Fransui Kevork
see
Sevan, Sevda, 1945-

Bakhchisaraĭ
see
Bakhchisaray.

Bakhchisaraĭtseva, Margarita Emmanuilovna.
Energetics. Dopushcheno v kachestve ucheb. posobiíà po angliĭskomu íàzyku dlíà energ. vuzov i fakul'tetov. Izd. 3., ispr. i dop. Moskva, Gos. energ. izd-vo, 1958.
287 p. illus. 23 cm.
1. Power (Mechanics) 2. Electric engineering. I. Title.
OU NUC74-38251

Bakhchisaray. Istoriko-arkheologicheskiĭ muzeĭ.
(Bakhchisaraĭ)
Бахчисарай : Ист.-археол. музей : Фотоальбом / [Авт. фото Е. Л. Векслерчик, Ю. А. Нейман ; Авт. текста И. И. Чурилов]. — 2-е изд. — Киев : Мистецтво, 1976.
[96] p. : ill. ; 21 cm. USSR 76
1.33rub
1. Bakhchisaray. Istoriko-arkheologicheskiĭ muzeĭ. I. Vekslerchik, E. L. II. Neĭman, ÍÙ. A. III. Churilov, I. I. IV. Title.
GN36.R92B342 76–530904

Bakhchisaray. Istoriko-arkheologicheskiĭ muzeĭ.
Bakhchisaraĭ, istoriko-arkheologicheskiĭ muzeĭ; [fotoal'bom. Avt. teksta I. I. Churilov. Avt. fotografii E. L. Vekslerchikh & ÍU. A. Neĭman. Kiev, Mystetstvo, 1973]
[96] p. front., illus.
I. Churilov, I. I.
MH NUC75-135230

Bakheit, Awad El-Kariem Mohomed.
Responses of sixteen warm-season grasses to nitrogen and phosphorous fertilization, submitted by Awad El-Kariem Mohamed [sic] Bakheit. Fort Collins, 1972.
xv, 111 l. illus. 28 cm.
Typescript (photocopy)
Thesis (Ph. D.)—Colorado State University.
Bibliography: leaves [77]-82.
1. Grasses. 2. Fertilizers and manures. I. Title.
CoFS NUC74-122632

Bakheit, Jaafar Muhammad Ali.
(al-Fa''ālīyah al-idārīyah wa-ḥarakat al-taghyīr fī al-Sūdān)
الفعالية الادارية وحركة التغيير فى السودان [تأليف] جعفر محمد على بخيت. — [الخرطوم] 1969.
23 l. 26 cm. (جامعة الخرطوم. شعبة ابحاث السودان. سلسلة سمنار الدراسات الافريقية، ورقة رقم 8)
Bibliography: leaves 21–23.
1. Decoration and ornament, Architectural—Sudan. I. Title. II. Series: Silsilat saminār al-dirāsāt al-Afrīqīyah, waraqah raqm 8.
NA3587.8.A1B3 72–210874
rev

Bakheit, Jaafar Muhammad Ali.
(al-Idārah al-Barīṭānīyah wa-al-ḥarakah al-waṭanīyah fī al-Sūdān, 1919–1939)
الادارة البريطانية والحركة الوطنية فى السودان، ١٩١٩– ١٩٣٩. تأليف جعفر محمد علي بخيت. نقله من الانجليزية الى العربية هنرى رياض. [الطبعة 1.] بيروت دار الثقافة [1972]
318 p. 24 cm. £S1.00 (Sudan)
Includes bibliographical references.
1. Sudan—History—1899–1956. I. Title.
DT108.6.B36 1972 72–982555

Bakheit, Jaafar Muhammad Ali.
(al-Thawrah al-idārīyah)
الثورة الادارية [تأليف جعفر محمد على بخيت. الخرطوم، المطبعة الحكومية] 1971.
97 p. ports. 24 cm.
At head of title: جمهورية السودان الديمقراطية. وزارة الحكومة المحلية.
«سلسلة من المقالات والاحاديث التى كتبها والقاها الدكتور جعفر محمد على بخيت وزير الحكومة المحلية.»
1. Local government—Sudan—Addresses, essays, lectures. I. Title.
JS7819.2.B33 78–981636
rev

Bakher, A
see
Behar, A

Bakher, Benjamin Zeeb
see
Bacher, Wilhelm, 1850-1913.

Bakhilina, Natal'íà Borisovna.
(Istoriíà ťsvetooboznachenii v russkom íàzyke)
История цветообозначений в русском языке / Н. Б. Бахилина. — Москва : Наука, 1975.
286 p. ; 20 cm. USSR 75
At head of title: Akademiíà nauk SSSR. Institut russkogo íàzyka.
Includes bibliographical references and index.
1.01rub
1. Russian language—Semantics. 2. Russian language—Etymology. 3. Colors, Words for. I. Title.
PG2585.B3 76–509378

Bakhirko, Boris Antonovich.
(Ėkonomika khimicheskoĭ promyshlennosti)
Экономика химической промышленности : [Учебник для вузов по специальности "Экономика и организация хим. пром-сти"] / Б. А. Бахирко, А. Ф. Колосов, В. Ф. Москвин ; Под ред. Л. А. Костандова и А. Ф. Румянцева. — Москва : Высш. школа, 1975.
479 p. ; 22 cm. USSR 76
Includes bibliographical references.
1.36rub
1. Chemical industries—Russia. I. Kolosov, Aleksandr Fomich, joint author. II. Moskvin, Viktor Fedorovich, joint author. III. Title.
HD9656.R92B34 76–522093

Bakhīt, Ja'far Muḥammad 'Alī.
see
Bakheit, Jaafar Muhammad Ali.

Bakhit, Muhammad Adnan Salamah.
The Ottoman Province of Damascus in the sixteenth century / by Muhammad Adnan Salamah Bakhit. — London? : [s.n.], 1972.
xi, 314 leaves ; 31 cm. GB***
Thesis - University of London.
Bibliography: leaves 292-314.
1. Syria—History—1516-1918. 2. Damascus—History. I. Title.
DS97.5.B24 956.91'03 76-378997
76 MARC

Bakhitov, Mukhetdin Sharafutdinovich.
(Kritika sovremennykh tendentsiĭ antikommunizma)
Критика современных тенденций антикоммунизма. Москва, Наука, 1973.
149 p. 20 cm. (Академия наук СССР. Научно-популярная серия) 0.26rub USSR***
At head of title: М. Ш. Бахитов.
Includes bibliographical references.
1. Communism—1945– 2. Propaganda, Anti-communist. 3. Communist revisionism. I. Title.
HX44.B29 74–303212

Bakhle, Y. S.
see Metabolic functions of the lung. New York, M. Dekker, c1977.

Bakhmat, Yehudah
see
Bachmat, Y

Bakhmatiuk, Oleksa, 1820–1882.
(Oleksa Bakhmatiuk)
Олекса Бахматюк : альбом / [вступна стаття та впорядкування Ю. П. Лащука]. — Київ : Мистецтво, 1976.
18, 95 p. : ill. (some col.) ; 21 cm. USSR***
Summary in English; list of illustrations also in English.
1.68rub
1. Bakhmatiuk, Oleksa, 1820–1882. 2. Pottery, Ukrainian.
I. Lashchuk, IU. P.
NK4210.B28L37 77–515123

Bakhmatskii, V.G.
see Partgruporg. [Khabarovsk] Khabarovskoe kn. izd-vo, 1968.

Bakhmetev, Boris Aleksandrovich
see Thompson, Dorothy, 1893-1961. Russia today... New York, Foreign policy association [1929]

Bakhmet'ev, Vladimir Matveevich, 1885–1963.
[Nastuplenie]
Наступление; роман. [Москва?] Худож. лит-ра, 1934–
v. 20 cm.
At head of title, v. 1– : Вл. Бахметьев.
1. Russia—History—Revolution, 1917–1921—Fiction. I. Title.
PG3476.B258N3 1934 73–205469

Bakhmet'ev, Vladimir Matveevich, 1885–1963.
[Prestuplenie Martyna]
Преступление Мартына; роман. 9. изд. Москва, Гос. изд-во худож. лит-ры, 1931.
278 p. 21 cm. (His Собрание сочинений, т. 3)
I. Title.
PG3476.B258 1931, t. 3 72–228097

Bakhmet'ev, Vladimir Matveevich, 1885–1963.
(Shagi)
Шаги; избранные произведения. [Москва] Гос. изд-во худож. лит-ры, 1933.
437 p. port. 20 cm.
CONTENTS: Шаги.—Последние дни его превосходительства.—Повести о прошлом.—Огненный ветер.
I. Title.
PG3476.B258A6 1933 74–201742

Bakhmet'ev, Vladimir Matveevich, 1885–1963.
[Sobranie sochinenii]
Собрание сочинений. Москва, Земля и фабрика, 19
v. 20 cm.
CONTENTS:
т. 2. Железная трава.
PG3476.B258 1929 73–203058

Bakhmet'ev, Vladimir Matveevich, 1885–1963.
[Sobranie sochinenii]
Собрание сочинений. Москва, Гос. изд-во худож. лит-ры, 19
v. 21 cm.
CONTENTS:
т. 3. Преступление Мартына.
PG3476.B258 1931 72–228098

Bakhmet'ev, Vladimir Matveevich, 1885–1963.
(Stupeni)
Ступени; рассказы о женщине и революции. [Москва] Московское т-во писателей, 1932.
197 p. port. 18 cm.
CONTENTS: Алена.—Воскресенье.—Гудки.—Люди и вещи.—Тень в пламени.—Случай.—Ее победа.
I. Title.
PG3476.B258S8 1932 74–201959

Bakhmet'ev, Vladimir Matveevich, 1885–1963.
[Zheleznaia trava]
Железная трава. Изд. 3. Москва, Земля и фабрика, 1929.
253 p. 20 cm. (His Собрание сочинений, т. 2)
I. Title.
PG3476.B258 1929, t. 2 73–203057

Bakhmut, A.I., comp.
see Muzei istorii Korsun'-Shevchenkivs'koi bytvy. Putivnyk po ekspozytsii. Dnipropetrovs'k, Promin', 1969.

Bakhmutova, Elena Aleksandrovna.
Vyrazitel'nie sredstva russkogo iazyka. Leksika i frazeologiia. Uchebnoe posobie. [Kazan'] Izd-vo Kazanskogo universiteta, 1967.
163 p. port.
1. Russian language–Lexicology. 2. Russian language–Words. I. Title.
UU NUC74-38254

Bakhmutova, V.
see Sverdlovsk, Russia. Literaturnyi muzei im. D.N. Mamina-Sibiriaka. Sverdlovskii literaturnyi muzei im. D.N. Mamina-Sibiriaka; putevoditel'. [Sverdlovsk] Sverdlovskoe knizhnoe izd-vo, 1959.

Bakhmutskaia, Sarra Abramovna
see Ozdorovlenie truda i byta v kolkhozakh. 1931.

Bakhnov, Vladlen Efimovich, 1924–
(Taina, pokrytaia mrakom)
Тайна, покрытая мраком. Юморист. рассказы. [Ил.: Е. Буров. Москва, "Сов. писатель," 1973].
286 p. with illus. 16 cm. 0.30rub USSR 73
At head of title: Владлен Бахнов.
CONTENTS: О:О в мою пользу.—Тайна, покрытая мраком.—Метаморфозы.—Наука и жизнь.—За гранью фантастики (Фантастические пародии)
I. Title.
PG3479.K48T3 74–344403

Bakhori, Abdumalik
see
Bahorī, Abdumalik.

Bakhorī, Somadatta, 1921–
(Bīca meṃ bahatī dhārā)
बीच में बहती धारा; कविता-संग्रह. [लेखक] सोमदत्त बखोरी. [पोर्ट लुई? Printed by Luxmi Print., 1971]
94 p. 18 cm.
In Hindi.
I. Title.
PK2098.B318B5 73–220009

Bakhorī, Somadatta, 1921–
(Gaṅgā kī pukāra)
गंगा की पुकार; एक प्रवासी भारतीय की भारत-यात्रा. [लेखक] सोमदत्त बखोरी. [1. संस्करण] दिल्ली, आभा प्रकाशन, 1972.
[11], 260 p. illus. 19 cm. Rs8.70
In Hindi.
1. India—Description and travel—1947– I. Title.
DS414.B335 72–902837

Bakhov, Anatolii
see Vakhov, Anatolii Alekseevich.

Bakhov, Anatolii Sergeevich.
На заре советской дипломатии; органы советской дипломатии в 1917–1922 гг. Москва, Международные отношения, 1966.
173, [2] p. illus., ports. 20 cm.
At head of title: А. С. Бахов.
Bibliographical references included in "Примечания" (p. 157–[174])
1. Russia—Diplomatic and consular service. 2. Russia—Foreign relations—1917–1945. I. Title.
Title transliterated: Na zare sovetskoi diplomatii.
JX1807.B3 67–46203
rev

Bakhov, Anatolii Sergeevich.
The Warsaw Treaty Organisation and European security / Anatoly Bakhov. — Moscow : Novosti Press Agency Pub. House, 1975.
54 p. ; 17 cm. USSR***
Includes bibliographical references.
0.16rub
1. Organizatsiia stran Varshavskogo dogovora. 2. Warsaw pact, 1955. I. Title.
JX1393.W2B32 341.72 76-364288
76 MARC

Bakhov, Eredzhib.
Dolgii put'. [By] Bakhov Eredzhib Pshimafovich. Maikop, Adygeiskoe otdelenie Krasnodarskogo knizhnogo izd-va, 1970.
182 p. port.
Title page and text in Adyghe.
Russian title from colophon.
A novel.
MH NUC74-55414

Bakhov, Oleg Petrovich, joint author
see Esaulov, Sergei IUr'evich. (Vertolet kak ob"ekt upravleniia) 1977.

Bakhovaddinov, A M
see
Bogoutdinov, Alautdin Makhmudovich.

Bakhoven, A. F.
see De Economie van de sociale zekerheid. Deventer, Kluwer, 1974.

Bakhoven, A. F.
see Sociale zekerheid... 's-Gravenhage : Martinus Nijhoff, 1974.

Bakhoven, P Sahertian-
see Sahertian-Bakhoven, P

Bakhovkina, L N
(Gosudarstvennye zakupki sel'skokhoziaistvennoi produktsii)
Государственные закупки сельскохозяйственной продукции. (Анализ правоотношений). Москва, "Юрид. лит.," 1972.
216 p. 20 cm. 0.69rub USSR 72–VKP
At head of title: Институт государства и права Академии наук СССР. Л. Н. Баховкина.
Includes bibliographical references.
1. Farm produce—Russia. I. Title.
74–332138

Bakhrakh, Dem'ian Nikolaevich.
(Administrativno-pravovye mery bor'by s p'ianstvom)
Административно-правовые меры борьбы с пьянством / Д. Н. Бахрах ; отв. ред. д-р юрид. наук Ю. М. Ткачевский. — Москва : "Юрид. лит.," 1973.
53 p. ; 20 cm. — (Законодательство об ответственности за пьянство) USSR 73
Includes bibliographical references.
0.09rub
1. Drunkenness (Criminal law)—Russia. 2. Alcoholism and crime. 3. Sanctions, Administrative—Russia. I. Title.
74–352281

Bakhrakh, Dem'ian Nikolaevich.
(Otvetstvennost' za narushenie obshchestvennogo poriadka)
Ответственность за нарушение общественного порядка / Д. Н. Бахрах, А. В. Серегин. — Москва : Юрид. лит., 1976.
80 p. ; 20 cm. — (Библиотечка народного дружинника) USSR 76
Series romanized: Bibliotechka narodnogo druzhinnika.
Includes bibliographical references.
0.12rub
1. Sanctions, Administrative—Russia. 2. Auxiliary police—Russia. 3. Public policy (Law)—Russia. I. Seregin, Alekseĭ Vasil'evich, joint author. II. Title.
77–509307

Bakhrakh, Dem'ian Nikolaevich.
Sovetskoe zakonodatel'stvo ob administrativnoi otvetstvennosti; uchebnoe posobie. Perm', 1969.
340 p. 23 cm.
At head of title: Permskii gosudarstvennyi universitet im. A. M. Gor'kogo.
Bibliographical footnotes.
1. Administrative law–Russia. I. Title.
CSt-H NUC74-55436

Bakhrakh, Dem'ian Nikolaevich, ed.
see Administrativnaia otvetstvennost'... Perm', 1972.

Bakhrakh, Dem'ian Nikolaevich, ed.
see Pravovye voprosy upravleniia. Perm', 1973.

Bakhrakh, **Dem'ian Nikolaevich, ed.**
see **Pravovye voprosy upravleniia promyshlennost'iu. [1972]**

Bakhrakh, G'erom
see
Bachrach, Jerome C

Bakhrakh, Lev Davidovich
see Sovremennoe sostoīanie i perspektivy razvitiīa golografii. 1974.

Bakhrakh, Ye E
Somatic polysaccharide-containing antigens of Pasteurella pestis. Translated from: Zhurnal mikrobiologii, epidemiologii i immunobiologii, 1972, 3: 12-16. [n.p., 1972?]
1 v.
JPRS 56551.
I. Veynblat, V.I. II. Title.
DNAL NUC74-1284

Bakhrakh, Yehoshuʻa
see
Bachrach, Yehoshuʻa.

Bakhren'kov, Nikolaĭ Pavlovich.
(Spravochnik po santekhnike na predprīiatīiakh bytovogo obsluzhivaniīa)
Справочник по сантехнике на предприятиях бытового обслуживания. Минск, "Беларусь," 1973.
272 p. with diagrs. 20 cm. 0.58rub USSR 73
At head of title: Н. П. Бахреньков, Б. В. Кузнецов.
Bibliography: p. 269.
1. Sanitary engineering—Handbooks, manuals, etc. I. Kuznetsov, Boris Vladimirovich, electrical engineer, joint author. II. Title.
TH6024.B34 74-317866

Bakhrevskiĭ, Vladislav Anatol'evich.
(Dorogoe solnt͡se)
Дорогое солнце. [Рассказы. Для сред. школьного возраста. Ил.: С. Калачев]. Москва, "Сов. Россия," 1972.
87 p. with illus. 20 cm. 0.19rub USSR 73-VKP
At head of title: Владислав Бахревский.
CONTENTS: Карельская береза.—"Море, а сколько времени?"—Анвар и большая страна.—Тетрадка, которой не было.—Дорогое солнце.—Старожилово.—Ему все легко дается.—Зеленая игрушечная шишка.—Зимний лагерь капитана Грина.
I. Title.
PZ63.B257 74-332209

Bakhrevskiĭ, Vladislav Anatol'evich.
Kruzhka sily. Moskva, Detskaīa lit-ra, 1969.
110 p. illus. 21 cm.
At head of title: Vladislav Bakhrevskiĭ.
"Dlīa srednego vozrasta."
I. Title.
PSt NUC74-38257

Bakhrevskiĭ, Vladislav Anatol'evich.
(Spoloshnyĭ kolokol)
Сполошный колокол. Ист. роман. [Для сред. и ст. школьного возраста]. Худож. Ю. Иванов. Москва, "Дет. лит.," 1972.
238 p. with illus. 21 cm. 0.52rub USSR 72-VKP
At head of title: Владислав Бахревский.
1. Pskov, Russia (City)—History—Juvenile fiction. I. Title.
PZ63.B273 74-316247

Bakhronov, A., joint author
see Malikov, M (Odamlar uchun khavfli gizhzhalar) 1973.

Bakhrushin, Alekseĭ Petrovich, 1853-1904
see Moscow. Gosudarstvennyĭ istoricheskiĭ muzeĭ. Katalog knig bibliīoteki Aleksīeīa Petrovicha Bakhrushina. 1912.

Bakhrushin, Īuriĭ Alekseevich.
(Istoriīa russkogo baleta)
История русского балета. [Учеб. пособие для ин-тов культуры, театр., хореогр. и культ.-просвет. училищ]. Изд. 2-е. Москва, "Просвещение," 1973.
254 p. with illus., 28 l. of illus. 22 cm. 1.07rub USSR 73
At head of title: Ю. А. Бахрушин.
Includes bibliographical references.
1. Ballet—History. 2. Dancing—Russia—History. I. Title.
GV1787.B22 1973 74-303205

Bakhrushin, Sergeĭ Vladimirovich, 1882-
Dukhovnyīa i dogovornyīa gramoty knīazeĭ velikikh i udīel'nykh. Pod redakt͡sieĭ S. V. Bakhrushina. Moskva, Izdanie N. N. Klochkova, 1909. [Ann Arbor, Mich., 1963]
x, 11-148, 4 p. 27 cm. (Pamīatniki russkoĭ istorii, izdavaemye pod redakt͡sieĭ... V. O. Klīuchevskogo, M. K. Līubavskago... S. V. Bakhrushina... [i dr.])
On double leaves.
Photocopy (positive) made by University Microfilms.
1. Russia–Hist.–To 1533–Sources. I. Title.
MiU NUC74-38246

Bakhrushin, Sergeĭ Vladimirovich, 1882–1950.
(Ocherki po istorii kolonizat͡sii Sibiri v 16. i 17. vv.)
Очерки по истории колонизации Сибири в XVI и XVII вв. / С. В. Бахрушин. — Москва : Изд. М. и С. Сабашниковых, 1927.
198 p., [1] fold. leaf of plates : map ; 24 cm.
Includes bbiliographical references and index.
1. Siberia—History. I. Title.
DK764.B3 1927 77-510372

Bakhrushin, Sergeĭ Vladimirovich, 1882-
Pamīatniki istorii Velikago Novgoroda. Moskva, Izd. N. N. Klochkova, 1909. [Ann Arbor, Mich., 1963]
87 p. (on double leaves) (Pamīatniki russkoĭ istorii)
Photocopy (positive) made by University Microfilms.
1. Novgorod, Russia (City)–Hist.–Sources. I. Title.
MiU NUC74-38245

Bakhrushin, Sergeĭ Vladimirovich, 1882-1950
see Historia dyplomacji. Warszawa, Ksiazka i Wiedza, 1973.

Bakhrushin, Sergeĭ Vladimirovich, 1882-1950, ed.
see Müller, Gerhard Friedrich, 1705-1783. Istoriīa Sibiri. [New York, Public Library, 1963-

Bakhrushin State Central Theatre Museum
see
Moscow. Gosudarstvennyĭ t͡sentral'nyĭ teatral'nyĭ muzeĭ.

Bakhsh, Ahmad, ed.
see Life insurance nationalisation in Pakistan. [Karachi, Sunrise Publications, 1972]

Bakhsh, Husain
see Husain Bakhsh.

Bakhsh, Ilahi.
With the Quaid-i-Azam during his last days. Lahore, Maktaba-tul-Maarif [1949?]
118 p. illus. 19 cm.
1. Jinnah, Mahomed Ali, 1876–1948. I. Title.
DS385.J5B34 73-205811

Bakhsh, Muḥammad.
(Sangīt vidyā nidhi)
سنگیت ودیا نیدھی. مصنف محمد بخش. لاہور، رشید پبلشرز
[1964]
214 p. 22 cm. Rs11.00
In Urdu.
Includes music in letter notation.
1. Music, Indic—History and criticism. I. Title.
ML338.B22 72-930108

Bakhsh, Muhammad
see also
Muhammad Bakhsh, 1830-1906?

Bakhsh, Muhammad Rahim
see Rahim Bakhsh, Muhammad.

Bakhsh, S Karim.
Urdu made easy; a simplified Urdu grammar specially prepared for elementary B. O. R.'s test, army special colloquial examinations in Urdu, by S. Karim Bakhsh. [Lucknow, Printed by R. S. Bhargava, 1941]
2, 241 p. 19 cm.
1. Urdu language—Grammar. I. Title.
PK1973.B3 491'.439'5 74-184471
MARC

Bakhsh, Salahuddin Khuda
see Khuda Bakhsh, Salahuddin, 1877-1931.

Bakhshălīīev, Oruj.
[Mirzā Melkum khan]
Мирзә Мелкум хан. Һәјатı вә әдәби фәалијјәти. Бакы, Азәрнәшр, 1970.
76 p. 16 cm. 0.15rub USSR 71-22194
Includes bibliographical references.
1. Mirzā Malkum Khān, 1833-1908.
PL314.M5Z57 72-227914

Bakhshāpurī, Faiẓu
see
Faiẓu Bakhshāpurī.

Bakhshi, N. K.
see PACT; a panorama of industry, agriculture, commerce & trade. New Delhi.

Bakhshi, Padumlal Punnalal, *comp.*
साहित्य-शिक्षा; उच्च श्रेणीके विद्यार्थियों, उदीयमान कलाकारों और आलोचकोंके लिए साहित्य और उसके अंगोंको स्पष्ट करनेवाले निबन्धोंका क्रमबद्ध संग्रह. सम्पादक पदुमलाल पुन्नालाल बख्शी [तथा] हेमचन्द्र मोदी. बम्बई, हिन्दी-ग्रन्थ-रत्नाकर [1962]
176 p. 19 cm. (नवयुग पाठ्य-ग्रन्थावली, नं. 6)
In Hindi.
1. Hindi literature—Addresses, essays, lectures. I. Modi, Hemachandra. II. Title.
Title romanized: Sāhitya śikshā.
PK2033.B298 S A 68-10987
PL 480 : I-H-5717

Bakhshiev, Nikolaĭ Grigor'evich.
(Spektroskopiīa mezhmolekulīarnykh vzaimodeĭstviĭ)
Спектроскопия межмолекулярных взаимодействий. Ленинград, "Наука," Ленингр. отд-ние, 1972.
263 p. with diagrs. 22 cm. 1.25rub USSR 72-VKP
At head of title: Академия наук СССР. Отделение общей физики и астрономии. Н. Г. Бахшиев.
Includes bibliographies.
1. Molecular spectra. I. Title.
QC454.M6B33 73-326199

Bakhshiev, Nikolaĭ Grigor'evich.
(Vvedenie v molekulīarnuīu spektroskopiīu)
Введение в молекулярную спектроскопию : [учеб. пособие для хим. фак. ун-тов и хим.-технол. ин-тов] / Н. Г. Бахшиев. — Ленинград : Изд-во Ленингр. ун-та, 1974.
181 p. : ill. ; 23 cm. USSR 74
At head of title: Leningradskiĭ gosudarstvennyĭ universitet imeni A. A. Zhdanova.
Bibliography: p. 165–[167]
Includes index.
0.62rub
1. Molecular spectra—Addresses, essays, lectures. I. Title.
QD96.M65B34 75-533736

Bakhshiev, Nikolaĭ Grigor'evich
see Spektrokhimiīa vnutri- i mezhmolekulīarnykh vzaimodeĭstviĭ. 1975-

Bakhshilev, I., joint author
see Pashaiev, A Măktăbli—radio hăvăskary. 1970.

Bakhshish Singh.
The Supreme Court of India as an instrument of social justice / Bakhshish Singh. — 1st ed. — New Delhi : Sterling Publishers, 1976.
303 p. ; 22 cm.
A revision of the author's thesis, Meerut University, 1973.
"Bibliography of books and table of cases": p. [277]-293.
Includes index.
Rs60.00
1. India (Republic). Supreme Court. 2. Sociological jurisprudence. 3. India—Constitutional law. I. Title.
347'.54'035 76-903696
77 MARC

Bakhshu.
(Sahasarasa)
सहसरस; नायक बख्शू के ध्रुपदों का संग्रह. लिप्यंतरण और संपादन: प्रेमलता शर्मा. [1. संस्करण] नयी दिल्ली, संगीत नाटक अकादेमी [1972]
139, 298 p. facsim. 25 cm. Rs25.00
Text in Braj; introd. in Persian and Hindi; critical apparatus in Hindi.
Includes bibliographical references.

1. Songs, Braj—Texts. I. Śarmā, Premalatā, ed. II. Title.

M1808.B336S2 73-904653

Bakhshyan, Step'an Tigrani Melik'-
see Melik'-Bakhshyan, Step'an Tigrani.

Bakhśī, Locana.
(Merī khushī moṛa de)
ਮੇਰੀ ਖ਼ੁਸ਼ੀ ਮੋੜ ਦੇ. [ਕਹਾਣੀਕਾਰ] ਲੋਚਨ ਬਖਸ਼ੀ. [ਜਲੰਧਰ, ਨਿਊ ਬੁੱਕ ਕੰਪਨੀ, 1970]
124 p. 19 cm. Rs5.00
In Panjabi.

I. Title.

PK2659.B287M4 72-906264

Bakhsī, Yogendra, comp.
see Jaitley, Lal Chand, comp. Gaila-gaila. [1970]

Bakhśī Haṃsarāja, 18th cent.
बख्शी हंसराज और उनका काव्य; १८वीं शताब्दी के बुन्देलखंडी कृष्णभक्त कवि बख्शी हंसराज की जीवनी एवं कृतित्व की शोध तथा सनेह-सागर का समग्र सम्पादन. लेखक [i.e. सम्पादक] वासुदेव गोस्वामी. 1. संस्करण. दतिया, म.प्र., गोस्वामी पुस्तक सदन; प्रमुख विक्रेता: लायल बुक डिपो, ग्वालियर, 1970.
211 p. geneal. table. 23 cm. Rs10.00
In Braj; introductory matter and commentary in Hindi.
Biographical sketch of the author: p. 13–34.
I. Gosvāmī, Vāsudeva, ed.
Title romanized: Bakhśī Haṃsarāja aura unakā kāvya.

PK1967.9.B3S3 1970 77-915184

Bakhśī Haṃsarāja, 18th cent.
(Śrī Miharāja caritra)
श्री मिहराज चरित्र / रचयिता बकसी हंसराज ; संपादक देवकृष्ण शर्मा. — प्रथमावृत्ति. — जामनगर : श्री संतसभा, वि.सं. 2021 [1964]
12, 451 p., [2] leaves of plates : ill. ; 25 cm.
In Braj.
Rs10.00

1. Prāṇanātha, 1618–1694—Poetry. I. Śarmā. Devakṛshṇa. II. Title.

PK1967.9.B3S7 1964 76-901508

Bakhśīdāsa Jāṭava
see
Jāṭava, Bakhśīdāsa.

Bakhśū
see
Bakhshu.

Bakht, Zaid.
Comparative cost structure of manufacturing industries of Bangladesh / by Zaid Bakht and Siddiqur Rahman Osmani. — Dacca : Bangladesh Institute of Development Economics, 1973.
26, 8 [21] leaves (18 fold.) ; 29 cm. — (Research report series ; new ser., no. 12)
Bibliography: leaf 26.
1. Manufactures—Costs. 2. Bangladesh — Manufactures. I. Osmani, Siddiqur Rahman, joint author. II. Title. III. Series: Bangladesh Institute of Development Economics. Research report series ; no. 12.
HF5686.M3B12 338.4'3 74-902294
MARC

Bakht Singh
see Singh, Bakht, 1904-

Bakhta, Fedor Mikhaĭlovich.
(Spravochnik brigadira-takelazhnika po montazhu tekhnologicheskogo oborudovaniía)
Справочник бригадира-такелажника по монтажу технологического оборудования / Ф. М. Бахта, Ю. Н. Левицкий. — Москва : Стройиздат, 1974.
187 p. : ill. ; 20 cm. USSR 75
At head of title: Ministerstvo montazhnykh i spetsial'nykh stroitel'nykh rabot SSSR. Glavkhimmontazh i Glavnoe upravlenie kadrov i uchebnykh zavedeniĭ.
0.69rub
1. Hoisting machinery—Rigging—Handbooks, manuals, etc. 2. Installation of industrial equipment—Handbooks, manuals, etc. I. Levitskiĭ, ÍÛriĭ Nikolaevich, joint author. II. Title.
II. Title.
TJ1367.B34 76-521047

Bakhta, Fedor Mikhaĭlovich.
(Spravochnik brigadira-takelazhnika po montazhu tekhnologicheskogo oborudovaniía)
Справочник бригадира-такелажника по монтажу технологического оборудования / Ф. М. Бахта, Ю. Н. Левицкий. — Изд. 2., испр. — Москва : Стройиздат, 1976.
183 p. : ill. ; 20 cm. USSR***
At head of title: Ministerstvo montazhnykh i spetsial'nykh stroitel'nykh rabot SSSR. Glavkhimmontazh i Glavnoe upravlenie kadrov i uchebnykh zavedeniĭ.
0.42rub
1. Hoisting machinery—Rigging—Handbooks, manuals, etc. 2. Installation of industrial equipment—Handbooks, manuals, etc. I. Levitskiĭ, ÍÛriĭ Nikolaevich, joint author. II. Title.
TJ1367.B34 1976 77-508590

Bakhtadze, Boris.
Pis'ma o literature. [By] Boris Nikolaevich Bakhtadze. Tbilisi, Nakaduli, 1968.
108 p.
Title page and text in Georgian.
Russian title from colophon.
1. Literature.
MH NUC74-55437

Bakhtadze, Kseniía Ermolaevna.
[Biologicheskie osnovy kul'tury chaía]
Биологические основы культуры чая. Тбилиси, "Мецниереба," 1971.
367 p. with illus. 22 cm. 2.15rub USSR 72-VKP
At head of title: К. Е. Бахтадзе.
Added t. p. in Georgian.
On leaf preceding t. p.: Академия наук Грузинской ССР.
Bibliography: p. 360–[365]
1. Tea. I. Title.
SB271.B14 72-361432

Bakhtadze, Kseniía Ermolaevna.
[Biologiía, selektsiía i semenovodstvo chaĭnogo rasteniía]
Биология, селекция и семеноводство чайного растения. Москва, Пищепромиздат, 1947.
230 p. illus. 23 cm.
At head of title: Всесоюзный научно-исследовательский институт чайной промышленности и субтропических культур.
Bibliography: p. 227–230.
1. Tea. I. Title.
SB271.B15 55-40908
rev

Bakhtaev, Shabden Abdovich, joint author
see Grinman, Isaak Grigor'evich.
Gazorazrîadnye mikrometry. 1967.

Bakhtamîan, I ÎA Melik-
see
Melik-Bakhtamîan, I ÎA

Bakhtamov, Rafail Borisovich.
[Zakon est' zakon. Azerbaijani]
Ганун ганундур / Рафаил Бахтамов ; [тәрчүме едәни Емин Маһмудов]. — Бакы : Кәнчлик, 1974.
292 p. : ill. ; 21 cm. USSR***
1. Law—Russia—Juvenile literature. I. Title.
Title romanized: Ganun ganundur.
75-549421

Bakhtamova, Z. I.
see Erewani Fizikayi Institowt. (Bibliograficheskiĭ ukazatel' trudov sotrudnikov Erevanskogo fizicheskogo instituta) 1974.

Bakhtānī, 'Abd Allāh, 1926 or 7-
(Mīrzā 'Abd al-Raḥīm Raḥīmī)
میرزا عبد الرحیم رحیمی / تالیـــف عبد الله بختانی. —
[کابل] : انجمن تاریخ افغانستان، [—19]
62 p. ; 26 cm.
Cover title.
1. 'Abd al-Raḥīm Raḥīmī—Biography. 2. Poets, Persian—Biography. I. 'Abd al-Raḥīm Raḥīmī. II. Title.
PK6561.A17Z57 77-970885

Bakhteîarov, Vladimir Dmitrievich
see Spravochnik po derevoobrabotke. 1975.

Bakhteriîarov, V.D.
see ÎArmolinskii, Aleksandr Stepanovich.
Lesnoe tovarovedenie. 1972.

Bakhti, al-Hasan ibn Musa al Nau
see
al-Nawbakhtī, al-Ḥasan ibn Mūsá, fl. 900-913.

Bakhti, Mekhmon.
Vechnoe mgnoven'e; p'esy. Dushanbe, Irfon, 1972.
121 p. port. (Molodye rostki literaturnogo sada)
Title page and text in Tajik.
Russian title from colophon.
MH NUC76-14938

Bakhtiar, Laleh.
Sufi : expressions of the mystic quest / [by] Laleh Bakhtiar. — London : Thames and Hudson, 1976.
120 p. : ill. (some col.), plans, ports. (chiefly col.) ; 26 cm. — (Art and imagination) GB76-20360
Bibliography: p. 120.
ISBN 0-500-81015-X : £2.50
1. Sufism. I. Title.
BP189.3.B34 297'.4 76-377195
76 MARC

Bakhtiar, Laleh, joint author.
see Ardalan, Nader. The sense of unity ... Chicago, University of Chicago Press, 1973.

Bakhtiar, Laleh
see International Congress of Architects, Isfahan, 1970. The interaction of tradition... Teheran, Iran, Shahrivar Press, 1970.

Bakhtiar, Yahya.
Attorney General Yahya Bakhtiar's opening address in the Supreme Court of Pakistan in the reference by the Islamic Republic of Pakistan on dissolution of National Awami Party, Rawalpindi, June 19, 20, and 23, 1975. — Islamabad : Directorate of Research, Reference & Publications, Information & Broadcasting Division, Govt. of Pakistan, 1975.
55 p. ; 25 cm.
Cover title.
1. Awami League. I. Title: Attorney General Yahya Bakhtiar's opening address in the Supreme Court of Pakistan ...
342'.5491'087 75-930549
77 MARC

Bakhtiari, Hamid.
The hydrogeologic behaviour of an unconfined aquifer [Winnipeg, Agassiz Center, University of Manitoba, 1972
xix, 176 p. illus. 28 cm. (Agassiz Center for Water Studies Research report, no. 5) C**
Bibliography: p. 133–137.
1. Aquifers—Manitoba. I. Title. II. Series.
HD1696.C2A7 no. 5 333.9'1'00971 s 73-15485
[GB1030.M35] [627'.56'0971273] MAR

Bakhtiarov, Anatoliĭ Aleksandrovich, 1851–
(Brîukho Peterburga)
Брюхо Петербурга; общественно-физіологическ очерки, А. Бахтіарова. С.-Петербургъ, Изд. Ф. Павленкова, 1888.
316 p. 23 cm.
1. Leningrad. I. Title.
DK551.B27 73-21518

Bakhtiarov, N I
[Povyshenie nadezhnosti raboty pretsizionnykh par toplivnoĭ apparatury dizeleĭ]
Повышение надежности работы прецизионных па топливной аппаратуры дизелей. Москва, "Машино строение," 1972.
200 p. with illus. 22 cm. 0.79rub USSR 72-VK
At head of title: Н. И. Бахтиаров, В. Е. Логинов, И. И. Лихаче
Bibliography: p. 193–[198]
1. Diesel motor—Fuel systems—Reliability. I. Loginov, Vasil Egorovich, joint author. II. Likhachev, Igor' Ivanovich, joint author. III. Title.
TJ797.B28 73-3158

Bǎkhtiîa Il'îa-
see
Il'îa-Bakhtiîa.

Băkhtiiarov, A S
(Ieni măishăt vă kommunist shûuru).
Јени мәишәт вә коммунист шүуру. Бакы, Азәрнәшр, 1970.
96 p. 20 cm. 0.14rub USSR 71-13159
Includes bibliographical references.

1. Azerbaijan—Social conditions. 2. Communism—Azerbaijan. I. Title.
HN530.A9B34 73-207918

Bakhtiiarov, Al'frid Kambarovich, joint author
see Shamsiev, Ubaĭdulla Shamsievich. (Seĭsmostoĭkost' zdaniĭ s uchetom prostranstvennykh faktorov) 1974.

Bakhtin, A. E., ed.
see Ekonomiko-matematicheskie modeli i metody otraslevogo planirovaniia. Novosibirsk, Izd-vo "Nauka"; Sibirskoe otd-nie, 1967.

Bakhtin, A. E., ed.
see Programmy na ĖVM dlia reshenia zadach optimizatsii. 19

Bakhtin, B. B.
see Vakhtin, B. B.

Bakhtin, I. A., ed.
see Nekotorye voprosy vyssheĭ matematiki. Voronezh, 1971.

Bakhtin, Ivan Aleksandrovich
see Metodicheskie rekomendatsii po inkubatsii iaits. 1975.

Bakhtin, Mikhail Ivanovich
see Nekotorye voprosy istorii KPSS i partiĭnoĭ raboty sredi rechnikov. [Gor'kiĭ] Volgo-Viatskoe kn. izd-vo, 1967-

Bakhtin, Mikhail Ivanovich, ed.
see Nekotorye voprosy marksizma-leninizma... Gor'kiĭ, Volgo-Viatskoe knizhnoe izd-vo, 1968.

Bakhtin, Mikhail Mikhaĭlovich.
Dostoevskij; poetica e stilistica [di] Michail Bachtin. Trad. di Giuseppe Garritano. Torino, Einaudi, 1968.
355 p. 19 cm. (Piccola biblioteca Einaudi, 109)
Translation of Problemy poetiki Dostoevskogo.
1. Dostoevskiĭ, Fedor Mikhaĭlovich, 1821-1881.
NjP NUC76-16422

Bakhtin, Mikhail Mikhaĭlovich.
Dostojevskij umělec. K poetice prózy. [Autor:] Michail Bachtin. Z rus. orig. Problemy poetiki Dostojevskogo přel. Jiří Honzík. Doslov: Radegast Parolek. 1. vyd. Praha, Čs. spis., t. Stráž, Vimperk, 1971.
367, [3] p. 21 cm. (Edice Dílna, sv. 37) Kčs28.00 Cz 72-229
Translation of: Problemy poetiki Dostoevskogo.
Includes bibliographical references.
1. Dostoevskiĭ, Fedor Mikhaĭlovich, 1821-1881—Criticism and interpretation. I. Title.
PG3328.Z6B2412 73-348409

Bakhtin, Mikhail Mikhaĭlovich.
Épopée et roman / [Mikhaïl Bakhtine]. — Paris : Éditions de la Nouvelle critique, 1973.
40 p. ; 23 cm. — (Recherches internationales à la lumière du marxisme ; no 76) F***
Cover title.
Includes bibliographical references.
6.00F
1. Fiction. I. Title. II. Series.
AP20.R142 no. 76 74-195343
[PN3331] MARC

Bakhtin, Mikhail Mikhaĭlovich.
François Rabelais a lidová kultura středověku a renesance. Michail Michajlovič Bachtin [přel., obrazovou přílohu uspoř. a dosl. naps. Jaroslav Kolár] Vyd. 1. Praha, Odeon, 1975.
406 p., [24] leaves of plates. col. ill. 22 cm.
Translation of Tvorchestvo Fransua Rable i narodnaia kul'tura srednevekov'ia i Renessansa.
Includes bibliographical references and index.
1. Rabelais, Francois, 1490 (ca)-1553? 2. Wit and humor.
MH NUC77-89740

Bakhtin, Mikhail Mikhaĭlovich.
L'œuvre de François Rabelais et la culture populaire au Moyen Age et sous la Renaissance [par] Mikhaïl Bakhtine. Traduit du russe par Andrée Robel. [Paris] Gallimard [1972, c1970]
471 p. 23 cm. (Bibliothèque des idées) F***
Translation of Tvorchestvo Fransua Rable i narodnaia kul'tura srednevekov'ia i Renessansa.
Includes bibliographical references.
1. Rabelais, François, 1490 (ca.)-1553? I. Title.
PQ1694.B314 72-368256
NjR NcD ViU MiU WMM CtY MWelC AU NcU InU CSt NBuU

Bakhtin, Mikhail Mikhaĭlovich.
Problems of Dostoevsky's poetics [by] Mikhail Bakhtin. Translated by R. W. Rotsel. [Ann Arbor, Mich.] Ardis [c1973]
vii, 249 p. 24 cm. $8.95
Translation of Problemy poėtiki Dostoevskogo.
Bibliography: p. 230-243.
1. Dostoevskiĭ, Fedor Mikhaĭlovich, 1821-1881 — Criticism and interpretation. I. Title.
PG3328.Z6B2413 891.7'3'3 74-152737
ISBN 0-88233-040-3 ; 0-88233-041-1 (pbk.) MARC

Bakhtin, Mikhail Mikhaĭlovich.
(Problemy poėtiki Dostoevskogo)
Проблемы поэтики Достоевского. Изд. 2., перер. и доп. Москва, Сов. писатель, 1963.
361 p. 21 cm.
At head of title: М. Бахтин.
First ed. published in 1929 under title: Проблемы творчества Достоевского.
Bibliographical footnotes.
1. Dostoevskiĭ, Fedor Mikhaĭlovich, 1821-1881—Criticism and interpretation. I. Title.
PG3328.Z6B24 1963 68-45409
rev

Bakhtin, Mikhail Mikhaĭlovich.
(Problemy poėtiki Dostoevskogo)
Проблемы поэтики Достоевского. Изд. 3-е. Москва, "Худож. лит.," 1972.
470 p. 17 cm. 0.98rub USSR 72-VKP
At head of title: М. Бахтин.
First ed. published in 1929 under title: Проблемы творчества Достоевского.
Includes bibliographical references.
1. Dostoevskiĭ, Fedor Mikhaĭlovich, 1821-1881—Criticism and interpretation. I. Title.
PG3328.Z6B25 1972 73-304487

Bakhtin, Mikhail Mikhaĭlovich.
(Problemy tvorchestva Dostoevskogo)
Проблемы творчества Достоевского. Ленинград, Прибой, 1929.
243 p.
At head of title: М. М. Бахтин.
Later editions published under title: Проблемы поэтики Достоевского.
Bibliographical footnotes.
Photo-offset. Ann Arbor, Mich., University Microfilms, 1961. 22 cm.
1. Dostoevskiĭ, Fedor Mikhaĭlovich, 1821-1881—Criticism and interpretation. I. Title.
PG3328.Z6B24 1961 75-201365
rev

Bakhtin, Mikhail Mikhaĭlovich.
(Voprosy literatury i ėstetiki)
Вопросы литературы и эстетики : Исследования разных лет / М. Бахтин. — Москва : Худож. лит., 1975.
502 p., [1] leaf of plates : port. ; 21 cm. USSR 75
Includes index.
1.45rub
1. Fiction—Addresses, essays, lectures. 2. Literature—Addresses, essays, lectures. I. Title.
PN3331.B25 76-516041

Bakhtin, Nikolaĭ Ivanovich.
(Gorod i derevnia)
Город и деревня : экономические аспекты / Н. И. Бахтин. — Минск : Беларусь, 1974.
190 p. ; 17 cm. USSR***
Includes bibliographical references.
0.28rub
1. Russia—Rural conditions. 2. Communism and society. 3. Agriculture—Economic aspects—Russia. I. Title.
HN523.5.B33 75-569661

Bakhtin, Vladimir Solomonovich
see Novye golosa. 1973.

Bakhtin, Vladimir Solomonovich
see Skazki Leningradskoi oblasti ser'eznye i neser'eznye, ozornye i ne ochen' ... 1976.

Bakhtinskiĭ, Mikhail Iosifovich
see
Bakhtyns'kyĭ, Mykhaĭlo Iosypovych, 1934-

Bakhtiyar, Muzaffar
see Congress of Iranian Studies, 1st, Teheran University, 1970. Proceedings... Teheran, 1972-

Bakhtiyār, Muzaffar, ed.
see Yādnāmah-'i Duktur Mu'īn. [1972]

Bakhtiyārī, Abū al-Fatḥ Awzhan
see
Awzhan Bakhtiyārī, Abū al-Fatḥ, 1906 or 7-

Bakhtiyārī, ʻAlī Qulī Maḥmūdī
see
Maḥmūdī Bakhtiyārī, ʻAlī Qulī.

Bakhtiyārī, Husayn Pazhmān
see Pazhmān Bakhtiyārī, Husayn.

Bakhtiyārī, Pazhmān.
(Andarz-i yak mādar)
اندرز يك مادر ، از پژمان بختيارى . [تهران] انتشارات ادارهٔ كل نگارش ، وزارت فرهنگ و هنر [1347 i. e. 1968]
67 p. illus. 25 cm.
«بمناسبت جشن فرهنگ و هنر»
Poems.
I. Title.
PK6561.B324A8 74-213118

Bakhtyns'kyĭ, Mykhaĭlo Iosypovych, 1934–
(Materyns'ki zori)
Материнські зорі; поезії. Київ, Рад. письменник, 1973.
70 p. illus., port. 17 cm. 0.21rub USSR***
At head of title: Михайло Бахтинський.
I. Title.
PG3949.12.A37M3 74-343939

Bakhtyrev, Anatoliĭ Ivanovich, 1928–1968?
(Ėpokha pozdnego reabilitansa)
Эпоха позднего реабилитанса; рассказы, дневник, письма. Иерусалим, Изд. П. Гольдштейна, Академия пресс, 1973.
125 p. port. 22 cm.
I. Title.
PG3479.K55E6 1973 75-564740

Bakhuizen, S C
Chalcis-in-Euboea, iron and Chalcidians abroad / by S. C. Bakhuizen, with a contribution by R. Kreulen. — Leiden : Brill, 1976.
vi, 100 p. : ill., maps ; 28 cm. — (Chalcidian studies ; 3) (Studies of the Dutch Archaeological and Historical Society ; v. 5) Ne76-25
Bibliography: p. [xi].
Includes indexes.
ISBN 9004045465 : fl 36.00
1. Khalkís, Greece—History. 2. Iron mines and mining—Greece—Khalkís. 3. Iron industry and trade—Khalkís, Greece. 4. Khalkís, Greece—Emigration and immigration. I. Kreulen, R. II. Title. III. Series. IV. Series: Dutch Archaeological and Historical Society. Studies ; v. 5.
DF261.C4B34 938'.4 76-383370
*77 MARC

Bakhuizen, Th.
see Utrecht. Rijksuniversiteit. Instituut voor Staats- en Administratiefrecht. Projectgroep Bestuurskunde. Enige beschouwingen over het verkeersbeleid in het algemeen en de rijkswegenplanning in het bijzonder. [IJmuiden, Vermande, 1973].

Bakhuizen van den Brink, Jan Nicolaas, 1896–
Constantijn de Grote / J. N. Bakhuizen van den Brink. — Amsterdam : Noord-Hollandsche Uitg. Mij., 1975.
53 p., [1] leaf of plates : ill. ; 24 cm. — (Mededelingen der Koninklijke Nederlandse Akademie van Wetenschappen, Afd. Letterkunde : Nieuwe reeks ; deel 38, no. 6) Ne 76-5
Pages also numbered 227-275 continuing the paging of the preceding number.
Includes bibliographical references and index.
fl 15.00
1. Constantinus I, the Great, Emperor of Rome, d. 337. I. Title. II. Series: Akademie van Wetenschappen, Amsterdam. Afdeling Letterkunde. Mededelingen ; Nieuwe reeks ; deel 38, no. 6.
AS244.A512 deel 38, no. 6 76-527651
[DG315]

Bakhuizen van den Brink, Jan Nicolaas, 1896-
see Ratramnus, monk of Corbie, d. ca. 868.
De corpore et sanguine Domini... Ed. renouvelée. Amsterdam: North-Hollad, 1974.

Bakhuizen van den Brink, Jan Nicolaas, 1896-
see Wat vindt u van het getuigenis? Wageningen, Zomer & Keuning [1972]

Bakhur, Viktor Timofeevich.
(Ėmotsii—plíusy i minusy)
Эмоции—плюсы и минусы / В. Т. Бахур. — Москва : Знание, 1975.
93 p. : ill. ; 17 cm. — (Народный университет : Факультет здоровья ; 2/1975) USSR 75
0.15rub
1. Emotions. I. Title. II. Series: Narodnyĭ universitet : Fakul'tet zdorov'ía ; 1975, 2.
RA773.N3 1975, vol. 2 75-534019
[BF566]

Bakhurov, Vasiliĭ Gerasimovich.
[Khimicheskaía dobycha poleznykh iskopaemykh]
Химическая добыча полезных ископаемых. (Основы процесса, характеристика месторождений, исследования и изыскания, пром. опыт). Под ред. Д. Т. Десятникова. Москва, "Недра," 1972.
134 p. with diagrs. 21 cm. 0.86rub USSR 72-VKP
At head of title: В. Г. Бахуров, И. К. Руднева.
Bibliography: p. 130-[132]
1. Leaching. 2. Nonferrous metals. I. Rudneva, Irina Konstantinovna, joint author. II. Title.
TN292.B337 73-313944

Bakhutov, Aleksandr Mikhaĭlovich.
(Bezrabotitsa i bor'ba s neĭ)
Безработица и борьба с ней / А. Бахутов. — Москва : Московский рабочий, 1928.
70 p. ; 18 cm.
Bibliography: p. 70.
"Народное хозяйство СССР в 1927/28 г."
1. Unemployed—Russia. I. Title.
HD5796.B33 75-529330

Bakhvalov, Aleksandr Aleksandrovich.
(Nezhnost' k revushchemu zveríu)
Нежность к ревущему зверю. Роман. Москва, "Современник," 1973.
277 p. 20 cm. (Новинки Современника) 0.59rub USSR 73
At head of title: Александр Бахвалов.
I. Title.
PG3479.K56N4 74-343973

Bakhvalov, ÍU. A., ed.
see Vychislitel'naía tekhnika i kibernetika. 1971.

Bakhvalov, N S
(Chislennye metody)
Численные методы; анализ, алгебра, обыкновенные дифференциальные уравнения. Допущено в качестве учеб. пособия для студентов вузов, обучающихся по специальности "Прикладная математика." Москва, Наука, 1973-
v. illus. 23 cm. 1.47rub (v. 1) USSR***
At head of title, : Н. С. Бахвалов.
Bibliography, : p. [622]-[627]
1. Numerical analysis. I. Title.
QA297.B33 74-308566

Bakhvalov, N S
(Chislennye metody)
Численные методы : анализ, алгебра, обыкновенные дифференциальные уравнения : [учеб. пособие для вузов, по специальности "Прикл. математика"] / Н. С. Бахвалов. — Изд. 2-е, стереотип. — Москва : Наука, 1975-
v. : ill. ; 22 cm. USSR 75
Bibliography: v. 1, p. [622]-627.
Vol. 1 includes index.
1.47rub (v. 1)
1. Numerical analysis. I. Title.
QA297.B33 1975 75-402964

Bakhytzhan Momysh-uly
see
Baurdzhan Momysh-Uly.

Bâkî, 1526 or 7-1600.
Baki : hayatı, sanatı, şiirleri / hazırlayan, Nevzat Yesirgil. — 2. basılış. — İstanbul : Varlık Yayınevi, 1963.
104 p. ; 17 cm. — (Türk klâsikleri ; 22) (Varlık yayınları ; sayı 1001)
Includes bibliographical references.
1. Bâkî, 1526 or 7-1600. I. Kudret, Cevdet, ed.
PL248.B26Z52 1963 75-587484

Bâkî, 1526 or 7-1600.
Baki [hazırlayan] İsmet Zeki Eyüboğlu. [İstanbul, Kitaş, 1972]
191 p. (Doğunun ve batının büyük ustaları, 2)
1. Eyüboğlu, Zeki.
MH NUC74-1291

Baki, R
see
Bachi, Roberto, 1909-

Bakić, Dragoljub N 1898-1968.
(Pet vekova Kragujevca)
Пет векова Крагујевца. Чланци и успомене, преводи и преписка. 〈Живомир. Спасић: Драгољуб Бакић и његово дело〉. Крагујевац, Народна библиотека "Вук Караџић," 1972.
390, [2] p. with illus., facsims., ports. 20 cm. (Завичајна библиотека, књ. 1) 60.00Din Yu 73
At head of title: Драгољуб Н. Бакић.
Summary in French, English, Italian, and Russian.
Bibliography: p. 366-367.
1. Kragujevac, Yugoslavia—History. I. Title.
DR396.K7B34 1972 73-970390

Bakić, Vojislav S
Porodično pravo. 1., dop. i izm. izd. Beograd, Savremena administracija, 1974.
346 p. illus. 24 cm. Yu***
At head of title: Vojislav S. Bakić.
1. Domestic relations—Yugoslavia. I. Title.
74-970653

Bakić, Vojislav S
Porodično pravo Vojislav S. Bakić. 8., dop. i izm. izd. Beograd, Savremena administracija, 1975.
xvi, 376 p. 24 cm.
Includes index.
1. Domestic relations--Yugoslavia. I. Title.
ViU NUC77-89736

Bakić, Vojislav S
see Najnoviji zakoni iz porodičnog prava. Osnovi zakonodavstva SSSR... Beograd, Institut za uporedno,pravo, 1969.

Bakić, Vojislav S.
see Serbia (Federated Republic, 1945-). Laws, statutes, etc. Zbirka novih porodičnopravnih i naslednopravnih propisa SR Srbije. Beograd : Savremena administracija, 1975.

Bakidsky, Jan
see Bratislava. Vysoká škola ekonomická. Študijný program Vysokej školy ekonomickej v Bratislave. [Bratislava] 1967.

Bakiev. A
see
Boqiev, Osim.

Bakiev, Abdushukur Rakhimovich
see
Boqiev, A

Bakikhanov, Abbas-Kuli, 1794-1847.
(Gulistān-i Iram)
گلستان ارم [از] عباسقلی آقا باکیخانوف. متن علمی، انتقادی بسعی و اهتمام عبد الکریم علی‌زاده [و دیگران] باکو، ادارهٔ انتشارات علم، 1970.
xix, 287, 39 p. 23 cm.
At head of title: فرهنگستان علوم جمهوری شوروی سوسیالیستی آذربایجان. انستیتوی تاریخ.
Added title pages in Russian and Azerbaijani; Russian t. p.: Аббас-Кулу Ага Бакиханов. Гюлистан-и Ирам; Azerbaijani t. p.: Аббасгулу Ага Бакыханов. Кулустани-Ирәм.
Introd. in Azerbaijani, English, and Persian.
1. Azerbaijan—History. I. Alizade, Abdul-Kerim, ed. II. Title.
DS324.A9B34 1970 74-219130

Bâkiler, Yavuz Bülent.
Duvak; şiirler. Ankara, Hisar Yayınları, 1971.
64 p. illus. (Hisar yayınları, 14)
MH NUC73-126351

(Bakin)
馬琴 / 水野稔編. — 東京 : 角川書店, 昭和34 [1959]
380 p. : ill. ; 20 cm. — (日本古典鑑賞講座 ; 第25巻)
Bibliography: p. 367-380.
1. Takizawa, Bakin, 1767-1848—Criticism and interpretation. I. Mizuno, Minoru, 1911- II. Takizawa, Bakin, 1767-1848. Nansō Satomi hakken den. Selections. 1959. III. Takizawa, Bakin, 1767-1848. Chinsetsu yumiharizuki. Selections. 1959. IV. Series: Nihon koten kanshō kōza ; dai 25-kan.
PL798.4.Z5B28 75-789836

(Bakin)
馬琴 / 日本文学研究資料刊行会編. — 東京 : 有精堂, 昭和49 [1974]
2, 308 p. : ill. ; 22 cm. — (日本文学研究資料叢書) Ja ***
Bibliography: p. 307-308.
CONTENTS: 藤村作 馬琴研究—水野稔 馬琴の文学と風土—森潤三郎 曲亭馬琴翁と和漢小説の批評—荒木良雄 小説批評家としての馬琴—中村幸彦 滝沢馬琴の小説観—重友毅 馬琴の隠微—後藤丹治 馬琴の読本と雨月物語—鵜月洋 馬琴文学の基本的課題—浜田啓介 馬琴の所謂稗史七法則について—国領不二男 黄表紙よりみた馬琴の教訓性—学海居士 椿説弓張月細評—中村幸彦 椿説弓張月の史的位置—学海居士 南総里見八犬伝—和田万吉 南総里見八犬伝—浜田啓介 八犬伝の構想に於ける対管領戦の意義—橋本四郎 里見八犬伝の文体とその文語—平出鏗二郎 五嶋恵迪及び其馬琴論—浜田啓介 馬琴に於ける書肆、作者、読者の問題—柴田光彦 滝沢家訪問往来人名簿—鈴木重三 馬琴読本諸版書誌ノート—木村三四吾 馬琴遺稿流伝始末項記—徳田武 解説
¥2600
1. Takizawa, Bakin, 1767-1848—Criticism and interpretation—Addresses, essays, lectures. I. Nihon Bungaku Kenkyū Shiryō Kankōkai. II. Series: Nihon bungaku kenkyū shiryō sōsho.
PL798.4.Z5B29 75-803846

(Bakin hyōtō shū)
馬琴評答集 天理 天理大学出版部 東京 八木書店(発売) 昭和48(1973)
604, 56 p. illus. 22 cm. (天理図書館善本叢書 和書之部 12)
¥8600 Ja 73-7245
Photoreproduction of MS. copies.
CONTENTS: 小津桂窓・曲亭馬琴 侠客傳第二集愚評 八犬傳九輯愚評—石川畳翠・典亭馬琴 侠客傳四輯評—小津桂窓・曲亭馬琴 八犬傳九輯再評并答書 侠客傳四輯評 里見八犬傳九輯中帙愚評 八犬傳九輯下帙上評并答 八犬傳九輯下帙中之中愚評 金瓶梅五集 里見八犬傳第九輯下帙之下上徧略評 八犬傳第九輯下帙之下中徧愚評—曲亭馬琴 稗說虎之巻 水滸後傳國字評追考 三遂平妖傳國字評—濱田啓介 解題

1. Takizawa, Bakin, 1767-1848—Correspondence—Facsimiles. 2. Japanese fiction—Edo period, 1600-1868—History and criticism. 3. Chinese fiction—History and criticism. I. Takizawa, Bakin, 1767-1848. II. Ozu, Keisō. III. Ishikawa, Jōsui, d.? 1841. IV. Series: Tenri Toshokan. Tenri Toshokan zempon sōsho, Washo no bu, 12.
PL798.4.Z5B3 1973 74-810350

Baking; an American tradition; a bicentennial publication from the publishers of Baking Industry. [Editor: Laurie A. Gorton. Chicago, Putnan, c1976]
76 p. ill. (some col.) 42 cm.
Cover title.
1. Baking. 2. Bakers and bakeries--U. S. --History. I. Baking industry.
IU NUC77-89739

Baking industry
see Baking; an American tradition... [Chicago, Putnan, c1976]

Baking industry magazine
see Formula book of cakes, fillings & icings, v. 2. Chicago [1970]

Bakinovskiĭ, L. V.
see Khimiía uglevodov. 1975.

Bakinovskiĭ, L. V.
see Khimiía uglevodov. 1976.

Bakinskiĭ, Viktor Semenovich.
Istoriía chetyrekh brat'ev; roman. [Leningrad, "Sovetskiĭ pisatel' ", 1971]
324 p. illus. 21 cm.
At head of title: Viktor Bakinskiĭ.
I. Title.
NIC NUC76-63338

Bakinskiĭ nauchno-issledovatel'skiĭ institut travmatologii i ortopedii
see T͡Sentral'nyĭ nauchno-issledovatel'skiĭ institut travmatologii i ortopedii. Materialy ob"edinennoĭ nauchnoĭ sessii... Baku, 1963.

(Bakinskiĭ okrug protivovozdushnoĭ oborony)
Бакинский округ противовоздушной оборны : ист. очерк : 1920–1974 гг. / [ред. коллегия А. У. Константинов (пред.) ... et al. ; предисл. Героя Сов. Союза, Маршала Сов. Союза П. Батицкого]. — Баку : Азернешр, 1974.
362 p., [15] leaves of plates : ill. ; 22 cm. USSR 75
Includes bibliographical references.
1.60rub
1. Baku—Air defenses, Military—History. I. Konstantinov, A. U.
UG635.R9B34 76–507093

Bakīr, Amīn.
(Masraḥīyat fajr wa-ramād)
مسرحية فجر ورماد : ثلاثة فصول فى مشاهد / تأليف امين بكير. — [القاهرة] : المجلس الأعلى لرعاية الفنون والآداب والعلوم الاجتماعية، 1971]
134 p. ; 20 cm. — (مطبوعات المجلس الاعلى لرعاية الفنون والاداب والعلوم الاجتماعية ؛ 135 : الكتاب الاول ؛ 48)
I. Title. II. Title: Fajr wa-ramād. III. Series: United Arab Republic. al-Majlis al-Aʻlá li-Riʻāyat al-Funūn wa-al-Ādāb wa-al-ʻUlūm al-Ijtimāʻīyah. al-Maṭbūʻāt ; 135.
PJ7816.A46M3 74–960664

Bakīr, Najīb.
(Dawr al-Niyābah al-ʻĀmmah fī Qānūn al-murāfaʻāt)
دور النيابة العامة فى قانون المرافعات : دراسة تأصيلية مقارنة / تأليف نجيب بكير. — الطبعة 1. — [القاهرة] : مكتبة عين شمس، 1974.
726 p. ; 24 cm.
Bibliography: p. [704]–719.
£E2.25
1. Public prosecutors. I. Title.
74–960453

Bakir, Tomris.
Der Kolonnettenkrater in Korinth und Attika zwischen 625 und 550 v. Chr. / Tomris Bakir. — Würzburg : K. Triltsch, 1974.
81 p., [8] leaves of plates : ill. ; 25 cm. — (Beiträge zur Archäologie ; 7) GFR***
Bibliography: p. 69–77.
1. Corinth, Greece—Antiquities. 2. Attica—Antiquities. 3. Kraters—Greece—Corinth. 4. Kraters—Greece—Attica. 5. Pottery dating. I. Title. II. Series.
DF261.C65B34 938'.7'02 75–563487

Bakirci, Nebile
see Turkey. Talim ve Terbiye Dairesi. Ilk ve orta dereceli okullarda... Ankara, 1961.

Bakirov, Abdulkhalat Abdullatypovich.
(Geologicheskie osnovy prognozirovanii͡a neftegazonosnosti nedr)
Геологические основы прогнозирования нефтегазоносности недр. Москва, "Недра," 1973.
344 p. with diagrs. and maps, 1 l. of maps. 25 cm. 3.05rub USSR 73
At head of title: А. А. Бакиров.
Bibliography: p. 333–[342]
1. Petroleum—Geology. 2. Gas, Natural—Geology. I. Title.
TN870.5.B27 73–365729

Bakirov, Abdulkhalat Abdullatypovich
see Teoreticheskie osnovy i metody poiskov i razvedki skoplenii nefti i gaza. 1976.

Bakirov, Apash Bakirovich.
(Metamorficheskie kompleksy Vostochnoĭ chasti Sredneĭ Azii)
Метаморфические комплексы Восточной части Средней Азии. Фрунзе, "Илим," 1972.
137 p. with diagrs., 3 l. of diagrs. 21 cm. 0.58rub USSR 72
At head of title: Академия наук Киргизской ССР. Институт геологии. Академия наук СССР. Сибирское отделение. Институт геологии и геофизики. А. Бакиров, Н. Л. Добрецов.
Bibliography: p. 129–[135]
1. Rocks, Metamorphic. 2. Petrology—Soviet Central Asia. I. Dobret͡sov, Nikolaĭ Leont'evich, joint author. II. Title.
QE475.A2B33 73–347981

Bakirov, F S
(I͡Uridik terminlar lughati)
Юридик терминлар луғати. Х. С. Сулаймонова таҳрири остида. Тошкент, Ўзбекистон ССР Фанлар академияси нашриёти, 1959.
118 p. 21 cm.
At head of title: Ўзбекистон ССР Фанлар академияси. Философия ва ҳуқуқ институти. Ф. Бакиров.
Added t. p.: Словарь юридических терминов.
1. Law—Terms and phrases. I. Title. II. Title: Slovar' i͡uridicheskikh terminov.
74–224401

Bakirov, F S
(Khalq maslaȟatchisi)
Халқ маслаҳатчиси : халқ маслаҳатчиларига ёрдам / Ф. Бакиров. — Тошкент : Ўздавнашр, 1960.
78 p. ; 20 cm.
Includes bibliographical references.
1. Lay judges—Uzbekistan. I. Title.
75–549858

Bakirov, F S
(Khalq maslaȟatchisi)
Халқ маслаҳатчиси : қўлланма : ўзгартилган ва тўлдирилган / Ф. Бакиров. — 2. нашри. — Тошкент : Ўзбекистон, 1964.
93 p. ; 20 cm.
Includes bibliographical references.
1. Lay judges—Russia. 2. Lay judges—Uzbekistan. I. Title.
75–532646

Bakirov, Fatikh
see
Bakirov, F S

Bakirov, Urkhan Khakimzhanovich.
[Prognozirovanie nauchno-tekhnicheskogo progressa v oblasti okhrany truda]
Прогнозирование научно-технического прогресса в области охраны труда. Свердловск, 1970.
134 p. with diagrs. 20 cm. (Охрана труда и техника безопасности) 0.60rub USSR 71–VKP
At head of title: Центральный научно-исследовательский и проектно-конструкторский институт профилактики пневмокониозов и техники безопасности. У. Х. Бакиров, В. С. Заверткин.
Bibliography: p. 130–[134]
1. Mine safety. I. Zavertkin, V. S., joint author. II. Title.
TN295.B34 72–360073

Bakirtzēs, Giōrgos
see
Vakirtzēs, Giōrgos.

Bakis, Karl I͡Anovich.
(Ėkonomicheskai͡a ėffektivnost' avtomaticheskikh stanochnykh liniĭ v mashinostroenii)
Экономическая эффективность автоматических станочных линий в машиностроении. Москва, "Машиностроение," 1972.
144 p. 21 cm. 0.51rub USSR 72–VKP
At head of title: К. Я. Бакис.
Bibliography: p. [143]
1. Machinery, Automatic. I. Title.
TJ213.B12 73–318574

Bakis, Raimo.
Theoretical considerations in the design of an electron gun and the evaluation of measured excitation functions. [n.p.] 1959.
77 l.
Thesis (Ph.D.)—Kansas State University.
I. Title.
KMK NUC73-119559

Bakish, David.
Richard Wright. New York, Ungar [1973]
xiv, 114 p. 20 cm. (Modern literature monographs)
Bibliography: p. 107–109.
1. Wright, Richard, 1908–1960.
PS3545.R815Z56 813'.5'2 71–190353
ISBN 0–8044–2015–7 MARC

Bakish, Robert A., ed
see International Conference on Electron and Ion Beam Science and Technology, 5th, Houston, Tex., 1972. Electron and ion beam science and technology. Princeton, N.J, [1972]

Bakish, Robert A., ed.
see Practice of desalination. Park Ridge, N. J., Noyes Data Corp., 1973.

Bakitov, Kalau Bakitovich, joint author
see Kanlybaeva, Zhamal Musagalievna. Fiziko-mekhanicheskie svoĭstva gornykh porod i ikh vlii͡anie na prot͡sess sdvizhenii͡a massiva. 1972.

Bakjian, Andy, 1915–
A hitch in Hell. San Antonio, Oliver Co. [1974]
174 p. 22 cm. $6.95
I. Title.
PZ4.B16974Hi 813'.5'4 74–18340
[PS3552.A437] MARC
ISBN 0–8111–0542–3

Bakjidarov, L S
see Barkhudarov, Leonid Semenovich.

Bakk, Ann, 1942- joint author
see Grunewald, Karl, 1921- Omsorgsboken. Stockholm, Esselte studium, 1973.

Bakkady, Laszlo.
10 [i.e. Tíz] ev aranyermes trofeai ... 1960-1969. Budapest, Mezogazdasagi Kiado, 1971.
469 p. illus.
Preface and captions also in German.
1. Hunting. Hungary. I. Szidnai, Laszlo. II. Szabolcs, Jozsef. III. Title.
DNAL NUC73-41426

Bakkala, Richard G
Synopsis of biological data on the chum salmon, Oncorhynchus keta (Walbaum) 1792. Washington, U.S. Bureau of Commercial Fisheries, 1970.
89 p. illus. (U.S. Fish and Wildlife Service. Circular 315) (FAO Fisheries synopsis no. 41)
1. Chum salmon. I. United States. Bureau of Commercial Fisheries. II. Title. III. Series. IV. Series: Food and Agriculture Organization of the United Nations. FAO Fisheries synopsis no. 41.
DI NUC76-16420

Bakkan, Engvald, 1897-
Ei kvern som mel : noveller / Engvald Bakkan. — Oslo : Gyldendal, 1976.
122 p. ; 22 cm. N76-Oct.
CONTENTS: Ei kvern som mel.—Vilbør.—Brevet frå Solskinsøyane.—Takk for Gro.
ISBN 8205089442 : kr59.00
I. Title.
PT9067.B3K84 77-483618
•77 MARC

Bakkan, Engvald, 1897–
Noveller i utval. Oslo, Gyldendal, 1972.
179 p. 19 cm. kr49.50 N 72–38
CONTENTS: Åklæet og spjotet.—Skuggar i lauv.—Fiskaren og lykka hans.—Ein husmann.—Slumpehøvet.—Stjernene skal danse.—Pehrsen—med h.—"Kramellen."—Det blinde hjarta.—Virgo.—Eit brev.—Nei, at du kom hit—?—I natt får du sove—!—Ingenting.—Mellom røvarar.—Levande vatn over turr mold.
I. Title.
PT9067.B3N69 72–370834
ISBN 0–82–05–00968–6

Bakkār, Zubayr ibn
see Zubayr ibn Bakkār, d. 870.

Bakkay, László.
10 [i. e. Tíz] év aranyérmes trófeái = Goldmedaillen-Trophäen des letzten Jahrzehntes (1960–1969) / Bakkay László, Szidnai László, Szabolcs József ; [szerk., Kattinger Gusztáv]. — Budapest : Mezőgazdasági Kiadó, 1971.
469 p. : ill. ; 21 x 30 cm.
Hungarian and German; introd. also in French.
1. Hunting trophies. 2. Deer hunting—Europe. I. Szidnai, László, joint author. II. Szabolcs, József, joint author. III. Title. IV. Title: Goldmedaillen-Trophäen des letzten Jahrzehntes (1960–1969)
SK301.B27 75–553470

Bakke, Arnt. Folkemusikken i Vefsn. 1974
in Svare, Reidar. Frå gamal tid : tru og tradisjon. Mosjøen : [Vefsn bygdeboknemnd], 1973.

Bakke, Arnt.
Fridthjov Anderssen; mennesket og musikeren [av] Arnt Bakke og Haavard Hanssen. Bodø, H. Sundem, 1947.
170 p. illus. 23 cm.
1. Anderssen, Fridthjov, 1876–1937. I. Hanssen, Haavard.
ML410.A556B3 73–211767

Bakke, Edward Wight, 1903-
Organizational factors in productivity. [n.p., 1961]
22 l. illus.
Paper for Conference on Labor Productivity, Cadenabbia, Italy, 1961, under the auspices of the International Economic Association.
Title may vary from final version.
1. Productivity. I. Conference on Labor Productivity, Cadenabbia, Italy, 1961. II. Title.
MH-IR NUC74-40207

Bakke, Egil, 1927–
Økonomisk politikk / Egil Bakke. — Oslo : Universitetsforlaget, c1975.
101 p. : graphs. ; 21 cm. N 75–May
ISBN 82–00–01446–0 : kr42.00
1. Norway—Economic policy. 2. Norway—Commercial policy. I. Title.
HC365.B28 75–537164

Bakke, Jan.
The chemistry of some nitrogen-containing organic compounds. Trondheim, Norway, University of Trondheim, 1971.
1 v. (various pagings) illus. 24 cm. (Trondheim. Norges tekniske høgskole. Doktoravhandling, no. 104)
Includes bibliographical references.
1. Nitro compounds. 2. Aromatic compounds. I. Title. II. Series.
AAP NUC73-120146

Bakke, Jeannette Anderson.
The lion and the lamb and the children; Christian childhood education through The chronicles of Narnia. [Minneapolis] c1975.
viii, 357 l. illus. 29 cm.
Thesis (Ph. D.)--University of Minnesota.
Bibliography: leaves 278-292.
MnU NUC77-89732

Bakke, John Paul, 1938-
The debates on the Fox and Pitt East India Bills, 1783, 1784: a case study in the rhetoric of the House of Commons. [Iowa City] University of Iowa, 1966. Ann Arbor, Mich., University Microfilms [1967]
v, 626 l. 22 cm.
Thesis—University of Iowa.
Bibliography: leaves 620-626.
"... authorized facsimile ... produced by microfilm xerography ..."
1. Great Britain—Politics and government—1760-1820. 2. Great Britain. Parliament. House of Commons. 3. East India Company (English) I. Title.
OkU NUC74-124854

Bakke, Karen.
The sewing machine as a creative tool / Karen Bakke. — Englewood Cliffs, N.J. : Prentice-Hall, c1976.
xiii, 113 p., [4] leaves of plates : ill. ; 24 cm. — (The Creative handcrafts series) (A Spectrum book)
Bibliography: p. 108-110.
Includes index.
ISBN 0-13-807255-8. ISBN 0-13-807248-5 pbk.
1. Sewing. 2. Needlework. I. Title.
TT713.B34 746.4'028 75-26868
75 MARC

Bakke, Kari.
Gråspurven : utvalg, 1962–1974 / Kari Bakke. — Oslo : Aschehoug, 1974.
72 p. ; 19 cm. N 74–Nov
Poems.
ISBN 82–03–05399–3 : kr24.00
I. Title.
PT8951.12.A4G7 75–576661

Bakke, Marit.
Nyheder i radio og TV. Sammenligning mellem Norge og Danmark. Af Marit Bakke og Karen Siune. Arhus C, Arhus universitet, Institut for statskundskab, Eksp.: Universitetsparken, [1972.
iv, 70, [12] l. 30 cm. kr10.00 D 73–27
Bibliography : leaf [82]
1. Radio journalism — Denmark. 2. Radio journalism — Norway. 3. Television broadcasting of news—Denmark. 4. Television broadcasting of news—Norway. I. Siune, Karen, joint author. II. Title.
PN5287.R3B3 73–359717

Bakke, Marit.
Radio and TV news in Denmark and Norway by Marit Bakke and Karen Siune. Aarhus, Denmark, Institute of Political Science, University at Aarhus, 1974.
9 l. 30 cm.
IU NUC76-18068

Bakke, Marit.
Sentrum og periferi i radio- og fjernsynsnyheter. En innholdsanalyse av innenriksnyheter. Oslo, 1973.
6, 87 l. tables, diagrs. 30 cm. (Universitetet i Oslo. Institutt for presseforskning. Stensil nr. 26) N 73
Bibliography : p. 85–87.
1. Radio journalism — Norway. 2. Television broadcasting of news—Norway. 3. Content analysis (Communication) I. Title. II. Series: Oslo. Universitetet. Institutt for Presseforskning. Stensil nr. 26.
PN5291.O75 nr. 26 73–364954
[P92.N6]
ISBN 82–570–6007–0

Bakke, Marit.
Utenrikstelegrammer fra NTB. En analyse av nyhetskriterier. Oslo, 1970.
1 v. (various pagings) maps, tables, diagrs. 30 cm. (Institutt for presseforskning. Stensil nr. 14) N 71–4/5
Includes bibliography.
1. Norsk telegrambyrå. I. Title. II. Series: Oslo. Universitet. Institutt for presseforskning. Stensil nr. 14.
PN5291.O75 nr. 14 73–342110
[HE8260.N65]

Bakke, Mary Sterling.
A sampler of lifestyles : womanhood & youth in colonial Lyme / by Mary Sterling Bakke. — Lyme, Conn. : Lyme Bicentennial Commission, c1976.
vii, 152 p. : ill. ; 22 cm.
$3.50
1. Women—Connecticut—Lyme. 2. Youth—Connecticut—Lyme. I. Lyme Bicentennial Commission. II. Title.
HQ1438.C8B25 974.6'5 76-40503
76 MARC

Bakke, Robert J
Contingency employment research & development program for the Sierra Economic Development District (SEDD) / by Robert J. Bakke. — [Boulder, Colo.] : Resources Development Internship Program, Western Interstate Commission for Higher Education, 1974.
i, 78 p. : ill. ; 28 cm.
Includes bibliographical references.
1. Manpower policy—California—Sierra Economic Development District. 2. Labor supply—California—Sierra Economic Development District. 3. Sierra Economic Development District—Economic conditions. I. Western Interstate Commission for Higher Education. Resources Development Internship Program. II. Title: Contingency employment research & development program ...
HD5726.S54B33 331.1'1'097943 76-620844
76 MARC

Bakke, Robert Lauman.
Removing contextual constraints to innovation in education: differentiated stuffing in a junior college. [Cambridge] 1972.
v, 169 l.
Thesis (Ed. D.)—Harvard University Graduate School of Education.
1. Teaching teams—U.S. 2. Junior colleges—U.S.—Case studies. 3. Differentiated teaching staffs. I. Title.
MH-Ed NUC73-120431

Bakke, Torgeir.
see Symposium on the Phylogeny and Systematic Position of the Pogonophora, University of Copenhagen, 1973. The phylogeny and systematic position of pogonophora ... Hamburg, Parey, 1975.

The Bakke symposium / Mary Ten Thor, [editor] ; A. M. Aabenberg, I. Kraft, F. Montmorency-Tedesco, [participants]. — Sacramento, Calif. : Uncommon Lawyers Workshop, 1977.
283 p. ; 22 cm.
Bibliography: p. 256-266.
Includes index.
1. Medical education—Law and legislation—United States—Congresses. 2. Discrimination in education—Law and legislation—United States—Congresses. 3. Bakke, Allan Paul. I. Thor, Mary Ten. II. Aabenberg, A. M. III. Kraft, Ivor. IV. Montmorency-Tedesco, F.
KF2907.E3B3 344'.73'0798 77-89940
77 MARC

Bakkeh, Clarence J
The legal basis for college student personnel work. 2d ed. Washington, American College Personnel Association [1968]
65 p. 28 cm. (Student personnel series, no. 2)
Bibliography; p. 58-65.
1. Student counselors—Law and legislation—U.S. 2. Personnel service in higher education. I. Title. II. Series.
OKentU NUC73-119541

Bakken, Clarence J
The legal basis for college student personnel work. Washington, American College Personnel Association [1966]
55 p. 28 cm. (Student personnel series, no. 2)
Bibliography: p. 58-65.
1. Student counselors—Law and legislation—U.S. 2. Personnel service in higher education. I. Title. II. Series.
TxU NUC76-70996

Bakken, Craig J
An evaluation of patient compliance with aftercare instructions given in an emergency department... [n. p.] 1975.
1 v.
MnU-B NUC77-89735

Bakken, Douglas A.
see Nebraska State Historical Society. A guide to the archives and manuscripts of the Nebraska State Historical Society. Lincoln, 1967.

Bakken, Gordon Morris, 1943-
Rocky Mountain constitution-making, 1850-1912. Gordon Morris Bakken. [Madison, Wis.] 1970.
511 l.
Thesis—University of Wisconsin.
Vita.
Bibliography: leaves 488-511.
Microfilm (positive) Ann Arbor, Mich., University Microfilms, 1970. 1 reel. 35 mm. (Publication no. 8260)
NNC NUC76-70997

Bakken, Hallvard S
Bergen i bilder. [Av] Hallvard S. Bakken. Utg. av Bergen billedgalleri. Bergen, Utgiveren, 1970.
24 p. 26 cm. N 71–35
"Katalog" : [4] p. inserted.
1. Bergen, Norway — Description — Views. 2. Bergen, Norway. Billedgalleriet. I. Title.
N8214.5.N8B34 72–360519

Bakken, Hallvard S.
see Biskop Jacob Neumann, en humanist. [Bergen : Wilhelm Neumann, 1974].

Bakken, Harald Carl.
Political Pan-racialism and the black American elite 1918-1934, by Harald Carl Bakken. [n. p.] 1976.
2 v. (695 leaves) 29 cm.
Thesis--Harvard.
Bibliography: v. 2, leaves 677-695.
1. Negroes--Race identity. 2. Negroes--United States.
MH NUC77-89734

Bakken, Harold S.
see Drammens sparebank. Hvor Drammenselven iler ... Drammen : Harald Lyche & co., 1973.

Bakken, Henry Harrison, 1896-
The hills of home : a family history / by Henry H. Bakken. — 1st ed. — Madison, Wis. : Mimir Publishers, c1976.
xii, 399 p. : ill. ; 29 cm.
1. Bakken family. 2. United States—Genealogy. I. Title.
CS71.B175 1976 929'.2'0973 76-151158
77 MARC

Bakken, Henry Harrison, 1896-
Historical evaluation, theory, and legal status of futures trading in American agricultural commodities. Madison, Wis., Mimir Publishers, 1960.
28 p. 24 cm. (Futures Trading Seminar, Chicago. Futures Trading Seminar; principal papers, v. 1 [pt. 1])
1. Commodity exchanges. 2. Short selling. 3. Produce trade—United States. I. Series.
IMacoW NUC75-69051

Bakken, Lavola J
Land of the North Umpquas, peaceful Indians of the West, by Lavola J. Bakken. Grants Pass, Or., Te-Cum-Tom Publications [1973]
40 p. illus. 22 cm.
Bibliography : p. 38.
1. Umpqua Indians. I. Title.
E99.U45B34 970.3 73–84954
ISBN 0–913508–03–9 MARC

Bakken, Lloyd A., joint author.
see Wright, Boyd L. Convention profile and individual biographies. Grand Forks, Bureau of Governmental Affairs, University of North Dakota, 1971.

Bakken, Ove, 1910- comp.
see Eldre essayistiske tekster. Trondheim, Tapir, 1973.

Bakken, Ove, 1910- ed.
see Uppdal, Kristofer, 1878-1961. Tretten brev. Brotstykke av ei livshistorie. [Trondheim] 1972.

Bakken, Petter M
Feedforward linearization of communication transmitters, by Petter M. Bakken. Trondheim, Norwegian Institute of Technology, Electronics Research Laboratory, 1975.
viii, 253 p. ill., graphs. 30 cm. (Doktoravhandling. Universitetet i Trondheim, Norges tekniske høgskole, nr. 116)
"ELAB report STF44 A75120."
Includes bibliographies.
1. Amplifiers (Electronics) I. Title. II. Series: Trondheim. Norges tekniske høgskole. Doktoravhandling, nr. 116.
AAP NUC77-89741

Bakken, Svein
see Sanitaerforhold i hytteområder. Oslo, Landbruksforlaget, 1971.

Bakken, Terry, joint author
see Monahan, Evelyn. Put your psychic powers to work... Chicago, Nelson-Hall Co. [1973]

Bakken, Timothy H 1951-
Hinsdale / by Timothy H. Bakken. — [Hinsdale, Ill.] : Hinsdale Doings, 1976.
ix, 302 p. : ill. ; 29 cm.
$18.95
1. Hinsdale, Ill.—History. I. Title.
F549.H68B34 978.8'39'02 76-150926
77 MARC

Bakkenhoven, John, ed.
see Fleur. Amsterdam, Amsterdam Boek, 1974-75.

Bakkenist, Spits en Co.
Aansluiting onderwijs-beroepspraktijk : samenvatting van het onderzoek naar de mogelijkheden om functie-eisen te confronteren met onderwijsdoelstellingen / uitg. door Bakkenist, Spits & Co. en het Instituut voor Toegepaste Sociologie te Nijmegen. — 's-Gravenhage : Staatsuitgeverij, 1974.
50 p. ; 24 cm. — (Sociale zaken ; jaarg. 1973, 7) Ne***
Bibliography : p. 49-50.
ISBN 90-12-00332-6
1. Education—Netherlands. 2. Education—Aims and objectives. 3. Occupational training—Netherlands. I. Instituut voor Toegepaste Sociologie. II. Title. III. Series: Sociale zaken (Hague) ; jaarg. 1973, 7.
LA822.B34 75-575202

Bakkensen, Ralph.
A comparative analysis of the impact on social welfare of Oregon's "Bottle Bill" and Washington's "Model Litter Control Act". [Stanford, Calif.] 1973.
ix, 184 p. illus. 28 cm.
Cover title.
Bibliography: p. 179-184.
1. Litter (Trash)—Washington (State). 2. Litter (Trash)—Oregon. 3. Refuse and refuse disposal—Law and legislation. I. Title..
Wa NUC75-17357

Bakker, A
An experimental integrated system for application of a computer in shipbuilding industry [by] A. R. Bakker. Wageningen, Netherlands Ship Model Basin [1971?]
157 p. illus. 25 cm. (Netherlands Ship Model Basin. Publication no. 341) Ne***
Summary in Dutch.
Bibliography : p. 154.
1. Electronic data processing—Naval architecture. I. Title. II. Series: Wegeningen. Nederlandsch Scheepsbouwkundig Proefstation. Publicatie no. 341.
VM156.B314 623.82'0028'54 74-194832
MARC

Bakker, A P Margadant-
see
Margadant-Bakker, A P

Bakker, Bert, 1912- ed.
see A. Roland Holst: zeventig jaar. Den Haag, B. Bakker/Daamen [1958?]

Bakker, Bert, 1912-
see Huygens, M H Beroemde strafzaken. Den Haag, Joachimsthal, [1972]

Bakker, Bert, 1912- ed.
see Visioen en werkelijkheid ... Den Haag, Daamen, 1963.

Bakker, Boudewijn.
see Amsterdam in the eighteenth century. Delft, Elmar, [1976?]

Bakker, Cornelis B
No trespassing! Explorations in human territoriality [by] Cornelis B. Bakker and Marianne K. Bakker-Rabdau. San Francisco, Chandler & Sharp Publishers [1973]
xiv, 284 p. 24 cm. $8.95
Bibliography : p. 273-279.
1. Interpersonal relations. I. Bakker-Rabdau, Marianne K., joint author. II. Title.
[DNLM: 1. Spatial behavior. 2. Territoriality. BF 469 B168n 1973]
HM132.B3 158'.2 73-7326
ISBN 0-88316-500-7 MARC

Bakker, Dirk J.
see The Neuropsychology of learning disorders ... Baltimore, University Park Press, c1976.

Bakker, Doris L., joint author
see Power, Lawrence, 1928- Diabetes outpatient care... Springfield, C. C. Thomas [1973]

Bakker, Douwe Jan, 1943-
see Douwe Jan Bakker, Jeroen Henneman, Pieter Holstein ... ... [Luzern, Kunstmuseum, 1976]

Bakker, Eduard Meine van Zinderen
see Zinderen Bakker, Eduard Meine van.

Bakker, Elna S., joint author.
see Cowles, Raymond Bridgman, 1896-1975. Desert journal ... Berkeley, University of California Press, c1977.

Bakker, G.
see Measurement of the base... Delft, 1972.

Bakker, G majoor b. d.
Helleense krijgsgeschiedenis. [Door] G. Bakker. Nijmegen, Dekker & Van de Vegt, 1972.
265 p. illus. 24 cm. fl 25.00 Ne 72-49
Bibliography : p. 246-247.
1. Greece—History, Military. I. Title.
DF89.B34 73-316814
ISBN 90-255-9771-8

Bakker, Geert, 1927-
Wymbritseradiel : skiednis fan in greidgritenij / under red. fan G. Bakker. — Bolsward : Osinga, 1974.
188 p. : ill., maps (1 fold. in pocket) ; 24 cm. — ([Utjeften] - Fryske Akademy ; nr. 459) (Sudwesthoekerige ; nr. 11) Ne 74-47
Includes bibliographical references.
ISBN 90-6066-254-7 : fl 17.50
1. Wymbritseradeel, Netherlands. I. Title. II. Series: Fryske Akademy. Utjeften ; nr. 459.
DJ411.W93B34 75-553117

Bakker, H de.
De Nederlandse bodem in kleur / H. de Bakker en A. W. Edelman-Vlam. — Wageningen : Stichting voor Bodemkartering : Pudoc, 1976.
148 p., [32] leaves of plates : ill. ; 25 cm. Ne76-42
Bibliography: p. 143-147.
ISBN 9022005763 : fl 35.00
1. Soils—Netherlands. 2. Soils—Netherlands—Pictorial works. I. Edelman-Vlam, A. W., joint author. II. Title.
S599.4.N4B34 76-489385
*77 MARC

Bakker, Hans.
Bonkige skûtsjes, bondige schippers. Geschiedenis van het skûtsjesilen in Friesland. Leeuwarden, Miedemapers, 1971.
196 p. with illus. 21 cm. fl 10.90 Ne 71-31
Bibliography : p. [6]
1. Sailboat racing. 2. Sailing barges. I. Title.
GV811.5.B34 73-363452
ISBN 90-6149-961-5

Bakker, Hans.
Tracer diffusion in face centered cubic metals. [n.p., 1970?]
59 p. ill. 25 cm.
Thesis—Universiteit van Amsterdam.
In English, summary and 'Stellingen' in Dutch only.
'Stellingen' tipped in.
Bibliography: p. 58-59.
1. Crystal lattices. 2. Solids. 3. Diffusion. I. Title.
KU NUC76-71048

Bakker, Hendrik Dirk, 1938-
'Tyrosinosis'; tyrosinemie en tyrosylurie. Utrecht, Drukkerij Elinkwijk [1973]
109 p. illus.
Proefschrift—Utrecht.
Title also in English.
Summary in English.
Vita.
Includes bibliography.
1. Tyrosinosis. 2. Tyrosine metabolism. I. Title.
MiU NUC75-17358

Bakker, Ina Boudier-
see Boudier-Bakker, Ina, 1875-1966.

Bakker, J
Welzijnsvoorzieningen in de stadswijk Assen-Noord. Rapporteur: J. Bakker. Assen, Stichting Opbouw Drenthe, Afdeling Onderzoek, Voorlichting en Dokumentatie [1971-
v. illus. 30 cm. Ne*** (v. 1)
1. Social services—Drenthe, Netherlands. I. Stichting Opbouw Drenthe. Afdeling Onderzoek, Voorlichting en Dokumentatie. II. Title.
HV310.D7B34 72-362459

Bakker, J
see also
Bakker, Jan.
Ernest Hemingway.

Bakker, J., 1927- ed.
see Door de wereld. Dagboek. Kampen, Kok, 1972.

Bakker, J. H.
see also
Bakker, Joris Hendricus, 1940-

Bakker, J. H. Ing., joint author
see Boer, C Ing. Opbouw en afwerking van gebouwen. Amsterdam, Agon Elsevier, 1972-

Bakker, J J M
Constant en variabel. De fonematische structuur van de Nederlandse woordvorm. Asten N.-Br., Schriks' Drukkerij N.V., 1971.
184 p. tables (in pocket) 24 cm.
Academisch proefschrift—Amsterdam.
"Stellingen" ([2] p.) inserted.
Summary in English.
Bibliography: p. 180-184.
1. Dutch language—Phonology. 2. Dutch language—Word formation. I. Title.
IU NUC76-70903

Bakker, J.J.M., ed.
see Herman van den Bergh bij zijn zeventigste verjaardag. [Utrecht, Ambo, 1967]

Bakker, Jacobus Theodorus.
Eschatologische prediking bij Luther [door] J. T. Bakker. Kampen, J. H. Kok, 1964.
105 p. 22 cm.
Includes bibliographical references.
1. Eschatology—History of doctrines. 2. Preaching—History—Germany. 3. Luther, Martin, 1483-1546—Theology. I. Title.
BR333.5.E75B3 72-225046

Bakker, Jacobus Willem de.
A calculus for recursive program schemes [by] J.W. de Bakker and W.P. de Roever. Amsterdam, Stichting Mathematisch Centrum, 1972.
61 p. 28 cm. (Amsterdam. Mathematisch Centrum. Rekenafdeling. [Publicatie] MR 131/72)
Bibliography: p. 59-61.
1. Recursive programming. I. Roever, W.P. de. II. Title. III. Series.
CaBVaU NUC73-41424

Bakker, Jacobus Willem de.
Recursive procedures, by J. W. de Bakker. Amsterdam, Mathematisch Centrum, 1971.
108 p. 24 cm. (Mathematical Centre tracts, 24) Ne***
Bibliography : p. 106-108.
1. Formal languages. 2. Recursive functions. I. Title. II. Series: Amsterdam. Mathematisch Centrum. Mathematical Centre tracts, 24.
QA267.3.B34 001.6'42 74-150249
MARC

Bakker, Jacobus Willem de.
see Foundations of computer science. Amsterdam, Mathematisch Centrum, 1975.

Bakker, Jacobus Willem de
see MC-25 Informatica Symposium, Amsterdam, 1972. MC-25 Informatica Symposium... Amsterdam, Mathematisch Centrum, 1971.

Bakker, Jan.
Ernest Hemingway. The artist as man of action. ⌐By⌐ J. Bakker. Assen, Van Gorcum, 1972.
302 p. 24 cm. (Van Gorcum's Literaire Bibliotheek, 21) fl 38.00 Ne 72-25
Bibliography: p. 284-289.
1. Hemingway, Ernest, 1899-1961.
PS3515.E37Z5822 813'.5'2 73-168703
ISBN 90-232-0989-3 MARC

Bakker, Jan Adrianus.
Verslag Mondsee Seminar, methoden en technieken van volksontwikkeling. ⌐'s-Gravenhage, 1951⌐
36 p. 29 cm.
1. International Seminar on Methods and Techniques of Adult Education, Unterach, Austria, 1950. I. Title.
LC5209.B3 65-52118 ‡
rev

Bakker, Jan Adrianus
see Doctor Wiardi Beckman Stichting. Sociale dienstverlening. Deventer, Kluwer, 1971.

Bakker, Jan Pieter, 1906-
A forgotten factor in the interpretation of glacial stairways. J.P. Bakker. Berlin, 1965.
⌐18⌐-34 p. ill. 25 cm.
Reprint from Annals of Geomorphology.
"References": p. 33-34.
1. Glaciers. 2. Erosion. I. Title.
NcU NUC76-70889

Bakker, Jant Visser
see Visser-Bakker, Jant

Bakker, Jim.
Move that mountain / by Jim Bakker with Robert Paul Lamb. — 1st ed. — Plainfield, N.J. : Logos International, 1976.
vii, 183 p., ⌐4⌐ leaves of plates : ill. ; 21 cm.
ISBN 0-88270-164-9 : $5.95
1. Bakker, Jim. 2. Evangelists—United States—Biography. 3. Television in religion. I. Lamb, Robert Paul, joint author. II. Title.
BV3785.B3A35 269'.2'0924 76-10532
76 MARC

Bakker, Johanna Gertruida, joint author.
see Lier, H. N. van. Onderzoek op de spartelvijver de Oldemeyer. ⌐s.l.⌐ Staatsbosbeheer, Afd. Recreatie-Onderzoek, 1973.

Bakker, Joris Hendricus, 1940-
Noordierland ⌐door⌐ Joris Bakker. ⌐Den Haag⌐ Nederlands Instituut voor Vredesvraagstukken, 1973.
100 p. illus. 21 cm. Ne***
Bibliography: p. 76-81.
1. Northern Ireland—History.
DA990.U46B223 74-324519

Bakker, Jozephus Wilhelmus Maria, 1946-
Tunneling experiments with superconductors. Nijmegen, Stichting Studentenpers, 1973.
168 p. illus. 22 cm.
Proefschrift-Nijmegen.
Vita.
Bibliography: p. 153-158.
1. Superconductors. 2. Tunneling (Physics) 3. Superconductivity. I. Title.
DCU NUC76-70904

Bakker, K
Is bekeering voor ieder noodig? [Amsterdam, druk van Ipenbuur & Van Seldam, n. d.]
19 p. 22 cm.
1. Psychology, Religious.
MH-AH NUC76-18038

Bakker, K
see Meijendel... Den Haag: W. van Hoeve, 1974.

Bakker, L.A.R., joint author
see Thiadens, Albertus Joannes Henricus. Doodgaan is nog geen sterven. [Baarn, Het Wereldvenster, 1972].

Bakker, L.A.R.
see Thiadens, Albertus Joannes Henricus. Het sterven dat ons toe-komt. [Groningen, Wolters-Noordhoff, 1972]

Bakker, Leo
see La Teologia di Piet Schoonenberg. Brescia, Queriniana, 1973.

Bakker, Lothar.
see Bonn. Rheinisches Landesmuseum. Graffiti auf römischer Keramik im Rheinischen Landesmuseum Bonn. Köln, Rheinland-Verlag, 1975.

Bakker, Marilyn.
Plastics sheet versus flat glass / revision by Marilyn Bakker. — Stamford, Conn. : Business Communications Co., ⌐1977⌐
v, 116 leaves ; 28 cm. — (Business opportunity report ; P-036)
Based on Plastics as a glazing substitute, by Business Communications Co., published in 1973.
1. Plastics industry and trade—United States. 2. Glass trade—United States. 3. Plastic windows. 4. Glazing. I. Business Communications Co. Plastics as a glazing substitute. II. Title. III. Series.
HD9661.U62B34 1977 338.4'7'66840973 77-368633
77 MARC

Bakker, Nicolaas Tjepko, 1934-
In der Krisis der Offenbarung : Karl Barths Hermeneutik, dargestellt an seiner Römerbrief-Auslegung / Nico T. Bakker ; ⌐übers. von⌐ Wolfgang Bunte. — Neukirchen -Vluyn : Neukirchener Verlag, 1974.
180 p. ; 24 cm. GFR***
"Die vorliegende Arbeit erschien in vorläufiger Form unter dem Titel De Hermeneutiek van der Römerbrief van Karl Barth, Alphen van den Rijn, 1972, als Dissertation für die Theologische Fakultät der Universität Leiden."
1. Barth, Karl, 1886-1968. Der Römerbrief. I. Title.
BS2665.B343B34 76-512233

Bakker, P
Bedrijfsbeleid en budgettering. De betekenis van de budgettering als bestuursinstrument in het bedrijf. 2e geheel nieuw bew. druk. ⌐Door⌐ P. Bakker. Den Haag, NIVE; Leiden, Stenfert Kroese, 1971.
xviii, 365 p. 23 cm. (NIVE publikatie, no. 518) fl 55.00 Ne 71-33
Fold. diagr. in pocket.
First ed. published in 1948 under title: De grondslagen van de bedrijfsbudgetering.
Includes bibliographies.
1. Budget in business. I. Title. II. Series: Nederlands Instituut voor Efficiency. Publicatie, no. 518.
T58.A2N4 nr. 518 73-344878
[HF5550]
ISBN 90-207-0247-5

Bakker, P
Inflation and profit control : how to account for inflation in business / P. Bakker. — Toronto : Methuen, ⌐1974?⌐
x, 148 p. ; 24 cm. C***
Includes bibliographical references and index.
ISBN 0-458-91140-2
1. Inflation (Finance) and accounting. I. Title.
HF5657.B32 657'.3 75-314139
75 MARC

Bakker, P
Pengantar rekeningstelsel dan administrasi perusahaan modern ⌐oleh⌐ P. Bakker. Saduranerdjemahan R. Soemita Adikoesoema. Tjet. 1. ⌐Djakarta⌐ Budi Kemuning ⌐1964⌐
262 p. 32 cm.
Translation of Inleiding tot het rekeningstelsel en de moderne bedrijfsadministratie.
——— Djawaban soal-soal. Bandung, Budi Kemuning ⌐1964?⌐
188 p. 32 cm. HF5645.B2515 Suppl.
1. Accounting. 2. Cost accounting. I. Adikoesoema, R. Soemita, tr. II. Title.
HF5645.B2515 S A 64-6306
rev PL 480: Indo-472

Bakker, Piet.
Ciske-trilogie. Ciske de rat. Ciske groeit op. Cis de man. 11. ed. Amsterdam, Elsevier, 1964.
720 p.
I. Title.
CU-SB NUC74-124873

Bakker, Piet.
Cisko el rata; novela. ⌐Traducción de Enrique Molina. 2. ed.⌐ Buenos Aires, Companía General Fabril Editora ⌐1961⌐
373 p. 20 cm. (Colección Anaquel)
Translation of Ciske de rat, first volume of a trilogy by the same title; the subsequent volumes are: Ciske groeit op; Cis de man.
I. Title.
MB NUC73-119493

Bakker, Reinout.
De geschiedenis van het fenomenologisch denken. ⌐Door⌐ R. Bakker. ⌐4. herz. en uitgebreide dr.⌐. Utrecht, Spectrum, ⌐1974⌐.
571 p. 18 cm. (Aula-boeken, 174) fl 9.50 Ne 74-20
Includes bibliographical references.
1. Phenomenology—History. I. Title.
B829.5.B33 1974 74-346238
ISBN 90-274-4881-7

Bakker, Reinout
see Graaf, Johannes de, 1911- De mondige mens tussen goed en kwaad. Utrecht, Bijleveld, 1966.

Bakker, Sjoerd, 1915-
Geef mij maar de vrije natuur ... De natuur onder handbereik. Den Haag, Scheltens & Giltay, ⌐1974⌐.
192 p., 48 p. of photos. 23 cm. Ne 74-26
Bibliography: p. 235-237.
ISBN 90-6158-291-1 : fl 27.50
1. Natural history—Netherlands. 2. Birds—Netherlands. I. Title.
QH159.B34 75-591032

Bakker, W
Dengan pahlawan perwira di Benua es utara, oleh W. Bakker. Disadur oleh E. Suanda Mihardja. Djakarta, Penerbitan Dan Balai Buku Indonesia ⌐n.d.⌐
⌐207⌐ p. illus., fold. map. 23 cm.
1. Indonesian language-Readers. 2. Nansen, Fridtjof, 1861-1930-Juv. literature. I. Mihardja, E. Suanda. II. Title.
Mi NUC76-50644

Bakker, W O
Molens in Groningen in oude ansichten / door W. O. Bakker. — Zaltbommel : Europese Bibliotheek, 1977.
76 p. : ill. ; 15 x 21 cm. Ne77-21
fl 26.90
1. Windmills—Netherlands—Groningen—History. I. Title.
TJ823.B18 77-484199
*77 MARC

Bakker, Wijbren.
Kent u ze nog ... de Beilers : met afbeeldingen uit Drijber, Hijken, Holthe, Hooghalen, Klatering, Oranje, Smalbroek, Spier en Wijster / samengesteld door W. Bakker. — Zaltbommel : Europese Bibliotheek, 1974.
38 leaves : ill. ; 15 x 21 cm. Ne 74-23
fl 17.90
1. Beilen, Netherlands—History—Pictorial works. I. Title.
DJ411.B33B35 74-353582

Bakker, Willem Frederick, 1934-
Pronomen abundans and pronomen coniunctum. A contribution to the history of the resumptive pronoun within the relative clause in Greek. ⌐By⌐ W. F. Bakker. Amsterdam, North-Holland Pub. Co., 1974.
120 p. 26 cm. (Verhandelingen der Koninklijke Nederlandse Akademie van Wetenschappen, afd. letterkunde. Nieuwe reeks, deel 82) fl 50.00 Ne 74-10
Includes bibliographical references.
1. Greek language, Modern—Pronoun. 2. Greek language—Pronoun. I. Title. II. Series: Akademie van Wetenschappen, Amsterdam. Afdeling Letterkunde. Verhandelingen. Nieuwe reeks, deel 82.
PA1085.B3 489'.3'5 72-96838
ISBN 0-7204-8248-8 MARC

Bakker, Willem Frederik, 1934-
Studia Byzantina et Neohellenica Neerlandica. Ed. by W. F. Bakker, A. F. van Gemert en W. J. Aerts. Leiden, Brill, 1972.
345 p., 10 p. of photos. 25 cm. (Byzantina Neerlandica. ⌐Series B: Studia⌐ fasc. 3) fl 68.00 Ne 72-47
English, French, German, or Latin.
Includes bibliographical references.
1. Byzantine Empire—Civilization—Addresses, essays, lectures. I. Gemert, F. A. J. van. II. Aerts, W. J. III. Title. IV. Series.
DF521.B24 914.95'03 73-160424
ISBN 90-04-03552-4 MARC

Bakker, Willem Frederik, 1934-
see Phalieros, Marinos, ca. 1395-1474. [Logoi didaktikoi] Logoi didaktikoi. Leiden: E. J. Brill, 1977.

Bakker-Arkema, F. W., joint author
see Brooker, Donald B Drying cereal grains. Westport, Conn., AVI Pub. Co., 1974.

Bakker-Arkema, F. W.
see Institute for Simulation of Cooling and Drying Beds of Agricultural Products, Michigan State University, 1970. Proceedings. East Lansing, Agricultural Engineering Dept., Michigan State University, 1970 [i.e. 1971]

Bakker-Rabdau, Marianne K., joint author
see Bakker, Cornelis B No trespassing! San Francisco, Chandler & Sharp Publishers [1973]

Bakker Schut, P. H.
see Coornhert-Liga. Alternatieve justitiebegroting 1972. Deventer, Kluwer, 1971.

Bakker Schut, P. H.
see Coornhert-Liga... Utrecht, Ars aequi, 1973.

Bakker Schut, P. H., joint author.
see Lehning, Arthur. Duitsland... Baarn, Wereldvenster, [1976]

Bakkeren, Henk.
Hakken in hout : scheepsversieringen, naamborden, decoraties / Henk Bakkeren. — [Bussum : De Boer, 1976]
136 p. : ill. ; 25 cm. — (De Boer maritiem) Ne77-6
Bibliography: p. 136.
ISBN 9022811786 : fl 35.00
1. Ship decoration. 2. Wood-carving. I. Title.
VM308.B34 77-474884
•77 MARC

Bakkes, C M
Die Britse deurbraak aan die Benede-Tugela op Majubadag 1900 / deur C. M. Bakkes. — Pretoria : Sentrale Dokumentasiediens, S. A. W., 1973.
iv, 106 p., [6] leaves of plates : ill. ; 31 cm. — (Publikasie - Sentrale Dokumentasiediens, S. A. W. ; no. 3) SA***
Originally presented as the author's thesis, University of Pretoria, 1971.
Summary in English.
Bibliography : p. 92–97.
Includes index.
ISBN 0–621–0–1316–1
1. South African War, 1899–1902. I. Title. II. Series: South Africa. Army. Sentrale Dokumentasiediens. Publikasie - Sentrale Dokumentasiediens, S. A. W. ; no. 3.
DT930.B34 1973 74–351291

Bakkes, Margaret.
Waar jou skat is / Margaret Bakkes. — Kaapstad : Human en Rousseau, 1975.
176 p. ; 22 cm. SA
Originally published in Die Huisgenoot.
ISBN 0–7981–0438–4 : R3.85
I. Title.
PT6592.12.A4W3 75–406045

Bakketeig, Leiv Sigmund, 1938- joint author
see Bjerkedal, Tor, 1926- Endringer i forekomsten av medfødte misdannelser, prematuritet go dødfødsel. Bergen [1971]

Bakketeig, Leiv Sigmund, 1938-
see Bjerkedal, Tor, 1926- Medical registration of births in Norway, 1967-68. Bergen, University of Bergen, 1972.

Bakkmoen, Per Kr.
see Fremad og aldri glemme... [Oslo]: Pax [1974].

Bakksh, Ataollah Azadi-
see Azadi-Bakksh, Ataollah, 1944-

Bakkum, P.
see Aardrijkskunde, biologie, vaderlandse geschiedenis en natuurkunde. Groningen, Wolters, 1966.

al-Bakkūsh, al-Ṭayyib.
(al-Taṣrīf al-ʻArabī min khilāl ʻilm al-aṣwāt al-ḥadīth)
التصريف العربي من خلال علم الأصوات الحديث / الطيب البكوش ؛ تقديم صالح القرمادي. — [تونس : توزيع محلات ع. ابن عبد الله]، 1973.
199 p. ; 21 cm.
Errata slip inserted.
Bibliography : p. 194–196.
1TD
1. Arabic language—Phonology. I. Title.
PJ6121.B3 76–970184

Bakkūshah, Muḥammad
see al-Mindāsī, Saʻīd ibn ʻAbd Allāh, d. 1677? [Dīwān] Dīwān Saʻīd al-Mindāsī. [1970?]

Bakla-Şenalp, Leman.
Cumhuriyetimizin 50. [i. e. elli'nci] yılı bibliyografyası ve elli'nci yılla ilgili çalışmalar / hazırlayan Leman Şenalp. — İstanbul : [İstanbul Üniversitesi, Rektörlüğü]. 1975.
182 p. ; 24 cm. — (Yayın - İstanbul Üniversitesi, Rektörlüğü ; nu. 2070)
Includes index.
1. Turkey—History—1918–1960—Bibliography. 2. Turkey—History—1960– —Bibliography. I. Title: Cumhuriyetimizin 50. [i. e. elli'nci] ...
Z2850.B34 77–970488
[DR590]

Baklacıoğlu, S
Kamu iktisadi teşebbüslerinin ve kamu iştiraklerinin özel kesime devredilmesi olanakları. Ankara, Ayyıldız Matbaası, 1973.
40 p. (Türkiye Ekonomi Kurumu İktisadi Araştırmalar Enstitüsü konferanslar, seri 1973/2)
1. Turkey—Econ. condit.
MH NUC76-70905

Baklaev, Ikov Petrovich.
Geologicheskoe stroenie i perspektivy Tur'inskikh kontaktovo-metasomaticheskikh mestorozhdeniĭ medi na Severnom Urale. Sverdlovsk, 1959.
141 p. illus. (Akademiia nauk SSSR. Ural'skiĭ filial. Trudy Gorno-geologicheskogo in-ta, vyp. 37)
ICRL NUC74-38256

Baklaev, Iakov Petrovich.
(Kontaktovo-metasomaticheskie mestorozhdeniia zheleza i medi na Urale)
Контактово-метасоматические месторождения железа и меди на Урале. (Закономерности их размещения и локализации). Москва, "Недра," 1973.
231 p. with diagrs. and maps, 2 l. of diagrs. 27 cm. 2.80rub USSR 73
At head of title: Академия наук СССР. Уральский научный центр. Институт геологии и геохимии им. академика А. Н. Заварицкого. Я. П. Баклаев.
Bibliography : p. 218–[229]
1. Metamorphism (Geology). 2. Iron ores—Russia—Ural Mountain region. 3. Copper ores—Russia—Ural Mountain region. I. Title.
QE475.A2B35 73–363085

Baklaev, Iakov Petrovich
see Mineralogiia i geokhimiia zhelezorudnykh mestorozhdeniĭ Urala. 1974.

Baklanoff, Eric N
Chile's balance of payments, economic development, and foreign economic policy. [n.p.] 1958.
279 l.
Thesis—Ohio State University.
Vita.
Includes bibliography.
Microfilm of typescript. Ann Arbor, Mich., University Microfilms, 1959. 1 reel.
1. Chile—Econ. condit.—1918- 2. Chile—Commerce. 3. Chile—Economic policy. I. Title.
MiU NUC74-175377

Baklanoff, Eric N
Expropriation of U.S. investments in Cuba, Mexico, and Chile / Eric N. Baklanoff. — New York : Praeger, 1975.
xviii, 170 p. ; 25 cm. — (Praeger special studies in international economics and development)
Includes bibliographical references and index.
ISBN 0-275-09780-3 : $15.00
1. Investments, American—Chile. 2. Investments, American—Cuba. 3. Investments, American—Mexico. I. Title.
HG5160.5.A3B34 332.6'7373 74-6731
74 MARC

Baklanoff, Eric N.
see Mediterranean Europe and the Common Market ... University, Published for the Office for International Studies and Programs by the University of Alabama Press, c1976.

Baklanov, Gleb Ivanovich.
(Chem zanimaetsia statistika)
Чем занимается статистика. Москва, "Статистика," 1974.
86 p. 20 cm. (Статистика для всех) 0.14rub USSR 74
At head of title: Г. И. Бакланов.
Includes bibliographical references.
1. Statistics. I. Title.
HA29.5.R9B34 74–343737

Baklanov, Gleb Ivanovich.
Measurement of labour productivity in Soviet industry. [n. p., 1961]
19 l.
Paper for Conference on Labor Productivity, Cadenabbia, Italy, 1961, under the auspices of the International Economic Association.
Title may vary from final version.
1. Productivity—Russia. I. Conference on Labor Productivity, Cadenabbia, Italy, 1961. II. Title.
MH-IR NUC75-1060

Baklanov, Gleb Ivanovich.
(Sbornik zadach po statistike promyshlennosti)
Сборник задач по статистике промышленности. [Для вузов по специальности "Статистика"]. Под ред. Г. И. Бакланова. Изд. 2-е, испр. и доп. Москва, "Статистика," 1971.
232 p. 22 cm. 0.66rub USSR 71-VKP
By A. I. Ivanov and others.
1. Industrial statistics—Problems, exercises, etc. I. Ivanov, Alekseĭ Ivanovich, fl. 1971– II. Title.
HA40.I 6B255 1971 74–332106

Baklanov, Gleb Ivanovich.
(Statistika promyshlennosti)
Статистика промышленности / Г. И. Бакланов, В. Е. Адамов, А. Н. Устинов ; под ред. Г. И. Бакланова. — Изд. 3., перер. и доп. — Москва : Статистика, 1976.
415 p. : ill. ; 22 cm. USSR***
"Допущено ... в качестве учебника для студентов вузов, обучающихся по специальности 'Статистика.'"
Bibliography : p. 412.
1.25rub
1. Industrial statistics. I. Adamov, Vladimir Evgen'evich, joint author. II. Ustinov, Arkadiĭ Nilovich, joint author. III. Title.
HA40.I 6B258 1976 76–528473

Baklanov, Gleb Ivanovich, ed.
see Moscow. Ėkonomiko-statisticheskiĭ institut. Promyshlennaia statistika. Moskva, 1965.

Baklanov, Gleb Ivanovich, ed.
see Moscow. Ėkonomiko-statisticheskiĭ institut. Sbornik stateĭ kafedry promyshlennoĭ statistiki. Moskva, 1968.

Baklanov, Gleb Ivanovich
see Moscow. Ėkonomiko-statisticheskiĭ institut. 2 [i.e. Vtoraia] konferentsiia po itogam nauchnykh rabot kafedr za 1954 [i.e. 1964] g. Moskva, 1965.

Baklanov, Gleb Ivanovich, ed.
see Nekotorye sovremennye problemy promyshlennoĭ statistiki... Moskva, 1969.

Baklanov, Gleb Ivanovich, ed.
see O nektorykh problemakh razvitiia ekonomicheskikh naul. 1971.

Baklanov, Gleb Ivanovich, ed.
see Statisticheskie issledovaniia v otrasliakh narodnogo khoziaĭstva. 1974.

Baklanov, Gleb Vladimirovich.
Tochka opory. Moskva, Molodaia gvardiia, 1971.
317 p. illus. 17 cm. (Seriia "Sport i lichnost'", kn. 12)
1. Sports—Russia—Biography. I. Title.
MdU NUC76-14935

Baklanov, Gleb Vladimirovich.
(Veter voennykh let)
Ветер военных лет / Г. В. Бакланов. — Москва : Воениздат, 1977.
286 p., [1] leaf of plates : port. ; 21 cm. — (Военные мемуары) USSR***
Series romanized: Voennye memuary.
1.22rub
1. World War, 1939–1945 — Campaigns — Eastern. 2. Baklanov, Gleb Vladimirovich. 3. World War, 1939–1945—Personal narratives, Russian. 4. Generals—Russia—Biography. 5. Russia (1923– U. S. S. R.). Armiia—Biography. I. Title.
D764.B213 77-510600

Baklanov, Grigoriĭ IAkovlevich.
[Byl mesiats maĭ]
Был месяц май ... [Киносценарий.—О том, что предшествовало фильму. Москва, "Искусство," 1971].
127 p. with illus. 16 cm. (Библиотека кинодраматургии)
0.30rub USSR 72-VKP
At head of title: Г. Бакланов.
PARTIAL CONTENTS: Хуциев, М. Сбывшееся ожидание.—Ошеров, В. Испытание хроникой.—Шитова, В. Вкус победы.
I. Title.
PN1997.B9B3 72-374027

Baklanov, Grigoriĭ IAkovlevich.
(Druz'ia)
Друзья : Роман / Григорий Бакланов. — Москва : Сов. писатель, 1976.
271 p. : port. ; 17 cm. USSR 76
0.49rub
I. Title.
PG3476.B28635D7 76-522528

Baklanov, Grigorii IAkovlevich. IUzhnee glavnogo udara
see Baklanov, Grigorii IAkovlevich. (Pushki strelaiut na rassvete) 1974.

Baklanov, Grigoriĭ IAkovlevich.
(Izbrannoe)
Избранное / Григорий Бакланов ; [предисл. А. Бочарова ; ил. В. Медведев]. — Москва : Моск. рабочий, 1974.
461 p. : port. ; 21 cm. USSR 74
Short stories.
CONTENTS: Пядь земли.—Мертвые сраму не имут.—Карпухин.—Темп вечной погони.
0.95rub
PG3476.B28635A6 1974 75-572035

Baklanov, Grigoriĭ IAkovlevich.
(Piad' zemli)
Пядь земли. Повести, рассказ, очерки. [Ил.: С. Соколов]. Москва, "Худож. лит.," 1973.
575 p. with illus. port. 21 cm. 1.20rub USSR 74
At head of title: Григорий Бакланов.
CONTENTS: Южнее главного удара.—Пядь земли.—Мертвые сраму не имут.—Почем фунт лиха.—Карпухин.—Темп вечной погони (Месяц в Америке).
I. Title.
PG3476.B28635P5 1973 74-315332

Baklanov, Grigoriĭ IAkovlevich.
(Pushki strelaiut na rassvete)
Пушки стреляют на рассвете : из повести "Южнее главного удара" : [для ст. возраста] / Григорий Бакланов ; [ил., Е. Грибов]. — Москва : Дет. лит., 1974.
63 p. : ill. ; 21 cm. — (Слава солдатская) USSR 74
0.19rub
1. World War, 1939–1945—Fiction. I. Baklanov, Grigoriĭ IAkovlevich. IUzhnee glavnogo udara. II. Title.
PG3476.B28635P8 77-515813

Baklanov, Grigoriĭ IAkovlevich.
(Temp vechnoĭ pogoni)
Темп вечной погони. (Месяц в Америке). Москва, "Сов. писатель," 1972.
223 p. with illus. 16 cm. 0.32rub USSR 73-VKP
At head of title: Григорий Бакланов.
1. United States—Description and travel—1960– 2. United States—Social conditions—1960– I. Title.
E169.02.B325 73-335161

Baklanov, Grigoriĭ IAkovlevich.
(Voennye povesti)
Военные повести / Григорий Бакаланов. — Москва : Сов. писатель, 1975.
495 p. : ill. ; 21 cm. USSR***
CONTENTS: Piad' zemli. — IUzhnee glavnogo udara. — Mertvye sramu ne imut.—Temp vechnoĭ pogoni.
0.88rub
1. World War, 1939–1945—Russia—Fiction. I. Title.
PG3476.B28635V6 1975 75-358218

Baklanov, Nikolaĭ Borisovich, 1881–
(Arkhitekturnye pamiatniki Dagestana)
Архитектурные памятники Дагестана. Ленинград, Изд-во Всерос. академии художеств, 1935–
v. illus. (part col.) 36 cm. (Материалы по истории архитектуры Кавказа)
At head of title, v. 1– : Всероссийская академия художеств. Научно-исследовательский институт архитектуры. Н. Б. Бакланов.
1. Architecture—Daghestan. I. Title. II. Series: Materialy po istorii arkhitektury Kavkaza.
NA1492.8.B34 75-534245

Baklanov, Nikolaĭ Borisovich, 1881- ed.
see Arkhitekturnye pamiatniki Turkmenii. 1939-

Baklanov, Viktor Mykolaĭovych
see Gorodskaia gazeta. 1975.

Baklanova, Elena Nikolaevna.
(Krest'ianskiĭ dvor i obshchina na russkom Severe)
Крестьянский двор и община на русском Севере : Конец XVII—начало XVIII в. / Е. Н. Бакланова ; АН СССР, Ин-т истории СССР. — Москва : Наука, 1976.
221 p. ; 21 cm. USSR 77
Includes bibliographical references.
0.98rub
1. Land tenure—Russia, Northern. 2. Peasantry—Russia, Northern. I. Title.
HD719.N6B34 77-512253

Baklanova, Natal'ia Apollinar'evna
see Ocherki po istorii torgovli i promyshlennosti v Rossii. 1928.

Baklashov, Igor' Vladimirovich.
(Mekhanika gornykh porod)
Механика горных пород / И. В. Баклашов, Б. А. Картозия. — Москва : Недра, 1975.
272 p. : ill. ; 22 cm. USSR 75
Bibliography: p. 264–[270]
1.09rub
1. Rock mechanics. I. Kartoziia, Boris Arnol'dovich, joint author. II. Title.
TA706.B33 76-533210

Baklashov, Igor' Vladimirovich.
(Raschet, konstruirovanie i montazh armirovki stvolov shakht)
Расчет, конструирование и монтаж армировки стволов шахт. Москва, "Недра," 1973.
248 p. 22 cm. 0.90rub USSR 74
At head of title: И. В. Баклашов.
Bibliography: p. 243–[246]
1. Mine timbering. 2. Mine shafts. I. Title.
TN289.B29 74-321391

Baklien, Kåre
see Brandtzaeg, Per. Immunohistochemical studies... -- Oslo : Universitetsforlaget, 1976.

Bakliwal, Bhaurilal, 1898-1967
see Srī Bhaṃvarīlāla Bākalīvāla smārikā. [1968]

Bakman, Tanfel' Borisovich.
(Kyïv)
Київ : Kiev : фотоальбом / [фото Т. Б. Бакмана ; художник Б. И. Бродський]. — Київ : Мистецтво, 1974.
[116] p. : chiefly col. ill. ; 23 x 33 cm. USSR 74-44525
Ukrainian, Russian, English, French, German, and Spanish.
4.19rub
1. Kiev—Description—Views. I. Brods'kyĭ, B. I., joint author.
DK651.K37B28 75-532553

Bakman, Tanfel' Borisovich.
(Ul'ianovsk—rodina Lenina)
Ульяновск—родина Ленина = Ulyanovsk—Lenin's native city : [Фотоальбом / Авт. альбома и фотогр. Т. Б. Бакман]. — Ульяновск : Приволж. кн. изд-во. Ульян. отд-ние, 1976.
[93] p. : chiefly col. ill. ; 16 x 21 cm. USSR 76
Russian and English.
2.05rub
1. Lenin, Vladimir Il'ich, 1870–1924—Homes and haunts—Russian Republic—Ul'ianovsk. 2. Ul'ianovsk, Russia—Description—Views. I. Title. II. Title: Ulyanovsk—Lenin's native city.
DK254.L446B264 77-514436

Bakman, Tanfel' Borisovich
see Sevastopol'. 1971.

Bakó, Agnes
see A Szocialista forradalomért ... [Budapest] Kossuth Könyvkiadó, 1975.

Bako, Audu, 1924–
Kano State local government reform. [Kano, Information Division, Office of the Secretary to the Military Govt., 1968?]
13, [8] p. illus. 22 cm.
Cover title.
English and Hausa.
1. Local government—Kano State, Nigeria. I. Title.
JS7656.9.K3B3 352.0669'5 73-171603
MARC

Bako, Audu, 1924-
see Kano, Nigeria (State). Military Governor. Policy statement broadcast by the Military Governor, Kano State, His Excellency Alhaji Audu Bako, April 1969. Zaria, Nigeria, Information Division, Office of the S. M. G., Kano State, and printed by Gaskiya Corporation, [1969]

Bako, Audu, 1924-
see Kano, Nigeria (State). Military Governor. Policy statement broadcast by the Military Governor, Kano State, His Excellency Alhaji Audu Bako, on Monday, 1st April, 1968. [Kano] Distributed by Information Division, Military Government Office, Kano State, Nigeria [1968]

Bako, Elemer.
Guide to Hungarian studies. Stanford, Calif., Hoover Institution Press [1973]
2 v. (xv, 1218 p.) illus. 29 cm. (Hoover Institution bibliographical series, 52)
1. Hungary—Bibliography. 2. Hungary—History—Chronology. I. Title. II. Series: Stanford University. Hoover Institution on War, Revolution, and Peace. Bibliographical series, 52.
Z2146.B3 016.91439 79-152422
ISBN 0-8179-2521-X MARC

Bakó, Ferenc
see Módszerek és feladatok. Eger, 1968.

Bakó, Ferenc
see Múzeumi kiállítóhelyek Heves megyében. Eger, 1972.

Bakó, Ferenz
see Dely, Károly. Bükk; útikalauz. Budapest, Sport [c1971]

Bako, Ján
see Sborník prác z ochrany prírody v Zapadoslovenskom kraji. Bratislava, Krajské stredisko Štátnej pamiatkovej starostlivosti a ochrany prírody, 1962.

Bako, Usuve.
Osen'. [By] Usuve Bako (Bakoev) Erevan, Aĭastan, 1971.
167 p. port.
Title page and text in Kurdish.
Russian title from verso of t. p.
MH NUC75-129133

Bako-zade, Dzhura Khamidovich.
(Cherty novogo)
Черты нового : современность и проза / Дж. Бако-Заде ; под ред. чл.-кор. АН СССР, проф. Г. И. Ломидзе. — Душанбе : Дониш, 1974.
115 p. ; 22 cm. USSR 74
At head of title: Академия наук Таджикской ССР. Институт языка и литературы им. Рудаки.
Includes bibliographical references.
0.60rub
1. Tajik prose literature—History and criticism. I. Title.
PK6978.4.B3 75-568298

Bakočević, Aleksandar.
(Putevi kulturne politike)
Путеви културне политике. ⟨Милош Јевтић: [Предговор]. Нацрт корица: Јелена Грујичић, Милош Мајсторовић⟩. Београд, ⟨Културно просветна заједница Србије⟩, 1972.
237, [1] p. 20 cm. (Библиотека Култура и друштво) 30.00Din
Yu 73-1702
1. Serbia—Intellectual life. 2. State encouragement of science, literature and art. I. Title.
DR381.S44B34 73-971009

Bakočević, Aleksandar, ed.
see Savez komunista Srbije. Centralni komitet. Neka pitanja kadrovske politike, organizovanja i metoda rada Saveza komunista Srbije. 1966.

Bakočević, Aleksandar
see Savez komunista Srbije. Centralni komitet. Plenum. Aktivnost Saveza... Beograd, Sedma sila, 1964.

Bakočević, Aleksandar
see Savez komunista Srbije. Centralni komitet. Plenum. Organizacija rukovodstva SK Srbije. [Beograd, Sedma sila, 1965]

Bakóczi, Antal.
Vadászszenvedély, vadászati fegyelem. Budapest, Táncsics Könyvkiadó, 1971.
295 p. illus. 19 cm. 22.00Ft
1. Hunting. I. Title.
SK35.B26 72-226261

Bakoev, Mamadvafo
see Nasihat ba farzangd. [1971].

Bakoev, Usuve
see Bako, Usuve.

Bakojannis, Pavlos, 1935-
Militärherrschaft in Griechenland; eine Analyse zu Parakapitalismus und Spätfaschismus. Stuttgart, W. Kohlhammer [c1972]
218 p. 21 cm. (Reihe Kohlhammer) GDB***
A revision of the author's thesis, Constance.
Bibliography: p. 173-179.
1. Greece, Modern—Politics and government—1967- 2. Greece, Modern—Economic conditions—1918- 3. Greece, Modern—Social conditions. I. Title.
DF852.B34 73-313417
ISBN 3-17-231251-8

Bakok, N Lalong.
Menudju dunia baru; uraian agama Katolik, karangan N. Lalong Bakok. Ende, Pertjetakan "Arnoldus/Nusa Indah" [1966?]
314 p. 24 cm.
1. Catholic Church—Doctrinal and controversial works—Catholic authors. I. Title.
BX1751.2.B23 S A 68-20321
PL 480 : Indo-6399

Bakolak Inpres 6/1971
see
Indonesia. Badan Koordinasi Pelaksana Inpres no. 6/1971
for publications by and about this body.
Titles and other entries beginning with this acronym are filed following this card.
75-589093

Bakolas, Nikoy, tr.
see Faulkner, William, 1897-1962. Hē voulē kai to pathos. Athēnai, Ekdoseis Gkonē, 1963.

Bakom servicefasaden : en studie i socialhjälpens irrgångar / Mats Björling ... [et al.]. — Stockholm : LiberFörlag, [1976]
56, [1] p. : ill. ; 19 cm. S76-19/20
"Lag om socialhjälp den 4 januari 1956 (nr 2)": p. 53-[57]
Bibliography: p. 52.
ISBN 9138028247 : kr15.00
1. Public welfare—Sweden—Law. I. Björling, Mats, 1945- II. Sweden. Laws, statutes, etc. Lag om socialhjälp. 1976.
344'.485'03 76-469594
•76 MARC

Bakony, Leo Irwin, 1922-
Household demand for telecommunications services—a projection to 1980, by L. I. Bakony. [Ottawa, Dept. of Communications, 1971]
128 p. illus. 28 cm. (Telecommission study 2b, ii) $1.75 C***
Includes bibliographical references.
1. Telecommunication—Canada. I. Canada. Dept. of Communications. II. Title. III. Series.
HE7814.B34 384 73-157373
MARC

Bakony, Leo Irwin, 1922-
A statistical study of trade inventory behavior, by L. I. Bakony. [Rotterdam] Netherlands School of Economics, Econometric Institute, 1964.
21 l. illus. 33 cm. (Netherlands School of Economics. Econometric Institute. Report 6416)
Cover title.
Bibliography: leaf 18.
MoKU NUC76-70906

Bakony, Lucien
Pratique du fer forgé et de la ferronnerie décorative : pour l'artisan et l'amateur : outillage, traçage, techniques d'exécution / par Lucien Bakony et Jean Rovière. — 4. éd. mise à jour. — Paris : Éditions Eyrolles, 1975.
127 p. : ill. ; 18 cm. F***
Includes index.
30.00F
1. Blacksmithing. 2. Architectural ironwork. I. Rovière, Jean, joint author. II. Title.
TT240.B3 1975 682'.4 75-514065
75 MARC

Bakonyi, Aliette
see Jules César et ses contemporains. [Ottawa] Université d'Ottawa [1972]

Bakonyi Múzeum
see Molnár, Zsuzsa P Borsos József, 1821-1883... [Veszprém]: Veszprém Megyei Múzeumok Igazgatósága, [1971]

Bakonyi Múzeum
see Thomas, Edit B A nagydémi, lararium. Veszprém [A Veszprém Megyei Múzeumi Igazgatoság] 1965.

Bakopda.
Initials of Badan Koordinasi Pembangunan Daerah, the name of many Indonesian local development boards. Publications by or about any one of these boards are found under the name written in full and entered under the jurisdiction in which it is located, e.g.
Sumatera Barat, Indonesia. Badan Koordinasi Pembangunan Daerah.
S A 68-18849

Bakorlantik DKI Jakarta Raya
see
Badan Koordinasi Penanggulangan Masalah Kenakalan Remaja dan Penyalah Gunaan Narkotika Daerah Khusus Ibu Kota Jakarta Raya
for publications by and about this body.
Titles and other entries beginning with this acronym are filed following this card.

Bakos, Eva.
Central European cooking; original recipes from Switzerland, Austria. Czechoslovakia, Hungary and Rumania [by] Eva Bakos and Albert Kofranek. New York, Galahad Books [1973]
100 p. col. illus. (Round the world cooking library)
1. Cookery, European. I. Kofranek, Albert, joint author. II. Title.
RP NUC75-17347

Bakos, Eva.
Heirate nur keine Wienerin / Eva Bakos. — Wien ; Hamburg : Zsolnay, c1975.
279 p. ; 21 cm. Au75-21-195
ISBN 3-552-02719-X : S180.00
I. Title.
PT2662.A44H4 75-522828
•76 MARC

Bakos, Eva.
Savoir vivre in Wien. (Vorw. u. engl. Bearb.: Alice Greenidge Hall; franz. Bearb.: Francoise Sköldebrand u. Marianne Ewerlöf. Fotos, [teilw. farb.]: Alfred Cermak.) Wien, P. Müller (1973).
188 p. illus. (part. col.) 22 cm. S 210.00 Au 74-4-270
German, English, and French.
1. Vienna—Description—Guide-books. I. Title.
DB849.B35 914.36'13'045 74-314903

Bakos, Eva.
Witwe à la carte. Roman. Wien, Hamburg, Zsolnay (1973).
323 p. 23 cm. S180.00 Au 73-8-153
I. Title.
PT2662.A44W5 74-183636

Bakos, Ferenc.
Csonttollú madarak tele / Bakos Ferenc. — Budapest : Szépirodalmi Könyvkiadó, c1975.
135 p. ; 19 cm.
ISBN 9631503569 : 9.50Ft
I. Title.
PH3213.B2132C75 77-477794
77 MARC

Bakos, Ferenc, fl. 1957-
Idegen szavak és kifejezések szótára. Szerk., Bakos Ferenc. Főmunkatárs, Fábián Pál. Budapest, Akadémiai Kiadó, 1973.
xvi, 927 p. 21 cm.
130.00Ft
1. Hungarian language—Foreign words and phrases—Dictionaries. I. Fábián, Pál. II. Title.
PH2670.B3 75-565818

Bakos, Ferenc, fl. 1957-
Idegen szavak és kifejezések szótára / szerk. Bakos Ferenc, főmunkatárs Fábián Pál. — Budapest : Akadémiai Kiadó, 1974, c1973.
xvi, 927 p. ; 21 cm.
ISBN 9630504618 : 130.00Ft
1. Hungarian language—Foreign words and phrases—Dictionaries. I. Fábián, Pál, joint author. II. Title.
PH2670.B3 1974 77-467271
77 MARC

Bakos, Ferenc, fl. 1957-
Román-magyar szótár. Budapest, Terra, 1961.
816 p. 15 cm. (Kisszótár sorozat)
Added t. p. : Dicționar romîn-maghiar.
1. Romanian language—Dictionaries—Hungarian. I. Title.
PC781.H8B3 63-27473

Bakos, Ferenc, fl. 1957-
see Idegen szavak szótára. 4. kiad. Budapest, Terra, 1975.

Bakos, Jack D
Structural analysis for engineering technology [by] Jack D. Bakos, Jr. Columbus, Ohio, Merrill [1973]
ix, 316 p. illus. 26 cm.
Bibliography: p. 303-304.
1. Structures, Theory of. I. Title.
TA645.B32 624'.171 72-81673
ISBN 0-675-09063-6 MARC

Bakos, Jack D
Structural design for engineering technology [by] Jack D. Bakos, Jr. Columbus, Ohio, Merrill [1974]
xii, 450 p. illus. 26 cm.
Bibliography: p. 429-432.
1. Structural design. I. Title.
TA658.B34 624'.1771 73-91052
ISBN 0-675-08850-X MARC

Bakos, Lajos.
Hiszem és vallom / Bakos Lajos. — Budapest : Református Zsinati Iroda Sajtóosztálya, 1973.
258 p. ; 20 cm.
65.00Ft
1. Theology, Doctrinal—Popular works. 2. Reformed Church—Doctrinal and controversial works. I. Title.
BT77.B28 75-573367

Bakoš, Ľudovít.
Teória výchovy. ... učebnica pre štúdium učiteľstva pre ZDŠ. Sprac. Ľudovít Bakoš a kol. 2. vyd. Bratislava, SPN, t. Svornosť, 1972.
306, [6] p. tables, front. 21 cm. Kčs22.50 CzS 72-MS
Includes bibliographies.
1. Communist education. 2. Teaching. I. Title.
LC1030.B29 1972 73-301939

Bakoš, Ludovit
see Štúrovci a slovenská škola v prvej polovici 19. storočia... [1. vyd.] Bratislava, Slovenské pedagog. nakl., 1960.

Bakoš, Ludovít
see Zborník družobných univerzít... V Bratislave : Univerzita Komenského, 1975.

Bakos, Miklós.
see Szabó, Zoltán, 1908- Contact catalysis. Amsterdam, Elsevier Scientific Pub. Co., 1976-

Bakos, Miklós.
see Szabó, Zoltan, 1908- Contact catalysis. Budapest, Akadémiai Kiadó, 1976.

Bakoš, Mikuláš.
Literárna história a historická poetika. Príspevky k metodológii literárnej vedy. [Doslov:] Oskár Čepan. 1. vyd. Bratislava, Slov. spis., t. Pravda, Žilina, 1973.
256, [4] p. diagrs., port. 21 cm. (Horizonty, zv. 25) Kčs18.00 CzS 73
Includes bibliographical references.
1. Literature—History and criticism—Theory, etc. 2. Poetics. I. Title.
PN441.B26 73-337475

Bakoš, Mikuláš, ed.
see Pred tvárou vštekých... [Vyd. 1.] Bratislava, Tatran Slovenské vyd. beletrie a umenia, 1965.

Bakoš, Mikuláš, ed.
see O svetovom románe... Bratislava, Vydavatel'stvo Slovenskej akadémie vied, 1967.

Bakoš, Oliver
see Gwerk, Edmund, 1895-1956. O umení... Bratislava : Pallas, 1975.

Bakoš, Oliver
see Meštánek, Ľubomír. Génius. Bratislava, Slov. filmový ústav, 1970-

Bakos, Zsigmond.
Pártmunka az értelmiségi pártszervezetekben / Bakos Zsigmond. — Budapest : Kossuth Könyvkiadó, 1973.
65 p. ; 21 cm.
3.00Ft
1. Magyar Szocialista Munkáspárt—Party work. I. Title.
JN2191.S92B32 76-520651

Bakosová, D.
see Vademecum medici. [Martin] Osveta, 1974.

Bakotan
see
Badan Kerjasama Otomatisasi Administrasi Negara
for publications by and about this body.
Titles and other entries beginning with this acronym are filed following this card.
74-233165

Bakou
see
Baku.

Bakouma, ville nouvelle; études préliminaires d'urbanisme. Paris, Secrétariat des Missions d'Urbanisme et d'Habitat, 1970.
104, xx p. illus., maps (4 fold. in pocket), plans.
At head of title: République Centrafricaine. URBA, Compagnie des Mines d'Uranium de Bakouma. Secrétariat d'État aux Affaires Etrangères.
In portfolio.
1. Cities and towns–Planning–Bakouma, Central African Republic. I. Compagnie des Mines d'Uranium de Bakouma, Bangui. II. France. Secrétariat d'État aux affaires étrangères chargé de la cooperation. III. France. Secrétariat des Missions d'Urbanisme et d'Habitat. IV. Central African Republic.
CLU NUC76-16253

Bakounine, **Michel**
see Bakunin, Mikhail Aleksandrovich, 1814-1876.

Bakourēs, Michaēl Geōrgiou.
(Hellenikē physis kai Hellēnikos politismos kai anthrōpismos)
Ἑλληνικὴ φύσις καὶ Ἑλληνικὸς πολιτισμὸς καὶ ἀνθρωπισμός / Μιχ. Γ. Μπακουρῆ. — 2. ἔκδ. — Ἀθῆναι : Ἑλληνικὴ Ἀνθρωπιστικὴ Ἑταιρεία, 1967.
9 p. ; 25 cm. — (Ἀρχαιότης καὶ σύγχρονα προβλήματα ; 16)
Includes bibliographical references.
1. Greece, Modern—Description and travel—1951- 2. Humanism. I. Title. II. Series: Archaiotēs kai synchrona provlēmata ; 16.
DF727.B29 1967 75-585031

Bakov, I͡Akym
see Lektyra. Novy Sad, Pokraínsky zavod za vydavanie uchebnikokh, 1967-68.

Bakovi͡a, Dzhordzhe
see
Bacovia, George, 1881-1957.

Bakovljev, Milan.
Interpunkcija i pravopisni znaci; programirani udžbenik. Beograd, Zavod za izdavanje udžbenika Socijalističke Republike Srbije [1971]
314 p.
CaOTU NUC74-38222

Bakovljev, Milan.
Terijske osnove programirane nastave. Beograd, "Duga," 1972.
120, [2] p. 17 cm. (Biblioteka XX vek, 7) 25.00Din Yu 72-2125
Bibliography: p. [109]-118.
1. Programmed instruction. I. Title.
LB1028.5.B26 72-971012

Bakow, Harry Anthony, 1947-
Individual differences and conditioning in the human newborn, by Harry Anthony Bakow. [n. p.] 1974 [i. e. 1976]
viii, 118 l. 29 cm.
Thesis (Ph. D.)--University of Rochester.
Vita.
Bibliography: leaves 110-116.
1. Infants (Newborn) 2. Infant psychology. 3. Individuality. I. Title.
NRU NUC77-89733

Bąkowa, Joanna
Szlachta województwa krakowskiego wobec opozcji Jerzego Lubomirskiego w latach 1661-1667 / Joanna Bąkowa. — Wyd. 1. — Warszawa : Państwowe Wydawn. Naukowe, 1974.
191, [3] p. ; 24 cm. — (Prace Krakowskiego Oddziału Polskiego Towarzystwa Historycznego ; nr. 12)
Summary in French.
Bibliography: p. 181-[192]
zł45.00
1. Krakow (Voivodeship)—History. 2. Lubomirski, Jerzy Sebastian, książę, 1616-1667. 3. Poland — History — Rebellion of Lubomirski, 1665-1666. I. Title. II. Series: Polskie Towarzystwo Historyczne. Oddział Krakowski. Prace ; nr. 12.
DK511.K58B34 75-583291

Bakownts', Aksel, 1899-1938.
[Works]
Երկեր : [Կազմեց և խմբագրեց Սերգեյ Գայադյան] Երևան, Հայպետհրատ, 1955 :
xx, 686 p. port. 23 cm.
Title romanized: Erker.
PK8548.B24 1955b 74-235201

Bakownts', Aksel, 1899-1938.
[Works]
Երկեր / Ակսել Բակունց. — Երևան : Հայկական ՍՍՀ ԳԱ Հրատարակչություն, 1976-
v. : port. ; 22 cm.
At head of title: Haykakan SSH Gitut'yunneri Akademia, M. Abeghiani anvan Grakanut'yan Institut.
Added t. p.: Sochinenii͡a.
Errata slip inserted in v. 1.
Includes bibliographical references.
2.16rub (v. 1)
Title romanized: Erker.
PK8548.B24 1976 77-970551

Bąkowski, Klemens.
Kronika Krakowa z lat 1918-1923. Kraków, Gebethner i Wolff, 1925.
vi, 136 p. plates. 22 cm.
1. Kraków—History. I. Title.
DK4725.B34 77-500972

Bąkowski, Klemens.
Teatr Krakowski, 1780-1815. W Krakowie, w Druk. Czasu, 1907.
95 p. illus. 22 cm. (Biblioteka krakowska, nr. 37)
Bound with Müller, Eugeniusz. Żydzi w Krakowe w drugiej połowie XIV stulecia. W Krakowie, 1906.
1. Krakow. Teatr Krakowski. I. Title. II. Series.
DB879.K8B48 nr. 37 74-207505
[PN2616.K72]

Bakowski, Marie T., joint author.
see Carter, Stephen K. Chemotherapy of cancer. New York, Wiley, c1977.

Bakowski, Stefan.
Fizyka dla klasy VI [napisali] S. Bakowski, Cz. Scisłowski. [5. wyd.] Warszawa, Państwowe Zakłady Wydawnictw Szkolnych, 1961.
223 p. illus. 22 cm.
English translation of Physics for the 6th grade, by S. Bakowski, Cz. Fotyma, Cz. Scisłowski.
"Spis tabel przydatnych do rozwiazywania zadań: p. [219]"
1. Physics—Textbooks. I. Fotyma, Czesław, joint author. II. Scisłowski, Czesław, joint author. III. Title.
IEdS NUC75-51684

Bakowsky, Herbert.
Das Notgeld der Stadt Flensburg, 1914-1923 / Herbert Bakowsky. — 1. Aufl. — Berlin : Verlag Pröh, 1975.
70 p. : ill. ; 21 cm. — (Schriftenreihe Die Münze ; Bd. 49) GFR***
"Auslieferung in USA: Hans und Beate Rauch, Los Angeles, Calif. 90060, USA."
1. Inflation (Finance)—Germany—Flensburg—History. 2. Paper money—Flensburg—History. I. Title. II. Series.
HG1010.F54B34 76-461381
76 MARC

Bakr, 'Abd al-Muhaymin.
(al-Wasīṭ fī sharḥ qānūn al-jazā' al-Kūwaytī)
الوسيط في شرح قانون الجزاء الكويتى : القسم الخاص / تاليف عبد المهيمن بكر سالم . — الطبعة 1. — [الكويت] : جامعة الكويت ، 1972-1973.
436 p. ; 24 cm. — (مطبوعات جامعة الكويت)
Bibliography: p. 435-436.
1. Criminal law—Kuwait. I. Title. II. Series: Jāmi'at al-Kuwayt. Maṭbū'āt Jāmi'at al-Kuwayt.
75-972746

al-Bakr, Aḥmad Ḥasan, 1914-
(Khiṭāb al-Ra'īs al-munāḍil Aḥmad Ḥasan al-Bakr bi-munāsabat al-awwal min Ayyār 1973)
خطاب الرئيس المناضل احمد حسن البكر بمناسبة الأول من ايار ١٩٧٣ . — [بغداد] : الجمهورية العراقية ، وزارة الاعلام ، مديرية الاعلام العامة ، 1973.
19 p. : port. ; 17 cm. — (السلسلة الوثائقية — مديرية الاعلام العامة ; 24)
Cover title: Khiṭāb al-Sayyid al-Ra'īs Aḥmad Ḥasan al-Bakr bi-munāsabat al-awwal min Ayyār.
1. Iraq — Politics and government — Addresses, essays, lectures. I. Title. II. Title: Khiṭāb al-Sayyid al-Ra'īs Aḥmad Ḥasan al-Bakr bi-munāsabat al-awwal min Ayyār.
DS79.65.B29 75-587895

al-Bakr, Aḥmad Ḥasan, 1914-
(Khiṭāb al-Sayyid al-ra'īs Aḥmad Ḥasan al-Bakr fī al-dhikrá al-khāmisah li-thawrat al-sābi' 'ashar min Tammūz, 1973)
خطاب السيد الرئيس أحمد حسن البكر فى الذكرى الخامسة لثورة السابع عشر من تموز ١٩٧٣ . — [بغداد] : الجمهورية العراقية ، وزارة الاعلام ، مديرية الاعلام العامة ، 1973.
51 p. : port. ; 16 cm. — (السلسلة الوثائقية ; 25)
Series romanized: al-Silsilah al-wathā'iqīyah.
1. Iraq—Politics and government—Addresses, essays, lectures. I. Title.
DS79.65.B295 75-973161

al-Bakr, Aḥmad Ḥasan, 1914-
(Masīrat al-thawrah)
مسيرة الثورة ، فى خطب وتصريحات السيد رئيس الجمهورية العراقية احمد حسن البكر ، ١٩٦٨ - ١٩٧٠ . [بغداد ، مديرية التأليف والترجمة والنشر ، 1971]
266 p. 22 cm.
1. Iraq—Politics and government—Addresses, essays, lectures. I. Title.
DS79.65.B3 73-220841

al-Bakr, Ahmad Hasan, 1914-
President Ahmed Hassan Al-Bakr's speech on the occasion of May Day, 1973. [Baghdad, Ministry of Information, 1973]
18 p.
MH NUC76-70907

Bakr, M Abu.
Fluorspar deposits in the northern part of Koh-i-Maran Range, Kalat Division, West Pakistan, by Muhammad Abu Bakr. Karachi, Printed by the Manager, Govt. of Pakistan Press, 1962.
7 p. fold. map. 28 cm. (Records of the Geological Survey of Pakistan, v. 9, pt. 2)
Cover title.
"References": p. 3.
1. Fluorspar—Pakistan—Kalāt. I. Title. II. Series: Pakistan. Geological Survey. Records, v. 9, pt. 2.
QE295.P3 vol. 9, pt. 2 555.49'08 s 72-939582
[TN948.F6] [549'.4] MARC

Bakr, M Abu.
Fluorspar deposits of Pakistan, by M. Abu Bakr. Issued by the Director General, Geological Survey of Pakistan. Karachi, Printed by the Manager, Govt. of Pakistan Press, 1965.
5 p. map. 28 cm. (Records of the Geological Survey of Pakistan, v. 16, pt. 2)
Cover title.
"References": p. 4.
1. Fluorspar—Pakistan. I. Title. II. Series: Pakistan. Geological Survey. Records, v. 16, pt. 2.
QE295.P3 vol. 16, pt. 2 72-939583
[TN948.F6] MARC

Bakr, M Abu.
Geology of parts of trans-Himalayan region in Gilgit and Baltistan, West Pakistan, by M. Abu Bakr. Issued by the Director General, Geological Survey of Pakistan. Karachi, Printed by Manager, Govt. of Pakistan Press, 1965.
iii, 17 p. illus., maps. 28 cm. (Records of the Geological Survey of Pakistan, v. 11, pt. 3)
Cover title.
"References": p. 14.
1. Geology—Pakistan—Gilgit. 2. Geology—Pakistan—Baltistan. I. Title. II. Series: Pakistan. Geological Survey. Records, v. 11, pt. 3.
QE295.P3 vol. 11, pt. 3 555.49'08 s 72-939584
[555.49'122] MARC

Bakr, M Abu.
Geology of the Western Ras Koh Range, Chagai and Kharan Districts, Quetta and Kalat divisions, West Pakistan. Karachi, Manager of Publications, 1964.
28 p. illus., maps. (Records of the Geological Survey of Pakistan, v. 10, pt. 2-A)
Cover title.
Includes bibliography.
1. Geology—Pakistan—West Pakistan. I. Title. II. Series: Pakistan. Geological Survey. Records, v. 10, pt. 2-A.
CU-A NUC75-84604

Bakr, M Abu.
Thermal springs of Pakistan, by M. Abu Bakr. Issued by the Director General, Geological Survey of Pakistan. Karachi, Printed by the Manager, Govt. of Pakistan Press, 1965.
4 p. 28 cm. (Records of the Geological Survey of Pakistan, v. 16, pt. 3)
Cover title.
"References": p. 3.
1. Springs—Pakistan. 2. Springs—Bangladesh. I. Title. II. Series: Pakistan. Geological Survey. Records, v. 16, pt. 3.
QE295.P3 vol. 16, pt. 3 555.49'08 s 72-939585
[GB1159.P2] [551.2'3] MARC

Bakr, M Abu.
Vermiculite deposits in the Doki River Area Ras Koh Rang, Kalat Division, West Pakistan, by Muhammad Abu Bakr. Karachi, Printed by the Manager, Govt. of Pakistan Press, 1962.
5 p. maps. 27 cm. (Records of the Geological Survey of Pakistan, v. 9, pt. 1)
Cover title.
"References": p. 5.
1. Vermiculite—Pakistan—Kalāt. I. Title. II. Series: Pakistan. Geological Survey. Records, v. 9, pt. 1.
QE295.P3 vol. 9, pt. 1 555.49'08 s 72-939581
[TN948.V4] [553'.67] MARC

Bakr, M Abu.
Vermiculite deposits of Pakistan, by M. Abu Bakr. Issued by the Director General of the Geological Survey of Pakistan. Karachi, Manager of Publications, 1965.
9 p. 28 cm. (Records of the Geological Survey of Pakistan, v. 16, pt. 1)
Cover title.
"References": p. 8.
1. Vermiculite—Pakistan. I. Title. II. Series: Pakistan. Geological Survey. Records, v. 16, pt. 1.
QE295.P3 vol. 16, pt. 1 555.49'08 s 72-939586
[TN948.V4] [553'.67] MARC

Bakr, Mamdūh Abū
see Abū Bakr, Mamdūh.

Bakr, Mohammed A., ed.
see Energy and development: a case study. Cambridge, Mass., MIT Press [1973]

Bakr, Muhammad Abu
see Bakr, M Abu.

Bakr, Sa'īd, Abū
see Abū Bakr, Sa'īd, 1899-1948.

Bakr, al-Sayyid Ya'qūb
see Hourani, George Fadlo. [Arab seafaring in the Indian Ocean in ancient and early medieval times. Arabic] al-'Arab wa-al-milāhah fī al-Muhīt al-Hindī fī al-'usūr al-qadimah wa-awa'il al-qurun al-wustá. [1958]

Bakr Darwīsh
see
Darwīsh, Bakr.

Bakr Miṣbāḥ Tunayrah
see
Tunayrah, Bakr Miṣbāḥ.

Bakr Mūsá
see
Mūsá, Bakr, 1935-

Bakr Tunayrah
see
Tunayrah, Bakr Miṣbāḥ.

Bakradze, K S
(Izbrannye filosofskie trudy)
Избранные философские труды : [в 4-х т.] / К. С. Бакрадзе. — 2-е изд. — Тбилиси, Изд-во Тбил. ун-та, 19
v. ; 22 cm. USSR 73
CONTENTS:
—3. Очерки по истории новейшей и современной буржуазной философии.—
Includes bibliographical references and index.
2.58rub (v. 3)
1. Philosophy—Collected works. I. Title.
B29.B242 74-355322

Bakrān, Muḥammad ibn Najīb, fl. 1208.
(Jahān'nāmah)
جهان نامه، متن جغرافیائی تالیف شده در ٦٠٥ هجری. از محمد بن نجیب بکران. با ٢ مقدمه و ٥ فهرست. بکوشش محمد امین ریاحی. [تهران، انتشارات کتابخانه ابن سینا، 1342 i. e. 1963]
24, 139 p. 25 cm.
1. Geography, Medieval. I. Riyāḥī, Muḥammad Amīn, ed. II. Title.
G93.B3 1963 73-218736

al-Bakrī, 'Abd al-Bāqī.
(al-Madkhal li-dirāsat al-qānūn wa-al-sharī'ah al-Islāmīyah)
المدخل لدراسة القانون والشريعة الاسلامية، تأليف عبد الباقي البكري. النجف، مطبعة الآداب -1972.
v. 24 cm. 2 ID (v. 1)
CONTENTS: جزء 1. نظرية القاعدة القانونية والقاعدة الشرعية. المراجع العامة للكتاب (p. 811-821)—
1. Islamic law. I. Title.
74-213198

al-Bakrī, 'Abd al-Bāqī.
(Tanfīdh al-iltizām)
تنفيذ الالتزام، دراسة مقارنة. تأليف عبد الباقي البكري. بغداد، مطبعة الزهراء، 1971.
544 p. 24 cm. (His شرح االقانون المدني العراقي، 3) 2 ID
Includes bibliographical references.
1. Executions (Law) I. Title.
74-207001

al-Bakrī, Abū 'Ubayd 'Abd Allāh ibn 'Abd al-'Azīz, 1040-1094.
(Faṣl al-maqāl fī sharḥ Kitāb al-amthāl)
فصل المقال في شرح كتاب الأمثال / لأبي عبيد البكري ؛ حققه وقدم له احسان عباس وعبد المجيد عابدين. — بيروت : دار الامانة، 1971.
20, 619 p., [2] leaves of plates : facsims. ; 25 cm. — (مكتبة الامثال العربية ؛ 2)
Added t. p.: Faṣl al-maqāl fī sharḥ al-Amthāl (Commentary on Ibn Sallām's Book of proverbs)
«وهو شرح لكتاب «الأمثال» لأبي عبيد القاسم بن سلام»
Bibliography: p. [605]-610.
Includes indexes.
1. Abū 'Ubayd al-Qāsim ibn Sallām, ca. 773-ca. 837. al-Amthāl. 2. Proverbs, Arabic. I. Abū 'Ubayd al-Qāsim ibn Sallām, ca. 773-ca. 837. al-Amthāl. 1971. II. 'Abbās, Iḥsān. III. 'Ābidīn, 'Abd al-Majīd. IV. Title.
PN6519.A7A632 1971 75-549899

al-Bakri, Abū Ubayd 'Abd Allāh ibn 'Abd al-Aziz, 1040-1094. al-Mamālik waal-masālik
see Ibrāhīm ibn Ya'qūb al-Isrā'īlī al-Turtūshī, fl. 965. Relacja Ibrāhīma ibn Ja'kūba z podrózy do krajów słowiańskich, w przekazie al-Bekriego. Kraków, Skł. gł. w księg. Gebethnera i Wolffa, 1946.

al-Bakrī, 'Ādil.
(Ma'a 'Uthmān al-Mawṣilī fī fannihi wa-'abqarīyatih)
مع عثمان الموصلى فى فنه وعبقريته / عادل البكرى. — [بغداد] : وزارة الاعلام، مديرية الفنون العامة، 1973.
43 p. : ill. ; 20 cm.
«مهراجان الموسيقار عثمان الموصلى»
«بمناسبة ذكرى مرور نصف قرن على وفاته»
1. 'Uthmān al-Mawṣilī, 1854-1923—Addresses, essays, lectures. I. Title.
CT1919.I 7U823 75-587866

al-Bakrī, Aḥmad.
(al-'Uyūn al-ja'ānīn)
العيون الجعانين : اشعار بالعامية المصرية / احمد البكرى ؛ الغلاف والرسوم الداخلية بريشة محمد جاد. — [القاهرة] : دار ابن عروس للنشر، [1976?]
94 p. : ill. ; 16 cm.
£E0.10
I. Title.
PJ7816.A467U9 76-961147

Bakrī, 'Aṭā.
(al-Kindī fī mawkib al-ḥaḍārah)
الكندي فى موكب الحضارة / تأليف عطا بكري. — [بغداد : s. n., 1962]
64 p. : ill. ; 22 cm.
Cover title: al-Kindi and precis of the history of Baghdad.
1. al-Kindī, d. ca. 873—Addresses, essays, lectures. 2. Bagdad—History—Addresses, essays, lectures. I. Title.
B753.K54B34 75-549836

al-Bakrī, Fuḍayl ibn ʿAlī al-Jamālī
see
al-Jamālī al-Bakrī, Fuḍayl ibn ʿAlī, d. 1583 or 4.

al-Bakrī, Ḥāzim.
(Dirāsāt fī al-alfāẓ al-'āmmīyah al-Mawṣilīyah wa-muqāranatuhā ma'a al-alfāẓ al-'āmmīyah fī al-aqālīm al-'Arabīyah)
دراسات في الألفاظ العامية الموصلية ومقارنتها مع الألفاظ العامية في الاقاليم العربية، تأليف حازم البكري. بغداد، مطبعة اسعد، 1972.
523 p. 24 cm. 1.25 ID
Bibliography: p. 513-518.
1. Arabic language—Dialects—Mosul. I. Title.
PJ6830.M6B3 74-217313

al-Bakrī, Muḥammad Hamdī, 1906- joint author
see Kāmil, Murād. (Tārikh al-adab al-Siryānī min nash'atihi ilá al-'aṣr al-ḥāḍir) 1974.

al-Bakrī, Muhammad Tawfīq.
[Ṣahārīj al-lu'lu']
كتاب صهاريج اللؤلؤ، تأليف السيد محمد توفيق البكرى. وشرحه احمد بن امين الشنقيطى وابو بكر محمد لطفى المصرى. الطبعة 2، منقحة مصححة على النسخة الاصلية للمؤلف. [مصر] ملتزم الطبع محمود حجاج الكتبى [1907?]
388 p. 24 cm.
Text is vocalized.
I. al-Shinqīṭī, Aḥmad ibn al-Amīn, d. 1912 or 13. II. Abū Bakr Muḥammad Luṭfī. III. Title: Ṣahārīj al-lu'lu'.
Title romanized: Kitāb ṣahārīj al-lu'lu'.
PJ7816.A47S2 1907 73-211156

Bakrow, William
see Gibson, Raymond C Resources and needs for higher education in Iowa. Des Moines, 1960.

Bakrū, Muhammad, joint author
see Khayyāt, Kamāl Muhammad Sa'īd. (Mash iqtiṣādī—ijtimā'ī li-ihda qurá Muhāfazat al-Sulaymānīyah: qaryat Hasil) [1973]

Bakry, Hasan S K
Ancient Egypt abroad, by H. K. Bakry. [Cairo, Dept. of International Organizations, the Foreign Press and Information Service, Ministry of Culture and Information, 1973]
101 p. illus. 17 cm. (Prism. Supplement, 6)
1. Folk-lore, Egyptian. 2. Legends—Egypt. 3. Mythology, Egyptian. I. Title. II. Series: Prism (Cairo, Egypt) Supplement, 6.
NIC NUC76-70925

Bakry, Hasbullah.
Problematik hukum Islam dan negara Islam di Indonesia [oleh] H. Hasbullah Bakry. [Tjet. 1.] Djakarta, Widjaya [1967]
33 p. 17 cm.
1. Islamic law. 2. Islamic law—Indonesia. 3. State, The. I. Title.
76-949792

Bakry, Hasbullah.
Systematik filsafat / oleh Hasbullah Bakry. — Sala : AB. Siti Sjamsiah, [1964]
93 p. ; 22 cm.
1. Philosophy—Introductions. I. Title.
B28.I 5B34 75-949655

Bakry, Hasbullah
see Warsito S Disekitar kebatinan. Jakarta, Bulan Bintang [1973]

Bakša, Ján.
Základy psychológie a sociológia poľnohospodárskych podnikov : učebný text pre posl. VŠP a postgraduálneho štúdia : [určené pre smer ASR a AF / autori] J. Bakša, M. Antošová, V. Grausová. — 1. vyd. — Nitra : VŠP, 1975.
215 p. : ill. ; 29 cm. CzS 75
At head of title: Vysoká škola poľnohospodárska v Nitre. Rektorát VŠP n Nitre. Katedra pedagogiky a sociológie.
Bibliography: p. 213–215.
Kčs13.00
1. Agricultural education — Czechoslovak Republic. 2. Psychology—Methodology. 3. Sociology—Methodology. I. Antošová, M., joint author. II. Grausová, V., joint author. III. Title.
S539.C95B34 76–526373

Baksa, Ottóné.
A juhtartás költség és jövedelem alakulása. [Írták: Baksa Ottóné és Kovács Tiborne. Készült a Gazdaságelemző Igazgatóság, Költség- és Árelemző Osztályán] Budapest, Statisztikai és Gazdaságelemző Központ, 1972.
25 p. 28 cm.
"1972, 12."
1. Sheep—Economic aspects—Hungary. I. Kovács, Tiborné, joint author. II. Hungary. Statisztikai és Gazdaságelemző Központ. Költség- és Árelemző Osztály. III. Title.
SF375.5.H9B34 75–566185

Bakşan, Ziya M
Çocuklara Karagöz / hazırlayan, Ziya M. Bakşan. — 1. baskı. — [İstanbul] : Milliyet Yayınları, 1971.
344 p. ; ill. ; 15 cm. — (Çocuk kitapları dizisi ; 23)
Bibliography: p. 343-344.
1. Puppets and puppet-plays—Turkey—Juvenile literature. I. Karagöz. II. Title.
PN1978.T8B34 75–587907

Baksheev, Nikolaĭ Sergeevich.
(Klinicheskie lektŝii po akusherstvu)
Клинические лекции по акушерству. (Избр. главы). Москва, "Медицина," 1972.
512 p. with illus., 2 l. of illus. 21 cm. USSR 72–VKP
At head of title: Н. С. Бакшеев.
2.00rub
1. Obstetrics. I. Title.
[RG524.B27] 75–579291

Baksheev, Nikolaĭ Sergeevich.
(Preduprezhdenie zhenskikh bolezneĭ)
Предупреждение женских болезней. Москва, "Знание," 1972.
78 p. with illus. 21 cm. (Народный университет: Факультет здоровья, 10) 0.15rub USSR 72–VKP
At head of title: Н. С. Бакшеев.
1. Woman—Health and hygiene. 2. Woman—Diseases. I. Title. II. Series: Narodnyĭ universitet: Fakul'tet zdorov'ia, 1972, 10.
RA773.N3 1972, vol. 10 73–324842
[RG121]

Baksheev, Nikolaĭ Sergeevich, joint author
see Kurskiĭ, Mikhail Dmitrievich. (Biokhimicheskie osnovy mekhanizma deĭstviia serotonina) 1974.

Baksheev, Nikolaĭ Sergeevich, ed.
see Respublikanskoe obshchestvo akusherov-ginekologov Ukrainskoĭ SSR. Matochnye krovotecheniia v akusherstve i ginekologii. Kiev, Zdrov'ia, 1966.

Baksheeva, Galina.
Mosty, cherez kotorye oni shli, [by] Galina Baksheeva. Minsk, Mastatskaia literatura, 1973.
91 p. illus. [6] l. of plates, ports.
1. Russia (1923- U.S.S.R.). Armiia—Biography. 2. Generals—Russia. 3. World War, 1939-1945—Russia. I. Title.
CaOTU NUC75-138736

Bakshi, Bimal Kumar, 1919-
Accelerated laboratory investigations on durability of wood; final technical report. Dehra Dun, India, Forest Research Institute & Colleges [1968?]
57, 20 p. illus.
Grant no. FG–IN–106; reporting period June 23, 1962 to June 22, 1967.
Bibliography: p. 54-57.
1. Wood. Deterioration. 2. Wood research. I. Dehra Dūn. Forest Research Institute. II. Title.
DNAL NUC76-70899

Bakshi, Bimal Kumar, 1919–
Studies on four species of Ceratocystis, with a discussion on fungi causing sap-stain in Britain. Kew, Surrey, Commonwealth Mycological Institute, 1951.
16 p. 25 cm. (Mycological papers, no. 35)
Cover title.
Bibliography: p. 15–16.
1. Ceratocystis. 2. Wood-staining fungi—Great Britain. 3. Blue stain. I. Title. II. Series: Commonwealth Mycological Institute, Kew, Eng. Mycological papers, no. 35.
QK623.O6B37 74–196570
MARC

Bakshi, Bimal Kumar, 1919-
see Survey of the diseases of important native and exotic forest trees... Dehra, India [1972]

Bakshī, Candrakānta, 1932–
(Atītavana)
અતીતવન. [લેખક] ચંદ્રકાંત બક્ષી. [1. આવૃત્તિ. મુંબઈ, અશોક પ્રકાશન]; પ્રાપ્તિસ્થાન: નવભારત સાહિત્ય મંદિર [1974]
319 p. 19 cm. Rs10.25
"આ નવલ ૮ સપ્ટેમ્બર ૧૯૭૧ થી ૩ મે ૧૯૭૨ સુધી દૈનિક 'જન્મભૂમિ' માં ધારાવાહિક સ્વરૂપે પ્રકટ થઈ હતી."
In Gujarati.
A novel.
I. Title.
PK1859.B3A9 74–903297

Bakshī, Candrakānta, 1932–
[Ayanavṛtta]
અયનવૃત્ત; ઐતિ-ભૌગોલિક નવલકથા. [લેખક] ચંદ્રકાંત બક્ષી. [પ્રથમાવૃત્તિ] મુંબઈ, અશોક પ્રકાશન [1972]
186 p 19 cm. Rs5.00
In Gujarati.
I. Title.
PK1859.B3A98 72–902249

Bakshī, Candrakānta, 1932–
(Hanīmūna)
હનીમૂન. [લેખક] ચન્દ્રકાન્ત બક્ષી. [પ્રથમાવૃત્તિ] સુરત, સાહિત્ય સંગમ; મુખ્ય વિક્રેતા રૂપાલી પ્રકાશન, અમદાવાદ [1972]
248 p. 19 cm. Rs7.25
Distributor statement stamped on t. p.
"આ નવલ ... દૈનિક 'જનસત્તા'માં ધારાવાહિક સ્વરૂપે પ્રકટ થઈ હતી."
In Gujarati.
A novel.
List of the author's works: p. [4]
I. Title.
PK1859.B3H3 72–903928

Bakshī, Candrakānta, 1932–
(Lagnanī āgalī rāte)
લગ્નની આગલી રાતે. [લેખક] ચંદ્રકાન્ત બક્ષી. [પ્રથમાવૃત્તિ. મુંબઈ, અશોક પ્રકાશન]; પ્રાપ્તિસ્થાન : નવભારત સાહિત્ય મંદિર [1973]
208 p. 19 cm. Rs6.00
In Gujarati.
A novel.
I. Title.
PK1859.B3L3 73–906847

Bakshī, Candrakānta, 1932–
મશાલ. [લેખક] ચંદ્રકાન્ત બક્ષી. [પ્રથમાવૃત્તિ] સૂરત, સાહિત્ય સંગમ [1968]
272 p. 19 cm. (સાહિત્ય સંગમ પ્રકાશન, નં. 105)
In Gujarati.
Short stories.
I. Title.
Title romanized: Maśāla.
PK1859.B3M3 S A 68–9874
PL 480 : I-Gu-1192

Bakshī, Candrakānta, 1932–
(Pêrêlisisa)
પૅરૅલિસિસ / चन्द्रकान्त बक्षी. — પ્રથમાવૃત્તિ. — સુરત : સાહિત્ય સંગમ, [19]67.
210 p. ; 17 cm. — (રમ્યકથા પેપરબેક સિરિઝ ; 1)
In Gujarati.
Series romanized: Ramyakathā peparaboka sirijha.
A novel.
Rs6.75
I. Title.
PK1859.B3P4 75–904904

Bakshī, Candrakānta, 1932–
(Surakhāba)
સુરખાબ / ચંદ્રકાંત બક્ષી. — 1. આવૃત્તિ. — મુંબઈ : અશોક પ્રકાશન : પ્રાપ્તિસ્થાન, નવભારત સાહિત્ય મંદિર, 1974.
191 p. ; 19 cm.
In Gujarati.
A novel.
Rs6.00
I. Title.
PK1859.B3S8 75–901727

Bakshi, Dhani Ram, 1896-1965
see Goswami, Shrawan Kumar, 1938- Nāgapurī aura usake bṛhat-traya. [1971]

Bakshi, Lalit Kumar, 1929–
(Jaṅga)
જંગ; ઐતિહાસિક નવલકથા. [લેખક] લલિતકુમાર બક્ષી. [1. આવૃત્તિ. મુંબઈ] ત્રિલોચન પ્રિન્ટિંગ પ્રેસ; મુખ્ય વિતરક નવભારત સાહિત્ય મંદિર [1972]
230 p. 19 cm. Rs6.50
In Gujarati.
1. India-Pakistan Conflict, 1965—Fiction. I. Title.
PK1859.B313J3 72–903330

Bakshi, O P
Politics and prejudice : notes on Aristotle's political theory / O. P. Bakshi. — [1st ed.] — Delhi : Publication Division, University of Delhi, 1975.
iii, 189 p. ; 23 cm.
Includes bibliographical references and index.
Rs45.00
1. Aristoteles. Politica. 2. Political science—History—Greece. I. Title.
JC71.A7B34 320.1'01 75-907918
76 MARC

Bakshi, Oskar Aleksandrovich
see Voprosy svarochnogo proizvodstva. 1974.

Bakshi, Padumlal Punnalal, comp.
साहित्य-शिक्षा; उच्च श्रेणीके विद्यार्थियों, उदीयमान कलाकारों और आलोचकोंके लिए साहित्य और उसके अंगोंको स्पष्ट करनेवाले निबन्धोंका क्रमबद्ध संग्रह. सम्पादक पदुमलाल पुन्नालाल बख्शी [तथा] हेमचन्द्र मोदी. बम्बई, हिन्दी-ग्रन्थ-रत्नाकर [1962]
176 p. 19 cm. (नवयुग पाठ्य-ग्रन्थावली, नं. 6)
In Hindi.
1. Hindi literature — Addresses, essays, lectures. I. Modī, Hemacandra. II. Title.
Title romanized: Sāhitya śikshā.
PK2033.B298 S A 68–10987
PL 480 : I-H-5717

Bakshi, Parvinrai Mulwantrai, 1921–
An introduction to legislative drafting [by] P. M. Bakshi. [2d ed.] Bombay, N. M. Tripathi, 1972.
111 p. 23 cm. Rs15.00
Running title: Legislative drafting.
Includes bibliographical references.
1. Bill drafting—India. I. Title. II. Title: Legislative drafting.
328.54'07'73 73–902193
MARC

Bakshī, Rameśa.
(Baisākhiyoṃvālī imārata)
बैसाखियोंवाली इमारत. [लेखक] रमेश बक्षी. 1. संस्करण. दिल्ली, प्रवर प्रकाशन, 1966.
168 p. 19 cm. Rs5.00
In Hindi.
A novel.
I. Title.
PK2098.13.A373B3 S A 67–6243

Bakshī, Rameśa.
(Calatā huā lāvā)
चलता हुआ लावा. [लेखक] रमेश बख्शी. [दिल्ली] राधाकृष्ण प्रकाशन [1968]
110 p. 19 cm.
In Hindi.
A novel.
4.50

I. Title.
PK2098.13.A373C3 73-904402

Bakshī, Rameśa.
(Devayānī kā kahanā hai)
देवयानी का कहना है. [नाटककार] रमेश बक्षी. [दिल्ली] इन्द्रप्रस्थ प्रकाशन; [वितरक विद्यार्थी प्रकाशन, 1972]
135 p. illus. 19 cm. Rs6.50
In Hindi.

I. Title.
PK2098.13.A373D4 72-908769

Bakshī, Rameśa.
(Eka amūrta takalīfa)
एक अमूर्त तकलीफ़. [कहानीकार] रमेश बक्षी. [1. संस्करण. इलाहाबाद, नीलाभ प्रकाशन, 1972]
175 p. 19 cm.
In Hindi.
Rs6.00

I. Title.
PK2098.13.A373E4 72-900066

Bakshī, Rameśa.
(Hama tinake)
हम तिनके. [लेखक] रमेश बक्षी. [कलकत्ता] न्यू एज पब्लिशर्स [1963]
301 p. 19 cm.
In Hindi.
A novel.

I. Title.
PK2098.13.A373H3 S A 66-3003

Bakshī, Rameśa.
(Kaṭatī huī zamīna)
कटती हुई ज़मीन; रमेश बक्षी का दूसरा कहानी-संग्रह. [1. संस्करण] जबलपुर, लोकचेतना प्रकाशन [1966]
215 p. 19 cm.
In Hindi.
Rs5

I. Title.
PK2098.13.A373K3 S A 67-6300
PL 480: I-H-4592

Bakshī, Rameśa.
(Khuleāma)
खुलेआम / रमेश बक्षी. — 1. संस्करण. — दिल्ली : इन्द्रप्रस्थ प्रकाशन, 1975.
95 p. ; 19 cm.
In Hindi.
A novel.
Rs8.00

I. Title.
PK2098.13.A373K5 75-907677

Bakshī, Rameśa.
(Merī priya kahāniyāṁ)
मेरी प्रिय कहानियाँ / रमेश बक्षी. — 1. संस्करण. — दिल्ली : राजपाल, 1975.
124 p. ; 19 cm.
In Hindi.
CONTENTS: शबरी.—खाली.—उत्तर.—एक अमूर्त तकलीफ.—तलघर.—पैरोडी.—हे राम!
Rs7.00
I. Title.
PK2098.13.A373M44 75-905834

Bakshī, Rameśa.
(Mezapara ṭikī huī kuhaniyāṁ)
मेज़पर टिकी हुई कुहनियाँ. [लेखक] रमेश बक्षी. [प्रथम संस्करण] काशी, भारतीय ज्ञानपीठ [1963]
204 p. 19 cm. (ज्ञानपीठ लोकोदय ग्रन्थमाला: हिन्दी ग्रन्थांक, १६५)
In Hindi.
Short stories.

I. Title.
PK2098.13.A373M47 S A 65-1193
PL 480: I-H-1132

Bakshi, Rameśa.
(Pitā-dara-pitā)
पिता-दर-पिता और दो कहानियां. [लेखक] रमेश बक्षी. [1. संस्करण] कलकत्ता, रूपाम्बरा प्रकाशन [1971]
103 p. 23 cm. (नये रचनाकार, 12)
In Hindi.
Rs6.00
CONTENTS.—पिता-दर-पिता.—पितृऋण.—उत्तर.

I. Title.
PK2098.13.A373P5 75-921728

Bakshī, Rameśa.
(Qisse ūpara qissā)
क़िस्से ऊपर क़िस्सा, कथा प्रयोग. [लेखक] रमेश बक्षी. जयपुर, अपोलो पब्लिकेशन, १९६३ [1963]
95 p. illus. 23 cm.
In Hindi.

I. Title.
PK2098.13.A373Q5 S A 63-3720
PL 480: I-H-1009

Bakshī, Rameśa.
(Sattāīsa dāuna)
27 डाउन / रमेश बक्षी. — दिल्ली : पंजाबी पुस्तक भंडार ; नई दिल्ली : एकमात्र वितरक, हिन्दी बुक सेन्टर, 1974.
131 p. ; 19 cm.
In Hindi.
A novel.
Rs8.00

I. Title.
PK2098.13.A373S2 74-904277

Bakshī, Rameśa.
(Tīsarā hāthī)
तीसरा हाथी / रमेश बक्षी. — 1. संस्करण. — दिल्ली : इन्द्रप्रस्थ प्रकाशन, 1975.
112 p., [1] leaf of plates : ill. ; 19 cm.
In Hindi.
A play.
Rs8.50

I. Title.
PK2098.13.A373T5 75-907180

Bakshī, Rameśa, ed.
see Sharma, Achala, 1952- [Blaikaāuṭa] [New Delhi] [1972]

Bakshi, Ramprasad Premshanker, 1894–
(Vāṅmaya vimarśa)
વાઙ્મય વિમર્શ. [લેખક] રામપ્રસાદ પ્રે. બક્ષી. [2. આવૃત્તિ] મુંબઈ, એન. એમ. ત્રિપાઠી [1970]
470, 6 p. 19 cm. Rs9.00
In Gujarati.

1. Gujarati literature—Addresses, essays, lectures. I. Title.
PK1850.B3 1970 70-921362

Bakshi, Sri Ram.
Kalidasa: a new interpretation. [Lawrence, 1970]
iv, 254 l. 28 cm.
Thesis (Ph. D.)—University of Kansas.
1. Kālidāsa. I. Title.
KU NUC73-81600

Bakshi, Svarup Kumari, 1919–
(Cunāva kī ghuṛadauṛa)
चुनाव की घुड़दौड़; प्रतिनिधि कहानियों का संग्रह. [लेखिका] स्वरूप कुमारी बक्शी. [1. संस्करण] लखनऊ, भारतीय ग्रन्थमाला [1972]
102 p. illus. 23 cm. Rs7.00
In Hindi.
CONTENTS: मूर्ख बालक.—बच्चों का राज.—पेन खो गया.—चमेली रानी.—हब्शी मेम साहब.—कुरूप कन्या.—माला.—चुनाव की घुड़दौड़.

I. Title.
PK2098.B338C8 72-900755

Bakshi, Svarup Kumari, 1919–
कौड़ियों का नाच; कहानी संग्रह. [लेखिका] स्वरूप कुमारी बक्शी. [2. संस्करण] लखनऊ, भारतीय ग्रन्थमाला [1965]
86 p. 22 cm. 3.75
In Hindi.

I. Title.
Title romanized: Kauṛiyoṁ kā nāca.
PK2098.B338K3 1965 78-905308

Bakshi, Svarup Kumari, 1919–
(Maiṃ māyake calī jāūṅgī)
मैं मायके चली जाऊंगी; हास्य व्यंग से परिपूर्ण एकांकी संग्रह. [लेखिका] स्वरूप कुमारी बक्शी. [1. संस्करण] लखनऊ, भारतीय ग्रन्थमाला [1971]
87 p. 22 cm. Rs5.00
In Hindi.
CONTENTS: मैं मायके चली जाऊंगी.—विवाह का विज्ञापन.—मनपसन्द की शादी.—नई पड़ोसिन.—अधिकारों का युग.
I. Title.
PK2098.B338M3 72-905116

Bakshiev, Nikolaĭ Grigor'evich.
(Vvedenie v molekuliarnuiu spektroskopiiu)
Введение в молекулярную спектроскопию : [учеб. пособие для хим. фак. ун-тов и хим.-технол. ин-тов] / Н. Г. Бахшиев. — Ленинград : Изд-во Ленингр. ун-та, 1974.
181 p. : ill. ; 23 cm. USSR 74
At head of title: Leningradskiĭ gosudarstvennyĭ universitet imeni A. A. Zhdanova.
Bibliography: p. 165-[167]
Includes index.
0.62rub
1. Molecular spectra—Addresses, essays, lectures. I. Title.
QD96.M65B34 75-533736

Baksht, F. G.
see Termoemissionnye preobrazovateli i nizkotemperaturnaia plazma. 1973.

Bakshtanovskiĭ, Vladimir Iosifovich.
(Printsipy moral'nogo vybora)
Принципы морального выбора / В. И. Бакштановский. — Москва : Знание, 1974.
63 p. ; 20 cm. — (Новое в жизни, науке, технике : Серия Этика ; 10/1974) USSR***
Bibliography: p. [58]
0.10rub
1. Decision-making (Ethics) I. Title. II. Series: Novoe v zhizni, nauke, tekhnike : Seriia Ėtika ; 1974, 10.
BJ1468.5.B34 75-558232

Bakshtanovskiĭ Vladimir Iosifovich
see Vladimirskiĭ gosudarstvennyĭ pedagogicheskiĭ institut. (Formirovanie professional'noĭ napravlennosti studentov pedagogicheskikh vuzov) 1976.

Bakshutov, Vladimir Kuz'mich.
Studencheskoe dvizhenie v stranakh kapitala. [By] V.K. Bakshutov & V.I. Chuprov. Moskva, Znanie, 1971.
45 p. (V pomoshch' lektoru)
1. Student movements. I. Chuprov, Vladimir Il'ich.
MH NUC75-129132

Bakshy, Alexander, 1885- tr.
see Bor'kii, Maksim, 1868-1936. The lower depths, and other plays. New Haven, Yale University Press [1971, c1945]

Bakśī, Dhanīrāma
see
Bakshi, Dhani Ram, 1896-1965.

Baksi, Ranajit Kumar.
Humanity and God. Calcutta [1956]
76 p.
1. God. I. Title.
NSyU NUC73-59274

Baksi, Samarendra N
Thyrocalcitonin relationships with thyroid hormone secretion rate and lactation in rats. [Columbia] 1971.
167 l. illus.
Thesis (Ph.D.)–University of Missouri.
Vita.
Includes bibliography.
MoU NUC73-44460

Baksi, Samarendra N
Thyrocalcitonin relationships with thyroid hormone secretion rate and lactation in rats. [Columbia] 1971.
167 l. illus.
Thesis (Ph.D.)–University of Missouri.
Vita.
Includes bibliography.
Microfilm copy.
MoU NUC73-44459

Baksi, Sudhangshu. 1928–
ভালবাসা. [লেখক] সুধাংশু বক্সী. কলিকাতা, বুক ব্যাঙ্ক [1957]
236 p. 23 cm.
In Bengali.
A novel.

I. Title.
Title romanized: Bhālabāsā.
PK1730.13.A4B5 73-204476

Baksi, Subhendu Kumar.
On the foraminiferas from Raghavapuram mudstone, West Godavari District, Andhra Pradesh, India. Calcutta, 1966.
19 p. illus. 25 cm. (Geological, Mining and Metallurgical Society of India. Bulletin no. 37)
Bibliography: p. 17-18.
1. Foraminifera (fossil)–India–Andhra Pradesh. 2. India–Paleontology–Andhra Pradesh. I. Title.
DI-GS NUC74-122423

Bakst, Allan
see How to plan for tax savings... Rev. ed. [Greenvale, N.Y.] Panel Publishers [c1973]

Bakst, Allan
see How to save taxes and increase your wealth... [Greenvale, N.Y.] Panel Publishers [1971]

Bakst, Allan.
see How to take money out of a closely-held corporation... Rev. ed. Greenvale, N.Y., Panel Publishers, 1976.

Bakst, David A., joint author
see Morrison, Robert M 1904- Insurance agency purchases and mergers. Addendum. [Santa Monica, Calif., Insurors Press [c1972-

Bakst, James.
A history of Russian-Soviet music / by James Bakst. — Westport, Conn. : Greenwood Press, [1977] c1966.
x, 406 p., [8] leaves of plates : ill. ; 24 cm.
Reprint of the ed. published by Dodd, Mead, New York.
Bibliography: p. 391-393.
Includes index.
ISBN 0-8371-9422-9
1. Music—Russia—History and criticism. 2. Music—Russian Republic—History and criticism. I. Title.
[ML300.B28 1977] 780'.947 76-55406
76 MARC

Bakst, Lev Samoĭlovich, 1866-1924.
Bakst. — New York : Rizzoli, 1977.
[103] p. : chiefly ill. (some col.) ; 24 cm.
ISBN 0-8478-0072-5 : $4.95
1. Bakst, Lev Samoĭlovich, 1866-1924.
ND699.B3A43 792.8'025'0924 76-51470
77 MARC

Bakst: an exhibition... [London, 1973]
see under Fine Art Society, London.

Bakstad, Pål, 1935-
Difference-differential approximations to a first order partial differential equation describing the hydraulics of boiling water reactors, by P. Bakstad. Kjeller, Institutt for atomenergi, 1963.
[18] p. illus. (Kjeller report 54)
ICRL NUC74-122422

Bakstad, Pål, 1935-
"RAMONA I;" a FORTRAN code for transient analysis of boiling water reactors and boiling loops, by P. Bakstad and K. O. Solberg. Kjeller, Institutt for atomenergi, 1968.
1 v. (various pagings) illus. (Kjeller report 135)
ICRL NUC74-122421

Bakšytė, I
see Vaistiniai augalai. Vilnius, Mintis, 1973.

Băktashi, S. Ă., joint author
see Zahiri, M J (Nadir element iataglarynyn geologiiasy) 1974.

Baktay, Ervin.
Indiai regék és mondák / feldolgozta Baktay Ervin ; Harmatta János előszavával ; [a képeket válogatta Tóth Edit]. — 2. kiad. — Budapest : Móra, 1977.
426 p. : ill. ; 24 cm. — (Regék és mondák) H77
Adapted selections from the Mahābhārata and Rāmāyaṇa.
ISBN 963110544X : 35.00Ft
1. Mythology, Hindu. I. Mahābhārata. Hungarian. Selections. II. Vālmīki. Rāmāyaṇa. Hungarian. Selections. III. Title.
BL2001.2.B28 1977 77-476108
*77 MARC

Baktay, Ervin.
Rámájana és Mahábhárata. Elbeszéli Baktay Ervin. Budapest, Európa, 1960.
715 p. 19 cm.
A shortened modern prose version of the two Indian epics.
"Szanszkrit nevek és szavak jegyzéke": p. 697-[710]
I. Valmiki. Ramayana. II. Mahābhārata. III. Title.
NNC NUC76-69359

Bakteriĭnye i virusnye preparaty; posobie dlia vracheĭ i studentov meditsinskikh i farmatsevticheskikh institutov. [Pod obshcheĭ red. S. P. Karpova] Izd. 2., perer. i dop. Tomsk, Izd-vo Tomskogo univ., 1971.
305 p. illus.
At head of title: Tomskiĭ nauchno-issledovatel'skiĭ institut vaktsin i syvorotok. Tomskiĭ ordena Trudovogo Krasnogo Znameni meditsinskiĭ institut.
1. Bacterial vaccines. 2. Viral vaccines. I. Karpov, Sergeĭ Petrovich, ed.
DNLM NUC75-129915

Bakteriologické vyšetrovanie tuberkulózy. Praktická príručka určená pre stred. zdravot. pracovníkom v tuberkuloznych laboratóriách a strediskách ... Autori: Ružena Grígelová ... 1. vyd. Martin, Osveta, t. Tlač. SNP, B. Bystrica, 1972.
301, [2] p. 19 p. of col. plates, tables, photos, graphs, diagrs. 21 cm. (Edícia pre stredných zdravotníckych pracovníkov)
CzS 72-MS
Bibliography: p. 288–[289]
Kčs20.00
1. Mycobacterium tuberculosis. 2. Antitubercular agents. I. Grigelová, Ružena.
[QR201.T6B27] 75-406053

"Bakteriologie und Biochemie der Mykobakterien", Internationales Symposium
see Internationales Symposium "Bakteriologie und Biochemie der Mykobakterien"

Bakthavatsalan, K M 1927–
ராணி மங்கம்மாள். [எழுதியவர்] கி. மா. பக்தவத்சலன். [2. பதிப்பு] சென்னை, அருணோதயம் [1963]
72 p. 18 cm. (அருணோதயம் வெளியீடு 59) Rs1.50
In Tamil.
A play.
1. Mangammal, Queen, fl. 1689–1706—Drama. I. Title.
Title romanized: Rāṇi Maṅkammāḷ.
PL4758.9.B2R3 1963 S A 68-580
rev PL 480 : I-T-1647

(Baktriĭskie drevnosti)
Бактрийские древности : Предварит. сообщ. об археол. работах на юге Узбекистана : [Сборник статей] / АН СССР, Ин-т археологии, Науч. совет по проблемам археологии Сред. Азии и Казахстана, Ин-т археологии АН УзССР ; [Отв. ред. В. М. Массон]. — Ленинград : Наука, Ленингр. отд-ние, 1976.
126 p. : ill. ; 28 cm. USSR 77
Includes bibliographies.
0.67rub
1. Uzbekistan—Antiquities. 2. Bactria—History. I. Masson, Vadim Mikhaĭlovich. II. Akademiia nauk SSSR. Institut arkheologii. III. Akademiia nauk SSSR. Nauchnyĭ sovet po problemam arkheologii Sredneĭ Azii i Kazakhstana. IV. Akademiia nauk Uzbekskoĭ SSR, Tashkend. Institut arkheologii.
DK945.B34 77-510983

Baktygulov, Dzhumadil Sapalovich.
Из истории перехода киргизского крестьянства к оседлости и социалистическим способам хозяйствования. Фрунзе, "Кыргызстан," 1971.
112 p. 20 cm. 0.38rub USSR 71-VKP
At head of title: Дж. С. Бактыгулов.
Includes bibliographical references.
1. Land settlement—Kirghizistan. 2. Migration, Internal—Kirghizistan. 3. Kirghizistan—Rural conditions. I. Title.
Title romanized: Iz istorii perekhoda kirgizskogo krest'ianstva k osedlosti.
HD1516.R8B33 72-370272

Baku. Azerbaidzhanskaia respublikanskaia biblioteka
see Abdullaiev, Shamil. (Sovet Ittifagy Kommunist Partiiasy tarikhina dair na okhumaly) 1972.

Baku. Azerbaidzhanskaia respublikanskaia biblioteka
see Nadzhafova, M IU (Molla Panakh Vagif) 1970.

Baku. Azerbaĭdzhanskiĭ gosudarstvennyĭ meditsinskiĭ institut.
(Materialy Nauchnoĭ konferentsii)
Материалы Научной конференции, посвященной 50-летию образования СССР. (18–21 сент. 1972). Баку, 1972.
255 p. 21 cm. 1.00rub USSR 73
At head of title: Министерство здравоохранения Азербайджанской ССР.
1. Medicine—Congresses.
R106.B34 1972 73-360103

Baku. Azerbaĭdzhanskiĭ gosudarstvennyĭ muzeĭ iskusstv
see Azerbaidzhanskiĭ gosudarstvennyĭ muzeĭ iskusstv.

Baku. Azerbaĭdzhanskiĭ gosudarstvennyĭ nauchno-issledovatel'skiĭ institut pedagogiki
see
Azerbaĭdzhanskiĭ gosudarstvennyĭ nauchno-issledovatel'skiĭ institut pedagogiki.

Baku. Azerbaĭdzhanskiĭ gosudarstvennyĭ pedagogicheskiĭ institut iazykov.
Zhizn' i tvorchestvo M. F. Akhundova; posviashchaetsia 150-letiiu so dnia rozhdeniia. [Glav. red. Mamedov, G. K.] Baku, 1962.
271 p. illus. (Its Uchenye zapiski, 18, spetsial'nyi vyp.)
Added t.-p. in Azerbaijani. Russian or Azerbaijani with Azerbaijani or Russian summaries.
1. Ahund-zâde, Feth Ali, 1812-1878. I. Mamedov, G.K. II. Ahund-zâde, Feth Ali, 1812-1878. III. Title.
MH NUC76-42115

Baku. Azerbaĭdzhanskiĭ gosudarstvennyĭ pedagogicheskiĭ institut i͡azykov
see Almanja-azărbaĭjanja lùghăt. 1971.

Baku. Azerbaĭdzhanskiĭ gosudarstvennyĭ pedagogicheskiĭ institut i͡azykov
see Fransyzja-azărbaĭjanja lùghăt. 1965.

Baku. Azerbaĭdzhanskiĭ gosudarstvennyĭ universitet.
Материалы Научной конференции молодых ученых, посвященной 50-летию Азербайджанского государственного университета им. С. М. Кирова. (22–26 сент.) Баку, Изд. АГУ, 1969.
125 p. 22 cm. 0.56rub USSR 69–VKP
At head of title: Министерство высшего и среднего специального образования Азербайджанской ССР.
1. Science—Congresses. I. Title.
Title romanized: Materialy nauchnoĭ konferent͡sii molodykh uchenykh.
Q101.B34 72–374039

Baku. Azerbaĭdzhanskiĭ gosudarstvennyĭ universitet
see Akademiia nauk Azerbaĭdzhanskoĭ SSR, Baku. ⌈400, i.e. Chetyrekhsot-letie so dnia smerti velikogo azerbaidzhanskogo poeta Fizuli. Baku⌉ 1958.

Baku. Azerbaĭdzhanskiĭ gosudarstvennyĭ universitet
see Ălimirzăīev, Khălil. Azerbaĭdzhanskiĭ gosudarstvennyĭ universitet za 50 let. Baku, Azerbaĭdzhanskoe gos. izd-vo, 1969.

Baku. Azerbaĭdzhanskiĭ gosudarstvennyĭ universitet
see Tezisy dokladov Nauchnoĭ konferent͡sii, posvi͡ashchennoĭ pi͡atidesi͡atiletii͡u obrazovanii͡a SSSR. 1972.

Baku. Azerbaĭdzhanskiĭ gosudarstvennyĭ universitet. I͡Uridicheskiĭ fakul'tet
see Istorii͡a gosudarstva i prava Azerbaĭdzhanskoĭ SSR, 1920-1934 gg. Baku, ELM, 1973.

Baku. Azerbaĭdzhanskiĭ institut nefti i khimii
see Issledovanii͡a po nekotorym voprosam konstruktivnoĭ teorii funkt͡siĭ i different͡sial'nykh uravneniĭ. 1974.

Baku. Azerbaĭdzhanskiĭ institut nefti i khimii
see Năbiīev, T A (Azărabaĭjanda agrar munasibătlari) 1970.

Baku. Azerbaĭdzhanskiĭ institut nefti i khimii
see Neft vă gaz iataglarynyn ishlănmăsindă ămăk muhafizăsi vă ťanghyn profilaktikasy. 1974.

Baku. Azerbaĭdzhanskiĭ institut nefti i khimii
see Rukovodstvo po primenenii͡u matematicheskoĭ teorii eksperimenta pri issledovanii svoĭstv gornykh porod i prot͡sessa ikh razrushenii͡a. 1973.

Baku. Azerbaĭdzhanskiĭ institut nefti i khimii
see Vsesoi͡uznai͡a konferent͡sii͡a po dinamike i prochnosti neftepromyslovogo oborudovanii͡a, 1st, Baku, 1973. (Materialy pervoi Vsesoi͡uznoi konferent͡sii po dinamike i prochnosti neftepromyslovogo oborudovanii͡a) 1974

Baku. Azerbaĭdzhanskiĭ institut nefti i khimii. Fundamental'nai͡a biblioteka
see Kubrak, L V
K. N. Kulizade. 1971.

Baku. Azerbaĭdzhanskiĭ nauchno-issledovatel'skiĭ i proektnyĭ institut neft͡ianoĭ promyshlennosti
see
Azerbaĭdzhanskiĭ nauchno-issledovatel'skiĭ i proektnyĭ institut neft͡ianoĭ promyshlennosti.

Baku. Azerbaĭdzhanskiĭ nauchno-issledovatel'skiĭ institut gidrotekhniki i meliorat͡sii
see Polat-Zade, Ali Asker oglu. Vodozabornye sooruzheniia na gornykh rekakh. Baku, Azerbaĭdzhanskoe gos. izd-vo, 1964.

Baku. Azerbaĭdzhanskiĭ nauchno-issledovatel'skiĭ institut neftepererabatyvai͡ushcheĭ promyshlennosti.
In 1958 the Institut nefti of the Akademii͡a nauk Azerbaĭdzhanskoĭ SSR and the Azerbaĭdzhanskiĭ nauchno-issledovatel'skiĭ institut neftepererabatyvi͡ushcheĭ promyshlennosti merged to form the Institut neftekhimicheskikh prot͡sessov of the Akademii͡a nauk Azerbaĭdzhanskoĭ SSR.
Works by these bodies are found under the following headings according to the name used at the time of publication:
Akademii͡a nauk Azerbaĭdzhanskoĭ SSR. Baku. Institut nefti.
Baku. Azerbaĭdzhanskiĭ nauchno-issledovatel'skiĭ institut neftepererabatyvai͡ushcheĭ promyshlennosti.

Akademii͡a nauk Azerbaĭdzhanskoĭ SSR, Baku. Institut neftekhimicheskikh prot͡sessov.
74–236469

Baku. Azerbaĭdzhanskiĭ nauchno-issledovatel'skiĭ institut po dobyche nefti.
For works by this body issued under its later name see
Azerbaĭdzhanskiĭ gosudarstvennyĭ nauchno-issledovatel'skiĭ i proektnyĭ institut neft͡ianoĭ promyshlennosti.

Baku. Azerbaĭdzhanskiĭ pedagogicheskiĭ institut
see
Azerbaĭdzhanskiĭ gosudarstvennyĭ nauchno-issledovatel'skiĭ institut pedagogiki.
rev74

Baku. Institut istorii partii.
Azărbaĭjan Kommunist partii͡asynyn tarikhi
see its
Istorii͡a Kommunisticheskoĭ partii Azerbaĭdzhana. Azerbaijani.

Baku. Institut istorii partii.
⌈Istorii͡a Kommunisticheskoĭ partii Azerbaĭdzhana. Azerbaijani⌉
Азәрбайҹан Коммунист партиясынын тарихи. Бакы, Азәрбайҹан Дөвләт Нәшрийяты, 1958–
v. 22 cm.
At head of title, v. 1– : Азәрбайҹан МК янында Партия тарихи институт—Сов. ИКП МК янында Марксизм-ленинизм институтнун филиалы.
Includes bibliographical references.
1. Kommunisticheskai͡a partii͡a Azerbaĭdzhana—History. I. Title.
Title romanized: Azărbaĭjan Kommunist partii͡asynyn tarikhi.
JN6598.K725B312 75–564843

Baku. Institut istorii partii.
⌈Kommunisticheskai͡a partii͡a Azerbaĭdzhana v t͡sifrakh. Azerbaijani⌉
Азәрбајҹан Коммунист Партијасы рәгәмләр. Стат. мәчмуәси. ⌈Бакы⌉, Азәрнәшр, ⌈1970⌉.
144 p. 21 cm. 0.38rub USSR 71–18454
At head of title: Азәрбајҹан КП МК-нын Иартија Тарихи Институту—Сов. ИКП МК јанында марксизм-ленинизм институтунун филиалы.
Issued also in Russian.
1. Kommunisticheskai͡a partii͡a Azerbaĭdzhana—Statistics. I. Title.
Title romanized: Azărbaĭjan Kommunist Partii͡asy rägămlăr.
JN6598.K725B31312 73–204952

Baku. Institut istorii partii
see Detishche leninskoi natsional'noi politiki. 1974.

Baku. Institut istorii partii
see Meshadi Azizbekov—plamennyĭ borets za vlast' Sovetov. 1976.

Baku. Institut istorii partii
see Pod leninskim znamenem sot͡sialisticheskogo internat͡sionalizma. 1972.

Baku. Institut istorii partii
see Sovet kandi——alli il. 1973.

Baku. Institut istorii partii
see T͡Sentral'naia bol'shevistskai͡a pechat' ob Azerbaĭdzhane. 1976.

Baku. Institut istorii partii
see Za obrazovanie Soi͡uza Sovetskikh Sot͡sialisticheskikh Respublik. 1972.

Baku. Institut istorii partii
see Za vlast' Sovetov. ⌈Baku, Azerneshr⌉ 1967.

Baku. Muzeĭ Azerbaĭdzhanskoĭ literatury im. Nizami
see
Muzeĭ Azerbaĭdzhanskoĭ literatury im. Nizami.

Baku. Muzeĭ istorii Azerbaĭdzhana.
(Azărbaĭjan tarikhi muzeĭinin ălli ildiĭi)
Азәрбајҹан тарихи музејинин 50 илдији / П. Ә. Әзизбәјованын редактәси алтында ; Азәрбајҹан Тарихи Музеји ; ⌈сост., П. А. Азизбекова ... et al.⌉. — Бакы : "Елм," 1973.
⌈184⌉ p. with ill. ; 27 cm. USSR 73–26623
At head of title: Азәрбајҹан ССР Елмләр Академијасы.
Added t. p.: Музею истории Азербайджана 50 лет.
Azerbaijani and Russian.
Includes indexes.
4.50rub
1. Baku. Muzeĭ istorii Azerbaĭdzhana. I. Azizbekova, Pista A., ed. II. Title. III. Title: Muzei͡u istorii Azerbaĭdzhana pi͡at'desi͡at let.
DK511.A95B34 1973 74–229046

Baku. Muzeĭ istorii Azerbaĭdzhana
see Azărbayjan tarihină dair materiallar. Baku, Elm Năshriyyatı, 197-

Baku. Muzeĭ istorii Azerbaĭdzhana
see Azerbaĭdzhanskai͡a nat͡sional'nai͡a odezhda. 1972.

Baku. Muzeĭ istorii Azerbaĭdzhana
see Materialy Nauchnoĭ sessii, posvi͡ashchennoĭ dvukhsotpi͡atidesi͡atiletii͡u Akademii nauk SSSR. 1974.

Baku. Muzeĭ istorii Azerbaĭdzhana
see Sessii͡a, posvi͡ashchennai͡a itogam polevykh arkheologicheskikh i ėtnograficheskikh issledovaniĭ 1971 g. v SSSR, Baku, 1972. (Materialy) 1972.

Baku. Nauchno-issledovatel'skiĭ institut klinicheskoĭ i ėksperimental'noĭ medit͡siny
see Nauchno-issledovatel'skiĭ institut klinicheskoĭ i ėksperimental'noĭ medit͡siny, Baku.

Baku. Nauchno-issledovatel'skiĭ institut kurortologii i fizicheskikh metodov lechenii͡a
see Nauchno-issledovatel'skiĭ institut kurortologii i fizicheskikh metodov lechenii͡a.

Baku. Respublikanskai͡a nauchnai͡a medit͡sinskai͡a biblioteka
see Respublikanskai͡a nauchnai͡a medit͡sinskai͡a biblioteka.

Baku. S. M. Kirov adyna Azărbaĭjan Dövlăt Universiteti
see
Baku. Azerbaĭdzhanskiĭ gosudarstvennyĭ universitet.

Baku. Universitet
see Baku. Azerbaidzhanskii gosudarstvennyi universitet.

Baku. Vsesoi͡uznyĭ nauchno-issledovatel'skiĭ institut po tekhnike bezopasnosti v neftīanoĭ promyshlennosti.
(Instrukt͡sii͡a po tekhnike bezopasnosti pri ėkspluatat͡sii skvazhin beskompressornym gazliftnym sposobom)
Инструкция по технике безопасности при эксплуатации скважин бескомпрессорным газлифтным способом. Москва, "Недра," 1971.
55 p. with diagrs. 20 cm. 0.14rub — USSR 71
At head of title: Министерство нефтяной промышленности СССР. Всесоюзный нефтяной научно-исследовательский институт по технике безопасности.
1. Oil wells—Gas lift—Safety measures. I. Title.
TN871.B252 1971 — 73-360485

Baku. [Fotoal'bom by, avt. D. Dal'nev; foto V. Volodkina... i dr.] Moskva, "Progress" [1973]
[80] p. (chiefly illus.)
Title also in Azerbaijani, English, German, French, and Arabic.
Azerbaijani, Russian, English, German, French and Arabic.
1. Baku–Views. I. Dal'nev, D.
MH — NUC75-128307

(Baku s vertoleta)
Баку с вертолета : [фотоальбом / авт. Т. Мелик-Аббасов, А. Гашумов ; фото С. Кулешов, Р. Нагиев]. — Баку : Упр. по иностр. туризму при Совете Министров АзССР, 1973.
[87] p. : chiefly col. ill. ; 21 x 22 cm. — USSR 73
On cover: Baku s ptich'ego poleta.
Russian, English, French, and German.
3.50rub
1. Baku — Description, Aerial. 2. Baku — Description — Views. I. Melik-Abbasov, T. II. Title: Baku s ptich'ego poleta.
DK651.B29B32 — 75-569645

Bakucz, József.
Kövesedő ég [irta] Bakucz József. Párizs, [Montrouge] (139, Av. Jean-Jaurès, 92120), Magyar Mühely, 1973.
68 p. 21 cm. 20.00F — F 73-12064
Poems.
I. Title.
PH3213.B214K6 — 74-332978

(Bakufu seichō kiroku)
幕府征長記錄　日本史籍協會編　[東京]　東京大學出版會　[昭和48 i. e. 1973]
2, 37, 667 p. illus. 22 cm. (日本史籍協會叢書 169) ¥3000 — Ja ***
Reprint of the 1919 ed.
1. Japan—History—Restoration, 1853-1870—Sources. I. Nihon Shiseki Kyōkai. II. Series: Nihon Shiseki Kyōkai. Nihon Shiseki Kyōkai sōsho, 169.
DS881.3.B32 1973 — 73-808682

(Bakuha jishin ni yoru jishinha sokudo no jikanteki henka ni kansuru kenkyū)
爆破地震による地震波速度の時間的変化に関する研究. — 川崎：地質調査所, 昭和50 [1975]
74 p. : ill. ; 26 cm. — (地質調査所報告 ; 第254号) — Ja ***
On p. [4] of cover: Precies measurements of changes in seismic wave velocities [sic] by means of explosion-seismic method.
Summaries in English.
Includes bibliographies.
CONTENTS: 地震波速度変化研究グループ　観測報告—飯塚進...et al. 走時の解析結果
1. Seismic waves. 2. Blast effect. I. Chishitsu Chōsajo. II. Jishinha Sokudo Henka Kenkyū Gurūpu. III. Title: Precies measurements of changes in seismic wave velocities by means of explosion-seismic method. IV. Series: Chishitsu Chōsajo. Report ; no. 254.
QE304.C54a no. 254 — 76-802368
[QE538.5]

(Bakuhan taisei ron)
幕藩体制論 / 佐々木潤之介 ... [et al.]. — 東京：学生社, 昭和49 [1974]
285 p. ; 19 cm. — (シンポジウム日本歴史 ; 11) — Ja 74-18801
Bibliography: p. [270]-273.
Includes index.
¥1250
1. Japan—Politics and government—1600-1868—Addresses, essays, lectures. 2. Japan—Economic conditions—To 1868—Addresses, essays, lectures. I. Sasaki, Junnosuke, 1929- II. Series: Shimpojūmu Nihon rekishi ; 11.
DS871.B32 — 75-800357

(Bakuhansei no dōyō)
幕藩制の動揺 / 津田秀夫 ... [et al.]. — 東京：学生社, 昭和49 [1974]
352 p. ; 19 cm. — (シンポジウム日本歴史 ; 13) — Ja 74-15687
Bibliography: p. [340]-342.
Includes index.
¥1400
1. Japan—History—Tokugawa period, 1600-1868—Addresses, essays, lectures. 2. Japan—Economic conditions—Early to 1868—Addresses, essays, lectures. I. Tsuda, Hideo, 1918- II. Series: Shimpojūmu Nihon rekishi ; 13.
DS871.B34 — 74-810121

Bakul', Valentin Nikolaevich
see Mezhdunarodnai͡a konferent͡sii͡a po primenenii͡u sineteticheskikh almazov v promyshlennosti, Kiev, 1971. (Sinteticheskie almazy v promyshlennosti) 1974.

Bakul', Valentin Nikolaevich
see Sinteticheskie sverkhtverdye materialy i tverdye splavy. 1973, c1974.

Bakul Raval
see
Raval, Bakul, 1930-

Bákula, Juan Miguel
see
Bákula Patino, Juan Miguel.

Bakula, K G 1917-
ནང་པའི་བསྟན་པ་ལ་འཇུག་པའི་སྒོ་དང་པོ་བཞུགས་སོ་, by K. G. Bakula. Delhi, Printed at Khanna Litho Press, 1967.
63 p. illus. 18 cm. 2.00
In Tibetan.
1. Mahayana Buddhism—Introductions. I. Title.
Title romanized: Nañ pa'i bstan pa la...
BQ7420.B34 — S A 68-20574
PL 480: I-Tib-178

Bakula, Kushok
see
Bakula, K. G 1917-

Bakuła, Leszek, 1930-
Połów horyzontu. [Wyd. 1. Łódź] Wydawn. Łódzkie [1972]
50 p.
On leaf facing t.p.: Korespondencyjny Klub Młodych Pisarzy przy Zarządzie Głównym ZMW.
Poems.
MH — NUC73-120425

Bakula, William J., joint author
see Rudelius, William. An introduction to contemporary business. New York, Harcourt Brace Jovanovich [1973]

Bakula, William J., joint author.
see Rudelius, William. An introduction to contemporary business. 2d ed. New York, Harcourt, Brace, Jovanovich, c1976.

Bákula Patiño, Juan Miguel.
La politica estera del Perù / Juan Miguel Bákula. — Roma : IILA, 1973.
29 p. ; 22 cm. — (Documenti e punti di vista ; 1) — It 74-Jan
L600
1. Peru—Foreign relations—Addresses, essays, lectures.
I. Title.
F3433.B34 — 327.85 — 74-351545

Bakule, Lubomír.
see Formator Symposium on Mathematical Methods for Analysis of Large Scale Systems, 2d, Prague, 1974. Proceedings of a symposium held in Prague, June 18-21, 1974. Prague, Academia, 1975.

Bakule, Václav.
A short introduction into international and world finances. Prague, University of 17th November of Prague, 1972.
275 p. 25 cm. 0.12rub — Cz***
Includes bibliographical references.
1. International finance. I. Title.
HG3881.B26 — 332.4'5 — 73-178040
MARC

Bakule, Václav.
Světové finance : [vysokošk. učebnice] / Václav Bakule. — 1. vyd. — Praha : SNTL ; Bratislava : Alfa, 1976.
245 p. ; 25 cm. — Cz 76
Bibliography : p. 235-242.
Includes index.
Kčs24.00
1. International finance. I. Title.
HG3881.B27 — 76-527689

Bakuleśa, pseud.
(Īśkanī khuśbū)
ઈશ્કની ખુશ્બૂ / લેખક બકુલેશ. — 1. આવૃત્તિ. — મુંબઈ : આર. આર. શેઠની કં., 1942.
7, 252 p. ; 19 cm. — (આનંદ ગ્રંથાવલિ ; પુસ્તક 8)
In Gujarati.
Short stories.
Series romanized: Ānanda granthāvali.
I. Title.
PK1859.B32I8 — 76-984452

Bakulīa, M. F.
see Praktikum la farmakolojie. 1972.

Bakulin, B.
see Khleb. 1975.

Bakulin, Pavel Ivanovich.
(Kurs obshcheĭ astronomii)
Курс общей астрономии : [для ун-тов по специальности "Астрономия"] / П. И. Бакулин, Э. В. Кононович, В. И. Мороз. — Изд. 3-е, испр. — Москва : Наука, 1974.
512 p., [2] fold. leaves of plates : ill. ; 22 cm. — USSR 74
Bibliography : p. [501]
1.33rub
1. Astronomy. I. Kononovich, Ėdvard Vladimirovich. II. Moroz, Vasiliĭ Ivanovich. III. Title.
QB43.2.B33 1974 — 75-574213

Bakulin, Pavel Ivanovich, ed.
see Astronomicheskiĭ kalendar. 1973.

Bakulin, Sergeĭ Nikolaevich, 1893-
Statistika vneshneĭ torgovli. Moskva, Mezhdunarodnai͡a kniga, 1940. [Ann Arbor, Mich., 1961]
317 p. (on double leaves)
At head of title: Kon'īunkturnyĭ institut Narkomvneshtorga SSSR. S. N. Bakulin, D. D. Mishustin.
Photocopy (positive) made by University Microfilms.
1. Commercial statistics. 2. Russia–Comm. I. Mishustin, Dmitriĭ Dmitrievich, joint author.
MiU — NUC74-41035

Bakulin, Viktor Ivanovich.
(Vnutrennie ėlektroprovodki)
Внутренние электропроводки. Москва, Россельхозиздат, 1973.
95 p. with illus. 22 cm. (Библиотечка сельского электрика) 0.16rub — USSR 73
At head of title: В. И. Бакулин, А. П. Бодин, Ф. И. Московкин.
1. Electric wiring, Interior. 2. Rural electrification. I. Bodin, Aleksandr Platonovich, joint author. II. Moskovkin, Fedor Ivanovich, joint author. III. Title.
TK3271.B26 — 73-353969

Bakulin, Vladimir Georgievich, joint author
see Panov, Boris Dmitrievich. Sovershenstvovanie tekhnologii vskrytīa i oprobovanīa produktivnykh plastov v skvazhinakh. 1973.

Bakulov, Igor' Alekseevich, ed.
see (Ėpizootologiia s mikrobiologieĭ) 1972.

Bakulov, Igor' Alekseevich
see Listerioz zhivotnykh. 1972.

Bakulov, Igor' Alekseevich
see Sibirskai͡a i͡azva zhivotnykh. 1975.

Bakulov, Igor' Alekseevich
see Slovar' ėpizootologicheskikh terminov. 1975.

Bakuma, P. F.
see Inzhenernye izyskanii͡a v stroitel'stve. 1975.

Bakuma, P. F.
see Spravochnik po obshchestroitel'nym rabotam. 1975.

(Bakumatsu ishin)
幕末・維新. — 東京：研秀出版, [昭和50 i. e. 1975]
219 p., [1] leaf of plates : ill. ; 30 cm. — (日本の歴史 ; 12)
Ja 76-7768

1. Japan—History—Restoration, 1853-1870. 2. Japan—History—1787-1868. I. Series: Nihon no rekishi (Tokyo, Kenshū Shuppan) ; 12.
DS835.N5537 vol. 12 77-800096
[DS881.3]

Bakumatsu Ishin Kenkyūkai
see Katsū, Yasuyoshi, 1823-1899. [Katsu Kaishu no kotoba] 47 (1972)

(Bakumatsu ishin ki Mino chihō no murakata sōdō kankei shiryō)
幕末維新期美濃地方の村方騒動関係史料 / 岐阜大学教育学部. — 岐阜：同学部, 昭和51 [1976]
67 p. ; 22 cm. — (郷土資料 ; 7) Ja ***
Cover title.

1. Peasant uprisings—Japan—Gifu (Prefecture)—Sources. 2. Gifu, Japan (Prefecture)—History—Sources. I. Gifu Daigaku. Kyōiku-gakubu. II. Series: Kyōdo shiryō (Gifu, 1971-) ; 7.
DS894.59.G537B34 77-814997

(Bakumatsu ishin Shushigakusha shokan shū)
幕末維新朱子學者書簡集. — 東京：明徳出版社, 昭和50 [1975]
468 p. ; 22 cm. — (朱子學大系 ; 第14巻) Ja ***
CONTENTS: 大橋訥菴書簡—楠本端山書簡—楠本碩水書簡—並木栗水書簡—楠本碩水・並木栗水論學書
¥6500

1. Philosophers—Japan—Correspondences. 2. Neo-Confucianism—Japan. 3. Chu, Hsi, 1130-1200. I. Series: Shushigaku taikei : dai 14-kan.
B128.C54S54 vol. 14 77-814998
[B5241]

(Bakumatsu keizai shi kenkyū)
幕末經濟史研究 日本經濟史研究所編 [京都] 臨川書店 [昭和48 i.e. 1973]
2, 8, 420 p. illus. 22 cm. ¥3500 Ja ***
Reprint of the 1935 ed. published by Yūhikaku.
Includes bibliographical references.

1. Japan—Economic conditions—To 1868. I. Nihon Keizaishi Kenkyūjo, Kyoto.
HC462.6.B34 1973 74-802198

(Bakumatsu kinnō shisō no kenkyū)
幕末勤皇思想の研究 [編輯者・國學院大學道義學會 東京 青年教育普及會 昭和12 i.e. 1937]
1, 193 p. 23 cm. (道義論叢 第4輯)

1. Philosophy, Japanese. 2. Kokutai. I. Kokugakuin Daigaku Dōgi Gakkai. II. Series: Dōgi ronsō, dai 4-shū.
B5241.B34 73-817381

(Bakumatsu kyōgen shū)
幕末狂言集 / [編纂者 渥美清太郎]. — 東京：春陽堂, 昭和5 [1930]
628 p., [1] leaf of plates : ill. ; 20 cm. — (日本戯曲全集 [歌舞伎篇] ; 第22巻)
本巻には…三世櫻田治助の作を主として収めた
"非賣品"
CONTENTS: 花觀臺大和文庫—月梅攝景清—新造鯉奇談—名譽仁政銖—韜聚海駒量傳記—新板越白浪—隅田川對高賀紋—解説
1. Kabuki plays. I. Atsumi, Seitarō, 1892-1959, comp. II. Sakurada, Jisuke, 1802-1877. III. Series: Nihon gikyoku zenshū, kabuki-hen ; dai 22-kan.
PL767.N54 dai 22 74-820004

(Bakumatsu Meiji jitsurekidan)
幕末明治実歴譚 綿谷雪編 東京 青蛙房 昭和46 (1971)
421 p. 22 cm. (青蛙選書 37) ¥1500 Ja 71-17707
「名家談叢」第1号(明治28年9月)-第40号(明治31年12月)より4編を選び校訂したもの
CONTENTS: 青木弥太郎 青木弥太郎懺悔談—薄井竜之 筑波騒動実歴談—村田経芳 村田銃発明談—桃川燕林 桃川如燕の伝
1. Japan—History—Restoration, 1853-1870—Anecdotes, facetial, satire, etc. 2. Japan—History—Meiji period, 1868-1912—Anecdotes, facetial, satire, etc. I. Watatani, Kiyoshi, 1903- ed. II. Meika dansō.
DS881.3.B347 74-806863

(Bakumatsu Meiji kaikaki no nishikie hanga)
幕末明治開花期の錦繪版畫 / 樋口弘編著. — 東京：味燈書屋, 昭和18 [1943], 昭和19 [1944] printing.
6, 9, 80 p., [116] leaves of plates : 320 ill. (6 col.) ; 31 cm.
Bibliography: p. 54-55.
"浮世繪師歌川系圖" (1 fold. leaf) inserted at end.

1. Color prints, Japanese—Edo period, 1600-1868. 2. Color prints, Japanese—Meiji period, 1868-1912. 3. Higuchi, Hiroshi, 1905- —Art collections. I. Higuchi, Hiroshi, 1905-
NE1321.8.B34 77-800296

(Bakumatsu no bungaku)
幕末の文学 / 出席者 前田愛…[et al.]. — 東京：学生社, 昭和52 [1977]
226 p. : ill. ; 22 cm. — (シンポジウム日本文学 ; 11) Ja 77-9130
"昭和四十九年四月八日.九日の両日にわたる討論を整理したもの"
Includes index.
¥1900

1. Japanese literature—Edo period, 1600-1868—Congresses. 2. Japanese literature—Meiji period, 1868-1912—Congresses. I. Maeda, Ai, 1932- II. Series: Shimpojūmu Nihon bungaku ; 11.
PL703.S47 vol. 11 77-812438
[PL726.5]

(Bakumatsu no eiketsu)
幕末の英傑. — 東京：暁教育図書, 昭和49 [1974]
195 p. : ill. ; 31 cm. — (人物探訪日本の歴史 ; 15) Ja ***
Includes index.
¥2000

1. Japan—History—19th century—Biography. 2. Japan—Biography. I. Series: Jimbutsu tambō Nihon no rekishi ; 15.
DS881.5.A1B3 75-806008

(Bakumatsu no nomin ikki)
幕末の農民一揆 変革期野州農民の闘い 大町雅美 長谷川伸三編著 東京 雄山閣 昭和49(1974)
253 p. 22 cm. ¥1800 Ja 74-3930
Colophon inserted.
Includes bibliographical references.

1. Peasant uprisings—Tochigi, Japan (Prefecture) 2. Tochigi, Japan (Prefecture)—History. I. Ōmachi, Masami, 1927- ed. II. Hasegawa, Shinzō, 1937- ed.
DS894.49.T627B34 74-804418

(Bakumatsu no onna)
幕末のおんな / [新人物往来社編]. — 東京：新人物往来社, 昭和49 [1974]
242 p. : ill. ; 20 cm. Ja 74-13303
Bibliography: p. 242.
¥980

1. Japan—History—Restoration, 1853-1870—Biography. 2. Women—Japan—Biography. I. Shinjimbutsu Ōraisha.
DS881.5.A1B34 75-801305

(Bakumatsu seiji ron shū)
幕末政治論集 / [校注者 吉田常吉, 佐藤誠三郎]. — 東京：岩波書店, 1976.
585, 5 p. ; 22 cm. — (日本思想大系 ; 56) Ja 76-13790
Includes bibliographies.
¥2800

1. Japan—History—Restoration, 1853-1870—Sources. I. Yoshida, Tsunekichi, 1910- II. Satō, Seizaburō, 1932- III. Series: Nihon shisō taikei ; 56.
DS881.3.B348 76-804817

Bakumenko, Danylo Oleksandrovych, 1918–
(Vohnepad)
Вогнепад. Поезії. [Київ, "Рад. письменник," 1973]
71 p. 14 cm. 0.26rub USSR 73-14049
At head of title: Данило Бакуменко.
I. Title.
PG3949.12.A4V6 74-300742

Bakumenko, Igor' Timofeevich.
Закономерные кварц-полевошпатовые срастания в пегматитах и их генезис. Москва, Наука, 1966.
171 p. illus., 12 plates. 22 cm.
At head of title: Академия наук СССР. Сибирское отделение. Институт геологии и геофизики. И. Т. Бакуменко.
Bibliography: p. 157-[169]
1. Pegmatites. 2. Quartz. 3. Feldspar. I. Title.
Title romanized: Zakonomernye kvart͡s-polevoshpatovye srastanii͡a v pegmatitakh.
QE462.P4B34 74-222827

Bakumenko, Igor' Timofeevich, joint author
see Mel'gunov, Sergeĭ Vladimirovich. (Mineralogii͡a i geokhimii͡a metamorfogennykh segregat͡sionnykh pegmatoidov) 1975

Bakun, A. S.
see Vyborg. [1972]

Bakun, Andrew.
Coastal upwelling indices, west coast of North America, 1946-71. Seattle, Wash., National Marine Fisheries Service, 1973.
103 p. illus., tables. 26 cm. (United States. National Marine Fisheries Service. Special scientific report - fisheries no. 671)
Includes bibliography.
1.Upwelling (Oceanography)—Indexes. 2.Ocean currents—Pacific coast (North America)—Indexes. 3.Marine fauna. 4.Aquatic biology. I.United States. National Marine Fisheries Service. II.Title. III.Series.
DI NUC75-23986

Bakun, William Henry.
Empirical transfer functions for stations in the central California seismological network, by William H. Bakun and Jay Dratler, Jr. Menlo Park, Calif., U.S. Geological Survey, 1976.
77, [80] l. ill. 27 cm. (Reports-Open file series. United States Geological Survey ; 76-259)
Transmittal sheet dated March 19, 1976.
Bibliography: leaf 76.
I.Dratler, Jay. II.Title.
DI-GS NUC77-89747

Bakunin, Aleksandr Vasil'evich, ed.
see Iz istorii razvitii͡a promyshlennosti Urala. 1972.

Bakunin, Aleksandr Vasil'evich
see Iz istorii stroitel'stva sot͡sializma i kommunizma. 1974.

Bakunin, Aleksandr Vasil'evich, ed.
see Ocherki istorii Sverdlovska, 1723-1973. 1973.

Bakunin, Aleksandr Vasil'evich
see V bor'be za nauchno-tekhnicheskiĭ progress. 1975.

Bakunin, Jack.
Pierre Leroux and the birth of democratic socialism. New York, 1973.
383 l. 29 cm.
Thesis—CUNY.
Bibliography: leaves 365-283.
NNCU NUC76-70902

Bakunin, Jack.
Pierre Leroux and the birth of democratic socialism, 1797-1848 / by Jack Bakunin. — New York : Revisionist Press, 1976.
p. cm.
Bibliography: p.
Includes index.
ISBN 0-87700-221-5
1. Leroux, Pierre, 1797-1871. I. Title.
HX263.L35B34 335'.2 75-44403
75 MARC

Bakunin, M M
(Tropicheskaia Gollandiia)
Тропическая Голландия : пять лѣтъ на островѣ Явѣ / М. М. Бакунинъ. — С.-Петербургъ : Тип. А. С. Суворина, 1902.
viii, 455, xii, ⌜6⌝ leaves of plates : maps (some fold.) ; 23 cm.
1. Java. I. Title.
DS646.18.B27 75–568695

Bakunin, Mikhail Aleksandrovich, 1814-1876.
Bakunin on anarchy; selected works by the activist-founder of world anarchism. Edited, translated and with an introd. by Sam Dolgoff. Pref. by Paul Avrich. New York, Vintage Books [c1971, 1972]
xxvii, 405, vii p. 20 cm.
"First Vintage Books edition, May 1972."
1. Anarchism and anarchists—Collected works. I. Title.
MsU NUC75-35245

Bakunin, Mikhail Aleksandrovich, 1814–1876.
Bakunin's writings. ⌜Edited⌝ by Guy A. Aldred. New York, Gordon Press, 1973.
x, 107 p. 23 cm.
1. Anarchism and anarchists—Addresses, essays, lectures.
[HX915.B165 1973] 335'.83 72–94725
ISBN 0–87967–049–0 MARC

Bakunin, Mikhail Aleksandrovich, 1814-1876.
Confession : 1851 / Bakounine ; traduit par Paulette Brupbacher ; avant-propos de Boris Souvarine ; introduction de Fritz Brupbacher ; annotations de Max Nettlau. — ⌜Paris⌝ : Presses universitaires de France, 1974.
235 p. ; 20 cm. — (Virages) F 74-17767
Translation of Ispoved'.
1. Bakunin, Mikhail Aleksandrovich, 1814-1876. I. Nettlau, Max, 1865-1944. II. Title.
HX915.B22314 1974 335'.83'0924 75-513410
75 MARC

Bakunin, Mikhail Aleksandrovich, 1814-1876.
The confession of Mikhail Bakunin : with the marginal comments of Tsar Nicholas I / translated by Robert C. Howes ; introduction and notes by Lawrence D. Orton. — Ithaca, N.Y. : Cornell University Press, 1977.
200 p. : port. ; 22 cm.
Translation of Ispoved'.
Includes bibliographical references and index.
ISBN 0-8014-1073-8
1. Bakumin, Mikhail Aleksandrovich, 1814-1876. 2. Anarchism and anarchists—Biography. I. Orton, Lawrence D. II. Title.
HX915.B22313 335'.83'0924 76-25646
77 MARC

Bakunin, Mikhail Aleksandrovich, 1814–1876.
(Edna programa za osvobozhdenie na chovechestvoto)
Една програма за освобождение на човечеството. Sydney, Наш пъть, 1971.
94 p. 21 cm. (Библиотека "Документация-Ориентация," № 4) 1.00(U.S.). 5.00F (France) Aus***
1. Social history—19th century. 2. Europe—Politics—1789–1900. 3. Utopias. 4. Anarchism and anarchists. I. Title.
HN15.5.B34 1971 73–324490

Bakunin, Mikhail Aleksandrovich, 1814-1876.
Fédéralisme, socialisme et antithéologisme Lettres sur le patriotisme. Dieu et l'état. Paris, P.V. Stock, 1895. Didot, 1972.
357 p. 18 cm. (His Oeuvres, t. 1) (Bibliothèque sociologique, no. 4)
At head of title: Michel Bakounine.
1. Anarchism and anarchists. 2. Atheism. I. Title.
MdU IaU NUC75-104984

Bakunin, Mikhail Aleksandrovich, 1814–1876.
Frühschriften/ Michail Bakunin. Eingel., übers. u. mit Anm. versehen von Rainer Beer. — Köln; Hegner, 1973.
221 p.; 17 cm. — (Hegner-Bücherei) DM17.80 GFR 73–A40
1. Philosophy—Collected works. I. Beer, Rainer, 1931- ed.
B4238.B232G42 74–315805
ISBN 3–7764–0206–7

Bakunin, Mikhail Aleksandrovich, 1814-1876.
Ispoved'. French. 1974.
see Duclos, Jacques, 1896- Bakounine et Marx, ombre et lumière. [Paris] Plon [1974]

Bakunin, Mikhail Aleksandrovich, 1814–1876.
(Izbrannye sochineniia)
Избранные сочинения. С предисл. Дж. Гильома. Петербург, Голос труда, 19
v. in port. 22 cm.
1. Bakunin, Mikhail Aleksandrovich, 1814–1876.
HX915.B1637 1920b 74–202217

Bakunin, Mikhail Aleksandrovich, 1814–1876.
Избранные сочинения. С биографическим очерком В. Черкезова. Петербург, Голос труда, 1919–22.
5 v. port. 20–23 cm.
Includes bibliographical references.
CONTENTS: т. 1. Государственность и анархия.—т. 2. Кнуто-Германская империя и социальная революция.—т. 3. Бернские медведи и Петербургский медведь. Речи и статьи по славянскому вопросу. Народное дело. Речи на конгрессах Лиги мира и свободы. Федерализм, социализм и антитеологизм.—т. 4. Политика Интернационала. Письмо к французу. Парижская коммуна.—т. 5. "Альянс" и Интернационал. Интернационал и Мадзини.
1. Anarchism and anarchists—Russia. 2. Europe—Politics—1815-1871. 3. Socialism.
Title romanized: Izbrannye sochineniia.
HX914.B33 72–226500

Bakunin, Mikhail Aleksandrovich, 1814–1876.
Избранныя сочиненія. Подъ ред. В. Черкезова. ⌜n. p.⌝ Изд. Ф. А. К. Г., 1920–
v. port. 19 cm.
Includes bibliographical references.
1. Anarchism and anarchists.
Title romanized: Izbrannyia sochineniia.
HX915.B1637 1920 72–226428

Bakunin, Mikhail Aleksandrovich, 1814–1876.
(Izbrannye sochineniia)
Избранные сочинения. С биографическим очерком В. Черкезова. 2. изд. Петербург, Голос труда, 1922–
v. in 22 cm.
Vol. 1-2 bound with Михаил Бакунин. Москва, 1926.
CONTENTS: т. 1. Государственность и анархия.—т. 2. Кнуто-германская империя и социальная революция.
1. Bakunin, Mikhail Aleksandrovich, 1814–1876.
HX915.B3M54 74–202530

Bakunin, Mikhail Aleksandrovich, 1814–1876.
La Liberté. Choix de textes, présentation et notes de François Munoz. Paris, J.-J. Pauvert, 1972.
327 p. 18 cm. (Libertés nouvelles, 20) 11.80F F 72–9706
At head of title: Bakounine.
"Sources pour le choix des textes": p. 307–⌜319⌝
1. Socialism. I. Munoz, François, ed. II. Title.
HX915.B1658 1972b 335'.83 74–163892
MARC

Bakunin, Mikhail Aleksandrovich, 1814–1876.
Michel Bakounine et l'Italie : 1871–1872 / ⌜Michel Bakounine⌝ ; introduction et annotations de Arthur Lehning. — (Nouvelle éd.⌝. — Paris : Éditions Champ liber, 1973–
v. ; 27 cm. — (His Œuvres complètes ; 1)
F 74–5531 (v. 1)
Includes index.
CONTENTS: 1. ptie. La polémique avec Mazzini. Écrits et matériaux.
ISBN 2–85184–005–3 (v. 1) : 59.00F (v. 1)
1. Italy—Politics and government—1870–1915. 2. The International. 3. Bakunin, Mikhail Aleksandrovich, 1814–1876. 4. Mazzini, Giuseppe, 1805–1872. I. Title.
DG557.5.B342 320.9'45'09 74–194564
MARC

Bakunin, Mikhail Aleksandrovich, 1814-1876.
Michel Bakounine et les conflits dans l'Internationale 1872 : la question germano-slave, le communisme d'État : écrits et matériaux / ⌜Michel Bakounine⌝ ; introd. et annotations de Arthur Lehning. — Paris : Éditions Champ libre, c1975.
lxvii, 492 p. ; 27 cm. — (His Œuvres complètes ; v. 3) F***
Chiefly French; some Italian or German.
Includes bibliographical references and index.
ISBN 2-85184-040-1
1. The International—Addresses, essays, lectures. 2. Socialism in Europe—Addresses, essays, lectures. 3. Europe—Politics and government—1848-1871—Addresses, essays, lectures. I. Lehning, Arthur. II. Title.
HX11.I5B23 1975 335'.0094 76-453337
76 MARC

Bakunin, Mikhail Aleksandrovich, 1814-1876.
Michel Bakounine et ses relations slaves, 1870-1875 / textes établis et annotés par Arthur Lehning. — Leiden : E. J. Brill, 1974.
lxxxix, 586 p., ⌜20⌝ leaves of plates : ill. ; 27 cm. — (Archives Bakounine ; 5) Ne75-6
Chiefly French or Russian; some German or Italian.
Appendices (p. ⌜385⌝-485): 1. Documents sur les conflits dans l'Internationale relatifs à l'Alliance et au Congrès de La Haye.—2. Documents concernant les relations de Michel Bakounine avec les Polonais et les Serbes de Zurich.—3. Table des matières et introduction du recueil Istoričeskoe Razvitie Internacionala, 1873.—4. Correspondance.—5. Michail Sažin (Arman Ross)—Écrits autobiographiques.—6. A propos du Mémoire du comte Palen, 1875.
Errata slip for all volumes in series inserted.
Includes bibliographical references and index.
ISBN 9004041745 : fl 220
1. Anarchism and anarchists—Collected works. I. Lehning, Arthur. II. Title. III. Series.
HX915.B1564 1974 335'.83 75-506918
75 MARC

Bakunin, Mikhail Aleksandrovich, 1814–1876.
(Nauka i nasushchnoe revoliutsionnoe dielo)
Наука і насущное революціонное дѣло. ⌜Genève, 1870–
v. 18 cm.
Caption title.
1. Labor and laboring classes—Russia. 2. Russia—Social conditions. 3. Socialism. I. Title.
HD8526.B255 74–224538

Bakunin, Mikhail Aleksandrovich, 1814–1876.
Les Ours de Berne et l'Ours de Saint-Pétersbourg. ⌜Par⌝ Michel Bakounine. Lausanne, Éditions l'Age d'homme,) La Cité-éditeur, (1972).
64 p. 18 cm. (Collection La Suisse en question) 7.70F
Sw 73–A–2471
1. Switzerland—Politics and government—1848– 2. Nechaev, Sergei Gennadievich, 1847–1882. 3. Extradition—Switzerland. I. Title.
JN8762 1970.B34 323.6'4 74–166908
MARC

Bakunin, Mikhail Aleksandrovich, 1814-1876.
The Paris Commune and the idea of the state ⌜by⌝ Michael Bakunin. ⌜London, Centre International de Recherches sur l'Anarchisme, 1971⌝
⌜8⌝ p. 27 cm.
Cover title.
Translation of La Commune de Paris et la notion de l'etat.
"A biographical and bibliographical note": p. ⌜7-8⌝
1. Anarchism and anarchists. 2. Paris—Hist.-Commune, 1871. I. Centre International de Recherches sur l'Anarchisme. II. Title.
NjR NUC73-77639

Bakunin, Mikhail Aleksandrovich, 1814-1876.
La révolution sociale ou la dictature militaire. 1972
see European socialism and the problems of war and militarism... New York, Garland, 1972.

Bakunin, Mikhail Aleksandrovich, 1814–1876.
Selected writings ⌜of⌝ Michael Bakunin, edited and introduced by Arthur Lehning; translations from the French by Steven Cox; translations from the Russian by Olive Stevens. London, Cape, 1973.
288 p. 21 cm. (Writings of the Left) £4.95 GB 73–26491
Bibliography: p. 287–288.
1. Anarchism and anarchists—Collected works. I. Lehning, Arthur, ed.
HX915.B165 1973b 320'.08 74–162390
ISBN 0–224–00893–5; 0–224–00898–6 (pbk.) MARC

Bakunin, Mikhail Aleksandrovich, 1814–1876.
Selected writings / Michael Bakunin ; edited and introduced by Arthur Lehning ; translations from the French by Steven Cox, translations from the Russian by Olive Stevens. — 1st Evergreen ed. — New York : Grove Press : distributed by Random House, ⌜1974⌝
288 p. ; 21 cm. — (Writings of the left) (An Evergreen book ; E–629)
Bibliography: p. 287–288.
ISBN 0–8021–0020–1 : $4.95
1. Anarchism and anarchists—Collected works.
[HX915.B165 1974] 335'.83'0924 73–21013
MARC

Bakunin, Mikhail Aleksandrovich, 1814-1876.
Sobranie sochineniĭ i pisem 1828-1876. Pod red. i s primechaniiami IU. M. Steklova. [Moskva] Izd-vo Vsesoiunogo ob-va politikatorzhan i ssylino-poselentsev [1934-35; Dusseldorf, Brücken-Verlag, 1970]
4 v. illus., ports. 23 cm. (Klassiki revoliutsionnoĭ mysli domarksistskogo perioda, 1) (Slavica-reprint nr. 60/1)
No more published.
TxU IEN NcU NUC74-55453

Bakunin, Mikhail Aleksandrovich, 1814–1876.
Le socialisme libertaire ⌜par⌝ Michel Bakounine. Textes établis et présentés par Fernand Rude. ⌜Paris⌝ Denoël/Gonthier ⌜1973⌝
217 p. 18 cm. (Bibliothèque Médiations, 111) F***
1. Bakunin, Mikhail Aleksandrovich, 1814–1876. 2. Socialism in Europe. I. Rude, Fernand, ed. II. Title.
HX915.B3A3 1973 335'.83'094 74–161402
MARC

Bakunin, Mikhail Aleksandrovich, 1814–1876.
Staatlichkeit und Anarchie und andere Schriften/ Michail Bakunin. Hrsg. u. eingel. von Horst Stuke. — Frankfurt (M.), Berlin, Wien: Ullstein, 1972.
xxi, 885 p.; 18 cm. — (Ullstein-Buch; Nr. 2846) DM9.80
GFR 73–A
Bibliography: p. 857–864.
1. Anarchism and anarchists—Collected works. I. Title.
HX915.B1659 1972 74–330952
ISBN 3–548–02846–2

Bakunin, Mikhail Aleksandrovich, 1814-1876.
Vosemnadt͡sat' pisem M. A. Bakunina.
[Mikh. Lemke. n. p., n. d.]
183-214 p.
I. Lemke, Mikhail Konstantinovich, 1872-1923, ed.
InU NUC74-91171

Bakunin, Mikhail Aleksandrovich, 1814-1876
see Confino, Michael, 1926- comp.
Daughter of a revolutionary ... LaSalle, Ill., Library Press, 1973.

Bakunin, Mikhail Aleksandrovich, 1814-1876
see Confino, Michael, 1926- Violence dans la violence... Paris, F. Maspero, 1973.

Bakunin, Mikhail Aleksandrovich, 1814-1876
see Herber, Lewis. Anarchy. [Buffalo, N.Y., Friends of Malatesta, 1969?]

Bakunin, Mikhail Aleksandrovich, 1814-1876
see Kornilov, Aleksandr Aleksandrovich, 1862-1926. (Gody stranstviĭ Mikhaila Bakunina)
1925.

Bakunin, Mikhail Aleksandrovich, 1814-1876
see Kornilov, Aleksandr Aleksandrovich, 1862-1926. (Molodye gody Mikhaila Bakunina)
1915.

Bakunin, Mikhail Aleksandrovich, 1814-1876
see Kornilov, Aleksandr Aleksandrovich, 1862-1926. (Semeĭstvo Bakuninykh) [1915-25]

Bakunin, Mikhail Aleksandrovich, 1814-1876
see Mikhail Bakunin. 1876-1926; 1926.

Bakunin, Mikhail Aleksandrovich, 1814-1876.
see Socialisme autoritaire ou libertaire?. Paris, Union générale d'éditions, 1975.

Bakunina, Tat'i͡ana A
Périodiques en langue russe publiés en Europe de 1855 à 1917. [Paris, La Haye,] Mouton et Cie, 1970.
629-709 p. 24 cm. F 72-9254
At head of title: Tatiana Ossorguine, Eugénie Lange, Paul Chaix.
Caption title.
"Cahiers du monde russe et soviétique, volume XI ... 4e cahier. Tirage à part."
"Bibliographies et catalogues": p. 636.
1. Russian periodicals in foreign countries—Bibliography. I. Lange, Eugénie, joint author. II. Chaix, Paul, joint author. III. Title.
Z6956.R9B26 73-313137

Bakunina, Tat'i͡ana A., joint author
see Barmache, Nicolas. (Mikhail Andreevich Osorgin) Paris, Institut d'études slaves, 1973.

Bakunov, V. S.
see Praktikum po tekhnologii keramiki i ogneuporov. 1972.

Bakuradze, Aleksandr Nikolaevich, joint author
see Asatiani, Archil Vladimirovich. (Neĭro-gumoral'nye mekhanizmy pishchevoĭ dei͡atel'nosti) 1975.

Bakuradze, Aleksandr Nikolaevich
see Vsesoi͡uznoe fiziologicheskoe obshchestvo imeni I. P. Pavlova. (Dvenadt͡satyĭ s"ezd Vsesoi͡uznogo fiziologicheskogo obshchestva imeni I. P. Pavlova) 1975.

Bakuradze, Bidzina Varlamovich.
(Narodnye universitety Sovetskoĭ Gruzii)
Народные университеты Советской Грузии. Тбилиси, "Мецниереба," 1970.
110 p. 21 cm. 0.58rub USSR 71-VKP
At head of title: Научно-методический кабинет народных университетов Грузинской ССР. Б. В. Бакурадзе.
Includes bibliographical references.
1. University extension—Georgia (Transcaucasia) I. Title.
LC6257.G46B34 73-336589

Bakurdzhiev, Georgi.
see Pencheva, Bela. Guéorgui Bakardjiev. [Sofia] Sofia-presse, [1971?]

Bakŭrdzhiev, Petŭr.
National income and living standards [by] Peter Bakurdjiev. [Sofia] Sofia Press, 1974.
48 p. with illus. 20 cm. (30 years since the socialist revolution in Bulgaria) Bu 74-1359
1. National income—Bulgaria. 2. Cost and standard of living—Bulgaria. I. Title.
HC407.B93 I 512 339.4'7'094977 74-187099
MARC

Bakŭrdzhiev, Petŭr.
see Bulgaria ... Sofia, Sofia-Press, 1977.

Bakurevich, I͡Uriĭ L'vovich.
(Ėkspluatat͡sii͡a avtomobileĭ na Severe)
Эксплуатация автомобилей на Севере. Под ред. канд. техн. наук Ф. Н. Шевелева. Изд. 2-е, перераб. и доп. Москва, "Транспорт," 1973.
180 p. with illus. and maps. 21 cm. 0.65rub USSR 74
At head of title: Ю. Л. Бакуревич, С. С. Толкачев, Ф. Н. Шевелев.
First ed. published in 1964 under title: Эксплуатация автомобилей зимой.
Bibliography: p. 175-[178]
1. Motor-trucks—Cold weather operation. I. Tolkachev, Sergeĭ Sergeevich, writer on automotive transportation, joint author. II. Shevelev, Fedor Nikolaevich, joint author. III. Title.
TL230.B26 1973 74-313586

Bakurskiĭ, Aleksandr Ivanovich, ed.
see Ėkonomicheskai͡a rol' mestnykh Sovetov v period razvitogo sot͡sializma. 1973.

Bakūshah, Muḥammad
see
Bakkūshah, Muḥammad.

(Bakushin Kahoku no sōkyō)
驀進華北の剿共 / 華北宣傳聯盟編. — 北京：同聯盟, 昭和17 [1942]
2, 9, 351 p., [4] leaves of plates : ill. ; 19 cm.

1. China—Economic policy—Addresses, essays, lectures. 2. Anti-communist movements—China—Addresses, essays, lectures. 3. China—Politics and government—1912-1949—Addresses, essays, lectures. I. Kahoku Senden Remmei.
HC427.8.B38 76-800845

(Bakushin no oka ni te)
爆心の丘にて 山里浜口地区原爆戦災誌 長崎市山里浜口地区原爆復元の会·高谷重治[著 長崎] 長崎の証言刊行委員会 [昭和47 i.e. 1972]
377 p. illus. 20 cm. ¥500 Ja ***
Bibliography: p. 374.

1. Nagasaki—Bombardment, 1945—Personal narratives. I. Takatani, Shigeji, 1896- ed. II. Nagasaki-shi Yamazato Hamaguchi Chiku Gembaku Fukugen no Kai.
D767.25.N3B34 74-800648

Bakushinskai͡a, Ol'ga Anatol'evna, joint author
see Zhvirbli͡anskai͡a, Adel'geĭda I͡Ul'evna. (Mikrobiologii͡a v pishchevoĭ promyshlennosti) 1975.

Bakushinskiĭ, Anatoliĭ Vasil'evich, 1883-1939.
(N. A. Andreev)
Н. А. Андреев, 1873-1932. Москва, Искусство, 1939.
91, [4] p. illus. 30 cm. (Мастера советского искусства)
"Списокъ работъ Н. А. Андреева": p. 79-[92]
1. Andreev, Nikolaĭ Andreevich, 1873-1932. I. Series: Mastera sovetskogo iskusstva.
NB699.A47B34 74-222666

Bakushinskiĭ, Anatoliĭ Vasil'evich, 1883-1939.
(Vladimir Nikolaevich Domogat͡skiĭ)
Владимир Николаевич Домогацкий; статья А. В. Бакушинского. Москва, Всекохудожник, 1936.
66, [2] p. illus. 26 cm. (Серия монографий: Советские художники, 8)
Bibliography: p. 66-[67]
1. Domogat͡skiĭ, Vladimir Nikolaevich, 1876-1939. I. Title.
NB699.D6B34 73-215822

Bakusui
see
Hori, Bakusui, 1718-1783.

Bakutis, Alice R
Nurse anesthetists continuing education review : 700 essay questions and referenced answers / by Alice R. Bakutis. — Flushing, N. Y. : Medical Examination Pub. Co., 1975.
166 p. ; 22 cm.
Bibliography: p. 158-161.
Includes index.
ISBN 0-87488-356-3
1. Anesthesiology—Examinations, questions, etc. I. Title.
RD81.B33 617'.96 74-15787
MARC

Bakutis, Alice R
Self-assessment of current knowledge for the nurse anesthetist : 1200 multiple choice questions and referenced answers / by Alice R. Bakutis. — 2d ed. — Flushing, N.Y. : Medical Examination Pub. Co., 1976.
172 p. ; 22 cm.
Includes bibliographical references.
ISBN 0-87488-715-1 : $7.50
1. Anesthesiology—Examinations, questions, etc. I. Title.
RD82.3.B34 1976 617'.96'076 76-711
76 MARC

al-Bākuwī, 'Abd al-Rashīd ibn Ṣāliḥ, fl. 1403.
[Talkhīṣ al-āthār wa-'ajā'ib al-malik al-qahhār. Russian & Arabic]
كتاب تلخيص الاثار وعجائب الملك القهار ، تأليف عبد الرشيد صالح بن نورى الباكوى. ترجمه وعلق عليه ضياء الدين ابن موسى بونياتوف. موسكو ، دار النشر «العلم» ، ادارة التحريرة الرئيسية للآداب الشرقية ، 1971.

192, 162 p. facsims. 27 cm.

Added t. p.: 'Абд ар-Рашӣд ал-Ба̄кувӣ. Кита̄б талх̮ӣс̧ ал-а̄с̱а̄р ва 'аджа̄'иб ал-малик ал-к̦ахха̄р.

Text reproduced in facsimile from ms. arab. 585 in the Bibliothèque nationale, Paris.

1. Geography, Arabic. 2. Islamic Empire—Description and travel. I. Bunii͡atov, Zii͡a M., ed. II. Paris. Bibliothèque nationale. Mss. (Arab. 585) III. Title: Talkhīṣ al-āthār wa-'ajā'ib al-malik al-qahhār. IV. Title: Kitāb talkhīṣ al-āṣār ba 'adzhā'ib al-malik al-ḳakhkhār.
Title romanized: Kitāb talkhīṣ al-āthār wa-'ajā'ib al-malik al-qahhār.

G93.B36 1971 74-220862

Bakuzis, Egolfs Voldemars.
Foundations of forest ecosystems : lecture and research notes / Egolfs V. Bakuzis. — St. Paul : College of Forestry, University of Minnesota, 1974-
v. : ill. ; 28 cm.
Previous drafts were prepared in 1966 and 1970 under title: Forest synecology lecture notes.
Includes bibliographies.
CONTENTS: Chapter 1. Scientific method.—Chapter 2. Mathematics, measurements, and statistical methods.—Chapter 3. Concepts of systems in general.—Chapter 4. Systems theories.—Chapter 5. Systematics.—Chapter 6. Physical, biological, and ecological theory.
1. Forest ecology. 2. Forests and forestry. I. Title.
QH541.5.F6B28 574.5'264 75-623271
75 MARC

Bakwesegha, Christopher J 1943-
Modernization and national integration in Uganda. [n. p.] 1973.
xix, 312 l. illus.
Thesis–Rutgers University, The State University of New Jersey.
Vita.
Bibliography: leaves [277]-297.
Photocopy of typescript. Ann Arbor, Mich., University Microfilms, 1974. 21 cm.
1. Civilization, Modern. 2. Social integration. 3. Uganda–Economic conditions. I. Title.
WvU NUC76-31160

Bakwin, Harry, 1894-
see Developmental disorders of motility and language. Philadelphia, Saunders [c1968]

Bakwin, Harry, 1894-
see Wildenstein and Company, inc., New York. An exhibition of paintings and sculpture...
[New York, c1967]

Bakx, Pieter
see
Asselbergs, Willem Jan Marie Anton, 1903-1968.

Baky, Adly Abdel, 1915-
Daniel and the kings of Babylon; a prophet in a pagan city [by] Adly A. Baky. [1st. ed.] New York, Exposition Press [c1971]
211 p. 21 cm.
1. Daniel, the prophet–Fiction. I. Title.
OU NUC73-120414

Baky, Gyuláné.
see Jókaitól, Jókairól ... Budapest, Tankönyvkiadó, 1975.

Bal, A. G., joint author
see Henry, J fl. 1965-
Thésaurus des symboles agrobioclimatiques, géographiques et techniques. [Tervuren, Musée royal de l'Afrique centrale] 1971.

Bal, C
Scheveningen in oude ansichten, door C. Bal. Zaltbommel, Europese Bibliotheek, 1972.
[120] p. illus. 15 x 21 cm. (In oude ansichten) Ne***
1. Scheveningen, Netherlands—Description—Views. I. Title.
DJ411.S32B3 73-304804

Bal, Claude Michel.
Si la foule nous voit ensemble; pièce en cinq actes, de Claude Bal. Paris, 1960.
42 p. illus. (L'avant-scène, no. 216)
Microcard edition.
ICRL NUC74-33052

Bal, Gangadhar, 1927-
ଆଲୋକ ଓ ଆଲୋଚନା. [ଲେଖକ] ଗଙ୍ଗାଧର ବଲ. [କଟକ, ଫ୍ରେଣ୍ଡସ ପବ୍ଲିଶର୍ସ, 1970]
3, 177, ii p. 19 cm. Rs5.00
In Oriya.
Includes bibliographical references.

1. Oriya literature—Addresses, essays, lectures. I. Title.
Title romanized: Āloka o ālocanā.

PK2570.5.B3 70-917723

Bal, Gangadhar, 1927-
[Sāhitya jijñāsā]
ସାହିତ୍ୟ ଜିଜ୍ଞାସା. [ଲେଖକ] ଗଙ୍ଗାଧର ବଲ. [କଟକ, ଓଡ଼ିଶା ବୁକ୍ ଷ୍ଟୋର, 1971]
4, 256 p. 19 cm. Rs5.00
In Oriya.

1. Oriya literature—Addresses, essays, lectures. I. Title.

PK2570.5.B35 72-902583

Bal, Józef.
Formacje przysłówkowe z sufiksalnym j i k typu dzisiaj, wczoraj, dzisiak, tamok w historii i dialektach języka polskiego. Wrocław, Zakl. Narodowy im. Ossolińskich, Wydawn. Polskiej Akademii Nauk, 1974.
115 p. (Polska Akademia Nauk. Oddział w Krakowie. Prace Komisji Językoznawstwa, Nr. 38)
Summary in English.
Includes bibliography.
MiU NUC76-18184

Bal, Karol.
Rozum i historia; historiozofia Hegla wobec Oświecenia. Wrocław, Zakład Narodowy im. Ossolińskich, 1973.
273 p. 21 cm. zł42.00
Summary in French and German.
Bibliography: p. [238]-255.
1. Hegel, Georg Wilhelm Friedrich, 1770-1831. 2. History—Philosophy. 3. Enlightenment. I. Title.
B2949.H5B34 73-221933

Bal, L
Micromorphological analysis of soils; lower levels in the organization of organic soil materials. Wageningen, 1973.
174 p. illus. (Stichting voor Bodemkartering, Wageningen. Soil survey papers no. 6)
Bibliography: p. 119-134.
I. Title.
DNAL NUC75-22663

Bal, Marcel Bolle de
see Bolle de Bal, Marcel.

Bal, Mieke, 1946-
La complexité d'un roman populaire : ambiguïté dans "La chatte" / Mieke Bal. — Paris : La Pensée universelle, [1974]
92 p. ; 18 cm. F***
Bibliography: p. [91]-92.
17.20F
1. Colette, Sidonie Gabrielle, 1873-1954. La chatte. I. Title.
PQ2605.O28C4893 75-511903
75 MARC

Bal, Mrutyunjaya Narayan, 1946-
(Ākāśara svaralipi)
ଆକାଶର ସ୍ୱରଲିପି; [ଆଧୁନିକ ଓଡ଼ିଆ କ୍ଷୁଦ୍ରଗଳ୍ପ ସଂଚୟନ. ଗାଳ୍ପିକ] ମୃତ୍ୟୁଞ୍ଜୟ ନାରାୟଣ ବଲ. [ସଂଯୋଜକ ଅପୂର୍ବ ରଞ୍ଜନ ରାୟ. କଲିକତା, ଜଗନ୍ନାଥ ପଢ଼ିହାରୀ, 1968]
4, 111 p. 19 cm. Rs2.00
In Oriya.
Short stories.

I. Rāya, Apūrba Rañjana, ed. II. Title.

PK2579.B255A78 72-904077

Bal, Peggy.
Fairchild : heritage of the Spokane plains / by Peggy Bal ; illustrated by Jacqueline M. Rappe. — [Spokane?] : Bal, c1976.
iii, 103 p. : ill. ; 22 cm.
Includes bibliographical references.
1. Spokane Co., Wash.—History. 2. Fairchild Air Force Base—History. I. Title.
F897.S7B34 979.7'37 76-150922
77 MARC

Bal, Sarjit Singh, 1927-
A brief history of the modern Punjab / Sarjit Singh Bal ; with a foreword by M. S. Randhawa. — Ludhiana : Lyall Book Depot, 1974.
48 p. ; 22 cm.
Based on the presidential address delivered to the modern section of the eighth Punjab History Conference, Patiala, 1973.
Bibliography: p. 45-48.
Rs5.50
1. Punjab—History. I. Title.
DS485.P2B28 954'.5 74-903056
75[r76]rev MARC

Bal, Sarjit Singh, 1927- joint author.
see Grewal, J. S. Guru Gobind Singh ... Chandigarh, Dept. of History, Panjab University, 1967.

Bal', V M
Rezekt͡sii͡a zheludka v klinike i eksperimente; uchenye zapiski. Sbornik nauchnykh rabot Kafedry gospital'noĭ khirurgii. Astrakhan, 1966.
107 p. illus.
At head of title: Astrakhanskiĭ gosudarstvennyĭ medit͡sinskiĭ institut imeni A. B. Lunacharskogo.
1. Duodenal ulcer. 2. Gastrectomy. 3. Postgastrectomy syndromes. I. Astrakhanskiĭ gosudarstvennyĭ medit͡sinskiĭ institut. Kafedra gospital'noĭ khirurgii. II. Title.
MBCo NUC76-42196

Bal, Vidya, 1937-
(Kamalākī)
कमलाकी. [लेखिका] विद्या बाळ. [1. आवृत्ती] मुंबई, मौज प्रकाशन गृह [1972]
19, 227 p. illus. 22 cm. (मौज प्रकाशन 211) Rs17.50
In Marathi.

1. Deshpande, Kamalabai (Kelkar) 1898-1965. I. Title.

LA2383.I 62D472 72-906597

Bal, Willy, 1916-
O destino de palavras de origem portuguesa num dialecto quicongo. Willy Bal. Louvain, Centre d'études portugaises et brésiliennes, Université catholique de Louvain, 1974.
54 p. 25 cm.
French summary: p. 54.
"Separata da Revista portuguesa de filologia, Vol. XV, tomos I e II."
Bibliography: p. [52]-53.
1. Ki-Kongo language—Foreign words and phrases—Portuguese. I. Title.
CaBVaU NUC76-18029

Bal, Willy, 1916-
La faillite de 1830? : Élie Baussart, "La Terre wallonne" et le mouvement régionaliste / Willy Bal ; introduction biographique de Jean Quériat ; avec la collaboration de Suzanne-Élie Baussart. — Bruxelles : Vie ouvrière, dép., 1973.
120 p., [14] leaves of plates : ill. ; 18 cm. Be 74-1574
Includes bibliographical references.
ISBN 2-87003-089-4 : 150F
1. Baussart, Élie, 1887-1965. 2. La Terre wallonne. I. Title.
DH492.W3B34 949.3'4'004916 75-500069
[B] MARC

Bal Dewan
see
Dewan, Bal.

Bal Gangadhar Tilak
see Tilak, Bal Gangadhar, 1856-1920.

Bāl-Khayr, Muḥammad.
Étendard interdit : poèmes de guerre et d'amour de Mohamed Belkheir / recueillis, présentés et traduits par Boualem Bessaïh ; préf. de Jacques Berque. — Éd. bilingue. — Paris : Sindbad, c1976.
161 p. : ill. ; 23 cm. — (La Bibliothèque arabe) (Collection Littératures) F***
French or Arabic.
ISBN 2-7274-0000-4 : 40.00F
I. Bessaïh, Boualem. II. Title.
PJ7816.A49E84 892'.7'15 77-466231
77 MARC

Bāl Krishan Qamar Lakhnavī
see
Qamar Lakhnavī, Bāl Krishan, 1864-1937.

Bal Patil
see
Patil, Bal.

Bal-po A-su
see
A-su, Bal-po.

Bal Raj Varma
see
Varma, Bal Raj.

Bāl-Ruwīn, Muḥammad Muḥammad.
(Dirāsāt fī falsafat Mā ba'da al-ṭabī'ah)
دراسات فى فلسفة ما بعد الطبيعة / محمد محمد بالروين. — بنغازى : دار ليبيا للنشر والتوزيع ، [1975?]
126 p. ; 24 cm. — (منشورات الجامعة الليبية)
Bibliography: p. 125-126.
1. Metaphysics. I. Title. II. Series: al-Jāmi'ah al-Lībīyah. Manshūrāt al-Jāmi'ah al-Lībīyah.
BD118.A7B34 75-961083

Baḷa, Aung
see
Aung Baḷa, 1925-

Baḷa, Baishṇaba Caraṇa.
(Cintāmaṇi : Sāmantasiṃhāra)
ଚିନ୍ତାମଣି: ସାମନ୍ତସିଂହାର. ଲେଖକ ବୈଷ୍ଣବ ଚରଣ ବଳ. ଭଦ୍ରକ, କୃଷ୍ଣଚରଣ ବେହେରା [1964]
2, 88 p. 19 cm. Rs1.50

1. Abhimanyu Sāmanta Siṃhāra, 1757-1806. Bidagdha cintāmaṇi. I. Title.

PK2579.A2B532 72-903627

Baḷa, Baishṇaba Caraṇa.
ଗଙ୍ଗାଧର ମେହେର. ଲେଖକ ବୈଷ୍ଣବ ଚରଣ ବଳ. ଭଦ୍ରକ, ଚିନ୍ତାମଣି ମିଶ୍ର [1964]
2, 82 p. 19 cm. Re1.50
In Oriya.

1. Meher, Gangadhar, 1862-1924.
Title romanized: Gaṅgādhara Mehera.
PK1569.M46Z6 S A 68-9714
PL 480 : I-O-940

Baḷa, Baishṇaba Caraṇa.
ଉପେନ୍ଦ୍ରଭଞ୍ଜ କବିସମ୍ରାଟ କାହିଁକି? [ଲେଖକ] ବୈଷ୍ଣବ ଚରଣ ବଲ. [କଟକ?] କଶୋରୀ ମୋହନ ପରିଡ଼ା [1963]
103 p. 19 cm. Rs2
In Oriya.

1. Upendra Bhañja, 1670–1720. I. Title.
Title romanized: Upendrabhañja kabisamrāṭa kāhinki.
PK2579.U6Z58 S A 68–9716
PL 480 : I–O–937

Bālā, Bhai, 1466–1544.
(Janamasākhī Bhāī Bālā)
ਜਨਮਸਾਖੀ ਭਾਈ ਬਾਲਾ / ਸੰਪਾਦਕ ਸੁਰਿੰਦਰ ਸਿੰਘ ਕੋਹਲੀ, ਸਹਾਇਕ ਸੰਪਾਦਕ ਜਗਜੀਤ ਸਿੰਘ. — ਚੰਡੀਗੜ੍ਹ : ਪਬਲੀਕੇਸ਼ਨ ਬਿਉਰੋ, ਪੰਜਾਬ ਯੂਨੀਵਰਸਿਟੀ, 1975.
318 p. ; 25 cm.
In Panjabi.
Bibliography: p. 317–318.
Includes index.
Rs45.00
1. Nānak, 1st Guru of the Sikhs, 1469–1538. 2. Sikh gurus—Biography. I. Kohli, Surinder Singh, 1920– II. Jagjit Singh, 1928– III. Title.
BL2017.9.N3B29 1975 76–902301

Bāla, Jagannātha Nārāyaṇa Siṃha
see
Siṃha, Jagannātha Nārāyaṇa, 1887?-1950?

Bała, Marian, illus.
see Nyka, Józef. In the Polish Tatra mountains. Warsaw, Interpress Publishers, 1971.

Bâlă, Mihai.
Mecanica rocilor şi tuneluri hidrotehnice. Bucureşti, Oficiul de documentare şi publicaţii tehnice, 1973.
2 v. (502 p.) with figs. 24 cm. R 74–481
At head of title: Ministerul Minelor, Petrolului şi Geologiei. Mihai Bâlă, Gheorghe Popa, Michael Ion.
Includes bibliographies.
lei150 per vol.
1. Tunnels. 2. Rock mechanics. I. Popa, Gheorghe, joint author. II. Ior, Michael, joint author. III. Title.
TC174.B33 75–408379

Bâlă, Paul.
Mitul creştin. Filiaţii şi paralele. Bucureşti, Editura enciclopedică română, 1972.
191 p. 19 cm. (Enciclopedia de buzunar) lei 6.75 R 73–744
At head of title: Paul Bâlă, Octavian Cheţan.
Bibliography: p. 175–178.
1. Salvation—Comparative studies. 2. Christianity and other religions. I. Cheţan, Octavian, joint author. II. Title.
BL476.B34 73–346439

Bala, Vehbi.
Jeta e Fan S. Nolit; portret-monografi. [Tiranë] Shtëpia Botuese e Librit Politik [1972]
188 p. illus.
1. Noli, Fan Stylian, Bp., 1882-1965.
MH NUC76-70888

Bāla, Vidyā
see
Bal, Vidya, 1937-

Bala, Władysław.
Technologia zmechanizowanych robót wodnomelioracyjnych; podręcznik dla studentów wydziału melioracji wyższych szkół rolniczych. Władysław Bala, Władysław Pichór. [Wyd. 1.] Warszawa, Państwowe Wydawn. Rolnicze i Leśne, 1972.
467, [1] p. illus. 25 cm. zł52.00
Bibliography: p. 467–[468]
1. Hydraulic engineering—Poland. 2. Drainage—Poland. I. Pichór, Władysław, joint author. II. Title.
TC95.P7B34 74–208946

Bala Devāna
see
Dewan, Bal.

Bāla-kṛishṇa Dīkshita
see
Bālakṛṣṇa Bhaṭṭa.

Bāla Kṛshṇa Miśra
see
Mishra, Balkrishna, 1934-

Bala Mbarga, Henri.
Instruction civique: 5 ème année, classe de seconde [par] Henri Bala Mbarga [et] Gatien Ebanga. Yaoundé, Center d'Edition et de Production de Manuels et d'Auxiliares de l'Enseignement, 1973.
186 p. illus.
1. Cameroon—Economic conditions. 2. Civics, Cameroon. I. Ebanga, Gatien. II. Title.
ScU NUC75-24828

Bala Mbarga, Henri.
Instruction civique: 7ème année [par] Henri Bala Mbarga [et] Joseph Dessap. Yaoundé, Centre d'Edition et de Production de Manuels et d'Auxiliares de l'Ensiggnement, 1973.
109 p. illus.
1. Cameroon—Economic conditions. 2. Civics, Cameroon. I. Dessap, Joseph. II. Title.
ScU NUC75-24827

Bala Mbarga, Henri.
J'aime mon pays: le Cameroun. Manuel d'instruction civique et d'education nationale. [Nouv. éd. Yaoundé, Centre d'édition et de production de manuels et d'auxiliares de l'enseignement, 1970]
264 p. illus.
1. Cameroun (Fed. Rep.)—Pol. & govt.—1960- I. Title.
InU IU NUC74-22969

Bala Ramavarma, Maharaja of Travancore, 1912-
see Memorial submitted by the Christians of Travancore to H. H. The Maharaja of Travancore. [s.l.: s.n.], 1946.

बाल-सखा.
[प्रयाग, इंडियन प्रेस]
v. illus. 25 cm. monthly.
In Hindi.

Title romanized: Bāla-sakhā.
AP215.H5B33 73–201599

Bālā Saroja
see Saroja Bālā.

Bāla Sāvarakara
see
Savarkar, S S 1923-

Balaam, L N
Fundamentals of biometry, [by] L. N. Balaam. London, Allen and Unwin, 1972.
xiv, 259 p. illus. 23 cm. index. (The Science of biology series, no. 3) £4.90 B 72–18739
With answers.
Includes bibliographies.
1. Biometry. I. Title.
QH323.5.B35 1972b 574'.01'5195 72–305558
ISBN 0–04–519007–0; 0–04–519008–9 (pbk.) MARC

Balaam, L N
Fundamentals of biometry [by] L. N. Balaam. New York, Wiley [1972]
xiv, 259 p. illus. 23 cm.
"A Halsted Press book."
1. Biometry. I. Title.
QH323.5.B35 574'.01'5195 72–4170
ISBN 0–470–04571–X MARC

Balaam, L. N., joint author
see Federer, Walter Theodore, 1915-
Bibliography on experiment and treatment design, pre-1968. Edinburgh, Oliver and Boyd, 1972.

Balaam, L. N., joint author
see Federer, Walter Theodore, 1915-
Bibliography on experiment and treatment design, pre-1968. New York, Hafner Pub. Co., 1973 [c1972]

Balaam, L. N.
see Federer, Walter Theodore, 1915-
Bibliography of experiment design, 1950-1967. Madison, University of Wisconsin, Mathematics Research Center, 1971.

Balabaev, Gennadiĭ Viktorovich
see Chigirev, Alekseĭ. Odna zhizn' u kazhdogo. Saransk, Mordovskoe knizhnoe izd-vo, 1973.

Balaban, A. T.
see Chemical applications of graph theory. London, Academic Press, 1976.

Balaban, Abraham, 1944– comp.
(Amir Gilbo'a)
אמיר גלבע; מבחר מאמרי ביקורת על יצירתו. ליקט וצירף מבוא וביבליוגרפיה אברהם בלבן. [תל אביב] עם עובד [1972]
192 p. 22 cm. (פני הספרות) IL6.80
On verso of t. p.: Amir Gilboa; a selection of critical essays of his writings.
Bibliography: p. 189–190.
CONTENTS: שמיר, מ. היוצר וכיבוש היוצר.—צורית, א. שירת אמיר גלבע.—זך, נ. מובנותו של אמיר גלבע.—שביד, א. אל המלים הפשוטות.—מוקד, ג. אמיר גלבע—כינוס בתום עשרים שנה.—מירון, ד. הרהורים על שירת גלבע.—לוז, צ. מרחבים ומרכז—אמיר גלבע.—גורפיין, ר. ספרו החדש של אמיר גלבע.—באר, ח. דברים על אמיר גלבע.—מגד, מ. דובב שפתי ישנים.—האפרתי, י. על שני שירים של אמיר גלבע.—גורפיין, ר. שאול.—בר־יוסף, ח. יצחק לאמיר גלבע.
1. Gilboa, Amir.
PJ5054.G5Z57 73–950117

Balaban, Grigoriĭ I͡U
Реальный мир в свете универсальной теории подвижного равновесия. Hamilton, Ont., 1960.
47 p. port. 21 cm.
At head of title: Г. Ю. Балабан.
1. Physics—Philosophy. I. Title.
Title romanized: Real'nyĭ mir v svete universal'noĭ teorii podvizhnogo ravnovesii͡a.
QC6.B3 73–203100

Balaban, Grigoriĭ IU
Real'nyĭ mir v svete universal'noĭ teorii podvizhnogo ravnovesii͡a. [By] G. I͡U. Balaban. 2. izd. perer. i dop. Hamilton, Ont., 1970.
76 p. port.
1. Cosmology.
MH NSyU CoU NUC74-55398

Balaban, John, 1943–
After our war. [Pittsburgh] University of Pittsburgh Press [1974]
84 p. 21 cm. (Pitt poetry series)
I. Title.
PS3552.A44A7 813'.5'4 73–13313
ISBN 0–8229–5247–5 MARC

Balaban, John, 1943– comp.
Vietnamese folk poetry / translated by John Balaban. — Greensboro, [N. C.] : Unicorn Press, [1974]
47 p. [1] leaf of plates : ill. ; 23 cm. — (Unicorn keepsake series ; v. 7)
ISBN 0–87775–063–7 : $5.00. ISBN 0–87775–066–1 pbk.
I. Title.
PL4378.6.B34 895.9'22'1008 74–82762
MARC

Balaban, John, 1943-
The Year of the Monkey; winning hearts and minds in Vietnam. [n.p., 1968?]
35 l. 29 cm.
Cover title.
Photocopy of typescript.
Experiences of a field representative for the Committee of Responsibility, inc., a private American organization.
1. Vietnamese Conflict, 1961- —Personal narratives, American. I. Title.
NIC NUC73-81599

Balaban, Majer, 1877-1943, ed.
see Kahal, Krakow. Takanot Kraka. [729 i. e. 1968]

Balaban, P., joint author
see **Deutsch, Sarah.** Pseudo-random dot scan television systems. Brooklyn, 1964.

Balaban, Romulus.
Pelerin în lumea sportului. ⌊Comentarii sportive. Prefață de Dumitru Radu Popescu⌋. București, „Stadion," 1972.
235 p., errata. 20 cm. lei 9.00 R 72-2462
Includes bibliographical references.
1. Sports—Addresses, essays, lectures. I. Title.
GV706.B34 73-360893

Balaban, Viktor.
(Ukraïntsi v Teksasi)
Українці в Тексасі : матеріяли до історії 200-річча ЗСА і 100-річчя українців в Америці / Віктор Балабан, Богдан Гірка ; упорядкував Іван Овечко. — Юстон : Балабан, 1976.
160 p. : ill. ; 22 cm.
Added t. p.: Ukrainians in Texas.
Ukrainian or English.
1. Ukrainian Americans—Texas—Biography. 2. Ukrainian Americans — Texas — Genealogy. 3. Texas — Biography. 4. Texas — Genealogy. I. Hirka, Bohdan, 1911- joint author. II. Title. III. Title: Ukrainians in Texas.
F395.U5B34 77-508103

Balaban, Vojislav
see Yugoslavia. Savezni zavod za statistiku. Statistički album SFR Jugoslavije 1945-1973. Beograd: 1974.

Balabanē, Helenē G
see
Valavanē, Helenē G

Balabanian, David M.
see Law and motion practice; a two-hour discussion. [Sound recording] [Berkeley] California Continuing Education of the Bar, p1976.

Balabanian, Norman, 1922-
Electrical science ⌊by⌋ Norman Balabanian ⌊and⌋ Wilbur R. Le Page. New York, McGraw-Hill ⌊1970-
v. 23 cm.
CONTENTS: book 1. Resistive and diode networks.—book 2. Dynamic networks.
1. Electronic networks—Programmed instruction. I. Le Page, Wilbur R., joint author. II. Title.
TK454.2.B35 621.319′2′077 75-116658
ISBN 0-07-003544-X (v. 2) MARC
rev

Balabanian, Norman, 1922-
Fourier series : a programmed text / Norman Balabanian. — Syracuse, N.Y. : Alternative Publishers, c1976.
xii, 114 p. : ill. ; 23 cm.
1. Fourier series—Programmed instruction. I. Title.
QA404.B33 515′.2433 75-30569
77 MARC

Balabanis, Homer P
The classical ideal of the good man. [Berkeley, Calif.] Diablo Press [1972]
118 p.
1. Good and evil. I. Title.
InU NUC75-31657

Balabanoff, Angelica, 1878-1965.
My life as a rebel ⌊by⌋ Angelica Balabanoff. Bloomington, Indiana University Press ⌊1973, c1938⌋
ix, 324 p. 21 cm. (Classics in Russian studies) $3.50
1. Communism—History. 2. Socialism—History. 3. Balabanoff, Angelica, 1878-1965. I. Title.
HX312.B3 1973 335.43′092′4 [B] 72-88914
ISBN 0-253-15485-5 MARC

Balabanoff, Angelica, 1878-1965.
Il traditore. Roma, Napoleone, 1973.
294 p. 17 cm. (Universale Napoleone, 1) L1200 It 73-Sept
On cover: Mussolini e la conquista del potere.
Contains the Italian portion of 8 fascicles originally published in a bilingual edition in New York in 1942.
1. Mussolini, Benito, 1883-1945. I. Title.
DG575.M8B24 73-356914

Balabanoff, Angelica, 1878-1965.
Die Zimmerwalder Bewegung 1914-1919. ⌊Frankfurt, Verlag Neue Kritik, 1969⌋
160 p. 21 cm. (Archiv sozialistischer literatur, 16)
Facsimile reprint, with reproduction of original title page, of 1928 edition.
1. International Socialist Congress. I. Title.
CSt-H NUC73-119532

Balabanov, Aleksandŭr Mikhaĭlov, 1879-1955.
(Studii, statii, retsenzii, spomeni)
Студии, статии, рецензии, спомени. Под ред. ⌊с предг.⌋ на Тодор Боров. ⌊Т. 1- София, Бълг. писател, 1973-
v. port. 19 cm. (Библиотека Български критици) 4.27 lv (v. 1) Bu 73-2345 (v. 1)
Bibliography: v. 1, p. 675-⌊687⌋
1. Bulgarian literature—Addresses, essays, lectures. 2. Criticism—Bulgaria — Addresses, essays, lectures. 3. The arts — Bulgaria — Addresses, essays, lectures. I. Title.
PG1008.B33 1973 73-366092

Balabanov, Boĭan.
⌊Izbrani piesi⌋
Избрани пиеси: Пред буря, Пътища, Птиците летят по две, Щастието не идва само. София, Бълг. писател, 1972.
307 p. port. 21 cm. 2.40 lv Bu 72-2743
PG1038.12.A4A6 1972 73-302870

Balabanov, Boĭan.
(Oblatsite minavat, nebeto ostava)
Облаците минават, небето остава : комедия / Боян Балабанов. — София : Бълг. писател, 1975.
9J p. ; 21 cm. — (Съвременна българска драма) Bu 75-1645
Series romanized: Sŭvremenna bŭlgarska drama.
0.75 lv
I. Title.
PG1038.12.A4O2 75-594251

Balabanov, Boĭan.
Putishta; piesa. Sofiia, Bŭlgarski pisatel, 1965.
81 p. (Sŭvremenna bŭlgarska drama)
MH NUC75-129135

Balabanov, Boĭan.
(Zrelosten izpit)
Зрелостен изпит : ⌊пиеса в 5 к.⌋ / Боян Балабанов. — София : Бълг. писател, 1976.
83 p. ; 21 cm. — (Съвременна българска драма) Bu 76-2717
Series romanized: Sŭvremenna bŭlgarska drama.
0.70 lv
I. Title.
PG1038.12.A4Z36 77-506747

Balabanov, Ĭordan.
(Lesopark "Sinite kamŭni")
Лесопарк "Сините камъни" : излетни маршрути / ⌊състав. Йордан Балабанов⌋. — София : ДСП Реклама, 1975.
32 p., ⌊1⌋ fold. leaf : ill. ; 17 cm. Bu 75-911
1. Sinite Kamuni Forest Park, Bulgaria. I. Title.
SB484.B9B34 76-528536

Balabanov, Mikhail Solomonovich, 1873-
(Istoriia rabocheĭ kooperatsii v Rossii)
История рабочей кооперации в России; очерки по истории рабочего кооперативного движения, 1864-1917. Изд. 3. Москва, Экон. жизнь, 1925.
265 p. 23 cm.
At head of title: М. Балабанов.
Includes bibliographical references.
1. Cooperation—Russia. 2. Labor and laboring classes—Russia. I. Title.
HD3355.B3 1925 74-201813

Balabanov, Mikhail Solomonovich, 1873-
Ob"edinennyĭ kapital protiv rabochikh, 1905-1917. [Leningrad] Priboĭ, 1930.
77 p. (Istoriia v populiarnykh ocherkakh: Rossiia i SSSR)
Microfilm copy. New York, N.Y., International Micro-Print Preservation, 1972. 1 reel.
CaOTU NUC76-90412

Balabanov, Mikhail Solomonovich, 1873-
(Obshchee uchenie o kooperatsii)
Общее учение о кооперации, по курсу лекций, читанных в Ленинградском институте народного хозяйства. Москва, Гос. изд-во, 1928.
368 p. 24 cm.
At head of title: М. Балабанов.
Bibliography: p. ⌊367⌋-368.
1. Cooperation. I. Title.
HD2956.B32 73-216138

Balabanov, Mikhail Solomonovich, 1873-
(Ocherki po istorii rabochego klassa v Rossii)
Очерки по истории рабочего класса в России. Изд. 4., испр. и доп. Москва, Экон. жизнь, 1925-26 ⌊v. 1, 1926⌋
3 v. in 1. 23 cm.
At head of title: М. Балабанов.
Includes bibliographical references.
CONTENTS: ч. 1. Крепостная Россия.—ч. 2-3. Капиталистическая Россия.
1. Labor and laboring classes—Russia. I. Title.
HD8526.B26 74-224478

Balabanov, Mikhail Solomonovich, 1873-
Ot 1905 k 1917 gody; massovoe rabochee dvizhenie. M. Balabanov. Moskva, Gosudarstvennoe izd-vo, 1927.
455 p.
Includes bibliography.
Xerox copy. Ann Arbor, Mich., University Microfilms, 1971.
1. Labor and laboring classes-Russia. I. Title.
MU NUC75-129143

Balabanov, Mikhail Solomonovich, 1873-
Ot 1905 [i. e. tysiacha deviatsot piatogo] k 1917 godu; massovoe rabochee dvizhenie. Moskva, Gos. izd-vo, 1927.
455 p.
Includes bibliographical references.
Microfilm. New York, N.Y. International Micro-Print Preservation, 1972. 1 reel.
1. Labor and laboring classes-Russia-History. I. Title.
CaOTU NUC76-90410

Balabanov, Mikhail Solomonovich, 1873-
(Ot tysiacha deviat'sot piatogo k tysiacha deviat'sot semnadtsatomu godu)
От 1905 к 1917 году : массовое рабочее движение / М. Балабанов. — Москва : Гос. изд-во, 1927.
455 p. ; 23 cm.
Includes bibliographical references.
1. Labor and laboring classes—Russia. I. Title.
HD8526.B27 75-569953

Balabanov, N. P
see Plovdiv, Bulgaria. Universitet. (Dokladi na Dvanadeseta nauchna sesiia) 1976.

Balabanov, P. I.
see Evpatoriia. 1974.

Balabanov, Rumen
see Kare momcheta. 1974.

Balabanov, V. G.
see Primenenie élektronnykh vychislitel'nykh mashin v sudostroenii. 19

Balabanov, Vladimir Aleksandrovich.
(Nekrobakterioz zhivotnykh)
Некробактериоз животных. Москва, "Колос," 1971.
136 p. with illus. 20 cm. (Библиотека практического ветеринарного врача) 0.26rub USSR 71-VKP
At head of title: В. А. Балабанов.
Bibliography: p. 127-⌊135⌋
1. Communicable diseases in animals. 2. Actinomyces necrophorus. I. Title.
[SF781.B34] 74-331977

Balabanovich, Evgeniĭ Zinov'evich.
Чехов и Чайковский. Москва, "Моск. рабочий," 1970.
184 p., 16 l. of illus. 20 cm. USSR 70-VKP
At head of title: Е. Балабанович.
Includes bibliographical references.
0.55rub
1. Chekhov, Anton Pavlovich, 1860-1904. 2. Chaĭkovskiĭ, Petr Il'ich, 1840-1893.
Title romanized: Chekhov i Chaĭkovskiĭ.
PG3458.B27 1970 70-541377
rev

Balabanovich, Evgeniĭ Zinov'evich.
(Chekhov i Chaĭkovskiĭ)
Чехов и Чайковский. 2-е изд. Москва, "Моск. рабочий," 1973.
182 p., 16 l. of illus. 20 cm. USSR 73
At head of title: Е. Балабанович.
Includes bibliographical references.
0.56rub
1. Chekhov, Anton Pavlovich, 1860-1904. 2. Chaĭkovskiĭ, Petr Il'ich, 1840-1893.
PG3458.B27 1973 73-349535
rev

Balabanovich, Evgeniĭ Zinov'evich.
(Iz zhizni A. P. Chekhova)
Из жизни А. П. Чехова : Дом в Кудрине / Е. Балабанович. — 4-е изд., доп. — Москва : Моск. рабочий, 1976.
288 p. : ill. ; 16 cm. USSR 76
First ed. published in 1958 under title: Dom A. P. Chekhova v Moskve; 2d ed. published in 1961 under title: Dom v Kudrine.
0.40rub
1. Moscow. Dom-muzeĭ A. P. Chekhova. I. Title.
PG3458.Z7B32 1976 76-531956

Balabanovo, Russia (Kaluga). Vsesoiuznyĭ nauchno-issledovatel'skiĭ institut derevo-obrabatyvaiushcheĭ promyshlennosti
see
Vsesoiuznyĭ nauchno-issledovatel'skiĭ institut derevoobrabatyvaiushcheĭ promyshlennosti.

Balabekov, M. T., ed.
see Tashkend. Tashkentskiĭ politekhnicheskiĭ institut. Mekhanicheskiĭ fakul'tet. (Sbornik materialov po itogam nauchno-issledovatel'skikh rabot ...) 1972.

Balabhadra, 17th cent.
[Hāyanaratna]
अथहायनरत्नःप्रारम्यते / श्रीमद्दैवज्ञाचार्यपंडितदामोदरात्मजबलभद्रविरचिते. — [s.l. : s.n.], संवत् 1924 [1867] (वाराणसी : काशीसंस्कृत मुद्रायामङ्कितेयंविचक्षणैः)
70 p. (on double leaves) ; 29 x 13 cm.
In Sanskrit.
1. Astrology, Hindu. I. Title.
Title romanized: Athahāyanaratnaḥprārabhyate.
BF1714.H5B34 1867 76–985179

Baḷabhadra Bhañja, fl. 1764–1784.
ଅମ୍ବିକା ବିଳାସ. ବଳଭଦ୍ର ଭଞ୍ଜଦେବ ପ୍ରଣୀତ. ସଂକଳକ, ଟୀକାକାର,ଓ ମୁଖବନ୍ଧ ଲେଖକ ବାନାମ୍ବର ଆଚାର୍ଯ୍ୟ. [2. ସଂସ୍କରଣ] କଟକ, କଳିଙ୍ଗ ଗ୍ରନ୍ଥ ମନ୍ଦିର [1970]
25, 272 p. 23 cm. 8.00
First published in 1937.
In Oriya.
"ବାମଜ୍ଞା କୋଇଲ": [266]–272.
1. Siva (Hindu deity)—Poetry. 2. Baḷabhadra Bhañja, fl. 1764–1784—Poetry. I. Acharya, Banambar, ed. II. Title.
Title romanized: Ambikā biḷāsa.
PK2579.B2574A8 1970 78–915282

Balabin, Stanislav Prokop'evich.
Doch' taĭgi; povesti. Moskva, Sovremennik, 1973.
190 p. 21 cm. (Novinki-sovremennika)
I. Title.
MB NUC75-139794

Balabina, Galina Vasil'evna.
(Kontrol' kachestva svarnykh soedineniĭ iz plastmass v stroitel'stve)
Контроль качества сварных соединений из пластмасс в строительстве / Г. В. Балабина, И. Ф. Истратов. — Москва : Стройиздат, 1975.
192, [1] p. : ill. ; 20 cm. USSR***
Bibliography : p. 190–[193]
0.71rub
1. Plastics—Welding. 2. Welding—Quality control. 3. Plastics in building. I. Istratov, Igor' Fedorovich, joint author. II. Title.
TP1160.B33 76–511815

Balabīra Ātasha
see
Ātasha, Balabīra.

Balabkins, Nicholas.
Entrepreneur in a small country : a case study against the background of the Latvian economy, 1919-1940 / Nicholas Balabkins and Arnolds Aizsilnieks. — 1st ed. — Hicksville, N.Y. : Exposition Press, [1975]
xiv, 143 p. : map ; 21 cm. — (An exposition-university book)
Includes bibliographical references and index.
ISBN 0-682-48158-0 : $6.50
1. Latvia—Economic conditions. 2. Entrepreneur. I. Aizsilnieks, Arnolds P., joint author. II. Title.
HC337.L3B24 330.9'47'43084 74-21436
75 MARC

Balabolkin, Remir Konstantinovich.
(Ėkspluatatsiia avtomobileĭ i gusenichnykh transporterov)
Эксплуатация автомобилей и гусеничных транспортеров / Р. К. Балаболкин, В. М. Купцов. — Москва : Транспорт, 1975.
95 p. : ill. ; 17 cm. — (В помощь строителям БАМ) USSR 75
0.18rub
1. Motor-trucks. 2. Tracklaying vehicles. I. Kuptsov, Viktor Mikhaĭlovich, joint author. II. Title.
TL232.B34 75–535670

Balabushevich, Vladimir Vasil'evich, ed.
see Andreĭ Evgen'evich Snesarev. 1973.

Bālacandra.
see Yogāmrtam. Hindi & Kannada. (Yogamrta) [2492 i. e. 1965 or 6]

Balacciu, Jana.
see Calistrat Hogaş ... [Bucureşti] Editura Eminescu, 1976.

Balacco, Hugo Roberto
see Mendoza, Argentine Republic (Province). Dirección de Estadísticas e Investigaciones Económicas. Censo de empleados publicos. Mendoza, 1969.

Balacco, Hugo Roberto
see Mendoza, Argentine Republic (Province). Dirección de Estadísticas e Investigaciones Económicas. Censo nacional de problación, familias y viviendas, 1970: Mendoza, 1973.

Balacco, Hugo Roberto
see Mendoza, Argentine Republic (Province). Dirección de Estadísticas e Investigaciones Económicas. Censo nacional de viviendas—1970. Mendoza, 1972.

Bălăceanu, Constantin.
Personalitatea umană, o interpretare cibernetică. [Iaşi], „Junimea," 1972.
247 p. with figs. 20 cm. lei 6.25 R 72-2742
At head of title: C. Bălăceanu, Edm. Nicolau.
Bibliography : p. 235–242.
1. Personality. 2. Information theory in psychology. I. Nicolau, Edmond, joint author. II. Title.
BF698.B312 72–356985

Bălăceanu, Constantin
see Nicolau, Edmond. Elemente de neurocibernetică. Bucureşti, Editura ştiinţifică, 1967.

Bălăceanu, Valentin.
Munţii Făgăraş : ghid turistic / Valentin Bălăceanu, Mihai Cicotti, Emilian Cristea ; [cartografia, Nicolau Constantin]. — Bucureşti : Editura pentru turism, 1974.
70 p. : ill., fold. col. map ; 18 cm. — (Munţii noştri ; 1)
R 74-3443
lei 8.00
1. Făgăraş Mountains, Romania—Description and travel—Guide-books. I. Cicotti, Mihai, joint author. II. Cristea, Emilian, joint author. III. Title. IV. Series.
DR210.M85 no. 1 75–593066
[DR281.F]

Bălăceanu, Valentin.
Munţii Făgăraşului : [ghid turistic] / V. Bălăceanu, M. Cicotti, Em. Cristea ; [coperta, Keri Eugen ; cartografia, L. Marinache, V. Marinache]. — [Bucureşti] : "Sport-Turism," 1975.
337, [3] p., [11] leaves of plates : ill. (some col.), maps (3 fold. in pocket) ; 20 cm. R 76–198
Bibliography : p. 337–[338]
lei 20.00
1. Făgăras Mountains, Romania—Description and travel—Guide-books. I. Cicotti, Mihai, joint author. Cristea, Emilian, joint author. III. Title.
DR281.F18B34 76–507333

Balachan, Vladimir Fedorovich, 1939-
Dobraia pogoda; stikhi. [By] Vladimir Balachan. Novosibirsk, Zapadno-Sibirskoe knizhnoe izd-vo, 1971.
68 p. port.
MH NUC75-129136

Balachan, Vladimir Fedorovich, 1939-
Teplyn'; [stikhotvoreniia. By] Vladimir Balachan. [Predisl.: Il'ia Fonīakov] Novosibirsk, Zapadno-Sibirskoe knizhnoe izd-vo, 1969.
84 p. port.
MH NUC75-129137

Balachan, Vladimir Fedorovich, 1939-
Zerno k zernu. [Moskva] Molodaia gvardiia, 1972.
32 p. (Molodye golosa)
Poems.
MH CU NUC75-129122

Balachander, K
see
Pālacantar, K

Balachandra, J., joint author
see Elayaperumal, K
Electrochemical factors of stress corrosion cracking of zirconium in CH_3OH- HCl solution. Bombay, Bhabha Atomic Research Centre, 1971.

Balachandra, Mysore.
A study of gyroscopic systems. [Minneapolis] 1971.
vi, 233 l. illus. 29 cm.
Thesis (Ph.D.)—University of Minnesota.
Bibliography: leaves 212-215.
MnU NUC73-44392

Balachandra Shastri
see
Shastri, Balchandra, 1905-

Balachandran, Krishnan, 1944-
Effects of curvature on pulsatile viscous flow in thin-walled elastic tubes. St. Louis, 1972.
ix, 99 l. illus.
Thesis—Washington University.
Binding title: Pulsatile flow in curved tubes.
Vita.
Bibliography: leaves 79-81.
1. Blood—Circulation. 2. Viscosity. 3. Fluid dynamics.
MoSW NUC73-44457

Balachandran, Lakshmi Bai.
A case grammar of Hindi : with a special reference to the causative sentences / Lakshmi Bai Balachandran. — [1. संस्करण]. — Agra : Central Institute of Hindi, [1973]
76, 40 p. ; 25 cm. — (Decennary publication series ; no. 7)
Added t.p. in Hindi: हिन्दी का कारक-व्याकरण : प्रेरणार्थक वाक्यों के विशेष संदर्भ में.
English or Hindi.
"A thesis presented to the faculty of the graduate school of Cornell University for the degree of doctor of philosophy, January, 1971."
Bibliography: p. [39]–40.
Rs10.00 ($5.00U.S.)
1. Hindi language—Grammar, Generative. 2. Hindi language—Case. I. Title: A case grammar of Hindi. II. Title: Hindī kā kāraka-vyākaraṇa. III. Series.
PK1933.B28 75–906574

Balachandran, M
Basic economic statistics / M. Balachandran. — Monticello, Ill. : Council of Planning Librarians, 1976.
37 p. ; 28 cm. — (Exchange bibliography ; 971)
Cover title.
$4.00
1. United States—Statistics—Bibliography. 2. Economic indicators—United States—Bibliography. I. Title. II. Series: Council of Planning Librarians. Exchange bibliography ; 971.
Z5942.C68 no. 971 016.3092'08 s 76-358887
[Z7554.U5] 76 MARC
[HA205]

Balachandran, M
Contruction, housing and real estate statistics / M. Balachandran. -- Monticello, Ill. : Council of Planning Librarians, 1976.
30 p. ; 28 cm. -- (Exchange bibliography - Council of Planning Librarians ; 997)
Cover title.
1. Construction industry--U.S.--Statistics--Bibliography. 2. Housing--U.S.--Statistics--Bibliography. 3. Real estate business--U.S.--Statistics--Bibliography. I. Title. II. Series: Council of Planning Librarians. Exchange bibliography ; 997.
OrPS NUC77-83283

Balachandran, M
Malls and shopping centers : a selected bibliography, 1970-1975 / M. Balachandran. — Monticello, Ill. : Council of Planning Librarians, 1976.
35 p. ; 28 cm. — (Exchange bibliography ; 1123)
Cover title.
$3.50
1. Shopping malls—Bibliography. 2. Shopping-centers—Bibliography. I. Title. II. Series: Council of Planning Librarians. Exchange bibliography ; 1123.
Z5942.C68 no. 1123 016.3092 s 76-150155
[Z7164.C81] 76 MARC
[HF5434]

Balachandran, M
Manpower statistics & related data for planners / M. Balachandran. — Monticello, Ill. : Council of Planning Librarians, 1976.
34 p. ; 29 cm. — (Exchange bibliography - Council of Planning Librarians ; 1063)
Cover title.
$3.50
1. Labor and laboring classes— United States—1970- —Bibliography. I. Title. II. Series: Council of Planning Librarians. Exchange bibliography ; 1063.
Z5942.C68 no. 1063 016.3092 s 77-471137
[Z7164.L1] 77 MARC
[HD8072]

Balachandran, Sarojini.
Airport planning (1965-1975) / by Sarojini Balachandran. — Monticello, Ill. : Council of Planning Librarians, 1976.
51 p. ; 29 cm. — (Exchange bibliography - Council of Planning Librarians ; no. 1140)
Caption title.
$5.00
1. Airports—Planning—Bibliography. I. Title. II. Series: Council of Planning Librarians. Exchange bibliography ; no. 1140.
Z5942.C68 no. 1140 016.3092'08 s 77-362648
[Z5064.A28] 77 MARC
[TL725.3.P5]

Balachandran, Sarojini.
Employee communication : a bibliography / Sarojini Balachandran. — Urbana : American Business Communication Association, University of Illinois, 1976.
55 p. ; 23 cm.
1. Communication in personnel management—Bibliography. I. Title.
Z7164.C81B26 016.6584'5 77-361396
[HF5549.5.C6] 77 MARC

Balachandran, Sarojini.
Energy statistics : a guide to sources / Sarojini Balachandran. — Monticello, Ill. : Council of Planning Librarians, 1976.
51 p. ; 28 cm. — (Exchange bibliography ; 1065)
Cover title.
Includes index.
$5.00
1. Power resources—United States—Statistics—Bibliography. I. Title. II. Series: Council of Planning Librarians. Exchange bibliography ; 1065.
Z5853.P83B34 016.3092'08 s 76-369694
[HD9502.U5] 76 MARC

Balachandran, Sarojini.
Energy statistics : an update to bibliography no. 1065 / Sarojini Balachandran. — Monticello, Ill. : Council of Planning Librarians, 1977.
22 p. ; 28 cm. — (Exchange bibliography - Council of Planning Librarians ; 1247)
Cover title.
Includes index.
$2.00
1. Power resources—United States—Statistics—Bibliography. I. Title. II. Series: Council of Planning Librarians. Exchange bibliography ; 1247.
Z5942.C68 no. 1247 016.3092 s 77-360255
[Z5853] 77 MARC
[HD9502.U5]

Balachandran, Sarojini.
Social accounting / Sarojini Balachandran. — Monticello, Ill. : Council of Planning Librarians, 1977.
41 p. ; 28 cm. — (Exchange bibliography - Council of Planning Librarians ; 1276)
Cover title.
$4.00
1. Industry—Social aspects—Bibliography. I. Title. II. Series: Council of Planning Librarians. Exchange bibliography ; 1276.
Z5942.C68 no. 1276 016.3092 s 77-151689
[Z7164.C81] 77 MARC
[HD60]

Balachandran, Sarojini.
Transportation statistics / Sarojini Balachandran. — Monticello, Ill. : Council of Planning Librarians, 1976.
43 p. ; 29 cm. — (Exchange bibliography - Council of Planning Librarians ; 1177)
Cover title.
Includes index.
$4.50
1. Transportation—Statistics—Bibliography. 2. Transportation—United States—Statistics—Bibliography. I. Title. II. Series: Council of Planning Librarians. Exchange bibliography ; 1177.
Z5942.C68 no. 1177 016.3092 s 77-352178
[Z7164.T8] 77 MARC
[HE191.5]

Balachandran, Venkataraman, 1937-
The generalized transportation problem - an operator theory of parametric programming, stochastic programming with recourse, and boolean requirements. Ann Arbor, Mich., University Microfilms, 1973.
1 reel. 35 mm.
Thesis—Carnegie-Mellon University, 1973.
Collation of the original: 272 leaves. illus.
1. Electronci data processing—Transporation. I. Title.
ViBlbV NUC76-70898

Balachandran Nayar, K.
see In quest of Kerala. Trivandrum, Accent Publications, 1974.

Balaci, Alexandru.
Alessandro Manzoni. [Viața și opera], de Alexandru Balaci. Monografie. [Coperta de Sergiu Dinculescu]. București „Univers," 1974.
216 p. 20 cm. lei 11.50 R 74-1881
Bibliography: p. [209]-214.
1. Manzoni, Alessandro, 1785-1873.
PQ4715.B28 74-337688

Balaci, Alexandru.
Boccaccio : [monografie] / Alexandru Balaci. — [București] : "Albatros", 1976.
204, [3] p. ; 20 cm. R76-4172
Bibliography: p. 201-[205]
lei7.50
1. Boccaccio, Giovanni, 1313-1375.
PQ4277.B28 77-459189
•77 MARC

Balaci, Alexandru.
Jurnal italian. [Coperta: Gh. Coclitu]. București, „Albatros," 1973.
232 p. 20 cm. lei 8.75 R 73-5139
1. Italy—Description and travel—1945- 2. Italian literature—Addresses, essays, lectures. I. Title.
DG430.B24 74-307092

Balaci, Alexandru.
Ludovico Ariosto, contemporanul nostru / Alexandru Balaci ; [coperta de Gh. Marinescu]. — București : "Albatros," 1974.
232, [4] p. : 20 cm. R 75-1662
Bibliography: p. 229-[233]
lei 9.00
1. Ariosto, Lodovico, 1474-1533.
PQ4587.B25 75-534770

Balaci, Anca.
Cetăți și himere : Italia de la Tarquinia la Siracuza / Anca Balaci ; cuvînt înainte de Francesco Gligora ; fotografii de Dan Eremia Grigorescu ; [prezentarea grafică János Bencsik]. — București : "Sport-Turism," 1975.
142 p., [16] leaves of plates : ill. ; 21 cm. R 75-2965
lei 11.50
1. Italy—Description and travel—1945- 2. Italy—Antiquities. I. Title.
DG430.B247 76-502834

Balaci, Anca.
Mic dicționar mitologic greco-roman / Anca Balaci. — Ed. a 2-a. — București : Editura științifică, 1969.
447 p., [22] leaves of plates : ill. ; 17 cm.
Includes index.
1. Mythology—Dictionaries—Romanian. I. Title.
BL715.B34 1969 76-526543

Balacs, Peter, joint author
see Balogh, Thomas, Baron Balogh, 1905- Fact and fancy in international economic relations... Oxford, New York, Pergamon Press [1973]

Balada, Eduardo
see
Costa Clavell, Javier.

Balade istorice / [antologie și bibliografie alcătuite de Mihai Dascăl] ; prefață de Valeriu Cristea ; [coperta seriei, Constantin Gluță]. — București : "Minerva," 1975.
xv, 173 p. ; 20 cm. — (Meșterul Manole) R 76-249
Bibliography : p. 167-[171]
lei 7.75
1. Ballads, Romanian—Text. I. Dascăl, Mihai.
PC821.B3 76-519952

Balade populare maghiare / în versiunea românească a lui Petre Șaitiș ; prefață de Ion Șeuleanu ; [ilustrațiile și grafica volumului de Mircea Bălău]. — Cluj-Napoca : "Dacia," 1975.
175 p. : ill. ; 23 x 25 cm. R 76-849
Added t. p.: Magyar népballadák.
In Romanian and Hungarian.
lei 23.00
1. Ballads, Hungarian—Texts. 2. Ballads, Hungarian—Translations into Romanian. 3. Ballads, Romanian—Translations from Hungarian. I. Șaitiș, Petre. II. Title: Magyar népballadák.
PH3125.B3 76-519073

Balade populare românești. [București] Ed. pentru literatură, 1967.
2 v. 17 cm.
Bibliography: p. 383-387.
1.Romanian ballards and songs. I.Title.
IU NUC73-119560

Baladeva. BaladevĪ. 1970
see Gaṅgeśa, 13th cent. [Tattvacintāmaṇi. Sāmānyanirukti] Sāmānyanirukti. [Darbhanga] 1970.

Baladeva Caralā
see
Caralā, Baladeva, 1940-

Baladeva Caudharī
see
Chaudhry, Baldev, 1945-

Baladeva Prasāda Sāhu
see
Sāhu, Baladeva Prasāda.

Baladeva Upadhyaya, Pandit
see Upadhyaya, Baladeva, 1899-

Baladeva Vidyābhūṣaṇa, 1720-1790. Baladevabhāṣya. 1910-1912.
in **Bādarāyaṇa.** **The Vedânta-sûtras of Bâdarâyaṇa, with the commentary of Baladeva.** Allahabad, Pâṇini Office, 1912 [i.e. 1910-1912]

Baladeva Vidyābhuṣaṇa, 1720-1790. Baladevabhāṣya. English. 1974.
in Bādarāyaṇa. The Vedânta sûtras of Bâdarâyaṇa. [New York, AMS Press, 1974]

Baladeva Vidyābhusana, 1720-1790. Gītabhûshana
see Mahābhārata. Bhagavadgītā. Śrīśrīmadbhagabadgīta. [1967-68]

Baladeva Vidyābhūṣana, 1720-1790. Govindabhāsya
see Bādarāyana. Bedāntasūtram. [1968-70]

Baladeva Vidyābhūṣaṇa, 1720-1790. Īśāvasyopaniṣadbhāṣya. 1970
see Upanishads. Īśopaniṣad. Bengali & Sanskrit. Śuklayajurbbedīyā Bājasaneya-saṃhitopanishaṭ. [1970]

Baladeva Vidyābhūṣaṇa, 1720-1790.
(Prameyaratnavalī)
प्रमेयरत्नावली : गौड़ीयवैष्णवदर्शनप्रकरणग्रन्थ: / बलदेवविद्याभूषणविरचिता ; कृष्णदेववेदान्तवागीशविरचित-कान्तिमालाख्यटीकोपेता ; प्रभाख्य-नवीनटीकया वङ्गानुवादेन च समलङ्कृत्य उपदेशसहस्रांवेदान्तदर्शनादि-विविध-ग्रन्थसम्पादयित्रा विद्यारत्नोपनाम-भारद्वाज-श्रीमद्-अक्षयकुमारशर्मशास्त्रिणा सम्पादिता ; श्रीमदगौरसुन्दरशर्म-भागवतदर्शनाचार्येण परिद्दष्टा. — Calcutta : संस्कृतसाहित्यपरिषद, [1927]
24, 138 p. ; 22 cm. — (संस्कृतसाहित्यपरिषद्ग्रन्थमालायाम्, 18)
Added cover title in English.
Bengali and Sanskrit; commentaries in Sanskrit; foreword in English.
Series romanized: Saṃskṛtasāhityapariṣadgranthamālāyām.
1. Vaishnavism. I. Kṛṣṇadevavedântavāgīśa. Kāntimālā. 1927 II. Akṣayakumāraśarmaśāstri. Prabhā. 1927. III. Akṣayakumāraśarmaśāstri. IV. Gaurasundaraśarma Bhāgavatadarśanācārya. V. Title.
BL1245.V3B33 76-984766

Baladeva Vidyābhuṣaṇa, 1720-1790. Prameyaratnāvalī. English & Sanskrit, 1974.
see Bādarāyaṇa. The Vedânta sûtras of Bâdarâyaṇa. [New York, AMS Press, 1974]

Baladevadāsa.
(Anubhava Rāmāyaṇa)
अनुभव रामायण / बलदेवदासकृत. मुबई : शिवदुलारे वाजपयी, 1922.
24 p. ; 17 cm.
Cover title.
In Hindi.
I. Title.
PK2098.B3385A8 75-986022

Baladevānanda Sārada
see Upanishads. Isādi dvādasopanisadah. [1970]

Baladevānanda Śārada, ed.
see Vidyanand Giri, Swami, 1922- Brahmasūtram Vidyānandavṛttih. [1969]

Baladevaprasāda Miśra
see
Mishra, Baldeo Prasad, 1913-1965.

Baladevasiṃha
see
Langeh, Baldev Singh, 1934-

Baladewa Bala, pseud.
ਹੱਕ ਪਰਾਇਆ; [ਨਾਵਲ. ਲੇਖਕ] ਬਲਦੇਵ ਬਲ. [ਨਵੀਂ ਦਿਲੀ, ਮਿਰਜਨਾ ਪ੍ਰੈਸ, 1969]
147 p. 19 cm. 5.00
In Panjabi.

1. Nānak, 1st guru of the Sikhs, 1469-1538—Fiction. I. Title.
Title romanized: Hakka parāiā.
PK2659.B29H3 71-908020

Baladewa Dhiloṃ
see
Dhiloṃ, Baladewa, 1934-

Baladewa Siṅgha.
(Jīwana saṅgharasha)
ਜੀਵਨ ਸੰਘਰਸ਼; ਨਾਵਲ. ਲੇਖਕ ਬਲਦੇਵ ਸਿੰਘ. ਅੰਮ੍ਰਿਤਸਰ, ਲੋਕ ਸਾਹਿੱਤ ਪ੍ਰਕਾਸ਼ਨ [1972]
267 p. 19 cm. Rs15.00
In Panjabi.

I. Title.
PK2659.B2914J5 72-907424

Baladewa Siṅgha Buṭara
see
Buṭara, Baladewa Siṅgha.

al-Baladhuri, Ahmad ibn Yahyá, d. 892. Ansab al-ashraf. Khilafat al-Walid ibn Yazid. 1974
see Derenk, Dieter. Leben und Dichtung des Omaiyadenkalifen Al-Walid Ibn Yazid ... Freiburg im Breisgau : K. Schwarz, 1974.

al-Baladhuri, Ahmad ibn Yahyá, d. 892. Ansab al-ashraf. Maqtal al-Walid ibn Yazid. 1974
see Derenk, Dieter. Leben und Dichtung des Omaiyadenkalifen Al-Walid Ibn Yazid ... Freiburg im Breisgau : K. Schwarz, 1974.

Baladi, George Y., joint author
see Phillips, Bruce R Results of two free-field code calculations... Vicksburg, Miss., 1973.

al-Baladī, Ḥusayn.
('Ishtu fī Amrīkā al-Lātīnīyah)
عشت فى امريكا اللاتينية / بقلم حسين البلدى. — [القاهرة : s. n., 19
v. : ill. ; 19 cm. — (كتب سياسية ؛ الكتاب)
Series romanized: Kutub siyāsīyah ; al-kitāb
1. Latin America. I. Title.
F1408.25.B34 75-972001

Baladī, Muḥammad ibn Aḥmad al-Khabbāz al-
see
al-Khabbāz al-Baladī, Muḥammad ibn Aḥmad, 10th cent.

Baladi, Naguib.
[Dīkārt]
ديكارت ، بقلم نجيب بلدى. الطبعة 2. مصر ، دار المعارف [1968]
223 p. 22 cm. (نوابغ الفكر الغربى ، 12)
Bibliography: p. 222-223.
1. Descartes, René, 1596-1650.
B1875.B26 1968 72-225569

Baladni pisni. [Upor. ta vstup. stattīa H. A. Nud'hy] Kyïv, Muzychna Ukraïna, 1969.
270 p. illus. (Iz dzherel ukraïns'koï pisni)
1. Ballads—Ukrainian. I. Nud'ha, Hryhoriĭ Antonovych, ed.
MH MiU NUC74-56447

Balado, Carmen L., joint author
see Valle, Emérita S del. Manual de dietas del Distrito Noreste de Salud y Bienestar. [Río Piedras, P.R., 196]

Balado, José Luis González-
see González-Balado, José Luis.

Balado, Juan F García
see García Balado, Juan F

Baladon, Andres N Acosta
see Acosta Baladon, Andres N

Baladouni, Vahé, 1925- comp.
(T'argmanowt'iwnner)
Թարգմանութիւններ : քերթուած եւ արձակ / [Թարգմանեց եւ կազմեց] Վահէ Պալատունի. — Պէյրութ : Sevan Print. House, 1973.
72 p. ; 25 cm.
£L5.00 ($2.00U.S.)
1. Armenian literature—Translations from foreign languages. 2. Literature, Modern—Translations into Armenian.
PK8701.B3 74-299046

Baladouni, Vahe, 1925-
Toward a comprehensive theoretical framework of accountancy. Ann Arbor, University Microfilms, 1965.
1 reel. 35 mm.
Thesis—University of Illinois.
1. Accounting. I. Title.
MsU NUC74-122427

al-Balady, Mohammad ibn Ahmad al-Khabbaz
see
al-Khabbāz al-Baladī, Muḥammad ibn Aḥmad, 10th cent.

(Balady muzhnosti ĭ vidvahy)
Балади мужності й відваги = Баллады мужества и отваги = Балады мужнасці і адвагі : вибрані балади російських, українських та білоруських письменників : 1941-1945 / [відп. редактор С. А. Крижанівський]. — Київ : Наук. думка, 1975.
294 p. ; 21 cm. USSR***
On leaf preceding t. p.: Akademiia nauk URSR. Instytut suspil'nykh nauk.
Includes bibliographical references.
1.59rub

1. Ballads, Russian—Texts. 2. Ballads, Ukrainian—Tests. 3. Ballads, White Russian—Texts. 4. World War, 1939-1945—Poetry. I. Kryzhanivs'kyĭ, Stepan Andriĭovych, 1910- II. Akademiia nauk URSR, Kiev. Instytut suspil'nykh nauk. III. Title: Ballady muzhestva i otvagi. IV. Title: Balady muzhnastsi i advahi.
PG3235.W36B3 76-527592

Baladzhiian, Khristofor
see Adygeia—piat'desiat. 1972.

Balaeïshchik, Faniia Bentsianovna
see Avtomaticheskaia mezhdugorodnaia i sel'skaia telefonnaia sviaz'. 1976.

Bălăeț, Dumitru.
Ce rămîne : poezii / Dumitru Bălăeț ; coperta, Ion Nedelcu. — București : Editura Eminescu, 1974.
90 p. ; 20 cm. R 74-4049
lei 6.00
I. Title.
PC840.12.A48C4 75-576702

Bălăeț, Drumitru, ed.
see Ionescu, Radu, 1834-1872. Scrieri alese. Bucuresti, "Minerva," 1974.

Balaev, Igor' Tembolatovich.
Romanticheskaia poėma Kosta Khetagurova "Fatima". K voprosu o sviazi s romanticheskimi poėmami Lermontova. Ordzhonikidze, Izd-vo "Ir", 1970.
71 p.
1. Khetagurov, Konstantin Levanovich, 1859-1906.
InU NUC74-38255

Balaev, Tembol.
Mlechnyĭ put'; stikhi. Ordzhonikidze, Ir, 1971.
279 p. illus.
Title page and text in Ossetian.
Russian title from verso of t.p.
MH NUC75-129134

Balaev, Tembulat Il'ich, comp.
see (Ir Leninyl zaryntš) 1970.

Balaev, Tembulat Il'ich.
see Osetiia o Lenine poet. Ordzhonikidze, Izd-vo Ir, 1970.

Balafon.
[Abidjan] Air Afrique
no. illus. 27 cm.
1. Africa, West—Description and travel—1951- —Periodicals. I. Air Afrique.
DT470.B27 72-625306

Balafoutis, Christos J
Cooling power and weather types in Thesaloniki / by Christos J. Balafoutis. — Thessaloniki : [Meteorological Institute of the University of Thessaloniki], 1974.
p. 49-62 : graphs ; 25 cm. — (Meteōrologika ; 37) (Publications of the Meteorological Institute of the University of Thessaloniki)
Summary in Greek.
Bibliography: p. 61-62.
1. Thessaloniki—Climate. 2. Climatic classification—Greece—Thessaloniki. 3. Cooling power (Meteorology)—Greece—Thessaloniki. I. Title. II. Series. III. Series: Thessalonike. Panepistēmion. Ergastērion Meteōrologias kai Klimatologias. Publications.
QC989.G98T42 551.6'9'4956 76-357096
76 MARC

Balafoutis, Christos J
The cooling power of Thessaloniki-Greece III, by Christos J. Balafoutis and George C. Livadas. Thessaloniki, 1972.
227-240 p. illus. 24 cm. (Thessaloniki. Panepistemion. Ergasterion Meteorologias. Meteorologika 21)
Reprint of Scientific Annales of the Faculty of Math & Physics of the Univ. of Thessaloniki, v. 12, p. 227-240 (1972)
1. Atmospheric temperature—Thessaloniki, Greece—Observations. 2. Atmospheric temperature—Thessaloniki, Greece—Measurement. I. Title. II. Series.
DAS NUC75-84377

Bālagangādhararāvu, Yārlagadda
see Kāsula Purusōttamakavi, 18th cent. [Āndhranāyakśatakamu] Āndhranāyaka satakam. 1975.

Balaganov, Bal'zhinima Balaganovich, joint author
see Dagbatsyrenov, TSydyp Darmaevich. (Ekonomicheskie problemy povysheniia kachestva zhivotnovodcheskoĭ produktsii) 1975.

Balagezian, IUrik Garnikovich.
(Uskorennye ispytaniia na nadezhnost' i faktornyĭ analiz rezul'tatov nabliudeniĭ)
Ускоренные испытания на надежность и факторный анализ результатов наблюдений. Ленинград, 1972.
23 p. 21 cm. (Ленинградский дом научно-технической пропаганды. Серия: Улучшение качества промышленной продукции (стандартизация, повышение надежности, защитные покрытия, техническая эстетика)) 0.13rub USSR 72-VKP
At head of title: Ленинградская организация общества "Знание" РСФСР. Ю. Г. Балагезян, Ж. С. Мельницкая.
Bibliography: p. [22]
1. Machinery — Reliability. 2. Machinery — Testing. 3. Factor analysis. I. Mel'nitskaia, Zhanna Sigizmundovna. II. Title.
TJ153.B22 73-325822

(al-Balāgh)

البلاغ.
راولپنڈی ؍غلام حسین کھوکھر؎
v. ill. 28 cm. weekly.
Other title : Al Balagh.
In Urdu.
1. Pakistan—Politics and government—Periodicals. I. Title: Al Balagh.
DS376.B3 74–930534 (MARC–S)

(al-Balāgh)

البلاغ.

كراچى، محمد تقى عثمانى.

v. 24 cm. monthly.
In Urdu.

1. Islam—Periodicals. I. ʻUs̲mānī, Muḥammad Taqī.
BP1.B32 72–930371 (MARC–S)

al-Balāghī, Muḥammad Jawād, d. 1933.
(Ālāʼ al-Raḥmān fī tafsīr al-Qurʼān)
آلاء الرحمن فى تفسير القرآن ؍تأليف؎ محمد جواد البلاغي النجفي. الطبعة 2. قم، مكتبة الوجدانى ؍1936؟؎
2 v. in 1. 25 cm.
1. Koran—Commentaries. I. Title.
BP130.4.B279 1936 74–211442

al-Balāghī, Muḥammad Jawād, d. 1933.
(ʻIqd fī ilzām ghayr al-Imāmī bi-aḥkām niḥlatih)
عقد فى الزام غير الامامى باحكام نحلته، تصنيف جواد البلاغى. طهران، مكتبة الصدوق ؍(1958 or 9) cover 1378؎
37 p. 23 cm.
Bibliographical footnotes.
1. Contracts (Islamic law) I. Title.
73–222480

Balāghī, Ṣadr al-Dīn.
(Burhān-i Qurʼān)
برهان قران و رد مهمترين شبهات پيروان كمونيزم و ساير معاندين اسلام، شامل جالبترين مباحث اجتماعى و نظامات اقتصادى و قضائى قرآن. نوشتهٔ سيد صدر الدين بلاغى. ؍تهران؎ مرتضى فتى، مركز فروش: انتيم ؍1958؎ 1336.
266 p. 25 cm.
1. Islam and economics. 2. Communism and Islam. I. Title.
BP173.75.B34 74–204867

Balāghī, Ṣadr al-Dīn.
(Qaṣaṣ-i Qurʼān)
قصص قرآن با فرهنك قصص قران، تاليف صدر الدين بلاغى. ؍تهران؎ چاپ تابان ؍1951؎ 1330.
6, 446 p. illus., ports., maps. 22 cm.
1. Koran stories. 2. Koran—Dictionaries. I. Title.
BP130.58.B34 74–200760

Balagin, Ivan I͡Akovlevich.
(Peredacha diskretnoĭ informat͡sii i telegrafii͡a)
Передача дискретной информации и телеграфия. ₍Учебник для вузов ж.-д. транспорта₎. Москва, "Транспорт," 1971.
352 p. with illus. 22 cm. 0.93rub USSR 71–VKP
At head of title: И. Я. Балагин, В. А. Кудряшов, Н. Ф. Семенюта.
Bibliography: p. 347.
1. Data transmission systems. 2. Railroads—Telegraph. I. Kudri͡ashov, Vladimir Aleksandrovich. II. Semeni͡uta, Nikolaĭ Filippovich. III. Title.
TK5102.5.B33 73–305525

Bāḷagōpāḷa, Kavi, 1830–1930.
₍Lāvaṇigaḷu₎
ಕವಿ ಬಾಳಗೋಪಾಳನ ಲಾವಣಿಗಳು / ಸಂಪಾದಕರು ನಿಂಗಣ್ಣ ಸಣ್ಣಕ್ಕಿ. — ಧಾರವಾಡ : ಸಮಾಜ ಪುಸ್ತಕಾಲಯ, 1974.
15, 135 p. ; 20 cm.
In Kannada.
Poems.
Rs4.50
I. Sannakki, Ninganna, 1939– II. Title.
Title romanized: Kavi Bāḷagopāḷana lāvaṇigaḷu.
PL4659.B18L3 1974 75–906840

Balagué, Miguel.
El testamento de Jesús : los discursos de la Ultima Cena, (Jn. 13-17) / Miguel Balagué. — Madrid : Studium : distribuye, Difusoria del Libro, 1976.
216 p. ; 20 cm. Sp76-June
Includes bibliographical references.
ISBN 8430412301 : 250ptas
1. Bible. N.T. John XIII-XVII—Criticism, interpretation, etc. I. Title.
BS2615.2.B29 77-482169
77 MARC

Balaguer, Ana S
Reflexiones urgentes para religiosas sobre el evangelio de San Marcos, ₍por₎ Ana S. Balaguer. Bilbao, Mensajero ₍1972₎
284 p. 20 cm. (Colección Vida religiosa, 59) Sp***
1. Bible. N. T. Mark I–IX—Meditations. I. Title.
BS2585.4.B34 74–328349

Balaguer, Enrique.
Firmes de carreteras / E. Balaguer Camphuis, J. A. Fernández del Campo. — Madrid : Gráf. J. San Martín, ₍1973₎
455 p., 4 leaves : ill. ; 23 cm. Sp 74
Includes bibliographies.
ISBN 84–400–6808–5
1. Pavements. I. Fernández del Campo, J. Antonio, joint author. II. Title.
TE250.B27 75–542670

Balaguer, Irene
see
Balaguer i Felip, Irene.

Balaguer, João Carlos B., 1949- joint author.
see Malta, Christovão Piragibe Tostes. Você conhece processo civil?. Rio de Janeiro, Editora Rio, 1975-

Balaguer, Joaquín, 1906–
Apuntes para una historia prosódica de la métrica castellana / Joaquín Balaguer. — Santo Domingo, República Dominicana : ₍s. n.₎, 1974.
269 p. ; 24 cm.
1. Spanish language—Versification. I. Title.
PC4511.B3 1973 75–532008

Balaguer, Joaquín, 1906-
El centinela de la frontera, vida y hazañas de Antonio Duvergé. Santo Domingo, Librería Hispaniola, 1970.
202 p. (Colección Pensamiento dominicano, 47)
1. Duvergé, Antonio, 1807-1853. I. Title.
ICU NUC75-36306

Balaguer, Joaquín, 1906–
El centinela de la frontera : vida y hazañas de Antonio Duvergé / Joaquín Balaguer. — 2. ed. — Santo Domingo : ₍s. n.₎, 1974.
190 p., ₍18₎ leaves of plates : ill. ; 22 cm.
1. Duvergé, Antonio. 2. Dominican Republic—History—1844–1930. I. Title.
F1938.4.D872B34 1974 75–544803

Balaguer, Joaquín, 1906–
Colón, precursor literario / Joaquín Balaguer. — 2. ed. — Santo Domingo : ₍s. n.₎, 1974.
150 p. ; 22 cm.
Includes bibliographical references.
1. Colombo, Cristoforo. 2. Dominican literature—History and criticism. I. Title.
E112.B15 1974 75–546741

Balaguer, Joaquín, 1906–
Discursos / ₍Joaquín Balaguer₎. — 1. ed. — Santo Domingo : ₍s. n.₎, 19
v. : ill. ; 22 cm.
CONTENTS:
—t. 2. La marcha hacia el capitolio.
1. Dominican Republic—Politics and government—1961– —Addresses, essays, lectures.
F1938.55.B29 75–553468

Balaguer, Joaquín, 1906–
Guía emocional de la ciudad romántica. Santo Domingo, República Dominicana, Ediciones ALPA ₍1969₎
140 p. illus. 28 cm.
1. Santo Domingo—Description. I. Title.
F1939.S4B34 72–362219

Balaguer, Joaquín, 1906–
Guía emocional de la ciudad romántica / Joaquín Balaguer. — Santo Domingo, República Dominicana : ₍s. n.₎, ₍1974?₎
220 p. : ill. (some col.) ; 28 cm.
Includes index.
1. Santo Domingo—Description. 2. Santo Domingo—Poetry. I. Title.
F1939.S4B34 1974 972.93 75–568176

Balaguer, Joaquín, 1906-
Historia de la literatura dominicana; premio nacional de obras didacticas, 1956. 5. ed. [corregida] Santo Domingo, J. D. Postigo, 1970.
370 p. illus. 22 cm.
1. Dominican literature–History and criticism. I. Title.
TxU NB GU NUC74-122431

Balaguer, Joaquín, 1906–
Historia de la literatura dominicana / Joaquín Balaguer. — 5. ed., corr. y aumentada. — ₍s. l. : s. n., 1972?₎ (B₍ueno₎s A₍ire₎s : Gráfica Guadalupe) 1972?
372 p. : ports. ; 23 cm.
Includes indexes.
1. Dominican literature—History and criticism. I. Title.
PQ7400.B26 1972 75–544814

Balaguer, Joaquín, 1906–
La marcha hacia el Capitolio : ₍temas políticos : dos campañas electorales 1966–1970 y 1970–1974₎ / Joaquín Balaguer. — 1. ed. — Santo Domingo : ₍s. n.₎, 1973.
477 p., ₍27₎ leaves of plates : ill. ; 22 cm. — (His Discursos ; t. 2)
1. Dominican Republic—Politics and government—1961– —Addresses, essays, lectures. I. Title.
F1938.55.B29 t. 2 75–553466

Balaguer, Joaquín, 1906-
Los próceres escritores. 2. ed. [Buenos Aires, Gráfica Guadalupe, 1971]
309 p.
1. Dominican literature–History and criticism. 2. Dominican Republic–Biography. I. Title.
PPiU NUC74-122428

Balaguer, Joaquín, 1906–
Temas educativos y actividades diplomáticas / Joaquín Balaguer. — 1. ed. — Santo Domingo : ₍s. n.₎, 1973.
326 p. ; 22 cm. — (His Discuros ; t. 3)
1. Dominican Republic—Foreign relations—Addresses, essays, lectures. 2. Education—Dominican Republic—Addresses, essays, lectures. 3. Latin America—Addresses, essays, lectures. I. Title.
F1938.55.B29 t. 3 75–546147
[F1938.2]

Balaguer, Jorge Rubió y
see Rubió y Balaguer, Jorge, 1887-

Balaguer, José María Escrivá de
see Escrivá de Balaguer, José María, 1902-1975.

Balaguer, Luis, 1934-
Libro titulado de primera mano las coplas de nuestros santos patronos San Servando y San Germán, vulgo de las dos Españas / ₍por₎ Luis Balaguer. — 1. ed. — Madrid : Rialp, D.L. 1976.
80 p., 2 leaves ; 18 cm. — (Adonais ; 337) Sp77-Mar
On cover: Las coplas de nuestros patronos San Servando y San Germán.
Poems.
ISBN 8432118966 : 75ptas
I. Title. II. Title: Las coplas de nuestros patronos San Servando y San Germán.
PQ6652.A37L5 77-471592
77 MARC

Balaguer, Manuel.
Une Oasis en Périgord : la Double de Dordogne, pays de conquêtes, terre de beauté / Manuel Balaguer, ... ; illustrations de Lilian Longaud ; ₍publié par₎ la Double du Périgord et les amis de la forêt. — ₍Montpon-Ménestérol₎ : la Double du Périgord et les amis de la forêt ; ₍Périgueux₎ : ₍P. Fanlac₎, 1974.
342 p., ₍6₎ leaves of plates : ill. ; 23 cm. F75-10410
Bibliography: p. 339-340.
60.00F
1. Dordogne, France (Dept.) I. Title.
DC611.D7B34 75-519101
76 MARC

Balaguer, Pedro Bohigas
see Bohigas Balaguer, Pedro, 1901-

Balaguer, Soledad, 1947-
Frente Polisario : la última guerrilla / Soledad Balaguer, Rafael Wirth. — 1. ed. — Barcelona : Editorial Laia, 1976.
157 p., ₍4₎ leaves of plates : ill. ; 20 cm. — (Laia/paperback ; 24) Sp***
ISBN 8472228738
1. Frente Popular para la Liberación de Saguía El Hamra y Río de Oro. 2. Spanish Sahara—Politics and government. I. Wirth, Rafael, 1943- II. Title.
JQ3701.S346F733 329.9′64′8 77-458739
77 MARC

Balaguer, Vicente Nicolau
see
Nicolau Balaguer, Vicente.

Balaguer, Víctor, 1824-1901.
Don Juan de Serrallonga. Victor Balaguer. Madrid, TEBAS, 1975.
287 p. 19 cm. (La novela histórica española, 17)
ISBN 84-7273-089-1.
I. Title. II. Series.
CaBVaU NUC77-82678

Balaguer, Víctor, 1824–1901.
Guía de Barcelona a Arenys de Mar por el ferro-carril. Barcelona, Imp. Nueva de J. Jepús y R. Villegas, 1857. [Mataró, Caja de Ahorros Layetana, 1973]
104 p. illus. 18 cm. Sp***
1. Barcelona (Province)—Description and travel—Guide-books. I. Title.
DP302.B36B24 1973 914.6'72'047 74–320134

Balaguer Albás, José María Escrivá de
see
Escrivá de Balaguer, José María, 1902- rev73

Balaguer Camphuis, Enrique
see
Balaguer, Enrique.

Balaguer i Felip, Irene.
Com equipar una guarderia infantil / Irene Balaguer i Felip, Adela Boix i Junquera, Pepa Odena i Savé. — 1. ed. — Barcelona : Editorial Nova Terra, 1974.
95 p. : ill. ; 20 cm. — (Quaderns d'Educació ; no. 10) Sp***
Bibliography: p. 67–70.
ISBN 84–280–0818–3 : 120ptas
1. Kindergartens. 2. Schools—Furniture, equipment, etc. I. Boix i Junquera, Adela, joint author. II. Odena i Savé, Pepa, joint author. III. Title.
LB3325.K5B34 75–553335

Balaguer Perigüell, Emilio.
La introducción del modelo físico-matemético en la medicina moderna. Análisis de la obra de G. A. Borelli (1608–1679): De motu animalium. Valencia, etc. [Cátedra de Historia de la Medicina. Facultad de Medicina, etc.] 1974.
163 p., illus. 21 cm. (Cuadernos hispánicos de historia de la medicina y de la ciencia, 14. Serie A: Monografías) Sp 74–Apr
Bibliography: p. [151]–163.
1. Borelli, Giovanni Alfonso, 1608–1679. De motu animalium. 2. Medicine—History. I. Title. II. Series.
QP301.B63B34 74–351824
ISBN 84–600–6055–1

Balaguer Vintró, Ignacio.
Hiperlipidemias : tratamiento dietético y farmacológico / por Balaguer Vintró y A. Corominas Vilardell. — 1. ed. — Barcelona : Jims, 1975.
xi, 282 p. : ill. ; 25 cm. Sp75-Oct
Includes bibliographies and index.
ISBN 8470921185 : 1500ptas
1. Hyperlipemia. I. Corominas Vilardell, Augusto, joint author. II. Title. [DNLM: 1. Hyperlipemia—diet therapy. 2. Hyperlipemia—drug therapy. WD200 B171h 1975]
[RC632.H87B34] 616.3'99 75-675571
Shared Cataloging with •76 MARC
DNLM

Balaguer y Albás, José María Escrivá de
see
Escrivá de Balaguer, José María, 1902-

Balaguer y Ricardo, Joaquín
see
Balaguer, Joaquín, 1906-

Balagueró Lladó, L
El carcinoma in situ del cuello uterino, por L. Balagueró Lladó. [1. ed.] Barcelona, Editorial Espaxs [1971]
xv, 255 p. illus. 27 cm. Sp***
Bibliography: p. [221]–250.
1. Cervix uteri—Cancer. I. Title.
[DNLM: 1. Carcinoma in Situ-Pathology. 2. Cervix neoplasms—Pathology. WP 460 B171c 1971]
[RC280.U8B34] 73–595411
Shared Cataloging with DNLM

Balagura, Saul.
Hunger; a biopsychological analysis. New York, Basic Books [1973]
vii, 181 p. illus. 22 cm. (Basic topics in physiological psychology series) $8.95
Includes bibliographies.
1. Hunger. 2. Psychology, Physiological.
QP141.B258 599'.01'32 73–78464
ISBN 0–465–03190–0 MARC

Balahuri, Éduard Adal'bertovich
see
Balahuri, Eduard Adal'bertovych.

Balagurov, Íàkov Alekseevich.
(Bor'ba za Sovety v Karel'skom Pomor'e)
Борьба за Советы в Карельском Поморье. Изд. 2-е, перераб. и доп. Петрозаводск, "Карелия," 1973.
160 p. with illus., 1 l. of diagrs. 20 cm. 0.43rub USSR 73
At head of title: Я. А. Балагуров.
Includes bibliographical references.
1. Karelia—History. I. Title.
DK265.8.K35B3 1973 74–313546

Balagurov, Íàkov Alekseevich.
(Karelii͡a v gody pervoĭ russkoĭ revoli͡ut͡sii (1905–1907))
Карелия в годы первой русской революции (1905–1907) / Я. А. Балагуров. — Петрозаводск : Карелия, 1977.
110 p. : ill. ; 21 cm. USSR 77
Includes bibliographical references.
0.19rub
1. Karelia—History. 2. Russia—History—Revolution of 1905. I. Title.
DK265.8.K35B33 77–514440

Balagurov, Íàkov Alekseevich
see Ocherki istorii Karel'skoĭ organizat͡sii KPSS. 1974.

Balagurov, Vladimir Aleksandrovich.
(Beskontaktnye dvigateli postoi͡annogo toka s postoi͡annymi magnitami)
Бесконтактные двигатели постоянного тока с постоянными магнитами / В. А. Балагуров, В. М. Грилин, В. К. Лозенко. — Москва : Энергия, 1975.
127 p. : ill. ; 20 cm. USSR 76
Bibliography: p. 123–[124]
0.40rub
1. Electric motors, Direct current. 2. Commutation (Electricity) 3. Transistor circuits. 4. Magnets. I. Gridin, Vladimir Mikhaĭlovich, joint author. II. Lozenko, Valeriĭ Konstantinovich, joint author. III. Title.
TK2681.B27 76–517762

Balagurov, Vladimir Aleksandrovich, ed.
see Postoi͡annye magnity. [1972]

Balagurunathan, C S 1930–
குலநிதி. [எழுதியவர்] செ. சு. பாலகுருநாதன். [1. பதிப்பு] சென்னை, தமிழ் எழுத்தாளர் கூட்டுறவுச் சங்கம் [1970]
136 p. (p. [133]–136 advertisements) 19 cm. (தமிழ் உறவு, 59)
In Tamil.
A novel.
I. Title. Title romanized: Kulaniti.
PL4758.9.B22K8 72–922159

Balagurunathan, C S 1930–
ஓடி விளையாடு பாப்பா. [எழுதியவர்] செ. சு. பாலகுருநாதன். [1. பதிப்பு] சென்னை, கலைமகள் காரியாலயம் [1971]
68 p. col. illus. 22 cm. Rs3.50
"இந்திய அரசாங்கத்தின் பரிசுபெற்ற புத்தகம்."
In Tamil.
1. Sports for children. I. Title.
Title romanized: Ōṭi viḷaiyāṭu pāppā.
GV709.2.B34 74–923892

Balahur, Paul.
Anotimpul corăbiilor : [versuri] / Paul Balahur. — Iași : "Junimea" 1974.
71 p. ; 20 cm. — (Colecția Lyra) R 75–289
lei 5.50
I. Title.
PC840.12.A485A8 75–577848

Balahur, Paul.
Făt-Frumos din grai : poezii / Paul Balahur ; [coperta, Dumitru Verdeș]. — [București] : Editura Eminescu, 1976.
110 p. ; 20 cm. R76-3670
lei7.75
I. Title.
PC840.12.A485F3 77-460488
•77 MARC

Balahuri, Eduard Adal'bertovych.
(Zakarpatti͡a—zemli͡a slov'i͡ans'ka)
Закарпаття—земля слов'янська : з історії слов'янських племен Закарпаття VI–XIII ст. : нариси / Е. А. Балагурі, С. І. Пеняк. — Ужгород : Карпати, 1976.
156, [4] p. : ill. ; 17 cm. USSR***
Bibliography: p. 156–[157]
0.27rub
1. Zakarpatskaya oblast—Antiquities. 2. Ethnology—Russia—Zakarpatskaya oblastĭ. I. Peni͡ak, Stephan Ivanovich, joint author. II. Title.
DK511.Z3B34 76–525934

Balai, 5th cent.
see Ephraem Syrus, Saint. Wybrane pieśni i poematy syryjskie. Warszawa, Akademia Teologii katolickiej, 1973.

Balai Bahasa.
The Instituut voor Taal- en Cultuuronderzoek of Universitas Indonesia was established in 1946. The name was changed in 1950 to Lembaga Penjelidikan Bahasa dan Kebudajaan. In 1952 it merged with Balai Bahasa to form Lembaga Bahasa dan Budaja. The latter was separated from the University in 1959 and reorganized as Lembaga Bahasa dan Kesusastraan. In 1966 the name of the latter was changed to Direktorat Bahasa dan Kesusastraan, in 1969 to Lembaga Bahasa Nasional, and in 1975 to Pusat Pembinaan dan Pengembangan Bahasa.
Works by these bodies are found under the following headings according to the name used at the time of publication:
Universitas Indonesia. Instituut voor Taal- en Cultuuronderzoek.
Universitas Indonesia. Lembaga Penjelidikan Bahasa dan Kebudajaan.
Balai Bahasa.
Universitas Indonesia. Lembaga Bahasa dan Budaja.
Lembaga Bahasa dan Kesusastraan.
Indonesia. Direktorat Bahasa dan Kesusastraan.
Lembaga Bahasa Nasional.
Pusat Pembinaan dan Pengembangan Bahasa.

Balai Besar Penjelidikan Kehutanan.
In 1913 the Proefstation voor het Boschwezen was established. In 1928 the name was changed to Bosbouwproefstation; during the period 1942–45 the body was known as Ringyoo Sikenzyoo, and in 1945 the Indonesian form of name, Balai Penjelidikan Kehutanan, came into use. In 1956 the name was changed to Balai Besar Penjelidikan Kehutanan, and in 1957, to Lembaga Pusat Penjelidikan Kehutanan. This body was abolished in 1961; its subordinate research agencies continued to exist as separate institutes.
Works by this body are found under the name used at the time of publication.
73–212815

Balai Geografi.
In 1955 the Instituut Geografi of the Republic of Indonesia became Balai Geografi and, in 1961, Dinas Geografi. In 1968 its functions were assumed by Lembaga Geografi.
Works by these bodies are found under the following headings according to the name used at the time of publication:
Instituut Geografi.
Balai Geografi.
Indonesia. Dinas Geografi.
Lembaga Geografi.

Balai Hidrologi dan Hidrometri.
Angka² aliran sungai² di Djawa dan Sumatra. Bandung [1958?]
58 l. illus. 34 cm. (Its Penerbitan 1)
Title from label mounted on cover.
1. Stream measurements—Java. 2. Stream measurements—Sumatra. I. Title. II. Series.
GB1345.B34 S A 68–20129
PL 480: Indo–6588

Balai Hidrologi dan Hidrometri
see also
Indonesia. Dinas Hidrologi.

Balai Kursus Tertulis Pendidikan Guru.
Didaktik dan metodik. -- Bandung : Balai Kursus Tertulis Pendidikan Guru, 195-
v. : ill. ; 27 cm.
Caption title.
"Kursus Guru B-B IV."
1. Education--Study and teaching. 2. Education--Indonesia. I. Title.
NIC NUC77-94473

Balai Kursus Tertulis Pendidikan Guru.
Ilmu djiwa anak. -- Bandung : Balai Kursus Tertulis Pendidikan Guru, 195-
v. : ill. ; 27 cm.
Cover title.
"Kursus guru A-C V."
Contents:--1. Masa sekolah.
1. Child study. I. Title.
NIC NUC77-94521

Balai Kursus Tertulis Pendidikan Guru.
Ilmu djiwa : bag. ilmu djiwa umum. -- Bandung : Balai Kursus Tertulis Pendidikan Guru, 195-
v. : ill. ; 27 cm.
Cover title.
"Kursus pengadjar A IV/K. G. B. -D IV."
1. Psychology. I. Title.
NIC NUC77-94472

Balai Kursus Tertulis Pendidikan Guru.
Ilmu pendidikan umum. -- Bandung : Balai Kursus Tertulis Pendidikan Guru, 195-
v. : ill. ; 27 cm.
Caption title.
"Kursus Guru B-B IV."
1. Education--Study and teaching. 2. Education--Indonesia. I. Title.
NIC NUC77-94522

Balai Kursus Tertulis Pendidikan Guru.
Menggambar dalam praktek di S. R. -- Bandung : Balai Kursus [Tertulis] Pendidikan Guru, 195-.
64 p. : ill. ; 27 cm
Cover title.
"K. G. A. -C V."
Cover title.
"Kursus guru A-A VI."
1. Drawing. 2. Child study. 3. Children as artists. I. Title.
NIC NUC77-94520

Balai Kursus Tertulis Pendidikan Guru.
Metodik berhitung : bahan peladjaran kelas 4 sampai kelas 6. -- Bandung : Balai Kursus Tertulis Pendidikan Guru, 195-.
[23] p. : ill. ; 27 cm.
Caption title.
"Kursus pengadjar-B I."
"Nomor istimewa."
1. Arithmetic--Study and teaching (Primary)
I. Title.
NIC NUC77-94490

Balai Kursus Tertulis Pendidikan Guru.
Pendidikan djasmani : teori, tudjuan dan sistimatik. -- Bandung : Balai Kursus Tertulis Pendidikan Guru, 195-.
28 p. : ill. ; 27 cm.
Cover title.
"Kursus guru B-D IV."
1. Physical education and training--Indonesia.
I. Title.
NIC NUC77-94519

Balai Kursus Tertulis Pendidikan Guru.
Pengadjaran bahasa : bagaimana kita mengadjarkan bahasa kepada anak2 di S. R. -- Bandung : Balai Kursus Tertulis Pendidikan Guru, 195-.
76 p. : ill. ; 27 cm.
Cover title.
"Kursus pengadjar-D IV."
1. Teaching. 2. Education of children.
I. Title.
NIC NUC77-94518

Balai Kursus Tertulis Pendidikan Guru.
Pengadjaran membatja dan menulis permulaan. -- Bandung : Balai Kursus Tertulis Pendidikan Guru, 195-.
48 p. : ill. ; 27 cm.
Cover title.
"Kursus Guru Atas-B V."
1. Reading. 2. Writing. I. Title.
NIC NUC77-94480

Balai Kursus Tertulis Pendidikan Guru.
Pengadjaran membatja landjutan. -- Bandung : Balai Kursus Tertulis Pendidikan Guru, 195-.
[23] p. : ill. ; 27 cm.
Caption title.
"Kursus pengadjar."
"Nomor istimewa."
1. Reading. 2. Writing. I. Title.
NIC NUC77-94481

Balai muhibbah.
[Kuala Lumpur] Kementerian Perpaduan Negara.
no. illus. 38 cm.
1. Malaysia—Periodicals. I. Malaysia. Kementerian Perpaduan Negara.
DS591.B34 78-942895
MARC-S

Balai Pendidikan Guru Bandung.
Ilmu bumi Indonesia. -- Bandung : Balai Pendidikan Guru, 195-
v. : ill. ; 27 cm. -- ([Its publication] 84)
Cover title.
Vol. 4B: Tjet. 3.
1. Physical geography--Text-books--1945- I. Title.
NIC NUC77-94488

Balai Pendidikan Guru Bandung.
Ilmu ukur bidang. -- Bandung : Balai Pendidikan Guru, 195-
v. : ill. ; 27 cm. -- ([Its publication] 111)
Cover title.
1. Geometry. I. Title.
NIC NUC77-94489

Balai Pendidikan Guru Bandung.
Menggambar. -- Bandung : Balai Pendidikan Guru, 195-
v. : ill. ; 27 cm. -- ([Its publication] 101, 161)
Cover title.
Vol. 4B: Tjet. 2.
1. Drawing--Instruction. I. Title.
NIC NUC77-94487

Balai Pendidikan Guru Bandung.
Pekerdjaan tangan. -- Bandung : Balai Pendidikan Guru, 195-
v. : ill. ; 27 cm. -- ([Its publication] 223)
Cover title.
Contents. --3. Pekerdjaan teknis.
1. Handicraft. I. Title.
NIC NUC77-94486

Balai Pendidikan Guru Bandung.
Seni suara. -- Bandung : Balai Pendidikan Guru, 195-
v. : ill. ; 27 cm. -- ([Its publication] 109)
Cover title.
1. Music--Instruction and study--Juvenile.
I. Title.
NIC NUC77-94485

Balai Penelitian dan Peninjauan Sosial.
Balai Persiapan Pekerdjaan Sosial was established in 1952. In 1956 the name was changed to Balai Penjelidikan dan Penjandraan Sosial; and in 1961 to Balai Penelitian dan Peninjauan Sosial.
Works by this body are found under the name used at the time of publication.

Balai Penelitian dan Penindjauan Sosial.
Facts and figures on social work in Indonesia, 1966-1970. — Jogjakarta : Dept. of Social Affairs, Institute of Social Research and Observation, [1971]
47 leaves : ill. ; 35 cm.
1. Public welfare—Indonesia—Statistics. 2. Indonesia—Social conditions. I. Title.
HV403.B34 1971 362'.9598 76-941000
77 MARC

Balai Penelitian dan Peninjauan Sosial.
Fertility levels of women from a variety of personal, social, economic, and educational conditions. Jogjakarta, 1971.
84 p. 32 cm.
Translation of Tingkat[2] fertilita wanita dalam pelbagai kondisi pribadi, sosial, ekonomi dan pendidikan.
Includes bibliographical references.
1. Fertility, Human—United States. 2. Indonesia—Population. I. Title.
HB903.F4B34 1971 301.32'1'09598 72-941555
73[r77]rev MARC

Balai Penelitian dan Peninjauan Sosial.
Kumpulan ringkasan hasil penelitian sosial B. P. P. S., tahun 1966–1969. Jogjakarta, 1970.
143 p. 21 cm.
Cover title.
1. Social science research—Indonesia. I. Title.
H62.5.I 6B34 1969 74–940487

Balai Penelitian dan Peninjauan Sosial.
Laporan hasil survey bidang sosial ekonomi daerah parameter II kotamadya Yogyakarta, th. 1975 dalam rangka Kampong Improvement Program (K.I.P.) / oleh kerjasama antara BPPS Departemen Sosial, [Direktorat Jenderal] Direktorat Tata Kota dan Tata Daerah, Cipta Karya dengan Unicef. — [Yogyakarta : s.n., 1975]
ix, 133 p. : maps ; 33 cm.
1. Yogyakarta, Indonesia—Economic conditions. 2. Yogyakarta, Indonesia—Social conditions. I. Indonesia. Direktorat Tata Kota dan Tata Daerah. II. United Nations. Children's Fund. III. Title: Laporan hasil survey bidang sosial ekonomi daerah parameter II ...
HC448.Y63B34 1975 76-941720
77 MARC

Balai Penelitian dan Peninjauan Sosial.
Pandangan singkat tentang maksud dan tudjuan Balai Penelitian dan Penindjauan Sosial. A short view of the scope and aim of the Institute for Social Research and Observation. Jogjakarta [1967?]
18 p. 21 cm.
Cover title.
English and Indonesian.
1. Social service—Research—Indonesia.
HV11.B27 1967 S A 68–15987
PL 480 : Indo–8252

Balai Penelitian Industri
see Seminar Container, Jakarta, Indonesia, 1974. Hasil Seminar Container Balai Penelitian Industri dan Lembaga Penelitian... Jakarta: Proyek Balai Penelitian Industri, 1974.

Balai Penelitian Keramik.
Hasil-hasil penelitian atas survey bahan-bahan mentah keramik didaerah Djawa Barat; laporan. [Bandung] 1971–
v. fold. maps (in pocket) 33 cm.
Cover title.
Abstract in English.
Bibliography: v. 1, leaf 174.
1. Ceramic materials—Testing. I. Title.
TA430.B34 1971 73–940368

Balai Penelitian Keramik
see Lokakarya Keramik, Bandung, Indonesia, 1972. Paper[s] untuk Lokakarya Keramik. [Bandung, 1972-

Balai Penelitian Kimia.

For works by this body issued under its earlier name see

Bogor, Indonesia. Balai Penjelidikan Kimia.

Balai Penelitian Perkebunan Banda Atjeh
see Dinas Perkebunan Rakjat Atjeh. Survey pengusahaan nilam rakjat didaerah Atjeh... [n.p., 1971?]

Balai Penelitian Perkebunan Bogor.
Balai Penjelidikan Perkebunan Besar and Balai Penjelidikan dan Pemakaian Karet merged on Dec. 31, 1968, to form Balai Penelitian Perkebunan Bogor.
Works by these bodies are found under the following headings according to the name used at the time of publication:
Bogor, Indonesia. Balai Penjelidikan Perkebunan Besar.
Bogor, Indonesia. Balai Penjelidikan dan Pemakaian Karet.
Balai Penelitian Perkebunan Bogor.
73–203963

Balai Penelitian Perkebunan Bogor.
Beberapa panadangan mengenai standard Indonesian rubber (SIR). — [Bogor] : Balai Penelitian Perkebunan Bogor, [1969]
14 leaves ; 30 cm. — (Bulletin - Balai Penelitian Perkebunan Bogor ; no. 6)
1. Rubber—Indonesia. I. Title. II. Series: Balai Penelitian Perkebunan Bogor. Bulletin - Balai Penelitian Perkebunan Bogor ; no. 6.
TS1885.I 55B35 1969 76–940564

Balai Penelitian Perkebunan Bogor.
Laporan perkembangan. Bogor, 1973.
[30] l. 29 cm.
1. Balai Penelitian Perkebunan Bogor. 2. Plantations—Indonesia.
HD1471.I 5B34 1973 73–942317

Balai Penelitian Perkebunan Bogor.
Statistik coklat. 1970/72–
[Bogor] Balai Penelitian Perkebunan Bogor.
v. 33 cm.
Vols. for 1970–72 issued together.
Continues: Balai Penelitian Perkebunan Bogor. Statistik tjoklat.
English and Indonesian.
Vols. for 1970/72– issued in cooperation with Biro Pusat Statistik.
1. Cocoa — Indonesia — Statistics — Periodicals. I. Indonesia. Biro Pusat Statistik.
HD9200.I 5B33 75–645440
MARC-S

Balai Penelitian Perkebunan Bogor.
Statistik karet.
[Bogor] Balai Penelitian Perkebunan Bogor.
v. 21 x 33 cm.
English and Indonesia.
Vols. for issued in cooperation with Biro Pusat Statistik.
1. Rubber industry and trade—Indonesia—Statistics. I. Indonesia Biro Pusat Statistik.
HD9161.I 6B34a 76–640110
MARC-S

Balai Penelitian Perkebunan Bogor.
Statistik kopi. 1968–
[Bogor. Indonesia] Balai Penelitian Perkebunan Bogor.
v. 34 cm. annual.
English and Indonesian.
Vols. for 1968– issued in cooperation with Biro Pusat Statistik of Indonesia and Direktorat Djendral Perkebunan of Indonesia.
1. Coffee trade—Indonesia—Statistics—Periodicals. 2. Coffee—Indonesia—Statistics—Periodicals. I. Indonesia. Biro Pusat Statistik. II. Indonesia. Direktorat Djenderal Perkebunan. III. Title.
HD9199.I 45B34a 74–941637
MARC-S

Balai Penelitian Perkebunan Bogor.
Statistik teh. 1970/71– Bogor.
v. 33 cm.
Volume for 1970/71 covers period 1970–71.
English and Indonesian.
Vols. for issued in cooperation with Biro Pusat Statistik.
1. Tea trade—Indonesia—Statistics—Periodicals. I. Indonesia. Biro Pusat Statistik. II. Title.
HD9198.I 52B34a 74–646962
MARC-S

Balai Penelitian Perkebunan Bogor
see Lamb, James. Technical cooperation scheme of Colombo plan. Bogor [1972]

Balai Penelitian Perkebunan Bogor
see Laporan penyelenggaraan Simposium International Rubber Research and Development Board... Bogor : Balai Penelitian Perkebunan Bogor [1973]

Balai Penelitian Perkebunan Bogor
see McIntyre, G A Report on biometrical services... Bogor, 1971.

Balai Penelitian Perkebunan Bogor
see Pertemuan Teh, Bogor, Indonesia, 1973. Perumusan, Bogor, 1-3 Maret 1973. Bogor [1973]

Balai Penelitian Perkebunan Bogor
see Technical Meeting Standard Indonesian Rubber, 1st, Bogor, Indonesia, 1970. Technical Meeting Standard Indonesian Rubber, Bogor, 4–5 Mei 1970... [Bogor, 1970]

Balai Penelitian Perkebunan Medan
see
Sumatra Planters Association. Research Institute.

Balai Penelitian Perkebunan Tjabang Djember
see Jahmadi, M Budidaja dan pengolahan kopi. [Djember] 1972.

Balai Penelitian Perkebunan Tjabang Djember
see Situmorang, Sangap. Budidaja dan pengolahan tjoklat. ₍Djember, 1972₎

Balai Penelitian Tembakau Deli.
Kultura tembakau Deli. Medan [1969?]
14 l.
1. Tobacco. Indonesia. I. Title.
DNAL NUC75-108514

Balai Penerbitan Adabi. Unit Pengajian Ekonomi.
see Kamus ekonomi. Edisi 1. Kota Bharu, Balai Penerbitan Adabi, 1973.

Balai Penjelidikan Beras
see Cultivation, manuring & watering "sawah-rice". [n. p.] Multiplied and circulated by the Service of Agricultural Extension, 1st Grade Territory West-Java, Section: Publication, Documentation and Agricultural Information, 1962.

Balai Penjelidikan dan Pemakaian Karet
see
Bogor, Indonesia. Balai Penjelidikan dan Pemakaian Karet.

Balai Penjelidikan dan Penjandraan Sosial.
Balai Persiapan Pekerdjaan Sosial was established in 1952. In 1956 the name was changed to Balai Penjelidikan dan Penjandraan Sosial: and in 1931 to Balai Penelitian dan Peninjauan Sosial.
Works by this body are found under the name used at the time of publication.

Balai Penjelidikan Kehutanan.
In 1913 the Proefstation voor het Boschwezen was established. In 1928 the name was changed to Bosbouwproefstation; during the period 1942-45 the body was known as Ringyoo Sikenzyoo, and in 1945 the Indonesian form of name, Balai Penjelidikan Kehutanan, came into use. In 1956 the name was changed to Balai Besar Penjelidikan Kehutanan, and in 1957, to Lembaga Pusat Penjelidikan Kehutanan. This body was abolished in 1961; its subordinate research agencies continued to exist as separate institutes.
Works by this body are found under the name used at the time of publication.
73-212809

Balai Penjelidikan Kehutanan.
Daftar pohon-pohonan Djambi (Sumatera) (telah diperbaiki) = Revised list of treespecies, collected in the division Jambi, Sumatra. — Bogor : Balai Penjelidikan Kehutanan, Djawatan Kehutanan, Kementerian Pertanian, 1954.
24 p. ; 29 cm. — (Seri daftar nama pohon-pohonan ; no. 14a) (Laporan Balai Penjelidikan Kehutanan ; no. 8a)
Cover title.
English and Indonesian.
1. Timber—Indonesia—Jambi (Propinsi). 2. Trees—Indonesia—Jambi (Propinsi). 3. Trees—Nomenclature (Popular). I. Title. II. Title: Revised list of treespecies, collected in the division Jambi, Sumatra. III. Series. IV. Series: Balai Penjelidikan Kehutanan. Rapport ; no. 8a.
SD97.J3B6 no. 8a 76-949573
₍SD527.I5₎ 76 MARC

Balai Penjelidikan Kehutanan. Laporan
see Balai Penjelidikan Kehutanan. Rapport. Bogor (Buitenzorg) 1948-

Balai Penjelidikan Kehutanan. Pelaporan
see Balai Penjelidikan Kehutanan. Rapport. Bogor (Buitenzorg) 1948-

Balai Penjelidikan Kehutanan.
Rapport. no. 1-
Bogor (Buitenzorg) 1948-
no. in v. 30 cm.
Supersedes Voorloopig rapport of Bosbouwproefstation.
Some issues have title and text also in English and Indonesian; some issues have summaries in English and Indonesian.
1. Forests and forestry—Indonesia—Collected works. 2. Forestry research—Indonesia—Collected works. I. Balai Penjelidikan Kehutanan. Report. II. Balai Penjelidikan Kehutanan. Laporan. III. Balai Penjelidikan Kehutanan. Pelaporan.
SD97.J3B6 52-41705
rev

Balai Penjelidikan Kehutanan. Report
see Balai Penjelidikan Kehutanan. Rapport. Bogor (Buitenzorg) 1948-

Balai Penjelidikan Kehutanan
see Serie Bosbijproducten. Bogor, Indonesia, Djawatan Kehutanan, Kementerian Kemakmuran R. I. S.

Balai Penjelidikan Padi
see also
Proefstation voor Rijst.

Balai Penjelidikan Penjakit Hewan. Library
see
Balai Penjelidikan Penjakit Hewan. Perpustakaan.

Balai Penjelidikan Penjakit Hewan. Perpustakaan.
Catalogue of publications on anaerobic bacteria in the Library of the Veterinary Institute, Bogor, Indonesia, collected and donated to the institute by F. C Kraneveld. Bogor, Veterinary Institute, 1954.
194 p. 34 cm.
Cover title.
1. Bacteria, Anaerobic—Bibliography—Catalogs. 2. Bacteriology—Bibliography—Catalogs. 3. Bacteria, Pathogenic—Bibliography—Catalogs. I. Kraneveld, F. C. II. Title.
Z5180.B34 1954 56-40143
rev

Balai Penjelidikan Perikanan Darat.

For works by this body issued under its later name see

Lembaga Penelitian Perikanan Darat.

Balai Penjelidikan Perusahaan Perkebunan Gula.
In 1887 the Proefstation voor de Java-Suikerindustrie was established. In 1959 its name was changed to Balai Penjelidikan Perusahaan-Perusahaan Gula. About 1965 it became Balai Penjelidikan Perkebunan Gula.
Works by this body published before the change of name around 1965 are found under
Pasuruan, Indonesia (City). Balai Penjelidikan Perusahaan-Perusahaan Gula.
Works published after that date are found under
Balai Penjelidikan Perusahaan Perkebunan Gula.

Balai Penjelidikan Perusahaan Perkebunan Gula.
Annual report—Indonesian Sugar Experiment Station. 1966-
Pasuruan, Balai Penjelidikan Perusahaan Perkebunan Gula ₍etc.₎
v. 25 cm.
1. Sugar-cane—Indonesia—Periodicals. 2. Sugar-cane—Periodicals. 3. Balai Penjelidikan Perusahaan Perkebunan Gula.
SB215.B34a 77-649321
MARC-S

Balai Penjelidikan Perusahaan Perkebunan Gula.
Bulletin Balai Penjelidikan Perusahaan Perkebunan Gula. no. 1- Sept. 1968-
Pasuruan, Indonesia ₍Balai Penjelidikan Perusahaan Perkebunan Gula₎
no. 35 cm.
Indonesian with summaries in English.
1. Sugar-cane—Indonesia—Collected works. 2. Sugar-cane—Collected works.
SB229.I 5B34a 76-646478
MARC-S

Balai Penjelidikan Perusahaan Perkebunan Gula
see Lauw, Ing Biauw. Statistik tentang tanaman tebu tahun 1962 dan 1963. [Pasuruan] 1966.

Balai Penjelidikan Perusahaan Perkebunan Gula
see Madjalah perusahaan gula. Djuni 1965- Pasuruan, B. P. U.-P. P. N.-Gula.

Balai Penjelidikan Tehnik Pertanian.
Laporan tahunan—Balai Penjelidikan Tehnik Pertanian. ₍Bogor₎ Balai Penjelidikan Tehnik Pertanian.
v. in 25 cm.
1. Balai Penjelidikan Tehnik Pertanian. 2. Agriculture—Indonesia—Periodicals. 3. Agriculture—Periodicals.
S297.B36a 75-647980
MARC-S

Balai Penlitian dan Penindjauan Sosial
see
Balai Penelitian dan Peninjauan Sosial.

Balai Perguruan Tinggi
see
Universitas Indonesia.

Balai Persiapan Pekerdjaan Sosial.
Balai Persiapan Pekerdjaan Sosial was established in 1952. In 1956 the name was changed to Balai Penjelidikan dan Penjandraan Sosial; and in 1931 to Balai Penelitian dan Peninjauan Sosial.
Works by this body are found under the name used at the time of publication.

Balai Pustaka, Djakarta
see Bina pantjasila. 10 Feb. 1966- [Djakarta]

Balai Seni Lukis Negara. Annual report
see Balai Seni Lukis Negara. Lapuran tahunan——Balai Seni Lukis Negara Malaysia. [Kuala Lumpur]

Balai Seni Lukis Negara.
Empat abad seni China dalam kumpulan persendirian = Four centuries of Chinese art in private collections / Balai Seni Lukis Negara, 28hb. Mei-17hb. Jun 1973. — Kuala Lumpur : Balai, ₍1973?₎
26 p. : ill. ; 25 cm.
English and Malay.
1. Art, Chinese—Exhibitions. 2. Art, Chinese—Ming-Ch'ing dynasties, 1368-1912—Exhibitions. 3. Art, Chinese—20th century—Exhibitions. 4. Art—Private collections. I. Title. II. Title: Four centuries of Chinese art in private collections.
N7343.5.B34 1973 73-942697
77 MARC

Balai Seni Lukis Negara.
Lapuran tahunan—Balai Seni Lukis Negara Malaysia. ₍Kuala Lumpur₎ Balai Seni Lukis Negara Malaysia.
v. 23 cm.
Added title page title : Annual report.
English and Malay.
1. Balai Seni Lukis Negara. I. Balai Seni Lukis Negara. Annual report.
N3750.K8A3 708'.9595'1 75-644067
MARC-S

Balai Seni Lukis Negara. Lembaga Amanah.
Annual report.
Kuala Lumpur.
v. in 25 cm.
Supersedes its Report.
N3750.K8B322 708'.95951 72-949511

Balai Seni Lukis Negara. Lembaga Amanah.
Report. 1964-
Kuala Lumpur.
v. in 25 cm. annual.
Supersedes its Penyata mengenal kerja² dan kejayaan²-nya; superseded by its Annual report.
N3750.K8B32 72-949510

Balaîan, B P
(Vosstaniîa plemen na îuge Irana)
Восстания племен на юге Ирана : 1922-1930 / Б. П. Балаян. — Ереван : Изд-во Ереван. ун-та, 1974.
112 p. ; 20 cm. USSR 75
At head of title: Erevanskiĭ gosudarstvennyĭ universitet. Fakul'tet vostokovedeniîa.
Includes bibliographical references.
0.30rub
1. Iran—History. 2. Peasant uprisings—Iran. I. Title.
DS315.B28 76-527358

Balaîan, R. A.
see Nagornyi Karabakh za piat'desiat let. 1973.

Balain
see
Balin and Balan.

Balaiș, Florin.
Îndrumătorul instructorului de volei / Florin Balaiș. — ₍București₎ : "Sport-Turism," 1975.
199, ₍5₎ p. : ill. ; 20 cm. R 75-2861
Bibliography: p. ₍201₎
lei 5.50
1. Volleyball. I. Title.
GV1017.V6B24 75-548141

Bălăiță, George, 1935-
Lumea în două zile : roman / George Bălăiță ; ₍coperta, Eugen Palade₎. — București : Editura Eminescu, 1975.
393 p. ; 20 cm. R 75-4079
lei 14.50
I. Title.
PC840.12.A487L8 75-406567

Bălaj, Teofil.
Autografe pariziene. ₍Coperta de: M. Baciu₎. Cluj, „Dacia," 1972.
276 p. 20 cm. lei 7.00 R 73-2
1. Paris—Intellectual life. I. Title.
DC715.B19 73-341045

Bălaj, Teofil.
Romania. The land and the people. Foreword by Șerban Cioculescu. Translated into English by Dumitru Chițoran. Bucharest, „Meridiane," 1972.
247 p. with graphs., 44 l. of illus. (part col.), ports, and map. 19 cm. lei 20.00 R 72-4256
Translation of România se prezintă.
1. Romania. I. Title.
DR205.B2213 914.68 73-154367
MARC

Balajīta Snehī
see
Baljit Snehi, 1950-

Balajka, Bohumil, Dr., ed.
see Wolker ve fotografii. ⌈V Praze, Státní pedagogické nakl., 1965⌉

Balajka, Jiří.
Kvapalné palivá v energetike / Jiří Balajka, Stanislav Malik, Jozef Šellej ; ⌈prebal a väzbu navrhol Svetozár Mydlo⌉. — 1. vyd. — Bratislava : Alfa, 1976.
266 p. : ill. ; 21 cm. — (Edícia energetickej literatúry) CzS 76
Bibliography: p. 260-266.
Kčs24.50
1. Liquid fuels. I. Malik, Stanislav, joint author. II. Šellej, Jozef, joint author. III. Title.
TP343.B27 76-528099

al-Balak, Fu'ād
see
al-Buluk, Fu'ād.

Balák, Jaromír, ed.
see 20 years of health education in the Czech Socialist Republic. ⌈Prague, Institute of Health Education, 1973⌉

(Bālaka)
बालक.
⌈काठमाडौं, नेपाल बाल संगठन⌉
v. illus., ports. 25 cm. monthly.
In Nepali.
I. Nepāla Bāla Saṅgaṭhana.
AP215.N4B3 S A 68-5810
PL 480: N-13-S

Bālaka, Bālakr̥shṇa Garga
see
Garga, Bālakr̥shṇa.

Balakaev, Alekseĭ Guchinovich.
(Saglar)
Саглар; повести и рассказы. Алексей Балакаев. ⌈Перевод с калмыцкого⌉ Москва, Сов. Россия, 1967.
110 p. illus., port. 21 cm. (Романы, повести, рассказы Советской России)
CONTENTS: Саглар; повесть.—Три рисунка; повесть.—Аав; рассказ.
I. Title.
PL430.9.B34S2 70-201424

Balakaev, Alekseĭ Guchinovich.
(Sudite meni͡a sami)
Судите меня сами. Повесть. Авториз. пер. с калм. Г. Садовникова. ⌈Москва, "Современник," 1972⌉.
271 p. with port. 17 cm. 0.56rub USSR 72-VKP
At head of title: А. Балакаев.
I. Title.
PL428.9.B27S8 74-316103

Balakaev, Alekseĭ Guchinovich.
(Sudite meni͡a sami)
Судите меня сами : повесть / А. Балакаев ; авторизованный перевод с калмыцкого Г. Садовникова. — Москва : Современник, 1975.
270 p. : port. ; 18 cm. USSR***
I. Title.
PL430.9.B34S8 1975 75-403093

Balakaev, Alekseĭ Guchinovich.
Sudite meni͡a sami; povest'. [By] Balakaev Alekseĭ Guchinovich. Ėlista, Kalmytskoe knizhnoe izd-vo, 1969.
317 p. port.
Title page and text in Kalmuck.
Russian title from colophon.
MH NUC74-55439

Balakaev, Alekseĭ Guchinovich.
(Zeleni͡a li͡ubov')
Зеленая любовь. Повести, рассказы. Пер. с калм. ⌈Ил.: А. Р. Косолапов⌉. Москва, "Сов. писатель," 1972.
343 p. with illus. 17 cm. 0.57rub USSR 72-VKP
At head of title: Алексей Балакаев.
CONTENTS: Зеленая любовь.—Саглар.—Некрасивая.—Аава.—Песня маленькой Намджал.—Чужое счастье.—Дорога.—Сибирская легенда.—Лотос.—Легенда о земле.
I. Title.
PL429.Z77 1972 74-344380

Balakaev, Maulen Balakaevich.
Grammatika sovremennogo kazakhskogo i͡azyka. Uchebnik dli͡a filologicheskikh institutov universitetov i pedagogicheskikh institutov. Sintaksis (na kazakhskom i͡azyke) Alma-Ata, Kazuchpedgiz, 1961.
290 p. 22 cm.
Title page and text in Kazakh.
1. Kazakh language—Grammar. 2. Kazakh language—Syntax. I. Kordabaev, T., ed. II. Title.
TNJ NUC74-56448

Balakaev, Maulen Balakaevich.
⌈Qazirgi qazaq tili grammatikasy⌉
Қазіргі қазақ тілі грамматикасы. Синтаксис. Университет пен педагогтық институттардың филология факультеттеріне арналған оқулық. Өнделіп, толықтырылып 3-басылуы. Алматы, "Мектеп," 1971.
339 p. 22 cm. 0.89rub USSR 71-42654
At head of title: М. Балақаев, Т. Қордабаев.
Bibliography: p. 334-⌈335⌉
1. Kazakh language—Syntax. I. Kordabaev, T. II. Title.
PL65.K43B316 73-204966

Balakaev, Maulen Balakaevich, ed.
see Qazaq tilining grammatikasy. 196

Balakaev, Tultaĭ Balakaevich.
(Sovet ȯkimetī zholyndaghy kȯresker)
Совет өкіметі жолындағы күрескер / Т. Балақаев. — Алматы : Қазақ ССР Ғылым академиясының баспасы, 1960.
71 p. : ill. ; 21 cm.
At head of title: Qazak SSR Ghylym akademii͡asynyn͡g Tarikh, arkheologii͡a zhăne ėtnografii͡a instituty.
Includes bibliographical references.
1. Ăĭtiev, Ăbdīrakhman, 1886-1936. I. Title.
DK909.A57B34 75-588053

Balakhan, Phra Sarasas
see Sarasas Balakhan, Phra.

Balakhnicheva, T.
see Ri͡adovye kommunizma. Kishinev, Karti͡a moldoveni͡aske, 1962.

Balakhonov, Viktor Evgen'evich.
(Romen Rollan i ego vremi͡a)
Ромен Роллан и его время. Ранние годы. Ленинград, Изд-во Ленингр. ун-та, 1972.
197 p. 21 cm. 0.96rub USSR 73-VKP
At head of title: Ленинградский государственный университет имени А. А. Жданова. В. Е. Балахонов.
Includes bibliographical references.
1. Rolland, Romain, 1866-1944. 2. French literature—19th century—History and criticism. 3. French literature—20th century—History and criticism. I. Title.
PQ2635.O5Z5573 74-303377

Balakhonov, Viktor Ivanovich.
(Feodosii͡a)
Феодосия : ист.-краевед. очерк / В. Балахонов. — Симферополь : Таврия, 1975.
115 p., ⌈20⌉ leaves of plates : ill. ; 18 cm. USSR 75
0.57rub
1. Feodosiya. I. Title.
DK651.F4B24 1975 76-528293

Balakhont͡sev, Vitaliĭ Grigor'evich.
(Sblizhenie v kosmose)
Сближение в космосе. Москва Воениздат, 1973.
240 p. with illus. 21 cm. 0.78rub USSR 73
At head of title: В. Г. Балахонцев, В. А. Иванов, В. И. Шабанов.
Bibliography: p. 235-⌈238⌉
1. Orbital rendezvous (Space flight) I. Ivanov, Vitaliĭ Aleksandrovich, joint author. II. Shabanov, Vladimir Ivanovich, joint author. III. Title.
TL1095.B34 73-362866

Balakhovskai͡a, L. G.
see Zhenshchiny mira v bor'be za sotsial'nyi progress. 1972.

Balakhovskiĭ, Igor' Sergeevich.
(Obmen veshchestv v ėkstremal'nykh uslovii͡akh kosmicheskogo poleta i pri ego imitat͡sii)
Обмен веществ в экстремальных условиях космического полета и при его имитации. Москва, "Наука," 1973.
211 p. with illus., 1 l. of illus. 22 cm. (Проблемы космической биологии, т. 22) 1.71rub USSR 73
At head of title: И. С. Балаховский, Ю. В. Наточин.
On leaf preceding t. p.: Академия наук СССР. Отделение физиологии.
Includes bibliographies.
1. Space flight—Physiological effect. I. Natochin, I͡U. V., joint author. II. Akademii͡a nauk SSSR. Otdelenie fiziologii. III. Title. IV. Series: Problemy kosmicheskoĭ biologii, t. 22.
QH327.P7 t. 22 73-366149
[RC1075]

Balakhovskiĭ, M. M.
see Mezhdunarodnyi t͡sentr nauchnoi i tekhnicheskoi informat͡sii. (Slovar' sokrashchenii po informatike) Dictionary of abbreviations in informatics. 1976.

Balakhovskiĭ, M. M.
see Periodicheskie i prodolzhai͡ushchiesi͡a izdanii͡a po informatike. 1973.

Balakian, Anna Elizabeth, 1915-
Surrealism: the road to the absolute. New York, Noonday Press [1959]
209 p.
Microfilm. Washington, D.C., Library of Congress, 1966.
1. French poetry—20th cent.—Hist. & crit. 2. Surrealism.
KyU NUC75-36305

Balakian, Anna Elizabeth, 1915-
Surrealism; the road to the absolute ⌈by⌉ Anna Balakian. Rev. and enl. London, Allen & Unwin ⌈1972, c1970⌉
256 p. illus., ports. 20 cm.
Includes bibliographical references.
1. French poetry—20th century—History and criticism. 2. Surrealism.
OrPS NUC76-70897

Balakian, Nona, ed.
The creative present; notes on contemporary American fiction. Edited by Nona Balakian and Charles Simmons. 2d ed. New York, Gordian Press, 1973 ⌈c1963⌉
xxvi, 269 p. 23 cm. $8.50
Bibliography: p. ⌈257⌉-265.
1. American fiction—20th century—Addresses, essays, lectures. I. Simmons, Charles, 1924- joint ed. II. Title.
[PS379.B29 1973] 813'.5'09 77-189247
ISBN 0-87752-158-1 MARC

Balakin, Georgiĭ Nikolaevich.
O povyshenii roli Sovetov. Vladivostok, Dal'nevostochnoe kn. izd-vo, 1967.
33 p. 20 cm.
1. Soviets. I. Title.
CSt-H NUC74-55460

Balakin, Nikolaĭ Grigor'evich.
(Risunok v nebe)
Рисунок в небе. ⌈О заслуж. мастере спорта СССР, летчике И. Н. Егорове⌉. Москва, Изд-во ДОСААФ, 1973.
48 p. with illus. 16 cm. (Чемпионы СССР, Европы и мира, вып. 2) 0.07rub USSR 73
At head of title: Н. Г. Балакин.
1. Egorov, Igor' Nikolaevich, 1939- 2. Stunt flying. I. Title.
TL540.E43B34 74-300935

Balakin, Petr Petrovich.
(Khudozhniki goroda Gor'kogo)
Художники города Горького / П. П. Балакин, В. П. Батуро. — Горький : Волго-Вят. кн. изд-во, 1974.
53 p., ⌈25⌉ leaves of plates : ill. (some col.) ; 27 cm. USSR 74
Bibliography: p. 41.
1.55rub
1. Art—Gorki, Russia. 2. Art, Modern—20th century—Gorki, Russia. 3. Artists—Russia—Gorki—Biography. I. Baturo, Vladimir Petrovich, joint author. II. Title.
N6997.G6B34 75-539486

Balakin, Valeriĭ Georgievich, joint author
see Danilov, Fedor Aleksandrovich. Gori͡achai͡a prokatka i pressovanie trub. 1972.

Balakin, Vi͡acheslav Alekseevich.
⌈Khozi͡aĭstvennai͡a reforma v transportnom stroitel'stve⌉
Хозяйственная реформа в транспортном строительстве. Москва, "Транспорт," 1972.
144 p. 20 cm. 0.43rub USSR 72-VKP
At head of title: В. А. Балакин, В. В. Богданов, М. Я. Кантор.
Includes bibliographical references.
1. Construction industry—Russia. I. Bogdanov, Viktor Vasil'evich, joint author. II. Kantor, Mark I͡Akovlevich, joint author. III. Title.
HD9715.R92B2835 72-367374

Balakin, Vi͡acheslav Alekseevich.
(Novye ėkonomicheskie uslovii͡a raboty transportnykh stroitel'nykh organizat͡siĭ)
Новые экономические условия работы транспортных строительных организаций / В. А. Балакин. — Москва : Транспорт, 1975.
207 p. ; 21 cm. USSR***
Bibliography: p. 206-207.
0.72rub
1. Construction industry—Russia. I. Title.
HD9715.R92B28354 75-538370

Balakin, Vîacheslav Alekseevich.
(Osnovnye fondy i proizvodstvennye moshchnosti transportnogo stroitel'stva)
Основные фонды и производственные мощности транспортного строительства. Москва, "Транспорт," 1973.
113 p. with diagrs. 21 cm. (Труды Всесоюзного научно-исследовательского института транспортного строительства, вып. 89. Отделение экономики и организации строительства) 0.85rub
USSR 73
At head of title: В. А. Балакин.
Includes bibliographical references.
1. Construction industry—Russia. 2. Transportation. I. Title. II. Series: Babushkin, Russia. Vsesoîuznyĭ nauchno-issledovatel'skiĭ institut transportnogo stroitel'stva. Trudy, vyp. 89.
HD9715.R92B2836 73-355440

Balakina, A.S., joint author
see Ismailov, Mamadzhan Ismailovich. Ŭzbekiston marmari. 1971.

Balakina, L.M.
see Pole uprugikh naprîazheniĭ Zemli i mekhanizm ochagov zemletrîaseniĭ. 1972.

Balakina, Natal'îa Vladimirovna.
(Novye zashchitnye materialy i tekhnologicheskie prot͡sessy dlîa konservat͡sii i upakovki detaleĭ toplivnoĭ apparatury)
Новые защитные материалы и технологические процессы для консервации и упаковки деталей топливной аппаратуры / Н. В. Балакина. — Ленинград : Ленингр. организация о-ва "Знание" РСФСР, ЛДНТП, 1974.
27 p. : ill. ; 22 cm. — (Серия Улучшение качества промышленной продукции (стандартизация, надежность, защитные покрытия, техническая эстетика)) USSR 74
At head of title: Ленинградская организация общества "Знание" РСФСР. Ленинградский дом научно-технической пропаганды.
0.17rub
1. Gas and oil engines—Fuel systems—Corrosion. I. Title.
TJ787.B28 75-535512

Balakina, Ol'ga Igorevna.
(Gran' malakhita)
Грань малахита : Стихи / Ольга Балакина ; Обществ. ред. А. Михайлов. — Москва : Современник, 1976.
63 p. : port. ; 16 cm. — (Первая книга в столице) USSR 76
Series romanized: Pervaîa kniga v stolit͡se.
0.23rub
I. Title.
PG3479.L34G7 77-500392

Balakir, Eduard Andreevich, joint author
see Krylov, ÎUrii Ivanovich. (Karbidno-okisnye sistemy) 1976.

Balakirev, N comp.
(Zhenshchina vo vsi͡ekh vidakh)
Женщина во всѣхъ видахъ; художественный юмористическій сборникъ. Сост. Н. Балакиревъ. [С.-Петербургъ] Т-во худож. печати [1903]
161 p. illus. (part col.) 28 cm.
1. Woman—Anecdotes, facetiae, satire, etc. I. Title.
PN6231.W6B3 1903 20-23968
rev

Balakirev, Valentin Sergeevich.
(Primenenie sredstv pnevmo- i gidroavtomatiki v khimicheskikh proizvodstvakh)
Применение средств пневмо- и гидроавтоматики в химических производствах. [Учеб. пособие для вузов по специальности "Автоматизация и комплексная механизация хим.-технол. процессов"]. Москва, "Химия," 1973.
176 p. with illus. 21 cm. (Химическая кибернетика) 0.36rub
USSR 73
At head of title: В. С. Балакирев, А. Э. Софиев.
Bibliography: p. [176]
1. Chemical process control. 2. Pneumatic control. 3. Hydraulic control. I. Sofiev, Aleksandr Ėl'khananovich, joint author. II. Title.
TP155.75.B34 74-334138

Balakirov, ÎUriĭ Aĭrapetovich.
[Termodinamicheskie svoĭstva nefti i gaza]
Термодинамические свойства нефти и газа. Москва, "Недра," 1972.
190 p. with diagrs. 20 cm. 1.00rub USSR 72-VKP
At head of title: Ю. А. Балакиров.
Bibliography: p. 134-[138]
1. Petroleum—Thermal properties. 2. Gas, Natural—Thermal properties. I. Title.
TN871.B269 72-368750

Balakirov, ÎUriĭ Aĭrapetovich, joint author
see Krivonosov, Ivan Vasil'evich. (Osvoenie, issledovanie i ekspluatat͡siîa mnogoplastovykh skvazhin) 1975.

Balakrishna, S
see
Balkrishna, S

Balakrishna Panicker, V. C., 1889-1914. Oru vilāpam
see George, Irumbayam P V 1938-
[Cru vilāpam] [1971]

Balakrishna Pillai, P
മാനുഷോദയം. ഗ്രന്ഥകർത്താ പി. ബാലകൃഷ്ണപിള്ള. തിരുവനന്തപുരം, തിരുവിതാംകൂർ സർവ്വകലാശാല, പ്രസിദ്ധീകരണവകുപ്പ്, 1120 [1944 or 5]
ii, 178 p. illus. 19 cm. (Travancore University series, no. 3. Popular science series, no. 3)
In Malayalam.
1. Man—Origin. 2. Man, Prehistoric. I. Title. II. Series: Trivandrum, India (City). University of Kerala. Kerala University series, no. 3. III. Series: Popular science series, no. 3.
Title romanized: Mānuṣōdayaṃ.
GN743.B32 72-287509

Balakrishnan, A. S., ed.
see All India Conference of Dravidian Linguists, 1st, Trivandrum, 1971. Souvenir released on the occasion of the first Conference of Dravidian Linguists... [Trivandrum, 1971?]

Balakrishnan, A V
Applied functional analysis / A. V. Balakrishnan. — New York : Springer-Verlag, 1976.
x, 309 p. ; 24 cm. — (Applications of mathematics ; v. 3)
"Revised and enlarged version of the author's Introduction to optimization theory in a Hilbert space."
Bibliography: p. 305-306.
Includes index.
ISBN 0-387-90157-4
1. Hilbert space. 2. Mathematical optimization. I. Title.
QA322.4.B34 515'.73 75-25932
75 MARC

Balakrishnan, A V
Stochastic differential systems [by] A. V. Balakrishnan. Berlin, New York, Springer-Verlag, 1973-
v. 26 cm. (Lecture notes in economics and mathematical systems, v. 84 DM22.00 GDB***
Includes bibliographical references.
CONTENTS: 1. Filtering and control: a function space approach.
1. Control theory. 2. Stochastic processes. 3. Differential games. I. Title. II. Series.
QA402.3.B29 519.2 73-79363
ISBN 0-387-06303-X (v. 1) (New York) MARC

Balakrishnan, C.
see Symposium on Drag Reduction in Polymer Solutions, St. Louis, 1972. Drag reduction in polymer solutions. New York, American Institute of Chemical Engineers, 1973.

Balakrishnan, Kalppatta.
[Akalcca]
അകൽച്ച; നോവൽ. [എഴുതിയത്] കൽപററ ബാലകൃഷ്ണൻ. [തൃശ്ശൂർ?]; വിതരണം: നാഷനൽ ബുക്ക്സ്റ്റാൾ, കോട്ടയം [1971]
221 p. 19 cm. Rs4.25
In Malayalam.
I. Title.
PL4718.9.B2342A8 74-927142

Balakrishnan, Kalppata. Nōval, enta ennae?
see Vijayan, Karot. (Agnippura) 1971.

Balakrishnan, M P 1951-
മായാ മാന്ത്രികൻ; നോവൽ. [എഴുതിയത്] എം. പി. ബാലകൃഷ്ണൻ. കുന്നംകുളം, എച്ച്. & സി. സ്റ്റോഴ്സ് [1969]
174 p. 19 cm. Rs2.75
In Malayalam.
I. Title.
Title romanized: Māyā māntrikan.
PL4718.9.B235M3 73-916803

Balakrishnan, M R 1939-
Nuclear cross-section calculations using R-matrix by M. Balakrishnan. Bombay, Bhabha Atomic Research Centre, 1973.
35 p. 29 cm.
B.A.R.C.-663.
Includes bibliographical references.
1. Neutrons—Scattering. 2. Neutron cross sections. I. Title.
WU NUC76-70896

Balakrishnan, Manamadurai Ramaswamisivan, 1899-
புன்னகை பூத்த நாடு. [எழுதியவர்] எம். ஆர். பாலகிருஷ்ணன். சென்னை, வாசகர் வட்டம் [அங்கத்தினர்களுக்கென, அதன் பதிப்பாளரான 'புக்வென்சர்' (Bookventure) நிறுவனத்தினரால் வெளியிடப்பட்டது, 1968]
vii, 234 p. illus. (part col.) map. 19 cm. (வாசகர் வட்டப் பிரசுரம் 20)
6.00
In Tamil.
1. Thailand—Description and travel. 2. Agriculture—Thailand. I. Title.
Title romanized: Puṉṉakai pūtta nāṭu.
DS566.B27 74-900386

Balakrishnan, Manamadurai Ramaswamisivan, 1899-
வாழை; முக்கனிகளில் முதன்மை. [எழுதியவர்] எம். ஆர். பாலகிருஷ்ணன். [1. பதிப்பு] சென்னை, நியூ செஞ்சுரி புக் ஹவுஸ் [1968]
xiv, 167 p. illus. 18 cm. (விழித்தெழும் விவசாயம் வரிசை, 5)
In Tamil.
Bibliography: p. 165-167.
1. Banana. I. Title.
Title romanized: Vāḻai.
SB379.B2B34 S A 68-11724
PL 480: I-T-2626

Balakrishnan, Muriyad.
അഹല്യ; നോവൽ. [എഴുതിയത്] ബാലകൃഷ്ണൻ. തൃശ്ശിവപേരൂർ, മംഗളോദയം, 1969.
132 p. 19 cm. Rs2.50
Added t. p. in English.
In Malayalam.
I. Title.
Title romanized: Ahalya.
PL4718.9.B236A7 71-918601

Balakrishnan, Muriyad.
[Atithi]
അതിഥി; കഥകം. [എഴുതിയത്] ബാലകൃഷ്ണൻ. തൃശ്ശൂർ, കറൻറ് ബുക്ക്സ് [1971]
93 p. 19 cm. Rs2.50
In Malayalam.
CONTENTS: അതിഥി.—തീർത്ഥയാത്ര.—നാളെ.—ചിരി.—പഴയ കാമുകി, പുതിയ സ്നേഹം.—ആർദ്രത.—മരണം.
I. Title.
PL4718.9.B236A9 72-901851

Balakrishnan, Muriyad.
[Kaṇṇikal]
കണ്ണികം; നോവൽ. [എഴുതിയത്] ബാലകൃഷ്ണൻ. കോഴിക്കോട്, പൂർണ്ണാ പബ്ലിക്കേഷൻസ്; വിതരണം: ടൂറിങ്ങ് ബുക്ക്സ്റ്റാൾ, 1971.
327 p. 19 cm. Rs8.00
In Malayalam.
I. Title.
PL4718.9.B236K3 72-900808

Balakrishnan, Muriyad.
മൃഗതൃഷ്ണ; നോവൽ. [എഴുതിയത്] ബാലകൃഷ്ണൻ. തൃശ്ശൂർ, കറൻറ് ബുക്ക്സ് [1970]
370 p. 19 cm. Rs7.50
In Malayalam.
I. Title.
Title romanized: Mṛgatṛṣṇa.
PL4718.9.B236M7 74-913918

Balakrishnan, P 1947-
(Kālam kaṉiyaṭṭum)
காலம் கனியட்டும். [எழுதியவர்] பெ. பாலகிருஷ்ணன். [1. பதிப்பு] சென்னை, வைரம் பதிப்பகம் [1972]
85 p. 18 cm. Rs2.00
In Tamil.
A novel.

I. Title.

PL4758.9.B24K3 72-901404

Balakrishnan, P 1947-
மன்னியுங்கள்! [எழுதியவர்] பெ. பாலகிருஷ்ணன். [1. பதிப்பு] சென்னை, அறிவுச் சுடர் நிலையம் [1970]
47 p. 18 cm. Rs1.25
In Tamil.
A novel.

I. Title.
Title romanized: Maṉṉiyuṅkaḷ.

PL4758.9.B24M3 75-918294

Balakrishnan, P 1947-
(Tēṉ tuḷikaḷ)
தேன் துளிகள். எழுதியவர் பெ. பாலகிருஷ்ணன். [1. பதிப்பு. சென்னை] சத்யா பதிப்பகம்; விற்பனை உரிமை: வைரம் பதிப்பகம் [1973]
100 p. 19 cm. Rs2.50
In Tamil.
Short stories.

I. Title.

PL4758.9.B24T4 73-904772

Balakrishnan, P Kesavan, 1924-
(Ini ñān uṟaṅṅaṭṭe)
ഇനി ഞാൻ ഉറങ്ങട്ടെ; നോവൽ. [എഴുതിയത്] പി. കെ. ബാലകൃഷ്ണൻ. കോട്ടയം, സാഹിത്യപ്രവർത്തക സഹകരണസംഘം; [sales dept.] നാഷനൽ ബുക്ക്സ്റ്റാം [1973]
261 p. 22 cm. Rs8.00
In Malayalam.

I. Title.

PL4718.9.B26 I 5 73-903197

Balakrishnan, **P. Kesavan, 1924-** ed.
see Nārāyanaguru. [Rev. ed.] [1969]

Balakrishnan, R comp.
மாணாக்கரின் காந்தி. தொகுப்பாசிரியர் ஆர். பாலகிருஷ்ணன் [மற்றும்] ரி.எல்.எம். புகாரி. [1st ed.] கொழும்பு, அரசு வெளியீடு [1969]
66 p. ports. 19 cm. (காந்தி நூல்கள் [1]) (அரசு வெளியீடு, 22)
In Tamil.

1. Gandhi, Mohandas Karamchand, 1869-1948—Anniversaries, etc. I. Buhari, T. L. M., joint comp. II. Title.
Title romanized: Māṇākkariṉ Kānti.

DS481.G3B32 70-913693

Balakrishnan, R
see also
Pālakiruṣṇan, R

Balakrishnan, S K 1915-
[Kēraḷa jyōtissā]
കേരള ജ്യോതിസ്സ്; ശ്രീനാരായണഗുരുദേവന്റെ സംക്ഷിപ്ത ജീവിതചരിത്രം. ഗ്രന്ഥകാരൻ എസ്. കെ. ബാലകൃഷ്ണൻ. Tellicherry, Balakrishnan Grandhalayam, 1971.
iv, iv, 58 p. 19 cm. Rs1.50
In Malayalam.

1. Sree Narayanan, Swami, 1856-1928. I. Title.

BL1175.S67B33 72-900469

Balakrishnan, S K 1915-
നീലസാരി; എട്ട് ചെറുകഥകൾ. കഥാകൃത്ത് എസ്. കെ. ബാലകൃഷ്ണൻ. തലശ്ശേരി, ബാലകൃഷ്ണ ഗ്രന്ഥാലയം; [distributors: Modern Book House, Cannanore] 1970.
93 p. 19 cm. Rs2.00
In Malayalam.

I. Title.
Title romanized: Nīlasāri.

PL4718.9.B27N5 76-916600

Balakrishnan, Sangoli.
(Jaṉatā ekspiras)
ஜனதா எக்ஸ்பிரஸ் / சங்கொலி பாலகிருஷ்ணன். — 1. பதிப்பு. — பம்பாய் : பாலன் பதிப்பகம், 1975.
104 p. ; 19 cm.
In Tamil.
Short stories.
CONTENTS: மாணிக்கம் கூழாங்கல் ஆவதில்லை.—இரு மொட்டுகள்.—கடவுளைக் கண்டேன்.—ஒரு விவசாயியின் பார்வையில்.—சிறு மீன்கள்.—துஷ்ட-தேவதை?—பெரிய வீட்டுப்பிள்ளை.—பணம் படுத்திய பாடு.—பெற்ற மனம்.—அலங்காரம் எதுக்கடி ...?—ஊருக்கு புதுசு.—ஜனதா எக்ஸ்பிரஸ்.
Rs3.00

I. Title.

PL4758.9.B265J3 76-901720

Balakrishnan, T R
Fertility and family planning in a Canadian metropolis / T. R. Balakrishman, K. F. Kantner, J. D. Allingham. — Montreal : McGill-Queen's University Press, 1975.
xvi, 217 p. ; 24 cm. C***
Bibliography: [209]-213.
Includes index.
1. Birth control—Toronto. 2. Fertility, Human. 3. Family size. 4. Contraceptives. I. Kantner, K. F., joint author. II. Allingham, John D., joint author. III. Title.
HQ766.5.C3B34 301.32'1 75-332127
76 MARC

Balakrishnan, V
Genetic diversity among Australian Aborigines / V. Balakrishnan and L. D. Sanghvi and R. L. Kirk. — Canberra : Australian Institute of Aboriginal Studies, 1975.
ix, 115 p. : diagrs., graphs, maps ; 25 cm. — (Research and regional studies) (Australian Aboriginal studies ; no. 3) Aus
Bibliography: p. 106-115.
ISBN 0-85575-043-X
1. Australian aborigines—Anthropometry. 2. Human population genetics—Australia. I. Sanghvi, L. D., joint author. II. Kirk, Robert L., joint author. III. Title. IV. Series: Regional and research studies. V. Series: Australian Aboriginal studies ; no. 3. VI. Series: Australian Aboriginal studies ; no. 3.
GN57.A9B34 573.2'1'0994 77-352804
77 MARC

Balakrishnan, V 1933-
(Agnidēvata)
അഗ്നിദേവത; നോവൽ. [എഴുതിയത്] വി. ബാലകൃഷ്ണൻ. ആലപ്പുഴ, ശ്രീ കൃഷ്ണവിലാസം ബുക്കഡിപ്പോ [1973]
276 p. 19 cm. Rs7.00
In Malayalam.

I. Title.

PL4718.9.B28A7 73-901804

Balakrishnan, V 1933-
(Avaḷ sundariyāṇā)
അവൾ സുന്ദരിയാണ്; നോവൽ. [എഴുതിയത്] വി. ബാലകൃഷ്ണൻ. ആലപ്പുഴ, ശ്രീകൃഷ്ണവിലാസം ബുക്കഡിപ്പോ [1972]
79 p. 19 cm. Rs2.00
In Malayalam.

I. Title.

PL4718.9.B28A95 73-900230

Balakrishnan, V 1933-
ഇലഞ്ഞിപ്പൂമണം; നോവൽ. [എഴുതിയത്] വി. ബാലകൃഷ്ണൻ. [Champakulam] ബി. കെ. എം. പ്രസിദ്ധീകരണം [1970]
67 p. 19 cm. Rs1.25
In Malayalam.

I. Title.
Title romanized: Ilaññippūmaṇam.

PL4718.9.B28 I 4 76-916450

Balakrishnan, V 1933-
ഉത്തരഭാരതത്തിലൂടെ. [എഴുതിയത്] വി. ബാലകൃഷ്ണൻ. [1st ed.] കോഴിക്കോട്, പി. കെ. ബ്രദേർസ് [1971]
154 p. 19 cm. Rs2.50
In Malayalam.

1. India—Description and travel—1947- I. Title.
Title romanized: Uttarabhāratattilūṭe.

DS414.B343 70-927985

Balakrishnan, V., 1933-
see Iesdi Inglīsa-Hindi-Malayālam nighantu. [1968]

Balakrishnan, V., 1933-
see Malayāḷaṃ Malayāḷaṃ Ingḷiṣ Hindi nighaṇṭu. [1970]

Balakrishnan Nair, A
Parliamentary control of the administrative function in India : a study in procedure / A. Balakrishnan Nair. — Trivandrum : [s. n.], 1973.
xiv, 276 p. ; 22 cm.
Title on jacket: Parliamentary control over administration.
"Written on the basis of [the author's] dissertation for which the degree of doctor of philosophy was awarded by the University of Kerala."
"Published under the auspices of the Kerala Academy of Political Science."
"Foot notes": p. [235]-276.
1. Legislative bodies — India. 2. Legislative auditing — India. I. Title. II. Title: Parliamentary control over administration.
JQ254.B34 328.54'07'456 74-902246
MARC

Balakrishnan Nair, G
[Śivāravindaṃ]
ശ്രീനാരായണഗുരുദേവന്റെ കുണ്ഡലിനിപ്പാട്ട് 'ശിവാരവിന്ദം' വ്യാഖ്യാനം. വ്യാഖ്യാതാ ജി. ബാലകൃഷ്ണൻ നായർ. [1st ed.] തിരുവനന്തപുരം, ശ്രീനാരായണ പബ്ളിഷിംഗ് ഹൗസ് [1972]
xxx, 105 p. 19 cm. Rs2.50
Cover title: കുണ്ഡലിനിപ്പാട്ട്.
In Malayalam.

1. Yoga, Haṭha. I. Sree Narayanan, Swami, 1856-1928. Kuṇḍalinippāṭṭā. II. Title: Kuṇḍalinippāṭṭā. III. Title: Śivāravindaṃ.
Title romanized: Śrīnārāyaṇagurudēvanṟe Kuṇḍalinippāṭṭā 'Śivāravindaṃ' vyākhyānaṃ.

B132.Y6B33 72-906941

Balakrishnan Nair, G. Sivāravindam
see Balakrishnan Nair, G (Srīnārāyanagurudēvanṟe Municaryāpañcakam 'Sivāravindam' vyākhyānam) '971]

Balakrishnan Nair, G
[Śrīnārāyaṇagurudēvanṟe Daivadaśakaṃ]
ശ്രീനാരായണഗുരുദേവന്റെ ദൈവദശകം 'ശിവാരവിന്ദം' വ്യാഖ്യാനം. വ്യാഖ്യാതാ ജി. ബാലകൃഷ്ണൻ നായർ. [1st ed.] തിരുവനന്തപുരം, ശ്രീനാരായണ പബ്ളിഷിംഗ് ഹൗസ് [1970]
vi, 150 p. 19 cm. Rs2.50
In Malayalam; foreword in English.

1. Sree Narayanan, Swami, 1856-1928. Daivadaśakam. I. Title.

PL4718.9.S64D332 77-928523

Balakrishnan Nair, G
(Śrīnārāyaṇagurudēvanṟe Municaryāpañcakaṃ 'Śivāravindaṃ' vyākhyānaṃ)
ശ്രീനാരായണഗുരുദേവന്റെ മുനിചര്യാപഞ്ചകം 'ശിവാരവിന്ദം' വ്യാഖ്യാനം. വ്യാഖ്യാതാവ് ജി. ബാലകൃഷ്ണൻ നായർ. [1. പതിപ്പ്] കണ്ണൂര്, ശ്രീനാരായണഗുരുസേവാസംഘം [1971]
65 p. 19 cm. Re1.00
Cover title: മുനിചര്യാ പഞ്ചകം.
Malayalam and Sanskrit; commentary in Malayalam.
1. Sree Narayanan, Swami, 1856-1928. Municaryāpañcakaṃ. 2. Asceticism—Hinduism. I. Sree Narayanan, Swami, 1856-1928. Municaryāpañcakaṃ. 1971. II. Balakrishnan Nair, G. Sivāravindaṃ.
BL2015.A8B34 72-908701

Balakrishnan Nair, K.
see Symposium on Cropping Patterns in India, Indian Agricultural Research Institute, 1968. Cropping patterns in India. New Delhi [1972]

Balakrishnan Nair, N
(Svarājyabhimāni)
സ്വരാജ്യാഭിമാനി; അഥവാ, വേലുത്തമ്പിദളവാ, ഒരു ജീവിതചരിത്രം. ഗ്രന്ഥകർത്താ എൻ. ബാലകൃഷ്ണൻ നായർ. [2d ed.] തിരുവനന്തപുരം, ഉള്ളൂർ പബ്ലിഷേഴ്സ് [1967]
xvi, 359 p. port. 21 cm. Rs6.00
In Malayalam.
Bibliographical footnotes.
1. Velu Thampi, 1765–1809. I. Title.
DS479.V4B3 1967 S A 68-7565
PL 480: I-Mal-1285

Bālakr̥sṇa Bhaṭṭa.
(Prameyaratnārṇava)
प्रमेयरत्नार्णव. श्रीबालकृष्णभट्टविरचित. हिन्दी अनुवाद सहित. सम्पादक एवं अनुवादक केदारनाथ मिश्र. नागरदास का. बाँभणिया द्वारा लिखित आमुख सहित. [1. संस्करण] वाराणसी, आनन्द प्रकाशन; [प्रमुख वितरक भारतीय विद्या प्रकाशन, 1971]
46, 280 p. 19 cm. Rs10.00
Added t. p. in English.
Hindi and Sanskrit; introductory matter and notes in English, Hindi, or Sanskrit.
Bibliography: p. [275]-277.
1. Vallabhācārya, 1479–1531? 2. Vaishnavism. 3. Vedanta. I. Mishra, Kedar Nath, 1936– ed. II. Title.
B133.V32B34 72-903710

Bālakr̥sṇa Tripāṭhī.
(Praśastikāśikā)
प्रशस्तिकाशिका. Praśastikāśikā of Bālakr̥ṣṇa Tripāṭhin. Critically edited with introd. by K. V. Sarma. [1. संस्करणम्] होशियारपुरम्, विश्वेश्वरानन्द-संस्थानम् 1967.
xxv, 60 p. 24 cm. (विश्वेश्वरानन्द-भारतभारती-ग्रन्थमाला, 39) (विश्वेश्वरानन्द-संस्थान-प्रकाशनम् 412)
In Sanskrit; introd. in English.
1. Letter-writing, Sanskrit. I. Sarma, K. Venkateswara, 1919– ed. II. Title. III. Series: Vishveshvaranand Indological series, 39. IV. Series: Vishveshvaranand Institute. Publication, 412.
PK840.B33 S A 68-20797
PL 480: I-San-1116

Bālakr̥snamūrti, Paṅganāmala.
(Rāmanāṭaka vimarśanamu)
రామనాటక విమర్శనము : పది రామాయణనాటకములపైన విమర్శ / రచయిత పంగనామల బాలకృష్ణమూర్తి. — తిరుపతి : తిరుమల తిరుపతి దేవస్థానములు, 1959.
xvi, 352 p. ; 22 cm. — (శ్రీ వేంకటేశ్వర ప్రాచ్యపరిశోధనాలయ గ్రంథమాల ; సంఖ్య 62)
In Telugu.
1. Sanskrit drama—History and criticism. 2. Rama (Hindu deity) in literature. I. Title. II. Series: Sri Venkateswara University, Tirupati, India. Oriental Research Institute. S.V. University oriental series ; 62.
PK2933.B25 75-928231

Bālakr̥snan, Kalpaṭṭa
see
Balakrishnan, Kalppatta.

Bālakr̥snan, Vāppālaśśēri.
(Snēhattinte kaittiri)
സ്നേഹത്തിന്റെ കൈത്തിരി. [എഴുതിയത്] ബാലകൃഷ്ണൻ വാപ്പാലശ്ശേരി. [Ernakulam? K.V. Kochumadhavi]; വിതരണക്കാർ എം. എസ്സ്. ബുക്ക്ഡിപ്പോ, കൊല്ലം [1962]
128 p. 19 cm. Rs1.50
In Malayalam.
CONTENTS: ഐസ്ക്രീം പ്രേമം.—ഒരു പൂമൊട്ടുകളുടെ വിരിയാതായി.—ഓമ്മകം മരിക്കന്നില്ല.—ഞാൻ നിന്നെ സ്നേഹിക്കുന്നു.—സ്നേഹത്തിന്റെ കൈത്തിരി.—ഒരു കൊട്ടകാററാരം ഭിക്കുന്നു.—ദുഃഖത്തിന്റെ ചുരുളുകൾ.
I. Title.
PL4718.9.B295S5 73-900238

Bālakr̥snan Nāyar, G
see
Balakrishnan Nair, G

Bālakr̥snatripāṭhī
see
Bālakr̥sṇa Tripāṭhī.

Balakshin, Boris Sergeevich.
Fundamentals of manufacturing engineering, by Boris Balakshin. Translated from the Russian by Nicholas Weinstein. Moscow, Mir Publishers, 1971.
574 p. illus. 22 cm. 2.97rub USSR***
Translation of Osnovy tekhnologii mashinostroeniia.
1. Machine-shop practice. 2. Production engineering. I. Title.
TJ1160.B22513 621.7′5 73-179055
MARC

Balakshin, Boris Sergeevich, ed.
see Adaptivnoe upravlenie stankami. 1973.

Balakshin, Boris Sergeevich
see Vzaimozameniaemost' i tekhnicheskie izmereniia v mashinostroenii. 1972.

Balalaev, A. S.
see Klintsam 250 let. [Klintsy] Brianskiĭ rabochiĭ, 1959.

Balalaev, German Aleksandrovich.
(Proizvodstvo antikorrozionnykh rabot)
Производство антикоррозионных работ. [Учебник для проф.-техн. училищ и подгот. рабочих на производстве] Изд. 3-е, перераб. и доп. Москва, "Высш. школа," 1973.
383 p. with illus. 21 cm. (Профтехобразование. Строительные работы) 0.60rub USSR 73
At head of title: Г. А. Балалаев.
Bibliography: p. [380]
1. Corrosion and anti-corrosives. I. Title.
TA418.74.B3 1973 74-343941

Balalaev, German Aleksandrovich.
(Proizvodstvo antikorrozionnykh rabot v promyshlennom stroitel'stve)
Производство антикоррозионных работ в промышленном строительстве. Москва, Стройиздат, 1973.
270 p. with illus. 20 cm. 0.88rub USSR 73-VKP
At head of title: Г. А. Балалаев, Ю. В. Дерешкевич, Б. С. Горина.
Bibliography: p. 265–[268]
1. Industrial equipment—Corrosion. 2. Plastics. I. Dereshkevich, IUliĭ Vladislavovich, joint author. II. Gorina, Basia Sanderovna, joint author. III. Title.
TS191.B34 73-335045

Balalaev, IU. F.
see Prikladnaia mekhanika. 1972.

Balalaev, Vladimir Alekseevich.
(Izobarnye iadra s massovym chislom A-169)
Изобарные ядра с массовым числом A-169 : 169Ho 169Er169Tm169Yb / В. А. Балалаев, Б. С. Джелепов, В. Е. Тер-Нерсесянц. — Ленинград : Наука, 1976.
222 p., [1] fold. leaf : ill. ; 26 cm. — (Свойства атомных ядер ; вып. 19) USSR***
At head of title: Akademiia nauk SSSR. Otdelenie iadernoĭ fiziki.
Includes bibliographies.
1.80rub
1. Nuclear isobars—Charts, diagrams, etc. I. Dzhelepov, Boris Sergeevich, joint author. II. Ter-Nersesiants, Vavik Egishevich, joint author. III. Title. IV. Series: Svoĭstva atomnykh iader ; vyp. 19.
QC770.S8 vyp. 19 77-500814
[QC795.8.N8]

Balalaeva, N. M.
see Voprosy vseobshcheĭ istorii. Khabarovsk, 1972.

Balali, Renate, 1940–
Wandlungen und Differenzierungen der Kulturlandschaft beiderseits der linksniederrheinischen Lössgrenze. [Bonn, 1971?]
266, [88] p. maps (6 fold. in pocket) 21 cm. GDB***
Inaug.-Diss.—Bonn.
Vita.
Bibliography: p. 236–263.
1. Agricultural geography—North Rhine-Westphalia. 2. Physical geography—North Rhine-Westphalia. 3. Land settlement—North Rhine-Westphalia. 4. Loess—North Rhine-Westphalia. I. Title.
S466.N6B34 75-586307

Balalov, Viktor Dmitrievich
see Tekhpromfinplan predpriiatiia bytovogo obsluzhivaniia. 1972.

Balam, Karam Singh, 1923–
(Piāra kurabānīāṃ)
ਪਿਆਰ ਕੁਰਬਾਨੀਆਂ. ਕਰਤਾ ਕਰਮ ਸਿੰਘ 'ਬਾਲਮ.' ਅੰਮ੍ਰਿਤਸਰ, ਭਾਈ ਬੂਟਾ ਸਿੰਘ ਪ੍ਰਤਾਪ ਸਿੰਘ [1966]
152 p. 19 cm. Rs3.00
In Panjabi.
Poems.
I. Title.
PK2659.B292P5 70-924234

Balamani Amma, Nalappat, 1909–
Thirty poems / Balamani Amma. — Bombay : Orient Longmans, 1970.
60 p. ; 23 cm.
"Readings from Indian poetry."
Rs17.50
I. Title.
PL4718.9.B3T5 894′.812′16 74-902937
75[r76]rev MARC

Balamani Amma, Nalappat, 1909–
(Veyilārumpōḷ)
വെയിലാറുമ്പോൾ. ഗ്രന്ഥകർത്രി ബാലാമണിയമ്മ. [1. പതിപ്പ്] കോഴിക്കോട്, മാതൃഭൂമി പ്രിന്റിംഗ് ആൻഡ് പബ്ലിഷിംഗ് കമ്പനി, 1971.
45 p. 19 cm. Re1.00
In Malayalam.
Poems.
I. Title.
PL4718.9.B3V4 72-900468

Balamanoharan, A 1942–
(Kumārapuram)
குமாரபுரம் / அ. பாலமனோகரன். — 1st ed. — கொழும்பு : வீரகேசரி, 1974.
131 p. ; 19 cm. — (வீரகேசரி பிரசுரம் ; 28)
Series romanized: Vīrakēcari piracuram.
In Tamil.
A novel.
Rs3.40
I. Title.
PL4758.9.R276K8 76-900271

Balamanoharan, A 1942–
(Nilakkiḷi)
நிலக்கிளி. [எழுதியவர்] அ. பாலமனோகரன். [1st ed.] கொழும்பு, வீரகேசரி; [sole distributors: Express Newspapers (Ceylon), 1973.
150 p. 19 cm. Rs2.25
In Tamil.
A novel.
I. Title.
PL4758.9.B276N5 73-905752

Balamezov, Stefan G 1883–1959.
[Krizata v săvremenniia parlamentarizm]
Кризата в съвременния парламентаризъм; беседа по сравнително държавно право. София, Акация, 1923.
23 p. 21 cm.
Bibliography: p. 22.
Bound with the author's Парламентарното управление въ славянскитѣ страни. София, 1926. Copy 2; his Нашата конституция и нашиятъ парламентаризъмъ, ч. 1. София, 1919; Kirov, Stefan. Кратъкъ курсъ по българско конституционно право. София, 1920. Copy 2; Kirov, Stefan. Кратъкъ курсъ по общо държавно право. София, 1918; and Sokolov, K. N. Държавно право, ч. 1. София, 1923. Copy 3.
1. Representative government and representation. I. Title.
JF1051.B25 73-201440

Balamezov, Stefan G 1883–1959.
[Nashata konstitutsiia i nashiiat parlamentarizŭm]
Нашата конституция и нашиятъ парламентаризъмъ. София, Право, 1919–
v. 23 cm.
Bound with the author's Кризата в съвременния парламентаризъм. София, 1923.
Includes bibliographical references.
CONTENTS: ч. 1. Търновската конституция; история на първоначалния текстъ отъ 1879 год.
1. Bulgaria—Constitutional history. I. Title.
JF1051.B25 73-201901

Bal'amī, Abū 'Alī Muḥammad ibn Muḥammad, fl. 946–973, tr.
see al-Ṭabarī, 838?-923. [Tārīkh al-rusul wa-al-mulūk. Persian] Tārīkh-i Bal'amī. 1341– [1952 or 3–

Balamoan, G Ayoub, 1931-
History of human tragedies on the Nile : 1884 to 1975 / by G. Ayoub Balamoan. — Cambridge : Harvard University Center for Population Studies, 1976-
v. : ill. ; 28 cm.
Bibliography: v. 1, p. 462-470.
CONTENTS: pt. 1. Migration policies in the Anglo-Egyptian Sudan, 1884-1956.
1. Sudan—Emigration and immigration. 2. Sudan—Population. 3. Nile Valley—Emigration and immigration. 4. Nile Valley—Population. I. Title.
HB3673.S8B34 301.32′9′62 76-10276
76 MARC

Balamoan, G Ayoub, 1931-
Migration policies in the Anglo-Egyptian Sudan, 1884 to 1956 / by G. Ayoub Balamoan. — Cambridge : Harvard University Center for Population Studies, 1976.
xxviii, 470 p. : ill. ; 28 cm. — (History of human tragedies on the Nile: 1884 to 1975 ; pt. 1)
Bibliography: p. 462-470.
1. Sudan—Emigration and immigration. I. Title.
HB3673.S8B34 pt. 1 301.32′9′62 s 76-10005
76 MARC

Balamoan, G Ayoub, 1931-
Preliminary demographic research notes on Inter-African migration; are there 6,000,000 West Africans in the Upper Nile Valley? By G. A. Balamoan. Ibadan, Balamoan, 1968.
1 v. (various pagings)
1. Sudan—Emig. & immig.
MH NUC73-119626

Bālamukunda Bharatiyā
see
Bharatiyā, Bālamukunda.

Bālamukunda Gupta
see
Gupta, Balmukand, 1909-

Balamurali Krishṇa, M 1930-
[Janakarāgakṛtimañjari. Telugu & Sanskrit]
ஜனகராகக்ருதிமஞ்சரி. [கவிஞர்] எம். பாலமுரளீக்ருஷ்ண. [1. பதிப்பு. Madras, Srirangam Printers, 1973?]
208 p. (முரளீ ரவளீ வெளியீடு 2) 23 cm. Rs9.00
First published in 1952.
Prefatory matter in English.
Includes music in letter notation.
1. Music, Karnatic. I. Title: Janakarāgakṛtimañjari.
Title romanized: Jaṉakarākakrutimañcari.
M1808.B345J3 74-902704

Balamutov, Vladislav Georgievich
see Study Tour on Standardization of Radiation Dosimetry, 1971. Standardization of radiation dosimetry in the Soviet Union... Vienna, International Atomic Energy Agency, 1973.

Balan, A. G.
see Armizin, D V Meliorativnoe zemledelie. 1966.

Balán, Américo Abraham
see Martín Fierro; cinco xilografías originales... [Buenos Aires] Empresa Líneas Marítimas Argentinas [1972]

Balan, C A
(Tūkkumarattinṭe niḻalil)
തൂക്കമരത്തിന്റെ നിഴലിൽ; സ്മരണകരം. [ഗ്രന്ഥകർത്താ] സി. എ. ബാലൻ. കോട്ടയം, സാഹിത്യപ്രവർത്തക സഹകരണസംഘം; [Sales Dept.] നാഷനൽ ബുക്ക്സ്റ്റാൾ [1967]
136 p. 19 cm. Rs2.00
In Malayalam.
Autobiographical.
1. Prisoners—India—Personal narratives. I. Title.
HV9792.B3 S A 68-8573
Library of Congress PL 480: I-Mal-1231

Balan, Dušan, 1939–
Put do ploda / Dušan Balan. — Zrenjanin : Centar za kulturu, 1974.
43 p. ; 21 cm. — (Biblioteka Ulaznica : Savremena poezija)
Yu***
Poems.
I. Title.
PG1419.12.A45P8 75-970877

Balan, Evelyn U
Vacances à Nouméa. [Adelaide] Rigby [1970]
82 p. illus.
1. New Caledonia—Description and travel. 2. French language—Readers. I. Title.
CLU NUC76-70895

Bălan, George.
Cazul Schoenberg : (un geniu rău al muzicii?) / George Bălan ; [coperta de Eugen Nicolcev]. — București : Editura muzicală, 1974.
272 p. with music, 4 leaves of ports. and facsims. ; 21 cm.
R 74-2760
1. Schönberg, Arnold, 1874-1951. I. Title.
ML410.S283B2 74-350626

Bălan, George.
Înnoirile muzicii. București, Editura Muzicală a Uniunii Compozitorilor din Republica Socialistă România, 1966.
227 p. illus. 21 cm.
1. Music—History and criticism. I. Title.
ML160.B11 74-215589

Bălan, George.
Mică filosofie a muzicii urmată de La hotarul dintre muzică și cuvînt / George Bălan. — [București] : Editura Eminescu, 1975.
334 p. ; 20 cm. — (Sinteze) R 75-3801
Summary in French and German.
lei 10.00
1. Music—Philosophy and aesthetics. I. Title: Mică filosofie a muzicii ... II. Title: La hotarul dintre muzică și cuvînt.
ML3800.B207M5 75-407963

Bălan, George.
Muzica și lumea ideilor. București, Editura muzicală, 1973.
383 p. 20 cm. lei 24.50 R 74-328
Includes bibliographical references.
1. Music—Philosophy and aesthetics. I. Title.
ML3800.B207M95 74-311900

Bălan, George.
O istorie a muzicii europene : epoci și curente : personalități și capodopere / George Bălan. — [București] : "Albatros," 1975.
455 p., [18] leaves of plates : ill., ports. ; 21 cm. R 75-2860
Includes index.
lei 27.00
1. Music—Europe—History and criticism. I. Title.
ML240.B25 75-547795

Bălan, Gheorghe, joint author.
see Oancea, Corneliu. 1950-1975, 25 [i.e. O mie nouă sute cincizeci-o mie nouă sute șaptezeci și cinci, douăzeci și cinci] ani [de activitate a] I.C.M.J. Sibiu ... [Sibiu, s.n., 1975]

Bălan, Ion.
Drumuri și nori / Ion Bălan. — Vîrșeț : Libertatea, 1960.
160 p. ; 21 cm.
I. Title.
PC840.12.A5D78 77-456374
77 MARC

Bălan, Ion.
Ninalb : povestiri / Ion Bălan ; prefață de Octav Păun ; [coperta, Ivan Lacković]. — București : "Minerva," 1975.
xii, 121 p. ; 20 cm. R 75-4998
Includes bibliographical references.
lei 8.25
I. Title.
PC840.12.A5N5 1975 76-509220

Bălan, Ion
see Flora, Radu. (Tišina svitanja) 1975.

Bălan, Ion
see Societatea de Limbă Română din P. S. A. Voivodina. Contribuții la istoria culturală a românilor din Voivodina, I ... Zrenjanin: [s.n.], 1973.

Bălan, Ion Dodu, 1929–
Artă și ideal : [critică literară] / Ion Dodu Bălan. — București : Editura Eminescu, 1975.
326 p. ; 20 cm. R 75-2068
Includes bibliographical references.
lei 9.25
1. Romanian literature—History and criticism—Collected works.
PC803.B3 75-542802

Bălan, Ion Dodu, 1929–
Copilăria unui Icar : [Aurel Vlaicu] / Ion Dodu Bălan ; [copertă și ilustrații de Damian Petrescu]. — București : Editura Ion Creangă, 1974.
93 p. : ill. ; 24 cm. R 75-816
lei 5.75
1. Vlaicu, Aurel, 1882-1913. I. Title.
TL540.V59B34 75-410395

Bălan, Ion Dodu, 1929-
Copilăria unui Icar : [Aurel Vlaicu] / Ion Dodu Bălan ; [copertă și ilustrații, Damian Petrescu]. — Ediția a 2-a adăugită. — București : Editura Ion Creangă, 1976.
172 p. : ill. ; 21 cm. R76-3644
lei8.75
1. Vlaicu, Aurel, 1882-1913. 2. Aeronautics—Romania—Biography. I. Title.
TL540.V59B34 1976 77-452001
•77 MARC

Bălan, Ion Dodu, 1929-
Cultural policy in Romania / Ion Dodu Balan ; with the cooperation of the Directorates of the Council of Socialist Culture and Education. — Paris : Unesco Press, 1975.
70 p., [4] leaves of plates : ill. ; 25 cm. — (Studies and documents on cultural policies) F***
"[B.10]SHC.74/XIX.29/A."
Includes bibliographical references.
ISBN 923101188X
1. Arts—Romania—Management. I. Title. II. Series.
NX770.R6B35 354'.498'0085 75-308807
75 MARC

Bălan, Ion Dodu, 1929–
Ethos și cultură sau vocația tinereții. [Studii. Coperta: Gh. Marinescu]. [București], „Albatros," 1972.
432 p. 20 cm. (Atitudini) lei 11.50 R 72-4033
Includes bibliographical references.
1. Romanian literature—Addresses, essays, lectures. 2. Aesthetics. 3. Ethics. I. Title.
PC808.B27 73-306908

Bălan, Ion Dodu, 1929– comp.
Hej, zöld levél; román népdalok. Válogatta Ioan Dodu Bălan. Szerk, és a bevezetőt írta Faragó József. [A köt. fordítói: Fényi István, et al.] Bukarest, Ifjusági Könyvkiadó, 1966.
246 p. 23 cm.
Translation of Foale verde foicică.
Bibliography: p. 231–[241]
1. Romanian ballads and songs. 2. Romanian poetry—Translations into Hungarian. 3. Hungarian poetry—Translations from Hungarian. I. Faragó, József, ed. II. Fényi, István, tr. III. Title.
PC872.H8B3 79-252898
rev

Balan, Ion Dodu, 1929-
Octavian Goga. Monografie. [Bucuresti] "Minerva," 1971.
426 p. 31 l. of plates, ports., and facsims.
Summary in French.
Bibliography: p. 357-[403]
1. Goga, Octavian, 1881-1938. I. Title.
CU-SB NUC74-124872

Bălan, Ion Dodu, 1929– comp.
Octavian Goga / [interpretat de Sorin Alexandrescu, Ion Dodu-Bălan, Mihai Beniuc, ...] ; ediție îngrijită de Ion Dodu-Bălan ; [coperta colecției, Ion Dogar-Marinescu]. — București : Editura Eminescu, 1974.
287 p. ; 20 cm. — (Biblioteca critică) R 74-2084
Bibliography: p. 277–[282]
lei 10.50
1. Goga, Octavian, 1881–1938.
PC839.G6Z6 1974 74-356067

Bălan, Ion Dodu, 1929–
Octavian Goga : monografie / Ion Dodu Bălan. — Ediția a 2-a revăzută și adăugită. — [București] : "Minerva," 1975.
468 p., [32] leaves of plates : ill., ports. ; 20 cm. R 75-4514
Summary in French.
Bibliography: p. 350–[398]
Includes indexes.
lei 21.50
1. Goga, Octavian, 1881–1938.
PC839.G6Z6 1975 76-501913

Bălan, Ion Dodu, 1929-
Valori literare. [București] Editura pentru Literatură, 1966.
337 p. 21 cm.
1. Romanian literature–Addresses, essays, lectures. I. Title.
NNC NUC75-31696

Bălan, Ion Dodu, 1929-
see Cartea înțelepciunii populare ... București : "Minerva," 1974.

Balán, Jorge, 1940–
Centro e periferia no desenvolvimento brasileiro / Jorge Balán, org. ; textos de Antônio Octávio Cintra ... [et al.]. — São Paulo : Difusão Européia do Livro, 1974.
251 p. ; 21 cm. — (Corpo e alma do Brasil)
Essays prepared for the Primeiro Curso de Atualização para Professores de Ciências Sociais, organized by the Departamento de Ciência Política da Universidade Federal de Minas Gerais, and held in Belo Horizonte, July 1972.
Includes bibliographies.
CONTENTS: Balán, J. Introdução. — Cintra, A. O. A política tradicional brasileira: uma interpretação das relações entre o centro e a periferia.—Schwartzman, S. Um enfoque teórico do regionalismo político.—Balán, J. Migrações internas no desenvolvimento capitalista no Brasil: ensaio histórico-comparativo.—Reis, F. Wanderley. Solidariedade, interesses e desenvolvimento político: um marco teórico e o caso brasileiro.—Bacha, E. Lisboa. Sobre a dinâmica de crescimento da economia industrial subdesenvolvida.
Cr$35.00
1. Brazil—Economic conditions—1945– —Addresses, essays, lectures. 2. Regionalism—Brazil—Addresses, essays, lectures. I. Cintra, Antônio Octávio. II. Title.
HC187.B19 75–557564

Balán, Jorge, 1940–
Men in a developing society; geographic and social mobility in Monterrey, Mexico [by] Jorge Balán, Harley L. Browning [and] Elizabeth Jelin, with the assistance of Waltraut Feindt. Austin, Published for the Institute of Latin American Studies by the University of Texas Press [1973]
xix, 384 p. 23 cm. (Latin American monographs, no. 30) $11.50
Bibliography: p. [359]–373.
1. Social mobility—Monterey, Mexico. 2. Occupational mobility. 3. Migration, Internal—Mexico—Monterey. I. Browning, Harley L., joint author. II. Jelin, Elizabeth, 1941– joint author. III. Texas. University at Austin. Institute of Latin American Studies. IV. Title. V. Series: Latin American monographs (Austin, Tex.) no. 30.
HN120.M6B34 301.44'044'09721 72–6282
ISBN 0–292–75004–8 MARC
Library of Congress 73 [4]

Balán, Jorge, 1940– comp.
Migración, estructura ocupacional y movilidad social : el caso de Monterrey / Jorge Balán, Harley L. Browning, Elizabeth Jelin. — 1. ed. — México : Universidad Nacional Autónoma de México, Instituto de Investigaciones Sociales, 1973.
287 p. ; 23 cm.
"Los estudios ... se originaron con el proyecto de investigación sobre 'Movilidad social, migración y fecundidad en Monterrey.' Dicho proyecto fue iniciado por el Centro de Investigaciones Económicas de la Facultad de Economía de Nuevo León (Monterrey) y el Population Research Center, Department of Sociology, University of Texas (Austin)."
Includes bibliographies.
CONTENTS: Balán, J. Introducción.—Balán, J. ... et al. El uso de computadoras en el análisis de historias vitales.—Browning, H. L. y Feindt, W. El contexto económicos-social de la migración a Monterrey. Selectividad de migrantes a una metrópoli en un país en desarrollo: estudio de un caso mexicano. Status migratorio y posición socioeconómica en una metrópoli de un país en desarrollo: el caso de Monterrey.—Land, K. C. Duración de la residencia y probabilidad de migrar.—Feindt, W. y Browning, H. L. La migración de retorno: su significado en una metrópoli industrial y una localidad agrícola en México.—Alvírez, D. Consecuencias de la migración a los Estados Unidos: los migrantes que regresan a México.—Vaughan, D. R. y Feindt, W. Residencia inicial y movilidad residencial de los migrantes en Monterrey.—Balán, J. Determinantes del nivel educacional en Monterrey: un análisis multivariado. — Jelin, E. Cambios ocupacionales en Monterrey: ciclo vital y cohortes. Trabajadores por cuenta propia y asalariados: ¿distinción vertical u horizontal?—Balán, J. Movilidad social de los hijos de agricultores en la ciudad.—Balán, J. y Jelin, E. Migración a Monterrey y movilidad social.—Mir, A. Aspectos subjetivos de la movilidad social. — Muñoz, H., Oliveira, O. de y Stern, C. Categorías de migrantes y nativos y algunas de sus características socioeconómicas: comparación entre las ciudades de Monterrey y México.
1. Monterey, Mexico — Social conditions — Addresses, essays, lectures. 2. Migration, Internal—Mexico—Addresses, essays, lectures. 3. Social mobility—Monterey, Mexico—Addresses, essays, lectures. 4. Occupational mobility — Monterey, Mexico — Addresses, essays, lectures. I. Browning, Harley L., joint comp. II. Jelin, Elizabeth, 1941– joint comp. III. Title.
HN120.M6B35 309.1'72'1 75–553810

Balán, Jorge, 1940-
Regional urbanization under primary sector expansion in "neo-colonial" societies. [Austin, Tex., 1974]
41 l. 28 cm.
"Prepared for the Seminar on New Directions of Urban Research, Institute of Latin American Studies, University of Texas at Austin, May 16-18, 1974."
Includes bibliographical references.
1. Cities and towns—Argentine Republic. 2. Cities and towns—Growth. 3. Cities and towns—Latin America. I. Seminar on New Directions of Urban Research, University of Texas at Austin, 1974. II. Title.
TxU NUC76-52914

Balan, Jozef, ed.
see International Symposium on Ribosomes and Ribonucleic Acid Metabolism, 1st, Bratislava, 1973. Ribosomes and RNA metabolism... Bratislava, Pub. House of the Slovak Academy of Sciences, 1973.

Balan, Kantampulli.
(Sarkkass)
സർക്കസ്സ്. [എഴുതിയത്] കണ്ടമ്പുള്ളി ബാലൻ. കോട്ടയം, സാഹിത്യപ്രവർത്തക സഹകരണസംഘം; sales dept.: നാഷനൽ ബുക്ക്സ്റ്റാൾ, 1972.
211, [1] p. 19 cm. Rs5.00
In Malayalam.
Bibliography: p. [212]
1. Circus—India—Kerala. I. Title.
GV1805.I 5B34 72–904524

Balan, Maniyoor E 1937–
[Cuṭala]
ചുടല; നോവൽ. [എഴുതിയത്] മണിയൂർ ഇ. ബാലൻ. കോട്ടയം, സാഹിത്യപ്രവർത്തക സഹകരണസംഘം; [sales dept.] നാഷനൽ ബുക്ക്സ്റ്റാൾ [1971]
154 p. 19 cm. Rs3.25
In Malayalam.
I. Title.
PL4718.9.B324C8 72–900439

Bălan, Nicolae, Metropolitan of Transylvania
see
Nicolae, Metropolitan of Transylvania, 1882-

Balan, Punalur, 1929–
(Kōṭṭayile pāṭṭŭ)
കോട്ടയിലെ പാട്ട്; കവിതകൾ. [എഴുതിയത്] പുനലൂർ ബാലൻ. കോട്ടയം, സാഹിത്യപ്രവർത്തക സഹകരണസംഘം; [sales dept.] നാഷനൽ ബുക്ക്സ്റ്റാൾ [1973]
113 p. 18 cm. Rs3.50
In Malayalam.
I. Title.
PL4718.9.B326K6 74–901515

Balan, Punalur, 1929–
[Rāman Rāghavan]
രാമൻ രാഘവൻ; കവിതകൾ. [രചയിതാ] പുനലൂർ ബാലൻ. Trivandrum? V. N. Subhashini: വിതരണം: നാഷനൽ ബുക്ക്സ്റ്റാൾ, കോട്ടയം, 1971.
49 p. 19 cm. Rs1.25
In Malayalam.
I. Title.
PL4718.9.B326R3 72–901599

Balan, Punalur, 1929-
see Oru kālaghaṭṭantinṭe kavita. 1974.

Bălan, Ștefan.
Calculul structurilor în domeniul plastic : momente independente / Stefan Bălan, Valeriu Petcu. — București : Editura Academiei Republicii Socialiste România, 1976.
372 p. : ill. ; 25 cm. R76-1298
Summary in English.
Table of contents in Romanian and English.
Bibliography: p. [368]
lei 34.00
1. Plastic analysis (Theory of structures) I. Petcu, Valeriu, joint author. II. Title.
TA652.B29 76-467657
*76 MARC

Bălan, Ștefan.
Essai des constructions. Sous la direction de Ștefan Bălan [et] Mircea Arcan. Traduit du roumain par Radu Călinescu. Bucarest, Éditions Meridiane, 1972.
572 p. illus. 25 cm. 103F (France) R***
Translation of Încercarea construcțiilor.
Includes bibliographies.
1. Materials—Testing. I. Arcan, Mircea, joint author. II. Title.
TA410.B2314 72–356983

Bălan, Ștefan.
Scurtă istorie a mecanicii. [Coperta de Dumitru Ionescu]. București, „Albatros," 1972.
144 p., 14 l. of plates. 19 cm. (Lyceum, 132) lei 5.00 R 72–3422
At head of title: Stefan Bălan, Igor Ivanov.
Bibliography: p. 143.
1. Mechanics—History. I. Ivanov, Igor, joint author. II. Title.
QA802.B34 72–366355

Bălan, Theodor.
Prietenii mei muzicieni : Tiberiu Brediceanu, Constantin Silvestri, Constanța Erbiceanu, Ion Vasilescu : [micromonografii] / Theodor Balan. — București : Editura Muzicală, 1976.
382 p., [4] leaves of plates : ill., ports. ; 21 cm. R76-4121
lei20.50
1. Brediceanu, Tiberiu. 2. Silvestri, Constantin, 1913- 3. Erbiceanu, Constanța. 4. Vasilescu, Ion. 5. Composers—Romania—Biography. I. Title.
ML390.B23 780'.92'2 77-450759
*77 MARC

Balan Menon, P K
see
Menon, P K Balan.

Bălan-Osiac, Elena.
Sentimentul dorului în poezia română, spaniolă și portugheză. București, „Minerva," 1972.
268 p. 20 cm. (Confluențe) lei 8.00 R 73–801
Summary in French.
Bibliography: p. 245–[258]
1. Romance poetry—History and criticism. 2. Solitude in literature. I. Title.
PN814.B3 73–340117

Balananda, Swami.
Past, present, inevitable future of mankind [by] Swamy Balananda. Manchester, David Adams and friends, 1972.
[4], vi, 53 p. port. 22 cm. index. £0.30 B 72–19206
1. Spirituality. 2. Religions. I. Title.
BL624.B33 200 72–195934
ISBN 0–9502413–0–X MARC

al-Balanbūri, Sa'id Aḥmad ibn Muḥammad Yūsuf. al-'Awn al-kabīr fi ḥall al-Fawz al-kabīr. 1974
see Waliulla, Shah, 1702 or 3-1762 or 3. [al-Fawz al-kabīr fī uṣūl al-tafsīr. Arabic] al-Fawz al-kabīr fī uṣūl al-tafsīr. [1974]

La Balance.
Glashütten im Taunus, D. Auvermann
v. 22 cm.
"Revue allemande et française."
Reprint of a publication issued in Paris, by Ludwig Börne.
1. Arts—Periodicals. I. Börne, Ludwig, 1786–1837.
NX2.B34 72–87914
MARC–S

Balance Development, National Conference on
see National Conference on Balance Development, Wagga Wagga, New South Wales, 1962.

A balance for the measurement of film pressures.
see Freud, Benjamin B. I. The shapes of hanging and of detaching drops ... Chicago, 1927.

Balance (kit) A simulation of four families caught in ecological dilemmas [by] David Yount and Paul Dekock. Lakeside, California, Interact, 1970.
1 teacher guide (40 p. 28 cm.) 35 student guides (4 p. 28 cm.)
1. Ecology—Study and teaching—Aids and devices. I. Yount, David. II. Dekock, Paul.
CaBVaU NUC74-24151

Balance of power or hegemony : the interwar monetary system / Benjamin M. Rowland, editor ; W. H. Bruce Brittain ... [et al.]. — New York : New York University Press, 1976.
xvii, 266 p. ; 22 cm. — (A Lehrman Institute book)
"Essays ... originally presented as working papers at the [Lehrman] Institute's International Monetary Seminar which met over an eighteen-month period beginning in the spring of 1973."
Includes bibliographical references and index.
ISBN 0-8147-7368-0 : $10.95
1. Monetary policy—History—Congresses. 2. International economic relations—History—Congresses. 3. Economic history—1918-1945—Congresses. I. Rowland, Benjamin M. II. Brittain, W. H. Bruce. III. Lehrman Institute. IV. Series: Lehrman Institute. A Lehrman Institute book.
HG255.B33 332.4'5 75-27423
76 MARC

The Balance sheet of empire. [n.p., Time-Life International in co-operation with the British Broadcasting Corporation c1973]
2689-2716 p. illus. 30 cm. (Time-Life books) (The British Empire v. 97)
1. Great Britain—Colonies.
CtY NUC76-70892

Balance y Experiencias de la Reforma Agraria en América Latina, Seminario Latinoamericano sobre
see
Seminario Latinoamericano sobre Balance y Experiencias de la Reforma Agraria en América Latina.

A Balanced approach to resource extraction and creative land development associated with open-pit copper mining in Southern Arizona : ₍a joint project of the College of Architecture and the College of Mines of the University of Arizona / designed and prepared by Fred S. Matter, project coordinator ... et al.₎. — ₍Phoenix₎ : Arizona Board of Regents, ₍1974₎
v, 85 p. : ill. ; 22 x 30 cm.
Cover title.
Includes bibliographical references.
1. Copper mines and mining—Arizona. 2. Reclamation of land—Arizona. 3. Strip mining—Environmental aspects—Arizona. I. Matter, Fred S. II. Arizona. University. College of Architecture. III. Arizona. University. College of Mines.
TN443.A6B34 622'.4 74-188851
MARC

Balanced Development, National Conference on
see
National Conference on Balanced Development.

Balanced transportation planning for suburban and academic communities; a case study of the San Francisco Peninsula. Edited by Christopher H. Lovelock. 2d ed., rev. and enl. Stanford, Calif., Stanford Workshops on Political and Social Issues, 1973.
1 v. (various pagings) illus., maps. 28 cm. Political and Social Issues."
Includes bibliography.
I. Lovelock, Christopher H. II. Stanford Workshop on Transportation Planning, 1971. III. Stanford Workshop on Political and Social Issues.
Wa NUC75-24829

Balanchine, George.
101 stories of the great ballets / George Balanchine and Francis Mason. — 1st ed. — Garden City, N.Y. : Dolphin Books, 1975.
xiv, 541 p. ; 18 cm.
"A Doubleday Dolphin book."
Includes index.
ISBN 0-385-03398-2
1. Ballets—Stories, plots, etc. I. Mason, Francis, joint author. II. Title.
MT95.B3 1975 792.8'4 73-9140
75 MARC

Balanci, Bernard
see Lapicque, Charles René, 1898-
Charles Lapicque... Paris, Mayer, 1972.

Balanci Graham (Galerie)
see Galerie Balanci Graham.

The Balancing act. Quota hiring in higher education ₍by₎ George C. Roche III. Black studies revisited ₍by₎ Ernest Van den Haag ₍and₎ Alan Reynolds. LaSalle, Ill., Open Court ₍1974₎
viii, 251 p. 21 cm.
Includes bibliographical references.
ISBN 0-87548-295-3
1. Faculty integration—United States. 2. Higher education and state—United States. 3. Afro-American studies. I. Roche, George Charles. Quota hiring in higher education. 1974. II. Van den Haag, Ernest. Black studies revisited. 1974.
LB2332.6.B34 658.31'1 74-11131
MARC

The Balancing act / Jayme Curley ... ₍et al.₎ ; editor, Sydelle Kramer. — 1st ed. — Chicago : Chicago Review Press/Swallow Press : distributed by Swallow Press, c1976.
217 p. ; 22 cm.
ISBN 0-914090-19-4 : $8.95. ISBN 0-914090-20-8 pbk. : $4.95
1. Mother and child—Case studies. 2. Children of working mothers—United States—Case studies. 3. Mothers—Employment—United States—Case studies. I. Curley, Jayme. II. Kramer, Sydelle.
HQ759.B26 301.42'7 76-2201
76 MARC

Balancing act: a book of poems by Maine women, editors, Agnes Bushell ... [et al] Portland, Me., Littoral Books, c1975.
48 p. 23 cm.
"Published with the support of the Maine Commission on the Arts and Humanities."
I. Bushell, Agnes.
MeU NUC77-81895

Balanda, Gérard.
Le nouveau droit constitutionnel zaïrois. Paris (15ᵉ), Nouvelles éditions africaines, 21, rue Mademoiselle, 1972.
352 p. 23 cm. 70.00F F 72-8081
Includes legislation.
Bibliography : p. ₍340₎-346.
1. Zaire—Constitutional law. I. Title.
72-371075

Balanda, Gérard.
Statut juridique du Fonds belgo-congolais d'amortissement et de gestion; contribution à la théorie des établissements publics internationaux. ₍Lubumbashi, 1968₎
vi, 231 p. 24 cm. (Publications de l'Université officielle du Congo à Lubumbashi, v. 20)
Includes bibliographical references.
1. Fonds belgo-congolais d'amortissement et de gestion. I. Title. II. Series: Université officielle du Congo à Lubumbashi. Publications, v. 20.
74-207511

Balandier, Anne, joint author.
see Almasy, Elina. Comparative survey analysis ... Beverly Hills, Calif., Sage Publications, c1976.

Balandier, Georges.
Anthropo-logiques. ₍1. éd.₎. Paris, Presses universitaires de France, 1974.
278 p. 22 cm. (Sociologie d'aujourd'hui) 39.00F F***
Includes bibliographical references.
1. Social structure. 2. Social change. 3. Society, Primitive. I. Title.
GN490.B35 301.2 74-177843
MARC

Balandier, Georges.
Antropologia política. Traduçao de Octavio Mendes Cajado. [São Paulo] Difusão Europía do Livro, Editora da Universidade de São Paulo [1969]
192 p. 22 cm.
Translation of Anthropologie politique.
Bibliography: p. 183-184.
1. Government, Primitive. I. Title.
TxU NUC75-31697

Balandier, Georges.
Gurvitch. ₍Paris₎ Presses universitaires de France, 1972.
120 p. 18 cm. (Collection SUP. Philosophes) 7.50F F***
Bibliography : p. ₍118₎
1. Sociology. I. Gurvitch, Georges, 1894-1965. Gurvitch. 1972.
HM22.F8G83 72-367303

Balandier, Georges.
Gurvitch / by Georges Balandier ; translated from the French by Margaret A. Thompson ; with the assistance of Kenneth A. Thompson. — New York : Harper & Row, c1974.
vi, 110, ₍1₎ p. ; 23 cm. — (Explorations in interpretative sociology)
Translation of Gurvitch.
Includes extracts from Gurvitch's works.
"The works of Gurvitch": p. ₍40₎-42.
Bibliography: p. ₍111₎
ISBN 0-06-136171-2 : $12.50
1. Gurvitch, Georges, 1894-1965. 2. Sociology. I. Gurvitch, Georges, 1894-1965.
HM22.F8G8313 1974 301'.092'4 75-329852
75 MARC

Balandier, Georges.
Gurvitch / Georges Balandier ; translated from the French by Margaret A. Thompson, with the assistance of Kenneth A. Thompson. — Oxford ₍Eng.₎ : B. Blackwell, c1975.
vi, 110, ₍1₎ p. ; 23 cm. — (Explorations in interpretative sociology)
GB***
Translation of Gurvitch.
Includes extracts from Gurvitch's major works.
"The works of Gurvitch": p. ₍48₎-52.
Bibliography: p. ₍111₎
ISBN 0-631-15590-2 : £3.50
1. Gurvitch, Georges, 1894-1965. 2. Sociology. I. Gurvitch, Georges, 1894-1965.
HM22.F8G8313 1975 301'.092'4 73-94341
75₍r76₎rev MARC

Balandier, Georges.
Political anthropology. Translated from the French by A. M. Sheridan Smith. New York, Vintage Books ₍1972, c1970₎
viii, 214 p. 19 cm. $1.95
Translation of Anthropologie politique.
Includes bibliographies.
1. Government, Primitive. I. Title.
[GN490.B3413 1972] 321.1 72-766
ISBN 0-394-71818-6 MARC

Balandier, Georges.
Politische Anthropologie. ₍Nach der 2., durchgesehenen und erw. Aufl. aus dem Französischen von Friedrich Griese. München₎ Nymphenburger Verlagshandlung ₍c1972₎
226 p. illus. 21 cm. (Sammlung Dialog, 45) GDB***
Translation of Anthropologie politique.
Bibliography: p. 218-219.
1. Government, Primitive. I. Title.
GN490.B3415 72-375363
ISBN 3-485-3045-7

Balandier, Georges.
Sociologie actuelle de l'Afrique noire, dynamique sociale en Afrique centrale. ₍3ᵉ édition.₎ Paris, Presses universitaires de France, 1971.
xvi, 533 p. illus. 22 cm. (Bibliothèque de sociologie contemporaine) 32.00F F 71-6749
Bibliography: p. ₍521₎-524.
1. Fan (African people) 2. Bakongo (African tribe) I. Title.
DT530.B3 1971 73-333158

Balandier, Georges, ed.
see Dictionnaire des civilisations africaines. Paris, F. Hazan, 1968.

Balandier, Georges.
see Rencontres internationales, 25th, Geneva, 1975. Solitude et communication. Neuchâtel, Éditions de la Baconnière, ₍1975₎

Balandin, Alekseĭ Aleksandrovich, 1898-1967.
Izbrannye trudy
see
Balandin, Alekseĭ Aleksandrovich, 1898-1967.
Selected works.

Balandin, Alekseĭ Aleksandrovich, 1898–1967.
(Mul'tipletnai͡a teorii͡a kataliza)
Мультиплетная теория катализа. ₍Москва₎ Изд-во Московского университета, 1963–70.
3 v. illus. 22 cm.
At head of title: А. А. Баландин.
Includes bibliographies.
1. Catalysis. 2. Binding energy. I. Title.
QD501.B2 64-45449
rev 2

Balandin, Alekseĭ Aleksandrovich, 1898–1967.
₍Selected works₎
Избранные труды. ₍Ред. коллегия: д-р хим. наук Е. И. Клабуновский (отв. ред.) и др. Вступит. статья д-ра хим. наук Е. И. Клабуновского₎. Москва, "Наука," 1972.
584 p. with diagrs. port. 27 cm. 3.80rub USSR 72–VKP
On leaf preceding t. p.: Академия наук СССР. Институт органической химии имени Н. Д. Зелинского.
List of works by and about A. A. Balandin: p. 526–577.
Includes bibliographies.
1. Catalysis—Addresses, essays, lectures. I. Klabunovskiĭ, Evgeniĭ Ivanovich, ed.
Title romanized: Izbrannye trudy.
QD501.B19 1972 73-313089

Balandin, Arkadiĭ Ivanovich
see Fol'klor. 1977.

Balandin, Gennadiĭ Fedorovich.
(Formirovanie kristallicheskogo stroenii͡a otlivok)
Формирование кристаллического строения отливок. Кристаллизация в литейной форме. Изд. 2-е, перераб. и доп. Москва, "Машиностроение," 1973.
287 p. with illus. 22 cm. 2.07rub USSR 73
At head of title: Г. Ф. Баландин.
Bibliography: p. 274–₍281₎
1. Metal castings. 2. Crystallization. I. Title.
TN690.B26 1973 73-341627

Balandin, Igor' Grigor'evich, joint author
see Solov'ev, Valentin Dmitrievich, 1907- (Biokhimicheskie osnovy vzaimodeĭstvii͡a virusa i kletki) 1969.

Balandin, Igor' Grigor'evich, joint author
see Solov'ev, Valentin Dmitrievich, 1907-
Kletka i virus. 1973.

Balandin, Lolliĭ Aleksandrovich.
(Na st͡sene i za kulisami)
На сцене и за кулисами. Путь театра "Красный факел" (1920–1970). Новосибирск, Зап.-Сиб. кн. изд-во, 1972.
303 p. with illus., 10 l. of illus. 20 cm. 1.32rub USSR 72
At head of title: Лоллий Баландин.
1. Krasnyĭ fakel (Theater)—History. I. Title.
PN2726.N6B3 73-366141

Balandin, Rudol'f Konstantinovich. BAM—Aspekt geologicheskiĭ. 1976
see Po-khozi͡aĭski ispol'zovat' nedra planety. 1976.

Balandin, Rudol'f Konstantinovich.
(Po kholodnym sledam)
По холодным следам : ₍для ст. возраста₎ / Р. Баландин ; ₍рис. авт. и Б. Лаврова₎. — Москва : Дет. лит., 1974.
205, ₍2₎ p. : ill. ; 21 cm. — (Научно-художественная литература)
USSR 75
Bibliography : p. ₍207₎
0.49rub
1. Geology, Stratigraphic—Quaternary—Juvenile literature. I. Title.
QE696.B28 75-589979

Balandin, Rudol'f Konstantinovich.
(Podvizhnaia zemnaia tverd')
Подвижная земная твердь : динамика Земли / Р. К. Баландин. — Москва : Мысль, 1976.
69, [3] p. : ill. ; 20 cm. USSR***
Bibliography: p. [71]
0.12rub
1. Geodynamics. I. Title.
QE501.B257 77-501985

Balandin, Rudol'f Konstantinovich.
(Vremia—Zemlia—mozg)
Время—Земля—мозг / Р. К. Баландин ; [послесл. чл.-кор. АН СССР Н. Б. Вассоевича]. — Минск : Вышэйш. школа, 1973.
237 p. : ill. ; 21 cm. USSR 74
Bibliography: p. 226-[233]
Includes index.
0.72rub
1. Historical geology. 2. Evolution. I. Title.
QE28.3.B34 75-538278

Balandin, Sergeĭ Nikolaevich.
(Sibirskiĭ arkhitektor A. D. Kriachkov)
Сибирский архитектор А. Д. Крячков / С. Баландин, О. Ваганова. — Новосибирск : Зап.-Сиб. кн. изд-во, 1973.
55 p., 13 leaves of ill. ; 20 cm. USSR 73
0.32rub
1. Kriachkov, Andreĭ Dmitrievich, 1876-1950. 2. Architecture—Siberia. I. Vaganova, Ol'viia Petrovna, joint author. II. Title.
NA1199.K74B34 74-352455

Balandin, Sergeĭ Stepanovich.
[Besshatunnye dvigateli vnutrennego sgoraniia]
Бесшатунные двигатели внутреннего сгорания. [Изд. 2-е, доп.] Москва, "Машиностроение," 1972.
176 p. with illus. 22 cm. 0.82rub USSR 72-VKP
At head of title: С. С. Баландин.
First ed. published in 1968 under title: Бесшатунные поршневые двигатели внутреннего сгорания.
Bibliography: p. [174]
1. Gas and oil engines. I. Title.
TJ785.B25 1972 72-374049

Balandina, V. A.
see Metody issledovaniia udaroprochnykh polistirolov. 1975.

Balandrano, Guillermo Garza
see Garza Balandrano, Guillermo, 1943-

Balanenko, IUriĭ I
(Moia stolitsa, moia Moskva)
Моя столица, моя Москва ... : [фотоальбом] / Юрий Баланенко, Александр Березин ; [специальная цветная фотосъемка Николая Рахманова]. — Москва : Планета, 1974.
207 p. : chiefly col. ill. ; 35 cm. USSR 74
10.82rub
1. Moscow—Description—Views. I. Berezin, Aleksandr Davydovich, joint author. II. Rakhmanov, Nikolaĭ Nikolaevich, joint author. III. Title.
DK601.5.B33 75-591685

Balanenko, IUriĭ I
Moscow / Yury Balanenko, Alexander Berezin ; [colour photography, Nikolai Rakhmanov]. — Moscow : Planeta Publishers, 1974.
207 p. : chiefly ill. (some col.) ; 35 cm. USSR***
Translation of Moia stolitsa, moia Moskva.
10.82rub
1. Moscow—Description—Views. I. Berezin, Aleksandr Davydovich, joint author. II. Rakhmanov, Nikolaĭ Nikolaevich. III. Title.
DK601.5.B3313 947'.31 76-474547
76 MARC

Balanenko, IUriĭ I
(Moskva)
Москва. [Фотоальбом. Фотогр. Ю. Абрамочкина и др. Москва, "Планета," 1973].
511 p. with illus. 35 cm. 23.85rub USSR 73
At head of title: Юрий Баланенко, Александр Березин.
1. Moscow—Description—Views. I. Berezin, Aleksandr Davydovich, joint author.
DK601.5.B34 73-362898

Bălănescu, Caliţa.
Echipamente automatizate de transport uzinal : sinteză documentară. — Bucureşti : C. N. S. T. Consiliul Naţional pentru Ştiinţă şi Tehnologie, I. N. I. D. Institutul naţional de informare şi documentare ştiinţifică şi tehnică, 1974.
100 p. : ill. ; 24 cm. — (Informarea documentară în sprijinul realizării cincinalului înainte de termen) R 74-4209
"Elaborarea lucrării: ing. Bălănescu Caliţa."
Bibliography: p. 93-99.
lei 50.00
1. Conveying machinery—Automatic control. I. Title.
TJ1390.B29 75-567514

Balangoḍa Ānandamaitreya
see
Ānandamaitreya, Balangoḍa.

Balanin, Vasiliĭ Vasil'evich, ed.
see Vodnye puti i gidrotekhnicheskie sooruzheniia. 1973.

Balanos, Dēmētrios Simou, 1877-
Hē ekklēsia mas [hypo] Dem. Simou Balanou. Nea ekd. Athēnai, 1967.
108 p. 21 cm. (Syllogos pros diadosin ophelimōn, vivliōn, periodos deutera, 19)
1. Orthodox Eastern Church, Greek. I. Title. II. Series.
OCU NUC75-86754

Balanovskiĭ, Robert Mikhaĭlovich.
(IA—inspektor manezha)
Я—инспектор манежа : Повесть : [Для сред. и ст. возраста] / Р. Балановский ; [В соавторстве с А. Минчковским ; Рис. Ю. Шабанова]. — 2-е изд. — Ленинград Дет. лит., Ленингр. отд-ние, 1976.
175 p. : col. ill. ; 24 cm. USSR 76
0.73rub
I. Minchkovskiĭ, Arkadiĭ Mironovich. II. Title.
PZ63.B3 1976 76-527590

Balans, Jean Louis.
Autonomie locale et intégration nationale au Sénégal / Jean-Louis Balans, Christian Coulon, Jean-Marc Gastellu. — Paris : A. Pedone, c1975.
xv, 178 p. : maps ; 24 cm. — (Série Afrique noire ; 5) (Bibliothèque - Institut d'études politiques de Bordeaux) F***
Bibliography: p. 19-21.
ISBN 2-233-00018-8 : 35.00F
1. Senegal—Politics and government. 2. Local government—Senegal. 3. Senegal—Social conditions. 4. Tribes and tribal system—Senegal. I. Coulon, Christian, joint author. II. Gastellu, Jean Marc, joint author. III. Title. IV. Series. V. Series: Bordeaux. Université. Institut d'études politiques. Bibliothèque.
HC501.S4 no. 5 320'.08 s 77-452732
[JQ3396.A91] 77 MARC

(Balans na vŭtreshnootraslovite i mezhduotraslovite vrŭzki v mashinostroeneto)
Баланс на вътрешноотрасловите и междуотрасловите връзки в машиностроенето : [изследване] / Асен П. Найденов ... [et al. ; науч. ред. Радка Стефанова] — София : Техника, 1974.
131 p., fold. leaf ; 20 cm. Bu 74-1952
Bibliography: p. 130.
0.71 lv
1. Machinery—Trade and manufacture—Bulgaria. 2. Interindustry economics. I. Naĭdenov, Asen Pachev. II. Stefanova, Radka, ed.
HD9705.B852B35 75-568445

Balans narodnogo khoziaĭstva. Statisticheskie metody izucheniia proizvodstva. "Otv. redaktor: V.S. Nemchinov] Moskva, Izd-vo Akademii nauk SSSR, 1959.
280 p. illus. 27 cm. (Uchenye zapiski po statistike, 5)
At head of title: Akademiia nauk SSSR. Otdelenie ekonomicheskikh, filosofskikh i pravovykh nauk.
Cover title: Voprosy balansa narodnogo khoziaĭstva i teorii indeksov.
Includes bibliographies.
1. Statistics. 2. Econometrics. I. Nemchinov, Vasilii Sergeevich, 1894-1964, ed. II. Akademiia nauk SSSR. Otdelenie ekonomicheskikh, filosofskikh i pravovykh nauk. III. Series.
NjP NUC76-63228

Balans van de Nederlandse kerk : kritische evaluatie van wetenschap en praktijk / J. F. Lescrauwaet ... [et al.]. — Bilthoven : Ambo, [1975]
281 p. ; 21 cm. — (Annalen van het Thijmgenootschap ; jaarg. 63, afl. 1) (Amboboeken) Ne 75-25
Includes bibliographical references.
ISBN 90-263-0316-5 : fl 27.50
1. Catholic Church in the Netherlands—Addresses, essays, lectures. 2. Theology, Catholic—Netherlands—Addresses, essays, lectures. I. Lescmrauwaet, Josephus Franciscus. II. Series: Thijmgenootschap. Annalen ; jaarg. 63, afl. 1.
BX1551.2.B34 76-504520

(Balans vremeni naseleniia Latviiskoĭ SSR)
Баланс времени населения Латвийской ССР / [И. М. Гейдане ... et al.]. — Рига : Зинатне, 1976.
254 p., [2] fold. leaves : ill. ; 23 cm. USSR***
At head of title: Akademiia nauk Latviiskoĭ SSR. Institut ėkonomiki.
Bibliography: p. 250-[252]
Includes index.
1.31 rub
1. Time allocation surveys—Latvia. I. Geĭdane, I. M. II. Latvijas Padomju Socialistiskās Republikas Zinātnu akadēmija. Ekonomikas institūts.
HB199.B29 77-502996

al-Balansī, Muḥammad ibn Ghālib, d. 1177?
(Dīwān)
ديوان / الرصافي البلنسي، ابي عبد الله محمد بن غالب ؛ جمعه وقدم له احسان عباس. — الطبعة 1. — بيروت : دار الثقافة، 1960.
142 p. ; 25 cm. — (المكتبة الأندلسية ؛ 5)
Bibliography: p. 23.
I. Series: al-Maktabah al-Andalusīyah ; 5.
PJ7755.B32A17 1960 75-587613

Balanson, Richard David.
The total syntheses of cedrene, porantherine and perhydrohistrionicotoxin / by Richard David Balanson. -- [s.l. : s.n., 1975]
145, 29 leaves, [1] leaf of plates : ill. (some col.) ; 29 cm.
Thesis--Harvard, 1976.
Includes bibliographical references.
MH NUC77-86006

(Balansovyĭ metod vyvchenniia rozvitku narodnoho hospodarstva)
Балансовий метод вивчення розвитку народного господарства / за редакцією доктора економічних наук, професора В. В. Бондаренка. — Київ : Наукова думка, 1974.
350 p. ; 21 cm. USSR***
At head of title: Akademiia nauk Ukraïns'koï RSR. Instytut ekonomiky.
Includes bibliographical references.
2.12rub
1. Interindustry economics. 2. Ukraine—Economic conditions—1945- I. Bondarenko, Viktor Viktorovich. II. Akademiia nauk URSR, Kiev. Instytut ekonomiky.
HB142.B34 75-531745

Balantič, France, 1921-1943.
Zbrano delo / France Balantič ; uredil, vinjete narisal in opremil France Papež. — Buenos Aires : Slovenska kulturna akcija, 1976.
231 p. : ill. ; 20 cm.
Bibliography: p. 225-231.
PG1918.B3 1976 77-474706
77 MARC

Balantine-Scott, Nadoo.
Trail blazers of New Zealand : original narration / Nadoo Balantine-Scott ; compilation & editing, John Forbis ; design & graphics, John Pratt. — Wellington : Duf Syndications, 1974.
190 p. : ill. ; 18 x 23 cm. NZ***
"Extension to the radio series of the same name."
1. New Zealand—History—Miscellanea. 2. New Zealand—Biography. I. Forbis, John. II. Title.
DU420.B34 993 75-309886
75 MARC

Balantseva, I. A., ed.
see Russia (1923- U.S.S.R.). Glavnoe upravlenie geodezii i kartografii. Pochvennaia karta SSSR. Moskva, 1963.

Balanyi, György.
Histoire de la nation hongroise, par Georges Balanyi. [Traduction française de F. Gachot] Budapest, Éditions de l'Académie Saint-Étienne, 1930. [Nendeln, Kraus Reprint, 1973]
91 p. illus., 2 fold. maps. 25 cm. (Seeds of conflict. Series I: Irredentist and nationalist questions in Central Europe, 1913-1939. Hungary, 2)
No. 3 in series vol.
Pages also numbered 915-1005.
NIC NUC75-71159

Balanza, José.
Literatura española e hispanoamericana. Guatemala, Editorial Escolar "Piedra Santa" [19--]
122 p. 21 cm.
1. Spanish literature—Hist. & crit. 2. Spanish American literature—Hist. & crit. I. Title.
TxU NUC75-73752

Balanza, José.
Vida de Floridablanca. Guatemala [Imp. Minerva] 1961.
57 p. 23 cm.
1. Floridablanca, José Moñino y Redondo, conde de, 1782-1808.
TxU NUC74-173584

Balanzategui, Enrique Calderón
see
Calderón Balanzategui, Enrique.

Balaoritēs, Aristotelēs, 1824-1879.
A. Valaoritēs kai N. Thomazaios (anekdotos allēlographia) Athēnai, 1961.
34 p. 26 cm. (Athens. Panepistēmion. Spoudastērion Vyzantinēs kai Neoellēnikēs Philologias. [Dēmosieumata, 34)
1. Tommaseo, Niccolo, 1802-1874. I. Zōras, Geōrgios Theodorou, 1909- II. Series.
NN MH NUC74-119987

Balaōritēs, Aristotelēs, 1824-1879.
Aristotelēs Valaoritēs. Epimeleia Kl. Paraschou. Athēnai, Ekdot. Oikos I.N. Zacharopoulou [1959]
55, 276 p. (Vasikē vivliothēkē, 16)
CU WaU MnU NUC74-120087

Balaōritēs, Aristotelēs, 1824-1879.
Ta hapanta. Prologos Spyrou Mela. Eisagōgē Kl. Paraschou. Epimeleia Kl. Paraschou. Athēnai, Ekdoseis Delta; Genikē apokleistike polēsis: Ch. Ph. Giovanēs [196-?]
2 v. (880 p.) 22 cm. (Hapanta Neoellēnōn syngrapheōn)
MnU NUC74-120077

Balaōritēs, Aristotelēs, 1824-1879.
Hapanta. Prologos Ar. Kampanē. Kritikē analysis Kōstē Palama. [Thessalonikē] Philologikē, 1961-63.
2 v. 22 cm. (Neoellēnikē vivliothēkē)
1. Greek literature, Modern—Collected works. I. Palamas, Kōstēs, 1859-1943. II. Kabanēs, Aristos, 1883- III. Series.
NN NUC74-120059

Balaōritēs, Aristotelēs, 1824-1879.
Phōteinos. Epimeleia G.P. Savvidēs. Athēna [Ekdotikē Hermēs] 1970.
191 p. 17 cm. (Nea Hellēnikē vivliothēkē, 7)
I. Savidis, George, 1929- II. Title.
ICU NUC74-123162

Balaorites, Aristoteles, 1824-1879. Stichoi graphthentes kata tas teleutaias hemeras tes eis Helbetian anachoreseos mou. 1955
in Patriarcheas, Vasileios D (Ho Aritstoteles Balaorites peri tes Anglokratias ...) 1955.

Balaōritēs, Aristotelēs, 1824-1879
see Hapanta... Athēnai, Ekdot. Oikos E. PA. V. Ethnikē Paidagōgikē Vivliothēkē [196-?]

Balaōritēs, Nanos
see
Valaōritis, Nanos.

Balapanov, Zhumakhan Balapanovich.
Spetsializatsiia i proizvodstvennye tipy sel'skokhoziaĭstvannykh predpriiatiĭ. (Na primere khoziaĭstv Semirech'ia) Alma-Ata, Kaĭnar, 1970.
154 p. map. 21 cm.
At head of title: Zh. Balapanov.
Includes bibliographical references.
1. Agriculture. Economic aspects. Kazakhstan. I. Title.
NcD CU-SB CaOTU NUC74-43226

Balaphoutēs, Chrēstos I
see
Balafoutis, Christos J

Balapitiye Taruna Baudha Samitiya
see Vălitota. 1971.

Balapriya, 1937-
வான் மழை. [எழுதியவர்] பாலப்ரியா. [1. பதிப்பு] நாகப்பட்டினம், இமயப் பதிப்பகம் [1967]
188 p. 18 cm. (பெண் எழுத்தாளர் நாவல் வரிசை)
In Tamil.
A novel.

I. Title.
Title romanized: Vāṉ maḻai.
PL4758.9.B28V3 S A 68-9905
PL 480: I-T-2351

Bālāpūrakara, Viśvanātha Vyāsa
see
Viśvanātha Vyāsa Bālāpūrakara.

Balaqaev, M
see
Balakaev, Maulen Balakaevich.

Balar, Damodar, 1933-
(Behulā)
બેહુલા / દામોદર બલર. — 1. આવૃત્તિ. — વડોદરા : વિશ્વમાનવ સંસ્કાર શિક્ષણ ટ્રસ્ટ ; અમદાવાદ : પ્રાપ્તિસ્થાન ગુર્જર ગ્રંથરત્ન કાર્યાલય, 1975.
30, 179 p., [1] leaf of plates : ill. ; 19 cm.
In Gujarati.
A novel.
Rs10.00

I. Title.
PK1859.B33B4 75-905356

(Balarāja : jīwana te kalā)
ਬਲਰਾਜ : ਜੀਵਨ ਤੇ ਕਲਾ / ਸੰਪਾਦਕ ਨਰੇਸ਼. — ਚੰਡੀਗੜ੍ਹ : ਬਲਰਾਜ ਸਾਹਨੀ ਯਾਦਗਾਰ ਸਭਾ, 1974.
88 p. ; 19 cm.
In Panjabi.
CONTENTS: ਨਰੇਸ਼. ਬਲਰਾਜ ਮੇਰੀ ਨਜ਼ਰ ਵਿੱਚ.—ਕੰਵਲ, ਜ. ਸਿੰ. ਜੁਹੂ ਦਾ ਮੋਤੀ ਗਵਾਚ ਗਿਆ.—ਗੁਰਬਖ਼ਸ਼ ਸਿੰਘ. ਬਹੁ-ਪੱਖੀ ਸ਼ਾਨਦਾਰ ਸ਼ਖ਼ਸੀਅਤ.—ਅਣਖੀ, ਰਾ. ਸ. ਇਕ ਦਿਨ ਬਲਰਾਜ ਸਾਹਨੀ ਨਾਲ.—ਅਤਰ ਸਿੰਘ. ਬਲਰਾਜ ਸਾਹਨੀ ਦੀ ਦੇਣ.—ਆਹਲੂਵਾਲੀਆ, ਜ. ਸਿੰ. ਬਲਰਾਜ ਸਾਹਨੀ, ਪੰਜਾਬੀਅਤ ਦਾ ਪ੍ਰਤੀਕ.—ਗਾਰਗੀ, ਬ. ਬਲਰਾਜ ਸਾਹਨੀ, ਇਕ ਐਕਟਰ.—ਭੋਗਲ, ਪਿ. ਸਿੰ. ਸੌਂਝਿਆ ਪੰਜਾਬੀ, ਬਲਰਾਜ ਸਾਹਨੀ.—ਸੈਨੀ, ਪ੍ਰੀ. ਬਲਰਾਜ, ਇਕ ਅਗਾਂਹਵਧੂ ਅਭਿਨੈਤਾ.—ਹਸਰਤ, ਸੁ. ਵੀ. ਸਿੰ. ਬਲਰਾਜ ਸਾਹਨੀ ਦਾ ਪੰਜਾਬੀ ਸਾਹਿਤ ਵਿਚ ਸਥਾਨ.—ਨਰੇਸ਼. ਸੁਪਨਿਆਂ ਦਾ ਬਣਜਾਰਾ.—ਬਲਰਾਜ ਦੀ ਕਹਾਣੀ, ਬਲਰਾਜ ਦੀ ਜ਼ਬਾਨੀ.—ਤੇਜਿੰਦਰਾ ਆਦਰਸ਼. ਚੰਨਣ ਰੁੱਖ ਲਗਾ ਵਿਚ ਵਿਹੜੇ.
Rs5.00
1. Sahni, Balraj. I. Naresh, 1942-
PN2888.S15B28 75-901203

(Balarāja Sāhanī)
ਬਲਰਾਜ ਸਾਹਨੀ. [ਸੰਪਾਦਕ ਕਪੂਰ ਸਿੰਘ ਘੁੰਮਣ. ਪਟਿਆਲਾ, ਭਾਸ਼ਾ ਵਿਭਾਗ, ਪੰਜਾਬ, 1970]
110 p. illus. 25 cm. Rs5.00
In Panjabi.
CONTENTS: ਸੀਤਲ, ਜੀ. ਸਿੰ. ਪੰਜਾਬ ਦੀ ਜਿਉਂਦੀ ਜਾਗਦੀ ਤਸਵੀਰ.—ਜੀਵਨ ਦਰਪਨ.—ਸਾਹਨੀ, ਬ. ਸਾਹਿਤਕਾਰ ਤੇ ਪੰਜਾਬੀ.—ਬਲਰਾਜ ਦੀ ਕਹਾਣੀ, ਆਪਣੀ ਜ਼ਬਾਨੀ.—ਨਾਨਕ ਸਿੰਘ. ਬਲਰਾਜ ਦੀ ਸ਼ਖ਼ਸੀਅਤ.—ਸਾਹਨੀ, ਭੀ. ਨੇੜਿਉਂ ਤੱਕਿਆ ਬਲਰਾਜ.—ਕੰਵਲ, ਜ. ਸਿੰ. ਪੇਂਡੂ ਬਲਰਾਜ.—ਸਾਹਨੀ, ਅ. ਮੇਰੇ ਡੈਡੀ.—ਦਲਜੀਤ ਸਿੰਘ. ਬਹੁਮੁਖੀ ਸਾਹਿਤਕ ਪ੍ਰਤਿਭਾ ਦਾ ਸੁਆਮੀ.—ਘੁੰਮਣ, ਕ. ਸਿੰ. ਬਲਰਾਜ ਦੀ ਲੇਖਣੀ ਦਾ ਜਾਦੂ.—ਕਸੇਲ, ਕਿ. ਸਿੰ. ਬਲਰਾਜ : ਕਹਾਣੀਕਾਰ.—ਭਿੰਡਰ, ਚ. ਸਿੰ. ਬਲਰਾਜ : ਸਫ਼ਰਨਾਮਾ ਲੇਖਕ.—ਸੇਠੀ, ਨਿ. ਬਲਰਾਜ ਸਾਹਨੀ : ਸਟੇਜ ਐਕਟਰ.—ਘੁੰਮਣ, ਕ. ਸਿੰ. ਪੰਜਾਬੀ ਰੰਗ ਮੰਚ ਤੇ ਬਲਰਾਜ ਸਾਹਨੀ.—ਅਨੰਦ, ਜ. ਸਿੰ. ਇਪਟਾ ਦਾ ਆਸ਼ਕ.—ਕਿਰਪਾਲ, ਪ੍ਰੇ. ਪੰਜਾਬੀਅਤ ਦਾ ਉਪਾਸ਼ਕ.—ਸਾਹਨੀ, ਸੰ. ਪ੍ਰੇਰਣਾ ਸਰੋਤ.—ਸਾਹਨੀ, ਬ. ਰੱਖੜੀ.
1. Sahni, Balraj. I. Sahni, Balraj. II. Ghuman, Kapur Singh, 1927- ed. III. Punjab, India (State). Language Dept.
PN2888.S15B3 70-924782

Balaram, joint author.
see Urbanowski, Ferris. Yoga for new parents ... 1st ed. New York, Harper's Magazine Press, [1975]

Balaram, Nhalileveettil Edavalath, 1919-
Kerala: three years of UF government headed by C. Achutha Menon, by N. E. Balaram. [New Delhi, Communist Party of India, 1973]
54 p. 19 cm. (Communist Party publication no. 10; March 1973 (C87)) Re0.80
1. Kerala—Economic policy. 2. Kerala—Social policy. I. Achutha Menon, Chelat, 1913- II. Title. III. Series: Communist Party of India. Publication, no. 10: March 1973 (C 87)
JQ298.C6A23 1973, no. 10, C87 329.9'54 s 73-902906
[HC437.K4] [338.954'83] MARC

Balarām Dās
see
Balarāmadāsa.

Balarāma, Swami, ed.
see Dādūdayāla, 1544-1603. Sri Svāmī Dādū Dayālu. 1970.

Balarāma Bhādagāum̐le.
[Pushpāñjali]
पुष्पाञ्जली; कविता संग्रह. लेखक बलराम 'भादगाउँले.' [प्रथमावृत्ति. बिराटनगर? विमल कुमार चैनवाला, 2027, i.e. 1971]
2, 8, 68 p. 18 cm. Re1.00
In Nepali.

I. Title.
PK2598.B254P8 70-926885

Balarāma Dāsa
see
Dāsa, Balarāma.

Balarama Gupta, G S
Mulk Raj Anand : a study of his fiction in humanist perspective / by G. S. Balarama Gupta. — 1st ed. — Bareilly : Prakash Book Depot, 1974.
xi, 163 p. ; 23 cm.
Revision of the author's thesis, Karnatak University, with title, The artist as humanist: a study of Mulk Raj Anand's fiction.
Bibliography: p. [157]-163.
Includes index.
Rs15.00
1. Anand, Mulk Raj, 1905- I. Title.
PR9499.3.A5Z59 1974 823 74-901555
75 MARC

Balarama Gupta, G. S.
see The Journal of Indian writing in English. Jan. 1973- [Gulbarga]

Balarama Panicker, Kochukunjupanicker, 1911-
(Śrīnārayaṇaguru)
ശ്രീനാരായണഗുരു; പ്രബന്ധങ്ങളിലൂടെ. പ്രബന്ധകർത്താ കെ. ബാലരാമപ്പണിക്കർ. [1st ed.] വക്കല, ശ്രീനാരായണധർമ്മസംഘം ട്രസ്റ്റ്, 1969.
x, ii, 340, 117, 24 p. 23 cm. Rs10.00
In Malayalam.

1. Sree Narayanan, Swami, 1856-1928. I. Title.
BL1175.S67B35 72-909019

Balarama Panicker, Kochukunjupanicker, 1911-
(Śrīnārāyaṇavijayaḥ)
श्रीनारायणविजयः; सव्याख्यानः. के. बालरामप्पणिक्कर्नाम्ना विरचितः. प्रसाधकसमितिः वि. वि. शर्म [तथा अन्य. 1st ed.] श्रीमदनन्तपुरम्, 1971.
1 v. (various pagings) illus. 22 cm. Rs14.00
Added t. p.: The Sree Narayana vijayam, with commentary.
Additions and corrections in ms.
In Sanskrit; prefatory matter in English or Sanskrit.

1. Sree Narayanan, Swami, 1856-1928—Poetry. I. Title.
PK3799.B3S7 72-905843

Balaramacharya.
(Muraḷīravam)
మురళీరవం; లలిత సంగీత గీతమాల. [కవి] మడిపడగ బలరామాచార్యులు. విజయవాడ, క్వాలిటీ పబ్లిషర్స్ [1972]
iv, 64 p. 20 cm. Rs2.50
In Telugu.

I. Title.
PL4780.9.B257M8 72-903672

Balarāmadāsa.
[Poems]
বলরামদাসের পদাবলী / ব্রহ্মচারী অমরচৈতন্য সম্পাদিত ; ভূমিকা ও নিবন্ধ সুকুমার সেন, স্বামী প্রজ্ঞানানন্দ. — কলিকাতা : নবভারত পাবলিশার্স, 1362 [1956]
53, 175 p. : 23 cm.
In Bengali.
I. Amaracaitanya, Brahmachari, ed.
Title romanized: Balarāmadāsera padābalī.
PK1718.B2192A6 1956 75-985551

Balarāmāmūrti, Yēṭūkūri.
(Āndhrula saṅkṣipta caritra)
ఆంధ్రుల సంక్షిప్త చరిత్ర. రచన: ఏటుకూరు బలరామమూర్తి. విజయవాడ, విశాలాంధ్ర ప్రచురణాలయం [1966]
259, ii, ii p. 19 cm.
In Telugu.
Bibliography: p. i–ii (2d group)

1. Andhra Pradesh, India—History. I. Title.

DS485.A55B27 72-907182

Balarāmāmurti, Yēṭūkūri.
(Bhāratīya tatvaśāstramu)
భారతీయ తత్వశాస్త్రము. రచన: ఏటుకూరు బలరామమూర్తి. విజయవాడ, విశాలాంధ్ర పబ్లిషింగ్ హౌస్ [1971]
224 p. 19 cm. Rs4.00
In Telugu.

1. Philosophy, Indic—History. I. Title.

B131.B25 72-903363

Balaraman, K S
(Kaṇakku)
கணக்கு : புதுக் கவிதைகள் / கொ. ச. பலராமன். — 1st ed. — இராஜபாளையம் : விசுவசாந்தி பதிப்பகம், 1975.
52 p. ; 76 mm.
In Tamil.
Re1.00

I. Title.

PL4758.9.B292K3 76-903723

Balaraman, K S
(Racikaṉ)
ரசிகன் : புதுக் கவிதைகள் / கொ. ச. பலராமன். — 1st ed. — இராசபாளையம் : அன்னை பதிப்பகம், 1973.
43 p. ; 82 mm.
In Tamil.
Re0.25

I. Title.

PL4758.9.B292R3 76-903724

Bālarāmappaṇikkar, K
see
Balarama Panicker, Kochukunjupanicker, 1911-

Bālarāmavarmma, Maharaja of Travancore
see
Bala Ramavarma, Maharaja of Travancore, 1912-

Balarāmdās
see
Balarāmadāsa.

Balaramiah, V 1912–
(Muppū kuru)
முப்பு குரு. Elixir of life. ஆசிரியர் வி. பலராமய்யா. [2. பதிப்பு] சென்னை, அருட்பெருஞ்சோதி பதிப்பகம் [1971]
vi, 85 p. 19 cm. Rs3.00
In Tamil.

1. Medicine—India. 2. Alchemy. I. Title.

R606.B287 1971 73-902667

Balard, François
see Van Kote, Francis. Distribution de la radioactivité dans l'environnement... [Gif-sur-Yvette (S.-et.O.) Service de documentation du C.E.A. Centre d'études nucleaires de Saclay] 1972.

Balard, Michel.
Des barbares à la Renaissance : Moyen âge occidental / Michel Balard, ... Jean-Philippe Genêt, ... Michel Rouche, ... — [Paris] : Hachette, [1973]
279, [24] p. : ill. ; 21 cm. — (Initiation à l'histoire) (Collection Hachette université) (Classiques Hachette) F 74-11341
Includes bibliographies and index.
42.00F
1. Middle Ages—History. 2. Europe—History—476-1492. I. Genêt, Jean Philippe, joint author. II. Rouche, Michel, joint author. III. Title.
D118.B34 914'.03'1 74-193912
MARC

Balard, Michel, ed.
see Les Actes de Caffa du notaire Lamberto di Sambuceto, 1289-1290. Paris, Mouton, 1973.

Balard, Michel, ed.
see Gênes et l'outre-mer. Paris, La Haye, Mouton, 1973-

Balareva, Agapiia Dimitrova.
(Kompozitorŭt Georgi Dimitrov)
Композиторът Георги Димитров / Агапия Баларева. — София : Изд-во на Българската академия на науките, 1976.
157 p., [4] leaves of plates : ill., music ; 20 cm. Bu***
At head of title: Bŭlgarska akademiia na naukite. Institut za muzikoznanie.
Added t. p.: Der Komponist Georgi Dimitrov.
Summary in Russian and German.
Bibliography: p. 137-145.
1.19 lv
1. Dimitrov, Georgi Petrov, 1904– I. Title. II. Title: Der Komponist Georgi Dimitrov.
ML410.D55B3 77-506894

Balarezo Gamarra, Manuel.
see Peru. Laws, statutes, etc. Código civil (1936) Código civil peruano . . . 1. ed. Lima, Editorial Juris, 1974 [i.e. 1975]

Balarezo Gamarra, Manuel.
see Peru. Laws, statutes, etc. Código de procedimientos civiles del Perú . . . 1. ed. Lima, Editorial Juris, 1975.

Balarezo Gamarra, Manuel, ed.
see Peru. Laws, statutes, etc. [Código penal (1924)] Código penal peruano, Ley no. 4868 ... Lima : Editorial Litográfica América, 1973, 1974 printing.

Balarini, Sebastião José.
see Banco de Desenvolvimento do Espírito Santo. Departamento de Estudos Econômicos. A indústria de transformação no Espírito Santo . . . Vitória, O Banco, 1974.

Balart, Rafael L Díaz-
see
Díaz-Balart, Rafael L

Bālarwīn, Muḥammad Muḥammad
see
Bāl-Ruwīn, Muḥammad Muḥammad.

Balaryn, Jerzy.
Sytuacja demograficzna Opolszczyzny po II [i. e. drugiej] wojnie światowej : studium demograficzne / Jerzy Balaryn. — Wyd. 1. — Opole : Instytut Śląski w Opolu, 1975.
407 p. : ill. ; 24 cm.
Bibliography: p. 401-407.
zł60.00
1. Opole region, Poland—Population. I. Title.
HB3608.7.O65B35 75-410166

Balás, David L
(Metousia Theou)
Μετουσία Θεοῦ : man's participation in God's perfections according to Saint Gregory of Nyssa / by David L. Balás. — Romae : I. B. C. Libreria Herder, 1966.
xxii, 185 p. ; 25 cm. — (Studia Anselmiana philosophica theologica ; fasc. 55)
Text in English.
Bibliography: p. [xi]-xxii.
Includes indexes.
1. Gregorius, Saint, Bp. of Nyssa, fl. 379-394. 2. God—History of doctrines—Early church, ca. 30-600. 3. Participation—History. I. Title. II. Series.
BR65.G76B3 231 75-308647
(MARC)

Balas, Egon.
The intersection cut; a new cutting plane for integer programming. Pittsburgh, Management Sciences Research Group, Carnegie-Mellon University, 1969.
25 l. 28 cm. (Carnegie-Mellon University. Graduate School of Industrial Administration. Management sciences research report, no. 187)
"Working paper 33-69-7."
1. Integer programming. I. Title. II. Series.
MoKU NUC75-31698

Balás, Elemér.
Büntetőjogi reform-törekvések; adalékok a büntető-törvény módosításához. Budapest, Pátria Irod. Vállalat és Nyomdai Részvénytársaság, 1901.
143 p. 20 cm.
1. Criminal law—Hungary. I. Title.
74-216302

Balás, Elemér, ed.
see Hungary. Laws, statutes, etc. [Bünteto torvénykönyv] Az összes magyar bünteto törvények gyujteménye. Budapest, Kalmár A., 1900.

Balaş, Ion.
Ultimul obstacol. [Amintiri. Coperta: Cornel Ricman]. [Bucureşti], "Stadion," 1973.
224 p. 19 cm. R 73-4947
lei 5.75
1. Sports—Romania. I. Title.
GV645.B34 75-560015

Balás, János, Dr.
see Budapest. Müszaki Egyetem. Központi Könyvtár. Central Library of the Technical University of Budapest... [Budapest, 1972?]

Balas, Mark John.
see Conference on Control Theory of Systems Governed by Partial Differential Equations, Naval Surface Weapons Center (White Oak), 1976. Control theory of systems governed by partial differential equations. New York, Academic Press, 1977.

Balas, Mikhail
see
Ballas, Mikhail B

Balás, P Elemér, 1883–1947.
Degré Lajos és a végszükség problémája. Szeged, Városi Nyomda és Könyvkiadó, 1937.
32 p. 24 cm.
Includes bibliographical references.
1. Degré, Lajos, 1882–1915. I. Title.
74-216535

Balás, P Elemér, 1883–1947.
... Szerzői jogi reformtörekvések, irta Balás P. Elemér. Budapest, Cáthy Ferenc, 1927.
52 p. 22½ cm. (A sajtó könyvtára ... 2. szám)
1. Copyright—Hungary. I. Title.
35-37548

Bălaşa, Gheorghe.
Sportivi de seamă [români] : campioni olimpici, campioni mondiali, campioni europeni / Gheorghe Bălaşa. — Bucureşti : "Stadion," 1944.
176 p. : ill., ports. ; 21 cm. R 75-1447
Includes bibliographical references.
lei 7.25
1. Athletes—Romania—Biography. I. Title.
GV697.A1B34 77-504974

Bălaşa, Sabin, illus.
see Chiriac, Virgil. Lacrimile Lăcrămioarei. Bucureşti, Editura Ion Creangă, 1972.

Palasagunskiĭ, Iusuf khas-Khadzhib
see
Yūsuf, khāṣṣ-ḥājib, 11th cent.

Balasaheb Deoras
see
Deoras, Balasaheb.

Balasakēs, Paulos
see
Valasakēs, Paulos.

Balasani͡an, Sergeĭ Ishkhanovich.
(Magmaticheskie format͡sii Armi͡anskoĭ SSR)
Магматические формации Армянской ССР / С. И. Баласанян ; Ереван. гос. ун-т. — Ереван : Изд-во Ереван. ун-та, 1975.
217 p. : tables (2 fold. in pocket) ; 21 cm. USSR 76
Bibliography: p. 213–[216]
0.95rub
1. Rocks, Igneous. 2. Petrology—Armenia. I. Title.
QE461.B25 76-533249

Balasanyan, Grigor.
(Aprelow gaghtnik'ě)
Ապրելու գաղտնիքը: Երևան, Հայաստան Հրատարակչություն, 1971:
476 p. port. 18 cm. 0.64rub
I. Title.
PK8548.B25A8 1971 73-219900

Balasanyan, Grigor.
Taĭna zhizni. Erevan, Aĭastan, 1971.
476 p. port.
Title from verso of t.p.
Title page and text in Armenian.
I. Title.
CaOTU NUC74-43239

Balasanyasi, Rajarishi.
(Katampam)
கதம்பம். இயற்றியவர் ராஜரிஷி பால சன்யாசி. [3. பதிப்பு] பெங்களூர், ஸ்ரீ பராசக்தி ஆசிரமம், 1961 [i.e. 1973]
34 p. 19 cm. Re0.50
In Tamil.

1. Hindu hymns, Tamil. 2. Gods, Hindu. I. Title.

BL1226.3.B27 1973 73-903989

Balasanyasi, Rajarishi.
Life of Sri Sai Baba, the immortal saint of India / by Rajarshi Bala Sanyasi. — Bangalore : Sri Parasakthi Ashram, 1949.
vi, 66 p. : ill. ; 19 cm. — (Parasakthi series ; no. 24)
1. Sri Sai Baba, of Shirdi, Saint, d. 1918. I. Title.
BL1175.S7B34 294.5'6'1 [B] 74-195006
MARC

Balasch, Ramon Pinyol i
see
Pinyol i Balasch, Ramon.

Balaschev, Georgi Dimitrov, 1869–1936.
Бѣлѣжки върху веществената култура на Старо -българското ханство и основанието му въ Европа. София, 1902.
80 p. 1 col. illus. 24 cm.
1. Bulgaria—History—Early to 1393. I. Title.
Title romanized: Bi͡eli͡ezhki vŭrkhu veshtestvenata kultura na Staro-bŭlgarskoto khanstvo.
DR75.B34 74-201480

Balascio, Joseph Francis.
The growth and characterization of single crystal calcite. [n.p.] 1972.
97 l.
Thesis (Ph.D.)–Pennsylvania State University.
I. Title.
PSt NUC73-119840

Balasescu, Victor, joint author
see Secara, Eugeniu. Exploatarea retelelor de canalizare. Bucuresti, Editura tehnica, 1973.

Balash, Anatoliĭ Vikent'evich.
(Tekhnika oformlenii͡a gazetnoĭ polosy)
Техника оформления газетной полосы : [учеб. пособие для вузов по специальности "Журналистика"] / А. В. Балаш. — Минск : Изд-во БГУ, 1973.
175 p. with ill., 1 leaf of tables ; 20 cm. USSR 74
Bibliography: p. 146–[147]
0.37rub
1. Newspaper layout and typography. I. Title.
Z253.5.B27 75-581278

Balashch, Ramon Pinyol i
see Pinyol i Balasch, Ramon.

Balashenko, Sergeĭ Grigor'evich.
(Immunnye globuliny v veterinarii)
Иммунные глобулины в ветеринарии. Минск, "Ураджай," 1972.
144 p. with illus. 20 cm. 0.25rub USSR 72-VKP
At head of title: С. Г. Балашенко, В. П. Урбан.
Bibliography: p. 134–[143]
1. Gamma globulin. 2. Veterinary immunology—Russia. I. Urban, Valeriĭ Petrovich, joint author. II. Title.
[SF757.2.B34] 74-332360

Balashenko, Sergeĭ Grigor'evich.
(Planirovanie protivoėpizooticheskikh meropriiatiĭ)
Планирование противоэпизоотических мероприятий / С. Г. Балашенко. — Минск : Ураджай, 1974.
63 p. : ill. ; 20 cm. USSR 74
0.11rub
1. Veterinary medicine—Russia—Gomel' (Province) 2. Communicable diseases in animals—Russia—Gomel' (Province) I. Title.
SF686.G65B34 75-574062

Balashi͡avichi͡us, B.
see Dorogami druzhby. 1976.

Balashkand, Mikhail Ivanovich.
(Istochniki vozbuzhdenii͡a uprugikh voln pri seĭsmorazvedke na akvatorii͡akh)
Источники возбуждения упругих волн при сейсморазведке на акваториях / М. И. Балашканд, С. А. Ловля. — Москва : Недра, 1977.
129 p. : ill. ; 21 cm. USSR 77
Bibliography: p. 125–128.
0.42rub
1. Seismic prospecting. 2. Marine mineral resources. I. Lovli͡a, Sergeĭ Aleksandrovich, joint author. II. Title.
TN269.B26 77-511705

Balashov, Anatoliĭ Nikolaevich, joint author
see Kasimzade, Murad Salman Ogly. Ėlektrokineticheskie preobrazovateli informat͡sii. 1973.

Balashov, Andreĭ Semenovich.
(Potrebitel'skai͡a kooperat͡sii͡a v SSSR)
Потребительская кооперация в СССР : [по материалам IX Всесоюзного съезда кооператоров] / А. С. Балашов. — Москва : Знание, 1975.
63 p. ; 21 cm. — (Новое в жизни, науке, технике : Серия Торговля и бытовое обслуживание ; 11/1975) USSR***
0.11rub
1. Cooperation—Russia. I. Vsesoi͡uznyĭ s"ezd kooperatorov, 9th, 1974. II. Title. III. Series: Novoe v zhizni, nauke, tekhnike : Serii͡a Torgovli͡a i bytovoe obsluzhivanie ; 1975, 11.
HD3355.B33 76-502669

Balashov, Boris Serafimovich
see Parakhonskiĭ, Boris Mikhaĭlovich. Voprosy ekonomiki i planirovanii͡a gruzovykh perevozok vozdushnym transportom. 1972.

Balashov, Dmitriĭ Mikhaĭlovich.
Kak sobirat' fol'klor; rukovodstvo po sboru proizvedeniĭ ustnogo narodnogo tvorchestva. [By] D. M. Balashov. Moskva, Znanie, 1971.
37 p. illus. (Iz t͡sikla "Pami͡atniki russkoi kul'tury")
At head of title: Vsesoi͡uznoe obshchestvo "Znanie". Vserossiĭskoe obshchestvo okhrany pami͡atnikov istorii i kul'tury.
1. Folklore–Russia. 2. Folklore–Field work.
MH NUC75-129920

Balashov, Dmitriĭ Mikhaĭlovich.
(Marfa-posadnit͡sa)
Марфа-посадница. Роман. Москва, "Сов. Россия," 1972.
432 p. with illus. 22 cm. 0.95rub USSR 72-VKP
At head of title: Д. Балашов.
1. Boret͡skai͡a, Marfa Ivanovna, called Marfa Posadnit͡sa, 15th cent.—Fiction. I. Title.
PG3479.L35M3 72-370924

Balashov, Dmitriĭ Mikhaĭlovich.
(Marfa posadnit͡sa)
Марфа посадница : роман / Дмитрий Балашов. — Петрозаводск : Карелия, 1976.
503 p., [1] leaf of plates : port. ; 21 cm. — (Библиотека северной прозы) USSR***
Series romanized: Biblioteka severnoĭ prozy.
0.98rub
1. Boret͡skai͡a, Marfa Ivanovna, called Marfa Posadnit͡sa, 15th century—Fiction. I. Title.
PG3479.L35M3 1976 77-509759

Balashov, Evgeniĭ Pavlovich.
[Ot͡senka tekhnicheskoĭ rabotosposobnosti magnitno-poluprovodnikovykh ėlementov]
Оценка технической работоспособности магнитно-полупроводниковых элементов и устройств вычислительной техники. Ленинград, 1972.
32 p. with diagrs. 22 cm. (Ленинградский дом научно-технической пропаганды. Серия: Приборы и устройства радиоэлектронной техники и автоматики) 0.18rub USSR 72-VKP
At head of title: Ленинградская организация общества "Знание" РСФСР. Е. П. Балашов.
Bibliography: p. [31]
1. Computers—Reliability. I. Title.
TK7885.B26 73-312678

Balashov, Evgeniĭ Pavlovich.
(Proektirovanie magnitnoĭ sistemy zapominai͡ushchikh ustroĭstv na ferritovykh serdechnikakh)
Проектирование магнитной системы запоминающих устройств на ферритовых сердечниках с прямоугольной петлей гистерезиса; стенограмма лекции. Ленинград, 1963.
39, [1] p. illus. 22 cm. (Ленинградский дом научно-технической пропаганды. Серия: Приборы и элементы автоматики)
At head of title: Ленинградское областное отделение Общества "Знание" РСФСР. Е. П. Балашов.
Bibliography: p. 39–[40]
1. Magnetic memory (Calculating-machines) I. Title.
TK7895.M3B32 73-267667

Balashov, Evgeniĭ Pavlovich.
(Sovremennye sredstva vychislitel'noĭ tekhniki)
Современные средства вычислительной техники : единая система ЭВМ / Е. П. Балашов, В. Б. Смолов. — Москва : Ленингр. организация о-ва "Знание" РСФСР, ЛДНТП, 1973.
34 p. : diagrs. ; 21 cm. — (Серия Автоматизированные управления производством) USSR 74
0.21rub
1. Computers. I. Smolov, Vladimir Borisovich, joint author. II. Title.
TK7885.B28 74-354723

Balashov, Grigoriĭ Mikhaĭlovich, joint author
see Albi͡akov, Mikhail Petrovich. (Sistema mashin dli͡a ukhoda za nasazhdenii͡ami v zelenykh zonakh gorodov) 1975.

Balashov, I͡Uriĭ Aleksandrovich, joint author
see Berliner, I͡Uriĭ Iosifovich. (Tekhnologii͡a khimicheskogo i neft͡ianogo apparatostroenii͡a) 1976.

Balashov, I͡Uriĭ Andreevich.
(Geokhimii͡a redkozemel'nykh ėlementov)
Геохимия редкоземельных элементов / Ю. А. Балашов ; АН СССР, Ин-т геохимии и аналит. химии им. В. И. Вернадского. — Москва : Наука, 1976.
267 p. : ill. ; 22 cm. USSR 76
Bibliography: p. 234–[266]
2.64rub
1. Rare earth metals. I. Title.
QE516.R2B34 77-506127

Balashov, I͡Uriĭ Sergeevich.
(Krovososushchie chlenistonogie i rikketsii)
Кровососущие членистоногие и риккетсии. Ленинград, "Наука," Ленингр. отд-ние, 1973.
250 p. with illus., 6 l. of illus. 27 cm. 2.92rub USSR 73
At head of title: Академия наук СССР. Зоологический институт. Ю. С. Балашов, А. Б. Дайтер.
Bibliography: p. 213–[247]
1. Rickettsii͡a. 2. Insects as carriers of disease. I. Daĭter, Arkadiĭ Borisovich, joint author. II. Title.
QR353.B34 74-308732

Balashov, I͡Uriĭ Sergeevich.
A translation of Bloodsucking ticks (Ixodoidea)—vectors of diseases of man and animals [by] Yu. S. Balashov. Translated by Olga G. Strekalovsky. Translation edited by Harry Hoogstraal and Roger J. Tatchell. [College Park, Md., Entomological Society of America, 1972]
161–376 p. illus. 27 cm. (Miscellaneous publications of the Entomological Society of America, v. 8, no. 5) $8.00
Translation of Krovososushchie kleshchi (Ixodoidea)
Bibliography: p. 362–376.
1. Ticks. 2. Ticks as carriers of disease. I. Title. II. Title: Bloodsucking ticks (Ixodoidea). III. Series: Entomological Society of America. Miscellaneous publications, v. 8, no. 5.
QL461.E563 vol. 8, no. 5 595.7'008 s 72-170346
[QL458.I 9] [595'.42] MARC

Balashov, M.
see Polipshennia pleminnykh i͡akosteĭ sil's'kohospodars'kykh tvarin. Kyiv, Vydavnitstvo Ukrains'koĭ akademii sil's'kohospodars'kykh nauk, 1961.

Balashov, N. T.
see Raboty po akklimatizat͡sii i gibridizat͡sii... Kiev, Gos. izd-vo s.-kh. lit-ry Ukrainskoĭ SSR, 1963.

Balashov, Nikolaĭ Ivanovich.
(Ispanskai͡a klassicheskai͡a drama v sravnitel'no-literaturnom i tekstologicheskom aspektakh)
Испанская классическая драма в сравнительно-литературном и текстологическом аспектах / Н. И. Балашов ; АН СССР, Ин-т мировой литературы им. А. М. Горького. — Москва : Наука, 1975.
335 p. : ill. ; 20 cm. USSR 75
Includes bibliographical references and index.
1.85rub
1. Spanish drama—Classical period—1500-1700—History and criticism. I. Title.
PQ6105.B3 76-516713

Balashov, Nikolaĭ Ivanovich, ed.
see Akademii͡a nauk SSSR. Institut mirovoĭ literatury. (Istorii͡a nemet͡skoĭ literatury) 1962-76.

Balashov, Nikolaĭ Ivanovich, ed.
see Geroĭ khudozhestvennoĭ prozy. 1973.

Balashov, Nikolaĭ Ivanovich
see Obshchee i osobennoe v literaturakh sot͡sialisticheskikh stran Evropy. 1977.

Balashov, Petr Stepanovich
see Literatura v izmeni͡ai͡ushchemsi͡a mire. 1975.

Balashov, V. A., comp.
see Predprii͡atii͡a vysokoĭ kul'tury. 1974.

Balashov, Yu S
see
Balashov, I͡Uriĭ Sergeevich.

Balashov, Russia (City). Gosudarstvennyĭ pedagogicheskiĭ institut.
(Vchenye zapiski)
Ученые записки. т. 1.–
Балашов, 1956–
v. 21 cm.
Microfilm. [Moskva] Gosudarstvennai͡a biblioteka SSSR imeni V. I. Lenina, 1968– reels. 35 mm.
1. Education—Russia—Periodicals.
Microfilm Slavic S–2034 LA 77–640192 (MARC–S)

Balashov, Russia (City). Gosudarstvennyĭ pedagogicheskiĭ institut
see Vidishchev, B V O khudozhestvennom masterstve pisateleĭ klassidov. Balashov [Gor. tipografii͡a] 1961.

Balashova, E. L.
see Detal'nai͡a gravirazvedka v rudnykh raionakh. 1974.

Balashova, Evrosinii͡a Antonovna
see Tremadokskie i smezhnye s nimi otlozhenii͡a Kazakhstana. Moskva, Izd-vo Akademii nauk SSSR, 1961.

Balashova, L. P.
see Moscow. Publichnai͡a biblioteka. Otdel rukopiseĭ. (Vospominanii͡a i dnevniki vosemnadt͡satogo—dvadt͡satogo vv.) 1976.

Balashova, Renata Konstantinovna, joint author
see Nakhalov, Viktor Aleksandrovich. (Regulirovka kreplenii truboprovodov teplovykh ėlektrostant͡siĭ. 1975.

Balashova, T.V.
see Sovremennyĭ revoli͡ut͡sionnyĭ prot͡sess i progressivnai͡a literatura. 1976.

Balashova, Valentina Vasil'evna.
(Mikoplazmy i zhelezobakterii)
Микоплазмы и железобактерии / В. В. Балашова. — Москва : Наука, 1974.
63, [2] p. : ill. ; 21 cm. USSR 75
At head of title: Akademii͡a nauk SSSR. Institut mikrobiologii.
Bibliography: p. 59-[64]
0.44rub
1. Mycoplasmatales. 2. Iron bacteria. I. Title.
QR352.B34 75–533988

Balasingham, C 1917-
Sai Baba and the Hindu theory of evolution / C. Balasingham. — Delhi : Macmillan Co. of India, c1974.
x, 71, [1] p. ; 23 cm.
Bibliography: p. [72]
Rs18.00
1. Evolution. 2. Philosophy, Hindu. 3. Sathya Sai Baba, 1926- I. Title.
B132.E9B34 116 75-901110
75 MARC

Balaskas, Arthur.
Bodylife / Arthur Balaskas ; foreword by R. D. Laing. — London : Sidgwick & Jackson, c1977.
192 p. : ill. ; 26 cm. GB***
Includes index.
ISBN 0-283-98309-4 : £6.50. ISBN 0-283-98368-X pbk.
1. Exercise. 2. Human mechanics. 3. Movement, Psychology of. I. Title.
RA781.B22 613.7'1 77-363832
77 MARC

Balaskas, Arthur.
see Every body knows . . . London, British Broadcasting Corporation, 1975.

Balasko, John Allan, 1941-
1972 West Virginia hybrid corn performance trials. [Morgantown] 1973.
20 p. (West Virginia. Agricultural Experiment Station, Morgantown. Current report 62)
I. Title.
DNAL NUC74-125599

Balasquide, L A
Compendio intrahistórico de Peñuelas [por] L. A. Balasquide. San Juan de Puerto Rico, Editorial Cordillera, 1972.
292 p. 19 cm.
1. Peñuelas, Puerto Rico. I. Title.
CtY NUC74-125956

Balassa, Bálint, báró, 1551–1594.
Összes költemények, Szép magyar komédia. [Irta] Balassi Bálint. [Szigeti József előszavával]. Bukarest, „Kriterion," 1972.
248 p. 21 cm. (Magyar klasszikusok) lei 14.00 R 72–2514
PH3194.B3A6 1972 73–303671

Balassa, Bela, 1899-
Foot-and-mouth disease; a guide to reference sources, comprehensive works, review articles, bibliographies. Greenport, L. I., USDA, Agricultural Research Service [1969]
7 l.
1. Foot-and-mouth disease. Bibliography. I. United States. Animal Disease Laboratory, Plum Island, N. Y. II. Title.
DNAL NUC75-107741

Balassa, Bela A
The economic reform in Hungary [by] Bela Balassa. [n. p.] 1969.
34 l. 28 cm. (Final working paper, no. 25)
"Undertaken as part of a consultant arrangement with the World Bank."
Includes bibliographical references.
1. Hungary. Economic policy. I. International Bank for Reconstruction and Development. II. Title.
NcD NUC75-31634

Balassa, Bela A
Indicators of protection and other incentive measures, by Bela Balassa and Daniel M. Schydlowsky. Cambridge, Mass., 1972.
29 p. (Harvard University. Institute of Economic Research. Discussion paper no. 229)
Includes bibliographical references.
1. Free trade and protection—Protection. 2. Commercial policy. I. Schydlowsky, Daniel M., 1940- II. Harvard University. Institute of Economic Research. III. Title.
MH-PA NUC73-43787

Balassa, Bela A
Papers on policy reform in developing countries. Bela Balassa. [n. p.] 1975.
179 p. in various paginations. 28 cm.
Includes bibliography.
1. Underdeveloped areas—Economic policy—Addresses, essays, lectures. I. Title.
CtY NUC77-81749

Balassa, Bela A
Protection industrielle dans les pays en voie de développement. [n. p.] Banque internationale pour la réconstruction et le développement, Association internationale de développement [1970]
63 p. (Rapport no. EC-175)
Cover title.
1. Underdeveloped areas—Commerce. 2. Free trade and protection—Protection. 3. Tariff. I. International Bank for Reconstruction and Development. II. Title.
MoSW NUC74-133760

Balassa, Bela A
La segunda década del desarrollo y la integración económica regional, por Bela Balassa. Bogotá, Fundación para la Educación Superior y el Desarrollo, 1973.
15, 17 p. 28 cm.
Cover title.
"Documento de trabajo preparado para el Simposio sobre Uruguay y la ALALC (Montevideo, septiembre de 1972)"
TxU NUC76-70891

Balassa, Bela A
Tariffs and trade policy in the Andean common market. [n. p.] International Bank for Reconstruction and Development, 1973.
26 p. (Bank staff working paper, No. 150)
1. Tariff—Adean Common Market—Law. I. International Bank for Reconstruction and Development. II. Title.
CU-L NUC76-70321

Balassa, Bela A
The theory of economic integration, by Bela Balassa. London, Allen and Unwin, 1973.
iii–xiii, 304 p. 22 cm. (Unwin university books, 113) £2.85
GB 73–18553
Bibliography: p. 274–289.
Includes index.
1. International economic integration. I. Title.
HF1408.B2 1973 338.91 74–159529
ISBN 0–04–330235–1 MARC

Balassa, Bela A.
see Bornstein, Morris, 1927- Economia di mercato ed economia pianificata . . . Milano; F. Angeli, c1973.

Balassa, Béla A
see Economic progress, private values, and public policy: essays in honor of William Fellner. Amsterdam; New York: North-Holland Pub. Co., 1977.

Balassa, Bela A.
see European economic integration. Amsterdam, North-Holland, 1975.

Balassa, Imre, 1886–
Operák könyve [írta] Balassa Imre [és] Gál György Sándor. Átdolg. és bőv. új kiad. Budapest, Zeneműkiadó, 1971.
799 p. 19 cm.
1. Operas—Stories, plots, etc. I. Gál, György Sándor, joint author. II. Title.
MT95.B32 74–230783

Balassa, Imre, 1886–
Operák könyve / Balassa Imre, Gál György Sándor. — Átdolg. és bőv. kiad. 2. kiad. — Budapest : Zeneműkiadó, 1975.
799 p. ; 19 cm.
Includes indexes.
ISBN 963–330–050–9 : 74.00Ft
1. Operas—Stories, plots, etc. I. Gál, György Sándor, joint author. II. Title.
MT95.B32 1975 76–530360

Balassa, Imre, 1886-
see Ethnographische Sammlungen der Museen in Ungarn. [Budapest, 1964?]

Balassa, Iván.
Az eke és a szántás története Magyarországon. Budapest, Akadémiai Kiadó, 1973.
630 p. illus. 25 cm.
Summary in German.
Bibliography: p. 543-574.
115.00Ft
1. Plows—Hungary—History. 2. Plowing—History. I. Title.
S683.B34 75-566268

Balassa, Iván.
Getreidebau in Ost- und Mitteleuropa. Hrsg. von I. Balassa. Budapest, Akadémiai Kiadó, 1972.
653 p. illus. 25 cm.
Includes bibliographies.
1. Agriculture—Europe. 2. Agricultural implements—Europe. 3. Grain—Europe. I. Title.
S452.B34 73-206975

Balassa, Iván.
Lápok, falvak, emberek : Bodrogköz / Balassa Iván ; [az illusztrációkat Czinke Ferenc rajzolta]. — Budapest : Gondolat, 1975.
302 p. : ill. ; 25 cm.
ISBN 9632801423 : 45.00Ft
1. Folk-lore—Hungary. 2. Ethnology—Hungary. 3. Hungary—Social life and customs. I. Title.
GR154.5.B34 77-470598
77 MARC

Balassa, Iván, joint author
see Béni, Gyöngyi. Magyar múzeumok. Budapest, Népmüvelési Propaganda Iroda, 1969.

Balassa, Iván
see Csikós Tóth, András, 1902-1963. Csikós Tóth András emlékkiállítás. Túrkeve [Damjanich Múzeum] 1970.

Balassa, Iván
see Georgikon Majormúzeum, Kezthely. Georgikon Majormúzeum, Keszthely. Keszthely : Magyar Mezogazdasági Muzeum, 1972.

Balassa, József, 1864-1945.
Helyes magyarság. Budapest, Genius Könyvkiadó [n.d.]
128 p. (Szabad Iskola, 7)
1. Hungarian language--Grammar. I. Title. II. Series.
CLU NUC77-87923

Balassa, József, 1864-1945.
Magyar-angol zsebszótár; a mindennapi társalgás és utazás közben előforduló szavak, szólások és beszélgetések gyüjteménye, az angol kiejtés magjelölésével Balassa József, közreműködésvel szerkesztette Honti Rezső. Budapest, Az Athenaeum irodalmi és nyomdai r.t. kiadás [19-?]
318 p. 16 cm. (Az Athenaeum angol zsebszótára)
1. Hungarian language—Dictionaries—English. 2. English language—Dictionaries—Hungarian. I. Honti, Rezső, joint author. II. Title.
N NUC76-18196

Balassa, Lóránt, ed.
see Hungary. Laws, statutes, etc. Az állami egyenesadók jogszabálygyüjteménye. Budapest, A Magyar Királyi Állami Nyomda nyomása, 1941.

Balassagyarmat a Tanácsköztársaság idején. [Közreadja a balasagyarmati Palóc Muzeum Történeti és Néprajzi Munkaközössége. Az előszót írta Manga János. Budapest] Muzeumok Központi Propaganda Irodája, 1959.
177 p. illus., 24 plates, facsims., port. 20 cm.
1. Balassagyarmat, Hungary—Hist. 2. Hungary—Hist.—Revolution, 1918-1919. I. Manga, János. II. Palóc Muzeum Történeti és Néprajzi Munkaközössége, Balassagyarmat.
CSt-H NUC76-25758

Balasse, Willy
see Klep van Velthoven, Norbert. Grande vente aux enchères publiques, 27-31 mars 1956. Bruxelles, 1956.

Balássy, László, comp.
Haldokló bilincsek; szemelvények Afrika és Ázsia irodalmából. [Válogatták Balássy László és Csanád Béla. fordították Balássy László, et al. Az előszót írta Szeghalmi Elemér. Budapest] Ecclesia Könyvkiadó, 1968.
389 p. illus. 20 cm.
80.00
1. Hungarian literature—Translations from foreign literature. 2. Literature—Translations into Hungarian. I. Csanád, Béla, comp. II. Title.
PH3421.A8B3 74-230558

Balaster, Ammon Nazareth, 1943-
A time-shared analog computer system in hybrid configuration using high speed automatic patching. [n.p.] 1972.
162 l.
Thesis (Ph.D.)—Pennsylvania State University.
I. Title.
PSt NUC75-36303

Balastèr-von Wartburg, Anna-Maria.
Das literarische Werk von Roman Boos : 9. Jan. 1889-10. Dez. 1952 : Bibliographie / zusgest. unter Verwendung von Vorarbeiten von Edith Boos und Michaela Gäch-Boos durch Anna-Maria Balastèr-von Wartburg ; biographische Notiz verfasst von Robert Friedenthal. — Basel : Verlag Die Pforte, 1973.
87 p. : port. ; 21 cm. Sw 74-A-4975
10.00F
1. Boos, Roman, 1889-1952—Bibliography. I. Friedenthal, Robert. II. Title.
Z8109.2.B34 75-591232
[PT2603.O656]

Balaštík, Jaroslav.
Konzervace ovoce a zeleniny : [určeno také studentům stř. prům. škol s potrav. zaměřením] / Jaroslav Balaštík. — 1. vyd. — Praha : SNTL, 1975.
335 p. : ill. ; 25 cm. Cz 75
Bibliography : p. 332.
Includes index.
Kčs40.00
1. Fruit processing. 2. Vegetable processing. I. Title.
TP440.B34 75-410822

Balaštík, Jaroslav.
Konzervovanie ovocia, zeleniny, húb, mäsa a vajec v domácnosti. Ilustr. ... Ada Jakabová. 5. vyd. Bratislava, Príroda, t. Tlač. SNP, Banská Bystrica, 1973.
389, [10] p. illus., tables, diagrs. 21 cm. (Rastlinná výroba) (Edícia Knižnica záhradkára) Kčs28.00 CzS 73
Fourth ed. published in 1970 under title: Konzervovanie ovocia, zeleniny, mäsa a vajec v domácnosti.
Bibliography: p. 389.
1. Food—Preservation. I. Title.
TX601.B26 1973 74-330167

Balastreire, Luiz Antonio, 1943-
Relaxation modulus and fracture parameters for corn endosperm in bending. [n.p.] 1974.
133 l.
Thesis—Ohio State University.
Includes bibliographical references.
1. Maize—Harvesting. 2. Endosperm. I. Title.
OU NUC76-18030

Balasubrahmaniam, V
Law & practice of estate duty, wealth tax & gift tax / V. Balasubramanian. — 3d ed. — Madras : Vishwanath Publications, 1974.
xxviii, 1103 p. ; 25 cm.
Title on spine: Estate duty, wealth tax & gift tax.
Earlier editions entered under: India (Republic). Laws, statutes, etc., have title: Law & practice of estate duty.
Includes index.
Rs85.00
1. Inheritance and transfer tax—India. 2. Property tax—India. 3. Gifts—Taxation—India. I. India (Republic). Laws, statutes, etc. Estate duty act, 1953. 1974. II. Title. III. Title: Estate duty, wealth tax & gift tax.
343'.54'053 75-901699
75 MARC

Balasubrahmanyam, Maddali.
The law of charitable and Hindu religious institutions and endowments in Andhra Pradesh : containing commentary and notes on the latest integrated enactment, the Andhra Pradesh charitable and Hindu religious institutions and endowments act (17 of 1966), with appendices of Court fees and suits valuation act applicable to Andhra Pradesh ... / Balasubrahmanyam, M. — 2d [rev.] enl. ed. — Hyderabad : New India Publications, 1974.
439 p. in various pagings ; 26 cm.
Cover title: Law of charitable and Hindu religious institutions and endowments; with commentaries on the Andhra Pradesh act.
1. Charitable uses, trusts and foundations—Andhra Pradesh, India. 2. Religious trusts—Andhra Pradesh, India. I. Andhra Pradesh, India. Laws, statutes, etc. Andhra Pradesh charitable and Hindu religious institutions and endowments act, 1966. 1974. II. Title.
346'.5484'064 75-900131
75 MARC

Balasubrahmanyam, S R
Middle Chola temples : Rajaraja I to Kulottunga I, A.D. 985-1070 / S. R. Balasubrahmanyam. — Faridabad : Thomson Press (India), Publication Division, 1975.
xxxii, 424 p., [102] leaves of plates : ill. (some col.), map ; 25 cm.
Includes bibliographical references and index.
Rs180.00
1. Temples, Hindu—India—South India. 2. Temples—India—South India. 3. Architecture, Chola. I. Title.
NA6007.S6B34 726'.1'4509548 76-902102

Balasubrahmanyam, T K
(Kaṇṇīrp pukai)
கண்ணீர்ப் புகை. [எழுதியவர்] 'மகரிஷி.' [1. பதிப்பு] சென்னை, தமிழ்ப் புத்தகாலயம் [1973]
143 p. 19 cm. Rs3.00
In Tamil.
Novels.
CONTENTS: கண்ணீர்ப் புகை.—வட்டத்துக்குள் ஒரு சதுரம்.
I. Balasubrahmanyam, T. K. Vaṭṭattukkuḷ oru caturam. 1973. II. Title. III. Title: Vaṭṭattukkuḷ oru caturam.
PL4758.9.B3K26 73-904806

Balasubrahmanyam, T K
(Kaṭal nurai)
கடல் நுரை. [எழுதியவர்] மகரிஷி. [1. பதிப்பு] மதுரை, மீனுட்சி புத்தக நிலையம் [1972]
159 p. 19 cm. (மீனுட்சி, 107)
In Tamil.
Novels.
CONTENTS: கடல் நுரை.—பனிப்போர்.
I. Title. II. Title: Paṉippōr.
PL4758.9.B3K3 72-905695

Balasubrahmanyam, T K
(Nīccal kuḷam)
நீச்சல் குளம். [எழுதியவர்] மகரிஷி. [1. பதிப்பு] சென்னை, தமிழ்ப் புத்தகாலயம் [1972]
200 p. 19 cm. Rs4.00
In Tamil.
Novels.
CONTENTS: நீச்சல் குளம்.—மண்புழு.
I. Title. II. Title: Maṇpuḻu.
PL4758.9.B3N5 72-906099

Balasubrahmanyam, T K
(Patrakāḷi)
பத்ரகாளி / மகரிஷி [i.e. டி. கே. பாலசுப்ரஹ்மணியன்]. — 1. பதிப்பு. — சென்னை : தமிழ்ப் புத்தகாலயம், 1975.
98 p. ; 19 cm.
In Tamil.
A novel.
Rs3.00
I. Title.
PL4758.9.B3P35 76-900801

Balasubrahmanyam, T. K. Vattattukkul oru caturam. 1973
see Balasubrahmanyam, T K (Kannirp pukai). [1973]

Balasubrahmanyam, V 1926-
Verse with prose [by] V. Balasubrahmanyam. Calcutta, Writers Workshop publication, 1972.
28 p. 23 cm. Rs20.00
"A Writers Workshop redbird book."
I. Title.
PR9480.9.B25V4 72-901584
MARC

Balasubramania Iyer, K comp.
[Upanayaṉa mantrārttaṅkaḷ]
உபநயன மந்த்ரார்த்தங்கள். ஸ்ரீகாஞ்சீ ஜகத்குரு ஸ்ரீசங்கராசார்ய ஸ்வாமிகள் ஸ்ரீமுகத்துடனும் கி. பாலசுப்ரஹ்மண்ய ஐய்யர் அவர்களின் தமிழ், ஆங்கில அனுவாதத்துடனும் கூடியது. [1. பதிப்பு] சென்னை, ஸ்ரீ காமகோடி கோசஸ்தானம் [1971]
117 p. 19 cm. Rs1.50
English, Sanskrit, and Tamil.
1. Sacred thread ceremony. I. Title.
BL1226.82.S2B34 71-923981

Balasubramania Iyer, K comp.
விவாஹ மந்த்ரார்த்தங்கள். ஸ்ரீகாஞ்சி ஜகத்குரு ஸ்ரீசங்கராசார்ய ஸ்வாமிகள் ஸ்ரீமுகத்துடனும் கி. பாலசுப்ரஹ்மண்ய ஐய்யர் அவர்களின் தமிழ், ஆங்கில அனுவாதத்துடனும் கூடியது. [1. பதிப்பு] சென்னை, ஸ்ரீ காமகோடி கோசஸ்தானம் [1971]
14, 221 p. 18 cm. Rs3.00
English, Sanskrit, and Tamil.
Previously published in Śrī Kāmakōṭi pratīpam.
1. Marriage—Hinduism. I. Title.
Title romanized: Vivāha mantrārttaṅkaḷ.
BL1226.82.M3B33 75-923982

Balasubramania Mudaliar, M 1896–1958.
(Civañāṉapōtam Tamil mutal nūlē, molipeyarppalla)

சிவஞானபோதம் தமிழ் முதல் நூலே, மொழிபெயர்ப்பல்ல; 120 காரணங்கள். ம. பாலசுப்பிரமணிய முதலியார் அவர்கள் எழுதியது. சென்னை, சைவ சித்தாந்த மகா சமாஜம், 1965.

xx, 32 p. 19 cm. Re0.50
First published in 1949.
"சமாஜ வைர விழா வெளியீடு."
In Tamil; introductory matter in English, or Tamil.
1. Maykaṇṭatēvar. Civañāṉapōtam. I. Title.

PL4758.9.M43C572 1965 73–903926

Balasubramaniam, A
The need for pesticide legislation in Malaysia / by A. Balasubramaniam. — Kuala Lumpur, Malaysia : Ministry of Agriculture and Fisheries, 1974.
8, [1] p. ; 23 cm. — (Information booklet - Ministry of Agriculture and Fisheries ; no. 1)
Bibliography: p. 8-[9]
1. Pesticides—Law and legislation—Malaysia. I. Title. II. Series: Malaysia. Kementerian Pertanian dan Perikanan. Information booklet — Ministry of Agriculture and Fisheries ; no. 1.
346'.595'042 74-940831
76 MARC

Balasubramaniam, A., joint author
see Yunus, Ahmad. Major crop pests in Peninsular Malaysia. -- Malaysia : Ministry of Agriculture and Rural Development, 1975.

Balasubramaniam, K. M., 1908-
see Māṇikkavācakar, 9th cent. Tiruvembavai in Tamil. Madras, South India Saiva Siddhanta Works Pub. Society, Tinnevelly, [pref. 1954]

Balasubramaniam, Ku Ma 1920–
(Atirṣṭak kuḻantai)
அதிர்ஷ்டக் குழந்தை. [எழுதியவர்] கு. மா. பாலசுப்பிரமணியன். [1. பதிப்பு] சென்னை, சங்கரி பதிப்பகம் [1971]
80 p. 19 cm. Rs2.00
In Tamil.
A novel.

I. Title.

PL4758.9.B295A9 72–900901

Balasubramaniam, M 1908–
(Maraṇattai vellum mārkkam)
மரணத்தை வெல்லும் மார்க்கம் : சித்தர்கள் திருவாய் மலர்ந்தருளியது / இயற்றியவர் சித்தாந்தி பாலசுப்பிரமணியம். — [s.l. : s.n., 1974 – ([பெங்களூர் : வேல் முருகன் அச்சகம்])
v. : ill. ; 15 cm.
Cover title.
Includes index.
CONTENTS: 1. பொது விஷயங்கள்.
Rs2.50 (v. 1)
1. Self-realization. I. Title.
BJ1470.B28 75–906334

Balasubramaniam, Ponnuswamy, 1936–
நிலவுப் பூ. [எழுதியவர்] 'சிற்பி' பாலசுப்பிரமணியம். [முதற் பதிப்பு] சிதம்பரம், விற்பனை உரிமை: மணிவாசகர் நூலகம் [1963]
146 p. illus. 19 cm. (செந்தில் வெளியீடு 1)
In Tamil.
Poems.

I. Title.
Title romanized: Nilavup pū.
PL4758.9.B32N5 S A 65–6754
PL 480 : I–T–740

Balasubramaniam, Ponnuswamy, 1936–
[Oḷipparavai]
ஒளிப்பறவை. [கவிஞர்] சிற்பி பாலசுப்பிரமணியம். [1. பதிப்பு] சிதம்பரம், மணிவாசகர் நூலகம் [1971]
126 p. 19 cm. (சக்தி வெளியீடு 1) Rs2.75
In Tamil.

I. Title.
PL4758.9.B32O4 72–927155

Balasubramaniam s/o Arumugam, 1940-
Effect of certain organochlorines on reproduction in chickens and mallard ducks... [n. p.] 1971.
xiii, 196 l. 29 cm.
Thesis (Ph. D.)—Louisiana State University.
Vita.
Bibliography: leaves 115-126.
1. Poultry. 2. Mallard. 3. Insecticides. I. Title.
LU NUC73-71306

Balasubramanian, C 1935–
(Ilakkiya aṇikaḷ)
இலக்கிய அணிகள். [எழுதியவர்] சி. பாலசுப்பிரமணியன். [1. பதிப்பு] சென்னை, விற்பனை உரிமை: பாரி நிலையம் [1972]
296 p. 19 cm. Rs7.00
"நறுமலர்ப் பதிப்பக வெளியீடு."
In Tamil.
Includes bibliographical references.
1. Tamil literature—Addresses, essays, lectures. 2. Tamils—Addresses, essays, lectures. I. Title.
PL4758.05.B27 72–905224

Balasubramanian, Kamakshi, 1948-
A comparison of social universals in Russian and Tamil literature: a typological study. [Providence] 1975.
vi, 155 l. 28 cm.
Thesis (Ph.D.)--Brown University.
Vita.
Bibliography: leaves 151-155.
1. Tamil literature--20th century--History and criticism. 2. Russian literature--19th century--History and criticism.
RPB NUC77-85537

Balasubramanian, Krishnamurthy, 1940-
Fast electrochemical studies with capillary microcells; and, Effects of adsorption on diffusion limited electrode reactions under potentiostatic conditions. [New York] 1971.
vii, 169 l. diagrs., tables. 29 cm.
Thesis—Columbia University.
Bibliographical footnotes.
1. Electrochemistry. 2. Electrodes. 3. Adsorption. I. Title: Fast electrochemical studies with capillary microcells. II. Title: Effects of adsorption on diffusion limited electrode reactions under potentiostatic conditions.
NNC NUC74-134563

Balasubramanian, Krishnamurthy, 1948–
Bibliography on agrarian tensions and land reforms, by K. Balasubramanian. New Delhi, Documentation Centre, Gandhi Peace Foundation [1972?]
2, 68, xxix l. 29 cm. Rs5.00
Cover title.
1. Land reform—India—Bibliography. 2. Land tenure—India—Bibliography. I. Title.
Z7165.I 6B34 016.3333'23'0954 73–902470
MARC

Balasubramanian, N., 1945-
see Coherent optics in mapping . . . Palos Verdes Estates, Calif., SPIE, c1974.

Balasubramanian, Naragana, 1939-
Dislocation dynamics and the deformation of alpha-brass. [New York] 1970.
122 l. diagrs. 29 cm.
Thesis—Columbia University.
Bibliography: leaves 67-62.
1. Brass. 2. Deformations (Mechanics) I. Title.
NNC NUC76-70894

Balasubramanian, R
see Suresvarācarya. The Taittirīyopanisad bhāsya-vārtika of Suresvara. Madras: University of Madras, 1974.

Balasubramanian, S. C.
see National Institute of Nutrition (India). Nutritive value of Indian foods. Hyderabad, India, National Institute of Nutrition, Indian Council of Medical Research, 1971, 1972 printing.

Balasubramanian, Thiripuramadevi Venkatesan, 1933-
Finite element stress analysis of turbine blade hooks. [Ithaca, N.Y.] 1970.
vii, 319 l. illus. 29 cm.
Thesis (Ph.D.)—Cornell University.
1. Gas-turbines. 2. Blades. 3. Strains and stresses. I. Title.
NIC NUC74-5498

Balasubramanian, Vethaiya.
Adaptability of nitrate specific ion electrode for nitrate analysis in tropical soils [by] V. Balasubramanian and Y. Kanehiro. [Honolulu] Hawaii Agricultural Experiment Station [1974]
15 p. graphs, tables. ([Hawaii. Agricultural Experiment Station, Honolulu] Department paper 19)
1. Soils—Nitrogen content. 2. Soils—Analysis. I. Kanehiro, Yoshinori, joint author. II. Title. III. Series.
HU NUC76-18159

Balasubramanyam, K., 1916-
see India (Republic). Superintendent of Census Operations, Mysore. District census hand book, Mysore State. Bangalore, Director of Print., Stationery and Publications, 1967-[74?]

Balasubramanyam, V N
International transfer of technology to India [by] V. N. Balasubramanyam. New York, Praeger [1973]
xiv, 143 p. 25 cm. (Praeger special studies in international economics and development)
Includes bibliographical references.
1. Technology transfer. 2. India—Economic conditions. I. Title.
T174.3.B35 029'.9'60954 73–163925
MARC

Balasubramanyam, V. N., joint author.
see MacBean, Alasdair I. Meeting the Third World challenge. London, Macmillan Press for the Trade Policy Research Centre, 1976.

Balasubramanyan, R
Fishing crafts of India and the different timbers for their construction, by R. Balasubramanyan. Bangkok, FAO Regional Office for Asia and the Far East [1964]
7 p. illus. (Indo-Pacific Fisheries Council. Occasional paper 64/6)
ICRL NUC74-125661

Balasubramanyan, R
Studies on fish baits - Part I: A note on the use of different baits for sea-fishing, by R. Balasubramanyan. Bangkok, FAO Regional Office for Asia and the Far East [1964]
8 p. illus. (Indo-Pacific Fisheries Council. Occasional paper 64/7)
ICRL NUC74-125662

Balasubramanyan, R
Studies on fish baits - Part II: Preliminary experiments to evaluate the relative efficiency of different natural baits in line fishing, by R. Balasubramanyan. Bangkok, FAO Regional Office for Asia and the Far East [1964]
9 p. illus. (Indo-Pacific Fisheries Council. Occasional paper 64/8)
ICRL NUC74-125655

Balasubramanyan, R
The technological characteristics of wood as a building material for fishing boats, by R. Balasubramanyan. Bangkok, FAO Regional Office for Asia and the Far East [1964]
4 p. (Indo-Pacific Fisheries Council. Occasional paper 64/9)
ICRL NUC74-125660

Balasundaram, C 1924-
(Pulavar uḷḷam)
புலவர் உள்ளம் (தொண்டு); கவிதை நாடகம். ஆசிரியர் ச. பால சுந்தரம். [3. பதிப்பு] தஞ்சாவூர், தாமரை வெளியீட்டகம்; [கிடைக்கு மிடம் பாரி நிலையம், சென்னை, 1971]
176 p. 19 cm. Rs3.00
In Tamil; introd. in English.

I. Title.
PL4578.9.B324P8 1971 73-906997

Balasundaram, C 1924-
(Yāṉkaṇṭa Aṇṇā)
யான்கண்ட அண்ணா; கவிதைகள். [எழுதியவர்] ச. பாலசுந்தரம். [1. பதிப்பு] தஞ்சாவூர், தாமரை வெளியீட்டகம் [1971]
52 p. 20 cm. Rs1.75
In Tamil.

1. Annadurai, C.N., 1909-1969. I. Title.
DS481.A64B34 74-929607

Balasundaram, M S
Applied geochemistry in mineral exploration, by M. S. Balasundaram. [Calcutta, Manager of Publications] 1972.
iii, 50 p. 1 fold. map. 24 cm. (Geological Survey of India. Miscellaneous publication no. 21) $0.94.
"PGSI. 71/1500."
"References": p. [47]-50.
1. Geochemical prospecting. 2. Mines and mineral resources—India. I. Title. II. India (Republic). Geological Survey. Miscellaneous publications no. 21.
TN270.B27 555.4 74-187963
MARC

Balasundaram, M. S.
see India (Republic). Geological Survey. Geodynamics Project ... [Calcutta] Geological Survey of India, 1972.

Balasundaram, M. S.
see India (Republic). Geological Survey. Geodynamics project ... Calcutta, The Survey, 1973.

Balasundaram Pillai, T S 1904-
(Caṅkanūṟ kaṭṭuraikaḷ)
சங்கநூற் கட்டுரைகள், அல்லது பழந்தமிழர் நாகரிகம். தி. சு. பால சுந்தரன் (இளவழகனுர்) எழுதியவை. [7th ed.] திருநெல்வேலி, திருநெல்வேலித் தென்னிந்திய சைவசித்தாந்த நூற்பதிப்புக் கழகம், 1966-
v. in 19 cm. — (கழக வெளியீடு, 273, 336
In Tamil.
Series romanized: Kaḻaka veḷiyīṭu.
Vol. 2: 2d ed., 1957.
1. Tamil literature—Addresses, essays, lectures. I. Title.
PL4758.B35 S A 68-20814
PL 480: I-T-2349

Balasundaram Pillai, T S 1904-
பண்டைத்தமிழர் பொருளியல்வாழ்க்கை. தி. சு. பாலசுந்தரம் பிள்ளை (இளவழகனுர்) எழுதியது. [1st ed.] திருநெல்வேலி, திருநெல்வேலித் தென்னிந்திய சைவசித்தாந்த நூற்பதிப்புக் கழகம், 1963.
8, 187 p. illus. 19 cm. (கழக வெளியீடு, 392)
In Tamil.
1. Tamil literature—Hist. & crit. 2. Economics in literature. 3. Politics in literature. I. Title.
Title romanized: Paṇṭaittamiḻar poruḷiyalvāḻkkai.
PL4758.05.B33 1963 S A 68-9897
PL 480: I-T-2249

Balasundaram Pillai, T S 1904-
(Tirukkuṟaḷ aṟam)
திருக்குறள் அறம். ஆசிரியர் தவத்திரு அழகரடிகள். [1st ed.] சென்னை, திருநெல்வேலித் தென்னிந்திய சைவசித்தாந்த நூற்பதிப்புக் கழகம், 1970.
17, [3], 479 p. 19 cm.(டாக்டர் மு. வ. திருக்குறள் பரிசு சொற்பொழிவு. நூல் 1) (கழக வெளியீடு 1392) Rs8.75
In Tamil.
Bibliography: p. [19]-[20] (1st group)
1. Tiruvaḷḷuvar. Tirukkuṟaḷ. I. Title. II. Series: Dr. Mu. Va. Tirukkural Endowment lectures, 1.
PL4758.9.T5B3 78-915361

Balasundaram Pillai, T.S., 1904- ed.
see Kīlkkanakku. Patinen Kikkanakku. 1963,

Balasundaram Pillai, T.S., 1904- ed.
see Kīlkkanakku. Patinen Kīlkkanakku. 1966.

Balasundaram Pillai, T.S., 1904- ed.
see Nālatiyār. **Patinen kīlkkanakku: Nālatiyār urai.** 1968.

Balasunderarao, Gali, 1913-
[Apōha]
అపోహ; సాంఘిక నాటకము. రచన: గాలి బాలసుందరరావు. మ[ద్రాస్, మధురా పబ్లికేషన్స్ [1966]
103 p. 19 cm. Rs2.00
In Telugu.

I. Title.
PL4780.9.B264A8 70-924348

Balasunderarao, Gali, 1913-
సత్యాగ్రహి; సాంఘిక నాటకము. రచన: గాలి బాలసుందర రావు. మ[ద్రాసు, మధురా పబ్లికేషన్స్ [1965]
112 p. 19 cm. 2.00
In Telugu.

I. Title.
Title romanized: Satyāgrahī.
PL4780.9.B264S3 79-901281

Balasuriya, Ellangakoon, 1928-
ප්‍රජා සංවර්ධනය. Community development. කතෘ ඉලංගකෝන් බාලසූරිය විසිනි. [කොළඹ] ඇම්. ඩී. ගුණසේන [1970]
99 p. 18 cm. Rs2.80
In Sinhalese.

1. Community development. I. Title. II. Title: Community development.
Title romanized: Prajā saṃvardhanaya.
HN17.5.B3 78-916220

Bālasūriya, Gunasēkara.
(Kapruka Sindemi)
කප්රුක සින්දෙමි. [කර්තෘ] ගුණසේකර බාලසූරිය. [කොළඹ, පුබුදු ප්‍රකාශකයෝ] 1973.
183 p. 19 cm. Rs4.00
In Sinhalese.
A novel.

I. Title.
PK2859.B28K3 73-903215

Balasy, François Moreau de
see
Moreau de Balasy, François.

Balász, Anna, 1907-
Tettének oka ismeretlen; regény. Budapest, Szépirodalmi Könyvkiadó [1971]
224 p.
I. Title.
InU NUC73-119680

Bałaszewicz, Julian Aleksander.
Raporty szpiega. Wybór, opracowanie i studium wstępne Rafał Gerber. [Warszawa] Państwowy Instytut Wydawniczy [1973]
2 v. illus.
At head of title: Albert Potocki (Julian Aleksander Bałaszewicz)
Translated from the Russian.
Includes bibliographical references in "Przypisy", v. 1 & 2.
1. Russia–History–Alexander II, 1855-1881. 2. Bałaszewicz, Julian Aleksander. 3. Espionage. Russian. I. Gerber, Rafal, ed. II. Title.
MiEM NUC76-70325

Balat, Alain.
Sens et formes de l'économie monétaire; le langage de la monnaie. Paris, Flammarion [1973]
487 p. 21 cm. (Nouvelle bibliothèque scientifique) 50.00F F***
Bibliography: p. [473]-475.
1. Money. 2. Economics. I. Title.
HG221.B189 332.4 73-181033
MARC

Balāṭah, ʻĪsá.
(Badr Shākir al-Sayyāb)
بدر شاكر السياب؛ حياته وشعره. [تأليف] عيسى بلاطه.
بيروت، دار النهار [1971]
222 p. 21 cm.
Bibliography: p. 215-222.
1. al-Sayyāb, Badr Shākir, 1926-1965.
PJ7862.A93Z59 74-220414

Balatka, Břetislav.
Geomorfologický vývoj dolního Poohří / Břetislav Balatka, Jaroslav Sládek. — Praha : Academia, 1975.
69 p., [4] leaves of plates : ill., (some col.) [3] maps (in pocket) ; 24 cm. — (Rozpravy Československé akademie věd ; Řada matematických a přírodních věd ; roč. 85/1975, seš. 5) Cz***
Summary in English.
Bibliography: p. 62-64.
Kčs25.00
1. Geomorphology—Czechoslovak Republic—Ohře Valley. I. Sládek, Jaroslav, joint author. II. Title. III. Series: Československá akademie věd. Rozpravy: Řada matematických a přírodních věd ; 1975, roč. 85, seš. 5.
Q44.C4 1975, roč. 85, ses. 5 75-543173
[GB436.C95]

Balaton Symposium on Particle Physics, High Energy Hadron Interactions, 9th, Balatonfüred, 1974.
Proceedings of the IX Balaton symposium on particle physics, : high energy hadron interactions, 12-18 June 1974, Balatonfüred / editors: I. Montvay, G. Pocsik, A Sebestyén. -- Budapest : [Kultura Hungarian Trading Co.], 1975.
2 v. ; ill. ; 29 cm.
Organized by the Hungarian Academy of Sciences, the Central Research Institute of Physics, the Eötvös Lorand University, and the Eötvös Lorand Physical Society.
Includes bibliographies.
1. Hadrons--Congresses. I. Montvay, I. II. Pocsik, G. III. Sebestyén, A.
OU NUC77-90957

Balatoni almanach. [Csoóri Sándor, et al. versei a Balatonról. Veszprém, 1970]
[28] l. 23 cm.
Catalog of an exhibition of manuscripts of Hungarian poets in Badacsonyi Irodalmi Múzeum, held in 1967.
1. Poetry of places—Hungary—Balaton Lake. 2. Balaton Lake, Hungary—Description and travel—Poetry. I. Csoóri, Sándor. II. Badacsonyi Irodalmi Múzeum.
PH3404.B3B3 74-230333

Balatoni Beszélgetések, Siófok, Hungary, 1969.
Diákszínjátszó csoportvezetők és irodalom szakos tanárok országos tanácskozása. [Előadások. Szerk. Ujvári Jenőné és Klujber László. Kaposvár, Somogy Megyei Tanács VB. Művelődésügyi Osztálya, 1970]
51 p. 29 cm.
1. College and school drama—Congresses. 2. Amateur theatricals—Hungary—Congresses. I. Ujvári, Jenőné, ed. II. Klujber, László, ed. III. Title.
PN3191.H9B33 1969 72-227476

Balatoni Beszélgetések, Siófok, Hungary, 1970.
Helytörténeti bizottságok országos tanácskozása, Siófok, 1970. julius 9-11./ szerk., Kanyar József. — Kaposvár : Somogy Megyei Tanács VB. Művelődésügyi Osztálya, 1971.
98 p., [1] leaf of plates : ill. ; 29 cm.
Cover title: Balatoni Beszélgetések, Siófok, 1970. Helytörténeti bizottságok országos konferenciája.
Includes bibliographical references.
1. Somogy, Hungary (Comitat)—History—Congresses. 2. Hungary — History, Local — Congresses. 3. Local history — Congresses. I. Kanyar, József. II. Title.
DB975.S65B34 1970 76-517499

Balatoni Beszélgetések, Siófok, Hungary, 1972.
A könyv és a könyvtár szerepe a nevelő-oktató munkában. [Szerk.: Kelemen Elemér és Kisfaludi Sándor] Budapest [Országos Pedagógiai Könyvtár és Múzeum] 1973.
116 p. 26 cm.
Summary in English and Russian.
1. School libraries—Congresses. 2. Libraries and schools—Congresses. 3. Books and reading for youth—Congresses. I. Kelemen, Elemér, ed. II. Kisfaludi, Sándor, ed. III. Title.
Z675.S3B22 1972 74-234596

Balatoni Kisgrafikai Bennále, 1973, Balatoni Múzeum, Keszthely
see Második Balatoni Kisgrafikai Biennálé, 1973, Balatoni Múzeum, Keszthely. Veszprém, Veszprém Megyei Múzeumi Igazgatóság, 1973.

Balatoni Múzeum
see Második Balatoni Kisgrafikai Biennálé, 1973, Balatoni Múzeum, Keszthely. Veszprém, Veszprém Megyei Múzeumi Igazgatóság, 1973.

Balátová-Tuláčková, Emilie.
Flachmoorwiesen in mittleren und unteren Opava-Tal (Schlesien). Prag, Academia, 1972.
201 p. 14 charts (in pocket) illus. 25 cm. (Vegetace ČSSR, A4)
"Literatur": p. 181-201.
1. Marshes–Opava Valley, Czechoslovak Republic. 2. Marsh flora–Opava Valley, Czechoslovak Republic. I. Title.
CtY-KS NUC74-151818

Balátová-Tuláčková, Emilie.
Grundwasserganglinien und Wiesengesellschaften. Vergleichende Studie der Wiesen aus Südmähren und der Südwestslowakei. In memoriam Jaroslav Drastich. Praha, Academia, Nakl. Československé akademie věd, 1968.
37 p. illus., tables (in pocket) (Přírodovědné práce ústavů Československé akademie věd, 22, nova ser. 2)
Summary in English.
Includes bibliography.
1. Drastich, Jaroslav. 2. Meadow ecology–Moravia. 3. Meadow ecology–Slovakia. I. Title. II. Series: Československá akademie věd. Přírodovědné práce, 2, nova ser. 2.
ICU NUC76-25689

Balat͡skiĭ, Leonid Timofeevich.
(Ėkspluatat͡sii͡a i remont deĭdvudnykh ustroĭstv morskikh sudov)
Эксплуатация и ремонт дейдвудных устройств морских судов / Л. Т. Балацкий, Т. Н. Бегагоен. — Москва : Транспорт, 1975.
158, [2] p. : ill. ; 22 cm. — (Библиотечка судомеханика) USSR***
Series romanized: Bibliotechka sudomekhanika.
Bibliography: p. 157-[159]
0.58rub
1. Shafting. I. Begagoen, Timofeĭ Naftulovich, joint author. II. Title.
VM758.B33 75-407413

Balat͡skiĭ, Leonid Timofeevich.
Повреждения гребных валов. Москва, "Транспорт," 1970.
141 p. with illus. 21 cm. 0.50rub USSR 70-VKP
At head of title: Л. Т. Балацкий, Г. Н. Филимонов.
Bibliography: p. 135-[140]
1. Shafting—Defects. I. Filimonov, German Nikolaevich, joint author. II. Title.
Title romanized: Povrezhdenii͡a grebnykh valov.
VM758.B34 73-353947

Balat͡skiĭ, Leonid Timofeevich.
(Ustalost' valov v soedinenii͡akh)
Усталость валов в соединениях. Киев, "Техніка," 1972.
179 p. with illus. 20 cm. 1.36rub USSR 72-VKP
At head of title: Л. Т. Балацкий.
Bibliography: p. 171-[178]
1. Shafting—Fatigue. I. Title.
TJ1057.B3 73-313979

Balat͡skiĭ, Leonid Timofeevich
see Filimonov, German Nikolaevich. Fretting v soedinenii͡akh sudovykh detaleĭ. 1973.

Balat͡skiĭ, Oleg Fedorovich.
(Ėkonomika zashchity vozdushnogo basseĭna)
Экономика защиты воздушного бассейна / О. Ф. Балацкий. — Харьков : Вища школа, 1976.
98 p. : ill. ; 20 cm. USSR***
Bibliography: p. 95-97.
0.60rub
1. Air—Pollution—Economic aspects. I. Title.
HC79.A4B34 77-505668

Balat͡skii, Sergeĭ Petrovich, joint author
see Baĭbolov, Urkalyĭ Baĭbolovich. Pensionnoe obespechenie kolkhoznikov. 1972.

Balat͡skiĭ, Vasiliĭ Grigor'evich.
(Muzeĭ v katakombakh)
Музей в катакомбах. Музеят в катакомбите. [Автор на текста Василий Григорьевич Балацкий. Превод на български Лиляна Димитрова Кръстева] 2. изд., перер. и доп. Одесса, Маяк, 1972.
30 p. illus. 21 cm. 0.29rub
Russian or Bulgarian.
1. Muzeĭ partizanskoĭ slavy. I. Title. II. Title: Muzei͡at v katakombite.
D733.R92O33 1972 73-216959

Balat͡skova-Podol'skova, Svetlana Ivanovna.
(Fortran ĖVM "Minsk-32")
Фортран ЭВМ "Минск-32" / С. И. Балацкова-Подольскова, И. М. Булко, В. И. Цагельский. — Москва : Статистика, 1976.
174 p. : ill. ; 22 cm. USSR***
0.56rub
1. Minsk computer—Programming. 2. FORTRAN (Computer program language) I. Bulko, Inna Mechislavovna, joint author. II. T͡Sagel'skiĭ, Vladimir Iosifovich, joint author. III. Title.
QA76.8.M5B34 76-523547

Bălău, Gheorghe, 1904–
Cîntecele mele. Culegere îngrijită de Mihai Deleanu și Vasile Ioniță. [Coperta: Nicolae Lengher. Ilustrația: Ștefan Szekely]. Reșița, Comitetul pentru cultură și educație socialistă al județului Caraș-Severin. Centrul județean de îndrumare a creației populare și a mișcarii artistice de masă, Asociația folcloriștilor și etnografilor „George Cătană," 1973.
112 p. with illus. and port. 20 cm. lei 22.40 R 74-705
I. Title.
PC840.12.A533C5 74-339606

Balaur, N. S.
see Problemy fotoėnergetiki rasteniĭ. 1974.

Bălăuță, Lidia.
Gazele naturale pe glob. București, Ministerul Minelor, Petrolului și Geologiei, Oficiul de documentare și publicații tehnice, 1973.
87 p. with figs. and maps. 24 cm. (Studiu de sinteză) lei 60.00 R 73-5211
1. Gas, Natural. I. Title.
TN880.B34 74-303004

Balavadze, B K
(Nabli͡udenii͡a zemnykh prilivov v Tbilisi)
Наблюдения земных приливов в Тбилиси. 1- Тбилиси, "Мецниереба," 1972-
v. with illus. 22 cm. 0.63rub (v. 1) USSR 73-VKP (v. 1)
At head of title, v. 1- : Б. К. Балавадзе, К. З. Картвелишвили.
Added t. p. in Georgian.
On leaf preceding t. p., v. 1- : Академия наук Грузинской ССР. Институт геофизики.
Summary also in English.
Bibliography: v. 1, p. 132-[136]
1. Earth tides—Russia—Tiflis—Observations. 2. Gravimeter (Geophysical instrument) I. Kartvelishvili, Karlo Zakhar'evich, joint author. II. Title.
QC809.E2B26 73-331328

Balavanta G Kuḷakarṇī
see
Kulkarni, Balwant G 1907-

Balavanta Sāṅgale
see
Sāṅgale, Balavanta.

Balavanta Siṃha
see
Balwant Singh, 1926?-

Balavensky, A., tr.
see Nossalsky, C comp. Recueil de chants populaires russes traduits en langue française. 1892.

Balavoine, Claudie.
see Musae reduces ... Leiden, E. J. Brill, c1975.

Balawanta Siṅgha Nūra
see
Noor, Balwant Singh, 1913-

Balawindarajīta.
(Badalā)
ਬਦਲਾ : [ਨਾਵਲ] / ਬਲਵਿੰਦਰਜੀਤ. — ਦਿੱਲੀ : ਆਰਸੀ ਪਬਲਿਸ਼ਰਜ਼, 1976.
62 p. ; 19 cm.
In Panjabi.
Rs5.00

I. Title.

PK2659.B2924B3 76-903711

Balawyder, A
Canadian-Soviet relations between the world wars [by] Aloysius Balawyder. [Toronto] University of Toronto Press [1972]
ix, 248 p. 23 cm. $12.50 C***
Revision of the author's thesis, McGill University.
Bibliography: p. [225]-231.
1. Canada—Foreign relations—Russia. 2. Russia—Foreign relations—Canada. I. Title.
F1029.5.R9B3 1972 327.71'047 70-163802
ISBN 0-8020-1768-1; 0-8020-0073-8 (microfiche) MARC
rev

Balay, R
Mission interdisciplinaire d'étude sur le développement intégré du bassin du Niger (octobre-novembre 1969). Rapport sectoriel "élevage" [par] R. Balay. Paris, 1970.
83 p. 27 cm. F***
1. Stock and stock-breeding—Niger Valley. I. Title.
SF55.A32B34 338.1'7'60883 74-178382
MARC

Balayo, Joe.
Faces of the Philippines. [Text by Joe Balayo. Fotos by Milo Ramos and Joe Sarmiento. Manila?, National Media Production Center, 1967?-
v. illus. 27 cm.
Cover title.
CONTENTS: 1. The Ilocos region.
1. Philippine Islands—Description and travel—Views. 2. Ethnology—Philippine Islands—Pictorial works. I. Ramos, Milo, illus. II. Sarmiento, Joe, illus. III. Title.
DS656.2.B34 959.9 76-364526
76 MARC

Balayogi, Mummidivaram, 1930-
see Appa Rao, Borusu, 1909- (Bhagavanu Sribalayogi sukti muktavali) 1968.

Balaž, Arpad G 1887-
Arpad Balaž. Slike, grafike, crteži, 1920-1970. Izložbene prostorije Galerija Matice srpske 26. IV - 11. V 1970. [Katalog. Odgovorni urednik Slobodan S. Sanader] Novis Sad, Galerija savremene likovne umetnosti [1971]
[31] p. illus., port. 21 cm. (Galerija savremene likovne umetnosti. Izdanje 8)
Serbocroatian, French, and Hungarian.
Bibliography: p. [27]-[30]
I. Snanader, Slobodan S., ed. II. Matica srpska, Novi Sad. Galerija.
NNC NUC74-135820

Baláž, Jozef, illus.
Dvanásť grafík Jozefa Baláža / [autorka textu Eva Trojanová ; autorka fot. Ľudmila Mišurová]. — 1. vyd. — Bratislava : Pallas, 1975.
1 portfolio ([4] p., 12 leaves of plates) : ill. (some col.) ; 34 cm. — (Albumy ; zv. 1) CzS 75
Kčs30.00
1. Baláž, Jozef, illus. I. Trojanová, Eva. II. Title.
NE2371.C9B34 76-515285

Baláž, Jozef, illus.
see Rázus, Martin, 1888-1937. Maroško študuje. Bratislava, Mladé letá, t. Tlač. SNP, B. Bystrica, 1968.

Baláž, Ondrej.
Učiteľ a spoločnosť. 1. vyd. Bratislava, SPN, t. Pravda, 1973.
191, [4] p. tables. 21 cm. (Základné pedagogické a psychologické diela) Kčs18.50 CzS 73-MS
Summary in Russian and German.
Bibliography: p. 184-187.
1. Teacher-student relationships. 2. Educational sociology. I. Title.
LB1033.B34 73-344844

Baláž, Peter.
Lehrbuch der slowakischen Sprache für Slawisten. ... vysokoškolská učebnica pre Letný seminár slovenského jazyka a kultúry. Autori: Peter Baláž a Miloslav Darovec. 1. vyd. Bratislava, SPN, t. Svornosť, 1972.
238, [8] p. 21 cm. Kčs17.00 CzS 72-MS
1. Slovak language—Text-books for foreigners. I. Darovec, Miloslav, joint author. II. Title.
PG5239.3.S5B3 73-314892

Baláž, Peter.
Manuel de slovaque à l'usage des slavisants. ... vysoškol. učebnica pre Letny seminár slovenského jazyka a kultúry Studia Academica Slovaca. Autori: Peter Baláž, Jozef Bartoš, Miloslav Darovec. 1. vyd. Bratislava, SPN, t. Svornost, 1973.
285, [8] p. illus. 21 cm. Kčs19.50 CzS 73
1. Slovak language—Text-books for foreigners—French. I. Bartoš, Jozef, joint author. II. Darovec, Miloslav, joint author. III. Title.
PG5239.3.F7B3 74-178868 MARC

Baláž, Vincent.
Dodávateľsko-odberateľské vzťahy v investičnej výstavbe : [určená predovšetkým stred. odb. techn. a ekon. kádrom ... i pre štud. priem. škôl ... / autori] Vincent Baláž, Marián Kodoň, Viliam Porázik. — 1. vyd. — Bratislava : Alfa, 1974.
134 p. ; 21 cm. — (Edícia ekonomickej literatúry) CzS 74
Bibliography: p. 134.
Kčs15.00
1. Delivery of goods (Law)—Czechoslovak Republic. 2. Czechoslovak Republic—Economic policy. I. Kodoň, Marián, joint author. II. Porázik, Viliam, joint author. III. Title.
75-562508

Balazard, Simone.
Deux femmes à la rencontre / Simone Balazard. — Paris : B. Grasset, [1975]
270 p. ; 21 cm. F***
ISBN 2-246-00163-3 : 32.00F. ISBN 2-246-00164-1 luxe : 120F
I. Title.
PQ2662.A37D4 843'.9'14 75-503805
75 MARC

Balazard, Yves.
Préparation d'un chantier de travaux publics : évaluation des moyens et des coûts, ordonnancement des tâches / par Yves Balazard. — Paris : Éditions Eyrolles, 1976.
ix, 198 p. : ill. ; 24 cm. F***
80.00F
1. Public works—Management. 2. Industrial engineering. I. Title.
TD159.5.B34 76-452283
76 MARC

Balázs, András.
Az élet meghosszabbítható / Balázs András ; [az ábrákat Bernáth Sándor készítette] — 2., átdolg. kiad. — Budapest : Gondolat, 1973, c1962.
371 p., [52] leaves of plates : ill. ; 25 cm.
Bibliography: p. 325-354.
Includes index.
70.00Ft
1. Aging. I. Title.
QP86.B24 1973 75-566066

Balázs, András
see Reproduction & aging. New York, MSS Information Corp. [1974]

Balázs, Anna.
Boldog ifjuságom. [Budapest] Kossuth Könyvkiadó, 1972.
278 p. 21 cm. 18.00Ft
I. Title.
PH3213.B218B6 73-200630

Balázs, Anna.
Egy orvos az autóbuszon. Budapest, Szépirodalmi Könyvkiadó [1973]
387 p. 19 cm.
CONTENTS: Egy orvos az autóbuszon.—Napló.—A művész úr.—A tízes szoba kulcsa.—Monológ.—A férjek.—A barátnő.—Virágok.—A csúnya lány.—Irigység.—Özvegyen.—Száz lottószelvény.—Az új lakás.—Halpaprikás.—A feleség.—Vakság.—A gyilkos.—A tépéscsináló.—A házmesterfiú.—A professzor.—Az utolsó ember.—Testvérek.
25.50Ft
I. Title.
PH3213.B218O7 75-580044

Balázs, Anna.
Három történet : kisregények / Balázs Anna. — Budapest : Szépirodalmi Könyvkiadó, 1976.
522 p. ; 19 cm.
CONTENTS: Maris.—Homályban.—Májusi lakodalom.
ISBN 9631507068 : 32.00Ft
I. Title.
PH3213.B218H3 77-554661
77 MARC

Balázs, Béla, 1884-1949.
Álmodó ifjúság / Balázs Béla. — Budapest : Magvető, 1976.
442 p. : port. ; 20 cm. — (30 [i.e. Harminc] év)
ISBN 9632702395 : 38.00Ft
1. Balázs, Béla, 1884-1949—Biography. 2. Authors, Hungarian—20th century—Biography. I. Title.
PH3213.B22Z513 1976 77-477809
77 MARC

Balázs, Béla, 1884–1949.
Béla Balázs : Essay, Kritik 1922–1932 / Zusammenstellung und Redaktion, Gertraude Kühn, Manfred Lichtenstein, Eckart Jahnke. — Berlin : Staatliches Filmarchiv der DDR, 1973.
396 p. : port. ; 21 cm. GFR***
Includes indexes.
1. Moving-pictures—Addresses, essays, lectures.
PN1994.B256 1973 75-559879

Balázs, Béla, 1884-1948.
A film. [A benczetést és a jegyzeteket irta: Nemeskürty Istvan.] Budapest, Gondolat, 1961.
270 p. port. 20 cm.
1. Moving-pictures Aesthetics. I. Title.
NNC NUC74-33090

Balázs, Béla, 1884–1948.
Der Film. Werden u. Wesen einer neuen Kunst. (3. Aufl., erw.) Wien, Globus Verl. (1972).
309 p. 21 cm. S80.00 Au 73-3-280
Translation of Filmkultúra.
1. Moving-pictures. I. Title.
PN1994.B268 1972 73-311255
ISBN 3-85364-005-2

Balázs, Béla, 1884-1949.
Der Film : Werden und Wesen einer neuen Kunst / Béla Balázs. — 4. Aufl. — Wien : Globus Verlag, c1972.
309 p. ; 21 cm. Au***
Third and 4th ed. has been enlarged by selected chapters of the author's filmtheoretical works : Filmkultura, Der Geist des Fims, and Der sichtbare Mensch.
Includes indexes.
ISBN 3-85364-005-2
1. Moving-pictures. I. Title.
PN1994.B257 1972 76-465662
76 MARC

Balázs, Béla, 1884–1949.
Der Geist des Films/ Béla Balázs. Einl.: Hartmut Bitomsky. — Neuausg. 1.-2. Tsd. — Frankfurt (am Main) : Makol-Verlag, 1972.
55, 216 p.; 21 cm. GFR 73-A
1. Moving-pictures. I. Bitomsky, Hartmut, 1942– ed. II. Title.
PN1994.B27 1972 74-319323

Balázs, Béla, 1884–1949.
Halálos fiatalság : drámák, tanulmányok / Balázs Béla ; [válogatta és szerk. Fehér Ferenc és Radnóti Sándor ; az előszót Fehér Ferenc írta]. — [Budapest] : Magyar Helikon, 1974.
368 p. ; 20 cm.
CONTENTS: Doktor Szélpál Margit.—Az utolsó nap.—Halálos fiatalság.—Heláleszté tika.—A líraí érzékenységről.
ISBN 963-207-184-0 : 50.00Ft
I. Title.
PH3213.B22H3 1974 77-502801

Balázs, Béla, 1884–1949.
The mantle of dreams / Béla Baláza ; translated by George Leitmann. — 1st ed. — Tokyo : Kodansha International ; New York : distributed by Harper & Row, 1974.
123 p. : ill. ; 22 cm.
"Translated from the German limited edition of 1922 published by D. & R. Bischoff, Munich, as Der Mantel der Träume."
CONTENTS: The mantle of dreams.—Li Tai-pe and the thief.—The parasols.—The clumsy god.—The opium smokers.—The flea.—The old child.—The god robbers.—Li Tai-pe and springtime.—The ancestors.—The moon fish.—The friends.—The revenge of the chestnut tree.—The tearful glance.—The child of clay.—The victor.
I. Title.
ISBN 0-87011-203-1 : ¥2,500 ($10.00U.S.) Ja***
PZ3.B18Man 3 833'.9'12 73-79760
[PT2603.A35] MARC

Balázs, Béla, 1884–1949.
Theory of the film; character and growth of a new art. New York, Arno Press, 1972.
291 p. illus. 24 cm. (The Arno Press cinema program. The Literature of cinema)
Translation of Filmkultúra.
Reprint of the 1952 ed. published by D. Dobson, London, in series: International theatre and cinema.
1. Moving-pictures. I. Title. II. Series: The Arno Press cinema program. III. Series: The Literature of cinema. III. Series: The IV. Series: International library of theatre and cinema.
PN1994.B266 1972 791.43 71-169347
ISBN 0-405-03910-7 MARC

Balázs, Béla, 1884–1949.
A vándor énekel : versek és novellák / Balázs Béla ; [válogatta, szerk. és az előszót írta Radnóti Sándor]. — [s. n.] : Magyar Helikon, 1975.
335 p. ; 20 cm.
ISBN 963-207-434-3 : 45.00Ft
I. Title.
PH3213.B22V36 1975 77-502621

Balazs, Bela, 1884-1949
see "Antifashizm - nash stil'". Moskva, Progress, 1971.

Balázs, Béla, 1884-
see A Fakó lovacska... Budapest, Európa, 1958.

Balázs, Béla, 1918–1959, ed.
A klerikális reakció, a Horthy-fasizmus támasza. Budapest, Művelt Nép Könyvkiadó, 1953–
v. illus., fold. map. 21 cm.
At head of title: A Magyar Tudományos Akadémia Történettudományi Intézete.
CONTENTS: 1. 1919–1930.
1. Church and state in Hungary. I. Title.
BR817.H8B28 55-21707

Balázs, Béla, 1918–1959.
A klerikális reakció szerepe a Horthy-fasizmus uralomrajutásában és konszolidálásában. Budapest, Szikra, 1954.
71 p. 19 cm.
Bibliography: p. 66–69.
1. Hungary — Politics and government — 1918–1945. 2. Catholic Church in Hungary. I. Title.
DB955.B28 67-52315

Balázs, Béla, 1918–1959.
A középrétegek szerepe társadalmunk fejlődésében; egy évszázad magyar történelmének néhány sajátosságáról 1849–1945. [Budapest] Kossuth Könyvkiadó, 1958.
234 p. 20 cm.
1. Middle classes—Hungary. I. Title.
HT690.H8B3 60-30723

Balázs, Béla, 1918–1959.
Népmozgalom és nemzeti bizottságok, 1945–1946. [Sajtó alá rendezte és a bevezetést írta Lackó Miklós. Budapest] Kossuth Könyvkiadó, 1961.
231 p. 21 cm.
At head of title: A Magyar Tudományos Akadémia Történettudományi Intézete.
1. Local government—Hungary. I. Lackó, Miklós, ed. II. Title.
JS4668.B3 62-27699

Balázs, Béláné.
Négynyelvű közgazdasági szótár : magyar, angol, német, orosz / Balázs Béláné, Kelen Zsuzsa. — Budapest : Közgazdasági és Jogi Könyvkiado, 1974.
494 p. ; 21 cm.
Bibliography: p. [493]-494.
Includes indexes.
ISBN 963-220-105-1 : 66.00Ft
1. Economics—Dictionaries—Polyglot. 2. Hungarian language—Dictionaries—Polyglot. I. Kelen, Zsuzsa, joint author. II. Title.
HB61.B325 76-508476

Balázs, Dénes.
Galápagos. Budapest, Gondolat, 1973.
215, [1] p. illus. (part col.) 26 cm. 57.00Ft
Bibliography: p. 213-[216]
1. Natural history—Galápagos Islands. I. Title.
QH198.G3B34 73-220199

Balázs, Dénes.
Hátizsákkal Alaszkától a Tűzföldig. Budapest [Táncsics Könyvkiadó] 1972.
2 v. illus. 19 cm. (Utikalandok 111–112)
CONTENTS: 1. rész. Észak-Amerika.—2. rész. Dél-Amerika.
32.00Ft per vol.
1. America—Description and travel—1951– 2. Backpacking. I. Title.
E27.2.B34 74-230111

Balázs, Dénes.
Tájfun Manila felett / Balázs Dénes. — Budapest : Gondolat, 1975.
233 p., [40] leaves of plates : ill. (some col.), maps ; 21 cm. — (Világjárók ; 99)
ISBN 963-280-293-4 : 47.00Ft
1. Philippine Islands—Description and travel. 2. Balázs, Dénes. I. Title.
DS660.B34 77-505250

Balazs, Etienne, 1905-1963
see Aubin, Françoise. Études Song. [Paris] Mouton [19

Balazs, Étienne, 1905-1963
see Aubin, Françoise. In memoriam Étienne Balazs. [Paris] Mouton [c1970]

Balázs, Éva H
Karl von Zinzendorf et ses relations avec la Hongrie à l'epoque de l'absolutisme éclairé. É. H. Balázs. Budapest, Akadémiai Kiadó, 1975.
22 p. 24 cm. (Studia historica—Academiae Scientiarum Hungaricae, 104)
"Publié dans Études historiques 1975. I."
Summary in Russian.
Bibliographical footnotes.
1. Zinzendorf, Karl, Graf von, fl. 1785. 2. Hungary—History—Joseph II, 1780-1790. I. Title. II. Series: Magyar Tudományos Akadémia, Budapest. Studia historica, 104.
NIC NUC77-81748

Balazs, Eva K 1928-
A psycho-social study of outstanding female athletes. [n. p.] 1974.
viii, 181 p. illus., tables.
Thesis–Boston University.
Bibliography: p. 177-180.
1. Athletes, Women. 2. Athletes, American.
I. Title.
MBU NUC76-18031

Balázs, Ferenc.
Bejárom a kerek világot : (1923–1928) / Balázs Ferenc ; [a bevezető tanulmányt írta és a jegyzeteket összeállította Mikó Imre]. — Bukarest : Kriterion, 1975.
305 p. : port. ; 20 cm. R 75-4760
lei 9.50
1. Balázs, Ferenc—Biography. I. Title.
PH3213.B225Z515 76-502352

Balázs, Ferenc.
Mesék. [Az utószót Marosi Ildikó irta]. Bukarest, „Kriterion," 1973.
80 p. with facsims. and port. 15 cm. lei 5.25 R 73-5490
PH3213.B225M4 74-333436

Balazs, Ferenc.
A novenyvedelem gepei. Balazs Ferenc, Dimitrievits Gyorgy. Budapest, Mezogazdasagi Kiado, 1975.
202 p. ill.
Bibliography: p. 194.
1. Spraying and dusting in agriculture.
2. Spraying equipment. 3. Plants, Protection of. Hungary. I. Dimitrievits, Gyorgy. II. Title.
DNAL NUC77-82728

Balázs, G Árpád.
Bolyongó paletta; önéletrajz [írta] Balázs G. Arpád. [Szabadka, A Szabadkai Munkásegyetem] 1969.
40 p. illus. 15 cm. (Életjel miniatűrök, 5)
MH NUC73-119533

Balázs, György, Dr.
Betonburkolatok hibái és javitása műgyantával / Balázs György, Ludányi Tibor, Varga Ferencné. — Budapest : Közlekedési Dokumentációs Vállalat, 1973.
118 p., [2] fold. leaves of plates : ill. ; 24 cm. — (Tudományos közlemények—Budapesti Műszaki Egyetem Építőmérnöki Kar, Építőanyagok Tanszék ; 4)
Summary also in English, German, and Russian.
Includes bibliographical references.
1. Concrete construction—Maintenance and repair. 2. Concrete—Defects. I. Ludányi, Tibor, joint author. II. Varga, Ferencné, joint author. III. Title. IV. Series: Budapest. Műszaki Egyetem. Építőanyagok Tanszék. Tudományos közlemények ; 4.
TA681.B185 75-402714

Balázs, György, Dr., joint author
see Boros, Jánosné. C_3A - $CaSO_4$ - $CaCL_2$ - H_2O rendszer hidratációja. Budapest, Közlekedési Dokumentációs Vállalat, 1972.

Balázs, István, ed.
see Népművelési szervek ellenőrzése. Budapest, Közgazdasági és Jogi Könyvkiadó, 1967.

Balázs, János.
Funktionswerte der Pronominalität. [Übers. von Péter Lieber] Budapest, Akadémiai Kiadó, 1973.
240 p. 25 cm.
Bibliography: p. 225–235.
1. Grammar, Comparative and general—Pronoun. I. Title.
P279.B315 74-232795

Balázs, József, 1930–
A magyar bűnugyi statisztika kialakulása és fejlődése, különös tekintettel annak módszertani kérdéseire. Szeged, 1969.
62 p. 24 cm. (Acta Universitatis Szegediensis de Attila József nominatae. Acta juridica et politica, t. 16, fasc. 1)
Summary in German and Russian.
Includes bibliographical references.
1. Criminal statistics—Hungary. 2. Crime and criminals—Hungary. I. Title. II. Series: Acta juridica et politica, t. 16, fasc. 1.
74-215704

Balázs, József, 1944-
Fábián Bálint találkozása Istennel / Balázs József. — Budapest : Magvető, 1976.
240 p. ; 19 cm.
ISBN 9632702263 : 14.00Ft
I. Title.
PH3213.B227F3 77-554346
77 MARC

Balázs, József, 1944-
Koportos : kisregény / Balázs József. — Budapest : Szépirodalmi Könyvkiadó, 1976.
91 p. ; 19 cm.
ISBN 9631505294 : 9.00Ft
I. Title.
PH3213.B227K6 77-474384
77 MARC

Balazs, Klara.
Bogyos gyumolcsuek vedelme. Budapest, Mezogazdasagi Kiado, 1971.
243 p. illus.
Bibliography: p. 229-236.
1. Berries. Diseases. 2. Berries. Pests.
I. Vajna, Laszlo. II. Title.
DNAL NUC73-42808

Balazs, Klara.
Kiskertek es hazikertek novenyvedelmi naptara. Budapest, Mezogazdasagi Kiado, 1972.
205 p. illus.
Bibliography: p. 204.
1. Gardening. Hungary. Handbooks, manuals, etc. 2. Plants, Protection of. Hungary.
I. Bodor, Janos. II. Lelkes, Lajos. III. Title.
DNAL NUC74-151816

Balazs, Marianne E
Sheldon Peck / [by Marianne E. Balazs]. — New York : Whitney Museum of American Art, [1975]
p. 273-282 : ill. (some col.) ; 31 cm.
Cover title.
"Reprinted from the magazine Antiques, August 1975."
1. Peck, Sheldon, 1797-1868. 2. Primitivism in art—United States. I. Peck, Sheldon, 1797-1868. II. Whitney Museum of American Art, New York.
ND1329.P42B34 759.13 76-351651
76 MARC

Balazs, Mary.
The voice of thy brother's blood : poems / by Mary Balazs. — New Wilmington, Pa. : Dawn Valley Press, c1976.
60 p. ; 22 cm.
$3.00
I. Title.
PS3552.A445V6 811'.5'4 76-18590
76 MARC

Balazs, Mary.
see Touching this earth ... New Wilmington, Pa., Dawn Valley Press, c1977.

Balazs, Mary
see I, that am ever stranger... [New Wilmington, Pa., Globe Printing Co., 1974]

Balázs, Mihály, ed.
see Felkészülés a hivatásra... Budapest, Felsőoktatási Pedagógiai Kutatóközpont, 1971.

Balazs, Phillip Terry.
Network models of broadband cable communication systems. [Stanford, Calif.] 1973.
xii, 130 l.
Thesis (Engineer)—Stanford University.
Includes bibliographical references.
1. Community antenna television. I. Title.
CSt NUC74-125597

Balázs, R., ed.
see Metabolic compartmentation in the brain... New York, Wiley [1972]

Balázs, Sándor.
Elmélkedés a célszerűségről. Bukarest, „Kriterion," 1972.
247 p. 21 cm. lei 12.00 R 72-3521
1. Teleology. I. Title.
BD548.H8B34 73-310435

Balazs, Sandor.
Gombatermesztes. Budapest, Mezogazdasagi Kiado, 1973.
239 p. illus.
Bibliography: p. 235-236.
1. Mushroom culture. I. Title.
DNAL NUC75-22665

Balázs, Sándor.
Tájékoztató a nagyobb ipari szakkönyvtárakról. (Összeállította Balázs Sándor és Szabolcska Ferenc) Budapest, 1961.
227 p. 24 cm. (Országos Műszaki Könyvtár és Dokumentációs Központ módszertani kiadványsorozata, 5)
1. Libraries, Special—Hungary—Directories. I. Szabolcska, Ferenc, joint author. II. Title. III. Series: Budapest. Országos Műszaki Könyvtár és Dokumentációs Központ. Az Országos Műszaki Knöyvtár és Dokumentációs Központ módszertani kiadványsorozata, 5.
Z794.3.B34 74-231099

Balazs, Sandor.
Zoldsegkulonlegessegek. Budapest, Mezogazdasagi Kiado, 1973.
191 p. illus.
Bibliography: p. 191.
1. Vegetables. Hungary. 2. Vegetables. Varieties. I. Filius, Istvan. II. Title.
DNAL NUC74-125596

Balázs, Sándor
see Látóhatár. Kolozsvár, "Dacia," 1973.

Balázs, Sándor, 1883- Reng a föld Itáliában. 1973.
in Balázs, Sándor, 1883- Viharfelhők Róma felett ... Budapest, Móra Könyvkiadó, 1973.

Balázs, Sándor, 1883-
Viharfelhők Róma felett : Hannibal és Spartacus élete / Balázs Sándor. — Budapest : Móra Könyvkiadó, 1973.
328 p., [16] leaves of plates : ill. ; 19 cm. — (Nagy emberek élete)
CONTENTS: Hannibál a kapuk elött. 2. kiad.—Reng a föld Itáliában. 3. kiad.
18.50Ft
1. Hannibal. 2. Punic War, 2d, 218-201 B.C. 3. Generals—Carthage—Biography. 4. Spartacus, d. 71 B.C. 5. Rome—History—Servile War, 73-71 B.C. 6. Gladiators—Biography. I. Balázs, Sándor, 1883- Reng a föld Itáliában. 1973. II. Title.
DG249.B33 1973 77-483124
77 MARC

Balázs, Sándor, fl. 1959–
Kiegészítő műszaki könyvtárosi ismeretek [írta] Balázs Sándor [és] Jánszky Lajos. Budapest, Országos Műszaki Könyvtár és Dokumentációs Központ, 1962.
81 p. 24 cm. (A Könyvtárosképzés füzetei)
1. Technical libraries. I. Jánszky, Lajos, joint author. II. Title.
Z675.T3B27 70-266484
rev

Balázs, Sándor, fl. 1959–
A szakirodalom és a műszaki dokumentáció szolgáltatásainak terjesztése és felhasználása az iparban [írták] Balázs Sándor [és] Szabolcska Ferenc. [Budapest] 1961.
18 p. 24 cm. (Az Országos Műszaki Könyvtár kiadványai, 5)
Summary in English.
Includes bibliographical references.
1. Communication of technical information. 2. Technology—Information services—Hungary. I. Szabolcska, Ferenc, joint author. II. Title. III. Series: Budapest. Országos Műszaki Könyvtár és Dokumentációs Központ. Az Országos Műszaki Könyvtár kiadványai, 5.
T10.5.B34 79-294630
rev

Balázs, Sándor, fl. 1959–
Tájékoztató a nagyobb ipari szakkönyvtárakról. [Összeállította Balázs Sándor és Szabolcska Ferenc, szerk. Jánszky Lajos. Budapest [Országos Műszaki Könyvtár és Dokumentációs Központ] 1961.
227 p. 24 cm. (Országos Műszaki Könyvtár és Dokumentációs Központ módszertani kiadványsorozata, 5, 1961)
1. Technical libraries—Hungary. 2. Information services—Hungary. I. Szabolcska, Ferenc, joint author. II. Jánszky, Lajos, ed. III. Title. IV. Series: Budapest. Országos Műszaki Könyvtár és Dokumentációs Központ. Az Országos Műszaki Könyvtár és Dokumentációs Központ módszertani kiadványsorozata, 1961, 5.
Z675.T3B32 72-220211
rev

Balázs, Sándor, fl. 1959- ed.
see Gépi lyukkártyákkal végzett munkák a magyarországi műszaki tájékoztatásban; cikkgyűjtemény. Budapest, Országos Műszaki Könyvtár és Dokumentációs Központ, 1966.

Balázs-Piri, Balázs, joint author
see Palásti, László. Ma mi is fúrunk. [Budapest] Kossuth Könyvkiadó, 1969.

Balázsová, K
Kalendár ochrany rastlín v záhradke / [autori] K. Balázsová, [J. Bodor, L. Lelkes ; z maď. orig. Kiskertek ... prel. a na slov. podm. uprav. Zlatica Vaneková]. — 1. vyd. — Bratislava : Príroda, 1975.
232 p. : ill. ; 21 cm. — (Edícia Rastlinná výroba) (Knižnica záhradkára) CzS 75
Kčs20.00
1. Garden pests. 2. Plants, Protection of. I. Bodor, J., joint author. II. Lelkes, L., joint author. III. Title.
SB603.5.B3417 75-529860

Balba', 'Abd al-Ḥakīm.
(Ḥarakat al-tajdīd al-shi'rī fī al-mahjar bayna al-naẓarīyah wa-al-taṭbīq)
حركة التجديد الشعرى فى المهجر بين النظرية والتطبيق /
تأليف عبد الحكيم بلبع. — [القاهرة] : مكتبة الشباب، [1974]
387 p. ; 24 cm.
Bibliography: p. 375-382.
£E1.50
1. Arabic poetry—America—History and criticism. I. Title.
PJ8510.B3 75-960102

Balba, Abd el Monem, 1919–
(al-Arḍ wa-al-insān fī al-waṭan al-'Arabī)
الأرض والانسان فى الوطن العربى؛ عرض لدور الأرض فى
توحيد الأمة العربية ونشاطها الحضارى على مر العصور [تأليف]
عبد المنعم بلبع. [اسكندرية] دار المطبوعات الجديدة
[cover 1973]
256 p. illus. 24 cm. £E0.60
Includes bibliographical references.
1. Anthropo-geography—Arab countries. I. Title.
GF698.B34 73-960363

Balba, Abd el Monem, 1919–
(Aḍwā' 'alá al-zirā'āh al-'Arabīyah)
اضواء على الزراعة العربية / عبد المنعم بلبع. — اسكندرية :
دار المطبوعات الجديدة، [1975]
181 p. : maps ; 25 cm.
Includes bibliographical references.
£E1.20
1. Agriculture—Arab countries. 2. Agriculture—Egypt. I. Title.
HD2123 1975.B35 75-961037

Balba, Abd el Monem, 1919–
(Istiṣlāḥ wa-taḥsīn al-arāḍī)
استصلاح وتحسين الاراضى =
Land reclamation and improvement /
عبد المنعم بلبع. — الاسكندرية : دار المطبوعات الجديدة،
[1974]
7, 575 p. : ill. ; 24 cm.
Bibliography: p. 563-575.
£E2.50
1. Reclamation of land. I. Title. II. Title: Land reclamation and improvement.
HD1714.B34 74-960832

Balbach, Alfons.
As hortalicas na medicina domestica Alfons Balbach. 6. ed. Sao Paulo, Edicoes "A Edificacao do Lar", 1975.
398 p., [12] leaves of plates. ill., (some col.)
1. Materia medica, Vegetable. I. Title.
DNAL NUC77-81747

Balbach, Anatol B
Syllabus for money and banking. Northridge, Calif., Bureau of Business Services and Research, School of Business Administration and Economics, San Fernando Valley State College [1965?]
51 l. illus. 29 cm.
Reproduction of typescript.
1. Banks and banking–Study and teaching. 2. Finance–Outlines, syllabi, etc. I. Title.
CNoS NUC76-70319

Balbach, Daniel R., joint author
see Wiesner, Glenn R Orthodontics and wind instrument performance. [Washington, Music Educators National Conference, 1973]

Balbach, Margaret K
A laboratory manual for general botany / Margaret K. Balbach, Lawrence C. Bliss, Harry J. Fuller. — 5th ed. — New York : Holt, Rinehart and Winston, c1977.
xii, 393 p. : ill. ; 28 cm.
Includes index.
ISBN 0-03-089749-1
1. Botany—Laboratory manuals. I. Bliss, Lawrence C., joint author. II. Fuller, Harry James, 1907- joint author. III. Title.
[QK53.B22 1977] 581'.028 76-30542
76 MARC

Balbach, Stanley B.
see Basic real estate practice ... [3d ed.]. Springfield, Illinois Institute for Continuing Legal Education, 1976-

Balbachan, Irina Pavlovna.
(Rykhlenie merzlykh gruntov vzryvom)
Рыхление мерзлых грунтов взрывом / И. П. Балбачан, Г. А. Шлойдо, А. А. Юрко. — Москва : Недра, 1974.
102 p. : ill. ; 21 cm. USSR 75
Bibliography: p. 101-102.
0.35rub
1. Frozen ground. 2. Earthwork — Cold weather conditions. 3. Blasting. I. Shloĭdo, Gennadiĭ Andreevich, joint author. II. Ĭurko, Alekseĭ Akakievich, joint author. III. Title.
TA713.B33 76-503856

Balbakov, M
(Ėffektivnost' ispol'zovaniia osnovnykh fondov i tekhniki v sel'skom khoziaĭstve Kirgizii)
Эффективность использования основных фондов и техники в сельском хозяйстве Киргизии. Фрунзе, "Илим," 1972.
175 p., 1 l. of tables. 21 cm. 0.67rub USSR 72
At head of title: Академия наук Киргизской ССР. Институт экономики. М. Балбаков, Д. Давлетов, Ш. Мусакожоев.
Includes bibliographical references.
1. Agriculture—Kirghizistan. 2. Agricultural machinery—Kirghizistan. I. Davletov, Dzh., joint author. II. Musakozhoev, Sh., joint author. III. Title.
S471.R92K53 74-328788

Balbakov, M
(Nauchno-tekhnicheskiĭ progress i povyshenie ėffektivnosti zemel'nykh resursov v Kirgizii)
Научно-технический прогресс и повышение эффективности земельных ресурсов в Киргизии. Фрунзе, "Илим," 1973.
84 p. 22 cm. USSR 73
At head of title: Академия наук Киргизской ССР. Институт экономики. М. Б. Балбаков, К. А. Абдымаликов, А. К. Кожогулов.
Includes bibliographical references.
0.32rub
1. Reclamation of land—Kirghizistan. 2. Agriculture—Kirghizistan. I. Abdymalikov, K., joint author. II. Kozhogulov, Alym Kozhogulovich, joint author. III. Title.
S616.R9B34 74-328898
rev

Balbakov, M., ed.
see Povyshenie ėffektivnosti proizvodstva v otrasliakh narodnogo khoziaĭstva Kirgizskoĭ SSR. 1970.

Balbar, George, illus.
see Historic homes of Niagara-on-the-Lake... [Fonthill, Ont., Stonehouse Publications, c1971]

Balbás, Leopoldo Torres
see Torres Balbás, Leopoldo.

Balbashov, A M
(Magnitnye kristally v tekhnike)
Магнитные кристаллы в технике / А. М. Балбашов, А. Я. Червоненкис. — Москва : Знание, 1974.
62, [1] p. : ill. ; 20 cm. — (Новое в жизни, науке, технике : Серия Радиоэлектроника и связь ; 9, 1974) USSR 74
Bibliography: p. [63]
0.10rub
1. Magnetic memories (Calculating-machines) 2. Magnetic devices. 3. Crystals. I. Chervonenkis, Andreĭ Ĭakovlevich, joint author. II. Title. III. Series: Novoe v zhizni, nauke, tekhnike : Seriia Radioėlektronika i sviaz' ; 1974, 9.
TK7800.N65 1974, 9 74-359381
[TK7895.M3]

Balbashova, Natal'ia Borisovna.
(Miniatiurnye impul'snye transformatory na ferritovykh serdechnikakh)
Миниатюрные импульсные трансформаторы на ферритовых сердечниках / Н. Б. Балбашова. — Москва : Энергия, 1976.
119 p. : ill. ; 20 cm. — (Библиотека по автоматике ; вып. 562)
Series romanized: Biblioteka po avtomatike.
Bibliography: p. 117-[118]
0.41rub
1. Pulse transformers. 2. Magnetic cores. I. Title.
TK7872.T7B29 77-504689

Balbastre i Ferrer, Josep.
Recull de modismes i frases fetes. Català-castellà, castellà-català. [1 ed. Barcelona] E[ditorial] P[òrtic, 1973]
254 p. 18 cm. (Col·lecció Llibre de butxaca, no. 66) 175ptas Sp***
1. Catalan language—Idioms, corrections, errors. 2. Catalan language—Dictionaries—Spanish. 3. Spanish language—Dictionaries—Catalan. I. Title.
PC3879.B3 74-311384
ISBN 84-300-5747-1

Balbernie, Richard.
Residential work with children. Revised ed. London, Human Context Books [1972].
xii, 240 p. 1 illus. 22 cm. index. £3.50
Bibliography: p. [224]-230.
1. Child psychotherapy—Residential treatment. 2. Socially handicapped children—Great Britain. I. Title.
[DNLM: 1. Child guidance. 2. Child, Institutionalized. 3. Residential treatment—In infancy and childhood. WS 350 B172r 1972]
[HV887.G5B3 1972] 362.7'4 72-305982
ISBN 0-903137-40-2 ; 0-903137-50-X (pbk.) MARC
Shared Cataloging with DNLM

Balberova, L A
(Setevoe planirovanie v stroitel'stve)
Сетевое планирование в строительстве. Библиогр. указатель литературы за 1966–1968 гг. и половину 1969 г. Москва, 1969.
108 p. 21 cm. 0.45rub USSR 70-VKP
At head of title: Госстрой СССР. Гипротис.
By L. A. Balberova, I. A. Pavlova, and K. S. Vorob'eva.
1. Construction industry—Management—Bibliography. 2. Network analysis (Planning)—Bibliography. I. Pavlova, I. A., joint author. II. Vorob'eva, K. S., joint author. III. Moscow. Gosudarstvennyĭ institut tipovogo proektirovaniia i tekhnicheskikh issledovaniĭ. III. Title.
Z7914.B9B34 73-311136

Balbert, Peter Henry, 1942–
D. H. Lawrence and the psychology of rhythm : the meaning of form in The rainbow / by Peter Balbert. — The Hague : Mouton, 1974.
130 p. ; 22 cm. — (Studies in English literature ; v. 99) Ne 74-46
Bibliography: p. [127]-128.
Includes index.
fl 24.00
1. Lawrence, David Herbert, 1885-1930. The rainbow. 2. Lawrence, David Herbert, 1885-1930—Style. I. Title.
PR6023.A93R332 74-84240
MARC

Balbes, Raymond.
Distributive lattices / Raymond Balbes and Philip Dwinger. — Columbia : University of Missouri Press, [1975] c1974.
xiii, 294 p. : ill. ; 27 cm.
Bibliography: p. 261-283.
Includes indexes.
ISBN 0-8262-0163-6 : $25.00
1. Lattices, Distributive. I. Dwinger, Philip, joint author. II. Title.
QA171.5.B29 1975 511'.33 73-94309
75 MARC

Balbi, Ettore.
Genova oggi e allora : alla ricerca del volto perduto di una città / a cura di Ettore Balbi ; (da un'idea di Stefano Bertorello). — Genova : Programma, [1975?]
177 p. : ill. ; 24 cm. It 76-Feb
L10000
1. Genoa—Description—Views. I. Title.
DG632.5.B4 76-524779

Balbi, Francesco, 16th cent.
The Siege of Malta, 1565 / Francesco Balbi di Corregio; translated from Spanish by Henry Alexander Balbi; with a foreword by Harry Luke. — Copenhagen, O. F. Gollcher and O. Rostock, 1961.
227 p., 11 leaves of plates : ill., port. ; 24 cm.
Translation of La verdadera relacion de todo lo que este año de MDLXV ha sucedido en la isla de Malta.
1 Malta—Siege, 1565. I. Balbi, Henry Alexander, 1867-1937, tr. II. Title.
DG992.2.B313 1961 945.8'5 75-315390
MARC

Balbi, Giorgio
see Cisari, Giulio. Ex libris. [Savona, Liguria, 19--]

Balbi, Giovanna
see
Petti Balbi, Giovanna.

Balbi, Giovanni.
La donazione. Milano, F. Vallardi [1964]
ix, 130 p. 24 cm. (Trattato di diritto civile, v. 2, fasc. 4)
Includes bibliographical references.
1. Gifts—Italy. I. Title.
74-205267

Balbi, Giovanni, d. 1298.
Catholicon. [1 leaf, on paper. Mainz, Printer of the Catholicon (Johann Gutenberg?) 1460]
[1] l. 40.2 cm.
Hain. Repertorium, *2254; Gesamtkat. d. Wiegendr., 3182; Goff. Third census, B-20.
In a portfolio (40.5 cm.) On cover: J. B. de Janua. Catholicon. Maguntia. 1460.
Initials and paragraph-marks supplied in red and blue.
Incun. 1460.B32 76-516260
[PA2361]

Balbi, Giovanni, d. 1298.
Catholicon. [Strassburg, The R-Printer (Adolf Rusch), ca. 1470]
[372] l., the first and the last (wanting) blank. f°. 49.8 cm.
Hain. Repertorium (with Copinger's Supplement) *2251; Brit. Mus. Cat. (XV cent.) I, p. 65 (IC. 660); Gesamtkat. d. Wiegendr., 3185; Goff. Third census, B-23.
Contemporary brown blind-tooled calf. Covers lined with leaves from a 14th?-cent. ms. of the Digesta.
Rubricated in red, blue, and purple. Chief initials supplied in various colors.
Inscription: Bibl. publ. Civ. Trev. 1803.
1. Latin language—Dictionaries. 2. Latin language—Grammar—Early to 1500. I. Title.
Incun. X.B212 75-571587
[PA2361]

Balbi, Giovanni, d. 1298.
Catholicon. [Strassburg, The R-Printer (Adolf Rusch), ca. 1470]
[400] l. (leaves [1] and [400] blank, leaves [85-86] and [400] wanting) bound in 2 v. f°. 49 cm.
Hain. Repertorium (with Copinger's Supplement) 2253; Brit. Mus. Cat. (XV cent.) I, p. 64 (IC. 663); Gesamtkat. d. Wiegendr., 3184; Goff. Third census, B-22.
Leaves [85-86] supplied in ms.
Rubricated (partly in red and blue) Borders on leaf [2ª] and chief initials supplied in various colors.
Bibliographical note written on an inserted leaf signed: Buttmann. From the Berlin Royal Library.
1. Latin language—Dictionaries. 2. Latin language—Grammar—Early to 1500. I. Title.
Incun. X.B213 75-571588
[PA2361]

Balbi, Giovanni, d. 1298.
Catholicon. Nuremberg, Anton Koberger, 18 Feb. (XII Kal. Mart.) 1483.
[60], iiii-xii, [325] l., the first (wanting) and last blank. f°. 35 cm.
Hain. Repertorium (with Copinger's Supplement) *2256; Brit. Mus. Cat. (XV cent.) II, p. 424 (IB. 7285); Gesamtkat. d. Wiegendr., 3187; Goff. Third census, B-25.
Partly rubricated in red and blue. 2 initials (1 with gold and silver) and border supplied in various colors on leaf [2ª] Old blind-tooled pigskin, with 2 clasps.
Title written inside upper cover, in a cartouche, beneath the date 1543. Inscription on leaf [2ª]: Convent⁹ Balberg. (?) ord. Praed.
1. Latin language—Dictionaries. 2. Latin language—Grammar—Early to 1500. I. Title.
Incun. 1483.B34 75-571586
[PA2361]

Balbi, Giovanni, d. 1298.
Catholicon. [Strassburg, Printer of the 1483 Jordanus de Quedlinburg, not after 1483]
[57], xii, [325] l., the first and the last (wanting) blank. f°. 42 cm.
Hain. Repertorium (with Copinger's Supplement) *2252; Brit. Mus. Cat. (XV cent.) I, p. 130 (IC. 1932); Gesamtkat. d. Wiegendr., 3186; Goff. Third census, B-24.
Old blind-tooled pigskin. Leaves [43-50] misbound after leaf [10]
Donated by the burgermeister of Frankfurt an der Oder to the university library in 1521 (inscription at end) Bookplate: Liber Biblioth. Academ. Francof. Stamps: Ex Bibl. Univ. Viad. Vrat.; Ex Biblioth. Regia Berolinensi.
1. Latin language—Dictionaries. 2. Latin language—Grammar—Early to 1500. I. Title.
Incun. X.B2 75-571589
[PA2361]

Balbi, Giovanni, d. 1298.
Catholicon. Venice, Hermannus Liechtenstein, 24 Sept. (VIII Kal. Oct.) 1483.
[356] l., the first blank. f°. 32 cm.
Hain. Repertorium (with Copinger's Supplement) *2257; Brit. Mus. Cat. (XV cent.) V, p. 356 (IB. 21971); Gesamtkat. d. Wiegendr., 3188; Goff. Third census, B-26.
Initials supplied in red.
1. Latin language—Dictionaries. 2. Latin language—Grammar—Early to 1500. I. Title.
Incun. 1483.B343 Thacher Coll. 75-571594
[PA2361]

Balbi, Giovanni, d. 1298.
Catholicon. Venice, Bonetus Locatellus for Octavianus Scotus, 20 Nov. (XII Kal. Dec.) 1495.
312 l. woodcuts: initials, publisher's device. f°. 29.7 cm.
Leaf [1ª] (t. p.): Catholicon.
Hain. Repertorium, *2264; Brit. Mus. Cat. (XV cent.) V, p. 445 (IB. 22928); Gesamtkat. d. Wiegendr., 3201; Goff. Third census, B-33.
1. Latin language—Dictionaries. 2. Latin language—Grammar—Early to 1500. I. Title.
Incun. 1495.B15 Thacher Coll. 75-571593
[PA2361]

Balbi, Giovanni, d. 1298.
Catholicon / Joannes Balbus — Westmead, England : Gregg International Publishers, 1971.
ca. 450 p. ; 33 cm.
Reprint of the 1460 ed. published in Mainz.
ISBN 0-576-72240-5
1. Latin language—Dictionaries. 2. Latin language—Grammar—To 1500. I. Title.
PA2361.B3 1971 473 76-479047
76 MARC

Balbi, Giovanni Francesco, 16th cent.
Tractatus fecūdus ꝛ perutilis profunde subtilisq; ac quottidiane materie omnis prescriptionis tam ciuilis q̃; canonice, qui De presciptionibus inscribitur. Editus per Ioānemfranciscum Balbum. Cui pro materie complemento annectitur copiosa repetitio solēnis ꝛ peculiaris l. Celsus ff. De vsucapio. p eūdē edita. Supadditis vbiq; opportūis multisq; alijs additiōib⁹ ꝛ apostilis vna cū dictis Hostiē. in Sūma de prescriptōib⁹ ꝛ vsucapiōib⁹ ꝛ cū Reptorio seu tabula Hieronymi de Marliāo nouissime edita. [Mediolani, Impressa p I. A. Scinzenzeler impensis I. I. ꝛ fratrū de Lignano mercatorum, 1515]
97, [20] l. 42 cm.
Repertorium ([20] l.) has special t. p.
1. Prescription (Roman law) 2. Prescription (Canon law) I. Henricus de Segusia, Cardinal, d. 1271. II. Marliano, Hieronymus de. III. Title: Tractatus fecundus et perutilis profunde subtilisque ac quottidiane materie omnis prescriptionis. IV. Title: De prescriptionibus.
76-506068

Balbi, Girolamo, ca. 1460–ca. 1535.
Epigrammata. Vienna, Johann Winterburg, 1 Aug. (Kal. Aug.) 1494.
[22] l. 4°. 21 cm.
Hain. Repertorium (with Copinger's Supplement) *2250; Brit. Mus. Cat. (XV cent.) III, p. 811 (IA. 51517); Gesamtkat. d. Wiegendr., 3181; Goff. Third census, B-18.
Leaves [19-20] misbound after leaf [1]
I. Title.
Incun. 1494.B35 Thacher Coll. 75-580657
[PA8462.B25]

Balbi, Henry Alexander, 1867-1937, tr.
see Balbi, Francesco, 16th cent. The Siege of Malta, 1565. Copenhagen, O. F. Gollcher and O. Rostock, 1961.

Balbi, Lermo Rafael.
El hombre transparente. Santa Fe [Arg.] Ediciones Colmegna [1966]
68 p. 18 cm.
I. Title.
MU NUC74-125634

Balbi, Lermo Rafael.
La tierra viva; poemas. Santa Fe, Argentina, Librería y Editorial Colmegna [1972]
47 p. 18 cm. (Colección Apertura, 7)
LACAP 73-1127
I. Title.
PQ7798.12.A48T5 73-334289

Balbi, Raffaele.
Quaestio de lucidis intervallis / Raffaele Balbi. — Napoli : M. D'Auria, 1974.
30 p. ; 25 cm. — (Bibliotheca "Monitor ecclesiasticus" ; 45)
It***
Includes bibliographical references.
1. Insanity—Jurisprudence (Canon law) I. Title. II. Series: Monitor ecclesiasticus. Bibliotheca ; 45.
BX880.M58 no. 45 75-539197

Balbi, Renato.
L'evoluzione stratificata. [Napoli] Edizioni Scientifiche Italiane [1965]
497 p. 25 cm.
Includes bibliography.
1. Evolution. I. Title.
DeU NUC76-70909

Balbi, Selmar
see Hernández, José, 1834-1886. Martín Fierro... Montevideo, Fundación Editorial Unión del Magisterio, 1973.

Balbiani, Antonio.
L'archeologia - sentiero delle antiche civiltà; appendice con pianta e note illustrative del Museo di Lecco. Como, Antonio Noseda [1963]
17 [xii] p. incl. illus. on 3 plates, plan. 24 cm.
"Note bibliografiche", p. 17.
OClMA NUC76-70908

Balbiani, Antonio.
Le fortificazioni di Lecco, del Mandellasco e della Valsassina. [Como] Pietro Cairoli [1972?]
195-208 p. incl. 3 plates. 23 cm.
"Estratto da Le fortificazioni del Lago di Como".
"Note, p. 207.
"Bibliografia", p. 207.
OClMA NUC76-70890

Balbiani, Antonio.
I maestri comacini in Europa, con particolare riguardo all'architettura romanica comasca. Como, A. Noseda [1962]
19 p. 24 cm.
"Conferenza tenuta per il Comitato di Roma della Società Dante Alighieri nella sala di Palazzo Firenze."
I. Società Dante Alighieri. Comitato di Roma.
OClMA NUC76-70447

Balbín, Armando.
¿Hacia dónde vamos? [Buenos Aires, 1973]
xi, 232 p. 20 cm.
1. Justice, Administration of—Argentine Republic. I. Title.
74-212129

Balbín, Bohuslav Alois, 1621-1688.
Krásy české země. (Výbor) z lat. přel. Helena Businská. Praha, Památník nár. písemnictví, t. ST 5, 1970.
55, [1] p. port. 30 cm. Cz 71-2707
1. Czechoslovak Republic—Description and travel. I. Businská, Helena, tr. II. Title.
DB197.B34 73-300401

Balbin, Bohuslav Alois, 1621-1688.
Verisimilia hvmaniorvm disciplinarum; seu, Judicium privatum de omni litterarum (quas humaniores appellant) artificio; quo in libello praecepta epistolarum, latinitatis, grammaticae, poeseos (generatim & speciatim) emblematum, symbolorum, historiae, rhetoricae (sacrae & profane) aliaque hujusmodi, summa brevitate adferuntur, & quid in singulis verisimile sit, proponitur... Pragae, typis Universitatis Carolo Ferdinandeae, 1966.
[23], 297 p. 14 cm.
1. Humanities. 2. Latin language. 3. Latin literature. 4. Imprints—17th century (checklist) I. Title.
KAS NUC76-25690

Balbín, Rafael María de.
Sacrificio y alegría. Madrid, Ediciones Rialp [1973]
240 p. 19 cm. (Patmos, 147) Sp***
Includes bibliographical references.
1. Christian life—Catholic authors. I. Title.
BX2350.2.B317 74-340236
ISBN 84-321-1607-6

Balbín A , William.
Censo minero del carbón, por William Balbín A. Bogotá, Ministerio de Minas y Energia, División de Minas, Fomento Minero, 1975.
56, [20] p. 28 cm.
1. Coal mines and mining—Colombia. I. Title.
TxU NUC77-82714

Balbín Guadalupe, Augusto Juan.
see Peru. Laws, statutes, etc. Código de procedimientos penales... 1. ed. [s.l., s.n.] 1976 (Concepción : Eswelra)

Balbín Lucas, Rafael de.
Sistema de rítmica castellana. 3. ed. aum. Madrid, Editorial Gredos [1975]
420 p. 21 cm. (Biblioteca románica hispánica. 2. Estudios y ensayos, 64)
1. Spanish language—Rhythm. 2. Spanish language—Versification. I. Title. II. Series.
KU NUC77-82717

Balbin Ordaya, Bertha Olga.
Aprovechamiento de las tierras aridas del departamento de Lima. Lima, Universidad Nacional Mayor de San Marcos, Dept. de Geografia, 1970.
126 p. illus. 27 cm.
1. Reclamation of land—Lima (Dept.) 2. Arid regions—Lima (Dept.) 3. Land—Lima (Dept.) I. Title.
CtY InU NUC74-33909

Balbín Pechuán, Vicente.
Los contratos municipales / Vicente Balbín Pechuán ; prólogo del Profesor Eduardo García de Enterría. — 1. ed. — [Madrid] : Civitas, 1976.
284 p. ; 21 cm. — (Manuales prácticos) Sp76-June
Includes index.
ISBN 8473980190
1. Public contracts—Spain. I. Title.
346'.46'023 76-485671
*76 MARC

Balbino Filho, Nicolau.
Registro de imóveis : doutrina, prática, jurisprudência / Nicolau Balbino Filho ; [índice remissivo de Sônia M. M. Zuccarino]. — 1. ed. — [São Paulo] : Editora Atlas, 1975.
340, 56, [3] p. : forms ; 21 cm.
"Registros públicos" (p. [1]-[59], 2d group) contains text of Lei no. 6.015, de 31 de dezembro de 1973.
Bibliography: p. [315]-318.
Includes index.
Cr$90.00
1. Land titles—Registration and transfer—Brazil. I. Brazil. Laws, statutes, etc. Lei no. 6.015, de 31 de dezembro de 1973. 1975. II. Title.
76-451342
76 MARC

Balbino Filho, Nicolau.
Registro de imóveis : doutrina, prática, jurisprudência / Nicolau Balbino Filho. — 3. ed. — São Paulo : Editora Atlas, 1976.
412, 56, [4] p. : forms ; 21 cm.
"Registros públicos" (p. [5]-[59], 2d group) contains text of Lei no. 6.015, de 31 de dezembro de 1973.
Bibliography: p. 389-392.
Includes index.
Cr$130.00
1. Land titles—Registration and transfer—Brazil. I. Brazil. Laws, statutes, etc. Lei no. 6.015, de 31 de dezembro de 1973. 1976. II. Title.
77-567981
77 MARC

Balbir, J. K.
see Wedemeyer, Charles A Evaluation of extension... Paris, Unesco, 1973.

Balbīr Rāṭhī
see
Rāṭhī, Balbīr.

Balbir Sahai Sinha
see Sinha, Balbir Sahai.

Balbir Singh, 1896–
(Kalama di karāmāta)
ਕਲਮ ਦੀ ਕਰਾਮਾਤ. ਕ੍ਰਿਤ: ਬਲਬੀਰ ਸਿੰਘ. ਅੰਮ੍ਰਿਤਸਰ, ਖਾਲਸਾ ਸਮਾਚਾਰ [for Bhai Vir Singh Sahitya Sadan] 1969.
328 p. 19 cm. Rs4.00
Cover title.
In Panjabi.
Includes bibliographical references.

1. Sikhism—Addresses, essays, lectures. I. Title.

BL2018.B27 75-919082

Balbir Singh, 1896–
(Nirukta Srī Gurū Grantha Sāhiba)
ਨਿਰੁਕਤ ਸ੍ਰੀ ਗੁਰੂ ਗ੍ਰੰਥ ਸਾਹਿਬ. [ਲੇਖਕ] ਬਲਬੀਰ ਸਿੰਘ, ਮਹਿੰਦਰ ਕੌਰ [ਤੇ] ਜੀ.ਐਸ. ਅਨੰਦ. ਪਟਿਆਲਾ, ਪੰਜਾਬੀ ਯੂਨੀਵਰਸਿਟੀ, 1972–
v. 29 cm. Rs30.00 (v. 1)
In Panjabi.
CONTENTS: 1. ੳ ਤੋਂ ਅਖੋਟ, ਪਰਚੀ ਨੰਬਰ ੧ ਤੋਂ ੧੭੯੬ ਤਕ.

1. Ādi-Granth—Dictionaries—Panjabi. I. Mahindara Kaura, joint author. II. Ananda, G. S., joint author. III. Title.

BL2017.45.B3 74-900625

Balbir Singh, 1896–
ਬੁਧ ਸਰੂਪ. ਲਿਖਤ ਬਲਬੀਰ ਸਿੰਘ. 1. ਵਾਰ. ਅੰਮ੍ਰਿਤਸਰ, ਮੈਨੇਜਰ, ਖਾਲਸਾ ਸਮਾਚਾਰ, 1966.
8, 306 p. 19 cm. Rs4
Cover title.
Added t. p. in English.
In Panjabi.
Bibliographical footnotes.

I. Title.
Title romanized: Shuddha sarūpa.

PK2659.B293S5 S A 68-2564
rev PL 480: I-Pu-975

Balbir Singh, 1896–
(Śrī Gurū Grantha Sāhiba jī dī antalī bāṇi Rāgamālā dā sawāla te Jodha Kawī ate Ālama bāre pura zora)
ਸ੍ਰੀ ਗੁਰੂ ਗ੍ਰੰਥ ਸਾਹਿਬ ਜੀ ਦੀ ਅੰਤਲੀ ਬਾਣੀ ਰਾਗਮਾਲਾ ਦਾ ਸਵਾਲ ਤੇ ਜੋਧ ਕਵੀ ਅਤੇ ਆਲਮ ਬਾਰੇ ਪੁਰ ਜ਼ੋਰ, ਪੁਰ ਦਲੀਲ, ਖੋਜ ਪੂਰਤ ਵਾਕਫੀ. ਲਿਖਤ: ਬਲਬੀਰ ਸਿੰਘ. ਅੰਮ੍ਰਿਤਸਰ, ਖਾਲਸਾ ਸਮਾਚਾਰ [for Bhai Vir Singh Sahitya Sadan, 1969]
3, 216 p. 19 cm. Rs2.00
Cover title.
In Panjabi.
1. Ādi-Granth—Criticism, interpretation, etc. 2. Ālam, Shaikhh, fl 1583. I. Title.
BL2017.45.B33 70-919149

Balbir Singh, 1930-
The conceptual framework of Indian philosophy / Balbir Singh. — Delhi : Macmillan Co. of India, 1976.
xiv, 354 p. ; 23 cm.
Bibliography: p. [317]-342.
Includes index.
Rs65.00
1. Philosophy, Indic. I. Title.
B131.B26 181'.4 76-904196
77 MARC

Balbir Singh, 1938-
see
Singh, Balbir, 1938-

Balbis, Cesare, 1934–
I monti dal cielo / Cesare Balbis ; sotto gli auspici del Club alpino italiano. — [Ivrea] : Priuli & Verlucca, [1975]
190 p. : ill ; 24 cm. — (Collana La Montagna è vita) It 75-Sept
Bibliography: p. 190.
L7000
1. Aeronautics—Alps. I. Title.
TL526.A45B34 75-594494

Balbloo Dasgupta
see
Dasgupta, Babloo, 1941-

Balbo, Anselmo.
Guida alla fauna parmense. 30 itinerari di caccia. Parma. L. Battei, 1971.
143 p. illus.; plate inserted. 21 cm. It 72-Feb
Name of author on t. p.: A. Balbo.
L1400
1. Hunting—Italy—Parma (Province) 2. Game and game-birds—Italy—Parma (Province) I. Title.
SK207.B34 75-582924

Balbo, Laura.
La inferma scienza : tre saggi sulla istituzionalizzazione della sociologia in Italia / di Laura Balbo, Giuliana Chiaretti, Gianni Massironi. — Bologna : Il mulino, [1957]
314 p. ; 22 cm. — (Studi e ricerche ; 45) It***
Includes bibliographical references.
L3000
1. Sociology—History—Italy. I. Chiaretti, Giuliana, joint author. II. Massironi, Gianni, joint author. III. Title.
HM22.I 55B34 76-509331

Balbo, Laura.
La scuola del capitale. Classi sociali e scuola di massa. Padova, Marsilio, 1973.
211 p. 21 cm. (Ricerche sociologiche, 9) L3000 It 74-Jan
At head of title: A cura di Laura Balbo e Giuliana Chiaretti.
Includes bibliographical references.
1. Educational sociology—Italy—Addresses, essays, lectures. 2. Students' socio-economic status—Italy—Addresses, essays, lectures. I. Chiaretti, Giuliana. II. Title.
LC191.B25 370.19'341'0945 74-342507

Balbo, Prospero, conte, 1762–1837.
Catalogo delle opere di Giambattista Beccaria. Firenze, Edizioni Sansoni antiquariato, 1961.
17 p. 25 cm. (Biblioteca degli eruditi e dei bibliofili, 69)
"Trecentotrentatrè esemplari." No. 31.
1. Beccaria, Giovanni Battista, 1716–1781—Bibliography. I. Title.
Z8086.25.B3 1961 74-208222

Balbo, Teresio.
Gli effetti dell'età sull'elettrocardiogramma del bovino [per] Dr. Teresio Balbo e Dr. Utillio Dotta. [Milan, Società Farmaceutici Italia] 1966.
89 p. illus. (Veterinaria, v. 15, no. 6)
ICRL NUC73-60913

Balboa, Alfonso.
El indio que le gustaba la música y otros cuentos / Alfonso Balboa. — México : B. Costa-Amic Editor, 1974.
181 p. ; 21 cm.
CONTENTS: El indio que gustaba la música.—El indio que cruzó las piernas.—El indio y su perro.—Post mortem.—San Pascualito.—Ceferina.—Declaración penal.—Los dos curanderos.—El espectacular suicidio de Raúl.—El hombre misterioso del Parque.
I. Title.
PQ7298.12.A45 I 5 75-558046

Balboa, Iolanda Tecla de.
O cordeiro da meia noite [por] Iolanda de Balboa. [1. ed.] Luanda, Angola: Editora Argos [1970?]
441 p. 21 cm.
I. Title.
CtY NUC74-125633

Balboa, Miguel Cabello de
see Cabello de Balboa, Miguel, 16th cent.

Balboa, Calif. Pavilion Gallery
see Fine Arts Patrons of Newport Harbor. Morris Graves, retrospective. [Balboa? 1963]

Balboni, Arturo, ed.
see Yaoundé II. [Roma, 1969?]

Balboni, Dante
see La Cattedra lignea di S. Pietro in Vaticano. [Roma] Tipografia poliglotta vaticana, 1971.

Balboni, Elena, illus.
see Savorelli Tosi, Aurora. La palla medica. Bologna, C.S.E.F., 1971.

Balboni, Giuseppe Carlo.
see Anatomia umana. Milano, E.E., 1975-1976.

Balbontín, José Antonio.
Reflexiones sobre la no violencia. [1. ed.] Madrid, Sala [1973]
155 p. 24 cm. Sp 74-Jan
1. Nonviolence. 2. Violence. I. Title.
HM278.B34 74-320653
ISBN 84-358-0047-4

Balbontín, José Miguel Losada
see Losada Balbontín, José Miguel.

Balbontín Moreno, Manuel G
Manuel Rodríguez en Yerbas Buenas. Apendice: Cuatro cartas del prócer a San Martín y parte séptima del libro "Los restos de Manuel Rodríguez. [Por] Manuel G. Balbontín M. 2. ed. Santiago de Chile, Orbe, 1964.
72 p.
Bibliography: p. 67-69.
1. Chile—History—War of Indepence, 1810-1824. 2. Rodríguez, Manuel, 1785-1818. 3. Yerbas Buenas, Chile—History.
DGU NUC75-84376

Balbuena, Bernardo de
see Valbuena, Bernardo de, 1568-1627.

Balbuena Rojas, Dionisio.
Sucesos inéditos de la Batalla de "El Carmen" / Dionisio Balbuena Rojas. — Asunción : [Dirección de Publicaciones de las FF.AA.NN., Impr. Militar], 1976.
270, [2] p. : ill., (8 fold. in pocket) ; 21 cm.
On spine: Batalla de "El Carmen."
Bibliography: p. [272]
1. El Carmen, Battle of, 1934—Personal narratives. 2. Chaco War, 1932-1935—Personal narratives. 3. Balbuena Rojas, Dionisio. 4. Paraguay. Ejército. Regiment no. 3 Corrales. I. Title. II. Title: Batalla de "El Carmen."
F2688.5.B25 77-458622
77 MARC

Bal'burov, Afrikan Andreevich.
(Belyĭ mesiaŝ)
Белый месяц : Повести и рассказы / Африкан Бальбуров ; [Худож. В. Шорц]. — Москва : Современник, 1975.
301 p. ; 16 cm. — (Наш день) USSR 75
Series romanized: Nash den'.
CONTENTS: Zarevo.—Belyĭ mesiaŝ.—Chau-Chau.—Obidy.—Vstrecha.—Nasha Raia.—Strashnaia mest'.
0.49rub
I. Title.
PG3476.B28665B4 76-507044

Bal'burov, Afrikan Andreevich.
(Dvenadtsat' moikh dragotsennosteĭ)
Двенадцать моих драгоценностей / Африкан Бальбуров. — Москва : Сов. Россия, 1975.
222 p., [8] leaves of plates : ill. ; 20 cm. — (В семье российской, братской) USSR 75
Series romanized: V sem'e rossiĭskoĭ, bratskoĭ.
0.67rub
1. Buriat-Mongolia. 2. Bal'burov, Afrikan Andreevich—Biography. I. Title.
DK771.B8B25 76-509407

Bal'burov, Afrikan Andreevich.
O druzhbe i schast'e. [By] Afrikan Bal'burov. Moskva, Sovetskaia Rossiia, 1973.
221 p. illus.
Short stories.
MH InU NUC75-128321

Balbus, Isaac D
The dialectics of legal repression; Black rebels before the American criminal courts [by] Isaac D. Balbus. New York, Russell Sage Foundation [1973]
xv, 269 p. illus. 24 cm. (Publications of Russell Sage Foundation)
Based on the author's thesis, University of Chicago.
Includes bibliographical references.
1. Criminal justice, Administration of — United States. 2. Los Angeles—Riots, 1965. 3. Detroit—Riot, 1967. 4. Chicago—Riot, April 1968. I. Title.
KF9223.B3 345'.73'05 73-76762
ISBN 0-87154-081-9 MARC

Balbus, Joannes
see
Balbi, Giovanni, d. 1298.

Balbus, Stanislaw, ed.
see Lektury obowiązkowe... Wroclaw, Zaklad Narodowy im. Ossolińskich, 1973.

Balbusso, Gian Paolo, 1941–
Luogo comune. Con cinque disegni di Enzo Bontempi. Milano, I dispari, 1971.
53 p. illus. 19 cm. (Sisifo, 4) It 71–Sept
Poems.
I. Title.
PQ4862.A353L8 74–326239

Balbuts͡kiĭ, Mikhail Makarovich.
(T͡Senoobrazovanie na bytovye uslugi)
Ценообразование на бытовые услуги / М. М. Балбуцкий ; под ред. канд. экон. наук А. Н. Шклярика. — Минск : Наука и техника, 1974.
157 p. ; 20 cm. USSR 74
At head of title: Академия наук БССР. Институт экономики.
Includes bibliographical references.
0.77rub
1. Service industries — Russia — Costs. 2. Service industries — Prices—Russia. I. Title.
HD9986.R92B34 75–560816

Balbyshev, Ivan Nikolaevich.
(Rodnai͡a priroda)
Родная природа / И. Н. Балбышев. — Ленинград : Лениздат, 1975.
240 p. : ill. ; 20 cm. USSR 75
Bibliography: p. 237–[238]
0.41rub
1. Phenology—Russian Republic. 2. Zoology—Russian Republic. I. Title.
QH544.B34 77–513486

Balcácer, Juan Daniel, 1949-
Pedro Santana : historia política de un déspota / Juan Daniel Balcácer ; prólogo del docotor J. I. Jiménes-Grullón. — 1. ed. — [Santo Domingo, República Dominicana : Taller, 1974]
195 p. ; 20 cm. — (Biblioteca Taller)
Bibliography: p. 192-195.
1. Santana, Pedro, Pres. Dominican Republic, 1801-1864. 2. Dominican Republic—History—1844-1930.
F1938.4.S32B34 76-454818
76 MARC

Balcanii, zonă a păcii, cooperării și bunei vecinătăți / coordonarea volumului și prefața, George Macovescu. — București : Editura Politică, 1976.
295 p. ; 19 cm. R76-3538
Includes bibliographical references.
lei9.00
1. Balkan Peninsula—Foreign relations—Romania—Sources. 2. Romania—Foreign relations—Balkan Peninsula—Sources. I. Macovescu, George.
DR38.3.R6B34 77-465515
*77 MARC

Balcanoslavica. 1– 1972–
Прилеп, Центар за исражување на старословенската култура.
v. ill. 24 cm. annual.
English, French, German, Macedonian, and/or Serbo-Croatian.
Issued by Centar za istražuvanje na staroslovenskata kultura (with Sojuz na arheološkite društva na Jugoslavija, 1972–73; Narodni muzej Krajine—Negotin, 1974–
1. Balkan Peninsula—Antiquities, Slavic—Periodicals. 2. Slavs in the Balkan Peninsula—History—Periodicals. I. Centar za istražuvanje na staroslovenskata kultura. II. Savez arheoloških društava Jugoslavije. III. Narodni muzej Krajine—Negotin.
DR20.B34 76–640892
(MARC–S)

Balcar, Luboš.
Historia magistra. Výběr z rozhlasových pořadů Historia magistra, zvukový archiv pěti tisíciletí. [Autoři:] Luboš Balcar—Ladislav Cvekl. 1. vyd. Praha, Svoboda, t. Rudé právo 1972–
v. 21 cm. Kčs30.00 (v. 1) Cz 72 (v. 1)
"Ve spolupráci s československým rozhlasem."
CONTENTS: 1. Od pravěku k vrcholům středověku.
1. World history—Sources. I. Cvekl, Vladislav, joint author. II. Title.
D5.B3 73–347110

Balcarce, Argentine Republic (Buenos Aires). Facultad de Agronomía
see Facultad de Agronomía, Balcarce, Argentine Republic.

Balcázar, José María Vivas
see Vivas Balcázar, José María.

Balcázar, Rafael Naranjo
see Naranjo Balcázar, Rafael.

Balcázar de Bucher, Cecilia
see Bucher, Cecilia Balcázar de, 1940-

Balcells, Albert, comp.
El arraigo del anarquismo en Cataluña (textos de 1926–1932). Introducción y selección de Albert Balcells. Barcelona, A. Redondo [1973]
175 p. 18 cm. (Colección Beta, 35) Sp***
Articles previously published in L'Opinió.
Includes bibliographical references.
1. Anarchism and anarchists—Spain—Catalonia. I. L'Opinió. II. Title.
HX928.C35B3 73–328171
ISBN 84–7159–080–8

Balcells, Albert.
Cataluña contemporánea / por Albert Balcells. — 1. ed. — Madrid : Siglo Veintiuno de España Editores, 19
v. ; 18 cm. — (Estudios de historia contemporánea) Sp***
"Documentos": v. 2, p. [57]–165.
Bibliography: v. 2, p. 55–56.
CONTENTS:
2. 1900–1936.
ISBN 84–323–0160–4
1. Catalonia—History. 2. Catalonia—History—Sources. I. Title.
DP302.C68B27 946'.7 75–574859

Balcells, Albert, comp.
La polèmica de 1928 [i. e. mil nou-cents vint-i-vuit]; entorn de l'anarquisme a Catalunya. [1. ed.] Barcelona, Editorial Nova Terra [1973]
183 p. 19 cm. (Síntesi, 35) Sp***
Includes bibliographical references.
1. Anarchism and anarchists—Spain—Catalonia. I. Title.
HX928.C35B32 73–337583
ISBN 84–280–0719–5

Balcells, Albert.
El sindicalismo en Barcelona, 1916-1923. [2. ed.] Barcelona, Editorial Nova Terra [1968]
191 p. 17 cm. (Colección "Síntesis," 12)
Translation of El sindicalisme a Barcelona, 1916-1923.
Bibliography: p. 185-190.
1. Trade unions—Barcelona. 2. Spain—Politics and government—20th cent. I. Title.
ViU NUC76-70918

Balcells, Albert.
Trabajo industrial y organización obrera en la Cataluña contemporánea, 1900–1936 / Albert Balcells. — 1. ed. — Barcelona : Editorial Laia, 1974.
320 p. ; 19 cm. — (Ediciones de bolsillo ; 386) Sp***
Includes bibliographical references.
ISBN 84–7222–286–1
1. Trade-unions—Catalonia—History. 2. Women—Employment—Spain—Catalonia—History. 3. Socialism in Catalonia. I. Title.
HD6765.C3B34 75–562241

Balcells, Albert, ed.
see Campalans, Rafael, 1887-1933. Ideari de Rafael Campalans. [Barcelona] E[ditorial] P[òrtic, 1973]

Balcells, Albert.
see El Estatuto de Cataluña de 1932 y su puesta en práctica. Barcelona, M. Arimany, 1977.

Balcells, Anton Cañellas i
see
Cañellas, Anton, 1923-

Balcells, Fernando Morales
see Morales Balcells, Fernando.

Balcells, José María.
Las figuraciones. [Toledo, Imp. Gómez Menor] 1971.
98 p., 3 l. 21 cm. (Biblioteca Toledo, no. 23) Sp 72–May/June
I. Title.
PQ6652.A38F5 74–306268

Balcells, José María.
Márgenes de la curiosidad : estudios de literatura española / José María Balcells ; edición, Angel Caffarena. — Málaga : Librería Anticuaria El Guadalhorce, 1974.
128 p. ; 22 cm. — (Colección Almoraduj ; 17) Sp***
"Edición de 150 ejemplares."
Includes bibliographical references.
1. Spanish literature—History and criticism—Addresses, essays, lectures. I. Title.
PQ6039.B23 75–578128

Balcells, José María.
Mi viejo Henry y otros tropicotópicos / José María Balcells. — Carboneras de Guadazaón : El Toro de Barro, [1975?]
74 p. ; 20 cm. Sp75-Oct.
ISBN 8440088523 : 100ptas.
I. Title.
PQ6652.A38M5 76-467020
76 MARC

Balcells, José María.
Miguel Hernández, corazón desmesurado / José María Balcells. — 1. ed. — Barcelona : Editorial DIROSA, 1975.
229 p. ; 22 cm. — (Colección Documentación y ensayo ; no. 10) Sp***
Bibliography: p. 207-228.
ISBN 8473580222
1. Hernández, Miguel, 1910-1942.
PQ6615.E57Z58 75-518293
75 MARC

Balcells, José María
see Expresión : antología de textos comunicación, literatura ... 2. reedición. Barcelona : V. Vives, 1973, 1974 printing.

Balcells, José María.
see Poesía castellana de cárcel . . . [1. ed.]. [Barcelona] Editorial DIROSA, [1976]

Balcells Gené, Jordi.
Programa de trabajo para una pedagogía integral vivenciada / Jordi Balcells Gené, Anna M.a Muñoz Vicén. — Madrid : Ciencias de la Educación Preescolar y Especial, [1976]
192 p. : ill. ; 24 cm. — (Colección Educación especial ; 6) Sp***
Bibliography: p. [191]-192.
ISBN 8485252020 : 550ptas
1. Creative activities and seat work—Handbooks, manuals, etc. 2. Nature study—Handbooks, manuals, etc. I. Muñoz Vicén, Anna María, joint author. II. Title. III. Title: Para una pedagogía integral vivenciada.
LB1537.B25 77-461847
77 MARC

Balcells Gorina, Alfonso, ed.
see Marañón, Gregorio, 1887-1960. Manual de diagnóstico etiológico. 12. ed., rev. y puesta al día. Madrid : Espasa-Calpe, 1974.

Balcells Junyent, José. Aspectos sociológicos de la persuasión. 1973
in Bermejo y Gironés, Juan Ignacio. Sobre el carácter gerencial de la función pública. [Barcelona] : Patronato Municipal de la Vivienda Excmo. [1973]

Balcells Junyent, José. La indagación sociológica al servicio de la vivienda. 1973
in Bermejo y Gironés, Juan Ignacio. Sobre el carácter gerencial de la función pública. [Barcelona] : Patronato Municipal de la Vivienda del Excmo. [1973]

Balcells Riba, Manuel.
see Simposio Internacional de Actualidades Neurológicas, 3d, Barcelona, 1971. Erfermedades musculares. Barcelona, Salvat, c1971.

Balcer, Bogdan.
Krzemień świeciechowski w kulturze pucharów lejkowatych : eksploatacja, obróbka i rozprzestrzenienie / Bogdan Balcer. — Wrocław : Zakład Narodowy im. Ossolińskich, 1975.
371 p., [3] fold. leaves : ill. ; 24 cm.
At head of title: Polska Akademia Nauk. Instytut Historii Kultury Materialnej.
Summary in English.
Bibliography: p. [350]–360.
zł85.00
1. Funnel-beaker culture—Poland. 2. Stone implements—Poland. 3. Poland—Antiquities. I. Title.
GN776.2.F8B34 76–513394

Balcer, Yves Michel.
Optimal advertising and inventory policy with random demand. [Stanford, Calif.] 1973.
vi, 139 l.
Thesis (Ph.D.)—Stanford University, 1974.
Bibliography: leaves 135-139.
1. Inventories—Mathematical models. 2. Advertising—Mathematical models. I. Title.
CSt NUC75-22666

Balcerak, Wiesław.
Powstanie państw narodowych w Europie Środkowo-Wschodniej / Wiesław Balcerak. — Wyd. 1. — Warszawa : Państwowe Wydawn. Naukowe, 1974.
501 p. ; 21 cm.
Includes bibliographical references and index.
zł56.00
1. Europe, Eastern—History. 2. Central Europe—History. I. Title.
DR47.B34 75–586117

Balcerek, Józef.
Samorząd robotniczy a systemy społecznogospodarcze. Warszawa, Instytut Wydawn. CRZZ, 1973.
259 p. 20 cm.
Bibliographical footnotes.
1. Works councils. 2. Employees' representation in management. I. Title.
CSt-H NUC75-22635

Balcerkiewicz, Stanislaw, joint author
see Celinski, Florian. Zespoly muraw psamofilnych w Wielkopolskim Parku Narodowym pod Poznaniem. Warszawa [Panstwowe Wydawn. Naukowe] 1973.

Balcerowski, Witold.
Wybór kształtu próbek do pomiaru wytrzymałości filców na rozciąganie. ⌊Łódź⌋ 1966.
21 p. illus. (Prace In-tu Włókiennictwa. Seria B. Zesz. 5, 1966)
ICRL NUC74-126823

Balcerzak, Alojzy, illus.
see Korczakowska, Jadwiga. Pałac pod grusza. ⌊Wyd. 3.⌋. Warszawa, Pax, 1973.

Balcerzak, Edwin A., joint author.
see Mayer, Morris Fritz. Group care of children ... New York, Child Welfare League of America, c1977.

Balcerzak, Ewa.
Stanisław Lem. ⌊Wyd. 1.⌋. Warszawa, Państwowy Instytut Wydawniczy, 1973.
177 p. port. 18 cm. (Portrety współczesnych pisarzy polskich) zł20.00
1. Lem, Stanisław.
PG7158.L39Z6 74–212480

Balcerzak, Hanna, illus.
see Beylin, Karolina. W Warszawie w latach 1900-1914. [Warszawa] Państwowy Instytut Wydawniczy [1972]

Balcerzan, Edward.
Któż by nas takich pięknych; tryptyk. ⌊Wyd. 1. Poznań Wydawn. Poznańskie, 1972.
239 p. 20 cm. zł20.00
CONTENTS: Henerał.—Rynien flet.—Któż by nas takich pięknych.
I. Title.
PG7161.A44K9 73–214566

Balcerzan, Edward, comp.
Lata siedemdziesiąte; almanach najmłodszej poezji Wielkopolski. Edward Balcerzan wybrał wiersze i napisał przedm. Wojeiech Korytowski oprac. graficznie. [Wyd. 1. Poznań] Wydawn. Poznańskie, 1973.
119 p. illus.
1. Polish poetry—Wielkopolska. 2. Polish poetry—20th cent.—Coll. I. Title.
MH NUC76-70920

Balcerzan, Edward.
Przez znaki; granice autonomii sztuki poetychiej na marginesie polskiej poezji wspólczesnej. ⌊Wyd. 1.⌋. Poznań, Wydawn. Poznańskie, 1972.
307 p. 20 cm. zł35.00
Summary in Russian.
Includes bibliographical references.
1. Poetry, Modern—20th century—History and criticism. 2. Polish poetry—20th century—History and criticism. I. Title.
PN1117.B3 73–214881

Balcerzan, Edward
see Inspiracja twórcza... Warszawa, 1973.

Balcerzan, Edward
see Rzecz poetycka; festiwale. Łódź, Wydawn. Łodzkie, 1970.

Bălcescu, Nicolae, 1819–1852.
Opere / N. Bălcescu ; ediţie critică de G. Zane şi Elena G. Zane. — Bucureşti : Editura Academiei Republicii Socialiste România, 1974–
v. : ill. ; 25 cm. R 75–500 (v. 1)
Includes bibliographical references and indexes.
CONTENTS: 1. Scrieri istorice, politice şi economice, 1844–1847.
lei 36.00 (v. 1)
1. Romania—History—Collected works. I. Zane, G. II. Zane, Elena G.
DR217.B22 1974 75–586295

Bălcescu, Nicolae, 1819–1852.
Românii supt Mihai-Voievod Viteazul / Nicolae Bălcescu. — Ediţie îngrijită de Andrei Rusu ; postfaţă de G. C. Nicolescu. — Bucureşti : Editura pentru literatură, 1967.
451 p., ⌊1⌋ leaf of plates : port. ; 21 cm. R***
First ed. published in 1878 under title: Istoria Românilor sub Michaiu Voda Vitézul.
Includes bibliographical references.
1. Romania—History—To 1711. 2. Mihai II, Viteazul, Voivode of Wallachia, 1558–1601. I. Rusu, Andrei. II. Title.
DR240.B34 1967 75–405631

Bălcescu, Nicolae, 1819–1852.
Românii supt Mihai-Voievod Viteazul. Studiu introductiv de Paul Cornea. Ediţie îngrijită, glosar şi bibliografie de Andrei Rusu. Ediţia a 2-a. Bucureşti, „Albatros," 1973.
xxxii, 480 p. 17 cm. (Lyceum, 1–2) lei 6.00 R 73–4404
First ed. published in 1878 under title: Istoria Românilor sub Michaiu Voda Vitézul.
Bibliography: p. 467–478.
1. Romania—History—To 1711. 2. Mihai II, Viteazul, Voivode of Wallachia, 1558–1601. I. Rusu, Andrei, ed. II. Title.
DR240.B34 1973 73–363891

Bălcescu, Nicolae, 1819–1852.
Românii supt Mihai-Voievod Viteazul / Nicolae Bălcescu ; ⌊ediţie îngrijită şi repere istorico-literare de Andrei Rusu ; coperta seriei, Constantin Guluţă⌋. — Bucureşti : "Minerva," 1975.
485 p. ; 21 cm. R 75–4798
First ed. published in 1878 under title: Istoria Românilor sub Michaiu Voda Vitézul.
Includes bibliographical references and index.
lei 14.00
1. Romania—History—To 1711. 2. Mihai II, Viteazul, Voivode of Wallachia, 1558–1601. I. Title.
DR240.B34 1975 76–502836

Balcescu, Nicolae, 1819-1852.
Romînii supt Mihai-Voievod Viteazul. Editie îngrijită de Andrei Rusu. Prefată de G.C. Nicolescu. Bucuresti, Editura Minerva, 1970.
449 p.
First edition published in 1878 under title: Istoria Românilor sub Michaiu Voda Vitézul.
1. Rumania—History. 2. Mihai II, Viteazul, Voivode of Wallachia, 1558-1601. I. Rusu, Andrei, ed. II. Title.
CU NUC74-30161

Bălcescu, Nicolae, 1819–1852.
Scrieri / N. Bălcescu ; antologie şi prefaţă de D. Păcurariu. — Bucureşti : Editura Ion Creangă, 1974.
222 p. ; 17 cm. — (Biblioteca şcolarului ; 80) R 76–767
Includes bibliographical references.
lei 3.50
1. Romania—History—Collected works.
DR217.B229 1974 76–513423

Bălcescu, Nicolae, 1819–1852.
Scrieri alese. Ediţie de Andrei Rusu. Prefaţă de Paul Cornea. Cronologie de Horia-Nestorescu-Bălceşti. ⌊Coperta: Cristea Müller⌋. Bucureşti, „Minerva," 1973.
lxiv, 383 p. 20 cm. lei 13.50 R 73–3191
Includes bibliographical references.
1. Romania—History—Addresses, essays, lectures. I. Title.
DR217.B23 1973 74–340250

Balcesti, Horia Nestorescu-
see Nestorescu-Balcesti, Horia.

Balch, Alan Frederick.
All honor to Jefferson ...; an inquiry into American legislative-executive relations, 1870-1900, by Joshua F. Speed ⌊pseud. n.p.⌋ 1970.
Bowdoin Prize (Graduate English)—Harvard.
1. Separation of powers—U.S.
MH NUC74-85637

Balch, Ann Renker.
Ancient Lake Cahuilla's fish trappers / by Ann Renker Balch and John W. Balch. — ⌊s. l. : s. n., 1974⌋
92 p. : ill. ; 22 cm.
1. Indians of North America—California—Antiquities. 2. Imperial Co., Cal.—Antiquities. 3. Indians of North America—California—Fishing. 4. California—Antiquities. I. Balch, John W., joint author. II. Title.
E78.C15B15 979.4'99 74–27266
MARC

Balch, Ann Renker.
The ancient Rock-Circle people of the Borrego Valley / by Ann Renker Balch and John W. Balch. — ⌊s.l.⌋ : Balch, c1976.
69 p., ⌊1⌋ fold. leaf of plates : ill. ; 22 cm.
1. Indians of North America—California—Borego Valley. 2. Borego Valley, Calif.—Antiquities. I. Balch, John W., joint author. II. Title.
E78.C15B16 979.4'98'00497 76-5106
76 MARC

Balch, Clayton.
see Shakespeare, William, 1564-1616. Othello... Woodbridge, Conn., Apollo Books ⌊1971⌋

Balch, Earl W
Serials processing system reference manual, by Earl Balch. La Jolla, Calif., University Library, University of California, San Diego, 1972.
16 ⌊71⌋ p. illus. 28 cm. (The Larc reports, v. 5, issue 3)
1. Electronic data processing—Cataloging of serial publications. 2. California. University, San Diego. Library. I. Title. II. Series: Larc Association. The Larc reports, v. 5, issue 3.
Z695.7.B35 025.3'4'302854 73–157156
ISBN 0–88257–015–3 MARC

Balch, Emily Tapscott Clark, 1893-1953.
Innocence abroad / Emily Clark. — Westport, Conn. : Greenwood Press, 1975, c1931.
270 p., ⌊13⌋ leaves of plates : ports. ; 22 cm.
Reprint of the ed. published by Knopf, New York.
CONTENTS: The Reviewer.—James Branch Cabell.—Ellen Glasgow.—Amélie Rives.—Joseph Hergesheimer.—H. L. Mencken.—Carl van Vechten.—Ernest Boyd.—Elinor Wylie.—Frances Newman.—Julia Peterkin.—Dubose Heyward.—Paul Green and Gerald Johnson.
ISBN 0-8371-7433-3
1. The Reviewer. 2. Authors, American. 3. American literature—Southern States—History and criticism. I. Title.
PN4900.R4B3 1975 810'.5 74-2796
74 MARC

Balch, Emily Tapscott Clark, 1893-1953
see Sherman, Stuart Pratt, 1881-1926. Ellen Glasgow; critical essays. Folcroft, Pa., Folcroft Press ⌊1969⌋

Balch, Glenn, 1902- Indian paint
see Burton, Ardis E Indian paint. St. Louis, Webster Division, McGraw-Hill, 1962.

Balch, John W., joint author.
see Balch, Ann Renker. The ancient Rock-Circle people of the Borrego Valley. ⌊s.l.⌋ Balch, c1976.

Balch, Michael, ed.
see Essays on economic behavior under uncertainty. Amsterdam: North-Holland Pub. Co.; New York: American Elsevier Pub. Co., 1974.

Balch, Philip, 1947-
Social class and paths to treatment, expectations, and case outcome of patients at a mental health guidance center. ⌊Tallahassee, Fla.⌋ 1973.
vi, 141 l.
Thesis (Ph.D.)—Florida State University.
Bibliography: leaves 137-140.
Vita.
1. Psychiatric clinics—Florida—Leon Co. I. Title.
FTaSU NUC75-22636

Balch, Robert William, 1944-
Negative reactions to delinquent labels in a junior high school. [n.p.] 1972.
207 l.
Thesis (Ph. D.)—University of Oregon.
Vita.
Bibliography: leaves 198-207.
1. Juvenile delinquency. I. Title.
OrU NUC73-119593

Balch, Stephen Howard.
Party government in the United States House of Representatives, 1911-1919. [Berkeley] 1972.
1 v. (various pagings)
Thesis (Ph. D.)—University of California.
Includes bibliography.
CU NUC73-119841

Balch, Thomas, 1821–1877.
The French in America during the War of Independence of the United States, 1777–1783. With a new introd. and pref. by George Athan Billias. Boston, Gregg Press, 1972.
2 v. illus. 24 cm. (The American Revolutionary series. American and French accounts of the American Revolution)
Reprint of the 1891–95 ed. published by Porter & Coates, Philadelphia.
Translation of Les Français en Amérique pendant la Guerre de l'indépendance.
Includes bibliographical references.
1. United States—History—Revolution—French participation. I. Title. II. Series: American and French accounts of the American Revolution.
E265.B172 973.3'47 72–8702
ISBN 0–8398–0185–8 MARC

Balch, William Ralston, 1852-1923.
The complete compendium of universal knowledge, containing all you want to know of language, history, government, business and social forms, and a thousand and one other useful subjects. [New York, Syntonic Research, inc., 1973]
438 p. illus., tables. 20 cm.
Copyrighted by F. Oldach, Sr., 1895.
Facsimile ed. of a rare 1895 reference book.
1. Encyclopedias and dictionaries. I. Title.
DI NUC77-81

Balch, William Stevens, 1806-1887.
A peculiar people; or, Reality in romance. By William S. Balch. Chicago, H.A. Sumner, 1881 [1973]
xi-xii, 13-452 p. 19 cm.
Micro-transparency (negative) Louisville, Ky., Lost Cause Press, 1973. 6 sheets. 10.5 x 14.8 cm. (L.H. Wright. American fiction, 1876-1900, no. 251)
I. Title.
PSt NUC75-24831

Balch Institute.
see Immigrants in industrial America ... Charlottesville, Published for Eleutherian Mills-Hagley Foundation and Balch Institute by University Press of Virginia, [1977]

Balchand, Asandas.
The salvific value of non-Christian religions, according to Asian Christian theologians writing in Asian-published theological journals, 1965-1970. Manila, East Asian Pastoral Institute, 1973.
81 p. 23 cm.
Reprinted from Teaching all nations, 1973, no. 1-2.
Bibliography: p. 70-81.
1. Salvation-Comparative studies. 2. Christianity and other religions. I. Title.
NRCR NUC74-133746

Balchandra Shastri
see
Shastri, Balchandra, 1905-

Balchen, Bernt, 1899-
The next fifty years of flight, as visualized by Bernt Balchen and told to Erik Bergaust. Foreword by James H. Doolittle. Explorer books edition. [Ann Arbor, Xerox University Microfilms 1975]
214 p. illus. 22 cm.
This is an authorized facsimile of the original book, published by Viking, 1960, and was produced ... by microfilm-xerography.
1. Aeronautics. I. Bergaust, Erik. II. Title.
MsSM NUC77-84371

Balchev, Georgi
see Natsionalen kongres na bŭlgarskite ortopedi i travmatolozi, 1st, Varna, Bulgaria, 1972.
Pŭrvi Natsionalen kongres na bŭlgarskite ortopedi i travmatolozi. Sofiia, Meditsina i fizkultura, 1973.

Balchin, Nigel, 1908-1970.
The Borgia testament. Original illus. by Janet Archer. [Geneva, Edito-Service, c1973]
249 p. illus. 21 cm. Sw***
1. Borgia, Cesare, 1476?-1507—Fiction. I. Title.
PZ3.B191Bo 5 823'.9'12 74-170442
[PR6003.A52] MARC

Balchin, Nigel, 1908-
Kings of infinite space. New York, Modern Literary Editions [c1967]
191 p. 18 cm. (Curtis books)
I. Title.
OU NUC76-70317

Balchin, Paul N
Urban land economics / Paul N. Balchin and Jeffrey L. Kieve. — London : Macmillan, 1977.
xviii, 278 p. : ill. ; 23 cm. — (Macmillan building and surveying series) GB***
Bibliography: p. [262]-263.
Includes index.
ISBN 0-333-18083-6 : £6.95
1. Land use, Urban—Great Britain. 2. Urban economics. 3. City planning—Great Britain. I. Kieve, Jeffrey, joint author. II. Title.
HD596.B34 333.7'7'0941 77-362917
77 MARC

Bal'chitis, Al'girdas Al'binovich
see
Balčytis, Algirdas.

Bal'chiunene, Galina Iosifovna.
(M. K. Chiurlenis)
М. К. Чюрленис : к 100-летию со дня рождения / Г. И. Бальчюнене. — Москва : Знание, 1975.
29 p., [8] leaves of plates : ill. (some col.) ; 20 cm. — (Новое в жизни, науке, технике : Серия Искусство ; 5/1975) USSR***
Includes bibliographical references.
0.15rub
1. Čiurlionis, Mikolajus Konstantinas, 1875-1911. I. Series: Novoe v zhizni, nauke, tekhnike : Serifa Iskusstvo, 1975, 5.
NX6.N6 1975, no. 5 75-546923
[ND1978.C58]

Bal'chugov, A D
(Muzei i vystavki)
Музеи и выставки. Путеводитель по музеям и выставкам Свердловска и обл. Свердловск, Сред.-Уральск. кн. изд-во, 1971.
137 p. with illus. 17 cm. 0.59rub USSR 71
"Составитель ... А. Д. Бальчугов."
1. Museums—Russia—Sverdlovsk (Province) 2. Sverdlovsk, Russia—Exhibitions. I. Title.
AM60.S9B34 73-348169

Bal'chugov, A. D.
see Sverdlovsk. 1975.

Balchum, Oscar J
Chest diseases: case studies; a compilation of 61 case histories related to chest diseases, by Oscar J. Balchum and Ralph C. Jung. Flushing, N. Y., Medical Examination Pub. Co. [1973]
227 p. illus. 22 cm.
1. Chest—Diseases—Cases, clinical reports, statistics. I. Jung, Ralph C., joint author. II. Title.
RC941.B18 617'.54'0077 73-156686
ISBN 0-87488-012-2 MARC

Balchunis, Robert James, 1949-
Studies in photochemical methods of uracil and azauracil functionalization. [n.p.] 1975.
152 l.
Thesis-Ohio State University.
Includes bibliographical references.
1. Photochemistry. 2. Uracil. I. Title.
OU NUC77-82715

Balci, A Nihat.
Timber trends and prospects in Turkish forestry / by A. Nihat Balci. — Istanbul : Kutulmus Matbaasi, 1968.
vi, 55, [1] p. : ill. ; 24 cm. — (O. F. yayin ; no. 122) (I.Ü. yayin ; no. 1269)
Errata slip inserted.
Bibliography: p. [56]
1. Forest products—Turkey. I. Title. II. Series: Istanbul. Üniversite. Orman Fakültesi. Orman Fakültesi yayinlari ; no. 122.
HD9766.T82B34 76-350266
76 MARC

Balci, Metin, 1939-
An econometrics study of monetary sector of Turkey: 1948-1970. [n.p.] 1973.
183 p.
Thesis (Ph.D.)-New York University.
I. Title.
NNU NUC76-70316

Balcı, Perihan.
Eski İstanbul evleri ve Boğaziçi yalıları / Perihan Balcı. — [İstanbul? : s. n.], 1975.
98 p., [1] leaf of plates : chiefly ill. ; 28 cm.
1. Architecture, Domestic—Turkey—Istanbul. 2. Architecture—Details. 3. Istanbul—Buildings. I. Title.
NA7396.I 85B34 77-970075

Balčikonis, Juozas, 1885- comp.
see Drabužiai. Vilnius: Vaga, 1974.

Balcıoğlu, Beşir.
Protokol ve sosyal davranış. Ankara, Başnur Matbaası, 1969.
133 p. illus. 17 cm.
1. Diplomatic etiquette—Turkey. I. Title.
JX1679.B26 76-971011
rev

Balcıoğlu, Semih, comp.
50 [i. e. Elli] yılın Türk mizah ve karikatürü. [Hazırlayanlar] Semih Balcıoğlu [ve] Ferit Öngören. [1. baskı. İstanbul] Türkiye İş Bankası Kültür Yayınları [1973]
356, 264 p. illus. 25 cm. (Cumhuriyetin ellinci yılı dizisi, 4) (İş Bankası kültür yayınları, 125)
Cover title.
CONTENTS: Balcıoğlu, S. 50 yılın Türk karikatürü.—Öngören, F. 50 yılın Türk mizahı.
1. Turkish wit and humor, Pictorial. 2. Turkish wit and humor. I. Öngören, Ferit, comp. II. Title. III. Series.
NC1660.T9B34 74-211425

Balčiūnas, Juozas, 1891-
Karnavalo aikšteje; novelės. [London] Nida [1972]
284 p.
I. Title.
InU NUC75-36315

Balčiuniene, Taida
see Mousie goes for water; Lithuanian rhymes. [Moscow, Progress pub., 197-?]

Balcke, Gernot, joint author.
see Albrecht, Günter E. R. Modellbahnlexikon ... Düsseldorf, Alba, 1975.

Balcken, Andrea L.
see American Library Association. Children's Services Division. School and public library relations... Chicago, 1970.

Balcom, E Joan.
Fundy tales, by E. Joan Balcom. [Kentville, N. S., distributed by G. R. Saunders, c1969]
27 p. 22 cm C***
1. Legends—Canada—Fundy, Bay of. I. Title.
GR113.B27 398.2'09716'3 72-172619
MARC

Balcomb, D.
see Solar heating handbook for Los Alamos. Los Alamos, N.M., Los Alamos Scientific Laboratory of the University of California; Springfield, Va.: distributed by National Technical Information Service, 1975.

Balcomb, Dorothy M
History of Toogong: commemorating the centenary of St. Alban's Church of England, Toogong by Dorothy Balcomb. Canowindra, N. S. W. Canowindra and District Historical Society, 1972.
i, 58 p. ill., facsims., map. 21 cm. Aus
Bibliography: p. [1]
1. Toogong, Australia—History. 2. St. Alban's Church of England, Toogong, Australia. I. Canowindra & District Historical Society. II. Title.
DU180.T66B34 919.44 74-170732
ISBN 0-9598975-0-X MARC

Balcomb, J Douglas
The crosscorrelation method of measuring system dynamic response. Los Alamos, New Mexico, University of California, Los Alamos Scientific Laboratory; [distributed by the Clearinghouse for Federal Scientific and Technical Information, Springfield, Va.] 1963.
14 l.
Presented as a Summary Paper at the Symposium on Noise Analysis in Nuclear Systems at the University of Florida, Gainesville, Fla.
"LADC-5876."
Bibliography: leaf [15]
1. System analysis. 2. Automatic control. 3. Frequency response (Dynamics) 4. Feedback control systems. I. Title.
MsSM NUC76-26031

Balcomb, Kenneth C
A boy's Albuquerque, 1898-1912, by Kenneth C. Balcomb. [Albuquerque, N.M.] Balcomb [197-?]
123 l. 28 cm.
Cover title.
1. Balcomb, Kenneth C. 2. Albuquerque, N.M.-History. I. Title.
NmU NUC77-82713

Balcomb, Mary N
Nicolai Fechin / by Mary N. Balcomb ; with a foreword by Eya Fechin Branham. — 1st ed. — [Flagstaff, Ariz.] : Northland Press, c1975.
xxiv, 167 p. : chiefly ill. (some col.) ; 32 cm.
Bibliography: p. 165-167.
ISBN 0-87358-140-7 : $40.00
1. Feshin, Nikolaĭ Ivanovich, 1881-1955. I. Feshin, Nikolaĭ Ivanovich, 1881-1955.
ND699.F43B34 759.13 75-11161
76 MARC

Balcon, Jill
see Early Victorian poetry. Argo PLP 1044. [1968]

Balcon, Jill
see Poems for several voices. [Sound recording] Folkways Records FL 9894. c1973.

Balcon, Jill
see Yeats, Willian Butler, 1865-1939. Poems. [Sound recording] Folkways Records FL 9894. c1973.

Balcou, Jean.
Fréron contre les philosophes / Jean Balcou. — Genève : Droz, 1975.
493 p., ⌊1⌋ fold. leaf of plates : geneal. table ; 24 cm. — (Histoire des idées et critique littéraire ; no 151) Sw75-A-7792
Bibliography: p. ⌊473⌋-484.
Includes index.
80.00F
1. Fréron, Élie Catherine, 1718-1776. 2. Voltaire, François Marie Arouet de, 1694-1778—Contemporaries. I. Title.
PQ2105.F7B3 070.4'092'4 76-469184
*76 MARC

Balcou, Jean.
see Le dossier Fréron ... Genève, Droz, ⌊1975⌋

Balcou, Jean, ed.
see Racine, Jean Baptiste, 1639-1699. Phèdre, tragédie, 1677. [Paris] Hachette [c1968]

Balcou, Jean Pierre.
see Études sur Édouard et Tristan Corbière. ⌊Brest⌋ Centre de recherche bretonne et celtique, Université de Brest, ⌊1976⌋

Balcou, Yves.
Etude de la dynamique des réorientations moléculaires à l'intérieur des réseaux cristallins de dérivés benzèniques penta ou hexa substitués. [Rennes, 1970]
190 p. illus. (Bulletin de la Société Scientifique de Bretagne, fasc. hors sér., t. 4)
Bibliography: p. 177-186.
1. Benzene. 2. Crystal lattices. 3. Molecular dynamics. I. Title.
CtY NUC75-36307

Balčytis, Algirdas.
(Emkostnaiâ podoblast' indukfšionnykh profšessov preobrazovaniâ potokov ėnergii)
Емкостная подобласть индукционных процессов преобразования потоков энергии / А. Бальчитис. — Вильнюс : Минтис, 1973.
306 p. : ill. ; 23 cm. USSR 74
Added t. p.: Energijos srautų indukcinių keitimo procesų talpuminė posritė.
On leaf preceding t. p.: LTSR Aukštojo ir specialiojo vidurinio mokslo ministerija. Kauno politechnikos institutas.
Includes bibliographies and index.
2.17rub
1. Electrohydrodynamic generators. 2. Magnetohydrodynamic generators. I. Title. II. Title: Energijos srautų indukcinių keitimo procesų talpuminė posritė.
TK2975.B34 75-591480

Bald,
see Organization for Economic Cooperation and Development. Library. Problèmes de la main-d'œuvre ... ⌊Paris⌋ Organisation de coopération et de développement économiques, 1974.

Bald, Detlef.
Das Forschungsinstitut Amani; Wirtschaft und Wissenschaft in der deutschen Kolonialpolitik Ostafrika, 1900-1918, von Detlef und Gerhild Bald. München, IFO-Institut für Wirtschaftsforschung, 1972.
115 l. illus., map. 30 cm.
1. Biologisch-Landwirtschaftliches Institut, Amani, Tanzania. 2. Agricultural research—Tanzania. I. Bald, Gerhild, joint author. II. Title.
IEN NUC75-84381

Bald, Frederick Clever, 1897-
see A History of Michigan in paintings. [Lansing] 1964-67.

Bald, Gerhild, joint author
see Bald, Detlef. Das Forschungsinstitut Amani; Wirtschaft und Wissenschaft... München, IFO-Institut für Wirtschaftsforschung, 1972.

Bald, James, 1910-
Over my shoulder : poems / by James Bald. — Ilfracombe : Stockwell, 1975.
64 p. ; 15 cm. GB75-12732
ISBN 0-7223-0716-0 : £0.95
I. Title.
PR9619.3.B28O9 821 75-333184
76 MARC

Bald, Kenneth.
see Fritz, Jean. The secret diary of Jeb & Abigail ... Pleasantville, N.Y., Reader's Digest Association, c1976.

Bald, Robert Cecil, 1901-
Bibliographical studies in the Beaumont & Fletcher folio of 1647, by R. C. Bald. ⌊Folcroft, Pa.⌋ Folcroft Library Editions, 1974.
vi, 114 p. 26 cm.
Reprint of the 1938 ed. printed at the Oxford University Press for the Bibliographical Society, which was issued as no. 13 of the Supplement to the Bibliographical Society's Transactions for 1937.
Includes bibliographical references.
1. Beaumont, Francis, 1584-1616. Comedies and tragedies—Bibliography. 2. Fletcher, John, 1579-1625. Comedies and tragedies—Bibliography. I. Title. II. Series: Bibliographical Society, London. Transactions. Supplement no. 13.
Z8086.B17 1974 016.822'3'09 73-1600
ISBN 0-8414-1790-3 MARC

Bald, Robert Cecil, 1901-
see Davis, Herbert John, 1893-1967, ed. Nineteenth-century studies. Norwood, Pa., Norwood Editions, 1976 ⌊c1940⌋

Bald, Robert Cecil, 1901- joint ed.
see Davis, Herbert John, 1893-1967, ed. Nineteenth-century studies. Philadelphia, R. West, 1976, ⌊c1940⌋

Bald, Robert Cecil, 1901- ed.
see Middleton, Thomas, d. 1627. A game at chesse. [Ann Arbor, Mich., University Microfilms, 1971]

Bald, Wolf-Dietrich.
Die Behandlung grammatischer Probleme in Lehrwerken für den Englischunterricht/ Wolf-Dietrich Bald; Broder Carstensen, Marlis Hellinger. — 1. Aufl. — Frankfurt (am Main⌋, Berlin, München: Diesterweg, 1972.
151 p.; 21 cm. — (Schule und Forschung; Heft 19) DM16.80 GDB 73-A14
Bibliography: p. 135-151.
1. English language—Study and teaching—German students. I. Carstensen, Broder, joint author. II. Hellinger, Marlis, joint author. III. Title.
PE1068.G4B27 74-350962
ISBN 3-425-04219-X

Bald, Wolf-Dietrich.
Studien zu den kopulativen Verben des Englischen. (München) Hueber (1972).
183 p. 21 cm. (Commentationes Societatis Linguisticae Europaeae, 5) DM20.00 GDNB 72-A49
A revision of the author's thesis, Hamburg.
Bibliography: p. 173-183.
1. English language—Verb. I. Title. II. Series: Societas Linguistica Europaea. Commentationes, 5.
PE1319.B3 1972 73-313793

Bald, Wolf Dietrich.
see Linguistisches Kolloquium, 11th, Aachen, 1976. Akten des 11. Linguistischen Kolloquiums, Aachen 1976. 1. Aufl. Tübingen, Niemeyer, 1977.

Bald, Wolf-Dietrich.
see Linguistisches Kolloquium, 11th, Aachen, 1976. Grammatik und interdisziplinäre Bereiche der Linguistik. 1. Aufl. Tübingen, Niemeyer, 1977.

Bald, Wolf-Dietrich.
see Linguistisches Kolloquium, 11th, Aachen, 1976. Semantik und Pragmatik. 1. Aufl. Tübingen, Niemeyer, 1977.

Bald Eagle Nest Survey Workshop, Twin Cities, Minn., 1973.
Notes on a bald eagle nest survey workshop, Twin Cities, Minnesota, August 15, 1973. Edited by Carl R. Madsen. Fort Snelling, Minn., U. S. Bureau of Sport Fisheries and Wildlife, 1973.
iii, 47, [1] p. illus.
1. Bald eagle—Congresses. 2. Birds—Eggs and nests—Congresses. I. Madsen, Carl R., ed. II. United States. Bureau of Sport Fisheries and Wildlife. III. Title.
DI NUC75-65847

Bald Knob, Ark. City Planning Commission
see Arkansas. University. City Planning Division. A planning report for Bald Knob, Arkansas. Fayetteville, Ark., 1964.

Balda, Martín Iturbe
see
Iturbe Balda, Martín.

Balda, Russell P.
see Carothers, Steven W Breeding birds of the San Francisco Mountain area... Flagstaff, Ariz., Northern Arizona Society of Science and Art, 1973.

Baldacci, Antonio, 1867-
Le Somaliland italien / par A. Baldacci. — Bruxelles : J. Goemaere, Imp. du Roi, 1910.
34 p. : map ; 25 cm.
"Extrait du Bulletin de colonisation comparée, janvier 1910."
Somaliland, Italian.
I. Title.
DT416.B27 967'.7303 75-505143
75 MARC

Baldacci, Luigi.
Libretti d'opera e altri saggi / Luigi Baldacci. — Firenze : Vallecchi, ⌊1974⌋
vii, 269 p. : ill. ; 18 cm. — (Tascabili Vallecchi ; 52) It 75-Jan
Includes bibliographical references and index.
L1400
1. Libretto. I. Title: Libretti d'opera ...
ML2110.B26 75-576420

Baldacci, Luigi.
Il petrarchismo italiano nel Cinquecento / Luigi Baldacci. — Nuova ed. accresciuta. — Padova : Liviana, 1974.
274 p. ; 23 cm. — (Guide di cultura contemporanea) It 74-Nov
Includes bibliographical references and index.
L5000
1. Italian literature—16th century—History and criticism.
2. Petrarca, Francesco, 1304-1374—Influence. I. Title.
PQ4080.B3 74-355700

Baldacci, Luigi, ed.
see Carducci, Giosuè, 1835-1907. Poesie scelte. ⌊Milano⌋: A. Mondadori, 1974.

Baldacci, Luigi
see Foscolo, Ugo, 1778-1827. Opere. Firenze : L. Pugliese, [1974]

Baldacci, Luigi, ed.
see Imbriani, Vittorio, 1840-1886. Dio ne scampi dagli Orsenigo e altri racconti. Firenze, Vallecchi, 1972.

Baldacci, Luigi
see Lirici del Cinquecento. Milano: Longanesi, ⌊1975⌋

Baldacci, Luigi, ed.
see Marchi, Emilio de, 1851-1901. Demetrio Pianelli. Novara, Edizioni per il Club del libro, 1970.

Baldacci, Luigi, ed.
see Pascoli, Giovanni, 1855-1912. Poesie. Milano : Garzanti, 1974.

Baldacci, Osvaldo.
Geografia generale. Con 34 tavole fuori testo e 237 figure nel testo. Torino, Unione tipografico-editrice torinese, ⌊1972⌋.
xxviii, 940 p. illus., 44 plates. 24 cm. (Manuali di geografia, 3)
L20000 It 73-Mar
Includes bibliographies.
1. Geography. I. Title.
G115.B32 73-324538

Baldacci, Osvaldo.
L'incidenza geografico-culturale del gruppo etnico italiano nel contesto urbano di Toronto ... Roma, 1972.
43 p. illus. 24 cm. (Università di Roma. Facoltà di lettere e filosofia. Pubblicazioni dell'Istituto di geografia. Serie A: Antropica e fisica, 15) L1500 It 73-Feb
Title also in English.
Bibliography: p. 10.
1. Italians in Toronto. 2. Toronto—Social conditions. I. Title. II. Title: The geographical and cultural impact of Italian ethnic group in metropolitan Toronto. III. Series: Antropica e fisica, 15.
F1059.5.T689 I 82 73-346261

Baldacci, Osvaldo.
Il pensiero geografico / Osvaldo Baldacci. — Brescia : La scuola, c1975.
231 p. ; 21 cm. — (Analisi e sintesi ; 22) It 76-May
Bibliography: p. [223]-228.
Includes index.
L3300
1. Geography—Philosophy. I. Title.
G70.B35 76-516298

Baldacci, Osvaldo.
Puglia. 2. ed. riveduta e aggiornata. Con una carta geografica e 6 tavole a colori fuori testo, 303 figure e 26 cartine geografiche nel testo. Torino, Unione tipografico -editrice torinese, [1972].
x, 564 p. illus., 6 plates, map. 28 cm. (Le Regioni d'Italia, v. 14)
L15000 It 72-July
Bibliography: p. 539-543.
1. Apulia—Description and travel. I. Series.
DG975.A65B3 1972 72-366507

Baldacci, Paolo
see Recherches sur les amphores romaines... Rome, École française de Rome, 1972.

Baldacci, Riccardo.
Dinamica e stabilità. [A cura di] R. Baldacci, G. Ceradini, E. Giangreco. Genova, Italsider, Gruppo Finsider, [1972?].
xi, 730 p. illus., plates. 21 cm. (Collana tecnico scientifica per la progettazione di strutture in acciaio, v. 2 b) It 73-Jan
Includes bibliographies.
1. Structural dynamics. 2. Structural stability. I. Ceradini, G., joint author. II. Giangreco, Elio, joint author. III. Title.
TA654.B34 624'.171 74-320538

Baldacci, Riccardo.
Scienza delle costruzioni ... [Torino], Unione tipografico -editrice torinese, 1970-1976.
2 v. illus. 24 cm. (Scienze) It 71-May (v. 1)
Includes bibliographies.
CONTENTS: v. 1. Fondamenti di meccanica dei solidi.—v. 2. Fondamenti di meccanica delle strutture.
L12000 (v. 1) ; L28000 (v. 2)
1. Structures, Theory of. I. Title.
TA645.B34 624'.17 74-869603

Baldaccini, César, 1921-
César. Rotonda di via Besana, marzo 1974. Comune di Milano, Ripartizione cultura. Milano, Arti grafiche Fiorin, 1974.
[23] l. illus. 24 cm. It 74-July
Introductory text by P. Restany also in French.
Includes bibliography.
1. Baldaccini, César, 1921- I. Rotonda di via Besana.
NB623.B26R67 74-324009

Baldaccini, César, 1921-
César: compressions d'or [par James Baldwin et Françoise Giroud. Paris, Hachette, 1973]
93 p. (chiefly illus. (part col.)) 27 cm. 70.00F F***
1. Baldaccini, César, 1921- 2. Goldsmithing—France. I. Baldwin, James, 1924- II. Giroud, Françoise. III. Title: Compressions d'or.
NK7198.B27B34 730'.92'4 74-164875 MARC

Baldaccini, César, 1921-
César; [exposition] 3 au 30 janvier 1972, Musée Cantini. Marseille, 1972.
[58] p. illus. 18 cm.
I. Marseille. Musée Cantini.
WU NUC75-84606

Baldaccini, César, 1921-
César : [exposition] Arles, 5 juillet-30 septembre 1973 : salles romanes du cloître Saint-Trophime. — [s.l. : s.n., 1973?] ([Arles] : Impr. L'Homme de bronze)
[8] p., [16] leaves of plates : chiefly ill. ; 21 cm.
1. Baldaccini, César, 1921-
NB553.B22A46 730'.92'4 75-504184
75 MARC

Baldaccini, César, 1921-
César : rétrospective des sculptures = Overzichtstentoonstelling van sculpturen : [exposition itinérante], Musée d'art et d'histoire, Musée Rath, Genève, 26.2-11.4.1976, Grenoble, Knokke, Rotterdam, Paris : [catalogue / réd. Rainer Michael Mason]. — [Genève : s.n., 1976]
130 p. : ill. ; 25 cm. Sw77-2503
Text in French; prefaces also in Dutch.
Bibliography: p. 113-114.
1. Baldaccini, César, 1921- I. Mason, Rainer Michael. II. Musée Rath.
NB553.B22M37 730'.92'4 77-479478
•77 MARC

Baldaccini, César, 1921-
see Restany, Pierre. César. New York, H. N. Abrams, 1976, c1975.

Baldaeus, Philippus, 1632-1672.
A true and exact description of the great island of Ceylon. Being the section relating to Ceylon of the "Beschrijving der Oost Indische kusten Malabar en Choromandel der Zelver aangrenzende ryken en het machtige Eyland Ceylon nevens een onstandige en grondigh doorzochte ontdekking en wederlegginge van de afgoderye den Oost-Indische heydenen," by Phillipus Baldaeus published in Dutch in Amsterdam, 1672. A new and unabridged translation into English by Pieter Brohier. With an introd. by S. D. Saparamadu. [Dehiwala] Ceylon Historical Journal [1960]
lxvi, 403, lxxiii p. illus., maps (part fold.) ports. 21 cm.
"First edition in present translation."
Comprises v. 8, nos. 1-4, July 1958 to April 1959 of the Ceylon Historical Journal.
Includes bibliographical references.
1. Ceylon—History—1505-1948. 2. Ceylon—Description and travel. 3. Tamils in Ceylon. I. Ceylon historical journal. II. Brohier, Pieter, b. 1792, tr. III. Title.
DS489.7.B3413 1960 915.49'3'031 74-182589 MARC

Baldaev, Khristofor Fokeevich, joint author
see Efremov, Petr Grigor'evich. Ryby rek i ozer Mariĭskoĭ ASSR. 1971.

Baldaev, Vil Evgrafovich
see Kalinin, Arkadiĭ Vasil'evich. Shushenskiĭ pereval. [Irkutsk] Vostochno-Sibirskoe knizhnoe izd-vo, 1971.

Baldamus, Wilhelm.
The consumption imperative: structural change in advanced industrial capitalism. [Birmingham, University of Birmingham, Faculty of Commerce and Social Science] 1971.
15 p, [9] l., ii, i-x, [1] p. illus. 30 cm. (University of Birmingham. Faculty of Commerce and Social Science. Discussion paper. Series E, no. 18)
Includes bibliographies.
1. Industry—Social aspects. 2. Industrial sociology. 3. Social change. I. Title. II. Series: Birmingham, England. University. Faculty of Commerce and Social Science. Discussion papers. Series E: Social science methodology, no. 18.
IEdS NUC75-84394

Baldamus, Wilhelm.
Implicit observation: further notes on cross-classification, by W. Baldamus. Birmingham, University of Birmingham, Faculty of Commerce and Social Science, 1973.
17, ix p. illus. 30 cm. (University of Birmingham. Faculty of Commerce and Social Science. Discussion papers. Series E, no. 24.) GB***
Bibliography: p. i-ix.
1. Sociology—Methodology. 2. Sociology—Terminology. I. Title. II. Series: Birmingham, Eng. University. Faculty of Commerce and Social Science. Discussion papers. Series E: Social science and methodology, no. 24.
H31.B63 no. 24 300'.1'8 s 74-172396
[HM24] [301'.01'4] MARC

Baldamus, Wilhelm.
The role of discoveries in social science / by W. Baldamus. — [Birmingham, Eng.] : University of Birmingham, Faculty of Commerce and Social Science, 1966.
53 p. ; 28 cm. — (Discussion papers : Series E, social science methodology ; no. 2)
Includes bibliographical references.
1. Sociology—Methodology. 2. Serendipity. I. Title. II. Series: Birmingham, Eng. University. Faculty of Commerce and Social Science. Discussion papers : Series E, social science methodology ; no. 2.
H31.B63 no. 2 76-374405
[HM24] 76 MARC

Baldamus, Wilhelm.
The structure of sociological inference / W. Baldamus. — London : M. Robertson, 1976. GB***
x, 238 p. ; 23 cm.
Bibliography: p. [215]-230.
Includes indexes.
ISBN 0-85520-130-4 : £7.45
1. Sociology—Methodology. 2. Inference (Logic) I. Title.
HM24.B32 1976b 301'.01'8 77-354250
77 MARC

Baldamus, Wilhelm.
The structure of sociological inference / W. Baldamus. — New York : Barnes & Noble Books, 1976.
x, 238 p. : ill. ; 23 cm.
Bibliography: p. [215]-230.
Includes indexes.
ISBN 0-06-490285-4 : $17.50
1. Sociology—Methodology. I. Title.
HM24.B32 1976 301'.01'8 76-17219
76 MARC

Baldani, Arcidio.
Opera decima : poesie / Arcidio Baldani. — Milano : Europa unita, c1975.
126 p. ; 20 cm. It 75-Dec
L3500
I. Title.
PQ4862.A355O54 76-501040

Baldani, Arcidio.
Opera nona : poesie / Arcidio Baldani. — Milano : Europa unita, 1974.
159 p. ; 20 cm. It 75-Apr
Poems.
L3500
I. Title.
PQ4862.A355O56 75-578048

Baldani, Arcidio.
Opera ottava, poesie / Arcidio Baldani. — Milano : Europa unita, 1973.
140 p. ; 20 cm. It 74-Feb
L2500
I. Title.
PQ4862.A355O57 75-528927

Baldani, Arcidio.
Opera settima: poesie. Milano, Europa unita, 1972.
112 p. 20 cm. L2000 It 73-Feb
"300 esemplari."
I. Title.
PQ4862.A355O66 74-345937

Baldani, Arcidio.
Opera undicesima : poesie / Arcidio Baldani. — Milano : Europa unita, [c1976]
143 p. ; 20 cm. It76-Nov
L4000
I. Title.
PQ4862.A355O67 851'.9'14 77-470409
•77 MARC

Baldano, Namzhil Garmaevich.
Izbrannoe; p'esy; avtorizovannyĭ perevod s buriâtskogo. Moska, Sovetskiĭ pisatel', 1969.
354 p.
WaU NUC74-21953

Baldano, Namzhil Garmaevich.
Plamîâ; drama. Moskva, Gos. Izd-vo "Iskusstvo", 1959.
89 p.
WaU NUC74-21951

Baldano, Namzhil Garmaevich
see Gesar (Romances, etc.). Russian. (Geser) 1973.

Baldanza, Frank.
Iris Murdoch. New York, Twayne Publishers [1974]
187 p. port. 21 cm. (Twayne's English authors series, TEAS 169)
Bibliography: p. 179-184.
1. Murdoch, Iris.
PR6063.U7Z58 823'.9'14 73-22302
ISBN 0-8057-1410-3 MARC

Baldanza, Giuseppe
see Vatican Council, 2d, 1962-1965. [Decretum de institutione sacerdotali. 1967] Torino-Leumann, Elle di Ci [1967]

Baldanzhapov, Purbo Baldanovich
see Altan tobči. Russian & Mongolian. Selections. (Altan tobchi) 1970.

Baldanzi, Giampiero.
Efeito da queimada sôbre a fertilidade do solo. Curitiba, 1959.
56 p. tables. 22 cm. (Boletim técnico do Departamento de produção vegetal, Secretaria de agricultura do Paraná, no. 1)
Cover title.
Summary in English.
Bibliography: p. 47-56.
1. Burning of land. I. Title II. Series.
NNBG NUC74-175378

Baldares Carazo, Manuel, joint author
see González de Wong, Maria Isabel. La promoción en la Escuela de Ciencias Económicas... Ciudad Universitaria Rodrigo Facio, Instituto de Investigaciones Económicas, 1969.

Baldaro Verde, Jole.
Compendio di scienze dell'educazione. Genova, Tilgher, 1973.
220 p. 24 cm. L3500 It 73-Sept
At head of title: Jole Baldaro Verde, Michele Schiavone.
Includes bibliographical references.
1. Education—1965- 2. Family. I. Schiavone, Michele, joint author. II. Title.
LB1025.2.B28 73-364446

Baldaro Verde, Jole.
La psicologia nel momento educativo / Jole Baldaro Verde. — Genova : Tilgher, [1974]
214 p. ; 22 cm. It***
Includes bibliographies.
L4500
1. Educational psychology. 2. Child development. I. Title.
LB1051.B185 75-404961

Baldass, Peter von.
Romanische Kunst in Österreich / Baldass, Buchowiecki, Mrazek. — 3., verm. u. textlich überarb. Aufl. — Wien : Forum Verl., 1974.
96 p., [62] leaves of plates : ill. (some col.) ; 28 cm. Au 75-4-205
Includes bibliographical references.
S360.00
1. Art, Romanesque—Austria. 2. Art, Austrian. I. Buchowiecki, Walther, joint author. II. Mrazek, Wilhelm, joint author. III. Title.
N6803.B3 1974 75-536989

Baldassare, Mark.
Crowding and human behavior: are cities behavioral sinks? [Monticello, Ill., 1974]
15 p. 28 cm. (Council of Planning Librarians. Exchange bibliography, no. 631)
Cover title.
1. Crowding stress—Bibliography. 2. Cities and towns—Growth—Bibliography. I. Title. II. Series.
NBuU NUC75-22637

Baldassare, Mark, joint author.
see Feller, Susan. Theory and methods in urban anthropology ... Monticello, Ill., Council of Planning Librarians, 1975.

Baldassare, Mark, joint author.
see Fischer, Claude S., 1948- Crowding studies and urban life ... Berkeley, Institute of Urban & Regional Development, University of California, 1974.

Baldassari, Maurizio, joint author
see Mossa, Giovanni. La vita economica di Roma nel Medioevo. Roma, Liber, 1971.

Baldassari, Tommaso.
Frutticoltura pratica. 12. ed. Firenze, Vallecchi [1965]
226 p. (Collana practica dell'agricoltore, 1)
1. Fruit-culture. Italy. I. Title. II. Series.
DNAL NUC75-36316

Baldassaro, Lawrence Anthony, 1943-
Dante's participation in the sins of the Inferno. [Bloomington, Ind.] 1972.
196 p.
Thesis (Ph.D.)–Indiana University.
Vita.
InU NUC73-44390

Baldassarre, Antonio.
Privacy e costituzione : l'esperienza statunitense / Antonio Baldassarre. — Roma : Bulzoni, [1974]
482 p. ; 24 cm. It 75-Apr
Includes bibliographical references.
L8500
1. Privacy, Right of. 2. Common law. I. Title.
75-568869

Baldassarre, Elia.
Lo psichiatra disadattato. Roma, Napoleone, 1973.
182 p. 17 cm. (Universale Napoleone, 7) L1200 It 74-Mar
1. Baldassarre, Elia. 2. Child psychiatry. I. Title.
RC339.52.B34A33 74-312830

Baldassarre-Guégan, Jacqueline.
Au gré du vent : janvier 74-août 75 / Jacqueline Baldassarre-Guégan. — Paris : Éditions Saint-Germain-des-Prés, c1976.
113 p. ; 21 cm. — (Collection La Poésie, la vie) F***
Poems.
ISBN 2-243-00301-5 : 25.00F
I. Title.
PQ2662.A3716A93 841'.9'14 77-462804
77 MARC

Baldassarre-Guégan, Jacqueline.
Envolée : février-décembre 1973 / Jacqueline Baldassarre-Guégan. — Paris (184, Brd Saint-Germain, 75006) : la Grisière, 1974.
120 p. ; 19 cm. — (Balises) F75-887
Poems.
18.00F
I. Title.
PQ2662.A3716E5 841'.9'14 75-505299
75 MARC

Baldassarre Olimpo da Sassoferrato, frate
see
Olimpo da Sassoferrato, 1486?-1540.

Baldassarre Olimpo degli Alessandri da Sassoferrato, frate
see
Olimpo da Sassoferrato, 1486?-1540.

Baldassarri, Mario.
Algebraicheskie mnogoobrazii͡a. Perevod s angliĭskogo I͡U.I. Manina. Pod red. M.M. Postnikova. Moskva, Izd-vo inostrannoĭ lit-ry, 1961.
315 p. 21 cm.
At head of title: M. Bal'dassarri.
Translation of Algebraic varieties.
Bibliography: p. [290]-307.
1. Geometry, Algebraic. I. Title.
NBuU NUC74-21963

Baldassarri, Rita.
Lucini / di Rita Baldassarri. — Firenze : La nuova Italia, 1974.
119 p. ; 17 cm. — (Il Castoro ; 91-92) It 74-Dec
Cover title.
Bibliography: p. 104-114.
L1100
1. Lucini, Gian Pietro, 1867-1914.
PQ4827.U45Z59 74-350979

Baldassini, Girolamo, 1720-1780.
Memorie istoriche dell'antichissima e regia città di Jesi / Girolamo Baldassini. — Bologna : Forni, 1972.
699 p. in various pagings ; 24 cm. — (Biblioteca istorica della antica e nuova Italia ; n. 98) It 73-June
Reprint of the 1765 ed. printed by P. P. Bonelli, Jesi.
"Appendice di tutte le bolle, brevi, lettere, privilegj ed istromenti cavati quasi tutti da pergamene antiche, che si conservano nell'Archivo segreto di quella segreraria priorale, e altrove e che si citano nelle memorie istoriche della città di Jesi distribuite per ordine cronologico": p. [1]-cxxviii (3d group).
Includes index.
1. Iesi, Italy—History. I. Title.
DG975.I4B34 1972 945'.671 75-555821

Baldauf, Anita, comp.
Dagobert und der Zauberdraht: Geschichten von heute/ Hrsg.: Anita Baldauf; Hans Schmidt.—1. Aufl.—Berlin: Verlag Tribüne, 1973.
170 p.; 21 cm. 6.80M GDR 74-A
1. German literature—20th century. 2. Labor and laboring classes—Germany (Democratic Republic, 1949-) I. Schmidt, Hans, fl. 1970- joint comp. II. Title.
PT1334.B3 74-304471

Baldauf, Anita, joint comp.
see Schmidt, Hans, fl. 1970- comp. Verflixte Gedanken. Berlin, Tribüne, 1970.

Baldauf, Ethel
see Pilgrim Presbyterian Church, Trenton, N. J. 50th anniversary, 1911-1961... [Trenton, N. J., 1961]

Baldauf, Günther.
Zum Verbandsprinzip in Verdichtungsräumen : ein Beitr. z. kommunalen Neugliederung im Ruhrgebiet u. in anderen Ballungsräumen / von Günther Baldauf. — Köln ; Berlin ; Bremen ; München ; Hamburg ; Hannover ; Kiel ; Mainz ; München ; Wiesbaden : Deutscher Gemeindeverlag, 1974.
v, 94 p. ; 23 cm. — (Abhandlungen zur Kommunalpolitik ; Bd. 7) GFR 74-A37
Includes bibliographical references.
ISBN 3-555-30077-6 : DM32.00
1. Local government—North Rhine-Westphalia. 2. North Rhine-Westphalia—Administrative and political divisions. I. Title. II. Series.
75-536308

Baldauf, Josef.
Ein experimenteller Beitrag zur Analyse der negativ chronotropen und dromotropen Wirkung der Hypoxie am isolierten Meerschweinchen-Herzen / Josef Baldauf. — Saarbrücken : Universitäts- und Schulbuchverlag, c1975.
97 p. : graphs ; 26 cm. — (Annales universitatis Saraviensis : Medizin ; v. 22, fasc. 2) GFR***
Habilitationsschrift—Universität des Saarlandes, Saarbrücken.
Bibliography: p. 95-97.
1. Anoxemia. 2. Cardiology, Experimental. 3. Heart conduction system. 4. Bradycardia. I. Title: Ein experimenteller Beitrag zur Analyse der negativ chronotropen und dromotropen Wirkung ... II. Series: Saarbrücken. Universität des Saarlandes. Annales : Medizin ; v. 22, fasc. 2.
R55.S214 vol. 22, fasc. 2 75-510520
[RC103.A4] 75 MARC

Baldauf, Lucia, 1916- comp.
Litauische Lyrik; eine Anthologie. Litauisch-deutsch. Ausgewählt und übers. von Lucia Baldauf. München, W. Fink, 1972.
306 p. 23 cm. GDB***
1. Lithuanian poetry (Collections) 2. Lithuanian poetry—Translations into German. 3. German poetry—Translation from Lithuanian. I. Title.
PG8715.B27 73-335691

Baldauf, R J
A study of selected chemical and biological conditions of the lower Trinity River and upper Trinity Bay. [Austin] 1970.
168 p. illus. (TR-26)
Research project completion report, project no. A-007-TEX, Feb. 1, 1966-June 30, 1969; agreement nos. 14-01-0001-814, 14-01-0001-989, 14-01-0001-1412, 14-01-0001-1864.
Bibliography: p. 85-92.
PB 190 269.
1. Water quality—Texas—Trinity River. 2. Water quality—Texas—Trinity Bay. 3. Shrimps—Texas—Trinity Bay. 4. Shrimps—Texas—Trinity River. 5. Menhaden fisheries. 6. Blue crabs. I. Title. II. Series: Texas. Agricultural and Mechanical University, College Station. Water Resources Institute. Technical report no. 26.
DI DLC NUC76-24572

Baldazzi, Anna.
Bibliografia della critica dannunziana nei periodici italiani dal 1880 al 1938 / Anna Baldazzi. — Roma : Cooperativa scrittori, 1977.
271 p. ; 24 cm. — (Archivio italiano) It77-July
Includes index.
L6000
1. Annunzio, Gabriele d', 1863-1938—Criticism and interpretation—Bibliography. I. Title.
Z8037.3.B34 77-484489
[PQ4804] •77 MARC

Baldazzi, Enrico
see Facchino, Carlo Alberto. Zavattarello. Zavattarello, Associazione Amici di Zavattarello-Pro loco, 1972.

Balde, Jakob, 1604-1668.
De eclipsi solari anno M. DC. LIV. die XII. Augusti, in Europa, a pluribus spectata tvbo optico: nunc itora à Jacobo Balde ... tubo satyrico por lustrata, libri dvo. Monachii, Typis L. Stravb., sumptibus J. Wagneri, 1662.
232 p. illus.
Microprint. New York, Readex Microprint, 1974. 3 cards. (Landmarks of science)
1. Eclipses–Solar–1654. I. Title.
InU NUC76-18035

Balde, Mamadou Saliou
see Cros, Claude. Les migrations rurales vers la zone arachidière orientale. Dakar, Direction de l'aménagement du territoire, 19

Baldeck, Charles Marvin, 1938-
The solvent extraction of aluminum, lead and some transition metals with 2, 2, 6, 6-tetramethyl-3, 5-heptanedione. [n.p.] 1973.
260 l.
Thesis–Ohio State University.
Bibliography: leaves 355-360.
1. Extraction (Chemistry) 2. Aluminum. 3. Lead. I. Title.
OU NUC74-125952

Baldelli, Bruna Rolandi
see
Rolandi Baldelli, Bruna.

Baldelli, Giovanni.
Itinerario. Parma, Guanda, 1973.
168 p. 18 cm. (Piccola Fenice) L2000 It 73-Oct
Poems.
I. Title.
PQ4862.A363 I 8 74-314537

Baldelli, Giovanni.
La pied a l'étrier; poèmes. Rodez, Éditions Subervie [1969]
93 p. 20 cm.
I. Title.
IU NUC76-70315

Baldelli, Giovanni.
Social anarchism. [Harmondsworth, Eng.] Penguin Books [1972, c1971]
192 p.
1. Anarchism and anarchists. I. Title.
ViBlbV NUC74-125951

Baldelli, Ignazio.
San Francesco e Manzoni, realtà spirituale nuova e lingua nuova : conversazione tenuta nella Sala francescana di cultura il 26 aprile 1974 / Ignazio Baldelli. — Assisi : Sala francescana di cultura P. Antonio Giorgi, 1974.
16 p. ; 24 cm. It75-Oct
1. Italian language—Dialects—Assisi. 2. Francesco d'Assisi, Saint, 1182-1226. Cantico de lo frate sole. 3. Italian language—Dialects—Florence. 4. Manzoni, Alessandro, 1785-1873. I promessi sposi. I. Title.
PC1826.Z9A83 76-477520
•76 MARC

Baldelli, Ignazio.
Vocabolario minimo della lingua italiana per stranieri : 1741 parole con frasi ed esempi di uso frequente con traduzione in inglese, francese, tedesco e spagnolo / Ignazio Baldelli, Alberto Mazzetti. — Firenze : Le Monnier, 1974.
iv, 194 p. ; 21 cm. — (Pubblicazioni dell'Università italiana per stranieri di Perugia) It 75-Aug
L2500
1. Italian language—Dictionaries—Polyglot. 2. Italian language—Conversation and phrase books—Polyglot. I. Mazzetti, Alberto, joint author. II. Title. III. Series: Perugia. Università italiana per stranieri. Pubblicazioni dell'Università italiana per stranieri di Perugia.
PC1635.B3 75-591919

Baldelli, Pio.
Charlie Chaplin / Pio Baldelli. — 1. ed. — Firenze : La nuova Italia, 1977.
244 p., [4] leaves of plates : ill. ; 21 cm. — (Dimensioni ; 42) It77-Apr
Bibliography: p. 229-230.
Appendices (p. 233-242): La psicologia della comica cinematografica.—Intervista di Theodore Dreiser a Mack Sennett.
L4000
1. Chaplin, Charles, 1889-
PN2287.C5B25 77-472047
77 MARC

Baldelli, Pio.
El cine y la obra literaria. [Traducción: Alejandro Saderman. Buenos Aires] Editorial Galerna [1970]
436 p. (Teoría y crítica literaria. Serie mayor)
1. Moving-pictures and literature. 2. Moving-picture plays—Hist. & crit. 3. Moving-pictures—Production and direction. I. Title.
DeU NUC74-5497

Baldelli, Pio.
Cinema dell'ambiguità. 2. ed. Roma, Samona e Savelli, 1971.
2 v. 20 cm. (Saggistica, 20, 21)
"Filmografia a cura di Pietro Angelini": v. 1, p. [381]-400, v. 2, p. [265]-273.
Includes bibliographical references.
Contents.—v. 1. Rossellini, De Sica e Zavattini, Fellini.—v. 2. Bergman, Antonioni.
1. Moving-pictures. Italy. I. Title.
NcD NUC73-119794

Baldelli, Pio.
Film e opera letteraria. Padova, Marsilio [1964]
412 p. 22 cm. (Biblioteca di cultura cinematografica, 4)
Includes bibliographical references.
1. Moving-pictures and literature. I. Title.
PN1995.3.B3 74-208015

Baldelli, Pio.
Informazione e controinformazione. Milano, G. Mazzotta, 1972.
405 p. illus. 19 cm. (Biblioteca di nuova cultura, 4) L1900 It 72-Sept
Includes bibliographical references.
1. Communication — Social aspects. 2. Communication — Political aspects. I. Title.
HM258.B35 73-303977

Baldelli, Pio.
Informazione e controinformazione. [3. ed.] Milano, G. Mazzota [1973, c1972]
431 p. illus. 19 cm. (Biblioteca di nuova cultura, 4)
Includes bibliographical references.
1. Communication—Social aspects. 2. Communication—Political aspects. I. Title.
MdBJ NUC76-70314

Baldelli, Pio.
Luchino Visconti. Milano, G. Mazzotta, 1973.
352 p. illus., plates. 24 cm. (Cinema e informazione visiva, 4) L6000 It 74-Mar
Bibliography: p. 339-347.
1. Visconti, Luchino, 1906-
PN1998.A3V583 74-305971

Baldelli, Pio.
Roberto Rossellini. I film (1936-1972) e la filmografia nella più completa analisi del cinema del grande regista. In appendice brani critici di A. Bazin e J. Rivette e la sceneggiatura inedita del Caligola. Roma, La nuova sinistra, [1972].
393 p. 21 cm. (Saggistica, 39) L3800 It 72-Aug
Cover title.
Includes documents in French.
"Filmografia": p. [305]-313.
1. Rossellini, Roberto, 1906- I. Caligola.
PN1998.A3R6625 72-362217

Baldelli, Pio, ed.
see I Compagni. [Bologna] Capelli [1963]

Baldelli, Pio.
see Le Istituzioni in Italia ... Roma, Savelli, c1976.

Baldelló, Francisco, 1887-
Los "Goigs de la Mare de Deu." Barcelona, Balmesiana (Biblioteca Balmes) 1956.
15 p. 25 cm.
Offprint from Analecta Sacra Tarraconensia, v. 28 (1955) p. 183-197.
Besutti (1959) 3992.
ODaU-M NUC74-173583

Baldelló, Francisco, 1887-
Petit historial dels "Amics dels Goigs" [de] Francesc de P. Baldelló. Pròleg de Carles Babot i Boixeda. Barcelona, Torrell de Reus, 1959.
55 p. facsims. 18 cm.
"70 exemplare en paper de fil, numerats a mà. 250 exemplars en paper corrent. Exemplar núm 23."
"Publicació dels "Amics dels Goigs."
ODaU-M NUC74-37784

Baldellou, Miguel Angel.
[Alejandro de la Sota / Miguel Angel Baldellou]. — [Madrid : Servicio de Publicaciones del Ministerio de Educación y Ciencia, 1975]
120 p. : ill. ; 17 cm. — (Colección Artistas españoles contemporáneos ; 103 : Serie arquitectos) Sp76-Mar
Includes bibliographical references.
ISBN 843690463X
1. Sota, Alejandro de la, 1913- 2. Architects—Spain—Biography.
NA1313.S63B34 720'.92'4 77-451600
•77 MARC

Baldellou, Miguel Angel.
Luis Gutiérrez Soto. [Madrid] Dirección General de Bellas Artes [1973]
93 p. plates (part col.) 17 cm. (Artistas españoles contemporáneos, 38. Serie arquitectos) 60ptas Sp•••
1. Gutiérrez Soto, Luis, 1900-
NA1313.G87B34 73-339488

Baldellou, Vicente, joint author
see Junyent, Emilio. Una vivienda ibérica de Mas Boscà. Barcelona, 1972.

Baldellou Vazquez, Antonio, joint author
see Ballesta Martinez, Francisca. Cromosomopatias autosomicas.. Barcelona, Editorial Espaxs, 1971.

Balden, Theo, 1904-
Theo Balden, Plastik und Graphik. [Exhibition] Staatliche Museen zu Berlin, National-Galerie. [Berlin, 1963]
1 v. (chiefly illus.) 23 cm.
I. Berlin. National-Galerie (East Berlin) II. Berlin. Staatliche Museen.
KyLoU NUC76-25660

Balden, Theo, 1904-
Theo Balden. Plastik u. Graphik. (Ausstellg. aus Anlass s. 65. Geburtstages. [Katalog]) Berlin, Staatliche Museen National-Galerie [1971]
32 l. with illus. 21 cm. DM4.00 GDNB 71-B24-229
I. Berlin. National-Galerie (East Berlin).
N6888.B29B47 72-360925

Balden, Theo, 1904-
Theo Balden / Raimund Hoffmann. — 1. Aufl. — Berlin : Henschelverlag, 1976.
46 p. : chiefly ill. (some col.) ; 27 cm. — (Welt der Kunst) GDR•••
Includes bibliographical references.
7.00M
1. Balden, Theo, 1904- I. Hoffmann, Raimund.
NB588.B32H63 77-468631
77 MARC

Baldensperger, Denis.
Les Armes secrètes. Préface d'Alain Decaux. Paris, Rouff, 1969.
183 p. plates. 17 cm. (Dossiers de l'histoire, 16) 5.50 F 69-10521
Illustrated cover.
Bibliography: p. [175]-[176]
1. Atomic bomb—History. 2. Guided missiles—History. 3. Weapons systems—History. I. Title.
UF767.B28 74-311981

Baldensperger, Fernand, 1871-1958.
Bibliographie critique de Goethe en France. New York, B. Franklin [1972]
ix, 251 p. 23 cm. (Burt Franklin bibliography & reference series, 455. Selected essays and texts in literature and criticism, 177)
Reprint of the 1907 ed.
1. Goethe, Johann Wolfgang von, 1749-1832—Bibliography. 2. Baldensperger, Fernand, 1871-1958. Goethe en France. I. Title.
Z8350.B25 1972 016.831'6 72-81937
ISBN 0-8337-3961-1

Baldensperger, Fernand, 1871-1958.
Études d'histoire littéraire. Genève, Slatkine Reprints, 1973.
4 v. in 2. 18 cm. Sw•••
Reprint of the Paris, 1907-1910, 1939 editions.
Includes bibliographical references.
1. French literature—Addresses, essays, lectures. 2. Literature—Addresses, essays, lectures. I. Title.
PQ139.B28 1973 840'.9 74-169471
MARC

Baldensperger, Fernand, 1871-1958.
Goethe en France; étude de littérature comparée. 2. éd. rev. New York, B. Franklin [1973]
398 p. 22 cm. (Burt Franklin research & source works series. Selected essays and texts in literature and criticism, 200)
Reprint of the 1920 ed. published by Hachette, Paris.
1. Goethe, Johann Wolfgang von, 1749-1832—Appreciation—France. I. Title.
PT2173.F7B3 1973 831'.6 72-81938
ISBN 0-8337-3961-1 rev MARC

Baldensperger, J
Carte pédologique de moyenne Casamance [République du Sénégal] dressée par J. Baldensperger, J.P. Staimesse et C. Tobias. [Dakar] Centre O.R.S.T.O.M. de Dakar, 1968.
col. map. 66 x 86 cm.
Scale 1:200,000.
Inset: Carte de situation.
1. Soils—Senegal—Casamance—Maps. I. Staimesse, J.P. II. Tobias, C. III. France. Office de la recherche scientifique et technique outre-mer. Centre de Dakar. IV. Title.
NIC NUC76-84421

Baldeo Prasad Mishra
see
Mishra, Baldeo Prasad, 1913-1965.

Baldeón, Amelia. Los niveles sin cerámica del Montico de Charratu. 1974.
in Dos estudios sobre Prehistoria del País Vasco. Bilbao, Universidad, 1974.

Balder, Bruno.
Der glaubenslose Christ; eine kritische Auseinandersetzung mit der christlichen Ideologie. 2., verbesserte Aufl. Darmstadt, Melzer [1973, c1972]
143 p. 21 cm. GFR***
Includes bibliographical references.
1. Catholic Church—Doctrinal and controversial works. I. Title.
BX1765.2.B26 1973 73-348876
ISBN 3-7874-0005-2

Balder Schauffelen, Konrad.
Raus mit der Sprache. (Frankfurt a. M.) Suhrkamp (1969).
71 p. 20 cm. 22.80 GDB 69-A17-229
Poems.
I. Title.
PT2662.A45R3 70-398060
rev

Balderas-Moreno, Juventino.
Production functions, technology and functional income distribution in Mexico: A cross-section analysis of the manufacturing sector in 1960 and 1965. [Boulder] 1973.
xiii, 132 l. illus.
Thesis (Ph. D.)—University of Colorado.
Bibliography: leaves [114]-118.
1. Mexico—Economic conditions-1945- 2. Mexico—Manufactures. 3. Income—Mexico. I. Title.
CoU NUC76-70313

Balderi, Iginio
see Amsterdam. Stedelijk Museum. Iginio Balderi; zeven variaties... [Amsterdam, 1974]

Baldermann, Ingo.
Die Sache des Religionsunterrichts : zwischen Curriculum u. Biblizismus / Ingo Baldermann, Gisela Kittel. — Göttingen : Vandenhoeck und Ruprecht, 1975.
190 p. ; 21 cm. GFR76-A
Includes bibliographical references.
ISBN 3-525-61172-2 : DM22.00
1. Christian education—Addresses, essays, lectures. I. Kittel, Gisela, joint author. II. Title.
BV1473.B28 76-456975
76 MARC

Baldermann, Joachim.
Wanderungsmotive und Stadtstruktur : empir. Fallstudie zum Wanderungsverhalten im Grossstadtraum Stuttgart / Joachim Baldermann, George Hecking, Erich Knauss. — Stuttgart : Krämer, 1976.
157, [14] p. : numerous ill., maps ; 30 x 33 cm. — (Schriftenreihe des Städtebaulichen Instituts der Universität Stuttgart ; 6) GFR76-A
"Eine Untersuchung der Abteilung Forschung des Städtebaulichen Instituts der Universität Stuttgart in Zusammenarbeit mit der Stadtverwaltung Stuttgart."
Bibliography: p. 155-156.
ISBN 3-7828-1431-2 : DM32.00
1. Migration, Internal—Germany, West—Stuttgart region. 2. Residential mobility—Germany, West—Stuttgart region. 3. Stuttgart region—Population. 4. Stuttgart—Suburbs and environs. I. Hecking, Georg, joint author. II. Knauss, Erich, joint author. III. Stuttgart. Universität. Städtebauliches Institut. Abteilung Forschung. IV. Stuttgart. V. Title. VI. Series: Stuttgart. Universität. Städtebauliches Institut. Schriftenreihe des Städtebaulichen Instituts der Universität Stuttgart ; 6.
HB2266.S78B34 76-486043
76 MARC

Balderrama, Alfonso.
La conexion de los rios navegables de la Hoya Amazonica Boliviana con el sistema vial del Centro y Sur. Cochabamba, 1960.
25 l.
1. Transportation—Bolivia. 2. Roads—Bolivia. I. Title.
MiEM NUC76-69360

Balderrama, Alfonso.
Plan de integración de la red primaria de transportes. Cochabamba, 1960.
43 l.
Cover title.
1. Transportation—Bolivia. 2. Railroads—Bolivia. I. Title.
MiEM NUC76-69361

Balderrama, Joel.
El puerto imposible para Bolivia / [Joel Balderrama]. — Cochabamba, Bolivia : UMSS, Editorial Universitaria, 1976.
128 p. ; 20 cm.
"Anexos" (p. 79-128) contain treaties, protocols, etc.
1. Tacna-Arica question. 2. Bolivia—Foreign relations. 3. Harbors—Bolivia. I. Title.
F3097.3.B226 77-473847
77 MARC

Balderrama C., Maritza, joint author
see Payne, Ruth. Contenido y metodos de la ensenanza en Bolibia. La Paz, Comision Episcopal de Educacion, 1972.

Balderrama C , Teresa.
Costos y financiamiento de la educación pública en Bolivia / Teresa Balderrama C., Jorge Rivera P. — La Paz : Comisión Episcopal de Educación, Secretariado Nacional, 1973.
217 p. ; 29 cm. — (Estudios educacionales ; no. 3)
1. Education—Bolivia—Finance—Statistics. I. Rivera P., Jorge, joint author. II. Title. III. Series: Estudios educacionales (La Paz) ; no. 3.
LB2899.B6B35 75-526391

Baldersheim, Harald, 1944-
Forvaltningsorganisasjon og samfunnsstruktur : ei orientering om teorier og synsmåtar / Harald Baldersheim. — Oslo : Universitetsforlaget, [1975]
126 p. : ill. ; 22 cm. N 75-Nov
Includes bibliographical references.
ISBN 82-00-01480-0
1. Public administraton. I. Title.
JF1358.N6B34 76-503047

Balderson, Bo.
Statsrådets verk. [Detektivroman] Stockholm, Bonnier, 1973.
227, (1) p. 21 cm. kr43.00 S 73-36
I. Title.
PT9876.12.A4S85 74-331086
ISBN 91-0-038567-0; 91-0-038566-2 (pbk.)

Balderson, James H., joint author
see Nagle, John M Group problem solving... Eugene [Or.] 1974.

Balderson, Jay Russell
see Brackenridge, Hugh Henry, 1748-1816. A critical edition of Hugh Henry Brackenridge's Modern chivalry, part I. [Iowa City] 1972 [c1973]

Balderston, Frederick E
Academic demand for new Ph. D.'s 1970-90: its sensitivity to alternative policies [by] F. E. Balderston [and] Roy Radner. [Berkeley, Calif.] 1971.
61 l. 28 cm. (California. University. Office of the Vice President-Planning. Ford Foundation program for research in university administration. Paper, P-26)
1. Doctor of philosophy degree. 2. College graduates—Employment. I. Radner, Roy, 1927- II. Title. III. Series.
CaBVaU NUC73-43789

Balderston, Frederick E
Cost analysis in higher education [by] F.E. Balderston. [Berkeley, Calif.] 1972.
37 l. 28 cm. (California. University. Office of the Vice President-Planning. Ford Foundation program for research in university administration, paper, P-33)
Includes bibliography.
1. Education, Higher—Costs. I. Title. II. Series.
CaBVaU CU-L NUC73-119679

Balderston, Frederick E
Hē exelixis tēs epistēmēs tēs dioikēseōs [hypo] F.E. Balderston. Athēnai, c1962.
35 p. 21 cm. (Kentron Programmatismou kai Oikonomikōn Ereunōn. Lecture series, 2)
1. Management. I. Title. II. Series.
CaBVaU NUC75-31189

Balderston, Frederick E
Financing postsecondary education. Berkeley, University of California, Office of Vice-President-Planning, 1972.
i, 33 l.
1. Universities and colleges—Finance. I. Title.
CU-L CaBVaU NUC73-119590

Balderston, Frederick E
Managing today's university / Frederick E. Balderston. — 1st ed. — San Francisco : Jossey-Bass, 1974.
xvi, 307 p. : ill. ; 24 cm. — (The Jossey-Bass series in higher education)
"Reports of the Ford Foundation Program for Research in University Administration": p. 289-291.
Bibliography: p. 293-299.
Includes index.
ISBN 0-87589-236-1
1. Universities and colleges—Administration. I. Title.
LB2341.B26 658'.91'3781 74-9111
MARC

Balderston, Frederick E
The repayment period for loan-financed college education [by] F.E. Balderston. Berkeley, Office of the Vice President-Planning, University of California, 1970.
i, 11 l. (For Foundation program for research in university administration. Paper P-15)
1. Student loan funds—United States. 2. Student aid—United States. I. Title.
CU NUC76-70402

Balderston, Frederick E
Thinking about the outputs of higher education [by] F.E. Balderston. [Berkeley, Calif.] 1970.
15 l. 28 cm. (California. University. Office of the Vice President-Planning and Analysis. Research projects in university administration. Paper P-5)
1. Education, Higher. I. Title. II. Series.
CaBVaU NUC74-125658

Balderston, Frederick E
Varieties of financial crisis [by] Frederick E. Balderston. [Berkeley, Calif., Office of the Vice President - Planning, University of California] 1972.
29 l. 28 cm. (California. University. Office of the Vice President - Planning. Ford Foundation Program for Research in University Administration, paper P-29)
Bibliographical footnotes.
1. Universities and colleges—U. S.—Finance. I. Title. II. Series.
CaBVaU NUC73-119834

Balderston, Jean Merrill, 1936-
The Edward Dickinsons of Amherst, a family analysis. New York, Teachers college, Columbia University, 1969.
247 p.
Microfilm.
Thesis (Ed.D.)—Columbia University.
Bibliography: p. 226-235.
1. Dickinson family.
NN NUC73-119558

Balderston, John Lloyd, 1889-
Berkeley Square, a play in three acts by John L. Balderston (in collaboration with J. C. Squire)... London, Samuel French limited [n. d.]
88 p. illus. 22 cm. (French's acting edition)
Microfilm.
I. Title.
CaBVaU NUC75-22634

Balderston, John Lloyd, 1889-1954. Berkeley Square
see [Berkeley Square] [Sound recording] American Forces Radio and Television Service RU 46-2, 3B [1972]

Balderston, John Lloyd, 1889-1954, joint author
see Deane, Hamilton. Dracula. New York, S. French [c1960]

Balderston, Judith B., joint author.
see Ritzen, Jozef M. Methodology for planning technical education ... New York, Praeger, 1975.

Balderston, Katharine Canby, 1895-
A census of the manuscripts of Oliver Goldsmith / by Katharine Canby Balderston. — Folcroft, Pa. : Folcroft Library Editions, 1976 [c1926]
xii, 73 p. ; 23 cm.
Reprint of the ed. published by E. B. Hackett, The Brick Row Book Shop, New York.
Includes index.
ISBN 0-8414-1789-X lib. bdg. : $15.00
1. Goldsmith, Oliver, 1728-1774—Manuscripts—Bibliography. I. Title.
Z8353.B18 1976 016.828'6'09 76-41731
[PR3493] 76 MARC

Balderston, Katharine Canby, 1895-
A census of the manuscripts of Oliver Goldsmith / by Katharine Canby Balderston. — Norwood, Pa. : Norwood Editions, 1977, c1926.
xii, 73 p. ; 23 cm.
Reprint of the ed. published by E. B. Hackett, New York.
Includes index.
ISBN 0-8482-0223-6 : $12.50
1. Goldsmith, Oliver, 1728-1774—Manuscripts—Bibliography. I. Title.
Z8353.B18 1977 828'.6'09 77-767
77 MARC

Balderston, Katharine Canby, 1895- ed.
see Goldsmith, Oliver, 1728-1774. The collected letters of Oliver Goldsmith. Cambridge [Eng.] The University press, 1928. New York, Kraus Reprint Co., 1969.

Balderston, Katharine Canby, 1895-
see Goldsmith, Oliver, 1728-1774. The collected letters of Oliver Goldsmith. Folcroft, Pa., Folcroft Library Editions, 1975.

Balderston, Katharine Canby, 1895- ed.
see Goldsmith, Oliver, 1728-1774. The collected letters of Oliver Goldsmith. Norwood, Pa., Norwood Editions, 1975.

Balderston, Katharine Canby, 1895-
see Wellesley College, 1875-1975 ... Wellesley, Mass., Wellesley College, [1975]

Balderston, M.B.
see Van den Driessche, R. Trials with selective herbicides... -- Victoria, B.C. : Research Division, British Columbia Forest Service, [1974]

Balderston, Marion.
Balderston family history [by Marion Balderston and Hortense B. C. Gibson. n. p., 1973]
50 p. illus. 23 cm.
Includes bibliographical references.
1. Balderston family. I. Gibson, Hortense B. C., joint author. II. Title.
CS71.B187 1973 929'.2'0973 73-91162
MARC

Balderston, Marion.
see The Lost war ... New York, Horizon Press, c1975.

Balderstone, Greg.
Where the words are unspoken [by] Greg Baldersone [sic] [Fredericton, N. B.] Fiddlehead Poetry Books, 1972.
20 p. 22 cm. C***
Limited ed. of 500 copies.
I. Title.
PR9199.B3W4 811'.5'4 73-330761
MARC

Baldes, Derek W
Non-monetary (subsistence) activities in the national accounts of developing countries, by Derek W. Baldes. Paris, Development Centre of the Organization for Economic Co-operation and Development, 1975.
99 p. (Development Centre Studies)
Bibliography: p. 95-99.
1. Underdeveloped areas—Economic indicators. 2. Economic research. I. Organization for Economic Co-operation and Development. Development Centre. II. Title. III. Series.
NbU NUC77-84370

Baldes, J. James, joint author
see Latham, Gary P Assigned versus participative goal setting with independent producer-contractors... Tacoma, Wash.: Human Resources Planning and Development, Weyerhaeuser Co., 1974.

Baldeschi, Paolo.
L'analisi dei sistemi applicata al territorio. Critiche e contributi ... Firenze, CLUSF, 1972.
174 p. illus. 23 cm. L2500 It 73-Apr
CONTENTS: Baldeschi, P. Introduzione: Note metodologiche sull'analisi dei sistemi applicata al fenomeni territoriali. Dragonas, T. Lineamenti di un modello territoriale. Montanari, F. Urbanistica e atteggiamento scientifico.
Includes bibliographical references.
1. Land—Mathematical models. I. Dragonas, Teodoro. II. Montanari, Flaminia. III. Title.
HD111.B22 73-347710

Bâldescu, Emil.
Din istoria legăturilor revoluţionare româno-bulgare, 1909-1916 / Emil Bâldescu. — [Bucureşti] : Editura ştiinţifică, 1966.
181 p. ; 20 cm.
Summary in English, Russian, and Bulgarian.
Includes bibliographical references.
1. Communism—Romania—History. 2. Communism—Bulgaria—History. 3. Romania—Relations (general)—Bulgaria. 4. Bulgaria—Relations (general)—Romania. I. Title.
HX372.B3 76-521730

Bâldescu, Emil.
Simion Mehedinţi; gînditor social-politic şi pedagog. Bucureşti, Editura Ştiinţifică, 1969.
132 p. 20 cm.
Includes bibliographical references.
1. Mehedinţi, Simion, 1868 or 9-1962. I. Title.
LA2375.R62M432 74-221464

Bâldescu, Emil.
Spiru Haret în ştiinţă, filozofie, politică, pedagogie, învăţămînt. Bucureşti, Editura didactică şi pedagogică, 1972.
347 p. with facsims., port. on leaf. 20 cm. lei 15.00 R 72-4268
Bibliography: p. 339-[344]
1. Haret, Spiru C. I. Title.
LB775.H362B34 73-313273

Baldessari, John, 1931-
Four events and reactions / John Baldessari. — [Florence : Centro Di, c1975]
[52] p. : chiefly ill. ; 13 x 18 cm. — (Cat[aloghi] ; 62) It***
Cover title.
Published on the occasion of the exhibition held at the Stedelijk Museum, Amsterdam, Nov. 21st, 1975-Jan. 4th, 1976.
1. Photography, Artistic—Exhibitions. I. Amsterdam. Stedelijk Museum. II. Title.
TR647.B33 1975 709'.2'4 77-364251
77 MARC

Baldessari, John, 1931-
Ingres and other parables. [London, Studio International Publications] 1971 [i. e. 1972]
22 p. illus. 31 cm. GB***
ISBN 0-902063-10-3
English, French, German and Italian.
1. Baldessari, John, 1931- I. Title.
N6512.B26 709'.2'4 74-192675
MARC

Baldessari, John, 1931-
see Contemporary Arts Museum. John Baldessari, Frances Barth, Richard Jackson, Barbara Munger, Gary Stephen... [Houston, Tex., c1972]

Baldessari, John, 1931-
see "Konzept"—Kunst. Art & language. Basel, Kunstmuseum [1972]

Baldessari, Roberto Iras
see Iras-Baldessari, Roberto.

Baldessarini, Ross J 1937-
Chemotherapy in psychiatry / Ross J. Baldessarini. — Cambridge, Mass. : Harvard University Press, 1977.
xiii, 201 p. ; 22 cm.
Includes index.
Bibliography: p. [163]-196.
ISBN 0-674-11380-2
1. Psychopharmacology. I. Title.
[DNLM: 1. Mental disorders—Drug therapy. 2. Psychopharmacology. QV77 B176c]
RC483.B26 616.8'918 76-30322
76 MARC

Baldet, Marcel.
Les armes à feu. Paris, Gründ [1972]
190 p. illus. (part col.) 30 cm. (Collection de l'amateur) F***
Bibliography: p. 189-190.
1. Firearms—Collectors and collecting. I. Title.
TS532.4.B33 73-310595

Baldev Bhatia
see
Bhatia, Baldev.

Baldev Charla
see
Caralā, Baladeva, 1940-

Baldev Dhillon
see
Dhilom, Baladewa, 1934-

Baldev Kumar
see
Kumar, Baldev, 1913-

Baldev Raj Sharma
see
Sharma, Baldev Raj, 1939-

Baldev Singh Langeh
see
Langeh, Baldev Singh, 1934-

Baldev Vanshi, 1938-
(Upanagara meiṇ vāpasī)
उपनगर में वापसी / बलदेव वंशी. — 1. संस्करण. — दिल्ली : साहित्य भारती ; नई दिल्ली : एकमात्र वितरक हिन्दी बुक सेन्टर, 1974.
96 p. ; 23 cm.
In Hindi.
Poems.
Rs12.00

I. Title.
PK2098.13.A377U6 75-900660

Baldewyns, Albert, 1919-
Les batteries de Walcheren / Albert Baldewyns [&] André Herman-Lemoine. — Bruxelles ; Paris : Rossel, dép. 1974.
208 p., [12] leaves of plates : ill., maps. ; 24 cm. — (Collection Des temps et des hommes ; 3) Be74-2336
Bibliography: p. 203-204.
250F
1. World War, 1939-1945—Campaigns—Scheldt. 2. Scheldt—History. I. Herman-Lemoine, André, 1938- joint author. II. Title.
D763.N42S33 940.54'21 75-506805
75 MARC

Baldi, Agnello.
Aristide Gabelli: filosofia, pedagogia, metodo, colloqui, questionari, parallelismi, riassunti delle opere [di] Agnello Baldi [e] Corrado Ciranna. Roma, Ciranna [1970]
117 p. (I Cirannini)
1. Gabelli, Aristide, 1830-1891. I. Gabelli, Aristide, 1830-1891. II. Ciranna, Corrado, joint author. III. Title. IV. Series.
CU-SB NUC74-127243

Baldi, Agnello.
Guittone d'Arezzo fra impegno e poesia / Agnello Baldi. — [Salerno] : Società editrice salernitana, [1975]
142 p. ; 21 cm. — (Collana di saggistica Letteratura e società ; 2) It 76-Jan
Bibliography: p. 137-139.
Includes index.
L3500
1. Guittone d'Arezzo, d. 1294—Criticism and interpretation. I. Title.
PQ4472.G7B33 75-410233

Baldi, Angela.
Stato e scuola materna in Italia : profilo storico-legislativo / Angela Baldi. — Brescia : La scuola, c1974.
256 p. ; 21 cm. It 75-June
"Documenti": p. [151]-245.
1. Nursery schools—Law and legislation—Italy. I. Title.
75-590535

Baldi, Bernardino, 1553-1617.
Cronica de matematici overo Epitome dell'-istoria delle vite loro. Opera di Monsignor Bernardino Baldi da Urbino, abate di Guastalla. Urbino, A.A. Monticelli, 1707.
156 p.
Microprint. New York, Readex Microprint, 1974. 2 cards. (Landmarks of science)
1. Mathematicians. I. Title.
InU NUC76-18032

Baldi, Bernardino, 1553-1617.
In mechanica Aristotolis problemata exercitationes: adiecta svccincta narratione de autoris vita & scriptis. Mogvntiae: I. Albini, 1621.
[20], 194 p. diagrs.
Microprint. New York, Readex Microprint, 1969. 3 chards. (Landmarks of science)
1. Aristoteles—Mechanica. I. Title.
InU NUC76-70900

Baldi, Bernardino, 1553-1617.
Memorie concernenti la città di Urbino... Roma, G.M. Salvioni, 1724.
1 reel. 35 mm. (Manuscripta. Microfilms of rare and out-of-print books. List 82: History-sources, no. 7)
Microfilm (positive) St. Louis, St. Louis University, 1969.
Collation of the original: 4 p. l., 147, [1] p. front., 146 p. l. 42 cm.
1. Urbino. I. Title. II. Series.
PSt NUC74-125645

Baldi, Bruno.
Dizionario di storia: dalle origini ai nostri giorni. [Per] Bruno Baldi [e] Luigi Troisi. Roma, Edizioni San Giorgio [1974?]
876 p. 25 cm.
ICN NUC75-27459

Baldi, Bruno
see Letture geografiche : (i paesi extra-europei) Milano : L. Trevisini, [1961]

Baldi, Carlo.
Una Mamma di Galilea. Vicenza, Luigi Favero [1964]
97, [5] p. col. plates. 25 cm.
ODaU-M NUC73-60948

Baldi, Gianni.
I potenti del sistema, o il sistema dei potenti / Gianni Baldi ; introduzione di Giorgio Galli. — 1. ed. — Milano : A. Mondadori, 1976.
226 p. ; 19 cm. — (L'Immagine del presente ; 31) It77-Jan
Includes index.
L2500
1. Industry—Social aspects—Italy. 2. Italy—Social conditions. 3. Businessmen—Italy—Biography. I. Title.
HC305.B27 77-452675
*77 MARC

Baldi, Gianni
see Il Libro della caccia. [1. ed. Milano] Mondadori [1967]

Baldi, Giorgio.
Confronto fra comportamento del polline e dell'endosperma nella mutagenesi del locus wx del riso. [Milano] Ente Nazionale Risi [1966]
11 p. illus.
At head of title: Ente Nazionale Risi. Istituto di Allevamento Vegetale, Bologna.
"Contributo all' 'Anno internazionale del riso' indetto dalla F.A.O. 1966."
Summary in English.
Includes bibliographical references.
CU-A NUC74-24757

Baldi, Giorgio.
Introduzione al miglioramento genetico qualitativo. A cura di G. Baldi, M. Buiatti, F. Salamini. Bologna, Edagricole, 1972.
61 p. illus. 26 cm. (Trattato di genetica agraria speciale. Quaderno, 10) L2000 It 73-Jan
Bibliography: p. 49-60.
1. Plant-breeding. 2. Plant genetics. I. Buiatti, M. II. Salamini, Francesco. III. Title. IV. Series.
SB123.T68 no. 10 73-322893

Baldi, Guido, ed.
see Catone, Angelo, d. 1495. Il Liber de epidimiis. Roma, 1968.

Baldi, Guido, 1942-
Carlo Emilio Gadda. Milano, U. Mursia, 1972.
183 p. port. 20 cm. (Civiltà letteraria del Novecento. Profili, n. 24) It 72-June
Bibliography: p. 177-179.
L2500
1. Gadda, Carlo Emilio, 1893-1973.
PQ4817.A33Z62 72-341585

Baldi, Guido, 1942-
Giuseppe Rovani e il problema del romanzo nell'Ottocento. Firenze, L. S. Olschki, 1967.
236 p. 21 cm. (Saggi di "Lettere italiane," 11) It 67-7921
L2800
1. Rovani, Giuseppe, 1818-1874. 2. Italian prose literature—19th century—History and criticism. I. Title.
PQ4731.R7Z6 853'.7 76-350047
rev

Baldi, Guido, 1942-
see Manzoni ... Torino: Paravia, c1975.

Baldi, Guido Maria
see L'Anziano nella società. Roma, Tip. Loffari [1967]

Baldi, Giuseppe, Dott.
Sintesi storica dei vaccini antitubercolari. Roma, Arti grafiche E. Cossidente, 1967.
12 p. 24 cm. It 70-June
At head of title: Istituto di storia della medicina dell'Università di Roma.
Bibliography: p. 11-12.
1. Tuberculosis—Preventive innoculation—History. I. Title.
RC311.3.S4B34 73-334216

Baldi, Henry Victor, 1942-
The relationship between administrative succession and organizational instability in four selected schools of education, by H. Victor Baldi. [n.p.] 1973.
222 l. 29 cm.
Thesis (Ph. D.)—University of Wisconsin.
Vita.
Includes bibliography.
1. Education, Higher—Management. I. Title.
WU NUC74-125955

Baldi, Marino.
Die Freistellung vom EWG-Kartellverbot. Funktion und Inhalt von Art. 85 Abs. 3 EWGV. Bern, Stämpfli, 1972.
470 p. 23 cm. (Schweizerische Beiträge zum Europarecht, Bd. 12) 66.00F Sw 72-A-6793
Originally presented as the author's thesis, Hochschule für Wirtschafts- und Sozialwissenschaften, St. Gall.
Bibliography: p. 456-470.
1. Trusts, Industrial—European Economic Community countries—Law. I. Title. II. Series.
73-302682
ISBN 3-7272-0076-6

Baldi, Paolo.
see Roggero, G. A. Le relazioni pubbliche. 1. ed. Milano, F. Angeli, c1968.

Baldi, Peter.
Über die Gewährleistungspflicht des Verkäufers von Aktien, insbesondere beim Verkauf aller Aktien einer Gesellschaft...von Peter Baldi... Zürich, Schulthess, 1975.
1 p.l., 151 p., 1 l. 23 cm.
Diss.–Zürich.
Vita.
"Literatur": p. 7-11.
1. Stock and stockholders–Switzerland. I. Title.
MH-L NUC77-82712

Baldi, Peter.
Über die Gewährleistungspflicht des Verkäufers von Aktien, insbesondere beim Verkauf aller Aktien einer Gesellschaft / Peter Baldi. — Zürich : Schulthess Polygraphischer Verlag, 1975.
ii, 151 p. ; 23 cm. — (Zürcher Beiträge zur Rechtswissenschaft ; 468)
Sw75-A-6079
Originally presented as the author's thesis, Zürich.
Bibliography: p. 7-11.
ISBN 3-7255-1652-9 : 32.00F
1. Stocks—Switzerland. 2. Stock purchase agreements (Close corporations)—Switzerland. 3. Warranty—Switzerland. I. Title: Über die Gewährleistungspflicht des Verkäufers ... II. Series.
75-517246
*75 MARC

Baldi, Philip, 1946-
Deponent and middle in Latin. [n.p.] 1973.
vii, 174 l. 29 cm.
Thesis (Ph. D.)—University of Rochester.
Vita.
Bibliography: leaves 126-133.
1. Latin language—Verb. I. Title.
NRU NUC74-125954

Baldi, Roberto.
Il contratto di agenzia / Roberto Baldi. — 2. ed. completamente rielaborata, ampliata e aggiornata. — Milano : A. Giuffrè, 1977.
348 p. ; 25 cm. It77-Apr
Bibliography: p. [319]-327.
L9000
1. Agency (Law)—Italy. 2. Conflict of laws—Agency—Italy. 3. Commercial agents—Italy. 4. Conflict of laws—Commercial agents—Italy. I. Title.
77-469107
*77 MARC

Baldi, Sergio.
Etnologia sociale delle popolazioni dell'Africa occidentale / S. Baldi, G. Del Gaudio. — [Napoli] : Edizioni del delfino, [1975]
411 p. ; 22 cm. It 76-July
Bibliography: p. 395-402.
L7000
1. Ethnology—Africa, West. 2. Slavery in Africa, West. I. Del Gaudio, Giovanni, joint author. II. Title.
GN652.5.B34 76-523018

Baldi, Sergio.
Sir Thomas Wyatt. Translated by F. T. Prince. [Harlow, Eng.] Published for the British Council by Longman Group [c1971]
42 p. port. 22 cm. (Writers & their work, no. 139)
Minor amendments to text and additions to bibliography of the 1961 ed.
Bibliography: p. [39]-42.
1. Wyatt, Sir Thomas, 1503?-1542. I. Title.
IaU NUC75-36304

Báldi, Tamás.
Mollusc fauna of the Hungarian upper Oligocene (Egerian) studies in stratigraphy, palaeoecology, palaeogeography, and systematics. Budapest, Akadémiai Kiadó, 1973.
511 p. illus. 25 cm.
Bibliography: p. 369-393.
1. Mollusks, Fossil. 2. Paleontology—Oligocene. 3. Paleontology—Hungary. I. Title.
QE801.B25 564'.09439 74-192085
MARC

Báldi, Tamás
see Colloquium on Neogene Stratigraphy, Budapest, 1969. Geological excursions in the Neogene areas of Hungary... [Budapest, Hungarian Geological Society, 1969]

Baldi, Vincenzo.
Parole di salute per grandi e piccini. Pagine di pedagogia serena. Foggia, Tipo-lito Adriatica, [1972?].
105 p. 21 cm. L750 It 73-Feb
Bibliography: p. [108].
1. Education—Addresses, essays, lectures. I. Title.
LB41.B25617 73-346554

Baldicer; a simulation game... [n.p.] 1970
see under Wilcoxon, Georgeann.

Baldick, Robert.
Les diners Magny. Traduit de l'anglais par l'auteur. [Paris] Denoël [1972]
264 p. 8 plates. illus., facsim., ports. 21 cm.
Original title: Dinner at Magny's.
Bibliography: p. [243]-246.
1. Authors, French—Correspondence, reminiscences, etc. I. Title.
NBuU NUC74-125962

Baldick, Robert, ed.
see Chateaubriand, Francois Auguste Rene, vicomte de, 1768-1848. Memoirs of Chateaubriand. London, Hamish Hamilton [1961]

Baldick, Robert
see Éon de Beaumont, Charles Geneviève Louis Auguste André Timothée d', 1728-1810. The memoirs of Chevalier d'Eon. [London] Anthony Blond [1970]

Baldieri, Vincenzo.
Quando c'é chi ascolta ... Gli ex voto di Montenero. Montenero, 1969.
161 p. illus. 24 cm. (Collana Marilux, n. 7) It Suppl-7
1. Montenero, Madonna di. 2. Santuario di Montenero. I. Title.
BT660.M655B35 73-318325

Baldigo, Jeanne McGee, 1944-
An exploration of elementary school children's conceptions of family roles. [Bloomington, Ind.] 1975.
209 p. illus.
Thesis (Ph.D.)–Indiana University.
Vita.
InU NUC77-82711

Baldin, A
(Tri pokolīenīīa)
Три поколѣнія; поэма. Харьковъ, Тип. Губ. правленія, 1883-
v. 23 cm.
I. Title.
PG3453.B19T7 53-50707

Baldin, Asturio
see Manuale della manutenzione degli impianti industriali. Milano : F. Angeli, c1975.

Baldin, Georgiĭ Alekseevich.
(Komanda SPP)
Команда СПП. Рассказы о славных делах детей железнодорожников. [Для детей]. Москва, "Транспорт," 1971.
184 p. with illus. 20 cm. 0.32rub USSR 71-VKP
At head of title: Г. Балдин, П. Сосков.
Previous editions published under title: Юные друзья железнодорожников.
I. Soskov, Pavel Petrovich, joint author. II. Title.
PZ63.B323 1971 74-341715

Baldin, Georgiĭ Alekseevich
see Na stal'nykh magistraliakh. 1975.

Baldin, Giuliana.
Còredo in Val di Non. San Romedio-Castel Braghèr. Origini, storia, turismo. A cura di Memmo Caporilli. Testo di Giuliana Baldin. Còredo, Ufficio turistico, 1972.
176 p. illus. 24 cm. It***
Second enl. ed.
Bibliography: p. [178]-[179]
1. Còredo, Italy. I. Title.
DG975.C737B3 1972 914.5'385 74-345062

Baldin, Leonid Vasil'evich.
[Obshchestvennaia sobstvennost' na sredstva proizvodstva]
Общественная собственность на средства производства. Характер труда. Основной экономический закон социализма. Москва, "Высш. школа," 1972.
70 p. 20 cm. (В помощь изучающим политическую экономию в средних специальных учебных заведениях) 0.08rub USSR 72-VKP
At head of title: Л. В. Балдин.
Includes bibliographies.
1. Marxian economics—Outlines, syllabi, etc. I. Title.
HB97.5.B235 73-303177

Baldin, Leonid Vasil'evich, joint author
see Mineev, Vladimir Nikolaevich. (Tvorcheskoe uchastie trudiashchikhsia v upravlenii) 1974.

Baldin, Leonid Vasil'evich, joint author
see Zhalina, Elizaveta Aleksandrovna. Leninskie printsipy upravleniia narodnym khoziaistvom. 1973.

Baldin, Sergeĭ Alekseevich
see Prikladnaia spektrometriia s poluprovodnikovymi detektorami. 1974.

Baldin, Viktor Ivanovich.
(Arkhitekturnyĭ ansambl' Troitse-Sergievoĭ lavry)
Архитектурный ансамбль Троице-Сергиевой лавры / В. Балдин. — Москва : Искусство, 1976.
143 p. : chiefly ill. (some col.) ; 26 cm. USSR 76
On leaf preceding t. p.: The architectural ensemble of the Trinity-St. Sergius Lavra.
Summary in English; legends and list of illustrations also in English.
Bibliography: p. 142.
4.00rub
1. Troitskaia Sergieva lavra. I. Title. II. Title: The architectural ensemble of the Trinity-St. Sergius Lavra.
NA5697.T7B34 77-505811

Baldina, Ol'ga Dmitrievna.
(Russkie narodnye kartinki)
Русские народные картинки. Москва, "Мол. гвардия," 1972.
207 p. with illus. 22 cm. 0.96rub USSR 73-VKP
At head of title: Ольга Балдина.
1. Engravings, Russian. 2. Folk art—Russia. I. Title.
NE675.B34 73-325703

Baldine, Ronald Peter.
Drug abuse and preventive law enforcement in selective counties of Ohio. [n.p., n.d.]
1 v.
OClW NUC75-63817

Baldinelli, Armando, 1908-
Armando Baldinelli / Albert Werth. — London : Gallery Twenty-One Book Publishers, 1974.
126 p. : ill. (some col.) ; 31 cm. GB***
Bibliography: p. 116-118.
1. Baldinelli, Armando, 1908- I. Werth, Albert Johannes, 1927-
N6923.B26W47 709'.2'4 75-312846
75 MARC

Baldinelli, Armando, 1908-
Baldinelli [a cura di] Umbro Apollonio. Roma, Edizioni d'Arte moderna [c1964]
75 p. (chiefly illus. part col.) 29 cm.
Text and captions in Italian and English.
Leaf tipped in: All enquiries in connection with this work should be addressed ... Hugh Keartland (Publishers) ... Johannesburg.
First published 1965.
Bibliography: p. 72-73.
1. Baldinelli, Armando, 1908- I. Apollonio, Umbro, 1911-
N6923.B26A85 74-231783

Balding, Gary O
Data for wells in the Modesto-Merced area, San Joaquin Valley, California, by Gary O. Balding and R.W. Page. Menlo Park, U.S. Dept. of the Interior, Geological Survey, Water Resources Division, 1971.
iv, 122 p. illus., maps. 27 cm.
"Open-file report."
Prepared in cooperation with the California Dept. of Water Resources.
1. Water, Underground—California. 2. Water-supply—California—San Joaquin Valley. I. Page, R. W., joint author. II. United States. Geological Survey. Water Resources Division. III. California. Dept. of Water Resources. IV. Title.
CLSU NUC73-44504

Balding, Gary O., joint author
see Hotchkiss, William R Geology, hydrology, and water quality of the Tracy-Dos Palos area... Menlo Park, Calif., 1971.

Balding, Peter, joint author.
see Gold, Edwin Richard. Receptor-specific proteins ... Amsterdam, Excerpta Medica, 1975.

Balding & Mansell, ltd.
Synopsis of type faces. [London, 1962?]
1 v. (unpaged) specimens. 21 x 27 cm.
Cover title.
Includes "New types/1962 list" (51 x 34 cm. fold. to 17 x 26 cm.)
1. Printing—Specimens. 2. Type and type-founding—Display type. I. Title.
NNC NUC74-24756

Baldinger, Annemarie Seiler-
see Seiler-Baldinger, Annemarie.

Baldinger, Françoise.
Orée. [Paris] Chambelland [1973]
79 p. 19 cm. F***
Poems.
I. Title.
PQ2662.A373O7 841'.9'14 75-503415
75 MARC

Baldinger, Kurt, 1919–
Dictionnaire étymologique de l'ancien français / Kurt Baldinger ; avec la collaboration de Jean-Denis Gendron et Georges Straka. — Québec : Presses de l'Université Laval ; Tübingen : Niemeyer ; Paris : Klincksieck, 19
v. ; 28 cm. C 74-4619-5 (fasc. G1-3)
On cover: DEAF.
Fascicle G1 called "seconde édition" replacing a provisional ed. issued in 1971.
Issued in parts.
ISBN 0-7746-6606-4 (fasc. G1) : $14.00 (fasc. G1-3)
——— Index. — Québec : Presses de l'Université Laval ; Tübingen : Niemeyer ; Paris : Klincksieck, 19
v. ; 28 cm. C 74-4619-5 (fasc. G1-3)
Issued in parts.
ISBN 0-7746-6718-4 (fasc. G1-G3)
PC2883.B3 1974 Suppl. 1
——— Complément bibliographique / rédigé par Frankwalt Möhren. — Québec : Presses de l'Université Laval ; Tübingen : Niemeyer ; Paris : Klincksieck, 1974–
v. ; 28 cm. C 74-4619-5 (v. 1)
Issued in parts.
"[Cette] première livraison ... sera remplacée par des versions révisées et augmentées qui paraîtront à des intervalles de plus en plus longs au fur et à mesure qu'elles seront plus complètes ... chacune remplacera entièrement la précédente."
PC2883.B3 1974 Suppl. 2
1. French language—To 1500—Etymology—Dictionaries. I. Gendron, Jean Denis, joint author. II. Straka, Georges, joint author. III. Möhren, Frankwalt, ed. IV. Title. V. Title: DEAF.
PC2883.B3 1974 447'.01 75-513620
(MARC)

Baldinger, Kurt, 1919–
Dictionnaire étymologique de l'ancien français : DEAF : [fascicule G 1] / Kurt Baldinger, avec la collaboration de Jean Denis Gendron et Georges Straka. — Québec : Les Presses de l'Université Laval, [1971]
xxxi p., 152 columns : ill. ; 25 cm. C***
"Fascicule d'expérimentation."
No more published in this ed.
1. French language—To 1500—Etymology—Dictionaries. I. Gendron, Jean Denis, joint author. II. Straka, Georges, joint author. III. Title. IV. Title: DEAF.
PC2883.B3 72-334121

Baldinger, Kurt, 1919-
Dictionnaire onomasiologique de l'ancien gascon : DAG / Kurt Baldinger ; réd. avec le concours de Inge Popelar ; [Heidelberger Akad. d. Wiss., Komm. für d. Altokzitan. u. Altgaskogn. Wörterbuch]. — Tübingen : Niemeyer, 1975-
v. ; 24 cm. GFR75-A (v. 1)
Index inserted in v. 1.
ISBN 3-484-50075-1 (v. 1) : DM50.00 (v. 1)
1. Gascon dialect—Glossaries, vocabularies, etc. I. Title. II. Title: DAG.
PC3426.B3 76-455575
76 MARC

Baldinger, Kurt, 1919-
Dictionnaire onomasiologique de l'ancien occitan = DAO / Kurt Baldinger ; rédigé avec le concours de Inge Popelar. -- Tübingen : M. Niemeyer, c1975.
1 v. ; 24 cm.
On verso of t.p.: Heidelberger Akademie der Wissenschaften, Kommission für das Altokzitanische und Altgaskonische Wörterbuch.
"Index alphabétique des articles (concepts)" and "Bibliographie provisoire" ([7] p.) laid in in fasc. 1.
ISBN 3-484-50076-x.
1. Provençal language. Dictionaries. French. I. Popelar, Inge. II. Heidelberger Akademie der Wissenschaften. Kommission für das Altokzitanische und Altgaskonische Wörterbuch. III. Title.
MnU NUC77-94347

Baldinger, Kurt, 1919–
La formación de los dominios lingüísticos de la Península Ibérica. Versión ... de Emilio Lledó y Montserrat Macau. 2. ed. corr. y muy aum. Madrid, Gredos [1972]
496 p. 20 cm. (Biblioteca románica hispánica. 1. Tratados y monografías, 10) Sp 72-Apr
Translation of Die Herausbildung der Sprachräume auf der Pyrenäenhalbinsel.
Bibliography: p. [257]-385.
1. Spain—Languages. 2. Portugal—Languages. I. Title.
P381.S6B318 1972 73-350571

Baldinger, Kurt, 1919–
Introduction aux dictionnaires les plus importants pour l'histoire du français; recueil d'études publié sous la direction de Kurt Baldinger. [Paris] Klincksieck, 1974.
184 p. 22 cm. (Bibliothèque française et romane. Sér. D: Initiation, textes et documents, 8) 50.00F F***
1. French language—Etymology—Addresses, essays, lectures. 2. French language—Lexicography—Addresses, essays, lectures. I. Title. II. Series.
PC2571.B3 442 74-193119
ISBN 2-252-01655-8 MARC

Baldinger, Kurt, 1919–
Zum Einfluss der Sprache auf die Vorstellungen des Menschen: (Volksetymologie u. semant. Parallelverschiebung) / Kurt Baldinger. — Heidelberg: Winter, 1973.
56 p.: ill.; 25 cm. — (Sitzungsberichte der Heidelberger Akademie der Wissenschaften, Philosophisch-Historische Klasse; Jahrg. 1973, Abh. 2) DM18.00 GFR 74-A
"Vorgetragen am 11. November 1972."
Includes bibliographical references.
1. Language—Psychology. 2. Semantics. I. Title. II. Series: Heidelberger Akademie der Wissenschaften. Philosophisch-Historische Klasse. Sitzungsberichte, Jahrg. 1973, Abh. 2.
P106.B34 74-318622
ISBN 3-533-02289-7

Baldinger, Kurt, 1919-
Zur hochschul-politischen Lage. Heidelberg, Ruprecht-Karl-Universität, 1968.
13 p. 24 cm. (Heidelberg. Universität. Dokumentation nr. 1)
1. Education—Germany. I. Title. II. Series.
TxU NUC74-125654

Baldinger, Kurt, 1919- ed.
see Walther von Wartburg (1888-1971). Tübingen, M. Niemeyer [c1971]

Baldinger, Milton Irving.
Cases and materials on Federal income taxation, by Milton I. Baldinger. Washington, National Tax Press, 1947–
1 v. (loose-leaf) 26 cm.
On spine: Federal taxation. Income tax, vol. 1.
1. Income tax—United States—Cases. I. Title. II. Title: Federal taxation.
KF6368.B34 343'.73'052 74-157309
MARC

Baldinger, Wallace Spencer, 1905-
The development of form in American painting of the twentieth century, by Wallace Spencer Baldinger. Chicago, 1938.
viii, 239 l. illus. 32 cm.
Thesis—University of Chicago.
Bibliography: leaves 206-216.
1. Painting, American. 2. Painting, Modern—20th century—United States. 3. Composition (Art) I. Title.
ND212.B29 759.13 75-318496
75 MARC

Baldinger, Wallace Spencer, 1905-
see Oregon. University. Museum of Art. A group of four Japanese Buddhist sculptures. Eugene [1963?]

Baldinger, Wallace Spencer, 1905-
see Oregon. University. Museum of Art. Japanese netsuke and inro. [Eugene, 1961 ?]

Baldinger, Wallace Spencer, 1905- ed.
see Oregon. University. Musuem of Art. Rolf Klep--a retrospective. Eugene, Or., 1969.

Baldini, Angel A
New short method for the precise determination of time and azimuth. New short method for latitude determination. Washington, D.C., Georgetown College Observatory, 1958.
15, 7 p. (Georgetown Observatory monograph, no. 7)
1. Azimuth. 2. Geodesy.
ICU NUC74-33089

Baldini, Angel A
Satellite goedesy based on stellar orientation of lines between unknown stations. Fort Belvoir, Va., 1969.
58 p. illus. 26 cm. (United States. Army Engineer Topographic Laboratories. Research note no. 32)
1. Artificial satellites in geodesy. 2. Satellite triangulation. I. Title. II. Series.
DME NUC75-31699

Baldini, Antonio, 1889-1962.
La strada delle meraviglie / Antonio Baldini ; illustrazioni di Maria De Matteis. — Torino : Einaudi, [1974]
vi, 77 p. : ill. ; 24 cm. — (Libri per ragazzi ; 41) It 75-Jan
Children's stories.
L2000
1. Fairy tales. I. De Matteis, Maria, ill. II. Title.
PZ44.B25 1974 75-555624

Baldini, Antonio, 1889-1962
see Schnitzler, Arthur, 1862-1931. La signorina Elsa. Milano, Dall'Oglio, 1967.

Baldini, Attilio, ed.
see Addison, Joseph, 1672-1719. The spectator. Napoli, Morano, 1973.

Baldini, Baccio, d. 1585.
La mascherata della genealogia degl'iddei, Florence, 1565 / Baccio Baldini. Discorso sopra li dei de' gentili, Rome, 1602 / Jacopo Zucchi. — New York : Garland Pub., 1976.
131, 170 p., [7] leaves of plates : ill. ; 24 cm. — (The Renaissance and the gods)
The first work is a reprint of the ed. published by Appresso i Giunti, under titel: Discorso sopra la mascherata della geneologia degl'iddei de' gentili; the second work is a reprint of the ed. published by D. Gigliotti.
Includes index.
ISBN 0-8240-2059-6 : $40.00
1. Francesco Maria de' Medici, grand duke of Tuscany, 1541-1587. 2. Giovanna, of Austria, consort of Francesco Maria de' Medici, grand duke of Tuscany, d. 1578? 3. Florence—History—1421-1737. 4. Rome (City). Palazzo Ruspoli. 5. Painting, Renaissance. 6. Mythology, Classical. I. Zucchi, Jacopo, ca. 1541-ca. 1589. Discorso sopra li dei de' gentili. 1976. II. Title. III. Series.
DG738.19.B27 1976 945'.5'060924 75-27852
76 MARC

Baldini, Ennio.
Considerazioni sul momento evolutivo dell'organizzazione aziendale. Milano, Celuc, [1973].
120 p. 21 cm. (Ricerche, 36) It 73-Dec
At head of title: Ennio Baldini, Lucia Giudetti.
Bibliography: p. [117]-120.
L1300
1. Management. 2. Organization. 3. Psychology, Industrial. I. Giudetti, Lucia, joint author. II. Title.
HD37.I 8B29 75-583841

Baldini, Enrico
see Indagine sulle cultivar... Bologna, 1973.

Baldini, Gabriele, 1919-1969.
Memorietta sul colore del vento, e altri scritti del capitano B. N. Cizico. A cura di Gabriele Baldini. [Milano], A. Mondadori, 1973.
xix, 148 p. 20 cm. (Scrittori italiani e stranieri) L2000
It 73-Nov
I. Title.
PQ4807.A47M4 1973 73-357466

Baldini, Gabriele, 1919-1969
see Arte e letteratura. Scritti in ricordo di Gabriele Baldini. Roma, Edizioni di storia e letteratura, 1972.

Baldini, Mario G., ed.
see Platelets: production, function, transfusion, and storage. New York, Grune & Stratton [1974]

Baldini, Massimo, 1947-
Epistemologia contemporanea e clinica medica / Massimo Baldini. — Firenze : Città di vita, 1975.
110 p. ; 17 cm. It76-May
Includes bibliographical references.
L3000
1. Medicine—Philosophy. 2. Knowledge, Theory of. I. Title.
[DNLM: 1. Philosophy, Medical. W61 B177e 1975]
[R723.B27] 76-676236
Shared Cataloging with •77 MARC
DNLM

Baldini, Massimo, 1947-
Epistemologia e storia della scienza / Massimo Baldini. — Firenze : Città di vita, 1974.
91 p. ; 24 cm. — (Università degli studi di Siena, Facoltà di magistero. Sede di Arezzo, Quaderni dell'Istituto di scienze filosofiche ; 3) It 74-Dec
Includes bibliographical references and index.
L2100
1. Science—Philosophy. 2. Knowledge, Theory of. I. Title. II. Series: Siena. Università. Facoltà di magistero. Sede di Arezzo. Istituto di scienze filosofiche. Quaderni ; 3.
Q175.B174 75-555699

Baldini, Massimo, 1947-
I fondamenti epistemologici dell'educazione scientifica / Massimo Baldini. — Roma : A. Armando, 1976.
93 p. ; 21 cm. It77-Feb
Includes bibliographical references and index.
L1500
1. Science—Study and teaching. 2. Knowledge, Theory of. I. Title.
Q181.B193 77-468935
•77 MARC

Baldini, Massimo, 1947-
Il linguaggio delle utopie : utopia e ideologia, una rilettura epistemologica / Massimo Baldini. — Roma : Studium, [1974]
ix, 265 p. ; 21 cm. — (La Cultura ; 3) It 75-Sept
Bibliography: p. [263]-265.
L5000
1. Utopias. 2. Ideology. I. Title.
HX806.B25 76-506592

Baldini, Massimo, 1947-
Teoria e storia della scienza / Massimo Baldini. — Roma : A. Armando, 1975.
214 p. ; 22 cm. — (Filosofia e problemi d'oggi ; 46) It 75-Oct
Bibliography: p. 205-214.
L3000
1. Science—History. 2. Science. I. Title.
Q125.B295 75-403404

Baldini, Massimo, 1947-
see Il Pensiero utopico. Roma : Città nuova [1974]

Baldini, Massimo, 1947-
see La Semantica generale. Roma, Città nuova, 1976.

Baldini, Raffaello.
Gifts from Italy; design and colour, by Raffaello Baldini and Luigi Massoni. Milan, Alfieri and Lacroix [1971]
176 p. illus.
1. Handicraft. 2. Design. 3. Art, Italian. I. Title.
OClSA NUC75-36317

Baldini, Rolando, illus.
see Vicini Marri, Noemi. I giorni della Resistenza. Roma, Editori riuniti, 1973.

Baldini, Rudolph A 1930-
Student science activities for grades 6-9 [by] Rudolph A. Baldini. Photography by J. Rutherford Ferrill. West Nyack, N. Y., Parker Pub. Co. [c1973]
208 p. illus. 24 cm.
Bibliography: p. 200-202.
1. Science — Study and teaching (Elementary) 2. Science — Experiments. 3. Project method in teaching. I. Title.
[LB1585.B24] 372.3'5'044 72-6755
ISBN 0-13-855817-5 MARC

Baldini, Umberto.
Mostra di opere d'arte restaurate; nona esposizione, Firenze, ottobre-novembre, 1958. Catalogo a cura di Umberto Baldini. [Firenze, Tip. Giuntina, 1958]
29 p. 16 plates. 17 cm.
At head of title: Soprintendenza alle gallerie per le provincie di Firenze, Arezzo e Pistoia. Gabinetto del restauri.
Title on cover: Dodici capolavori restaurati.
1. Paintings, Italian—Exhibitions. 2. Paintings—Italy—Conservation and restoration. I. Title. Soprintendenza alle gallerie per le provincie di Firenze, Arezzo e Pistoia. Gabinetto del restauri. II. Title. III. Title: Dodici capolavori restaurati.
ND1651.I 8F582 73-208117

Baldini, Umberto.
II [i. e. Seconda] mostra di affreschi staccati, Firenze, Forte di Belvedere, 1958. [Catalogo a cura di Umberto Baldini e Luciano Berti. Firenze, Tip. Giuntina, 1958]
vi, 83 p. 40 plates. 22 cm.
Includes bibliographical references.
1. Mural painting and decoration, Italian—Exhibitions. 2. Mural painting and decoration—Italy—Conservation and restoration. I. Berti, Luciano, joint author. II. Title. III. Title: Mostra di affreschi staccati.
ND2755.B34 74-206745

Baldini, Umberto.
El taller de los Della Robbia. [Traducción de Andrés Soria. Granada] Albaicín/Sadea [1968]
[7] p. illus., col. plates. 36 cm. (Forma y color; los grandes ciclos del arte, 38)
Bibliography: p. [7]
1. Robbia, Luca della, 1400?-1487. 2. Robbia, Della, Family. I. Title. II. Series.
OrU NUC74-5510

Baldini, Umberto, ed.
see Buonarroti, Michel Angelo, 1475-1564. L'opera completa di Michelangelo scultore. Milano, Rizzoli, 1973.

Baldini, Umberto
see Cavallini, Sauro. Sculture e disegni di Cavallini. [Viareggio, Galleria d'arte moderna, 1972]

Baldini, Umberto
see Fantoni, Marcello. Fantoni... [Firenze, Mirteto, 1973]

Baldini, Umberto
see Fresques de Florence. [Bruxelles, Crédit communal de Belgique], 1969.

Baldini, Umberto
see Galleria d'arte La stanzina. Meriti e momenti della pittura toscana dell'Ottocento. Firenze, Galleria d'arte La stanzina, 1973.

Baldini, Umberto
see Guidi, Ugo. Ugo Guidi. Firenze, L'Indiano, [1972]

Baldini, Umberto
see Lippi, Fra Filippo, 1412?-1469. Filippo Lippi. [Milano] Fratelli Fabbri [c1964]

Baldini, Umberto, ed.
see Soprintendenza alle gallerie per la province di Firenze e Pistoia. Firenze restaura. Firenze, Sansoni, 1972.

Baldini, Umberto
see Toscana. [Milano] Electa [1975?]

Baldini, Umberto.
see Zagaglia, Beppe. Ritorno a Firenze. Modena, Artioli, 1976.

Baldini, Vittorio Alessandro.
Operations research problems in the motion picture industry, by Vittorio Alessandro Baldini. Cambridge, Operations Research Center, Massachusetts Institute of Technology, 1975.
v, 118 p. ill. 28 cm. (Technical report no., 110)
Work performed under Grant-in-aid, Coca-Cola, U.S.A., M.I.T. OSP 27857.
Bibliography: p. 117-118.
1. Operations research. 2. Moving picture industry. I. Title. II. Series: Massachusetts Institute of Technology. Operations Research Center Technical report, no. 110.
MCM NUC77-82697

Baldino Balaguer, João Carlos
see
Balaguer, João Carlos B 1949-

Baldinucci, Francesco Saverio, 18th cent.
Vite di artisti dei secoli XVII ⌐i.e. diciassettesimo⌐-XVIII / Francesco Saverio Baldinucci. — 1. ed. integrale del Codice Palatino 565 / trascrizione, note, bibliografia e indici a cura di Anna Matteoli. — Roma : De Luca, 1975.
514 p. ; 24 cm. — (Raccolta di fonti per la storia dell'arte ; 2. ser., 3) It77-Feb
Bibliography: p. 441-463.
Includes index.
1. Art, Italian. 2. Art, Modern—17th-18th centuries—Italy. 3. Artists—Italy—Biography. I. Matteoli, Anna. II. Title. III. Series.
N6911.A1R3 ser. 2, t. 3 77-464495
⌐N6916⌐ •77 MARC

Baldión, Félix Salcedo
see Salcedo Baldión, Félix.

Baldirāmā Martīnith, Firnāndū
see
Valderrama Martínez, Fernando.

Baldirio, Ismenia R de.
Dos análisis parciales de los resultados obtenidos en la aplicación del test de inteligencia de Kuhlmann-Anderson a una muestra de alumnos de educación primaria / Ismenia R. de Baldirio, Dríades Sanabria G., Jorge Nunes. — Caracas : Ministerio de Educación, Dirección de Planeamiento, Departamento de Investigaciones Educacionales, 1974.
81 p. : 21 graphs ; 22 cm. — (Serie 2, Análisis e interpretación de datos ; no. 5)
At head of title: Programa Nacional de Investigaciones Educacionales.
Summary in Spanish and English.
Bibliography: p. 63.
1. Education, Elementary—Venezuela—Caracas Metropolitan area. 2. Kuhlmann-Anderson test. I. Sanabria G., Dríades, joint author. II. Nunes, Jorge, 1941- joint author. III. Title: Dos análisis parciales ... IV. Series: Análisis e interpretación de datos ; no. 5.
LA607.B34 77-454698
77 MARC

Baldis, Elba Diana Pothé de
see Pothé de Baldis, Elba Diana.

Baldisseri, Miranda.
Bibliography on pollution in selected tropical biota. Rome, 1972.
v, 30 p. 28 cm.
1. Marine pollution—Bibliography. 2. Biotic communities—Tropics—Bibliography. I. Title.
DI NUC75-31658

Baldivia, José
see Alcázar, José Luis. Bolivia... [1. ed.] México, Ediciones Era [1973]

Baldivia de Bettachini, Marina Lely Lijerón
see Lijerón Baldivia de Bettachini, Marina Lely.

Baldivia Galdo, José María, 1884–
La política argentina en Bolivia : reminiscencias históricas ⌐por⌐ José María Baldivia G. La Paz, Impr. Eléctrica, 1933.
67 p. 22 cm.
"Conferencias dictadas en sesiones de 'Los Amigos de la Ciudad.'"
1. Argentine Republic—Foreign relations—Bolivia. 2. Bolivia—Foreign relations—Argentine Republic. 3. Chaco Boreal, Paraguay. I. Title.
F2833.5.B5B34 74-207203

Baldivieso, Valentin Abecia
see Abecia Baldivieso, Valentin.

Baldivieso G., Alberto
see Bolivia. Laws, statutes, etc. [Decreto ley no. 10267] Ley de organización judicial. Sucre: Tall. Gráf. Onda, 1973.

Baldivieso Molina, Nora.
Manejo de oficinas [por] Nora Baldivieso M. La Paz [Editora Novedades] 1966.
75 p. 19 cm.
1. Office management. I. Title.
TxU NUC75-31653

Baldizón de Castroconde, Norma.
A ti, maestro que naces. 2. ed. ⌐Guatemala⌐ Editorial "José de Piñeda Ibarra," 1966.
17 p. 20 cm.
1. Teachers—Poetry. I. Title.
TxU NUC74-127254

Baldner, Gaby.
Joba und das Wildschwein. Bilder von Gerhard Oberländer. ⌐Hamburg, H. Ellermann, 1960⌐
26 p. col. illus. 21 x 30 cm.
I. Oberländer, Gerhard, illus. II. Title.
MB NUC74-173567

Baldner, Leonhardt.
Vogel-, Fisch- und Thierbuch : ⌐recht natürl. Beschreibung u. Abmahlung d. Wasser Vögel, Fischen, vierfüsigen Thier, Insecten, u. Gewürm, so by Strassburg in d. Wassern gefunde werden, die ich selber geschossen u. d. Fisch gefangen, auch alles in meiner Handt gehabt / Leonhardt Baldner⌐. — Nachdr. — Stuttgart : Müller und Schindler, 1973–
v. : col. ill. ; 20 x 32 cm. GDB 74-A2
Facsimile reprint of the 1666 manuscript.
Vol. 1 describes birds only.

——— Handschrift Ms. fol. phys. et hist. nat. 3 der Murhardschen Bibliothek der Stadt Kassel und Landesbibliothek : Einführung / von Robert Lauterborn. — Stuttgart : Müller und Schindler, 1973.
63 columns ; 20 x 32 cm.
Reprint from the 1903 edition published by Lauterborn, Ludwigshafen a. Rh.
DM280.00 (v. 1 and Einführung)
QL41.B3 1666a Suppl.
1. Zoology — Pre-Linnaean works. 2. Zoology — Pictorial works I. Lauterborn, Robert. II. Murhardtsche Bibliothek der Stadt Kassel und Landesbibliothek. Mss. (Folio phys, et hist, nat. 3)
QL41.B3 1666a 591 75-526356

Baldo degli Ubaldi, 1327?–1400.
Ad tres priores libros decretalium commentaria. Collatione vetustissimorum exemplarium nunc recens summo labore suae integritati restituta et ab innumeris mendis vindicata; quibus accesserunt Francisci a Perona et Petri Crassi adnotamenta. Neudr. d. Ausg. Lyon 1585. Aalen, Scientia-Verl., 1970.
285, 32 l. 39 cm. DM220.00 GDB 71-148-160
At head of title: Baldo degli Ubaldi (Baldus Perusinus)
1. Canon law. I. Title.
73-366821
ISBN 3-511-00416-0

Baldo degli Ubaldi, 1327?-1400.
Baldi Vbaldi Pervsini ... In Decretalivm volvmen commentaria, Francisci de Parona, alias excvsis, Vincentiiqve Godemini nouissimis, nunc primum additis, adnotationibus illustrata. Venetiis, Apud Iuntas, 1595. [Torino, Bottega d'Erasmo, 1971]
318 l., [319]-418 p. 35 cm.
Text in double columns.
"Ristampa anastatica."
1. Canon law. I. Parona, Francesco de. II. Godeminus, Vincentius. III. Title: In Decretalium volumen commentaria.
MnU NUC73-44413

Baldo degli Ubaldi, 1327?-1400.
Consiliorvm, sivre responsorvm, volumen primum (-sextum). Hac novissima editione recognitum, pluribusq in locis accuratissime castigatum; cvm qvaestionibvs, svmmariis et indice locupletissimo. Venetiis ⌐apud Hieronymum Polum⌐ 1575-1576. ⌐Ristampata anastatica⌐ Torino, Bottega d'Erasmo, 1970⌐
6 v. in 3.
1. Canon law. 2. Roman law—Consilium.
CU-L NUC73-33738

Baldo degli Ubaldi, 1327?-1400.
see Durantis, Gulielmus, Bp. of Mende, 1237 (ca.)-1296. Speculum judiciale. Padua, Johannes Herbort, de Seligenstadt, 1479.

Baldo degli Ubaldi, 1327?-1400
see Durantis, Gulielmus, Bp. of Mende, 1237 (ca.)-1296. Speculum judiciale. Venice, Georgius Arrivabenus and Paganinus de Paganinis, 1488.

Baldo degli Ubaldi, 1327?-1400
see Durantis, Gulielmus, Bp. of Mende, 1237 (ca.)-1296. Specvli pars prima[-quarta] Lvgdvni [Impressa per Dominicū Verardum] 1543 (i.e. 1544)

Baldo degli Ubaldi, 1327?-1400
see Durantis, Gulielmus, Bp. of Mende, 1237 (ca.)-1296. Specvlum ivris Gvlielmi Dvrandi cvm Ioan. Venetiis, Apvd Ivntas, 1577.

Baldo, Adriano.
Osservando i funghi coltivati. (Cariche elettriche e sviluppo). Verona, 1973.
106 p. 21 cm. L2500 It 73-July
1. Mushroom culture. I. Title.
SB353.B26 73-343857

Baldo, Frank V
Changes in rate-making for railroad freight. [n.p.] 1968.
129 p.
Thesis (Ph. D.)—Pennsylvania State University.
Includes abstract.
1. Railroads—Freight. 2. Railroads—Rates. 3. Freight and freightage. I. Title.
OClJC NUC75-31654

Baldo, Frank V., ed.
see American Society of Traffic and Transportation. Ohio Chapter. The effect of productivity on transportation cost and pricing... Akron, Ohio, University of Akron ⌐1973⌐

Baldo, Frank V., ed.
see American Society of Traffic and Transportation. Ohio Chapter. Improving transportation cost and corporate profit... Akron, Ohio, Bureau of Business and Economic Research, University of Akron, 1970.

Baldo, John Holland.
Nuclear magnetic resonance and temperature jump studies on the interaction of small molecules with proteins, by John Holland Baldo. [n.p., 1975]
vi, 192 l., [5] p. ill. 29 cm.
Thesis—Harvard.
Includes bibliographical references.
MH NUC77-82698

Baldó, Ricardo
see
Baldó García, Ricardo, 1911-

Baldó del Castaño, Vicente.
Conceptos fundamentales de derecho mercantil. Las relaciones jurídicas empresariales. Barcelona, Marcombo ⌐1974⌐
267 p. 22 cm. Sp 74-Mar
1. Commercial law—Spain. I. Title.
74-334854
ISBN 84-267-0258-9

Baldó del Castaño, Vicente.
Prácticas de derecho civil (obligaciones y contratos) Dirigidas por Vicente Baldó del Castaño. ⌐Valencia, Librerías M. Real, 1969?⌐
73 p. 21 cm.
Exercises with blank pages for notes.
1. Obligations (Law)—Spain—Examinations, questions, etc. I. Title.
73-211797

Baldó del Castaño, Vicente.
Régimen jurídico de las ventas a plazos : particular estudio de sus garantías / Vicente Baldó del Castaño ; prólogo de Luis Díez-Picazo. — Madrid : Tecnos, ⌐1974⌐
280 p. ; 22 cm. — (Biblioteca Tecnos de estudios jurídicos) Sp***
Bibliography: p. ⌐277⌐-280.
ISBN 84-309-0536-7
1. Sales, Conditional—Spain. 2. Sales, Conditional. I. Title.
75-562222

Baldó García, Ricardo, 1911–
Del negro al amarillo. Relatos de exilio. Alcoy ⌐Imp. La Victoria⌐ 1972.
171 p., 1 l. 20 cm. 100ptas Sp 73
I. Title.
PQ6603.A43D4 73-351827

Baldocchi, M. A., ed.
see Congresso di cibernetica, Casciana Terme, Italy, 1971. Atti del Congresso di cibernetica. Pisa, Lito Felici, 1971.

Baldoceda, Blas Puente
see
Puente Baldoceda, Blas.

Baldock (Bob) and Son
see Bob Baldock and Son.

Baldock, Cora Vellekoop, 1935–
Sociology in Australia and New Zealand; theory and methods ₍by₎ Cora V. Baldock and James Lally. Westport, Conn., Greenwood Press ₍1974₎
xii, 328 p. 21 cm. (Contributions in sociology, no. 16)
Bibliography: p. 291–314.
1. Sociological research—Australia. 2. Sociological research—New Zealand. I. Lally, James, joint author. II. Title.
HM48.B34 301'.07'20931 72–778
ISBN 0–8371–6126–6 MARC

Baldock, E D
Manual of map reproduction techniques ₍by₎ E. D. Baldock. ₍Ottawa, R. Duhamel, Queen's printer, 1964₎
32 p. illus. (part col.), maps (part col.) 25 cm.
On cover: Surveys and Mapping Branch, Mines and Technical Surveys, Ottawa.
1. Map printing. I. Canada. Surveys and Mapping Branch. II. Title.
GA150.B34 74–230375

Baldock, J. W.
see Botswana. Geological Survey Dept. Coal exploration records of boreholes. ₍Gaborone₎ Botswana, Geological Survey Dept., Ministry of Mineral Resources and Water Affairs, 19

Baldock, Peter.
Community work and social work / Peter Baldock. — London ; Boston : Routledge & K. Paul, 1974.
ix, 130 p. ; 22 cm. — (Library of social work) GB***
Bibliography: p. 125–130.
ISBN 0–7100–8026–3. ISBN 0–7100–8027–1 pbk.
1. Social service. 2. Community organization. 3. Social case work. I. Title.
HV41.B255 1974 361'.941 75–306460
MARC

Baldock, Eng. Services Electronics Research Laboratory
see Symposium on Electron Bombardment Floating-Zone Melting and Allied Electron Bombardment Techniques, Baldock, Herts., Eng., 1959. Electron bombardment floating-zone melting... Baldock, S.E.R.L. ₍1960₎

Baldomero, Enrique Baca
see Baca Baldomero, Enrique.

Baldomero Sanín Cano. ₍Medellín, Editorial Granamérica, 1973₎
133 p. 17 cm. (Colección "Academia antioqueña de historia," 23)
CONTENTS: Maya, R. Baldomero Sanín Cano.—Villegas, S. López de Mesa.—González, F. J. Críticas al profesor López de Mesa.—Bronx, H. Comentarios a unos escritos del profesor López de Mesa.
1. Sanín Cano, Baldomero, 1861–1957—Addresses, essays, lectures. 2. López de Mesa, Luis, 1888–1967—Addresses, essays, lectures.
PQ8179.S37Z58 74–219548

Baldonado, Lisa, 1927-
Developing language competence in children from Spanish language backgrounds: an analysis of an oral language field-test through oral language assessment instruments. [Amherst] 1974.
xiii, 157 l. illus. 28 cm.
Thesis (Ed. D.)–University of Massachusetts.
1. Education, Bilingual. 2. Puerto Ricans in the U. S.–Education. I. Title.
MU NUC76-19274

Baldone, Salvatore.
Produzione e distribuzione del reddito : appunti di economia politica / Salvatore Baldone. — Bologna : Il mulino, 1976.
227 p. ; 21 cm. — (La Nuova scienza : Serie di economia) It77-Feb
Bibliography: p. ₍215₎-227.
L4000
1. Economics. 2. Income distribution. I. Title.
HB177.B19 77-461766
•77 MARC

Baldoni, Remigio.
see Gruppo di lavoro sulle piante foraggere. Risultati della sperimentazione collegiale sulle colture foraggere. Roma, Consiglio nazionale delle ricerche, 1975.

Baldor, Aurelio.
Algebra elemental; con gráficos y 6523 ejercicios y problemas con respuestas. Guatemala, Cultural Centroamericana, 1970.
576 p. col. illus.
1. Algebra. 2. Spanish language books.
RB UNC73-122495

Baldor, Aurelio.
Aritmética; teórico-práctica. Guatemala, Cultural Centroamericana, 1970.
639 p. illus.
I. Title.
LN NUC73-122496

Baldor, Aurelio.
Geometría plana y del espacio, con una introducción a la Trigonometría. ₍2. ed.₎ Texto rev. por Marcelo Santaló Sors y Pablo E. Suardíaz Calvet. Guatemala, Cultural Centroamericana ₍c1967-
v. illus.
I. Title.
LN NUC74-5496

Baldovi, Chusep B
see
Bernat y Baldoví, José, 1810-1864.

Baldoví, José Bernardo
see
Bernat y Baldoví, José, 1810-1864.

Baldoví, José Bernat y
see
Bernat y Baldoví, José, 1810-1864.

Baldovinos de la Pena, Gabriel.
La administración de empresas de investigación. ₍Mexico, 1971₎
250 p. illus.
1. Research. Management. I. Title.
DNAL NUC73-123852

Baldovinos de la Peña, Gabriel.
El ejercicio profesional agronómico. Prólogo de Armando Bejarano Pedroza. Mexico ₍Editorial Agronómica Mexicana₎ 1971.
111 p. 24 cm.
1. Agriculture as a profession. I. Title.
TxU NUC74-125651

Baldovinos de la Peña, Gabriel.
La política económica para la agricultura. ₍México, Editorial Agronómica Mexicana, 1969-70₎
2 v. 23 cm.
TxU NUC74-125650

Baldovinos de la Peña, Gabriel.
Posiciones agropecuarias a 1974 en la producción y el consumo. [México, Editorial Agronómica Mexicana, 1974?]
94 l. 29 cm.
Imprint from label mounted on last page.
1. Farm produce–Mexico–Stat. 2. Food consumption–Mexico–Stat. I. Title.
TxU NUC76-18980

Baldovinos de la Peña, Gabriel.
Principios de la educación agrícola. [1. ed. México, Federación Editorial Mexicana, 1973]
94 p. 23 cm. (Colección Pensamiento actual, 8)
1. Agricultural education–Mexico. I. Title.
TxU CtY NUC74-125604

Baldovinos de la Peña, Gabriel.
Los próximos veinticinco años serán de progreso en la agricultura?... ₍México, Editorial Agronómica Mexicana, 1970?₎
80 p. 20 cm.
"Edición conmemorativa con motivo del XXV aniversario de nuestro ejercicio profesional agronómico (1945-1970), Escuela Nacional de Agricultura, Chapingo, Méx."
1. Agriculture–Mexico. 2. Agriculture–Economic aspects–Mexico. I. Title.
TxU NUC74-125659

Baldovius, Samuel, 1646-1720.
Christlicher Zeit-vertreiber für Männer und für Weiber... Bey Anfang des 1683. Jahres... zur Seelen-Lust und christlicher Ergetzung... gewiesen vom... Hoff-Prediger L. Samuele Baldovio... Bremen, gedruckt bey Herman Brauer ₍1683₎
1 reel. 35 mm. (German Baroque literature, reel 83, no. 422 q)
Poems.
Microfilm (positive) Research Publications, New Haven, Conn., 1970.
Collation of the original: 135 p.
I. Title.
PSt NUC74-127933

Baldrian, Johann.
Kleine Charakteristik von Hamburg / von e. Kosmopoliten, drey Treppen hoch. — Neue mit dazu gehörigen Anm. verm. Ausg. Nachdr. ₍d. Ausg. Hamburg u. Leipzig 1783₎. — Hamburg : Kötz, 1975.
94 p. ; 17 cm. GFR75-A27
Author's signature at end of text: Johann Baldrian.
ISBN 3-920569-08-3 : DM16.00
1. Hamburg. I. Ein Kosmopolit. II. Title.
DD901.H27B34 1975 76-464814
76 MARC

Baldrich, Fernando
see Arnold, Prudencio, 1809-1896. Un soldado argentino. [2. ed.] Buenos Aires, Eudeba [1970]

Baldrich, Gregori Satorres
see
Satorres Baldrich, Gregori.

Baldrich, J Amadeo.
Historia de la guerra del Brasil : contribución al estudio razonado de la historia militar argentina / J. Amadeo Baldrich. — 2. ed. — Buenos Aires : Editorial Universitaria de Buenos Aires, 1974 ₍i.e. 1975₎
xx, 472 p. : map ; 23 cm. — (Cuestiones de geopolítica)
"Anexos: Documentos principales comprobatorios": p. 337-466.
Bibliography: p. 335-336.
1. Argentine-Brazilian War, 1825-1828. I. Title.
F2725.B3 1975 76-472210
76 MARC

Baldrich Caballe, Juan.
Apuntes sobre plagas del almendro. Madrid, 1972.
135 p. illus. (Publicaciones de Extension Agraria)
1. Fruits. Diseases and pests. 2. Almond. I. Title.
DNAL NUC74-125950

Baldridge, Cyrus Le Roy, 1889- joint author
see Singer, Caroline, 1888- Boomba lives in Africa. Freeport, N. Y., Books for Libraries Press, 1972.

Baldridge, Cyrus Le Roy, 1889- ed.
see Singer, Caroline, 1888-1963. Night blooming cereus, a memory. ₍n.p., Printed for Friends of Caroline Singer, 1963₎

Baldridge, Donald Carl, 1932-
Mexican petroleum and United States-Mexican relations, 1919-1923. ₍n. p.₎ 1971.
ix, 255 l.
Thesis—University of Arizona.
Bibliography: leaves 242-255.
Microfilm. Ann Arbor, Mich. University Microfilms, 1971. 1 reel. 35 mm.
1. U. S.—Relations (general) with Mexico. 2. Mexico—Relations (general) with the U. S. I. Title.
TxU NUC76-71714

Baldridge, Donald Carl, 1932-
Mexican petroleum and United States-Mexican relations, 1919-1923. ₍Ann Arbor, University Microfilms, 1974₎
ix, 255 l. 22 cm.
Thesis—University of Arizona, 1971.
Authorized facsimile produced by microfilm-xerography.
Bibliography: leaves 242-255.
1. U. S.—For. rel.—Mexico. 2. Mexico—For. rel.—U. S. 3. Petroleum—Mexico. I. Title.
LU ScU NcU NUC75-22633

Baldridge, Henry David, 1924-
Shark attack / H. David Baldridge. — London : Everest Books Limited, 1976.
278 p., [16] p. of plates : ill., ports. ; 18 cm. GB76-10793
ISBN 0-905018-30-3 : £0.60
1. Shark attacks. I. Title.
QL638.9.B34 1976 614.8'1 76-375656
76 MARC

Baldridge, Henry David, 1924-
Shark attack : a definitive analysis of the world's best information on attacks by sharks against men, including excerpts from over 200 case histories / by H. David Baldridge. — Anderson, S.C. : Droke House/Hallux, c1974.
297 p. : ill. ; 24 cm.
Includes index.
ISBN 0-8375-6780-7 : $8.95
1. Shark attacks. I. Title.
QL638.9.B34 614.8'1 74-79073
76 MARC

Baldridge, Henry David, 1924-
Shark attack: a program of data reduction and analysis. Sarasota, Fla., Mote Marine Laboratory, 1974.
x, 98 p. ill. 27 cm.
Submitted to the Office of Naval Research, Oceanic Biology Programs.
1. Sharks. 2. Sharks—Behavior. I. Mote Marine Laboratory. II. United States. Office of Naval Research. III. Title.
NWM NUC76-52932

Baldridge, Henry David, 1924-
Shark attack against man; a program of data reduction and analysis, by H. David Baldridge. Sarasota, Fla., Mote Marine Laboratory, 1973.
69 l. 28 cm.
"A report submitted to the United States Navy Office of Naval Research, Oceanic Biology Programs."
Bibliography: leaves 66-69.
1. Sharks. I. Title.
CSt NUC75-22615

Baldridge, J Victor, comp.
Academic governance; research on institutional politics and decision making. Compiled and edited by J. Victor Baldridge. Berkeley, Calif., McCutchan Pub. Corp. [1971]
vii, 579 p. 24 cm.
Includes bibliographies.
1. Universities and colleges—U. S.—Administration—Collections. 2. Decision-making in school management. I. Title.
LA226.B26 378.1 79-146313
ISBN 0-8211-0118-8 rev MARC

Baldridge, J Victor.
The adoption of innovations: the effect of organizational size, differentiation, and environment [by] J. Victor Baldridge and Robert Burnham. Stanford, Calif., School of Education, Stanford University, 1973.
iv, 32 p. 28 cm. (Stanford University. Center for Research and Development in Teaching. Research and development memorandum no. 108)
Bibliography: p. 29-32.
1. Educational innovations. 2. Diffusion of innovations. I. Burnham, Robert. II. Title. III. Series.
Mi NUC74-133756

Baldridge, J Victor.
Environmental pressure, professional autonomy, and coping strategies in academic organizations [by] J. Victor Baldridge. Stanford, Calif., Stanford Center for Research and Development in Teaching, 1971.
21 l. 28 cm. (Stanford University. Center for Research and Development in Teaching. Research and development memorandum, no. 78)
Bibliography: leaves 20-21.
1. Universities and colleges—Administration. 2. Faculty participation in administration. 3. Community and college. I. Title. II. Series.
Mi NUC73-43788

Baldridge, J Victor.
An experiential course for teaching social science [by] J. Victor Baldridge, with Robert Cotrell [and others] Stanford, Calif., School of Education, Stanford University, 1972.
iv, 38 p. 28 cm. (Stanford University. Center for Research and Development in Teaching. Research and development memorandum no. 99)
Bibliography: p. 31-32.
1. Social sciences—Study and teaching. I. Cotrell, Robert. II. Title. III. Series.
Mi NUC74-126027

Baldridge, J Victor.
Models of university governance; bureaucratic, collegial, and political. Stanford, School of Education, Stanford University, 1971.
iv, 15 l. (Stanford University. Center for Research and Development in Teaching. Research and development memorandum no. 77)
1. Universities and colleges—Administration. I. Title. II. Series.
MH-Ed NUC73-44384

Baldridge, J Victor.
Power and conflict in the university; theory and research in the sociology of complex organizations. [n.p.] 1968.
381 l.
Thesis—Yale University.
Includes bibliography.
Microfilms of typescript. Ann Arbor, Mich., University Microfilms, 1969. 1 reel.
1. Universities and colleges—Administration. 2. New York University—Administration. I. Title.
MiU NUC75-31655

Baldridge, J Victor.
Social science paradigms and the study of complex organizations. Stanford, School of Education, Stanford University, 1971.
iv, 24 l. (Stanford University. Center for Research and Development in Teaching. Research and development memorandum no. 76)
1. Associations, institutions, etc. I. Title. II. Series.
MH-Ed NUC73-44383

Baldridge, J Victor.
Sociology: a critical approach to power, conflict, and change [by] J. Victor Baldridge. New York, Wiley [1975]
xii, 497 p. illus. 25 cm.
Includes bibliographies.
ISBN 0-471-04573-X
1. Sociology. 2. Social history—20th century. I. Title.
HM51.B18 301 74-19065
MARC

Baldridge, J. Victor
see Action: an experiential approach to sociology... New York, Wiley, c1975.

Baldridge, J. Victor.
see Governing academic organizations ... Berkeley, Calif., McCutchan Pub. Corp., c1977.

Baldridge, J. Victor, joint author.
see Kemerer, Frank R. Unions on campus. 1st ed. San Francisco, Jossey-Bass, 1975.

Baldridge, J. Victor.
see Managing change in educational organizations ... Berkeley, Calif., McCutchan Pub. Corp., [1975]

Baldridge, J. Victor
see Stam, James. The dynamics of conflict on campus... Stanford, School of Education, Stanford University, 1971.

Baldridge, Kenneth Wayne, 1926-
Nine years of achievement; the civilian conservation corps in Utah. Ann Arbor, University Microfilms, 1971.
1 reel. 35 mm. (University Microfilms 71-24265)
Microfilm (positive) of typescript.
Thesis (Ph. D.)—Brigham Young University.
Collation of the original: vi, 389, [6] l.
Bibliography: leaves 382-389.
I. Title.
PSt NUC76-71749

Baldridge, Mary Humphrey.
Bride of the gorilla / by Mary Humphrey Baldridge. — 1st ed. — [Toronto : Playwrights Co-op, 1974]
17 leaves ; 29 cm. C***
Cover title.
$1.25
I. Title.
PR9199.3.B35B7 812'.5'4 76-383483
77 MARC

Baldridge, Mary Humphrey.
The photographic moment / by Mary Humphrey Baldridge. — 1st ed. — Toronto : Playwrights Co-op, 1975.
61, ii leaves ; 28 cm. C***
Cover title.
$2.25
I. Title.
PR9199.3.B35P5 812'.5'4 76-355313
76 MARC

Baldridge, Pat.
Headline recipes from your State-Times and Morning Advocate. Edited by Pat Baldridge. Art by David I. Norwood. Cover photo by Art Kleiner. Baton Rouge, La., Franklin Press, c1972.
47 p. illus. 27 cm.
Recipes drawn from the newspapers published by the Capital City Press.
1. Cookery, American—Louisiana. 2. Cookery, Creole. I. Norwood, David I., illus. II. Kleiner, Art. III. State-Times. IV. Morning Advocate. V. Title.
LU NUC75-101212

Baldridge, Robert Lee, 1919-
see U. S. Congress. Senate. Library. Index of congressional committee hearings... Washington, Govt. print. off., 1935.

Baldridge, William John, 1944-
Simulated core polarization in the lead region. [n.p., 1975]
238 l.
Thesis (Ph. D.)—Pennsylvania State University.
I. Title.
PSt NUC77-82699

Baldridge Reading Instruction Materials, inc.
see Reading and study techniques for academic subjects. Greenwich, Conn. [c1966]

Baldrige, Edwin Rockefeller, 1930-
Talleyrand in the United States, 1794 to 1796 by Edwin Rockefeller Baldrige, Jr. [n.p.] 1963.
ix, 168 l. illus.
Thesis-Lehigh University.
Bibliography: leaves 151-167.
Microfilm (positive) Ann Arbor, Mich., University Microfilms, 1963. 1 reel. (Publication no. 7857)
NNC NUC73-122504

Baldrige, Letitia.
Juggling : the art of balancing marriage, motherhood, and career / Letitia Baldrige. — New York : Viking Press, c1976.
270 p. ; 22 cm.
ISBN 0-670-41043-8
1. Baldrige, Letitia. I. Title.
CT275.B316A29 1976 301.41'2'0924 75-41400
75 MARC

Baldrige, Letitia.
Roman candle. The life of an embassy social secretary. London, Hale, 1957.
256 p. ill. 22 cm.
1. Italy—Social life and customs. 2. United States Embassy, Italy. I. Title.
KU NUC76-70881

Baldry, George.
The rabbit skin cap : a tale of a Norfolk countryman's youth / written in his old age by George Baldry ; edited by Lilias Rider Haggard ; illustrated by Edward Seago. — Ipswich : Boydell Press ; Bungay : Waveney Publications, 1974.
258 p., [12] p. of plates : ill. ; 25 cm. — (The Norfolk library)
GB75-02588
Reprint of the 1939 ed. published by Collins, London.
ISBN 0-85115-045-4 : £2.75
1. Country life—England—Norfolk (County) 2. Baldry, George. 3. Norfolk, Eng. (County) I. Title.
S522.G7B35 1974 942.6'19'0810924 75-325924
75 MARC

Baldry, H C
A Grécia antiga; cultura e vida [por] H. C. Baldry. [Lisboa] Editorial Verbo [1969, c1968]
138 p. illus. (part col.) 21 cm. (Biblioteca das civilzações primitivas, 4)
1. Greek literature—Hist. & crit. I. Title.
CtY NUC74-5509

Baldry, P E
The battle against bacteria : a fresh look : a history of man's fight against bacterial disease with special reference to the development of antibacterial drugs / Peter Baldry. — Cambridge, [Eng.] ; New York : Cambridge University Press, 1976.
x, 179 p. : ill. ; 22 cm.
Includes indexes.
ISBN 0-521-21268-5
1. Bacteriology, Medical—History. I. Title.
QR46.B28 1976 616.01'4'09 76-639
76 MARC

Balduc, Elizabeth Fenn
see Walker, Ara F The descendants of Edward Fenn of Wallingford, Conn., 1688. [Cleveland? Ohio] 1971.

Balducci, Carlo Alberto.
Aspetti religiosi e polictici del Concilio di Rimini. Rimini, Tip. Gattei, 1960.
1 v.
Microfilm: original in Cornell Univ. Library.
1. Rimini, Council of, 359. 2. Church history—Primitive and early church. 3. Arianism.
ICU NUC75-108905

Balducci, Carolyn.
Earwax. Boston, Houghton Mifflin, 1972.
151 p. 21 cm. $4.95
SUMMARY: Twenty-year-old Norma, in Europe to make a film, finds romance and adventure.
I. Title.
PZ7.B1818Ear [Fic] 72-2760
ISBN 0-395-14328-4 MARC

Balducci, Carolyn.
Earwax. Boston, G. K. Hall, 1973 [c1972]
189 p. 25 cm. $5.95
SUMMARY: Twenty-year-old Norma, in Europe to make a film, finds romance and adventure.
Large print ed.
1. Sight-saving books. [1. Sight-saving books] I. Title.
[PZ7.B1818Ear 3] [Fic] 72-12922
ISBN 0-8161-6077-5 MARC

Balducci, Carolyn.
A self-made woman : biography of Nobel-prize-winner Grazia Deledda / Carolyn Balducci. — Boston : Houghton Mifflin, 1975.
200 p. : port. ; 22 cm.
SUMMARY: A biography of a Sardinian woman who determinedly rose above the restrictions of her environment to win the Novel Prize for literature in 1926.
Bibliography: p. 196-200.
ISBN 0-395-21914-0 : $6.95
1. Deledda, Grazia, 1871-1936—Biography—Juvenile literature. [1. Deledda, Grazia, 1871-1936. 2. Authors, Italian] I. Title.
PQ4811.E6Z58 853'.9'12 75-17032
75 MARC

Balducci, Corrado.
La possessione diabolica / Corrado Balducci ; prefazione di Emilio Servadio. — 1. ed. — Roma : Edizioni mediterranee, 1974.
245 p., [8] leaves of plates : ill. ; 22 cm. It 75-Sept
Bibliography: p. [239]-245.
L4000
1. Demoniac possession. 2. Personality, Disorders of. I. Title.
BF1555.B27 75-402397

Balducci, Ernesto, 1922-
La chiesa come eucaristia: saggi sulla chiesa locale Ernesto Balducci. 2. ed. Brescia, Queriniana, 1971.
153 p. 24 cm. (Theologia publica, 15)
1. Church—Catholic authors. 2. Lord's Supper—Catholic authors. I. Title. II. Series.
MChB-W NUC76-71713

Balducci, Ernesto, 1922–
5 [i. e. Cinque] conferenze di cultura teologica: "Aspetti dell'esistenza cristiana" (anno III) Firenze, Scuola di guerra aerea, 1959.
85 p. 25 cm.
1. Theology—Addresses, essays, lectures. I. Title: Aspetti dell'esistenza cristiana.
BR85.B385 73-207396

Balducci, Ernesto, 1922-
Cristianismo y cristiandad. [Tr. de J. Llopis] Barcelona, Juventud [c1966]
176 p.
I. Title.
LN NUC74-125653

Balducci, Ernesto, 1922-
La politica della fede : dall'ideologia cattolica alla teologia della rivoluzione / Ernesto Balducci ; introduzione e premesse storiche di Lodovico Grassi. — 1. ed. — Rimini ; Firenze : Guaraldi, 1976.
235 p. ; 21 cm. — (Presente e imperfetto ; nuova ser. 16) It76-Dec
L4000
1. Christianity and politics. I. Title.
BR115.P7B15 261.7 77-451486
•77 MARC

Balducci, Ernesto, 1922–
Vietnam collera di Dio. Torino, Gribaudi, 1973.
117 p. 19 cm. L1200 It 74-May
1. Catholic Church in Vietnam. I. Title.
BX1650.A7B34 74-316356

Balducci, Ernesto, 1922-
see L'Arte di Romanino e il nostro tempo ... Brescia, Grafo, 1976.

Balducci, Ernesto, 1922-
see Decidere per la speranza. Assisi, Cittadella editrice, 1972.

Balducci, Ernesto, 1922-
see Famiglia aperta nella Chiesa e nella società. Milano, Ancora, 1973.

Balducci, Ernesto, 1922-
see Francesco e altro. Roma, Borla, 1977.

Balducci, Ernesto, 1922-
see Un Risque appelé prière. [Paris] Desclée de Brouwer, c1972.

Balducci, Gioacchino.
Italia moderna. New York, Holt, Rinehart and Winston [1973]
viii, 230 p. illus. 24 cm.
1. Italian language—Readers. I. Title.
PC1117.B277 458'.6'421 72-90215
ISBN 0-03-091224-5

Balducci, Giovanni
see Zingarelli, Nicola, 1860-1935. Vocabolario della lingua italiana. Nuova ed. Bologna, Zanichelli, c1962.

Balducci, Richard.
Le Café des veuves : roman / Richard Balducci. — Paris : J. Dullis, 1976.
213 p. ; 21 cm. F76-7889
ISBN 2-7083-0034-2 : 29.90F
I. Title.
PQ2662.A374C27 843'.9'14 77-463890
77 MARC

Balducci, Richard.
Tu seras le plus riche de ton cimetière. Paris, Presses de la Cité [1974]
218 p. 20 cm. F***
I. Title.
PQ2662.A374T8 843'.9'14 74-178818
MARC

Balducci, Silverio, 1922–
I canti dell'amarezza e della solitudine. Presentazione di Raffaello Bertoli. Pisa, Giardini editori e stampatori, 1972.
50 p. 23 cm. (Biblioteca Giardini) L1300 It 73-June
I. Title.
PQ4862.A367C3 73-343445

Balduf, Emery Winfield, 1889- ed.
see Kant, Immanuel, 1724-1804. Prize essay on natural theology and morals... 1926.

Balduf, Walter Valentine, 1889–
The bionomics of entomophagous Coleoptera, by Walter Valentine Balduf ... St. Louis, Chicago [etc.] John S. Swift co., inc., c1935-39.
2 v. illus., diagrs. 28 x 21½ cm.
"Planographed."
Parts II has title: The bionomics of entomophagous insects.
Includes bibliographies.
1. Beetles. 2. Zoology—Ecology. I. Title. II. Title: The bionomics of entomophagous insects.
QL497.B33 595.7 36-3652

Balduf, Walter Valentine, 1889-1969.
The bionomics of entomophagous Coleoptera. Hampton (Middlesex), E. W. Classey, 1969-1974.
2 v. illus. 28 cm. 18.00 B***
Reprint of 1935 ed., New York.
Part 2 has title: The bionomics of entomophagous insects.
Includes bibliographies.
1. Entomophagous insects. 2. Beetles. 3. Zoology—Ecology. I. Title. II. Title: The bionomics of entomophagous insects.
QL497.B34 595.7'6 74-424784
69[r75]rev MARC

Balduino, Armando.
Corrado Alvaro. 2. ed. riveduta e ampliata. Milano, U. Mursia, 1972.
275 p. port. 20 cm. (Civiltà letteraria del Novecento. Profili, n. 11) L2500 It 72-Dec
Bibliography: p. 231-270.
1. Alvaro, Corrado, 1895-1956.
PQ4801.L75Z58 1972 73-308760

Balduino, Armando.
Messaggi e problemi della letteratura contemporanea / Armando Balduino. — 1. ed. — Venezia : Marsilio, 1976.
254 p. ; 22 cm. — (Ricerche ; 17) It77-Mar
Includes bibliographical references and index.
L6500
1. Italian literature—20th century—History and criticism—Addresses, essays, lectures. I. Title.
PQ4088.B32 77-463216
•77 MARC

Balduinus, Antonius.
Assertiones in vniversam logicam Aristotelis ... Praeside M. Antonio Balduino ... Respondente D. F. Balthasaro Schellio ... Monachij, Excudebat Adamus Berg, 1575.
6 l.
See also Wilhelm Risse, Bibliographia logica, 1965. v. 1, p. 79, different ed.
Microfilm (negative) of original in the University of Pennsylvania Library, Philadelphia. 1 reel. 35 mm.
TxU NUC74-127941

Baldung, Hans, called Grien, d. 1545.
Baldung Grien : [monografie] / Viorica Guy Marica. — București : "Meridiane", 1976.
79 p. : ill. (some col.) ; 20 cm. — (Maeștrii artei universale) R76-4725
Bibliography: p. 76-77.
1. Baldung, Hans, called Grien, d. 1545. 2. Painters—Germany—Biography. I. Guy Marica, Viorica. II. Title.
ND588.B2G9 77-462146
•77 MARC

Baldung, Hans, called Grien, d. 1545.
Hans Baldung Grien. Hrsg. von der Freien Lehrer-Vereinigung für Kunstpflege, Berlin, mit einem Geleitwort von Alexander Troll. Berlin, Dom [19--]
4 p. 12 plates. 29 cm. (Dom-Kunstgaben)
Caption title.
1. Baldung, Hans, called Grien, d. 1545. I. Troll, Alexander, ed. II. Freie Lehrervereinigung für Kunstpflege, Berlin.
ViU NUC75-24830

Baldung, Hans, called Grien, d. 1545
see Aquarelle und Zeichnungen... Wien, A. Schroll [19--]

Baldung, Hans, called Grien, d. 1545.
see Walther, Sigrid. Baldung Grien. Dresden, Verlag der Kunst, 1975.

Baldus, David C
Proposed abandoned railroad right-of-way re-use act; interim report (final edition) by David C. Baldus and Stephen W. Grow. Iowa City, Institute of Urban and Regional Research, 1975.
22 l. 28 cm. (Iowa. University. Institute of Urban and Research. Technical report, no. 36)
Prepared for Department of Transportation, Office of University Research, Washington, D.C. Contract no. DOT-OS-40019.
1. Railroads—Abandonment. 2. Railroads—Right of way. 3. Regional planning. I. Grow, Stephen W., joint author. II. Title.
IaU NUC77-82700

Baldus, Hans Roland.
Uranius Antoninus, Münzprägung und Geschichte. Bonn, R. Habelt, 1971.
324 p. illus., xiii plates. 28 cm. (Antiquitas. Reihe 3: Abhandlungen zur Vor- und Frühgeschichte, zur klassischen und provinzial-römischen Archäologie und zur Geschichte des Altertums, Bd. 11) GDB***
Bibliography: p. [277]-290.
1. Coins, Roman—Syria. 2. Uranius Antoninus. I. Series: Antiquitas. Reihe 3 (Serie in 4to): Abhandlungen zur Vor- und Frühgeschichte, zur klassischen und provinzial-römischen Archäologie und zur Geschichte des Altertums, Bd. 11.
CJ1094.B3 73-356972
ISBN 3-7749-1112-6

Baldus, Herbert, 1899-
A contribuição de Anchieta ao conhecimento dos indios do Brasil. Asunción [1968?]
[7]-13 p. 22 cm.
1. Anchieta, José de, 1534-1597. 2. Indians of South America—Brazil. I. Title.
TxU NUC74-125652

Baldus, Paulheinz.
see Germany (Federal Republic, 1949-). Laws, statutes, etc. Strafgesetzbuch ... 9., völlig neu bearb. Aufl. Berlin, de Gruyter, 1974-

Baldus, Rolf D
Zur operationellen Effizienz der Ujamaa Kooperative Tansanias / Rolf D. Baldus. — Göttingen : Vandenhoeck und Ruprecht, 1976.
xii, 275 p., : graphs, map ; 21 cm. — (Marburger Schriften zum Genossenschaftswesen : Reihe B, Veröffentlichungen des Instituts für Kooperation in Entwicklungsländern der Philipps-Universität Marburg, Lahn ; Bd. 13) GFR76-A51
Summary and table of contents also in English.
Originally presented as the author's thesis, Marburg, 1976.
Bibliography: p. 245-275.
ISBN 3-525-86093-5 : DM31.00
1. Agriculture, Cooperative—Tanzania. 2. Cooperative societies—Tanzania. I. Title. II. Title: Ujamaa Kooperatives Tansanias. III. Series: Marburger Schriften zum Genossenschaftswesen : Reihe B, Veröffentlichungen des Institutes für Kooperation in Entwicklungsländer der Philipps-Universität Marburg (Lahn) ; Bd. 13.
HD1491.T3B34 1976 77-468333
77 MARC

Baldussi, Rosa Boldori de
see
Boldori de Baldussi, Rosa.

Balduzzi, Edoardo.
see L'Assistenza psichiatrica ... 1. ed. Roma, Il pensiero scientifico, 1975.

Balduzzi, Franco.
Der AASHO-Strassentest; Dokumente und Auswertung, von F. Balduzzi. Düsseldorf, Beton-Verlag [1964?]
221 p. illus. 21 cm. (Mitteilungen der Versuchsanstalt für Wasserbau und Erdbau an der Eidgenössischen Technischen Hochschule, Nr. 64)
Hrsg. vom Fachverband Zement e.V., Köln im Betonstrassenjahrbuch 1962/64.
1. Road materials—Testing. I. American Association of State Highway Officials. II. Fachverband Zement. III. Title.
FU NUC73-51331

Baldwin, Abp. of Canterbury, d. 1190.
Traités [de] Baudouin de Ford. [Édités par] Robert Thomas. [Chimay, 1973-
v. 21 cm. (Pain de Cîteaux, 35- N. T. Be**
Latin and French on opposite pages.
1. Theology — Addresses, essays, lectures. 2. Catholic Church — Doctrinal and controversial works—Catholic authors—Addresses, essays, lectures. I. Thomas, Robert, O. C. S. O., ed.
BX1756.B334T7 230'.2 74-165605
MARC

Baldwin, Agnes
see Brett, Agnes (Baldwin) 1876-1955.

Baldwin, Agnes Leland.
A re-examination of the 1928 Cape Romain decision in South Carolina. Summerville, S.C., 1972.
1 v. (various pagings) illus. maps (part fold.)
1. Marshes, Tide. 2. Cape Romain National Wildlife Refuge. 3. Submerged lands—S. C.
ScU NUC74-125953

Baldwin, Alan.
A place called Dimbaza / [by Alan Baldwin and Anthony Hall ; illustrations by Kitty Lloyd-Lawrence]. — London : Africa Publications Trust, 1973.
[3], 31 p. : ill., facsims., maps, ports. ; 30 cm. — (Studies in the mass removal of population in South Africa) GB 74-16493
Cover title: A place called Dimbaza; a case study of a rural resettlement township in South Africa.
Includes bibliographical references.
ISBN 0-900033-14-2 : £0.50
1. Dimbaza, South Africa — Social conditions. 2. Land settlement—South Africa. 3. Migrant labor—South Africa. I. Hall, Anthony, joint author. II. Title. III. Series.
HN800.S63D553 301.45'19'680687 74-186532
MARC

Baldwin, Alan.
The Section ten people : a study of the urban Africans in South Africa / written by Alan Baldwin. — London : Africa Publications Trust, 1975.
32 p. : ill. ; 21 cm. — (Studies in the mass removal of population in South Africa ; no. 4 ISSN 0305 0106) GB***
£0.50
1. Land settlement—South Africa. 2. South Africa—Race relations. I. Title. II. Series.
HD991.Z63B34 301.36'3'0968 77-369042
77 MARC

Baldwin, Alan.
Uprooting a nation : the study of 3 million evictions in South Africa / Alan Baldwin. — London : Africa Publications Trust, 1974.
[1], 37 p. : ill., maps ; 30 cm. — (Studies in the mass removal of population in South Africa ; no. 2) GB74-17645
Includes bibliographical references.
ISBN 0-900033-15-0 : £0.50
1. Land settlement—Africa, South. 2. Bantus—Economic conditions. 3. Migrant labor—Africa, South. I. Title. II. Series.
HD989.S6B3 301.45'1'0420968 75-314951
75 MARC

Baldwin, Alan, joint author
see Arnold, Guy. Rhodesia... London, Africa Bureau, 1972.

Baldwin, Alexinia Young.
The effect of a process-oriented curriculum on advancing higher levels of thought processes in high potential students. [Storrs, Conn.] 1971.
viii, 189 l. illus., tables.
Typescript.
Thesis (Ph.D.)—University of Connecticut, 1972.
Bibliography: leaves 81-87.
1. Gifted children—Education. 2. Curriculum enrichment. I. Title.
CtU NUC73-34795

Baldwin, Alfred Lee, 1914-
see The Measurement of social expectations and their development in children. [Chicago, University of Chicago Press, 1969]

Baldwin, Alice Blackwood, 1845-
An army wife on the frontier : the memoirs of Alice Blackwood Baldwin, 1867-1877 / edited and with an introd. by Robert C. and Eleanor R. Carriker. — Salt Lake City : Tanner Trust Fund, University of Utah Library, [1975]
118 p. : ill. ; 24 cm. — (Utah, the Mormons, and the West ; no. 6)
Reprint of pt. 3 (Memoirs of (Mrs. Frank D.) Alice Blackwood Baldwin) of the author's Memoirs of the late Frank D. Baldwin, major general, U.S.A. published in 1929 by Wetzel Pub. Co., Los Angeles.
Includes bibliographical references and index.
1. Frontier and pioneer life—The West. 2. The West—History—1848-1950. 3. Indians of North America—Wars—1866-1895. 4. Baldwin, Alice Blackwood, 1845- I. Title. II. Series.
F594.B18A33 978'.02'0924 75-14983
75 MARC

Baldwin, Andrew Bennett, 1930-
A study of the Precambrian hematite ore deposits at Fort Gouraud, Mauritania. [Ann Arbor, Mich., University Microfilms, 1974]
159 l. illus., diagrs. (part fold.) 22 cm.
Thesis—University of Toronto.
Includes bibliography.
Photocopy of typescript.
1. Mines and mineral resources—Africa. 2. Ore-deposits—Mauritania. 3. Hematite—Mauritania. I. Title.
CNoS NUC76-18979

Baldwin, Anne Norris.
A friend in the park. Illustrated by Ati Forberg. New York, Four Winds Press [1973]
[38] p. col. illus. 25 cm. $4.88 (lib. bdg.)
SUMMARY: Newly-arrived in Paris, a little boy has trouble making friends until the day an unusual and amusing boy appears in the park where he plays.
[1. Friendship—Fiction] I. Forberg, Ati, illus. II. Title.
PZ7.B1818Fr [E] 73-77538
MARC

Baldwin, Anne Norris.
Jenny's revenge. Illustrated by Emily Arnold McCully. New York, Four Winds Press [1974]
[38] p. illus. 23 cm. $3.95
SUMMARY: A little girl decides to be very bad to gain some attention from her working mother.
[1. Behavior—Fiction. 2. Mothers—Fiction] I. McCully, Emily Arnold, illus. II. Title.
PZ7.B1819Je [E] 73-88071
MARC

Baldwin, B S
Flinders and the French, by B. S. Baldwin. Adelaide, South Australia, 1965.
[53]-67 p. 25 cm.
Cover title.
"Reprinted with original page numbers from Proceedings of the Royal Geographical Society of Australasia, South Australian Branch, vol. 65 (1964)
Includes bibliographical references.
OCU NUC74-127934

Baldwin, Barry.
Studies in Aulus Gellius / by Barry Baldwin. — Lawrence, Kan. : Coronado Press, 1975.
130 p. ; 22 cm.
Spine title: Aulus Gellius.
Includes bibliographical references and indexes.
ISBN 0-87291-071-7
1. Gellius, Aulus. 2. Authors, Latin—Biography. I. Title.
PA6391.B34 878'.01 77-352699
77 MARC

Baldwin, Barry.
Studies in Lucian. Toronto, Hakkert, 1973.
xv, 123 p. 24 cm. $8.00 C***
Bibliography: p. ix-xv.
1. Lucianus Samosatensis—Biography. I. Title.
PA4236.B3 887'.01 [B] 73-83516
ISBN 0-88866-524-5 MARC

Baldwin, Billy.
Billy Baldwin decorates. [1st ed.] New York, Holt, Rinehart and Winston [1972]
219 p. illus. (part col.) 30 cm. $15.00
"A House & Garden book."
1. Baldwin, Billy. 2. Interior decoration—United States. I. Title.
NK2135.B34A42 1972 747'.213 74-161814
ISBN 0-03-001021-7 MARC

Baldwin, Billy.
Billy Baldwin decorates. New York, Holt, Rinehart and Winston [1973, c1972]
221 p. illus. 30 cm. $15.00
"A House & garden book."
1. Baldwin, Billy. 2. Interior decoration—United States. I. Title.
NK2135.B34A42 747'.213 72-78105
ISBN 0-03-001021-7 MARC

Baldwin, Billy.
Billy Baldwin remembers. New York, Harcourt Brace Jovanovich [1974]
232 p. illus. 29 cm.
1. Baldwin, Billy. 2. Interior decorators—United States—Correspondence, reminiscences, etc. I. Title.
NK2004.3.B34A22 747'.21'3 74-8712
ISBN 0-15-112070-6 MARC

Baldwin, Brewster.
Santa Fe, New Mexico, by Brewster Baldwin and Frank E. Kottlowski. 2d ed. Socorro, N.M., 1968.
51 p. illus., maps, diagrs. 23 cm. (New Mexico. State Bureau of Mines and Mineral Resources. Scenic trips to the geologic past, no. 1)
1. Geology—New Mexico—Santa Fe. 2. Santa Fe, N.M. I. Kottlowski, Frank Edward, joint author. II. Title. III. Series.
INS NUC76-71843

Baldwin, Burt Russell, 1938-
The prevalence of formal volunteer organizations: an analysis of the international level. Ann Arbor, Mich., University Microfilms, c1971.
xvii, 322 l.
Thesis—Boston College.
1. Volunteer workers in social service. 2. Volunteer workers in education. I. Title.
NSyU NUC74-127970

Baldwin, C E
The history and development of the port of Blyth / by C. E. Baldwin. — Newcastle Upon Tyne : A. Reid, 1929.
viii, 188 p., [13] leaves of plates : ill. (1 fold. map in pocket) ; 26 cm.
1. Blyth, Eng. (Northumberland)—Harbor—History. I. Title.
HE558.B55B34 77-355229
77 MARC

Baldwin, C. Stephen, joint author.
see Badrud Duza, M. Nuptiality and population policy . . . New York, Population Council, c1977.

Baldwin, Carl R.
see New York (City). Metropolitan Museum of Art. The Impressionist epoch. ⌈New York, 1974⌉

Baldwin, Carol.
The buses roll. Photos. by Carol Baldwin and Peter T. Whitney. Text by Robert Coles. Pref. by Erik H. Erikson. Edited by Linn Underhill. ⌈1st ed.⌉ New York, Norton ⌈1974⌉
109 p. illus. 21 cm.
1. School integration—Berkeley, Calif.—Pictorial works. 2. Berkeley, Calif.—Schools. I. Whitney, Peter T., illus. II. Coles, Robert. III. Title.
LA245.B4B34 370.19'342 74-11072
ISBN 0-393-05529-9; 0-393-05535-3 (pbk.) MARC

Baldwin, Carolyn W
Denominational publishing: a study of major Protestant Church-owned publishing houses in the United States. Chicago, 1971.
iii, 116 l.
Microfilm (positive)
Thesis—University of Chicago.
Bibliography: leaves 113-116.
1. Religious literature—Publication and distribution—United States. 2. Publishers and publishing—United States. I. Title.
CU NUC74-125646

Baldwin, Charlene M., joint author.
see Baldwin, David E. The Yoruba of southwestern Nigeria . . . Boston, G. K. Hall, c1976.

Baldwin, Charles Crittenton, 1888-
Stanford White / by Charles C. Baldwin ; with an introd. by Paul Goldberger. — New York : Da Capo Press, 1976, c1931.
xii, 399 p., ⌈31⌉ leaves of plates : ill. ; 23 cm. — (A Da Capo paperback)
Reprint, with new introd., of the ed. published by Dodd, Mead, New York.
Includes bibliographical references and index.
ISBN 0-306-80031-4
1. White, Stanford, 1853-1906.
⌈NA737.W5B3 1976⌉ 720'.92'4 75-31800
75 MARC

Baldwin, Charles Green.
Effects of media presentation mode and learner personality in the teaching of a factual learning task, by Charles Green Baldwin III. [Los Angeles] 1975.
vi, 134 l. ill. 28 cm.
Thesis—University of Southern California.
Bibliography: leaves 107-119.
1. Audio-visual education. I. Title.
CLSU NUC77-82701

Baldwin, Charles Henry, 1902–
The Asheton family. ⌈Washington? 1972⌉
14 p. 30 cm.
1. Ashton family. I. Title.
CS71.A82 1972 929'.2'0973 73-156926
MARC

Baldwin, Charles L
Higher education; its economic potential in the San Diego area, 1960-1975, by Charles L. Baldwin, Joan S. Shaheen ⌈and Imre Barlai. ⌈San Diego, Calif., Copley Press, Economic Research Dept. ⌈1960?⌉
⌈6⌉ p. diagrs., tables. 28 cm.
Cover title.
I. Copley Press, inc. Economic Research Dept. II. Title.
CU-S NUC74-127075

Baldwin, Charles Sears, 1867-1935.
An introduction to English Medieval literature / by Charles Sears Baldwin. — Norwood, Pa. : Norwood Editions, 1975, ⌈c1914⌉
xii, 261 p. ; 23 cm.
Reprint of the 1922 ed. published by Longmans, Green, New York.
Includes bibliographical references and index.
ISBN 0-88305-072-2 lib. bdg. : $25.00
1. Anglo-Saxon literature—History and criticism. 2. English literature—Middle English, 1100-1500—History and criticism. I. Title.
⌈PR166.B2 1975⌉ 820'.9'001 75-26983
75 MARC

Baldwin, Christina.
One to one : self-understanding through journal writing / Christina Baldwin. — New York : M. Evans, c1977.
xvi, 186 p. : 22 cm.
Bibliography: p. 181-186.
ISBN 0-87131-232-8 : $6.95
1. Diaries—Therapeutic use. 2. Self-perception. I. Title.
RC489.D5B34 616.8'916'6 76-58537
77 MARC

Baldwin, Christopher Columbus, 1800-1835.
Diary. Worcester, Mass., Published by the Society, 1901. ⌈New York, Johnson Reprint Corp., 1971⌉
xx, 380 p. illus. 23 cm. (American Antiquarian Society, Worcester, Mass. Transactions and collections, no. 8)
TxU NUC73-34781

Baldwin, Clare Charles, 1904–
Organization and administration of substitute-teaching service in city school systems. New York, Bureau of Publications, Teachers College, Columbia University, 1934. ⌈New York, AMS Press, 1972⌉
vii, 115 p. forms. 22 cm.
Reprint of the 1934 ed., issued in series: Teachers College, Columbia University. Contributions to education, no. 615.
Originally presented as the author's thesis, Columbia.
Bibliography: p. 99-101.
1. Substitute teachers. 2. School management and organization—United States. I. Title. II. Series: Columbia University. Teachers College. Contributions to education, no. 615.
LB2844.1.S8R3 1972 371.1'4 75-176533
ISBN 0-404-55615-9 MARC

Baldwin, Clarence W
Crossroads on the Cedar; a story of two cities. 4th printing. Waterloo, Iowa, Pioneer Advertising Co., 1975.
83 p. illus., maps (1 col. fold.) 22 cm.
Includes bibliographical references.
1. Waterloo, Iowa—Hist. 2. Cedar Falls, Iowa—Hist. 3. Black Hawk Co., Iowa—Hist. I. Title.
IaU NUC77-81855

Baldwin, Clifford Thomas.
Fundamentals of electrical measurements, by C. T. Baldwin. 2nd ed., revised and enlarged. London, Harrap, 1973.
349 p. illus. 22 cm. £1.95 GB 74-12980
Bibliography: p. 344.
Includes index.
1. Electric measurements. 2. Measuring instruments. I. Title.
TK275.B29 1973 621.37 74-181825
ISBN 0-245-51990-4 MARC

Baldwin, D. A.
see Dudley, William W Analysis of aquifer response for the Sterling Event. [Oak Ridge, Tenn., U.S. Atomic Energy Commission, Technical Information Center] 1973.

Baldwin, D. L.
see Jennings, Donald Alfred, 1930-
Construction of a flashlamp-pumped dye laser... Washington, 1971.

Baldwin, David.
Puritan aristocart in the age of Emerson; a study of Samuel Gray Ward. [Ann Arbor, Mich., University Microfilms, 1973, c1961]
xvii, 315 l. 22 cm.
Thesis (Ph. D.)—University of Pennsylvania.
Facsimile reprint.
Bibliography: leaves vii-xiii.
1. Ward, Samuel Gray. I. Title.
PSt NUC74-125595

Baldwin, David Allen, 1936-
see America in an interdependent world . . . Hanover, N.H., Published for Dartmouth College by University Press of New England, 1976.

Baldwin, David E
The Yoruba of southwestern Nigeria : an indexed bibliography / David E. Baldwin and Charlene M. Baldwin. — Boston : G. K. Hall, c1976.
xxiii, 269 p. ; 24 cm.
Includes index.
ISBN 0-8161-7857-7
1. Yorubas—Bibliography. I. Baldwin, Charlene M., joint author. II. Title.
Z3597.B34 016.9669'2'004963 76-1935
⌈DT513⌉ 76 MARC

Baldwin, David R
Definitions of common terms used in Pennsylvania state fiscal affairs, by David R. Baldwin. [Harrisburg] Pennsylvania State Treasury Dept., 1964.
1 v. (unpaged) 28 cm.
Cover title.
1. Finance, Public—Pennsylvania—Dictionaries. I. Pennsylvania. Treasury Dept. II. Title.
PSt NUC74-12630

Baldwin, Dean Richard, 1942-
Sir Perceval of Galles: an edition. [n.p.] 1972 [c1973]
320 l.
Thesis—Ohio State University.
Includes text of the romance.
Bibliography: leaves 308-320.
1. Perceval of Galles. I. Title.
OU NUC74-125603

Baldwin, Donald M
The North Carolina Outer Banks: a geography of tourist attraction. Knoxville, 1971.
83 l. col. photos. (mounted) 27 cm.
Thesis—University of Tennessee.
1. Outer Banks, North Carolina—Descr. & trav. I. Title.
NcRS NUC73-34780

Baldwin, Donald N 1923–1972.
The quiet revolution: grass roots of today's wilderness preservation movement ⌈by⌉ Donald N. Baldwin. With an introd. by Orville L. Freeman. ⌈1st ed.⌉ Boulder, Colo., Pruett Pub. Co. ⌈c1972⌉
xxii, 295 p. illus. 23 cm.
Bibliography: p. 257–271.
1. Wilderness areas—United States—History. 2. Nature conservation—United States—History. I. Title.
QH76.B35 333.9'5 72-90480
ISBN 0-87108-062-1 MARC

Baldwin, Dorothy.
Understanding your baby : a course in child development 0-3 years / ⌈by⌉ Dorothy Baldwin ; with a foreword by W. D. Wall. — London : Ebury Press, 1975.
144 p. : ill. ; 22 cm. GB75-15246
ISBN 0-85223-075-3 : £2.00
1. Infants—Care and hygiene. 2. Child development. 3. Parent and child. I. Title.
RJ61.B216 155.4'22 76-354914
76 MARC

Baldwin, Doug.
The fur trade in the Moose-Missinaibi River Valley, 1770-1917 / Doug Baldwin. — ⌈Toronto?⌉ : Ontario Ministry of Culture and Recreation, Historical Planning & Research Branch, ⌈1976?⌉
iv, 93 leaves : ill. maps ; 30 cm. — (Research report - Ontario Ministry of Culture and Recreation ; 8) C***
Bibliography: leaves 90-93.
1. Fur trade—Ontario—Moose River watershed—History. I. Title. II. Series: Ontario. Ministry of Culture and Recreation. Research report - Ontario Ministry of Culture and Recreation ; 8.
HD9944.C23O573 381'.43'9 76-375301
76 MARC

Baldwin, Douglas Owen.
Political and social behaviour in Ontario, 1879-1891; a quantitative approach. ⌈n.p.⌉ 1973.
337 l.
Thesis—York University.
Bibliography: leaves 321-337.
Microfilm of typescript. Ottawa, National Library of Canada, 1973. 1 reel. 35 mm. (Canadian theses on microfilm, no. 15679)
1. Ontario—Politics and government—1867-1905. I. Title.
CaOTY NUC75-24826

Baldwin, Duane E
An inquiry into the feasibility of auditing published financial projections, by Duane E. Baldwin. ⌈n. p.⌉ 1975.
vi, 187 l. 29 cm.
Thesis—University of Southern California.
Bibliography: leaves 171-187.
1. Financial statements. 2. Auditing. I. Title.
CLSU NUC77-81853

Baldwin, E.C., joint author
see The Airborne ITPR brassboard experiment. Washington, 1972.

Baldwin, Edward Franklin, 1930-
Trade between Mexico and the United States, 1945-1962: a case study of the applicability of the Prebisch hypothesis on the trade prospects of developing nations. ⌈n.p.⌉ 1970.
xvi, 248 l. illus. 20 cm.
Thesis—University of Houston.
Bibliography: leaves 184-190.
Appendix (Tables): leaves 191-248.
Photocopy of typescript. Ann Arbor, Mich., University Microfilms, 1974.
FU-L NUC76-32095

Baldwin, Edward R
The cross-country skiing handbook, by Edward R. Baldwin. Toronto, Modern Canadian Library, c1972.
160 p. ill. 20 cm. (Modern Canadian Library. MCL [publication] 110) $3.50 C 73-1290
Bibliography: p. 133-134.
1. Cross-country skiing. I. Title.
GV854.9.C7B34 1972b 796.9'3 74-154923
ISBN 0-919364-18-7 MARC

Baldwin, Edward R
The cross-country skiing handbook; a detailed instruction book on cross-country Nordic skiing for both beginners and experts, by Edward R. Baldwin. New York, Scribner [c1972]
160 p. illus. 19 cm. (The Scribner library. Emblem editions) $3.50
Bibliography: p. 133-134.
1. Cross-country skiing. I. Title.
GV854.9.C7B34 796.9'3 73-155569
ISBN 0-919364-18-7 MARC

Baldwin, Edward R
The cross-country skiing handbook; a detailed instruction book on cross-country Ski touring for both beginners and experts, by Edward R. Baldwin. Spec. rev. ed. New York, Scribner [c1973]
159 p. illus. 21 cm. (The Scribner library. Emblem editions)
Bibliography: p. 157-159.
1. Cross-country skiing. I. Title.
PSt NUC75-22616

Baldwin, Edward R
The family guide to cross-country skiing : a complete manual on the latest techniques and equipment / Edward R. Baldwin. — Toronto : Pagurian Press, c1976.
159 p. : ill. ; 23 cm.
"A Christopher Ondaatje publication." C***
Bibliography: p. 157-158.
ISBN 0-88932-029-2 : $4.95
1. Cross-country skiing. 2. Family recreation. I. Title.
GV854.9.C7B35 796.9'3 77-357101
77 MARC

Baldwin, Elaine.
Differentiation and co-operation in an Israeli veteran moshav; with a foreword by Max Gluckman. Manchester, Manchester University Press, 1972.
xxv, 240 p. 23 cm. index. £3.60 B 73-00591
Distributed in the U. S. A. by Humanities Press, New York.
Bibliography: p. [235]-236.
1. Agriculture, Cooperative—Israel. 2. Villages—Israel. I. Title.
HD1491.I 7B34 301.29'5694 73-157219
ISBN 0-7190-0438-1 MARC

Baldwin, Ernest Hickock, 1869-1922.
see Galloway, Joseph, 1731-1803. Selected tracts. New York, Da Capo Press, 1974.

Baldwin, Eugene F
Doctor Cavallo, by Eugene F. Baldwin and Maurice Eisenberg. Peoria, Ill. [Press of J.W. Franks & sons] 1895 [1972]
317 p. 19 cm.
Micro-transparency (negative). Louisville, Ky., Lost Cause Press, 1972. 8 cards. 7.5 x 12.5 cm. (L.H. Wright. American Fiction, 1876-1900, no. 253)
I. Eisenberg, Maurice. II. Title.
PSt NUC73-123850

Baldwin, Ewart Merlin, 1915-
Eocene stratigraphy of southwestern Oregon / Ewart M. Baldwin. — Portland, Or. : State of Oregon, Dept. of Geology and Mineral Industries, 1974.
vi, 40 p. : ill., maps (1 fold. col. in pocket) ; 28 cm. — (Bulletin - State of Oregon, Department of Geology and Mineral Industries ; 83)
Errata slip inserted.
Bibliography: p. 37-40.
1. Geology, Stratigraphic—Eocene. 2. Geology—Oregon. I. Title. II. Series: Oregon. State Dept. of Geology and Mineral Industries. Bulletin ; 83.
QE155.A3 no. 83 553'.09795 s 75-621399
[QE692.2] 75 MARC

Baldwin, Ewart Merlin, 1915-
Geology of Oregon / Ewart M. Baldwin. — Rev. ed. — Dubuque, Iowa : Kendall/Hunt Pub. Co., c1976.
xi, 147 p. : ill. ; 28 cm.
Bibliography: p. 137-143.
Includes index.
ISBN 0-8403-1435-3 : $5.95
1. Geology—Oregon. I. Title.
QE155.B3 1976 557.95 76-4346
76 MARC

Baldwin, Ewart Merlin, 1915-
see Oregon. State Dept. of Geology and Mineral Industries. Geology and mineral resources of Coos County, Oregon. Portland [1973]

Baldwin, Faith
see Cuthrell, Faith Baldwin, 1893-

Baldwin, Ford L
Chemical control of cocklebur and morning glory in soybeans. Rev. Little Rock, 1975.
folder. illus. (Arkansas. University. Cooperative Extension Service. Leaflet 446)
I. Title.
DNAL NUC77-81863

Baldwin, Ford L
Control weeds early in soybeans. Rev. Little Rock, 1975.
folder. (Arkansas. University. Cooperative Extension Service. Leaflet 444)
I. Title.
DNAL NUC77-81862

Baldwin, Ford L
Weed your pasture and hay crops with chemicals. Rev. Little Rock, 1975.
folder. (Arkansas. University. Cooperative Extension Service. Leaflet 295)
I. Title.
DNAL NUC77-81861

Baldwin, Foy Spencer, 1870- ed.
see Bosworth, Louise Marion, ed. The living wage of women workers ... New York [etc.] Longmans, Green, and co., 1911.

Baldwin, Foy Spencer, 1870-1934, ed.
see Bosworth, Louise Marion. ... The living wage of women workers ... Philadelphia, The American academy of political and social science, 1911.

Baldwin, Frances.
How unemployment insurance operates in the labor market, by Frances Baldwin... [Montreal?] 1957.
[5] p. (Canadian business. Sept. 1957) (In Pamphlets, Vol. 1016)
Caption title.
At head of title: Government.
1. Insurance, Unemployment—Canada. 2. Unemployed. Canada. I. Title.
NcD-L NUC74-33182

Baldwin, Frances, comp.
That way and this; poetry for creative dance; chosen by Frances Baldwin and Margaret Whitehead. London, Chatto & Windus, 1972.
128 p. 23 cm. £1.25 GB 72-25418
Bibliography: p. 128.
1. English poetry. 2. American poetry. I. Whitehead, Margaret, joint comp. II. Title.
PR1175.B253 821'.008 74-189228
ISBN 0-7011-1856-3 ; 0-7011-1857-1 (pbk.) MARC

Baldwin, Frank.
The March First Movement; Korean challenge, and Japanese response. [New York] 1969 [c1972]
343 l. tables. 29 cm.
Thesis—Columbia University.
Bibliography: leaves 335-343.
1. Korea—Hist.—Independence movement, 1919. I. Title.
NNC NUC76-71712

Baldwin, Frank.
The March First Movement: Korean challenge and Japanese response [by] Frank Prentiss Baldwin, Jr. [New York] 1972.
343 l.
Thesis—Columbia University.
Microfilm. Ann Arbor, Mich., University Microfilms, 1972. 1 reel. 35 mm.
1. Korea—History—Independence movement, 1919. 2. Korea—For. rel.—Japan. 3. Japan—For. rel.—Korea. I. Title.
NIC NUC74-125594

Baldwin, Frank.
Without parallel; the American-Korean relationship since 1945. Edited by Frank Baldwin. [1st ed.] New York, Pantheon Books [1974]
376 p. 21 cm. (The Pantheon Asia library) $12.95
Includes bibliographical references.
1. United States—Foreign relations—Korea—Addresses, essays, lectures. 2. Korea—Foreign relations—United States—Addresses, essays, lectures. 3. Korea—History—1945- —Addresses, essays, lectures. I. Title.
E183.8.K7B34 1974 327.73'0519 73-18718
ISBN 0-394-47546-1 ; 0-394-70642-0 (pbk.) MARC

Baldwin, Frank Arnold.
Simple short-wave receivers, by F.A. Baldwin. London, Data Publications [1970]
148 p. illus. (Data book series, no. 19)
1. Radio, Short wave—Receivers and reception. I. Title. II. Series.
NmU NUC74-125656

Baldwin, Frank B 1939-
Delaware criminal code [by] Frank B. Baldwin, III. Wilmington, Delaware Law Center, 1973.
66 p. 23 cm.
Cover title: Delaware criminal law; an outline of the Delaware criminal code of 1973.
1. Criminal law—Delaware. I. Title.
KFD561.Z9B3 345'.751 73-161204
MARC

Baldwin, Frank B 1939-
Delaware criminal code / Frank B. Baldwin, III, and Arlen B. Mekler. — Wilmington : Delaware Law Center, 1974.
xx, 250 p. ; 22 cm.
Cover title: Delaware criminal law; an outline of the Delaware criminal code of 1973.
1. Criminal law—Delaware. I. Mekler, Arlen B., joint author. II. Delaware Law Center. III. Title.
KFD561.Z9B3 1974 345'.751 75-327205
75 MARC

Baldwin, Fred Davis, 1937-
The American enlisted man in World War I. [n.p.] 1964 [c1965, 1973]
v, 253 p.
Thesis—Princeton University.
Bibliography: leaves 242-253.
Photocopy of typescript. Ann Arbor, Mich., University Microfilms, 1973. 22 cm.
1. European War, 1914-1918. U.S. 2. U.S. Army. A.E.F., 1917-1920.
NcD NUC75-22614

Baldwin, George Curriden, 1917-
An introduction to nonlinear optics [by] George C. Baldwin. [New York, Plenum Pub. Corp., 1974, c1969]
x, 155 p. illus. 23 cm.
"A Plenum/Rosetta edition."
Bibliography: p. 145-148.
1. Nonlinear optics. I. Title.
[QC446.2.B34 1974] 535 73-23074
ISBN 0-306-20004-X MARC

Baldwin, George Curriden, 1917-
A review of non-linear optics. Schenectady, N.Y. General Electric, Research and Development Center, 1965.
91, 4 p. diagrs. 29 cm. (General Electric. Research and Development Center. Report no. 65GL94)
Cover title.
Includes bibliography.
1. Nonlinear optics. I. Title. II. Series.
IEdS NUC75-31656

Baldwin, George Lewis, ed.
see Texas Tech University. Dept. of Mathematics. Visiting scholars' lectures. [Lubbock, 1971?]

Baldwin, George M.
see Arnold, E R Report to the Port of Portland Commission on commercial aviation development... [Portland, Or., 1968]

Baldwin, George Walter, 1928-
Some notes on the history of Nechako Lodge No. 86 A.F. and A.M. and on Freemasonry in the city of Prince George, by George W. Baldwin. [Prince George, B.C., 1970.
36 p. illus. 22 cm.
Cover title.
1. Freemasons. Nechako Lodge, No. 86, Prince George, B.C. I. Title.
CaBVaU CaOTU NUC73-47754

Baldwin, Godfrey.
Estimates and projections of the population of the U.S.S.R. by age and sex: 1950 to 2000. Washington, GPO, 1973.
29 p. (U.S. Bureau of Economic Analysis International population reports. Series P-91, no. 23)
1. Population—USSR. 2. Population forecasting—USSR. I. Title. II. Series.
DS NUC74-125602

Baldwin, Godfrey.
Projections of the population of the Communist countries of Eastern Europe, by age and sex: 1972 to 2000. Prepared by Godfrey Baldwin, Foreign Demographic Analysis Division, Bureau of Economic Analysis. Washington, D.C., U.S. Dept. of Commerce, Social and Economic Statistics Administration, Bureau of Economic Analysis, For sale by Supt. of Docs., U.S. Govt. Print. Off., 1972.
48 p. (International population reports, series P-91, no. 22)
A United States Department of Commerce publication.
Cover title.
I. United States. Bureau of Economic Analysis. Foreign Demographic Analysis Division.
MH NUC76-11155

Baldwin, Gordon Cortis, 1908-
Ambush basin [by] Gordo Baldwin. New York, Avalon Book, T. Bouregy and Co. [c1960]
222 p. 21 cm.
I. Title.
AzU NUC74-179822

Baldwin, Gordon Cortis, 1908-
Ambush basin. New York, Airmont Publishing Co. [1964]
128 p. 18 cm. (Airmont, W12)
First published 1960.
I. Title.
MiEM NUC76-71702

Baldwin, Gordon Cortis, 1908-
Brand of Yuma [by] Gordo Baldwin. New York, Bouregy [c1960]
222 p. 20 cm. (Avalon books)
I. Title.
MiEM NUC75-69985

Baldwin, Gordon Cortis, 1908–
Inventors and inventions of the ancient world, by Gordon C. Baldwin. New York, Four Winds Press [1973]
251 p. illus. 24 cm. $6.50
SUMMARY: Discusses some of the inventions of the ancient world and the cultures which produced them.
Bibliography: p. [218]-[220]
1. Man, Prehistoric—Juvenile literature. 2. Inventions—Juvenile literature. [1. Man, Prehistoric. 2. Inventions] I. Title.
GN741.B27 73-76461
MARC

Baldwin, Gordon Cortis, 1908-
Powdersmoke justice. London, R. Hale [1957]
154 p. 19 cm.
I. Title.
AzU NUC74-173582

Baldwin, Gordon Cortis, 1908-
Roundup at Wagonmound. [New York] Arcadia House [c1960]
222 p. 20 cm.
I. Title.
AzU NUC74-173581

Baldwin, Gordon Cortis, 1908-
Sundown country. [New York] Arcadia House [c1959]
222 p. 20 cm.
I. Title.
AzU NUC74-173589

Baldwin, Gordon Cortis, 1908-
Trouble range. [New York] Arcadia House [c1959]
223 p. 20 cm.
I. Title.
MiEM NUC75-61636

Baldwin, Gordon Cortis, 1908-
Wyoming rawhide, by Gordo Baldwin. New York, Avalon Books, T. Bouregy and Co. [c1961]
221 p. 20 cm.
I. Title.
AzU NUC74-178011

Baldwin, Gratia Eaton.
The new Beatrice; or, The virtue that counsels: a study in Dante. New York, AMS Press, 1966.
88 p. 23 cm.
1. Dante Alighieri, 1265-1321—Characters—Beatrice. 2. Dante Alighieri, 1265-1321—Allegory and symbolism. I. Title. II. Title: The virtue that counsels: a study in Dante.
PQ4410.B3B3 1966 851.1 66-6098
rev

Baldwin, H. P.
see Hawaiian Islands. Legislature. Committee on Foreign Relations. Hoike a ka hapauuku o ke Komite o na Aina E... [Honolulu, 1890]

Baldwin, Hanson Weightman, 1903-
The crucial years, 1939-1941 : the world at war / Hanson W. Baldwin. — London : Weidenfeld & Nicolson, 1976.
vi, 499 p., [8] leaves of plates : ill. ; 24 cm. GB***
Includes bibliographical references and index.
ISBN 0-297-77089-6 : £12.50
1. World War, 1939-1945—Campaigns. I. Title.
D755.B27 1976b 940.54'2 77-355781
77 MARC

Baldwin, Hanson Weightman, 1903-
The crucial years, 1939-1941 : the world at war / Hanson W. Baldwin. — 1st ed. — New York : Harper & Row, c1976.
499 p., [8] leaves of plates : maps ; 25 cm. — (A Cass Canfield book)
Includes bibliographical references and index.
ISBN 0-06-010186-5 : $20.00
1. World War, 1939-1945—Campaigns. I. Title.
D755.B27 1976 940.54'2 74-15808
75 MARC

Baldwin, Hanson Weightman, 1903-
Grosse Schlachten des Zweiten Weltkrieges. [Aus dem Amerikanischen übersetzt von Thomas M. Höpfner] Düsseldorf, Econ Verlag [1968]
429 p. maps.
Translation of Battles lost and won.
Bibliography: p. 411-420.
1. World War, 1939-1945—Campaigns.
I. Title.
CLU NUC73-47879

Baldwin, Hanson Weightman, 1903-
The price of power / Hanson W. Baldwin. — New York : Da Capo Press, 1976, c1948.
xii, 361 p. ; 22 cm. — (Franklin D. Roosevelt and the era of the New Deal)
Reprint of the 1st ed. published for the Council on Foreign Relations by Harper, New York.
Bibliography: p. 329-333.
Includes index.
ISBN 0-306-70803-5
1. United States—Foreign relations—1945-1953. 2. United States—Defenses. 3. World politics—1945-1955. I. Council on Foreign Relations. II. Title. III. Series.
E744.B2 1976 327.73 76-990
76 MARC

Baldwin, Hanson Weightman, 1903- joint author.
see Lowenthal, Abraham F. A new treaty for Panama? Washington, American Enterprise Institute for Public Policy Research, c1977.

Baldwin, Harmon Arthur, 1922-
School law and the Indiana teacher : a manual for Indiana teachers, school administrators, and school board members. — Rev. 3d ed. / by Harmon A. Baldwin. — [Bloomington, Ind. : Beanblossom Publishers, c1975]
112 p. ; 23 cm.
First-2d ed. by L. A. Burt.
Bibliography: p. 106-112.
$4.00
1. Teachers—Legal status, laws, etc.—Indiana. I. Burt, Lorin A. School law and the Indiana teacher. II. Title.
KFI3393.B3 1975 344'.772'078 75-331078
75 MARC

Baldwin, Harold Westcott.
The logic of reflexive refutations. [Boulder] 1973.
v, 199 l.
Thesis (Ph.D.)–University of Colorado.
Bibliography: leaves [197]-199.
1. Knowledge, Theory of. 2. Metaphysics. 3. Logic. I. Title.
CoU NUC76-71703

Baldwin, Helen Hayes Green, tr.
see Binet, Alfred, 1857-1911. Alterations of personality. Ann Arbor, Mich., Univ. Microfilms, 1973.

Baldwin, Henry, 1780-1844
see [Cambreleng, Churchill Caldom] 1786-1862. An examination of the new tariff. New York, Gould & Banks, 1821 [1974]

Baldwin, Henry Ives, 1896-
Annals of the class of 1922, Yale Forest School, by Henry I. Baldwin, with an introduction by George A. Garratt. [New Haven? Conn.] 1972.
ix, 86 l. illus. 28 cm.
I. Yale University. School of Forestry. Class of 1922.
CtY NUC74-154614

Baldwin, J M
Structure and function of haemoglobin. New York, Pergamon Press [c1975]
225-320 p. (Progress in biophysics & molecular biology, v. 29, no. 3)
1. Hemoglobins. I. Title. II. Series.
PPWM NUC77-81864

Baldwin, J. R.
see also
Baldwin, John Raymond, 1918-
Baldwin, John Richard.
Baldwin, John Russel.

Baldwin, James, 1841-1925.
The horse fair / by James Baldwin. — Great Neck, N.Y. : Core Collection Books, 1976.
418 p. : ill. ; 23 cm.
Reprint of the 1895 ed. published by Century Co., New York.
ISBN 0-8486-0201-3
I. Title.
PZ3.B193 Ho 15 813'.4 76-9890
[PS1059.B48] 76 MARC

Baldwin, James, 1924-
Al encuentro del hombre; cuentos. [Traducción de Patricio Canto. Buenos Aires] Editorial Tiempo Contemporáneo [1971]
222 p. 20 cm. (Colección Ficciones)
Translation of Going to meet the man.
I. Title.
MB NUC73-123825

Baldwin, James, 1924-
The amen corner; a play. [London] Transworld [1970, c1968]
126 p. (Corgi books)
I. Title.
CLU NUC73-122502

Baldwin, James, 1924-
Een ander land [door] James Baldwin. [Vertaling: Oscar Timmers] Utrecht, A.W. Bruna [1973]
253 p. 18 cm.
"9. druk."
Translation of Another country.
I. Title.
TxU NUC76-71715

Baldwin, James, 1924-
Beale Street Blues. Roman. Deutsch von Nils Thomas Lindquist. [1.-30. Tausend. Reinbek bei Hamburg] Rowohlt, 1974.
186 p. 22 cm.
Translation of If Beale Street could talk.
I. Title.
MB NUC76-18978

Baldwin, James, 1924-
Blues for Mister Charlie, a play by James Baldwin. London, Michael Joseph [1965]
124 p. 18.4 cm.
"First published by Michael Joseph Ltd.... 1965."
InU NUC74-125640

Baldwin, James, 1924-
Blues für Mr. Charlie. Amen Corner. Zwei Schauspiele. [Reinbek bei Hamburg] Rowohlt [1971]
155 p. 19 cm.
Translation of Blues for Mr. Charlie and The amen corner.
1. American drama–Translations into German. 2. German drama–Translations from English. I. Title.
NN NUC76-71720

Baldwin, James, 1924-
Blues für Mr. Charlie. Amen corner. Zwei schauspiele. [Reinbek bei Hamburg] Rowohlt [1971]
156 p. 19 cm.
"Deutsch von Kai Molving."
Microcard copy.
I. Title.
CaBVaU NUC73-123831

Baldwin, James, 1924-
El cuarto de Giovanni. [Traducción de Estela Canto. Buenos Aires] Editorial Tiempo Contemporáneo [1970]
167 p. 20 cm. (Colección Ficciones)
Translation of Giovanni's room.
I. Title.
MB NUC73-122461

Baldwin, James, 1924-
The devil finds work : an essay / by James Baldwin. — New York : Dial Press, 1976.
122 p. ; 22 cm.
ISBN 0-8037-1916-7 : $6.95
1. Baldwin, James, 1924- —Knowledge—Performing arts. 2. Moving-picture plays—History and criticism. 3. Negroes in moving-pictures. I. Title.
PS3552.A45Z515 791.43'09'73 76-28
76 MARC

Baldwin, James, 1924–
A dialogue [by] James Baldwin [and] Nikki Giovanni. Foreword by Ida Lewis. Afterword by Orde Coombs. [1st ed.] Philadelphia, Lippincott [1973]
112 p. 21 cm. $2.45
Developed from the transcript of a conversation, taped for the television program "Soul," and first shown in the United States on WNET–TV, Dec. 1971.
1. Negroes — Psychology. 2. United States — Race question. 3. Baldwin, James, 1924– 4. Giovanni, Nikki. I. Giovanni, Nikki, joint author. II. Title.
E185.625.B34 301.45'19'6073 73–4388
ISBN 0–397–00916–X ; 0–397–00948–8 (pbk.) MARC

Baldwin, James, 1924-
Gehe hin und verkünde es vom Berge; Roman. [Aus dem Amerikanischen übertragen von Jürgen Manthey. Reinbek bie Hamburg] Rowohlt [1971, c1966]
197 p. 19 cm.
Translation of Go tell it on the mountain.
1. Negroes–New York (City)–Fiction. 2. Negroes–Southern States–Fiction. I. Title.
NN NUC76-71716

Baldwin, James, 1924-
L'homme qui meurt. Traduit de l'anglais par Jean Autret. [Paris] Gallimard [1970]
446 p. 21 cm. (Du monde entier)
Translation of Tell me how long the train's been gone.
I. Autret, Jean, tr. II. Title.
TxU NUC76-71709

Baldwin, James, 1924–
If Beale Street could talk. London, M. Joseph [1974]
230 p. 20 cm. £3.00 GB***
I. Title.
PZ4.B18 If 3 813'.5'4 74–180874
[PS3552.A45] MARC

Baldwin, James, 1924–
If Beale Street could talk. New York, Dial Press, 1974.
197 p. 22 cm. $6.95
I. Title.
PZ4.B18 If 813'.5'4 74–1161
ISBN 0–8037–4169–3 MARC

Baldwin, James, 1924-
If Beale Street could talk. [New York] New American Library [1975, c1974]
242 p. 18 cm.
"A Signet book."
I. Title.
UU NUC77-82204

Baldwin, James, 1924-
Inny kraj. James Baldwin; przełożył Tadeusz Jan Dehnel. [Wiersze przełożyła Ludmiła Marjańska; posłowiem opatrzył Wacław Sadkowski] Wyd. 2. [Warszawa] Państwowy Instytut Wydawn, 1975.
465 p. 19 cm. (Proza wzpólozesna)
Translation of Another country.
I. Title.
MB NUC77-81849

Baldwin, James, 1924-
Le jour où j'étais perdu ... l'autobiographie de Malcolm X. Traduit de l'américain par Magali Berger. Scénario de James Baldwin d'après le livre d'Alex Haley. [Paris] Stock [1973]
315 p. 22 cm. (Collection Eugène Clarence Braun-Munk)
1. Little, Malcolm, 1925-1965–Drama. I. Little, Malcolm, 1925-1965. The autobiography of Malcolm X. II. Title.
TxU NUC76-71841

Baldwin, James, 1924-
Little man, little man : a story of childhood / by James Baldwin ; illustrated by Yoran Cazac. — London : Joseph, 1976.
GB76-27180
95 p. : ill. (chiefly col.) ; 26 cm.
ISBN 0-7181-1374-8 : £2.95
I. Cazac, Yoran. II. Title.
PZ4.B18 Li 4 813'.5'4 77-352241
[PS3552.A45] 77 MARC

Baldwin, James, 1924-
Malcolm X; een filmscript naar Alex Haley's Autobiografie van Malcolm X. Utrecht/Antwerpen, A. W. Bruna & Zoon [1973]
160 p. 21 cm.
1. Little, Malcolm, 1925-1965–Drama. 2. Little, Malcolm, 1925-1965 The autobiography of Malcolm X. I. Title.
TxU NUC76-71719

Baldwin, James, 1924-
One day, when I was lost; a scenario. Based on Alex Haley's The autobiography of Malcolm X. London, Michael Joseph. [1972]
167 p. 23 cm.
1. Little, Malcolm, 1925-1965–Drama. I. Little, Malcolm, 1925-1965. The autobiography of Malcolm X. II. Title.
CSt WU NUC73-121279

Baldwin, James, 1924–
One day, when I was lost; a scenario. Based on Alex Haley's "The autobiography of Malcolm X." New York, Dial Press, 1973.
280 p. illus. 22 cm. $7.50
1. Little, Malcolm, 1925–1965—Drama. I. Little, Malcolm, 1925–1965. The autobiography of Malcolm X. II. Title.
PN1997.O45B3 812'.5'4 72–10572
MARC

Baldwin, James, 1924-
Otro país. Traducción de Luis Echávarri. Buenos Aires, Editorial Sudamericana [c1971]
468 p. 18 cm. (Colección horizonte.)
Translation of Another country.
1. Negro musicians–Fiction. 2. New York (City)–Fiction. 3. Miscegenation–Fiction. I. Title.
NN NUC76-71718

Baldwin, James, 1924-
Rassenkrapf-Klassenkampf; ein Streitgespräch [von] James Baldwin [und] Margaret Mead. Deutsch von Monika Kulow. [Reinbeck bei Hamburg] Rowohlt [1973]
188 p. 19 cm.
Translation of A rap on race.
1. United States–Race question. 2. Race problems. I. Mead, Margaret, 1901- joint author. II. Title.
NN NUC76-71707

Baldwin, James, 1924-
Sano minulle milloin juna lähti. [Suomentanut Irmeli Sallamo] Helsinki, Kirjayhtymä [1970]
490 p. 21 cm. (Arena-sarja)
Translation of Tell me how long the train's been gone; a novel.
I. Title.
MB NUC73-122501

Baldwin, James, 1924–
[Selected works. Russian]
Выйди из пустыни : рассказы и публицистика / Джеймс Болдуин ; пер. с англ. ; [вступ. статья В. Большакова, с. 5–22 ; составитель Р. Рыбкин]. — Москва : Мол. гвардия, 1974.
202 p. ; 21 cm. USSR 74
CONTENTS: Выйди из пустыни. — Всего-навсего утро да вечер ... — Скала. — Скажи, когда ушел поезд. — Блюз Сонни. — Имени его не будет на улицах.—Открытое письмо моей сестре Мисс Анджеле Дэвис.
0.58rub
I. Title.
Title romanized: Vyĭdi iz pustyni.
PS3552.A45A56 75–558742

Baldwin, James, 1924-
Eine Strasse und kein Name. Deutsch von Irene Ohlendorf. [Reinbeck bei Hamburg] Rowohlt [1973]
133 p. 19 cm. (Das neue Buch.)
Translation of No name in the street.
1. Negroes. 2. United States–Race question. I. Title.
NN NUC76-71699

Baldwin, James, 1924-
see Baldaccini, César, 1921–
César: compressions d'or. [Paris, Hachette, 1973]

Baldwin, James, 1924-
see Bondy, François, 1915- Gespräche mit James Baldwin... Wien, Europaverl. (1972).

Baldwin, James, 1924- joint author
see Mead, Margaret, 1901- Le racisme en question. [Paris] Calmann-Lévy [1972]

Baldwin, James, 1924-
see Mead, Margaret, 1901- A rap on race. [1st ed.] New York, Dell [1972, c1971]

Baldwin, James, 1924-
see Mead, Margaret, 1901- A Rap on race... [Phonodisc] CMS 641/2. [1972]

Baldwin, James Gordon, 1945-
The fine structure of the anterior region of males of Heterodera glycines and Meloidogyne incognita (nematoda: tylenchoidea) with emphasis on amphids and papillae. Raleigh, N.C., 1973.
169 l. plates. 29 cm.
Thesis (Ph.D.)–North Carolina State University at Raleigh.
Vita.
Bibliography: leaves 162-169.
NcRS NUC75-22618

Baldwin, James Mark, 1861-1934, ed.
Dictionary of philosophy and psychology; including many of the principal conceptions of ethics, logic, aesthetics, philosophy of religion, mental pathology, anthropology, biology, neurology, physiology, economics, political and social philosophy, philology, physical science, and education; and giving a terminology in English, French, German, and Italian. Written by many hands and edited by James Mark Baldwin... with the co-operation and assistance of an international board of consulting editors... With illustrations and extensive bibliographies...
New York, London, Macmillan, 1901-05.
3 v. in 4. illus., plates (part col.) diagrs. 27 cm.
The volumes for 1901 to 1908 of the Psychological index form bibliographical supplements no. 1-8 to the Dictionary of philosophy and psychology.
Ultra microfiche. Dayton, Ohio, National Cash Register, 1970. 1st title of 1. 10.5 x 14.8 cm. (PCMI library collection, 998)
1. Philosophy–Dictionaries. 2. Psychology–Dictionaries. I. Title.
KEmT NUC76-40663

Baldwin, James Mark, 1861-1934.
Handbook of psychology. New York, H. Holt, 1889-91. [Ann Arbor, Mich., Published on demand by University Microfilms, 1974]
2 v. illus.
1. Psychology.
MH NUC75-22617

Baldwin, James Mark, 1861-1934.
The individual and society; or, Psychology and sociology, by James Mark Baldwin... Boston, R. G. Badger, 1911.
10 p., 2 l., 13-210 p. 20 cm.
"The French edition bears the title, 'Psychologie et sociologie (l'Individu et la société).'"
One chapter (VI) has been added to the book in the English form.
"The material of the book has also served as a basis for a course of twenty-five lectures on 'Psycho-sociology,' delivered in the National university of Mexico, October to December, 1910."
Ultra microfiche. Dayton, Ohio, National Cash Register, 1970. 1st title of 7. 10.5 x 14.8 cm. (PCMI library collection, 166-1)
1. Social psychology. I. Title.
KEmT NUC75-108878

Baldwin, James Mark, 1861-1934.
The individual and society. New York, Arno Press, 1974 [c1911]
210 p. 21 cm. (Perspectives in social inquiry)
Reprint of the ed. published by R. G. Badger, Boston.
1. Social psychology. I. Title. II. Series.
HM51.B2 1974 301.1 73-14145
ISBN 0-405-05492-0 MARC

Baldwin, James Mark, 1861-
Social and ethical interpretations in mental development, a study in social psychology. 4th ed. New York, Macmillan, 1906.
xxvi, 606 p.
"Work crowned with the gold medal of the Royal Academy of Denmark."
Ultra microfiche. Dayton, Ohio, National Cash Register, 1970. 2d title of 7. 10.5 x 14.8 cm. (PCMI library collection, 166-2)
1. Social psychology. 2. Social ethics. I. Title.
KEmT NUC73-122034

Baldwin, James Mark, 1861-1934.
Social and ethical interpretations in mental development. New York, Arno Press, 1973 [c1897]
xx, 580 p. 23 cm. (Classics in psychology)
Reprint of the 2d ed. published in 1899 by Macmillan, New York.
Includes bibliographical references.
1. Social psychology. 2. Social ethics. I. Title. II. Series.
[DNLM: HMB181s 1897F]
HM251.B3 1973 301.1 73-2960
ISBN 0-405-05133-6 MARC

Baldwin, James Mark, 1861-1934.
Social and ethical interpretations in mental development. A study in social psychology, by James Mark Baldwin. New York, Macmillan, 1897. Ann Arbor, Mich., Xerox University Microfilms, 1974.
xiv, 574 p. 19 cm.
1. Social psychology. 2. Social ethics.
PSt NUC75-22619

Baldwin, James Mark, 1861-1934.
Thought and things : a study of the development and meaning of thought or genetic logic / by James Mark Baldwin. — New York : Arno Press, 1975.
4 v. in 2 ; 24 cm. — (Classics in child development)
Reprint of the 1906-1915 ed.; v. 1-2 were published by S. Sonnenschein, London; v. 3 by G. Allen, London; and v. 4 by Putnam, New York.
Original ed. issued in series: Library of philosophy.
Includes bibliographical references and indexes.
ISBN 0-405-06451-9
1. Logic. 2. Thought and thinking. I. Title. II. Series. III. Series: Library of philosophy.
BC121.B2 1975 160 74-21397
74 MARC

Baldwin, James Mark, 1861- ed.
see Binet, Alfred, 1857-1911. Alterations of personality. Ann Arbor, Mich., Univ. Microfilms, 1973.

Baldwin, James Willis, 1888-
The social studies laboratory; a study of equipment and teaching aids for the social studies, by J. W. Baldwin. New York, Bureau of Publications, Teachers College, Columbia University, 1929. [New York, AMS Press, 1972]
vi, 98 p. 22 cm.
Reprint of the 1929 ed., issued in series: Teachers College, Columbia University. Contributions to education, no. 371.
Originally presented as the author's thesis, Columbia.
Bibliography: p. 95-98.
1. Social sciences—Study and teaching. 2. Teaching—Aids and devices. I. Title. II. Series: Columbia University. Teachers College. Contributions to education, no. 371.
LB1584.B25 1972 300'.7'8 79-176534
ISBN 0-404-55371-0 MARC

Baldwin, Jane.
The Lightning Creek site, Nw-8, Nowara County, Oklahoma. Norman, Oklahoma, University of Oklahoma Research Institute, 1970.
48 p. illus. (Oklahoma. University. Oklahoma River Basin Survey Project. Archaeological site report, no. 18)
Bibliography: p. 45-48.
I. Title. II. Series.
DAU NUC73-46825

Baldwin, Janice
see Wisconsin. Legislative Council. Constitutional and statutory provisions... Madison, 1972.

Baldwin, Janice.
see Wisconsin. Legislative Council. County home rule. Rev. Madison, The Council, 1972.

Baldwin, Janice
see Wisconsin. Legislative Council. Municipal services. Madison, 1972.

Baldwin, Janice.
see Wisconsin. Legislative Council. Town government incorporation. Madison, The Council, 1974.

Baldwin, Jean Marshall, 1926-
Observational learning following operantly conditioned imitation in severely and profoundly retarded children. Milwaukee, 1973.
Microfilm copy (positive) of typescript by University Microfilms, Ann Arbor, Mich. (74-18219)
Thesis (Ph. D.)—Marquette University.
Collation: viii, 81 p. illus.
List of references: p. 77-80
WMM NUC76-71708

Baldwin, Joan.
Listen! It's poetry. Give it a go, by Joan Baldwin and Lyn Brown. Sydney, Independent Poets, 1973.
70 p. 22 cm. $1.00 Aus
I. Brown, Lyn Ingoldsby. II. Title.
PR9619.3.B3L5 821 74-164149
ISBN 0-9599188-0-9 MARC

Baldwin, John, ed.
see Johnson and Johnson, inc. [Pharmacy management] Revised... [New Brunswick, N. J., c1971]

Baldwin, John, ed.
see Johnson and Johnson, inc. Stock management manual. Rev. [New Brunswick? N. J., c1973]

Baldwin, John, of Pennsylvania.
Claims of John Baldwin, against the Mexican government, for damages which resulted to him, for outrages committed upon his person by the authorities of that government, etc., etc. Submitted to the Board of Commissioners under the convention with Mexico of April 11, 1838. Washington, P. Force, printer, 1841.
2 p. l., 38 p. 25 cm.
1. Baldwin, John, of Pennsylvania—Claims vs. Mexico.
JX238.M6B4 1841 CA 25-1143
rev

Baldwin, John, of Pennsylvania.
Memorial and accompanying documents, relating to the claim of John Baldwin, addressed to the Board of Commissioners, under the convention of April 11, 1839, between the United States and the Republic of Mexico. Washington, Printed by P. Force, 1841.
31 p. 23 cm.
1. Baldwin, John, of Pennsylvania—Claims vs. Mexico.
JX238.M6B4 1841a CA 25-1484
rev

Baldwin, John, of Pennsylvania.
Memorial and accompanying documents, relating to the claim of John Baldwin, addressed to the Board of Commissioners under the convention of April 11, 1839, between the United States of America and the Republic of Mexico. Submitted to the board, September 27, 1841. Washington, P. Force, printer, 1841.
2 p. l., 35 p. 24½ cm.
1. Baldwin, John, of Pennsylvania—Claims vs. Mexico.
JX238.M6B4 1841b CA 25-1144
rev

Baldwin, John, of Pennsylvania.
Memorial of John Baldwin, of Pennsylvania, in relation to his claims on Mexico. [Washington 1852]
7 p. 22 cm.
1. Baldwin, John, of Pennsylvania—Claims vs. Mexico.
JX238.M6B4 1852 CA 25-1483
rev

[**Baldwin, John,** of Pennsylvania]
To the Senate and House of Representatives of the United States. [Washington, 1848]
5 p. 23 cm.
Caption title.
Signed: John Baldwin for himself and various other claimants. Washington city, July 7, 1848.
Petition that the Mexican claims be considered as finally adjudicated, and provision be made for their immediate payment.
1. Baldwin, John, of Pennsylvania—Claims vs. Mexico. I. Title.
JX238.M6B4 1848 CA 25-1180
rev

Baldwin, John, Ph.D.
The urban criminal : a study in Sheffield / John Baldwin and A. E. Bottoms, in collaboration with Monica A. Walker. — London : Tavistock Publications, 1976.
ix, 262 p. : ill. ; 23 cm. GB***
Bibliography: p. 242-255.
Includes indexes.
ISBN 0-422-74860-9 : £6.50. ISBN 0-422-74870-6 pbk.
1. Crime and criminals—Sheffield, Eng. I. Bottoms, A. E., joint author. II. Walker, Monica A., joint author. III. Title.
HV6950.S5B35 364'.9428'21 76-361940
76 MARC

Baldwin, John, 1939-
A group problem-solving method for teaching and decision-making / [by] John Baldwin. — Accrington : [The author], 1975.
[4] p. ; 21 cm. GB76-03687
ISBN 0-9504674-0-5 : £0.15
1. Group work in education. 2. Decision-making. I. Title.
LB1084.B34 001.4'2 76-362687
76 MARC

Baldwin, John, 1944-
An uninhibited approach to Indianology; "early American artistry." Illustrated [by] John Baldwin. [St. Louis, Printed by Messenger Print. Co., 1974-
v. illus. 29 cm.
Bibliography: p. 124.
1. Indians of North America—Antiquities. 2. Indians of North America—Antiquities—Collectors and collecting. 3. North America—Antiquities. I. Title.
E77.9.B32 970.1 74-177224
MARC

Baldwin, John L
Climates of the United States [by] John L. Baldwin. Washington, U. S. Dept. of Commerce; [for sale by the Supt. of Docs., U. S. Govt. Print. Off.] 1973.
vi, 113 p. illus., maps. 26 cm. $1.15
1. United States—Climate. I. Title.
QC983.B34 551.6'973 74-600969
MARC

Baldwin, John L
An experimental investigation of water entry. [College Park, Md.] 1972.
213 l. illus. 29 cm.
Typescript.
Thesis—University of Maryland.
Vita.
Includes bibliography.
1. Projectiles. 2. Water. 3. Waves. I. Title.
MdU NUC73-123829

Baldwin, John L.
see United States. Environmental Data Service. Weather atlas of the United States... Detroit, Gale Research Co., 1975.

Baldwin, John N.
John Marshall. An address delivered before the State university of Iowa and the Iowa state bar association, Iowa City, Iowa, February 4th, 1901. By John N. Baldwin. [n. p., 1901]
cover-title, 26 p. 22½ cm. (In Dillon, J. F., comp. Centenary and memorial addresses and proceedings ... on Marshall day, 1901. [New York, 190-] 27½ cm. v. 6)
Errata slip attached to p. [1]
1. Marshall, John, 1755-1835.
KF8745.M3D47 vol. 6 CA 15-1076

Baldwin, John R
A positive theory of regulation and the "public" corporation in the context of the Canadian air transport industry. [n. p.] 1973.
1 v.
Thesis—Harvard.
1. Independent regulatory commissions—Canada. 2. Air lines—Canada. 3. Corporations—Government—Canada.
MH NUC76-71700

Baldwin, John R
The regulatory agency and the public corporation : The Canadian air transport industry / John R. Baldwin. — Cambridge, Mass. : Ballinger Pub. Co., c1975.
xvi, 252 p. : ill. ; 24 cm.
A revision of the author's thesis, Harvard, 1973.
Bibliography: p. 239-247.
Includes index.
ISBN 0-88410-262-9
1. Aeronautics and state—Canada—Case studies. 2. Government business enterprises—Canada—Case studies. 3. Independent regulatory commissions—Canada—Case studies. I. Title.
HE9815.A4B34 1975 387.7'0971 75-8916
75 MARC

Baldwin, John Raymond, 1918- joint author.
see Mavrodineanu, Radu, 1910- Glass filters as a standard reference material for spectrophotometry ... Washington, U.S. Dept. of Commerce, National Bureau of Standards : for sale by the Supt. of Docs., U.S. Govt. Print. Off., 1975.

Baldwin, Joseph B
Kenneth Grahame's The wind in the willows, dramatized by Joseph Baldwin. Chicago, Dramatic Pub. Co. [c1966]
118 p. illus. 19 cm.
I. Grahame, Kenneth, 1859-1932. The wind in the willows.
OrPS NUC75-84379

Baldwin, Joseph Clark, 1897-1957.
Reminiscences. ꞁGlen Rock, N.J., Microfilming Corporation of America, 1972ꞁ
76, 32 l. on 2 sheets. (N.Y.T.O.H.P. ꞁi.e. New York times oral history program ꞁ1ꞁ Columbia University. Oral History Research Office. ꞁOral historyꞁ collection, 1)
Title from first frame.
Microfiche copy.
MH NUC73-123830

Baldwin, Joseph Glover, 1815-1864.
Party leaders; sketches of Thomas Jefferson, Alex'r Hamilton, Andrew Jackson, Henry Clay, John Randolph, of Roanoke, including notices of many other distinguished American statesmen. By Jo. G. Baldwin... New York, D. Appleton and company, 1855.
2 p.l., ꞁ7ꞁ-369 p. 19 cm.
Microfilm. Ann Arbor, Mich., University Microfilms, 1962. 1 reel. (American culture series 213:3)
1. Jefferson, Thomas, pres. U.S., 1743-1826. 2. Hamilton, Alexander, 1757-1804. 3. Jackson, Andrew, pres. U.S., 1767-1845.
MiU NUC76-71717

Baldwin, Joseph K
A collector's guide to patent and proprietary medicine bottles of the nineteenth century ꞁbyꞁ Joseph K. Baldwin. Nashville, T. Nelson ꞁc1973ꞁ
540 p. illus. 24 cm. $15.00
1. Medicine bottles—Catalogs. I. Title. II. Title: Patent and proprietary medicine bottles.
NK5440.B6B33 615'.1 72-13899
ISBN 0-8407-4322-X MARC

Baldwin, Joyce G
Haggai, Zechariah, Malachi; an introduction and commentary, by Joyce G. Baldwin. [1st ed.] Downers Grove, Ill., Inter-varsity Press [1972]
253 p. 19 cm. (The Tyndale Old Testament commentaries.)
Includes bibliographical references.
1. Bible. O. T. Haggai—Commentaries. 2. Bible. O. T. Zechariah—Commentaries. 3. Bible. O. T. Malachi—Commentaries. I. Title.
NN DAU NUC75-84603

Baldwin, Joyce G
Haggai, Zechariah, Malachi: an introduction and commentary, by Joyce G. Baldwin. London, Tyndale Press, 1972.
253 p. 19 cm. (The Tyndale Old Testament commentaries) £1.20
B 72-20593
1. Bible. O. T. Haggai—Commentaries. 2. Bible. O. T. Zechariah—Commentaries. 3. Bible. O. T. Malachi—Commentaries. I. Title.
BS1655.3.B34 1972 224'.9 73-155348
ISBN 0-85111-624-8; 0-85111-825-9 (pbk.) MARC

Baldwin, Joyce G
Women likewise. London, Falcon ꞁ1973ꞁ
32 p. 18 cm. (A Falcon booklet)
Includes bibliographical references.
1. Ordination of women. 2. Women as ministers. I. Title.
MBU-T NUC75-22622

Baldwin, Joyce Karen.
Mechanics of respiration in euthermic and hyperthermic Gallus domesticus. ꞁDavis, Calif.ꞁ 1973.
52 l. illus.
Thesis (Ph.D.)—University of California, Davis.
Typescript.
CU-A NUC75-22621

Baldwin, K D S
Demography for agricultural planners, by K.D.S. Baldwin. Rome, Development Research and Training Service, Policy Analysis Division, Food and Agriculture Organization of the United Nations, 1975.
viii, 185 p. graphs. 28 cm.
Includes bibliographies.
1. Rural population—Handbooks, manuals, etc. 2. Demography—Handbooks, manuals, etc. 3. Agriculture—Economic aspects—1945- Handbooks, manuals, etc. I. Title.
TU NUC77-82203

Baldwin, Karl Ferguson, 1885-1967.
Everyman's handbook of Japan. With the collaboration of Ida A. Van Tyne. ꞁWashington? 1933?ꞁ
132 l. maps 35 cm.
Illustrative matter in pocket.
Includes bibliographies.
1. Japan. I. Van Tyne, Ida A., joint author. II. Title.
DS806.B25 952 75-303545
75 MARC

Baldwin, Kenneth Huntress, 1943-
Enchanted enclosure : the Army Engineers and Yellowstone National Park : a documentary history / by Kenneth H. Baldwin. — Washington : Historical Division, Office of the Chief of Engineers, U.S. Army : for sale by the Supt. of Docs., U.S. Govt. Print. Off., 1976.
xiii, 111 p. : ill. ; 28 cm.
Includes bibliographical references.
$1.90
1. Yellowstone Valley—Discovery and exploration. 2. United States. Army. Corps of Engineers. 3. Yellowstone National Park—History. I. Title.
F737.Y4B34 978.7'52 76-602549
77 MARC

Baldwin, Kenneth Huntress, 1943-
see Individual and community... Durham, N. C.: Duke Univ. Press, 1975.

Baldwin, Kent Francis.
Estimation of the biasing parameter in ridge regression. ꞁNewark, Del.ꞁ 1974.
vii, 95 l. illus. 28 cm.
Thesis (Ph.D.)—University of Delaware.
Includes bibliography.
1. Regression analysis. I. Title.
DeU NUC75-22620

Baldwin, Lawrence Martindale.
Children's structuring of American-English kinship. ꞁn.p.ꞁ 1973.
1 v.
Thesis—Harvard.
1. Kinship—United States. 2. Kinship—Great Britain.
MH NUC76-71701

Baldwin, Leland Dewitt, 1897-
The American quest ꞁbyꞁ Leland D. Baldwin ꞁandꞁ Erling A. Erickson. Belmont, Calif., Wadsworth Pub. Co. ꞁ1973ꞁ
2 v. (808 p.) illus. 26 cm.
Chapter 11 (p. 388-443) and bibliography included in each volume.
1. United States—History. I. Erickson, Erling A., 1934- joint author. II. Title.
E178.1.B155 973 72-84790
ISBN 0-534-00200-5 (v. 1) MARC

Baldwin, Leona.
Mingo-Pike : disaster! / By Leona Baldwin. — ꞁCanada, Ky.ꞁ : Baldwin, c1977.
62 p. : ill. ; 27 cm.
$4.50
1. Tug Fork, W. Va.-Ky.—Flood, 1977. 2. Disaster relief—West Virginia—Mingo Co. 3. Disaster relief—Kentucky—Pike Co. I. Title.
F247.M57B34 976.9'1 77-375539
77 MARC

Baldwin, Lewis M., joint comp.
see Harth, Dorothy E comp. Voices of Aztlan; Chicano literature of today. New York, New American Library [1974]

Baldwin, Lindley J. The march of faith
see Umuganwa w'umunyafirika. [Gitege] Centre évangélique du Burundi, 1969.

Baldwin, Mabel.
A history of the Mississippi Business Education Association, 1917-1972. Hattiesburg, Miss., 1974.
1 v. illus.
1. Mississippi Business Education Association. 2. Business education—Mississippi—Societies, etc. I. Mississippi Business Education Association. II. Title.
MsSM NUC76-50510

Baldwin, Malcolm F 1940-
The off-road vehicle and environmental quality; an updated report on the social and environmental effects of off-road vehicles, particularly snowmobiles, with suggested policies for their control. 2d ed. Washington, Conservation Foundation [1973]
61 p.
Includes chart of state regulations for off-road vehicles in pocket in back.
1. Snowmobiles. 2. Tracklaying vehicles. 3. Environmental policy. I. Title.
ViBlbV ICarbS NUC75-18525

Baldwin, Malcolm F 1940-
Public policy on oil: an ecological perspective. Washington, D.C., Conservation Foundation, 1971.
63 p.
Reprinted from Ecology Law Quarterly.
1. Petroleum industry and trade—U.S. 2. Petroleum conservation. I. Conservation Foundation. II. Title.
DI NUC73-34777

Baldwin, Malcolm F 1940-
The Santa Barbara oil spill -- a discussion paper. Washington, Conservation Foundation, 1969.
81 l. map. 29 cm.
Photocopy of typescript. Prepared for Conference on Law and the Environment, Airlie House, 1969.
Bibliographical footnotes: leaves 68-81.
1. Oil pollution of rivers, harbors, etc. 2. Environmental law. I. Conference on Law and the Environment, Airlie House, 1969. II. Conservation Foundation. III. Title.
WaU-L NUC75-125390

Baldwin, Malcolm F 1940-
The Southwest energy complex: a policy evaluation, by Malcolm F. Baldwin. Washington, Conservation Foundation ꞁ1973ꞁ
ii, 73 p. map. 28 cm. $3.50
Includes bibliographical references.
1. Electric power-plants—Southwest, New—Environmental aspects. 2. Coal mines and mining—Southwest, New. I. Title.
TD195.E4B34 333.7'2'0979 73-79429
MARC

Baldwin, Malcolm F., 1940- joint author.
see Baldwin, Pamela L Onshore planning for offshore oil ... Washington, D.C. Conservation Foundation, 1975.

Baldwin, Malcolm F., 1940-
see Environmental Impact Assessment Project. A scientific and policy review... Washington, D.C., 1973.

Baldwin, Mary, 1908- comp.
see Goudge, Elizabeth, 1900- The ten gifts. ꞁLondonꞁ Hodder and Stoughton ꞁ1969ꞁ

Baldwin, Mary Alice.
Archaeological evidence of cultural continuity from Chumash to Salinan Indians in California. San Luis Obispo, San Luis Obispo County Archaeological Society [196-?]
ii, 71 p. illus. (San Luis Obispo County Archaeological Society. Occasional paper no. 6)
Bibliography: p. 59-71.
1. Chumashan Indians. 2. Salinan Indians. 3. Indians of North America—Calif.—San Luis Obispo Co., Calif. I. Title. II. Series.
CU-SB NUC74-137604

Baldwin, Mary Newton, 1903-
Time's wingèd chariot / Mary Newton Baldwin. — Francestown, N.H. : Golden Quill Press, c1975.
80 p. ; 21 cm.
ISBN 0-8233-0218-0 : $5.00
I. Title.
PS3503.A5535T5 811'.5'4 74-33874
75 MARC

Baldwin, Maynard Martin, 1904-
see Portraits of complexity... [Columbus, Ohio] Battelle, 1975.

Baldwin, Michael.
Buried god; selected poetry. London, Hodder & Stoughton, 1973.
3-215 p. 22 cm. £2.50 GB 73-30898
I. Title.
PR6052.A39B8 823'.9'14 74-163855
ISBN 0-340-16601-0 MARC

Baldwin, Michael.
The cellar: a fable. London, Hodder and Stoughton, 1972.
187 p. 23 cm. £1.90 B 72-12761
I. Title.
PZ4.B1816Ce 823'.9'14 72-195707
[PR6052.A39] MARC
ISBN 0-340-15822-0

Baldwin, Michael.
Double image; five poems by Michael Baldwin, John Fairfax and Brian Patten. Illustrated by Ken Turner; edited by John Fairfax. [London] Longman [1972]
[6] l. illus.
I. Fairfax, John, 1930- II. Patten, Brian, 1946- III. Title.
InU NUC73-123854

Baldwin, Michael, joint author
see Atkinson, Terry. Air-conditioning show/Frameworks. 1966-7. [Chipping Norton, Oxon, Art and Language Press, 1967?]

Baldwin, Monica.
Ho salto il muro; romanzo. [Traduzione dall' inglese di Bruno Tasso. 1. ed. Milano] Garzanti [1967]
378 p. 19 cm. (Collezione "I Rossi e i blu")
Translation of I leap over the wall.
1. Monasticism and religious orders for women. I. Title.
MB NUC74-137605

Baldwin, Neil.
The bared and bended arm. [Dennis, Mass.] Salt-Works Press [1974]
[10] p. 20 cm.
Poems.
First edition.
One of an edition of 250 copies.
I. Title.
CU-B NUC76-18977

Baldwin, Neil E.
see New York (State). State University, Buffalo Lockwood Memorial Library. The manuscripts and letters of William Carlos Williams... [Buffalo? University of Buffalo? 1973]

Baldwin, Nick.
Heavy goods vehicles 1919-1939 / by Nick Baldwin. — London : Almark Pub. Co., 1976.
96 p. : ill. ; 21 cm. GB***
Includes index.
ISBN 0-85524-266-3 : £3.25
1. Motor-trucks, British. I. Title.
TL230.B27 629.22'4'0941 76-382657
76 MARC

Baldwin, Nick.
Light vans and trucks, 1919-1939 / by Nick Baldwin and Arthur Ingram. — London : Almark Pub. Co., 1977.
96 p. : ill. ; 21 x 22 cm. GB***
Includes index.
ISBN 0-85524-262-0 : £3.50
1. Motor trucks—Great Britain—History. I. Ingram, Arthur, joint author. II. Title.
TL230.B272 629.22'4'0941 77-366846
77 MARC

Baldwin, Nick.
see A Motoring heritage. Edinburgh, Bartholomew in association with Leyland Historic Vehicles, 1976.

Baldwin, Norman Cecil.
The Lisbon story. [Sutton Coldfield, Eng., ca. 1960?]
[12] p. illus. 21.5 cm. (A "Popular pamphlet")
"Reprinted from 'The Aero field'."
On early Portuguese air mail flights.
1. Air mail service—Portugal—Hist. I. Title.
MB NUC76-69503

Baldwin, Orrel T
Makers of American history [by] Orrel Baldwin. Educational consultant: Clyde Vochatzer. Illustrated by Victor Mays. Teacher's annotated ed. New York, Noble and Noble [1972]
vii, 472 p. illus. 25 cm.
SUMMARY: Traces the history of the United States through events in the lives of individuals instrumental in shaping it, from Columbus to Nixon.
Bibliography: p. 458-463.
1. United States—History—Juvenile literature. [1. United States—History] I. Mays, Victor, 1927- illus. II. Title.
E178.1.B185 372.8'973 72-172750
ISBN 0-8107-2542-8 MARC

Baldwin, Pamela L
Onshore planning for offshore oil : lessons from Scotland / Pamela L. Baldwin and Malcolm F. Baldwin. — Washington, D.C. : Conservation Foundation, 1975.
183 p. : ill. ; 23 cm.
Bibliography: p. 181-183.
$5.00
1. Oil well drilling, Submarine. 2. Petroleum in submerged lands—Scotland. I. Baldwin, Malcolm F., 1940- joint author. II. Title.
TN871.3.B34 333.8'2 75-606
75 MARC

Baldwin, Patricia J
Congruence between the expectations of the clinical nurse specialist as perceived by the nurse specialist, the nurse educator, and the nurse administrator with implications for curriculum development in graduate nursing programs, by Patricia J. Baldwin. [n.p.] 1975.
xi, 135 l. 28 cm.
Thesis (D.N.Sc.)—Catholic University of America.
Bibliography: leaves 86-88.
1. Graduate nursing education. 2. Nursing audit. I. Title.
DCU NUC77-81848

Baldwin, Petie W 1927-
Winds of imagination / [poet, Petie W. Baldwin ; illustrator, R. Brian Regehr. — 1st ed. — Visalia, Calif. : Creative Ventures, 1976.
[46] p. : ill. ; 24 cm.
ISBN 0-917166-00-0. ISBN 0-917166-01-9 pbk.
I. Regehr, R. Brian. II. Title.
PS3552.A4514W5 811'.5'4 76-17537
76 MARC

Baldwin, R
Economics of structural fire protection. R. Baldwin. Garston, Eng., Building Research Establishment, 1975.
11 p. 30 cm. (Current paper—Building Research Establishment, CP 45/75)
Based on lectures given at Edinburgh University, course on Quantitative methods of risk management April, 1974, and at BRE Symposium on Cost-Effectiveness and Fire Protection, October, 1974.
Bibliography: p. 10-11.
1. Building, Fireproof. 2. Fire Prevention. I. Building Research Establishment. II. Title.
DHUD NUC77-81843

Baldwin, R., joint author.
see Waverman, Leonard. Determinants of interlocking directorates in Canada. Toronto, Institute for the Quantitative Analysis of Social and Economy Policy, University of Toronto, 1975.

Baldwin, R P
Mapping / by R. P. Baldwin. — [Saskatoon, Sask. : Churchill River Study], 1975.
x, 24 p. : maps ; 28 cm. — (Final report - Churchill River Study ; 26) C***
"Prepared for the Churchill River Study Board."
Bibliography: p. 22.
1. Churchill River watershed, Sask. and Manitoba—Maps. I. Churchill River Study. Board. II. Title. III. Series: Churchill River Study. Final report - Churchill River Study ; 26.
GA475.C48B34 627'.81 76-383998
77 MARC

Baldwin, R W
The great comprehensive gamble : statistics of secondary education examinations, 1966-1973 / [compiled] by R. W. Baldwin. — Macclesfield : Helios Press ; [London] : [Distributed by Independent Schools Information Service], [1975]
13 p. ; 26 x 38 cm. GB76-27511
Caption title.
ISBN 0-905639-00-6 : £0.30
1. Examinations—Great Britain—Statistics. 2. Comprehensive schools—Great Britain—Statistics. I. Title.
LB3056.G7B34 373.1'2'620941 77-353196
77 MARC

Baldwin, Ralph.
The unity of the Canterbury tales. [Folcroft, Pa.] Folcroft Library Editions, 1973 [c1955]
112 p. 26 cm.
Reprint of the ed. published by Rosenkilde and Bagger, Copenhagen, which was issued as v. 5 of Anglistica; originally issued as thesis, Johns Hopkins University.
Bibliography: p. [111]-112.
1. Chaucer, Geoffrey, d. 1400. Canterbury tales. I. Title. II. Series: Anglistica, v. 5.
PR1874.B3 1973 821'.1 73-16142
ISBN 0-8414-9885-7 (lib. bdg.) MARC

Baldwin, Ralph.
The unity of the Canterbury tales / by Ralph Baldwin. — Norwood, Pa. : Norwood Editions, 1975 [c1955]
112 p. ; 26 cm.
Reprint of the ed. published by Rosenkilde and Bagger, Copenhagen, which was issued as v. 5 of Anglistica.
Originally presented as the author's thesis, Johns Hopkins University.
Bibliography: p. [111]-112.
ISBN 0-88305-970-3 : $13.50
1. Chaucer, Geoffrey, d. 1400. Canterbury tales. I. Title. II. Series: Anglistica ; v. 5.
[PR1874.B3 1975] 821'.1 75-41311
75[r76]rev MARC

Baldwin, Randall Richardson, 1943-
The idealist theory of tragedy: tragic poetry as the vehicle of transcendental idea in the theoretical writings of Schiller, Schelling, Schlegal and Hölderlin, by Randall Richardson Baldwin. [Toronto?] c1975.
viii, 184, [15] l.
Vita.
Thesis—University of Toronto.
Bibliography: leaves 183-184 (2d group)
1. German drama (Tragedy)—History and criticism. 2. German poetry-19th century—History and criticism. 3. Philosophy in literature. I. Title.
CaOTU NUC77-82696

Baldwin, Richard A., joint author
see Harl, Neil E An analysis of the economic implications of the permit system... Ames, Iowa State Water Resources Research Institute, 1971.

Baldwin, Richard F
Plywood manufacturing practices / Richard F. Baldwin. — [San Francisco] : M. Freeman Publications, [1975]
xii, 260 p. : ill. ; 24 cm.
"A Forest Industries book."
Includes bibliographical references and indexes.
ISBN 0-87930-030-2 : $22.50
1. Plywood. I. Title.
TS870.B33 674'.834 74-20161
MARC

Baldwin, Robert Charles.
An investigation of the configurational stability of some α-substituted radicals. [Stanford, Calif.] 1971.
xi, 60 l.
Thesis (Ph.D.)—Stanford University, 1972.
Includes bibliographical references.
1. Carbon radicals. I. Title.
CSt NUC73-34782

Baldwin, Robert D
Sources of variability in missile unit evaluations, by Robert D. Baldwin and Harry E. Anderson. [Alexandria, Va.] George Washington University, Human Resources Research Office, 1966.
vii, 19 p. graphs. (George Washington University, Washington, D.C. Human Resources Research Office. Technical report 66-13)
Bibliographical footnotes.
1. Nike rocket. 2. Fire control (Gunnery) I. Anderson, Harry E., joint author. II. Title.
CU NUC76-71710

Baldwin, Robert E
Desarrollo económico; un análisis introductorio. [Traducción por Silvia Salinas] Buenos Aires, Amorrotu editores [1970]
146 p. graph, tables. (Biblioteca de economía política. Serie introductoria)
Translation of Economic development and growth.
Bibliography: p. 140-142.
1. Economic development. I. Title.
PrU NUC73-122462

Baldwin, Robert E comp.
International trade and finance; readings. ₍Compiled by₎ Robert E. Baldwin ₍and₎ J. David Richardson. Boston, Little, Brown ₍1973, c1974₎
x, 486 p. 23 cm. (Little, Brown series in economics)
Includes bibliographical references.
1. International economic relations—Addresses, essays, lectures. 2. Commerce—Addresses, essays, lectures. 3. International finance—Addresses, essays, lectures. I. Richardson, J. Davis, joint comp. II. Title.
HF1411.B233 1974 382.1 73-8326 MARC

Baldwin, Robert E. Nontariff distortions of international trade
see Reducing nontariff barriers to world trade... Washington, Brookings Institution [c1970]

Baldwin, Robert E
The Philippines / by Robert E. Baldwin. — New York : National Bureau of Economic Research : distributed by Columbia University Press, 1975.
xix, 165 p. ; 24 cm. — (Foreign trade regimes and economic development ; v. 5)
Includes bibliographical references and index.
ISBN 0-87014-505-3
1. Philippine Islands Economic conditions 1946 2. Philippine Islands—Commercial policy. 3. Foreign trade regulation—Philippine Islands. I Title. II. Series.
HC10.F58 vol. 5 330.9 s 74-82373
₍HC455₎ 75 MARC

Baldwin, Robert E., joint author.
see Meier, Gerald M. Economic development ... Huntington, N.Y., R. E. Krieger Pub. Co., 1976, c1957.

Baldwin, Robert Harrison, 1931-
A quest for unity: an analysis of the educational theories of Alexander Meiklejohn. ₍Pittsburgh₎ 1967.
306 p.
Thesis (Ph.D.)—University of Pittsburgh.
Microfilm edition (1 reel) Positive; filmed by University Microfilms.
Bibliography: p. 293-306.
1. Meiklejohn, Alexander, 1872-1964. I. Title.
OOxM NUC73-122032

Baldwin, Robert S
see Portland, Or. City Planning Commission. Planning guidelines; Portland downtown plan, February, 1972. [Portland, Or., 1972]

Baldwin, Robert William.
see Homburger, Freddy, ed. The physiopathology of cancer. 3d. ed. Basel, S. Karger, 1974-1976.

Baldwin, Robin
see Fresno, Calif. Redevelopment Agency. The case for governmental cooperation... [Fresno] 1969.

Baldwin, Roger E
Genetics ₍by₎ Roger E. Baldwin. New York, Wiley ₍1973₎
viii, 296 p. illus. 26 cm. (Self-teaching guides)
1. Genetics—Programmed instruction.
[QH430.B35] 575.1′07′7 73-5765
ISBN 0-471-04588-8 MARC

Baldwin, Roger Edwin.
The development and evaluation of voluntary choice programmed instruction in mathematics. ₍Minneapolis₎ 1964 ₍c1965₎
v, 280 l.
Thesis—University of Minnesota.
Includes bibliography.
Microfilm copy of typescript. Ann Arbor, University Microfilms.
1. Mathematics—Programmed instruction. I. Title.
CaBVaU NUC75-29480

Baldwin, Roger Nash, 1884–
The Japanese reminiscences of Roger Baldwin. — 1961.
118 p.
Transcript of interviews conducted for the Occupation of Japan Project of the Oral History Research Office of Columbia University in 1961.
Includes index.
Microfiche of typescript. Glen Rock, N. J. : Microfilming Corp. of America, 1975. — 2 sheets ; 11 x 15 cm. — (Columbia University oral history collection ; pt. 2, no. 10)
ISBN 0-88455-015-X : $8.00
1. Japan—History—Allied occupation, 1945-1952—Sources. 2. Baldwin, Roger Nash, 1884- I. Series: Columbia University oral history collection ; pt. 2, no. 10.
Microfiche DS889.15 952.04′092′4 74-30443

Baldwin, Roger Nash, 1884-
The reminiscences of Roger Nash Baldwin. Glen Rock, N.J., Microfilming Corp. of America ₍c1972₎
11 sheets. 105 x 147 mm.
Micro-transparency (positive) of typescript.
Transcription of interviews by H.B. Phillips in 1953-1954.
Collation of the original: 2 v. (New York Times Oral History Program. Columbia University Oral History Collection)
1. Baldwin, Roger Nash, 1884- I. Phillips, H. B. II. Series.
PSt MH NUC74-793

Baldwin, Roger Nash, 1884-
see Civil liberties. [Sound recording] Pleasantville, N. Y.] Educational Audio Visual LE 7008. p1976.

Baldwin, Roger Nash, 1884-
see Talmadge, Irving DeWitt, ed. Whose revolution? ... Westport, Conn., Hyperion Press, 1975, c1941.

Baldwin, Ronald F
The effect of teacher in-service training and knowledge of research on spelling instruction and achievement of elementary school children. [Iowa City, c1975]
xi, 392 l. 28 cm.
Thesis (Ph.D.)--University of Iowa.
1. Elementary school teachers--In-service training. 2. English language--Orthography and spelling--Study and teaching (Elementary) 3. Spelling reform. I. Title.
IaU NUC77-85697

Baldwin, Ronald Martin.
Biosynthesis of vitamin K. [Berkeley] 1974.
xxiv, 348 l. illus.
Thesis (Ph. D.)—University of California.
Includes bibliographical references.
CU NUC76-18976

Baldwin, Ruth Elizabeth, 1918-
Palatibility of Missouri fish ₍by₎ Ruth E. Baldwin. ₍Springfield, Va., National Technical Information Service, 1972₎
31 l. illus. (COM - 72 - 11310)
Completion report for period June 1967- May 1969 prepared for Missouri Dept. of Conservation and National Oceanic and Atmospheric Administration, National Marine Fisheries Service.
1. Food preferences. 2. Cookery (Fish). 3. Fishes—Missouri. I. Title.
MoU NUC75-26590

Baldwin, Ruth Elizabeth, 1918-
A study of flavor and aroma of three species of fish taken from different fresh water sources, by Ruth E. Baldwin. ₍n. p.₎ 1961.
136 l. illus. 29 cm.
Thesis (Ph. D.)—University of Wisconsin.
Vita.
Includes bibliography.
I. Title.
WU NUC73-9454

Baldwin, Ruth Marie, 1918-
Alexander Gill, the Elder, High Master of St. Paul's School; an approach to Milton's intellectual development. 1955. [Ann Arbor, Mich., University Microfilms, 1974]
v, 202 l.
Thesis—University of Illinois.
Vita.
Bibliography: leaves [195]-202.
1. Gill, Alexander, 1564-1635. 2. Milton, John, 1608-1674. I. Title.
NGenoU NUC75-17399

Baldwin, Samuel Davies.
Armageddon; or, The overthrow of Romanism and monarchy; the existence of the United States foretold in the Bible ... Cincinnati, Applegate ₍1854₎
480 p. 20 cm.
1. Bible—Prophecies. 2. Bible—Prophecies—United States. I. Title.
BS647.B33 1854 73-157432 MARC

Baldwin, Samuel Davies.
Armageddon; or, The overthrow of Romanism and monarchy; the existence of the United States foretold in the Bible ... Rev. ed. Cincinnati, Applegate ₍1854₎
480 p. 21 cm.
1. Bible—Prophecies. 2. Bible—Prophecies—United States. I. Title.
BS647.B33 1854b 73-156680 MARC

Baldwin, Sidney, 1885-
Marjorie of Monhegan; a year in a girl's life on a Maine coast island, by Sidney Baldwin. Illustrated by Ann Watson. Monhegan, Me., J.B. Day [1973]
300 p. illus., map. 21 cm.
I. Watson, Ann, illus. II. Title.
MeU NUC76-71684

Baldwin, Sidney, 1922- joint author.
see Richardson, Ivan L. Public administration ... Columbus, Ohio, C. E. Merrill Pub. Co., c1976.

Baldwin, Spurgeon W., ed.
see Bible. N. T. Spanish (Old Spanish). Escorial. Biblioteca. MSS. (I-I-6) Nuevo Testamento [según el manuscrito escurialense I-I-6. Madrid, 1970.

Baldwin, Stanley C
Bad Henry, by Stan Baldwin and Jerry Jenkins in collaboration with Hank Aaron. ₍1st ed.₎ Radnor, Pa., Chilton Book Co. ₍1974₎
205 p. illus. 22 cm.
1. Aaron, Henry, 1934– 2. Baseball. I. Jenkins, Jerry B., joint author. II. Aaron, Henry, 1934– III. Title.
GV865.A25B34 796.357′092′4 74-5035
ISBN 0-8019-5960-8 MARC

Baldwin, Stanley C
What did Jesus say about that? / Stanley C. Baldwin. — Wheaton, Ill. : Victor Books, c1975.
156 p. ; 21 cm. — (An Input book)
ISBN 0-88207-718-X : $1.95
1. Jesus Christ—Teachings. I. Title.
BS2415.B333 232.9′54 74-28510
75 MARC

Baldwin, Stanley C
Will the real good guys please stand. Wheaton, Ill., Victor Books [c1971]
32 p. (Youth today book)
1. Revolutionists. I. Title. II. Series.
WHi NUC73-34835

Baldwin, Stanley C., joint author.
see MacGregor, Malcolm, 1945- Your money matters ... Minneapolis, Bethany Fellowship, 1977.

Baldwin, Stanley C.
see Mallory, James D The kink and I... ₍Wheaton, Ill.₎ Victor Books ₍1973₎

Baldwin, Sterling T.
see Kipps, Paul Henry, 1932- Trends in poultry slaughter, 1967-1972. Harrisonburg, Va., Bureau of Business and Economic Research, Madison College School of Business, 1973.

Baldwin, Sterling T
see Kipps, Paul Henry, 1932- Valley poultry slaughter, January-March, 1973. Harrisonburg, Va., Bureau of Business and Economic Research, Madison College School of Business, 1973.

Baldwin, Sterling T.
see Mills, Neil B Transportation development planning activities... [Harrisonburg, Va.] Madison College School of Business, Bureau of Business & Economic Research, 1973.

Baldwin, Teresa.
Impacts of Federal outlays in Washington State, 1966 to 1975 : report / prepared by Teresa Baldwin, Wendy Holden ; Washington State Office of Community Development, Office of the Governor. — ₍Olympia₎ : Office of Community Development, 1976.
120 p. ; 29 cm.
Bibliography: p. 119-120.
1. Grants-in-aid—Washington (State) I. Holden, Wendy, joint author. II. Washington (State). Office of Community Development. III. Title.
HJ755.B34 336.1′85 77-622014
77 MARC

Baldwin, Thelma L
Children's communication accuracy related to race and socioeconomic status [by] Thelma L. Baldwin, Paul T. McFarlane [and] Catherine J. Garvey. Baltimore, Center for the Study of Social Organization of Schools, Johns Hopkins University, 1970.
23 l. (Johns Hopkins University. Center for the Study of Social Organization of Schools. Report no. 62)
Includes bibliography.
1. Child study. 2. Communication—Social aspects. 3. Language arts (elementary). I. McFarlane, Paul T., joint author. II. Garvey, Catherine J., joint author. III. Title.
MiU NUC74-24142

Baldwin, Thelma L., joint author
see Garvey, Catherine J Studies in communication... Baltimore, Johns Hopkins University, 1970.

Baldwin, Thomas, b. 1750?
Narrative of the massacre of my wife and children / Thomas Baldwin. — New York : Garland Pub., 1977.
24 p., [1] fold. leaf of plates : ill. ; 23 cm. — (The Garland library of narratives of North American Indian captivities ; v. 52)
Issued with the reprint of the 1833 ed. of Priest, J. The captivity and sufferings of Gen. Freegift Patchin. New York, 1977.
Reprint of the 1835 ed. published by Martin and Wood, New York, under title: Narrative of the massacre, by the savages, of the wife and children of Thomas Baldwin ....
ISBN 0-8240-1676-9 (set) : $25.00
1. Indians of North America—Captivities. 2. Frontier and pioneer life—Kentucky. 3. Baldwin family. 4. Baldwin, Thomas, b. 1750? 5. Kentucky—Biography. I. Title. II. Series.
E85.G2 vol. 52 973'.04'97 76-51390
[E87] 76 MARC

Baldwin, Thomas, b. 1750?
Narrative of the massacre of my wife and children / Thomas Baldwin. — New York : Garland Pub., 1977.
24 p., [1] fold leaf of plates : ill. ; 23 cm. — (The Garland library of narratives of North American Indian captivities ; v. 52)
Issued with the reprint of the 1833 ed. of Priest, J. The captivity and sufferings of Gen. Freegift Patchin. New York, 1977.
"2nd edition."
Reprint of the 1836 ed. published by Martin & Perry, New York, under title: Narrative of the massacre, by the savages, of the wife and children of Thomas Baldwin ...
ISBN 0-8240-1676-9 (set) : $25.00
1. Indians of North America—Captivities. 2. Frontier and pioneer life—Kentucky. 3. Baldwin family. 4. Baldwin, Thomas, b. 1750? 5. Kentucky—Biography. I. Title. II. Series.
E85.G2 vol. 52 973'.04'97 s 76-51393
[E87] 76 MARC

Baldwin, Thomas, 1753-1826.
A catechism; or, compendium of Christian doctrine and practice, by Thomas Baldwin. 4th ed. Boston, Printed by Lincoln & Edmands, 1818.
34 p. illus. 15 cm.
Includes 5 hymns, without music.
L.C. copy imperfect: various pages mutilated; p. [[1]-[2], 15-16, and 33-34 wanting.
1. Baptists—Catechisms and creeds—English. I. Title.
BX6336.B34 1818 77-464358
77 MARC

Baldwin, Thomas, 1753-1826.
A catechism; or, compendium of Christian doctrine and practice, by Thomas Baldwin. 6th ed. Boston, Printed by Lincoln & Edmands, 1824.
34 p. illus. 15 cm.
Cover title: Dr. Baldwin's catechism.
Includes 5 hymns, without music.
1. Baptists—Catechisms and creeds—English. I. Title.
BX6336.B34 1824 77-358098
77 MARC

Baldwin, Thomas E
Municipal structure and expenditure change: the interaction of legislative insulation and racial socioeconomic dissimilarity in community decision making. [Cincinnati] 1973.
xxiii, 219 l. 29 cm.
Thesis (Ph.D.)—University of Cincinnati.
Bibliography: leaves 211-219.
OCU NUC76-71666

Baldwin, Thomas Frederick, 1933-
The Lansing Mexican-American community: a study of general problems and radio programming preferences [by] Thomas F. Baldwin, Ramon L. Merlos [and] Steven K. Meuche. [East Lansing, Michigan State University] 1970.
[28] l. 28 cm.
1. Radio audiences—Lansing, Mich. 2. Mexican Americans—Lansing, Mich. I. Merlos, Ramon L. II. Meuche, Steven K. III. Title.
Mi NUC75-108670

Baldwin, Thomas Frederick, 1933-
The WKAR and WKAR-FM audiences, November-December 1970. Prepared by Thomas F. Baldwin. Research assistants: Craig Stillwell [and] Gary Steinke. [East Lansing, ca. 1971]
1 v. (unpaged) 27 cm.
On cover: A survey of the audiences, 1970.
1. WKAR (Radio station) East Lansing, Mich. I. Michigan. State University, East Lansing. Continuing Education Service. II. Title.
Mi NUC73-123853

Baldwin, Thomas Oakley, 1947-
Structural studies on bullfrog hemoglobin. [Austin, Tex.] 1971.
iv, 195 l. illus. 29 cm.
Thesis (Ph.D.)—University of Texas at Austin.
Vita.
Bibliography: leaves 189-195.
1. Rana catesbeiana. 2. Bullfrog. 3. Hemoglobin.
TxU NUC73-123828

Baldwin, Thomas Pratt, 1941-
Hugo von Hofmannsthal and the grotesque. [n.p.] c1972.
285 l. 29 cm.
Thesis (Ph.D.)—University of Wisconsin.
Vita.
Includes bibliography.
1. Hofmannsthal, Hugo Hofmann, Edler von, 1874-1929.
WU NUC73-34783

Baldwin, Victor L
Isn't it time he outgrew this? Or, A training program for parents of retarded children, by Victor L. Baldwin, H. D. Bud Fredericks [and] Gerry Brodsky. Illus. by Mari VanDyke. Springfield, Ill., Thomas [1973]
xix, 209 p. illus. 24 cm.
1. Mentally handicapped children—Care and treatment. I. Fredericks, H. D. Bud, joint author. II. Brodsky, Gerry, joint author. III. Title. IV. Title: A training program for parents of retarded children.
RJ506.M4B35 649'.15'2 72-84136
ISBN 0-398-02626-X MARC

Baldwin, Victor L., joint author
see Frederick, H D Bud. A validity study of the diagnosis and placement of certified EMR pupils in Oregon... [Monmouth, 1969?]

Baldwin, Wayne J
Longer life for nehu, prepared by W.J. Baldwin, J.W. Struhsaker [and] G. Akiyama. Translated into the Japanese by Seiyei Wakukawa. Honolulu, University of Hawaii Sea Grant Program, 1972.
24 p. illus. (UNIHI-SEAGRANT-MS-71-01A)
English and Japanese on opposite pages.
"Study funded by the National Science Foundation Sea Grant Program and the State of Hawaii Fisheries Research Program."
1. Nehu. 2. Bait. I. Struhsaker, Jeannette W., joint author. II. Akiyama, Gerald S., joint author. III. Wakukawa, Seiyei, tr. IV. Title. V. Series: Hawaii. University, Honolulu. Sea Grant Program. UNIHI-SEAGRANT-MS-71-01A.
HU NUC74-132283

Baldwin, William A
Christian Science and vital Christianity : a lecture delivered at Germantown, Philadelphia, May 28, 1888 / by Wm. A. Baldwin. — Chicago : Wm. T. Baldwin, c1888.
23 p. ; 23 cm.
1. Christian Science—Addresses, essays, lectures. I. Title.
BX6945.B3 77-361811
77 MARC

Baldwin, William Edward, 1883-1966.
Baldwin's Ohio township law : with text and forms. — 4th ed. / rev. by William B. Shimp and Dennis S. Pines. — Cleveland : Banks-Baldwin Law Pub. Co., c1977-
1 v. : forms ; 27 cm. — (Baldwin's Ohio practice series)
First ed. published in 1939 under title: Ohio township officers manual.
Loose-leaf for updating.
Includes index.
1. Local government—Ohio. I. Shimp, William B. II. Pines, Dennis S. III. Banks-Baldwin Law Publishing Company, Cleveland. IV. Title. V. Title: Ohio township law.
KFO430.A3 1977 342'.771'09 77-371433
77 MARC

Baldwin, William Edward, 1883-1966.
see Bouvier, John, 1787-1851. Bouvier's Law dictionary. Baldwin's century ed. Cleveland, Banks-Baldwin Law Pub. Co., 1948, c1934.

Baldwin, William Edward, 1883-1966, ed.
see Ohio. Laws, statutes, etc. Baldwin's Ohio revised code ... 4th (50th anniversary) ed. Cleveland, Banks-Baldwin Law Pub. Co., [1971-

Baldwin, William Lee.
Structure and performance in a vertical market network : some policy implications for the Thai rice trade / by William L. Baldwin. -- [Bangkok : Thammasat University, Faculty of Economics, 1971?]
31 leaves : diagrs. ; 35 cm. -- ([Discussion paper series - Thammasat University, Faculty of Economics ; no. 2])
Caption title.
1. Rice--Thailand. 2. Rice--Marketing. 3. Rice--Prices. I. Title.
NIC NUC77-101196

Baldwin, William Lee.
see The Role of foreign financial assistance to Thailand in the 1980's ... Lexington, Mass., Lexington Books, [1975]

Baldwin, William W
Social problems of the Ojibwa Indians in the Collins area in Northwestern Ontario. [n.p., 1956?]
51-123 p. 29 cm.
Caption title.
1. Chippewa Indians—Social life and customs. 2. Acculturation. I. Title.
DeU NUC76-69502

Baldwin, William Walter, 1940-
Growth and phospholipid metabolism of Lineola longa. [Bloomington, Ind.] 1973.
173 p. illus.
Thesis (Ph.D.)—Indiana University.
Vita.
InU NUC75-17396

Baldwin-Ford, Pamela.
see Gordon, Bernard L. If an auk could talk. New York, H. Z. Walck, c1977.

Baldwin-Scarborough, Mayra.
Bicentennial bibliography, Essex County, New Jersey, 1973; basic history sources for boroughs, cities, towns, townships, and villages of Essex County, New Jersey, as selected by librarians from the public libraries. Mayra Baldwin-Scarborough, editor. [Nutley, N. J., American Revolution Bicentennial Committee, Special Libraries Association, N. J. Chapter, 1973]
1 v. (unpaged) 30 cm. $1.00
"The Essex County ID & beyond [slide program] by Mayra Baldwin-Scarborough" inserted at end.
1. Essex Co., N. J.—History—Bibliography—Union lists. 2. Catalogs, Union—Essex Co., N. J. 3. Libraries—Essex Co., N. J. I. Special Libraries Association. New Jersey Chapter. American Revolution Bicentennial Committee. II. Title.
Z1314.E8B35 016.91749'03'3 73-163983
MARC

Baldwin, Mich. Township Planning Commission.
Subdivision ordinance, Baldwin Township, Iosco Co., Michigan. Baldwin, Mich., 1968.
12 l. (HUD 701 Report)
1. Subdivision regulation—Baldwin, Mich.
DHUD NUC74-7439

Baldwin, Mich. Township Planning Commission.
Zoning ordinance, Baldwin Township, Iosco County, Michigan. Baldwin, Mich., 1968.
73 l. (HUD 701 Report)
1. Zoning legislation—Baldwin, Mich.
DHUD NUC74-7440

Baldwin, Mich. Township Planning Commission
see Raymond W. Mills and Associates. Capital improvements program, comprehensive community plan, Baldwin Township, Iosco County, Michigan. Midland, Mich., 1967.

Baldwin Bird Club
see Miller, Raymond F Biographies of people for whom birds have been named. Baldwin City, Kan., 1966-

Baldwin centennial historical album. Chippewa Falls, Wis., Culbert Swan Productions [1974]
164 p. illus.
1. Baldwin, Wis.—History.
WHi NUC76-18975

The Baldwin Consurvey, Starkville, Mississippi; consurvey city directory. Quality edition. Volume 5. -- Chillicothe, Ohio : Baldwin Consurvey Co., 1973.
505 p. ; 24 cm.
1. Starkville, Mississippi--Directories.
MsSM NUC77-101127

Baldwin-Lima-Hamilton Corporation.
The Baldwin Locomotive Works; catalogue of locomotives. An historic reprint. Ocean, N. J. Specialty Press [1972?]
125 p. illus. 16 x 24 cm.
Reprint of the 1915? ed. published by Rand McNally, New York.
1. Baldwin locomotives — Catalogs. I. Title: Catalogue of locomotives.
TJ625.B2B34 1972 625.2′61′0974811 72-96486
ISBN 0-913556-02-5 MARC

Baldwin-Lima-Hamilton Corporation.
History of the Baldwin Locomotive Works, 1831-1923. [Milwaukee, Old Line Publishers, 1971?]
210 p. illus. 24 cm.
1. Baldwin locomotives. I. Title.
MU NUC76-43478

Baldwin-Lima-Hamilton Corporation.
Locomotive number 60,000, an experimental locomotive. Omaha, Kratville Publications, 1969.
80 p. illus. 17 x 24 cm.
Reprint of 1928 edition.
"This book from the collection of William C. King."
1. Baldwin locomotives. I. Title.
IaU NUC74-24697

Baldwin-Lima-Hamilton Corporation.
The story of Eddystone / the Baldwin Locomotive Works, Philadelphia. — Felton, Calif. : Glenwood Publishers, [1974]
75 p., [1] leaf of plates : ill. ; 29 cm.
$8.95
1. Baldwin-Lima-Hamilton Corporation—History. I. Title.
TJ625.B2B34 1974 338.7′62′5261 74-193260
MARC

Baldwin-Lima-Hamilton Corporation
see Bell, Joseph Snowden, 1843- The development of the eight driving wheel locomotive. Philadelphia, Baldwin Locomotive Works, 1917, 1963.

Baldwin locomotives
see Duke, Donald, 1929- Southern Pacific steam locomotives... [Rev. ed.] San Marino, Calif., Golden West Books [1962]

The Baldwin M. Baldwin collection... [San Diego, 1972]
see under San Diego, Calif. Fine Arts Gallery.

Baldwin Park, Calif. Ordinances, local laws, etc.
[Municipal code. Baldwin Park, 1959]
1 v. (unpaged)
CLL NUC75-69984

Baldwin Park, Calif. Ordinances, local laws, etc.
Municipal code; ordinance no. 691. Adopted December 18, 1974. [Baldwin Park, Calif., City Clerk, 1975-
1 v. (Loose-leaf)
Cover title.
Caption title: Baldwin Park municipal code.
CLL NUC76-18951

Baldwin Piano & Organ Company
see The Keynote. Cincinnati.

Baldwin-Wallace College, Berea, Ohio
see MacLeod, William J Contagious ideas and dynamic events. [Berea, Ohio?] c1959.

Baldwin-Wallace College, Berea, Ohio. Emilie and Karl Riemenschneider Memorial Bach Library.
Supplemental catalog, no. 3. Compiled by Janet B. Winzenburger, Music Librarian, Baldwin-Wallace College. Berea, Ohio, Riemenschneider Bach Institute, Baldwin-Wallace College, 1972.
12 l. 28 cm.
1. Music—Bibliography—Catalogs. I. Winzenburger, Janet B. II. Title.
GU NUC76-82934

Baldwin-Wallace College, Berea, Ohio. Emilie and Karl Riemenschneider Memorial Bach Library.
Supplemental catalog of the Emilie and Karl Riemenschneider Memorial Bach Library. Compiled by Janet B. Winzenburger. Berea, Ohio, Riemenschneider Bach Institute, 1970.
46 l. 28 cm.
1. Bach, Johann Sebastian, 1685-1750—Bibl. I. Winzenburger, Janet B.
IU NUC74-12632

Baldwin-Whitehall School District
see Pittsburgh. Baldwin-Whitehall School District.

Baldwin's Ohio legislative service. 1971-
Cleveland, Banks-Baldwin Law Pub. Co.
v. 28 cm.
"Monthly reports ... with full text of all laws."
1. Legislation — Ohio. 2. Ohio. General Assembly. I. Banks-Baldwin Law Publishing Company, Cleveland. II. Title: Ohio legislative service.
KFO15.B34 348′.771′026 73-645782
ISSN 0092-0959 MARC-S

Baldwinsville, N. Y.
see Syracuse-Onondaga County Planning Agency. Planning reports. [Syracuse, N. Y., 1973-

Baldwinsville, N. Y. Ordinances, local laws, etc.
Code of the village of Baldwinsville, Onondaga County. Editor in Chief, H. H. J. Stoll. Spencerport, N. Y., General Code publishers, 1971-
2 pts. in 1 v. (loose-leaf) 26 cm.
Serial no. 48.
Contents.—pt. 1. Administrative ordinances.—pt. 2. General ordinances.
I. Stoll, H. H. J.
N NUC73-84629

Baldy, Alice Montgomery.
The romance of a Spainsh nun. By Alice Montgomery Baldy. Philadelphia, J. B. Lippincott Company, 1891.
199 p. 19 cm.
On cover: American novels.
Micro-transparency (negative). Louisville, Ky., Lost Cause Press, 1973. 4 sheets. 10.5 x 14.8 cm. (L. H. Wright. American fiction, 1876-1900, no. 255)
I. Title.
PSt NUC75-18514

Baldy, José Luis da Silveira, ed.
see Amato Neto, Vicente. Doenças transmissíveis. [Rio de Janeiro] Livraria Atheneu, 1972.

Baldy, Robert, joint author
see Barry, Michael Kaneti. 2,100 sixth formers... [London] Hutchinson Educational [c1971]

Baldzhiev, Iliía.
(Storete pŭt)
Сторете път. Стихотворения. (Худож. Георги Ковачев). (София) Профиздат, 1972.
103 p. with illus. 20 cm. 0.83 lv Bu 72-2858
I. Title.
PG1038.12.A43S8 74-316287

Bale, C G
Materials on wills and estate planning, compiled by C. G. Bale & C. W. Alexandrowicz. Kingston, Ont., Faculty of Law, Queen's University [1971?]
iv, 297 l. 36 cm.
Cover title.
On cover: Part II. Estate Planning.
Bibliographical footnotes.
1. Wills—Ontario. 2. Estate planning—Ontario. I. Alexandrowicz, G. W. II. Title.
CaBVaU NUC73-123882

Bale, Gurunanjappa S
Indentification of high risk Navaho children at birth ... Oklahoma City, 1972.
ix, 109 l. tables. 28 cm.
Bibliography: leaves 95-98.
Thesis (Ph. D.)—University of Oklahoma.
1. Infants—Mortality. 2. Navaho Indians. I. Title.
OkU-M NUC73-123826

Bale, Harvey Edgar, 1944-
The role of price and redistributional factors in the adjustment to exchange - rate devaluation. [College Park, Md.] 1972.
153 l. illus.
Typescript.
Thesis—University of Maryland.
Vita.
Includes bibliography.
1. Foreign exchange problem—Finland. 2. Foreign exchange problem—France. 3. Foreign exchange problem—Gt. Brit. 4. Currency question. I. Title.
MdU NUC73-123824

Bale, Jack B
Coastal and shore landforms of Baja California, Del Norte, Mexico, by Jack B. Bale and John A. Minch. Riverside, Calif. [1971]
85 p. col. illus., maps. 28 cm. (California. University, Riverside. Dept. of Geography. Technical report 0-71-2)
1. Coasts—Baja California. 2. Landforms—Baja California. I. Title. II. Series.
DME NUC75-26579

Bale, John.
Industrial estates : a bibliography and geographical introduction / John R. Bale. — Monticello, Ill. : Council of Planning Librarians, 1976.
17 p. ; 28 cm. — (Exchange bibliography ; 1022)
Cover title.
$1.50
1. Industrial districts—Bibliography. I. Title. II. Series: Council of Planning Librarians. Exchange bibliography ; 1022.
Z5942.C68 no. 1022 016.3092′08 s 76-367553
[Z7164.L9] 76 MARC
[HD1393.5]

Bale, John.
Perspectives in geographical education, edited by John Bale, Norman Graves [and] Rex Walford. [Edinburgh] Oliver & Boyd [1973]
307 p. illus. 22 cm. (Geography for teachers) £2.00 GB***
Includes bibliographies.
1. Geography—Study and teaching.—Addresses, essays, lectures. I. Graves, Norman John, joint author. II. Walford, Rex, joint author. III. Title.
G73.B17 910′.7′1042 74-158088
ISBN 0-05-002736-0 MARC

Bale, John, Bp. of Ossory, 1495-1563.
The epistle exhortatory of an English Christian, by Henry Stalbrydge (John Bale). 'Reply to Gosson,' by Thomas Lodge. Introductory notes by Peter Davison. New York, Johnson Reprint Corp., 1972.
28 l., 48 p. 16 cm. (Theatrum redivivum)
Reprint of The epistle exhortatorye of an Englyshe Christiane, published at Antwerp, 1544 (STC 1291), and of A reply to Stephen Gosson's Schoole of abuse in defense of poetry, musick, and stage plays, published 1579-80 (STC 16663).
1. Theater—Moral and religious aspects. I. Lodge, Thomas, 1558?-1625. A reply to Stephen Gosson's Schoole of abuse. 1972. II. Gosson, Stephen, 1554-1624. The schoole of abuse. III. Title. IV. Title: Reply to Gosson.
PN2047.B43 1972 792′.013 70-175662
MARC

Bale, John, Bp. of Ossory, 1495-1563.
The image of bothe churches, after the moste wonderfull and heauenly Reuelacion of Sainct John the Euangelist, contayning a very frutefull exposicion or paraphrase upon the same. Wherein it is conferred with the other scripturs, and most auctorised historyes. Compyled by John Bale. [Amsterdam, Theatrum Orbis Terrarum; New York, Da Capo Press, 1973]
1 v. (unpaged) 16 cm. (The English experience, its record in early printed books published in facsimile, no. 498)
Reprint of the 1548? ed. printed by R. Jugge, London.
"S. T. C. no. 1297."
Text of Revelation included.
1. Bible. N. T. Revelation—Commentaries. 2. Bible. N. T. Revelation—Paraphrases, English. I. Bible. N. T. Revelation. English. 1548. II. Title. III. Series.
BS2825.A2B34 1548a 228'.07 72-5965
ISBN 90-221-0498-2 MARC

Bale, John, Bp. of Ossory, 1495-1563.
Kynge Johan, a play in two parts. Edited by J. Payne Collier from the ms. of the author in the library of His Grace the Duke of Devonshire. London, Printed for the Camden Society by J.B. Nichols, 1838. New York, Johnson Reprint Corp. [1968]
xiv, 110 p. 23 cm. ([Camden Society. Publication no. 2])
1. John, King of England, 1167?-1216—Drama. I. Collier, John Payne, 1789-1883, ed. II. Title. III. Series: Camden Society, London. [Publications] Series, no. 1, v. 2.
MCE NUC74-158607

Bale, John, Bp. of Ossory, 1495-1563.
Kynge Johan, a play in two parts. Edited by J. Payne Collier from the ms. of the author in the library of His Grace the Duke of Devonshire. London, Printed for the Camden Society by J.B. Nichols, 1838 [1971]
xiv, 110 p. 22 cm. ([Camden Society, London. Publications, no. 2])
Microfilm. [New York, AMS Press, 1971] Partial reel. 35 mm.
1. John, King of England, 1167?-1216—Drama. I. Collier, John Payne, 1789-1883, ed. II. Title. III. Series.
OrPS NUC73-123851

Bale, John, Bp. of Ossory, 1495-1563.
Scriptorum illustrium Maioris Brytanniae catalogus. Basle 1557, 1559. Farnborough, Gregg, 1971.
2 v. illus., port. 28 cm.
Facsimile of the British Museum Grenville Library copy.
1. English literature—Early modern (to 1700)—Bibliography. 2. Gt. Brit.—Bio-bibliography. I. Title.
NhD NUC73-34785

Bale, Joy.
The storm's eye : a narrative in verse celebrating Cassius Marcellus Clay, man of freedom, 1810-1903 / by Joy Bale ; edited by Wade Hall, Alice Scott, Gregg Swem. — Louisville : Kentucky Poetry Press, [1974]
[32] p. ; 22 cm. — (Poets of Kentucky series ; no. 7)
1. Clay, Cassius Marcellus, 1810-1903—Poetry. I. Title.
PS3552.A452S8 811'.5'4 74-18658
MARC

Bale, Judith Robyn, 1945-
Chemical and physical studies of iron-sulfur proteins. [n. p.] 1974.
220 l. illus. 29 cm.
Thesis (Ph. D.)—University of Wisconsin.
Vita.
Includes bibliography.
I. Title.
WU NUC76-18972

Bale, Malcolm D., joint author.
see Ryan, Mary Ellen, 1928- An analysis of the relationship between U.S. wheat exports and Montana farm prices. Bozeman, Montana Agricultural Experiment Station, Montana State University, 1976.

Bale, Michael H.
Bale catalogue of Palestine & Israel postage stamps. Ilfracombe, Eng., Michael H. Bale.
v. ill. 24 cm.
Continues: Bale catalogue of Israel.
1. Postage-stamps—Israel—Catalogs—Periodicals. I. Title.
HE6185.P14B3 769'.5695694 75-643830
MARC-S

Bale, Michael H.
see Bale catalogue of Israel. 1969- Ilfracombe, Eng.

Bale, Robert.
Die Jagdberggemeinden. Bevölkerung u. Wirtschaft. [Mit Diagr. u. Tab.] Innsbruck, Wagner'sche Univ. Buchhandlung in Komm., 1972.
153 p. 21 cm. (Beiträge zur alpenländischen Wirtschafts- und Sozialforschung, Folge 154) S152.00 Au 73-4-66
Bibliography: p. 149-153.
1. Villages—Austria—Vorarlberg. 2. Vorarlberg—Economic conditions—Case studies. I. Title.
HT431.B32 73-317680

Bale, Ronald Mark.
The effect of task difficulty and incentive on the manifestation of learned helplessness in humans / Ronald Bale. -- [Cincinnati] 1975.
vii, 149 leaves ; 29 cm.
Thesis (Ph. D.)--University of Cincinnati, 1975.
Bibliography: leaves 109-115.
OCU NUC77-85724

Bale, Shelby G., ed.
see Conference on United States Polar Exploration, Washington, D. C., 1967. United States polar exploration. Athens, Ohio Univ. Press [1970]

Balē, Tilla.
Elegeies. Athēnai, 1957.
95 p. port. 25 cm.
I. Title.
OCU NUC74-120073

Bale catalogue of Israel. 1st- ed.; 1969-
Ilfracombe, Eng.
v. illus. 22 cm.
Compiled and published by M. H. Bale.
Continued by: Bale, Michael H. Bale catalogue of Palestine & Israel postage stamps.
1. Postage-stamps—Israel—Catalogs. I. Bale, Michael H.
HE6185.P14B3 72-615812
380.1'45'7695695694

Balea, Ilie.
Dialogul artelor; studii și eseuri. București, Editura pentru Literatură, 1969.
343 p. 21 cm.
Includes bibliographical references.
1. Music and literature. I. Title.
ML3849.B167D5 74-230801

Băleanu, Andrei.
see Cultura spectacolului teatral ... [București] "Meridiane" 1976.

Baleares. — 1. ed. — Barcelona : Editorial Noguer, 1974.
369 p. : ill. (some col.) ; 30 cm. — (Tierras de España) (Publicaciones de la Fundación Juan March)
Bibliography: p. 319-333.
Includes indexes.
CONTENTS: Rosselló Verger, V. M. Introducción geográfica.—Santamaría, A. Introducción histórica.—Moll, F. de B. Introducción literaria.—Sebastián, S. Arte.
ISBN 84-279-8004-3
1. Art — Balearic Islands — History. I. Roselló Verger, Vicente M.
N7109.B25B34 75-560618

Balearic Islands. Ilustre Colegio de Abogados
see
Ilustre Colegio de Abogados de Baleares.

Balearic Islands. Ilustre Colegio de Procuradores
see
Ilustre Colegio de Procuradores de Baleares.

Balearic Islands. Jefatura Agronomica de Baleares
see Pons Canals, Antonio. Planificación del cultivo del almendro. Palma de Mallorca [1970]

The Balearic Islands. [Edited by Jacques Heers] 2d rev. ed. Geneva, Nagel Publishers [1969, c1970]
127 p. illus. 16 cm. (Nagel's encylopedia guide)
1. Balearic Islands—Description and travel—Guide-books. I. Heers, Jacques. II. Nagel Publishers.
NNC NUC76-71706

Balech, Enrique.
Algunas especies nuevas o interesantes de tintinnidos del Golfo de Mexico y Caribe. Buenos Aires, Impr. y Casa Editora "Coni," 1968.
166-197 p. illus. (Revista del Museo Argentino de Ciencias Naturales "Bernardino Rivadavia" e Instituto Nacional de Investigación de las Ciencias Naturales. Hidrobiología, t. 2, no. 5)
"Trabajo de la Estación Hidrobiológica de Puerto Quequén."
Summary in English.
Includes bibliography.
1. Tintinnidae. I. Title.
CU DLC NUC73-122002

Balech, Enrique.
Cuarta contribución al conocimiento del género Protoperidinium. Buenos Aires, Coni, 1973.
[347]-368 p. 6 plates. 28 cm. (Revista del Museo Argentino de Ciencias Naturales "Bernardino Rivadavia" e Instituto Nacional de Investigación de las Ciencias Naturales. Hidrobiología, t. 3, no. 5)
Bibliography: p. 367-368.
1. Peridinium. I. Title.
IaU NUC76-71663

Balech, Enrique.
Dinoflagelados nuevos o interesantes del Golfo de Mexico y Caribe. Buenos Aires, Impr. y Casa Editora "Coni," 1967.
78-126 p. illus. (Revista del Museo Argentino de Ciencias Naturales "Bernardino Rivadavia" e Instituto Nacional de Investigación de las Ciencias Naturales. Hidrobiología, t. 2, no. 3)
"Trabajo de la Estación Hidrobiológica de Puerto Quequén."
Summary in English.
Includes bibliography.
1. Dinoflagellata. I. Title.
CU NUC73-124486

Balech, Enrique.
El género Cladopyxis (Dinoflagellata). Buenos Aires, Coni, 1964.
[27]-39 p. illus. 24 cm. (Comunicaciones del Museo Argentino de Ciencias Naturales "Bernardino Rivadavia" e Instituto Nacional de Investigación de las Ciencias Naturales. Hidrobiología, t. 1, no. 4)
At head of title: Ministerio de Educación y Justicia de la Nación. Subsecretaría de Cultura.
Summary in French.
Bibliography: p. 39.
1. Cladopyxis. I. Title.
IaU NUC76-71664

Balech, Enrique.
Microplancton de la campaña oceanográfica Productividad III. Buenos Aires, Coni, 1971.
202 p. map, 39 plates. 28 cm. (Revista del Museo Argentino de Ciencas Naturales "Bernardino Rivadavia" e Instituto de Investigación de las Ciencias Naturales. Hidrobiología, t. 3, no. 1)
"Trabajo de la estación hidrobiológica de Puerto Quequén."
Summary in English.
Bibliography: p. 196-201.
1. Marine plankton—Atlantic Ocean. I. Title.
IaU NUC76-71665

Balech, Enrique.
Microplancton del atlántico ecuatorial oeste (Equalant I) Buenos Aires, Servicio de Hidrografía Naval, 1971.
103 p. illus. 26 cm. $480
Summary in English.
"500 ejemplares."
"H. 654. Público."
Bibliography: p. 101-103.
1. Marine plankton—Atlantic Ocean. I. Title.
QH91.8.P5B28 574.92'4'6 73-205875

Balech, Enrique.
Notas históricas y críticas de la oceanografía biológica argentina. Buenos Aires, Servicio de Hidrografía Naval, 1971.
57 p. illus. 26 cm. $4.50
"H. 1027. Público."
Bibliography: p. 55-57.
1. Marine biology—Argentina. I. Argentine Republic. Servicio de Hidrografía Naval. II. Title.
QH91.25.A7B34 574.92'4'68 73-214405

Balech, Enrique.
Observaciones sobre dinoflagelados fósiles / Enrique Balech. -- Buenos Aires : Imprenta y casa editora "Coni", 1967.
20 p. : ill. ; 25 cm. -- (Comunicaciones : Paleontologia - Instituto Nacional de Investigación de las Ciencias Naturales ; t. 1, no. 2)
Summary in English.
Work by the Hydrobiologic Station of Puerto Quequén.
Bibliography: p. 19-20.
1. Dinoflagellata (fossil). I. Estación Hidrobiológica de Puerto Quequén. II. Title.
DI-GS NUC77-94500

Balech, Enrique.
Planktono kaj mara produktado / E. Balech. -- Liège, Belgium : Someraj Universitataj Kursoj, 1974.
88 leaves : ill. ; 29 cm. -- ([Someraj Universitataj Kursoj. ¶Kursotekstoj, KT 07])
Bibliography: leaves 75-81.
1. Marine plankton. 2. Esperanto--Technical Esperanto. I. Title. II. Series.
CU-S NUC77-101192

Baledón Gil, Arturo.
La Academia Nacional de Medicina ante los problemas médico-forenses [por] Arturo Baledón Gil, Alfonso Quiroz Cuarón y Javier Piña y Palacios. [1. ed.] México, Ediciones Botas, 1971.
64 p. 17 cm.
1. Academia Nacional de Medicina de México. 2. Medical jurisprudence—Mexico. I. Quiroz Cuarón, Alfonso, joint author. II. Piña y Palacios, Javier, joint author.
CU-B NUC73-34786

Baleeiro, Aliomar.
Cinco aulas de finanças e política fiscal / Aliomar Baleeiro. — 2. ed., rev., com autorização da Universidade Federal da Bahia. — São Paulo : J. Bushatsky, c1975.
160 p. ; 22 cm.
Includes bibliographies and index.
1. Fiscal policy. 2. Finance, Public. I. Title.
HJ181.B27 1975 75-520474
76 MARC

Baleeiro, Aliomar.
Direito tributário brasileiro. 4. ed., rev. e acrescida de um apêndice. Rio [de Janeiro] Forense, 1972.
xxiv, 600 p. 22 cm. Cr$60.00
Includes text of the Código tributário nacional.
Bibliography: p. [573]-[576]
1. Taxation—Brazil—Law. I. Brazil. Laws, statutes, etc. Código tributário nacional. 1972. II. Title.
73-203402

Baleeiro, Aliomar.
Direito tributário brasileiro. 6. ed. rev. e acrescida de um apêndice. Rio [de Janeiro] Forense, 1974 [c1970]
xxiv, 606 p. 22 cm. Cr$80.00
Includes text of the Código tributário nacional.
Bibliography: p. [573]-577.
1. Taxation—Brazil—Law. I. Brazil. Laws, statutes, etc. Código tributário nacional. 1974. II. Title.
74-223473

Baleeiro, Aliomar.
Direito tributário brasileiro / Aliomar Baleeiro. — 8. ed., rev. e acrescida de um apêndice. — Rio de Janeiro : Forense, 1976.
xx, 626 p. ; 22 cm.
Includes text of the Código tributário nacional.
Bibliography: p. 589-594.
Includes index.
Cr$130.00
1. Taxation—Brazil—Law. I. Brazil. Laws, statutes, etc. Código tributário nacional. 1976. II. Title.
343'.81'04 76-486424
76 MARC

Baleeiro, Aliomar.
Uma introdução à ciência das finanças. 10. ed. rev. e adaptada à Constituiçao de 1969, ao Código Tributário Nacional e à legislação posterior. Rio [de Janeiro] Forense, 1974.
517 p. illus. 24 cm.
Bibliography: p. [501]-505.
1. Finance, Public. 2. Finance, Public—Brazil. I. Title.
TxU NUC76-18974

Baleeiro, Aliomar.
Limitações constitucionais ao poder de tributar / Aliomar Baleeiro. — 3. ed. rev., de acordo com a Emenda constitucional no. 1, de 1969, e com o C. T. N. — Rio [de Janeiro] : Forense, 1974.
419 p. ; 24 cm.
Includes bibliographical references and index.
Cr$100.00
1. Taxation—Brazil—Law. I. Title.
75-533594

Baleeiro, Aliomar.
Limitações consitutionais ao poder de tributar / Aliomar Baleeiro. 4. ed. rev. de acordo com a Emenda Constitucional no. 1, de 1969, e com o C.T.N. -- Río de Janeiro : Forense, 1974.
420 p. ; 24 cm.
Includes bibliographical references and index.
1. Taxation--Brazil--Law. I. Title.
FU-L NUC77-101193

Baleeiro, Aliomar
see Aspectos de impôsto único sôbre minerais. Salvador, Brazil [Editôra Mensageiro] 1971.

Baleeiro, Aliomar
see Motta, Cândido. Rui, homem de letras... Brasília, Academia Brasiliense de Letras, 1972.

Baleen whales in eastern North Pacific and Arctic waters. [Compiled by Alice Seed. Cover sketch and drawings by Maxine Morse. Seattle, Pacific Search [1972]
44 p. illus. 21 cm. (Pacific search books)
Cover title.
Bibliography: p. 43.
1. Whales—North Pacific Ocean. 2. Whales—Arctic Ocean. I. Seed, Alice, ed.
QL737.C42B34 599'.51'091643 72-98717
MARC

Baleful beasts and eerie creatures / Introd. by Andre Norton ; illustrated by Rod Ruth. — Chicago : Rand McNally, c1976.
124 p. : ill. (some col.) ;
CONTENTS: Butler, B. The patchwork monkey.—Gessner, L. The Yamadan.—Land, C. Monster blood.—Lightner, A. M. Tigger.—Wellman, A. The spell of spirit stones.—Smith, R. R. The night creature.—Rathjen, C. H. To face a monster.—Bednarz, W. You a what you eat.—Ritchie, R. Nightmare in a box.
ISBN 0-528-82171-7 : $5.95. ISBN 0-528-80211-9 lib. bdg. : $5.97
1. Horror tales, American. [1. Horror stories. 2. Short stories] I. Ruth, Rod.
PZ5.B216 813'.0872 76-20529
76 MARC

Baleha, IUriĭ Ivanovych
see Vishchyĭ vohon'. 1974.

Baleiko, Marc O
The molecular theory of transport processes in dense polyatomic gas mixtures. [Minneapolis] 1971.
vii, 256 l. 29 cm.
Thesis (Ph.D.)—University of Minnesota.
Bibliography: leaves 255-256.
MnU NUC73-34787

Bálek, Alexej.
Dlouhodobý vývoj investic, počtu obyvatelstva, pracujících a národního důchodu v ČSSR v číslech / Alexej Bálek, Dagmar Škodová. — Praha : Ekonomický ústav ČSAV, 1972.
51 p. ; 20 cm. — (Informační publikace - Československá akademie věd, Ekonomický ústav ; č. 101) Cz***
1. Czechoslovak Republic—Statistics. I. Škodová, Dagmar, joint author. II. Title. III. Series: Československá akademie věd. Ekonomický ústav. Informační publikace : č. 101.
HB9.C38 č. 101 75-546506
[HA1196]

Bálek, František.
Poslední šance. 1. vyd. Praha, NV, t. SG, Most, 1973.
147, [2] p. front. 20 cm. (Stopa, sv. 11) Kčs13.00 Cz 73
I. Title.
PG5039.12.A36P6 74-333484

Bálek, František.
Smrtihlav. Il. Josef Jícha. 1. vyd. Plzeň, Západočes nakl., t. Stráž, Vimperk, 1972.
192, [1] p. illus. 21 cm. Kčs18.00 Cz 72-SKČ
Illustrated t. p.
I. Title.
PG5039.12.A36S6 73-307982

Bálek, František.
Spiknutí stínů / František Bálek. — 1. vyd. — Plzeň : Západočes. nakl., 1975.
208 p. ; 21 cm. Cz 75
Kčs17.50
I. Title.
PG5039.12.A36S65 76-518304

Balek, J
On extreme flood in Zambia [by] J. Balek. Lusaka, 1971.
9, [8] l. illus. 33 cm. (Zambia. National Council for Scientific Research. Water Resources research report WR 11) (NCSR/TR 19)
Bibliography: leaf [8]
1. Floods–Zambia. I. Title.
DI-GS NUC76-71748

Balek, J
Water balance of the Zambesi Basin / J. Balek. — Lusaka : National Council for Scientific Research, Zambia, 1971.
21, [9] leaves (2 fold.), [13] leaves of plates (3 fold.) ; 30 cm. — (Water resources research report ; WR 8)
"NCSR/TR 15."
Bibliography: leaf 20 (1st group)
1. Water balance (Hydrology)—Zambesi River watershed. I. Title. II. Series.
GB809.Z35B34 551.4'8'096894 77-360930
77 MARC

Balekchîan, Georgiĭ Grigor'evich.
(Otsenka kachestva produktsiĭ v promyshlennom proizvodstve)
Оценка качества продукции в промышленном производстве. Минск, Изд-во БГУ, 1973.
88 p. with diagrs. 20 cm. 0.48rub USSR 73
At head of title: Г. Г. Балекчян.
Bibliography: p. 86-[87]
1. Quality control. I. Title.
TS156.B36 74-312356

Balella, Giovanni.
see Mussolini giurista. [Roma] Il Diritto fascista, [1937?]

Balen, A. Th. M. van, joint author.
see Henkes, Harold E. Oogheelkunde... Amsterdam, Elsevier, 1976.

Balen, Loraine Maria Ferla.
O sentir interior : [poesias] / Loraine Maria Ferla Balen. — Caxias do Sul [Brasil : s. n.], 1974.
59 p. ; 22 cm.
Cr$10.00
I. Title.
PQ9698.12.A42S4 75-580925

Balen Blanken, Gerard Cornelis van, 1852-1939
see Veurman, B W E Dokter in West-Friesland. [Hoorn, "West-Friesland", 1964?]

Balen-Chavannes, A E van.
Bibliografie van de geschiedenis van Zuid-Holland tot 1966, samengesteld door A. E. van Balen-Chavannes. Met indices van J. H. Rombach en J. E. H. Rombach-de Kievid. Delft, Culturele Raad van Zuid-Holland, 1972.
310 p. 25 cm. Ne***
1. Holland, South (Province)—History—Bibliography. I. Title.
Z2454.H64B34 73-336010

Balendran, V S
Ground water in Ceylon / by V. S. Balendran. — [Moratuwa? : Published for the Geological Survey Dept. by the Documentation & Publications Division of the Industrial Development Board of Ceylon], 1970.
17 p. : ill., map ; 26 cm. — (Mineral information series ; no 1)
At head of cover title: Ministry of Industries & Scientific Affairs.
Includes bibliographical references.
Rs2.50
1. Water, Underground—Ceylon. I. Title. II. Series.
GB1159.C4B34 551.4'9'095493 75-907831
76 MARC

Balendu Sekaram, Kandavalli, 1909-
The Andhras through the ages / by K. Balendu Sekharam. — Hyderabad, India : Sri Saraswati Book Depot, 1973.
2 v. in 1 ; 22 cm.
Bibliography: p. [265]-266.
Includes index.
Rs40.00
1. Andhra Pradesh, India—History. I. Title.
DS485.A55B3 954'.84 74-902721
76 MARC

Balendu Sekaram, Kandavalli, 1909-
The Nayaks of Madura, by Khandavalli Balendusekharam. [1st ed.] Hyderabad, Andhra Pradesh Sahithya Akademi [1975]
30 p. 22 cm.
"World Telugu Conference publication."
1. Madura—Kings and rulers. I. Title.
IaU NUC77-84373

Balendu Sekaram, Kandavalli, 1909–
Nayaks of Tanjore / by Khandavalli Balendusekharam. — Hyderabad : Andhra Pradesh Sahitya Akademi, 1975.
vi, 44 p. ; 22 cm. — (ప్రపంచ తెలుగు మహాసభల ప్రచురణ)
Prefatory matter in Telugu.
Rs2.00

1. Tanjore, India (District)—History. I. Title. II. Series: World Telugu Conference, Hyderabad, India, 1975. World Telugu series.
DS485.T3B34 954′.82 75–904043

Balenko, I͡Uriĭ Kornilovich
see Spravochnik po korabel'noĭ avtomatike. 1974.

Balensi, Yvan.
Les conventions entre les sociétés commerciales et leurs dirigeants / Yvan Balensi ; préf. de Jean Hémard. — Paris : Economica, 1975.
vii, 194 p. ; 22 cm. — (Collection Études juridiques) (Série Droit des affaires) F***
Bibliography: p. [181]-184.
ISBN 2-7178-0089-1
1. Directors of corporations—France. I. Title.
346′.44′0664 75-517101
76 MARC

Balent, Boris
see Bardejovské katechizmy z rokov 1581 a 1612. [Turčiansky sv. Martin. Nákladom P. Fábryho, 1947]

Balent, Boris
see Bratislava. Slovenská národná galéria. Exlibrisy Martina Benku... [V Bratislave, 1968]

Balentović, Ivo.
Gole priče. ⟨Ilustracije: Josip Babogredac [i dr.]⟩. Umag, Za ⟨izdavača: Ivo Balentović⟩, 1973.
131, [3] p. 19 cm. (Mala biblioteka "Susreti," sv. 2) Yu 74
I. Title.
PG1619.12.A45G6 74–970354

Balentović, Ivo.
Preko devet brda i dolina. Novele. Oprema i crteži u tekstu: Ivo Balentović. Crtež naslovne strane: Zora Balentović. Umag, Naklada: Ivo Balentović, 1973.
125 p. with illus. 19 cm. (Mala biblioteka "Susreti," sv. 1)
22.00Din Yu 73
I. Title.
PG1619.12.A45P7 73–970394

Balentović, Ivo
see Osamljeni svirač. Umag, Matica hrvatska, 1970.

Baleōzian, Nshan S
see
Paleōzian, Nshan S 1873-1923.

Balerdi, Fermin Francisco, 1931-
The response by sweet potatoes to various calcium salts applied to providence silt loam and stough very fine sandy loam soils ... [n.p.] 1971.
xi, 118 l. illus. 29 cm.
Thesis (Ph.D.)–Louisiana State University, Baton Rouge.
Vita.
Bibliography: leaves 113-117.
Includes abstract.
1. Sweet potatoes. I. Title.
LU NUC73-123837

Bales, Carol Ann, 1940–
Chinatown Sunday: the story of Lilliann Der. Chicago, Reilly & Lee Books [1973]
[32] p. illus. 29 cm.
SUMMARY: A ten-year-old Chinese-American girl describes her family and their life in a Chicago suburb.
1. Der, Lilliann—Juvenile literature. 2. Chinese in the United States—Juvenile literature. [1. Chinese in the United States] I. Title.
E184.C5B185 917.3′06′951 73–6481
MARC

Bales, Carol Ann, 1940-
see Cloud, Kevin. Kevin Cloud... Chicago, Reilly & Lee Books [1972]

Bales, Charles F 1897-
Twice a boy / by Charles F. Bales. — Terre Haute, Ind. : Sycamore Press, c1976.
xi, 127 p. : ill. ; 23 cm.
1. Bales, Charles F., 1897- 2. United States—Biography. I. Title.
CT275.B344A37 973.9′092′4 77-150224
77 MARC

Bales, Eugene.
Plotinus: A critical examination. [Columbia] 1973.
228 l.
Thesis (Ph.D.)—University of Missouri.
Vita.
Includes bibliography.
MoU NUC76-71674

Bales, Eugene.
Plotinus: A critical examination. [Columbia] 1973.
228 l.
Thesis (Ph.D.)—University of Missouri.
Vita.
Microfilm copy.
Includes bibliography.
MoU NUC76-71675

Bales, Harold W.
see Basic surgery. New York, Macmillan, c1977.

Bales, James D 1915–
Instrumental music and New Testament worship, by James D. Bales. Searcy? Ark. [1973]
299 p. 22 cm.
Bibliography: p. 281–294.
1. Music in churches. I. Title.
ML3001.B2 264′.2 73–169351
MARC

Bales, James D 1915-
Modernism: Trojan horse in the church [by] James D. Bales. Searcy, Ark., c1971.
234 p.
Bibliographical references included in "Footnotes" (p. 228-234)
1. Modernism. I. Title.
TNDC NUC73-34788

Bales, James D 1915-
Pentecostalism in the church / by James D. Bales. -- Shreveport, Louisiana : Lambert Book House, c1972.
112 p.
1. Pentecostal churches. 2. Gifts, Spiritual. I. Title.
IObT NUC77-101194

Bales, James D 1915-
Prophecy and premillennialism : the cross before the crown / James D. Bales. -- Searcy, Arkansas : Bales, c1972.
236 p.
1. Millennium. 2. Bible--Prophecy. I. Title.
IObT NUC77-101189

Bales, James D 1915-
The sower goes forth, by James D. Bales. Shreveport, La., Lambert Book House, c1973.
173 p.
Includes bibliographical references.
1. The sower (Parable) 2. Jesus Christ–Parables. I. Title.
TNDC NUC76-71685

Bales, James D 1915-
Studies in Hebrews / by James D. Bales. -- Shreveport, Louisiana : Lambert Book House, c1972.
172 p.
Bibliography: p. 170-172.
1. Bible. N. T. Hebrews--Study--Outlines, syllabi, etc. I. Title.
IObT NUC77-101195

Bales, James D 1915-
The sufficiency of the Scriptures. Searcy, Ark., Bales Bookstore [n.d.]
64 p. illus.
Cover title.
1. Fundamentalism. I. Title.
CtHC NUC73-78960

Bales, James D., 1915- comp.
see Hoover, John Edgar, 1895-1972. J. Edgar Hoover speaks concerning communism. [Nutley, N.J.] Craig Press [c1970]

Bales, James D., 1915- comp.
see Hoover, John Edgar, 1895-1972. J. Edgar Hoover speaks concerning communism. Washington, Capitol Hill Press [1971, c1970]

Bales, Kent Roslyn.
Nathaniel Hawthorne's use of the sublime. [n.p.] 1967 [c1968. Ann Arbor, Mich., University Microfilms, 1972]
204 l.
Thesis—University of California.
Bibliography: leaves 200-204.
Photocopy. 21 cm.
1. Hawthorne, Nathaniel, 1804-1864. 2. Sublime, The. I. Title.
CSt NUC73-34778

Bales, Milton M
Types of the Holy Spirit and other addresses. New York, Alliance Press [n.d.]
148 p. frontis. 19 cm.
1. Holy spirit—Addresses, essays, lectures. 2. Sanctification. 3. Typology (Theology) I. Title.
IEG NUC73-71302

Bales, Richard.
Proust and the Middle Ages / Richard Bales. — Genève : Droz, 1975.
vi, 165 p. : facsims. ; 24 cm. — (Histoire des idées et critique littéraire ; 147) Sw75-A-6430
Based on thesis, University of London.
Bibliography: p. 147-159.
Includes index.
48.00F
1. Proust, Marcel, 1871-1922—Knowledge—History. 2. Middle Ages in literature. I. Title.
PQ2631.R63Z4635 843′.9′12 76-355678
76 MARC

Bales, Robert Freed, 1916-
A set of categories for the analysis of small group interaction / Robert F. Bales. -- (Indianapolis : Bobbs-Merrill, 197-?]
[251]-263 p. : ill. ; 28 cm. -- (Bobbs-Merrill reprint series in the social sciences, S-5)
Caption title.
"Paper read at the annual meeting of the American Sociological Society held in New York, December 28-30, 1949."
Reprinted from American sociological review, vol. 15, April, 1950.
Issued with Channels of communication in small groups. [Indianapolis, Bobbs-Merrill, 19-?]
1. Small groups. 2. Social interaction. I. Title.
PSt NUC77-86723

Bales, Robert Freed, 1916, joint author
see Parsons, Talcott, 1902- Apuntes sobre la teoría de la acción. Buenos Aires, Amorrortu [1970]

Bales, Ronald E.
see Producers Creamery Company. Removing radionuclides from fresh milk. Rockville, Md., 1966.

Bales, Vivian D., joint author
see Ball, Bonnie (Sage) The Dickenson families of England and America ... Searcy, Ark., Mrs. L. E. Presley, [1972]

Bales, William Alan.
The seeker / William Alan Bales. — New York : McGraw-Hill, c1976.
130 p. ; 22 cm.
ISBN 0-07-003557-1
I. Title.
PZ4.B1819 Se 813′.5′4 75-34415
[PS3552.A4524] 75 MARC

Balescu, R
Equilibrium and nonequilibrium statistical mechanics / Radu Balescu. — New York : Wiley, [1975]
xiv, 742 p. : ill. ; 23 cm.
"A Wiley-Interscience publication."
Includes bibliographies and indexes.
ISBN 0-471-04600-0
1. Statistical mechanics. I. Title.
QC174.8.B34 1975 530.1′3 74-20907
74 MARC

Balesdent, R
Grammaire méthodique de l'espagnol moderne, avec exercices : à l'usage de l'enseignement secondaire et du premier cycle de l'enseignement supérieur / R. Balesdent et N. Marotte. — [Paris] : Ophrys, c1975.
281 p. ; 24 cm. F***
Includes index.
ISBN 2-7080-0415-8
1. Spanish language—Text-books for foreigners—French. I. Marotte, N., joint author. II. Title.
PC4129.F7B27 468'.2'441 76-485495
76 MARC

Baleshwar Ramyadav
see
Yādava, Bāleśvara Rāma, 1937-

Baleste, Marcel.
L'économie française / par Marcel Baleste. — 3. éd. entièrement refondue. — Paris : Masson, 1974.
244 p. : ill. (some col.) ; 24 cm. — (Collection Géographie) F***
Includes bibliographies.
ISBN 2-225-39941-7
1. France—Economic conditions—1945- I. Title.
HC276.2.B26 1974 330.9'44'083 74-76396
MARC

Baleste, Marcel.
L'économie française / par Marcel Baleste. — 4. éd. entièrement refondue. — Paris ; New York : Masson, 1976.
263 p. : ill. (some col.) ; 24 cm. — (Collection Géographie ISSN 0338-2664) F***
Includes bibliographies.
ISBN 2-225-45694-1 : 52.00F
1. France—Economic conditions—1945- I. Title.
HC276.2.B26 1976 330.9'44'083 77-455748
77 MARC

Baleste, Marcel
see Ambrosi, Christian. Les grandes puissances du monde contemporain... [Paris] Delagrave, 1973-

Balestier, Wolcott, 1861-1891
see Kipling, Rudyard, 1865-1936. The naulahka... New York and London, Macmillan, 1892 [1973]

Balestin, Gary Gene, 1949-
Effects of unilateral cerebral trauma on language and cognitive structure / by Gary Gene Balestin. --[s.l. : s.n.], 1976.
vii, 181 leaves : ill. ; 28 cm.
Thesis (Ph.D.)--University of Chicago.
Bibliography: leaves 162-181.
1. Aphasia. 2. Speech, Disorders of. I. Title.
ICU NUC77-85148

Balestra, Carlos Fontan
see Fontan Balestra, Carlos.

Balestra, Cesare.
I servizi postali della Marina italiana nella seconda guerra mondiale : contenente il catalogo degli annulli delle navi da guerra che presero parte al conflitto con la loro valutazione / C. Balestra, A. Cecchi ; con la collaborazione di B. Cadioli. — Firenze : G. Orlandini, c1974.
219 p. : ill. ; 27 cm. It 75-Oct
Bibliography : p. 211.
Includes index.
1. Cancellations (Philately) — Italy. 2. Italy. Marina — Postal service. 3. World War, 1939-1945—Postal service. I. Cecchi, Aldo, joint author. II. Title.
VG65.I 8B34 75-404861

Balestra, Fernando.
Pirandello e il teatro dei problemi / [Fernando Balestra]. — Roma : Cremonese, 1975.
128 p. ; 19 cm. — (Uomini e problemi ; 27) It76-June
Bibliography: p. 127-128.
L1500
1. Pirandello, Luigi, 1867-1936—Criticism and interpretation. 2. Pirandello, Luigi, 1867-1936—Influence. 3. Italian drama—20th century—History and criticism. I. Title.
PQ4835.I7Z5347 77-564279
*77 MARC

Balestra, Juan, 1861-
El noventa; una evolución política argentina. 4. ed. [Buenos Aires] Luis Farina [1971]
252 p. 20 cm.
1. Argentine republic—Pol. & govt.—1860- I. Title.
PPT NUC73-34794

Balestra, Pietro, 1935–
Calcul matriciel pour économistes. ([Avec la collab. de] Aurelio Mattei.) Albeuve, Éditions Castella (1972).
xii, 243 p. 24 cm. 21.00F Sw 72-A-3266
Bibliography: p. 238-240.
1. Matrices. I. Title.
QA188.B34 73-339311

Balestra, Pietro, 1935-
Industrial labor in Western Europe : a research report / by the Long Range Planning Service, Stanford Research Institute ; [by Pietro Balestra]. — Menlo Park, Calif. : The Service, 1974.
20 p. ; 28 cm. — (Report - Long Range Planning Service, Stanford Research Institute ; no. 516)
Cover title.
"Report group: European."
Includes bibliographical references.
1. Labor supply—Europe. 2. Labor and laboring classes—Europe. I. Stanford Research Institute. Long Range Planning Service. II. Title. III. Series: Stanford Research Institute. Long Range Planning Service. Report ; no. 516.
HC101.S77 no. 516 330'.08 s 76-374417
[HD5764.A6] 76 MARC

Balestra, Pietro, 1935-
Pooling cross-section and time-series data in the estimation of a dynamic model: the demand for natural gas by Pietro Balestra and Marc Nerlove. Stanford, California, Stanford University, 1964.
47 p. (Stanford University-Institute for Mathematical studies in the Social Sciences. Technical report no. 8)
"Prepared under the auspices of National Science Foundation Grant GS-142."
Includes bibliographical references.
1. Time-series analysis. 2. Gas, Natural. I. Nerlove, Marc, 1933-
MH-PA NUC76-71687

Balestra, Réginald
see Kramer, Daniel. Nyon. Genève, Editions générales S.A., Benjamin Laederer [1967]

Balestra, René H 1929–
Las oligarquías zurdas / René H. Balestra ; prólogo de Alfredo Orgaz. — Buenos Aires : Ediciones Líbera, [1974]
149 p. ; 20 cm.
1. Political science. 2. Totalitarianism. 3. Justice. I. Title.
JA69.S6B35 75-574929

Balestra, Tito.
Quiproquo / Tito Balestra. — 1. ed. — Milano : Garzanti, 1974.
153 p. ; 22 cm. It***
Poems.
L4000
I. Title.
PQ4862.A369Q5 75-551646

Balestrazzi, Giuseppe.
Vecchia Parma cara al cuore ... Parma, Artegrafica Silva, 1971.
124 p. plates. 24 cm. N. T. It 72-May
Articles previously published in the Gazzetta di Parma.
1. Parma—Biography—Anecdotes, facetiae, satire, etc. I. Title.
DG975.P25B33 72-361586

Balestreri, Leonida.
Brigata G. Balilla. (Pagine della lotta partigiana). Presentazione de Vittorio Pertusio. Novi Ligure, Quaderni de Il novese, 1971.
182 p. illus. 21½ cm. (Quaderni de "Il Novese," n. 4) L2000 It 71-Nov
"IIa edizione riveduta."
Supplement to Il Novese, 1971, no. 3.
1. World War, 1939-1945—Underground movements—Genoa (Province) 2. Brigata G. Balilla. I. Series: Il Novese. Quaderni, n. 4.
D802.I 82G442 1971 73-312431

Balestreri, Roberto, joint author
see Scopinaro, Domenico. Gli ormoni della corteccia surrenale... Genova, Pagano, 1963.

Balestrieri, Antonio
see Etologia e psichiatria. Bari: Laterza, [1974]

Balestrieri, Giovanni.
Alcuni interventi di assistenza tecnica nella zona di Capua. Di Giovanni Balestrieri e Carlo Perone Pacifico. Portici, Della Torre, 1969.
53 p. 24½ cm. (Centro di specializzazione e ricerche economico-agrarie per il Mezzogiorno. Assistenza tecnica, 3) It Suppl-4
At head of title: Cassa per il Mezzogiorno; Università di Napoli; Centro di Specializzazione e ricerche economico-agrarie per il Mezzogiorno.
Summaries in English.
Includes bibliographical references.
CONTENTS: Balestrieri, G. Intervento per l'introduzione di nuove colture.—Perone Pacifico, C. Un problema di organizzazione per la commercializzazione: il latte.
1. Plant introduction—Italy—Addresses, essays, lectures. 2. Milk trade—Italy—Addresses, essays, lectures. I. Perone Pacifico, Carlo. II. Title.
SB108.I 8B34 72-371100

Balestrieri-Terrasi, Marinella
see La Produttività delle aziende agrarie in comprensori irrigui del Mezzogiorno... Portici, Della Torre, 1971-

Balestrini, Bruno, illus.
see 1200 years of Italian sculpture. New York, H. N. Abrams [1973]

Balestrini, Nanni.
Poesie pratiche, 1954-1969 / Nanni Balestrini. — Torino : G. Einaudi, c1976.
158 p. ; 18 cm. — (Collezione di poesia ; 133) It76-July
"Le poesie comprese in questa raccolta fanno parte dei libri Come si agisce ... Ma noi facciamone un'altra ... Senza lacrime per le rose ... è inedita."
L2500
I. Title.
PQ4862.A37P6 76-472197
*76 MARC

Balestrini, Nanni.
Prendiamoci tutto. Conferenza per un romanzo: letteratura e lotta di classe. Milano, Feltrinelli, 1972.
34 p. 17 cm. (Libelli) L200 It 73-Sept
1. Balestrini, Nanni. Vogliamo tutto. 2. Labor and laboring classes in literature. I. Title.
PQ4862.A37V632 73-366602

Balestrini, Nanni.
La violenza illustrata / Nanni Balestrini. — Torino : Einaudi, c1976.
131 p. ; 22 cm. It76-May
L3000
I. Title.
PQ4862.A37V5 76-461505
*76 MARC

Balestrini, Nanni.
Vogliamo tutto : romanzo / Nanni Balestrini. — Milano : Feltrinelli, 1973.
155 p. ; 18 cm. — (Universale economica ; 677) It 73-Nov
L1000
I. Title.
PQ4862.A37V6 1973 75-582441

Balestrini, Nanni, joint author
see Argento, Dario. Le cinque giornate. Milano: Bompiani [1974]

Balestrini, Nanni
see Argento, Dario. Profondo thrilling. Milano: Sonzogno, 1975.

Balestrini, Nanni
see Parmiggiani, Claudio. Alfabeto. Milano, L'uomo e l'arte, 1974.

Balestrini C , César.
Los precios del petróleo y la participación fiscal de Venezuela / César Balestrini C. — Caracas : Universidad Central de Venezuela, Facultad de Ciencias Económicas y Sociales, División de Publicaciones, 1974.
131 p. : graphs ; 19 cm. — (Colección Esquema)
"Anexos de las Gacetas oficiales que contienen las resoluciones sobre valores de exportación": p. 49-130.
Bibliography: p. 131.
1. Petroleum industry and trade—Venezuela. 2. Petroleum products—Prices—Venezuela. I. Title.
HD9574.V42B28 74-228527

Balestrino, Philip.
Fat and skinny. Illustrated by Pam Makie. New York, Crowell [1975]
33 p. col. illus. 21 x 23 cm. (Let's-read-and-find-out science books)
SUMMARY: Briefly explains how metabolism affects how fat or skinny a person is.
ISBN 0-690-00454-0. ISBN 0-690-00665-9 (lib. bdg.).
1. Metabolism—Juvenile literature. [1. Metabolism] I. Makie, Pam, illus. II. Title.
QP171.B315 1975 612'.39 74-12306
74 MARC

Balestro, Piero.
Dialogo o ideologia? J. B. von Hirscher: l'idea del regno di Dio tra illuminismo e romanticismo. Torino, Borla, 1971 [i. e. 1972].
253 p. 21 cm. (Le Idee e la vita, 64) L2700 It 72-Nov
Includes bibliographical references.
1. Kingdom of God—History of doctrines. 2. Hirscher, Johann Baptist von, 1788-1865. I. Title.
BT94.B32 1972 73-318637

Bāleśvara Prasāda, Rai Bahadur, comp.
[Loka paraloka hitakārī]
लोक परलोक हितकारी; जिसमें सौ से अधिक स्वदेशी और विदेशी संतों महात्माओं, विद्वानों, और ग्रंथों के अनुमान साढ़े छः सौ चुने हुए बचन दिए गये हैं. सम्पादक बालेश्वर प्रसाद, उर्फ प्रेम प्रसाद. [आगरा, राधास्वामी सतसंग] 1968.
10, 245 p. port. 19 cm. (संतबानी पुस्तक-माला) Rs2.00
In Hindi.
1. Conduct of life. I. Title.
BJ1588.H5B35 72-923357

Bāleśvara Rāma Yādava
see
Yādava, Bāleśvara Rāma, 1937

Baleswari, N 1928–
[Cumaitāṅki]
ந. பாலேஸ்வரி எழுதிய சுமைதாங்கி. 1. பதிப்பு. [யாழ்ப்பாணம்?] நரேசி வெளியீடு, 1973.
71 p. 19 cm. Rs1.90
In Tamil.
Short stories.
CONTENTS: சுமைதாங்கி.—இது தான் உலகம்.—மகா தியாகி.—எல்லைக் கோடு.—டெரலின் ஷேட்.—ஜெயந்தியின் தந்தி.
I. Title.
Title romanized: Na. Pālēsvari eḷutiya Cumaitāṅki.
PL4758.9.B34C78 73-905753

Baleswari, N 1928–
(Pūjaikku vanta malar)
பூஜைக்கு வந்த மலர்; [சமூக நாவல். எழுதியவர்] ந. பாலேஸ்வரி. 1. பதிப்பு. கொழும்பு, வீரகேசரி பிரசுரம், 1972.
159 p. Rs2.25
In Tamil.
Previously published serially in Mittiraṉ.
I. Title.
PL4758.9.B34P8 72-904729

Balet, Jan B 1913-
Joanjo; eine Geschichte aus Portugal. Erzählt und gemalt von Jan Balet. München, A. Betz Verlag [c1965]
[30] p. col. illus. 25 x 31 cm. (Bilderbücher der Sechs)
I. Title.
MB NUC74-137602

(Balet i ėstetika)
Балетъ и эстетика / составилъ N. — [s. l. : s. n.], 1896 (С.-Петербургъ : Тип. В. М. Курочкина)
45 p., [1] leaf of plates : port. ; 22 cm.
1. Dancing. 2. Ballet. I. N.
GV1795.B28 75-559097

Baletas, Geōrgios, 1907–
[Iōannēs Gryparēs ho prōtos metasolōmikos]
Ἰωάννης Γρυπάρης ὁ πρῶτος μετασολωμικός· βίος, ἔργο, ἐποχή [ἔγραψε] Γ. Βαλέτας. Ἀθήνα, Ἐκδόσεις Πηγῆς, 1970.
599 p. illus. 22 cm. (Μεγάλες μορφές τῆς Ἑλληνικῆς λογοτεχνίας)
Bibliography: p. 562–578.
1. Gryparēs, I. N., 1870–1942. I. Title.
PA5610.G78B3 72-225022

Baletas, Geōrgios, 1907-
Iōannēs Polemēs; hē zōē kai to ergo tou. 2. symplērōmenē ekd. Athēna, Dōrikos, 1970.
77 p. port. illus. 22 cm.
1. Polemēs, Iōannēs, 1862-1924. I. Title.
ICU NUC74-120040

Baletas, Geōrgios, 1907–
(Lexiko Neoellēniko philologiko)
Λεξικὸ Νεοελληνικὸ φιλολογικό: βιογραφίες ποιητῶν καὶ συγγραφέων· κατάλληλο βοήθημα τῶν μαθητῶν τοῦ δημοτικοῦ καὶ τοῦ γυμνασίου [ὑπὸ] Γ. Βαλέτα. Ἀθήνα, Ἐκδόσεις Παρνασσὸς Γ. Μπατζακίδη [196–]
191 p. ports. 22 cm.
1. Authors, Greek (Modern)—Biography. 2. Greece, Modern—Biography. I. Title.
PA5240.B3 77-513880

Baletas, Geōrgios, 1907-
Papadiamantēs; hē zōē, to ergo, hē epochē tou, philologikē meletē. Ekd. 2. [Athēna, Archaios Ekdot. Oikos Dēmētrakou, 1957.]
685 p. illus., ports.
1. Papadiamantēs, Alexandros, 1851-1911.
CLU OCU NUC74-123154

Baletas, Geōrgios, 1907- ed.
see Aiolika grammata. 1971-

Baletas, Geōrgios, 1907- ed.
see Ephtaliōtēs, Argyrēs, 1849-1923. [Works] Hapanta. 1952-

Baletas, Geōrgios, 1907-
see Gryparēs, I N 1870-1942. Hapanta ta prōtotypa me ta merika metaphrasmata. 2. ekd. symplērōmenē. Athēna, Dōrikos, 1967.

Baletas, Geōrgios, 1907- ed.
see Hellenike nomarchia. 1948-49 [cover 1949]

Baletas, Geōrgios, 1907- ed.
see Karkabitsas, Andreas, 1866-1923. Ta hapanta... Athēnai, Ch. Giovanēs, 1973.

Baletas, Geōrgios, 1907- ed.
see Koraēs, Adamantios, 1748-1833. (Koraēs, hapanta ta prōtotypa erga) [1964-65]

Baletas, Georgios, 1907- ed.
see Malakasēs, Miltiadēs, 1869-1913. Hapanta. Athēna, A. Redman (Hellas) [1964]

Baletas, Georgios, 1907- ed.
see Nirbanas, Paulos, pseud., 1866-1937. Ta hapanta... Athenai, Ekdot. Oikos Ch. Giovane, 1968.

Baletas, Geōrgios, 1907-
see Petrōph, Iōannēs, 1849-1922. Atlas tou hyper anexartesias hierou ton Hellenon agonos. 1971.

Baletas, Georgios, 1907-
see Tertsetēs, Geōrgios, 1800-1874. Works. [1954]

Baletas, Kōstas G
see
Valetas, Kōstas G

Baletić, Alica Wertheimer-
see Wertheimer-Baletić, Alica, 1937-

Baletka, Ladislav.
Kunovice. 1272–1972. Minulost a přítomnost valašské obce. Kunovice, MNV, t. MTZ 26, Valašské Meziříčí, 1972.
95, [1] p. [16] p. of plates. 20 cm. Cz 72
1. Kunovice, Czechoslovak Republic (Vsetín)
DB879.K976B3 73-350462

Baletka, Ladislav, joint author
see Borovička, Milan. Valašské Meziřiči. Ostrava, Profil, Čes. Těšin, 1973.

Baletoman
see
Skal'kovskiĭ, Konstantin Apollonovich, 1843-1905.

Balett Intézet
see
Állami Balett Intézet.

Balettas, Spyridōn
see Valettas, Spyridōn.

Balette, Bernard, joint author
see Guerrée, Henri. Pratique de l'assainissement des agglomérations urbaines et rurales. 6. éd. mise à jour. Paris, Eyrolles, 1972 [c1961]

Balety Birgit Cullberg / [red. Zbigniew Krawczykowski]. — [Warszawa : Teatr Wielki, 1975?]
1 portfolio (4 pamphlets) : ill. ; 24 cm. P***
Cover title.
Summaries also in French.
CONTENTS: Birgit Cullberg.—Adam i Ewa.—Księżowy renifer.—Panna Julia.
zł14.00
1. Ballet. 2. Birgit Cullberg. I. Krawczykowski, Zbigniew.
GV1790.A1B34 77-510344

Balev, Boris.
(Nash Dimitrovski komsomol)
Наш Димитровски комсомол : за учениците от VII и VIII кл. / Борис Балев. — София : Нар. младеж, 1975.
213 p. ; 20 cm. — (В помощ на политическата учебна година в Димитровския комсомол) Bu 76-471
Series romanized: V pomosht na politicheskata uchebna godina v Dimitrovskiia komsomol.
Bibliography: p. 208–[210]
0.52 lv
1. Dimitrovski komunisticheski mladezhki sŭiuz. I. Title.
HQ799.B8B35 76-514965

Balev, Boris.
Спътник на комсомолския активист в дружеството. [Автор Борис Балев] София, 1970.
52 p. 20 cm. Bu***
At head of title: Димитровски комунистически младежки съюз. Централен комитет. Отдел "Организационен."
1. Dimitrovski komunnisticheski mladezhki suiuz. I. Dimitrovski komunisticheski mladezhki sŭiuz. Otdel Organizatsionen. II. Title.
Title romanized: Spŭtnik na komsomolskiia aktivist v druzhestvoto.
HQ799.B82D542 73-322513

Balev, Milko, ed.
see Zhivkov, Todor. Ausgewählte Reden und Aufsätze. Wien, Globus Verl. (1973).

Balev, Viktor
see Radev, Radi Iankov. (Tekhniko-ikonomicheski vŭprosi na tsenoobrazuvaneto pri vŭglishtata) 1963.

Balevičius, K
Lietuvos gamtos paminklai. Vilnius, "Mintis," 1971.
192 p. with illus. 16 cm. (Lietuvos gamta) 0.33rub. USSR 72-203
At head of title: K. Balevičius.
1. Nature conservation—Lithuania. 2. Natural history—Lithuania. I. Title.
QH77.L5B34 72-370600

Balevics, Zigmunds
see Latvian S.S.R. Valsts centrālais archīvs. Reliģiskais sektantism Latvijā, 1920-1940 ... Rīgā, Latvijas valsts izdevniecība, 1962.

Balevics, Zigmunds
see Psihologija un religija... Riga, Zinatne, 1973.

Balevska, Elka.
(Bŭlgarska leksikologiia i leksikografiia)
Българска лексикология и лексикография. 1944–1968. Библиогр. София, БАН, 1973.
166 p. 22.5 cm. 1.47 lv Bu 73-2869
At head of title: Българска академия на науките. Институт за български език.
1. Bulgarian language—Lexicology—Bibliography. 2. Bulgarian language—Lexicography—Bibliography. 3. Lexicology—Bibliography. 4. Lexicography—Bibliography. I. Title.
Z2898.L5B34 74-320954

Balevska, P.
see International Colloquium on Bioenergetics and Mitochondria, 5th, Varna, Bulgaria, 1975. Bioenergetics and mitochondria ... Sofia, Pub. House of the Bulgarian Academy of Sciences, 1976.

Balevska, R K
Номенклатура и систематика на дивите и история на прадомашните животни в нашите земи. София, Изд-во на Българската академия на науките, 1968.
175 p. illus. 21 cm. 1.38 (pbk.)
At head of title: Академия на селскостопанските науки. Р. К. Балевска, Ал. Петров.
Bibliography: p. 158–166.
1. Domestic animals—History. 2. Zoology—Classification. I. Petrov, Aleksandŭr, joint author. II. Title.
Title romanized: Nomenklatura i sistematika na divite i istoriia na pradomashnite zhivotni v nashite zemi.
SF41.B33 72-228212

Balevski, Angel.
(Problemi na naukata i obrazovanieto)
Проблеми на науката и образованието. ⟨Избрани докл., статии и изказвания⟩. Под ред. [с предг.] на Пантелей Зарев. София, БАН, 1974.
202 p. 24.5 cm. 2.28 lv Bu 74-1533
Added t. p.: Problèmes de la science et de l'éducation.
Summary in Russian, French, English and German.
Table of contents also in Russian, French, English and German.
Includes bibliographical references.
1. Science—History—Bulgaria. 2. Engineering—Study and teaching—Bulgaria. 3. Bŭlgarska akademiia na naukite, Sofia. 4. Science and state—Bulgaria. I. Title. II. Title: Problèmes de la science et de l'éducation.
Q127.B9B34 74-353290

Balevski, Angel.
(V proslava na 250-godishninata na Akademiiata na naukite na SSSR)
В прослава на 250-годишнината на Академията на науките на СССР : докл. пред тържественото заседание на общото събрание на БАН, състояло се на 19 апр. 1974 г. в столичната зала Г. Кирков / Ангел Балевски. — София : Бан, 1975.
33 p. : ill. ; 20 cm. Bu 75-295
0.30 lv
1. Akademiia nauk SSSR—History. 2. Bulgaria—Relations (general) with Russia. 3. Russia—Relations (general) with Bulgaria. I. Title.
AS262.A68B34 75-531694

Balevski, Angel, ed.
see Nemsko-bŭlgarski mashinostroitelen rechnik. 1972.

Balevski, Boris.
Chiprovtsi; [istoricheski ocherk. By] B. Balevski. Sofiia, Izd-vo na Natsionalniia sŭvet na Otechestveniia front, 1968.
55 p. illus. (Bashtino ognishte)
1. Chiprovtsi, Bŭlgaria.
MH NUC74-21946

Balevski, Dano.
(Prebroiavane)
Преброяване : 1975 : резултати, перспективи / Дано Балевски. — 1. изд. — София : Партиздат, 1976.
119 p. : ill. ; 17 cm. — (Въпроси на деня) Bu 76-1444
Series romanized: Vŭprosi na deniia.
0.34 lv
1. Bulgaria—Census, 1975. I. Title.
HA1626.B34 76-531097

Balevski, Krŭst'o.
(Novi nasoki na kontsentratsiiata, spetsializatsiiata i integratsiiata na selskostopanskoto proizvodstvo i prerabotvashtata promishlenost vŭv Vrachanski okrŭg)
Нови насоки на концентрацията, специализацията и интеграцията на селскостопанското производство и преработващата промишленост във Врачански окръг : доклад, изнесен от Кръстьо Балевски - председател на ОНС на съвместното заседание на ОК на БКП, БЗНС, ОНС и ОКС - гр. Враца. — Враца : [s. n.], 1970.
79 p. ; 20 cm.
At head of title: Okrŭzhen Komitet na BKP - Vratsa, and other organizations.
1. Agriculture—Bulgaria—Vratsa (Okrŭg) I. Title.
S469.B82V733 75-590253

Balewa, Abubakar Tafawa, Sir, 1912-1966.
Shaihu Umar / na Sir Abubakar Tafawa Balewa. — Zaria : Northern Nigerian Pub. Co., c1966.
49 p. : ill. ; 22 cm.
I. Title.
PL8234.B3S5 1966 75-402431

Balewa, Abubakar Tafawa, Sir, 1912-1916. Shaihu Umar.
see Ladan, Umaru. Shaihu Umar. London, Longman, 1975.

Balewicz, Aleksander.
Analiza ekonomiczna nowych rozwiazań w budynkach doswiadczalnych i przykładowych na wsi. [Wyd. 1] Warszawa, Arkady, 1967.
59 p. illus. (Prace In-tu Techniki Budowlanej, nr. 293)
Seria II. Konstrukcje budowlane i inzynieryjne, nr. 39.
At head of title: Aleksander Balewicz, Zygmunt Racięcki.
Summaries in English, Polish, and Russian.
ICRL NUC74-137610

Baley, James A. Gymnastics in the schools
see Baley, James A Handbook of gymnastics in the schools... Boston, Allyn and Bacon [1974]

Baley, James A
Handbook of gymnastics in the schools: instructional, exhibitional, and competitive gymnastics for men and women [by] James A. Baley. Boston, Allyn and Bacon [1974]
x, 340 p. illus. 26 cm.
"Portions of this book were published previously in Gymnastics in the schools," in 1965.
Includes bibliographical references.
1. Gymnastics—Study and teaching. I. Baley, James A. Gymnastics in the schools. II. Title. III. Title: Gymnastics in the schools.
GV461.B32 796.4'07 73-84244
MARC

Baley, James A
Illustrated guide to developing athletic strength, power, and agility / James A. Baley. — West Nyack, N.Y. : Parker Pub. Co., c1977.
223 p. : ill. ; 23 cm.
ISBN 0-13-450999-4 : $10.95
1. Physical education and training. 2. Exercise. I. Title. II. Title: Developing athletic strength, power, and agility.
GV711.5.B34 796.4'07 76-23440
76 MARC

Baley, James A
Physical education and the physical educator / James A. Baley, David A. Field. — 2d ed. — Boston : Allyn and Bacon, c1976.
ix, 390 p. : ill. ; 24 cm.
Includes bibliographical references and index.
ISBN 0-205-05052-2 : $10.95
1. Physical education and training—Philosophy. I. Field, David Albert, 1917- joint author. II. Title.
[DNLM: 1. Physical education and training. 2. Teaching. QT255 B184p]
GV342.B3 1976 613.7 75-20056
75 MARC

Baley, John Dennis.
Cost-effectiveness of three methods of remedial instruction in mastery learning and the relationship between aptitude and achievement. [n.p.] 1972.
iv, 95 l. illus. 28 cm.
Thesis (Ed.D.)—University of Southern California.
Typewritten.
1. Remedial teaching. 2. Academic achievement. I. Title.
CLSU NUC73-123836

Balezin, S H
Mechanism for the formation of sugars from formaldehyde. II; K voprosu o mekhaninzme obrazovaniya skharov iz pormal'degida. II. Translated from: Zhurnal obshchey khimii, 1968. 17 (12): 2288-2291. [n.p., 1968?]
1 v.
Translated by National Aeronautics and Space Administration.
I. Title.
DNAL NUC73-47468

Balezin, Stepan Afanas'evich.
(Praktikum po fizicheskoĭ i kolloidnoĭ khimii)
Практикум по физической и коллоидной химии. [Для биол.-хим. фак. пед. ин-тов]. Изд. 4-е, доп. Москва, "Просвещение," 1972.
278 p. with illus. 21 cm. 0.50rub USSR 72-VKP
At head of title: С. А. Балезин.
Bibliography: p. [276]
1. Chemistry, Physical and theoretical—Laboratory manuals. I. Title.
QD457.B3 1972 73-322952

Balezin, Stepan Afanas'evich.
(Vydaiushchiesia russkie uchenye-khimiki)
Выдающиеся русские ученые-химики / С. А. Балезин и С. Д. Бесков. — Изд. 2-е, перераб. — Москва : Просвещение, 1972.
220, [4] p. : ill., ports. ; 21 cm. — (Пособие для учителей) USSR 72
Bibliography: p. 219-[221]
0.46rub
1. Chemists—Russia. I. Beskov, Sergeĭ Dmitrievich, joint author. II. Title.
QD21.B3 1972 75-558779

Balezin, Stepan Afanas'evich
see Ingibitory korrozii metallov. 1972.

Balezin, Vadim Pavlovich.
[Pravovoĭ rezhim zemel' sel'skikh naselennykh punktov]
Правовой режим земель сельских населенных пунктов. Москва, Изд-во Моск. ун-та, 1972.
224 p. 22 cm. 1.17rub USSR 72-VKP
At head of title: В. П. Балезин.
Includes bibliographical references.
1. Land tenure—Russia—Law. I. Title.
73-303801

Balezin, Vadim Pavlovich
see Abramova, Aleksandra Afanas'evna. Osnovy sovetskogo grazhdanskogo, trudovogo, zemel'nogo i kolkhoznogo prava. 1968.

Baleztena, Ignacio
see
Premin de Iruña.

Baleztena Ascárate, Ignacio
see
Premin de Iruña.

Balf, Mary.
The mighty company; Kamloops and the H. B. C. [Kamloops, B. C.] Kamloops Museum, 1973.
15 p. 22 cm.
Cover title.
1. Hudson's Bay Company—Hist. 2. Kamloops, B. C.—Hist. I. Title.
CaBVaU NUC75-18526

Balf, Mary.
The overlanders and other North Thompson travellers. [Kamloops, B. C.] Kamloops Museum, 1973.
15 p.
Cover title.
1. Frontier and pioneer life—Kamloops, B. C.
CaOTP CaBVaU NUC75-18511

Balf, Mary.
Ship ahoy! Paddlewheelers of the Thompson waterway. [Kamloops, B. C.] Kamloops Museum, 1973.
12 p. 22 cm.
Cover title.
1. British Columbia—Hist—1871-1918. 2. Thompson River, B. C. I. Title.
CaBVaU CaOTP NUC75-17398

Balf, Miriam, joint comp.
see Corbin, Richard K comp. Twelve American plays. Alternate ed. New York, Scribner [c1973]

Balfe, Margaret
see Analysis of international Great Lakes shipping and hinterland. Milwaukee, Center for Great Lakes Studies, University of Wisconsin--Milwaukee, 1975.

Balfe, Richard G
Charles P. Neill and the United States Bureau of Labor; a study in progressive economics, social work and public administration, by Richard G. Balfe. [n.p.] 1956.
v, 237 l.
Thesis—University of Notre Dame.
Vita.
Bibliography: leaves 214-236.
Photocopy of typescript. Ann Arbor, Mich., University Microfilms, 1974. 22 cm.
1. Neill, Charles Patrick, 1865-1942. 2. United States. Bureau of Labor. I. Title.
ViU NUC76-27463

Balfet, H.
see Pratiques et représentations de l'espace dans les communautés méditerranéennes. Paris, Éditions du Centre national de la recherche scientifique, 1976.

Balfet, Hélène.
Céramique ancienne en Proche-Orient, Israël et Liban, VIe-IIIe millénaire; étude technique. Paris [École pratique des hautes études] 1962.
200 p.
Thèse—École pratique des hautes études, Paris.
Microfiche (negative) Paris, Institut d'ethnologie, 1971. 4 sheets, 11 x 15 cm.
1. Pottery, Ancient—Near East. I. Title.
WU NUC75-26577

Balfi, Éric.
Artefact / Éric Balfi. — Paris : Éditions Saint-Germain-des-Prés, c1976.
59 p. ; 19 cm. — (Collection A l'écoute des sources) F***
ISBN 2-243-00245-0 : 14.00F
I. Title.
PQ2662.A377A9 841'.9'14 77-450992
77 MARC

Balfoort, Dirk Jacobus, 1886- ed.
see Wasielewski, Wilhelm Joseph von, 1822-1896. De viool en hare meesters... 's Gravenhage, J. P. Kruseman [n.d.]

Balfoort, Maurits.
De vorstinnen van Brugge. Naar de vertellingen van Maurits Sabbe. Met vele foto's uit het gelijknamige televisiefeuilleton. Antwerpen, Utrecht, Standaard Uitgeverij, [1973].
142 p. illus. 25 cm. Be 73-Nov
ISBN 90-02-12083-4 : 125F
I. Sabbe, Maurits, 1873-1938. II. Title.
PT6466.12.A43V6 74-354397

Balfour of Inchrye, Harold Harington Balfour, Baron
see
Balfour, Harold Harington, Baron Balfour of Inchrye, 1897-

Balfour, Alexander.
Basic numerical analysis with Algol. [By] A. Balfour [and] W. T. Beveridge. London, Heinemann Educational Books [c1972]
239 p. illus.
Bibliography: p. [235]
1. Numerical analysis—Computer programs. 2. ALGOL (Computer program language). I. Beveridge, Walter Thomson, joint author. II. Title.
ScU NUC75-26592

Balfour, Alice Blanche.
Twelve hundred miles in a waggon. Salisbury, Pioneer Head, 1970.
265 p. illus. (The Heritage series, v. 2)
1. Africa, South—Description and travel. 2. Africa, East—Description and travel. I. Title.
MiEM NUC73-47467

Balfour, Arthur James Balfour, 1st Earl of, 1848-1930.
Criticism and beauty, a lecture rewritten ... by the Right Honourable Arthur James Balfour, M.P. Oxford, The Clarendon press, 1910.
48 p. 25 cm. (Romanes lecture, 1909)
Ultra microfiche. Dayton, Ohio, National Cash Register, 1970. 3d title of 8. 10.5 x 14.8 cm. (PCMI library collection, 104-3)
1. Aesthetics. I. Title.
KEmT NUC73-122031

Balfour, Arthur James Balfour, 1st Earl of, 1848-1930.
Essays and addresses. Freeport, N. Y., Books for Libraries Press [1972]
vi, 314 p. 22 cm. (Essay index reprint series)
Reprint of the 1893 ed.
CONTENTS: The pleasures of reading.—Bishop Berkeley's life and letters.—Handel.—Cobden and the Manchester school.—Politics and political economy.—A fragment on progress.—The religion of humanity.
I. Title.
PR4057.B135E7 1972 824'.8 72-3422
ISBN 0-8369-2890-3 MARC

Balfour, Arthur James Balfour, 1st Earl of, 1848-1930.
Speeches on Zionism, by the Right Hon. the Earl of Balfour. Edited by Israel Cohen; with a foreword by the Rt. Hon. Sir Herbert Samuel. New York, Kraus Reprint, 1971.
128 p. 24 cm.
"First published in 1928."
1. Zionism. I. Cohen, Israel, 1879- ed.
NBuU NUC73-34834

Balfour, Boyce Burton, 1943-
Spatial planning and analysis of the location of public school facilities / by Boyce Burton Balfour, II. -- Raleigh : North Carolina State University, 1974.
xi, 163 leaves : ill. ; 29 cm.
Bibliography: leaves 114-116.
Vita.
Thesis--North Carolina State University.
I. Title.
NcRS NUC77-101190

Balfour, Campbell.
Incomes policy and the public sector. London, Routledge and Kegan Paul, 1972.
xiii, 276 p. 23 cm. index. £3.50 B 72-27742
Bibliography: p. [265]-272.
1. Wage-price policy—Great Britain. 2. Wages—Great Britain. 3. National Board for Prices and Incomes. I. Title.
HC260.W24B3 331.2'1'0942 72-171225
ISBN 0-7100-7306-2 MARC

Balfour, Campbell.
Industrial relations in the Common Market, London, Boston, Routledge and Kegan Paul, 1972.
xi, 132 p. 22 cm. £2.00 B 72-26386
Bibliography: p. 131-132.
1. Industrial relations—European Economic Community countries. 2. European Economic Community. I. Title.
HD8380.5.B24 1972 331'.094 72-90115
ISBN 0-7100-7436-0; 0-7100-7437-9 (pbk.) MARC

Balfour, Campbell.
Participation in industry, edited by Campbell Balfour. London, Croom Helm [1973]
217 p. 22 cm. £4.00 GB***
Bibliography: p. 213-214.
1. Employees' representation in management—Great Britain. 2. Employees' representation in management—European Economic Community countries. I. Title.
HD5660.G7B27 331 73-178521
ISBN 0-85664-030-1; 0-85664-058-1 (pbk.) MARC

Balfour, Campbell.
Participation in industry. Edited by Campbell Balfour. Totowa, N. J., Rowman and Littlefield [1973]
217 p. 23 cm. $13.50
Bibliography: p. 213-214.
1. Employees' representation in management—Great Britain. 2. Employees' representation in management—European Economic Community countries. I. Title.
HD5660.G7B27 1973b 331 73-178337
ISBN 0-87471-429-X

Balfour, Campbell.
Unions and the law. Farnborough, Saxon House Lexington, Mass., Lexington Books, 1973.
vii, 141 p. 24 cm. £3.00 GB 73-25254
Bibliography: p. 135-136.
Includes index.
1. Trade-unions—Great Britain. I. Title.
KD3050.Z9B34 344'.42'01 73-5248
ISBN 0-347-01003-2 MARC

Balfour, Charlotte Cornish, tr.
see Clara of Assisi, Saint, d. 1253. The life and legend of the Lady Saint Clare. London, New York [etc.] Longmans, Green and co., 1910.

Balfour, Conrad, 1928-
A sack full of sun. Minneapolis, Dillon Press [1974]
169 p. facsim. 21 cm.
Autobiographical.
1. Balfour, Conrad, 1928- I. Title.
E185.97.B2A36 977.6'05'0924 [B] 74-8763
ISBN 0-87518-074-4 MARC

Balfour, D. M.
see Roodnat, A C A tour of the Anne Frank House in Amsterdam. [Amsterdam] Anne Frank Foundation [1971]

Balfour, David E.
see McIntosh, Eduard. Islas Galapagos; notes on anchorages. [Guayaquil, Ecuador, Impreso en Cromos Cia., Ltda., 197-?]

Balfour, E
Orkney birds—status and guide, by E. Balfour; with a note on rarities by Roy H. Dennis. Stromness, C. Senior, 1973.
64 p. illus., maps. 22 cm. £0.65 B 73-05147
Bibliography: p. 62-63.
1. Birds—Scotland—Orkney Islands. I. Dennis, Roy H. II. Title.
QL690.S4B34 598.2'9411'2 73-160096
ISBN 0-9502648-0-6 MARC

Balfour, Edward Green, 1813-1889.
Encyclopaedia Asiatica, comprising Indian Subcontinent, eastern and southern Asia : commercial, industrial, and scientific / by Edward Balfour. — New Delhi : Cosmo Publications, 1976.
9 v. ; 29 cm.
"The present work was originally published with the title Cyclopaedia of India and of eastern and southern Asia in 1858 ..."
Reprint of the 3d ed., 1885, published by Bernard Quaritch, London.
CONTENTS: v. 1. A-Boehmeria.—v. 2. Boehmeria-Cumin.—v. 3. Cumin-Gyrocarpus.—v. 4. H. Jangtang.—v. 5. Japan-Maibee.—v. 6. Maidah-Nysa.—v. 7. O-Rhamneae.—v. 8. Rhapis-Tanglal.—v. 9. Tangal-Zymoosht.
Rs150.00 per vol.
1. India—Dictionaries and encyclopedias. 2. Asia—Dictionaries and encyclopedias. I. Title.
DS405.B18 1976 950'.03 76-911330
77 MARC

Balfour, Evelyn Barbara, Lady, 1898- The Haughley experiment. 1975.
in Balfour, Evelyn Barbara, Lady, 1898- The living soil and The Haughley experiment. New rev. ed. London, Faber and Faber, 1975.

Balfour, Evelyn Barbara, Lady, 1898-
The living soil and The Haughley experiment / E. B. Balfour. — New rev. ed. — London : Faber and Faber, 1975.
383 p. : ill. ; 23 cm. GB***
"Part one was first published as The living soil, in 1943."
Bibliography: p. [371]-373.
Includes index.
ISBN 0-571-10713-3 : £5.25
1. Soils. 2. Compost. 3. Soil micro-organisms. 4. Nutrition. 5. Organic gardening. I. Balfour, Evelyn Barbara, Lady, 1898- The Haughley experiment. 1975. II. Title. III. Title: The Haughley experiment.
S591.B16 1975 631.4 76-353925
76 MARC

Balfour, Evelyn Barbara, Lady, 1898-
The living soil and the Haughley Experiment / E. B. Balfour. — New York : Universe Books, 1976, c1975.
383 p. ; 23 cm.
Reprint of the first seven chapters of The living soil (first published in 1943) forms Part 1 of the present book. Part 2, The story of the Haughley Experiment, was written with the colaboration of R. F. Milton.
Bibliography: p. [371]-373.
Includes index.
ISBN 0-87663-269-X : $15.00
1. Soils. 2. Nutrition. 3. Organic gardening. 4. Haughley research farms limited, Ipswich, Eng. I. Title. II. Title: The Haughley Experiment.
S591.B158 1976 631.4 75-27030
76 MARC

Balfour, Francis Maitland, 1851-1882.
A treatise on comparative embryology, by Francis M. Balfour... London, Macmillan and co., 1880-81.
2 v. illus. 24 cm.
Forms v. 2-3 of the "Memorial ed." of the author's works, published London, 1885.
Bibliography: xxii p. at end of v. 1 and xxii p. at end of v. 2.
Microprint. New York, Readex Microprint, 1969. 13 cards. (Landmarks of Science)
1. Embryology. I. Title.
InU NUC76-71681

Balfour, Frederic Henry.
see Taoist texts ... New York, Gordon Press, 1975.

Balfour, Gerald Alan, 1944-
Unit determination and representation procedures in state employment / by Gerald Alan Balfour. -- [East Lansing] : Balfour : [s.n.], 1975.
[4], vii, 252 leaves : ill. ; 29 cm.
Thesis (Ph.D.)--Michigan State University.
Bibliography: leaves 236-252.
1. Collective bargaining--Government employees--United States--States. 2. Collective bargaining--Government employees--Michigan. 3. Collective bargaining--Municipal employees--United States--States. I. Title.
MiEM NUC77-86498

Balfour, Gyneth S., joint author
see Lepschat, May Ringle. Washington County, Oregon records. [Portland] Genealogical Forum of Portland, Oregon, 1972.

Balfour, Harold Harington, Baron Balfour of Inchrye, 1897-
An airman marches, by H. H. Balfour ... with 16 illustrations. London, Hutchinson & co., ltd. [1933]
282 p. incl. front. (port.) plates, ports., map, facsim. 23½ cm.
Autobiography.
1. Balfour, Harold Harington, Baron Balfour of Inchrye, 1897- I. Title.
DA574.B28A3 1933 923.242 33-37661
rev

Balfour, Harold Harington, Baron Balfour of Inchrye, 1897-
Wings over Westminster [by] Harold Balfour. London, Hutchinson, 1973.
224, [11] p. illus., facsims., ports. 23 cm. index. £3.00
B 73-10851
1. Balfour, Harold Harington, Baron Balfour of Inchrye, 1897- I. Title.
DA89.6.B34A3 942.082'092'4 73-164356
ISBN 0-09-114370-5 MARC

Balfour, Henry, 1863-1939.
The natural history of the musical bow : a chapter in the developmental history of stringed instruments of music / by Henry Balfour. — Portland, Me. : Longwood Press, 1976.
viii, 87 p. : ill. ; 22 cm.
Reprint of the 1899 ed. published by Clarendon Press, Oxford.
ISBN 0-89341-006-3 : $12.50
1. Stringed instruments, Bowed—History. 2. Stringed instruments, Bowed—Bow. 3. Musical instruments, Primitive. I. Title.
ML755.B18 1976 787 76-22326
76 MARC

Balfour, James.
The tiny tots. London, Hutchinson [1972]
206, [1] p. 21 cm.
I. Title.
IaU NUC73-34771

Balfour, Margaret.
The problems of post-secondary education for Manitoba Indians and Metis. [Winnipeg] The Task Force on Post-secondary Education, 1973.
39 p. 28 cm. C***
Cover title.
"Staff background paper."
1. Indians of North America—Manitoba—Education. I. Manitoba. Task Force on Post-secondary Education. II. Title.
E78.M25B3 371.9'7'9707127 73-173157
MARC

Balfour, Michael David, 1939–
The A to Z of health food terms; edited by Michael Balfour & Judy Allen. London, Garnstone Press, 1973.
140 p. 21 cm. £1.60 GB 73-11669
1. Food—Dictionaries. I. Allen, Judy, joint author. II. Title.
TX349.B35 641.1'03 73-595496
ISBN 0-85511-150-X MARC

Balfour, Michael David, 1939- ed.
see The Health food guide... 2nd ed. London, Garnstone Press, 1972.

Balfour, Michael Leonard Graham, 1908-
Four-power control in Germany and Austria, 1945-46 / by Michael Balfour, John Mair. London, New York, Oxford University Press, 1956. New York, Johnson Reprint Corp., 1972.
390 p. (Survey of International Affairs, 1939-46, 8)
1. Germany–Hist.–Allied occupation, 1945- 2. Austria–Hist.–Allied occupation, 1945- I. Mair, John. II. Title. III. Series.
KMK NUC73-123855

Balfour, Michael Leonard Graham, 1908-
Helmuth James von Moltke, 1907-1945 : Anwalt der Zukunft / Freya von Moltke, Michael Balfour, Julian Frisby. -- Stuttgart : Deutsche Verlags-Anstalt, 1975.
368 p. : ill., ports ; 22 cm.
Translation by Freya von Moltke of Helmut von Moltke, a leader against Hitler by M. Balfour and J. Frisby.
Includes bibliographical notes and index.
1. Moltke, Helmuth James Wilhelm Ludwig Eugen Heinrich, Graf von, 1907-1945. 2. Anti-Nazi movement. I. Frisby, Julian, joint author. II. Moltke, Freya von, 1911- III. Title.
NSbSU NUC77-84508

Balfour, Michael Leonard Graham, 1908–
Helmuth von Moltke; a leader against Hitler, by Michael Balfour and Julian Frisby. [London] Macmillan [1972]
x, 388 p. illus. 22 cm. £5.95 B***
Includes bibliographical references.
1. Moltke, Helmuth James Wilhelm Ludwig Eugen Heinrich, Graf von, 1907-1945. 2. Anti-Nazi movement. I. Frisby, Julian, joint author. II. Title.
DD247.M6B34 943.086'092'4 [B] 72-86789
ISBN 0-333-14030-3 MARC

Balfour, Michael Leonard Graham, 1908–
Helmuth von Moltke; a leader against Hitler, by Michael Balfour and Julian Frisby. [New York] St. Martin's Press [1973, c1972]
x, 388 p. illus. 23 cm. $16.95
Includes bibliographical references.
1. Moltke, Helmuth James Wilhelm Ludwig Eugen Heinrich, Graf von, 1907-1945. 2. Anti-Nazi movement. I. Frisby, Julian, joint author.
DD247.M6B34 1973 943.086'092'4 [B] 73-160777
MARC

Balfour, Michael Leonard Graham, 1908-
The Kaiser and his times / Michael Balfour. -- Harmondsworth : Penguin Books, 1975.
xi, 530 p., [7] leaves of plates : ill. ; 18 cm. -- (Pelican books)
Includes bibliographical references and indexes.
1. Wilhelm II, German Emperor, 1859-1941. I. Title.
NmU NUC77-85736

Balfour, Ralph C
Client orientation: an exploratory study of selected interview behaviors of seventh grade male students. [Iowa City] 1974.
vi, 75 l. illus. 28 cm.
Thesis (Ph. D.)–University of Iowa.
1. Counseling. 2. Personnel service in secondary education. 3. Interpersonal relations. I. Title.
IaU NUC76-18995

Balfour, Rex.
The Bryan Ferry story / as told by Rex Balfour. — London : M. Dempsey, 1976.
128 p. : ill. ; 20 cm. GB***
ISBN 0-86044-015-X : £1.50
1. Ferry, Bryan. 2. Rock musicians—England—Biography. I. Title.
ML420.F36B3 784'.092'4 77-360344
77 MARC

Balfour, Robert C
This land I have loved, by Robert C. Balfour, Jr. [Tallahassee, Fla., Printed by Rose Printing Co., c1975]
131 p. col. illus., col. maps.
1. Tallahassee–Description–Views. 2. Thomasville, Ga.–Description–Views. 3. Albany, Ga.–Description–Views. I. Title.
FTaSU NUC76-18973

Balfour, Robert Llewellyn.
A nobody gives hell to everybody, by Robert L. Balfour. New York, Vantage Press [1972]
235 p.
1. U.S.–Civilization–20th century–Addresses, essays, lectures. I. Title.
ScU NUC75-26591

Balfour Browne, John Hutton
see
Browne, John Hutton Balfour, 1845-1921.

Balfour-Melville, Barbara Gordon, 1846-
Musings in verse. Edinburgh, Privately printed by T. and A. Constable [n.d.]
38 p.
I. Title.
ScU NUC75-17264

Balfour-Melville, James Leslie, 1895-
The descendants of James Balfour-Melville of Mount Melville and Eliza Ogilvy Maitland-Heriot, 31st March, 1974 / [Editors : J. L. Balfour-Melville, and M. R. Balfour-Melville]. — [Forest Hills, Vic. : J. L. Balfour-Melville, 1974?]
9 leaves : geneal. table ; 30 cm. Aus
Cover title
Supplement to The Balfours of Pilrig.
ISBN 0-9599817-1-3 : $1.80
1. Balfour family. I. Balfour-Melville, Michael Ronald, 1942- joint author. II. The Balfours of Pilrig. III. Title: The descendants of James Balfour—Melville ...
CS2009.B34 1974 929'.2'0994 75-327805
76 MARC

Balfour-Melville, Michael Ronald, 1942- joint author.
see Balfour-Melville, James Leslie, 1895- The descendants of James Balfour-Melville of Mount Melville and Eliza Ogilvy Maitland-Heriot, 31st March, 1974. [Forest Hills, Vic., J. L. Balfour-Melville, 1974?]

Balfour-Nrowne, Frank, 1874-
British water beetles. London, Printed for the Ray Society, sold by Bernard Quaritch, 1950-1958.
3 v. illus. 23 cm. (The Ray Society. [Publications] no. 27, 134, 141)
Includes bibliographies.
I. Quaritch, Bernard, 1819-1889.
AAP NUC73-9418

Balfour declaration. 1973
see Montagu, Edwin Samuel, 1879-1924. Edwin Montagu and the Balfour declaration. London, Arab League Office [1972?]

Balfour, Guthrie & Co., ltd.
A first century of commerce, 1869-1969. San Francisco, 1969.
26 p. illus. 24 cm.
I. Title.
OrCS NUC73-112849

The Balfours of Pilrig.
see Balfour-Melville, James Leslie, 1895- The descendants of James Balfour-Melville of Mount Melville and Eliza Ogilvy Maitland-Heriot, 31st March, 1974. [Forest Hills, Vic., J. L. Balfour-Melville, 1974?]

Balgård, Gunnar, 1938–
Carl Jonas Love Almqvist—samhällsvisionären. Stockholm, Sveriges radio; [Solna, Seelig], 1973.
347, (1) p. 21 cm. kr45.00 S 73-9/10
Bibliography: p. 341–344.
1. Almquist, Carl Jonas Love, 1793–1866.
PT9729.Z5B35 1973 73-324579
ISBN 91-522-1321-8

Balgård, Matts.
Vår dagliga tidning. [Stockholm, Liberala studieförbundet, 1964]
79 p. illus. 22 cm.
Bibliography: p. 79.
1. Swedish newspapers. I. Title.
PN5304.B3 75-572943

Balgård, Matts.
Västerbotten, nutid, framtid [av] Matts Balgärd, Lennart Hartin [och] Ingvar Kvarnbrink. [Umeå] Västerbottens läns bildningsförbund [1962]
119 p. illus. 22 cm.
1. Västerbotten, Sweden. I. Hartin, Lennart, 1915– II. Kvarnbrink, Ingvar.
DL971.V3B34 74-210563

Balgård, Matts
see Kultur idag, i morgon? Stockholm : LT, 1975.

Balgaev, Iskander Kadyrkulovich
see Zherebt͡sov, Mikhail Ivanovich. Elektrifikat͡sii͡a Uzbekistana. Tashkent, Gos. izd-vo Uzbekskoĭ SSR, 1959.

Balgarnie, Robert, 1826–1899.
Sir Titus Salt, baronet [by] R. Balgarnie. Settle, Brenton Publishing, 1970.
[6], xv, 330, [2] p. 2 illus. 19 cm. index. £1.50 GB 72-28375
Reprint of 1st ed., London, Hodder and Stoughton, 1877.
1. Salt, Sir Titus, 1803–1876.
CT788.S16B3 1970 338'.092'4 73-165873
ISBN 0-902847-00-7 MARC

Balge, Russell John.
Seasonal variation in three carbohydrate fractions of the leaves of Ilex opaca Ait. cv. Miss Helen at three light reduction levels, and their possible relation to flowering and fruiting. [Newark, Del.] 1974.
viii, 134 l. illus. 28 cm.
Thesis (Ph. D.)–University of Delaware.
Includes bibliography.
1. Holly. I. Title.
DeU NUC75-18520

Balgley, E., ed.
see Computerization in chemical industry and General papers. [Chicago, American Chemical Society, 1974]

Balgley, E., ed.
see The Small chemical enterprise... [New York, American Chemical Society, 1973]

Balgooy, M M J van.
Plant-geography of the Pacific as based on a census of Phanerogam genera. Leyden, Rijksherbarium, 1971.
222 p. maps. (Blumea. Supplement v. 6)
1. Botany–Pacific area. 2. Phanerogams. I. Title. II. Series.
ICIU CaBVaU NcU NUC74-137606
NNBG

Balgooyen, Thomas G
Behavior and ecology of the American Kestrel (Falco sparverius) [Berkeley] 1972.
1 v. (various pagings) illus., maps.
Thesis (Ph. D.)–University of California.
Includes bibliography.
CU NUC73-123838

Balgooyen, Thomas G
Behavior and ecology of the American kestrel (Falco sparverius L.) in the Sierra Nevada of California / by Thomas G. Balgooyen. — Berkeley : University of California Press, 1976.
83 p., [2] leaves of plates : ill. ; 27 cm. — (University of California publications in zoology ; v. 103)
Bibliography: p. 75-83.
ISBN 0-520-09514-6
1. American kestrel. 2. Birds—Sierra Nevada. 3. Birds—California. I. Title: Behavior and ecology of the American kestrel ... II. Series: California. University. University of California publications in zoology ; v. 103.
QL696.F34B34 598.9'1 73-620224
76 MARC

Balgopal, Pallassana R
Sensitivity training; a study in theory and its applicability to social work education. [New Orleans, 1971, c1972]
145 l.
Thesis–Tulane University.
Includes bibliography.
1. Social work education. 2. Group relations training. I. Title.
ICIU NUC76-71711

Balgord, William D
Novel catalysts and catalyst supports for control of NOx in automobile exhaust [by] William D. Balgord [and] Kai-wen K. Wang. [Albany] New York State Dept. of Environmental Conservation, Environmental Quality Research and Development Unit, 1970.
ii, 17, [17] p. illus. 28 cm. (New York (State). Dept. of Environmental Conservation. Technical paper no. 2)
Cover title.
Includes bibliography.
1. Automobile exhaust gas. 2. Motor vehicles—United States. Pollution control devices. 3. Nitrogen oxides. I. Wang, Kai-wen K. II. New York (State). Environmental Quality Research and Development Unit. III. Title. IV. Series.
N NUC75-29478

Balguer, Pedro Bohigas
see Bohigas Balguer, Pedro, 1901-

Balgur, Raphael.
(Milon basisi 'ivri angli)
מילון מסיסי עברי אנגלי / ר. בלגור, מ. דגוט. — ת[ל]-א[ביב] : ספרית מעריב, [1975]
128 p. ; 24 cm.
Introd. in Hebrew and English.
Cover title: Basic dictionary Hebrew-English.
Bibliography: p. 5.
1. Hebrew language—Dictionaries—English. I. Dagut, M., joint author. II. Title. III. Title: Basic dictionary—Hebrew-English.
PJ4833.B25 75-950615

Balgur, Raphael.
(Milon basisi 'ivri romani)
מילון בסיסי עברי רומני / רפאל בלגור, איתן אמיר. — ת[ל-]א[ביב] : הוצאת ספרית מעריב, [1975]
128 p. ; 24 cm.
On cover: Dictionar de bază ebraic-român.
1. Hebrew language—Dictionaries—Romanian. I. Amir, Etan, joint author. II. Title. III. Title: Dictionar de bază ebraic-român.
PJ4835.R8B3 75-951071

Balgur, Raphael.
(Milon besisi 'Ivri Portugali)
מילון בסיסי עברי פורטוגלי / ר. בלגור, צ. יותם. — ת[ל-]א[ביב] : הוצאת ספרית מעריב, 1975.
127 p. ; 24 cm.
Includes introd. in Hebrew and Portuguese.
Cover title: Dictionario básico—hebraico português.
Includes bibliographical references.
1. Hebrew language—Dictionaries—Portuguese. I. Iusim, H., joint author. II. Title. III. Title: Dicionário básico—hebraico português.
PJ4835.P6B3 76-951008

Balguy, John, 1686-1748.
The foundation of moral goodness / John Balguy. — New York : Garland Pub., 1976.
68, 102 p. ; 19 cm. — (British philosophers and theologians of the 17th & 18th centuries)
Reprint of the 1728-29 editions printed for J. Pemberton, London.
ISBN 0-8240-1750-1
1. Virtue. 2. Ethics. I. Title. II. Series.
[BJ1520.B26 1976] 170 75-11194
76 MARC

Balhana, Altiva Pilatti.
Arquivo da paróquia de Santa Felicidade / [Altiva Pilatti Balhana]. -- Curitiba : Universidade Federal do Paraná, Departamento de História, 1971.
44 p. -- (Boletim da Universidade Federal do Paraná, Departamento de História ; no. 11)
CLU NUC77-101165

Balhana, Altiva Pilatti.
Levantamento e arrolamento de arquivos [por] Altiva Pilatti Balhana [e] Cecília Maria Westphalen. Curitiba, Universidade Federal do Paraná, Conselho de Pesquisas, 1970.
36 p. 23 cm. (Universidade Federal do Paraná. Departamento de História. [Boletim] no. 10) (Boletim da Universidade Federal do Paraná)
Caption title.
Summary in English.
1. Archives—Brazil—Paraná (State) I. Westphalen, Cecília Maria, joint author. II. Title. III. Series: Paraná, Brazil (State). Universidade Federal. Departamento de História. Boletim no. 10.
CD4077.P37B34 75-573083

Balhana, Altiva Pilatti. Mudança na estrutura agrária dos Campos Gerais. 1963
in Contribuicão ao estudo da história agrária do Paraná... Curitiba, 1963.

Balhana, Altiva Pilatti
see História do Paraná. 2. ed. [rev. e aumentada] edicão escolar. [Curitiba] : Gráfica Editôra Paraná Cultural, 1969.

Balhana, Altiva Pilatti, joint author
see Westphalen, Cecilia Maria. Nota prévia ao estudo da ocupação da terra no Parana moderno. Curitiba, 1968.

Balhar, Jan.
Skladba lašských nářečí. 1. vyd. Praha, Academia, rozmn. ST 5, 1974.
197, [1] p. with map. 24 cm. (Československá akademie věd. Česká nářečí, sv. 7) Kčs26.00 Cz 74
Summary in English.
Bibliography: p. 12-16.
1. Czech language—Dialects—Lašsko. I. Title. II. Series: Československá akademie věd. Sekce jazyka a literatury. Česká nářečí, sv. 7.
PG4771.L3B3 74-319819

al-Balhī, Muḥammad ibn Yūsuf
see
al-Ganjī, Muḥammad ibn Yūsuf.

al-Balhī, Šaqīq
see
al-Balkhī, Shaqīq ibn Ibrāhīm, d. 809 or 10.

Balhigfer
see
Fernández de la Vega, Baltasar-Higinio.

Balhoff, John Frederick, 1948-
Coupled radiating shock layers with finite rate chemistry effects... [n.p.] 1975.
2 v. (xiv, 447 l.) illus. 29 cm.
Thesis (Ph.D.)--Louisiana State University, Baton Rouge, La.
Vita.
Includes bibliographical references.
Includes abstract.
1. Ablation (Aerothermodynamics) 2. Aerodynamic heating. 3. Space vehicles--Atmospheric entry. I. Title.
LU NUC77-85696

Bālī, Balajīta Siṅgha, comp.
(Yugga krāntī)
ਯੁੱਗ ਕ੍ਰਾਂਤੀ. ਸੰਪਾਦਕ ਬਲਜੀਤ ਸਿੰਘ ਬਲੀ [ਤੇ] ਪੁਰਦਮਨ ਸਿੰਘ ਬੇਦੀ. ਚੰਡੀਗੜ੍ਹ, ਗੁਰੂ ਨਾਨਕ ਮਿਸ਼ਨਰੀ [1973]
80 p. 22 cm. Rs5.00
In Panjabi.
1. Sikhism—Addresses, essays, lectures. 2. Baisakhi (Festival)—Addresses, essays, lectures. I. Title.
BL2018.B28 74-902608

Bali, Dev Raj, 1936-
(Mānavavāda kī Paścātya aura Bhāratīya paramparā)
मानववाद की पाश्चात्य और भारतीय परम्परा : दार्शनिक निबन्ध / देवराज बाली. — 1. संस्करण. — जम्मू : युवा हिन्दी लेखक संघ, 1975.
59 p. ; 23 cm.
In Hindi.
Rs8.00
1. Humanism. 2. Philosophy, Comparative. I. Title.
B105.H8B34 76-902565

Bali, Gauri Nandan Singh
see
Abid Manawari, 1938-

Bālī, Indu.
टूटती-जुड़ती; नारी हृदय-मंथनपूर्ण कहानी संग्रह. [लेखिका] इन्दु बाली. [1. संस्करण] जयपुर, अर्चना प्रकाशन [1970]
4, 239 p. 19 cm. Rs10.00
In Hindi.
I. Title.
Title romanized: Ṭūṭatī-juṛatī.
PK2098.13.A38T8 74-918362

Bali, K
Bulan muda, hati muda, oleh K. Bali. [Chet. 1. Ipoh, Pustaka Muda, 1966]
60 p. 18 cm.
I. Title.
NIC NUC73-122500

Bali, K
Dari shurga ka-naraka, oleh K. Bali. [Kuching] Borneo Literature Bureau [1970]
iii, 32 p. illus. 19 cm. $0.50
CONTENTS: Dari shurga ka-naraka.—Bermacham² ribut.—Minat bukan bererti chinta.—Purnama dingin.—Rendah.
I. Title.
PL5139.B32D3 74-943737

Bali, K
Dari shurga ka-naraka, oleh K. Bali. [Kuching] Borneo Literature Bureau [1970]
iii, 32 p. illus. 19 cm.
Microfiche copy. 1 sheet. 11 x 15 cm. (NYPL FSN 15,662)
I. Title.
NN NUC76-71686

Bali, K.
Memperkenalkan Berunai, oleh K. Bali. [Chetakan 2. Kota Bharu] Penerbit PAP [1969]
80 p. illus., map, ports. 19 cm. 1.30
Bibliography: p. [5]
1. Brunei (State) I. Title.
DS646.35.B3 1969 74-202638

Bālī, L R
see
Balley, L R 1930-

Bali, Lekh Raj.
The factorial invariance of intelligence tests over grades, sex, and chronological age. [Berkeley] 1973.
xiv, 109 l.
Thesis (Ph.D.)–University of California.
Bibliography: leaves 105-109.
CU NUC75-17390

Bālī, Tārakanātha.
जयशंकर प्रसाद और अजातशत्रु. लेखक तारकनाथ बाली. [1. संस्करण] आगरा, विनोद पुस्तक मन्दिर [1955]
116 p. 18 cm.
In Hindi.
1. Prasad, Jai Shankar, 1889-1937. 2. Ajātaśatru, fl. ca. 494 B.C.-ca. 467 B.C. I. Title.
Title romanized: Jayaśaṅkara Prasāda aura Ajātaśatru.
PK2098.P7K31832 72-220075

Bālī, Tārakanātha.
कामायनी की टीका. [लेखक] तारकनाथ बाली. [1. संस्करण] आगरा, विनोद पुस्तक मन्दिर [1956]
3, 409 p. 19 cm.
In Hindi.
1. Prasad, Jai Shankar, 1889-1937. Kāmāyanī. I. Title.
Title romanized: Kāmāyanī kī ṭīkā.
PK2098.P7K31833 72-209114

Bālī, Tārakanātha.
युगद्रष्टा कबीर; आलोचनात्मक अध्ययन. लेखक तारकनाथबाली. ₍1. संस्करण₎ आगरा, विनोद पुस्तक मन्दिर ₍1957₎
6, 160 p. 19 cm.
In Hindi.
Bibliographical footnotes.

1. Kabīr, 15th cent. I. Title.
Title romanized: Yugadrashṭā Kabīra.
BL2020.K3A32 71–287506
S A

Bālī, Tārakanātha, joint comp.
see Kalelkar, Dattatraya Balkrishna, 1885– comp. Bhāratīya kāvya-siddhānta. ₍1969₎

Bali.
Initials of Badan Angkutan Laut Indonesia. Publications by and about this body are found under its name written in full.
Titles and other entries beginning with these initials are filed following this card.
73–217492

Bali.
Keterangan Pemerintah Daerah Propinsi Bali kepada D. P. R. D. Propinsi Bali, pada tgl. 6 September 1972. ₍Denpasar₎ 1972.
1 v. (various pagings) 32 cm.
Cover title.
1. Bali—Economic policy. I. Title.
HC448.B3B3 1972 73–942282

Bali.
Keterangan Pemerintah Daerah Propinsi Bali kepada D. P. R. D. Propinsi Bali, pada tgl. 4 Oktober 1973. ₍Denpasar, 1973₎
99, ₍20₎ p. 33 cm.
Cover title.
At head of title: Departemen Dalam Negeri, Daerah Prop. Bali.
1. Bali—Economic conditions. 2. Bali—Social conditions. 3. Bali—Politics and government. I. Title.
HC448.B3B3 1973 74–940305

Bali
see Workshop Peraturan-Peraturan Bangunan dan Zoning Daerah Bali, Sanur, Indonesia, 1971. Laporan hasil. ₍Djakarta₎ Pemerintah Daerah tingkat I Bali bekerdja sama dengan Direktorat Tata Kota & Daerah ₍1972?₎

Bali. Agama Wilajah Bali-Selatan, Kantor
see
Bali. Kantor Agama Wilajah Bali-Selatan.

Bali. Dewan Perwakilan Rakyat Daerah.
Pedoman kerja Pemerintah Daerah Propinsi Bali, menyongsong pelaksanaan Pelita ke II Republik Indonesia, 1973–1978. ₍Denpasar₎ Biro DPRD-Propinsi Bali ₍1972₎
148 p. 33 cm.
Cover title.
1. Bali—Economic policy. 2. Bali—Economic conditions. I. Title.
HC448.B3B33 1972 73–941218

Bali. Dinas Perindustrian.
Laporan—Dinas Perindustrian Propinsi Bali. Denpasar.
v. 33 cm.
1. Bali—Industries—Periodicals. 2. Bali. Dinas Perindustrian.
HC448.B3B34a 72–942342
MARC-S

Bali. Direktorat Pembangunan.
Program bantuan pembangunan kabupaten/kotamadya (Proyek Inpres no. 3, tahun 1971) Daerah Propinsi Bali. — ₍Denpasar₎ : Direktorat Pembangunan, ₍1974₎
92 leaves ; 21 x 33 cm.
Cover title.
1. Regional planning—Bali. I. Title: Program bantuan pembangunan kabupaten/kotamdya (Proyek Inpres no. 3, tahun 1971) ...
HT395.I 58B33 1974 74–941500

Bali. Direktorat Pembangunan Masyarakat Desa.
Lapuran dan evaluasi umum pelaksanaan bantuan pembangunan desa Propinsi Bali, tahun 1969/70 s/d 1972/73. ₍Denpasar₎ 1973.
₍78₎ l. 32 cm.
1. Community development—Bali. 2. Villages—Bali. I. Title.
HN710.B312B34 1973 73–941872

Bali. Kantor Agama Wilajah Bali-Selatan.
Tuntunan muspa / oleh Kantor Agama Wilajah Bali-Selatan. — ₍Denpasar : Kantor, 1967?₎
39 p. ; 15 cm.
1. Prayer (Hinduism) 2. Hinduism—Bali (Island) I. Title.
BL1215.P7B34 1967 S A 68–19212
PL 480 : Indo-6009

Bali. Kantor Sensus dan Statistik.
Bali dalam angka.
Denpasar.
v. 33 cm
1. Bali—Statistics—Periodicals. I. Title.
HA1817.B3B34a 73–942215
MARC-S

Bali. Kantor Sensus dan Statistik.
Djumlah penduduk Propinsi Bali th. 1971; hasil sementara sensus penduduk tahun 1971 (pentjatjahan lengkap) Singaradja ₍1972₎
viii, 151, ₍43₎ l. 33 cm.
Cover title.
1. Bali—Census, 1971. I. Title.
HA1817.B3A45 1972 73–942216

Bali Chopra
see
Chopra, Bali, 1931–

Bali, Insel der Tempel und Tänze. [Wien? 1971?]
see under Indonesia. Kedutaan Besar. Austria.

Bali Jee
see
Bālī Jī.

Bālī Jī.
(Lamḥon̲ kā dukh)
لمحوں کا دکھ / بالیؔ جی. — 1. ایڈیشن. — لاہور : لوک کلا پبلیکیشنز, ₍1974 or 1975₎
144 p. ; 21 cm.
In Urdu.
Poems.
Rs10.00

I. Title.
PK2200.B3244L3 75–938558

Baliabin, R. V.
see Stepanov, Valentin Vladimirovich. (Spravochnik svarshchika) 1974.

Bali͡abin, Vasiliĭ Ivanovich.
(Golubai͡a Argunʹ)
Голубая Аргунь : Роман / Василий Балябин ; ₍худож. В. Петров₎. — Иркутск : Вост.-Сиб. кн. изд-во, 1975.
399 p. : ill. ; 20 cm. USSR 76
0.72rub
I. Title.
PG3476.B2867G6 1975 77–505722

Bali͡abin, Vasiliĭ Ivanovich.
(Zabaĭkalʹt͡sy)
Забайкальцы; роман. Москва, Советский писатель, 1966–69.
3 v. in 2. port. 21 cm.
At head of title: Василий Балябин.
1.32rub (v. 1, 2) ; 0.75rub (v. 3)
I. Title.
PG3476.B2867Z2 67–42072

Bali͡abin, Vasiliĭ Ivanovich.
(Zabaĭkalʹt͡sy)
Забайкальцы : роман / Василий Балябин ; ₍ил. Н. А. Шеберстов₎. —Москва : Сов. писатель, 1974.
845 p. : ill. ; 22 cm. USSR 74
2.11rub
1. Siberia—History—Revolution, 1917–1921—Fiction. I. Title.
PG3476.B2876Z2 1974 75–581329

Bali͡akin, Oleg Konstantinovich.
(Tekhnologii͡a i organizat͡sii͡a sudoremonta)
Технология и организация судоремонта : ₍учеб. пособие для учащихся судомех. специальности вузов ММФ₎ / О. К. Балякин. — Москва : Транспорт, 1974.
350 p. : ill. ; 22 cm. USSR 74
Bibliography: p. ₍348₎
0.97rub
1. Ships—Maintenance and repair. I. Title.
VM901.B34 75–554139

Balian, Esther M
Captain Daniel Bishop, Jr., a brief genealogy / compiled by Esther M. Balian. — Baltimore : Gateway Press, 1974.
45 p. : ill. ; 22 cm.
Includes bibliographical references and index.
1. Bishop family. I. Title.
CS71.B6317 1974 929'.2'0973 74–21675
MARC

Bali͡an, Grigoriĭ Aĭkazovich.
(Prutni͡ak prostertyĭ i ego kulʹtura v Kirgizii)
Прутняк простертый и его культура в Киргизии. Фрунзе, "Кыргызстан," 1972.
262 p. with illus. 21 cm. 0.65rub USSR 72-VKP
At head of title: Г. А. Балян.
Bibliography: p. 250–₍261₎
1. Kochia prostrata. 2. Forage plants—Kirghizistan. I. Title.
SB207.K6B35 73–330511

Balʹi͡an, Khoren Vaganovich, joint author
see Petrov, Anatoliĭ Aleksandrovich. (Organicheskai͡a khimii͡a) 1973.

Balian, Lorna.
Bah! Humbug? / Lorna Baliaon. — Nashville : Abingdon, 1977.
₍32₎ p. : ill. (some col.) ; 29 cm.
SUMMARY: Two children set a trap for Santa Claus but only one of them manages to see him.
ISBN 0-687-02345-9
₍1. Santa Claus—Fiction. 2. Christmas stories₎ I. Title.
PZ7.B1978 Bah ₍E₎ 76 76-50625
MARC

Balian, Lorna.
Humbug rabbit. Nashville, Abingdon Press ₍1974₎
₍32₎ p. col. illus. 29 cm.
SUMMARY: Father Rabbit's reply of "Humbug" to the idea that he is the Easter Rabbit doesn't spoil Easter for his children or Granny's grandchildren.
₍1. Easter stories₎ I. Title.
PZ7.B1978Hq [E] 73–9555
ISBN 0-687-18046-5 MARC

Balian, Lorna.
Sometimes it's turkey, sometimes it's feathers. Nashville, Abingdon Press ₍1973₎
₍32₎ p. illus. 24 cm. $3.50
SUMMARY: When she finds a turkey egg, Mrs. Gumm decides to hatch it and have a turkey for Thanksgiving dinner.
₍1. Thanksgiving Day—Stories₎ I. Title.
PZ7.B1978So [E] 72–3867
ISBN 0-687-39074-5 MARC

Balian, Lorna.
The sweet touch / Lorna Balian. — Nashville : Abingdon Press, c1976.
₍40₎ p. : ill. (some col.) ; 21 x 27 cm.
SUMMARY: The genie Peggy's plastic ring conjures up is only a beginner who doesn't know how to put a stop to the one wish he can grant.
ISBN 0-687-40773-7
₍1. Magic—Fiction₎ I. Title.
PZ7.B1978 Sw ₍E₎ 74 74-34217
MARC

Balian, Pʿarhantsem
see
Palian, Pʿarhandzem.

Balʹi͡an, Roblen Khorenovich
see (Kratkiĭ spravochnik konstruktora radioėlektronnoĭ apparatury) 1972.

Balian, Roger.
see Aux frontières de la spectroscopie laser ... Amsterdam, North-Holland Pub. Co.,

Balian, Roger.
see Bloch, Claude. Scientific works ... Amsterdam, North-Holland Pub. Co., 1975.

Balian, Roger.
see Fluid dynamics ... London, Gordon and Breach Science Publishers, c1977.

Balian, Roger.
see Molecular fluids ... London, Gordon and Breach Science Publishers, c1976.

Balian, Roger.
see Physique atomique et moléculaire et matière interstellaire ... Amsterdam, North-Holland Pub. Co., 1975.

Bal'ían, Sarkis Vaganovich.
(Tekhnicheskaía termodinamika i teplovye dvigateli)
Техническая термодинамика и тепловые двигатели. ‹Учеб. пособие для неэнерг. специальностей втузов›. Изд. 2-е перераб. и доп. Ленинград, "Машиностроение," ‹Ленингр. отд-ние›, 1973.
302 p. with illus., 1 l. of diagrs. inserted. 27 cm. 1.14rub
USSR 73–VKP
At head of title: С. В. Бальян.
Bibliography: p. ‹297›
1. Thermodynamics. 2. Heat engines. I. Title.
TJ265.B19 1973 74–332442

Balian, Trdat
see
Palian, Trdat, 1850-1923.

Baliani, Marco.
see Roma Ovest lungo il Tevere ... Roma, Bulzoni, c1976.

Baliant, András.
English-Pidgin-French phrase book and sports dictionary. Inglis-Pisin-Frans tok save na spot diksineri. Anglais-pidgin-française dictionnaire phraseologique et sportif. [Port Moresby, c1969]
viii, 89 p.
Cover title: English, Pidgin and French dictionary of sports and phrase book.
1. English language–Dictionaries–Pidgin English. 2. Pidgin English–Dictionaries–English. 3. Sports–Terminology. I. Title.
CLU NUC76-71735

Baliarda, Luis.
La industria farmacéutica argentina / Luis Baliarda. -- Buenos Aires : Editorial Médica Panamericana, 1972.
182 p. : ill.
1. Drug trade--Argentine Republic. I. Title.
NbU NUC77-101191

Baliari, Eduardo.
Los monumentos. ‹Buenos Aires› Ministerio de Cultura y Educación ‹1972›
90 p. illus. 20 cm. (Colección Almario de Buenos Aires)
LACAP 72–4564
1. Buenos Aires—Statues. I. Title.
F3001.5.A2B34 73–310559

Balíasna, Ryva Naumivna.
(Chetvert' veka)
Четверть века. Книга лирики. Пер. с евр. Р. Заславского. ‹Ил.: Э. Б. Аронов›. Москва, "Сов. писатель," 1973.
120 p. with illus. 16 cm. 0.34rub USSR 73–VKP
At head of title: Рива Балясная.
I. Zaslavskiĭ, Ritaliĭ Zinov'evich, tr. II. Title.
PJ5129.B215C5 74–332189

Balíasna, Ryva Naumivna.
Chetvert' veka; kniga liriki. Perevod s evreĭskogo Ritaliía Zaslavskogo. [Khudozhnik E. B. Aronov] Moskva, Sov. pisatel', 1973.
219 p. illus., port. 17 cm.
Poems.
I. Title.
MB NUC75-138735

Balíasov, Pavel Dmitrievich.
(Szhatie tekstil'nykh volokon v masse i tekhnologiía tekstil'nogo proizvodstva)
Сжатие текстильных волокон в массе и технология текстильного производства / П. Д. Балясов. — Москва : Легкая индустрия, 1975.
175, ‹1› p. : ill. ; 20 cm. USSR 75
Bibliography: p. 173–‹176›
0.93rub
1. Textile fibers—Testing. 2. Textile industry. 3. Strains and stresses. I. Title.
TS1540.B25 76–509482

Balibar, Étienne.
Cinq études du matérialisme historique / Étienne Balibar. — Paris : F. Maspero, 1974.
295 p., ‹1› leaf of plates : ill. ; 22 cm. — (Théorie) F***
34.00F
1. Dialectical materialism. 2. Marx, Karl, 1818-1883. 3. Lenin, Vladimir Il'ich, 1870-1924. I. Title.
B809.8.B26 335.4'11 74-193450
74‹r75›rev MARC

Balibar, Etienne.
On the dictatorship of the proletariat / Etienne Balibar ; introd. by Grahame Lock ; afterword by Louis Althusser ; translated by Grahame Lock. — London : NLB ; Atlantic Highlands, N.J. : Humanities Press, 1977, c1976.
237 p. ; 22 cm.
Translation of Sur la dictature du prolétariat.
Includes bibliographical references and index
ISBN 0-391-00721-1
1. Dictatorship of the proletariat. I. Title.
JC474.B3413 1977 321.9'4 77-4068
77 MARC

Balibar, Étienne.
Sur la dictature du prolétariat / Étienne Balibar. — Paris : F. Maspero, 1976.
289 p. ; 22 cm. — (Théorie) F***
Includes bibliographical references.
ISBN 2-7071-0863-4 : 35.00F
1. Dictatorship of the proletariat. I. Title.
JC474.B34 77-477460
77 MARC

Balibar, Étienne
see Althusser, Louis. Das Kapital lesen I-II. ‹Reinbek bei Hamburg› Rowohlt ‹1972›

Balibar, Renée.
Les français fictifs : le rapport des styles littéraires au français national / Renée Balibar; avec la collaboration de Geneviève Merlin et Gilles Tret ; présentation de Étienne Balibar et Pierre Macherey. — ‹Paris› : Hachette, ‹1974›
295 p. ; 23 cm. — (Collection Analyse : Série Langue et littérature) (Hachette littérature) F***
Includes bibliographical references.
ISBN 2-01-000458-2 : 45.00F
1. French fiction—19th century—History and criticism. 2. French fiction—20th century—History and criticism. 3. French language—Style. 4. Languages—Political aspects. 5. Literature and society. I. Merlin, Geneviève, joint author. II. Tret, Gilles, joint author. III. Title.
PQ663.B3 843'.083 75-506283
75 MARC

Balibar, Renée.
Le français national : politique et pratiques de la langue nationale sous la Révolution française / Renée Balibar, Dominique Laporte ; présentation de Étienne Balibar et Pierre Macherey. — ‹Paris› : Hachette, ‹1974›
224 p. ; 23 cm. — (Collection Analyse : Série Langue et littérature) (Hachette littérature) F***
ISBN 2-01-000113-3 : 39.00F
1. French language—History. 2. Languages—Political aspects. I. Laporte, Dominique, 1949- joint author. II. Title.
PC2083.B3 440'.9 75-506280
75 MARC

Balibar, Renée.
see Péguy mis à jour ... Québec, Presses de l'Université Laval, 1976.

Balibouse, Guy.
L'équipe de Suisse : ‹l'histoire de 1905 à 1976 / Guy Balibouse, Pierre Tripod›. — ‹Lausanne› : Éditions Sporama : Diffusion Payot, ‹1976›
215 p. : ill. (some col.) ; 26 cm. Sw76-11278
45.00F
1. Soccer—Switzerland—History. I. Tripod, Pierre, joint author. II. Title.
GV944.S92B34 77-478692
•77 MARC

Balibutsa, Maniragaba.
see Thompson, Thomas L. The settlement of Sinai and the Negev in the Bronze Age. Wiesbaden, Reichert, 1975.

Balić, Branko.
see Nova tendencija 3 ... Zagreb, Galerija suvremene umjetnosti, ‹1965›

Balić, Carolus
see Balic, Charles, Father, 1899-

Balić, Charles, Father, 1899-
Die Corredemptrixfrage innerhalb der franzisch-kanischen Theologie. Werl/Westf., Dietrich Coelde ‹1957 ?›
‹218›-287 p. 24 cm.
"Sonderdruck aus Franziskanische Studien 39 (1957) H. 2-4."
Includes bibliography.
ODaU-M NUC73-59283

Balić, Charles, Father, 1899-
De regula mariologica Joannis Duns Scoti. Roma, Arti Grafiche A. Chicca ‹1956 ?›
‹110›-133 p. 25 cm.
"Estratto da Euntes Docete, anno IX, 1956, fasc. 1-3."
Includes bibliography.
ODaU-M NUC73-59275

Balić, Charles, Father, 1899-
Voraussetzungen für die Dogmatisierung einer Glaubenswahrheit (Gedanken zu zwei marianischen Bullen), von Karl Balic. München, K. Zink, 1957.
20 p. 24 cm.
Offprint from Auer, Johann and Volk, Hermann, eds. Theologie in Geschichte und Gegenwart.
ODaU-M NUC73-59279

Balic, Charles, Father, 1899- ed.
see Bibliotheca Assumptionis B. Virginis Mariae. Roma, Academia Mariana, 1948-1962.

Balić, Charles, Father, 1899-
see Studia mediaevalia et mariologioa. Roma, Antonianum, 1971.

Balić, Ismail
see Balić, Smail.

Balić, Lorenzo Carlo
see Balic, Charles, Father, 1899-

Balić, Olga. Prva pomoć. 1970
in Yugoslavia. Laws, statutes, etc. Osnovni zakon o bezbednosti saobraćaja na putevima. Nis, Zavod za izdavanje strucnih publikacija zastite na radu, 1970.

Balić, Smail.
Kultura Bošnjaka. Muslimanska komponenta. Wien, (Ungargasse 9/20: Balić) 1973.
col. plate, 247 p., xiii p. of illus. 24 cm. S250.00 Au 74–3–204
Added t. p.: Die Kultur der Bosniaken.
Errata slip inserted.
Summary in German.
Bibliography: p. 207–230.
1. Bosnia and Herzegovina—Intellectual life. 2. Muslims in Bosnia and Herzegovina. I. Title. II. Title: Die Kultur der Bosniaken.
DB240.5.B27 74–310492

Balić, Smail
see Bosanski pogledi, 1960-1967. Beč, (Smail Balić) 1971.

Balić, Smail
see Ilmihal za mladež i odrasle. Beč, S. Balić, 1973.

Balić, Smail, ed.
see al-Istakhrī, 10th cent. al-Istahrī und seine Landkarten im Buch "Suwar al-akālīm"... Wien, G. Prachner, 1965.

Balić, Smail, comp
see Die Muslims im Donauraum. Wien, (Moslemischer Sozialdienst) 1971.

Balice, Vincent Joseph, 1937-
Ibsen's feminine mystique / by Vincent J. Balice. 1st ed. -- New York : Vantage Press, c1975.
211 p. ; 21 cm.
Bibliography: p. 205-211.
1. Ibsen, Henrik, 1828-1906--Knowledge--Women. 2. Women in literature. I. Title.
AU NUC77-85737

Balice, Vincent Joseph, 1937-
A study of the female as wife and mother in Ibsen's dramas / by Vincent Joseph Balice. -- [s. l. : s. n.], 1971.
vi, 213 leaves.
Thesis--Purdue University.
Vita.
Photocopy. Ann Arbor, Mich. : Xerox University Microfilms, 1974. -- vi, 213 leaves; 22 cm.
Bibliography: leaves 207-212.
1. Ibsen, Henrik, 1828-1906--Criticism and interpretation. 2. Women in literature. I. Title.
WU NUC77-87086

Balick, Bruce, 1943-
Fine structure in H II regions. ‹Ithaca, N.Y.› 1971.
viii, 176 l. illus. 29 cm.
Thesis (Ph.D.)–Cornell University.
1. Interstellar hydrogen. 2. Nebulae. I. Title.
NIC NUC73-123839

Balicka-Knotz, Renata.
Ubiory kobiece i męskie : od XVIII do początku XX wieku w zbiorach Muzeum w Rzeszowie : katalog / Renata Balicka-Knotz. — Rzeszów : Muzeum Okręgowe, 1974.
214 p. : ill. ; 21 cm.
Errata slip inserted.
List of illustrations also in English and French; summaries in the same languages.
Bibliography: p. ₍98₎
zł30.00
1. Costume—Poland—Catalogs. I. Rzeszów, Poland. Muzeum Narodowe. II. Title.
GT1060.B26 77-502494

Balicki, Jan.
Dyskryminacja rasowa w świetle prawa międzynarodowego. Wrocław, Zakład Narodowy im. Ossolińskich, 1972.
294 p. 21 cm.
Summary in English.
Bibliography: p. ₍283₎–287.
zł45.00
1. Race discrimination—Law and legislation. 2. International convention on the elimination of all forms of racial discrimination. I. Title.
75-592736

Balicki, Stanisław Witold.
Cultural policy in Poland ₍by₎ Stanisław Witold Balicki, Jerzy Kossak and Mirosław Żuławski. Paris, Unesco, 1973.
67 p. illus. 24 cm. (Studies and documents on cultural policies)
$2.00 (U.S.) F***
"SHC.72/XIX.19/A."
Label mounted on t. p.: UNIPUB, Inc., New York.
Includes bibliographical references.
1. Poland—Intellectual life. I. Kossak, Jerzy, joint author. II. Żuławski, Mirosław, joint author. III. Title. IV. Series.
DK443.7.B34 301.29'438 73-79494
ISBN 92-3-101067-0 MARC

Balicki, Stanislaw Witold, ed.
see Zeleński, Tadeusz, 1874-1941. O Wyspiańskim. Kraków, Wydawn. Literackie [1973]

al-Balīdī, Muḥammad ibn Muḥammad
see
al-Bulaydī, Muḥammad ibn Muḥammad, d. 1762 or 1763.

Baliero Silva, Wáshington, joint author
see Carballo Lázaro, Roberto. Realidad y perspectivas de los procesos de integración económica. Montevideo, Ediciones Jurídicas A.M. Fernández [1973]

Baliga, A. V., 1904-1964
see Science and society... Bombay, Lalvani Pub. House [1972]

Baliga, B S
Studies in Madras administration. [Rev. ed.] Madras, Printed at the India Press, for the Controller of Stationery and Printing, 1960.
2 v. on 1 reel.
Negative; microfilmed by the Library Photographic Service, University of California.
1. Madras (State)—Pol. & govt. 2. Madras (State—Econ. condit. 3. Madras (State)—Hist.
ICU NUC74-178482

Baliga, B. S.
see Madras (State) Madras district gazetteers. Madras, Printed by the Superintendent, Govt. Press, 1957-

Baliga, Bantval Vittaldas, 1943-
Intermediate-range peak-load demand forecasting. ₍n.p.₎ 1971.
117 l. illus.
I. Title.
ViBlbV NUC73-34773

Baliga, Bantwal Rabindranath.
Flammability limits and the oscillatory burning of solid propellants at low pressure. [n. p.] 1974.
1 v.
Thesis.
OClW NUC76-18983

Baliga, Bhaskar B 1930-
(p,γ) reactions in the giant resonance region in Li^7, B^{11}, Na^{23} and K^{39} / Bhaskar B. Baliga. — ₍New York : s.n.₎, 1963.
vii, 72, ₍28₎ leaves : ill. ; 29 cm.
Thesis—Columbia University.
Includes bibliographical references.
1. Cross sections (Nuclear physics) 2. Photonuclear reactions. 3. Gamma rays—Spectra. 4. Nuclear magnetic resonance. I. Title.
QC794.6.C7B34 76-359111
76 MARC

Baligand, Pierre.
see Échanges et dialogue ... Paris (18, rue des Quatres-Vents, 75006) IDOC-France, 1975.

Baligand, Renée A
Les poèmes de Raymond Queneau; étude phonostylistique ₍par₎ Renée A. Baligand. Montréal, Didier ₍1972₎
xii, 124 p. 23 cm. (Studia phonetica, 6) C***
Bibliography: p. ₍121₎–124.
1. Queneau, Raymond, 1903- I. Series.
P215.S78 no. 6 73-364465
₍PQ2633.U43₎

Baligar, Veeranna
see
Veeranna Baligar, 1941-

Baligar, Virupax C
The physical, chemical and micromorphological properties of soil and their influence on soybean and sorghum root growth. -- [s.l. : s.n.], 1975.
[xvi], 123 l. : ill. ; 28 cm.
Thesis (Ph.D.)--Mississippi State University.
Bibliography: leaves [114]-123.
1.Soils--Analysis. 2.Soy-bean. 3.Sorghum. I.Title.
MsSM NUC77-84509

Balīghuddīn, Shāh.
(Razm-i ḥaq o bāṭil)
رزم حق و باطل (ہماری کہانی تاریخ کی زبانی). ₍مصنف₎ شاہ بلیغ‌الدین. ₍اشاعت 1. کراچی، پیراڈائز سبسکرپشن ایجنسی،
₍1973-
v. illus., maps. 25 cm. Rs30.00 (v. 1)
In Urdu.
CONTENTS: 1. پہلی صدی ہجری کے معرکے.
1. Islamic Empire—History, Military. 2. Islamic Empire—History—622-661. I. Title.
DS38.1.B34 73-930590

Balík, Hubert
see Komunistická strana Československa. Ustřední výbor. Oddělení propagandy, agitace a kultury. ČSSR... Praha, ÚV KSČ, 1971.

Balikçisi, Halikarnas
see Halikarnas Balikçisi, 1886-

Balikhin, Mikhail Ivanovich.
Анализ производственно-хозяйственной деятельности строительных организаций. ₍Техн.-экон. анализ произв.-хоз. деятельности строит.-монтажных организаций). ₍Учебник для вузов по специальности "Экономика и организация стр-ва"₎. Москва, Стройиздат, 1971.
304 p. with diagrs. 22 cm. 0.91rub USSR 71-VKP
At head of title: М. И. Балихин.
1. Construction industry—Russia—Auditing and inspection. I. Title.
Title romanized: Analiz proizvodstvenno-khozíàĭstvennoĭ deíàtel'nosti stroitel'nykh organizaíàiĭ.
HD9715.R92B284 1971 72-361690

Balikhin, Mikhail Ivanovich.
Новое в планировании капитального строительства и строительного производства. Москва, Стройиздат, 1971.
80 p. with diagrs. 20 cm. 0.22rub USSR 72-VKP
At head of title: М. И. Балихин.
1. Construction industry—Russia—Management. I. Title.
Title romanized: Novoe v planirovanii kapital'nogo stroitel'stva i stroitel'nogo proizvodstva.
HD9715.R92B314 73-314505

Balikían, O. S.
see Admiral flota Sovetskogo Soíùza Ivan Stepanovich Isakov. 1975.

Balıklı Rum Hastanesi
see
Nosokomeia Valouklē.

Balikpapan, Indonesia.
Analisa & rencana garis besar Kotamadya Balikpapan, kerjasama Pemerintah Daerah Kotamadya Balikpapan dengan Direktorat Tata Kota dan Daerah. ₍Jakarta₎ 1973.
v, 108 l. 21 x 33 cm.
Cover title.
"Penyempurnaan Juni 1973."
1. Cities and towns—Planning—Balikpapan, Indonesia. I. Indonesia. Direktorat Tata Kota dan Daerah. II. Title.
HT169.I 54B33 1973 73-942619

Balikpapan, Indonesia
see Dasawarsa Kotamadya Balikpapan, 1960-1970. [Balikpapan] : Kotamadya Balikpapan [1970]

Balil Illana, Alberto.
C. Iulius versus Maximus "Thrax". Madrid, Imprenta y Editorial Maestre, 1965.
171 p. 24 cm.
"Publicado en el 'Boletín de la Real Academia de la historia', v. 157."
Bibliographical footnotes.
MWH NUC73-47466

Balil Illana, Alberto.
Casa y urbanismo en la España antigua / Alberto Balil. — Santiago de Compostela : Seminario de Arqueología, Facultad de Filosofía y Letras, Universidad, 1972-
v. : ill. ; 25 cm. — (Studia archaeologica ; 17 20, 28) Sp***
"Publicado en el Boletín del Seminario de Estudios de Arte y Arqueología de la Universidad de Valladolid, t. 36.
Includes bibliographical references.
1. Spain—Antiquities. 2. Architecture, Domestic—Spain—History. 3. Cities and towns, Ruined, extinct, etc.—Spain—History. I. Title. II. Series: Studia archaeologica (Santiago de Compostela) ; 17 ₍etc.₎
DP44.B28 75-407973

Balil Illana, Alberto.
Economía de la Hispania romana (S. I-III d.C.) / Alberto Balil. — Santiago de Compostela : Seminario de Arqueología, Facultad de Filosofía y Letras, Universidad, 1972.
119 p. ; 24 cm. — (Studia archaeologica ; 15) Sp74-Jan
Includes bibliographical references.
1. Spain—Economic conditions. 2. Spain—History—Roman period, 218 B.C.—414 A.D. 3. Romans in Spain. I. Title. II. Series: Studia archaeologica (Santiago de Compostela) ; 15.
HC384.B34 76-482316
*76 MARC

Balil Illana, Alberto.
Estudios de cerámica romana. [Por] A. Balil. Santiago de Compostela, Seminario de Argueología, Facultád de Filosofía y Letras, 1969 ₍i.e. 1970-
illus. (Studia archaeologica, 4)
Library has: v. 1.
1. Pottery, Roman. I. Title. II. Series: Studia archaeologica (Santiago de Compostela), 4.
ICU NUC74-24159

Balima, Salfo Albert, 1930-
Genèse de la Haute-Volta. ₍Ouagadougou, Presses africaines, 1970?₎
253 p. illus., music. 24 cm.
Bibliography: p. 252-253.
1. Upper Volta—History. 2. Upper Volta—History—Sources. I. Title.
DT553.U75B34 73-205694

Balin, Aleksandr, tr.
see Dzhalagoníià, Nodar Doment'evich, 1934- (Zemlia dlia tsvetov) 1972.

Balin, Aleksandr Ivanovich, 1890-1937.
(Liníià zhizni)
Линия жизни. ₍Ил.: Б. Шляпугин₎. Москва, "Сов. писатель," 1973.
159 p. with illus. 17 cm. (Книга стихов) 0.54rub USSR 73-VKP
At head of title: Александр Балин.
I. Title.
PG3476.B28675L5 1973 74-341598

Balin, Aleksandr Ivanovich, 1890-1937.
Postupok, kniga stikhov. Aleksandr Balin. Moskva, "Molodaia gvardiia, 1974.
111 p. illus. 15 cm.
MH MB NUC75-128323

Balin, Aleksandr Ivanovich, 1890-1937.
(Zatíàzhnoĭ pryzhok)
Затяжной прыжок : ₍Стихи₎ / Александр Балин ; ₍Ил. Б. Шляпугин₎. — Москва : Современник, 1975.
125 p. ; 17 cm. USSR 75
0.52rub
I. Title.
PG3476.B28675Z23 1975 77-514170

Balin, Howard.
Reproductive biology. Editors: Howard Balin ₍and₎ Stanley Glasser. Amsterdam, Excerpta Medica, 1972.
973 p. illus. 25 cm. Ne***
Includes bibliographies.
1. Reproduction. 2. Conception—Prevention. I. Glasser, Stanley, joint author. II. Title.
QP251.B27 591.2'16 73-163374
ISBN 90-219-2031-X MARC

Balin, Viktor Iosifovich.
(Premchand-novellist)
Премчанд-новеллист. Москва, Изд-во Ленингр. ун-та, 1973.
163 p. 20 cm. 0.66rub USSR 74
At head of title: Ленинградский государственный университет имени А. А. Жданова. В. И. Балин.
Includes bibliographical references.
1. Srivastava, Dhanpat Rai, 1881–1936. I. Title.
PK2098.S7Z56 74–319023

Balin and Balan. English.
The tale of Balain, from the Romance of the Grail, a 13th century French prose romance. Translated from the Old French by David E. Campbell. Evanston [Ill.] Northwestern University Press, 1972.
[33], 121 p. front. 24 cm. (Northwestern University Press medieval French texts)
Translation of the manuscript in the Cambridge University Library (Add. 7071) which comprises the Balain section of the Continuation of the Merlin from the Romance of the Grail.
Includes bibliographical references.
I. Title. II. Series.
PQ1496.M422E5 1972 843'.1 72–77830
ISBN 0–8101–0385–0 MARC

Balin and Balan. English
see Clarke, Graham, 1941- Balyn and Balan. [Boughton Monchelsea, Kent] Ebenezer Press [1970]

Balina, Aloys.
Sukuma expression of traditional religion in life / by Aloys Balina, Anthony Mayala, Justin M. Mabula. — [Kipalapala, Tanzania] : Kipalapala Seminary, 1971.
v, 74 p. : ill. ; 20 cm.
Bibliography: p.: 72-74.
1. Suku (African tribe)—Religion. I. Mayala, Anthony, joint author. II. Mabula, Justin M., joint author. III. Title.
BL2480.S8B34 299'.6 75-980130
76 MARC

Balina, Aloys.
Traditional marriage in Tanzania today. By Aloys Balina, Anthony Mayala [and] Justin M. Mabula. Kipalapala [Tanzania] Kipalapala Seminary, 1970.
vii, 58 p. illus. 20 cm.
1. Suku (African tribe) 2. Marriage customs and rites–Tanzania. I. Mayala, Anthony, joint author. II. Mabula, Justin M., joint author. III. Title.
IEN NUC76-71688

Balingit, Jesus E
Ang Kasalukuyang landas ng pag-ibig / isinalin ni Jesus Estrada Balingit. -- [s.l. : s.n.], 1974.
256 p. : ill. ; 21 cm.
I. Title.
MiU NUC77-101186

Balingit, Jesus E
The crusader of the cross, by Jesus E. Balingit. Philippines, 1972.
xxxii, 340 p. illus. 18 cm.
1. Meditations. I. Title.
BX2182.2.B3 242 75-304274
75 MARC

Balingit, Jesus E
I know mine and mine know me ... By Jesus E. Balingit. [Manila, Printed by Arnoldus Press, 1970]
160 p. illus. 23 cm.
CONTENTS: English poems.—Tagalog poems.—Other poems [in Pampango and Ilocano].—Thoughts.
I. Title.
PR9550.9.B3 I 22 821 73–170478
MARC

Balins, Arnolds, 1922–
Man's economic world; an introduction to economic geography [by] Arnolds Balins, Helen Sweet [and] Paul Thomas. Toronto, Holt, Rinehart and Winston of Canada [1971]
v, 426 p. illus. (part col.) maps. (part col.) 26 cm. $6.85
C 72–1655
Includes bibliographical references.
1. Geography, Economic. I. Sweet, Helen, joint author. II. Thomas, Paul, 1934– joint author. III. Title.
HC59.B3535 330.9 73–162679
ISBN 0–03–925570–0 MARC

al-Balinsī, Muḥammad ibn Ghālib
see
al-Balansī, Muḥammad ibn Ghālib, d. 1177?

Balińska, Irena Jomini-
see Jomini-Balińska, Irena.

Balinski, M L
A warehouse problem [by] M. L. Balinski [and] H. D. Mills. Prepared for Veterans Administration under Contract No. V1001P-116. [Princeton, Mathematica] 1960.
12 l. diagr.
1. Transportation–Mathematical models. I. Mills, Harlan D., 1919- joint author. II. Title.
MCM NUC74-27638

Balinski, M. L.
see Approaches to integer programming. Amsterdam, North-Holland Pub. Co., 1974.

Balinski, M. L.
see Computational practice in mathematical programming. Amsterdam, North-Holland, 1975.

Balinski, M. L.
see Nondifferentiable optimization. Amsterdam, North-Holland, 1975.

Balinski, M. L.
see Pivoting and extensions ... Amsterdam, North-Holland Pub. Co., 1974.

Baliński, Michał, 1794–1864.
Dawna Akademia Wileńska; próba jej historyi od założenia w roku 1579 do ostatecznego jej przekształcenia w roku 1803. Przez Michała Balińskiego. Petersburg, Nakł. i drukiem J. Ohryzki, 1862.
xi, 606 p. illus. 25 cm.
Includes bibliographical references.
1. Vilna. Akademia Wileńska—History. I. Title.
LF4446.V56B34 73–333960

Balinsky, Boris Ivan, 1905-
An introduction to embryology / B. I. Balinsky. — 4th ed. — Philadelphia : Saunders, 1975.
xvii, 648 p. : ill. ; 27 cm.
Bibliography: p. 605-633.
Includes index.
ISBN 0-7216-1518-X
1. Embryology. I. Title.
[DNLM: 1. Embryology. QL955 B186i]
QL955.B184 1975 591.3'3 74-17748
75 MARC

Balint, Andras.
A critique of English-Hungarian and Hungarian-English general lexicography. [New York] 1968. [c1971]
xvi, 344 l. tables. 29 cm.
Thesis–Columbia University.
Bibliography: leaves 315-332.
1. Hungarian language–Lexicography. 2. English language–Lexicography. I. Title.
NNC NUC73-123841

Bálint, András.
Florile lui Bálint András = Bálint András virágai / Bálint András, Seres András. — Sf. Gheorghe : Centrul județean de îndrumare a creației populare și a mișcării artistice de masă Covasna, 1974.
31 p. : ill. ; 22 cm. — (Meșteri populari) R 75–2328
Romanian and Hungarian.
lei 3.20
1. Bálint, Andras. 2. Wood-Carving—Romania. I. Seres, András, joint author. II. Title. III. Title: Bálint András virágai.
NK9798.B26S47 75–547392

Bálint, Csanád.
Hunok, avarok, magyarok; vezető a Szegedi Móra Ferenc Múzeum régészeti kiállításához. Szeged [Szegedi Nyomda, 1973?]
[38] p. illus. 20 cm.
Summary in German; captions also in German.
Bibliography: p. [33]
1. Magyars. 2. Avars. 3. Huns. 4. Hungary—Antiquities. I. Szeged, Hungary. Móra Ferenc Múzeum. II. Title.
DB920.B29 74–234686

Balint, Emery, 1911-
A university laboratory for building research [by] E. Balint. Kensington, N.S.W., Architecture and Building Research Laboratory, University of New South Wales [1971?]
23 p. illus. (Report no. 6)
Cover title.
1. Building research. 2. Building research–Study and teaching. I. Title. II. Series: New South Wales. University. Kensington. Architecture and Building Research Laboratory. Report no. 6.
CaMWU NUC76-36564

Bálint, Endre, 1914–
Hazugságok naplójából. Budapest, Magvető Könyvkiadó [1972]
238, [48] p. illus. 23 cm. 63.00Ft
1. Arts, Hungarian. 2. Arts, Modern—20th century—Hungary. I. Title.
NX571.H8B34 73–204776

Bálint, Endre, 1914-
see Pilinszky, János. A nap születése. Budapest, Móra, 1974.

Balint, Enid.
Six minutes for the patient; interactions in general practice consultation, edited by Enid Balint & J. S. Norell. London, Tavistock Publications, 1973.
xxi, 182 p. 23 cm. (Mind and medicine monographs, 23) £2.25
GB 74–03907
Distributed in the U. S. A. by Harper & Row Publishers, Barnes & Noble Import Division.
Bibliography: p. 176–177.
Includes index.
1. Physician and patient. 2. Medicine and psychology. 3. Physicians (General practice) I. Norell, Jacob Solomon, joint author. II. Title. III. Series.
R727.3.B29 616.08 74–165159
ISBN 0–422–74270–8 MARC

Balint, Enid
see Balint, Michael. Focal psychotherapy; an example of applied psychoanalysis. London, Tavistock Publications; Philadelphia, J. B. Lippincott, 1972.

Balint, George, 1923-
An iterative method for the analysis of multi-story frames. [New York] 1974.
iv, 95 l. illus. 29 cm.
Thesis–Columbia University.
Bibliography: leaves 91-95.
1. Structural frames. I. Title.
NNC NUC76-18994

Bálint, György.
Gyumolcsoskert. 2. jav. kiad. Budapest, Mezogazdasagi Kiado, 1974.
324 p. illus.
1. Fruit-culture. I. Title.
DNAL NUC76-18993

Bálint, György, 1906–1943.
Rejtsd el az örümöd / Bálint György ; [Az előszó és a szerkesztés Gondos Ernő munkája]. — Budapest : Szépirodalmi Könyvkiadó, 1974.
103 p., [1] leaf of plates : port. ; 19 cm.
ISBN 963–15–0107–8 : 14.50Ft
I. Title.
PH3213.B233R4 1974 75–579850

Bálint, Gyula, ed.
see A III. [i. e. Harmadik] ötéves terv eredményei megyénkben, 1966-1970. Szeged, 1971.

Bálint, István.
Sorsok, szenvedélyek / Bálint István. -- Budapest : Kiadja az Alkoholizmus Elleni Országos Bizottság, 1972?
169 p. ; 21 cm.
1. Alcoholism--Hungary. 2. Hungary--Social conditions. I. Title.
NjR NUC77-101187

Bálint, István.
Utmutató alkoholista betegek gondozásához. Budapest [Alkoholizmus Elleni Országos Bizottsag] 1975.
64 p.
1. Alcoholism--Therapy. I. Alkoholizmus Elleni Országos Bizottság. II. Title.
DNLM NUC77-87922

Balint, John A
Gsstrointestinal bleeding : diagnosis and management / John A. Balint, I. James Sarfeh, Martin B. Fried. — New York : Wiley, c1977.
xiii, 101 p. : ill. ; 26 cm. — (Clinical gastroenterology monograph series) (A Wiley medical publication)
Includes bibliographical references and index.
ISBN 0-471-04607-8
1. Gastrointestinal hemorrhage. I. Sarfeh, I. James, joint author. II. Fried, Martin Barry, 1946- joint author. III. Title. IV. Series.
[DNLM: 1. Hemorrhage, Gastrointestinal—Diagnosis. 2. Hemorrhage, Gastrointestinal—Therapy. WI143 B186g]
RC802.B34 616.3'3 77-4423
77 MARC

Bálint, József, ed.
see A Népgazdaság irányitási rendszere. Budapest, Közgazdasági és Jogi Könyvkiadó, 1970.

Bálint, József
see Sistema upravlenii͡a narodnym khozi͡aĭstvom v VNR. Budapesht, Izd-vo Akademii nauk Vengrii, 1972.

Bálint, Károly
see A Népi ülnök kézikönyve. 2. jav. kiad. Budapest, Közgazdasági és Jogi Könyvkiadó, 1966.

Bálint, Lajos, 1886–
Mind csak színház / Bálint Lajos. — Budapest : Szépirodalmi Könyvkiadó, 1975.
281 p., ⌊1⌋ leaf of plates : port. ; 19 cm.
CONTENTS: Jászai Mari.—A szőke csoda.—Szacsvay Imre.—Tóth Imre.—Újházi Ede.—A legszebb színésznő.—A Thália Társaság.—Hevesi.—Pethes Imre.—Bevezető.—A Latabárok.—Egy család százötven éve.—Gózon Gyula.—Somogyi Erzsi.—Rajnay Gábor.—Gombaszögi Frida.—Boldogtalan boldogság.—A titokzatos ember.—Testvérharc.—Az igazi hős óbudán.—Magamról.
ISBN 963-15-0258-9 : 20.00Ft
1. Actors, Hungarian—Biography. I. Title.
PN2859.H85B3 75-401771

Bálint, Lea.
Boldogsagom erdeje. Budapest, Magvető Kiadó [1972]
105 p.
I. Title.
InU DLC NUC73-121096

Balint, Magda.
Greater London's economically active population / by Magda Balint. — London : Greater London Council, c1975.
89 p. : ill. ; 30 cm. — (Research memorandum - Intelligence Unit, Greater London Council ; RM441) GB***
Bibliography: p. 89.
ISBN 0-7168-0696-7 : £1.00
1. Labor supply—England—London metropolitan area—Statistics. I. Title. II. Series: Greater London Council. Intelligence Unit. Research memorandum - Intelligence Unit, Greater London Council ; RM441.
HD5768.L8B25 331.1'1'09421 76-364639
76 MARC

Balint, Michael.
The doctor, his patient, and the illness. Rev. ed. New York, International Universities Press ⌊1972⌋
395 p.
1. Psychotherapy. 2. Physicians. 3. Medicine—Cases, clinical reports, statistics. I. Title.
ViBlbV NUC73-123844

Balint, Michael.
Focal psychotherapy; an example of applied psychoanalysis ⌊by⌋ Michael Balint, Paul H. Ornstein & Enid Balint. London, Tavistock Publications; Philadelphia, J. B. Lippincott, 1972.
vii, 166 p. 23 cm. index. (Mind & medicine monographs, 22) £2.50 B 72-31181
Bibliography: p. 160–⌊161⌋
1. Psychotherapy—Cases, clinical reports, statistics. I. Ornstein, Paul H. II. Balint, Enid. III. Title. IV. Series.
RC480.5.B28 616.8'914 73-159491
ISBN 0-422-74040-3 MARC

Balint, Michael.
Les Voies de la régression. Avec une étude de Enid Balint: Distance dans l'espace et dans le temps. Traduit de l'anglais par Myriam Viliker et Judith Dupont. Paris, Payot, 1972.
191 p. 23 cm. (Bibliothèque scientifique. Collection Science de l'homme) 28.70F F 72-7540
Translation of Thrills and regressions.
1. Psychoanalysis. I. Title.
BF175.B214 72-364604

Balint, P S
Reinforcement detailing of frame corner joints with particular reference to opening corners ⌊by⌋ P. S. Balint and H. P. J. Taylor. ⌊London⌋ Cement and Concrete Association, 1972.
16 p. (Technical report, 42.462)
Cover title.
1. Structural frames. I. Taylor, H. P. J. II. Title.
CU-A NUC73-123856

Bálint, Sándor.
Szeged reneszánsz kori műveltsége / Bálint Sándor. — Budapest : Akadémiai Kiadó, 1975.
185 p. : ill. ; 25 cm. — (Humanizmus és reformáció ; 5)
Some of the text in Latin.
Summary in French.
Includes bibliographical references and index.
ISBN 963-05-0685-8 : 44.00Ft
1. Szeged, Hungary—Intellectual life—History. 2. Renaissance—Hungary—Szeged. I. Title. II. Series.
DB999.S93B34 77-505085

Bálint, Sárosi.
Cigányzene ... Budapest, Gondolat, 1971.
247 p. illus. (part col.), music. 20 cm.
Bibliography: p. 227-[232]
1. Folk music, Gipsy—Hist. & crit. I. Title.
CaBVaU NUC74-137607

Bálint, Stefan, joint author.
see Hentschel, Uwe. Plausible diagnostic taxonomy in the field of neurosis. Lund, Lund University, 1974.

Balint, Stephen V
Identifying parameters of heterogeneously mixed normal populations using curve fitting techniques research report / by Stephen V. Balint. -- Texarkana, Texas : Production Design Engineering Division, U.S. Army Material Command, Intern Training Center, 1971.
v, 65, [1] p. : ill. ; 27 cm. -- (USAMC-ITC Report ; no. 2-71-25)
Bibliography: p. 65-[66]
1. Manpower--Evaluation. 2. Population--Statistical methods. I. Title.
DI-GS NUC77-101188

Bálint, Tibor, 1932–
Kenyér és gyertyaláng : arcképek, vallomások, tanulmányok / Bálint Tibor. — Kolozsvár-Napoca : Dacia, 1975.
214 p. ; 20 cm. R 75-2349
lei 7.75
I. Title.
AC95.H9B332 75-548581

Bálint, Tibor, 1932–
Nekem már fáj az utazás. ⌊Novellák⌋. Bukarest, „Kriterion," 1973.
279 p. 20 cm. lei 13.50 R 74-1102
I. Title.
PH3213.B234N4 74-323678

Bálint-Izsák, László.
Holdsütésben : három kisregény / Bálint Izsák László ; ⌊fedélterv Kazinczy G.⌋. — ⌊Timişoara⌋ : Facla, 1976.
187 p. ; 20 cm. R76-4774
CONTENTS: Garzonlakás.—Holdsütésben.—Csöppi.
lei8.50
I. Title.
PH3213.B2344H65 77-551550
*77 MARC

Balint Society.
see Patient-centred medicine ... London, Regional Doctor Publications Ltd. ⌊for⌋ the Balint Society, 1972.

Balintescu, Alexandru
see Arhiva generalului Gheorghe Magheru... Bucuresti: [s.n.] 1968.

Balintfy, Joseph L
Mathematical models and analysis of certain stochastic processes in general hospitals, by Joseph L. Balintfy. Baltimore, Md., 1962.
165 l. illus.
Thesis—Johns Hopkins University.
Bibliography: leaves 161-164.
Microfilm (positive) Ann Arbor, Mich., University Microfilms, 1963. 1 reel. (Publication no. 3616)
NNC NUC74-178483

Balintfy, Joseph L
see Tulane University of Louisiana. Computer System Research Group. Computerized dietary information system. New Orleans ⌊1966?-67⌋

Bálintné Hegyesi, Júlia.
Szolnok helyismereti bibliográfiája / Bálintné Hegyesi Júlia. — Szolnok : ⌊Verseghy Ferenc Megyei Könyvtár⌋, 1974–
v. ; 20 cm. — (A Verseghy Ferenc Megyei Könyvtár bibliográfiái)
Includes indexes.
19.50Ft (v. 1)
1. Szolnok, Hungary—Bibliography. I. Title. II. Series: Verseghy Ferenc Megyei Könyvtár. Verseghy Ferenc Megyei Könyvtár bibliográfiái.
Z2147.S96B34 75-401161
[DB879.S937]

Balio, Tino.
United Artists : the company built by the stars / Tino Balio. — Madison : University of Wisconsin Press, 1976.
xviii, 323 p. : ill. ; 24 cm.
Includes bibliographical references and index.
ISBN 0-299-06940-0 : $15.00
1. United Artists Corporation. I. Title.
PN1999.U5B3 791.43'06'579494 75-12208
75 MARC

Balio, Tino.
see The American film industry. Madison, University of Wisconsin Press, 1976.

Baliobov, M. Gh., joint author
see Guliamov, I͡Akh'i͡a Guli͡amovich. (Uzbekiston SSR tarikhi) 1958.

Balioniene, Emilija, 1931-
Palaukių vasara. Vilnius, Vaga, 1967.
57 p. 17 cm.
Short stories.
1. Fiction, Lithuanian. I. Title.
NN NUC73-47469

Balionienė, Emilija, 1931-
Prieblandos valanda; apsakymai. Vilnius, Vaga, 1972.
129 p.
Russian title in colophon: Sumerechnyi chas.
Lithuanian text.
I. Title: Sumerechnyi chas.
MH NUC75-26589

Baliotti, Dan, illus.
see Fischler, Stan. The blazing North Stars. Englewood Cliffs, N. J., Prentice-Hall ⌊c1972⌋

Baliotti, Dan, illus.
see Fischler, Stan. The burly Bruins... Englewood Cliffs, N. J., Prentice-Hall ⌊c1971⌋

Baliotti, Dan, illus.
see Fischler, Stan. The champion Bruins... Englewood Cliffs, N. J., Prentice-Hall ⌊c1972⌋

Baliotti, Dan, illus.
see Fischler, Stan. Chicago's Black Hawks. Englewood Cliffs, N.J., Prentice-Hall [c1972]

Baliotti, Dan, illus.
see Fischler, Stan. The conquering Canadiens, Stanley Cup champions. Scarborough, Ont., Prentice-Hall of Canada [c1971]

Baliotti, Dan, illus.
see Fischler, Stan. Go Leafs, go! The Toronto hockey story. Scarborough, Ont., Prentice-Hall of Canada [1971]

Baliotti, Dan, illus.
see Fischler, Stan. The roaring Rangers and the Emile Francis years. Englewood Cliffs, N.J., Prentice-Hall [c1971]

Baliotti, Dan.
see Fischler, Stan. This is hockey. Englewood Cliffs, N.J., Prentice-Hall, c1975.

Balioulēs, Stergios
see
Valioulēs, Stergios, 1916-

Baliozian, Ara.
The Armenians : their history and culture : a short introduction / by Ara Baliozian. — Toronto : Kar Pub. House, 1975.
211 p. ; 21 cm. C***
Bibliography: p. [195]-[204]
Includes index.
1. Armenians. I. Title.
DS165.B27 956.6'2 76-361732
76 MARC

Balirama Hiramana Patila
see
Patila, Balirama Hiramana, 1898-1973.

Balis, Jan.
see Bibliothèque royale Albert Ier. 100e [i.e. Centième] anniversaire du Jardin botanique national de Belgique. Bruxelles, 1970.

Balis, Jan
see Bibliothèque royale Albert Ier. 100 [i.e. Hunderd] jaar Nationale Plantentuin van België. Brussel, Koninklijke Bibliotheek Albert I, 1970.

Balis, M Earl.
Antagonists and nucleic acids. [By] M. Earl Balis. With a chapter by George B. Brown. New York, American Elsevier, 1968.
x, 293 p. 25 cm. (Frontiers of biology, v. 10)
Includes bibliographies.
1. Nucleic acids. 2. Antimetabolites. I. Title. II. Series.
NNC NUC73-122030

Balisong, Benito V 1932-
The history and present status of education in the Province of Abra, by Benito V. Balisong. [Cebu City] 1962.
xiv, 260 l. 28 cm.
Thesis–University of San Carlos.
Bibliography: leaves [252]-258.
1. Education–Philippine Islands. 2. Abra, Philippines (Province) I. Title.
CtY NUC74-175379

Balitskiĭ, Andreĭ Vasil'evich.
(Tekhnologiia izgotovleniia vakuumnoĭ apparatury)
Технология изготовления вакуумной аппаратуры / В. А. Балицкий. — Изд. 3-е, перераб. и доп. — Москва : Энергия, 1974.
312 p. : ill. ; 20 cm. USSR 74
Bibliography: p. 306-[309]
1.05rub
1. Vacuum. 2. Physical instruments. I. Title.
QC166.B26 1974 75-529141

Balitskiĭ, D. K., ed.
see Veprosy paleogeografii, vulkanizma i metallogenii podnego dokembriia i paleozoia iuga Srednei Sibiri. 1972.

Balitskiĭ, Vitaliĭ Grigor'evich
see Voprosy istorii Dal'nego Vostoka. Khabarovsk, Khabarovskii gos. ped. institut, 1972.

Baliukonytė, Onė.
Laukinės vaivorykštės. Vilnius, "Vaga," 1971.
75 p. 17 cm. 0.24rub USSR 71-37714
Poems.
I. Title.
PG8722.12.A35L3 72-372690

Balius Artau, Jaime.
Hay dinero en el champiñon... Barcelona, Editiorial Sintes [c1971]
155 p.
1. Mushroom culture. I. Title.
InLP NUC76-71689

Balivānī, Hūndrāju
see
Balwani, Hundraj, 1946-

Baliyāṭika, Vijaya, 1933-
(Jai jajamāna)
जै जजमान; भोजपुरी कहानी संग्रह. लेखक विजय बलियाटिक. [1. संस्करण] वाराणसी, भोजपुरी संसद [सं. 2030 i.e. 1973]
2, 106 p. 20 cm. Rs3.50
In Bhojpuri.

I. Title.

PK1828.B3J3 73-907799

Baliyāṭika, Vijaya, 1933-
(Visphoṭa)
विस्फोट; हास्य-व्यंग्य के भ्रान्तेय शब्दायुधों का. [कवि] विजय बलियाटिक. [1. संस्करण. वाराणसी, समकालीन प्रकाशन, 1973]
6, 94 p. port. 22 cm. Rs4.50
In Hindi.

I. Title.

PK2098.13.A42V5 73-903355

Balize
see
British Honduras.

Baljeu, Joost.
Joost Baljeu : [tentoonstelling] Haags Gemeentemuseum, 13 december 1975-14 februari 1976. — [Den Haag : Haags Gemeentemuseum, 1976]
[84] p. : ill. ; 21 cm. Ne***
Dutch or English.
Bibliography: p. [81]-[82].
1. Baljeu, Joost. I. Hague. Gemeentemuseum.
NB653.B34H34 77-462041
77 MARC

Baljeu, Joost.
Morgen kan het architectuur zijn = It can be architecture tomorrow / Joost Baljeu. — [s.l. : s.n., 1975?] (Den Haag : Combigraph Drukkerijen)
[32] p., [12] leaves of plates : ill. ; 21 cm. Ne***
Cover title.
Issued in portfolio.
Dutch and English.
"This publication ... appears on the occasion of a retrospective exhibition of works by the author, to be held in the Haags Gemeentemuseum ... from December 13th 1975 to February 14th 1976."
1. Baljeu, Joost. I. Title. II. Title: It can be architecture tomorrow.
NB653.B34A5 709'.2'4 77-478624
77 MARC

Baljeu, Joost.
Theo van Doesburg / Joost Baljeu. — London : Studio Vista, 1974.
232 p. : ill. (some col.), facsims., plans, ports. ; 26 cm. GB75-13711
Bibliography: p. 205-219.
Includes index.
ISBN 0-289-70358-1 : £8.50
1. Doesburg, Theo van, 1883-1931. I. Doesburg, Theo van, 1883-1931. Selected works. 1974.
N6953.D57B34 1974b 709'.2'4 75-325382
75 MARC

Baljeu, Joost.
Theo van Doesburg. [1st American ed.] New York, Macmillan [1974]
232 p. illus. (part col.) 26 cm.
Bibliography: p. 205-219.
ISBN 0-02-506440-1 : $15.95
1. Doesburg, Theo van, 1883-1931. I. Doesburg, Theo van, 1883-1931. Selected works. 1974.
N6953.D57B34 1974 709'.2'4 [B] 74-7400
MARC

Baljeu, Joost.
see Annely Juda Fine Art. Joost Baljeu ... London, Annely Juda Fine Art, [1975]

Baljit Snehi, 1950-
(Kalaṅkita rākhī)
कलंकित राखी; एक सामाजिक उपन्यास. [लेखक] बलजीत 'स्नेही.' [1. संस्करण] नई दिल्ली, अजय पब्लिशर्स [1972]
190 p. 18 cm. Rs8.00
In Hindi.

I. Title.

PK2098.13.A43K3 72-903113

Baljon, Johannes Marinus Simon, tr.
see Waliullah, Shah, 1702 or 3-1762 or 3. A mystical interpretation of prophetic tales by an Indian muslim... Leiden, Brill, 1973.

Balk, Alfred
see Twentieth Century Fund. A free and responsive press... New York, 1973 [c1972]

Balk, Alfred.
see Twentieth Century Fund. A free and responsive press ... Millwood, N.Y., Kraus Reprint Co., 1975, c1972.

Balk, D. O.
see Ocherki istorii Rudnogo Altaia. Ust'-Kamenogorsk, 1970 [vyp. dan. 1971]

al-Balk, Fu'ād
see
al-Buluk, Fu'ād.

Balk, Greta.
Internationale forumkeuze voor en na de inwerkingtreding van het EEG-executieverdrag / Greta Balk. — [Groningen] : H. D. Tjeenk Willink ; [Leiden] : A. W. Sijthoff, 1975.
31 p. ; 24 cm. — (Studentenscripties internationaal privaatrecht ; 5)
Ne76-29
At head of title: Interuniversitair Instituut voor Internationaal Recht T. M. C. Asser Instituut.
Bibliography: p. 30-31.
ISBN 9001048501 : fl 4.00
1. Jurisdiction—European Economic Community countries. 2. Judgments—European Economic Community countries. 3. Executions (Law)—European Economic Community countries. I. Title. II. Series.
77-475598
*77 MARC

Balk, H Wesley.
The dramatization of 365 days [by] H. Wesley Balk. Based on the book by Ronald J. Glasser. Minneapolis, University of Minnesota Press [1972]
vii, 148 p. illus. 22 cm. $5.95
"Song for 365 days by, Tom Johnson" (unacc. melody) : p. 28-29.
1. Vietnamese Conflict, 1961- —Drama. I. Glasser, Ronald J. 365 days. II. Title.
PS3552.A454D7 812'.5'4 72-85756
ISBN 0-8166-0670-6 MARC

Balk, Mark Benevich.
(Sbornik zadach po nebesnoĭ mekhanike i kosmodinamike)
Сборник задач по небесной механике и космодинамике. [Учеб. пособие для вузов]. Под общ. ред. В. Г. Демина. Москва, "Наука," 1972.
336 p. with diagrs. 22 cm. 0.95rub USSR 73-VKP
At head of title: М. Б. Балк, В. Г. Демин, А. Л. Куницын.
Includes bibliographies.
1. Astrodynamics—Problems, exercises, etc. 2. Mechanics, Celestial—Problems, exercises, etc. I. Demin, Vladimir Grigor'evich, joint author. II. Kunitsyn, Andreĭ Leonidovich, joint author. III. Title.
TL1050.B317 74-341744

Balk, Mark Benevich
see Polianaliticheskie i reguliarnye kvaternionnye funktsii. 1973.

Balk, Walter L
Improving government productivity : some policy perspectives / Walter L. Balk. — Beverly Hills, Calif. : Sage Publications, c1975.
70 p. : ill. ; 22 cm. — (Sage professional papers in administrative and policy studies ; ser. no. 03-025)
Bibliography: p. 67-70.
ISBN 0-8039-0626-9 : $3.00
1. Civil service—Labor productivity. 2. United States—Officials and employees. I. Title.
HD8001.B35 331.1'18 75-38319
76 MARC

Balk, Walter L
see Adams, Harold. Planning for change in the Division of Vocational Education. Albany, 1968.

Balk, Walter L.
see Administering state government productivity improvement programs ... Albany, The Project, [1975]

Balk, Walter L.
see Motivating state government productivity improvement programs ... [Albany] Productivity Research Project for State Government, State University of New York at Albany, [1975]

Balk, Walter L.
see Symposium on Productivity and Managerial Assessment, Albany, 1975. Public utility productivity ... Albany, New York State Dept. of Public Service, [1975?]

Balk-Smit Duyzentkunst, F
Een referentiële identiteitskrisis. Door F. Balk-Smit Duyzentkunst. Assen, Van Gorcum, 1972.
26 p. 23 cm. fl 3.90 Ne 72-45
Rede—Amsterdam.
Bibliography: p. 25-26.
1. Grammar, Comparative and general—Syntax. 2. Logic. I. Title.
P39.B28 73-337348
ISBN 90-232-1055-7

Balk-Smit Duyqentkunst, F
see Controversen in de taal- en literatuurwetenschap. Wassenaar: Servire, 1974.

Balka
see
Tokombaev, Aaly.

Balka, Aaly
see Tokombaev, Aaly.

Balka, Austra.
Vaŗviksnēm skanot : dzejoļi / Austra **Balka.** — [s. l.] : Dzilna, 1974.
109 p. : ill. ; 22 cm.
I. Title.
PG9119.B3V3 74-236597

Balka, Don
see College algebra. 2d ed. Menlo Park, Calif., Cummings Pub. Co. [1973]

Balka, Marie.
Les mains nues : [roman] / M. Balka. — [Paris] : Gallimard, [1975]
365 p. ; 21 cm. F***
39.00F
I. Title.
PQ2662.A38M3 843'.9'14 75-510689
75 MARC

Balka, Marie.
Oratorio [par] M. Balka. [Paris] Gallimard [1973]
235 p. 21 cm. 25.00F F***
I. Title.
PQ2662.A38O7 843'.9'14 74-183940
MARC

Balka, Marie.
Outpost [by] M. Balka. Translated by the author. New York, Delacorte Press [1973]
167 p. 21 cm. $6.00
Translation of La rançon du silence.
I. Title.
PZ4.B1837Ou 843'.9'14 70-180049
[PQ2662.A38] MARC

Balkam, H. S.
see Community planning act 1972... [Fredericton] New Brunswick, Dept. of Municipal Affairs [1972]

Balkan, Behire.
Türkiye özetli nüfus bibliografyası. cilt 1- 1970-
[Ankara]
v. 24 cm. (Hacettepe Üniversitesi yayınları)
Turkish or English.
1. Turkey—Population—Bibliography. I. Title. II. Series: Hacettepe Üniversitesi. Hacettepe Üniversitesi yayınları.
Z7165.T9B342 72-207051
rev MARC-S

Balkan, Katherine Shelly, 1945-
Sir Joshua Reynolds' theory and practice of portraiture: a reevaluation. Los Angeles, 1972.
529 l.
Thesis (Ph. D.)—University of California, Los Angeles.
Includes abstract.
Appendix B. Illustrations. leaves 225-529.
Bibliography: leaf 183.
Vita.
1. Reynolds, Sir Joshua, 1723-1792. I. Title.
CLU NUC76-71690

Balkan, Kemal.
İnandık'ta 1966 [i. e. bin dokuz yüz altmış altı] yılında bulunan Eski Hitit çağına ait bir bağış belgesi = Eine Schenkungsurkunde aus der althethitischen Zeit, gefunden in İnandık, 1966 / Kemal Balkan. — Ankara : [Anadolu Medeniyetlerini Araştırma Vakfı], 1973.
xii, 103 p. : ill. ; 24 cm. — (Anadolu Medeniyetlerini Araştırma Vakfı yayınları ; no. 1)
German and Turkish.
Errata slip inserted.
Includes bibliographical references.
1. Gifts (Hittite Law) 2. Deeds, Hittite. 3. Inscriptions, Hittite. I. Title: İnandık'ta bin dokuz yüz altmış altı yılında ... II. Title: Eine Schenkungsurkunde aus der althethitischen Zeit ... III. Series: Anadolu Medeniyetlerini Araştırma Vakfı. Anadolu Medeniyetlerini Araştırma Vakfı yayınları ; no. 1.
76-970129

Balkan, Kemal
see Ankara Arkeoloji Müzesi. Ankara Arkeoloji Müzesinde bulunan Bogazköy tabletleri. Istanbul : Milli Eğitim Basimevi, 1948.

Balkan, Kemal, ed.
see Anum-hirbi, King of Mama. Mama kirali Anum-Hirbi'nin kaniş kirali Warşama'ya Gönerdiği mektup. Ankara, Türk Tarih Kurumu Basimevi, 1957.

Balkan Conference, International
see
International Balkan Conference, University of California at Los Angeles, 1969.

Balkan Medical Union
see
Union médicale balkanique.

The Balkan range : a Bulgarian reader / edited by John Robert Colombo and Nikola Roussanoff. — Toronto : Hounslow Press, c1976.
343 p. : ill. ; 24 cm. C***
Bibliography: p. 339-343.
ISBN 0-88882-011-9
1. Bulgarian literature—Translations into English. 2. English literature—Translations from Bulgarian. 3. Bulgaria—History—Literary collections. I. Colombo, John Robert, 1936- II. Roussanoff, Nikola.
PG1145.E1B3 891.8'1'08 76-377077
76 MARC

The Balkan states...specially prepared for, and with the assistance of, the Information Department of the Royal Institute of International Affairs. London, Oxford University Press, H. Milford, 1936- New York, Johnson Reprint Corporation [1970-
v. map, tables. 22 cm.
Includes bibliographical references.
Contents.-1.Economic.
1. Balkan peninsula—Econ. condit. I. Royal Institute of International Affairs. Information Dept.
NcD NUC77-34222

Balkanikus.
[Makedonskata osvoboditelna borba]
Македонската освободителна борба и превратa отъ 19 май, 1934 год. въ България. Индианаполисъ, Изд. на Центр. ком-т на Македонскитѣ полит. организации въ Съединенитѣ Щати, Канада, и Австралия, 1936.
20 p. 30 cm.
At head of title: Балканикус.
1. Macedonia—History. 2. Macedonian question. I. Title.
DR701.M4B28 66-96973
rev 2

Balkanistica. no. 1-
[Cambridge, Mass.] Slavica Publishers, 1974-
no. ill. 23 cm.
"Occasional papers in Southeast European studies."
No. 1- published for the American Association for South Slavic Studies.
ISSN 0360-2206
1. Balkan States—Collected works. I. American Association for South Slavic Studies.
DR1.B34 949.6 75-648409
MARC-S

Balkanistické symposium
see Celostátní balkanistické symposium, 1st, Brno, 1969.

Bałkanistyka polska; materiały z posiedzeń naukowych Komisji Bałkanistycznej przy Komitecie Słowianoznawstwa PAN w latach 1972-1973. [Komitet redakcyjny tomu: Zdzisław Stieber, Kazimierz Feleszko, Jan Reychman] Wrocław, Zakład Narodowy im. Ossolińskich Wydawn. Polskiej Akademii Nauk, 1974.
156 p.
At head of title: Polska Akademia Nauk. Komitet Słowianoznawstwa.
Summaries in German, French, English and Russian.
Bibliographical footnotes.
I. Stieber, Zdzisław.
MiU NUC76-22707

The Balkans; useful information for all those interested in the situation of the Balkans. An authoritative Turkish document. [Indianapolis, Central Committee of the Macedonian Patriotic Organization of the United States and Canada, 1969]
16 p. illus. 22 cm.
Caption title.
I. Macedonian Patriotic Organization of the United States and Canada. Central Committee.
IEdS NUC76-24463

Balkanska medicinska nedelja, 10th, Belgrad, 1970.
Recueil des communications de la X semaine médicale balkanique. Zbornik radova X balkanske medicinske nedelje. Belgrade, le 13-17 septembre, 1970. <Ljubljana, Zveza Zdravniških društev SFRJ; "Lek," tovarna farmacevtskih in kemičnih izdelkov, 1972>.
1226, [5] p. with illus. 25 cm. Yu72-9360
Includes bibliographies.
1. Medicine—Congresses. I. Title.
[R106.B36 1970] 610 73-970582
76 MARC

Balkanski, Gr
(Parizhkata komuna i bŭdeshteto obshtestvo)
Парижката комуна и бъдещето общество. Sydney, Наш път, 1971.
59 p. 21 cm. (Библиотека "Документация-Ориентация," № 5)
$1.00 (U.S.) 5.00F (France) Aus***
1. Paris—History—Commune, 1871. I. Title.
DC318.B34 73-325431

Balkanski, Gr
(Zadruzhno stopanisvane)
Задружно стопанисване : обществото, икономиката, формите на стопанисване, техниката са средства, инструменти, целта е човекът—неговото благоденствие и щастие ... / Гр. Балкански. — [Sydney] : Наш път, 1974.
49 p. ; 21 cm. — (Библиотека Документация—ориентация ; № 8) Aus***
Cover title.
Series romanized: Biblioteka Dokumentatsiia-orientatsiia.
1. Collective farms—Europe, Eastern. 2. Socialism. 3. Cooperation. I. Title.
HD1492.E8B28 76-506527

Balkanski, Minko, 1927-
see International Conference on Light Scattering in Solids, 3d, Campinas, Brazil, 1975. Proceedings of the third International Conference on Light Scattering in Solids, Campinas, Brazil, July 25-30, 1975. Paris, Flammarion, 1975.

Balkanski, Minko, 1927-
see Photonics. [Paris] Gauthier-Villars, c1973.

Balkanski, Nenko Dimitrov, 1907- ed.
see Sofia. Vissh institut za izobrazitelni izkustva "Nikolai Pavlovich." Dŭrzhavna khudozhestvena akademiia. (1972).

(Balkanski kulturni i literaturni vrŭzki)
Балкански културни и литературни връзки. [Сб. изследвания]. София, БАН, 1974.
262 p. 24 cm. (Studia Balcanica, 8) 2.50 lv Bu 74-1072
At head of title: Българска академия на науките. Институт за балканистика.
Added t. p.: Relations culturelles et littéraires des peuples balkaniques.
Edited by P. Rusev and others.
Summaries in Russian and French; table of contents also in Russian and French.
Includes bibliographical references.
1. Balkan Peninsula—Literatures—Addresses, essays, lectures. 2. Balkan Peninsula—Civilization—Addresses, essays, lectures. I. Rusev, Pen'o, ed. II. Bŭlgarska akademiia na naukite, Sofia. Institut za balkanistika. III. Title: Relations culturelles et littéraires des peuples balkaniques. IV. Series.
HT131.S8 no. 8 74-343346
[PN849.B3]

(Balkanski pisateli)
Балкански писатели; сборник с произведения на участниците в първата среща на балканските писатели. Отговорни редактори: Лиляна Ацева, Николай Янков. София, Нар. култура, 1965.
541 p. illus., ports. 21 cm.
1. Balkan Peninsula—Literatures. 2. Literature, Modern—20th century—Translations into Bulgarian. 3. Bulgarian literature—Translations from foreign literature. 4. Bulgarian literature—20th century. I. Atseva, Liliana, ed. II. Iankov, Nikolaĭ, ed.
PN849.B3B3 75-581579

(Balkanski prouchvaniia)
Балкански проучвания. XX век. София, БАН, 1972.
302 p. 24 cm. (Studia balcanica, 6) 2.87 lv Bu 72-925
At head of title: Българска академия на науките. Институт за балканистика.
Added t. p.: Recherches balkaniques.
Edited by N. Todorov and others.
Summaries in French; table of contents also in Russian and French.
Includes bibliographical references.
1. Balkan Peninsula—History—20th century—Addresses, essays, lectures. 2. Bulgaria—Relations (general) with the Balkan Peninsula—Addresses, essays, lectures. 3. Balkan Peninsula—Relations (general) with Bulgaria—Addresses, essays, lectures. I. Todorov, Nikolaĭ, ed. II. Bŭlgarska akademiia na naukite, Sofia. Institut za balkanistika. III. Title: Recherches balkaniques. IV. Series.
HT131.S8 no. 6 73-366018
[DR45]

Balkanski simpozium Formi za povishavane kvalifikatsiíata na nauchnite rabotnitsi, Varna, Bulgaria, 1972.
(Balkanski simpozium "Formi za povishavane kvalifikatsiíata na nauchnite rabotnitsi")
Балкански симпозиум "Форми за повишаване квалификацията на научните работници." ⌈Доклади. 14–16 окт.⌉. 1972 г. ⌈София⌉ Съюз на науч. работници в България (1973).
164 p. with diagrs. 20 cm. Bu 73-2640
Edited by K. Dimov and others.
Includes bibliographies.
1. Universities and colleges — Bulgaria — Graduate work — Congresses. I. Dimov, Kiril, ed. II. Sŭiûz na nauchnite rabotnitsi v Bŭlgariíà.
LA958.B34 1972 74-329854

(Balkanskiĭ istoricheskiĭ sbornik)
Балканский исторический сборник. ⌈Ред. коллегия: канд. ист. наук В. Я. Гросул, И. Э. Левит и Е. Е. Чертан. Сб.⌉ 1– Кишинев "Картя молдовеняскэ," 1968–
v. 21 cm. USSR 69-VKP (v. 1)
At head of title: v. : Академия наук Молдавской ССР. Институт истории.
Added t. p. in Moldavian and French.
Includes bibliographical references.
1.33rub (v. 1)
1. Balkan Peninsula—History—Collected works. I. Grosul, Vladislav Íàkimovich, ed. II. Levit, I. É., ed. III. Chertan, Evgeniĭ Evgen'evich, ed. IV. Akademiíà de Shtiintse a RSSM. Institutul de Istorie.
DR2.B33 76-517180

(Balkanskiĭ lingvisticheskiĭ sbornik)
Балканский лингвистический сборник / АН СССР, Ин-т славяноведения и балканистики ; ⌈Ред. коллегия ... Т. В. Цивьян (отв. ред.)⌉. — Москва : Наука, 1977.
324 p. : ill. ; 22 cm. USSR 77
Bibliography: p. 271–⌈274⌉
1.63rub
1. Balkan Peninsula — Languages — Addresses, essays, lectures. I. Tŝiv'íàn, Tat'íàna Vladimirovna. II. Akademiíà nauk SSSR. Institut slavíànovedeniíà i balkanistiki.
P381.B3B28 77-511860

(Balkanskoe íàzykoznanie)
Балканское языкознание. ⌈Сборник статей. Ред. коллегия: д-р филол. наук, проф. С. Б. Бернштейн и канд. филол. наук Г. П. Клепикова⌉. Москва, "Наука," 1973.
332 p. with maps. 22 cm. 1.20rub USSR 73
At head of title: Академия наук СССР. Институт славяноведения и балканистики.
Includes bibliographical references.
1. Balkan Peninsula — Languages — Addresses, essays, lectures. I. Bernshteĭn, Samuil Borisovich, 1910– ed. II. Klepkova, G. P., ed. III. Akademiíà nauk SSSR. Institut slavíànovedeniíà i balkanistiki.
P381.B3B34 73-342733

Balkanton Record
see
Zavod Balkanton.

Balkanturist.
Autokarte von Bulgarien. ⌈Sofia, Kartproekt, 1958⌉
⌈14⌉, 18 p. (chiefly illus., col. maps) 17 cm.
Scale of road maps 1 : 750,000
1. Bulgaria—Road maps. 2. Cities and towns—Bulgaria—Maps. I. Title.
G2041.P2B25 1958 **Map 64-213**
rev

Balkanturist.
Automobile map of Bulgaria. ⌈Sofia, Kartproekt, 1958⌉
⌈32⌉ p. illus., col. maps. 17 cm.
Scale of road maps (numbered 1 to 18) 1 : 750,000.
1. Bulgaria—Road maps. I. Title.
G2041.P2B2 1958 **Map 60-478**
rev

Balkareĭ, I. M.
see Dinamika stroitel'nykh konstruktŝiĭ. 1976.

Balkarov, Boris Khazeshevich.
Фонетика адыгейских языков. (Синхронно-диахронное исследование). Нальчик, "Эльбрус," 1970.
334 p. with diagrs. 21 cm. 1.40rub USSR 70-VKP
At head of title: Б. Х. Балкаров.
Bibliography: p. 323–⌈328⌉
1. Adyghe language — Phonetics. 2. Kabardian language — Phonetics. I. Title.
Title romanized: Fonetika adygeĭskikh íàzykov.
PK9201.A4B3 73-326012

Balkarova, Fousat Guzerovna.
Pesnía na skale; stikhi. Perevod s kabardinskogo Mariny Tarasovoĭ. Moskva, Sovremennik, 1973.
59 p. 17 cm. (Novinki sovremennika)
Poems.
Translated from the Kabardian.
I. Title.
MB NUC75-138734

Balkavi Bairagi.
(Do ṭūka)
दो टूक. ⌈कवि⌉ बालकवि बैरागी. ⌈1. संस्करण⌉ दिल्ली, राजपाल ⌈1971⌉
113 p. 22 cm. Rs6.00
In Hindi.

I. Title.
PK2098.13.A44D6 71-926139

Balke, Bruno
see Burdick Corporation. Advanced exercise procedures... Milton, Wis. [1973?]

Balke, Klaus-Dieter
see Beiträge zur Hydrogeologie... Krefeld: Geolog. Landesamt Nordrhein-Westfalen, 1974.

Balke, Marianne.
Registerband, Handbuch des Büchereiwesens / bearb. von Marianne Balke. — Wiesbaden : Harrassowitz, 1976.
xii, 76 p. ; 29 cm. GFR76-A
ISBN 3-447-01732-5 : DM48.00
1. Library science—Collected works—Indexes. 2. Libraries—Collected works—Indexes. 3. Langfeldt, Johannes. Handbuch des Büchereiwesens—Indexes. I. Langfeldt, Johannes. Handbuch des Büchereiwesens.
Z674.B27 76-477582
76 MARC

Balke, Peter Thomas, 1932-
see Peter Blake. Amsterdam, Stedelijk Museum, 1973.

Balke, Siegfried
see Gespräch über Internationale Zusammenarbeit in der Neuen Technik, Hanover, 1966. Bericht. [Hannover, Buchdr. und Verlag "Niedersachsen," 1966]

Balke, Thomas Edward.
An analysis of interperiod income tax allocation. Ann Arbor, University Microfilms, 1970.
1 reel. 35 mm.
Thesis—University of Missouri.
1. Accounting. I. Title.
MsU NUC76-71692

Balke, Turid, 1921–
Det begynte en fredag i Finvik / tegnet og fortalt av Turid Balke. — ⌈Oslo⌉ : Tiden, 1974.
44 p. : ill. ; 19 x 23 cm. N 74-Dec
ISBN 82-10-00996-6 : kr23.00
I. Title.
PZ54.5.B28 75-576731

Balke, W
Calvijn en de doperse radikalen. Door W. Balke. Amsterdam, Van Bottenburg, 1973.
400 p. with illus. 24 cm. fl 39.50 Ne 73-29
Title also in English: Calvin and the anabaptist radicals.
Dissertatie—Utrecht.
Vita.
Summary in English and German.
Includes bibliographical references.
1. Calvin, Jean, 1509–1564. 2. Anabaptists. I. Title. II. Title: Calvin and the anabaptist radicals.
BX9418.B15 73-354266
ISBN 90-70057-15-8

Balke, Winfried.
Konkurrenzwerbung und Werbeerfolg/ Winfried Balke. ⌈1. Aufl.⌉ — Wiesbaden: Betriebswirtschaftlicher Verlag Gabler 1972.
216 p.: ill.; 25 cm. DM32.00 GDB 72-A43
Bibliography: p. ⌈213⌉–216.
1. Advertising research. 2. Marketing research. I. Title.
HF5822.B244 73-350493
ISBN 3-409-36412-9

Balkema, A A
Monotone transformations and limit laws [by] A. A. Balkema. Amsterdam, Mathematisch Centrum, 1973.
170 p. 24 cm. (Amsterdam. Mathematisch Centrum. Mathematical centre tracts, no. 45)
1. Transformations (Mathematics) 2. Limit theorems (Probability theory) I. Title. II. Series.
PSt NRU NUC75-18524

Balkema, John B
The aged in minority groups: a bibliography. Compiled by John B. Balkema. Washington, National Council on the Aging, 1973.
19 p. 28 cm.
1. Aged — United States — Bibliography. 2. Minorities — United States—Bibliography. I. Title.
Z7165.U5B34 016.30143'5'0973 73-158203
MARC

Balkema, John B
A general bibliography on aging, compiled by John B. Balkema. Washington, National Council on the Aging, 1972.
52 p. 28 cm.
"Covers the years 1967–1972."
1. Aging—Bibliography. I. National Council on the Aging. II. Title.
Z6663.A3B34 016.30143'7 72-170017
MARC

Balkema, John B
Housing and living arrangements for older people; a bibliography. Compiled by John B. Balkema. Washington, National Council on the Aging, 1972.
20 p. 28 cm.
1. Aged—Bibliography. 2. Aged—Dwellings—Bibliography. 3. Old age homes—Bibliography. I. Title.
Z7164.O4B34 016.3015'4 73-155963
MARC

Balken, Eva Ruth, 1901-
see Psicología, semántica y patología del lenguaje... [1. ed.] Buenos Aires, Paidós [1966]

Balken, Gerrit, 1935–
Das Verhältnis des nationalen Kartellrechts zu dem der EWG und die Zuständigkeit der beiderseitigen Behörden. ⌈Köln, 1966⌉
xv, 235 p. 21 cm.
Inaug.-Diss.—Cologne.
Vita.
Bibliography: p. 201–218.
1. Antitrust law—European Economic Community countries. I. Title.
75-405516

Balkenende, Lidia.
Enciclopedia del ser. Buenos Aires, F. A. Colombo ⌈1972⌉
94 p. 21 cm.
LACAP 73-0218
Poems.
I. Title.
PQ7798.12.A497E5 73-320831

Balkenhol, Heinz.
Die Ausdrucksgestaltung des Rakugo : eine phonetische Untersuchung / von Heinz Balkenhol. — Hamburg : Gesellschaft für Natur- und Völkerkunde Ostasiens, 1972.
v, 392 p. : ill., graphs ; 21 cm. — (Mitteilungen der Gesellschaft für Natur- und Völkerkunde Ostasiens ; Bd. 54⌈a⌉) GFR***
Bibliography: p. 274–292.
1. Rakugo—History and criticism. 2. Japanese language—Phonetics. 3. Japanese language—Rhetoric. I. Title. II. Series: Deutsche Gesellschaft für Natur- und Völkerkunde Ostasiens. Mitteilungen ; Bd. 54a.
DS501.D4 Bd. 54 76-504093
[PL746]

Balkenohl, Manfred.
Der Antitheismus Nietzsches : Fragen und Suchen nach Gott : eine sozialanthropologische Untersuchung / Manfred Balkenohl. — München : F. Schöningh, 1976.
270 p. ; 24 cm. — (Abhandlungen zur Sozialethik ; Bd. 12) GFR***
Originally presented as the author's thesis, Münster.
Bibliography: p. 255-262.
Includes indexes.
ISBN 3-506-70212-2
1. Theism—History. 2. God—History of doctrines. 3. Nietzsche, Friedrich Wilhelm, 1844-1900. I. Title. II. Series.
BT98.B26 1976 76-464922
76 MARC

Balker, Habakuk II de
see
Habakuk II de Balker.

Balkevičius, Jonas, ed.
see Vardai ir žodžiai. Vilnius, [Mintis] 1971.

Balkhavdarov, Khalimbek Arslanbekovich.
(Dvizhenie i istechenie rudy pri vypuske)
Движение и истечение руды при выпуске / Х. А. Балхавдаров. — Ленинград : Наука, Ленингр. отд-ние, 1975.
108 p. : ill. ; 22 cm. USSR 75
At head of title: Akademiíà nauk SSSR. Kol'skiĭ filial im. S. M. Kirova. Gornyĭ institut.
Bibliography: p. 104–⌈107⌉
0.68rub
1. Mining engineering. 2. Ore handling. 3. Apatite—Russia—Khibiny. 4. Bulk solids flow. I. Title.
TN292.B345 76-502570

al-Balkhī, 'Abd Allāh ibn Ahmad, d. 931.
Maqālat al-Islāmīyīn. Dhikr al-Mu'tazilah. 1974
see Fadl al-i'tizāl wa-ṭabaqāt al-Mu'tazilah) [1974]

al-Balkhī, Abū Bakr ʿAbd Allāh ibn ʿUmar al-Wāʿiẓ
see
al-Wāʿiẓ al-Balkhī, Abū Bakr ʿAbd Allāh ibn ʿUmar, 12th cent.

al-Balkhī, Muqātil ibn Sulaymān
see
Muqātil ibn Sulaymān al-Balkhī, d. 767.

al-Balkhī, Shaqīq ibn Ibrahīm, d. 809 or 10. Ādāb al-'ibādāt. 1973
see Nusūs sūfīyah ghayr manshūrah. [1973]

Balkhuver, Aría, 19th cent.
ספר שם אריה ... שאלות ותשובות ... כסדר ארבעה חלקי
הש"ע וגם ... קונטרס רוב וספק בממון וקונטרס הזמה ... מאתי
... אריה ליבוש באלחובר. ווילנא, בדפוס האלמנה והאחים ראם
[v. 1, 1874] 1873–74.
2 v. in 1. 34 cm.
1. Responsa—1800- I. Title: Shem Aryeh.
Title romanized: Sefer Shem Aryeh.
BM522.24.L54 73-206734

Balkhuver, Aría, 19th cent.
ספר שם אריה ... שאלות ותשובות ... כסדר ארבעה חלקי
הש"ע וגם ... קונטרס רוב וספק בממון וקונטרס הזמה ...
מאתי ... אריה ליבוש באלחובר. ווילנא, בדפוס האלמנה והאחים
ראם [i. e. 1873–74; v. 1, 1874] 633. ירושלים, מכון חתם סופר,
730 [1969 or 70]
2 v. 31 cm. IL46.00
Cover title: שו"ת שם אריה
1. Responsa—1800- I. Title: Shem Aryeh.
Title romanized: Sefer Shem Aryeh.
BM522.24.L542 75-953202

Balkhy, Hassan O 1939-
International trade and income distribution: a 3 x 3 model. Albuquerque, 1973.
xii, 81 l. illus.
Thesis (Ph. D.)—University of New Mexico.
Bibliography: leaves 77-79.
1. International economic relations—Mathematical models. I. Title.
NmU NUC75-18516

Balkin, Alfred.
Involvement with music : essential skills and concepts / Alfred Balkin, Jack A. Taylor. — Boston : Houghton, Mifflin Co., [1975]
xiv, 342 p. : ill. ; 29 cm.
Includes index.
ISBN 0-395-16989-5
1. Music—Theory, Elementary—Programmed instruction. I. Taylor, Jack A., joint author. II. Title.
MT7.B145 I 6 781'.07'7 73-9408
MARC

Balkin, Alfred.
The operas of Hugo Weisgall. [New York] 1968.
547 l. illus. music.
Thesis—Columbia University.
Microfilm. Univ. Microfilms, Ann Arbor, Mich.
1. Weisgall, Hugo—Operas.
InU NUC73-122463

Balkin, Jeffrey Gilbert.
Nonresident individuals, U.S. income taxation / by Jeffery [i.e. Jeffrey] Gilbert Balkin ; Leonard L. Silverstein, chief editor. — Washington : Tax Management Inc., c1977-
1 v. : forms ; 28 cm. — (Tax management portfolios ; 340)
"Revises and supersedes 138-3rd T.M., Nonresident individuals, U.S. income taxation and withholding, part I only."
Loose-leaf for updating.
Includes bibliography.
1. Taxation of aliens—United States. I. Title. II. Series.
KF6289.A1T35 no. 340 343'.73'04 s 77-150987
[KF6441] 77 MARC

Balkin, Jeffrey Gilbert.
Nonresident individuals—U. S. income taxation and withholding. Washington, Tax Management Inc. [1974-
1 v. (loose-leaf) 28 cm. (Tax management portfolios; foreign income, 138-3d)
"Revises and supersedes 138-2nd T. M., Nonresident individuals—U. S. income taxation (Part I)."
Includes bibliography.
1. Taxation of aliens—United States. I. Title. II. Series: Tax management portfolios, 138-3d.
KF6289.A1T35 no. 138-3d 343'.73'04 s 74-167252
[KF6441] [343'.73'052] MARC

Balkin, M. Kh.
see Valkin, M. Kh.

Balkin, Richard.
A writer's guide to book publishing / by Richard Balkin, with two chapters by Jared Carter. — New York : Hawthorn Books, c1977.
xiv, 236 p. ; 25 cm.
Bibliography: p. 221-224.
Includes index.
ISBN 0-8015-8935-5 : $9.95
1. Authors and publishers. 2. Publishers and publishing. I. Carter, Jared. II. Title.
PN155.B3 808'.025 76-24230
77 MARC

Balking, Eng.
see
Baulking, Eng.

Balkır, Hikmet Saim
see
Hikmet Saim.

Balkır, S Edip.
Dipten gelen ses : Arifiye Köy Enstitüsü, 1940-1946 / S. Edip Balkır. — İstanbul : Hür Yayınevi, 1974.
525 p. : ill. ; 20 cm. — (Hür yayınlar ; 76)
Includes bibliographical references and index.
1. Education, Rural—Arifiye, Turkey. 2. Arifiye Köy Enstitüsü. I. Title. II. Title: Arifiye Köy Enstitüsü.
LC5148.T82A742 75-549366

Balko, Bohdan, 1939-
The study of relaxation in solids by Selective Excitation Double Mossbauer techniques. [n.p.] 1973.
xvi, 224 p. illus., tables.
Thesis—Boston University.
Bibliography: p. 212-223.
1. Solids. I. Title.
MBU NUC76-71693

Balko, Ján.
Sultánova pomsta / Ján Balko ; [ilustr. Igor Rumanský]. — 1. vyd. — Bratislava : Tatran, 1975.
278 p. ; ill. ; 21 cm. (Edícia Meteor zv. 63) CzS 75
Kčs21.00
I. Title.
PG5439.12.A44S9 76-501094

Balkov, Kim Nikolaevich.
Na pīatachke; povesti. Ulan-Ude, Burīatskoe knizhnoe izd-vo, 1969.
156 p. illus.
I. Title.
CaOTU NUC74-45554

Balkov, Kim Nikolaevich.
Rosstan'; povesti. [By] Kim Balkov. Ulan-Ude, Burīatskoe knizhnoe izd-vo, 1971.
167 p. illus.
MH NUC 75-129138

Balkov, Vladimir Aleksandrovich, ed.
see Geograficheskie problemy i voprosy prirodopol'zovanīa. 1972 [1973]

Balkowski, Dieter.
Funktionsgerechte Wandkonstruktionen: Wandaufbau nach bauphysikalischen Eigenschaften/ Frank Dieter Balkowski. — Köln-Braunsfeld: R. Müller, 1971.
189 p.: ill., 2 maps; 30 cm. DM58.00 GFR 72-A
Bibliography: p. 189.
1. Exterior walls—Thermal properties—Tables. I. Title.
TH2235.B34 73-361571
ISBN 3-481-10971-7

Balkowski, Dieter.
Modernes Wohnen in alten Häusern; durch Ausbau und Umbau zur Wertsteigerung [von] D. Balkowski. Wiesbaden, Bauverlag [1973]
115 p. illus. 20 x 21 cm. (Wohnen + [i. e. und] Werken) GFR***
1. Dwellings—Remodeling. I. Title.
TH4816.B35 73-339196
ISBN 3-7625-0303-6

Balkrishan Akinchan, 1932-
(Bhāratīya nīti-kāvya paramparā aura Rahīma)
भारतीय नीति-काव्य परम्परा और रहीम / लेखक बालकृष्ण 'अकिंचन' ; भूमिका सावित्री सिन्हा. — 1. संस्करण. — दिल्ली : अलंकार प्रकाशन, 1974.
22, 581 p. : 23 cm.
"सागर विश्वविद्यालय की पी-एच. डी. उपाधि के लिए स्वीकृत शोध-प्रबन्ध."
In Hindi.
Bibliography: p. [556]-563.
Rs50.00
1. Abdur Rahim Khan, Khan Khanan, 1556-1627—Criticism and interpretation. I. Title.
PK2095.A2Z57 75-900061

Balkrishan Akinchan, 1932-
(Rahīma kā nīti-kāvya)
रहीम का नीति-काव्य. [लेखक] बालकृष्ण 'अकिंचन.' भूमिका : विजयेन्द्र स्नातक. [दिल्ली, अलंकार प्रकाशन, 1972]
4, 2, 9, 6, 388 p. 22 cm. Rs30.00
"सागर विश्वविद्यालय द्वारा पी-एच. डी. की उपाधि के लिए स्वीकृत शोध-प्रबन्ध का रहीम सम्बन्धी भाग."
In Hindi.
Bibliography: p. [385]-388.
1. Abdur Rahim Khan, Khan Khanan, 1556-1627. I. Title.
PK2095.A2Z58 72-902993

Balkrishna, S., ed.
see Seminar on Geophysical Investigations in the Peninsular Shield, Osmania University, 1963. Seminar on Geophysical Investigations in the Peninsular Shield... [Hyderabad, India, Krishnarao International Press, 1963?]

Balkrishna Mishra
see
Mishra, Balkrishna, 1934-

Balkrishna Narayan Datar
see
Datar, Balkrishna Narayan, 1899-

Balkrishna Shripad Dandage
see
Junnedadāsa, 1915-

Balks, Jānis, illus.
see Arums, Kaldejs. Ganu zēns un velns, un citas pasakas. [n. p. Dzilnas izdevums, 1973.

Balkt, Herman Hendrik ter
see
Habakuk II de Balker.

Balkundi, S. V., 1938- joint author
see Saolapurkar, V K 1935-
Rice. [Rev. ed.] New Delhi, Fertiliser Association of India, 1972.

Balkwell, James William, 1942-
Social choice behavior: a theoretical and empirical study. [n. p.] 1973.
6, xii, 131, [i. e. 133] l. illus.
Thesis (Ph. D.)—Michigan State University.
Bibliography: leaves 128-131.
1. Decision-making. I. Title.
MiEM NUC76-71745

Balkwill, H R
Brock River map-area, District of Mackenzie (97 D) [by] H. R. Balkwill and C. J. Yorath. [Ottawa] Dept. of Energy, Mines and Resources [1970]
v, 25 p. illus. 25 cm. (Geological Survey of Canada. Paper 70-32)
Bibliography: p. 23-25.
1. Geology—Northwest Territories, Can.—Mackenzie District. I. Yorath, C. J., joint author. II. Canada. Dept. of Energy, Mines and Resources. III. Title. IV. Series: Canada. Geological Survey. Paper 70-32.
QE185.A42 no. 70-32 557.1'08 s 73-171806
[QE196.N7] [557.12'21] MARC

Balkwill, H R
Brock River map-area, District of Mackenzie (97D) [by] H. R. Balkwill and C. J. Yorath. [Ottawa] Dept. of Energy, Mines and Resources, [1971]
v, 25 p. illus. 25 cm. (Geological Survey of Canada. Paper 70-32) C***
Part of illustrative matter in pocket.
Bibliography: p. 23-25.
$2.00
1. Geology—Northwest Territories, Can.—Brock River watershed. I. Yorath, C. J., joint author. II. Title. III. Series: Canada. Geological Survey. Paper 70-32.
QE185.A42 no. 70-32 1971 557.1'08 s 75-305968
[QE195] [557.193] MARC

Balkwill, H R
Reconnaissance geology, Southern Great Bear Plain, District of Mackenzie (96SE and part of 86SW) [by] H. R. Balkwill. [Ottawa] Dept. of Energy, Mines and Resources [1971]
v, 47 p. illus., maps (1 fold. col. in pocket) 25 cm. (Geological Survey of Canada. Paper 71-11) $1.50 C***
Bibliography: p. 30-34.
1. Geology—Northwest Territories, Can.—Mackenzie District. I. Title. II. Series: Canada. Geological Survey. Paper 71-11.
QE185.A42 no. 71-11 557.1'08 s 74-169900
[QE195] [557.19'3] MARC

Balkwill, H R
Simpson Lake map-area, District of Mackenzie (97 B) [by] H. R. Balkwill and C. J. Yorath. [Ottawa] Dept. of Energy, Mines and Resources [1970]
v, 10 p. illus., fold. map (in pocket) 25 cm. (Geological Survey of Canada. Paper 69-10) $1.50 C***
Bibliography: p. 9-10.
1. Geology—Northwest Territories, Can.—Simpson Lake region. I. Yorath, C. J., joint author. II. Title. III. Series: Canada. Geological Survey. Paper 69-10.
QE185.A42 no. 69-10 557.1'08 s 72-194723
[QE195] [557.12'21] MARC

Balkwill, H R
Structural analysis of the western ranges, Rocky Mountains, near Golden, British Columbia. Austin, Tex., 1969. Ann Arbor, Mich., University Microfilms, 1972.
xi, 166 l. illus., maps (part fold.) 22 cm.
Thesis—University of Texas at Austin, 1969.
1. Geology, Structural. 2. Geology—British Columbia—Golden. I. Title.
CaBVaU NUC73-34772

Balkwill, H. R., joint author
see Hopkins, W S Description, palyndogy and paleoecology of the Hassel Formation (Cretaceous) on eastern Ellef Ringnes Island... [Ottawa] Dept. of Energy, Mines and Resources [1973]

Balkwill, H. R., joint author.
see Yorath, C. J. Franklin Bay and Malloch Hill map-areas, district of Mackenzie, 95 C,F. Ottawa, Dept. of Energy, Mines and Resources, 1975.

Ball, A fl. 1967-
The effect of room-temperature prestrain on the tensile properties of the intermetallic compound Ni Ti in the temperature range 150°-370°C, by A. Ball, S. G. Bergersen and M. M. Hutchison. Melbourne, Dept. of Supply, Australian Defence Scientific Service, Aeronautical Research Laboratories, 1967.
8, [6] l. illus., graphs, tables. 29 cm. (Aeronautical Research Laboratories, Fisherman's Bend, Vic. Metallurgy note, 50) Aus69-764
Bibliography: p. 7.
1. Nickel-titanium alloys—Testing. 2. Martensite. I. Bergersen, S. G., joint author. II. Hutchison, M. M., joint author. III. Title. IV. Series: Fisherman's Bend, Australia. Aeronautical Research Laboratories. Metallurgy note, 50.
TA459.F54 no. 50 669'.008 s 73-164655
[TA480.N63] 73[r75]rev MARC

Ball, A fl. 1967-
Pressurization effects in chromium, by A. Ball and F. P. Bullen. Melbourne, Dept. of Supply, Australian Defence Scientific Service, Aeronautical Research Laboratories, 1969.
10, [7] l. illus. 30 cm. (Metallurgy report 79) Aus***
Bibliography: leaves 8-9.
1. Chromium. 2. Dislocations in metals. I. Bullen, F. P., joint author. II. Title. III. Series.
TN4.M357 no. 79 669'.008 s 72-516391
70[r75]rev MARC

Ball, A fl. 1967-
Unusual lattice defects in non-stoichiometric NiAl, by A. Ball. Melbourne, Dept. of Supply, Australian Defence Scientific Service, Aeronautical Research Laboratories, 1969.
7, [5] l. illus. 30 cm. (Metallurgy note 60) Aus***
Includes bibliographical references.
1. Nickel-aluminum alloys. 2. Crystals—Defects. I. Title. II. Series: Fishermen's Bend, Australia. Aeronautical Research Laboratories. Metallurgy note 60.
TA459.F54 no. 60 669'.008 s 72-190720
[TN693.N5] 72[r75]rev MARC

Ball, Abraham, 1908-
The price guide to Baxter prints / [text] by A. Ball and M. Martin. — Woodbridge : Antique Collectors' Club, 1974.
[8], 275 p. : chiefly ill. (some col.), port., 28 cm. GB74-27244
Includes index.
ISBN 0-902028-23-5 : £8.75
1. Baxter, George, 1804-1867. 2. Color prints—Catalogs. I. Martin, Michael, 1935- joint author. II. Baxter, George, 1804-1867. III. Title. IV. Title: Baxter prints.
NE1860.B2B35 769'.92'4 75-310254
75 MARC

Ball, Abraham, 1908–
The price guide to pot-lids and other underglaze colour prints on pottery, by A. Ball. Woodbridge, Antique Collectors' Club, 1970.
[37], 496 p. (chiefly illus. (some col.)). 22 cm. £4.20 B 71-04584
1. Pot-lids—Great Britain. I. Title.
NK4695.L5B34 738.3'83 73-158851
ISBN 0-902028-03-0 MARC

Ball, Abraham, 1908–
So you think you know your antiques : the Leslie Crowther quiz book / compiled by A. Ball ; edited by L. Crowther. — Clopton, Eng. : Antique Collectors' Club, 1974.
80 p. ; 19 cm. GB***
ISBN 0-902028-19-7 : £0.75
1. Art—Miscellanea. I. Crowther, Leslie, ed. II. Title.
N7438.B33 745.1'076 75-302601
MARC

Ball, Abram Naumovich
see Pestitsidy... Kishinev, "Kartia Moldoveniaskė", 1970.

Ball, Adrian.
Yesterday in Bath: a camera record, 1849-1949. Designed by Douglas Merritt. London, Pitman, 1972.
144 p. chiefly illus. ports. 29 cm. £3.00 B 72-21204
1. Bath, Eng.—Description—Views. I. Title.
DA690.B3B18 914.23'8 73-157586
ISBN 0-273-31854-3 MARC

Ball, Adrian, ed.
see My greatest race. London, Hart-Davis, Mac-Gibbon, [1974]

Ball, Adrian
see My greatest race. New York : Dutton, 1974.

Ball, Alan Egerton, 1944- Professor Fuddle's fantastic fairy-tale machine. 1974.
in Kemp, David. King Grumbletum & the magic pie. [Toronto, Simon & Pierre Pub. Co., c1974]

Ball, Alan William.
Street and place names in Watford [by] Alan W. Ball. Watford, Watford Borough Council, 1973.
104 p. illus., coat of arms, maps. 25 cm. £1.50 GB 74-02079
Bibliography: p. 100-103.
1. Watford, Eng.—Streets. 2. Names, Geographical—England—Watford. 3. Watford, Eng.—History. I. Title.
DA690.W34B32 914.25'8 74-176520
ISBN 0-903403-02-3; 0-903408-03-1 (pbk.) MARC

Ball, Alan William.
Watford: a pictorial history, 1922-1972 [by] Alan W. Ball. Watford, Watford Borough Council, 1972.
80 p. chiefly illus., coats of arms, facsims., ports. 31 cm. £2.00 B 72-21961
1. Watford, Eng.—History—Pictorial works.
DA690.W34B34 914.25'8 73-158676
ISBN 0-903408-00-7; 0-903408-01-5 (pbk.) MARC

Ball, Alpheus Messerly, 1905-1968.
Solid propellants, by A. M. Ball. [Washington, Headquarters, U. S. Army Materiel Command, 1964–
pts. illus. 26 cm. (U. S. Army Materiel Command. Engineering design handbook: explosives series)
AMC pamphlet, AMCP 706-175.
Includes bibliographies.
1. Solid propellants. I. United States. Army Materiel Command. II. Series: United States. Army Materiel Command. Engineering design handbook: Ammunition and explosives series.
TP270.B25 66-61474
rev MARC

Ball, Amos Entheus.
Tenderfoot to sourdough : the true adventures of Amos Entheus Ball in the Klondike gold rush as told in his own words / by Hazel T. Procter. — New Holland, Pa. : E. C. Procter, 1975.
xii, 94 p. : ill. ; 22 cm.
1. Klondike gold fields. 2. Ball, Amos Entheus. I. Procter, Hazel T. II. Title.
F931.B33 971.9'1'020924 74-31818
76 MARC

Ball, Arthur Cecil, 1941-
A comparison of counting methods for the determination of strontium-90 in milk. Raleigh, N.C., 1974.
41 l. illus., tables. 29 cm.
Bibliography: leaf 35.
Vita.
Thesis—North Carolina State University at Raleigh.
NcRS NUC76-18992

Ball, Berenice M 1903–
Barns of Chester County, Pennsylvania / by Berenice M. Ball. — 1st ed. — West Chester, Pa. : Chester County Day Committee of the Women's Auxiliary, Chester County Hospital, 1974.
xii, 241 p. : ill. (some col.) ; 27 cm.
Bibliography: p. 239.
Includes index.
1. Barns—Pennsylvania—Chester Co. I. Title.
NA8230.B26 917.48'13 74-82632
MARC

Ball, Bona W 1937-
Rhetoric in the plays of George Peele. Lexington, Kentucky, 1966. [Ann Arbor, University Microfilms, 1972]
iv, 363 l. 20 cm.
Thesis—University of Kentucky, 1966.
Xerox copy.
Vita.
Bibliography: leaves 353-363.
1. Peele, George, 1558?-1597? I. Title.
RPB NUC73-123842

Ball, Bonnie Sage
Bonnie's rhythmic verse / by Bonnie Ball ; illustrated by Nancy G. Ball. -- [s.l. : s.n.], c1975 (Richlands, Va. : Hankins Print. Service)
19 p. : ill. ; 28 cm.
Poems.
"Fireflies (poem) mounted on p. [3] of cover.
I. Title.
Vi NUC77-85695

Ball, Bonnie Sage
The Dickenson families of England and America (Dickinson, Dickerson, Dickson, Dixon, etc.) [by] Bonnie S. Ball [and] Vivian D. Bales. Searcy, Ark., Mrs. L. E. Presley, [1972]
152 p. 28 cm.
1. Dickinson family. I. Bales, Vivian D., joint author. II. Title.
CS71.D553 1972 929'.2'0973 73-152737
MARC

Ball, Bonnie Sage
The Melungeons: their origin and kin. 3d ed. [n.p.] 1971.
71 p. 21 cm.
1. Melungeons.
TU NUC73-34779

Ball, Bonnie Sage.
Scott County, Virginia, U.S. census, 1850 / compiled by Bonnie S. Ball and Samuel B. Shumate. — Berryville : Virginia Book Co., [1963?]
[182] leaves ; 29 cm.
Includes index.
1. Scott Co., Va.—Census, 1850. 2. Scott Co., Va.—Genealogy. I. Shumate, Samuel B., joint author. II. United States. Census Office. 7th census, 1850. III. Title.
F232.S3B36 929'.3'09755732 75-324865
75 MARC

Ball, Bonnie Sage.
Stickleyville : its early history, people, and schools / by Bonnie Ball. -- [Aransas Pass, Tex.] : Biography Press, [1975?]
76 p. : ill. ; 22 cm.
Cover title.
1. Stickleyville, Va.--History. 2. Schools--Virginia--Lee County.
Vi NUC77-85342

Ball, Brian.
The effect of temperature on interfacial properties of the quartz-dodecylammonium acetate-aqueous solution interface. [Berkeley] 1971.
xi, 205 l.
Thesis (Ph.D.)—University of California.
Bibliography: leaves 168-173.
CU NUC73-34775

Ball, Brian N
Keegan, the no-option contract. London, A. Barker, c1975.
127 p.
I. Title.
ViBlbV NUC77-84305

Ball, Brian N
The probability man. New York, Daw Books [1972]
175 p. 18 cm.
I. Title.
CNoS NUC76-71726

Ball, Brian N
The regiments of night. New York, Daw Books [c1972]
188 p. 18 cm.
I. Title.
CNoS NUC76-71725

Ball, Brian N
Singularity station [by] Brain N. Bell. New York, Daw Books, inc. [1973]
176 p. 18 cm. (Daw books, no. 84)
First printing.
I. Title.
OU NUC75-18521

Ball, Brian N
Sundog, by B. N. Ball. London, D. Dobson [1965]
216 p. 21 cm.
I. Title.
TxHR NUC76-71724

Ball, Brian N
Timepiece, by Brian N. Ball. New York, Ballantine Books [1970, c1968]
153 p. 18 cm.
I. Title.
CNoS NUC76-71723

Ball, Brian N
Timepit; a science fiction novel, by Brian N. Ball. London, Dobson [1971]
188 p. (Dobson science fiction)
ISBN 0-234-77600-5.
I. Title.
CaOTY NUC73-34776

Ball, Brian N
Timepivot, by Brian N. Ball. New York, Ballantine Books [c1970]
186 p. 18 cm.
I. Title.
CNoS NUC76-71746

Ball, Brian N
Zeitpunkt Null. Timepit. Utopischertechnischer Roman. [Aus dem Englischen übertragen von Wulf Bergner] München, W. Goldmann [1973]
123 p. 18 cm. (Goldmann Science fiction, Bd. 0169)
"Ungekürzte Ausgabe."
Translation of Timepit; a science fiction novel.
I. Title.
MB NUC76-71722

Ball, Bryan W
A great expectation : eschatological thought in English Protestantism to 1660 / by Bryan W. Ball. — Leiden : Brill, 1975.
x, 281 p. ; 25 cm. — (Studies in the history of Christian thought ; v. 12) Ne76-1
Bibliography: p. p. [247] - 263.
Includes indexes.
ISBN 9004043152 : f. 62.00
1. Eschatology—History of doctrines. 2. Theology, Protestant—England. 3. Religious thought—England. I. Title. II. Series.
BT819.5.B3 236'.0942 76-352732
•76 MARC

Ball, Charles, Negro slave.
Slavery in the United States: a narrative of the life and adventures of Charles Ball, a black man, who lived forty years in Maryland, South Carolina and Georgia, as a slave. New York, J.S. Taylor, 1837 [1974]
xii, [13]-517 p. 18 cm.
Prepared by ---- Fisher from the verbal narrative of Ball. cf. Introd.
A later edition (New York, 1859) published under title: Fifty years in chains.
Micro-transparency (positive) La Crosse, Wisconsin, Northern Micrographics, Inc., 1974.
7 sheets. 10.5 x 14.5 cm. (American autobiographies)
Kaplan no. 271.
Copied from the original located in the Library of Congress.
1. Ball, Charles, Negro slave. 2. Slavery in the U.S.—Maryland. 3. Slavery in the U.S.—South Carolina. 4. Slavery in the U.S.—Georgia. I. Fisher, ----, of Lewistown? Pa.
PSt NUC75-128657

Ball, Charles Edward.
Lafcadio Hearn: an appreciation, by Chas. E. Ball. [Folcroft, Pa.] Folcroft Library Editions, 1974.
12 p. 26 cm.
Reprint of the 1926 ed. published by the Caxton Book Shop, London.
1. Hearn, Lafcadio, 1850-1904.
PS1918.B28 1974 813'.4 74-13639
ISBN 0-8414-3251-1 (lib. bdg.) 74 MARC

Ball, Charles Edward.
Lafcadio Hearn : an appreciation / by Chas. E. Ball. — Norwood, Pa. : Norwood Editions, 1976.
12 p. ; 26 cm.
Reprint of the 1926 ed. published by the Caxton Book Shop, London.
ISBN 0-8482-0201-5 lib. bdg. : $8.50
1. Hearn, Lafcadio, 1850-1904. 2. Authors, American—19th century—Biography.
[PS1918.B28 1976] 813'.4 76-30639
76 MARC

Ball, Charles H
Musical structure and style : an introduction / Charles H. Ball. — Morristown, N.J. : General Learning Press, [1975]
viii, 253 p. : music ; 21 cm.
Bibliography: p. [235]-236.
Discography: p. [241]-249.
Includes index.
ISBN 0-382-18052-6
1. Music—Analysis, appreciation. I. Title.
MT6.B1847M8 781 74-24464
75 MARC

Ball, Charles S
Remembering our heritage; studies in Friends beliefs [by] Charles S. Ball. [Whittier, Calif., California Yearly Meeting, Pref. 1964]
26 p. 18 cm.
PSC-Hi NUC73-121005

Ball, Clyde L
The General Assembly of North Carolina; a handbook for legislators [by] Clyde L. Ball and Milton S. Heath, Jr. 3d ed. Chapel Hill, Institute of Government, University of North Carolina, 1972.
iv, 118 p. 23 cm. (The Law and government series)
——— Supplement / prepared by Michael Crowell. — [S. l. : s. n.], 1974.
17 p. ; 23 cm.
KFN7821.B3 1972 Suppl.
1. North Carolina. General Assembly. I. Health, Milton Sydney, 1928- joint author. II. Crowell, Michael. III. Title. IV. Series: North Carolina. University. Institute of Government. Law and government.
KFN7821.B3 1972 328.756'05 73-622790
(MARC)

Ball, Colin.
Education for a change: community action and the school [by] Colin and Mog Ball; illustrations by Jeremy Long. Harmondsworth, Penguin, 1973.
212 p. illus. 18 cm. (Penguin education specials) £0.50
B 73-09363
Includes bibliographical references.
1. Community and school. I. Ball, Mog, joint author. II. Title.
LC215.B26 361.7 73-163478
ISBN 0-14-080360-2 MARC

Ball, D B C
see Ball, Doris Bell Collier.

Ball, D. F.
see Welsh Soils Discussion Group. Land classification in relation to productivity. Aberystwyth, Welsh Soils Discussion Group, 1964.

Ball, D. F.
see also
Ball, Derrick Frank.

Ball, David.
The mutant daughter, David Ball. New York, Buffalo Press, c1975.
[21] leaves. 28 cm.
I. Title.
TxU NUC77-84297

Ball, David.
Praise of crazy. Providence, R.I., c1975.
[15] p.
I. Title.
ViBlbV NUC76-18662

Ball, David G 1942-
Descendants of Ezekiel Ball, Woodbury, Vermont; representing seven generations and including families with surnames: Ball, Bruce, Burnham, Clark, Goodell, Guyette, Hersey, Hill, Kimball, Lyford, Martin, Mason, McKay, Parmenter, Putnam, Ranttila, Scott, Taylor [and] Tebbetts. David G. Ball (compiler). [Omaha] 1972.
[26] p. 28 cm.
1. Ball family. I. Title.
CS71.B2 1972 929'.2'0973 74-151362
MARC

Ball, Derek.
An introduction to real analysis, by Derek G. Ball. [1st ed.] Oxford, New York, Pergamon Press [1973]
xvii, 305 p. illus. 21 cm. (The Commonwealth and international library. Mathematical topics)
1. Mathematical analysis. 2. Numbers, Real. I. Title.
QA300.B25 1973 515 72-84200
ISBN 0-08-016936-8; 0-08-016937-6 (pbk.) MARC

Ball, Derrick Frank.
Some aspects of technological economics [by] D. F. Ball. London, Chemical Society [1974]
v, 90 p. maps. 22 cm. (Chemical Society. Monographs for teachers, no. 25) GB***
Bibliography : p. 90.
ISBN 0-85186-7 : £1.00
1. Industry—Social aspects—Great Britain. 2. Chemical industries—Management. 3. Mineral industries—Management. I. Title. II. Series: Monographs for teachers, no. 25.
QD1.R6785 no. 25 540'.8 s 74-194618
[HD60.5.G7] [338'.0942] MARC

Ball, Derrick Frank
see Agglomeration of iron ores. London, Heinemann Educational, 1973.

Ball, Derrick Frank
see Agglomeration of iron ores. New York, American Elsevier Pub. Co., 1973.

Ball, Desmond.
Déjà vu : the return to counterforce in the Nixon Administration / Desmond Ball. — [Los Angeles?] : California Seminar on Arms Control and Foreign Policy, 1974, c1975.
iii, 73 p. ; 28 cm. — (Foreign scholar series)
Cover title.
Includes bibliographical references.
1. United States—Military policy—Addresses, essays, lectures. 2. Intercontinental ballistic missiles—Addresses, essays, lectures. 3. Deterrence (Strategy)—Addresses, essays, lectures. 4. United States. President, 1969-1974 (Nixon)—Addresses, essays, lectures. I. Title. II. Series.
UA23.B274 355.03'35'73 76-353977
76 MARC

Ball, Don.
Portrait of the rails; from steam to diesel, by Don Ball, Jr. Introd. by David P. Morgan. Greenwich, Conn., New York Graphic Society [1972]
295 p. illus. 30 cm. $19.95
1. Railroads — United States — History. 2. Locomotives — United States—History. I. Title.
TF23.B34 385'.36'0973 72-80413
ISBN 0-8212-0448-3 MARC

Ball, Don.
Portrait of the rails, from steam to diesel / by Don Ball, Jr. ; introd. by David P. Morgan. — New York : Galahad Books [1974?], c1972.
295 p. : ill. ; 29 cm.
Originally published by New York Graphic Society, Greenwich, Conn.
Includes index.
ISBN 0-88365-100-9 : $19.95
1. Railroads—United States—History. 2. Locomotives—United States—History. I. Title: Portrait of the rails.
[TF23.B34 1974] 385'.36'0973 74-77007
MARC

Ball, Don.
Railroads : an American journey / Don Ball, Jr. — Boston : New York Graphic Society, 1975.
286 p. : ill. ; 29 cm.
ISBN 0-316-73300-8 : $19.95
1. Railroads—United States—History. 2. Locomotives—United States—History. I. Title.
TF23.B35 385'.0973 74-78769
75 MARC

Ball, Donald.
Other worlds, edited by Donald Ball. [Harmondsworth, Eng.] Penguin Books [1971]
108 p. illus. 21 cm. (Penguin English project stage one)
1. Literature—Collections. I. Title.
IEN NUC73-34833

Ball, Donald Alton, 1923-
The economic impact of the American retiree in Jalisco, Mexico, on the Mexican economy. [n.p.] 1971.
151 l.
Thesis—University of Florida.
Vita.
Microfilm. Ann Arbor, Mich., University Microfilms.
1. Jalisco, Mexico—Econ. condit. 2. Tourist trade—Mexico. I. Title.
InU NUC74-137609

Ball, Donald B
Florida Indians and Spanish occupation, by Donald B. Ball. Chattanooga, Tribute Press, 1973.
21 p. illus., map.
1. Indians of North America—Florida—History. 2. Apalachee Indians. 3. Calusa Indians. I. Title.
WHi NUC75-18518

Ball, Donald W
An application of a confidence weighting system to the items on a multiple-choice achievement test. [Lawrence] 1970.
vii, 117 l. tables. 28 cm.
Thesis (Ed. D.)—University of Kansas.
1. Educational tests and measurements. I. Title.
KU NUC73-47470

Ball, Donald W
Biography, attitude or situation: approaches to standing, sitting, and definitions of self. [n.p.] 1969 [c1970]
xvi, 299 l. tables.
Thesis—University of California, Los Angeles.
Vita.
Bibliography: leaves 267-299.
Microfilm of typescript. Ann Arbor, Mich., University Microfilms, 1970. 1 reel. 35 mm.
1. Cognition. 2. Social interaction. 3. Personal space. I. Title.
IEdS NUC73-46837

Ball, Donald W
Microecology: social situations and intimate space [by] Donald W. Ball. Indianapolis, Bobbs-Merrill [1973]
38 p. 23 cm. (The Bobbs-Merrill studies in sociology)
Bibliography: p. 33-38.
1. Interpersonal relations. 2. Personal space. I. Title.
HM132.B33 301.11 72-10541
ISBN 0-672-61209-7 (pbk.) MARC

Ball, Donald W.
see Sport and social order ... Reading, Mass., Addison-Wesley Pub. Co., c1975.

Ball, Doris Bell Collier.
The dark and the light [by] Josephine Bell. London, G. Bles [1971]
250 p. 21 cm.
Third book of a trilogy, preceded by Jacobean adventure and Over the seas.
I. Title.
CoU NUC74-145592

Ball, Doris Bell Collier.
Death of a con man [by] Josephine Bell. New York, J. B. Lippincott [1968]
187 p. 20 cm.
I. Title.
CtY MB NUC73-33682

Ball, Doris Bell Collier.
In the king's absence [by] Josephine Bell. London, Bles, 1973.
251 p. 21 cm. £1.95 GB 73-14820
1. Charles II, King of Great Britain, 1630-1685—Fiction. 2. Cromwell, Oliver, 1599-1658—Fiction. I. Title.
PZ3.B1987 In 823'.9'12 74-162271
[PR6003.A525] MARC
ISBN 0-7138-0700-8

Ball, Doris Bell Collier.
Over the seas; an historical novel. Josephine Bell [i. e. D. B. C. Ball]. London, G. Bles, 1970.
253 p. 21 cm.
I. Title.
CoU NUC76-71704

Ball, Doris Bell Collier.
A pigeon among the cats / Josephine Bell [i. e. D. B. C. Ball] — London : Hodder & Stoughton, 1974.
190 p. ; 20 cm. GB 74-07493
ISBN 0-340-17931-7 : £1.95
I. Title.
PZ3.B1987Pi 823'.9'12 74-196698
[PR6003.A525] MARC

Ball, Doris Bell Collier.
A question of loyalties / Josephine Bell [i.e. D. B. C. Ball]. — London : Bles, 1974.
245 p. ; 21 cm. GB75-00227
ISBN 0-7138-0810-1 : £2.75
1. Marlborough, John Churchill, 1st Duke of, 1650-1722—Fiction. I. Title.
PZ3.B1987 Qe 823'.9'12 76-356088
[PR6003.A525] 76 MARC

Ball, Doris Bell Collier.
To serve a queen [by] Josephine Bell. London, Bles, 1972.
255 p. 21 cm. £1.95 GB 73-04723
PZ3.B1987Tp 73-175008
[PR6003.A525] MARC
ISBN 0-7138-0510-2

Ball, Doris Bell Collier.
The trouble in Hunter Ward / by Josephine Bell [i.e. D. B. C. Ball]. — New York : Walker and Co., c1976.
191 p. ; 22 cm.
ISBN 0-8027-5361-2 : $6.95
I. Title.
PZ3.B1987 Ts 3 823'.9'12 76-53947
[PR6003.A525] 77 MARC

Ball, Doris Bell Collier.
The upfold witch, by Josephine Bell [pseud.] London, White Lion Publishers [1973]
190 p.
ISBN 85617-041-0.
I. Title.
CaOTP NUC75-18517

Ball, Doris Bell Collier.
Victim / by Josephine Bell [i. e. D. B. C. Ball]. — New York : Walker, 1976, c1975.
192 p. ; 22 cm.
ISBN 0-8027-5348-5 : $6.95
I. Title.
PZ3.B1987 Vi 3 823'.9'12 75-42827
[PR6003.A525] 76 MARC

Ball, Dorothy Whitney.
Don't drive up a dirt road; a novel. New York, Lion Press [1970]
157 p. 24 cm.
I. Title.
PZ4.B1839Do 813'.5'4 73-112653
[PS3552.A4546] MARC
ISBN 0-87460-076-6; 0-87460-144-4 (lib. bdg.)

Ball, Duane E
Open space preservation: some recent efforts by state governments. [By] Duane E. Ball. Philadelphia, Institute for Environmental Studies [University of Pennsylvania] 1970.
37, ix l. 28 cm.
Bibliographical footnotes.
1. Open spaces. U.S. States. I. Title.
MnU-L NUC74-145557

Ball, Edward C
The American strategy and French role in the Fort Stanwix treaty of 1784, by Edward C. Ball. [Rome? N.Y., c1972]
21 p. illus. 22 cm.
Cover title.
Bibliography: p. 9-10.
1. Fort Stanwix, Treaty of, 1784. 2. Indians, Iroquois. I. Title.
CtY NUC76-71721

Ball, Ellen M
Serological tests for the identification of plant viruses / Ellen M. Ball, with sections contributed by A. I. E. Aapola ... [et al.]. — St. Paul : American Phytopathological Society, Plant Virology Committee, 1974.
31 p., [1] leaf of plates : ill. ; 28 cm.
Includes bibliographies.
1. Plant viruses—Identification. 2. Serology—Technique. I. Title.
QR351.B34 576'.6483'028 76-357996
76 MARC

Ball, Eric Glendinning.
Energy metabolism [by] Eric G. Ball. Reading, Mass., Addison-Wesley Pub. Co., 1973.
xi, 84 p. illus. 25 cm.
Bibliography: p. 81-82.
1. Energy metabolism.
QP171.B32 574.1'33 72-4389
ISBN 0-201-00406-2; 0-201-00407-0 (pbk.) MARC

Ball, Evelyn V. Lowdermilk
see Okmulgee Genealogical Society. Okmulgee County, Oklahoma, marriage records. Okmulgee, Okla., 1974-

Ball, F D
Carboniferous compilation : volume IV: uranium and base metals / compiled by F. D. Ball, D. E. Gemmell. -- [s.l.] : New Brunswick Dept. of Natural Resources, Mineral Resources Branch, 1975.
60 leaves ; 29 cm. -- (Topical report - New Brunswick Mineral Resources Branch ; 75-22)
Bibliography: leaves 3-5.
1. Uranium--New Brunswick. 2. Geology, Stratigraphic--Carboniferous. I. Gemmell, D. E. II. Title.
DI-GS NUC77-85714

Ball, Frances S T
Mrs. Tatnall and her school. [n.p., 1972?]
72 p. illus. 24 cm.
1. Tatnall School, Wilmington, Del. I. Title.
DeU NUC75-26578

Ball, Francis Elrington, d. 1928.
Swift's verse; an essay. [Folcroft, Pa.] Folcroft Library Editions, 1974.
xv, 402 p. 26 cm.
Reprint of the 1929 ed. published by J. Murray, London.
Includes bibliographical references.
1. Swift, Jonathan, 1667-1745. I. Title.
PR3726.B3 1974 821'.5 74-8049
ISBN 0-8414-3196-5 (lib. bdg.) 74 MARC

Ball, Francis Elrington, d. 1928.
Swift's verse : an essay / by F. Elrington Ball. — Norwood, Pa. : Norwood Editions, 1976.
xv, 402 p. ; 26 cm.
Reprint of the 1929 ed. published by J. Murray, London.
Includes bibliographical references and index.
ISBN 0-8482-0170-1 : $30.00
1. Swift, Jonathan, 1667-1745. I. Title.
[PR3726.B3 1976] 821'.5 76-18084
76 MARC

Ball, Frank Norman.
Metatopia [by] F. N. Ball. Ipswich [Eng.] Thames Bank Pub. Co. [c1961]
244 p. 21 cm.
I. Title.
MB NUC74-33088

Ball, Frederic Cyril.
One of the damned; the life and times of Robert Tressell, author of The Ragged trousered philanthropists [by] F. C. Ball. London, Weidenfeld and Nicolson [1973]
xiii, 266 p. illus. 22 cm. £5.00 GB***
Bibliography: p. 256.
1. Tressall, Robert—Biography. I. Title.
PR5671.T85Z6 823'.9'12 [B] 74-159463
ISBN 0-297-76651-1 MARC

Ball, Frederick Carlton.
Syllabus for advanced ceramics [by] F. Carlton Ball. Bassett, Calif., Keramos Books [1974, c1972]
v, 68 p. illus.
1. Ceramics. I. Title.
MoWgW NUC76-18931

Ball, Frederick Carlton.
Syllabus for beginning pottery [by] F. Carlton Bell. [1st ed.] Bassett, Calif., Keramos Books [c1971]
vi, 76 p. illus. 28 cm.
1. Pottery—Study and teaching. I. Title.
ViU NUC74-145655

Ball, Gene V
Self-assessment of current knowledge in rheumatology, by Gene V. Ball and Joe G. Hardin. Flushing, N. Y., Medical Examination Pub. Co., 1972.
144 p. 22 cm.
1. Rheumatism—Examinations, questions, etc. I. Hardin, Joe G., joint author. II. Title.
RC927.B34 616.7'2'0076 73-159117
ISBN 0-87488-258-3 MARC

Ball, Gene V. Self-assessment of current knowledge in rheumatology.
see Pieroni, Robert E. Self-assessment of current knowledge in rheumatology ... 2d ed. Flushing, N.Y., Medical Examination Pub. Co., 1976.

Ball, Geoffrey.
Hints for pianists on sight reading. [n.p., n.d.]
[4] p. 21 cm.
1. Sight-reading (Music) I. Title.
KyLoS NUC75-16660

Ball, Geoffrey H
A comparison of some cluster seeking techniques. [Griffiss Air Force Base, N.Y., Rome Air Development Center, 1966]
vi, 47 l. (Technical report no. RADC-TR-66-514)
Includes bibliographies.
1. Cluster analysis. I. United States. Air Development Center, Rome, N.Y. II. Title.
MoSW NUC75-26605

Ball, George.
Baxter's flat-picking manual, with complete instruction and annotations by George Ball. [New York, Amsco Music Pub. Co., c1967]
ii, 49 p. illus. 29 cm.
1. Guitar—Instruction and study. I. Title.
TxHR NUC73-121189

Ball, George E., ed.
see Rohdendorf, Boris. The historical development of diptera. Edmonton: Univ. of Alberta Press, 1974.

Ball (George J.) inc., West Chicago, Ill.
The Ball red book. Vic Ball, editor. 10th ed. [West Chicago] 1960.
288 p. illus. 21 cm.
1. Floriculture. 2. Plants, Ornamental. I. Ball, Vic, ed. II. Title.
IU NUC74-37786

Ball (George J.) inc., West Chicago, Ill.
The Ball red book. Produced by Geo. J. Ball, inc. Revised by Ed Harthun. Vic Ball, editor [and others] 13th ed. [n.p.] 1976.
501 p. illus. 23 cm.
1. Floriculture. 2. Plants, Ornamental. I. Ball, Vic. II. Title.
SdB NUC77-87244

Ball, George W
Diplomacy for a crowded world : an American foreign policy / George W. Ball. — 1st ed. — Boston : Little, Brown, c1976.
x, 356 p. ; 24 cm.
"An Atlantic Monthly Press book."
Includes bibliographical references and index.
ISBN 0-316-07953-7
1. United States—Foreign relations—1945- 2. United States—Foreign relations administration. I. Title.
JX1417.B34 327.73 76-6928
76 MARC

Ball, George W
The international monetary system. [Sound recording] Encyclopedia Americana/CBS News Audio Resource Library 09723. [1972]
1 cassette. 2 1/2 x 4 in. (Vital history cassettes, Sept. '72, no. 3)
Distributed by Grolier Educational Corp., New York.
Recorded Sept. 27, 1972 in New York.
Duration: 6 min., 23 sec.
1. Foreign exchange. 2. International finance. 3. Currency question. I. Title. II. Series.
NjP NUC77-64008

Ball, George W.
see Taylor, Maxwell Davenport, 1901- Vietnam peace developments. [Phonotape] Encyclopedia Americana/CBS News Audio Resource Library 10722 [1972]

Ball, George Williams, 1941-
The Schur Index. Syracuse, N.Y., 1972.
119 l.
Thesis–Syracuse University.
Vita.
Bibliography: leaves [117]-118.
Microfilm of typescript. Ann Arbor, Mich., University Microfilms, 1973. 1 reel. (Doctoral dissertation series, 73-9505)
NSyU NUC76-71750

Ball, Georgiĭ Aleksandrovich.
(Toropun-Karapun i taĭny moego detstva)
Торопун-Карапун и тайны моего детства : повесть -сказка : [для мл. школьного возраста] / Георгий Балл ; рис. В. Чапля. — Москва : Дет. лит., 1974.
156 p. : ill. ; 22 cm. USSR 74
0.70rub
I. Title.
PZ63.B3275 75-581200

Ball, Georgiĭ Aleksandrovich.
(Trubiashchiĭ v tishine)
Трубящий в тишине : рассказы и повесть / Георгий Балл. — Москва : Сов. писатель, 1977.
212 p. : port. ; 20 cm. USSR***
CONTENTS: Мастер из Озерок.—Майя.—Взгляд в прошлое.
0.70rub
I. Title.
PG3479.L4T7 77-515192

Ball, Gerald T., 1939- joint author.
see Owens, Elisabeth A. The indirect credit ... Cambridge [Mass.] International Tax Program, Law School of Harvard University, 1975-

Ball, Gordon.
see Ginsberg, Allen, 1926- Journals ... 1st ed. New York, Grove Press : distributed by Random House, 1977.

Ball, Harris Hartwell.
An examination of the major efforts for organizational effectiveness in the Department of State from 1924–1971, by Harris Hartwell Ball, Jr. [Washington] 1971.
v l., 164 p. 28 cm.
Thesis (M. B. A.)—George Washington University.
Bibliography: p. 149–164.
1. United States. Dept. of State. 2. United States—Foreign relations administration. I. Title.
JX1706.A4 1971b 353.1 74-156655
MARC

Ball, Helen.
Person to person; poems. [Toronto, Coach House Press, 1970]
47 p. 22 cm.
I. Title.
CaBVaU CaQMM NUC73-121234

Ball, Helen H., joint author.
see Meyers, Elizabeth S. The kindergarten teacher's handbook. Los Angeles, Gramercy Press, c1973.

Ball, Herbert Dean.
Experimental investigation of eddy diffusivities of air in turbulent annular flow. [n.p.] 1972.
250 l. (K.S.U. Doctor of Philosophy Dissertation, 1972)
I. Title.
KMK NUC73-34762

Ball, Howard, 1937-
The vision and the dream of Justice Hugo L. Balck : an examination of a judicial philosophy / Howard Ball. — University : University of Alabama Press, [1975]
vii, 232 p. ; 22 cm.
Includes bibliographical references and index.
ISBN 0-8173-5165-5 : $8.50
1. Black, Hugo Lafayette, 1886-1971. I. Title.
KF8745.B55B3 340'.0973 74-22710
75 MARC

Ball, Howard, 1937-
The Warren Court's conceptions of democracy: an evaluation of the Supreme Court's apportionment opinions. New Brunswick, N.J., 1970.
xii, 212 l. illus. 29 cm.
Typewritten.
Thesis (Ph. D.)–Rutgers University.
Vita.
1. U.S. Supreme Court. 2. Apportionment (Election law) I. Title.
NjR NUC73-47472

Ball, Howard G 1930-
Educable mentally retarded students' perceptions of the teachers' nonverbal behavior, by Howard G. Ball. [n.p.] 1972.
202 l.
Thesis—Ohio State University.
Bibliography: leaves 190-202.
1. Mentally handicapped children—Education. 2. Nonverbal communication. 3. Interaction analysis in education. I. Title.
OU NUC75-35253

Ball, Howard George, 1921-
A congruency study of the training needs of middle management in department stores as perceived by post-secondary marketing educators and business in the department store industry. Madison, 1970.
214 p.
Thesis–University of Wisconsin.
Microfilm. Ann Arbor, Mich., University Microfilms. 1 reel. 35 mm.
CLSU NUC73-47471

Ball, Hugo, 1886–1927.
Flametti; oder, Vom Dandysmus der Armen. Roman. Nachdruck der Ausg. Berlin 1918. Nendeln, Kraus Reprint, 1973.
224 p. 23 cm. (Bibliothek des Expessionismus)
Cover title.
I. Title. II. Title: Vom Dandysmus der Armen.
GU NUC74-132029

Ball, Hugo, 1886-1927.
Flametti; oder, vom Dandysmus der Armen : Roman / Hugo Ball. — 1. Aufl. — [Frankfurt (Main)] : Suhrkamp, 1975.
182 p. ; 19 cm. — (Bibliothek Suhrkamp ; Bd. 442) GFR75-A
ISBN 3-518-01442-0 : DM10.80
I. Title. II. Title: Vom dandysmus der armen.
PT2603.A37F6 1975 75-517838
76 MARC

Ball, Hugo, 1886–1927.
Flight out of time : a Dada diary / by Hugo Ball ; edited with an introd., notes, and bibliography by John Elderfield ; translated by Ann Raimes. — New York : Viking Press, 1974.
lxiv, 254 p., [6] leaves of plates : ill. ; 22 cm. — (The Documents of 20th-century art)
Translation of Die Flucht aus der Zeit.
Bibliography: p. 238–246.
Includes index.
ISBN 0-670-31841-8 : $20.00
1. Dadaism—History—Sources. I. Title. II. Series.
NX600.D3B3413 1974 838'.9'1203 72-75755
[B] MARC

Ball, Hugo, 1886–1927.
Die Kulisse. Das Wort und das Bild. (Tagebuchaufzeichnungen. [Einsiedeln,] Zürich, Köln,) Benziger, (1971).
193 p. 18 cm. (Benziger Broschur) 9.80F Sw 71-A-6552
Contains the first 2 chapters, which constitute part 1, of the author's Die Flucht aus der Zeit.
I. Title.
PT2603.A37Z522 1971 72-363652
ISBN 3-545-36141-1

Ball, Hugo, 1886-1927
see Cabaret Voltaire... Roma, G: Mazzotta, 1970.

Ball, Ian G
May we recommend; a graded series of radio plays adapted from a selection of well-known stories, by Ian Ball and Marion MacWilliam. [London] Longmans [1959-
v. 20 cm.
1. Radio plays. 2. Children's plays. I. MacWilliam, Marion, joint author. II. Title.
CaBVaU NUC75-2982

Ball, Ian M
Pitcairn: children of mutiny ₍by₎ Ian M. Ball. ₍1st ed.₎ Boston, Little, Brown ₍1973₎
xvi, 380 p. illus. 21 cm.
1. Pitcairn Island. 2. Bounty (Ship) I. Title.
DU800.B24 919.6'18 72-11513
ISBN 0-316-07938-3 MARC

Ball, Ian R
The morphology, karyology and taxonomy of a new freshwater planarian of the genus Phagocata from California (Platyhelminthes : Turbellaria) / Ian R. Ball, N. Gourbault. -- Toronto : Royal Ontaria Museum, 1975.
19 p. ; 26 cm. -- (Royal Ontario Museum. Life sciences contributions ; no. 105)
Bibliography: p. 17-19.
1. Phagocata. I. Gourbault, Nicole, joint author. II. Title. III. Series: Toronto. Royal Ontario Museum. Life Science Division. Contributions; no. 105.
AzFU NUC77-85693

Ball, Ian R
A new genus of freshwater Triclad from Tasmania, with reviews of the related genera Cura and Neppia (Turbellaria, Tricladida) / Ian R. Ball. — Toronto : Royal Ontario Museum, 1974.
48 p. : ill. ; 26 cm. — (Life sciences contributions ; no. 99) C***
Summaries in English, French, German, and Spanish.
Bibliography: p. 38-41.
ISBN 0-88854-167-8 : $2.00
1. Neppia. 2. Cura. 3. Romankenkius. 4. Platyhelminthes—Classification. 5. Platyhelminthes—Australia—Tasmania. I. Title. II. Series: Toronto. Royal Ontario Museum. Life Sciences Division. Contributions ; no. 99.
QL1.T65 no. 99 574'.08 s 77-360884
₍QL391.P7₎ 77 MARC

Ball, Ian R
Systematic and biogeographical relationships of some Dugesia species (Tricladida, Paludicola) from Central and South America. New York, American Museum of Natural History, 1971.
25 p. illus. 24 cm. (American Museum novitates, no. 2472)
Bibliography: p. 21-24.
1. Dugesia. I. Title. II. Series.
NNM NUC74-145653

Ball, Ian Traquair.
Institution building for development: OEO community action programs on two, North Dakota Indian reservations. [Ann Arbor, Mich., University Microfilms, 1968]
164 l. 21 cm.
Thesis–Indiana University.
Microfilm xerography copy made in 1973.
1. Indians of North America–North Dakota. 2. Community development. I. Title.
OkU NUC76-62643

Ball, Ian Traquair.
Regional environmental management : implementation and institutional strategy in the Twin Cities metropolitan area : a case study of the Metropolitan Council of the Twin Cities Area as an environmental management organization / by Ian Traquair Ball. — ₍s.l. : s.n.₎, 1975.
v, 124 p. : maps ; 27 cm.
Includes bibliographical references.
"Prepared for the U.S. Environmental Protection Agency, grant no. R803906-01-0, through the University of Minnesota, School of Public Affairs."
1. Environmental policy—Twin Cities metropolitan area. 2. Metropolitan Council of the Twin Cities Area. I. United States. Environmental Protection Agency. II. Title.
HC107.M62T93 301.31'09776'579 76-351656
76 MARC

Ball, Irvin Joseph.
Ecology of duck broods in a forested region of north-central Minnesota. [Minneapolis] 1973.
67 l. illus. 29 cm.
Thesis (Ph. D.)–University of Minnesota.
Bibliography: leaves 62-65.
I. Title.
MnU-A NUC75-18513

Ball, Ivan Jay.
A rhetorical study of Zephaniah, by Ivan Jay Ball, Jr. Berkeley, Calif., 1972.
iv, 308 l. 29 cm.
Typescript.
Thesis (Th. D.)—Graduate Theological Union.
Bibliography: leaves 296-308.
1. Bible. O. T. Zephaniah—Criticism, interpretation, etc. I. Title.
PPiPT NUC74-132094

Ball, Ivan Jay.
A rhetorical study of Zephaniah, by Ivan Jay Ball, Jr. Berkeley, Calif., 1972.
iv, 308 l. 29 cm.
Thesis--Graduate Theological Union.
Typescript.
Bibliography: leaves 296-308.
Microfilm of typescript. ₍Ann Arbor, Mich., University Microfilms, 1972₎ 1 reel. 35 mm.
1. Bible. O. T. Zephaniah--Criticism, interpretation, etc. I. Title.
CBGTU NUC75-26584rev.

Ball, J B
Working plan for Kasyoha-Kitomi Forest Reserve, period 1.7.68 to 30.6.78. Prepared by J. B. Ball. ₍Entebbe, Uganda Forest Dept., 1968₎
10, ₍7₎ p. maps. 33 cm.
Bibliography: p. 17.
1. Kashoya-Kitomi Forest Reserve, Uganda. I. Title.
SD664.U36B34 333.7'5'096761 73-179723
MARC

Ball, J N
Merchants and merchandise : the expansion of trade in Europe 1500-1630 / J. N. Ball. — London : Croom Helm, 1977.
226 p. : map ; 23 cm. GB77
Bibliography: p. 207-220.
Includes index.
ISBN 0-85664-493-3 : £7.95
1. Europe—Commerce—History. 2. Merchants—Europe—History. I. Title.
HF493.B34 382'.094 77-368722
77 MARC

Ball, J. N.
see also
Ball, John N

Ball, J T 1932-
A proposal to substitute a progressive tax credit for deductions from adjusted gross income in the Federal individual income tax. ₍Austin, Tex.₎ 1971.
xiv, 190 l. charts. 29 cm.
Thesis (Ph.D.)—University of Texas at Austin.
Vita.
Bibliography: leaves 183-190.
1. Income tax—U.S.
TxU NUC73-34763

Ball, J T 1932-
A proposal to substitute a progressive tax credit for deductions from adjusted gross income in the federal individual income tax. Ann Arbor, University Microfilms, 1972.
1 reel. 35 mm.
Thesis—University of Texas at Austin, 1971.
1. Accounting. I. Title.
MsU NUC75-26593

Ball, James H
Energy conservation through building design. [Kent, Ohio] Kent State University, School of Architecture and Environmental Design, 1973.
1 v. (unpaged) 29 cm.
1. Architectural design. 2. Force and energy. I. Title.
OKentU NUC76-35257

Ball, James Hammond, 1942-
The design, development, testing, and modeling of a vibratory marine sediment coring sampler / by James H. Ball. -- [s.l. : s.n.], c1975.
284 l. : ill. ; 29 cm.
Thesis (Ph.D.)--University of Wisconsin.
Vita.
Includes bibliography.
I. Title.
WU NUC77-86047

Ball, James Wooley.
Wave action in Mission Bay Harbor, California; hydraulic model investigation by J. W. Ball ₍and₎ C. W. Brasfield. Conducted by U. S. Army Engineer Waterways Experiment Station, Corps of Engineers, Vicksburg, Miss. ₍n.p.₎ 1969.
ix, 15, ₍37₎, 6 p. illus., photos, 11 plates, tables. (U. S. Waterways Experiment Station, Vicksburg, Miss. Technical report no. H-69-8)
Bibliography: p. 14-15.
"Sponsored by U. S. Army Engineer District."
1. Hydraulic engineering–Mission Bay Harbor, California. 2. Waves, Calming of. I. Brasfield, Charles W., joint author. II. Title. III. Series.
MsSM NUC75-26597

Ball, James Wooley, joint author
see Brasfield, Charles W Expansion of Santa Barbara Harbor, California. ₍n.p.₎ 1967.

Ball, Jane Eklund, 1921- comp.
Short stories. Boston, Houghton Mifflin ₍c1969₎
250 p. 21 cm. (Houghton books in literature. Designs for reading)
1. Short stories.
FU NUC74-145556

Ball, Jean M.
see A Gift of heritage. 1st ed. ₍St. John's₎ Vahalla Press by arrangement with the Newfoundland Historic Trust, 1975.

Ball, Jerald.
Speaking of math: a study guide ₍by₎ Jerald Ball and Philip Daro. ₍Cupertino, Calif.₎ J. E. Freel ₍1973₎
199 p. illus. 29 cm.
1. Mathematics—1961- I. Daro, Philip, joint author. II. Title.
QA39.2.B36 510'.7'7 73-168318
MARC

Ball, John Charles.
Social deviancy and adolescent personality; an analytical study with the MMPI, by John C. Ball. Westport, Conn., Greenwood Press ₍1973, c1962₎
xv, 119 p. illus. 22 cm. (A University of Kentucky study)
Includes bibliographical references.
1. Adolescent psychology. 2. Deviant behavior. 3. Minnesota multiphasic personality inventory. I. Title.
[BF724.B28 1973] 155.5 72-12308
ISBN 0-8371-6687-X MARC

Ball, John Charles, joint author
see Snarr, Richard W Involvement in a drug subculture... Richmond, Ky., Law Enforcement Dept., Eastern Kentucky University ₍and₎ Dept. of Psychiatry, Temple University, Philadelphia, Pa., 1969.

Ball, John Dudley, 1911-
The eyes of Buddha / John Ball. — 1st ed. — Boston : Little, Brown, c1976.
viii, 244 p. ; 22 cm.
ISBN 0-316-07952-9
I. Title.
PZ4.B187 Ey 813'.5'4 76-205
₍PS3552.A455₎ 76 MARC

Ball, John Dudley, 1911-
The fourteenth point, by John Ball. ₍1st ed.₎ Boston, Little, Brown ₍1973₎
327 p. 22 cm. $7.95
I. Title.
PZ4.B187Fo 813'.5'4 73-10460
[PS3552.A455] MARC
ISBN 0-316-07949-9

Ball, John Dudley, 1911-
Last plane out; a novel by John Ball. New York, Bantam Books [1971]
246 p.
OClUr NUC76-62644

Ball, John Dudley, 1911-
Mark one: the dummy ₍by₎ John Ball. ₍1st ed.₎ Boston, Little, Brown ₍1974₎
x, 239 p. 22 cm.
I. Title.
PZ4.B187Mar 813'.5'4 74-7365
ISBN 0-316-07950-2 MARC

Ball, John Dudley, 1911-
Misión de salvamento. ₍Traducción de E. Riamban. Barcelona₎ Editorial Molino ₍1970₎
205 p. 20 cm. (Juvenil ciencia y aventura, 25)
Translation of Rescue Mission.
I. Title.
MB NUC75-81130

Ball, John Dudley, 1911-
Phase three alert : a novel / by John Ball. — 1st ed. — Boston : Little, Brown, c1977.
311 p. ; 22 cm.
ISBN 0-316-07937-5
I. Title.
PZ4.B187 Ph 813'.5'4 76-56162
₍PS3552.A455₎ 76 MARC

Ball, John Dudley, 1911-
Police chief / John Ball. — 1st ed. — Garden City, N.Y. : Published for the Crime Club by Doubleday, 1977.
182 p. ; 22 cm.
ISBN 0-385-12883-5 : $6.95
I. Title.
PZ4.B187 Po 813'.5'4 76-56264
[PS3552.A455] 77 MARC

Ball, John Dudley, 1911-
The winds of Mitamura : a novel / by John Ball. — 1st ed. — Boston : Little, Brown, [1975]
271 p. ; 22 cm.
ISBN 0-316-07951-0
I. Title.
PZ4.B187 Wi 813'.5'4 75-2291
[PS3552.A455] 75 MARC

Ball, John Dudley, 1911-
see The Mystery story. San Diego, University Extension, University of California, c1976.

Ball, John E
Carpenters and builders library / by John E. Ball. — 4th ed. — Indianapolis : T. Audel, c1976.
4 v. : ill. ; 23 cm.
Third ed., by H. F. Ulrey, published in 1970 under the same title.
Includes indexes.
CONTENTS: no. 1. Tools, steel square, joinery.—no. 2. Builder math, plans, specifications.—no. 3. Layouts, foundations, framing.—no. 4. Millwork, power tools, painting.

ISBN 0-672-23240-5 (v. 1) : $5.95 per vol.
1. Carpentry. 2. Building. I. Ulrey, Harry F. Carpenters and builders library. II. Title.
TH5604.U44 1976 694 76-24079
76[r77]rev MARC

Ball, John E
Exterior and interior trim / John E. Ball. — Albany : Delmar Publishers, c1975.
192 p. : ill. ; 26 cm.
Includes index.
ISBN 0-8273-1120-6
1. Building—Details. 2. Carpentry. I. Title.
TH153.B34 694'.69 75-6060
75 MARC

Ball, John E
Exterior and interior trim / John E. Ball. — New York : Van Nostrand Reinhold, c1975.
v, 192 p. : ill. ; 27 cm.
Includes index.
ISBN 0-442-20543-0
1. Building—Details. 2. Carpentry. I. Title.
TH2025.B34 1975 694'.69 75-41497
75 MARC

Ball, John E
Practical problems in mathematics for masons [by] John E. Ball. Albany, N. Y., Delmar Publishers [1973]
v, 105 p. illus. 26 cm.
1. Mathematics—Problems, exercises, etc. I. Title.
[QA43.B25] 513'.02'4693 73-3726
MARC

Ball, John E
see Blueprint reading and sketching for carpenters—residential. Albany, N.Y., Delmar Publishers, [1975]

Ball, John E., joint author.
see Jones, Raymond P. Framing, sheathing, and insulation. New York, Van Nostrand Reinhold, [1976] c1973.

Ball, John Edward.
Effects of original vegetation on reservoir water quality / John Ball, Clark Weldon, Ben Crocker. -- [College Station] : Texas Water Resources Institute, Texas A & M University, 1975.
viii, 120 p. : ill., maps ; 28 cm. --(Technical report - Texas Water Resources Institute, Texas A & M University ; no. 64)
At head of title: Research project completion report.
Project Number A-025-TEX.
Bibliography: p. 92-93.
1. Water quality. 2. Reservoirs. 3. Plant-Water relationships. I. Weldon, Clark. II. Crocker, Ben. III. Title.
DI-GS NUC77-87274

Ball, John Edward.
The kinetics and settleability of activated sludge developed under pure oxygen conditions. [Austin, Tex.] 1972.
xv, 173 l. illus. (part col. plates) 29 cm.
Thesis (Ph. D.)—University of Texas at Austin.
Vita.
Bibliography: leaves 164-173.
1. Water-aeration. 2. Oxygen—Industrial applications. 3. Kinematics.
TxU NUC74-132109

Ball, John Edward.
The kinetics and settleability of activated sludge developed under pure oxygen conditions [by] John E. Ball, Michael J. Humenick [and] Richard E. Speece. Austin, Center for Research in Water Resources, University of Texas, 1972.
xv, 173 l. illus. 28 cm. (University of Texas. Center for Research in Water Resources. CRWR-94)
"EHE-72-18."
Bibliography: leaves 164-173.
1. Sewage—Purification—Activated sludge process. I. Humenick, Michael J., joint author. II. Speece, Richard E., joint author. III. Title. IV. Series: Texas. University at Austin. Center for Research in Water Resources. CRWR 94.
TD756.B34 628'.354 72-612625
MARC

Ball, John Edwin.
A study to determine the effect of industrial arts experience on the attitude changes of university freshmen. Denton, Tex., 1971.
119 p.
Thesis—North Texas State University.
Microfilm. Ann Arbor, Mich., University Microfilms. 1 reel. 35 mm.
CLSU NUC73-34764

Ball, John Edwin.
A study to determine the effect of industrial arts experience on the attitude changes of university freshmen. Denton, Tex., 1971.
119 l. tables. 21 cm.
Thesis (Ed.D.)—North Texas State University.
Bibliography: leaves 104-110.
Microfilm xerography facsimile by University Microfilms, Ann Arbor, Michigan, 1973.
1. Industrial arts—U.S. I. Title.
IMacoW NUC76-62585

Ball, John L
Fisheries and the state of Hawaii input to the National Fisheries plan / John L. Ball, Jr. -- Honolulu : Sea Grant College Program, University of Hawaii, 1975.
80 p. -- (Working paper - Sea Grant College Program, University of Hawaii ; no. 4)
Research sponsored by NOAA Office of Sea Grant under grant no. 04-5-158-17.
Bibliography: p. 79-80.
1. Fishery policy--Hawaii. 2. Marine resources and state--Hawaii. I. Title. II. Series: Hawaii. University, Honolulu. Sea Grant College Program. Working paper ; no. 4.
HU NUC77-86422

Ball, John L
Marine Advisory Program input - 1974. [Honolulu, Sea Grant College Program, University of Hawaii] 1974.
v, 13 p. (Miscellaneous report. UNIHI-SEAGRANT-MR-74-03)
Research sponsored by NOAA Office of Sea Grant under grant no. 04-3-158-29.
"References cited": p. 13.
NUC75-18512

Ball, John L., joint author
see Ahsan, Abu Ekram. Costs and earnings of tuna vessels in Hawaii. [Honolulu] University of Hawaii Sea Grant Program, 1972.

Ball, John Leslie, 1933-
A bibliography of Canadian theatre history, 1583-1975 / John Ball, Richard Plant ; general editor, Anton Wagner. — Toronto : Playwrights Co-op, 1976.
160 p. : ill. ; 24 cm. C76-6606-X
Includes index.
ISBN 0-919834-02-7 : $6.95. ISBN 0-919834-03-5 pbk.
1. Theater—Canada—History—Bibliography. I. Plant, Richard, joint author. II. Title.
Z1377.D7B33 016.792'0971 76-383197
[PN2301] 76 MARC

Ball, John N
see Functional capacity of ectopic pituitary transplants... London, 1965.

Ball, John N., joint author
see Holmes, Robert Lewis. The pituitary gland... Cambridge [Eng.] Univ. Press, 1974.

Ball, John Rice, 1881-
The faunas of the Brassfield and Bainbridge limestones of southeastern Missouri. 1927.
v, 425 l. illus. 29 cm.
Typescript (carbon copy)
Thesis—University of Chicago.
Includes bibliographical references.
1. Invertebrates, Fossil. 2. Paleontology—Silurian. 3. Paleontology—Missouri—Ste. Genevieve Co. I. Title.
QE770.B34 73-171879
MARC

Ball, John Richard, 1929-
Allied health education: its development and potential role in health and social change. [Durham, N.C.] 1971 [1972]
1 v.
Thesis (Ed. D.)—Duke University.
Microfilm of typescript. Ann Arbor, Mich., University Microfilms, 1972. 1 reel. 35 mm.
1. Medical care—U.S. 2. Medical personnel—U.S. 3. Medical education—U.S. I. Title.
FMU NUC75-26594

Ball, John T
A study of the utility of data from Experimental Environmental Reporting Buoy-1 (XERB-1) and, analogously, Ocean Weather Station (OWS) HOTEL during the period February 1, 1970 - July 31, 1971, by John T. Ball and Gaylord M. Northrop. Hartford, Conn., 1971.
1 v. (various pagings) illus. 29 cm. (National Data Buoy Center. NDBCM WO 145-1) (CEM 4116-452)
Prepared for National Data Buoy Center, National Ocean Survey, contract NAS8-27743.
1. Automatic meteorological stations. 2. Oceanographic buoys. 3. Oceanographic research stations. I. Title. II. Series. III. Series: Center for the Environment and Man, inc., Hartford, Conn. CEM 4116-452.
DAS NUC76-35256

Ball, Johnson.
William Caslon, 1693-1766: the ancestry, life and connections of England's foremost letter-engraver and type-founder. Kineton, Roundwood Press, 1973.
xxviii, 494, [63] p. (2 fold.) illus., facsims., geneal. tables, ports. (1 col.) 25 cm. £8.50 GB 73-23405
Bibliography: p. 462-478.
Includes index.
1. Caslon, William, 1692-1766. 2. Printing—History—England. 3. Type and type-founding—History.
Z250.A2C372 1973 686.2'24'0924 [B] 73-181202
ISBN 0-900093-13-7 MARC

Ball, Joseph Anthony.
Unitary pertubations of contractions. [Charlottesville, Va.] 1973.
iii, 122 l. 29 cm.
Thesis—University of Virginia, 1973.
Bibliography: leaves 121-122.
1. Perturbations (Mathematics) 2. Hilbert space. I. Title.
ViU NUC75-17391

Ball, Joseph Hurst, 1905-
The implementation of Federal manpower policy, 1961-1971; a study in bureaucratic competition and intergovernmental relations. [New York] 1972.
288 p.
PB 210 656.
Photocopy of thesis, Columbia University.
1. Labor bureaus—U.S. 2. U.S.—Dept. of Labor—Manpower Administration. I. Title.
InU MH-Ed NUC74-132247

Ball, Joseph Hurst, 1905-
The implementation of federal manpower policy, 1961-1971: a study in bureaucratic competition and intergovernmental relations. Springfield, Va., distributed by National Technical Information Service, 1972.
[x], 288 columns. 28 cm.
"PB-210 656."
Originally issued as thesis, Columbia Univ.; prepared under grant no. 91-34-70-39 from the Manpower Administration, U.S. Dept. of Labor.
Bibliography: columns 277-288.
1. Manpower policy—United States. 2. United States—Politics and government. I. Title.
NjP NUC75-29479

Ball, Joseph W
The archaeological ceramics of Becan, Campeche, Mexico / Joseph W. Ball. — New Orleans : Middle American Research Institute, Tulane University, 1977.
xiii, 190 p. : ill. ; 27 cm. — (Publication - Middle American Research Institute, Tulane University ; 43)
At head of title: National Geographic Society-Tulane University program of research in Campeche.
Bibliography: p. 188-190.
$12.50
1. Becan site, Mexico. 2. Mayas—Pottery. 3. Indians of Mexico—Pottery. 4. Indians of Central America—Pottery. I. Title. II. Series: Tulane University of Louisiana. Middle American Research Institute. Publication ; 43.
F1421.T95 no. 43 738.3'7 77-151772
[F1219.1.B43] 77 MARC

Ball, Joseph W
Ceramic sequence at Becan, Campeche, Mexico. Madison, 1973.
1 v.
Thesis (Ph.D.)—University of Wisconsin.
Microfilm. 1 reel. 35 mm. c. 650 frames.
MH-P NUC76-62586

Ball, Kay, joint author
see Jones, Deborah. Education for management... London, H. M. Stationery Off., 1972.

Ball, Kenneth.
Alfa Romeo Giulia, 1750, 2000, 1962-73 autobook: [workshop manual for] Alfa Romeo Giulia 1300TI, GT, 1967-72; Alfa Romeo Giulia 1600TI, Super, 1962-72; Alfa Romeo Giulia 1600 Sprint, GT, GTV, 1963-68; Alfa Romeo Giulia 1600 Spyder, 1962-68; Alfa Romeo Giulia 1600 Spyder Duetto, 1962-68; Alfa Romeo Giulia Super 1.6, 1972-73; Alfa Romeo 1750, GT Veloce, 1968-72; Alfa Romeo 1750, Spyder Veloce, 1968-72; Alfa Romeo 2000, GT Veloce, 1971-73; Alfa Romeo 2000, Spyder Veloce, 1971-73 by Kenneth Ball and the Autopress team of technical writers. 4th ed. fully rev. Brighton, Autopress, 1973.
162 p. illus. 25 cm. (Autobook series of workshop manuals, 724)
1st ed. 1971.
1. Alfa Romeo automobile. I. Title.
LLafS NUC76-40400

Ball, Kenneth.
Audi 70, 80, Super 90, 1966-72 autobook: [workshop manual for] Auto Union Audi 70, 1966-69; Auto Union Audi 70L, 1967-69; Auto Union Audi 70L, 1967-69; Auto Union Audi Variant 80, 1966-69; Auto Union Audi Variant 75, 1969; Auto Union Audi Super 90, 1966-69; Audi NSU Audi Variant 75, 1970-72 by Kenneth Ball and the Autopress team of technical writers. 1st ed. Brighton, Autopress, 1973.
176 p. illus. 25 cm. (Autobook series of workshop manuals 701)
1. Audi automobile. 2. NSU automobile. I. Title.
LLafS NUC76-62587

Ball, Kenneth.
Audi 100 1969-72 autobook; workshop manual for Auto Union Audi 100, 1969-70, Audi 100S 1969-72, Audi 100LS 1969-72, Audi 100GL 1971-72, Audi 100 Coupé S 1971-72. [2d ed.] Brighton, Eng., Autopress [c1972]
177 p. illus. (Autopress series of workshop manuals, no. 332)
1. Automobiles, foreign—Maintenance and repair—Handbooks, manuals, etc. 2. Audi automobile. I. Title.
LN NUC74-132160

Ball, Kenneth.
Austin A30, A35, A40 autobook: a workshop manual for Austin A30, A35 models, 1951-62 and A40 Farina Mk I and II, 1958-1967 by Kenneth Ball and the Autopress team of technical writers. 2d ed. fully rev. Brighton, Autopress, 1969.
150 p. illus. 25 cm. (Autobook series of workshop manuals)
Imprint covered by label: New York, Drake publishers.
1st ed. 1969.
1. Austin automobile. 2. B.M.C. automobile. I. Title.
LLafS NUC76-62588

Ball, Kenneth.
Austin Allegro 1973-74 autobook: [workshop manual for] Austin Allegro 1100, 1973-74; Austin Allegro 1300, Super 1973-74; Austin Allegro 1500 Super, Special, 1973-74; Austin Allegro 1750 Sport, Special, 1973-74 by Kenneth Ball and the Autopress team of technical writers. 1st ed. Brighton, Autopress, 1974.
208 p. ill. 25 cm. (Autobook series of workshop manuals, 771)
1. Austin automobile. 2. B. M. C. automobile. I. Title.
LLafS NUC76-21317

Ball, Kenneth.
Austin-Healey 100/6, 3000 1956-68 autobook; workshop manual for Austin-Healey 100 six 1956-59, Austin-Healey 3000 Mk 1 1959-61, Austin-Healey 3000 Mk 2 1961-64, Austin-Healey 3000 Mk 3 1964-68. Brighton, Autopress [c1971]
164 p. illus. 26 cm. (The Autobook series of workshop manuals)
Pub. 1969 under title: Austin-Healey 100/6 and 3000, 1956-1968 autobook.
CoD NUC76-63217

Ball, Kenneth.
Austin, Morris 1800 1964-71 autobook. Workshop manual for Austin 1800 Mk 1 1964-68, Austin 1800 Mk 2 1968-71, Austin 1800S 1969-71, Morris 1800 Mk 1 1966-68, Morris 1800 Mk 2 1968-71, Morris 1800S 1968-71, Wolseley 18/85 Mk 1 1967-69, Wolseley 18/85 Mk 2 1969-71, Wolseley 18/85 Mk 2 S 1969-71, by Kenneth Ball and the Autopress team of technical writers. [3d ed., rev.] Brighton, Eng., Autopress Ltd. [1971]
184 p. illus. (The Autobook series of workshop manuals)
SBNO 85147 236 2.
1. Austin automobile. 2. Morris automobile. 3. Wolseley automobile. I. Autopress Ltd. II. Title.
CaOTP NUC75-79989

Ball, Kenneth.
BMW 1600, 1966-70 autobook: workshop manual for the BMW 1600, 1600-2, 1600 T1, 1966-70 by Kenneth Ball and the Autopress team of technical writers. 1st ed. Brighton, Autopress, 1970, 1971 print.
181 p. illus. 25 cm. (Autobook series of workshop manuals, 125)
1. BMW automobile. I. Title.
LLafS NUC76-62590

Ball, Kenneth.
BMW 1800 1964-70 autobook: workshop manual for all models of the BMW 1800 1964-70, by Kenneth Ball and the Autopress team of technical writers, 2nd ed. fully revised. Brighton, Autopress, 1970.
169 p. illus. 25 cm. (Autobook series of workshop manuals)
£2.00 GB 71-24022
1. BMW automobile. I. Title.
TL215.B25B34 1970 629.28'8'22 74-176434
ISBN 0-85147-180-3 MARC

Ball, Kenneth.
BMW 2000, 1966-73 autobook: workshop manual for BMW 2000, 1966-73; BMW 2000 CS, 1967-70; BMW 2000 CA, 1967-70; BMW 2002, 1968-73 by Kenneth Ball and the Autopress team of technical writers. 4th ed. fully rev. Brighton, Autopress, 1973.
176 p. illus. 25 cm. (Autobook series of workshop manuals, 707)
1st ed. 1970.
1. BMW automobile. I. Title.
LLafS NUC76-62591

Ball, Kenneth.
Chevrolet corvair 1960-69 autobook. Workshop manual for Chevrolet Corvair 140 cu in 1960-61, Chevrolet Corvair 145 cu in 1961-64 [and] Chevrolet Corvair 164 cu in 1964-69. 1st ed. Brighton Eng., Autopress [1972]
176 p. illus. (Autobook series of workshop manuals)
ISBN 0-85147-268-0.
CaOTP NUC74-132097

Ball, Kenneth.
Chevrolet Corvette V 8, 1957-65 autobook; workshop manual... [1st ed.] Brighton, Eng., Autopress [c1972]
181 p. illus.
1. Corvette automobile.
OC LN RP NUC74-132043

Ball, Kenneth.
Chevrolet Corvette V 8, 1965-71 autobook; workshop manual... [1st ed.] Brighton, Eng., Autopress [c1972]
177 p. illus.
1. Corvette automobile.
LN RP NUC74-132183

Ball, Kenneth.
Chevrolet Vega 2300, 1970-71; autobook; workshop manual... [1st ed. Brighton, Eng., Autopress [c1972]
171 p. illus.
1. Vega automobile.
LN CaOTP RP NUC75-80105

Ball, Kenneth.
Citroen DS19, ID19 1955-66 autobook; workshop manual for Citroen 2 litre DS19 1955-65 [and] Citroen 2 litre ID19 1955-66 by Kenneth Ball and the Autopress team of technical writers. Brighton, Eng., Autopress [1972]
176 p. illus. (Autobook series of workshop manuals)
ISBN 0-85147-130-7.
1. Citroen automobile. I. Autopress Limited II. Title.
CaOTP NUC75-56271

Ball, Kenneth.
Citroen Dyane, Ami, 1964-74 autobook: [workshop manual for] Citroen 2CV, 425cc., 435cc., 1964-72; Citroen Dyane 4, 435cc., 1970-74; Citroen Dyane 6, 602cc., 1968-74; Citroen Ami, 602cc., 1964-69; Citroen Ami 8, 602cc., 1969-74; Citroen 7 1/4cwt Van, 602cc., 1969-74 by Kenneth Ball and the Autopress team of technical writers. 1st ed. Brighton, Autopress, 1974.
144 p. ill. 25 cm. (Autobook series of workshop manuals, 789)
1. Citroën automobile. I. Title.
LLafS NUC76-21298

Ball, Kenneth.
Citroen 19, 20, 21, 1966-72, autobook; workshop manual for Citroen ID, 19, D 19, D Speciale, 1966-72; Citroen ID 20, D 20, D Super 1968-72; Citroen DS 19, 1966-68; Citroen DS 20, 1968-72; Citroen DS 21, 1966-72, by Kenneth Ball and the Autopress team of technical writers. Brighton, Eng., Autopress [c1972]
184 p. illus.
ISBN 0-85147-260-5.
1. Citroen automobile.
CaOTP NUC74-132101

Ball, Kenneth.
Datsun 240 Z, 1970-72 autobook; workshop manual... [2d ed.] Brighton, Eng., Autopress [c1972]
160 p. illus.
1. Datsun automobile.
OC LN RP NUC74-132185

Ball, Kenneth.
Datsun 240Z, 1970-73 autobook: [workshop manual for] Datsun 240Z, 1970-73 by Kenneth Ball and the Autopress team of technical writers. 3d ed. fully rev. Brighton, Autopress, 1973.
160 p. illus. 25 cm. (Autobook series of workshop manuals, 705)
1st ed. 1972.
1. Datsun automobile. I. Title.
LLafS NUC76-62592

Ball, Kenneth.
Datsun 510 series, 1300, 1600 1968-72 autobook; workshop manual for Datsun 1300, 1968-70, Datsun 1600, 1968-72, Datsun 1600 SSS, 1968-72, by Kenneth Ball and the Autopress team of technical writers. 2d ed., fully rev. Brighton, Eng., Autopress [1972]
176 p. illus.
ISBN 0-85147-308-3.
1. Datsun automobile. I. Title.
CaOTP NUC74-132095

Ball, Kenneth.
Datsun 1200, 1970-73 autobook: workshop manual for Datsun B110 Series, 1200 cc., 1970-73; Datsun KB110 Series, 1200 cc., 1970-73; Datsun VB110 Series, 1200 cc., 1970-73; Datsun 1200 Pickup, 1973 by Kenneth Ball and the Autopress team of technical writers. 3d ed. fully rev. Brighton, Autopress, 1973.
153 p. illus. 25 cm. (Autobook series of workshop manuals, 753)
1st ed. 1972.
1. Datsun automobile. I. Title.
LLafS NUC76-62589

Ball, Kenneth.
1100 MK 2, 3, 1300 MK 1, 2, 3, America 1968-73 autobook; workshop manual... [4th ed., rev.] Brighton, Eng., Autopress [1973]
177 p. illus.
1. Austin automobile. 2. Morris automobile. 3. Riley automobile. 4. Vanden-Plas automobile. 5. Wolseley automobile.
LN RP NUC74-132188

Ball, Kenneth.
1100 Mark I, 1962-67 autobook : workshop manual for Austin 1100 Mk I, 1963-67 ; Austin 1100 Countryman Mk I, 1966-67 ; Morris 1100 Mk I, 1962-67 ; Morris 1100 Traveller Mk I, 1966-67 ; MG 1100 Mk 1, 1962-67 ; Riley Kestrel 1100 Mk I, 1965-67 ; Vanden Plas Princess 1100 Mk I, 1963-67 ; Wolseley 1100 Mk I, 1965-67 / by Kenneth Ball and the Autopress team of technical writers. -- 6th ed. fully rev. -- Brighton : Autopress, 1971.
154 p. : ill. ; 25 cm. -- (Autobook series of workshop manuals ; 211)
1st ed. 1968.
1. Austin automobile. 2. Morris automobile. 3. M. G. automobile. I. Title.
LLafS NUC77-101108

Ball, Kenneth.
Fiat 124 1966-72 autobook: workshop manual for Fiat 124A, 1966-73; Fiat AF, 1967-73; Fiat 124 Special, 1969-73; Fiat 124 Special T, 1971-73 by Kenneth Ball and the Autopress team of technical writers. 5th ed. fully rev. Brighton, Autopress, 1973.
184 p. illus. 25 cm. (Autobook series of workshop manuals, 835)
1st ed. 1970.
1. Fiat automobile. I. Title.
LLafS NUC76-62593

Ball, Kenneth.
Fiat 124 sport, 1966-72 autobook; workshop manual... [2d ed., rev.] Brighton, Eng., Autopress [c1972]
157 p. illus.
1. Fiat automobile.
LN OC RP NUC74-132184

Ball, Kenneth.
Fiat 127 1971-74 autobook: [workshop manual for] Fiat 127 Series A, 1971-74; Fiat 127 Series AF, 1972-74 by Kenneth Ball and the Autopress team of technical writers. 1st ed. Brighton, Autopress, 1974.
128 p. ill. 25 cm. (Autobook series of workshop manuals, 737)
1. Fiat automobile. I. Title.
LLafS NUC76-21393

Ball, Kenneth.
Fiat 128 1969-72 autobook; workshop manual for Fiat 128 1969-72 by Kenneth Ball and the Autopress team of technical writers. Brighton, Eng., Autopress [1973]
136 p. illus. (Autobook series of workshop manuals)
ISBN 0-85147-318-0.
1. Fiat automobile. I. Autopress Ltd. II. Title.
CaOTP NUC75-26710

Ball, Kenneth.
Fiat 128 1969-73 autobook: workshop manual for Fiat 128, 1969-1972; Fiat 128S, 1972-73; Fiat 128SL, 1972-73; Fiat 128 Rally, 1972-73 by Kenneth Ball and the Autopress team of technical writers. 2d ed. fully rev. Brighton, Autopress, 1973.
137 p. illus. 25 cm. (Autobook series of workshop manuals, 725)
1st ed. 1972.
1. Fiat automobile. I. Title.
LLafS NUC76-62594

Ball, Kenneth.
Fiat 500 1957-73 autobook: [workshop manual for] Fiat 'New 500' (110), 1957-60; Fiat 500 D (110 D) 1960-65; Fiat Giardiniera (120) 1960-68; Fiat 500F (110 F) 1965-73; Fiat 500 L (110 F/L) 1969-73; Autobianchi Giardiniera, 1968-72 by Kenneth Ball and the Autopress team of technical writers. 3d ed. fully rev. Brighton, Autopress, 1973.
176 p. illus. 25 cm. (Autobook series of workshop manuals, 751)
1st ed. 1970.
1. Fiat automobile. 2. Autobianchi automobile.
LLafS NUC76-62595

Ball, Kenneth.
Fiat 850, 1964-71 autobook; workshop manual for Fiat 850, 1964, Fiat 850S, 1964-71, Fiat 850S Coupé, 1965-68, Fiat 850S Special, 1968-71, Fiat 850S Spyder, 1965-68, Fiat 850 Sport 903 cc., 1968-71, by Kenneth Ball and the Autopress team of technical writers. [3d ed. fully rev. Brighton, Eng., Autopress [1972]
176 p. illus.
ISBN 0-85147-271-0.
1. Fiat automobile. I. Title.
CaOTP NUC73-120487

Ball, Kenneth.
Fiat 850, 1964-72; workshop manual... [4th ed., rev.] Brighton, Eng., Autopress [c1972]
178 p. illus.
1. Fiat automobile.
LN RP NUC74-132189

Ball, Kenneth.
Fiat 1100 1957-69 autobook; workshop manual for Fiat 1100, 1957-62; Fiat 1100 D, 1962-66; Fiat 1100 R, 1966-69; Fiat 1200, 1957-63 by Kenneth Ball and the Autopress team of technical writers. 1st ed. Brighton, Autopress, 1972.
168 p. illus. 25 cm. (Autobook series of workshop manuals, 201)
1. Fiat automobile. I. Title.
LLafS NUC76-62598

Ball, Kenneth.
Fiat 1300, 1500 1961-67 autobook: workshop manual for Fiat 1300 1961-66; Fiat 1500 1961-67 by Kenneth Ball and the Autopress team of technical writers. 1st ed. Brighton, Autopress, c1972.
168 p. illus. 25 cm. (Autobook series of workshop manuals, 214)
1. Fiat automobile. I. Title.
LLafS NUC76-62597

Ball, Kenneth.
Ford Anglia, Prefect 100 E 1953-62 autobook: a workshop manual for the Ford Anglia, Prefect and Popular 100E, including Escort, Squire, and Thames 5 and 7 cwt. vans, 1953-62 by Kenneth Ball and the Autopress team of technical writers. 1st ed. Brighton, Autopress, 1969.
151 p. illus. 25 cm. (Autopress series of workshop manuals)
1. Anglia automobile. 2. Prefect automobile. 3. Popular automobile. I. Title.
LLafS NUC76-62596

Ball, Kenneth.
Ford Capri 1300, 1600 OHV 1968-73 autobook. Workshop manual for Ford Capri 1300 OHV 1968-73, Ford Capri 1300 OHV GT 1968-71, Ford Capri 1600 OHV 1968-72, Ford Capri 1600 OHV GT 1968-72 by Kenneth Ball and the Autopress team of technical writers. [4th ed., rev.] Brighton, Eng., Autopress [1973]
178 p. illus. (Autobook series of workshop manuals)
SNB 0 85147 324 5.
CaOTP NUC74-132099

Ball, Kenneth.
Ford Cortina Mark 3, 1970-73 autobook: workshop manual for Ford Cortina Mk 3, 1300 cc. GT OHV, 1970-73; Ford Cortina Mk 3, 1600 cc. GT, 2000cc. OHC, 1970-73; Ford Taunus 1300cc., 1600cc GT OHC, 1970-73 by Kenneth Ball and the Autopress team of technical writers. 2d ed. fully rev. Brighton, Autopress, 1973.
184 p. illus. 25 cm. (Autobook series of workshop manuals, 730)
1st ed. 1972.
1. Cortina automobile. 2. Taunus automobile. I. Title.
LLafS NUC76-62601

Ball, Kenneth.
Ford Cortina Mk3 1970-75 autobook: Ford Cortina Mk3 1300, 1600 OHV 1970-75; Ford Cortina Mk3 1600, 2000, GT, OHC 1970-75; Ford Taunus 1300, 1600, GT, OHC 1970-75, by Kenneth Ball and the Autopress team of technical writers. [4th ed. Fully rev.] Brighton, Eng., Autopress [1975]
186 p. ill. (Autobook series of workshop manuals, 730)
Includes index.
ISBN 0-85147-549-3.
CaOTP NUC77-84219

Ball, Kenneth.
Ford Cortina, 1969-70 autobook: workshop manual for Ford Cortina 1300, 1969-70; Ford Cortina 1600, 1969-70; Ford Cortina 1600E, 1969-70; Ford Cortina GT, 1969-70; Ford Cortina-Lotus 1969-70 by Kenneth Ball and the Autopress team of technical writers. 2d ed. Brighton, Autopress, 1973.
168 p. illus. 25 cm. (Autobook series of workshop manuals, 810)
1st ed. 1970.
1. Cortina automobile. I. Title.
LLafS NUC76-62599

Ball, Kenneth.
Ford Escort 1967-72 autobook; workshop manual for Ford Escort 1100 1967-72, Ford Escort 1100 de luxe 1967-72, Ford Escort 1100 Super 1967-70, Ford Escort 1100 Estate de luxe 1968-72, Ford Escort 1100 Estate Super 1969-72, Ford Escort 1300 Super 1967-72, Ford Escort 1300 GT 1967-72, Ford Escort 1300 Estate de luxe 1968-72, Ford Escort 1300 Estate Super 1969-72, Ford 6 cwt Escort Van 1098cc 1968-72, Ford 8 cwt Escort Van 1298cc 1968-72, Ford 8 cwt Escort Van 1098cc 1968-72. [5th ed. fully rev.] Brighton, Eng., Autopress [c1972]
147 p. illus.
ISBN 0-85147-275-3.
Previously published as Escort autobook one.
CaOTP NUC74-649

Ball, Kenneth.
Ford Falcon series XK, XL, 1960-63 autobook: workshop manual for Ford Falcon XK, 1960-62; Ford Falcon XL, 1962-63; Ford Futura, 1962-63; Ford Squire, 1962-63, including panel vans and utilities by Kenneth Ball and the Autopress team of technical writers. 1st ed. Brighton, Autopress, 1972.
159 p. illus. 25 cm. (Autobook series of workshop manuals, 325)
1. Falcon automobile. I. Title.
LLafS NUC76-62600

Ball, Kenneth.
Ford Falcon straight six 1964-70 autobook; workshop manual... [1st ed.] Brighton, Eng., Autopress [c1972]
200 p.
1. Falcon automobile.
LN OC RP NUC74-132042

Ball, Kenneth.
Ford falcon V8 1965-1971 autobook; workshop manual... [1st ed.] Brighton, Eng., Autopress [c1972]
212 p. illus.
1. Falcon automobile.
LN OC RP NUC74-132046

Ball, Kenneth.
Ford maverick straight six 1969-71 autobook; workshop manual... [1st ed.] Brighton, Eng., Autopress [c1972]
198 p. illus.
1. Maverick automobile.
LN RP OC NUC74-132047

Ball, Kenneth.
Ford Maverick V8 1970-72 autobook: [workshop manual for] Ford Maverick V8 302 CID, 1970-72 by Kenneth Ball and the Autopress team of technical writers. 1st ed. Brighton, Autopress, 1973.
192 p. illus. 25 cm. (Autobook series of workshop manuals, 416)
1. Maverick automobile. I. Title.
LLafS NUC76-62554

Ball, Kenneth.
Ford Mustang Straight Six, 1965-72 autobook: [workshop manual for] Ford Mustang Straight Six, 200 CID, 1965-70; Ford Mustang Straight Six, 250 CID, 1968-72 by Kenneth Ball and the Autopress team of technical writers. 1st ed. Brighton, Autopress, 1973.
210 p. illus. 25 cm. (Autobook series of workshop manuals, 866)
1. Mustang automobile. I. Title.
LLafS NUC76-62602

Ball, Kenneth.
Ford Mustang V8 1965-71 autobook; workshop manual for Ford Mustang, all models, with V8 engines of 289 cu in, 302 cu in, 351 cu in, 390 cu in, 427 cu in and 428 cu in, 1965-71, by Kenneth Ball and the Autopress team of technical writers. Brighton, Eng., Autopress [1972]
248 p. illus. 25 cm. (Autobook series of workshop manuals)
1. Mustang automobile.
LN OC NUC74-132048

Ball, Kenneth.
Ford Pinto 1970-72 autobook; workshop manual... [1st ed.] Brighton, Eng., Autopress [c1973]
172 p. illus.
1. Pinto automobile.
LN OC RP NUC74-132045

Ball, Kenneth.
Hillman Hunter 1966-72 autobook; workshop manual for Hillman Hunter 1, 2, GT, 1966-70, Hillman New Hunter, GT, 1970-72; Humber Sceptre 2, 1966-7; Humber New Sceptre 1967-72; Singer Vogue, 1966-70; Sunbeam Rapier, Rapier, H120, 1967-72; Sunbeam Alpine, GT, 1969-72; Sunbeam Arrow Sedan, 1969-72. [3d ed. fully rev.] Brighton, Eng., Autopress [c1972]
178 p. illus.
ISBN 0-85147-298-2.
1. Hillman automobile. I. Title.
CaOTP NUC74-132100

Ball, Kenneth.
Hillman Super Minx 1, 2, 3, 1961-65 autobook: workshop manual for Hillman Super Minx Mk 1, 1961-62; Hillman Super Minx Mk 2, 1962-64; Hillman Super Minx Mk 3, 1964-65; Singer Vogue 1, 1961-62; Singer Vogue 2, 1962-64; Singer Vogue 3, 1964-65; Humber Sceptre Mk 1, 1963-65 by Kenneth Ball and the Autopress team of technical writers. 2d ed. fully rev. Brighton, Autopress, 1971, 1972 print.
188 p. illus. 25 cm. (Autobook series of workshop manuals, 192)
1st ed. 1970.
1. Hillman automobile. 2. Singer automobile. 3. Humber automobile. I. Title.
LLafS NUC76-62603

Ball, Kenneth.
Jaguar E type 1961-72 autobook; workshop manual for Jaguar E type 3.8 litre 1961-65, Jaguar E type 4.2 litre 1964-68, Jaguar E type 4.2 litre 2 + 2 1966-68, Jaguar E type 4.2 litre series 2 1968-71, Jaguar E type 4.2 litre 2 + 2 series 2 1968-71, Jaguar E type 4.2 litre 2 + 2 series 3 1971-72. [2d ed.] Brighton, Autopress [1972]
194 p. illus. (Autobook series of workshop manuals)
1. Jaguar automobile. I. Title.
OCl NUC76-62605

Ball, Kenneth.
Jaguar E type 1961-72 autobook; workshop manual... [3d ed.] Brighton, Eng., Autopress [c1972]
194 p. illus.
1. Jaguar automobile.
LN OC RP NUC74-132036

Ball, Kenneth.
Jaguar Mark I, 2 1955-69 autobook: workshop manual for Jaguar 2.4 Mk 1 1955-59; Jaguar 2.4 Mk 2 1959-67; Jaguar 240 1967-69; Jaguar 3.4 Mk 1 1957-59; Jaguar 3.4 Mk 2 1959-67; Jaguar 340 1959-68; Jaguar 3.8 Mk 2 1959-67 by Kenneth Ball and the Autopress team of technical writers. 1st ed. Brighton, Autopress, 1969, c1973 print.
201 p. illus. 25 cm.
1. Jaguar automobile. I. Title.
LLafS NUC76-62607

Ball, Kenneth.
Jaguar S Type, 420 1963-68 autobook: [workshop manual for] Jaguar 3.4S, 1963-68; Jaguar 3.8S, 1963-68; Jaguar 420, 1966-68 by Kenneth Ball and the Autopress team of technical writers. 1st ed. Brighton, Autopress, 1970, 1973 print.
184 p. illus. 25 cm. (Autobook series of workshop manuals, 703)
1. Jaguar automobile. I. Title.
LLafS NUC76-62604

Ball, Kenneth.
Jaguar XJ6 1968-73 autobook: [workshop manual for] Jaguar XJ6, 2.8 litre, 1968-73; Jaguar XJ6, 4.2 litre, 1968-73 by Kenneth Ball and the Autopress team of technical writers. 3d ed. fully rev. Brighton, Autopress, 1973.
169 p. illus. 25 cm. (Autobook series of workshop manuals, 799)
1st ed. 1970.
1. Jaguar automobile. I. Title.
LLafS NUC76-62606

Ball, Kenneth.
Jaguar XK120, XK140, XK150, Mark 7, 8, 9 1948-61 autobook: [workshop manual for] Jaguar XK120 1948-54; Jaguar XK140, 1954-57; Jaguar XK150, 1957-61; Jaguar Mk 7, 1950-54; Jaguar Mk 7M, 1954-57; Jaguar Mk 8, 1956-61; Jaguar Mk 9, 1958-61 by Kenneth Ball and the Autopress team of technical writers. 1st ed. Brighton, Autopress, 1969, 1973 print.
215 p. illus. 25 cm. (Autobook series of workshop manuals, 702)
1. Jaguar automobile. I. Title.
LLafS NUC76-62608

Ball, Kenneth.
Land Rover 1, 2, 1948-61 autobook; workshop manual for Land-Rover 1 1595 cc petrol engine; 1948-51, Land-Rover 1 1997 cc petrol engine; 1952-58, Land-Rover 1 2052 cc diesel engine; 1957-58, Land-Rover 2 2052 cc diesel engine, 1959-61. Brighton, Eng., Autopress [1970]
206 p. illus.
ISBN 0-85147-128-5.
1. Rover automobile. I. Title.
CaOTP NUC74-160596

Ball, Kenneth.
Land Rover 2, 2A, 3 1959-72 autobook; workshop manual for Land Rover 2 2286 cc petrol engine 1959-61; Land Rover 2A 1961-71; Land Rover 3 1971-72. Brighton, Autopress [1972]
215 p. illus.
1. Rover automobile. I. Title.
CaOTP NUC73-120457

Ball, Kenneth.
MG Midget TA-TF, 1936-55 autobook: workshop manual for MG Midget TA, TB, TC, TD, TF 1500, 1936-55 by Kenneth Ball and the Autopress team of technical writers. 2d ed. fully rev. Brighton, Autopress, 1969, 1972 print.
166 p. illus. 25 cm. (Autobook series of workshop manuals, 062)
1st ed. 1968.
1. MG automobile. I. Title.
LLafS NUC76-62609

Ball, Kenneth.
MGA, MGB, 1955-68 autobook; workshop manual... [2d ed.] Brighton, Eng., Autopress [c1971]
196 p. illus.
1. MG automobile.
RP LN NUC75-108471

Ball, Kenneth.
MGB 1969-73 autobook; workshop manual... [5th ed.] Brighton, Eng., Autopress [c1973]
184 p. illus.
1. MG automobile.
LN OC NUC74-132128

Ball, Kenneth.
Mazda 808, 818, 1972-73 autobook: [workshop manual for] Mazda 808, 1972-73; Mazda 818, 1972-73 by Kenneth Ball and the Autopress team of technical writers. 1st ed. Brighton, Autopress, 1973.
152 p. illus. 25 cm. (Autobook series of workshop manuals, 877)
1. Mazda automobile. I. Title.
LLafS NUC76-62611

Ball, Kenneth.
Mazda 1500, 1800 1967-73 autobook: workshop manual for Mazda 1500, 1967-69; Mazda 1800 1969-73 by Kenneth Ball and the Autopress team of technical writers. 1st ed. Brighton, Autopress, 1972.
185 p. illus. 25 cm. (Autobook series of workshop manuals, 717)
1. Mazda automobile. I. Title.
LLafS NUC76-62612

Ball, Kenneth.
Mazda R100, Rx-3 1970-74 autobook: [workshop manual for] Mazda R100, 1970-72; Mazda Rx-3, 1972-74 by Kenneth Ball and the Autopress team of technical writers. 2d ed. fully rev. Brighton, Autopress, 1974.
160 p. ill. 25 cm. (Autobook series of workshop manuals, 757)
1st ed. 1973.
1. Mazda automobile. I. Title.
LLafS NUC76-21398

Ball, Kenneth.
Mazda RX-2 1971-73 autobook: [workshop manual for] Mazda RX-2 Saloon, 1971-73; Mazda RX-2 Coupé, 1972-73 by Kenneth Ball and the Autopress team of technical writers. 1st ed. Brighton, Autopress, 1973.
144 p. illus. 25 cm. (Autobook series of workshop manuals, 729)
1. Mazda automobile. I. Title.
LLafS NUC76-62610

Ball, Kenneth.
Mercedes-Benz 190 1958-68 autobook: workshop manual for Mercedes-Benz 190B, 1959-61; Mercedes-Benz 190C, 1961-65; Mercedes-Benz 200, 1965-68 by Kenneth Ball and the Autopress team of technical writers. 1st ed. Brighton, Autopress, 1971.
186 p. illus. 25 cm. (Autobook series of workshop manuals, 177)
1. Mercedes automobile. I. Title.
LLafS NUC76-62614

Ball, Kenneth.
Mercedes-Benz 220B 1959-65 autobook: workshop manual for Mercedes-Benz 220B 1959-65; Mercedes-Benz 220SB, 1959-65; Mercedes-Benz 220SEB, 1959-65; Mercedes-Benz 220SEBC, 1961-65 by Kenneth Ball and the Autopress team of technical writers. 1st ed. Brighton, Autopress, 1971.
200 p. illus. 25 cm. (Autobook series of workshop manuals, 185)
1. Mercedes automobile. I. Title.
LLafS NUC76-62434

Ball, Kenneth.
Mercedes-Benz 220/8 1968-72 autobook: workshop manual for Mercedes-Benz 220/8, 1968-72 by Kenneth Ball and the Autopress team of technical writers. 1st ed. Brighton, Autopress, 1972.
177 p. illus. 25 cm. (Autobook series of workshop manuals, 291)
1. Mercedes automobile. I. Title.
LLafS NUC76-62613

Ball, Kenneth.
Mercedes-Benz 230 1963-68 autobook: workshop manual for Mercedes-Benz 230, 1965-67; Mercedes-Benz 230S, 1965-68; Mercedes-Benz 230SL, 1963-67 by Kenneth Ball and the Autopress team of technical writers. 1st ed. Brighton, Autopress, 1971, 1972 print.
194 p. illus. 25 cm. (Autobook series of workshop manuals, 194)
1. Mercedes automobile. I. Title.
LLafS NUC76-62430

Ball, Kenneth.
Mercedes-Benz 250 1965-68 autobook: workshop manual for Mercedes-Benz 250S, 1965-68; Mercedes-Benz 250SE, 1965-67; Mercedes-Benz 250SEBC, 1965-67; Mercedes-Benz 250SL, 1967 by Kenneth Ball and the Autopress team of technical writers. 1st ed. Brighton, Autopress, 1971, 1972 print.
192 p. illus. 25 cm. (Autobook series of workshop manuals, 206)
1. Mercedes automobile. I. Title.
LLafS NUC76-62431

Ball, Kenneth.
Mercedes-Benz 250 1968-72: workshop manual for Mercedes-Benz 250, 1968-72 by Kenneth Ball and the Autopress team of technical writers. 1st ed. Brighton, Autopress, 1972.
176 p. illus. 25 cm. (Autobook series of workshop manuals, 292)
1. Mercedes automobile. I. Title.
LLafS NUC76-62432

Ball, Kenneth.
Mercedes-Benz 280, 1968-72 autobook: Workshop manual for Mercedes-Benz 280 S 1968-72; Mercedes-Benz 280 SE 1968-72; Mercedes-Benz 280 SEL 1968-69; Mercedes-Benz 280 SL 1968-71 by Kenneth Ball and the Autopress team of technical writers. 1st ed. Brighton, Autopress, 1972.
200 p. illus. 25 cm. (Autobook series of workshop manuals, 293)
1. Mercedes automobile. I. Title.
LLafS NUC76-62433

Ball, Kenneth.
Mini Cooper 1961-72 autobook. Workshop manual for Mini Cooper 997cc 1961-63, Mini Cooper 998cc 1964-69, Mini Cooper 'S 1000' 1964-65, Mini Cooper 'S' 1071cc 1963-64, Mini Cooper 'S 1275' Mk 1, 2 1964-70, Mini Cooper 'S' Mk 3 1970-72 by Kenneth Ball and the Autopress team of technical writers. [2d ed., rev.] Brighton, Eng., Autopress [1972]
152 p. illus. (Autobook series of workshop manuals)
SBN 0 85147 301 6.
1. Mini Cooper automobile. I. Autopress Ltd. II. Title.
CaOTP NUC75-80097

Ball, Kenneth.
Morris Marina 1971-75 autobook: Morris Marina 1.3 Super 1971-75, Morris Marina 1.8 Super TC 1971-75, Morris Marina 1.17 cwt van 1972-75, Morris Marina 1.37 cwt, 10 cwt van, 1972-75, Austin Marina 1.8 1973-75, by Kenneth Ball and the Autopress team of technical writers. 3rd ed., fully rev. Brighton, Autopress, 1975.
192 p. ill. (The Autobook series of workshop manuals, 850)
ISBN 0-85147-546-9.
CaOTP NUC77-84220

Ball, Kenneth.
Morris Minor 1952-71 autobook: [workshop manual for] Morris Minor series 2, 1952-56; Morris Minor 1000 with 948 cc engine, 1956-62; Morris Minor 1000 with 1098 cc engine, 1962-70; Morris 1/4 ton Van, 1956-62; Morris 6 cwt. Van and Pick-up, 1962-70; Morris Minor Traveller, 1953-71 by Kenneth Ball and the Autopress team of technical writers. 4th ed. fully rev. Brighton, Autopress, 1970, 1973 print.
136 p. illus. 25 cm. (Autobook series of workshop manuals, 770)
Previous editions: 1967, 1968, 1969.
1. Morris Minor automobile. I. Title.
LLafS NUC76-62435

Ball, Kenneth.
NSU 1000 1963-1972 autobook: workshop manual for NSU Prinz 1000L, 1000LS, 1000TT, 1963-67; NSU TYPLLO, 110SC, 1966-67; NSU 1000C, 1000C Super, 1000TTS, 1967-72; NSU 1200, 1200C, 1200C Super, 1200TT, 1967-72 by Kenneth Ball and the Autopress team of technical writers. 2d ed. fully rev. Brighton, Autopress, 1972.
160 p. illus. 25 cm. (Autopress series of workshop manuals, 282)
First ed. 1971.
1. NSU automobile. I. Title.
LLafS NUC76-62437

Ball, Kenneth.
NSU Prinz, 1957-72 autobook: workshop manual for NSU Prinz 1, 1957-58; NSU Prinz 2, 1958-60; NSU Prinz 3, 1960-62; NSU Prinz 4, 1961-69; NSU Prinz 4L, 1967-68; NSU Prinz Super L, 1968-72; NSU Sport Prinz, 1960-68 by Kenneth Ball and the Autopress team of technical writers. 2d ed. fully rev. Brighton, Autopress, 1972.
185 p. illus. 25 cm. (Autobook series of workshop manuals, 342)
1st ed. 1972.
1. NSU automobile. I. Title.
LLafS NUC76-62436

Ball, Kenneth.
Opel Ascona, Manta 1970-73 autobook: [workshop manual for] Opel Ascona 1.6S, 1900SR, 1971-73; Opel Ascona Voyage, 1971-73; Opel Mana 1.6S, 1.9S, 1970-73; Opel 1900, 1970-73 by Kenneth Ball and the Autopress team of technical writers. 2d ed. fully rev. Brighton, Autopress, 1973.
161 p. illus. 25 cm. (Autobook series of workshop manuals, 811)
1st ed. 1972.
1. Opel automobile. I. Title.
LLafS NUC76-62438

Ball, Kenneth.
Opel Ascona, Manta 1970-75 autobook: Opel Ascona 1.6S, 1900, 1900SR 1971-75; Opel Ascona Voyage 1971-75; Opel Manta 1.6S, 1.9S, Rallye 1970-75; Opel 1900 1970-75; Opel Manta Berlinetta 1972-75, by Kenneth Ball and the Autopress team of technical writers. [4th ed., rev.] Brighton, Eng., Autopress, 1975.
168 p. ill. (Autobook series of workshop manuals)
Includes index.
ISBN 0-85147-567-1.
CaOTP NUC77-84221

Ball, Kenneth.
Opel Kadett, Olympia, 1492, 1698 or 1897 cc., 1967-72 autobook; workshop manual... [3d ed.] Brighton, Eng., Autopress [c1972]
144 p. illus.
1. Opel automobile.
RP LN OC NUC74-132129

Ball, Kenneth.
Peugeot 204 1965-72 autobook; workshop manual for Peugeot 204, 1965-72, Peugeot 204 B 1966-72; Peugeot 204 C, 1966-70; Peugeot 204 GL, 1966-72, by Kenneth Ball and the Autopress team of technical writers. Brighton, Eng., Autopress [1972]
136 p. illus.
ISBN 0-85147-184-6.
1. Peugeot automobile. I. Title.
CaOTP NUC74-132106

Ball, Kenneth.
Peugeot 404, 1960-73 autobook: [workshop manual for] Peugeot 404 1618cc, 1960-73 by Kenneth Ball and the Autopress team of technical writers. 2d ed. fully rev. Brighton, Autopress, 1972, 1973 print.
135 p. illus. 25 cm. (Autobook series of workshop manuals, 995)
1st ed. 1970.
1. Peugeot automobile. I. Title.
LLafS NUC76-62439

Ball, Kenneth.
Peugeot 504, 1968-70 auto book; workshop manual for Peugeot 504, 1968-70; Peugeot 504 fuel injection, 1968-70. Brighton, Eng., Autopress [1972]
176 p. illus.
ISBN 0-85147-229-X.
1. Peugeot automobile. I. Title.
CaOTP NUC74-132108

Ball, Kenneth.
Porsche 356A, B, C, 1957-65 autobook: [workshop manual for] Porsche 356A, 1957-59; Porsche 356B, 1959-63; Porsche 356C, 1963-65 by Kenneth Ball and the Autopress team of technical writers. 1st ed. Brighton, Autopress, 1970, 1974 print.
170 p. illus. 25 cm. (Autobook series of workshop manuals, 827)
1. Porsche automobile. I. Title.
LLafS NUC76-22244

Ball, Kenneth.
Porsche 911, 1964-69 autobook: workshop manual for Porsche 911, 1964-67; Porsche 911L, 1967-68; Porsche 911S, 1966-69; Porsche 911T, 1967-69; Porsche 911T Luxe, 1968-69; Porsche 911 1968-69 by Kenneth Ball and the Autopress team of technical writers. 1st ed. Brighton, Autopress, 1971, 1972 print.
176 p. illus. 25 cm. (Autobook series of workshop manuals, 166)
1. Porsche automobile. I. Title.
LLafS NUC76-62420

Ball, Kenneth.
Porsche 912, 1965-69 autobook: workshop manual for Porsche 912, 1965-69 by Kenneth Ball and the Autopress team of technical writers. 1st ed. Brighton, Autopress, 1971, 1972 print.
145 p. illus. 25 cm. (Autobook series of workshop manuals, 167)
1st ed. 1970.
1. Porsche automobile. I. Title.
LLafS NUC76-62421

Ball, Kenneth.
Reliant Regal 1952-73 autobook. Workshop manual for Reliant Regal Mk 1 to 6 1952-62, Reliant Vans 1955-63, Reliant Regal 3/25 1962-68, Reliant Regal 21E, 21E-700 1967-73, Reliant Regal 3/30 1968-73, Reliant Super Van Mk 3 1968-73, by Kenneth Ball and the Autopress team of technical writers. [3d ed., rev.] Brighton, Eng., Autopress [1973]
168 p. illus. (Autobook series of workshop manuals)
SBN 0 8514 333 4.
CaOTP NUC74-132030

Ball, Kenneth.
Renault 5, 1972-73 autobook: [workshop manual for] Renault 5L, 1972-73; Renault 5TL, 1972-73, Kenneth Ball and the Autopress team of technical writers. 1st ed. Brighton, Autopress, 1973.
153 p. illus. 25 cm. (Autobook series of workshop manuals, 739)
1. Renault automobile. I. Title.
LLafS NUC76-62422

Ball, Kenneth.
Renault 6 1968-72 Autobook; workshop manual for Renault 6 - 850 1968-72 Renault 6 - 1100 1970-72. [2d ed., fully rev.] Brighton, Autopress [1972]
176 p. illus. (Autobook series of workshop manuals)
ISBN 0-85147-286-9.
1. Renault automobile. I. Title.
CaOTP NUC73-120525

Ball, Kenneth.
Renault 15, 17, 1971-74 autobook: [workshop manual for] Renault 15TL (R1300), 1289cc, 1971-74; Renault 15TS (R1302), 1565cc, 1971-74; Renault 17TL (R1312, R1322), 1565cc, 1971-74; Renault 17TS (R1313, R1323), 1565cc, 1971-74 by Kenneth Ball and the Autopress team of technical writers. 1st ed. Brighton, Autopress, 1973.
200 p. illus. 25 cm. (Autobook series of workshop manuals, 741)
1. Renault automobile. I. Title.
LLafS NUC76-62423

Ball, Kenneth.
Renault 16, 1965-71 autobook; workshop manual for Renault 16 1965-71, Renault 16TS 1968-71. [2d ed. rev.] Brighton, Eng., Autopress [1971]
174 p. illus. 25 cm. (Autobook series of workshop manuals)
1. Renault automobile. I. Title.
CoFS NUC73-121323

Ball, Kenneth.
Renault 16 1965-71 autobook; workshop manual for Renault 16 1965-71, Renault 16 TL 1970-71, Renault 16 TS 1968-71. [3d ed. fully rev.] Brighton, Eng., Autopress [c1971]
202 p. illus.
ISBN 0-85147-244-3.
1. Renault automobile. I. Title. II. Title: Workshop manual for Renault 16.
CaOTP NUC73-34832

Ball, Kenneth.
Renault 16, 1965-73 autobook: [workshop manual for] Renault 16, 1965-72; Renault 16TL, 1970-73; Renault 16TS, 1968-73; Renault 16L, 1972-73 by Kenneth Ball and the Autopress team of technical writers. 5th ed. fully rev. Brighton, Autopress, 1973.
200 p. illus. 25 cm. (Autobook series of workshop manuals, 755)
1st ed. 1970.
1. Renault automobile. I. Title.
LLafS NUC76-62424

Ball, Kenneth.
Renault Dauphine, Floride, 1957-67 autobook: workshop manual for Renault Dauphine, 1957-64; Gordini, 1959-67; Floride, 1959-63 by Kenneth Ball and the Autopress team of technical writers. 1st ed. Brighton, Autopress, 1971, 1973 print.
168 p. illus. 25 cm. (Autobook series of workshop manuals, 801)
1. Renault automobile. I. Title.
LLafS NUC76-62418

Ball, Kenneth.
Renault R4, R4L, 4, 1961-72 autobook: workshop manual for Renault R4, 1961-65; Renault R4L, 747cc, 1961-63; Renault R4L, 845cc, 1963-65; Renault 4, 1965-72 by Kenneth Ball and the Autopress team of technical writers. 2d ed. fully rev. Brighton, Autopress, 1972.
160 p. illus. 25 cm. (Autobook series of workshop manuals, 289)
1st ed. 1970.
1. Renault automobile. I. Title.
LLafS NUC76-62419

Ball, Kenneth.
SAAB 99, 1969-74 autobook: [workshop manual for] SAAB 99, 1709cc., 1969-71; SAAB 99, 1854cc., 1971-74; SAAB 99, 1985cc., 1972-74 by Kenneth Ball and the Autopress team of technical writers. 3d ed. fully rev. Brighton, Autopress, 1974.
183 p. ill. 25 cm. (Autobook series of workshop manuals, 798)
1st ed. 1971.
1. Saab automobile. I. Title.
LLafS NUC76-21406

Ball, Kenneth.
Simca 1300, 1301, 1500, 1501, 1963-73 autobook; Simca 1300 GL, LS 1963-66; Simca 1301, GL, GLS, LS, Special 1966-73; Simca 1500 L, GL, GLS 1963-66; Simca 1501 GL, GLS, Special 1966-73. 3d rev. ed. Brighton, Eng., Autopress, 1973.
193 p. ill. (Autobook series of workshop manuals, 970)
ISBN 0 85147 372 5.
1. Simca automobile. I. Title.
CaOTP NUC76-62417

Ball, Kenneth.
Sprite, Midget 1958-69 autobook; workshop manual covering all models of the Austin Healey Sprite and MG Midget 1958-69. [2d ed. fully rev.] Brighton, Eng., Autopress [c1970]
143 p. illus.
ISBN 0-85147-106-4.
1. Sprite automobile. 2. Midget automobile. I. Title.
CaOTP NUC73-121251

Ball, Kenneth.
Sprite, Midget 1958-72 autobook; workshop manual... [5th ed., rev.] Brighton, Eng., Autopress [c1972]
158 p. illus.
1. Sprite automobile. 2. Midget automobile.
LN RP NUC74-132190

Ball, Kenneth.
Sunbeam Rapier, Alpine, 1955-65 autobook : workshop manual for Sunbeam Rapier 1, 1955-58 ; Sunbeam Rapier 2, 1958-59 ; Sunbeam Rapier 3, 1959-61 ; Sunbeam Rapier 3A, 1961-63 ; Sunbeam Rapier 4, 1963-65 ; Sunbeam Alpine 1, 1959-60 ; Sunbeam Alpine 2, 1960-63 ; Sunbeam Alpine 3, 1963-64 ; Sunbeam Alpine 4, 1964-65 / by Kenneth Ball and the Autopress team of technical writers. -- 2d ed. fully rev. -- Brighton : Autopress, 1970, 1972 print.
168 p. : ill. ; 25 cm. -- (Autobook series of workshop manual ; 181)
1st ed. 1969.
1. Sunbeam automobile. I. Title.
LLafS NUC77-101109

Ball, Kenneth.
Toyota Corona 1900, 1969-70 autobook; workshop manual for the Toyota Corona Mk2 1900, 1969-70. [1st ed.] Brighton, Eng., Autopress [c1971]
200 p. illus. 25 cm. (Autobook series of workshop manuals)
1. Toyota automobile. I. Title.
CoFS NUC74-145654

Ball, Kenneth.
Toyota Corona 1900 MK 2 1969-71 autobook; workshop manual for Toyota Corona 1900 MK 2 1969-71, Toyota Corona 1900 SL MK 2 1970-71. Brighton, Eng., Autopress [1971]
193 p. illus.
1. Toyota automobile—Handbooks, manuals, etc. 2. Automobiles—Maintenance and repair—Handbooks, manuals, etc. I. Title.
ViBlbV NUC73-120568

Ball, Kenneth.
Toyota Corono 1900 Mk 2, 1969-72 autobook : workshop manual for Toyota Corona 1900 Mk 2, 1969-72 ; Toyota Corona 1900 SL Mk 2, 1970-72 / by Kenneth Ball and the Autopress team of technical writers. -- 3d ed. fully rev. -- Brighton : Autopress, 1972.
194 p. : ill. ; 25 cm. -- (Autobook series of workshop manuals ; 311)
1st ed. 1970.
1. Toyota Corona Mark II automobile. I. Title.
LLafS NUC77-101110

Ball, Kenneth.
Triumph Dolomite 1972-75 autobook: Triumph Dolomite 1854cc 1972-75, by Kenneth Ball and the Autopress team of technical writers. [2d ed., rev.] Brighton, Eng., Autopress [1975]
202 p. (Autopress series of workshop manuals)
Includes index.
ISBN 0-85147-554-X.
1. Triumph automobile. I. Title.
CaOTP NUC77-84218

Ball, Kenneth.
Triumph GT 6, Vitesse 2 litre 1969-72 autobook; workshop manual... [2d ed., rev.] Brighton, Eng., Autopress [c1972]
170 p. illus.
1. Triumph automobile. 2. Vitesse automobile.
LN OC RP NUC74-132187

Ball, Kenneth.
Triumph Stag, 1970-74 autobook: [workshop manual for] Triumph Stag, 1970-74 by Kenneth Ball and the Autopress team of technical writers. 1st ed. Brighton, Autopress, 1974.
170 p. ill. 25 cm. (Autobook series of workshop manuals, 808)
1. Triumph automobile. I. Title.
LLafS NUC76-21411

Ball, Kenneth.
Triumph TR2, TR3, TR3A, 1952-62, autobook: workshop manual for the Triumph TR2, TR3, and TR3A, 1952-62. Brighton, Autopress [c1972]
176 p. illus. (The Autobook series of workshop manuals)
1. Triumph automobile. I. Title.
LN NUC74-132107

Ball, Kenneth.
Triumph TR4, TR4A 1961-67 autobook, by Kenneth Ball and the Autopress team of technical writers. Brighton, Eng., Autopress [c1969]
152 p. illus.
"Workshop manual for Triumph TR4, 1961-65; Triumph TR4A, 1965-67."
1. Triumph automobile. I. Title.
LN NUC74-145599

Ball, Kenneth.
Triumph TR 4, TR 4 A, 1961-67 autobook; workshop manual. [1st ed.] Brighton, Eng., Autopress [c1971]
150 p. illus.
1. Triumph automobile.
RP NUC74-145600

Ball, Kenneth.
Triumph TR5, TR250, TR6 1967-70 autobook; workshop manual for the Triumph TR5, TR250, TR6 1967-70. Brighton, Eng., Autopress [c1970]
168 p. illus.
ISBN-0-85147-115-3.
1. Triumph automobile. I. Title.
CaOTP NUC73-121250

Ball, Kenneth.
Triumph TR5, TR250, TR6, 1967-73 autobook; workshop manual... [5th ed.] Brighton, Eng., Autopress [c1973]
162 p. illus.
1. Triumph automobile.
LN OC RP NUC74-132186

Ball, Kenneth.
Triumph Toledo, 1970-73 autobook: workshop manual for Triumph Toledo 1300cc., 1970-73; Triumph Toledo 1500cc., 1970-73 by Kenneth Ball and the Autopress team of technical writers. 2d ed. fully rev. Brighton, Autopress, 1973.
184 p. illus. 25 cm. (Autobook series of workshop manuals, 975)
1st ed. 1972.
1. Triumph automobile. I. Title.
LLafS NUC76-35268

Ball, Kenneth.
Triumph Toledo 1970-75 autobook; Triumph Toledo 1300 1970-75; Triumph Toledo 1500 1970-75 by Kenneth Ball and the Autopress team of technical writers. [3d ed. rev.] Brighton, Autopress [1975]
186 p. ill. (The Autobook series of workshop manuals)
Includes index.
ISBN 0-85147-550-7.
CaOTP NUC77-84217

Ball, Kenneth.
Vauxhall Victor 3300, Ventora, 1968-72, autobook; workshop manual for Vauxhall Victor 3300, 1968-69, Vauxhall Victor 3300 SL, 1969-72, Vauxhall Ventora Mk 1, 1968-69, Vauxhall Ventora Mk 2, 1969-72, by Kenneth Ball and the Autopress team of technical writers. Brighton, Eng., Autopress [c1972]
170 p. illus.
ISBN 0-85147-204-4.
1. Vauxhall automobile.
CaOTP NUC74-132159

Ball, Kenneth.
Vauxhall Victor FD 1600, 2000 1967-72 autobook; workshop manual for Vauxhall Victor 1600 FD 1967-69, Vauxhall Victor 1600 Super 1969-72, Vauxhall Victor 2000 FD 1967-69, Vauxhall Victor 2000 SL 1969-72, Vauxhall VX 4/90 1969-72. [3d ed. fully rev.] Brighton, Eng., Autopress [c1972]
192 p. illus.
ISBN 0-85147-279-6.
CaOTP NUC73-120590

Ball, Kenneth.
Vauxhall Viva HA 1963-66 autobook. Workshop manual for the Vauxhall Viva HA series 1963-66 including 90 and SL90, Bedford Beagle and 8 cwt. van. [4th ed.] Brighton, Eng., Autopress [1971]
190 p. illus. (Autobook series of workshop manuals)
SBN 085147 157 9.
1. Vauxhall Viva automobile. I. Title.
CaOTP NUC74-160595

Ball, Kenneth.
Vauxhall Viva HA, 1963-66 autobook: workshop manual for Vauxhall Viva HA, 1963-66; Vauxhall Viva 90, 1965-66; Vauxhall Viva SL, 1965-66; Vauxhall Viva SL90, 1965-66; Bedford Beagle, 1964-66; Bedford 6 cwt Van, 1964-66; Bedford 8 cwt Van, 1964-66 by Kenneth Ball and the Autopress team of technical writers. 4th ed. fully rev. Brighton, Autopress, 1970, 1973 print.
184 p. illus. 25 cm. (Autobook series of workshop manuals, 157)
1st ed. 1968, under title: Vauxhall autobook two.
1. Vauxhall automobile. I. Title.
LLafS NUC76-40395

Ball, Kenneth.
Vauxhall Viva HB, 1966-70 autobook: [workshop manual] Vauxhall Viva HB, 1966-70; Vauxhall Viva HB90, 1966-70; Vauxhall Viva HBSL, 1966-70; Vauxhall Viva HB SL90, 1966-70 by Kenneth Ball and the Autopress team of technical writers. 6th ed. fully rev. Brighton, Autopress, 1971, 1973 print.
160 p. illus. 25 cm. (Autobook series of workshop manuals, 880)
1st ed. 1968 under title: Viva autobook Two.
1. Vauxhall automobile. I. Title.
LLafS NUC76-40396

Ball, Kenneth.
Vauxhall Viva HC, Firenza 1971 autobook; Workshop manual for Vauxhall Viva HC 1159cc, 1971, Vauxhall Viva HC SL 1159cc, 1971, Vauxhall Firenza 1159cc, 1971, Vauxhall Firenza SL 1159cc, 1971. Brighton, Eng., Autopress [c1971]
153 p. illus.
ISBN 0-85147-252-4.
1. Vauxhall automobile. I. Title.
CaOTP NUC74-160598

Ball, Kenneth.
Volkswagen 411, 1968-72 autobook: [workshop manual for] Volkswagen 411, 1968-69; Volkswagen 411L, 1968-69; Volkswagen 411E, 1969-70; Volkswagen 411 LE, 1969-72 by Kenneth Ball and the Autopress team of technical writers. 1st ed. Brighton, Autopress, 1972, 1973 print.
161 p. illus. 25 cm. (Autobook series of workshop manuals, 353)
1. Volkswagen automobile. I. Title.
LLafS NUC76-35267

Ball, Kenneth.
Volkswagen 1600 fastback, 1965-70 autobook: workshop manual for Volkswagen 1600 TL, 1965-70; Volkswagen 1600 Variant, 1965-66; Volkswagen 1600 L, 1966-67; Volkswagen 1600 Variant L, 1966-70; Volkswagen 1600 T, 1968-70; Volkswagen 1600 TA, 1969-70; Volkswagen 1600 Variant A, 1969-70; Volkswagen 1600 Variant M, 1969-70; Volkswagen 1600 Variant L, 1965-70; Karmann Ghia 1600 Coupé, 1965-69 by Kenneth Ball and the Autopress team of technical writers. 1st ed. Brighton, Autopress, 1971.
176 p. illus. 25 cm. (Autobook series of workshop manuals, 220)
1. Volkswagen automobile. I. Title.
LLafS NUC76-40398

Ball, Kenneth.
Volkswagen Beetle, 1954-67 autobook: workshop manual for Volkswagen 1200, 1954-65; Volkswagen 1200A, 1965-66; Volkswagen 1300, 1965-67; Volkswagen 1500, 1965-67; Karmann-Ghia 1200, 1955-65; Karmann-Ghia 1300, 1965-66; Karmann-Ghia 1500, 1966-67 by Kenneth Ball and the Autopress team of technical writers. 4th ed. fully rev. Brighton, Autopress, 1970, 1971a print.
184 p. illus. 25 cm. (Autobook series of workshop manuals, 133)
1st ed. 1969.
1. Volkswagen. I. Title.
LLafS NUC76-35418

Ball, Kenneth.
Volkswagen beetle, super beetle 1968-73 autobook; workshop manual. [4th ed., rev.] Brighton, Eng. [c1973]
165 p. illus.
1. Volkswagen automobile.
LN OC RP NUC74-132182

Ball, Kenneth.
Volkswagen Transporter, 1968-73 autobook: [workshop manual for] Volkswagen 1 ton FC 1600cc., 1700 cc. Van, 1968-73; Volkswagen 1 ton FC 1600 cc., 1700 cc. Pick-up, 1968-73; Volkswagen 1 ton FC 1600 cc., 1700 cc. Kombi, 1968-73; Volkswagen 1 ton FC 1600 cc., 1700 cc. Micro-bus, 1968-73. Kenneth Ball and the Autopress team of technical writers. 2d ed. fully rev. Brighton, Autopress, 1973.
169 p. illus. 25 cm. (Autobook series of workshop manuals, 733)
1st ed. 1971.
1. Volkswagen automobile. I. Title.
LLafS NUC76-40399

Ball, Kenneth.
Volvo 120 series 1961-70 autobook; workshop manual for Volvo 121 1961-67, Volvo 122 1961-67, Volvo 123 GT 1967-68, Volvo 131 1963-70, Volvo 132 1963-68, Volvo 133 1968-70, Volvo 221 1962-68, Volvo 222 1962-68, Volvo 223 1967-68. Brighton, Eng., Autopress [1972]
192 p. illus. (Autobook series of workshop manuals 276)
CaOTP NUC73-120488

Ball, Kenneth.
Volvo 140 1966-71 autobook; workshop manual for Volvo 142, 1967-69, Volvo 142S, 1967-69, Volvo 144, 1966-71, Volvo 144S, 1966-71, Volvo 144GL, 1970-71, Volvo 145, 1968-71, Volvo 145S, 1968-71, by Kenneth Ball and the Autopress team of technical writers. [2d ed., fully rev.] Brighton, Eng., Autopress [1972]
176 p. illus.
ISBN 0-85147-270-2.
1. Volvo automobile. I. Title.
CaOTP NUC74-132096

Ball, Kenneth.
Volvo 160 series, 1968-72 autobook: workshop manual for Volvo 164, 1968-72; Volvo 164E, 1971-72 by Kenneth Ball and the Autopress team of technical writers. 1st ed. Brighton, Autopress, 1972, 1973 print.
153 p. illus. 25 cm. (Autobook series of workshop manuals, 782)
1. Volvo automobile. I. Title.
LLafS NUC76-35269

Ball, Kenneth.
Volvo 1800 1960-71 autobook; workshop manual for Volvo P1800, 1961-63, Volvo 1800S, 1963-69, Volvo 1800E, 1961-71. Brighton, Eng., Autopress [c1972]
168 p. illus.
ISBN 0-85147-258-S.
1. Volvo automobile. I. Title.
CaOTP NUC74-132102

Ball, L. B., joint author
see Kuba, Dennis. A Univac 1108 program for obtaining rigorous error estimates... Madison, University of Wisconsin, Mathematics Research Center, 1972.

Ball, Larry Durwood.
The office of the United States marshal in Arizona and New Mexico territories, 1851-1912. Ann Arbor, Mich., University Microfilms, 1970.
1 reel. 35 mm.
Thesis (Ph. D.)—University of Colorado.
Microfilm of typescript.
1. United States marshals—Hist. I. Title.
WHi NUC76-35270

Ball, Leonard, joint author.
see Howard, T. William. A dictionary of psychiatric drugs for non-medical mental health workers. [s.l., s.n.] c1977 (Gulfport [Miss.?] : B. Weaver)

Ball, Leslie David, 1944-
Defining computer security needs in a university data base environment. [Amherst] 1975.
xii, 202 l. 28 cm.
Thesis (Ph. D.)—University of Massachusetts.
1. Electronic data processing departments—Security measures. 2. Massachusetts. University. I. Title.
MU NUC77-84241

Ball, Linda Virginia.
Student contracting for achievement grades in ninth grade general mathematics. [Storrs, Conn.] 1972.
viii, 133 l. illus.
Typescript.
Thesis (Ph. D.)—University of Connecticut.
Bibliography: leaves [86]-90.
1. Mathematics—Study and teaching (Secondary) I. Title.
CtU NUC73-121320

Ball, Lucille, 1911-
see [A Shroud for Sarah] [Sound recording] American Forces Radio and Television Service RU 14-6, 5B [1975]

Ball, Margaret Elizabeth, 1947-
Variations in the assimilation of Arabic and English loans into the Swahili of Mombasa, Kenya. [Austin, Tex.] 1971.
iii, 97 l. 29 cm.
Thesis (Ph. D.)—University of Texas at Austin.
Vita.
Bibliography: leaves 95-97.
TxU NUC73-121086

Ball, Margaret Elizabeth, 1947-
Variations in the assimilation of Arabic and English loans into the Swahili of Mombasa, Kenya. [Austin] 1971 [1972]
iii, 97 l.
Microfilm copy. Ann Arbor, Mich., University Microfilms, 1972. 1 reel. 35 mm.
IU FMU NUC74-132044

Ball, Marion J
How to select a computerized hospital information system, compiled and edited by Marion J. Ball. Basel, New York, S. Karger, 1973.
77 p. illus. 31 cm. (Data processing in medicine, v. 2) 59.00F ($16.55U.S.) Sw***
Includes bibliographical references.
1. Electronic data processing—Hospitals—Administration. I. Title. II. Series: Datenverarbeitung in der Medizin. [Monographie] v. 2.
RA971.B23 651.8 73-160667
MARC

Ball, Mary Margaret, 1909–
NATO and the European union movement, by M. Margaret Ball. Westport, Conn., Greenwood Press [1974, c1959]
xi, 486 p. illus. 22 cm.
"Published under the auspices of the London Institute of World Affairs."
Reprint of the ed. published by Stevens, London, which was issued as no. 45 of the Library of world affairs.
Bibliography: p. 428–457.
ISBN 0-8371-7642-5
1. European federation. 2. North Atlantic Treaty Organization. I. Title. II. Series: The Library of world affairs, no. 45.
JN15.B3 1974 341.24'2 74–9319
MARC

Ball, Mary Margaret, 1909-
Native Americans bibliography. [Lawrence, Kansas?] 1973.
1 v. (various pagings) 30 cm.
A compilation of various pricelists and bibliographies published by the Bureau of Indian Affairs.
1. Indians of North America–Bibliography. I. United States. Bureau of Indian Affairs. II. Title.
MoKU NUC76-35261

Ball, Matthew Curry.
Physical data for inorganic chemists / M. C. Ball and A. H. Norbury. — London : Longman, 1974.
xiv, 175 p. ; 22 cm. GB***
Includes bibliographies and index.
ISBN 0-582-44092-0 : $5.95
1. Chemistry, Inorganic—Handbooks, manuals, etc. 2. Chemistry, Physical and theoretical—Handbooks, manuals, etc. I. Norbury, A. H., joint author. II. Title.
QD475.B28 541 73–90717
MARC

Ball, Mia, 1942-
The Worshipful Company of Brewers : a short history / [by] Mia Ball. — London : Hutchinson, 1977.
143 p., [4] p. of plates : ill. (some col.), facsims., (1 col.), ports. ; 24 cm.
GB77-11121
Bibliography: p. 133-134.
Includes index.
ISBN 0-09-127850-3 : £5.00
1. Worshipful Company of Brewers—History. I. Title.
HD9397.G72W672 338.6'32 77-366475
77 MARC

Ball, Michael.
The economics of an urban housing market, Bristol Area Study / by Michael Ball and Richard Kirwan. — London : Centre for Environmental Studies, 1975.
315 p. (10 fold.) : ill., 2 maps ; 30 cm. — (Research paper - Centre for Environmental Studies ; CES RP 15) GB75-17326
Bibliography: p. 313-315.
ISBN 0-85980-024-5 : £2.40
1. Housing—England—Bristol. I. Kirwan, Richard Martin, joint author. II. Title. III. Series: Centre for Environmental Studies. Research paper ; CES RP 15.
HD7334.B65B35 301.5'4'0942393 76-357824
76 MARC

Ball, Michael.
Housing policy in a socialist country : the case of Poland / Michael Ball and Michael Harloe. — London : Centre for Environmental Studies, 1974.
58 p. : 1 ill. ; 30 cm. — (Research paper - Centre for Environment Studies ; CES RP8) GB74-26288
Includes bibliographical references.
ISBN 0-85980-019-9 : £0.50
1. Housing—Poland. I. Harloe, Michael, joint author. II. Title. III. Series: Centre for Environment Studies. Research paper ; CES RP8.
HD7345.7.A3B34 301.5'4'09438 75-311913
75 MARC

Ball, Mog.
Death / Mog Ball. — London : Oxford University Press [for] Chameleon/Ikon, 1976.
[2], 66 p. : ill., facsims. ; 21 x 22 cm. — (Standpoints) GB76-32894
Cover title.
Includes bibliographical references.
ISBN 0-19-913235-6 : £0.75
1. Death. I. Title. II. Series.
GT3150.B33 128'.5 77-361220
77 MARC

Ball, Mog.
Young people as volunteers / [by] Mog Ball. — [Berkhamsted] : Volunteer Centre, 1976.
[1], 60 p. : ill. ; 30 cm. GB77-04680
Cover title.
Bibliography: p. 60.
ISBN 0-904647-07-2 : £1.00
1. Youth volunteers in social service—Great Britain. 2. Youth volunteers in community development—Great Britain. I. Title.
HV243.B34 361.7 77-363545
77 MARC

Ball, Mog, joint author
see Ball, Colin. Education for a change... Harmondsworth, Penguin, 1973.

Ball, Morris H., ed.
see Rochester, N. Y. University. Economic Education Workshop. The work we do in the Rochester region. [Rochester, N. Y.] University of Rochester, University school of liberal and applied studies [1960?]

Ball, Murray Hone, 1939–
Bruce the barbarian [by] Murray Ball. London, Quartet Books, 1973.
[128] p. of illus. 18 cm. £0.30 GB 73–30252
I. Title.
PN6738.B7B3 741.5'9931 74–172321
ISBN 0-7043-1060-0 MARC

Ball, Nelson,
Dry spell. [Poem by Nelson Ball; serigraph by Barbara Caruso. Toronto, Seripress, 1973]
1 fold. p. 1 col. plate.
Edition limited to 80 numbered and signed copies.
1. Canadian poetry, English. I. Caruso, Barbara, illus. II. Title.
CaOTP NUC75-18523

Ball, Nelson,
Our arms are featherless wings. [Poem by Nelson Ball; serigraph by Barbara Caruso. Toronto, Seripress, 1973]
1 fold. p. 1 col. plate.
Edition limited to 80 numbered and signed copies.
1. Canadian poetry, English. I. Caruso, Barbara, illus. II. Title.
CaOTP NUC75-17400

Ball, Nelson.
The shore: a poem [by] Nelson Ball & 2 prints [by] Barbara Caruso. [Toronto, Seripress, 1974]
3 l. in folder. illus. 23 cm.
"Edition of 50."
1. Canadian poetry. I. Caruso, Barbara, illus. II. Title.
RPB NUC76-21062

Ball, Nelson
see Poetry of Canada. [Buffalo] Intrepid Press [1969]

Ball, Nicole.
Regional conflicts and the international system : a case study of Bangladesh / Nicole Ball. — [Brighton] : Institute for the Study of International Organisation, 1974.
[3], 88 p. ; 30 cm. — (ISIO monographs ; 1st ser., no. 9 ISSN 0306-560X)
GB75-16030
Errata slip inserted.
Bibliography: p. 85-88.
ISBN 0-900479-09-4 : £1.50 ($4.00 U.S.)
1. Bangladesh—Politics and government—1971- 2. Bangladesh—Economic conditions. 3. South Asia—Politics and government. I. Title. II. Series: Brighton, Eng. University of Sussex. Institute for the Study of International Organisations. ISIO monographs ; ser. 1, no. 9.
DS395.5.B34 320.9'549'205 76-353765
76 MARC

Ball, Nina
see Crouch, Andraé. Through it all. Waco, Tex. : Word Books, [1974]

Ball, Norbert Louis, 1940- joint author
see McCrossan, Robert G 1924-
An evaluation of surface geochemical prospecting for pertoleum, Olds-Caroline area, Alberta. [Ottawa] Dept. of Energy, Mines and Resources [1972]

Ball, Norbert Louis, 1940- joint author
see Price, L L Stratigraphy of Cominco Potash shaft no. 1 Vanscoy, Saskatchewan. [Ottawa] Dept. of Energy, Mines, and Resources [1973]

Ball, Norman R., joint comp.
see Sinclair, Bruce, comp. Let us be honest and modest... Toronto: Oxford Univ. Press, 1974.

Ball, Patricia M
The heart's events : the Victorian poetry of relationships / Patricia M. Ball. — London : Athlone Press, 1976.
[7], 227 p. ; 23 cm. GB76-22901
Distributed in the U.S. by Humanities Press, Atlantic Highlands, N.J.
Includes index.
ISBN 0-485-11163-2 : £6.25
1. English poetry—19th century—History and criticism. 2. Interpersonal relations in literature. I. Title.
PR591.B3 821'.8'09354 76-383151
76 MARC

Ball, Perry Columbus, 1851-1933.
Letters and poems, by Perry Columbus Ball. Compiled by Wilbur P. Ball. [n.p., 1969]
vi, 24 p. port.
1. Ball, Perry Columbus, 1851-1933. I. Ball, Wilbur P., 1923- comp. II. Title.
WHi NUC73-47871

Ball, Peter John Hannaford, 1948-
Ovulation, egg collection and transfer and oviduct fluids in ewes with permanent oviducal cannulae. -- [Ithaca, N.Y.] : Ball, 1975.
viii, 118 leaves : ill. ; 29 cm.
Thesis (Ph.D.)--Cornell University.
Bibliography: leaves 109-117.
1. Sheep breeding. 2. Ovulation. I. Title.
NIC NUC77-86046

Ball, Rachel Stutsman, joint author
see Stott, Leland Hyrum, 1897- The identification and assessment of thinking ability... [Washington] 1968.

Ball, Richard, 1900-
Congregationalism in Cornwall : a brief survey / by Richard Ball. — [London : s.n., 1955]
54 p., [1] leaf of plates : port. ; 19 cm.
1. Congregational churches in Cornwall, Eng. 2. Cornwall, Eng.—Church history. I. Title.
BX7177.C67B34 77-364404
77 MARC

Ball, Richard Edward, 1919- joint author.
see Schwartzman, Sylvan David. Elements of financial analysis. New York, D. Van Nostrand, c1977.

Ball, Richard Henry, 1935-
Interpretation of the first-order correction to the magnetic moment invariant [by] R.H. Ball. [Santa Monica, Calif., Rand Corp.] 1966.
4 p. 28 cm. (Rand Corporation. Paper, P-3350)
Cover title.
Bibliography: p. 4.
1. Particles (Nuclear physics) I. Title. II. Series.
MB NUC73-46824

Ball, Richard Henry, 1935- joint author.
see Vestine, Ernest H. Nature of surface flow in the earth's central core ... Santa Monica, Calif., Rand Corp., 1967.

Ball, Richard Neal, 1944-
Full convex l-subgroups of a lattice ordered group. [n. p.] 1974.
69 l. 29 cm.
Thesis (Ph. D.)–University of Wisconsin.
Vita.
Includes bibliography.
I. Title.
WU NUC76-21410

Ball, Rick A.
see Indianapolis architecture. [Indianapolis?] Indiana Architectural Foundation, c1975.

Ball, Robert, 1937-
see United States. Bureau of Labor Statistics. Labor and material requirements for construction of private single-family houses. Washington, Govt. Print. Off., 1972.

Ball, Robert C 1912-
An action program for water quality management. Prepared by Robert C. Ball, Howard A. Tanner [and] Marvin E. Stephenson. East Lansing, Mich., Michigan State University [1972]
14 l. illus.
1. Water quality management. I. Tanner, Howard A., joint author. II. Stephenson, Marvin Eugene, joint author. III. Title.
MiEM NUC75-56274

Ball, Robert C 1912-
Culture and agriculture importance of earthworms. [East Lansing] 1973.
27 p. illus. (Michigan State University. Cooperative Extension Service. Extension bulletin E-766)
Bibliography: p. 26-27.
I. Title.
DNAL NUC75-29798

Ball, Robert C 1912-
An ecological evaluation of stream eutrophication [by] Robert C. Ball, Niles R. Kevern [and] Terry A. Haines. East Lansing, Institute of Water Research, Michigan State University, 1973.
1 v. (various pagings) illus. (Michigan. State University, East Lansing. Institute of Water Research. Technical report, no. 36)
At head of title: Project completion report for Title II project.
"OWRR Project C-1663, C-2205 and C-3381."
Includes bibliographies.
1. Stream ecology. 2. Eutrophication. I. Kevern, Niles R. II. Haines, Terry Alan, 1943- III. Title. IV. Series.
MiEM NUC75-17389

Ball, Robert C., 1912- An ecological evaluation of stream eutrophication
see Moncrief, Lewis W The demand for and value of the sport fishery... East Lansing. Institute of Water Research, Michigan State University [1972]

Ball, Robert C., 1912- An ecological evaluation of stream eutrophication
see Moncrief, Lewis W User related study of three Michigan Rivers... East Lansing, Institute of Water Research, Michigan State University [1973]

Ball, Robert C., 1912- An ecological evaluation of stream eutrophication
see Pearce, James W Economic evaluation of the sport fishery... East Lansing [1973]

Ball, Robert C 1912-
Evaluation of lake dredging as a lake restoration technique; a research proposal to: Environmental Protection Agency, Water Quality Office. Prepared by: Robert C. Ball, Thomas G. Hahr and Niles R. Kevern. East Lansing, Institute of Water Research, Michigan State University, 1971.
69, 10 l. illus.
Reproduced from typescript.
Includes bibliographies.
1. Dredging. 2. Lansing, Lake. 3. Water resources development—Michigan—Ingham County. I. Bahr, Thomas Gordon, joint author. II. Kevern, Niles R., 1931- joint author. III. Title.
MiEM NUC73-34750

Ball, Robert C 1912-
The Red Cedar River report, by Robert C. Ball, Kenneth J. Linton [and] Niles R. Kevern. East Lansing, Museum, Michigan State University, 1968-69.
2 v. illus., maps. 25 cm. (Publications of the Museum, Michigan State University. Biological series, v. 4, no. 2, 4)
Includes bibliographies.
CONTENTS: 1. Chemistry and hydrology.—2. Bioecology.
1. Fresh-water biology—Michigan—Red Cedar River. 2. Red Cedar River, Mich. I. Linton, Kenneth J., joint author. II. Kevern, Niles R., 1931- joint author. III. Title. IV. Series: Michigan. State University, East Lansing. Museum. Publications. Biological series, v. 4, no. 2, 4.
QH1.M58 vol. 4 no. 2, etc. 70-625199
574'.08 s
[QH105.M5] 70[r75]rev2 MARC

Ball, Robert C., 1912-
see Grzenda, Alfred Richard, 1932- Primary production, energetics, and nutrient utilization in a warm-water stream. [East Lansing, Institute of Water Research, Michigan State University] 1968.

Ball, Robert James.
Inflation and the theory of money, by R. J. Ball. With a new introd. [2d ed.] London, Allen & Unwin [1973]
313 p. illus. 22 cm.
Bibliographical footnotes.
1. Inflation (Finance) I. Title.
PPT NUC76-62517

Ball, Robert James.
The international linkage of national economic models, edited by R. J. Ball. Amsterdam, North-Holland Pub. Co.; New York, American Elsevier Pub. Co., 1973.
xii, 467 p. 23 cm. (Contributions to economic analysis, 78) $31.50 (U.S.) Ne***
Includes bibliographical references.
1. International economic relations—Mathematical models. I. Title. II. Series.
HF1411.B236 1973 382.1 72-88287
ISBN 0-444-10464-X (American Elsevier) MARC

Ball, Robert Jerome, 1941-
The structure of Tibullus's elegies. [New York] 1971.
376 l. 29 cm.
Thesis—Columbia University.
Bibliography: leaves 355-376.
1. Tibullus, Albius. I. Title.
NNC NUC73-34793

Ball, Robert Jerome, 1941-
The structure of Tibullus's elegies. [New York] 1971 [1973]
3, 376 l.
Thesis—Columbia University.
Bibliography: leaves 362-376.
Photocopy. Ann Arbor, Mich., University Microfilms, 1973. 21 cm.
OCU NUC74-132111

Ball, Robert Jonathan, 1942-
Teaching teachers in the seventies: the search for meaning; the history of the creation of the 1971-72 Master of Arts in Teaching program at the University of Massachusetts. [Amherst] University of Massachusetts, 1974.
viii, 278 l. illus. 28 cm.
Thesis (Ed. D.)—University of Massachusetts.
1. Teachers, Training of. 2. Massachusetts. University. School of Education. I. Title.
MU NUC76-21073

Ball, Robert R
The "I feel" formula / Robert R. Ball. — Waco, Tex. : Word Books, c1977.
120 p. ; 23 cm.
Includes bibliographical references.
ISBN 0-8499-0001-8 : $5.95
1. Christian life—Presbyterian authors. 2. Psychology, Religious. I. Title.
BV4501.2.B382 248'.48'52 77-152880
77 MARC

Ball, Sir Robert Stawell, 1840-1913.
The cause of an ice age, by Sir Robert Ball... New York, D. Appleton and Company, 1891.
xii, 180 p. incl. front. diagrs. 19 cm. (Modern science series, ed. by Sir J. Lubbock. [I])
Micro-opaque. New York, Readex Microprint, 1973. 2 cards. 23 x 15 cm. (Landmarks of science)
1. Glacial epoch. I. Title.
IaAS NUC75-17403

Ball, Sir **Robert Stawell,** 1840–1913.
Great astronomers. Plainview, N. Y., Books for Libraries Press [1974]
xii, 372 p. illus. 22 cm. (Essay index reprint series)
Reprint of the 1895 ed. published by Isbister, London.
CONTENTS: Ptolemy. — Copernicus. — Tycho Brahe. — Galileo. — Kepler. — Isaac Newton. — Flamsteed. — Halley.—Bradley.—William Herschel. — Laplace. — Brinkley. — John Herschel. — The Earl of Rosse.—Airy.—Hamilton.—Le Verrier.—Adams.
1. Astronomers. 2. Astronomy—History. I. Title.
QB35.B18 1974 520'.92'2 [B] 74-994
ISBN 0-518-10142-8 MARC

Ball, Sir Robert Stawell, 1840-1913.
The theory of screws: a study in the dynamics of a rigid body. By Robert Stawell Ball. Dublin, Hodges, Foster, and Co., 1876.
194 p. 23 cm.
Micro-opaque. New York, Readex Microprint, 1973. 3 cards. 23 x 15 cm. (Landmarks of science)
1. Screws—Theory, 1876. I. Title.
IaAS NUC75-17404

Ball, Robert Stawell, Sir, 1840-1913
see Tissandier, Gaston, 1843-1899. Wonders of water... London, Paris, and New York, Cassell, Petter, & Galpin [n.d.]

Ball, Rodney Jack, 1943-
The feasibility of determining success criteria for educational research and development projects. [n. p.] 1974.
180 l.
Thesis (Ph. D.)—Ohio State University.
Bibliography: leaves 176-180.
1. Educational research. 2. Project management. I. Title.
OU NUC76-21409

Ball, S.F., joint author
see Pucci, P F Heat transfer and flow friction... [Monterey, Calif.] U.S. Naval Postgraduate School, 1967.

Ball, S.J.
see Delene, J G A digital computer code for simulating large multistage flash evaporator desalting plant dynamics. Oak Ridge, Tenn., Oak Ridge National Laboratory, Union Carbide Corp., U.S. Atomic Energy Commission, 1971.

Ball, Samuel.
Assessing the attitudes of young children toward school. [n.p.] Head Start Test Collection, Educational Testing Service [1971]
11 p. (Head Start Test Collection report)
1. Attitude (Psychology)—Testing. 2. Students—Attitudes. I. Title. II. Series.
MH-Ed NUC73-34761

Ball, Samuel,
Improving classroom instruction through educational psychology. New York, Associated Educational Services Corp. [c1967]
1 v. (various pagings) (Selected Academic Readings)
1. Educational psychology. I. Title. II. Series.
NSyL NUC76-62489

Ball, Samuel.
Reading with television: an evaluation of the Electric Company, by Samuel Ball and Gerry Ann Bogatz. Princeton, Educational Testing Service, 1973.
2 v.
A report to the Children's Television Workshop.
1. Electric Company (Television program) 2. Television in elementary education. I. Bogatz, Gerry Ann. II. Children's Television Workshop. III. Title.
MH-Ed IaU NUC74-132246

Ball, Samuel.
Research on Sesame Street; some implications for compensatory education, by Samuel Ball [and] Gerry Ann Bogatz. Princeton, N.J., Educational Testing Service [1972?]
29 p. 28 cm.
"Proceedings of the Second Annual Hyman Blumberg Symposium on Research in Early Childhood Education, Johns Hopkins Press, 1972."
Cover title.
TxU NUC74-132084

Ball, Samuel, joint author
see Anderson, Scarvia B Encyclopedia of educational evaluation. San Francisco: Jossey-Bass Publishers, 1975.

Ball, Samuel
see Bogatz, Gerry Ann. The second year of Sesame Street... Princeton, N. J., Educational Testing Service, 1971.

Ball, Samuel.
see Motivation in education. New York, Academic Press, 1977.

Ball, Sandra J
see
Ball-Rokeach, Sandra.

Ball, Sarah Lee
see Simpson County Sesquicentennial Celebration, 1974. Historical Booklet Committee. Simpson county "Honoring the Past"... [n. p., 1974?]

Ball, Sidney, 1857-1918.
The moral aspects of socialism, by Sidney Ball. London, The Fabian Society, 1901 [Nendeln, Liechtenstein, Kraus Reprint, 1969]
23 p. 22 cm. (Fabian tract no. 72)
1. Socialism. 2. Social ethics. I. Title.
MB NUC75-96098

Ball, Stanley Crittenden, 1885-
Jungle fowls from Pacific islands, by Stanley C. Ball. Honolulu, The Museum, 1933. New York, Kraus Reprint, 1971.
121 p. illus., 7 plates. 23 cm. (Bernice P. Bishop Museum. Bulletin 108)
Reprint of the 1933 ed.
Bibliography: p. 118-119.
1. Poultry—Oceanica. I. Title.
IaU NUC75-58871

Ball, Stanley William.
Finance in the marketing function. London, Industrial and Commercial Techniques, 1972.
106 l.
1. Accounting—Study and teaching. 2. Finance. I. Title.
ViBlbV NUC74-132103

Ball, Terence.
Civil disobedience and civil deviance. Beverly Hills, Calif., Sage Publications [1973]
49 p. 22 cm. (Sage professional papers in American politics, ser. no. 04-012) $2.25
Bibliography: p. 45-49.
1. Government, Resistance to. I. Title.
JC328.2.B34 322'.01 73-92214
ISBN 0-8039-0359-6 MARC

Ball, Terence.
Laws and explanation in political science. [Berkeley] 1973.
1 v. (various pagings)
Thesis (Ph. D.)—University of California.
Includes bibliographical references.
CU NUC75-18522

Ball, Thomas, 1819-1911.
My threescore years and ten : an authobiography / by Thomas Ball. — 2d ed. — New York : Garland Pub., 1977, c1891.
13, xi, 379 p., [5] leaves of plates : ill. ; 19 cm. — (The Art experience in late nineteenth-century America)
Reprint of the 1892 ed. published by Roberts Bros., Boston; with new introd.
ISBN 0-8240-2242-4 : $25.00
1. Ball, Thomas, 1819-1911. 2. Sculptors—United States—Biography. I. Title. II. Series.
NB237.B3A25 1977 730'.92'4 75-28884
76 MARC

Ball, Thomas Michael, 1940-
Proposed evaluative criteria constructed from selected factors essential to a sound broadcast education program in Florida's community colleges. [Gainesville] 1971.
x, 249 l. 28 cm.
Manuscript copy.
Thesis—University of Florida.
Vita.
Bibliography: leaves 236-247.
1. Radio broadcasting—Study and teaching. 2. Television broadcasting—Study and teaching. I. Title.
FU NUC73-34765

Ball, Timothy Horton, 1826-
Encyclopedia of genealogy and biography of Lake County, Indiana, with a compendium of history, 1834-1904. A record of the achievements of its people in the making of commonwealth and the founding of a nation. Chicago, Lewis Pub. Co., 1904. [Evansville, Ind., Unigraphic, Inc., 1974]
[8], 674 p. illus., plates. 26 cm.
Reprint of the 1904 edition.
ICN NUC75-17402

Ball, Valentine, 1843-1895.
see **Tavernier, Jean Baptiste, 1605-1689. Travels in India. Lahore, al-Biruni, 1976.**

Ball, Vaughn C. Rules regarding scientific evidence
see Seminar for State Trial Judges and Solicitors Association of Georgia, 7th, Georgia Center for Continuing Education, 1975. Program materials for seventh seminar... Athens, Ga., Institute of Continuing Legal Education in Georgia, 1975.

Ball, Vic, ed.
see Ball (George J.) inc., West Chicago, Ill. The Ball red book. 10th ed. [West Chicago] 1960.

Ball, Vic
see Ball (George J.) inc., West Chicago, Ill. The Ball red book. 13th ed. [n.p.] 1976.

Ball, Victoria Kloss.
Opportunities in interior design / Victoria Kloss Ball. — Rev. ed. — Louisville, Ky. : Vocational Guidance Manuals, c1977.
v, 122 p. : ill. ; 21 cm.
First ed. published in 1963 under title: Opportunities in interior design and decoration.
Bibliography: p. [118]-119.
Includes index.
ISBN 0-89022-228-2. ISBN 0-89022-229-0 pbk.
1. Interior decoration—Vocational guidance. I. Title.
NK2116.B3 1977 729 76-51706
77 MARC

Ball, Virgil Eldon.
The cost of buffalo depletion; A study of the economics of natural resource utilization in relation to property rights. Raleigh, N.C., 1972.
72 l. illus., tables. 29 cm.
Thesis—North Carolina State University at Raleigh.
Bibliography: leaves 70-72.
Vita.
NcRS NUC73-121319

Ball, Virginia A 1928-
Managing the dental practice; a guide for the dental assistant [by] Virginia A. Ball [and] Edwin W. Halvorson. San Francisco, Rinehart Press [1974]
xi, 189 p. illus. 24 cm.
Includes bibliographical references.
1. Dentistry—Practice. 2. Dental assistants. I. Halvorson, Edwin W., 1909- joint author. II. Title.
[DNLM: 1. Dental assistants. 2. Practice management, Dental. WU 90 B187m 1974]
RK60.5.B34 651'.9'6176 74-602
ISBN 0-03-010416-5 MARC

Ball, Walter Savage.
Amherst life. Selections from the under-graduate publications at Amherst College. Ed. by Walter Savage Ball. Illustrated by William Cary Duncan. Amherst. W.C. Howland, 1896.
xii, 139 p. incl. front., illus. 18 cm.
Micro-transparency (negative). Louisville, Ky., Lost Cause Press, 1973. 3 sheets. 10.5 x 14.8 cm. (L.H. Wright. American fiction, 1876-1900, no. 260)
1. Amherst College. I. Title.
PSt NUC75-26803

Ball, Walter Savage, ed.
Amherst life; selections from the under-graduate publications at Amherst College. Edited by Walter Savage Ball. Illustrated by William Cary Duncan. Amherst, W. C. Howland, 1896 [1974]
xii, 139 p. illus.
Microfilm (positive) Ann Arbor, Mich., University Microfilms, 1974. 2d title of 15. 35 mm. (American fiction series, reel 254.2)
I. Title.
KEmT NUC75-120006

Ball, Walter William Rouse, 1850-1925.
Fun with string figures. New York, Dover Publications [1970]
viii, 80 p. 21 cm.
"Unabridged republication of the third edition of the work first published ... in 1920 under title: An introduction to string figures."
Includes bibliographical references.
SUMMARY: Discusses the history of string figures and gives directions for making cat's cradle, the ebbing tide, and many other designs.
ISBN 0-486-22809-6 : $1.00
1. String figures. [1. String figures] I. Title.
GV1218.S8B35 1971 793'.9 76-173664
rev MARC

Ball, Walter William Rouse, 1850-1925.
A history of the study of mathematics at Cambridge, by W. W. Rouse Ball... Cambridge, University Press, 1889.
xvli, 264 p. 20 cm.
Micro-opaque. New York, Readex Microprint, 1973. 3 cards. 23 x 15 cm. (Landmarks of science)
1. Mathematics—Hist. 2. Mathematics—Study and teaching. 3. Cambridge University—Hist.
IaAS NUC75-17405

Ball, Walter William Rouse, 1850-1925.
Mathematical recreations and essays / by W. W. Rouse Ball. — 7th ed. — London : Macmillan, 1917.
xvi, 506 p. (p. 493-506 advertisements) : ill. ; 21 cm.
First-3d ed. published under title: Mathematical recreations and problems of past and present times.
Includes index.
1. Mathematical recreations. 2. Geometry—Problems, Famous. 3. Cryptography. 4. Ciphers. I. Title.
QA95.B2 1917 77-351716
77 MARC

Ball, Walter William Rouse, 1850-1925.
Mathematical recreations & essays / by W. W. Rouse Ball and H. S. M. Coxeter. — 12th ed. — Toronto ; Buffalo : University of Toronto Press, [1974]
xvii, 428 p. : ill. ; 20 cm. C***
First-3d ed. published under title: Mathematical recreations and problems of past and present times.
Bibliography: p. 418.
Includes index.
ISBN 0-8020-1844-0 : $12.50. ISBN 0-8020-6138-9 pbk.
1. Mathematical recreations. 2. Geometry—Problems, Famous. 3. Cryptography. 4. Ciphers. I. Coxeter, Harold Scott Macdonald, 1907- II. Title.
QA95.B2 1974 793.7'4 72-186276
MARC

Ball, Walter William Rouse, 1850-1925.
A short account of the history of mathematics, by W.W. Rouse Ball... 2d ed. London and New York, Macmillan and co., 1893.
xxiv, 520 p. diagrs. 20 cm.
"First edition printed 1888."
Micro-opaque. New York, Readex Microprint, 1973. 6 cards. 23 x 15 cm. (Landmarks of science)
1. Mathematics—Hist.
IaAS NUC75-16659

Ball, Wilbur N.
see The Report of the visitation committee reviewing the evaluative criteria for South High School... [Salt Lake City] 1956.

Ball, Wilbur P 1923-
Sons of Asel F. Ball [by] Wilbur P. Ball. Clovis, Calif. [1971]
ii, 26 p. illus. 22 cm.
Bibliography: p. 23.
1. Ball family. I. Title.
CS71.B2 1971 929'.2'0973 73-153307
MARC

Ball, Wilbur P., 1923- comp.
see Ball, Perry Columbus, 1851-1933. Letters and poems. [n.p., 1969]

Ball, Wilfried, ed.
see Arbeitsgemeinschaft Gebrauchswert-Kosten-Analyse. Höchste Effektivität durch Gebrauchswert-Kosten-Analyse; Tafelwerk. Berlin, Dietz, 1971.

Ball, William J.
see Indiana Canal Company. Charter and organization of the Indiana Canal Company. Cincinnati, Printed by E. Shepard, 1850.

Ball, William Lee, 1892-1972.
Genealogy of William Ball born 1812, Loudon County, Virginia / compiled by William Lee Ball. — Honolulu, Hawaii : ⌈E. B. Carr⌉, 1974.
x, 60 p. ; 23 cm.
1. Ball family. I. Title.
CS71.B2 1974 929'.2'0973 75-303661
75 MARC

Ball, Zachary, pseud.
Pseudonym of Kelly R. Masters writing by himself, as well as the joint pseudonym of Kelly R. Masters and Frankie Lee Griggs Zelley. For other works by Zelley writing by herself see entries under
Zelley, Frankie Lee Griggs, 1908–

Ball, Zachary, pseud.
Bar pilot, by Zachary Ball ⌈pseud.⌉ Drawings by Arthur Shilstone. New York, Holiday House ⌈1955⌉
218 p. illus. 21 cm.
SUMMARY: Suffering from anmesia incurred brom a blow during a shipping accident, a young boy sets out to discover his identity in midnineteenth century New Orleans.
⌈1. River life—Fiction. 2. River boats—Fiction. 3. New Orleans⌉ I. Title.
PZ7.B1992 Bar ⌈Fic⌉ 55-1794
⌈r76⌉rev MARC

Ball, Zachary, pseud.
Bristle face ⌈by⌉ Zachary Ball ⌈pseud.⌉ New York, Holiday House ⌈1962⌉
206 p. illus. 22 cm.
SUMMARY: Half-dog, half porcupine in appearance, Bristle Face becomes an outstanding hunting dog and a good friend of the fourteen-year-old orphan boy who adopts him.
⌈1. Mississippi—Fiction. 2. Fox-hunting—Fiction. 3. Dogs—Fiction⌉ I. Title.
PZ7.B1992 Br ⌈Fic⌉ 62-2219
⌈r76⌉rev MARC

Ball, Zachary, pseud.
Joe Panther, by Zachary Ball ⌈pseud.⌉ Illustrated by Elliott Means. New York, Holiday House ⌈1950⌉
241 p. illus. 21 cm.
I. Title.
PZ7.B1992Jo 50-10209

Ball, Zachary, pseud.
Kep ⌈by⌉ Zachary Ball ⌈pseud.⌉ New York, Holiday House ⌈1961⌉
207 p. 22 cm.
SUMMARY: After a family tragedy, a boy starts a new life with a couple who have a serious personal problem of their own to contend with.
⌈1. Family life—Fiction. 2. Adoption—Fiction. 3. Nature—Fiction⌉ I. Title.
PZ7.B1992 Kg ⌈Fic⌉ 61-16063
⌈r75⌉rev3 MARC

Ball, Zachary, pseud.
North to Abilene, by Zachary Ball ⌈pseud. New York⌉ Holiday House ⌈1960⌉
190 p. illus. 22 cm.
SUMMARY: An orphaned frontier lad and his pet bull meet up with a rancher who teaches the boy to ride, rope, shoot and to become a cattleman.
⌈1. Ranch life—Fiction. 2. The West—Fiction. 3. Cattle trade—Fiction⌉ I. Title.
PZ7.B1992 No ⌈Fic⌉ 60-2172
⌈r76⌉rev MARC

Ball, Zachary, pseud.
Piney, by Zachary Ball ⌈pseud. 1st ed.⌉ Boston, Little, Brown, 1950.
273 p. 20 cm.
I. Title.
PZ7.B1992Pi 50-7647

Ball, Zachary, pseud.
Salvage diver, by Zachary Ball ⌈pseud. New York⌉ Holiday House ⌈1961⌉
220 p. 21 cm.
SUMMARY: Two Seminole youths and their boat are hired for the summer by two men who want to search for sunken ships off the Florida Keys.
⌈1. Underwater exploration—Fiction. 2. Salvage—Fiction⌉ I. Title.
PZ7.B1992 Sal ⌈Fic⌉ 61-65036
⌈r75⌉rev MARC

Ball, Zachary, pseud.
Skin diver, by Zachary Ball ⌈pseud. New York⌉ Holiday House ⌈1956⌉
251 p. 21 cm.
SUMMARY: Two young skin divers are hired to help a researching biochemist working off the coast of Florida.
⌈1. Skin diving—Fiction⌉ I. Title.
PZ7.B1992 Sk ⌈Fic⌉ 56-14156
⌈rev⌉rev/AC/ MARC

Ball, Zachary, pseud.
Sky diver, by Zachary Ball. New York, Holiday House ⌈1967⌉
213 p. 22 cm.
I. Title.
PZ7.B1992 Sm 67-1937
⌈r75⌉rev MARC

Ball, Zachary, pseud.
Sputters ⌈by⌉ Zachary Ball ⌈pseud.⌉ New York, Holiday House ⌈c1963⌉
220 p. front. 21 cm.
SUMMARY: A dog proves his worth in a badger fight, a dog fight, and in the sheriff's hunt for moonshiners.
⌈1. Dogs—Fiction. 2. Mississippi—Fiction⌉ I. Title.
PZ7.B1992 Sp ⌈Fic⌉ 63-6534
⌈r76⌉rev MARC

Ball, Zachary, pseud.
Swamp chief, by Zachary Ball ⌈pseud.⌉ New York, Holiday House ⌈1952⌉
212 p. 21 cm.
SUMMARY: Through the eyes of a young man, the traditional life-style of the Seminole Indian and the vicissitudes of modern existence are recounted.
⌈1. Seminole Indians—Fiction. 2. Indians of North America—Fiction⌉ I. Title.
PZ7.B1992 Sw ⌈Fic⌉ 52-9567
⌈r76⌉rev MARC

Ball, Zachary, pseud.
Tent show, by Zachary Ball. New York, Holiday House ⌈1964⌉
186 p. illus. 22 cm.
SUMMARY: Based on the author's youthful experiences in a traveling tent show, this story of a young comedian and his performing dog portrays the life of traveling entertainers in early twentieth-century America.
⌈1. Acting as a profession—Fiction. 2. Theater—Fiction⌉ I. Title.
PZ7.B1992 Te ⌈Fic⌉ 64-7315
⌈r76⌉rev MARC

Ball, Zachary, pseud.
Wilderness teacher, by Zachary Ball ⌈pseud.⌉ and Myra Fowler. Illus. by Leonard Vosburgh. New York, Rand McNally ⌈1956⌉
224 p. illus. 22 cm.
SUMMARY: A fifteen-year-old girl travels with her aunt and uncle to their Florida homestead where a lonely existence inspires her to fulfill her hopes of becoming a school teacher.
⌈1. Frontier and pioneer life—Florida—Fiction. 2. Teaching as a profession—Fiction⌉ I. Fowler, Myra, joint author. II. Vosburgh, Leonard W., illus. III. Title.
PZ7.B1992 Wi ⌈Fic⌉ 56-6052
⌈r76⌉rev MARC

Ball Lima, Guillermo.
Contrato y régimen del trabajo : Ley 20.744, explicada y comentada / Guillermo Ball Lima. — Buenos Aires : Editorial El Coloquio, ⌈1975⌉
223 p. ; 22 cm.
"Este trabajo es un capítulo de la obra Derecho empresarial argentino, actualmente en preparación."
Includes bibliographical references.
1. Labor laws and legislation—Argentine Republic. 2. Labor contract—Argentine Republic. I. Title.
344'.82'01891 76-455098
76 MARC

Ball Lima, Guillermo.
Obligaciones patrimoniales laborales : soluciones prácticas / Guillermo Ball Lima. — Buenos Aires : Editorial El Coloquio, ⌈1975⌉
94 p. : ill. ; 22 cm.
1. Labor contract—Argentine Republic. I. Title.
344'.82'01891 76-451406
76 MARC

Ball-Rokeach, Sandra, joint author.
see De Fleur, Melvin Lawrence, 1923- Theories of mass communication. 3d ed. New York, D. McKay Co., c1975.

Ball del Sant Crist de Salomó : versió renovada / per Marcial Martínez. — ⌈s.l. : s.n., 1973⌉ (Barcelona : Impr. Fidel)
31 p. ; 20 cm.
Sp73
I. Martínez, Marcial.
PC3937.B34 76-480628
•76 MARC

Ball line of Virginia. -- [Baltimore? : Genealogical Pub. Co., 1975?]
38 [i.e. 39] p. : ill., coat of arms ; 27 cm.
Bibliography: p. [39]
1. Ball family (William Ball, 1615-1680)
Vi NUC77-84512

The Ball-room instructer : containing a complete description of cotillons and other popular dances : written and arranged for amateurs in dancing. — New York : Huestis & Cozans, 1851.
48 p. : ill. ; 12 cm.
1. Square dancing.
GV1763.B18 1851 77-351734
77 MARC

Ball State University
see
Indiana. Ball State University, Munice.

Ballā Īśvarudu
see
Īśvarudu, Ballā.

Balla, Andrés.
Los dueños de la selva. Buenos Aires, Trenti Rocamora ⌈1972⌉
191 p.
Novel.
I. Title.
InU NUC74-132085

Balla, Andrés.
El Inca Tupac Amaru. Buenos Aires, Instituto Lucchelli Bonadeo, 1971.
100 p. 18 cm.
1. Tupac-Amaru, José Gabriel, originally Condorcanqui, d. 1781, in fiction, drama, poetry, etc. I. Title.
CtY NUC73-121087

Balla, Andrés.
Los que respondieron al fuego : drama en tres actos / Andrés Balla. — ⌈Buenos Aires?⌉ : Autores Argentinos Asociados, 1975.
77 p. ; 19 cm.
I. Title.
PQ7797.B2717Q4 76-480291
76 MARC

Balla, Andrés.
Sala de niños; novela. [2d ed.] Madrid, Ediciones Literoy [1969]
258 p. 20 cm. (Colección Voz del tiempoo, no. 1)
I. Title.
WU OU CSf NUC73-47474

Balla, Bálint.
Kaderverwaltung; Versuch zur Idealtypisierung der Bürokratie sowjetisch-volks-demokratischen Typs. Stuttgart, F. Enke, 1972.
viii, 282 p. 25 cm. (Soziologische Gegenwartsfragen, n.F., Nr. 37) DM49.00 GDB***
Habilitationsschrift—Technische Universität, Berlin.
Bibliography: p. ⌈277⌉–279.
1. Bureaucracy. 2. Russia — Politics and government — 1953– 3. Communism—Russia. I. Title. II. Series.
JF1353.B34 73-307580
ISBN 3-432-01784-7

Balla, Bálint
see Historische Entwicklung und sozialer Wandel. Stuttgart: Enke, 1974.

Balla, Bálint
see Sozialisation durch Massenkommunikation. Stuttgart, F. Enke Verlag, 1971.

Balla, Bálint
see Soziologie und Gesellschaft in Ungarn ... Stuttgart: Enke, 1974-

Balla, Bálint
see Vom Agrarland zur Industriegesellschaft. -- Stuttgart : F. Enke, 1974.

Balla, David A., joint author.
see Lewis, Dorothy Otnow. Delinquency and psychopathology. New York, Grune & Stratton, c1976.

Balla, Demeter
see Budapest. [Budapest, Corvina, c1972]

Balla, Demeter
see Budapest in 64 colour photographs. Budapest, Hungary, Kossuth Print House, Distributed by Kulture, Budapest, c1972.

Balla, Demeter, ill.
see Huszár, Tibor. Contemporary Hungarian society. [Budapest]: Corvina Press, 1974.

Balla, Demeter, illus.
see Thousand-year-old Budapest. [Budapest, Kossuth Print. House, c1970]

Balla, Gábor Tamás, comp.
Sugarak 71; az agrárfelsőoktatási intézmények irodalmi antológiája. Gödöllő, KISZ Agrártudományi Egyetemi Bizottsága, 1971.
133 p. illus. 21 cm.
1. Hungarian literature—20th century. I. Title.
PH3136.B27 74–208402

Balla, Gergely.
Nagykörösi krónikája a honfoglalástol 1758-ig. Nagykörös város megbízásából új kiadásban közrebocsátja Dr. Törös László. Nagykörös, 1970.
193 p. illus.
1. Nagy-Körös, Hungary. I. Title.
MiEM NUC74-145657

Balla, Giacomo, 1871-1958.
Balla. [Exposition] du 24 mai au 2 juil. 1972, Musée d'art moderne de la ville de Paris. [Rome] De Luca [1972]
155 p. illus., col. plates. 24 cm.
I. Paris. Musée d'art moderne de la ville de Paris. II. Title.
CaBVaU NUC73-121293

Balla, Giacomo, 1871–1958.
Balla / [a cura di] Enrico Crispolti. — [Roma] : Editalia, [c1975]
18 p., [16] leaves of plates : ill. ; 24 cm. It***
On spine: 5.
Bibliography: p. 16.
1. Balla, Giacomo, 1871–1958. I. Crispolti, Enrico.
ND623.B19C74 759.5 76–523658

Balla, Giacomo, 1871-1958.
Giacomo Balla. [Mostra, 19 maggio-luglio 1971] Galleria d'arte 'Peccolo', Livorno. [Livorno, 1971]
[20] p. (chiefly illus.) group port. 24 cm.
Text by Luigi Lambertini. Also includes an interview with Francesco Cangiullo.
1. Balla, Giacomo, 1871-1958. I. Lambertini, Luigi. II. Galleria d'arte Peccolo.
TxU NUC75-26599

Balla, Giacomo, 1871-1958.
Giacomo Balla (1871-1958) [Mostra] Galleria Nazionale d'Arte Moderna, Roma, Valle Giulia, 23 dic., 1971-27 febbr., 1972. [Roma] De Luca [1971]
197 p. plates., port. 24 cm.
At head of title: Soprintendenza alle gallerie Roma II. Arte Contemporanea.
I. Rome (City). Galleria nazionale d'arte moderna.
CtY NUC73-43819

Balla, Giacomo, 1871-1958.
Giacomo Balla : studi, ricerche, oggetti, Verona, Museo di Castelvecchio, febbraio-marzo 1976 / [schede e notazioni a cura di Luigi Marcucci]. — Verona : Grafiche AZ, [1976]
150 p. : ill. ; 24 cm. It76-May
1. Balla, Giacomo, 1871-1958. I. Marcucci, Luigi. II. Verona. Museo di Castelvecchio.
N6923.B27M37 76-463595
*76 MARC

Balla, Giacomo, 1871–1958.
Giacomo Balla: trenta esempi. [Torino, Galleria d'arte Martano, 1974?]
51 p. illus. 23 cm. (Documenti Martano/due, 47) It***
Exhibition held in Turin from May 6 to May 31, 1974.
CONTENTS: Fagiolo, M. Analisi e sintesi. Un taccuino di Balla: trenta esempi.
1. Balla, Giacomo, 1871–1958. I. Fagiolo dell'Arco, Maurizio, 1939– II. Gallerie d'arte Martano.
N6923.B27F32 74–354606

Balla, Giacomo, 1871–1958.
Omaggio a Giacomo Balla : 26 dicembre 1974–10 gennaio 1975 : Galleria d'arte moderna F. Falsetti, Cortina d'Ampezzo / [testo introdutivo di Enrico Crispolti]. — Prato : Galleria d'arte Falsetti, [1974]
31 p., [19] leaves of plates : ill. ; 25 cm. It 75–Dec
Bibliography: p. 27.
L2000
1. Balla, Giacomo, 1871–1958. I. Galleria d'arte Falsetti, Cortina d'Ampezzo. II. Title.
ND623.B19A56 75–405285

Balla, Giacomo, 1871-1958
see Turin. Galleria d'arte moderna. Giacomo Balla. [Torino, 1963]

Balla, John Coleman, 1936-
The relationship of Laramide stocks to regional structure in central Arizona. [Tucson] 1972.
132 l. illus. (part col., part fold. in pocket), maps (part col., part fold.) 29 cm.
Thesis (Ph.D.)—University of Arizona.
Includes bibliography.
1. Geology—Arizona—Pinal Co. I. Title.
AzU NUC74-132082

Balla, László
see Petőfi az iskolában. Szeged : [s.n.], 1972.

Balla, László, Dr.
Az alföldi homoki szőlőtermelés és forgalmazás főbb közgazdasági problémái. [Készítették; Balla László, Szücs István és Kozma József. Készült a Gazdaságelemző Igazgatóság Ágazati Osztályán] Budapest, Statisztikai és Gazdaságelemző Központ, 1972.
75 p. 28 cm.
"1972, 6."
1. Grapes—Hungary. I. Szücs, István, Dr., joint author. II. Kozma, József, joint author. III. Hungary. Statisztikai és Gazdaságelemző Központ. Ágazati Osztály. IV. Title.
HD9259.G7H82 76–522379

Balla, Laszlo, 1927–
[Selected works. Russian]
Жар в снегу : рассказы / Ласло Балла ; авторизованный перевод с венгерского Е. Терновской. — Москва : Сов. писатель, 1975.
198 p. : ill. ; 17 cm. USSR***
CONTENTS: Peshkom.—Glaza skul'ptury.—Portret.—Vlfublennye.—Feri.—Varshani.—Teatr i kulisy.—Studencheskaia svad'ba.—Horror vacui.—Lili Marlen.—Solo na barabane.—Tabak.—Samosval no. BB9299.—Chertopolokh.—Chto ostaetsia.—Kriuk.—Siniĭ Sneg.—Tridtsat' sekund.—Stuk chasov vselennoĭ.—Stul.—Zhatva.—Luchi.—Zhar v snegu.
0.27rub
I. Title.
Title romanized: Zhar v snegu.
PH3213.B236A57 75–401537

Balla, Mykola Ivanovych
see Podvez'ko, M L (Anhlo-ukraïns'kyĭ slovnyk) 1974.

Balla, Olena Mykhaĭlivan Cherneha-
see
Cherneha-Balla, Olena Mykhaĭlivna.

Balla, Zsófia.
Vízláng : versek / Balla Zsófia. — Bukarest : Kriterion, 1975.
83 p. ; 20 cm. R 76-930
lei 7.75
I. Title.
PH3213.B237V5 76–526703

Balla. Musée d'art moderne de la ville de Paris du 24 mai au 2 juillet 1972. [Rome] De Luca [1972]
155 p. illus., plates (part col.) 24 cm. 22.00F F***
Translation of Giacomo Balla.
"Le plan du catalogue et la sélection des œuvres ont été établis par Giorgio de Marchis avec la collaboration de Livia Velani ... Bernardina Sani ... et de Annamaria del Monte."
Bibliography: p. 35–46.
Balla, Giacomo, 1871–1958.
I. De Marchis, Giorgio. II. Paris. Musée d'art moderne de la ville de Paris.
ND623.B19G514 73–318925

Bałłaban, Jerzy.
Opole; 1945 i dziś. [Wyd. 1.]. Warszawa, Interpress, 1970.
143 p. illus. 16 cm.
At head of title: Jerzy Bałłaban, Zdzisław Jaeschke, Stanisław Racławicki.
"Opole; informator turystyczny" (24 p.) laid in.
CONTENTS: Opole, Opole, to jest piękne miasto.—Od pradziejów do terazniejszości.—1945–1950.—Opole; 1945 i dziś.—Stolica regionu.
zł55.00
1. Opole, Poland. I. Jaeschke, Zdzisław, joint author. II. Racławicki, Stanisław, joint author. III. Title.
DK4800.O624B34 76–505325

Bałłaban, Jerzy.
Rok 1945 [i. e. tysiącdziewięćset czterdziesty piąty] w Opolu we wspomnieniach pierwszych działaczy PPR. Opole, Nakł. własny, 1962.
37, xxiii p. 20 cm. (Wydawnictwa Instytutu Śląskiego w Opolu. Komunikaty. Seria monograficzna, 29)
At head of title: Instytut Śląski w Opolu.
Bibliographical references included in "Przypisy" (p. i–v)
1. Polska Partia Robotnicza—History. I. Title. II. Series: Oppeln. Instytut Śląski. Komunikaty. Seria monograficzna, 29.
DK4600.O66A25 nr. 29 65–43145
[JN6769.A53]

Bałłaban, Jerzy.
Województwo Oploskie; przewodnik. [Autorzy:] Jerzy Bałłaban, Stanislaw Michalak, Korneliusz Pszczyński. Warszawa, Sport i Turystyka [1967]
261 p. maps (1 fold. col. in pocket) 17 cm.
At head of title: Wojewódzki Komitet Kultury Fizycznej i Turystyki w Opolu.
1. Oppeln (Voivodeship)—Description—Guide-books. I. Michalak, Stanisław, joint author. II. Pszczyński, Korneliusz, joint author. III. Title.
IEN NUC73-47489

Ballabio, Camillo Benso.
La malattia di s. [i. e. sant'] Ambrogio e in s. Ambrogio. Milano, A cura dell'Istituto ortopedico G. Pini, 1973.
42 p. 27 cm. It 74–Sept
Bibliography: p. 41–42.
1. Ambrosius, Saint, Bp. of Milan. I. Title.
BR1720.A5B34 74–347236

Ballabio, Camillo Benso
see International Symposium on Rheumatology, San Remo, Italy, 1972. Atti ... Milano : Fondazione Carlo Erba, 1974.

Ballabriga, A
Some aspects of the use of biopsy in paediatrics, by A. Ballabriga and A. Moragas. Abstracts: contribution of biopsy to clinical examination. Dietetic notes: how much vitamin D should infant foods contain? [Lindau-Budensee] Nestlé Scientific Services [c1970]
110 p. illus. 24 cm. (Annales Nestlé, no. 25)
Includes bibliography.
1. Biopsy—Abstracts. 2. Pediatrics—Abstracts. 3. Biopsy—In infancy & childhood—Abstracts. 4. Vitamin D. I. Moragas, A. II. Title. III. Title: Contribution of biopsy to clinical examination. IV. Series.
CaBVaU NUC75-108470

Ballachey, Egerton L 1908-
Country report: psychological factors, Jordan prepared under the direction of Egerton L. Ballachey. [Washington, D.C.] American University, Washington, D.C., Special Operations Research Office [196-?]
2 v. 39 cm.
"Operating under contract with the Department of the Army."
1. Jordan. I. American University, Washington, D.C. Special Operations Research Office.
WU NUC76-62957

Ballachey, Egerton L 1908-
Country report: psychological factors, Saudi Arabia prepared under the direction of Egerton L. Ballachey. [Washington, D.C.] American University, Washington, D.C., Special Operations Research Office [196-?]
2 v. 39 cm.
"Operating under contract with the Department of the Army."
1. Saudi Arabia. I. American University, Washington, D.C. Special Operations Research Office.
WU NUC76-62958

Ballachey, Egerton L 1908-
"Specific" vs. "general" orientation factors in maze running / by E.L. Ballachey and I. Krechevsky. -- [New York : Kraus Reprint, 1976]
[83]-97 p. : diagrs. ; 24 cm. -- (University of California publications in psychology ; v. 6, no. 7)
Reprint of 1932 ed. published by the University of California Press, Berkeley.
Bibliography: p. 97.
1. Animal intelligence. 2. Rats. I. Krechevsky, Isadore, 1909- joint author. II. Title.
NSbSU NUC77-85980

The ballad of Barko Khan... [Little Valley, N.Y., George Straight, 1961]
see under Drew, DeSilver George.

The Ballad of Black Bess. [Lexington, Kentucky, 1958]
[4] p. illus. ([Kentucky culture series])
Typed note at end: "By Bruce F. Denbo, Director, University of Kentucky Press, February 1958."
Microfiche copy (2 cds.)
1. Morgan, John Hunt, 1825-1864. 2. Sculpture, American. 3. Lexington, Ky.—Description. I. Denbo, Bruce F. II. Title.
OOxM NUC75-69052

Ballad of Master Manole
see
Meşterul Manole.

The ballad of Peggy Flynn. Dublin, St. Sepulchre's Press, 1974
see under [Kenelly, Brendan]

Ballad of the Argesh Monastery
see
Meşterul Manole.

The Ballad of the Bethel: the ruse of a New England skipper. A ballad of the seafaring men of old Boston, and young America, written from memory with added verse lines and an historic commentary by William C. H. Dowson. [Boston] Boston Public Library, 1972.
5 l. illus. 30 cm.
Originally written previous to 1915.
1. Bethel (Ship)–Poetry. I. Dowson, William C. H.
MB NUC74-2274

The Ballad opera; a collection of 171 original texts of musical plays printed in photo-facsimile. [Selected and arranged by Walter H. Rubsamen] [New York, Garland Pub., 1974]
v. illus. 22 cm.
1. Ballad operas—To 1800—Librettos. I. Rubsamen, Walter Howard, 1911–1973, comp.
ML48.B18 782.8′1′208 74–3145
MARC

Ballad studies / edited by E. B. Lyle. — Cambridge [Eng.] : D. S. Brewer ; Totowa, N.J. : Rowman and Littlefield for the Folklore Society, 1976.
212 p. ; 23 cm. — (Mistletoe series) GB***
Includes bibliographical references.
ISBN 0-87471-898-8 (Rowman and Littlefield) : $8.50 (U.S.)
1. Ballads, English—History and criticism—Addresses, essays, lectures. 2. Ballads, American—History and criticism—Addresses, essays, lectures. I. Lyle, E. B. II. Folk-lore Society, London. III. Series: Mistletoe books.
PR507.B32 1976 821′.04 77-360676
77 MARC

Ballada o donskom krae 1920-1970. [Sostavitel' Z.I. Prosvirnova. Rostov-na-Donu, Rostovskoe kn. izd-vo, 1970]
196 p. illus. 27 cm.
1. Don Cossacks, Province of the. 2. Rostov on the Don, Russia (Province) I. Prosvirnova, Z.I., comp.
CSt-H NUC74-21961

Ballade d'ech grand bon Diu d'bous
see Debrie, René. Une chanson picarde inédite ... Amiens, Archives départementales de la Somme, 1973.

Ballade vom schönen Tag; Liebesgeschichten polnischer Autoren. Ausgewählt und bearbeitet von Danuta Łukawska und Barbara Olszańska. [1. Aufl. Hamburg] Claassen Verlag [1972]
354 p. 19 cm. (Bibliotheca polonica)
"Originaltitel: Po prostu miłość."
1. Short stories, Polish—Translations into German. 2. Short stories, German—Translations from Polish. I. Łukawska, Danuta, ed. II. Olszanska, Barbara, ed.
MB PPT NUC74-132249

Ballades, fabliaux et traditions du moyen âge. [n.p., n.d.]
clxvi, 48 p.
Microfilm (positive. Literature of folklore, reel 284)
1. Folk-lore—France. 2. Legends—France.
UU NUC73-71301

Balladine, Roman.
The secrets of belly dancing [by] Roman Balladine & Sula. Millbrae, Calif., Celestial Arts Pub. [c1972]
96 p. illus. 22 cm. $2.95
1. Belly dance. I. Sula, joint author. II. Title.
GV1798.B25 793.3 72–91977
MARC

Balladine, Roman. The secrets of belly dancing
see Vergara, Adela. The new art of belly dancing. Completely rev. ed. Millbrae, Calif.: Celestial Arts, 1974.

Balladine, Roman, joint author
see Vergara, Adela. The new art of belly dancing. Completely rev. ed. Millbrae, Calif.: Celestial Arts, 1974.

Balladore-Pallieri, Giorgio, 1905–
Diritto costituzionale / G. Balladore Pallieri. — 8. ed. — Milano : Giuffrè, 1965.
xv, 473 p. ; 22 cm. — (Manuali Giuffrè)
Bibliography: p. [xiii]–xv.
1. Italy—Constitutional law. I. Title.
75–566021

Balladore-Pallieri, Giorgio, 1905–
Diritto costituzionale. 10 ed. Milano, A. Giuffrè, 1972.
xiii, 491 p. 22 cm. (Manuali Giuffrè) L5200 It 72–July
At head of title: G. Balladore-Pallieri.
Bibliography: p. [xv].
1. Italy—Constitutional law. I. Title.
73–321837

Balladore-Pallieri, Giorgio, 1905–
Il diritto internazionale ecclesiastico. Padova, CEDAM, 1940.
vii, 231 p. 25 cm. (Trattato di diritto internazionale, v. 12)
Includes bibliographical references.
1. Ecclesiastical law. 2. Church and state. 3. Religious liberty. 4. Papacy. I. Title. II. Series.
75–548080

Balladore-Pallieri, Giorgio, 1905–
Diritto internazionale privato italiano / Giorgio Balladore Pallieri. — Milano : A. Giuffrè, 1974.
xii, 372 p. ; 24 cm. — (Trattato di diritto civile e commerciale, 45) It 75–Jan
Bibliography: p. [xi]–xii.
L6400
1. Conflict of laws—Italy. I. Title.
74–356098

Balladore-Pallieri, Giorgio, 1905–
Dottrina dello Stato / Giorgio Balladore Pallieri. — 2. ed. — Padova : CEDAM, 1964.
viii, 318 p. ; 25 cm.
Bibliography: p. [xi]
1. State, The. 2. Sovereignty. 3. Law—Philosophy. I. Title.
76–501530

Ballads. [Phonodisc. New York] Holt, Rinehart and Winston [1969] 4809406.
2 s. 12 in. 33⅓ rpm.
At head of title: The Oregon curriculum: Literature I.
"This record accompanies Literature I ... Albert R. Kitzhaber, General Editor."
Performed by Barre Toelken and others.
Program notes on slipcase.
CONTENTS: The tenderfoot.—Get up and bar the door.—Babylon.—The Wife of Usher's well.—Lord Randall.—The Devil and the farmer's wife.—Edward, Edward.—Barbara Allen's cruelty.—How ballads change; an illustrated lecture by Barre Toelken.
1. Ballads, American. 2. Ballads, English. I. Kitzhaber, Albert Raymond, 1915– comp. Literature I. II. Toelken, Barre. How ballads change. Phonodisc. 1969. III. Title: The Oregon curriculum.
[M1629] 74–760121

Ballads: Scottish and English. With illus. by J. Lawson. London, W. P. Nimmo, 1878.
viii, 472 p. illus. 19 cm.
Cover title: The book of ballads.
1. Scottish ballads and songs. I. Title: The book of ballads.
PR1181.B4 1878 821′.04 73–172606
MARC

Ballaer, R. van, joint author
see Neesen, V Vraag en aanbod van geschoolde arbeidskrachten in Limburg. Hasselt, Limburgse Economische Raad, 1971.

Ballagas, Emilio, 1908-1954.
Emilio Ballagas. Prólogo de Angel Augier. Selección y notas de Rosario Antuña. [2. ed. Habana, U.N.E.A.C., 1972]
294 p. (Colección Orbita)
Originally published under title: Orbita de Emilio Ballagas.
I. Antuña, Rosario, ed.
MH NUC74-132028

Ballagas, Emilio, 1908-1954.
Emilio Ballagas. [Introducción y selección de textos: Emilio de Armas. La Habana] Dirección Nacional de Educación General, MINED [1973]
75 p. 27 cm. (El autor y su obra)
Includes bibliography.
I. Armas, Emilio de, ed.
PPiU NUC76-35259

Ballagas, Emilio, 1908-1954.
Lira negra: selecciones Afroamericanas y españolas [by Emilio Ballagas] Recopilación, prólogo y notas biocríticas de Jose Sanz y Diaz. 2. ed. Madrid, Aguilar, c1962.
423 p. (Coleccion Crisol, no. 21)
I. Title.
KMK NUC75-61622

Ballagh, James Curtis.
White servitude in the Colony of Virginia; a study of the system of indentured labor in the American colonies. Baltimore, Johns Hopkins Press, 1895. [New York, Johnson Reprint Corp., 1973]
99 p. 22 cm.
Pages also numbered 266–357.
Original ed. issued as no. 6–7 of South Carolina, Maryland, and Virginia, which forms the 13th series of Johns Hopkins University studies in historical and political science.
Bibliography: p. [96]–99.
1. Indentured servants. 2. Slavery in the United States—Virginia. I. Title: II. Series: Johns Hopkins University. Studies in historical and political science, 13th ser., 6–7. III. Series: South Carolina, Maryland, and Virginia, no. 6–7.
JA37.S58 no. 6–7 320.9′73′02 s 72–14346
[HD4875.U5] [301.44′44′09755] MARC
ISBN 0–384–03146–3

Ballagi, Aladár.
Buda és Pest a világirodalomban. [Budapest] Budapest Székesfőváros, 1925–
v. illus. 26 cm.
Introductory matter in English and Hungarian; text in English, French, German, Italian, Latin, and Spanish; commentary in Hungarian.
Bibliography: v. 1, p. [453]–480.
CONTENTS: 1. 1473–1711.—
1. Buda—Bibliography. 2. Pest—Bibliography. I. Title.
Z2147.B9B34 73–219432

Ballaguer, Josemaría Escrivá de
see
Escrivá, José María.

Ballai, János.
Épületek vízellátása, csatornázása és gázellátása [írta] Ballai János [és] Marton Pál. 5. kiad. Budapest, Műszaki Könyvkiadó, 1971 [c1969]
775 p. illus. 24 cm.
Bibliography: p. 767–[768]
1. Water-supply engineering. 1971. 2. Gas engineering. I. Marton, Pál, joint author.
NN NUC76-2362

Ballaine, Jerrold F.
see Anderson, Charles E Appraisal of property located at 1306-1318 Capitol Way, Olympia, Washington... [Olympia, 1969]

Ballaine, Wesley Charles, 1906–
Development and economic aspects of the laws regulating investments of mutual savings banks / by Wesley Charles Ballaine. 1940.
viii, 273 leaves ; 32 cm.
Typescript (carbon copy).
Thesis—University of Chicago.
On spine: Mutual savings bank investment laws.
Bibliography: leaves 268–273.
1. Savings-banks—United States. 2. Investments—Law and legislation—United States. I. Title. II. Title: Mutual savings bank investment laws.
KF1004.B3 346′.73′082 75–306025
MARC

Ballaira, Guglielmo, ed.
see Demosthenes. L'orazione sulla corona. Torino, Loescher, 1971.

Ballaira, Guglielmo, ed.
see Octavia (Praetexta) Ottavia. Torino : G. Giappichelli, [1974]

Ballaira, Gugielmo, ed.
see Tiberius (rhetor) Tiberii de figuris Demosthenicis. [Roma, Ed. dell'ateneo, c1968]

Ballal, N Narayana, 1937–
(Kempudīpa)
ಕೆಂಪುದೀಪ. [ಲೇಖಕ] ಎನ್. ನಾರಾಯಣ ಬಲ್ಲಾಳ. ಬೆಂಗಳೂರು, ಪುರೋಗಾಮಿ ಸಾಹಿತ್ಯ ಸಂಘ [1967]
138 p. 19 cm. Rs2.00
In Kannada.
A novel.

I. Title.

PL4659.B22K4 SA 68–9553
PL 480: I-Kan-1096

Ballal, Vyasaraya, 1923–
(Anurakte)
ಅನುರಕ್ತೆ : ಕಾದಂಬರಿ / ವ್ಯಾಸರಾಯ ಬಲ್ಲಾಳ. — ಮೈಸೂರು : ಗೀತಾ ಬುಕ್ ಹೌಸ್, 1953, 1974 printing.
238 p. ; 19 cm.
In Kannada.
Rs6.75

I. Title.
PL4659.B223A83 1974 75–902515

Ballal, Vyasaraya, 1923–
(Mañjari)
ಮಂಜರಿ : ಕಥಾ ಸಂಗ್ರಹ / ವ್ಯಾಸರಾಯ ಬಲ್ಲಾಳ. — ಬೆಂಗಳೂರು : ಕರ್ನಾಟಕ ಸಹಕಾರೀ ಪ್ರಕಾಶನ ಮಂದಿರ, 1975.
v, 441 p. ; 22 cm.
In Kannada.
Rs18.00

I. Title.
PL4659.B223M3 75–908734

Ballal, Vyasaraya, 1923–
ಉತ್ತರಾಯಣ; ಕಾದಂಬರಿ. ಲೇಖಕರು ವ್ಯಾಸರಾಯ ಬಲ್ಲಾಳ. ಬೆಂಗಳೂರು, ಶಾರದಾ ಪ್ರಕಟನಾಲಯ [1969]
vi, 447 p. 19 cm. (ಕನ್ನಡ ಸಾಹಿತ್ಯದ ಪ್ರಕಟನೆ 18) Rs6.50
In Kannada.

I. Title.
Title romanized: Uttarāyaṇa.
PL4659.B223U8 72–919908

Ballāla, of Benares, fl. 1600.
भोज-कालिदास; नेपाली श्लोक र भा.टी. सहित. अनुवादक रामप्रसाद सत्याल. वाराणसी, कृष्ण कुमारी देवी; [पाइने ठेगाना: माधवप्रसाद शर्मा] सं. 2018 [1962]
3, 241 p. 18 cm. Rs2.25
In Sanskrit; commentary in Nepali.

1. Bhojaraja, King of Dhara—Poetry. 2. Kālidāsa—Poetry. I. Satyāla, Rāmaprasāda, ed. II. Title.
Title romanized: Bhoja-Kālidāsa.
PK3791.B186B4 1962b 71–913392

Ballāla, of Benares, fl. 1600.
[Bhojaprabandhaḥ]
भोजप्रबन्धः. श्रीबल्लालविरचितः. [व्याख्याकार] पारसनाथ द्विवेदी. [1. संस्करण] आगरा, विनोद पुस्तक मन्दिर [1972]
6, 272 p. 19 cm. Rs3.50
Hindi and Sanskrit; pref., notes, and glosses in Hindi.

I. Dwivedi, Paras Nath, 1929– ed. II. Title.
PK3791.B186B4 1972 78–928621

Ballam, Harry.
The story of a thread of cotton. Written by Harry Ballam; drawn by Stanley Herbert. [Harmondsworth, Penguin Books, n. d.]
23 p. illus. (part col.) 18 x 23 cm. ([Puffin picture books])
Cover title.
1. Thread—Juvenile literature. I. Herbert, Stanley. II. Title.
MB NUC76-77181

Ballamy, Gailord.
Complete guide to the Split-Pro defense. West Nyack, N.Y., Parker [1971]
225 p. illus.
1. Football. I. Title.
ViBlbV NUC73-34766

Ballanca, Faik.
Pritësit e rrufeve : tregime / Faik Ballanca. — Tiranë : Naim Frashëri, 1975.
194 p. ; 17 cm.
CONTENTS: Pritësit e rrufeve.—Qitësi me qeleshe të bardhë.—Im ungj Saliu.—Pse s'qëllon kjo pushka ime?—Një çast i vogël harrese.—Dy hapa larg vdekjes.—Një pëllëmbë tokë.—Gjah me thëllëzë.—Ai burrë që desh m'u bë dhëndër.—Dehje.—Në Rrëfim.—Kënga e fundit e Marko Boçarit.
L3.00
I. Title.
PG9621.B32P7 76–518807

Ballance, Bill.
The Bill Ballance hip handbook of nifty moves ... and how to cope in situations of utter copelessness. Los Angeles, Nash Pub. [1973]
xiii, 250 p. illus. 23 cm. $6.95
I. Title. II. Title: Hip handbook of nifty moves ... and how to cope in situations of utter copelessness.
PN6162.B28 301.41'02'07 73–83523
ISBN 0–8402–1320–4 MARC

Ballance, Frank C
Zambia and the East African community, by Frank C. Ballance. [Syracuse, N. Y.] Program of Eastern African Studies, Syracuse University, 1971.
139, 4 l. 28 cm. (Eastern African studies, 1)
Bibliography: leaves 135–139.
1. East African Community—Zambia. I. Title. II. Series.
HC517.E2B34 380.1'09689'4 74–151837
MARC

Ballance, Frank C.
see United States. Congress. Senate. Committee on Foreign Relations. Subcommittee on Foreign Assistance. The political and economic crisis in southern Africa ... Washington, U.S. Govt. Print. Off., 1976.

Ballance, George.
From tourism to reality : a collection of poems based on the exhibition "Poetry Illustrated" / [by] George Ballance. — Symington : G. B. Books, 1976.
40 p. : ill. ; 21 cm. GB76-27155
ISBN 0-905491-00-9 : £0.75
I. Title. II. Title: Poetry illustrated.
PR6052.A45F7 821'.9'14 76-383202
76 MARC

Ballance, John B.
see The Hot deformation of austenite. [New York] Metallurgical Society, AIME, c1977.

Ballance, Milford R
The hands of time [by] Milford R. Ballance. [1st ed.] New York, Vantage Press [1972]
208 p. illus. 21 cm. $6.95
1. Albemarle region, N. C. I. Title.
F262.A33B34 917.56'1 72–171260
ISBN 0–533–00183–8 MARC

Ballance, Robert Howard, 1941-
Recent development in Mexican agriculture; a study of economic considerations and environmental constraints. [Knoxville, Tenn.] 1969.
xi, 171 l.
Thesis–University of Tennessee.
Vita.
Bibliography: leaves 161-164.
Microfilm. Ann Arbor, Mich., University Microfilms. 1 reel. 35 mm.
TxU NUC74-145656

Ballance, Wilbur C
Ground-water levels in Wyoming, 1974 / Wilbur C. Ballance and Pamela B. Freudenthal. -- Cheyenne, Wyoming : U.S. Geological Survey, Water Resources Division, 1975.
iii, 186 p. : ill., maps ; 28 cm.
Open-file report.
Prepared by the United States Geological Survey in cooperation with the Wyoming State Engineer and the city of Cheyenne.
Bibliography: p. 6.
1. Water, Underground--Wyoming. 2. Wyoming--Water-supply. I. United States. Geological Survey. Water Resources Division. II. Title.
DI-GS NUC77-86505

Ballance, Wilbur C
Radiochemical monitoring of water after the Cannikin event, Amchitka Island, Alaska, August 1973. By Wilbur C. Ballance. Lakewood, Colo., United States Geological Survey, 1974.
1 card. maps. 11 x 15 cm.
"Amchitka-42."
"USGS-474-205."
Microfiche (Negative) Springfield, Va., National Technical Information Service, 1974.
1. Cannikin Project. 2. Radioactive pollution of water. I. United States. Geological Survey. II. Title.
DI NUC76-21307

Ballance, Wilbur C.
see Koopman, Francis Christian, 1921- Hydrologic test in hole GB-1. [Washington] 1968.

Ballanche, Pierre Simon, 1776-1847.
Du sentiment considéré dans ses rapports avec la littérature et les arts. Lyon, Ballanche et Barret, 1801 [1972]
344 p.
Xerox copyflo reproduction. **Ann Arbor,** University Microfilms.
1. Art and literature. I. Title.
MiEM NUC73-121092

Balland, André
see Les Architectures (1962-1967). Rome, École française de Rome; en depot aux E. de Boccard, Paris, 1971.

Ballande, Henri, 1901–
De l'Amirauté à Bikini; souvenirs des jours sans joie. Paris, Presses de la Cité [1972]
314 p. plates. 21 cm. 26.90F F***
Autobiographical.
1. Ballande, Henri, 1901– I. Title.
DC373.B25A33 940.54'23'0924 73–342238
[B] MARC

Ballande, Henri, 1901-
Histoires de famille. [Val-de-Marne, Impr. Foucault, 1970]
189 p. illus.
1. Ballande family.
MH NUC73-121186

Ballande, Henri, 1901-
Midship en Chine / Henri Ballande. — Paris : Éditions France-Empire, c1977.
285 p., [6] leaves of plates : ill. ; 19 cm. F***
32.00F
1. China—Description and travel—1901-1948. 2. Ballande, Henri, 1901- I. Title.
DS710.B33 77-468863
77 MARC

Ballanti, Graziella, 1927-
Il comportamento insegnante / Graziella Ballanti. — Roma : A. Armando, 1975, 1976 printing.
309 p. : ill. ; 20 cm. — (Educazione comparata e pedagogie ; 15) It77-Jan
Includes bibliographical references.
L5000
1. Comparative education. I. Title.
LA132.B25 77-466449
•77 MARC

Ballanti, Graziella, 1927–
Correnti e problemi della psicologia scientifica. Teramo, EIT, 1973.
2 v. 21 cm. (Collana di psicologia, 2) L5000 It 73–Sept
Bibliography: v. 2, p. [113]–132.
1. Psychology, Experimental. I. Title.
BF184.B36 74–307035

Ballantine, Betty.
see Gallardo Villaseñor, Gervasio, 1934- The fantastic world of Gervasio Gallardo. 1st U.S. ed. Bearsville, N.Y., Peacock Press, c1976.

Ballantine, Christopher John.
Music and society : the forgotten relationship / by C. J. Ballantine. — Pietermaritzburg : University of Natal Press, 1974.
23 p. ; 22 cm. SA
Inaugural lecture delivered in the University of Natal, Durban on 9th Oct., 1974.
Includes bibliographical references.
ISBN 0-86980-049-3 : R0.75
1. Music and society.
ML3795.B27 780'.07 77-354481
77 MARC

Ballantine, David, joint author.
see Haney, Robert. Woodstock handmade houses. New York, Ballatine Books, 1974.

Ballantine, David Stephen, 1922-
see United States. Brookhaven National Laboratory, Upton, N.Y. Radiation Division. Bibliography of technical publications and reports ... 1951-1962, inclusive. New York, 1963.

Ballantine, Derek.
The horse in Australia / [by] Derek Ballantine. — Melbourne : Macmillan, 1976.
128 p., [4] leaves of plates : ill. ; 28 cm. Aus
ISBN 0-333-21066-2
1. Horses—Australia. 2. Horsemanship—Australia. I. Title.
SF284.A78B34 636.1'00994 77-364906
77 MARC

Ballantine, Derek.
see The Australasian book of thoroughbred racing. Abbotsford, Vic., Stockwell Press, 1974.

Ballantine, Harden Parke, 1938-
A study of the public's attitudes concerning student rights in Dayton, Ohio. [Bloomington, Ind.] 1973.
133 p.
Thesis (Ed.D.)—Indiana University.
Vita.
InU NUC74-132083

Ballantine, Henry Winthrop, 1880–1951.
Ballantine's Problems in law for law school and bar examination review : a collection of concrete problems with solutions, covering principal legal topics / William E. Burby, editor and twenty-eight other contributors. — 5th ed. — St. Paul : West Pub. Co., 1975.
xxvii, 767 p. ; 27 cm. — (American casebook series)
Includes index.
1. Law—United States—Examinations, questions, etc. I. Burby, William Edward, 1893- ed. II. Title: Problems in law. III. Series.
KF388.B3 1975 340'.076 74-20437
MARC

Ballantine, Hepburn.
A crusade into Catalonia. 1894. — Liverpool : H. Young, 1913.
xii, 132 p., [1] leaf of plates : port. ; 23 cm.
1. Catalonia—Description and travel. I. Title.
DP302.C61B32 77-363942
MARC

Ballantine, John W
The human side of economics and its significance for enterprise management, by John W. Ballantine. [Madison, Wis., Mimir Publishers Inc., 1973]
170 p.
"Notes on sources": p. 163-166.
1. Economics. 2. Management—Case studies. I. Title.
MH-BA NSyU NUC75-18515

Ballantine, Joseph William, 1888–
American Far Eastern policy, by Joseph Ballantine. [Jamaica, N. Y., Center of Asian Studies, St. John's University, 1968?]
12 l. 29 cm. (St. John's papers in Asian studies, no. 4)
"A lecture given on May 13, 1968, under the auspices of the Department of History and the Center of Asian Studies, St. John's University, New York."
1. United States—Foreign relations—East (Far East) 2. East (Far East)—Foreign relations—United States. I. Title. II. Series.
DS518.B32 327.73'05 73-171718
MARC

Ballantine, Joseph William, 1888-
Reminiscences. [Glen Rock, N.J., Microfilming Corporation of America, 1972]
263 l. on 3 sheets. (N.Y.T.O.H.P. [i.e. New York times oral history program [1] Columbia University. Oral History Research Office. [Oral history] collection, 1)
Title from first frame.
MH NUC73-121321

Ballantine, Joseph William, 1888-
Reminiscences. [New York, New York Times, 1972]
3 sheets. 11 x 15 cm. (New York times oral history program)
Microfiche.
Compiled from interviews sponsored by the Oral History Research Office, Columbia University.
1. Diplomats, American—Correspondence, reminiscences, etc. I. Columbia University. Oral History Research Office. II. Series.
TxU NUC76-35260

Ballantine, Richard.
Richard's bicycle book. Illustrated by John Batchelor. New York, Ballantine Books [1972]
248 p. illus. 21 cm. $1.95
1. Bicycles and tricycles. I. Title.
TL410.B24 629.22'72 72-172763
ISBN 0-345-02813-9 MARC

Ballantine, Richard, joint author
see Griffiths, Joel. Silent slaughter. Chicago, Regnery [1972]

Ballantyne, Bryan, ed.
see Forensic toxicology... Bristol : J. Wright, 1974.

Ballantyne, David John, 1931- joint author
see Binder, Wolfgang D Pollen viability testing... [Victoria? B.C.] Dept. of the Environment, 1974.

Ballantyne, David Watt, 1924-
Sydney bridge upside down [by] David Ballantyne. London, Hale; [Christchurch] Whitcombe & Tombs [1968]
223 p. 21 cm.
Novel.
I. Title.
CLU NUC76-35271

Ballantyne, Dorothy Dunning.
George Earle and family of Hobart, Indiana. [Merriville, Ind., Lake County Public Library, n.d.]
9 p. port.
1. Earle family. 2. Earle, George, 1807-1876. I. Title.
WHi NUC75-26623

Ballantyne, George H.
see Society of Writers to H. M. Signet, Edinburgh. Library. Checklist of periodical publications in the Signet Library, Edinburgh. [Edinburgh] [The Library] 1975.

Ballantyne, James Robert, 1813-1864
see Kapila. A lecture on the Sa'nkhya philosophy ... Mirzapore: Orphan School Press, 1850.

Ballantyne, James Robert, 1813-1864, ed.
see Patañjali. Yoga-sutra of Patanjali. [2d ed.] Delhi, Indological Book House, 1971.

Ballantyne, James Robert, 1813-1864, tr.
see Patañjali. [Yogasútra. English and Sanskrit] Yoga sutras of Patanjali... [2d ed.] Calcutta, Susil Gupta, [1952]

Ballantyne, John Chalmers, ed.
see Scott-Brown, Walter Graham. Diseases of the ear, nose and throat. 3d ed. London, Butterworths [1971]

Ballantyne, Ken E
Reflections; a selection of poems, by Ken. E. Ballantyne. Kingstown, St. Vincent, Printed at the Graphic Printery, c1969.
16 p. 20 cm.
I. Title.
NN NUC76-35264

Ballantyne, Ned.
Your horoscope and your dreams; 25,000 interpretations of the predictions of the sun, moon, and stars and of the messages received in sleep, by Ned Ballantyne and Stella Coeli. [Rev. ed.]. New York, Franconia Pub. Co. [1973]
768 p. illus. 22 cm. $5.95
1. Astrology. 2. Dreams. I. Coeli, Stella, joint author. II. Title.
BF1708.1.B34 1973 135.3 73-173486
MARC

Ballantyne, Paul, 1909-
see Gurney, Albert Ramsdell, 1930-
The old one two. [Sound recording] [St. Paul] Minnesota Public Radio, p1976.

Ballantyne, Robert Michael, 1825-1894.
Chasing the sun; or, Rambles in Norway [by] R. M. Ballantyne. New York, Mershon Company [n.d.]
182 p.
I. Title.
MoU NUC77-84290

Ballantyne, Robert Michael, 1825-1894.
The dog Crusoe. [n.p., n.d.]
381 p. 19 cm.
Title page and p. 13-16 missing; caption title.
I. Title.
MB NUC76-21414

Ballantyne, Robert Michael, 1825-1894.
The dog Crusoe and his master; a story of adventure in the American prairies, by R. M. Ballantyne. Dublin, Browne and Nolan [n.d.]
207 p. illus. 19 cm. (The Sterling Stories)
I. Title.
MB NUC73-121318

Ballantyne, Robert Michael, 1825-1894.
The garret and the garden, or, Low life high up, and Jeff Benson, or, The young coastguardsman, by R. M. Ballantyne. New York, T. Whittaker [n.d.]
260 p. plates. 19 cm.
I. Title.
MB NUC75-16658

Ballantyne, Robert Michael, 1825-1894.
Gascoyne, the sandal-wood trader. [n.p., n.d.]
356 p. illus. 17 cm.
Title page missing; caption title.
I. Title.
MB NUC76-21413

Ballantyne, Robert Michael, 1825-1894.
Hudson's Bay; or, Every-day life in the wilds of North America, during six years' residence in the territories of the honourable Hudson's Bay Company... Edinburgh, For private circulation, and copies to be had of Blackwood & Sons, 1848.
x, 328 p. illus., 4 pl. (incl. front.) 20 cm.
Micro-opaque. Louisville, Ky., Lost Cause Press, 1961. 5 cards. 7.5 x 12.5 cm. (Plains and Rockies, 144a)
NIC NUC74-178484

Ballantyne, Robert Michael, 1825-1894.
Martin Rattler; or, A boy's adventures in the forests of Brazil. London, Blackie [19--]
222 p. col. illus. 19 cm. (Blackie's crown library)
I. Title. II. Series.
CaBVaU NUC75-17674

Ballantyne, Robert Michael, 1825-1894.
The Red Eric: or, The whaler's last cruise. R. M. Ballantyne. London, Ward, Lock, 19--?
319 p. 20 cm.
I. Title.
AkU NUC76-21412

Ballantyne, Sheila.
Norma Jean, the termite queen / Sheila Ballantyne. — 1st ed. — Garden City, N.Y. : Doubleday, 1975.
278 p. ; 22 cm.
ISBN 0-385-03264-1 : $7.95
I. Title.
PZ4.B1875 No 813'.5'4 74-27448
[PS3552.A464] 75 MARC

Ballantyne, Verne, 1904-
How and where to find gold : secrets of the '49ers / Verne Ballantyne. — New York : Arco Pub. Co., c1976.
124 p. : ill. ; 24 cm.
Bibliography: p. 117-122.
Includes index.
ISBN 0-668-03859-4 lib. bdg. : $8.95
1. Prospecting. 2. Gold. I. Title.
TN271.G6B34 622'.18'41 75-18878
77 MARC

The Ballantyne-Lockhart controversy, 1838-1839. New York, Garland Pub. Inc., 1974.
88, 122, 125, 97 p. 22 cm. (The English book trade, 1660-1853)
Reprint of Refutation of the mistatements and calumnies contained in Mr Lockhart's Life of Sir Walter Scott, bart., respecting the Messrs Ballantyne, by the trustees and son of the late Mr James Ballantyne, first published in 1838 by Longman, Orme, Brown, Green, and Longmans, London; of The Ballantyne-humbug handled, in a letter to Sir Adam Fergusson, by J. G. Lockhart, first published in 1839 by R. Cadell, Edinburgh; and of Reply to Mr Lockhart's pamphlet, entitled, "The Ballantyne-humbug handled," by the authors of a Refutation of the mistatements and calumnies contained in Mr Lockhart's Life of Sir Walter Scott, bart., respecting the Messrs Ballantyne, first published in 1839 by Longman, Orme, Brown, Green, and Longmans, London.
1. Scott, Walter, Sir, bart., 1771-1832—Friends and associates. 2. Ballantyne, James, 1772-1833. 3. Ballantyne, John, 1774-1821. 4. Lockhart, John Gibson, 1794-1854. Life of Sir Walter Scott. 5. Lockhart, John Gibson, 1794-1854. The Ballantyne-humbug handled. I. Refutation of the mistatements and calumnies contained in Mr Lockhart's Life of Sir Walter Scott, bart., respecting the Messrs. Ballantyne. 1974. II. Lockhart, John Gibson, 1794-1854. The Ballantyne-humbug handled. 1974. III. Reply to Mr. Lockhart's pamphlet, entitled, "The Ballantyne-humbug handled." 1974. IV. Series.
PR5338.B35 1974 828'.7'09 74-13211
ISBN 0-8240-0986-X 74 MARC

Ballarat, Australia. Fine Art Public Gallery
see Fine Art Public Gallery, Ballarat, Australia.

Ballarat Historical Society.
Roll book, Ballarat pioneers. — [Ballarat, Australia] : Ballarat Historical Society, [1974]
[73] leaves ; 21 x 30 cm. Aus***
Cover title.
1. Ballarat, Australia—Genealogy. 2. Registers of births, etc.—Ballarat, Australia. I. Title.
CS2008.B34B34 1974 929'.3945 76-372192
76 MARC

Ballard, Adolphus, 1867-1915.
The Domesday inquest, by Adolphus Ballard ... With twenty-seven illustrations. London, Methuen & Co. [1906]
xvi, 283, [1] p. front. (facsim.) illus., 18 pl., 2 maps, plan. 23 cm. (The antiquary's books ...)
Ultra microfiche. Dayton, Ohio, National Cash Register, 1970. 1st title of 5. 10.5 x 14.8 cm. (PCMI library collection, 115-1)
1. Domesday book. 2. Agriculture—England—Hist. 3. Land tenure—Gt. Brit.—Hist.
KEmT NUC74-160597

Ballard, Adolphus, 1867-1915, joint author
see Levett, Ada Elizabeth. The black death. New York, Octagon Books, 1974.

Ballard, Alan.
PL/C: the Cornell compiler for PL/1/ adapted by Alan Ballard from Cornell University documentation. Rev. Vancouver, B.C.: Computing Centre, University of British Columbia, 1975.
ii, 79 p. 28 cm.
At head of title: UBC PLC.
"Subject code 03.2."
1. PL/1 (Computer program language) I. Cornell University.
CaBVaU NUC77-84266

Ballard, Allen B
The education of Black folk; the Afro-American struggle for knowledge in white America [by] Allen B. Ballard. [1st ed.] New York, Harper & Row [1973]
vi, 173 p. 22 cm. $6.95
"Portions of this work appeared in Change."
Includes bibliographical references.
1. Negroes—Education—History. I. Title.
LC2741.B34 1973 378.73 73-156504
ISBN 0-06-010222-5 MARC

Ballard, Bettina.
In my fashion. New York, D. McKay [1960]
312 p. 21 cm.
Xeroxed copy. Ann Arbor, University Microfilms, 1971.
1. Fashion. 2. Vogue. I. Title.
GU NUC73-59286

Ballard, Bill, 1928-
The illustrated guide to platform tennis / by Bill Ballard and Jim Hevener. — 1st ed. — New York : Mason/Charter, 1977.
115 p. : ill. ; 28 cm.
ISBN 0-88405-616-3 : $12.95. ISBN 0-88405-617-1 pbk. : $7.95
1. Paddle tennis. I. Hevener, Jim, 1927- joint author. II. Title.
GV1006.B3 796.34'6 77-24688
77 MARC

Ballard, Bobby Joe, 1930-
A proposed program budgeting model and its application for an American-sponsored overseas school / by Bobby J. Ballard. -- [East Lansing] : Ballard, 1975.
[3], vii, 146 leaves : ill. ; 29 cm.
Thesis (Ph.D.)--Michigan State University.
Bibliography: leaves 139-146.
1. Schools, American. 2. Schools, American--Athens. I. Title.
MiEM NUC77-84519

Ballard, Buena, S.
see Gunter, Gordon, 1909- Salinity problems of organisms... Vicksburg, Miss. U.S. Army Engineer Waterways Experiment Station, 1973.

Ballard, Charles Rollin, 1828?-1906.
The book I've read before, by Charles R. Ballard. New York, Limited Editions Club, 1972.
[8] p. illus. 16 cm.
"From the Literary world, Boston, 1890."
I. Limited Editions Club, inc., New York. II. Title.
LU NUC73-120460

Ballard, Charles S
Modernized denture technic. Seattle [n.d.]
16 p. illus.
Cover title.
1. Prosthodontics. 2. Complete dentures. I. Title.
WaU NUC76-54082

Ballard, D. E., joint author.
see Ledbetter, William Burl. Evaluation of full-scale experimental concrete highway finishes. College Station, Texas Transportation Institute, Texas A&M University, 1974.

Ballard, D Lee.
More on the deep and surface grammar of interclausal relations, by D. Lee Ballard, Robert J. Conrad [and] Robert E. Longacre. Santa Ana, Calif., Summer Institute of Linguistics [c1971]
v, 61 p. 23 cm. (Language data. Asian Pacific series, no. 1)
Bibliography: p. [58]-59.
1. Grammar, Comparative and general—Syntax. 2. Grammar, Comparative and general—Sentences. 3. Generative grammar. I. Conrad, Robert J., joint author. II. Longacre, Robert E., joint author. III. Title. IV. Series.
P295.B3 415 75-310899
75 MARC

Ballard, Dana Harry.
Hierarchic recognition of tumors in chest radiographs with computer / Dana H. Ballard. — Basel ; Stuttgart : Birkhäuser, 1976.
xv, 192 p. : ill. ; 23 cm. — (ISR, Interdisciplinary systems research ; 15) Sw76-4145
Originally presented as the author's thesis, University of California, Irvine, 1974.
Includes bibliographical references and indexes.
ISBN 3-7643-0800-1 : 28.00F
1. Chest—Tumors—Radiography—Data processing. 2. Optical data processing. 3. Medical screening. I. Title. II. Series.
RC280.C5B34 1976 616.9'92'712 76-469285
*76 MARC

Ballard, David Pitt.
Ethnicity and political behavior. [n.p.] 1972.
1 v.
Honors thesis—Harvard.
1. Political participation—United States. 2. Minorities—United States.
MH NUC76-35263

Ballard, Dennis D., joint author.
see Miller, Martin G. Youth services systems of Iowa ... Ames, Dept of Sociology and Anthropology, Iowa State University, 1973.

Ballard, Dorothy.
Horseback honeymoon : the vanishing Old West of 1907 through the eyes of two young artists in love / Dorothy Ballard ; with drawings and photos. by Ella and Quincy Scott. — New York : Two Continents Pub. Group, c1975.
ix, 246 p. : ill. ; 22 cm.
Includes index.
ISBN 0-8467-0105-7 : $8.95
1. Northwestern States—Description and travel. 2. Overland journeys to the Pacific. 3. Scott, Ella. 4. Scott, Quincy, 1882- I. Title.
F597.B35 917.7'04'30924 75-15042
75 MARC

Ballard, Edward G comp.
Martin Heidegger: in Europe and America. Ed. by Edward G. Ballard and Charles E. Scott. The Hague, Martinus Nijhoff, 1973.
210 p. 1 p. of photos. 24 cm. fl 32.50 Ne 74-12
"Most of the articles ... first appeared in The Southern journal of philosophy, v. 8, no. 4, 1970."
Includes bibliographical references.
1. Heidegger, Martin, 1889- —Influence. I. Scott, Charles E., joint comp. II. The Southern journal of philosophy. III. Title.
B3279.H49B26 193 74-174268
ISBN 90-247-1534-2 MARC

Ballard, Ellis Ames, 1861-1938.
Equity in Pennsylvania. Philadelphia, Rees Welsh, 1895-
v. 24 cm.
On spine: Pennsylvania equity.
1. Equity — Pennsylvania — Digests. 2. Equity pleading and procedure—Pennsylvania—Digests. I. Title. II. Title: Pennsylvania equity.
KFP85.B34 347'.748'072 74-160652
MARC

Ballard, Ernesta Drinker.
Growing plants indoors; a garden in your house. Photos. by Edmund B. Gilchrist & others. New York, Barnes & Noble [c1973]
258 p. illus.
First published in 1958.
1. House-plants. I. Title.
RP NUC75-17240

Ballard, Ernesta Drinker.
see The Philadelphia area green pages ... Philadelphia, Pennsylvania Horticultural Society, [1975]

Ballard, Evelyn.
Council/board proceedings, by Evelyn Ballard and Georgia Cobb. [Mississippi State, Miss.] Cooperative Extension Service, Mississippi State University [n.d.]
1 v. (unpaged) (Mississippi. Cooperative Extension Service, Mississippi State. Public administration series)
1. Municipal government--Mississippi--Handbooks, manuals, etc. I. Cobb, Georgia, joint author. II. Title. III. Series: Mississippi. Cooperative Extension Service, Mississippi State. Public administration series.
MsSM NUC77-85124

Ballard, George Alexander, 1862-1948.
The influence of the sea on the political history of Japan. Westport, Conn., Greenwood Press [1972]
xix, 311 p. illus. 23 cm.
Reprint of the 1921 ed.
1. Japan—History. 2. Japan—History, Naval. I. Title.
DS835.B3 1972 952 74-136516
ISBN 0-8371-5435-9 MARC

Ballard, Gerald, 1931-
Aleatory music of the twentieth century and its relationship to the social and cultural theories of Pitirim A. Sorokin and Baker Brownell. Ann Arbor, Mich., University Microfilms, 1971.
1 reel. 35 mm. (University Microfilms 71-29450)
Microfilm (positive) of typescript.
Thesis (Ed. D.)—University of Tennessee.
Collation of the original: vi, 171 p.
Bibliography: leaves 166-170 l.
1. Music—20th century. 2. Sorokin, Pitirim Aleksandrovich, 1889-1968. 3. Brownell, Baker, 1887- I. Title.
PSt NUC75-26529

Ballard, Grace Bruton, joint comp.
see Moore, Elizabeth Darby. The Bruton family circle cookbook. [n.p.] 1972.

Ballard, Harold N.
see Atmospheric tidal measurements... Fort Monmouth, N. J., 1971.

Ballard, J G 1930-
The burning world. [New York] Berkley Pub. Corp. [1964]
160 p. 18 cm. (A Berkley Medallion book)
I. Title.
GU NUC75-26598

Ballard, J G 1930-
Concrete island [by] J. G. Ballard. London, Cape, 1974.
176 p. 21 cm. £1.95 GB 74-09901
I. Title.
PZ4.B1893Co 823'.9'14 74-171375
[PR6052.A46] MARC
ISBN 0-224-00970-2

Ballard, J G 1930-
Concrete island [by] J. G. Ballard. New York, Farrar Straus and Giroux [1974, c1973]
176 p. 21 cm.
I. Title.
PZ4.B1893Co 3 823'.9'14 73-87699
[PR6052.A46] MARC
ISBN 0-374-12807-3

Ballard, J G 1930-
Crash [by] J. G. Ballard. London, Cape [1973]
224 p. 21 cm. £2.25 GB***
I. Title.
PZ4.B1893Cp 823'.9'14 73-177443
[PR6052.A46] MARC
ISBN 0-244-00782-3

Ballard, J G 1930–
Crash [by] J. G. Ballard. New York, Farrar, Straus and Giroux [1973]
223 p. 21 cm. $6.95
I. Title.
PZ4.B1893Cp 3 823'.9'14 73–84112
[PR6052.A46] MARC
ISBN 0-374-13072-8

Ballard, J G 1930–
Crash [by] J. G. Ballard. [Paris] Calmann-Lévy [1974]
253 p. 22 cm. (Dimensions)
I. Title.
OU NUC76-21388

Ballard, J G 1930–
The day of forever [by] J.G. Ballard. [London] Panther Books [c1967]
146 p. (Panther science fiction)
I. Title.
CaOTP NUC73-2353

Ballard, J G 1930-
High-rise / J. G. Ballard. — London : J. Cape, 1975.
204 p. ; 21 cm. GB***
ISBN 0-224-01168-5 : £2.95
I. Title.
PZ4.B1893 Hi 823'.9'14 75-332844
[PR6052.A46] 76 MARC

Ballard, J G 1930-
High-rise / J. G. Ballard. — New York : Holt, Rinehart and Winston, 1977, c1975.
204 p. ; 22 cm.
ISBN 0-03-020651-0 : $6.95
I. Title.
PZ4.B1893 Hi 3 823'.9'14 76-29899
[PR6052.A46] 76 MARC

Ballard, J G 1930–
Kristallwelt. Roman. [Frankfurt a. M.] Fischer Taschenbuch Verlag [1971]
142 p. 18 cm. (In Fischer Bücherei, no. 1228)
Translation of 'The Crystal world'.
I. Title.
NBuU NUC73-34774

Ballard, J G 1930-
Low-flying aircraft, and other stories / [by] J. G. Ballard. — London : Cape, 1976.
191 p. ; 21 cm. GB77-01841
CONTENTS: The ultimate city.—Low-flying aircraft.—The dead astronaut.—My dream of flying to Wake Island.—The life and death of God.—The greatest television show on Earth.—A place and a time to die.—The Comsat angels.—The beach murders.
ISBN 0-224-01311-4 : £3.50
I. Title.
PZ4.B1893 Lp 823'.9'14 77-357909
[PR6052.A46] 77 MARC

Ballard, J G 1930–
El mundo sumergido. [Traducción de Francisco Abelenda. 2. ed. Buenos Aires] Minotauro [1971]
184 p. 20 cm. (Colección otros mundos)
Translation of The drowned world.
I. Title.
MB NUC73-121091

Ballard, J G 1930–
The overloaded man. [London] Panther [c1967]
158 p. (Panther science fiction)
I. Title.
CaOTP NUC73-121187

Ballard, J G 1930–
Playa terminal. [Traducción de Aurora Bernárdez. Buenos Aires] Minotauro [1971]
199 p. 20 cm.
Translation of Terminal beach.
I. Title.
MB NUC73-121090

Ballard, J G 1930–
The terminal beach, by J.G. Ballard. [Harmondsworth, Middlesex] Penguin Books [c1964]
223 p. (Penguin science fiction, 2499)
I. Title.
CaOTP NUC73-2354

Ballard, J G 1930–
Der unmögliche Mensch, und andere Stories. Deutsch von Alfred Scholz. [1. Aufl. Hamburg] Marion von Schröder Verlag [1971]
179 p. 21 cm. (Science fiction & fantastica)
Translation of The impossible man and other stories.
I. Title.
MB NUC73-121317

Ballard, J G 1930–
Vermilion sands. [New York] Berkley Publishing Corp. [c1971]
192 p. (Berkley medallion book, S1980)
I. Title.
MiEM NUC73-34767

Ballard, J G 1930–
Vermilion sands [by] J. G. Ballard. London, Cape, 1973.
208 p. 21 cm. £2.25 GB 73-30403
I. Title.
PZ4.B1893Ve 823'.9'14 74–154893
[PR6053.A46] MARC
ISBN 0-224-00894-3

Ballard, J G 1930–
The wind from nowhere [by] J. G. Ballard. [Harmondsworth, Eng.] Penguin Books [1974, c1962]
185 p. 18 cm.
"Published in Penguin Books 1967."
I. Title.
INS NUC76-21387

Ballard, J. G., 1930-
see J. G. Ballard, the first twenty years. Hayes, Bran's Head Books Ltd, 1976.

Ballard, Jack S.
see The United States Air Force in Southeast Asia ... Washington, Office of Air History : for sale by the Supt. of Docs., U.S. Govt. Print. Off., 1977.

Ballard, Jack Stokes, 1928–
The shock of peace: military and economic demobilization after World War II. Los Angeles, University of California, 1974.
viii, 317 l.
Thesis—University of California, Los Angeles.
Vita.
Bibliography: leaves 276-317.
Photocopy of typescript. Ann Arbor, Mich., University Microfilms, 1975. 20 cm.
1. United States—History—1945– 2. United States—Economic policy—1945-1960. I. Title.
NmLcU NUC76-21316

Ballard, James, 1921-
Rolling all the time : stories / by James Ballard. — Urbana : University of Illinois Press, c1976.
168 p. ; 20 cm. — (Illinois short fiction)
CONTENTS: Introductory aeronautics.—Wild honey.—The feast of Crispian.—Down by the riverside.—Rolling all the time.—In the city.—Hundred to one.
ISBN 0-252-00613-5 : $6.95. ISBN 0-252-00614-3 pbk.
I. Title.
PZ3.B2121 Ro 813'.5'4 76-13475
[PS3503.A5507] 76 MARC

Ballard, James Harold, 1934–
Leading new church members in a study of the Christian life / by James H. Ballard. -- Wake Forest, N.C. : [s.n.], 1975.
180 l. ; 29 cm.
Project in Ministry report (D. Min.)--Southeastern Baptist Theological Seminary.
Appendices: leaves 84-176.
Bibliography: leaves 177-180.
1. Church membership. 2. Christian life--Study and teaching. I. Title.
NcWFSB NUC77-84514

Ballard, James Moses.
The effect of syntactical transformations on the performance of a conservation of meaning task by urban black and white high school students [Minneapolis] 1972.
iv, 93 l. 29 cm.
Thesis (Ph. D.)—University of Minnesota.
Bibliography: leaves 81-88.
MnU NUC73-121089

Ballard, James T
Rapid tensile tests of six intermediate-grade steel reinforcing bars by J. T. Ballard [and] J.R. Hossley. [Rev. ed.] Conducted by U.S. Army Engineer Waterways Experiment Station, Corps of Engineers, Vicksburg, Miss. [n. p.] 1967.
1 v. (various pagings) illus., photos, plates. (U.S. Waterways Experiment Station, Vicksburg, Miss. Miscellaneous paper no. 1-837)
"Sponsored by Air Force Weapons Laboratory."
1. Steel bars—Testing. 2. Reinforcing bars. I. Hossley, James R., joint author. II. Title. III. Series.
MsSM NUC76-35266

Ballard, James T., joint author
see Carre, Gary L Evaluation of end wall designs for underground protective military structures. Vicksburg, Miss., 1968.

Ballard, Jerry.
To the regions beyond: an introduction to Southern Methodist foreign missions. With a foreword by Frank McLellan. [Orangeburg, S. C.] Southern Methodist Church, Board of Foreign Missions [1970]
69 p. 21 cm.
Bibliography: p. 66-69.
1. Missions, Foreign—Hist. 2. Southern Methodist Church—Missions. I. Southern Methodist Church. Board of Foreign Missions. II. Title.
IEG NUC73-126137

Ballard, Jim.
see Timmermann, Tim. Strategies in humanistic education. Amherst, MA, Mandala, 1975-

Ballard, John.
Preliminary estimate, Missouri land in public ownership, 1974-1976 / John Ballard. — Columbia : University of Missouri—Columbia, Extension Division, 1976.
52 p. : maps ; 28 cm.
Cover title.
"Governmental Affairs Program, UED 39."
1. Missouri—Public lands—Statistics. I. University of Missouri—Columbia. University Extension Division. II. University of Missouri—Columbia. Governmental Affairs Program. III. Title.
HD243.M8B34 333.1'09778 77-622428
77 MARC

Ballard, John Addison.
The development of political parties in French Equatorial Africa. Medford, Mass., 1963.
vi, 675 l.
Thesis—Tufts University.
Microfilm copy. Cambridge, Mass., MIT Libraries, 1973. 1 reel. 35 mm.
1. Africa, French Equatorial—Pol. & govt. I. Title.
ScU NUC76-35262

Ballard, John Thomas, joint author
see Buell, Murray Fife, 1905– Evaporation from lowland vegetation... New Brunswick, N. J., 1972.

Ballard, John Wesley, 1944–
On the principal indecomposable modules of finite Chevalley groups. [n. p.] 1974.
109 l. 29 cm.
Thesis (Ph. D.)—University of Wisconsin.
Vita.
Includes bibliography.
I. Title.
WU NUC76-21076

Ballard, Keith Emerson.
Study guide for Copi: Introduction to logic. 4th ed. New York, Macmillan [c1972]
vii, 274 p. illus. 24 cm.
On cover: A self-instructional supplement.
1. Logic. I. Copi, Irving M. Introduction to logic.
WaU NjP NUC74-132157

Ballard, Kelley B
Analysis of variance and co-variance with unequal treatment groups; methods for desk calculation [by] Kelley B. Ballard and Don M. Gottfredson. Vacaville, California Medical Facility, 1965.
1 v. (various pagings) illus. (Institute for the Study of Crime and Delinquency, Sacramento, Calif. Report, no. 7)
Cover title.
"Social Agency Effectiveness Study."
Includes bibliography.
1. Analysis of variance. 2. Rehabilitation of criminals—Research. I. Gottfredson, Don M., joint author. II. Title. III. Series.
MiEM NUC76-35265

Ballard, L F
Instrumentation for measurement of moisture; literature review and recommended research [by] L. F. Ballard. [Washington] Highway Research Board, National Research Council, 1973.
60 p. illus. 28 cm. (National Cooperative Highway Research Program. Report 138) $4.00
Bibliography: p. 50-59.
1. Moisture—Measurement—Instruments. 2. Highway engineering. I. Title. II. Series.
TE7.N25 no. 138 625.7'08 s 72-9486
[TA418.64] [625.7] MARC
ISBN 0-309-02023-9

Ballard, L. F.
see Field evaluation of new air pollution monitoring systems... Research Triangle Park, N. C., Research Triangle Institute, 1971.

Ballard, Lloyd V 1887-1969.
Beloit College, 1917-1923; the Brannon years, by Lloyd V. Ballard. [Beloit? Wis.] Brannon family and Beloit College, 1971.
144 p. illus. (1 fold.), ports. 23 cm.
1. Beloit College, Beloit, Wis. 2. Brannon, Melvin Amos, 1865-1950. I. Title.
WHi NUC74-145652

Ballard, Loys.
Ways of establishing an environmental background for reading experiences. [North Newton, Kan., Mennonite Press, 1974]
24 p. port. 24 cm.
1. Reading. I. Title.
LB1050.B32 372.4'1 74-77982
MARC

Ballard, Margaret Byrnside.
Bishop Matthew W. Clair, Sr. : a biography, by Margaret B. Ballard. Buckhannon, W. Va., 1973.
34 p. illus., facsims. 23 cm.
"Prepared under the auspices of the Commission on Archives and History of the West Virginia Conference of the United Methodist Church and Monroe County Historical Society."
1. Clair, Matthew Walker, 1865-1943.
WvU NUC75-18396

Ballard, Martin.
Dockie. London, Longman, 1972.
160 p. 22 cm. £1.50 B 73-06688
I. Title.
PZ7.B2118Do 73-160035
ISBN 0-582-15498-7 MARC

Ballard, Martin.
Dockie. [1st American ed.] New York, Harper & Row [1973]
214 p. 22 cm. $3.95
SUMMARY: Through with school at age fourteen, Moggy figures he can always continue working on the docks if his boxing ambitions don't materialize. Then as a result of a strike he is blackballed from the docks.
[1. London—Social life and customs—Fiction] I. Title.
PZ7.B2118Do 3 [Fic] 73-5476
ISBN 0-06-020400-1; 0-06-020401-X (lib. bdg.) MARC

Ballard, Martin.
Scholars and ancestors; China under the Sung Dynasty [by] Martin Ballard. Editorial consultant: Peter Mathias. Maps by Stuart Jordan. London, Methuen Educational [1973]
76, [1] p. illus., maps. 22 cm. (ERA histories, 10)
1. China—History—Sung dynasty, 960-1279. I. Title.
NIC NUC76-35258

Ballard, Martin.
The story of teaching. London, Longmans Young, 1969.
[10], 101 p. illus. 23 cm. index. 20/- B 70-00785
Bibliography: p. 95-96.
1. Education—History. I. Title.
LA11.B27 371.1'009 78-472349
SBN 582-15500-6 rev MARC

Ballard, Martin.
Who am I? A book of world religions...
[London] Hutchinson Educational [1971]
175 p. illus. 22 cm.
NjPT NUC73-121135

Ballard, Patti.
Cabbage... a variety of ways. [Spartanburg, S. C.] Wofford College Press, 1974.
[11] p.
Edition of 50 copies.
1. Cookery. I. Title. II. S. C. publications—Spartanburg—Wofford College Press, 1974.
ScU NUC75-18398

Ballard, Paul.
A guide to maps in the Newcastle-Tweed River area, 1770-1971 [by] P. Ballard. Newcastle, N. S. W., University of Newcastle [1971?]
76, 9 p. illus., facsims., maps, tables. 26 cm. (University of Newcastle publications in geography, no. 1) ANL
Bibliography: p. 74.
1. Newcastle, Australia—Maps—Bibliography. 2. Tweed Valley, Australia—Maps—Bibliography. I. Title. II. Series: Newcastle, Australia. University. Publications in geography, no. 1.
Z6027.A89B34 016.912'944 73-160116
ISBN 0-7259-0008-3 MARC

Ballard, Paul H., ed.
see Psychedelic religion? Cardiff, University College Cardiff [1972]

Ballard, Paul H.
see The Valleys call... Ferndale, Ron Jones Publications, 1975.

Ballard, Philip Boswood, 1865-
Teaching and testing English [by] P. B. Ballard. London, University of London Press [1964]
xi, 167 p. 19 cm.
First published in 1939.
1. English language—Study and teaching. 2. Thought and thinking. I. Title.
NBuU NUC75-26582

Ballard, Ralph.
Tales of early Niles. [Niles, Mich.] Fort St. Joseph Historical Society [n.d.]
96 p. front. 23 cm.
OClU NUC76-50643

Ballard, Richard Lee.
Spin refrigerator dynamics. [Berkeley] 1971.
v, 189 l. illus.
Thesis (Ph. D.)—University of California.
Bibliography: leaves 123-128.
CU NUC73-121134

Ballard, Robert Burford, 1921-
Brain waves: a personnel management tool? [n. p.] 1974.
283 l.
Thesis (Ph. D.)—University of Oregon.
Vita.
Bibliography: leaves 280-283.
1. Electroencephalography. 2. Ability—Testing. I. Title.
OrU NUC76-21075

Ballard, Robert E
A biosystematic and chemosystematic study of the Bidens pilosa complex in north and central America. [Iowa City, c1975]
xiv, 268 l. illus., plates, maps. 28 cm.
Thesis (Ph. D.)—University of Iowa.
1. Bidens pilosa. I. Title.
IaU NUC77-84272

Ballard, Robert F
Effect of antenna operation on structure and foundation behavior, AMRAD and RAMPART radar towers, White Sands Missile Range, New Mexico by R. F. Ballard [and] Jack Fowler. Vicksburg, Miss., U. S. Army Engineer Waterways Experiment Station, Corps of Engineers, 1967.
xi, 25 p. illus. (U. S. Waterways Experiment Station, Vicksburg, Miss. Miscellaneous paper no. 4-955)
"Sponsored by Office, Chief of Engineers, U. S. Army."
1. Radar—Antennas. I. Fowler, Jack, joint author. II. Title. III. Series.
MsSM NUC76-40392

Ballard, Robert F
Effect of antenna operation on structure and foundation behavior, FPS-26 Towers, Bellefontaine Air Force Station, Ohio, and Keesler Air Force Base, Mississippi, by R. F. Ballard [and] Jack Fowler. Conducted by U. S. Army Engineer Waterways Experiment Station, Corps of Engineers Vicksburg, Miss. [n. p.] 1964.
1 v. (various pagings) illus., plates, tables. (fold.) (U. S. Waterways Experiment Station, Vicksburg, Miss. Miscellaneous paper no. 4-694)
"Sponsored by Office, Chief of Engineers, U. S. Army."
1. Foundations—Testing. 2. Radar—Antennas. I. Fowler, Jack, joint author. II. Title. III. Series.
MsSM NUC76-40394

Ballard, Robert F
Rapid subsurface exploration; review of selected geophysical techniques, by R. F. Ballard, F. K. Chang. Vicksburg, Miss., U. S. Army Engineer Waterways Experiment Station, Soils and Pavements Laboratory, 1973.
ix, 17 p. figures, illus. (U. S. Waterways Experiment Station, Vicksburg, Miss. Miscellaneous paper, no. S-73-36, report, no. 1)
Sponsored by Office, Chief of Engineers, U. S. Army.
Bibliography: p. 17.
1. Geophysics. 2. Seismology. I. Chang, Frank K., joint author. II. Soils and Pavements Laboratory. III. Title. IV. Series.
MsSM NUC76-88813

Ballard, Robert F
Seismic field methods for in situ moduli / Robert F. Ballard, Jr., Francis G. McLean. -- Vicksburg, Miss. : U.S. Army Engineer Waterways Experiment Station, Soils and Pavements Laboratory, 1975.
39 [1] p. : ill. ; 28 cm. -- (United States. Waterways Experiment Station, Vicksburg, Mississippi. Miscellaneous paper ; S-75-10)
Prepared for Office, Chief of Engineers, U.S. Army.
1. Seismology. 2. Finite element methods. 3. Earthquakes and buildings. I. McLean, Francis G., joint author. II. Title. III. Series.
MsSM NUC77-84513

Ballard, Robert Melvyn.
A follow-up study of the academic record and career experiences of students enrolled for the A. M. L. S. degree at the Department of Library Science, the University of Michigan, 1960-61. [Ann Arbor] 1972.
208 p.
Thesis—University of Michigan.
Microfilm.
1. Educational research. I. Title.
InU KEmT NcU NNC NUC74-132251

Ballard, Robert Melvyn.
A follow-up study of the academic record and career experiences of students enrolled for the A. M. L. S. Degree at the Dept. of Library Science, the University of Michigan, 1960-61. [Ann Arbor] 1972.
x, 208 l. tables.
Thesis (Ph. D.)—University of Michigan.
Bibliography: leaves 203-208.
Vita.
Microfilm. Ann Arbor, Mich., University Microfilms. 1 reel.
1. Library science as a profession—Research. I. Title.
MsSM NUC76-62513

Ballard, Robert Melvyn.
A job history of the Atlanta University School of Library Service graduates, 1948-1959. Atlanta, 1961.
iii, 42 l.
Thesis (M. S. L. S.)—Atlanta University.
Bibliography: leaves 41-42.
Microfilm (negative) of typescript. Baton Rouge, Louisiana State University Library, 1962. 1 reel. 35 mm.
1. Atlanta University. School of Library Service—Alumni. I. Title.
LU NUC73-33087

Ballard, Sarah Cherry.
Literature on library administration, 1959-1963: a bibliographic essay. Washington, The Catholic University of America, 1970.
ii, 74 l. 28 cm.
A research paper ... Department of Library Science, The Catholic University of America. In partial fulfillment ... degree of Master of Librar Science.
1. Library administration. I. Title.
TNJ-P NUC73-121999

Ballard, Stanley Newton.
The effects of motivational group techniques upon selected personality and behavioral variables. Denton, Tex., 1971.
145 p.
Thesis—North Texas State University.
Microfilm. Ann Arbor, Mich., University Microfilms. 1 reel. 35 mm.
CLSU NUC73-34753

Ballard, W L
Essays on African literature. Edited by W. L. Ballard. Atlanta, School of Arts and Sciences, Georgia State University, 1973.
iv, 195 p. 23 cm. (Spectrum. Monograph series in the arts and sciences, v. 3)
1. Nigerian literature—Addresses, essays, lectures. I. Title. II. Series.
PL8014.N6B3 896 74-158476 MARC

Ballard, William Wayne, 1932-
see Balster, Clifford A Catalog of stratigraphic names for Montana. Butte, Montana College of Mineral Science and Technology, 1971.

Ballard, Willis Todhunter, 1903-
Chance Elson. New York, Pocker Books, inc. [1959, c1958]
298 p. (Cardinal edition, C277)
I. Title.
KEmT NUC76-69348

Ballard, Willis Todhunter, 1903-
Gunman from Texas [by] Todhunter Ballard. New York, Popular Library [1960]
144 p. 18 cm. (Popular giant, G484)
Copyright 1956.
I. Title.
MiEM NUC76-69347

Ballard, Willis Todhunter, 1903-
Guns of the lawless, by Todhunter Ballard. New York, Popular Library [1963]
142 p. 18 cm. (Western heritage library book, SP 259)
Copyright 1956.
I. Title.
MiEM NUC76-62954

Ballard, Willis Todhunter, 1903-
Home to Texas [by] Todhunter Ballard. [1st ed.] Garden City, N. Y., Doubleday, 1974.
159 p. 22 cm. (A Double D western)
I. Title.
PZ3.B2126Ho 813'.5'2 74-2502
[PS3503.A5575] MARC
ISBN 0-385-09595-3

Ballard, Willis Todhunter, 1903-
Loco and the Wolf [by] Todhunter Ballard. [1st ed.] Garden City, N. Y., Doubleday, 1973.
160 p. 22 cm. (DD western) $4.95
I. Title.
PZ3.B2126Ll 813'.5'2 73-79642
[PS3503.A5575] MARC
ISBN 0-385-05076-3

Ballard, Willis Todhunter, 1903-
Look to your guns [by] Parker Bonner [pseud.] New York, Paperback Library [c1969]
128 p. 18 cm. (Paperback library original western, 63-167)
I. Title.
MiEM NUC76-62956

Ballard, Willis Todhunter, 1903-
Nowhere left to run [by] Todhunter Ballard. Boston, G. K. Hall, 1973 [c1972]
288 p. 25 cm. $7.95
Large print ed.
I. Title.
[PZ3.B2126No 4] 813'.5'2 72-14104
[PS3503.A5575] MARC
ISBN 0-8161-6084-8

Ballard, Willis Todhunter, 1903-
Outlaw brand [by] Todhunter Ballard, writing as Parker Bonner. [New York] Avon [1972, c1954]
143 p. 18 cm. (Avon, 19231)
"A shorter version...appeared serially in Ranch romances under the title 'Railroad doctor'."
I. Title.
CoFS NUC76-62955

Ballard, Willis Todhunter, 1903-
Rawhide gunman [by] Todhunter Ballard. [New York] Avon [1972]
159, [1] p. 18 cm. (Avon, S446)
Copyright 1954.
I. Title.
MiEM NUC76-62953

Ballard, Willis Todhunter, 1903-
The sheriff of Tombstone / Todhunter Ballard. — 1st ed. — Garden City, N.Y. : Doubleday, 1977.
187 p. ; 22 cm.
ISBN 0-385-12694-4 : $6.95
I. Title.
PZ3.B2126 Sh 813'.5'2 76-53410
[PS3503.A5575] 77 MARC

Ballard, Willis Todhunter, 1903-
Trails of rage / Todhunter Ballard. — 1st ed. — Garden City, N.Y. : Doubleday, 1975.
184 p. ; 22 cm.
ISBN 0-385-09941-X : $5.95
I. Title.
PZ3.B2126 Tp 813'.5'2 75-6150
[PS3503.A5575] 75 MARC

Ballard, Willis Todhunter, 1903-
Trails of rage / Todhunter Ballard. — Boston : G. K. Hall, 1976, c1975.
262 p. ; 24 cm.
"Published in large print."
ISBN 0-8161-6351-0
1. Sight-saving books. I. Title.
[PZ3.B2126 Tp 4] 813'.5'2 76-101
[PS3503.A5575] 76 MARC

Ballard County, Ky. Planning Commission
see Scruggs and Hammond. Existing land use analysis, population, and economic factors... Lexington, Ky., 1970.

Ballardini, Gaetano, 1878-1953.
La maiolica italiana : dalle origini alla fine del Cinquecento / Gaetano Ballardini. — Faenza : Faenza editrice, c1975.
207 p. : ill. (some col.) ; 25 cm. — (Serie Arte e storia della ceramica) It 75-Dec
1. Majolica—Italy. I. Title.
NK4315.B24 1975 75-406526

Ballardini, Romeo.
Studio della metodologia per l'analisi e l'intervento in due centri storici minori / Romeo Ballardini. — Bologna : Tip. SAB, 1974.
90 leaves, [48] fold. leaves of plates : ill. ; 29 cm. It 75-July
Includes bibliographies.
L2000
1. Urban renewal—San Giorgio di Piano, Italy. 2. Urban renewal—Camerano, Italy. I. Title.
HT178.I 82S253 76-514924

Ballari, Aldo.
Eritrea '41 [i. e. quarantuno]. (1941-1948). Roma, G. Volpe, 1973.
301 p. illus. 24 cm. (I Racconti di Ba'Al, t. 1) L2900 It 74-Jan
Errata slip inserted.
Bibliography: p. 257-258.
1. World War, 1939-1945—Eritrea. 2. Eritrea—History. I. Title.
D766.84.B27 74-351304

Ballāri Jilleya Kannaḍa Sāhitya Sammēḷana
see
Bellary District Kannada Sahitya Sammelana.

Ballāri Jilleya Sāhitya Sammēḷana
see
Bellary District Kannada Sahitya Sammelana.

Ballarian, Anna.
Fabric collage : contemporary stitchery and appliqué / Anna Ballarian. — Worcester, Mass. : Davis Publications, c1976.
80 p., [4] leaves of plates : ill. ; 27 cm.
Bibliography: p. [77]
ISBN 0-87192-089-1
1. Applique. 2. Needlework. I. Title.
NK9104.B34 746.4'4 76-29553
77 MARC

Ballarin, Andreina
see Ludovico degli Arrighi, Vicentino, fl. 1522. La operina/di Ludovico Vicentino... Vicenza: Officine grafiche STA, 1974.

Ballarin, Andreina
see Vicenza. Museo civico. Recenti acquisizioni... [Vicenza, Officine grafiche STA, 1967]

Ballarin, Eduardo.
Administrative implications of a cross-product subsidization scheme / Eduardo Ballarin. -- [Boston] : Graduate School of Business Administration, George F. Baker Foundation, Harvard University, 1976.
iii, 220 leaves : ill. ; 29 cm.
Thesis--Harvard University.
Appendices (leaves 207-220).
Includes bibliographical references.
1. New products. 2. Industrial organization. I. Title.
MH-BA NUC77-85991

Ballarin, John Zabalo
see
Txiki, 1892-1948.

Ballarín, José María Poal
see
Poal Ballarín, José María.

Ballarin, S
The construction of the gravimetric map of Italy, by S. Ballarin, B. Palla and C. Trombetti. Firenze, 1972.
31 p. illus. (8 fold. maps in pocket) 28 cm. (Italy. Commissione geodetica. Pubblicazioni, 3rd serie. Memoria, no. 19)
1. Gravity—Italy—Maps. I. Title. II. Series.
DME NUC75-31781

Ballarín Cornel, Angel.
Civilización pirenaica; vestigios ancestrales, toponimia, leyendas, refranes, adivinanzas y dichos. [Zaragoza] 1972.
187 p. illus., maps. 22 cm. Sp***
1. Benasque Valley, Spain—Civilization. I. Title.
DP302.B616B35 73-306514

Ballarín Cornel, Angel.
Vocabulario de Benasque. Zaragoza, Institución "Fernando el Católico," 1971.
220 p., 2 l. 24 cm. (Publicación de la Institución Fernando el Católica, no. 518) 200ptas Sp 72-Jan
1. Spanish language—Provincialisms—Benasque. I. Title. II. Series: Saragossa. Institución Fernando el Católico. Publicación, no. 518.
PC4815.B4B3 72-363606

Ballarín Marcial, Alberto.
Estudios de derecho agrario y política agraria / Alberto Ballarín Marcial. -- Madrid : [s.n.], 1975.
1026 p. ; 25 cm.
Includes bibliographical references and indexes.
1. Agricultural laws and legislation--Spain. 2. Agriculture and state--Spain. I. Title.
ViU NUC77-84511

Ballarini, Klaus.
Über Konsum in disaggregierten Ökonomien / Klaus Ballarini. — Meisenheim am Glan : Hain, 1976.
77 p. ; 23 cm. — (Schriften zur wirtschaftswissenschaftlichen Forschung ; Bd. 112)
Originally presented as the author's thesis, Universität Karlsruhe.
Bibliography: p. 74-77.
ISBN 3-445-01442-6 : DM19.00
1. Consumption (Economics)—Mathematical models. I. Title.
HB801.B28 1976 339.4'7'0184 77-459489
77 MARC

Ballarini, Klaus.
Über Wachstumsgleichewicht, technischen Fortschritt und Akkumulation des Kapitals / Klaus Ballarini, Christian Winterberg. — Meisenheim (am Glan) : Hain, 1975.
62 p. : 7 ill. ; 23 cm. — (Mathematical systems in economics ; 14) GFR75-A
Bibliography: p. 61-62.
ISBN 3-445-01226-1 : DM11.50
1. Economic development—Mathematical models. 2. Technological innovations—Mathematical models. 3. Capital—Mathematical models. I. Winterberg, Christian, joint author. II. Title: Über Wachstumsgleichgewicht ... III. Series.
HD82.B263 75-518516
75 MARC

Ballarini, Teodorico.
Introduzione alla Bibbia, con antologia esegetica. [2. ed. Torino] Marietti [1968, c1964]
2 v. illus., maps. 25 cm.
Bibliographical footnotes.
Contents.—v.1. Atti degli Apostoli. San Paolo e le sue lettere Tessalonicesi, 1 e 2 Corinzi, Galati, Romani.—v.2. Epistole della prigionia, Pastorali, Ebrei, Cattoliche, Apocalisse.
1. Bible—Introductions. I. Title.
PPT NUC73-122053

Ballarini, Teodorico, ed.
see Introduzione alla Bibbia... [Torino] M Marietti [1962-

Ballarino, Tito.
Costituzione e diritto internazionale privato / Tito Ballarino. — Padova : CEDAM, 1974,
ix, 188 p. ; 25 cm. — (Pubblicazioni della Università di Pavia. Studi nelle scienze giuridiche e sociali ; nuova ser., v. 12) It***
Includes bibliographical references and index.
L4500
1. Conflict of laws—Italy. 2. Italy—Constitutional law. I. Title. II. Series: Parma. Università. Istituto di esercitazioni nelle scienze giuridiche e sociali. Studi nelle scienze giuridiche e sociali ; nuova ser., v. 12.
75-560099

Ballarino, Tito.
Il governo dello stato nel diritto internazionale. Pavia, Tipografia del libro [1961]
149 p. (Pubblicazioni della Università di Pavia, Studi nelle scienze giuridiche e sociali, 138)
Bibliographical footnotes.
1. State, The. 2. International law. I. Title.
CU-L NUC76-69346

Ballarino, Tito.
Organizzazione internazionale. (Aspetti giuridici). Milano, Celuc, 1973.
267 p. 21 cm. (Richerche, 34) L3000 It 73-Dec
1. International agencies. I. Title.
JX1995.B27 74-301545
rev

Ballario, Mario, comp.
50 [i.e. Cincuenta] años de poesía en Mendoza; 1922-1972. Responsable: Mario Ballario. [Mendoza? Argentina] Ediciones Azor [1972]
261 p. 23 cm.
1. Argentine poetry—Mendoza (Province) 2. Argentine poetry—20th cent. I. Title.
CtY NUC75-31783

Ballario, Pina.
I canti della mia solitudine. Milano, Casa Ed. "La Vittoriosa" [n.d.]
90 p. 21 cm.
I. Title.
CtU NUC73-71303

Ballario Yoshida, Celia
see
Yoshida, Celia Ballario.

Ballart, Gilberto Toste
see Toste Ballart, Gilberto.

Ballart, Rafael Viver
see
Viver Ballart, Rafael.

Ballas, Gila Cohen
see Cohen Ballas, Gila.

Ballas, Jack A.
see Houston-Galveston Area Council. Regional atlas, 1972. [Houston?] 1972.

Ballas, Mikhail B
(Istoriko-statisticheskiĭ ocherk vinodělīia v Rossii)
Историко-статистическій очеркъ винодѣлія въ Россіи (Кавказъ и Крымъ). М. Баласа. Санктпетербургъ, Тип. Т-ва "Общественная польза," 1877.
xvii, 143 p. 23 cm.
Bibliography: p. [xiii]-xvii.
1. Wine and wine making—Russia—Caucasus. 2. Wine and wine making—Crimea. I. Title.
TP559.R8B3 74-237089

Ballas, Nikolaos
see Vallas, Nikolaos, 1871-1932.

Ballas, Samir K
Self-assessment of current knowledge in hematology / by Samir K. Ballas. — Flushing, N.Y. : Medical Examination Pub. Co., 1974-1975.
2 v. : ill. ; 22 cm.
Part 2 edited by F. S. Morrison.
Bibliography: v. 1., p. 172.
CONTENTS: pt. 1. Textbook review.—pt. 2. Literature review.
ISBN 0-87488-248-6 (v. 1)
1. Hematology—Examinations, questions, etc. 2. Blood—Diseases—Examinations, questions, etc. I. Morrison, Francis S. II. Title.
RC636.B26 616.1'5'0076 74-22986
75[r75]rev MARC

Ballas, Samir K
Self-assessment of current knowledge in hematology / by Samir K. Ballas. — 2d ed. — Flushing, N.Y. : Medical Examination Pub. Co., 1977-
v. : ill. ; 22 cm.
Bibliography: v. 1, p. 260-261.
CONTENTS: pt. 1. Textbook review.
1. Hematology—Examinations, questions, etc. 2. Blood—Diseases—Examinations, questions, etc.
RC636.B26 1977 616.1'5'0076 77-89727
77 MARC

Ballas, Shimon, 1930–
[Hitbaharut]
התבהרות; רומן [מאת] שמעון בלס. מרחביה, ספרית פועלים [1972]
202 p. 22 cm. IL10.00
I. Title.
PJ5054.B23H5 72-950469

Ballasis, Edward
see Bellasis, Edward, 1852-1922.

Ballatore, Gian Pietro.
Commento alla carta dei suoli della Sicilia in scala 1:250.000. Palermo, Industria Grafica Nazionale, 1968.
38 p. 25 cm.
At head of title: Ballatore Gian Pietro, M. Fierotti Giovanni.
Summary in English.
Includes bibliography.
1. Soils—Sicily—Maps. I. Fierotti, Giovanni. II. Title.
DI-GS NUC75-108664

Ballauff, Theodor.
Pädagogik. Eine Geschichte der Bildung und Erziehung. Unter Mitarbeit von Gert Plamböck. Freiburg (i. Br.), München, Alber (1969–73)
3 v. 23 cm. (Orbis academicus; Problemgeschichten der Wissenschaft in Dokumenten und Darstellungen, Bd. 1. [Geisteswissenschaftliche Reihe] 11-13) DM78.00 (pt. 1) GDB 69-A43-406 (pt. 1)
Vol. 2-3 by Theodor Ballauff und Klaus Schaller.
Includes bibliographies.
CONTENTS: Bd. [1. e. T.] 1. Von der Antike bis zum Humanismus.—Bd. 2. Vom 16. bis zum 19. Jahrhundert.—Bd. 3. 19./20. Jahrhundert.
1. Education—Philosophy—History. I. Plamböck, Gert. II. Schaller, Klaus, 1925- joint author. III. Title. IV. Series: Orbis academicus; problemgeschichten der Wissenschaft in Dokumenten und Darstellungen, Bd. 1/11-1/13.
LA11.B28 73-443574
rev

Ballay, Jozef.
Hodiny slohu v 3.-5. ročníku základných deväťročných škôl. Autori: Jozef Ballay, Gustáv Janáček. Ilustr. Jozef Cesnak. 2. vyd. Bratislava, SPN, t. Svornosť, 1973.
297, [5] p. tables, front. 21 cm. (Knižnica metodickej literatúry) Kčs19.50 CzS 73
Bibliography: p. 297.
1. Slovak language—Composition and exercises. I. Janáček, Gustav, joint author. II. Title.
PG5335.B3 1973 74-339445

Ballaz, Bernard
see La Simulation de gestion... Paris, Presses universitaires de France, 1974.

Ballaz, Jesús.
Lucha y contemplación; concilio de los jóvenes. Barcelona, Ediciones Don Bosco [1974]
63 p. illus. 22 cm. (Cuadernos edebé, 1) Sp***
ISBN 84-236-0654-6
1. Youth—Religious life—Congresses. I. Title.
BV4536.B34 75-580467

Ballaz, Jesús.
Peligro de salvación / Jesús Ballaz. La encuesta / Ventura Porta. — Barcelona : Ediciones Don Bosco, [1974?]
61 p. : ill. (2 fold. inserted) ; 21 cm. — (Cuadernos edebé ; 7) Sp***
Plays.
ISBN 84-236-0665-1
I. Porta Roses, Ventura. La encuesta. 1974. II. Title.
PZ77.B28 862'.6'4 75-552811

Ballbach, Nathan Anthony, 1905-1974.
The Gooseneck tidings / by Nathan Anthony Ballbach. — East Lansing, Mich. : Northlands Press, c1977.
98 p. ; 21 cm.
ISBN 0-918808-01-4 : $4.50
I. Title.
PS3503.A5576G6 1977 811'.5'2 75-28578
77 MARC

Balle, C G
Wills and estate planning, by C.G. Bale, G.W. Alexandrowicz [and] C.T. Asplund. [Kingston, Ont., Faculty of Law, Queen's University, 1971?]
362 p. 36 cm.
Cover title.
1. Wills—Ontario. 2. Estate planning—Ontario. I. Alexandrowicz, G.W. II. Asplund, C.T. III. Title.
CaBVaU NUC73-34784

Ballé, Catherine.
Informatique et changement dans l'entreprise [par] Catherine Ballé [et] Jean-Louis Peaucelle. Sous la direction de Michel Crozier. Paris [Copedith] 1970.
126 p.
At head of title: Centre national de la recherche scientifique. Groupe de sociologie des organisations.
I. Groupe de sociologie des organisations.
MH NUC76-24501

Ballé, Catherine.
Le pouvoir informatique dans l'entreprise [par] Catherine Ballé [et] Jean-Louis Peaucelle. Préf. de Michel Crozier. Paris, Éditions d'organisation, 1972.
168 p. 24 cm. (Collection Sociologie des organisations) 28.00F F***
Bibliography: p. [167]-168.
1. Electronic data processing—Business. 2. Management information systems. I. Peaucelle, Jean Louis, joint author. II. Title.
HF5548.2.B32 73-301393

Balle, Claus, joint author.
see Nissen, Christian S. Olie- og energipolitik ... [København] Akademisk forlag : [eksp., DBK] 1976.

Balle, Francis.
Institutions et publics des moyens d'information: presse, radiodiffusion, télévision. Paris, Montchrestien [1973]
vi, 696 p. 19 cm. (Collection Université nouvelle. Précis Domat) 40.00F F***
Includes bibliographies.
1. Communication. 2. Mass media. I. Title.
P90.B265 74-155072
ISBN 2-7076-0132-2 MARC

Balle, Francis.
"Pour comprendre les média," Mac Luhan, analyse critique par Francis Balle ... Paris, Hatier, 1972.
80 p. 18 cm. (Profil d'une œuvre, 202. Sciences humaines) 3.80F F 72-11088
Bibliography: p. 77-[80]
1. McLuhan, Herbert Marshall. Understanding media. I. Title.
P90.M263B3 301.2 73-305565

Balle, Francis, comp.
Sociologie de l'information; textes fondamentaux, par Francis Balle et Jean G. Padioleau. Préf. de Jean Cazeneuve. Paris, Larousse [1973]
371, [1] p. illus. 21 cm. (Sciences humaines et sociales) (Larousse université) 36.00F F***
Bibliography: p. 349-[372]
Errata slip inserted.
1. Communication—Social aspects—Addresses, essays, lectures. 2. Mass media—Addresses, essays, lectures. I. Padioleau, Jean G., joint comp. II. Title.
HM258.B355 301.16 73-154065
MARC

Balle, Francis.
see Encyclopédie de la sociologie ... Paris, Larousse, c1975.

Balle, Mogens, 1921-
see Dotremont, Christian, 1922- Ja og nej, måske. [Vaerløse, Grafodan, 1968]

Balle, Malle, Hupe und Artur. Ein Spiel fur Kinder, von Dagmar Dorsten [et al.] Frankfurt, Verlag der Autoren, 1970.
87 p. 15 cm.
Microcard Copy.
I. Dorsten, Dagmar.
CaBVaU NUC74-22758

Ballegeer, Jan Piet.
see Landuyt, Octave. 1922- Octave Landuyt. [Brussel] Arts & Voyages. c1970.

Ballegeer, Johan.
Barbele slaet den trommele. Antwerpen, Utrecht, Standaard Uitgeverij [1972]
94 p. illus. 22 cm. (Zegelvikings, 16)
I. Title.
MB NUC75-31782

Ballegeer, Johan.
De visserij langs Vlaanderens kust in oude prentkaarten / door Johan Ballegeer en Jean-Pierre Braems. — Zaltbommel : Europese Bibliotheek, 1976.
116 p. : ill. ; 15 x 21 cm. Ne76-50
fl 24.90
1. Fisheries—Belgium—History—Pictorial works. 2. Flanders—Views. I. Braems, J. P., joint author. II. Title.
SH265.B34 77-460252
•77 MARC

Ballegeer, Yves.
Approximation de fonctions de poisson généralisées par une fonction des sinistres extrêmes. (Louvain, Impr. Offset Frankie, 1972).
[iv], 111 p. diagrs., tables. 25 cm. (Publications de la Faculté des sciences économiques, sociales et politiques de l'Université de Louvain, nouv. sér., no 98) Be 73-611
Bibliography: p. 110.
1. Poisson distribution. 2. Approximation theory. I. Title. II. Series: Louvain. Université catholique. Faculté des sciences économiques, sociales et politiques. Publications, nouv. sér., no 98.
QA273.6.B35 73-336155

Ballegoijen de Jong, J P A van.
Hofjes in de Hofstad / J. P. A. van Ballegoijen de Jong ; foto's Barry de Vos. — Baarn : Wereldvenster, [1976]
104 p. : ill. ; 24 cm. Ne76-1
"Gebaseerd op een rubriek in de 'Haagsche courant,' die in 1971... verscheen."
ISBN 9029307471 : fl 21.50
1. Hague—Courtyards. I. Vos, Barry de. II. Title.
DJ411.H337B34 76-453129
76 MARC

Balleine, George Reginald, 1873-1966.
The tragedy of Philippe d'Auvergne, Vice-Admiral in the Royal Navy and last Duke of Bouillon / by G. R. Balleine. — Chichester : Phillimore, 1973.
xiv, 145 p., leaf of plate, [4] p. of plates : ill., geneal. table, map, port. ; 23 cm. GB75-00335
Maps on lining papers.
Bibliography: p. 133-135.
Includes index.
ISBN 0-85033-124-2 : £3.50
1. d'Auvergne, Philippe, 1754-1816. 2. Jersey—History. I. Title.
DA670.J5D352 941.07'3'0924 75-308244
75 MARC

Balleine, John Arthur.
The story of St. Brelade Church, Jersey; as told by the late John A. Balleine. 9th ed. Gloucester, British Publishing, [1972].
33 p. illus. 19 cm. B 72-17762
1. Jersey. St. Brelade. I. Title.
NA5471.J4B3 1972 914.23'4 73-331153
ISBN 0-7140-0720-X MARC

Ballek, Ladislav.
Južná pošta / Ladislav Ballek. — 1. vyd. — Bratislava : Slov. spis., 1974.
199 p., [1] leaf of plates : ill. ; 21 cm. — (Nová próza) CzS 74
Kčs16.00
I. Title.
PG5439.12.A45J8 75-589768

Ballem, John Bishop.
The devil's lighter: a novel by John Ballem. Don Mills, Ont., General Pub. Co., 1973.
237 p. 23 cm. $7.95 C 74-730-0
I. Title.
PZ4.B1918De 813'.5'4 74-181321
[PR9199.3.B36] MARC
ISBN 0-7736-0025-6

Ballem, John Bishop.
The dirty scenario : a novel / by John Ballem. — Don Mills, Ont. : General Pub. Co. Ltd., 1974.
256 p. ; 23 cm. C***
ISBN 0-7736-0035-3 : $8.95
I. Title.
PZ4.B1918 Di 813'.5'4 75-321926
[PR9199.3.B36] 75 MARC

Ballem, John Bishop.
The Judas conspiracy / by John Ballem. — Don Mills, Ont. : Musson Book Co., 1976.
303 p. ; 19 cm. C76-017003-7
ISBN 0-7737-0028-5 : $6.95. ISBN 0-7737-7129-8 pbk.
I. Title.
PZ4.B1918 Ju 813'.5'4 77-352126
[PR9199.3.B36] 77 MARC

Ballem, John Bishop.
The oil and gas lease in Canada. [Toronto, Buffalo] University of Toronto Press [1973]
viii, 336 p. 25 cm. $25.00 C***
Includes bibliographical references.
1. Oil and gas leases—Canada. I. Title.
346'.71'04682 72-75734
ISBN 0-8020-1879-3; 0-8020-0218-8 (microfiche) MARC

Ballén, Humberto Murcia
see Murcia Ballén, Humberto.

Ballén de Garay, Parhelia.
El Panamá de ayer / Parhelia Ballén de Garay. -- Los Angeles : Writers Guild of America, 1975.
59 p. : ill. ; 22 cm.
1. Panama--Description and travel. 2. Panama--History. I. Title.
CU-BANC NUC77-85460

Ballenberger, Gerhard.
Die Schwäbische Alb in Farbe; ein Reiseführer f. Naturfreunde/ Gerhard Ballenberger, Eduard Haas. [Mit 112 Farbfotos von G. Ballenberger u. a. Die Kt. d. Schwäb. Alb zeichnete Maria Bertsch]. — Stuttgart: Franckh, 1972.
72 p.: 112 ill. (col.), maps; 20 cm. — (Bunte Kosmos-Taschenführer) DM7.80 GDB 72-A51
Bibliography: p. 70.
1. Physical geography—Germany—Alps, Swabian. 2. Alps, Swabian—Description and travel. I. Haas, Eduard, joint author. II. Title.
GB214.S95B34 914.3'46 73-305285
ISBN 3-440-03933-1

Ballendas, Petros G
Eisagōgē eis tēn epistēmēn tou dikaiou [5. ekd.] Thessalonikē, E. P. Sakkoulas, 1958.
249 p. 25 cm.
Reproduced from typescript.
MiU-L NUC74-118443

Ballēndas, Petros G
Engrapha ek tēs nomikēs praktikēs. Athēnai, Aphoi. P. Sakkoula, 1959.
131 p. 23 cm.
1. Forms—Greece.
MH-L NUC74-120075

Ballēndas, Petros G
Hē epharmogē allodapou dikonomikou dikaiou. Athēnai, 1957.
177 p. 22 cm.
Added t.p. in French.
1. Civil procedure (International law)
MH-L NUC74-120067

Ballēndas, Petros G
To idiōtikon diethnes dikaion eis ton Hellēnikon kōdika idiōtikou nautikou dikaiou. Athēnai, 1959.
23 p. 24 cm.
Added t.p. in French.
1. Maritime law.
MH-L CU NUC74-118463

Ballenden, P. St.
see Swaziland. Committee on Housing Needs. Report on credit for housing and agriculture. Mbabane, 1964.

Ballendorf, Dirk A
The development of a regional plan for the North Africa, Near East, Asia and Pacific Region of the Peace Corps. Cambridge, 1973.
46 l.
Thesis (Ed. D.)—Harvard University.
Project report: Planning.
1. U. S. Peace Corps. 2. Technical assistance, American. I. Title.
MH-Ed NUC75-18394

Ballendorf, Dirk A.
see Shiba, Shoji, 1933- A heuristic approach to educational planning. Cambridge? Harvard University Center for Studies in Education and Development? [196—]

Ballendorf, Dirk A.
see Shiba, Shoji, 1933- The K. J. method. [n. p., 196—?]

Ballenegger, Jacques, 1945-
La pollution en droit international : la responsabilité pour les dommages causés par la pollution transfrontière / Jacques Ballenegger. — Genève : Droz, 1975.
268 p. ; 22 cm. — (Travaux de droit, d'économie, de sociologie et de sciences politiques ; no 105) Sw75-A-7430
Bibliography: p. 251-259.
Includes index.
50.00F
1. Pollution—Law and legislation. 2. Pollution—International cooperation. I. Title.
76-450789
•76 MARC

Ballenger, Marcus.
see Primary school potpourri. Washington, Association for Childhood Education International, c1976.

Ballenger, Thomas Lee.
Story of the banking business in Tahlequah, Oklahoma / by T. L. Ballenger. — Tahlequah : Tahlequah Print. Co., 1968.
19 p. : ill. ; 24 cm.
1. Banks and banking—Oklahoma—Tahlequah. I. Title.
HG2613.T33B34 76-373062
76 MARC

Ballenpflanzungen. [Oslo?] A/S Jiffy-Pot [196-?]
see under Internationale Forstkonferenz, Náchod, Czechoslovak Republic, 1964.

Ballentine, George Derrill, 1936-
An analysis of the modal split of work trips in Texas cities. [Austin, Tex.] 1972.
xiii, 147 l. illus. 29 cm.
Thesis (Ph. D.)—University of Texas at Austin.
Vita.
Bibliography: leaves 146-147.
1. Local transit—Texas. 2. Motor bus lines.
TxU NUC75-31786

Ballentine, J Gregory.
On the general equilibrium analysis of tax incidence, by J. Gregory Ballentine and Ibrahim Eris. Houston, Tex., Program of Development Studies, William Marsh Rice University, 1973.
34 p. 28 cm. (William Marsh Rice University, Houston, Tex. Program of Development Studies. Paper no. 38)
"AID contract no. AID/csd-3302."
Includes bibliographical references.
1. Taxation—Mathematical models. 2. Equilibrium (Economics) I. Eris, Ibrahim, joint author. II. Title. III. Series.
HD82.W535 no. 38 338'.008 s 74-173170
[HJ2321] [336.2'001] MARC

Ballentine, Jene.
see Unexpected ... Honolulu, Otherworlds Media, c1976.

Ballentine, John Jennings, 1896-1970.
Reminiscences. [Glen Rock, N.J., Microfilming Corporation of America, 1972]
759 l. on 8 sheets. (N.Y.T.O.H.P. [i.e. New York times oral history program [1] Columbia University. Oral History Research Office. [Oral history] collection, 1)
Title from first frame.
MH NUC73-121316

Ballentine, Nadra.
see Unexpected ... Honolulu, Otherworlds Media, c1976.

Ballentine, Richard K., joint author
see Guarraia, Leonard J Influences of microbial populations... Washington, Environmental Protection Agency, 1972.

Ballentine, Richard K., joint author
see Warner, Richard W Black-water impoundment investigations. Cincinnati, Ohio, 1969.

Ballentine, Rudolph, 1941- joint author.
see Rama, Swami, 1925- Yoga and psychotherapy ... Glenview, Ill., Himalayan Institute, c1976.

Ballentine, Rudolph, 1941-
see Science of breath. Glenview, Ill., Himalayan Institute, c1976.

Ballentine, Rudolph, 1941-
see The Theory & practice of meditation. Glenview, Ill., Himalayan Institute, c1975.

Ballentine, Rudolph M Mrs.
Himalayan Mountain cookery / compiled by Mrs. Rudolph M. Ballentine, Sr. — Glenview, Ill. : Himalayan International Institute of Yoga Science and Philosophy, c1976.
185 p. : ill. ; 23 cm.
Includes index.
ISBN 0-89389-015-4 : $3.50
1. Cookery, India. 2. Cookery, Yoga. I. Title.
TX724.5.I5B34 641.5'954 77-362033
77 MARC

Ballentyne, Denis William George.
A dictionary of named effects and laws in chemistry, physics and mathematics [by] D. W. G. Ballentyne D. R. Lovett. 3rd ed. London, Chapman and Hall, 1972.
iii, viii, 355 p. illus. 22 cm. (Science paperbacks, no. 81) £1.50
GB 73-01870
Distributed in the U. S. A. by Harper & Row Publishers.
1. Chemistry—Dictionaries. 2. Physics—Dictionaries. 3. Mathematics—Dictionaries. I. Lovett, D. R., joint author. II. Title.
Q123.B3 1972 500.2'03 73-595044
ISBN 0-412-20970-5 MARC

Balleny Islands, Reconnaissance Party, 1963-1964
see Quartermain, L B The Balleny Islands... Rev. [Wellington, N. Z.] Antarctic Division, 1964.

Baller, Ėleazar Aleksandrovich.
(Chelovek i svoboda)
Человек и свобода. Москва, "Сов. Россия," 1972.
283 p. with illus. 17 cm. (Советский образ жизни) 0.76rub
USSR 73-VKP
At head of title: Э. А. Баллер.
Includes bibliographical references.
1. Liberty. I. Title.
B824.4.B33 73-353838

Baller, Ėleazar Aleksandrovich.
Socialist democracy and the individual / E. Baller. — Moscow : Novosti Press Agency Pub. House, 1974.
62 p., [8] leaves of plates : ill. ; 17 cm. USSR***
0.21rub
1. Communism and society. I. Title.
HX542.B344 335.43 75-330202
75 MARC

Baller, Eleazar Aleksandrovich, ed.
see Aktual'nye filosofskie problemy obshchestvennogo razvitiia. Moskva, 1973.

Baller, Eleazar Aleksandrovich
see Maslin, Aleksandr Nikiforovich. Lenin. Moskva, Znanie, 1972.

Baller, Frederick William, 1852-1922. A Mandarin primer
see Wilder, George Durand, 1869- Analysis of Chinese characters. New York: Dover Publications, 1974.

Baller, Hinrich.
see Berlin. Technische Universität. Planungskollektiv SHF 3. SHF 3 [i.e. drei] ... [3. Aufl.]. Berlin, Das Kollektiv, Vorwort, 1972.

Baller, Uffe
see Nørgaard, Jørgen. Introduktion til formueretten. 3. udg. København, Juristforbundet, 1972.

Baller, Warren Robert, 1900-
Bed-wetting: origins and treatment [by] Warren R. Baller. With a foreword by Theodore H. Blau. New York, Pergamon Press [1975]
xiii, 124 p. illus. 23 cm. (Pergamon general psychology series, 38)
Bibliography: p. 112-120.
ISBN 0-08-017859-6. ISBN 0-08-017860-X (Pbk.). ISBN 0-08-017861-8 (Text ed.)
1. Enuresis. I. Title.
[DNLM: 1. Enuresis—Etiology—Popular works. 2. Enuresis—Therapy—Popular works. WS322 B191b]
RC564.B34 1975 616.8'49 74-8771
74 MARC

Ballerina : portraits and impressions of Nadia Nerina / edited by Clement Crisp ; designed by Barney Wan. — London : Weidenfeld & Nicolson, [1975]
ca. 200 p. : ill. ; 30 cm. GB***
ISBN 0-297-76951-0 : £6.00
1. Nerina, Nadia. 2. Ballet. I. Crisp, Clement.
GV1785.N47B34 792.8'028'0924 75-330284
75 MARC

Ballerini, Carlo.
see Convegno di Nimega sul Boccaccio, 1975. Atti del Convegno di Nimega sul Boccaccio (28-29-30 ottobre 1975) Bologna, Pàtron, 1976.

Ballerini, Enrico.
Aspetti tecnici ed organizzativi della banca di credito ordinario. Milano, Celuc, 1972.
353 p., incl. plate. illus. 20½ cm. (Ricerche, 17) L4000
It 72-Dec
1. Bank management. 2. Banks and banking — Accounting. 3. Electronic data processing—Banks and banking. I. Title.
HG1607.I 8B34 72-374863

Ballerini, Luigi, 1940-
Eccetera. E. Parma, Guanda, 1972.
56 p. 18 cm. (Piccola fenice) L1300 It 72-July
Poems.
I. Title.
PQ4862.A443E25 72-362975

Ballerini, Luigi, 1940-
La piramide capovolta : scritture visuali a d'avanguardia / Luigi Ballerini. — 1. ed. — Venezia : Marsilio, 1975.
112 p., [26] leaves of plates : ill. ; 21 cm. — (Saggi ; n. 42)
It 76-Apr
L4800
1. Italian literature—20th century—History and criticism. 2. Visual poetry, Italian—History and criticism. I. Title.
PQ4088.B33 76-531562

Ballerini, Luigi, 1940-
Scrittura visuale in Italia. 1912-1972. Catalogo do Luigi Ballerini. Introduzione di Aldo Passoni. Galleria civica d'arte moderna, Torino, 27 settembre-28 ottobre 1973. Torino, Galeria civica d'arte moderna, [1973]
120 p. illus., plates. 30 cm. It 74-Jan
Bibliography: p. [63]-78.
1. Visual poetry, Italian—Exhibitions. I. Turin. Galleria d'arte moderna. II. Title.
PQ4220.V57B3 76-532628

Ballerini, Luigi, 1940- ed.
see Finch College, New York. Museum of Art. Contemporary Study Wing. Italian visual poetry, 1912-1972. [New York, 1973]

Ballerini, Luigi, 1940-
see Logical space. New York, Out of London Press, 1975.

Ballerini, Michel, 1947-
Le roman de montagne en France. [Paris] Arthaud [1973]
325 p. illus. 21 cm. (Sempervivum, 53) 36.00F F***
Bibliography: p. 251-[289]
1. French fiction—History and criticism. 2. Mountains in literature. I. Title.
PQ637.M6B3 843'.03 73-176837
MARC

Ballero, Felice
see La Spiga 1974 [i.e. millenovecentosettantaquattro] Firenze: Edizioni Città di vita, [1974]

Ballero, Mireille
see Le Corfec, Jean Michel. Le petrole. [Paris] Éditions des Deux coqs d'or [1973]

Ballero, Mireille, joint author
see Le Corfec, Jean Michel. Le sens de l'histoire. Bruxelles: H. Fagne, 1973.

Ballero, Mireille, joint author
see Sauvageot, Claude, 1935- Inde. Paris : A. Michel, 1974.

Ballerstedt, Eika.
see Soziologischer Almanach ... Frankfurt, Herder & Herder, c1975.

Ballerstedt, Gustav.
Wahlordnung zum Bayerischen Personalvertretungsgesetz. Für die Praxis erläutert von Gustav Ballerstedt und Helmut Engelhard. [Neuwied] H. Luchterhand [1959]
xiv, 142 p. 21 cm.
"Abkürzungsverzeichnis" (bibliographical) : p. xi-xiv.
1. Bavaria—Officials and employees. 2. Works councils—Bavaria. I. Engelhard, Helmut, joint author. II. Bavaria. Laws, statutes, etc. Wahlordnung zum Bayerischen Personalvertretungsgesetz. 1959. III. Title.
61-24658

Ballerstedt, Gustav.
Wahlordnung zum bayerischen Personalvertretungsgesetz /f. d. Praxis erl. von Gustav Ballerstedt, Helmut Engelhardt, Hans Werner Schleicher. — 3., neu bearb. u. erw. Aufl. — Neuwied ; Berlin : Luchterhand, 1974.
xvi, 152 p. ; 21 cm. GFR 74-A
Includes the text of the Wahlordnung zum bayerischen Personalvertretunsgesetz and the Bayerisches Personalvertretungsgesetz.
Includes bibliographical references and index.
ISBN 3-472-12307-9 : DM16.80
1. Bavaria—Officials and employees. 2. Works councils—Bavaria. I. Englehard, Helmut, joint author. II. Schleicher, Hans Werner, joint author. III. Bavaria. Laws, statutes, etc. Wahlordnung zum bayerischen Personalvertretungsgesetz. 1974. IV. Bavaria. Laws, statutes, etc. Personal- vertretungsgesetz. 1974. V. Title.
75-551570

Ballerstedt, Gustav
see Engelhard, Helmut. Personalvertretungsgesetz für das Land Neidersachsen... 3., vollständig neubearb. Aufl. [Neuwied] Luchterhand [1973]

Ballerstedt, Kurt.
In memoriam Schmidt-Rimpler : Reden gehalten am 26. November 1975 bei d. Gedenkfeier d. Rechts- u. Staatswiss. Fak. d. Rhein. Friedrich-Wilhelms-Univ. Bonn / von Kurt Ballerstedt u. Walter Gerhardt. — Bonn : Hanstein, 1976.
47 p. : 1 ill. ; 21 cm. — (Alma mater, Beiträge zur Geschichte der Universität Bonn ; 38) GFR77-A
Includes bibliographical references.
ISBN 3-7756-9134-0
1. Schmidt-Rimpler, Walter, 1885-1975. 2. Lawyers—Germany, West—Biography. I. Schmidt-Rimpler, Walter, 1885-1975. II. Gerhardt, Walter, 1934- III. Title. IV. Series.
340'.092'4 77-466345
77 MARC

Ballerstedt, Kurt
see Beiträge zum Zivil- und Wirtschaftsrecht ... Berlin : Duncker und Humblot, 1975.

Ballerstedt, Kurt, ed.
see Festschrift für Ernst Gessler. Zum 65. Geburtstag am 5. März 1970. München, F. Franz [1971]

Ballesio, Roland.
Étude stratigraphique du Pliocène rhodanien / par Roland Ballesio. — Lyon : Département des sciences de la terre de l'Université Claude Bernard, 1972 [i.e. 1973]
333 p. : ill. ; 30 cm. — (Documents des Laboratoires de géologie de la Faculté des sciences de Lyon ; no 53) F74-1019
Bibliography: p. 299-315.
Includes index.
Summaries in English, German, and Russian.
1. Geology, Stratigraphic—Pliocene. 2. Geology—Rhone Valley. I. Title. II. Series: Lyons. Université. Département des sciences de la terre. Documents ; no 53.
QE1.L98 no. 53 550'.8 s 75-506751
[QE695] 75 MARC

Ballesta, Juan Cano
see Cano Ballesta, Juan.

Ballesta Martínez, Francisca.
Cromosomopatías autosómicas, por Francisca Ballesta Martínez [y] Antonio Baldellou Vázquez. [1. ed.] Barcelona, Editorial Espaxs, 1971.
167 p. illus. 23 cm. (Monografías de la Cátedra de Pediatría de Barcelona, 2) Sp***
Bibliography: p. [147]-164.
1. Chromosome abnormalities. I. Baldellou Vázquez, Antonio, joint author. II. Title. III. Series: Barcelona. Universidad. Cátedra de Pediatría. Monografías, 2.
[DNLM: Chromosome Abnormalities. W1 MO5418 v. 2 1971]
[RB155.B22] 73-595410
Shared Cataloging with DNLM

Ballesté, Sol López-Gómez
see
López-Gómez Ballesté, Sol.

Ballester, Alexandre.
Dins un gruix de vellut, facem comèdia. Farsa en tres actes. Palma de Mallorca, Editorial Moll, 1973.
112 p. 16 cm. (Biblioteca Les Illes d'or, 105) 50 ptas Sp***
I. Title.
PC3942.12.A42D5 1973 73-336247
ISBN 84-273-0337-8

Ballester, Antonio.
Análisis automático y continuo de las características físicas, químicas y biológicas del mar / por Antonio Ballester ... [et al.]. — Madrid : Consejo Superior de Investigaciones Científicas, 1972.
71 p. : ill. ; 24 cm. — (Publicaciones técnicas - Patronato de Investigación Científica y Técnica Juan de la Cierva ; 1) Sp***
Caption title.
On cover: Suplemento Investigación pesquera.
Bibliography: p. 71.
Summary in English.
1. Oceanography—Automation. 2. Oceanographic instruments. I. Investigación pesquera. II. Title. III. Series: Spain. Consejo Superior de Investigaciones Científicas. Patronato Juan de la Cierva Codorniú. Publicaciones técnicas - Patronato de Investigación Científica y Técnica Juan de la Cierva ; 1.
GC41.B34 75-568942

Ballester, Carlos.
Poemas de Sitges, primer libro, 1965 a 1971. [Madrid, 1972]
250 p. plate. 22 cm. Sp***
1. Sitges, Spain — Description — Poetry. 2. Poetry of places — Spain—Sitges. I. Title.
PQ6603.A45P6 73-318359

Ballester, César.
Misterio, magía y ocultismo / [texto, César Ballester]. — Barcelona : Salvat, c1973, 1975 printing.
143 p. : ill. ; 20 cm. — (Biblioteca Salvat de grandes temas ; 82) Sp***
Bibliography: p. [142]
ISBN 8434574411
1. Occult sciences. 2. Psychical research. I. Title.
BF1415.B33 75-512816
75 MARC

Ballester, César Sentías.
see Sentías Ballester, César.

Ballester, Gonzalo Torrente
see Torrente Ballester, Gonzalo.

Ballester, José
see
Ballester Nicolás, José.

Ballester, José María.
La reforma cultural en Francia : el Ministerio de Asuntos Culturales / José María Ballester y Jorge Demerson. — Madrid : Editora Nacional, 1974, c1975.
158 p. ; 22 cm. — (Mundos abiertos) Sp***
ISBN 8427612206 : 125ptas
1. France. Ministère d'État chargé des affaires culturelles. 2. Arts—France—Management. I. Demerson, Georges, joint author. II. Title.
NX770.F7B35 75-512911
75 MARC

Ballester, Juan Morey
see
Morey Ballester, Juan.

Ballester, Lorenzo Campins y
see Campins y Ballester, Lorenzo, ca. 1732-1785.

Ballester, Luis Alberto.
Las oscuras hazañas : cuentos / Luis Alberto Ballester. — [Buenos Aires] : Ediciones Buenos Aires Secreto, [1973]
111 p. ; 20 cm.
CONTENTS: Oscuridad resplandeciente.—Ciclos.—La cena.—Trenes.—Un suceso común.—Avalón.—Los espejos velados.—En el colectivo 38.—El comienzo de la Edad de Oro.—Tiempo de balada.—El invernadero.—La ciudad en la ciudad, el tiempo en el tiempo.—Verano.—La ventana.
I. Title.
PQ7798.12.A5O7 863 77-480832
77 MARC

Ballester, Luis Alberto.
Techos de Buenos Aires. Buenos Aires, Ediciones Buenos Aires Secreto [1972]
88 p. illus.
I. Title.
InU NUC74-132089

Ballester, Luis García
see García Ballester, Luis.

Ballester, Pedro
see
Ballester y Pons, Pedro.

Ballester, Rosa.
Colección historicomédica de la Facultad de Medicina de Valencia / [por] Rosa Ballester, Francesc Bujosa, Guillermo Olagüe. — Valencia : Cátedra e Instituto de Historia de la Medicina, [etc.], 1976.
54 p. : ill. ; 21 cm. — (Cuadernos valencianos de historia de la medicina y de la ciencia ; 18 : Serie A, Monografías) Sp77-Jan
Includes bibliographical references.
ISBN 8460005119
1. Medicine—Spain—Valencia—History—Exhibitions. 2. Valencia (City). Universidad. Facultad de Medicina. I. Bujosa i Homar, Francesc, joint author. II. Olagüe de Ros, Guillermo, joint author. III. Title. IV. Series.
R557.V3B34 77-480061
77 MARC

Ballester, Santiago Rodríguez
see Rodríguez Ballester, Santiago.

Ballester Escalas, Rafael.
El Alcázar de Toledo / Rafael Ballester Escalas. — 1. ed. — Barcelona : Editorial Bruguera, 1975.
187 p. ; 18 cm. — (La Guerra civil española ; 2) (Libro amigo ; 298) Sp***
Bibliography: p. 7-8.
ISBN 8402041418 : 60ptas
1. Toledo, Spain. Alcázar—Siege, 1936. 2. Moscardó Ituarte, José, 1878- I. Title.
DP269.2.A4B3 946'.43 75-504188
75 MARC

Ballester Escalas, Rafael.
La batalla del Ebro / Rafael Ballester Escalas. — Barcelona : Editorial Bruguera, 1974.
253 p. ; 18 cm. — (La Guerra civil española ; 1) (Libro amigo ; 285) Sp***
Includes bibliographical references.
ISBN 84-02-03795-X : 60ptas
1. Ebro River, Battle of the, 1938. I. Title.
DP269.2.E27B34 946.08'1 74-355405

Ballester Escalas, Rafael.
El fabuloso mundo romano. [1. ed. Barcelona, Ediciones AFHA, 1973]
74 p. illus. 31 cm. (Selecciones Auriga) Sp***
ISBN 84-201-0377-2
1. Rome—History—Juvenile literature. I. Title.
DG209.B318 937 75-579535

Ballester Escalas, Rafael.
Historia de los Papas. Rafael Ballester ... Barcelona, etc., Bruguera [1972]
222 p., 1 l. 18 cm. (Colección Sí no, no. 18) 30ptas Sp 73-Feb
First ed.
1. Papacy—History. I. Title.
BX955.2.B27 74-335117

Ballester Escalas, Rafael.
El Imperio Romano [por] Rafael Ballester. [1. ed.] Barcelona, Bruguera [1973]
219 p. 18 cm. (Colección Sí no, no. 30) 30ptas Sp***
Bibliography: p. 215-[216]
1. Rome—History. I. Title.
DG209.B32 73-321890
ISBN 84-02-02630-3

Ballester Escalas, Rafael.
Simón Bolívar. R. Crossbow [Seud.] Barcelona, etc., Bruguera [1973]
155 p., 2 l. 11 cm. (En 25000 palabras, 34) 10ptas Sp 74-Mar
First ed.
1. Bolívar, Simon, 1783-1830. 2. Latin America—History—Wars of Independence, 1806-1830.
F2235.3.B232 980'.02'0924 74-337349
ISBN 84-02-02805-5 [B]

Ballester Escalas, Rafael, joint author
see Pericot García, Luis, 1899-
Historia de Roma. Barcelona, Montaner y Simón, 1963.

Ballester Escalas, Rafael, joint author
see Pericot Garcia, Luis, 1899- Historia de Roma. 2. ed. Barcelona, Mantaner y Simón [c1970]

Ballester Escalas, Rafael
see Shakespeare, William, 1546-1616.
Coriolano. Barcelona, Editorial Lumen, 1973.

Ballester Nicolás, José.
... Alma y cuerpo de una ciudad, guía de Murcia. Murcia, Imp. suc. de Nogués, 1944.
210 p., 3 l. plates, fold. map. 14 cm.
1. Murcia, Spain (City)—Description—Guide-books. I. Title.
DP402.M9B3 914.6'773 47-24040
rev

Ballester Nicolás, José.
Amanecer de la prensa periódica en Murcia. Panorama de una pequeña ciudad. [Murcia] Academia de Alfonso X El Sabio, 1971.
172 p., 1 l. 22 cm. Sp 71-Dec
1. Press — Murcia, Spain (City) — History. 2. Murcia, Spain (City)—History. I. Title.
PN5319.M82B3 73-367228
rev

Ballester Nicolás, José.
Guía de Murcia. 1. ed. Madrid, Patronato Nacional del Turismo, 1930.
143 p. illus., maps. 17 cm. (Guías "España")
Fold. col. map mounted on lining-paper.
"Bibliografía": p. [132]-135.
1. Murcia, Spain (City)—Description—Guide-books. I. Series.
DP402.M9B35 914.6'773 48-40487
rev

Ballester Nicolás, José.
Murcia en dos tiempos. Dos conferencias] por José Ballester y Francisco Alemán Sainz. [Murcia] Cátedra "Saavedra Fajardo" Universidad de Murcia, 1954.
73 p. illus. 22 cm.
CONTENTS: Mi Murcia entre dos siglos, por J. Ballester.—Semblante y talante de Murcia, por F. Alemán Sainz.
1. Murcia, Spain (City) I. Alemán Sainz, Francisco.
DP402.M9B38 57-18093 ‡
rev

Ballester Nicolás, José.
La Virgen de la Fuensanta y su Santuario del monte. Murcia, Ayuntamiento, 1972.
144 p., 1 l., plates. 25 cm. Sp 73-Apr
At head of title: José Ballester.
Includes bibliographical references.
1. Santuario de Nuestra Señora de la Fuensanta, Murcia, Spain. I. Title.
BT660.F7B34 73-362213

Ballester Nicolás, José.
see Homenaje a José Ballester. Murcia, [s.n.] 1972.

Ballester Ros, Ignacio
see España es así: hechos y cifras. [Madrid, 1965]

Ballester Viu, Francisco de Borja.
Luz en la monotonía. [Bilboa, Ed. Vizcaina, 1968-
v.
I. Title.
NcU NUC74-145602

Ballester y Peris, Eduardo.
De Valencia a Tokio. Valencia [Artes Gráf. Soler] 1973.
104 p. 22 cm. Sp 74
1. Japan—Description and travel—1945- I. Title.
DS811.B26 915.2'04'4 74-347076
ISBN 84-400-6729-1

Ballester y Pons, Pedro.
De re cibaria : cocina, pastelería, repostería menorquinas / Pedro Ballester. — 3. ed. / con un prólogo de Juan Hernández Mora. — Barcelona : Sintes, 1973.
xvii, 215 p., [6] leaves of plates : ill. ; 21 cm. Sp 74-Dec
Bibliography: p. [4]-6.
ISBN 84-302-0492-X
1. Cookery, Spanish. I. Title.
TX723.5.S7B33 1973 75-542785

Ballestero, Enrique.
El balance : una introducción a las finanzas / Enrique Ballestero. — Madrid : Alianza, [1974]
159 p. ; 20 cm. — (Alianza universidad ; 91) Sp***
Includes index.
ISBN 84-206-2091-2
1. Financial statements. 2. Accounting. I. Title.
HF5681.B2B27 657'.3 75-563870

Ballestero, Enrique.
Contabilidad agraria. Madrid, Mundi-Prensa, 1969.
261 p.
1. Agriculture. Accounting. I. Title.
DNAL NUC73-2351

Ballestero, Enrique.
Contabilidad agraria. 2. ed. rev. y ampl. Madrid, Mundi-Prensa, 1973.
294 p. 22 cm. (Biblioteca agropecuaria Mundi-Prensa) 340ptas Sp 73-Dec
1. Agriculture—Accounting. I. Title.
S567.B225 1973 74-344754
ISBN 84-7114-037-3

Ballestero, Enrique.
Critica del Camino. [Madrid, Talleres Gráficos Montaña, 1972]
217 p. 19 cm. (Un ensayo sobre una obra capital de la literatura ascetica contemporanea)
Bibliographical footnotes.
1. Escrivá, José María. Comino. I. Title.
MChB NUC74-132110

Ballestero, Enrique.
La nueva contabilidad / Enrique Ballestero. — Madrid : Alianza Editorial, 1975.
147 p. : ill. ; 20 cm. — (Alianza universidad : 116) Sp***
Bibliography: p. [143]-144.
Includes index.
ISBN 8420621161
1. Accounting. I. Title.
HF5651.B36 75-508813
75 MARC

Ballestero, Enrique.
Principios de economía de la empresa. [Madrid] Alianza Editorial (1971)
480 p. 20 cm. (Alianza universidad) 140ptas Sp 71-July/Aug/Sept
Bibliography: p. 469-472.
1. Industrial management. 2. Business. I. Title.
HD37.S66B33 73-350857
NNC

Ballestero, Enrique.
Principios de economía de la empresa. [2. ed. Madrid] Alianza Editorial (1973)
492 p., illus. 20 cm. (Alianza universidad, 4) 200ptas Sp 73-Nov
Bibliography: p. 479-483.
1. Industrial management. 2. Business. I. Title.
HD37.S66B33 1973 74-304960
ISBN 84-206-2004-1

Ballestero, Luis-Martin
see Martín-Ballestero y Costea, Luis.

Ballestero, Manuel.
Crítica y marginales; compromiso y trascendencia del símbolo literario. [1. ed. Barcelona] Barral Editores, 1974.
132 p. 20 cm. (Breve biblioteca de respuesta) (Series de respuesta, 104) Sp***
Includes bibliographical references.
1. Literature—Addresses, essays, lectures. I. Title.
PN37.B28 74-334593
ISBN 84-211-0304-0

Ballestero, Manuel.
Marx; o, La crítica como fundamento. Madrid, Editorial Ciencia Nueva [1967]
230 p. 20 cm. (Colección "Los complementarios," de ensayistas españoles contemporáneos)
Includes bibliographical references.
CONTENTS: Elementos criticos de la filosofía de la existencia.—Marx; o, La crítica como fundamento.
1. Marx, Karl, 1818-1883. 2. Criticism (Philosophy) 3. Sartre, Jean Paul, 1905- I. Title. II. Title: La crítica como fundamento.
B3305.M74B22 74-203841

Ballestero y Costea, Luis Martín-
see Martín-Ballestero y Costea, Luis.

Ballesteros, Alberto Montoro-
see
Montoro-Ballesteros, Alberto, 1941-

Ballesteros, Antonio Gullón
see Gullón Ballesteros, Antonio.

Ballesteros, Antonio Martínez
see Martínez Ballesteros, Antonio.

Ballesteros, David.
Arturo Uslar Pietri: renovador de la conciencia nacional. [Los Angeles] 1968.
270 l.
Thesis—University of Southern California.
Microfilm. Ann Arbor, Michigan, University Microfilms, 1969.
1. Uslar Pietri, Arturo, 1906-
InU NUC73-47481

Ballesteros, Emilio Zapatero
see Zapatero Ballesteros, Emilio.

Ballesteros, Faustino Zapatero
see
Zapatero Ballesteros, Faustino.

Ballesteros, Francisco de Ramón y
see Ramón y Ballesteros, Francisco de.

Ballesteros, Francisco Fernández
see
Fernández Ballesteros, Francisco.

Ballesteros, Héctor Sainz
see Sainz Ballesteros, Héctor.

Ballesteros, Iris Lérou
see Lérou Ballesteros, Iris.

Ballesteros, Jesús.
La filosofía jurídica de Giuseppe Capograssi. Con un prólogo de José Corts Grau. Roma, 1973.
xix, 216 p. 25 cm. (Cuadernos del Instituto Jurídico Español, 23) Sp***
Includes bibliographical references.
1. Capograssi, Giuseppe, 1889-1956. 2. Law—Philosophy. I. Title. II. Series: Instituto Jurídico Español. Cuadernos, 23.
74-301946
ISBN 84-00-03903-3

Ballesteros, Jesús M Carrillo
see
Carrillo Ballesteros, Jesús M

Ballesteros, Jorge Bernales
see
Bernales Ballesteros, Jorge.

Ballesteros, Jorge Santos
see Santos Ballesteros, Jorge.

Ballesteros, José Antonio García
see
García Ballesteros, José Antonio.

Ballesteros, José Ramón, 1901–
Origen y evolución del charro mexicano. Bibliografía de Manuel Porrúa. México, Librería de M. Porrúa [1972]
206 p. illus. 20 cm. (Biblioteca mexicana, 43) LACAP 78-0165
Bibliography: p. [185]-206.
1. Horses—Mexico. 2. Horsemen—Mexico. 3. Horsemanship. 4. Mexico—Social life and customs. I. Title.
SF284.M6B34 73-328166

Ballesteros, Juan de Tapia y
see Tapia y Ballesteros, Juan de.

Ballesteros, Laura Esther Garza
see Garza Ballesteros, Laura Esther.

Ballesteros, Miguel
see
Ballesteros Viana, Miguel, 1866-1910.

Ballesteros, Octavio A 1936-
The effectiveness of public school education for Mexican-American students as perceived by principals of elementary schools of predominantly Mexican-American enrollment / by Octavio A. Ballesteros. — San Francisco : R and E Research Associates, 1976.
x, 97 p. ; 28 cm.
Originally presented as the author's thesis, East Texas State University.
Bibliography: p. 71-77.
ISBN 0-88247-372-7
1. Mexican Americans—Education—United States. 2. Public schools—United States. I. Title: The effectiveness of public school education for Mexican-American students ...
LC2682.B34 1976 371.9'7'6872 75-36575
76 MARC

Ballesteros, Paulino Algo, 1923-
External capital in Puerto Rico's industrial development. [n.p.] 1959.
viii, 242 l.
Thesis—University of Illinois.
Bibliography: leaves 228-242.
Photocopy of typescript. Ann Arbor, Mich., Xerox University Microfilms, 1974. 21 cm.
1. Investments, American—Puerto Rico. 2. Economic assistance, American—Puerto Rico. 3. Puerto Rico—Econ. condit. I. Title.
NBNC NUC76-22243

Ballesteros, Rafael, 1938–
Turpa. Carboneras de Guadazaón (Cuenca) [Madrid, Gráf. Do-Mo, 1972]
41 p., 3 l. 18 cm. (El Toro de barro, 25) Sp 73-Mar
Poems.
I. Title.
PQ6652.A48T8 73-334630

Ballesteros, Rafael, 1938-
see [Colección de poemas y cuentos] Montevideo [1066]

Ballesteros de Gaibrois, Mercedes.
El personal / Mercedes Ballesteros. — 1. ed. — Barcelona : Ediciones Destino, 1975.
222 p. ; 19 cm. — (Colección Ancora y delfín ; v. 476) Sp***
ISBN 8423309266
I. Title.
PQ6603.A473P44 863'.6'2 76-469728
76 MARC

Ballesteros Gaibrois, Manuel.
Escritores de Indias. Selección, estudio y notas por el dr. Manuel Ballesteros. 4. ed. illustrada. Zaragoza, Editorial Ebro [1969]
2 v. illus. 18 cm. (Biblioteca clasica "Ebro". Clasicos españoles. [Ser. prosa. 3, 10])
Bibliography: v. 1, p. [15]-16; v. 2, p [11]-12.
NcGU NUC73-47936

Ballesteros Gaibrois, Manuel.
España desde el siglo XV hasta nuestros dias. 3. ed. Madrid, Ediciones La Ballesta, 1967.
261 p. illus.
1. Spain—Hist.
MiU NUC73-121145

Ballesteros Gaibrois, Manuel.
Isabel de Castilla, Reina Católica de España. 2. ed. Madrid, Editora Nacional, 1970.
281 p., 1 l., plates. 24 cm. (Mundo cientifico. Serie historia) 250ptas Sp 71-Jan
"Apéndice documental": p. [203]-278.
Bibliography: p. 193-202.
1. Isabel I, la Católica, Queen of Spain, 1451-1504. I. Title.
DP163.B24 1970 73-337259

Ballesteros Gaibrois, Manuel.
Vida y obra de Fray Bernardino de Sahagún. León, Institución "Fray Bernardino de Sahagún" [1973]
139 p. illus., plates (part col.) 24 cm. Sp***
Bibliography: p. 127-139.
1. Sahagún, Bernardino de, d. 1590. I. Title.
F1231.S33B34 907'.202'4 [B] 74-308056
ISBN 84-00-03907-6

Ballesteros Gaibrois, Manuel, joint author.
see Gómez Acevedo, Labor. Culturas indígenas de Puerto Rico. 1. ed. Madrid, Samarán, 1975.

Ballesteros Gallardo, Angel, 1940–
No sabe la muerte que se llama muerte / Angel Ballesteros Gallardo. — ₍Algeciras? : s. n., 1974?₎
58 p. ; 17 cm. — (Separatas Bahía de Algeciras : 7) Sp***
Poems.
60ptas
I. Title.
PQ6652.A42N6 75-585800

Ballesteros Jaime, Lucio.
Poemas de infancia. Valencia ₍Sucesor de Vives Mora. Artes Gráf.₎ 1972.
88 p. 20 cm. Sp 72–July
1. Children—Poetry. I. Title.
PQ6652.A44P57 72–374259

Ballesteros Jaime, Lucio.
Los sueños y otros poemas. Valencia ₍Suc. de Vives Mora, Gráf.₎ 1969.
17 l. 20 cm. Sp 71–Feb
I. Title.
PQ6652.A44S8 72–374260

Ballesteros Jaime, Lucio.
Villancicos.
Valencia.
v. 18 cm. annual.
1. Christmas—Poetry. I. Title.
PQ6652.A44V5 72–626295

Ballesteros Llopart, Jesús
see
Ballesteros, Jesús.

Ballesteros López, Doris.
Biblioteca Nacional de Colombia : bibliografía sobre la Biblioteca Nacional / por Doris Ballesteros López. — Bogotá : ₍s.n.₎, 1975.
vii, 38 leaves ; 28 cm.
Thesis (licenciatura en bibliotecología y archivística)—Universidad Social Católica de La Salle, Bogotá.
1. Bogotá. Biblioteca Nacional—Bibliography. I. Title: Bibliografía sobre la Biblioteca Nacional.
Z774.B72B28 016.05 76-484914
76 MARC

Ballesteros R., Leopoldo
see Rodriguez Estrada, Mauro. La cultura mixe... [1. ed.] Mexico, Editorial Jus [1974]

Ballesteros Viana, Miguel, 1866–1910.
Historia de Utiel. Prólogo del Iltmo. Sr. Dr. D. José Martínez Ortiz. Nueva ed. Utiel, 1973.
803 p. illus. 23 cm. 500ptas Sp***
1. Utiel, Spain—History. I. Title.
DP402.U8B34 1973 914.6'763 74–312600
ISBN 84-500-5814-7
Includes bibliographical references.

Ballesteros y Beretta, Antonio, 1880-
see Santander, Spain (Province). Diputación Provincial. La marina cántabra... Santander, 1968.

Ballestrasse, Flavio, comp.
Studi sul Settecento medico. Pisa, Giardini, 1970.
99 p. 24 cm. (Scientia veterum, 153) It***
CONTENTS: Contro i dommatici e i galenisti, di G. Gazola.—Intorno all'aria e ai vermiccioli quali cause delle pestilenze.—Testi medici della Biblioteca Vaticana.
1. Medicine—Italy—History. 2. Medicine—15th-18th centuries. I. Gazola, Giuseppe. Contro i dommatici e i Galenisti. II. Corte, Bartolomeo. Intorno all'aria e ai vermiccioli quali cause delle pestilenze. III. Title. IV. Series.
R131.A1S27 no. 153 73–301645
[R517]

Ballestrasse, Flavio, ed.
see ₍Marinis, Tammaro de₎ 1878-1969. Le antiche opere di medicina manoscritte e stampate della raccolta "Vittorio Putti." Pisa, Giardini, 1969.

Ballestrasse, Flavio, joint author
see Oberti, Andrea. Evoluzione storica della chirurgia plastica, dagli albori al XX secolo ... Montecatini Terme, Tip. editrice Pierini, 1965.

Ballestrem, Agnes, joint author
see Derveaux-Van-Ussel, Ghislaine. Le retable malinois de l'eglise d'Odeby. Bruxelles Musées royaux d'art et d'histoire, 1973.

Ballestrem, Ferdinand, Graf von.
Standortwahl von Unternehmen und Industriestandortpolitik; ein empirischer Beitrag zur Beurteilung regionalpolitischer Instrumente. Berlin, Duncker & Humblot ₍1974₎
158 p. 24 cm. (Finanzwissenschaftliche Forschungsarbeiten, n. F., Heft 44) GFR***
Bibliography: p. ₍148₎-158.
1. Industries, Location of. 2. Regional planning. I. Title.
HD58.B24 74–180119
ISBN 3-428-030097-4 MARC

Ballestrero, Bianca
see Da immagine a piano... Firenze, Teorema, 1973.

Ballestrero, Maria Vittoria Gentili
see
Gentili Ballestrero, Maria Vittoria.

Ballet, Guy.
Dilbeek in oude prentkaarten. Dilbeek en cartes postales anciennes, door Guy Ballet & Anna Abeels. Zaltbommel, Europese Bibliotheek, 1973.
₍80₎ p. illus. 15 x 21 cm. Ne***
1. Dilbeek, Belgium—Description—Views. I. Abeels, Anna, joint author. II. Title. III. Title: Dilbeek en cartes postales anciennes.
DH811.D49B34 73–342598

Ballet, René.
Dérive; roman. ₍Paris₎ Calmann-Levy ₍1972₎
251 p. 21 cm. 20.50F F***
I. Title.
PQ2662.A4D4 72–365518

Ballet, René
see Vailland, Roger. Roger Vailland... Paris, P. Seghers, 1973.

Ballet and dance. London, Macdonald and Co., 1973.
₍3₎, 35 p. col. illus. 20 cm. (Macdonald first library, 54) £0.40
GB 73–00584
Includes index.
1. Dancing—Juvenile literature. 2. Ballet—Juvenile literature.
GV1599.B34 793.3 73–169094
ISBN 0-356-04278-2 MARC

Ballet and modern dance; with contributions by leading choreographers, dancers and critics. London, Octopus Books, 1974.
144 p. illus. (some col.), ports. 29 cm. £1.95 GB 74-13116
1. Ballet — Addresses, essays, lectures. 2. Modern dance — Addresses, essays, lectures.
GV1787.B245 792.8'2 74–179852
ISBN 0-7064-0322-3 MARC

Ballet collection ₍solos for girls, advanced technique, Notated by Ann Hutchinson₎ New York, Dance Notation Bureau ₍1961-63₎
₍7₎ l. 28 cm.
1. Dance notation–Scores. 2. Ballets–Excerpts–Dance Scores. I. Hutchinson, Ann.
OU NUC74-19040

Le Ballet de cour en France, 1581-1671. Préf. de M. P. de Mirimonde. Commentaires du catalogue de M. F. Christout. Aix en Provence, Pavillon de Vendôme, 1971.
₍48₎ p. illus. 19 cm. F***
At head of title: Une des origines du spectacle contemporain.
Catalog of an exhibition held in 1971 at the Pavillon de Vendôme, Aix-en-Provence.
1. Ballet—Exhibitions. I. Christout, Marie Françoise. II. Pavillon de Vendôme.
ML141.A5P3 792.8'0944 73–198133

Le Ballet en langage forésien, 1605 : étude linguistique, traduction, notes et lexique / par Simone Escoffier ; étude littéraire par Claude Longeon. — Saint-Étienne : Centre d'études foréziennes, 1974.
107 p. ; 24 cm. — (Inventaires et documents - Centre d'études foréziennes ; 4) F***
Poem.
Bibliography: p. ₍39₎-41.
ISBN 2-85145-025-5 : 29.00F
I. Escoffier, Simone. II. Longeon, Claude, 1941- III. Series: Centre d'études foréziennes. Inventaires et documents ; 4.
PQ1711.B34 1974 841'.4 75-515886
75 MARC

The Ballet exhibition 1959, held at the Army and Navy stores, Westminster, London, July 30th to August 21st. Exhibition designed by Tom Lingwood. ₍London, 1959₎
32 p. illus., ports. 22 cm.
Bibliography, p. 29-31.
1. Ballet–Exhibitions–Gt. Br.–London, 1959. I. Lingwood, Tom. II. Army and Navy Stores, ltd.
NN NUC76-31469

Ballet Nacional de Cuba
see Cuba en el ballet. set. 1970-
[La Habana]

El Ballet Nacional de Cuba en Europa; criticas. ₍Havana₎ 1969.
72 p. 20 cm.
1. Cuba. Ballet Nacional.
CtY NUC73-122038

Ballet reading materials. New York, Dance Notation Bureau, c1970.
3 l. 28 cm.
1. Dance notation–Scores. 2. Ballet–Studies and exercises. I. Dance Notation Bureau.
OU NUC74-23253

Ballet Society.
The Ballet Society. v. 1–
1946/47–
₍New York₎
v. illus. 25 cm.
1. Ballet Society.
ML28.N5B28 792.8'06'27471 74–643269
ISSN 0094-355X MARC-S

Ballet Theatre, New York.
For works by this body issued under its later name see
American Ballet Theatre.

Ballet Theatre Foundation.
see American Ballet Theatre ... ₍New York₎ Ballet Theatre Foundation, c1976.

Ein Ballett in Deutschland. Die Compagnie d. Dt. Oper a. Rh. Mit Beitr. von Klaus Geitel u. Horst Koegler sowie e. Vorw. von Grischa Barfuss. (Schwarzweissfotos: Hermann Weisweiler. Farbfotos: Rudolf Einke.) (Düsseldorf, Wien, Econ-Verl., 1971.)
55 p., 32 l. of illus. 30 cm. DM30.00 GDB 71–A
1. Deutsche Oper am Rhein. Ballett. I. Geitel, Klaus.
GV1786.D48B34 74–319995
ISBN 3-430-11156-0

Balletta, Francesco.
Il Banco di Napoli e le rimesse degli emigrati (1914–1925) / Francesco Balletta. — Napoli : Institut international d'histoire de la banque, 1972.
211 p., ₍4₎ leaves of plates : ill. ; 25 cm. — (Gens d'affaires, banques, monnaies, finances ; 2) It***
Bibliography: p. 185–206.
Includes index.
1. Emigrant remittances—Italy—History. 2. Banco di Napoli—History. I. Title.
HG3951.B34 75–530101

Balletti, Andrea.
Le Quattro Castella : memoria storica / Andrea Balletti. — Ristampa anastatica. — ₍Bologna₎ : A. Forni, ₍1973₎
vi, 94 p., ₍8₎ leaves of plates : ill. ; 24 cm. It 75–Feb
"Ristampa anastatica dell'edizione di Reggio Emilia, 1937."
1. Quattro Castella, Italy.
DG975.Q37B34 1973 75–535132

Balletto, Cesare.
Saggio di flora micologica analitica. Con particolare riguardo per la flora ligustica. Note sulla biologia e sulla sistematica discussione di specie rare o critiche. Prefazione di Henri Romagnesi. Genova, 1972.
526 p. 20 cm. It 72–Sept
On spine: Flora micologica analitica.
On cover: Funghi superiori.
Bibliography: p. 36–46.
1. Fungi. 2. Fungi—Liguria. I. Title. II. Title: Flora micologica analitica.
QK603.B25 72–374549

Balletto, Giovanni, 1905–1972.
Kilimanjaro, montagna dello splendore. Dai ricordi di un medico alpinista. Bologna, Tamari, 1974.
243 p. plates, port. 19 cm. It 74–Aug
L3000
1. Balletto, Giovanni. 2. Physicians — Correspondence, reminiscences, etc. 3. Africa, East — Description and travel — 1951– I. Title.
R520.B34A34 75–551284

Balletto, Laura.
Genova, Mediterraneo, Mar nero (Secc. XII-XV) / Laura Balletto. — Genova : Civico istituto colombiano, 1976.
293 p. ; 25 cm. — (Studi e testi - Civico istituto colombiano ; 1. Serie storica) It***
Italian or Latin.
Includes bibliographical references.
1. Genoa—History—To 1339. 2. Genoa—History—1339-1528. 3. Genoa—Relations (general) with the Mediterranean region. 4. Mediterranean region—Relations (general) with Genoa. 5. Genoa—Relations (general) with the Black Sea region. 6. Black Sea region—Relations (general) with Genoa. 7. Feodosia, Russia—History. I. Title. II. Series: Genoa. Civico istituto colombiano. Stuti e testi - Civico istituto colombiano ; 1.
DG637.4.B34 77-470272
77 MARC

Balletto, Laura, ed.
see Savona. Laws, statutes, etc. Statuta antiquissima Saone. Bordighera, Istituto internazionale di studi liguri-Museo Bicknell, 1971.

Balletto, Maria Luisa, ed.
see Genoa (Republic) Navi e navigazione a Genova nel Quattrocento. Genova, 1973.

Ballevāra, Śrīdhara
see
Sagar, 1946-

Ballew, Gary I
Quantitative geologic analysis of multiband photography from the Mono Craters area, California, by Gary I. Ballew. Stanford, Calif., Remote Sensing Laboratory, Stanford University, 1969.
iv, 56 l. illus. 28 cm. (Stanford RSL technical report, 69-2)
Cover title.
Bibliography: leaves 32-33.
1. Remote sensing systems. 2. Geology—Calif. Mono Craters area. 3. Aerial photography in geology. I. Title.
CSt NUC74-123552

Ballew, Hunter.
Teaching children mathematics. Columbus, Ohio, Merrill [1973]
xvi, 479 p. illus. 24 cm.
Includes bibliographies.
1. Mathematics—Study and teaching (Elementary) I. Title.
QA135.5.B25 372'.72 73-75000
ISBN 0-675-08982-4 MARC

Ballew, Ralph J
Parker Branch; two decades of progress [by Ralph J. Ballew and Harold C. Young. Knoxville? Tenn., Published cooperatively by the North Carolina Agricultural Extension Service and the Tennessee Valley Authority, 1972]
[16] p. illus. 28 cm.
Cover title.
1. Parker Branch watershed. 2. Watershed management. 3. Reclamation of land. I. Young, Harold C., joint author. II. North Carolina. State University, Raleigh. Agricultural Extension Service. III. Tennessee Valley Authority. IV. Title.
GU NUC74-127109

Ballew, Steven Early, 1945-
Faulkner's psychology of individualism: a fictional principle and Light in August. [Bloomington, Ind.] 1974.
185 p.
Thesis (Ph. D.)–Indiana University.
Vita.
InU NUC76-21074

Ballewar, Shridhara
see
Sagar, 1946-

Balley, L R 1930–
(Ḍākaṭara Ambeḍakara)
ਡਾਕਟਰ ਅੰਬੇਡਕਰ: ਜੀਵਨ ਅਤੇ ਮਿਸ਼ਨ. ਲੇਖਕ ਲਾਹੌਰੀ ਰਾਮ ਬਾਲੀ. ਜਲੰਧਰ; ਭੀਮ ਪੱਤ੍ਰਕਾ ਪ੍ਰਕਾਸ਼ਨ, 1971.
xii, 452 p. port. 19 cm. Rs12.00
In Panjabi.
Includes bibliographical references.
1. Ambedkar, Bhimrao Ramji, 1892–1956. I. Title.
DS481.A6B34 72–905712

Ballhaus, William Francis.
Interaction between the ocean surface and underwater spherical blast waves. [Berkeley] 1971.
v, 68 l.
Thesis (Ph.D.)—University of California.
Bibliography: leaves 49-50.
CU NUC73-34745

Ballhausen, Carl Johan, 1926-
Lectures on ligand field theory, delivered at the Summer School in Ligand Field Theory held at Bangalore, 1970 / by C. J. Ballhausen ; notes by B. S. Prabhananda, V. R. Marathe. — Bombay : Tata Institute of Fundamental Research, 1970, cover 1972.
82 leaves ; 28 cm. — (Tata Institute of Fundamental Research lectures on mathematics and physics : Physics ; 46)
Rs5.00
1. Ligand field theory—Addresses, essays, lectures. I. Title. II. Series: Lectures on mathematics and physics : Physics ; 46.
QD475.B32 541'.2242 75-901711
75 MARC

Ballhausen, Carl Johan, 1926- joint author
see Dingle, Robert B Polarized crystal spectra of optically active ions. København, (Munksgaard), 1967

Balli, Antonio.
Le mie api : verità e misteri / Antonio Balli ; pref. di Otto Morgenthaler. — Bologna : Edizioni agricole, c1955.
viii, 287 p. ; 22 cm.
Bibliography : p. [285]–287.
1. Bees. I. Title.
QL568.A6D3 76–517957

Ballı, Edibe.
Abaques pour le calcul des profondeurs de formation = Teşekkül derinliklerinin hesaplanması için abaklar / Edibe Ballı, Adnan Kıral, Jean-Claude Pecker. — İstanbul : Observatoire de l'Université d'Istanbul], 1965.
3, [4] p., [17] fold. leaves of plates : graphs ; 27 cm. — (İstanbul Üniversitesi Observatuarı yazıları ; sayı 83)
Cover title.
In French with summary in English and Turkish.
Bibliography: p. [7]
1. Spectrum, Solar—Charts, diagrams, etc. I. Kıral, Adnan, joint author. II. Pecker, Jean Claude, joint author. III. Title. IV. Title: Teşekkül derinliklerinin hesaplanması için abaklar. V. Series: Istanbul. Üniversite. Observatoryum. İstanbul Üniversitesi Observatuarı yazıları ; sayı 83.
QB551.B3 523.7'2 76-468685
76 MARC

Balli, Kristaq.
Varka dhe ura : tregime / Kristaq Balli. — Tiranë : Naim Frashëri, 1975.
107 p. ; 17 cm.
CONTENTS: Erërat e dëborës.—Kali i botës.—Gurë të rëndë.—Vajza nga qyteti i bardhë.—Dy djem nga fshati.—Varka dhe ura.—Vegimet e dimrit qe shkoi.
L2.00
I. Title.
PG9621.B325V3 77–506679

Balliano, Adolfo, joint tr.
see Henry, Joseph, 1870-1947. Vecchi nomi dialettali di località valdostane... [Milano] Centro universitario di studi alpini-G. U. F. Milano [1941]

Balliano, Piera.
Studio sull'evoluzione della concentrazione dell'industria cartaria in Italia : [indagine svolta per incarico della Commissione delle communità europee] / Piera Balliano, Renato Lanzetti. — Luxembourg : Ufficio delle pubblicazioni ufficiali delle Comunità europeè, 1976.
189 p. ; 28 cm. It***
At head of title: Commissione delle comunità europee.
L3300
1. Paper making and trade—Italy. 2. Industrial concentration—Italy. I. Lanzetti, Renato, joint author. II. Commission of the European Communities. III. Title.
HD9835.I82B34 77-471768
77 MARC

Balliano, Piera.
Studio sull'evoluzione della concentrazione nel settore della costruzione di macchine per l'industria tessile in Italia / [Gruppo di lavoro SORIS, Piera Balliano, Renato Lanzetti]. — [Bruxelles] : Commissione delle Comunità europee, 1976.
159 p. : graphs ; 27 cm. Be***
At head of title: Commissione delle Comunità europee.
$5.20 (U.S.)
1. Textile machinery industry—Italy. 2. Industrial concentration—Italy. I. Lanzetti, Renato, joint author. II. Commission of the European Communities. III. Title.
HD9865.I82B34 77-472297
77 MARC

Balliano, Piera.
Studio sull'evoluzione della concentrazione nell'industria cotoniera italiana (N.I.C.E. 233) / di Piera Balliano, Giovanni Bertone, Filippo Mosini. — [Luxembourg : Ufficio delle pubblicazioni ufficiali delle Comunità europee], 1975.
149 p. : graphs ; 30 cm. It***
At head of title: Commissione delle Comunità europee.
On spine: La concentrazione nell'industria cotoniera italiana.
1. Cotton trade—Italy—Consolidation. 2. Consolidation and merger of corporations—Europe. I. Bertone, Giovanni, joint author. II. Mosini, Filippo, joint author. III. Commission of the European Economic Communities. IV. Title. V. Title: La concentrazione nell'industria cotoniera italiana.
HD9885.I82B25 76-479483
76 MARC

Ballico, Pietro.
L'opera di avvaloramento agricolo e zootecnico della Tripolitania e della Cirenaica. Testi di P. Ballico e G. Palloni. Roma, ABETE, 1971.
xvii, 405 p. plates. 24 cm. (L'Italia in Africa; serie economico-agraria, v. 1: L'Avvaloramento e la colonizzazione, t. 3) It 74–Sept
At head of title: Ministero degli affari esteri. Comitato per la documentazione delle attività italiane in Africa.
Includes bibliographies.
1. Agriculture and state—Libya—Tripolitania. 2. Agriculture and state—Libya—Cyrenaica. 3. Agriculture—Economic aspects—Libya—Tripolitania. 4. Agriculture—Economic aspects—Libya—Cyrenaica. I. Palloni, Giuseppe. II. Title. III. Series: L'Italia in Africa; serie economico-agraria, v. 1. IV. Series: L'avvaloramento e la colonizzazione, t. 3.
HD2139.L522T742 75–557016

Balliet, Conrad Arthur, 1927-
The verse technique of Matthew Arnold. [Ithaca, N. Y.] 1961. [Ann Arbor, University Microfilms, 1972]
236 l.
Thesis (Ph. D.)–Cornell University.
Vita.
Photocopy. 20 cm.
1. Arnold, Matthew, 1822-1888. 2. English language–Versification. I. Title.
CU NUC73-59710

Balliet, Thomas M., ed.
see Swift, Jonathan, 1667-1745. Gulliver's travels. Taipei, Commercial Press, 1970.

Balliett, Thomas David.
American laborism, 1886-1914 : an essay / presented by Thomas David Balliett. -- [s.l. : s.n., 1975]
124 leaves ; 28 cm.
Honors thesis--Harvard.
Includes bibliographies.
1. Trade unions--United States.
MH NUC77-84518

Balliett, Whitney.
Alec Wilder and his friends; the words and sounds of Marian McPartland, Mabel Mercer, Marie Marcus, Bobby Hackett, Tony Bennett, Ruby Braff, Bob and Ray, Blossom Dearie, and Alec Wilder. Illustrated with photos. by Geoffrey James. Boston, Houghton Mifflin Co., 1974.
ix, 205 p. ports. 23 cm.
1. Jazz musicians. 2. Wilder, Alec. I. Title.
ML385.B24 813'.5'4 74–6272
ISBN 0-395-19398-2 MARC

Balliett, Whitney.
Improvising : sixteen jazz musicians and their art / Whitney Balliett. — New York : Oxford University Press, 1977.
vi, 263 p. ; 22 cm.
Includes index.
ISBN 0-19-502149-5 : $10.95
1. Jazz music. 2. Jazz musicians. I. Title.
ML3561.J3B245 785.4'2'0922 76-42635
77 MARC

Balliett, Whitney.
New York notes : a journal of jazz, 1972-1975 / Whitney Balliett. — Boston : Houghton Mifflin, 1976.
250 p. ; 22 cm.
ISBN 0-395-24296-7
1. Jazz music—New York (City) I. Title.
ML3561.J3.B247 785.4'2 75-40213
75 MARC

Balliett, Whitney.
New York notes : a journal of jazz, 1972-1975 / Whitney Balliett. — New York : Da Capo Press, [1977] c1976.
250 p. ; 22 cm.
Reprint of the 1976 ed. published by Houghton Mifflin, Boston.
ISBN 0-306-80037-3
1. Jazz music—New York (City) I. Title.
[ML3561.J3B247 1977] 785.4'2 76-51396
76 MARC

Ballieu, Robert.
Notes de géometrie projective, par Robert F. Ballieu. 4. ed. Louvain, Vander, 1970.
147 p. 24 cm.
Bibliography: p. 147.
1. Geometry, Projective. I. Title.
PSt NUC73-121188

Ballieux, R. E., ed.
see Federation of European Biochemical Societies. Immunoglobulins: cell bound receptors and humoral antibodies. [Amsterdam] North-Holland Pub. Co., [New York] American Elsevier, 1972, [1973].

Ballif, Bonnie L., joint author
see Adkins, Dorothy Christina, 1912-
Final report on continuation of research on teaching preschool children motivation... Honolulu, 1972.

Ballif, Claude.
Nicolas Obouhow: l'harmonie totale. Ivan Wyschnegradsky: l'ultrachromatisme et les espaces non octaviants. Paris, La revue musicale [1972]
141 p. illus. (La revue musicale, double numéro 290-291)
MH NUC75-32783

Ballif, Claude
see Journée Claude Ballif, Paris, 1968. Claude Ballif, journée du 7 mars 1968, l'A. R. C. Paris, "la Revue musicale," [1968.]

Ballif, Sergiu, joint author.
see Stăncescu, Ioan D. Meteorologie şi drumeţie. Bucureşti, "Sport-Turism" 1976.

Ballin, Michael Gerald.
D.H. Lawrence and William Blake: a comparative and critical study, by Michael G. Ballin. [Toronto] c1972.
iv, 386 l.
Thesis—University of Toronto.
Bibliography: leaves 374-386.
1. Lawrence, David Herbert, 1885-1930. 2. Blake, William, 1757-1827. I. Title.
CaOTU NUC73-121315

Ballin, Paul Frédéric Jean Grunebaum-
see Grunebaum-Ballin, Paul Frédéric Jean, 1871-1969.

Ballin, Peter J 1946-
Geographic variation in courtship behaviour of the guppy, Poecilia reticulata. [Vancouver, B.C.] University of British Columbia, 1973.
xiv, 135 l. illus. 28 cm.
Thesis (M.Sc.)—University of British Columbia, 1974.
Vita.
Bibliography: leaves 118-130.
1. Guppies. I. Title.
CaBVaU NUC75-18565

Balling, Claus.
B for Børge. Brudstykker af en dansker. København, Borgen, 1974.
109 p. 22 cm. kr44.00 D 74-19
I. Title.
PT8176.12.A39B2 74-345480
ISBN 87-418-1363-4

Balling, Claus.
Mordet. København, Borgen, 1973.
87 p. 22 cm. kr38.00 D 73-12
I. Title.
PT8176.12.A39M6 74-313022
ISBN 87-418-1820-2

Balling, Erik, 1924–
Samtale med Erik Balling / Ib Lindberg ; med filmografi udarb. af Per Calum. — København : Det Danske Filmmuseum, 1974.
64 p. : ill. ; 21 cm. — (Monografier - Det Danske filmmuseum ; 6)
Bibliography of the author's works: p. 53–64. D 75–21
kr25.00
1. Balling, Erik, 1924– I. Lindberg, Ib, 1944– II. Title. III. Series: Copenhagen. Danske filmmuseum. Monografier ; 6.
PN1998.A3B355 75–534668

Balling, Fredda Dudley, joint author
see Garnett, Tay. Light your torches and pull up your tights. New Rochelle, N. Y., Arlington House [1973]

Balling, Frederick J
Sister Carrie: notes. Lincoln, Nebr., Cliff's notes [c1967]
97 p. 21 cm.
Bibliography: p. 96-97.
1. Dreiser, Theodore, 1871-1945. Sister Carrie. I. Title.
CoU NUC76-35240

Balling, Heinz.
Nettolohnberechnung. Lohnsteuer, Sozialversicherg, Ausgleichszahlgn u. Lohnausgleich, Lohn-, Kinder- u. Ehegattenzuschläge, Kindergeld mit Tabellen. (2., überarb. Aufl.) Berlin, Staatsverl. d. Deutschen Demokratischen Republik, 1971.
607 p. 22 cm. 7.80M GDNB 71-A49-127
Pages 600–607 blank for "Notizen."
1. Wages—Accounting. 2. Payroll deductions—Germany (Democratic Republic, 1949–) I. Title.
HF5681.W3B33 1971 72–367461

Balling, John D 1945-
Habituation as a measure of perceptual integration. [Amherst] 1972.
vii, 101 l. tables. 28 cm.
Thesis (Ph.D.)—University of Massachusetts.
1. Auditory perception. I. Title.
MU NUC74-127749

Balling, Morten.
Børsens økonomiske leksikon / red. af Morten Balling, Niels Strange Nielsen og Bo Stærmose. — [København] : Børsen, 1974.
249 p. : ill. ; 24 cm. D 75-3
ISBN 87-7553-015-5 : kr166.75
1. Economics—Dictionaries—Danish. I. Strange Nielsen, Niels, joint author. II. Stærmose, Bo, joint author. III. Title.
HB61.B327 75–567551

Balling, Morten.
Merværdiafgift, kundetilgodehavender og leverandørgæld. En undersøgelse af behovet for den såkaldte betalingsmetode ved opgørelsen af merværdiafgiften. København, Statens Trykningskontor, (D. B. K.), 1971.
128 p. 30 cm. kr25.30 D 72-4
Bibliography: p. 48.
1. Value-added tax—Denmark. I. Title.
HJ5715.D4B34 73–352414
ISBN 87-503-1202-2

Balling, Morten.
The missing price effect of lottery bond redemptions / Morten Balling, Erik Gørtz. — [Odense : Odense Universitet, Institut for Historie og Samfundvidenskab, eksp., Niels Bohrs Allé 75, 1975]
10 leaves : 30 cm. — (Skrifter fra Institut for Historie og Samfundsvidenskab, Odense Universitet : Samfundsvidenskab ; no. 28) D76-5
Cover title.
Includes bibliographical references.
1. Mortgage bonds—Denmark. 2. Lotteries—Denmark. I. Gørtz, Erik, joint author. II. Title. III. Series: Odense universitet. Institut for historie og samfundsvidenskab. Skrifter : Samfundsvidenskab ; no. 28.
HG5599.M6B34 332.6'323 76-375329
•76 MARC

Ballinger, Bill S
see Ballinger, William Sanborn, 1912-

Ballinger, Carter M., 1922- ed.
see Blood transfusion. Boston, Little, Brown, 1967.

Ballinger, Carter M., 1922- ed.
see Western Conference on Anesthesiology, 11th, Salt Lake City, 1969. Endocrines and enzymes in anesthesiology. Springfield, Ill., Thomas [1973]

Ballinger, Charles Edwin, 1935-
Drug education: some guidelines for development of instructional programs for students: K-12. [Columbus, Ohio] 1971 [1972]
1 v.
Thesis–Ohio State University.
Microfilm of typescript. Ann Arbor, Mich., University Microfilms, 1972. 1 reel. 35 mm.
1. Drug abuse–Study and teaching. I. Title.
FMU NUC73-121132

Ballinger, Charles Edwin, 1935-
Educating for intercultural understanding; the role of the teacher [by] Charles E. Ballinger. [Columbus, Ohio] Ohio Association of Supervision and Curriculum Development [1970 ?]
8 l. 28 cm. (Innovative curriculum series)
Cover title.
Includes bibliographical references.
1. Intercultural education. I. Title.
II. Series: Ohio Association of Supervision and Curriculum Development. Innovative curriculum series.
OU NUC74-122370

Ballinger, Harry Russell, 1892–
Painting landscapes [by] Harry R. Ballinger. A new, enl. ed. New York, Watson-Guptill Publications [1973, c1965]
192 p. illus. (part col.) 27 cm. $14.95
1. Landscape painting—Technique. I. Title.
ND1342.B28 1973 758'.1 72–8335
ISBN 0-8230-3651-0 MARC

Ballinger, Jerrold, joint author.
see Aldouby, Zwy. The shattered silence ... New York, Coward, McCann & Geoghegan, [1971]

Ballinger, Margaret, 1894–
Britain in Southern Africa, by Margaret L. Hodgson and W. G. Ballinger. [Lovedale, South Africa] Lovedale Press [1932–
v. 22 cm.
CONTENTS:
—no. 2. Bechuanaland Protectorate.
1. Africa, Southern—Politics and government. 2. British in Southern Africa. I. Ballinger, William George, 1893– joint author. II. Title.
DT746.B34 55–54440

Ballinger, Martha Sherman Bacon
see
Bacon, Martha Sherman, 1917-

Ballinger, R. Maxil
see The Conference Board. Renegotiation in peace and war. New York [c1950, 1971]

Ballinger, Raymond A 1907-
Art and reproduction : graphic-reproduction techniques / Raymond A. Ballinger. — New York : Van Nostrand Reinhold, 1977.
112 p. : ill. ; 27 cm.
Bibliography: p. 110.
Includes index.
ISBN 0-442-20550-3 : $7.95
1. Printing, Practical. 2. Graphic arts. I. Title.
Z244.B2 686.2'24 76-5070
76 MARC

Ballinger, Richard M
The illustrated guide to the houses of America / edited by Richard M. Ballinger and Herman York. — New York : Galahad Books, c1971.
xii, 260 p. : ill. ; 29 cm.
Includes index.
ISBN 0-88365-177-7 : $13.95
1. Architecture, Domestic—United States. I. York, Herman H., 1908– joint author. II. Title.
[NA7205.B34 1971b] 728'.0973 73–92079

Ballinger, Ronald B
Detente in Southern Africa : two views / Ronald Ballinger and Gerrit Olivier. — [Braamfontein] : South African Institute of International Affairs, [1976]
29 p. ; 30 cm. SA***
Cover title.
"These papers were read on the occasion of the 46th annual council meeting of the South African Institute of Race Relations in Johannesburg on 21 January 1976."
Includes bibliographical references.
ISBN 0-909239-18-5
1. South Africa—Politics and government—1961- —Addresses, essays, lectures. 2. South Africa—Race question—Addresses, essays, lectures. 3. Africa, Southern—Politics and government—1975- —Addresses, essays, lectures. 4. Africa, Southern—Race question—Addresses, essays, lectures. I. Olivier, Gerrit, joint author. II. South African Institute of Race Relations. III. Title.
DT779.9.B34 327'.0968 76-383658
77 MARC

Ballinger, Ronald B
Dr. Moynihan and the Amalekites : the United States and the United Nations / Ronald Ballinger. — Braamfontein : South African Institute of International Affairs, 1976.
17 p. ; 30 cm. SA***
Cover title.
"This paper contains the text of a talk given to the Witwatersrand Branch of the Institute on 15 March, 1976."
Includes bibliographical references.
ISBN 0-909239-20-7
1. United Nations—United States—Addresses, essays, lectures. 2. Moynihan, Daniel Patrick—Addresses, essays, lectures. I. Title.
JX1977.2.U5B26 341.23'73 77-356342
77 MARC

Ballinger, Royce E
Systematics and evolution of the genus Uta (Sauria: Iguanidae) by Royce E. Ballinger and Donald W. Tinkle. Ann Arbor, Museum of Zoology, University of Michigan, 1972.
83 p. illus. 26 cm. (University of Michigan. Museum of Zoology. Miscellaneous publications, no. 145)
Bibliography: p. 79-83.
1. Uta. I. Tinkle, Donald W., joint author. II. Title. III. Series: Michigan. University. Museum of Zoology. Miscellaneous publications, no. 145.
QL666.L2B16 598.1'12 72-612603
MARC

Ballinger, Walter F
The management of trauma. Edited by Walter F. Ballinger II, Robert B. Rutherford [and] George D. Zuidema. 2d. ed. Philadelphia, Saunders, 1973.
xiv, 795 p. illus. 26 cm.
Includes bibliographies.
1. Wounds. I. Rutherford, Robert B., joint author. II. Zuidema, George D., joint author. III. Title.
RD93.B33 1973 617'.1 73-77933
ISBN 0-7216-1521-X MARC

Ballinger, Walter F., ed.
see Alexander, Edythe Louise. Alexander's Care of the patient in surgery. 5th ed. St. Louis, C. V. Mosby Co., 1972.

Ballinger, Walter F.
see American College of Surgeons. Committee on Pre and Postoperative Care. Manual of surgical nutrition. Philadelphia, Saunders, 1975.

Ballinger, Walter F.
see Practice of surgery ... Saint Louis, C. V. Mosby Co., 19

Ballinger, William George, 1893- joint author
see Ballinger, Margaret, 1894- Britain in Southern Africa. [Lovedale, South Africa] Lovedale Press [1932-

Ballinger, William Sanborn, 1912-
The Corsican [by] Bill S. Ballinger. New York, Dodd, Mead [1974]
ix, 342 p. 24 cm. $7.95
I. Title.
PZ3.B21394Co 813'.5'4 73-19085
[PS3552.A47] MARC
ISBN 0-396-06918-5

Ballinger, William Sanborn, 1912-
The heir hunters [by] Bill S. Ballinger. London, T. V. Boardman [1967]
168 p. 21 cm.
I. Title.
CoU NUC76-62952

Ballinger, William Sanborn, 1912-
Puinen enkeil. [Kirj.] Bill S. Ballinger. [Suomentanut Juhani Pietilainen] Helsinki, Tammi [1971]
199 l. 20 cm.
Translation of The body in the bed.
I. Title.
MB NUC73-121314

Ballinger, William Sanborn, 1912-
La source de la peur [par] Bill S. Ballinger. Traduit de l'Américan par Marcel Frère. [Paris] Gallimard [1971]
249 p. 18 cm. (Série noire, 1426)
Translated from The source of fear.
I. Title.
NcRS CtY NUC74-122415

Ballinger, William Sanborn, 1912-
Triptych: Portrait in smoke, The longest second, The tooth and the nail. Los Angeles, Sherbourne Press [c1971]
646 p.
I. Title.
ICarbS NUC76-62951

Ballinger ledger
see Interesting facts about Ballinger, Texas. [Ballinger, Tex., 1972?]

Ballington, James Ralph, 1942-
The breeding biology of the purported diploid ancestors of Vaccinium ashei Reade / James Ralph Ballington, Jr. -- Raleigh : North Carolina State University, 1975.
iv, 48 leaves : ill., graphs ; 29 cm.
Includes bibliographical references.
Vita.
Thesis--North Carolina State University.
I. Title.
NcRS NUC77-87600

Ballion, Robert.
Étude des conséquences de l'échec scolaire sur le devenir socio-professionnel dans les milieux favorisés / Robert Ballion, avec la collaboration de Claude Bellan et de Marie Carole de Buhan. — [Paris] : C.O.R.D.E.S., 1974.
268 leaves ; 30 cm. F***
At head of title: Commissariat du plan, C.O.R.D.E.S., C.N.R.S.-E.P.H.E., Centre d'éthnologie sociale et de psychosociologie.
"Rapport de recherche. Convention C.O.R.D.E.S. no 20/73 du 5 juillet 1974."
"Fiche de synthèse": 6 leaves inserted.
Bibliography: leaves 266-268.
1. Professional education—France. 2. Vocational guidance—France. I. Bellan, Claude, joint author. II. Buhan, Marie Carole de, joint author. III. Title: Étude des conséquences de l'échec scolaire sur le devenir socio-professionnel ...
LC1060.B34 378'.01'30944 76-487162
77 MARC

Ballis, George, illus.
see Oakland Economic Development Council. Discover the friendly city - Oakland. [Oakland, Calif., 1970]

Ballis, Giovanni
see La Famiglia nella società secolarizzata... Milano: Ancora, c1974.

Ballis, William Belcher, 1908-
The legal position of war: changes in its practice and theory from Plato to Vattel, by William Ballis. With a new introd. for the Garland ed. by Wayne K. Patterson. New York, Garland Pub., 1973 [c1937]
6, xi, 188 p. 22 cm. (The Garland library of war and peace)
Originally presented as the author's thesis, University of Chicago.
Bibliography: p. [174]-184.
1. War (International law)—History. I. Title. II. Series.
JX4508.B33 1973 341.6 75-147596
ISBN 0-8240-0357-8 MARC

Ballistic-range technology. London, Harford House, 1970.
xii, 508 p. (AGARDograph 138)
1. Ballistic missiles. I. Canning, Thomas N., ed. II. Series.
NBuU NUC71-63845rev.

(Ballisticheskie ustanovki i ikh primenenie v ėksperimental'nykh issledovaniíàkh)
Баллистические установки и их применение в экспериментальных исследованиях / под ред. Н. А. Златина и Г. И. Мишина. — Москва : Наука, 1974.
344 p. : ill. ; 23 cm. USSR***
Bibliography: p. [327]-341.
Includes index.
2.22rub
1. Ballistics. 2. Projectiles. I. Zlatin, N. A. II. Mishin, G. I.
UF820.B258 75-529297

Ballistocardiograph Research Society.
Ballistocardiography: research and computer diagnosis. Ed.: Ernst K. Franke. Basel ..., S. Karger, 1973.
vi, 121 p. illus. 25 cm. (Bibliotheca cardiologica, No. 32)
42.00F Sw 73-A-6457
Proceedings of the 16th annual meeting of the Ballistocardiograph Research Society, Atlantic City, N. J., April 1972.
Includes bibliographies.
1. Ballistocardiography—Congresses. 2. Electronic data processing—Electrocardiography—Congresses. I. Franke, Ernst, K., ed. II. Title. III. Series.
RC683.5.B3B36 1973 616.1'2'0754 74-161079
ISBN 3-8055-1376-3 MARC

Ballistocardiograph Research Society.
Ultrasound and ballistocardiography in cardiovascular research : proceedings of the 17th annual meeting of the Ballistocardiograph Research Society, Altantic City, N.J., April 1973 / editor, Jan Baan. — Basel ; New York : S. Karger, 1974.
117 p. : ill. ; 26 cm. — (Bibliotheca cardiologica ; no. 34) Sw***
Includes bibliographies and index.
ISBN 3-8055-1763-7
1. Cardiovascular research—Congresses. 2. Ultrasonic cardiography—Congresses. 3. Ballistocardiography—Congresses. I. Baan, Jan. II. Title. III. Series.
RC669.B25 1974 616.1'07'54 75-314938
75 MARC

Ballistocardiography and Cardiovascular Dynamics, European Congress on
see
European Congress on Ballistocardiography and Cardiovascular Dynamics.

Ballīūzek, Feliks Vladimirovich, joint author
see Filatov, Antonin Nikolaevich. Upravlīāemaīā gemodilīūtsiia. 1972.

Balliviān, José Arturo, ed.
see Haenke, Thaddäus, 1761-1816. Tadeo Hænke ... La Paz, Impr. y litografía de "EL Nacional" de I. V. Vila [etc.] 1898-1900.

Balliviān, Manuel Vicente, 1848-1921
see Haenke, Thaddäus, 1761-1816. Tadeo Hænke ... La Paz, Impr. y litografía de "El Nacional" de I. V. Vila [etc.] 1898-1900.

Ballivián, Mario Bedoya
see
Bedoya Ballivián, Mario.

Balliviān, Vicente, 1810-
Claudio y Elena. La Paz [J. Camarlinghi] 1969.
48 p. (Colección Popular. Serie 6, v. 18)
First published in his Recreos juveniles (London, 1834)
I. Title.
PPiU NUC73-2350

Ballivián Calderón, René.
El capitalismo en las ideologías económicas contemporáneas; su presente y su destino según el moderno pensamiento económico. Buenos Aires, Editorial Paidós [1972]
222 p. 23 cm. (Biblioteca de economía, política, sociedad. Serie mayor, 11)
LACAP 73-0247
Includes bibliographical references.
1. Economics. 2. Capitalism. I. Title.
HB87.B24 73-324224

Ballivián Calderón, René.
Principios de economía minera. 2. ed. La Paz, Librería Editorial "Juventud", 1973.
290 p. 22 cm.
1. Mining industry and finance. I. Title.
TxU PSt NUC75-18391

Ballivián Calderón, René.
Relaciones humanas en una nueva dimensión, a la luz de las ideas de Teilhard de Chardin / René Ballivián Calderón. — La Paz : Librería Editorial Juventud, 1974.
89 p. ; 19 cm.
Includes bibliographical references.
1. Teilhard de Chardin, Pierre. 2. Interpersonal relations. I. Title: Relaciones humanas en una nueva dimensión ...
B2430.T374B25 75-558118

Ballivián Calderón, René.
Teoría del desarrollo : texto introductorio / René Ballivián Calderón. — 1. ed. — La Paz : Editorial Los Amigos del Libro, 1976.
240, x p. : ill. ; 20 cm.
"Curso dictado ... entre los meses de noviembre y abril de 1976 en la Universidad Boliviana de San Andrés, La Paz."
Bibliography: p. 234-240.
1. Economic development. 2. Economic development—Social aspects. 3. Economics—History. I. Title.
HD85.S7B34 77-556634
77 MARC

Ballke, Wolfgang, 1948-
Umfang und Intensität der Verfassungsgerichtlichen Überprüfung von Gesetzen zur kommunalen Gebietsreform / vorgelegt von Wolfgang Ballke. — [s.l. : s.n.], 1975.
xxviii, 214 p. ; 21 cm. GFR***
Thesis—Münster.
Vita.
Bibliography: p. xii-xxvi.
1. Germany, West—Administrative and political divisions. 2. Judicial review—Germany, West. 3. Local government—Germany, West. I. Title: Umfang und Intensität ...
76-457613
76 MARC

Ballman, Jacqueline.
Zona make-up. Met een tekening van Jan Burssens. Brussel, Le Marronnier-fleur, (1969).
64 p. illus. 24 cm. (Le Marronnier-Fleur, nr. 3) 100F
Be 70-1729
Poems.
I. Title.
PQ2662.A42Z42 73-329598

Ballmann, Gottfried.
Hinweise für den heimatkundlichen Deutschunterricht in Mehrstufenklassen unter besonderer Berücksichtigung der Stufen 1 und 2. Berlin, Volk und Wissen, 1967.
132 p. 22 cm. (Methodik des Deutschunterrichts in der Unterstufe) DM3.30 GDNB 67-A17-331
Bibliography: p. 128-130.
1. German language—Study and teaching (Elementary)
I. Title.
LB1577.G4B26 73-304292

Ballmann, P
Fossile Vögel aus dem Neogen der Halbinsel Gargano (Italien) ₍von₎ P. Ballmann. Leiden, Rijksmuseum van Geologie en Mineralogie, 1973.
75 p. illus. 27 cm. (Scripta geologica, 17) fl 20.50 Ne***
Cover title.
Summary in English.
Bibliography: p. 60-61.
1. Birds, Fossil. 2. Paleontology—Tertiary. 3. Paleontology—Italy—Gargano Promontory. I. Title. II. Series.
QE871.B34 74-310530

Ballmann, P
Fossile Vögel aus den Neogen der Halbinsel Gargano (Italien), zweiter Teil / P. Ballmann. — Leiden : Rijksmuseum van Geologie en Mineralogie, 1976.
59 p. : ill. ; 26 cm. — (Scripta geologica ; 38) Ne***
Cover title.
Continues the author's work published under the same title in 1973.
Summary in English.
Bibliography: p. 44-45.
fl 22.00
1. Birds, Fossil. 2. Paleontology—Tertiary. 3. Paleontology—Italy—Gargano Promontory. I. Title. II. Series.
QE871.B342 77-471824
77 MARC

Ballmann, Wilhelm.
Betriebswirtschaftliche Überwachungsarten; was der Unternehmer und der Revisor von der betriebswirtschaftlichen Überwachung und insbesondere von der Revision wissen müssen. ₍Berlin₎ E. Schmidt ₍c1973₎
48 p. 23 cm.
"Erscheint auch in der 'Zeitschrift Interne Revision' Bd. 7 (1972) H. 4."
Includes bibliographical references.
1. Auditing. 2. Auditors—Germany (Federal Republic, 1949–) 3. Business enterprises—Valuation—Germany (Federal Republic, 1949–) I. Title.
HF5667.B238 73-207329
ISBN 3-503-01032-7

Ballmark Business Forms
see The Ballmark plan of industrial democracy... [Regina, Sask., c1973]

The Ballmark plan of industrial democracy; a universal economic system. ₍Regina, Sask., Ballmark Business Forms, c1973₎
10 p. 22 cm. $1.25 C***
Running title: Industrial democracy.
1. Full employment policies. 2. Welfare economics. I. Ballmark Business Forms. II. Title: Industrial democracy.
HD82.B265 331.1'377 74-169620
MARC

Ballmer, André Aug E
La barrière de feu : roman / André Aug. E. Ballmer. — Genève : Perret-Gentil, c1975.
263 p. ; 21 cm. Sw75-A-3508
25.00F
I. Title.
PQ2662.A425B3 843'.9'14 75-516683
•76 MARC

Ballmer, André Aug E
La fin du jour ou Le temps d'Alexandre. Roman. (Genève, Éditions) Perret-Gentil, (1972).
174 p. 21 cm. 20.00F Sw 72-A-3919
At head of title: André Aug. E. Ballmer.
I. Title.
PQ2662.A425F5 72-361907

Ballmer, André Aug E
L'hostellerie du désert. Récit dialogué ₍par₎ André Aug. E. Ballmer. (Genève,) Perret-Gentil, (1973).
295 p. 21 cm. 25.00F Sw73-A-5770
I. Title.
PQ2662.A425H6 76-456933
76₍r76₎rev MARC

Ballmer, André Aug. E.
see Présentation originale des poètes du mardi. Genève, Perret-Gentil, 1974.

Ballmer, Roger, 1947-
Versuch einer Erfassung der Strassenverkehrs- unfallfolgekosten für die Schweiz 1972 / par Roger Ballmer. — Berne : H. Lang ; Francfort/M. : P. Lang, 1975.
224 p. : ill. ; 23 cm. Sw75-A-6384
Thesis—Geneva.
Vita.
Bibliography: p. 213-224.
ISBN 3-261-01681-7 : 38.00F
1. Traffic accidents—Economic aspects—Switzerland. I. Title.
HE5614.5.S9B34 76-482045
•76 MARC

Ballmer, Thomas T
Sprachrekonstruktionssysteme und einige ihrer Anwendungsmöglichkeiten in Satz- und Textlinguistik / Thomas T. Ballmer. — Kronberg/Ts. : Scriptor Verlag, 1975.
378 p. ; 21 cm. — (Skripten Linguistik und Kommunikationswissenschaft ; 15) GFR***
Originally presented as the author's thesis, Technische Universität Berlin, 1974.
Bibliography: p. 366-377.
ISBN 3-589-20074-X
1. Discourse analysis. 2. Formal languages. I. Title: Sprachrekonstruktionssysteme und einige ihrer Anwendungsmöglichkeiten ...
P302.B3 1975 75-516053
75 MARC

Ballmer, Thomas T
see Konstanzer Textlinguistik-Kolloquium, 1972. Testlinguistik und Pragmatik... Hamburg: Buske, 1974.

Ballmoos, Kurt von.
Les aventures de Célèstin, le petit moine : ₍dessins₎ / Kurt von Ballmoos. — ₍Lausanne, Av. du Théâtre 16 : Pierre-M.₎ Favre, ₍1973₎
₍42₎ leaves : all ill. ; 17 cm. Sw 74-A-2578
9.00F
1. Swiss wit and humor, Pictorial. I. Title.
NC1659.B28A44 741.5'9494 75-501626
MARC

Ballmoos, Kurt von.
Tell 73 ₍i. e. soixante-treize.₎ ₍Dessins.₎ Lausanne, (Av. du Théâtre 16, Pierre-M., Favre,) 1973.
18 l. illus. 12 x 17 cm. 6.00F Sw 74-A-2579
1. Swiss wit and humor, Pictorial. I. Title.
NC1659.B28A56 74-179534
MARC

Ballner, William G
The effects of emotional stress upon levels of anxiety and oral dependence as measured in the Holtzman inkblot and TAT protocols of matched groups of heroin addicts, alcoholics, and controls / by William G. Ballner. -- ₍s.l. : s.n.₎, 1975.
vii, 84 leaves ; 28 cm.
Thesis (Ph.D.)--Catholic University of America.
Bibliography: leaves 66-74.
1. Stress (Psychology) 2. Narcotic addicts. 3. Alcoholics. I. Title.
DCU NUC77-85963

Ballnerová, Ruth.
Městské hejtmanství a policejní ředitelství Praha, 1769–1855; inventář. ₍Zprac.₎ Ruth Ballnerová. Praha, Archivní správa Ministerstva vnitra, 1960.
340 p. 29 cm. (Inventáře a katalogy fondů Státního ústředního archivu v Praze, 11)
1. Státní ústřední archiv v Praze. I. Title. II. Series: Státní ústřední archiv v Praze. Inventáře a katalogy fondů, 11.
CD1167.P7B34 75-573084

Ballo, Ferdinando.
Arlecchino di Ferruccio Busoni; Volo di notte di Luigi Dallapiccola; Coro di morti di Goffredo Petrassi. ₍Milano, La Lampada, 1942₎
46 p. illus. 17 cm. (Collezione di guide musicali, 6)
1. Busoni, Ferruccio Benvenuto, 1866-1924. Arlecchino. 2. Dallapiccola, Luigi, 1904– Volo di notte. 3. Petrassi, Goffredo, 1904– Coro di morti. I. Title: Arlecchino. II. Title: Volo di notte. III. Title: Coro di morti.
MT95.B335A7 74-221412

Ballo, Ginés Maragall
see
Maragall Ballo, Ginés.

Ballo, Guido, 1914–
Alfabeto solare. Prefazione di Francesco Leonetti. Milano, Palazzi, 1973.
124 p. 20 cm. (Poeti d'oggi, 5) L1800 It 73-July
"Nota bio-bibliografica": p. ₍113₎-119.
CONTENTS: Metràpolis. — Alfabeto solare. — Spartito degli uccelli.—Acre.—Radicàrio.
I. Title.
PQ4862.A444A8 73-337099

Ballo, Guido, 1914–
La chiave dell'arte moderna ... Duecentoquattordici illustrazioni in biano e nero. Sessanta illustrazioni a colori. Impaginato da Mario Monti. Milano, Longanesi, 1968.
474 p. illus. 22½ cm. (His Occhio critico, 2) (La Vostra via, v. 70) 5000 It 68-Nov
Bibliography: p. ₍447₎-452.
1. Art, Modern—20th century. I. Title. II. Series.
N7477.B36 vol. 2 70-400218
[N6490] rev

Ballo, Guido, 1914-
La mano e la macchina : dalla serialità artigianale ai multipli / Guido Ballo. — Milano : Jabik & Colophon : Sperling & Kupfer, 1976.
271 p. : ill. ; 21 cm. It77-Apr
Includes bibliographical references and index.
L12000
1. Art—Reproduction. 2. Multiple art. I. Title.
N8580.B34 77-466645
•77 MARC

Ballo, Guido, 1914–
Mario Radice. Torino, ILTE, 1973.
205 p. illus. 29 cm. L18000 It 73-Sept
Text also in English.
Bibliography: p. 196-205.
1. Radice, Mario.
ND623.R16B34 759.5 74-305796

Ballo, Guido, 1914–
Il nuovo sistema per vedere l'arte. Duecento illustrazioni in bianco e nero, trenta illustrazioni a colori. Impaginato da Mario Monti. Milano, Longanesi ₍1973₎
289 p. illus. (part col.) 23 cm. (His Occhio critico, 1) (La Vostra via, v. 64) L7000 It***
Second ed.
Bibliography: p. ₍281₎-284.
1. Art—Psychology. 2. Visual perception. I. Title. II. Series.
N7477.B36 vol. 1 74-324390
[N71]

Ballo, Guido, 1914–
Occhio critico. Impaginazione di Mario Monti. Milano, Longanesi ₍1968–1973, v. 1 1973₎
2 v. illus. (part col.) 23 cm. (La Vostra via, v. 64, 70) L7000 (v. 1) L5000 (v. 2) It***
Vol. 1: 2 ed., v. 2: 1st ed.
Includes bibliographies.
1. Art appreciation. I. Title.
N7477.B36 74-323633

Ballo, Guido, 1914-
La scuola italiana di Parigi. Milano, Centro d'arte Annunciata, 1971.
1 v. (unpaged) illus. (part col.) (₍Collana dell'Angelo₎ Anno 30, n. 10)
At head of title: Galleria Annunciata.
1. Paintings, Italian. I. Galleria Annunciata. II. Title. III. Series.
CU NUC75-32100

Ballo, Guido, 1914–
Sicilia controcanti / Guido Ballo. — 1. ed. — Parma : Guanda, 1975.
160 p. ; 23 cm. — (Collana Fenice : Sezione poeti) It 75-July
Prose and verse.
Bibliography: p. 149-155.
L4200
1. Sicily—Description and travel—Poetry. 2. Sicily—Social life and customs—Poetry. 3. Poetry of places—Sicily. I. Title.
PQ4862.A444S5 75-532750

Ballo, Guido, 1914-
see Cascella, Andrea. Andrea Cascella. Milano, Edizioni del Naviglio, 1972.

Ballo, Guido, 1914-
see Tadini, Emilio. Emilio Tadini ... Parma: Università di Parma [1975]

Ballo Moreno, Alejandro
Alejandro Balló Moreno, servidor de la Palabra. [Sevilla, Esc. Gráf. Salesiana, 1972]
111 p., 2 l., plates. 22 cm. Sp 73
Bibliography: p. 107-111.
1. Balló Moreno, Alejandro.
BX4705.B158A63 73-359250

Ballocco, Mario, 1913–
Mario Ballocco. Werke, 1949-1972. Neue Galerie am Landesmuseum Joanneum, 13. 1. – 11. 2. 73. (Ausstellung u. Katalog: Wilfried Skreiner. Werkskatalog u. Katalogred.: Ulla Herrgesell, Werner Fenz. [Einf.:] Umbro Apollonio. Übers.: Maria Kiefer-Tarlao, Franz Holzer.) (Graz, Neue Galerie am Landesmuseum Joanneum [19]73.)
10 l., 18 plates (part col.) 24 cm. S36.00 Au 73-13-168
1. Ballocco, Mario, 1913– I. Skreiner, Wilfried. II. Graz. Neue Galerie.
ND623.B193S57 73-351019

Ballod, Carl, 1864–1931.
K. Baloȝcha Latwijas i ȝweidoȝchana; indiwiduālā u ȝoziālā Latwija. Rigâ, J. Treimans, 1919.
24 p. 22 cm.
1. Latvia—History—1918-1940. 2. Latvia—Economic policy. I. Title. II. Title: Latwijas i weido chana.
DK511.L18B26 72-245092

Ballod, F V
(Privolzhskie "Pompei")
Приволжские "Помпеи"; опыт художественно-археологического обследования части правобережной Саратовско-Царицынской приволжской полосы. Москва, Гос. изд-во, 1923.
131 p. illus. 27 cm.
1. Volga Valley—Antiquities. I. Title.
GN824.V58B34 74-224456

Ballod, F V
Старый и Новый Сарай, столицы Золотой Орды; результаты археологических работ летом 1922 года. Казань [Изд. Комбината изд-ва и печати] 1923.
62 p. illus. (part col.) 26 cm.
At head of title: В. Ф. [sic] Баллод.
Includes bibliographical references.
1. Saraĭ Staryĭ, Russia—Antiquities. 2. Excavations (Archaeology)—Russia—Saraĭ Staryĭ. 3. Golden Horde. I. Title.
Title romanized: Staryĭ i Novyĭ Saraĭ, stolit͡sy Zolotoĭ Ordy.
DK651.S387B34 73-215683

Ballois, Pierre.
Les Escoumins. Suivi de Chicoutimi et de Le Coureur. Hull, Que., 1973.
88 p. 21 cm. C***
At head of title: Paraboles I-III.
I. Title. II. Title: Paraboles I-III.
PQ3919.2.B25E8 74-194311
MARC

[**Ballon,**] directeur des jardins du roi.
Nouveau traité des orangers et citronniers, contenant la maniére de les connoître, les façons qu'il leur faut faire pour les bien cultiver, & la vraie methode qu'on doit garder pour les conserver. Paris, C. de Sercy, 1692.
6 p. l., 187, [5] p. 15 cm.
By Ballon and Garnier.
1. Orange. 2. Lemon. 3. Fruit-culture—Early works to 1800. I. Garnier, ——, jardinier du roi, joint author. II. Title.
SB370.O7B34 Agr 17-33
rev

Ballón, Eduardo.
see La Publicidad ... Lima, Centro de Estudios y Promoción del Desarrollo, Area de Educación : [distribuye Mosca Azul] 1974.

Ballón, Milagro Luna
see
Luna Ballón, Milagro.

Ballón, Oscar Urteaga
see Urteaga Ballón, Oscar.

Ballon, Robert J
Financial reporting in Japan / by Robert J. Ballon, Iwao Tomita, Hajime Usami ; with a preface by Takeshi Watanabe. — 1st ed. — Tokyo ; New York : Kodansha International ; New York : distributed by Harper & Row, 1976.
xxii, 305 p. ; 24 cm. Ja***
Includes bibliographical references and index.
ISBN 0-87011-269-4 : Y3,000 ($15.00 U.S.)
1. Financial statements—Japan. 2. Accounting—Japan. 3. Corporations—Japan—Finance. I. Tomita, Iwao, 1924- joint author. II. Usami, Hajime, joint author. III. Title.
HF5681.B2B275 658.1'512'0952 75-30179
76 MARC

Ballon, Robert J
Japan's market and foreign business. Robert J. Ballon, editor. Tokyo, Sophia University; in cooperation with EncyclopÆdia Britannica (Japan) [1971]
xii, 304 p. 23 cm. Y18,000 ($8.50 U.S.) Ja***
Rev. ed. published in 1973 under title: Marketing in Japan.
1. Marketing—Japan—Addresses, essays, lectures. 2. Consumers—Japan—Addresses, essays, lectures. I. Title.
HF5415.12.J3B3 1971 658.8'00952 72-176014
72[r75]rev MARC

Ballon, Robert J
Japan's salary system / by R. J. Ballon and H. Inohara. — Tokyo : Sophia University, 1976.
28 p. ; 28 cm. — (Bulletin - Sophia University Socio-Economic Institute ; 60) Ja76-30
Includes bibliographical references.
1. Wages—Dismissal wage—Japan. 2. Retirement—Japan. I. Inohara, Hideo, joint author. II. Title. III. Series: Jochi Daigaku, Tokyo. Shakai Keizai Kenkyujo. Bulletin - Sophia University Socio-Economic Institute ; 60.
HD4928.D5B34 331.2'52'0952 77-360404
*77 MARC

Ballon, Robert J
Marketing in Japan : revised edition of Japan's market and foreign business / Robert J. Ballon, editor. — Rev. ed. — Tokyo : Sophia University ; New York : Kodansha International, 1973, 1974 printing.
xvi, 200 p. ; 24 cm. Ja***
Rev. ed. of Japan's market and foreign business published in 1971.
Includes bibliographical references and index.
ISBN 0-87011-200-7 : $12.50
1. Marketing—Japan—Addresses, essays, lectures. 2. Consumers—Japan—Addresses, essays, lectures. I. Title.
HF5415.12.J3B33 1974 658.8'00952 73-79771
MARC

Ballon, Victorine, tr.
see Potter, Beatrix, 1866-1943. La famille Flopsaut. London, Warne [n. d.]

Ballon, Victorine, tr.
see Potter, Beatrix, 1866-1943. Histoire de Pierre Lapin. London, Warne [n. d.]

Ballón Aguirre, Enrique, 1940–
Vallejo como paradigma : un caso especial de escritura / Enrique Ballón Aguirre. — Lima : Instituto Nacional de Cultura, 1974.
213 p. ; 18 cm.
A revision of the author's thesis, Universidad Nacional Mayor de San Marcos de Lima, 1971.
On spine: 4.
Bibliography: p. 199-213.
1. Vallejo, César Abraham, 1892-1938—Language. I. Title.
PQ8497.V35Z58 1974 75-557345

Ballone, Edoardo.
Viaggio fra i vini del Monferrato ... Villanova Monferrato, Donna e Giachetti, [1972?].
174 p. illus., plates. 31 cm. It 72-Dec
"Di Edoardo Ballone e Riccardo Di Corato."
1. Wine and wine making—Monferrato. 2. Monferrato—Description and travel. I. Di Corato, Riccardo, 1927– joint author. II. Title.
TP559.I 8B34 73-308656

Ballone, Edoardo.
Viaggio fra i vini della Toscana ... Milano, S. E. D. D., [1973?].
184 p. illus. 31 cm. (Viaggio fra i vini d'Italia) L6500 It 74-Feb
Bibliography: p. [191]
1. Tuscany—Description and travel. 2. Wine and wine making—Tuscany. I. Title.
DG734.2.B27 74-306028

Balloni, Augusto.
Criminologia. Quaderno di appunti delle lezioni del prof. Augusto Balloni. Anno accademico 1971-72. Bologna, Cooperativa libraria universitaria, 1972.
230 p. 24 cm. L3100 It 73-Mar
Includes bibliographies.
1. Crime and criminals. I. Title.
HV6025.B24 73-345391

Balloni, Augusto.
Criminologia e psicopatologia : analisi di 110 perizie psichiatriche / Augusto Balloni ; presentazione del prof. Renzo Canestrari. — Bologna : Pàtron, c1976.
xii, 255 p. ; 22 cm. — (Collana di studi criminologici ; 1) It76-Oct
Includes bibliographical references and index.
L4500
1. Criminal psychology. 2. Psychology, Pathological. I. Title.
HV6080.B34 76-487890
*76 MARC

Balloni, Augusto.
La fabbrica dei disadattati. Infanzia abbandonata e gioventù deviante. Presentazione di Achille Ardigò. Milano-Roma, Sapere, 1974.
144 p. 20 cm. (Contro lo sfruttamento, 4) L1500 It 74-Sept
At head of title: Augusto Balloni, Luigi Fadiga.
Bibliography: p. 143-144.
1. Child welfare—Italy. 2. Juvenile delinquency—Italy. 3. Children—Law—Italy. I. Fadiga, Luigi, joint author. II. Title.
HV774.A6B34 74-342608

Balloni, Valeriano, comp.
Lezioni sulla politica economica in Italia. A cura di Valeriano Balloni. Milano, Edizioni di Comunità, 1972.
viii, 413 p. 22½ cm. (Studi e ricerche di scienze sociali, 51) L5000 It 72-Dec
At head of title: Istituto superiore di studi economici Adriano Olivetti (ISTAO).
Includes bibliographies.
1. Italy—Economic policy—Addresses, essays, lectures. 2. Finance, Public—Italy — Addresses, essays, lectures. 3. Monetary policy — Italy—Addresses, essays, lectures. I. Title.
HC305.B286 72-373950

Ballonoff, Paul A comp.
Genetics and social structure: mathematical structuralism in population genetics and social theory. Edited by Paul Ballonoff. Stroudsburg, Pa., Dowden, Hutchinson & Ross [1974]
xv, 504 p. illus. 26 cm. (Benchmark papers in genetics, v. 1)
CONTENTS: Macfarlane, A. Analysis of relationships of consanguinity and affinity.—Kroeber, A. L. Classificatory systems of relationship. — Pearl, R. The measurement of the intensity of inbreeding. — Bernstein, S. Démonstration mathématique de la loi d'hérédité de Méndel. — Bernstein, S. Principe de stationarité et généralisations de la loi de Mendel.—Etherington, I. M. H. On non-associative combinations.—Etherington, I. M. H. Genetic algebras.—Etherington, I. M. H. Duplication of linear algebras.—Etherington, I. M. H. Non-associative algebra and the symbolism of genetics.—Reiersöl, O. Genetic algebras studied recursively and by means of differential operators.—Cotterman, C. W. A calculus for statistics-genetics.—Livingstone, F. B. A formal analysis of prescriptive marriage systems among the Australian aborigines.—Courrège, P. A. A mathematical model of the structure of kinship. — White, H. C. Models of kinship systems with prescribed marriage. — Liu, P. H. Formal analysis of prescriptive marriage system: the Murngin case.—Maruyama, T. Analysis of population structure, II. — Haldane, J. B. S. and Jayakar, S. D. An enumeration of some human relationships.—Wright, S. The interpretation of population structure by F-statistics with special regard to systems of mating.—Cavalli-Sforza, L. L., Kimura, M., and Barrai, I. The probability of consanguineous marriages.—Jacquard, A. Genetic information given by a relative.—Schull, W. J. and Neel, J. V. The interpretation of the effects of inbreeding.—Bibliography: (p. 497-500)
1. Population genetics—Addresses, essays, lectures. 2. Kinship—Addresses, essays, lectures. I. Title.
[DNLM: 1. Genetics, Population. 2. Mathematics. W1 BE516 v. 1 1974/QH 431 G3285 1974]
GN289.B34 301.42'1'0157321 73-20412
ISBN 0-87933-067-8 MARC

Ballonoff, Paul A
Mathematical foundations of social anthropology / Paul A. Ballonoff. — The Hague : Mouton, [1976].
xv, 131 p. ; 24 cm. — (Publications of the Maison des sciences de l'homme) Ne76-11
Bibliography: p. [129]-131.
1. Kinship. 2. Marriage. 3. Demographic anthropology. 4. Mathematical anthropology. I. Title. II. Series: Maison des sciences de l'homme, Paris. Publications of the Maison des sciences de l'homme.
GN487.B34 301.42'01'51 76-461637
76 MARC

Ballonoff, Paul A.
see Demographic genetics. Stroudsburg, Pa., Dowden, Hutchinson & Ross, c1975.

Ballonoff, Paul A.
see MSSB Conference on Genealogical Mathematics, Houston, 1974. Genealogical mathematics ... Paris, Mouton, c1974.

Ballonoff, Paul A., ed.
see Mathematical models of social and cognitive structures... Urbana, Univ. of Illinois Press [1974]

Ballorain, Rolande.
Le nouveau féminisme américain; essai. Étude historique et sociologique du Women's Liberation Movement. [Paris] Denoël/Gonthier [1972]
430 p. illus. 22 cm. (Collection Femme) 38.00F F***
Includes bibliographical references.
1. Women's Liberation Movement—United States. 2. Women in the United States. I. Title.
HQ1426.B26 72-374788
rev

Ballot, George Muller.
Floris Jespers en die vlaamse ekspressionisme. Pretoria, 1969.
ix, 316 l. 30 cm.
Proefskrif–Pretoria.
Reproduced from typescript.
Summary in English.
Bibliography: leaves 305-316.
1. Jespers, Floris, 1889-1965. 2. Expressionism (Art)–Flanders. I. Title.
CtY NUC74-122371

Ballot, Helmut, 1917-
Irrlicht am Nadelkap. 2. Aufl. Recklinghausen, Paulus Verlag, c1963.
112 p. illus.
I. Title.
CaBVaU NUC73-2355

Ballot, Michael H., joint author
see Fischer, Robert B Chico housing market... Chico, Calif., 1970.

Ballot, Michael Harvey, 1940-
The time-phasing and size of computer installations. [Ann Arbor, Mich., University Microfilms, 1973]
1 reel. 35 mm.
Thesis—Stanford University, 1973.
Collation of the original: 249 l. illus.
Microfilm copy.
1. Computer input-ouput equipment. 2. Replacement of industrial equipment. I. Title.
ViBlbV NUC75-18397

Ballot, Paul, professeur.
L'énergie des temps présents / Paul Ballot. — [Gray] : La presse de Gray, [1974]
45 p. : ill. ; 27 cm. F***
Cover title.
13.00F
1. Power resources. 2. Power (Mechanics) I. Title.
TJ153.B224 333.7 75-506840
75 MARC

Ballot Box, joint author.
see Holland, Henry Edmund, 1868-1933. The tragic story of the Waihi strike. Dunedin, N. Z., Hocken Library, University of Otago, 1975.

Ballot-Lena, Brigitte.
L'Enfant au masque de Jardin / Brigitte Ballot-Lena. — Paris : P.J. Oswald, 1973.
29 p. ; 18 cm. F75-13023
9.00F
I. Title.
PQ2662.A428E5 841'.9'14 76-454255
76 MARC

Ballots Project.
BALLOTS system reference manual. Project BALLOTS. 2d ed. Stanford, Calif., The Project, 1973.
1 v.
At head of title: Stanford University Libraries.
Loose-leaf for updating.
1. Project BALLOTS. I. Title.
CU NUC77-26613

Ballots Project
see Epstein, A H A user's view of BALLOTS... Stanford, Calif., BALLOTS Project, 1972.

Ballots Project
see Stanford University. Libraries. Bibliographic automation of large library operations... [Washington, ERIC Document Reproduction Service] 1971.

Ballots Project
see Stanford University. Libraries. Final report of the Ballots Project... [Stanford, Calif., 1975]

Ballots Project
see User's view of BALLOTS: nos. 4, 5, 6 and 7. Stanford, Calif., 1973-74.

BALLOTS II: reference digest. Stanford, Calif., Stanford University Libraries, 1975.
18 p. 29 cm.
1. Ballots Project. 2. Stanford University Libraries. I. Stanford University. Libraries.
CSt NUC76-21083

Ballotta, Paolo.
Le déchiffrement du Disque de Phaestos / Paolo Ballotta. — Bologna : Libreria editrice Minerva, 1974.
ix, 245 p. : ill. ; 24 cm. It75-Oct
Bibliography: p. 193-245.
L6000
1. Phaistos Disk.
P1036.B3 76-463840
*76 MARC

Ballotta, Paolo.
Le poème du Disque de Phaestos / Paolo Ballotta. — Bologna : Libreria editrice Minerva, 1974.
39 p. : ill. ; 21 cm. It75-Oct
Includes the author's romanized transcription and French translation of text from the Phaestus disc.
1. Phaistos Disk. I. Title.
P1036.B34 76-481580
*76 MARC

Ballotto, Francesco.
Storia della letteratura greca, dalle origini al 529 d.C. Nuova [i.e. 3.] ed. Milano, Signorelli [1972]
942 p. fold. col. map, plates. 24 cm.
Bibliography: p. [821]-910.
1. Greek literature—Hist. & crit. I. Title.
IU NUC74-127739

Ballou, Adin, 1803-1890.
Autobiography of Adin Ballou, 1803-1890, containing an elaborate record and narrative of his life from infancy to old age : with appendixes / completed and edited by William S. Heywood. — Philadelphia : Porcupine Press, 1975.
xviii, 586 p. : ports. ; 22 cm. — (The American utopian adventure : series two)
Reprint of the 1896 ed. published by Vox Populi Press, Lowell, Mass.
"Published works of Adin Ballou": p. [573]-574.
Includes index.
ISBN 0-87991-033-X
1. Ballou, Adin, 1803-1890. I. Heywood, William Sweetzer, 1824-1903.
BX9969.B27A3 1975 288'.092'4 74-26603
74 MARC

Ballou, Adin, 1803-1890. Christian non-resistance defended against Rev. Henry Ward Beecher. 1972
in Ballou, Adin, 1803-1890. Christian non-resistance in all its important bearings... New York, Garland Pub., 1972.

Ballou, Adin, 1803–1890.
Christian non-resistance, in all its important bearings, illustrated and defended. Philadelphia, J. M. M'Kim, 1846. [New York, J. S. Ozer, 1972]
240 p. 22 cm. (The Peace movement in America)
Facsimile reprint.
1. Evil, Non-resistance to. I. Title. II. Series.
BT736.6.B34 1846a 171 76–137527
MARC

Ballou, Adin, 1803–1890.
Christian non-resistance in all its important bearings, illustrated and defended, together with A discourse on Christian non-resistance in extreme cases, and Christian non-resistance defended against Rev. Henry Ward Beecher, by Adin Ballou, and Non-resistance, a critical review of Adin Ballou's Christian non-resistance, by C. H. With an introd. for the Garland ed. by Larry Gara. New York, Garland Pub., 1972.
12, xv, 278, 32, 20, 87–113 p. 22 cm. (The Garland library of war and peace)
Reprint of 3 works by the author originally published in 1910, 1860, and 1862, respectively, and Non-resistance by C. H. originally published in the Christian examiner, v. 44, Jan. 1848.
1. Evil, Non-resistance to. 2. Christian ethics. 3. War and religion. I. Ballou, Adin, 1803–1890. A discourse on Christian non-resistance in extreme cases. 1972. II. Ballou, Adin, 1803–1890. Christian non-resistance defended against Rev. Henry Ward Beecher. 1972. III. Title. IV. Series.
BT736.6.B34 1972 241'.4 77–147697
ISBN 0–8240–0225–3 MARC

Ballou, Adin, 1803-1890. A discourse on Christian non-resistance in extreme cases. 1972
in Ballou, Adin, 1803-1890. Christian non-resistance in all its important bearings... New York, Garland Pub., 1972.

Ballou, Adin, 1803–1890.
History of the Hopedale Community, from its inception to its virtual submergence in the Hopedale Parish. William S. Heywood, editor. Philadelphia, Porcupine Press, 1972.
xvii, 415 p. port. 22 cm. (The American utopian adventure)
Reprint of the 1897 ed.
"Constitution by-laws, rules, and regulations of the Hopedale Community": p. [368]–396.
1. Hopedale Community. I. Heywood, Willliam Sweetzer, 1824–1905, ed.
HX656.H7B2 1972 335'.9'7443 76–187467
ISBN 0–87991–007–0 MARC

Ballou, Adin, 1803–1890.
History of the Hopedale Community, from its inception to its virtual submergence in the Hopedale Parish. William S. Heywood, editor. Lowell, Mass., Thompson & Hill, 1897. [New York, AMS Press, 1974]
xvii, 415 p. port. 23 cm. (Communal societies in America)
"Constitution, by-laws, rules, and regulations of the Hopedale Community": p. [368]–396.
1. Hopedale Community. I. Title.
HX656.H7B2 1974 335'.9'7443 72–2935
ISBN 0–404–10701–X MARC

Ballou, Adin, 1803-1890.
Practical Christian socialism: a conversational exposition of the true system of human society; in three parts, viz: I. Fundamental principles. II. Constitutional policy. III. Superiority to other systems. Hopedale [Mass.] New York, Fowlers and Wells, 1854.
xxi, 655 p. front. (port.) 24 cm.
Microfilm. Ann Arbor, Mich., University Microfilms, 1963. 1 reel. 35 mm. (American culture series, 222:4)
1. Socialism, Christian. 2. Social sciences. I. Title.
FU NUC74-124851

Ballou, Adin, 1803–1890.
Practical Christian socialism: a conversational exposition of the true system of human society ... Hopedale [Mass.] 1854. [New York, AMS Press, 1974]
655 p. port. 23 cm. (Communal societies in America)
ISBN 0–404–10702–8
1. Socialism, Christian. 2. Social sciences. I. Title.
HX51.B2 1974 335'.7 72–2936
MARC

Ballou, Adin, 1803-1890.
The towpath. New York, Uphill Pr. [1966]
12, [1] p. illus. 21 cm.
Limited ed.
I. Title.
NjP NN NUC75-32739

Ballou, Clara E
Ethelind. By "Carlottah" [pseud.] New York, J.S. Ogilvie [c1885]
179 p. 19 cm.
Micro-transparency (negative). Louisville, Ky., Lost Cause Press, 1973. 4 sheets. 10.5 x 14.8 cm. (L.H. Wright. American fiction, 1876-1900, no. 262)
I. Title.
PSt NUC75-17242

Ballou, David Penfield, 1942-
Instrumentation for the study of rapid biological oxidation-reduction reactions by EPR and optical spectroscopy / by David Penfield Ballou. -- Ann Arbor, Mich. : University Microfilms, 1976.
243 leaves : ill.
Thesis--University of Michigan, 1971.
KMK NUC77-87601

Ballou, Eleanor F
When to buy what; a buying calendar for annual publications. Prepared by Eleanor Ballou [and] Gloria D. Dean. San Francisco, PACAF Library Service, 1971.
ii, 141 p. 27 cm.
At head of title: PACAF basic bibliographies for base libraries.
On cover: Pacific Air Forces.
1. Yearbooks—Bibliography. 2. Book buying (Libraries) 3. Bibliography—Best books. 4. Military libraries. I. Title.
IEN NUC74-124037

Ballou, Hosea, 1771-1852.
A treatise on atonement; in which the finite nature of sin is argued, its cause and consequences as such, the necessity and the nature of atonement, and its glorious consequences in the final reconciliation of all men to holiness and happiness. Randolph, Vt., Printed by Sereno Wright, 1805 [1971]
216 p.
Microfilm (positive) Ann Arbor, Mich., University Microfilms, 1971. 1st title of 13. 35 mm. (American culture series, reel 468.1)
1. Universalism. 2. Atonement. I. Title.
KEmT NUC73-124008

Ballou, Hubbard W.
see Guidelines for use in producing facsimiles of rare books and related materials. [Washington, C.M. Spaulding, 1972]

Ballou, Hubbard W.
see Readers, reader-printers; 1971 supplement to the Guide to microreproduction equipment. 5th ed. Silver Spring, Md., c1971.

Ballou, John
see Newbrough, John Ballou, 1828-1891.

Ballou, John E.
see Hanford Biology Symposium, 14th, Richland, Wash., 1974. Radiation and the lymphatic system ... [Oak Ridge, Tenn.] Technical Information Center, Office of Public Affairs, Energy Research and Development Administration, 1976.

Ballou, Maturin Murray, 1820-1895.
The child of the sea; or, The smuggler of colonial times and The love test, by Lieutenant Murray [pseud.] Boston, U.S. Publishing Co., 1846 [1972]
100 p.
Added t.p., engraved.
"The gipsey girl": p. 94-100.
Microfilm (positive) Ann Arbor, Mich., University Microfilms, 1972. 6th title of 18. 35 mm. (American fiction series, reel 173.6)
I. Title. II. Title: The smuggler of colonial times. III. Title: The love test.
KEmT NUC73-126010

Ballou, Maturin Murray, 1820-1895.
The duke's prize; a story of art and heart in Florence, by Lieutenant Murray. New York, S. French [185-?]
100 p.
Microfilm (positive) Ann Arbor, Mich., University Microfilms, 1966. 11th title of 20. 35 mm. (American fiction series, reel 11.11)
I. Title.
MiU NUC76-37219

Ballou, Maturin Murray, 1820-1895.
Miralda; or, The justice of Tacon. A drama in three acts, written by M.M. Ballou. Boston, W.V. Spencer [1858]
29 p.
Microfilm (positive) Ann Arbor, Mich., University Microfilms, 1974. 4th title of 50. 35 mm. (American culture series, reel 552.4)
I. Title.
KEmT NUC75-16640

Ballou, Maturin Murray, 1820-1895.
The protege of the grand duke; a tale of Italy, by Frank Forester [pseud.] Boston, F. Gleason, 1845.
50 p.
Microfilm (positive) Ann Arbor, Mich., University Microfilms, 1974. 3d title of 11. 35 mm. (American fiction series, reel 233.3)
I. Title.
KEmT NUC76-5218

Ballou, Maturin Murray, 1820-1895.
The sea-witch; or, The African quadroon. A story of the slave coast, by Lieutenant Murray. New York, S. French [1855?]
77 p.
Microfilm (positive) Ann Arbor, Mich., University Microfilms, 1966. 12th title of 20. 35 mm. (American fiction series, reel 11.12)
I. Title.
MiU NUC76-37220

Ballou, Maturin Murray, 1820-1895.
The Spanish musketeer; a tale of military life, by Lieutenant Murray [pseud.] Boston, Gleason's Publishing Hall, 1852, c1846 [1974]
100 p. illus.
Added t.p., illus.
Microfilm (positive) Ann Arbor, Mich., University Microfilms, 1974. 4th title of 11. 35 mm. (American fiction series, reel 233.4)
I. Title.
KEmT NUC74-44229

Ballou, Mercedes Perrier, 1934-
Oral responses of fifth grade girls to selected storybooks. [n.p.] 1975.
251 l.
Thesis--Ohio State University.
Bibliography: leaves 248-251.
1. Children's literature. 2. Books and reading for children. 3. Comprehension. I. Title.
OU NUC77-85582

Ballou, Robert.
Early Klickitat valley days, by Robert Ballou [Goldendale, Wash., Printed by the Goldendale Sentinel, 1938]
496 p. illus., ports. 24 cm.
——— Index to names of persons and subjects, compiled by Jean Allyn Smeltzer. Portland, Or. [1972]
16 p. 22 cm.
F897.K6B3 Suppl.
1. Klickitat Co., Wash.—History. 2. Frontier and pioneer life—Washington (State)—Klickitat Co. I. Smeltzer, Jean Allyn. II. Title.
F897.K6B3 979.7 38-32579
rev

Ballou, Robert Oleson, 1892- ed.
see James, William, 1842-1910. William James on psychical research. Clifton [N.J.] A. M. Kelley, 1973 [c1960]

Ballou, Robert Oleson, 1892-
see The Portable world Bible. [New York] Penguin Books, 1976.

Ballou, Robert Oleson, 1892- ed.
see World bible. New York, Viking Press [1965, c1944]

Ballou, Ronald H 1937-
Business logistics management [by] Ronald H. Ballou. Englewood Cliffs, N. J., Prentice-Hall [c1973]
xiii, 514 p. illus. 25 cm. (Prentice-Hall international series in management) $14.95
Includes bibliographical references.
1. Physical distribution of goods—Management. I. Title.
HF5415.7.B34 658.7'8 72-1338
ISBN 0-13-104802-3 MARC

Ballou, Ronald H 1937-
Time delay effects in computerised physical distribution systems / by Ronald H. Ballou. -- Bradford, Eng. : MCB, [1976]
182-211 p. ; 24 cm. -- (International journal of physical distribution ; v. 6, no. 4)
1. Physical distribution of goods--Data processing. I. Title. II. Series.
CaBVaU NUC77-88158

Ballou, Stephen V., joint author
see Campbell, William Giles, 1902- Form and style... 4th ed. Boston, Houghton Mifflin [1973, c1974]

Balloun, Joe L
A cross-sectional test of Maslow's need hierarchy theory. [Berkeley] 1971.
127 l.
Thesis (Ph.D.)—University of California.
Bibliography: leaves 70-71.
CU NUC73-34752

Ballová, L'uba, ed.
see Internationales Musikologisches Symposium, 2d, Piešťany, Czechoslovak Republic, 1970. Tagungsbericht... [Bratislava, Slowakisches Nationalmuseum, c1970]

Ballová, L'uba
see Slovenské národne múzeum. Hudobné zbierky Slovenskeho narodného muzea. Bratislava: Opus pre Slovenské národné muzeum a Slovenský hudobný fond, 1975.

Ballow, E. Vernon.
see Niosh Solid Sorbents Roundtable, 2d, Cincinnati, 1973. Second NIOSH Solid Sorbents Roundtable ... Cincinnati, Ohio, U.S. Dept. of Health, Education, and Welfare, Public Health Service, Center for Disease Control, National Institute for Occupational Safety and Health, 1976.

Ballow, Henry, 1707-1782.
A treatise of equity. [n.p. 1973]
iv.
NjP NUC74-121691

Ballowe, James.
see A Sampler ... Winthrop, Ill., Dunes House, 1976.

Balls, Bryan.
Travellers' guide to Malta : a concise guide to the Mediterranean islands of Malta, Gozo and Comino. — 2nd ed. / text by Brian Balls and Richard Cox ; drawings by Guy Magnus ; maps by Tom Stalker-Miller. — London : Thornton Cox Ltd., 1975.
110 p., [8] p. of plates : ill. (some col.), maps ; 22 cm. GB75-25064
Cover title: Thornton Cox's travellers' guide to Malta, Gozo, and Comino.
Distributed by Hastings House, New York.
Includes index.
ISBN 0-902726-20-X : £1.40
1. Malta—Description and travel—Guide-books. I. Cox, Richard. II. Title. III. Title: Thornton Cox's travellers' guide to Malta, Gozo, and Comino.
DG989.B23 1975 914.58'5'04 76-360224
76 MARC

Balls, Michael, ed.
see British Society for Developmental Biology. The cell cycle in development and differentiation... Cambridge [Eng.] Univ. Press, 1973.

Balls, Michael.
see British Society for Developmental Biology. The early development of mammals ... Cambridge [Eng.] Cambridge University Press, 1975.

Balls, Michael.
see Organ culture in biomedical research ... London, Cambridge University Press, 1976.

Ballstadt, Carl, 1931-
see Major John Richardson ... Montreal, Lawrence M. Lande Foundation, 1972.

Ballstadt, Carl, 1931-
see The Search for English-Canadian literature ... Toronto, University of Toronto Press, [1975]

Ballstaedt, Mark T.
see Fabulous gold. 1st ed. Salt Lake City, Utah, Publishers House, c1975.

Ballu, Eugène Belin de
see Belin de Ballu, Eugène.

Ballu, Jacques Nicolas Belin de
see Belin de Ballu, Jacques Nicolas, 1753-1815.

Ballu-Loureiro, Nicole.
Portugese kunst. Schilder- en beeldhouwkunst van het naturalisme tot op heden. [Tentoonstelling ingericht door de vereniging "De Vrienden van Portugal" te Brussel en de Calouste Gulbenkian Stichting, met de medewerking van het Nationaal Voorlichtingssecretariaat van Portugal. Paleis voor Schone Kunsten, Brussel, oktober-november 1967. Catalogus door Nicole Ballu-Loureiro. Nederlandse vertaling: Bob Lebacq. Brussel, Paleis voor Schone Kunsten, 1967]
1 v. (unpaged) illus. 25½ cm. Be 68-1594
Translation of Art portugais.
1. Art, Portuguese—Exhibitions. 2. Art, Modern—19th century—Portugal. 3. Art, Modern—20th century—Portugal. I. Amis du Portugal. II. Fundação Calouste Gulbenkian. III. Brussels. Palais des beaux-arts. IV. Title.
N7128.B314 709'.469 rev 68-102283

Balluat, Paul, Baron de Constant de Rebecque d'Estournelles
see
Estournelles de Constant, Paul Henri Benjamin, baron d', 1852-1924.

Balluet, Paul Henri Benjamin, baron d'Estournelles de Constant
see
Estournelles de Constant, Paul Henri Benjamin, baron d', 1852-1924.

Balluseck, Lothar von.
Die CDU; Kurskorrektur oder mehr? Bad Godesberg, Hohwacht [1974?]
32 p. 21 cm. (Schriftenreihe Zündung, Anregungen, Programme, Initiativen, Heft 1) GFR***
1. Christlich-Demokratische Union (Germany (Federal Republic)) I. Title. II. Series.
JN3971.A98C4142 74-327201

Balluseck, Lothar von.
Erläuterungen für Deutsche / von Lothar von Balluseck. — Bonn-Bad Godesberg : Hohwacht-Verlag, [1975]
104 p. ; 21 cm. GFR75-A
Includes bibliographical references and index.
ISBN 3-87353-018-X : DM12.00
1. Germany, West—Intellectual life. 2. Ideology. 3. Civilization—Philosophy. I. Title.
DD259.2.B334 76 75-517118 MARC

Balluseck, Lothar von.
Frei sein wie die Väter?: eine Bilanz nach 25 Jahren Bundesrepublik/ Lothar von Balluseck. — 8., erw. Aufl. — Bonn-Bad Godesberg: Hohwacht-Verlag, 1974.
239 p.: numerous ill.; 21 x 29 cm. GFR 74-A
Bibliography: p. 236-237.
ISBN 3-87353-010-4 : DM36.00
1. Germany—History—Philosophy. I. Title.
DD94.B3 1974 943 75-571511

Balluseck, Lothar von, comp.
Die guten und die bösen Deutschen: das Freund-Feind-Bild im Schrifttum d. DDR/ Lothar von Balluseck. — Bonn-Bad Godesberg: Hohwacht-Verlag, 1972.
165 p.: ill.; 24 cm. — (Politische Text- und Bildsammlungen für Schule und Unterricht; Bd. 2) DM19.80 GDB 72-A19
Includes bibliographical references.
1. Civics, German—Study and teaching. 2. Communism—Germany (Democratic Republic, 1949-) I. Title. II. Series.
JN3971.5.A3 1972 72-365070

Balluseck, Lothar von.
Die Unternehmer; sind sie noch zu retten? Bad Godesberg, Hochwacht-Verlag [1974?]
16 p. 21 cm. GFR***
Lecture held at the Kiwanis-Club Köln on October 8, 1973.
1. Entrepreneur. I. Title.
HB601.B285 74-347168

Balluseck, Lothar von
see Auto heute im menschlichen Getriebe ... Bonn-Bad Godesberg : Hohwacht-Verlag, 1974.

Ballvé, Faustino.
Formulario procesal civil, por Faustino Ballvé. Con un índice alfabético por materias, redactado por Andrés Botas A. 2. ed. México, Ediciones Botas, 1970.
241 p. 22 cm.
1. Civil procedure—Mexico—Forms. I. Title.
MiU-L CSt-Law NUC73-121233

Ballwahn, Larry Lee, 1943-
Teacher perspectives of individualized instruction, by Larry L. Ballwahn. [n. p.] c1975.
166 l. 29 cm.
Thesis (Ph. D.)—University of Wisconsin.
Vita.
Includes bibliography.
1. Individualized instruction. I. Title.
WU NUC77-85559

Ballweg, Joachim.
see Beiträge zur Grammatik und Pragmatik. Kronberg/Ts., Scriptor Verlag, 1975.

Ballweg, John A
Social class differences in friend and kin relationships of the Negro conjugal unit. [Lincoln, Neb.] 1967.
125 l. tables.
Microfilm of typescript. Ann Arbor, Mich., University Microfilms, 1967. 1 reel. 35 mm.
Thesis—University of Nebraska.
Bibliography: leaves 110-117.
1. Negro families. 2. Negroes—Social life and customs. I. Title.
NN NUC76-37217

Ballweg, John A 1926-
Measuring attitudes toward water use priorities [by] John A. Ballweg. Blacksburg, Water Resources Research Center, Virginia Polytechnic Institute and State University, 1972.
ix, 135 p. 23 cm. (VPI-WRRC-Bull. 50)
Bibliography: p. 103-107.
1. Water resources development—Smith Mountain Lake, Va.—Public opinion. 2. Attitude (Psychology)—Testing. I. Title. II. Series: Virginia Polytechnic Institute and State University. Water Resources Research Center. Bulletin 50.
TD201.V57 no. 50 551.4'8'08 s 72-612520
[HD1695.S57] [301.15'43'33391] MARC

Ballweg, Manfred.
Bruckmann's Uhren-Lexikon / Manfred Ballweg. — München : Bruckmann, 1975.
232 p., [23] leaves of plates : numerous ill. (some col.) ; 25 cm. GFR 75-A
Bibliography: p. 232.
ISBN 3-7654-1559-6 : DM54.00
1. Clocks and watches—Dictionaries—German. I. Title.
NK7484.B28 75 75-510934 MARC

Ballweg, Ottmar.
Zu einer Lehre von der Natur der Sache. 2. Aufl. Basel, Helbing, 1963.
75 p. 23 cm. (Basler Studien zur Rechtswissenschaft, 57)
"Literaturverzeichnis: p. 71-75.
1. Philosophy of law. I. Title.
NjP NUC74-124038

Bally, A W
Structure, seismic data, and orogenic evolution of southern Canadian Rocky Mountains [by] A.W. Bally, P.L. Gordy, and G.A. Stewart... and Exploration in the Canadian Rockies and foothills [by] L.F. Keating. [Calgary, Alta.] Alberta Society of Petroleum Geologists [1970]
337-381, [1]-14 p. maps, 13 plates (in pocket) 24 cm.
Special reprinting from the Bulletin of Canadian petroleum geology, v. 14, no. 3, September 1966...and the Canadian journal of earth sciences, v. 3, 1966.
Cover title.
1. Geology—Alberta. 2. Geology—Rocky Mountains. I. Gordy, P. L. II. Stewart, George Alan. III. Keating, L. F. Exploration in the Canadian Rockies and foothills. IV. Title.
CaBVaU NUC73-47497

Bally, Charles, 1865-1947.
El lenguaje y la vida. Traducción de Amado Alonso. 6. ed. Buenos Aires, Editorial Losada [1972]
236 p.
Original French title: Le language et la vie.
1. Language and languages. I. Title.
ScU NUC75-32811

Bally, Charles, 1865-1947.
Tableau synoptique des termes d'identification et de leurs principaux synonymes, tiré de Traité de stylistique française, t. 2 [de] Charles Bally. [Montréal] Université de Montréal, Faculté des lettres, Département de linguistique et Faculté des arts B. A. pour adultes, 1964.
3, 226-264 p. 28 cm.
Cover title.
1. French language—Synonyms and antonyms. 2. French language—Terms and phrases. I. Bally, Charles, 1865-1947. Traité de stylistique française. II. Montréal. Université. Département de linguistique. III. Title.
CaQMM NUC76-36573

Bally, Charles, 1865-1947. Traité de stylistique française
see Bally, Charles, 1865-1947. Tableau synoptique des termes... [Montréal] Faculté des arts B.A. pour adultes, 1964.

Bally, Charles, 1865-1947, ed.
see Saussure, Ferdinand de, 1857-1913. Course in general linguistics. Revised ed. London: Fontana, 1974.

Bally, Dorel.
Difracția razelor X și a neutronilor. București, Editura tehnică, 1972.
455 p. with figs. 21 cm. lei 33.00 R 72-3029
At head of title: Dorel Bally, Ludmila Beneș, Rodica Mănăilă.
Includes bibliographies.
1. X-rays—Diffraction. 2. Neutrons—Diffraction. 3. X-ray spectroscopy. I. Beneș, Ludmila, joint author. II. Mănăilă, Rodica, joint author. III. Title.
QC482.B28 72-361798

Bally, Ralph Edward, 1944-
The effects of levels of word familiarity on tests of auditory discrimination and its relationship with socioeconomic level and race / by Ralph Edward Bally. -- [s.l. : s.n.], 1976.
vi, 84 leaves ; 28 cm.
Thesis (Ph. D.)--Catholic University of America.
Bibliography: leaves 64-[70]
1. Auditory perception. 2. Word recognition. I. Title.
DCU NUC77-86705

Bally, René Jacques.
Procedee actuale pentru îmbunătățirea stabilității pămînturilor. București, Centrul de informare și documentare hidrotehnică, 1972.
75 p. illus. 30 cm. (Studii de sinteză) lei 100 R***
At head of title: Ministerul Agriculturii, Industriei Alimentare și Apelor. Consiliul Național al Apelor.
"Elaborator: R. J. Bally."
Bibliography: p. 69-75.
1. Soil stabilization. 2. Grouting. I. Title.
TA710.B28 73-342173

Bally, René Jacques.
Procedee moderne pentru executarea infrastructurilor construcțiilor hidrotehnice. [Elaborator: dr. ing. R. J. Bally. București], C. I. D. H., Centrul de informare și documentare hidrotehnică, 1973.
84 p. with figs. and graphs. 30 cm. (Studii de sinteză, 4) lei 120 R 73-4766
At head of title: Ministerul Agriculturii, Industriei Alimentare și Apelor. Consiliul Național al Apelor.
Bibliography: p. 75-83.
1. Hydraulic structures—Foundations. I. Title
TC180.B34 74-301360

Bally, Théodore, 1896-
Theodor Bally. Retrospektive. (Ausstellung) Aargauer Kunsthas, Aarau, 9. März-14. April 1973. (Katalog). Aarau, 1973.
56 p. illus. (part col.) 30 cm. 5.00F Sw 73-B-1520
Introduction also in French.
1. Bally, Théodore, 1895- I. Aargauer Kunsthaus.
N7153.B28A62 74-330719

Bally, Théodore, 1896-
Théodore Bally: Schwarz-weiss Photos, Collagen, Zeichnungen. [Ausstellung] Kunstmuseum Basel, 29. Januar-12. März 1972. [Basel, Kunstmuseum, 1972]
[20] p. illus.
1. Bally, Théodore, 1896- I. Basel. Öffentliche Kunstsammlung.
InU NUC73-120532

Bally Case and Cooler, inc.
Working data catalog: sectional prefab walk-in coolers and freezers, refrigerated buildings. Bally, Pa. [1973]
1 v. (loose-leaf) illus. 30 cm.
"Current [3rd?] edition."
1. Refrigerators. 2. Cold-storage lockers. I. Title.
NIC NUC76-37218

Ballymena; consultants' proposals for the new town centre. Prepared for the Antrim and Ballymena Development Commission [by] Austin Smith. Lord, Drivers Jonas, Jamieson and MacKay, and Nigel Rose and Partners. London, 1970.
viii, 92 p. illus., maps. 30 cm.
1. Cities and towns—Planning—Ballymena. I. Austin Smith, Lord Partnership. II. Antrim and Ballymena Development Commission.
NIC CaBVaU NUC76-24901

Balma, Francis Octave.
Sept contes de Noël / Francis-Octave Balma. — Lyon : Maison rhodanienne de poésie ; Sète (15, rue des Rosiers, 34200) : F. Balma, 1973.
115 p. ; 19 cm. F76-10179
CONTENTS: Un songe.—François-Jean le Violoneux.—Un Noël a l'auberge du Poisson qui parle.—Murmure et Gâcheur.—Les sept Pères Noël.—Camomille de Balaruc.—Un amour de petit cireur.—Belzébuth.
15.00F
1. Christmas stories. I. Title.
PQ2603.A2813S4 843'.9'14 77-463891
77 MARC

Balmaceda, Angela Elena Luchenio de Rey
see
Luchenio de Rey Balmaceda, Angela Elena.

Balmaceda, Estela A 1944-
The spinning of edible protein fibers. [Amherst] 1973.
xiv, 104 l. illus. 28 cm.
Thesis (Ph.D.)—University of Massachusetts.
1. Textile fibers, Synthetic. 2. Food texture. I. Title.
MU NUC74-127741

Balmaceda, José Manuel, Pres. Chile, 1840-1891.
Pensamiento de Balmaceda [compilado por] Fernando Vargas. [1. ed. Santiago de Chile, Editora Nacional G. Mistral, 1974]
196 p. (Colección Ideario)
I. Silva Vargas, Fernando. II. Title.
InU NUC76-31607

Balmaceda, Raúl Rey
see Rey Balmaceda, Raúl.

Balmaceda, Virginia Cox
see
Cox Balmaceda, Virginia.

Balmaceda Agüero, Manuel José.
Evolución constitucional de Chile en la patria vieja. [Santiago] 1969.
95 l.
Licenciado—Universidad Catolica de Chile.
Bibliography: leaves 91-93.
1. Chile—Constitutional history. I. Title.
CLU NUC74-123550

Balmain Teachers College.

For works by this body issued under its later name see

William Balmain College.

Bālmakand, Mahtah, fl. 1719-1720.
Letters of the king-maker of the eighteenth century = (Bālmukund Nāma) / by Mehta Bālmukund ; English translation [from the Persian] with introduction and notes by Satish Chandra. — London : Asia Publishing House for Aligarh Muslim University, Department of History, The Centre of Advanced Study, 1972.
131, iv, [72] p. ; 25 cm. GB73-27857
English and Persian text; notes in English.
Letters written on behalf of Saiyid Abdullah Khan.
Bibliography: p. i-iv.
Includes index.
ISBN 0-210-22254-9 : £3.00
1. Mogul Empire—History—Sources. 2. Abdullah Khan, Saiyid, d. 1723. 3. Mogul Empire—Kings and rulers—Correspondence. I. Chandra, Satish. II. Abdullah Khan, Saiyid, d. 1723. III. Title. IV. Title: Bālmukund Nāma.
DS461.8.B3413 954.02'9'0924 77-354679
77 MARC

Balmaña, Ramón María Mullerat
see
Mullerat Balmaña, Ramón María.

Balmanno, M.
see Moore, Thomas, 1779-1852. The poetical works of Thomas Moore. New York, Johnson, Fry [19--?]

Balmanno, Mary.
Pen and pencil. By Mrs. Balmanno. New York, D. Appleton, 1957.
299 p. illus. 24 cm.
I. Title.
OKentU NUC73-57833

Balmas, Enea Henri.
La commedia francese del Cinquecento [di] Enea Balmas. Milano, Editrice Viscontea [1969]
159 p. 18 cm.
Includes bibliographical references.
1. French drama—16th cent.—Hist. & crit. 2. French drama (Comedy)—Hist. & crit. I. Title.
OU NUC73-2386

Balmas, Enea Henri.
Paul Melissus. Viaggiatore italiano. Verona, Tip. Bettinelli, 1969.
52 p. illus. 25 cm. (Quaderni del Seminario di lingue e letterature moderne straniere dell'Università di Padova, 1)
Includes bibliographical references.
1. Melissus, Paul, 1539-1602. 2. Italy—Description and travel—1501-1800. 3. Italy in literature. I. Series: Padua. Università. Seminario di lingue e lettere moderne straniere. Quaderni, 1.
NIC NUC76-38175

Balmas, Enea Henri.
Pramollo / Enea Balmas. — Torre Pellice : Società di studi valdesi, 1975.
49 p. : ill. ; 24 cm. It***
"Supplemento al Bollettino della Società di studi valdesi n. 135, 1. semestre '75."
L500
1. Pramollo, Italy—History. 2. Waldenses in Pramollo, Italy. I. Società di studi valdesi. Bollettino. II. Title.
DG975.P873B33 75-405626

Balmas, Enea Henri.
La Renaissance II, 1548-1570. [Paris] Arthaud [1974]
296 p. illus. (Littérature française, 4)
1. French literature—16th Cent.—Hist. & crit. 2. Renaissance. I. Title.
WMM NUC76-21120

Balmas, Enea Henri.
Situazioni e profili, con una prefazione di Diego Valeri. Milano, Istituto editoriale cisalpino [1968]-
v. 21 cm. (Collana Università commerciale L. Bocconi. Lingue e letterature straniere, 9) It***
At head of title: Enea Balmas.
CONTENTS: [1] Gide, Sartre, Jouhandeau, Gracq, Camus.
1. French literature—20th century—Addresses, essays, lectures. I. Title. II. Series: Lingue e letterature straniere, 9.
PQ306.B26 73-302484

Balmas, Enea Henri
see Antologia della letteratura francese. Milano: Fabbri, c1969.

Balmas, Enea Henri, ed.
see Gringore, Pierre, 1475 (ca.)-1538? Lettres nouvelles de Milan. [Milano] Cisalpino [1955, 1968]

Balmas, Enea Henri, ed.
see Histoire mémorable de la guerre faite par le Duc de Savoye... Torino, Claudiana, 1972.

Balmas, Enea Henri
see Storia della letteratura francese. Milano: Fabbri, c1969.

Balmas, Enea Henri
see Storia delle persecuzioni e guerre contro il popolo chiamato valdese che abita nelle valli del Piemonte, di Angrogna, Luserna, S. Martino, Perosa e altre, a far tempo dall'anno 1555 fino al 1561. Torino : Claudiana, c1975.

Balmaseda, Alfredo.
Cantando y adivinando / Alfredo Balmaseda ; ilus. de Darío Mora. — 1. ed. — La Habana : Unión de Escritores y Artistas de Cuba, [1975]
44 p. : col. ill. ; 24 cm.
1. Riddles, Spanish—Juvenile literature. I. Title.
PN6375.B3 398.6 76-469478
76 MARC

Balmaseda, Beatriz.
La mujer, la pata quebrada y en casa / Beatriz Balmaseda. — 1. ed. — Barcelona : DOPESA, 1977.
312 p. ; 19 cm. — (Documento periodístico ; 52) Sp***
Bibliography: p. 309-312.
ISBN 847235296X : 375ptas
1. Women. 2. Women—Sexual behavior. I. Title.
HQ1154.B265 77-475341
77 MARC

Balmaseda, Cesar de.
Momentos, 1925 a 1928. Madrid [1951]-1966.
2 v. 21 cm.
I. Title.
MU NUC76-37225

Balmaseda, Manuel.
Primer cancionero flamenco [por] M. Balmaseda. [Bilbao] Z[ero; distribuidor exclusivo: Madrid, ZYX, 1973]
149 p. 17 cm. (Colección Se hace camino al andar. Serie S, no. 32) 45ptas Sp***
Includes bibliographical references.
I. Title.
PQ6603.A477P7 74-302707
ISBN 84-317-0202-8

Balmasov, Evgeniĭ I͡Akovlevich.
(Avtomatizat͡sii͡a prot͡sessov proizvodstva drevesnykh plit)
Автоматизация процессов производства древесных плит. Москва, "Лесная пром-сть," 1973.
224 p. with diagrs. 22 cm. 0.86rub USSR 73
At head of title: Е. Я. Балмасов.
Bibliography: p. 221-[223]
1. Particle board. 2. Wood-using industries—Automation. I. Title.
TS875.B34 74-303562

Balmasov, Evgeniĭ I͡Akovlevich, ed.
see Avtomatizat͡sii͡a lesnoĭ i derevoobrabatyvai͡ushcheĭ promyshlennosti. 1973.

Balmasova, Marii͡a Vasil'evna
see Bekesh, Vladimir Iosifovich. Sot͡siologii͡a i propaganda. 1971.

Balme, B E
Palynology of Permian and Triassic strata in the Salt Range and Surghar Range, West Pakistan. [Lawrence, University Press of Kansas, 1970]
306-453 p. illus., maps. 25 cm.
"Reprinted ... from Stratigraphic boundary problems: Permian and Triassic. Bernard Kummel and Curt Teichert, editors," 1970.
1. Palynology—West Pakistan. 2. Geology, Stratigraphic—Triassic. 3. Geology, Stratigraphic—Permian. I. Title.
OkU NUC76-71852

Balme, D. M., ed.
see Aristoteles. Aristotle's De partibus animalium I... Oxford, Clarendon Press, 1972.

Balme, M G
Cupid and Psyche : an adaptation from The golden ass of Apuleius / [by] M. G. Balme, J. H. W. Morwood. — London : Oxford University Press, 1976.
80 p. : ill. ; 23 cm. GB76-17473
Latin text, English introd. and notes.
ISBN 0-19-912047-1 : £0.95
1. Latin language—Readers. I. Morwood, J. H. W., joint author. II. Apuleius Madaurensis. Psyche et Cupido. 1976. III. Title.
PA2095.B22 478'.6'421 77-366500
77 MARC

Balme, M G
The millionaire's dinner party; an adaptation of the Cena Trimalchionis of Petronius [by] M. G. Balme. [London, New York] Oxford University Press [1974, c1973]
95 p. illus. 23 cm. $2.50(U.S.) GB***
Text in Latin; notes in English.
1. Latin language—Readers. I. Petronius Arbiter. Saturae: Cena Trimalchionis. II. Title.
PA2095.B23 1974 478'.6'421 74-167294
ISBN 0-19-912025-0 MARC

Balme, M G
Scrutanda; [by] M. G. Balme and M. C. Greenstock. London, Oxford University Press, 1973.
96 p. maps. 21 cm. £0.50 GB 73-31312
Latin text, English comprehension questions.
1. Latin language—Readers. I. Greenstock, M .C., joint author. II. Title.
PA2095.B24 478'.6'421 74-158574
ISBN 0-19-831777-8 MARC

Balme, Pierre.
La basilique Notre Dame du Port [par] P. Balme et R. Crégut. [Clermont-Ferrand, G. de Bussac, 1971]
38, [2] p. illus., plans. 22 cm. (Le touriste en Auvergne, no. 3)
Cover title.
ODaU-M NUC75-32812

Balmer (Charles F.) and Company
see Charles F. Balmer and Company.

Balmer, Donald Gordon, 1926-
State election services in Oregon [by] Donald G. Balmer. Princeton, N.J., Citizens' Research Foundation [1972]
60 p. illus. 23 cm. (Citizens' Research Foundation. Study no. 21) $1.00
1. Elections—Oregon—Costs. I. Title. II. Series.
JK1966.O7B35 324'.795 75-307915
75 MARC

Balmer, Dres, 1949-
see Kurzwaren ... Gümligen, Zytglogge-Verlag, 1975.

Balmer, Edwin, joint author
see Wylie, Philip, 1902- When worlds collide. [New rev. ed. New York, Dell Pub. Co., c1933, 195-?]

Balmer, Hans, 1935- joint author.
see Wolff, Gunther, 1932- Atmung und Beatmung ... Berlin, Springer-Verlag, 1975.

Balmer, Hans Peter, 1945-
Nietzsches Aufloesung der Teleologie im Grundverhaeltnis von Mensch und Welt. [n. p.] 1972.
166 p.
Diss.-Tuebingen.
Bibliography: p. [153]-166.
1. Nietzsche, Friedrich, 1844-1900.
CSt NUC76-37227

Balmer, Hans Rudolf.
Robert Leu & [und] Söhne. Es Mundartspiel i dreine Ufzüge. Elgg, Volksverlag, [1971].
55 p. 20 cm. 6.50F Sw 71-A-6031
I. Title.
PT2603.A383R6 74-332758

Balmer, Hans Rudolf.
Der Strassewüscher Gregor : bärndütschi Gschichte / Hans Rudolf Balmer. — Bern : Francke, c1974.
141 p. ; 21 cm. Sw 75-A-154
CONTENTS: Der Strassewüscher Gregor.—E Läbeskrise.—Der neu Sigerischt.—Ds Grosschind.—Ohni Aasähe vor Pärson.—D Annonce.—Der Lerchebüelwäg.—Dür d Zytig gheilt.—Sinnlosi Treui.—Gryggere.
19.80F
I. Title.
PT2603.A383S8 75-527524

Balmer, Henry Scott, 1922-
A study of the variations in value orientation of Negro and white lower and middle socio-economic class students in the fifth and sixth grades. [Syracuse, N.Y.] 1971.
xiv, 337 l.
Thesis—Syracuse University.
Vita.
Bibliography: leaves 319-337.
Microfilm of typescript. Ann Arbor, Mich., University Microfilms, 1971. 1 reel. (Doctoral dissertation series, 72-6657)
NSyU NUC73-34751

Balmer, Jon.
Pasión volcanica. Buenos Aires, Ediciones Malinca [1959]
127 p. 18 cm. (Colección Nueva pandora, no. 57)
Translation of Moment of rapture.
I. Title.
MB NUC74-173588

Balmer, Joseph.
Artikel aus den Dakota-Scout Heften der Jahre 1956 bis 1958. Neuaufl. [Eddersheim, Interessengemeinschaft für Indianerkunde, 1967]
159 p. illus., ports. (Kalumet. Sonderheft, nr. 1)
1. Dakota Indians-Wars. 2. Dakota Indians. 3. Little Big Horn, Battle of the, 1876. I. Interessengemeinschaft für Indianerkunde, Deutschland. II. Title. III. Series.
CU-SB NUC76-17574

Balmer, Joseph.
So lebten die Prärie-Indianer. [Frankfurt-am-Main, Interessengemeinschaft für Indianerkunde, 1967]
159 p. ports. 22 cm. (Kalumet Sonderheft, 1)
A collection of essays published in the Dakota Scout from 1956 through 1958.
ICN NUC73-121146

Balmer, K. R., joint author.
see Ewers, J. W. Review of federal recreation research activities. Ottawa, Ministry of State for Urban Affairs, 1974.

Balmer, Louis Edward.
The influence of superintendents and teachers upon attitudes of elementary school principals. Chapel Hill, 1971.
149 p.
Thesis—University of North Carolina at Chapel Hill.
Microfilm. Ann Arbor, Mich., University Microfilms. 1 reel. 35 mm.
CLSU NUC73-34741

Balmer, N. Alfred, comp.
see Bible. O. T. Apocrypha. Ecclesiasticus. English. Revised Standard. Selections. 1973. Wisdom from the Apocrypha... St. Louis, Concordia Pub. House [1973]

Balmès, François, joint author.
see Badiou, Alain. De l'idéologie. Paris, F. Maspero, 1976.

Balmes, Jaime Luciano, 1810-1848.
Consideraciones políticas sobre la situación de España, 1840 / Jaime Balmes. — 1. ed. — Madrid : Doncel, 1975.
257 p. ; 18 cm. — (El Libro de bolsillo Doncel ; 61) Sp75-Oct
ISBN 8432505145 : 160ptas
1. Spain—History—Carlist War, 1833-1840. I. Title.
DP219.2.B34 1975 76-467431
*76 MARC

Balmes, Jaime Luciano, 1810-1848.
El criterio / Jaime Luciano. — 11. ed. — Madrid : Espasa-Calpe, 1973, c1939.
240 p. ; 18 cm. — (Colección austral ; 71) Sp74-Jan
ISBN 8423900711
I. Title.
B4568.B23C7 1973 76-451839
*76 MARC

Balmes, Jaime Luciano, 1810-1848.
El criterio / Jaime Balmes. — 1. ed. en Obras inmortales. — Barcelona : Bruguera, 1974, c1967.
335 p. ; 20 cm. — (Obras inmortales) Sp***
Bibliography: p. 29-31.
ISBN 8402037690
1. Philosophy. I. Title.
B4568.B23C7 1974 100 77-456855
77 MARC

Balmes, Jaime Luciano, 1810-1848.
De las ideas. Prólogo de Manuel Fuentes Benot. [3d ed.] Madrid, Aguilar [1963]
201 p. (Biblioteca de iniciacion filosofica, no. 33)
1. Philosophy. I. Title. II. Series.
UU NUC76-37226

Balmes, Jaime Luciano, 1810-1848.
Filosofía elemental. [Notas prologales y revisón texto; Jaime Uyá. 1. ed. Barcelona] Zeus [c1968]
449 p. cover illus. (Podium; obras significativas)
Originally published under title: Curso de filosofía elemental.
I. Uya, Jaime, ed. II. Title. III. Series.
CU-SB NUC73-2322

Balmforth, C K
Interface: library automation with special reference to computing activity; edited by C. K. Balmforth and N. S. M. Cox. Cambridge, Mass., M. I. T. Press [1971]
ix, 251 p. 25 cm. $15.00
Includes papers presented at the Newcastle Seminar on the Management of Computing Activities in Academic Libraries, 10-13 January 1969.
Bibliography: p. 232-240.
1. Libraries—Automation—Congresses. I. Cox, Nigel S. M., joint author. II. Newcastle Seminar on the Management of Computing Activity in Academic Libraries, 1969. III. Title.
Z678.9.A1B35 1971b 025'.028'5 70-158649
ISBN 0-262-02084-X rev MARC
IU Wa DNAL GAT DHUD NjR CSt OU InU NjMD PSt NSyU MiEM

Balmforth, E Lynn.
Rock 'n' reality; mirrors of rock music: it's relationship to sex, drugs, family and religion. Salt Lake City, Hawkes Publications [1971]
137 p.
1. Jazz music. I. Title.
UU NUC73-34754

Balmforth, Ramsden.
Evolution vs. religion. Girard, Kan., Haldeman-Julius Co. [19--]
64 p. 13 cm. (Ten cent pocket series no. 191)
1. Evolution. 2. Religion. I. Title. II. Series.
KU-RH NUC76-21119

Balmforth, Ramsden.
The problem-play and its influence on modern thought and life / by Ramsden Balmforth. — Brooklyn : Haskell House, 1977.
155 p. ; 21 cm.
Reprint of the 1928 ed. published by G. Allen & Unwin, London.
Includes index.
ISBN 0-8383-2129-2
1. Drama—History and criticism. 2. Theater—Moral and religious aspects. I. Title.
PN1647.B32 1977 809'.933'5 76-52915
76 MARC

Bālmīki
see
Vālmīki.

Bal'mont, Konstantin Dmitrievich, 1867-1943.
Bi͡elyĭ zodchiĭ; tainstvo chetyrekh svi͡etil'nikov. S.-Peterburg, Izdatel'stvo "Sirin", 1914.
2 p.l., 324 p. 32 x 25 cm.
At head of title: K. Bal'mont.
Poems.
Microfiche. Tumba, Sweden, International Documentation Centre, 196-.
I. Title.
TxU NUC76-3985

Bal'mont, Konstantin Dmitrievich, 1867-1943.
Bi͡elyĭ zodchiĭ; tainstvo chetyrekh svi͡etil'nikov. S.-Peterburg, Izdatel'stvo "Sirin", 1914.
2 p.l., 324 p. 32 x 25 cm.
At head of title: K. Bal'mont.
Poems.
Microfilm. Zug, Switzerland, Inter Documentation Co. 1973. 6 cards. 10.5 x 15 cm.
I. Title.
IU NUC75-138748

Bal'mont, Konstantin Dmitrievich, 1867-1943.
Bi͡elyi͡a zarnit͡sy; mysli i vpechatli͡enii͡a. [By] K. D. Bal'mont. S.-Peterburg, Izd. M. V. Pirozhkova, 1908.
217 p.
Photocopy. Ann Arbor, Mich. Xerox University Microfilms, 1975. 23 cm.
I. Title.
ViU NUC76-527

Bal'mont, Konstantin Dmitrievich, 1867-1943.
Bielyi͡a zarnit͡sy; mysli i vpechatlienii͡a.
S.-Peterburg, Izd. M. V. Pirozhkova, 1908.
[Ann Arbor, Mich., University Microfilms, 1970]
217 p. 21 cm.
At head of title: K. D. Bal'mont.
"Authorized facsimile ... produced in 1970 by microfilm-xerography."
I. Title.
NPV NUC76-14816

Bal'mont, Konstantin Dmitrievich, 1867-1943.
Gamai͡un; izbrannye stikhi. Stokkhol'm, Si͡evernye ogni, 1921.
109 p. 16 cm.
Microfiche. Tumba, Sweden, International Documentation Centre, 196-.
I. Title.
TxU NUC76-90395

Bal'mont, Konstantin Dmitrievich, 1867-1943.
Gdi͡e moĭ dom; ocherki, 1920-1923. Praga, 1924.
182 p. 18 cm.
Microfiche. Tumba, Sweden, International Documentation Centre, 196-.
I. Title.
TxU NUC76-90396

Bal'mont, Konstantin Dmitrievich, 1867-1943.
Gori͡ashchii͡a zdanii͡a; lirika sovremennoĭ dushi. Moskva, Tipo-lit. T-va I. N. Kushnerev, 1900.
213 p. 22 cm.
Microfiche. Tumba, Sweden, International Documentation Centre, 196-.
I. Title.
TxU NUC76-90397

Bal'mont, Konstantin Dmitrievich, 1867-1943.
Gornyi͡a vershiny; sbornik stateĭ. Moskva, Grif, 1904-
v.
Microfilm. Tumba, Sweden, International Documentation Centre, 1970. 6 cards.
9 x 12 cm.
1. Russian literature—Addresses, essays, lectures. I. Title.
IU NUC74-45553

Bal'mont, Konstantin Dmitrievich, 1867-1943.
I͡Asen'. Vidi͡enie dreva. Moskva, Izd-vo K. F. Nekrasova, 1916.
237 p. 19 cm.
Microfilm. Tumba, Sweden, International Documentation Centre [1974] 3 sheets.
9 x 12 cm.
I. Title.
WU TxU NUC75-128322

Bal'mont, Konstantin Dmitrievich, 1867-1943.
Iz chuzhezemnykh poėtov. S.-Peterburg, Prosvieshchenie [1909]
118 p.
Microfilm. Tumba, Sweden, International Documentation Centre [1974] 2 sheets
9 x 12 cm.
1. Russian poetry—Translations from foreign literature. I. Title.
WU NUC75-128314

Bal'mont, Konstantin Dmitrievich, 1867-1943.
Izbrannyi͡a stikhotvorenii͡a. N'i͡u-Ĭork [Izd. M. Gurevicha, 19-?]
94 p.
MH IaU NUC74-74173

Bal'mont, Konstantin Dmitrievich, 1867-1943.
Kraĭ Ozirisa; egipetskie ocherki. Moskva, 1914.
323 p. 19 cm.
Microfilm. Tumba, Sweden, International documentation Centre [1972] 5 cards. 9 x 12 cm.
I. Title.
IU NUC75-139784

Bal'mont, Konstantin Dmitrievich, 1867-1943.
Kraĭ Ozirisa; egipetskie ocherki. Moskva, 1914.
323 p. 19 cm.
Microfilm. Zug, Switzerland, Inter Documentation Co. AG [1974] 5 sheets.
9 x 12 cm.
I. Title.
WU NUC75-128316

Bal'mont, Konstantin Dmitrievich, 1867-1943.
Marevo. Parizh, Franko-russkai͡a pechat', 1922.
130 p. 22 cm.
Poems.
Microfilm. Tumba, Sweden, International Documentation Centre [1972] 3 cards.
9 x 12 cm.
I. Title.
IU NUC76-90385

Bal'mont, Konstantin Dmitrievich, 1867-1943.
Moe-eĭ. Rossii͡a. Praga, Plami͡a, 1924.
125 p. 18 cm.
Poems.
Microfilm. Tumba, Sweden, International Documentation Centre [1972] 3 cards.
9 x 12 cm.
I. Title.
IU NUC76-90384

Bal'mont, Konstantin Dmitrievich, 1867-1943.
Pi͡esni mstiteli͡a. Parizh, 1907.
64 p.
Microfilm. Tumba, Sweden, International Documentation Centre [1974] 2 sheets.
9 x 12 cm.
I. Title.
WU NUC75-128317

Bal'mont, Konstantin Dmitrievich, 1867-1943.
Pod novym serpom; roman. Berlin, Slovo, 1923.
381 p. 20 cm.
Microfiche. Tumba, Sweden, International Documentation Centre, 196-.
I. Title.
TxU NUC76-90387

Bal'mont, Konstantin Dmitrievich, 1867-1943.
Pod si͡evernym nebom; ėlegii, stansy, sonety. S.-Peterburg, Tip. M. Stasi͡ulevicha, 1894.
81, iii p. 20 cm.
Microfiche. Tumba, Sweden, International Documentation Centre, 196-.
I. Title.
TxU NUC76-90386

Bal'mont, Konstantin Dmitrievich, 1867-1943.
[Poems]
Избранные стихотворения и поэмы = Ausgewählte Versdichtungen / К. Д. Бальмонт ; Ausw., Vorw. u. Kommentar von Vladimir Markov ; with an introd. by Rodney L. Patterson. — München : Fink, 1975.
764 p. ; 19 cm. — (Centrifuga ; vol. 24) GFR 76-A
Preliminaries in English or German, poems and commentary in Russian.
Includes bibliographical references.
DM120.00
Title romanized: Izbrannye stikhotvorenii͡a i poėmy.
PG3453.B2A17 1975 76-518875

Bal'mont, Konstantin Dmitrievich, 1867-1943.
Poėzii͡a kak volshebstvo. Poetry as enchantment. Letchworth, Prideaux Press [1973]
93 p. port. 18 cm. (Russian titles for the Specialist, 49)
Reprint of the Moscow, 1915, ed.
I. Title.
TU NUC75-128313

Bal'mont, Konstantin Dmitrievich, 1867-1943.
Polnoe sobranie stikhov. [Moskva] Skorpion, 1907-14.
10 v. in 5. 23 cm.
Microfilm. Zug, Switzerland, Inter-Documentation Co. [1970] 27 cards. 9 x 12 cm.
IU NUC74-48814

Bal'mont, Konstantin Dmitrievich, 1867-1943.
Ptit͡sy v vozdukhi͡e; stroki napi͡evnyi͡a.
S.-Peterburg, Shipovnik, 1908.
228 p. 26 cm.
Microfilm. Tumba, Sweden, International Documentation Centre [1974] 5 sheets.
9 x 12 cm.
I. Title.
WU NUC75-128315

Bal'mont, Konstantin Dmitrievich, 1867-1943.
Si͡evernoe sii͡anie; stikhi o Litvi͡e i Rusi. Parizh, Rodnik, 1931.
180, [9] p. 18 cm.
"Knigi K. D. Bal'monta": 3 p. at end.
Microfilm. Tumba, Sweden, International Documentation Centre [1972] 4 cards.
9 x 12 cm.
I. Title.
IU NUC76-90388

Bal'mont, Konstantin Dmitrievich, 1867-1943.
Solnechnai͡a pri͡azha; izbornik, 1890-1918. Moskva, Izdanie M. i S. Sabashnikovykh, 1921.
271, [1] p. port. 19 cm. (On cover: Pushkinskai͡a biblioteka)
At head of title: K. D. Bal'mont.
Microfilm. Tumba, Sweden, International Documentation Centre [1972] 5 cards.
9 x 12 cm.
I. Title.
IU NUC76-90389

Bal'mont, Konstantin Dmitrievich, 1867-1943.
Sonety solnt͡sa, meda i luny. Pi͡esni͡a mirov. Moskva, Izdanie V. V. Pashukanisa, 1917.
272 p., 1 l. 17 x 13 cm.
At head of title: K. D. Bal'mont.
Microfiche. Tumba, Sweden, International Documentation Centre, 196-.
I. Title.
TxU NUC76-3974

Bal'mont, Konstantin Dmitrievich, 1867-1943.
Svietlyĭ chas; izbrannye stikhi. Paris, J. Povolozky [1921]
69 p.
Microfilm Tumba, Sweden, International Documentation Centre [1974] 1 sheet.
9 x 12 cm.
I. Title.
WU NUC75-128318

Bal'mont, Konstantin Dmitrievich, 1867-1943.
V razdvinutoĭ dali; poėma o Rossii. [Bi͡elgrad] 1929 [cover 1930]
199 p. port. 21 cm. (Russkai͡a biblioteka. kn., 11)
Microfiche. Tumba, Sweden, International Documentation Centre, 196-.
1. Russia—Descr. & trav.—Poetry. 2. Poetry of places—Russia. I. Title. II. Series: Russkai͡a biblioteka. Bi͡elgrad, kn. 11.
TxU NUC76-3975

Bal'mont, Konstantin Dmitrievich, 1867-1943.
Vozdushnyĭ put'; razskazy. Berlin, Ogon'ki, 1923.
199 p. 21 cm.
Microfiche. Tumba, Sweden, International Documentation Centre, 196-.
I. Title.
TxU NUC76-90408

Bal'mont, Konstantin Dmitrievich, 1867-1943.
Zelenyĭ vertograd. Slova pot͡sielui͡nyi͡a.
S.-Peterburg, Shipovnik, 1909.
248, v p. 24 cm.
Microfiche. Tumba, Sweden, International Documentation Centre, 196-.
I. Title.
TxU NUC76-3976

Bal'mont, Konstantin Dmitrievich, 1867-1943.
Zhar-ptit͡sa; svirīel' slavi͡anina. Moskva, Skorpion, 1907.
234 p. 23 cm.
Microfilm. Tumba, Sweden, International Documentation Centre [1974] 6 sheets.
9 x 12 cm.
I. Title.
WU TxU NUC75-128320

Bal'mont, Konstantin Dmitrievich, 1867-1943.
Zlyíà chary; kniga zaklíatiĭ. [Moskva, Izd. zhurnala "Zolotoe runo"] 1906.
116 p. 26 cm.
Microfilm. Tumba, Sweden, International Documentation Centre [1974] 3 sheets. 9 x 12 cm.
I. Title.
WU NUC75-128319

Bal'mont, Konstantin Dmitrievich, 1867-1943.
Zmîeinye t͡svîety. [Moskva] Skorpion, 1910.
248 p. 24 cm.
Microfiche. Tumba, Sweden, International Documentation Centre, 196-.
I. Title.
TxU NUC76-90390

Bal'mont, Konstantin Dmitrievich, 1867-1943.
Zovy drevnosti; gimny, pîesni i zamysly drevnikh. [Novoe izd., znachitel'no dop. i perer. Berlin] Slovo, 1923.
319 p. 20 cm.
Microfiche. Tumba, Sweden, International Documentation Centre, 196-.
I. Title.
TxU NUC76-3983

Bal'mont, Konstantin Dmitrievich, 1867-1943.
Zovy drevnosti; gimny, pîesni i zamysly drevnikh. [Novoe izd., znachitel'no dop. i perer. Berlin] Slovo, 1923.
319 p. 20 cm.
Microfilm. Zug, Switzerland, Inter Documentation Co. [1973] 7 cards. 9 x 12 cm.
I. Title.
IU NUC75-138747

Bal'mont, Konstantin Dmitrievich, 1867-1943, tr.
see Kālidāsa. Dramy. Moskva, Izd. M.I.S. Sabashnikovykh, 1916.

Bal'mont, Konstantin Dmitrievich, 1867-1943
see Kniga razdumiĭ. 1974.

Bal'mont, Konstantin Dmitrievich, 1867-1943
see Kruglikova, Elizaveta Sergeevna. (Parizh nakanunîe voĭny) 1916.

Balmonte, Ana María.
Herencia, medio y educación / ⌜Personalidad entrevistada René Zazzo ; texto Ana M.a Balmonte⌝. — Barcelona : Salvat Editores, 1974, c1973.
142 p. : col. ill. ; 20 cm. — (Biblioteca Salvat de grandes temas ; 33) Sp***
Bibliography: p. ⌜141⌝
ISBN 84-345-7391-1
1. Intelligence levels. I. Zazzo, René. II. Title.
BF431.B32 1974 74-351868

Balmoral Castle. ⌜Derby? Pilgrim Press, 1972⌝
24 p. illus.
1. Balmoral Castle.
MiEM NUC74-127745

Balmoral Recreation Committee
see ⌜William, Dorothy Anne⌝ 1954- Balmoral, 1872-1972. ⌜Stonewall, Man., Interlake Pub., 1972⌝

Balmukand Gupta
see
Gupta, Balmukand, 1909-

Balmukhanov, Saim Baluanovich, ed.
see Voprosy tkanevoĭ radiochuvstvitel'nosti. 1970.

Balmukund, Mehta
see
Bālmakand, Mahtab, fl. 1719-1720.

Balmukund Virottam
see
Virottam, Balmukund, 1935-

Balmus, Elvira
see Dictionar român-francez. Editia a 2-a. Bucuresti, Editura stiintifică, 1972.

Balnaves, John.
Australian libraries. — 2d ed. completely rev. and rewritten by John Balnaves & Peter Biskup. — ⌜Hamden, Conn.⌝ : Linnet Books, ⌜1975⌝
191 p. ; 23 cm. — (Comparative library studies)
Includes bibliographies and index.
ISBN 0-208-01361-X
1. Libraries—Australia. I. Biskup, Peter, joint author. II. Title.
Z870.A1B3 1975 021'.00994 75-1258
75 MARC

Balnaves, John.
Australian libraries. — 2nd ed. / completely revised and re-written by John Balnaves & Peter Biskup. — London : Bingley, 1975.
191 p. ; 23 cm. — (Comparative library studies) GB75-14573
Includes bibliographies and index.
ISBN 0-85157-181-6 : £4.75
1. Libraries—Australia. I. Biskup, Peter, joint author. II. Title.
Z870.A1B3 1975b 021'.00994 75-323919
75 MARC

Balnaves, John.
A workbook in information retrieval / by John Balnaves. — Canberra : Canberra College of Advanced Education, 1974.
vi, 183 p. ; 30 cm. Aus
Bibliography: p. 183.
ISBN 0-85889-005-4 : $1.30
1. Information storage and retrieval systems—Handbooks, manuals, etc. 2. Documentation—Handbooks, manuals, etc. I. Title.
Z699.B25 029 75-308612
75 MARC

Balneaves, Elizabeth.
Mountains of the Murgha Zerin: between the Hindu Khush and the Karakoram. London, Gifford, 1972.
239, ⌜16⌝ p. illus. (some col.), ports. (1 col.). 23 cm. £2.25
B 73-08587
Bibliography: p. 234.
1. Chitral—Description and travel. 2. Gilgit—Description and travel. 3. Swāt, Pakistan—Description and travel. I. Title.
DS392.C47B34 915.49'122'045 73-330706
ISBN 0-7071-0213-8 MARC

Balneoekonomické kolokvium, 3d, Karlovy Vary, Czechoslovakia, 1974.
III. ⌜i. e. Třetí⌝ Balneoekonomické kolokvium, Karlovy Vary, 14.-15. listopadu 1974 : sborník referátů příspěvků a projevů / ⌜redigoval Bořivoj V. Černý⌝. — V Mariánských Lázních : Výzkumný ústav balneologický, 1975.
166 p. : ill. ; 29 cm. Cz***
Cover title.
Includes bibliographies.
1. Health resorts, watering-places, etc.—Economic aspects—Congresses. 2. Balneology—Congresses. I. Černý, Bořivoj V. II. Výzkumný ústav balneologický.
RA791.B34 1974 76-530155

Balneologia Bohemica. Jahrg. 1-
1972-
⌜Praha, Verlag Avicenum⌝
v. 24 cm. quarterly.
"Zeitschrift des Forschungsinstituts für Balneologie."
German with summaries in English, French and Russian.
1. Balneology—Periodicals. I. Výzkumný ústav balneologický.
RM801.B17 73-646189
MARC-S

Balneologia polska.
Poznań, Polskie Towarzystwo Balneologii, Bioklimatologii i Medycyny Fizykalnej.
v. illus. 24 cm.
"Kwartalnik poświęcony zagadnieniom uzdrowiskowym, fizykoterapii oraz bioklimatologii."
Began in 1951. Cf. New serial titles.
Summaries in English or German.
1. Balneology—Periodicals. 2. Baths—Poland—Periodicals. I. Polskie Towarzystwo Balneologii, Bioklimatologii i Medycyny Fizykalnej.
RM801.B175 72-626210

Balneotherapia gynaecologica. Proceedings of the 1. symposium with international participation of gynaecological balneotherapy, held in Frantiskovy Lázne, Czechoslovakia, October 10.-14. 1967. Symposium was organized by Czechoslovak Society of Gynaecology and Obste⌜t⌝rics ⌜aj. Sborník.⌝ Edited by Miroslav Vojta. Praha, Merkur, Balnea, 1971.
286, ⌜1⌝ p. ⌜6⌝ col. plates, with tables and graphs. 21 cm. Cz 71
English or German with summaries in the other language.
Organized by the Czechoslovak Society of Gynaecology and Obstetrics, the Central Administration of Spa and Mineral Springs, and the Czechoslovak State Spas.
Includes bibliographical references.
1. Hydrotherapy—Congresses. 2. Gynecology—Congresses. 3. Baths, Moor and mud—Congresses. I. Vojta, Miroslav, ed. II. Czechoslovak Society of Gynaecology and Obstetrics. III. Czechoslovak Republic. Ústřední správa lázní a zřídel. IV. Czechoslovak State Spas.
RG126.B34 618.1'065'3 75-301497
MARC

Balner, Hans, ed.
see International Symposium on Infections and Immunosuppression in Subhuman Primates, Rijswijk, Netherlands, 1969. Infections and immunosuppression in subhuman primates. Baltimore, Williams & Wilkins [c1970]

Balner, Hans, ed.
see Transplantation genetics of primates. New York, Grune & Stratton [1972]

Balny d'Avricourt, Adrien.
L'enseigne Balny et la conquête du Tonkin: Indochine 1973 ⌜par⌝ A. Balny d'Avricourt. Paris, Éditions France-Empire ⌜1973⌝
324 p. illus. 19 cm. 24.50F F***
Bibliography: p. ⌜317⌝-321.
1. Vietnam—History—1858-1945. 2. Balny d'Avricourt, Adrien. I. Balny, d'Avricourt, Adrien, 1849-1873. II. Title.
DS557.A566B34 959.7'03 74-160553
MARC

Balny d'Avricourt, Adrien, 1849-1873
see Balny d'Avricourt, Adrien. L'enseigne Balny et la conquête du Tonkin... Paris, Éditions France-Empire [1973]

(Bal'nye tant͡sy)
Бальные танцы / ⌜составитель А. Н. Беликова⌝. — Москва : Сов. Россия, 1975.
107 p. : ill. ; 22 cm. — (Библиотечка В помощь художественной самодеятельности ; № 8, 1975) USSR***
Includes music.
0.30rub
1. Ballroom dancing. I. Belikova, Alla Nikolaevna. II. Series: Bibliotechka "V pomoshch' khudozhestvennoĭ samodeíatel'nosti" ; 1975, no. 8.
PG3242.B5 1975, no. 8 75-592293
[GV1751]

Baló, József.
Logika / Baló József. — 3. kiad. — Budapest : Tankönyvkiadó, 1974.
187 p. ; 24 cm. — (Tanárképző főiskolai tankönyvek)
ISBN 9631700119 : 16.00Ft
1. Logic. I. Title.
BC117.H8B34 1974 77-480223
77 MARC

Baló, Jozsef, 1895-
... Warzen, papillome und krebs ... von dr. Joseph Baló ... und dr. Béla Korpássy ... Budapest, K. Rényi; ⌜etc., etc.⌝ 1936.
303 p. illus. (incl. tables, diagrs.) 24½ cm. (Acta litterarum ac scientiarum Reg. universitatis hung. Francisco-Josephinae. Sectio medicorum ... tom. VII)
"Schrifttum" interspersed.
1. Cancer. 2. Papilloma. 3. Warts. I. Korpássy, Béla, joint author.
[RC261.B283] Agr 38-314

Baloarek, Józef.
Samorząd robotniczy a systemy społeczno-gospodarcze. Warszawa, Instytut Wydawniczy CRZZ, 1973.
259 p. 20 cm. zł23.00
Includes bibliographical references.
1. Employees' representation in management. 2. Works councils. I. Title.
HD5650.B15 73-213453

Balobanov, Oleg Maksimovich.
(Pravovoe regulirovanie morskoĭ perevozki passazhirov)
Правовое регулирование морской перевозки пассажиров. Москва, Рекламбюро ММФ, 1972.
50 p. 20 cm. 0.16rub USSR 72-VKP
At head of title: Одесский институт инженеров морского флота. Факультет повышения квалификации руководящих и инженерно-технических работников ММФ. Кафедра коммерческой эксплуатации морского транспорта.
"Автор: Балобанов Олег Максимович."
Includes bibliographical references.
1. Maritime law—Russia. I. Odessa. Institut inzhenerov morskogo flota. Fakul'tet povyshenii͡a kvalifikat͡sii rukovodi͡ashchikh i inzhenerno-tekhnicheskikh rabotnikov MMF. II. Odessa. Institut inzhenerov morskogo flota. Kafedra kommercheskoĭ ėkspluatat͡sii morskogo transporta. III. Title.
73-342757

Baloc, 'Abdul'azīz.
('Azīzān-i muḥtaram)
عزیزان محترم : خاکے / از عبدالعزیز بلوچ. — ⌜ملتان؟⌝ : حبیب الرحمٰن بٹالوی ; ملتان : ملنے کا پتہ، مرکز ادب، 1975.
152 p. ; 19 cm.
In Urdu.
Rs4.00
1. Baloch, 'Abdul 'azīz—Biography. 2. Authors, Urdu—20th century Biography. I. Title.
PK2200.B3247Z513 76-938760

Baloc, ʻAlī Muḥammad
see
Baloch, Ali Muhammad, 1911-

Baloc, Maulā Bakhsh Mushtāq
see
Mushtāq, Maulā Bakhsh, 1944-

Balocchi, Luigi, 1766-1832. Moïse
see Rossini, Gioacchino Antonio, 1792-1868. [Moïse. Libretto. English & Italian] Moses : opera ... New York : Greenstone & Landsman, [1935]

Balocchi, Luigi, 1766-1832. Moïse.
see Rossini, Gioacchino Antonio, 1792-1868. [Moïse. Libretto. Italian] Mosè... Venezia, Tip. di commercio [1836]

Balocchi, Luigi, 1766-1832. Moïse
see Rossini, Gioacchino Antonio, 1792-1868. [Moïse. Libretto. Italian] Mosè ... Sesto S. Giovanni, Cass editrice Madella, 1915.

Balocchi, Luigi, 1766-1832. Moïse
see Rossini, Gioacchino Antonio, 1792-1868. [Moïse. Libretto. Italian] Mosè ... Sesto San Giovanni, Casa per edizioni popolari [1934]

Balocchi, Luigi, 1766-1832. Moïse
see Rossini, Gioacchino Antonio, 1792-1868. [Moïse. Libretto. Italian] Mosè ... Milano, New York, G. Ricordi [1937]

Balocchi, Luigi, 1766-1832. Moïse et Pharaon
see Rossini, Gioacchino Antonio, 1792-1868. [Moïse. Libretto. Italian] Mosé e Faraone ... Firenze, Calasanziani, 1853.

Balocchi, Luigi, 1766-1832. Le siège de Corinthe
see Rossini, Gioacchino Antonio, 1792-1868. [Le siège de Corinthe. Libretto. English & Italian] The siege of Corinth : lyric tragedy in three acts. New York : G. Schirmer, c1974.

Baloch, Ali Muhammad, 1911–
(Āsān aur mukammal Urdū-Sindhī bol cāl)
آسان اور مکمل اردو سندھی بول چال. مصنف علی محمد بلوچ.
کراچی، اقبال بک ڈپو [1972?]
159 p. 19 cm. Rs4.00

1. Urdu language—Conversation and phrase books—Sindhi. I. Title.

PK1975.B374 72–930083

Baloch, Bashir Ahmed, 1935– comp.
لله گراناز. درگیجوک: بشیر احمد. کوئٹه، بلوچی اکیڈمی [1970]
50, 6 p. 22 cm. Rs1.25
Added title: Lallah and Granaz, a Baluchi folk tale.
In Baluchi, introd. in English.

I. Title. II. Title: Lallah and Granaz.
Title romanized: Lallah Grānāz.

PK6858.9.B3L3 71–932729

Baloch, M S
Comprehensive survey of the Monongahela River, by M. S. Baloch, E. N. Henry, and J. C. Burchinal. Charleston, West Virginia Dept. of Natural Resources, Division of Water Resources, 1973–
v. illus. 29 cm.
Cover title.
Vol. 1 has also special title: Inventory.
"Prepared by the West Virginia Department of Natural Resources, Division of Water Resources, Charleston, West Virginia in cooperation with West Virginia University and assistance of United States Department of Agriculture."
1. Physical geography—Monongahela River watershed. I. Henry, Edgar N., joint author. II. Burchinal, Jerry C., joint author. III. West Virginia. Division of Water Resources. IV. Title.
GB126.W4B34 917.54'5'02 74–621120
MARC

Baloch, M S
Flow characteristics of Greenbrier River, by M. S. Baloch, E. N. Henry [and] W. H. Dickerson. Charleston, W. Va., Division of Water Resources, 1969.
95 l. illus., maps. 28 cm.
Cover title: Stream flow characteristics of: Greenbrier River sub -basin.
Prepared in cooperation with the U. S. Geological Survey.
1. Stream measurements—West Virginia—Greenbrier River. I. Henry, Edgar N., joint author. II. Dickerson, Walter Howard, 1914– joint author. III. West Virginia. Division of Water Resources. IV. U. S. Geological Survey. V. Title. VI. Title: Stream flow characteristics of: Greenbrier River sub-basin.
GB1225.W4B3 551.4'83'097548 78–631634
MARC

Baloch, M S
Potomac River Basin / by M. S. Baloch, M. U. Islam, and J. C. Burchinal ; prepared by the West Virginia Dept. of Natural Resources, Division of Water Resources, in cooperation with the West Virginia University. — Charleston : West Virginia Dept. of Natural Resources, Division of Water Resources, 1973–
v. : maps (some col.) ; 29 cm.
Includes bibliographical references.
CONTENTS: v. 1. Inventory.
1. Water resources development—West Virginia. 2. Water resources development—Potomac River watershed. I. Islam, M. Nurul, joint author. II. Burchinal, Jerry C., joint author. III. West Virginia. Division of Water Resources. IV. West Virginia. University. V. Title.
TC424.W4B35 333.9'102'097549 74–623356
MARC

Baloch, M S
Streamflow characteristics of the Potomac River / by M. S. Baloch, E. N. Henry and W. H. Dickerson ; prepared by the West Virginia Dept. of Natural Resources, Division of Water Resources, in cooperation with West Virginia University. — Charleston : [West Virginia Dept. of Natural Resources, Division of Water Resources], 1971.
276 p. : ill. ; 28 cm.
Cover title.
1. Stream measurements—Potomac River. I. Henry, Edgar N., joint author. II. Dickerson, Walter Howard, 1914– joint author. III. West Virginia. Division of Water Resources. IV. Title.
GB1227.P7B34 551.4'83'09752 74–621861
MARC

Baloch, M. S., joint author.
see Adkins, James R. New River Basin. Charleston, W. Va., Dept. of Natural Resources, Division of Water Resources, 1976-

Baloch, M. S., joint author.
see Islam, M. Nural. Little Kanawha River Basin. Charleston, Division of Water Resources, West Virginia Dept. of Natural Resources, 1974-

Baloch, M.S.
see West Virginia. Division of Water Resources. Monongahela River. [Charleston, W.Va., 1973-

Baloch, Manzoor Ahmad A.
see Medicinal plants. Tandojam, Dept. of Botany and Plant Breeding, College of Agriculture, [1968?]

Baloch, Mir Khudabux Bijarani Marri.
Searchlights on Baloches and Balochistan / Mir Khuda Bakhsh Bijarani Marri Baloch ; [edited by M. Jaffer Hussain]. — 1st ed. — Karachi : Royal Book Co., 1974.
x, 387 p. : ill., maps ; 23 cm.
Bibliography: p. [371]-378.
Includes index.
Rs65.00
1. Baluchistan—History. 2. Baluchis—History. I. Title.
DS392.B28B34 954.9'15 75-930017
76 MARC

Baloch, Nabi Bakhsh, comp.
(Baita)
بيت. مرتب نبي بخش خان بلوچ. حيدرآباد، سنڌ، سنڌي ادبي بورڊ؛ [ملڻ جو هنڌ: سنڌي ادبي بورڊ بڪ اسٽال، 1971 :1970–71; v. 1]
2 v. 22 cm. (لوڪ ادب سلسلي جو ڪتاب، 19–18) Rs8.00 per vol.
Added t.p.: v. 1. Baita compositions.–v. 2. Narra ja baita, the long 'bait' poems sung to the accompaniment of narru (reed), composed by Sawan and his contemporaries.
Vol. 2 has title: نڙ جا بيت
In Sindhi.
Includes biographical sketch of the contributors.

1. Sindhi poetry. 2. Poets, Sindhi—Biography. I. Sawan Khaskheli. II. Title. III. Series: Sindhi folklore & literature, 18–19.

PK2788.6.B3 72–930470

Baloch, Nabi Bakhsh.
Development of music in Sind, by N. A. Baloch. Hyderabad [Pakistan] Sind University Press, 1973.
32 p. 25 cm. Rs20.00
Bibliography: p. 31–32.
"Prepared and published on the occasion of the International Symposium on Moenjodaro (23–25 February, 1973) as part of the Sindhi folk music festival held on February 23, 1973."
1. Music—Pakistan—Sind. I. Title.
ML345.P28B3 781.7'549'18 73–930242
MARC

Baloch, Nabi Bakhsh.
(Dori)
ڏور. مرتب نبي بخش خان بلوچ. [ڇاپو 1.] حيدرآباد، پاڪستان، سنڌي ادبي بورڊ، 1970.
4, 9–32, 738 p. ports. 23 cm. (سنڌي لوڪ ادب، 15) Rs14.00
Added t. p. in English: Doar; allegorical riddles.
In Sindhi.

1. Riddles, Sindhi. I. Title. II. Title: Doar. III. Series: Sindhi folklore & literature, book 15.

PN6377.S45B27 78–931692

Baloch, Nabi Bakhsh, comp.
The education policy, 1972: implications and implementation; containing address to the nation by the President of Pakistan, statement of the policy by the Minister of Education and Provincial Co-ordination, and the papers read at the seminar organised by the Institute of Education, University of Sind, Hyderabad, Sind, March 29, 1972. Edited by N. A. Baloch. Hyderabad, Institute of Education, University of Sind, 1972.
107 p. ports. 22 cm. (Sind University. Institute of Education. Research & publication series, no. 3) Rs5.00
1. Education—Pakistan—Addresses, essays, lectures. I. Title. II. Series: Sind University, Hyderabad, Pakistan. Institute of Education. Research & publication series, no. 3.
LA1156.B28 370'.9549'1 72–931020
MARC

Baloch, Nabi Bakhsh.
(Gujhāratūn)
ڳجهارتون. مرتب نبي بخش خان بلوچ. حيدرآباد، پاڪستان، سنڌي ادبي بورڊ، 1969.
4, 5, 78, 820, 4 p. illus. 23 cm. (سنڌی لوڪ ادب، 13) Rs16.00
Added t.p.: Gujharatoon: the literary-cum-cultural riddles.
In Sindhi.

1. Riddles, Sindhi. I. Title. II. Series: Sindhi folklore & literature, 13.

PN6377.S45B28 74–931817

Baloch, Nabi Bakhsh, comp.
(Loku gīta)
لوڪ گيت. مرتب نبي بخش خان بلوچ. حيدر آباد، سنڌ، سنڌي ادبي بورڊ، 1965.
6, 14, 405, 12 p. 23 cm. (لوڪ ادب سلسلي جو ڪتاب 17) Rs5.40
Added t.p.: Folk songs.
In Sindhi.
Without the music.

1. Folk-songs, Sindhi-Texts. I. Title. II. Title: Folk songs. III. Series: Sindhi folklore & literature, book 17.

PK2788.4.B3 S A 68–20742
PL 480: P–Si–240

Baloch, Nabi Bakhsh.
(Proliyūn, ḍiṭhūn, ma'mā'ūn, 'ain ḅola)
پروليون، ڏٺون، معمائون، ۽ ٻول. مرتب نبي بخش خان بلوچ. حيدرآباد، سنڌ، سنڌي ادبي بورڊ، 1965.
3, 12, 292, 6 p. 23 cm. (سنڌي لوڪ ادب، 12) Rs4.50
Added t. p.: Riddles and enigmas.
In Sindhi.

1. Riddles, Sindhi. I. Title. II. Title: Riddles and enigmas.

PN6377.S45B3 70–930780

Baloch, Nabi Bakhsh.
(Shāha je risāle jā sarcashmā)
شاه جي رسالي جا سرچشما. تحقيق نبي بخش خان بلوچ. [ڇاپو 1.] ڀٽ شاه، حيدرآباد، سنڌ، شاه عبداللطيف ڀٽ شاه ثقافتي مرڪز، 1972.
6, 29, [9]–159, 4 p. facsims. 22 cm. (شاه جي رسالي ۽ سوانح بابت
Added t. p.: Source materials for the poetic compendium (Risalo) of Shah Abdul Latif of Bhit; a study based on thirty one manuscripts and thirteen published editions of Shah-jo-risalo.
In Sindhi.

1. 'Abd al-Laṭīf, Shah, ca. 1689–ca. 1752—Sources. I. Title. II. Series: Research project on Shah-jo Risalo & Shah Abdul-Latif's biography, book 4. III. Series: Shah Abdul Latif Cultural Centre Committee. Publication, no. 10.

PK2788.9.A2Z6 72–930347

Baloch, Nabi Bakhsh.
(Shāhu je risāle jī tartību)
شاهہ جي رسالي جي ترتيب. تحقيق: نبي بخش خان بلوچ.
[حاپو 1.] ڀٽ شاه، حيدرآباد، سند، شاه عبداللطيف ڀٽ
شاه ثقافتي مرڪز، 1974.
212 p. 22 cm.
(شاه صاحب جي رسالي ۽ سوانح بابت جامع تحقيقي رٿا جو ڪتاب 6)
Added t. p.: A study of the internal arrangement and compilation of the poetic compendium (Risalo) Shah Abdul Latif of Bhit.
In Sindhi.
Rs6.00

1. ʻAbd al-Laṭīf, Shah, ca. 1689–ca. 1752. Risālo. I. Title. II. Title: A study of the internal arrangement and compilation of the poetic compendium (Risalo) of Shah Abdul Latif of Bhit. III. Series: Research project on Shah-jo Risalo & Shah Abdul-Latif's biography, book 6.

PK2788.9.A2R542 74-930085

Baloch, Nabi Bakhsh.
(Sindh meṉ Urdū shāʻirī)
سندھ میں اردو شاعری، از عہد شاہ جہاں تا قیام پاکستان.
مؤلف نبی بخش خان بلوچ. [2. اشاعت. حیدرآباد، سندھ، ممتاز
مرزا؛ ملنے کا پتہ: زیب ادبی مرکز] 1970.
11, 268 p. 22 cm. Rs5.00
In Urdu.
Includes bibliographical references.

1. Urdu poetry—Sind. 2. Poets, Urdu—Biography. I. Title.

PK2197.S5B3 72-930080

Baloch, Nabi Bakhsh
see 'Abd al-Latif, Shah, ca. 1689-1ca. 1752. (Shāha jo risālo) 1974.

Baloch, Nabi Bakhsh, ed.
see 'Ali Muhammadu Shahu, Sayyidu, 1811-1870. (Muslih al-miftah). 1970.

Baloch, Nabi Bakhsh
see Ḥaẓrata Shāha 'Abdullaṭīfa Bhiṭā'īa Sindhī bolī'a jo ma'māru. 1969.

Baloch, Nabi Bakhsh, ed.
see 'Inayatullah, Shah, 17th cent. (Miyunu Shahu 'Inata jo kalamu) 1963.

Baloch, Nabi Bakhsh, ed.
see Kalichbeg Faridunbeg, Mirza, Khan Bahadur. (Ahaval-i Shahu 'Abdullatifu Bhita'i). 1972.

Baloch, Nabi Bakhsh, ed.
see Muhammad Ja'far ibn 'Abd al-Karīm al-Būbakānī, 16th cent. (Ḥāṣil al-Nahj) 1969.

Baloch, Nabi Bakhsh, ed.
see Qādrī, Shāhu Lutifullāh, ca. 1611-ca. 1679. (Sindhī rasālo) 1968.

Baloch, Nabi Bakhsh
see Sabhu ranga. 1968.

Baloch, Nabi Bakhsh, ed.
see Sangi, 'Abd al-Husayn Khan, ca. 1851-1924. (Kulliyyat-i Sangi) 1969.

Baloch, Nabi Bakhsh, ed.
see Seminar on the Traditional Arts and Crafts of Sind Region, Hyderabad, India, 1966. The traditional arts & crafts of Hyderabad region... Hyderabad, Pakistan, 1966.

Baloch, Nabi Bakhsh
see Shaha 'Abdullatifa Bhita'ia je kalama men insani akhlaqa 'ain kirdara jo ma'iyaru. 1968.

Baloch, Nabi Bakhsh
see Shāhu Sharīfu Bhāḍā'i jo risālo. 1972.

Baloch, Nabi Bakhsh, ed.
see Sind University, Hyderabad, Pakistan. Decade of reforms & development, 1958-68... [Hyderabad] 1968.

Baloch, Nabi Bakhsh
see Sura kaliyāṇa jo mutāli'o. 1970.

Baloch, Nabi Bakhsh
see Sura khanbhāta jo mutāli'o. 1972.

Baloch, Nabi Bakhsh
see Sura sariraga jo mutali'o. 1973.

Baloch, Nabi Bakhsh
see Vijayanandī, 10th cent. [Karaṇatilaka. Arabic] Ghurrat al-zījāt. 1973.

Baloch, Taju
see
Taj Baloch, 1940-

Balocho, Antonius de
see
Antonio da Vercelli, d. 1483.

Balocu, Ghulāmu Rasūlu, 1935–
(Sindhī marṣiyah navīsī)
سنڌي مرثيہ نويسي. مولف غلام رسول بلوچ. [چاپو 1.]
حيدرآباد، سنڌ، انسٽيٽيوٽ آف سنڌالاجي، سنڌ يونيورسٽي [1970]
2, 3, 102 p. 18 cm. Rs2.50
Includes bibliographical references.
"سنڌ يونيورسٽيءَ جي سنڌي شعبي م. اي. اي. لاءِ پيش ڪيل
مونوگراف."
In Sindhi.

1. Elegiac poetry, Sindhi—History and criticism. I. Title.

PK2788.2.B3 72-930636

Balocu, Muḥammadu Bakhshu.
(Miskīnu Jahānu Khānu Khoso)
مسڪين جهان خان کوسو. تصنيف: محمد بخش بلوچ مجنون.
تعارف: نبي بخش خان بلوچ. ميرپورخاص، جميل پبليڪيشنس؛
[ملڻ جو هنڌ: ادبيات، حيدرآباد، پاڪستان، 1967]
7, 104 p. illus. 18 cm. Rs2.00
In Sindhi.

I. Khoso, Miskīnu Jahānu Khānu.

HV28.K37B34 76-930736

Balocu, Saḥaru, joint author
see Ḥusainī, Imdādu. Sindhu jī dinī adaba jo ka' talāgu. [1971

Balode, L.
see Latvian S.S.R. Laws, statutes, etc. [Biedru tiesu nolikums. Russian] Kommentariĭ k Polozheniīu o tovarishcheskikh sudakh Latviĭskoiĭ SSR. 1973.

Balodis, Andrejs.
Miķeļtornis. Dzeja. [Mākslinieks: Z. Zuze]. Rīgā, "Liesma," 1973.
135 p. with illus. 17 cm. 0.53rub USSR 73-6769
I. Title.
PG9048.B3M5 74-333065

Balodis, Andrejs, ed.
see Dzejas diena. Rīgā, "Liesma," 1969.

Balodis, Andrejs, comp.
see (V granite vechnosti) [1969].

Balodis, Juris, 1911-
see Latvijas Padomju Socialistiskas Republikas Zinātnu akadēmija. Neorganiskas kimijas institut. (Chetvertaīa konferentsiīa molodykh nauchnykh rabotnikov Instituta neorganicheskoĭ khimii) 1975.

Balodis, V
The transformation from growth ring and internode number to distances from pith and height in stem. [Melbourne] Australia, Commonwealth Scientific and Industrial Research Organization, 1972.
10 p. (Forest Products Laboratory, Division of Applied Chemistry Technological paper, no. 67)
1. Growth (Plants) 2. Tree-rings. I. Title. II. Series: Australia. Commonwealth Scientific and Industrial Research Organization. Division of Applied Chemistry. Forest Products Laboratory. Technological paper, no. 67.
NcU DI NUC74-127490

Balog, Cyril Edward, 1944-
Adolf A. Berle, Jr.; the intellectual as modern priest. [n.p., c1973]
1 reel. 35 mm.
Thesis (Ph. D.)—University of Illinois at Urbana-Champaign.
Microfilm of typescript. Ann Arbor, Mich., University Microfilms [1973]
1. Berle, Adolf Augustus, 1895-1971. I. Title.
WHi NUC76-37223

Balog, Galina Pavlovna
see Muzei i parki Pushkina. 1976.

Balog, Győző.
A tulajdonjogfenntartásról, különös tekintettel a veszélyviselésre. Szeged, M. Kir. Ferencz József-Tudományegyetem Barátainak Egyesülete, 1937.
26–92 p. 26 cm. (Acta litterarum ac scientiarum Reg. Universitatis Hung. Francisco-Iosephinae Sectio juridico-politica, t. 10, fasc. 3)
Cover title.
Summary in German.
Bibliography: p. 83–86.
1. Sales, Conditional—Hungary. 2. Security (Law)—Hungary. I. Title. II. Series: Cluj, Transylvania. Tudományegyetem. Acta litterarum ac scientiarum Reg. Universitatis Hung. Francisco-Iosephinae. Sectio juridico-politica, t. 10, fasc. 3.
AS142.C6233 t. 10, fasc. 3 75–572531

Balog, Mikhal'
see
Balogh, Mihály.

Balog, Nikola
see Ustav Socijalističke Federativne Republike Jugoslavije ... Beograd: Institut za političke studije Fakulteta političkih nauka, 1975.

Balog, Paul.
Umayyad, ʻĀbbasid, and Ṭūlūnid glass weights and vessel stamps / by Paul Balog. — New York : American Numismatic Society, 1976.
322, lv p., : ill. ; 29 cm. — (Numismatic studies ; no. 13)
Bibliography: p. 39-42.
Includes indexes.
1. Weights and measures, Arabic. 2. Glass weights. I. Title. II. Series.
CJ3413.B34 681′.2 77-359885
77 MARC

Balog, Zvonimir, 1932–
Preporučena ptica : [pjesme] / Zvonimur Balog. — Zagreb : Znanje, 1975.
151 p. ; 20 cm. — (Biblioteka Itd) Yu***
I. Title.
PG1619.12.A47P7 76–518157

Balog, Zvonimir, 1932-
see Od doseljenja Hrvata do najnovijih debata... Zagreb: Društvo hrvatskih humorista, 1975.

Balogh, András
see A Fővárosi Kertészet száz éve. [Budapest] Mezőgazdasági Kiadó, 1967.

Balogh, Beatrix.
Röpülj madárka : tanulmányok, vars és népdal feldolgozások / Balogh Beatrix ; [illusztrálta, Balogh Beatrix ; szerk., a Népművelési Intézet]. — Budapest : Népművelési Propaganda Iroda, 1966, cover 1967.
107 p. : ill. (some col.) ; 29 cm.
Includes unacc. melodies.
1. Puppets and puppet-plays in education. I. Népművelési Intézet. II. Title.
PN1979.E4B3 1967 75–408410

Balogh, Béni.
Éleskővár kincse; bükki mondák. Budapest, Móra Könyvkiadó, 1971.
101 p. illus. 21 cm. 12.00Ft
CONTENTS: Uróz Ilona.—Kőrózsa.—Kecsketúró.—Paprakás.—Bélkő.—Éleskövár kincse.—A szegény ember vára.—Nekézseny.—A bölényvadász.—A defterdár és az ördög.—Repül a török.—Szalacsikő.—A Strázsa-hegy.—Szepessy kuruckapitány.—A görög nemzetőrleány.—Az egri vándordeák.—A tardonai papírmalom.—A csendbiztos puttonyosa.—Szombaton virradóra.—Szamaras vitézek.
I. Title.
PZ90.H8B342 73-204938
rev

Balogh, Brian Henry.
Coordination in a metropolitan government : rapid transit planning for metropolitan Dade County / by Brian Henry Balogh. -- [s.l. : s.n., 1975]
137 leaves ; 28 cm.
Honors thesis--Harvard.
Bibliography: leaves 132-137.
1. Metropolitan government--Dade County, Fla. 2. Urban transportation--Dade County, Fla.
MH NUC77-85667

Balogh, Edgár, 1906–
Duna-völgyi párbeszéd : cikkek, tanulmányok, dokumentumok, 1929–1972 / Balogh Edgár ; [válogatta, az előszót és a jegyzeteket írta, Sándor László]. — Budapest : Szépirodalmi Könyvkiadó, 1974.
612 p. ; 21 cm.
Includes bibliographical references.
ISBN 963-15-0160-4 : 33.00Ft
1. Hungarian literature—20th century—Addresses, essays, lectures. 2. Hungarians in Eastern Europe—Addresses, essays, lectures. I. Title.
PH3017.B33 75-528883

Balogh, Edgár, 1906-
Intelmek. Bukarest, Kriterion, 1972.
157 p. 20 cm.
1. Hungarians in Transylvania. 2. Transylvania—Intellectual life. I. Title.
NNC NUC74-127740

Balogh, Edgár, 1906–
Mesterek és kortársak : tanulmányok, jegyzetek, emlékezések / Balogh Edgár ; [válogatta és a bevezetöt írta Kántor Lajos]. — Bukarest : Kriterion, 1974.
506 p. : port. ; 21 cm. R 75-907
Includes index.
lei 16.00
1. Hungarian literature—Transylvania—History and criticism—Addresses, essays, lectures. 2. Hungarian literature—History and criticism—Addresses, essays, lectures. I. Title.
PH3402.T7B3 75-527909

Balogh, Elemér, 1881–
A háborús jogalkotás főbb irányelvei, írta Balog Elemér. Budapest, Magyar Jogélet, 1916.
71 p. 24 cm. (A Magyar jogélet könyvtára)
Includes bibliographical references.
1. War and emergency legislation—Hungary. I. Title.
74-216415

Balogh, Elemér, 1881-
Political refugees in ancient Greece from the period of the tyrants to Alexander the Great [by] Elemér Balogh with the collaboration of F. M. Heichelheim. Roma, "L'Erma" di Bretschneider, 1972.
133 p. (Studia juridica, 74)
Reprint of the 1943 ed.
Includes bibliography.
1. Greece—Exiles. I. Heichelheim, Fritz, 1901- II. Title.
MiU NUC74-127115

Balogh, Elemér, 1938–
Ússzatok, halacskák : regény / Balogh Elemér. — Budapest : Szépirodalmi Könyvkiadó, 1975.
150 p. ; 19 cm.
ISBN 963-15-0320-8 : 14.50Ft
I. Title.
PH3213.B2394U8 77-502455

Balogh, Endre.
Tanári kézikönyv a történelem tanításához a középiskolák IV. osztályában. Budapest, Tankönyvkiadó [1972]
387 p. 20 cm. 30.00Ft
"Készült a művelődésügyi miniszter rendeletére, az MM Közoktatási Főosztálya és az Országos Pedagógiai Intézet irányításával."
Includes bibliographies.
1. Hungary—History—Study and teaching. 2. History—Study and teaching—Hungary. I. Title.
DB923.8.B34 74-210240

Balogh, Gyula
see Hungary. Művelődésügyi Minisztérium. Tananyagbeosztási javaslatok a kisegíto iskola összevont osztályai számára. Budapest: Tankönyvkiado, 1973.

Balogh, István.
A cívisek világa (Debrecen néprajza) Budapest, Gondolat, 1973.
306, [1] p. illus. 19 cm. 25.50Ft
Bibliography: p. 300–[307]
1. Debrecen, Hungary—Social life and customs. I. Title.
DB879.D4B32 74-209723

Balogh, István.
Hordás, nyomtatás, cséplés / Bałogh István, Végh József. — Budapest : Néprajzi Muzeum Ethnologiai Adattár, 19
v. : ill. ; 21 cm. — (A Hagyományos paraszti gazdálkodás ismeretanyaga és szókincse ; 3) (Útmutató füzetek a néprajzi adatgyüjtéshez ; 14)
Bibliography: v. 2, p. 93–96.
1. Harvesting—Hungary. 2. Harvesting—Terminology. 3. Threshing—Hungary. 4. Threshing—Terminology. I. Végh, József. II. Title. III. Series. IV. Series: Útmutató füzetek a néprajzi adatgyüjtéshez ;
GN36.H8U7 no. 14 75-593007
[S469.H9]

Balogh, István.
A parasztság művelődése a két világháború között. Budapest, Akadémiai Kiadó, 1973.
103 p. 20 cm. (Értekezések a történeti tudományok köréből, új sorozat, 66) 14.00Ft
Includes bibliographical references.
1. Hungary—Politics and government—1918–1945. 2. Peasantry—Hungary. 3. Hungary—Intellectual life. I. Title. II. Series.
AS142.M323 new ser., 662köt 74-234043
[DB955]

Balogh, István
see A Hagyományos paraszti gazdálkodás ismeretanyaga és szókincse. Budapest, Magyar Nemzeti Múzeum, Néprajz Múzeum Ethnologiai Adattár, 1962-

Balogh, János.
The Oribatid genera of the world [by] J. Balogh. [Translated by L. Gozmány] Budapest, Akadémiai Kiadó, 1972.
188 p. 71 plates. 25 cm.
1. Oribatei—Classification. I. Title.
QL458.A2B173 595'.42 73-156927
MARC

Balogh, Jenő, 1864-1953
see Büntetőjogi dolgozatok ... Pécs : Wessely és Horvath Könyvnyomdajából, [1916]

Balogh, Jolán.
Die Anfänge der Renaissance in Ungarn : Matthias Corvinus und die Kunst / Jolán Balogh ; [Übersetzung aus dem Ungarischen, Hildegard Baranyai]. — Graz : Akademische Druck- u. Verlagsanstalt, 1975.
xviii, 453 p. : ill. (some col.) ; 28 cm. — (Forschungen und Berichte des Kunsthistorischen Institutes der Universität Graz ; 4) Au***
Bibliography: p. xvii-xviii.
Includes indexes.
ISBN 3-201-00931-8
1. Art, Renaissance—Hungary. 2. Art, Hungarian. 3. Matthias I, King of Hungary, 1440?-1490—Art patronage. I. Title. II. Series: Graz. Universität. Kunsthistorisches Institut. Forschungen und Berichte ; 4.
N6817.B34 76-456802
76 MARC

Balogh, Jolán.
Katalog der ausländischen Bildwerke des Museums der Bildenden Künste in Budapest, IV.-XVIII. Jahrhundert / Jolán Balogh. — Budapest : Akadémiai Kiadó, 1975.
2 v. : ill. ; 25 cm.
Includes bibliographical references and indexes.
CONTENTS: 1. Textband.—2. Bildband.
ISBN 9630500949
1. Art—Budapest—Catalogs. 2. Budapest. Szépművészeti Múzeum. I. Budapest. Szépművészeti Múzeum. II. Title.
N1620.B34 76-459404
76 MARC

Balogh, József.
A szociológiai szemlélet és módszer szerepe az agitációs és propagandamunkában / Balogh József. — [Budapest] : Kossuth Könyvkiadó, 1974.
42 p. ; 20 cm.
ISBN 963-09-0281-8 : 3.00Ft
1. Propaganda. I. Title.
HM263.B32 76-522366

Balogh, Kálmán, ed.
see Conférence internationale sur le Mésozoïque, Budapest, 1959. Excursions de la Conférence sur le Mésozoïque... Budapest, Felsőoktatási Jegyzetellátó Vállalat, 1959]

Balogh, Károly.
Vetomag-gazdalkodasunk vertikuma a fobb teruleti (regionalis) problemak tukreben. Budapest, 1971.
92 p. illus. (Agrargazdasagi Kutato Intezet fuzetei, no. 11)
Bibliography: p. 91-92.
I. Title.
DNAL DLC NUC73-123886

Balogh, Károly.
see Organization and operation of the vertical system in food economy ... Budapest, Research Institute for Agricultural Economics, 1973.

Balogh, László.
Halastavi pecsenyekacsa / Balogh Laszlo, Kozma Lajos, Mosonyi Geza. -- Budapest : Mezogazdasagi Kiado, 1975.
210 p. : ill.
Includes a chapter by Gooderham K. K.
Bibliography: p. 205-206.
1. Ducks. 2. Fish-culture. Hungary. I. Kozma, Lajos, 1924- II. Mosonyi, Geza. III. Title.
DNAL NUC77-86680

Balogh, László.
A munkaszervezési tartalékok feltárása és hasznosítása / Balogh László, Kápolnai György, Parányi György. — Budapest : Közgazdasági és Jogi Könyvkiadó, 1975.
197, [1] p. ; 19 cm. — (Munkaszervezési sorozat)
Bibliography: p. 197-[198]
ISBN 9632201973 : 15.00Ft
1. Production management. I. Kápolnai, György, joint author. II. Parányi, György, joint author. III. Title.
TS155.B244 77-461671
77 MARC

Balogh, László, 1919–
Békebeli históriák; pesti pitaval. [Írták] Balogh László, Czéh György [és] Lantos László. [Budapest] Minerva, 1970.
437 p. 20 cm. 41.00
1. Criminal law—Hungary—Cases. I. Czéh, György, joint author. II. Lantos, László, joint author. III. Title.
74-229429

Balogh, Laszlo, 1919- ed.
see Nemzetközi Didaktikai Munkaértekezlet, Budapest, 1969. Méres, értekelés, osztályozás. Budapest, 1970.

Balogh, Mihály
see Pomoshch' Sovetskogo Soíuza razvivaíushchimsía stranam. 1968.

Balogh, Mihály
see A Szovjetunió segítsége a fejlődő országok számára. Budapest, Magyar Tudományos Akadémia, Afro-Ázsiai Kutató Csoport, 1968.

Balogh, Pál
see A Magyar Országos Horgász Szövetség 20 éve. Budapest, 1965.

Balogh, Sándor.
Parlamenti és pártharcok Magyarországon, 1945–1947 / Balogh Sándor ; [szerk., Kukk Györgyné]. — [Budapest] : Kossuth Könyvkiadó, 1975.
631 p. ; 25 cm.
Includes bibliographical references and index.
ISBN 963-09-0173-0 : 90.00Ft
1. Hungary—Politics and government—1945– 2. Political parties—Hungary. I. Title.
DB956.B364 76-511171

Balogh, Sándor
see Nógrád megye története. [Salgótarján] Nógrád Megyei Tanács Végrehajtó Bizottsága [1969-1974?]

Balogh, Thomas, Baron Balogh, 1905–
The economics of poverty. 2d ed. London, Weidenfeld & Nicolson [1974]
vii, 291 p. 22 cm. £4.50 GB***
Includes bibliographical references.
1. Underdeveloped areas. 2. Economic development. 3. Economic assistance. I. Title.
HC59.7.B3 1974 330.9'172'4 74–165719
ISBN 0–297–76694–5 ; 0–297–76702–X (pbk.) MARC

Balogh, Thomas, Baron Balogh, 1905-
The economics of poverty / Thomas Balogh. — 2d ed. — White Plains, N.Y. : International Arts and Sciences Press, 1974.
vii, 291 p. ; 23 cm.
Includes bibliographical references and index.
ISBN 0-87332-049-2 : $12.50
1. Underdeveloped areas. 2. Economic development. 3. Economic assistance. I. Title.
HC59.7.B3 1974b 330.9'172'4 73-90495
75 MARC

Balogh, Thomas, Baron Balogh, 1905–
Fact and fancy in international economic relations; an essay on international monetary reform, by Thomas Balogh in collaboration with Peter Balacs. [1st ed.] Oxford, New York, Pergamon Press [1973]
xiv, 116 p. 22 cm.
"The text of this book is reissued from World development, volume 1, February and March 1973."
Includes bibliographical references.
1. International economic relations. 2. International finance. I. Balacs, Peter, joint author. II. Title.
HF1411.B24 1973 382.1 73–7993
ISBN 0–08–017740–9 MARC

Balogh, Thomas, Baron Bologh, 1905-
Partenaires inégaux dans l'échange international; analyse théorique. Traduit par Michel Chatelus. Paris, Dunod, 1971.
xx, 268 p. 24 cm. (Collection du Centre d'économétrie de la Faculté de droit et des sciences économiques de Paris. Association Cournot, 8)
Translation of Unequal partners.
1. Relations économiques internationales. I. Title. II. Series: Paris. Université. Faculté de droit et des sciences économiques. Centre d'économétrie. Association Cournot. Collection, 8)
CaOOU NUC73-126105

Balogh, Thomas, Baron Balogh, 1905–
(Siyāsat al-i'mār al-iqtiṣādī fī al-'Irāq)
سياسة الاعمار الاقتصادى فى العراق / الفه توماس بالوك ؛ ساعده فى البحث وقدمه للعربيـــة محمد سلمان حســن. — [بغداد] : الثقافة الجديدة ، 1958.
208 p. ; 25 cm.
Includes bibliographical references.
1. Iraq—Economic policy. I. Title.
HC497.I 7B34 74–235129

Balogh, Thomas, Baron Balogh, 1905-
Socios desiguales. Versión española de José M.a Montoya. Madrid, Editorial Gredos, S.A., [c1969]
557 p. 25 cm. (Biblioteca de ciencias económicas, 2. Politica económica.)
Translation of: Unequal partners.
1. International foreign relations. I. Title.
MiAlbC NUC74-122367

Balogh, Zoltán, 1930–
Die Welt des Es; die philosophische Begrifflichkeit des Martin Buber. [München] 1968.
115 p. 21 cm. GDB***
Inaug.-Diss.—Munich.
Vita.
Bibliography: p. [111]–115.
1. Buber, Martin, 1878–1965. I. Title.
B3213.B84B32 73–888294
rev

Balogh Ádám Múzeum.
A Szekszárdi Balogh Ádám Múzeum évkönyve. 1970–
[Szekszárd]
v. illus. 24 cm.
1. Balogh Ádám Múzeum. 2. Tolna, Hungary (Comitat) — History—Collections. I. Title.
DB975.T6B34 73–641738
MARC-S

Balogun, Ekundayo E 1937-
A study of satellite-observed cloud patterns of tropical cyclones. [n.p.] 1972.
248 l.
Thesis (Ph.D.)—University of Chicago.
1. Cyclones. 2. Clouds—Photographs from space. 3. Clouds—Mathematical models. I. Title.
ICU NUC74-127744

Balogun, Isaac Ojo Bolarinwa, 1937-
The intellectual and residential correlates of reading achievement in Nigerian secondary schools. [n.p.] 1972.
113 p.
Thesis (Ph.D.)—New York University.
I. Title.
NNU NUC74-127743

Balogun, Isaac Ojo Bolarinwa, 1937-
The intellectual and residential correlates of reading achievement in Nigerian secondary schools. New York, 1972.
vi, 113 l. tables.
Microfilm of typescript. Ann Arbor, Mich., University Microfilms, 1972. 1 reel. 35 mm.
Thesis—New York University.
Bibliography: leaves 94-101.
1. Education, Secondary—Nigeria. 2. Reading (Secondary education) I. Title.
NN NUC76-71851

Balogun, Ismail A B
The life and works of 'Uthmān dan Fodio : the Muslim reformer of West Africa / Ismail A. B. Balogun. — Lagos, Nigeria : Islamic Publications Bureau, 1975.
105 p., [2] leaves of ill. : ill. ; 22 cm.
Some quotations also in Arabic.
Bibliography: p. 84-85.
Includes index.
1. Usuman dan Fodio, 1754-1817. 2. Muslims in Nigeria—Biography. 3. Fulah Empire—Biography. I. Title.
BP80.U83B34 297'.092'4 77-366367
77 MARC

Balogun, Ismail A. B., ed.
see Usuman da Fodio, 1744-1817. A critical edition of the Ihya... London, 1967.

Balogun, Kolawole.
My country Nigeria. Ibadan, Africanus [pref. 1971]
100 p. map. 19 cm.
Includes bibliographical references.
1. Nigeria—Pol. & govt. 2. Nigeria—Hist. I. Title.
NRU ViBlbV NUC73-123904

Balogun, Kolawole.
My country Nigeria. [2d ed.] Ibadan, Nigeria, Africanus and Co. [1971]
100 p. map. 19 cm.
1. Nigeria—Hist. 2. Nigeria—Politics and government. I. Title.
CNoS NUC76-71850

Balogun, Kolawole.
Village boy: my own story. Ibadan, Nigeria, Africanus Publishers [1969]
148 p. illus. 21 cm.
1. Balogun, Kolawole, 1926- I. Title.
ViU NUC76-37222

Balogun, Kolawole.
What Nigeria wants; a close study of Indian struggles with special references to Nigerian problems. [Yaba, Chuks, n.d.]
12 p. 19 cm.
1. Nationalism—India. 2. Nationalism—Nigeria. I. Title.
IEN NUC73-78962

Balogun, Lekan.
Nigeria... social justice or doom. [London] Yemisi Pub. Concern [1970?]
48 p. 21 cm.
1. Socialism in Nigeria. 2. Nigeria—Pol. & govt. I. Title.
CSt-H NUC73-122823

Balogun, Ola, 1945-
The tragic years : Nigeria in crisis, 1966-1970 / Ola Balogun. — Benin City, Nigeria : Ethiope Pub. Corp., 1973.
vi, 125 p., [4] leaves of plates : ill. ; 23 cm.
Bibliography: p. 125.
1. Nigeria—History—Civil War, 1967-1970. I. Title.
DT515.9.E3B34 966.9'05 75-307919
75 MARC

Balogun, Saka Adegbite.
Gwandu emirated in the nineteenth century with special reference to political relations, 1817-1903. Ibadan, 1970.
547 p. 29 cm.
Thesis—Ibadan University.
Includes bibliography.
Microfilm (negative) of typescript. Ibadan University Library, Photocopying Section, 1972? 1 reel.
1. Gwandu, Nigeria—Hist. I. Title.
WU NUC74-120837

Baloi-Islamic Institute
see English-Maranao self-study guide. Baloi, Philippines [196-?]

Baloković, Joyce (Borden)
Singing wings; an autobiographical biography of Zlatko Baloković, concert violinist and citizen of the world, by Joyce Borden Baloković. [Camden, Me.? Camden Herald Publishing Company? 1973?]
378 p. 23 cm.
1. Baloković, Zlatko, 1885-1965. I. Title.
MeU NUC76-74354

Balomenos, Geōrgios Periklēs
see Valomenos, Geōrgios Periklēs.

Balon, Eugen K
Domestication of the carp Cyprinus carpio L. [by] Eugene K. Balon. [Toronto] Royal Ontario Museum, Life Sciences, 1974.
37 p. illus. 26 cm. (Royal Ontario Museum. Life Sciences miscellaneous publication) $3.00 C***
Summary in French and Russian.
Bibliography: p. 27–34.
1. Carp. 2. Fish-culture. 3. Domestication. I. Title. II. Series: Toronto. Royal Ontario Museum. Life Sciences Division. Miscellaneous publications.
QL638.C94B32 597'.52 74–186560
ISBN 0–88854–147–3 MARC

Balon, Eugen K
Die embryonale und larvale Entwicklung der Donauzope (Abramis ballerus Subsp.). Bratislava, Slovenskej Adadémie Vied, 1959.
78 p. illus. 24 cm. (Biologické práce, V/6)
Bibliography: p. 76-78.
I. Series.
AAP NUC74-33086

Balon, Eugen K
Expedícia Cayo Largo; prírodopis koralcvého sveta Antíl. [Vyd. 1.] Bratislava, Vydavateľstvo Slovenskej akadémie vied, 1967.
231 p. illus. 25 cm. 35.00
At head of title: Augen Balon, Ján Seneš.
Bibliography: p. [215]–219.
1. Marine fauna—Caribbean Sea. 2. Marine fauna—Cuba. I. Seneš, Ján, joint author. II. Title.
QL134.5.B34 73–209650

Balon, Eugen K
Lake Kariba : a man-made tropical ecosystem in Central Africa / edited by E. K. Balon & A. G. Coche. — The Hague : Junk, 1974.
xii, 767 p. : ill. ; 25 cm. — (Monographiae biologicae ; v. 24) Ne***
Includes bibliographies.
ISBN 90–6193–076–6
1. Fishes—Kariba, Lake, Zambia and Southern Rhodesia. 2. Kariba, Lake, Zambia and Southern Rhodesia. 3. Reservoir ecology. 4. Fish populations. I. Coche, A. G., joint author. II. Title. III. Series.
QP1.P37 vol. 24 574'.08 s 75–300246
[QL635.Z28] [597'.0929'6891] MARC

Balon, Eugen K
Vek a rast neresového stáda Dunajaského kapra - sazana (Cyprinus carpio morpha Hungaricus heck.) z Malého Dunaja nad Kolárovom. [Bratislava, Slovenská akadémia vied, 1957.
961-986 p. illus. 24 cm.
Separátny odtlačok: Pol'nohospodárstovo. Landwirtschaft, Rocník IV, 1957.
Reprinted from Pol'nohospodárstovo. Landwirtschaft, Ročník IV, Číslo 5. 1957.
Includes bibliography.
AAP NUC75-8563

Balon, Joseph.
Grand dictionnaire de droit du moyen âge. Namur, les Anciens Ets Godenne, 1972–
v. 25 cm. (His Ius Medii Aevi, 5) 680F (v. 1) Be 72–4268 (v. 1)
French or Latin.
Bibliography: v. 1, p. [ix]–xlii.
1. Law, Medieval—Dictionaries—French. 2. Law, Medieval—Dictionaries—Latin. 3. Latin language—Dictionaries—French. I. Title.
73–334555

Balon, Joseph.
Tables générales des "Anciens Pays et assemblées d'États." T. I–L. Algemene inhoudstafel [van] "Standen en landen." Delen I–L. [Par. Door] J(oseph) Balon [&] É(mile) Lousse. (Namur, les Anciens Ets Godenne, 1970).
62 p. 25 cm. (Anciens pays et assemblées d'États, 51. Standen en landen) Be 71–3958
1. Political science research—Belgium. 2. International Commission for the History of Representative and Parliamentary Institutions, Belgian Section. I. Lousse, Émile, 1905– joint author. II. Title: Algemene inhoudstafel Standen en landen. III. Series: Anciens pays et assemblées d'États, 51.
JN5718.A7 no. 51 73–327262
[JA88.B4]

Balon, Karl-Heinz.
Planspiel : soziales Lernen in simulierter Wirklichkeit / Karl-Heinz Balon, Detlef Sokoll. — Starnberg : Raith, 1974.
125 p. ; 19 cm. — (Projekte im Unterricht) GFR 74–A
Bibliography: p. 124–125.
ISBN 3-921121-68-X : DM8.80
1. Group work in education. 2. Social sciences—Study and teaching. I. Sokoll, Detlef, joint author. II. Title.
LB1032.B29 75–590858

Balonek, Frank J
1869-1969; centennial history of the First United Presbyterian Church of Mumford. Edited by Frank J. Balonek. Mumford, N.Y., Centennial Committee, 1969.
vi, 44 p. illus.
Centennial program tipped in.
1. First United Presbyterian Church, Mumford, N.Y.—History. I. First United Presbyterian Church, Mumford, N.Y. II. Title.
NGenoU NUC75-75166

Balonov, Lev ÎAkovlevich.
(Slukh i rech' dominantnogo i nedominantnogo polushariĭ)
Слух и речь доминантного и недоминантного полушарий / Л. Я. Балонов, В. Л. Деглин ; АН СССР, Ин-т эволюц. физиологии и биохимии им. И. М. Сеченова. — Ленинград : Наука, Ленингр. отд-ние, 1976.
218 p., [1] fold. leaf : ill. ; 21 cm. USSR 77
Bibliography: p. 196–[215]
1.17rub
1. Hearing. 2. Speech. 3. Cerebral hemispheres. I. Deglin, Vadim L'vovich, joint author. II. Title.
QP461.B27 77–511823

Balory, Louise.
Memini / Louise Balory. — Paris : la Pensée universelle, 1973.
126 p. ; 18 cm. F74-11342
17.12F
1. Ascq, France—Massacre, 1944. 2. World War, 1939-1945—Atrocities. I. Title.
D762.A8B34 940.53'37 75-504039
75 MARC

Balossini, Cajo Enrico.
Aspetti operativi negli statuti delle banche popolari italiane : ricerca promossa dal Servizio studi della Banca popolare di Novara / Cajo Enrico Balossini. — Milano : A. Giuffrè, 1975.
461 p. ; 26 cm. It 75-May
Bibliography: p. 422–443.
Includes indexes.
L8000
1. Banking law—Italy. 2. Banks and banking, Cooperative—Law and legislation—Italy. I. Title.
75–583226

Balossini, Cajo Enrico.
Il diritto delle consuetudini e degli usi. Milano, A. Giuffrè, 1974.
362 p. 25 cm. It 74–May
Includes bibliographical references.
L5200
1. Customary law—Italy. 2. Customary law. I. Title.
75–560696

Balossini, Cajo Enrico.
Sonetti da Shakespeare e per Maria / Cajo Enrico Balossini. — Milano : A. Giuffrè, 1976.
vii, 311 p. ; 21 cm. It76-Mar
L5000
I. Shakespeare, William, 1564-1616. Sonnets. II. Title.
PQ4862.A455S6 76-488765
•77 MARC

Baloste-Fouletier, Irène.
Chronique de l'ordre asilaire. Paris, F. Maspero, 1973.
171 p. 22 cm. (Textes à l'appui. Série Psychiatrie) 20.00F F***
Includes bibliographical references.
1. Mental illness—Personal narratives. I. Title.
RC463.B34 362.2'092'4 [B] 74–190097
MARC

Balotă, Nicolae, 1925-
Arte poetice ale secolului XX [i.e. douăzeci] : ipostaze românești și străine / Nicolae Balotă. — București : "Minerva", 1976.
481 p. ; 20 cm. — (Confluențe) R77-730
Summary in German.
Includes bibliographical references and index.
lei17.50
1. Romanian poetry—20th century—History and criticism. 2. European poetry—20th century—History and criticism. I. Title.
PC810.B3 77-554246
•77 MARC

Balotă, Nicolae, 1925–
De la Ion la Ioanide : prozatori români ai secolului XX / Nicolae Balotă. — București : Editura Eminescu, 1974.
539 p. ; 20 cm. — (Sinteze) R 75–1615
Summary in English and German.
Includes bibliographical references and index.
lei 21.00
1. Romanian literature—20th century—History and criticism. I. Title.
PC808.B28 75–409868

Balotă, Nicolae, 1925–
Introducere în opera lui Al. Philippide / Nicolae Balotă ; [coperta, Dumitru Verdeș]. — București : "Minerva," 1974.
333 p. ; 17 cm. — (Introducere în opera lui ; 10) R 75–880
Includes bibliographical references.
lei 7.25
1. Philippide, Alexandru—Criticism and interpretation. I. Title.
PC840.26.H5Z58 75–584073

Balotă, Nicolae, 1925–
Jakob Burckhardt, un umanist modern / Nicolae Balotă. — București : "Albatros," 1974.
202 p. ; 20 cm. — (Contemporanul nostru) R 75–1659
Includes bibliographical references.
lei 7.00
1. Burckhardt, Jakob Cristoph, 1818–1897. I. Title.
D15.B8B32 75–534616

Balotă, Nicolae, 1925-
Labirint; eseuri critice. [București] Editura Eminescu, 1970.
425 p. 20 cm.
1. Literature, Modern—Addresses, essays, lectures. I. Title.
NNC NUC75-31788

Balotă, Nicolae, 1925–
Lupta cu absurdul. [Coperta colecției: Sergiu Georgescu]. București, „Univers," 1971.
564 p. 20 cm. (Colecția Studii) lei 16.00 R 71–4605
Bibliography: p. [532]–546.
1. Literature, Modern—20th century—History and criticism. I. Title.
PN779.R6B3 73–304612

Balotă, Nicolae, 1925–
Umanităţi. Eseuri. Bucureşti, Editura Eminescu, 1973.
487 p. 21 cm. lei 19.00 R 73–2233
I. Title.
AC95.R8B27 73–354274

Balotă, Nicolae, 1925-
Universul prozei : [critică literară] / Nicolae Balotă. — București : Editura Eminescu, 1976.
499 p. ; 20 cm. R76-1341
Includes bibliographical references.
lei17.00
1. Romanian literature—20th century—History and criticism—Addresses, essays, lectures. 2. Literature, Modern—History and criticism—Addresses, essays, lectures. I. Title.
PC808.B284 76-467360
•76 MARC

Balotă, Nicolae, 1925- ed.
see Dan, Pavel, d. 1937- Urca bătrînul. Bucuresti, "Minerva," 1973.

Balough, Teresa.
A complete catalogue of the works of Percy Grainger / edited, catalogued, and with a foreword, afterword, and explanatory notes, by Teresa Balough. — Nedlands, W.A. : Dept. of Music, University of Western Australia, 1975.
xvi, 255 p. : port. ; 22 cm. — (Music monograph ; 2) Aus
American distributors: T. Front Musical Literature, Beverly Hills, Calif.
ISBN 0-9599791-2-3 : $7.50
1. Grainger, Percy Aldridge, 1882-1961—Bibliography. I. Title. II. Series.
ML134.G78B2 016.78'092'4 76-377434
76 MARC

Baloušková, Zdeňka, joint author
see Heřman, Miroslav. Úvod do odborného stylu českeho jazyka a chemické terminologie pro zahraniční posluchače VŠCHT ... Praha, SNTL, rozmn., 1971.

Balova, Elizaveta Fedorovna.
(Sovershenstvovanie ėkonomicheskogo stimulirovaniâ stroitel'nogo proizvodstva v usloviâkh khoziâĭstvennoĭ reformy)
Совершенствование экономического стимулирования строительного производства в условиях хозяйственной реформы. Москва, Стройиздат, 1974.
127 p. 20 cm. (Хозяйственная реформа в действии) 0.37rub USSR 74
At head of title: Е. Ф. Балова, Д. А. Шапочкин, П. С. Захарова.
Includes bibliographical references.
1. Construction industry—Russia. 2. Incentives in industry—Russia. I. Shapochkin, Dmitriĭ Aleksandrovich. II. Zakharova, Polina Sergeevna. III. Title.
HD9715.R92B335 74–329794

Balovnev, Vladilen Ivanovich.
(Metody fizicheskogo modelirovaniâ rabochikh prot͡sessov dorozhno-stroitel'nykh mashin)
Методы физического моделирования рабочих процессов дорожно-строительных машин / В. И. Баловнев. — Москва : Машиностроение, 1974.
231 p. : ill. ; 23 cm. USSR 74
Bibliography: p. 226–[228]
Includes index.
1.57rub
1. Road machinery. 2. Engineering models. I. Title.
TE223.B263 75–554548

Balovnev, Vladilen Ivanovich.
(Novye metody rascheta soprotivleniĭ rezaniû gruntov)
Новые методы расчета сопротивлений резанию грунтов. Рекомендовано в качестве учебно-методического пособия. [Москва] Росвузиздат, 1963.
94, [2] p. illus. 22 cm.
At head of title: Московский автомобильно-дорожный институт. Отделение усовершенствования руководящих и инженерно-технических работников. В. И. Баловнев.
Bibliography: p. [65]
1. Excavating machinery—Dynamics. 2. Soil mechanics. I. Title.
TA735.B27 72–207523

Balovnev, Vladilen Ivanovich.
The utilization of methods of similitude and modeling for optimization of parameters and prediction of the trend of development of highway construction machines; Ispolzovanie metodov podobiya i modelirovaniya dla optimizatsii parametrov i prognozirovaniya tendentsii razvitiya dorozhno-stroitelnykh mashin. Translated from: Stroitel'nye i dorozhnye mashiny, 1971, by William R. Gill. [n.p., n.d.]
20–23 p.
Includes bibliographies.
I. Title.
DNAL NUC72-102435

Balovnev, Vladilen Ivanovich, joint author
see Karaban, Georgiĭ L'vovich. (Mashiny dlîâ soderzhaniîâ i remonta avtomobil'nykh dorog i aėrodromov) 1975.

Balow, Tom, joint author
see Carpenter, John Allan, 1917- Botswana. Chicago, Childrens Press [1973]

Balow, Tom, joint author.
see Carpenter, John Allan, 1917- Lesotho. Chicago, Childrens Press, [1975]

Balowitz, Victor Chaim, 1931-
Personal identity and bodily identity. Ann Arbor, Mich., University Microfilms, 1970.
1 reel. 35 mm.
Microfilm of typescript.
Collation of original: 93 leaf.
Thesis—Columbia University.
Bibliography: leaf 93.
1. Identity. I. Title.
NBuC NUC74-124040

Balowitz, Victor Chaim, 1931-
Personal identity and bodily identity. [New York] 1969 [c1970]
93 l. 29 cm.
Thesis—Columbia University.
Bibliography: leaf 93.
1. Identity. I. Title.
NNC NUC73-122814

Balows, Albert.
Clinical microbiology : how to start and when to stop / edited by Albert Balows. — Springfield, Ill. : Thomas, [1975]
ix, 90 p. : ill. ; 24 cm. — (American lecture series ; publication no. 981 : A monograph in the Bannerstone division of American lectures in clinical microbiology)
Includes bibliographies and indexes.
ISBN 0-398-03389-7
1. Medical microbiology—Technique. 2. Microbiological laboratories. I. Title.
[DNLM: 1. Microbiology—Laboratory manuals. QW25 C641]
QR46.B314 616.01 74-30204
74 MARC

Balows, Albert, ed.
see Current techniques for antibiotic susceptibility testing. Springfield, Ill., Thomas [1974]

Balows, Albert, ed.
see International Conference on Anaerobic Bacteria, Atlanta, 1972. Anaerobic bacteria: role in disease... Springfield, Ill., Thomas, [1974]

Balows, Albert, ed.
see International Conference on Opportunistic Fungal Infections, 2d, Lexington, Ky., 1972. Opportunistic fungal infections... Springfield, Ill., Thomas, [1976, c1975]

Baloyi, Samuel Jonas.
Murhandziwani; hi Sam Baloyi. [2d ed] Johannesburg, Swiss Mission in South Africa, 1967.
32 p. 18 cm.
Story in Thonga.
I. Title.
MdU NUC73-47493

Baloyi, Samuel Jonas.
Xaka. [Johannesburg, Afrikaanse Pers Booksellers, 195-?]
109 p. 18 cm.
1. Chaka, Zulu chief, 1787?-1828—Drama. I. Title.
PL8731.B3 73-200505

Baloyra, Enrique A 1942-
Political leadership in the Cuban Republic, 1944-1958. [Gainesville, Fla.] 1971 [c1972]
1 v.
Thesis—University of Florida.
Microfilm of typescript. Ann Arbor, Mich., University Microfilms, 1969. 1 reel. 35 mm.
1. Cuba—Politics and government—1933-1959. I. Title.
FMU NUC73-123887

Baloyra, Enrique A 1942-
Problemas del hombre nuevo en Cuba: la dirigencia. [Chapel Hill, 1973]
51 p.
"Versión preliminar."
1. Cuba—Politics and government—1959- —Addresses, essays, lectures. I. Title.
NcU NUC74-127755

Baloyra, Enrique A., 1942- joint author.
see Martz, John D. Electoral mobilization and public opinion... Chapel Hill, University of North Carolina Press, c1976.

Balpe, Jean Pierre, comp.
Le bestiaire fantastique / par Jean-Pierre Balpe. — Paris : Larousse, [1974]
143 p. : ill. ; 16 cm. — (Textes pour aujourd'hui) F***
ISBN 2-03-038001-6
1. Animals—Literary collections. I. Title.
PN6071.A7B34 808.8'036 75-500433
MARC

Balpe, Jean Pierre.
Les moments de poésie à l'école élémentaire / par Jean-Pierre Balpe ; avec la collaboration de Mme F. Clément-Bolayron. — Paris : A. Colin, [1974]
2 v. : ill., music ; 21 cm. — (Pratique pédagogique ; 17) F***
Vol. 2 has title: Poèmes en liberté.
1. French poetry—Study and teaching—France. I. Clément-Bolayron Mme F., joint author. II. Title. III. Title: Poèmes en liberté.
PQ63.F8B34 841'.007'1244 75-504600
75 MARC

Balqīs Fāṭimah.
(Suhel)
سہیل. [مصنفہ] بلقیس فاطمہ. بنگلور، بک سینٹر [1970]
487 p. 18 cm. Rs18.00
In Urdu.
A novel.

I. Title.
PK2200.B327S8 79-926114

Balraj Komal, 1928-
[Balrāj Komal]
بلراج کومل؛ انتخاب کلام بلراج کومل. علی‌گڑھ، انجمن ترق
اردو، ہند [1971]
62 p. 18 cm. (اردو شاعروں کا انتخابی سلسلہ) Rs1.00
In Urdu.

PK2200.B328A17 1971 70-927149

Balraj Komal, 1928-
(Nizhād-i sang)
نژاد سنگ / بلراج کومل. — اشاعت 1. — لکھنؤ : نصرت پبلشرز,
.1975
136 p. ; 23 cm.
In Urdu.
Poems.
Rs10.00

I. Title.
PK2200.B328N5 75-907806

Balraj Mehta
see
Mehta, Balraj.

Balrāmpūrī, Qamar
see
Qamar Balrāmpūrī, 1937-

Bālruwīn, Muḥammad Muḥammad
see
Bāl-Ruwīn, Muḥammad Muḥammad.

Bals, Christel, 1930-
see Institut für Raumforschung. Gutachten zu raumordnungspolitischen Problemen... Bad Godesberg, Selbstverlag der Bundesanstalt für Landeskunde und Raumforschung, 1966.

Bals, Hansjürgen.
Kriterien für die Produktionsplanung im Energiesektor aus gesamtwirtschaftlicher Sicht; Probleme des energiewirtschaftlichen Strukturwandels unter besonderer Berücksichtigung des Steinkohlenbergbaus. Münster, 1971.
iv, 192 p. illus. 21 cm.
Inaug.-Diss.—Münster.
Vita.
1. Power resources—Mathematical models. I. Title.
NjR NUC73-34742

Balş, M G
Imunofluorescența și aplicațiile ei în inframicrobiologie [de] M. G. Balş. București, Editura Academiei Republicii Socialiste România, 1966.
283, [2] p. illus. 25 cm.
Bibliography: p. 259-[284]
1. Immunofluorescence. 2. Microbiology—Technique. I. Title.
QR187.I 48B34 76-511686

Balş, Teodor, 1924-
Pasărea de sunet : [versuri] / Teodor Balş ; [coperta și ilustrațiile, Janos Bencsik]. — București : Editura Ion Creangă, 1975.
93 p. : ill. ; 23 cm. R 75-4939
lei 4.75
I. Title.
PC840.12.A55P3 76-508969

Balsa, J V Frías
see
Frías Balsa, J V

Balsam, Alan, joint author
see Balsam, Rosemary Marshall. Becoming a psychotherapist... Boston: Little, Brown [1974]

Balsam, M S
Cosmetics, science and technology. Editorial board: M. S. Balsam [and others] Edited by M. S. Balsam and Edward Sagarin. 2d ed. New York, Wiley-Interscience [1972-74]
3 v. 23 cm.
1957 ed. edited by E. Sagarin.
Includes bibliographical references.
ISBN 0-471-04646-9 (set)
1. Cosmetics. I. Sagarin, Edward, 1913- ed. Cosmetics, science and technology. II. Sagarin, Edward, 1913- joint author. III. Title.
TP983.B282 668'.55 75-177888
rev MARC

Balsam, Peter D
The effects of varying the trace interval, cs duration, and inter reinforcement interval on key pecking in the pigeon / by Peter D. Balsam. -- Greensboro : University of North Carolina at Greensboro, 1975.
vii, 91 leaves ; 28 cm. (North Carolina. University at Greensboro. [Dept. of Psychology.] Dissertation; 75-2.)
Thesis--University at Greensboro.
Bibliography: leaves 89-91.
I. Title. II. Series.
NcGU NUC77-85681

Balsam, Rosemary Marshall.
Becoming a psychotherapist : a clinical primer / Rosemary Marshall Balsam, Alan Balsam ; [contributing authors : Iza S. Erlich, Henry Grunebaum] ; foreword by Roy Schafer. — 1st ed. — Boston : Little, Brown, [1974]
xviii, 319 p. ; 24 cm.
Bibliography: p. 307-308.
Includes index.
1. Psychotherapy. I. Balsam, Alan, joint author. II. Erlich, Iza S. III. Title.
RC480.5.B29 616.8'914 74-125
MARC

Balsama, George D
The decomposition and rebirth of post-reformation France [by] George D. Balsama. Dubuque, Iowa, Kendall/Hunt Pub. Co. [1974]
xi, 187 p. 22 cm.
Includes bibliographical references.
1. France—Politics and government—16th century. 2. France—Politics and government—17th century. I. Title.
DC111.5.B34 320.9'44'028 73-90902
ISBN 0-8403-0876-0 MARC

Balsamer, Aloys.
Ein Grantler sagt ... : Selbstgespräche e. Bayern / Aloys Balsamer ; ill. von Helmut Heimmerl. — Regensburg : Walhalla- und-Praetoria-Verlag, 1975.
219 p. : ill. ; 20 cm. GFR76-A
Articles which originally appeared in the author's column Selbstgespräch eines Grantlers published in the Mittelbayerische Zeitung.
I. Heimmerl, Helmut. II. Selbstgespräch eines Grantlers. III. Title.
PT2662.A49G7 77-470682
77 MARC

Balsamo, Francesco, ed.
see Tortora, Filippo, 1669-1738? Breve notizia della città... Noto, Jonica, 1972.

Balsamo, Ignatius.
Con Maria e la Chiesa. 2. ed. [Borgetto (Palermo)] Edizioni Romitelliane [1968]
159 [1] p. 21.5 cm.
ODaU-M NUC73-47494

Balsamo, Ignatius.
An instruction how to pray and meditate well, 1622 [by] Ignacio Balsamo; [translated out of French into English John Heigham]. Menston, Scolar Press, 1972.
[4], 336 p. 20 cm. (English recusant literature, 1558–1640, v. 102)
B 72–21312
Facsim. of 1st ed. of this translation, St Omer, 1622.
S. T. C. no. 1341.
1. Prayer. 2. Meditation. I. Title. II. Series: Rogers, David Morrison, comp. English recusant literature, 1558–1640, v. 102.
BX1750.A1E5 vol. 102 230′.2 s 73–157408
[BV209] [248′.3] MARC
ISBN 0–85417–813–9

Balsamo, Joseph
see
Cagliostro, Alessandro, conte di, assumed name of Giuseppe Balsamo, 1743-1795.

Balsamo, Larry Thomas, 1939-
Theodore G. Bilbo and Mississippi politics, 1877-1932. [Columbia, Mo.] 1967.
288 l.
Thesis—University of Missouri.
Vita.
Bibliography: leaves [280]-288.
Microfilm of typescript. Ann Arbor, Mich., University Microfilms, 1968. 1 reel. 35 mm.
1. Mississippi—Pol. & govt.—1865- 2. Bilbo, Theodore Gilmore, 1877-1947. I. Title.
LU NUC76-74353

Balsamo, Luigi.
La lettura pubblica in Sardegna; documenti e problemi. Firenze, L. S. Olschki, 1964.
vi, 79 p. illus. 21 cm. (Biblioteconomia e bibliografia, saggi e studi, 1)
1. Books and reading—Sardinia. 2. Public libraries—Sardinia. I. Title.
Z1003.5.S23B34 74–232849

Balsamo-Crivelli, Riccardo, marchese, 1874-
La pietra al collo : romanzo / di Riccardo Balsamo Crivelli ; prefazione di Francesco Flora. — Milano : Gentile, [1945]
xvi, 231 p. ; 18 cm. — (Il Divano ; v. 1)
I. Title.
PQ4807.A57P5 1945 76-482615
76 MARC

Balsan, Alain.
Valence au Grand Siècle. Préf. de Gilbert Tournier. [Valence, Éditions Sorepi, 1973]
207 p. illus. 24 cm. F***
Bibliography: p. [171]–185.
35.00F
1. Valence, France (Drôme)—Economic conditions. 2. Valence, France (Drôme)—Social conditions. I. Title.
HC275.B26 309.1′44′98 75–501091
MARC

Balsan, François, 1902–
Au Registan inexploré (Sud-afghan) Photos. de l'auteur. [Paris] Berger-Levrault [1973, c1972]
226 p. illus. 21 cm. 27.00F F***
1. Rigestān region, Afghanistan—Description and travel. I. Title.
DS374.R53B34 1973 915.81 74–178341
MARC

Balsan, François, 1902–
Embuscades en Éthiopie. [Illustrations de F. Boudignon.] Paris, Éditions de l'Amitié, 1971.
156 p. illus., col. plates. 19 cm. (Bibliothèque de l'amitié, 79. Aventure) 9.20F F 72–7924
At head of title: F. Balsan.
I. Title.
PZ23.B27E5 73–311909

Balsan, François, 1902–
Explorări în Kalahari / François Balsan ; în românește de Florica-Eugenia Condurachi. — [București : Editura ştiinţifică, 1969]
423 p., [20] leaves of plates : ill., maps, ports. ; 21 cm.
Translation of L'étreinte du Kalahari.
1. Kalahari Desert. I. Title.
DT995.K2B316 76–516789

Balsan, François, 1902-
Poursuite au Wallega. [Paris, Les Éditions du Temps, 1962]
142 p. illus. 19 cm. (Aujourd'hui l'aventure)
1. Ethiopia—Descr. & trav. 1901-1945. I. Title.
CtY NUC75-61624

Balsan, Louis
see Larzac, terre méconnue. Paris, Éditions ouvières [1973]

Balsara, Jimmy P
Similitude study of reinforced concrete deep beams, by J. P. Balsara [and] L. E. Roggenkamp. Conducted by U. S. Army Engineer Waterways Experiment Station, Vicksburg, Miss., 1971. [n.p., n.d.]
44 p. illus. (U.S. Waterways Experiment Station, Vicksburg, Miss. Miscellaneous paper, no. N-71-2)
"Sponsored by Defense Atomic Support Agency."
Bibliography: p. 33.
1. Concrete beams—Testing. I. Roggenkamp, Larry, E., joint author. II. United States. Defense Atomic Support Agency. III. Title. IV. Series.
MsSM NUC76-74356

Balsara, Pestanji Phirozshah.
Ancient Iran, its contribution to human progress / by Pestanji Phirozshah Balsara. — Bombay : Iran League, 1936.
viii, 125 p. ; 22 cm. — (Iran League propaganda publication ; no. 18)
"Reprint from the Iran League Quarterly."
Originally presented as the author's thesis (M. A.), Bombay University.
Bibliography: p. [115]–119.
Includes index.
1. Iran—Civilization—Addresses, essays, lectures. I. Title. II. Series: Iran League, Bombay. Propaganda publication ; no. 18.
DS266.B35 1936 915.5′03 74–187971
MARC

Balsara, Pestanji Phirozshah.
Highlights of Parsi history / by P. P. Balsara. — 3d ed., [rev. and enl.]. — Bombay : Published by C. B. Trikannad for K. & J. Cooper, 1964.
92 p. ; 19 cm.
Includes index.
Rs6.00
1. Parsees. I. Title.
DS432.P3B25 1964 954′.7 75-907050
76 MARC

Balsari, Ketki, 1926–
શ્રી કિશોરલાલ મશરૂવાળા; એક અધ્યયન. [લેખિકા] કેતકી બલસારી. [1. આવૃત્તિ] અમદાવાદ, નવજીવન પ્રકાશન મંદિર [1970]
10, 386 p. port. 19 cm. Rs8.00
In Gujarati.
"પીએચ.ડી. માટે લખેલો મહાનિબંધ ..."
Bibliography: p. 386.
1. Mashruwala, Kishorlal Ghanshyamlal, 1890–1952.
Title romanized: Śrī Kiśoralāla Maśarūvalā.
PK1859.M36Z57 74–919682

Balsas, Héctor.
Flecha al viento; selección de lecturas para 5° y 6° año [por] Héctor Balsas [y] Anáis Pereira. Montevideo, ARCA [1973]
180 p. 20 cm.
"Prosa y verso."
1. Spanish language—Readers—1950- I. Pereira, Anáis, joint author. II. Title.
TxU NUC75-18393

Balsas, Héctor.
Leyendas del mundo; segunda selección. [1. ed. Montevideo] Editorial Ejido [1973]
27 p. 19 cm.
1. Legends—Juvenile literature. I. Title.
TxU NUC76-74352

Balsas, Héctor.
see Montevideo siempre ... Montevideo, Arca, 1976.

Balsaver, Sudhir
see Movement. [New Delhi, India]

Balsbaugh, Edward U
The leaf beetles of Alabama (Coleoptera: Chrysomelidael. Auburn, Ala., 1972.
223 p. illus. (Alabama. Agricultural Experiment Station. Bulletin 441)
Bibliography: p. 209-214.
I. Title.
DNAL NUC74-127756

Balscheit-Osmer, Elisabeth, 1943-
Prosper Merimee als Historiker. Bamberg, 1972.
295 p.
Dis.—Basel.
1. Merimee, Prosper, 1803-1870.
CSt NUC76-71864

Balsdon, John Percy Vyvian Dacre, 1901-
The Emperor Gaius (Caligula) / by J. P. V. D. Balsdon. — New York : AMS Press, 1976.
xix, 243 p. : geneal. table ; 19 cm.
Reprint of the 1934 ed. published by Clarendon Press, Oxford.
Bibliography: p. 222-228.
Includes index.
ISBN 0-404-14503-5
1. Caligula, Emperor of Rome, 12-41. I. Title.
DG283.B3 1976 937′.07′0924 75-41014
76 MARC

Balsdon, John Percy Vyvian Dacre, 1901-
Julius Caesar and Rome [by] J. P. V. D. Balsdon. [Harmondsworth, Eng.] Penguin Books [1971]
191 p. (A Pelican book)
American ed. has title: Julius Caesar; a political biography.
1. Caesar, C. Julius. I. Title.
OCl NUC73-123888

Balsdon, John Percy Vyvian Dacre, 1901–
Oxford now and then [by] Dacre Balsdon. New York, St. Martin's Press [1971, c1970]
xi, 267 p. illus., map (on lining paper) 23 cm. $8.95
1. Oxford. University—History. I. Title.
LF509.B3 1971 378.425′72 73–135035
MARC

Balsdon, John Percy Vyvian Dacre, 1901-
Roman women : their history and habits / J. P. V. D. Balsdon. — Revised [ed]. — London : Bodley Head, 1974.
355 p., fold. leaf, leaf of plate, 16 p. of plates : ill., geneal. tables, ports. ; 23 cm. GB75-03975
Bibliography: p. 337-340.
Includes index.
ISBN 0-370-00226-1 : £3.50
1. Women—Rome. I. Title.
HQ1136.B34 1974 301.41′2′0937 75-330450
75 MARC

Balsdon, John Percy Vyvian Dacre, 1901-
Roman women : their history and habits / J. P. V. D. Balsdon. — Westport, Conn. : Greenwood Press, 1975, c1962.
355 p., [8] leaves of plates : ill. ; 22 cm.
Reprint of the ed. published by Bodley Head, London.
Bibliography: p. 337-340.
Includes index.
ISBN 0-8371-8040-6
1. Women—Rome. I. Title.
[DG91.B3 1975] 301.41′2′0937 75-8718
75 MARC

Balse, Mayah.
The Indian female : attitude towards sex / Mayah Balse. — 1st ed. — New Delhi : Chetana Publications, 1976.
124 p. ; 22 cm.
Includes index.
Rs30.00
1. Women—India. 2. Women—Sexual behavior. I. Title.
HQ1742.B35 301.41′2′0954 76-901666
76 MARC

Balse, Mayah.
Just a matter of mistresses. Bombay, Jaico Publishing House, 1972.
208 p.
I. Title.
AzU NUC76-74351

Balse, Mayah.
Mystics and men of miracles in India / Mayah Balse. — New Delhi : Heritage Publishers, 1976.
185 p., [4] leaves of plates : ill. ; 23 cm.
Rs40.00
1. Occult sciences—India. 2. Mysticism—India. I. Title.
BF1434.I4B34 133′.092′2 76-901438
77 MARC

Balse, Mayah.
Of gods and demons. Illustrated by Nandkumar M. Muzumdar. [Bombay] IBH Pub. Co. [1968]
92 p. col. illus. 19 cm. (Echo)
1. Mythology, Indic—Juvenile literature. I. Title.
MBU-T NUC74-124054

Balse, Mayah.
The sensuous saint / Mayah Balse. — New Delhi : Sterling Publishers, 1975.
322 p. ; 17 cm.
"Sterling paperbacks, S 40."
Rs7.00
I. Title.
PZ4.B198 Se 823 75-901531
[PR9499.3.B23] 76 MARC

Balsebre, Enrique Freijo
see Freijo Balsebre, Enrique.

Balseiro, José Agustín, 1900-
see The Hispanic presence in Florida ... Miami, Fla., E. A. Seemann Pub., [1977], c1976.

Balseiro, José Agustín, 1900-
see Presencial hispánica en la Florida ... Miami, Fla., Ediciones Universal, c1976.

Balsells Morera, Pablo.
Cárceles soviéticas, por Pablo Balsells. Barcelona, Bosch [1937]
296 p. 22 cm. (Temas jurídicos soviéticos)
"Código de trabajo correccional de R. S. F. S. R.": p. [257]-290.
Includes bibliographical references.
1. Prisons — Russia — Laws and regulations. 2. Forced labor — Russia. I. Russia (1917- R. S. F. S. R.). Laws, statutes, etc. Ispravitel'no-trudovoĭ kodeks RSFSR. Spanish. 1937. II. Title. III. Title: Código de trabajo correccional de R. S. F. S. R.
73-202443

Balsemão, Francisco C P
Informar ou depender? [por] Francisco C. P. Balsemão. Lisboa, Ediçóes Atica [1971]
329 p. 23 cm.
1. Communication. 2. Mass media. 3. Government publicity. 4. Selective dissemination of information. I. Title.
TxU DLC NUC74-124039

Balsemão, Jayme de.
Endymius e Séleneia (contos). Lisboa, Impr. Libanio da Silva [19--]
189 p.
I. Title.
NcU NUC76-26877

Balsemo, Iacopo da
see
Balsamo, Giacomo, ca. 1425-ca. 1503.

Balser, Heinrich.
Die GmbH: ein Handbuch f. d. wirtschaftl. notarielle u. gerichtl. Praxis; mit Erl., Beisp., Formularen/ von Heinrich Balser; Witold Meyer; Vincent Pichura. — 5., durchges. u. erg. Aufl. — Freiburg (im Breisgau): Haufe, 1972.
362 p.; 22 cm. DM34.80 GFR 73-A13
1. Private companies—Germany (Federal Republic, 1949-)—Handbooks, manuals, etc. I. Meyer, Witold, joint author. II. Pichura, Vincent, joint author. III. Title.
73-351928
ISBN 3-448-00250-X

Balser, James L
A survey of the impact of the Uniform commercial code on businessmen in West Virginia, by James L. Balser. Morgantown, Bureau of Business Research, West Virginia University, 1969.
viii, 49 p. 30 cm. (Graduate research monographs in business and economics, v. 1, no. 4)
West Virginia University bulletin, ser. 70, no. 4-4.
Bibliography: p. [45]-46.
1.50
1. Commercial law—West Virginia. I. Title. II. Series.
KFW1352.Z9B34 658.1'2 77-631666
MARC

Balser, K.
see Jayme, Georg. Contribution to the electron-microscopy... [n.p., n.d.]

Balser, Otto.
Conrad Ferdinand Meyers Renaissancenovellen / Otto Blaser. — Reprograph. Nachdr. d. Ausg. Bern 1905. — Hildesheim : Gerstenberg, 1975.
ix, 150 p. ; 19 cm. — (Untersuchungen zur neueren Sprach- und Literaturgeschichte ; Heft 8) GFR75-A
Reprint of the ed. published by A. Francke.
Includes bibliographical references.
ISBN 3-8067-0501-1 : DM28.00
1. Meyer, Conrad Ferdinand, 1825-1898—Criticism and interpretation. 2. Meyer, Conrad Ferdinand, 1825-1898—Knowledge—History. I. Title. II. Series.
PT2432.Z9B55 1975 76-488771
77 MARC

Balser, Peter
see Ott, Heinrich. Die Antwort des Glaubens; systemat. Stuttgart, Kreuz-Verlag, 1972.

Balser, Richard P comp.
Die casting plant [an accumulation of data on die casting, by] Richard Balser [and] Harry Thomas. [n.p., 1971]
1 v. (various pagings) illus. (part col.), maps (part col., part fold., part in pockets) 29 cm.
Cover title.
In loose-leaf.
Submitted as part of the course requirements for IE 343, Plant Layout and Handling.
Includes bibliographical references.
NcRS NUC73-34743

Balser S , Carlos.
El jade de Costa Rica : un album arqueológico con reproducciones en color = an archaeological picture book with color reproductions / Carlos Balser S. — [s.l. : s.n.], 1974 (San José : Lehmann)
88 p. : ill. ; 22 cm.
Spanish and English.
Bibliography: p. 85-88.
1. Indians of Central America—Costa Rica—Antiquities. 2. Costa Rica—Antiquities. 3. Jade art objects—Costa Rica. 4. Indians of Central America—Costa Rica—Sculpture. I. Title.
F1545.B34 77-475206
77 MARC

Balsevich, J 1951-
Studies related to the insect control potential of thujone derivatives / by J. Balsevich. -- [Vancouver, B. C.] : University of British Columbia, 1975.
xi, 80 leaves : ill. ; 28 cm.
Thesis (M.Sc.)--University of British Columbia.
Vita.
Bibliography: leaves 79-80.
1. Insect control--Biological control. 2. Insect hormones. I. Title. II. Series.
CaBVaU NUC77-85882

Balsham, Joel, 1935-
A conceptual undergraduate teacher-training program in the philosophical context of community development. Amherst, 1971.
ii, 120 l. illus., append. 28 cm.
Thesis (Ed.D.)—University of Massachusetts.
Microfilm no. 1455.
1. Teacher, Training of. 2. Community development. I. Title.
MU NUC73-34735

(Balshanut ḥishuvit)
בלשנות חישובית : ערב-עיון שנתי של קבוצת-איל״א לבלשנות חישובית, אוניברסיטה בר-אילן, רמת-גן, כ״ו בכסלו תשכ״ח / עורכים, אסא כשר, יעקב שויקה. — ירושלים : איל״א, c1969.
183 p. : ill. ; 22 cm. — (פרסומי איל״א : סדרה כללית ; כרך 2-3)
Added t. p.: Computational linguistics.
Errata, p. 93-115 inserted.
Bibliography: p. 87-91.
1. Linguistics—Data processing—Congresses. I. Choueka, Y. II. Kasher, Asa. III. Igud Yiśre' eli le-'ibud informatsyah. Ḳevutsat-Ila le-valshanut ḥishuvit. IV. Title: Computational linguistics. V. Series: Igud Yiśre'eli le-'ibud informatsyah. Pirsume Ila : Sidrah kelalit ; kerekh 2-3.
QA76.I 3 vol. 2-3 75-951354
[P98]

Balshastri Jambhekar, 1810-1846.
[Works]
आचार्य बाळ गंगाधर शास्त्री जांभेकर (१८१२-१८४६) यांचें जीवनवृत्त व लेखसंग्रह, पश्चिम भारतांतील नवयुगप्रवर्तक आणि आधुनिक महाराष्ट्राचे जनक / संशोधक व संपादक गणेश गंगाधर जांभेकर; पुरस्कर्ते बाळ गंगाधर खेर. — पुणें : गणेश गंगाधर जांभेकर, 1950-
v. : ill., maps, ports. ; 23 cm. — (शताब्दी-स्मारक-ग्रंथ ; 1-
Added t.p.: Memoirs and writings of Acharya Bal Shastri Jambhekar.
Marathi or English.
Includes indexes.
CONTENTS: v. 1. उपोद्घात, अर्थात् गेल्या शंभर वर्षांतील चरित्रसाहित्याचें सिंहावलोकन (१८४६-१९४३).—v. 2. इंग्रजी व मराठी निवडक लेख. —v. 3. चरित्र-साहित्य (सटिक) परिशिष्टें, १-६.
1. Balshastri Jambhekar, 1810-1846. I. Jambhekar, Ganesh Gangadhar, 1889- II. Series: Śatābdi-smāraka-grantha ; 1-3
Title romanized: Ācārya Bāḷa Gaṅgādhara Śāstrī Jambhekara (1812-1846) yāñcẽ jīvanavṛtta va lekhasaṅgraha.
CT1508.B33A34 1950 75-986379

Bal'shin, M IŪ
[Nauchnye osnovy poroshkovoĭ metallurgii]
Научные основы порошковой металлургии и металлургии волокна. Москва, "Металлургия," 1972.
335 p. with illus. 21 cm. 2.48rub USSR 72-VKP
At head of title: М. Ю. Бальшин.
Includes bibliographies.
1. Powder metallurgy. 2. Metallic whiskers. I. Title.
TN695.B33 73-302914

Balshin, Michael, 1941-
Absorption of amino acids In vitro by the rectum of the desert locust (Schistocerca gregaria). [Vancouver, B. C.] 1973.
xiv, 147 l. illus. 28 cm.
Thesis—University of British Columbia.
Vita.
Bibliography: leaves 140-147.
1. Desert locust. 2. Amino acids. 3. Absorption (Physiology). I. Title.
CaBVaU NUC75-18400

Balshone, Benjamin M
America the beautiful : this great country, good and evil, as seen through my eyes / by Benjamin Balshone. -- 1st ed. -- New York : Vantage Press, 1975.
374 p. : ill., ports. ; 22 cm.
1. Balshone family. I. Title.
OU NUC77-85437

Balshone, Bruce L
Bicycle transit : its planning and desing / Bruce L. Balshone, Paul L. Deering, Brian D. McCarl ; foreword by Tom McCall. — New York : Praeger, 1975.
xv, 164 p. : ill. ; 24 cm. — (Praeger special studies, design/environmental planning series)
Bibliography: p. 124-147.
ISBN 0-275-05410-1
1. Cycling paths—Design and construction. I. Deering, Paul L., joint author. II. McCarl, Brian D., joint author. III. Title.
TE301.B34 711'.7 75-55
75 MARC

Balsiger, Dave.
In search of Noah's ark / by Dave Balsiger & Charles E. Sellier, Jr. — Los Angeles : Sun Classic Books, c1976.
218 p., [16] leaves of plates : ill. ; 18 cm.
Bibliography: p. 216-217.
ISBN 0-917214-01-3 : $1.95
1. Noah's ark. 2. Deluge. I. Sellier, Charles E., joint author. II. In search of Noah's ark. [Motion picture]
BS658.B34 222'.11 76-151887
77 MARC

Balsiger, Dave.
see Bullock, Randy. It's good to know. Milford, Mi., Mott Media, [1975]

Balsiger, Dave
see Musgraves, Don, 1935- One more time. Minneapolis, Bethany Fellowship [1974]

Balsiger, Dave
see Warnke, Mike. The Satan-seller. Plainfield, N. J., Logos International [c1972]

Balsiger, James Walter.
A computer simulation model for the eastern Bering Sea king crab population. [Seattle] 1974.
197 l. illus.
Thesis (Ph. D.)—University of Washington.
Bibliography: leaves 194-197.
1. Theses—Individual program. 2. King crabs. 3. Crabs—Bering Sea. I. Title.
WaU NUC75-18392

Balsillie, A D
That was my line / [by] A. D. Balsillie. — Ilfracombe : Stockwell, 1976.
34 p. : ill. ; 19 cm. GB76-26413
ISBN 0-7223-0894-9 : £0.75
1. Balsillie, A. D. 2. Railroads—Employees—Biography.
TF140.B34A34 1976 385'.092'4 76-381169
76 MARC

Balsillie, David, 1944-
The formation of heartwood phenols in red pine (pinus resinosa Ait.) and white elm (ulmus america L.) [by] D. Balsillie. [Toronto] 1972.
181 l. illus.
Thesis—University of Toronto.
Bibliography: leaves 174-181.
1. Red pine. 2. American elm. 3. Phenols. I. Title.
CaOTU NUC73-123889

Balsillie, David, 1944-
see McGovern, P C Sulphur dioxide levels... Sudbury, 1972.

Balsillie, J H
Analysis and interpretation of Littoral Environment Observation (LEO) and profile data along the western panhandle coast of Florida / by James H. Balsillie. -- Fort Belvoir, Va. : U.S. Coastal Engineering Research Center, 1975.
104 p. : ill., maps ; 26 cm. -- (Technical memorandum--U.S. Coastal Engineering Research Center ; no. 49)
1. Coasts--Florida--Panhandle region. 2. Beach erosion--Florida--Panhandle region. 3. Sedimentation and deposition--Florida--Panhandle region. I. Title.
DI-GS NUC77-85881

Balsillie, J H
Surf observations and longshore current prediction / by James H. Balsillie. -- Fort Belvoir, Va. : U.S. Army, Corps of Engineers, Coastal Engineering Research Center ; Springfield, Va. : available from National Technical Information Service, 1975.
39 p. : ill. ; 26 cm. -- (Technical memorandum--U.S. Coastal Engineering Research Center ; 58)
Bibliography: p. 19-20.
1. Ocean waves. 2. Coasts--California--Point Mugu. 3. Ocean currents. I. Title.
DI-GS NUC77-85880

Balsing, Randy.
Great lengths / Randy Blasing. -- Providence, R.I. : First Editions, 1975.
42 p. ; 22 cm.
Poems.
I. Title.
NmLcU NUC77-94626

Balsinger, H., joint author
see Freeman, John Wright. Preliminary results from the lunar ionosphere detector. Houston, Tex., 1970.

Bal'sis, A B
see
Balsys, Antanas.

Balskus, Pat.
Mary's pilgrim; life of St. Peregrine. Illustrated by the Daughters of St. Paul. [Boston] St. Paul Editions [1972]
92 p. illus. 22 cm. (Encounter books) $1.50
SUMMARY: The life of the thirteenth-century Italian priest who became the patron against cancer after being miraculously cured of that disease.
1. Laziosi, Pellegrino, Saint, 1265-1345—Juvenile literature. [1. Laziosi, Pellegrino, Saint, 1265-1345. 2. Saints] I. Daughters of St. Paul. II. Title.
BX4700.L43B34 282'.092'4 [B] [92] 68-58160 MARC

Balskus, Pat.
Trailblazer for the Sacred Heart / by Pat Balskus. — Boston : St. Paul Editions, c1976.
120 p., [8] leaves of plates : ill. ; 22 cm.
SUMMARY: The life of the founder of the Enthronment of the Sacred Heart of Jesus.
$3.00
1. Crawley-Boevey, Mateo, 1875-1960—Juvenile literature. [1. Crawley-Boevey, Mateo, 1875-1960. 2. Clergy. 3. Catholic Church—Biography] I. Title.
BX4705.C7817B34 271'.7 75 75-37947 MARC

Balslev, Benjamin.
De danske Jøders historie [af] Benj. Balslev. København, O. Lohse, 1932.
138 p. 24 cm.
Includes bibliographical references.
1. Jews in Denmark—History. I. Title.
DS135.D4B34 74-206692

Balslev, Erik.
Schrodinger operators with symmetries [by] E. Balslev. Marseille, Centre de physique théorique, 1972.
92 l. 30 cm. 30.00F F***
Bibliography: leaves 89-92.
1. Schrödinger operator. 2. Symmetry (Physics) I. Title.
QC174.17.S3B34 530.1'24 73-168573 MARC

Balslev, I.
see Interdisciplinary Symposium on the Measurement of Oxygen, Odense University, 1974. Measurement of oxygen ... Amsterdam, Elsevier Scientific Pub. Co., 1976.

Balslev, N
Elektriske måleinstrumenter [af] N. Balslev. [n. p.] Akademisk forlag, 1964.
130 p. illus. 23 cm.
1. Electric meters. 2. Electric measurements. I. Title.
TK301.B28 74-206754

Balslev, Vilhelm.
Danske plantesamfund [af] Vilhelm Balslev og Kristen Simonsen. 4. ændrede udg. ved Bodil lange. Med tegninger af Vagn Petersson. København, P. Haase, 1961.
114, [9] p. illus. 22 cm.
Bibliography: p. [115]-[118]
1. Plant communities—Denmark. 2. Botany—Denmark—Ecology. I. Simonsen, Kristen, joint author. II. Lange, Bodil. III. Title.
QK956.D4B34 1961 74-206505

Balsley, Ben Burton.
Ionosperic drift velocity measurements at Jimarca, Peru (July 1967-March 1970) by Ben B. Balsley and Ronald F. Woodman. Asheville, N.C., U.S. Dept. of Commerce, National Oceanic and Atmospheric Administration Environmental Data Service, 1971.
44 p. (chiefly charts) 28 cm. (World Data Center A. Upper Atmosphere Geophysics. Report UAG-17)
"Prepared by World Data Center A, Upper Atmosphere Geophysics, NOAA, Boulder, Colorado."
1. Ionospheric drift—Charts, diagrams, etc. I. Woodman, Ronald F. II. IGY World Data Center A: Upper Atmosphere Geophysics. III. Title.
NIC NUC74-124849

Balsley, Howard Lloyd, 1913- joint author
see Clover, Vernon T Business research methods. [Columbus, Ohio, Grid, inc., 1974]

Balsley, Irol Verneth Whitmore, 1912-
Homestyle baking, by Irol Whitmore Balsley, Larhylia Whitmore Wood [and] Nanna Carson Whitmore. Philadelphia, Dorrance [c1973]
464 p. 23 cm. $10.00
1. Baking. I. Wood, Larhylia Whitmore, joint author. II. Whitmore, Nanna Carson, joint author. III. Title.
TX763.B33 641.7'1 73-83485
ISBN 0-8059-1894-9 MARC

Balsley, Irol Verneth Whitmore, 1912-
Shorthand transcription studies [by] Irol Whitmore Balsley [and] S. J. Wanous. Shorthand plates written by Grace A. Bowman. 4th ed. (Jubilee) Cincinnati, South-Western Pub. Co. [1968]
vii, 249 p. illus., forms. 21 x 28 cm.
1. Shorthand. I. Wanous, Samuel James, 1907- joint author. II. Title.
Z56.B18 1968 653'.427 68-26343 [r77]rev MARC

Balsley, Irol Verneth Whitmore, 1912-
see **Century 21 shorthand: collegiate series. Cincinnati, South-Western Pub. Co., [1974-**

Balsmeier, Phillip W 1938-
The development of an induced course load matrix for the University of Arkansas; a case study. Ann Arbor, Mich., University Microfilms, 1973.
1 reel. 35 mm.
Thesis—University of Arkansas.
Collation of the original: 160 leaves. illus.
1. Universities and colleges—Business management—Case studies. I. Title.
ViBlbV NUC76-74350

Balsnes, Sigurd, 1901-
"Og ljos over landet strøymde." Førde, [1972]
61 p. 22 cm. N 73-25
1. Libraries—Norway—Addresses, essays, lectures. I. Title.
Z825.A1B34 74-304803

Balson, Diane.
Yo-yo / by Diane Balson. — New York : Morrow, 1976.
288 p. ; 22 cm.
ISBN 0-688-02979-5
I. Title.
PZ4.B199 Yo 813'.5'4 75-25723
[PS3552.A4715] 75 MARC

Balss, Heinrich, 1886-
Die Zeugungslehre und Embryologie in der Antike: eine Ubersicht, von Heinrich Balss. Würzburg, JAL-reprint, 1973.
82 p. (Quellen und Studien zur Geschichte der Naturwissenschaften und der Medizin, Bd. 5, Hft. 2-3)
Caption title.
Reprint of the 1936 ed. published in Berlin.
1. Zoology—Hist. 2. Reproduction. 3. Embryology—Hist. I. Title. II. Series.
InU NUC76-74349

Balss un atbalsis; lasámgrámata 6. klasei. Lidijas Ziemeles un Eduarda Silkalna redakcijā. Sastadītaji: Gerhards Brēmanis [et al.] Mārtiņa Gaujas ilustrācijas un vāka zīmējums. [Washington?] Amerikas latviešu apvieniba, 1972.
179 p. illus. 24 cm.
1. Latvian language—Readers.
MB NUC74-121688

Balster, Clifford A
Catalog of stratigraphic names for Montana. Clifford A. Balster, editor. A cooperative project of the Montana Bureau of Mines and Geology, and the Montana Geological Society. Contributing members of the Society: W. W. Ballard [and others] Butte, Montana College of Mineral Science and Technology, 1971.
iii, 448 p. 29 cm. (State of Montana, Bureau of Mines and Geology, special publication 54) $1.50
"A cooperative project of the Montana Bureau of Mines and Geology, and the Montana Geological Society."
1. Geology, Stratigraphic—Nomenclature—Montana. I. Ballard, William Wayne, 1932- II. Montana. State Bureau of Mines and Geology. III. Montana Geological Society. IV. Title. V. Series: Montana. State Bureau of Mines and Geology. Special publication 54)
QE645.B34 551.7'009786 70-636592 MARC

Balster, Clifford A
Geomorphology and soils, Willamette Valley, Oregon [by C.A. Balster and R.B. Parsons] Corvallis, 1968.
31 p. illus., maps (1 fold. in pocket) 28 cm. (Oregon. Agricultural Experiment Station, Corvallis. Special report, no. 265)
Bibliography: p. 17.
1. Geomorphology-Oregon-Willamette River watershed. 2. Soils-Oregon-Willamette River watershed. I. Parsons, Robert Bruce. II. Title.
DI-GS NUC74-122414

Balster, Clifford A
Structure contour map, upper cretaceus, southeastern Montana. [n.p., 1973?]
map 44 x 74 cm. (Montana. Bureau of mines and geology. Special publication 60.)
Scale 1:316,800.
1. Geology, Structural. 2. Montana—Maps. I. Series.
NIC NUC76-74348

Balster, Robert Eden, 1925-
An exploratory study of strategies and tactics used to introduce planned innovations in selected community services programs. [n.p.] 1971.
[4] vii, 243 l.
Thesis (Ph.D.)—Michigan State University.
Bibliography: leaves 198-205.
1. Community. I. Title.
MiEM NUC73-34736

Balston, Thomas.
John Martin, 1789-1854, illustrator and pamphleteer. London, Bibliographical Society, 1934.
[383]-432 p. 23 cm.
"Reprinted ... from the transactions of the Bibliographical Society, The Library, Mar. 1934."
"Check lists": p. 400-432.
1. Martin, John, 1789-1854. 2. Martin, John, 1789-1954—Bibliography.
NC978.5.M38B34 741'.092'4 74-191868 MARC

Balsvig, K E
Historisk geografi / K.-E. Balsvig. — [København] : Gyldendal, 1976.
43, [1] p. : ill. ; 30 cm. — (Samfundsgeografi) D76-18
Bibliography: p. [44]
ISBN 8700091510 : kr38.50
1. Ørslev, Denmark—Historical geography. I. Title.
DL291.O382B34 77-460693
77 MARC

Balswick, Jack O., joint author
see Layne, Norman R Ascension at the cross roads: a case study of a church caught in the turbulence of rapid social change. Athens, University of Georgia, 1973.

Balswick, Jack Orville, 1938-
The family as a factor in vocational rehabilitation success, by Jack O. Balswick. [Iowa City] 1967.
191 l.
Thesis—University of Iowa.
Microfilm copy. Ann Arbor, Mich., University Microfilms, 1967. 1 reel. 35 mm.
1. Family. 2. Vocational rehabilitation.
I. Title.
MoU NUC73-122816

Balsys, Antanas.
(Stanovlenie nauchnogo mirovozzreniia lichnosti)
Становление научного мировоззрения личности : пресса в системе формирования научного мировоззрения личности / Антанас Бальсис. — Вильнюс : Периодика, 1974.
346 p. ; 20 cm. USSR 75
At head of title: Akademiia nauk Litovskoĭ SSR. Otdel filosofii, prave i sotsiologii pri Institute istorii.
Includes bibliographical references.
1.50rub
1. Atheism — Study and teaching — Lithuania. 2. Communism — Study and teaching — Lithuania. 3. Journalism — Social aspects — Lithuania. I. Title.
BL2747.3.B253 75-526939

Balt, John.
By reason of insanity. [London] Panther [1972, c1966]
223 p.
1. Mental illness–Personnal narratives.
I. Title.
ViBlbV NUC74-121686

Baltă, Eugenia, joint author.
see Baltă, Petru. Introduction to the physical chemistry of the vitreous state. București, România, Editura Academiei, 1976.

Balta, Paul, 1929–
La politique arabe de la France; de De Gaulle à Pompidou [par] Paul Balta [et] Claudine Rulleau. Paris, Sindbad [1973]
279 p. 23 cm. (La Bibliothèque arabe. Collection L'Actuel)
32.90F F***
Bibliography: p. [277]–279.
1. France—Foreign relations—Arab countries. 2. Arab countries—Foreign relations—France. I. Rulleau, Claudine, joint author. II. Title.
DS63.2.F8B34 327.44'017'4927 73–173132
MARC

Baltá, Pedro.
Las urnas. Barcelona, Ediciones Rondas [1972]
304 p. 19 cm. (Colección Actualidad) Sp***
I. Title.
PQ6652.A5U7 73–316275

Baltă, Petru.
Introduction to the physical chemistry of the vitreous state / P. Baltă and E. Baltă ; [translated from Romanian by Tatiana Nichitin]. — București, România : Editura Academiei, 1976.
287 p. : ill. ; 25 cm. R***
Rev. and enl. translation of Introducere în chimia fizică a stării vitroase.
Includes bibliographical references.
ISBN 0-85626-088-6
1. Glass. I. Baltă, Eugenia, joint author. II. Title.
QD471.B2613 541'.3 77-351467
77 MARC

Balta, Tahsin Bekir.
İdare hukuku. Ankara, Ankara Üniversitesi Basımevi, 1972–
v. 24 cm. (Ankara Üniversitesi Siyasal Bilgiler Fakültesi yayınları, no. 326
Includes bibliographical references.
CONTENTS: 1. Genel konular.
1. Administrative law—Turkey. 2. Administrative law. I. Title. II. Series: Ankara. Üniversite. Siyasal Bilgiler Fakültesi. Siyasal Bilgiler Fakültesi yayınlarından, no. 326 [etc.]
73–202017

Baltabaev, Arystangali Baltabaevich.
(Agrotekhnika vyrashchivaniia lesnykh kul'tur v zasushlivykh usloviiakh)
Агротехника выращивания лесных культур в засушливых условиях : из опыта работы жанааркин. лесхоза / А. Б. Балтаваев. — Алма-Ата : Кайнар, 1975.
68, [1] p. : ill. ; 17 cm. USSR 75
Bibliography: p. 68–[69]
0.11rub
1. Afforestation—Kazakhstan. I. Title.
SD409.B28 76–527572

Baltabaev, Mukash Baltabaevich.
Nekotorye problemy vseobshchego srednego obrazovaniia v Kirgizskoi SSR. Frunze [Mektep] 1970.
116 p.
Title page and text in Kirghiz.
Russian title from colophon.
1. Secondary education–Kirghizistan.
MH NUC75-129139

Baltabaeva, Kh
see
Boltaboeva, Ḣ

Baltac, Th
Redresoare pentru material rulant electric. [Sinteză documentară elaborată de dr. ing. Th. Baltac, ing. P. Ciortan, ing. C. Banu]. [București], Ministerul Transporturilor și Telecomunicațiilor, Centrul de documentare și publicații tehnice, 1971.
91 p. with figs. and graphs. 21 cm. lei 30.00 R 71–3739
Bibliography: p. 83–88.
1. Semiconductor rectifiers. 2. Electric locomotives. I. Ciortan, Petre, joint author. II. Banu, C., joint author. III. Title.
TF368.B32 72–370801

Baltac, Vasile.
Optimizarea sistemelor de operare ale calculatoarelor numerice / Vasile Baltac. — [Timișoara] : "Facla," 1974.
208 p. : ill. ; 21 cm. R 75–454
Summary in English.
Bibliography: p. 195–198.
Includes index.
lei 17.50
1. Electronic digital computers—Programming. I. Title.
QA76.6.B344 75–544929

Baltac, Vasile
see Felix C-256 [i. e. două sute cincizeci si sase]. Bucuresti, Editura tehnică, 1974.

Baltacioğlu, İsmail Hakki, 1887-
Atatürk; başlangiç, yetişmesi, kişiliği, devrim metodu, ilkeleri. Erzurum, Atatürk Üniversitesi Basimevi, 1973.
110 p. (Atatürk Üniversitesi yayinlari)
Cumhuriyetin 50. yili aramağani.
1. Atatürk, Kemal, 1881-1938.
MH NUC76-71849

Baltacıoğlu, İsmail Hakkı, 1887–
Türk plâstik sanatları / yazan Ismayıl Hakkı Baltacıoğlu. — Ankara : [Millî Eğitim Bakanlığı], 1971.
136 p., [8] leaves of plates : ill. ; 28 cm.
Includes bibliographical references.
1. Arts, Turkish. I. Title.
NX565.A1B34 76–970441

Baltacıoğlu, İsmail Hakkı, 1887-
Türke doğru. [Ankara, 1972]
482 p. port. (Türkiye Iş Bankası Kültür yayınları, 116. Sosyal ve Felsefi eserler dizisi, 14)
"Türke doğru ilk defa 1942 yılında yayınlanmıştır."
I. Title.
ICU NUC74-120836

Baltadoros, Antōnios A., ed.
see Baltadōros, Giōrgos A 1897-1930. Hapanta. Athēnai, 1966.

Baltadōros, Giōrgos A 1897-1930.
Hapanta; logotechnika diegēmata, dēmosiographika grammata, zōgraphikē, lexilogion. Eisagōgē-epi meleia Antōniou A. Baltadorou. Kritikēs. Athēnai, 1966.
334 p. plates (part col.), ports., facsims. 30 cm.
1. Greek literature, Modern—Collected works. I. Baltadoros, Antōnios A., ed.
NN NUC74-120049

Baltadzhieva, Zhivka, 1947-
Slunchevo splitane; stikhotvoreniia. Sofiia, Narodna mladezh, 1971.
52 p. front. (Biblioteka Smiana. Pŭrvi knigi na mladi avtori. Lirika, 98)
MH NUC75-129140

Baltag, Cezar.
Madona din dud. [Versuri. Coperta: Ion Dogar Marinescu]. București, Editura Eminescu, 1973.
80 p. 19 cm. lei 5.00 R 73–2239
I. Title.
PC840.12.A56M3 74–326047

Baltag, Cezar.
Șah orb. [Eseuri. Coperta: Ion Petrescu]. București, Editura Eminescu, 1971.
116 p. 19 cm. lei 5.50 R 71–3314
I. Title.
PC840.12.A56S2 74–326289

Baltag, Cezar.
Unicorn în oglindă : [versuri] / Cezar Baltag. — București : Editura Eminescu, 1975.
127 p. ; 20 cm. R 75–931
lei 7.00
I. Title.
PC840.12.A56U5 76–526472

Baltag, Cezar.
see Ion Barbu ... [București] Editura Eminescu, 1976.

Baltagi, Paul, joint author
see Cernescu, Alexandru. Avioane românești străbat Africa ... București: Editura militară, 1975.

Baltaĭtis, IUliĭ Viktorovich, joint author
see Matiashin, Ignat Mikhaĭlovich. (Oslozhneniia appendektomii) 1974.

Baltājī, Muḥammad
see
Bultājī, Muḥammad.

Baltake, Joe.
The films of Jack Lemmon / by Joe Baltake ; tribute by Walter Matthau ; foreword by Judith Crist. — 1st ed. — Secaucus, N.J. : Citadel Press, c1977.
255 p. : ill. ; 29 cm.
ISBN 0-8065-0560-5 : $14.95
1. Lemmon, Jack. 2. Moving-picture actors and actresses—United States—Biography. I. Title.
PN2287.L42B3 791.43'028'0924 77-636
77 MARC

Baltakis, Algimantas, 1930- Akimirkos
see Paškauskaitė, Lili, 1925- Lili Paškauskaitės akvafortai A. Baltakio eilėraščių rinkiniui "Akimirkos". [Vilnius, Vaga, 1970]

Baltakis, Algimantas, 1930-
Duona ir debesys; lyrika. [Dailininkė Lili Paškauskaitė] Vilnius, Vaga, 1973.
151 p. front.
Russian title in colophon: Khleb i oblaka.
Lithuanian text.
MH NUC76-74347

Baltakis, Algimantas, 1930–
[Pėsčias paukštis. Russian]
Пешая птица. Избранное. Вильнюс, Vaga, 1969.
270 p. 18 cm. 0.80rub USSR***
At head of title: Альгимантас Балтакис.
I. Title.
Title romanized: Peshaia ptitsa.
PG8722.12.A4P417 73–315856

Baltakis, Algimantas, 1930–
Stebuklinga žolė. Eilėraščiai. Vilnius, "Vaga," 1971.
422 p. with illus. 13 cm. 1.29rub USSR 71–42763
I. Title.
PG8722.12.A4S7 74–345357

Baltakis, Algimantas, 1930- ed.
see Poezijos pavasaris. Vilnius, Vaga, 1967.

Baltakis, Frank P
Determination of the performance parameters of a fluttering vane-type fuze-arming device using a controlled-geometry wind tunnel. Prepared by: Frank P. Baltakis, Gary D. Senechal [and] Paul J. Dawson. White Oak, Silver Spring, Md., Naval Ordnance Laboratory [1970]
iv, 14, [36], 20 p. illus. 28 cm. (U.S. Naval Ordnance Laboratory, White Oak, Md. NOLTR 70-255)
Caption title.
1. Flutter (Aerodynamics) I. Senechal, Gary D. II. Dawson, Paul J. III. Title.
NIC NUC74-135810

Baltan, Ben-Zion.
(ha-Nevi'im bi-delatot)
הנביאים בדלתות : בצרוף נבואות מקבילות : קונצפציה חדשה במדע התנ"ך / ערוך ומבואר ע"י בן ציון בלצן. — קישינוב : הוצאת מקור, ‎‏[1936 or 1937]-‏‎ ‎697.‏-
v. : maps ; 24 cm.
Cover title.
Added cover title: A new conception in the science of the Bible.
Biblical texts vocalized.
CONTENTS: חוברת 1. האזינו. נבואות יואל ועמוס. משא בבל אשר חזה ישעיהו בן־אמוץ.
1. Bible. O. T. Prophets—Commentaries. I. Bible. O. T. Prophets. Hebrew. Selections. 1936 or 7. II. Title. III. Title: A new conception in the science of the Bible.
BS1505.B28 75-951068

Baltanov, Ravil' Gubaĭdullovich.
(Sotsiologicheskie problemy v sisteme nauchno-ateisticheskogo vospitaniia)
Социологические проблемы в системе научно-атеистического воспитания. (Проблемы конкретно-социол. анализа религии и атеизма в СССР). Казань, Изд-во Казан. ун-та, 1973.
251 p. 21 cm. 1.00rub USSR 73
At head of title: Р. Г. Балтанов.
Bibliography: p. 234-[249]
1. Atheism—Study and teaching—Russia. 2. Russia—Religion—1917- I. Title.
BL2747.3.B254 74-328819

Baltar, Antonio Bezerra.
Control de la ejecución de proyectos por el metodo del camino critico (Pert). Antonio Baltar. Santiago de Chile, Cuadernos del Instituto Latinoamericano de Planificación Economica y Social, 1968.
51 p. 27 cm. (Latin American Institute for Economic and Social Planning. Cuadernos. Ser. I. Apuntes de clase, no. 4)
Bibliography: p. 51.
1. Critical path analysis. 2. Project management. I. Title.
WU DLC NUC76-74973

Baltar, Antonio Bezerra.
Control de la ejecución de proyectos por el metodo del camino critico (PERT). [2. ed. rev.] Santiago de Chile, 1971.
60 p. (Cuadernos del Instituto Latinoamericano de Planificación Económica y Social. Serie 1: Apuntes de clases, 4)
1. Critical path analysis.
MH NUC74-124041

Baltar Dominguez, Ramon
see Opusculos medicos gallegos del siglo XVIII. Santiago de Compostela, Bibliofilos Gallegos, 1961.

Baltard, Louis Pierre, 1764-1846.
see [Legrand, Jacques Guillaume] 1743-1807. A series of lithographic drawings illustrative of the relation between the human physiognomy and that of the brute creation. London, Printed for the proprietor, I. P. Blanquet, and published by J. Carpenter, 1827.

Băltărețu, Aurelian.
Aventuri in lumea chimiei. [Copertă și ilustrații: Ionescu Dumitru. Coperta colecției: A. Olsufiev]. [București], Editura Ion Creangă, 1972.
96 p. with illus. 17 cm. (Colecția Alfa) R 72-3622
lei 6.00
1. Chemistry—Juvenile literature. I. Title.
QD35.B34 75-575886

Băltărețu, Constantin.
see Cultura spectacolului teatral ... [București] "Meridiane" 1976.

Băltărețu, Ernest.
Les pompes centrifuges : conditions fonctionnelles-constructives, chaînes de cotes / par Ernest Băltărețu. — București : Editura technică ; Paris : Éditions Eyrolles, 1975.
87 p. : ill. ; 24 cm. R75-2835
Translation of Pompe centrifuge.
Part of illustrative matter in pocket.
Bibliography: p. 77-[78]
lei8.80
1. Centrifugal pumps. I. Title.
TJ919.B3414 75-520837
*76 MARC

Bǎltarǎetu, Florica, joint author
see Matei, Ion. Metode de proiectare și realizare a aerajului general și parțial. București, Oficiul de documentare și publicații tehnice, 1973.

Baltarusių ir moldavų šokiai. Vilnius, LTSR Kultūros ministerijos Liaudies meno rūmai, 1972.
116 p. with illus. and music 20 cm. 0.36rub USSR 72-33739
1. Folk dancing, Lithuanian. 2. Folk dancing, White Russian.
GV1664.L55B34 74-348130

Baltas, Sotērēs.
Kosmas ho Aitōlos; ho Hagios epanastatēs (1714-1779) Athēna, Ekdoseis Kypros [1966]
55 p. illus.
1. Kosmas Aitōlos, 1714-1779.
MH NUC74-123678

Baltasar, Francisco
see
Baltazar, Francisco, 1788-1862.

Baltasar Gracián en su tercer centenario, 1658-1958. Madrid, Universidad, 1958.
272-445 p. 24 cm. (Revista de la Universidad de Madrid, v. 7, no. 27)
1. Gracián y Morales, Baltasar, 1601-1658. I. Gracián y Morales, Baltasar, 1601-1658.
IaU NUC76-74269

Băltățeanu, Miron.
Economisirea materialului lemnos în construcții. Sinteză documentară elaborată de ing. Miron Băltățeanu. [București], Centrul de documentare pentru construcții, arhitectură și sistematizare, 1971.
38 p. with figs. 30 cm. (Sinteză documentară) lei 50.00 R 72-2051
Bibliography: p. 32-38.
1. Construction industry—Romania. 2. Building materials industry—Romania. I. Title.
HD9715.R82B34 72-356418

Băltățeanu, Miron.
Investițiile și eficiența lor economică. [Sinteză documentară întocmită de ing. Miron Băltățeanu. [București], Centrul de documentare pentru construcții, arhitectură și sistematizare, 1973.
28 p. 29 cm. (Ciclul de sinteze documentare. Organizarea, planificarea și economia construcțiilor) lei 50.00 R 74-1259
Bibliography: p. 25-28.
1. Capital investments—Europe. 2. Capital investments—Romania. I. Title.
HC240.9.C3B34 74-323643

Bălțatu, V I
Cartea cineastului amator. [București] Editura Tineretului [1967]
225 p. illus. (part col.) 24 cm.
1. Cinematography. 2. Amateur moving-pictures. I. Title.
MB NUC74-121664

Baltaxe, Christiane Anna-Maria, 1934-
N.S. Trubetzkoy and the theory of distinctive features. Los Angeles, 1970.
xii, 290 l.
Microfilm copy. Ann Arbor, Mich., University Microfilms, 1972. 1 reel. 35 mm.
IU NUC74-126582

Baltaxe, Christiane Anna-Maria, 1934-
N. S. Trubetzkoy and the theory of distinctive features. Los Angeles, 1970. [Ann Arbor, Michigan, University Microfilms, 1970]
290 l. diagrs.
Thesis—University of California.
Photocopy of typescript.
1. Linguistic research. 2. Grammar, Comparative and general—Phonology. I. Title.
GAT NUC73-47491

Baltaxe, Harold A
Coronary angiography, by Harold A. Baltaxe, Kurt Amplatz [and] David C. Levin. Springfield, Ill., Thomas [1973]
xi, 239 p. illus. 24 cm.
Includes bibliographical references.
1. Coronary arteries—Radiography. 2. Coronary heart disease. I. Amplatz, Kurt, joint author. II. Levin, David C., joint author. III. Title.
RC685.C6B26 616.1'23'07572 72-88439
ISBN 0-398-02709-9 MARC

Baltay, Charles, 1937- ed.
see International Conference on Neutrino Physics and Astrophysics, 4th, Downingtown, Pa., 1974. Neutrinos—1974 (Philadelphia). New York : American Institute of Physics, 1974.

Baltay, Maureen S.
see United States. Congressional Budget Office. Long-term care ... Washington, The Office : for sale by the Supt. of Docs., U.S. Govt. Print. Off., 1977.

Baltay, Maureen S.
see United States. Congressional Budget Office. Projected acute-care bed needs of Veterans Administration hospitals. Washington, The Office : for sale by the Supt. of Docs., U.S. Govt. Print. Off., 1977.

Baltay, Michael L., joint author
see Rogers, Paul, 1909- Reinforced concrete design for buildings. New York, Van Nostrand Reinhold [1973]

Baltazar, de Corvaõ e.
Horas amargas / de Corvão e Baltazar. — [s. l.] : Baltazar ; [Beira, Moçambique : pedidos a M. Salema É Carvalho, 1974?]
64 p. ; 19 cm.
I. Title.
PQ9909.2.B33H6 869'.1 76-521960

Baltazar, Apcar, 1880-1909.
Convorbiri artistice / [de] Apcar Baltazar ; prefață și antologie de Radu Ionescu. — București : "Meridiane," 1974.
169 p. ; 20 cm. R 74-3515
Includes bibliographical references.
lei 5.25
1. Art—Addresses, essays, lectures. I. Title.
N7445.8.R6B34 74-356479

Baltazar, Camil, 1902-
Austria. București, Editura Științifică, 1965.
250, [5] p. illus. 20 cm. (Pe harta lumii)
Bibliography: p. 247-[251]
1. Austria.
DB17.B34 75-580046

Baltazar, Camil, 1902-
Evocări și dialoguri literare / Camil Baltazar. —București : "Minerva," 1974.
308 p. ; 20 cm. — (Seria Memoralistică) R 74-4072
Includes bibliographical references.
lei 10.50
1. Baltazar, Camil, 1902- —Biography. 2. Authors, Romanian—Correspondence, reminiscences, etc. I. Title.
PC840.12.A57Z52 75-565489

Baltazar, Camil, 1902-
Ghirlanda iubirii : [versuri] / Camil Baltazar ; [coperta, Tia Peltz]. — [București] : Editura Eminescu, 1975.
75 p. : port. ; 20 cm. R 75-4062
lei 11.50
I. Title.
PC840.12.A57G5 76-500235

Baltazar, Camil, 1902-
Glorie iubirii. [Versuri. Coperta de Tia Peltz]. [București], „Albatros", 1973.
136 p., port. on leaf. 19 cm. lei 8.75 R 73-4930
I. Title.
PC840.12.A57G58 73-367234

Baltazar, Camil, 1902-
Reculegeri în nemurirea ta. Elegii de dragoste. [Coperta de Andrei Olsufiev]. București, „Cartea Românească," 1972.
140 p. 19 cm. lei 7.25 R 72-2472
I. Title.
PC840.12.A57R4 72-361571

Baltazar, Camil, 1902–
Soare pe culmi. [Versuri]. Cuvînt înainte de Ovid S. Crohmălniceanu. [Coperta: Petre Vulcănescu. Desene: Tudor Marinescu-Calovia]. București, „Minerva," 1972.
288 p. 19 cm. (Retrospective lirice) lei 12.00 R 73-1110
Bibliography: p. [25]
I. Title.
PC840.12.A57S6 74-347656

Baltazar, Camil, 1902–
Violoncel solar. [Versuri. Coperta de: Andrei Olsufiev]. București, Editura Eminescu, 1972.
80 p. 20 cm. lei 6.25 R 73-1111
I. Title.
PC840.12.A57V5 74-327970

Baltazar, Clare R 1927-
A catalogue of Philippine Hymenoptera : (with a bibliography, 1758-1963) / by Clare R. Baltazar. — Honolulu : Entomology Dept., Bernice P. Bishop Museum, 1966.
488 p. ; 26 cm. — (Pacific insects monograph ; 8)
Cover title.
Includes index.
1. Hymenoptera—Philippine Islands. 2. Hymenoptera—Philippine Islands—Bibliography. 3. Insects—Philippine Islands. I. Title. II. Series.
QL461.P218 no. 8 595.7'0909'823 s 76-375094
[QL567.5.P6] 76 MARC

Baltazar, Eulalio R
The dark center; a process theology of Blackness [by] Eulalio R. Baltazar. New York, Paulist Press [1973]
181 p. 23 cm. $4.95
Includes bibliographical references.
1. Race (Theology) 2. Black (in religion, folk-lore, etc.) 3. Symbolism. I. Title.
BT734.B3 261.8'34'5196 73-83811
ISBN 0-8091-1788-6 MARC

Baltazar, Francisco, 1788-1862. Florante at Laura
see Monleon, Fernando B Si Balagtas at ang kanyang obra maestra ... [Maynila] Pambansang Komisyon ng Unesco sa Pilipinas sa tulong ng Unesco [1969]

Baltazar, Francisco, 1788–1862.
Mabini's version of "Florante at Laura." With a pref. by Carlos Quirino and a new English translation by Tarrosa Subido. Manila, National Heroes Commission, 1964.
xx, 119 p. illus. 26 cm. (Mabini centenary series, v. 1)
Title on cover: Apolinario Mabini's hand-written version of Francisco Baltasar's Florante at Laura.
Manuscript copy in Tagalog and printed English translation on opposite pages.
Includes bibliographical references.
I. Mabini, Apolinario, 1864–1903. II. Subido, Tarrosa, trans. III. Title. IV. Title: Florante at Laura. V. Series.
PL6058.9.B36F613 899'.211'12 73-171320

Baltazar Pérez, José, 1862-1942.
El convento de monjas; novela histórica yucateca. 3. ed. Mérida, México, distribuidora de Libros Yucatecos, 1970.
196 p. port. 23 cm. ([Publicaciones] v. 4)
I. Title.
PPiU NUC75-26583

Baltazar Pérez, José, 1862-1942.
Ocho años entre salvajes; novela histórica yucateca. 3. ed. Mérida, México, distribuidora de Libros Yucatecos, 1970.
208 p. port. ([Publicaciones] v. 2)
1. Aguilar, Jerónimo de, d. 1526?—Fiction. I. Title.
PPiU PPT NUC75-32089

Baltazar Pérez, José, 1862-1942.
La venganza de X'Zazil; novela histórica yucateca. 4. ed. Mérida, México, distribuidora de Libros Yucatecos, 1971.
284 p. 23 cm. ([Publicaciones] v. 3)
I. Title.
PPiU NUC75-31790

Baltazzi, Evan S.
Kickboxing : a safe sport, a deadly defense / by Evan S. Baltazzi. — Rutland, Vt. : C. E. Tuttle Co., 1976.
vii, 72 p. : ill. ; 28 cm.
ISBN 0-8048-1171-7 : $6.50
1. Boxing. I. Title.
GV1133.B34 796.8'3 75-33439
76 MARC

Baltazzis, Nikos, joint comp.
see Wagner, Leslie, comp. Readings in applied microeconomics. Oxford, Clarendon Press, 1973.

Bălteanu, Dan.
Piatra Mare : ghid turistic / Dan Bălteanu ; [cartografia, Vasile Marinache]. — București : "Sport-Turism," 1975.
39 p. : ill., fold. col. map (in pocket) ; 18 cm. — (Colecția Munții noștri ; 10) R 75-4118
lei 7.00
1. Piatra Mare Mountain, Romania — Description and travel — Guide-books. I. Title. II. Series: Munții noștri ; 10.
DR210.M85 no. 10 76-501720
[DR281.P42]

Baltensweiler, Armin.
Die Convair CV-990 [i.e. neunhundertneunzig] Coronado : ein aussergewöhnliches Flugzeug = The Convair CV-990 Coronado : an exceptional aircraft / A. Baltensweiler, R. Krähenbühl, A. Waldis. — Luzern : Verkehrshaus der Schweiz, [1975]
52 p. : ill. ; 21 cm. — (Veröffentlichungen - Verkehrshaus der Schweiz ; Heft Nr. 24) Sw***
German and English.
ISBN 3-85954-024-6
1. Convair 990 (Jet transport) I. Krähenbühl, Rolf, joint author. II. Waldis, Alfred, joint author. III. Title. IV. Series: Verkehrshaus der Schweiz. Veröffentlichungen ; Heft 24.
HE363.S9V4 Heft 24 76-483088
[TL686.C59] 76 MARC

Baltensweiler, Heinrich.
Kirchgemeinde in der Vorstadt; das Binninger Modell. Zürich, Theologischer Verlag, 1971.
153 p.
1. Suburban churches. I. Title.
InU NUC76-74346

Baltensweiler, Heinrich, ed.
see Neues Testament und Geschichte. Zürich, Theologischer Verlag (1972)

Balter, Harry Graham.
Tax fraud and evasion : a guide to civil and criminal practice under Federal law / by Harry Graham Balter. — 4th ed. — Boston : Warren, Gorham & Lamont, c1976.
1 v. in various pagings ; 26 cm.
First-2d eds. published under title: Fraud under Federal tax law.
Includes index.
ISBN 0-88262-038-X : $56.00
1. Tax evasion—United States. I. Title.
KF6334.B3 1976 345'.73'0233 76-10629
76 MARC

Balter, Harry Graham.
see Tax fraud. Springfield, Illinois Institute for Continuing Legal Education, c1975.

Balter, Lucjan.
Nieomylność encyklik papieskich : studium teologiczno-historyczne / Lucjan Balter. — Warszawa : Akademia Teologii Katolickiej, 1975.
525 p. ; 24 cm.
Summary in French; table of contents also in French.
Bibliography: p. [473]–507.
Includes index.
1. Popes—Infallibility—History of doctrines. 2. Encyclicals, Papal. I. Title.
BX1806.B36 76-508963

Bal'termants, Dmitriĭ Nikolaevich.
(Vogograd)
Волгоград = Volgograd / [автор фото и текста Д. Бальтерманц]. — Москва : Прогресс, [1975?]
[24] p. : chiefly col. ill. ; 13 cm. USSR***
Cover title.
Russian, English, French, German, and Spanish.
1.00rub
1. Volgograd, Russia (City)—Description—Views.
DK651.S7B33 75-400362

Bal'termants, Dmitriĭ Nikolaevich.
(Vstrecha s Chukotkoĭ)
Встреча с Чукоткой. Фотогр. Д. Бальтерманца. Текст Ю. Рытхэу. [Москва, "Планета," 1971].
127 p. with illus. 24 cm. 2.42rub USSR 72-VKP
Added t. p. in English and German: Glimpses of Chukotka; Begegnung mit TSchukotka.
Russian, English and German.
1. Chukotskiy natsional'nyy okrug, Russia—Description and travel—Views. I. Rytkhèu, IUriĭ Sergeevich, 1930- II. Title. III. Title: Glimpses of Chukotka. IV. Title: Begegnung mit TSchukotka.
DK771.C42B34 73-303862

Bal'termants, Dmitriĭ Nikolaevich
see Moskva. [1971]

Bal'termants, Dmitriĭ Nikolaevich
see Zorin, Valentin Sergeevich. (Protivorechivaia Amerika) 1976.

Baltes, Eugenia
see Bucharest. Biblioteca Centrală de Stat. Laboratorul de Patologie si Restaurare a Cărtii. Recomandări pentru conservarea colectiilor bibliotecilor. [Fotografii: Panait Dunitru]. Bucuresti, 1972.

Baltes, Heinrich P
Spectra of finite systems : a review of Weyl's problem, the eigenvalue distribution of the wave equation for finite domains and its applications on the physics of small systems / Heinrich P. Baltes, unter Mitarb. von Eberhard R. Hilf. — Mannheim ; Wien ; Zürich : Bibliographisches Institut, 1976.
116, 20 p. ; 21 cm. GFR76-A
Bibliography: p. [105]-112.
Includes index.
ISBN 3-411-01491-1 : DM24.00
1. Weyl's problem. I. Hilf, Eberhard R., joint author. II. Title.
QC174.26.W28B34 77-465744
77 MARC

Baltes, Helmut.
Environmental statistics : an instrument of environmental planning / by H. Baltes and W. Nowak. — Stuttgart : W. Kohlhammer, 1975.
17 p. : ill. ; 30 cm. — (Studies on statistics ; no. 31) GFR***
Caption title.
Translation of Umweltstatistik, ein Instrument der Umweltplanung, published in Wirtschaft und Statistik, v. 4, April 1974.
Includes bibliographical references.
DM4.00
1. Environmental protection—Germany, West—Statistics. I. Nowak, Werner, Dr., joint author. II. Title. III. Series: Germany (Federal Republic, 1949-). Statistiches Bundesamt. Studies on statistics ; no. 31.
TD171.5.G3B3413 301.31 76-376863
76 MARC

Baltes, Joachim.
Die Neutralität des Berufsbeamten : exemplar. Bestimmung e. hergebrachten Grundsatzes d. Berufsbeamtentums / von Joachim Baltes. — Würzburg : Schmitt und Meyer, 1973.
159 p. ; 21 cm. — (Schriften zur öffentlichen Verwaltung ; Bd. 3) GFR 74-A38
Originally presented as the author's thesis, Würzburg.
Bibliography: p. 131–155.
Includes index.
DM11.80
1. Civil service—Germany, West. I. Title.
75-545106

Baltes, Josef.
Gewinnung und Verarbeitung von Nahrungsfetten / von Josef Baltes. — Berlin : P. Parey, 1975.
255 p. : ill. ; 24 cm. — (Grundlagen und Fortschritte der Lebensmitteluntersuchung ; Bd. 17 ISSN 0432-7454) GFR***
Revised and updated ed. of the second part of Öle und Fette by W. Wachs first published in 1964.
Bibliography: p. [248]-249.
Includes index.
ISBN 3-489-78914-8
1. Oils and fats, Edible. I. Wachs, Werner. Öle und Fette. Pt. 2. II. Title. III. Series.
TP670.W122 1975 75-512596
75 MARC

Baltes, Matthias.
Über die Natur des Kosmos und der Seele [von] Timaios Lokros, kommentiert von Matthias Baltes. Leiden, Brill, 1972.
xiv, 252 p. 25 cm. (Philosophia antiqua; a series of monographs on ancient philosophy, v. 21)
Bibliography: p xi-xiv.
1. Timaeus Locrus. Peri physiōs kosmō kai psychas. I. Title. II. Series.
CaBVaU NUC74-127491

Baltes, Matthias.
Die Weltentstehung des Platonischen Timaios nach den antiken Interpreten / von Matthias Baltes. — Leiden : E. J. Brill, 1976-
v. ; 25 cm. — (Philosophia antiqua ; v. 30-) Ne***
Presented in part as the author's Habilitationsschrift, Münster, 1974.
Includes bibliographical references and index.
ISBN 9004047204
1. Plato. Timaeus. 2. Astronomy, Greek. I. Title. II. Series.
B387.B34 1976 77-454811
77 MARC

Baltes, Paul B
Life-span developmental psychology : introduction to research methods / Paul B. Baltes, Hayne W. Reese, John R. Nesselroade. — Monterey, Calif. : Brooks/Cole Pub. Co., c1977.
xv, 272 p. : ill. ; 23 cm. — (Life-span human development series)
Bibliography: p. 249-265.
Includes indexes.
ISBN 0-8185-0232-0 : $7.95
1. Developmental psychology. 2. Psychological research. I. Reese, Hayne Waring, 1931- joint author. II. Nesselroade, John R., joint author. III. Title.
BF713.B34 155 77-2342
77 MARC

Baltes, Paul B., ed.
see Life-span developmental psychology... New York, Academic Press, 1973.

Baltes, Paul B., joint author
see Nesselroade, John R Adolescent personality development and historical change, 1970-1972. [Chicago]: Univ. of Chicago Press, 1974.

Baltes, Peter.
Berufsfelder des Diplompädagogen : ein empirischer Beitrag zur Analyse pädagogischer Berufsfelder und ihrer Ausbildungserfordernisse / Peter Baltes und Alfred E. Hoffmann. — Heidelberg : Quelle & Meyer, c1975.
200 p. ; 22 cm. — (Q & M aktuell) GFR***
Bibliography: p. 177-178.
ISBN 3-494-00777-2
1. Teachers, Training of—Germany, West. 2. Teaching as a profession. I. Hoffmann, Alfred, 1937- joint author. II. Title.
LB1725.G4B35 75-510399
75 MARC

Baltes, Tudor, comp.
see Orele țării XXV [i.e. douăzeci și cinci]. Antologie de poezie patriotică închinată aniversării Republicii. Tîrgu-Mureș, 1972.

Băltescu, Mircea, ed.
see Tara Bîrsei. Bucuresti, Editura Academiei Republicii Socialiste România, 1972-

Baltev, Dimitur.
(Georgi Kolarov)
Георги Коларов. Моногр. очерк. София, Бълг. художник, 1973.
128 p. with illus. 23.5 cm. 5.00 lv Bu 74-47
Summary in Russian and German; list of illustrations also in Russian and German.
Bibliography: p. 30.
1. Kolarov, Georgi Petrov, 1909- 2. Pottery, Bulgarian.
NK4210.K56B34 74-307869

Balthán, Renzis
see
Sanhueza Beltrán, Enrique.

Balthasar de Porta, fl. 1487-1499.
Expositio Canonis Missae. [Leipzig] Conrad Kachelofen, 1497.
[20] l. 4°. 19.4 cm.
Leaf [1a] (t. p.) : Expositio canōis sacratissime misse. Leaf [1b]: Canon sacratissime misse, vna cū expositiōe eiusdē vbi imprimis premittit pulchra cōtemplatio ante missam habēda de xp̄i pulchritudine ...
Text of the Canon varies from standard version.
Gesamtkat. d. Wiegendr., 3219; Brit. Mus. Gen. cat., v. 139, column 383 (IA. 12339); Goff. Third census, B-41.
Rubricated. Initials supplied in colors.
1. Mass—Early works to 1800. I. Catholic Church. Liturgy and ritual. Roman canon. 1497. II. Title: Expositio Canonis sacratissime Misse.
Incun. 1497.B34 Thacher Coll. 77-516008

[**Balthasar de Porta**] fl. 1487-1499.
Expositio mysteriorum Missae. Leipzig, Melchior Lotter [14]99.
[20] l. 4°. 21 cm.
Leaf [1a] (t. p.) : Expositio misteriorum misse cristi passionē deuotissime figurantiū, metrice atq3 psayce posita. Et verus modus rite celebrandi ...
An adaptation, with additions, of the work with same title by Guilelmus de Gouda, interspersed with extracts, typographically emphasized, from Girolamo dalle Valli's poem Jesuida.
"Carmen Werhee [sic] de vita diui onuffrij": leaf [19b]-[20b]
Hain. Repertorium (with Copinger's Supplement) *6807; Brit. Mus. Cat. (XV cent.) III, p. 651 (IA. 12122); Gesamtkat. d. Wiegendr., 3224; Goff. Third census, B-44.
One initial supplied in ink.
1. Mass—Early works to 1800. I. Guilelmus de Gouda. Expositio mysteriorum Missae. II. Valli, Girolamo dalle. Jesuida. Selections. 1499. III. Faber de Werdea, Johannes, d. 1505. Carmen de vita Sancti Onuphrii. 1499. IV. Title.
Incun. 1499.B32 77-516003
[BX2230]

Balthasar, Hans Urs von, 1905-
Der antirömische Affekt. [Freiburg im Breisgau, Herder, 1974]
302 p. 18 cm. (Herderbücherei, 492) GFR***
"Originalausgabe."
Includes bibliographical references.
1. Catholic Church—Doctrinal and controversial works—Catholic authors. 2. Papacy. I. Title.
BX1751.2.B233 74-338497
ISBN 3-451-01902-2

Balthasar, Hans Urs von, 1905-
Cordula oder der Ernstfall. Mit einem Nachwort zur 3. Aufl. (Einsiedeln), Johannes Verlag [c1966, 1967]
132 p. 19 cm. (Kriterien, 2)
1. Christian life—Catholic authors. I. Title.
IEG NUC74-121665

Balthasar, Hans Urs von, 1905-
Dante / Hans Urs von Balthasar. — Brescia : Morcelliana, [1973]
129 p. ; 21 cm. It 74-Apr
Cover has subtitle: Viaggio attraverso la lingua, la storia, il pensiero della Divina commedia.
Translation of Dante, from the author's Herrlichkeit, II; translated by G. Magagna.
Includes bibliographical references.
L2000
1. Dante Alighieri, 1265-1321—Criticism and interpretation. 2. Dante Alighieri, 1265-1321. Divina commedia.
PQ4390.B23416 75-552953

Balthasar, Hans Urs von, 1905-
Elucidations / Hans Urs von Balthasar ; translated [from the German] by John Riches. — London : S. P. C. K., 1975.
viii, 216 p. ; 23 cm. GB 75-07098
Translation of Klarstellungen.
ISBN 0-281-02768-4 : £3.50
1. Catholic Church—Doctrinal and controversial works—Catholic authors. 2. Theology—Addresses, essays, lectures. I. Title.
BX1751.2.B2413 230'.2 75-323101
75 MARC

Balthasar, Hans Urs von, 1905-
Engagement with God / Hans Urs von Balthasar ; translated [from the German] by John Halliburton ; foreword by E. L. Mascall ; introductory essay by D. M. MacKinnon. — London : S.P.C.K., 1975.
x, 100 p. ; 23 cm. GB75-07523
Translation of In Gottes Einsatz leben.
Includes bibliographical references.
ISBN 0-281-02769-2 : £3.25
1. Meditations. 2. Balthasar, Hans Urs von, 1905- I. Title.
BX2184.B3313 230'.2 76-351692
76 MARC

Balthasar, Hans Urs von, 1905-
Hans Urs von Balthasar [compiled by Martin Redfern] London, New York, Sheed & Ward, 1972.
126 p. 20 cm. (Theologians today; a series selected and edited by Martin Redfern) £1.25 GB 73-09848
CONTENTS: Scripture as the Word of God.—Thérèse of Lisieux: the Church and the contemplative life.—The perfectibility of man.—The last five Stations of the Cross.
1. Theology—Collected works—20th century. 2. Catholic Church—Collected works. I. Series: Redfern, Martin. Theologians today.
BX891.B33 230'.2'08 72-2166
ISBN 0-7220-7240-6 MARC

Balthasar, Hans Urs von, 1905-
Henri de Lubac : sein organisches Lebenswerk / Hans Urs von Balthasar. — Einsiedeln : Johannes Verlag : [Auslfg., Benziger], 1976.
100 p., [1] leaf of plates : port. ; 19 cm. — (Kriterien ; 38) Sw76-5249
Includes bibliographical references.
ISBN 3-265-10173-8 : 14.00F
1. Lubac, Henri de, 1896-
BX4705.L7918B34 230'.2'0924 76-472482
76 MARC

Balthasar, Hans Urs von, 1905-
Katholisch : Aspekte des Mysteriums / Hans Urs von Balthasar. — Einsiedeln : Johannes-Verlag : [Auslfg., Benziger], 1975.
93 p. ; 19 cm. — (Kriterien ; 36) Sw75-A-6882
ISBN 3-265-10166-5 : 12.00F
1. Catholicity—Addresses, essays, lectures. I. Title.
BX9.B325 75-521795
*76 MARC

Balthasar, Hans Urs von, 1905-
Das Katholische an der Kirche. Eine Meditation. Köln, Wienand (1972).
19 p. 21 cm. (Kölner Beiträge, Heft 10) DM1.00 GDR 73-A32
Speech given in Cologne, Sept. 13, 1972.
1. Church—Catholicity. I. Title.
BV601.3.B3 1972 74-302512

Balthasar, Hans Urs von, 1905-
Le Mystère pascal, par H. Urs von Balthasar et A. Grillmeier. Paris, Cerf, 1972.
369 p. 21 cm. (Mysterium salutis; dogmatique de l'histoire du salut, 12)
1. Jesus Christ—Passion. 2. Jesus Christ—Resurrection. 3. Salvation. I. Grillmeier, Alois, 1910- joint author. II. Title. III. Series.
NNF NUC75-31789

Balthasar, Hans Urs von, 1905-
Pneuma und Institution / Hans Urs von Balthasar. — Einsiedeln : Johannes-Verlag : [Auslfg., Benziger, 1974]
456 p. ; 23 cm. — (Skizzen zur Theologie ; 4) Sw 74-A-6816
ISBN 3-265-10157-6 : 49.00F
1. Theology—Addresses, essays, lectures. I. Title.
BR85.B393 75-529498

Balthasar, Hans Urs von, 1905-
Points de repère pour le discernement des esprits. Traduction de l'allemand par Bernard Kapp. Revue par l'auteur. [Paris] Fayard [1973]
iii, 252 p. 22 cm.
Translation of Klarstellungen zur Prüfung d. Geister.
1. Catholic Church—Doctrinal and controversial works—Catholic authors. 2. Theology—addresses, essays, lectures. I. Title.
NNF NUC76-71900

Balthasar, Hans Urs von, 1905-
Prayer / [by] Hans Urs von Balthasar ; translated [from the German] by A. V. Littledale. — [1st ed., reprinted] / foreword by Kenneth Woollcombe. — London : S. P. C. K., 1973.
246 p. ; 23 cm. GB 74-06019
Translation of Das betrachtende Gebet.
ISBN 0-281-02771-4 : £2.25
1. Contemplation. I. Title.
BV5091.C7B33 1973 248'.3 75-501106
MARC

Balthasar, Hans Urs von, 1905-
La prière contemplative. Traduit de l'allemand par Bernard Kapp. [Paris] Fayard [1972]
v, 297 p. 22 cm. (Le signe)
Translation of Das betrachtende Gebet.
1. Prayer. 2. Contemplation. I. Title.
MBtS NUC75-31785

Balthasar, Hans Urs von, 1905-
Retour au centre. [Traduit par Robert Givord.] Paris [Bruges,] Desclée, De Brouwer, 1971.
159 p. 19 cm. 18.00F F 72-2437
Translation of Einfaltungen.
Includes bibliographical references.
1. Theology—Addresses, essays, lectures. I. Title.
BR85.B3914 72-358530

Balthasar, Hans Urs von, 1905-
Theodramatik. Einsiedeln, Johannes-Verlag. [Auslfg.: Benziger, Einsiedeln.] (1973-
v. 23 cm. 59.00 (v. 1) Sw 74-A-493 (v. 1)
Includes bibliographical references.
CONTENTS: 1. Bd. Prolegomena.
1. Religion and drama. I. Title.
PN1647.B33 74-323309
ISBN 3-265-10137-1 (v. 1)

Balthasar, Hans Urs von, 1905-
The theology of Karl Barth. Translated by John Drury. [Anchor Books ed.] Garden City, N.Y., Doubleday, 1972.
vii, 302 p. 18 cm. (A Doubleday Anchor book)
Translation of Karl Barth: Darstellung und Deutung seiner Theologie.
Bibliography: p. [291]-295.
1. Barth, Karl, 1886-1968. I. Title.
ViU NUC73-34737

Balthasar, Hans Urs von, 1905-
Die Wahrheit ist symphonisch. Aspekte des christlichen Pluralismus. Einsiedeln, Johanne-Verlag. [Auslfg.: Benziger, Einsiedeln.] (1972).
165 p. 19 cm. (Kriterien, 29) 9.50F Sw 73-A-441
1. Theology. 2. Pluralism. I. Title.
BR118.B25 73-310929
ISBN 3-265-10134-7

Balthasar, Hans Urs von, 1905- Warum ich noch ein Christ bin
in Zwei Plädoyers. München, Kösel (1971)

Balthasar, Hans Urs von, 1905- Warum ich noch ein Christ bin. English. 1971
see Two say why. London, Search Press; Chicago, Franciscan Herald Press [1971]

Balthasar, Hans Urs von, 1905-
see Barth, Karl, 1886-1968. Rinnovamento e unità della Chiesa. [Roma] Silva Editore [c1969]

Balthasar, Hans Urs von, 1905-
see Baumgartner, Wilfrid, 1902- Installation de M. Hans Urs von Balthasar comme associé étranger ...... [Paris] Institut de France, 1975.

Balthasar, Hans Urs von, 1905-
see Beierwaltes, Werner. Grundfragen der Mystik. Einsiedeln : Johannes-Verlag : [Auslfg., Benziger, 1974]

Balthasar, Hans Urs von, 1905- ed.
see Catholic Church. Synodus Episcoporum. Das Priesteramt. [Einsiedeln] Johannes Verlag [c1972]

Balthasar, Hans Urs von, 1905-
see Civilisations et Christianisme. Venise, Société Européenne de culture, 1957.

Balthasar, Hans Urs von, 1905-
see Diskussion über Hans Küngs Christ sein. Mainz, Matthias-Grünewald-Verlag, c1976.

Balthasar, Hans Urs von, 1905-
see Kirche aus lebendigen Steinen. Mainz, Matthias-Grünewald-Verlag, c1975.

Balthasar, Hans Urs von, 1905- joint author.
see Ratzinger, Joseph. Prinzipien christlicher Moral. Einsiedeln, Johannes-Verlag : [Auslfg., Benziger] 1975.

Balthasar, Hans Urs von, 1905-
see Thérèse von Lisieux... Leutesdorf (am Rhein): Johannes-Verlag [1973?].

Balthasar, Karl.
see Die Oberbayerische Pechkohle. München, Bayer. Geologisches Landesamt, 1975.

Balthasar, Louis.
Die Reservenbesteuerung bei der Verlegung juristischer Personen. Bern, Herbert Lang; Frankfurt/M., Peter Lang, 1973.
x, 165 p. 21 cm. (Europäische Hochschulschriften. Reihe 2: Rechtswissenschaft, Bd. 81) 32.00F Sw 74-A-778
Originally presented as the author's thesis, Bern.
Bibliography: p. 3-12.
1. Corporate reorganizations—Taxation—Switzerland. 2. Corporation reserves—Taxation—Switzerland. 3. Domicile in taxation—Switzerland. 4. Liquidation—Taxation—Switzerland. I. Title. II. Series.
ISBN 3-261-01021-5 74-309071

Balthasar, Vladimír.
Grabwespen—Sphecoidea. [Autor:] Vladimír Balthasar. Praha, Academia, 1972.
471 p., [9] p. of illus. 25 cm. (Fauna ČSSR, Bd. 20) Kčs110.00 Cz 73-SKČ
Bibliography: p. 457-459.
1. Sphecidae. 2. Hymenoptera—Czechoslovak Republic. I. Title. II. Series.
QL298.C8F3 Bd. 20 73-345152
[QL568.S7]

Balthasar, Vladimír.
Neue Arten der Familien Scarabaeidae und Aphodiidae. (124. Beitrag zur Kenntnis der Scarabaeoidea, Col.) [München] 1967.
8 p. 24 cm. (Opuscula zoologica, hrsg. von der Zoologischen Staatssammlung in München, Nr. 91)
1. Scarabaeidae. 2. Aphodiidae. 3. Scarabaeoidea.
ICF NUC73-2352

Balthasar, Vladimir.
Eine neue Dynamopus-Art. 138. Beitrag zur Kenntnis der Scarabaeoidea, Coleoptera. München, 1971.
3 p. (Opuscula zoologica, no. 121)
I. Title.
DNAL NUC73-34738

Balthasar Neumann in Baden-Württemberg: Bruchsal, Karlsruhe, Stuttgart, Neresheim : Ausstellung zum europäischen Denkmalschutzjahr, Staatsgalerie Stuttgart, 28. Sept. bis 30. Nov. 1975. — [Stuttgart : Staatsgalerie, 1975]
144 p. : ill. (some col.), plans ; 33 cm. GFR***
Includes bibliographies.
1. Neumann, Balthasar, 1687-1754. 2. Architecture, Baroque—Baden-Württemberg—Exhibitions. I. Neumann, Balthasar, 1687-1754. II. Stuttgart. Staatsgalerie.
NA1088.N4B34 75-521577
76 MARC

Balthazar, André, joint author
see Besset, Maurice. Calder. [Paris, Maeght, 1973]

Balthazar, André
see Bury, Pol, 1922- Alentour, par André Balthazar. [Paris, Maeght, 1969]

Balthazar, André
see Miró, Joan, 1893- Miró, sculptures. [Paris, Maeght, 1970]

Balthazar, Earl Edward, 1918–
The emotionally disturbed, mentally retarded: a historical and contemporary perspective [by] Earl E. Balthazar [and] Harvey A. Stevens. Englewood Cliffs, N. J., Prentice-Hall [1974, c1975]
xiv, 333 p. 24 cm. (Prentice-Hall series in special education)
Bibliography: p. 275-327.
1. Mental deficiency. 2. Psychology, Pathological. I. Stevens, Harvey A., joint author. II. Title.
[DNLM: 1. Affective disturbances. 2. Affective disturbances—History. 3. Mental retardation. 4. Mental retardation—History. WM 100 B197e]
RC570.B23 616.8'588 74-8866
ISBN 0-13-274969-6 MARC

Balthazar, Earl Edward, 1918-
Managing the mentally retarded through interdisciplinary action [by] Earl E. Balthazar [and] Harvey A. Stevens. [Madison, Wis.] Central Wisconsin Colony and Training School Research Department, 1971.
23 l. 28 cm. (ED 052-560)
"Paper presented at the 90th annual meeting of the American Association on Mental Deficiency, 1966."
1. Mentally handicapped—Care and treatment. I. Stevens, Harvey A., joint author. II. Title. III. Series: Educational Resources Information Center. ERIC document, ED 052-560.
NBuC NUC76-74137

Balthazar, Earl Edward, 1918-
Programs for the developmentally disabled: a multidisciplinary approach; a monograph series by Earl E. Balthazar. Madison, Division of Mental Hygiene, Dept. of Health and Social Services, Central Wisconsin Colony and Training School [c1975-
v. 28 cm. (Central Wisconsin Colony and Training School Research Dept. [Publication] v. 12, no. 1-3]
Includes bibliographies.
Contents: 1. Developmental disabilities and their relationships to general development.-- 2. Mental retardation; descriptions and definitions.--3. General programs for the mentally retarded.
1. Mental retardation services. 2. Mentally handicapped--Care and treatment. 3. Mental deficiency. 4. Nervous system--Diseases. I. Title.
IaU NUC77-90067

Balthazar, Herman
see Centre de recherches et d'études historiques de la Seconde Guerre Mondiale. Archief H. de Man. Brussel, Navorsings- en Studeicentrum, 1971.

Balthazar, Hugo, ed.
see Maeterlinck, Maurice, 1862-1949. Pelléas et Mélisande. Anvers, Éditions de Sikkel, 1968.

Balthazarszoon, Floris, 1562?-1616.
Kaart van Rijnland, door Floris Balthasar, 1610-1615. Herdrukt van de origineele koperen platen en opnieuw uitgegeven met medewerking van het Hoogheemraadschap van Rijnland en voorafgegaan van een inleiding door mr. S. J. Fockema Andreae. 's-Gravenhage, M. Nijhoff, 1929.
10 p., 3 l. illus. (coats of arms) maps, diagr. 53½ cm.
In portfolio.
Bibliographical foot-notes.
1. Rijnland—Map—To 1800. 2. Maps, Early—Facsimiles. I. Fockema Andreae, Sybrandus Johannes, 1904-1968, ed. II. Hoogheemraadschap van Rijnland.
G1862.R5B3 1929 40-17792

Balthazarszoon, Floris, 1562?-1616.
Kaarten van Delfland 1611. [Alphen aan den Rijn, Canaletto, 1972]
[40] p. maps. 48 cm. Ne***
First ed. published under title: Caert van Delfland.
Bibliography: p. [7]-[8]
1. Delfland, Netherlands—Maps—To 1800. 2. Maps, Early—Facsimiles. I. Title.
G1862.D4B3 1972 74-650143

Balthazarszoon, Floris, 1562?-1616.
Kaarten van Rijnland 1615. [Alphen aan den Rijn, Canaletto, 1972]
[54] p. illus., maps. 48 cm. Ne***
First ed. published under title: Caert van Rijnland.
Bibliography: p. [8]
1. Rijnland—Maps—To 1800. 2. Maps, Early—Facsimiles. I. Title.
G1862.R5B3 1972 74-650142

Balthazarszoon, Floris, 1562?-1616.
Kaarten van Schieland 1611. [Alphen aan den Rijn, Canaletto, 1972]
[36] p. illus., maps. 48 cm. Ne***
First ed. published under title: Caert van Schieland.
Bibliography: p. [6]
1. Schieland, Netherlands—Maps — To 1800. 2. Maps, Early — Facsimiles. I. Title.
G1862.S3B3 1972 74-650141

Balthes, Heinz, 1937- ill.
see Cordan, Wolfgang, 1909-1966. Tage mit Antonio. Düsseldorf : Verlag Eremiten-Presse, 1974.

Balthes, Heinz, 1937- ill.
see Frorath, Günter, 1946- Das geit zu weit... Düsseldorf: Eremiten-Presse, 1973.

Balthes, Heinz, 1937-
see Wohmann, Gabriele, 1932- Ein Fall von Chemie ... Erstausg. Düsseldorf, Verlag Eremiten-Presse, 1975.

Balthrope, Bill.
"On how to do nothing well" : a history of the San Antonio Conopus Club / by Bill Balthrope. — San Antonio : Naylor Co., c1975.
viii, 66 p. ; 22 cm.
1. Conopus Club. San Antonio Branch. I. Title.
HS2330.C663B34 367'.9764'351 76-354719
76 MARC

Balthus, 1908–
Balthus. Marseille [Musée] Cantini, 1973.
1 v. (unpaged) illus. (part col.) 17 cm. F***
Catalog, by M. Latour, of an exhibition held from July to Sept. 1973.
Includes bibliography.
1. Balthus, 1908– I. Latour, Marie L. II. Marseille. Musée Cantini.
ND553.B23L37 759.4 74-168930
MARC

Balti ārini, melni jerini, gudram ganinam izganit. [Latviešu tautas mīklas, sastādījūsi Anna Graubina. Ilustrējis Talivaldis Banis] Rīgâ, "Liesma," 1970.
1 v. (unpaged) col. illus. 28 cm.
1. Riddles, Latvian—Juvenile literature.
I. Graubina, A.
MB NUC74-123551

Baltić, Aleksandar.
Osnovi radnog prava Jugoslavije, sistem samuopravnih međusobnih radnih odnosa i osnovni problemi sociologije rada / Aleksandar Baltić, Milan Despotović. — 4., izm. i dop. izd. — Beograd : Savremena administracija, 1975.
497 p. ; 24 cm. Yu***
Includes bibliographical references.
1. Labor laws and legislation—Yugoslavia. 2. Insurance, Social—Yugoslavia. I. Despotović, Milan, joint author. II. Title: Osnovi radnog prava Jugoslavije.
75-970598

Baltič, Aleksandar. Pravna izgradnja samoupravnih sporazuma i društvenih dogovori u oblasti rada. Zagreb: Ekonomski institut, 1971, cover 1972.

Baltić, Aleksandar
see Brajic, Vlajko. Problemi zapošljavanja u uslovima tehnoloskog progresa. Beograd, Institut za uporedno pravo, 1972.

Baltić, Svetozar, 1936–
(Balade o očevini)
Баладе о очевини / [аутор] Светозар Балтић. — Београд : Просвета, 1974.
77 p. ; 21 cm. — (Савремена поезија 1974) Yu 75-361
Poems.
Series romanized: Savremena poezija 1974.
I. Title.
PG1419.12.A47B3 76-527282

Baltic and International Maritime Conference
see Puchta, Karl-Ferdinand. Die Gencon-Charter. Hamburg, Deutscher Verkehrs-Verlag, 1968.

Baltic Committee in Scandinavia.
The Baltic States 1940-1972 : documentary background and survey of developments presented to the European Security and Cooperation Conference. — Stockholm : Baltic Committee in Scandinavia, 1972.
120 p. ; 21 cm. S***
Bibliography: p. 118-120.
1. Baltic States—History. I. Title.
DK511.B3B282 1972 947'.4'0842 76-370672
76 MARC

Baltic Provinces. Laws, statutes, etc.
Сборникъ узаконеній и распоряженій о крестьянахъ Прибалтійскихъ губерній. Составилъ и издалъ А. П. Василевскій. Москва, Унив. тип., 189
v. 28 cm.
1. Peasantry—Baltic States. 2. Law—Baltic States. I. Vasilevskiĭ, Alekseĭ Petrovich, 1841-1893, ed. II. Title.
Title romanized: Sbornik uzakoneniĭ i rasporiazheniĭ o krest'ianakh Pribaltiĭskikh guberniĭ.
75-561618

Baltic Provinces. Laws, statutes, etc.
(Sbornik uzakoneniĭ o krest'ianakh Pribaltiĭskikh guberniĭ)
Сборникъ узаконеній о крестьянахъ Прибалтійскихъ губерній. Составилъ В. Е. Рейтернъ. С.-Петербургъ, Общественная польза, 1898.
3 v. 21 cm.
"Изданіе неоффиціальное."
CONTENTS: т. 1. ч. 1–2. Положенія о крестьянахъ Курляндской и Лифляндской губерній.—т. 2. ч. 3. Положеніе о крестьянахъ Эстляндской губерніи.—т. 3. ч. 4–5. Положеніе о крестьянахъ Лифляндской губерніи (1860 г.) и Общая часть.
1. Peasantry—Baltic States. I. Reitern, V. E., d. 1897, ed.
58-53523

Baltic States... Buffalo, N.Y., W.S. Hein, 1972.
see under Kavass, Igor I

The Baltic States 1940–1972; documentary background and survey of developments, presented to the European Security and Cooperation Conference. [2d. ed.] Stockholm, Baltic Committee in Scandinavia, 1972.
120, [1] p. map. 21 cm. S***
Bibliography: p. 118–[121]
1. Baltic States—Annexation to Russia. 2. Baltic States—History. I. Conference on Security and Cooperation in Europe.
DK511.B3B283 1972 947'.4'0842 74-150072
MARC

Baltierra, Luis Guillermo Alvarez
see
Alvarez B , Luis, 1939-

Baltiĭskaia vesna; sbornik [o Kaliningradskom krae. Sost. A. L'vov, S. Snegov] Moskva, "Sovremennik", 1974.
531 p. illus. 18 cm. (Nash den')
1. Kaliningrad (Province) in literature.
2. Russian literature–20th cent.–Coll.
I. L'vov, Arkadiĭ L'vovich, comp. II. Snegov, Sergeĭ Aleksandrovich, comp.
MH NUC75-128306

(Baltiĭskie iazyki i ikh vzaimosviazi so slovianskimi, finno-ugorskimi i germanskimi iazykami)
Балтийские языки и их взаимосвязи со славянскими, финно-угорскими и германскими языками. Тезисы докл. науч. конф., посвящ. 100-летию со дня рождения акад. Я. Эндзелина. [г. Рига, 21–22 февр. 1973 г. Отв. ред. чл.-кор. АН ЛатвССР Р. Я. Грабис]. Рига, "Зинатне," 1973.
130 p. 20 cm. 0.34rub USSR 73
At head of title: Академия наук Латвийской ССР. Латвийский государственный университет им. П. Стучки.
Includes bibliographies.
1. Baltic languages—Congresses. 2. Languages in contact—Congresses. 3. Endzelins, Jānis, 1873–1961. I. Endzelins, Jānis, 1873–1961. II. Grabis, Rūdolfs, ed. III. Latvijas Padomju Socialistiskās Republikas Zinātņu akadēmija. IV. Riga. Universitāte.
PG8001.B28 74-303692

(Baltiĭskie moriaki v bor'be za vlast' Sovetov v 1919 g.)
Балтийские моряки в борьбе за власть Советов в 1919 г. [Документы и материалы]. Сост. Н. А. Маркина, Т. С. Федорова (отв. сост.) Ред. коллегия: ... А. Л. Фрайман (отв. ред.) [и др.]. Ленинград, "Наука," Ленингр. отд-ние, 1974.
391 p. 27 cm. 1.51rub USSR 74
On leaf preceding t. p.: Академия наук СССР. Ленинградское отделение Института истории СССР. Центральный государственный архив Военно-Морского Флота СССР.
Bibliography: p. 386–[387]
1. Russia—History—Revolution, 1917–1921—Sources. 2. Russia (1923– U. S. S. R.). Voeno-Morskoĭ Flot. Baltiĭskiĭ flot—History—Sources. I. Markina, N. A., comp. II. Fedorova, T. S., comp. III. Fraĭman, Anton L'vovich, ed. IV. Akademiia nauk SSSR. Institut istorii SSSR. Leningradskoe otdelenie. V. Russia (1923– U. S. S. R.). TSentral'nyĭ gosudarstvennyĭ arkhiv Voenno-Morskogo Flota.
DK265.A5146 74-324654

Baltiĭsko-Leningradskoe bazovoe morskoe O. V. N. O.
see Voenno-morskaia nauchnaia mysl'. 1926-

(Baltika pomnit, 1941–1945)
Балтика помнит, 1941–1945 **: фотоальбом / [фото Н. П. Янова ; авт. вступит. статьи и стихов Б. Азаров ; ред.-сост. М. А. Горенков]. — Калининград : Калининградское кн. изд-во,** 1973.
14, [138] p. : chiefly ill., ports. (some col.) ; 18 x 23 cm. USSR 74
2.36rub
1. World War, 1939–1945—Naval operations, Russian—Pictorial works. 2. Russia (1923– U. S. S. R.). Voenno-Morskoĭ flot. Baltiĭskiĭ flot—Pictorial works. I. Ianov, Nikolaĭ Pavlovich. II. Azarov, Vsevolod Borisovich. III. Gorenkov, Mikhail Alekseevich, ed.
D779.R9B34 75-558361

Baltimoore, G.
see Calanchi, Giuseppe, 1927-

Baltimore, David.
see Animal virology. New York, Academic Press, 1976.

Baltimore, David.
see Nobel lectures in molecular biology, 1933-1975. New York, Elsevier North-Holland, c1977.

Baltimore, Lester Bruce.
Southern nationalists and Southern nationalism, 1850-1870, by Lester B. Baltimore. [Ann Arbor, Mich., University Microfilms, 1968?]
3,270 l. ([University Microfilms. Publication no.] 69-3359. [Doctoral dissertation series])
Thesis–University of Missouri, 1968.
Microfilm copy.
1. Nationalism–United States (Southern)
MH NUC76-71886

Baltimore, Lester Bruce.
Southern nationalists and southern nationalism, 1850-1870. [Columbia] University of Missouri, 1968.
3, 270 l. 22 cm.
Thesis—University of Missouri.
Vita.
Bibliography: leaves [251]-270.
Photocopy (positive) Ann Arbor, Mich., University Microfilms, 1969.
1. U.S.—Hist.—Civil War—Causes. I. Title.
KyU NUC76-71863

Baltimore.
Baltimore land use coding system : a proposed system for coding land use activities. — Baltimore : Dept. of Planning, Research Section, 1974.
iv, 67 leaves ; 28 cm.
"Developed through the combined efforts of the Department of Assessments, the Bureau of Management Information Systems, the Department of Housing and Community Development, and the Department of Planning."
Includes index.
1. Urban land use—Classification—Data processing. I. Baltimore. Dept. of Planning. Research Section.
HD111.B24 1974 333.7'7'097526 76-374566
76 MARC

Baltimore.
The city hall, Baltimore. History of construction and dedication. Baltimore, The Mayor and city council, 1877.
vi, 1 p.l., pp. [9]-141, 10 p.l., [1]-v. 11 plates.
Micropublished as no. 462 on Reel 34, in "American Architectural Books," based on the Henry-Russell Hitchcock bibliography of the same title. New Haven: Research Publications, Inc., 1972.
1. Baltimore. City hall. I. Forrester, Allen E.
UU NUC76-105073

Baltimore. Annunciation Greek Orthodox Community.
Fiftieth anniversary souvenir book; 1906-1956. Baltimore [1956?]
157 p. (chiefly illus. and advertising) 28 cm.
On cover: 50th anniversary, 1906-1956, Greek Orthodox Church "Evangelismos".
1. Baltimore. Annunciation Greek Orthodox Community. Anniversaries, etc.
NcD NUC74-22372

Baltimore. Bureau for Opening Streets.
Annual report. 1st–3d; 1947–49. [Baltimore]
3 v. 23 cm.
First report includes the 87th Annual report of the Commissioners for Opening Streets (the earlier name of the bureau); later issued with the Report of the Dept. of Assessments.
1. Baltimore. Bureau for Opening Streets. 2. Baltimore—Streets. I. Baltimore. Commissioners for Opening Streets. Annual report.
HE356.5.B28A25 72-620830
MARC-S

Baltimore. Bureau of Accounts and Disbursements.
Financial report, city of Baltimore, Maryland. Baltimore.
v. 26 cm. annual.
Continues a publication with the same title issued by the Bureau of Control and Accounts and continued by Annual financial report of the city of Baltimore, Maryland issued by the Dept. of Finance.
1. Finance, Public—Baltimore—Accounting. I. Title.
HJ9777.M32B33 72-625329

Baltimore. Bureau of Accounts and Disbursements
see also
Baltimore. Bureau of Control and Accounts.

Baltimore. Bureau of Building Inspection.
In 1968 the Baltimore Bureau of Building Inspection and the Urban Renewal and Housing Agency merged to form the Baltimore Dept. of Housing and Community Development.
Works by these bodies are found under the following headings according to the name used at the time of publication:
Baltimore. Bureau of Building Inspection.
Baltimore. Urban Renewal and Housing Agency.
Baltimore. Dept. of Housing and Community Development.
74-236464

Baltimore. Bureau of Control and Accounts.
Financial report, city of Baltimore, Maryland. Baltimore.
v. 27 cm. annual.
Continued by a publication with the same title issued by the Bureau of Accounts and Disbursements.
1. Finance, Public—Baltimore—Accounting. I. Title.
HJ9777.M32B33 72-625330

Baltimore. Bureau of Control and Accounts
see also
Baltimore. Bureau of Accounts and Disbursements.

Baltimore. Bureau of Opening Streets.
Annual report. 1st–3d; 1947–49. [Baltimore]
3 v. 23 cm.
First report includes the 87th Annual report of the Commissioners for Opening Streets (the earlier name of the bureau); later issued with the Report of the Dept. of Assessments.
1. Baltimore—Streets. I. Baltimore. Commissioners for Opening Streets. Annual report.
HE356.5.B28A25 72-620830

Baltimore. Business Opportunities Center
see Business Opportunities Center, Baltimore.

Baltimore. Charters.
Charter and Public local laws of Baltimore city (article 4 of the Code of public local laws of Maryland) with all amendments and additions thereto down to and including the Acts of 1937, with an appendix containing the acts establishing the city's boundaries and the agreement between Baltimore city and Baltimore county, as to the use of the out-fall sewer by Baltimore county, as to the use of the out -fall sewer by Baltimore county, and with references to, and annotations of, decided cases. Compiled under the direction of R. E. Lee Marshall, city solicitor by Horace E.

Flack, Department of legislative reference. Baltimore [King bros., printers and publishers] 1938.
xii, 787 p. 23½ cm.
1. Municipal charters—Baltimore. I. Flack, Horace Edgar, 1879- II. Baltimore. Ordinances, etc. III. Maryland. Laws, statutes, etc. (Baltimore)
KFX1101.A6 1938 352.07526 39-8668

Baltimore. Charters.
Charter of Baltimore City, 1964 revision; with amendments to July 1, 1973. Compiled and indexed by Leon A. Rubenstein. [Baltimore, 1973]
iv, 166 p. 23 cm.
1. Baltimore. Charters. I. Rubenstein, Leon A., comp. II. Title.
KFX1101.A6 1973 342'.7526'02 74-184634
MARC

Baltimore. City Dept. of Planning
see Baltimore. Dept. of Planning.

Baltimore. City Planning Commission
see Baltimore. Planning Commission.

Baltimore. Civic Center Commission
see Greater Baltimore Committee. Planning Council. Report. [Baltimore] 1958.

Baltimore. Commissioners for Opening Streets.
Annual report
see Baltimore. Bureau for Opening Streets. Annual report. 1st.-3d ; 1947-49. [Baltimore]

Baltimore. Community College
see Community College of Baltimore.

Baltimore. Comptroller's Dept. Bureau of Accounts and Disbursements
see
Baltimore. Bureau of Accounts and Disbursements.

Baltimore. Control and Accounts, Bureau of
see
Baltimore. Bureau of Control and Accounts.

Baltimore. Coppin State College
see Coppin State College.

Baltimore. Council for International Visitors
see
Baltimore Council for International Visitors.

Baltimore. Dept. of Finance.
Annual financial report of the city of Baltimore, Maryland.
Baltimore.
v. 28 cm.
Report year ends June 30.
Continues Financial report, city of Baltimore, Maryland issued by the Bureau of Accounts and Disbursements.
1. Finance, Public—Baltimore—Accounting. I. Title.
HJ9777.M32B33 336.752'6 72-625327

Baltimore. Dept. of Finance. Bureau of Control and Accounts
see
Baltimore. Bureau of Control and Accounts.

Baltimore. Dept. of Housing and Community Development.
In 1968 the Baltimore Bureau of Building Inspection and the Urban Renewal and Housing Agency merged to form the Baltimore Dept. of Housing and Community Development.
Works by these bodies are found under the following headings according to the name used at the time of publication:
Baltimore. Bureau of Building Inspection.
Baltimore. Urban Renewal and Housing Agency.
Baltimore. Dept. of Housing and Community Development.
74-236462

Baltimore. Dept. of Housing and Community Development.
see Baltimore. Dept. of Planning. Baltimore community renewal program interim report ... [Baltimore, Dept. of Planning] 1972-

Baltimore. Dept. of Housing and Community Development. Planning Division.
Design guide; exterior residential rehabilitation. City of Baltimore, Dept. of Housing and Community Development, Division of Planning. Baltimore, The Dept., 1974.
22 p. ill. 22 x 28 cm.
1. Urban renewal—Baltimore. I. Title.
CaBVaU NUC76-21084

Baltimore. Dept. of Housing and Community Development. Planning Division.
The people of Upton; their characteristics, housing, needs, attitudes. [Baltimore] 1969.
iii, 78 p. map. 28 cm.
1. Urban renewal—Baltimore. I. Title.
IU NUC73-124301

Baltimore. Dept. of Housing and Community Development. Research and Analysis Section.
Homesteading : the second year, 1975. — — Baltimore : Research and Analysis Section, Planning Division, Dept. of Housing and Community Development, 1976.
32 p. : maps ; 28 cm.
Written by S. Hartman.
1. Urban homesteading—Maryland—Baltimore. I. Hartman, Sara S. II. Title.
HD7304.B2B29 1976 301.5'4 77-620949
77 MARC

Baltimore. Dept. of Housing and Community Development. Research and Analysis Section.

For works by this body issued under its earlier name see

Baltimore. Dept. of Housing and Community Development. Research Section.

Baltimore. Dept. of Housing and Community Development. Research Section.
Housing needs of the elderly, 1970-1980. [Baltimore] 1972.
18 l. maps, tables. 28 cm.
1. Housing—Baltimore. 2. Aged—Baltimore. I. Title.
TxU NUC75-31794

Baltimore. Dept. of Housing and Community Development. Research Section.

For works by this body issued under its later name see

Baltimore. Dept. of Housing and Community Development. Research and Analysis Section.

Baltimore. Dept. of Legislative Reference
see Baltimore. Ordinances, etc. The Baltimore city code of 1927... [Baltimore, King bros., inc., printers and publishers] 1928.

Baltimore. Dept. of Legislative Reference
see Maryland. Constitution. Constitution of Maryland... [Annapolis] Secretary of State of Maryland [1969 ?]

Baltimore. Dept. of Legislative Reference
see Maryland. Constitution. Constitution of Maryland with amendments to January 1, 1971... [Annapolis] Secretary of State of Maryland [1972]

Baltimore. Dept. of Legislative Reference
see also
Maryland. State Dept. of Legislative Reference.

Baltimore. Dept. of Planning.
Baltimore, community facilities and services / [prepared by the Department of Planning]. — [Baltimore : Planning Commission, 1974?]
136 p. : ill., map (fold. col. in pocket) ; 23 cm.
Cover title.
1. Social service—Baltimore. 2. Municipal services—Baltimore. 3. Baltimore—Social policy. I. Baltimore. Planning Commission. II. Title.
HV87.B2B35 1974 361.6'3'0975271 74-76073
75 MARC

Baltimore. Dept. of Planning.
Baltimore's development program: 1972, 1973, 1974, 1975, 1976, 1977, as approved and adopted by the Board of Estimates, August 4, 1971. Baltimore, City Planning Commission [1971 ?]
256 p. illus., col. maps (1 fold. in pocket) 29 x 28 cm.
1. Cities and towns—Planning—Baltimore. 2. Baltimore—Public works. I. Title.
IU NUC73-125116

Baltimore. Dept. of Planning.
Baltimore's development program, 1976, 1977, 1978, 1979, 1980, 1981 : capital improvement program, comprehensive plan / Baltimore City Planning Commission/Department of Planning. — [Baltimore] : The Department, [1975 or 1976]
252 p. : ill., fold. map (in pocket) ; 29 cm.
1. Cities and towns—Planning—Baltimore. 2. Urban renewal—Baltimore. 3. Capital budget—Maryland—Baltimore. I. Title.
HT168.B35B34 1975 711'.4'097526 75-39413
76 MARC

Baltimore. Dept. of Planning.
MetroCenter/ Baltimore; a presentation to the American Institute of Planners, Jury of Awards, April, 1972. Baltimore, 1972.
1 v. (unpaged) illus., 3 photos. in pocket.
Commentaries and reproduced articles mounted on blank pages.
1. Cities and towns—Planning—Baltimore. I. American Institute of Planners. II. Title.
CU NUC76-74344

Baltimore. Dept. of Planning. Metro center/Baltimore
see Wallace, McHarg, Roberts and Todd. MetroCenter/Baltimore technical study... [Baltimore, City Dept. of Planning, 1970 ?]

Baltimore. Dept. of Planning.
The Mund Plan. [Baltimore, 1971?]
92 p. illus. 8 x 27 cm.
1. Cities and towns—Planning—Baltimore. I. Cornell University. School of Architecture, Art and Planning. II. Title.
MiEM NUC75-72765

Baltimore. Dept. of Planning.
Neighborhood services : inventory. — [Baltimore] : Baltimore City Dept. of Planning, 1969.
120 p. : maps ; 22 x 29 cm.
1. Municipal services—Maryland—Baltimore. I. Title.
HD4606.B2B32 1969 363.5 76-374258
76 MARC

Baltimore. Dept. of Planning.
see Baltimore. Planning Commission. Baltimore's development program, as recommended by the Planning Commission, February 23, 1973. Baltimore, Planning Commission/-Dept. of Planning, [1973]

Baltimore. Dept. of Planning
see **Maryland. Baltimore Regional Planning Council. Regional core study. Phase one working papers. Baltimore, 1968-**

Baltimore. Dept. of Planning. Research Section.
see Baltimore. Baltimore land use coding system ... Baltimore, Dept. of Planning, Research Section, 1974.

Baltimore. Dept. of Traffic Engineering.
Annual report. 19 -56
Baltimore.
v. illus. 23 cm.
Continued by the Annual report issued under the later name of the dept.: Dept. of Transit and Traffic.
1. Traffic engineering—Baltimore.
HE356.5.B28A3 72-624278

Baltimore. Dept. of Transit and Traffic.
Annual report. 1957-
[Baltimore]
v. illus. 23-29 cm.
Continues the Annual report issued under the earlier name of the dept.: Dept. of Traffic Engineering.
1. Traffic engineering—Baltimore.
HE356.5.B28A3 72-624277

Baltimore. Dept. of Transit and Traffic.
TOPICS: traffic operations program to increase capacity and safety. [Baltimore] 1971.
113 l. diagrs. (part fold.) maps. 28 cm.
1. Traffic engineering–Baltimore metropolitan area. I. Title.
IU NUC75-31787

Baltimore. Dept. of Transit and Traffic.
Urban mass transportation demonstration project; final report. [Baltimore] 1971.
iii, 147 l. illus., maps. 28 cm.
Cover title: Job express transportation, Baltimore, Maryland; final report.
1. Urban transportation–Baltimore. I. Title.
IU NUC73-125117

Baltimore. East Baltimore Baptist Church.
Second and Fourth Baptist church history, 1651-1972. [n.p.] 1972.
[ii], 49 p. illus. 29 cm.
1. Baltimore, Md. Fourth Baptist Church–History.
KyLoS NUC74-13992

Baltimore. Enoch Pratt Free Library
see Enoch Pratt Free Library, Baltimore.

Baltimore. Fidelity and Guaranty Company
see Fidelity and Guaranty Company.

Baltimore. Goucher College
see Goucher College, Baltimore.

Baltimore. Har Sinai Congregation
see Jews. Liturgy and ritual. [Sabbath prayers (Reform, Har Sinai Congregation). German & Hebrew] Gebetbuch für israelitische Reform-Gemeinden. New York, Gedruckt bei H. Frank, 1856-

Baltimore. John F. Kennedy Institute for the Habilitation of the Mentally and Physically Handicapped Child
see
John F. Kennedy Institute for the Habilitation of the Mentally and Physically Handicapped Child.

Baltimore. John Hopkins Hospital
see Johns Hopkins Hospital, Baltimore.

Baltimore. Mayor.
Report to the citizens of Baltimore, by Thomas D'Alesandro, Jr., Mayor. May 20th, 1947 to May 20th, 1948. [Baltimore, 1948]
113 p. illus. 23 cm.
Cover title.
Caption title: First report; a summary of city administration of Baltimore during the year ... [including] reports of officials and chiefs of city departments, bureaus, agencies, and commissions.
1. Baltimore—Politics and government. 2. Baltimore—Executive departments.
JS13.B18 352'.008'097526 74-154116
MARC

Baltimore. Mayor's Advisory Committee on Herring Run.
A plan for improvement and conservation: Herring Run Stream Valley. Baltimore [1973]
1 v. (unpaged) maps, ports. 36 cm.
Cover title.
1. Herring Run watershed, Baltimore. 2. Cities and towns—Planning—Baltimore. 3. Watershed management—Baltimore.
IU NUC76-66795

Baltimore. Mayor's Committee on Cable Television.
Cable communications for Baltimore; report of the Mayor's Committee on Cable Television. Baltimore, 1973.
1 v. (various pagings) maps. 28 cm.
Includes bibliography.
1. Community antenna television—Baltimore. I. Title.
IU NUC76-66796

Baltimore. Medical College. Dental Dept.
The Department of Dentistry of the University of Maryland was founded in 1882. In 1913 it absorbed the Dental Department of the Baltimore Medical College. In 1920 it became the School of Dentistry. In 1923 it was absorbed by the Baltimore College of Dental Surgery when that college became a division of the university.
Works by these bodies are found under the following headings according to the name used at the time of publication:
Maryland. University. Dept. of Dentistry.
Baltimore. Medical College. Dental Dept.
Maryland. University. School of Dentistry.

Maryland. University. Baltimore College of Dental Surgery.
73-210760

Baltimore. Model Cities Agency.
Second action year, comprehensive demonstration plan. Baltimore, 1971.
487 l. 30 cm.
1. Cities and towns–Planning–Baltimore. 2. Urban renewal–Baltimore.
IU NUC74-122411

Baltimore. Model Cities Agency.
Third action year, comprehensive demonstration plan. Baltimore, 1972.
635 l. 30 cm.
1. Cities and towns—Planning—Baltimore. 2. Urban renewal—Baltimore.
IU NUC74-126587

Baltimore. Model Cities Agency. Information & Evaluation Division.
Third action year evaluation report: education component [by] Information & Evaluation Division, Baltimore Model Cities Agency. [Baltimore, 1973]
54 l. 28 cm.
Cover title.
1. Cities and towns–Planning–Baltimore. 2. Urban renewal–Baltimore.
IU NUC77-14294

Baltimore. Model Cities Agency. Information & Evaluation Division.
3rd action year evaluation report of the Information & Evaluation Division: recreation component. [Baltimore, 1973]
33 l. 28 cm.
Cover title.
1. Cities and towns–Planning–Baltimore. 2. Urban renewal–Baltimore.
IU NUC77-14295

Baltimore. Model Cities Section
see The Mund plan. [Baltimore? 1970 or 1]

Baltimore. Model Urban Neighborhood Demonstration Program
see United States. Office of Economic Opportunity. The Mund plan. Washington [1973?]

Baltimore. Mount Royal Station Gallery
see
Mount Royal Station Gallery.

Baltimore. Municipal Museum
see Dorsey, John R 1938- A guide to Baltimore architecture. Cambridge, Md., Tidewater Publishers, 1973.

Baltimore. Municipal Museum.
see Van Devanter, Ann C. "Anywhere so long as there be freedom" ... Baltimore, Baltimore Museum of Art, c1975.

Baltimore. Museum of Art.
200 [i.e. Duecento] anni di pittura americana (1776-1976) : mostra organizzata dal Baltimore Museum of Art, Galleria d'arte moderna, Valle Giulia, Roma, 1-26 ottobre 1976. — Roma : De Luca, 1976.
21 p., 60 leaves of plates : ill. ; 24 cm. It77-Jan
At head of title: Soprintendenza alla Galleria nazionale d'arte moderna e contemporanea.
Text on verso of plates.
1. Painting, American—Exhibitions. 2. Painting, Colonial—United States—Exhibitions. 3. Painting, Modern—19th century—United States—Exhibitions. 4. Painting, Modern—20th century—United States—Exhibitions. I. Rome (City). Galleria nazionale d'arte moderna. II. Title.
ND205.B23 1976 77-471670
•77 MARC

Baltimore. Museum of Art.
Eighteenth and nineteenth century Maryland silver in the collection of the Baltimore Museum of Art / text by Jennifer Faulds Goldsborough ; edited by Ann Boyce Harper. — Baltimore : The Museum, 1975.
ix, 204 p. : ill. ; 26 cm.
"A project supported by the Stieff Company, Baltimore."
Bibliography: p. 201-204.
1. Silverwork—Maryland—Catalogs. 2. Baltimore. Museum of Art. I. Goldsborough, Jennifer F. II. Title: Eighteenth and nineteenth century Maryland silver ... III. Title: Maryland silver.
NK7112.B26 1975 75-15344
739.2'3'775207401526
76 MARC

Baltimore. Museum of Art.
The inspired copy : artists look at art ; [catalogue of] an exhibition [held] April 25–June 29, 1975 [at] the Baltimore Museum of Art. -- [Baltimore, Md. : The Museum, 1975?]
[14] p. : ill. ; 24 x 21 cm.
Cover title.
Bibliography: p. [14]
1. Prints--Exhibitions. 2. Imitation (in art). I. Title.
CtY NUC77-87888

Baltimore. Museum of Art.
Lea Halpern : dates of the exhibition, January 27-March 21, 1976. — [Baltimore] : Baltimore Museum of Art, [1976?]
[24] p., [8] leaves of plates : ill. (8 col. in pocket) ; 26 cm.
"Catalogue of the exhibition": p. [1]-[24]
1. Halpern, Lea Henny, 1901- 2. Pottery, Dutch—Exhibitions. I. Halpern, Lea Henny, 1901-
NK4210.H3B34 1976 738'.092'4 76-359580
76 MARC

Baltimore. Museum of Art.
Picasso : drawings and watercolors, 1899-1907 / by Victor I. Carlson. — Baltimore : Baltimore Museum of Art, c1976.
xxiv, 111 p. : ill. (some col.) ; 26 cm.
Half title: Picasso, drawings and watercolors, 1899-1907, in the collection of the Baltimore Museum of Art.
Bibliography: p. 109-111.
$15.00
1. Picasso, Pablo, 1881-1973. I. Carlson, Victor I.
NC248.P5B27 1976 741.9'44 76-41022
77 MARC

Baltimore. Museum of Art. Record, v. 3, no. 1
see Baltimore. Museum of Art. Saidie A. May Collection. [Baltimore, 1972]

Baltimore. Museum of Art.
Saidie A. May Collection. [Catalogue of an exhibition. Baltimore, 1972]
87 p. illus. (part col.) 26 cm.
"An issue of the Baltimore Museum of Art Record, v. 3, no. 1, 1972."
Includes bibliographical references.
1. Art—Exhibitions. 2. May, Saidie Adler, 1879-1951—Art collections. I. Baltimore. Museum of Art. Record, v. 3, no. 1. II. Title.
N5220.M54B34 1972 708'.152'6 74-171020
MARC

Baltimore. Museum of Art.
Still life and flowers; an exhibition sponsored by the Maryland Arts Council, organized by the Baltimore Museum of Art, on tour from May 11-November 12, 1967. [n.p., 1967?]
16 p. front., plates. 19 cm.
1. Still life painting. 2. Flower painting and illustration. I. Maryland Arts Council. II. Title.
MdBJ NUC76-36301

Baltimore. Museum of Art.
2,000 years of calligraphy; a three-part exhibition organized by the Baltimore Museum of Art, the Peabody Institute Library [and] the Walters Art Gallery. [Compiled by Dorothy E. Miner, Victor I. Carlson, and P.W. Filby. London] F. Muller Ltd. [1972]
201 p. illus., facsims. 29 cm.
"A facsimile edition."
"This edition, reprinted from the original plates in 1972 and published in the United Kingdom ... is limited to 250 numbered copies."
I. Miner, Dorothy Eugenia.
TxU CtY KU NUC74-127489

Baltimore. Museum of Art.
2,000 years of calligraphy; a three-part exhibition organized, by The Baltimore Museum of Art, [The] Peabody Institute Library [and The] Walters Art Gallery. June 6 - July 18, 1965. A comprehensive catalog. Totowa, N.J., Rowman and Littlefield [1972]
201 p. illus., facsims. 28 cm.
"Compiled by Dorothy E. Miner ..., Victor I. Carlson ... [and] P.W. Filby."
Reprint edition.
I. Miner, Dorothy Eugenia. II. Peabody Institute, Baltimore, Library. III. Walters Art Gallery, Baltimore.
ICN NUC73-120493

Baltimore. Museum of Art.
Washington: twenty years. [Essays by Diana F. Johnson and Ellen Hope Gross] Baltimore [c1970]
51 p. 22 cm.
Includes catalog of the exhibition held at the Baltimore Museum of Art from May 12 to June 21, 1970.
1. Art, Modern—20th cent.—Washington, D.C. I. Johnson, Diana F. II. Gross, Ellen. III. Title.
DSI NUC76-74135

Baltimore. Museum of Art.
see American prints, 1870-1950. Chicago, University of Chicago Press, c1976.

Baltimore. Museum of Art.
see Asia Society. Gods, thrones, and peacocks ... New York, Arno Press, 1976, c1965.

Baltimore. Museum of Art
see Bannard, Walter Darby, 1934- Walter Darby Bannard. [Baltimore] Baltimore Museum of Art [1973]

Baltimore. Museum of Art
see Clisby, Roger D 19th & 20th century prints & drawings... [Sacramento, Calif.] E. B. Crocker Art Gallery, 1973.

Baltimore. Museum of Art
see Corning, N.Y. Museum of Glass. Tales from a king's book of kings... [Corning, c1973]

Baltimore. Museum of Art
see 200 [i.e. Dve stotine] godina američkog slikarstva ... Beograd: Američka ambasada, [1976]

Baltimore. Museum of Art.
see Embry, Norris, 1921- Norris Embry. Baltimore, Baltimore Museum of Art, c1975.

Baltimore. Museum of Art.
see 14 American photographers ... Baltimore, Baltimore Museum of Art, [1975] c1974.

Baltimore. Museum of Art
see Gogh, Vincent van, 1853-1890. Vincent van Gogh... [Baltimore, 1961]

Baltimore. Museum of Art.
see Katzen, Lila. Sculpture and site ... Syracuse, N.Y., Published by Visual Artis Publications for the Everson Museum of Art and the Baltimore Museum of Art, 1975.

Baltimore. Museum of Art
see Katzenberg, Dena S Blue traditions... [Baltimore, c1973]

Baltimore. Museum of Art.
see Richardson, Brenda. Frank Stella ... Baltimore, Baltimore Museum of Art, c1976.

Baltimore. Museum of Art.
see Richardson, Brenda. Mel Bochner ... Baltimore, Baltimore Museum of Art, c1976.

Baltimore. Museum of Art
see Robinson, Theodore, 1852-1896. Theodore Robinson, 1852-1896. [Baltimore] Baltimore Museum of Art [1973]

Baltimore. Museum of Art.
see Saint-Aubin, Gabriel Jacques de, 1724-1780. Prints and drawings by Gabriel de Saint-Aubin, 1724-1780, Davison Art Center, Wesleyan University, Middletown, Connecticut, March 7-April 13, 1975, Baltimore Museum of Art, Baltimore, Maryland, April 25-June 8, 1975. [Middletown, Conn.] The Center, [1975?]

Baltimore. Museum of Art
see Segal, George, 1924- George Segal, environments... -- Philadelphia : [1976]

Baltimore. Museum of Art
see Studies on Thomas Cole, an American romanticist. Baltimore, Museum of Art, 1967.

Baltimore. Museum of Art
see Turner, Joseph Mallord William, 1775-1851. J.M.W. Turner, illustrations for books. [Baltimore, 1975]

Baltimore. Museum of Art.
see Van Devanter, Ann C. "Anywhere so long as there be freedom" ... Baltimore, Baltimore Museum of Art, c1975.

Baltimore. Museum of Art
see Wight, Frederick Stallknecht, 1902- Milton Avery. [Baltimore, n.d.]

Baltimore. Ordinances, etc.
The Baltimore city code of 1927 containing the general ordinances of the mayor and city council in force on May 21, 1928. Codified by Horace E. Flack, Department of legislative reference. [Baltimore, King bros., inc., printers and publishers] 1928.
1430 p. 23½ cm.
1. Ordinances, Municipal—Baltimore. I. Baltimore. Dept. of Legislative Reference. II. Title.
KFX1101.A6 1928 28-28660

Baltimore. Ordinances, etc.
see Baltimore. Charters. Charter and Public local laws of Baltimore city... Baltimore [King bros., printers and publishers] 1938.

Baltimore. Peabody Institute
see Peabody Institute, Baltimore.

Baltimore. Planning Commission.
Baltimore's development program, as recommended by the Planning Commission, February 23, 1973. — Baltimore : Planning Commission/Dept. of Planning, [1973]
160 p., [1] fold. leaf of plates : map ; 29 cm.
1. Baltimore—Public works. 2. Baltimore—Economic policy. 3. Baltimore—Social policy. 4. Baltimore—Appropriations and expenditures. I. Baltimore. Dept. of Planning. II. Title: Baltimore's development program ...
HD4606.B2B34 1973a 338.9752'6 76-371672
76 MARC

Baltimore. Planning Commission.
Baltimore's development program, 1973, 1974, 1975, 1976, 1977, 1978, as approved and adopted by the Board of Estimates, November 1, 1972. Baltimore [1973]
255 p. illus. 29 cm.
Part of illustrative matter in pocket.
1. Baltimore—Public works. I. Title.
HD4606.B2B34 1973 711'.4'097526 74-184732
MARC

Baltimore. Planning Commission.
Baltimore's development program: 1974, 1975, 1976, 1977, 1978, 1979 as approved by the Board of Estimates, May 16, 1973. Baltimore, City Planning Commission/Department of Planning [1973]
186 p. fold. col. map (in pocket) 29 x 28 cm.
1. Cities and towns—Planning—Baltimore. 2. Baltimore—Public works. I. Title.
IU NUC76-74345

Baltimore. Planning Commission.
Recommended capital improvement program, 1964-1969. Baltimore, 1963.
242 p.
1. Baltimore—Public works. I. Title.
CaOTP DLC NUC76-74343

Baltimore. Planning Commission.
see Baltimore. Dept. of Planning. Baltimore, community facilities and services. [Baltimore, Planning Commission, 1974?]

Baltimore. Planning Commission. Dept. of Planning
see
Baltimore. Dept. of Planning.

Baltimore. Public Schools.
1974 reorganization of the Baltimore City Public Schools. — Rev. ed. — Baltimore, Md. : Baltimore City Public Schools, c1974.
vi, 116 leaves ; 29 cm.
1. Schools—Decentralization—Maryland—Baltimore. 2. Baltimore. Public schools. I. Title.
LB2862.B34 1974 379'.1535 75-328952
75 MARC

Baltimore. Regional Planning Council
see Regional Planning Council, Baltimore.

Baltimore. Roland Park Presbyterian Church
see Roland Park Presbyterian Church.

Baltimore. Stock Exchange.
The Philadelphia Board of Brokers was established in 1790. In 1875 the name was changed to the Philadelphia Stock Exchange. In 1949 the Philadelphia Stock Exchange and the Baltimore Stock Exchange merged to form the Philadelphia-Baltimore Stock Exchange. In 1953 the Philadelphia-Baltimore Stock Exchange merged with the Washington Stock Exchange to form the Philadelphia-Baltimore-Washington Stock Exchange. In 1972 the name was changed to the PBW Stock Exchange, on May 10, 1976, to the Philadelphia Stock Exchange.
Works by the Philadelphia Stock Exchange before the 1949 merger are found under
Philadelphia. Stock Exchange.

Works by the Philadelphia Stock Exchange after the name change in 1976, and by the other bodies are found under the following headings according to the name used at the time of publication:
Philadelphia Board of Brokers.
Baltimore. Stock Exchange.
Philadelphia-Baltimore Stock Exchange.
Washington, D.C. Stock Exchange.
Philadelphia-Baltimore-Washington Stock Exchange.
PBW Stock Exchange.
Philadelphia Stock Exchange.

Baltimore. University. School of Law.
University of Baltimore law review.
Baltimore, Md.
v. 26 cm. semiannual.
1. Law—Periodicals—Maryland. I. Title.
K2.A46 340'.05 73-643578
ISSN 0091-5440 MARC-S

Baltimore. University. School of Law
see The Forum. [Baltimore]

Baltimore. University. School of Law
see The Forum law journal. Baltimore.

Baltimore. Urban Observatory
see Baltimore Urban Observatory.

Baltimore. Urban Renewal and Housing Agency.
In 1968 the Baltimore Bureau of Building Inspection and the Urban Renewal and Housing Agency merged to form the Baltimore Dept. of Housing and Community Development.
Works by these bodies are found under the following headings according to the name used at the time of publication:
Baltimore. Bureau of Building Inspection.
Baltimore. Urban Renewal and Housing Agency.
Baltimore. Dept. of Housing and Community Development.
74-236463

Baltimore. Urban Renewal and Housing Agency.
A demonstration of rehabilitation, Harlem Park, Baltimore, Maryland. [Baltimore] 1965.
iv, 95 p. illus. 22 x 28 cm.
1. Urban renewal—Baltimore—Case studies. I. Title.
HT177.B35A5 72-224592
MARC
IU OrU PSt MiU NcD MB NBuU-L MsSM NNC ViU DHHF TU OOxM

Baltimore. Urban Renewal and Housing Agency.
Highlights.
[Baltimore]
v. maps. 28 cm. annual.
1. Urban renewal—Baltimore. 2. Housing—Baltimore. I. Title.
HT177.B35A33 72-620585

Baltimore. Urban Renewal and Housing Agency.
Inventory of residential blight; findings.
Baltimore, 1964.
33, xi p. illus., maps. 28 cm. (Its Community renewal program)
"Interim report no. 1."
1. Urban renewal–Baltimore. I. Title.
NIC NUC74-122417

Baltimore. Urban Renewal and Housing Agency
see Hartman, Sara S Selected housing... [Baltimore] 1964.

Baltimore. Urban Renewal and Housing Agency. Planning Dept.
see Hartman, Sara S Baltimore's housing situation in 1960. Baltimore, 1962.

Baltimore. Urban Renewal and Housing Agency. Renewal Planning Dept.
The people of Mount Winans; their characteristics, needs, attitudes. [Baltimore] 1968.
66 p. illus. 28 cm.
1. Baltimore—Social conditions. I. Title.
HN80.B3B37 1968 309.1'752'71 74-185166
MARC

Baltimore. Walters Art Gallery
see
Walters Art Gallery, Baltimore.

Baltimore. Wilmer Ophthalmological Institute
see
Johns Hopkins Hospital, Baltimore. Wilmer Ophthalmological Institute.

Baltimore (Archdiocese). Liturgical Commission.
Repent and believe. Baltimore, Md. [1971]
64 p. 22 cm.
1. Confession, Communal—Liturgy. 2. Penance (Sacrament). I. Title.
IMunS NUC73-71299

Baltimore Afro-American.
see Best short stories by Afro-American writers, 1925-1950. Milwood, N.Y., Kraus Reprint Co., 1977, c1950.

Baltimore and Ohio Railroad Company.
Concerning the blue china. [n.p., n.d.]
12 p. illus.
Originally prepared for the Baltimore and Ohio Centenary Exposition and Pageant held in 1927, Baltimore, Md.
1. Porcelain. I. Title.
WHi NUC73-71300

Baltimore and Ohio Railroad Company.
Report of the engineers on the reconnoissance [sic] and surveys, made in reference to the Baltimore and Ohio rail road. Baltimore, Printed by W. Wooddy, 1828.
188 p. illus.
Reports signed by Wm. Howard [and others]
Microfilm (positive) Ann Arbor, Mich., University Microfilms, 1974. 3d title of 11. 35 mm. (American culture series, reel 568.3)
KEmT PSt NUC75-16612

Baltimore and Ohio Railroad Company.
Suburban homes along the line of the Baltimore and Ohio Southwestern R. R. Cincinnati, A. H. Pugh Printing Co., 1891. [Cincinnati, Ohio, Miami Purchase Association, 1973]
28 p. illus.
1. Cincinnati, Ohio.–Suburbs and environs –Description and travel–Guidebooks. 2. Baltimore and Ohio Railroad Company. I. Title.
WHi NUC74-121687

Baltimore and Ohio Railroad Company
see Hollifield, William. Casualties on the Baltimore and Ohio Railroad, 1854-1855... Lutherville, Md., 1974.

Baltimore Association for the Improvement of the Condition of the Poor.
Housing conditions in Baltimore; report of a special committee of the Association for the Improvement of the Condition of the Poor and the Charity Organization Society. New York, Arno Press, 1974 [c1907]
96 p. illus. 23 cm. (Metropolitan America)
Reprint of the ed. published in Baltimore.
Bibliography: p. [95]-96.
1. Housing—Baltimore. 2. Baltimore—Poor. I. Charity Organization Society of Baltimore City. II. Title. III. Series.
HD7304.B2B34 1974 301.5'4'097526 73-11915
ISBN 0-405-05384-3 MARC

Baltimore bibliophiles
see Alberts, Robert C Connoisseur's haven. [Pittsburgh, 1967?]

Baltimore bibliophiles
see The Baltimore Bibliophiles Library. [Baltimore, E. Heyl, 1970]

The Baltimore Bibliophiles Library. [Baltimore, E. Heyl, 1970]
[12] p. 23 cm.
"Limited to 125 copies."
1. Baltimore. Bibl. I. Baltimore bibliophiles.
NcD NUC76-24462

Baltimore catechism
see Schumacher, Magnus Ambrose, 1885– My way to God; a teacher's manual for the grades: grade seven. St. Paul, Catechetical Guild [1960]

Baltimore City Hospitals
see United States. National Heart Institute. Section on Gerontology. [Publications, 1940-1969. Washington? 1970?]

Baltimore College of Dental Surgery
see
Maryland. University. Baltimore College of Dental Surgery.

Baltimore Council for International Visitors.
1975 Maryland, our Maryland : an ethnic and cultural directory : a roster of over 400 organizations belonging to the many ethnic groups in Maryland / compiled by the Baltimore Council for International Visitors ; sponsored by the Maryland Bicentennial Commission. — [Baltimore] : The Council, c1975.
71 p. ; 22 cm.
1. Minorities—Maryland—Societies, etc.—Directories. 2. Minorities—Maryland—Baltimore—Societies, etc.—Directories. 3. Maryland—Societies, etc.—Directories. 4. Baltimore—Societies, etc.—Directories. I. Title. II. Title: Maryland, our Maryland.
F190.A1B34 1975 301.45'1'062752 76-358660
76 MARC

Baltimore Co., Md.
Baltimore County publications. 2d ed. [Towson? Md., 1972]
23 p. 23 cm.
Cover title.
"Prepared by Richard Parsons, Baltimore County Public Library, with the cooperation of the Office of Information & Research, Baltimore County, Maryland."
1. Baltimore Co., Md.—Government publications—Bibliography. I. Parsons, Richard. II. Title.
Z1294.B35B34 1972 015'.752'71 73-162796
MARC

Baltimore Co., Md. Board of Education.
Handbook for elementary instrumental music teachers. [n.p.] 1969.
[40] l. charts, music. 29 cm.
1. School music–Instruction and study–Baltimore Co., Md.
MdBP NUC73-47480

Baltimore Co., Md. Charter Board.
Proposed home rule charter for Baltimore County, Maryland : to be submitted to the voters of Baltimore County at the general election on Tuesday, November 6, 1956. — [s.l. : s.n., 1955 or 1956]
xxxiii, 105 p. : ill. ; 24 cm.
Includes index.
1. County charters—Maryland—Baltimore Co. I. Title.
KFM1799.B32A35 1956 77-363007
77 MARC

Baltimore Co., Md. Dept. of Public Safety. Police Bureau
see
Baltimore Co., Md. Police Bureau.

Baltimore Co., Md. Office of Information and Research.
Baltimore County, Maryland, at a glance, 1969. Rev. ed. [n.p., 1969]
44 p. illus.
1. Baltimore Co., Md. 2. Maryland: Counties: Baltimore. I. Title.
WHi NUC73-47479

Baltimore Co., Md. Office of Planning.
New zoning tools, Baltimore County.
[n.p.] 1971.
10 p.
1. Zoning legislation—Baltimore County, Md. I. Title.
DHUD NUC76-74342

Baltimore Co., Md. Office of Planning.
1980 guideplan for Baltimore County, Maryland. Adopted June 15, 1972. [Towson, Md.] Baltimore County Office of Planning and Zoning [1972]
12 p. col. illus., col. maps (1 fold.) 29 cm.
Bibliography: p. 12.
1. Regional planning—Baltimore Co., Md.
IU NUC75-32807

Baltimore Co., Md. Office of Planning.
1973-76 overall program design for planning and zoning activities in Baltimore County, Maryland. [Towson, Md., 1973]
iv, 124 p. 28 cm.
"Adopted by the Baltimore County Planning Board on July 19, 1973."
1. Regional planning–Baltimore Co., Md. 2. Zoning–Baltimore Co., Md.
IU NUC74-127108

Baltimore Co., Md. Office of Planning.
Report of the Baltimore County Planning Board to the Zoning Commissioner on zoning reclassification petitions, cycle V, April-October, 1973. Towson, Md., Baltimore County Office of Planning and Zoning, 1973.
vi, 81 p. maps. 28 cm.
"Adopted July 19, 1973."
1. Zoning—Baltimore Co., Md.
IU NUC75-23090

Baltimore Co., Md. Ordinances, etc.
Title 22. Planning, zoning and subdivision control. [Baltimore, 1970?]
78 p. 28 cm.
Caption title.
1. Regional planning—Law and legislation—Baltimore Co., Md. I. Title: Planning, zoning and subdivision control.
IU NUC75-32101

Baltimore Co., Md. Police Bureau.
Baltimore County, Maryland, complete street directory. [Towson?] Produced by the Baltimore County Police Bureau, 1963.
299 l. map. 28 cm.
1. Baltimore Co., Md.—Streets. I. Title.
F187.B2B25 1963 63-25649
rev

Baltimore Co., Md. Police Bureau.
Baltimore County street directory. [Towson?] Produced by Baltimore Co. Police Bureau, c1962–
v. 29 cm.
CONTENTS: Sectors A-1 through A-6.—Sectors B-1 through B-7.
1. Baltimore Co., Md.—Streets. I. Title.
F187.B2B25 1962 62-53436
rev

Baltimore Co., Md. Police Bureau.

For works by this body issued under its later name see

Baltimore Co., Md. Police Dept.

Baltimore Co., Md. Police Dept.
Street guide of Baltimore County. [Towson] Baltimore County Public Library, 1972.
vi, 234 p. maps. 18 cm. $3.00
1. Baltimore Co., Md.—Streets—Directories. I. Title.
F187.B2B25 1972 917.52'71'044 73-166453
73[r75]rev MARC

Baltimore Co., Md. Police Dept.
Street guide of Baltimore County. [Rev. issue. Towson] Baltimore County Public Library, 1974.
ii, 287 p. 18 cm.
1. Baltimore Co., Md.—Streets—Directories. I. Title.
F187.B2B25 1974 917.52'71'044 74-174436
MARC

Baltimore Co., Md. Police Dept.
For works by this body issued under its earlier name see
Baltimore Co., Md. Police Bureau.

Baltimore Co., Md. Public Library
see Gambit; selected strategies... [n.p.] c1973.

Baltimore Co., Md. Public Schools.
Elementary school physical education; a guide for physical education teachers. Towson, Md., 1970.
1 v. (loose-leaf) 30 cm.
Cover title: A guide for elementary school physical education teachers.
1. Physical education for children. I. Title.
MoKU NUC73-47485

Baltimore Co., Md. Public Schools.
Probing with a microscope; a teaching manual for elementary school science, level three. Towson, Md., Board of Education of Baltimore County, 1972.
50, vi p. 28 cm.
Includes bibliographies.
1. Microscope and microscopy–Study and teaching (Elementary) I. Title.
MoKU NUC76-74372

Baltimore Co., Md. Public Schools.
A search for structure; a student manual for junior high school science. Grade seven. Towson, Md., Board of Education of Baltimore County, 1969-1970.
3 v. in 4. illus. 28 cm.
Cover title.
1. Science—Study & teaching (Secondary) I. Title.
OU NUC75-32088

Baltimore Criminal Justice Commission, inc.
Survey analysis: organization and operations of Baltimore City State's Attorney's Office. Baltimore, 1969.
1 v. (various pagings) diagrs. 29 cm.
1. Baltimore, Md. State's Attorney.
C NUC74-146355

Baltimore Feminist Project
see Sexism and racism in popular basal readers, 1964-1976... -- New York : c1976.

Baltimore Hebrew College.
see National Symposium on the Integration of Soviet Jews into the American Jewish Community, Baltimore Hebrew College, 1976. The Soviet Jewish emigre . . . Baltimore, Baltimore Hebrew College, c1977.

Baltimore Metropolitan Meals on Wheels.
Organization manual for meals on wheels. Rev. ed. Baltimore, Meals on Wheels, 1970.
1 v. (various pagings) illus.
1. Aged—Nutrition. 2. Cookery for the sick. I. Meals on Wheels. II. Title.
LN NUC76-24902

Baltimore Model Cities Agency
see Baltimore. Model Cities Agency.

Baltimore Museum of Art
see Baltimore. Museum of Art.

Baltimore National Bank
see Fidelity-Baltimore National Bank.

Baltimore Regional Planning Council
see Maryland. Baltimore Regional Planning Council.
(for dates prior to 1964)

Baltimore, slavery, and constitutional history. Baltimore, Johns Hopkins Press, 1896. [New York, Johnson Reprint Corp., 1973]
8 v. (588 p.) in 1. 22 cm.
Each vol. also paged separately.
Originally issued as 14th series of the Johns Hopkins University studies in historical and political science.
Includes bibliographical references.
1. United States—Politics and government—Collections. 2. Slavery in the United States—Collections.
JA37.B35 320.9'73 72-14331
MARC

Baltimore Stock Exchange
see
Baltimore. Stock Exchange.

Baltimore Union for Jobs or Income Now.
Baltimore U-Join; the summer report. New York, Students for a Democratic Society and its Economic Research and Action Project [1964?]
1 v. (various pagings)
Cover title.
1. Baltimore Union for Jobs or Income Now. 2. Unemployed-Baltimore, Md. 3. Baltimore, Md.—Poor. I. Students for a Democratic Society. Economic Research and Action Project. II. Title.
WHi. NUC75-79038

Baltimore Urban Design Concept Associates.
Housing relocation and compensation related to the interstate highway system, Baltimore, Maryland. [Baltimore] 1968.
1 v. (various pagings)
"Confidential draft."
"To be submitted, after revision, to the Maryland State Roads Commission."
1. Relocation (Housing)–Baltimore. 2. Compensation (Law)–Baltimore. I. Maryland. State Roads Commission. II. Title.
CU NUC76-89142

Baltimore Urban League. Consumer Services Division.
This way to a better home; a training manual designed for use with residents moving into new or renovated apartments or homes. Rev.
New York, Soap and Detergent Association, 1972.
1 v. (unpaged) illus. 28 cm.
1. Moving, Household. I. Title.
CaBVaU NUC75-35252

Baltimore Urban Observatory
see FHA policies and the Baltimore City housing market. Baltimore, 1974.

Baltimore Urban Observatory
see The Housing market and code enforcement in Baltimore. Baltimore, Md., 1972.

Baltimore Urban Observatory
see Nicholsonne, W William. Citizens speak. Baltimore, 1972.

Baltimore Urban Observatory
see Oakland, William Horace. Incidence and other fiscal impacts of the reform of educational finance... Baltimore, 1974.

Baltimore Urban Observatory
see Stough, Roger R The effect of inner city open space... Baltimore, 1973.

Baltimore Yearly Meeting
see Friends, Society of. Baltimore Yearly Meeting.

Baltimorski muzej likovnih umetnosti
see
Baltimore. Museum of Art.

Baltin, Eckhardt
see Die Fabrik von morgen ... München: Siemens AG, Bereich Datenverarbeitung, [1972]

Baltinis, Andrius, 1909–1975.
Vyskupo Vincento Borisevičiaus gyvenimas ir darbai / Andrius Baltinis. — Roma : Lietuvių katalikų mokslo akademija, 1975.
ix, 178 p., [6] leaves of plates : ill. ; 26 cm. — (Negęstantieji žiburiai ; 6 t.) It***
At head of title: Lietuvių katalikų mokslo akademija.
Title also in English: Bishop Vincentas Borisevičius, his life and works.
Summary in English.
Bibliography: p. [157]–158.
Includes index.
1. Borisevičius, Vincentas, 1887–1947. 2. Catholic Church—Bishops—Biography. 3. Bishops—Lithuania—Biography. I. Title. II. Title: Bishop Vincentas Borisevičius, his life and works.
BX4705.B655B34 76-526521

Baltinos, Thanasēs
see
Valtinos, Thanasēs.

Baltiņš, Andris.
Elektriskie tīkli. Rīgā, "Zvaigzne," 1973.
318 p. with illus. 21 cm. 0.64rub USSR 74-7588
At head of title: A. Baltiņš.
Bibliography: p. [313]
1. Electric networks. 2. Electric power distribution. I. Title.
TK3226.B265 74-338084

Baltiņš, G
Latvijas PSR tautas saimniecības izaugsme. Rīgā, "Liesma," 1971.
98 [2] p. with illus. 20 cm. 0.17rub USSR 72-5549
At head of title: G. Baltiņš, T. Ieva.
Bibliography: p. [70]
1. Latvia—Economic conditions. I. Ieva, Teodors, joint author. II. Title.
HC337.L3B28 72-373339

Baltische Gesellschaft in Deutschland
see Baltisches Burschentum. Die student. Korporationen... [München] Balt. Ges. in Deutschland (1968).

Baltische Monatshefte
see Wittram-Hoffmann, Renate. Baltische Monatsschrift. Register 1859-1939. Marburg/Lahn, 1973.

Baltische Monatsschrift
see Wittram-Hoffmann, Renate. Baltische Monatsschrift. Register 1859-1939. Marburg/Lahn, 1973.

Baltisches Burschentum. Die student. Korporationen d. Deutschbalten, Esten, u. Letten einst u. jetzt. Hrsg. unter d. Red. von Hans von Rimscha. [München] Balt. Ges. in Deutschland (1968).
63 p. with illus. 21 cm. DM6.00 GDB 71-B18-1
1. Students' societies—Baltic States—History. 2. Students' societies—Germany—History. I. Rimscha, Hans von, 1899– ed. II. Baltische Gesellschaft in Deutschland.
LA853.B25B34 73-337130

Baltistica.
Vilnius, Mintis.
v. 22 cm. 2 no. a year. (4– : Lietuvos TSR aukštųjų mokyklų mokslo darbai)
English, French, German, Latvian, Lithuanian or Russian, with summaries in one of the other languages.
Vols. for issued by Lietuvos TSR aukštojo ir specialiojo vidurinio mokslo ministerija.
1. Baltic languages—Periodicals. I. Lithuanian S. S. R. Aukštojo ir specialiojo vidurinio mokslo ministerija. II. Series.
PG8001.B33 74-644880
MARC-S

Baltkalnis, L
Ateistis gimsta siandiena. Vilnius, Valstybine Politines ir Mokslines Literaturos Leidykla, 1959.
107 p. illus. 20 cm.
1. Ukraine—Econ. condit. 2. Lithuanian collection. I. Title.
OKentU NUC75-67081

Baltl, Hermann.
Österreichische Rechtsgeschichte : von den Anfängen bis zur Gegenwart / Hermann Baltl. — 3., wesentl. erw. Aufl. — Graz : Leykam, 1977.
363 p. ; 25 cm. Au77-12-24
Errata slip inserted.
Bibliography: p. 9-14.
Includes indexes.
ISBN 3-7011-7025-8 : S345.00
1. Law—Austria—History and criticism. I. Title.
77-481052
•77 MARC

Baltner, Howard A
Acting-in; practical applications of psychodramatic methods [by] Howard A. Baltner. [New York] Springer Pub. Co. [1973]
152 p. illus.
Bibliography.
1. Psychodrama. I. Title.
F NUC76-74371

(Balto-slavíanskie issledovaníia)
Балто-славянские исследования / ₍отв. редактор Т. М. Судник₎. — Москва : Наука, 1974.
263 p., ₍1₎ fold. leaf : ill. ; 22 cm. USSR***
At head of title: Akademiia nauk SSSR. Institut slavíanovedeniia i balkanistiki.
Includes bibliographical references.
1.14rub
1. Baltic languages—Grammar, Comparative—Slavic. 2. Slavic languages—Grammar, Comparative—Baltic. 3. Balto-Slavic linguistic unity. I. Sudnik, T. M. II. Akademiia nauk SSSR. Institut slavíanovedeniia i balkanistiki.
PG8018.B28 75-584733

(Balto-slavíanskiĭ sbornik)
Балто-славянский сборник. ₍Отв. ред. В. Н. Топоров₎. Москва, "Наука," 1972.
423 p., 3 l. of tables. 22 cm. 1.95rub USSR 72-VKP
At head of title: Академия наук СССР. Институт славяноведения и балканистики.
Includes bibliographies.
1. Baltic languages—Grammar, Comparative—Slavic. 2. Slavic languages—Grammar, Comparative—Baltic. 3. Balto-Slavic linguistic unity. I. Toporov, Vladimir Nikolaevich, ed. II. Akademiia nauk SSSR. Institut slavíanovedeniia i balkanistiki.
PG8018.B3 73-315833

Baltov, Angel, joint author
see Kolarov, Dobromir. (Mekhanika na plastichnite sredi) 1975.

Baltpurviņš, Augusts, 1871-1930.
Klusumam; dzejas un prozas izlase. ₍Mākslinieks Harijs Purviņš₎ Rīgā, Liesma, 1972.
348 p. port.
Russian title in colophon: Tishine.
Compiled by Valdemārs Ancītis.
MH NUC74-126574

Baltra Cortés, Alberto.
Crecimiento económico de América Latina; problemas fundamentales. Santiago, Pacifico [1969]
301 p.
1. Latin America–Economic conditions.
I. Title.
UU NUC73-47490

Baltra Cortés, Alberto.
Crecimiento económico de América Latina; problemas fundamentales. ₍6. ed.₎ Santiago de Chile, Editorial del Pacífico ₍1970, c1964₎
306 p. 19 cm.
Bibliographical footnotes.
1. Latin America–Economic conditions–1945- I. Title.
NN NUC76-41095

Baltra Cortés, Alberto.
El futuro económico de Chile y de América Latina ₍por₎ Alberto Baltra, Felipe Herrera ₍y₎ René Silva. ₍1. ed. Santiago de Chile₎ Editorial universitaria ₍1957₎
129 p. (Colección Saber, no. 8)
Microfiche (neg.) 3 sheets. 11 x 15 cm.
Three papers presented at a Spring 1956 Symposium on Economic Development in Chile and Latin America.
Bibliographical footnotes.
1. Economic history—Chile. 2. Economic history—Latin America.
NN NUC74-64255

Baltra Cortés, Alberto.
Gestión económica del Gobierno de la Unidad Popular / Alberto Baltra Cortés. — Santiago de Chile : Editorial Orbe, ₍1973 or 1974₎
143 p. ; 18 cm. — (Colección Encuentro : Testimonio)
Errata slip inserted.
Includes bibliographical references.
1. Chile—Economic conditions—1918- 2. Chile—Economic policy. I. Title.
HC192.B263 330.9′83′064 75-562390

Baltra Cortés, Alberto.
Teoría económica. 3. ed. ₍Santiago de Chile₎ Editorial Andrés Bello, 1973-
v. 25 cm.
Bibliography: v. 1, p. 487-500.
1. Economics. I. Title.
TxU NUC76-41580

Baltrėnas, Vilius
see Iš mūsų išeivijos dešimtmečių... Vilnius: Gintaras, 1973.

Baltrūnas, A
Šviesos gimimas : apsakymai / Aleksas Baltrunas. — Vilnius : Vaga, 1974.
124 p. ; 17 cm. USSR 74-34364
CONTENTS: Poilsis.—Kareivis ieško motinos.—Traukiniai išeina iš pirmo kelio.—Kaktusai mėgsta pienà?—Rožių šerkšnas.—Sielos alkis.—Kultūrinė atvanga.—Žiedai.—Laiškai algebros vadovėlyje.—Viktutė.—Šviesos gimimas.—Iš vaikystės etiudų.
0.30rub
I. Title.
PG8721.B28S9 75-403790

Baltrūnas, A
Tolimi keliai. Apysaka. ₍2-ras pataisytas leidimas₎. Vilnius, "Vaga," 1973.
421 p. 21 cm. 1.02rub USSR 73-17187
I. Title.
PG8721.B28T6 1973 74-333372

Baltrūnas, A
Traukiniai išeina iš pirmo kelio / Aleksas Baltrūnas. — Vilnius : Vaga, 1975.
359 p. ; 21 cm. USSR 75-35262
CONTENTS: Tu mane šauki?—Pavasario srautas.—Albinutė—Konfliktas su dievu.—Mašenka—Baltoji kalija.—Mėlynieji lubinai.—Lietus.—Įtarimas.—Poilsis.—Kareivis ieško motinos.—Traukiniai išeina iš pirmo kelio.—Kaktusai mėgsta pieną?—Laiškai algebros vadovėlyje—Šviesos gimimas.—Rožių šerkšanas.—Sielos alkis.—Viktutė.—Vaikystės etiudai.
0.72rub
I. Title.
PG8721.B28A15 1975 76-528179

Baltrušaitienė, Irena.
Pietryčių Lietuvos hidrografija : upės / I. Baltrušaitienė, J. Jablonskis, M. Lasinskas. — Vilnius : Mintis, 1975.
141, ₍3₎ p., ₍2₎ fold. leaves : ill. ; 23 cm. USSR***
LTSR Mokslų akademija. Fizinių-techninių energetikos problemų institutas.
Summary in Russian and English.
Bibliography: p. 140-₍142₎
1.42rub
1. Hydrology—Lithuania. I. Jablonskis, Jonas, joint author. II. Lasinskas, Mykolas, joint author. III. Title.
GB747.L5B34 76-511677

Baltrušaitis, Jurgis, 1873-1944. Gornaía tropa. Lithuanian. 1973
see Baltrušaitis, Jurgis, 1873-1944. Žemės laiptai. Vilnius, "Vaga," 1973.

Baltrušaĭtis, Jurgis, 1873-1944.
Gornaía tropa; vtoraía kniga stikhov. Moskva, Skorpion, 1912. ₍Ann Arbor, Mich., Univ. Microfilms, 1972₎
167 p. 24 cm.
At head of title: ÍU. Baltrushaĭtis.
I. Title.
CaBVaU NUC74-43229

Baltrušaitis, Jurgis, 1873-1944.
Gornaía tropa; vtoraía kniga stikhov. Moskva, Skorpion, 1912.
181 p.
Microfilm. Tumba, Sweden, International Documentation Centre [1973] 4 sheets 9 x 12 cm.
I. Title.
WU NUC75-128942

Baltrušaitis, Jurgis, 1873-1944.
Žemės laiptai. Kalnų takas. ₍Eilerasciai₎. Vertė L. Broga. Vilnius, "Vaga," 1973.
278 p. port. 17 cm. 0.42rub USSR 73-37596
Translation of Zemnye stupeni and Gornaía tropa.
I. Broga, L. tr. II. Baltrušaitis, Jurgis, 1873-1944. Gornaía tropa. Lithuanian. 1973. III. Title. IV. Title: Kalnų takas.
PG8721.B3Z416 74-345214

Baltrušaitis, Jurgis, 1873-1944.
Zemnyía stupeni; ėlegii, píesni, poėmy. Moskva, Skorpion, 1911.
212 p.
Microfilm. Tumba, Sweden, International Documentation Centre [1973] 3 sheets 9 x 12 cm.
I. Title.
WU NUC75-128941

Baltrušaitis, Jurgis, 1903-
see Anamorfosen; spel met perspectief. Köln, DuMont Schauberg, c1975.

Baltrush, Michael Allen.
Speech bit rate reduction using HCM wave functions as the data base. ₍Storrs, Conn.₎ 1976.
₍3₎, xvi, 205 l. illus., photos., tables.
Thesis (Ph.D.)--University of Connecticut.
Bibliography: leaves 204-205.
1. Speech processing systems. 2. Automatic speech recognition. I. Title.
CTU NUC77-87440

Baltruszajtis, Grażyna
see Wiek XVIII ₍i. e. osiemnasty₎... Warszawa: Państwowy Instytut Wydawniczy, 1974.

Bal'ts, Aleksandr Fedorovich, b. 1841.
(Opisanie dieistvii Zapadnago otriada dieistvuiushchei armii, pod nachal'stvom general-ad"iutanta Gurko)
Описаніе дѣйствій Западнаго отряда дѣйствующей арміи, подъ начальствомъ генералъ-адъютанта Гурко съ 25 декабря 1877 года до Филиппопольскаго боя включительно / составлено Бальцемъ. — С.-Петербургъ : Въ Тип. Второго Отд-нія Собственной Е. И. В. канцеляріи, 1880.
288 p., ₍10₎ leaves of plates (5 fold.) : plans, col. map. ; 23 cm.
1. Russo-Turkish War, 1877-1878—Regimental histories—Russia.—2. Gvardeiskaia pekhotnaia diviziia. 2. Russia. Armiia. 2. Gvardeiskaia pekhotnaia diviziia. 3. Gurko, Iosif Vladimirovich, 1828-1901. I. Title.
DR573.3.B34 75-529363

Baltsan, Ben Zion
see
Baltsan, Ben-Zion.

Baltsan, Iosif L'vovich, 1923-
Lik mgnoven'ía; stikhi. [By] Baltsan Iosif L'vovich. [Kishinev] Kartía moldoveniaske, 1973.
360 p. illus.
Title page and text in Moldavian.
Russian title from colophon.
MH NUC75-128305

Baltsan, Iosif L'vovich, 1923-
Nochi razdum'ía; stikhi. [By] Baltsan Iosif L'vovich. [Kishinev] Kartía moldoveníaské, 1971.
130 p.
Title page and text in Moldavian.
Russian title from colophon.
MH NUC75-129146

Baltsan, Iosif L'vovich, 1923-
₍Nopts' de vege₎
Нопць де веге. Версурь. ₍Кишинэу₎, "Картя Молдовеняскэ," 1971.
131 p. 16 cm. 0.35rub USSR 71-49663
At head of title: Иосиф Балцан.
I. Title.
PC794.M69B274 73-306391

Baltsan, Iosif L'vovich, 1923- tr.
see Broniewski, Władysław, 1897-1962. Poeziĭ shi poeme. 1971.

Baltsan, Iosif L'vovich, 1923-
see Storozhevye ogni. [Kishinev] Kartía moldoveníaske [1970]

Baltschieder, Switzerland
see Geschichte und Chronik von Baltschieder. (Glis, Paul Heldner, 1971)

Baltų ir slavų kalbų ryšiai. ⌈Atsak. redaktorius: K. Morkūnas⌉. Vilnius, Mintis, 1968.
205 p. 27 cm. (Lietuvių kalbotyros klausimai, 10)
At head of title: Lituvos TSR Mokslų Akademija. Lituvių kalbos ir litertūros institutas.
Summaries in German and Russian.
Includes bibliographical references.
1. Baltic languages—Addresses, essays, lectures. 2. Baltic-Slavic linguistic unity—Addresses, essays, lectures. 3. Slavic languages—Addresses, essays, lectures. I. Morkūnas, Kazys, 1929- ed. II. Lituvos TSR Mokslų akademija, Vilna. Lietuvių kalbos ir literatūros institutas. III. Series.
PG8501.L5 no. 10 74-232134
[PG8002]

Baltų kalbų veiksmažodžio tyrinėjimai. ⌈Red. kolegija: A. Sabaliauskas (ats. redaktorius)⌉ Vilnius, "Mintis," 1973.
262 p. 27 cm. (Lietuvių kalbotyros klausimai, 14) 1.49rub
USSR 73-13070
At head of title: Lietuvos TSR Mokslų akademija. Lietuvių kalbos ir literatūros institutas.
Title also in Russian: Исследования по балтийскому глаголу.
"VII Tarptautiniam slavistų suvažiavimui."
English, German, Latvian, Lithuanian, or Russian.
Summaries in English, Lithuanian, or Russian.
Includes bibliographical references.
1. Baltic languages—Verb—Addresses, essays, lectures. I. Sabaliauskas, Algirdas, ed. II. Lietuvos TSR Mokslų akademija, Vilna. Lietuvių kalbos ir literatūros institutas. III. International Congress of Slavists, 7th, Warsaw, 1973. IV. Title: Issledovanii͡a po baltiĭskomu glagolu. V. Series: Lietuvių kalbotyros klausimai, 14.
PG8501.L5 no. 14 74-318910
[PG8061]

Baltun, Petr Kazimirovich
see Tomskiĭ, Nikolaĭ Vasil'evich, 1900-
Nikolaĭ Vasil'evich Tomskiĭ. Moskva, "Izobrazitel'noe iskusstvo", 1974.

Baltus, Bernd.
Bedingungen visuellen Verhaltens in pädagogischer Kommunikation : eine experimentelle Studie / Bernd Baltus. — Hamburg : H. Lüdke, c1976.
158 p. : graphs ; 21 cm. — (Geistes- und sozialwissenschaftliche Dissertationen ; 39) GFR***
Bibliography: p. 156-158.
ISBN 3-920588-42-8
1. Interaction analysis in education. 2. Teacher-student relationships. I. Title.
LB1033.B35 76-485601
76 MARC

Baltus, Dale Frank, 1937-
Kentucky Association of School Administrators (1949-1971) : the accommodation of an organization to a changing society. ⌈Bloomington, Ind.⌉ 1972.
1 v.
Thesis (Ed. D.)—Indiana University.
Vita.
InU NUC73-123890

Baltus, Jacques, 1690-1760. Annales de Baltus. 1974.
in François, Jean, 1722-1791. Histoire de Metz. Paris, Éditions du Palais royal, ⌈1974⌉

Baltus, Rita K
Personal psychology for life and work / Rita K. Baltus. -- New York : McGraw-Hill Book Co., c1976.
iv, 284 p. : ill. ; 24 cm.
Includes bibliographies.
1. Psychology. I. Title.
DCU NUC77-85507

Baltušis, Juozas, 1909-
Abišalė : apsakymai / Juozas Baltušis. — Vilnius : Vaga, 1974.
325 p. ; 21 cm. USSR 74-24272
CONTENTS: Cukriniai runkeliai. — Aš jau ne piemenė. — Kurie išeina.—Savaitė prasideda gerai.—Posūkis iš vieškelio.—Taip praėjo vasara.—Nežvyruotu vieškeliu.—Partizanas Daura.—Baltieji dobiliukai.—Tylos sekundės.—Abišalė.—Valiusei reikia Alekso.—Paskutinis tylus džiaugsmas.—Ko nepasakė Laukys.—Tolimas aidas.—Praėjo mergina.—Gėlės.
0.72rub
I. Title.
PG8721.B32A64 75-565246

Baltušis, Juozas, 1909-
Gieda gaideliai : dramos ir feljetonai / Juozas Baltušis. — Vilnius : Vaga, 1975.
403 p. ; 21 cm. USSR 75-28827
1.17rub
I. Title.
PG8721.B32G5 76-526939

Baltušis, Juozas, 1909-
Kas dainon nesudita. Vilnius, Valstybine Grozines Literaturos Leidykla, 1959.
93 p. illus. 17 cm.
1. Lithuania. 2. Lithuanian collection. I. Title.
OKentU NUC76-62496

Baltušis, Juozas, 1909-
Nežvyruotu vieškeliu. Apsakymų rinktinė. Vilnius, "Vaga," 1971.
451 p. 17 cm. 0.65rub USSR 71-45604
I. Title.
PG8721.B32N4 74-326083

Baltušis, Juozas, 1909-
Prodannye gody; roman v novellakh. Iuozas Baltushis. [khud. K. Skromanas] per. s litovskogo K. Kela i Z. Fedorova. Vil'nius, Vaga, 1974.
712 p. ill. 21 cm.
Translation of Parduotos vasaros.
MH NUC76-21085

Baltušis, Juozas, 1909-
Su kuo valgyta druska / Juozas Baltušis. — Vilnius : Vaga, 1973-
v. : ill. ; 21 cm. USSR 73-33526
CONTENTS: 1. Saulėta vaikystė.
0.82rub (v. 1)
I. Title.
PG8721.B32S8 75-567155

Baltušis, Juozas, 1909-
⌈Su kuo valgyta druska. Russian⌉
Пуд соли / Юозас Балтушис ; авторизованный перевод с литовского В. Чепайтиса. — Москва : Сов. писатель, 1976-
v. : ill. ; 21 cm. USSR***
CONTENTS: 1. Солнечное детство.
0.63rub (v. 1)
I. Title.
Title romanized: Pud soli.
PG8721.B32S817 77-514485

Baltušis, Juozas, 1909-
see Emigranto dalia ... Vilnius : Vaga, 1973.

Baltusnikas, Zenonas.
Kaunas / Zenonas Baltušnikas ; ⌈translated by M. Ginsburgas ; edited by A. Medonis and V. Grodzenskis⌉. — Vilnius : Gintaras, 1973.
40 p. : ill. (some col.) : 20 cm. USSR***
0.32rub
1. Kaunas.
DK651.K125B3513 914.7'5 75-500140
MARC

Baltušnikas, Zenonas.
Kaunas. ⌈By⌉ Zenonas Baltušnikas. ⌈Per. s litovskogo: R. Shturo⌉ Vil'nius, Mintis, 1973.
30 p. chiefly illus.
1. Kaunas—Descr.
MH NUC76-74355

Baltušnikas, Zenonas.
⌈Kaunas. Russian⌉
Каунас / Зенонас Балтушникас ; ⌈пер. с литов.⌉. — Изд. 2-е, испр. — Вильнюс : Минтис, 1974.
63 p. : ill. ; 20 cm. USSR 75
0.32rub
1. Kaunas.
DK651.K125B3517 1974 75-545978

Baltvilks, Jānis.
Putnu gredzenošana / J. Baltvilks. — Riga : Zinatne, 1974.
33 p. : ill. ; 20 cm. USSR***
At head of title: Latvijas PSR Zinātņu akadēmija. Bioloģijas institūts.
0.07rub
1. Bird-banding—Latvia. I. Title.
QL677.5.B32 76-510055

Balty, Janine, ed.
see Apamée de Syrie ... Bruxelles, Centre belge de recherches archéologiques à Apamée de Syrie, 1969.

Balty, Janine, ed.
see Colloque Apamée de Syrie, Brussels, 1972. Apamée de Syrie ... Bruxelles, Centre belge de recherches archéologiques à Apamée de Syrie, 1972.

Balty, Jean Charles, joint author
see Napoleone-Lemaire, Jacqueline. L'église a atrium de la grande colonnade. Bruxelles, Centre Belge de recherches archéologiques a Apamée de Syrie, 1969.

Baltz, Claude.
Essai sur le capital idéologique / Claude Baltz. — Lille : Atelier Reproduction des thèses, Université Lille III ; Paris : diffusion, H. Champion, 1976.
2 v. (x, ix, 825 p.) : ill. ; 24 cm. F***
Thesis—Paris VIII.
Bibliography: p. 801-825.
ISBN 2-252-01690-6 : 80.00F
1. Economics. 2. Economic policy. 3. Ideology. 4. Linguistics. 5. System analysis. I. Title.
HB199.B314 330 76-486672
77 MARC

Baltz, Lewis, 1945-
Lewis Baltz : The Corcoran Gallery of Art, Washington, D.C., June 19-September 12, 1976. — Washington : The Gallery, 1976.
⌈21⌉ p. : chiefly ill. ; 21 cm. — (The Nation's Capital in photographs, 1976)
Bibliography: p. ⌈21⌉
1. Photography, Artistic—Exhibitions. 2. Washington, D.C.—Description—Views. I. Corcoran Gallery of Art, Washington, D.C. II. Series.
TR647.B34 1976 779'.9'9753 76-19239
76 MARC

Baltz, Shirley V
The quays of the city : an account of the bustling eighteenth century port of Annapolis / by Shirley V. Baltz. — Annapolis, Md. : Liberty Tree, ⌈1975⌉
viii, 63 p. : maps ; 28 cm.
Includes bibliographical references.
1. Annapolis—History—Colonial period, ca. 1600-1775. 2. Annapolis—Harbor. I. Title.
F189.A6B34 975.2'56'02 75-317823
75 MARC

Baltzan, B
see
Baltan, Ben-Zion.

Baltzan, P
Abbreviations used in medical literature, collected by P. Baltzan. ⌈Tel-Aviv⌉ Israel Medical Association ⌈1972?⌉
56 p. 12 cm. IL1.00
On cover: נוטריקון רפואי
Introd. also in Hebrew.
1. Medicine—Abbreviations. I. Title.
R121.B24 610'.1'48 72-950522
MARC

Baltzar, Veijo.
Mari. Helsinki, Tammi, 1973.
158 (1) p. 21 cm. Fmk21.00 Fi 73
I. Title.
PH355.B3M3 74-331032
ISBN 951-30-2449-0; 951-30-2448-2 (pbk.)

Baltzarek, Franz.
Die Geschichte der Wiener Börse. Öffentl. Finanzen u. privates Kapital im Spiegel einer österr. Wirtschaftsinstitution. ⌈Mit Tab.⌉ Wien, Verl. d. Österr. Akad. d. Wiss., 1973.
173 p. tables. 24 cm. (Österreichische Akademie der Wissen- Sozial- und Stadtgeschichte, 1) S240.00 Au 74-1/2-64
Bibliography: p. 163-169.
1. Vienna. Börse. I. Title. II. Series: Akademie der Wissenschaften, Vienna. Kommission für Wirtschafts-, Sozial- und Stadtgeschichte. Veröffentlichungen, 1.
HG4592.B34 74-304816
ISBN 3-7001-0033-7

Baltzarek, Franz.
Die Städte Vorarlbergs. Redigiert von Franz Baltzarek und Johanne Pradel, unter Mitarbeit von Roman Sandgruber. Wien, In Kommission bei Verlag Brüder Hollinek, 1973.
137 p. illus. (Österreichische Akademie der Wissenschaften. Kommission für Wirtschafts-, Sozial- und Stadtgeschichte. Osterreichisches Städtebuch, 3)
1. Cities and towns—Vorarlberg, Aus. I. Pradel, Johanne, ed. II. Title.
MH NUC75-19666

Baltzarek, Franz.
Wirtschaft und Gesellschaft der Wiener Stadterweiterung / von Franz Baltzarek, Alfred Hoffmann, Hannes Stekl. -- Wiesbaden : F. Steiner, 1975.
xii, 432 p., [13] leaves of plates : ill., plans (1 col., in pocket) ; 24 cm. (Die Wiener Ringstrasse, ; Bd. 5)
Bibliography: p. 404-415.
I. Hoffmann, Alfred, 1937- II. Stekl, Hannes, 1944- III. Title. IV. Series.
RPB NUC77-89766

Baltzarek, Franz
see Wien an der Schwelle der Neuzeit ...
Wien : Wiener Stadt- u. Landesarchiv (MA 8), 1974.

Baltzell, Edward Digby, 1915-
Philadelphia gentlemen; the making of a national upper class. With a new afterword by the author. Chicago, Quadrangle Books [1971]
466 p. (Quadrangle paperbacks, QP 236)
"First Quadrangle paperback edition."
1. Philadelphia—Soc. life & cust. 2. Class distinction—Case studies. I. Title.
NcU NUC73-34740

Baltzer, Annie.
Fremmedsprogspsykologi / Annie Baltzer. — [København, K] : Københavns Universitet, Institut for Anvendt og Matematisk Lingvistik, [eksp., Nørre Voldgade 96], 1974.
173 p. ; 30 cm. D 75-7
Summary in English.
Bibliography: p. 152-173.
free
1. Languages—Psychology. 2. Language and languages—Study and teaching—Psychological aspects. I. Title.
[DNLM: 1. Language. 2. Psycholinguistics. BF455 B197f 1974]
[P37.B3 1974] 75-594822
Shared Cataloging with DNLM

Baltzer, Christiane.
Trois communes du nord de l'Alsace, Drusenheim, Herrlisheim, Offendorf : leur évolution socio-économique : un second Fos en Alsace? / Par Christiane Baltzer. — Strasbourg : Institut national de recherche et de documentation pédagogiques, CRDP, 1973.
92 p., [17] leaves of plates : ill., maps ; 30 cm. — (Annales du Centre régional de recherche et de documentation pédagogiques de Strasbourg) F***
"Mémoire de maîtrise présenté en 1972 à l'Institut de géographie, Université Louis Pasteur, Strasbourg."
Bibliography: p. 83-86.
1. Drusenheim, France—Economic conditions. 2. Herrlisheim, France—Economic conditions. 3. Offendorf, France—Economic conditions. I. Title. II. Title: Drusenheim, Herrlisheim, Offendorf.
HC278.D7B34 75-517927
76 MARC

Baltzer, Claude Grynblat-
see
Grynblat-Baltzer, Claude.

Baltzer, Eduard, 1814-1887.
Pythagoras, der Weise von Samos: e. Lebensbild/ nach d. neuesten Forschungen bearb. von Eduard Baltzer. — Unveränd. Neudr. d. Ausg. von 1868. — Walluf (bei Wiesbaden) : Sändig, 1973.
viii, 180 p. : map; 21 cm. DM34.00 GFR 74-A6
Originally published by F. Förstemann, Nordhausen.
Includes bibliographical references.
1. Pythagoras. I. Title.
B243.B3 1973 74-350223

Baltzer, Friedrich, 1884-
see Czihak, G. The sea urchin embryo—biochemistry and morphogenesis. Berlin, Springer-Verlag, 1975.

Baltzer, Fritz.
Theodor Boveri, life and work of a great biologist, 1862-1915. Berkeley, Univ. of California Press, 1967.
165 p. illus., ports.
Translation of Theodor Boveri; Leben und Werk eines grossen Biologen.
1. Biology—Hist. 2. Boveri, Theodor, 1862-1915.
OCU-M NUC76-39176

Baltzer, Hans, 1900- illus.
see David, Kurt, 1924- Black Wolf of the steppes. Boston, Houghton Mifflin, 1972 [c1971]

Baltzer, Hans, 1900- illus.
see Pludra, Benno. Die Reise nach Sundevit. Stuttgart, Thienemann (1972).

Baltzer, Hans, 1900- illus.
see The Sandalwood box; folk tales from Tadzhikistan. Chalfont St. Giles, Sadler, 1972.

Baltzer, Hans, 1900- illus.
see Strittmatter, Erwin, 1912- Pony Pedro. [11. Aufl.] Berlin, Kinderbuchverlag [1970?]

Baltzer, Klaus, 1928-
Die Biographie der Propheten / Klaus Baltzer. — Neukirchen-Vluyn : Neukirchener Verlag, c1975.
220 p. ; 21 cm. GFR76-A
Bibliography: p. [199]-208.
Includes indexes.
ISBN 3-7887-0436-5 : DM34.00
1. Bible. O.T. Prophets—Criticism, interpretation, etc. 2. Bible. O.T. Historical books—Criticism, interpretation, etc. I. Title.
BS1505.2.B34 224'.06 76-458201
76 MARC

Baltzer, Otto, 1863-
Beiträge zur Geschichte des christologischen Dogmas im 11. [elften] und 12. [zwölften] Jahrhundert/ Otto Baltzer. — Neudr. d. Ausg. Leipzig 1898. — Aalen, Scientia-Verlag, 1972.
78 p.; 21 cm. DM18.00 GFR 73-A22
Reprint of the ed. published by Deichert, Leipzig, in series: Studien zur Geschichte der Theologie und der Kirche, Bd. 3, Heft 1.
1. Jesus Christ—History of doctrines—Middle Ages. I. Title. II. Series: Studien zur Geschichte der Theologie und der Kirche, Bd. 3, Heft 1.
BT198.B2 1972 73-359606
ISBN 3-511-04227-5

Baltzer, Otto, 1863-
Die Sentenzen des Petrus Lombardus; ihre Quellen und ihre dogmengeschichtliche Bedeutung. Aalen, Scientia, 1972.
164 p. 21 cm. (Studien zur Geschichte der Theologie und der Kirche, Bd. 8, Heft 3)
"Neudruck der Ausgabe Leipzig 1902."
1. Petrus Lombardus, Bp. of Paris, 12th century. Sententiarum libri IV. I. Title. II. Series.
NjR NUC73-123903

Baltzer, Ralf Alexander, 1941-
Autobiographie zwischen Belletristik und Sachbuch zur Wirklichkeitserfassung von Selbstdarstellungen. [n.p.] 1972.
252 p.
Thesis (Ph.D.)—New York University.
1. Dissertations, Academic—N.Y.U.—1972. I. Title.
NNU NUC74-131295

Baltzer, Rebecca Anne, 1940-
Notation, rhythm and style in the two-Notre Dame clausula. [n.p.] 1974.
2 v. (viii, 546 p.) music.
Thesis—Boston University.
Bibliography: v. 2, p. 534-545.
1. Musical notation. 2. Cadence (Music) I. Title.
MBU NUC76-21144

Baltzo, C. Howard, 1913- joint author.
see Baker, Ralph C The northern fur seal. Washington, 1963.

Bălu, Ion.
G. Călinescu : 1899-1965 : biobibliografie / Ion Bălu. — București : Editura științifică și enciclopedică, 1975.
xxix, 680 p., [8] leaves of plates : ill., ports. ; 21 cm. R 76-924
Includes index.
lei 36.00
1. Călinescu, George, 1899-1965—Bibliography.
Z8140.64.B34 76-517908
[PC839.C25]

Bălu, Ion.
Marin Preda / Ion Bălu ; [coperta colecției, Teodor Bogoi ; portret, Radu Duma]. — [București] : "Albatros", 1976.
192 p. ; 17 cm. — (Monografii) R77-566
Bibliography: p. 186-[189]
lei5.50
1. Preda, Marin—Criticism and interpretation.
PC840.26.R4Z58 77-551404
•77 MARC

Balu, K., joint author
see Satya Brat, 1942- Syntheses of phyllitic minerals; their utilisation in radioactive waste treatment. Bombay, Bhabha Atomic Research Centre, 1970-

Balu Lal Achha
see
Achha, Balu Lal, 1950-

Balu und seine Gefährten : Märchen d. Südsee / mit Ill. von Günther Lawrenz ; [Red., Ulf Diederichs]. — 1. Aufl. — Düsseldorf ; Köln : Diederichs, 1974.
168 p. : ill. ; 20 cm. — (Diederichs Löwenbücher ; 5) GFR 74-A
ISBN 3-424-00490-1 : DM9.80
1. Tales, Oceanian.
PZ34.B22 74-356748

Baluarte, Amparo.
Cáliz de amor / Amparo Baluarte. — Lima : [Baluarte], 1975.
138 p. : ill. ; 21 cm.
I. Title.
PQ8497.B22C3 861 76-484705
76 MARC

Baluba et Lulua; une ethnie à la recherche d'un nouvel équilibre. Nendeln, Kraus Reprint, 1970.
106 p. (Collection "Études congolaises," no. 2)
OClW NUC74-137768

Balūc, Muḥammad Akbar.
(Balūc qaum apnī tārīkh ke ā'īnah meṉ)
بلوچ قوم اپنی تاریخ کے آئینہ میں. تالیف محمد اکبر نوتی زئی بلوچ. [کراچی، انٹرنیشنل پریس] 1973.
272 p. 19 cm. Rs6.50
Cover title: قوم بلوچ تاریخ کے آئینے میں
In Urdu.
1. Baluchis—History. 2. Baluchistan—History. I. Title. II. Title: Qaum-i Balūc tārīkh ke ā'īne meṉ.
DS380.B3B27 74-930002

Balūc, Muḥammad Ḥusain 'Anqā, 1907-
(Inqilābī Balūcī tārīkh)
انقلابی بلوچی تاریخ؛ مختلف زمانوں میں مختلف ناموں سے حکومت، ۲۶۰۰ قبل مسیح سے ۱۹۵۶ بعد مسیح تک. مؤلف میر محمد حسین عنقا بلوچ. مچھ، 1974.
8, 5-301 p. illus., maps. 21 cm. Rs15.00
Cover title: بلوچ قوم کے دور قدیم کی تاریخ
In Urdu.
Includes bibliographical references.
1. Baluchis. 2. Baluchistan—History. I. Title. II. Title: Balūc qaum ke daur-i qadīm kī tārīkh.
DS380.B3B29 74-930286

Balucani, Lanfranco.
Profili sistematici dell'ordinamento scolastico / Lanfranco Balucani. — Roma : Bulzoni, c1975.
178 p. : 24 cm. It 76-Feb
Bibliography : p. [169]-174.
L4500
1. School management and organization—Italy. 2. Education and state—Italy. I. Title.
LB2917.B26 76-507270

Baluch, Jacek.
Literatura czeska, 1918-1968 r.; wykłady. [Wyd. 1] Kraków, Nakł. Uniw. Jagiellońskiego, 1973.
185 p. (Wydawnictwa [jubileuszowe] Uniwersytetu Jagiellońskiego, 186)
At head of title: Uniwersytet Jagielloński. Katedra Filologii Słowiańskiej.
Limited ed., 300 cop.
1. Czech literature—20th cent.
MH NUC76-74138

Baluch, Jacek
see Halas, František, 1901-1949. Wybór poezji. Wrocław, Zakł. Narod. im. Ossolinskich, 1975.

Baluch, Mir Ahmad Yar Khan
see
Ahmad Yar Khan, 1904-

Baluch, Muhammad Sardar Khan.
پلنگ و بلوچ. [لیکوک] میر محمد سردار خان بلوچ. کوئٹہ، بلوچی اکیڈمی [1970]
154 p. 23 cm. Rs3.50
In Baluchi.
Includes bibliographical references.
1. Baluchis. 2. Baluchistan—History. I. Title.
Title romanized: Pulang va Balūch.
DS485.B2B33 74-932[illegible]

Baluch, Stephen James.
Estimates of genetic variance in Coronilla varia L. cv. 'Chemung'. [n.p.] 1973.
34 l.
Thesis (Ph.D.)—Pennsylvania State University.
I. Title.
PSt NUC74-131291

Baluchistan.
Baluchistan district gazetteer series. Bombay, Printed at the Bombay Education Society's Press, 1906-08.
9 v. in 18. illus.
Imprint varies.
Vol. 9: index and Appendix to v. 1-8.
Bibliography at end of each part.
Microfiche. Tumba, Sweden, International Documentation Centre, 1964 ? 91 sheets in 2 boxes. 9 x 12 cm.
1. Baluchistan—Gazetteers.
MiU NUC76-71888

Baluchistan.
Baluchistan district gazetteer series, B. Volume: States, village statistics. Compiled by Jamiat Rai, superintendent of census operations. Allahabad, Pioneer Press, 1922.
319 p. 22 cm.
CONTENTS: Sarawan.—Jhallawan.—Makran.—Kharan.
1. Baluchistan—Statistics. 2. Villages—Baluchistan—Statistics. I. Rai, Jamiat. II. Title.
LC copy replaced by microfilm
[HA1728.B24B34 1922] 74-206167
Microfilm 46143 HA

Baluchistan.
Speech by Governor delivered at the time of releasing the budget and the annual development programme. 1971/72-
[Karachi?]
v. 25 cm.
1. Budget—Baluchistan. 2. Baluchistan—Economic policy. 3. Baluchistan—Social policy. I. Title.
HJ67.5.Z5B3542 354'.549'1500722 78-939938
MARC-S

Baluchistan.
Statistical analysis of the tribes of Bāluchistān, 1921 / by Diwan Bahadur Diwan Jamiat Rai, late Superintendent of Census Operations. — [2d ed.]. — [s.l. : s.n.], 1926 (Allahabad : Pioneer Press)
83 p. ; 42 cm.
1. Ethnology—Pakistan—Baluchistan (Province) I. Rai, Jamiat. II. Title.
GN635.P27B34 1926 572.9'549'15 76-362888
76 MARC

Baluchistan.
Supplementary budget statement.
[Quetta]
v. 28 cm.
1. Budget—Baluchistan.
HJ67.5.Z5B3543a 354'.549'1500722 74-647648
MARC-S

Baluchistan.
Temporary establishment provided in the budget.
[Quetta]
v. 28 cm. annual.
1. Baluchistan, Pakistan (Province)—Appropriations and expenditures—Periodicals. I. Title.
HJ67.5.Z5B356 76-939916
rev

Baluchistan. Bureau of Statistics.
Development statistics of Baluchistan Province. Quetta, Govt. of Baluchistan, Planning and Development Dept., Bureau of Statistics.
v. 31 cm.
1. Baluchistan—Statistics. I. Title.
HA1730.5.Z9B343a 315.49'15 75-930189
MARC-S

Baluchistan. Finance Dept.
Annual development programme of Baluchistan.
[Quetta]
v. 21 x 34 cm.
1. Baluchistan—Appropriations and expenditures. 2. Baluchistan—Economic policy. I. Title.
HJ67.5.Z5B3512 338.9549'15 72-939567

Baluchistan. Finance Dept.
Speech by Finance Minister, Government of Baluchistan delivered at the time of announcing the budget proposals and the annual development programme.
[Quetta, Govt. of Baluchistan, Finance Dept.]
v. 27 cm.
1. Budget—Baluchistan. I. Title.
HJ67.5.Z5B36a 354'.549'1500722 75-644595
MARC-S

Baluchistan. Finance Dept.
White paper on the budget, 1973-74. [Quetta, 1973]
86 p. 27 cm.
Cover title.
1. Budget—Baluchistan. I. Title.
HJ67.5.Z5B36 1973 354'.549'1500722 74-191284
MARC

Baluchistan. Intelligence Bureau.
Notes on the tribes of Afghan descent in Baluchistan, compiled by the Baluchistan Intelligence Bureau, Quetta, 1937. New Delhi, Printed by the Manager, Govt. of India Press, 1938.
iv, 56 p. map. (fold. col. in pocket) 36 cm.
"Ref. no. B-41950."
1. Ethnology—Baluchistan. 2. Pushtuns. I. Title.
GN635.P27B36 1938 572.9'549'15 77-356951
77 MARC

Baluda, Viktor Petrovich
see Gemorragicheskiĭ sindrom pri ostroĭ luchevoĭ bolezni. 1969.

Baluev, Boris Petrovich.
(Lenin polemiziruet s burzhuaznoĭ pressoĭ)
Ленин полемизирует с буржуазной прессой / Б. П. Балуев. — Москва : Политиздат, 1977.
252 p. ; 20 cm. USSR***
Includes bibliographical references.
0.99rub
1. Lenin, Vladimir Il'ich, 1870-1924. 2. Press. 3. Journalism. I. Title.
DK254.L46B34 77-514383

Baluev, Boris Petrovich
see Sofsialisticheskoe sorevnovanie i pechat'. 1975.

Baluev, P. N., ed.
see Issledovaniia po voprosam istorii KPSS i partiinogo stroitel'stva. [Novosibirsk, 1970-

Baluja, Kasturi Lal, 1945-
Excitation and ionization of heliums by electron impact using distorted-wave theory. Tallahassee, Fla., 1973.
xi, 210 l.
Thesis (Ph. D.)—Florida State University.
Bibliography: leaves 204-209.
Vita.
1. Collisions (Nuclear physics) 2. Helium ions. 3. Wave functions. I. Title.
FTaSU NUC76-39174

Bałuk, Wacław.
Lower Tortonian gastropods from Korytnica, Poland = Ślimaki Dolnotortońskie z Korytnicy / by Wacław Bałuk. — Warszawa : Państwowe Wydawn. Naukowe, 1975-
v. : ill., maps ; 30 cm. — (Paleontologia Polonica ; no. 32)
Bibliography: v. 1, p. [181]-186.
1. Gasteropoda, Fossil. 2. Paleontology—Miocene. 3. Paleontology—Poland—Korytnica (Kielce) I. Title. II. Title: Ślimaki Dolnotortońskie z Korytnicy. III. Series.
QE808.B34 75-327354
76 MARC

Balukhatyĭ, Sergeĭ Dmitrievich, 1893-1945.
Chekhov - dramaturg. Leningrad, Gosudarstvennoe izdatel'stvo "Khudozhestvennaia literatura", 1936. [Ann Arbor, Mich., University Microfilms, 1970]
318, [2] p. front. (port.) plates, facsims. 18 x 14 cm.
At head of title: S. Balukhatyĭ.
Errata slip mounted on p. 318.
Bibliographical references included in "Primechaniia" (p. 289-[317])
Xerox copy.
1. Chekhov, Anton Pavlovich, 1860-1904. I. Title.
CLSU NUC76-4334

Balukhatyĭ, Sergeĭ Dmitrievich, 1893-1945.
Problemy dramaturgiecheskogo analiza: Chekhov. Leningrad, "Academia", 1927. [Ann Arbor, University Microfilms, Inc., 1961]
184 p. 20 cm. (Gosudarstvennyĭ institut istorii iskusstv. Voprosy poetiki, vyp. 9)
Xerox copy.
Bibliographical references included in "Primechaniia": p. 169-[184]
1. Chekhov, Anton Pavlovich, 1860-1904.
RPB MiU NRU NUC74-21969

Balukhatyĭ, Sergeĭ Dmitrievich, 1893-1945.
Russkie pisateli o literature (xvii-xx vv.) otryvki iz pisem, dnevnikov, stateĭ, zapisnykh knizhek, khudozhestvennykh proizvedeniĭ... pod obshcheĭ redaktsieĭ S. Balukhatogo. Leningrad, Sovetskiĭ pisatel', 1939.
2 v. 22 cm.
Vols. 1-2 have also special t.p. "Organizatsiia i redaktura vsego truda... pri neposredstvennom uchastii A. G. Ostrovskogo." v. 1, p. VIII.
Includes bibliographies.
Xerographic reproduction. Ann Arbor, Mich., University Microfilms, 1967. 21 cm.
1. Criticism. 2. Authorship. 3. Literature—Esthetics. 4. Russian literature (Selections: Extracts, etc.) I. Ostrovskiĭ, Arseniĭ Georgievich, 1897- ed. II. Title.
MeB NUC74-62938

Balukhatyĭ, Sergeĭ Dmitrievich, 1893-1945.
Spravochnik po Tolstomu; daty zhizni i tvorchestva, khronologiia i sistematika sochineniĭ, bibliografiia. Sostavili S. Balukhatyĭ i O. Pisemskaia. Moskva, Gos. izd-vo, 1928. [Ann Arbor, Mich., 1961]
123 p. (on double leaves)
Photocopy (positive) made by University Microfilms.
1. Tolstoĭ, Lev Nikolaevich, graf, 1828-1910. I. Pisemskaia, O.
MiU CU-S NUC74-62928

Balukhatyĭ, Sergeĭ Dmitrievich, 1893-1945.
Teoriia literatury; annotirovannaia bibliografiia. [Leningrad] Priboĭ, 1929-
[Ann Arbor, University Microfilms, inc. 1961-
v. 22 cm.
At head of title: Slovarno-bibliograficheskiĭ kabinet (SBIK) slovesnogo otdeleniia Gos. instituta istorii iskusstv.
Contents.—v. 1. Obshchie voprosy.—
1. Literature—Philosophy—Bibl.
RPB NUC76-17988

Balukhatyĭ, Sergeĭ Dmitrievich, 1893-1945
see Leningrad. Universitet. Trudy iubileinoi nauchnoi sessii. Leningrad, 1946.

Balukhatyĭ, Sergeĭ Dmitrievich, 1893-1945.
see Moderne Dramentheorie. Kronberg/Ts., Scriptor Verlag, 1975.

Balukhatyĭ, Sergeĭ Dmitrievich, 1893-1945
see Moscow. Moskovskiĭ khudozhestvennyĭ akademicheskiĭ teatr. Chaĭka v postanovke Moskovskogo khudozhestvennogo teatra. [Ann Arbor, Mich., 1962]

Balukhovs'kyĭ, Mykola Pylypovych.
(Novye geologicheskie metody v neftegazrazvedke).
Новые геологические методы в нефтегазразведке. Киев, "Наук. думка," 1972.
139 p. with diagrs. and maps, 2 l. of diagrs. 21 cm. 0.94rub
USSR 72-VKP
At head of title: Академия наук УССР. Институт геологических наук. Н. Ф. Балуховский.
Bibliography: p. 132-[136]
1. Geochemical prospecting. 2. Petroleum—Geology—Russia. 3. Gas, Natural—Geology—Russia. I. Title.
TN271.P4B33 73-330494

Balukhovs'kyĭ, Mykola Pylypovych
see Nauchno-tekhnicheskaia konferentsiia po razvitiiu proizvoditel'nykh sil Khar'kovskogo ėkonomicheskogo administrativnogo raĭona, Kharkov, 1958. Geologiia i poleznye iskopaemye Khar'kovskogo ėkononicheskogo raĭona. Kiev, Izd-vo Akademii nauk Ukrainskoĭ SSR, 1960.

Balukiewicz, Irena
see Barański, Rajmund. Pediatria. [Wyd. 2.] Warszawa, Państwowy Zakład Wydawn. Lekarskich, 1974.

Balukov, V. A., comp.
see Pervyĭ Sovet rabochikh deputatov. 1971.

Balūlah, ʻAlī ʻĪd.
(al-ʻAlāqah bayna al-muwāzanah al-ʻāmmah wa-al-muwāzanah al-istithmārīyah wa-al-khiṭṭah al-iqtiṣādīyah)
العلاقة بين الموازنة العامة والموازنـــة الاستثماريـــة والخطة الاقتصادية ، بقلم على عيد بلوله . [الخرطوم] معهد الادارة العامة ، 1969.
25 l. 28 cm. (بحوث دورية ، 20)
Includes bibliographical references.
1. Budget—Sudan. 2. Sudan—Economic policy. I. Title. II. Series: Maʻhad al-Idārah al-ʻĀmmah, Khartum. Buḥūth Dawrīyah, 20.
HJ2189.S84B33 74-214765

Balūlah, ʻAlī ʻĪd.
المشكلة الادارية والاكتفاء الذاتى فى السودان ، بقلم على عيد بلوله . [الخرطوم] معهد الادارة العامة ، 1967.
27, [2] l. 28 cm. (معهد الادارة العامة . بحوث دورية ، 21)
Bibliography: leaf [28]
1. Sudan—Politics and government—Addresses, essays, lectures. I. Title.
Title romanized: al-Mushkilah al-idārīyah wa-al-iktifāʼ al-dhātī fī al-Sūdān.
JQ3981.S82B33 75-549680

Balūlah, ʻAlī ʻĪd.
(al-Taʻlīm wa-al-tadrīb al-idārī fī al-Sūdān)
التعليم والتدريب الادارى فى السودان ، اعداد على عيد بلولة . الخرطوم ، معهد الادارة العامة ، 1970.
59, [1] l. 28 cm. (بحوث دورية ، 33)
Bibliography: leaf [60]
1. Sudan—Politics and government. I. Title. II. Maʻhad al-Idārah al-ʻĀmmah, Khartum. Buḥūth dawrīyah, 33.
JQ3981.S82B34 74-228197

Balūlah, ʻAlī ʻĪd.
تمويل المنازل السكنية فى العاصمة المثلثة ، بقلم على عيد بلوله . الخرطوم ، معهد الادارة العامة ، 1967.
30, [3] l. 28 cm. (معهد الادارة العامة . بحوث دورية ، 22)
Bibliography: leaf [32]
1. Housing—Khartum—Finance. I. Title.
Title romanized: Tamwīl al-manāzil al-sakanīyah.
HD7378.S8B3 75-972420

Bālūlāla Acchā
see
Achha, Balu Lal, 1950-

Balunas, Leonard Charles.
A study of the relationship of acceptance of disability in self and presence of disability in others to subordination of physique in the social perceptions of men with physical disabilities. Buffalo, 1971.
77 l.
Thesis (Ph.D.)—State University of New York at Buffalo.
1. Physically handicapped—Psychological aspects. 2. Social perception. 3. Personality. I. Title.
NBuU NUC73-34731

Balusamy, N
Studies in Maṇimēkalai, by N. Balusamy. [1st ed.] Madurai, Āthirai Pathippakam; copies can be had of A. T. N. Nagalingam, 1965.
242 p. 19 cm. Rs10.00
Half t. p.: Maṇimēkalai.
"Thesis approved for the M. Litt. degree of the University of Madras."
Bibliography: p. [239]-242.
1. Cāttaṉār. Maṇimēkalai. I. Title. II. Title: Maṇimēkalai.
PL4758.9.C3M333 894'.811'11 70-916821
MARC

Baluschek, Hans, 1870-1935.
Hans Baluschek : 1870-1935 : Gemälde, Zeichnungen, Graphik : [Ausstellung] Staatliche Kunsthalle Karlsruhe 8. Juni bis 3. August 1975 : [Katalog]. — Karlsruhe : Staatliche Kunsthalle, 1975.
63 p., [28] leaves of plates : ill. ; 22 cm. GFR***
Cover title.
Includes bibliographical references.
1. Baluschek, Hans, 1870-1935. I. Karlsruhe. Staatliche Kunsthalle.
N6888.B3K37 75-518941
75 MARC

Baluss, Mary E 1945-
Integrated services for victims of crime : a county-based approach. -- Washington : National Association of Counties Research Foundation, 1975.
24 p. ; 28 cm.
Bibliography: p. 22-24.
1. Victims of crime. I. National Association of Counties. II. Title.
NIC NUC77-87626

Băluţă, Crişan.
see Pe poteci cu bănuţei de piatră ... Bucureşti, "Sport-Turism" 1976.

Baluti Katukandany le Ossambala, 1940-
Profil d'une romance : poèmes / Baluti Katukandany Le Ossambala. — Kinshasa : Édition Sivi, [1973?]
44 p. ; 19 cm.
I. Title.
PQ3989.2.B28P7 75-506733
75 MARC

Balutis, Alan P
Public administration and the legislative process / Alan P. Balutis, James J. Heaphey. — Beverly Hills : Sage Publications, c1974.
58 p. ; 22 cm. — (Sage professional papers in administrative and policy studies ; ser. no. 03-024)
Bibliography: p. 56-58.
ISBN 0-8039-0459-2 : $2.50
1. New York (State). Legislature—Officials and employees. I. Heaphey, James J., 1930- joint author. II. Title.
JK3471.B32 328.747'07'6 74-21613
76 MARC

Balutis, Alan P
The role of national legislatures in civilian control of the military in developing nations / by Alan P. Balutis. -- Buffalo : Council on International Studies, State University of New York at Buffalo, 1975.
39 leaves : charts ; 29 cm. -- (Special studies ; no. 64)
"Presented to the Conference 'Civilian Control of the Military: Myth and Reality in Developing Countries', sponsored by the State University of New York at Buffalo and the Inter-University Seminar on Armed Forces and Society, Buffalo, N.Y., Oct. 18-19, 1974."
Includes bibliographical references.
1. Civil supremacy over the military--Underdeveloped areas. 2. Underdeveloped areas--Politics. I. Title. II. Series: New York (State). State University, Buffalo. Council on International Studies. Special studies; no. 64.
ICarbS NUC77-86687

Balutis, Alan P.
see Legislative staffing ... [Beverly Hills] Sage Publications, c1975.

Balutis, Alan P.
see The Political pursestrings ... [Beverly Hills] Sage Publications, [1975]

Balvanović, Vladimir, 1930-1970.
Magija slike / Vladimir Balvanović. — Sarajevo : Sineast, 1975.
159, [4] p., [7] leaves of plates : ill. ; 19 x 21 cm. — (Biblioteka Prvi plan ; knj. 2) Yu***
"Sineast 28."
Bibliography: p. [163]
1. Moving-pictures. I. Title.
PN1994.B272 1975 75-971497

Balvanović, Vladimir, 1930-1970.
Razgovori sa Žakom. 〈Risto Trifković: "Još jedna generacija (Uz smrt Vladimira Balvanovića)"〉. Sarajevo, "Svjetlost," 1972.
104 p. 19 cm. 20.00Din Yu 72
I. Title.
PG1619.12.A55R3 1972 72-970576

A Bálvány; mai észt kisregények. Ford. Bereczki Gábor, Fehérvári Győző, Kálmán Béla, Rab Zsuzsa. Válogatta és az életrajzi jegyzeteket írta Fehérvári Győző. Budapest, Europa, 1973.
538 p.
1. Hungarian literature. 2. Estonian literature—Translations into Hungarian. I. Fehérvári, Győző.
CLU NUC76-74139

Balvé, Beba.
see Los Asalariados ... [Buenos Aires?] Centro de Investigaciones en Ciencias Sociales, [1975?]

Balverde, Alberto Bergeret
see
Bergeret Balverde, Alberto.

Balvert, J H
On-line datatransmissie / J. H. Balvert, G. Lansink. — Alphen aan den Rijn : Samsom, 1975.
201 p. : ill. ; 25 cm. — (Reeks automatische informatieverwerking) Ne 75-32
Bibliography: p. 183-184.
Includes index.
ISBN 90-14-02414-2 : fl 33.25
1. Data transmission systems. I. Lansink, G., joint author. II. Title.
TK5105.B34 75-548545

Balvert, J. H.
see Data base en accountant. Alphen aan den Rijn, Samsom, 1977.

Balvig, Flemming.
Tyveriet af en by : lov-og-orden tendenser i en dansk provinsby / Flemming Balvig. — [s.l. : s.n., 1976?]
98, 16, 20 leaves : ill. ; 30 cm. D***
Includes bibliographical references.
1. Crime and criminals—Horsens, Denmark—Public opinion. 2. Public opinion—Horsens, Denmark. I. Title.
HV7025.H67B34 76-479852
76 MARC

Balvín, Josef
see Prague. Mestské divadlo, Královské Vinohrady. Divadlo na Vinohradech 1907-1967 ... Prahá: Divadelní ústav, 1968.

Balwani, Hundraj, 1946-
('Ain hū'a ro'e veṭhī)
۽ هوءِ روئي ويٺي؛ ڇهن ڪهاڻين جو مجموعو. ليک هوندراج بلواڻي. احمدآباد، اپسرا پبليڪيشن [1968]
17 (i. e. 71) p. 18 cm. 1.50
In Sindhi.

I. Title.
PK2859.B32A7 71-903347

Balwani, Hundraj, 1946- comp.
(Hiku sona jo rupayo)
هڪ سون جو روپيو؛ لاڏن، لولين، ۽ گيتن جو نئون ڪتاب. گڏ ڪندڙ هوندراج بلواڻي. بڙودا، لوڪ ڪي. نوتاڻي؛ ملڻ جو هنڌ: شرميلا آفيس، احمدآباد، 1972.
38 p. 19 cm. (اپسرا بوڪ سيريز) Re1.00
In Sindhi.
Without the music.
1. Songs, Sindhi—Texts. I. Title.
M1808.B348H5 72-903511

Balwant Bhaneja
see
Bhaneja, Balwant, 1941-

Balwant G Kulkarni
see
Kulkarni, Balwant G 1907-

Balwant Singh
see also
Gujrati, Balwant Singh, 1912-
Singh, Balwant.
Singh, Balwant, 1903-

Balwant Singh, 1893-
The army of Maharaja Ranjit Singh. Lahore, Lahore Book Shop [1945?]
xii, 80 p. 19 cm.
Includes bibliographical references.
1. Sikhs—History. 2. Punjab—History, Military. I. Title.
DS485.P3B28 1945 72-208106
72[r75]rev MARC

Balwant Singh, 1908-
An easy approach to map reading (in Hindi) by Balwant Singh. [With] numerous exercises. 1st ed. Bareilly, Prakash Book Depot [1964]
v, 6, 176 p. illus., fold. map. 19 cm.
English or Hindi.
1. Maps, Military. I. Title.
UG470.B26 912'.014 S A 65-3544
rev PL 480: I-H-1566

Balwant Singh, 1926?-
आग की कलियां. ₍लेखक₎ बलवन्त सिंह. इलाहाबाद, उर्दू साहित्य प्रकाशन ₍1962₎
128 p. 20 cm.
In Hindi.
A novel.

I. Title.
Title transliterated: Āga kī kaliyāṃ.
PK2098.B3394A7 S A 63-3303 ‡
rev PL 480: I-H-845

Balwant Singh, 1926?-
औरत और आबशार. ₍लेखक₎ बलवन्त सिंह. ₍प्रथम संस्करण₎ इलाहाबाद, प्रगति प्रकाशन ₍1962₎
119 p. 19 cm.
In Hindi.
A novel.

I. Title.
Title transliterated: Aurata aura ābaśāra.
PK2098.B3394A9 S A 63-3396 ‡
rev PL 480: I-H-892

Balwant Singh, 1926?-
बासी फूल. ₍लेखक₎ बलवन्त सिंह. ₍1. संस्करण₎ दिल्ली, राजपाल ₍1967₎
188 p. 18 cm. **Rs4**
In Hindi.
A novel.

I. Title.
Title romanized: Bāsī phūla.
PK2098.B3394B3 S A 68-4718
rev PL 480: I-H-5062

Balwant Singh, 1926?-
चिलमन. ₍लेखक₎ बलवन्त सिंह. ₍1. संस्करण₎ दिल्ली, राजकमल प्रकाशन ₍1970₎
188 p. 19 cm. Rs6.00
In Hindi.
Short stories.

I. Title.
Title romanized: Cilamana.
PK2098.B3394C5 74-918015
rev

Balwant Singh, 1926?-
दो अकालगढ़. ₍उपन्यासकार₎ बलवन्त सिंह. ₍1. संस्करण₎ इलाहाबाद, लोकभारती प्रकाशन ₍1969₎
624 p. 19 cm.
In Hindi.

I. Title.
Title romanized: Do Akālagaṛha.
PK2098.B3394D6 76-908505
rev

Balwant Singh, 1926?-
काले कोस. ₍लेखक₎ बलवन्त सिंह. ₍1. संस्करण₎ बनारस, सरस्वती प्रेस ₍1957₎
392 p. 22 cm.
In Hindi.
A novel.

I. Title.
Title transliterated: Kāle kosa.
PK2098.B3394K3 S A 65-3221
rev

Balwant Singh, 1926?-
(Merī priya kahāniyāṁ)
मेरी प्रिय कहानियाँ. ₍लेखक₎ बलवन्तसिंह. ₍1. संस्करण₎ दिल्ली, राजपाल ₍1971₎
153 p. 19 cm. Rs5.00
In Hindi.

I. Title.
PK2098.B3394M4 73-921564

Balwant Singh, 1926?-
₍Pahalā patthara₎
पहला पत्थर और अन्य कहानियाँ. ₍लेखक₎ बलवन्त सिंह. ₍1. संस्करण₎ इलाहाबाद, लोकभारती प्रकाशन ₍1971₎
199 p. 19 cm. Rs6.50
In Hindi.
CONTENTS.—पहला पत्थर.—चकोरी.—मैं ज़रूर रोऊँगी.—पेपर वेट.—कुछ क्षण.—तीन बातें.—वेश्या.—तावीज़.—निहालचन्द.—अपरिचित.—बाबा मंहगासिंह.—सूरमासिंह.
I. Title.
PK2098.B3394P3 74-926441

Balwant Singh, 1926?-
राका की मंज़िल; ₍उपन्यास. लेखक₎ बलवन्त सिंह. ₍1. संस्करण₎ दिल्ली, राजकमल प्रकाशन ₍1971₎
322 p. 22 cm. Rs15.00
In Hindi.

I. Title.
Title romanized: Rākā kī mañzila.
PK2098.B3394R3 78-920150

Balwant Singh, 1926?-
(Rāta, cora aura cāṁda)
रात, चोर और चाँद / बलवन्तसिंह. — नई दिल्ली : प्रोग्रेसिव पब्लिशर्स, ₍19--₎
467 p. ; 19 cm.
In Hindi.
A novel.

I. Title.
PK2098.B3394R35 76-987092

Balwant Singh, 1926?-
सूना आसमान. ₍लेखक₎ बलवन्त सिंह. ₍1. संस्करण. इलाहाबाद, लोकभारती प्रकाशन, 1967₎
630 p. illus. 19 cm. **Rs14**
In Hindi.
A novel.

I. Title.
Title romanized: Sūnā āsamāna.
PK2098.B3394S9 S A 68-4168
rev PL 480: I-H-4952

Balwant Singh Anand
see
Anand, Balwant Singh.

Balwant Singh Johar
see
Johar, Balwant Singh, 1909-

Balwant Singh Nag
see
Nag, Balwant Singh, 1906-

Balwant Singh Noor
see
Noor, Balwant Singh, 1913-

Balwinder Singh, joint author
see Kahlon, A S 1923-
Marketing of groundnut... Ludhiana, Punjab Agricultural University [1968]

Baly, A D
Jordan and Israel, by A.D. Baly. ₍n.p., n.d.₎
iii, 128 l. 32 cm.
1. Jordan–Description. 2. Israel–Description. I. Title.
PPiPT NUC73-103097

Baly, Denis.
The geography of the Bible / Denis Baly. — New and revised ed. — Guildford : Lutterworth Press, 1974.
xv, 288 p., fold. leaf : ill., maps (some col.) ; 24 cm. GB75-11467
Bibliography: p. 257-262.
Includes indexes.
ISBN 0-7188-2151-3 : £4.00
1. Bible—Geography. I. Title.
BS630.B34 1974b 220.9′1 75-320061
75 MARC

Baly, Denis.
The geography of the Bible. New and rev. ed. New York, Harper & Row ₍1974₎
xv, 288 p. illus. 24 cm.
Bibliography: p. 257–262.
1. Bible—Geography. I. Title.
BS630.B34 1974 220.9′1 73–6340
ISBN 0-06-060371-2 MARC

Baly, Edward Charles Cyril, 1871-
Spectroscopy, by E.C.C. Baly ... 3d ed. London, New York ₍etc.₎ Longmans, Green and co., 1924-
v. illus., plates, diagrs. 22 cm. (Half-title: Textbooks of physical chemistry)
Ultra microfiche. Dayton, Ohio, National Cash Register, 1970. 2d title of 6. 10.5 x 14.8 cm. (PCMI library collection, 077-2)
1. Spectrum analysis.
KEmT NUC74-23484

Baly, Monica Eileen.
Nursing and social change / by Monica E. Baly. — London : Heinemann Medical, 1973.
x, 285 p. : ill. ; 22 cm. GB73-29999
Includes bibliographies and index.
ISBN 0-433-01160-2 : £2.75
1. Nurses and nursing—Social aspects—History. I. Title.
₍RT31.B34 1973₎ 362.1′04′25 75-594559
75 MARC

Baly, Monica Eileen.
Professional responsibility in the community health services / ₍by₎ Monica E. Baly. — Aylesbury : HM & M, 1975.
viii, 95 p. : ill. ; 20 cm. — (Topics in community health) GB76-24998
Bibliography: p. 90-91
Includes index.
ISBN 0-85602-040-0 : £1.50
1. Community health nursing. 2. Nursing ethics. 3. Nurse practitioners. I. Title.
₍DNLM: 1. Community health services. 2. Nurse practitioners. WY128 B198p 1975₎
₍RT98.B34₎ 362.1′4′023 76-677137
Shared Cataloging with DNLM 77 MARC

Baly, Steven J
Connecticut regional medical program. Health library services [by] Steven J. Baly. [n.p., 1972]
17, [13] l. map. 28 cm.
Bibliography: leaves 17.
1. Connecticut Regional Medical Program. 2. Medical libraries–Conn. I. Title.
CtY-M NUC76-37248

Balyeat, Ralph E
see Pearson, William W A model for the examination of existing and potential employment opportunities for residents of a model neighborhood area. Athens, 1970.

Balyeat, Ralph R., joint author.
see Burt, Marvin R. A comprehensive emergency services system for neglected and abused children. 1st ed. New York, Vantage Press, c1977.

Balygin, Ivan Efimovich.
(Ėlektricheskie svoĭstva tverdykh dielektrikov)
Электрические свойства твердых диэлектриков / И. Е. Балыгин. — Ленинград : Энергия, Ленингр. отд-ние, 1974.
189 p. : ill. ; 21 cm. USSR 74
Bibliography: p. 181–₍188₎
0.82rub
1. Dielectrics. I. Title.
QC585.B29 74-359515

Balyka, D A
Biblioteka v mynulomu; kul'turno-istorychnyĭ narys. Kyïv, Derzh. vyd-vo Ukraïny, 1925.
115 p. illus. 18 cm. (Naukovo-populîarna biblioteka knyhoznavstva, vyp. 3)
At head of title: Ukraïns'kyĭ instytut knyhoznavstva. D. Balyka.
Photocopy. Ann Arbor, University Microfilms, 1973. 19 cm.
1. Libraries–Hist. I. Title.
IU NUC75-138746

Balykov, V E
(Bukhgalterskiĭ uchet v sel'skokhozîaĭstvennykh predprîatiîakh pri polnom i vnutrikhozîaĭstvennom raschete)
Бухгалтерский учет в сельскохозяйственных предприятиях при полном и внутрихозяйственном расчете. Под ред. В. Е. Балыкова и Н. Г. Белова. Москва, Колос, 1972.
280 p. illus. 21 cm. (Учебники и учебные пособия для факультетов повышения квалификации)
At head of title: В. Е. Балыков ⌈и др.⌉
"Допущено ... в качестве учебного пособия для факультетов повышения квалификации высших сельскохозяйственных учебных заведений."
0.41rub
1. Agriculture—Russia—Accounting. I. Belov, Nikolaĭ Grigor'evich, ed. II. Title.
S567.B23 75–581405

Balyn and Balan
see Balin and Balan.

Balyogeshwar
see
Guru Maharaj Ji, 1957-

Balys, Jonas, 1909-
Lietuvių dainos Amerikoje; pasakojamosios dainos ir baladės. Surinko ir suredagavo Jonas Balys. Boston, Lietuvių enciklopedijos leidykla, 1958.
xlii, 326 p. music. 22 cm. (Lietuvių tausakos lobynas, 5)
Added t. p.: Lithuanian folksongs in America.
1. Lithuanian ballads and songs. 2. Folksongs, Lithuanian. 3. Lithuanians in the U.S. I. Title. II. Title: Lithuanian folksongs in America.
NIC NUC73-58156

Balys, Jonas, 1909-
see Haussig, Hans Wilhelm. Götter und Mythen im alten Europa. Stuttgart, E. Klett Verlag ⌈1973⌉

Balys, Jonas, 1909- joint author.
see Thompson, Stith, 1885- The oral tales of India. Westport, Conn., Greenwood Press, 1976, c1958.

Balyshev, O. A., joint author
see Pampura, Viktor Dmitrievich. Fiziko-matematicheskie modeli prirodnykh gidrotermal'nykh sistem. 1973.

Balyts'kyĭ, Kostîantyn Petrovych.
(Reaktivnost' organizma i khimioterapiîa opukholeĭ)
Реактивность организма и химиотерапия опухолей / К. П. Балицкий, И. Г. Векслер. — Киев : Наук. думка, 1975.
251, ⌈3⌉ p. : ill. ; 21 cm. USSR 75
At head of title: Akademiîa nauk Ukrainskoĭ SSR. Institut problem onkologii.
Bibliography: p. 217–⌈252⌉
1.60rub
1. Cancer—Chemotherapy. I. Veksler, Il'îa Grigor'evich, joint author. II. Title.
RC271.C5B34 75–546000

Balyudz, Binyamin
see
Bliudz, Benjamin, 1893-

Balyuzi, H M
'Abdu'l-Bahá: the centre of the Covenant of Bahá'u'lláh, by H. M. Balyuzi. London, Ronald, 1971.
xv, 560, ⌈13⌉ p. illus., facsim., ports. 21 cm. Index. £1.75 ($5.00 U. S.) B 72–01858
Bibliography: p. ⌈518⌉–521.
1. 'Abd ul-Bahā ibn Bahā Ullāh, 1844–1921. I. Title.
BP393.B33 297'.896'3 [B] 72–196284
ISBN 0–85398–029–2 MARC
CtY

Balyuzi, H M
The Báb; the herald of the day of days, by H. M. Balyuzi. Oxford, ⌈Eng.⌉ G. Ronald ⌈1973⌉
xiv, 255 p. illus. 21 cm. £1.60 ($5.25U.S.) B***
Includes bibliographical references.
1. Bāb, 'Alī Muḥammad Shīrāzī, 1820–1850.
BP391.B34 297'.88'0924 [B] 73–167688
ISBN 0–85398–048–9 MARC

Balyuzi, H M
Muḥammad and the course of Islám / by H. M. Balyuzi. — Oxford ⌈Eng.⌉ : G. Ronald, c1976.
xviii, 457 p., ⌈8⌉ leaves of plates : ill., maps ; 22 cm. GB***
Bibliography: p. ⌈430⌉-432.
Includes index.
ISBN 0-85398-060-8 : $14.75
1. Islamic Empire—History. 2. Muḥammad, the prophet. I. Title.
DS38.3.B34 909'.097'671 76-362857
76 MARC

Balz, F.
see Informationen zum Sport in der Bundesrepublik Deutschland ... Stand, Februar 1975. Schorndorf, Hofmann, 1975.

Balz, Gunther W
The feasting eye : ⌈poems⌉ / Gunther W. Balz. — ⌈s. l. : s. n., 1974⌉ (San Francisco : Greenwood Press)
97 p. ; 23 cm.
"Edition of 500 copies."
I. Title.
PS3552.A472F4 811'.5'4 75–306810
MARC

Balz, Horst Robert.
Die "Katholischen" Briefe; die Briefe des Jakobus, Petrus, Johannes und Judas. Übersetzt und erklärt von Horst Balz und Wolfgang Schrage. [11. Aufl.] Göttingen, Vandenhoeck & Ruprecht, 1973.
240 p. 24 cm. (Das Neue Testament deutsch neues Göttinger Bibelwerk, 10)
1. Bible. N. T. Catholic Epistles–Commentaries. I. Schrage, Wolfgang, joint author. II. Title. III. Series: Das Neue Testament deutsch, 10.
NNF NUC76-71889

Balz, Horst Robert, ed.
see Das Wort und die Wörter... Stuttgart, W. Kohlhammer [c1973]

Balz, Manfred Wilhelm.
Invention and innovation under Soviet Law : a comparative analysis / Manfred Wilhelm Balz. — Lexington, Mass. : Lexington Books, ⌈1975⌉
ix, 187 p. ; 24 cm.
Includes bibliographical references and index.
ISBN 0-669-92668-X
1. Patent laws and legislation—Russia. I. Title.
346'.47'0486 73-20152
73 MARC

Balz, W.
see Orgel dynamics. ⌈Ispra, Italy⌉ 1969.

Balza, José.
Setecientas palmeras plantadas en el mismo lugar; ejercicio. Caracas, Sintesis Dosmil, 1974.
157 p. (Colección Los vasos comunicantes)
I. Title.
NcU NUC76-21138

Balza Donatti, Camilo. Relámpago sur. 1972
in Oropeza, José Napoleón. Cuento[s]... [Maracaibo, Universidad del Zulia, 1972]

Balza Donatti, Camilo, joint author.
see Barceló Sifontes, Lyll. El Zulia, la ciudad y su mundo ... Caracas, ⌈Instituto Zuliano de la Cultura⌉ 1973.

Balzac, Basil de.
Varios momentos de poesía. ⌈Montevideo, 1967⌉
44 p.
I. Title.
CLU NUC73-2345

Balzac, Gabrielle.
Laudate Mariam : poèmes / Gabrielle Balzac. ⌈Paris⌉ : La Croix de gueules, 1965.
32 p. ; 22 cm.
I. Title.
PQ2662.A46L3 841'.9'14 75-505716
75 MARC

Balzac, Honoré de, 1799-1850.
Der alchimist. Berlin, E. Rowohlt [n. d.]
278 p. (Gesammelte werke)
I. Title.
NmU NUC76-21143

Balzac, Honoré de, 1799-1850.
Another study of women. Girard, Kan., Haldeman-Julius Co. ⌈19--⌉
60 p. 13 cm. (Little blue book no. 1044, ed. by E. Haldeman-Julius)
I. Title. II. Series.
KU-RH NUC75-63818

Balzac, Honoré de, 1799-1850.
Un asunto tenebroso. Prologo de Carlos Ollero. ⌈Barcelona⌉ Salvat con la colaboracion de Alianza Editorial ⌈c1969⌉
176 p. 19 cm. (Biblioteca basica Salvat de libros RTV, 37)
Translation of: Une ténébreuse affaire.
I. Title.
NdU NUC74-137767

Balzac, Honoré de, 1799-1850.
The atheist's mass ⌈and⌉ an accursed house ⌈by⌉ Honore de Balzac, edited by E. Haldeman-Julius. Girard, Kan., Haldeman-Julius Co. ⌈n. d.⌉
64 p. 13 cm. (Little Blue Book no. 15)
I. Haldeman-Julius Co. II. Series.
KU-RH NUC73-103865

Balzac, Honoré de, 1799–1850.
Balzac ; ⌈choix de textes⌉ / par René Guise. — Paris : Hatier, ⌈1972–1973⌉
2 v. ; 19 cm. — (Collection Thema anthologie ; 1, 7) F***
Bibliography: v. 2, p. ⌈123⌉–124.
Includes index.
CONTENTS: 1. La société.—2. L'individu.
ISBN 2–218–02027–0
I. Guise, René, ed.
PQ2159.A2G8 1972 843'.7 74–189166
MARC

Balzac, Honoré de, 1799–1850.
Balzac, 1799–1850, maximes et pensées. Paris, A. Silvaire, 1973.
159 p. 12 cm. (Maximes et pensées) 6.00F F 74–2136
PQ2160.S5 74–169305
MARC

Balzac, Honoré de, 1799-1850.
Balzac's Contes drolatiques; droll stories collected from the abbeys of Touraine; translated into English, complete and unabridged. London, Priv. Print. ⌈n. d.⌉
366 p. illus.
"The first English version ever brought before the public."—Translator's pref.
1. Contes drolatiques. 2. Droll stories.
MoU NUC74-9887

Balzac, Honoré de, 1799-1850.
The black sheep = La rabouilleuse / Honoré de Balzac ; translated with an introduction by Donald Adamson. — Harmondsworth ; Baltimore ⌈etc.⌉ : Penguin, 1976.
339 p. ; 18 cm. — (The Penguin classics) GB76-18561
First published in 1842 under title: Les deux frères.
ISBN 0-14-044237-5 : £0.75 ($2.25 U.S.)
I. Title. II. Title: La rabouilleuse.
PZ3.B22 Bl. 5 843'.7 77-357255
⌈PQ2165.D3⌉ 77 MARC

Balzac, Honoré de, 1799-1850.
La busqueda de lo absoluto. ⌈Por⌉ Honorato de Balzac. Traducido para esta colección por María Eugenia de Puerto. ⌈Bogota, Instituto Colombiana de Cultura, 1971⌉
2 v. (Biblioteca colombiana de cultura, colección popular, 17, 18)
I. Title.
InU NUC74-137766

Balzac, Honoré de, 1799-1850. Le cabinet des antiques. 1966
in Balzac, Honoré de, 1799-1850. La veille fille. [Paris] Le Livre de poche [1966, c1964]

Balzac, Honoré de, 1799-1850.
La casa del gato que pelotea y otros relatos. [Traducción de Milena Fabiani. Buenos Aires] Centro Editor de América Latina [1971]
142 p. illus. 18 cm. (Biblioteca fundamental del hombre moderno, 25)
I. Title.
MB NUC74-137765

Balzac, Honoré de, 1799-1850.
The centenarian : or, The two Beringhelds / (Honoré de Balzac) Horace de Saint-Aubin, pseud. ; translated from the original 1822 French ed. by George Edgar Slusser. — [New York] : Arno Press, 1976.
vi, 454 p. ; 24 cm. — (Supernatural and occult fiction)
Translation of Le centenaire : ou, Les deux Béringheld.
ISBN 0-405-08110-3
I. Title. II. Series.
PZ3.B22 Cd 3 843'.7 75-46250
[PQ2163] 76 MARC

Balzac, Honoré de, 1799-1850.
César Birotteau, préface de Pierre Barbéris. Paris, Livre de Poche, 1973.
xlviii, 353 p., [4] leaves of plates. ill. 18 cm. (Livre de poche classique, 1605)
"Note bibliographique": p. [xlvii]-xlviii.
I. Barberis, Pierre. II. Title.
NjP NUC76-39175

Balzac, Honoré de, 1799-1850.
The Chouans. A new translation from the French. New York, F. M. Lupton Pub. Co. [n. d.]
362 p. illus. 19 cm.
I. Title.
GU NUC76-21142

Balzac, Honoré de, 1799-1850.
Les chouans. Une passion dans le désert. Illus. de Édouard Toudouze et Pierre Vidal. Paris, A. Michel [19--?]
502 p. illus. 21 cm. (His Oeuvres complètes de H. de Balzac. Scènes de la vie militaire)
I. Title.
CaBVaU NUC75-63819

Balzac, Honoré de, 1799–1850.
Les Chouans. Préf. de Pierre Gascar. Notice de Roger Pierrot. [Paris] Gallimard [1972]
508 p. 18 cm. (Collection Folio, 84) F***
1. Chouans—Fiction. I. Title.
PQ2163.C5 1972 73-309508

Balzac, Honoré de, 1799–1850.
Les Chouans. Introduction et commentaires de René Guise. Paris, le Livre de poche, 1972.
xxii, 424 p. illus. 16 cm. (Le Livre de poche classique, 705)
4.30F F 72-13162
1. Chouans—Fiction. I. Title.
PQ2163.C5 1972b 843'.7 73-178507
MARC

Balzac, Honoré de, 1799-1850.
Les chouans, ou, La Bretagne en 1799. Paris, Imprimerie nationale [1958]
409 p. 22 cm. (His La comédie humaine: Scenes de la vie militaire) (Collection nationale des grands auteurs)
I. Title.
MU NUC73-57830

Balzac, Honoré de, 1799-1850.
Christ in Flanders and other stories. Girard, Kan., Haldeman-Julius Co. [19--]
63 p. 13 cm. (Little blue book no. 318, ed. by E. Haldeman-Julius)
I. Title. II. Series.
KU-RH NUC75-16343

Balzac, Honoré de, 1799-1850.
Los Chuanes: escenas de la vida militar. [Traducción del francés por Fernando G. Vela] Madrid, Espasa-Calpe [1971, c1923]
254 p. 18 cm. (Colección Austral, 1488)
Translation of Les Chouans.
I. Title.
IU NUC74-137781

Balzac, Honoré de, 1799-1850.
Le colonel Chabert. Paris, Ollendorff [n. d.]
1 v. (Scènes de la vie privée)
KEmT NUC76-23087

Balzac, Honoré de, 1799-1850.
Le Colonel Chabert ; (suivi de) El Verdugo ; Adieu ; Le Réquisitionnaire / Honoré de Balzac ; préface de Pierre Gascar ; édition établie et annotée par Patrick Berthier. — [Paris] : Gallimard, 1974.
308 p. ; 18 cm. — (Collection Folio ; 93) F75-1398
Includes bibliographical references.
6.70F
I. Berthier, Patrick. II. Title.
PQ2159.A2B47 843'.7 75-504042
75 MARC

Balzac, Honoré de, 1799-1850.
Le Colonel Chabert suivi de Ferragus, chef des Dévorants / Honoré de Balzac ; introduction et commentaires de Rose Fortasier. — Paris : le Livre de poche, 1973.
xx, 256 p. : ill. ; 17 cm. — (Le Livre de poche classique ; 1140)
F74-3517
5.50F
I. Fortassier, Rose. II. Balzac, Honoré de, 1799-1851. Ferragus, chef des Dévorants. 1973. III. Title: Le Colonel Chabert.
PQ2163.C7 1973 843'.7 75-506053
75 MARC

Balzac, Honoré de, 1799-1850.
La comédie humaine. Préface et notes de Roland Chollet. [Genève, Edito-Service S.A.] Distribué par le Cercle du Bibliophile [19-?]-
v. illus. 21 cm.
Contents.— t. 13 Mémoires de deux jeunes mariées. Une ténébreuse affaire.
I. Title.
PSt NUC76-21303

Balzac, Honoré de, 1799-1850.
La comédie humaine / Balzac ; éd. publiée sous la direction de Pierre-Georges Castex ; avec la collaboration de Pierre Citron ... [et al.]. — [Paris] : Gallimard, c1976-
v. ; 18 cm. — (Bibliothèque de la Pléiade ; 26) F***
Includes bibliographical references.
CONTENTS: 1-2. Études de mœurs. Scènes de la vie privée.
120F (v. 2)
I. Castex, Pierre Georges, 1915- II. Title.
PQ2159.C7 1976 843'.7 76-478711
76 MARC

Balzac, Honoré de, 1799-1850. La confession. 1972
in Balzac, Honoré de, 1799-1850. Le Médecin de campagne. Paris, le Livre de poche, 1972.

Balzac, Honoré de, 1799-1850. La confidence des Ruggieri
see Crain, William Leeper, 1897- A critical edition of Balzac's "Le secret des Ruggieri." Chicago, 1937.

Balzac, Honoré de, 1799-1850.
Les contes drolatiques. Dessins originaux d'Alice Huertas. [Fribourg, Suisse] Éditions du Lac [c1972]
586 p. illus. 22 cm.
I. Title.
WU NUC76-39173

Balzac, Honoré de, 1799-1850.
Contes philosophiques. Introduction par Paul Bourget. Londres, J. M. Dent; Paris, G. Crès [19--]
xv, 400 p. 17 cm.
Contains the twelve stories following La peau de chagrin in the series "Romans et contes philosophiques."
I. Title.
MeB NUC74-10395

Balzac, Honoré de, 1799–1850.
Le Contrat de mariage. Précédé de Une Double famille. Et suivi de L'Interdiction [par] Honoré de Balzac; préface de Jean-Louis Bory; notice et notes de Samuel S. [Silvestre] de Sacy. [Paris], Gallimard, 1973.
434 p. 18 cm. (Collection Folio, 302) 5.80F F 73-7533
I. Balzac, Honoré de, 1799–1850. Une double famille. 1973. II. Balzac, Honoré de, 1799–1850. L'interdiction. 1973. III. Title. IV. Title: Une double famille. V. Title: L'interdiction.
[PQ2165.C3 1973] 843'.7 74-179024
MARC

Balzac, Honoré de, 1799-1850.
A coquette versus a wife (The peace of a home) Girard, Kan., Haldeman-Julius Co. [19--]
64 p. 13 cm. (Little blue book no. 1046, ed. by E. Haldeman-Julius)
I. Title. II. Series.
KU-RH NUC75-16344

Balzac, Honoré de, 1799-1850.
Cousin Pons. Translated from the French, by Norman Cameron. New York, Pantheon Books [n. d.]
397 p. 18 cm. (The Novel Library)
I. Cameron, J. Norman, tr. II. Title.
NcRS NUC73-71269

Balzac, Honoré de, 1799-1850.
Le cousin Pons... Vienne, Manz [19-?]
476 p. 18 cm. (Collection Manz)
At head of title: H. de Balzac. Les parents pauvres.
I. Title.
IU NUC73-80378

Balzac, Honoré de, 1799–1850.
Le cousin Pons. Préf. de Jacques Thuillier. Postface et notes d'André Lorant. [Paris] Gallimard [1973]
439 p. 18 cm. (Collection Folio, 380) F***
I. Lorant, André, ed. II. Title.
PQ2165.C4 1973 843'.7 74-183824
MARC

Balzac, Honoré de, 1799–1850.
Le cousin Pons. Présenté par Maurice Ménard. [Paris] Le Livre de poche [1973]
395 p. 17 cm. (Le Livre de poche classique, 989) 4.50F F***
I. Ménard, Maurice, ed. II. Title.
PQ2165.C4 1973b 74-154658
MARC

Balzac, Honoré de, 1799–1850.
Le cousin Pons. [Éd. de A.-M. Meininger] Paris, Garnier [1974]
lxxxi, 444 p. plates. 19 cm. (Classiques Garnier) 32.00F
F***
Bibliography: p. [424]-425.
I. Meininger, Anne Marie, éd. II. Title.
PQ2165.C4 1974 843'.7 74-178997
MARC

Balzac, Honoré de, 1799-1850.
La cousine Bette. Paris, Librairie Gründ [n. d.]
2 v. 19 cm. (La bibliothèque précieuse)
I. Title.
TxU NUC76-21141

Balzac, Honoré de, 1799–1850.
La Cousine Bette. Préface et notes de Pierre Barbéris. [Paris,] Gallimard, 1972.
512 p. 18 cm. (Collection Folio, 138) 6.00F F 72-12272
I. Barbéris, Pierre, ed. II. Title.
PQ2165.C5 1972 73-323934

Balzac, Honoré de, 1799–1850.
La cousine Bette. Introd. de Roger Pierrot. [Paris] Le Livre de poche [1972]
527 p. 17 cm. (Le Livre de poche classique, 952) F***
I. Title.
PQ2165.C5 1972b 843'.7 74-150517
MARC

Balzac, Honoré de, 1799–1850.
Le Curé de village [par] Honoré de Balzac. Préface de Pierre Barbéris. Paris, le Livre de poche, 1972.
331 p. 17 cm. (Le Livre de poche classique, 1563) 4.30F
F 73-4084
I. Title.
PQ2165.C8 1972 843'.7 73-178512
MARC

Balzac, Honoré de, 1799-1850.
Le curé de village suivi de Véronique et de Véronique au tombeau / H. de Balzac ; avant propos de Ki Wist. — 1. éd. intégrale conforme à la publication des feuilletons de 1839. — Bruxelles : Éditions Henriquez, 1961.
A-D, xxxvii, 115 p. : facsims. ; 22 cm.
Includes bibliographical references.
I. Balzac, Honoré de, 1799-1850. Véronique. 1961. II. Balzac, Honoré de, 1799-1850. Véronique au tombeau. 1961. III. Title.
PQ2165.C8 1961 843'.7 75-513922
75 MARC

Balzac, Honoré de, 1799-1850.
Le député d'Arcis. Paris, Imprimerie nationale [1958]
378 p. 22 cm. (His La comédie humaine: Scènes de la vie politique) (Collection nationale des grands auteurs)
I. Title.
MU NUC73-58155

Balzac, Honoré de, 1799-1850. Le député d'Arcis. German. 1967
in Balzac, Honoré de, 1799-1850. Eine Episode aus der Zeit der Schreckensherrschaft. München, Goldmann [1967]

Balzac, Honoré de, 1799-1850.
La dernière fée : ou, La nouvelle lampe merveilleuse / par Horace de Saint-Aubin [i.e. H. de Balzac]. — Paris : Bibliophiles de l'originale, [1963]
2 v. in 1 ; 19 cm. — (Le Cabinet romantique ; no 6)
Facsim. of the 1823 ed., Paris.
I. Title.
PQ2165.D27 1963 76-450155
76 MARC

Balzac, Honoré de, 1799-1850.
La dernière fée : ou, La nouvelle lampe merveilleuse / Honoré de Balzac. — Genève : Slatkine Reprints, 1976.
139 [i.e. 239], 206, 211 p. ; 23 cm. Sw***
Reprint of the 1825 ed., published by Delongchamps, Paris.
Original t.p. has pseud.: H. de Saint-Aubin.
I. Title.
PQ2165.D27 1976 843'.7 76-488411
76 MARC

Balzac, Honoré de, 1799-1850.
Don Juan [and] A passion in the desert. Girard, Kan., Haldeman-Julius Co. [19--]
63 p. 13 cm. (Little blue book no. 344, ed. by E. Haldeman-Julius)
I. Title. II. Series.
KU-RH NUC75-16345

Balzac, Honoré de, 1799-1850.
Un drame au bord de la mer / Honoré de Balzac. — La Baule : Éditions des Paludiers, c1976.
63 p. : ill. ; 16 cm. F***
I. Title.
PQ2165.D7 1976 843'.7 76-477990
76 MARC

Balzac, Honore de, 1799-1850.
Droll stories; collected in the monasteries of Touraine and given to the light by Honore de Balzac. Translated into modern English by Alec Brown, with engravings by Gustave Dore. New York, Citadel Press [1958]
528 p. illus.
I. Title.
KEmt NUC76-62497

Balzac, Honoré de, 1799-1850.
Droll stories, collected in the monasteries of Touraine and given to the light by Honoré de Balzac. Translated into modern English by Alec Brown. With engravings by Gustave Doré. London, Elek Books [1958] 1972 printing.
528 p. illus. 21 cm. (Masterpieces of world literature, 2)
Translation of Les contes drolatiques.
Label mounted on t.p.: Paul Elek Inc., Salem, N. H.
I. Brown, Alec, 1900-1962, tr. II. Doré, Gustave, 1832-1883, illus-tration. III. Title.
PQ2164.A423 65-7365

Balzac, Honoré de, 1799-1850.
La duquesa de langeais. Una hija de Eva. Traducción de Ramon de la Rosa Olivera. Con introducción de Alejandro Cioranescu. Santa Cruz de Tenerife, Romerman Ediciones [1969]
300 p. 18 cm. (Flor de Romero)
I. Title. II. Title: Una hija de Eva.
CtY NUC73-47484

Balzac, Honoré de, 1799-1850.
Les Employés. Introduction, notice et notes de Samuel S. [Silvestre] de Sacy. Paris, le Livre de poche, 1970.
380 p. 16 cm. (Le Livre de poche classique, 2666) 3.90F
F 70-10864
Includes bibliographical references.
I. Silvestre de Sacy, Samuel, ed. II. Title.
PQ2165.E46 1970 73-179390
MARC

Balzac, Honoré de, 1799-1850.
Eine Episode aus der Zeit der Schreckensherrschaft. Un épisode sous la terreur. Der Abgeordnete von Arcis. Le député d'Arcis. Z. Marcas. (Übertragen von Irma Schauber und herausgegeben von Ernst Sander.) München, Goldmann [1967].
185 p. 18 cm. (His Menschliche Kommödie, Sittenstudie. Szenen aus dem politischen Leben) (Goldmanns gelbe Taschenbücher, Bd. 1928) DM2.80 GDB 68-A10-166
I. Sander, Ernst Leo, 1898- ed. II. Schauber, Irma, tr. III. Balzac, Honoré de, 1799-1850. Le député d'Arcis. German. 1967. IV. Balzac, Honoré de, 1799-1850. Z. Marcas. German. 1967.
PQ2170.S8G45 73-332546

Balzac, Honoré de, 1799-1850.
Eugenia Grandet. [n.p., c1966]
1 v.
Translated from the French.
I. Title.
NB NUC75-26581

Balzac, Honoré de, 1799-1850.
Eugénie Grandet. Paris, Librairie Gründ [n.d.]
252 p.
I. Title.
KMK NUC73-72783

Balzac, Honoré de, 1799-1850.
Eugénie Grandet. Chronologie et préface par Pierre Citron. [Paris] Garnier-Flammarion [c1964]
189 p. 18 cm. (Garnier-Flammarion texte integral 3)
Bibliography: p. 24.
I. Title.
CoU NUC75-26556

Balzac, Honoré de, 1799-1850.
Eugénie Grandet; translated by Ellen Marriage, introd. by Marcel Girard. London, Dent; New York, Dutton [1968]
235 p. (Everyman's library)
An Everyman paperback.
I. Title.
InU NUC73-122822

Balzac, Honoré de, 1799-1850.
Eugénie Grandet. Translated by Marion Ayton Crawford. [Harmondsworth, Middlesex] Penguin Books [1971]
247 p. 18 cm. (The Penguin classics, L50)
I. Title.
CLSU NUC73-34727

Balzac, Honoré de, 1799-1850.
Eugénie Grandet. Présentation et commentaires de Maurice Bardèche. [Paris] Le Livre de poche [1974, c1972]
xvii, 292 p. 17 cm. (Le Livre de poche classique, 1414) F***
I. Bardèche, Maurice, ed. II. Title.
PQ2166.A1 1974 843.7 74-190600
ISBN 2-253-00386-7 MARC

Balzac, Honoré de, 1799-1850.
Eugénie Grandet / Honoré de Balzac. Harmondsworth, England ; Baltimore : Penguin books, [1975, c1955]
xv, 247 p. ; 19 cm. (Penguin classics, L50)
Translated by Marion Crawford.
I. Title.
MiEM NUC77-87668

Balzac, Honoré de, 1799-1850.
Eugénie Grandet et Une ténébreuse affaire. (2 romans.) Introd. par Jean-Paul Pellaton. (Genève, Édito-Service.) Distribué par le Cercle du bibliophile, [Genève, Évreux, Bruxelles,] (1971).
xiv, 416 p. 6 plates. 20 cm. (Les Classiques de la jeunesse) Sw 72-B-401
I. Balzac, Honoré de, 1799-1850. Une ténébreuse affaire. 1971. II. Title. III. Title: Une ténébreuse affaire.
PQ2166.A1 1971 73-320484

Balzac, Honoré de, 1799-1850.
Facino Cane. Sarrasine. [Übertragen von Hedwig Lachmann] Leipzig, Insel-Verlag [19--?]
82 p. 19 cm. (Insel-Bücherei, Nr. 19)
I. Title. II. Title: Sarrasine.
ICarbS NUC75-26719

Balzac, Honoré de, 1799-1850.
Le faiseru. Adaptation [par] Pierre Franck. Paris, 1973.
52 p. illus. (L'Avant-scène, no. 524)
I. Franck, Pierre. II. Title. III. Series.
ICarbS NUC75-17245

Balzac, Honoré de, 1799-1850. Le faiseur.
see Hammel, Claus, 1932- Le Faiseur. Berlin, Eulenspiegel Verlag [1972]

Balzac, Honoré de, 1799-1850.
La femme de trente ans. Paris, Imprimerie nationale [1958]
248 p. 22 cm. (His La comédie humaine: Scènes de la vie privée) (Collection nationale des grands auteurs)
I. Title.
MU WU NUC73-58140

Balzac, Honoré de, 1799-1850.
La femme de trente ans. Chronologie et préf. par Pierre Citron. Paris, Garnier-Flammarion [1967]
242 p. 18 cm. (Texte integral GF 69)
I. Citron, Pierre. II. Title.
NjP NUC75-26555

Balzac, Honoré de, 1799-1850. Ferragus, chef des Dévorants. 1973.
in Balzac, Honoré de, 1799-1850. Le Colonel Chabert suivi de Ferragus, chef des Dévorants. Paris, le Livre de poche, 1973.

Balzac, Honoré de, 1799-1850.
Die Frau von dreissig Jahren. [Ubersetzt von Erich Noether] Berlin, E. Rowohlt [n.d.]
286 p. (Gesammelte Werke)
NmU NUC75-16352

Balzac, Honoré de, 1799-1850.
Die Frau von 30 Jahren; Roman von Honoré de Balzac. Übersetzt von Edmund Th. Kauer. Berlin, Verlag der Schillerbuchhandlung [n.d.]
320 p. 19 cm.
Title of French original: La femme de trente ans.
I. Title.
TU NUC75-16347

Balzac, Honoré de, 1799-1850.
The girl with the golden eyes. London, Sphere [1972]
126 p. 18 cm. £0.30 B***
Translation of La fille aux yeux d'or.
I. Title.
PZ3.B22Gi 10 843'.7 73-331295
[PQ2167.F5] MARC

Balzac, Honoré de, 1799-1850.
Histoire de la grandeur et de la décadence de César Birotteau, Marchand perfumeur, adjoint du maire du deuxième arrondissement de paris, Chevalier de la Légion d'honneur, etc. Paris, Imprimerie nationale [1958]
357 p. 22 cm. (His La comédie humaine: Scènes de la vie parisienne) (Collection nationale des grands auteurs)
I. Title: César Birotteau. II. Title.
MU NUC76-24678

Balzac, Honoré de, 1799-1850.
History of the thirteen / Honoré de Balzac ; translated and introduced by Herbert J. Hunt. — Harmondsworth, Eng. : Penguin Books, 1974.
390 p. ; 19 cm. — (Penguin classics) GB***
Translation of Histoire des Treize.
Bibliography: p. [19]
CONTENTS: Ferragus.—The Duchesse de Langeais.—The girl with the golden eyes.
ISBN 0-14044-301-0 : £0.60
I. Title.
PZ3.B22Hl 5 843'.7 74-195973
[PQ2167.H5] MARC

Balzac, Honoré de, 1799-1850.
Illusions perdues. Paris, Editions G. P., Département des Presses de la Cité [1970]
570 p. 21 cm. (Fleuve d'or)
I. Title.
CaOOU NUC73-47486

Balzac, Honoré de, 1799-1850.
Illusions perdues. [Introduction par Pierre Gallet. Fribourg] Éditions du Lac [c1972]
3 pts. in 2 v. 22 cm.
I. Title.
WU NUC76-39165

Balzac, Honoré de, 1799–1850.
Illusions perdues [par] Honoré de Balzac. Présenté par Maurice Ménard. Paris, le Livre de poche, 1972.
xv, 605 p. 17 cm. (Le Livre de poche classique. Texte intégral, 862) 5.00F F 73-1406
I. Ménard, Maurice, ed. II. Title.
PQ2167.I 6 1972 843'.7 73-180691
MARC

Balzac, Honoré de, 1799–1850.
Illusions perdues / Honoré de Balzac ; préf. de Gaëtan Picon. — [Paris] : Gallimard, [1974]
699 p. ; 18 cm. — (Collection Folio ; 62) F***
8.00F
I. Title.
PQ2167.I 6 1974 843'.7 74-189087
MARC

Balzac, Honoré de, 1799-1850.
In the time of the terror and other stories. Girard, Kan., Haldeman-Julius Co. [19--]
64 p. 13 cm. (Little blue book no. 143, ed. by E. Haldeman-Julius)
I. Title. II. Series.
KU-RH NUC75-16346

Balzac, Honoré de, 1799–1850.
Jésus Christ en Flandre / Honoré de Balzac. — Chicago : [s. n.], 1941 ([Chicago?] : R. DaBoll ... [et al.]) "Privately printed."
26 p., [1] leaf of plates : ill. ; 18 cm.
Text in English.
I. Title.
PQ2167.J4 1941 843'.7 75-302365
MARC

Balzac, Honoré de, 1799-1850.
Louis Lambert. [Traducción de Aníbal Leal. 1. ed.] Buenos Aires, Juarez Editor [1970]
xxvii, 133 p. 21 cm. (Colección Literaria: raros y olvidados)
I. Title.
MB NUC73-122817

Balzac, Honoré de, 1799-1850.
Le lys dans la vallée. Paris, Imprimerie [1958]
344 p. 22 cm. (His La comédie humaine: scenes de la vie de province) (Collection nationale des grands auteurs)
I. Title.
MU NUC73-57831

Balzac, Honoré de, 1799-1850.
Le lys dans la vallée. Avec une notice sur la vie de Balzac, une présentation générale, une étude littéraire et une analyse méthodique du roman, des notes, des questions et des thèmes de réflexion, par Gérard Roubichou. Paris, Bordas [1967]
256 p. illus. (Sélection littéraire Bordas)
Includes bibliography.
I. Roubichou, Gérard, ed. II. Title.
MiU NUC76-25746

Balzac, Honoré de, 1799–1850.
Le lys dans la vallée. Préf. de Paul Morand. Postface, dossier, et notes d'Anne-Marie Meininger. [Paris] Gallimard [1972]
435 p. 18 cm. (Collection Folio, 112) F***
I. Meininger, Anne Marie, ed. II. Title.
PQ2167.L8 1972 73-315478

Balzac, Honoré de, 1799–1850.
Le lys dans la vallée. Chronologie, préf. et archives de l'œuvre par Nicole Mozet. [Paris] Garnier-Flammarion [1972]
314 p. 18 cm. F***
Bibliography: p. [37]-38.
I. Mozet, Nicole, ed. II. Title.
PQ2167.L8 1972 73-319283

Balzac, Honoré de, 1799–1850.
Le Lys dans la vallée. Introduction et commentaires de Roger Pierrot. Paris, le Livre de poche, 1972.
xviii, 491 p. plates. 17 cm. (Le Livre de poche, 1461) (Le Livre de poche classique) 5.00F F 72-11877
I. Pierrot, Roger, ed. II. Title.
PQ2167.L8 1972b 843'.7 73-178514
MARC

Balzac, Honoré de, 1799-1850.
La maison Nucingen. Paris, Ollendorff [n.d.]
1 v. (Scènes de la parisienne)
KEmT NUC76-23106

Balzac, Honoré de, 1799-1850.
Maximes et pensées. Paris, A. Silvaire [1973]
159 p. 12 cm.
RPB NUC76-39164

Balzac, Honoré de, 1799-1850.
Le médecin de campagne. Paris, Imprimerie nationale [1958]
290 p. 22 cm. (His La comédie humaine: Scènes de la vie de campagne) (Collection nationale des grands auteurs)
I. Title.
MU NUC73-57832

Balzac, Honoré de, 1799–1850.
Le Médecin de campagne. Suivi de La Confession [par] Honoré de Balzac. Préface de Pierre Barbéris. Paris, le Livre de poche, 1972.
xlvii, 357 p. 17 cm. (Le Livre de poche classique, 1997) 4.30F F 73-4614
I. Balzac, Honoré de, 1799–1850. La confession. 1972. II. Title. III. Title: La confession.
PQ2167.M45 1972 843'.7 73-178511
MARC

Balzac, Honoré de, 1799-1850.
Le Médecin de campagne / Honoré de Balzac ; préface d'Emmanuel Le Roy Ladurie ; édition établie et annotée par Patrick Berthier. — [Paris] : Gallimard, 1974.
472 p. ; 18 cm. — (Collection Folio ; 633) F75-1911
Includes bibliographical references.
8.00F
I. Berthier, Patrick. II. Title.
PQ2167.M45 1974 843'.7 76-459727
76 MARC

Balzac, Honoré de, 1799-1850.
Le médecin de campagne / Balzac ; [introd., bibliographie et dossier de l'œuvre par Pierre Barbéris ; notes et relevés de variantes par Maurice Allem]. — Paris : Garnier, c1976.
lx, 382 p. : ill. ; 19 cm. — (Classiques Garnier) F***
Bibliography: p. [lix]-lx.
40.00F
I. Barbéris, Pierre. II. Allemand, Maurice, 1872- III. Title.
PQ2167.M45 1976 843'.7 76-475208
76 MARC

Balzac, Honoré de, 1799-1850.
Middle classes, with introduction by George Saintsbury. New York, President Pub. Co. [n. d.]
iii-vi, 364 p. 20 cm.
Translation of: Les Petits Bourgeois.
I. Title.
OKentU NUC75-16351

Balzac, Honoré de, 1799–1850.
A murky business. (Une ténébreuse affaire) Translated and introduced by Herbert J. Hunt. [Harmondsworth, Eng., Baltimore] Penguin Books [1972]
222 p. 19 cm. (Penguin classics) $1.95 (U.S.) B***
I. Title.
PZ3.B22Mr 8 843'.7 72-171388
[PQ2161] MARC
ISBN 0-14-044271-5

Balzac, Honoré de, 1799-1850.
The mysterious exiles. Girard, Kan., Haldeman-Julius Co. [19--]
60 p. 13 cm. (Little blue book no. 1047, ed. by E. Haldeman-Julius)
I. Title. II. Series.
KU-RH NUC75-16348

Balzac, Honoré de, 1799-1850.
Œuvres complètes. Texte revisé et annoté par Marcel Bouteron et Henri Longnon; illus. de Charles Huard, gravées sur bois par Pierre Gusman. Paris, L. Conard, 1925-56.
40 v. front., illus. 22 cm.
Original publication of this set was first started 1912. This is a reprint edition.
I. Bouteron, Marcel, 1877-1962.
OrCS NUC73-33699

Balzac, Honoré de, 1799-1850.
Old Goriot; The abbé Birotteau; with introduction by George Saintsbury. New York, President Pub. Co. [n.d.]
vi, 273, iv, 68 p. 20 cm.
NBuU NUC74-131292

Balzac, Honoré de, 1799-1850.
Papa Goriot [por] Honorato de Balzac. Prólogo de Manuel Peyrou. [Traducción de Oscar Hermes Villordo. Buenos Aires, Compañía General Fabril Editora, 1965]
313 p. front. 17 cm. (Los Libros del mirasol)
Translation of Le père Goriot.
I. Title.
MB NUC73-122818

Balzac, Honoré de, 1799-1850.
Papá Goriot [por] Honorato de Balzac. [Traducción del francés por Joaquín de Zuazagoitia] Madrid, Espasa-Calpe [1973]
238 p. 18 cm. (Colección austral, no. 1543)
Translation of Le père Goriot.
I. Title.
IU NUC76-71866

Balzac, Honoré de, 1799-1850.
Les Paysans. L'envers de l'histoire contemporaine. Préf. et notes de Roland Chollet. Paris, Cercle du Bibliophile, 1967.
583 p. illus. 21 cm. (His La Comédie humaine et autres oeuvres, v. 24)
I. Title. II. Title: L'envers de l'histoire contemporaine.
NIC NUC73-122824

Balzac, Honoré de, 1799-1850.
Les Paysans / Honoré de Balzac ; préface de Louis Chevalier, ... ; édition établie et annotée par S. de Sacy. — [Paris] : Gallimard, 1975.
495 p. ; 18 cm. — (Collection Folio ; 675) F75-15698
10.00F
I. Silvestre de Sacy, Samuel. II. Title.
PQ2167.P2 1975 843'.7 76-477913
76 MARC

Balzac, Honoré de, 1799-1850.
La Peau de chagrin, Le Curé de Tours et Le Colonel Chabert. Introduction par Henry Mazel. Paris, Nelson [n.d.]
551 p. front. 16 cm.
I. Title. II. Title: Le Curé de Tours. III. Title: Le Colonel Chabert.
NBuU NUC74-131280

Balzac, Honoré de, 1799–1850.
La Peau de chagrin: texte de l'édition originale, 1831 [par] Honoré de Balzac. Préface de Pierre Barbéris. Paris, le Livre de poche, 1972.
xlvii, 366 p. 17 cm. (Le Livre de poche classique, 1701) 4.50F F 73-4615
I. Title.
PQ2167.P5 1972 73-180465
MARC

Balzac, Honoré de, 1799-1850.
La Peau de chagrin / Honoré de Balzac ; préface d'André Pieyre de Mandiargues ; édition établie et annotée par S. [Samuel Silvestre] de Sacy. — [Paris] : Gallimard, [1974]
437 p. ; 18 cm. — (Collection Folio ; 555) F74-13635
6.00F
I. Silvestre de Sacy, Samuel. II. Title.
PQ2167.P5 1974 843'.7 75-503796
75 MARC

Balzac, Honoré de, 1799-1850.
Le père Goriot. With an introd. by Horatio Smith. New York, Scribner [c1956]
xxxv, 321 p. 17 cm. (The Modern student's library)
"The text... is that of the Conrad Edition (Oeuvres Complètes, vol. VI, Paris, 1912)"
Includes bibliographical references.
I. Title.
OU NUC73-58106

Balzac, Honoré de, 1799-1850.
Le père Goriot. Présenté par Beatrix Beck. [Paris] Livre de poche [1967]
442 p. (Livre de poche classique)
Copyright 1961.
I. Title.
MiEM NUC76-39166

Balzac, Honoré de, 1799–1850.
Le Père Goriot. Préface de Félicien Marceau. Notice et notes de Thierry Bodin. [Paris] Gallimard, 1971.
445 p. 18 cm. (Collection Folio, 8) 6.00F F 72-5983
I. Title.
PQ2168.A1 1971 72-359559

Balzac, Honoré de, 1799–1850.
Le Père Goriot. Introduction d'André Maurois ... Commentaires de Nicole Mozet. Paris, le Livre de poche, 1972.
xviii, 359 p. plates. 17 cm. (Le Livre de poche classique, 757) 4.30F F 72–8759
I. Title.
PQ2168.A1 1972 843'.7 73–178510
MARC

Balzac, Honoré de, 1799-1850.
Le père Goriot. [Fribourg, Suisse] Éditions du Lac [c1974]
302 p. 22 cm.
I. Title.
WU NUC76-21140

Balzac, Honoré de, 1799-1850.
Père Goriot / Honoré de Balzac ; with the ill. of Eugène Abot. — Limited ed. — Franklin Center, Pa. : Franklin Library, 1977.
387 p. : ill. ; 24 cm. — (The 100 greatest books of all time)
"Notes from the editors" (22 p.) inserted in pocket.
I. Title.
PZ3.B22 Per 1977 843'.7 77-563394
[PQ2168] 77 MARC

Balzac, Honore de, 1799-1850. Le pere Goriot
see Zeiz, A H Väter... [Zürich, c1940]

Balzac, Honoré de, 1799–1850.
Physiologie du mariage. Préface, notice et notes de Samuel S. [Silvestre] de Sacy. Paris, le Livre de poche, 1971.
446 p. 17 cm. (Le Livre de poche, 3254) 4.10F F 71–12586
Includes bibliographical references.
1. Marriage. I. Silvestre de Sacy, Samuel, ed. II. Title.
HQ737.B3 1971 73–317100

Balzac, Honoré de, 1799-1850.
The physiology of marriage; the petty troubles of married life. New York, Société des Beaux-Arts [19--?]
496 p.
1. Marriage. I. Title.
TxU NUC76-22699

Balzac, Honoré de, 1799-1850.
The plays of Honoré de Balzac. — New York : H. Fertig, 1976.
xv, 437, 307 p. ; 24 cm.
Reprint of v. 34 and 35 of The works of Honore de Balzac published in 1901 by Avil Pub. Co., Philadelphia, under title: The dramas.
CONTENTS: Vautrin.—The resources of Quinola.—Pamela Giraud.—The stepmother.—Mercadet.
I. Title.
PQ2161.F46 1976 vol. 34-35 76-25511
[PQ2158] 77 MARC

Balzac, Honoré de, 1799-1850.
La prima bela / Traducción del francés por José García Mercadal. -- Madrid, Espasa-Calpe, 1975.
391 p. ; 18 cm. -- (Coleccion Austral. No. 1574)
Translation of La cousine Bette.
I. Title.
OU NUC77-86832

Balzac, Honoré de, 1799-1850.
Les proscrits, Louis Lambert, Séraphîta. Paris, Imprimerie Nationale [1958]
376 p. 22 cm. (His La comédie humaine: Études philosophiques) (Collection nationale des grandes auteurs)
I. Title: Louis Lambert. II. Title: Séraphîta. III. Title.
MU NUC73-58105

Balzac, Honoré de, 1799–1850.
La rabouilleuse. Texte présenté, établi, et annoté par René Guisde. [Paris] Gallimard [1972]
439 p. 18 cm. (Collection Folio, 163) F***
First published in 1842 under title: Les deux frères.
I. Guisde, René. II. Title.
PQ2165.D3 1972 843'.7 73–302018

Balzac, Honoré de, 1799–1850.
La Rabouilleuse [par] Honoré de Balzac. Introduction et commentaires de Roger Pierrot. Paris, le Livre de poche, 1972.
xvi, 415 p., [6] l. illus. 17 cm. (Le Livre de poche classique, 543) 4.00F F 73–1948
First published in 1842 under title: Les deux frères.
I. Title.
PQ2165.D3 1972b 843'.7 73–178509
MARC

Balzac, Honoré de, 1799–1850.
[Razskazy]
Разсказы Онорэ Бальзака. Переводъ Ел. Вл. Штейнъ. С.-Петербургъ, Изд. М. М. Ледерле, 1894–
v. port. 18 cm. (Моя библіотека, №№ 97 и 98
CONTENTS: т. 1. Фачино Кане. Полковникъ Шаберъ. Миньона.
I. Series: Moia biblioteka, no. 97, 98.
PQ2162.R8S5 73–202983

Balzac, Honoré de, 1799-1850.
The Red Inn. Girard, Kan., Haldeman-Julius Co. [19--]
64 p. 13 cm. (Little blue book no. 1042, ed. by E. Haldeman-Julius)
Cover title: Crime at the Red Inn.
I. Title. II. Series.
KU-RH NUC75-16349

Balzac, Honoré de, 1799-1850.
Romans et contes. [Edition établie et annotée par Jean A. Ducourneau.] Paris, Les Bibliophiles de l'originale [1972-
v. (His Oeuvres complètes, 24-
MH NUC73-32188

Balzac, Honoré de, 1799-1850. Sarrasine. 1976.
in Barthes, Roland. S-Z. Paris, Éditions du Seuil, 1976.

Balzac, Honoré de, 1799-1850. Sarrasine. English. 1974
see Barthes, Roland. S/Z. New York, Hill and Wang [1974]

Balzac, Honoré de, 1799-1850.
Selected short stories [of] Honore de Balzac / selected and translated with an introduction by Sylvia Raphael. — Harmondsworth ; New York : Penguin, 1977.
271 p. ; 18 cm. — (Penguin classics) GB77-12173
ISBN 0-14-044325-8 : £1.00 ($2.95 U.S.)
I. Raphael, Sylvia. II. Title.
PZ3.B22 Sc 1977 843'.7 77-366318
[PQ2161] 77 MARC

Balzac, Honoré de, 1799–1850.
Séraphîta. Paris, P. J. Oswald [1973]
168 p. 18 cm. (Collection La Source de la liberté; ou, La solution intégrale, 5) 15.00F F***
I. Title.
PQ2172.A1 1973 73–180462
MARC

Balzac, Honoré de, 1799-1850.
Seraphita / by Honoré de Balzac ; introd. by Paul M. Allen. — Blauvelt, N.Y. : Steinerbooks, c1976.
179 p. ; 18 cm.
ISBN 0-8334-1757-6 : $2.50 ($2.75 Can)
I. Title.
PZ3.B22 Se 9 843'.7 76-12203
[PQ2172] 77 MARC

Balzac, Honoré de, 1799-1850.
Short stories, by Honore de Balzac. New York, The Modern Library [n. d.]
252 p. 17 cm. (The modern library of the world's best books [no.] 40)
TxU NUC76-21086

Balzac, Honoré de, 1799–1850.
[Sobranie sochinenii]
Собраніе сочиненій Бальзака. С.-Петербургъ, Тип. бр. Пантелеевыхъ, 1896–99.
20 v. port. 21 cm. (Собраніе сочиненій избранныхъ иностранныхъ писателей)
CONTENTS: т. 1. Горіо; романъ. Разсказы.—т. 2. Бѣдные родственники: Кузина Бета.—т. 3. Бѣдные родственники: Кузенъ Понсъ.—Т. 4. Модеста Миньонъ.—т. 5. Беатриса.—т. 6. Деревенскій докторъ. Тридцатилѣтняя женщина.—т. 7. Крестьяне.—т. 8. Исторія тринадцати.—т. 9. Евгенія Гранде. Деревенскій священникъ. — т. 10. Погибшія мечтанья. — т. 11. Погибшія мечтанья. Послѣднее воплощеніе Вотрена.—т. 12. Сцены изъ военной жизни: Шуаны или Бретань въ 1799 г. Любовь въ пустынѣ.—т. 13. Исторія величія и паденія Цезаря Бирото. Брачный договоръ.—т. 14. Первый шагъ; романъ. Разсказы: Проклятый сынъ. Гамбара, Массимилла Дони.—т. 15. Сцены изъ провинціальной жизни: Старая дѣва. Кабинетъ древностей. Опека. Онорина.—т. 16. Шагреневая кожа. Пьерэтта.—т. 17–19. Разсказы.—т. 20. Мелкіе невзгоды супружеской жизни. Записки двухъ новобрачныхъ.
I. Series: Sobranie sochinenii izbrannykh inostrannykh pisatelei.
PQ2162.R8P3 1896 72–228137

Balzac, Honoré de, 1799-1850.
La Société par René Guise. Paris, Hatier [c1972]
127 p. 19 cm. (Collection Thema/Anthologie, 1)
I. Guise, René. II. Title.
TxDaM NUC74-131277

Balzac, Honoré de, 1799-1850.
La solterona. [n. p., c1968]
1 v.
1. Spanish language books. I. Title.
RP NUC76-39170

Balzac, Honoré de, 1799–1850.
(Sozertsatel'naia zhizn' Ludviga Lamberta)
Созерцательная жизнь Лудвига Ламберта. Соч. Бальзака. Переводъ съ французскаго Александры Зражевской. С.-Петербургъ, Въ Тип. Имп. Россійской академіи, 1835.
xx, 200, xxiv p. 21 cm.
Translation of Louis Lambert.
I. Title.
PQ2167.L7R8 1835 73–215713

Balzac, Honoré de, 1799-1850.
Splendeurs et misères des courtisanes [par] Balzac. Préf. de Félicien Marceau. Notes de J.-A. Ducourneau. [Paris] Livre de poche [1965, c1963]
638 p. (Le Livre de poche classique, 1085-1087)
I. Title.
MoU NUC73-40896

Balzac, Honoré de, 1799–1850.
Splendeurs et misères des courtisanes. Préf. et notes de Pierre Barbéris. [Paris] Gallimard [1973]
698 p. 18 cm. (Collection Folio, 405) F***
Bibliography: p. [697]–698.
I. Barbéris, Pierre, ed. II. Title.
PQ2173.S6 1973 74–183746
MARC

Balzac, Honoré de, 1799–1850.
Splendeurs et misères des courtisanes, extraits. Avec une notice ... une étude ... des notes ... par Jacques Gautreau ... Paris, Montréal, Bordas, 1972.
256 p. illus. 17 cm. (Univers des lettres, 409. Sélection) 5.00F F 72–9008
I. Gautreau, Jacques, ed. II. Title.
PQ2173.S62 1972 72–364758

Balzac, Honoré de, 1799-1850.
Splendeurs et misères des courtisanes : texte intégral / H. de Balzac ; préf. de Maurice Cazeneuve. — Paris : Garnier, c1975.
464 p., [16] leaves of plates : ill. ; 24 cm. F***
ISBN 2-7050-0001-1
I. Title.
PQ2173.S6 1975 843'.7 76-466276
76 MARC

Balzac, Honoré de, 1799-1850.
The splendors and miseries of a courtesan. Compressed by Ralph Oppenheim. Girard, Kan., Haldeman-Julius Co. [19--]
64 p. 13 cm. (Little blue book no. 1067, ed. by E. Haldeman-Julius)
I. Oppenheim, Ralph, ed. II. Title. III. Series.
KU-RH NUC75-16342

Balzac, Honoré de, 1799-1850.
A study of a woman, and Comedies of the counter. Girard, Kan., Haldeman-Julius Co. [19--]
32 p. 13 cm. (Little blue book no. 1043, ed. by E. Haldeman-Julius)
I. Title. II. Series.
KU-RH NUC75-16350

Balzac, Honoré de, 1799-1850. Une ténébreuse affaire. 1971
in Balzac, Honore de, 1799-1850. Eugénie Grandet et Une ténébreuse affaire. (Genève, Édito-Service, 1971)

Balzac, Honoré de, 1799-1850.
Une Ténébreuse affaire / Honoré de Balzac ; texte présenté, établi et annoté par René Guise. — [Paris] : Gallimard, 1973.
307 p. ; 18 cm. — (Collection Folio ; 468) F74-7112
6.00F
I. Guise, René. II. Title.
PQ2170.S8 1973b 843'.7 75-506421
75 MARC

Balzac, Honoré de, 1799–1850.
Une Ténébreuse affaire / Honoré de Balzac. — [Nouvelle éd.] / introduction et commentaires de Rose Fortassier. — Paris : le Livre de poche, 1973.
346 p. ; 17 cm. — (Le Livre de poche ; 611 : Le Livre de poche classique) F 74–13267
4.50F
I. Title.
PQ2170.S8 1973 843'.7 74–195545
MARC

Balzac, Honoré de, 1799-1850.
Le théâtre inédit de Honoré de Balzac. Édition critique d'après les manuscrits de Chantilly [par] Douchan Z. Milatchitch. Genève, Slatkine Reprints, 1973.
405 p.
Reprint of the Paris, 1930 edition.
Bound as issued, with Milatchitch, Douchan Z. Le theatre de Honoré de Balzac. Genève, 1973.
1. Milatchitch, Douchan Z., ed.
MH NUC76-39168

Balzac, Honoré de, 1799-1850.
Ursule Mirouët [par] H. de Balzac. Paris, Calmann Lévy [n. d.]
309 p. 19 cm. (His Oeuvres complètes. Scènes de la vie de province)
I. Title.
CLSU NUC76-21139

Balzac, Honoré de, 1799-1850.
Ursule Mirouët, par H. de Balzac. Paris, Nelson, Éditeurs [n. d.]
380 p.
At head of title: scènes de la vie de province.
OClUr NUC76-21115

Balzac, Honoré de, 1799-1850.
Ursule Mirouët / [by] Honoré de Balzac ; translated and with an introduction by Donald Adamson. — Harmondsworth ; Baltimore : Penguin, 1976.
266 p. ; 18 cm. — (The Penguin classics) GB76-30538
Translation of Ursule Mirouët.
ISBN 0-14-044316-9 : £0.80 ($2.95 U.S.)
I. Adamson, Donald. II. Title.
PZ3.B22 U 30 843'.7 77-455640
[PQ2175.U8] 77 MARC

Balzac, Honoré de, 1799-1850. Véronique. 1961.
in Balzac, Honoré de, 1799-1850. Le curé de village suivi de Véronique et de Véronique au tombeau. 1. éd. intégrale conforme à la publication des feuilletons de 1839. Bruxelles, Éditions Henriquez, 1961.

Balzac, Honoré de, 1799-1850.
La vieille fille. Suivie de Le cabinet des antiques. Préf. de Jean Dutourd. [Paris] Le Livre de poche [1966, c1964]
446 p. 17 cm. (Le Livre de poche classique, 1269-1270) 3.90F F***
Collectively entitled Les rivalités.
I. Balzac, Honoré de, 1799-1850. Le cabinet des antiques. 1966. II. Title. III. Title: Le cabinet des antiques. IV. Title: Les rivalités.
PQ2175.V52 1966 843'.7 73-176612 MARC

Balzac, Honoré de, 1799-1850.
Werke. Wien, Kurt Desch [1961]
2 v. 19 cm. (Klassiker im Verlag Kurt Desch; Honoré de Balzac)
Contents–I. Bd. Das Chagrin–Leder, Oberst Chabert, Vater Goriot, Verlorene Illusiones; v. 1. Chagrin leather, Colonel Chabert, Old Goriot, Lost illusions; II. Bd. Glanz und Elend der Kurtisanen, Eugenie Grandet, Cäsar Birotteau, Vetter Pons; v. 2. Splendor and need of courtesans, Eugenie Grandet, César Biretteau. Cousin Pons.
IEdS NUC73-39296

Balzac, Honoré de, 1799-1850. Z. Marcas. German. 1967
in Balzac, Honoré de, 1799-1850. Eine Episode aus der Zeit der Schreckensherrschaft. München, Goldmann [1967]

Balzac, Honoré de, 1799-1850
see Beaumont, Pierre de, 1910- Eugenie Grandet. [Paris, Hatier, 1972, c1968]

Balzac, Honoré de, 1799-1850
see Nadezhdin, Nikolaĭ Ivanovich, 1804-1856, comp. (Sorok odna povîest' luchshikh inostrannykh pisateleĭ) 1836.

Balzac, Jean Louis Guez, sieur de, d. 1654.
Les entretiens (1657). Éd. critique avec introd., notes et documents inédits établie par B. Beugnot. Paris, M. Didier, 1972.
2 v. (xlv, 659 p.) 19 cm. F***
At head of title: Société des textes français modernes.
Includes bibliographical references.
I. Beugnot, Bernard, 1932- ed. II. Title.
PQ1713.E3 1972 73-349037 MARC

Balzac, Jean Louis Guez, sieur de, d. 1654.
Oeuvres. Publiées par Valentin Conrart. Genève, Slatkine Reprints, 1970-
v. 31 cm.
GU MiEM LU IaAS NUC73-47426

Balzac, Jean Louis Guez, sieur de, d. 1654.
Œuvres ... Publ. par Valentin Conrart. (Réimpr. de l'éd. de Paris, 1665.) Genève, Slatkine Reprints, 1971.
2 v. 31 cm. 700F ($164.50U.S.) Sw 72-A-89
PQ1713.A1 1971 74-161058 MARC

Balzac [par Béatrix Beck et al. Paris] Hachette [1970, c1959]
295 p. illus. (part mounted col.), ports. (part mounted col.) facsims. 25 cm. (Collection Génies et réalités)
1. Balzac, Honoré de, 1799-1850. I. Beck, Béatrix.
NjMD NUC73-48312

Balzac and the nineteenth century: studies in French literature presented to Herbert J. Hunt by pupils, colleagues, and friends; edited by D. G. Charlton, J. Gaudon and Anthony R. Pugh. Leicester, Leicester University Press, 1972.
[11], 399, [5] p. illus., port. 24 cm. £6.00 B 72-18396
"Distributed in North America by Humanities Press, New York."
English and French.
"Select bibliography of the works of Herbert J. Hunt [by] Constance B. West": p. [7]-18.
Includes bibliographical references.
1. Balzac, Honoré de, 1799-1850. 2. French literature—19th century—Addresses, essays, lectures. 3. Hunt, Herbert James. I. Hunt, Herbert James. II. Charlton, Donald Geoffrey, ed. III. Gaudon, Jean, ed. IV. Pugh, Anthony R., ed.
PQ2177.A2B28 840'.9'007 73-160050
ISBN 0-7185-1106-9 MARC

Balzac and the nineteenth century; studies in French literature presented to Herbert J. Hunt by pupils, colleagues, and friends. Edited by D. G. Charlton, J. Gaudon, and Anthony R. Pugh. [New York] Humanities Press, 1972 [i. e. 1973]
399 p. illus. 24 cm. $18.00
Imprint covered by label: Distributed in the U. S. A. by Humanities Press, New York.
English or French.
"Select bibliography of the works of Herbert J. Hunt [by] Constance B. West": p. [7]-18.
Includes bibliographical references.
1. Balzac, Honoré de, 1799-1850—Addresses, essays, lectures. 2. French literature—19th century—Addresses, essays, lectures. 3. Hunt, Herbert James. I. Charlton, Donald Geoffrey, ed. II. Gaudon, Jean, ed. III. Pugh, Anthony R., ed. IV. Hunt, Herbert James.
PQ2181.B3 843'.7 73-152546
ISBN 0-391-00189-2 MARC

Balzac, la novela, el realismo y Papa Goriot / Rogelio Mirza, Jorge González Bouzas. -- Montevideo : Ediciones de la Banda Oriental, 1975.
63 p. ; 19 cm. -- (Colección "Horas de estudio" ; 13)
1. Balzac, Honoré de, 1799-1850--Criticism and interpretation. 2. Balzac, Honoré de, 1799-1850. Le père Goriot. I. Mirza, Rogelio. II. González Bouzas, Jorge.
TxU NUC77-87889

Balzamo, Rosario.
Come un romanzo ... / di Rosario Balzamo. — Napoli : A. Berisio, [1976]
148 p. ; 21 cm. It76-June
I. Title.
PQ4862.A463C6 76-466812
*76 MARC

Balzán, Freddy
see Labana Cordero, Efraín. TO3 - Campo antiguerrillero. 3. ed. Caracas, Ediciones Bárbara, 1970, c1969.

Balzana, Leodino
see Socialità, principi e tecniche dell'infermiere unico. Perugia, Stab. Grafica, 1973.

Balzani, Elde, joint author
see Fabbri, Tebaldo. Nuova grammatica italiana. Bologna, Casa Editrice Patrón [c1972]

Balzani, Ugo, conte, 1874-1916.
Le cronache italiane nel medio evo. Hildesheim, New York, G. Olms, 1973.
xiv, 333 p. 20 cm. GFR***
Reprint of the ed. published in Milan by U. Hoepli in 1909.
Includes bibliographical references.
1. Italy—History—476-1268—Historiography. I. Title.
DG503.B4 1973 73-351771
ISBN 3-487-04671-7

Balzano, Jeanne.
Wanted ... a brother, by Gina Bell. Pictures by George Wilde. New York, Abingdon Press, [1959]
31 p. illus. (part col.) 21 cm.
SUMMARY: Timothy longs for a brother, but in time he comes to appreciate his sister.
[1. Brothers and sisters—Fiction] I. Wilde, George A. II. Title.
PZ7.B2146 Wan [E] 59-7503
[r77]rev2 MARC

Balzano, Michael P
Reorganizing the Federal bureaucracy : the rhetoric and the reality / Michael P. Balzano. — Washington : American Enterprise Institute for Public Policy Research, c1977.
43 p. ; 23 cm. — (Studies in political and social processes) (AEI studies ; 165)
Includes bibliographical references.
ISBN 0-8447-3264-8 : $2.25
1. Action (Service Corps) 2. Administrative agencies—United States. I. Title. II. Series. III. Series: American Enterprise Institute for Public Policy Research. AEI studies ; 165.
HC110.P63B34 353.04 77-84326
77 MARC

Balzano, Oscar Alberto Fernández
see
Fernández Balzano, Oscar Alberto.

Balzarek, Mauriz, 1872-1945
see Linz, Austria. Stadtmuseum. Der Architekt Mauriz Balzarek, 1872-1945... Linz [1972 ?]

Balzarevičius, P
(Osushenie i osvoenie kul'turnykh pastbishch)
Осушение и освоение культурных пастбищ. Москва, "Колос," 1969.
96 p. with illus. and maps. 20 cm. USSR 69-VKP
At head of title: П. Балзаравичюс, П. Аксомайтис.
Bibliography : p. 94-[95]
0.14rub
1. Pastures—Lithuania. 2. Drainage—Lithuania. I. Aksomaitis, P. K., joint author. II. Title.
SB199.B35 78-548625

Balzarevičius, P., ed.
see Kaunas. Lietuvos hidrotechnikos ir melioracijos mokslinio tyrimo institutas. Lietuvos hidrotechnikos ir melioracijos mokslinio tyrimo instituto ... Vilnius : Periodika, 1973.

Balzarini, Guido.
La retribuzione del lavoro subordinato ... Chieti, Edizioni dell'Università, 1971-
v. 24½ cm. (Università degli studi G. D'Annunzio, Chieti. [Pubblicazioni] Serie giuridica, 4) L3500 (v. 1) It 72-Nov (v. 1)
Includes bibliographical references.
CONTENTS: 1. Principi generali.
1. Labor contract—Italy. 2. Master and servant—Italy. 3. Wages—Italy. I. Title. II. Series: Università degli studi G. D'Annunzio. Pubblicazioni. Serie giuridica, 4.
73-304110

Balzarino, Angel, 1943-
El hombre que tenía miedo : cuentos / Angel Balzarino. — Rafaela [Argentina] : Ediciones E.R.A., 1974.
61 p. ; 21 cm. — (Colección El hombre y la palabra ; no. 1)
CONTENTS: El hombre que tenía miedo.—Un cuarto para los otros.—El desplazado.—Tiempo de odio y soledad.—Cena de honor.—El ordenanza.
I. Title.
PQ7798.12.A54H6 76-474990
76 MARC

Balzarotti, A
Effetto della temperatura sugli spettri di termoriflettanza del silicio [di] A. Balzarotti, M. Grandolfo [e] P. Vecchia. Roma, 1969.
20 l. illus. (Istituto superiore di sanità. Laboratori di fisica. Rapporti ISS 69 32)
Summary in English.
1. Silicon. 2. Spectrum Analysis. 3. Temperature. I. Grandolfo, Martino. II. Vecchia, P. III. Title. IV. Series.
DNLM NUC76-39169

Balzarotti, Rodolfo
see Rodolfo Balzarotti e Angelo Stabin hanno preso i seguenti appunti su... Milano, Jaca Book [1969]

Balzekas Museum of Lithuanian Culture.
Progress report. [Chicago, n. d.]
1 v. (unpaged) 28 cm.
1. Lithuanians in the United States. 2. Lithuanian collection. I. Title.
OKentU NUC75-92695

Balzer, Bernd.
Bürgerliche Reformationspropaganda; die Flugschriften des Hans Sachs in den Jahren 1523–1525. Stuttgart, J. B. Metzler, 1973.
vi, 236 p. illus. 24 cm. (Germanistische Abhandlungen, 42) GDB***
Originally presented as the author's thesis, Freie Universität, Berlin.
Bibliography: p. [219]–231.
1. Sachs, Hans, 1494–1576. 2. Reformation—Germany. I. Title.
PT1781.R4B3 1973 73–339505
ISBN 3-476-00262-4

Balzer, Brigitte.
Sozialtherapie mit Eltern Behinderter : Orientierungen für eine Konzeption im Rahmen eines psychohygienischen Gemeindeprogramms / Brigitte Balzer, Susanne Rolli. — Weinheim : Beltz, 1975.
230 p. ; 21 cm. — (Beltz Monographien : Sozialpädagogische Reihe ; Bd. 11) GFR***
Bibliography: p. [218]-230.
ISBN 3-407-55501-6
1. Mentally handicapped children—Family relationships. 2. Problem family—Germany, West. 3. Family social work—Germany, West. I. Rolli, Susanne, joint author. II. Title.
HV901.G3B34 75-517253
75 MARC

Balzer, Carmen.
Arte, fantasía y mundo / Carmen Balzer. — Buenos Aires : Plus Ultra, c1975.
271 p. : ill. ; 20 cm. — (Psicología) (Colección Mundo presente ; v. 6)
Includes bibliographical references.
1. Imagination. 2. Art—Psychology. I. Title.
N71.B27 701'.15 77-450825
77 MARC

Balzer, Eileen Hsü
see
Hsü-Balzer, Eileen.

Balzer, F
Fünfstellige natürliche Werte der Sinus- und Tangentenfunktionen und Tachymetertafeln neuer Teilung für Maschinenrechnen/ bearb. von F. Balzer u. H. Dettwiler. — 7. Aufl. — Stuttgart: Wittwer, 1972.
152 p.; 25 cm. DM10.50 GFR 73-A16
1. Trigonometry—Tables, etc. I. Dettwiler, H., joint author. II. Title.
QA55.B23 1972 516'.24'0212 74–322089
ISBN 3-87919-100-X

Balzer, Friedrich-Martin.
Klassengegensätze in der Kirche: Erwin Eckert u. d. Bund d. Religiösen Sozialisten Deutschlands/ Friedrich-Martin Balzer. Mit e. Vorw. von Wolfgang Abendroth. — Köln: Pahl-Rugenstein, 1973.
296 p.; 23 cm. (Kleine Bibliothek: Politik, Wissenschaft, Zukunft, 36) DM14.80 GFR 73-A
A revision of the author's thesis, Marburg.
Bibliography: p. 293–296.
1. Eckert, Erwin, 1893–1972. 2. Bund der Religiösen Sozialisten Deutschlands. 3. Lutheran Church in Germany. 4. Germany—Politics and government—1918–1933. I. Title.
HN39.G3B33 1973 73–357968
ISBN 3-7609-0083-6

Balzer, Georg.
Goethe als Gartenfreund / Georg Balzer. — München : Heyne, 1976.
227 p. : numerous ill. ; 18 cm. — (Heyne ex libris ; 11) GFR76-A18
ISBN 3-453-42014-4 : DM6.80
1. Goethe, Johann Wolfgang von, 1749-1832—Knowledge—Botany. I. Title.
PT2208.B7B3 1976 77-467968
77 MARC

Balzer, J LeRoy.
Aerodynamic behavior of fibrous aerosols: relationship to selective sampling. [Berkeley] 1971.
xii, 144 l. illus.
Thesis (Ph. D.)—University of California.
Bibliography: leaves 138-144.
CU NUC73-32190

Balzer, Jürgen, 1906–
Béla Bartók; en portrætskitse. Udg. af Folkeuniversitetsforeningen. København, Rhodos [c1962]
112 p. 20 cm. (Folkeuniversitetets bibliotek. Musik, bd. 2)
1. Bartók, Béla, 1881–1945.
ML410.B26B24 74–209487

Balzer, Karl.
Sabotage gegen Deutschland : der heimtück. Kampf gegen d. dt. Frontsoldaten / Karl Balzer. — 1. Aufl. — Preussisch Oldendorf : Schütz, 1974.
336 p., [4] leaves of plates : ill. ; 21 cm. GFR 75-A
Bibliography: p. 335–336.
Includes index.
ISBN 3-87725-072-6 : DM29.80
1. World War, 1939–1945—Underground movements—Europe. 2. Europe—Sabotage. I. Title.
D802.A2B33 75–594283

Balzer, Oswald Marian, 1858–1933.
Urywek nieznanego Promptuarza praw Michała Chwałkowskiego. [Lwów, 1890]
1 v. (various pagings) 23 cm.
Caption title.
Detached from Przewodnik naukowy i literacki, 1890.
1. Chwałkowski, Mikołaj, d. ca. 1700. I. Chwałkowski, Mikołaj, d. ca. 1700. Promptuarz praw.
72–360610

Balzer, R M
Block programming in O/S-360 assembly code. Santa Monica, Rand Corporation [1968]
9 l. 28 cm. (Rand Corporation. [Paper] P-3810)
1. Programming languages (Electronic computers) I. Title. II. Series.
MB NUC73-122819

Balzer, R M
The ISPL language specifications [by] R. M. Balzer. A report prepared for Advanced Research Projects Agency. Santa Monica, Calif., Rand, 1971.
x, 39 p. 28 cm. ([Rand Corporation] R-563-ARPA)
Contract no. DAHC15 67 C 0141.
ARPA order no. 189–1.
Bibliography: p. 39.
1. ISPL (Electronic computer system) I. United States. Advanced Research Projects Agency. II. Title. III. Series: Rand Corporation. Rand report R-563-ARPA.
AS36.R3 R–563 081 s [001.6'424] 73–170480
[QA76.6] MARC

Balzer, R M
The ISPL machine: principles of operation [by] R. M. Balzer. Santa Monica, Calif., Rand, 1971.
ix, 27 p. 28 cm. ([Rand Corporation. Rand report] R-562-ARPA)
"Report prepared for Advanced Research Projects Agency."
Bibliography: p. 27.
1. ISPL (Electronic computer system) I. United States. Advanced Research Projects Agency. II. Title. III. Series.
QA76.6.B345 001.6'44'04 73–170479
MARC

Balzer, R M
An overview of the ISPL computer system design [by] R. M. Balzer. [Santa Monica, Calif., Rand Corp.] 1971.
18 p. 28 cm. ([Rand Corporation. Paper] P-4734)
Cover title.
"Presented at the third Operating Systems Conference, Palo Alto, California, 18–20 October 1971."
Bibliography: p. 18.
1. ISPL (Electronic computer system) I. Title. II. Series.
AS36.R28 no. 4734 081 s 73–152561
[QA76.6] [001.6'44'04] MARC

Balzer, R M
Ports—a method for dynamic interprogram communication and job control [by] R. M. Balzer. Santa Monica, Calif., Rand, 1971.
vii, 16 p. illus. 28 cm. ([Rand Corporation. Rand report] R-605-ARPA)
"Research ... supported by the Advanced Research Projects Agency under Contract no. DAHC15-67-C-0141."
Includes bibliographical references.
1. Ports (Electronic computer system) I. Title. II. Series.
AS36.R3 R–605 081 s 74–151489
[QA76.6] [001.6'44'04] MARC

Balzer, Richard.
Clockwork : life in and outside an American factory / Richard Balzer. — 1st ed. — Garden City, N.Y. : Doubleday, 1976.
xii, 333 p. : ill. ; 24 cm.
ISBN 0-385-11036-7 : $10.00
1. Electric industry workers—Massachusetts—North Andover. 2. Western Electric Company. 3. Industrial sociology—Massachusetts—North Andover. I. Title.
HD8039.E32N673 331.7'62'13097445 75-21209
76 MARC

Balzer, Richard.
Next door, down the road, around the corner; a family album. Garden City, N. Y., Doubleday, 1973.
188 p. illus. 29 cm. $12.95
1. United States—Civilization—1970– —Pictorial works. I. Title.
E169.12.B29 1973 917.3'03'9240222 73–76449
ISBN 0-385-05345-2; 0-385-05407-6 (pbk.) MARC

Balzer, Richard, illus.
see Hsü-Balzer, Eileen. China day by day. New Haven, Yale Univ. Press, 1974.

Balzer, Robert Lawrence.
Robert Lawrence Balzer's book of wines & spirits. [Los Angeles] Ward Ritchie Press [1973]
118 p. illus. 28 cm. $7.95
On spine: Book of wines & spirits.
1. Alcoholic beverages. I. Title: Book of wines & spirits.
TP507.B3 641.2 78–166301
ISBN 0-378-01141-3 MARC

Balzer, Rolf
see 100 [i.e. Hundert] Fragen, 100 Antworten... Berlin: Panorama DDR [1974]

Balzer, Rolf.
see 100 questions, 100 answers ... 2d ed., rev. and brought up to date. [Berlin] Panorama DDR, [1975]

Balzer, Rolf
see 100 questions, 100 answers : GDR. Berlin : Panorama DDR, [1974]

Balzer, Rudolf, 1942–
Der Einfluss Vergils auf Curtius Rufus. München, 1971.
157 p. 21 cm. GDB***
Inaug.-Diss.—Munich.
Vita.
Bibliography: p. 155–157.
1. Vergilius Maro, Publius—Influence—Curtius Rufus. I. Title.
PA6825.B35 73–345821

Balzerano, A
L'educazione fisica nella sua evoluzione storica. Dal Medio-Evo ai nostri tempi. Napoli, Istituto grafico italiano, 1972.
167 p. 25 cm. It 72-Sept
At head of title: A. e G. Balzerano.
1. Physical education and training—History. I. Balzerano, G., joint author. II. Title.
GV217.B34 74–340930

Balzerano, G., joint author
see Balzerano, A L'educazione fisica nella sua evoluzione storica. Napoli, Istituto grafico italiano, 1972.

Balzert, Monika.
Die Komposition des Claudianischen Gotenkriegsgedichtes c. 26 / Monika Balzert. — Hildesheim ; New York : Olms, 1974.
vii, 158 p. ; 21 cm. — (Spudasmata ; Bd. 23) GFR 75-A
Originally presented as the author's thesis, Tübingen, 1970.
Bibliography: p. 147–151.
ISBN 3-487-05134-6 : DM24.80
1. Claudianus, Claudius. De bello gothico. I. Title.
PA6372.D3B3 1974 76–500006

Balzhi, Mikhail Fedorovich, ed.
see Avtomobili, traktory i dvigateli. 1971.

Bal'zhinova, L. B.
see Akademiia͡ nauk SSSR. Sibirskoe otdelenie. Institut geografii Sibiri i Dal'nego Vostoka. (Prirodnye rezhimy stepeĭ Minnusinskoĭ kotloviny) 1976.

Balzhiser, Richard E
Engineering thermodynamics / Richard E. Balzhiser, Michael R. Samuels. — Englewood Cliffs, N.J. : Prentice-Hall, c1977.
xii, 612 p. : ill. ; 24 cm.
Includes indexes.
ISBN 0-13-279570-1 : $19.95
1. Thermodynamics. I. Samuels, Michael R., joint author. II. Title.
TJ265.B23 621.4'021 76-25440
76 MARC

Balzhiser, Richard E
Termodinámica química para ingenieros [por] Richard E. Balzhiser, Michael R. Samuels [y] John D. Eliassen. Traducción y adaptación: Juan L. Hernández Sánchez. Englewood Cliffs [N. J.] Prentice/Hall International [1973, c1974]
xvii, 733 p. illus. 24 cm.
Translation of Chemical engineering thermodynamics.
Includes bibliographical references.
1. Chemical engineering. 2. Thermodynamics. I. Samuels, Michael R., joint author. II. Eliassen, John D., joint author. III. Title.
[TP155.B37418] 660.2'9'69 73–8453
ISBN 0-13-906776-0 MARC

Balzli, Ernst, 1902-1959.
Bärnerchoscht : syner schönschte Gschichte / Ernst Balzli. — Ostermundigen-Bern : Viktoria-Verlag, 1975.
192 p. ; 21 cm. Sw75-A-7523
CONTENTS: Fürabe.—Reisgäld.—Ds Gutschi.—Ds Meitli.—Ds Chnächtebett.—Halblyn.—Der Rosenchranz.—Bureglück.—Chnächtemärit.—Chummer Fritzlis Reischorb.—Der Näschtlibutz.
I. Title.
PT2603.A394B3 1975 76-466667
*76 MARC

Balzli, Ernst, 1902-1959.
Bärnerchoscht : zwöite Gang / Ernst Balzli. — Ostermundigen-Bern : Viktoria-Verlag, c1976.
192 p. ; 21 cm. Sw77-191
CONTENTS: D'Stächpalme.—Unterwysig.—Büehlme Chrischtes Ougschtered.—Herbärgsuechi.—Der Stündeler.—Ds Gnadebrot.—Der Süchel.—Ds Rütteli.—Huslüt.—D'Säimaschine.—Dokterruschtig.
24.80F
I. Title.
PT2603.A394B34 1976 77-481417
*77 MARC

Balzli, Ernst, 1902-1959.
Zwüsche Tür u Angle; Geschicht us der "gueten alte Zyt" zum eine dreiaktige Stück umgmödelet. Aarau, A. Breuninger [1956]
59 p. 20 cm.
Microfiche (negative) 2 sheets. 11 x 15 cm. (NYPL FSN-02461)
1. Drama, German. 2. German language–Dialects–Switzerland–Texts.
NN NUC73-66927

Balzo, Carlo del, 1853-1908.
L'Italia nella letteratura francese dalla caduta dell' impero romano alla morte di Enrico IV. Genève, Slatkine Reprints, 1971.
416 p. 22 cm.
On spine: I.
Reprint of 1905 Turin-Rome ed.
1. Literature, Comparative—Italian and French. 2. French Literature—Hist. & crit. I. Title.
CaQMM DCU NUC74-145334

Balzo, Carlo del, 1853–1908.
Napoli e i napoletani. A cura di Giulia Malato Mastrangeli. Introduzione di Enrico Malato. Napoli, La nuova cultura, 1972.
237 p. 21 cm. (Collana di scrittori napoletani) L4000
It 73–May
1. Naples—Social life and customs. I. Title.
DG845.6.B33 1972 73–340002

Balzo, Carlo del, 1853–1908.
Napoli e i napoletani. Con note di Domenico Capecelatro Guadioso. Introduzione di **Max Vajro** e note di Domenico Capecelatro Guadioso. Roma, Edizioni dell'Ateneo, 1972.
xv, 318 p. illus. 24 cm. (Cultura e storia del nostro paese, 4)
It 73–May
1. Naples—Social life and customs. I. Title.
DG845.6.B34 73–332651

Balzola, Ana.
La ardilla blanca. Ilustraciones de Pablo Ramírez. [1. ed. Barcelona] Editorial Juventud [1967]
1 v. (unpaged) col. illus. 20 cm. (Colección Jardin de infancia, I)
I. Title.
MB NUC76-71555

Bama, James.
The western art of James Bama / introd. by Ian Ballantine. — New York : Scribner, 1975.
45 leaves of plates : 45 col. ill. ; 29 cm.
"An original Peacock Press/Bantam book."
ISBN 0-684-14410-7 : $10.00
1. Bama, James. 2. The West in art. I. Title.
ND237.B235A57 1975 759.13 75-7782
76 MARC

Bama, James.
Western paintings : [exhibitions] / James Bama. — New York : Coe Kerr Gallery, c1977.
[44] p. : ill. (some col.) ; 28 cm.
Held at the Coe Kerr Gallery, New York, March 15-April 16, 1977 and at the Buffalo Bill Historical Center, Cody, Wyoming, May 1-July 18, 1977.
1. Bama, James. 2. The West in art. I. Coe Kerr Gallery. II. Buffalo Bill Historical Center. III. Title.
ND237.B235C63 759.13 77-151080
77 MARC

Bāma, Śaṅkara.
काल के कंपन; ऐतिहासिक कहानियाँ. [लेखक] शंकर बाम. [1. संस्करण] दिल्ली, जीवन-ज्योति प्रकाशन [1971, i.e. 1970]
205 p. 22 cm. Rs15.00
In Hindi.
I. Title. Title romanized: Kāla ke kampana.
PK2098.13.A49K3 70–917380

Bāma, Śaṅkara.
रीत और गीत. लेखक शंकर बाम. [नई दिल्ली] युनेस्को की ओर से नेशनल बुक ट्रस्ट, इंडिया, 1967.
108 p. illus. 19 cm. (नवसाक्षर पुस्तक-माला, 4)
In Hindi.
1. Hindi language—Readers for new literates. I. Title.
Title romanized: Rīta aura gīta.
PK1935.B3 S A 68–9054
PL 480 : I-H-5825

Bama
see
Bamah
for publications by and about this body.
Titles and other entries beginning with this acronym are filed following this card.

Bạma Pyi Ạlok-thạmā Ạsi Ạyōn Ạhpwẹ-chok.
(Ạchei hkan thạbāw htā hsōn hpyat chet myā)
အခြေခံသဘောထားဆုံးဖြတ်ချက်များ : အထွေထွေလုပ်ငန်းစဉ်နှင့်ဖွဲ့စည်းပုံဥပဒေ,-- [ရန်ကုန်] : ဗမာပြည်အလုပ်သမားအစည်းအရုံးအဖွဲ့ချုပ်, [1952]
62 p. ; 19 cm.
Cover title.
In Burmese.
1. Trade-unions—Burma—Congresses. I. Title.
HD6805.7.B3 1952 76–985076

Bạma Pyi Hsoshelit Pati.
For works by this body issued before 31 Dec. 1951 see
Burma Socialist Party.

Bāmadeba Pandita
see
Pandita, Bāmadeba.

Bamah.
see Symposium on Current Problems in Civil Aviation, 1st, Tel-Aviv, 1972. Airports of the future ... [Tel-Aviv] BAMA, [1973?]

Bamah le-Yahadut va-ruah.
Jewry and Judaism in the modern world ...; third annual symposium, Monday Elul 20, 5725-September 5, 1966, F. Mann Auditorium, Hechal Hatarbut, Tel Aviv. Tel Aviv, Forum for Jewish Thought [1967]
38, 36 p. illus., ports. 25 cm.
Added t.p. in Hebrew.
Text in English and Hebrew.
MeB NUC74-145680

Bamah le-Yahadut va-ruah
see 'Am yehudi-ayekah?! 1972.

Bamah le-Yahadut va-ruaḥ
see Diyun pumbi 'al Yisrael ben ha'amim, Tel-Aviv, 1971. (Diyun pumbi 'al Yisrael ben ha-'amim, Hekhal ha-tarbut—Tel-Aviv' 1973.

Bamajana, Hariśa.
(Jindagī ra vādhyatā)
जिन्दगी र वाध्यता; कथा संग्रह. लेखक हरीश बमजन. [1. संस्करण] काठमाडौं, रत्न पुस्तक भण्डार [सं. 2030 i.e. 1973]
62 p. 20 cm. Rs1.25
In Nepali.
CONTENTS: अनि एउटा मान्छे घरभित्र पस्छ.—कुरूप समयलाई पाइताला पाइताला छोड्दै ....—जिन्दगी र वाध्यता.—कान्छी.—बाक्लिदै गएको साँझ र छरपस्टिएको आकाश.—शोकेस भित्रको जिन्दगी.—सिम्फोनी.
I. Title.
PK2598.B26J5 73–906227

Bamako. Centre Djoliba
see
Centre Djoliba.

Bamako. Chambre de commerce, d'agriculture et d'industrie.
Élements du bilan économique.
Bamako, Chambre de commerce, d'agriculture et d'industrie de Bamako.
v. ill. 31 cm. annual.
1. Mali — Economic conditions — Periodicals. 2. Mali—Economic policy—Periodicals. I. Title.
HC547.M25B35a 330.9'66'2305 75–640580
MARC–S

Bamako. Chambre de commerce, d'agriculture et d'industrie.
Gouvernement assemblée nationale et représentations diverses de la république du Mali. Représentations étrangèrs au Mali. [Bamako, 1963]
1 v. (various pagings) 31 cm.
Microfilm.
Cover title.
1. Mali—Registers.
NN NUC73-124281

Bamako. Chambre de commerce, d'agriculture et d'industrie.
Précis fiscal, commercial, des changes et des échanges.
Bamako, Chambre de commerce, d'agriculture et d'industrie de Bamako.
v. 31 cm.
1. Trade regulation — Mali. 2. Business tax — Mali. 3. Excise tax—Mali. I. Title.
336.2'71 76–642376
MARC–S

Bamako. Chambre de commerce, d'agriculture et d'industrie.
Recueil des principaux textes législatifs et réglementaires promulgues en République du Mali du 1er janvier 1959 au 31 décembre 1964. [Bamako] Chambre de commerce [1965]
4, 49 l. 31 cm.
Cover title.
1. Mali—Law—Indexes.
CtY-L NUC76-71545

Bamako. Chambre de commerce, d'agriculture et d'industrie
see Annuaire des entreprises du Mali. 1972- [Bamako]

Bamako. Chambre de commerce, d'agriculture et d'industrie
see also
Chambre de commerce et d'industrie du Mali.

Bamako. Jardin zoologique
see
Parc biologique, Bamako.

Bamako. Parc biologique
see
Parc biologique, Bamako.

Bamako. Protestant Mission
see Protestant Mission, Bamako.

Bamako ... [Paris (10e),] Éditions "Continent 2000," [18, rue du Faubourg Poissonnière,] 1971.
32 p. illus. (part col.) 27 cm. (Capitales d'Afrique. Capitals of Africa) F 72–12674
Cover title.
English and French.
1. Bamako—Description—Guide-books.
DT551.9.B35B35 73–314792

Bamali, Nuhu.
Bala da Babiya; lafiya uwar jiki. Zaria ₍Nigeria₎ Gaskiya Corp., 1961 ₍i.e. 1966₎
82 p. illus. 22 cm.
Title translated: Bala and Babiya.
1. Hausa language—Readers. I. Title.
CSt NUC74-137770

Bamali, Nuhu, ed.
see Park, Mungo, 1771-1806. Mabudin Kwara... Zariya ₍Gaskiya Corp.₎ 1962.

Bamangwato Concessions, ltd. Treaties, etc. International Development Association, 1970.
Reimbursement agreement between International Development Association and Bamangwato Concessions Limited... ₍Washington, D.C., 1970₎
16 p. 27 cm. (Credit number 172 BT)
At head of title: Conformed copy.
1. Debts, Public—Botswana. I. International Development Association. Treaties, etc. Bamangwato Concessions, ltd., 1970.
MH-L CLL NUC76-24315

Bamashmous, Said M
A study of the 1967 baccalaureate graduates of the independent colleges of Kansas with respect to their major areas of study. ₍Lawrence, 1974₎
v, 75 l. 28 cm.
Thesis (Ph.D.)—University of Kansas.
Bibliography: leaves 73-75.
1. College students. Kansas. I. Title.
KU NUC76-25341

Bāmaṭraf, Muḥammad ʻAbd al-Qādir
see
Bā Maṭraf, Muḥammad ʻAbd al-Qādir.

Bamatter, Fréd
see Tagung für Kinderheilkunde, Geneva, 1969. Tagung für Kinderheilkunde... ₍Lindau-Bodensee₎ Wissenschaftliche Abteilung Nestlé ₍1970₎

Bamattre, Robert.
An annotated bibliography on the life of Pierre Fauchard, his influence on endodontics and periodontics, and the developments made in these disciplines since the 17th century. [n.p., n.d.]
23 l. 29 cm.
1. Fauchard, Pierre—Bibl. 2. Endodontics—Bibl. 3. Periodontia—Bibl.
CLSU NUC73-32204

Bamba, Kaichirō, 1909-
see (Gendai kaikeigaku no kihon kadai) 47 (1972)

Bamba, Kaichirō, 1909-
see Inoue, Tatsuo, 1907- (Reikai genka keisan seigi) [26 i.e. 1951]

Bamba, Kaichirō, 1909-
see Numata, Yoshiho. (Rijun tosei to genka keisan). 15₍1940₎

Bamba, Masatomo.
(Nihon Jukyō ron)
日本儒教論 萬羽正朋著 ₍東京₎ 三笠書房 ₍昭和14 i. e. 1939₎
328 p. 17 cm. (日本歴史全書 18)

1. Philosophy, Confucian—Japan—History. I. Title.
B5243.C6B35 75-791189

Bamba, Nobuya, 1937-
Japanese diplomacy in a dilemma; new light on Japan's China policy, 1924–1929. Kyoto, Minerva Press ₍1972₎
440 p. illus. 22 cm. ¥3500 Ja***
Bibliography: p. ₍401₎–425.
1. Japan—Foreign relations—1912–1945. 2. Japan—Foreign relations—China. 3. China—Foreign relations—Japan. I. Title.
DS888.5.B34 327.52′051 73–154366
MARC

Bamba, Nobuya, 1937–
Japanese diplomacy in a dilemma; new light on Japan's China policy, 1924–1929. Vancouver, University of British Columbia Press ₍1972₎
440 p. illus. 22 cm. C***
Bibliography: p. ₍401₎–425.
1. Japan—Foreign relations—1912–1945. 2. Japan—Foreign relations—China. 3. China—Foreign relations—Japan. I. Title.
DS888.5.B34 1972b 327.52′051 73–169397
ISBN 0-7748-0018-6 MARC

Bamba, Nobuya, 1937–
(Manshū jihen e no michi)
満州事変への道 幣原外交と田中外交 馬場伸也著 東京 中央公論社 昭和47(1972)
243 p. 18 cm. (中公新書 302) ¥300 Ja 72-19147
Bibliography: p. 240–243.

1. Japan—Foreign relations—1912–1945. 2. Japan—Foreign relations—China. 3. China—Foreign relations—Japan. I. Title.
DS888.5.B35 73–800760

Bambach, Richard Karl, 1934-
Bivalvia of the Siluro-Devonian Arisaig group, Nova Scotia, by Richard Karl Bambach. ₍New Haven₎ 1969 ₍1973₎
376 l. 85 plates with descriptions.
Thesis (Ph.D.)–Yale University.
Xerox copy of microfilmed typescript. Ann Arbor, University Microfilms, 1973.
1. Lamellibranchiata, Fossil. 2. Paleobiology—Nova Scotia. I. Title.
KMK NUC74-131294

Bambacus, John N
Needs assessment of municipal government in Allegany County, Maryland : report submitted to the United States Department of Housing and Urban Development and to the Community Development Administration, State of Maryland Department of Economic and Community Development / prepared by John N. Bambacus ; project assistants, David M. Miltenberger, Stanley W. Parrott, Jr. — Frostburg, Md. : Dept. of Political Science, Frostburg State College, ₍1973₎
iii, 21 leaves : ill. ; 28 cm.
Bibliography: leaves 12–14.

1. Municipal government—Allegany Co., Md. I. United States. Dept. of Housing and Urban Development. II. Maryland. Community Development Administration. III. Title.
JS451.M39A43 352.0752′94 74–623461
MARC

Bambakarēs, Markos
see
Vamvakarēs, Markos, 1905-

Bambang Riyanto
see Evaluasi program modernisasi desa tahun ke-I–IV Pelita I Propinsi Jawa Tengah. Yogyakarta : Fakultas Ekonomi Universitas Gadjah Mada, 1973.

Bambang Soetrisno, R
see
Soetrisno, R Bambang.

Bambara, Antonino.
Il dirigente d'azienda. Figura giuridica, capacità, compiti, competenze, responsabilità, poteri, anzianità, orario di lavoro, ferie, trattamento economico e giuridico, tutela giurisdizionale dei diritti, risoluzione del rapporto di lavoro. Milano, L. di G. Pirola, 1970.
126 p. 24 cm. (Del lavoro, 1) L1600 It 70–Feb
At head of title: Antonino Bambara, Antonio Gualtieri.
Cover title: Il dirigente di azienda.
Includes legislation and jurisprudence.
Bibliography: p. 117–119.
1. Executives—Italy. 2. Business enterprises—Italy. I. Gualtieri, Antonio, joint author. II. Title. III. Title: Il dirigente di azienda.
74–338664

Bambara, Antonino.
Gli illeciti tributari in sede di accertamento ... Milano, L. di G. Pirola, 1971.
164 p. 24 cm. It 71–Sept
L2300
1. Tax evasion—Italy. I. Title.
75–552476

Bambara, Antonino.
Soci, amministratori, sindaci. Compatibilità con il lavoro subordinato, figure giuridiche, assunzioni, licenziamenti, anzianità, competenze, delibere, responsabilità, poteri, rappresentanza. Milano, L. di G. Pirola, 1971.
94 p. 24 cm. (Del lavoro, 2) L1500 It 71–Jan
At head of title: Antonio Bambara, Giacomo Deodato.
Bibliography: p. 87–89.
1. Directors of corporations — Italy. 2. Respondent superior — Italy. I. Deodato, Giacomo, joint author. II. Title.
74–347195

Bambára, Antonino.
see Italy. Laws, statutes, etc. Codice degli onorari e delle spese giudiziarie ... Milano, Pirola, 1975.

Bambara, Toni Cade.
The seabirds are still alive : collected stories / by Toni Cade Bambara. — 1st ed. — New York : Random House, c1977.
208 p. ; 22 cm.
CONTENTS: The organizer's wife.—The apprentice.—Broken field running.—The sea birds are still alive.—The long night.—Medley.—A tender man.—A girl's story.—Witchbird.—Christmas Eve at Johnson's Drugs N Goods.
ISBN 0-394-48143-7 : $7.95
I. Title.
PZ4.B2116 Se 813′.5′4 76-53533
₍PS3552.A473₎ 76 MARC

Bambara, Toni Cade, comp.
Tales and stories for Black folks. ₍1st ed.₎ Garden City, N. Y., Zenith Books, 1971.
164 p. 22 cm. (Zenith anthologies) $3.95
CONTENTS: Raymond's run, by T. C. Bambara.—Thank you, M'am, by L. Hughes.—Train whistle guitar, by A. Murray.—To hell with dying, by A. Walker.—The day the world almost came to an end, by P. Crayton.—The sky is gray, by E. J. Gaines.—Let me hang loose, by V. Howard.—The wages of good, by B. Diop.—Straighten up and fly right, by J. Blackamore.—The parable of the eagle, by J. Aggrey.—The toad and the donkey, by T. C. Bambara.—Little Black Riding Hood, by W. Figueroa.—The three little panthers, by G. Powell and T. C. Bambara.—The three little brothers, by B. Pearson.—Billy goat's turf, by G. Powell.—The true story of Chicken Licken, by L. Holmes.—Jack and the beanstalk, by E. Spencer.
1. American fiction—Negro authors. 2. Negroes—Juvenile fiction. ₍1. Negroes—Fiction. 2. Short stories₎ I. Title.
PZ5.B218Tal 813′.5′08 [Fic] 79–144248
[PS647.N35] rev MARC

Bambarende, Siri Sivali
see Siri Sivali Bambarende.

Bambas, Maraine H
"Arisen"; an Easter chancel drama, by "Rae" Bambas. Boston, Baker's Plays [c1970]
28 p. 19 cm.
1. Easter—Drama. I. Title.
RPB NUC76-71556

Bambas, Neophytos, 1770–1855.
(Syntaktikon tēs archaias Hellēnikēs glōssēs)
Συντακτικὸν τῆς ἀρχαίας Ἑλληνικῆς γλώσσης. Ἔκδ. 2. Ἀθήνησι, Τύποις: Χ. Νικολαΐδου Φιλαδελφέως, 1846.
10, 319 p. 22 cm.
Includes bibliographical references.
1. Greek language—Syntax. I. Title.
PA367.B27 1846 76–526846

Bambas, Neophytos, 1770-1855, tr.
see Bible. N. T. Greek, Modern. 1956. Bambas. Hē kainē Diathēkē tou Kyriou kai Sōtēros hēmōn Iēsou Christou. [1956]

Bambauer, Hans Ulrich
see Tröger, Walther Ehrenreich, 1910-1963. Optische Bestimmung der gesteinsbildenden Minerale. 4., neu bearb. Aufl. Stuttgart: Schweizerbart 1971-

Bambayashi, Mitsuhira
see
Tomobayashi, Mitsuhira, 1813-1864.

Bambeck, Manfred.
Göttliche Komödie und Exegese / Manfred Bambeck. — Berlin ; New York : de Gruyter, 1975.
253 p. ; 23 cm. GFR75-A
Bibliography: 8th prelim. page.
Includes indexes.
ISBN 3-11-004874-4 : DM76.00
1. Dante Alighieri, 1265-1321. Divina commedia. 2. Bible—Criticism, interpretation, etc. 3. Dante Alighieri, 1265-1321—Allegory and symbolism. 4. Symbolism in literature. I. Title.
PQ4419.B5B3 75-512628
75 MARC

Bambeck, Manfred.
see Philologica Romanica ... München, W. Fink, 1975.

Bambenek, Mark, joint author
see Anbar, Michael. Selected specific rates of reactions of transients from water in aqueous solution. [Washington] National Bureau of Standards, 1973-
—— ——Supplemental data. Washington: Dept. of Commerce, 1975-

Bamber, Charles James, 1855-
Plants of the Punjab : a descriptive key to the flora of the Punjab, North-west Frontier Province, and Kashmir / by C. J. Bamber. — Dehra Dun : Bishen Singh Mahendra Pal Singh ; Delhi : Periodical Experts, 1976.
iii, 652, xxviii p., ⌈6⌉ leaves of plates : ill. ; 25 cm.
Includes a reproduction of the original t.p.
Reprint of the 1916 ed. printed by the Superintendent, Govt. Print., Punjab, Lahore.
Includes index.
Rs175.00
1. Botany—Punjab. 2. Botany—North-west Frontier Province. 3. Botany—Kashmir. I. Title.
QK358.B3 1976 582'.09'545 76-911101
76 MARC

Bamber, Chrissie, joint author.
see Sandow, Stuart A. Durations ... New York, Times Book, c1977.

Bamber, E W
Description of Carboniferous and Permian stratigraphic sections, Northern Yukon Territory and northwestern district of Mackenzie (N. T. S. 106 M; 116 C, F, G, H, I, J, P; 117 A, B, C) ⌈by⌉ E. W. Bamber ⌈Ottawa⌉ Dept. of Energy, Mines and Resources ⌈1973⌉
161 p. illus. 25 cm. (Geological Survey of Canada, paper 72-19)
$2.00 C***
Bibliography: p. 161.
1. Geology, Stratigraphic—Permian. 2. Geology, Stratigraphic—Carboniferous. 3. Geology—Yukon Territory. 4. Geology—Northwest Territories, Can.—Mackenzie District. I. Title. II. Series: Canada. Geological Survey. Paper, 72-19.
QE185.A42 no. 72-19 557.1'08 s 73-164747
[QE674] [551.7'5'097121] MARC

Bamber, E W
Mississippian corals from northeastern British Columbia, Canada [by] E. W. Bamber. [n. p., Princeton University, 1962. Ann Arbor, Mich., University Microfilms, 1972]
199 l. illus. 22 cm.
Photocopy.
Thesis–Princeton University.
Bibliography: leaves 195-199.
1. Corals, Fossil. 2. Paleontology. I. Title.
CaBVaU NUC73-59711

Bamber, R. N., joint author
see Gallivan, B
Computer listing of a reserve collection. [Lancaster] University of Lancaster Library, 1972.

Bamber, Roy Thomas.
Play, interest, domestication, and creativity. [Columbia] 1973.
207 l. illus.
Thesis (Ph. D.)—University of Missouri.
Vita.
Includes bibliography.
MoU NUC76-71558

Bamber, Roy Thomas.
Play, interest, domestication, and creativity. [Columbia] 1973.
207 l. illus.
Thesis (Ph. D.)—University of Missouri.
Vita.
Includes bibliography.
Microfilm copy.
MoU NUC76-71557

Bamberg, David, 1904- joint author
see Albo, Robert J The Oriental magic of the Bambergs. ⌈1st ed. San Francisco⌉ San Francisco Book Co., 1973.

Bamberg, Günter, 1940-
Lineare Bayes-Verfahren in der Stichprobentheorie / Günter Bamberg. — Meisenheim am Glan : Hain, 1976.
viii, 132 p. ; 23 cm. — (Mathematical systems in economics ; Heft 27)
GFR76-A
Bibliography: p. 124-128.
Includes index.
ISBN 3-445-01400-0 : DM21.00
1. Sampling (Statistics) 2. Bayesian statistical decision theory. 3. Estimation theory. I. Title. II. Series.
QA276.6.B35 77-450142
77 MARC

Bamberg, Günter, 1940-
Statistische Entscheidungstheorie / Günter Bamberg. — Würzburg ; Wien : Physica-Verlag, 1972.
149 p. : 24 graphs. ; 21 cm. — (Physica Paperback) GFR 74-A
Bibliography : p. 138-145.
Includes index.
ISBN 3-7908-0099-6 : DM20.00
1. Statistical decision. I. Title.
QA279.4.B35 75-556613

Bamberg, Günter, 1940-
see Deutsche Gesellschaft für Operations Research. Arbeitsgruppe Prognoseverfahren im Marketing. Information und Prognose ... Meisenheim/Glan, A. Hain, c1975.

Bamberg, Günter, 1940-
see Förstner, K Einführung in die Wahrscheinlichkeitsrechnung. Meisenheim am Glan, Anton Hain, 1973.

Bamberg, Hans-Dieter.
Politisches Lesebuch: f. Arbeiter, Schüler, Lehrlinge, Sozialarbeiter, Gewerkschafter u. progressive Lehrer/ Hrsg. von Hans-Dieter Bamberg; Manfred Bosch. ⌈Beitr.: W. Ahlmann u. a.⌉. — Starnberg: Raith, 1973.
446 p.; 19 cm. — (Reihe Gesellschaft und Erziehung) DM11.80
GFR 73-A
Includes bibliographical references.
1. Social sciences—Addresses, essays, lectures. 2. Civics, German—Addresses, essays, lectures. I. Bosch, Manfred, joint author. II. Title.
H35.B226 74-310363
ISBN 3-921121-56-6

Bamberg, Hans-Dieter.
Über Werdegang, Aktivitäten und Ansichten des Rainer Barzel/ Hans-Dieter Bamberg. — Köln: Pahl-Rugenstein, 1972.
48 p.; 23 cm. — (Hefte zu politischen Gegenwartsfragen; 1)
DM3.00 GFR 73-A32
Includes bibliographical references.
1. Barzel, Rainer. 2. Germany (Federal Republic, 1949-)—Politics and government. I. Title.
DD259.7.B3B35 73-361685
ISBN 3-7609-0069-0

Bamberg, Hans-Dieter.
see Handbuch Gruppenarbeit ... München, Weismann, 1975.

Bamberg, Hans-Dieter, joint author
see Koch, Hans-Gerhard, 1913- CDU/CSU : verhinderte Staatspartei. Starnberg : Raith, 1974.

Bamberg, Robert D., ed.
see James, Henry, 1843-1916. The portrait of a lady ... ⌈1st ed.⌉. New York, Norton, ⌈1975⌉

Bamberg Oetomo, Raden
see Oetomo, Bambang, Raden.

Bamberg. Bayerisches Staatsarchiv
see Bavaria. Staatsarchiv, Bamberg.

Bamberg. Gesamthochschule
see
Gesamthochschule Bamberg.

Bamberg. Historisches Museum.
Bildheft; zusammengestellt im Auftrag der Stadt Bamberg von Joachim Meintzschel. Bamberg, 1971.
⌈3⌉ p. 44 plates. (1 double) 21 cm.
I. Meintzschel, Joachim.
MWiCA NUC74-44526

Bamberg. Hoffmann (E.T.A.)-Theater
see
Hoffmann (E.T.A.)-Theater.

Bamberg. Neue Residenz
see Donauwaldgruppe. Donauwaldgruppe... [s.l.: s.n., 1974]

Bamberg. Neue Residenz
see Matulla, Oskar, 1900- (Ausstellung.) (Wiener Neustadt, Kunstverein Wiener Neustadt, 1970.)

Bamberg. Staatliche Bibliothek. MSS.
see also
Bamberg. Staatsbibliothek. MSS.

Bamberg. Staatliche Bibliothek. MSS. A. I. 47
see Dobbie, Elliott Van Kirk, 1907-1970. The manuscripts of Caedmon's hymn... Ann Arbor, Univ. Microfilms [1970]

Bamberg. Staatliche Bibliothek. MSS. (Med. 2, fol. 93v-232r)
see Medicina Plinii. Physica Plinii Bambergensis (Cod. Bamb. med. 2, fol. 93v-232r). Hildesheim, G. Olms, 1975.

Bamberg. Staatsbibliothek.
Schrifttum zur Geschichte des Bistums und Hochstifts Bamberg: 1945–1971/ für d. Berichte d. Hist. Vereins Bamberg 90 (1950)–107 (1971) zusammengestellt u. systemat. geordnet in d. Staatsbibliothek Bamberg. — Bamberg: Staatsbibliothek ⌈1971⌉.
66 columns; 36 cm. GFR 73-B9
Caption title.
1. Bamberg (Diocese)—Bibliography. 2. Bamberg (Ecclesiastical principality)—Bibliography. I. Title.
Z7778.B34B34 1971 74-323597

Bamberg. Staatsbibliothek.
see Krafft, Barbara, 1764-1825. Barbara Krafft nata Steiner, Iglau 1764-1825 Bamberg ... 1. Aufl. Bamberg, Kunstverein, 1976.

Bamberg. Staatsbibliothek. MSS.
see also
Bamberg. Staatliche Bibliothek. MSS.

Bamberg. Staatsbibliothek. MSS. Misc. (580a)
see Freytag, Frantz Melchior. Die Ebermannstadter Liederhandschrift... Kulmbach, Freunde der Plassenburg, 1972.

Bamberg (Ecclesiastical principality). Laws, statutes, etc.
Des Lantgerichts zu Bamberg Reformation. ⌈Bamberg? J. Pfeyl? 1503?⌉
⌈23⌉ p. 29 cm.
Caption title.
1. Bamberg (Ecclesiastical principality). Landgericht. I. Title.
54-52794
rev

Bamberg, S. C. Planning Commission.
Comprehensive planning: 1, Community facilities plan and public improvements program; 2, Recommended comprehensive zoning ordinance; 3, Recommended subdivision regulations; 4, Preliminary thoroughfare plan and future land use plan; 5, Population and economic study. Bamberg, 1969.
5 v. (HUD 701 Report)
1. City planning–Bamberg, S. C.
DHUD NUC76-11161

Bamberg, S.C. Planning Commission.
Existing land use survey analysis. Bamberg, 1969.
23 l. (HUD 701 Report)
1. Land use—Bamberg, S.C.
DHUD NUC74-7441

Bamberg, S. C. Planning Commission
see South Carolina. State Planning and Grants Division. Project completion report UPA Project no. SPC 17... Bamberg, 1970.

Bamberg Co., S. C.
see also
Orangeburgh District, S. C.

Bamberg County Committee.
Bamberg County celebrating South Carolina's Tricentennial, 1670-1970. Souvenir program. ⌈n.p.⌉ 1970.
40 p. illus.
1. Bamberg County, S.C.—History.
ScU NUC74-7442

Bamberg heute: Zur 1000-Jahr-Feier d. Stadt Bamberg im Jahre 1973/ [Schriftl. u. Zusammenstellung: Willi Braun.] In Zusammenarb. mit d. Stadt Bamberg. — Berlin, Basel: Länderdienst-Verlag, 1972.
102 p.: ill. (part col.), map; 30 cm. — (Deutschlands Städtebau, Kommunal- und Volkswirtschaft) DM18.00 GDB 73-A10
1. Bamberg—Economic conditions. 2. Bamberg—Social conditions. I. Braun, Willi.
HC289.B24B34 73-340240
ISBN 3-87455-017-6

Bamberger, Bernard Jacob, 1904-
Recollections of William Rosenau. New York, Temple Oheb Shalom [1965]
7 p. 22 cm.
"Centennial sabbath in honor of 100th anniversary of the birth of the Rev. Dr. William Rosenau."
1. Rosenau, William, 1865-1943. I. Title.
OCH NUC74-137769

Bamberger, Catherine, 1935-
L'Ensorceleé de Barbey d'Aurevilly; thematologie. [New York] 1973 [c1974]
310, [4] l. 29 cm.
Thesis—Columbia University.
Introduction in French and English; Conclusion in English.
Bibliography: leaves 307-310.
1. Barbey d'Aurevilly, Jules Amédée, 1808-1889. L'ensorceleé. I. Title.
NNC NUC76-30147

Bamberger, David. A functional teacher's guide
see Gordis, David. A conceptual teacher's guide. New York, Behrman House [c1971]

Bamberger, David
see Siegel, Seymour. Teacher's guides for When a Jew prays... [New York, Behrman, c1973-

Bamberger, David S., tr.
see Murger, Henri, 1822-1861. [Scenes de la vie de Bohème. Selections. English] Sources of Puccini's "La Boheme". [n. p.] 1973.

Bamberger, E. Clinton
see Association of American Law Schools. Curriculum Study Project. Training for the public professions of law, 1971. [n. p.] 1971.

Bamberger, E. N.
see American Society of Mechanical Engineers. Rolling-Elements Committee. Life adjustment factors for ball and roller bearings... New York, American Society of Mechanical Engineers [c1971]

Bamberger, Günter G 1943–
Gestörte Ehen und ihr soziologischer Kontext Günter G. Bamberger. — Kevelaer : Butzon und Bercker, 1974.
124 p. : ill. ; 20 cm. — (Familie in der Diskussion ; 6) GFR 76-A
Bibliography: p. 121-123.
ISBN 3-7666-8809-X : DM9.80
1. Marriage—Germany, West. 2. Divorce—Germany, West. I. Title. II. Series.
HQ5.F35 no. 6 76-502103
[HQ625]

Bamberger, Ingolf, 1943-
Budgetierungsprozesse in Organisationen. [n. p.] 1971.
296, xxxiii p. illus. 21 cm.
Inaug.-Diss.—Mannheim (Wirtschaftshochschule)
Vita.
Bibliography: p. [i]-xxxiii. Bibliographical footnotes.
1. Budget in business. I. Title.
MdU NUC73-32203

Bamberger, Jeanne Shapiro.
The art of listening; developing musical perception, by Jeanne Shapiro Bamberger and Howard Brofsky. With a foreword by Roger Sessions. 2d ed. New York, Harper & Row [1972]
xxii, 357 p. illus. 24 cm.
In the 1969 ed. Brofsky's name appeared first on t. p.
ISBN 0-06-040962-2
1. Music — Analysis, appreciation. 2. Music — Instruction and study—Audio-visual aids. I. Brofsky, Howard, joint author. II. Title.
MT150.B74 1972 780'.15 75-186223
rev MARC

Bamberger, Jeanne Shapiro.
The art of listening : developing musical perception / Jeanne Shapiro Bamberger, Howard Brofsky ; with a foreword by Roger Sessions. — 3d ed. — New York : Harper & Row, [1975]
xxvi, 403 p. : ill. ; 24 cm.
Includes indexes.
ISBN 0-06-040948-7
1. Music—Analysis, appreciation. 2. Music—Instruction and study—Audio-visual aids. I. Brofsky, Howard, joint author. II. Title.
MT150.B74 1975 780'.15 74-14347
74 MARC

Bamberger, Jeanne Shapiro.
Developing a musical ear: a new experiment. [Cambridge] M. I. T. A. I. Laboratory, 1972.
18 p. illus. (M. I. T. Artifical Intelligence Laboratory. Artificial intelliegence memo, no. 264)
Contract no. N00014-70-A-0362-0002.
1. Music—Analysis, appreciation. I. Title. II. Series.
MCM NUC76-71529

Bamberger, Joan
see Rosaldo, Michelle Zimbalist. Woman, culture, and society. Stanford, Calif., Stanford Univ. Press, 1974.

Bamberger, John Eudes, ed.
see Evagrius Ponticus, 345?-399? The praktikos. Chapters on prayer. Spencer, Mass., Cistercian Publications, 1970 [c1972]

Bamberger, Paul.
Eating is to till the earth; poems. Milwaukee, Wis., Shore Pub. Co., c1972.
92 p.
I. Title.
CLU NcD CU-A NUC74-133884

Bamberger, Richard.
Buchpädagogik. [Hrsg. vom Internationalen Institut für Jugendliteratur und Leseforschung und vom Österreichischen Buchklub der Jugend. Wien, Leinmüller, 1972]
171 p. (Schriften zur Jugendlektüre, Bd. 13)
Bibliography: p. 165-[172]
1. Reading. I. Internationales Institut für Jugendliteratur und Leseforschung. II. Title. III. Series.
CLU NUC76-71552

Bamberger, Richard.
Freedom through education; [life and work of Booker Washington] Wien, Verlag für Jugend und Volk [19--]
43 p. (United World Library, 3)
1. Washington, Booker Taliaferro, 1859?-1915. I. Title.
MiU NUC74-6938

Bamberger, Richard.
Jugendschriftenkunde / Richard Bamberger. — [1. Aufl.]. — Wien ; München : Jugend & Volk, c1975.
204 p. ; 21 cm. Au76-11-224
Bibliography: p. 189-193.
Includes indexes.
ISBN 3-7141-5170-2 : S88.00
1. Children's literature—History and criticism. I. Title.
PN1009.A1B33 76-475730
*76 MARC

Bamberger, Richard.
Lese-Erziehung. [Mit Diagr. u. Tab.] Wien, München, Jugend & Volk, (1973–
v. 21 cm. (Pädagogik der Gegenwart, 903) S 108.00 (v. 1.)
Au 73-16-162 (v. 1.)
1. Reading. I. Title.
LB1050.B33 73-350110
ISBN 3-7141-5340-3 (v. 1)

Bamberger, Richard.
Promoting the reading habit / by Richard Bamberger. — Paris : Unesco ; New York : distributed by Unesco Publications Center, c1975.
52 p. ; 27 cm. — (Reports and papers on mass communication ; no. 72) F***
Bibliography: p. 47-52.
ISBN 9231012185
1. Books and reading. I. Title. II. Series.
Z1003.B1853 028'.9 75-328349
76 MARC

Bamberger, Richard.
Reading and children's books; essays and papers, a collection of reprints. [Vienna, International Institute for Children's, Juvenile and Popular Literature, 1971?]
108 p. illus. 21 cm. Au***
1. Books and reading for children—Addresses, essays, lectures. I. International Institute for Children's, Juvenile and Popular Literature. II. Title.
Z1037.B263 028.52 73-150798
MARC

Bamberger, Richard.
20 years of the International Board on Books for Young People, 1973 / editors Richard Bamberger, Lucia Binder, Bettina Hürlimann. — Prague : Společnost přátel knihy pro mládež, 1973.
235 p. : ill. ; 21 cm. Cz***
English, French and German.
1. International Board on Books for Young People. I. Binder, Lucia, joint author. II. Hürlimann, Bettina, 1909- joint author. III. International Board on Books for Young People. IV. Title.
Z1037.A1B23 028.5 74-196527
MARC

Bamberger, Richard
see International Board on Books for Young People. Report... [Sofia? 1963?]

Bamberger, Richard, ed.
see International Institute for Children's, Juvenile and Popular Literature. 1000 & 1 [i. e. Tausendundein] Buch. Wien, Jugend & Volk, 1970.

Bamberger, Richard.
see Internationales Institut für Jugendliteratur und Leseforschung. Jugendbuch und Jugendbuchtheorie heute ... Wien, Internat. Inst. f. Jugendliteratur u. Leseforschung : Österr. Buchklub d. Jugend, [1976]

Bamberger, Richard, ed.
see Die Lesesituation in Österreich. Wien, Selbstverl. des Österr. Buchklubs d. Jugend [19]72.

Bamberger, Richard, 1911-
see Beiträge zur Didaktik und Erziehungswissenschaft... Paderborn, F. Schöningh, 1971.

Bamberger, Richard Edwin, 1930-
A study of organizational climate, faculty belief systems, and their relation to the rate of adoption of educational innovations in selected school districts. [Albany] 1970.
Microfilm of typescript. Ann Arbor, Mich., University Microfilms, 1970.
Collation of original: vi, 121 l.
Thesis-State University of New York at Albany.
Includes bibliography.
1. Education innovations. 2. School environment. 3. Teacher-administrator relationships. I. Title.
N NUC73-38947

Bamberger, Richard H., joint author
see Katz, Lewis R Justice is the crime... Cleveland, Press of Case Western Reserve University, 1972.

Bamberger, Rudolf, 1888-1945
see Rudolf Bamberger: Skizzen aus Leben u. Werk... Berlin: Dt. Kinemathek Berlin [1972]

Bamberger, Ruth E 1937-
Determinants of policy orientations and likemindedness of local party elites: the case of Franklin County, Ohio, by Ruth E. Bamberger. [n. p.] 1973.
129 l.
Thesis—Ohio State University.
Bibliography: leaves 127-129.
1. Political parties—Ohio—Franklin County. I. Title.
OU NUC75-16642

Bamberger, Seckel, 1863-1934, editor and tr.
see Aboth. 1914. Pirke Aboth. 2. Aufl. Frankfurt a. M., J. Kauffmann, 1914.

Bamberger, Selig, tr.
see Jews. Liturgy and ritual. [Hagadah. German & Hebrew] Seder ha-Hagadah le-lel shimurim. 8. Aufl. der Neuausg. Frankfurt a. M., M. Lehrberger, 1934.

Bamberger, Selig, ed.
see Kohn, J H (Otsar ha-Torah veha-Talmud) Bibel- und Talmudschatz... 9. Aufl., neu bearb. Hamburg, G. Kramer, 5670—1910.

Bamberger, Selig, ed.
see Kohn, J H [Otsar ha-Torah veha-Talmud] Bibel- und Talmudschatz... 12. Aufl., neu bearb. Hamburg, G. Kramer, 1924.

Bamberger, Seligman Baer, 1807-1878. Neti'ah shel Simhah. 1972
in Bamberger, Seligman Baer, 1807-1878. She'elot u-teshuvot Yad ha-Levi. 725-32 [1965-72]

Bamberger, Seligman Baer, 1807–1878.
(She'elot u-teshuvot Yad ha-Levi)
שו"ת יד הלוי; כולל תשובות בד' חלקי שו"ע אשר השיב לשואליו יצחק דוב הלוי במברגר. [ומצורף אליו שו"ת נטיעה של שמחה להגאון [המחבר] ושו"ת זכר של שמחה לבנו נשמחה הלוי במברגר] מובא לדפוס ברובו עפ"י כתבי־יד ובמיעוטו עפ"י דפוסים פזורים. ערך שלמה אדלר. ירושלים, 725–32 [1965–72]
2 v. 25 cm.
"שו"ת נטיעה של שמחה." and "שו"ת זכר שמחה" have special title pages.
1. Responsa—1800– I. Bamberger, Seligman Baer, 1807–1878. Neti'ah shel Simḥah. 1972. II. Bamberger, Simon, 1832–1897. Zekher Simḥah. 1972. III. Adler, Shelomoh, ed. IV. Title: Yad ha-Levi. V. Title: Neti'ah shel Simḥah. VI. Title: Zekher Simḥah.
BM522.24.M3 HE 65–1353
rev PL 480 : Is–1730

Bamberger, Simḥah, 1899–1957.
(She'elot u-teshuvot She'erit Simḥah)
שו"ת שארית שמחה : תשובות בארבעה חלקי שו"ע / מאת שמחה הלוי במברגר ; ונלוו אליהן כמה תשובות, מאת יצחק (זעקל) הלוי במברגר. ירושלים : [1968 or 1969] 729, [s. n.]
111 p. ; 25 cm.
1. Responsa—1800– I. Title: She'erit Simhah.
BM522.24.M317 1968 76–951227

Bamberger, Simon, 1832-1897. Zekher Simhah. 1972
in Bamberger, Seligman Baer, 1807-1878. She'elot u-teshuvot Yad ha-Levi. 725-32 [1965-72]

Bamberger, Simon Simcha
see
Bamberger, Simḥah, 1899-1957.

Bamberger, Y
Torseurs sur un espace affine [par] Y. Bamberger [et] J. P. Bourguignon. Paris, Centre de mathématiques, École polytechnique [196-?]
46 p.
1. Geometry, Affine. I. Bourguignon, J. P., joint author. II. Title.
MiU NUC73-39798

Bamberger, Y. Torseurs sur un espace affine. 1975.
in Schwartz, Laurent. Les Tenseurs. Paris, Hermann, 1975.

Bambergs, Kārlis, 1894-
see Agronomijas terminu vārdnīca ... Rīgā : Zinatne, 1973.

Bambergs, Kārlis, 1894-
see Rušināmaugu un pākšaugu razības kāpināšana. Rīgā, Latvijas PSR Zinātņu akadēmijos izdevniecība, 1963.

Bambergs christliche Sendung... München, 1966
see under Bavaria. Staatsarchiv, Bamberg.

Bambetsos, Alexandros Basileiou, 1890-
Eisēgēseis pros tēn 4. Anatheōrētikēn Voulēn tou Vouleutou Trikkalōn. Athēnai, 1961.
538 p. illus. 26 cm.
1. Greece. Constitution. I. Title.
OCU NUC74-120085

Bambey, Senegal. Centre de recherches agronomiques
see also the later heading
Centre national de recherches agronomiques.

Bambey, Senegal. Centre national de recherches agronomiques
see
Centre national de recherches agronomiques.

Bambi (Motion picture)
see Miller, Albert G 1905- Walt Disney's Bambi gets lost. New York, Random House [1972]

Bambiger, Michael.
The liberated man's natural foods cookbook / Michael Bambiger. — 1st ed. — Port Washington, N.Y. : Ashley Books, [1974]
240 p. ; 22 cm.
Includes index.
ISBN 0-87949-013-6 : $6.95
1. Cookery (Natural foods) I. Title.
TX741.B35 1974 641.6 73-83920
75 MARC

Bambiger, Michael S
Major commercial airport location: a methodology for the evaluation of potential sites [by] Michael S. Bambiger and Hugo L. Vandersypen. Evanston, Ill., Transportation Center, Northwestern University, 1969.
ix, 153 p. illus. 28 cm. (Evanston, Ill. Transportation Center at Northwestern University. Research report)
Includes bibliography.
1. Airports—Location. I. Evanston, Ill. Transportation Center at Northwestern University. II. Title.
CLSU NUC77-73633

I Bambini e la TV : la prima ricerca sull'esperienza televisiva dai 3 ai 6 anni / [di] P. Bertolini, M. Dallari, F. Frabboni, V. Gherardi, M. Manini, R. Massa ; a cura di Piero Bertolini e Riccardo Massa. — 1. ed. — Milano : Feltrinelli economica, 1976.
273 p., [6] leaves of plates : ill. ; 18 cm. — (I Nuovi testi ; 122)
It77-Mar
L3000
1. Television and children. 2. Television broadcasting—Italy. I. Bertolini, Piero. II. Massa, Riccardo, 1945-
HQ784.T4B33 77-468098
•77 MARC

Bambini in manicomio / [a cura di] Psichiatria democratica. — Roma : Bulzoni, [1975]
109 p. ; 17 cm. — (Psichiatria ; 1) (Psychon) It 75-Sept
L1500
1. Child psychotherapy—Residential treatment—Italy.
I. Psichiatria democratica.
RJ504.5.B35 75-546044

Bambini per chi? : immagine dell'infanzia e della pedagogia parentale nel Ferrarese / A. Bassi ... [et al.]. — 1. ed. — Milano : Feltrinelli, 1975.
132 p. ; 18 cm. — (I Nuovi testi ; 86) It 75-Sept
Bibliography: p. 131-[133]
L1700
1. Parent and child. 2. Children in Ferrara (Province) 3. Children—Management. I. Bassi, Amleto.
HQ755.85.B35 76-508912

Il Bambino e l'ambiente socio-culturale. — Brescia : Centro didattico nazionale per la scuola materna, 1974.
199 p. : ill. ; 21 cm. It 75-Feb
At head of title: Ministero della pubblica istruzione. Centro didattico nazionale per la scuola materna.
1. Students' socio-economic status—Italy. I. Brescia. Centro didattico nazionale per la scuola materna.
LC206.I 8B35 75-540336

Il Bambino non visto : una esperienza di formazione degli educatori per una nuova scuola dell'infanzia / [Alberto Alberti ... et al.] ; a cura del Dipartimento dei servizi sociali del Comune di Foligno ; introduzione di Alberto Alberti. — 1. ed. — Roma : Editori riuniti, 1975.
163 p., 1 fold. leaf of plates : facsim. ; 19 cm. — (Paideia ; 44)
It 75-Sept
L1500
1. Education, Preschool—Foligno, Italy. I. Alberti, Alberto, 1907- II. Foligno, Italy. Dipartimento dei servizi sociali.
LB1140.2.B25 75-542402

Bambirra, Vania.
Capitalismo dependiente latinoamericano. Santiago de Chile, Editorial Prensa Latinoamericana, c1973.
157 p. 23 cm. (Chile. Universidad, Santiago. Centro de Estudios Socio-Economicos. Cuadernos, no. 16)
1. Latin America—Foreign economic relations. 2. Latin America—Econ. condit.—1945- I. Title. II. Series.
CtY NUC75-17442

Bambirra, Vania, comp.
L'esperienza rivoluzionaria latino-americana ... / a cura di Vania Bambirra ; premessa di Saverio Tutino. — Milano : G. Mazzotta, 1973.
410 p. ; 19 cm. — (Biblioteca di nuova cultura ; 15) It 74-July
Essays.
Includes bibliographical references.
L2800
1. Revolutions—Latin America—Addresses, essays, lectures. 2. Latin America—Politics and government—1948- —Addresses, essays, lectures. I. Title.
F1414.2.B28 76-508457

Bambirra, Vania.
Integración monopólica mundial e industrialización sus contradicciones / Vania Bambirra. — Caracas : Universidad Central de Venezuela, Facultad de Ciencias Económicas y Sociales, División de Publicaciones, 1974.
31 p. ; 21 cm. — (Colección Esquema)
Includes bibliographical references.
1. Corporations, Foreign—Latin America. 2. Monopolies—Latin America. 3. Latin America—Economic conditions—1945. I. Title.
HD2810.5.B34 75-579425

Bambirra, Vania.
La revolución cubana: una reinterpretación. [1. ed. en México. México] Editorial Nuestro Tiempo [1974]
172 p. 19 cm. (Colección: Latinoamérica Hoy)
Bibliography: p. 169-172.
1. Cuba—Pol. & govt.—1959- 2. Movimiento Revolucionario de 26 de Julio (Cuba) 3. Guerrillas—Cuba. I. Title.
CSt-H NUC76-25304

Bambirra, Vania.
La revolución cubana; una reinterpretación. [2. ed. México] Editorial Nuestro Tiempo [1974]
172 p. (Latinoamérica Hoy)
1. Cuba—Politics and government—1959- I. Title.
InU NUC76-25342

Bamboat, Zenobia.
Les voyageurs français dans l'Inde aux XVIIe et XVIIIe siecles. Avec une introduction de M. A. Martineau. New York, B. Franklin [1972]
197 p. illus. 24 cm. (Burt Franklin research and source works series. Geography & discovery series: the literature of travel and exploration, 15)
Reprint of the 1933 ed., issued in series: Bibliothèque d'histoire coloniale.
Bibliography: p. [189]-193.
1. India—Description & travel—1498-1761. 2. Travelers, French. 3. Missions—India. I. Title.
DS411.5.B3 1972 72-83617

Bamborough, J B
The little world of man / by J. B. Bamborough. — Norwood, Pa. : Norwood Editions, 1975.
187 p. ; 26 cm.
Reprint of the 1952 ed. published by Longmans, Green, London, New York.
Bibliography: p. [178]-182.
Includes indexes.
ISBN 0-88305-919-3 : $15.00
1. Psychology—History. 2. Mind and body. 3. English literature—Early modern, 1500-1700—History and criticism. 4. Shakespeare, William, 1564-1616—Knowledge—Psychology. I. Title.
BF98.B2 1975 820'.9'003 75-40126
75 MARC

Bamborough, Philip.
Treasures of Islam / [by] Philip Bamborough. — Poole : Blandford Press, 1976.
160 p. : ill. (some col.), facsims. (some col.), map, ports. ; 23 cm.
Ill. on lining papers.
Includes index.
ISBN 0-7137-8503-9 : £3.50. ISBN 0-7137-8505-5 pbk.
1. Art, Islamic. I. Title.
N6260.B35 709'.1'7671 76-376890
76 MARC

Bamborough, Philip.
Treasures of Islam / Philip Bamborough. — New York : Arco Pub. Co., 1977, c1976.
160 p. : ill. (some col.) ; 22 cm.
Includes index.
ISBN 0-668-04178-1 : $8.95
1. Art, Islamic. I. Title.
N6260.B35 1977 709'.1'7671 76-55808
76 MARC

Bamboté, Pierre.
La poésie est dans l'histoire. Paris, P.J. Oswald [1960]
40 p. 22 cm. (Collection Janus)
I. Title.
MdU NUC73-2344

Bamboté, Pierre.
Princesse Mandapu; roman [par] Bamboté. Paris, Présence africaine [1972]
187 p. 20 cm. (Écrits) F***
I. Title.
PQ3989.2.B3P7 73-318866

Bamboté, Pierre.
Technique pour rien : suivi de Civilisation des autres / Makombo Bamboté. — Paris : Librairie Saint-Germain-des-Prés, [1973]
142 p. ; 21 cm. — (Poésie sans frontière) F***
I. Title.
PQ3989.2.B3T4 841 74-195526
MARC

Bambou, Pierre.
Tim-tim. [Port-au-Prince] 1973.
60 p. 21 cm. (Colection Coucouille)
Poems in Haitian creole dialect.
I. Title. II. Series.
TxU NUC76-71530

Bambra, Audrey.
Teaching folk dancing [by] Audrey Bambra and Muriel Webster. London, Batsford, 1972.
128 p. illus., music. 26 cm. index. £2.20 B 72-28017
Includes bibliographical references.
1. Folk dancing. I. Webster, Muriel, joint author. II. Title.
GV1743.B35 793.3'1 73-160068
ISBN 0-7134-2164-9 MARC

Bambra, Audrey.
Teaching folk dancing, by Audrey Bambra and Muriel Webster. New York, Theatre Arts Books [c1972]
128 p. illus., music.
Bibliographical references.
1. Folk dancing. I. Webster, Muriel, joint author. II. Title.
RP NUC77-50034

Bambrick, Susan.
The changing relationship : the Australian government and the mining industry / by Susan Bambrick. — [Melbourne] : Committee for Economic Development of Australia, 1975.
v, 93 p. : maps ; 24 cm. — (M. series ; no. 42) Aus***
Includes bibliographical references.
ISBN 0-85801-043-7 : $8.00
1. Mineral industries—Australia. 2. Industry and state—Australia. I. Title. II. Series: Committee for Economic Development of Australia. Monograph series ; no. 42.
HC601.C57 no. 42 330.9'94 s 75-331248
[HD9506.A72] 76 MARC

Bambrick, Susan.
see The Multinational corporation and international investment in Australia ... Sydney, Sydney University Extension Board, 1974.

Bambrough, Renford.
Conflict and the scope of reason; the St John's College, Cambridge, lecture, 1973–74, delivered at the University of Hull, 8 March 1973, by J. R. Bambrough. Hull, University of Hull, 1974.
[4], 20 p. 22 cm. (St. John's College lecture, 1973–74) £0.30
GB 74-13922
Bibliography: p. 19–20.
1. Reason—Addresses, essays, lectures. 2. Reasoning—Addresses, essays, lectures. I. Title. II. Series: The St. John's College, Cambridge, lecture, 1973–74.
BC177.B26 168 74-182777
ISBN 0-900480-77-7 MARC

Bambrough, Renford, ed.
see Wisdom: twelve essays. Oxford, Blackwell [1974]

Bambrough, Renford, ed.
see Wisdom: twelve essays. Totowa, N. J., Rowman and Littlefield [1974]

La bambufluto. Japanese.
竹笛：南ベトナム短篇集 / [金沢エスペラント会婦人部共訳]. — 金沢：[金沢エスペラント会婦人部], 昭和49 [1974]
230 p. : ill. ; 18 cm. Ja 75-12783
Translated from the Esperanto.
¥600
CONTENTS: ズウン・ティ・ミン・フォン 野の花—ホアイ・ブウ 竹笛—レイ・ビイン・ホア 帰順者—アイン・ドク 風の季節—グェン・テイ 母ちゃんの留守に—ファン・ヴォ 爆弾の穴の側で—チャン・フォン・チャ 水牛—ツウ・ニヤン・ヴイ ビェン・チャインの母—アイン・ドク 私と同じ村の人の話
¥600

1. Esperanto fiction—Translations into Japanese. 2. Japanese fiction—Translations from Esperanto. 3. Vietnamese Conflict, 1961–1975—Fiction. I. Kanazawa Esuperantokai. Fujinbu. II. Title.
Title romanized: Takebue.
PL780.E8L3 76-811156

Bamburgh Castle official guide-book. [New ed.]. Morpeth, W. H. Watson-Armstrong, 1972.
48 p. illus. 23 cm. GB 73-02796
Cover title.
1. Bamburgh. Castle.
DA664.B25B35 1972 914.28'2 74-178921
ISBN 0-9502676-0-0 MARC

Bamburkin, Alekseĭ Petrovich.
(Nazemnye radiosvetotekhnicheskie sredstva obespechenii͡a poletov)
Наземные радиосветотехнические средства обеспечения полетов. [Учеб. пособие для сред. учеб. заведений гражд. авиации]. Москва, "Транспорт," 1973.
244 p. with illus. 22 cm. 0.68rub USSR 73
At head of title: А. П. Бамбуркин, В. А. Кузнецов.
1. Airports—Traffic control. 2. Airports—Lighting. I. Kuznet͡sev, Vladimir Aleksandrovich. II. Title.
TL725.3.T7B35 74-344105

Bamburov, Vitalii Grigor'evich
see Fiziko-khimicheskie issledovanii͡a zhidkikh metallov i splavov. 1974.

Bamburov, Vitaliĭ Grigor'evich
see Sintez i svoĭstva soedineniĭ redkikh ėlementov chetvertykh-shestykh grupp. 1975.

Bāmdād,
see
Shāmlū, Aḥmad.

Bāmdād, Badr al-Mulūk.
From darkness into light : women's emancipation in Iran / by Badr ol-Moluk Bámdád ; edited and translated by F. R. C. Bagley. — 1st ed. — Hicksville, N.Y. : Exposition Press, c1977.
xx, 140 p., [1] leaf of plates ; 22 cm. — (An Exposition-university book)
Translation of Zan-i Īrānī az inqilāb-i mashrūṭīyat tā inqilāb-i safīd.
Includes bibliographical references.
ISBN 0-682-48705-8 : $8.00
1. Women—Iran—History. 2. Feminism—Iran. 3. Women's rights—Iran. I. Bagley, Frank Ronald Charles. II. Title.
HQ1768.B3513 301.41'2'0955 76-50308
77 MARC

Bāmdād, Badr al-Mulūk.
طباخی ، ایرانی ، فرنگی ، ترکی. تالیف بدر الموك [sic] بامداد.
[چاپ 3. تهران ، شرکت مطبوعات ، 1326 i. e. 1947 or 8]
299, 6 p. illus. 21 cm.
Cover title.
1. Cookery, Iranian. 2. Cookery, Turkish. 3. Cookery, French. I. Title.
Title romanized: Tabbākhī.
TX724.5.I7B35 1947 74-216769

Bāmdād, Mahdī.
(Sharḥ-i ḥāl-i rijāl-i Īrān)
شرح حال رجال ایران ، در قرن ۱۲ و ۱۳ و ۱۴ هجری.
نگارش مهدی بامداد. [تهران ، کتابفروشی زوار ،
1347– i. e. 1968 or 9–]
v. ports. 25 cm.
Added t. p.: Dictionary of national biography of Iran, 1700–1960, by Mahdi Bamdad.
Cover title: تاریخ رجال ایران
1. Iran—Biography. I. Title. II. Title: Tārīkh-i rijāl-i Īrān. III. Title: Dictionary of national biography of Iran.
DS271.B35 78-279974
rev

Bamdas, Aleksandr Markovich.
(Analogovoe modelirovanie ispolnitel'nykh ferromagnitnykh ustroĭstv)
Аналоговое моделирование исполнительных ферромагнитных устройств / А. М. Бамдас, Ю. П. Разуваев, С. В. Шапиро. — Москва : Наука, 1975.
439 p. : ill. ; 22 cm. USSR 75
Bibliography: p. [430]–439.
2.49rub
1. Magnetic devices—Electromechanical analogies. 2. Magnetic devices — Data processing. 3. Electronic apparatus and appliances — Electromechanical analogies. 4. Electronic apparatus and appliances—Data processing. I. Razuvaev, I͡Uriĭ Petrovich, joint author. II. Shapiro, Semen Vol'fovich, joint author. III. Title.
TK7872.M25B35 76-507163

Bamdes, Ḥayim.
[Matsa Ḥayim]
ספר מצא חיים ... כולל מאמרים ... מאתי חיים במדם.
ווילנא, בדפום ש. פ. גארבער, 1905.
96 p. 22 cm.
1. Bible. O. T.—Commentaries. I. Title.
Title romanized: Sefer Matsa Ḥayim.
BS1158.H4B33 75-950317

Bame, Edgar Allen, 1936-
Concepts of the interface between technology and the environment: implications for industrial arts education. Raleigh, N.C., 1973.
176 l. tables. 29 cm.
Thesis (Ph.D.)—North Carolina State University at Raleigh.
Vita.
Bibliography: leaves 131-143.
NcRS NUC75-16641

Bameĭko, Taras.
От Карпат до Донца или еще дальше? [n. p., 19—]
26 p. 30 cm.
1. Ukraine—Foreign relations—Russia. 2. Ukraine—History. 3. Russia—Foreign relations—Ukraine. I. Title.
Title transliterated: Ot Karpat do Dont͡sa ili eshche dal'she?
DK508.57.R9B35 74-213808

Bamert, Ursula
see Althaus, Hans. Schweizer Ski-Nationalmannschaft 1972. Derendingen-Solothurn, Habegger [1971]

Bamesberger, Velda Christena, 1896–
An appraisal of a social studies course, in terms of its effect upon the achievement, activities, and interests of pupils, by Velda C. Bamesberger. New York, Bureau of Publications, Teachers College, Columbia University, 1928. [New York, AMS Press, 1972]
91 p. 22 cm.
Reprint of the 1928 ed., issued in series: Teachers College, Columbia University. Contributions to education, no. 328.
Originally presented as the author's thesis, Columbia.
Bibliography: p. 90–91.
1. Social sciences—Study and teaching (Elementary) I. Title. II. Series: Columbia University. Teachers College. Contributions to education, no. 328.
LB1584.B3 1972 372.8'3'043 72-176535
ISBN 0-404-55328-1 MARC

Bamfield, J A N
A consumer's guide to the Common Market [by J. A. N. Bamfield] Loughborough, Co-operative Union, Education Department [1973]
52 p. 21 cm. (Topic for today, no. 3) £0.25 GB 73-05594
1. Consumers—European Economic Community countries. I. Title. II. Series.
HC240.B26 338.91'4 74-179952
ISBN 0-85195-080-9 MARC

Bamfield, Veronica, 1908-
On the strength : the story of the British army wife / Veronica Bamfield. — London : C. Knight, c1974.
223 p. : ill. ; 22 cm. GB***
Includes bibliographies and index.
ISBN 0-85314-231-9 : £3.25
1. Great Britain. Army—Military life. 2. Army wives. I. Title.
U767.B28 355.1'2 75-315719
75 MARC

Bamford, A J
Upper air observations, 1922–23, by A. J. Bamford. With appendices by H. Jameson. Colombo, Printed by A. C. Richards, Acting Govt. Printer, 1924.
32 p. illus. 34 cm. (Ceylon Survey Dept. Bulletins of the Colombo Observatory, no. 5)
Cover title.
1. Atmosphere, Upper—Ceylon—Colombo—Rawinsonde observations. I. Title. II. Series: Colombo, Ceylon. Observatory. Bulletins, no. 5.
QC990.C42C62 551.5'14'095493 73-151493
MARC

Bamford, Brian Reginald.
The law of shipping and carriage in South Africa, by B. R. Bamford. 2d ed. Cape Town, Juta, 1973.
xxxiii, 283 p. 26 cm. SA***
First ed. published in 1961 under title: The law of shipping in South Africa.
Bibliography: p. xiii.
1. Maritime law—Africa, South. 2. Carriers—Africa, South. I. Title.
343'.68'0968 74-170527
ISBN 0-7021-0480-9 MARC

Bamford, Brian Reginald
see South Africa. Laws, statutes, etc. [Electoral consolidation act, 1946. Afrikaans and English] Handboek oor die Wet tot konsolidasie van die kieswette ... Kaapstad, Juta, 1964.

Bamford, C H
Addition and elimination reactions of aliphatic compounds. Edited by C. H. Bamford and C. F. H. Tipper. Amsterdam, New York, Elsevier Scientific Publishing Co., 1973.
xiii, 515 p. 25 cm. (Their Comprehensive chemical kinetics, v. 9)
fl 166.40 Ne 73-14
Includes bibliographies.
1. Elimination reactions. 2. Addition reactions. I. Tipper, Charles Frank Howlett, joint author. II. Title.
QD501.B242 vol. 9 541'.39'08 s 72-83195
[QD281.E4] [547'.4] MARC
ISBN 0-444-41051-1

Bamford, C H
Degradation of polymers / edited by C. H. Bamford and C. F. H. Tipper. — Amsterdam ; New York : Elsevier Scientific Pub. Co., 1975.
xv, 562 p. ; 25 cm. — (Their Comprehensive chemical kinetics ; v. 14)
Includes bibliographies and index.
ISBN 0-444-41155-0 (American Elsevier) : fl 200.00
1. Polymers and polymerization—Deterioration. I. Title.
QD501.B242 vol. 14 541'.39'08 s 73-85218
[TA455.P58] *75[r76]rev MARC

Bamford, C H
Electrophilic substitution at a saturated carbon atom. Edited by C. H. Bamford and C. F. H. Tipper. Amsterdam, New York, Elsevier Scientific Pub. Co., 1973.
xiii, 256 p. 25 cm. (Their Comprehensive chemical kinetics, v. 12) Ne***
Includes bibliographical references.
1. Substitution reactions. 2. Aliphatic compounds. I. Tipper, Charles Frank Howlett, joint author. II. Title.
QD501.B242 vol. 12 541'.39'08 s 72-83196
[QD281.S67] [541'.393] MARC
ISBN 0-444-41052-X

Bamford, C H
Ester formation and hydrolysis and related reactions, edited by C. H. Bamford and C. F. H. Tipper. Amsterdam, New York, Elsevier, 1972.
x, 309 p. illus. (Comprehensive chemical kinetics. Section 4: Organic reactions, v. 10)
Includes bibliographies.
1. Esterification. 2. Hydrolysis. 3. Chemical reactions. I. Tipper, Charles Frank Howlett, joint author. II. Title.
DGU MiEM AzTeS NjP NUC73-116533

Bamford, C H
Free-radical polymerisation / edited by C. H. Bamford and C. F. H. Tipper. — Amsterdam ; New York : Elsevier Pub. Co., 1976.
xiii, 594 p. : ill. ; 25 cm. — (Their Comprehensive chemical kinetics ; v. 14A)
Includes bibliographical references and index.
ISBN 0-444-41486-X
1. Polymers and polymerization. 2. Radicals (Chemistry) I. Tipper, Charles Frank Howlett, joint author. II. Title.
QD501.B242 vol. 14A 541'.39'08 76-28370
[QD381] 76 MARC

Bamford, C. H.
see Non-radical polymerisation. Amsterdam, Elsevier Scientific Publishing Co., 1976.

Bamford, C.H.
see Selected elementary reactions. -- Amsterdam ; New York ; Elsevier Scientific Pub. Co., 1976.

Bamford, G. S. T., joint author
see Bennion, Edmund Baron. The technology of cake making. [5th. ed.] Aylesbury, L. Hill, 1973.

Bamford, Georgia Loring.
The mystery of Jack London, some of his friends, also a few letters, a reminiscence. With illus. by the author and also from photos. [Folcroft, Pa.] Folcroft Library Editions, 1973 [c1931]
252 p. illus. 23 cm.
Reprint of the ed. published by the author, Oakland, Calif.
1. London, Jack, 1876-1916. I. Title.
PS3523.O46Z6 1973 818'.5'209 [B] 73-15997
ISBN 0-8414-9856-3 (lib. bdg.) MARC

Bamford, Georgia Loring.
The mystery of Jack London : some of his friends, also a few letters : a reminiscence / by Georgia Loring Bamford. — Norwood, Pa. : Norwood Editions, 1976 [c1931]
252 p. : ill. ; 22 cm.
Reprint of the ed. published by G. L. Bamford, Oakland, Calif.
Includes index.
ISBN 0-8482-0269-4 lib. bdg. : $22.50
1. London, Jack, 1876-1916—Biography. 2. Authors, American—20th century—Biography. I. Title.
PS3523.O46Z6 1976 818'.5'09 76-27654
76 MARC

Bamford, Joan.
Collecting antiques for the future / Joan Bamford. — Guildford [Eng.] : Lutterworth, 1976.
184 p. : ill. ; 23 cm. GB***
Bibliography: p. 173.
Includes index.
ISBN 0-7188-7008-5 : £4.50
1. Antiques. 2. Collectors and collecting. I. Title.
NK1125.B353 745.1'075 77-350619
77 MARC

Bamford, John M
The burning heart. London, C.H. Kelly [n.d.]
188 p. 18 cm.
1. Holy Spirit. 2. Sanctification. I. Title.
IEG NUC74-928

Bamford, P C
Histories of the non-co-operation and Khilafat movements / by P. C. Bamford. — Delhi : Deep Publications, 1974.
xiv, 270 p. ; 22 cm.
Includes a reproduction of the t. p. of the 1925 ed., published by Govt. of India Press, Delhi.
Includes bibliographical references and index.
Rs50.00
1. India—Politics and government—1919-1947. 2. Khilafat Movement. I. Title.
DS480.45.B27 1974 320.9'54'035 74-903099
MARC

Bamford, Paul Walden, 1921-
The Barbary Pirates: victims and the scourge of Christendom, by Paul W. Bamford. Minneapolis, Associates of the James Ford Bell Library, University of Minnesota, 1972.
21 p. 20 cm. (James Ford Bell lectures, no. 10)
1. Africa, North-Hist.-1517-1882. 2. Pirates. I. Title. II. Series.
ScU ICN CaBVaU KU NUC74-16790

Bamford, Paul Walden, 1921-
Fighting ships and prisons; the Mediterranean galleys of France in the age of Louis XIV [by] Paul W. Bamford. With drawings by John W. Ekstrom. Minneapolis, University of Minnesota Press [1973]
x, 380 p. illus. 24 cm. $16.50
Bibliography: p. 357-361.
1. Galleys. 2. Louis XIV, King of France, 1638-1715. I. Title.
VM71.B35 387.2'1 72-92334
ISBN 0-8166-0655-2 MARC

Bamford, Samuel, 1788-1972.
Walks in South Lancashire and on its borders; with letters, descriptions, narratives, and observations, current and incidental [by] Samuel Bamford. With an introd. by J. D. Marshall. [Brighton] Harvester Press, 1972.
xvii, 288 p. 18 cm. (Society and the Victorians)
Reprint of the 1844 ed.
1. Labor and laboring classes-Lancashire, Eng. 2. Weavers-Lancashire, Eng. 3. Lancashire, Eng.-Description and travel. I. Title. II. Series.
TxHR NUC76-71452

Bamford, Samuel, 1788-1872.
Walks in South Lancashire and on its borders; with letters, descriptions, narratives, and observations, current and incidental [by] Samuel Bamford. With an introd. by J. D. Marshall. Clifton [N. J.] A. M. Kelley, 1972.
xvii, 288 p. 18 cm. (Society and the Victorians)
Reprint of the 1844 ed.
1. Labor and laboring classes—Lancashire, Eng. 2. Weavers—Lancashire, Eng. 3. Lancashire, Eng.—Description and travel. I. Title. II. Series.
HD8399.L36B35 1972 301.44'42'094272 72-80019
ISBN 0-678-8023-2 MARC

Bamford, T. J.G.
see Wigan, M Ramsay. The effects of network structure... Crowthorne, Berkshire, Urban Transport Division, Transport Systems Dept., Transport and Road Research Laboratory, 1973.

Bamford, T W
Public school data : a compilation of data on public and related schools (boys) mainly from 1866 / T. W. Bamford. — [Hull] : University of Hull, Institute of Education, 1974.
79 p. : ill., maps ; 22 cm. — (Aids to research in education ; no. 2)
GB75-11583
Bibliography: p. 69-71.
Includes index.
ISBN 0-85958-200-0 : £1.25
1. Public schools, Endowed (Great Britain)—Statistics. I. Title. II. Series.
Z5811.A35 no. 2 373.2'24'0941 76-378816
[LA632] 76 MARC

Bamford, W. E., ed.
see Symposium on Raise and Tunnel Boring, University of Melbourne, 1970. Symposium on Raise and Tunnel Boring... [Melbourne, University of Melbourne] 1970.

Bamforth, Frederic Richard, 1899-
A classification of boundary value problems for a system of ordinary linear differential equations of the second order / by Frederic Richard Bamforth. — 1927.
ii, 47 leaves ; 29 cm.
Typescript (carbon copy).
Thesis—University of Chicago.
Vita.
1. Boundary value problems. 2. Differential equations, Linear. I. Title: A classification of boundary value problems ...
QA379.B35 515'.352 76-362482
76 MARC

Bamgbala, E O
Merchantable yields and stand projection in Akure Natural High Forest Reserve, Western Nigeria. Ibadan, 1973.
21 p. (Nigeria. Dept. of Forest Research. Research paper. Forest series no. 21)
Bibliography: p. 8.
I. Title.
DNAL NUC76-71531

Bamgboṣe, Ayọ.
Linguistics in a developing country : an inaugural lecture delivered at the University of Ibadan on 27 October 1972 / by Ayọ Bamgboṣe. — [Ibadan] : University of Ibadan, 1973.
20 p. ; 22 cm.
Bibliography: p. 19-20.
1. Linguistic research—History—Nigeria. 2. Nigeria—Languages. 3. Languages—Political aspects. I. Title.
P81.N5B3 410'.9669 75-312646
75 MARC

Bamgboṣe, Ayọ.
The novels of D. O. Fagunwa / Ayọ Bamgboṣe. — Benin City, Nigeria : Ethiope Pub. Corp., 1974.
ix, 132 p. ; 22 cm.
Bibliography: p. 131-132.
1. Fagunwa, D. O.—Criticism and interpretation. I. Title.
PL8824.F27Z6 896'.333'3 75-324528
75 MARC

Bamgboṣe, Ayọ.
see Mother tongue education ... London, Hodder and Stoughton, 1976.

Bamgbose, Ayo
see Yoruba Orthography Committee. Report. Ibadan, Ministry of Education [1972]

Bamigboye, D L
Kwara State schools board. Speech delivered by his Excellency the Military Governor of Kwara State, Colonel D. L. Bamibgoye, at the official launching of the Kwara State schools board in Ilorin, state capital, on 3/7/72. Ilorin, 1972.
14 p. front. (port.)
1. Education—Nigeria. Kwara State.
MBU NUC76-71546

Bamigboye, D L
Speech on the occasion of the launching of the Kwara State 1970-74 development plan delivered at Ilorin on Thursday 17th December, 1970. Ilorin, 1970.
20 p. illus. tables.
Cover title: 4 year development plan. 1970-1974.
1. Economic development—Nigeria—Kwara State.
MBU NUC73-39797

Bamigboye, D. L.
see Budget confidence... [Llorin, Nigeria, Information Division, Military Governor's Office, 1970 ?]

বাংলা, আমার বাংলা; ⌜বায়ান্নর একুশে ফেব্রুয়ারী ও বাংলা দেশের মুক্তি সংগ্রামের শহীদের স্মরণে⌝ মোহাম্মদ লিয়াকতউল্লাহ্ সম্পাদিত. ⌜সহ-যোগী সম্পাদনায়: নুরুল করিম নাসিম ⌜ও⌝ নার্গিস আরা হাওয়া. ঢাকা, সপ্তর্ষি সংঘ, 1972⌝
50 p. 22 cm. Re1.00
In Bengali.
1. Bangladesh—Languages—Addresses, essays, lectures. I. Liẏākataullāh, Mohāmmada, ed. II. Nāsima, Nurula Karima, ed. III. Nārgisa Ārā Hāoẏā, ed.
Title romanized: Bāṃlā, āmāra Bāṃlā.
DS485.B44B27 72-901814

(Bāṃlā-bidyā carcā)
বাংলা-বিদ্যা চর্চা : উচ্চ পর্যায়ে বাংলা ভাষা-সাহিত্যের শিক্ষা ও পাঠক্রম বিষয়ক আলোচনা বিবরণী / সম্পাদক নীলরতন সেন. — কল্যাণী : বাংলা বিভাগ, কল্যাণী বিশ্ববিদ্যালয়, 1974.
158, ⌜92⌝ p. ; 22 cm.
Comprises proceedings and papers of a seminar held at Kalyani University, Dec. 30, 1972–Jan. 1, 1973.
Bengali or English.
1. Bengali philology—Study and teaching—India—Congresses. I. Sen, Nilratan.
PK1657.B3 75-904691

(Bāṃlā kabitā)
বাংলা কবিতা / মযহারুল ইসলাম সম্পাদিত. — 1. সংস্করণ. — ঢাকা : বাংলাদেশ বুক কর্পোরেশন্, 1975.
300, ⌜73⌝ p. ; 22 cm.
In Bengali.
Includes biographical sketches of the contributors.
Tk16.50
1. Bengali poetry. I. Islam, Mazharul.
PK1714.B3 1975 75-907776

বাংলা নামে দেশ. ⌜সম্পাদনা: অভীক সরকার. 1. সংস্করণ⌝ কলিকাতা, আনন্দ পাবলিশার্স ⌜1972⌝
151 p. (chiefly illus., maps) 29 cm. Rs10.00
In Bengali.
1. Bangladesh—Politics and government—1971– I. Sarkar, Aveek, 1945– ed.
Title romanized: Bāṃlā nāme deśa.
DS485.B492B268 72-902431

(Bāṃlā prabāda pariciti)
বাংলা প্রবাদ পরিচিতি / মোহাম্মদ হানীফ পাঠান সংকলিত. — ঢাকা : বাংলা একাডেমী, 1976.
9, 580 p. ; 22 cm.
In Bengali.
Tk35.00
1. Proverbs, Bengali. I. Pathan, Mohammad Hanif.
PN6519.B42B28 76-900546

(Bāṃlā sāhitye choṭa galpera dhārā)
বাংলা সাহিত্যে ছোঠ গল্পের ধারা / শ্রীকুমার বন্দ্যোপাধ্যায়, প্রফুল্লচন্দ্র পাল সম্পাদিত. — কলিকাতা : মহাজাতি ⌜pref. 13 i.e. 19
v. ; 22 cm.
In Bengali.
1. Short stories, Bengali. I. Banerjee, Srikumar. II. Pāla, Praphullacandra.
PK1716.B24 75-985591

Bāṃlādeśa
see
Bangladesh.

Bāṃlādeśa Bāṃlā-sikshaka Samiti
see Bāṅalādeśa. 1974.

Bamladésa Bhashattva Samāja
see Bāṅalādeśa. 1974.

Bāṃlādeśa Chātra Iuniẏana
see
Bangladesh Students Union.

Bāṃlādeśa Kamiuniṣṭa Pārṭi
see
Communist Party of Bangladesh.

(Bāṃlādeśa kathā kaẏa)
বাংলাদেশ কথা কয় / সম্পাদক আবদুল গাফ্ফার চৌধুরী. — ঢাকা : মুক্ত-ধারা, 1974.
6, 192 p. ; 22 cm.
In Bengali.
CONTENTS: বড়ুয়া, বি. সাদা কফিন.—গুণ, নি. শেষ যাত্রা নয়.—হাফিজ, আ. লাল পল্টন.—বড়ুয়া, সু. বুলি তোমাকে লিখছি.—হক, ফ. চরিত্র.—আসফ-উজ-জামান. রক্ত প্রজন্ম.—ওসমান, বু. সোলেমান ভাই.—মাহবুব, কা. নীল নক্শা.—ইসলাম, অ. শব্দ তাড়িত.—চৌধুরী, আ. কমলা রঙের রোদ.—সেন, স. পারিবাম্নুর কাহনা.—আহ্মদ, ই. অন্যের ডায়েরি থেকে.—রায়হান, জ. সময়ের প্রয়োজনে.—আহ্মেদ, কা. শেষ বাজি.—ওসমান, শ. আলোক অন্বেষা.—চৌধুরী, আ. গ. রোদের অন্ধকারে বৃষ্টি.
Tk9.00
1. Short stories, Bengali. 2. Bangladesh—History—Revolution, 1971—Fiction. I. Chaudhury, Abdul Gaffar.
PK1716.B25 75-900376

Bāṃlādeśa Lokagaṇanā uniśacuẏāttara Semināra
see
Census of Bangladesh 1974 Seminar, Dacca, 1973.

Bāṃlādeśa Śilpa Byāṃka
see
Bangladesh Shilpa Bank.

বাংলাদেশের মুক্তিযুদ্ধ. কলিকাতা বিশ্ববিদ্যালয় বাংলাদেশ সহায়ক সমিতির পক্ষে যতীন্দ্র চট্টোপাধ্যায় সম্পাদিত. ⌜কলিকাতা⌝ মুক্তধারা ⌜1971⌝
⌜19⌝, 121 p. port. 22 cm. Rs3.50
In Bengali.
Includes bibliographies.
1. Bangladesh—Politics and government—1971– 2. Bangladesh—History—Revolution, 1971. I. Caṭṭopādhyāẏa, Yatīndra, comp. II. Calcutta University Bangladesh Sahayak Samiti.
Title romanized: Bāṃlādeśera muktiyuddha.
DS395.5.B35 72-928014

(Bāṃlādeśera muktiyuddha)
বাংলাদেশের মুক্তিযুদ্ধ / কলিকাতা বিশ্ববিদ্যালয় বাংলাদেশ সহায়ক সমিতির পক্ষে যতীন্দ্র চট্টোপাধ্যায় সম্পাদিত. — ঢাকা : মুক্তধারা, 1972.
144 p. : ill. ; 22 cm.
In Bengali.
Includes bibliographies.
Reprint of the 1971 ed. published in Mujibnagar.
Tk3.50
1. Bangladesh—History—Revolution, 1971—Personal narratives. I. Caṭṭopādhyāẏa, Yatīndra. II. Calcutta University Bangladesh Sahayak Samiti.
DS395.5.B35 1972 75-929512

Bāmlāra Krshaka Sabhā
see Rasul, Md. Abdullah. Krshakasabhāra itihāsa. [1969]

Bāṃlāra Lokasaṃskṛti Ālocanā Cakra, Calcutta, 1970.
(Paścimabaṅgera lokasaṃskṛti)
পশ্চিমবঙ্গের লোকসংস্কৃতি. ⌜কলিকাতা, পশ্চিমবঙ্গ সরকারের তথ্য ও জনসংযোগ বিভাগের উদ্যোগে প্রকাশিত, 1973?⌝
2, 2, 234 p. 26 cm. Rs5.50
"পবসমু-৭৩/৭৪-৫৫৬ এফ-১ হাঃ."
In Bengali.
Includes bibliographical references.
1. Ethnology—India—West Bengal. 2. West Bengal—Social life and customs. I. West Bengal. Information and Public Relations Dept. II. Title.
DS485.B493B335 1970 73-906563

(Bāṃlāra māṭi, durjaẏa ghāṅṭi)
বাংলার মাটি, দুর্জয় ঘাঁটি. ঢাকা, অগ্নিবীনা খেলাঘর আসর ⌜1970⌝
28 p. 21 cm. Re0.50
"একুশের অমর শহীদদের স্মৃতির উদ্দেশ্যে."
In Bengali.
1. Bengali language—Addresses, essays, lectures. 2. East Pakistan—Languages—Addresses, essays, lectures. 3. Pakistan—Languages—Addresses, essays, lectures.
DS485.B44B28 75-931292

(Bāṃlāra saṃskṛti o aitihya)
বাংলার সংস্কৃতি ও ঐতিহ্য / জ্যোতির্ময় ঘোষ সম্পাদিত. — কলকাতা : জাতীয় শিক্ষা পরিষৎ, 1975.
12, 154 p. ; 22 cm.
In Bengali.
Rs10.00
1. Bengal—Civilization—Addresses, essays, lectures. I. Ghosha, Jyotirmaẏa.
DS485.B44B285 75-907656

Bamm, Peter
see Emmrich, Kurt, 1897-

Bamman, Henry A
Bearcat ⌜by⌝ Henry A. Bamman ⌜and⌝ Robert J. Whitehead. Illus. ⌜by⌝ James Andrews. Palo Alto, Calif., Field Educational Publications ⌜1967⌝
89 p. illus. (part col.) 22 cm. (The checkered flag series)
I. Whitehead, Robert J., joint author. II. Title.
MB NUC74-137753

Bamman, Henry A
500 ⌜by⌝ Henry A. Bamman ⌜and⌝ Robert J. Whitehead. Illus. ⌜by⌝ James Andrews. Palo Alto, Calif., Field Educational Publications ⌜1968⌝
90 p. illus. (part col.) 22 cm. (The checkered flag series)
I. Whitehead, Robert J., joint author. II. Title.
MB NUC74-137755

Bamman, Henry A
Flea ⌜by⌝ Henry A. Bamman ⌜and⌝ Robert J. Whitehead. Illus. ⌜by⌝ James Andrews. Palo Alto, Calif., Field Educational Publications ⌜1969⌝
89 p. illus. (part col.) 22 cm. (The checkered flag series)
I. Whitehead, Robert J., joint author. II. Title.
MB NUC74-137754

Bamman, Henry A
Free to read : a guide to effective reading / Henry A. Bamman, Midori F. Hiyama, Delbert L. Prescott. — Rev. ed. — Menlo Park, Calif. : Cummings Pub. Co., ⌜1975⌝
266 p. : ill. ; 24 cm.
Includes index.
ISBN 0-8465-5835-1
1. Readers—1950– 2. English language—Grammar—1950– I. Hiyama, Midori, joint author. II. Prescott, Delbert L., joint author. III. Title.
PE1121.B362 428′.6 74-84819
MARC

Bamman, Henry A
Fundamentals of basic reading instruction ⌜by⌝ Henry A. Bamman, Mildred A. Dawson ⌜and⌝ James J. McGovern. 3d ed. New York, Mckay ⌜1973⌝
vi, 280 p. 22 cm.
First–2d ed. written by M. A. Dawson and H. A. Bamman.
Bibliography: p. 271–272.
1. Reading (Elementary) I. Dawson, Mildred Agnes, 1897– joint author. II. McGovern, James Joseph, 1946– joint author. III. Dawson, Mildred Agnes, 1897– Fundamentals of basic reading instruction. IV. Title.
LB1573.B357 1973 372.4′1 72-90925
MARC

Bamman, Henry A
Grand prix [by] Henry A. Bamman [and] Robert J. Whitehead. Illus. [by] James Andrews. Palo Alto, Calif., Field Educational Publications [1969]
90 p. illus. (part col.) 22 cm. (The checkered flag series)
I. Whitehead, Robert J., joint author. II. Title.
MB NUC74-137746

Bamman, Henry A
Riddler [by] Henry A. Bamman [and] Robert J. Whitehead. Illus. [by] James Andrews. Palo Alto, Calif., Field Educational Publications [1967]
89 p. illus. (part col.) 22 cm. (The checkered flag series)
I. Whitehead, Robert J., joint author. II. Title.
MB NUC74-137750

Bamman, Henry A
Scramble [by] Henry A. Bamman [and] Robert J. Whitehead. Illus. [by] James Andrews. San Francisco, Field Educational Publications [1969]
90 p. illus. (part col.) 22 cm. (The checkered flag series)
I. Whitehead, Robert J., joint author. II. Title.
MB NUC74-137749

Bamman, Henry A
Smashup [by] Henry A. Bamman [and] Robert J. Whitehead. Illus. [by] James Andrews. Palo Alto, Calif., Field Educational Publications [1967]
89 p. illus. (part col.) 22 cm. (The checkered flag series)
I. Whitehead, Robert J., joint author. II. Title.
MB NUC74-137748

Bamman, Henry A.
see New reading skill builder. Montreal, 1966-

Bammatova, P. A., comp.
see Kalinin i Dagestan. Makhachkala, Dagestanskoe knizhnoe izd-vo, 1967.

Bammel, Christian.
see Portugal auf dem Weg zum Sozialismus? ... 1. Aufl. Offenbach, Verlag Zweitausend, 1975.

Bammel, Ernst.
Die Reichsgründung und der deutsche Protestantismus / Ernst Bammel. — Erlangen : Universitätsbund Erlangen-Nürnberg ; Auslfg., Universitätsbibliothek, 1973.
86 p. ; 24 cm. — (Erlanger Forschungen ; Reihe A ; Bd. 22) GDR 74-B29
Includes bibliographical references and index.
1. Germany—History—1866-1871. 2. Protestant churches—Germany. 3. Bismarck, Otto, Fürst von, 1815-1898. I. Title.
DD222.B32 322'.1'0943 75-550488

Bammer, Anton.
Die Architektur des jüngeren Artemision von Ephesos. Wiesbaden, F. Steiner, 1972.
72 p. illus. (1 fold.), 12 plates. 35 cm. GDB***
Bibliography: p. [68]-69.
1. Ephesus. Temple of Diana. I. Title.
NA285.E6B34 72-357317

Bammer, Anton.
Architektur und Gesellschaft in der Antike : zur Deutung baulicher Symbole / Anton Bammer. — Wien : Österr. Ges. f. Archäologie, 1974.
148 p. : ill. ; 21 cm. — (Archäologisch-soziologische Schriften) Au 75-6-243
"Wichtige Abschnitte dieses Buches sind bereits in einem Aufsatz: Zur soziologischen Deutung ephesischer Architektur, Ist. Mitt. 25, 1975, als Beitrag zur Festschrift für G. Kleiner, enthalten."
Bibliography: p. 130.
Includes index.
S80.00
1. Architecture—Greece. 2. Architecture and society—Greece. 3. Symbolism in architecture. I. Title. II. Series.
NA270.B3 75-580531

Bammer, Anton.
Führer durch das Archäologische Museum in Selçuk-Ephesos / A. Bammer, R. Fleischer, D. Knibbe. — [Wien] : Österr. Archäolog. Inst., 1974.
191 p., [14] leaves of plates : ill. ; 20 cm. Au 74-23-262
Includes bibliographical references.
S80.00
1. Asia Minor—Antiquities. 2. Classical antiquities—Catalogs. 3. Efes Müzesi. I. Fleischer, Robert, joint author. II. Knibbe, Dieter, joint author. III. Title.
DS155.B35 75-531870

Bammert, Jacques Joseph.
La Grande histoire du Château-Lambert et de Le Thillot : duché de Lorraine / J.-J. Bammert, ... — [Remiremont] (Les Genêts, 88200) : [J.-J. Bammert], 1974.
24 p. ; 22 cm. F77-514
1. Château-Lambert, France—History. 2. Le Thillot, France—History. I. Title.
DC801.C483B35 77-479356
77 MARC

Bammert, Jean Jacques.
Contes de Lourres du Nonon Batisse [par] J.-J. Bammert, ... [Remiremont] (Les Genêts, 88200), [J.-J. Bammert], [1973].
56 p. ill. 14 x 22 cm. F 73-10745
On cover: Série 1.
10.00F
I. Title.
PQ2662.A47C6 843'.9'14 74-192479
MARC

Bammert, Jean Jacques.
L'histoire du chapitre des nobles dames de Remiremont, 620-1791 [par] J.-J. Bammert. [Remiremont, Impr. Lalloz-Perrin, 1971]
1 v. (unpaged) illus. 27 cm. F***
On cover: Les nobles dames de Remiremont.
Includes bibliography.
1. Remiremont, France (Abbey)—History. I. Title. II. Title: Les nobles dames de Remiremont.
BX2615.R4B35 70-497181
rev

Bammert, Jean Jacques.
Remiremont : ville princière, duché de Lorraine / J.-J. Bammert, ... — [Remiremont] (les Genêts, 88200) : [J.-J. Bammert], 1974.
48 p., [4] p. of plates : ill. ; 21 cm. F77-1422
Cover title.
14.00F
1. Remiremont, France (Abbey). 2. Remiremont, France—History. I. Title.
BX2615.R4B36 77-478369
77 MARC

Bammert, Karl.
A general review of closed-cycle gas turbines using fossil, nuclear, and solar energy / by Karl Bammert. — München : Thiemig, 1975.
xi, 75 p. : 47 ill. ; 18 cm. — (Thiemig-Taschenbücher ; Bd. 57) GFR75-A
Bibliography: p. 69-75.
ISBN 3-521-06101-9
1. Gas-turbines. 2. Electric power-plants. I. Title.
TJ778.B28 621.43'3 76-384071
77 MARC

Bammert, Karl.
Die Strömung in vielstufigen Axialturbinen mit gerader Beschaufelung [von] K. Bammert. Braunschweig, 1961.
18 p. illus. (Deutsche Forschungsanstalt für Luftfahrt. Institut für Strahltriebwerke. Bericht Nr. 135)
ICRL NUC74-173587

Bammert, Karl.
Zur Berechnung der Strömung in vielstüfigen azialen Turbomaschinen mit beliebiger Beschaufelung, von K. Bammert. Düsseldorf, VDI-Verlag [1960]
6 p. illus. (Deutsche Forschungsanstalt für Luftfahrt. Institut für Strahltriebwerke. Bericht Nr. 137)
"Sonderdruck aus 'Forschung auf dem Gebiete des Ingenieurwesens,' Bd. 26, Nr. 6, 1960."
Cover imprint: Braunschweig.
ICRL NUC74-178485

Bammes, Gottfried.
Der Akt in der Kunst / Gottfried Bammes. — Leipzig : E. A. Seemann, 1975.
17 p., [46] leaves of plates : ill. (some col.) ; 21 cm. GDR***
1. Nude in art. 2. Art—Themes, motives. I. Title.
N7572.B35 76-453069
76 MARC

Bammes, Gottfried.
Die Gestalt des Menschen : ein Handbuch der Anatomie für Künstler / Gottfried Bammes. — 2., erw. Aufl. — Ravensburg : O. Maier, 1973.
429 p. : ill. (some col.) ; 30 cm. GFR***
First ed. published in 1969 under title: Der nackte Mensch.
Bibliography : p. 416-[418]
Includes index.
1. Nude in art. 2. Anatomy, Artistic. I. Title.
NC765.B18 1973 75-551127

Bammes, Gottfried.
Die Gestalt des Tieres : [Lehr- u. Handbuch d. Künstleranatomie typ. Landsäugetiere] / Gottfried Bammes. — Leipzig : Seeman, VEB, 1975.
502 p. : numerous ill. (some col.) ; 30 cm. GFR76-A
Bibliography: p. 492-494.
Includes index.
120.00M
1. Morphology (Animals) 2. Anatomy, Comparative. 3. Animal mechanics. I. Title.
QL799.B35 599'.04'7 76-463179
76 MARC

Bammes, Gottfried.
Das zeichnerische Aktstudium; seine Entwicklung in Werkstatt, Schule, Praxis u. Theorie. [2. Aufl.] Leipzig, Seemann [1973]
340 p. 229 ill. (part col.). 25 cm. GDR***
Summary in English, French and Russian.
Bibliography : p. 336-[339]
1. Nude in art. I. Title.
NC765.B19 1973 74-317498

Bammesberger, Alfred, 1938-
Abstraktbildungen in den baltischen Sprachen/ Alfred Bammesberger. — Göttingen: Vandenhoeck und Ruprecht, 1973.
157 p.; 25 cm. — (Ergänzungshefte zur Zeitschrift für vergleichende Sprachforschung auf dem Gebiet der indogermanischen Sprachen; Nr. 22) DM24.00 GFR 74-A
An abridgement of the author's Habilitationsschrift, Freiburg i. B., 1970.
Includes bibliographical references.
1. Baltic languages—Word formation. I. Title. II. Series: Zeitschrift für vergleichende Sprachforschung auf dem Gebiet der indogermanischen Sprachen. Ergänzungshefte, Nr. 22.
PG8061.B3 1973 74-320077
ISBN 3-525-26208-6

Bamotrā, Kr̥shṇa
see
Bumotra, Krishan, 1947-

Bampakos, Antōnios M
Praxeis koinēs diatheseōs kai alla syngenē phainomena kata to dikaion tēs archaias Thessalias. Athēnai, 1961.
271 p. 25 cm.
Bibliography: p. [9]-16.
OCU NUC74-123168

Bampfield, Thomas, 1623?-1693.
An enquiry whether the Lord Jesus Christ made the world. 1692. English books, 1641-1700. Ann Arbor, Mich., University Microfilms, 1961-
reels. 35 mm.
Microfilm copy of books included in Wing's Short-title catalogue of... English books printed... 1641-1700.
1. English literature—Early modern (to 1700)—Collections. I. Wing, Donald Goddard, 1904- Short-title catalogue of books.
CaBVaU NUC73-771

Bampilē, Maria G
To phōs tēs psychēs mou; poiēmata. Athēna, 1956.
49 p. 22 cm.
I. Title.
OCU NUC74-123161

Bampo, Gustavo, 1849-1927.
Contributo quinto alla storia dell'arte in Friuli ed alla vita dei pittori, indoratori, intagliatori e scultori friulani dal XV al XVII secolo / di Gustavo Bampo. — Udine : Tip. Doretti, 1962.
viii, 243 p. : 30 cm.
At head of title: Accademia di scienze, lettere e arti, Udine.
Italian or Latin.
Includes indexes.
1. Art—Friuli—History. 2. Artists—Friuli—Biography. I. Title: Contributo quinto alla storia dell'arte in Friuli ...
N6919.F7B35 1962 75-403760

Bampoe, David Opare.
A guide to the despatches from and to the Gold Coast of the British administration, 1850-1902. London, 1967.
Microfilm copy (positive) of typescript made by University Microfilms, Tylers Green, High Wycombe, England.
Collation: 2 reels (unpaged in original)
Thesis, submitted for the Fellowship of the Library Association.
1. Gt. Britain. Colonial Office. Despatches from and to the Gold Coast of the British administration, 1850-1902—Bibl.
CSt-H NUC77-51437

Bampoe, David Opare.
A guide to the despatches from and to the Gold Coast of the British administration, 1850-1902, by David Opare Bampoe. [n. p.] 1967.
2 v. in 5. maps. 24 cm.
"Thesis submitted for the Fellowship of the Library Association."
Photocopy of typescript. Tylers Green, High Wycombe [Eng.] University Microfilms, Ltd.
1. Ghana—History—Sources. I. Title.
IEN NUC76-71532

Bampos, Miltiadēs A
Stoicheiōdēs paidiatrikē [hypo] Miltiadou A. Bampou. En Athēnais, Typois Sōt. Spyropoulou, 1957.
1275 p. illus. (part col.) 25 cm.
1. Pediatrics. I. Title.
CtY NUC75-86730

Bamps, Paul.
Cornaceae. Bruxelles, Jardin botanique national de Belgique, (rue Royale, 236), 1971.
5 p. illus. 25 cm. (Flore du Congo, du Rwanda, et du Burundi: Spermatophytes) 25.00F Be 72-134
1. Afrocrania volkensii. 2. Botany—Africa, Eastern. I. Title. II. Series.
QK495.C785B3 73-301412

Bamps, Paul.
Flacourtiaceae. Par P. Bamps. Bruxelles, Jardin botanique national de Belgique, r. Royale, 236, 1968–
v. illus. 25 cm. (Flore du Congo, du Rwanda et du Burundi: Spermatophytes) 70.00F (v. 1) Be 69-880 (v. 1)
CONTENTS: 1. ptie. Tribus Oncobeae, Scolopieae, Phyllobotryeae et Flacourtieae.
1. Flacourtiaceae. 2. Botany—Zaire. I. Series.
QK495.F55B35 73-311181

Bamps, Paul.
Flore d'Afrique Centrale (Zaire-Rwanda-Burundi): Spermatophytes; Araliaceae. [Bruxelles] Jardin botanique national de Belgique, 1974.
30 p. illus.
1. Araliaceae. 2. Botany–Zaire. 3. Botany–Rwanda. I. Title.
MiEM NUC76-25320

Bamps, Paul.
Flore du Congo du Rwanda et du Burundi. Spermatophytes: Ochnaceae, par P. Bamps. Genres Idertia, Rhabdophyllum et Campylospermum, par C. Farron. Bruxelles, Jardin botanique national de Belgique, 1967.
66 p. illus.
1. Ochnaceae. 2. Botany–Congo (Democratic Republic) 3. Botany–Rwanda. 4. Botany–Burundi. I. Farron, C., joint author. II. Title.
MiEM NUC73-39453

Bams, Robert A
Evaluation of gravel incubators on first "hatchery" generation Tsolum River pink salmon, 1970-72, by Robert A. Bams. Nanaimo, B.C., Fisheries Research Board of Canada, Pacific Biological Station, 1973-
v. 28 cm. (Technical report–Fisheries Research Board of Canada, no. 405)
Includes bibliography.
Contents: pt. 2. Evaluation at the adult stage.
1. Fish-culture. 2. Pink salmon. 3. Salmon. I. Canada. Fisheries Research Board. Biological Station, Nanaimo, B.C. II. Title. III. Series: Canada. Fisheries Research Board. Technical report, no. 405.
Wa NUC76-71467

Baṃśa, Bhikkhu Ārya
see Ārya Baṃśa, Bhikkhu, joint author.

Baṃsala, Pramodakumāra.
(Adhūrā citra)
अधूरा चित्र; डायरी शैली में रचित प्रेरणापूर्ण लघु उपन्यास. [लेखक] प्रमोद बंसल. [1. संस्करण] नई दिल्ली, शारदा प्रकाशन [1972]
136 p. 19 cm. Rs6.00
In Hindi.
I. Title.
PK2098.13.A5A66 72-907882

Baṃsala, Pushpā.
(Mohana Rākeśa kā nāṭya-sāhitya)
मोहन राकेश का नाट्य-साहित्य / पुष्पा बन्सल. — 5. संस्करण. — दिल्ली : सूर्य प्रकाशन, 1976.
4, 114 p. ; 22 cm.
In Hindi.
Rs15.00
1. Rakesh, Mohan, 1925–1972—Dramatic works. I. Title.
PK2098.R36Z59 1976 77-900261

Baṃsala, Raghubīra Śaraṇa.
(Ārya samājī netā)
आर्य समाजी नेता; जिसमें प्रसिद्ध-प्रसिद्ध आर्य समाजी नेताओं का जीवन-चरित्र बड़ी सरल-भाषा में दिया गया है. लेखक रघुबीर शरण बंसल. देहली, प्राप्तिस्थान: राष्ट्रीय प्रकाशन मण्डल [1964]
292 p. 19 cm.
In Hindi.
1. Arya-samaj—Biography. I. Title.
BL1255.A2B35 75-984525

Baṃśidhara Senāpati
see
Senapati, Bongshidhar, 1942-

Baṃśidhārī Dāsa
see
Dāsa, Baṃśidhārī.

Bamuinikile-Mudiasa, Symphorien.
La mort et l'au-delà chez les Baluba du Kasai; position traditionnelle et perspectives catéchétiques. [Lubumbashi, CEPSI, 1971]
120 p. illus. maps. 24 cm. (Centre d'étude des problèmes sociaux indigènes. Collection de mémoires, 29)
Mémoire présenté et soutenu pour l'obtention de la maîtrise en pastorale catéchétique.
1. Baluba (Tribu africaine)—Religion. I. Title.
CaOOU NUC73-32193

Bamunas
see Indonesia. Laws, statutes, etc. Peraturan-peraturan tentang Badan Musjawarah Pengusaha Nasional Swasta... Makassar, Jajasan penerbitan Universitas Hasanuddin [1964?]

Bamunas Djaya.
Aneka warta Bamunas Djaya.
Djakarta, Bamunas Djaya.
v. 34-36 cm.
1. Indonesia—Commercial policy—Periodicals. 2. Indonesia—Commerce—Periodicals.
HF1597.B35a 75-648210
MARC-S

Bamunuacci, Sōmasiri.
(Oba enaturu balā siṭimi)
ඔබ එනතුරු බලා සිටිමි. [කර්තෘ] සෝමසිරි බමුනුඇච්චි. [ගම්පහ? ඩී. ඩී. රණසිංහ, 1969]
40 p. 19 cm.
In Sinhalese.
Poems.
I. Title.
PK2859.B33O2 78-925279
SA

Bamus Sutera
see
Badan Musjawarah Persuteraan Alam Nasional.

Bamwisho, Jean.
Les adolescents et la compréhension des textes écrits. Contribution méthodologique à l'élaboration d'instruments destinés à mesurer, à long terme, l'efficacité des méthodes d'apprentissage de la lecture. Berne, Herbert Lang; Francfort/M., Peter Lang, 1972.
238 p. illus. 23 cm. (Publications universitaires européennes. Série 11: Pédagogie, v. 3) 44.00F Sw 73-A-1392
Bibliography: p. 203-207.
1. Reading. I. Title. II. Series: Europäische Hochschulschriften. Reihe 11: Pädagogik, Bd. 3.
LB1050.B34 73-175730
ISBN 3-261-00192-5 MARC

Bamzai, Prithivi Nath Kaul, 1910–
A history of Kashmir: political, social, cultural, from the earliest times to the present day. Introd. by Jawaharlal Nehru. [2d rev. ed.] New Delhi, Metropolitan Book Co. [1973]
xxii, 866 p. illus. (part col.) 25 cm. Rs85.00
Bibliography: p. 843-844.
1. Kashmir—History. I. Title.
DS485.K2B23 1973 915.4'6 72-908048
MARC

Bamzai, Prithivi Nath Kaul, 1910–
Jammu and Kashmir [by] P. N. K. Bamzai. [New Delhi] Publications Division, Ministry of Information and Broadcasting, Govt. of India [1973]
62 p. illus., fold. map. 22 cm. (States of our Union, 15) Rs2.40
1. Kashmir.
DS485.K2B232 915.49'13 74-900539
MARC

Ban, A W van den.
Inleiding tot de voorlichtingskunde. [Door] A. W. van den Ban. Meppel, Boom, [1974].
255 p. 22 cm. (Teksten agologie) Ne 74-17
Includes bibliographical references.
ISBN 90-6009-133-7 : fl 19.90
1. Communication in agriculture. 2. Agricultural innovations. I. Title.
S494.5.C6B36 75-565532

Bán, Alzira Dornelles.
A nova escola: gerência científica [por] Alzira Dornelles Bán [e] Halina Brzezinska. Porto Alegre, Sulina [1973, c1972]
289 p. illus. 22 cm. (Coleção Organização) Cr$28.00
Bibliography: p. 287-289.
1. School management and organization. I. Brzezinska, Halina, joint author. II. Title. III. Series.
LB2805.B25 73-213708

Ban, Arline J
Life is a gift. By Arline and Joseph D. Ban. Teacher's guide, semester 1. [Valley Forge, American Baptist Board of Education and Publication, 1970]
127 p. illus. 28 cm. (Perspective 2 - Junior, grades 5-6)
1. Children–Elementary 5-6. I. Title.
IEG NUC73-112416

Ban, Arline J
Life is a gift. By Arline and Joseph D. Ban. [Learner's book, first semester] Cover and major illus. by Jack Kershner. Valley Forge, American Baptist Board of Education and Publication, 1970.
139 p. illus., plates, music. 28 cm. (Perspective 2 - Junior, grades 5-6)
1. Children–Elementary 5-6. I. Title.
IEG NUC73-112430

Ban, Arline J
The new disciple / Arline J. Ban and Joseph D. Ban. — Valley Forge, Pa. : Judson Press, c1976.
93 p. : ill. ; 22 cm.
SUMMARY: A discussion of what it means to be a disciple of Christ in today's world aimed at young people who are thinking about joining an American Baptist church.
ISBN 0-8170-0658-3 : $1.50
1. Baptists—Membership—Juvenile literature. 2. Christian life—Baptist authors—Juvenile literature. 3. Baptists—Doctrinal and controversial works—Juvenile literature. [1. Baptists—Membership. 2. Christian life—Baptist authors] I. Ban, Joseph D., joint author. II. Title.
[BX6219.B35] 248'.48'61 75-35898
75 MARC

Ban, Hisao
see
Hari, Hisao, 1918-

Bán, Imre, 1905–
Eszmék és stílusok : irodalmi tanulmányok / Bán Imre. — Budapest : Akadémiai Kiadó, 1976.
275 p. ; 25 cm.
Includes index.
CONTENTS: Dante és a joachimizmus.—Dante Ulixese.—Janus Pannonius és a magyar irodalmi hagyomány.—Ariosto "Orlando furioso"-ja, a reneszánsz irodalmi stílusának mintája. — Melius Juhász Péter.—Az olasz reneszánsz irodalomelmélete.—Károlyi Péter poétikája.—Balassi Bálint platonizmusa.—"Fejedelmeknek serkentő órája."—Comenins és a magyar szellemi élet.—A magyar manierista irodalom.—A magyar barokk próza változatai.—Apáczai Csere János doktori értekezése.—Losontzi István poétikája és a kései magyar barokk költészet.—Kazinczy Ferenc klasszicizmusa.—Debreceni diákirodalom a XVIII–XIX. század fordulóján.—Csokonai és Debrecen.
1. Hungarian literature—History and criticism—Addresses, essays, lectures. 2. Dante Alighieri, 1265–1321—Criticism and interpretation—Addresses, essays, lectures. I. Title.
PH3017.B337 76–526667

Bán, Imre, 1905–
Irodalomelméleti kézikönyvek Magyarországon a XVI–XVIII. században. Budapest, Akadémiai Kiadó, 1971.
109 p. 19 cm. (Irodalomtörténeti füzetek, 72. sz.) 11.00Ft
Includes bibliographical references.
1. Literature—History and criticism—Theory, etc. 2. Literature—Study and teaching—Hungary. I. Title. II. Series.
PN441.B27 72–227251

Bán, Imre, 1905-
Istorija mađarske književnosti / Imre Ban, Janoš Barta, Mihalj Cine ; [preveo s mađarskog Sava Babić]. — [Novi Sad] : Matica srpska, 1976.
430 p., [32] leaves of plates : ill. ; 25 cm. Yu***
Translated from Hungarian.
"Bibliografija knjiga iz mađarske književnosti prevedenih na srpskohrvatski jezik" by M. Čurčić: p. 349-423.
Includes index.
1. Hungarian literature—History and criticism. I. Barta, János, joint author. II. Czine, Mihály, joint author. III. Čurčić, Marija. IV. Title.
PH3012.B2619 77-461034
77 MARC

Bán, Imre, 1905-
A Karthausi Névtelen műveltsége / Bán Imre. — Budapest : Akadémiai Kiadó, 1976.
137 p. ; 19 cm. — (Irodalomtörténeti füzetek ; 88. sz)
Includes bibliographical references and index.
ISBN 963050698X : 15.00Ft
1. Karthauzi Névtelen—Criticism and interpretation. I. Title. II. Series.
PH3194.K33Z59 77-554274
77 MARC

Ban, I[illegible]an Albert
see
Bannius, Joannes Albertus. [illegible].

Ban, Istvan.
Uj utak a novenyvedelmi vizsgalatokban. Budapest, Mezogazdasagi Kiado, 1973.
274 p. tables.
Bibliography: p. 267-271.
1. Plants, Protection of. 2. Biomathematics. I. Title.
DNAL NUC76-71533

Ban, Itsuki, 1916–
(Sōtaisei riron gaisetsu)
相對性理論概説　時空構成の論理　伴五紀著　[東京]　目黑書店　[昭和25 i.e. 1950]
2, 3, 140 p. illus. 22 cm.
1. Relativity (Physics) I. Title.
QC173.55.B36 74–808425

Ban, Jan Albert
see
Bannius, Joannes Albertus, 1597 or 98-1644.

Bán, Jenö.
The tactics of end-games. London, Pitman [c1963]
214 p. illus.
1. Chess–End games. I. Title.
UU NUC73-38946

Ban, Joan Albert
see
Bannius, Joannes Albertus, 1597 or 98-1644.

Ban, Joseph D
Deepen the revolution [by] Joseph D. Ban. [n.p., 1969]
7 p. 28 cm.
"...presented as part of the National Honor Society program at the McMinnville High School, September 25, 1969."
1. Revolutions—Addresses, essays, lectures. I. Title.
KyLoS NUC73-2347

Ban, Joseph D
"Facing new demands;" three Bible studies, by Joseph D. Ban. [McMinnville, Oregon, Linfield College, c1968]
[35] p. 22 cm.
"...Prepared for and presented to the Oregon Conference of American Baptist Women."
1. Baptists—Addresses, essays, lectures. 2. Church and social problems—Addresses, essays, lectures. I. Title.
KyLoS NUC73-2348

Ban, Joseph D
When dissent is unavoidable [by] Joseph D. Ban. [n.p., 1969]
8 l. 28 cm.
"This sermon was presented in the First Baptist Church of McMinnville, Oregon on Sunday, October 19, 1969."
1. Baptists—Sermons. 2. Sermons, American. I. Title.
KyLoS NUC73-2349

Ban, Joseph D., joint author.
see Ban, Arline J. The new disciple. Valley Forge, Pa., Judson Press, c1976.

Ban, Kokei, 1733-1806.
(Kinsei kijin den)
近世畸人伝　伴蒿蹊著　森銑三校註　東京　岩波書店　昭和46(1971)
271 p. 15 cm. (岩波文庫 2196-2198) ¥150 Ja 71-18608
第5刷(第1刷: 昭和15年)
1. Japan—Biography. 2. Japan—History—Tokugawa period, 1600-1868—Biography. 3. Eccentrics and eccentricities. I. Mori, Senzo, 1895- ed. II. Title.
CT1835.B3 1971 74–811097
J

Bàn, Magdolna, 1940-
Magdolna Bàn, Hongrie. — Morges : Éditions "K", Galerie Pro arte Kasper, [1976]
[8] p. : ill. ; 21 cm. — (Collection des meilleurs peintres naïfs d'aujourd'hui ; no 4) Sw76-10569
Cover title.
1. Bàn, Magdolna, 1940- 2. Primitivism in art—Hungary. I. Series.
ND522.5.B35A5 77-472172
•77 MARC

Ban, Michael.
Local compliance with Mapp v. Ohio: the power of the Supreme Court; a case study. [n.p.] 1973.
1 v.
Thesis—Harvard.
1. Cincinnati, Ohio—Police. 2. Boston, Mass.—Police. 3. United States. Supreme Court.
MH NUC76-71534

Ban, Michio.
(Edojō shi)
江戸城史：増補·東京城史 / [伴三千雄]. — 東京：名著出版，昭和49[1974]
396, 20, 4 p. : ill. ; 22 cm. Ja 74-4661
"大正八年…刊行された「東京城史」に、新らたに巻頭写真と江戸城年表とを増補し…復刊"
Accompanied by maps (3 fold. col.) in pocket.
Limited edition; 500 copies printed.
¥5000
1. Tokyo. Edojō. I. Title. II. Title: Tōkyōjō shi.
NA7758.T57B36 74–808732

Bán, Miklós, joint author
see Császár, József. Optikai szinkép, ligandumtér-elmélet, komplex szerkezet. Budapest, Akadémiai Kiadó, 1972.

Ban, Nobutomo, 1773-1846. Chuko zassho shu. 1973
see Chusei kayo shu. 48 (1973)

Ban, Nobutomo, 1773-1846.
(Wakasa kyūji kō)
若狭舊事考　伴信友著　小浜　若狭学術振興会　昭和46(1971)
1 v. 26 cm. Ja 72-4380
原本: 藤山宗一所蔵(天保七年) 複製
限定50部
Colophon inserted.
1. Fukui, Japan (Prefecture)—History—Sources. 2. Fukui, Japan (Prefecture)—Description and travel. I. Title.
DS894.59.F83A32 1836a 73–804638

Ban, Nobutomo, 1773-1846
see Hirata, Atsutane, 1776-1843. (Hirata Atsutane, Ban Nobutomo, Okuni Takamasa) 1973.

Ban, Nobutomo, 1773-1846, ed.
see Wakasa no Kuni shugoshiki shidai. 47 (1972)

Ban, Rando.
(Kindaika ni yoru ginkō torihiki kakuchō)
近代化による銀行取引擴張　伴蘭土著　[大阪]　產業經濟社　[1956]
2, 3, 308 p. illus. 19 cm.
Colophon inserted.
1. Banks and banking—United States. I. Title.
HG2481.B28 73–818107

Ban, S
Research on prestressed structures in earthquake zones; methods and results. General reporter: S. Ban. London [Cement and Concrete Association] 1972.
9 p. 30 cm. (Seismic structures, theme 2)
"Report presented at the Fip Symposium on Seismic Structures."
Includes bibliography.
1. Earthquakes and building. I. Fédération internationale de la précontrainte. II. Symposium on Seismic Structure, Tbilisi, 1972. III. Title. IV. Series.
CaBVaU NUC76-71566

Ban, Satoe, ed.
see (Indoneshia shiryō shū) 47- (1972-

Ban, Satoe
see Kokusai kankei ron kogi. 1974.

Ban, Shizuo, 1896–
(Tekkin konkuritogaku kyōtei)
鐵筋コンクリート學教程 / 坂靜雄著. — 東京：產業圖書，昭和23 [1948]
8, 371 p. : ill. ; 22 cm.
Includes index.
1. Reinforced concrete. 2. Reinforced concrete construction. I. Title.
TA444.B23 76–801633

Ban, Shizuo, 1896–
(Tekkin konkuritogaku kyōtei)
鐵筋コンクリート學教程 / 坂靜雄著. — 修正版. — 東京：產業圖書，昭和26 [1951]
8, 371 p. : ill. ; 22 cm.
Includes index.
1. Reinforced concrete. 2. Reinforced concrete construction. I. Title.
TA444.B23 1951 77–812556

Ban, Sukeyoshi
see
Ban, Kōkei, 1733-1806.

Ban, Thomas A
Recent advances in the biology of schizophrenia, by Thomas A. Ban. Springfield, Ill., Thomas [1973]
ix, 119 p. illus. 24 cm. (American lecture series, publication no. 863. A monograph in American lectures in objective psychiatry) $12.50
An expansion of the author's presentations at a symposium on schizophrenia at the Arizona State Hospital in Phoenix on Nov. 12, 1971.
Bibliography: p. 94-105.
1. Schizophrenia. 2. Schizophrenia—Chemotherapy. I. Title.
RC514.B356 616.8'982 72-86995
ISBN 0-398-02571-1 MARC

Ban, Thomas A.
see The Butyrophenones in psychiatry. [n. p., 1964?]

Ban, Thomas A., ed.
see Collegium Internationale Neuro-psycho-pharmacologicum. Psychopharmacology... Amsterdam, North-Holland Pub. Co., 1973.

Ban, Thomas A., ed.
see International Symposium on Trazodone, 1st, Montreal, 1973. Trazodone. Basel, New York, S. Karger [1974]

Ban, Velimir.
Koraci. Zagreb, Izdavač: Velimir Ban, 1973.
45 p. 20 cm. Yu 73-3715
Poems.
I. Title.
PG1619.12.A6K6 74-970697

Bản ánNích-Xơ'n. Hà-nội, Sự Thật, 1972.
88 p. 19 cm.
Includes bibliographical references.

1. United States—Foreign relations—Vietnam. 2. Vietnam—Foreign relations—United States. 3. Nixon, Richard Milhous, 1913-

E183.8.V5B27 73-215370

Bản anh hùng ca tháng Chạp. Tập thơ. Hà Nội, Quân Đội Nhân Dân, 1973.
59 p.
1. Vietnamese poetry—Collections.
ICarbS NUC76-71535

Ban Công Nghê Nhât-nam.
Sách day làm 42 [i.e. bốn mu'o'i hai] nghề ít vốn. In lần 4. Hà-nôi, Thế Gió'i [1960?]
440, xii p. illus. 19 cm. (Tu sách Công Nghê)
1. Vietnam—Occupations. I. Title.
CtY NUC75-26373

Ban dân.
Xuân Nhâm Dần. [Saigon, 1961]
82 p. illus. 31 cm.
1. Vietnamese literature (Collections)
I. Title.
NIC **NUC73-57653**

Ban giáo su' vạn vật
see Vạn vật... [Saigon] Alpha [1969]

Ban' Gu
see
Pan, Ku, 32-92.

Ban Jaketto, Kabushiki Kaisha
see Asobi no kenkyu. 1974.

Ban Nghiên Cứ'u Hiến Pháp Quốc-Hội Lập-Hiến Việt Nam Cộng-Hòa
see Thuyết-trình về hiến-pháp... -- [Saigon?] : So' Tài Liệu, 1967.

Ban Nghiên cu'u văn sử'dia Viet-Nam
see Tập san nghiên cu'u văn sử'dia. [Hà-noi]
Ban nghiên cú'u van sử'dia Viêt Nam.

Ban Ser Corp.
The risk and insurance management guide for savings institutions / Ban Ser Corp. — New York : Professional Services Division, Canfield Press, c1975-
1 v. ; 30 cm.
Loose-leaf for updating.
1. Risk (Insurance) 2. Insurance. 3. Savings-banks. I. Title.
HG8053.B33 1975 658.1'5 75-18654
76 MARC

Bàn Tài Đoàn.
Muối của cụ Hồ; thơ. [Hà-nội] Văn Học, 1960.
76 p. 19 cm.

I. Title.

PL4378.9.B28M8 76-984831

Bàn Tài Đoàn.
Sáng cả hai miền : thơ / Bàn Tài Đoàn. — [Hà nội] : Văn Học, 1975.
93 p. ; 18 cm.
Errata slip inserted.
I. Title.
PL4378.9.B28S2 77-986457
77 MARC

Ban Tu Thu' Khai Trí.
Tự'-điển Việt-Nam. Saigon, Khai-Trí [1971]
956 p.
1. Vietnamese language—Dictionaries.
I. Title.
ICarbS NUC76-35409

Ban tu thu' Tuấn-Tú
see Anh Viêt tù' diến. [Saigon] Tuan-Tu [1970]

Ban Tuyên Huấn Trung Ương Đoàn Thanh niên Lao động Viêt-Nam.
Tìm hiểu nghị quyết Đại hội Đoàn toàn quốc lần thứ ba. Hà-nội, Nhà xuất bản Thanh Niên, 1961.
59 p.
Microfilm of the original in the Library of Congress. Washington, D.C., Library of Congress, Photoduplication Service, 1971. 35 mm.
No. 75 on film titled Communist Vietnamese publications.
1. Youth movement—Vietnam (Democratic Republic, 1946-) I. Title.
NIC NUC75-128426

Bāṇa.
[Caṇḍīśataka]
महाकवि-बाणभट्ट-विरचितं चण्डीशतकम्. महाराणा-कुम्भकर्णप्रणीतया अज्ञातकर्तृकतया टीकया च संवलितम्. सम्पादक श्रीगोपालनारायण बहुरा. प्रथमावृत्ति. जोधपुर, राजस्थान प्राच्यविद्या प्रतिष्ठान (Rajasthan Oriental Research Institute), 1968.
43, 160 p. 25 cm. (राजस्थान पुरातन ग्रन्थमाला, ग्रन्थाङ्क 94) Rs5.25
In Sanskrit; critical apparatus in Hindi or Sanskrit.

1. Parvati (Hindu deity)—Poetry. I. Kumbha, Maharana of Mewar, fl. 1433-1468. Caṇḍīśatakamahākāvyavṛtti. II. Bahura, Gopal Narayan, ed. III. Title: Caṇḍīśataka. IV. Series: Rajasthan Oriental Research Institute, Jodhpur, India. Rajasthan puratana granthamala, 94.
Title romanized: Mahākavi-Bāṇabhaṭṭa-viracitaṃ Caṇḍīśatakam.

PK3791.B188C3 72-905031

Bāṇa.
[Harṣacarita. Hindi & Sanskrit]
हर्षचरितम् / महाकविबाणभट्टविरचितं ; श्रीशङ्करकविरचित 'सङ्केत' व्याख्योपेतम् ; हिन्दीव्याख्याकार: श्रीजगन्नाथपाठक:. — वाराणसी : चौखम्बा विद्याभवन, 1958.
33, 5, 455 p. ; 19 cm. — (विद्याभवन संस्कृत ग्रन्थमाला ; 36)
Introd. in Hindi; commentary in Sanskrit.
1. Harṣavardhana, King of Thānesar and Kanauj, fl. 606-647. I. Śaṅkarakavi. Harṣacaritasaṅketa. 1958. II. Pāṭhaka, Jagannātha. III. Title: Harṣacarita. IV. Series: Vidyabhawan Sanskrit granthamala ; 36.
Title romanized: Harṣacaritam.
DS451.9.H3B316 1958 76-984768

Bāṇa.
(Kādambarī)
कादम्बरी / [श्रीवाणभट्टविरचित: ; edited by Madana Mohana Tarkālaṁkāra]. — [Calcutta : Sanskrit Press, 1850]
2 v. in 1 ; 21 cm.
Includes ms. notes by Albrecht Weber.
Vol. 2 has separate t.p.
L.C. copy imperfect : t.p. wanting; caption title.
In Sanskrit.
The Kādambarī of Bāṇa was completed by his son, Bhūṣana Bhaṭṭa.
I. Bhūṣana Bhaṭṭa. Kādambarī. II. Tarkalankar, Madanmohan, 1815-1857. III. Weber, Albrecht Friedrich, 1825-1901. IV. Title.
PK3791.B188K3 1850 76-984767

Bana. Kadambari
see Nagavarma, 10th cent. (Karnataka Kadambari sangraha). 1970.

Bāṇa. Kādambarī
see Nāgavarma, 12th cent. (Karnātaka Kādambari saṅgraha) 1944.

Bāṇa. Kādambarī
see Trivikrama, son of Rajaraja. Kādambarī-kathāsāra. Tirupati, Tirumala-Tirupati Devasthanams Press, 1957.

Bāṇa. Kādambarī
see Turamari, Gaṅgādhara Maḍivaḷēśvara, 1827-1877. (Bāṇa Kādambari) 1975.

Bāṇa.
(Kādambarī)
कादम्बरी. श्रीमद्बाणभट्टप्रणीता. श्रीभानुचन्द्र-सिद्धचन्द्रगणिविरचितया संस्कृतटीकया संवलिता हिन्दीभाषानुवादेन चालंकृता. सम्पादक: श्रीमोहन-देवपन्त:. अनुवादक: श्रीहरिश्चन्द्रविद्यालङ्कार:. [1. संस्करण] दिल्ली, मोतीलाल बनारसीदास [1971-
v. 24 cm. Rs30.00 (v. 1)
Hindi and Sanskrit; commentary in Sanskrit (introd. in Hindi.
The Kādambarī of Bāṇa was completed by his son, Bhūṣaṇa Bhaṭṭa.
I. Bhūṣaṇa Bhaṭṭa. II. Bhānucandragaṇi, 16th cent. Kādambarīṭīka. III. Siddhacandra, 16th cent. Kādambarīṭīka. IV. Pant, Mohandev, 1905- ed. V. Vidyalankar, Harishchandra, tr. VI. Title.
PK3791.B188K3 1971 72-903711

Bāṇa.
कादम्बरी, कथामुख भाग. बाणभट्ट-रचित. आलोचनात्मक भूमिका, संस्कृत टीका, हिन्दी अनुवाद, अँग्रेजी अनुवाद, शब्दार्थ, टिप्पणी, आदि के सहित. टीकाकार रामस्वरूप शास्त्री. Translated into English by Debi Prasad Malviya. सम्पादक तथा हिन्दी अनुवादक प्रकाशनारायण शर्मा. 3. संस्करण. इलाहाबाद, रामनारायणलाल बेनीमाधव, 1968.
37, 412, 17 p. 19 cm. Rs5.00
English., Hindu., and Sanskrit.
I. Malviya, Debi Prasad, tr. II. Śarmā, Prakāśanārāyaṇa, ed. III. Śāstri, Rāmasvarūpa, ed. IV. Title.
Title romanized: Kādambarī, kathāmukha bhāga.
PK3791.B188K3 1968b 77-907176

Bāna.
The Kādambarī of Bāṇa / translated with occasional omissions and accompanied by a full abstract of the continuation of the romance by the author's son Bhūshaṇabhaṭṭa, by C. M. Ridding. — 1st Indian ed. — New Delhi : Oriental Books Reprint Corp. : distributed by Munshiram Manoharlal Publishers, 1974.
xxiv, 231 p. ; 23.
Reprint of the 1896 ed. published by Royal Asiatic Society, London, as Oriental translation fund : New ser., v. [7]
Includes bibliographical references and indexes.
Rs40.00
I. Bhūṣana Bhaṭṭa. II. Ridding, Caroline Mary. III. Title. IV. Series: Oriental Translation Fund, London. Publications : new ser. ; v. 7.
PK3791.B188K33 1974 891'.2'3 75-928024
76[r77]rev MARC

Bāṇa Bhaṭṭa, son of Citrabhānu
see
Bāṇa.

Bāṇabhaṭṭa, son of Citrabhānu
see
Bāṇa.

Banach, Andrzej.
Erotyzm po polsku. Andrzej Banach. Wyd. 1. Warszawa, Wydawn. Artystyczne i Filmowe, 1974.
205 p. chiefly ill. 19 cm.
1. Sex in art. 2. Sex in literature. 3. Erotica.
MH NUC76-25343

Banach, Andrzej.
Lekcja z nut. ₍Wyd. 1. Krakow₎ Polskie Wydawn. Muzyczne ₍1971₎
327 p. illus. 22 cm. zł65.00
1. Music title-pages. I. Title.
ML112.5.B3 74–218237

Banach, Andrzej.
Nauka pisania. Kraków ₍Wydawn. Literackie₎ 1971.
366 p. illus. 18 cm. zł45.00
1. Arts—Addresses, essays, lectures. I. Title.
NX65.B36 73–214552

Banach, Andrzej.
Nikifor, mistrz z Krynicy. Karaków, Wydawn. Literackie, 1957.
123 p. illus. (part col.) 18 cm.
1. Nikifor, painter. I. Title.
CtY NUC74-33085

Banach, Andrzej.
Zbierajmy pieniądze. Kraków ₍Wydawn. Literackie₎ 1970.
405 p. illus. 20 cm.
38.00
1. Numismatics. I. Title.
CJ75.B36 75–573840

Banach, Andrzej
see Banach, Ela. Dziennik podrozy po Hiszpanii. Krakow : Wydawn. Literackie, 1974.

Banach, Andrzej, joint author
see Banach, Ela. Odkrycie Amsterdamu. -- Wyd. 1. --Kraków : Wydawn. Literackie, 1975.

Banach, Andrzej, joint author
see Banach, Ela. Podróż na Sycylię, czyli koniec świata. Kraków, Wydawn. Literackie, 1971.

Banach, Andrzej
see Druzychi, Jerzy, 1930- 20 [Zwanzig Exlibris. Köbenhavn, Exlibristen, 1973.

Banach, Czeslaw
see Program i metody pracy inspekcji szkolnej. Warszawa: Wydawnictwa Szkolne i Pedagogiczne, 1974.

Banach, Ela.
Dziennik podróży po Hiszpanii / Eli i Andrzeja Banachów. — Wyd. 1. — Kraków : Wydawn. Literackie, 1974.
378 p., ₍10₎ leaves of plates : ill. (some col.) ; 17 cm.
Includes index.
zł70.00
1. Spain—Description and travel—1951– I. Banach, Andrzej. II. Title.
DP43.B34 75–582143

Banach, Ela.
Odkrycie Amsterdamu / Ela i Andrzej Banachowid ; [układ graf. Andrzej Banach]. -- Wyd. 1. -- Kraków : Wydawn. Literackie, 1975.
369 p., [13] leaves of plates : ill. ; 18 cm.
1. Amsterdam--Description. 2. Art--Amsterdam. I. Banach, Andrzej, joint author.
MH NUC77-87667

Banach, Ela.
Podróż na Sycylię, czyli koniec świata. Kraków, Wydawn. Literackie, 1971.
2 v. illus. (part col.) 18 cm. zł85.00 (2 v.)
At head of title: Ela i Andrzej Banach.
1. Sicily—Description and travel. I. Banach, Andrzej, joint author. II. Title.
DG864.2.B35 72–208489
rev

Banach, Jerzy.
Kraków; cztery pory roku. Wstep i opracowanie Jerzego Banacha. W fotografii Henryka Hermanowicza. Kraków, Wydawn. Literackie, 1959.
xii p. 160 plates. 33 cm.
Appendix in English, French, German, and Russian in pocket.
1. Kraków—Descr.—Views.
PCamA NUC74-33077

Banach, Jerzy, ed.
see Zabytki architektury Krakowa. Kraków, 1960.

Banach, John A
The Cape Midlands: its demography, 1911-1960 and regional income, 1954/55-59/60. Pietermaritzburg, 1969.
x, 255 p. 33 cm. (Rhodes University, Grahamstown, South Africa. Institute of Social & Economic Research. Occasional paper, no. 14)
Processed.
Thesis (Master of Commerce)–Rhodes University)
Includes bibliography.
1. Cape of Good Hope–Population.
CSt-H NUC73-40897

Banach, Stefan, 1892-1945.
Differentsial'noe i integral'noe ischislenie
see
Banach, Stefan, 1892-1945.
Rachunek różniczkowy i całkowy. Russian.

Banach, Stefan, 1892–1945.
₍Rachunek różniczkowy i całkowy. Russian₎
Дифференциальное и интегральное исчисление. Пер. с польск. и ред. С. И. Зуховицкого. Изд. 3-е, **испр. Москва, "Наука,"** 1972.
423 p. with diagrs. 22 cm. 0.93rub USSR 72–VKP
1. Calculus. I. Title.
Title romanized: Differentsial'noe i integral'noe ischislenie.
QA303.B2417 1972 73–322960

Banach, Stefan, 1892-1945
see Fast, H comp. The new Scottish book, Wrocław, 1946-1958. [Wrocław? 1958?]

Banachi, Raymond.
The cadaver. [New York, 1971]
1 v. (unpaged) 30 cm.
Produced at Playbox, N. Y. C., June 11, 1971.
1. American drama. 2. Drama—Promptbooks and typescripts, One-act. I. Title.
NN NUC76-71536

Banachowska, Lucja, ed.
see Spory filozoficzne w literature radzieckiej lat dwudziestych. [Wybor tekstow tlumaczyly z rosyjskiego: Hanna Gumpricht i Ruta Swiatlo. [Warszawa] Ksiazka i Wiedza, 1972.

Banachowska, Lucja, ed.
see Strukturalizm a marksizm. Warszawa, Książka i Wiedza, 1969.

Baňacká, Ol'ga, joint author
see Stančíková, Alžbeta. Charakter plaveninového režimu ... Bratislava : Veda, 1974.

Banacki, J. Robert
see National Opinion Research Center. Readership of the news; a special report... Chicago, 1961.

Banacki, Raymond.
Games; a nightmare comedy in one act. ₍New York, 1969₎
1 v. (unpaged) 29 cm.
Typescript.
Produced by New York Theatre Ensemble, N.Y.C., Dec. 26, 1969.
1. Drama, American. 2. Drama—Promptbooks and typescripts—One-act. I. Title.
NN NUC73-2343

Banacloche Pérez, Julio.
Las exenciones en el impuesto de tráfico / Julio Banacloche Pérez. — Madrid : Editorial de Derecho Financiero, 1974.
xv, 254 p. ; 20 cm. — (Series Monografías tributarias ; v. 8) Sp***
ISBN 84–7379–002–2
1. Business tax—Spain. 2. Taxation, Exemption from—Spain. I. Title.
343'.46'068 75–556357

Banacos, Charles.
Voicing: tonal paralipsis, techniques by Charles Banacos for pianists, composers, & arrangers. Dracut, Mass., 1973.
2 v. music. 22 cm.
1. Tonality. 2. Musical intervals and scales. 3. Music—Theory, Elementary. I. Title.
OO NUC76-71539

Banacos, Charles.
Voicings: voicings in fifths, techniques by Charles Banacos for pianists, composers, & arrangers. Dracut, Mass., 1973.
1 v. (unpaged) music. 22 cm.
1. Musical intervals and scales. 2. Music—Theory, Elementary. I. Title.
OO NUC76-71538

Banacos, Charles.
Voicings: voicings in fourths, techniques by Charels Banacos for pianists, composers & arrangers. Dracut, Mass., 1973.
1 v. (unpaged) music. 22 cm.
1. Musical intervals and scales. 2. Music—Theory, Elementary. I. Title.
OO NUC76-71537

Banacos, Charles.
Voicings: voicings using clusters, techniques by Charles Banacos for pianists, composers, & arrangers. Dracut, Mass., 1973.
1 v. (unpaged) music. 22 cm.
1. Musical intervals and scales. 2. Music—Theory, Elementary. I. Title.
OO NUC76-71540

Banacre
see
Banco do Estado do Acre
for publications by and about this body.
Titles and other entries beginning with this acronym are filed following this card.

Banad, S S 1931–
(Vacanakāra Dēvaradāsimayya)
ವಚನಕಾರ ದೇವರದಾಸಿಮಯ್ಯ. ₍ಲೇಖಕ₎ ಎಸ್. ಎಸ್. ಬಾಣದ. ಧಾರವಾಡ, ಕರ್ನಾಟಕ ವಿಶ್ವವಿದ್ಯಾಲಯ, 1971.
vi, 68 p. 16 cm. (ಉಪನ್ಯಾಸ ಗ್ರಂಥಮಾಲೆ, 115)
In Kannada.
1. Dēvaradāsimayya, fl. 1008–1050. 2. Lingayats. I. Title.
BL1245.L5B26 73–927044

Banādāsa, Mahatma, 1821 or 2–1892 or 3.
(Guru-mahātmya)
गुरु-महात्म्य. रचयिता महात्मा बनादास. संपादक भगवतीप्रसाद सिंह. ₍1. संस्करण. गोरखपुर, महात्मा बनादास स्मारक समिति, सं. 2028 i.e. 1972₎
19, 86 p. port. 19 cm. Rs1.25
In Awadhi.
I. Siṃha, Bhagavatī Prasāda, ed. II. Title.
PK1947.9.B3G8 1972 73–906840

Banados, Carlos Vattier
see Vattier Banados, Carlos.

Banaim
see
Bureau d'aménagement du nouvel aéroport international de Montréal
for publications by and about this body.
Titles and other entries beginning with this acronym are filed following this card.

Banaitis, Daiva Audenas.
The professionalization of physical therapy and the educational preparation of physical therapists for professional autonomy / by Daiva Audenas Banaitis. -- Carbondale, Ill. : [s.n.], 1975.
vi, 193 leaves ; 29 cm.
Thesis--Southern Illinois University.
Vita.
Bibliography: leaves 182-188.
1. Physical therapy as a profession. I. Title.
ICarbS NUC77-87593

Banaitis, Jurgis.
Vaisiu ir Darzoviu Perdirbimas. Vilnius, Valstybine Politines ir Mokslines Literaturos Leidykla, 1956.
145 p. illus. 21 cm.
Bibliography: p. 143-₍144₎
1. Canning and preserving. 2. Lithuanian Collection. I. Title.
OKentU NUC74-173586

Baṇakara, Mahadēva, 1932–
(Baṇṇada kārañji)
ಬಣ್ಣದ ಕಾರಂಜಿ; ಪ್ರೇಮಗೀತೆಗಳು. [ಕವಿ] ಮಹದೇವ ಬಣಕಾರ. ಬೆಂಗಳೂರು, ಅನುಭವ ಮಂಟಪ ಪ್ರಕಾಶನ; [ಅಧಿಕೃತ ಮಾರಾಟಗಾರರು ಬೆಂಗಳೂರು ಬುಕ್ ಬ್ಯೂರೊ, [1972]
120 p. illus. 19 cm. Rs4.00
In Kannada.
Poems.
"ಮುಂಬೈ ಕರ್ನಾಟಕ ಶ್ರೇಷ್ಠ ಗ್ರಂಥವೆಂದು ಮುಂಬೈ ಸರ್ಕಾರದಿಂದ ಪರಿಗಣಿಸಲ್ಪಟ್ಟು, ೧೯೫೭ರಲ್ಲಿ ಮೈಸೂರು ಸರ್ಕಾರದಿಂದ ಐದುನೂರು ರೂಪಾಯಿಗಳ ಬಹುಮಾನ ಪಡೆದ ಪುಸ್ತಕ."
I. Title.
PL4659.B26B3 73–903069
SA

(Bāṅalā bhāshā)
বাঙলা ভাষা. সম্পাদনাঃ মনসুর মুসা. [ঢাকা, খান ব্রাদার্স, 1971]
5, 171 p. 22 cm.
In Bengali.
Includes bibliographical references.
Rs5.00

1. Bengali language—Addresses, essays, lectures. I. Musa, Mansur. II. Title.
PK1658.B26 73–932515
rev SA

(Bāṅalādeśa)
বাঙলাদেশ / সম্পাদনায়, মনসুর মুসা. — ঢাকা : নওরোজ কিতাবিস্তান, 1974.
iiiii (i.e. v), 520 p. : maps ; 22 cm.
"বাংলাদেশ বাংলা-শিক্ষক সমিতি, বাংলাদেশ ভাষাতত্ত্ব সমাজ, এবং ঢাকা বিশ্ববিদ্যালয়ের বাংলা বিভাগের যৌথ উদ্যোগে আয়োজিত 'একুশে ফেব্রুয়ারী বক্তৃতামালা'."
Imprint on cover: বাঙলা বিভাগ, ঢাকা বিশ্ববিদ্যালয়.
In Bengali.
Includes bibliographies.
Tk33.00

1. Bengal—Civilization—Addresses, essays, lectrues. I. Musa, Mansur. II. Bāṃlādeśa Bāṃlā-śikshaka Samiti. III. Bāṃlādeśa Bhāshātattva Samāja. IV. University of Dacca. Dept. of Bengali.
DS485.B44B29 75–902538

Banaladesa Lekhaka Sibira
see He svadesa. [1378, i.e. 1972]

Bañales, F L Valer
see
Valer Bañales, F L

Bañales Baranda, Ramiro, joint author
see Planas Gómez, José. Manual de procedimientos de la Seguridad Social. [Bilbao, Imp. R. G. M.] (1972)

Banamāḷī Dāsa, 16th cent.
(Cāṭa Icchābatī)
ଚାଟ ଇଚ୍ଛାବତୀ; ପ୍ରାଚୀନ କାବ୍ୟ. କବି ବନମାଳୀ ଦାସ. ସଂପାଦକ କେଦାରନାଥ ମହାପାତ୍ର. [ଭୁବନେଶ୍ୱର] ଓଡ଼ିଶା ସରକାରଙ୍କ ଶିକ୍ଷା ବିଭାଗ, 1961.
20, 68 p. 19 cm. Re0.75
Added t.p. in English.
In Oriya.
Includes bibliographical references.

I. Title. II. Title: Chata-Ichhavati.
PK2579.B264C3 1961 75–985469

Banamali Misra
see
Vanamālimiśra, 17th cent.

Banamali Sahu
see
Sahu, Banamali, 1923-

Banamali Senapati
see
Senapati, Banamali, 1928-

Bananal, Eduardo.
Camilo Osias, educator and statesman / by Eduardo Bananal ; foreword by Diosdado Macapagal. — Quezon City [Philippines] : Manlapaz Pub. Co., 1974.
xvi, 208, [10] p. : ports. ; 23 cm.
Bibliography: p. [211]-[212]
Includes index.
1. Osias, Camilo, 1889-
LA2383.P62O832 370'.92'4 75-322306
75 MARC

Bananuka, Biregyeya-
see
Biregyeya-Bananuka.

Banaras Hindu University.
Descriptive catalogue of Samskrit manuscripts in Gaekwada Library, Bhārat Kalā Bhavana Library, and Samskrit Mahā-Vidyālaya Library, Banaras Hindu University / Ramā Śaṅkar Tripāṭhī. — [Varanasi] : Banaras Hindu University, 1971.
x, 1099 p. ; 25 cm. — (Banaras Hindu University Sanskrit series ; v. 6) (B.H.U. research publication)
Includes indexes.
Rs100.00
1. Manuscripts, Sanskrit—Catalogs. 2. Banaras Hindu University. I. Tripathi, Ramashankar, 1936- II. Sayaji Rao Gaekwad Library. III. Bharat Kala Bhavan. IV. Banaras Hindu University. Samskrit Mahavidyalaya. Library. V. Title. VI. Series: Banaras Hindu University. Sanskrit series ; v. 6. VII. Series: Banaras Hindu University. B.H.U. research publication.
Z6621.B243S353 016.091'0954 75-900817
76 MARC

Banaras Hindu University
see Udupa, K N 1920-
Advances in research in Indian medicine... Varanasi, 1970.

Banaras Hindu University. Centre of Advanced Study in Philosophy.
Year book.
Varanasi.
v. 26 cm.
1. Philosophy, Indic—Yearbooks. 2. Philosophy, Comparative—Yearbooks.
B130.B34a 107'.11'542 72–908442
MARC-S

Banaras Hindu University. Centre of Advanced Study in Philosophy
see Anviksiki. Varanasi.

Banaras Hindu University. Centre of Advanced Study in Philosophy
see Seminar on the Concept of Philosophy, Banaras Hindu University, 1965. The concept of philosophy. Varanas, Banaras Hindu University [1968]

Banaras Hindu University. College of Agriculture
see National Symposium on Maximization of Agricultural Production, Banaras Hindu University, 1968. Maximization of agricultural production. Calcutta, 1969.

Banaras Hindu University. Dept. of Ancient Indian History, Culture, and Archaeology
see Seminar papers on the chronology of the punch-marked coins. Varanasi [1966]

Banaras Hindu University. Dept. of Ancient Indian History, Culture, and Archaeology
see Seminar papers on the problem... Varanasi [India, 1969]

Banaras Hindu University. Dept. of Botany
see Misra, Ramdeo, 1908- Ecological studies of noxious weeds... Varanasi, India, Banaras Hindu University [1969?]

Banaras Hindu University. Dept. of Metallurgical Engineering.
see International Symposium on Fifty Years of Metallurgy, Varanasi, 1973. International Symposium on Fifty Years of Metallurgy ... [s.l., s.n., pref. 1973] (Delhi : INSDOC)

Banaras Hindu University. Dept. of Psychology.
Research brochure. 1968–
Varanasi.
v. 25 cm. annual
1. Psychology—Periodicals.
BF1.B35a 150'.8 72–907557
MARC-S

Banaras Hindu University. Dept. of Sociology.
see Seminar on Tradition and Modernization. Tradition and modernization ... Allahabad, Indian International Publications, 1976 [i.e. 1975]

Banaras Hindu University. Dept. of Spectroscopy
see Symposium on Spectroscopy and Allied Problems, Banaras Hindu University, 1963. Proceedings. Varanasi [1964]

Banaras Hindu University. Farm Management Studies Centre.
Studies in economics of farm management in Deoria, Uttar Pradesh : combined report 1966-69 / Gauri Shankar Lavania [Officer-in-Charge]. — [New Delhi] : Directorate of Economics and Statistics, Ministry of Agriculture, Govt. of India, [1974]
ix, 294 p. ; 30 cm.
Sponsored by the Directorate of Economics and Statistics, Govt. of India.
On back cover: Published by the Controller of Publications, Delhi.
"PDES. 131. 66-69/700."
Rs18.50 ($6.66 U.S.)
1. Agriculture—Economic aspects—India—Uttar Pradesh. I. Lavania, Gauri Shankar, 1928- II. Title.
HD2075.U6B35 1974 338.1'0954'2 75-902093
76 MARC

Banaras Hindu University. Post Graduate Institute of Indian Medicine
see The Journal of research in Indian medicine. July 1966- Varanasi, Banaras Hindu University.

Banaras Hindu University. Samskrit Mahavidyalaya. Library.
see Banaras Hindu University. Descriptive catalogue of Samskrit manuscripts in Gaekwada Library, Bhārat Kalā Bhavana Library, and Samskrit Mahā-Vidyālaya Library, Banaras Hindu University. [Varanasi] Banaras Hindu University, 1971.

Banaras Hindu University. Sayaji Rao Gaekwad Library
see Sayaji Rao Gaekwad Library.

Banaras Hindu University Inquiry Committee
see India (Republic). Banaras Hindu University Inquiry Committee.

Banaras Hindu University Library
see Sayaji Rao Gaekwad Library.

Banārasī, Bebasa
see
Bebasa Banārasī, 1938-

Bañares, Gregorio.
Filosofía farmacéutica o la farmacia en 1800 del Dr. D. Gregorio Bañares, con notas de archivo sobre la vida profesional en Cádiz hace más de cien años. Cádiz, 1971.
[1] l., 15 p. 28 cm. Sp 71-June
Cover title.
At head of title: Mariano de Rétegui Bensusan.
1. Pharmacology—Early works to 1800. 2. Pharmacy—Early works to 1800. I. Rétegui Bensusan, Mariano de, ed. II. Title.
RM88.B36 1971 615'.1 75–557114

Bănărescu, Petru.
Biogeografie. Perspectivă genetică și istorică. București, Editura științifică, 1973.
304 p. with maps. 24 cm. lei 19.00 R 73-2165
At head of title: P. Bănărescu, N. Boșcaiu.
Bibliography: p. 293–299.
1. Geographical distribution of animals and plants. I. Boșcaiu, Nicolae, joint author. II. Title.
QH84.B36 73–349838

Bănărescu, Petru.
Pisces, Teleostei; Cyprinidae (Gobioninae). Bearb. von Petru Banarescu und Teodor T. Nalbant. Berlin, New York, de Gruyter, 1973.
vii, 304 p. illus., maps. 28 cm. (Das Tierreich, Lfg. 93)
DM320.00 GFR***
Text in English.
Bibliography: p. [291]–298.
1. Cyprinidae. 2. Fishes—Classification. I. Nalbant, Teodor T., joint author. II. Title. III. Series.
QL638.C94B34 597'.53 74–300275
ISBN 3-11-004627-X

Bănărescu, Petru.
Principii și probleme de zoogeografie / P. Bănărescu. — ⌈București⌉ : Editura Academiei Republicii Socialiste România, 1970.
260 p. : ill., maps ; 24 cm.
Summary in English.
Bibliography: p. ⌈255⌉–260.
1. Zoogeography. 2. Zoogeography—Romania. I. Title.
QL101.B35 76–524812

Bănărescu, Petru.
Principiile și metodele zoologiei sistematice. ⌈București⌉, Editura Academiei Republicii Socialiste România, 1973.
220 p. with figs. 24 cm. lei 13.00 R 73–3636
Summary in English.
Bibliography: p. 211–⌈214⌉
1. Zoology—Classification. I. Title.
QL351.B36 73–359601

Bănărescu, Petru.
Principles and problems of zoogeography = Principii și probleme de zoogeografie / P. Bănărescu ; translated from Roumanian. -- Belgrade : Translated and published for U.S. Department of Commerce and the National Science Foundation, Washington, D.C., by the NOLIT Pub. House ; available from U.S. Dept. of Commerce, National Technical Information Service, Springfield, Va., 1975.
214 p. : ill. ; 24 cm. -- (TT 71-56006)
1. Zoogeography. I. Title.
FMU NUC77-88176

Banarlı, Nihat Sami, 1908–
Resimli Türk edebiyatı tarihi; destanlar devrinden zamanımıza kadar. ⌈İstanbul⌉ Yedigün Neşriyatı ⌈1948⌉
424, ⌈16⌉ p. illus., ports. 29 cm.
On cover: Türk edebiyatı tarihi.
Bibliography: p. ⌈425⌉–⌈429⌉
1. Turkish literature—History and criticism. I. Title.
PL205.B3 1948 N E 62–1023
rev

Banarlı, Nihat Sami, 1908–
Resimli Türk edebiyatı tarihi; destanlar devrinden zamânımıza kadar. ⌈Yazan⌉ Nihad Sâmi Banarlı. İstanbul, M. E. B. Devlet Kitapları, 1971–
v. illus. (part col.) 29 cm.
Issued in parts.
Rev. and enl. 2d ed.
Includes bibliographical references.
1. Turkish literature—History and criticism. I. Title. II. Title: Türk edebiyatı tarihi.
PL205.B3 1971 73–211090

Banarlı, Nihat Sami, 1908–
Türkçenin sırları ⌈yazan⌉ Nihad Sâmi Banarlı. ⌈İstanbul⌉ 1972.
viii, 319 p. 19 cm. (İstanbul Fetih Cemiyeti'nin 66., İstanbul Enstitüsü'nün 53. kitabıdır)
1. Turkish language. I. Title. II. Series: İstanbul Enstitüsü. İstanbul Enstitüsü neşriyatı, 53.
DR719.I 77 no. 53 74–202855
[PL113]

Banārsī, Muḥammad Asad Ashk
see
Ashk Banārsī, Muḥammad Asad.

Banārsī, Muḥammad Kāẓim
see Kāẓim Banārsī, Muḥammad, 1912-

Banarsi Dass Arora
see
Arora, Banarsi Dass.

Banáry, Boris.
Súpis redakčného archívu slovenských spevov. Zost. Boris Banáry. Martin, Matica slovenská, rozmn., 1972.
216, ⌈3⌉ p. 20 cm. (Fondy Literárneho archívu Matice slovenskej, č. 70) CzS 72
Includes bibliographical references.
1. Songs, Slovak—Bibliography. 2. Songs—Indexes. I. Title. II. Series: Matica slovenská, Turčiansky sv. Martin. Literárny archív. Fondy, č. 70.
ML120.C9B3 73–351132

Bañas, Eliseo P., joint author
see Siega, Gorgonio D Selected Philippine periodical index ... Dumaguete City [196-]

Banaś, Jan.
Zielony wiatr; wiersze. Andrzej Basaj: grafika. ⌈W Warszawie⌉ Ludowa Spółdzielnia Wydawnicza ⌈1970⌉
33 p. illus. 19 cm.
Cover title.
I. Title.
CaBVaU NUC73-91930

Banaś, Marian, ed.
see Wybrane zagadnienia z zakresu geologii złóz surowców skalnych i nauk pomocniczych. Kraków : Akademia Górniczo-Hutnicza im. S. Staszica, 1974.

Banas, Norma.
Identifying early learning ga‿ps : a guide to the assessment of academic readiness / Norma Banas, I. H. Wills. — Atlanta : Humanics Press, c1975.
v, 77 p. : ill. ; 23 cm.
Includes bibliographies.
1. Learning disabilities. 2. Readiness for school. I. Wills, Isabel Hayes, 1917– II. Title.
LC4704.B36 371.9′1 75–13794 (MARC)

Banas, Norma.
New approaches to success in the classroom : closing learning gaps / Norma Banas, I. H. Wills ; ill. by Sharon Henderson. — Atlanta : Humanics Ltd., c1976.
130 p. (p. 128-130 blank) : ill. ; 28 cm.
ISBN 0-89334-000-6
1. Language arts (Elementary) 2. Mathematics—Study and teaching (Elementary) I. Wills, I. H., joint author. II. Title.
LB1576.B28 372.6 76-15126
77 MARC

Banas, Norma.
Prescriptive teaching : theory into practice / by Norma Banas, I. H. Wills ; with ill. by Sharon S. Henderson. — Springfield, Ill. : Thomas, c1977.
xi, 270 p. : ill. ; 26 cm.
Bibliography: p. 265.
Includes index.
ISBN 0-398-03546-6
1. Perceptual-motor learning. 2. Slow learning children. I. Wills, I. H., joint author. II. Title.
LB1067.B27 371.9′043 76-4963
76 MARC

Banas, Norma.
Success begins with understanding : a guide to prescriptive teaching programs illustrated with the Wechsler intelligence scale for children and the Detroit tests of learning aptitude / Norma Banas, I. H. Wills ; with contributions by Sandra Felton. — San Rafael, Calif. : Academic Therapy Publications, 1974, c1972.
82 p. : ill. ; 23 cm.
Includes bibliographical references.
ISBN 0-87879-039-X : $2.00
1. Learning disabilities. 2. Wechsler intelligence scale for children. 3. Learning ability—Testing. I. Wills, I. H., joint author. II. Felton, Sandra, joint author. III. Title.
LC4704.B38 1974 371.9 72-85687
77 MARC

Banas, Paul Anthony, 1929-
see Human Sciences Research, inc. A study of local leadership in community economic planning. McLean, Va., 1966.

Bañas, Raymundo C
see Bañas y Castillo, Raymundo, 1894-

Bañas y Castillo, Raymundo, 1894–
Pilipino music and theater, by Raymundo C. Bañas. Quezon City, Manlapaz Pub. Co., 1969 ⌈c1970⌉
264 p. illus. 27 cm.
1. Music—Philippine Islands. 2. Musicians, Philippine. 3. Theatre—Philippine Islands. I. Title.
ML3758.P5B3 780′.955 74–184143
MARC

Banas classificado industrial brasileiro. Who produces what in Brazil 1974–
⌈São Paulo, Editora Banas⌉
v. 28 cm.
English, French, German, Portuguese, and Spanish.
1. Brazil — Commerce — Directories — Periodicals. 2. Commercial products—Brazil—Directories—Periodicals. I. Title: Who produces what in Brazil.
HF3403.B35 338.4′025′81 75–640380
MARC-S

Banaschewski, Peter.
Macaulay und Acton. Ein Beitrag zum Freiheitsbegriff in der englischen Geschichtsschreibung. Miesbach, Mayr, 1960.
1 reel.
Microfilm copy (negative)
1. Macaulay, Thomas Babington Macaulay, 1st Baron, 1800-1859. 2. Acton, John Emerich Edward Dalberg Acton, 1st Baron, 1834-1902. I. Title.
TNJ NUC73-57834

Banaschik-Ehl, Christa.
Scharnhorsts Lehrer, Graf Wilhelm von Schaumburg-Lippe, in Portugal : die Heeresreform 1761–1777 / Christa Banaschik-Ehl. — Osnabrück : Biblio-Verlag, 1974.
vii, 261 p., ⌈12⌉ leaves of plates : ill. (some col.), maps ; 23 cm. — (Studien zur Militärgeschichte, Militärwissenschaft und Konfliktforschung ; Bd. 3) GFR 74–A
Originally presented as the author's thesis, Universität des Saarlandes, Saarbrücken, 1969.
Bibliography: p. 195–209.
ISBN 3–7648–0929–9 : DM48.00
1. Portugal. Exército — Organization — History. 2. Schaumberg-Lippe, Wilhelm, Graf zu, 1724–1777. 3. Portugal—History, Military. I. Title. II. Series.
UA762.B36 1974 75–561784

Banasco, Rocco R 1934-
Lingua e tecnica delle canzoni di Giacomo da Lentini. ⌈n.p.⌉ 1973.
184 l.
Thesis (Ph.D.)—University of Chicago.
1. Giacomo da Lentini, 13th cent. I. Title.
ICU NUC74-131293

Banasević, Nikola.
Etudes d'histoire littéraire et de littérature comparée / Nikola Banasević. -- Beograd : Izdavačko-informativni centar studenata, 1975.
138 p. ; 24 cm. -- (Univerzitetski udžbenici ; 21)
Bibliographical footnotes.
1. Literature--Addresses, essays, lectures. 2. Literature, Comparative--Addresses, essays, lectures. 3. Yugoslav literature--Addresses, essays, lectures. I. Title. II. Series.
CaBVaU NUC77-86128

Banašević, Nikola
see Petar II, Prince Bishop of Montenegro, 1813-1851. (Gorski vijenac) 1973.

Banašević, Nikola
see Petar II, Prince Bishop of Montenegro, 1813-1815. [Works] Celokupna dela Petra Petrovića Njegoša. 1967.

Banašević, Nikola
see Petar II, Prince Bishop of Montenegro, 1813-1851. [Works] Celokupna dela Petra II Petrovića Njegoša. 1975.

Banašević, Nikola
see Petar II, Prince Bishop of Montenegro, 1813-1851. [Works] Celokupna djela P. P. Njegoša. 1951-1955.

Banasiak, Stefan.
Początki władzy ludowej w Łodzi. Łódź, 1973.
31 p. (Biblioteczka wiedzy o Łodzi, zesz. 15)
On verso of t. p.: Prezydium Łódzkiego Komitetu Frontu Jedności Narodu. Uniwersytet Łódzki.
"550 rocznica nadania Łodzi praw miejskich."
"150 rocznica powstania Łodzi przemysłowej."
MH NUC76-71543

Banasiak, Stefan, ed.
see Polska Zjednocznoa Partia Robotnicza. Komitet Wojewódzki, Lódź. Wydzial Propagandy. Za ojczyzne i za lud. [Lódź] Wydawn. Lódzkie [1973]

Banasiewicz, Maria.
Źródła do dziejów Uniwersytetu im. Adama Mickiewicza w Poznaniu. Poznań ⌈Wydawn. Uniwersytetu im. A. Mickiewicza⌉ 1973–
v. 24 cm. (Uniwersytet im. Adama Mickiewicza w Poznaniu. Seria: Dzieje UAM, nr. 10) zł36.00
At head of title, v. 1– : Maria Banasiewicz, Antoni Czubiński.
Includes bibliographical references.
CONTENTS: t. 1. Organizacja i rozwój uczelni od listopada 1918 roku do inauguracji w maju 1919 roku.
1. Posen. Universytet—History. I. Czubiński, Antoni, joint author. II. Title. III. Series: Posen. Uniwersytet. Seria: Dzieje UAM, nr. 10.
LF4207.P6B36 74–222068

Banasik, Robert C 1942-
Partitioning the regulator: an investigation of the relationship between regulator part functions and the patient state, by Robert C. Banasik. [n.p.] 1974.
121 l.
Thesis (Ph.D.)–Ohio State University.
Bibliography: leaves 118-121.
1. Medical care–United States. 2. Medical care, Cost of–United States. 3. Electronic data processing–Medicine. I. Title.
OU NUC76-25321

Banasiński, Antoni.
Nowoczesne metody przygotowywania decyzji kierowniczych. Warszawa, 1970.
119 p. 29 cm. (Zakład Administracji Państwowej. Materiały i studia, nr. 86) zł40.00
Added t. p.: The modern methods of managerial decision-making.
Table of contents also in English.
Bibliography: p. 100–102.
1. Decision-making—Mathematical models. I. Title. II. Series.
HD38.B24 73–204729

Banasiński, Antoni, joint author
see Lange, Oscar Richard, 1904-1965.
Teoriia statistiki. 1971.

Banasree Roy
see
Roy, Banasree, 1936-

Banassat, Marcel.
Paris aux cent villages / Marcel Banassat. — 1. éd. — Paris : P.C.V. éditions, c1976-
v. : ill. (some col.) ; 30 cm. F***
Bibliography: v. 1, p. 160.
Includes index.
65.00F (v. 1)
1. Paris—Description. 2. Paris—History. I. Title.
DC707.B298 944'.361 77-471193
77 MARC

The Banasthali patrika.
[Jaipur, Banasthali Vidyapith]
v. 22–25 cm.
I. Banasthali Vidyapith.
AS471.B35 79–928151

Banaszak, Konrad J
Genesis of the Mississippi Valley-type lead-zinc ores. [n.p., 1975]
1 v.
Thesis (Ph.D.)--Northwestern University.
1. Lead ores--Mississippi Valley. 2. Zinc ores--Mississippi Valley. 3. Geology--Mississippi Valley. I. Title.
IEN NUC77-86107

Banaszak, Konrad J
Interaction of bulk precipitation, stream water, and sewage in a small watershed near Oxford, Mississippi, by Konrad J. Banaszak, Charlie B. Whitten and Dan A. Thompson. [n.p.] Water Resources Research Institute, Mississippi State University, 1973.
70 l. illus.
1. Watersheds–Research. 2. Water–Analysis. 3. Hydrologic cycle. I. Mississippi. State University. Water Resources Research Institute. II. Title.
GAT NUC75-72329

Banaszak, Konrad J
Relative throughfall enrichment by biologic and by aerosol-derived materials in loblolly pines / by Konrad J. Banaszak. -- Mississippi State : Water Resources Research Institute, Mississippi State University, 1975.
ii, 28 leaves : ill. ; 28 cm.
"Supported in part by funds provided by the Office of Water Resources Research."
Bibliography: leaves 27-28.
1. Loblolly-pine. I. Mississippi, State University. Water Resources Research Institute. II. United States. Office of Water Resources Research. III. Title.
DI NUC77-89205

Banaszczyk, Eugeniusz, comp.
Pierwsze skrzydła. Zebrał i opracował Eugeniusz Banaszczyk. [Wyd. 2., popr. i uzup.]. Warszawa, Wydawn. Ministerstwa Obrony Narodowej, 1972.
366 p. illus. 20 cm. zł25.00
Includes bibliographical references.
1. Aeronautics—Poland. I. Title.
TL526.P57B3 1972 73–204690

Banaszczyk, Eugeniusz.
Skrzydlata dywizja / Eugeniusz Banaszczyk. — Wyd. 1. — Warszawa : Polska i Wiedza, 1975.
194 p., [8] leaves of plates : ill. ; 20 cm. — (Biblioteka pamięci pokoleń - Rada Ochrony Pomników Walki i Męczeństwa) P*** zł20.00
1. World War, 1939–1945 — Aerial operations, Polish. 2. Poland. Wojsko Polskie. Samodzielna Eskadra Lotnicza. I. Title.
D792.P6B36 77–505069

Banaszczyk, Eugeniusz.
W bitwie o Anglię. [Wyd. 1.]. Warszawa, Książka i Wiedza, 1973.
199 p. illus. 20 cm. (Biblioteka pamięci pokoleń) zł20.00
1. Britain, Battle of, 1940. 2. World War, 1939–1945—Aerial operations, Polish. 3. World War, 1939–1945—Aerial operations, British. I. Title.
D756.5.B7B3 74–200283

Banaszewski, Tadeusz, joint author
see Battaglia, Andrzej. Maszyny do przeróbki wegla... Warszawa, Państwowe Wydawn. Naukowe, [1972-

Banaszkiewicz, Henryk.
Kliniczne i społeczne aspekty kiły późnej. Warszawa, 1972.
183 p.
1. Syphilis, Latent. I. Title.
DNLM NUC74-131296

Banaszkiewicz, Jakub.
Państwo i partia w systemie kapitalistycznym. [Wyd. 1.]. Warszawa, Państwowe Wydawn. Naukowe, 1972.
292 p. 21 cm. zł28.00
Includes bibliographical references.
1. State, The. 2. Political parties. I. Title.
JC11.B35 73–200101

Banaszkiewicz, Jakub
see Filozofia marksistowska... Wyd. 3., rozsz. i popr. Warszawa: Państwowe Wydawn, Naukowe, 1975.

Banaszkiewicz, Władysław, comp.
Lenin na ekranie. [Opracowali: Władysław Banaszkiewicz i Grażyna Hartwig. Teksty z języka rosyjskiego przełożył Stefan Atlas. Wyd. 1.]. Warszawa, Wydawnictwa Artystyczne i Filmowe, 1973.
179 p. illus. 20 cm. zł30.00
Includes bibliographical references.
1. Lenin, Vladimir Il'ich, 1870–1924, in moving pictures. I. Hartwig, Grażyna, joint comp.
DK254.L46B35 74–210742

Banaszkiewicz, Wladyslaw
see Sesja Awangarda Filmowa Lat Dwudziestych, Sosnowiec, 1975. Z dziejów awanagardy filmowej ... Katowice: US, 1976.

Bănătan, Octavian.
50 [al Cincizecilea] de ani de sport la Institutul de Medicină si Farmacie, Bucureşti. [Bucureşti] Editura Stadion [1970]
220 p. illus., ports.
Summaries in French, English, Russian, and German.
1. Physical education and training—History—Rumania. 2. Sport medicine—History—Rumania. 3. Sports—History—Rumania. 4. Institutul de Medicină şi Farmacie, Bucharest. I. Title.
DNLM NUC74-137777

Bănăţan, Octavian.
Educaţia fizică şi sportul în învătămîntul superior. [București], „Stadion", 1973.
298 p., 12 l. of plates, errata. 20 cm. lei 9.50 R 73–2400
At head of title: Octavian Bănăţan, Marin Bîrjega, Alexe Nicu.
Bibliography: p. 205–[207]
1. Physical education and training. 2. College sports. I. Bîrjega, Marin. II. Nicu, Alexe. III. Title.
GV347.B36 73–341225

Bănăţan, Octavian.
Pregătirea fizică a studenților. [București], „Stadion," 1972.
391 p. with figs., errata. 20 cm. lei 11.00 R 72–2001
Bibliography: p. 383–[388]
1. Physical education and training—Romania—Statistics. I. Title.
GV285.B36 74–328364

Bănăţeanu, Ion Constantin, 1928- joint author
see Bărbulescu, Nicolae. Chimie pentru muncitori ... București, Editura Tehnică, 1962.

Bănăţeanu, Tancred.
Arta populară bucovineană / Tancred Bănăţeanu ; [prefață, acad. Em. Condurachi ; prezentarea grafică, Vladimir Șetran, Ion Bițan]. — [Suceava] : Centrul de îndrumare a creației populare și a mișcării artistice de masă a județului Suceava, 1975.
501 p. : ill. (some col.) ; 23 x 29 cm. R 75–4033
Summary in English, French, German, and Russian.
Table of contents and legends in Romanian, English, French, German, and Russian.
Bibliography: p. 433–440.
lei 60.00
1. Folk art—Bukowina. I. Title.
NK1028.B84B25 75–409198

Bănăţeanu, Tancred.
Arta populară din nordul Transilvaniei. [Prezentare grafica: Vladimir Setran. Fotografii executate de Dan Er. Grigorescu. Red. artistica: Gabriela Dumitrescu. Baia Mare] Casa Creaţiei Populare a Judeţului Maramures, 1969.
293, [8] p. illus., plates (part col.) 24 x 29 cm.
In Romanian; summary in French, Russian, and English.
Bibliographical footnotes.
TxU NUC74-137751

Bănăţeanu, Tancred.
Ceramica din Glogova, Regiunea Oltenia. Bucureşti, 1966.
95 p. illus. 24 cm. (Studii și cercetări, 1)
Summaries in English, French and Russian.
1. Pottery — Oltenia, Romania. 2. Oltenia, Romania — Industries. I. Title. II. Series: Muzeul de Artă Populară al Republicii Socialiste România. Studi şi cercetări, 1.
TP803.R6B36 72–375085

Bănăteanu, Tancred
see Bucharest. Muzeul de Artă al Republicii Populare Romîne. Mobilier si feronerie populara. [Bucureşti, "Artis," 1971]

Bănăteanu, Tancred, joint author
see Zderciuc, Boris. Die Volkskunst in Rumänien. Bukarest, Verlag Meridiane, 1964.

Bănăţeanul, Ion Popovici-
see Popovici-Bănăţeanul, Ion, 1869-1893.

Banathy, Bela H
Design, development and validation of a transportable instructional system for the training of educational diffusion/evaluation personnel. Final report, by Bela H. Banathy [and others] Berkeley, Calif., Far West Laboratory for Educational Research and Development, 1971.
115 [i.e. 127] p.
1. Teachers—Training. I. Title.
InU NUC74-137745

Banathy, Bela H
A design for foreign language curriculum [by] Bela H. Banathy [and] Dale L. Lange. Lexington, Mass., Heath [1972]
128 p. illus. 24 cm.
Bibliography: p. 121–128.
1. Languages, Modern—Study and teaching. I. Lange, Dale L., joint author. II. Title.
LB1578.B36 375'.418 72–3690
ISBN 0–669–82073–3 MARC

Banathy, Bela H
Developing a systems view of education; the systems-model approach [by] Bela H. Banathy. Belmont, Calif., Lear Siegler/Fearon Publishers [c1973]
vi, 90 p. diagrs. 26 cm.
1. Education—Mathematical models. I. Title.
TxU UU NUC75-16639

Banathy, Bela H.
see Love, William D Options and perspectives... New York, Modern Language Association of America, 1973.

Banātvālā, Ghulām Maḥmud, 1933–
(Muslim Lig, āzādī ke ba'd)
مسلم لیگ، آزادی کے بعد. ﹝مصنف﹞ غلام محمود بنات والا.
﹝بمبئی، محمد حسین سلیمان پٹیل؛ سول ڈسٹریبیوٹرز علوی بک ڈپو،
﹝1971
11, 123 p. illus., ports. 23 cm. Rs7.50
In Urdu.
Includes bibliographical references.

1. All-India Muslim League. I. Title.

DS480.84.B248 72–902068
S A

al-Banaurī, Muḥammad Zakariyyā.
(Mas'alah-yi rūḥ o nafs)
مسئلہ روح و نفس، از سید محمد زکریا البنوری. کراچی، اداره
مجلس علمی ﹝1971﹞
176 p. 22 cm. (سلسلہ مطبوعات، 51) Rs4.00
In Urdu.
Series romanized: Silsilah-yi maṭbū'āt.

1. Soul (Islam) I. Title.

BP166.73.B36 76–932887
S A

Banavalikap, A S
A report on the labour conditions in textile industry in Holkar State. ﹝Indore, Printed by Modern Printery, 1948?﹞
ii, 127 p. 24 cm.
On cover: A study of industrial dissatisfactions, being the report of an enquiry.
1. Textile workers—Indore, India (State) 2. Textile industry and fabrics—Indore, India (State) I. Title.
HD8039.T42 I 32 331.7'67'7009543 74–175144
MARC

Banavalkar, Prabodh Vaman, 1939-
Analysis and behavior of light gage hyperbolic paraboloid shells. [Ithaca, N.Y.] 1971.
vii, 251 l. illus. 29 cm.
Thesis (Ph. D.)—Cornell University.
1. Shells (Engineering) 2. Elastic plates and shells. 3. Hyperboloid. I. Title. II. Title: Light gage hyperbolic paraboloid shells.
NIC NUC73-32200

Banavārī Lāla Miśra, 1923-
see
Misra, Banwarilal, 1923-

Banavārīlāla Handā
see
Handā, Banavārīlāla.

Banavārīlāla Miśra, 1923-
see
Misra, Banwarilal, 1923-

Banay, Yaakov, 1896–
﹝Bi-netive psikhologyah ve-ḥinukh﹞
בנתיבי פסיכולוגיה וחינוך ﹝מאת﹞ יעקב בנאי. תל-אביב, אל"ף
﹝1972﹞
116 p. 21 cm. IL7.00
1. Psychology. 2. Education—Israel. I. Title.
BF38.B26 72–950591

Banay, Yaakov, 1896–
הרקע להתפתחות הנפשית של ילדינו ﹝מאת﹞ יעקב בנאי. תל
-אביב, תרבות וחינוך, 725 ﹝1965﹞
31 p. 17 cm. IL1.00
"נדפס ב'אורים להורים,' חוב' 10, 11–12, 1964."
1. Child study. I. Title.
Title romanized: ha-Reka' la-hitpatḥut ha-nafshit shel yeladenu.
LB1131.B3213 HE 68–4664
PL 480 : Is–5785

Banay, Yaakov, 1896–
הילד והספר; טיפוח אהבת הקריאה ומשמעותה ﹝מאת﹞ יעקב
בנאי. תל-אביב, תרבות וחינוך, 727 ﹝1967﹞
30 p. 16 cm. (הוברת הסבוה להורים) IL1.00
1. Books and reading for children. I. Title.
Title romanized: ha-Yeled veha-sefer.
Z1037.A1B24 HE 68–4341
PL 480 : Is–6396

Ang Banay nga Cristohanon. Visayan ed. ﹝Manila﹞ Dept. of Audio-Visual Work, Philippine Federation of Christian Churches ﹝196-?﹞
﹝12﹞ p. ill. 24 cm.
Issued also in English under title: The Christian family.
1. Family--Religious life. I. Philippine Federation of Christian Churches. Dept. of Audio-Visual Work.
NIC NUC77-90862

Banayan, A.
see Pouyanne, H Les anévrysmes sacculaires multiples du système carotidien supra-clinoïdien. [Paris, Masson] 1973.

(Banayung)
באנייונג; פראגראמאטישע באהאנדלונגען ערב דער 8-טער וועלט
-קאנפערענץ. רעדאגירט: הורוויץ. תל-אביב, איהוד עולם
פועלי ציון—צ. ס.—התאחדות, 1964–65.
2 v. 24 cm.
On back cover: Banaiung.
Vol. 2 has subtitle: באהאנדלונגען אויף דער וועלט-קאנפערענץ אין "בית בערל."
1. World Union of Poalei Zion—Hitachdut. 2. Labor Zionism—Addresses, essays, lectures. I. Horvits, Mosheh, ed. II. World Union of Poalei Zion—Hitachdut. III. Title: Banaiung.
DS150.L484B36 HE 68–4676
PL 480 : Is–4342

Banazol, Luís Ataíde da Silva, 1919-
Guiné-Bissau, três vezes vinte cinco / Luís Ataíde Banazol. — Lisboa : Prelo, 1974.
94 p. ; 19 cm. — (Documentos ; ﹝21﹞)
1. Guinea-Bissau—Politics and government. 2. Partido Africano da Independência da Guiné e Cabo Verde. I. Title.
DT613.75.B35 76-472137
76 MARC

Banazol, Luís Ataíde da Silva, 1919-
Portugal : el origen del movimiento de las fuerzas armadas ; Los capitanes / Luís Ataíde Banazol ; traducción : Biviana Goday. -- Barcelona : Avance, 1975.
146 p. ; 20 cm. -- (Avance, serie popular, 3)
"Titulo original: A origem do movimento das forças armadas - Os capitães."
I. Goday, Biviana. II. Title.
OU NUC77-86109

Banba, Kaichirō
see
Bamba, Kaichirō, 1909-

Banbenko, Konstantin Ivanovich.
The theory of extremal problems for univalent functions of class S / by K. I. Babenko. — Providence, R. I. : American Mathematical Society, 1975.
iii, 327 p. ; 26 cm. — (Proceedings of the Steklov Institute of Mathematics ; no. 101 (1972))
Translation of K teorii ėkstremal'nykh zadach dli͡a odnolistnykh funkt͡siĭ klassa S.
Includes bibliographical references.
ISBN 0–8218–3001–5
1. Univalent functions. 2. Maxima and minima. I. Title. II. Series: Akademii͡a nauk SSSR. Matematicheskiĭ institut. Proceedings ; no. 101.
QA1.A413 no. 101 515'.64 74–23425
[QA331] MARC

Banbery, Fred, joint author.
see Bond, Michael. Paddington at the circus. London, Collins, 1973.

Banbery, Fred, joint author
see Bond, Michael. Paddington at the circus. New York, Random House, 1974, c1973.

Banbery, Fred, illus.
see Bond, Michael. Paddington bear. London, Collins, 1972.

Banbery, Fred, illus.
see Bond, Michael. Paddington Bear. New York, Random House, 1973, c1972.

Banbery, Fred, joint author.
see Bond, Michael. Paddington goes shopping. London, Collins, 1973.

Banbery, Fred, illus.
see Bond, Michael. Paddington's garden. London, Collins, 1972.

Banbery, Fred, illus.
see Bond, Michael. Paddington's garden. New York, Random House, 1973, c1972.

Banbery, Fred, joint author
see Bond, Michael. Paddington's lucky day. New York, Random House, 1974, c1973.

Banbuck, Cabuzel Andréa.
Histoire politique, économique et sociale de la Martinique sous l'Ancien Régime, 1635-1789 ﹝par﹞ C.A. Banbuck. Paris, M. Rivière, 1935; réédité par La Société de distribution et de culture. Port-de-France, Martinique, 1972.
335 p. map. 25 cm. (Bibliothèque d'histoire économique)
1. Martinique—Hist. 2. Martinique—Econ. condit. 3. Martinique—Soc. condit. I. Title.
CtY NUC75-26562

Banbury, E. E.
see Selected trees and shrubs evaluated... -- Peoria, Ill. : Agricultural Research Service, U.S. Dept. of Agriculture, 1976.

Banbury, Philip.
Man and the sea : from the Ice Age to the Norman Conquest / Philip Banbury. — London : Adlard Coles, 1975.
269 p. : ill., maps ; 24 cm. GB***
Bibliography: p. ﹝254﹞-258.
Includes index.
ISBN 0-229-11506-3 : £8.50
1. Navigation—Europe—History. 2. Boat-building—History. 3. Shipbuilding—History. I. Title.
VK55.B36 1975 387'.094 75-329998
75 MARC

Banbury, Eng. Ornithological Society
see
Banbury Ornithological Society.

Banbury Ornithological Society.
A study of birds in the South Midlands : the decennial report of the Banbury Ornithological Society / ﹝edited by﹞ A. Brownett ; illustrations, Liz Blundell. — ﹝Oxford : The Society﹞, 1974.
58 p. : ill. ; 22 cm. GB 75-08191
Bibliography: p. 57-58.
ISBN 0-9500216-1-X : £0.60
1. Birds—England—Banbury. I. Brownett, Anthony. II. Title.
﹝QL690.G7B29 1974﹞ 598.2'9425'73 75-318420
75 MARC

Banbury wills and inventories / transcribed, abstracted and edited by E. R. C. Brinkworth and J. S. W. Gibson. — Banbury : Banbury Historical Society, 19 -
v. ; 21 cm. — (﹝Records publications﹞ - Banbury Historical Society ; v. 14 ISSN 0552-0823) GB76-36495 (v. 2)
Includes indexes.
CONTENTS:
—pt. 2. 1621-1650.

ISBN 0-900129-14-X (v. 2) : £2.50 (v. 2)
1. Banbury, Eng.—History—Sources. 2. Wills—England—Banbury. I. Brinkworth, Edwin Robert Courtney. II. Gibson, Jeremy Sumner Wycherley. III. Series: Banbury Historical Society, Banbury, Eng. Records publications ; v. 14.
DA690.B22B33 929'.3425'73 77-355983
77 MARC

Banca Catalana. Departamento de Extranjero
see
Banca Catalana. Servicio Extranjero.

Banca Catalana. Servei d'Estudis.
Evolució econòmica.
﹝Barcelona﹞
v. illus. 27 cm.
1. Spain—Economic conditions—1918– 2. Catalonia—Economic conditions. I. Title.
HC381.B29a 73–364635
MARC–S

Banca Catalana. Servei d'Estudis.
Localització i dinàmica de l'activitat econòmica. Barcelona, 1968 ﹝i. e. 1970﹞
222 p. maps. 24 cm. (Estudis d'economia catalana)
1. Catalonia—Economic conditions. 2. Catalonia—Industries. I. Title. II. Series.
HC387.C25B258 74–200615

Banca Catalana. Servei d'Estudis
see Evolució de les àrees de trànsit dels autobusos de línia [sic] a Catalunya... [Barcelona] Banca Catalana, Servei d'Estudis [1970]

Banca Catalana. Servicio Extranjero.
Exportación: regimen de comercio y procedimientos de tramitación. [Barcelona, 1971?]
208 p. 22 cm. Sp***
"Modificaciones legales producidas con posterioridad a la edición de la presente publicación" [18] p. inserted.
1. Export controls—Spain. I. Title.
74-336599

Banca commerciale italiana.
The Italian stock market; structure, workings and impact of taxation for foreign investors. [Milan, 1972]
[86] p. illus. 28 cm.
1. Stock exchange—Italy. I. Title.
MiDW NUC76-71571

Banca commerciale italiana.
Il portolano del mondo economico. Cifre e notizie sistematicamente ordinate paese per paese. Paesi socialisti. [Milano], Banca commerciale italiana, Ufficio studi, 1972.
xxi, 482 p. 26½ cm. It 72-July
Bibliography: p. 479-482.
1. Communist countries—Economic conditions. I. Title.
HC59.B354 73-305100

Banca commerciale italiana
see Algorismus; trattato di aritmetica pratica... Verona, Italy, 1972.

Banca commerciale italiana
see Articles of agreement of the International Monetary Fund. Italian. Gli accordi di Bretton Woods ... [Roma, Tipografia editrice Italia, 1945?]

Banca commerciale italiana
see England and Italy a century ago, a new turn in economic relations. Milan, 1967.

Banca commerciale italiana
see Italy. Laws, statutes, etc. Decreto del Presidente della Repubblica 20 gennaio 1958, n. 645. Milano, 1971

Banca commerciale italiana
see Italy. Laws, statutes, etc. Decreto del Presidente della Repubblica 20 gennaio 1958, n. 645. Milano, 1972.

Banca commerciale italiana.
see The New inflation and monetary policy ... London, Macmillan, 1976.

Banca commerciale italiana.
see The "New inflation" and monetary policy ... New York, Holmes & Meier Publishers, 1976.

Banca d'Italia.
Bollettino—Banca d'Italia.
[Roma, Italy] Banca d'Italia.
v. 28 cm.
Bimonthly -1975; quarterly
Vol. for 1975 complete in one issue.
Continues: Banca d'Italia. Bollettino mensile del Servizio studi economici.
1. Banca d'Italia. 2. Banks and banking, Central—Italy—Statistics—Periodicals.
HG3084.B318 332.1'1'0945 77-640046
MARC-S

Banca d'Italia.
Fine dell'autarchia e miracolo economico. (1946-1959). Nelle relazioni di Luigi Einaudi e Donato Menichella. Roma, Janus, [1973?].
550 p. 26 cm. (Documenti di economia italiana, 1) L7000
It 73-Nov
Cover title.
1. Banca d'Italia. 2. Italy—Economic conditions—1945- —Addresses, essays, lectures. I. Einaudi, Luigi, Pres. Italy, 1874-1961. II. Menichella, Donato. III. Title.
HG3084.B33 1973 73-355775

Banca d'Italia
see Seminar on Commercial Banking in a Modern Economy, Rome, 1969. Commercial banking in a modern economy. Milano, A. Giuffrè, 1971

Banca d'Italia. Biblioteca.
Indice delle pubblicazioni cessate e delle raccolte interrotte. [n. p.], 1970.
101 p. 24 cm. It 71-Feb
1. Periodicals—Bibliography—Catalogs. 2. Banca d'Italia. Biblioteca. I. Title.
Z6945.B34 73-345864

Banca d'Italia. Gruppo per lo studio della politica monetaria e fiscale.
Bilancia dei pagamenti dell'Italia (1947-1967), [a cura di Francesco Masera con collaborazione di Maria Buoninconti. Roma, 1970?-
v. 28 cm (Its [Pubblicazioni], fasc. 11) It***
CONTENTS: pt. 1. Dati annuali.
1. Balance of payments—Italy. I. Masera, Francesco, ed. II. Title. III. Series: Banca d'Italia. Gruppo per lo studio della politica monetaria e fiscale. Pubblicazioni—Banca d'Italia, Gruppo per lo studio della politica monetaria e fiscale, fasc. 11.
HG3883.I 8B35 1970 74-337361

Banca d'Italia. Gruppo per lo studio della politica monetaria e fiscale.
Bilancia dei pagamenti dell'Italia (1947-1969). [Roma, 1974?]
275 p. 28 cm. (Its [Pubblicazioni], fasc. 12) It***
"A cura di Francesco Masera con la collaborazione di Maria Buoniconti."
1. Balance of payments—Italy. I. Masera, Francesco, ed. II. Title. III. Series: Banca d'Italia. Gruppo per lo studio della politica monetaria e fiscale. Pubblicazioni—Banca d'Italia, Gruppo per lo studio della politica monetaria e fiscale, fasc. 12.
HG3883.I 8B35 1974 74-325635

Banca d'Italia. Gruppo per lo studio della politica monetaria e fiscale.
Un modello econometrico dell'economia italiana (M1 BI) (Stesura provvisoria) [Roma, Centro stampa della Banca d'Italia, 1970-
v. 28 cm. It***
CONTENTS: fasc. 1. Carli, G. Presentazione. Masera, F. [et al.] Relazione generale.—
fasc. 4. Vicarelli, F. Settore rapporti finziari con l'estero.
1. Italy—Economic conditions—Mathematical models. I. Masera, Francesco, ed. II. Title.
HC305.B354 1970 73-310237
rev

Banca d'Italia. Gruppo per lo studio della politica monetaria e fiscale.
Situazioni della Banca d'Italia (1936-1968). A cura di Francesco Masera. [Roma, Centro stampa della Banca d'Italia, 1970?-
v. 28 cm. (Its [Pubblicazioni], fasc. 9) It***
CONTENTS: pt. 1. Situazioni contabili.
1. Banca d'Italia. I. Masera, Francesco, ed. II. Title. III. Series: Banca d'Italia. Gruppo per lo studio della politica monetaria e fiscale. Pubblicazioni—Banca d'Italia, Gruppo per lo studio della politica monetaria e fiscale, fasc. 9.
HG3084.B33 1970 74-337360

Banca d'Italia. Servizio studi
see Fratianni, Michele. Proposta per la ridefinizione del problema della liquidità internazionale. Roma, 1970.

Banca di credito finanziario, Milan.
Dati cumulativi di 500 [i. e. cinquecento] società italiane. (1965-1966-1967-1968-1969). A cura di Mediobanca. Milano, O. Capriolo, [1970?].
85 p., incl. table. 24 cm. It 70-June
1. Corporations—Italy—Finance. I. Title.
HG4166.B33 1970 73-557235
rev

Banca di credito finanziario, Milan.
Dati cumulativi di 520 [i.e. cinquecentoventi] società italiane (1965-1970) / a cura di Mediobanca. — Milano : O. Capriolo, [1971?]
143 p. ; 24 cm. It***
Chiefly tables.
1. Corporations—Italy—Finance. I. Title.
HG4166.B33 1971 77-452026
77 MARC

Banca di credito finanziario, Milan.
Dati cumulativi di 555 [i. e. cinquecentocinquantacinque] società italiane. [1968-1971]. A cura di Mediobanca. [Milano, O. Capriolo, 1972?]
157 p. 24 cm. It***
1. Corporation—Italy—Finance. I. Title.
HG4166.B33 1972 74-317266

Banca di credito finanziario, Milan.
Dati cumulativi di 655 [i. e. seicentocinquantacinque] società italiane (1968-1972). A cura di Mediobanca. Milano, O. Capriolo, 1973.
169 p. 24 cm. It 74-June
1. Corporations—Italy—Finance. I. Title.
HG4166.B33 1973 74-318301

Banca di credito finanziario, Milan.
Dati cumulativi di 668 [i. e. seicentosessantaotto] società italiane, (1968-1973) / a cura di Mediobanca. — [s. l. : s. n., 1974?] (Milano : O. Capriolo)
173 p. ; 24 cm. It***
1. Corporations—Italy—Finance. I. Title.
HG4166.B33 1974 76-519605

Banca di credito finanziario, Milan.
La finanza pubblica; Stato ed amministrazioni autonome (1966-1970). A cura di Mediobanca. [Milano, 1972-
v. 29 cm. It***
——— Appendici. [Milano, 1972-
v. ; 29 cm. It***
HJ1185.B33 1972 Suppl.
1. Finance, Public—Italy. I. Title.
HJ1185.B33 1972 73-324205

La Banca española en la Restauración / por Rafael Anes Alvarez ... [et al.] ; dirigido por Gabriel Tortella Casares ; edición y revisión a cargo de Pedro Schwartz. — Madrid : Servicio de Estudios del Banco de España, 1974.
2 v. : ill. ; 25 cm. Sp***
Bibliography: v. 1, p. 537-551.
Includes index.
CONTENTS: t. 1. Política y finanzas.—t. 2. Detos para una historia económica.
ISBN 84-500-0296-6 : 1000ptas
1. Money supply—Spain—History. 2. Banco de España, Madrid—History. 3. Banks and banking—Spain—History. I. Anes Alvarez, Rafael. II. Tortella Casares, Gabriel.
HG1134.B35 332.1'1'0946 75-570950

Banca interamericana per lo sviluppo
see Inter-American Development Bank.

Banca Internaţională pentru Reconstrucţie şi Dezvoltare
see
International Bank for Reconstruction and Development.

Banca Mas Sardá. Servicio de Estudios.
Diccionari de banca i borsa : [català-castellà] = diccionario de banca y bolsa : [castellano-catalán] / [Banca Mas Sardà Servei d'Estudis]. — Barcelona : Edicions Alba, [1975?]
69 p. ; 16 x 24 cm. — (Publicacions de Banca Mas Sardà : Serie D)
Sp***
ISBN 8438300081
1. Banks and banking—Dictionaries—Catalan. 2. Investments—Dictionaries—Catalan. 3. Catalan language—Dictionaries—Spanish. 4. Banks and banking—Dictionaries—Spanish. 5. Investments—Dictionaries—Spanish. 6. Spanish language—Dictionaires—Catalan. I. Title. II. Title: Diccionario de banca y bolsa.
HG151.B265 1975 76-454176
76 MARC

Banca Mas Sardá. Servicio de Estudios.
see Diccionario de banca y bolsa. [Barcelona] Banca Mas Sardá, Servicio de Estudios, [1976?]

Banca Natională a Republicii Socialiste Romania
see Studii, probleme, comentarii bancare. Bucuresti, Editura Academiei Republicii Socialiste Romania, 1972.

Banca Naţională a Republicii Socialiste România.
For works by this body issued under its earlier name see
Banca Naţională a României, Bucharest.

Banca Naţională a României, Bucharest.
For works by this body issued under its later name see
Banca Naţională a Republicii Socialiste România.

Banca nazionale del lavoro.
A Guide for foreign investors in Italy. 3. ed. Rome, Tip. A. Staderini, 1969.
157 p. illus. 26 cm. It Suppl-6
1. Investments, Foreign—Law and legislation—Italy. 2. Taxation—Italy—Law. 3. Corporation law—Italy. I. Title.
346'.45'092 73-156085
MARC

Banca nazionale del lavoro.
Perù / Banca nazionale del lavoro. — ₍s. l.₎ : La Banca, 1955.
vii, 75 p. : map ; 28 cm.
1. Peru—Economic conditions—1918– 2. Peru—Commerce—Italy. 3. Italy—Commerce—Peru. I. Title.
HC227.B29 1955 76-519922

Banca nazionale del lavoro
see Liguria. [Milano, 1967]

Banca nazionale somala.
Economic report. 1963/64–
Mogadiscio, Somali National Bank.
v. ill. 30 cm. annual.
1. Somalia—Economic conditions—Periodicals.
HC567.S7B35a 330.9'67'7305 75-642825
MARC-S

Banca popolare cooperativa di San Paolo di Civitate.

For works by this body issued under its later name see

Banca popolare di San Paolo Civitate.

La Banca popolare di Apricena nel 50° anniversario della sua costituzione. San Severo, Cromografica moderna ₍1961₎
33 p. plates. 24 cm.
1. Banca popolare di Apricena.
HG3090.A584B3513 74-234716

Banca popolare di Bergamo
see I Pittori bergamaschi... Bergamo, Poligrafiche Bolis, 1975-

Banca popolare di Lecco.
La Banca popolare di Lecco cent'anni dopo. 1872-1972. Lecco, Grafiche Stefanoni, 1972.
₍154₎ l. illus. 29 cm. It 73-Mar
1. Banca popolare di Lecco.
HG3090.L44P632 73-338487

Banca popolare di Lecco.
Banca popolare di Lecco; la nuova residenza della sede di Milano, ottobre 1965. ₍Lecco, 1965₎
23 p. col. illus., 12 col. plates. 17 x 24 cm.
Cover title.
Caption title: Inaugurazione della nuova residenza della sede di Milano.
1. Banca popolare di Lecco. I. Title: Inaugurazione della nuova residenza della sede di Milano.
HG3090.L44P634 74-210024

Banca popolare di Lecco.
I novant'anni della Banca popolare di Lecco, 1872-1962. ₍Lecco, 1964?₎
₍44₎ p. (chiefly illus., part col.) 22 x 24 cm.
Cover title.
"Commento 'parlato' del documentario filmato" (₍11₎ p.) inserted at end.
1. Banca popolare di Lecco. I. Title.
HG3090.L44P635 74-205623

Banca popolare di Lecco
see Laghi di Brianza. ₍Lecco₎, 1972.

Banca popolare di Lecco
see Per il traforo ferroviario dello Spluga. Lecco, A cura della Banca popolare de Lecco, 1970.

Banca popolare di Milano
see L'Abbazia di Viboldone. [Milano] Banca popolare di Milano [1959]

Banca popolare di Novara.
La moneta italiana. Un secolo dal 1870. Novara, Banca popolare di Novara, 1971.
558 p. illus. 35 cm. It 72-Oct
——— Supplemento ... Novara, Banca popolare di Novara, ₍1973–
v. illus. 35 cm.
HG1029.B3 1971 Suppl.
1. Money—Italy—History. 2. Paper money—Italy—History. I. Title.
HG1029.B3 1971 74-308025

Banca San Paolo, Brescia.
La Banca S. ₍i. e. San₎ Paolo nel LXXV° ₍i. e. settantesimo quinto₎ di fondazione, Brescia, 1888-1963. — ₍s. l. : s. n., 1963₎ (Brescia : La Scuola)
77 p. : ill. ; 25 cm.
1. Banca San Paolo, Brescia. I. Title: La Banca San Paolo nel settantesimo quinto di fondazione ...
HG3090.B74S315 1963 75-580830

Banca y finanzas. no. 152–
₍Bogotá₎ Asociación Bancaria de Colombia, 1976–
no. 25 cm.
"Revista de la Asociación Bancaria de Colombia."
Continues: Asociación Bancaria de Colombia. Información financiera.
1. Finance—Colombia—Periodicals. 2. Banks and banking—Colombia—Periodicals. I. Asociación Bancaria de Colombia.
HG185.C6A86a 76-648529
MARC-S

Bancal, Jean.
L'économie des sociologues : objet et projet de la sociologie économique / par Jean Bancal. — 1. éd. — Paris : Presses universitaires de France, 1974.
329 p. ; 22 cm. — (Sociologie d'aujourd'hui) F***
Bibliography: p. ₍317₎-323.
49.00F
1. Sociology. 2. Economics. I. Title.
HM35.B35 301 75-502407
75 MARC

Bancari e banchieri : istituti finanziari e rapporti sociali di produzione : saggi / Corsetti ... ₍et al.₎ ; a cura di Renzo Stefanelli. — Bari : De Donato, c1976.
223 p. ; 21 cm. — (Riforme e potere ; 8) It76-Apr
L3000
1. Banks and banking—Italy—Addresses, essays, lectures. 2. Bank employees—Italy—Addresses, essays, lectures. I. Corsetti, Renato,. II. Stefanelli, Renzo, 1937-
HG3080.B29 332.1'0945 76-466509
*76 MARC

Bancaud, Jean
see E. E. G. et S. E. E. G. dans les tumeurs cérébrales et l'épilepsie. Paris, Édifor ₍1973₎

Bancaud, Jean
see Stereoelectroencephalography. Amsterdam, Elsevier, c1975.

Bances Candamo, Francisco Antonio, 1662-1709?
La gran comedia, El esclavo en grillos de oro. ₍n.p., n.d.₎
20 p.
Numbered on one side of page only.
I. Title. II. Title: El esclavo en grillos de oro.
ICU NUC73-103099

Bances Candamo, Francisco Antonio, 1662-1709?
La piedra filosofal / Francisco Bances Candamo. — Milano : Cisalpino-Goliardica, ₍1974₎
xvii, 145 p. ; 24 cm. It 75-May
A play.
Introduction in Italian.
L2400
I. Title.
PQ6279.B25P5 1974 75-532280

Bances Candamo, Francisco Antonio, 1662-1709?
Qvien es qvien premia al amor. Comedia famosa, fiesta a svs magestades, para el domingo de carnestolendas, en el gran salon de su real palacio. ₍Sevilla, F. de Leefdael, n.d.₎
36 p.
I. Title.
ICU NUC73-103098

(Bancha kurabu)
番茶クラブ / NHK編 ; 緒方富雄 ... ₍et al.₎. — 東京 : 要書房, 昭和28 ₍1953₎
204 p. ; 19 cm.
Colophon inserted.
Originally broadcasted once a week, Jan. 8, 1952-Apr. 5, 1953.
1. Interviews. I. Ogata, Tomio, 1901- II. Nippon Hōsō Kyōkai.
AC145.B36 77-802164

Banchefsky, Howard, 1929-
An analysis of the differential in service training needs of new bachelor degree workers in the Jewish Center field. ₍n.p.₎ 1975 ₍i.e. 1976₎
158 l.
Thesis--Ohio State University.
Bibliography: leaves 155-158.
1. Social work education. 2. Community centers, Jewish. I. Title.
OU NUC77-86108

Bancher, Engelbert, ed.
see Vienna. Technische Hochschule. Der Ingenieur; ein Beruf mit Zukunft. [Wien, Rektorat der Technischen Hochschule, 1972]

Banchero, Anderssen, 1925-
Triste de la calle cortada / Anderssen Banchero ; ₍fotografía, Julio Navarro₎. — Montevideo : EBO, ₍1975₎
79 p. ; 20 cm. — (Colección Acuarimántima ; 5)
CONTENTS: Una luna de perros.—La casa del lago.—Triste de la calle cortada.—Magnolias.—Cierto sol del invierno.—Pampero.—Para un jugador de fútbol.
I. Title.
PQ8520.12.A5T7 863 77-456041
77 MARC

Banchero, Julius Thomas, 1914-
see Hengstebeck, R J Disproportionation of toluene. ₍Notre Dame, Ind.₎ 1969.

Banchero Castellano, Raúl.
Lima y el mural de Pachacamilla. Lima ₍Editorial Jurídica₎ 1972.
359 p. illus.
"Historia del Señor de los Milagros de Nazarenas, del Monasterio y de la Hermandad."
1. Lima—Church history. I. Title.
InU NUC73-113950

Banchetti, Silvestro.
Attivismo, attualismo, personalismo. Bologna, Cooperativa libraria universitaria, 1973.
353 p. 24 cm. It 74-Apr
Includes bibliographical references.
1. Educational psychology. 2. Child study. 3. Personality. I. Title.
LB1051.B2428 74-337189

Banchetti, Silvestro.
L'educazione alla democrazia e la pedagogia dell'impegno / Silvestro Banchetti. — Bologna : Cooperativa libraria universitaria editrice, ₍1975₎
391 p. ; 24 cm. It76-June
Includes bibliographical references.
L7500
1. Education and state—Italy. I. Title.
LC93.I8B36 76-478017
*76 MARC

Banchev, Blazho, comp.
see Bulgaria. Laws, statutes, etc. (Sbornik normativni aktove po ikonomicheskiia mekhanizum prez 1971-1975...) 1972.

Bancheva, Nonka D.
see Kosev, Dimitŭr. (Faktori za povishavane na porizvoditelnostta na truda v mashinostroeneto) 1974.

Banchi, Luciano, 1837-1887, ed.
see Silvestro Cartaio. Batecchio, commedia di maggio... Bologna, Commissione per i testi di lingua, 1968.

Banchi, Luciano, 1837-1887, ed.
see Silvestro Cartaio. Profezia sulla guerra di Siena. Bologna, Commissione per i testi di lingua, 1968.

Banchieri, Adriano, d. 1634.
Adriano Banchieri's Conclusioni nel suono dell'organo of 1609: a translation and commentary by Lee Raymond Garrett. ₍n.p.₎ 1972.
124 l.
Thesis (D.M.A.)—University of Oregon.
Translator's vita.
Bibliography: leaves ₍121₎-124.
1. Organ. 2. Music. Theory. 16th-17th centuries. I. Garrett, Lee Raymond, 1943- tr.
OrU NUC73-116930

Banchieri, Adriano, d. 1634.
Adriano Banchieri's Conclusioni nel suono dell' organo of 1609: a translation and commentary. Ann Arbor, University Microfilms, 1973.
Microfilm copy (positive) of typescript.
Collation of the original, as determined from the film: ix, 124 l. music.
The editor's thesis (D.M.A.)—University of Oregon, 1972.
Vita.
Bibliography: leaves ₍121₎-124.
I. Garrett, Lee Raymond, 1943-
OO OCU NUC75-75604

Banchieri, Adriano, d. 1634. Cacasenno
see Croce, Giulio Cesare, 1550-1609. Bertoldo e Bertoldino... [3. ed.] Milano, U. Mursia [1965]

Banchieri, Adriano, d. 1634. Cacasenno. 1973
see Croce, Giulio Cesare, 1550-1609. Bertoldo e Bertoldino. Milano, Mursia, 1973.

Banchieri, Adriano, d. 1634.
Cartella musicale nel canto figurato, fermo & contrapunto. Nouamente in questa Terza impressione ridotta dall'antica alla moderna pratica, & dedicata. Venetia, G. Vincenti, 1614. [Ann Arbor, Mich., University Microfilms, 1969]
246, [1] p. illus., music. 19 cm.
TNJ-P NUC73-112428

Banchieri, Adriano, d. 1634.
Conclusioni nel suono dell'organo / Adriano Banchieri. -- New York : Broude Brothers, 1975.
71 p. : ill. ; 25 cm. -- (Monuments of music and music literature in facsimile. 2d ser. : Music literature ; 101)
A facsimile reprint of the Bologna, 1609 edition.
1. Organ. 2. Music--Theory--16th-17th century. I. Title. II. Series.
NcGU NUC77-86306

Banchieri, Annamaria.
Le dame di Francia / Annamaria Banchieri. — Milano : Virgilio, 1974.
363 p. ; 21 cm. It 75-Feb
Bibliography: p. 363.
L5800
1. France—History—Louis XV, 1715-1774. 2. France—Princes and princesses. 3. Women—Biography. I. Title.
DC36.7.B25 75-584373

Banchieri, Annamaria.
Venti o trenta braccia di vita, romanzo. Roma, A. Colla [1946]
211 p. 18 cm.
I. Title.
PQ4807.A67V4 47-29290

Banchieri, G. C., joint author
see Alcozer, Guilio. Le cisti aeree disontogenetiche del polmone. Genova, Pagano [1961]

Banchieri, Giuseppe, 1927-
see Aspetti della giovane pittura in Italia. Ovada [1972?].

Banchieri, Giuseppe, 1927-
see Guidacci, Margherita. Quindici poesie e sette disegni. [Milano: Edizioni 32, 1973]

Banchini, Ferdinando.
Bianco e nero / Ferdinando Banchini. — Roma : Gesualdi, 1974.
47 p. ; 21 cm. It 74-Oct
Poems.
L2000
I. Title.
PQ4862.A467B5 74-355615

Banchini, Ferdinando.
La lunga strada. (Liriche). Firenze, Il Fauno, 1971.
43 p. 21 cm. (Novecento poetico, n. 3)
Microfiche (negative) 1 sheet. 11 x 15 cm. (NYPL FSN 16, 011)
I. Title.
NN NUC76-71541

Banchini, Ferdinando.
La sosta ambigua. Con prefazione di Vitulio Margaritelli. [Roma], Il Campidoglio, 1973.
62 p. 21 cm. (Collana di cultura Le Nove muse. Poesia, 18)
L1000 It 73-May
I. Title.
PQ4862.A467S6 74-341066

Banchini, Ferdinando.
Le théâtre de Montherlant. Roma, Fratelli Palombi, 1971.
266 p. 24 cm. L4500 It 72-May
Bibliography: p. 261-263.
1. Montherlant, Henry de, 1896- I. Title.
PQ2625.O45Z554 842'.9'12 73-309561

Banchio, Enrique Carlos.
Responsabilidad obligacional indirecta; hechos de los representantes y auxiliares del deudor en el cumplimiento de las obligaciones. Buenos Aires, Editorial Astrea de R. Depalma, 1973.
151 p. 21 cm.
Bibliography: p. [147]-151.
1. Liability (Law)—Argentine Republic. 2. Debtor and creditor—Argentine Republic. 3. Liability (Law) 4. Debtor and creditor. I. Title.
75-592720

Banchong, Wānit
see
Wānit Banchong.

Banchs, Enrique, 1888-1968. Antología viva de su poesía. 1975.
in Martínez, David, 1921- Enrique Banchs, poeta del sentimiento humano... Buenos Aires, Editorial Plus Ultra, c1975.

Banchs, Enrique, 1888-
Obra poética (1907-1955) Buenos Aires, Academia Argentina de Letras, 1973.
570 p. facsims., port. 21 cm.
"Textos completos de los cuatro libros publicados por Enrique Banchs: Las barcas, El libro de los elogios, El cascabel del halcón y La urna, y las poesías aparecidas en diarios y revistas a partir de la edición de la primera de las obras citadas."
PQ7797.B275A17 1973 74-207247

Bancik, L
Zaklady pol'nohospodarstva a pridruzenej lesnej vyroby. Zvolen, 1965.
188 p. (Zvolen. Vysoka skola lesnicka a drevarska. Docasne vysokoskolske ucebnice, no. 6/65)
1. Agriculture. Text-books. 2. Forestry. Text-books. I. Zvolen. Czecholovak Republic (City). Vysoka skola lesnicka a drevarska. Katedra zoologie a ochrany lesov. II. Title. III. Series.
DNAL NUC75-105125

Bancík, Ľudovít.
Základy poľovníctva. Autori: Ľudovít Bancík a kol. 1. vyd. Bratislava, Príroda, t. Tlač. SNP, Martin, 1973.
358, [8] p. 16 p. of col. plates, illus., tables, photos, graphs, diagrs. 21 cm. (Edícia Poľovníctvo) Kčs30.00 CzS 73
Bibliography: p. 358.
1. Hunting—Slovakia. I. Title.
SK223.C9B36 74-313269

Băncilă, Ileana.
Dan Simonescu. Biobibliografie. Cuvînt înainte de Dan Zamfirescu. București, 1972.
xxxii, 190 p., 3 l. of ports. 21 cm. lei28.50 R 73-1165
At head of title: Biblioteca Centrală Universitară București.
"Lucrare elaborată în cadrul Serviciului de Informare și Documentare condus de Ileana Băncilă."
1. Simonescu, Dan—Bibliography. I. Bucharest. Universitatea. Biblioteca Centrală. Serviciul de Informare și Documentare.
Z8819.43.B36 73-347436

Băncilă, Ileana, ed.
see Bucharest. Universitatea. Biblioteca Centrală. Sectorul de Documentare. Constiinta socialistă. Cercetare bibliografică. Bucuresti, 1973.

Băncilă, Ileana, ed.
see Bucharest. Universitatea. Biblioteca Centrală. Sectorul de Documentare. Probleme de pedagogie universitară contemporană. Bucuresti, 1972.

Băncilă, Ileana
see Bucharest. Universitatea. Biblioteca Centrală. Serviciul de Informare si Documentare. Cartea veche romănească în colecțiile... Bucuresti, Centrul de Multiplicare al Universitătii din Bucuresti, 1972.

Băncilă, Ileana
see Bucharest. Universitatea. Biblioteca Centrală. Serviciul de Informare si Documentare. Opera lui Mihai Eminescu... Bucuresti, Biblioteca Centrala Universitara, 1973.

Băncilă, Ileana, ed.
see Bucharest. Universitatea. Biblioteca Centrală. Serviciul de Informare si Documentare. Sociologia grupurilor mici. Bucuresti, 1972.

Băncilă, Ioan.
Algoritmi și metode de optimizare a resurselor. [București], C. N. S. T. Consiliul Național pentru Știință și Tehnologie, I. N. I. D. Institutul Național de Informare și Documentare Științifică și Tehnică, 1973.
80 p. with figs. 24 cm. (Informarea documentară în sprijinul realizării cincinalului înainte de termen) (Sinteză documentară, 1973) lei 50.00 R 74-1457
At head of title: Ioan Băncilă, Gheorghe Ciobanu.
Bibliography: p. 76-79.
1. Industrial project management. 2. Mathematical optimization. I. Ciobanu, Gheorghe, conf. dr., joint author. II. Title.
T56.8.B35 74-337657

Băncilă, Octav, 1872-1944.
Octav Băncilă. 1872-1972. Catalog[ul] expoziție[i] organizată cu prilejul împlinirii a 100 de ani de la nașterea artistului. Întocmit de Mihai Pocloș și Hariton Clonaru. [Prezentare de Demostene Botez]. București, 1972.
xxxii p. with ports., 94 p. with illus. (part col.) 24 cm. lei 15.00 R 73-1316
At head of title: Consiliul Culturii și Educației Socialiste. Comitetul de Cultură și Educație Socialistă al Municipiului București. Muzeul de Artă al Republicii Socialiste România.
Introductory matter and legends also in English.
Bibliography: p. xxx-xxxi.
1. Băncilă, Octav, 1872-1944. I. Pocloș, Mihai, ed. II. Clonaru, Hariton, joint author. III. Muzeul de Artă al Republicii Socialiste România.
ND933.B33P62 74-326319

Bancilhon, Line.
Étude expérimentale de la morphogenèse et plus spécialement de la floraison d'un groupe de Phyllanthus (Euphorbiacées) a rameaux dimorphes. Paris, Masson, 1969.
127-224 p. illus. (Repr. from Annales des sciences naturelles; Botanique, 12. ser., t. 10, 1969)
Thèse—Paris.
MH-G NUC74-137775

Banciu, Mircea, joint author
see Pogany, Iuliu. Metode fizice în chimia organică. Bucuresti, Editura stiintifică, 1972.

Banciu, Vasile.
Aplicații ale cercetării operaționale în industria minieră. București, Oficiul de documentare și publicații tehnice, 1973.
218 p. with figs. 24 cm. lei 100 R 73-4303
At head of title: Ministerul Minelor, Petrolului și Geologiei. Vasile Banciu, Imre Kiss.
Bibliography: p. [215]-216.
1. Mineral industries—Management. 2. Operations research. I. Kiss, Imre, joint author. II. Title.
TN153.B3 74-357007

Banciu, Vasile.
Normarea muncii în industria minieră / Vasile Banciu. — Ediția a 2-a, revăzută și completată. — București : Editura tehnică, 1975.
274 p. : ill. ; 21 cm. R76-1093
Published in 1966 under title: Normarea tehnică a muncii în industria minieră.
Bibliography: p. 251-253.
lei12.50
1. Mineral industries—Romania—Production standards. I. Title.
TN95.R8B35 1975 77-469615
*77 MARC

Banciu, Vasile
see Îndrumar privind calculul salariilor în industria miniera si petrolieră. Bucuresti, Oficiul de documentare si publicatii tehnice, 1972.

Bănciulescu, Victor.
Acest straniu secol al sportului / Victor Bănciulescu ; [coperta, Val Munteanu]. — București : "Sport-Turism", 1976.
165 p. ; 20 cm. R77-988
Includes bibliographical references.
lei6.50
1. Sports—History. I. Title.
GV576.B28 77-484500
*77 MARC

Bănciulescu, Victor.
Mexico 68; breviar olimpic. [București] Editura Consiliului Național pentru Educație Fizică și Sport, 1968.
247 p. 17 cm.
"Codul olimpic": p. 46-107.
"Bibliografiile marilor campioni": p. 157-[170]
Bibliography: p. 242-245.
1. Olympic Games, Mexico City, 1968. I. International Olympic Committee. Olympic rules. Romanian. Selections. 1968. II. Title.
GV722 1968.B36 75-566117

Bănciulescu, Victor.
Olimpiadele albe. [Documentarea privind sportivii romîni a fost întocmită cu concursul specialistului Dorin Șteflea. Prefață de Monique Berlioux]. [București], „Stadion," 1973.
236 p., 8 l. of plates. 20 cm. lei 8.00 R 73-2225
Includes bibliographical references.
1. Olympic games (Winter) I. Title.
GV841.5.B36 73-364639

Bănciulescu, Victor.
Sport și legendă. Ediţia a 2-a. ⌈București⌉, "Stadion," 1973.
208, xxxiv p. with illus. 17 cm. R 73-3129
Bibliography: p. 201-⌈203⌉
lei 6.00
1. Sports in literature. 2. Epic poetry—History and criticism. I. Title.
PN1323.B3 1973 75-400907

Bănciulescu, Victor, joint author
see Goga, Ilie. Jocurile olimpice de la München 1972. Burcurești, "Stadion," 1973.

Banck, Majt, ed.
see Andersson, Dan, 1888-1920. Ur Dan Anderssons diktning. Stockholm, Läromedelsförlagen, c1972.

Bancke, Linda Lee.
Background antecedents of aggressiveness and assertiveness found in academically achieving women, by Linda Bancke. ⌈Cincinnati⌉ 1972.
v, 144 l. 29 cm.
Thesis (Ph.D.)—Univ. of Cincinnati.
Bibliography: leaves 90-92.
1. Cincinnati. University—Theses. Ph.D., 1972. I. Title.
OCU NUC74-131276

Bancke, Peter.
Brushanen. Udgivet i samarbejde med Dansk naturhistorisk forening ⌈et al.⌉ København⌉ Rhodos ⌈1965⌉
86, ⌈1⌉ p. illus. 22 cm. (Dyrenes liv, 3)
Bibliography: p. ⌈87⌉
1. Ruff (Bird) I. Dansk naturhistorisk forening, Copenhagen. II. Title. III Series.
QL696.C48B36 75-591638

Banco, Irmela.
Studien zur Verteilung und Entwicklung der Bevölkerung von Griechenland / von Irmela Banco. — Bonn : Dümmlers ⌈in Komm.⌉, 1976.
xxi, 297, ⌈24⌉ p. : ill. (some col.), graphs, maps (13 fold. in pocket) ; 23 cm. — (Bonner geographische Abhandlungen ; Heft 54) GFR77-A
Bibliography: p. 258-297.
ISBN 3-427-75541-X : DM38.00
1. Greece, Modern—Population. I. Title. II. Series.
G58.B6 Heft 54 77-454311
⌈HB3597⌉ 77 MARC

Banco, Leonard Irving.
The treatment of acute lymphoblastic leukemia in mice with L-asparaginase and radioactive colloidal gold^{198}. New Haven, 1974.
v, 79 l. illus. 29 cm.
Thesis (M.D.)—Yale University.
Bibliography: leaves 75-79.
1. Leukemia. 2. Asparaginase. 3. Gold, Colloidal. I. Title.
CtY-M NUC76-25323

Banco, Maso di
see Maso di Banco, 14th cent.

Banco Agrícola, La Paz, Bolivia.
La ganadería boliviana; situación de la comercialización de la carne y posibilidades para su desarrollo. Versión española del inglés. La Paz, Bolivia, 1970.
129 p. tables, graphs.
Papers submitted by various authors.
1. Meat industry and trade—Bolivia. 2. Bolivia—Industries. I. Title.
PPiU NUC74-137776

Banco Agricola de Bolivia. Treaties, etc. International Development Association, Jan. 13, 1970.
Project agreement (interim second Beni livestock development project) between International Development Association and Banco Agricola de Bolivia, dated January 13, 1970. ⌈Washington, D.C., 1970⌉
9 p. 27 cm. (Credit number 171 BO)
At head of title: Conformed copy.
1. Debts, Public—Bolivia. I. International Development Association. Treaties, etc. Banco Agricola de Bolivia, Jan. 13, 1970.
MH-L NUC76-24316

Banco Agrícola de la República Dominicana.
Memoria sobre las actividades desarrolladas—Banco Agrícola de la República Dominicana.
Santo Domingo, Banco Agrícola de la República Dominicana.
v. 28 cm.
1. Banco Agrícola de la República Dominicana. 2. Banks and banking—Dominican Republic.
HG2819.B36B36a 76-649240
MARC-S

Banco Agrícola del Paraguay, Asunción.
El Banco Agrícola del Paraguay en la Exposición Internacional de Agricultura de Buenos Aires. Asunción, Taleres nacionales de H. Kraus ⌈1910⌉
xxiii, 277 p. illus., maps. (1 fold.) 30 cm.
At head of title: Centenario de la Revolución de mayo—República Argentina, 1910.
1. Buenos Aires. Exposición Internacional de Agricultura, 1910. 2. Paraguay—Industries ⌈and resources⌉
255.7.B22 1910 ed.
Arg 14-1693
rev
U. S. Nat'l Agr. Libr. 255.7.B22 1910 ed.

Banco Agrícola Hipotecario, Bogotá. Caja de Crédito Agrario
see
Caja de Crédito Agrario, Bogotá.

Banco Agrícola y Pecuario, Caracas.
El B. A. P. y la descentralización administrativa. Caracas, 1967.
28 l.
Cover title.
"Informe presentado ante la XXIII Asamblea Anual de Fedecamaras."
I. Title.
NcU NUC74-137771

Banco Agrícola y Pecuario, Caracas.
El Banco Agrícola y Pecuario en el Estado Zulia. Caracas, 1974.
24 l. 28 cm.
Cover title.
1. Banco Agrícola y Pecuario, Caracas. 2. Agriculture—Economic aspects—Venezuela—Zulia. I. Title.
TxU NUC76-25302

Banco Agrícola y Pecuario, Caracas.
El Banco Agrícola y Pecuario en sus 45 años, 1928/1973. ⌈Caracas, 1973⌉
63, ⌈25⌉ p. illus. 28 cm.
Half title: BAP/45 años.
"Estadísticas históricas": p. ⌈3⌉-⌈23⌉ (2d group)
1. Banco Agricola y Pecuario, Caracas—History. I. Title.
HG2051.V4B29 1973 74-211906

Banco Agrícola y Pecuario, Caracas.
El crédito agario en Venezuela; informe presentado al Seminario de Programación y Administración de la Reforma Agraria. ⌈Caracas? 1965⌉
43 p. charts. 19 cm.
Cover title.
1. Agricultural credit—Venezuela. I. Title.
PPiU NUC74-137772

Banco Agrícola y Pecuario, Caracas.
Créditos ganaderos en función del productor campesino. Caracas, 1973.
27 l. 32 cm.
Cover title.
"IX asamblea de la Confederación Interamericana de Ganaderos."
1. Agricultural credit—Venezuela. 2. Banco Agrícola y Pecuario, Caracas. 3. Animal industry—Venezuela. I. Title.
TxU NUC76-71544

Banco Agrícola y Pecuario, Caracas.
Gestion crediticia del B.A.P., año 1972 y programas de creditos para 1973 a nivel de regiones y entidades federales. Caracas, 1973.
43 l.
Cover title.
"Informe que presenta el Banco Agricola y Pecuario a la XVI Convención de Gobernadores."
1. Agricultural credit—Venezuela. I. Title.
NcU NUC75-26804

Banco Agrícola y Pecuario, Caracas.
Información presentada a la primera convención nacional de productores de café. [San Cristobal] 1962.
53 l.
At head of title: "Banco Agricola y Pecuario. Gerencia de Crédito Empresarial."
1. Coffee—Venezuela. I. Title.
InU NUC75-67080

Banco Agrícola y Pecuario, Caracas.
Informe que presenta el Banco Agrícola y Pecuario a la 1° Convención Nacional de la Federación Campesina de Venezuela a celebrarse en Los Caracas entre los días 17 y 20 de abril. -- Los Caracas : El Banco, 1975.
20 leaves ; 27 cm.
Cover title: Informe presentado a la I Convención Nacional de la Federación Campesina.
1. Banco Agrícola y Pecuario, Caracas. 2. Agricultural credit--Venezuela.
TxU NUC77-86126

Banco Agrícola y Pecuario, Caracas.
Manual de tramitacion de creditos. [Caracas, 19--?]
44 p. illus.
1. Agricultural credit. Venezuela. I. Title.
DNAL NUC76-25324

Banco Agrícola y Pecuario, Caracas.
Produccion, consumo y mercadeo de productos agropecuarios en Venezuela. Caracas, 1963.
136 l. illus., maps.
Bibliography: leaves 134-136.
1. Agriculture. Economic aspects. Venezuela. I. Title.
DNAL NUC76-71554

Banco Agrícola y Pecuario, Caracas.
Programa de reforma administrativa. Caracas, 1972.
38, 44, 40 l. 32 cm.
Cover title.
1. Banco Agrícola y Pecuario, Caracas. I. Title.
TxU NUC75-26559

Banco Agricola y Pecuario, Caracas
see Informe presentado a la Junta Administradora del Banco Agrícola y Pecuario... ⌈Caracas, 1966⌉

Banco Agrícola y Pecuario, Caracas.

For works by this body issued under its later name see

Instituto de Crédito Agrícola y Pecuario.

Banco Agrícola y Pecuario, Caracas. Oficina de Programación y Presupuesto.
Proyecto de presupuesto 1974. Caracas, 1973.
2 v. 32 cm.
1. Banco Agrícola y Pecuario, Caracas. I. Title.
TxU NUC75-73902

Banco América do Sul.
(Kabushiki Kaisha Nambei Ginkō nijūnenshi)
株式會社南米銀行二十年史 / ⌈編集 南米銀行⌉. — サンパウロ：同銀行, 昭和35 ⌈1960⌉
16, 3, 159 p., ⌈16⌉ leaves of plates : ill. ; 22 cm.
Colophon inserted.
"非売品"

1. Banco América do Sul. I. Title.
HG2890.S34B272 1960 75-791266

Banco Andrade Arnaud.
As maiores emprêsas brasileiras de 1968; um análise de todos os setores da economia, do compartamento das maiores firmas e do seu papel no desenvolvimento do pais ⌊apresentado pelo⌋ Banco Andrade Arnau ⌊e⌋ Visão. ⌊São Paulo, 1969⌋
93-272 p. illus., ports. (Visão, 29 de agosto de 1969)
On cover: Quem e quem na economia brasileira.
1. Brazil—Industries. 2. Brazil—Economic policy. I. Visão. II. Title. III. Title: Quem e quem na economia brasileira.
InU NUC73-126138

Banco Asturiano.
Polo de desarrollo de Oviedo. ⌊San Sebastian, Valverde⌋ 1969.
2 v. illus.
1. Oviedo, Spain (Province). Economic conditions. I. Banco de Bilbao. II. Title.
DNAL NUC76-24903

Banco Atlantida
see Honduras, bella tierra de pinares. [3. ed. San Pedro Sula, 1968?]

Banco Central.
Boletín informativo—Banco Central.
Madrid, Banco Central.
no. 28 cm.
Continues: Banco Central. Departamento Extranjero. Boletín informativo.
English and Spanish.
1. Banco Central. 2. Spain—Economic conditions—1918- 3. Finance—Spain.
HC381.B332 75-648122
MARC-S

Banco Central da República do Brasil
see
Banco Central do Brasil.

Banco Central de Bolivia.
XXV [Veinte cinco] años de labor bancaria al servicio del pais, 1945-1970. La Paz [1970]
26 p. tables. 30 cm.
"Estudios economicos y estadistica."
1. Banks and banking—Bolivia. 2. Finance—Bolivia—Statistics. I. Banco Central de Bolivia. División de Estudios Economicos y Estadistica. II. Title.
CtY-E NUC 76-24272

Banco Central de Bolivia División de Estudios Economicos y Estadistica
see Banco Central de Bolivia. XXV [Veinte cinco] años de labor bancaria... La Paz [1970]

Banco Central de Chile, Santiago.
Directorio de exportadores de Chile. Exporter directory of Chile: 1967, gerencia de fomento de exportaciones. [Santiago, 1967]
1 v. (various pagings) map. 22 cm.
Cover title.
Introduction and indexes in Spanish and English.
1. Chile—Comm.—Direct. I. Title.
LNHT NUC73-112462

Banco Central de Chile, Santiago
see Articles of agreement of the International Monetary Fund. Spanish. ... Convenios sobre el Fondo monetario internacional ... Santiago de Chile, Imprenta universitaria, 1946.

Banco Central de Costa Rica.
Cifras de cuentas nacionales de Costa Rica, serie 1957-1970; estimación 1971. ⌊San José, 1971?⌋
15 l. tables. 22 x 33 cm.
Cover title.
1. Costa Rica—Stat.
LNHT NUC74-137773

Banco Central de Costa Rica.
Estadísticas económicas, 1966-1971. ⌊San José, 1972?⌋
iii, 31 l. 28 cm.
Cover title.
"EE/2034/Sec. Estadística: mar/7-abril-72/250."
1. Banks and banking—Costa Rica—Statistics. 2. Costa Rica—Economic conditions. 3. Costa Rica—Commerce. I. Title.
TxU NUC75-26567

Banco Central de Costa Rica.
Estadísticas económicas 1967 a 1972. ⌊San José, 1973⌋
iii, 31 l. 28 cm.
Cover title.
At head of title: Banco Central de Costa Rica. Departamento de Estudios Económicos. EE/2273/Sec. Estadística: edem/9-abril-73/250.
1. Banks and banking—Costa Rica—Stat. 2. Costa Rica—Econ. condit. 3. Costa Rica—Comm. I. Title.
TxU NUC75-20033

Banco Central de Costa Rica.
Importaciones CIF. Indices de valor precios y quantum para los años 1968/1970. Año de referencia 1967 100. ⌊San José, 1971?⌋
5, 16 l. 21 x 28 cm.
1. Commercial statistics. I. Title.
NIC NUC74-137774

Banco Central de Costa Rica.
Información estadística mensual.
San José.
no. in v. 28 cm.
Issued by its Departamento de Comercio Exterior.
1. Finance—Costa Rica—Statistics.
HG185.C7B35a 73-647455
MARC-S

Banco Central de Costa Rica
see Aguilar Piedra, Carlos H Colección de objetos indigenas de oro del Banco Central de Costa Rica. Ciudad Universitaria "Rodrigo Facio", Universidad de Costa Rica, 1972.

Banco Central de Costa Rica. Departamento de Transacciones Internacionales.
Información estadística mensual — Banco Central de Costa Rica, Departamento de Transacciones Internacionales.
San José, Banco Central de Costa Rica, Departamento de Transacciones Internacionales.
no. 28 cm.
Issues for published in 2 or more pts.
1. Finance—Costa Rica—Statistics. 2. Costa Rica—Commerce.
HG185.C7B35b 76-648730
MARC-S

Banco Central de Costa Rica. Departamento de Transacciones Internacionales.
Información estadística mensual — Banco Central de Costa Rica, Departamento de Transacciones Internacionales. no. 283- enero 1975-
San José, Banco Central de Costa Rica, Departamento de Transacciones Internacionales.
no. 28 cm.
Issues for published in 2 or more pts.
Continues: Banco Central de Costa Rica. Información estadística mensual.
1. Finance—Costa Rica—Statistics. 2. Costa Rica—Commerce.
HG185.C7B35a 76-648731
MARC-S

Banco Central de Costa Rica. Departamento Monetario.
Balanza de pagos: Costa Rica.
San José, Departamento Monetario.
v. ill. 25 cm. annual.
1. Balance of payments—Costa Rica—Periodicals. I. Title.
HG3883.C64B34a 77-648572
MARC-S

Banco Central de Costa Rica. Departamento Monetario.
Crédito y cuentas monetarias.
⌊San José⌋ Banco Central de Costa Rica, Departamento Monetario.
v. 28 cm.
Continues: Banco Central de Costa Rica. Crédito y cuentas monetarias.
Vols. for includes comparative data for the four previous years.
1. Banks and banking—Costa Rica—Statistics. 2. Credit—Costa Rica—Statistics. I. Title.
HG2734.B35a 332.1′097286 76-642284
MARC-S

Banco Central de Honduras, Tegucigalpa.
Boletín estadístico.
Tegucigalpa.
v. 28 cm.
1. Banks and banking—Honduras—Statistics.
HG2754.B35 72-623699

Banco Central de Honduras, Tegucigalpa.
Indice general de precios al consumidor, 1965 - 1970. Tegucigalpa, 1971.
67 p. illus. tables. 28 cm.
Issued by its Departamento de Estudios Economicos.
At head of title: Republica de Honduras.
1. Price indexes—Honduras. 2. Prices—Honduras. I. Title.
CtY-E NUC74-137752

Banco Central de Honduras, Tegucigalpa.
Informe económico.
Tegucigalpa.
v. 28 cm.
Vols. for prepared by its Departamento de Estudios Económicos.
1. Honduras—Economic conditions—1918-
HC145.A1B25 72-626627

Banco Central de Honduras, Tegucigalpa.
Reseña de los acontecimientos monetarios y financieros de Honduras.
Tegucigalpa.
v. 28 cm.
Issued by its Departamento de Estudios Económicos.
1. Finance—Honduras. 2. Honduras—Economic conditions—1918- 3. Money—Honduras. I. Title.
HG185.H6B35a 73-644749
MARC-S

Banco Central de Honduras, Tegucigalpa.
Revista.
Tegucigalpa.
v. 30 cm.
1. Banks and banking—Honduras—Statistics. 2. Honduras—Commerce. 3. Finance, Public—Honduras—Statistics. 4. Economic indicators—Honduras.
HG2754.B352a 74-641145
MARC-S

Banco Central de Honduras, Tegucigalpa
see Cámara de Compensación Centroamericana. Tres años de compensación multilateral centroamericana. Tegucigalpa [1964?]

Banco Central de Honduras, Tegucigalpa
see Historia financiera de Honduras... Tegucigalpa ⌊1957⌋

Banco Central de Honduras, Tegucigalpa. Sección de Seguros.
Boletín de estadísticas de seguros.
Tegucigalpa, Banco Central de Honduras, Superintendencia de Bancos, Sección de Seguros.
v. 28 cm.
1. Insurance—Honduras—Statistics. I. Title.
HG8555.H62B3a 76-648361
MARC-S

Banco Central de la República Argentina, Buenos Aires. Boletín estadístico
see Banco Central de la República Argentina, Buenos Aires. Estadística bancaria por partido o departamento y por localidad. Buenos Aires.

Banco Central de la República Argentina, Buenos Aires. Boletín estadístico.
see Banco Central de la República Argentina, Buenos Aires. Sistema de cuentas del producto e ingreso de la Argentina. ⌊Buenos Aires⌋ Banco Central de la República Argentina, Gerencia de Investigaciones Económicas, 1975.

Banco Central de la República Argentina, Buenos Aires.
Descripción de las características de las monedas y billetes. Buenos Aires ⌊1967?⌋
⌊9⌋ p. 29 cm.
"Suplemento del Boletín estadístico no. 21, diciembre de 1967."
1. Coins, Argentine. 2. Bank-notes—Argentine Republic. II. Title.
TxU NUC73-47440

Banco Central de la República Argentina, Buenos Aires.
Distribución funcional del ingreso en la República Argentina (excluído los sectores industrias, manufactureras y comercio), años 1950-1968. Buenos Aires [1970]
15 p. illus. 29 cm.
"Suplemento del Boletín estadístico, no. 4, abril de 1970."
1. Income—Argentine Republic—Stat. I. Title.
TxU NUC74-137778

Banco Central de la República Argentina, Buenos Aires.
Estadística bancaria por partido o departamento y por localidad.
Buenos Aires.
v. 29 cm.
Vols. for issued as a suppl. to its Boletín estadístico.
Earlier statistical information issued in its Boletín estadístico.
1. Banks and banking—Argentine Republic—Statistics. I. Banco Central de la República Argentina, Buenos Aires. Boletín estadístico.
HG2864.B32a 73-642523
MARC-S

Banco Central de la República Argentina, Buenos Aires.
Sistema de cuentas del producto e ingreso de la Argentina / Banco Central de la República Argentina. — [Buenos Aires] : Banco Central de la República Argentina, Gerencia de Investigaciones Económicas, 1975.
2 v. : ill. ; 26 cm.
Supplement to the Boletín estadístico nos. 11-12, Nov.-Dec. 1974.
CONTENTS: v. 1. Metodología y fuentes.—v. 2. Cuadros estadísticos.
1. Gross national product—Argentine Republic. 2. National income—Argentine Republic. 3. Cost and standard of living—Argentine Republic. I. Banco Central de la República Argentina, Buenos Aires. Boletín estadístico. II. Title.
HC180.I5B35 1975 339.382 76-460383
76 MARC

Banco Central de la República Argentina, Buenos Aires
see Argentine Republic. Congreso. Biblioteca. Servicio de Referencia. Bancos centrales. Buenos Aires, 1964-

Banco Central de la República Argentina, Buenos Aires
see Argentine Republic. Laws, statutes, etc. [Ley no. 18.061] Ley de entidades financieras... Buenos Aires, 1969.

Banco Central de la República Argentina, Buenos Aires
see La Creación del Banco Central... [Buenos Aires, 1972]

Banco Central de la República Argentina, Buenos Aires. Departamento de Finanzas Públicas.
La experiencia del Banco Central como agente financiero del Gobierno Nacional en la captación del ahorro interno.
Buenos Aires, 1971.
23 l. 30 cm.
LACAP 72-4407
Cover title.
1. Banco Central de la República Argentina, Buenos Aires. 2. Stocks—Argentine Republic. 3. Saving and investment—Argentine Republic. I. Title.
HG2866.B34 73-327520
rev

Banco Central de la República Dominicana.
Cuentas nacionales : producto nacional bruto, 1960-1971. — Santo Domingo : Banco Central de la República Dominicana, Departamento de Estudios Económicos, División de Cuentas Nacionales, 1973.
xiii, 164 p. : ill. ; 28 cm.
Cover title.
1. Gross national product—Dominican Republic. I. Title.
HC157.D63 I 512 1973 75-544812

Banco Central de la Republica Dominicana.
Ingresos y gastos de las familias en la Santo Domingo, 1971.
133 p. tables, fold. map. 26 cm. (Its Estudio sobre presupuestos familiares, I.)
Cover title.
Published by the Banco Central de la Republica Dominicana, the Oficina Nacional de Estadistica and the Agencia Internacional para el Desarrollo (USAID)
1. Income statistics—Dominican Republic. 2. Cost and standard of living—Dominican Republic. 3. Dominican Republic—Economic conditions. I. Dominican Republic. Oficina Nacional de Estadística. II. United States. Agency for International Development. III. Title.
CtY-E NUC76-71453

Banco Central de la República Dominicana.
see En una bella isla del Caribe ... [Santo Domingo, Banco Central de la República Dominicana, 1975]

Banco Central de la República Dominicana
see Grupo Conjunto de Ingreso Nacional. Cuentas nacionales de la República Dominicana. Santo Domingo, 1966.

Banco Central de la República Dominicana
see Grupo Conjunto de Ingreso Nacional. Cuentas nacionales de la República Dominicana. Santo Domingo, 1968-

Banco Central de la República Dominicana
see Wallich, Henry Christopher, 1914- Conference dictada... Santo Domingo, 1965.

Banco Central de la República Dominicana. Departamento de Estudios Economicos.
Distribución del gasto de las familias en la ciudad de Santo Domingo, 1969. Santo Domingo, Banco Central de la República Dominicana, Oficina Nacional de Estadística [y] Agencia Internacional para el Desarrollo (USAID) 1972.
145 p.
Monograph no. 2.
At head of title: Estudio sobre presupuestos familiares.
1. Cost of living—Santo Domingo. I. Dominican República. Oficina Nacional de Estadística. II. United States. Agency for International Development. III. Title. IV. Title: Estudio sobre presupuestos familiares.
DS NUC74-131268

Banco Central de la República Dominicana. Departamento de Estudios Economicos.
Indice de precios al consumidor en la ciudad de Santo Domingo, 1960-1970. Santo Domingo, Banco Central de la República Dominicana, Oficina Nacional de Estadística [y] Agencia Internacional para el Desarrollo (USAID) 1972.
158 p. illus.
Monograph no. 4.
At head of title: Estudio sobre presupuestos familiares.
1. Prices—Santo Domingo. I. Dominican Republic. Oficina Nacional de Estadística. II. United States. Agency for International Development. III. Title. IV. Title: Estudio sobre presupuestos familiares.
DS NUC74-131267

Banco Central de la República Dominicana. División de Cuentas Nacionales.
Cuentas nacionales: producto nacional bruto.
Santo Domingo, Banco Central de la República Dominicana, Departamento de Estudios Económicos, División de Cuentas Nacionales.
v. 28 cm.
1. Gross national product—Dominican Republic—Periodicals. I. Title.
HC157.D63 I 513 77-640956
MARC-S

Banco Central de Nicaragua
see Nicaragua. Dirección General de Estadistica y Censos. Comercio exterior de Nicaragua, 1969. [Managua? 1970?]

Banco Central de Nicaragua.
see Nicaragua. Laws, statutes, etc. Principales leyes económicas y sociales de Nicaragua. [Managua] Banco Central de Nicaragua, 1963.

Banco Central de Nicaragua
see Nicaragua. Laws, statutes, etc. Principales leyes económicas y sociales de Nicaragua. 2. ed., [ampliada. Managua] 1970 [i.e. 1971]

Banco Central de Nicaragua. Departamento de Estudios Económicos.
Boletín semestral—Banco Central de Nicaragua, Departamento de Estudios Económicos.
[Managua]
v. 28 cm.
Continues Boletín trimestral issued by the Banco Central de Nicaragua.
1. Nicaragua—Economic conditions—1918- —Periodicals. 2. Finance—Nicaragua—Periodicals. 3. Nicaragua—Statistics—Periodicals.
HC146.A1B32 330.9'7285'05 74-646122
MARC-S

Banco Central de Nicaragua. Departamento de Estudios Económicos.
Estudio sobre cambio estructural en Centro-america, 1960-1969. [Managua] Banco Central de Nicaragua [1971]
67 p.
1. Central America—Economic condit.—Stat. 2. Central America—Economic policy. I. Title.
MiEM NUC73-126457

Banco Central de Nicaragua. Departamento de Estudios Económicos.
Indicadores económicos.
[Managua] Departamento de Estudios Económicos.
v. 28 cm.
Spine title : Indicadores económicos de Nicaragua.
1. Economic indicators—Nicaragua. I. Title. II. Title: Indicadores económicos de Nicaragua.
HC146.A1B33a 330.9'7285'05 76-646130
MARC-S

Banco Central de Nicaragua. Departamento de Estudios Económicos.
Presentación de avances sobre el estudio de actitudes en la actividad algodonera / Banco Central de Nicaragua, Departamento de Estudios Económicos. — [Managua] : El Departamento, 1976.
89 p. in various pagings : forms ; 29 cm.
"DEE-UEE-Doc. No. 1."
1. Cotton trade—Nicaragua. 2. Cotton growing—Nicaragua. 3. Agricultural estimating and reporting—Nicaragua. I. Title: Presentación de avances sobre el estudio de actitudes ...
HD9084.N52B36 1976 338.1'7'351097285 76-473119
76[r77]rev MARC

Banco Central de Nicaragua. Departamento de Estudios Económicos
see Nicaragua. Dirección General de Estadistica y Censos. Nicaragua, resultados del censo experimental de poblacion, agosto 1969. San José, Costa Rica : Naciones Unidas, 1972.

Banco Central de Nicaragua. Departamento de Investigaciones Tecnológicas.
Situación de la artesanía nicaragüense. — [Managua] : División Industrial, Departamento de Investigaciones Tecnológicas, Banco Central de Nicaragua, 1976.
91 p. : ill. ; 28 cm.
1. Artisans—Nicaragua. 2. Handicraft—Nicaragua. I. Title.
HD2346.N48B36 1976 77-467925
77 MARC

Banco Central de Reserva de El Salvador, San Salvador.
Gráficas del Banco Central de Reserva sobre moneda, crédito bancario y otras materias relacionadas.
1945-
[San Salvador] Central de Reserva de El Salvador.
v. 22 x 28 cm. annual.
The first two vols. cover figures up to 1945 and 1948 respectively; in the next 3 from 1939 forward and beginning with the 6th vol., each covers a 20 year period, e. g. 1940/59, 1941/60, etc.
1. Money—Salvador—Periodicals. 2. Credit—Salvador—Periodicals. 3. Salvador—Economic conditions—1918- —Periodicals. I. Title.
HG734.B22a 332'.097284 79-287228
MARC-S

Banco Central de Reserva de El Salvador, San Salvador
see Union Monetaria Centroamericana. Acuerdo para el establecimiento de la Union Monetaria Centroamericana... [Sal Salvador] Secretaria Ejecutiva [1964]

Banco Central de Reserva de El Salvador, San Salvador
see Union Monetaria Centroamericana. Agreement for establishment of the Central American Monetary Union... [San Salvador, 1964]

Banco Central de Reserva del Perú.
Actividad agropecuaria, situación acutal y perspectivas de promoción económica y social. Lima, Peru, Sociedad Nacional Agraria [1961?]
175 p.
"Separativa de Actividades Productivas del Peru, Banco Central de Reserva del Peru, 1961."
1. Peru–Economic policy. 2. Peru–Social policy. 3. Peru–Indus. I. Sociedad Nacional Agraria. II. Title.
TxHU NUC73-74941

Banco Central de Reserva del Perú.
El desarrollo económico y financiero del Perú, 1968-1973 / Banco Central de Reserva del Perú. — [Lima : El Banco, 1974?]
xii, 296 p. : graphs ; 30 cm.
1. Peru—Economic conditions—1968- 2. Financial institutions—Peru. 3. Peru—Economic policy. I. Title.
HC227.B297 1974 330.9'85'063 77-451852
77 MARC

Banco Central de Reserva del Perú.
El desarrollo económico y financiero del Perú de 1969 a 1972. [Lima] 1972.
vi, 186 p. illus. 29 cm.
1. Peru—Economic conditions—1918- I. Title.
TxU NUC75-26566

Banco Central de Reserva del Perú.
Estatutos. Aprobados por Resolución Suprema No. 0056-69/HC/DH de 14 de enero de 1969, en cumplimiento del artículo 111 de la Ley Orgánica del Banco Central de Reserva del Perú. Lima, Imp. Casa Nacional de Moneda, 1969.
60 p. 20 cm.
1. Banking law—Peru. I. Peru. Laws, statutes, etc. II. Title.
NNC NUC73-126243

Banco Central de Reserva del Perú.
Informe de la balanza de pages no. 9 (G-9). [Lima] División de Estudios Económicos, Departamento de Estadísticas Económicos, Sección de Balanza de Pagos Internacionales, 1973.
2 v. 30 cm.
On cover of v. 1: Desarrollo de la balanza de pagos del Perú.
Contents. — v. 1. Balanza de pagos global, 1971-1972. v. 2. Balanza de pagos regional, 1968-1972.
DPU NUC75-76769

Banco Central de Reserva del Perú.
Trabajo piloto de cuentas regionales; investigacion de las zonas II y III del proyecto de desarrollo de las cuencas de los rios Huallaga central, Chicayacu y Nieva, ingreso y producto. [Lima?] 1970-
v. illus.
1. Water resources development–Huallaga River Valley. 2. Peru–Water resources development–Huallaga River Valley. I. Title.
DS NUC73-38949

Banco Central de Reserva del Perú
see Cusco monumental. [Lima, 1971?]

Banco Central de Reserva del Perú. Departamento de Análisis Externo. División de Estudios Económicos.
Estudio económico del comercio exterior del Perú con los países del grupo sub-regional andino, 1960-1969. — Lima : Banco Central de Reserva del Perú, División de Estudios Económicos, Departamento de Análisis Externo, 1970.
v, 2, 95, [29] leaves : map ; 29 cm.
Cover title.
1. Peru—Commerce—Andes region. 2. Andes region—Commerce—Peru. I. Title: Estudio económico del comercio exterior del Perú ...
HF3468.A5B35 1970 77-474851
77 MARC

Banco Central de Reserva del Perú. Sección **Balanza de Pagos.**
Desarrollo de la balanza de pagos del Perú, **1966, 1967, 1968, y 1969.** Lima, 1970.
166 l. illus. 29 cm. (Informe G8)
1. Balance of payments—Peru. I. Title.
TxU NUC73-112906

Banco Central de Venezuela, Caracas.
Algunas estadisticas de los paises de ALALC. [Caracas] 1968.
121 p. 21 x 35 cm.
At head of title: Sección ALALC.
1. Latin America—Statistics. 2. Latin America—Commerce. 3. Latin America—Economic conditions—1918- 4. Asociación Latinoamericana de Libre Comercio. I. Title.
INS NUC74-137780

Banco Central de Venezuela, Caracas. Anexo estadístico
see Banco Central de Venezuela, Caracas. Series estadísticas—Banco Central de Venezuela. [Caracas]

Banco Central de Venezuela, Caracas.
La economía venezolana en los últimos treinta años. [Caracas, 1971]
30, 14 l. illus. 28 cm. (Colección XXX Aniversario)
1. Venezuela—Econ. condit. I. Title.
CLSU NUC74-137779

Banco Central de Venezuela, Caracas.
La economía venezolana en los últimos treinta años. [Caracas, 1971]
318 p. illus. (part col.) (Colección XXX Aniversario)
Includes bibliographical references.
1. Venezuela—Economic conditions. I. Title.
MH-BA DPU NcU NRU NUC73-32189
NBrockU MiEM CtY-E DNAL

Banco Central de Venezuela, Caracas.
Estudio sobre presupuestos familiares e índices de costo de vida, área metropolitana de Maracaibo. Caracas, 1972.
198 p. 23 cm.
At head of title: Banco Central de Venezuela. Universidad del Zulia.
1. Cost and standard of living—Maracaibo metropolitan area, Venezuela. 2. Consumption (Economics)—Maracaibo metropolitan area, Venezuela. I. Zulia, Venezuela. Universidad. II. Title.
HD7021.B26 73-203568

Banco Central de Venezuela, Caracas.
Estudio sobre presupuestos familiares e índices de costo de vida para el área Puerto La Cruz-Barcelona. Caracas, 1971.
104 p. 2 fold. maps. 23 cm.
1. Consumption (Economics)—Puerto La Cruz (Anzoátegui) 2. Consumption (Economics)—Barcelona, Venezuela (City) 3. Cost and standard of living—Puerto La Cruz (Anzoátegui) 4. Cost and standard of living—Barcelona, Venezuela (City) I. Title.
HD7021.B33 1971 74-208263

Banco Central de Venezuela, Caracas.
Memoria especial, correspondiente al período 1966-1970. [Caracas, 1971?]
136 p.
I. Title.
PPiU CtY MiU NUC73-32194

Banco Central de Reserva del Perú. Departamento de Estudios Economicos. División de Investigaciones Especiales.
Importaciones, 1960-64. Lima, 1966.
44 p.
1. Peru–Commerce. I. Title.
MH NUC76-71527

Banco Central de Venezuela, Caracas.
Series estadísticas—Banco Central de Venezuela. [Caracas] Banco Central de Venezuela.
v. 30 cm.
Running title : Anexo estadístico—Banco Central de Venezuela.
1. Finance—Venezuela—Statistics—Periodicals. 2. Finance, Public—Venezuela—Statistics—Periodicals. 3. Venezuela—Statistics—Periodicals. I. Banco Central de Venezuela, Caracas. Anexo estadístico.
HG185.V4B35a 75-643561
MARC-S

Banco Central de Venezuela, Caracas.
Sistema de cuentas nacionales, 1968-1969; adaptadas al ST/STAT/SER. F/2/REV. 3. Naciones Unidas. Caracas, Departamento de Cuentas Nacionales, 1971.
241 p. 24 cm.
1. Fiscal policy–Venezuela. I. Title.
CSt NUC75-26576

Banco Central de Venezuela, Caracas
see García Mendez, Guillermo. Maracaibo. Caracas, 1970.

Banco Central de Venezuela, Caracas
see Venezuela. Laws, statutes, etc. Libro de decretos del Poder Ejecutivo de Venezuela ... Caracas, Banco Central de Venezuela, 1973.

Banco Central de Venezuela, Caracas. Departamento de Investigaciones Económicas. Sección Integración.
Acuerdo de Cartagena. [Caracas, 1973?]
27 p. 30 cm.
"Trabajo realizado por la Sección Integración del Departamonto de Investigaciones Económicas del Banco Central de Venezuela."
1. Acuerdo de Cartagena. 2. Andes region–Economic integration.
LNT NUC76-89150

Banco Central de Venezuela, Caracas. Grupo de Trabajo de la ALALC.
Problemas de pagos en la zona Latinoamericana de libre comercio. Realizado por Augusto Lange Sayago [y] Helly Tineo Salazar. Caracas, 1965.
134 l. (Its Estudio ALALC, no. 1)
Bibliography: leaves 130-134.
1. Balance of payments—Latin America. 2. Asociación Latinoamericana de Libre Comercio. I. Lange Sayago, Augusto. II. Tineo Salazar, Helly. III. Title. IV. Series.
MCM NUC76-25895

Banco Central de Venezuela, Caracas. Grupo de Trabajo de la ALALC.
see Lange S , Augusto. Financiamiento de las exportaciones en América Latina. Caracas, Banco Central de Venezuela, Departamento de Investigaciones Económicas y Estadísticas, Grupo de Trabajo de la ALALC, 1966.

Banco Central de Venezuela, Caracas. Sección A. L. A. L. C.
Algunas estadísticas de los países de ALALC. 1960/66– [Caracas]
v. 21 x 35 cm.
1. Asociación Latinoamericana de Libre Comercio countries—Commerce. 2. Asociación Latinoamericana de Libre Comercio countries—Statistics. I. Title.
HF130.5.A3B33a 74-644242
MARC-S

Banco Central de Venezuela, Caracas. Sección A. L. A. L. C.
Manual sobre el sistema de compensación multilateral de saldos bilaterales y créditos recíprocos. [Caracas] 1972.
74 p.
1. Asociación Latinoamericana de Libre Comercio countries–Commercial policy–Handbooks, manuals, etc. 2. International clearing–Asociación Latinoamericana de Libre Comercio countries–Handbooks, manuals, etc. 3. Credit–Asociación Latinoamericana de Libre Comercio countries–Handbooks, manuals, etc. I. Title.
CLU NUC76-71521

Banco Central de Venezuela, Caracas. Sección A.L.A.L.C.
Sistema de compensación multilateral de saldos bilaterales y creditos reciprocos. [Caracas] 1970.
1 v. (various pagings)
1. Latin America–Econ. policy. 2. Inter-American Development Bank. I. Asociación Latinoamericana de Libre Comercio. II. Title.
NcU MCM NUC71-36297rev.

Banco Central de Venezuela, Caracas. Sección A. L. A. L. C.
see Informaciones relacionadas con la integración económica latinoamericana. [Caracas] 1968.

Banco Central del Ecuador
see Ecuador. Junta Monetaria. No. 555 [i. e. Número quinientos cincuenta y cinco. Quito, 1970?]

Banco Central del Ecuador
see Goode, Richard B Finanzas públicas en el Ecuador... Quito-Ecuador, Imprenta del Banco Central, 1956.

Banco Central del Ecuador
see Tratados, convenios, acuerdos y modus vivendi de comercio suscritos por el gobierno de la República del Ecuador... Ed. reservada. Quito, Impr. Banco Central del Ecuador, 1970.

Banco Central del Ecuador. Departamento de Comercio Internacional
see Acuerdo de integración subregional. Intergración subregional andina ... [Quito] 1970.

Banco Central del Ecuador. Departamento de Comercio Internacional
see Definición de las condiciones de venta en comericio exterior. Quito, Impr. Banco Central del Ecuador, 1970.

Banco Central del Ecuador. Departamento de Investigaciones Economicas.
La industria textil ecuatoriana: problemas y perspectivas. Ed. reservada. Quito, 1964.
135 [14] l. 31 cm.
Cover title.
1. Textile industry and fabrics—Ecuador. I. Title.
PPiU NUC74-137747

Banco Central del Ecuador. Museo.
see Richesses de l'Équateur ... [Paris] Petit Palais, 1973.

Banco Central del Ecuador. Museo
see Schätze aus Ecuador. Koln, 1974.

Banco Central del Ecuador. Museo
see Tesori dell'Ecuador. [Roma, 1973?]

Banco Central del Ecuador. Museo.
see Trésors de l'Équateur ... Genève, Le Musée, 1974.

Banco Central del Uruguay.
Recopilación sistemática de normas de regulación y contralor del sistema financiero dictadas por el Banco Central del Uruguay hasta el 23 abril de 1975. -- Montevideo : Diario oficial, 1975.
140 p. ; 19 cm. -- (Separatas del Diario oficial; s. B-975)
"Aprobadas por el Directorio del Banco Central del Uruguay en su sesión del 13 de marzo de 1975 y actualizada, de acuerdo a lo dispuesto por esa misma resolución, al 23 de abril de 1975."
"Separata del Diario oficial de fecha 20 de mayo de 1975."
1. Banking law--Uruguay. 2. Banks and banking, Central--Uruguay. I. Uruguay. Diario oficial.
CLL NUC77-87174

Banco Central del Uruguay.
Reseña de la actividad económico-financiera. [Montevideo] Banco Central del Uruguay.
v. 28 cm.
1. Uruguay—Economic conditions—1945- —Periodicals. 2. Finance—Uruguay—Periodicals. I. Title.
HC231.B272a 75-644943
MARC-S

Banco Central del Uruguay. Asesoría Económica y Estudios.
see Seminario sobre Mercado de Capitales en el Uruguay, Montevideo, 1973. Seminario, Mercado de Capitales en el Uruguay, Montevideo, diciembre de 1973. [Montevideo] Banco Central del Uruguay, Asesoría Económica y Estudios, [1974]

Banco Central del Uruguay. Asesoría Legal.
Antecedentes de la reforma financiera : estudios y proyectos de ley sobre Banco Central, regulación del sistema financiero, cheques y sistema financiero del Estado / Banco Central del Uruguay, Asesoría Legal. — Montevideo : La Asesoría, 1973.
326 p. ; 24 cm.
1. Banking law—Uruguay. 2. Banco Central del Uruguay. 3. Checks—Uruguay. 4. Finance, Public—Uruguay—Law. I. Title.
346'.895'082 77-451809
77 MARC

Banco Central del Uruguay. Asesoría Legal
see Uruguay. Laws, statutes, etc. [Ley no. 14.095] Delitos economicos ... Montevideo, 1973-1974.

Banco Central del Uruguay. Asesoría Legal
see Uruguay. Laws, statutes, etc. Normas vigentes sobre materia, bancocentralista, 1971. Montevideo, Banco Central del Uruguay, 1972.

Banco Central del Uruguay. Departamento de Investigaciones Economicas.
Cuentas nacionales. [Montevideo] 1969.
1 v. (unpaged) 28 cm.
1. Uruguay–Economic conditions–1945- 2. Uruguay–Statistics. I. Title.
MU NUC73-112429

Banco Central del Uruguay. Departamento de Investigaciones Económicas.
Importaciones cumplidas, estado por país, rubro y subrubro.
[Montevideo] Banco Central del Uruguay, Departamento de Investigaciones Económicas.
v. 42-45 cm. monthly.
"Cuadro 26."
1. Uruguay—Commerce—Periodicals. I. Title.
HF177.B33a 75-645273
MARC-S

Banco Central del Uruguay. Departamento de Investigaciones Económicas.
Importaciones cumplidas, estado por rubro y subrubro. [Montevideo] Banco Central del Uruguay, Departamento de Investigaciones Económicas.
v. 42-45 cm. monthly.
"Cuadro no. 27."
1. Uruguay—Commerce—Periodicals. I. Title.
HF177.B33c 75-645272
MARC-S

Banco Central del Uruguay. Departamento de Investigaciones Económicas.
La lana en el Uruguay y en los principales mercados mundiales, 1967-1972 / Banco Central del Uruguay, Departamento de Investigaciones Económicas, Roberto Muñoz Durán. — Montevideo : El Departamento, 1973.
101 p. : graphs ; 25 cm.
1. Wool trade and industry—Uruguay. 2. Wool trade and industry. I. Muñoz Durán, Roberto. II. Title.
HD9904.U82B35 1973 76-474444
76 MARC

Banco Central del Uruguay. Departamento de Investigaciones Económicas.
Producto e ingresos nacionales. [Montevideo?] 1971.
77 p.
1. Income—Uruguay—Statistics. I. Title.
DS NUC73-32175

Banco Central del Uruguay. Departamento de Investigaciones Economicas
see Munoz Duran, Roberto. La lana en el Uruguay y en los principales mercados mundiales, 1967--1972. Montevideo, 1973.

Banco Central del Uruguay. Departamento de Investigaciones Economicas
see Munoz Duran, Roberto. El mercado mundial de la carne vacuna... [Montevideo?] 1971.

Banco Central del Uruguay. Departamento de la Deuda Pública.
Memoria.
[Montevideo]
v. 25 cm.
Includes legislation.
1. Debts, Public—Uruguay. I. Uruguay. Laws, statutes, etc.
HJ8609.B35 72-626292

Banco Central del Uruguay. Departamento de Personal.
Bases para el llamado a concurso de oposición y méritos entre estudiantes de ciencias económicas / Banco Central del Uruguay, Departamento de Personal. — Montevideo : El Banco, [Oficina de Publicaciones], 1973.
77 p., [1] fold. leaf of plates : forms ; 24 cm.
1. Banks and banking—Uruguay. 2. Banco Central del Uruguay. 3. Bank employees—Recruiting. I. Title.
HG2955.B35 1973 75-547909

Banco Central del Uruguay. Directorio.
Nota cursada por el Directorio Interventor al ministro de economía y finanzas con motivo de la interpelación llevada a cabo en el Senado el día 15 de abril de 1971. Montevideo, 1971.
17 p. 23 cm.
Microfiche (negative) 1 sheet. 11 x 15 cm. (NYPL FSN 15, 679)
1. Banco Central del Uruguay. 2. Banks and banking—Uruguay. I. Title.
NN NUC76-71547

Banco Central del Uruguay. División Asesoría Económica y Estudios.
Boletín estadístico mensual—Banco Central del Uruguay, División Asesoría Económica y Estudios.
Montevideo.
no. 28 cm.
1. Finance—Uruguay—Statistics—Periodicals. 2. Finance, Public—Uruguay—Statistics—Periodicals. 3. Uruguay—Statistics—Periodicals.
HG185.U8B35a 330.9'895'06 74-647915
MARC-S

Banco Central del Uruguay. División Asesoría Económica y Estudios.
Indicadores de la actividad económico-financiera / Banco Central del Uruguay, Asesoría Económica y Estudios. -- [Montevideo] : La División, 1975.
[51] leaves : 23 x 35 cm.
Cover title.
Tables.
1. Finance--Uruguay--Statistics. 2. Finance, Public--Uruguay--Statistics. 3. Uruguay--Economic conditions--1945- I. Title.
TxU NUC77-86124

Banco Central do Brasil.
Becebê: informativo econômico e financeiro. [Rio de Janeiro, Becebê Editora, 1973-
v. 32 cm. Cr$3.000.00 (v. 1-15)
Cover title.
CONTENTS: v. 1. Resoluções, 1965 e 1966.—v. 2. Resoluções, 1967 e 1968.—v. 3. Circulares, 1965 e 1966.—v. 4. Circulares, 1967 e 1968.—v. 5. SUMOC: legislação.—v. 6. Índice, 1964 a 1972.—v. 7. 1o. semestre, 1969.—v. 8. 2o. semestre, 1969.—v. 9. 1o. semestre, 1970.—v. 10. 2o. semestre, 1970.—v. 11. 1o. semestre, 1971.—v. 12. 2o. semestre, 1971.—v. 13. 1o. semestre, 1972.—v. 14. 2o. semestre, 1972.—v. 15. 1o. semestre, 1973.
1. Banco Central do Brasil. I. Title.
HG2886.B34 1973 74-210320

Banco Central do Brasil.
Coletânea de resoluções e circulares do Banco Central; Leis 4595 de 31.12.64 [e] 4728 de 14.07.65. [Coordenação: Marcílio Duarte Lima. Rio de Janeiro] Casa Carreiro Editora [1973]
297 p. 29 cm. Cr$90.00
1. Banking law—Brazil. I. Lima, Marcílio Duarte, comp. II. Brazil. Laws, statutes, etc. Lei no. 4.595, de 31 de dezembro de 1964. III. Brazil. Laws, statutes, etc. Lei no. 4.728, de 14 de julho de 1965. IV. Title.
74-210553

Banco Central do Brasil.
Documentos do meio circulante. ₍Rio de Janeiro, 1971₎
ii, 93 p. 26 cm.
Cover title.
"Boletim do Banco Central do Brasil, outubro 1971, anexo: publicação especial."
Includes legislation.
1. Money—Brazil. I. Title.
TxU NUC75-26565

Banco Central do Brasil.
Investimentos e reinvestimentos de capitais estrangeiros. ₍Brasilia, 1974₎
391 p. (Its Anexo especial II ₍ao Boletim₎ 1974)
1. Investments, Foreign—Brazil. I. Title. II. Series: Banco Central do Brasil. Boletim.
DS NUC76-50590

Banco Central do Brasil.
Manual do credito rural. [São Paulo, Secretaria da Agricultura, 1972?]
56 p.
Transcription of the Manual de credito rural prepared by the Banco Central do Brasil with some omissions.
1. Agricultural credit. Brazil. I. Brazil. Ministerio da Agricultura. II. Title.
DNAL NUC76-103551

Banco Central do Brasil.
Manual do crédito rural, MCR. [Brasilia] Gerencia de Coordenação do Crédito Rural e Industrial [1974]
1 v. (various pagings) illus.
Cover title.
1. Agricultural credit–Brazil. I. Title.
PPiU NUC76-25330

Banco Central do Brasil.
Setor externo e desenvolvimento da economia nacional; análise período 1968/71 e año 1972. ₍Brasilia? 1973₎
52 p. illus. (Its Anexo especial II ao boletim, 1973)
1. Brazil—Foreign trade. 2. Brazil—Econ. condit.—1945- I. Title. II. Series.
DS NUC75-33100

Banco Central do Brasil
see Brazil. Laws, statutes, etc. Legislação. Belém [Brasil] : Centro de Documentação e Biblioteca, 1974.

Banco Central do Brasil
see Brazil. Laws, statutes, etc. Legislação sôbre mercado de capitais e bôlsas de valores. 3 ed., rev. e atualizada. [Rio de Janeiro] : Bôlsa de Valores do Rio de Janeiro, 1972.

Banco Central do Brasil
see Brazil. Laws, statutes, etc. Leis nos. 4595, de 31-12-64... ₍Rio de Janeiro? 1967?₎

Banco Central do Brasil
see Minas Gerais, Brazil. Conselho Estadual do Desenvolvimento. Diretrizes para a aplicacão do crédito rural ... Belo Horizonte [19]70.

Banco Central do Brasil
see Trigueiros, Florisvaldo dos Santos, 1919- Iconografia do meio circulante do Brasil. Brasília, 1972.

Banco Central do Brasil
see Valor das moedas em relação ao ouro... [Rio de Janeiro? 1970]

Banco Central do Brasil. Departamento Econômico.
Fluxo de fundos na economia Brasileira, 1959/1969; estudo preliminar. ₍Rio de Janeiro? 1973₎
27 p. illus. (Its Anexo especial ao boletim; vol. 9, no. 1)
1. Finance—Brazil. 2. Capital—Brazil. I. Title. II. Series.
DS NUC75-33092

Banco Central do Brasil. Fiscalização e Registro de Capitais Estrangeiros
see Capitais estrangeiros no Brasil; legislação. [Rio de Janeiro] 1970.

Banco Central Hipotecario, Bogotá.
El crédito y el Banco Central Hipotecario; conmemoración del vigésimoquinto aniversario del establecimiento. ₍Bogotá, Antares Impr. Fotograbado₎ 1957.
90 p. illus., ports. 25 cm.
1. Banco Central Hipotecario, Bogotá. I. Title.
TxU NUC75-66307

Banco Central Hipotecario del Perú, Lima.
Nueva guía de procedimientos del Banco Central Hipotecario del Perú. ₍Lima, 1971₎
15 p. 23 cm.
At head of title: Sector: economía y finanzas.
1. Banco Central Hipotecario del Perú, Lima. I. Title.
TxU NUC75-62033

Banco Central Hipotecario del Perú, Lima.
see Peru. Laws, statutes, etc. Legislación del Banco Central Hipotecario del Perú, 1975 ... ₍Lima₎ BCHP, ₍1975₎

Banco centrale della Repubblica dell'Ecuador
see
Banco Central del Ecuador.

Banco Centroamericano de Integración Económica.
Articles of agreement and by-laws. Teguciagalpa, Hondouras, Central American Bank for Economic Integration, 1963.
1 v. (various pagings) 28 cm.
1. Banks and banking—Central America.
TNJ NUC73-2161

Banco Centroamericano de Integración Económica.
Función del Banco Centroamericano de Integración Económica, BCIE. 2. ed. rev. Tegucigalpa, 1965.
ii, 36, 11, 7 p. illus. 28 cm.
I. Title.
HG3881.B286 1965 72-223773

Banco Centroamericano de Integración Económica.
Organismo financiero de la integración económica; el Banco Centroamericano. ₍Tegucigalpa, 1973?₎
45 p. illus.
Based on a report by Dr. Enrique Ortez Colindres presented to the Tercer Seminario sobre Problemática Jurídica e Institucional de la Integración Centroamericana, Tegucigalpa, 1968, entitled El Banco Centroamericano, Organismo Financiero de la Integración Económica, and with the statistics brought up to date to June 1973.
1. Banks and banking, International. 2. Health and development—Central America. I. Ortez Colindres, Enrique. II. Title.
DPAHO NUC75-30563

Banco Centroamericano de Integración Económica.
Statute: Central American Fund for Economic Integration. [Tegucigalpa? Honduras, 1965?]
[7] p. 22 cm. (Its Resolution no. AG-1/65)
1. Central American Fund for Economic Integration. I. Central American Fund for Economic Integration.
NcD NUC76-93165

Banco Centroamericano de Integración Económica.
Towards physical integration of Central America; main projects for 1969-1973. ₍Tegucigalpa? 1969?₎
1 v. (various pagings)
1. Central America–Economic integration. I. Title.
NcU NUC73-47438

Banco Centroamericano de Integración Económica.
see T.S.C. Consortium. Central American transportation study, 1964-1965 ... ₍Washington₎ The consortium, ₍1965₎

Banco Centroamericano de Integración Económica. Asamblea de Gobernadores, 1st, Tegucigalpa, 1961.
Informe de la reunión; Primera Reunión de la Asamblea de Gobernadores, Tegucigalpa, D. C., Honduras, 30 de mayo a 1 de junio de 1961. ₍Tegucigalpa₎ Banco Centroamericano de Integración Económica, 1961.
1 v. (various pagings) 28 cm.
"BCIE/AG/1."
1. Banco Centroamericano de Integración Económica—Congresses.
HG3881.B2863 1961 74-205833

Banco Centroamericano de Integración Económica. Departamento de Fomento de Inversiones.
Investment opportunities in the Central American Common Market. Tegucigalpa, Central American Bank for Economic Integration, Investment Development Dept., 1967.
65 p. 28 cm.
1. Central America—Economic conditions. 2. Mercado Común Centroamericano. 3. Investments—Central America. I. Title.
HC141.B35 1967 332.6'73'09728 74-185332
MARC

Banco Centroamericano de Integración Económia. Research and Development Dept.
Investment opportunities in the Central American common market. 3d rev. ed. Tegucigalpa, Honduras, 1971.
"With figures of 1970."
1. Central America—Economic conditions. 2. Investments—Central America. I. Title.
OU NUC75-58892

Banco Continental, Lima.
Peruvian import trade; a graphic revue of the Peruvian import market. Lima, 1956.
₍6₎ p. illus. 14 x 20 cm.
Cover title.
1. Peru—Comm. 2. Peru—Econ. condit. I. Title.
TxU NUC74-168011

Banco Continental, Lima. Galería.
Art nouveau en Lima : Galería del Banco Continental, Miraflores, septiembre 1973. — ₍Lima₎ : La Galería, ₍1973?₎
₍8₎ p. : ill. ; 21 cm.
Includes "Nota sobre el art nouveau" by J. García Bryce and catalog of the exhibition.
1. Art objects, Peruvian—Exhibitions. 2. Art nouveau—Lima. I. García Bryce, José. II. Title.
NK917.L5B35 75-569510

Banco Continental, Lima. Galería.
Figurillas del antiguo Perú : ₍exhibición₎ 8 nov 1973, Galería Banco Continental : colección del Arqto. Santiago Agurto Calvo. — ₍Lima₎ : La Galería, ₍1973?₎
₍8₎ p. : ill. ; 21 cm.
Includes essay by Agurto Calvo and catalog.
1. Indians of South America—Peru—Pottery—Exhibitions. 2. Indians of South America—Peru—Antiquities—Exhibitions. 3. Peru—Antiquities—Exhibitions. I. Agurto Calvo, Santiago. II. Title.
F3429.3.P8B36 1973 75-586468

Banco Continental, Lima. Galería.
see Jiménez Borja, Arturo. Máscaras peruanas ... ₍s.l., s.n., 1975₎ (Lima : Industrialgráfica)

Banco Continental, Lima. Galería.
see Lima. Universidad de San Marcos. Sección de Geografía. Quilcas, arte rupestre en el Perú. ₍Lima₎ La Galería, ₍1976₎

Banco Continental, Lima. Galeria
see McElroy, Keith. Fotografía en el Perú, siglo XIX ... [Lima]: Galeria del Banco Continental [1975]

Banco Continental, Lima. Galería.
see Miró Quesada Garland, Luis. Arquitectura en la cerámica precolombina ... ₍Lima₎ La Galería, ₍1976₎

Banco Cooperativo Agrario Argentino
see Seminario Interamericano de Bancos de Cooperativas, 2d, Buenos Aires, 1969. Antecedentes, trabajos y conclusiones. [Buenos Aires, 1969]

Banco Cooperativo Comunal: anteproyecto de ley. Lima, Federación Nacional de Campesinos del Perú [1963]
11 p. 34 cm.
Informe presentado al primer Congreso Nacional de Comunidades Campesinas del Perú, Lima, 1963.
1. Banks and banking, Cooperative—Peru. I. Congreso Nacional de Comunidades Campesinas, 1st, Lima, 1963. II. Federación Nacional de Campesinos del Peru.
TxU NUC75-49479

Banco da Amazônia. Anuário
see Banco da Amazônia. Divisão de Estatística e Econometria. Amazônia: Estatísticas básicas. Belém, Divisão de Documentação e Divulgacão.

Banco da Amazônia.
Fundo de desenvolvimento urbano da Amazônia. Belem; Centro de Documentação e Biblioteca, 1973.
1 v. (unpaged) 26 cm.
1. Regional development—Amazon. I. Title.
CtY-L NUC76-72873

Banco da Amazônia.
Programa especial de crédito rural proterra. Belém, 1971.
82 l. illus. 28 cm.
1. Agriculture—Economic aspects—Brazil—Amazon Valley. 2. Amazon Valley—Economic conditions. I. Title.
TNJ NUC75-97852

Banco da Amazônia
see Brazil. Laws, statutes, etc. Legislação. Belém [Brasil] : Centro de Documentação e Biblioteca, 1974.

Banco da Amazônia. Biblioteca.
Catálogo de periódicos da Biblioteca do BASA. — Belém : Ministério do Interior, Banco da Amazônia S.A., Departamento de Estudos Econômicos, Divisão de Documentação e Divulgação, 1972.
64 p. ; 23 cm.
1. Periodicals—Bibliography—Catalogs. 2. Banco da Amazônia. Biblioteca. I. Title.
Z6945.B33 1972 77-483461
[PN4832] 77 MARC

Banco da Amazônia. Centro de Documentação e Biblioteca.
see Amazônia, legislação desenvolvimentista. Belém, Ministério do Interior, Banco da Amazônia, Departamento de Estudos Econômicos, 19

Banco da Amazônia. Departamento de Estudos Econômicos.
Amazônia; perfis industriais. Belem, Departamento de Estudos Econômicos, Divasão de Documentação e Divulgação, 1971.
462 p. 23 cm.
1. Brazil—Industry. 2. Brazil—Industries—Statistics. 3. Industry—Brazil. I. Title.
CtY-E TNJ NUC73-113948

Banco da Amazônia. Departamento de Estudos Econômicos.
BASA : atuação e política / Banca da Amazônia, Departamento de Estudos Econômicos. — Belém : O Departamento, 1972.
59 p. : graphs ; 24 cm.
Includes bibliographical references.
1. Banco da Amazônia. I. Title.
HG2890.B44B314 1972 76-469057
76 MARC

Banco da Amazonia. Departamento de Estudos Econômicos.
see Amazônia, legislação desenvolvimentista. Belém, Ministério do Interior, Banco da Amazônia, Departamento de Estudos Econômicos, 19

Banco da Amazônia. Departamento de Estudos Econômicos. Divisão de Assistência Técnica
see
Banco da Amazônia. Divisão de Assistência Técnica.

Banco da Amazônia. Departamento de Estudos Econômicos. Divisão de Estatística e Econometria
see
Banco da Amazônia. Divisâo de Estatística e Econometria.

Banco da Amazônia. Departamento Jurídico
see Brazil. Laws, statutes, etc. Legislação. Belém [Brasil] : Centro de Documentação e Biblioteca, 1974.

Banco da Amazônia. Divisão de Assistência Técnica.
Amazônia—perfis industriais. Belém, Departamento de Estudos Econômicos, Divisão de Documentação e Divulgação, 1971.
462 p. 23 cm.
1. Amazon Valley—Industries. I. Title.
HC188.A5B35 1971 74-231742

Banco da Amazônia. Divisão de Estatística e Econometria.
Amazônia: Estatísticas básicas.
Belém, Divisão de Documentação e Divulgacão.
v. 28 cm. annual.
Cover title : Anuário BASA.
1. Amazon Valley—Statistics. I. Banco da Amazônia. Anuário. II. Title.
HA988.A48B36 73-641846

Banco da América do Sul
see
Banco América do Sul.

Banco de Albacete.
Estudio económico de la provincia de Albacete. [Albacete] (1970)
147 p., 1 l., illus. 27 cm. Sp 72-Jan
1. Albacete, Spain (Province)—Economic conditions. I. Title.
HC387.A55B35 72-360009

Banco de Alicante.
see Coloquios de Divulgación Bursatil, 2d, Alicante, Spain, 1974. II [i.e. Segundos] Coloquios de Divulgación Bursatil, 1974. Alicante, Banco de Alicante, 1975.

Banco de Angola, Lisbon.
Angola: economic and financial survey; annual report, 1972. [Lisboa] Banco de Angola, Economic Studies Dept. [1973]
179 p. col. diagrs. 25 cm.
Translated from Portuguese by G. F. W. Dykes and J. B. Conefrey Jr.
1. Angola—Econ. condit. I. Title. II. Title: Economic and financial survey of Angola.
CLSU NUC76-75612

Banco de Angola, Lisbon.
Angola 1970: economic and financial survey. [Translated by G. F. W. Dykes and J. B. Conefrey, Jr. Lisbon, 1971?]
171 p. 25 cm.
"Banco de Angola annual report."
1. Angola—Econ. condit. I. Title.
AAP NUC75-26563

Banco de Angola, Lisbon.
Banco de Angola.
[Lisbon]
v. ill. 22 cm.
In English.
Consists of its financial report.
1. Banco de Angola.
HG3429.A53B3a 332.1'1'09673 74-646901
MARC-S

Banco de Angola, Lisbon.
Economic and financial survey of Angola.
[Lisbon, Portugal] Banco de Angola.
v. 24 cm.
Published 1960-65.
1. Angola — Economic conditions — Periodicals. 2. Finance — Angola—Periodicals. I. Title.
HC578.A5B32a 330.9'67'303 76-648951
MARC-S

Banco de Angola, Lisbon
see Almeida e Vasconcellos Alvares, Pedro de. Notas sobre o problema das transferências de Angola. [Lisboa? 1956]

Banco de Angola, Lisbon. Economic Studies Dept.
Angola, economic and financial survey: Banco de Angola, annual report. 1970–
[Lisboa, Portugal] Banco de Angola, Economic Studies Dept.
v. in 25 cm.
Continues: Banco de Angola, Lisbon. Economic Studies Dept. Annual report and economic and financial survey of Angola.
1. Angola — Economic conditions — Periodicals. 2. Finance — Angola—Periodicals. 3. Banco de Angola, Lisbon. I. Title.
HC578.A5B33a 330.9'67'303 76-649026
MARC-S

Banco de Angola, Lisbon. Economic Studies Dept.
Annual report and economic and financial survey of Angola. 19 –69.
[Lisboa, Portugal] Banco de Angola, Economic Studies Dept.
v. in 25 cm.
Began with vol. for 1966.
Continued by: Banco de Angola, Lisbon. Economic Studies Dept. Angola, economic and financial survey: Banco de Angola, annual report.
1. Angola—Economic conditions—Periodicals. 2. Finance—Angola—Periodicals. I. Title.
HC578.A5B33a 330.9'67'303 76-649027
MARC-S

Banco de Bilbao.
Arancel de aduanas de 1960; disposiciones complementarias y acuerdo preferencial España-C. E. E. 5. ed. actualizado al 1-12-1970. [Bilboa] Banco de Bilbao, Servicio de Estudios, 1970.
cii, 332, 15 p. 21 x 26 cm. Sp***
"Legislación": p. [xi]-cii.
1. Tariff—Spain—Law. 2. Tariff—European Economic Community countries—Law. I. Spain. Laws, statutes, etc. II. Title.
75-583230

Banco de Bilbao.
El Bierzo : estudio económico de una comarca natural. — [Bilbao] : Banco de Bilbao, [1973]
146 p., [3] leaves of plates (1 fold.) : ill. ; 23 cm. Sp 74-Nov
1. Villafranca del Bierzo region, Spain—Economic conditions. 2. Villafranca del Bierzo region, Spain—Social conditions. I. Title.
HC387.V45B35 1973 75-526751

Banco de Bilbao.
España-Europa este : nueva era comercial / [Banco de Bilbao]. — Bilbao : El Banco, Servicio de Estudios, 1973.
119 p. : ill. ; 26 cm. Sp 74
1. Spain—Commerce—Europe, Eastern. 2. Europe, Eastern—Commerce—Spain. 3. Europe, Eastern—Commerce—Directories. 4. Europe, Eastern—Economic conditions. I. Title.
HF3688.E2B33 1973 382'.0946'04 74-352489

Banco de Bilbao.
Mercados extranjeros, Africa : guía del exportador / [Banco de Bilbao]. — [Bilbao] : Servicio de Estudios del Banco de Bilbao, 1974.
133 p., [2] leaves of plates : ill. ; 26 cm. Sp 75-Mar
1. Africa — Economic conditions — 1945- 2. Africa — Commerce. 3. Africa — Commerce — Spain. 4. Spain — Commerce — Africa. I. Title.
HC502.B24 1974 76-502003

Banco de Bilbao.
Panorama económico. Aragón. [Bilbao] (1971)
176 p., illus., fold. col. map. 23 cm. Sp 72-July/Aug/Sept
1. Aragon—Economic conditions. I. Title.
HC387.A68B35 73-324199

Banco de Bilbao.
Panorama económico. Asturias [Bilbao, 1972]
204 p., 1 l., illus., col. plates. 22 cm. Sp 72
1. Oviedo, Spain (Province)—Economic conditions. 2. Service industries—Oviedo, Spain (Province) I. Title.
HC387.O9B36 1972 73-347082

Banco de Bilbao.
Panorama económico. La Mancha. Albacete, Ciudad Real, Cuenca, Toledo. [Bilbao] (1972)
202 p., illus., plates (part col.) 23 cm. Sp 72
1. Mancha, La, Spain—Economic conditions. 2. Service industries—Mancha, La, Spain. I. Title.
HC387.M33B35 1972 73-347305

Banco de Bilbao
see Arteta, Aurelio, 1879-1940. Arteta en el Banco de Bilbao. (Bilbao, 1973)

Banco de Bilbao
see Banco Asturiano. Polo de desarrollo de Oviedo. [San Sebastian, Valverde] 1969.

Banco de Bilbao
see Boletín de Londres. [Bilbao, España] Banco de Bilbao.

Banco de Bilbao
see Exposición de Iconografía Bizantina y Rusa, Madrid, 1972. Exposición de iconografía bizantina y rusa. (Madrid, 1972)

Banco de Bilbao
see Gutierrez-Solana, Jose, 1886-1945. J. Solana. Noviembre-diciembre 1972. Madrid (1972).

Banco de Bilbao
see Joven Cámara de Valencia. "Problematica actual de la naranja." Valencia, 1973.

Banco de Bilbao
see Spain. Laws, statutes, etc. Arancel de 1960 y disposiciones complementarias... [Bilbao] [1968]

Banco de Bilbao. Economic Research Department
see
Banco de Bilbao. Servicio de Estudios.

Banco de Bilbao. Research Department
see
Banco de Bilbao. Servicio de Estudios.

Banco de Bilbao. Servicio de Estudios.
Como invertir en España / ⌈preparado y editado por el Servicio de Estudios del Banco de Bilbao⌉. — ⌈Bilbao⌉ : El Servicio, 1975.
80 p. ; 20 x 21 cm. Sp75-Dec
Includes index.
1. Investments, Foreign—Law and legislation—Spain. I. Title.
346'.46'07 76-471646
•76 MARC

Banco de Bilbao. Servicio de Estudios.
Economic report—Banco de Bilbao.
⌈Bilbao⌉ Research Department ⌈etc.⌉
v. 27 cm.
Vols. for issued by the banks' service variant name: Economic Research Department.
1. Spain — Economic conditions — 1918- — Periodicals. 2. Finance—Spain—Periodicals.
HG3190.B54B313 330.9'46'08 75-649117
MARC-S

Banco de Bilbao. Servicio de Estudios.
Informe económico—Banco de Bilbao.
⌈Bilbao⌉ Servicio de Estudios.
v. ill. 27 cm. annual.
Continues: Banco de Bilbao. Informe.
1. Spain — Economic conditions — 1918- — Periodicals. 2. Finance—Spain—Periodicals. 3. Economic history—1945- —Periodicals.
HG3190.B54B3 75-649116
MARC-S

Banco de Bilbao. Servicio de Estudios.
Panorama economico: Caceres. Bilbao, 1974.
226 p. col. illus., col. maps.
Includes bibliographical references.
1. Caceres, Spain (Province)—Economic conditions. I. Title.
DNAL NUC76-50619

Banco de Bilbao. Servicio de Estudios
see Boletín de Londres. ⌈Bilbao, España⌉ Banco de Bilbao.

Banco de Bilbao en Londres
see Boletín de Londres. ⌈Bilbao, España⌉ Banco de Bilbao.

Banco de Bogotá.
Informe.
⌈Bogotá⌉
v. 28 cm. annual.
Continues its Balance e informe.
1. Banco de Bogotá.
HG2910.B64B252 73-642442
MARC-S

Banco de Boston.
Algunos principios básicos de la exportación. [Buenos Aires, 197-]
94 p. 29 cm.
Cover title.
1. Commerce—Handbooks, manuals, etc. 2. Argentine Republic—Commerce—Handbooks, manuals, etc. I. Title.
TxU NUC76-92172

Banco de Construccion y Desarrollo
see Desarrollo de las obras publicas en Colombia. ⌈Bogota, 1969⌉

Banco de Crédito a la Construcción.
Memoria—Banco de Crédito a la Construcción.
⌈Madrid, Gabinete de Estudios⌉
v. ill. 22 cm.
1. Banco de Crédito a la Construcción.
HG3190.M64C6824 75-642773
MARC-S

Banco de Crédito Balear.
Banco de Crédito Balear, 1872–1972 : primer centenario. — Palma de Mallorca : Banco de Crédito Balear, 1973.
262 p., ⌈17⌉ leaves of plates : ill ; 28 cm. Sp***
ISBN 84-85048-10-5
1. Banco de Crédito Balear.
HG3189.B3B35 1973 75-557070

Banco de Crédito del Perú, Lima
see Pintura virreynal. [Lima] c1973.

Banco de Crédito del Perú, Lima.
see Platería virreinal. ⌈Lima, Banco de Crédito del Perú⌉ c1974.

Banco de Crédito del Perú, Lima
see Realidad, perspectivas y problemas de la selva peruana. Lima, 1972.

Banco de Crédito do Amazônia. Grupo Executivo de Coordenação do Crédito Rural.
Política de crédito rural; diretrizes e medidas. Relatorio do Grupo de trabalho criado pelo memorando presidencial GP-MF-38, de 3-3-61. Rio de Janeiro, Depart. de Imprensa Nacional, 1961.
124 p.
1. Agricultural credit—Brazil. I. Title.
ICU NUC76-17663

Banco de Crédito Industrial Argentino
see Banco Industrial de la República Argentina.

Banco de Crédito Local de España, Madrid.
Boletín bimestral informativo—Banco de Crédito Local de España.
⌈Madrid⌉ Banco de Crédito Local de España.
no. ill. 28 cm.
Title varies slightly.
1. Banco de Crédito Local de España, Madrid.
HG3190.M34C7393 75-647462
MARC-S

Banco de Crédito Local de España, Madrid.
Resumen informativo [sobre sus orígenes, desarrollo y actual funcionamiento] y [parte seleccionada de la] Memoria y balance del ejercicio 1960. [Madrid] 1961.
57 p.
"Para enviar a los participantes en la Conferencia Mundial de Gobiernos Locales, Washington, junio de 1961."
1. Banco de Crédito Local de España, Madrid. I. Title.
PPiU NUC75-1331

Banco de Crédito Real de Minas Gerais.
Relatório—⌈Banco de Crédito Real de Minas Gerais⌉
⌈Juiz de Flora, Banco de Crédito Real de Minas Gerais⌉
v. ill. 26 cm.
1. Banco de Crédito Real de Minas Gerais. 2. Banks and banking—Brazil—Minas Gerais.
HG2889.M55B36a 76-641046
MARC-S

Banco de Desenvolvimento de Minas Gerais, Belo Horizonte.
Bases para uma ação integrada na Região IV; síntese.
⌈Belo Horizonte, 1973⌉
56 l. illus. 31 cm.
Cover title.
1. Minas Gerais Brazil — Economic policy. 2. Agriculture and state—Brazil—Minas Gerais. I. Title.
HC188.M6B34 1973 73-219458

Banco de Desenvolvimento de Minas Gerais, Belo Horizonte.
Programa de desenvolvimento da pecuária de corte. [Belo Horizonte? 1970?]
2 v. illus. 31 cm.
1. Stock and stock-breeding—Brazil—Minas Gerais. 2. Stock and stock-breeding—Brazil—Bahia. 3. Stock and stock-breeding—Brazil—Espírito Santo. I. Title.
NIC NUC73-113170

Banco de Desenvolvimento de Minas Gerais, Belo Horizonte.
Programa de expansão e modernização da indústria de laticínios. ⌈Belo Horizonte⌉ 1972.
199 l. maps. 30 cm.
Cover title.
At head of title: Governo do Estado de Minas Gerais.
Includes bibliographical references.
1. Milk trade—Minas Gerais, Brazil. 2. Dairy products—Minas Gerais, Brazil. 3. Industrial promotion—Minas Gerais, Brazil. I. Title.
HD9282.B73M562 1972 73-212367

Banco de Desenvolvimento de Minas Gerais, Belo Horizonte.
Programa estratégico de desenvolvimento; resumo do documento preliminar elaborado pelo Ministério do Planejamento e Coordenação Geral. ⌈Belo Horizonte⌉ 1968.
1 v. (various pagings) 32 cm.
Cover title: Resumo do Programa estratégico de desenvolvimento.
"Texto para circulação interna, sujeito a revisão."
1. Brazil—Economic policy. 2. Brazil—Social policy. I. Brazil. Ministério do Planejamento e Coordenação Geral. Programa estratégico de desenvolvimento, 1968–1970. II. Title. III. Title: Resumo do Programa estratégico de desenvolvimento.
HC187.B247 1968 73-217764

Banco de Desenvolvimento de Minas Gerais, Belo Horizonte
see Congresso Brasileiro de Desenvolvimento Regional, 1st, Araxá, 1965. Anais. Araxá, 1965.

Banco de Desenvolvimento de Minas Gerais, Belo Horizonte. Departamento de Crédito Rural.
Programa agropecuário de exportação : subprograma de crédito integrado à produção agropecuária e conservação de solos / Banco de Desenvolvimento de Minas Gerais, Departamento de Crédito Rural. — ⌈Belo Horizonte⌉ : Departamento, 1972.
216 leaves in various foliations : ill. ; 34 cm.
Cover title.
Includes bibliographies.
1. Agricultural credit—Brazil—Minas Gerais. I. Title.
HG2051.B72M52 1972 75-532254

Banco de Desenvolvimento de Minas Gerais, Belo Horizonte. Departamento de Desenvolvimento Industrial.
Programa de recuperação e expansão da indústria acucareira em Minas Gerais. ⌈Belo Horizonte⌉ 1973.
35, ⌈43⌉ l. 29 cm.
Cover title: Programa de recuperação da indúsaçucareira em Minas Gerais.
1. Sugar trade—Minas Gerais, Brazil. I. Title.
HD9114.B7M562 1973 74-225225

Banco de Desenvolvimento de Minas Gerais, Belo Horizonte. Departamento de Desenvolvimento Mineral.
Oportunidades de investimento. ⌈Belo Horizonte⌉ 1973.
5 v. maps. 31 cm.
Cover title.
Vols. 2 and 5: introductory material in Portuguese and English.
CONTENTS: v. ⌈1⌉ Programa pó calcário; incentivo ao uso e aumento de produção de corretivos de solo.—v. ⌈2⌉ Mineralizações associadas às rochas básico-ultrabásicas e alcalinas.—v. ⌈3⌉ Siderurgia em Minas Gerais.—v. ⌈4⌉ Incentivos à indústria de mineração.—v. ⌈5⌉ Ouro, prata, platina.
1. Mineral industries—Minas Gerais, Brazil. 2. Investments—Minas Gerais, Brazil. 3. Investment tax credit—Minas Gerais, Brazil. I. Title.
HD9506.B73M562 1973 74-207674

Banco de Desenvolvimento de Minas Gerais, Belo Horizonte. Departamento de Desenvolvimento Mineral.
Programa de apoio à indústria de gusa, Minas Gerais / Banco de Desenvolvimento de Minas Gerais, ⌈Departamento de Desenvolvimento Mineral⌉, Centro Tecnológico de Minas Gerais. — ⌈Belo Horizonte⌉ : O Departamento, ⌈19⌉74.
2 v. : ill. ; 30 cm.
1. Charcoal—Brazil—Minas Gerais. I. Centro Tecnológico de Minas Gerais. II. Title.
HD9559.C45B733 77-465861
77 MARC

Banco de Desenvolvimento de Minas Gerais, Belo Horizonte. Departamento de Desenvolvimento Mineral. Gerência do Setor II.
Programa pedra preciosas; ⌈um novo enfoque ao setor. Belo Horizonte⌉ 1973.
32 l. 29 cm.
Cover title.
1. Precious stones—Brazil. I. Title.
HD9676.B72B36 1973 74-225260

Banco de Desenvolvimento do Ceará.
Relatório de atividades.
⌈Fortaleza⌉
v. 28 cm.
1. Banco de Desenvolvimento do Ceará.
HG2889.C4B32a 73-647532
MARC-S

Banco de Desenvolvimento do Ceará. Assessoria Técnica.
Ceará, polo textil / Banco de Desenvolvimento do Ceará S/A, BANDECE, Assessoria Técnica. — ⌜Fortaleza⌝ : A Assessoria, 1973.
⌜68⌝ leaves ; 33 cm.
Bibliography: leaf ⌜21⌝
1. Textile industry—Ceará, Brazil (State) I. Title.
HD9864.B83C43 1973 75-530136

Banco de Desenvolvimento do Espírito Santo.
Alguns indicadores econômicos e sociais do Espírito Santo, 1950-1968; produto real/renda interna. ⌜Vitória, 1970 or 71⌝
1 v. (various pagings) 27 cm.
Cover title.
1. Economic indicators—Espírito Santo, Brazil (State) 2. Social indicators—Espírito Santo, Brazil (State) I. Title.
HC188.E7B38 1970 74-205947

Banco de Desenvolvimento do Espírito Santo.
Incentivos fiscais e creditícios no Estado do Espírito Santo. Vitória, Brasil, 1971.
1 v. (various pagings) 27 cm.
Cover title: Catálogo dos incentivos; coletânea de legislação de inventivos fiscais e creditícios no Estado do Espírito Santo.
1. Investments—Espírito Santo, Brazil (State) 2. Sales tax—Espírito Santo, Brazil (State) 3. Espírito Santo, Brazil (State)—Economic policy. I. Title. II. Title: Catálogo dos incentivos.
73-222254

Banco de Desenvolvimento do Espírito Santo.
Plano de ação, 1975-1979 / Banco de Desenvolvimento do Espírito Santo S.A., BANDES. — Vitória : BANDES, 1975.
211 leaves : ill. ; 33 cm.
Includes bibliographical references.
1. Banco de Desenvolvimento do Espírito Santo. 2. Espírito Santo, Brazil (State)—Economic policy. I. Title.
HG2889.E86B36 1975 76-480180
76 MARC

Banco de Desenvolvimento do Espírito Santo
see Cadastro industrial. [Vitória]

Banco de Desenvolvimento do Espírito Santo.

For works by this body issued under its earlier name see

Companhia de Desenvolvimento Econômico do Espírito Santo.

Banco de Desenvolvimento do Espírito Santo. Departamento de Estudos e Programação.
Alguns indicadores econômicos e sociais do Espírito Santo.
Vitória.
v. 28 cm.
1. Economic indicators—Espírito Santo, Brazil (State) 2. Espírito Santo, Brazil (State)—Social conditions. I. Title.
HC188.E7B37 72-623970

Banco de Desenvolvimento do Espírito Santo. Departamento de Estudos e Programação.
Análise e projeção da população do Estado do Espírito Santo. Elaborado sob a responsabilidade de: Gilberto José Secomandi. Vitória, 1971.
40, ⌜1⌝ l. 28 cm.
Bibliography: leaf ⌜41⌝
1. Espírito Santo, Brazil (State)—Population. 2. Population forecasting—Espírito Santo, Brazil (State). I. Secomandi, Gilberto José. II. Title.
HB3564.E8B3 1971 73-213459

Banco de Desenvolvimento do Espírito Santo. Departamento de Estudos e Programação.
Crescimento e atraso relativo da economia do Espírito Santo, 1950/1968. Elaborado sob a responsabilidade de: Guilherme Henrique Pereira. Vitória, 1970 ⌜i. e. 1972⌝
29 l. 27 cm.
1. Gross national product—Espírito Santo, Brazil (State) 2. Espírito Santo, Brazil (State)—Economic conditions. I. Pereira, Guilherme Henrique. II. Title.
HC188.E7B36 1972 73-213482

Banco de Desenvolvimento do Espírito Santo. Departamento de Estudos e Programação.
Exportações em trânsito no Espírito Santo / Banco de Desenvolvimento do Espírito Santo, Departamento de Estudos e Programação. — Vitória : O Banco, 1971.
150 p. : graph ; 28 cm.
1. Espírito Santo, Brazil (State)—Commerce. I. Title.
HF3409.E7B35 1971 75-408561

Banco de Desenvolvimento do Espírito Santo. Departamento de Estudos e Programaçao.
População do Estado do Esprito Santo a nível de distritos, 1940-1970 / Banco de Desenvolvimento do Espírito Santo S. A., Departamento de Estudos e Programaçao. — Vitória : O Departamento, 1972.
66 leaves : maps ; 28 cm.
Bibliography: leaf 66.
1. Espírito Santo, Brazil (State)—Population. 2. Espírito Santo, Brazil (State)—Administrative and political divisions. I. Title.
HB3564.E8B3 1972 75-545598

Banco de Desenvolvimento do Espírito Santo. Departamento de Estudos e Programação.
O setor exportador da economia do Espírito Santo. Elaborado sob a responsabilidade de: Ricardo Ferreira dos Santos. Vitória, 1970.
56 l. 28 cm.
1. Espírito Santo, Brazil (State)—Commerce. I. Santos, Ricardo Ferreira dos. II. Title.
HF3409.E7B35 1970 74-227819

Banco de Desenvolvimento do Espírito Santo. Departamento de Estudos Econômicos.
A indústria de transformação no Espírito Santo : pesquisa, resultados preliminares / Banco de Desenvolvimento do Espírito Santo S.A., Departamento de Estudos Econômicos ; ⌜coordenadores, Sebastião José Balarini, Sandra Quintaes Freitas Lima, colaboradores, Antônio Caetano Gomes ... et al.⌝. — Vitória : O Banco, 1974.
84 leaves ; 27 cm.
Chiefly tables.
1. Espírito Santo, Brazil (State)—Manufactures. I. Balarini, Sebastião José. II. Title.
HD9734.B73E843 1974 338'.0981'5 76-474420
76 MARC

Banco de Desenvolvimento do Estado de Pernambuco

For works by this body issued under its later name see

Banco do Estado de Pernambuco.

Banco de Desenvolvimento do Estado de São Paulo.
Activities report—Banco de Desenvolvimento do Estado de São Paulo. 1973-
⌜São Paulo⌝ Banco de Desenvolvimento do Estado de São Paulo.
v. ill. 30 cm. annual.
Continues: Banco de Desenvolvimento do Estado de São Paulo. Yearly report.
Other title, 1973- : Report on activities—Banco de Desenvolvimento do Estado de São Paulo.
1. Banco de Desenvolvimento do Estado de São Paulo. I. Banco de Desenvolvimento do Estado de São Paulo. Report on activities.
HG2889.S25B34b 75-646024
MARC-S

Banco de Desenvolvimento do Estado de São Paulo.
Relatório anual.
⌜São Paulo⌝
v. illus. 29 cm.
1. Banco de Desenvolvimento do Estado de São Paulo.
HG2889.S25B34a 74-642814
MARC-S

Banco de Desenvolvimento do Estado de São Paulo.
Report on activities
see Banco de Desenvolvimento do Estado de São Paulo. Activities report. 1973-
[São Paulo]

Banco de Desenvolvimento do Estado de São Paulo.
Yearly report.
⌜São Paulo⌝
v. illus. 30 cm.
1. Banco de Desenvolvimento do Estado de São Paulo.
HG2889.S25B34b 332.1'1'09816 74-642813
MARC-S

Banco de Desenvolvimento do Estado do Maranhão.
Relatório da diretoria—Banco de Desenvolvimento do Estado do Maranhão.
São Luís ⌜Brasil⌝ Banco de Desenvolvimento do Estado do Maranhão.
v. ill. 28 cm.
1. Banco de Desenvolvimento de Estado do Maranhão.
HG2889.M35B36a 77-641987
MARC-S

Banco de Desenvolvimento do Paraná.
Atividades—Banco de Desenvolvimento do Paraná S. A. 1969-
⌜Curitiba⌝ Banco de Desenvolvimento do Paraná S. A.
v. ill. 29 cm.
1. Banco de Desenvolvimento do Paraná. 2. Banks and banking—Paraná, Brazil (State)—Periodicals.
HG2889.P33B35a 75-645961
MARC-S

Banco de Desenvolvimento do Paraná.
Atividades — Banco de Desenvolvimento do Paraná S. A. English.
Annual report — Banco de Desenvolvimento do Parana S. A.
Curitiba, Banco de Desenvolvimento do Parana S. A.
v. ill. 29 cm.
1. Banco de Desenvolvimento do Paraná. 2. Banks and banking—Paraná, Brazil (State)—Periodicals.
HG2889.P33B3513a 332.1'53 75-645962
MARC-S

Banco de Desenvolvimento do Paraná.
Dos precursores à escola Andersen : ⌜de 25 de setembro a 15 de outubro de 1975, salão de Exposições do BADEP / coordenação, Domício Pedroso⌝. — ⌜Curitiba : BADEP, 1975⌝
36 p. : ports. ; 21 cm. — (Panorama da arte no Paraná ; 1)
Cover title.
Bibliography: p. 34.
1. Art, Modern—19th century—Paraná, Brazil (State)—Exhibitions. 2. Art, Modern—20th century—Paraná, Brazil (State)—Exhibitions. 3. Art—Paraná, Brazil (State)—Exhibitions. 4. Artists—Brazil—Paraná (State)—Biography. I. Pedroso, Domício. II. Title. III. Series.
N6656.P3B36 1975 76-486741
76 MARC

Banco de Desenvolvimento do Paraná.
Information on Paraná. 1973-
⌜Curitiba⌝
v. illus. 23 x 31 cm.
1. Paraná, Brazil (State)—Economic conditions. 2. Paraná, Brazil (State)—Social conditions. 3. Paraná, Brazil (State)—Economic conditions—Maps. I. Title.
HC188.P35B25b 330.9'81'6 74-640798
MARC-S

Banco de Desenvolvimento do Paraná.
Paraná informações. 1973-
⌜Curitiba⌝
v. illus. 23 x 31 cm.
1. Paraná, Brazil (State)—Economic conditions. 2. Paraná, Brazil (State)—Social conditions. 3. Paraná, Brazil (State)—Economic conditions—Maps. I. Title.
HC188.P35B25a 74-640799
MARC-S

Banco de Desenvolvimento do Paraná.
Parana now. ⌜Curitiba, 1972⌝
⌜38⌝ p. col. illus. 31 cm.
Cover title.
1. Paraná, Brazil (State)—Economic conditions. 2. Paraná, Brazil (State)—Social conditions. I. Title.
HC188.P35B24 1972 330.9'81'6 73-166387
MARC

Banco de Desenvolvimento do Paraná.
Relatório—Banco de Desenvolvimento do Paraná S. A.
⌜Curitiba⌝ Banco de Desenvolvimento do Paraná S. A.
v. 28 cm.
1. Banco de Desenvolvimento do Paraná. 2. Banks and banking—Paraná, Brazil (State)—Periodicals.
HG2889.P33B35b 75-645963
MARC-S

Banco de Desenvolvimento do Paraná

see also the earlier heading

Companhia de Desenvolvimento Econômico do Paraná.

Banco de Desenvolvimento do Paraná. Centro de Promoções Econômicas
see Seminário Empresarial do Paraná, Curitiba, 1973. Anais do Seminário Empresarial do Paraná... ⌜Curitiba, 1973 or 4⌝

Banco de Desenvolvimento do Paraná. Departamento de Estudos Econômicos.
Aspectos gerais da infraestrutura paranaense. ⌜Curitiba⌝ 1970.
⌜56⌝ l. maps. 28 cm.
1. Transportation—Brazil—Paraná (State) 2. Electric utilities—Paraná, Brazil (State) 3. Communication and traffic—Brazil—Paraná (State) I. Title.
HE233.Z7P3725 74-206408

Banco de Desenvolvimento do Rio Grande do Norte
see
Banco do Desenvolvimento do Rio Grande do Norte.

Banco de España, Madrid.
Banco de España. Una visita a la planta noble del edificio de Madrid. (Madrid) ⌜1970⌝
29 l. col. illus., fold. plates. 30 cm. Sp 71-July/Aug/Sept
1. Banco de España, Madrid. 2. Banco de España, Madrid—Art collections.
HG3190.M34E733 1970 74-340799

Banco de España, Madrid.
Banco de España, único de emisión, 1874-1974. — Madrid : Banco de España, 1975.
112 p. : ill. ; 24 cm. Sp***
ISBN 8450067588
1. Banco de España, Madrid. I. Title.
HG3186.B29 1975 332.1'1'094641 76-458621
76 MARC

Banco de España, Madrid.
Los billetes del Banco de España, 1782-1974. — ⌜Madrid⌝ : Banco de España, ⌜1974⌝
xvi p., 1 leaf, 404 p. : col. ill. ; 29 cm. Sp74
ISBN 8450064546 : 3000ptas
1. Bank-notes—Spain—History. I. Title.
HG1137.B35 1974 77-454666
77 MARC

Banco de España, Madrid.
Boletín estadístico. Indicadores económicos. 4. trimestre 1974–
[Madrid] Banco de España.
v. 27 cm. quarterly.
Continues: Banco de España, Madrid. Boletín estadístico. Suplemento.
1. Finance—Spain—Statistics—Periodicals. 2. Economic indicators—Spain—Periodicals. I. Banco de España, Madrid. Indicadores económicos. II. Title.
HG3186.B29a 76-648497
MARC-S

Banco de España, Madrid.
Boletín estadístico. Suplemento. 1. trimestre 1973-3. trimestre 1974. [Madrid] Banco de España.
2 v. 27 cm. quarterly.
First issue preceded by an undated supplement covering 1962/72 with title: Boletín estadístico. Suplemento: indicadores económicos.
Continued by: Banco de España, Madrid. Boletín estadístico. Indicadores económicos.
1. Finance—Spain—Statistics—Periodicals. 2. Economic indicators—Spain—Periodicals.
HG3186.B29a 76-648498
MARC-S

Banco de España, Madrid. Indicadores económicos
see Banco de España, Madrid. Boletín estadístico. 4. trimestre 1974- [Madrid]

Banco de España, Madrid.
Mapa bancario.
[Madrid]
v. illus. 22 x 28 cm.
1. Banks and banking—Spain—Directories. 2. Banks and banking—Spain.
HG3183.B26 73-646950
MARC-S

Banco de España, Madrid.
Mapa bancario. Anexo.
[Madrid]
v. 22 x 29 cm.
1. Banks and banking—Spain—Directories—Periodicals.
I. Title.
HG3183.B25a 332.1'025'46 74-646996
MARC-S

Banco de España, Madrid
see Plan anual de expansión bancaria ; memoria. [Madrid]

Banco de España, Madrid
see Spain. Laws, statutes, etc. Spanish credit and banking legislation. [Madrid] Banco de España, 1968.

Banco de Estado do Rio Grande do Sul. Diretoria.
Relatório da Diretoria.
Porto Alegre, Diretoria, Banco do Estado do Rio Grande do Sul.
v. in 15-26 cm. annual.
Title varies slightly.
1. Banco do Estado do Rio Grande do Sul. 2. Banks and banking—Brazil—Rio Grande do Sul (State)—Periodicals.
HG2889.R5B3a 76-642143
MARC-S

Banco de Expansión Industrial
see
Exbank.

Banco de Financiación Industrial.
La banca privada.
[Madrid, etc., Servicio de Estudios]
v. illus. 24 cm.
1. Banks and banking—Spain. 2. Spain—Economic conditions—1918- I. Title.
HG3184.B32a 73-646973
MARC-S

Banco de Fomento Agrícola e Industrial de Cuba, Havana.
Regulations for the issue, custody, redemption drawing and cancellation of securities / Agricultural and Industrial Development Bank of Cuba. — Havana : [s. n.], 1953 (La Habana : Editorial Lex)
31 p. ; 24 cm.
1. Securities—Cuba. I. Title.
HG5252.B35 1953 332.6'32'097291 74-191178
MARC

Banco de Fomento Agropecuario.
Memoria anual—Banco de Fomento Agropecuario.
San Salvador, Banco de Fomento Agropecuario.
v. ill. 28 cm.
1. Banco de Fomento Agropecuario. 2. Agricultural credit—Salvador—Periodicals.
HG2051.S2B28a 75-645994
MARC-S

Banco de Fomento Agropecuario
see Franke, Enrique. The banknotes of the Republica of El Salvador ... San Salvador, 1974.

Banco de Fomento Agropecuario
see also the earlier heading
Salvador. Administración de Bienestar Campesino.

Banco de Fomento Agropecuario del Perú.
Ley organica. Lima, 1968.
47 p.
1. Agricultural credit. Peru. I. Peru. Laws, statutes, etc. II. Title.
DNAL NUC76-71520

Banco de Fomento Nacional.
Investments in Portugal. [3d ed.] Lisbon, 1972.
241 p. illus. 30 cm.
1. Portugal—Economic conditions.—1918- 2. Portugal—Industries. 3. Investments—Portugal. I. Title.
HC392.B26 1972 338'.09469 74-191376
MARC

Banco de Fomento Regional Zulia, Maracaibo
see Guerrero Matheus, Fernando. En la ciudad y el tiempo. [Maracaibo, 1968-70]

Banco de Granada
see Angeles Ortiz, Manuel. Manuel Angeles Ortiz ; obra retrospectiva... Granada [1973]

Banco de Granada.
see El Arbol, a través de un siglo de pintura española, 1874-1974 ... Granada, Banco de Granada, 1974.

Banco de Granada
see Los Artistas por el Sureste de España ... [Granada] Banco de Granada [1973]

Banco de Granada.
see García-Ochoa, Luis. García-Ochoa ... Granada, Banco de Granada, 1975.

Banco de Granada
see Villaseñor, Manuel L , 1924- Villasenor: [exposición], Galería de Exposiciones... [Granada] 1974.

Banco de Guatemala (Founded 1945)
Balanco mensual—Banco de Guatemala.
Guatemala, Banco de Guatemala.
v. in 24 cm.
1. Banco de Guatemala (Founded 1945) 2. Banks and banking—Guatemala—Finance—Periodicals.
HG2746.B34b 76-641556
MARC-S

Banco de Guatemala (Founded 1945)
Estudio económico y memoria de labores.
Guatemala, Banco de Guatemala.
v. 21 cm.
1. Banco de Guatemala (Founded 1945) 2. Guatemala—Economic conditions—1918- —Periodicals. I. Title.
HG2746.B34a 330.9'7281'05 75-642278
MARC-S

Banco de Guatemala (Founded 1945)
Guatemala: sector externo, 1963-1972. [Guatemala, 1973?]
31 p. 21 x 28 cm.
Cover title.
1. Guatemala—Commerce. I. Title.
TxU NUC76-71542

Banco de Guatemala (Founded 1945)
see Guatemala. Laws, statutes, etc. Leyes bancarias y financieras de Guatemala. 2. ed. corr. y aumentada. [Guatemala] 1972.

Banco de Guatemala (Founded 1945). Departamento de Estudios Económicos
see Banco de Guatemala (Founded 1945).

Banco de Investimento do Brasil
see Brazilian performance. Apr. 1975- [São Paulo]

Banco de Italia y Río de la Plata.
100 [i. e. Cien] años al servicio del país, 1872-1972. [Investigación y redacción: Enrique Olmedo Jaquenod. Buenos Aires, 1972]
333, [8] p. illus. 27 cm.
Bibliography: p. [339]-[340] LACAP 72
1. Banco de Italia y Río de la Plata. I. Olmedo Jaquenod, Enrique. II. Title.
HG2870.B84 I 83 73-320681

Banco de la Nación (Peru)
see Peru. Laws, statutes, etc. Reforma tributaria ... [Lima] El Banco, 1973-

Banco de la Nación Argentina, Buenos Aires.
Banco de la Nación Argentina, 1969.
[Buenos Aires, 1970?]
40 p. col. illus., col. maps. 30 cm.
Cover title.
1. Banks and banking-Argentine Republic. I. Title.
TxU NUC73-47437

Banco de la Nación Argentina, Buenos Aires.
El Banco de la Nación Argentina en su 75° aniversario, 1891-1966. [Buenos Aires, 1970]
370, [13] p. illus. 30 cm.
Bibliography: p. [381]-[382]
1. Banco de la Nación Argentina, Buenos Aires. 2. Argentine Republic—Economic conditions. I. Title.
HG2866.B35 73-205749

Banco de la Nación Argentina, Buenos Aires.
Museo Histórico y Numismático. Buenos Aires, 1972.
[28] p. illus. 24 cm. (Its Publicación no. 2) LACAP 73-0750
1. Banco de la Nación Argentina, Buenos Aires. Museo Histórico y Numismático. I. Title. II. Series.
HG2866.B35 1972 73-352754

Banco de la Nación Argentina, Buenos Aires.
Préstamos para actividades agropecuarias, comercio, industria, pesca, actividades diversas. [Buenos Aires, 197-]
70 p. 21 cm.
1. Bank loans--Argentine Republic. I. Title.
TxU NUC77-85477

Banco de la Nación Argentina, Buenos Aires.
Préstamos para las actividades agropecuarias.
[Buenos Aires, 1970]
85 p. 21 cm.
1. Agricultural credit—Argentine Republic. I. Title.
NcD NUC75-19128

Banco de la Nación Argentina, Buenos Aires
see Argentine Republic. Consejo Agrario Nacional. Convenio celebrado... Buenos Aires, 1968.

Banco de la Nación Argentina, Buenos Aires. Museo Histórico y Numismático.
La moneda metálica argentina. [Texto: Arnaldo J. Cunietti-Ferrando, Director del Museo Histórico y Numismático del Banco] Buenos Aires, 1972.
39 p. illus. 26 cm.
LACAP 73-0738
1. Numismatics—Argentine Republic. I. Cunietti-Ferrando, Arnaldo J. II. Title.
CJ2226.B36 73-334198

Banco de la Nación Argentina, Buenos Aires. Subgerencia General de Comercio Exterior.
Cómo iniciarse en las exportaciones. Compaginación, coordinación y comentarios de Osvaldo F. Rando, gerente departamental de comercio exterior. [Buenos Aires, 1973]
67 p. 30 cm.
Errata slip inserted.
1. Export sales-Argentine Republic-Handbooks, manuals, etc. I. Rando, Osvaldo F. II. Title.
TxU NUC76-89159

Banco de la Provincia de Buenos Aires. Archivo y Museo Históricos
see Manuel Belgrano: aportes documentales para la historia de las escuelas que fundo. Buenos Aires, 1970.

Banco de la Provincia de Córdoba.
Consejos de promoción. Córdoba [Argentina] 1967.
43 p. illus. 22 cm.
Microfiche (negative) 1 sheet. 11 x 15 cm. (NYPL FSN 16,337)
1. Córdoba, Argentine Republic (Province)–Economic conditions. 2. Regional planning–Córdoba, Argentine Republic (Province) I. Title.
NN NUC76-71526

Banco de la Provincia de Córdoba. Departamento de Promoción, Publicidad y Estadística.
Córdoba y su banco; breve reseña. [Córdoba] 1961.
15 p. map. 19 cm.
1. Banco de la Provincia de Córdoba. I. Title.
NIC NUC73-59588

Banco de la República, Bogotá.
América Latina y la situación monetaria internacional. Bogotá [1971?]
85 p.
Cover title.
1. Foreign exchange problem–Latin America. 2. Currency question. I. Title.
InU NUC73-113976

Banco de la República, Bogotá.
Analisis preliminar de las cuentas de flujo de fondos financieros de la economia colombiana, 1962-1969. Bogota, 1971.
127 p.
1. Finance–Colombia. 2. Colombia–Econ. condit.–1960- 3. Colombia–Stat. I. Title.
DAU NUC74-27267

Banco de la República, Bogotá.
Catálogo de billetes, 1923-1973; ed. conmemorativa del cincuentenario de la fundación del Banco de la República, Bogotá, Colombia, julio 20 de 1973. Bogotá, Litografía Arco [1973]
1 v. (unpaged) illus. 22 x 30 cm.
1. Paper money–Colombia–Catalogs. I. Title. I. Title.
TxU NUC75-26805

Banco de la República, Bogotá.
El mercado de capitales en Colombia. Bogotá, 1971.
446 p. 28 cm.
1. Capital–Argentine Republic. I. Title.
MU NUC75-26564

Banco de la República, Bogotá
see Barriga Villalba, A M El empréstito de Zea... Bogotá [1969?]

Banco de la República, Bogotá
see Colombia. Laws, statutes, etc. Reforma administrativa 1968 [i.e. mil novecientos sesenta y ocho. Bogotá, Editorial Andés, 1970]

Banco de la Republica, Bogota
see Inversiones extranjeras en Colombia. [Bogotá, Ediciones Continente, 1973?]

Banco de la República, Bogotá.
see Santa Marta 1525-1975 [i.e. mil quinientos veinticinco-mil novecientos setenta y cinco] [Bogotá, Banco de la República, 1975 or 1976]

Banco de la República, Bogotá.
see Simposio sobre Mercado de Capitales, 4th, Medellín, Colombia, 1975. El mercado de capitales en Colombia, 1975. 1. ed. Bogotá, El Banco, 1976.

Banco de la Republica, Bogotá
see Simposio sobre Mercado de Capitales en Colombia a Nivel Técnico, Bogotá, 1971. Documentos producidos. [Bogotá? 1971?]

Banco de la República, Bogotá
see Weitz-Hettelsater Engineers. Economic and engineering study... Kansas City, Mo., Engineers, 1965.

Banco de la República, Bogotá. Biblioteca Luis-Angel Arango.
Catálogo de la Biblioteca Luis-Angel Arango, Fondo Colombia. — Bogotá : Banco de la República, [1972?-
v. ; 28 cm.
Includes indexes.
CONTENTS: v. 1. Comprende: 010 a 339.4986. —v. 4. Comprende: 900 a 987.
1. Banco de la República, Bogotá. Biblioteca Luis-Angel Arango. I. Title.
Z907.B22 1975 75-519527
75 MARC

Banco de la Republica, Bogota. Biblioteca Luis-Angel Arango
see Boletin cultural y bibliografico. 1971- Bogota.

Banco de la Republica, Bogota. Departamento de Credito Agricola.
Estudio de productividad y costo de produccion de cultivos anuales en siete zonas de pais; semestre B - 1970. Elaborado por: Dpto. de Credito Agricola. Coordinacion: Gilberto Idarraga H. Bogota, 1971.
22, 24 l. maps.
At head of title: Fondo Financiero Agrario.
1. Agriculture–Colombia–Costs. 2. Agriculture–Economic aspects–Colombia. I. Idarraga H., Gilberto. II. Banco de la Republica, Bogota. Fondo Financiero Agrario. III. Title.
AzU NUC75-49478

Banco de la República, Bogotá. Departamento de Crédito Agrícola.
Estudio de productividad y costo de producción de cultivos anuales en siete zonas del país, semestre B—1971. Bogotá, 1972.
25, [37] l. map. 28 cm.
LACAP 72-5164
At head of title: Fondo Financiero Agrario.
1. Agriculture—Economic aspects—Colombia. I. Banco de la República, Bogotá. Fondo Financiero Agrario. II. Title.
HD1882.B35 1972 73-335644

Banco de la República, Bogotá. Departamento de Crédito Agrícola.
Estudio de productividad y costo de producción de cultivos anuales en siete zonas del país, semestre A--1972. Bogotá, 1973.
28, [40] l. map. 28 cm.
At head of title: Fondo Financiero Agrario.
1. Agriculture–Economic aspects–Columbia. I. Banco de la República, Bogotá. Fondo Financiero Agrario. II. Title.
TxU NUC75-75510

Banco de la República, Bogotá. Departamento de Crédito Agrícola. Fondo Financiero Agrario
see
Banco de la República, Bogotá. Fondo Financiero Agrario.

Banco de la Republica, Bogota. Departamento de Credito Externo
see Fondo de Promoción de Exportaciones. Directorio de exportadores, Colombia 1973. Bogotá [1973]

Banco de la República, Bogotá. Departamento de Investigaciones Económicas.
Colombia, the investor's guide. — Bogotá : Banco de la Republica, Economic Research Dept., 1974.
138 p. : ill., maps (1 fold. in pocket) ; 13 cm.
1. Colombia—Economic conditions—1970- I. Title.
HC197.B273 1974 330.9'861 76-381044
76 MARC

Banco de la República, Bogotá. Departamento de Investigaciones Económicas.
Cuentas nacionales, 1950-1967. [Bogotá? 1968?]
59 l. illus. 24 x 33 cm.
1. Colombia–Economic conditions–1918–Statistics. I. Title.
NjP TxU NNC PPT CLU NUC73-2186

Banco de la República, Bogota. Departamento de Investigaciones Económicas.
Cuentas nacionales, 1967 a 1969. Bogotá [1970?]
32 l. 22 x 28 cm.
Cover title.
DPU NUC73-112461

Banco de la República, Bogotá. Departamento de Investigaciones Económicas.
Disposiciones económicas.
Bogotá.
v. 25 cm. annual.
1. Industrial laws and legislation—Colombia—Digests. 2. Law—Colombia—Digests.
58-35898
MARC-S

Banco de la República, Bogotá. Departamento de Investigaciones Económicas.
Indice económico : selección de artículos de las publicaciones recibidas por la Biblioteca y Hemeroteca durante el año de 1971. — [Bogotá] : Banco de la República, Departamento de Investigaciones Económicas, [1975]
276 p. ; 28 cm.
Includes indexes.
1. Economic history—1945- —Periodicals—Indexes. 2. Economics—Periodicals—Indexes. I. Banco de la República, Bogotá. Departamento de Investigaciones Económicas. Biblioteca y Hemeroteca. II. Title.
Z7164.E2B23 1975 75-514745
75 MARC

Banco de la República, Bogotá. Departamento de Investigaciones Económicas.
Metodología del índice de precios al por mayor del comercio en general, base 1970=100 / Banco de la República, Departamento de Investigaciones Económicas. -- Bogotá : El Departamento, 1975.
173 p. : ill. ; 23 cm.
1. Price indexes. 2. Prices--Colombia. I. Title.
TxU NUC77-86646

Banco de la República, Bogotá. Departamento de Investigaciones Económicas.
Registros de exportación e importación.
[Bogotá]
v. 20 x 28 cm.
"Plan Vallejo y demás."
1. Colombia—Commerce. 2. Commercial products—Colombia—Classification. I. Title.
HF167.B33a 74-642952
MARC-S

Banco de la República, Bogotá. Departamento de Investigaciones Económicas.
Series estadísticas y gráficos.
v. illus. 20 x 28 cm.
LACAP 68-2828
1. Colombia—Economic conditions—1918- 2. Colombia—Statistics. I. Title.
HC197.B274a 330.9'861 78-380298
rev MARC-S

Banco de la República, Bogotá. Departamento de Investigaciones Económicas. Biblioteca y Hemeroteca.
see Banco de la República, Bogotá. Departamento de Investigaciones Económicas. Indice económico ... [Bogotá] Banco de la República, Departamento de Investigaciones Económicas, [1975]

Banco de la República, Bogotá. División Jurídica
see Colombia. Junta Monetaria. Disposiciones vigentes sobre moneda y cambio exterior... [Bogotá] Tall. Gráf. Banco de la Repúlica, 1971.

Banco de la República, Bogotá. División Jurídica
see Colombia. Laws, statutes, etc. Compilación de disposiciones orgánicas de las instituciones financieras. Bogotá, 1972-

Banco de la República, Bogotá. Fondo de los Empleados.
Informes estatutarios a la Asamblea General del Fondo de los Empleados del Banco de la República. [Bogotá] 1968.
46 p. illus. 24 cm.
1. Banks and banking, Cooperative–Colombia. 2. Bank employees–Colombia. I. Title.
TxU NUC76-36321

Banco de la Republica, Bogotá. Fondo de Promoción de Exportaciones.
Compilación de documentos relacionados con el Acuerdo de Cartagena. Bogotá, 1971.
158 p. 25 cm.
Cover title.
1. Acuerdo de Cartagena. I. Title.
MU NUC75-26573

Banco de la Republica, Bogota. Fondo Financiero Agrario
see Banco de la Republica, Bogota. Departamento de Credito Agricola. Estudio de productividad... Bogota, 1971.

Banco de la República, Bogotá. Fondo Financiero Agrario
see Banco de la República, Bogotá. Departamento de Crédito Agrícola. Estudio de productividad ... Bogotá, 1973.

Banco de la República, Bogotá. Fondo Financiero Agrario
see Banco de la República, Bogotá. Departamento de Crédito Agrícola. Estudio de productividad y costo de producción de cultivos anuales en siete zonas del país, semestre B—1971. Bogotá, 1972.

Banco de la República, Bogotá. Junta Directiva
see Colombia. Junta Monetaria. Disposiciones vigentes sobre moneda y cambio exterior... [Bogotá] Tall, Gráf. Banco de la República, 1971.

Banco de la República, Bogotá. Museo del Oro.
100 [i. e. Cien] obras maestras del Museo de Oro de Colombia. México [Museo Nacional de Antropología] 1967.
34 p. illus.
1. Goldsmithing—Colombia. 2. Colombia—Antiq. I. Title.
UU NUC75-26568

Banco de la República, Bogotá. Museo del Oro.
El Dorado. Bogotá [1973]
1 v. (unpaged) illus. 25 cm.
Includes bibliography.
1. Indians of South America—Colombia—Gold-smithing. 2. Colombia—Antiquities. I. Title.
F2270.1.G57B36 1970 739.2'27801 74-219624

Banco de la República, Bogotá. Museo del Oro
see Colombian Center. The treasures of El Dorado. [New York, 196-]

Banco de la República, Bogotá. Museo del Oro
see El Dorado, the gold of ancient Colombia from El Museo del Oro, Banco de la República, Bogotá, Colombia... [New York, Center for Inter-American Relations, 1974]

Banco de la República, Bogotá. Museo del Oro
see Le Musée de l'or de Bogota. [Paris] Petit Palais [1973]

Banco de la República, Bogotá. Museo del Oro
see Seiler-Baldinger, Annemarie. El Dorado ... Basel: Schweizerischer Bankverein, 1974.

Banco de la República Oriental del Uruguay.
Boletín trimestral. v. 1-
jun. 1970-
[Montevideo]
v. 26 cm.
LACAP 70-4980
1. Uruguay—Economic conditions—1945- —Periodicals.
HC231.B276 73-612726
rev MARC-S

Banco de la República Oriental del Uruguay.
see Morató, Octavio, 1871-1943. Al servicio del Banco de la República y de la economía uruguaya, 1896-1940. Montevideo, [s.n.,] 1976.

Banco de la Vivienda (Puerto Rico)
see Puerto Rico. Laws, statutes, etc. Compilación de leyes... [San Juan, P. R., 1968?]

Banco de Londres y México
see La Ciudad de México. México, D. F. [1969?]

Banco de Londres Y Río de la Plata
see
Bank of London and South America Limited.

Banco de los Trabajadores, Guatemala.
Banco de los Trabajadores. Guatemala [Secretaría de Información] 1965.
16 p. 21 cm.
Cover title.
At head of title: Obra del Gobierno Militar.
1. Banks and banking—Guatemala.
TxU NUC75-58864

Banco de México (Founded 1925)
Annual report.
Mexico.
v. 23 cm.
"Submitted by the Board of Directors of the Bank of Mexico, to the ... General Stockholders' Meeting."
HG2720.M44B3 332.1'0972 72-625245

Banco de México (Founded 1925)
El crédito al consumo en Monterrey, N. L., 1967. [Trabajo realizado bajo la dirección de Consuelo Meyer L.] México, Banco de México, Oficina Técnica de la Dirección, Estudios Monetarios y Crediticios de Carácter Especial, 1973.
2 v. (cxxxii, 1050 p.) 28 cm.
Bibliography: v. 2, p. 991-1009.
— —Apéndice estadístico. México, Banco de México, Oficina Técnica de la Dirección, Estudios Monetarios y Crediticios de Carácter Especial, 1972.
3 v. 28 cm.
TxU NUC75-128461

Banco de México (Founded 1925)
Disposiciones sobre divisas, oro, plata, pagos al amparo de convenios, financiamientos del extranjero y comercio exterior. [México, 1972-
v. (loose-leaf) 22 cm.
Cover title.
1. Commerce—Mexico. 2. Foreign exchange—Mexico. I. Title.
MH-L NUC73-113983

Banco de México (Founded 1925). Biblioteca.
Bibliografía monetaria y bancaria de México (1943-1958). México, 1965.
64 p. 21 cm. (Its Serie de bibliografías especiales, no. 6)
1. Money—Mexico—Bibliography. 2. Banks and banking—Mexico—Bibliography. 3. Finance—Mexico—Bibliography. I. Title. II. Series.
Z7165.M45B273 72-226823

Banco de Mexico (Founded 1925). Departamento de Investigaciones Industriales.
Bibliografía industrial de Mexico, 1970. México, Oficina Editorial, 1971.
432 p. 20 cm.
1. Mexico—Industries—Bibliography. I. Title.
IEN NUC73-113984

Banco de México (Founded 1925). Departamento de Investigaciones Industriales. Oficina de Economía Industrial
see
Banco de México (Founded 1925). Oficina de Economía Industrial.

Banco de Mexico (Founded 1925). Departamento de Investigaciones Industriales. Oficina de Planeación Industrial
see Banco de México (Founded 1925). Oficina de Planeación Industrial.

Banco de México (Founded 1925). Gerencia de Investigación Económica.
Indicadores económicos. v. 1-
dic. 1972-
[México]
v. 22 x 28 cm. monthly.
1. Economic indicators—Mexico—Periodicals. I. Title.
HC131.B28a 330.9'72'082 74-646614
MARC-S

Banco de México (Founded 1925). Investigaciones Industriales, Departamento de
see
Banco de México (Founded 1925). Departamento de Investigaciones Industriales.

Banco de México (Founded 1925). Oficina de Economía Industrial.
La estructura industrial de México en 1960. [México, 1967]
285 p. illus. 28 cm.
1. Mexico—Industries. I. Title.
HC135.B2185 1967 74-204655

Banco de México (Founded 1925). Oficina de Planeación Industrial.
La estructura industrial de México en 1950. México [1958?]
159 p. illus. (part col.)
"Director de la investigación: Fausto Urencio."
1. Mexico—Indus.—Stat. I. Urencio, Fausto. II. Title.
PPiU NUC73-109067

Banco de México (Founded 1925). Subdirección de Investigación Económica y Bancaria.
Indicadores económicos. v. 4-
dic. 1975-
México, Subdirección de Investigación Económica y Bancaria.
v. 22 x 29 cm. monthly.
Continues: Banco de México (Founded 1925). Gerencia de Investigación Económica. Indicadores económicos.
1. Economic indicators—Mexico—Periodicals. I. Title.
HC131.B28a 330.9'72'082 76-645001
MARC-S

Banco de Nordeste do Brasil, Fortaleza. Departamento de Estudos Economicos do Nordeste.
Crescimento demográfico dos estados do Nordeste, 1940-1970. Fortaleza-Ceará, 1971.
104 p. 21 cm. (P[ublicação] 203)
"Monografias elaboradas pelo TDE Hélio Augusto de Moura, coordenador do grupo."
1. Brazil, Northeast—Population. 2. Brazil—Population. I. Moura, Helio Augusto de. II. Title. III. Series: Banco do Nordeste do Brasil, Fortaleza. Publicação, 203.
NNC NUC74-160208

Banco de Previsión Social (Uruguay)
Manual de funciones y procedimientos de capacitación. Elaboración y redacción: Néfert Amorín de Carro [et al.] Montevideo, Departamento de Prensa y Propaganda del Banco de Previsión Social, 1973.
31 p. illus. 19 cm. (Gerencia General Técnica. Manual, 1)
I. Amorín de Carro, Néfert.
TxU NUC75-65848

Banco de Previsión Social (Uruguay)
Manual: reglamentos de certificaciones y de expedición de constancias y certificados. Elaboración y redacción: Enrique Arezo, Pedro Calero [y] Narciso Graña. Montevideo, 1972.
15 p. 19 cm. $2.00
LACAP 73-0670
Cover title: Manual: certificados.
1. Legal documents—Uruguay. I. Arezo, Enrique. II. Calero, Pedro. III. Graña, Narciso. IV. Title. V. Title: Manual: certificados.
74-319403

Banco de Previsión Social (Uruguay)
see Ferreria Badaró, Roberto, comp. Régimen policial. Montevideo, Departamento de Prensa y Propaganda del Banco de Previsión Social, 1972.

Banco de Previsión Social (Uruguay)
see Uruguay. Laws, statutes, etc. Leyes, decretos y resoluciones... [Montevideo, 1973]

Banco de Previsión Social (Uruguay). Departamento de Prensa y Propaganda
For publications of
the Banco de Previsión Social
issued by this body see
Banco de Previsión Social (Uruguay).

Banco de Río Negro. [Fray Bentos, 1959?]
[8] p. illus. 27 cm.
1. Banks and banking—Rio Negro, Uruguay (Dept.)
TxU NUC74-166313

Banco de Río Negro y Neuquén.
Estatutos. General Roca, 1970.
12 p. 20 cm.
1. Banco de Río Negro y Neuquén.
TxU NUC76-84411

Banco de Santander.
Foreign investments in Spain. [Santander, 1973]
38 p. 21 cm. Sp***
Cover title.
Translation of Inversiones extranjeras en España.
1. Investments, Foreign—Spain. 2. Investments, Foreign—Law and legislation—Spain. I. Title.
HG5632.B3213 1973 332.6'73'0946 74-150149
MARC

Banco de Santander.
El impuesto sobre los rendimientos del trabajo personal y los profesionales. — [Santander] : Banco de Santander, [1974]
27 p. ; 30 cm. Sp***
Cover title.
1. Professions—Taxation—Spain. 2. Professions—Licenses—Spain. I. Title.
76-505054

Banco de Santander
see Botín, Emilio. Informe de Emilio Botín a la Junta General, el 17 de junio de 1972 ... [Santander] [1972]

Banco de Santander
see Topeza, Victor H Business opportunities in Spain. [Santander, 1972]

Banco de Seguros del Estado, Montevideo. Gestión del directorio. Montevideo [n.d.]
1 v. 24 cm.
TxU NUC75-26698

Banco de Venezuela, Caracas.
Economía y finanzas.
[Caracas] Banco de Venezuela.
v. ill. 28 cm.
"Boletín Mensual."
Continues: Banco de Venezuela, Caracas. Boletín de economía y finanzas.
1. Venezuela—Economic conditions—1918- —Periodicals. 2. Finance—Venezuela—Periodicals. 3. Banks and banking—Venezuela—Periodicals. I. Title.
HC236.B33 75-647863
MARC-S

Banco de Venezuela, Caracas
see Sucre, Antonio José de, Pres. Bolivia, 1795-1830. Archivo de Sucre. Caracas, 1973-

Banco de Vizcaya.
Dividendos e intereses, ampliaciones de capital.
[Bilbao] Banco de Vizcaya.
v. 21 cm.
"Impuesto general sobre la renta de las personas físicas."
1. Dividends—Spain. 2. Corporations—Spain—Finance. I. Title.
HG4216.B35a 75-647945
MARC-S

Banco de Vizcaya.
Informe de la OCDE sobre la situación y perspectivas de la economía española.
[Bilbao]
v. 21 cm.
1. Spain—Economic conditions—1918- —Periodicals. 2. Spain—Economic policy—Periodicals. I. Organization for Economic Cooperation and Development. II. Title.
HC381.B3355a 74-647084
MARC-S

Banco de Vizcaya.
see Cámara Oficial de Comercio, Industria y Navegación de Santa Cruz de Tenerife. En torno a la bolsa. [Santa Cruz de Tenerife] Instituto Tinerfeño de Expansión Económica, [1975?]

Banco del Caribe, Caracas.
Venezuela: su economía en hechos y cifras. 1960/63-
[Caracas, Ediciones Banco del Caribe]
v. 24 cm.
Began with vol. for 1960/63.
1. Venezuela—Economic conditions—1918- I. Title.
HC236.B34a 66-52900
MARC-S

Banco del Estado de Chile.
Revista—Banco del Estado de Chile.
[Santiago de Chile]
v. illus. 29 cm.
1. Chile—Economic conditions—1918- —Periodicals. 2. Banks and banking—Chile—Periodicals. 3. Chile—Social conditions—Periodicals.
HC191.B33a 74-643294
MARC-S

Banco del Estado de Chile. Departamento de Política Financiera y Económica
see Morales, Marcelo. Evolución de las reformas financieras en Chile. [Santiago de Chile : Banco del Estado de Chile], 1971.

Banco del Libro.
Informe bienal.
Caracas.
v. 28 cm.
1. Banco del Libro.
Z786.B3514 74-642294
MARC-S

Banco del Libro. Biblioteca Pedagógica Daniel Navea
see
Biblioteca Pedagógica Daniel Navea.

Banco del Norte.
Estudio económico de la provincia de Málaga. (Madrid) Banco del Norte (1972)
186 p. 28 cm. Sp 73-Feb
Cover title.
1. Málaga, Spain (Province)—Economic conditions. 2. Málaga, Spain (Province)—Social conditions. I. Title.
HC387.M3B35 1972 73-347016

Banco di Chiavari e della Riviera Ligure.
1911/1925 [i.e. Mille e novecento undici/mille e novecento venticinque] Genova; cultura di una città, 30 magg.-30 giugno 1973 [Banco di Chiavari e della Riviera Ligure. Comitato organizzatore: Giuseppe Capone (et al.). Genova] 1973.
102 p. illus.
1. Art, Italian—Exhibitions. 2. Art, Modern—20th century—Genoa. I. Capone, Giuseppe. II. Title.
ViBlbV NUC76-84415

Banco di Napoli.
L'archivio storico del Banco di Napoli. Una fonte preziosa per la storia economica sociale e artistica del Mezzogiorno d'Italia. [Napoli], Banco di Napoli, 1972.
181 p. illus., plates, tables. 24 cm. It 73-Apr
Bibliography: p. 179-181.
1. Banco di Napoli. 2. Banks and banking—Naples—History. I. Title.
HG3090.N44B36 1972 73-353458

Banco di Napoli.
Il Centro elettronico. — [Napoli] : Banco di Napoli, 1962.
78 p. : ill. ; 23 cm.
1. Banco di Napoli. 2. Electronic data processing—Banks and banking. I. Title.
HG3090.N4B24 1962 75-575280

Banco di Napoli.
La collezione del Banco di Napoli. — Napoli : Soprintendenza alle gallerie della Campania, 1960.
23 p. ; 24 cm.
At head of title: Museo e gallerie nazionali di Capodimonte.
1. Paintings, Italian — Catalogs. 2. Paintings, Modern — Italy — Catalogs. 3. Banco di Napoli—Art collections. I. Naples. Museo e gallerie nazionali di Capodimonte. II. Title.
ND614.B3 75-537574

Banco di Napoli
see La Rassegna economica del Banco di Napoli, 1931-1971. [Napoli, 1975]

Banco di Napoli
see Xenion: nature morte e paesaggi campani. [Napoli, 1958]

Banco di Roma
see Euro cooperation; economic studies on Europe. [Paris]

Banco di Roma
see Heltzer, Harry. International integration... [Roma] 1974.

Banco di Roma
see The Journal of European economic history. spring 1972- Rome.

Banco di Roma
see Tributi delle società in Italia... Roma, 1971.

Banco di Roma per la Svizzera
see Donati, Ugo. Artisti Ticinesi a Venezia dal XV al SVIII secolo. Lugano [1961]

Banco di Sardegna.
see Le Garanzie reali e personali nei contratti bancari. Milano, A. Giuffrè, 1976.

Banco di Sicilia. Galleria
see
Galleria del Banco di Sicilia.

Banco di Sicilia. Saloni d'esposizioni
see Ente zolfi italiani. Premio Ente zolfi italiani... [Palermo, 1961]

Banco di Sicilia. Servizio studi.
see 50 [i.e. Cinquanta] anni di commercio estero della Sicilia 1924-1973. Palermo, Servizio studi del Banco di Sicilia, [1976]

Banco do Brasil (1905-)
Diretrizes para uma política de desenvolvimento rural. [Brasilia] 1967.
95 p. illus.
1. Agricultural policies and programs. Brazil. 2. Agriculture. Economic aspects. Brazil. I. Jost, Nestor. II. Title.
DNAL NUC74-29742

Banco do Brasil (1905-)
Resenha econômico financeira do Estado de São Paulo. [Rio de Janeiro] Banco do Brasil.
v. 24 cm.
1. São Paulo, Brazil (State)—Economic conditions. 2. Finance—Brazil—São Paulo (State) 3. Banco do Brazil (1905-) I. Title.
HC188.S3B36a 76-647809
MARC-S

Banco do Brasil (1905-)
see Brazil. Laws, statutes, etc. Capitais estrangeiros no Brasil. [Rio de Janeiro, 1968]

Banco do Brasil (1905-)
see Brazil. Laws, statutes, etc. Legislação de capitais estrangeiros. [Rio de Janeiro, 1966?]

Banco do Brasil (1905-). Carteira de Comercio Exterior
see Brazil. Carteira de Comercio Exterior.

Banco do Brasil (1905-). Departamento Geral de Importação.
Manual do importador brasileiro. [Rio de Janeiro] Banco do Brasil S.A., Carteira de Comércio Exterior [1973]
vii, 98 p. 25 cm.
1. Brazil—Commerce—Handbooks, manuals, etc. 2. Foreign trade regulation—Brazil. I. Brazil. Carteira de Comercio Exterior. II. Title.
TxU NUC76-102622

Banco do Brasil (1905–). Museu, Arquivo Histórico e Biblioteca.
A cultura grega através da moeda. — ⌐Rio de Janeiro⌐ : Banco do Brasil, Museu, Arquivo Histórico e Biblioteca, ⌐1970 or 1971⌐
88 p. : ill. ; 23 cm.
1. Civilization, Greek—Exhibitions. 2. Coins, Greek—Exhibitions. I. Title.
DF79.B25 1970 76-514654

Banco do Desenvolvimento do Espírito Santo
see Rodrigues, Lelio. Perspectivas de modernização da agricultura no Estado do Espírito Santo/Brasil. Vitoria [i.e. 1972]

Banco do Desenvolvimento do Rio Grande do Norte.
Implantação de um parque têxtil no Estado do Rio Grande do Norte / Banco do Desenvolvimento do Rio Grande do Norte S. A. — BDRN. — Natal : o Banco, 1971.
114 p. : ill. ; 28 cm.
Includes bibliographical references.
1. Textile industry—Rio Grande do Norte, Brazil (State) I. Title.
HD9864.B83R582 1971 75-529646

Banco do Estado da Guanabara.
Relatórios do exercício—BEG, COPEG.
⌐Rio de Janeiro⌐ BEG.
v. ill. 28 cm.
1. Banco do Estado da Guanabara. 2. Companhia Progresso do Estado da Guanabara. I. Companhia Progresso do Estado da Guanabara. Relatórios do exercício—BEG, COPEG.
HG2889.G8B35a 332.1'224'09815 75-640749
MARC-S

Banco do Estado de Goiás.
Relatório anual—Banco do Estado de Goiás.
⌐Goiânia⌐ Banco do Estado de Goiás.
v. ill. 22 x 31 cm.
1. Banco do Estado de Goiás.
HG2889.G6B35a 75-648520
MARC-S

Banco do Estado de Mato Grosso. Diretoria.
Relatório anual—Banco do Estado de Mato Grosso, Diretoria.
⌐Cuiabá⌐ Banco do Estado de Mato Grosso, Diretoria.
v. ill. 23 x 31 cm.
1. Banco do Estado de Mato Grosso.
HG2889.M37B36a 75-647558
MARC-S

Banco do Estado de Pernambuco.
BANDEPE relatório.
⌐Recife⌐
v. illus. 27 cm. annual.
Summary in English.
1. Banco do Estado de Pernambuco. I. Title.
HG2889.P47B35 73-642209
MARC-S

Banco do Estado de Pernambuco

For works by this body issued under its earlier name see

Banco de Desenvolvimento do Estado de Pernambuco.

Banco do Estado de Santa Catarina.
Relatório—Banco do Estado de Santa Catarina.
⌐Florianópolis⌐ Banco do Estado de Santa Catarina.
v. ill. 28 cm.
1. Banco do Estado de Santa Catarina. 2. Santa Catarina, Brazil—Economic conditions—Periodicals.
HG2889.S27B35a 75-643391
MARC-S

Banco do Estado de Santa Catarina.
Santa Catarina: Desempenho da economia.
⌐Florianópolis, s. n.⌐
v. ill. 21 cm.
Vols. for issued with the Secretaria da Fazenda, and the Secretaria do Desenvolvimento.
1. Santa Catarina, Brazil—Economic conditions—Periodicals. I. Santa Catarina, Brazil. Secretaria da Fazenda. II. Santa Catarina, Brazil. Secretaria do Desenvolvimento Econômico. III. Title.
HC188.S26B3a 75-645013
MARC-S

Banco do Estado de São Paulo.
Annual report—Banco do Estado de São Paulo.
⌐São Paulo⌐ Banco do Estado de São Paulo.
v. in ill. 30 cm.
1. Banco do Estado de São Paulo.
HG2890.S34B38a 75-646756
MARC-S

Banco do Estado de São Paulo
see Simonsen Associados. Trends in the automotive industry. [São Paulo] 1973.

Banco do Estado do Acre.
Relatório—Banco do Estado do Acre.
⌐Rio Branco⌐ Banco do Estado do Acre.
v. 23 x 33 cm.
1. Banco do Estado do Acre.
HG2889.A25B35a 75-648985
MARC-S

Banco do Estado do Amazonas.
BEA, Banco do Estado do Amazons / Banco do Estado do Amazonas. — ⌐Manaus⌐ : B.E.A., ⌐1974 or 1975⌐
48, ⌐15⌐ p. : chiefly col. ill. ; 28 cm.
Cover title.
1. Banco do Estado do Amazonas. 2. Banks and banking—Amazonas, Brazil.
HG2889.A5B36 1974 75-512718
75 MARC

Banco do Estado do Piauí.
Programa especial de financiamento da cultura do algodão no Estado do Piauí / Banco do Estado do Piauí S. A. — Teresina : O Banco, 1974.
⌐37⌐ leaves : ill. ; 26 cm.
1. Cotton trade—Piauí, Brazil. 2. Agricultural credit—Brazil—Piauí. I. Title.
HD9084.B62P52 1974 75-584623

Banco do Estado do Piauí.
Relatório—Banco do Estado do Piauí.
⌐Teresina⌐ Banco do Estado do Piauí.
v. ill. 24-28 cm.
1. Banco do Estado do Piauí.
HG2889.P5B35a 75-644508
MARC-S

Banco do Estado do Rio Grande do Sul. Assessoria Técnica.
Estrutura do sistema financeiro nacional. ⌐Pôrto Alegre, 1969⌐
82 l. 32 cm.
Cover title.
"Trabalho elaborado pela Assessoria Técnica do Banco do Estado do Rio Grande do Sul, S. A., destinado ao I Curso de Aperfeiçoamento para Administradores, de caráter interno, promovido pelo Centro de Estudos de Administração e Finanças."
1. Financial institutions—Brazil. I. Title.
HG185.B7B35 72-223076

Banco do Nordeste do Brasil, Fortaleza.
Abacaxi nordestino : pesquisa de mercado na Europa e Estados Unidos / Banco do Nordeste do Brasil. — Fortaleza : O Banco, 1973.
230 p., ⌐8⌐ leaves of plates : ill. ; 23 cm. — (Its ⌐Publicações⌐ ; 224)
1. Pineapple—Brazil, Northeast. I. Title. II. Series: Banco do Nordeste do Brasil, Fortaleza. Publicações ; 224.
HD9259.P53B36 1973 75-553579

Banco do Nordeste do Brasil, Fortaleza.
BNB, 21 [i. e. vinte e um] anos; maioridade no desenvolvimento. [Fortaleza, 1973?]
30 p. 21 cm.
1. Banco do Nordeste do Brasil, Fortaleza. I. Title.
TxU NUC76-71548

Banco do Nordeste do Brasil, Fortaleza.
O Banco do Nordeste e o desenvolvimento regional. ⌐Fortaleza, 19⌐72.
55 p. illus. 22 cm.
"Contribuição do BNB ao IX Congresso Nacional de Bancos, São Paulo, out/72."
1. Banco do Nordeste do Brasil, Fortaleza. 2. Brazil, Northeast—Economic conditions. I. Title.
HG2890.F64B3 1972 74-223238

Banco do Nordeste do Brasil, Fortaleza.
Distribuição espacial dos serviços de crédito agrícola / Banco do Nordeste do Brasil S. A. — ⌐Fortaleza⌐ : BNB, ⌐1967?⌐
67 p. : chiefly ill. (some col.) ; 44 cm.
Cover title.
Portuguese and English.
Part of illustrative matter in pocket.
Bibliography: p. 67.
1. Agricultural credit—Brazil, Northeast. 2. Agriculture—Economic aspects—Brazil, Northeast. I. Title.
HG2051.B7B28 1967 332.7'1'09813 75-573126

Banco do Nordeste do Brasil, Fortaleza.
Estudo economico do Municipio de Caruaru. Fortaleza, 1965.
63 p. tables. 28 cm.
At head of title: ETENE.
1. Caruaru, Brazil—Economic conditions. I. Banco do Nordeste do Brasil, Fortaleza. Departemento de Estudos Econômicos do Nordeste.
CtY-E NUC75-9274

Banco do Nordeste do Brasil, Fortaleza.
Investment opportunities in Northeast Brazil / Banco do Nordeste do Brasil. — Fortaleza : O Banco, 1975.
52 p. : ill. ; 21 cm.
At head of title: Superintendência do Desenvolvimento do Nordeste-SUDENE (Superintendency for the Development of the Northeast)
1. Brazil, Northeast—Economic conditions. 2. Investments, Foreign—Brazil, Northeast. 3. Brazil, Northeast—Industries. I. Brazil. Superintendência do Desenvolvimento do Nordeste. II. Title.
HC187.B266 1975 338'.0981'3 76-465893
76 MARC

Banco do Nordeste do Brasil, Fortaleza.
Oportunidades de investimentos no Nordeste, indústria de confecções. — ⌐Fortaleza⌐ : Banco do Nordeste do Brasil, ⌐1975?⌐
58 leaves ; 28 cm.
Cover title.
On cover: SEPLAN, SUDENE.
1. Clothing trade—Brazil, Northeast. 2. Brazil, Northeast—Industries. 3. Industrial promotion—Brazil, Northeast. I. Brazil. Secretaria de Planejamento. II. Brazil. Superintendência do Desenvolvimento do Nordeste. III. Title.
HD9940.B82B35 1975 77-483502
77 MARC

Banco do Nordeste do Brasil, Fortaleza.
Oportunidades de investimentos no Nordeste, indústria de couros e peles. — ⌐Fortaleza⌐ : Banco do Nordeste do Brasil, ⌐1975?⌐
65 leaves ; 28 cm.
Cover title.
On cover: SEPLAN, SUDENE.
1. Hides and skins industry—Brazil, Northeast. 2. Brazil, Northeast—Industries. 3. Industrial promotion—Brazil, Northeast. I. Brazil. Secretaria de Planejamento. II. Brazil. Superintendência do Desenvolvimento do Nordeste. III. Title.
HD9778.B72B35 1975 77-483504
77 MARC

Banco do Nordeste do Brasil, Fortaleza.
Oportunidades de investimentos no Nordeste, produtos alimentares. — ⌐Fortaleza⌐ : Banco do Nordeste do Brasil, ⌐1975?⌐
60 leaves ; 28 cm.
Cover title.
On cover: SEPLAN, SUDENE.
1. Food industry and trade—Brazil, Northeast. 2. Agriculture and state—Brazil, Northeast. 3. Brazil, Northeast—Industries. 4. Industrial promotion—Brazil, Northeast. I. Brazil. Secretaria de Planejamento. II. Brazil. Superintendência do Desenvolvimento do Nordeste. III. Title.
HD9014.B82B35 1975 77-483503
77 MARC

Banco do Nordeste do Brasil, Fortaleza.
Perspectivas de desenvolvimento do Nordeste até 1980; síntese. ⌐Fortaleza, 1972?–
v. 23 cm.
Includes bibliographical references.
1. Brazil, Northeast—Economic conditions. 2. Brazil, Northeast—Economic policy. I. Title.
HC187.B266 1972 73-213951

Banco do Nordeste do Brasil, Fortaleza.
Plano trienal.
⌐Fortaleza⌐ Banco do Nordeste do Brasil.
v. 29 cm.
1. Banco do Nordeste do Brazil, Fortaleza.
HG2890.F64B326a 75-648562
MARC-S

Banco do Nordeste do Brasil, Fortaleza
see Costa, Rubens Vaz da. O desenvolvimento regional no Brasil e no mundo Fortaleza-Ceará, 1969.

Banco do Nordeste do Brasil, Fortaleza
see Costa, Rubens Vaz da. A economia do Nordeste... Fortaleza, 1968.

Banco do Nordeste do Brasil, Fortaleza
see Costa, Rubens Vaz da. Financial evaluation of the fiscal incentives system... Fortaleza-Ceara, 1968.

Banco do Nordeste do Brasil, Fortaleza
see Costa, Rubens Vaz da. O Nordeste em marcha. 3. ed. Fortaleza, 1972.

Banco do Nordeste do Brasil, Fortaleza
see Costa, Rubens Vaz da. Política monetária. [2. impressão. Fortaleza-Ceará, 1968]

Banco do Nordeste do Brasil, Fortaleza
see Mais capital para o desenvolvimento do Nordeste... ⌐Rio de Janeiro, 1968?⌐

Banco do Nordeste do Brasil, Fortaleza. Departamento de Estudos Econômicos do Nordeste.
A agro-indústria do caju no Hordeste: situação atual e perspectivas. Fortaleza, 1973.
220 p. illus., fold. maps. 23 cm.
Summary in English.
Bibliography: p. 191–193.
1. Cashew nut industry—Brazil, Northeast. I. Title.
HD9259.C33B72 1973 74–223032

Banco do Nordeste do Brasil, Fortaleza. Departamento de Estudos Econômicos do Nordeste.
Análise conjuntural da economia Nordestina.
Fortaleza.
no. ill. 21 cm.
1. Brazil, Northeast—Economic conditions—Periodicals.
I. Title.
HC186.B325a 330.9'81'306 74–647277
MARC-S

Banco do Nordeste do Brasil, Fortaleza. Departamento de Estudos Econômicos do Nordeste.
Bacia leiteira de Alagoas; análise de uma função de produção de leite. ₍Elaborado pelo economista J. Josi da Silva₎ Fortaleza, 1969.
43 p. 28 cm. (Banco do Nordeste do Brasil, S. A. P₍ublicações₎ 173)
"Segunda etapa do Relatório sôbre Aspectos econômicos da bacia leiteira de Alagoas."
1. Dairying—Brazil—Alagoas (State) I. Silva, José Josi da. II. Title. III. Series: Banco do Nordeste do Brasil, Fortaleza. Publicações, 173.
SF233.B7B3 1969 76–523673

Banco do Nordeste do Brasil, Fortaleza. Departamento de Estudos Econômicos do Nordeste.
Café, uma nova oportunidade agrícola no Nordeste / Banco do Nordeste do Brasil S. A., Departamento de Estudos Econômicos do Nordeste (ETENE). — Fortaleza : Banco do Nordeste do Brasil S. A., 1973.
94 p. : ill. ; 22 cm.
Bibliography: p. 78.
1. Coffee trade—Brazil. 2. Coffee—Brazil. I. Title.
HD9199.B7B35 1973 75–584619

Banco do Nordeste do Brasil, Fortaleza. Departamento de Estudos Econômicos do Nordeste.
A carnaubeira e seu papel como uma planta econômica. Fortaleza ₍1972₎
104 p. illus. 22 cm. (Banco do Nordeste do Brasil. P₍ublicação₎ 207)
Bibliography: p. 97–104.
1. Wax palm of Brazil. I. Title. II. Series: Banco do Nordeste do Brasil, Fortaleza. Publicações, 207.
SB299.W3B27 1972 73–213552

Banco do Nordeste do Brasil, Fortaleza. Departamento de Estudos Econômicos do Nordeste.
Consumo de produtos industriais na Cidade de Arapiraca. Fortaleza, 1972.
122 p. illus. 22 cm. (Banco do Nordeste do Brasil, S. A. P₍ublicações₎ 221)
Cover title: Cidade de Arapiraca: consumo de produtos industriais.
1. Consumption (Economics) — Arapiraca, Brazil. 2. Cost and standard of living—Arapiraca, Brazil. I. Title. II. Cidade de Arapiraca; consumo de produtos industriais. III. Series: Banco do Nordeste do Brasil, Fortaleza. P₍ublicações₎ 221.
HD7013.B385 1972b 74–219967

Banco do Nordeste do Brasil, Fortaleza. Departamento de Estudos Econômicos do Nordeste.
Consumo de produtos industriais na Cidade de Campina Grande. Fortaleza, 1968 ₍i. e. 1969₎
124 p. map. 23 cm. (Banco do Nordeste do Brasil. P₍ublicações₎ 167)
At head of title: ETENE.
1. Consumption (Economics)—Campina Grande, Brazil. 2. Cost and standard of living—Campina Grande, Brazil. I. Title. II. Series: Banco do Nordeste do Brasil, Fortaleza. Publicações, no. 167.
HD7013.B363 72–222275
rev

Banco do Nordeste do Brasil, Fortaleza. Departamento de Estudos Econômicos do Nordeste.
Consumo de produtos industriais na cidade de Feira de Santana-Ba. Fortaleza, 1971.
119 p. illus. 23 cm. (Banco do Nordeste do Brasil, S. A. P₍ublicações₎ 198)
1. Consumption (Economics)—Feira de Santana, Brazil. 2. Cost and standard of living—Feira de Santana, Brazil. 3. Feira de Santana, Brazil—Economic conditions. I. Title. II. Series: Banco do Nordeste do Brasil, Fortaleza. Publicações, 198.
HD7013.B385 1971b 73–214517

Banco do Nordeste do Brasil, Fortaleza. Departamento de Estudos Econômicos do Nordeste.
Consumo de produtos industriais na cidade de Fortaleza. Fortaleza, 1972.
127 p. illus. 22 cm. (Banco do Nordeste do Brasil, S. A. P₍ublicações₎ 142)
At head of title: ETENE.
1. Consumption (Economics)—Fortaleza, Brazil. 2. Cost and standard of living—Fortaleza, Brazil. I. Title. II. Series: Banco do Nordeste do Brazil, Fortaleza. Publicações, 142.
HD7013.B385 1972d 74–223232

Banco do Nordeste do Brasil, Fortaleza. Departamento de Estudos Econômicos do Nordeste.
Consumo de produtos industriais na cidade de Garanhuns. Fortaleza, 1970.
120 p. illus. 22 cm. (Banco do Nordeste do Brasil. P₍ublicação₎ 201)
1. Consumption (Economics)—Garanhuns, Brazil. 2. Cost and standard of living—Garanhus, Brazil. I. Title. II. Series: Banco do Nordeste do Brasil, Fortaleza. Publicações, 201.
HD7013.B385 1970 73–214495

Banco do Nordeste do Brasil, Fortaleza. Departamento de Estudos Econômicos do Nordeste.
Consumo de produtos industriais na cidade de João Pessoa (PB). Fortaleza ₍1968₎
119 p. illus. 23 cm.
1. Consumption (Economics)—João Pessoa, Brazil. 2. Cost and standard of living—João Pessoa, Brazil. I. Title.
HD7013.B365 72–222647
TxU NNC

Banco do Nordeste do Brasil, Fortaleza. Departamento de Estudos Econômicos do Nordeste.
Consumo de produtos industriais na cidade de Maceió (Al). Fortaleza, 1968.
124 p. illus. 23 cm. (Banco do Nordeste do Brasil, S. A. P₍ublicações₎ 176)
1. Consumption (Economics)—Maceió, Brazil. 2. Cost and standard of living—Maceió, Brazil. I. Title. II. Series: Banco do Nordeste do Brasil Fortaleza. Publicações 176.
HD7013.B367 72–223185

Banco do Nordeste do Brasil, Fortaleza. Departamento de Estudos Econômicos do Nordeste.
Consumo de produtos industriais na Cidade de Mossoró (RN). Fortaleza, 1972.
116 p. 24 cm. (Banco do Nordeste do Brasil, S. A. P₍ublicações₎ 215)
At head of title: ETENE.
Cover title: Cidade de Mossoró; consumo de produtos industriais.
1. Consumption (Economics)—Mossoró, Brazil. 2. Cost and standard of living—Mossoró, Brazil. I. Title. II. Title. Cidade de Mossoró; consumo de produtos industriais. III. Series: Banco do Nordeste do Brasil, Fortaleza. P₍ublicações₎ 215.
HD7013.B385 1972c 74–219969

Banco do Nordeste do Brasil, Fortaleza. Departamento de Estudos Econômicos do Nordeste.
Consumo de produtos industriais na cidade de Parnaíba. Fortaleza, 1969.
124 p. illus. 23 cm. (Banco do Nordeste do Brasil, S. A. ₍Publicações₎ 164)
1. Consumption (Economics)—Parnaíba, Brazil. 2. Cost and standard of living—Parnaíba, Brazil. I. Title. II. Series: Banco do Nordeste do Brasil, Fortaleza. Publicações, 164.
HD7013.B385 1969 74–210561

Banco do Nordeste do Brasil, Fortaleza. Departamento de Estudos Econômicos do Nordeste.
Consumo de produtos industriais na cidade de Propriá. Fortaleza, 1972.
118 p. illus. 21 cm. (Banco do Nordeste do Brasil, S. A. P₍ublicações₎ 211)
1. Cost and standard of living—Propriá, Brazil. 2. Consumption (Economics)—Propriá, Brazil. I. Title. II. Series: Banco do Nordeste do Brasil, Fortaleza. Publicações, 211.
HD7013.B385 1972 74–219906

Banco do Nordeste do Brasil, Fortaleza. Departamento de Estudos Econômicos do Nordeste.
Consumo de produtos industriais nas cidades de Crato e Juazeiro do Norte. Fortaleza, 1971.
126 p. illus. 22 cm. (Banco do Nordeste do Brasil. P₍ublicação₎ 205)
1. Consumption (Economics)—Crato, Brazil. 2. Cost and standard of living—Crato, Brazil. 3. Consumption (Economics)—Juazeiro do Norte, Brazil. 4. Cost and standard of living—Juazeiro do Norte, Brazil. I. Title. II. Series: Banco do Nordeste do Brasil, Fortaleza. Publicações, 205.
HD7013.B385 1971 73–214443

Banco do Nordeste do Brasil, Fortaleza. Departamento de Estudos Econômicos do Nordeste.
Consumo de produtos industriais no Nordeste : resumo de pesquisas em trinta e quatro cidades / Banco do Nordeste do Brasil S. A., Departamento de Estudos Econômicos do Nordeste (ETENE). — Fortaleza : O Departamento, 1973.
51 p. : 24 cm. — (Banco do Nordeste do Brasil, S. A. P₍ublicações₎ ; 223)
1. Consumption (Economics) — Brazil, Northeast. I. Title. II. Series: Banco do Nordeste do Brasil, Fortaleza. Publicações ; 223.
HC190.C6B3 1973 339.4'8'6709813 75–558157

Banco do Nordeste do Brasil, Fortaleza. Departamento de Estudos Econômicos do Nordeste.
Custo de produção do algodão arbóreo no Seridó Cearense ₍elaborado pelo economista José Josi da Silva₎. Fortaleza, 1971.
66 l. illus. 28 cm. (Banco do Nordeste do Brasil. ₍Publicação₎ 200)
1. Cotton growing — Brazil — Ceará (State) 2. Cotton trade — Ceará, Brazil (State) I. Silva, José Josi da. II. Title. III. Series: Banco do Nordeste do Brasil, Fortaleza. Publicações, 200.
HD9084.B62C43 1971 73–213983

Banco do Nordeste do Brasil, Fortaleza. Departamento de Estudos Econômicos do Nordeste.
A indústria de cimento no Nordeste; tendências do consumo e da oferta. Fortaleza, 1970.
46 l. illus. 28 cm. (Banco do Nordeste do Brasil S. A. P₍ublicações₎ 185)
Bibliography: leaf 46.
1. Cement industries—Brazil, Northeast. I. Title. II. Series: Banco do Nordeste do Brasil, Fortaleza. Publicações, 185.
HD9622.B72B34 1970 74–210639

Banco do Nordeste do Brasil, Fortaleza. Departamento de Estudos Econômicos do Nordeste.
Indústria hoteleira do Nordeste. ₍Elaborado pelo economista Afonso César Coelho Ribeiro₎ Fortaleza, 1969.
108 l. 28 cm. (Banco do Nordeste do Brasil. P₍ublicações₎ 162)
Cover title: Indústria hoteleira no Nordeste.
I. Ribeiro, Afonso César Coelho.
TxU DLC NUC73-39809

Banco do Nordeste do Brasil, Fortaleza. Departamento de Estudos Econômicos do Nordeste.
Manual de estatísticas básicas do Nordeste. Fortaleza, 1958.
254, 8 p. illus., map.
I. Title.
MH NUC76-89166

Banco do Nordeste do Brasil, Fortaleza. Departamento de Estudos Econômicos do Nordeste.
Mercado consumidor de aves e ovos em Natal. Fortaleza-Ceará, 1969.
47 l.
1. Poultry industry—Brazil. 2. Egg trade—Brazil. I. Title.
MiEM NUC74-144041

Banco do Nordeste do Brasil, Fortaleza. Departamento de Estudos Econômicos do Nordeste.
Mercado consumidor de aves e ovos em São Luís. ₍Por José Maria Eduardo Nobre e Antônio Rocha Magalhães₎ Fortaleza, 1969.
43 l. illus. 28 cm. (Banco do Nordeste do Brasil, S.A. ₍Publicações₎ 161.
1. Poultry industry—São Luis do Maranhão, Brazil. I. Nobre, José Maria Eduardo. II. Magalhães, Antônio Rocha. III. Title.
FU NUC75-29481

Banco do Nordeste do Brasil, Fortaleza. Departamento de Estudos Econômicos do Nordeste.
Nordeste, análise conjuntural. no. 7–
1. semestre 1975–
₍Fortaleza, Banco do Nordeste do Brasil, Departamento de Estudos Econômicos do Nordeste₎
no. ill. 21 cm. semiannual.
Continues: Banco do Nordeste do Brasil, Fortaleza. Departamento de Estudos Econômicos do Nordeste. Análise conjuntural da economia Nordestina.
1. Brazil, Northeast—Economic conditions—Periodicals.
I. Title.
HC186.B325a 77–647620
MARC-S

Banco do Nordeste do Brasil, Fortaleza. Departamento de Estudos Econômicos do Nordeste.
Oportunidades de investimento no Nordeste : perfis das empresas / Banco do Nordeste do Brasil, Departamento de Estudos Econômicos do Nordeste (ETENE). — Fortaleza : O Departamento, 1975.
223 p. ; 24 cm.
Includes bibliographical references and indexes.
1. Corporations—Brazil, Northeast—Finance. 2. Investments—Brazil, Northeast. 3. Brazil, Northeast—Industries. I. Title.
HG4109.B25 1975 76-464524
76 MARC

Banco do Nordeste do Brasil, Fortaleza. Departamento de Estudos Econômicos do Nordeste.
Sondagem conjuntural na indústria de transformação do nordeste.
Fortaleza, Banco do Nordeste do Brasil, Departamento de Estudos Econômicos do Nordeste.
no. 21–30 cm. quarterly.
1. Brazil — Manufactures — Periodicals. 2. Brazil — Industries — Periodicals. I. Title.
HD9734.B7B35a 75–645631
MARC-S

Banco do Nordeste do Brasil, Fortaleza. Departamento de Estudos Econômicos do Nordeste.
Turismo no Nordeste; relatório da pesquisa de avaliação da I Campanha de Incentivo ao Turismo no Nordeste ₍elaborado pelo economista Afonso Cesar Coelho Ribeiro₎ Fortaleza, 1972.
75 p. 22 cm.
Includes bibliographical references.
1. Tourist trade—Brazil, Northeast. I. Ribeiro, Afonso Cesar Coelho. II. Title.
G155.B7B36 73–214421

Banco do Nordeste do Brasil, Fortaleza. Departamento de Estudos Economicos do Nordeste
see Banco do Nordeste do Brasil, Fortaleza. Estudo economico do Municipio de Caruaru. Fortaleza, 1965.

Banco do Nordeste do Brasil, Fortaleza. Departamento de Organização e Processamento.
Uma experiência em processamento de dados. Fortaleza, 1971.
96 p. illus. (part col.) 23 cm.
1. Banco do Nordeste do Brasil, Fortaleza. 2. Electronic data processing—Banks and banking. I. Title.
HG2890.F64B335 1971 74-232478

Banco do Nordeste do Brasil, Fortaleza. Departamento Industrial e de Investimentos.
Financiamento industrial. [3. ed.] Fortaleza, 1970.
60 p. 23 cm.
1. Industrial promotion–Brazil. I. Title.
OU NUC73-38950

Banco do Nordeste do Brasil, Fortaleza. Departamento Industrial e de Investimentos.
Financiamento industrial e serviços básicos / Banco do Nordeste do Brasil, S. A., Departamento Industrial e de Investimentos (CARIN). — 4. ed., rev. e atualizada / pelo Setor de Planejamento e Estudos—SEPLA ; com a colaboração de Maria Leônia Viana do Amaral ... [et al.]. — Fortaleza : BNB, 1974.
139 p. ; 21 cm.
First-3d eds. published under title: Financiamento industrial.
1. Industrial promotion—Brazil. I. Banco do Nordeste do Brazil, Fortaleza. Setor de Planejamento e Estudos. II. Title.
HG2890.F64B335 1974 75-580841

Banco do Nordeste do Brasil, Fortaleza. Departamento Industrial e de Investimentos.
Realizações em crédito industrial e serviços básicos / Banco do Nordeste do Brasil, S. A., Departamento Industrial e de Investimentos, CARIN. — 2. ed., rev. e atualizada / pelo Setor de Planejamento e Estudos, SEPLA ; com a colaboração de Francisco Leandro da Silva, Leanardo Antônio de Moura. — Fortaleza : CARIN, 1974.
143 p. ; 21 cm.
First ed published in 1972 under title: Aplicacões em crédito industrial.
1. Banco do Nordeste do Brasil, Fortaleza. 2. Credit — Brazil, Northeast. 3. Industrial promotion—Brazil, Northeast. I. Banco do Nordeste do Brasil, Fortaleza. Setor de Planejamento e Estudos. II. Title.
HG2890.F64B335 1974a 75-530835

Banco do Nordeste do Brasil, Fortaleza. Departamento Jurídico.
Pareceres.
Fortaleza.
v. 22 cm.
1. Banking law—Brazil.
74-641698
MARC-S

Banco do Nordeste do Brasil, Fortaleza. Departamento Rural.
Financiamento a cooperativas / Banco do Nordeste do Brasil, Departamento Rural. — Fortaleza : O Departamento, 1973.
42 p. ; 22 cm.
1. Agricultural credit—Brazil, Northeast. 2. Agriculture, Cooperative—Brazil, Northeast—Finance. I. Title.
HG2051.B7B28 1973 76-486353
77 MARC

Banco do Nordeste do Brasil, Fortaleza. Departamento Rural.
Programa especial de crédito rural; documento elaborado pelo Setor de Investigações Agricolas de DERUR. Fortaleza-Ceará, 1970 [i.e. 1971]
181 p. illus., maps (part. fold.) 23 cm. (P[ublicação do Banco do Nordeste do Brasil] 196)
Includes bibliographical references.
1. Agricultural credit–Brazil–Northeast. 2. Brazil, Northeast–Economic policy. I. Title.
NNC NUC75-26574

Banco do Nordeste do Brasil, Fortaleza. Departamento Rural. Divisão de Programas Especiais.
Mercados agrícolas: Informações.
Fortaleza, Banco do Nordeste do Brasil, Departamento Rural, Divisão de Programas Especiais.
v. 29 cm.
1. Produce trade—Brazil, Northeast—Statistics. I. Title.
HD9014.B8B35a 76-641391
MARC-S

Banco do Nordeste do Brazil, Fortaleza. Divisão de Agricultura.
Aspectos da agro-indústria canavieira do Nordeste [elaborado pelo economista Francisco Aubismar Costa Silveira]. Fortaleza, 1970 [cover 1971]
89 p. 22 cm. (Banco do Nordeste do Brasil. P[ublicação] 202)
Includes bibliographical references.
1. Sugar trade—Brazil, Northeast. 2. Sugar-cane—Brazil, Northeast. I. Silveira, Francisco Aubismar Costa. II. Title. III. Series: Banco do Nordeste do Brasil, Fortaleza. Publicações, 202.
HD9114.B6B35 1971 73-214511

Banco do Nordeste do Brasil, Fortaleza. Divisão de Agricultura.
A cultura do gergelim e suas possibilidades no Nordeste [elaborado pelo engo.-agro. José Almar Almeida Franco] Fortaleza, 1970.
69 p. 22 cm. (Banco do Nordeste do Brazil. P[ublicação] 199)
Includes bibliographical references.
1. Sesame. 2. Plant introduction—Brazil, Northeast. I. Franco, José Almar Almeida. II. Title. III. Banco do Nordeste do Brasil, Fortaleza. Publicações, 199.
SB299.S4B36 1970 73-214326

Banco do Nordeste do Brasil, Fortaleza. Divisão de Agricultura.
Mercado consumidor de aves e ovos em Maceió. Fortaleza, 1972.
77 p. illus. 22 cm. (Banco do Nordeste do Brasil, S. A. [Publicações] 214)
Cover title: Consumo de aves e ovos na cidade de Maceió.
1. Poultry industry—Maceió, Brazil. 2. Egg trade—Maceió, Brazil. I. Title. II. Title: Consumo de aves e ovos na cidade de Maceió. III. Series: Banco do Nordeste do Brasil, Fortaleza. Publicações, 214.
HD9437.B73M33 1972 74-223240

Banco do Nordeste do Brasil, Fortaleza. Divisão de Agricultura.
Mercado consumidor de aves e ovos em Parnaíba. Fortaleza, 1973.
57 p. 22 cm. (Banco do Nordeste do Brasil, S. A. [Publicações] 219)
Cover title: Consumo de aves e ovos na cidade de Parnaíba.
1. Poultry industry—Parnaíba, Brazil. 2. Egg trade—Parnaíba, Brazil. I. Title. II. Title: Consumo de aves e ovos na cidade de Parnaíba. III. Series: Banco do Nordeste do Brasil, Fortaleza. Publicações, 219.
HD9437.B73P373 1973 74-223231

Banco do Nordeste do Brasil, Fortaleza. Divisão de Agricultura.
Mercado consumidor de aves e ovos em Teresina. Fortaleza, 1972.
62 p. illus. 21 cm. (Banco do Nordeste do Brasil, S. A. [Publicações] 210)
Cover title: Consumo de aves e ovos na cidade de Teresina.
1. Poultry industry,—Teresina, Brazil. 2. Egg trade—Teresina Brazil. I. Title. II. Title: Consumo de aves e ovos na cidade de Teresina. III. Series: Banco do Nordeste do Brazil, Fortaleza. Publicações, 210.
HD9437.B73T473 1972 74-223239

Banco do Nordeste do Brasil, Fortaleza. Divisão de Agricultura.
Perspectivas da cultura do algodão no Nordeste. Fortaleza, 1973.
38 p. illus. 21 cm. (Banco do Nordeste do Brasil, S. A. P[ublicações] 220)
1. Cotton trade—Brazil, Northeast. 2. Cotton growing—Brazil, Northeast. I. Title. II. Series: Banco do Nordeste do Brasil, Fortaleza. P[ublicações] 220.
HD9084.B6B35 1973 74-219525

Banco do Nordeste do Brasil, Fortaleza. Divisão de Agricultura.
Possibilidades da caprinocultura e ovinocultura do Nordeste / Ministério do Interior, Banco do Nordeste do Brasil S. A., Departamento de Estudos Econômicos do Nordeste (ETENE), Divisão de Agricultura. — Fortaleza : O Divisão, 1974.
131 p., [12] leaves of plates : ill. ; 23 cm.
Bibliography: p. 131.
1. Goats—Brazil, Northeast. 2. Sheep—Brazil, Northeast. I. Title.
SF383.5.B7B36 1974 76-519106

Banco do Nordeste do Brasil, Fortaleza. Escritorio Tecnico de Estudos Economicos do Nordeste.
Balas, bombons e caramelos; análise de dados estatísticos [apresentado pelo Econ. A. Taumaturgo Nogueira] Fortaleza, 1957.
15 l. 28 cm. (Banco do Nordeste do Brasil, S.A. P[ublicações] 44)
At head ot title: Banco do Nordeste do Brasil, S.A. Escritório Técnico de Estudos Econômicos do Nordeste. ETENE.
I. Nogueira, Antônio Taumaturgo.
TxU NUC76-11235

Banco do Nordeste do Brasil, Fortaleza. Escritorio Tecnico de Estudos Economicos do Nordeste.
A indústria de fósforos de segurança e suas possibilidades de implantação no Nordeste; análisis de dados estatísticos [apresentado pelo Econ. A. Taumaturgo Nogueira] Fortaleza, 1957.
11 l. chart. 27 cm. (Banco do Nordeste do Brasil, S.A. P[ublicações] 20)
At head ot title: Banco do Nordeste do Brasil, S.A. Escritório Técnico de Estudios Econômicos do Nordeste. ETENE.
"Circulação externa."
I. Nogueira, Antônio Taumaturgo.
TxU NUC76-11234

Banco do Nordeste do Brasil, Fortaleza. Escritório Técnico de Estudos Econômicos do Nordeste.
Irrigação na área pernambucana do São Francisco; estudo preliminar. Fortaleza, 1957.
34 p. tables. (Banco do Nordeste do Brasil [Publicações] 30)
"Apêndices."
"Contribuição à I Reunião dos Técnicos de Irrigação e Drenagem, Sorocaba-São Paulo, dezembro 1957."
1. Irrigation—Brazil—São Francisco Valley. I. Title.
InU NUC75-67730

Banco do Nordeste do Brasil, Fortaleza. Escritório Técnico de Estudos Econômicos do Nordeste.
Isenção de impostos para novas indústrias. Comentários e sugestões ao Projeto da Comissão de Desenvolvimento de Pernambuco. Traduzido por José M. Cavalcante, e revisto por Diogo A.N. de Gaspar. Fortaleza, 1956.
18 p. 28 cm. (Banco do Nordeste do Brasil, S.A. P[ublicações] 10)
At head of title: ETENE.
Bibliographical footnotes.
1. Taxation, Exemption from—Pernambuco, Brazil (State) 2. Pernambuco, Brazil (State)—Indus. I. Title.
FU NUC75-66308

Banco do Nordeste do Brasil, Fortaleza. Escritório Técnico de Estudos Econômicos do Nordeste.
Mamona no Ceará [por Diogo Adolpho Nunes de Gaspar e Carlos Brandão da Silva] Fortaleza, 1956.
86 p. illus., maps (part fold.) 23 cm.
1. Castor bean—Marketing—Brazil. 2. Castor seed—Marketing—Brazil. I. Gaspar, Diogo Adolpho. II. Title.
NNC NUC74-145478

Banco do Nordeste do Brasil, Fortaleza. Escritório Técnico de Estudos Econômicos do Nordeste.
Manual de estatísticas básicas do Nordeste. [Fortaleza, Ceará] ETENE, Departamento de Estudos Econômicos do Nordeste, 1968.
176 p. (chiefly tables)
Explanatory notes in English and Portuguese.
1. Brazil, Northeast—Econ. condit. 2. Brazil, Northeast—Statistics. I. Title.
ICU NUC73-2187

Banco do Nordeste do Brasil, Fortaleza. Escritorio Técnico de Estudos Econômicos do Nordeste.
Possibilidades da indústria de cerveja no Nordeste, análise de dados estatísticos [apresentado pelo Econ. A. Taumaturgo Nogueira] Fortaleza, 1957.
16 l. 27 cm. (Banco do Nordeste do Brasil, S.A. P[ublicações] 23)
At head of title: Banco do Nordeste do Brasil, S.A. Escritório Técnico de Estudos Econômicos do Nordeste. ETENE.
I. Nogueira, Antônio Taumaturgo.
TxU NUC76-11236

Banco do Nordeste do Brasil, Fortaleza. Escritorio Técnico de Estudos Econômicos do Nordeste.
Velas de ignição para motores; [análises de dados estatísticos, apresentado pelo Econ. A. Taumaturgo Nogueira] Fortaleza, 1958.
31, 3, 4 l. 27 cm. (Banco do Nordeste do Brasil, S.A. P[ublicações] 43)
At head of title: Banco do Nordeste do Brasil, S.A. ETENE.
I. Nogueira, Antônio Taumaturgo.
TxU DLC NUC77-67414

Banco do Nordeste do Brasil, Fortaleza. Setor de Documentação e Biblioteca.
Banco do Nordeste, origens. [Rio de Janeiro, Editor Borsoi] 1958-
v. 23 cm.
"Trabalho de pesquisas e organização de Ismael Pordeus."
1. Banks and banking—Brazil. I. Pordeus, Ismael.
NNC NUC73-122847

Banco do Nordeste do Brasil, Fortaleza. Setor de Investigações Agrícolas.
Possibilidades de expansão da cultura do cajueiro. Fortaleza, 1970.
31 l. 28 cm.
1. Cashew nut—Brazil. I. Title.
SB401.C3B36 1970 338.1'7'45750981 74-207732

Banco do Nordeste do Brasil, Fortaleza. Setor de Investigações Agrícolas.
Programa especial de crédito rural. Fortaleza, 1970 [i. e. 1971]
184 p. illus. 23 cm. (Banco do Nordeste do Brasil, S. A. P[ublicações] 196)
1. Agricultural credit—Brazil, Northeast. 2. Agriculture—Economic aspects—Brazil, Northeast. I. Title. II. Series: Banco do Nordeste do Brasil, Fortaleza. Publicações, 196.
HG2051.B7B28 1970 73-214394

Banco do Nordeste do Brasil, Fortaleza. Setor de Planejamento e Estudos
see Banco do Nordeste do Brasil, Fortaleza. Departamento Industrial e de Investimentos. Financiamento industrial e servicos basicos. 4. ed., rev. e atualizada Fortaleza : BNB, 1974.

Banco do Nordeste do Brasil, Fortaleza. Setor de Planejamento e Estudos
see Banco do Nordeste do Brasil, Fortaleza. Departament Industrial e de Investimentos. Realizações em crédito industrial e serviços básicos. 2. ed., rev. e atualizada. Fortaleza: CARIN, 1974.

Banco Econômico da Bahia.
Cidade do Salvador. [Salvador, 19--]
col. map 38 x 58 cm. fold. to 14 x 10 cm.
Scale 1:20,000.
Issued in folder; title on folder: Salvador, Bahia, Brasil; guia turistico.
Inset: Zona central.
1. Salvador, Brazil—Maps.
TxU NUC73-77462

Banco Ecuatoriano de la Vivienda
see Ecuador. Laws, statutes, etc. [Decreto supremo no. 19 (1971)] El gobierno nacional y el mutualismo: Decreto supremo no. 19... Quito, 1971.

Banco Español de Crédito.
see Impuesto general sobre la renta de las personas físicas. Madrid, Banesto, 1974.

Banco Español de Crédito. Foreign Dept.
see Arboleya, Antonio G Spanish corporate taxation. [Madrid, 1966]

Banco Espírito Santo e Comercial de Lisboa.
A guide to investment and business in Portugal. [2d ed. Lisbon, 1970]
99 p. illus. (part col.), maps.
Bibliographical footnotes.
1. Commercial law—Portugal. 2. Investments, Foreign—Portugal. 3. Portugal—Economic policy. 4. Taxation—Portugal—Law. I. Title.
MH-BA NUC74-23525

Banco Espírito Santo e Comercial de Lisboa.
A guide to investment and business in Portugal. [Lisbon, 1973]
104 p. maps.
1. Investments—Foreign—Portugal. 2. Commercial law—Portugal. 3. Taxation—Portugal. I. Title.
InU NUC76-71565

Banco Exterior de España, Madrid.
Memoria.
[Madrid]
v. illus. 27 cm.
1. Banco Exterior de España, Madrid.
HG3190.M34E924a 74-642389
MARC-S

Banco Fonsecas & Burnay.
How to invest in Portugal. [Lisboa] 1971.
191 p.
1. Investments, Foreign—Portugal. 2. Industrial laws and legislation—Portugal. I. Title.
CLL NUC75-58863

Banco Ganadero.
Corrales para ganado de carne. Bogotá, 1967.
11 l. fold. illus. 28 cm.
Cover title.
At head of title: Banco Ganadero y Alianza para el progreso.
1. Cattle pens. I. Title.
TxU NUC76-71513

Banco Ganadero
see Instituto Colombiano de la Reforma Agraria. Subgerencia de Desarrollo Agricola. Manual tecnico... Bogota, 1969.

Banco Ganadero
see Velasquez Q , Jose. El ganado "San Martinero"; notas sobre su origen. Bogota, Banco Ganadero [1965]

Banco Ganadero Argentino.
[Evolución de los precios corrientes al productor por provincias: cereales. Buenos Aires, 1972?]
1 v. (unpaged) 28 cm. (Serie: Cereales)
Caption title.
1. Grain—Prices—Argentine Republic. I. Title.
TxU NUC75-26575

Banco Ganadero Argentino.
Temas de economía argentina, el sector agropecuario, 1964/1973 : Banco Ganadero Argentino, 10o aniversario. — [Buenos Aires] : Banco Ganadero Argentino, [1974]
95 p. : ill. ; 29 cm.
Cover title.
Errata slip inserted.
1. Agriculture—Economic aspects—Argentine Republic. I. Title.
HD1862.B36 1974 75-543720

Banco Ganadero Argentino. Servicio de Investigaciones Economicas.
La produccion rural Argentina en 1970 y once anos de economia agropecuaria regional. Buenos Aires, 1971.
81 p. illus.
1. Agriculture—Economic aspects—Argentine Republic—Statistics. I. Title.
DNAL NUC74-145515

Banco Gubernamental de Fomento para Puerto Rico
see Government Development Bank for Puerto Rico.

Banco Guipuzcoano. Departamento de Estudios.
Panorama de la industria guipuzcoana en 1972. — San Sebastián : Departamento de Estudios del Banco Guipuzcoana, 1973.
32 p. : ill. ; 24 cm. Sp 74
Cover title.
1. Guipúzcoa, Spain—Industries. I. Title.
HC387.G8B35 1973 74-346973

Banco Hipotecario de Chile.
see Valdivieso, Rauúl. Exposición de esculturas Raúl Valdivieso... [s.l., s.n.] 1976 (Santiago : Editorial Universitaria)

Banco Hipotecario de El Salvador, San Salvador.
see El Crédito agrícola en El Salvador, 1966. [San Salvador, s.n., 1967-

Banco Hipotecario de El Salvador, San Salvador
see Estudio del Crédito Agrícola de la República de El Salvador. Grupo Permanente de Trabajo. El crédito agrícola en el Salvador. [San Salvador, 1967]

Banco Hipotecario del Uruguay, Montevideo.
Casa propia sobre cimientos de ahorro. [n.p., n.d.]
[9] p. 20 cm.
1. Mortgages—Uruguay. I. Title.
TxU NUC75-26746

Banco Hipotecario del Uruguay, Montevideo. Departamento Financiero de la Habitación.
Carta organica. [Montevideo?] 1971.
81 p. 26 cm.
1. Banco Hipotecario del Uruguay. 2. Mortgage loans—Uruguay. I. Uruguay. Laws, statutes, etc. II. Title.
MU NUC76-88808

Banco Hipotecario Nacional, Buenos Aires.
Centro Habitacional Avellaneda; trabajo presentado al Comité de Selección de Paris para el Congreso Mundial de Arquitectos a celebrarse en octubre 1969. [Buenos Aires? 1969?]
[22] p. illus. 24 cm.
1. Architecture, Domestic—Avellaneda, Argentine Republic. I. Title.
TxU NUC74-144039

Banco Hispano Americano. Departamento de Relaciones Exteriores
see Disposiciones legales ... [Madrid] 1973.

Banco Industrial de Bilbao
see Joven Cámara de Valencia. "Problematica actual de la naranja." Valencia, 1973.

Banco Industrial de la República Argentina.
La práctica de o[rganización] y m[etodos. Buenos Aires?] Instituto Superior de Administración Pública, 1962.
iii, 30 l. 35 cm.
1. Public administration.
IU NUC74-33075

Banco Industrial de la República Argentina
see Dovey, H O Manual de sistemas de organización y métodos. [La Paz?] 1962.

Banco Industrial de la República Argentina. División Economía.
Actividades de nivel medio industrial en Alemania occidental. [Buenos Aires] Banco Industrial de la República Argentina, División Económica [1965]
98 l. illus. 35 cm.
Microfilm copy.
1. Industries, Small—Germany. 2. Artisans—Germany. I. Paulsen, Ewaldo G.
NN NUC74-81192

Banco Industrial de la Republica Argentina. División Economía.
Desarrollo económico regional: sus problemas geográficos; alqunas observaciones sobre una experiencia europea de interés para la Argentina. [Buenos Aires, 1965]
38 l. maps. 35 cm.
Microfilm.
Prepared by its División Economía.
Bibliography: leaf 38.
1. Economic planning—France. 2. Economic planning—Argentine.
NN NUC76-40029

Banco Industrial de la República Argentina. Gerencia de Investigaciones Tecnicas
see Barrios, Pedro Aníbal. La industria lechera en la República Argentina. [Buenos Aires] Banco Industrial de la República Argentina, 1959.

Banco Industrial de Venezuela
see Pocaterra, José Rafael, 1890-1955.
Archivo de José Rafael Pocaterra: la oposición a Gómez. Caracas, 1973.

Banco Industrial del Perú.
Annual report—Banco Industrial del Perú.
[Lima] Banco Industrial del Perú.
v. 25 cm.
1. Banco Industrial del Perú. 2. Peru—Industries.
HG2950.L54B283a 75-643622
MARC-S

Banco Industrial del Perú.
Memoria.
[Lima.
v. 24½ cm.
Cover-title.
1. Banco Industrial del Perú. 2. Peru—Industries.
HG2950.L54B282 43-27925
MARC-S

Banco Industrial del Perú.
Memoria. English. Annual report—Banco Industrial del Perú.
[Lima] Banco Industrial del Perú.
v. 25 cm.
1. Banco Industrial del Perú.
HG2950.L54B283a 75-643622
MARC-S

Banco Industrial del Perú
see Fuente, Alejandro de la. Aceros especiales — posibilidades. Lima, 1966.

Banco Industrial del Peru
see Instituto Nacional de Promoción Industrial. Industrial projects with an immediate market... Lima, 1966.

Banco Industrial del Perú
see Instituto Nacional de Promoción Industrial. Proyecto de instalación... Lima, 1965.

Banco Industrial del Perú.
see Instituto Nacional de Promoción Industrial Recursos y posibilidades industriales del Departamento de Huánuco. Lima, INPI, 1965.

Banco Industrial del Perú.
see Instituto Nacional de Promoción Industrial. Recursos y posibilidades industriales del Departamento de Ica. Lima, INPI, 1966.

Banco Industrial del Perú
see Instituto Nacional de Promoción Industrial. Recursos y posibilidades industriales del Departamento de La Libertad. Lima, 1966-

Banco Industrial del Perú
see Mercado de productos alimenticios y bebidas en 1962 y algunos productos industrializables,.. Lima, 1965.

Banco Industrial del Perú
see Metex (Firm) Posibilidades de establecer una industria... Lima, 1967.

Banco Industrial del Perú
see Serie: Recursos y posibilidades industriales de los departamentos del Perú. Lima, 1966-

Banco Industrial del Perú. Biblioteca.
Pequeña industria y artesanía; bibliografía. Lima, 1972.
vi, 59 p. 28 cm. (Its Serie bibliográfica, no. 1)
1. Small business—Bibliography. 2. Artisans—Bibliography. I. Title. II. Series.
Z7164.C81B28 1972 73-214520

Banco Industrial del Perú. Departamento de Estudios Económicos.
Peru: mercado de abrasivos moldeados. [Preparada por Willy Pérez Barreto R. y María Eugenia Tuesta H.] Lima, 1970.
20 p. tables, graphs. (Serie: Investigaciones económicas, v. 8)
1. Abrasives industry—Peru. 2. Peru—Industries. I. Pérez Barreto Rebatta, Willy. II. Tuesta Houghton, María Eugenia. III. Title. IV. Series: Banco Industrial del Perú. V. Serie: Investigaciones económicas, v. 8.
PPiU NUC73-40518

Banco Industrial del Perú. Departamento de Estudios Económicos.
Peru: mercado de alfombras. [Preparada por Luis Alcázar Osorio y Marco A. Aranaga Morales] Lima, 1970.
42 p. illus., tables. (Serie: Investigaciones económicas, v. 9)
1. Rug and carpet industry—Peru. 2. Peru—Industries. I. Alcázar Osorio, Luis. II. Aranga Morales, Marco A. III. Title. IV. Series: Banco Industrial del Perú. Serie: Investigaciones económicas, v. 9.
PPiU NUC73-47525

Banco Industrial del Perú. Departamento de Estudios Económicos.
Peru: mercado de papeles. [Preparada por Willy Pérez Barreto Rebatta, et al.] Lima, 1970.
142 p. tables, graphs. (Serie: Investigaciones económicas, v. 4)
1. Paper making and trade—Peru. 2. Peru—Industries. I. Pérez Barreto Rebatta, Willy. II. Title. III. Series: Banco Industrial del Peru. Serie: Investigaciones económicas, v. 4.
PPiU NUC73-39800

Banco Industrial del Perú. División de Comercio Exterior.
Manual para el exportador. 2. ed. [Lima, 1971]
128 p. 21 cm.
DPU NUC73-32173

Banco Industrial del Perú. División de Comercio Exterior.
Perú: Estadísticas de exportación.
[Lima] Banco Industrial del Perú, División de Comercio Exterior.
v. 28 cm.
1. Peru—Commerce—Periodicals. I. Title. II. Title: Estadísticas de exportación.
HF175.B34a 75-645996
MARC-S

Banco Industrial del Perú. Division de Comercio Exterior.
Peru: estadisticas de exportacion hasta 1968. [Lima, 1969?]
294 p. 28 cm. (Serie E-1)
Cover title.
"Presentación" dated 1969.
1. Peru—Commerce. I. Title.
TxU NUC74-144070

Banco Industrial del Perú. División de Comercio Exterior
see Acuerdo de Cartagena. Acuerdo de integración subregional andino. [Lima, Fondo del Libro] 1969.

Banco Industrial del Perú. División de Promoción Industrial
see Tarnawiecky, Rafael. Proyecto para la industrialización de la naranja... Lima, 1968.

Banco Inmobiliario
see Mory, Mario. The interest rate... Guatemala [1964]

Banco Interamericano de Desenvolvimento
see
Inter-American Development Bank.

Banco Interamericano de Desarrollo
see Inter-American Development Bank.

Banco Internacional de Reconstrucción y Fomento
see International Bank for Reconstruction and Development.

Banco La Caja Obrera.
Banco La Caja Obrera, 1905-1955. — [Montevideo] : El Banco, [1955]
[70] p. : ill. ; 31 cm.
Cover title.
1. Banco La Caja Obrera.
HG2960.M84B35 1955 76-471572
76 MARC

Banco Minero del Perú, Lima.
Exportaciones mineras del Perú.
[Lima]
v. 28 cm.
Vols. for prepared by its División de Planeamiento.
Includes comparative figures for the previous decade.
1. Mineral industries—Peru—Statistics. 2. Peru—Commerce. I. Banco Minero del Perú, Lima. División de Planeamiento. II. Title.
HD9506.P4B33a 74-642810
MARC-S

Banco Minero del Perú, Lima. División de Planeamiento
see Banco Minero del Perú, Lima. Exportaciones mineras del Perú. [Lima]

Banco Mundial
see
International Bank for Reconstruction and Development.

Banco Municipal Autónomo.
Memoria del Banco Municipal Autónomo.
Tegucigalpa, Banco Municipal Autónomo.
v. ill. 28 cm.
1. Banco Municipal Autónomo. 2. Banks and banking—Honduras—Periodicals.
HG2760.T44M823a 75-640557
MARC-S

Banco Municipal de la Ciudad de Buenos Aires
see Argentine Republic. Comisión Liquidadora Decreto-Ley No. 8. 124/57. Joyas, marfiles y armas antiguas... Buenos Aires [1957]

Banco Nacional da Habitação.
BNH-70 [i. e. setenta. Rio de Janeiro, Secretaria de Divulgação do BNH, 1971]
3 v. (in case) illus. 22 x 25-31 cm.
Vol. [2] has title: Resultados BNH-70; v. [3]: Resumo técnico-financiero, BNH-70.
1. Banco Nacional da Habitação. I. Title. II. Title: Resultados BNH-70. III. Title: Resumo técnico-financiero, BNH-70.
HG2888.H3B34 1971 73-356263

Banco Nacional da Habitacão.
BNH: solução brasileira de problemas brasileiros. [Rio de Janeiro, Secretaria de Divulgação do BNH, 1973]
34 p. col. illus. 22 cm.
1. Housing—Brazil—Finance. 2. Banco Nacional da Habitação. 3. Housing—Brazil. I. Title.
HD7323.A3B3 1973 73-219355

Banco Nacional da Habitação.
Banco Nacional da Habitação : documenta. — [Rio de Janeiro : Secretaria de Divulgação, Banco Nacional da Habitação, Ministério do Interior, 1974]
184 p. : ill. ; 27 cm.
1. Banco Nacional da Habitação. I. Title.
HG2888.H3B34 1974 75-557424

Banco Nacional da Habitação.
Banco Nacional da Habitação: FIMACO, RECON, REINVEST, REGIR. [Rio de Janeiro, 1969]
80 p. forms. 23 cm.
1. Housing—Brazil—Finance. I. Title.
HD7323A3B3 1969 74-231973

Banco Nacional da Habitação.
Banco Nacional da Habitação, 1974. — [Rio de Janeiro : BNH], 1974.
62 p. : graphs ; 27 cm.
Cover title: BNH 1974.
1. Banco Nacional da Habitação. I. Title.
HG2888.H3B34 1974a 75-557425

Banco Nacional da Habitaçao.
CHISAM: Coordenaçao de Habitaçao de Interêsse Social da Area Metropolitana do Grande Rio. [Rio de Janeiro?] Ministério do Interior [1969?]
103 p. illus., fold. col. map.
1. Public housing—Brazil. I. Title: Coordenaçao de Habitaçao de Interesse Social da Area Metropolitana do Grande Rio.
NcU NIC NUC73-113157

Banco Nacional da Habitacão.
Compre sua casa ou apartamento; sabendo o que de quem como está comprando. Manual do comprador de casa. [Rio de Janeiro, 1966?]
47 p.
1. Apartment houses—Brazil. 2. Mortgage finance—Brazil.
DHUD NUC73-39445

Banco Nacional da Habitação.
Considerações sobre crescimento urbano. [Rio de Janeiro, Banco Nacional da Habitação, Secretaria de Divulgação, 1973]
83 p. illus. 22 cm.
1. Urbanization—Brazil. 2. Cities and towns—Growth. I. Title.
NmU NUC76-71549

Banco Nacional da Habitação.
FGTS; ordem de serviço—FGST-POS. no. 01/71 do Banco Nacional da Habitação. [Contagem, Brasil, Centro das Indústrias das Cidades Industriais de Minas Gerais] 1971.
35 p. forms. 24 cm.
1. Non-wage payments—Brazil. I. Title.
73-221904

Banco Nacional da Habitação.
Instruções para reformulação dos créditos do S.F.H. e utilização dos saques nas contas vinculadas do F.G.T.S. [Rio de Janeiro, 1971]
107 p. 30 cm.
1. Mortgage loans—Brazil. 2. Sistema Financeiro da Habitação. I. Title.
CSt NUC73-116605

Banco Nacional da Habitação.
National Housing Bank: a Brazilian solution to Brazilian problems. [Rio de Janiero? BNH Information Office, 1973?]
32 p. col. diagrs. 22 cm.
1. Banco Nacional da Habitacao. 2. Housing—Brazil.
NNC NUC75-17243

Banco Nacional da Habitação.
Orçamento plurianual—BNH.
[Rio de Janeiro, Secretaria de Divulgação]
v. 22 cm.
1. Banco Nacional da Habitação. 2. Housing—Brazil—Finance—Periodicals.
HG2888.H3B34a 74-647112
MARC-S

Banco Nacional da Habitação.
Relatorio das atividades do BNH, 1970. Rio de Janeiro, Ministerio do Interior, 1970.
v.
Contents: v. 1. Resultados obtidos v. 2. Programacao plurianual.
1. Banks and banking—Brazil.
DHUD NUC74-24724

Banco Nacional da Habitação.
Uso do solo urbano; projeto para legislação tributária. [Rio de Janeiro, Secretaria de Divulgação do BNH, 1973]
85 p. 23 cm.
1. Local taxation—Brazil. I. Title.
73-220172

Banco Nacional da Habitação
see Brazil. Laws, statutes, etc. The national housing act of 1964. Rio de Janeiro, 1965.

Banco Nacional da Habitacão
see Centro das Indústrias do Estado de São Paulo. Relatório da Coordenacão Industrial para o Plano Habitacional, CIPHAB. [São Paulo] 1967.

Banco Nacional da Habitação
see Costa, Rubens Vaz da. Economic development and urban growth... Rio de Janeiro, 1972.

Banco Nacional da Habitação
see Costa, Rubens Vaz da. Fast urban growth... 4th ed., rev. [n.p.] 1972.

Banco Nacional da Habitacão
see Costa, Rubens Vaz da. Urban growth: the foundation of economic development. Rio de Janeiro, 1973.

Banco Nacional da Habitacao
see Plano nacional da habitacao popular. Rio de Janeiro : [Secretaria de Divulgacao do BNH], 1973.

Banco Nacional da Habitação
see Symposium on Urban Development, Rio de Janeiro, 1974. Simpósio sobre Desenvolvimento Urbano, Rio de Janeiro, 1974. [Rio de Janeiro : Secretaria de Divulgação do BNH], 1974.

Banco Nacional da Habitação. Assessoria de Planejamento e Coordenação.
BNH, avaliação e perspectivas / [Assessoria de Planejamento e Coordenação]. — Rio de Janeiro : [Secretaria de Divulgação do BNH], 1974.
117 p. : 1 graph ; 21 cm.
1. Banco Nacional da Habitação. I. Title.
HG2888.H3B34 1971 75-553515

Banco Nacional da Habitação. Assessoria de Planejamento e Coordenação.
Mercado habitacional.
[Rio de Janeiro] Banco Nacional da Habitacional, Assessoria de Planejamento e Coordenação.
v. 29 cm.
1. Housing—Brazil—Rio de Janeiro. 2. Real estate business—Brazil—Rio de Janeiro. 3. Construction industry—Brazil—Rio de Janeiro. I. Title.
HD7323.R5B36a 75-649482
MARC-S

Banco Nacional da Habitação. Assessoria Técnica de Documentação.
Boletim bibliográfico. v. 1-
jan. 1976-
Rio de Janeiro [Brasil] Ministério do Interior, Banco Nacional da Habitação, Área de Administração e Controle Operacional, Assessoria Técnica de Documentação.
v. 23 cm.
1. Cities and towns—Planning—Brazil—Bibliography. 2. Cities and towns—Planning—Bibliography. 3. Urbanization—Bibliography.
Z5942.B3a 016.3092'62'0981 76-647687
[HT169.B7] MARC-S

Banco Nacional da Habitacao. Conselho de Administracao. Resolucao do Conselho de Administracao, RC no. 1/73. 1973.
see Plano nacional da habitacao popular. Rio de Janeiro : [Secretaria de Divulgacao do BNH], 1973.

Banco Nacional da Habitação. Coordenação Geral do FGTS.
see Encontro Regional de Estudos sôbre o FGTS, 1st, Belém, 1970. 1°. [i.e. Primeiro] Encontro Regional de Estudos sôbre o FGTS, Belém, 11 a 14 de agôsto, 1970. [Belém, Secretaria de Divulgação do BNH] 1972.

Banco Nacional da Habitação. Coordenação Geral do FGTS.
see Seminário sobre Aspectos Jurídicos do FGTS, 1st, Brasília, 1968. 1o. [i.e. Primeiro] Seminário sobre Aspectos Jurídicos do FGTS, Brasília, 11 a 14 de março, 1968. [Rio de Janeiro, Secretaria de Divulgação do BNH] 1972.

Banco Nacional da Habitação. Coordenação Geral do FGTS.
see Seminário sobre Aspectos Jurídicos do FGTS, 2d, Recife, Brazil, 1972. 2° [i.e. Segundo] Seminário sobre Aspectos Jurídicos do FGTS, Recife, 28 a 30 de abril, 1972. [Rio de Janeiro, O Banco?] 1972.

Banco Nacional da Habitação. Coordenação Geral do FGTS.
see Simpósio Regional sobre Aspectos Jurídicos do FGTS, 1st, Porto Alegre, Brazil, 1968. 1o. [i.e. Primeiro] Simpósio Regional sobre Aspectos Jurídicos do FGTS, Porto Alegre, 19 a 22 de setembro, 1968. [Rio de Janeiro, Secretaria de Divulgação do BNH] 1972.

Banco Nacional da Habitação. Departamento da Receita.
Boletim informativo—BNH, Departamento da Receita.
[Rio de Janeiro] BNH, Departamento da Receita.
v. 29 cm. semiannual.
1. Non-wage payments—Brazil—Statistics—Periodicals.
HD4932.N6B35a 75-648227
MARC-S

Banco Nacional de Ahorro y Préstamo.
Memoria y cuenta.
[Caracas]
v. 27 cm. annual.
HG2970.Z6A55 72-624551

Banco Nacional de Comercio Exterior, S.A., Mexico.
ALALC, Reunión de ministros de relaciones exteriores, Montevideo, 3-6 de noviembre 1965 (documentación y resoluciones). México, Banco Nacional de Comercio Exterior, 1965.
24 p. (Suplemento de Comercio Exterior) Cover title.
1. Latin America—Economic integration—Addresses, essays, lectures. I. Asociacion Latinamericana de Libre Comercio. II. Title.
NcU NUC75-49477

Banco Nacional de Comercio Exterior, S. A., Mexico.
Annual report.
México.
v. illus. 27 cm.
1. Banco Nacional de Comercio Exterior, S. A., Mexico.
HG2720.M44B357a 74-641146
MARC-S

Banco Nacional de Comercio Exterior, S.A., Mexico.
El comercio exterior y el artesano mexicano (1825-1830). Introducción por Luis Chávez Orozco. México, 1965.
247 p. 20 cm. (Colección de documentos para la historia del comercio exterior de México, 2. serie, 1)
1. Mexico—Commerce. 2. Labor and laboring classes—Mexico. I. Title.
MU NUC73-40628

Banco Nacional de Comercio Exterior, S.A., Mexico.
Exporte a Mexico. Mexico, 1964.
141 p.
1. Mexico—Commerce. 2. Commercial products—Mexico. I. Title.
MiEM NUC76-71567

Banco Nacional de Comercio Exterior, S. A., Mexico.
México: la política económica para 1972. [1. ed.] México, 1972.
113, 353 p. 23 cm.
"Apéndice documental" (p. [1]-347 (2d group)), includes legislation.
Includes bibliographical references.
1. Mexico—Economic policy—1970- I. Title.
HC135.B2195 72-374993

Banco Nacional de Comercio Exterior, S.A., Mexico.
Mexico 1970: facts, figures and trend. [Edited by Jorge Eduardo Navarrete. Translated by Sara Susana L. de Gamboa. 5th ed.] Mexico, 1970.
246 p. col. illus.
1. Mexico—Economic conditions. 2. Mexico—Social conditions. I. Navarrete, Jorge Eduardo, ed. II. Title.
MsSM NUC73-47905

Banco Nacional de Comercio Exterior, S. A., México.
Mexico: the new government's economic policy. [Translated by Instituto de Intérpretes y Traductores. 1st ed.] Mexico City, 1971.
261 p. 17 cm.
Translation of México: la política económica del nuevo gobierno.
Includes bibliographical references.
1. Mexico—Economic policy—1970- I. Title.
HC135.B21913 330.9'72'082 73-155966
MARC

Banco Nacional de Costa Rica, San José.
Leyes, estatuos, etc. Colección de folletos publicado por el Banco Nacional de Costa Rica, con material suplemental insertado. Costa Rica [19--]
1 v. (various pagings) fold. tables. 27 cm.
1. Banks and banking—Costa Rica. 2. Banking law—Costa Rica. 3. Banco Nacional de Costa Rica.
IEdS NUC74-927

Banco Nacional de Costa Rica, San José
see La Ciudad de San José, 1871-1921. [San José, 1972]

Banco Nacional de Costa Rica, San José. Museo archeologico.
see Arte precolombiana ... Roma, Istituto italo-latino americano, [1976]

Banco Nacional de Crédito Agrícola y Ganadero. Oficina de Estadística e Información
see Estadísticas crediticias. México.

Banco Nacional de Crédito Cooperativo
see Brazil. Laws, statutes, etc. Repertório legal... Rio de Janeiro, 1967.

Banco Nacional de Crédito Cooperativo. Directoria.
Relatório da Diretoria.
[Brasília, Brazil, Banco Nacional de Crédito Cooperativo, Diretoria]
v. 33 cm.
1. Banco Nacional de Credito Cooperativo.
HG2890.B724B1726a 76-643831
MARC-S

Banco Nacional de Credito Ejidal, S. A., Mexico
see Mexico. Direccion General de Ektension Agricola. Programa de asistencia tecnica coordinado; Coahuila. [Chapingo] 1973.

Banco Nacional de Crédito Ejidal, S. A., México
see Sociedades Ejidales Ganaderas de Cananea, Sonora. Administración de los Ejidos Ganaderos de Cananea. Cananea, Sonora, Mexico, 1966.

Banco Nacional de Cuba (Founded 1948).
Development and prospects of the Cuban economy / [editor, Pedro Alvarez Tabío] — [s.l. : s.n.], 1975 (Havana : Experimental Graphic Unit of the Cuban Book Institute)
106 p., [1] fold. leaf of plates : ill. ; 27 cm.
"XXV anniversary of the National Bank of Cuba."
"The writing of this report has been a joint responsibility of the National Bank of Cuba and the Central Bureau of Statistics of the Central Planning Board."
1. Cuba—Economic conditions—1959- 2. Cuba—Social conditions—1959- I. Alvarez Tabío, Pedro. II. Cuba. Dirección Central de Estadística. III. Title.
HC157.C9B26 1975 330.9'7291'064 77-362234
77 MARC

Banco Nacional de Desarrollo Agrícola.
Estadísticas—BANDESA.
Guatemala, BANDESA.
v. 22 cm. monthly.
1. Banco Nacional de Desarrollo Agrícola. 2. Agricultural credit—Guatemala—Statistics—Periodicals.
HG2051.G95B33b 75-644113
MARC-S

Banco Nacional de Desarrollo Agrícola.
Memoria de labores. 1971-
Guatemala.
v. illus. 21 cm.
First report covers the months of May to Dec.
1. Banco Nacional de Desarrollo Agrícola.
HG2051.G95B33a 74-641195
MARC-S

Banco Nacional de Fomento (Honduras). División Técnica.
Boletín estadístico—Banco Nacional de Fomento.
Tegucigalpa, Banco Nacional de Fomento [etc.]
v. 27 cm.
Title varies slightly.
Issued quarterly with each no. cumulative for the year.
1. Banco Nacional de Fomento (Honduras) 2. Banks and banking—Honduras—Finance—Statistics.
HG2758.F65B34a 332.1'12'097283 76-641863
MARC-S

Banco Nacional de Fomento (Paraguay)
Política de crédito y normas operativas del Banco Nacional de Fomento. [Asunción, 1967]
26 l. 24 cm.
I. Title.
HG2938.F64A6 74-230078

Banco Nacional de Fomento (Paraguay). División de Promoción
see Martínez López, Digno. Estudio de viabilidad económica para la instalación de plantas industrializadoras de leche. [Asunción, 1965?]

Banco Nacional de Fomento, Quito.
Flota Mercante Grancolombiana, S. A. Quito, 1969.
23 p. 27 cm. (Its Informe)
1. Flota Mercante Grancolombiana, S. A. I. Series.
NIC NUC73-113162

Banco Nacional de Fomento, Quito.
II (Segundo) evaluación del programa de credito agricola de capacitacion para ayuda a la colonización espontanea de Santo Domingo de los Colorados. Quito, 1971.
37 l. tables. 32 cm.
Cover title.
Issued by its Division de Credito de Capacitación.
1. Development financing—Ecuador. 2. Development credit corporations—Ecuador. I. Title.
CtY-E NUC73-119129

Banco Nacional de la Vivienda, Santo Domingo
see Perez Montas, Hernando. Analisis de mercado para viviendas... Santo Domingo, Dominican Republic, 1965.

Banco Nacional de México.
Mexico statistical data.
[Mexico City, Banco Nacional de México]
v. 16 cm.
1. Mexico—Statistics. I. Title.
HA765.B35a 317.2 76-649123
MARC-S

Banco Nacional de Mexico
see Molina Zárate, Yolanda. Examen de la situación económica de México; indice analítico, 1925-1969. [2. ed. corregida y puesta al día] Mexico, Ediciones Banamex, 1970.

Banco Nacional de México
see Tenochtitlán, 1519-1521. [México, 1971]

Banco Nacional de Nicaragua.
El crédito rural en Nicaragua. — [Managua] : Banco Nacional de Nicaragua, [1975]
[40] p. : ill. ; 25 cm.
"Programa BNN/BID."
1. Agricultural credit—Nicaragua. I. Title.
HG2051.N5B36 1975 77-469299
77 MARC

Banco Nacional de Nicaragua.
Estudio de la economía del algodón en Nicaragua. [Managua] Asesoría de la Junta Directiva [196-]
123 p. 27 cm.
Cover title.
1. Cotton growing—Nicaragua. 2. Cotton trade—Nicaragua. I. Title.
TxU NUC73-126277

Banco Nacional de Nicaragua.
Informe anual—Banco Nacional de Nicaragua.
[Managua] Banco Nacional de Nicaragua.
v. ill. 27 cm.
1. Banco Nacional de Nicaragua. 2. Banks and banking—Nicaragua—Periodicals.
HG2766.B36a 76-640807
MARC-S

Banco Nacional de Obras y Servicios Públicos.
Banco Nacional de Obras y Servicios Públicos, S. A. : 40. aniversario, 1933-1973. — México : El Banco, Coordinación General de Prensa y Relaciones Públicas, [1973?]
[18] p., [13] leaves of plates : ill. (some col.), group port. ; 33 x 42 cm.
Cover title.
"Un hombre más allá del universo ..." ([2] p., [12] leaves of plates at end) includes reproductions of 12 sketches and paintings by Dr. Atl now in the collection of the Banco.
1. Banco Nacional de Obras y Servicios Públicos. I. Atl, Dr., 1875-1964.
HG2718.B35 1973 75-553422

Banco Nacional de Obras y Servicios Públicos.
Manual de autoconstruccion. [Mexico City, 1970]
217 p. illus., plans.
Cover title.
Bibliography: p. 217.
1. Building—Handbooks, manuals, etc. 2. House construction—Handbooks, manuals, etc. I. Title.
MCM NUC74-144040

Banco Nacional de Panamá.
Cuadernos. no. 6-
Panamá, Banco Nacional de Panamá, 1972-
no. 23 cm.
Earlier no. classified separately in L. C.
1. Panama—Economic conditions—Collected works. 2. Finance—Panama—Collected works.
HC147.A1B342 75-645426
MARC-S

Banco Nacional de Panamá.
[Cuatro temas de impacto en la problemática económica nacional] Panamá, 1972.
76 p. (Cuadernos del Banco Nacional de Panamá, no. 6)
MH-BA NUC75-26560

Banco Nacional de Panamá.
Investment opportunities in Panama. [Panamá] 1973.
76 p. illus. 23 cm. (Banco Nacional de Panamá. Brochure no. 7)
1. Panama—Economic conditions. 2. Taxation—Panama. 3. Investments—Panama. I. Title. II. Series.
HC147.B36 1973b 338'.09862 74-181648
MARC

Banco Nacional de Panamá.
Invierta en Panamá. [Panamá] 1973.
74 p. 23 cm. (Its Cuadernos, no. 7)
1. Panama—Economic conditions. 2. Taxation—Panama. 3. Investments—Panama. I. Title. II. Series.
HC147.B36 1973 74-215198

Banco Nacional de Panamá.
Memoria de la asamblea de gerentes y subgerentes del Banco Nacional de Panamá.
[Panamá, Banco Nacional de Panamá]
v. ill. 28 cm.
1. Banco Nacional de Panama. 2. Banks and booking. Central—Panama. I. Title.
HG2773.B35a 76-649078
MARC-S

Banco Nacional de Panamá
see Susto Lara, Juan Antonio, 1896- Evolucion historica del Banco Nacional de Panama. Edicion oficial. Panama, 1973.

Banco Nacional de Panamá. Asesoría Económica y Planificación.
Carta económica.
Panamá.
no. illus. 24 cm.
1. Panama—Economic conditions—Periodicals. 2. Economic history—1945- —Periodicals. I. Title.
HC147.A1B34a 74-641902
MARC-S

Banco Nacional do Desenvolvimento Econômico, Rio de Janeiro.
Action plan—BNDE.
[Rio de Janeiro, Brasil] BNDE.
v. 26 cm.
1. Banco Nacional do Desenvolvimento Econômico. Rio de Janeiro. 2. Industrial promotion—Brazil. 3. Small business—Brazil—Finance.
HG2890.R54B624 338'.0981 76-647777
MARC-S

Banco Nacional do Desenvolvimento Econômico, Rio de Janeiro.
FIPEME, apoio do BNDE às pequenas e médias indústrias no Brasil : trabalho apresentado na "Reunion Latinoamericana y el Caribe sobre la Pequeña y Mediana Indústria," Bogotá, novembro 26-30 de 1973 / Banco Nacional do Desenvolvimento Econômico. — [Rio de Janeiro] : BNDE, [1974?]
59 leaves ; 28 cm.
Cover title.
Bibliography: leaf 59.
1. Small business—Brazil—Finance. 2. Small business—Brazil. 3. Brazil—Industries. I. Title.
HG3729.B8B32 1974 75-553891

Banco Nacional do Desenvolvimento Econômico, Rio de Janeiro.
Manual de legislação; leis básicas do B. N. D. E., regimento e organização interna, pessoal. [Rio de Janeiro?] 1959-
v. 27 cm.
Cover title.
1. Banking law—Brazil. I. Title.
PPiU NUC76-71550

Banco Nacional do Desenvolvimento Econômico, Rio de Janeiro.
O que o BNDE tem feito para o Brasil crescer. [Rio de Janeiro, Artes Gráf., 196?]
[20] p. illus. (part col.) 20 x 24 cm.
Cover title.
1. Banco Nacional do Desenvolvimento Econômico, Rio de Janeiro. 2. Brazil—Econ. condit. 3. Brazil—Banks and banking. I. Title.
TxU NUC73-39305

Banco Nacional do Desenvolvimento Econômico, Rio de Janeiro.
Report of activities.
[Rio de Janeiro]
v. illus. 27 cm.
1. Banco Nacional do Desenvolvimento Econômico, Rio de Janeiro.
HG2890.R54B636a 332.1'223'0981 74-642223
MARC-S

Banco Nacional do Desenvolvimento Econômico, Rio de Janeiro
see Análise e projeções do desenvolvimento econômico. Rio, 1957.

Banco Nacional do Desenvolvimento Econômico, Rio de Janeiro
see Painéis internacionais sobre desenvolvimento socioeconomico. Rio de Janeiro: APEC, 1974.

Banco Nacional do Norte.
Relatório anual—BANORTE.
[Recife, Brasil] BANORTE.
v. ill. 27 cm.
1. Banco Nacional do Norte.
HG2890.R434B3623a 77-648402
MARC-S

Banco Nacional Ultramarino, Lisbon.
Some notes about Mozambique. [Lisboa] 1970.
39 l. illus. (part fold.)
On cover: Mozambique.
1. Mozambique–Economic conditions. I. Title.
PPiU NUC73-113163

Banco Nacional Ultramarino, Lisbon. Serviços Culturais e Técnicos de Documentação e Arquivo.
Boletim de imformação.
Lisboa.
no. illus. 30 cm.
HG3200.L74B32 72-626424

Banco Nacional Ultramarino, Lourenço Marquez
see Anacleto, António Neves, 1897- comp. Os actos abusivos do Banco Nacional Ultramarino e a teoria do abuso de direito. [Lisboa, Composto e impresso na Tipografia Tilusa, 1972]

Banco Nacional Ultramarino, Lourenço Marquez. Associação dos Empregados.
see Banco Nacional Ultramarino, Lourenço Marquez. Centro de Documentação e Informação. Livros interessando ao estudo do Distrito de Lourenço Marques ... Lourenço Marques, O Centro, 1972.

Banco Nacional Ultramarino, Lourenço Marquez. Centro de Documentação.
Catálogo da biblioteca organizada por J. A. de Carvalho e oferecida ao Banco Nacional Ultramarino pelos seus herdeiros. Lourenço Marques, 1972.
166 l. 30 cm. (Its Doc[umento de] trab[alho] no. 3)
——— Aditamento. Lourenço Marques, 1972.
12 l. 30 cm. (Its Doc[umento de] trab[alho] no. 4)
Z965.L632 1972 Suppl.
1. Banco Nacional Ultramarino, Lourenço Marquez. Centro de Documentação. I. Title. II. Series: Banco Nacional Ultramarino, Lourenço Marquez. Centro de Documentação. Documento de trabalho, no. 3-4.
Z965.L632 1972 73-327422

Banco Nacional Ultramarino, Lourenço Marquez. Centro de Documentação.

For works by this body issued under its later name see

Banco Nacional Ultramarino, Lourenço Marquez. Centro de Documentação e Informação.

Banco Nacional Ultramarino, Lourenço Marquez. Centro de Documentação e Informação.
Catálogo dos livros sobre Moçambique, existentes no CDI do Banco em Lourenço Marques. Lourenço Marques [1972]
232 l. 30 cm. (Centro de Documentação e Informação do Banco Nacional Ultramarino. Doc[umento de] trab[alho] no. 5)
1. Mozambique—Bibliography—Catalogs. 2. Banco Nacional Ultramarino, Lourenço Marques. Centro de Documentação e Informação. I. Title. II. Series: Banco Nacional Ultramarino, Lourenço Marques. Centro de Documentação e Informação. Documento de trabalho, no. 5.
Z3885.B34 1972 74-206406

Banco Nacional Ultramarino, Lourenço Marquez. Centro de Documentaçao e Informaçao.
Catálogo dos livros sobre Moçambique existentes no CDI do Banco em Lourenço Marques. Lourenço Marques, 1974.
281 p. 30 cm.
——— Aditamento. 1974.
61 p. 30 cm.
1. Mozambique–Bibl. I. Title.
MiEM NUC76-25306

Banco Nacional Ultramarino, Lourenço Marquez. Centro de Documentação e Informação.
Livros interessando ao estudo do Distrito de Lourenço Marques : catálogo : exposição organizada pelo Centro de Documentação e Informação do Banco Nacional Ultramarino, com a colaboração da Associação dos Empregados do Banco, de 21 a 30 de julho de 1972. — Lourenço Marques : O Centro, 1972.
61 leaves ; 30 cm. — (Doc. trab. - CDI.BNU Moçamb. ; no. 6)
1. Lourenço Marques, Mozambique (District)—Bibliography—Exhibitions. I. Banco Nacional Ultramarino, Lourenço Marquez. Associação dos Empregados. II. Title. III. Series: Banco Nacional Ultramarino, Lourenço Marquez. Centro de Documentação e Informação. Doc. trab. CDI.BNU Moçamb. ; no. 6.
Z3883.L68B36 1972 77-480211
[DT465.L3] 77 MARC

Banco Nacional Ultramarino, Lourenço Marquez. Centro de Documentação e Informação.

For works by this body issued under its earlier name see

Banco Nacional Ultramarino, Lourenço Marquez. Centro de Documentação.

Banco nazionale del lavoro.
Sicilia, by Andrea Caizzi [and others] With a foreword by Ugo La Malfa. [Venezia, Electa Editrice, 1971]
429 p. 427 illus. (part col.) 32 cm.
Bibliography: p. 419-422.
1. Sicily. I. Caizzi, Andrea. II. Title.
MB NUC73-77461

Banco Novo Mundo.
see Ciclo de Conferências sobre Comércio Internacional de Produtos Agrícolas e Agro-Industriais, 1st, São Paulo, Brazil, 1973. Anais do I [i.e. Primerio] Ciclo de Conferências sobre Comércio Internacional de Produtos Agrícolas e Agro-Industriais, 25 a 27 de abril de 1973. São Paulo, AEASP, [1973?]

Banco Obrero, Caracas.
Casas venezolanas. [Con fotos de George Steinheil y textos preparados y seleccionados por Pedro Grases y Manuel Perez Vila, todo bajo la dirección artistica de Jesus Emilio Franco. Caracas, Oficina de Relaciones Publicas del Banco Obrero, 1973]
8 p. 10 fold. sheets (in portfolio & case) illus. 33 cm.
Title from portfolio.
Each sheet folded to make 8 p. (4, text)
1. Venezuela–Historic houses. I. Steinheil, George. II. Grases, Pedro, 1909- III. Perez Vila, Manuel. IV. Title.
CLU NUC76-71451

Banco Obrero, Caracas.
Concurso de viviendas populares. [Caracas, 1973]
102 p. illus., plans. 20 x 30 cm.
1. Housing–Venezuela. 2. Labor and laboring classes–Dwellings–Venezuela. I. Title.
TxU NUC76-71514

Banco Obrero, Caracas.
Housing policy in Venezuela. Caracus, 1967.
17 l. 32 cm.
Cover title.
1. Housing—Venezuela. I. Title.
HD7331.A3B32 1967 74-184714
MARC

Banco Obrero, Caracas.
Manual de coordinacion modular. [Caracas] Banco Obrero, Oficina de Programacion y Presupuesto, Centro de Informacion y Documentacion, 1967.
1 v. (various pagings) illus. 31 cm.
Cover title.
1. Modular coordination (Architecture)–Handbooks, manuals, etc. 2. Building–Venezuela. I. Title.
FU NUC73-51204

Banco Obrero, Caracas.
Número especial. [Caracas] Banco Obrero, Oficina de Programación y Presupuesto, Centro de Información y Documentación [1969?]
1 v. (various pagings) illus.
Cover title.
Contains 6 documents, previously issued separately, combined to present at the II Congreso Interamericano de la Vivienda.
1. Housing–Venezuela. I. Congreso Interamericano de la Vivienda, 2d, Caracas, 1969. II. Title.
PPiU NUC73-40632

Banco Obrero, Caracas.
1ª [i.e. Primera] exposición nacional de manualidades de los adjudicatarios del Banco Obrero, Palacio de las Industrias (sede de pro-Venezuela) del 6 al 20 de octubre de 1966. [Caracas? 1966?]
[2] p. 21 cm.
1. Handicraft–Venezuela–Exhibitions.
TxU NUC74-145851

Banco Obrero, Caracas
see Simposium Latinoamericano sobre Racionalización de la Construcción, 1st, Caracas, 1973. Intercambio de conocimientos... Caracas, 1975?

Banco Obrero, Caracas. Centro de Información y Documentación

For publications of the Banco Obrero issued by this body see

Banco Obrero, Caracas.

Banco Obrero, Caracas. Oficina de Programación y Presupuesto.
Programa de viviendas para Valencia; estudio de las condiciónes y caracteristicas actuales y futuras de la población que se va a alojar. [2. ed. Valencia, Venezuela, 1965]
45 l. 32 cm.
Cover title.
1. Housing–Valencia, Venezuela. I. Title.
NNC NUC75-26561

Banco Peninsular
see España ante el Mercado Común. [Madrid] (1971)

Banco Popular, Bogotá. Museo Arqueológico
see Mora de Jaramillo, Yolanda. Cerámica y ceramistas de Ráquira. Bogota : Editora Arco, 1974.

Banco Popular Antiliano N.V.
The Netherlands Antilles. Aruba, Banco Popular Antiliano, 1971.
27 p. illus.
1. West Indies, Dutch–Description & travel. 2. West Indies, Dutch–Econ. conditions. I. Title.
MiEM NUC73-126458

Banco Popular de Puerto Rico, San Juan
see Guía para las elecciones, 1972. [San Juan, 1972]

Banco Popular Español. Centro de Estudios Bancarios.
Derecho civil. Madrid, Centro de Estudios Bancarios del Banco Popular Español, 1971.
83 p., illus. 21 cm. Sp 71-Mar
1. Civil law—Spain—Compends. I. Title.
73-349722

Banco Popular Español. Centro de Estudios Bancarios.
Derecho mercantil. Madrid, 1971.
194 p. 21 cm. Sp 72-Feb/Mar/Apr
1. Commercial law—Spain—Compends. I. Title.
73-349723

Banco Popular Español. Centro de Estudios Bancarios.
Economía política. Madrid, 1971.
182 p. 21 cm. Sp 71-Oct
1. Economics. I. Title.
HB178.5.B33 73-345941

Banco Popular Español. Centro de Estudios Bancarios.
Geografía económica. Madrid, Centro de Estudios Bancarios del Banco Popular Español, 1971.
119 p., illus. 21 cm. Sp 71-Apr
1. Spain—Economic conditions—1918- I. Title.
HC385.B319 73-345943

Banco Popular Español. Centro de Estudios Bancarios.
Operaciones bancarias de extranjero ... Madrid, Centro de Estudios Bancarios del Banco Popular Español, 1972.
166 p. 21 cm. Sp 72-July/Aug/Sept
Cover title: Operaciones extranjeras.
"Aclaraciones, ampliaciones y rectificaciones al texto Operaciones extranjeras, 1972" : [4] p. inserted.
1. Letters of credit. I. Title. II. Title: Operaciones extranjeras.
HG3745.B3 73-345948

Banco Popular Español. Centro de Estudios Bancarios.
Operaciones bancarias (extranjeras). Madrid, 1971.
112 p. 21 cm. Sp 71-Nov/Dec
1. Letters of credit. 2. Banks and banking. 3. Insurance, Credit. I. Title.
HG3745.B32 73-345949

Banco Popular Español. Centro de Estudios Bancarios.
Operaciones bancarias (nacionales) Madrid, 1971.
122 p. 21 cm. Sp 72-Jan
1. Banks and banking—Spain. I. Title.
HG3184.B34 73-345946

Banco Popular Español. Centro de Estudios Bancarios.
Organización bancaria. Madrid, 1972.
2 l., 185 p., illus. 21 cm. Sp***
1. Banks and banking—Spain. I. Title.
HG3184.B35 73-345947

Banco Popular Español. Servicio de Estudios Financieros.
Estudios financieros / Banco Popular Español, [Servicio de Estudios Financieros]. — [Madrid : El Servicio, [1968?]
1 v. : graphs ; 31 cm.
Cover title.
Loose-leaf for updating.
1. Corporations—Spain—Finance. I. Title.
HG4216.B36 1968 77-481443
77 MARC

Banco Português do Atlântico.
Summary of foreign exchange regulations in Portugal. [Lisbon] BPA [1975]
52 p. 21 cm.
Cover title.
1. Foreign exchange--Portugal. I. Title.
CLL NUC77-87858

Banco Regional de Brasília.
Relatório de atividades—Banco Regional de Brasília. [Brasília, Banco Regional de Brasília.
v. ill. 24 cm.
1. Banco Regional de Brasília.
HG2890.B724B22a 75-649047
MARC-S

Banco Regional de Brasília
see Fundação do Serviço Social do Distrito Federal. Sistema de crédito social orientado... [Brasília] 1971.

Banco Regional de Desenvolvimento do Extremo Sul.
Boletim estatístico.
Pôrto Alegre.
v. illus. 27 cm.
1. Bank loans—Brazil, South—Statistics.
HG2889.S6B36a 74-642098
MARC-S

Banco Regional de Desenvolvimento do Extremo Sul.
Estudo de pré-viabilidade para expansão e/ou implantação de indústrias de produtos cerâmicos estruturais na área da Grande Porto Alegre / Banco Regional de Desenvolvimento do Estremo [i.e. Extremo] Sul-BRDE. — Porto Alegre : BRDE, 1974.
155 leaves ; 31 cm. — (Estudos econômicos ; no. 5)
1. Ceramic industries—Brazil—Porto Alegre metropolitan area. I. Title. II. Series: Estudos econômicos (Porto Alegre) ; no. 5.
HD9615.B73P673 1974 76-469194
76 MARC

Banco Regional de Desenvolvimento do Extremo Sul.
Rio Grande do Sul: o futuro em ação. Rio Grande do Sul: the future in action. [Porto Alegre? 197-]
[24] p. 28 cm.
1. Rio Grande do Sul, Brazil (State). Economic conditions. I. Title.
TxU NUC76-25303

Banco Regional de Desenvolvimento do Extremo Sul. Agência de Porto Alegre.
Economia do Rio Grande do Sul : bibliografia / Banco Regional de Desenvolvimento do Extremo Sul, BRDE, Agência de Porto Alegre. — Porto Alegre : BRDE, 1974.
196 p. ; 31 cm.
Includes indexes.
1. Rio Grande do Sul, Brazil (State)—Economic conditions—Bibliography. I. Title.
Z7165.B7B28 1974 76-463640
[HC188.R4] 76 MARC

Banco Regional de Desenvolvimento do Extremo Sul. Agência de Porto Alegre.
A indústria de óleos vegetais comestíveis no Rio Grande do Sul / [realização da Agência de Porto Alegre, Banco Regional de Desenvolvimento do Extremo Sul]. — Porto Alegre : BRDE, 1973.
249 p. : ill. ; 31 cm. — (Estudos econômicos ; no. 4)
1. Oil industries—Brazil—Rio Grande do Sul (State) I. Title. II. Series: Estudos econômicos (Porto Alegre) ; no. 4.
HD9490.B82R53 75-580746

Banco Regional de Desenvolvimento do Extremo Sul. Gabinete de Estudos Econômicos.
Projeto para implantação de piqueladeiro em Alegrete. (versão preliminar). [Pôrto Alegre, 1968]
41 l. diagrs., tables. 31 cm.
Microfiche (negative) 11 x 25 cm. (NYPL FSN 15,574)
1. Wool trade and industry—Rio Grande do Sul, Brazil (State) I. Title.
NN NUC76-71515

Banco Totta-Aliança.
Portugal: some facts about its economy [edited by Banco Totta-Aliança. Lisbon, 1968?]
94 p. illus. 19 cm.
Cover title.
1. Portugal—Economic conditions—statistics. I. Title.
FU NUC74-144829

Banco Unión
see Anotaciones sobre la economía venezolana. [Caracas] Banco Unión, Oficina de Planificación [n.d.]

Banco Urquijo, Madrid.
Estudio general sobre inversiones en la economia cacereña, 1970-73. [Madrid] Iniciativas Extremeñas [1970]
4 v. illus.
1. Cáceres, Spain (Province)—Econ. condit. 2. Cáceres, Spain (Province)—Stat. I. Title.
NNU NUC73-38927

Banco Urquijo, Madrid. Servicio de Estudios Económicos.
El crecimiento de la industria española. — Madrid : Banco Urquijo, Servicio de Estudios Económicos, 1974.
101 p. : graphs ; 24 cm. Sp***
1. Spain—Industries. I. Title.
HC385.B335 1974 76-453386
76 MARC

Banco Urquijo, Madrid. Servicio de Estudios Económicos.
España: una economía en desarrollo. Madrid, Banco Urquijo, Servicio de Estudios Económicos, 1973.
37 p., illus. 24 cm. Sp 73-July
1. Spain—Economic conditions—1918- I. Title.
HC385.B335 1973 74-309294

Banco Urquijo, Madrid. Servicio de Estudios Económicos.
Spain; a developing economy. Madrid, Banco Urquijo, Economic Research Dept., 1973.
31 p. illus. 24 cm. Sp***
1. Spain—Economic conditions—1918- I. Title.
HC385.B335 1973b 330.9'46'082 74-172264
MARC

Banco Urquijo, Madrid. Servicio de Estudios en Barcelona.
El área metropolitana de Barcelona : su génesis y problemática. — Madrid : Editorial Moneda y Crédito, 1972.
576 p., [15] leaves of plates (6 fold.) : ill. ; 24 cm. Sp***
On spine: Génesis y problemática del área metropolitana.
Includes bibliographical references.
1. Cities and towns — Planning — Barcelona metropolitan area, Spain. 2. Barcelona metropolitan area, Spain. 3. Municipal services—Barcelona metropolitan area, Spain. I. Title. II. Title: Génesis y problemática del área metropolitana.
HT169.S652B28 1972 309.2'62'094672 75-557919

Banco Urquijo, Madrid. Servicio de Estudios en Barcelona.
Las fuentes de financiacion de la empresa en Espana. [2. edición. Madrid] Editorial Moneda y Credito, 1972.
527 p. tables. 24 cm.
1. Banks and banking—Spain. 2. Capital market—Spain. 3. Credit—Spain—Sources. 4. Development financing—Spain—Sources. I. Title.
CtY-E NUC74-139109

Banco Urquijo, Madrid. Servicio de Estudios en Barcelona.
Guía de fuentes estadísticas de España. Edición 1970. [Madrid] Editorial Moneda y Crédito [1970-
3 v. (loose-leaf) 27 cm.
"Primera edición."
——— Indices. Barcelona, Comisión Mixta de Coordinación Estadística, 1972-
v. 25 cm.
HA37.S77B3 Suppl.
ISBN 84-500-5696-9
1. Spain—Statistical services. I. Title.
HA37.S77B3 70-262820
rev

Banco Urquijo, Madrid. Servicio de Estudios en Barcelona.
International investment in Spain. Barcelona, 1971.
76 p. illus.
1. Investments, Foreign—Spain. 2. Spain—Economic conditions. I. Title.
MH-BA NUC73-32187

Banco Urquijo, Madrid. Servicio de Estudios en Barcelona.
Objetivos e instrumentos de la política económica española 1959-69. [Madrid] Editorial Moneda y Crédito, 1973.
iv, 309 p. illus. 23 cm. Sp***
"Estudio realizado ... bajo la supervisión ... de Pere Pi-Sunyer Bayó ..."
Bibliography: p. 309.
1. Spain—Economic policy. 2. Spain—Economic conditions—1918- I. Pi-Sunyer Bayó, Pere, ed. II. Title.
HC385.B336 1973 74-301624
ISBN 84-7110-064-9

Banco Urquijo, Madrid. Servicio de Estudios en Barcelona.
La oferta de servicios colectivos en Cataluña. [Madrid] Editorial Moneda y Crédito, 1972-
v. 24 cm.
Contents.—t. 1., v. 1. Introducción. t. 1, v. 2. Dotación escolar.
1. Public welfare—Catalonia. I. Title.
NN NUC76-89155

Banco Urquijo, Madrid. Servicio de Estudios en Barcelona.
see Reunión General de Servicios de Estudios Económicos, 1st, Madrid, 1973. Economía regional en España ... Madrid, Editorial Moneda y Crédito, 1975.

Banco Urquijo, Sevilla. Servicio de Estudios
see Iniciativas Extremenas, S. A. Estudio general sobre inversiones en la economia cacereña, 1970-73. [Madrid, Editorial Moneda y Credito, 1970]

Bancor.
Le confidenze di un banchiere. Milano, ETAS Kompass libri, 1973.
99 p. 19 cm. (Espresso/Documenti, 1) L1500 It 74-June
1. Banks and banking—Italy—Addresses, essays, lectures. 2. Currency question—Addresses, essays, lectures. I. Title.
HG3080.B33 1973 74-335238

Bancora.
మనం మనుష్యులం; స్త్రీ పాత్రలేని నాటిక. రచన: బంకోరా. [తొలికూర్పు] కె. సి. వర్క్స్, గుంటూరు Dist., బండపల్లి ప్రచురణలు [1970]
viii, 34 p. ports. 19 cm. Rs1.50
In Telugu.

I. Title.
Title romanized: Manaṃ manuṣyulaṃ.
PL4780.9.B29M3 77–918395

Bancos de Comercio System
see Sistema Bancos de Comercio.

Bancoseguros. año 1–
jul./agosto 1975–
[Montevideo] Agremiación de Funcionarios del Banco de Seguros.
v. ill. 28 cm.
"Publicación oficial de la Agremiación de Funcionarios del Banco de Seguros."
1. Agremiación de Funcionarios del Banco de Seguros. I. Agremiación de Funcionarios del Banco de Seguros.
HD6649.B262A473 76–647644
MARC-S

Bancquart, Marie Claire.
Mains dissoutes / Marie-Claire Bancquart. — Mortemart : Rougerie, [1975]
[31] p. ; 23 cm. F***
Poems.
I. Title.
PQ2662.A49M3 841'.9'14 76-452026
76 MARC

Bancquart, Marie Claire.
Paris des surréalistes. [Paris] Seghers [1972]
230 p. illus. 20 cm. (L'Archipel) 29.50F F***
Bibliography: p. [213]–216.
1. French literature—20th century—History and criticism. 2. Paris in literature. I. Title.
PQ307.P3B3 73–316278

Bancquart, Marie Claire.
Proche [par] Marie-Claire Bancquart. Paris, Librairie Saint-Germain-des-Prés, 1972.
42 p. 19 cm. (Poètes contemporains) 15.00F F 73–6913
Three hundred and thirty copies printed.
I. Title.
PQ2662.A49P68 74–183645
MARC

Bancquart, Marie Claire.
Projets alternés. [Mortemart] Rougerie [1972]
[35] p. 23 cm. 8.00F F***
"Édition ... tirée à 80 exemplaires sur Alfa-Mousse Navarre, numérotes de 1 à 80." No. 62.
Poems.
I. Title.
PQ2662.A49P7 74–328676
MARC

Bancquart, Marie Claire
see Bouilhet, Louis. Lettres à Louise Colet. Paris, Presses universitaires de France [1973]

Bancquart, Marie Claire
see Vallès, Jules Louis Joseph, 1832-1885. Correspondance avec Hector Malot. Paris, Éditeurs français réunis, 1968.

Bancquart, Marie Claire.
see Vallès, Jules Louis Joseph, 1832-1885. L'insurgé. [Paris] Gallimard, c1975.

Bancroft, Anne, 1923-
Religions of the East / [by] Anne Bancroft. — London : Heinemann, 1974.
256 p. : ill., ports. ; 26 cm. GB74-19837
Col. ill. on lining papers.
Bibliography: p. 250-252.
Includes index.
ISBN 0-434-90087-7 : £4.50
1. Religions. I. Title.
BL80.2.B36 1974b 291 75-306628
75 MARC

Bancroft, Anne, 1923–
Religions of the East. New York, St. Martin's Press [1974]
256 p. illus. 26 cm. $12.95
Bibliography: p. 250–252.
1. Religions. I. Title.
BL80.2.B36 1974 294 72–97352
MARC

Bancroft, Anne, 1923-
Twentieth century mystics & sages / Anne Bancroft. — London : Heinemann, 1976.
xv, 344 p. : ports. ; 22 cm. GB76-28710
Includes bibliographies and index.
ISBN 0-434-90088-5 : £5.00
1. Religions—Biography. I. Title.
BL72.B36 1976b 200'.92'2 77-354246
77 MARC

Bancroft, Arthur P
Gazetteer and directory of Clermont County, O., 1882. [By] Arthur P. Bancroft. Batavia, Ohio, Dale O. Cowen [n.d.]
122 p.
County histories of the "Old Northwest". Series II: Ohio. Reel 4, no. 15.
Advertising matter interspersed.
Microfilm copy.
1. Clermont Co., Ohio--Directories.
I. Title.
OOxM NUC77-87795

Bancroft, B Richard, 1936-
The historical development of the Music Department of the State University College at Fredonia, New York. [n.p., 1972]
2 v.
Final document (Ed.D.)—New York University.
1. Dissertations, Academic—N.Y.U.—1972.
I. Title.
NNU NUC74-139110

Bancroft, Betsy Barber.
Wild honeysuckle. Illustrated by Ruth Powers Bridges. Gretna [La.] Pelican Pub. Co., 1972 [c1966]
[29] p. illus. 23 cm.
Poems.
I. Title.
LU LN NUC74-144860

Bancroft, Catherine.
Satan and his witches: a battle for the Puritan mind; a study of the rationalization of Puritan ideology, 1684-1687. [n.p.] 1972.
1 v.
Honors thesis—Harvard.
1. Puritans—Massachusetts. 2. Witchcraft—Salem, Mass.
MH NUC76-71516

Bancroft, Darrell Stuart, 1941-
A multivariate analysis of the life cycle of policy loans. Ann Arbor, Mich., University Microfilms, 1974.
1 reel. 35 mm.
Thesis—University of Pennsylvania, 1973.
Collation of the original: 204 leaves. illus.
1. Insurance, Life—Finance. 2. Loans.
I. Title.
ViBlbV NUC76-25305

Bancroft, David.
Molière and the comedy of the imagination; some comments on Le malade imaginaire. [North Ryde, N. S. W.] Macquarie University, 1972.
ii, 45 p. 25 cm. (Monographs for teachers of French, v. 4, no. 3) Aus***
1. Molière, Jean Baptiste Poquelin, 1622–1673. Le malade imaginaire. I. Title. II. Series.
DC1.M62 vol. 4, no. 3 842'.4 73–178458
[PQ1835] MARC

Bancroft, David C.
see Arizona. Game and Fish Commission. Fishery investigations in Region III... [Phoenix, 1972?]

Bancroft, Edward, 1744-1821.
Experimental researches concerning the philosophy of permanent colours, and the best means of producing them by dying, callico printing, &c. London, T. Cadell and W. Davies, 1794.
xlvii, 456 p.
Microprint. New York, Readex Microprint, 1969. 6 cards. (Landmarks of science)
I. Title.
InU NUC76-71517

Bancroft, Edward, 1744-1821.
The history of Charles Wentworth, Esq. / Edward Bancroft. — New York : Garland Pub., 1975.
3 v. ; 18 cm. — (The Flowering of the novel)
Reprint of the 1770 ed. printed for T. Becket, London.
ISBN 0-8240-1192-9
I. Title. II. Series.
PZ3.B2224 Hi 20 813'.1 74-26666
[PS703.B34] 74 MARC

Bancroft, Emery Herbert.
Christian theology, systematic and Biblical / by Emery H. Bancroft. — 2d rev. ed. / edited by Ronald B. Mayers. — Grand Rapids : Zondervan Pub. House, c1976.
410 p. ; 23 cm.
Includes bibliographical references and index.
1. Theology, Doctrinal. I. Mayers, Ronald B. II. Title.
BT77.B3 1976 230 76-150619
76 MARC

Bancroft, F
Progress in O-E spinning : world literature survey, 1968-1974 / by F. Bancroft and C. A. Lawrence. — Manchester : Shirley Institute, 1975.
[2], ii, 138 p. (2 fold.) : ill. ; 30 cm. — (Publication—Shirley Institute ; S16)
GB75-24803
Includes bibliographical references.
ISBN 0-903669-14-5 : £15.00
1. Spinning. 2. Spinning machinery. I. Lawrence, Carl Anthony, joint author. II. Title. III. Series: Shirley Institute, Manchester, Eng. Publication ; S16.
TS1480.B3 677'.02822 76-356156
76 MARC

Bancroft, Frederic, 1860-1945.
A sketch of the Negro in politics, especially in South Carolina and Mississippi / by Frederic A. Bancroft. — New York : AMS Press, 1976.
92 p. ; 23 cm.
Reprint of the 1885 ed. published by J. F. Pearson, New York.
Originally presented as the author's thesis, Columbia College.
Bibliography: p. [91]-92.
ISBN 0-404-00003-7
1. Negroes—Politics and suffrage. 2. South Carolina—Politics and government—1865-1950. 3. Mississippi—Politics and government—1865-1950. I. Title.
JK1781.B24 1976 329 70-160007
75 MARC

Bancroft, G M
Mössbauer spectroscopy: an introduction for inorganic chemists and geochemists [by] G. M. Bancroft. London, New York, McGraw-Hill [c1973]
xii, 251 p. illus. 24 cm.
Includes bibliographical references.
1. Mössbauer spectroscopy.
CLU NUC76-71518

Bancroft, G M
Mössbauer spectroscopy: an introduction for inorganic chemists and geochemists [by] G. M. Bancroft. New York, Wiley [1973]
xii, 251 p. illus. 24 cm.
"A Halsted Press book."
Includes bibliographical references.
1. Mössbauer spectroscopy.
QC490.B35 537.5'352 73–3326
ISBN 0-470-04665-1 MARC

Bancroft, George, 1800-1891.
History of the battle of Lake Erie, and miscellaneous papers, by Hon. George Bancroft. Life and writings of George Bancroft, by Oliver Dyer ... New York, R. Bonner's sons, 1891.
1 reel. (On American culture series, reel 459, no. 2)
Microfilm (positive) 35 mm. Ann Arbor, Mich., University Microfilms, 1971.
Collation of the original: 264 p.
1. Erie, Lake, Battle of, 1813. 2. Perry, Oliver Hazard, 1785-1819. 3. Byron, George Gordon Noël Byron, baron, 1788-1824. 4. Everett, Edward, 1794-1865. 5. Washington, George, pres. U.S., 1732-1799. I. Dyer, Oliver, 1824-1907. Life and writings of George Bancroft. II. Title.
PSt NUC75-83792

Bancroft, George, 1800-1891.
History of the United States of America, from the discovery of the continent [to 1789] By Goerge Bancroft. The author's last revision... New York, D. Appleton and company, [c1882-86]
6 v. front. (port., v. 6) 23 cm.
Ultra microfiche. Dayton, Ohio, National Cash Register, 1970. 1st title of 1. 10.5 x 14.8 cm. (PCMI library collection, 956)
1. U.S.—Hist.—Colonial period. 2. U.S.—Hist.—Revolution. 3. U.S.—Hist.—Confederation, 1783-1789. I. Title.
KEmT NUC74-144864

Bancroft, George, 1800-1891.
Joseph Reed, a historical essay. New York, W. J. Widdleton, 1867.
64 p.
Microfilm (positive) Ann Arbor, Mich., University Microfilms, 1973. 6th title of 6. 35 mm. (American culture series, 514.6)
1. Reed, Joseph, 1741-1785.
KEmT PSt NUC74-144863

Bancroft, George, 1800-1891.
Literary and historical miscellanies. New York, Harper & brothers, 1855.
iv, 517 p. 24 cm.
Microfilm. Ann Arbor, Mich., University Microfilms, 1963. 1 reel. 35 mm. (American culture series, 223:1)
I. Title.
FU NUC75-107932

Bancroft, George, 1800-1891.
Martin Van Buren to the end of his public career, by George Bancroft. New York, Harper and brothers, 1889.
iv p., 1 l., 239 p. 21 cm.
Ultra microfiche. Dayton, Ohio, National Cash Register, 1970. 1st title of 4. 10.5 x 14.8 cm. (PCMI library collection, 74-1)
1. Van Buren, Martin, pres. U.S., 1782-1862.
KEmT NUC73-126324

Bancroft, George, 1800-1891
see Hunt, Charles Havens. Life of Edward Livingston. New York, D. Appleton and Company, 1864.

Bancroft, George Gilbert.
Genealogy of the Bancroft family. [n. p., 1966?]
23 l.
1. Bancroft family. I. Title.
WHi NUC76-71519

Bancroft, Gertrude.
The American labor force : its growth and changing composition / by Gertrude Bancroft. — New York : Russell & Russell, 1975, c1958.
xiv, 256 p. : ill. ; 25 cm.
Reprint of the ed. published by Wiley, New York, in series: Census monograph series.
Bibliography: p. 146-150.
Includes index.
ISBN 0-8462-1760-0 : $18.00
1. Labor supply—United States. I. Title. II. Series: Census monograph series.
HD5724.B33 1975 331.1'1'0973 73-86717
75 MARC

Bancroft, Griffing.
The white cardinal, by Griffing Bancroft. Illustrated by Charles Fracé. New York, Coward, McCann & Geoghegan [1973]
124 p. illus. 22 cm. $4.95
SUMMARY: Traces the first year in the life of a cardinal as he struggles to accept the fact that his rare albino coloring has destined him to be a loner.
Includes bibliographical references.
1. Cardinal-birds—Legends and stories. [1. Cardinals (Birds)—Fiction. 2. Birds—Fiction. 3. Albinos and albinism—Fiction] I. Title.
PZ7.B219Wh 3 [Fic] 72-89756
ISBN 0-399-20241-4; 0-399-20241-4 MARC

Bancroft, Hubert Howe, 1832–1918.
The book of the fair; an historical and descriptive presentation of the world's science, art, and industry, as viewed through the Columbian exposition at Chicago in 1893 ... By Hubert Howe Bancroft ... Chicago and San Francisco, The Bancroft company, 1895.
2 v. illus. (incl. ports., plans) 41 cm.
Paged continuously.
1. Chicago. World's Columbian exposition, 1893. I. Title.
T500.C1B2 1895 5-30158

Bancroft, Hubert Howe, 1832-1918.
The book of the fair; an historical and descriptive presentation of the world's science, art, and industry, as viewed through the Columbian exposition at Chicago in 1893, designed to set forth the display made by the congress of nations, of human achievement in material form, so as the more effectually to illustrate the progress of mankind in all the departments of civilized life, by Hubert Howe Bancroft ... New York, Bounty Books [1972? c1894]
v. illus. (incl. ports.) 28 cm.
1. Chicago. World's Columbian exposition, 1893. I. Title.
NjR NUC74-146067

Bancroft, Hubert Howe, 1832–1918.
... History of Central America ... San Franciso, A. L. Bancroft & company, 1882–87.
3 v. illus. (maps) fold. map. 24 cm. (The works of Hubert Howe Bancroft, v. VI–VIII)
"Authorities quoted": v. 1, p. xxv–lxxii.
CONTENTS: v. I. 1501–1530.—v. II. 1530–1800.—v. III. 1801–1887.
——— Microfilm.
1. Central America—History. 2. Central America—Bibliography. I. Series.
[F851.B215 vol. 6–8] 1–23104
Microfilm 9483 F

Bancroft, Hubert Howe, 1832–1918.
... History of the north Mexican states ... San Francisco, A. L. Bancroft & company [etc.] 1884–89.
2 v. illus. (incl. maps, plans) double map. 24 cm. (The works of Hubert Howe Bancroft. vol. xv–xvi)
"Authorities quoted": vol. I, p. xix–xlviii.
According to W. A. Morris, in Quarterly of the Oregon historical society, v. 4, p. 287–364, these volumes were the work of H. L. Oak, J. J. Peatfield, and William Nemos.
CONTENTS: v. 1. 1531–1800.—v. 2. "History of the North Mexican states and Texas," 1801–1889.
1. Mexico—History. 2. Southwest, New—History. 3. Texas—History. I. Oak, Henry Lebbeus, 1844–1905. II. Peatfield, Joseph Joshua, 1833– III. Nemos, William, 1848–
F851.B215 1–23109
——— Copy 2. F1226.B28

Bancroft, Hubert Howe, 1832–1918.
The native races [of the Pacific States] ... San Francisco, A. L. Bancroft & company, 1882.
5 v. illus., 11 fold. maps, fold. tab. 24 cm. (His Works v. I–V)
First issued separately, San Francisco, 1874–75.
"Authories quoted": v. 1, p. XVII–XLIX.
CONTENTS: v. 1. Wild tribes.—v. 2. Civilized nations.—v. 3. Myths and languages.—v. 4. Antiquities.—v. 5. Primitive history.
1. Indians of North American—Pacific States. 2. Indians of Mexico. 3. Indians of Central America. 4. Indians—Bibliography. I. Title.
[F851.B215 vol. 1–5] 3–6526
——— Microfilm copy. Microfilm 9483 E

Bancroft, John D
Histochemical techniques / J.D. Bancroft ; introductory chapter by A. Stevens ; with a foreword by A.G.E. Pearse. -- 2d ed. -- London ; Boston : Butterworths, 1975.
348 p. : ill.
First ed. published in 1967 under title: An introduction to histochemical techniques.
Includes bibliographies and index.
1. Histochemistry. Technique. I. Title.
DNAL NUC77-88179

Bancroft, John D
Histochemical techniques [by] J.D. Bancroft. Introductory chapter by A. Stevens, with a foreword by A.G.E. Pearse. 3d ed. London, Butterworths [1975]
ix, 348 p. illus. 23 cm.
First ed. published in 1967 under title: An introduction to histochemical techniques.
1. Histochemistry-- Technique. I. Title.
OkU-M NUC77-93153

Bancroft, John D
Histopathological stains and their diagnostic uses / John D. Bancroft, Alan Stevens ; photography by W. H. Brackenbury ; foreword by I. M. P. Dawson. — Edinburgh ; New York : Churchill Livingstone, 1975.
149 p. : ill. ; 24 cm. GB***
Label mounted on fly leaf which reads: Distributed in the U.S.A. by Longman Inc., New York.
Includes bibliographies and index.
ISBN 0-443-01226-1
1. Histology, Pathological—Technique. 2. Stains and staining (Microscopy) 3. Diagnosis, Cytologic. I. Stevens, Alan, joint author. II. Title.
RB43.B3 616.07'583 74-81753
75 MARC

Bancroft, John D
An introduction to histochemical techniques [by] J. D. Bancroft; with a foreword by A. G. E. Pearse. London, Butterworths, 1967.
ix, 268 p. plate, illus. (incl. 6 col.) 23 cm. 58/- B68-02399
Second ed. published in 1975 under title: Histochemical techniques.
1. Histochemistry—Technique. I. Title.
QH613.B36 1967 574.8'2'028 68-82580
[r75]rev MARC

Bancroft, John D.
see Theory and practice of histological techniques. Edinburgh, Churchill Livingstone, 1977.

Bancroft, John Henry Jeffries.
Deviant sexual behaviour : modification and assessment / by John Bancroft. — Oxford : Clarendon Press, 1974.
ix, 256 p., plate : ill. ; 23 cm. GB 74-19453
Bibliography: p. 235-252.
Includes index.
ISBN 0-19-857367-7 : £5.00
1. Sexual disorders. 2. Sexual deviation. I. Title.
RC556.B33 616.8'583'06 74-595055
75 MARC

Bancroft, Judith Ann, 1939-
Pedagogical moves and substantive meanings communicated in the verbal discourse of baccalaureate nursing classes. [n. p.] c1975.
323 l. 29 cm.
Thesis (Ph. D.)—University of Wisconsin.
Vita.
Includes bibliography.
1. Nurses and nursing—Study and teaching. I. Title.
WU NUC76-22105

Bancroft, Margaret Josephine, 1911-
see Bancroft family genealogy. [n.p., 1975]

Bancroft, Marie Effie (Wilton) Lady, 1839–1921.
The Bancrofts: recollections of sixty years [by] Marie Bancroft [and] Squire Bancroft. New York, B. Blom [1969]
xi, 462 p. illus. 24 cm.
Reprint of the 1909 ed. published by Dutton, New York.
1. Bancroft, Marie Effie (Wilton) Lady, 1839–1921. 2. Bancroft, Sir Squire Bancroft, 1841–1926. 3. Actors, English—Correspondence, reminiscences, etc. I. Bancroft, Sir Squire Bancroft, 1841–1926, joint author. II. Title.
PN2598.B3A3 1969 792'.028'0924 [B] 70–87117
MARC

Bancroft, Michael
see Canada. Immigration Appeal Board. Immigration appeal cases. Toronto, Carswell, 1972-

Bancroft, Michael, ed.
see Canadian encyclopedic degest, western... 2d ed. Calgary, Burroughs [1956-69]

Bancroft, Peggy.
Ringing axes and rocking chairs; the story of Barrett Township. With pen and ink sketches by Edna Palmer Engelhardt. [1st. ed. Mountainhome, Pa., Barrett Friendly Library, 1974]
xiii, 307 p. illus. 24 cm.
1. Barrett Township, Pa.—History. I. Title.
F159.B25B36 917.48'28 74–82144
MARC

Bancroft, Peggy.
This mountain land; in lore and legend, fact and fancy. Newfoundland, Pa., Newfoundland Area Public Library [1972]
45 p. illus.
1. Newfoundland, Pa., -History. 2. Pennsylvania- Cities and towns-Newfoundland. I. Title.
WHi NUC74-139111

Bancroft, Peter.
The world's finest minerals and crystals. London, Thames & Hudson [1973]
176 p. col. illus. 30 cm. £8.50 GB***
1. Mineralogy—Pictorial works. I. Title.
QE363.8.B36 1973b 549 74–150508
ISBN 0-500-01091-9 MARC

Bancroft, Peter.
The world's finest minerals and crystals. New York, Viking Press [1973]
176 p. col. illus. 29 cm. (A Studio book) $28.50
1. Mineralogy—Pictorial works. I. Title.
QE363.8.B36 1973 549 77–186742
ISBN 0-670-79022-2 MARC

Bancroft, Raymond L
America's mayors and councilmen: their problems and frustrations, by Raymond Bancroft. Washington, National League of Cities [1974]
96 p. illus. 28 cm. (NLC Research report) $10.00
1. Mayors — United States. 2. City councilmen — United States. I. Title. II. Series: National League of Cities. NLC research report.
JS323.B28 352'.008'0973 74–79000
MARC

Bancroft, Raymond L.
see National League of Cities. Municipal fire service trends: 1972. Washington, 1972.

Bancroft, Richard, Abp. of Canterbury, 1544-1610
see also
Canterbury Eng. (Province). Archbishop, 1604-1610 (Richard Bancroft)

Bancroft, Samuel, d. 1915
see Wilmington Society of the Fine Arts, Wilmington, Del. The Samuel and Mary R. Bancroft English pre-Raphaelite collection. Wilmington, c1962.

Bancroft, Sir Squire Bancroft, 1841-1926, joint author
see Bancroft, Marie Effie (Wilton) Lady, 1839-1921. The Bancrofts: recollections of sixty years. New York, B. Blom [1969]

Bancroft family genealogy, compiled and published by Margaret J. Bancroft. [n.p., 1975]
2 v. index, illus., facsims. 28 cm.
Title from index.
1. Bancroft family. I. Bancroft, Margaret Josephine, 1911-
NN NUC77-92573

Bancroft Library, Berkeley, Calif.
see California. University. Bancroft Library.

Bancroft-Whitney Company, San Francisco. California corporation manual.
see Dessent, Michael H. California corporation manual ... 2d ed. San Francisco, Bancroft-Whitney Co., 1974-1975.

Bancroft-Whitney Company, San Francisco
see American jurisprudence... 2d ed. Rochester, N. Y., Lawyers Co-operative Pub. Co., 1962-

Bancroft-Whitney Company, San Francisco
see American jurisprudence... 2d ed. San Francisco, Bancroft-Whitney Co., 1975.

Bancroft-Whitney Company, San Francisco
see American jurisprudence legal forms. 2. ed. Rochester, N. Y., Lawyers Co-operative Pub. Co. San Francisco, 1971-74.

Bancroft-Whitney Company, San Francisco
see American jurisprudence proof of facts, annotated ... San Francisco, Bancroft-Whitney Co. 1959-73.

Bancroft-Whitney Company, San Francisco
see American jurisprudence proof of facts quick index. Rochester, N.Y., Lawyers Co-operative Pub. Co. [and] Bancroft-Whitney Co., San Francisco, 1974.

Bancroft-Whitney Company, San Francisco
see American jurisprudence proof of facts, second series. Rochester, N. Y., Lawyers Co-operative Pub. Co [and] Bancroft-Whitney Co., San Francisco, 1974-

Bancroft-Whitney Company, San Francisco
see Anderson, Ronald Aberdeen, 1911-
Anderson's Uniform commercial code... San Francisco, Bancroft-Whitney Co., 1969 [c1968]

Bancroft-Whitney Company, San Francisco
see Cal jur, III. 3d ed. San Francisco, 1972-

Bancroft-Whitney Company, San Francisco
see Cal practice... San Francisco, 1967-71.

Bancroft-Whitney Company, San Francisco.
see California. Constitution. Constitution of the State of California, annotated ... San Francisco, Bancroft-Whitney Co., 1974.

Bancroft-Whitney Company, San Francisco,
see California. Laws, statutes, etc.
... Agricultural code... San Francisco, 1943.

Bancroft-Whitney Company, San Francisco.
see California. Laws, statutes, etc. Business and professions code annotated, of the State of California, adopted June 15, 1937, with amendments through the end of the 1975 sessions of the 1975-76 Legislature. San Francisco, Bancroft-Whitney Co., 1975-1976.

Bancroft-Whitney Company, San Francisco
see California. Laws, statutes, etc. Civil code annotated of the State of California. San Francisco, 1971-72.

Bancroft-Whitney Company, San Francisco
see California. Laws, statutes, etc. Code of civil procedure, annotated, of the State of California... San Francisco, 1972-

Bancroft-Whitney Company, San Francisco.
see California. Laws, statutes, etc. Corporations code annotated of the State of California ... San Francisco, Bancroft-Whitney Co., 1977.

Bancroft-Whitney Company, San Francisco
see California. Laws, statutes, etc. Deering's California codes... San Francisco, 1970.

Bancroft-Whitney Company, San Francisco
see California. Laws, statutes, etc. Deering's California practice codes... San Francisco, 1972 [c1971]

Bancroft-Whitney Company, San Francisco
see California. Laws, statutes, etc. Deering's California practice codes... San Francisco, 1973

Bancroft-Whitney Company, San Francisco
see California. Laws, statutes, etc.
Deering's California practice codes... San Francisco, Brancroft-Whitney Co., 1974 [c1973]

Bancroft-Whitney Company, San Francisco.
see California. Laws, statutes, etc. Deering's California practice codes, civil, civil procedure, evidence, probate ... San Francisco, Bancroft-Whitney Co., 1975, c1974.

Bancroft-Whitney Company, San Francisco.
see California. Laws, statutes, etc. Deering's California practice codes, civil, civil procedure, evidence, probate ... 1976 ed. San Francisco, Bancroft-Whitney Co., 1976, c1975.

Bancroft-Whitney Company, San Francisco.
see California. Laws, statutes, etc. Deering's California practice codes, civil, civil procedure, evidence, probate ... 1977 ed. San Francisco, Bancroft-Whitney Co., 1977, c1976.

Bancroft-Whitney Company, San Francisco
see California. Laws, statutes, etc. Deering's Penal code. San Francisco, 1973.

Bancroft-Whitney Company, San Francisco
see California. Laws, statutes, etc. Deering's Penal code. San Francisco, 1974.

Bancroft-Whitney Company, San Francisco.
see California. Laws, statutes, etc. Deering's Penal code ... San Francisco, Bancroft-Whitney Co., 1975, c1974.

Bancroft-Whitney Company, San Francisco.
see California. Laws, statutes, etc. Deering's Penal code ... 1976 ed. San Francisco, Bancroft-Whitney Co., 1976, c1975.

Bancroft-Whitney Company, San Francisco.
see California. Laws, statutes, etc. Deering's Penal code ... 1977 ed. San Francisco, Bancroft-Whitney Co., 1977, c1976.

Bancroft-Whitney Company, San Francisco
see California. Laws, statutes, etc.
Deering's Penal code, including enactments of the regular session of the 1971 legislature. San Francisco, 1972.

Bancroft-Whitney Company, San Francisco
see California. Laws, statutes, etc.
... Election code... San Francisco, 1945.

Bancroft-Whitney Company, San Francisco
see California. Laws, statutes, etc.
... Fish and game code... San Francisco, 1944.

Bancroft-Whitney Company, San Francisco.
see California. Laws, statutes, etc. Fish and game code annotated of the State of California, adopted May 21, 1957, with amendments through chapter 497 of the 1976 session of the 1975-76 legislature. [San Francisco] Bancroft-Whitney, 1976.

Bancroft-Whitney Company, San Francisco
see California. Laws, statutes, etc.
... Harbors and navigation code... San Francisco, Bancroft-Whitney company, 1944.

Bancroft-Whitney Company, San Francisco.
see California. Laws, statutes, etc. Health and safety code annotated of the State of California, adopted April 7, 1939, with amendments through the regular and second extraordinary sessions of 1973-74. San Francisco, Bancroft-Whitney Co., 1975.

Bancroft-Whitney Company, San Francisco
see California. Laws, statutes, etc.
... Health and safety code of the state of California. San Francisco, Bancroft-Whitney company, 1945.

Bancroft-Whitney Company, San Francisco
see California. Laws, statutes, etc.
... Insurance code of the state of California. San Francisco, 1944.

Bancroft-Whitney Company, San Francisco.
see California. Laws, statutes, etc. Insurance code of the State of California. Insurance code, annotated, of the State of California ... San Francisco, Bancroft-Whitney Co., 1976-

Bancroft-Whitney Company, San Francisco.
see California. Laws, statutes, etc. Labor code, annotated, of the State of California ... San Francisco, Bancroft-Whitney Co., 1976.

Bancroft-Whitney Company, San Francisco
see California. Laws, statutes, etc.
... Military and veterans code of the state of California. San Francisco, 1943 [c1944]

Bancroft-Whitney Company, San Francisco.
see California. Laws, statutes, etc. Probate code, annotated, of the State of California, adopted May 11, 1931, with amendments through July 11, 1974, of the regular session of 1973-74. San Francisco, Bancroft-Whitney Co., 1974.

Bancroft-Whitney Company, San Francisco.
see California. Laws, statutes, etc. Public resources code, annotated, of the State of California ... San Francisco, Calif, Bancroft-Whitney Co., 1976-

Bancroft-Whitney Company, San Francisco
see California. Laws, statutes, etc.
... Public resources code of the state of California. San Francisco, 1944.

Bancroft-Whitney Company, San Francisco.
see California. Laws, statutes, etc. Public utilities code, annotated, of the State of California ... San Francisco, Bancroft-Whitney Co., 1970.

Bancroft-Whitney Company, San Francisco
see California. Laws, statutes, etc.
... Streets and highways code of the state of California ... San Francisco, Bancroft--Whitney company, 1945.

Bancroft-Whitney Company, San Francisco
see California. Laws, statutes, etc. Uncodified initiative measures and statutes... San Francisco, 1973.

Bancroft-Whitney Company, San Francisco
see California. Laws, statutes, etc. Vehicle code, annotated, of the State of California. San Francisco, Bancroft-Whitney Co., 1972.

Bancroft-Whitney Company, San Francisco
see California. Laws, statutes, etc. ... Water code... San Francisco, 1945.

Bancroft-Whitney Company, San Francisco.
see California. Laws, statutes, etc. Water: uncodified acts of the State of California ... San Francisco, Bancroft-Whitney Co., 1970.

Bancroft-Whitney Company, San Francisco.
see California. Laws, statutes, etc. Welfare and institutions code, annotated, of the State of California, adopted May 25, 1937 ... San Francisco, Bancroft-Whitney Co., 1969.

Bancroft-Whitney Company, San Francisco
see California. Laws, statutes, etc. ... Welfare and institutions code of the state of California. San Francisco, Bancroft-Whitney company, 1944.

Bancroft-Whitney Company, San Francisco.
see California digest of official reports, third series. San Francisco, Bancroft-Whitney, 1974-1975.

Bancroft-Whitney Company, San Francisco
see California jurisprudence. 3. ed.... San Francisco, 1972-75.

Bancroft-Whitney Company, San Francisco.
see Lawyers Co-operative Publishing Company. Federal quick index to the total client-service library ... 2d ed. Rochester, N.Y., Lawyers Co-operative Pub. Co., 1975.

Bancroft-Whitney Company, San Francisco
see The living law; a guide to legal research through the pages of a modern system... [Rochester, N. Y., Lawyers Co-operative Pub. Co., c1972]

Bancroft-Whitney Company, San Francisco
see New Oregon digest; digest of Oregon legal authorities, State and Federal. San Francisco, Bancroft-Whitney Co. [1961-

Bancroft-Whitney Company, San Francisco
see Police evidence library. [Rochester] Aqueduct Books, 1965.

Bancroft-Whitney Company, San Francisco
see Texas. Laws, statutes, etc. [Penal code (1973)] Penal code of the State of Texas. Branch's 3d ed. San Francisco : Bancroft-Whitney Co., 197

Bancroft-Whitney Company, San Francisco
see Texas. Laws, statutes, etc. Texas annotated penal statutes with forms. Branch's 3d ed. San Francisco : Bancroft-Whitney Co., 1974-1975.

Bancroft-Whitney Company, San Francisco
see Texas jurisprudence pleading and practice forms. 2d ed. San Francisco, 1972-

Bancroft-Whitney Company, San Francisco
see United States. District Courts. USCS court rules... Rochester, N. Y.: Lawyers Co-operative Pub. Co., 1974.

Bancroft-Whitney Company, San Francisco
see United States. Laws, statutes, etc. United States code service. Rochester, N.Y., Lawyers Co-operative Pub. Co., 1972-

Bancroft-Whitney Company, San Francisco
see Washington (State). Courts. Washington court rules annotated. San Francisco, Bancroft-Whitney Co., 1968-

Bancroft-Whitney Company, San Francisco
see Workmen's compensation law... San Francisco, Bancroft-Whitney Co., 1960.

Bancroft Woodcock Silversmith : March 9, 1976 through April 15, 1976, The Historical Society of Delaware. -- Wilmington: Historical Society of Delaware, 1976.
[38] p. : ill.
1. Woodcock, Bancroft, 1732-1817. 2. Silversmithing--Delaware--Wilmington.
WHi NUC77-88832

Bancroftiana. no. 1-
Mar. 1950-
Berkeley, Friends of the Bancroft Library, University of California [1972?-
no. in v. illus. 24 cm.
Reprint.
INDEXES:
no. 1-50, Mar. 1950-Sept. 1971, in no. 1/50.
1. California. University. Bancroft Library—Periodicals.
I. Friends of the Bancroft Library.
Z881.C1522B35 021.7'09794'67 73-642029
ISSN 0090-7642 MARC-S

Band, Bernhand, 1940-
Überlegungen zur Lösung Betriebswirtschaftliche Entscheidungsprobleme mit diskreten Variablen durch Anwendung von Suchverfahren. Münster, Westfälische Wilhelms-Universität, 1971.
v, 232 p. 21 cm.
Photocopy.
Inaug. —Diss. —Münster, Westfalische Wilhelms-Universität.
1. Decision-making—Mathematical models.
I. Title.
NjR NUC73-32191

Band, Claire.
Two years with the Chinese Communists, by Claire and William Band. New Haven, Yale University Press, 1948.
xii, 347 p. illus., ports., maps. 23 cm.
London ed. (G. Allen & Unwin) has title: Dragon fangs.
University Microfilms facsimile reprint, 1975.
1. China--Hist.--1937-1945. 2. Communism--China. 3. World War, 1939-1945--Personal narratives, English. I. Band, William, 1906- joint author. II. Title.
DGW NUC77-87823

Band, Edward.
Barclay of Formosa, by Edward Band. Taipei, Ch'eng Wen Pub. Co., 1972.
212 p. illus. 19 cm.
Reprint of 1936 ed.
1. Barclay, Thomas, 1849-1935. 2. Missions.
I. Christian Literature Society of Japan.
FMU NUC73-118722

Band, Edward.
[Barclay of Formosa. Chinese]
巴克禮博士與台灣 / [author, Edward Band] ; 詹正義編譯. — 台北：長青文化事業股份有限公司, 1976.
176 p., [2] leaves of plates : ill. ; 20 cm. — (長青叢書)
Series romanized: Ch'ang ch'ing ts'ung shu.
1. Barclay, Thomas, 1849-1935. 2. Missionaries—Taiwan—Biography. 3. Missionaries—Scotland—Biography. I. Chan, Cheng-i, 1940- II. Title.
Title romanized: Pa-k'o-li po shih yü T'ai-wan.
BV3431.2.B37B3612 77-839266

Band, Edward.
Working his purpose out; the history of the English Presbyterian mission, 1847-1947. Taipei, Ch'eng Wen Pub. Co., 1972.
xix, 595 p. illus., maps. 20 cm. (The Man with the book)
Facsim. reprint 1948 ed.
1. Presbyterian Church—Missions. 2. Missions—China. 3. Missions—East (Far East) I. Title. II. Series.
CaBVaU NUC74-139108

Band, Inna Markovna.
(Anomalii v koėffitsientakh vnutrenneĭ konversii gamma-lucheĭ)
Аномалии в коэффициентах внутренней конверсии гамма-лучей / И. М. Банд, М. А. Листенгартен, А. П. Фересин ; АН СССР, Ленингр. ин-т ядерной физики им. Б. П. Константинова. — Ленинград : Наука, Ленингр. отд-ние, 1976.
175 p. : ill. ; 21 cm. USSR 77
Bibliography: p. 154-[163]
1.08rub
1. Gamma rays—Measurement. 2. Internal conversion (Nuclear physics)—Tables, etc. I. Listengarten, Mikhail Abramovich, joint author. II. Feresin, Anatoliĭ Petrovich, joint author. III. Title.
QC793.5.G327B36 77-513564

Band, Owd Linthrin
see Smith, Leah.

Band, P., 1935-
see National Conference on Breast Cancer, Montreal, Que., 1975. Breast cancer ... Berlin, Springer-Verlag, 1976.

Band, R B
Vunamoli manganese mine diamond drilling 1962-63, by R.B. Band. Suva, Govt. Press, 1965.
iii, 10 p. illus. (part fold.) map. 25 cm. (Fiji. Geological Survey Dept. Economic investigation no. 3)
Bibliography: p. 6.
1. Manganese mines—Fiji. 2. Fiji Islands—Geology, Economic—Viti Levu. 3. Borings—Fiji Islands—Viti Levu. I. Title.
DI-GS NUC76-75607

Band, William, 1906- joint author
see Band, Claire. Two years with the Chinese Communists. New Haven, Yale University Press, 1948, 1975.

Band music guide addendum. Evanston, Ill., The Instrumentalist Co. [c1973]
78 p. 22 cm.
Supplements the 5th edition of Band music guide published in 1970.
1. Band music—Bibliography. I. The Instrumentalist.
LLafS NUC75-17244

Band music guide : alphabetical listing of titles and composers of all band music. — 6th ed. — Evanston, Ill. : Instrumentalist Co., c1975.
ix, 360 p. ; 24 cm.
Previous editions edited by K. W. Berger.
1. Band music—Bibliography.
ML128.B23B4 1975 016.785'06 75-22534
75 MARC

Band of angels. [Motion picture] [n.p.] Warner Bros. [c1957]
18, [2] p. illus. 43 cm.
Movie pressbook for film starring Clark Gable and Yvonne DeCarlo.
InU NUC75-26531

Band of brothers. The story of a Keren Hayesod worker. [Ramat-Gan, Israel, designed and produced by Aharoni Advertising, 196-]
1 v. (unpaged) illus. 23 cm.
Cover title.
1. Keren Hayesod United Israel Appeal.
OCH NUC73-112423

Band record guide.
Evanston, Ill., Instrumentalist Co.
v. 28 cm. annual.
Key title: Band record guide, ISSN 0525-4612
1. Band music—Discography. I. Instrumentalist Company, Evanston, Ill.
ML156.4.B3B3 016.7899'12 75-647584
MARC-S

Band˙structure spectroscopy of metals and alloys. Edited by D. J. Fabian [and] L. M. Watson. London, New York, Academic Press, 1973.
xviii, 753 p. illus. 24 cm. GB***
"Based on the proceedings of the international meeting held at the University of Strathclyde, 26–30 September 1971, on electronic structure of metals and alloys."
Includes bibliographies.
1. Free electron theory of metals—Congresses. 2. Energy-band theory of solids—Congresses. 3. Alloys—Congresses. 4. Molecular spectra—Congresses. 5. X-ray spectroscopy—Congresses. I. Fabian, Derek J., ed. II. Watson, L. M., ed.
QC176.8.E4B36 530.4'1 72-12268
ISBN 0-12-247440-6 MARC

Banda, Aleke K
Speech at the opening of Malawi Young Pioneers training base at Neno on February 25, 1968. Blantyre, Republic of Malawi, Dept. of Information [1968]
13 p. 25 cm.
Cover title.
Processed.
1. Malawi Young Pioneers. 2. Youth movement–Malawi.
CSt-H NUC73-40627

Banda, Eldad J K Babwebona, 1943-
Studies of nearly second order structural phase transitions, by Eldad J. K. B. Banda. [n. p.] 1973 [i. e. 1974]
ix, 133 l. diagrs. 29 cm.
Thesis (Ph. D.)–University of Rochester.
Vita.
Bibliography: leaves 123-131.
I. Title.
NRU NUC76-30313

Banda, Hastings Kamuzu, 1905-
Closing address by H. E. the President, MCP Convention, Lilongwe, September [21st] 1968. [Zomba] Dept. of Information [1968]
18 p. 26 cm.
Cover title.
Processed.
1. Malawi–Pol. & govt. I. Malawi Congress Party. II. Title.
CSt-H NUC74-29738

Banda, Hastings Kamuzu, 1905-
His excellency the president's speeches; Malawi Congress Party convention, Mzuzu, September 1970. [Blantyre, Dept. of Information, Republic of Malawi, 1970]
1 v. (unpaged) illus.
1. Malawi–Politics and government. I. Malawi Congress Party. II. Title.
MiEM NUC75-56286

[Banda, Hastings Kamuzu, 1905-]
Malawi is a democratic state says P. M. [n. p., 1966?]
[4] p. port.
I. Malawi. President, 1966- (Banda) II. Title.
MH NUC74-179801

Banda, Hastings Kamuzu, 1905-
Malawi's attitude to events in Central and West Africa. Blantyre, 1966.
12 p.
1. Foreign policy—Malawi. I. Malawi. Office of the Prime Minister.
MBU NUC73-12244

Banda, Hastings Kamuzu, 1905-
Pioneers in inter-African relations. Speech at the State House Zomba, on Wednesday, 20th May, 1970. Blantyre, 1970.
18 p. illus.
Cover title.
1. Politics–Malawi.
MBU NUC73-38948

Banda, Hastings Kamuzu, 1905-
Republic celebrations, July, 1971. Blantyre, 1971.
[12] p. front. (port.)
Cover title.
On cover: His excellency the President's speeches.
1. Politics–Malawi.
MBU NUC73-32192

Banda, Hastings Kamuzu, 1905-
A threat to world peace; a great man speaks. [Yaba, Nigeria, Asroi Press, 1964?]
11 p. 18 cm.
Microfiche (negative) 1 sheet. 11 x 15 cm. (NYPL FSN 16,203)
Address to the members of the Zomba Debating Society.
1. Communism–Addresses, essays, lectures. I. Title.
NN NUC76-75583

Banda, Hastings Kamuzu, 1905-
see Malawi. President, 1966- (Banda) Chilika airport, January/February, 1971. Blantyre, 1971.

Banda, Hastings Kamuzu, 1905-
see Malawi. President, 1966- (Banda) The fruits of Independence... Zomba, 1968.

Banda, Hastings Kamuzu, 1905-
see Malawi, President, 1966- (Banda) Opening and closing of Parliament, March, 1971. Blantyre, 1971.

Banda, Hastings Kamuzu, 1905-
see Malawi. President, 1966- (Banda) The President speaks... [Zomba, Dept. of Information, 1968]

Banda, Hastings Kamuzu, 1905-
see Malawi. President, 1966- (Banda) Republic celebrations speeches... Blantyre, 1970.

Banda, Hastings Kamuzu, 1905-
see Malawi. President, 1966- (Banda) Speech to the Malawi Parliament... [Zomba] 1966.

Banda, Hastings Kamuzu, 1905-
see Malawi, President, 1966- (Banda) Speeches to Parliament, Malawi, July, 1970. Blantyre, 1970.

Banda, Hastings Kamuzu, 1905-
see Malawi, President, 1966- (Banda) State opening of Parliament July 2nd 1971... Blantyre, 1971.

Banda, Jerry N
Masautso a Kamnjira [by] Jerry N. Banda. [1st ed.] Lusaka, Northern Rhodesia Publications Bureau [1964]
63 p. 19 cm.
I. Title.
PL8593.9.B35M3 72-227367

Banda, M
The logic of coalition politics: Ceylon. Two articles by M. Banda and documents. [London, Socialist Labour League, 1964?]
[12] p. illus. 28 cm.
Cover title.
1. Ceylon—Pol. & govt. I. Socialist Labour League.
KU-RH NUC73-126242

Bandā, Prema Prakāśa.
वीर स्काउट; नाटक. [लेखक] प्रेम प्रकाश बनदा. [1. संस्करण] बनारस, हिन्दी प्रचारक पुस्तकालय [1955]
80 p. 18 cm.
In Hindi.
I. Title. Title romanized: Vīra skāuta.
PK2098.13.A53V5 72-203220

Banda y Vargas, Antonio de la.
El arquitecto andaluz Hernán Ruiz II / Antonio de la Banda y Vargas. — Sevilla : Universidad, 1974.
265 p., [10] leaves of plates : ill. ; 25 cm. — (Anales de la Universidad Hispalense : Serie Filosofía y letras ; no. 23) Sp***
Thesis—Seville, 1970.
Bibliography: p. 263–265.
ISBN 84-600-6023-4
1. Ruiz, Hernán, d. 1569. 2. Architecture—Andalusia. I. Title.
NA1313.R8B36 74-352030

Banda Aceh, Indonesia.
In 1962 the name of Kutaradja, Indonesia, was changed to Banda Atjeh. As a result of the orthographic reform in 1972 the name became Banda Aceh.
Works by this jurisdiction published before the orthographic reform of 1972 are found under the following headings according to the time of publication:
Kutaradja, Indonesia.
Banda Atjeh, Indonesia.
Works published after the orthographic reform are found under Banda Aceh, Indonesia.
74-224052

Banda Aceh, Indonesia. Wali Kota.
Masaalah pengembangan kota Kotamadya Banda Aceh : paper / Wali Kota/ Kepala Daerah Kotamadya Banda Aceh. — [Banda Aceh] : Wali Kota, 1974.
27 leaves ; 29 cm.
1. Banda Aceh, Indonesia—Economic conditions. I. Title.
HC448.B33B3 1974 74-940444

Banda Atjeh, Indonesia.
In 1962 the name of Kutaradja, Indonesia, was changed to Banda Atjeh. As a result of the orthographic reform in 1972 the name became Banda Aceh.
Works by this jurisdiction published before the orthographic reform of 1972 are found under the following headings according to the name used at the time of publication:
Kutaradja, Indonesia.
Banda Atjeh, Indonesia.
Works published after the orthographic reform are found under Banda Aceh, Indonesia.
74-224050

La Banda Casaroli di Florestano Vancini / a cura di Vincenzo Bassoli. — [Bologna] : Cappelli Editore, [1962]
250 p., [22] leaves of plates : ill. ; 21 cm. — (Dal soggetto al film ; 24)
1. La Banda Casaroli. [Motion picture] 2. Casaroli, Paolo. I. Bassoli, Vincenzo. II. Vancini, Florestano, 1926–
PN1997.B2452B3 75-548288

Bandā Kṛshṇa Satyanārāyaṇa
see
Satyanārāyaṇa, Bandā Kṛshṇa.

Bandacarya, Kanjalagi, comp.
see Jagarotsavada Madhvabhajanamanjari. 1973.

Bandai, Hisanao, 1914- joint author
see Yamazaki, Bunji, 1910- Nihon Shōken Hoyū Kumiai kiroku. 44 (1969)

Bandai-machi Chōshi Hensan Iinkai.
(Me de miru chōshi)
目でみる町史　福島県耶麻郡磐梯町　磐梯町（福島県）　磐梯町町史編纂委員会　1971.
73 p. (chiefly illus., maps) 26 cm. ¥300 Ja 73-4675
1. Bandai-machi, Japan—History. 2. Natural history—Japan—Bandai-machi. I. Title.
DS897.B28B26 1971 73-805209

Bandaiki
see
Tanabe-machi daichō.

al-Bandak, Māzin.
(Qiṣṣat al-nafṭ)
قصة النفط / مازن البندك. — الطبعة 1. — [بيروت] : دار القدس، 1974.
256 p. : ill. ; 24 cm.
Bibliography: p. 248–249.
Includes index.
1. Petroleum industry and trade. 2. Petroleum industry and trade—Near East. I. Title.
HD9576.N36B35 75-549258

Bandakov, Leonid Fedorovich, joint author
see Vorob'ev, Anatoliĭ Andreevich. (Bezygol'nyĭ sposob vvedenii͡a biologicheskikh preparatov v organizm) 1972.

Bandalī, Kūstī.
الله والتطور [تأليف] كوستي بندلي. [بيروت؟] منشورات النور [1968؟]
22 p. 17 cm.
Includes bibliographical references.
1. Islam and science—Addresses, essays, lectures. 2. Evolution—Addresses, essays, lectures. I. Title.
Title romanized: Allāh wa-al-taṭawwur.
BP190.5.S3B28 75-586765

Bandalī, Kūstī.
اله الالحاد المعاصر ، ماركس ـ سارتر ,تأليف, كوستي بندلي. بيروت ، منشورات النور ,1968,
9, 190 p. 22 cm.
Includes bibliographical references.
5.00
1. Philosophy and religion. 2. Marx, Karl, 1818–1883. 3. Sartre, Jean Paul, 1905– I. Title.
Title romanized: Ilāh al-ilḥād al-mu'āṣir.
BL51.B235 75–549726

Bandalī, Kūstī.
(al-Jins wa-ma'nāhu al-insānī)
الجنس ومعناه الانساني ,تأليف, كوستي بندلي. ,بيروت, منشورات النور ، 1971.
236 p. illus. 22 cm.
Bibliography: p. 219–232.
£L5.00
1. Sex. I. Title.
HQ21.B17 75–972547

Bandalī, Kūstī.
(Madkhal ilá al-'aqīdah al-Masīḥīyah: al-khalq — al-tajassud — al-fidā')
مدخل الى العقيدة المسيحية: الخلق — التجسد — الفداء. ,تأليف, كوستي بندلي. ,الطبعة 1. بيروت, منشورات النور ، 1967.
128 p. illus. 22 cm.
1. Theology, Doctrinal—Popular works. I. Title.
BT77.B32 73–221164

Bandalī, Kūstī.
(al-Ṭā'ifīyah, ra'y Masīḥī)
الطائفية ، راي مسيحي ,تأليف, كوستي بندلي. ,بيروت, منشورات النور ,1969?,
39 p. 17 cm.
Includes bibliographical references.
1. Sects—Lebanon. I. Title.
BR1115.L4B36 74–220890

Bandamanna saga. English.
The Confederates & Hen-Thorir / translated by Hermann Pálsson. — Edinburgh [Scot.] : Southside, 1975.
139 p. ; 22 cm. — (UNESCO collection of representative works : Icelandic series) (The New saga library) GB***
On spine: Two Icelandic sagas.
Includes bibliographical references.
ISBN 0-900025-17-4 : £2.95. ISBN 0-900025-18-2 pbk.
1. Icelandic and Old Norse literature—Translations into English. 2. English literature—Translations from Icelandic and Old Norse. 3. Sagas. I. Pálsson, Hermann, 1921- II. Hænsa-þóris saga. English. 1975. III. Title: The Confederates. IV. Series.
PT7269.B4E5 1975 76-374511
76 MARC

Bandammanavar, Kottūrēśa Mallēśappa, 1926- ed.
see Bhīmakavi, fl. 1369. (Bhīmakaviya Basava purāna) 1969.

Bandan Pimpinan Harian Pusat Korps Cacad Veteran R. I.
see Korps Cacad Veteran R. I. Badan Pimpinan Harian Pusat.

Bandara, H H
Cultural policy in Sri Lanka, by H. H. Bandara. Paris, Unesco, 1972.
70 p. illus. 25 cm. (Studies and documents on cultural policies)
$2.00(U.S.) F***
Includes bibliographical references.
1. Arts—Ceylon—Management. I. Title. II. Series.
NX770.C4B36 338.4'77'0095493 72–95233
ISBN 92-3-101004-2 MARC

Banḍara, H. R. P., ed.
see Aluthgama, Wijesiri, 1942- Sarasavi artha śāstraya. [1969]

Bandāra Mainikā Dasanāyaka
see
Dasanāyaka, Bandāra Mainikā, 1943-

Bandaranaike, Sirimavo R. D., 1916-
see Anāgataya upan davasa. [1970]

Bandaranaike, Solomon West Ridgeway Dias, 1899-1959.
The foreign policy of Sri Lanka : extracts from statements by the late Prime Minister Mr. S. W. R. D. Bandaranaike. — 3d ed. — [Colombo : Information Dept., Govt. of Sri Lanka], 1976.
122 p. ; 19 cm.
1. Sri Lanka—Foreign relations. I. Title.
DS489.8.B36 1976 327.549'3 77-900982
77 MARC

Bandaranaike, Solomon West Ridgeway Dias, 1899-1959
see Batipuda. Our days at Oxford, by K. P. S. Menon.—Death of a prime minister, by D. B. Dhanapala. Batipuda. 1970.

Bandaranaike, Soloman West Ridgeway Dias, 1899-1959
see Ceylon. Guvan Viduli ha Pravrtti Departamentuva. (Vimuktiye niyamuva) 1970.

Bandaranayake, Senake.
Sinhalese monastic architecture : the viháras of Anurádhapura / Senake Bandaranayake. — Leiden : Brill, 1974.
xviii, 438 p. : ill. ; 30 cm. — (Studies in South Asian culture ; v. 4) Ne 74–50
Bibliography: p. [386]–392.
Includes index.
ISBN 90-04-03992-9 : fl 175.00
1. Temples, Buddhist—Ceylon—Anuradhapura. 2. Temples—Ceylon—Anuradhapura. 3. Anuradhapura—Antiquities, Buddhist. I. Title. II. Series.
NA6008.A58B36 726'.78'43095493 75–501629
MARC

Bandarchyk, V. K.
see Narodnai͡a sel'skahaspadarchai͡a tėkhnika Belarusaŭ. 1974.

Bandarchyk, Vasiliĭ Kirylavich.
Belaruskai͡a ėtnahrafii͡a i fal'klor u pratsakh slavi͡anskikh vuchonykh ėpokhi ramantyzmu. Minsk, Navuka i tekhnika, 1973.
34 p.
At head of title: Akademii͡a navuk BSSR. Belaruski kamitėt slavistaŭ. V. K. Bandarchyk, L. A. Malash.
On cover: VII Mizhnarodny z'ezd slavistaŭ.
Summary in Polish.
Includes bibliographical references.
CaOTU NUC76-40773

Bandarchyk, Vasiliĭ Kirylavich.
(Historyi͡a belaruskaĭ ėtnahrafii—pachatak dvatstsataha st.)
Гісторыя беларускай этнаграфіі. Пачатак XX ст. Мінск, "Навука і тэхніка," 1970.
123 p. with illus. 20 cm. 0.38rub USSR 71–16429
At head of title: В. К. Бандарчык.
Includes bibliographical references.
1. Ethnology—Study and teaching. 2. Ethnology—White Russia. I. Title.
GN45.R8B32 73–330096

Bandarchyk, Vasiliĭ Kirylavich.
(Historyi͡a belaruskaĭ savetskaĭ ėtnahrafii)
Гісторыя беларускай савецкай этнаграфіі. Мінск, "Навука і тэхніка," 1972.
165 p. with illus. 20 cm. 0.55rub USSR 72–39207
At head of title: Акадэмія навук Беларускай ССР. Інстытут мастацтвазнаўства, этнаграфіі і фальклору. В. К. Бандарчык.
Includes bibliographical references.
1. Ethnology—Study and teaching. 2. Ethnology—White Russia. I. Title.
GN45.R8B33 73–337725

Bandarchyk, Vasiliĭ Kirylavich, ed.
see Belaruskae narodnae zhyllio͡. 1973.

Bandarchyk, Vasiliĭ Kirylavich, ed.
see Charadzeĭnyi͡a kazki. 1973-

Bandarchyk, Vasiliĭ Kirylavich, ed.
see Geograficheskoe obshchestvo SSSR. Belorusskiĭ otdel. Otdel ėtnografii. Pytanni belaruskaĭ ėtnahrafii, fal'klarystyki i tapanimiki. [Rėd. kalehii͡a: V.K. Bandarchyk i dr.] Minsk, 1967.

Bandarchyk, Vasiliĭ Kirylavich
see Izmenenii͡a v bytu i kul'ture gorodskogo naselenii͡a Belorussii. 1976.

Bandarchyk, Vasiliĭ Kirylavich
see Prozaicheskie zhanry fol'kloru narodov SSSR. 1974.

Bandarchyk, Vasiliĭ Kirylavich, ed.
see Pytanni belaruskaĭ ėtnahrafii, fal'klarystyki i tapanimiki. Minsk, 1967.

Bandarchyk, Vasiliĭ Kirylavich, ed.
see Radzinnai͡a paezii͡a. Minsk, Navuka i tekhnika, 1971.

Bandarchyk, Vasiliĭ Kirylavich
see Satsyi͡al'na-bytavyi͡a kazki. 1976.

Bandas, Rudolph George, 1896-
Modern questions in the light of Vatican II. St. Paul, Wanderer Press, inc., 1968.
163 p. 23 cm. (The faith of our fathers series)
1. Sociology, Christian—Study and teaching. 2. Sociology, Christian. 3. Apologetics—20th century—Popular works. I. Title.
MnCS NUC75-24024

Bandasch, Georg
see Germany (Federal Republic, 1949-) Laws, statutes, etc. Kommentar zum Handelsgesetzbuch, mit ausführlichen Erläuterungen der Nebengesetze ohne Seerecht. 2., überarb. Aufl. [Neuwied] Luchterhand [1973]

Bandau, Joachim, 1936–
Bandau. Figuren, Geräte, Monstren. (Ausstellg.) Kunsthalle Nürnberg, 29. Sept.–19. Nov. 1972. Kunstverein Freiburg, 10. Dez. 1972–21. Jan. 1973. (Nürnberg, Kunsthalle, 1972).
93 p. illus. 21 cm. (Kunsthalle Nürnberg. Katalog, 1972, Nr. 4) GDR 73–B3
Stamped on t. p.: Supplied by World Wide Books, Boston.
Bibliography: p. [103]–[104].
1. Bandau, Joachim, 1936– I. Nuremberg. Kunsthalle. II. Kunstverein Freiburg. III. Series: Nuremberg. Kunsthalle. Katalog, 1972, Nr. 4.
NB588.B33A43 74–198001

Bandau, Joachim, 1936-
Objekte auf Rädern und Zeichnungen : Kunsthalle Köln, 14. März bis 4. Mai 1975 : [Katalog] / Joachim Bandau ; [Manfred Schneckenburger]. — Köln : Kunsthalle Köln, 1975.
82 p. : ill. ; 27 cm. GFR***
Bibliography: p. 80-81.
1. Bandau, Joachim, 1936- I. Schneckenburger, Manfred. II. Cologne. Kunsthalle. III. Title.
NB588.B33S35 75-508158
75 MARC

Bandau, Joachim, 1936-
see Joachim Bandau, Hans Salentin, Erwin Wortelkamp... Ludwigshafen am Rhein, Städt. Kunstsammlungen, 1971.

Bandawe, Lewis Mataka.
Memoirs of a Malawian; the life and reminiscences of Lewis Mataka Bandawe. Edited and introduced by B. Pachai. Blantyre, Malawi, CLAIM, 1971.
143, xvi p. illus. 23 cm.
1. Bandawe, Lewis Mataka. I. Title.
DT859.6.B32A34 320.9'689'702 73–983563
[B] MARC

Bande, Alf, 1916–
Strövtåg i Karlskoga och Degerfors. Teckningar och layout: Tommy Gustavsson. Örebro, Ljungföretagen, 1972.
93 p. illus. 21 cm. kr29.50 S 73–35
1. Karlskoga, Sweden—Description. 2. Degerfors, Sweden (Västerbotten)—Description. I. Title.
DL991.K247B36 74–308289

Bande, Emilio.
Cristianos ahora. Madrid, Centro de Propaganda [1972]
166 p. 18 cm. Sp 72–June
1. Christianity—20th century. I. Title.
BR121.2.B2853 74–327299

Bande, José Manuel Martínez
see Martínez Bande, José Manuel.

Bande, Ushā.
मधुवन; सामाजिक उपन्यास. [लेखिका] उषा बन्दे. नई दिल्ली, विद्या प्रकाशन भवन [1970]
144 p. 18 cm. Rs4.50
In Hindi.

I. Title.
Title romanized: Madhuvana.

PK2098.13.A54M3 74–916995

Bande à Baader
see
Rote Armee Fraktion.

La Bande à Baader : ou, La violence révolutionnaire. — Paris : Éditions Champ libre, [1972]
218 p. ; 22 cm. — (Stratégie) F***
Translated from the German.
Includes bibliographical references.
CONTENTS: Marenssin, É. De la préhistoire à l'histoire.—Fraction Armée rouge. Sur la conception de la guérilla urbaine.—Fraction Armée rouge. Sur la lutte armée en Europe occidentale.
1. Communism—Germany, West. 2. Communist strategy. 3. Violence—Germany, West. 4. Baader, Andreas, 1943- I. Marenssin, Émile. II. Rote Armee Fraktion.
HX274.B3414 322.4'2'0943 75-518042
75 MARC

Bande mataram, Calcutta
see De Sarakāra, Pulakeśa. (Saratcandrera rajanaitika bhābanā) 1383 [1976]

Bande mataram, Calcutta
see Ghose, Aurobindo, 1872-1950. Bande Mataram; early political writings - 1. [Pondicherry, India, Sri Aurobindo Ashram, c1972]

Bandecchi, Pedro Brasil, 1917- comp.
Antologia histórica do Brasil [por] Brasil Bandecchi. São Paulo, 1973-
v. 23 cm. Cr$15.00 (v. 1)
Includes bibliography.
CONTENTS: Séculos XV e XVI.
1. Brazil—History—Sources. I. Title.
F2521.B183 73-221488

Bandecchi, Pedro Brasil, 1917-
Barqueiros do Tietê / Brasil Bandecchi. — 2. ed / [ilustrações de Marysia Portinari Maranca, Oswald de Andrade Filho, Oswaldo Sylveyra]. — [Franca, Brasil] : Empresa Comércio da Franca, 1975.
91 p. : ill. ; 19 cm.
Cr$10.00
I. Title.
PQ9698.12.A46B3 1975 869'.3 76-484503
76 MARC

Bandecchi, Pedro Brasil, 1917-
História de São Paulo [por] Brasil Bandecchi. [São Paulo] Serviço Nacional de Aprendizagem Comercial, Departamento Regional de São Paulo, Divisão de Formação para Turismo [1971 or 2]
32 p. 23 cm. (Cursos de turismo. Cadernos de estudos: 1-3)
"São Paulo—de cidade provinciana a metrópole. Toponímia dos municípios paulistas e alguns dados históricos (séculos XVI, XVII e XVIII) Toponímia brasílica dos municípios paulistas."
Bibliography: p. 9.
1. Names, Geographical—Brazil—São Paulo (State) 2. São Paulo, Brazil (City)—History. I. Title. II. Series.
F2631.B253 73-202249

Bandecchi, Pedro Brasil, 1917-
Historia econômica e administrativa do Brasil. 5. ed. rev. e ilus. São Paulo, Editôra Didática Irradiante [1970]
172 p. illus., maps.
1. Brazil—Economic conditions. 2. Brazil—Politics and government. I. Title.
DS NUC73-113161

Bandecchi, Pedro Brasil, 1917-
O município no Brasil e sua função política [por] Brasil Bandecchi. São Paulo, 1972.
125 p. 24 cms. (Coleção da Revista de história, 40)
Bibliography: p. [105]-117.
1. Municipal corporations—Brazil. I. Title.
75-537434

Bandecchi, Pedro Brasil, 1917-
O município no Brasil e sua função política / Brasil Bandecchi. — 3. ed., rev. — São Paulo : [s. n.], 1974.
110 p. ; 24 cm. — (Coleção da Revista de história ; 40)
Bibliography: p. [98]-110.
Cr$13.00
1. Local government—Brazil—History. I. Title.
JS2405.B35 1974 75-401877

Bandecchi, Pedro Brasil, 1917-
see Dicionário de história do Brasil ... 4. ed. São Paulo, Edições Melhoramentos, 1976, c1973.

Bandecchi, Pedro Brasil, 1917-
see São Paulo, Brazil (City). Departamento de Cultura. Divisão do Arquivo Histórico. Curso de história de São Paulo. [São Paulo, 1969]

Bandece
see
Banco de Desenvolvimento do Ceará
for publications by and about this body.
Titles and other entries beginning with this acronym are filed following this card.
75-589180

Bandeen, William R., ed.
see Symposium on Possible Relationships Between Solar Activity and Meteorological Phenomena, Goddard Space Flight Center, 1973. Possible relationships between solar activity... Greenbelt, Md., 1974.

Bandeen, William R.
see Symposium on Possible Relationships Between Solar Activity and Meteorological Phenomena, Goddard Space Flight Center, 1973. Possible relationship between solar activity and meteorological phenomena ... Washington, Scientific and Technical Information Office, National Aeronautics and Space Administration : for sale by the Supt. of Docs., U.S. Govt. Print. Off., 1975.

Bandeira, Antonio R
The ideological struggle in Chile : the middle class and the military / Antonio R. Bandeira. — [English ed., rev.] / [translated by Bonnie Shepard] — Toronto : Brazilian Studies, 1975.
70 p. ; 21 cm. C***
Revision of a translation of La lucha ideologica y la clase media en Chile.
Includes bibliographical references.
1. Middle classes—Chile—Political activity. 2. Chile—Armed Forces—Political activity. 3. Chile—Politics and government—1970- 4. Unidad Popular. I. Title.
HT690.C5B3613 1975 301.44'1 77-551761
77 MARC

Bandeira, Antônio Rangel.
Da liberdade de criação artística. [1. ed. Rio de Janeiro] Instituto Nacional do Livro, 1956.
103 p. 16 cm. (Biblioteca de divulgação cultural, 3)
Includes bibliographical references.
CONTENTS: Todos querem que a arte "colabore."—Onde se faz uma citação de Leibniz.—A grave acusação de Andrei Zhdanov.—De como escrevemos música "em brasileiro."—Ninguém aprende a ler n'Os lusíadas.—Lá bemol é apenas lá bemol.—A música pode levar ao adultério?—O cálculo integral não é antipopular.—No tempo de Palestrina também foi assim.—Por que não confiar no futuro?
1. Music—Addresses, essays, lectures. I. Title.
ML60.B154 780 74-200358

Bandeira, José Gomes.
Os trabalhadores e o lock-out em Vieira de Leiria / José Gomes Bandeira, Luís Humberto. — Porto [Portugal] : Afrontamento, 1974.
86 p. ; 19 cm. — (Movimento operário português ; 8)
1. Strikes and lockouts—Metal-workers—Portugal—Vieira de Leiria, Marinha Grande. I. Humberto, Luís, joint author. II. Title.
HD5409.M52 1974.V532 76-487303
76 MARC

Bandeira, Luiz Alberto Moniz.
Cartéis e desnacionalização : a experiência brasileira, 1964-1974 / Moniz Bandeira. — Rio de Janeiro : Civilização Brasileira, 1975.
xvii, 221 p. ; 21 cm. — (Coleção Retratos do Brasil ; v. 96)
Bibliography: 211-221.
Cr$40.00
1. Corporations, Foreign—Brazil. 2. Trusts, Industrial—Brazil. I. Title.
HD2834.B35 75-517073
75 MARC

Bandeira, Luiz Alberto Moniz.
Presença dos Estados Unidos no Brasil (dois séculos de história) [por] Moniz Bandeira. [Rio de Janeiro] Civilização Brasileira [1973]
xx, 497 p. 22 cm. (Coleção Retratos do Brasil, v. 87) Cr$50.00
Bibliography: p. 479-497.
1. United States—Relations (general) with Brazil. 2. Brazil—Relations (general) with the United States. I. Title.
E183.8.B7B36 73-219510

Bandeira, Manuel, 1886-1968.
Antologia poética. 6. ed. [Rio de Janeiro] Sabiá [1972, c1961]
242 p. 21 cm.
TxU NUC76-72855

Bandeira, Manuel, 1886-1968.
Antologia poética. 7. ed. Rio de Janeiro, Livraria J. Olympio Editora, 1974.
241 p. 22 cm. Cr$28.00
I. Title.
PQ9697.B27A6 1974 74-227311

Bandeira, Manuel, 1886-1968.
Noções de história das literaturas. [6. ed. Rio de Janeiro] Fundo de Cultura [1969]
398 p. illus. 21 cm. (Biblioteca fundo universal de cultura. Estante de literatura)
Includes bibliographies.
1. Literature—Hist. & crit. I. Title.
TxHR NUC76-72854

Bandeira, Manuel, 1886-
Seleta em prosa e verso de Manuel Bandeira. -- 2. ed. -- Rio de Janeiro : Livraria José Olympio, 1975.
176 p. : port. ; 19 cm. -- (Coleção Brasil moço)
I. Title.
TxU NUC77-87070

Bandeira, Manuel, 1886-1968
see Itinerarios... São Paulo : Livraria Duas Cidades, 1974.

Bandeira, Manuel, 1886-1968, tr.
see Mistral, Frédéric, 1830-1914. Miréia. Rio de Janeiro, Editôra Delta, 1962.

Bandeira, Manuel, 1886-1968, ed.
see Omar Khayyām. Rubaiyat. [Rio de Janeiro] Edições de Ouro [1965]

Bandeira, Manuel, 1886-1968, tr.
see Spitteler, Carl, 1845-1924. Prometeu e Epimeteu. Rio de Janeiro, Editora Delta, 1963.

Bandeira, Manuel, 1900-1964.
Alguns desenhos de Manoel Bandeira para o Arquivo Público Estadual. [Recife, Imprensa Oficial, 1967]
35 p., 31 plates (in portfolio) 34 cm.
LACAP 68-0096
1. Bandeira, Manuel, 1900-1964. I. Pernambuco, Brazil (State) Arquivo Público. II. Title.
NC200.B3A4 68-04220
rev

Bandeira, Maria de Lourdes.
Os Kariris de Mirandela: um grupo indígena integrado. [Salvador, Departamento Cultural da Reitoria da U. F. Ba., i. e. Universidade Federal da Bahia, 1972]
171 p. illus. 23 cm. (Estudos baianos, no. 6)
Bibliography: p. 169-171.
1. Kariri Indians. 2. Mirandela, Brazil. I. Title. II. Series: Estudos baianos (Salvador, Brazil, 1970-), no. 6.
F2520.1.K4B36 73-213794

Bandeira, Ricardo.
Pesadelo do alívio / de Ricardo Bandeira. — [s.l. : s.n., 1975]
(São Paulo : Copiadora e Indústria Gráfica Don Quixote)
43 p., [1] leaf of plates ; 21 cm.
Cr$30.00
I. Title.
PQ9698.12.A49P4 75-522665
76 MARC

Bandeira Coelho, Ernesto
see
Coelho, Ernesto Bandeira.

Bandeira de Mello, Agenor
see
Mello, Agenor Bandeira de.

Bandeira de Mello, Jorge Saldanha, 1903-
Epidemiologia da fome; [população, alimentação, saúde e a segurança nacional. Rio de Janeiro] Universidade do Estado da Guanabara, 1966.
150 p. (Coleção UEG 4)
1. Diet—Brazil. 2. Hunger. 3. Nutrition. I. Title.
MiU NUC73-113160

Bandeira de Mello, Lydio Machado, 1901-
A conquista do Reino de Deus / Lydio Machado Bandeira de Mello. — Belo Horizonte : [s.n.], 1975-
v. : 23 cm.
1. Theology—Addresses, essays, lectures. I. Title.
BR85.B394 75-512892
75 MARC

Bandeira de Mello, Lydio Machado, 1901–
Cosmologia do movimento; dedução a priori das leis físicas fundamentais. Belo Horizonte, 1965.
165 p. illus. 23 cm.
"Edição manuscrita pelo autor."
1. Mechanics, Analytic. 2. Motion. I. Title.
QA802.B36 78-403407
rev

Bandeira de Mello, Lydio Machado, 1901–
Crime e exclusão de criminalidade; legítima defesa, estado de necessidade, exercício regular de direito, estrito cumprimento de dever legal. 3. ed. rev. e ampliada Belo Horizonte, B Alvares [1962]
362 p. 24 cm. (His Tratado de direito penal, 1)
1. Criminal law—Brazil. 2. Criminal law. I. Title.
66-36076 ‡
rev

Bandeira de Mello, Lydio Machado, 1901–
O criminoso, o crime e a pena, segundo o Código penal de 21 de outubro de 1969. Belo Horizonte, Prisma Editôra Cultural [1970]
337 p. 24 cm. NCr$30.00
1. Crime and criminals—Brazil. 2. Punishment—Brazil. I. Title.
73-574224
rev

Bandeira de Mello, Lydio Machado, 1901–
Crítica cosmológica da física quântica; a prova termodinâmica da existencia de Deus. Belo Horizonte, 1969.
x, 292 p. 23 cm.
Cover title.
1. God—Proof. 2. Physics—Philosophy. I. Title.
BT102.B33 72-201746
rev

Bandeira de Mello, Lydio Machado, 1901–
Crítica do princípio de razão suficiente. Belo Horizonte, 1973.
220 p. illus. 23 cm.
1. Sufficient reason. I. Title.
BD591.B28 74-222252

Bandeira de Mello, Lydio Machado, 1901–
Da capitulação dos crimes e da fixação das penas; teoria a prática da capitulação dos crimes e da fixação das penas, o juiz criminal, a pena de morte. 4. ed., rev. e ampliada. Belo Horizonte, Editôra Bernardo Alvares [1963]
361 p. 23 cm. (His Tratado de direito penal, 3)
Third ed. published under title: Teoria e prática da capitulação dos crimes, da fixação das penas.
1. Punishment—Brazil. 2. Criminal law—Brazil. I. Title.
67-53392
rev

Bandeira de Mello, Lydio Machado, 1901–
Da responsabilidade penal e da isenção de pena; responsabilidade penal, das causas de isenção de pena, a embriaguez em direito penal, da co-autoria, das doenças mentais em criminosos, da maioridade penal 2. ed. rev. e ampliada. Belo Horizonte, B Alvares [1962]
377 p. 24 cm. (His Tratado de direito penal, 2)
1. Criminal liability. 2. Criminal liability—Brazil. I. Title.
66-36077
rev

Bandeira de Mello, Lydio Machado, 1901–
Dezessete aventuras no reino de Deus. Belo Horizonte, 1952.
239 p. 19 cm.
I. Title.
PQ9697.B314D4 57-25216 ‡
rev 2

Bandeira de Mello, Lydio Machado, 1901–
O direito penal hispano lusitano medieval; isto é: desde a invasão dos Suevos, capitaneados por Hermanerico, em 409, até as Ordenações afonsinas de 1446 (que foram o primeiro código europeu anterior à invenção da imprensa) e as Ordenações manuelinas de 1512 a 1514 (que foram o primeiro código europeu publicado) Belo Horizonte, 1960.
304 p. 24 cm.
1. Criminal law—Spain—History. I. Title.
66-32754 ‡
rev

Bandeira de Mello, Lydio Machado, 1901–
A divisibilidade por d na aritmética de base B; os caractéres de divisibilidade por qualquer número em tôdas as aritméticas de base inteira possíveis. Belo Horizonte, 1957, c1946.
104 p. 24 cm.
1. Numbers, Divisibility of. I. Title.
QA242.B4 1957 64-44820 ‡
rev

Bandeira de Mello, Lydio Machado, 1901–
Evangelho para bacharéis; oração de paraninfo. Belo Horizonte, 1969.
47 p. 23 cm.
Cover title.
1. Christian life. I. Title.
OU NUC74-21732

Bandeira de Mello, Lydio Machado, 1901–
A existência e a imortalidade da alma. Belo Horizonte, 1972.
xvii, 395 p. 24 cm.
Cover title.
"Edição manuscrita pelo autor."
1. Soul. 2. Immortality. I. Title.
CLSU InU KyLoS CaBVaU NUC74-70740

Bandeira de Mello, Lydio Machado, 1901–
Fórmulas gerais da distribuição de probabilidades pelas somas de pontos nos jogos com qualquer número de dados, de urnas com bolas numeradas ou rodas raios numerados. Belo Horizonte, 1967.
62 p. 23 cm.
Cover title.
"Edição manuscrita pelo autor."
1. Distribution (Probability theory) I. Title.
QA273.6.B37 519.2′4 68-119485
rev

Bandeira de Mello, Lydio Machado, 1901–
Homo triplex aut compositus. Belo Horizonte, 1955–
v. illus. 24 cm.
CONTENTS: 1. A origem dos sexos.
1. Sex (Biology) I. Title.
QH481.B3 66-37277 ‡
rev

Bandeira de Mello, Lydio Machado, 1901–
Manual de direito penal. Belo Horizonte, 1953–
v. 23 cm. (Manuais da Faculdade de Direito da Universidade de Minas Gerais, no. 2
1. Criminal law—Brazil. I. Title. II. Series: Belo Horizonte, Brazil. Universidade de Minas Gerais. Faculdade de Direito. Manuais, no. 2
55-42442
rev 2

Bandeira de Mello, Lydio Machado, 1901–
Meditações sôbre o direito e sôbre a origem das leis; notas para as aulas de Filosofia do Direito, dadas em 1952 e 1953, no curso de doutorado. Primeira série: Meditações sôbre o direito. Belo Horizonte, Of. Gráf. Faculdade de Direito, 1967.
234 p. 23 cm. unpriced BBM 68***
Cover title: Filosofia do direito; a fundamentação psicológica do direito natural.
Includes bibliographical references.
1. Law—Philosophy. 2. Natural law. I. Title. II. Title: Filosofia do direito.
70-359271
rev

Bandeira de Mello, Lydio Machado, 1901–
Memória, espaço e tempo. Belo Horizonte, 1963, c1962.
2 v. (306 p.) diagrs., tables. 23 cm.
Reproduced from manuscript copy.
I. Title.
B1044.B283M45 1963 64-47660
rev

Bandeira de Mello, Lydio Machado, 1901–
Metafísica do espaço; o problema da quarta dimensão. Ed. manuscrita pelo autor. Belo Horizonte, Of. Gráf. Faculdade de Direito, 1966.
xix, 275 p. 23 cm. unpriced BBM 68***
LACAP 68-5293
1. Fourth dimension. 2. Hyperspace. I. Title.
QA699.B3 73-363794
rev

Bandeira de Mello, Lydio Machado, 1901–
Metafísica do número. [Rio de Janeiro] 1945 [i. e. 1946]
161 p. 24 cm.
1. Symbolism of numbers. I. Title.
BF1623.P9B38 50-35720
rev 2

Bandeira de Mello, Lydio Machado, 1901–
Minutos de meditação. Rio de Janeiro, 1936.
205 p. 19 cm.
L. C. copy replaced by microfilm.
I. Title.
[AC75.B253] 70-230577
Microfilm 28220 AC rev

Bandeira de Mello, Lydio Machado, 1901–
No templo da sabedoria. Rio de Janeiro, 1937.
208 p. 19 cm.
1. Christian life—Addresses, essays, lectures. I. Title.
BV4510.B32 71-254543
rev

Bandeira de Mello, Lydio Machado, 1901–
A pluralidade de consciências, ¿monismo ou pluralismo? Edição manuscrita pelo autor. Belo Horizonte, 1966 [i. e. 1967]
xii, 254 p. 23 cm.
Added t. p.: Tratado de teologia matemática, 2.a parte. 1965.
Reproduced from manuscript.
1. Monism. 2. Pluralism. I. Title. II. Title: Tratado de teologia matemática.
B827.B36 70-362343
rev

Bandeira de Mello, Lydio Machado, 1901–
A predestinação para o bem; ensaio de uma metafísica do livre arbítrio humano. Rio de Janeiro, Leopoldina, 1947.
178 p. 24 cm.
1. Apologetics—20th century. I. Title.
BT1101.B18 61-59524
rev 2

Bandeira de Mello, Lydio Machado, 1901–
Prova matemática da existência de Deus. [3. ed.] Leopoldina [Brasil] 1942 [i. e. 1973]
95, [1] p. 23 cm.
"Suplemento a esta terceira edição": p. 81-[96]
1. God—Proof. I. Title.
BT102.B34 1942 74-229252

Bandeira de Mello, Lydio Machado, 1901–
Quadrados, círculos, esferas e cubos mágicos; um novo capítulo da teoria algébrica das permutações condicionadas. Edição manuscrita pelo autor. Belo Horizonte, Brasil, 1972.
65 p. diagrs. 24 cm.
On cover: Teoria algébrica das permutações condicionadas; círculos, esferas e cubos mágicos.
1. Permutations. 2. Magic squares.
RPB CaMWU NUC74-70731

Bandeira de Mello, Lydio Machado, 1901–
Quadrados mágicos; métodos gerais para a construção de quadrados mágicos propostos pelo autor: método dos determinantes; método do quadrado zéro. π em função do números figurados. Belo Horizonte, 1957.
142 p. illus. 24 cm.
1. Magic squares. I. Title.
QA165.B36 64-47074 ‡
rev

Bandeira de Mello, Lydio Machado, 1901–
O real e o possível; ontologia da possibilidade. A prova matemática e a prova estatística da existência de Deus. A natureza do possível. O possível não é creado: é intuido pelo homem. Deus é a realidade que torna possível a possibilidade. Belo Horizonte, 1954.
284 p. 23 cm.
1. Possibility. 2. God—Knowableness. I. Title.
B1044.B283R4 74-261528
rev

Bandeira de Mello, Lydio Machado, 1901–
Refutação científica do ateísmo teórico; as credenciais da razão. Belo Horizonte, 1973.
A 1-A 29, 299 p. illus. 24 cm.
Cover title: As credenciais da razão.
1. Atheism. I. Title. II. Title: As credenciais da razão.
BL2747.3.M42 74-205490

Bandeira de Mello, Lydio Machado, 1901–
Responsabilidade penal. Rio de Janeiro, Tip. Batista de Souza, 1941.
188 p. 23 cm.
"Tese apresentada à douta congregação da Faculdade Nacional de Direito da Universidade do Brasil, como candidato a uma cadeira de Direito Penal, de acôrdo com o edital de 20 de Agosto de 1940."
1. Criminal liability—Brazil. I. Title.
49-56132
rev 2

Bandeira de Mello, Lydio Machado, 1901–
Tabú, pecado e crime; tése sobre "a natureza, a origem e a finalidade da pena," apresentada à douta congregação da Faculdade de Direito da Universidade de Minas Gerais, no concurso para catedrático de Direito Penal ... Leopoldina, Gráfica Guimarães, 1949.
160 p. 24 cm.
1. Punishment. I. Title.
HV8675.B32 50-31272
rev 2

Bandeira de Mello, Lydio Machado, 1901–
Teoria algébrica das permutacoes condicionadas; algoritmia de posiçao, quadrados, círculos, esferas e cubos mágicos. Belo Horizonte, 1972.
65, [1] p. illus. 24 cm.
1. Mathematical recreations. 2. Permutations. I. Title.
NIC NUC75-14360

Bandeira de Mello, Lydio Machado, 1901–
Teoria e prática da capitulação dos crimes, da fixação das penas. 3. ed. Belo Horizonte, 1958 [i. e. 1959–
v. 23 cm. (His Tratado de direito penal, 2 [i. e. 3])
Fourth ed. published in 1963 under title: Da capitulação dos crimes e da fixação das penas.
1. Criminal law—Brazil. 2. Punishment—Brazil. I. Title.
65-56915 ‡
rev

Bandeira de Mello, Lydio Machado, 1901–
Trabalhos de algoritmia superior (Works of high algorithmy). Belo Horizonte, 1971.
xvi, 216 p. 22 cm.
"Teoria algébrica dos quadrados mágicos. O teorema-desafio de Goldbach. Teoria geral dos números perfeitos. Fórmula geral dos números figurados. Séries heteromorfas, porém equilvalentes. Os números amigos. Os teoremas clássicos da teoria dos números. Pequenos achados de matemática elementar."
"Como estabeleço a formação de todos os númerous pares por meio de somas de dois primos": 4 p. inserted.
1. Numbers, Theory of. I. Title. II. Title: Works of high algorithmy.
QA241.B26 74–208615

Bandeira de Mello, Lydio Machado, 1901–
Tratado de teologia matemática. Edição manuscrita pelo autor. Belo Horizonte, 1965.
285 p. illus. 23 cm.
Reproduced from manuscript.
1. God—Proof. I. Title.
BT175.B3 75–272932
rev

Bandeira de Mello, Oswaldo Aranha
see Aranha Bandeira de Mello, Oswaldo.

Bandeira Duarte, Oto Carlos, 1904–
Efemérides do teatro carioca [por] Bandeira Duarte. [Rio de Janeiro] Prefeitura do Distrito Federal, Secretaria Geral de Educação e Cultura [pref. 1958]
118 p. 24 cm. (Coleção Cidade do Rio de Janeiro, 7)
Bibliography: p. [115]–118.
1. Theater—Rio de Janeiro—History. I. Title.
PN2472.R5B3 70–248786

Bandeira Duarte, Oto Carlos, 1904-
A projeção fixa no ensino; produção, utilização e avaliação do material [por] Bandeira Duarte. Rio de Janeiro, Pongetti, 1961.
111 p. illus. 17 cm.
1. Audio-visual education. I. Title.
TxU NUC75-8322

Bandeira Duarte, Oto Carlos, 1904-
Rondon, o bandeirante do século XX; desenhos de A. Pacot. 3. ed. Rio de Janeiro, Gráf. N. S. de Fátima, 1957.
178 p. illus. 24 cm.
At head of title: Bandeira Duarte.
1. Rondon, Candido Mariano da Silva, 1865- 2. Indians of South America–Brazil. 3. Brazil–Exploring expeditions. 4. Roosevelt-Rondon scientific expedition. I. Title.
KU NUC75-6735

Bandeira Freire, Pedro
see
Freire, Pedro Bandeira.

Bandeira Vaughan, Raymundo
see
Vaughan, Raymundo Bandeira, 1889-

Bandeira de Nossa senhora da Oliveira, de Guimaraes; sua recepção em Goa. Goa, Imprensa nacional, 1956.
15 p. fold. plans. 19 cm.
Microfiche (neg.) 1 sheet. 11 x 15 cm.
Cover title.
1. Flags–Goa.
NN NUC74-33083

A Bandeira do Brasil / [organizado por Arthur Rabello Netto]. — [Curitiba : Fundação Educacional do Estado do Paraná, 1968]
24 p. : ill. ; 23 cm.
CONTENTS: Bandeira do Brasil.—Bilac, O. Oração à bandeira. Hino à bandeira nacional.—Dia da Bandeira: solenidade de culto à bandeira na Escola Superior de Guerra, 1967; alocução do Gen. José Campos de Aragão.—Lei que dispõe sôbre a bandeira, as armas e o sêlo nacionais: Lei n.º 5.389, de 22 de fevereiro de 1968.—Forma e apresentação dos símbolos nacionais: Lei n.º 5.443, de 28 de maio de 1968.—Estrada, J. Osorio Duque. Hino nacional.
1. Flags—Brazil. 2. Emblems, National—Brazil. I. Rabello Netto, Arthur, comp. II. Fundação Educacional do Estado do Paraná.
JC347.B7B28 74–234662

Bandekar, Dattu.
(Āvaḷyā bhopaḷyāñcī moṭa)
आंवळ्या भोपळ्यांची मोट. लेखक दत्तू बांदेकर. [2. आवृत्ति] मुंबई, भगवानदास हिरजी [1963]
146 p. 19 cm. Rs3.50
In Marathi.

I. Title.
PK2418.B323A9 1963 72–907362

Bandekar, Dattu.
(Cirīmirī)
चिरीमिरी. [लेखक] दत्तू बांदेकर. [2. आवृत्ति. मुंबई] भगवानदास हिरजी [1972]
172 p. 19 cm. Rs6.00
In Marathi.

I. Title.
PK2418.B323C5 1972 72–907363

Bandekar, Dattu.
(Premācā gulakanda)
प्रेमाचा गुलकंद / लेखक दतू बांदेकर. — 1. आवृत्ति. — मुंबई : भगवानदास हिरजी, 1959.
164 p. ; 19 cm.
In Marathi.
Short stories.

I. Title.
PK2418.B323P7 1959 75–986024

Bandekar, Dattu
see Atre, Prahlad Keshav, 1898-1969. (Pañcagavya) 1958.

Bandekar, Jagdeeshichandra Narayanrao.
A Monte Carlo normal coordinate analysis treatment of intermolecular vibrations in liquid water. [n.p., 1973]
145 l. (K.S.U. Doctor of Philosophy Dissertation, 1973)
Thesis (Ph.D.)—Kansas State University.
1. Water—Dipole moments. I. Title.
KMK NUC74-139112

Bandel, Betty, 1912- joint author.
see Wetzel, Ann B. Look around South Burlington, Vermont. Burlington, Vt., Chittenden County Historical Society, 1975.

Bandel, Ernst von, 1800-1876.
Ein Skizzenheft Ernst von Bandels / bearb. u. eingel. von Detlev Hellfaier. — Detmold : Lippische Landesbibliothek, 1975.
16 p., [28] leaves of plates : numerous ill. ; 22 cm. — (Kleine Faksimiles aus der Lippischen Landesbibliothek Detmold ; Heft 2) GFR75-B24
Bibliography: p. [6]
1. Bandel, Ernst von, 1800-1876. I. Hellfaier, Detlev. II. Title. III. Series: Lippische Landesbibliothek Detmold. Kleine Faksimiles aus der Lippischen Landesbibliothek Detmold ; Heft 2.
NC251.B316H44 741.9'43 76-466809
76 MARC

Bandel, Eugene, 1835–1889.
Frontier life in the Army, 1854–1861. Translated by Olga Bandel and Richard Jente; edited by Ralph P. Bieber. Philadelphia, Porcupine Press, 1974.
330 p. illus. 24 cm. (The Southwest historical series, 2)
Bandel's adventures as recorded in letters in German and a journal in English.
Reprint of the 1932 ed. published by A. H. Clark Co., Glendale, Calif.
Includes bibliographical references.
ISBN 0–87991–300–2
1. Frontier and pioneer life—The West. 2. The West—Description and travel—1848–1860. 3. Indians of North America—The West. 4. United States. Army—Military life. 5. Bandel, Eugene, 1835–1889. I. Title.
F786.S752 vol. 2 917.9'03'2 s 74–7156
[F593] [917.81'03'20924] [B] MARC

Bandel, Hannskarl
see Engel, Heinrich, fl. 1964- Tragsysteme. Structure systems. Stuttgart, Deutsche Verlags-Anstalt (1967).

Bandel, Klaus.
Embryonalgehäuse karibischer meso- und Neogastropoden (Mollusca) / von Klaus Bandel. — Mainz : Akademie der Wiss. u. d. Literatur ; Wiesbaden : Steiner [in Komm.], 1975.
133, [44] p. : numerous ill. ; 24 cm. — (Abhandlungen - Akademie der Wissenschaften und der Literatur, Mathematisch-Naturwissenschaftliche Klasse ; Jahrg. 1975, Nr. 1) GFR75-A
Summary also in English.
Bibliography: p. [129]-133.
ISBN 3-515-02022-5 : DM48.20
1. Pectinibranchiata—Caribbean area. 2. Neogastropoda—Caribbean area. 3. Embryology—Gasteropoda. I. Title. II. Series: Akademie der Wissenschaften und der Literatur, Mainz. Mathematisch-Naturwissenschaftliche Klasse. Abhandlungen ; Jahrg. 1975, Nr. 1.
Q49.M22 1975, Nr. 1 75-515468
[QL430.4] 75 MARC

Bandel, Klaus.
Isopod and limulid marks and trails in Tonganoxie Sandstone (Upper Pennsylvanian) of Kansas. Lawrence, 1967.
10 p. illus. 25 cm. (University of Kansas paleontological contributions. Paper 19)
Issued under same cover with no. 18 of the series.
Dated June 9, 1967.
Bibliography: p. 10.
1. Paleontology—Kansas. 2. Paleontology—Pennsylvanian.
ICF NUC73-2039

Bandel, P.R., ed.
see Netherlands (Kingdom, 1815-). Laws, statutes, etc. Waterstaatswetgeving. Zwolle, W.E.J. Tjeenk Willink, 1971.

Bandel, Peninah
see Meda' ge'ografi. [c1973]

Bandel, Vernon Allan, 1937-
The fertilizer value of broiler litter for topdressing small grains. College Park, Md., 1974.
19 p. illus. (Maryland. University. Agricultural Experiment Station. Miscellaneous publication 853)
Bibliography: p. 19.
I. Title.
DNAL NUC76-22388

Bandele
see Wiggins, Phil.

Bandelier, Adolph Francis Alphonse, 1840-1914.
Final report of investigations among the Indians of the Southwestern United States, carried on mainly in the years from 1880-1885 / by A. F. Bandelier. — New York : AMS Press, 1976.
2 v. : ill. ; 23 cm.
Reprint of the 1890-1892 ed. published by the University Press, Cambridge, which was issued as nos. 3-4 of Papers of the Archaeological Institute of America, American series.
ISBN 0-404-58053-X
1. Indians of North America—New Mexico. 2. Indians of North America—Arizona. 3. Indians of Mexico. I. Tile. II. Title. III. Series: Archaeological Institute of America. Papers of the Archaeological Institute of America : American series ; 3-4.
E78.N65B18 1976b 978.9'004'97 74-7918
76 MARC

Bandelier, Adolph Francis Alphonse, 1840-1914.
Hemenway Southwestern Archaeological Expedition : contributions to the history of the Southwestern portion of the United States / by A. F. Bandelier. — New York : AMS Press, 1976.
206 p. : map ; 23 cm.
Reprint of the 1890 ed. published by J. Wilson, Cambridge, which was issued as no. 5 of Papers of the Archaeological Institute of America, American series.
Includes bibliographical references.
ISBN 0-404-58057-2
1. Southwest, New—Description and exploration. 2. America—Discovery and exploration—Spanish. I. Hemenway Southwestern Archaeological Expedition, 1886-1894. II. Series: Archaeological Institute of America. Papers of the Archaeological Institute of America : American series ; 5.
F799.B26 1976b 917.9'04'1 74-7922
76 MARC

Bandelier, Adolph Francis Alphonse, 1840-1914.
Historical introduction to studies among the sedentary Indians of New Mexico ; Report on the ruins of the Pueblo of Pecos / by A. F. Bandelier. — New York : AMS Press, 1976.
133 p., 8 [i.e. 10] leaves of plates : ill. ; 23 cm.
Special t.p. for 2d article reads: A visit to the aborginal ruins in the valley of the Rio Pecos.
Reprint of the 1881 ed. published by A. Williams, Boston, which was issued as v. 1 of Papers of the Archaeological Institute of America, American series.
Includes bibliographical references.
ISBN 0-404-58051-3
1. Pueblo Indians. 2. Indians of North America—New Mexico. 3. New Mexico—Antiquities. 4. Pecos, N.M. I. Bandelier, Adolph Francis Alphonse, 1840-1914. A visit to the aboriginal ruins in the valley of the Rio Pecos. 1976. II. Title. III. Series: Archaeological Institute of America. Papers of the Archaeological Institute of America : American series ; 1.
[E99.P9B2 1976b] 970'.004'97 76-20788
76 MARC

Bandelier, Adolph Francis Alphonse, 1840-1914.
A history of the Southwest; a study of the civilization and conversion of the Indians in Southwestern United States and Northwestern Mexico from the earliest times to 1700, by Adolf F. Bandelier. Edited by Ernest J. Burrus. Rome, Jesuit Historical Institute; St. Louis, Mo., St. Louis University, 1969-
v. port. 25 cm. (Sources and studies for the history of the Americas, v. 7)
Translated from the author's ms. (Biblioteca Vaticana. Mss. (Lat. 1411-14116)) with title: Histoire de la colonisation et des missions de Sonora, Chihuahua, Nouveau-Mexique, et Arizona jusqu'à l'année 1700.
Contents.—v.1. A catalogue of the Bandelier collection in the Vatican Library.
1. Indians of North America—Southwest, New—History. 2. Indians of North America—Southwest, New—Antiquities. I. Burrus, Ernest J., ed. II. Title. III. Series.
OkU NUC76-75827

Bandelier, Adolph Francis Alphonse, 1840–1914.
Indians of the Rio Grande Valley, by Adolph F. Bandelier and Edgar L. Hewett. New York, Cooper Square Publishers, 1973.
274 p. illus. 24 cm.
Reprint of the 1937 ed. published by the University of New Mexico Press, Albuquerque, in series: Handbooks of archaeological history, by Edgar L. Hewett.
Includes bibliographical references.
CONTENTS: Hewett, E. L. The Rio Grande Pueblos today. — Bandelier, A. F. Documentary history of the Rio Grande Pueblos.
1. Pueblo Indians. I. Hewett, Edgar Lee, 1865–1946. II. Title.
E99.P9B22 1973 970.3 72–95268
ISBN 0-8154-0462-X MARC

Bandelier, Adolph Francis Alphonse, 1840-1914.
On the social organization and mode of government of the ancient Mexicans. New York, Cooper Square Publishers, 1975.
145 p. 24 cm.
"From the twelfth annual report of the Peabody Museum of Archaeology and Ethnology, Cambridge, 1879."
Reprint of the 1879 ed. printed at the Salem Press, Salem.
Includes bibliographical references.
1. Aztecs. 2. Indians of Mexico—Tribal government. 3. Indians of Mexico—Social life and customs. I. Title.
F1219.B224 1975 970.3 74-84547
ISBN 0-8154-0504-9 74 MARC

Bandelier, Adolph Francis Alphonse, 1840-1914.
Report of an archaeological tour in Mexico in 1881 / by A. F. Bandelier. — New York : AMS Press, 1976.
x, 326 p., 26 [i.e. 27] leaves of plates : ill. ; 23 cm.
Reprint of the 1884 ed. published by Cupples, Upham, Boston, which was issued as v. 2 of the Papers of the Archaeological Institute of America, American series.
Includes bibliographical references.
ISBN 0-404-58052-1
1. Indians of Mexico—Antiquities. 2. Mexico—Antiquities. I. Title. II. Series: Archaeological Institute of America. Papers of the Archaeological Institute of America : American series ; v. 2.
F1219.B2293 1976b 972'.004'97 76-24822
76 MARC

Bandelier, Adolph Francis Alphonse, 1840–1914.
... The unpublished letters of Adolphe F. Bandelier concerning the writing and publication of The delight makers, with an introduction by Paul Radin. El Paso, Tex., C. Hertzog, 1942.
2 p. l., vii–xv, 33 p. 1 l. incl. front. (port.) fold. facsim. 21 cm. (Southwestern archæologica)
"Two hundred ninety five numbered copies have been printed by Carl Hertzog ... 100 for Charles P. Everitt and 195 for the printer of which 145 are for sale." No. 203.
1. Bandelier, Adolph Francis Alphonse, 1840–1914. The delight makers. 2. Bandelier, Adolph Francis Alphonse, 1840–1914—Correspondence. 3. Janvier, Thomas Allibone, 1849–1913. I. Radin, Paul, 1883–1959, ed. II. Series.
PS1063.B8D43 813.49 43–184
——— Copy 2 (variant) New York, C. P. Everitt, 1942. No. 60.

Bandelier, Adolph Francis Alphonse, 1840-1914. A visit to the aboriginal ruins in the valley of the Rio Pecos. 1976.
in Bandelier, Adolph Francis Alphonse, 1840-1914. Historical introduction to studies among the sedentary Indians of New Mexico ; Report on the ruins of the Pueblo of Pecos. New York, AMS Press, 1976.

Bandelier, Alain
see Société jurassienne d'émulation. Cercle d'études historiques. Bibliographie jurassienne, 1928-1972... Porrentruy: Société jurassienne d'émulation, 1973.

Bandell, Dieter.
Die Aufsicht der Europäischen Gemeinschaften über die Mitgliedstaaten, verglichen mit der Bundesaufsicht und unter Berücksichtigung der internationalen Kontrolle. [Köln, W. Kleikamp, 1965]
xii, 113 p. 21 cm.
Thesis—Cologne.
Bibliography: p. ii-x.
1. European Communities. 2. Federal government—Germany (Federal Republic, 1949-) I. Title.
NNC NUC76-72872

Bandello, Matteo, 1485–1561.
Novelle. Prefazione di Francesco Picco. Milano, Bietti, 1973.
x, 254 p. illus. 20 cm. (Classici del ridere) L3000 It 74–Mar
PQ4606.A15 1973 74–321657

Bandello, Matteo, 1485–1561.
Novelle / di Matteo Bandello ; a cura di Giuseppe Guido Ferrero. — 1. ed. — [Torino] : Unione tipografico-editrice torinese, 1974.
968 p., [8] leaves of plates : ill. ; 23 cm. — (Classici italiani ; [n. 30]) (Classici UTET) It 74–Dec
"Edizione antologica."
Bibliography: p. [49]–52.
Includes index.
L12000
I. Ferrero, Giuseppe Guido.
PQ4606.A15 1974 75–528500

Bandello, Matteo, 1485-1561. Novelle. Selections. 1945.
in Amori, beffe e avventure. Roma, Atlantica, [1945]

Bandello, Matteo, 1485-1561. La sfortunata morte di dui infelicissimi amanti.
see Broke, Arthur, d. 1563. Brooke's 'Romeus and Juliet,' being the original of Shakespeare's 'Romeo and Juliet'. Norwood, Pa., Norwood Editions, 1975.

Bandello, Matteo, 1485-1561. La sfortunata morte di dui infelicissimi amanti
see Broke, Arthur, d. 1563. Romeus and Iuliet. Vaduz, Kraus Reprint, 1965.

Bandello, Matteo, 1485-1561.
see Novelle galanti del Cinquecento italiano. Venezia, Ateneo, [1945]

Bandello, Vincenzo, 1435–1506.
De singulari puritate et praerogativa conceptionis Salvatoris nostri Jesu Christi. Bologna, Ugo Rugerius, 12 Feb. 1481.
113 (i. e. 112), [5] l. 4°. 21.8 cm.
Leaf 4ᵃ: Ad illustrissimum ... ducem ... Herculem Estensem tractatus de singulari puritate : prerogatiua conceptionis saluatoris nostri iesu christi ... feliciter incipit.
The main work is preceded by the author's Epistola narrativa disputationis factae de conceptione B. V. Mariae.
"Epistola beati Bernardi de festo conceptionis Beate Virginis non faciendo": leaf [113ᵃ]–[114ᵇ]
Hain. Repertorium, *2353; Brit. Mus. Cat. (XV cent.) VI, p. 806 (IA. 28703); Gesamtkat. d. Wiegendr., 3238; Goff. Third census, B-49.
Rubricated.
Inscription, with owner's name erased, dated "153." Bookplate of Georg Kloss. From the library of Peter Force.
1. Immaculate Conception—Controversial literature. I. Bandello, Vincenzo, 1435–1506. Epistola narrativa disputationis factae de conceptione B. V. Mariae. 1481. II. Bernard de Clairvaux, Saint, 1091?–1153. Epistola de festo conceptionis B. Virginis non celebrando. 1481. III. Title.
Incun. 1481.B21 76–525207
[BT620]
——— Copy 2. 20 cm. Thacher Coll. Imperfect: 6 leaves wanting; 1st leaf mutilated.

Bandello, Vincenzo, 1435-1506. Epistola narrativa disputationis factae de conceptione B. V. Mariae. 1481
in Bandello, Vincenzo, 1435-1506. De singulari puritate... Bologna, Ugo Rugerius, 12 Feb. 1481.

Bandello, Vincenzo, 1435-1506
see also
Dominicans. Master General, 1501-1506 (Vincenzo Bandello)

Bandelloni, Enzo.
Elementi di architettura tecnica. Dalle lezioni del prof. E. Bandelloni. Ad uso degli allievi di ingegneria civile dell'Università di Padova. Padova, Cleup, 1970.
481 p. illus.; 5 plates inserted. 24 cm. It 72–Dec
Includes bibliographies.
1. Building. 2. Building materials. I. Title.
TH145.B25 73–338821

Bandelloni, Enzo.
Elementi di architettura tecnica, dalle lezioni del prof. Enzo Bandelloni : ad uso degli allievi di ingegneria civile dell'Università di Padova. — 2. ed. aggiornata. — Padova : CLEUP, 1975.
v, 505 p., [5] fold. leaves of plates : ill. ; 24 cm.
Includes bibliographies.
L6000
1. Building. 2. Building materials. I. Title: Elementi di architettura tecnica ...
TH145.B25 1975 721 76-480231
*76 MARC

Bandelow, Christoph.
Einführung in die Wahrscheinlichkeitstheorie / Christoph Bandelow. — Bochum : Studienverlag Brockmeyer, 1976.
vi, 198 p. ; 21 cm. GFR77-A
Based on the author's lectures given at Florida State University and Ruhr-Universität Bochum.
Bibliography: p. 186-187.
Includes indexes.
ISBN 3-921543-59-2 : DM11.80
1. Probabilities. I. Title.
QA273.B2555 77-553662
77 MARC

Bandemer, Hans
see Optimale Versuchsplanung... Berlin: Akademie-Verlag, 1973.

Bandemer, Hans.
see Optimale Versuchsplanung. 2., bearb. Aufl. Berlin, Akademie-Verlag, 1976.

Bandepe
see
Banco de Desenvolvimento do Estado de Pernambuco
Banco do Estado de Pernambuco
for publications by and about these bodies.
When this acronym occurs at the beginning of titles and other entries, it is filed as a word: Bandepe.
75–218640
rev

Bander, Carol Jean.
The reception of exiled German writers in the Nazi and conservative German-language press of California: 1933-1950, by Carol Bander. [n.p.] 1972.
vii, 362 l. 28 cm.
Thesis-University of Southern California.
Typewritten.
1. German literature-Émigré authors.
I. Title.
CLSU NUC73-113977

Bander, Edward J
Change of name and law of names, by Edward J. Bander. Dobbs Ferry, N. Y., Oceana Publications, 1973.
116 p. 19 cm. (Legal almanac series, no. 34) $4.00
"Revised and updated edition of How to change your name, and the law of names, by Lawrence G. Greene."
Bibliography: p. 111–114.
1. Names, Personal—United States—Law. I. Greene, Lawrence Gerard. How to change your name, and the law of names. II. Title.
KF468.Z9G7 1973 346'.73'012 73–11060
ISBN 0-379-11088-1 MARC

Bander, Edward J comp.
The corporation in a democratic society / edited by Edward J. Bander. — New York : H. W. Wilson Co., 1975.
202 p. ; 19 cm. — (The Reference shelf ; v. 46, no. 6)
Bibliography: p. 186–202.
SUMMARY: A compilation of articles by different authors discussing the various aspects of a corporation, including its development, functions, responsibilities, authority, and the corporate conscience.
ISBN 0-8242-0526-X
[1. Corporations—United States—Addresses, essays, lectures. 2. Industry—Social aspects—United States—Addresses, essays, lectures. [1. Corporations. 2. Industry—Social aspects] I. Title. II. Series.
HD2795.B25 338.7'4'0973 75–1164
MARC

Bander, Edward J
Supplemental index, August 1976, Collier bankruptcy manual ... / by Edward J. Bander. — New York : M. Bender, 1976.
192 p. ; 24 cm.
1. Bankruptcy—United States. I. Collier, William Miller, 1867-1956. Law and practice in bankruptcy. II. Title.
KF1524.C59 1954 Suppl 346'.73'078 77-350589
77 MARC

Bander, Edward J., joint author.
see Klein, Fannie J. Federal and State court systems ... Cambridge, Mass., Published for the Institute of Judicial Administration by Ballinger Pub. Co., c1977.

Bander, Karen Weiss.
The relationship between internal-external control and academic choice behavior. [Storrs, Conn.] 1975.
2, vii, 144 l. illus., tables.
Thesis (Ph.D.)--University of Connecticut, 1976.
Bibliography: leaves 95-100.
1. Academic achievement. 2. Personality and academic achievement. I. Title.
CtU NUC77-92276

Bander, Peter.
Carry on talking; how dead are the voices? Gerrards Cross, Smythe, 1972.
167, [8] p. illus., ports. 23 cm. index. £1.90 B 72-19187
1. Spiritualism. I. Title.
BF1261.2.B27 1972 133.9'3 72-169994
ISBN 0-900675-66-7 MARC

Bander, Peter.
Voices from the tapes; recordings from the other world. New York, Drake Publishers [1973]
167 p. illus. 23 cm. $6.95
1. Spirit writings. 2. Phonotapes in psychical research. I. Title.
BF1380.B36 133.9'3 73-181609
ISBN 0-88749-447-9 MARC

Bander, Robert.
see Sunset home remodeling guide to paneling, painting & wallpapering. 1st ed. Menlo Park, Calif., Lane Pub. Co., 1976.

Bander, Robert, ed.
see Sunset travel guide to Washington. [3d rev. ed.] Menlo Park, Calif., Lane Boosk [1973]

Bandera, Armando.
La Iglesia ante el proceso de liberación / por Armando Bandera. — Madrid : La Editorial Católica, 1975.
xiii, 382 p. ; 20 cm. — (Biblioteca de autores cristianos ; 373 : 10. Pensamiento social y político cristiano) Sp75-Apr
Includes bibliographical references.
ISBN 8422007096
1. Liberation theology. 2. Theology, Doctrinal—History—20th century. 3. Church. I. Title.
BT83.57.B36 75-516469
•76 MARC

Bandera, Armando.
La Iglesia, Sacramento del mundo. Guadalajara, OPE [1971]
397 p., 5 l. 21 cm. (Selección OPE, 13) 200ptas Sp 71-Oct
Includes bibliographical references.
1. Church. I. Title.
BX1746.B32 72-363247

Bandera, Armando.
María en el misterio de Cristo. Villava, España, Editorial OPE [1968]
83 p. 18 cm. (A la unidad por María, no. 2)
Includes bibliographical references.
1. Mary, Virgin—Theology. I. Title.
BT613.B34 72-227537

Bandera, Cesáreo.
Mimesis conflictiva : ficción literaria y violencia en Cervantes y Calderón / Cesáreo Bandera ; prólogo de René Girard. — Madrid : Gredos, [1975]
262 p. ; 20 cm. — (Biblioteca románica hispánica : 2. Estudios y ensayos ; 221) Sp75-Mar
Includes bibliographical references.
ISBN 8424906012
1. Cervantes Saavedra, Miguel de, 1547-1616—Criticism and interpretation. 2. Calderón de la Barca, Pedro, 1600-1681—Criticism and interpretation. I. Title.
PQ6353.B25 75-508756
•75 MARC

Bandera, Manuel M. de la
see Uruguay. Asamblea General. El reglamento... Montevideo [Imp. "Atenas"] 1963.

Bandera, Roberto Nuñez y
see Nuñez y Bandera, Roberto.

Bandera, Stepan, 1909-1959
see Za samostiĭnu Ukrainu... [Munich] Vyd. Zakordonnykh chastyn Orhanizatsiï ukraïns'kykh natsionalistiv, 1957.

Bandera, V.N., ed.
see The Soviet economy in regional perspective. New York, Praeger [1973]

Bandera de provincias : índices y selección de textos / por Rosella Gerini, Eugenia González Ricaño y Ofelia Gutiérrez García ; bajo la dirección de Adalberto Navarro Sánchez. — Guadalajara : Ediciones Et cætera, 1974.
294 p. ; 23 cm.
228 copies printed. "Doscientos numerados del 1 al 200 ... No. 42."
1. Mexican literature—20th century. 2. Bandera de provincias—Indexes. I. Gerini, Rosella. II. Navarro Sánchez, Adalberto.
PQ7244.B3 75-584221

Bandera County Historical Survey Committee
see Graves, Mrs. Howard, 1906- comp. History of Bandera County schools for over a century. Bandera, Tex. [1973]

Bandera Roja (Political party)
see No hay término medio. Caracas, América Rebelde, 1972.

La Bandera y el escudo nacional de Guatemala. Guatemala [Guatemala, 19--]
8 p. 19 cm.
1. Emblems, National—Guatemala.
TxU NUC76-22127

Banderier, Gaston.
Les revenus des ménages en 1970 / par Gaston Banderier et Pierre Ghigliazza. — Paris : Ministère de l'économie et des finances, Institut national de la statistique et des études économiques, 1974.
148 p. : graphs ; 30 cm. — (Collections de l'I.N.S.E.E. ; no 147 : Série M ; no 40) F***
Summary in English and Spanish.
1. Cost and standard of living—France—Statistics. 2. Income—France—Statistics. I. Ghigliazza, Pierre, joint author. II. Series: France. Institut national de la statistique et des études économiques. Collections ; no 147. III. Series: France. Institut national de la statistique et des études économiques. Ménages ; no 40.
HC271.A218 no. 147 330'.08 s 75-510844
[HD7028] 75 MARC

Banderier, Gaston, joint author.
see Perrot, Marguerite. Les revenus des personnes âgées. Paris, Institut national de la statistique et des études économiques, 1976.

Banderov, Aleksandùr.
България лето 893-то. Истор. поема за Олдамур Расате кхан [Владимир—син на княз Борис I]. Худож. Здравко Захариев. Пловдив, Хр. Г. Данов, 1970.
55 p. with illus. 20 cm. 0.51 lv Bu 70-2227
1. Vladimir, Prince of Bulgaria—Poetry. I. Title.
Title romanized: Bulgarii͡a leto osemstotin devetdeset i treto.
PG1038.12.A45B8 74-312035

Banderov, Aleksandŭr.
(Pŭtuvane kŭm planinata)
Пътуване към планината : стихове / Александър Бандеров. — 1. изд. — Пловдив : Хр. Г. Данов, 1974.
69 p. ; 20 cm. Bu 75-535
0.58 lv
I. Title.
PG1038.12.A45P8 **75-581934**

Bandes, Lucille Coleman, 1921-
The professional reading of teachers as a function of their personal characteristics in interaction with their school environment / Lucille Bandes. -- [New York : s.n.], 1975.
vii, 221 leaves : ill. ; 35 mm.
Thesis--Columbia University.
Bibliography: leaves 197-205.
Microfilm. Ann Arbor, Mich. : University Microfilms, 1976.
1. Reading research. I. Title.
InU NUC77-88819

Les Bandes de Picardie : le 1er régiment d'infanterie dans la Résistance / préf. du général Kœnig ; ill. de Périchon-Meslay. — Paris : Librairie Lamarre, [1946]
188 p., [4] fold. leaves of plates : ill. ; 24 cm.
1. World War, 1939-1945—Regimental histories—France—1er régiment d'infanterie. 2. France. Armée. 1er régiment d'infanterie. 3. World War, 1939-1945—Underground movements—France.
D761.3.B35 940.54'12'44 75-502789
75 MARC

Bandesa
see
Banco Nacional de Desarrollo Agrícola
for publications by and about this body.
Titles and other entries beginning with this acronym are filed following this card.
74-212957

Bandet, Jean Louis.
Adalbert Stifter; introduction à la lecture de ses nouvelles. [Paris] C. Klincksieck, 1974.
364 p. 24 cm. (Publications de l'Université de Haute Bretagne, 3) 52.00F F***
Bibliography: p. [359]-364.
1. Stifter, Adalbert, 1805-1868.
PT2525.Z5B3 833'.7 74-182099
ISBN 2-252-01641-8 MARC

Bandet, Jeanne.
L'enfant et les jouets, par Jeanne Bandet et Réjane Sarazanas. [Paris] Casterman [1972]
155 p. 18 cm. (Collection E 3, 18) 9.00F F***
Bibliography: p. 153-154.
1. Play. 2. Child study. I. Sarazanas, Réjane. II. Title.
BF717.B26 72-357573

Bandettini, Antonio.
I bilanci consolidati nei gruppi dell'I. R. I. e dell'E. N. I. Pisa, C. Cursi, 1969.
xii, 243 p. 25 cm. (Collana di studi economico-aziendali, pubblicazione n. 26) It Suppl-6
Bibliography: p. [239]-243.
1. Holding companies—Italy—Accounting. 2. Istituto per la ricostruzione industriale, Rome. 3. Ente nazionale idrocarburi. I. Title. II. Series.
HF5686.H6B35 73-303727

Bandettini, Antonio.
Le rilevazioni statistiche in economia aziendale / Antonio Bandettini. — Pisa : C. Cursi, 1972.
xxiii, 399 p. ; 25 cm. — (Collana di studi economico-aziendali ; pubblicazione n. 34) It 75-July
Summary in French and English.
Errata slip inserted.
Bibliography: p. [383]-399.
L8350
1. Auditing. I. Title. II. Series.
HF5667.B245 76-510153

Bandettini, Giuseppe.
Il cavaliere di Vittorio Veneto / G. Bendettini. — Firenze : P. Cipriani, [1973]
50 p. : ill. ; 21 cm. — (Collana di poesia ; 3) It 75-Apr
L1000
1. European War, 1914-1918—Campaigns—Italo-Austrian—Poetry. I. Title.
PQ4862.A468C3 75-527271

Bandhauer, Alfons.
Ich hab mich ergeben. (Ein Tatsachenbericht. Selbsterlebtes, f. die junge Generation geschrieben.) (Wels, Leopold-Bauer-Strasse 6) Selbstverl., 1971.
104 p. 21 cm. S64.00 Au 71-16-174
On cover: Das Pausezeichen.
1. World War, 1939-1945—Personal narratives, Austrian. 2. Bandhauer, Alfons. I. Title. II. Title: Das Pausezeichen.
D811.B326 74-340224

Bandhopādhyāya, Amiyakumāra
see Roy, Mohit, 1935- (Nadīyā Jelāra purākīrti) 1975.

Bandhu.
(Mukti-mārga)
મુક્તિ-માર્ગ : સામાજીક ત્રિઅંકી નાટક / લેખક બંધુ. — 1. આવૃત્તિ. — મુંબઈ : એન. એમ. ત્રિપાઠી લિમિટેડ, 1944.
168 p. ; 19 cm.
In Gujarati.

I. Title.

PK1859.B34M8 77-986001

Bandhu, C. M.
see Nepali segmental phonology. Kirtipur, Tribhuvan University, 1971.

Bandhu, Mānaka Tivārī
see
Tewari, Manak, 1941-

Bandhu, Vishva
see Vishva Bandhu, 1897-

Bandhu Pant
see
Pant, Bandhu, 1927-

Bandhu Śarmā
see
Śarmā, Bandhu, 1934-

Bandhudas Sen
see
Sen, Bandhudas.

Bandhukul, S
The Rastrelliger fishery research programme in Thailand, by S. Bandhukul. [Bangkok, FAO Regional Office for Asia and the Far East, 1961]
3 p. (Indo-Pacific Fisheries Council. Occasional paper 61/1)
ICRL NUC74-144591

Bandhula Śaraccandra
see
Śaraccandra, Bandhula.

Bandhurāmasiṃha.
(Sahakāra digdarśikā)
सहकार दिग्दर्शिका. लेखक बंधुरामसिंह. जबलपुर, मध्यप्रदेश राज्य सहकारी संघ ⌜1965?⌝
11, 306 p. 24 cm. Rs3.50
In Hindi.
1. Cooperation—India. 2. Community development—India. I. Title.
HD3538.B317 S A 68-9150
PL 480: I-H-5320

Bandhuvardhana, Priyaṃvadā M
(Heṭat davasak udāveyi)
හෙටත් දවසක් උදවෙයි. ⌜කර්තෘ⌝ ප්‍රියංවද ඇම්. බන්ධුවර්ධන. මහනුවර, කේ. එච්. බන්ධුවර්ධන ⌜1972⌝
237 p. 18 cm. Rs4.50
In Sinhalese.
A novel.
I. Title.
PK2859.B35H4 72-902511

Bándi, Gábor
see Baranya története az öskortól az Arpád-korig... Pécs: [Janus Pannonius Múzeum], 1973.

Bandi, Giorgio, joint author.
see Gavinelli, Corrado. Novara e Antonelli... ⌜Roma, Direzione generale degli archivi di Stato⌝ 1976, ⌜c1975⌝

Bandi, Giuseppe, 1834-1894.
I mille da Genova a Capua. Firenze, A. Salani ⌜1903⌝
373 p.
Microfilm (negative) Providence, R.I., Brown Photolab, 1970? 1 reel.
1. Garibaldi, Giuseppe, 1807-1882. 2. Italy—History—War of 1860-1861.
NNC NUC75-26602

Bandi, Hans-Georg.
Die Kunst der Eskimos auf der St.-Lorenz-Insel in Alaska / Hans-Georg Bandi ; Farbaufnahmen, Karl Buri. — Bern : Hallwag-Verlag, c1977.
63 p. : ill. ; 19 cm. — (Orbis pictus ; 65) Sw77-3865
Bibliography: p. 63.
ISBN 3-444-51062-4 : 10.80F
1. Eskimos—Alaska—St. Lawrence Island. 2. Eskimos—Alaska—St. Lawrence Island—Art. I. Title.
E99.E7B167 77-483085
•77 MARC

Bandi, Hans-Georg.
Originea eschimosilor; in lumina arheologiei. ⌜Bucuresti⌝ Editura Stiintifica, 1969.
202 p. illus., plates.
Translation from German.
Roumanian.
1. Eskimo—Art. 2. Indians of North America—Art. 3. Archeology. I. Title.
OCl NUC74-144830

Bandi, Hans-Georg.
Preliminary report on the St. Lawrence archaeological field project, 1967, of the University of Berne/Switzerland and the University of Alaska, by H. -G. Bandi. [n. p., 196?]
18 l. illus., maps. 28 cm.
1. St. Lawrence Island, Alaska. 2. Excavations (Archaeology)—Alaska. I. Title.
AkU NUC73-103965

Bandi, W.
see Leg length discrepancy ; The injured knee. Berlin, Springer-Verlag, 1977.

Bandi, Zoltan L
Metabolism of alkoxylipids in the rat. [Minneapolis] 1969.
134 l. illus. 29 cm.
Thesis (Ph. D.)—University of Minnesota.
Bibliography: leaves 129-134.
I. Title.
MnU-A NUC74-144590

Bándi, Zsuzsanna
see Hungary. Országos Levéltár. Ssehszlovákiai levéltri anyagról készült mikrofilmek (1973. január 1-én): repertórium. Budapest: 1974.

Bandi primer. ⌜n. p., 196-?⌝
34 p. illus. 31 cm.
Cover title.
Gbandi and English.
1. Primers, Gbandi.
PL8204.2.B3 73-206478

Bandić, Miloš I
Cvet i steg : književnost narodnooslobodilačke borbe / M. I. Bandić. — Beograd : Bandić, 1975.
104 p. ; 17 cm. — (Nezavisno izdanje ; 17) Yu***
Bibliography: p. 95-97.
Includes indexes.
35.00Din
1. Revolutionary literature, Yugoslav—History and criticism. 2. Yugoslav literature—20th century—History and criticism. 3. World War, 1939-1945—Literature and the war. I. Title.
PG1413.B3 76-501103

Bandić, Miloš I comp.
(Savremena proza)
Савремена проза / приредио ⌜и Предговор написао⌝ Милош И. Бандич. — 2. изд. — Београд : Нолит, 1973.
834 p. ; 21 cm. — (Српска књижевност у књижевној критици ; 10) Yu 73-8402
Bibliography: p. 829-⌜831⌝
1. Serbian prose literature—History and criticism. I. Title.
PG1412.B27 1973 74-352134

Bandiera, Luigi.
Palestrina ieri e oggi. Roma, 1972.
96 p. illus. 24 cm. L1000 It 72-Nov
1. Palestrina. I. Title.
DG975.P22B35 73-303559

Bandiera, Luigi.
Thomas Mann e i suoi legami con Palestrina / Luigi Bandiera. — Roma : Centro studi francescani del Lazio, 1975.
52 p. : ill. ; 21 cm. — (Collana di studi storici, religiosi, letterari ; n. 7) It76-Aug
L1200
1. Mann, Thomas, 1875-1955—Homes and haunts—Palestrina. 2. Authors, German—20th century—Biography. I. Title.
PT2625.A44Z5414 76-483256
•76 MARC

Bandiera, Luigi.
11+11 ⌜i. e. Undici più undici⌝ episodi della Resistenza / Luigi Bandiera. — Roma : Centro studi francescani del Lazio, 1974.
128 p. : 2 maps ; 22 cm. — (Collana di studi storici, religiosi, letterari ; n. 5) It 75-Dec
L1500
1. World War, 1939-1945—Underground movements—Italy. 2. Italy—History—German occupation, 1943-1945. I. Title.
D802.I 8B23 76-500923

Bandiera, Pasquale
see Le Sbarre del Concordato. Genova, Lanterna, 1973.

Bandieramonte, Rosetta, 1933–
Universo in amore / Rosetta Bandieramonte. — ⌜Catania⌝ : Libreria Minerva, 1975.
80 p. : port. ; 22 cm. It 76-Mar
Poems.
L2500
I. Title.
PQ4862.A475U5 76-508848

Bandilang pula.
Lumalawak ang pandaigdigang pakikibaka laban sa imperyalismong Amerikano. ⌜n.p.⌝ Samahang Demokratiko no Kabataan, 1972.
6 l. illus. 33 cm.
Caption title.
1. Vietnam—History. 2. United States—For. rel.—1961- 3. Imperialism. I. Title.
NIC NUC75-51735

Bandilang pula.
Tagumpay sa pakikibaka ng mga mamamayang Biyetnames! ⌜n.p.⌝ Samahang Demokratiko ng Kabataan, 1972.
2 l. 28 cm.
Caption title.
1. Vietnamese Conflict, 1961- I. Title.
NIC NUC75-51734

Bandilla, Rüdiger.
Das Klagrecht der Mitgliedstaaten der Europäischen Gemeinschaften gegen Durchagriffsakte. Wesen und Bedeutung für den Rechtsschutz des Einzelnen. Geleitwort von Hans Peter Ipsen. Hamburg, Christen, 1965.
139 p. 24 cm. (Schriftenreihe zur europäischen Intergration, Bd. 2) GDNB 67-A43-70
Issued also as thesis, Hamburg.
Bibliography: p. 132-139.
28.00
1. Parties to actions—European Economic Community countries. I. Title. II. Series.
75-560670

Bandin, Tomislav
see Tepšić, Radivoj. Poslovne financije... Zagreb, Informator, 1974.

Bandinelli, Mario.
La leva militare e gli appositi servizi comunali ; testo e commento critico-sistematico del D. P. R. 14 febbraio, 1964, n. 237, corredato di istruzioni, dell'elenco delle infermità (D. P. R. 28 maggio 1964, n. 496) e di indice generale alfabetico-analitico. 3. ed. Firenze, Noccioli ⌜1966⌝
xx, 182 p. 24 cm.
Bibliography: p. ⌜165⌝
1. Military service, Compulsory—Italy. I. Italy. Laws, statutes, etc. Decreto del Presidente della Repubblica 14 febbraio 1964, n. 237. 1966. II. Italy. Laws, statutes, etc. Decreto del Presidente della Repubblica 28 maggio 1964, n. 496. 1966. III. Title.
75-543222

Bandinelli, Ranuccio Bianchi
see Bianchi Bandinelli, Ranuccio, 1900-1975.

Bandini, Albert R
The miracle at Syracuse : the weeping Madonna. — Fresno, Calif. : Academy Library Guild, ⌜c1954⌝
93 p., ⌜1⌝ leaf of plates : ill. ; 21 cm.
1. Lacrime, La Madonna delle. 2. Mary, Virgin—Apparitions and miracles (Modern)—Italy—Syracuse, Sicily. I. Title.
BT660.S9B36 232.91 77-366772
77 MARC

Bandini, Alfredo.
Valores máximos das vazões médias diárias durante as enchentes na bacia do Rio Tietê. Maximum values of the average daily floods of the Tietê River drainage basin. ⌜By⌝ Alfredo Bandini ⌜and⌝ Angelo R. Cuomo. São Paulo, 1962.
15 p. illus. 28 cm.
"Separata da revista 'D.A.E.', no. 47 (Dezembro de 1962)."
1. Watersheds—Statistics. I. Cuomo, Angelo R. II. Title.
NTR NUC76-72874

Bandini, Angelo Maria, 1726-1803
see Vespucci, Amerigo, 1451-1512. Vita e lettere... Firenze, Nella Stamperia all' insegna di Apollo, 1745 [1973]

Bandini, Fernando, 1931–
see Ioannis XXIII somnium. Amstelodami, Academia Regia Desciplinarum Nederlandica, 1965.

Bandini, Fernando, 1931-
see Leopardi, Giacomo, conte, 1798-1837. Canti. Milano: Garzanti, 1975.

Bandini, Fernando, 1931-
see 1474 [i.e. Millequattrocentosettantaquattro], le origini della stampa a Vicenza ... [Vicenza] : N. Pozza, 1975.

Bandini, Fernando, 1931-
see Ricerche sulla lingua poetica contemporanea. Padova, Liviana, 1972.

Bandini, Franco.
Il mistero dei dischi volanti. Firenze, Centro internazionale del libro, 1971.
115 p. illus.; plate inserted. 28 cm. L3000 It Suppl-7
Bibliography: p. 111-112.
1. Flying saucers. I. Title.
TL789.B26 001.9'4 73-338943

Bandini, Franco.
Tecnica della sconfitta. Milano, Longanesi, 1969.
2 v. 18 cm. (I Libri Pocket, v. 208) (I Super pocket, v. 108) L900 It Suppl-4 (v. 2)
CONTENTS: v. 1. 1939: Storia di una guerra preventiva.—v. 2. 1940: Le sei incredibili settimane.
1. World War, 1939-1945—Causes. 2. World War, 1939-1945—Italy. I. Title.
D742.I 7B3 1969 72-357215

Bandini, Mirella.
Pinot Gallizio e il Laboratorio sperimentale d'Alba del Movimento internazionale per una Bauhaus immaginista (1955-57) e dell'Internazionale situazionista (1957-60). Introduzione e catalogo di Mirella Bandini. Prefazione di Aldo Passoni. Torino, Galleria civica d'arte moderna, 28 maggio-15 luglio 1974. Torino, Galleria civica d'arte moderna, [1974]
128, [52] p., incl. plates. illus. 23 cm. It 74-Sept
French or Italian.
1. Art, Italian—Exhibitions. 2. Art, Modern—20th century—Italy. 3. Internationale situationniste. Laboratorio sperimentale d'Alba. I. Gallizio, Pinot, 1902- II. Turin. Galleria d'arte moderna. III. Title.
N6918.B33 75-550926

Bandini, Mirella.
see Paolini, Giulio, 1940- Giulio Paolini. Parma, Università, 1976.

Bandini, Tullio.
Delinquenza giovanile. Analisi di un processo di stigmatizzazione e di esclusione. Prefazione di Giacomo Canepa. Milano, A. Giuffrè, 1974.
xi, 343 p. 21 cm. L5000 It 74-June
At head of title: Tullio Bandini, Umberto Gatti.
Bibliography: p. [317]-337.
1. Juvenile delinquency. 2. Juvenile justice, Administration of. 3. Rehabilitation of juvenile delinquents. I. Gatti, Umberto, joint author. II. Title.
HV9076.B2698 74-315505

Bandini Buti, Antonio, 1895-
Manuale di filatelia. Contiene la classificazione dei francobolli rari e rarissimi di Italia, San Marino e Vaticano. 3. ed. riveduta e aggiornata. Con 32 tavole fuori testo. Milano, U. Mursia, 1973.
279 p. 16 plates. 20 cm. (Il Bivio. Serie libri completi) It 73-June
At head of title: A. Bandini Buti.
1. Postage-stamps—Collectors and collecting. 2. Postage-stamps—Italy. I. Title.
HE6215.B34 1973 73-344789

Bandini Buti, Antonio, 1895-
see Mazzini, Giuseppe, 1805-1872. Educazione e democrazi ... Milano : Cisalpino -Goliardica, 1972.

Bandini Ramadoro, Mauro.
Guía para el mejoramiento de las condiciones de trabajo en la industria. Guatemala, 1974.
113 p. illus. 26 cm.
Tesis (ingeniería industrial)—Universidad Rafael Landívar, Guatemala.
Bibliography: p. 112-113.
1. Work environment. I. Title.
TxU NUC76-22103

Bandioli, Gianni.
Organizzazione e condotta della guerriglia. Torino, Litografia Massaza & Sinchetto, 1973.
vii, 107 p. 24 cm. L2500 It 73-July
1. Guerrilla warfare. I. Title.
U240.B25 73-348569

(Il) banditismo in Italia. Firenze, Sansoni, 1969.
202 p. (I problemi di Ulisse, no. 64)
Originally published in Ulisse.
1. Brigands and robbers—Italy. 2. Mafia. I. Ulisse.
CaOTP NUC74-17973

Il Bandito della Casbah, di Julien Duvivier / a cura di Glauco Viazzi. — 1. ed. — [Milano : Editoriale Domus, 1945]
xix, 122 p. : chiefly ill. ; 20 cm. — (Cineteca Domus in volumi ; 5)
Based on Pepé le Moko.
"I film di Duvivier": p. xvii-xix.
I. Duvivier, Julien, 1896-1967. II. Viazzi, Glauco. III. Pepé le Moko. [Motion picture]
PN1997.P4573B3 77-468229
77 MARC

The Banditti of the Rocky Mountains, and Vigilance Committee in Idaho. An authentic record of startling adventures in the gold mines of Idaho. Twentieth thousand. New York, Wilson & Co., 1865.
143 p. illus. 20 cm.
Micro-opaque. Louisville, Ky., Lost Cause Press, 1961. 2 cards. 7.5 x 12.5 cm. (Plains and Rockies, 413a)
NIC NUC74-172186

The Banditti of the Rocky Mountains and Vigilance Committee in Idaho; an authentic record of startling adventures in the gold mines of Idaho. [n.p., 197-?]
An account of Henry Plummer and the bandits organized and led by him.
Reprint of the New York, 1865 ed.
1. Plummer, Henry, d.1864. 2. Crime and criminals--Idaho. 3. Vigilance committees.
CU-SB NUC77-92275

Bandivadekar, Chandrakant Mahadeo, 1932-
'अज्ञेय' की कविता; एक मूल्यांकन. लेखक चन्द्रकान्त महादेव बांदिवड़ेकर. [1. संस्करण] इलाहाबाद, सरस्वती प्रेस [1971]
215 p. 22 cm. Rs12.00
In Hindi.
Includes bibliographical references.
1. Vatsyayan, Sachchidanand Hiranand, 1911- I. Title.
Title romanized: 'Ajñeya' kī kavitā.
PK2098.V34Z65 70-921227

Bandivadekar, Chandrakant Mahadev.
हिन्दी और मराठी के सामाजिक उपन्यासों का तुलनात्मक अध्ययन, 1920-47. लेखक चन्द्रकांत महादेव बांदिवडेकर. निर्देशक जगदीशचन्द्र जैन. [1. संस्करण] अजमेर, कृष्णा ब्रदर्स [1969]
xi, 7, 529 p. 23 cm. 25.00
"बम्बई विश्वविद्यालय की पी-एच. डी. की उपाधि के लिए स्वीकृत शोध-प्रबन्ध."
In Hindi.
List of Hindi novelists and their works: p. [525]-529.
Bibliography: p. [516]-524.
1. Hindi fiction—History and criticism. 2. Marathi fiction—History and criticism. 3. Literature, Comparative—Hindi and Marathi. 4. Literature, Comparative—Marathi and Hindi. I. Title.
Title romanized: Hindī aura Marāṭhī ke sāmājika upanyāsoṃ kā tulanātmaka adhyayana.
PK2042.B36 78-909926

Bandjar, Indonesia (Kabupaten)
Rentjana pembangunan lima tahun, 1969-1973. [Martapura] Dewan Perwakilan Rakjat Daerah Kabupaten Bandjar [1969]
[92] l. illus. 33 cm.
Cover title.
1. Bandjar, Indonesia (Kabupaten)—Economic conditions. 2. Bandjar, Indonesia (Kabupaten)—Economic policy. I. Title.
HC448.B34B35 1969 73-942011

Bandjaransari, Sudomo, ed.
see Panitya Peringatan Dua Ratus Tahun Kota Jogjakarta. Peringatan 200 [i.e. dua ratus] tahun Kota Jogjakarta. [Jogja, 1956]

Bandjarmasin, Indonesia. Universitas Lambung Mangkurat
see
Universitas Lambung Mangkurat.

Bandjarmasin, Indonesia (Kalimantan Selatan)
For works by this jurisdiction issued after the change of orthography in 1972 see
Banjarmasin, Indonesia (Kalimantan Selatan)
75-588710

Bandle, Catherine.
Obere Schranken für die Eigenwerte einer stueckweise freien Membran auf einem "Vierseit". [Geneva, Battelle Institute, Advanced Studies Center, 1970]
10 l. (Battelle Institute. Advanced Studies Center, Geneva. Mathematics report, no. 39)
Cover title.
Bibliography: leaves 9-10.
WaU NUC74-144594

Bandle, Oskar, 1926-
Die Gliederung des Nordgermanischen. Basel, Stuttgart, Helbing & Lichtenhahn, 1973.
117 p. 23 maps (in pocket) 24 cm. (Beiträge zur nordischen Philologie, Bd. 1) 36.00F Sw 73-A-2802
Based on the author's lecture presented before the Gesellschaft für Deutsche Sprache und Literatur, Zürich, February 1960.
Bibliography: p. 7-9.
1. Scandinavian languages—History. I. Title. II. Series.
PD1545.B3 73-354123
ISBN 3-7190-0623-9

Bandle, Oskar, 1926- ed.
see Festschrift für Siegfried Gutenbrunner: zum 65. Geburtstag am 26. Mai 1971 überreicht von seinen Freunden u. Kollegen. Heidelberg: Winter, 1972.

Bandler, Jane Yankovic.
Comic mechanisms in the cape and sword plays of Calderon de la Barca / by Jane Yankovic Bandler. -- [New Haven : s.n.], 1975.
iv, 227 leaves ; 29 cm.
Thesis--Yale.
Bibliography: leaves 223-227.
Microfilm of typescript. Ann Arbor, Mich. : University Microfilms, 1975. -- 1 reel ; 35 mm.
1. Calderón de la Barca, Pedro, 1600-1681. I. Title.
CtY NUC77-85508

Bandler, Richard.
Patterns of the hypnotic techniques of Milton H. Erickson, M.D. / by Richard Bandler and John Grinder. — Cupertino, Calif. : Meta Publications, 1975-
v. ; 24 cm.
Bibliography: v. 1, p. [263]-265.
1. Hypnotism—Therapeutic use. 2. Erickson, Milton H. I. Grinder, John, joint author. II. Title.
RC495.B32 615'.8512 75-24584
76 MARC

Bandler, Richard.
The structure of magic : a book about language and therapy / by Richard Bandler and John Grinder. — Palo Alto, Calif. : Science and Behavior Books, c1975-
v. : graphs ; 24 cm.
Bibliography: v. 1, p. [219]-225.
ISBN 0-8314-0044-7
1. Psychotherapy. 2. Languages—Psychology. I. Grinder, John, joint author. II. Title.
RC480.5.B32 616.8'914 75-12452
76 MARC

Bandlow, W., 1938-
see Genetics, biogenesis, and bioenergetics of mitochondria ... Berlin, W. de Gruyter, 1976.

Bandman, Everett.
Messenger RNA metabolism in animal cells grown in monolayer culture, differences found by comparing 3T3 cells in resting and growing states and SV40 virus-transformed 3T3 cells. [Berkeley] 1974.
xiv, 260 l. ill.
Thesis (Ph. D.)—University of California.
Bibliography: leaves 250-260.
CU NUC76-22104

Bandman, Mark Konstantinovich
see Akademiíà nauk SSSR. Sibirskoe otdelenie. Institut ėkonomiki i organizatšii promyshlennogo proizvodstva. (Modelirovanie formirovaniíà territorial'no-proizvodstvennykh kompleksov) Modelling of territorial-production complexes formation. 1976.

Bandman, Mark Konstantinovich
see Formirovanie territorial'no-proizvodstvennykh kompleksov Angaro-Eniseĭskogo regiona. 1975.

Bandman, Mark Konstantinovich
see Metodicheskie polozheniíà optimizatšii prostranstvennoĭ struktury ėkonomicheskogo raĭona. 1975.

Bandman, Mark Konstantinovich, ed.
see Modelirovanie formirovaniâ territorial'no-proizvodstvennykh kompleksov. Novosibirsk, 1971.

Bandman, Mark Konstantinovich, ed.
see Pol'sko-sovetskiĭ seminar na temu Primenenie modeleĭ dliâ razrabotki skhem formirovaniiâ TPK, Warsaw-Szymbark, 1973. (Primenenie modeleĭ dliâ razrabotki skhem formirovaniiâ TPK) 1973.

Bandmann, Günter.
Mittelalterliche Architektur als Bedeutungsträger. Berlin, Mann, 1965? c1951.
274 p. 16 plates, plans. 24 cm.
"Unveränderter Nachdruck im Offsetverfahren."
Bibliography: p. 261-269.
PPiU NUC73-126322

Bandmann, Günter
see Zum Wirklichkeitsbegriff. Wiesbaden: Steiner [in Komm.] 1974.

Bandmann, Hans-Jürgen.
Epicutantestung; Einführung in die Praxis [von] H.-J. Bandmann [und] S. Fregert. Im Namen der International Contact Dermatitis Research Group, H.-J. Bandmann [et al.] Berlin, New York, Springer-Verlag, 1973.
vii, 100 p. illus. 19 cm. (Kliniktaschenbücher) DM12.80 GFR***
Bibliography: p. 92.
1. Skin tests. I. Fregert, Sigfrid, joint author. II. International Contact Dermatitis Research Group. III. Title. IV. Series.
RC587.S6B32 616.9'7'075 73-77678
ISBN 3-540-06237-8

Bandmann, Hans-Jürgen.
Patch testing / S. Fregert, H.-J. Bandmann, published on behalf of the International Contact Dermatitis Research Group, H.-J. Bandmann ... [et al.]. — Berlin ; New York : Springer-Verlag, 1975.
vii, 78 p. : ill. ; 21 cm.
Translation of Epicutantestung.
In German ed. Bandmann's name appears first on title page.
Bibliography: p. 72.
Includes index.
ISBN 0-387-07229-2
1. Skin tests. I. Fregert, Sigfrid, joint author. II. International Contact Dermatitis Research Group. III. Title.
[DNLM: 1. Skin diseases—Diagnosis. 2. Skin tests. WR140 F858e]
RC587.S6B3213 616.9'7'075 75-2387
75 MARC

Bandmann, Hans-Jürgen
see Krebsvorsorge und Krebsfrüherkennung. München, Urban & Schwarzenberg, 1974.

The Bandmasters report. v. 1-
June 1973-
[Folcroft, Pa.]
v. in 28 cm. 5 no. a year.
1. Bands (Music)—Periodicals.
ML1.B42 785.1'2'05 73-645814
ISSN 0092-0819 MARC-S

Bandō, Eikichi.
(Hokubei Gasshūkoku narabini Eiryō Kanada ni okeru Nihonjin no genjō)
北米合衆國並に英領加奈陀に於ける日本人の現狀 [坂東榮吉著 神戸 日米時報社 大正4 i. e. 1915]
2, 5, 183 p. 22 cm.
Errata slip inserted.
1. Japanese in California. 2. Japanese in Hawaii. 3. Japanese in Canada. I. Title. II. Title: Nihonjin no genjō.
F855.2.J3B36 75-793455

Bando, Evgeniĭ Georgievich
see Revoliutsionnyĭ podvig sibiriakov. [1972]

Bando, Evgeniĭ Georgievich
see Silinskiĭ, Pavel Pavlovich. Puteshestvie v zavtra. Irkutsk, Vostochno-Sibirskoe knizhnoe izd-vo, 1972.

Bandō, Hiroshi.
(Pōrando ryūgaku ki)
ポーランド留学記 阪東宏著 東京 評論社 昭和43(1968)
257 p. illus. 18 cm. ¥320 Ja 68-9718
Colophon inserted.
1. Japanese students in Poland. 2. Poland—Description and travel—1945- 3. Education—Polsnf—1945- 4. Poland—History. I. Title.
LB2376.6.P6B36 73-801897

Bando, Hiroshi
see Minzoku no mondai. 1976.

Bandō, Kiyoyuki
see
Bandō, Shōu, 1918-

Bandō, Mitsugorō, 1882-1961.
(Mitsugorō geidan)
三津五郎藝談 / 井上甚之助. — 京都 : 和敬書店, 昭和25 [1950]
255 p., [6] leaves of plates : ill. ; 22 cm.
Colophon inserted.
1. Bandō, Mitsugorō, 1882-1961. 2. Kabuki—History and criticism—Addresses, essays, lectures. I. Inoue, Jinnosuke. II. Title.
PN2928.B3A35 75-791013

Bandō, Mitsugorō, 1906-1975.
(Kabuki hana to mi)
歌舞伎 花と実 / 坂東三津五郎. — 町田 : 玉川大学出版部, 昭和51 [1976]
262 p., [1] leaf of plates : ill. ; 19 cm. Ja 76-3839
Colophon inserted.
¥2200
1. Kabuki—Addresses, essays, lectures. I. Title.
PN2924.5.K3B27 1976 76-804186

Bandō, Mitsugorō, 1906-
(Kabuki uso to makoto)
歌舞伎 虚と実 坂東三津五郎著 町田 玉川大学出版部 昭和48(1973)
210 p. illus. 19 cm. ¥1800 Ja 73-19531
Colophon inserted.
1. Kabuki—Addresses, essays, lectures. I. Title.
PN2924.5.K3B28 74-801202

Bandō, Mitsugorō, 1906-
(Koke no tawagoto)
虚仮の戯言 坂東三津五郎著 京都 淡交社 昭和47(1972)
253 p. 19 cm. ¥800 Ja 72-10721
Colophon inserted.
1. Bandō, Mitsugorō, 1906- I. Title.
PN2928.B3A296 74-808611

Bandō, Mitsugorō, 1906-1975.
(Kuihōdai)
食い放題 / 坂東三津五郎. — 東京 : 日本経済新聞社, 昭和50 [1975]
262 p. : ill. ; 20 cm. Ja 75-11209
¥1600
1. Gastronomy—Addresses, essays, lectures. 2. Cookery, Japanese—Addresses, essays, lectures. I. Title.
TX641.B34 75-809592

Bandō, Mitsugorō, 1906-
(Tōkaidō kabukibanashi)
東海道歌舞伎話 坂東三津五郎著 東京 日本交通公社 昭和47(1972)
193 p. illus. 18 cm. (ベルブックス) ¥380 Ja 72-16002
1. Kabuki—Anecdotes, facetiae, satire, etc. 2. Tōkaidō—Anecdotes, facetiae, satire, etc. 3. Tōkaidō in literature—Addresses, essays, lectures. I. Title.
PN2924.5.K3B3 73-804007

Bandō, Mitsuo, 1906-1946
see Takano, Toshimi, 1929- Tonden sakka Bandō Mitsuo. 47(1972)

Bandō, Satoshi, 1931-
(Sengo rōdō kumiai undō shi)
戦後労働組合運動史 : 日本型労働組合の生態と問題 / 板東慧. — 東京 : 田畑書店, 1975.
278 p. ; 20 cm. Ja 75-3684
Includes bibliographical references.
¥1500
1. Trade-unions—Japan. 2. Industry and state—Japan. I. Title.
HD6832.B36 75-804891

Bandō, Shōu, 1918-
(Chōnin no sue)
町人の裔 : 坂東菖雨句集. — 東京 : 麻俳句会, 昭和50 [1975]
4, 221 p., [1] leaf of plates : port. ; 20 cm. — (麻叢書 ; 第1篇) Ja 76-2975
Poems.
Series romanized: Asa sōsho.
¥2000
I. Title.
PL823.A58C5 76-804282

Bando, Takeo, 1910- ed.
see Heikatsukin no seiri oyobi yakuri. 49[1974]

Bandō, Yūji, 1933-
(Shu no zetsumetsu to shinka)
種の絶滅と進化 : 恐竜はなぜ滅んだのか / 坂東祐司. — 東京 : 講談社, 昭和50 [1975]
238 p. : ill. ; 18 cm. — (ブルーバックス ; 267) Ja 75-11336
Series romanized: Burū bakkusu.
¥500
1. Paleontology. 2. Evolution. I. Title.
QE763.B36 75-808629

(Bandō sanjūsan kannon reijō nōkyō chō)
坂東三十三觀音靈場納經帖 札所研究会編輯 東京 久志本 昭和45 (1970)
1 v. (double leaves) 21 cm. Ja 71-34
Cover title.
1. Buddhist pilgrims and pilgrimages—Japan—Kantō region. 2. Avalokiteśvara—Cultus—Kantō region. I. Fudasho Kenkyūkai.
BQ6450.J32K363 75-805423
J

Bandodkar, Dayanand Balkrishna, 1911-1973
see Karnik, Dwarkanath Bhagwant, 1912- (Vṛtta sādhanā) [1974]

Bandoeng, Indonesia
see Bandung, Indonesia.

Bandoian, Charles Asa.
The Pliocene and Pleistocene rocks of Bonaire, Netherlands Antilles. New Brunswick, N. J., 1973.
iv, 54 l. illus. 29 cm.
Typewritten.
Thesis (Ph. D.)—Rutgers University.
1. Paleontology—Pilocene. 2. Paleontology—Pleistocene. 3. Paleontology—Netherlands Antilles. I. Title.
NjR NUC75-16662

[Bandol, Jean de, fl. 1368-1381]
La tappezzeria di Angers. Testo di Geneviève F. Souchal. [Milano] Fabbri; [Ginevra] A. Skira [1970]
72 p. illus. (part col.) 36 cm. (I Grandi decorati, 20)
1. Bible. N. T. Revelation–Pictures, illustrations, etc. I. Souchal, Geneviève. II. Angers, France. Château. III. Title.
PPT NUC76-93166

Bandomir, Andrzej.
Poczet uczonych polskich (pionierów nauk matematyczno -przyrodnuczych) / Andrzej Bandomir ; [ilustrowal Maciej Jędrysik. — Wyd. 1. — Warszawa : Nasza Ksieg., 1975.
282 p. : ports. ; 18 cm.
zł28.00
1. Mathematicians—Poland. I. Jędrysik, Maciej. II. Title.
QA28.B25 75-594434

Bandong, Francisco.
Effect of propylene glycol singly or in combinations with organic acids on mold development in high moisture corn by Francisco C. Bandong. [n. p.] 1974.
65 l. (K. S. U. Doctor of Philosophy Dissertation; 1974)
Thesis (Ph. D.)–Kansas State University.
1. Corn–Storage. 2. Fungicides. I. Title.
KMK NUC76-22387

Bandopadhay, Shyamal.
(Śūnya jānālā)
শূন্য জানালা / শ্যামল বন্দ্যোপাধ্যায়. — কলিকাতা : অভী প্রকাশন, 1976.
77 p. ; 22 cm.
In Bengali.
Poems.
Rs4.00

I. Title.

PK1718.B21925S8 76-903404

Bandopadhaya, Chabi, 1919–
चोर, एक सामाजिक नाटक. छवि बन्द्योपाध्याय-कृत. अनुवादक प्रबोध नारायण सिंह. [1. संस्करण. कलकत्ता, मिथिला दर्शन; प्राप्ति-स्थान: विशाल भारत बुक डिपो, 1965]
56 p. 21 cm. Re1
In Maithili.
Translation of Cora.

I. Siṃha, Prabodha Nārāyaṇa, tr. II. Title.
Title romanized: Cora.

PK1718.B2193C614 S A 68-8728
PL 480 : I-H-5509

Bandopadhaya, Nripendra Nath.
see Symposium on the Problems of the West Bengal Economy and Planning, Calcutta, 1974. Problems of the economy and planning in West Bengal ... Calcutta, Centre for Studies in Social Sciences, Calcutta, 1975.

Bandopadhya, Tarak Nath, 1901–
তীর্থ পথে. [লেখক] তারক নাথ বন্দ্যোপাধ্যায়. [1. সংস্করণ. কলিকাতা, গীতা গোস্বামী; পরিবেশক] সাহিত্য-কল্প [1378– , i.e. 1971–
v. 23 cm. Rs8.00
In Bengali.
CONTENTS: 1. উত্তরখণ্ড ও রাজস্থান.

1. India—Description and travel—1947– I. Title.
Title romanized: Tirtha pathe.

DS414.B347 75-924206

Bandopadhyay, Manohar.
Sighs and sorrows. [Delhi, New Age Publications]; sole distributor: Doaba House [1970]
vi, 62 p. 23 cm. Rs4.00
I. Title.
PR9480.9.B28S5 821 76-925789
MARC

Bandopadhyaya, Hari Benoy.
Hindu religion & culture; a scientific discussion. Mahesh [District] Hooghly; [distributors: Sahityasree, Calcutta] 1972.
181, [5] p. 23 cm. Rs10.00
Reviews of the author's work: p. [182]–[186]
1. Hinduism. I. Title.
BL1202.B28 294.5 72-906690
MARC

Bandopadhyaya, Madan.
[Madhyāhnera gāna]
মধ্যাহ্নের গান. [লেখক] শ্রীমদন বন্দ্যোপাধ্যায়. কলিকাতা, চলন্তিকা প্রকাশক [1371, i.e. 1964]
290 p. 23 cm. Rs6.50
In Bengali.
A novel.

I. Title.

PK1718.B23M3 77-924461

Bandopādhyāya, Pratāpa Kumāra
see Treda Iuniyanijam. [19--]

Bandopadhyaya, Saroj.
বাংলা উপন্যাসের কালান্তর. [লেখক] সরোজ বন্দ্যোপাধ্যায়. [পরিবর্তিত ও পরিবর্ধিত সংস্করণ] কলিকাতা, সাহিত্যশ্রী [1971]
375 p. 23 cm. Rs14.00
In Bengali.

1. Bengali fiction—History and criticism. I. Title.
Title romanized: Bāṃlā upanyāsera kālāntara.

PK1712.B28 73-924811

Bandopadhyaya, Saroj.
(Bāṅalā upanyāsera kālāntara)
বাঙলা উপন্যাসের কালান্তর / সরোজ বন্দ্যোপাধ্যায়. — পরিবর্তিত ও পরিবর্ধিত 3. সংস্করণ. — কলকাতা : সাহিত্যশ্রী, 1976.
6, 432 p. ; 23 cm.
In Bengali.
Includes bibliographical references.
Includes index.
Rs22.00

1. Bengali fiction—History and criticism. I. Title.

PK1712.B283 1976 76-901406

Bandopadhyaya, Saroj.
(Bikikinira hāṭa)
বিকিকিনির হাট / সরোজ বন্দ্যোপাধ্যায়. — 1. সংস্করণ. — কলিকাতা : নতুন সাহিত্য ভবন, 1364 [1957]
216 p. ; 23 cm.
In Bengali.
A novel.

I. Title.

PK1718.B235B5 75-985592

Bandopadhyaya, Saroj.
(Kabitā kalpanālatā)
কবিতা কল্পনালতা. [লেখক] সরোজ বন্দ্যোপাধ্যায়. [1. সংস্করণ] কলকাতা, এসেম পাবলিকেশনস্ [1379 i.e. 1972]
189 p. 22 cm. Rs9.00
In Bengali.

1. Bengali poetry—Addresses, essays, lectures. I. Title.

PK1710.B27 72-908006

Bandopadhyaya, Saroj.
(Komale gāndhāre Bishṇu De)
কোমলে গান্ধারে বিষ্ণু দে / সরোজ বন্দ্যোপাধ্যায়, পার্থপ্রতিম বন্দ্যোপাধ্যায়. — কলিকাতা : রুমা পাবলিকেশন, 1382 [1975]
141 p. ; 22 cm.
In Bengali.
Includes bibliographical references.
Rs15.00

1. Dey, Bishnu—Criticism and interpretation—Addresses, essays, lectures. I. Bandyopādhyāya, Pārthapratima, joint author. II. Title.

PK1718.D475Z59 76-900103

Bandopadhyaya, Saroj, ed.
see Basu, Samaresh, 1921- Samareśa Basura śreshthagalpa. [1967]

Bandopadhyaya, Shripada.
The music of India; a popular handbook of Hindustani music. With 25 half-tone plates (including 23 reproductions of Indian miniature paintings depicting ragas and raginis) and 30 line drawings of musical instruments. [3d ed.] Bombay, D. B. Taraporevala Sons [1970, c1958]
84 p. illus. 19 cm.
1. Music, Hindu. I. Title.
GU NUC73-126251

Bandopādhyāya, Sītārāma.
বন্ধন-হীন গ্রন্থি. [লেখক] শ্রীসীতারাম বন্দ্যোপাধ্যায়. কলিকাতা, প্রাপ্তিস্থান: পুঁথিঘর [1962]
167 p. 22 cm.
In Bengali.
A novel.

I. Title.
Title romanized: Bandhana-hina-granthi.

PK1718.B237B3 S A 63-4219
PL 480 : I-B-670

Bandor, Frank.
Hungary: extension of growth indexes to 1967 [by] Frank Bandor, Laszlo Czirjak [and] George Pall. Edited by Thad P. Alton. New York, Economic Studies, Riverside Research Institute, 1970.
ii, 58 p. 28 cm. (Occasional papers of the Research Project on National Income in East Central Europe, OP-33)
Includes bibliographical references.
1. Economic indicators—Hungary. 2. Hungary—Economic conditions—1945- 3. Index numbers (Economics) I. Czirjak, Laszlo, joint author. II. Pall, George, joint author. III. Title. IV. Series: Research Project on National Income in East Central Europe. Occasional papers, OP-33.
HC244.Z91534a OP-33 330.9'439'05 74-159917
74[r76]rev MARC

Bandorf, Helmut
see Verhalten und Lautausserungen. Berlin, Duncker & Humblot (1968)

Bandowryan, Garik.
Zhizn' protiv smerti. [Stikhi. By] Garik Avetisovich Bandurian. Erevan, Afastan, 1969.
28 p. illus.
Title page and text in Armenian.
Russian title from verso of t.p.
MH NUC74-21960

Bandrabur, Ionel.
Fiul primarului : [roman] / Ionel Bandrabur ; [coperta de Adrian Ionescu]. — [București] : "Albatros", 1976.
139 p. ; 19 cm. R76-3910
lei4.00
I. Title.
PC840.12.A58F52 77-460498
•77 MARC

Bandrabur, Toderiță.
Geologia cîmpiei Dunărene dintre Jiu și Olt. București, 1971.
146 p. illus. (part col.), 5 fold. col. maps. 24 cm. (Institutul Geologic. Studii tehnice și economice. Seria J: Stratigrafie, nr. 9)
R***
Originally presented as the author's thesis, Bucharest.
Summary in English and French.
Bibliography: p. 130-140.
1. Geology, Stratigraphic—Cenozoic. 2. Geology—Romania—Wallachia. I. Title. II. Series: Romania. Institutul Geologic. Studii tehnice și economice. Seria J: Stratigrafie, nr. 9.
QE690.B28 1971 72-362532

Bandrabur, Toderita, joint author
see Ghenea, C Guidebook for excursion inqua Prahova Valley-Brașov Basin. [Bucharest], Commission for Quaternary Map of Europe, 1972.

Bandreth, Roy H
Biomicroscopy, by Roy H. Bandreth. Berkeley, Univ. of California [1973]
279 p. illus. 28 cm.
Cover title.
Condensation of material taken from a book titled "Clinical slit lamp biomicroscopy."
Dept. of Health, Education, and Welfare, Health Professions Educational Improvement Program, Special Improvement Grant–5 D08 PE2036-02.
OU NUC76-75586

Bandrovs'kyĭ, Henrikh Īosypovych.
(Gorod shagaet v budushchee)
Город шагает в будущее : Из опыта экон. и социального планирования во Львове / Г. И. Бандровский. — Львов : Каменяр, 1975.
127 p., [14] leaves of plates ; 21 cm. USSR 76
0.61rub
1. Lvov—Social conditions. 2. Labor and laboring classes—Lvov. 3. Lvov—Industries. I. Title.
HN539.L9B26 76-516049

Bandrowska-Wróblewska, Jadwiga
see Stoi lipa, lipuleczka: pieśni mazurskie. [Warszawa]: Ludowa Spółdzielnia Wydawnicza, 1976.

Bandrowski, Juliusz Kaden-
see
Kaden-Bandrowski, Juliusz, 1885-1944.

Bandstetter, Alois.
Prosaauflösung; Studien zur Rezeption der höfischen Epik im frühneuhochdeutschen Prosaroman. [Frankfurt am Main] Athenäum Verlag, 1971.
252 p.
Habilitationsschrift—Universität des Saarlandes.
Appendix: Wigaleis vom Rade; Prosaroman.
InU NUC73-113632

Bandt, Carl I., joint author
see Zaki, H A Clean teeth brighten your smile! [Minneapolis?] University of Minnesota, 1971.

Bandt, Jacques de.
Les Prévisions en matière d'emploi : analyse critique et méthode / par Jacques De Bandt, ... — [Paris] : Éditions Cujas, 1974.
158 p. ; 23 cm. — (Théorie de la production ; cahier I.R.E.P. no 8 et 9) F75-7594
Summary in English.
Bibliography: p. 144-158.
24.00F
1. Employment forecasting. I. Title. II. Series: Théorie de la production ; cahier no 8 et 9.
HD5707.B3 75-516383
76 MARC

Bandt, Jacques de.
La Valeur ajoutée, mesure de l'activité; notes critiques sur l'utilisation de la notion de valeur ajoutée, par Jacques De Bandt,... [Paris], Éditions Cujas, 1973.
104 p. ill. 23 cm. (Théorie de la production, cahier no 5) 18.00F
F74-2247
Summary in English.
Includes bibliographical references.
1. Production (Economic theory) 2. Value. I. Title. II. Series.
HB241.B32 338'.001 75-506141
75 MARC

Bandt, Jacques de.
La Valeur économique du capital, par Jacques de Bandt, ... Paris, Éditions Cujas, 1973.
160 p. graphs. 23 cm. (Théorie de la production, cahier no 7) 20.00F F 74-9451
Summary in English.
Includes bibliographical references.
1. Capital. 2. Capital investments. 3. Production (Economic theory) I. Title. II. Series.
HB501.B24 658.1'52 74-188720
MARC

Bandt, Jacques de, joint author.
see Gray, Jean. Les misères de l'abondance . . . Paris, Éditions Entente, [1975]

Bandt, Jacques de.
see Institut de recherches en économie de la production. Analyse comparative des structures industrielles . . . [Paris, La Documentation française, c1975.

Bandt, Jacques de.
see The World economy in transition . . . Washington, Brookings Institution, 1975.

Bandt, Phillip L
A time to learn; a guide to academic and personal effectiveness [by] Phillip L. Bandt, Naomi M. Meara [and] Lyle D. Schmidt. New York, Holt, Rinehart and Winston [1974]
xi, 241 p. illus. 28 cm.
Bibliography: p. 175-182.
1. Learning, Psychology of. 2. Study, Method of. I. Meara, Naomi M., joint author. II. Schmidt, Lyle D., joint author. III. Title.
LB1051.B243 378.1'7'02812 73-7877
ISBN 0-03-086032-6 MARC

Bandtkie, Jerzy Samuel, 1768-1835.
Historya drukarn krakowskich, od zaprowadzenia drukow do tego miasta az do czasow naszych, wiadomoscia o wynalezieniu sztuki drukarskiey poprzedzona. W Krakowie, W Druk. Groeblowskiey J. Mateckiego, 1815. [Warszawa, Wydawn. Artystyczne i Filmowe, 1974]
504 p. 19 cm.
1. Printing—History—Krakow. I. Title.
CSt NUC76-23052

Bandtkie, Jerzy Samuel, 1768-1835.
Historya drukarń w Królestwie Polskiem i Wielkiem Xięstwie Litewskiem jako i w kraiach zagranicznych, w których polskie dzieła wychodziły. Przez Jerzego Samuela Bandtkie. [Warszawa, Wydawn. Artystyczne i Filmowe, 1974]
3 v.
Reprint of the 1826 ed. published by Drukarnia Józefa Mateckiego, Kraków.
Limited ed. of 300 numbered copies.
1. Printing—History—Poland.
MH NUC76-23335

Bandtlow, K
Medizin an Bord. Ärztl. Ratgeber f. d. Notfall. [Von] K. Bandtlow. Unter Mitarb. v. O. Bandtlow. Bielefeld, Berlin, Klasing (1970).
100 p. with illus. 19 cm. (Kleine Yacht-Bücherei, 27)
GDNB 70-A39-459
Bibliography: p. 96.
DM10.80
1. Medicine, Naval. 2. First aid in illness and injury. I. Bandtlow, O., joint author. II. Title.
RC986.B34 616.9'8024 76-516615

Bandtlow, O., joint author
see Bandtlow, K Medizin an Bord. Berlin, Klasing (1970)

Bandu, Oruvala.
(Biriyōsā)
බිරියෝසා. [කර්තෘ] ඔරුවල බන්දු. කොළඹ, පුබුදු ප්‍රකාශකයෝ [1972]
232 p. 19 cm. Rs4.50
In Sinhalese.
A novel.

I. Title.
PK2859.B34B5 73-901367

Bandu, Oruvala.
(Etera metera)
එතෙර මෙතෙර. [කර්තෘ] ඔරුවල බන්දු. නුගේගොඩ, මුද්‍රණය: දීපානී [1971]
103 p. 18 cm. Rs2.50
In Sinhalese.
A novel.

I. Title.
PK2859.B34E8 72-902199

Bandu, Oruvala.
(Gendagam polova)
ගෙන්දගම් පොළොව / ඔරුවල බන්දු. — කොළඹ : පුබුදු මුද්‍රණ ශිල්පියෝ සහ ප්‍රකාශකයෝ, 1974.
131 p. ; 18 cm.
In Sinhalese.
A novel.
Rs4.00

I. Title.
PK2859.B34G4 75-903265

Bandu, Oruvala.
[Gini kandu]
ගිනි කඳු. [කර්තෘ] ඔරුවල බන්දු. නුගේගොඩ, මුද්‍රණය: දීපානී [1971]
282 p. 18 cm. Rs5.00
In Sinhalese.
A novel.

I. Title.
PK2859.B34G5 72-900955

Bandu, Oruvala.
[Janapada andaraya]
ජනපද අන්දරය; නවකතාවකි. [කර්තෘ] ඔරුවල බන්දු. ගම්පහ, සරසවි ප්‍රකාශකයෝ [1967]
136 p. 19 cm.
In Sinhalese.
A novel.

I. Title.
PK2859.B34J3 70-928730

Bandu, Oruvala.
(Nirōdha)
නිරෝධ / ඔරුවල බන්දු. — කොළඹ : පුබුදු ප්‍රකාශකයෝ, 1973.
159 p. ; 20 cm.
In Sinhalese.
A novel.
Rs4.00

I. Title.
PK2859.B34N5 75-908925

Bandu, Oruvala.
පස් අවුරුද්ද. [කර්තෘ] ඔරුවල බන්දු. ගංගොඩවිල, දීපානී [1969]
300 p. 19 cm. 5.00
In Sinhalese.
A novel.

I. Title. Title romanized: Pas avurudda.
PK2859.B34P3 70-905349

Bandu, Oruvala.
(Yurōpā midivatta)
යුරෝපා මිදිවත්ත / ඔරුවල බන්දු. — [ගම්පහ : නව සාහිත්‍ය මණ්ඩලය, 1967?]
46, [2] p. ; 20 cm.
In Sinhalese.
Poems.
Rs1.00

I. Title.
PK2859.B34Y8 75-908811

Banduka, N M
The aspects of establishing ujamaa villages in Pare District, Tanzania, by Banduka, N. M. [Dar es Salaam, University of Dar es Salaam] 1971.
iii, 45 p. map. 33 cm.
Cover title.
At head of title: The University of Dar es Salaam, university examinations 1971. Political science—paper 7(a) dissertation.
Includes bibliographical references.
1. Community development—Tanzania—Case studies. 2. Villages—Tanzania—Case studies. I. Title.
HN814.T33C62 309.2'63'09678 72-983295
MARC

Bandula, Octavian, joint author
see Chirila, Eugen. Tezaurul monetar de la Baia Mare. [Baia Mare, Muzeul Regional Maramures, 1966]

Bandula Sri Sarachchandra
see
Sarachchandra, Bandula Sri.

Bandundu, Zaire. Centre d'études ethnologiques
see Centre d'études ethnologiques, Bandundu, Zaire.

Bandung, Hassan
see
Hassan, A

Bandung, Ibrahim.
Hukum pidana ta'zir. [Tanjungkarang] 1972.
[38] l. 34 cm.
"Diucapkan dalam dies natalis I. A. I. N. Raden Intan, Lampung."
Bibliography: leaf [38]
1. Punishment (Islamic law) I. Title.
72-942410

Bandung, Indonesia.
Perhitungan anggaran keuangan untuk dinas umum dan perusahaan-perusahaan Kotapradja Bandung.
[Bandung]
v. 31 cm.
1. Public utilities—Bandung, Indonesia—Finance—Periodicals.
I. Title.
HD4704.B35B36a S A 68-20527
MARC-S
PL 480: Indo-8323

Bandung, Indonesia
see Lembaga Penyelidikan Masalah Bangunan. Projek prototype perumahan Bandung '69. [Bandung: Dept. PU Tenaga Listrik, Direkt. Djend. Tjipta Karya, Lemb. Penj. Masalah Bang., Pemerintahan Daerah Kotamadya Bandung, 1970-

Bandung, Indonesia. Academy of Government
see
Akademi Pemerintahan Dalam Negeri, Bandung, Indonesia.

Bandung, Indonesia. Akademi Administrasi Negara Perguruan Tinggi Angkasa
see
Akademi Administrasi Negara Perguruan Tinggi Angkasa.

Bandung, Indonesia. Akademi Pemerintahan Dalam Negeri
see
Akademi Pemerintahan Dalam Negeri, Bandung, Indonesia.

Bandung, Indonesia. Balai Pendidikan Guru
see
Balai Pendidikan Guru Bandung.

Bandung, Indonesia. Balai Penelitian Keramik
see
Balai Penelitian Keramik.

Bandung, Indonesia. Building Research Institute
see
Lembaga Penyelidikan Masalah Bangunan.

Bandung, Indonesia. Institut Keguruan dan Ilmu Pendidikan.
Buku peringatan dwi dasa warsa IKIP Bandung, 1954-1974. — [Bandung : IKIP Bandung, 1974]
vi, 302 p. : ill. ; 28 cm.
Cover title.
Bibliography: p. 297-301.
1. Bandung, Indonesia. Institut Keguruan dan Ilmu Pendidikan.
LB2128.B34A54 75-940215

Bandung, Indonesia. Institut Keguruan dan Ilmu Pendidikan.
Laporan survey pendidikan kader koperasi / oleh team IKIP Bandung, Achmad Sanusi (ketua). — Djakarta : Direktorat Djendral Koperasi, Departemen Transkop, 1971.
100 p. in various pagings ; 28 cm.
1. Cooperation—Study and teaching—Indonesia. I. Sanusi, Achmad. II. Title.
HD2955.B35 1971 74-942563

Bandung, Indonesia. Institut Keguruan dan Ilmu Pendidikan.
Statuta IKIP-Malang. [Malang, 1971]
iv, 30 p. 21 cm.
1. Malay literature—Education.
NN NUC73-77267

Bandung, Indonesia. Institut Keguruan dan Ilmu Pendidikan
see Meulen, W J D V
Chryse Chersonesos dan Suvarnadvipa. Jogjakarta, 1970.

Bandung, Indonesia. Institut Keguruan dan Ilmu Pendidikan
see Mimbar pendidikan. Bandung.

Bandung, Indonesia. Institut Keguruan dan Ilmu Pendidikan
see Noer, Deliar. Hubungan tiga golongan. 1900-1942. Jogjakarta, 1970.

Bandung, Indonesia. Institut Keguruan dan Ilmu Pendidikan
see Seminar on South East Asian Studies, 1st, Bandung, Indonesia, 1968. Indonesia, prospects and problems... Bandung, Badan Penerbitan IKIP, 1968.

Bandung, Indonesia. Institut Keguruan dan Ilmu Pendidikan
see Seminar on South East Asian Studies, 2d, Bandung, 1969. Indonesia: prospects & problems. Bandung, IKIP Press, 1969.

Bandung, Indonesia. Institut Keguruan dan Ilmu Pendidikan
see Soejatno. Kolonailisme barat dan kemunduran rakjat Surakarta abad XIX. Jogjakarta, 1970.

Bandung, Indonesia. Institut Keguruan dan Ilmu Pendidikan
see Suratman, Darsiti. Politik pendidikan Belanda dan masjarakat di Djawa. Jogjakarta, 1970.

Bandung, Indonesia. Institut Keguruan dan Ilmu Pendidikan
see Umar, Mohammad. Prasasti munduan. Jogjakarta, 1970.

Bandung, Indonesia. Institut Keguruan dan Ilmu Pendidikan. Balai Penelitian Pendidikan.
In 1957 Lembaga Penjelidikan Pendidikan of Perguruan Tinggi Pendidikan Guru, Bandung came under Universitas Negeri Padjadjaran. In 1964 it became Balai Penelitian Pendidikan of Institut Keguruan dan Ilmu Pendidikan, Bandung.
Works by these bodies are found under the following headings according to the name used at the time of publication:
Perguruan Tinggi Pendidikan Guru, Bandung. Lembaga Penjelidikan Pendidikan.
Bandung, Indonesia. Universitas Negeri Padjadjaran. Lembaga Penjelidikan Pendidikan.
Bandung, Indonesia. Institut Keguruan dan Ilmu Pendidikan. Balai Penelitian Pendidikan.

Bandung, Indonesia. Institut Keguruan dan Ilmu Pendidikan. Balai Penelitian Pendidikan
see Indonesia. Direktorat Jenderal Pariwisata. Laporan survey wisatawan domestik. Bandung [1975-

Bandung, Indonesia. Institut Keguruan dan Ilmu Pendidikan. Balai Penelitian Pendidikan
see also
Bandung, Indonesia. Universitas Negeri Padjadjaran. Lembaga Penjelidikan Pendidikan.

Bandung, Indonesia. Institut Keguruan dan Ilmu Pendidikan. Fakultas Keguruan Sastra Seni. Badan Penerbit.

For publications of Institut Keguruan dan Ilmu Pendidikan, Bandung

issued by this body see

Bandung, Indonesia. Institut Keguruan dan Ilmu Pendidikan. Fakultas Keguruan Sastra Seni.

Bandung, Indonesia. Institut Teknologi.
Proceedings Institut Teknologi Bandung.
[Bandung, Institut Teknologi Bandung]
v. ill. 24 cm.
English or Indonesian.
1. Science—Collected works. 2. Technology—Collected works.
Q75.B28a 76-640692
MARC-S

Bandung, Indonesia. Institut Teknologi
see Industrial and technological research. [Bandung, Institut Teknologi Bandung, 1971]

Bandung, Indonesia. Institut Teknologi.
see Regional Centre for Education in Science and Mathematics. Steering Committee. Report of the second meeting of the Steering Committee for Education in Science and Mathematics, Bandung, Indonesia, 16th-19th October, 1967. Penang, Project Office, Malayan Teachers' College, [196-]

Bandung, Indonesia. Institut Teknologi
see Seminar Penerapan Teknologi Dalam Pertumbuhan dan Pengembangan Desa, Bandung, Indonesia, 1974. Seminar Penerapan Teknologi Dalam Pertumbuhan dan Pengembangan Desa ... [Jakarta] : Kerja sama Departemen Dalam Negeri Institut Teknologi Bandung, [1974-

Bandung, Indonesia. Institut Teknologi. Bagian Arsitektur
see Lembaga Penyelidikan Masalah Bangunan. Standard arsitektur di bidang perumahan. Bandung : Lembaga, 1972.

Bandung, Indonesia. Institut Teknologi. Bagian Planologi.
Konsep pemikiran dasar pembangunan regional daerah Lampung : laporan interim / Lembaga Penelitian Planologi Bagian Planologi, Institut Teknologi Bandung. — [Djakarta] : BAPPENAS, [1967]
24 leaves : col. maps ; 21 x 33 cm.
Includes bibliographical references.
1. Lampung, Indonesia—Economic conditions. 2. Lampung, Indonesia—Economic policy. I. Title.
HC448.L35B35 1967 75-949857

Bandung, Indonesia. Institut Teknologi. Bagian Planologi.
Laporan regional planning Sumatra Barat. [Bandung] Bagian Planologi ITB [between 1971 and 1973]
iv, 132 l. maps. 29 cm.
Cover title.
1. Sumatera Barat, Indonesia — Economic policy. 2. Sumatera Barat, Indonesia—Economic conditions. I. Title.
HC448.S788B37 72-942217

Bandung, Indonesia. Institut Teknologi. Bagian Sipil. Water Resources Research Centre
see
Bandung, Indonesia. Institut Teknologi. Water Resources Research Centre.

Bandung, Indonesia. Institut Teknologi. Dewan Mahasiswa
see Campus. Feb. 1968- [Bandung, Indonesia, DM. ITB]

Bandung, Indonesia. Institut Teknologi. Dewan Mahasiswa
see Presentasi kertas kerja desa. [Bandung]: Dewan Mahasiswa ITB [1975]

Bandung, Indonesia. Institut Teknologi. Ikatan Mahasiswa Arsitektur Gunadharma
see Pola. [Sept?] 1973- [Bandung]

Bandung, Indonesia. Institut Teknologi. Madjelis Permusjawaratan Mahasiswa
see Campus. Feb. 1968- [Bandung, Indonesia, DM. ITB]

Bandung, Indonesia. Institut Teknologi. Water Resources Research Centre
see Tem Survey Pelabuhan Samudera Muara-Sabak. Pelabuhan samudera Muara -Sabak, Propinsi Djambi ... Bandung: 1971.

Bandung, Indonesia. Institut Teknologi Tekstil
see
Institut Teknologi Tekstil.

Bandung, Indonesia. Lembaga Panjelidikan Masalah Bangunan
see Lembaga Penjelidikan Masalah Bangunan.

Bandung, Indonesia. Lembaga Pertjobaan Alat Peralatan
see
Lembaga Pertjobaan Alat Peralatan.

Bandung, Indonesia. Perguruan Tinggi Katolik Parahijangan
see
Perguruan Tinggi Katolik Parahijangan.

Bandung, Indonesia. Regional Housing Centre
see
Lembaga Penyelidikan Masalah Bangunan.

Bandung, Indonesia. Technische Hoogeschool
see also
Universitas Indonesia. Fakultas Teknik.

Bandung, Indonesia. Universitas Katolik Parahyangan
see
Universitas Katolik Parahyangan.

Bandung, Indonesia. Universitas Negeri Padjadjaran.
Rentjana pembinaan Universitas Padjadjaran tiga tahun, 1971-1973. — Bandung : Universitas, [1971]
xiv, 83 p. : graphs ; 22 cm.
1. Bandung, Indonesia. Universitas Negeri Padjadjaran. I. Title.
LG181.B3A74 77-940031
77 MARC

Bandung, Indonesia. Universitas Negeri Padjadjaran
see Buku peringatan tri-panca-warsa Universitas Negeri Padjadjaran, Bandung, Indonesia, 1957-1972. [Bandung, 1972]

Bandung, Indonesia. Universitas Negeri Padjadjaran
see Seminar Pengelolaan Lingkungan Hidup Manusia dan Pembangunan Nasional... [Bandung] Universitas Padjadjaran [1972]

Bandung, Indonesia. Universitas Negeri Padjadjaran. Bagian Kebidanan dan Penjakit Kandungan
see Simposium Kontrasepsi, Bandung, Indonesia, 1967. Kontrasepsi. [Bandung] Madjalah kedokteran Bandung [1967]

Bandung, Indonesia. Universitas Negeri Padjadjaran. Biro Penelitian Ekonomi dan Masyarakat.
Investigasi perindustrian di Jawa Barat. — [Bandung] : Kerjasama Biro Penelitian Ekonomi & Masyarakat, Fakultas Ekonomi, Universitas Padjadjaran Bandung, dan Biro Perencanaan dan Organisasi, Departemen Perindustrian, 1974.
xii, 224 leaves : maps ; 32 cm.
1. Jawa Barat, Indonesia—Industries. I. Indonesia. Departemen Perindustrian. Biro Perencanaan dan Organisasi. II. Title.
HC448.J42B35 1974 74-941375

Bandung, Indonesia. Universitas Negeri Padjadjaran. Biro Penelitian Ekonomi dan Masyarakat.
Pengaruh Proyek Inpres tahun 1970/1971 dan 1971/1972 terhadap kegiatan ekonomi & kesempatan kerja : (case study, Proyek Dam Parakan Raden, Rehabilitasi Jalan Salopa-Nariwati di Kabupaten Tasikmalaya, dan Proyek Dam Sindujaya dan Rehabilitasi Jalan Banyuresmi-Leuwigoong di Kabupaten Garut) / oleh Biro Penelitian Ekonomi dan Masyarakat, Fakultas Ekonomi, Universitas Padjadjaran. — Bandung : Universitas Padjadjaran, 1972.
iv [i. e. vii], 129 leaves ; 28 cm.
1. Roads—Economic aspects—Jawa Barat, Indonesia. 2. Dams—Economic aspects—Indonesia—Jawa Barat. 3. Labor supply—Jawa Barat, Indonesia. I. Title: Pengaruh Proyek Inpres tahun 1970/1971 dan 1971/1972 terhadap kegiatan ekonomi ...
HE365.I 54D472 1972 74-941388

Bandung, Indonesia. Universitas Negeri Padjadjaran. Biro Penelitian Ekonomi dan Masyarakat.
Survey potensi ekonomi Kabupaten Bandung / kerjasama Biro Penelitian Ekonomi & Masyarakat, Fakultas Ekonomi, Universitas Padjadjaran dan Pemda Kabupaten Bandung. — [Bandung] : Biro, 1973.
xix, 274 leaves, [11] leaves of plates : maps ; 31 cm.
Errata slip (2 leaves) inserted.
1. Bandung, Indonesia (Kabupaten)—Economic conditions. I. Bandung, Indonesia (Kabupten) II. Title.
HC448.B36B36 1973 75-940047

Bandung, Indonesia. Universitas Negeri Padjadjaran. Biro Pers dan Radio Mahasiswa
see Gema Padjadjaran. [Bandung]

Bandung, Indonesia. Universitas Negeri Padjadjaran. Fakultas Administrasi Negara dan Niaga.
For works by this body issued under its later name see
Bandung, Indonesia. Universitas Negeri Padjadjaran. Fakultas Sosial Politik.

Bandung, Indonesia. Universitas Negeri Padjadjaran. Fakultas Ekonomi.
Contour study Djawa Barat / susunan team survey Fakultas Ekonomi Universitas Padjadjaran, Hassan Poeradimadja ... [et al.]. — [Bandung] : Biro Penelitian Ekonomi dan Masjarakat, Fakultas Ekonomi, Universitas Padjadjaran, 1971.
i, 145 leaves ; 33 cm.
1. Jawa Barat, Indonesia—Economic conditions. I. Poeradimadja, Hassan. II. Title.
HC448.J42B35 1971 75-940571

Bandung, Indonesia. Universitas Negeri Padjadjaran. Fakultas Ekonomi.
Daya beli pedagang golongan ekonomi lemah dalam memperoleh kembali kios-kios/ruangan. — Bandung : Fakultas Ekonomi, Universitas Padjadjaran, 1973.
43 leaves ; 30 cm.
1. Markets—Indonesia—Bandung. 2. Bandung, Indonesia—Economic conditions. I. Title: Daya beli pedagang golongan ekonomi lemah ...
HF5475.I 52B353 75-940398

Bandung, Indonesia. Universitas Negeri Padjadjaran. Fakultas Ekonomi.
Laporan hasil penelitian keradjinan rakjat Djawa Barat, oleh Fakultas Ekonomi Universitas Padjadjaran dan Lembaga Penelitian, Pendidikan dan Penerangan Ekonomi dan Sosial. Djakarta, Lembaga Penelitian, Pendidikan & Penerangan Ekonomi dan Sosial, 1971.
xii, 56 l. 30 cm.
Includes summary in English.

——— Appendix. Djakarta, Lembaga Penelitian, Pendidikan & Penerangan Ekonomi dan Sosial, 1971.
152, 52 l. 21 x 30 cm.
English and Indonesian.
HD2346.I 62D52 Suppl. 1971
1. Small business—Djawa Barat, Indonesia. 2. Handicraft—Indonesia—Djawa Barat. I. Lembaga Penelitian, Pendidikan dan Penerangan Ekonomi dan Sosial. II. Title.
HD2346.I 62D52 1971 72-222157
rev

Bandung, Indonesia. Universitas Negeri Padjadjaran. Fakultas Ekonomi
see Indonesia. Direktorat Jenderal Koperasi. Tingkat pembentukah modal dalam rangka pengembangan koperasi di Jawa Barat. [s.l.: s.n., 1974]

Bandung, Indonesia. Universitas Negeri Padjadjaran. Fakultas Ekonomi. Jajasan Badan Penerbit.
For informational publications of Fakultas Ekonomi, Universitas Negeri Padjadjaran, issued by this body see
Bandung, Indonesia. Universitas Negeri Padjadjaran. Fakultas Ekonomi.

Bandung, Indonesia. Universitas Negeri Padjadjaran. Fakultas Hukum
see Padjadjaran. [Bandung, Penerbit Binatjipta]

Bandung, Indonesia. Universitas Negeri Padjadjaran. Fakultas Hukum
see Seminar Segi-Segi Hukum dari Pengelolaan Lingkungan Hidup, Bandung, Indonesia, 1976. Seminar Segi-Segi Hukum dari Pengelolaan Lingkungan Hidup. Cet. 1. [Jakarta] Badan Pembinaan Hukum Nasional : diedarkan oleh Binacipta, 1977.

Bandung, Indonesia. Universitas Negeri Padjadjaran. Fakultas Hukum. Lembaga Penelitian Hukum dan Kriminologi
see
Bandung, Indonesia. Universitas Negeri Padjadjaran. Lembaga Penelitian Hukum dan Kriminologi.

Bandung, Indonesia. Universitas Negeri Padjadjaran. Fakultas Hukum. Research Institute of Law and Criminology
see
Bandung, Indonesia. Universitas Negeri Padjadjaran. Lembaga Penelitian Hukum dan Kriminologi.

Bandung, Indonesia. Universitas Negeri Padjadjaran. Fakultas Ilmu Pasti dan Pengetahuan Alam. Djurusan Statistika
see Lembaga Penyelidikan Masalah Bangunan. Dinas Survey, Penjelidikan dan Perentjanaan. Buku petundjuk housing survey ... [Bandung, 1971]

Bandung, Indonesia. Universitas Negeri Padjadjaran. Fakultas Kedokteran.
Buku pedoman; peringatan lustrum ke III/usia 15 tahun. Edisi: H. Chasan Boesoirie [dan] Nagar Rasjid. [Bandung, 1972]
294 p. illus. 24 cm.
Cover title.
1. Bandung, Indonesia. Universitas Negeri Padjadjaran. I. Boesoirie, H. Chasan, ed. II. Rasjid, Nagar, ed.
LG181.B3A55 74-204828

Bandung, Indonesia. Universitas Negeri Padjadjaran. Fakultas Kedokteran. Bagian Kebidanan dan Penjakit Kandungan
see
Bandung, Indonesia. Universitas Negeri Padjadjaran. Bagian Kebidanan dan Penjakit Kandungan.

Bandung, Indonesia. Universitas Negeri Padjadjaran. Fakultas Pertanian.
Perbenihan padi varitas unggul di Propinsi Sumatera Utara dan Propinsi Sumatera Barat; laporan survey, Kerjasama antara Badan Pengendali Bimas dan Direktorat Pengembangan Produksi dengan Fakultas Pertanian, Universitas Padjadjaran. [Bandung] 1973.
xxvii, 225 l. maps. 29 cm.
Summary in English.
Errata slip inserted.
1. Rice—Indonesia—Sumatera Utara. 2. Rice—Indonesia—Sumatera Barat. I. Indonesia. Badan Pengendali Bimas. II. Indonesia. Direktorat Pengembangan Produksi. III. Title.
SB191.R5B28 1973 73-941971
SA

Bandung, Indonesia. Universitas Negeri Padjadjaran. Fakultas Publisistik.
Fakultas Publisistik Unpad kini. — Bandung : Fakultas Publisistik, Universitas Padjadjaran, 1970.
v, 48 p. : ports. ; 23 cm.
"Penerbitan chusus, th. 1970."
English or Indonesian.
Includes bibliographical references.
1. Communication—Study and teaching—Indonesia. 2. Bandung, Indonesia. Universitas Negeri Padjadjaran. Fakultas Publisistik. I. Title.
P91.5.I5B3 1970 76-941735
77 MARC

Bandung, Indonesia. Universitas Negeri Padjadjaran. Fakultas Sastra.
Abstraksi skripsi sarjana. — [Bandung] : Fakultas Sastra Universitas Padjadjaran, 1974.
v, 155 p. ; 21 cm.
1. Bandung, Indonesia. Universitas Negeri Padjadjaran. Fakultas Sastra—Dissertations. I. Title.
Z5055.I 66B332 1974 76-940001
[LB2391.I 5]

Bandung, Indonesia. Universitas Negeri Padjadjaran. Jurusan Antropologi
see Universitas Gadjah Mada. Lembaga Penelitian Ekonomi. Ijon di Jawa Barat. Yogyakarta, Universitas Padjadjaran, 1973.

Bandung, Indonesia. Universitas Negeri Padjadjaran. Jurusan Antropologi. Team Penelitian Antropologi
see
Bandung, Indonesia. Universitas Negeri Padjadjaran. Team Penelitian Antropologi.

Bandung, Indonesia. Universitas Negeri Padjadjaran. Lembaga Kebudayaan
see Tembang Sunda dan masalah-masalah yang dihadapinya dalam rangka pembinaan ... Bandung: Lembaga Kebudayaan Universitas Padjadjaran, 1974.

Bandung, Indonesia. Universitas Negeri Padjadjaran. Lembaga Penelitian Hukum dan Kriminologi
see Gautama, Sudargo, 1928- Agrarian law... Bandung, Universitas Padjadjaran, 1972.

Bandung, Indonesia. Universitas Negeri Padjadjaran. Lembaga Penjelidikan Kemasjarakatan
see Kumpulan karya-tak-berkala, 1959-1960. Bandung, [1960?]

Bandung, Indonesia. Universitas Negeri Padjadjaran. Lembaga Penjelidikan Pendidikan.
In 1957 Lembaga Penjelidikan Pendidikan of Perguruan Tinggi Pendidikan Guru, Bandung came under Universitas Negeri Padjadjaran. In 1964 it became Balai Penelitian Pendidikan of Institut Keguruan dan Ilmu Pendidikan, Bandung.
Works by these bodies are found under the following headings according to the name used at the time of publication:
Perguruan Tinggi Pendidikan Guru, Bandung. Lembaga Penjelidikan Pendidikan.
Bandung, Indonesia. Universitas Negeri Padjadjaran. Lembaga Penjelidikan Pendidikan.
Bandung, Indonesia. Institut Keguruan dan Ilmu Pendidikan. Balai Penelitian Pendidikan.

Bandung, Indonesia. Universitas Negeri Padjadjaran. Lembaga Penjelidikan Pendidikan.
Berita Lembaga Penjelidikan Pendidikan.
Bandung, F. K. I. P., Universitas Padjadjaran
no. 25 cm. (Lembaran sumbangsih - Lembaga Penjelidikan Pendidikan)
Summaries in English.
Began in 1957. Cf. New serial titles.
1. Educational research — Indonesia — Periodicals. I. Series: Bandung, Indonesia. Universitas Negeri Padjadjaran. Lembaga Penjelidikan Pendidikan. Lembaran sumbangsih.
LB1028.A1B34 subser. 74-648725
MARC-S

Bandung, Indonesia. Universitas Negeri Padjadjaran. Lembaga Penjelidikan Pendidikan.
Lembaran sumbangsih.
Bandung, 19
v. 22 cm.
1. Educational resetarch—Indonesia.
LB1028.A1B34 78-949506

Bandung, Indonesia. Universitas Negeri Padjadjaran. Research Institute of Law and Criminology
see
Bandung, Indonesia. Universitas Negeri Padjadjaran. Lembaga Penelitian Hukum dan Kriminologi.

Bandung, Indonesia. Universitas Negeri Padjadjaran. Team Penelitian Antropologi.
Studi tentang pembangunan daerah Pelabuhan Ratu; suatu hasil survey, oleh Team Penelitian Antropologi (staf ahli penelitian Pelabuhan Ratu, Jurusan Antropologi, Fakultas Sastra Universitas Padjadjaran) 1967. Bandung, Jurusan Antropologi, Universitas Padjadjaran, 1972.
193 l. 29 cm.
1. Djawa Barat, Indonesia—Social conditions. 2. Djawa Barat, Indonesia—Economic conditions. I. Title.
HN710.D53B35 1972 73-940304

Bandung, Indonesia. Universitas Negeri Padjadjaran. Team Psikologi Sosial.
Suatu penelitian mengenai studi perencanaan sosial dalam rangka program perbaikan lingkungan permukiman Kotamadya Cirebon : lingkungan Kasambi, lingkungan Jagasatru. — Bandung : Team Psikologi Sosial, Fakultas Psikologi Unpad, [1975?]
113 leaves in various foliations ; 29 cm.
Includes bibliographical references.
1. Cirebon, Indonesia—Social conditions. 2. Community development—Indonesia—Cirebon. I. Title: Suatu penelitian mengenai studi perencanaan sosial ...
HN710.C57Z42 76-941748
77 MARC

Bandung, Indonesia. Walikota.
Beberapa persoalan pokok dalam pembinaan dan pengembangan kota Kotamadya Bandung. Bandung, 1974.
81, [22] p. maps. 33 cm.
1. Bandung, Indonesia—Politics and government. I. Title.
JS7206.B36A33 1974 74-940441

Bandung, Indonesia (Kabupten)
see Bandung, Indonesia. Universitas Negeri Padjadjaran. Biro Penelitian Ekonomi dan Masyarakat. Survey potensi ekonomi Kabupaten Bandung ... [Bandung] : Biro, 1973.

Bandung Technological Institute
see
Bandung, Indonesia. Institut Teknologi.

Bandura, Albert, 1925–
Aggression: a social learning analysis. Englewood Cliffs, N. J., Prentice-Hall [1973]
ix, 390 p. illus. 24 cm. (The Prentice-Hall series in social learning theory) $8.95
Bibliography: p. 325–366.
1. Aggressiveness (Psychology) 2. Violence. I. Title.
HM281.B25 301.1 72–12990
ISBN 0–13–020743–8 MARC

Bandura, Albert, 1925-
A comparative test of the status envy, social power, and secondary reinforcement theories of identificatory learning [by] Albert Bandura, Dorothea Ross, and Sheila A. Ross. [Indianapolis] Bobbs-Merrill, 1963.
527-534 p. (Bobbs-Merrill reprint series in the social sciences, P-394)
"Reprinted from the Journal of abnormal and social psychology, v. 67, no. 6, 1963."
Caption title.
1. Identification (Psychology) 2. Imitation. I. Ross, Sheila Anne. II. Ross, Dorothea. III. Title.
MH-Ed NUC73-126247

Bandura, Albert, 1925-
Psychotherapy as a learning process. [Indianapolis] Bobbs-Merrill, 1961.
143-159 p. (The Bobbs-Merrill reprint series in the social sciences, P-395)
"Reprint from Psychological bulletin, v. 58, no. 2, March 1961."
Caption title.
1. Behavior modification. I. Title.
MH-Ed NUC74-33074

Bandura, Albert, 1925-
Relationship of family patterns to child behavior disorders. [n. p.] 1960.
36 l. 29 cm.
Caption title.
"Research grant reference number: M-1734."
1. Problem children. I. Title.
CSt NUC74-168012

Bandura, Albert, 1925-
Social-learning model of deviant behavior. New York, Holt, Rinehart & Winston, 1965.
117 l. 29 cm.
Caption title.
Bibliography: leaves [105]-117.
1. Psychology. 2. Human behavior. I. Title.
CSt NUC74-144053

Bandura, Albert, 1925-
Social learning theory. New York, General Learning Press, 1971.
46 p.
Includes bibliography.
1. Learning, Psychology of. I. Title.
MiU NUC73-113633

Bandura, Albert, 1925-
Social learning theory / Albert Bandura. — Englewood Cliffs, N.J. : Prentice Hall, c1977.
viii, 247 p. ; 24 cm.
Bibliography: p. 216-233.
Includes indexes.
ISBN 0-13-816751-6. ISBN 0-13-816744-3 pbk.
1. Learning, Psychology of. 2. Socialization. I. Title.
LB1084.B357 153.1'5 76-43024
76 MARC

Bandura, Albert, 1925-
see Analysis of delinquency and aggression. Hillsdale, N.J., L. Erlbaum Associates, 1976.

Bandura, Albert, 1925- joint author
see Mager, Robert Frank, 1923- Who did what to whom? Champaign, Ill., Research Press [c1972]

Bandura, I͡Uriĭ Nikolaevich.
(Imperii͡a "trekh brilliantov")
Империя "трех бриллиантов" / Ю. Бандура. — Москва : Политиздат, 1976.
63 p. ; 20 cm. — (Владыки капиталистического мира) USSR 76
Series romanized: Vladyki kapitalisticheskogo mira.
0.12rub
1. Big business—Japan. I. Title.
HD2907.B35 76-533417

Bandura, Jack Paul, 1943-
Non-uniformity of impulse propagation in the specialized Purkinje fiber system of the canine heart. [Bloomington, Ind.] 1972.
49 p. illus.
Thesis (Ph.D.)—Indiana University.
Vita.
InU NUC73-34526

Bandura, Ludwik.
O procesie uczenia się. Warszawa, Państwowe Zakłady Wydawnictw Szkolnych, 1972.
206 p.
Includes bibliography.
1. Study, Method of. 2. Learning, Psychology of. 3. Teaching. 4. Educational psychology. I. Title.
MiEM NUC76-72904

Bandura, Władysław
see Krakow. Uniwersytet Jagielloński. Biblioteka. Inwentarz rękopisów Biblioteki Jagiellońskiej. Nr. 8001-9000. [1. wyd.] Kraków, Nakl., 1971.

Bandurak, Volodymyr I͡Urii͡ovych.
Les' Martovych zblyz'ka; povist'. [By] Volodymyr Bandurak. Uzhhorod, Vyd-vo Karpaty, 1971.
121 p.
1. Martovych, Les', 1871-1916—Fiction.
MH InU CaOTU NUC74-21945

Bandurenko, I͡Evhen.
Vesela osin'; liryka, humor, satyra. [By] I͡Evhen Bandurenko. Odesa, Mai͡ak, 1971.
102 p. illus.
MH NUC74-21944

Banduri͡an, Garik Avetisovich
see Bandowryan, Garik.

Bandurka, Mieczysław.
Początki i rozwój ruchu robotniczego w Łodzi do 1918 r. Łódź, 1973.
38 p. (Biblioteczka wiedzy o Łodzi, zesz. 7)
On verso of t.p.: Prezydium Łódzkiego Komitetu Frontu Jeności Narodu. Uniwersytet Łódzki.
"550 rocznica nadania Łodzi praw miejskich".
"150 rocznica powstania Łodzi przemysłowej".
MH NUC76-66158

Bandurka, Mieczysław.
Zmiany administracyjne i terytorialne ziem województwa łódzkiego w XIX i XX wieku / Mieczysław Bandurka. — Wyd. 1. — Warszawa : Państwowe Wydawn. Naukowe, 1974.
210 p. : maps ; 24 cm.
At head of title: Naczelna Dyrekcja Archiwów Państwowych. Archiwum Państwowe Miasta Łodzi i Województwa Łódzkiego.
Includes bibliographical references and index.
zł64.00
1. Łódz, Poland (Voivodeship)—Administrative and political divisions. I. Title.
JS6139.L6B3 75-409419

Bandurka, Mieczysław
see Rosin, Ryszard. Łódź, 1423-1823-1973... Łódz : Wydział Kultury i Sztuki Urzędu Miasta Łodzi, 1974.

Bandurko, L.M.
see Pod pobednym znamenem Oktiabri͡a. Maĭkop, Adygeĭskoe otdelenie Krasnodarskogo knizhnogo izd-va, 1971.

Bandusch, Paul.
85 [i.e. Fünfundachtzig] Jahre Deutsche Eisschnellauf-Meisterschaften : 1891-1976 : e. Beitr. zur Geschichte d. Eisschnellaufs / Paul Bandusch. — 1. Aufl. — Berlin ; München ; Frankfurt a.M. : Bartels und Wernitz, 1977.
136 p. ; 21 cm. GFR77-A
Includes indexes.
ISBN 3-87039-004-2
1. Skating—Germany, West—Competitions. 2. Skating—Germany, West—Records. I. Title.
GV849.49.A2B36 77-475165
77 MARC

Bandy, Claude
see United States. Bureau of Domestic Commerce. The acquisition and maintenance of medical equipment. [Washington] U.S. Domestic and International Business Administration, Bureau of Domestic Commerce, 1975.

Bandy, Dalton Dale, 1945-
Federal taxation of private foundations. [Austin] 1972.
viii, 218 p. illus.
Thesis (Ph.D.)—University of Texas at Austin. Microfilm ed. (positive) by University Microfilms.
Vita: p. [219]
Bibliography: p. 214-218.
1. Charitable uses, trusts, and foundations—United States. I. Title.
OOxM NUC75-24078

Bandy, Dalton Dale, 1945-
Federal taxation of private foundations. [Austin, Tex.] 1972.
viii, 218 l. illus. 29 cm.
Thesis (Ph.D.)—University of Texas at Austin. Vita.
Bibliography: leaves 214-218.
TxU NUC74-139113

Bandy, David Brent, 1941-
see Heat transfer-Philadelphia. New York, American Institute of Chemical Engineers, 1969.

Bandy, Orville L.
see Paleoecology; [lectures]... Washington, American Geological Institute [1967?]

Bandy, Stephen Charles.
Caines Cynn; a study of Beowulf and the legends of Cain. [Princeton, N.J.] 1967.
245 l.
Thesis—Princeton University.
Abstract: leaves 244-245.
Bibliography: leaves 238-243.
1. Beowulf. 2. Cain in literature. I. Title.
CU-SB NUC74-144593

Bandy, William R
Cases and materials on business law [by] William R. Bandy [and] Eugene W. Nelson. Austin, Tex., Hemphill's, 1956.
355 p. 28 cm.
1. Commercial law—United States—Cases. I. Nelson, Eugene Walter, 1914- joint author. II. Title.
KF888.B27 346'.73'07 74-161675
MARC

Bandy, William Thomas, 1903-
Études baudelairiennes II, avec 10 illustrations. Neuchatel [Suisse] À la Baconnière [c1971]
223 p.
1. Baudelaire, Charles Pierre, 1821-1867. I. Title.
ViBlbV NUC73-113635

Bandy, William Thomas, 1903-
Index des rimes des Fleurs du mal [par] W.T. Bandy. Nashville, Vanderbilt University, 1972.
45 p. (Publications du Centre d'études Baudelairiennes, 1)
Limited edition of 100 copies.
1. Baudelaire, Charles, 1821-1867. Les épaves. 2. Baudelaire, Charles, 1821-1867. Les fleurs du mal.
MH NUC76-72875

Bandy, William Thomas, 1903- ed.
see Baudelaire, Charles Pierre, 1821-1867. Edgar Allan Poe... [Toronto, Buffalo] University of Toronto Press [1973]

Bandy, William Thomas, 1903- ed.
see Baudelaire im Urteil seiner Zeitgonossen. [Frankfurt a.M.] Insel Verlag [1969]

Bandy, William Thomas, 1903-
see Hommage à W. T. Bandy. Neuchâtel, (Éditions de) la Baconnière, (1973).

Bandy, William Thomas, 1903-
see Regards sur Baudelaire. Paris, Lettres modernes, 1974.

Bandyk, Il'ía Arkhipovich.
[Ekonomichnost' konstruktorskikh razrabotok]
Экономичность конструкторских разработок. Под ред. д-ра экон. наук, проф. М. М. Макеенко. Кишинев, "Картя молдовеняскэ," 1972.
160 p. with diagrs. 20 cm. 0.77rub USSR 72-VKP
At head of title: И. А. Бандык.
Includes bibliographical references.
1. Costs, Industrial. 2. Machinery—Design. I. Title.
TS167.B35 72-367721

Bandyk, Il'ía Arkhipovich.
(Tekhnicheskoe tvorchestvo—ego sut' i zadachi)
Техническое творчество—его суть и задачи / И. А. Бандык. — Кишинев : Картя Молдовеняскэ, 1976.
106 p. : ill. ; 20 cm. USSR***
Bibliography : p. 105-106.
0.20rub
1. Creative ability in technology. I. Title.
T173.8.B35 77-501548

Bandyopadhaya, Nilmani.
The golden flute. [Lucknow, 1972]
25 p. 17 cm. Rs10.00 ($1.50 U.S.)
I. Title.
PR9499.3.B26G6 821 73-903170
76 MARC

Bandyopadhyaẏ, Anandamay.
[Maṇikāñcana]
মণিকাঞ্চন; সামাজিক নাটক. শ্রীআনন্দময় বন্দ্যোপাধ্যায় প্রণীত. কলিকাতা, শ্রীমা বুক সিণ্ডিকেট, 1376 [1969 or 70]
156 p. 19 cm. Rs4.00
In Bengali.
I. Title.
PK1718.B243M34 72-903102

Bandyopadhyay, Atin.
(Alaukika jalayāna)
অলৌকিক জলযান / অতীন বন্দ্যোপাধ্যায়. — কলিকাতা : শঙ্খ প্রকাশন, 1382- [1975-
v. ; 22 cm.
In Bengali.
A novel.
I. Title.
PK1718.B245A8 75-906712

Bandyopadhyay, Atin.
(Cāru, Indra ebaṃ Kalakātā)
চারু, ইন্দ্র এবং কলকাতা / অতীন বন্দ্যোপাধ্যায়. — কলকাতা : জ্যোতি প্রকাশন, 1382 [1975]
159 p. ; 22 cm.
In Bengali.
Short stories.
Rs10.00
I. Title.
PK1718.B245C3 76-900177

Bandyopadhyay, Atin.
(Ḍākabāṃlo)
ডাকবাংলো / অতীন বন্দ্যোপাধ্যায়. — কলিকাতা : রামায়ণী প্রকাশ ভবন : পরিবেশক স্যাঙ্গুইন পাবলিশার্স কনসার্ন, 1973.
179 p. ; 22 cm.
In Bengali.
A novel.
Rs7.00
I. Title.
PK1718.B245D3 75-900429

Bandyopadhyay, Atin.
দুঃখিনী বর্ণমালা, মা আমার. [লেখক] অতীন বন্দ্যোপাধ্যায়. কলিকাতা, অনন্য প্রকাশন [1971]
156 p. 23 cm. Rs6.00
In Bengali.
A novel.
1. East Pakistan—History—Fiction. I. Title.
Title romanized: Duḥkhinī barṇamālā, mā āmāra.
PK1718.B245D8 79-928963

Bandyopadhyay, Atin.
(Ekajana daitya, ekaṭi lāla golāpa)
একজন দৈত্য, একটি লাল গোলাপ / অতীন বন্দ্যোপাধ্যায়. — 1. সংস্করণ. — কলিকাতা : রামায়ণী প্রকাশ ভবন, 1974.
149 p. ; 22 cm.
In Bengali.
A novel
Rs10.00
I. Title.
PK1718.B245E38 75-900431

Bandyopadhyay, Atin.
(Gambuje hātera sparśa)
গম্বুজে হাতের স্পর্শ. [লেখক] অতীন বন্দ্যোপাধ্যায়. কলকাতা, বিশ্ববাণী প্রকাশনী [1379 i.e. 1972]
173 p. 22 cm. Rs6.00
In Bengali.
A novel.
I. Title.
PK1718.B245G3 72-908348

Bandyopadhyay, Atin.
(Mānushera māmulī kecchā)
মানুষের মামুলী কেচ্ছা / অতীন বন্দ্যোপাধ্যায়. — কলিকাতা : দেবশ্রী সাহিত্য সমিধ, 1382 [1975]
92 p. ; 22 cm.
In Bengali.
A novel.
Rs5.00
I. Title.
PK1718.B245M3 75-908580

Bandyopadhyay, Atin.
[Nīlakaṇṭha pākhira khõje]
নীলকণ্ঠ পাখির খোঁজে. [লেখক] অতীন বন্দ্যোপাধ্যায়. [1. সংস্করণ] লিকাতা, রূপরেখা [1971-
2 v. 23 cm. Rs15.00 (v. 1) ; Rs10.00 (v. 2)
In Bengali.
A novel.
I. Title.
PK1718.B245N5 70-923288

Bandyopadhyay, Atin.
(Phoṭā padmera gabhīre)
ফোটা পদ্মের গভীরে / অতীন বন্দ্যোপাধ্যায়. — কলিকাতা : প্রফুল্ল গ্রন্থাগার, 1382 [1975]
219 p. ; 22 cm.
In Bengali.
A novel.
Rs14.00
I. Title.
PK1718.B245P48 75-906673

Bandyopadhyay, Atin.
(Pipāsā)
পিপাসা. [লেখক] অতীন বন্দ্যোপাধ্যায়. [1. সংস্করণ] কলিকাতা, গ্রন্থালয় [1379, i.e. 1972]
155 p. 22 cm. Rs5.00
In Bengali.
A novel.
I. Title.
PK1718.B245P5 72-905421

Bandyopadhyay, Atin.
(Rājā yāẏa banabāse)
রাজা যায় বনবাসে. [লেখক] অতীন বন্দ্যোপাধ্যায়. কলিকাতা, ডি.এম. লাইব্রেরী [1379 i.e. 1972]
491 p. 23 cm. Rs16.00
In Bengali.
A novel.
I. Title.
PK1718.B245R3 72-908882

Bandyopadhyay, Atin.
(Saba phula kine nāo)
সব ফুল কিনে নাও / অতীন বন্দ্যোপাধ্যায়. — কলিকাতা : সাহিত্য সংস্থা : প্রাপ্তিস্থান, সুহাস পাবলিশিং হাউস, 1974.
107 p. ; 22 cm.
In Bengali.
A novel.
Rs8.00

I. Title.

PK1718.B245S18 75–902361

Bandyopadhyay, Atin.
[Sādā jyotsnā]
সাদা জ্যোৎস্না. [লেখক] অতীন বন্দ্যোপাধ্যায়. কলিকাতা, গ্রন্থ-প্রকাশ [1378, i.e. 1972]
154 p. 23 cm. Rs6.00
In Bengali.
A novel.

I. Title.

PK1718.B245S2 72–903345

Bandyopadhyay, Atin.
(Samudra-mānusha)
সমুদ্র-মানুষ. [লেখক] অতীন বন্দ্যোপাধ্যায়. কলিকাতা, মিত্রালয় [1960]
186 p. 22 cm. Rs5.00
In Bengali.
A novel.

I. Title.

PK1718.B245S25 76–984012

Bandyopadhyay, Atin.
(Sukhī rājaputra)
সুখী রাজপুত্র. [লেখক] অতীন বন্দ্যোপাধ্যায়. কলিকাতা, ডি.এম. লাইব্রেরী [1380 i.e. 1973]
200 p. 22 cm. Rs7.00
In Bengali.
A novel.

I. Title.

PK1718.B245S8 73–907730

Bandyopadhyay, Atin.
[Takhana hemantakāla]
তখন হেমন্তকাল. [লেখক] অতীন বন্দ্যোপাধ্যায়. কলিকাতা, সাহিত্য প্রকাশ [1379, i.e. 1972]
155 p. 23 cm. Rs6.00
In Bengali.
A novel.

I. Title.

PK1718.B245T3 72–905103

Bandyopadhyay, Diptendranath, 1933–
(Tṛtīya bhubana)
তৃতীয় ভুবন. [লেখক] দীপেন্দ্রনাথ বন্দ্যোপাধ্যায়. কলিকাতা, মিত্রালয় [1958]
232 p. 19 cm. Rs4.50
In Bengali.
A novel.
"তেরশো চৌষট্টির শারদীয়া সংখ্যা 'নতুন সাহিত্য' পত্রিকায় তৃতীয় ভুবন প্রকাশিত হয়."
I. Title.

PK1730.13.A46T7 76–984014

Bandyopadhyay, Atin.
(Ṭukunera asukha)
টুকুনের অসুখ. [লেখক] অতীন বন্দ্যোপাধ্যায়. কলিকাতা, বর্ণালী [1380 i.e. 1973]
283 p. 22 cm. Rs12.00
In Bengali.
A novel.

I. Title.

PK1718.B245T8 74–901040

Bandyopadhyay, Bisva, 1916–
[Kābya-samāhṛti]
কাব্য-সমাহৃতি. [কবি] বিশ্ব বন্দ্যোপাধ্যায়. [কলিকাতা, তিলক মুখোপাধ্যায়]; পরিবেশক সিগনেট বুকশপ [1971–
v. 22 cm. Rs6.00 (v. 1)
In Bengali.

I. Title.

PK1718.B248K3 72–900609

Bandyopadhyay, Bisvanath, 1934–
বিহ্বল সিঁড়ি. [কবি] বিশ্বনাথ বন্দ্যোপাধ্যায়. [কলকাতা] কবিপত্র প্রকাশভবন [1378, i.e. 1971]
48 p. 23 cm. Rs3.00
In Bengali.

I. Title.
Title romanized: Bihvala siṅṛi.

PK1718.B25B5 76–925143

Bandyopadhyay, Bisvanath, 1934–
(Nihata pratimāguli)
নিহত প্রতিমাগুলি. [কবি] বিশ্বনাথ বন্দ্যোপাধ্যায়. কলিকাতা, মণি প্রকাশনী [1378 i.e. 1972]
43 p. 22 cm. Rs3.00
In Bengali.
Poems.

I. Title.

PK1718.B25N5 72–907748

Bandyopadhyay, Dipendranath, 1933–
[Haoẏā, nā-haoẏā]
হওয়া, না-হওয়া. [লেখক] দীপেন্দ্রনাথ বন্দ্যোপাধ্যায়. [1. সংস্করণ] কলিকাতা, মুকুন্দ পাবলিশার্স [1972]
162 p. 22 cm. Rs6.00
In Bengali.
Short stories.

I. Title.

PK1730.13.A459H35 72–902285

Bandyopadhyay, Ganesh Chandra, 1936–
A textbook of animal husbandry, by G. C. Banerjee. 3d ed. New Delhi, Oxford and IBH Pub. Co. [1971]
xxiii, 576 p. illus. 25 cm.
Bibliography: p. [565]-567.
1. Stock and stock-breeding. I. Title.
NIC NUC73-113588

Bandyopadhyay, Gautam.
Relations of processing parameters to the properties of lithium ferrite. [Berkeley] 1973.
1 v. (various pagings) illus.
Thesis (Ph.D.)—University of California.
Includes bibliography.
CU NUC75-16676

Bandyopadhyay, Gokul, 1921–1968.
(Āṅdhi)
আঁধি. [লেখক] স্বরাজ বন্দ্যোপাধ্যায়. কলিকাতা, মিত্র ও ঘোষ [1968]
260 p. 23 cm. Rs7.50
In Bengali.
A novel.

I. Title.

PK1718.B26A77 SA 68–8675

PL 480: I-B-3372

Bandyopadhyay, Gokul, 1921–1968.
[Bidyā bāulira bṛttānta]
বিদ্যা বাউলীর বৃত্তান্ত. [লেখক] স্বরাজ বন্দ্যোপাধ্যায়. [1. সংস্করণ] কলিকাতা, বাক্-সাহিত্য [1378, i.e. 1971]
225 p. 23 cm. Rs8.00
In Bengali.
A novel.

I. Title.

PK1718.B26B5 1971 77–928357

Bandyopadhyay, Gokul, 1921–1968.
(Duṭi hṛdaẏera gāna)
দুটি হৃদয়ের গান / স্বরাজ বন্দ্যোপাধ্যায়. — কলিকাতা : পলাশী : পরিবেশক, নব গ্রন্থ কুটির, 1368 [1961]
97 p. ; 23 cm.
In Bengali.
A novel.

I. Title.

PK1718.B26D85 75–985593

Bandyopadhyay, Gokul, 1921–
(Madhumatī)
মধুমতী. [লেখক] স্বরাজ বন্দ্যোপাধ্যায়. কলিকাতা, ক্যালকাটা পাবলিশার্স [1953]
165 p. 19 cm.
In Bengali.
A novel.

I. Title.

PK1718.B26M3 76–984015

Bandyopadhyay, Gokul, 1921–
(Rāta bhora)
রাত ভোর. [লেখক] স্বরাজ বন্দ্যোপাধ্যায়. কলিকাতা, বেঙ্গল পাবলিশার্স [1953]
126 p. 20 cm.
In Bengali.
A novel.

I. Title.

PK1718.B26R35 76–985016

Bandyopadhyay, Hari Benoy.
Hindu religion & culture; a scientific discussion. Mahesh [District] Hooghly [distributors: Sahityasree, Calcutta] 1972.
181, [5] p. 23 cm.
Reviews of the author's work: p. [182]-[186]
1. Hinduism. I. Title.
ICU NUC75-26607

Bandyopadhyay, Jamuna, 1931–
(Upala-byathita gati)
উপল-ব্যথিত গতি. [লেখিকা] যমুনা বন্দ্যোপাধ্যায়. [1. সংস্করণ] কলিকাতা, আনন্দ পাবলিশার্স [1971]
102 p. illus. 23 cm. Rs5.00
In Bengali.

1. Banerjee, Bibhuti Bhusan, 1896?–1950. I. Title.

PK1718.B298Z56 72–901518

Bandyopadhyay, Kanak, 1910–
রবীন্দ্রনাথের শেষের কবিতা. [লেখক] শ্রীকনক বন্দ্যোপাধ্যায়. [কলিকাতা, বাগর্থ, 1378, i.e. 1971]
2, 112 p. 22 cm. Rs5.00
In Bengali.
Includes bibliographical references.

1. Tagore, Sir Rabindranath, 1861–1941. Śeshera kabitā. I. Title: Śeshera kabitā.
Title romanized: Rabīndranāthera śeshera kabitā.

PK1723.S43B3 70–922433

Bandyopadhyay, Manik, 1908–1956.
অহিংসা. [লেখক] মানিক বন্দ্যোপাধ্যায়. কলকাতা, লেখাপড়া [1377, i.e. 1970]
250 p. 23 cm. Rs7.50
In Bengali.
A novel.

I. Title.
Title romanized: Ahiṃsā.

PK1718.B28A68 70–918988

Bandyopadhyay, Manik, 1908-1956.
[Correspondence]
অপ্রকাশিত মানিক বন্দ্যোপাধ্যায় : ডায়েরি ও চিঠিপত্র / ভূমিকা, নির্দেশপঞ্জি, ও সম্পাদনা, যুগান্তর চক্রবর্তী. — কলকাতা : অরুণা প্রকাশনী : পরিবেশক সিগনেট বুকশপ, 1976.
64, 349 p., [1] leaf of plates : port. ; 23 cm.
In Bengali.
Includes index.
Rs25.00
1. Bandyopadhyay, Manik, 1908-1956—Correspondence. 2. Bandyopadhyay, Manik, 1908-1956—Diaries. 3. Authors, Bengali—20th century—Biography. I. Cakrabarti, Yugāntara.
Title romanized: Aprakāśita Mānika Bandyopādhyāya.
PK1718.B28Z53 1976 76-905506

Bandyopadhyay, Manik, 1908-1956.
(Jibanera jaṭilatā)
জীবনের জটিলতা. [লেখক] মানিক বন্দ্যোপাধ্যায়. কলিকাতা, মৌসুমী প্রকাশনী [1968]
142 p. 22 cm. Rs4.00
In Bengali.
A novel.
I. Title.
PK1718.B28J5 1968 S A 68-8537
PL 480: I-B-3476

Bandyopadhyay, Manik, 1908-1956.
Lodochnik s reki Padmy. Roman. Perevod s bengal'skogo A. Gorbovskogo. Moskva, "Khudozhestvennaia literatura", 1969.
155 p. illus.
At head of title: Manik Bondopaddhai.
I. Gorbovskiĭ, A., tr. II. Title.
OClW NUC74-62937

Bandyopadhyay, Manik, 1908-1956.
[Mānika Bandyopādhyāyera cāraṭi upanyāsa]
মানিক বন্দ্যোপাধ্যায়ের চারটি উপন্যাস. কলিকাতা, গ্রন্থ প্রকাশ [1378, i.e. 1971]
226 p. 23 cm. Rs8.50
In Bengali.
CONTENTS: ধরা বাঁধা জীবন.—প্রতিবিম্ব.—চিন্তামণি.—আদায়ের ইতিহাস.
I. Title.
PK1718.B28A6 1971 72-900459

Bandyopadhyay, Manik, 1908-1956.
Padma River boatman [by] Manik Bandopadhyaya. Translated from the Bengali by Barbara Painter and Yann Lovelock. [St. Lucia] University of Queensland Press [1973]
xii, 142 p. 22 cm. (UNESCO collection of representative works: Indian series) (Asian and Pacific writing 4) Aus***
Translation of Padma nadir majhi.
Includes bibliographical references.
I. Title. II. Series. III. Series.
PZ4.B2145Pad 3 891'.44'37 74-160844
[PK1718.B28] MARC
ISBN 0-7022-0833-7; 0-7022-0834-5 (pbk.)

Bandyopadhyay, Manik, 1908-1956.
[Parādhīna prema]
পরাধীন প্রেম. [লেখক] মানিক বন্দ্যোপাধ্যায়. [1. সংস্করণ] কলিকাতা, রীডার্স কর্ণার [1362, i.e. 1955]
188 p. 19 cm.
In Bengali.
A novel.
I. Title.
PK1718.B28P38 1955 72-220041

Bandyopadhyay, Manik, 1908-1956.
(Pheriolā)
ফেরিওলা. [লেখক] মানিক বন্দ্যোপাধ্যায়. কলিকাতা, ক্যালকাটা পাবলিশার্স [1360, i.e. 1953]
143 p. 19 cm.
In Bengali.
Short stories.
I. Title.
PK1718.B28P5 1953 76-984017

Bandyopadhyay, Manik, 1908-1956. Reptile ways
see Ghose, Sukumar, 1935- comp. Contemporary Bengali literature: fiction. Calcutta, Academic Publishers [1972]

Bandyopadhyay, Manik, 1908-1956.
[Saharatalī]
শহরতলী. [লেখক] মানিক বন্দোপাধ্যায় [sic. নতুন সংস্করণ] কলিকাতা, মণ্ডল বুক হাউস [1379 i.e. 1972]
266 p. 22 cm. Rs9.00
In Bengali.
A novel.
I. Title.
PK1718.B28S2 1972 72-908167

Bandyopadhyay, Manilal, 1886-
জানি তুমি আসবে. [লেখক] মণিলাল বন্দ্যোপাধ্যায়. কলিকাতা] দেব সাহিত্য কুটীর [1375, i.e. 1968]
143 p. 23 cm. (যৌতুক সিরিজ, 14) 3.50
In Bengali.
A novel.
I. Title. Title romanized: Jāni tumi āsabe.
PK1718.B282J3 78-915274

Bandyopadhyay, Patitpaban, 1911- ed.
see Bose, Sukumar, 1931- (Manaspati Śrīarabinda) [1973]

Bandyopadhyay, Pranav.
(Ekaṭi nadī duṭi tīra)
একটি নদী দুটি তীর / প্রণব বন্দ্যোপাধ্যায়. — কলকাতা : বঙ্গগ্রন্থম, [19--]
111 p. ; 23 cm.
In Bengali.
Short stories.
I. Title.
PK1718.B283E4 76-984300

Bandyopadhyay, Pranav.
The eye lamp and other poems / Pranab Bandyopadhyay. — Calcutta : Epic Press, 1974.
79 p. : port. ; 19 cm.
"Most of these poems have been translated from the original Bengali version by Umanath Bhattacherjee."
Rs20.00
I. Title.
PK1718.B283A23 1974 891'.44'17 75-904206
76 MARC

Bandyopadhyay, Pranav.
(Istāhāra)
ইস্তাহার. [কবি] প্রণব বন্দ্যোপাধ্যায়. [1. সংস্করণ] কলিকাতা, বিশ্বজ্ঞান [1972]
63 p. 23 cm. Rs4.00
In Bengali.
I. Title.
PK1718.B283 I 7 72-904517

Bandyopadhyay, Pranav.
(Kādāmāṭira durga)
কাদামাটির দুর্গ. [কবি] প্রণব বন্দ্যোপাধ্যায়. কলিকাতা, বিশ্বজ্ঞান [1972]
47 p. 23 cm. Rs3.00
In Bengali.
Poems.
I. Title.
PK1718.B283K3 72-905918

Bandyopadhyay, Pranav.
The mud castles / Pranab Bandyopadhyay. — Calcutta : United Writers : selling agents, Firma KLM, 1976.
37 p. ; 23 cm.
Poems.
Rs20.00
I. Title.
PR9499.3.B25M8 821 76-904840
77 MARC

Bandyopadhyay, Pranav.
(Musāphira)
মুসাফির. [কবি] প্রণব বন্দ্যোপাধ্যায়. কলিকাতা, বিশ্বজ্ঞান [1972]
63 p. 23 cm. Rs3.00
In Bengali.
I. Title.
PK1718.B283M8 72-904888

Bandyopadhyay, Pranav.
(Nadīra ṭhikānā)
নদীর ঠিকানা / প্রণব বন্দ্যোপাধ্যায়. — কলিকাতা : জ্যোতি প্রকাশন, 1380 [1974]
179 p. ; 22 cm.
In Bengali.
A novel.
Rs8.00
I. Title.
PK1718.B283N3 76-900247

Bandyopadhyay, Pranav.
Portrait of love, and other poems / Pranab Bandyopadhyay. — Calcutta : United Writers : selling agents, Firma K. L. Mukhopadhyay, 1975.
38 p. ; 22 cm.
Rs15.00
I. Title.
PR9499.3.B25P6 821 75-906359
76 MARC

Bandyopadhyay, Pranav.
রং-তুলি. [লেখক] প্রণব বন্দ্যোপাধ্যায়. কলিকাতা, মিত্রালয় [195-]
175 p. 23 cm.
In Bengali.
A novel.
I. Title. Title romanized: Raṃ-tuli.
PK1718.B283R27 72-203200

Bandyopadhyay, Pranav.
Wherever you go, and other poems / Pranab Bandyopadhyay. — New Delhi : Oxford & IBH Pub. Co., 1975.
63 p., [1] leaf of plates : port. ; 22 cm.
"Translations from the original Bengali version from the poet's books, Istahar, Musafir, Kadamatir Durga, Sahar, Mukhosher rang & Jekhanei jao."
Rs20.00
I. Title.
PK1718.B283A26 891'.44'17 75-907220
76 MARC

Bandyopadhyay, Pranav.
(Yekhānei yāo)
যেখানেই যাও / প্রণব বন্দ্যোপাধ্যায়. — কলিকাতা : বিশ্বজ্ঞান, 1381 [1974]
47 p. ; 22 cm.
In Bengali.
Poems.
Rs3.00
I. Title.
PK1718.B283Y4 75-903811
S A

Bandyopadhyay, Pranav.
see Ancient ballads of India ... Calcutta, United Writers : selling agents, Firma KLM, 1976.

Bandyopadhyay, Pranav.
see Ghālib, 1796?-1869. Hundred ghazals of Mirza Ghalib. Calcutta, United Writers : selling agents, Firma K. L. Mukhopadhyay, 1975.

Bandyopadhyay, Pranav
see The Voice of the Indian poets... Calcutta, United Writers; selling agents, Firma K.L. Mukhopadhyay [1975]

Bandyopadhyay, Pratap.
A study of Vāmana's Kāvyālaṅkārasūtravṛtti. [Toronto] c1971.
2 v. (iii, 1208 l.)
Pt. 2 includes The sāhityasarvasa; a commentary on Vāmana's Kāvyālaṅkārasūtravṛtti, by Maheśvara Subuddhimiśra (leaves [636]-910) in Sanskrit.
Thesis—University of Toronto.
Bibliography: leaves [1153]-1177.
CaOTU NUC73-34513

Bandyopadhyay, S. C., joint author.
see Desai, Gunvant M. Dynamics of growth in fertiliser use at micro level. Ahmedabad, Centre for Management in Agriculture, Indian Institute of Management, 1973.

Bandyopadhyay, Sailesh Kumar, 1926–
(Biplabī bandhura prati)
বিপ্লবী বন্ধুর প্রতি. [লেখক] শৈলেশকুমার বন্দ্যোপাধ্যায়. কলিকাতা, অমর সাহিত্য প্রকাশন [1379 i.e. 1972]
96 p. 23 cm. Rs2.50
In Bengali.
Includes bibliographical references.
1. West Bengal—Politics and government. I. Title.
DS485.B493B34 72-908679

Bandyopadhyay, Samaresh, 1942-
Early foreigners on Indian caste system / by Samaresh Bandyopadhyay. — 1st ed. — Calcutta : Pilgrim Publishers, 1974.
vii, 56 p. (p. [55]-56 advertisements), [1] leaf of plates : ill. ; 22 cm.
Bibliography: p. [43]-48.
Includes index.
Rs16.00 ($4.00 U.S.)
1. Caste—India. 2. India—Social conditions. I. Title.
DS422.C3B34 301.44'0954 75-905932
76 MARC

Bandyopadhyay, Samaresh, 1942–
Foreign accounts of marriage in ancient India. Calcutta, Firma K. L. Mukhopadhyay, 1973.
xi, 76 p. 22 cm. Rs20.00 ($4.00U.S.)
Bibliography: p. [59]–65.
1. Marriage—India. 2. Divorce—India. I. Title.
HQ669.B36 301.42'0934 74–901124
MARC

Bandyopadhyay, Sanat, 1933–
(Nijera dike phire)
নিজের দিকে ফিরে. [কবি] সনৎ বন্দ্যোপাধ্যায়. [কলিকাতা, সীমান্ত প্রকাশনী]; পরিবেশক মনীষা গ্রন্থালয় [1971]
64 p. 22 cm. Rs3.50
In Bengali.
I. Title.
PK1730.13.A475N5 73-906362

Bandyopadhyay, Sanat, 1933–
[Praticchabi o anyānya kabitā]
প্রতিচ্ছবি ও অন্যান্য কবিতা. [লেখক] সনৎ বন্দ্যোপাধ্যায়. [পরিবর্ধিত সংস্করণ. কলিকাতা, অনুভব প্রকাশনী]; পরিবেশক মনীষা গ্রন্থালয় [1971]
64 p. 22 cm. Rs3.50
In Bengali.
I. Title.
PK1730.13.A475P7 74–928131

Bandyopadhyay, Santiranjan, 1920–
(Śubharātri)
শুভরাত্রি. [লেখক] শান্তিরঞ্জন বন্দ্যোপাধ্যায়. কলিকাতা, সাহিত্য [1362, i.e. 1955]
127 p. 23 cm.
In Bengali.
Short stories.
I. Title.
PK1718.B2847S9 76–984020
SA

Bandyopadhyay, Santiranjan, 1920–
(Timirābhisāra)
তিমিরাভিসার. [লেখক] শান্তিরঞ্জন বন্দ্যোপাধ্যায়. কলিকাতা, নবভারতী [1956]
286 p. 23 cm.
In Bengali.
A novel.
I. Title.
PK1718.B2847T5 76–984019

Bandyopadhyay, Saradindu, 1899–1970.
(Kahena kabi Kālidāsa)
কহেন কবি কালিদাস / শরদিন্দু বন্দ্যোপাধ্যায়. — 1. সংস্করণ. — কলিকাতা : আনন্দ পাবলিশার্স, 1368 [1961]
136 p. ; 23 cm.
In Bengali.
A novel.
I. Title.
PK1718.B285K27 1961 75–984078

Bandyopadhyay, Saradindu, 1899–
কল্পকুহেলি. [লেখক] শরদিন্দু বন্দ্যোপাধ্যায়. [1. সংস্করণ] কলিকাতা, আনন্দ পাবলিশার্স [1969]
287 p. 22 cm. Rs8.00
In Bengali.
Short stories.
I. Title.
Title romanized: Kalpakuheli.
PK1718.B285K35 78–913470

Bandyopadhyay, Saradindu, 1899–
(Kānu kahe rāi)
কানু কহে রাই. [লেখক] শরদিন্দু বন্দ্যোপাধ্যায়. কলিকাতা, গুরুদাস চট্টোপাধ্যায় [1955]
130 p. 19 cm.
In Bengali.
Short stories.
I. Title.
PK1718.B285K33 76–984022

Bandyopadhyay, Saradindu, 1899–1970.
কুমারসম্ভবের কবি. [লেখক] শরদিন্দু বন্দ্যোপাধ্যায়. [1. দে'জ সংস্করণ. কলিকাতা, দে'জ পাবলিশিং]; পরিবেশক দে বুক ষ্টোর [1377, i.e. 1970]
112 p. 23 cm. Rs4.00
In Bengali.
A novel.
1. Kalidāsa—Fiction. I. Title.
Title romanized: Kumārasambhabera kabi.
PK1718.B285K8 71–915571

Bandyopadhyay, Saradindu, 1899–1970.
শরদিন্দু অম্‌নিবাস. [লেখক] শরদিন্দু বন্দ্যোপাধ্যায়. শ্রীপ্রতুলচন্দ্র গুপ্ত সম্পাদিত. [1. সংস্করণ] কলিকাতা, আনন্দ পাবলিশার্স [1970–
v. port. 22 cm. Rs15.00 (v. 1)
In Bengali.
CONTENTS: 1. ব্যোমকেশ.
I. Gupta, Pratul Chandra, comp. II. Title.
Title romanized: Śaradindu amnibāsa.
PK1718.B285A6 1970 72–918805

Bandyopadhyay, Shibdas, 1927–
(Āgneya)
আগ্নেয়. [কবি] শিবদাস বন্দ্যোপাধ্যায়. কলিকাতা, অভীক পাবলিশার্স [1972]
63 p. 23 cm. Rs3.00
In Bengali.
Poems.
I. Title.
PK1718.B286A7 72–904097

Bandyopadhyay, Shibdas, 1927–
The shadows. Calcutta, Aveek Publishers [1971]
48 p. 23 cm. Rs3.00
I. Title.
PR9480.9.B3S5 821 74–928383
MARC

Bandyopadhyay, Shyamal
see
Bandopadhay, Shyamal.

Bandyopadhyay, Sunil, 1939–
(Bhāshāpathika Harinātha De)
ভাষাপথিক হরিনাথ দে. [লেখক] সুনীল বন্দ্যোপাধ্যায়. [কলিকাতা?] অভী প্রকাশন [1379, i.e. 1972]
12, 293 p. illus., ports. 22 cm. Rs15.00
On verso of t.p.: প্রকাশক সঞ্জীবকুমার বসু, কলিকাতা.
Bengali or English.
Works of Harinath De: p. [256]–265.
Bibliography: p. [266]–273.
1. De, Harinath, 1877–1911. I. Title.
PK109.D4B3 72–905603

Bandyopadhyay, Sunil, 1939– ed.
see De, Harinath, 1877–1911. Select papers... Calcutta, Sanskrit Pustak Bhandar [1972]

Bandyopadhyay, Susilkumar.
বাঙালিনী. [লেখক] সুশীল কুমার বন্দ্যোপাধ্যায়. কলিকাতা, রুবি প্রকাশনী [1971]
199 p. 22 cm. Rs5.50
In Bengali.
A novel.
I. Title.
Title romanized: Bāṅālinī.
PK1718.B287B3 71–924213

Bandyopadhyay, Susilkumar.
Sri Sri Bamakshepa / translated from Tarapith Bhairab by Sushil Kumar Bandopadhyay by Subodh Kumar Banerjee. — 1st ed. — Calcutta : Bamdev Sangha : available from Mahesh Library, 1971.
106 p., [2] leaves of plates : ill. ; 25 cm.
Rs5.00
1. Bāmākshepā, 1838-1911. I. Banerjee, Subodh Kumar. II. Title.
BL1175.B27B313 294.5'6'1 74-903940
75 MARC

Bandyopadhyay, Susilkumar.
(Tārāpīṭha bhairaba)
তারাপীঠ ভৈরব. [লেখক] সুশীল কুমার বন্দ্যোপাধ্যায়. কলিকাতা, বামদেব সংঘ [1955]
270, 8 p. geneal. table, ports. 26 cm.
In Bengali.
1. Bāmākshepā, 1838–1911. I. Title.
BL1175.B27B3 76–984023

Bandyopadhyay, Tapankumar.
রবীন্দ্রনাথের 'পুনশ্চ'-পর্ব. [লেখক] শ্রীতপনকুমার বন্দ্যোপাধ্যায়. কলিকাতা, বুক এক্সচেঞ্জ [1376, i.e. 1969]
192 p. 22 cm. Rs6.00
In Bengali.
1. Tagore, Sir Rabindranath, 1861–1941. Punaśca.
Title romanized: Rabīndranāthera 'Punaśca'-parba.
PK1723.P83B3 72–922439

Bandyōpadhyay, Taradas
see Bandyopādhyāya, Tārādāsa.

Bandyopadhyay, Tulasiprasad, 1917–
(Phāgunera paraśa)
ফাগুনের পরশ. [লেখক] তুলসীপ্রসাদ বন্দ্যোপাধ্যায়. কলিকাতা, আর্ট য়্যাণ্ড লেটার্স পাবলিশার্স [1957]
151 p. 19 cm. Rs2.75
In Bengali.
Short stories.
I. Title.
PK1718.B2875P5 76–984024

Bandyopādhyāy, Yogīndrakumar.
Laying the foundation of "One world;" the international text-book institute at Brunswick. [Braunschweig, Internationales Schulbuch-Institut, 1957]
32 p. illus. 24 cm.
Microfiche (neg.) 1 sheet. 11 x 15 cm.
1. History–Textbooks. 2. Cooperation, Intellectual.
NN NUC74-38765

Bandyopādhyāẏa, Ajiteśa, 1933–
(Bītaṃsa)
বীতংস. [নাট্যকার] অজিতেশ বন্দ্যোপাধ্যায়. [কলিকাতা] জাতীয় সাহিত্য পরিষদ [1379, i.e. 1972]
115 p. 19 cm. Rs4.00
In Bengali.
A play based on Joseph Kesselring's Arsenic and old lace.

I. Kesselring, Joseph, 1902–1967. Arsenic and old lace. II. Title.

PK1730.13.A49B5 72–903309

Bandyopādhyāẏa, Amarendranātha.
(Kākiẏāṭ)
কাকিয়াৎ / শ্রীঅমরেন্দ্রনাথ বন্দ্যোপাধ্যায়. — 1. সংস্করণ. — কলকাতা : আলোক চক্র, 1974.
244 p. ; 22 cm.
In Bengali.
Short stories.
CONTENTS: কাকিয়াৎ.—বালিস্ মার্কা হুকুম.—ব্লাক আণ্ড হোয়াইট.—বিস্ফোরণ.—আত্মজ.—মেলেনি উত্তর.—ছাড়পত্র.—কালো সোনা.—একটি সকাল.—প্রহরী.—ভূতাবিষ্ট.
Rs15.00
I. Title.
PK1730.13.A494K3 75–905364

Bandyopādhyāẏa, Amarendranātha.
(Subanaśiri)
সুবনশিরি / অমরেন্দ্রনাথ বন্দ্যোপাধ্যায়. — কলিকাতা : রবীন্দ্র লাইব্রেরী, 1381 [1974]
14, 455 p. ; 22 cm.
In Bengali.
A novel.
Rs20.00 ($3.00U.S.)

I. Title.

PK1730.13.A494S9 75–901166

Bandyopādhyāẏa, Amiẏa Rañjana
see
Banerjee, Amiya Ranjan, 1927-

Bandyopādhyāẏa, Amiẏakumāra.
বাঁকুড়া জেলার পুরাকীর্তি. [লেখক] অমিয়কুমার বন্দ্যোপাধ্যায়. [কলিকাতা] পূর্ত বিভাগ, পশ্চিমবঙ্গ সরকার [1971]
140 p. illus., facsim., map. 22 cm. Rs3.75
In Bengali.
Bibliography: p. [135]–136.

1. Bankura, India (District)—Antiquities. I. Title.
Title romanized: Bāñkuṛā Jelāra purākīrti.

DS485.B4B35 73–922301

Bandyopādhyāẏa, Amiẏakumāra.
(Bāñkuṛā Jelāra purākīrti)
বাঁকুড়া জেলার পুরাকীর্তি / অমিয়কুমার বন্দ্যোপাধ্যায়. — 2. পরিমার্জিত ও পরিবর্ধিত সংস্করণ. — [কলিকাতা] : পূর্ত (পুরাতত্ত্ব) বিভাগ, পশ্চিমবঙ্গ সরকার, 1975.
147 p., [25] leaves of plates : ill., 1 fold. map ; 22 cm.
In Bengali.
Bibliography: p. [138]–139.
Includes index.
Rs4.50
1. Bankura, India (District)—Antiquities. I. Title.
DS485.B19B36 1975 76–900517

Bandyopādhyāẏa, Amiẏakumāra.
(Dekhā haẏa nāi)
দেখা হয় নাই. [লেখক] অমিয়কুমার বন্দ্যোপাধ্যায়. [1. সংস্করণ] কলিকাতা, আনন্দ পাবলিশার্স [1380 i.e. 1973]
266 p. illus., maps. 23 cm. Rs20.00
In Bengali.

1. West Bengal—Description and travel. 2. Villages—India—West Bengal. I. Title.

DS485.B493B36 73–906167

Bandyopādhyāẏa, Amiẏakumāra
see Mukhopādhyāẏa, Śyāmacānda. (Kocabihāra Jelāra purākīrti) 1974.

Bandyopādhyāẏa, Bhānu.
চাটনী. [লেখক ভানু বন্দ্যোপাধ্যায়] সম্পাদক বিক্রম রায়চৌধুরী. [1. সংস্করণ. কলিকাতা, বিক্রম রায় চৌধুরী, 1955]
90 p. illus. 19 cm.
In Bengali.

1. Rāẏacaudhurī, Bikrama, ed. I. Title.
Title romanized: Cāṭnī.

PK1718.B2878C3 74–218668

Bandyopādhyāẏa, Bhavendra Nātha
see
Banerjee, Bhavendra Nath, 1951-

Bandyopādhyāẏa, Bijaẏabhūshaṇa.
(Bhāratīẏadarśane muktibāda)
ভারতীয়দর্শনে মুক্তিবাদ / বিজয়ভূষণ বন্দ্যোপাধ্যায়. — 1. সংস্করণ. — কলিকাতা : পরেশনাথ বন্দ্যোপাধ্যায় : প্রাপ্তিস্থান, সাধনসমর কার্য্যালয়, 1361 [1954]
241, 6 p. ; 25 cm.
In Bengali.
"Thesis approved for the degree of doctor of philosophy in the University of Calcutta in 1952."
Bibliography: p. [3]–6 (last group)
1. Soul. 2. Philosophy, Indic. I. Title.
B132.S55B35 75–985594

Bandyopādhyāẏa, Bimalendu.
(Agniyugera mānusha)
অগ্নিযুগের মানুষ. [লেখক] বিমলেন্দু বন্দ্যোপাধ্যায়. [হাওড়া, শ্রীরণজিতকুমার বন্দ্যোপাধ্যায়]; পরিবেশক শ্যামল ষ্টোর্স, চন্দননগর [1965]
103 p. 24 cm. Rs2.00
In Bengali.

1. Bandyopadhyay, Basantakumar, 1886– I. Title.

DS481.B35B36 73–902679
SA

Bandyopādhyāẏa, Bimalendu.
মানুষ শরৎচন্দ্র. [লেখক] বিমলেন্দু বন্দ্যোপাধ্যায়. [1. সংস্করণ] কলিকাতা, বিশ্বজ্ঞান [1971]
98 p. port. 22 cm. Rs3.00
In Bengali.

1. Chatterji, Saratchandra, 1876–1938. I. Title.
Title romanized: Mānusha Śaraṯcandra.

PK1718.C45Z575 79–925141

Bandyopādhyāya, Bīreśvara, tr.
see Teller, Edward, 1908– Āmādera paramānukendrika bhabishyat. [1959]

Bandyopādhyāẏa, Bīreśvara, 1924–
(Bāṃlādeśera saṅa prasaṅge)
বাংলাদেশের সঙ প্রসঙ্গে. [লেখক] বীরেশ্বর বন্দ্যোপাধ্যায়. সুনীতিকুমার চট্টোপাধ্যায়ের ভূমিকা সহ. [Calcutta] এশিয়াটিক সোসাইটি, 1972.
18, 398 p. illus. 23 cm. (Asiatic Society monograph series, v. 24) Rs20.00 ($3.50U.S.)
Preface, foreword, and added t.p. in English.
In Bengali.
Includes bibliographical references.
1. Festivals—Bengal. 2. Processions. I. Title. II. Series: Asiatic Society, Calcutta. Monograph series, v. 24.
GT4076.A3B462 73–907425

Bandyopadhyaya, Bisvanatha
see
Bandyopadhyay, Bisvanath, 1934-
Banerjee, Biswanath, 1926-

Bandyopādhyāẏa, Debabrata.
[Yakhana jībana yekhāne]
যখন জীবন যেখানে. [লেখক] দেবব্রত বন্দ্যোপাধ্যায়. কলিকাতা, সারবান; [পরিবেশক মিত্রালয়, 1971]
93 p. 23 cm. Rs3.00
In Bengali.
A novel.

I. Title.

PK1730.13.A5118Y3 72–903012

Bandyopādhyāẏa, Debadulāla, comp.
(Bāṃlādeśera galpa)
বাংলাদেশের গল্প; [বাংলাদেশের তেইশজন গল্পকারের বাছাই গল্পের সংকলন] দেবদুলাল বন্দ্যোপাধ্যায় ও প্রণবেশ সেন সম্পাদিত. কলিকাতা, গ্রন্থ প্রকাশ [1379 i.e. 1972]
291 p. 23 cm. Rs12.00
In Bengali.

1. Short stories, Bengali—Bangladesh. I. Sena, Praṇabeśa, joint comp. II. Title.

PK1717.B3B3 73–905830

Bandyopādhyāẏa, Debāśisa.
(Bīrabhūmera Yama-paṭa o paṭuẏā)
বীরভূমের যম-পট ও পটুয়া. [লেখক] দেবাশিস বন্দ্যোপাধ্যায়. কলকাতা, সুবর্ণরেখা [1972]
9, 37, [1] p. illus. geneal. table. 23 cm. Rs4.00
In Bengali.
Bibliography: p. 37–[38]

1. Patas (Art). 2. Patuas—India—Birbhum (District) 3. Yama (Hindu deity)—Art. I. Title.

ND2048.B57B36 73–904512

Bandyopādhyāẏa, Debīprasāda.
(Chuṭīra dinera kabitā)
ছুটীর দিনের কবিতা / দেবীপ্রসাদ বন্দ্যোপাধ্যায়. — কলিকাতা : পশ্চিমবঙ্গ শিক্ষা অধিকার, 1957.
25 p. : ill. ; 25 cm.
In Bengali.

I. Title.

PZ90.B4B32 75–984838

Bandyopādhyāẏa, Debīprasāda.
(Śikārera bicitra kāhinī)
শিকারের বিচিত্র কাহিনী / দেবীপ্রসাদ বন্দ্যোপাধ্যায়. — কলকাতা : নব সাহিত্য প্রকাশ, 1381 [1974]
184 p., [5] leaves of plates : ill. ; 23 cm.
In Bengali.
Rs8.00

1. Hunting—India. I. Title.

SK235.B36 75–929549

Bandyopādhyāẏa, Dibyendu, comp.
(Nāgakeśara)
নাগকেশর; [সাম্প্রতিক ছোটগল্পের সংকলন] সম্পাদনায়: দিব্যেন্দু বন্দ্যোপাধ্যায়, শংকর দাশগুপ্ত [ও] দিলীপকুমার বন্দ্যোপাধ্যায়. কলকাতা, আনন্দধারা প্রকাশন [1971]
82 p. 22 cm. Rs6.00
In Bengali.
Short stories.

1. Short stories, Bengali. I. Das Gupta, Sankar, joint comp. II. Bandyopādhyāẏa, Dilīpakumāra, joint comp. III. Title.

PK1716.B28 72–901708

Bandyopādhyāya, Dilīpakumāra.
চোখের বাইরে. ₍লেখক₎ দিলীপকুমার বন্দ্যোপাধ্যায়. ₍কলকাতা, বিশ্বমন্দির প্রকাশনী₎; পরিবেশক গ্রন্থালয় ₍1970₎
111 p. 23 cm. Rs4.00
In Bengali.
Short stories.

I. Title.
Title romanized: Cokhera bāire.

PK1730.13.A512C6 74–916132

Bandyopādhyāya, Dilipakumara, joint comp.
see Bandyopādhyāya, Dibyendu, comp. (Nāgakeśara) [1971]

Bandyopādhyāya, Gaurīśaṅkara
see
Banerjee, Gourisankar.

Bandyopādhyāya, Gobindalāla.
(Sīmāntahīrā)
সীমান্তহীরা. ₍লেখক₎ গোবিন্দলাল বন্দ্যোপাধ্যায়. কলিকাতা, বাসন্তী বুক ষ্টল ₍1954₎
151 p. 19 cm.
In Bengali.
A novel.

I. Title.

PK1718.B2888S5 76–984025

Bandyopādhyāya, Gopeśvara.
(Gīta-prabeśikā)
গীত-প্রবেশিকা / গোপেশ্বর বন্দ্যোপাধ্যায়. — 3. সংস্করণ. — কলিকাতা : বসুমতী-সাহিত্য-মন্দির, 1360 ₍1953₎
132 p., ₍1₎ leaf of plates : port. ; 25 cm.
In Bengali.
Includes music in letter notation.

1. Music, Indic—History and criticism. I. Title.

ML338.B27 75–985595

Bandyopādhyāya, Gopeśvara.
সঙ্গীতচন্দ্রিকা. ₍লেখক₎ গোপেশ্বর বন্দ্যোপাধ্যায়. ₍রমেশচন্দ্র বন্দ্যোপাধ্যায় সম্পাদিত. রবীন্দ্রভারতী সংস্করণ₎ কলিকাতা, রবীন্দ্রভারতী বিশ্ববিদ্যালয় ₍1374 i.e. 1967 or 8₎
16, 1115 p. 26 cm. Rs15.00
In Bengali and Hindi.
Includes short biographical sketches of the musicians.
Includes music in letter notation.
1. Songs, Bengali. 2. Songs, Hindi. I. Bandyopādhyāya, Rameśacandra, ed. II. Title.
Title romanized: Saṅgītacandrikā.

M1808.B349 73–919647

Bandyopādhyāya, Hārādhana.
(Bāṃlāra chele)
বাংলার ছেলে. ₍লেখক₎ শ্রীহারাধন বন্দ্যোপাধ্যায়. ₍কলিকাতা, শ্রীগুরু লাইব্রেরী, 1946?₎
251 p. 19 cm. Rs2.00
In Bengali.
A novel.

I. Title.

PK1718.B289B3 76–984026

Bandyopadhyaya, Haricharan.
(Pāliprabeśa)
পালিপ্রবেশ : শব্দানুশাসন / হরিচরণ বন্দ্যোপাধ্যায়. — কলিকাতা : মহাবোধি সোসাইটি, 1930–
v. ; 19 cm.
In Bengali.

1. Pali language—Grammar. I. Title.

PK1018.B4B3 75–985596

Bandyopādhyāya, Hemendranātha, 1931–
(Janmāntarabāda : rahasya o romāñca)
জন্মান্তরবাদ: রহস্য ও রোমাঞ্চ. ₍লেখক₎ হেমেন্দ্রনাথ বন্দ্যোপাধ্যায়. উপস্থাপক জ্যোতির্ময় দাশ. ₍কলিকাতা₎ অপরূপা; ₍একমাত্র পরিবেশক সুহাস পাবলিশিং হাউস, 1972₎
6, 201, 5 p. illus. 23 cm. Rs10.00
In Bengali.

1. Psychical research. I. Das, Jyotirmay, 1940– ed. II. Title.

BF1038.B4B36 72–907143

Bandyopādhyāya, Jānakīkumāra
see
Banerjee, Janaki Kumar, 1931-

Bandyopādhyāya, Jayanta.
(Jāhnabi Yamunāra utsa sandhāne)
জাহ্নবী যমুনার উৎস সন্ধানে. ₍লেখক₎ শ্রীজয়ন্ত বন্দ্যোপাধ্যায়. কলিকাতা, রীডার্স কর্ণার ₍1956₎
7, 182 p. 21 cm.
In Bengali.

1. Pilgrims and pilgrimages—Himalaya Mountains. I. Title.

DS485.H6B27 76–984027

Bandyopādhyāya, Jyotu.
(Citābhasma)
চিতাভস্ম. ₍নাট্যকার₎ জ্যোতু বন্দ্যোপাধ্যায়. কলিকাতা, রবীন্দ্র লাইব্রেরী ₍1379, i.e. 1972₎
88 p. 19 cm. Rs3.50
In Bengali.

I. Title.

PK1718.B267C5 72–904508

Bandyopādhyāya, Jyotu.
জ্যোতু বন্দ্যোপাধ্যায়ের চন্দ্রবিন্দু, বিসর্গ; দু'টি জনপ্রিয় একাঙ্ক একত্রে. কলকাতা, অপেরা; পরিবেশক নব গ্রন্থ কুটির ₍1378, i.e. 1971₎
85 p. 19 cm. Rs3.50
"সাংবাদিক ও নাট্য সমালোচকদের বিচারে ১৯৭০-এর শ্রেষ্ঠ নাট্যকার 'দিশারী' পুরস্কারপ্রাপ্ত."
In Bengali.
I. Title: Candrabindu. II. Title: Bisarga.
Title romanized: Jyotu Bandyopādhyāyera Candrabindu, Bisarga.

PK1718.B2895C3 77–925146

Bandyopādhyāya, Jyotu.
(Kabara theke balachi)
কবর থেকে বলছি; বাংলা দেশের মুক্তি যুদ্ধের পটভূমিকায় একাঙ্ক নাটক. ₍লেখক₎ জ্যোতু বন্দ্যোপাধ্যায়. কলিকাতা, লিপিকা ₍1971₎
29, 33 p. 23 cm. Rs3.00
In Bengali.
CONTENTS.—কবর থেকে বলছি.—বাজিকর.

I. Title. II. Title: Bājikara.

PK1718.B2895K3 70–928279

Bandyopādhyāya, Jyotu.
(Nihata niyati)
নিহত নিয়তি. ₍নাট্যকার₎ জ্যোতু বন্দ্যোপাধ্যায়. কলিকাতা, রবীন্দ্র লাইব্রেরী ₍1378, i.e. 1971₎
101 p. 19 cm. Rs3.00
In Bengali.

I. Title.

PK1718.B2895N5 72–900219

Bandyopādhyāya, Kāli Kumāra.
(Kenā golāma)
কেনা গোলাম. ₍লেখক₎ কালি কুমার বন্দ্যোপাধ্যায়. ₍কলিকাতা₎ নব বলাকা প্রকাশনী ₍1960₎
219 p. 22 cm.
In Bengali.
A novel.

I. Title.

PK1730.13.A514K4 76–984028

Bandyopadhyaya, Kalyani, 1935-
Agricultural development in China and India : a comparative study / Kalyani Bandyopadhyaya. — New Delhi : Wiley Eastern, c1976.
viii, 204 p. ; 23 cm.
Bibliography: p. ₍185₎-199.
Includes index.
Rs30.00
1. Agriculture and state—China. 2. Agriculture and state—India. I. Title.
HD2097.B36 338.1'851 77-901879
77 MARC

Bandyopadhyaya, Kalyani, 1935-
Agricultural development in China and India : a comparative study / Kalyani Bandyppadhyaya. — New York : Wiley, c1976.
viii, 204 p. ; 23 cm.
"A Halsted Press book."
Bibliography: p. ₍185₎-199.
Includes index.
ISBN 0-470-98931-9
1. Agriculture and state—China. 2. Agriculture and state—India. I. Title.
HD2067.B36 338.1'851 76-26958
76 MARC

Bandyopadhyaya, Kamal, 1912–
ভারত দর্শন. ₍লেখক₎ কমল বন্দ্যোপাধ্যায়. কলিকাতা, ক্লাসিক প্রেস ₍1963₎
v. illus., maps. 22 cm.
In Bengali.
PARTIAL CONTENTS.—[2] মাদ্রাজ.—[3] কেরল.

1. India—Description and travel—1947– I. Title.
Title transliterated: Bhārata darśana.

DS414.B37 S A 64-6423
PL 480 : I-B-1322

Bandyopādhyāya, Kaṇikā.
(Rabīndrasaṃgīta)
রবীন্দ্রসংগীত : কাব্য ও সুর / কণিকা বন্দ্যোপাধ্যায় ও বীরেন্দ্রচন্দ্র বন্দ্যোপাধ্যায়. — কলিকাতা : শঙ্খ প্রকাশন, 1382 ₍1975₎
14, 219, 4 p., ₍1₎ leaf of plates : port. ; 22 cm.
In Bengali.
Rs18.00

1. Tagore, Rabindranath, Sir, 1861–1941—Poetic works. I. Banerjea, Beerendra Chandra, 1917– joint author.

PK1727.P6B3 75–908167

Bandyopādhyāya, Kanikā, joint author
see Banerjea, Beerendra Chandra, 1917-
Rabīndra-saṅgītera nānādika. ₍1962₎

Bandyopādhyāya, Karuṇānidhāna.
(Trayī)
ত্রয়ী. ₍লেখক₎ শ্রীকরুণানিধান বন্দ্যোপাধ্যায়. ₍1. সংস্করণ₎ কলিকাতা, রঞ্জন পাবলিশিং হাউস ₍1360 i.e. 1954₎
8, 120 p. port. 23 cm.
In Bengali.
Poems.

I. Title.

PK1718.B2898T7 75–984499

Bandyopadhyaya, Krishnadhan, 1846–1904.
(Gītasūtrasāra)
গীতসূত্রসার : সংগীতের প্রকৃত উৎপত্তি এবং যাবতীয় মূলসূত্র ও সাধনোপদেশ সম্বলিত কণ্ঠে গান শিক্ষার সহজ উপায় / কৃষ্ণধন বন্দ্যোপাধ্যায়. — 4. সংস্করণ. — কলিকাতা : এ. মুখার্জী, 1382– ₍1976–
v. ; 23 cm.
First published in 1885.
In Bengali.
Rs20.00 (v. 1)

1. Music, Indic—History and criticism. I. Title.

ML338.B2752 76–901096

Bandyopādhyāya, Kṛśānu.
(Ādima lipsā)
আদিম লিপ্সা. ₍লেখক₎ কৃশানু বন্দ্যোপাধ্যায়. কলিকাতা, সাহিত্য প্রকাশ ₍1969₎
140 p. 23 cm. Rs4.50
In Bengali.
A novel.

I. Title.

PK1718.B29A67 70–905495

Bandyopādhyāya, Kṛśānu.
(Bibarṇa Bulabula)
বিবর্ণ বুলবুল. ₍লেখক₎ কৃশানু বন্দ্যোপাধ্যায়. কলিকাতা, রবীন্দ্র লাইব্রেরী ₍1378, i.e. 1972₎
141 p. 23 cm. Rs5.00
In Bengali.
Short stories.

I. Title.

PK1718.B29B53 72–904423

Bandyopādhyāya, Kṛśānu.
চুপি চুপি আঁধারে. ₍লেখক₎ কৃশানু বন্দ্যোপাধ্যায়. কলিকাতা, প্রফুল্ল গ্রন্থাগার ₍1969₎
156 p. 23 cm. 5.00
In Bengali.
A novel.

I. Title.
Title romanized: Cupi cupi ām̐dhāre.

PK1718.B29C8 78–906372

Bandyopādhyāya, Kṛśānu.
(Jānu, bhānu, kṛśānu)
জানু, ভানু, কৃশানু. ₍লেখক₎ কৃশানু বন্দ্যোপাধ্যায়. কলিকাতা, সাহিত্য প্রকাশ ₍1379 i.e. 1972₎
375 p. 23 cm. Rs12.50
In Bengali.

I. Title.

PK1718.B29J3 72–908638

Bandyopādhyāya, Kṛśānu.
ললিত পয়ার. ₍লেখক₎ কৃশানু বন্দ্যোপাধ্যায়. ₍কলিকাতা, সলিল-কুমার নন্দী₎; একমাত্র পরিবেশক জি. জি. বুক ডিস্ট্রিবিউটিং কোম্পানী ₍1377, i.e. 1970₎
118 p. 23 cm. Rs4.00
In Bengali.
A novel.

I. Title.
Title romanized: Lalita paẏāra.

PK1718.B29L25 71–916150

Bandyopādhyāya, Kṛśānu.
নিহত নায়িকা, নিহত নায়ক. ₍লেখক₎ কৃশানু বন্দ্যোপাধ্যায়. কলি-কাতা, দে'জ পাবলিশিং; ₍প্রাপ্তিস্থান: দে বুক স্টোর, 1971₎
262 p. 23 cm. Rs10.00
In Bengali.
Short stories.

I. Title.
Title romanized: Nihata nāẏikā, nihata nāẏaka.

PK1718.B29N5 71–923930

Bandyopādhyāya, Kṛśānu.
রক্তাক্ত খাইবার. ₍লেখক₎ কৃশানু বন্দ্যোপাধ্যায়. কলিকাতা, সাহিত্য প্রকাশ ₍1377, i.e. 1970₎
280 p. 23 cm. Rs9.00
In Bengali.
A novel.

1. Babar, Emperor of Hindustan, 1483–1530—Fiction. I. Title.
Title romanized: Raktākta Khāibāra.

PK1718.B29R36 79–916014

Bandyopādhyāya, Kṛśānu.
(Sedina śaila śikhare)
সেদিন শৈল শিখরে. ₍লেখক₎ কৃশানু বন্দ্যোপাধ্যায়. ₍1. সংস্করণ₎ কলিকাতা, রূপরেখা ₍1380 i.e. 1973₎
149 p. 22 cm. Rs6.00
In Bengali.
A novel.

I. Title.

PK1718.B29S4 73–905125

Bandyopādhyāya, Kṛśānu.
(Śuka naẏa, śāri naẏa)
শুক নয়, শারি নয়. ₍লেখক₎ কৃশানু বন্দ্যোপাধ্যায়. কলিকাতা, রবীন্দ্র লাইব্রেরী ₍1378, i.e. 1971₎
157 p. 23 cm. Rs5.00
In Bengali.
A novel.

I. Title.

PK1718.B29S8 72–900188

Bandyopādhyāya, Kṛśānu.
(Tūnera bāire tira)
তূণের বাইরে তীর. ₍লেখক₎ কৃশাণু বন্দ্যোপাধ্যায়. কলিকাতা, রোমাঞ্চ ₍1378, i.e. 1972₎
183 p. 23 cm. Rs6.00
In Bengali.
Short stories.
CONTENTS: তূণের বাইরে তীর.—ইন্দ্র, চন্দ্র, বরুণ.

I. Title.

PK1718.B29T75 72–904298

Bandyopādhyāya, Mānabendra.
(Ardheka śikārī)
অর্ধেক শিকারী / মানবেন্দ্র বন্দ্যোপাধ্যায়. — 1. সংস্করণ. — কল-কাতা : সিগনেট প্রেস, 1382 ₍1975₎
83 p. ; 22 cm.
In Bengali.
Poems.
Rs5.00

I. Title.

PK1730.13.A5143A9 75–907133

Bandyopādhyāya, Mānabendra.
রবীন্দ্রনাথ: শিশুসাহিত্য. ₍লেখক₎ মানবেন্দ্র বন্দ্যোপাধ্যায়. কল-কাতা, সংস্কৃত পুস্তক ভাণ্ডার ₍1377, i.e. 1970₎
103 p. 23 cm. 5.00
In Bengali.
Includes bibliographical references.

1. Tagore, Sir Rabindranath, 1861–1941. I. Title.
Title romanized: Rabīndranātha: śiśusāhitya.

PK1727.J8B3 77–913983

Bandyopādhyāya, Maṇikā Rahamāna, 1949–
(Bhālabāsāya mahāmārī)
ভালবাসায় মহামারী. ₍কবি₎ মণিকা রহমান বন্দ্যোপাধ্যায়. ভাট-পাড়া, ২৪ পরগণা ₍জেলা₎ সুমন্ত প্রকাশন ₍1973₎
36 p. 22 cm. Rs2.50
In Bengali.

I. Title.

PK1730.13.A5144B5 74–900614

Bandyopādhyāya, Nārāyaṇa.
(Biplabera sandhāne)
বিপ্লবের সন্ধানে. ₍লেখক₎ নারায়ণ বন্দ্যোপাধ্যায়. কলিকাতা, ডি. এন. বি. এ. ব্রাদার্স ₍1967₎
8, 400 p. 23 cm. Rs13.00
In Bengali.

1. Bengal—Hist. I. Title.

DS485.B49B3 S A 68–9828

PL 480: I-B-3507

Bandyopādhyāya, Narendranātha.
(Rakta-biplabera eka adhyāya)
রক্ত-বিপ্লবের এক অধ্যায় / নরেন্দ্রনাথ বন্দ্যোপাধ্যায়. — 1. সংস্করণ. — চন্দননগর : বিমলেন্দু বন্দ্যোপাধ্যায়, 1361 ₍1954₎
11, 154, 4 p. ; 19 cm.
In Bengali.

1. Chandernagor, India—History. I. Title.

DS486.C34B36 75–985597

Bandyopādhyāya, Nīlaratana.
(Ārya-Bhāratīya samājatantrabāda)
আর্য-ভারতীয় সমাজতন্ত্রবাদ = Indo-Aryan socialism / নীল-রতন বন্দ্যোপাধ্যায়. — কলিকাতা : কৃষ্ণরাণী দেবী : প্রাপ্তিস্থান সংসঙ্গী মিলনী, 1970.
82 p. ; 19 cm.
In Bengali.

1. Socialism in India. I. Title. II. Title: Indo-Aryan socialism.

HX392.B25 75–985598

Bandyopādhyāya, Nīlaratana.
(Sabhyatāra jaẏaẏātrā)
সভ্যতার জয়যাত্রা / নীলরতন বন্দ্যোপাধ্যায়. — কলিকাতা : অপূর্ব্ব কুমার ঘোষ, ₍pref. 1359 i.e. 1952₎
50 p. ; 18 cm.
In Bengali.
Errata slip inserted.

1. Anukūlacandra, 1888–1969. I. Title.

BL1175.A56B36 75–985599

Bandyopādhyāya, Nīlaratana.
(Śrīśrīṭhākura Anukūlacandrera jībana-kathā)
শ্রীশ্রীঠাকুর অনুকূলচন্দ্রের জীবন-কথা / নীলরতন বন্দ্যোপাধ্যায় প্রণীত. — রঙ্কিণী মহলা, বর্দ্ধমান : রাধানাথ বন্দ্যোপাধ্যায়, ₍pref. 1360–1361 i.e. 1953–1954₎
3 v. ; 19 cm.
In Bengali.

1. Anukūlacandra, 1888–1969, in fiction, drama, poetry, etc. I. Title.

PK1718.B2932S7 75–985600

S A

Bandyopādhyāya, Nīradabaraṇa, joint author
see Dasgupta, Santikumar, 1914– (Bāṃlādeśe naba sūryodaya) [1972]

Bandyopādhyāya, Nṛpendracandra
see
Banerji, Nripendra Chandra, 1885-1949.

Bandyopādhyāya, Paṅkajakumāra.
মুজিবরের বাংলা. ₍লেখক₎ পঙ্কজকুমার বন্দ্যোপাধ্যায়. ₍কলিকাতা, অপরূপা প্রকাশনী₎; পরিবেশক সুহাস পাবলিশিং হাউস ₍1378, i.e. 1971₎
1 v. (various pagings) illus. 23 cm. Rs10.00
In Bengali.

1. East Pakistan—Politics and government. 2. Pakistan—Politics and government. I. Title.
Title romanized: Mujibarera Bāṃlā.

DS485.B492B27 79–922994

Bandyopādhyāya, Paṅkajakumāra.
প্রেম দাও. ₍লেখক₎ পঙ্কজকুমার বন্দ্যোপাধ্যায়. কলিকাতা, অপ-রূপা ₍1970₎
143 p. 23 cm. Rs5.00
In Bengali.
Short stories.

I. Title.
Title romanized: Prema dāo.

PK1730.13.A5146P7 73–923037

Bandyopādhyāya, Pankajakumāra, joint author
see Caudhurī, Biśvanātha. (Hājara bacharera sādhu-santa.) 1972-

Bandyopādhyāya, Pareśa.
কী বেইমান. [কবি] পরেশ বন্দ্যোপাধ্যায়. [কলিকাতা, কবয়]; পরিবেশক সিগনেট বুক শপ [1377, i.e. 1970]
77 p. 19 cm. Rs3.00
In Bengali.

I. Title. Title romanized: Kī beimāna.

PK1730.13.A51465K5 79–922663

Bandyopādhyāya, Pārtha.
উজান; একাঙ্ক সংকলন. [নাট্যকার] পার্থ বন্দ্যোপাধ্যায়. [1. সংস্করণ] কলিকাতা, রবীন্দ্র লাইব্রেরী [1378, i.e. 1971]
142 p. 19 cm. Rs4.00
In Bengali.

I. Title. Title romanized: Ujāna.

PK1730.13.A5147U35 70–922319

Bandyopādhyāya, Pārthapratima, joint author
see Bandopadhyaya, Saroj. (Komale gāndhāre Bishṇu De) 1382 [1975]

Bandyopādhyāya, Patitapābana
see
Bandyopadhyay, Patitpaban, 1911-

Bandyopādhyāya, Rameśacandra, ed.
see Bandyopādhyāya, Gopeśvara. Saṅgītacandrikā. [1374 i. e. 1967 or 8]

Bandyopādhyāya, Raṅgalāla
see
Banerji, Rangalal, 1826-1887.

Bandyopadhyaya, Sachindranath, 1920–
(Bidiśāra niśā)
বিদিশার নিশা / শচীন্দ্রনাথ বন্দ্যোপাধ্যায়. — কলিকাতা : ক্লাসিক প্রেস, 1366 [1959]
163 p. ; 22 cm.
In Bengali.
A novel.

I. Title.

PK1718.B294B5 75–985601

Bandyopadhyaya, Sachindranath, 1920–
(Janapadabadhū)
জনপদবধূ : নাটক / শচীন্দ্রনাথ বন্দ্যোপাধ্যায়. — কলিকাতা : রবীন্দ্র লাইব্রেরী, 1381 [1974]
132 p. ; 18 cm.
In Bengali.
Rs5.00

I. Title.

PK1718.B294J36 1974 75–900702

Bandyopadhyaya, Sachindranath, 1920–
(Madhya dinera gāna)
মধ্য দিনের গান / শচীন্দ্রনাথ বন্দ্যোপাধ্যায়. — কলিকাতা : প্রাইমা পাবলিকেশনস, 1368 [1961]
154 p. ; 23 cm.
In Bengali.
A novel.

I. Title.

PK1718.B294M3 75–985603

Bandyopadhyaya, Sachindranath, 1920–
(Nagaranandinīra rūpakathā)
নগরনন্দিনীর রূপকথা. [লেখক] শচীন্দ্রনাথ বন্দ্যোপাধ্যায়. কলকাতা, গ্রন্থালয় [1973]
180 p. 23 cm. Rs6.00
In Bengali.
A novel.

I. Title.

PK1718.B294N2 73–904588

Bandyopadhyaya, Sachindranath, 1920–
(Patralekhāra upākhyāna)
পত্রলেখার উপাখ্যান / শচীন্দ্রনাথ বন্দ্যোপাধ্যায়. — কলিকাতা : রামায়ণী প্রকাশ ভবন : পরিবেশক স্যাঙ্গুইন পাবলিশার্স কনসার্ন, 1381 [1975]
143 p. ; 22 cm.
In Bengali.
A novel.
Rs10.00

I. Title.

PK1718.B294P3 75–905540

Bandyopadhyaya, Sachindranath. 1920–
সমুদ্রের গান. [লেখক] শচীন্দ্রনাথ বন্দ্যোপাধ্যায়. [কলিকাতা] ক্যালকাটা বুক ক্লাব [1362, i.e. 1955]
154 p. 19 cm.
In Bengali.
A novel.

I. Title. Title romanized: Samudrera gāna.

PK1718.B294S24 72–203198

Bandyopadhyaya, Sachindranath, 1920–
(Śāntira svākshara)
শান্তির স্বাক্ষর. [লেখক] শচীন্দ্রনাথ বন্দ্যোপাধ্যায়. কলকাতা, করুণা প্রকাশনী [1368, i.e. 1961]
127 p. 23 cm.
In Bengali.
A novel.

I. Title.

PK1718.B294S28 76–984018

Bandyopadhyaya, Sachindranath, 1920–
সীমাস্বর্গ. [লেখক] শচীন্দ্রনাথ বন্দ্যোপাধ্যায়. কলিকাতা, এসোসিয়েটেড পাবলিশার্স [195–]
137 p. 21 cm.
In Bengali.
A novel.

I. Title. Title romanized: Sīmāsvarga.

PK1718.B294S5 1950z 72–203197

Bandyopadhyaya, Sachindranath, 1920–
(Sūryera santāna)
সূর্যের সন্তান. [লেখক] শচীন্দ্রনাথ বন্দ্যোপাধ্যায়. [1. সংস্করণ] কলকাতা, গ্রন্থম্ [1968]
142 p. 22 cm. Rs5.00
In Bengali.
A novel.

I. Title.

PK1718.B294S85 S A 68–9028

PL 480: I-B-3393

Bandyopadhyaya, Sachindranath, 1920–
(Tomāra patākā)
তোমার পতাকা / শচীন্দ্রনাথ বন্দ্যোপাধ্যায়. — কলিকাতা : শঙ্কর প্রকাশন, 1382 [1975]
390 p. ; 22 cm.
In Bengali.
Bibliography: p. 389–390.
A novel.

1. India—History—19th century—Fiction. 2. India—History—20th century—Fiction. I. Title.

PK1718.B294T6 75–908535

Bandyopadhyaya, Sachindranath, 1920- ed.
see Mukhopadhyay, Balai Chand, 1899- [Works] Banaphula racanabali. [1973-

Bandyopādhyāya, Sanat
see
Bandyopadhyay, Sanat, 1933-

Bandyopādhyāya, Saṅkara
see
Banerjee, Sankar, 1937-

Bandyopādhyāya, Satya.
নহবত. [নাট্যকার] সত্য বন্দ্যোপাধ্যায়. কলি[কাতা] জাতীয় সাহিত্য পরিষদ [1377, i.e. 1971]
110 p. 19 cm. Rs4.00
In Bengali.

I. Title. Title romanized: Nahabata.

PK1718.B2964N3 77–920576

Bandyopādhyāya, Saurīndranātha, comp.
see Banerjee, Bibhuti Bhusan, 1896?-1950. (Sahaja mānusha Bibhūtibhūshaṇa) 1970.

Bandyopādhyāya, Śibadāsa
see
Bandyopadhyay, Shibdas, 1927-

Bandyopādhyāya, Sumitrā.
(Āphrikāra citra)
আফ্রিকার চিত্র / সুমিত্রা বন্দ্যোপাধ্যায় ; ভূমিকা সুনীতিকুমার চট্টোপাধ্যায়. — কলিকাতা : জিজ্ঞাসা, [pref. 1362 i.e. 1955]
53 p. : ill. ; 20 cm.
In Bengali.

1. Africa—Social life and customs. I. Title.

DT14.B33 75–985604

Bandyopādhyāya, Sunīla
see
Bandyopadhyay, Sunil, 1939-

Bandyopadhyaya, Suprasanna, ed.
see Cakrabarti, Santimaya. Riyam. 1968.

Bandyopādhyāya, Śyāmalendu.
(Samudrasnāna)
সমুদ্রস্নান / শ্যামলেন্দু বন্দ্যোপাধ্যায়. — 1. সংস্করণ. — কলিকাতা : আনন্দ পাবলিশার্স, 1976.
92 p. ; 23 cm.
In Bengali.
A novel.
Rs5.00

I. Title.

PK1730.13.A5237S2 76–901051

Bandyopādhyāya, Tapana.
[Bhābanāya sāmpratika śabdaguli]
ভাবনায় সাম্প্রতিক শব্দগুলি. [কবি] তপন বন্দ্যোপাধ্যায়. পূর্ব পুটিয়ারী, 24 পরগণা [জিলা] অর্ণব প্রকাশনী [1971]
48 p. 23 cm. Rs2.50
In Bengali.

I. Title.

PK1730.13.B524B5 1971 70–927953

Bandyopādhyāya, Tārādāsa.
Efficient optimum savings programme in a finite time horizon / Taradas Bandyopadhyay. -- Hamilton, Ont. : Dept. of Economics, McMaster University, 1975.
19 leaves. -- (Working paper - Dept. of Economics, McMaster University ; no. 75-10)
Bibliography: leaves 18-19.
1. Saving and investment--Mathematical models. I. Title. II. Series: McMaster University, Hamilton, Ont. Dept. of Economics. Working paper series ; no. 75-10.
CaOTU NUC77-87957

Bandyopādhyāẏa, Tārādāsa.
[Kājala]
কাজল. [লেখক] তারাদাস বন্দ্যোপাধ্যায়. কলিকাতা, গ্রন্থপ্রকাশ [1378, i.e. 1972]
12, 185 p. 23 cm. Rs7.00
In Bengali.
A novel.

I. Title.

PK1730.13.A525K3 72-902714

Bandyopādhyāẏa, Tārādāsa
see Banerjee, Bibhuti Bhusan, 1896?-1950. (Anaśvara). [1379 i. e. 1972]

Bandyopādhyāẏa, Tārādāsa, ed.
see Banerjee, Bibhuti Bhusan, 1896?-1950. Bibhuti-racanabali. [1377- , i. e. 1970-

Bandyopādhyāẏa, Tulasīkumāra
see
Banerjee, Tulshi Kumar.

Bandyopādhyāẏa, Tushāra, 1939-
(Ḍheu oṭhe Mekaṅe. Padmāẏa)
ঢেউ ওঠে মেকঙে, পদ্মায়. [কবি] তুষার বন্দ্যোপাধ্যায়. [1. সংস্করণ] কলিকাতা, বিশ্বজ্ঞান [1972]
32 p. 22 cm. Rs2.50
In Bengali.

I. Title.

PK1730.13.A527D5 73-900047

Bandyopādhyāẏa, Umāśaṅkara
see
Banerjee, Umasankar, 1948-

Bandyopādhyāẏa, Yamunā
see
Bandyopadhyay, Jamuna, 1931-

Bandyopadyaya, A.
see India (Republic). Laws, statutes, etc. Law of industrial disputes... Calcutta, Eastern book agency, 1972.

Bandyopadyaya, A.
see Jagadeesh, T K A guide to: the Employees' family pension scheme, 1971. Calcutta, Eastern Book Agency, 1971.

Bane, Allyne.
Creative clothing construction, [3d ed.] New York, McGraw-Hill [1973]
xiv, 529 p. illus. 24 cm.
First published in 1956 under title: Creative sewing.
1. Dressmaking. I. Title.
TT515.B33 1972 646.4 70-38730
ISBN 0-07-003615-2 MARC

Bane, Allyne.
Tailoring. 3d ed. New York, McGraw-Hill [1974]
xii, 538 p. illus. 24 cm. $12.95
1. Tailoring (Women's) I. Title.
TT519.5.B36 1974 646.4'5 74-5755
ISBN 0-07-003608-X MARC

Bane, Bernard M
Is President John F. Kennedy alive ... and well ? / by Bernard M. Bane. — 4th ed., rev. — Boston : BMB Pub. Co., 1974, c1973.
iv, 51 p. : ill. ; 23 cm.
ISBN 0-9600164-4-9 : $2.00
1. Bane, Bernard M. I. Title.
CT275.B173A33 1974 973.922 75-303177
MARC

Bane, Bernard M
Is President John F. Kennedy alive ... and well? / By Bernard M. Bane. -- 5th ed., rev. — Boston : BMB Pub. Co., 1975.
iv, 75 p. ; 23 cm.
Includes bibliographical references.
ISBN 0-9600164-4-9 : $3.00
1. Bane, Bernard M. I. Title.
CT275.B173A33 1975 973.922 75-328822
75 MARC

Bane, Bernard M
Is President John F. Kennedy alive ... and well? / By Bernard M. Bane. — 6th ed., rev. — Boston : BMB Pu[b]. Co., 1976.
iv, 99 p. ; 23 cm.
Includes bibliographical references.
ISBN 0-9600164-4-9 : $3.00
1. Bane, Bernard M. I. Title.
CT275.B36515A33 1976 001.9 76-21807
76 MARC

Bane, Charles A 1913-
The electrical equipment conspiracies; the treble damage actions [by] Charles A. Bane. New York, Federal Legal Publications [1973]
554 p. illus. 24 cm. $17.50
Includes bibliographical references.
1. Trusts, Industrial—United States—Law. 2. Electric machinery industry—Prices—United States. I. Title.
KF1890.E4B3 343'.73'078 73-75126
ISBN 0-87945-023-1 MARC

Bane, J. Donald.
see Death and ministry ... New York, Seabury Press, [1975]

Bane, John McGuire.
Barotropic and baroclinic coastal trapped waves in an upwelling frontal zone / by John McGuire Bane, Jr. -- [Tallahassee, Fla.] : Bane, 1975.
x, 112 leaves : ill. ; 29 cm.
Thesis (Ph.D.)--Florida State University.
Bibliography: leaves 107-112.
1. Dissertations, Academic--F.S.U.--Oceanography. 2. Ocean waves. I. Title.
FTaSU NUC77-88827

Bane, Mary Jo.
The effects of structure: a study of first grade children in open and traditional classrooms. Cambridge, 1972.
viii, 182 l.
Thesis (Ed.D.)—Harvard University.
1. Education—Experiment methods. 2. Education, Primary—Curricula. I. Title.
MH-Ed NUC73-34527

Bane, Mary Jo.
Here to stay : American families in the twentieth century / Mary Jo Bane. — New York : Basic Books, c1976.
xvi, 195 p. ; 24 cm.
Bibliography: p. [176]-186.
Includes index.
ISBN 0-465-02927-2 : $11.95
1. Family—United States. I. Title.
HQ536.B3 301.42'0973 76-44877
76 MARC

Bane, Mary Jo.
see The "Inequality" controversy ... New York, Basic Books, [1975]

Bane, Mary Jo
see Walker, Deborah Klein. The quality of the Head Start planned variation data. Cambridge, Huron Institute, 1973.

Bane, Pierre Cabiac de
see
Cabiac, Pierre.

Bane, Richard William.
The composition of the Roman Senate in 44 B.C. [n.p.] 1971.
iii, 133 l. 29 cm.
Thesis—University of Southern California.
Typewritten.
1. Rome. Senate. I. Title.
CLSU NUC74-128862

Bane, Suda Lorena, 1886-1952, ed.
The blockade of Germany after the armistice, 1918-1919; selected documents of the Supreme Economic Council, Superior Blockade Council, American Relief Administration, and other wartime organizations. Selected and edited by Suda Lorena Bane and Ralph Haswell Lutz. New York, H. Fertig, 1972 [c1970]
viii, 874 p. front. 24 cm.
Reprint of the 1942 ed., which was originally issued as Publication no. 16 of the Hoover Library on War, Revolution, and Peace.
Includes bibliographical references.

1. European War, 1914-1918—Blockades. 2. European War, 1914-1918—Food question—Germany. 3. European War, 1914-1918—Armistices. I. Lutz, Ralph Haswell, 1886-1968, joint ed. II. Title. III. Series: Stanford University. Hoover Institution on War, Revolution, and Peace. Publications, no. 16.
D581.B28 1972 940.4'52 79-80520
MARC

Bane, William, joint author
see Traylor, D Reginald. Creative teaching. [Houston, University of Houston, 1972]

Banea, Ion.
Opere complete. [München] Editia Monumentul MM, 1970.
1 v. (various pagings) illus., ports. (Colecţia "Omul nou")
Introduction by Horia Sima.
1. Legionary movement, Romania. 2. Romania—Hist.—Sources.
PPiU NUC73-126297

Banéat, Paul.
Le Département d'Ille-et-Vilaine : histoire, archéologie, monuments ... / Paul Banéat, ... — 3e [i. e. 2e] éd. / revue par Henri Queffélec. — Paris : Guénégaud, 1973.
4 v. : ill. ; 27 cm. F 74-6516
Reprint of the 1927 ed. published by Larcher, Rennes.
Includes bibliographical references.
1. Ille-et-Vilaine, France (Dept.) I. Queffélec, Henri, 1910- ed. II. Title.
DC611.I 3B36 1973 914.4'15'03 74-186647
MARC

Banegas, Estela Díaz
see Díaz Banegas, Estela.

Banek, Yvette Santiago.
see Saunders, Rubie. Quick and easy housekeeping. New York, F. Watts, 1977.

Banel, Joseph.
Lee Wong, boy detective. Drawings by Ed Malsberg. Champaign, Ill., Garrard Pub. Co. [1972]
62 p. col. illus. 23 cm. $2.89
SUMMARY: After a girl's personality changes drastically, a boy and his monkey investigate the mystery.
[1. Mystery stories] I. Malsberg, Edward, illus. II. Title.
PZ7.B2213Le [E] 72-1923
ISBN 0-8116-6967-X MARC

(Banenu)
בנינו. [בית אלפא, קיבוץ בית אלפא, 1968]
187 p. illus. 22 cm.
1. Bet-Alefa, Israel—Biography. I. Bet-Alefa, Israel.
DS110.B392B36 74-950461

Baner, Mabel.
Cocina vegetariana; 1.150 platos sanos y nutritivos. Las Fonts de Tarrasa, Editorial Sintes [1974]
271 p. 22 cm. (Biblioteca naturista) Sp***
1. Vegetarianism. I. Title.
TX837.B28 641.5'636 74-334537
ISBN 84-302-0504-7

Bañeres, Ignacio Segarra
see
Segarra Bañeres, Ignacio, 1929-

Banerjea, Beerendra Chandra, 1917-
আলোছায়া জানালায়. [লেখক] বীরেন্দ্র বন্দ্যোপাধ্যায়. কলিকাতা, মডেল পাবলিশিং হাউস [1377, i.e. 1971]
170 p. 22 cm. Rs5.00
In Bengali.
Short stories.

I. Title.
Title romanized: Ālochāẏā jānālāẏa.

PK1718.B2977A8 77-920698

Banerjea, Beerendra Chandra, 1917–
রবীন্দ্র-সঙ্গীতের নানাদিক. [লেখকগণ] বীরেন্দ্র বন্দ্যোপাধ্যায় ও কণিকা বন্দ্যোপাধ্যায়. কলিকাতা, মিত্রালয় [1962]
10, 103 p. illus., ports. 23 cm.
In Bengali.

1. Tagore, Sir Rabindranath, 1861-1941. I. Bandyopādhyāẏa, Kaṇikā, joint author.
Title transliterated: Rabīndra-saṅgītera nānādika.
PK1725.B275 S A 64-1117
PL 480 : I-B-136

Banerjea, Beerendra Chandra, 1917- joint author
see Bandyopādhyāya, Kaṇikā. (Rabīndrasaṃgīta) 1382 [1975]

Banerjea, Jitendra Nath.
The development of Hindu iconography. [3d ed. New Delhi] Munshiram Manoharlal [1974]
xxxvii, 653 p. XLVIII plates, front. 25 cm.
"Reprinted from 2d revised and enlarged edition of 1956."
Bibliography: p. [627]-632.
1. Mythology, Hindu. 2. Art, Hindu. 3. Idols and images. I. Title.
OrU NUC76-22118

Banerjea, N
Foreign exchange regulation act, 1973 / by N. Banerjea & S. K. Mukherjea. — Calcutta : International Law Book Centre, 1975.
839 p. in various pagings ; 25 cm. — (I.L.B.C. publication series ; no. 26)
Rs85.00 ($20.00 U.S.)
1. Foreign exchange—Law—India. I. India (Republic). Laws, statutes, etc. Foreign exchange regulation act, 1973. 1975. II. Mukherjea, S. K., joint author. III. Title.
343'.54'032 75-905171
75 MARC

Banerjea, N
Laws on gold control / by N. Banerjea and S. K. Mukherjea. — Calcutta : International Law Book Centre, [1975]
xviii, 322 p. ; 25 cm. — (I.L.B.C. publication series ; no. 27)
Includes the text of the Gold (control) act, 1968 as amended up to 1st September 1973.
Rs40.00
1. Gold—Law and legislation—India. I. Mukherjea, S. K., joint author. II. India (Republic). Laws, statutes, etc. Gold (control) act, 1968. 1975. III. Title.
343'.54'032 75-905167
76 MARC

Banerjea, N.
see India (Republic). Laws, statutes, etc. Central excise manual, amended upto June 1974. Calcutta, International Law Book Centre, 1974.

Banerjea, Surendranath, Sir, 1848-1925.
Speeches. Edited by Raj Jogeshur Mitter. 2d ed. Calcutta, S. K. Lahiri, 19
v. 20 cm.
1. India. Hist. 1765-1947. Addresses, essays, lectures. 2. India. Pol. & govt. 1765-1947. Addresses, essays, lectures. I. Mitter, Raj Jogeshur, ed.
NcD NUC73-77460

Banerjea, Surendranath, Sir, 1848–1925.
The trumpet voice of India; speeches of Surendranath Banerjea, delivered in England, 1909. 2d ed. Madras, Ganesh [1909?]
vi, 163 p. ports. 19 cm.
1. India—Politics and government—20th century—Addresses, essays, lectures. I. Title.
DS479.B36 1909 74–209883

Banerjee, A
Spirit above wars : a study of the English poetry of the two World Wars / A. Banerjee. — Delhi : Macmillan Co. of India, 1975.
232 p. ; 22 cm.
Bibliography: p. 213-224.
Includes index.
Rs55.00
1. English poetry—20th century—History and criticism. 2. European War, 1914-1918, in literature. 3. World War, 1939-1945, in literature. I. Title.
PR605.W3B3 821'.9'1209 75-908126
76 MARC

Banerjee, A
Spirit above wars : a study of the English poetry of the two World Wars / A. Banerjee. — London : Macmillan, 1976.
vii, 232 p. ; 22 cm. GB76-13612
Bibliography: p. [213]-224.
Includes index.
ISBN 0-333-17877-7 : £6.95
1. English poetry—20th century—History and criticisms. 2. European War, 1914-1918, in literature. 3. World War, 1939-1945, in literature. I. Title.
PR605.W3B3 1976 821'.9'1209 77-352833
77 MARC

Banerjee, Ajoy Kumar, 1945-
Analysis of orthotropic hyperbolic paraboloid shells. [Ithaca, N. Y.] 1973.
[3], vii, 175 l. 29 cm.
Bibliography: leaves 116-119.
Thesis (Ph. D.)—Cornell University.
1. Shells (Engineering) I. Title.
NIC NUC75-17673

Banerjee, Amiya Ranjan, 1927–
(Saṅgītera śilpadarśana)
সঙ্গীতের শিল্পদর্শন / অমিয় রঞ্জন বন্দ্যোপাধ্যায়. — কলিকাতা : কৃ. বন্দ্যোপাধ্যায় : পরিবেশক দে বুক ষ্টোর, 1975.
11, 170 p. ; 22 cm.
In Bengali.
Bibliography: p. [169]-170.
Includes index.
Rs15.00

1. Music—Philosophy and aesthetics. I. Title.
ML3845.B26 76-900260

Banerjee, Anandagopal.
Income-tax law and practice in India incorporating the Income-tax act, 1961 & Companies (profits) surtax act, 1964 (as amended upto the 30th June, 1972 and applicable for the assessment year 1972-73) [by] Anandagopal Banerjee... [16. ed.] Calcutta, Knowledge Home [1972]
[4], ix, 377 p. 24 cm.
1. Income tax—India. I. Title.
MH-L NUC74-141156

Banerjee, Anil Chandra.
Guru Nanak and his times. [1st ed.] Patiala, Punjabi University [1971]
245 p. 23 cm. Rs11.75
"Expanded version of Sitaram Kohli lectures delivered by [the author] at Punjabi University, Patiala, in March 1970, under the auspices of the Department of Punjab Historical Studies."
Bibliography: p. [233]-237.
1. Nānak, 1st guru of the Sikhs, 1469–1538. I. Title.
BL2017.9.N3B35 294.6'6'3 [B] 72–902581
MARC

Banerjee, Anil Chandra, ed.
Indian constitutional documents, 1757-1947. [Rev. 3d ed.] Calcutta, A. Mukherjee [1961-65]
4 v. 23 cm.
Vol. 4: 1st ed.
1. India—Constitutional history—Sources. I. Title.
NN NUC76-75611

Banerjee, Anil Chandra, ed.
see Cunningham, Joseph Davey, 1812-1851. Anglo-Sikh relations ... Calcutta : A Mukherjee, 1949.

Banerjee, Anukul Chandra, 1911–
Buddhism in India and abroad. Calcutta, World Press, 1973.
vii, 263 p. 22 cm.
Includes bibliographical references.
Rs30.00 ($5.50U.S.)
1. Buddha and Buddhism. I. Title.
BQ4012.B36 294.3 73–905994
MARC

Banerjee, Anukul Chandra, 1911-
Sarvāstivāda literature. Calcutta [D. Banerjee, 1957]
vii, 271 p.
Thesis—University of Calcutta.
Consists largely of an analytical study of the Vinayavastu, "The first work of the Tibetan Vinaya corresponding to the Pali Mahâvagga and portions of Cullavagga."
Bibliographical footnotes.
Microfilm (negative) Urbana, Ill., Photographic Services, University of Illinois Library, 1970. 1 reel. 35 mm.
IU NUC74-144592

Banerjee, Arun Kanti, 1942-
Plastic stress waves in prestressed thin-walled tubes: numerical analysis by rate dependent theories, by Arun K. Banerjee. [Gainesville] 1972.
xiii, 129 l. illus. 28 cm.
Typescript.
Thesis—University of Florida.
Vita.
Bibliography: leaves 123-128.
1. Stress waves. 2. Plasticity. I. Title.
FU NUC75-80096

Banerjee, Arun Kumar.
(Smitā)
স্মিতা / অরুণকুমার বন্দ্যোপাধ্যায়. — কলিকাতা : বিকল্প সাহিত্য ভবন, 1362 [1955]
56 p. : 19 cm.
In Bengali.
A play based on Joy, by John Galsworthy.

I. Galsworthy, John, 1867-1933. Joy. II. Title.
PK1718.B2979S5 75–984070

Banerjee, Asit Kumar, 1920–
বাংলা সাহিত্যে বিদ্যাসাগর. [লেখক] অসিতকুমার বন্দ্যোপাধ্যায়. কলিকাতা, মণ্ডল বুক হাউস [1377, i.e. 1970]
335 p. port. 23 cm. Rs12.00
In Bengali.
Includes bibliographical references.

1. Vidyasagar, Iswar Chandra, 1820-1891. I. Title.
Title romanized: Bāṃlā sāhitye Bidyāsāgara.
PK1729.V5Z63 72–915495

Banerjee, Asit Kumar, 1920–
(Dui nārī o tina nāẏikā)
দুই নারী ও তিন নায়িকা / অসিতকুমার বন্দ্যোপাধ্যায়. — কলিকাতা : পুস্তক বিপণি, 1976.
10, 123 p. ; 19 cm.
In Bengali.
Includes bibliographical references.
Rs6.00

1. Women—India—Calcutta—Social conditions. I. Title.
HQ1745.C3B35 76–901882

Banerjee, Asit Kumar, 1920–
সাহিত্যজিজ্ঞাসায় রবীন্দ্রনাথ. [লেখক] অসিতকুমার বন্দ্যোপাধ্যায়. কলকাতা, করুণা প্রকাশনী [1969–
v. 22 cm. 9.00 (v. 1)
In Bengali.
"কলকাতা বিশ্ববিদ্যালয়ে প্রদত্ত অধ্যাপক সুধীরকুমার দাশগুপ্ত বক্তৃতামালা."
Includes bibliographical references.
CONTENTS.—1. ভারতী পর্ব পর্যন্ত.
1. Tagore, Sir Rabindranath, 1861-1941. I. Title.
Title romanized: Sāhityajijñāsāẏa Rabīndranātha.
PK1726.B297 73–907901

Banerjee, Asit Kumar, 1920- ed.
see Chatterji, Sanjiv Chandra, 1834-1889. [Works] Sañjiba racanābali. [1973]

Banerjee, Asit Kumar, 1920- ed.
see Mitra, Peary Chand, 1814-1883. (Pyaricanda racanabali) [1971]

Banerjee, Asit Kumar, 1920-
see Purātana Bāṃlā nāṭaka saṅkalana. 1382 [1975]

Banerjee, Asit Kumar, 1920- ed.
see Sen, Nabin Chandra, 1847-1909. (Raibataka, Kurukshetra, Prabhāsa) [1960]

Banerjee, Asit Kumar, 1920-
see Subarṇalekhā. 1974.

Banerjee, Asit Kumar, 1946-
Bayesian inference for inverse Gaussian distribution and semi-Markov processes with emphasis on analysis of buying behavior. [n. p.] c1974.
146 l. illus. 29 cm.
Thesis (Ph. D.)—University of Wisconsin.
Vita.
Includes bibliography.
1. Consumers—Mathematical models. I. Title.
WU NUC76-22102

Banerjee, B. N., joint author
see Ghosh, G B Trends of information service in India. Calcutta: World Press, 1974.

Banerjee, Bhavendra Nath, 1951–
(Kshitija ke pāra)
क्षितिज के पार. लेखक 'अमिताभ' (भवेन्द्र नाथ बन्द्योपाध्याय). 1. संस्करण. इलाहाबाद, अमिताभ प्रकाशन [1972]
87 p. 19 cm. Rs5.00
In Hindi.

I. Title.

PK2098.13.A543K7 72–904395

Banerjee, Bibhuti Bhusan, 1896?–1950.
(Anaśvara)
অনশ্বর. [লেখক] বিভূতিভূষণ বন্দ্যোপাধ্যায় [ও] তারাদাস বন্দ্যোপাধ্যায়. কলিকাতা, মিত্র ও ঘোষ [1379 i.e. 1972]
135 p. 23 cm. Rs5.00
Completed by Tārādāsa Bandyopādhyāẏa.
In Bengali.
A novel.

I. Bandyopādhyāẏa, Tārādāsa. II. Title.

PK1718.B298A82 1972 72–905990

Banerjee, Bibhuti Bhusan, 1896?–1950.
(Araṇya pathika)
অরণ্য পথিক. [লেখক] বিভূতিভূষণ বন্দ্যোপাধ্যায়. কলিকাতা, গ্রন্থ প্রকাশ [1379 i.e. 1972]
183 p. 22 cm. Rs7.00
In Bengali.

1. Banerjee, Bibhuti Bhusan, 1896?–1950—Biography. I. Title.

PK1718.B298Z514 1972 73–905684

Banerjee, Bibhuti Bhusan, 1896?–1950.
(Āro ekaṭi)
আরো একটি. [লেখক] বিভূতিভূষণ বন্দ্যোপাধ্যায়. কলিকাতা, মিত্র ও ঘোষ [1379 i.e. 1972]
110 p. 19 cm. (মিত্র-ঘোষ বাংলা পকেট বই 6) Rs2.00
In Bengali.
Short stories.
"বিভূতিভূষণ বন্দ্যোপাধ্যায়; সংক্ষিপ্ত জীবনী": p. 108–110.

I. Title.

PK1718.B298A886 1972 72–905425

Banerjee, Bibhuti Bhusan, 1896?–1950.
অথৈ জল. [লেখক] বিভূতিভূষণ বন্দ্যোপাধ্যায়. [1. মিত্র-ঘোষ সংস্করণ] কলিকাতা, মিত্র ও ঘোষ [1966]
183 p. 23 cm. 5.50
In Bengali.
A novel.

I. Title.
Title romanized: Athai jala.

PK1718.B298A94 1966 70–909293

Banerjee, Bibhuti Bhusan, 1896?–1950.
বিভূতি বীথিকা. [লেখক] শ্রীবিভূতিভূষণ বন্দ্যোপাধ্যায়. কলিকাতা, সাহিত্যম্ [1377, i.e. 1971]
10, 338 p. illus. 23 cm. Rs8.00
In Bengali.

I. Title.
Title romanized: Bibhūti bīthikā.

PK1718.B298A6 1971 78–920954

Banerjee, Bibhuti Bhusan, 1896?–1950.
বিভূতি-রচনাবলী. [লেখক] শ্রীবিভূতিভূষণ বন্দ্যোপাধ্যায়. [সম্পাদক গজেন্দ্রকুমার মিত্র, চণ্ডীদাস চট্টোপাধ্যায়, ও তারাদাস বন্দ্যোপাধ্যায়] কলিকাতা, মিত্র ও ঘোষ [1377– , i.e. 1970–
v. ports. 25 cm. Rs14.00 per vol.
In Bengali.

I. Mitra, Gajendra Kumar, 1909– ed. II. Caṭṭopādhyāẏa, Caṇḍīdāsa, ed. III. Bandyopādhyāẏa, Tārādāsa, ed.
Title romanized: Bibhūti-racanābalī.

PK1718.B298 1970 74–921918

Banerjee, Bibhuti Bhusan, 1896?–1950.
(Bibhūtibhūshaṇa galpasamagra)
বিভূতিভূষণ গল্পসমগ্র / শ্রীবিভূতিভূষণ বন্দ্যোপাধ্যায় ; [সম্পাদনা, জিতেন্দ্রনাথ চক্রবর্তী, চন্ডীদাস চট্টোপাধ্যায়, মনীশ চক্রবর্তী]. — কলিকাতা : মিত্র ও ঘোষ পাব্লিশার্স, 1382– [1975–
v. : ill. ; 23 cm.
In Bengali.
Rs40.00 (v. 1)

I. Cakrabartī, Jitendranātha. II. Caṭṭopādhyāẏa, Caṇḍīdāsa. III. Cakrabartī, Manīśa. IV. Title.

PK1718.B298A6 1975 75–907871
SA

Banerjee, Bibhuti Bhusan, 1896?–1950.
(Bipinera saṃsāra)
বিপিনের সংসার / বিভূতিভূষণ বন্দ্যোপাধ্যায়. — 1. দে'জ সংস্করণ. — কলিকাতা : দে'জ পাবলিশিং, 1975.
199 p. ; 22 cm.
In Bengali.
A novel.
Rs10.00

I. Title.

PK1718.B298B5 1975 75–908595

Banerjee, Bibhuti Bhusan, 1896?–1950.
(Hīrāmānika jvale)
হীরামানিক জ্বলে. [লেখক] বিভূতিভূষণ বন্দ্যোপাধ্যায়. [1. অমর সংস্করণ] কলিকাতা, অমর সাহিত্য প্রকাশন [1380 i.e. 1973]
116 p. 22 cm. Rs5.00
In Bengali.
A novel.

I. Title.

PK1718.B298H5 1973 74–929598

Banerjee, Bibhuti Bhusan, 1896?–1950.
নীলগঞ্জের ফালমন্ সাহেব. [লেখক] বিভূতিভূষণ বন্দ্যোপাধ্যায়. [1. মিত্র ঘোষ সংস্করণ] কলিকাতা, মিত্র ও ঘোষ [1969]
119 p. 23 cm. 4.00
In Bengali.
Short stories.

I. Title.
Title romanized: Nīlagañjera Phālaman sāheba.
PK1718.B298N5 1969 74–908727

Banerjee, Bibhuti Bhusan, 1896?–1950.
নিশিপদ্ম. [লেখক] বিভূতিভূষণ বন্দ্যোপাধ্যায়. কলিকাতা, মণ্ডল বুক হাউস [1377, i.e. 1970]
170 p. 23 cm. Rs6.00
In Bengali.
A novel.

I. Title.
Title romanized: Niśipadma.

PK1718.B298N53 78–917583

Banerjee, Bibhuti Bhusan, 1896?-1950.
Pather panchali. Transcreated from the Bengali by Monika Varma. Calcutta, Writers Workshop, 1973.
3 v. 22 cm.
"A Writers Workshop greenbird book."
I. Varma, Monika, tr. II. Title.
PZ3.B22327 Pat 5 891′.44′36 73-903374
[PK1718.B298] 73[r76]rev2 MARC

Banerjee, Bibhuti Bhusan, 1896?-1950. Pathera pā̃ncalī
see Banerjee, Bibhuti Bhusan, 1896?-1950. (Zandan zhembúúr) 1964.

Banerjee, Bibhuti Bhusan, 1896?–1950.
(Sahaja mānusha Bibhūtibhūshaṇa)
সহজ মানুষ বিভূতিভূষণ. [সঙ্কলক] সৌরীন্দ্রনাথ বন্দ্যোপাধ্যায়. [কলিকাতা] আল্‌ফা-বিটা পাবলিকেশন্‌স্; [পরিবেশক বুক সারভিস] 1970.
56 p. 23 cm. Rs3.00
In Bengali.

1. Banerjee, Bibhuti Bhusan, 1896?–1950—Correspondence. I. Bandyopādhyāẏa, Saurīndranātha, comp. II. Title.

PK1718.B298Z53 1970 72–903296

Banerjee, Bibhuti Bhusan, 1896?–1950.
(Zandan zhembúúr)
Зандан жэмбүүр : повесть / [Б. Бондопадхай]. — Улаан-Удэ : Буряадай номой хэблэл, 1964.
176 p., [3] leaves of plates : ill. (some col.)] ; 21 cm.
A variant of the author's Pathera pā̃ncālī.
I. Title. II. Banerjee, Bibhuti Bhusan, 1896?–1950. Pathera pā̃ncālī.
PZ90.B77B3 1964 75–407373

Banerjee, Biswanath, 1926–
(Pāli o Prākṛta sāhityera itihāsa)
পালি ও প্রাকৃত সাহিত্যের ইতিহাস. [লেখক] বিশ্বনাথ বন্দ্যোপাধ্যায়. কলিকাতা, সারস্বত লাইব্রেরী [1379 i.e. 1972]
192, [4] p. 23 cm. Rs8.00
In Bengali.
Bibliography: p. [193]–[194]

1. Pali literature—History and criticism. 2. Prakrit literature—History and criticism. I. Title.

PK4503.B27 73–901324

Banerjee, Brajendra Nath.
(Rabīndra-grantha-paricaẏa)
রবীন্দ্র-গ্রন্থ-পরিচয় / ব্রজেন্দ্রনাথ বন্দ্যোপাধ্যায় ; সজনীকান্ত দাস্-লিখিত ভূমিকা. — পরিবর্তিত ও পরিবর্দ্ধিত 2. সংস্করণ. — কলিকাতা : সাহিত্য-নিকেতন, 1350 [1944]
8, 98 p. ; 19 cm. — (সাহিত্য-পরিষদ্‌গ্রন্থাবলী ; 89)
In Bengali.
Includes index.
1. Tagore, Rabindranath, Sir, 1861–1941—Bibliography. I. Title. II. Series: Sāhitya Parishad. Sāhitya-Parishad-granthābalī ; 89.
Z8857.9.B35 76–984302
[PK1725]

Banerjee, Brajendra Nath, comp.
সমসাময়িক দৃষ্টিতে শ্রীরামকৃষ্ণ পরমহংস. [সম্পাদক] ব্রজেন্দ্রনাথ বন্দ্যোপাধ্যায় [ও] সজনীকান্ত দাস. কলিকাতা, জেনারেল প্রিণ্টার্স য়্যাণ্ড পাব্লিশার্স [1968]
10, 208 p. illus. 23 cm. Rs5.00
"স্বামী বিজ্ঞানানন্দ শতবর্ষ-জয়ন্তী প্রকাশন."
Bengali or English.
Bibliography: p. [117]–145.
1. Ramakrishna, 1836–1886. I. Das, Sajani Kanta, 1900–1962, joint comp. II. Title.
Title romanized: Samasāmaẏika dṛshṭite Śrīrāmakṛshṇa Paramahaṃsa.

BL1175.R26B35 70–900125

Banerjee, Brojendra Nath, 1934-
Foreign aid to India / Brojendra Nath Banerjee. — Delhi : Agam Prakashan ; New Delhi : distributed by D.K. Publishers' Distributors, 1977.
xiii, 378 p. ; 23 cm.
Bibliography: p. [377]-378.
Rs80.00 ($16.00 U.S.)
1. Economic assistance, American—India. I. Title.
HC435.B334 338.91′54′073 77-900744
77 MARC

Banerjee, Brojendra Nath, 1934–
Management of Christian organisations in India. [1st ed.] New Delhi, Masihi Sahitya Sanstha [1973]
229 p. 22 cm. Rs8.00
Bibliography: p. 228–229.
1. Corporations, Religious—India. I. Title.
346′.54′064 73–907645
MARC

Banerjee, Brojendra Nath, 1934-
No flow of foreign money / Brojendra Nath Banerjee. — 1st ed. — Bombay : Gospel Literature Service, 1976, c1975.
154 p. ; 20 cm.
Bibliography: p. 154.
Rs10.00
1. Investments, Foreign—Law and legislation—India. 2. Charitable uses, trusts, and foundations—India. I. Title.
346′.54′07 76-902125
76 MARC

Banerjee, Charu Chandra.
Society : a scientific review / by Charu Chandra Banerjee ; foreword by Sheel Bhadra Yajee. — 1st ed. — Calcutta : D. Banerjee, 1973.
xv, 252 p., [4] leaves of plates : ill. ; 22 cm.
Rs10.00
1. Communism and society. 2. Socialism in India. I. Title.
HX542.B36 335.43′8′301 75-900365
75 MARC

Banerjee, Debabrata, 1928–
Personality characteristics of the unemployed youths of Calcutta; a socio-psychological study [by] D. Banerjee. [1st ed.] Calcutta, D. G. & Co. [1973]
ii, 77, iii p. 22 cm. Rs15.00
Running title: Personality characteristics of unemployed youths.
"This book is a revised version of the Ph. D. thesis entitled 'Attitudes and other personality traits of unemployed and employed undergraduates: a comparative study' which was approved by the University of Calcutta in 1964."
Bibliography: p. [45]–49.
1. Youth—Employment—Calcutta. 2. Unemployed—Calcutta. 3. Adolescent psychology—India—Calcutta. I. Title.
HD6276.I 4B35 155.9′3 73–902990
MARC

Banerjee, Debendranath.
Hormonal regulation of transcriptional and translational processes during normal and neoplastic development of mouse mammary gland. Lincoln, Neb., 1972.
vi, 175 l.
Thesis (Ph. D.)—University of Nebraska.
Bibliography: leaves 85-104.
Tables and figures: leaves 105-175.
I. Title.
NbU NUC74-139114

Banerjee, Digindra Chandra, 1910-
Digindra Chandra Banerjee's three-act play, None is responsible / translated by Abani Mukherjee. — Calcutta : Manisha Granthalaya, [1971?]
x, 80 p. ; 22 cm.
Translation of Keu dāyī naya.
Rs5.00
I. Title. II. Title: None is responsible.
PK1718.B2982K413 1971 75-901534
891′.44′27
76 MARC

Banerjee, Digindra Chandra, 1910–
মেঘের আড়ালে সূর্য. [নাট্যকার] দিগিন্দ্রচন্দ্র বন্দ্যোপাধ্যায়. কলিকাতা, বিশ্বজ্ঞান [1971]
26 p. 23 cm. Re1.00
In Bengali.

I. Title.
Title romanized : Meghera āṛāle sūrya.
PK1718.B2982M4 73–925145

Banerjee, Dipak K 1946-
Thermoelastic waves in anisotropic media, by Dipak K. Banerjee. [Ithaca, N.Y.] 1973.
[3], viii, 102 l. illus. 29 cm.
Includes bibliographical references.
Thesis (Ph.D.)—Cornell University.
1. Elastic waves. 2. Thermoelasticity. 3. Anisotropy. I. Title.
NIC NUC75-16657

Banerjee, Durga.
Designing and construction of 'Self-help' garments for the preschool children of Baroda. Baroda [India] Dept. of Clothing and Textiles, Faculty of Home Science, Maharaja Sayajirao University, 1964.
133 l. illus. (part fold.), photos. 30 cm.
Thesis (M.S.)—Maharaja Sayajirao University.
Bibliography: leaves [123]-125.
1. Children's clothing. I. Title.
IaAS NUC73-47932

Banerjee, Gauri Rani.
Papers on social work; an Indian perspective. [Bombay] Tata Institute of Social Sciences [1973]
xvi, 296 p. 25 cm. (TISS series, no. 23) Rs30.00
List of the author's works: p. 296.
1. Social service—India. I. Title. II. Series: Tata Institute of Social Sciences. Tata Institute of Social Sciences series, no. 23.
HV393.B35 362′.954 74–900210
MARC

Banerjee, Gobinda Lall.
In search of a new order / Gobinda Lall Banerjee ; foreword by Niharranjan Ray ; introd. by Sudhansu Mohan Banerjee. — Calcutta : B. Bhoumik, P. Das Gupta, N. Das Gupta, J. Chatterjee : to be had of Oxford Book & Stationery Co., [1973?]
48 p. ; 23 cm.
Rs5.00
1. Food supply—India. I. Title.
HD9016.I42B35 338.1′9′54 75-902116
76 MARC

Banerjee, Gourisankar, tr.
see Banerjee, Umasankar, 1948- (Bladakyanasara) [1970]

Banerjee, H N
Lives unlimited; reincarnation East and West [by] H. N. Banerjee and Will Oursler. [1st ed.] Garden City, N. Y., Doubleday, 1974.
187 p. 22 cm. $5.95
Includes bibliographical references.
1. Reincarnation. I. Oursler, William Charles, 1913- joint author. II. Title.
BL515.B26 133 73–9171
ISBN 0-385-03912-3 MARC

Banerjee, Hari Binoy
see
Bandopadhyaya, Hari Benoy.

Banerjee, Hemendra Nath, joint author
see Sinha, Sirajit, 1926- Ethnic groups... Calcutta, Anthropological Survey of India [1966]

Banerjee, Hiranmay, 1905–
(Āmarā phasala phalāi)
আমরা ফসল ফলাই / হিরণ্ময় বন্দ্যোপাধ্যায়. — কলিকাতা : শিশু সাহিত্য সংসদ, 1958.
106 p. : ill. ; 19 cm.
In Bengali.

1. Agriculture—India—West Bengal. I. Title.
S471.I32W472 75–985605

Banerjee, Hiranmay, 1905–
(Dui manīshī)
দুই মনীষী. [লেখক] হিরণ্ময় বন্দ্যোপাধ্যায়. কলিকাতা, জিজ্ঞাসা [1966]
189 p. 22 cm. Rs6.00
In Bengali.

1. Tagore, Sir Rabindranath, 1861-1941. 2. Vivekananda, Swami, 1863–1902. I. Title.
PK1726.B3 S A 68-9799
PL 480: I-B-3265

Banerjee, Hiranmay, 1905-
Experiments in rural reconstruction / by Hiranmay Banerjee. — Calcutta : Visva-Bharati, 1966.
157 p. ; 23 cm.
Includes bibliographical references.
Rs6.50
1. Community development—West Bengal. 2. West Bengal—Rural conditions. I. Title.
HN690.B4B26 309.2′63′095414 76-901139
76 MARC

Banerjee, Hiranmay, 1905-
The house of the Tagores. [Calcutta, Rabindra Bharati, 1963.
52 p.
1. Tagore family. 2. Tagore, Sir Rabindranath, 1861-1941. I. Title.
MiEM NUC73-47565

Banerjee, Hiranmay, 1905–
রবীন্দ্র দর্শন. [লেখক] শ্রীহিরণ্ময় বন্দ্যোপাধ্যায়. [3. সংস্করণ] কলিকাতা, সাহিত্য সংসদ [1369, i.e. 1962]
115 p. port. 22 cm. Rs2.50
In Bengali.
Includes bibliographical references.

1. Tagore, Sir Rabindranath, 1861–1941. I. Title.
Title romanized: Rabīndra darśana.
PK1725.B2897 1962 71–926285

Banerjee, Hiranmay, 1905–
[Rabīndra-śilpatattva]
রবীন্দ্র-শিল্পতত্ত্ব. [লেখক] হিরণ্ময় বন্দ্যোপাধ্যায়. কলিকাতা, রবীন্দ্রভারতী বিশ্ববিদ্যালয় [1377, i.e. 1970 or 71]
11, 304 p. 22 cm. Rs8.00
In Bengali.
Includes bibliographical references.

1. Tagore, Sir Rabindranath, 1861–1941. I. Title.
PK1725.B2898 73–928356

Banerjee, Hiranmay, 1905–
Rabindranath Tagore. [New Delhi] Publications Division, Ministry of Information & Broadcasting, Govt. of India [1971]
iv, 195 p. 22 cm. (Builders of modern India)
Includes bibliographical references.
1. Tagore, Sir Rabindranath, 1861–1941. I. Title. II. Series.
PK1725.B28977 891′.44′15 [B] 73–929536
MARC

Banerjee, Hiranmay, 1905–
উদ্বাস্তু. [লেখক] শ্রীহিরণ্ময় বন্দ্যোপাধ্যায়. কলিকাতা, সাহিত্য সংসদ্ [1970]
8, 344 p. 22 cm. Rs10.00
In Bengali.

1. Refugees, Pakistan. I. Title.
Title romanized : Udvāstu.
HV640.5.P25B35 78–926284

Banerjee, Indranil.
Sedimentology of Pleistocene glacial varves in Ontario, Canada; Nature of grain-size distribution of some Pleistocene glacial varves of Ontario, Canada, by Indranil Banerjee. Ottawa, Dept. of Energy, Mines and Resources, Canada, 1973.
ix, 60 p. ill., 2 fold. maps (in pocket). 25 cm. (Bulletin - Geological Survey of Canada, 226)
First title preceded by 'Part A' and second title preceded by 'Part B' on title page.
Includes bibliography.
1. Sediments (Geology)—Ontario. 2. Silt.

I. Title. II. Series: Canada, Geological Survey. Bulletin 226.
CaBVaU NUC76-75825

Banerjee, Janaki Kumar, 1931–
[Citrāṅkane Bāṃlāra meye]
চিত্রাঙ্কনে বাংলার মেয়ে. [লেখক] জানকীকুমার বন্দ্যোপাধ্যায়. কলিকাতা, ইণ্ডিয়া ইন্টারন্যাসানাল [1972]
viii, 140 p. illus., ports. 22 cm. Rs6.50
In Bengali.

1. Women as artists—Bengal. 2. Painting—Bengal. I. Title.
ND1007.B4B36 72–902719

Banerjee, Janaki Kumar, 1931- ed.
see Samajik Bharat... [Calcutta] Service and Goodwill Mission [195-]

Banerjee, Joydev.
Banerjee's Co-operative law and practice in West Bengal, with West Bengal co-operative societies act, 1973, and West Bengal co-operative societies rules, 1974 / by J. Banerjee. — 3d ed. — Calcutta : Eastern Law House, 1976.
xv, 446 p. : forms ; 22 cm.
Half title: Co-operative law and practice in West Bengal.
Bibliography: p. 446.
Rs35.00
1. Cooperative societies—India—West Bengal—Law. I. West Bengal. Laws, statutes, etc. West Bengal co-operative societies act, 1973. 1976. II. Title: Co-operative law and practice in West Bengal.
346′.5414′0668 77-900659
77 MARC

Banerjee, Kali S
Cost of living index numbers : practice, precision, and theory / Kali S. Banerjee. — New York : M. Dekker, [1975]
xiii, 179 p. : graphs ; 24 cm. — (Statistics, textbooks and monographs ; v. 11)
Bibliography: p. 171-175.
Includes index.
ISBN 0-8247-6266-5
1. Cost and standard of living. 2. Index numbers (Economics) I. Title.
HD6978.B25 339.4′7 75-985
75 MARC

Banerjee, Kali S
Weighing designs for chemistry, medicine, economics, operations research, statistics / Kali S. Banerjee. — New York : M. Dekker, [1975]
xiii, 141 p. ; 24 cm. — (Statistics, textbooks and monographs ; v. 12)
Bibliography: p. 133-138.
Includes index.
ISBN 0-8247-6287-8
1. Weighing designs. I. Title.
QA279.B36 519.8 75-194
75 MARC

Banerjee, Kamalesh.
Generalized Lagrange multipliers in dynamic programming. [Berkeley] 1971.
v, 97 l. illus.
Thesis (Ph. D.)—University of California.
Bibliography: leaves 95-97.
CU NUC73-113634

Banerjee, Kamalesh.
Generalized Lagrange multipliers in dynamic programming. ₍East Lansing, Dept. of Management, Michigan State University, 1971₎
97 l. illus.
"This is a reprint of the author's research report ORC 71-12, Operations Research Center, University of California, Berkeley, issued in 1971."
Includes bibliography.
1. Dynamic programming. 2. Mathematical optimization. I. Title.
MiEM NUC73-114293

Banerjee, Kshitish Chandra.
The effects of international re-alignments ₍by₎ K. C. Banerjee. Calcutta ₍1972₎
v, 100 p. 23 cm. Rs3.50
1. World politics—1945- I. Title.
D843.B254 327'.1'0904 73-906889 MARC

Banerjee, Kshitish Chandra.
India and international politics ₍by₎ K. C. Banerjee. Calcutta ₍1966₎
3, 80 p. 18 cm.
Rs2.00
1. India—Foreign relations. I. Title.
DS448.B32 327.54 74-900799 MARC

Banerjee, Monica Rahman
see
Bandyopādhyāya, Manika Rahamana, 1949-

Banerjee, Mrityunjoy.
Business administration : principles and techniques / Mrityunjoy Banerjee. — 4th rev. and enl. ed. — New York : Asia Pub. House, 1977.
xiv, 555 p. : ill. ; 22 cm.
Includes bibliographies and index.
ISBN 0-210-98179-1
1. Industrial management. I. Title.
HD31.B335 1977 658.4 77-363962 77 MARC

Banerjee, Mrityunjoy.
Inflation : causes and cures : with special reference to developing countries / Mrityunjoy Banerjee. — Calcutta : World Press, 1975.
xvi, 319 p. ; 22 cm.
Includes bibliographical references and index.
Rs30.00 ($6.00 U.S.)
1. Inflation (Finance) 2. Inflation (Finance)—India. 3. Underdeveloped areas—Inflation. I. Title.
HG255.B346 332.4'1'091724 75-905572 76 MARC

Banerjee, N.R. An introduction to Nepalese art
see Nepal. Dept. of Archaeology. Nepalese art... Kathmandu [1966]

Banerjee, Narayanchandra, d. 1943
see Kātyāyana. Kātyāyana-mata-saṅgraha... ₍Calcutta₎: University of Calcutta, 1927.

Banerjee, Nihar Ranjan, tr.
see Kṛshnadāsa Kavirāja, b. 1518 or 19. Shree Shree Chaitanya charitamritam. ₍Puri, Shree Gaurkishore Temple, 1926₎

Banerjee, Nikunja Vihari.
The concept of philosophy. ₍Calcutta₎ University of Calcutta, 1968.
88 p. 23 cm. (K. C. Bhattacharyya memorial lectures, 1964)
Rs5.00
"Delivered in the University of Calcutta, December 1964."
1. Philosophy. 2. Bhattacharyya, Krishnachandra, 1875-1949. I. Title.
B53.B26 101 74-901196 MARC

Banerjee, Nikunja Vihari.
The future of education / Nikunja Vihari Banerjee. — Calcutta : Progressive Publishers, 1976.
xxv, 200 p. ; 22 cm.
Includes bibliographical references and index.
Rs40.00 ($8.00 U.S.)
1. Education—Aims and objectives. 2. Education—History. 3. Education—Philosophy. I. Title.
LB41.B263 370.11 77-900610 77 MARC

Banerjee, Nikunja Vihari.
Indian experiments with truth. New Delhi, Arnold-Heinemann India ₍1973₎
48 p. illus. 14 x 22 cm. Rs15.00
1. Philosophy, Indic—Addresses, essays, lectures. 2. Philosophy, Indic—20th century—Addresses, essays, lectures. I. Title.
B5132.B3 181'.4 73-906814 MARC

Banerjee, Nikunja Vihari.
Kant's philosophy of the self / Nikunja Vihari Banerjee. — New Delhi : Arnold-Heinemann Publishers, 1974.
220 p., ₍1₎ leaf of plates : ill. ; 23 cm.
Rs35.00
1. Kant, Immanuel, 1724-1804. 2. Self (Philosophy) I. Title.
B2799.S37B36 126 75-901224 76 MARC

Banerjee, Nikunja Vihari.
Philosophical reconstruction. New Delhi, Arnold-Heinemann India ₍1973₎
155 p. 24 cm. Rs30.00
Includes bibliographical references.
1. Philosophy. 2. Knowledge, Theory of. I. Title.
B53.B27 121 73-905190 MARC

Banerjee, Nikunja Vihari.
The spirit of India philosophy / Nikunja Vihari Banerjee. — New Delhi : Arnold-Heinemann Publishers (India), 1974.
380 p. ; 25 cm.
Bibliography : p. ₍369₎-374.
Includes index.
Rs50.00
1. Philosophy, Indic. I. Title.
B131.B318 181'.4 74-901830 MARC

Banerjee, Nikunja Vihari.
The spirit of Indian philosophy / ₍by₎ Nikunja Vihari Banerjee. — London : Curzon Press, 1975.
380 p. ; 25 cm. GB75-17276
Bibliography: p. ₍369₎-374.
Includes index.
ISBN 0-7007-0078-1 : £5.00
1. Philosophy, Indic. I. Title.
B131.B318 1975 181'.4 75-327452 75 MARC

Banerjee, Nilratan
see
Bandyopādhyāya, Nīlaratana.

Banerjee, Nirendra Nath.
Stresses developed by granular materials in axisymmetric hoppers. Montreal, 1971.
xvi, 118 l. illus. 29 cm. (McGill University theses)
Typewritten ms.
Bibliography: leaves ₍110₎-115.
1. Granular materials. 2. Bins. 3. Silos. 4. Materials handling. I. Title.
CaQMM NUC73-34511

Banerjee, Nirmala.
see Symposium on the Problems of the West Bengal Economy and Planning, Calcutta, 1974. Problems of the economy and planning in West Bengal ... Calcutta, Centre for Studies in Social Sciences, Calcutta, 1975.

Banerjee, P
Early Indian religions ₍by₎ P. Banerjee. Delhi, Vikas ₍c1973₎
241 p. illus.
1. India—Religion—History. I. Title.
ViBlbV NjPT NjMD NUC75-16669

Banerjee, P
Early Indian religions ₍by₎ P. Banerjee. New York, Wiley ₍1973₎
xii, 241 p. illus. 23 cm.
"A Halsted Press book."
Bibliography : p. ₍225₎-234.
1. India—Religion—History. I. Title.
BL2001.2.B3 1973 294'.09 73-5869
ISBN 0-470-04670-8 MARC

Banerjee, P K
Geology and geochemistry of the Sukinda ultramafic field, Cuttack District, Orissa / by P. K. Banerjee. — Delhi : Manager of Publications, 1972.
171 p. : ill., maps ; 24 cm. — (Memoirs of the Geological Survey of India ; v. 103)
Bibliography: p. 159-171.
Rs12.40 ($4.47)
1. Geology—India—Cuttack (District) 2. Geochemistry. 3. Rocks, Ultrabasic. I. Title. II. Series: India (Republic). Geological Survey of India. Memoirs ; v. 103.
QE295.B36 555.4'13 75-310718 75 MARC

Banerjee, P.K., ed.
see Chatterjee, Chandi Charan. Human physiology. ₍6th ed.₎ Calcutta, Books & Allied Private ₍1966₎

Banerjee, Paresh Chandra.
A handbook of industrial employment / by P. C. Banerjee. — 2d ed. — Kalyani : Purna Pub. House, 1975.
159, 83 p. ; 23 cm.
"The Industrial disputes act, 1947": p. ₍1₎-83 (last group)
Includes index.
Rs18.00
1. Arbitration, Industrial—India. I. India (Republic). Laws, statutes, etc. Industrial disputes act, 1947. 1975. II. Title.
344'.54'018914 75-908792 76 MARC

Banerjee, Paresh Chandra.
The law of public servants / by Paresh Chandra Banerjee. — Kalyani, West Bengal : Purna Pub. House, 1974.
ii, 271 p. ; 23 cm.
To be kept up-to-date by the issue of annual supplements.
Rs15.00
1. Civil service—India. I. Title.
342'.54'068 74-903096 MARC

Banerjee, Paresh Chandra.
Wrongs and remedies / by Paresh Chandra Banerjee. — Kalyani, Dt. Nadia : Purna Pub. House, 1975.
147 p. ; 23 cm.
Includes index.
Rs15.00
1. Torts—India. 2. Damages—India. I. Title.
346'.54'03 75-904764 76 MARC

Banerjee, Pareshnath, 1897-
भारतरत्न. ₍लेखक₎ परेशनाथ वन्द्योपाध्याय. ₍छात्र संस्करण₎ कलकत्ता, कश्यप प्रकाशन ₍1968₎
149 p. facsim., ports. 2.00
In Hindi.

1. Bharat ratna. 2. India—Biog. I. Title.
Title romanized : Bhāratatratna.
CR6050.B315 S A 68-10758
PL 480 : I-H-5730

Banerjee, Prajnananda.
Calcutta and its hinterland : a study in economic history of India, 1833-1900 / Prajnananda Banerjee. — Calcutta : Progressive Publishers, 1975.
vi, 240, 2 p. ; 22 cm.
"This book has grown out a dissertation which was approved by the Rabindra Bharati University for Ph.D. degree."
Bibliography: p. ₍227₎-240.
Rs30.00 ($6.50 U.S.)
1. Calcutta metropolitan area—Economic conditions. I. Title.
HC438.C3B33 330.9'54'14 76-900656 76 MARC

Banerjee, Purnendu.
ঝড়ের সংকেত; কাল্পনিক নাটক. শ্রীপূর্ণেন্দু বন্দ্যোপাধ্যায় প্রণীত. ব্রজেন্দ্রকুমার দে কর্তৃক সংশোধিত. কলিকাতা, নির্মল-সাহিত্য-মন্দির, 1378 ₍1971₎
149 p. 19 cm. Rs4.00
In Bengali.

I. Title.
Title romanized : Jhaṛera saṃketa.
PK1730.13.A54J5 75-923138

Banerjee, Purnendu Kumar.
India and America; an alliance of values. [Washington, D.C., Information Service of India, 1967?]
34 p. 22 cm.
Cover title.
"Based on a keynote address delivered at the Conference on India, Bucknell University, Lewisburg, Pa., on March 9, 1967."
1. India—Relations (general) with U.S. 2. U.S.—Relations (general) with India. I. Conference on India, Bucknell University, 1967. II. Title.
FU NUC76-24784

Banerjee, R., joint author
see Ghosh, Jyotish Chandra, B. SC. (Manchester) Indian graphite, its benefication and probable uses. Delhi : Council of Scientific and Industrial Research ₍1951?₎

Banerjee, R N
An introduction to coal petrography; a technique for the Australian coal industry, by R.N. Banerjee, A.C. Cook [and] G.E. Edwards. [Sydney?] Joint Coal Board, 1973.
12, [8] l. illus.
Includes bibliographies.
1. Coal–Analysis. 2. Coal–Australia. I. Cook, A. C., joint author. II. Edwards, G. E., joint author. III. Joint Coal Board (Australia and New South Wales) IV. Title.
CU NUC76-75628

Banerjee, Rabin, 1925-
The welfare economics of India. [Rev. and enl. ed] Calcutta, H. Chatterji [1960]
111 p.
1. India–Economic policy. 2. India–Social conditions–1947- 3. Welfare economics. I. Title.
MoU NUC74-33084

Banerjee, Rubin, 1925–
মন্দা'-'নন্দার দেশে. [লেখক] শুভঙ্কর. কলিকাতা, প্রবর্ত্তক পাবলিশার্স [1961]
168 p. illus. 22 cm.
In Bengali.
1. Himalaya Mountains—Description and travel. I. Title.
Title romanized: Mandā'-'Nandāra deśe.
DS485.H6B277 72–219655

Banerjee, S
Arecanut tannins for leather industry [by] S. Banerjee, M.A. Ghani and Y. Nayudamma. Madras, Central Leather Research Institute [1968]
ii, 50 p. 34 cm.
"The work was done in the scheme sponsored both by Indian Central Arecanut Committee and Council of Scientific & Industrial Research."
Bibliography: p. 49-50.
1. Tannins. 2. Betel nut. I. Ghani, Muhammad Abdul, writer on agriculture, joint author. II. Nayudamma, Y., joint author. III. Indian Central Arecanut Committee. IV. India (Republic). Council of Scientific and Industrial Research. V. Title.
IU NUC73-126250

Banerjee, S.K.
see X-ray analysis of seeds. New Delhi [1973]

Banerjee, S N
Personal & company taxation in India (taxpayers' rights & obligations under Income-tax, Wealth-tax, Gift-tax & Estate duty acts) by S.N. Banerjee... Calcutta, International Law Book Centre [1973]
3 p.l., vi, 332 p. 24 cm.
1. Corporations—Taxation—India. 2. Income tax—India. 3. Taxation—India. I. Title.
MH-L NUC75-17671

Banerjee, S N
Principles & practice of taxation laws in India, by S.N. Banerjee... Calcutta, International Law Book Centre [1973]
3 p.l., vi, 332 p. forms. 24 cm.
1. Income tax—India. 2. Taxation—India. I. Title.
MH-L NUC75-17672

Banerjee, S. N.
see Laet, Joannes de, 1593-1649. The empire of the Great Mogol ... Delhi, Idarah-i Adabiyat-i Delli, 1975.

Banerjee, Sadhansu Mohan, 1899- tr.
see Banerjee, Tarasankar, 1898- The judge. Delhi, Hind Pocket Books [c1967]

Banerjee, Sankar, 1937- ed.
see Gaṅgāpada Basu smāraka-grantha. [1972]

Banerjee, Shyamananda, 1894–
A mystic sage: Ma Anandamayi. With a foreword by P. B. Mukharji. [Calcutta, 1973]
xix, 217 p. illus. 22 cm. (A mystic sage series, v. 1) Rs30.00 ($7.00U.S.)
Includes bibliographical references.
1. Anandamayi, 1896– I. Title.
BL1175.A49B36 294.5'42 73–906741
MARC

Banerjee, Srikumar.
Critical theories and poetic practice in the "Lyrical ballads" / by Srikumar Banerjee. — Norwood, Pa. : Norwood Editions, 1976.
205 p. ; 23 cm.
Reprint of the 1931 ed. published by Williams & Norgate, London.
Originally presented as the author's thesis, University of Calcutta.
Includes index.
ISBN 0-8482-0190-6 : $15.00
1. Wordsworth, William, 1770-1850. Lyrical ballads. I. Title.
[PR5869.L93B3 1976] 821'.7 76-20504
76 MARC

Banerjee, Srikumar.
Phases of Tagore's poetry / Srikumar Banerji. — Mysore : Prasārānga, University of Mysore, 1973.
49 p. ; 23 cm. — (Tagore memorial lectures ; 1968-69)
Rs3.00 ($2.00 U.S.)
1. Tagore, Rabindranath, Sir, 1861-1941—Poetic works—Addresses, essays, lectures. I. Title. II. Series.
PK1727.P6B33 891'.44'14 76-904286
77 MARC

Banerjee, Srikumar
see Bāmlā sāhitye chota galpera dhārā. [pref. 13 i.e. 19

Banerjee, Srikumar
see Sāhitya-samālocanā. [1974]

Banerjee, Subir K., joint author
see Stacey, Frank D The physical principles of rock magnetism. Amsterdam, New York, Elsevier Scientific Pub. Co., 1974.

Banerjee, Subodh Kumar.
see Bandyopadhyay, Susilkumar. Sri Sri Bamakshepa. 1st ed. Calcutta, Bamdev Sangha : available from Mahesh Library, 1971.

Banerjee, Sudhir, joint author.
see Mukherjee, Amitava. Chinese policy towards Asia. New Delhi, Sterling Publishers, c1975.

Banerjee, Sumanta.
India's monopoly press: a mirror of distortion. New Delhi [Indian Federation of Working Journalists, 1973]
95 p. 23 cm. Rs7.50
"An IFWJ publication."
1. Indic newspapers. 2. Press monopolies—India. I. Title.
PN5374.B3 323.44'5 73–905762
MARC

Banerjee, Sumanta.
India's monopoly press : a mirror of distortion / by Sumanta Banerjee. — [Prague] : International Organization of Journalists, 1974.
75 p. ; 21 cm. Cz***
1. Indic newspapers. 2. Press monopolies—India. I. Title.
PN5374.B3 1974 323.44'5 75-319365
75 MARC

Banerjee, Sunil Kumar, 1917–
(Biśa śatakera nayādarśana)
বিশ শতকের নয়াদর্শন. [লেখক] সুনীল কুমার বন্দ্যোপাধ্যায়. কলিকাতা, বিশশতক প্রকাশনী; প্রধান পরিবেষক রেনেসাঁ পাবলিশার্স্ [1973]
5, 70 p. 22 cm. Rs3.00
In Bengali.
1. Existentialism. 2. Philosophy, French—20th century. 3. Youth—Bengal. I. Title.
B819.B315 74–902742

Banerjee, Suresh Chandra.
(Pathera sandhāne)
পথের সন্ধানে. [লেখক] সুরেশচন্দ্র বন্দ্যোপাধ্যায়. কলিকাতা, রঞ্জন পাবলিশিং হাউস [1363 i.e. 1956]
362 p. 21 cm.
In Bengali.
A novel.
I. Title.
PK1718.B29847P3 74–218669

Banerjee, Tapan.
Sea grant report of marine technician training. South Portland, Maine, 1971.
28 l. illus. 28 cm. (Southern Maine Vocational Technical Institute. Publication no. 3)
Grant 2-35154.
1. Oceanography—Study and teaching—Southern Maine Vocational Technical Institute. 2. Marine biology—Study and teaching—Southern Maine Vocational Technical Institute. 3. National Sea Grant Program—Southern Maine Vocational Technical Institute. I. Title. II. Series.
DME NUC75-26587

Banerjee, Tarapada, 1907- joint author.
see Dhananjayan, N., 1929- Structure of electro-deposited manganese. Jamshedpur, National Metallurgical Laboratory, [c1969]

Banerjee, Tarasankar, 1898–
অভিনেত্রী. [লেখক] তারাশঙ্কর বন্দ্যোপাধ্যায়. কলকাতা, তুলি-কলম [1971]
182 p. 23 cm. Rs5.00
In Bengali.
A novel.
I. Title.
Title romanized: Abhinetrī.
PK1718.B2985A62 77–921104

Banerjee, Tarasankar, 1898–
বিচারক. [লেখক] তারাশঙ্কর বন্দ্যোপাধ্যায়. [1. তুলি-কলম সংস্করণ. কলকাতা, নব প্রকাশ]; পরিবেশক তুলি-কলম [1970]
123 p. 23 cm. Rs3.00
In Bengali.
A novel.
I. Title.
Title romanized: Bicāraka.
PK1718.B2985B48 75–92118[illegible]

Banerjee, Tarasankar, 1898–
[Bipāśā]
বিপাশা. [লেখক] তারাশঙ্কর বন্দ্যোপাধ্যায়. কলিকাতা, ডি.এম. লাইব্রেরী [1367, i.e. 1961]
193 p. 21 cm.
In Bengali.
A novel.
I. Title.
PK1718.B2985B49 73–202790

Banerjee, Tarasankar, 1898–1971.
(Byartha nāyikā)
ব্যর্থ নায়িকা. [লেখক] তারাশঙ্কর বন্দ্যোপাধ্যায়. [1. সংস্করণ] কলিকাতা, বাক্-সাহিত্য [1379, i.e. 1972]
129 p. 23 cm. Rs4.00
In Bengali.
A novel.
I. Title.
PK1718.B2985B9 1972 72–903758

Banerjee, Tarasankar, 1898–1971.
(Eka paśalā bṛshṭi)
এক পশলা বৃষ্টি. [লেখক] তারাশঙ্কর বন্দ্যোপাধ্যায়. কলকাতা, তুলি-কলম [1968]
127 p. 23 cm. Rs2.50
In Bengali.
"শেষ তিনটি গল্প পূর্বে 'এ্যাক্সিডেন্ট' নামক গল্পগ্রন্থে প্রকাশিত হয়েছিল."
I. Title.
PK1718.B2985E38 S A 68-9121
PL 480: I-B-3544

Banerjee, Tarasankar, 1898-1971. The eternal lotus
see Ghose, Sukumar, 1935- comp. Contemporary Bengali literature: fiction. Calcutta, Academic Publishers [1972]

Banerjee, Tarasankar, 1898-1971.
(Gabina Siṃ-yera ghoṛā)
গবিন সিং-য়ের ঘোড়া. [লেখক] তারাশঙ্কর বন্দ্যোপাধ্যায়. [1. সংস্করণ] কলিকাতা, শ্রী প্রকাশ ভবন [1968]
114 p. 23 cm. Rs3.00
In Bengali.
Short stories.

I. Title.
PK1718.B2985G24 S A 68-9810
PL 480: I-B-3386

Banerjee, Tarasankar, 1898
(Gaṇa-debatā)
গণ দেবতা / তারাশঙ্কর বন্দ্যোপাধ্যায়. — 3. সংস্করণ. — কলিকাতা : কাত্যায়নী বুক ষ্টল, 1350-1351 [1944]
2 v. ; 20 cm.
Vol. 2, 2d ed., published by মিত্রালয়.
In Bengali.
A novel.
CONTENTS: v. 1. চণ্ডীমণ্ডপ.—v. 2. পঞ্চগ্রাম.
I. Title.
PK1718.B2985G29 1944 76-984497

Banerjee, Tarasankar, 1898-1971.
গুরুদক্ষিণা. [লেখক] তারাশঙ্কর বন্দ্যোপাধ্যায়. [কলিকাতা] দেব সাহিত্য কুটীর [1968]
265 p. port. 23 cm. Rs5
In Bengali.
A novel.

I. Title.
Title romanized: Gurudakshiṇā.
PK1718.B2985G8 S A 68-8684
PL 480: I-B-3454

Banerjee, Tarasankar, 1898-
Internal market of India, 1834-1900. Calcutta, Academic Publishers [1966]
358 p.
Includes bibliographies.
1. India. Commerce. History. I. Title.
DNAL NUC73-2233

Banerjee, Tarasankar, 1898-1971.
(Janapada)
জনপদ. [লেখক] তারাশঙ্কর বন্দ্যোপাধ্যায়. কলিকাতা, ডি. এম. লাইব্রেরী [1380 i.e. 1973]
463 p. 22 cm. Rs16.00
"এই উপন্যাসখানি ধারাবাহিকভাবে বৈশাখ ১৩৫২ থেকে শ্রাবণ ১৩৫৫ 'শনিবারের চিঠি'তে প্রকাশিত হয়েছিল."
In Bengali.

I. Title.
PK1718.B2985J29 1973 73-907791

Banerjee, Tarasankar, 1898-
The judge [by] Tara Sankar Banerjee. Translated by Sudhansu Mohan Banerjee. Delhi, Hind Pocket Books [°1967]
103 p. 18 cm. Rs2
"Orient paperbacks."
Translation of বিচারক.
A novel.

I. Banerjee, Sadhansu Mohan, 1899- tr. II. Title.
PZ3.B22329Ju 891.4'4'37 S A 68-18674
[PK1718.B2985]
PL 480: I-E-9789

Banerjee, Tarasankar, 1898-1971.
(Kālāntara)
কালান্তর; উপন্যাস. [লেখক] তারাশঙ্কর বন্দ্যোপাধ্যায়. কলিকাতা, কাত্যায়নী বুক ষ্টল [1363, i.e. 1956]
278 p. 19 cm.
In Bengali.

I. Title.
PK1718.B2985K2 75-984500

Banerjee, Tarasankar, 1898-
কালরাত্রি. [লেখক] তারাশঙ্কর বন্দ্যোপাধ্যায়. কলকাতা, তুলি-কলম [1970]
270 p. 23 cm. Rs8.00
In Bengali.
A novel.

I. Title.
Title romanized: Kālarātri.
PK1718.B2985K27 76-914701

Banerjee, Tarasankar, 1898-
মানুষের মন. [লেখক] তারাশঙ্কর বন্দ্যোপাধ্যায়. কলকাতা, তুলি-কলম [1969]
168 p. 23 cm. 8.00
In Bengali.
Short stories.

I. Title.
Title romanized: Mānushera mana.
PK1718.B2985M315 79-903314

Banerjee, Tarasankar, 1898-
ना. [लेखक] ताराशंकर बन्द्योपाध्याय. [अनुवादक कमल जोशी. 1. संस्करण] कलकत्ता, अशोक पुस्तक मन्दिर [1958]
120 p. 19 cm. 2.00
In Hindi.
A novel.

I. Joshi, Kamal, 1920- tr. II. Title.
Title romanized: Nā.
PK1718.B2985N275 75-254753

Banerjee, Tarasankar, 1898-1971.
(Nāgarikā)
নাগরিকা / সম্পূর্ণ উপন্যাসটি লিখেছেন তারাশঙ্কর বন্দ্যোপাধ্যায় ... [et al.]. — কলিকাতা : অভিজিৎ প্রকাশনী, 1367 [1961]
181 p. ; 23 cm.
In Bengali.

I. Title.
PK1718.B2985N28 75-985606

Banerjee, Tarasankar, 1898-
पंचमूर्ति. [लेखक] ताराशंकर बन्द्योपाध्याय. [1. संस्करण. अनुवादक वेणी माधव सिंह] कलकत्ता, अशोक पुस्तक मन्दिर [1957]
243 p. 19 cm.
In Hindi.
A novel.

I. Siṃha, Veṇī Mādhava, tr. II. Title.
Title romanized: Pañcamūrti.
PK1718.B2985P27 72-220074

Banerjee, Tarasankar, 1898-1971.
Panchagram (Five villages). Translated by Marcus F. Franda & Suhrid K. Chatterjee. [Delhi] Manohar Book Service, 1973.
352 p. 23 cm. Rs35.00
Translation of the 2d pt. of the author's Gaṇadebatā.
A novel.
I. Franda, Marcus F., tr. II. Chatterjee, Suhrid K., tr. III. Title. IV. Title: Pañcagrama.
PZ4.B2147Pan 5 891'.443'7 73-900909
[PK1718.B2985] MARC

Banerjee, Tarasankar, 1898-
ফরিয়াদ. [লেখক] তারাশঙ্কর বন্দ্যোপাধ্যায়. কলিকাতা, মণ্ডল বুক হাউস [1378, i.e. 1971]
145 p. 23 cm. Rs5.00
In Bengali.
A novel.

I. Title.
Title romanized: Phariÿāda.
PK1718.B2985P5 71-921542

Banerjee, Tarasankar, 1898-1971.
(Rabīndranātha o Bāṃlāra pallī)
রবীন্দ্রনাথ ও বাংলার পল্লী. [লেখক] তারাশঙ্কর বন্দ্যোপাধ্যায়. কলিকাতা, সাহিত্য সংসদ্ [1971]
83 p. port. 23 cm. (নৃপেন্দ্রচন্দ্র বন্দ্যোপাধ্যায় স্মৃতি বক্তৃতামালা, 1971) Rs4.50
In Bengali.
1. Tagore, Sir Rabindranath, 1861-1941—Criticism and interpretation. I. Title. II. Series: Nṛpendracandra Bandyopādhyāya Smṛti baktṛtāmālā, 1971.
PK1725.B296 73-905455

Banerjee, Tarasankar, 1898-1971.
(Rādhā)
রাধা / তারাশঙ্কর বন্দ্যোপাধ্যায়. — 1. সংস্করণ. — কলিকাতা : ত্রিবেণী প্রকাশন, 1364 [1958]
319 p. ; 23 cm.
In Bengali.
A novel.

I. Title.
PK1718.B2985R3 1958 75-985607

Banerjee, Tarasankar, 1898-1971.
Râdhâ au lotus et autres nouvelles / par Tara Shankar Banerji ; traduction du bengali, introd. et glossaire de France Bhattacharya. — [Paris] : Gallimard, c1975.
177 p. ; 23 cm. — (Connaissance de l'Orient : collection UNESCO d'œuvres représentatives ; 41) (Série indienne) F***
Râdhâ au lotus is translation of Rāi-kamala.
I. Title. II. Series.
PK1718.B2985R3414 1975 75-517676
76 MARC

Banerjee, Tarasankar, 1898-1971.
(Sakhī ṭhākaruṇa)
সখী ঠাকরুণ. [লেখক] তারাশঙ্কর বন্দ্যোপাধ্যায়. কলিকাতা, মিত্র ও ঘোষ [1379, i.e. 1972]
131 p. 19 cm. (মিত্র-ঘোষ বাংলা পকেট বই 27)
In Bengali.
A novel.

I. Title.
PK1718.B2985S25 1972 72-905422

Banerjee, Tarasankar, 1898-1971.
শঙ্কর বাঈ. [লেখক] তারাশঙ্কর বন্দ্যোপাধ্যায়. [কলিকাতা] দেব সাহিত্য কুটীর [1967]
223 p. port. 23 cm. Rs5
In Bengali.
A novel.

I. Title.
Title romanized: Śakkara Bāī.
PK1718.B2985S27 S A 68-9017
PL 480: I-B-3449

Banerjee, Tarasankar, 1898-1971.
(Śatābdīra mṛtyu)
শতাব্দীর মৃত্যু. [লেখক] তারাশঙ্কর বন্দ্যোপাধ্যায়. কলিকাতা, মণ্ডল বুক হাউস [1378- i.e. 1971-
v. 23 cm.
In Bengali.
Vols. 2- : লেখক তারাশঙ্কর বন্দ্যোপাধ্যায় ও সনৎ কুমার বন্দ্যোপাধ্যায়.
Rs15.00
I. Title.
PK1718.B2985S38 1971 72-901512

Banerjee, Tarasankar, 1898-1971.
[Selected works]
তারাশঙ্কর বন্দ্যোপাধ্যায়ের স্ব-নির্বাচিত গল্প. — 1. সংস্করণ. — কলিকাতা : ইণ্ডিয়ান অ্যাসোসিয়েটেড্ পাবলিশিং কোং, 1361 [1954]
230 p. ; 23 cm.
In Bengali.

Title romanized: Tārāśaṅkara Bandyopādhyāyera sva-nirbācita galpa.
PK1718.B2985A6 1954 75-985608

Banerjee, Tarasankar, 1898–1971.
(Tārāśaṅkara-racanābalī)
তারাশঙ্কর-রচনাবলী. [লেখক] তারাশঙ্কর বন্দ্যোপাধ্যায়. [সম্পাদক শ্রীগজেন্দ্রকুমার মিত্র, শ্রীসুমথনাথ ঘোষ, ও শ্রীসনৎকুমার বন্দ্যোপাধ্যায়] কলিকাতা, মিত্র ও ঘোষ [1379– , i.e. 1972–
v. 25 cm. Rs15.00 per vol.
In Bengali.

I. Mitra, Gajendra Kumar, 1909– ed. II. Ghosh, Sumathanath, 1912– ed. III. Title.

PK1718.B2985 1972 72–905969

Banerjee, Tarasankar, 1898–1971.
(Unisaśo ekāttara)
১৯৭১. [লেখক] তারাশঙ্কর বন্দ্যোপাধ্যায়. কলিকাতা, মিত্র ও ঘোষ [1379 i.e. 1972]
178 p. 23 cm. Rs6.00
In Bengali.
Novels.
CONTENTS: একটি কালো মেয়ের কথা: ওপার বাংলা.—সুতপার তপস্যা: এপার বাংলা.
I. Title. II. Title: Ekaṭi kālo meyera kathā. III. Title: Sutapāra tapasyā.

PK1718.B2985U5 1972 72–905173

Banerjee, Tarasankar, 1898–
যাদুকরী. [লেখক] তারাশঙ্কর বন্দ্যোপাধ্যায়. কলকাতা, তুলি-কলম [1969]
152 p. 23 cm. 3.00
In Bengali.
Short stories.

I. Title. *Title romanized:* Yādukarī.

PK1718.B2985Y27 77–903319

Banerjee, Tarasankar, 1898–1971.
যোগভ্রষ্ট. [লেখক] তারাশঙ্কর বন্দ্যোপাধ্যায়. [1. সংস্করণ] কলিকাতা, মিত্র ও ঘোষ [1969]
6, 211 p. 23 cm. 7.00
In Bengali.
A novel.
"১৩৬৬ সালে এই রচনাটি পূজা-সংখ্যা 'উল্টোরথে' বের হয়েছিল. তখন নাম ছিল 'যবনিকা'."

I. Title. *Title romanized:* Yogabhrashṭa.

PK1718.B2985Y6 77–903430

Banerjee, Tarasankar, 1898–1971
see Mukherjee, Prabhatkumar, 1873–1932. (Prabhāta Kumāra Mukharjī kī kahāniyām) [1966]

Banerjee, Tarasankar, 1898–1971
see Sonāra malāṭa Tārāśaṅkara. 1973.

Banerjee, Tulshi Kumar, tr.
see Banerjee, Umasankar, 1948– (Blada kyanasara) [1970]

Banerjee, Tushar Kanti
see
Bandyopādhyāya, Tushāra, 1939–

Banerjee, Umasankar, 1948–
(Blāḍa kyānasāra)
ব্লাড ক্যান্সার. [কবি] উমাশঙ্কর বন্দ্যোপাধ্যায়. [Translated into English from the original Bengali by Gourisankar Banerjee and Tulshi Kumar Banerjee. Pref. by Kenneth S. Woodroofe] ভাটপাড়া, 24 পরগণা [জিলা] সুমন্ত প্রকাশন [1970]
55, [12] p. 23 cm. Rs3.00
Added title on cover: Blood cancer.
Bengali and English.
I. Banerjee, Gourisankar, tr. II. Banerjee, Tulshi Kumar, tr. III. Title. IV. Title: Blood cancer.

PK1730.13.A57B55 78–927884

Banerjee, Umasankar, 1948–
(Gulibiddha Rabīndranātha)
গুলিবিদ্ধ রবীন্দ্রনাথ. [কবি] উমাশঙ্কর বন্দ্যোপাধ্যায়. ভাটপাড়া, 24 পরগণা [জিলা] সুমন্ত প্রকাশন [1972]
36 p. 23 cm. Rs3.00
In Bengali.

I. Title.

PK1730.13.A57G8 73–901325

Banerjee, Umesh C
Morphology and fine structure of the pollen grains of maize and its relatives. [n.p.] 1973.
1 v.
Thesis—Harvard.
MH NUC76–75544

Banerjee, Umesh C., joint author.
see Rollins, Reed Clark, 1911– Atlas of the trichomes of Lesquerella (Cruciferae). [Jamaica Plain, Mass.] Bussey Institution of Harvard University, 1975.

Banerjee, Usha.
Health administration in a metropolis / Usha Banerjee. -- 1st ed. -- New Delhi : Abhinav Publications, 1976.
xiv, 256 p. : ill.
1.Community health services--India. 2.Health and welfare planning--India. 3.Public health administration--India. I.Title.
DNLM NUC77–87071

Banerjee-Schneider, Kornelia
see Curriculum-Materialien für die Vorschulschule... 2. Aufl. Weinheim, Beltz [1973, c1972].

Banerji, Adris.
Archaeological history of south-eastern Rajasthan. [1st ed.] Varanasi, Prithvi Prakashan, 1970.
viii, 198 p. illus., map. 23 cm. (Indian civilisation series no. 14, i. e. 15) Rs25.00
Includes bibliographical references.
1. Rajasthan, India—Antiquities. 2. Rajasthan, India—History. I. Title. II. Series.
DS485.R23B36 70–918665
MARC

Banerji, Anupam.
Illustration: techniques in felt-tip pen and charcoal drawing. [Illus. by Anupam Banerji. Fargo, North Dakota [North Dakota State University?] 1969.
[100] p. chiefly illus.
Cover title.
1. Pen drawing. 2. Drawing—Instruction. I. Title.
NbU NUC76–75610

Banerji, Aparna.
Traces of Buddhism in South India, c. 700-1600 A.D. / by Aparna Banerji. — Calcutta : Scientific Book Agency, 1970.
viii, 109 p. ; 22 cm.
On verso of t.p.: Published by Aparna Banerji, Calcutta.
Bibliography: p. [105]-109.
Includes index.
Rs12.00
1. Buddhism—India—South India—History. I. Title.
BQ306.B36 294.3'0954'8 75-906428
76 MARC

Banerji, Arun Prokash.
Keshub's place in the religious culture of Bengal. [Calcutta, n.d.]
1 fold. leaflet. 22 cm.
At head of title: 8th January jubilee year greetings.
1. San, Keshab Chandra, 1838–1884.
MH-AH NUC75–16674

Banerji, Asit.
Capital intensity and productivity in Indian industry / Asit Banerji. — Delhi : Macmillan Co. of India, 1975.
vi, 166 p. ; 22 cm. — (Delhi School of Economics: monograph in economics ; no. 2)
"Revised version of the author's Ph.D. dissertation submitted to the University of Delhi in 1969."
Bibliography: p. [159]-166.
Rs45.00
1. Capital—India. 2. Industrial productivity—India. I. Title. II. Series: Monograph in economics ; no. 2.
HC440.C3B35 1975 338.4'0954 75-908129
76 MARC

Banerji, Debabar, 1930–
Society, health problems, modern medicine, and social medicine; an analysis of their interrelationship in cross-cultural context. [Ithaca, N. Y.] 1963.
v, 187 p. 28 cm.
Thesis (M. A.)—Cornell University.
Includes bibliographies.
1. Social medicine. I. Title.
RA418.B29 362.1 73–171926
MARC

Banerji, H
Supply and demand for agricultural products / H. Banerji. — 1st ed. — Calcutta : Progressive Publishers, 1974.
vi, 108 p. ; 22 cm.
"Report on the research project on 'Derivation of the demand and supply coefficients of agricultural products in India.'"
"Published reports on research studies sponsored by the Research Programmes Committee, Planning Commission, New Delhi, as on 15th February, 1973." p. [91]-108.
Rs20.00
1. Agriculture—Economic aspects—India. 2. Supply and demand. I. Title.
HD2072.B26 338.1'0954 75-902544
76 MARC

Banerji, Hemchandra, 1838–1903.
[Hemacandra-racanāsambhāra]
হেমচন্দ্র-রচনাসম্ভার. [কবি] হেমচন্দ্র বন্দ্যোপাধ্যায়. শ্রীপ্রমথনাথ বিশী সম্পাদিত. কলিকাতা, মিত্র ও ঘোষ [1378, i.e. 1971]
10, 470 p. 23 cm. Rs12.00
In Bengali.

I. Bisi, Pramathanath, 1902– ed. II. Title.

PK1718.B29A17 1971 72–928424

Banerji, J. K., ed.
see Service and Goodwill Mission. National political economy of Bharatiya Samajik Republic. [Calcutta, Nilmadhab Gangooli, 195-?]

Banerji, Jayantanuja.
Mao Tse-tung and Gandhi: perspectives on social transformation [by] Jayantanuja Bandyopadhyaya. Bombay, Allied Publishers [1973]
vi, 156 p. 22 cm. Rs18.00
Includes bibliographical references.
1. Mao, Tse-sung, 1893– 2. Gandhi, Mohandas Karamchand, 1869–1948.
DS778.M3B35 301.24'8 73–904953
MARC

Banerji, Neil Bruniat, 1901–
Under two masters. With a foreword by Philip Mason. [Calcutta, Oxford University Press, Indian Branch, 1970.
xv, 317 p. illus., ports.
Includes bibliographical references.
1. India—Politics and government—1919–1947. 2. India—Politics and government—1947– I. Title.
ICU NUC73–47554

Banerji, Nripendra Chandra, 1885-1949.
At the cross-roads, 1885-1946 : the autobiography of Nripendra Chandra Banerji (Mastarmahasaya). — 2d ed. — Calcutta : Jijnasa, 1974.
viii, 282 p. : port. ; 23 cm.
First published in 1950, by A. Mukherjee, Calcutta.
Includes index.
Rs25.00 ($5.00 U.S.)
1. Banerji, Nripendra Chandra, 1885-1949. I. Title.
LA2383.I6B36 1974 370'.92'4 74-903444
75 MARC

Banerji, Nripendra Chandra, 1885–1949.
(Kārāra phula)
কারার ফুল / নৃপেন্দ্রচন্দ্র বন্দ্যোপাধ্যায়. — শান্তিনিকেতন : বি. বন্দ্যোপাধ্যায় ; কলিকাতা : প্রাপ্তিস্থান, জিজ্ঞাসা, 1382 [1975]
2 v. ; 22 cm.
In Bengali.
First published in 1930.
Poems.
CONTENTS: 1. সন্ধ্যামালতী.—2. রক্তজবা.
Rs8.00 (v. 1); Rs5.00 (v. 2)
I. Title.
PK1718.B2997K3 1975 76–900627

Banerji, R K
Environmental relationships and distribution of planktonic foraminifera in the equatorial and northern Pacific waters, by R.K. Banerji, C.T. Schafer and R. Vine. Dartmouth, N.S., Atlantic Oceanographic Laboratory, 1971.
65, [i.e. 81] p. illus. 25 cm. (Canada. Bedford Institute of Oceanography.
On cover: Dept. of Energy, Mines and Resources, Marine Sciences Branch, programmed by the Canadian Committee of Oceanography.
Includes bibliography.
1. Plankton—Pacific Ocean. I. Schafer, Charles Thomas. II. Vine, R. III. Canada. Marine Sciences Branch. IV. Canada. Committee on Oceanography. V. Title. VI. Series.
CaBVaU NUC73-77600

Banerji, R N 1921-
Economic progress of the East India Company on the Coromandel Coast, 1702-1746 / R. N. Banerji. — 1st ed. — Nagpur : Nagpur University, 1974.
xxiii, 243 p. ; 23 cm.
A revision of author's thesis, London University, 1965.
Bibliography: p. [228]-234.
Includes index.
Rs35.00
1. East India Company (English) 2. Coromandel coast—Commerce. I. Title.
HF486.E6B36 1974 382'.0954'82 75-900506
76 MARC

Banerji, Rakhal Das, 1885–1930.
[Bāṅgālāra itihāsa]
বাঙ্গালার ইতিহাস. [লেখক] রাখালদাস বন্দ্যোপাধ্যায়. শ্রীরমেশ-চন্দ্র মজুমদার কর্ত্তৃক সংশোধিত. [1. নবভারত সংস্করণ] কলিকাতা, নব-ভারত পাবলিশার্স [1971]
2 v. illus., geneal. tables. 23 cm. Rs12.50 per vol.
In Bengali.
Includes bibliographical references.
1. Bengal—History. I. Majumdar, Ramesh Chandra, ed. II. Title.
DS485.B47B3 1971 77–928452

Banerji, Rakhal Das, 1885–1930.
[Dhruvā. Hindi]
ध्रुवा. [उपन्यासकार] राखालदास वंद्योपाध्याय. अनुवादक शंभुनाथ वाज-पेयी. [1. संस्करण] वाराणसी, नागरीप्रचारिणी सभा [संवत् 2022 वि., i.e. 1965 or 6]
3, 3, 12, 157 p. 19 cm. (सूर्यकुमारी पुस्तकमाला, 32)
In Hindi.
1. Dhruvadevī, Queen of Magadha, fl. 380—Fiction. I. Vājapeyī, Śambhunātha, tr. II. Title.
Title romanized: Dhruvā.
PK1718.B3D515 1966 74–927607

Banerji, Rakhal Das, 1885-1930.
[Mayūkha. Hindi]
मयूख. [उपन्यासकार] राखालदास वंद्योपाध्याय. अनुवादक शंभुनाथ वाज-पेयी. [1. संस्करण] काशी, नागरीप्रचारिणी सभा [संवत् 2019, i.e. 1962 or 3]
1 v. (various pagings) 19 cm. (सूर्यकुमारी पुस्तकमाला, 29)
In Hindi.
Includes biographical sketch of the author: p. [1]-20 (2d group)
I. Vājapeyī, Śambhunātha, tr. II. Title. III. Title: Mayūkha. IV. Series: Sūryakumārī pustakamālā, 29.
Title romanized: Mayūkha.
PK1718.B3M315 71–927609

Banerji, Rakhal Das, 1885–1930
see Bangiya Sahitya Parishad, Calcutta. Museum. Descriptive list of sculptures & coins... Calcutta, R. K. Sinha, 1911.

Banerji, Ranadev.
Economic development and the patterns of manufactured exports, by R. Banerji and J. B. Donges. Kiel, Institut Für Weltwirtschaft, 1972.
24 p. 30 cm. (Kieler Diskussionsbeiträge zu aktuellen wirtschaftspolitischen Fragen, 16) GDB***
Cover title.
Bibliography: p. 24.
1. Economic development—Mathematical models. 2. Underdeveloped areas—Commerce. 3. Manufactures. I. Donges, Juergen B., joint author. II. Title. III. Series.
HB44.K45 no. 16 72–172516
[HD82] rev MARC

Banerji, Ranadev.
Exports of manufactures from India : an appraisal of the emerging pattern / Ranadev Banerji. — Tübingen : J. C. B. Mohr (P. Siebeck), 1975.
xvii, 347 p. : graphs ; 24 cm. — (Kieler Studien ; 130) GFR***
Bibliography: p. 330-347.
ISBN 3-16-336352-0 : DM58.00
1. India—Commerce. 2. India—Manufactures. 3. India—Industries. I. Title. II. Series.
HF3786.5.B35 382'.0954 75-315504
75 MARC

Banerji, Ranadev.
The "green revolution" and the trade prospects in selected cereals for the developing countries, by R. Banerji. Kiel, Institut für Weltwirtschaft, 1971.
22 p. illus. 30 cm. (Kieler Diskussionsbeiträge zu aktuellen wirtschaftspolitischen Fragen, 11)
Cover title.
1. Underdeveloped areas—Agriculture. 2. Grain trade—Underdeveloped areas. I. Title.
NIC NUC76-75625

Banerji, Rangalal, 1826–1887.
[Works]
রঙ্গলাল রচনাবলী : একখণ্ডে সম্পূর্ণ [sic] / সম্পাদক শ্রীশান্তিকুমার দাশগুপ্ত ও শ্রীহরিবন্ধু মুখটি. — কলিকাতা : দত্তচৌধুরী, 1381 [1974]
2, 28, 574 p., [1] leaf of plates : ill. ; 23 cm.
On verso of t.p.: নবীনচন্দ্র গ্রন্থ প্রচার সমিতির পক্ষে শ্রীসজীব দত্ত চৌধুরী কর্ত্তৃক সমিতির কার্যালয়, কলিকাতা, হইতে প্রকাশিত.
Bengali or English.
Rs25.00
Title romanized: Raṅgalāla racanābalī.
PK1718.B32 1974 75–903491

Banerji, Samir Kumar.
Micro-structural and solute effects on the megacycle damping of copper, by Samir Kumar Banerji. Stony Brook, N.Y., 1973.
xiv, 94 l. ill., graphs. 28 cm.
On spine: Structural correlations with dislocation damping.
Thesis—State University of New York at Stony Brook.
Vita.
Bibliography: leaves 48-50.
1. Damping (Mechanics) 2. Ultrasonics. 3. Copper alloys. I. Title.
NSbSU NUC76-75246

Banerji, Sanat Kumar, 1911–
Sri Aurobindo and the future of man : a study in synthesis / Sanat K. Banerji. — Pondicherry : Sri Aurobindo Society, 1974.
208 p. ; 22 cm.
"References": p. 199-208.
Rs20.00
1. Ghose, Aurobindo, 1872–1950. 2. Man.
B5134.G42B36 181'.45 74–902307
MARC

Banerji, Shanka K., comp.
see Water Resources Seminar, University of Delaware, 1966-1967. Second proceedings... Newark, University of Delaware, 1967.

Banerji, Srimati Aparna.
Traces of Buddhism in South India (c. 700-1600 A.D.) Calcutta, Scientific Book Agency, 1970.
109 p.
Bibliography: p. [105]-109 p.
1. Buddha and Buddhism—Deccan—Hist. I. Title.
CU-SB NUC76-75615

Banerji, Sukumer.
(Galpakāra Śaraṭcandra)
গল্পকার শরৎচন্দ্র / সুকুমার বন্দ্যোপাধ্যায় ও সুচরিতা রায়. — কলি-কাতা : বাণী-প্রকাশনী : প্রাপ্তিস্থান, সিগনেট বুকশপ্, [pref. 1361 i.c. 1954]
8, 42, 398 p. ; 20 cm.
In Bengali.
1. Chatterji, Saratchandra, 1876–1938—Criticism and interpretation. I. Rāya, Sucaritā, joint author. II. Title.
PK1718.C45Z585 75–985609

Banerji, Sures Chandra, 1917–
Aspects of ancient Indian life, from Sanskrit sources. [1st ed.] Calcutta, Punthi Pustak, 1972.
xi, 179 p. 23 cm. Rs35.00
Bibliography: p. 162.
1. India—Civilization. I. Title.
DS425.B27 915.4'03 72–905778
MARC

Banerji, Sures Chandra, 1917–
(Bhāratera jñānabijñāna)
ভারতের জ্ঞানবিজ্ঞান. [লেখক] শ্রীসুরেশচন্দ্র বন্দ্যোপাধ্যায়. কলি-কাতা, বুকল্যাণ্ড [1960–
v. 22 cm.
In Bengali.
Bibliography: v. 1, p. [205]-208.
1. India—Intellectual life. 2. Learning and scholarship—India. I. Title.
DS425.B28 75–984501

Banerji, Sures Chandra, 1917-
Contribution of Bihar to Sanskrit literature / Sures Chandra Banerji. — Patna : K. P. Jayaswal Research Institute, 1973.
x, 190 p. ; 25 cm. — (Historical research series ; no. 11)
Appendices (p. [139]-158): A. Supplementary list of naiyāyikas believed to have been Maithilas.—B. Nālandā and Vikramaśīlā.
Bibliography: p. [136]-138.
Includes index.
Rs15.00
1. Sanskrit literature—Bihar. I. Title. II. Series: Kashi Prasad Jayaswal Research Institute, Patna. Historical researches series ; no. 11.
PK3800.B5B3 891'.2'09 75-900272
76 MARC

Banerji, Sures Chandra, 1917-
Fundamentals of ancient Indian music and dance / by Sures Chandra Banerji. — 1st ed. — Ahmedabad : L.D. Institute of Indology, 1976.
viii, 120 p. ; 26 cm. — (L.D. series ; 57)
Includes the original Sanskrit text of Pañcamasāra-saṃhitā ascribed to Nārada.
Bibliography: p. [117]-120.
Rs25.00 ($3.50 U.S.)
1. Music, Indic—History and criticism. 2. Dance music, Indic—History and criticism. I. Nārada. Pañcamasāra-samḥitā. 1976. II. Title. III. Series: Lalbhai Dalpatbhai series. ; 57.
ML338.B28 781.7'34 77-901639
77 MARC

Banerji, Sures Chandra, 1917–
সংস্কৃত সাহিত্যের ইতিহাস: শ্রব্যকাব্য ও দৃশ্যকাব্য. [লেখক] শ্রীসুরেশ-চন্দ্র বন্দ্যোপাধ্যায়. [1. সংস্করণ] কলিকাতা, ঢাকা স্টুডেন্টস্ লাইব্রেরী [1377 বঙ্গাব্দ, i.e. 1971]
9, 256 p. 22 cm. Rs15.00
In Bengali.
Bibliography: p. [241]
1. Sanskrit literature—History and criticism. I. Title.
Title romanized: Saṃskṛta sāhityera itihāsa.
PK2903.B24 71–921183

Banerji, Sures Chandra, 1917- ed.
see Krsipaddhati. English and Sanskrit. Krsi-Parasara. Calcutta, Asiatic Society, 1960.

Banerji, Sures Chandra, 1917-
see Mahābhārata. Selections. Smrti material in the Mahābhārata... Calcutta, 1972-

Banerji, Sures Chandra, 1917-
see S.K. De memorial volume. Calcutta, Firma K.L. Mukhopadhyay, 1972.

Banerji, Sures Chandra, 1917-
see Śārṅgadeva. [Saṅgitaratnākara. Hindi] Saṅgitaratnākara. [1973 or 1974-

Banerji, Tara Shankar
see
Banerjee, Tarasankar, 1898-1971.

Banes, Daniel.
A chemist's guide to regulatory drug analysis. Washington, Association of Official Analytical Chemists [1974]
vi, 133 p. illus. 23 cm.
Includes bibliographical references.
1. Drugs—Adulteration and analysis. 2. Drugs—Law and legislation—United States. 3. United States. Food and Drug Administration. I. Title.
RS189.B29 615'.1901 74–75346
MARC

Banes, Daniel.
The provocative Merchant of Venice / by Daniel Banes. — Silver Spring, Md. : Malcolm House Publications, c1975.
vii, 111 p. : diagrs. ; 23 x 29 cm.
Bibliography: p. 111.
1. Shakespeare, William, 1564-1616. The merchant of Venice. I. Shakespeare, William, 1564-1616. The merchant of Venice. 1975. II. Title.
PR2825.B27 822.3'3 75-28622
76 MARC

Banes, Sally.
Sweet home Chicago : the real city guide / Sally Banes, Sheldon Frank & Tem Horwitz. — Chicago : Chicago Review Press, [1974]
267 p. : ill. ; 22 cm.
Includes index.
ISBN 0-914090-06-2
1. Chicago—Description—1951- —Guide-books. I. Frank, Sheldon, joint author. II. Horwitz, Tem, joint author. III. Title.
F548.18.B36 917.73'11'044 74-84707
MARC

Banes, Sally. Sweet home Chicago.
see Sweet home Chicago2. 2d ed., expanded & rev. Chicago, Chicago Review Press : distributed by the Swallow Press, c1977.

Banes, Sally.
see Our national passion ... Chicago, Follett Pub. Co., c1976.

Bănescu, A
Întreţinerea şi repararea utilajelor şi instalaţiilor din industria chimică / Andrei Bănescu, Doina Bănescu. — Bucureşti : Editura tehnică, 1975.
407 p. : ill. ; 21 cm. R 75-2855
Bibliography : p. 403-[404]
lei 15.00
1. Chemical plants—Equipment and supplies—Maintenance and repair. I. Bănescu, Doina, joint author. II. Title.
TP157.B34 75-591973

Bănescu, A., joint author
see Dimofte, Florin. Echilibrarea dinamică a maşinilor. Bucuresti, Consiliul Naţional pentru Ştiinţă şi Tehnologie, 1972.

Bănescu, A., joint author
see Dimofte, Florin. Utilizarea calculatoarelor electronice. Bucureşti, Consiliul National pentru Stiintă si Tehnologie, 1972.

Bănescu, Doina, joint author
see Bănescu, A Întretinerea si repararea utilajelor... Bucuresti: Editura tehnică, 1975.

Bănescu, Florin, 1939-
Anotimp al minsorilor albastre : [roman] / Florin Bănescu ; [coperta, Victor Creţulescu]. — [Bucureşti] : Editura Eminescu, 1975.
170 p. ; 20 cm. R 75-4741
lei 8.25
I. Title.
PC840.12.A583A83 76-502960

Bănescu, Florin, 1939-
Să arunci cu pietre în soare : [schiţe] / Florin Bănescu ; [coperta de Armand Crintea]. — Bucureşti : Editura Eminescu, 1974.
106 p. ; 20 cm. R 75-495
lei 5.25
I. Title.
PC840.12.A583S2 75-577766

Bănescu, Florin, 1939-
Seminţele dimineţii : roman / Florin Bănescu ; [coperta de Sergiu Dinculescu]. — Bucureşti : Editura Eminescu, 1976.
228 p. ; 17 cm. — (Colecţia Clepsidra) R77-349
lei6.25
I. Title.
PC840.12.A583S4 77-483856
•77 MARC

Banet, Anthony G.
see Creative psychotherapy ... La Jolla, Calif., University Associates, c1976.

Banet, Barbara, joint author.
see **Rozdilsky, Mary Lou. What now? ... New York, Scribner, [1975]**

Banet, Barbara
see The Scrap book. Ann Arbor, Mich. [1972]

Banff Conference on Pollution.

For works by this body issued under its later name see

International Banff Conference on Man and his Environment.

Banff Conference on Pollution, 1st, 1968.
Man and his environment; proceedings. Edited by M. A. Ward. [1st ed.] Volume 1. Oxford, New York, Pergamon Press [1970]
xi, 196 p. illus. 26 cm.
"Sponsored jointly by the University of Calgary and the Engineering Institute of Canada."
Includes bibliographical references.
1. Pollution—Congresses. I. Ward, M. A., ed. II. Calgary, Alta. University. III. Engineering Institute of Canada. IV. Title.
TD172.5.B3 1968 628'.5 70-113396
ISBN 0-08-015763-7 70[r76]rev MARC

Banff Conference on Theoretical Psychology, 3d, 1971.
Multivariate analysis and psychological theory. Edited by Joseph R. Royce. London, New York, Academic Press, 1973.
xvi, 567 p. illus. 24 cm. GB***
Held Sept. 27-Oct. 2, 1971 at the Banff School of Fine Arts; sponsored by the University of Alberta's Center for Advanced Study in Theoretical Psychology.
Includes bibliographies.
1. Multivariate analysis. 2. Psychometrics. I. Royce, Joseph R., ed. II. Alberta. University, Edmonton. Banff School of Fine Arts. III. Alberta. University, Edmonton. Center for Advanced Study in Theoretical Psychology. IV. Title.
BF39.B34 1971 150'.1'82 72-12278
ISBN 0-12-600750-0 MARC

Banff International Conference on Behavior Modification, 2d, 1970.
Behavior modification for exceptional children and youth; the proceedings ... Edited by Leo A. Hamerlynck [and] Frank C. [i. e. W.] Clark. Calgary, University of Calgary [1971]
148 p. illus. 23 cm. (Committee for Banff Conferences on Behavior Modification. Monograph no. 2) C***
Held April 2-3, 1970.
Includes bibliographies.
1. Exceptional children—Congresses. 2. Exceptional children—Education. I. Clark, Frank W., ed. II. Title. III. Series.
HQ773.B25 1970 371.9 73-160249
MARC

Banff International Conference on Behavior Modification. 4th. 1972.
Behavior change : methodology, concepts, and practice / the Fourth Banff International Conference on Behavior Modification ; edited and introduced by Leo A. Hamerlynck, Lee C. Handy, Eric J. Mash. — Champaign, Ill. : Research Press, 1974, c1973.
xiv, 358 p. : graphs ; 21 cm.
Conference held March 25-29 in Banff, Alberta, Canada.
Includes bibliographies.
ISBN 0-87822-089-5
1. Behavior modification—Congresses. I. Hamerlynck, Leo A., 1929- II. Handy, Lee C. III. Mash, Eric J. IV. Title.
BF637.B4B34 1972 153.8'5 75-318153
75 MARC

Banff International Conference on Behavior Modification, 5th, 1973.
Evaluation of behavioral programs in community, residential, and school settings. Edited by Park O. Davidson, Frank W. Clark [and] Leo A. Hamerlynck. Champaign, Ill., Research Press [1974]
xx, 448 p. illus. 21 cm.
Includes bibliographies.
1. Mental health services—Evaluation—Congresses. 2. Behavior modification—Congresses. I. Davidson, Park Olof, 1937- ed. II. Clark, Frank W., ed. III. Hamerlynck, Leo A., 1929- ed. IV. Title.
RA790.5.B28 1973 362.2'2 74-166405
ISBN 0-87822-090-9 74[r77]rev MARC

Banff International Conference on Behavior Modification, 6th, 1974.
Behavior modification and families / edited by Eric J. Mash, Leo A. Hamerlynck and Lee C. Handy. — New York : Brunner/Mazel, c1976.
xx, 362 p. : ill. ; 24 cm.
Proceedings of the conference held in March 1974 in Banff.
Includes bibliographies and index.
ISBN 0-87630-118-9
1. Behavior modification—Congresses. 2. Child psychology—Congresses. 3. Parent and child—Congresses. I. Mash, Eric J. II. Hamerlynck, Leo A., 1929- III. Handy, Lee C. IV. Title.
[DNLM: 1. Behavior therapy—Congresses. 2. Family therapy—Congresses. W3 BA203 1974b / WM420 B215 1974b]
BF637.B4B34 1974 618.9'28'915 75-37733
75 MARC

Banff International Conference on Behavior Modification, 6th, 1974.
Behavior modification approaches to parenting : [papers] / edited by Eric J. Mash, Lee C. Handy, and Leo A. Hamerlynck. — New York : Brunner/Mazel, c1976.
xviii, 254 p. : ill. ; 24 cm.
Includes bibliographies and index.
ISBN 0-87630-119-7
1. Behavior modification—Congresses. 2. Child psychology—Congresses. 3. Parent and child—Congresses. I. Mash, Eric J. II. Handy, Lee C. III. Hamerlynck, Leo A., 1929- IV. Title.
[DNLM: 1. Behavior therapy—Congresses. 2. Family therapy—Congresses. 3. Parent-child relations—Congresses. W3 BA203 1974ba / WM420 B215 1974ba]
BF637.B4B34 1974a 618.9'28'915 75-37993
75 MARC

Banff International Conference on Behavior Modification, 7th, 1975.
see The Behavioral management of anxiety, depression, and pain. New York, Brunner/Mazel, c1976.

Banff Leadership Conference on College Administration, 1st, 1970.
The community college in Canada: present status/future prospects; report of the proceedings, edited by the staff of the College Administration Project, Robert Bryce [and others] Edmonton, Alta., Dept. of Educational Administration, Faculty of Education, University of Alberta, 1971.
102 p. 28 cm.
1. Municipal junior colleges—Canada.
I. Bryce, Robert C., ed. II. Alberta. University, Edmonton. College Administration Project. III. Title.
CaBVaU NUC73-77601

Banff Regional Conference of School Administrators, 1970.
Board/administrator relationships; [proceedings of] the twelfth annual Banff Regional Invitational Conference for School Administrators, April 26, 27, 28, 1970. Edited by D. Friesen and C. S. Bumbarger. [Edmonton, Dept. of Educational Administration, Faculty of Education, University of Alberta, 1970]
iv, 78, [18] p. illus. 28 cm.
"Sponsored by the Department of Educational Administration, Faculty of Education, University of Alberta."
1. School management and organization—Canada—Congresses. I. Friesen, David, ed. II. Bumbarger, Chester S., ed. III. Alberta. University, Edmonton. Dept. of Educational Administration. IV. Title.
CaBVaU NUC75-9267

[Banff '74 Internation Conference]
Abstracts of papers to be presented at the International Conference, Sept. 4-7, the Banff Centre, Banff, Alta., Canada. [Hamilton? Ont., Canadian Association of Slavists? 1974?]
ca. 140 l.
"Sponsored by the American Association for the Advancement of Slavic Studies ... [et al.]"
I. American Association for the Advancement of Slavic Studies. II. Canadian Association of Slavists.
CaOTU NUC76-76213

Banff Workshop for Teachers of Family Medicine, 1st, 1970.
Proceedings. [n.p., 1970]
129 p. 28 cm.
Sponsored by the Society of Teachers of Family Medicine and the Division of Continuing Medical Education, Faculty of Medicine, the University of Calgary.
1. Family medicine—Study and teaching—Congresses. 2. Comprehensive health care—Education—Congresses. 3. General practice—Education—Congresses. I. Society of Teachers of Family Medicine. II. Calgary, Alta. University. Division of Continuing Medical Education. III. Title.
CaBVaU NUC76-11052

Bánffy, Eszter Gabriella.
Marxistische Ethik in der ungarischen Literatur / Eszter-Gabriella Bánffy. Christlicher Humanismus / Karl Rahner. — Wien ; München : [Ungarisches Kirchensoziolog. Inst.], 1976.
185 p. ; 21 cm. — (UKI-Berichte über Ungarn ; 1975/1-3) Au76-18-94
Bibliography: p. 168-185.
S120.00
1. Communist ethics. 2. Ethics, Hungarian. I. Rahner, Karl, 1904- Christlicher Humanismus. 1976. II. Title. III. Series: Ungarisches Kirchensoziologisches Institut. UKI-Berichte über Ungarn ; 1975, 1-3.
BJ1390.B26 76-482353
*76 MARC

Banfi, A., joint author
see Airoldi, Alberto. Proverbi brianzoli ascoltati da A. Airoldi e A. Banfi. [Erba], Licinium, 1970.

Banfi, Antonio, 1886-1957.
La crisi della civiltà borghese e il marxismo / Antonio Banfi ; introduzione, scelta e note a cura di Giovanni Mari. — Firenze : Cooperativa editrice universitaria, 1977.
346 p. ; 19 cm. It77-July
Includes bibliographical references.
L3500
1. Communism—Collected works. 2. Civilization, Modern—20th century—Collected works. I. Title.
HX291.B25 1977 77-550524
*77 MARC

Banfi, Antonio, 1886-1957.
Introduzione a Nietzsche : lezioni 1933-1934 / Antonio Banfi ; a cura di Dino Formaggio. — 1. ed. italiana. — Milano : Istituto editoriale internazionale, 1974.
187 p. ; 23 cm. — (Scienze dell'uomo ; 26) It***
Bibliography: p. [184]-187.
L5000
1. Nietzsche, Friedrich Wilhelm, 1844-1900—Addresses, essays, lectures. I. Title.
B3317.B27 1974 75-552300

Banfi, Antonio, 1886-1957.
Ricerche sull'amor famigliare e tre scritti inediti / Antonio Banfi ; presentazione di Vittorio Sereni. — Urbino : Argalìa, 1965.
50 p. ; 21 cm. — (Quaderni di Differenze)
1. Love. 2. Death. I. Title.
BD436.B35 1965 75-533505

Banfi, Antonio, 1886-1957.
Saggi sul marxismo / Antonio Banfi. — Roma : Editori Riuniti, c1960.
288 p. ; 22 cm. — (Nuova biblioteca di cultura ; 27)
1. Communism—Addresses, essays, lectures. I. Title.
HX56.B2 1960 76-519927

Banfi, Antonio, 1886-1957
see L'Accession de la Chine au rang de grande puissance. [Venise, 1958]

Banfi, Antonio, 1886-1957, ed.
see Galilei, Galileo, 1564-1642. Antologia. [Firenze] La Nuova Italia [1970]

Banfi, Luigi, ed.
see Croce, Giulio Cesare, 1550-1609. Bertoldo e Bertoldino. Milano, Mursia, 1973.

Banfi, Marzio.
Impotenza e stupore : romanzo / Marzio Banfi ; [illustrazioni di Silvia Banfi]. — Gentilino : Banfi, [1974]
167 p. : ill. ; 21 cm. Sw 75-A-2889
15.00F
I. Title.
PQ4862.A5 I 4 75-403273

Banfield, Alexander William Francis, 1918-
The mammals of Canada / A. W. F. Banfield ; ill. by Allan Brooks ... [et al.] ; cartography by Geoffrey Matthews and Jennifer Wilcox. — Toronto ; Buffalo : Published for the National Museum of Natural Sciences, National Museums of Canada by University of Toronto Press, [1974]
xxv, 438 p., [13] leaves of plates : ill. (some col.) ; 28 cm. C***
Includes bibliographies and index.
ISBN 0-8020-2137-9 : $19.95
1. Mammals—Canada. I. National Museum of Natural Sciences. II. Title.
QL721.B32 599'.0971 73-92298
MARC

Banfield, Ann M 1941-
Stylistic transformations; a study based on the syntax of Paradise Lost. [n.p.] c1973.
266 l. illus. 29 cm.
Thesis (Ph.D.)—University of Wisconsin.
Vita.
Includes bibliography.
1. Milton, John, 1608-1674. Paradise Lost. I. Title.
WU NUC74-116642

Banfield, Ann M 1941-
Stylistic transformations: a study based on the syntax of Paradise lost. [Madison] 1973.
xxiv, 266 l. illus.
Thesis–University of Wisconsin.
Bibliography: leaves 226-231.
Photocopy of typescript. Ann Arbor, Mich., University Microfilms, 1973. 22 cm.
1. Milton, John, 1608-1674. Paradise lost. 2. Milton, John, 1608-1674–Style. I. Title.
IU NUC76-75599

Banfield, Beryle.
Selected bibliography of materials for use in programs of African studies in elementary and secondary schools [by] Beryle Banfield. Prepared for the Conference on Teaching About Africa, Washington, D.C., May 15th and 16th, 1970. [n.p., 1970?]
16 l. 28 cm.
1. Africa. Study and teaching. 2. African studies. Bibl. I. Conference on Teaching About Africa, Washington, D.C., 1970. II. Title.
NcD NUC74-24053

Banfield, Beryle.
The teaching of Africa; instructional resources: a position paper. [New York, School Program Division, Center for Urban Education? 1970?]
12 l. 29 cm.
Caption title.
Includes bibliographical references.
Photocopy of typescript.
1. Africa. Study and teaching. 2. African studies. Bibl. I. Title.
NcD NUC73-126328

Banfield, Edward C
The city and the Revolutionary tradition [by] Edward C. Banfield. Delivered at Franklin Hall, Franklin Institute, Philadelphia, Pa., April 11, 1974. Washington, American Enterprise Institute for Public Policy Research [1974]
16 p. illus. 25 cm. (Distinguished lecture series on the Bicentennial) $1.00
Includes bibliographical references.
1. Cities and towns—United States—Addresses, essays, lectures. 2. Federal-city relations—United States—Addresses, essays, lectures. I. Title. II. Series.
HT123.B25 301.36'3'0973 74-83648
ISBN 0-8447-1309-0 MARC

Banfield, Edward C
The unheavenly city revisited, by Edward C. Banfield. Boston, Little, Brown [1974]
xii, 358 p. 21 cm.
A revision of The unheavenly city.
Bibliography: p. [291]-292.
1. Cities and towns—United States. I. Title.
HT123.B267 1974 301.36'0973 73-22876
MARC

Banfield, Edward C.
see Sindler, Allan P Policy and politics in America; six case studies. Boston, Little, Brown [1973]

Banfield, Edwin.
Antique barometers : an illustrated survey / [by] Edwin Banfield. — Bristol : Wayland Publications, [1977]
ix, 119 p. : ill. ; 23 cm. GB77-09827
Bibliography: p. 117.
Includes index.
ISBN 0-9505272-0-3 : £2.00
1. Barometer. I. Title.
QC886.B36 681'.753 77-366488
77 MARC

Banfield, J E
An introduction to mathematical organic chemistry / by J. E. Banfield. — [s.l.] : Gereng, c1972.
xiii, 690 p. : ill. ; 25 cm. Aus
Includes index.
1. Chemistry, Organic—Mathematics. I. Title.
QD255.5.M35B36 547'.001'51 76-355368
76 MARC

Banfield, Lorna L
The Ararat railway centenary : a history of the Ballarat to Ararat railway and lineside guide / by L. Banfield, K. W. Turton [and] R. K. Whitehead ; edited by R. K. Whitehead. — [Melbourne] : Australian Railway Historical Society, Victorian Division, 1975.
60 p. : ill., diagrs., maps ; 23 cm. Aus
"Issued by the Australian Railway Historical Society, Victorian Division, on the occasion of the centenary celebrations of the opening of the railway to Ararat, 5th April, 1975."
ISBN 0-85849-018-8
1. Railroads—Victoria, Australia. I. Turton, Keith W., joint author. II. Whitehead, R. K., joint author. III. Title.
TF122.V5B36 385'.09945 76-373149
76 MARC

Banfield, Lorna L
Green pastures and gold : a history of Ararat / [by] Lorna L. Banfield. — Canterbury, Vic. : Mullaya Publications, 1974.
xi, 146 p., 16 p. of plates : maps on lining papers ; 23 cm. Aus
Bibliography: p. 129-132.
Includes index.
ISBN 0-85914-008-3 : $7.50
1. Ararat, Australia—History. I. Title.
DU230.A7B29 994.5 75-305142
MARC

Banfield, Thomas Charles.
The organization of industry, explained in a course of lectures delivered in the University of Cambridge in Easter term 1844. 2d ed. Clifton [N. J.] A. M. Kelley, 1973.
viii, xvi, 166 p. 23 cm. (Reprints of economic classics)
Published in 1845 under title: Four lectures on the organization of industry.
Reprint of the 1848 ed.
1. Industrial organization. 2. Economics. I. Title.
HB161.B23 1973 338.6 68-55469
ISBN 0-678-00064-3 MARC

Banfield, Tom, joint author.
see Davies, Duncan. The humane technologist. London, Oxford University Press, 1976.

Banfield, William G., 1920- joint author
see Ohmori, Masaki, 1935- The ultrastructure of the mosquito, Aëdes aegypti (L.) Tokyo, Saikon Pub. Co., 1974.

Banfo, Bettino.
La stella del Kiber; una ragazza impareggiabile. Torino, Società Editrice Internazionale [1959]
159 p. illus. 22 cm.
I. Title.
MB NUC76-62499

Bang
see
Alving, Barbro, 1909-

Bang, Anton Christian, 1840-1913.
Hans Nielsen Hauge og hans samtid; en monografie. Christiania, J. Dybwad, 1875.
551 p. 22 cm.
Bibliography of works by and about H. Nielsen Hauge: p. 548-551.
1. Hauge, Hans Nielsen, 1771-1824.
BX8080.H3B3 74-216553

Bang, Anton Christian, 1840-1913.
Udsigt over den norske kirkes historie under katholicismen. Kristiania, Cammermeyer, 1887.
362 p. 20 cm.
1. Norway—Church history. 2. Catholic Church in Norway. I. Title.
BR1004.B36 74-230426

Bang, Bernhard Laurits Frederik, 1848-1932
see Engelsen, Christian, 1847-1906. Breve fra Chr. Engelsen til H. Krabbe og B. Bang, 1884-1906 ... København, V: Nordisk Veterinaermedicin, 1974.

Bang, Betsy.
The old woman and the red pumpkin; a Bengali folk tale. Translated and adapted by Betsy Bang. Illustrated by Molly Garrett Bang. New York, Macmillan [1975]
[32] p. col. illus. 26 cm.
SUMMARY: A retelling of an Indic folk tale in which a skinny old woman outwits the jackal, bear, and tiger who want to eat her.
ISBN 0-02-708360-8 : $6.95
[1. Folklore—India] I. Bang, Molly, illus. II. Title.
PZ8.1.B226Ol [398.2] [E] 74-13057
MARC

Bang, Betty
see
Mather, Betty Bang.

Bang, Bodil.
Roman/roman? : analyser / red. af Bodil Bang. — København : Vinten, 1974.
216 p. ; 19 cm. — (Stjernebøgernes kulturbibliotek) D 74-41
Bibliography: p. 212-215.
ISBN 87-414-3430-7 : kr34.50
1. Danish fiction—History and criticism. I. Title.
PT7862.B3 74-356562

Bang, Carl.
Nærmeste fortrolige / Carl Bang. — [København] : Gyldendal, 1976.
244 p. ; 24 cm. D76-19
ISBN 8701300911 : kr75.00
I. Title.
PT8175.B328N27 76-474141
76 MARC

Bang, Carl.
Naturspil. Digte. Ill. af Jørgen Brynjolf. København, (Borgen), 1972.
25 p. illus. 31 cm. kr28.00 D 72-51
I. Brynjolf, Jørgen, illus. II. Title.
PT8175.B328N3 74-328234
ISBN 87-418-1238-7

Bằng, Đú'c-
see Đú'c-Bằng.

Bằng, Đỳnh
see Đỳnh Bằng.

Bang, Elisabeth Wikborg, 1915–
Elsa Beskow : kunsten og livet / av Elisabeth Wikborg Bang. — Drammen : Lyche, [1975].
64, [2] p. : ill. ; 25 cm. N 75-Mar
Bibliography: p. [66]
ISBN 82-7008-084-5 : kr15.00
1. Beskow, Elsa Maartman, 1874-1953.
PT9875.B565Z558 75-590734

Bang, Garrett, comp.
Men from the village deep in the mountains and other Japanese folk tales, translated and illustrated by Garrett Bang. New York, Macmillan [1973]
84 p. illus. 23 cm. $4.95
CONTENTS: Men from the village deep in the mountains.—Patches.—The stone statue and the grass hat.—The grateful toad.—Raw monkey liver.—The crusty old badger.—The cloth of a thousand feathers.—The old woman in the cottage.—The two statues of Kannon.—The mirror.—Picking mountain pears.—The strange folding screen.
1. Tales, Japanese. [1. Folklore—Japan] I. Title.
PZ8.1.B227Me 398.2'0952 72-92431
ISBN 0-02-708350-0 MARC

Bang, Hải-
see Hải-Bang.

Bang, Herman Joachim, 1857-1912.
Aforismer. Samlet og udgivet af Harry Jacobsen. København, Nordisk Bogforlag [1973]
35 p. (Skrifter, udg. af Selskabet aforismens venner, 2)
1. Aphorisms and apothegms, I. Title. II. Series: Selskabet aforismens venner. Skrifter, 2.
CU NUC76-72877

Bang, Herman Joachim, 1857-1912.
Liv og død. København, Schubothe, 1899.
138 p. 19 cm.
CONTENTS: En fortælling om lykken.—En fortælling om elskov.—En fortælling om dem der skal dø.
I. Title.
PT8123.B3L5 74-230198

Bang, Herman Joachim, 1857-1912.
Min egen ven. Herman Bangs sidste brev til Betty Nansen. [Ved Per Busck-Nielsen]. København, Nyt Nordisk Forlag, 1974.
36 p. illus. 21 cm. kr18.50 D 74-20
1. Bang, Herman Joachim, 1857-1912—Correspondence. I. Nansen, Betty. II. Title.
PT8123.B3Z545 1974 74-337139
ISBN 87-17-01849-8

Bang, Herman Joachim, 1857-1912.
Sommerglæder. Ny. udg. Ill. af Svend Otto S. Med efterskrift af Hakon Stangerup. København, Lademann, [1970.]
175 p. illus. 25 cm. kr32.50 D 70-21
I. Svend Otto S., illus. II. Title.
PT8123.B3S6 1970 72-331559
ISBN 87-15-00017-6; 87-15-00016-8 (pbk.)
rev

Bang, Herman Joachim, 1857-1912.
Tien vieressä. Suomentanut: Anna-Maria Tallgren. Jyväskylä, K. J. Gummerus, 1918.
186 p. 21 cm.
Translation of Ved vejen.
Bound with Korpela, Simo. Elämän keskeltä. Jyväskylä, K. J. Gummerus, 1914.
I. Title.
PH355.K5943E4 75-400243
[PT8123.B3]

Bang, Herman Joachim, 1857-1912.
Tina. [Preložil a doslov napísal Jaroslav Kaňa. Bratislava, Vydal Slovenský spisovatel'] Spoločnost Priatel'ov Krásnych Knih, 1971.
168 p. 21 cm.
I. Title.
NcRS NUC74-115146

Bang, Herman Joachim, 1857-1912.
Tine. Udg. med efterskrift af Jacob Paludan. [2. opl. København, Gyldendal [1970]
222 p. 20 cm. (Gyldendals bibliotek. Dansk litteratur, bd. 19)
ISBN: 87-00-30387-9.
MnU NUC73-47552

Bang, Herman Joachim, 1857-1912.
Ved vejen [af] Herman Bang. Med vejledning ved Sven Møller Kristensen. Udg. af Dansklaererforeningen. 10. opl. [København] Gyldendal [1972]
159 p. 21 cm.
Bibliography: p. 156.
ISBN: 87-00-78011-1.
I. Kristensen, Sven Møller, 1909- ed. II. Title.
CaBVaU NUC76-72878

Bằng, Hoa
see Hoa Bằng.

Bang, Herman Joachim, 1857-1912.
Die Vier Teufel und andere novellen, von Herman Bang. Berlin, S. Fischer, n. d.
181 p. 18 cm. (Fischers bibliothek zeitgendssischer romane)
Translation of De fire djaevle.
I. Title. II. Series.
CaBVaU NUC76-22132

Bang, Hung Kyu, 1929-
Japan's colonial educational policy in Korea, 1905-1930. [Tucson, Ariz.] 1972.
xi, 229 l.
Thesis—University of Arizona.
Bibliography: leaves 218-229.
Microfilm. Ann Arbor, Mich., University Microfilms, 1972. 1 reel. 35 mm.
1. Education—Korea. 2. Korea—History—Chōsen, 1910-1945. I. Title.
NIC NUC76-75600

Bang, Hung Kyu, 1929-
Japan's colonial educational policy in Korea, 1905-1930. [Tucson] 1972 [Ann Arbor, Mich., University Microfilms, 1974]
xi, 229 l. 21 cm.
Thesis—University of Arizona.
Photocopy.
Bibliography: leaves 218-229.
1. Education—Korea. 2. Japan—Colonies—Administration. I. Title.
CaBVaU NUC76-22131

Bang, Inge Hofman-
see Hofman-Bang, Inge.

Bang, Inger.
En tyv i familien. København, Gyldendal, 1972.
117 p. 21 cm. kr23.50 D 72-18
I. Title.
PZ53.B328E5 72-349890
rev

Bang, James Suhil, 1921-
Social and social psychological correlates for community action potential. [n.p.] c1972.
2 v. (415 l.) 29 cm.
Thesis (Ph. D.)—University of Wisconsin.
Vita.
Includes bibliography.
1. Community life. 2. Sheboygan Falls, Wis.—Soc. condit. I. Title.
WU NUC73-113628

Bang, Jørgen.
Galliak salt : en Frankrigsmosaik / Jørgen Bang. — [København] : Gyldendal, 1975.
102 p., 20 leaves of plates : ill. ; 22 cm. D 75-40
Bibliography: p. [7]
Includes index.
ISBN 87-01-22971-0 : kr54.00
1. France—Antiquities, Roman. 2. France—Antiquities, Celtic. 3. France—Civilization. 4. Romans—France. 5. Celts—France. I. Title.
DC63.B23 75-409621

Bang, Jørgen.
Et ord er et ord / Jørgen Bang. — [København] : Schultz, 1967.
148 p. ; 21 cm. — (His De Svære ord ; 2)
Includes index.
1. Danish language—Idioms, corrections, errors. I. Title.
PD3460.B3 vol. 2 75-577192

Bang, Jørgen.
Som man siger / Jørgen Bang. — [København] : Gyldendal, [1969].
169 p. ; 21 cm. — (His De Svære ord ; 3)
Includes index for vols. 1-3.
1. Danish language—Idioms, corrections, errors. I. Title.
PD3460.B3 vol. 3 75-577191

Bang, Jørgen.
De sorte jomfruer. Oplevelser i Frankrig. København, Gyldendal. 1973.
116 p., 20 l. of plates. 22 cm. kr45.00 D 73-39
Bibliography: p. 109-[112]
1. France—Description and travel—1945- I. Title.
DC29.B27 74-300294
ISBN 87-00-68041-9

Bang, Jørgen.
Sproget og livet / Jørgen Bang. — [København] : Gyldendal, [1974].
154 p. : ill. ; 22 cm. — (His De Svære ord ; 5) D 74-38
Includes index.
ISBN 87-00-18871-9 : kr42.00
1. Danish language—Idioms, corrections, errors. I. Title.
PD3460.B3 vol. 5 75-568818

Bang, Jørgen.
De svære ord. [København] Schultz, 1965-
v. illus. 21 cm.
Collections of articles from the author's series "De Svære ord" in Berlingske tidende.
Vol. 2 has also special title: Et Ord er et ord; v. 3: Som man siger; v. 5: Sproget og livet.
Vols. 3 and 5 published by Gyldendal.
1. Danish language—Idioms, corrections, errors. I. Title.
PD3460.B3 68-76720

Bang, Jørgen, comp.
Synspunker på folkevisen. En antologi. København, Munksgaard, 1972.
391 p. 22 cm. (Munksgaards litterære antologier) kr57.50 D 72-41
Bibliography: p. 371-385.
1. Danish ballads and songs—History and criticism. I. Title.
PT7791.B3 72-369227
ISBN 87-16-00474-4

Bang, Jørgen, illus.
see Hejberg, Lars. Vestre fængsel. København, Rhodos, 1972.

Bang, Jørgen Chr
Lingva, lingvist, lingvistik / Jørgen Chr. Bang. — [Odense] : Odense universitet, 1974.
124 p. : diagrs. ; 21 cm. — (Skrifter fra Nordisk institut, Odense universitet ; v. 2) D***
Bibliography: p. 118-124.
kr4.00
1. Linguistics. 2. Language and languages. I. Title. II. Series: Odense universitet. Nordisk institut. Skrifter - Nordisk institut, Odense universitet ; v. 2.
P121.B314 75-546443

Bang, Kaj Nolsøe.
Færøerne—mine fædres land / Kaj Nolsøe Bang. — Svaneke : Eget Forlag : [eksp.] Nolsoyarstova, 1974.
205 p. ; 22 cm. D 74-49
ISBN 87-980322-0-8 : kr51.75
1. Faroe Islands—Social life and customs. I. Title.
DL271.F24B36 75-551988

Bang, Kaj Nolsøe.
Styrmænd til orlogs : optakten til 9. april / Kaj Nolsøe Bang. — København : Erichsen, 1976.
169 p. ; 22 cm. D76-52
Includes index.
ISBN 8755504841 : kr58.50
1. World War, 1939-1945—Personal narratives, Danish. 2. World War, 1939-1945—Denmark. 3. Bang, Kaj Nolsøe. 4. Seamen—Denmark—Biography. 5. Denmark—History—Christian X, 1912-1947. I. Title.
D811.5.B228 77-460595
77 MARC

Bang, Kap Soo, 1929–
(Ch'aesin pohŏmhak)
最新保險學 : 理論과實際 / 方甲洙著. — 서울 : 博英社, 1975.
641 p. : ill. ; 23 cm. — (大學全書 : 經濟學講義)
Includes legislation, bibliographies, and index.
W2900

1. Insurance. I. Title.
HG8051.B33 75–825995

Bang, Karin.
Arv og gjeld. Oslo, Dreyer, [1973–
v. 22 cm. kr35.00 (v. 1) N 73 (v. 1)
CONTENTS: 1. Bedremannsbarn.
I. Title.
PT8950.B357A77 74–314331
ISBN 82-09-01124-3 (v. 1)

Bang, Karin.
Bedremannsbarn. Oslo, Dreyer, [1973]
145 p. 22 cm. (Her Arv og gjeld, 1) kr35.00 N 73
I. Title.
PT8950.B357A77 vol. 1 74–314329
ISBN 82-09-01124-3; 82-09-01123-5 (pbk.)

Bang, Karin.
Borgersinn / Karin Bang. — Oslo : Dreyer, [1974]
183 p. ; 22 cm. — (Her Arv og gjeld ; 2) N***
ISBN 82-09-01199-5 : kr48.50. ISBN 82-09-01198-7 pbk.
I. Title.
PT8950.B357A77 vol. 2 75–563348

Bang, Karin.
Fugl blå : en gammeldags roman / Karin Bang. — Oslo : Dreyer, 1975.
136 p. ; 22 cm. N 75–Nov
ISBN 82-09-01303-3 : kr58.00. ISBN 82-09-01302-5 pbk.
I. Title.
PT8950.B357F8 76–504387

Bang, Karin.
Kort opphold. Dikt. Oslo, Dreyer, 1972.
3–42 p. 23 cm. kr22.50 N 72–45
Norwegian or English.
I. Title.
PT8950.B357K6 73–313257
ISBN 82-09-01011-5

Bang, Kirsten.
Drengen fra Cairo. København, Unitas, 1972.
152 p. 22 cm. kr20.70 D 72–43
I. Title.
PZ53.B33D7 73–306560
ISBN 87-7517-041-8

Bang, Kirsten.
Farlig færd til Mekka. København, Unitas, 1973.
118 p. 22 cm. kr20.70 D 73–46
I. Title.
PT8176.12.A5F3 74–339420
ISBN 87-7517-062-0

Bang, Kirsten.
Om Knud Rasmussen / Kirsten Bang. — [København] : Tranehuse, 1975.
44 p. : ill. ; 21 cm. D 76–6
ISBN 87-87563-04-5 : kr16.00
1. Rasmussen, Knud Johan Victor, 1879–1933. 2. Greenland—Discovery and exploration. I. Title.
G635.R3B28 76–515046

Bang, Kirsten.
Taru fra Nepal / Kirsten Bang. — København : Branner og Korch, 1976.
158 p. ; 21 cm. D76-22
ISBN 8741174755 : kr34.50
I. Title.
PZ53.B33T3 76-477416
76 MARC

Bang, Kirsten.
Tiggerdrengen Jugga. En fortælling fra Indien. Med tegninger af Kamma Svensson. København K., Abbé Pierre's Klunseres Forlag, Eksp.: Christianshavns Voldgade 43, 1972.
127 p. illus. 21 cm. kr19.50 D 72–47
I. Title.
PZ53.B33T5 73–307784
ISBN 87-980218-1-8

Bang, Molly, comp.
The goblins giggle, and other stories, selected and illustrated by Molly Bang. New York, Scribners [1973]
57 p. illus. 23 cm. $4.95
CONTENTS: The old man's wen.—The boy who wanted to learn to shudder.—Mary Culhane and the dead man.—A soccer game on Dung-Ting Lake.—The goblins giggle.
1. Tales. [1. Folklore] I. Title.
PZ8.1.B228Go 398.2'1 72–9033
ISBN 0-684-13226-5 MARC

Bang, Molly.
Wiley and the Hairy Man : adapted from an American folktale / Molly Garrett Bang. — New York : Macmillan, c1976.
64 p. : ill. ; 23 cm. — (Ready-to-read)
SUMMARY: With his mother's help, Wiley outwits the hairy creature that dominates the swamp near his home by the Tombigbee River.
ISBN 0-02-708370-5 lib. bdg. : $6.95
[1. Folklore—United States] I. Wiley and the Hairy Man. II. Title.
PZ8.1.B228 Wi 398.2'1'0973 75-38581
75 MARC

Bang, Molly, illus.
see Bang, Betsy. The old woman and the red pumpkin ... New York, Macmillan [1975]

Bang, Molly.
see The buried moon and other stories. New York, Scribner, c1977.

Bang, Preben.
Collins guide to animal tracks and signs; the tracks and signs of British and European mammals and birds; text, Preben Bang; illustrations, Preben Dahlstrom; translated and adapted by Gwynne Vevers. London, Collins [1974]
240 p. illus. (part col.) 21 cm. GB***
Illus. on lining papers.
Translation of Dyrespor.
Bibliography: p. 240.
1. Animal tracks. 2. Tracking and trailing. 3. Mammals—Europe. 4. Birds—Europe. I. Dahlstrom, Preben, illus. II. Vevers, Henry Gwynne, 1916– III. Title. IV. Title: Animal tracks and signs
QL768.B3613 599'.05 74–169035
ISBN 0-00-216106-0 MARC

Bang, Preben.
Dyrespor. Spor og sportegn efter pattedyr og fugle. Tegninger: Preben Dahlstrøm. København, Gad, 1972.
243 p. illus. 21 cm. kr69.00 D 72–47
Bibliography: p. 240.
1. Animal tracks. 2. Tracking and trailing. I. Dahlstrøm, Preben, illus. II. Title.
QL768.B36 73–334454
ISBN 87-12-23304-8; 87-12-23302-1 (pbk.)

Bảng, Trần-kim-
see Trần-kim-Bảng.

Bang, Vũ
see Vũ Bang, 1913-

Bang, W.
see Bang-Kaup, Willy, 1869-1934.

Bang Clausen, Helge
see
Clausen, Helge Bang.

Bang-Hansen, Odd
see Møte i musikk. [Oslo] : Tiden [1975]

Bang-Kaup, Willy, 1869-1934.
Vom Köktürkischen zum Osmanischen, Vorarbeiten zu einer vergleichenden Grammatik des türkischen ... / W. Bang. -- Berlin : G. Reimer, 1917-1921.
4 pts. in 3 v. ; 30 cm. -- (Abhandlungen der Königlich preussischen akademie der wissenschaften. -- Jahrg. 1917-21. -- Philosophisch-historische klasse, 1917, nr. 6 ; 1919, nr. 5 ; 1921, nr. 3)
Microfiche. Zug, Switzerland : Inter Documentation, 1975. -- 9 sheets ; 9 x 12 cm. 1. Turkish language--Grammar. 2. Turkish language--Etymology. I. Title. II. Series: Akademie der Wissenschaften, Berlin--Philosophisch-historische Klasse. Jahrg. 1917-21 Abhandlungen, 1917 nr. 6; 1919, nr. 5; 1921; nr. 3.
InU NUC77-86568

Bang Nielsen, Sophus
see
Nielsen, Sophus Bang.

Bang!
[Barcelona]
no. illus. 27 cm. bimonthly.
"Información estudios sobre la historieta."
1. Comic books, strips, etc.—Periodicals.
PN6700.B35 73–645229
MARC-S

Bàng Bá Lân, 1912–
Gàn bát sách; thời đàm [của] Đồ Gàn. [Saigon] Tiến Bộ [1969]
317 p. 21 cm.

1. Vietnam—Politics and government. I. Title.
DS557.A6B33 74–211280

Bằng Bá Lân, 1912–
Vào thu; thơ. Saigon, Ánh Sáng [1969]
106 p. illus. 27 cm.
I. Title.
NIC NUC73-2235

Bằng Giang.
Mảnh vụn văn-học sử / Bằng-Giang. — In lần thứ 1. — Saigon : Chân-Lưu, 1974.
300 p. ; 19 cm.
Bibliography: p. [299]–300.

1. Vietnamese literature—History and criticism. I. Title.
PL4378.B27 75–984861

Bằng Giang.
Từ thơ mới đến thơ tự do. Phụ thêm: Đi vào thi ca. [Saigon] Phù Sa [1969]
132 p. 19 cm.

1. Vietnamese poetry—History and criticism. I. Title.
PL4378.2.B3 73–220820

Bang Hansen, Folmer
see
Hansen, Folmer Bang.

Bang-Hansen, Kjetil.
Når det kommer til stykket. "En folkefiende" på Trøndelag teater. Red. av Kjetil Bang-Hansen, Erik Pierstorff og Ørjan Wiklund. Fotografiene er tatt av Grete Sandberg. Oslo, Grøndahl, [1972].
266 p. 21 cm. kr49.50 N 73–8
Includes bibliographical references.
1. Ibsen, Henrik, 1828–1906. En folkefiende. 2. Trondheim. Trøndelag teater. I. Ibsen, Henrik, 1828–1906. En folkefiende. 1972. II. Pierstorff, Erik, 1926– III. Wiklund, Ørjan. IV. Title.
PT8862.B3 73–314381
ISBN 82-504-0014-3

Bang-Hansen, Odd
see Fra Bach til Beatles : 17 epistler om musikk. Oslo : Tiden, [1973]

Bang-Kaup, Willy, 1869-1934, ed.
see Ford, John, 1586-ca. 1640. John Fordes Dramatische Werke... Nendeln, Liechtenstein, Kraus Reprinted, 1967.

Bằng-Phong.
Luận dề Nguyễn-công-Trứ và Cao-bá-Quát [dề tổng quát triết-lý, luân-lý và ky-thuật văn-chương. Saigon] A-Châu [19-?]
108 p. 22 cm. (Tủ sách Giáo khoa)
1. Nguyễn-công-Trứ, 1778-1858. 2. Cao-bá-Quát, d. 1854. I. Title.
CtY NUC73-107087

Bằng-Phong
see Nguyễn-duy-Diễn. Luân-dề về Đoan-tuyệt của Nhất-Linh. In lần 1. Saigon, Khai-Trí [1960]

Bàng Sĩ Nguyên.
Niềm vui; tập truyện. [Hà-nội] Thanh Niên [1961]
95 p. 19 cm.

I. Title.
PL4378.9.B3N5 73-210022

Bàng Thúc Long.
Ngư'ò'i trên núi cao; tập truyện ngắn. [Hà-nội] Văn Học, 1962.
88 p. 19 cm.

I. Title.
PL4378.9.B33N5 73-220829

Bàng Thúc Long, ed.
see Hầu phương thi dua vói tiên phương. Hanoi, Phổ Thông, 1968-69.

Banga, Dezider, comp.
Čierny vlas; Cigánske rozprávky. Z cigán. prel. a pre tlač. pripr. autor. Ilustr. ... Ferdinand Hložník. 1. vyd. Košice, Východoslov. tlač., 1969.
149, [3] p. col. illus. (also on lining paper), front. 24 cm. Kčs30.00
CzS 69
Illustrated t. p.
1. Tales, Gipsy. I. Title.
PZ70.S45B3 74-347375

Baṅgadarśana
see Baṅgadarśana. 1975.

(Baṅgadarśana)
বঙ্গদর্শন : নির্বাচিত রচনাসংগ্রহ / সম্পাদক রবীন্দ্র গুপ্ত ; দেবীপদ ভট্টাচার্যের মুখবন্ধ সংবলিত. — কলকাতা : চারুপ্রকাশ : পরিবেশন-কেন্দ্র, বিদ্যাসাগর পুস্তক মন্দির, 1975.
16, 471 p. ; 22 cm.
In Bengali.
Rs20.00
1. Bengali literature—History and criticism—Addresses, essays, lectures. 2. Bengal—Intellectual life—Addresses, essays, lectures. I. Gupta, Rabīndra. II. Baṅgadarśana.
PK1700.B3 76-901408

Bangalore, India (City). Christian Institute for the Study of Religion and Society
see Christian Institute for the Study of Religion and Society, Bangalore, India.

Bangalore, India (City). Dharmaram College
see
Dharmaram College.

Bangalore, India (City). Documentation, Research, and Training Centre.
Abstracting, indexing, and reviewing periodicals, pattern of use of documents by specialists, comparative study of schemes for library classification. — Bangalore : Documentation Research and Training Centre, Indian Statistical Institute, 1971-
v. ; 29 cm. — (Its Annual seminar ; 9)
Includes bibliographical references.
CONTENTS: pt. 1. Papers.
1. Documentation—Congresses. I. Title. II. Series.
Z1008.B27 no. 9 029 77-986081
77 MARC

Bangalore, India (City). Documentation, Research, and Training Centre.
Course leading to the master's degree in library science/documentation; orientation of readers. Bangalore, 1972.
2 v. 30 cm. (Its Annual seminar 10)
Includes bibliographical references.
1. Library schools and training—Addresses, essays, lectures. 2. Libraries and readers—Addresses, essays, lectures. I. Title.
WU NUC75-24022

Bangalore, India (City). Documentation, Research, and Training Centre.
Depth classification: subject heading. **Bangalore, 1965.**
569 p. 29 cm. (Its Annual seminar, 3)
1. Subject cataloging—Congresses. I. Title. II. Series.
OKentU NUC73-2234

Bangalore, India (City). Documentation, Research, and Training Centre.
Document retrieval: classification, subject heading, presentation of information. Bangalore Documentation Research and Training Centre, 1964.
1 v. (various pagings) 30 cm. (Its Annual seminar 2)
Annual seminar: Dec. 21-25, 1964.
Includes bibliographical references.
1. Classification—Addresses, essays, lectures. 2. Subject headings—Addresses, essays, lectures. 3. Information storage and retrieval systems—Addresses, essays, lectures. I. Title.
WU NUC75-29482

Bangalore, India (City). Documentation, Research, and Training Centre.
Rendering of names of corporate bodies; subject analysis, with sepecial reference to social sciences; documentation systems for industry. Bangalore, 1970.
2 v. (Its Annual seminar 8)
1. Cataloging. I. Title. II. Series.
OCIJC OCIW NUC73-126303

Bangalore, India (City). Documentation, Research, and Training Centre.
Subject analysis for document finding systems, quantification and librametric studies, management of translation service. Bangalore, 1969.
2 v. (834 p.) illus. (Its Annual seminar 7)
Includes bibliography.
1. Information storage and retrieval systems. I. Title.
MiU OCIJC OCIW NUC73-126302

Bangalore, India (City). Documentation, Research, and Training Centre.
Theory and practice of abstracting developments in classification technique of teaching documentation. Bangalore, 1968.
2 v. (Its Annual seminar 6)
1. Physics. 2. Textiles. 3. Leather. 4. Hindi literature. 5. Abstracting. I. Title. II. Series.
OCIJC NUC73-126304

Bangalore, India (City). Documentation, Research, and Training Centre
see Seminar on Cataloguing, 1st, Documentation, Research, and Training Centre, 1970. Working paper and proceedings. Bangalore, 1970.

Bangalore, India (City). Mysore State Botanical Garden.
Plant wealth in Lal-Bagh [by] M. H. Mari Gowda [and] M. Krishnaswamy. [Lalbagh, Bangalore? 1968]
166 p.
1. Botanical gardens—India. 2. Lal-Bagh—Catalogs. I. Mari Gowda, M. H.
KMK NUC77-15745

Bangalore, India (City). National Aeronautical Laboratory.
Current research programmes — National Aeronautical Laboratory.
Bangalore.
v. 28 cm.
1. Bangalare, India (City). National Aeronautical Laboratory. 2. Aeronautical research—India—Periodicals.
TL568.B3B35a 629.13'007'205487 74-648746
MARC-S

Bangalore, India (City). National Aeronautical Laboratory.
NAL news letter. v. 1-
Aug. 1973-
[Bangalore, National Aeronautical Laboratory]
v. in ill. 28 cm. monthly.
1. Bangalore, India (City). National Aeronautical Laboratory. I. Title.
TL500.B34a 629.13'007'205487 76-648485
MARC-S

Bangalore, India (City). Rashtrothana Parishat
see
Rashtrothana Parishat.

Bangalore, India (City). United Theological College of South India and Ceylon. Library.
Indian church history archives. Revised catalogue, 1968. [Bangalore, United Theological College Library, 1968]
48 p.
Cover title.
1. Church records and registers—India—Catalogs. 2. Library catalogs. I. Title.
CtHC NUC75-108024

Bangalore, India (City). University.
Research journal: humanities number.
Bangalore.
v. 23 cm. annual.
I. Title.
AS472.B3517 052 72-905270
MARC-S

Bangalore, India (City). University
see Gajendragadkar, Pralhad Balacharya, 1901- Search for industrial harmony. Bangalore [1972]

Bangalore, India (City). University
see Kavi Bendre. 1975.

Bangalore, India (City). University
see Mysore State year-book. Bangalore.

Bangalore, India (City). University
see Symposium on Strength and Deformation Behavior of Soils, Bangalore, India, 1972. Proceedings. [Bangalore] 1972-

Bangalore, India (City). University. Centre of Kannada Studies.
see Pampa, ondu adhyayana. 1974.

Bangalore, India (City). University. Dept. of Publications and Extension Lectures
see Vignana bharathi. Bangalore [India] 1975-

Bangalore, India (City). University. Kannada Adhyayana Kendrada
see
Bangalore, India (City). University. Centre of Kannada Studies.

Bangalore, India (City). University of Agricultural Sciences
see University of Agricultural Sciences.

Bangalore, India (City). Vallabhbhai Patel Institute
see
Vallabhbhai Patel Institute.

Bangalore Association of Teacher Educators.
see Conference of Teacher Educators of Mysore State, 1st, Bangalore, India, 1968. The first conference of teacher educators of Mysore State, Bangalore, January 6th and 7th, 1968. Bangalore, Bangalore Assocation of Teacher Educators, 1968.

Bangalore Civic Workers' Convention, 1960.
Our civic problems; incorporating the proceedings of the Bangalore civic workers' convention held on 26th June 1960, together with other articles of civic importance. Bangalore, Gokhale Institute of Public Affairs, 1961.
viii, 64 p. illus. 22 cm. (Gokhale Institute of Public Affairs, Bangalore. Public affairs pamphlet, 4)
1. Bangalore, India (City)—Politics and government—Congresses. I. Title. II. Series: Gokhale Institute of Public Affairs, Bangalore, India. Public affairs pamphlet, 4.
JS7030.B32B3 1960 74-204362

Bangalore Tamil Sangam.
(Peṅkaḷūrt Tamiḻc Caṅkam veḷḷi viḻā malar)
பெங்களூர்த் தமிழ்ச் சங்கம் வெள்ளி விழா மலர், 1950–1974. — பெங்களூர் : பெங்களூர்த் தமிழ்ச் சங்கம், [pref. 1975]
8, 104, 32 p. : ill. ; 27 cm.
English or Tamil.

1. Tamil literature—History and criticism—Addresses, essays, lectures. 2. Bangalore Tamil Sangam. I. Title.

PL4758.05.B35 77–900581

Bangalore University
see
Bangalore, India (City). University.

(Baṅgasāhitya sambhāra)
বঙ্গসাহিত্য সম্ভার / পরিকল্পনা প্রেমেন্দ্র মিত্র ; সম্পাদনা প্রতিভাকান্ত মৈত্র. — কলিকাতা : বুক ক্লাব, 1960–
v. ; 23 cm.
In Bengali.

1. Bengali literature. I. Mitra, Premendra. II. Moitra, Pratibha Kanto, 1926–

PK1713.B34 75–985741

Bangay, Garth E.
see Population estimates for the Great Lakes Basins... Burlington, Ont., Inland Waters Directorate, Canada Centre for Inland Waters, 1973.

Bangbose, Ayo
see Seminar on Yoruba Verb Phrase, University of Ibadan, 1971. The Yoruba verb phrase. [Ibadan] Ibadan University Press, 1972.

Bangdiwala, Ishver S
The effect of socio-economic levels on selected educational factors in Puerto Rico / by Ishver B. Bangdiwala. — [Río Piedras] : University of Puerto Rico, Río Piedras Campus, College of Education, Dept. of Graduate Studies, 1974.
v, 77 p. ; 28 cm.
Includes bibliographical references.
1. Students socio-economic status—Puerto Rico. I. Title.
LC205.5.P8B36 370.19'341 75-620926
75 MARC

Bange, G A
An analysis of floral wholesaling facilities in Los Angeles, California / by Gerald A. Bange. -- Washington : Agricultural Research Service, U.S. Dept. of Agriculture, 1976.
38 p. : ill., maps (1 part fold) -- (U.S. Dept. of Agriculture. Marketing research report ; no. 1042)
1. Flowers. Marketing. 2. Flowers. California. Los Angeles. Marketing. I. United States. Agricultural Research Service. II. Title.
DNAL NUC77-89204

Bange, G A
Planning and accounting for profit in floriculture. College Park, 1972.
35 p. (Maryland. Agricultural Experiment Station. Miscellaneous publication 806)
I. Title.
DNAL NUC73-113587

Bange, Hans.
Das Gladbacher Münster im 19. Jahrhundert : Wiederherstellung u. Neuausstattung / Hans Bange. — Mönchengladbach : Stadtarchiv Mönchengladbach, 1973.
208 p, 30 leaves of plates : ill. ; 23 cm. — (Beiträge zur Geschichte von Stadt und Abtei Mönchengladbach ; 4) GFR 74–B
Errata slip inserted.
Includes bibliographical references and index.
1. Mönchen-Gladbach, Ger. Münster. 2. Church architecture—Mönchen-Gladbach, Ger.—Conservation and restoration. I. Title. II. Series.
NA5586.M595B36 74–355898

Bange, Hans.
Das Münster zu Mönchengladbach / [von Hans Bange]. — Neuss : Gesellschaft für Buchdruckerei, [1974].
23 p. : ill. ; 21 cm. — (Rheinische Kunststätten ; Heft 1974, 5) GFR 74–A34
Cover title.
Bibliography : p. 23.
1. Mönchen-Gladbach, Ger. Münster. I. Title. II. Series.
N3.R45 1974, Heft 5 75–592204
[NA5586.M595]

Bange, Pierre.
Ironie et dialogisme dans les romans de Theodor Fontane. [Grenoble] Presses universitaires de Grenoble, 1974.
304 p. 24 cm. (Collection Theta) 65.00F F***
At head of title: Université Lyon II.
Bibliography: p. [291]–297.
1. Fontane, Theodor, 1819–1898—Technique. I. Title.
PT1863.Z7B34 833'.8 74–174297
ISBN 2-7061-0024-9 MARC

Bangemann, Martin, 1934-
Die Direktwahl, Sackgasse oder Chance für Europa? : Analysen u. Dokumente / Martin Bangemann, Roland Bieber. — 1. Aufl. — Baden-Baden : Nomos-Verlagsgesellschaft, 1976.
188 p. ; 18 cm.
Bibliography: p. 185-186. GFR77-A
Includes index.
ISBN 3-7890-0244-5
1. European Parliament—Elections. I. Bieber, Roland, joint author. II. Title.
JN36.B35 341.24'2 77-468537
77 MARC

Bangen, P
Hämatologische Untersuchungen nach "kritischer" Dekompression aus Überdruck, von P. Bangen. [Porz-Wahn, Deutsche Forschungs- und Versuchsanstalt für Luft-und Raumfahrt] 1973.
57 p. illus. (Deutsche Luft-und Raumfahrt. Forschungsbericht 73-63)
Summary in German and English.
ICRL NUC76-72879

Bangert, Albrecht, 1944-
Gründerzeit : Kunstgewerbe zwischen 1850 und 1900 / Albrecht Bangert. — Originalausg. — München : W. Heyne, c1976.
170 p. : ill. ; 18 cm. — (Heyne-Buch ; Nr. 4479 : Antiquitäten) GFR***
Bibliography: p. 163-164.
Includes index.
ISBN 3-453-41154-4
1. Art industries and trade, Victorian. 2. Antiques. I. Title.
NK775.B36 745.1'09'034 77-450862
77 MARC

Bangert, C. C., ed.
see Automotive Mower Associates. Power mower troubleshooting; a handbook. [2d rev. ed.] New York, Exposition Press [c1964]

Bangert, Charles W., tr.
see Eikeboom, Rogier, 1922- Programmed Latin grammar. [Glenview, Ill.] Scott, Foresman and Co. [1970]

Bangert, Dieter Ernst.
see Russia. Laws, statutes, etc. Artikul voinskiĭ. German & Russian. Krieges-Articuln mit kurtzen Anmerckungen. Faksimiledruck der 2. Ausg. 1935. Osnabrück, Biblio Verlag, 1976.

Bangert, Dieter Ernst.
see Russia. Laws, statutes, etc. Ustav voinskiĭ. German & Russian. Kriegs-Reglement von der Pflicht und Schuldigkeit der General-Feld-Marschälle und der gantzen Generalität (russisch-deutsch) Faksimiledruck der 2. Ausg. 1737. Osnabrück, Biblio Verlag, 1976.

Bangert, Ethel.
Nurse of the Sacramento. New York, Avalon Books [c1971]
189 p. 20 cm. (Avalon nurse stories)
I. Title.
OU NUC73-113627

Bangert, Harold W.
see America needs a new economic policy now. [Manila] Araneta U. Research Foundation for the 1971 Constitutional Convention, 1971.

Bangert, Hildebrand
see Neuzeitliche Verfahren der Werkstoffprufung. Düsseldorf, Verl. f. Stahleisen, 1973.

Bangert, Uwe.
Neumünster: Aquarelle u. Federzeichn/ von Uwe Bangert. — Neumünster: Wachholtz, 1972.
[54] p. (on double leaves) : chiefly ill. (part col.) ; 22 x 30 cm. DM30.00 GDB 72–A47
1. Neumünster, Ger.—Description—Views.
ND1954.B28A52 73–302671

Bangert, William V
A bibliographical essay on the history of the Society of Jesus : books in English / William V. Bangert. — St. Louis : Institute of Jesuit Sources, 1976.
xiv, 75 p. ; 23 cm. — (Study aids on Jesuit topics ; no. 6)
Includes index.
ISBN 0-912422-16-5 Smyth sewn pbk. : $2.50
1. Jesuits—Bibliography. I. Title. II. Series.
Z7840.J5B36 016.271'53 76-12667
[BX3702.2] 76 MARC

Bangert, William V
A history of the Society of Jesus [by] William V. Bangert. St. Louis, Institute of Jesuit Sources, 1972.
xii, 558 p. maps. 24 cm. $14.75
1. Jesuits—History. I. Title.
BX3706.2.B33 271'.53'009 78–188687
ISBN 0-912422-05-X MARC

Bangert, Wolfgang.
Die Mittelstadt. 3. Teil: Grundlagen und Entwicklungstendenzen der städtebaulichen. Struktur ausgewählter Mittelstädte. Hannover, Jänecke, 1972.
xi, 121 p. illus., maps (part col., 3 fold. in pocket) 25 cm. (Akademie für Raumforschung und Landesplanung, Hanover. Forschungs- und Sitzungsberichte, Bd. 70)
"Stadtforschung 3."
Bibliography: p. 116-121.
1. Cities and towns—Growth—Case studies. 2. Cities and towns—Germany.
NN NUC76-72857

Bangerter, Arnold.
Bear River investigations: Cache and Box Elder Counties, 1962–1965. [Salt Lake City] State of Utah, Division of Fish and Game [1967]
149 l. illus. 28 cm. (Utah. Division of Fish and Game. Publication no. 67–11)
Bibliography: leaf 149.
1. Fishes, Fresh-water—Utah—Bear River. 2. Limnology—Utah—Bear River. 3. Bear River, Utah-Idaho. I. Title. II. Series.
SH11.U78a no. 67–11 639'.08 s 74–163683
[QL628.U8] [597'.0929'79212] MARC

Bangerter, Arnold.
Fish Lake research project : final report / by Arnold Bangerter. — [Salt Lake City] : State of Utah, Dept. of Natural Resources, Division of Wildlife Resources, 1973.
38 leaves ; 28 cm. — (Publication - State of Utah, Division of Wildlife Resources ; no. 73-6)
1. Fishery management—Utah—Fish Lake. 2. Rainbow trout. 3. Fish Lake, Utah. I. Title. II. Series: Utah. Division of Wildlife Resources. Publication ; no. 73-6.
SK453.A25 no. 73-6 333.9'5 s 75-318958
75 MARC

Bangerter, Arnold.
Lower Strawberry River investigations 1966. [Salt Lake City] 1966.
31 l. graphs, tables.
Cover title.
1. Fishing—Utah. 2. Strawberry River, Utah. I. Title.
UU NUC73-2228

Bangerter, Charlotte.
We d Blüemli erwache : zwei Märchenspiele / von Charlotte Bangerter. -- Aarau : Sauerländer, 1975.
16 p. ; 21 cm. -- (Jugendborn-Sammlung ; Heft 172)
I. Title.
NmU NUC77-86589

Bangerter, Lowell A 1941-
Schiller and Hofmannsthal / Lowell A. Bangerter. — Madrid : Dos Continentes, 1974.
269 p. ; 21 cm. Sp***
Bibliography: p. 263-269.
ISBN 8485065190
1. Hofmannsthal, Hugo Hofmann, Edler von, 1874-1929—Criticism and interpretation. 2. Schiller, Johann Christoph Friedrich von, 1759-1805—Influence—Hofmannsthal. I. Title.
PT2617.O47Z7325 75-503721
75 MARC

Bangerter, Walter
see Afrikanische Kunstwerke. [Recklinghausen, A. Bongers, 1971]

Bangham, Ralph Vandervort, 1895–1966.
A resurvey of the fish parasites of western Lake Erie [by] Ralph V. Bangham. Columbus, Ohio State University, 1972.
vi, 23 p. 26 cm. (Bulletin of the Ohio Biological Survey, new ser., v. 4, no. 2)
Bibliography: p. 19–20.
1. Fishes—Erie, Lake—Diseases and pests. 2. Parasites—Fishes. I. Title. II. Series: Ohio Biological Survey. Bulletin, new ser., v. 4, no. 2.
QH105.O3A3 n. s., vol. 4, no. 2   574′.09771 s   73–621675
[QL628.E]   [597′.05′24]   MARC

Banghart, Frank William.
Educational planning [by] Frank W. Banghart [and] Albert Trull, Jr. New York, Macmillan [1972, c1973]
xi, 463 p. illus. 24 cm.
Bibliography: p. 451–457.
1. Educational planning. 2. Cities and towns—Planning—History. 3. Education—Economic aspects. I. Trull, Albert, joint author.
LB2805.B27   371.2′07   74–163613
MARC

Banghart, Frank William
see Florida. State University, Tallahassee. Educational Systems and Planning Center. Simulation for determining student station requirements... [Tallahassee, 1970 ?]

Banghart, Frank William
see Phi Delta Kappa Symposium on Educational Research, 1st, 1959. First annual Phi Delta Kappa Symposium on Educational Research. Bloomington, Ind. [c1960]

Bangia, T. R., joint author
see Joshi, Balwant Duttatraya, 1923– Chemical separation and spectrographic estimation of some common impurities in high purity selenium. Bombay, Bhabha Atomic Research Centre, 1971.

Bangia, T. R., joint author
see Joshi, Balwant Duttatraya, 1923– Spectrographic estimation of tellurium in high purity selenium after removing selenium by volatilization. Bombay, Bhabha Atomic Research Centre, 1971.

Bangini, L A
Aids to the study of the Ewe language, by L. A. Badini. [n.p., 197-?]
56 p. 19 cm.
1. Ewe language–Grammar. I. Title.
NRU   NUC73-113626

Bangiya Bijnan Parishad
see Jñāna o bijñāna.

বঙ্গীয় লোক-সঙ্গীত রত্নাকর; বাংলার লোক-সঙ্গীতের কোষ-গ্রন্থ. An encyclopaedia of Bengali folk-song. শ্রীআশুতোষ ভট্টাচার্য সম্পাদিত. [1. সংস্করণ] কলিকাতা, পশ্চিমবঙ্গ লোক-সংস্কৃতি গবেষণা পরিষদ [1966-67]
4 v. (13, 2047 p.) illus. 23 cm. 6.00 per vol.
In Bengali.
Vols. 2–4 include list of the author's works.
1. Folk-songs, Bengali—Texts. I. Bhattacharya, Asutosh, 1909– ed. II. Title. III. Title: An encyclopaedia of Bengali folk-song.
Title transliterated: Baṅgīya loka-saṅgīta ratnākara.
M1808.B35   S A 67–2333
PL 480 : I–B–2652
MN

Bangiya Sahitya Parishad, Calcutta
see Smāraka grantha. [1973?]

Bangiya Sahitya Parishad, Calcutta. Museum.
Descriptive list of sculptures & coins in the museum of the Bangiya Sahitya Parishad, by Rakhaldas Banerji. With an introd. by Ramendra Sundara Trivedi. Calcutta, R. K. Sinha, 1911.
7, 48, 5 p. 22 cm.
1. Bangiya Sahitya Parishad, Calcutta. Museum. 2. Sculpture—Calcutta—Catalogs. 3. Sculpture, Ancient—Catalogs. 4. Coins—Calcutta—Catalogs. 5. Coins, Ancient—Catalogs. I. Banerji, Rakhal Das, 1885–1930. II. Title.
NB71.C3B363   73–172072
MARC

Bangko sa Lupa ng Pilipinas
see
Land Bank of the Philippines.

Bangkok, Thailand. Asian Institute for Economic **Development and Planning.**
An approach to evolving guidelines for rural development : a report on the Expert Group meetin December 9-13, 1974. — Bangkok : United Nations Asian Development Institute, 1975.
iv, 67 p. ; 26 cm. — (Discussion paper series - United Nations Asian Development Institute ; no. 1)
1. Asia—Economic policy—Congresses. 2. Asia—Rural conditions—Congresses. 3. Community development—Asia—Congresses. I. Title. II. Series: Bangkok, Thailand. Asian Institute for Development and Planning. Discussion paper series - United Nations Asian Development Institute ; no. 1.
HC412.B322 1975   338.95   76-350348
76   MARC

Bangkok, Thailand. Asian Institute for Economic Development and Planning.
Education in Asia: a bibliography. [n.p.] 1969.
34 p. 28 cm. (Eric reports, Ed -49142)
"Supplements and up-dates the bibliography for A review of education in the Asian region which appeared in the Bulletin, v. 1, no. 1, Sept. 1966."
Photo-reproduction, 1969.
1. Education—Asia—Bibliography. I. Title. II. Series: U.S. Educational Resources Information Center. Eric reports, ED049142.
OO   NUC73-101656

Bangkok, Thailand. Asian Institute for Economic Development and Planning.
The UN Asian Institute for Economic Development and Planning; progress report on phase I, 1964–1968. Bangkok, 1969.
47 p. illus. 28 cm.
Cover title.
1. Economic research—Asia.
H64.B35B3   330′.07′205   73–171888
MARC

Bangkok, Thailand. Asian Institute for Economic Development and Planning.
The UN Asian Institute for Economic Development and Planning. — Bangkok : The Institute, 1971.
34 p. : ill. ; 28 cm.
Cover title.
1. Bangkok, Thailand. Asian Institute for Economic Development and Planning. 2. Economic research—Asia. I. Title.
H64.B35B32 1971   330′.07′205   75-310434
75   MARC

Bangkok, Thailand. Asian Institute for Economic Development and Planning
see Guzman, Raul P de. Achieving self-sufficiency in rice. Bangkok, Thailand, 1969.

Bangkok, Thailand. Asian Institute for Economic Development and Planning
see Mehta, Madhava Mal. Manpower and training requirements... [Bangkok? 1966]

Bangkok, Thailand. Asian Institute for Economic Development and Planning
see Sarkar, N K Industrial structure of Greater Bangkok. Bangkok, United Nations, Asian Institute for Economic Development and Planning, 1974.

Bangkok, Thailand. Asian Institute for Economic Development and Planning.
see Symposium on Development Aims and Socio-Cultural Values in Asia, Bangkok, Thailand, 1975. Asian rethinking on development . . . 1st ed. New Delhi, Abhinav Publications, 1976.

Bangkok, Thailand. Asian Institute for Economic Development and Planning
see Vietnam. Tổng Nha Kế-hoạch. Handbook of Vietnam country course... -- Saigon : [s.n., 1971?]

Bangkok, Thailand. Asian International Trade Fair, 1st, 1966
see Asian International Trade Fair, 1st, Bangkok, Thailand, 1966.

Bangkok, Thailand. Bank for Agriculture and Agricultural Co-operatives
see
Thanākhān phư̄a Kānkasēt lǣ Sahakō̜n Kānkaset, Bangkok, Thailand.

Bangkok, Thailand. Chulalongkorn University. German Section
see Festschrift zum 10. [i. e. zehnten] Jahrestage der Wiedereröffnung der Deutschkurse an der Chulalongkorn-Universität zu Bangkok am 12. Sept. 1967. Bangkok, 1967.

Bangkok, Thailand. English Language Center
see
English Language Center, Bangkok, Thailand.

Bangkok, Thailand. Hō samut hǣeng chāt
see Bangkok, Thailand. National Library.

Bangkok, Thailand. Institute for Child Study
see Bangkok Institute for Child Study.

Bangkok, Thailand. Mahamakuta Rajavidyalaya
see An Outline of Buddhism. [Bangkok] 1971.

Bangkok, Thailand. Marine Fisheries Laboratory
see Marine Fisheries Laboratory.

Bangkok, Thailand. Marut Bunnag International Law Office
see
Marut Bunnag International Law Office.

Bangkok, Thailand. Medical Research Laboratory
see Applied Scientific Research Corporation of Thailand. Identification of rats of Thailand. Bangkok, 1966.

Bangkok, Thailand. Medical Research Laboratory

see also the earlier heading

Thailand SEATO Cholera Research Laboratory.

Bangkok, Thailand. Military Research and Development Center.
Changwat handbook: Nakhon Phanom, Thailand. Bangkok, Joint Thai-U.S. Military Research and Development Center [1967]
v. illus., maps (part col.) 29 cm.
Cover title.
In Thai and English.
Prepared for Advanced Research Projects Agency, Office of the Secretary of Defense, Washington, D.C. Philco-Ford Project R-1040.
Bibliography: v. 1, p.1. 9.01-1.9.04.
Contents.—v.1. Physical environment.
1. Thailand—Physical geography—Nakhon Phanom. I. Title.
DI-GS   NUC76-72856

Bangkok, Thailand. Military Research and Development Center
see Christensen, Knud. Vegetation and soil analyses of AMPIRT forest test site. Bangkok, 1965.

Bangkok, Thailand. Military Research and Development Center
see Neal, Donald G Statistical description of the forests of Thailand. Bangkok, 1967.

Bangkok, Thailand. National Institute of Development Administration.
A note on economic development of Thailand; under the first national economic development plan, 1961-1966, and important features of the second national economic and social development plan, 1967-1971. Bangkok, Thailand, 1967.
51 p. tables.
1. Thailand—Econ. policy. I. Title.
ICU   NUC74-91850

Bangkok, Thailand. National Institute of Development Administration. Research Center.
Thai government organization charts.
[Bangkok] 1973.
34 p. 20 x 27 cm.
English and Thai.
1. Thailand—Executive departments.
I. Title.
CtY NUC77-21210

Bangkok, Thailand. National Institute of Development Administration. Research Center
see Boonkitticharoen, Virapong, 1939-
A proposed alternative for approximating cost of living index numbers. Bangkok, 1970.

Bangkok, Thailand. National Library.
Accession list of foreign language books [received by 31 January 1971. Bangkok, 1971]
15 l. 35 cm.
Cover title.
Mimeographed typescript.
NIC NUC73-41281

Bangkok, Thailand. National Library
see The Burney papers. Farnborough, Eng., **Gregg International Pub., 1971.**

Bangkok, Thailand. National Library. Fine Arts Dept.
see Amatayakul, Tri. The official guide to Ayutthaya and Bang Pa-In. 2. ed. Bangkok, 1973.

Bangkok, Thailand. National Museum
see Subhadradis Diskul, Prince. Masterpieces from private collections... [Bangkok, 1970]

Bangkok, Thailand. National Museum. Fine Arts Dept.
Guide to the National Museum, Bangkok, Thailand. [3d ed. Bangkok, 1970]
1 v. (unpaged) illus. 22 cm.
1. Art, Thai–Collections. I. Title.
TNJ NUC74-115151

Bangkok, Thailand. Office of the Municipal Advisor.
Administrative organization of the Bangkok Municipality / [prepared in the Office of the Municipal Advisor]. — [s.l. : s.n.], 1963 (Bangkok : Local Affairs Press, Dept. of Local Administration, Ministry of Interior)
48 p. ; 26 cm.
Cover title.
1. Municipal government—Bangkok, Thailand. I. Title.
JS7415.B32B35 1963 352.0593 76-379664
76 MARC

Bangkok, Thailand. Securities Exchange of Thailand
see
Securities Exchange of Thailand.

Bangkok, Thailand. Stock Exchange
see
Bangkok Stock Exchange.

Bangkok, Thailand. Sūn Bō̜rikān ʻEkkasān Kānwichai hǣng Prathēt Thai
see
Sūn Bō̜rikān ʻEkkasān Kānwichai hǣng Prathēt Thai.

Bangkok, Thailand. Thailand SEATO Cholera Research Laboratory
see
Thailand SEATO Cholera Research Laboratory.

Bangkok, Thailand. Thanākhān phūʻa Kānkasēt laē Sahakō̜n Kānkasēt
see
Thanākhān phūʻa Kānkasēt laē Sahakō̜n Kānkasēt, Bangkok, Thailand.

Bangkok, Thailand. Witthayalai Wicha Kansuksa see Witthayālai Wichā Kānsyksā, Bangkok.

Bangkok Bank Limited. Ch'ang nien pao kao shu
see Bangkok Bank Limited. [P'an-ku yin hang ch'ang nien pao kao shu, Bangkok]

Bangkok Bank Limited.
[P'an-ku yin hang ch'ang nien pao kao shu]
盤谷銀行常年報告書
[Bangkok]
v. 27 cm.
附泰國經濟簡明統計
Issued also in English.
1. Thailand—Economic conditions. I. Bangkok Bank Limited. Ch'ang nien pao kao shu.
HG3350.5.A8B3 72-836526

Bangkok Bank Limited. Economic Research Division
see Statistical data on commercial banks in Thailand. Bangkok, Thailand.

Bangkok First Investment and Trust Limited.
Investment guide to Thailand. [Bangkok, 1971]
32 p. illus.
Cover title.
[Information on National Executive Council] (1 l.) inserted.
1. Investments—Thailand. 2. Investments. Foreign—Thailand.
HU NUC75-58856

Bangkok Institute for Child Study.
Summaries of three studies concerning the socialization of Thai children. Bangkok, 1967.
16 p. 26 cm.
1. Children in Thailand. I. Title.
CtY NUC74-3278

Bangkok post. Supplement
see SEAMEO today. [Bangkok] 1971.

Bangkok post
see Southeast Asian Ministers of Education Organization. SEAMEO after seven years. [Bangkok, 1972]

Bangkok post
see Vista. Bangkok : T. Latchford, managing director for Post Pub. Co. -- [s.l. : s.n.], 1969.

Bangkok Stock Exchange

see also the later heading

Securities Exchange of Thailand.

Bangkok, the natural geographic and business centre of Southeast Asia. [Bangkok, Siam Publications, 1971]
[16] p. (chiefly illus., maps)
1. Bangkok, Thailand–Description. 2. Bangkok, Thailand–Economic conditions.
HU NUC74-115149

Bangla Academy.
In 1972 the Bengali Academy and the Central Board for Development of Bengali merged to form the Bangla Academy.
Works by these bodies are found under the name used at the time of publication.

బంగ్లా దేశ్ గీతాంజలి; తెలుగు కవులవీ, ఆంధ్రేతర భారతీయ కవులవీ, బంగ్లా దేశ్ కవులవీ ఉత్తమ గీతాల సంకలనం. మద్రాసు, వికాస సాహితి; [ప్రతులకు: విశాలాంధ్ర ప్రచురణాలయం, విజయవాడ, 1971]
71 p. 19 cm. Re1.00
In Telugu.
1. Tamil poetry. Title romanized: Baṅglā Dēś gītāñjali.
PL4758.6.B34 72-927896

Bangla Desh
see also headings filed as one word: Bangladesh.

Bangla Desh documents. [New Delhi, Ministry of External Affairs, 1971–73]
2 v. fold. col. map (in pocket) 25 cm. Rs25.00 per vol.
"List of refugee camps": xii p. in pocket in v. 2.
1. Bangladesh—Politics and government—Sources. 2. Pakistan—Politics and government—Sources.
DS395.B34 954.9′2 78–926706
rev MARC

Bangla Desh economy: problems and prospects. Edited by V. K. R. V. Rao. Delhi, Vikas Publications [1972]
vi, 199 p. 23 cm. (Studies in economic growth, no. 15) Rs24.00
Includes bibliographical references.
1. Bangladesh—Economic conditions—Addresses, essays, lectures. I. Rao, Vijendra Kasturi Ranga Varadaraja, 1908– ed. II. Title. III. Series.
HC440.8.B36 330.9′549′205 72–904282
ISBN 0–7069–0177–0 MARC

Bangla Desh: people's fight for democracy and secularism. [Calcutta, Hooghly Printing, 1971]
[24] p. illus. 24 cm.
Cover title.
1. India–Pakistan Conflict, 1971-
NIC NUC74-115144

బంగ్లాదేశ్; కవితా స్పందన. సమీకర్త [మరి ప్రతులకు] ఎస్. కె. వరంగల్ [1971]
62 p. 19 cm. Re1.00
In Telugu.
1. Prose poems, Telugu. I. N. K. II. K., N. Title romanized: Baṅglādeś.
PL4780.8.B33 72-925248

బంగ్లాదేశ్. హైద్రాబాద్, ఆంధ్రప్రదేశ్ కమ్యూనిస్టు సమితి; [ప్రతులు దొరకుచోటు: విశాలాంధ్ర ప్రచురణాలయం, విజయవాడ, 1971]
118 p. illus. 22 cm. Rs1.50
In Telugu.
1. Bangladesh—History. Title romanized: Baṅglādēś.
DS395.B35 72–901926

Bangladéš-zrození státu; fakta melze zamlčet. [Praha] Knihovna Rudého práva, 1972.
94 p. illus. 23 cm. (Fakta nelze zamlčet, 2/72.) (Knihovna Rudého práva.) Kčs3.00 Cz***
1. Bangladesh—Politics and government. I. Series.
DS485.B492B36 73–362446

Bangladesh.
In 1905 the eastern districts of Bengal were separated and merged with Assam to form Eastern Bengal and Assam. In 1912 these districts were reunited with Bengal, and Assam was restored as a separate jurisdiction. In 1947 Bengal was partitioned to form East Bengal, Pakistan and West Bengal, India. In 1956 East Bengal became East Pakistan, which in 1971 changed its name to Bangladesh as an independent nation.
Works by East Bengal and East Pakistan are found under **East Pakistan.**
Works by the other jurisdictions are found under the name used at the time of publication.
72–225003

Bangladesh.
The Bangladesh gazette. Dec. 23/30, 1971–
Dacca.
v. 35 cm. weekly
Includes extraordinary numbers.
1. Law—Bangladesh. 2. Bangladesh—Politics and government. I. Title.
340′.095492 72–908050
MARC-S

Bangladesh.
Bangladesh police regulations / edited by A. T. M. Kamru Islam. — 1st ed. — Dacca : Khoshroz Kitab Mahal, 197
v. ; 22 cm.
Tk35.00 (v. 1)
1. Police—Bangladesh. I. Kamrul Islam, A. T. M. II. Title.
345′.5492′052 75-9077
76 MAR

Bangladesh.
Police regulations, Bengal, 1943 / issued with the authority of the Government of the People's Republic of Bangladesh. — Dacca : Bangladesh Govt. Press, [19—]-19
v. ; 26 cm.
At head of title, v. 2: Govt. of the People's Republic of Bangladesh. Bangladesh Police.
CONTENTS:
—v. 2. Appendices. Forms.—v. 3. Index to Police regulations, Bengal, 1943.
Tk15.00 (v. 2) .Tk3.00 (v. 3)
1. Police—Bangladesh. I. Title.
345′.5492′052 75-90041
75 MAR

Bangladesh. Agriculture, Ministry of
see
Bangladesh. Ministry of Agriculture.

Bangladesh. Atomic Energy Commission
see
Bangladesh Atomic Energy Commission.

Bangladesh. Bureau of Statistics.
The Provincial Statistical Board and Bureau of Commercial and Industrial Intelligence of East Pakistan was reorganized in Jan. 1962 as the Bureau of Statistics. In 1971 the Bureau of Statistics of East Pakistan became the Bureau of Statistics of Bangladesh.
Works by these bodies are found under the following headings according to the name used at the time of publication:
East Pakistan. Provincial Statistical Board and Bureau of Commercial and Industrial Intelligence.
East Pakistan. Bureau of Statistics.
Bangladesh. Bureau of Statistics.
73-212803

Bangladesh. Bureau of Statistics.
Agricultural production levels in Bangladesh, 1947-1972. — [Dacca] : Bangladesh Bureau of Statistics, Statistics Division, Ministry of Planning, [1976]
xxv, 305 p. ; 26 cm.
Chiefly tables.
"Corrigenda" : (2 p.) inserted.
1. Field crops—Bangladesh—Statistics. I. Title.
SB187.B3B37 1976 338.1'09549'2 77-900980
77 MARC

Bangladesh. Bureau of Statistics.
Monthly statistical bulletin of Bangladesh. v. 1- Mar. 1972-
Dacca.
v. 25 cm.
Supersedes East Pakistan. Bureau of Statistics. Monthly bulletin of statistics.
1. Bangladesh—Statistics—Periodicals. 2. Bangladesh—Economic conditions—Periodicals. I. Title.
HA1730.8.A23 315.49'2 73-929599
MARC-S

Bangladesh. Bureau of Statistics.
Population projection of Bangladesh by age and sex from 1960 to 2005 A.D., January 1976. — [Dacca] : Bangladesh Bureau of Statistics, Statistics Division, Ministry of Planning, Govt. of the People's Republic of Bangladesh, [pref. 1976]
iii, 57 p. ; 29 cm. — (Population and demographic research series ; no. 1)
1. Population forecasting—Bangladesh. I. Title. II. Series.
HB3640.6.B36 1976 312'.09549'2 76-902568
76 MARC

Bangladesh. Bureau of Statistics
see Statistical digest of Bangladesh. no. 8- 1972- [Dacca]

Bangladesh. Census Commission.
Bangladesh census of population, 1974. — Dacca : Census Commission, Ministry of Home Affairs, Govt. of the People's Republic of Bangladesh, [1975]
ii, ii, 218 p. : ill. ; 24 cm. — (Bulletin - Census Commission ; no. 2) (Census publication ; no. 26)
Chiefly tables.
1. Bangladesh—Census, 1974. I. Title. II. Series: Bangladesh. Census Commission. Bulletin - Census Commission ; no. 2. III. Series: Census publication ; no. 26.
HA1730.8.A44 1975 312'.09549'2 77-151987
77 MARC

Bangladesh. Census Commission.
Bangladesh census of population, 1974 : provisional results. — Dacca : Census Commission, Ministry of Home Affairs, Govt. of the People's Republic of Bangladesh, [1974]
59 p. : maps ; 24 cm. — (Bulletin - Census Commission ; 1)
Tk10.00
1. Bangladesh—Census, 1974. I. Title. II. Series: Bangladesh. Census Commission. Bulletin - Census Commission ; 1.
HA1730.8.A44 312'.09549'2 75-902825
76 MARC

Bangladesh. Constitution.
Constitution of the People's Republic of Bangladesh. [Dacca] 1972.
91 p. 27 cm. Tk2.40
Caption title.
"Published in the Bangladesh Gazette, extraordinary, part I, dated the 14th December 1972."
1. Bangladesh—Constitutional law. I. Title.
342'.5492'023 73-900565
MARC

Bangladesh. Constitution.
The Constitution of the People's Republic of Bangladesh, as modified up to 25th January 1975. — [Dacca : Bangladesh Forms and Publications Office, pref. 1975]
viii, 203 p. ; 26 cm.
On cover: Government of the People's Republic of Bangladesh. Ministry of Law, Parliamentary Affairs and Justice.
Imprint from label mounted on back cover.
Tk13.42
1. Bangladesh—Constitutional law. I. Bangladesh. Ministry of Law, Parliamentary Affairs and Justice. II. Title.
342'.5492'023 76-901151
76 MARC

Bangladesh. Constitution.
The Constitution of the People's Republic of Bangladesh; passed by the Constituent Assembly of Bangladesh on the 4th Nov. 1972 and authenticated by the Speaker on the 14th Dec. 1972. [Dacca] Constituent Assembly of Bangladesh [1972]
vii, 83 p. 25 cm.
Cover title.
"Authorised English translation."
1. Bangladesh—Constitutional law. I. Title.
342'.5492'02 73-929582
MARC

Bangladesh. Constitution.
(Gaṇaprajātantrī Bāṃlādeśera saṃbidhāna)
গণপ্রজাতন্ত্রী বাংলাদেশের সংবিধান. — [ঢাকা] : বাংলাদেশ গণপরিষদ, [1972]
82 p. ; 26 cm.
Caption title.
In Bengali.
"১৯৭২ সালের ১৪ই ডিসেম্বর 'বাংলাদেশ গেজেটের অতিরিক্ত সংখ্যায়' প্রথম খন্ডে প্রকাশিত."
Tk2.25
1. Bangladesh—Constitutional law. I. Title.
76-903820

Bangladesh. Constitution.
(Gaṇaprajātantrī Bāṃlādeśera saṃbidhāna)
গণপ্রজাতন্ত্রী বাংলাদেশের সংবিধান : ১৯৭২ সালের ৪ঠা নভেম্বর তারিখে বাংলাদেশ গণপরিষদ কর্তৃক গৃহীত এবং ১৯৭২ সালের ১৪ই ডিসেম্বর তারিখে স্পীকার কর্তৃক প্রমাণীকৃত. — [ঢাকা] : বাংলাদেশ গণপরিষদ, [1973?]
8, 74 p. ; 25 cm.
Cover title.
In Bengali.
1. Bangladesh—Constitutional law. I. Title.
75-901843

Bangladesh. Constitution.
see Rahim, Syed Bazlur. Constitutional law in Bangladesh. Dacca, Publishers International, 1973.

Bangladesh. Dept. of Forest.
Progress report, 1966-72 : prepared for the tenth Commonwealth Forestry Conference, 1974 / by the Dept. of Forest of the People's Republic of Bangladesh. — [Dacca?] : The Dept., 1975.
26 p. ; 25 cm.
Cover title.
1. Forests and forestry—Bangladesh. I. British Commonwealth Forestry Conference, 10th, 1974.
SD235.B35B35 1975 338.1'7'49095492 75-325759
75 MARC

Bangladesh. Directorate of Agriculture (Extension and Management).
see Workshop on Experience with High Yielding Varieties of Rice Cultivation in Bangladesh, Bangladesh Rice Research Institute, 1975. Workshop on Experience with High Yielding Varieties of Rice Cultivation in Bangladesh. [Dacca] Bangladesh Rice Research Institute, [1975]

Bangladesh. Expert Committee on Pharmaceutical Industry.
Quantitative estimates of the requirement of drugs and medicines in Bangladesh : report of the sub-committee constituted by the Expert Committee on Pharmaceutical Industry. — [Dacca] : Dept. of Industries, Chemical Directorate, Govt. of the People's Republic of Bangladesh, [1976]
ii, [i.e. iv] 122 p. ; 26 cm.
On back cover: Published by the assistant controller-in-charge, Bangladesh Forms & Publications Office, Dacca.
Tk87.72
1. Drug trade—Bangladesh. I. Title.
HD9657.B362B36 1976 380.1'45'61510954 76-902709
77 MARC

Bangladesh. Export Promotion Bureau.
Major exportable products of Bangladesh. — [Dacca] : Export Promotion Bureau, Govt. of the People's Republic of Bangladesh, [pref. 1973]
ii, 27 p. ; 26 cm.
1. Foreign trade promotion—Bangladesh. 2. Commercial products—Bangladesh. I. Title.
HF1590.6.B36 1973 382'.6'095492 76-902518
77 MARC

Bangladesh. Finance, Ministry of
see
Bangladesh. Ministry of Finance.

Bangladesh. Forest, Dept. of
see
Bangladesh. Dept. of Forest.

Bangladesh. Home Affairs, Ministry of
see
Bangladesh. Ministry of Home Affairs.

Bangladesh. Industries, Ministry of
see
Bangladesh. Ministry of Industries.

Bangladesh. Information and Broadcasting, Ministry of
see
Bangladesh. Ministry of Information and Broadcasting.

Bangladesh. Jute Division.
The jute season. 1970/72-
[Dacca] Govt. of the People's Republic of Bangladesh, Jute Division.
v. ill. 25 cm. annual.
Report for 1970/72 covers the seasons 1970/71-1971/72.
1. Jute industry—Bangladesh. I. Title.
HD9156.J8B253a 76-640911
338.4'7'67713095492 MARC-S

Bangladesh. Laws, statutes, etc. Bangladesh laws (revision and declaration) act, 1973. 1974.
see Bangladesh. Laws, statutes, etc. The Bangladesh penal code. 1st ed. Dacca, Khoshroz Kitab Mahal, 1974.

Bangladesh. Laws, statutes, etc.
The Bangladesh penal code / Osman Ghani and Mozammel Haque. — 1st ed. — Dacca : Khoshroz Kitab Mahal, 1974.
234, vii p. ; 23 cm.
Includes text of Bangladesh laws (revision and declaration) act, 1973.
Tk13.00
1. Criminal law—Bangladesh. I. Bangladesh. Laws, statutes, etc. Bangladesh laws (revision and declaration) act, 1973. 1974. II. Ghani, Osman. III. Mozammel Haque. IV. Title.
345'.5492'002632 75-900223
75 MARC

Bangladesh. Laws, statutes, etc. Code of civil procedure, 1908. 1972.
in Sarkar, Subodh Chandra, 1886-1966. The law of civil procedure in India, Bangladesh & Pakistan. 5th ed. Calcutta, S. C. Sarkar, [1972-73]

Bangladesh. Laws, statutes, etc.
[Code of criminal procedure, 1898]
Criminal procedure code / Osman Ghani & Mozammel Haque. — 1st ed. — Dacca : Khoshroz Kitab Mahal, 1974.
465 p. in various pagings ; 22 cm.
Caption title: The code of criminal procedure, 1898.
Tk30.00
1. Criminal procedure—Bangladesh. I. Ghani, Osman. II. Mozammel Haque. III. Title.
345'.5492'0502632 75-900226
75 MARC

Bangladesh. Laws, statutes, etc.
The Contract act (IX of 1872), with up-to-date amendments & case-law. — 1st ed. — Dacca : Dacca Law Reports Office, 1975.
xi, 166 p. ; 25 cm.
On verso of t.p.: Published by Obaidul Huq Chowdhury.
Includes index.
Tk16.00
1. Contracts—Bangladesh. I. Title.
346'.5492'02 75-908927
76 MARC

Bangladesh. Laws, statutes, etc. Essential supplies (temporary powers) act, 1946. 1975.
in Bangladesh. Laws, statutes, etc. Law on paddy procurement ... 1st ed. Dacca, Dacca Law Reports Office, 1975.

Bangladesh. Laws, statutes, etc. Evidence act, 1872. 1974.
in Ghani, Osman. Evidence act. 1st ed. Dacca, Khoshroz Kitab Mahal, 1974.

Bangladesh. Laws, statutes, etc.
Finance (1971-72) order, 1972. [Dacca] 1972.
40 p.
"Published in the Bangladesh Gazette, Extraordinary, Part IIIA, dated the 24th May 1972."
1. Finance—Laws and legislation—Bangladesh. 2. Bangladesh—Finance—Laws and legislation.
DS NUC73-77459

Bangladesh. Laws, statutes, etc.
The General clauses act (X of 1897), with all Bangladesh amendments. — 1st ed. — Dacca : Dacca Law Reports Office, 1975.
iv, 34 p. ; 25 cm.
On verso of t.p.: Published by Obaidul Huq Chowdhury.
Tk4.50
1. Law—Bangladesh—Interpretation and construction. I. Title.
348'.5492'022 76-911011
76 MARC

Bangladesh. Laws, statutes, etc.
A hand book of criminal laws / by Hamza Hossain. — 1st ed. — Dacca : Khoshroz Kitab Mahal, 1974-75.
2 v. ; 23 cm. Tk50.00 per vol.
CONTENTS: v. 1. Major acts: Bangladesh penal code, Criminal procedure code, Evidence act.—v. 2 Minor acts.
1. Criminal law—Bangladesh. I. Hossain, Hamza. II. Title.
345'.5492'002632 75-900225
75[r76]rev MARC

Bangladesh. Laws, statutes, etc.
Jatiya rakkhi bahini act : [President's order no. 21 of 1972, as amended by act XI of 1974] / [edited by] Hamza Hossain ; rev. by Kamrul Islam. — 1st ed. — Dacca : Khoshroz Kitab Mahal, 1974.
68 p. ; 18 cm.
"Index of acts": p. [27]-35; "Index of President's order": p. [37]-68.
1. Bangladesh—Armed Forces. 2. Martial law—Bangladesh. I. Hossain, Hamza. II. Kamrul Islam, A. T. M. III. Title.
342'.5492'062 75-907465
76 MARC

Bangladesh. Laws, statutes, etc.
Law on paddy procurement : contains E.B. foodgrains (disposal & acquisition) order, 1948, Essential supplies (temporary powers) act, 1946, notifications, instructions, and with exhaustive commentary. — 1st ed. — Dacca : Dacca Law Reports Office, 1975.
32 p. ; 25 cm.
On verso of t.p.: Published by Obaidul Huq Chowdhury.
Tk4.00
1. Grain trade—Law and legislation—Bangladesh. 2. Surplus agricultural commodities—Bangladesh. I. Bangladesh. Laws, statutes, etc. Essential supplies (temporary powers) act, 1946. 1975. II. Title.
343'.5492'076 75-908928
76 MARC

Bangladesh. Laws, statutes, etc.
The Limitation act (IX of 1908), with up-to-date amendments & exhaustive case-law. — 1st ed. — Dacca : Dacca Law Reports Office, 1976.
263 p. ; 25 cm.
On verso of t.p.: Published by Obaidul Huq Chowdhury.
Includes index.
Tk23.00
1. Limitation of actions—Bangladesh. I. Title.
347'.5492'052 76-902519
76 MARC

Bangladesh. Laws, statutes, etc.
A manual of defence laws in Bangladesh / edited by A. T. M. Kamrul Islam. — 1st ed. — Dacca : Khoshroz Kitab Mahal, 1976-
v. ; 22 cm.
CONTENTS: v. 1. The Bangladesh Army act, 1952 (as adapted). The Bangladesh Air Force act, 1953 (as adapted). The Bangladesh Navy ordinance, 1961 (as adapted).
Tk20.00 (v. 1)
1. Military law—Bangladesh. I. Kamrul Islam, A. T. M. II. Title.
343'.5492'01 76-903641
76 MARC

Bangladesh. Laws, statutes, etc.
The Special powers act (act no. XIV of 1974) / [edited by] Hamza Hossain ; rev. by Kamrul Islam. — 1st ed. — Dacca : Khoshroz Kitab Mahal, 1974.
iv, 94 p. ; 19 cm.
PARTIAL CONTENTS: Index of acts.—Index of President order.
Tk3.00
1. Subversive activities—Bangladesh. 2. War and emergency powers—Bangladesh. I. Hossain, Hamza. II. Title.
345'.5492'0231 76-911010
77 MARC

Bangladesh. Ministry of Agriculture.
see Carruthers, I. D. A study of the needs and capacity for agro-economic planning and research in Bangladesh. Dacca, Ford Foundation, 1976.

Bangladesh. Ministry of Cabinet Affairs. Establishment Division.
Bangladesh district gazetteers. General editor: Muhammad Ishaq. Dacca, Bangladesh Govt. Press, 1971–
v. illus., fold. map. 26 cm.
Previous vols. published 1969–71 entered under East Pakistan. Services and General Administration Dept.
Bibliography: v. 1, p. 299–303.
CONTENTS: [1] Chittagong.
1. Bangladesh. I. Ishaq, Muhammad, 1918– ed. II. Title.
DS393.4.B36 915.49'2'035 73–169289
MARC

Bangladesh. Ministry of Finance.
Annual budget statement.
[Dacca]
v. 29 cm.
Cover title, : Budget estimates.
Vol. for 1971/73 cover period Dec. 16, 1971–June 30, 1973.
1. Budget—Bangladesh.
HJ67.8.B16a 354'.549'200722 74–640724
MARC–S

Bangladesh. Ministry of Finance. Annual financial statement
see Bangladesh. Ministry of Finance. Budget estimate. [Dacca]

Bangladesh. Ministry of Finance.
Budget estimate.
[Dacca]
v. 28 cm. annual.
Added title : Annual financial statement.
1. Budget—Bangladesh. I. Bangladesh. Ministry of Finance. Annual financial statement.
HJ67.8.B16b 336.549'2 74–647668
MARC–S

Bangladesh. Ministry of Finance.
Demands for grants and appropriations.
Dacca, Bangladesh Govt. Press.
v. 28 cm. annual.
1. Bangladesh—Appropriations and expenditures—Periodicals.
HJ67.8.C16a 336.549'2 74–647659
MARC–S

Bangladesh. Ministry of Finance.
Detailed estimates of revenue & receipts.
Dacca, Bangladesh Govt. Press.
v. 28 cm. annual.
1. Revenue—Bangladesh—Periodicals. 2. Bangladesh—Appropriations and expenditures—Periodicals.
HJ67.8.C16b 336'.02'5492 74–647656
MARC–S

Bangladesh. Ministry of Finance. Autonomous Bodies Wing.
Budget estimates of autonomous bodies.
Dacca, Govt. of the People's Republic of Bangladesh, Ministry of Finance, Finance Division, Autonomous Bodies Wing.
v. 29 cm.
1. Government business enterprises—Bangladesh—Finance—Periodicals. I. Title.
HD4295.6.A34a 354'.549'200722 76–913457
MARC–S

Bangladesh. Ministry of Finance. Economic Adviser's Wing.
Bangladesh economic survey. 1st–
1971/73–
Dacca, Ministry of Finance, Economic Adviser's Wing, Govt. of the People's Republic of Bangladesh.
v. in ill. 26 cm. annual.
First survey covers period Dec. 1971–June 1973.
1. Bangladesh—Economic conditions—Periodicals. I. Title.
HC440.8.A1B23a 330.9'549'205 76–913177
MARC–S

Bangladesh. Ministry of Finance. Implementation Cell.
National scales of pay as introduced by Government grades X to VII / Ministry of Finance, Implementation cell. — [Dacca] : The Cell, [1973?]
260 p. in various pagings ; 25 cm.
Cover title.
"MF (IC)-2/73/1."
Tk5.00
1. Bangladesh—Officials and employees—Salaries, allowances, etc. I. Title.
JQ636.Z2B36 1973 354'.549'2001232 75-900120
75 MARC

Bangladesh. Ministry of Finance. National Pay Commission
see
Bangladesh. National Pay Commission.

Bangladesh. Ministry of Foreign Affairs. External Publicity Division.
Bangladesh : contemporary events and documents . — [Dacca] : External Publicity Division, Ministry of Foreign Affairs, Republic of Bangladesh, [1971?]
viii, 119 p., [1] leaf of plates : port. ; 22 cm.
1. Bangladesh—History—Sources. I. Title.
DS393.2.B36 1971 954.9'2 75-312159
75 MARC

Bangladesh. Ministry of Forests, Fisheries and Livestock. Dept. of Forest
see
Bangladesh. Dept. of Forest.

Bangladesh. Ministry of Home Affairs. Census Commission
see
Bangladesh. Census Commission.

Bangladesh. Ministry of Industries.
(Agrādhikāra śilpa tālikā)
অগ্রাধিকার শিল্প তালিকা : প্রথম পঞ্চবার্ষিকী (১৯৭৩-৭৮) পরিকল্পনার শিল্প বিনিয়োগ তফসিলের অধীনে ১৯৭৪-৭৬ সালের জন্য. — ঢাকা : বাংলাদেশ ফরমস্ এণ্ড পাবলিকেশনস্ অফিস, [pref. 1974]
2, 9–32 p. ; 26 cm.
Cover title.
At head of title: Gaṇaprajātantrī Bāṃlādeśa Sarakāra.
In Bengali.
Tk2.00
1. Industry and state—Bangladesh. 2. Industrial promotion—Bangladesh. I. Title.
HD3616.B353B35 1974 76–902562

Bangladesh. Ministry of Industries.
Industrial investment schedule for the First five-year plan, 1973-78. — Dacca : Bangladesh Govt. Press, [1973?]
52 p. ; 28 cm.
Cover title.
Foreword signed: Syed Nazrul Islam, Minister for Industries.
Tk3.00
1. Industry and state—Bangladesh. 2. Investments—Bangladesh. I. Title.
HD3616.B353B35 1973 332.6'72'095492 75-900118
76 MARC

Bangladesh. Ministry of Industries
see Silpa dairektari, Eprila 1974 Im. [pref. 1974]

Bangladesh. Ministry of Industries. Expert Committee on Pharmaceutical Industry
see
Bangladesh. Expert Committee on Pharmaceutical Industry.

Bangladesh. Ministry of Information and Broadcasting.
This is Bangladesh. — [Dacca] : Dept. of Publications, Ministry of Information and Broadcasting, 1974.
32 p., [8] leaves of plates : col. ill. ; 22 cm.
1. Bangladesh. I. Title.
DS394.5.B36 1974 954.9'2 75-900451
75 MARC

Bangladesh. Ministry of Information and Broadcasting. Dept. of Publications.
Bangladesh progress.
[Dacca]
v. 25 cm.
1. Bangladesh—Economic conditions. 2. Bangladesh—Social conditions. 3. Bangladesh—Politics and government. I. Title.
HC440.8.A24a 330.9'549'205 74–648370
MARC–S

Bangladesh. Ministry of Information and Broadcasting. Dept. of Publications.
Bangladesh Progress, 1973. — [Dacca] : Dept. of Publications, Ministry of Information and Broadcasting, Govt. of the People's Republic of Bangladesh, [1974?]
111 p. ; 25 cm.
1. Bangladesh—Economic conditions. 2. Bangladesh—Social conditions. 3. Bangladesh—Politics and government. I. Title.
HC440.8.B34 1974 330.9'549'205 75-900448
75 MARC

Bangladesh. Ministry of Jute. Jute Division
see
Bangladesh. Jute Division.

Bangladesh. Ministry of Law, Parliamentary Affairs and Justice.
see Bangladesh. Constitution. The Constitution of the People's Republic of Bangladesh, as modified up to 25th January 1975. [Dacca, Bangladesh Forms and Publications Office, pref. 1975]

Bangladesh. National Board of Revenue.
Income-tax manual. / Government of the People's Republic of Bangladesh, National Board of Revenue. — Dacca : Bangladesh Forms & Publications Office, 1974-
v. ; 25 cm.
CONTENTS: pt. 1. Income-tax act, 1922, (XI of 1922), corrected up to July, 1974.
Tk.19.00 (v. 1)
1. Income tax—Bangladesh—Law. I. Title.
343'.5492'052 75-902539
75 MARC

Bangladesh. National Pay Commission.
Report of the National Pay Commission, Bangladesh. — [Dacca : Bangladesh Govt. Press], 1973-
Cover title.
Issued in parts.
Letter of transmittal signed: Ābdura Raba.
CONTENTS: v. 1. Main text.
Tk8.96
1. Civil service—Bangladesh—Salaries, allowances, etc. I. Rab, Abdur.
JQ636.Z2B37 1973 354'.549'200123 75-900119
76 MARC

Bangladesh. Planning Commission.
Annual development programme—Planning Commission. [Dacca] Planning Commission, Govt. of the People's Republic of Bangladesh.
v. in 34 cm.
1. Bangladesh—Economic policy.
HC440.8.A26b 309.2'3'09492 75-901783
MARC-S

Bangladesh. Planning Commission.
The annual plan, 1972-73; a report on the state of the Bangladesh economy and a programme for reconstruction and development for the year. Dacca, 1972.
66 p.
1. Bangladesh—Economic policy. 2. Bangladesh—Economic conditions.
DS NUC75-80104

Bangladesh. Planning Commission.
Annual plan—Planning Commission. -1973/74. [Dacca] Planning Commission, Govt. of the People's Republic of Bangladesh.
v. ill. 28 cm.
Continued by: Bangladesh. Planning Commission. Economic development and annual plan.
1. Bangladesh—Economic policy. 2. Program budgeting—Bangladesh.
HC440.8.A26a 338.9549'2 75-642112
MARC-S

Bangladesh. Planning Commission.
Economic development and annual plan. 1974/75- [Dacca] Planning Commission, Govt. of the People's Republic of Bangladesh.
v. ill. 28 cm.
Continues: Bangladesh. Planning Commission. Annual plan-Planning Commission.
Vols. for 1974/75- include economic development report for 1973/74-
1. Bangladesh—Economic policy—Periodicals.
HC440.8.A26a 338.9549'2 75-642134
MARC-S

Bangladesh. Planning Commission.
Economic review. 1974/75- [Dacca] Planning Commission, Govt. of the People's Republic of Bangladesh.
v. 25 cm. annual.
First report covers 10 months.
1. Bangladesh—Economic conditions—Periodicals. 2. Bangladesh—Economic policy—Periodicals. I. Title.
HC440.8.A1B26a 330.9'549'205 76-913460
MARC-S

Bangladesh. Planning Commission.
The First five year plan, 1973-78. — [Dacca] : The Commission, 1973.
549 p. ; 28 cm.
Tk50.00
1. Bangladesh—Economic policy. I. Title.
HC440.8.A4 1973 338.9549'2 75-900052
75 MARC

Bangladesh. Planning Commission
see Selsjord, M Report on the statistical situation in Bangladesh, .. Bergen, Norway, Chr. Michelsens Institute, Development Economics Research and Advisory Project (DERAP) 1972.

Bangladesh. Postpartum Family Planning Program
see Postpartum Family Planning Program.

Bangladesh. Revenue, National Board of
see
Bangladesh. National Board of Revenue.

Bangladesh. Śilpa Mantraṇālaẏa
see
Bangladesh. Ministry of Industries.

Bangladesh. Statistics, Bureau of
see
Bangladesh. Bureau of Statistics.

Bangladesh, Tea Board
see
Bangladesh Tea Board.

Bangladesh. Treaties, etc. Sweden, Nov. 6, 1972
see Sweden. Treaties, etc. Bangladesh, Nov. 6, 1972. Development credit agreement. [Washington, 1972]

Bangladesh. Treaties, etc. Sweden, May 18, 1973.
Development credit agreement (foodgrain storage project) between Kingdom of Sweden and People's Republic of Bangladesh, dated May 18, 1973. [n.p., 1973]
10 p.
1. Economic assistance, Swedish—Bangladesh. 2. Bangladesh—Economic assistance, Swedish. I. Sweden. Treaties, etc. Bangladesh, May 18, 1973. II. Title.
DS NUC76-102382

Bangladesh. Treaties, etc. United States
see
United States. Treaties, etc. Bangladesh.

Bangladesh, International Seminar on
see
International Seminar on Bangladesh, Calcutta, 1972.

Bangladesh; a brutal birth. Introduction by S. Mulgaokar. Photographed by Kishor Parekh. Hong Kong, Image Photographic Services [1972]
1 v. (unpaged) illus.
1. Bangladesh—Portraits. I. Mulgaokar, S. II. Parekh, Kishor.
CtHC NUC73-34514

Bangladesh: a brutal birth. Introduction by S. Mulgaokar. Photographed by Kishor Parekh. [Hongkong, Printed by Lee Fung Printers, 1972]
[96] p. (chiefly illus.) 29 cm.
1. East Pakistan. I. Parekh, Kishor.
NNC NUC75-13693

Bangladesh; a souvenir on the first anniversary of Victory Day, December 16, 1972. [Board of editors: Syed Ali Ahsan, Chairman, and others. Dacca, Ministry of Information and Broadcasting, Govt. of the People's Republic of Bangladesh, 1972?]
131 p. illus., maps. 28 cm.
1. Bangladesh. I. Ahsan, Syed Ali, 1922- ed.
DS393.4.B34 915.49'2'035 73-902479
MARC

Bangladesh Academy for Rural Development
see
Academy for Rural Development, Comilla, Bangladesh.

Bangladesh Agricultural Development Corporation.
Annual report.
[Dacca]
v. 29 cm.
Continues Annual report issued by the corporation under its earlier name: East Pakistan Agricultural Development Corporation.
1. Agriculture—Bangladesh—Periodicals. 2. Agriculture—Economic aspects—Bangladesh—Periodicals. 3. Agriculture and state—Bangladesh—Periodicals.
S322.B26E37a 630'.9549'2 74-930599
MARC-S

Bangladesh Agricultural Development Corporation.

For works by this body issued under its earlier name see

East Pakistan Agricultural Development Corporation.

Bangladesh Agricultural Research Council.
see Flora of Bangladesh. Dacca, Bangladesh Agricultural Research Council, [[19

Bangladesh Agricultural University

For works by this body issued under its earlier name see

East Pakistan Agricultural University.

Bangladesh Agricultural University
see Bangladesh journal of biological and agricultural sciences. 1972- Dacca.

Bangladesh Atomic Energy Commission.
see Nuclear power planning study for Bangladesh. Vienna, International Atomic Energy Agency, 1975.

Bangladesh Bank.
Annual report—Bangladesh Bank.
[Dacca, Dept. of Public Relations and Publications] Bangladesh Bank.
v. 25 cm.
Report year ends June 30.
1. Bangladesh Bank—Yearbooks. I. Bangladesh Bank. Dept. of Public Relations and Publications.
HG3290.6.A7B26a 332.1'1'095492 76-641639
MARC-S

Bangladesh Bank.
Bulletin—Bangladesh Bank.
[Dacca] Bangladesh Bank.
v. 24 cm.
1. Bangladesh—Economic conditions—Periodicals.
HC440.8.A1B28a 330.9'549'205 75-641825
MARC-S

Bangladesh Bank. Dept. of Public Relations and Publications
see Bangladesh Bank. Annual report—Bangladesh Bank. [Dacca]

Bangladesh Bank. Dept. of Research. Special Studies and Publications Division.
Report on currency and finance.
[Dacca, Director, Public Relations Dept., Bangladesh Bank]
v. 25 cm. annual.
1. Banks and banking—Bangladesh—Statistics—Periodicals. 2. Monetary policy—Bangladesh—Periodicals. I. Title.
HG3290.6.A5B32a 332'.09549'2 77-649490
MARC-S

Bangladesh Bank. Statistics Dept. Annual export receipts
see Bangladesh Bank. Statistics Dept. Yearly export receipts. [Dacca]

Bangladesh Bank. Statistics Dept.
Annual import payments.
[Dacca] Statistics Dept., Bangladesh Bank.
v. 25 cm.
1. Bangladesh—Commerce.
HF3790.6.A2a 382'.5'095492 75-649690
MARC-S

Bangladesh Bank. Statistics Dept.
Quarterly balance of payments.
[Dacca] Statistics Dept., Bangladesh Bank.
v. 25 cm.
1. Balance of payments—Bangladesh—Statistics—Periodicals.
HG3883.B33B36a 382.1'7'095492 76-913478
MARC-S

Bangladesh Bank. Statistics Dept.
Quarterly banking statistics.
[Dacca] Statistics Dept., Bangladesh Bank.
v. 25 cm.
1. Banks and banking—Bangladesh—Statistics.
HG3290.6.A5B34a 332.1'09549'2 75-649632
MARC-S

Bangladesh Bank. Statistics Dept.
Quarterly scheduled banks statistics. June 1975- [Dacca] Bangladesh Bank, Statistics Dept.
v. 25 cm.
Continues: Bangladesh Bank. Statistics Dept. Quarterly banking statistics.
Cover title, June 1975- : Scheduled banks statistics.
1. Banks and banking—Bangladesh—Statistics—Periodicals. I. Bangladesh Bank. Statistics Dept. Scheduled banks statistics. II. Title.
HG3290.6.A5B34a 332.1'09549'2 76-913479
MARC-S

Bangladesh Bank. Statistics Dept. Scheduled banks statistics
see Bangladesh Bank. Statistics Dept. Quarterly scheduled banks statistics. June 1975- [Dacca]

Bangladesh Bank. Statistics Dept.
Yearly export receipts.
[Dacca] Statistics Dept., Bangladesh Bank.
v. 26 cm.
Cover title : Annual export receipts.
1. Bangladesh—Commerce—Periodicals. I. Bangladesh Bank. Statistics Dept. Annual export receipts.
HF3790.6.A2b 382'.6'095492 76-913480
MARC-S

Bangladesh Darshan Samiti. General Conference, 1st, Dacca, 1974.
First General Conference, Bangladesh Darhsan [sic] Samiti, Dacca, January 21-23, 1974 / general president, D. M. Azraf ; edited by Abdul Jalil Mia. — [Dacca] : The Samiti, [1974?]
vii, 216 p., [4] leaves of plates : ill. ; 22 cm.
English or Bengali.
Tk12.50
1. Philosophy—Congresses. I. Azraf, Muhammad, 1906- II. Mia, Abdul Jalil, 1936-
B20.B36 1974 100 76-900165
76 MARC

The Bangladesh development studies. v. 2, no. 3-
July 1974-
[Dacca, Bangladesh Institute of Development Studies]
v. ill. 25 cm. quarterly.
Continues: The Bangladesh economic review.
"Journal of the Bangladesh Institute of Development Studies."
1. Bangladesh—Economic conditions—Periodicals. 2. Economic development—Periodicals. I. Bangladesh Institute of Development Studies.
HC440.8.A1B3 330.9'549'205 75-641512
MARC-S

Bangladesh directory & year book.
Calcutta, S. A. Hasnat.
v. 26 cm.
Vols. for published by S. A. Hasnat for the Associated Book Promoters.
1. Bangladesh—Commerce—Directories. 2. India—Commerce—Directories. 3. Commerce—Directories. I. Hasnat, S. A.
HF3790.6.A24 380.1'025'5492 76-913539
MARC-S

Bangladesh Economic Association
see Political economy. [Decca, 1974-

Bangladesh Economic Association. Annual Conference, 2d, University of Dacca, 1976.
see Alamgir, Mohiuddin, 1943- Economy of Bangladesh ... [Dacca] Bangladesh Economic Association, 1976.

Bangladesh economic review
see Talukder, Alauddin. Ten years of BER articles... Dacca, Bangladesh Institute of Development Economics, 1972.

The Bangladesh economic review. v. 1-
Jan. 1973-
[Dacca] Bangladesh Institute of Development Economics.
v. 25 cm. quarterly
Journal of the Bangladesh Institute of Development Economics.
1. Bangladesh — Economic conditions — Periodicals. 2. Economic development—Periodicals. I. Bangladesh Institute of Development Economics.
HC440.8.A1B3 330.9'549'205 73-901637
MARC-S

The Bangladesh economist. v. 1-
Mar. 1972-
Dacca.
v. 29 cm. monthly.
1. Bangladesh — Economic conditions — Periodicals. 2. Bangladesh—Periodicals.
HC440.8.A1B32 330.9'549'205 72-905867
MARC-S

The Bangladesh economist. v. 1-
Aug. 24, 1975-
Dacca [M. A. Wahab]
v. 42 cm. weekly.
Other title, 1975- : Weekly Bangladesh economist.
1. Bangladesh—Economic conditions—Periodicals. I. Title: Weekly Bangladesh economist.
HC440.8.A1B33 330.9'549'205 76-913158
MARC-S

Bangladesh establishment illegal; a legal study by International Commission of Jurists. Lahore, Fazalsons [1972]
78, 98 p. 22 cm. Rs15.00 ($2.00)
Cover title.
CONTENTS: pt. 1. Pakistan's viewpoint, by Rana Rehman Zafar.—pt. 2. Legal study of the events in East Pakistan, 1971, by the International Commission of Jurists, Geneva.
Includes bibliographical references.
1. Bangladesh—International status.
JX4084.B32B35 1972 341.2'9 73-930136
MARC

Bangladesh forges ahead; policies and measures. [Dacca] Dept. of Publications, Ministry of Information and Broadcasting, Govt. of the People's Republic of Bangladesh [1972 ?]
39 p. 24 cm.
Cover title.
1. Bangladesh.
NIC NUC75-26601

Bangladesh historical studies. v. 1-
1976-
[Dacca] Bangladesh Itihas Samiti.
v. 23 cm. annual.
"Journal of the Bangladesh Itihas Samiti."
1. Bangladesh—History—Periodicals. I. Bangladesh Itihas Samiti.
DS393.B35 954.9'205'05 76-913455
MARC-S

Bangladesh Institute of Development Economics.
The Pakistan Institute of Development Economics was established in 1957. In 1971 the name was changed to Bangladesh Institute of Development Studies, and in 1974 to Bangladesh Institute of Development Studies.
Works by this body are found under the name used at the time of publication.

Bangladesh Institute of Development Economics
see The Bangladesh economic review. Jan. 1973- [Dacca]

Bangladesh Institute of Development Economics
see Haque, Serajul. Economy of the Socialist countries... Dacca, Bangladesh Institute of Development Economics, 1972.

Bangladesh Institute of Development Economics
see Talukder, Alauddin. Ten years of BER articles... Dacca, Bangladesh Institute of Development Economics, 1972.

Bangladesh Institute of Development Economics.

For works by this body issued under its earlier name see

Pakistan Institute of Development Economics.

Bangladesh Institute of Development Studies.
The Pakistan Institute of Development Economics was established in 1957. In 1971 the name was changed to Bangladesh Institute of Development Economics and in 1974 to Bangladesh Institute of Development Studies.
Works by this body are found under the name used at the time of publication.

Bangladesh Institute of Development Studies.
A report on the background, current progammes and planned development of the Bangladesh Institute of Development Studies. 1975-
Dacca, Bangladesh Institute of Development Studies.
v. 28 cm. annual.
1. Bangladesh Institute of Development Studies—Periodicals. I. Title.
H62.5.B35B35a 338.9549'2 76-913174
MARC-S

Bangladesh Institute of Development Studies
see The Bangladesh development studies. v. 2, no. 3- July 1974- [Dacca]

Bangladesh Institute of Development Studies.
see Chowdhury, Nuimuddin, 1948- Tea industry of Bangladesh ... Dacca, Bangladesh Institute of Development Studies, 1974.

Bangladesh Institute of Law and International Affairs
see Law and international affairs. Jan. 1975- [Dacca]

Bangladesh Insurance Academy.
Journal—Bangladesh Insurance Academy. v. 1-
Mar. 1975-
Dacca, Bangladesh Insurance Academy.
v. 24 cm. monthly.
1. Insurance—Periodicals. 2. Insurance—Study and teaching—Bangladesh—Periodicals.
HG8013.B34a 368'.9'5492 75-907587
MARC-S

Bangladesh Itihas Samiti
see Bangladesh historical studies. 1976- [Dacca]

Bangladesh Jatiya Samabaya Union
see National Seminar on the Needs of the Cooperative Movement of Bangladesh, Dacca, 1972. The needs of the cooperative movement of Bangladesh... New Delhi, International Cooperative Alliance [1972]

Bangladesh journal of biological and agricultural sciences. v. 1-
1972-
Dacca.
v. 25 cm.
Supersedes Pakistan journal of biological and agricultural sciences.
"Published under the joint auspices of the Bangladesh Society for Biological and Agricultural Sciences and the Bangladesh Agricultural University."
1. Biology—Periodicals. 2. Agriculture—Periodicals. 3. Agriculture—Bangladesh—Periodicals. I. Bangladesh Society for Biological and Agricultural Sciences. II. Bangladesh Agricultural University.
QH301.P252 574'.05 72-906516
MARC-S

Bangladesh journal of zoology. v. 1-
Dec. 1973-
Dacca, Zoological Society of Bangladesh.
v. ill. 25 cm. semiannual.
1. Zoology—Bangladesh—Periodicals. 2. Zoology—Periodicals. I. Zoological Society of Bangladesh.
QL334.B34B35 591'.05 75-644003
MARC-S

Bangladesh Jute Mills Association.
Monthly summary of jute goods statistics.

Dacca.
v. 28 cm.
Continues the publication with the same title issued under the earlier name of the association: Pakistan Jute Mills Association.
1. Jute industry—Bangladesh—Statistics. I. Title.
HD9156.J8P45 73-647422
338.4'7'67713095492 MARC-S

Bangladesh Jute Mills Association

For works by this body issued under its earlier name see

Pakistan Jute Mills Association.

Bangladesh labour cases. v. 1-
Dec. 1974-
[Dacca, Srama Upadesta Kendra]
v. ill. 23 cm. monthly.
"Journal of labour laws and cases."
1. Labor laws and legislation—Bangladesh—Cases. 2. Labor laws and legislation—Bangladesh. I. Srama Upadesta Kendra.
344'.5492'010264 75-907586
MARC-S

Bangladesh National Scientific and Technical Documentation Centre.
Scientific & technological research institutions of Bangladesh / compiled and published by BANSDOC, Bangladesh National Scientific and Technical Documentation Centre ; editor, Ahsan A. Biswas. — Dacca : The Centre, 1975.
8 p. ; 29 cm. — (Its BANSDOC bibliography ; no. 98)
Cover title.
1. Research institutes—Bangladesh—Directories. I. Biswas, Ahsan A. II. Title. III. Series.
Q180.B3B36 1975 507'.20549'2 76-903598
77 MARC

Bangladesh National Scientific and Technical Documentation Centre.
see A Directory of scientists and technologists of Bangladesh. Dacca, BANSDOC (Bangladesh National Scientific and Technical Documentation Centre) 1976.

Bangladesh observer.
see Khan, Md. Shahabuddin. A subject index on articles published in the Pakistan Observer (now Bangladesh Observer) from 1959-1961. [s.l.] Directorate of Archives and Libraries, 1974-

Bangladesh observer
see also
Pakistan observer.

Bangladesh Rice Research Institute.
Chandina, a new cultivar for Bangladesh. — 1st ed. — Dacca : Bangladesh Rice Research Institute, 1972.
19 p. : ill. ; 27 cm.
1. Rice—Bangladesh—Varieties. 2. Rice—Bangladesh—Field experiments. I. Title.
[SB191.R5B29] 633'.18'23 76-911203
77 MARC

Bangladesh Rice Research Institute.
see Workshop on Experience with High Yielding Varieties of Rice Cultivation in Bangladesh, Bangladesh Rice Research Institute, 1975. Workshop on Experience with High Yielding Varieties of Rice Cultivation in Bangladesh. [Dacca] Bangladesh Rice Research Institute, [1975]

Bangladesh Rural Advancement Committee.
Sulla project : report on phase II, November 1, 1972-December 31, 1975. — Dacca : Bangladesh Rural Advancement Committee, [1976]
25, 12 p. ; 36 cm.
"Report on BRAC medical programme, by Dr. R. Arnholt": 12 p. (last group
1. Rural development—Bangladesh—Sylhet. I. Arnholt, R. Report o[n] BRAC medical programme. 1976. II. Title.
HD2075.6.Z9S92 338.9549'2 76-90334[7]
77 MAR[C]

Bangladesh Shilpa Bank.
Annual report and statement of accounts—Bangladesh Shilpa Bank.
Dacca, Bangladesh Shilpa Bank.
v. ill. 27 cm.
Report year ends June 30.
1. Bangladesh Shilpa Bank.
HG3290.6.A8B33a 332.1'1'095492 75-648917
MARC-S

Bangladesh Shilpakala Academy.
see Sculpture in Bangladesh. ⌈Dacca⌉ Bangladesh Shilpakala Academy, 1976.

Bangladesh shipping directory.
Chittagong, Bangladesh Ocean Publications.
v. ill. 26 cm. annual.
1. Shipping—Bangladesh—Directories.
HE880.6.B35 387.5′025′5492 76-913141
MARC-S

Bangladesh Society for Biological and Agricultural Sciences
see Bangladesh journal of biological and agricultural sciences. 1972- Dacca.

Bangladesh Students Union . Dacca College Branch
see Ninãda. [1378, i. e. 1972]

Bangladesh Students Union. Prakauśala Biśvabidyālaya Śākhā
see Ispāta. [1972]

Bangladesh Tea Board.
Statistics on tea. Dacca ⌈1972⌉
iv, 62 p. 26 cm.
1. Tea trade—Bangladesh—Statistics. 2. Tea—Bangladesh—Statistics. I. Title.
HD9198.B35B36 338.1′7′372095492 72-908823
MARC

Bangladesh Tea Board.

For works by this body issued under its earlier name see

Pakistan Tea Board.

Bangladesh Tea Research Station.
Annual report—Bangladesh Tea Research Station. 1969–
Srimangal, Bangladesh Tea Research Station.
v. in 26 cm.
Continues: Pakistan Tea Research Station. Annual report.
Reports for 1969– include data compiled by the station under its earlier name: Pakistan Tea Research Station.
1. Bangladesh Tea Research Station. 2. Tea—Bangladesh—Periodicals.
SB272.P3P35 354′.549′2008233 75-900768
MARC-S

Bangladesh Tea Research Station.

For works by this body issued under its earlier name see

Pakistan Tea Research Station.

Bangladeshiyo Cha Sangsad.
Annual report—Bangladeshiyo Cha Sangsad. 1971–
⌈Chittagong⌉
v. maps. 25 cm.
Supersedes in part Pakistan Tea Association. Report.
1. Bangladeshiyo Cha Sangsad — Periodicals. 2. Tea — Bangladesh—Statistics—Periodicals. 3. Tea trade—Bangladesh—Statistics—Periodicals.
SB272.B35B35a 633′.72′095492 74-647904
MARC-S

Bangladeshiyo Cha Sangsad
see also
Pakistan Tea Association.

Bangle, Edmond Dunsmoor.
The compensation of public school administrators based on the effectiveness of performance. [n. p.] 1974.
vii, 118 l. ill. 28 cm.
Thesis (Ed. D.)—University of Southern California.
1. School administrators—Salaries, pensions, etc. I. Title.
CLSU NUC76-22129

Bango, Jenö F 1934-
Changements dans les communautés villageoises de l'Europe de l'Est : exemple, la Hongrie / door Jenö Bango. — Leuven : Katholieke Universiteit te Leuven, Faculteit der sociale Wetenschappen, Département Sociologie, 1973.
vi, 434, 3 leaves : ill. ; 27 cm. Be***
Thesis—Katholieke Universiteit te Leuven.
At head of title: nr. 13.
Bibliography: leaves 421-434.
Includes index.
1. Hungary—Rural conditions. 2. Villages—Hungary. I. Title.
HN420.5.A8B36 309.2′63′09439 76-466213
76 MARC

Bango, Jenö F 1934–
Das neue ungarische Dorf : eine soziologische Untersuchung / Jenö F. Bango. — Bern : Verlag SOI, 1974.
viii, 88 p. : ill. ; 18 cm. — (Tatsachen und Meinungen ; 27)
Sw 74-A-5083
Includes bibliographical references.
ISBN 3-35913-073-0 : 11.60F
1. Hungary—Rural conditions. 2. Villages—Hungary. 3. Sociology, Rural. I. Title.
HN418.H92B36 74-350439

Bango, Jenö F 1934-
Les problèmes de la production collective et individuelle dans le village hongrois par J. Bango. Louvain ⌈Institut de recherches de l'Europe centrale⌉ 1973.
32 p. ill. 24 cm. (Cahiers de l'Institut de recherches de l'Europe centrale, 3)
"Notes": p. 31-32.
Cover title.
1. Hungary—Rural condit. 2. Agriculture and state—Hungary. I. Title. II. Series: Institut de recherches de l'Europe centrale. Cahiers, 3.
CaBVaU NUC76-72880

Bangor, Me. City Planning Board.
Documents relating to Hancock-York neighborhood development program, prepared by Planning Department, City of Bangor and Urban Renewal Authority of the City of Bangor ... ⌈Bangor? 1972⌉
1 v. 28 x 23 cm.
Cover-title.
1. Cities and towns—Planning—Bangor, Me. 2. Urban renewal. I. Bangor, Me. Urban Renewal Authority. II. Title.
MeBa NUC73-114289

Bangor, Me. Husson College
see
Husson College.

Bangor, Me. Public Library.
Bibliography of the State of Maine. Boston, G. K. Hall, 1962.
803 p. 37 cm.
CONTENTS: Author catalog.—Dictionary catalog.
1. Maine—Bibliography—Catalogs. I. Title.
Z1291.B32 018′.1 73-155965
MARC

Bangor, Me. Urban Renewal Authority
see Bangor, Me. City Planning Board. Documents relating to Hancock-York neighborhood development program. ⌈Bangor? 1972⌉

Bangor, Pa. Planning Commission.
A comprehensive plan. Bangor, Pa., 1968.
161 p. (HUD 701 Report)
1. Master plan—Bangor, Pa.
DHUD NUC74-2328

Bangor, Pa. Planning Commission.
A revitalization plan for the Bangor central business district. Bangor, Pa., 1967.
61 p. (HUD 701 Report)
1. Business districts—Bangor, Pa.
DHUD NUC74-2327

Bangor, Pa. Planning Commission.
Subdivision ordinance of 1968; zoning ordinance of 1967. Bangor Borough, Pa., 1967-68.
2 v. (HUD 701 Report)
1. Zoning—Bangor, Pa.
DHUD NUC74-2329

Bangor, Wales. University College of North Wales. Dept. of Agricultural and Forest Zoology.

For works by this body issued under its later name see

Bangor, Wales. University College of North Wales. Dept. of Applied Zoology.

Bangor, Wales. University College of North Wales. Institute of Economic Research.
Tourism in Gwynedd : an economic study : report to Wales Tourist Board / ⌈prepared by⌉ Brian Archer, Sheila Shea, Richard de Vane. — Cardiff : Wales Tourist Board, 1974.
iii-xv, 60 p. : ill. ; 30 cm. GB75-09483
"A Wales Tourist Board research study."
Includes bibliographical references.
ISBN 0-900784-33-4 : £2.00
1. Tourist trade—Gwynedd, Wales. I. Archer, Brian. II. Shea, Sheila. III. De Vane, Richard. IV. Wales Tourist Board. V. Title.
G155.G7B36 1974 75-327948
338.4′7′91429204857
75 MARC

Bangor, Wales. University College of North Wales. Institute of European Finance.
see Revell, Jack. Savings flows in Europe ... London, Financial Times, 1976.

Bangor abbey, Ireland.
Exhibition catalogue. 1400 years of Christian life in Bangor, Co. Down, June 1958. [Belfast, The Parish of Bangor Abbey] 1958.
22 p. 22 cm.
1. Bangor Abbey—Exhibitions. I. Title.
IEG NUC76-33553

Bangor Abbey; restoration 1960. [Belfast, Tradepress, 1960]
1 v. (unpaged, 20 p.) 22 cm.
Includes liturgy for service of Re-dedication, 26th November 1960.
Cover title page.
1. Bangor, Ireland. Bangor Abbey.
IEG NUC75-67072

Bangorey
see Braun jabulu. [Nellore, Visalandhra Pub. House, Vijayawada, 1973]

Bangpra Agricultural College, Cholburi, Thailand.
[Cholburi, Thailand, 1973]
11 p. 28 cm.
Caption title.
1. Witthayālai Kasēttrakam Bāngphra. 2. Agricultural colleges—Thailand.
NIC NUC76-75826

Bangs, David H
Business planning guide : a handbook to help you design, write, and use a business plan tailored to your specific business needs : includes worksheets for financial data / David H. Bangs, Jr., William R. Osgood. — Boston : Federal Reserve Bank of Boston, c1976.
iv, 85 p. ; 29 cm. — (The Business assistance monograph series)
Includes bibliographical references.
1. Business. 2. Corporate planning. I. Osgood, William, joint author. II. Title. III. Series.
HF5500.B236 658.4′01 76-55106
77 MARC

Bangs, Edward, 1756-1818.
Steven Kellogg's Yankee Doodle / written by Edward Bangs. — New York : Parents' Magazine Press, c1976.
⌈38⌉ p. : col. ill. ; 21 x 26 cm.
SUMMARY: An illustrated version of the well-known song of the American Revolution.
ISBN 0-8193-0833-1. ISBN 0-8193-0834-X lib. bdg.
⌈1. Songs, American⌉ I. Kellogg, Steven. II. Title.
PZ8.3.B223 St 4 784.7′19′73 75-19190
75 MARC

Bangs, Edward, 1756-1818.
Yankee Doodle. [n.p., c1976]
1 v.
An illustrated version of the well-known song of the American Revolution.
1. Songs, American. I. Title.
RP NUC77-87362

Bangs, F. Kendrick, ed.
see Bahr, Gladys. Foundations of education for business. Reston, Va., National Business Education Association [1975]

Bangs, Frank S.
see Lauber, Daniel. Zoning for family and group care facilities. [Chicago, American Society of Planning Officials, 1974]

Bangs, Frank S., joint author
see So, Frank S Planned unit development ordinances. ⌈Chicago, American Society of Planning Officials, 1973⌉

Bangs, John Kendrick, 1862-1922.
Coffee and repartee. Illustrated. New York and London, Harper & Brothers Publishers [n.d.]
[i]-viii, 1-123 [1] p. illus. 13 cm.
I. Title.
OKentU NUC73-103021

Bangs, John Kendrick, 1862-1922.
Coffee and repartee, by John Kendrick Bangs. New York, Harper & Brothers, publisher, 1893.
3 sheets. 11 x 15 cm. (L. H. Wright. American fiction, 1876-1900, no. 268)
Micro-transparency (negative) Louisville, Ky., Lost Cause Press, 1973.
Collation of the original: 123 p. illus.
I. Title.
PSt NUC75-17469

Bangs, John Kendrick, 1862-1922.
Coffee and repartee and the idiot. Illustrated. New York and London, Harper & brothers publishers [n.d.]
4 p., 1-221, [1] p. illus. 19 cm.
I. Title.
OKentU NUC73-103022

Bangs, John Kendrick, 1862-1922.
The dreamers; a club. Being a more or less faithful account of the literary exercises of the first regular meeting of that organization, reported by John Kendrick Bangs, with illustrations by Edward Penfield. New York, Harper & Brothers, 1899.
246 p. front., plates. 18 cm.
Micro-transparency (negative) Louisville, Ky., Lost Cause Press, 1973. 4 sheets. 10.5 x 14.8 cm. (L. H. Wright. American fictions, 1876-1900, no. 269)
I. Title.
PSt NUC75-17466

Bangs, John Kendrick, 1862-1922.
The enchanted typewriter, by John Kendrick Bangs; illustrated by Peter Newell. New York and London, Harper & Brothers, 1899.
4 sheets. 11 x 15 cm. (L. H. Wright. American fiction, 1876-1900, no. 270)
Micro-transparency (negative) Louisville, Ky., Lost Cause Press, 1974.
Collation of the original: 170 p.
I. Title.
PSt NUC75-17468

Bangs, John Kendrick, 1862-1922.
Ghosts I have met and some others. By John Kendrick Bangs. With illustrations by Newell, Frost, & Richards. New York, Harper & brothers, 1898.
4 sheets. 11 x 15 cm. (L. H. Wright. American fiction, 1876-1900, no. 271)
Micro-transparency (negative) Louisville, Ky., Lost Cause Press, 1973.
Collation of the original: 190 p.
I. Title.
PSt NUC75-17687

Bangs, John Kendrick, 1862-1922.
A house-boat on the Styx; being some account of the divers doings of the associated shades. By John Kendrick Bangs ... New York, Harper & Brothers, 1896.
4 sheets. 10.5 x 14.8 cm. (L.H. Wright. American fiction, 1876-1900, no. 272)
Micro-transparency (negative). Louisville, Ky., Lost Cause Press, 1973.
Collation of the original: viii, 171 p. front., plates. 18 cm.
I. Title.
PSt NUC74-173305

Bangs, John Kendrick, 1862-1922.
The idiot, by John Kendrick Bangs. New York, Harper, 1895.
vi, 115 p. front., plates. 17 cm.
Micro-transparency (negative) Louisville, Ky., Lost Cause Press, 1973. 3 sheets. 10.5 x 14.8 cm. (L.H. Wright. American fiction, 1876-1900, no. 273)
I. Title.
PSt NUC75-18543

Bangs, John Kendrick, 1862-1922.
The Idiot at home, by John Kendrick Bangs; illustrated by F. T. Richards. New York and London, Harper & brothers, 1900.
5 sheets. 10.5 x 14.8 cm. (L.H. Wright. American fiction, 1876-1900, no. 274)
Micro-transparency (negative) Louisville, Ky., Lost Cause Press, 1973.
Collation of the original: ix, 313, [1] p. incl. plates.
I. Title.
PSt NUC75-18554

Bangs, John Kendrick, 1862-1922.
Mr. Bonaparte of Corsica. New York, Harper & brothers, 1895.
4 sheets. 11 x 15 cm. (L. H. Wright. American fiction, 1876-1900, no. 275)
Illustrated by H. W. McVickar.
Micro-transparency (negative) Louisville, Ky., Lost Cause Press, 1973.
Collation of the original: xii, 265 p. incl. front., illus.
I. Title.
PSt NUC75-17470

Bangs, John Kendrick, 1862-1922.
Peeps at people, being certain papers from the writings of Anne Warrington Witherup [pseud.] Collected by John Kendrick Bangs ... with illustrations by Edward Penfield. New York, Harper & Brothers, 1899 [1973]
4 sheets. 11 x 15 cm. (L.H. Wright. American fiction, 1876-1900, no. 278)
Micro-transparency (negative) Louisville, Ky., Lost Cause Press, 1973.
Collation of the original: 184 p. plates.
1. American wit and humor. I. Witherup, Anne Warrington. II. Title.
PSt NUC75-50465

Bangs, John Kendrick, 1862-1922.
A rebellious heroine. A story. By John Kendrick Bangs. Illus. by W. T. Smedley. New York, Harper & brothers, 1896 [1974]
4 p.l., 255 p. front., plates. 18 cm.
Micro-transparency (negative) Louisville, Ky., Lost Cause Press, 1974. 4 sheets. 10.5 x 14.8 cm. (L.H. Wright. American fiction, 1876-1900, no. 280)
I. Title.
PSt NUC75-18552

Bangs, John Kendrick, 1862–1922.
Shylock Homes: his posthumous memoirs. Edited and introduced by Jon L. Lellenberg. [1st ed. Arlington, Va.] Dispatch-Box Press, 1973.
102 p. illus. 29 cm. (Dispatch-Box Press publication no. 1)
Three hundred copies. L. C. copy is not numbered.
Bibliography: p. 97–102.
1. Detective and mystery stories. I. Lellenberg, Jon L., ed.
PS1064.B3S57 813′.4 73–162788
MARC

Bangs, John Kendrick, 1862-1922.
Three weeks in politics, by John Kendrick Bangs. New York, Harper and brothers, 1894 [1974]
4 p.l., 82 p. front., plates. 14 cm.
On cover: Harper's black & white series.
Micro-transparency (negative) Louisville, Ky., Lost Cause Press, 1974. 3 sheets. 10.5 x 14.8 cm. (L.H. Wright. American fiction, 1876-1900, no. 282)
I. Title.
PSt NUC75-18553

Bangs, John Kendrick, 1862-1922.
The water ghost and others, by John Kendrick Bangs. New York, Harper & Brothers, 1894.
5 sheets. 11 x 15 cm. (L. H. Wright. American fiction, 1876-1900, no. 284)
Micro-transparency (negative) Louisville, Ky., Lost Cause Press, 1974.
Collation of the original: 296 p.
I. Title.
PSt NUC75-17467

Bangs, John Kendrick, 1862-1922.
see Harper's lost reviews ... Millwood, N.Y., Kraus-Thomson Organization Ltd., 1976.

Bangs, John Kendrick, 1862-1922
see Harper's weekly. Jan. 3, 1857- [New York, Harper's Magazine Co., etc.]

Bangs, R., joint author.
see Rourke, Robert Vincent. Chemical and physical properties of the Bangor, Dixmont, Caribou, Conant, Perham, and Daigle soil mapping units ... Orono, Life Sciences and Agriculture Experiment Station, University of Maine, 1975.

Bangs, Richard T., ed.
see Scotts Turfgrass Research Conference, Marysville, Ohio. Proceedings. Marysville, Ohio, O. M. Scott [1969-

Bangsberg, Harry Frederick, 1928-
see Wisconsin State University Foundation. Higher Education Survey Team. Public universities of the Republic of Viet-Nam. [n.p.] 1967.

Bangsbomuseet
see Bangsbomuseet 1946 [i. e. nitten hundrede og seksogfyrre]-1971. Frederikshavn, 1971.

Bangsbomuseet 1946 [i. e. nitten hundrede og seksogfyrre]–1971. Frederikshavn, [Bangsbomuseet], 1971.
48 p. illus. 21 cm. kr5.00 D 72-7
Published on the occasion of the 25th anniversary of Bangsbomuseet.
Includes bibliographies.
CONTENTS: Christensen, O. A. Frederikshavn museumsforenings stiftelse.—Michelsen, A. Glimt fra min barndoms Frederikshavn.—Erlandsen, A. Om guldsmede i Frederikshavn og en analyse af 2 af Bangsbomuseets sølvsmykker.—Andersen, K. Hårarbejde i Vendsyssel.—Laursen, P. Ellingåskibet.
1. Frederikshavn, Denmark—Social life and customs—Addresses, essays, lectures. 2. Frederikshavn, Denmark — Antiquities — Addresses, essays, lectures. I. Christensen, Obel A. II. Bangsbomuseet.
DL291.F72B36 74–315803

Bangsholm, Erik, joint author
see Blom, Torben. Tip og træf en tolver. København, Berlingske, 1971.

Bangsidhari Das
see
Dāsa, Baṃśidhārī.

Bangstad, Gary Philip, 1943-
Developing a choral rehearsal program designed to increase perception of form and style in choral music / by Gary Philip Bangstad. -- [s.l. : s.n.], 1975.
497 leaves : music.
Thesis--Arizona State University.
Vita.
Bibliography: leaves 453-457.
GU NUC77-86588

Bangui, Central African Republic. Chambre de commerce, d'agriculture et d'industrie.
For works by this body issued under its later name see
Chambre nationale de commerce.

Bangui, Central African Republic. Chambre nationale de commerce
see
Chambre nationale de commerce.

Bangui, Central African Republic. Institut Pasteur
see
Institut Pasteur, Bangui.

Banguoğlu, Tahsin, 1904-
Türkçenin grameri. İstanbul, Baha Matbaası, 1974.
630 p. col. map, tables (part fold.)
1. Turkish language—Grammar. I. Title.
MiU NUC76-22117

Banha de Andrade, António Alberto
see
Andrade, António Alberto de.

Banham, Katharine May, 1897-
Maturity level for school entrance and reading readiness; manual of directions, for kindergarten and first grade. Circle Pines, Minn., American Guidance Service, 1959.
⌊6⌋ p. 28 cm.
Bibliography: p. ⌊6⌋
1. Readiness for school. 2. Education tests and measurements. I. Title.
CaBVaU NUC74-172772

Banham, Martin.
African theatre today / ⌊by⌋ Martin Banham with Clive Wake. — London : Pitman, 1976.
vii, 103 p. ; 24 cm. — (Theatre today)
Bibliography: p. 93-99.
Includes index.
ISBN 0-273-00348-8 : £3.50
1. African drama—History and criticism. 2. Theater—Africa. I. Wake, Clive, joint author. II. Title.
PL8010.B3 809.2 77-350062
77 MARC

Banham, Martin, ed.
see Drama in education. ⌊London⌋ Pitman Publishing ⌊c1972-

Banham, Mary.
see A tonic to the nation . . . London, Thames & Hudson, 1976.

Banham, Reyner.
Age of the masters : a personal view of modern architecture / Reyner Banham. — Revised ed. — ⌊London⌋ : Architectural Press, 1975.
170 p. : ill. ; 21 cm. GB***
First ed. published in 1962 under title: Guide to modern architecture.
ISBN 0-85139-398-5 : £4.95
1. Architecture, Modern—20th century. I. Title.
NA680.B248 1975 724.9 75-324365
75 MARC

Banham, Reyner.
Age of the masters : a personal view of modern architecture / Reyner Banham. — 1st U.S. ed. — New York : Harper & Row, c1975.
170 p. : ill. ; 22 cm. — (Icon editions)
Edition for 1962 published under title: Guide to modern architecture.
Includes index.
ISBN 0-06-430369-1 : $15.00. ISBN 0-06-430064-1 pbk.
1. Architecture, Modern—20th century. I. Title.
NA680.B248 1975b 724.9 74-25276
75 MARC

Banham, Reyner, comp.
The Aspen papers; twenty years of design theory from the International Design Conference in Aspen, edited and with commentary by Reyner Banham. London, Pall Mall Press ⌊1974⌋
224 p. illus. 24 cm. £5.75 GB***
1. Design—Addresses, essays, lectures. 2. Industrial design—Addresses, essays, lectures. I. International Design Conference. II. Title.
NK1510.B26 1974b 745.4 74-174551
ISBN 0-269-02934-X MARC

Banham, Reyner, comp.
The Aspen papers; twenty years of design theory from the International Design Conference in Aspen. Edited and with commentary by Reyner Banham. New York, Praeger ⌊1974⌋
224 p. illus. 25 cm.
1. Design—Addresses, essays, lectures. 2. Industrial design—Addresses, essays, lectures. I. International Design Conference. II. Title.
NK1510.B26 745.4 73-14559
MARC

Banham, Reyner.
Los Angeles: the architecture of four ecologies. ⌊Harmondsworth, Eng.⌋ Penguin Books ⌊1973, c1971⌋
256 p. illus. 20 cm. (The Architect and society) (Pelican books, A1178) $3.95 (U.S.) GB***
Bibliography: p. 247-252.
1. Architecture—Los Angeles.
NA735.L55B3 1973 720'.9794'94 74-155302
ISBN 0-14-021178-0 MARC

Banhatti, Narayana Daso
see Poona, India (City). Government Manuscripts Library. Descriptive catalogue of the government collections of manuscripts... [Bombay] Government of Bombay, 1916-67.

Banhatti, Rajendra, 1938-
(Samānadharmā)
समानधर्मा; दहा कथांचा संग्रह. ⌊लेखक⌋ राजेन्द्र बनहट्टी. ⌊1. आवृत्ती. पुणे⌋ इनामदार बंधु प्रकाशन ⌊1971⌋
134 p. 19 cm. Rs5.00
In Marathi.

I. Title.

PK2418.B3237S2 72-900489

Banhatti, Shrinivas Narayan, 1901-
(Jñāneśvarīrahasya)
ज्ञानेश्वरीरहस्य. ⌊व्याख्याते⌋ श्रीनिवास नारायण बनहट्टी. ⌊प्रथमावृत्ति⌋ पुणे, कौशिक व्याख्यानमाला ⌊1971⌋
6, 136 p. 23 cm. (कौशिक व्याख्यान माला, सत्र 15) Rs6.75
On cover: शिक्षण प्रसारक मंडळी, पुणे.
In Marathi.

1. Jñānadeva, fl. 1290. Jñāneśvarī. I. Title.

PK2418.J48J633 73-903381

Banhatti, Shrinivas Narayan, 1901-
(Jñānopāsanā, va Bhāratīyāñcē kartavya)
ज्ञानोपासना, व भारतीयांचें कर्तव्य / लेखक श्रीनिवास नारायण बनहट्टी. — 2. आवृत्ति. — पुणें : सुविचार प्रकाशन मंडळ, 1940.
214 p. ; 19 cm. — (नवभारत ग्रंथमाला ; 1)
In Marathi.
Includes index.

1. World history. I. Title.

D21.B226 75-986380

Banhatti, Shrinivas Narayan, 1901-
(Joḍayātrā)
जोडयात्रा. ⌊लेखक⌋ श्री. ना. बनहट्टी. ⌊प्रथमावृत्ती. पुणे, सुविचार प्रकाशन मंडळ, 1974-
v. illus. 23 cm. Rs15.00 (v. 1)
In Marathi.

1. Hindu pilgrims and pilgrimages—India. 2. Hindu shrines—India. I. Title.

BL1227.A1B36 74-902375

Banhatti, Shrinivas Narayan, 1901-
(Vāṅgmayavimarśa)
वाङ्मयविमर्श / श्रीनिवास नारायण बनहट्टी. — 1. आवृत्ति. — पुणें : चित्रशाळा प्रकाशन, 1955.
16, 221, 4 p. ; 19 cm. — (प्रा. बनहट्टी लेखसंग्रह ; 3)
In Marathi.
Series romanized: Prā. Banahaṭṭī lekhasaṅgraha.

1. Marathi literature—History and criticism. I. Title.

PK2401.B3 76-984591

Banhatti, Shrinivas Narayan, 1901-
see Jñanadeva, fl. 1290. (Sri Jñānadevī: pratiśuddha sāhitā) 1973.

al-Banhawi, Muhammad Amin.
The Suez Canal: a descriptive bibliography. ⌊n.p.⌋ 1964.
vii, 309 l.
Thesis—University of Michigan.
Microfilm (positive) Ann Arbor, Mich., University Microfilms, 1964. 1 reel. (Publication no. 12588)
NNC KyU NUC75-22165

Banhazi, Janos.
A minimalis talajmuveles gepei / Banhazi Janos, Fulop Gabor. -- Budapest : Mezogazdasagi Kiado, 1975.
227 p. : ill.
Bibliography: p. 223-227.
1. Tillage. 2. Cultivators. 3. Agricultural machinery. I. Fulop, Gabor. II. Title.
DNAL NUC77-86569

Banhazi, Janos.
A szantofoldi talajmuveles korszeru gepei. Budapest, Mezogazdasagi Kiado ⌊1971⌋
287 p. illus.
1. Tillage machinery. Design. I. Fulop, Gabor. II. Title.
DNAL NUC73-34515

Banhazi, Janos
see Szantofoldi munkagepek. ⌊Budapest⌋ Mezogazdasagi Kiado, 1972.

Bánhidi, Zoltán.
Learn Hungarian, by Zoltán Bánhidi, Zoltán Jókay ⌊and⌋ Dénes Szabó, in collaboration with Jenö Tarján. 2d ed. Budapest, Tankönyvkiadó ⌊1966⌋
530 p.
1. Hungarian language-Composition and exercises. 2. Hungarian language-Grammar. 3. Hungarian language-Text-books for foreigners—English. I. Jókay, Zoltán. II. Szabó, Dénes, 1913- III. Title.
DAU NUC73-126249

Bánhidi, Zoltán.
Learn Hungarian. By Zoltán Bánhidi ⌊and⌋ Zoltán Jókai ⌊and⌋ Dénes Szabó, in collaboration with Jenö Tarjan ⌊drawings by Tamás Szecskó⌋ 3d ed. Budapest, Tankönyvkiadó ⌊1971, c1965⌋
531 p. illus.
1. Hungarian language—Grammar. 2. Hungarian language—Conversation and phrase books.
I. Title.
CLU NUC73-114290

Bánhidi, Zoltán.
Learn Hungarian / by Zoltán Bánhidi, Zoltán Jókay, Dénes Szabó; in collaboration with Jenö Tarján. ; ⌊drawings by Tamás Szecskó⌋. — 4th ed. — Budapest : Tankönyvkiadó, ⌊1975⌋ c1965.
531 p., ⌊3⌋ leaves of plates : ill. ; 25 cm.
On cover: Tanuljunk nyelveket.
Includes index.
ISBN 963170971X : 46.00Ft
1. Hungarian language—Composition and exercises. 2. Hungarian language—Grammar. I. Jókay, Zoltán, joint author. II. Szabó, Dénes, 1913- joint author. III. Title. IV. Title: Tanuljunk nyelveket.
PH2111.B33 1975 494'.511'82421 77-464052
77 MARC

Bánhidi, Zoltán.
A magyar sportnyelv története és jelene; sportnyelvtörténeti szótárral. Budapest, Akadémiai Kiadó, 1971.
323 p. 21 cm. (Nyelvészeti tanulmányok, 16) 50.00Ft
Bibliography: p. 191-202.
1. Sports—Dictionaries—Hungarian. 2. Sports—Hungary. I. Title. II. Series.
GV567.B36 74-203387

Banhos, Bernardino.
Sexo e sexto; psicologia e graça. Coimbra, 1972.
296 p.
1. Sex (Theology) 2. Chastity. I. Title.
CLU DLC NUC76-72881

Bani, 1932-
(Ḥarf-i mu'tabar)
حرف معتبر. ⌊شاعر⌋ بانی. ⌊انتخاب: چندر پرکاش شاد. ترتیب: مہدی حیدر زیدی. نئی دہلی، 1971⌋
128 p. 22 cm. Rs10.00
In Urdu.

I. Title.

PK2200.B3285H3 79-926051

al-Bānī, Muḥammad Sa'īd.
(Tanwīr al-baṣā'ir bi-sīrat (al-Shaykh Ṭāhir)
تنوير البصائر بسيرة (الشيخ طاهر) : تتضمن سيرة ... الشيخ طاهر الجزائري منذ نشأته الى وفاته واثبات عظمته وكونه عضوا عاملا في جثمان الهيئة الاجتماعية / بقلم محمد سعيد الباني. — ⌊s. l. : s. n.⌋, 1920 (⌊دمشق ؟⌋ : مطبعة الحكومة العربية السورية)
4, 159 p. : ports. ; 20 cm.
1. al-Jazā'irī, Ṭāhir, 1852-1920. I. Title.
BP80.J38B36 75-588393

Bani, Tina Baglini
see
Baglini Bani, Tina.

Banī Ādam, Ḥusayn.
(Kitābshināsī-i navishtah'hā-yi Fārsī)
کتابشناسی نوشته‌های فارسی برای کودکان و نوجوانان، از حسین بنی آدم. تهران، انجمن کتاب ⌊1968 or 9⌋ 1347.
182 p. 22 cm. (مجموعهٔ کتابشناسی‌های موضوعی فارسی، 3)
1. Children's literature, Persian—Bibliography. I. Title. II. Series: Majmū'ah-'i kitābshināsī'hā-yi mawẓū'ī-i Fārsī, 3.
Z1037.8.P47B35 73-209912

Banī Ādam, Ḥusayn.
('Unvān-i mawẓū'ī barāy-i āṡār-i Fārsī)
عنوان موضوعی برای آثار فارسی / گردآوری حسین بنی آدم. — تهران : دانشگاه تهران، [1973] 1352.
216 p. ; 24 cm. — (انتشارات کتابخانهٔ مرکزی و مرکز اسناد ؛ شمارهٔ 4)
Cover title: Subject headings for Persian works.
500 copies printed.
1. Subject headings, Persian. I. Title. II. Title: Subject headings for Persian works. III. Series: Teheran. Dānishgāh. Kitābkhānah-'i Markazī va Markaz-i Asnād. Intishārāt-i Kitābkhānah'i Markazī va Markaz-i Asnād ; shumārah-'i 4.
Z695.1.O7B36 77–970935

Banī Aḥmad, Aḥmad.
(Dimūkrāsī va mardum)
دموکراسی و مردم، نوشتهٔ احمد بنی احمد. تهران، مؤسسهٔ مطبوعاتی عطائی [1350 i. e. 1971 or 2]
242 p. ports. 22 cm.
1. India. I. Title.
DS407.B34 74–221012

Bāṇī Prabāsī.
মিনার. [লেখক] বাণী প্রবাসী. [1. সংস্করণ. মুর্শিদাবাদ, এ. বি. মোবাসী, 1361, i.e. 1954]
48 p. 19 cm.
Without the music.
In Bengali.

1. Songs, Bengali—Texts. I. Title.
Title romanized: Mināra.
M1808.B36M5 72–219982

Banī Riẓā'ī, Muḥammad
see Iran. Laws, statutes, etc. (Majmū'ah-i qavānīn va muqarrarāt-i ijrā'i dar zamīnah-i bihdāsht-i amākin-i 'umūmī...) 1352 [1973]

Banian, G., ed.
see Howshamatean Chipeyli Amerikean Orbanots'i. 1969.

Bānībrata Datta
see
Datta, Bānībrata.

Banič, Janez.
Eden / Janez Banič. — Maribor : Obzorja, 1974.
366 p. ; 19 cm. Yu***
I. Title.
PG1919.12.A5E3 75–970404

Banic, Janez
see Zivinozdravstveni nasveti. Ljubljana, Czp Kmecki glas, 1972.

Banic, M
Les réactions au contour pour une plaque encastrée, par M. Banic. Paris, Association française de recherches et d'essais sur les matériaux et les constructions [1964]
119, [6] p. illus. 27 cm. (Cahiers de la recherche théorique et expérimentale sur les matériaux et les structures, no. 17)
Thèse—Paris.
On cover: En vente chez Eyrolles, Paris.
Bibliography: p. [121]–[123]
1. Plates (Engineering) I. Title. II. Series.
TA492.P7B34 73–202348

Bănică, Constantin.
Algebraic methods in the global theory of complex spaces / Constantin Bănică and Octavian Stănăşilă. — Bucuresti : Editura Academiei ; London ; New York : Wiley, 1976.
296 p. ; 25 cm.
Rev. English version of Metode algebrice în teoria globală a spaţiilor complexe, published in 1974.
Bibliography: p. [293]-296.
ISBN 0-471-01809-0
1. Analytic spaces. 2. Homology theory. 3. Duality theory (Mathematics) I. Stănăşilă, Octavian, joint author. II. Title.
QA331.B25413 515'.7 76-5823
76 MARC

Bănică, Constantin.
Metode algebrice în teoria globală a spaţiilor complexe / Constantin Bănică şi Octavian Stănăşilă. — Bucureşti : Editura Academiei Republicii Socialiste România, 1974.
348 p. ; 25 cm. R***
Summary in English.
Bibliography: p. 343–[346]
lei 24.00
1. Analytic spaces. 2. Homology theory. 3. Duality theory (Mathematics) I. Stănăşilă, Octavian, joint author. II. Title.
QA331.B254 75–543147

Banichuk, Nikolaĭ Vladimirovich, joint author
see Chernous'ko, F L (Variafsionnye zadachi mekhaniki i upravlenifa) 1973.

Banícke listy. 1- 1974–
Bratislava, Veda.
no. ill. 24 cm.
"Zborník Ústavu vlastností hornín Slovenskej akadémie vied."
Added t. p. title: Folia montana.
Summaries in English, German, and Russian.
1. Mining engineering—Collected works. 2. Rock mechanics—Collected works. I. Slovenská akadémia vied. Ústav vlastností hornín. II. Title: Folia montana.
TN275.A1B3 75–649948
MARC-S

Banícke múzeum v Rožňave
see Labancz, Štefan. Banícky Gemer ... Martin : Osveta, 1973.

Banier, Antoine, 1673-1741.
The mythology and fables of the ancients explain'd from history : London, 1739-40 / Antoine Danier. — New York : Garland Pub., 1976.
4 v. ; 23 cm. — (The Renaissance and the gods ; 40)
Translation of La mythologie et les fables expliquées par l'histoire.
Reprint of the 1739-1740 ed. printed for A. Millar, London.
Includes bibliographical references and index.
ISBN 0-8240-2089-8 : $40.00 per vol.
1. Mythology. 2. Folk-lore. I. Title. II. Series.
BL305.B3 1976 292'.1'3 77-140
77 MARC

Banier, François Marie.
Hôtel du Lac : [théâtre] / François-Marie Banier. — [Paris] : Gallimard, [1975]
180 p. ; 21 cm. F***
29.00F
I. Title.
PQ2662.A53H6 842'.9'14 75-507909
75 MARC

Banier, François Marie.
La tête la première. Paris, B. Grasset [1972]
183 p. 19 cm. 16.00F F***
I. Title.
PQ2662.A53T47 72–364625

Banier, Madeleine.
Poupées de laine. Photos. de Yves Jannès. [Paris] Hachette [1974]
89 p. col. illus. 27 cm. (Collection Temps libre) F***
1. Dollmaking—Amateurs' manuals. I. Title.
TT175.B36 745.59'22 74–168612
ISBN 2-01-000289-X MARC

Banier, Madeleine.
Woollen dolls / by Madeleine Banier ; translated [from the French] by Christine Hauch ; photographs by Yves Jannès. — London : Angus and Robertson, 1975.
2-89 p. : chiefly ill. (chiefly col.) ; 27 cm. — (Family crafts)
GB76-03338
Translation of Poupées de laine.
Col. ill. on lining papers.
ISBN 0-207-95665-0 : £2.50
1. Dollmaking—Amateurs' manuals. I. Title.
TT175.B3613 1975 745.59'22 76-373155
76 MARC

Banigan, Sharon (Church) 1912-
see Tinkle and Twinkle. Kenosha, Wis., Samuel Lowe, c1956.

Banige, Mikhail Ĭŭr'evich.
(Dinamika sudovykh dvigateleĭ vnutrennego sgoraniĭa)
Динамика судовых двигателей внутреннего сгорания. (Учеб. пособие для студентов специальности "Судовые силовые установки"). Горький, 1971.
96 p. with diagrs. 20 cm. 0.18rub USSR 71-VKP
At head of title: Министерство высшего и среднего специального образования РСФСР. Горьковский политехнический институт им. А. А. Жданова. М. Ю. Баниге.
1. Marine engines. I. Title.
VM770.B33 73–325824

Banige, Vladimir Sergeevich.
(Kreml' Rostova Velikogo shestnadt͡satogo—semnadt͡satogo veka)
Кремль Ростова Великого XVI–XVII века / В. Баниге. — Москва : Искусство, 1976.
143 p. : ill. (some col.) ; 26 cm. USSR 76
Summary in English; list of illustrations also in English.
Bibliography: p. 143.
4.32rub
1. Rostov, Russia (City). Kreml'. I. Title.
DK651.R7B36 76–532092

Banige, Vladimir Sergeevich
see Bernshteĭn, Ėmmanuil Borisovich. Pamíatniki zodchestva Vologodskoĭ oblasti... Vologda, Vologodskoe kn. izd-vo, 1963.

Banijamali, Seyyed-Hossein.
The effect of a straining motion upon macromolecular conformation in dilute solution. [n. p.] 1974.
xviii, 239 l. illus., diagrs., tables. 30 cm.
Thesis (Sc. D.)—Massachusetts Institute of Technology.
Vita.
Bibliography: leaves 232-238.
1. Isobutylene. 2. Solution (Chemistry) 3. Macromolecules. 4. Polymers and polymerization. I. Title.
MCM NUC75-17680

Banik, Allen E
Your water and your health [by] Allen E. Banik with Carlson Wade. New Canaan, Conn., Keats Pub. [1974]
126 p. illus. 18 cm. (A Pivot original health book) $1.25
Bibliography: p. 124-126.
1. Water. 2. Water—Pollution. 3. Hygiene. I. Wade, Carlson, joint author. II. Title.
RA591.B36 613.3'1 74–79172
MARC

Banik, Sambhu N
Drugs and youth—it's impact on the community. [By] Sambhu N. Banik. [Bethesda, Md., ERIC Document Reproduction Service] 1969.
8 l. 22 cm.
Paper presented at World Mental Health Assembly, Washington, D.C., November 17-21, 1969.
1. Drugs and youth. I. Educational Resources Information Center. II. Title.
CMIG NUC74-115166

Banin, Aleksandr Petrovich.
(Ėffektivnost' meropriíatiĭ po okhrane prirodnykh resursov)
Эффективность мероприятий по охране природных ресурсов / А. П. Банин. — Москва : Стройиздат, 1977.
206 p. : ill. ; 20 cm. — (Защита окружающей среды) USSR***
Series romanized: Zashchita okruzhaíushcheĭ sredy.
Bibliography: p. 204.
0.71rub
1. Conservation of natural resources—Russia. 2. Environmental protection—Russia. 3. Building sites—Russia. I. Title.
S934.R9B36 77–513268

Banin, Aleksandr Petrovich.
(Ėkspertnaía ot͡senka ėffektivnosti novoĭ tekhniki v stroitel'stve)
Экспертная оценка эффективности новой техники в строительстве. Москва, Стройиздат, 1974.
112 p. with diagrs. 20 cm. (Экономика строительства)
USSR 74
At head of title: А. П. Банин.
0.40rub
1. Pipe-laying machinery. 2. Building—Russia. I. Title.
TJ933.B36 75–554837

Banin, Amos
see Anderson, Duwayne Marlo, 1927- The water-ice phase composition of clay water systems. Hanover, N.H., 1974-

Banini, L A
Aids to the study of the Eve language, by L.A. Banini. Ho (Ghana), E. P. Church Book Depot [1970]
56 p.
Cover title.
1. Ewe language—Grammar. I. Title.
CU NUC76-75601

Banino, George M
Origin of Roaring Brook, by George M. Banino. Trenton, N.J., Geological Survey, 1969.
8 p. illus., map. 28 cm.
1. Rivers—New Jersey. 2. New Jersey—Geology—Somerset Co. I. New Jersey. State Geologist.
DI-GS NUC74-25184

Baniol, Robert.
Le commentaire de texte composé : baccalauréats / Robert Baniol. — [Paris] : Delagrave, [1974]
127 p. ; 23 cm. — (Espaces et parcours littéraires) (Collection G. Belloc)
F***
1. French literature—Explication. I. Title.
PQ53.B26 840'.76 75-510620
75[r76]rev MARC

Baniol, Robert.
Le rêve vert : roman / Robert Baniol. — Paris : A. Michel, c1976.
310 p. ; 20 cm. F***
ISBN 2-226-00358-4 : 32.00F
I. Title.
PQ2662.A534R4 843'.9'14 77-455798
77 MARC

Baniol, Robert.
see La Condition ouvrière ... [Paris] Delagrave, [1974]

Baniol, Robert, ed.
see Flaubert, Gustave, 1821-1880. Madame Bovary: Flaubert. [Paris] Hatier [1973]

Baniol, Robert.
see La Ville ... [Paris] Delagrave, [1974]

Banis, Robert Joseph, 1943-
Solubilization, partial purification and properties of a microsomal long chain fatty acyl-CoA synthetase from the chicken. Raleigh, N. C., 1973.
129 l. illus., tables. 29 cm.
Bibliography: leaves 127-129.
Vita.
Thesis (Ph. D.)—North Carolina State University at Raleigh.
NcRS NUC76-75602

Banis, Tālivaldis, illus.
see Sakse, Anna, 1905- Varavīksne. Rīgā, "Liesma," 1968.

Banis, Victor J
Charms, spells, and curses for the millions [by] Victor Samuels [i. e. Banis]. Los Angeles, Sherbourne Press [c1970]
155 p. 21 cm. (For the millions series, FM37) $2.50
1. Talismans. 2. Incantations. I. Title.
BF1561.B3 133.4'4 71-99876
MARC

Banis, Victor J
The pussycat man [by] Victor J. Banis. Los Angeles, Sherbourne Press [c1969]
190 p. 22 cm.
"First printing."
I. Title.
OU NUC73-126299

Banisadr, Abol Hassan, joint comp.
see Vieille, Paul, comp. Pétrole et violence ... Paris, Éditions Anthropos, [1974]

Banish, Roslyn, 1942-
see City families ... 1st ed. New York, Pantheon Books, c1976.

Banister, Betty.
Trapped : a polio victim's fight for life / Betty Banister. -- Saskatoon, Sask. : Western Producer Prairie Books, 1975.
102 p. : ill. ; 21 cm.
"Originally published in serial form in The Western producer, August 15 to October 31, 1974."
ISBN 0-919306-49-7.
1. Banister, Betty. 2. Poliomyelitis--Personal narratives. I. Title.
CaMWU NUC77-86582

Banister, Gary, 1948-
My war with God. Grand Rapids, Zondervan Pub. House [c1973]
119 p. illus. 18 cm. $0.95
1. Polyradiculitis—Personal narratives. I. Title.
RC416.B36 248'.2 73-13062
MARC

Banister, Judith. Gli argenti inglesi
see Scheidt, Bernd. Englisches Silber. München: Schuler, c1973.

Banister, Judith.
Collecting antique silver. London, Ward Lock, 1972.
128 p. chiefly illus. 21 cm. index. (Concorde books) £1.25
B 72-31257
1. Silver articles, English. 2. Silver articles—Collectors and collecting. I. Title.
NK7143.B33 1972 739.2'3'742 73-160250
ISBN 0-7063-1332-1 ; 0-7063-1813-7 (pbk.) MARC

Banister, Judith.
Collecting antique silver / Judith Banister. — New York : Galahad Books, [1974] c1972.
128 p. : ill. ; 21 cm.
Includes index.
$4.95
1. Silver articles, English. 2. Silver articles—Collectors and collecting. I. Title.
NK7143.B33 1974 739.2'3'742 74-184819
MARC

Banister, Judith.
English silver hall-marks: with lists of English, Scottish and Irish hall-marks and makers marks; edited by Judith Banister. London, New York, Foulsham, 1970.
96 p. illus. 16 cm. £0.50 B 70-22524
1. Hall-marks. 2. Silver articles, British. I. Title.
NK7210.B36 739.2'3'742 73-165732
ISBN 0-572-00674-8 MARC

Banister, Judith.
Mid Georgian silver. [London], [Hamlyn], 1972.
64 p. illus. 19 cm. (Country Life collectors' guides) £0.65
B 72-25373
Caption title.
1. Silver articles, Georgian. I. Title.
NK7143.B348 739.2'3'742 73-153158
ISBN 0-600-43129-0 MARC

Banister, Keith Edward.
On the Cyprinid fish Barbus Allaudi Pellegrin: a possible intergeneric hybrid from Africa. Studies on African Cyprinidae, part II. London, British Museum, 1972.
[261]-290 p. 1 plate. 25 cm. (Bulletin of the British Museum (Natural History) Zoology, v. 24, no. 5)
1. Cyprinodnotes. I. Title. II. Series: British Museum (Natural History) Bulletin. Zoology, v. 24, no. 5.
NSyU NUC76-75605

Banister, Keith Edward.
A revision of the large Barbus (Pisces, Cyprinidae) of East and Central Africa. Studies on African Cyprinidae, part II. London, British Museum, 1973.
148 p. illus. 25 cm. (Bulletin of the British Museum (Natural History) Zoology, v. 26, no. 1)
1. Cyprinodontes. I. Title. II. Series: British Museum (Natural History) Bulletin. Zoology, v. 26, no. 1.
NSyU NUC76-75833

Banister, Keith Edward
see Studies on African cyprinidae. London, British Museum (Natural History) 1972-

Banister, Manly Miles, 1914-
Bookbinding as a handcraft / by Manly Banister ; photos. and drawings by the author. — New York : Sterling Pub. Co., c1975.
160 p. : ill. ; 27 cm.
Includes index.
ISBN 0-8069-5326-8. ISBN 0-8069-5327-6 lib. bdg.
1. Bookbinding. I. Title.
Z271.B199 686.3'02 75-14522
76 MARC

Banister, Manly Miles, 1914-
Etching and other intaglio techniques, by Manly Banister. Totowa, N. J., Littlefield, Adams, 1974 [c1969]
128 p. illus. 28 cm. (A Littlefield, Adams quality paperback, no. 286)
Reprint of the ed. published by Sterling Pub. Co., New York.
1. Etching—Technique. 2. Intaglio printing. I. Title.
[NE2135.B35 1974] 767'.2 74-10990
ISBN 0-8226-0286-5 MARC

Banister, Manly Miles, 1914-
Lithographic prints from stone and plate, by Manly Banister. Totowa, N. J., Littlefield, Adams, 1974 [c1972]
128 p. illus. 28 cm. (A Littlefield, Adams quality paperback, no. 285)
Reprint of the ed. published by Sterling Pub. Co., New York.
1. Lithography—Technique. I. Title.
[NE2425.B36 1974] 763 74-10971
ISBN 0-8226-0285-7 MARC

Banister, Manly Miles, 1914-
Making picture frames, by Manly Banister. With photos. by the author. New York, Sterling Pub. Co. [1973]
48 p. illus. 19 cm. (Little craft book series)
SUMMARY: Introduces the materials, tools, and techniques for constructing a variety of frames.
1. Picture frames and framing. [1. Picture frames and framing] I. Title.
N8550.B35 1973 749'.7 73-83451
ISBN 0-8069-5282-1 ; 0-8069-5283-0 (pbk.) MARC

Banister, Manly Miles, 1914-
Wood block cutting & printing / by Manly Banister ; photos, drawings, and prints by the author. — New York : Sterling Pub. Co., c1976.
72 p. : ill. (some col.) ; 22 cm.
Includes index.
ISBN 0-8069-5374-8. ISBN 0-8069-5375-6 lib. bdg.
1. Wood-engraving—Technique. I. Title.
NE1227.B27 761'.2 76-19813
76 MARC

Banister, Margaret S
Burn then, little lamp [by] Margaret Banister. Boston, Houghton Mifflin, 1967 [c1966]
314 p. 22 cm.
I. Title.
PZ4.B2163 Bu 67-10924
[PS3552.A477] [r77]rev MARC

Banister, Richard.
Case studies in multi-media instruction. Los Angeles, ERIC Clearinghouse for Junior Colleges, Graduate School of Education and the University Library, University of California, 1970.
57 p. (ERIC Clearinghouse for Junior Colleges. Topical paper no. 13)
Includes bibliography.
1. Audio-visual education. I. Title. II. Series.
CLU NUC73-126300

Banit, Feofan Gavrilovich.
Vnutripechnye pyleulavlivaîushchie ustroĭstva. Moskva, Gos. izd-vo lit-ry po stroitel'stvu, arkhitekture i stroitel'nym materialam, 1959.
126 p. illus. (Gos. vses. nauchno-issl. in-t tsementnoĭ promyshl. Trudy, vyp. 11)
ICRL NUC76-90409

Banítez, Fernando, 1911-
Los hongos alucinantes. [3. ed. Mexico, D. F., 1972, c1964]
125 p. illus. 18 cm. (Serie popular Era/2)
1. Mushrooms. Mexico. 2. Mushroom ceremony. 3. Hallucinogenic drugs. I. Title.
NB NUC76-72882

Banitt, Menahem, 1914-
see Sefer ha-pitronot mi-Bazel. Le glossaire de Bâle. Jérusalem: Académie nationale des sciences et des lettres d'Israël, 1972.

Banitz, Kalman, illus.
see Nash, Frederick C 1922-
Automatic technology. Toronto, New York, McGraw-Hill Ryerson [1973]

Baniukiewicz, Elżbieta.
Park w Łańcucie. [Wyd. 1. Warszawa] Arkady, 1972.
177 p. illus. map. 25 cm.
1. Łańcut—Descr.—Views. I. Title.
PCamA NUC75-24027

Baniukiewicz, Elżbieta.
Zamek w Łańcucie. Oprac. fotograficzne: Krzysztof Jabłoński. [Wyd. 2.]. Warszawa, Arkady, 1973.
108 p. illus. 16 cm.
At head of title: Elżbieta Baniukiewicz, Zofia Wiśniowska.
List of illus. and summaries in English, French, German, and Russian.
Bibliography: p. 35.
zł18.00
1. Łańcut, Poland (City). Castle. I. Wiśniowska, Zofia, joint author. II. Jabłoński, Krzysztof, illus.
DK4800.L36B36 1973 75-402055

Banja, Hasan.
La création de l'industrie socialiste en République populaire d'Albanie et ses perspectives de développement. Tirana, Naim Frasheri, 1968.
129 p. 17 cm.
1. Industry and state—Albania. 2. Albania—Economic conditions—1945- I. Title.
NNC NUC73-126326

Banja, Hasan.
Establishment and prospects of development of socialist industry in the People's Republic of Albania / Hasan Banja. — [Tirana] : Naim Frasheri, Pub. House, [1969].
127 p. ; 17 cm.
Includes bibliographical references.
1. Albania—Industries. I. Title.
HC402.B28 76 76-368533 MARC

Banja, Hasan.
Probleme aktuale të organizimit socialist të punës. [Tiranë] Shtëpia Botonjëse Naim Frashëri [1967]
199 p. 17 cm.
Includes bibliographical references.
1. Labor and laboring classes—Albania. 2. Labor productivity—Albania. I. Title.
HD8620.5.B35 74-209521

Banjaluka : pet godina poslije zemljotresa / [urednik Besim Karabegović ; autori tekstova Hare Beganović ... et al. ; fotografije Dušan Momčilović ... et al.]. — Banjaluka : Glas, 1974.
227 p., [1] leaf of plates : ill., maps ; 29 cm. Yu 76-540
1. Banja Luka, Yugoslavia. I. Karabegović, Besko. II. Beganović, Hare.
DR396.B355B33 76-530453

Banjanin, Thomas George, 1942-
The administration of justice in the United States district courts: an analysis of the impact of Rule 50(b) of the Federal rules of criminal procedure... Ann Arbor, Mich., Xerox University Microfilms, c1975.
[2], vii, 207 l. tables. 22 cm.
Thesis--George Washington University.
"Bibliography": leaves 203-207.
1. Criminal procedure--United States. 2. Justice, Administration of--United States. 3. U.S. District courts. I. Title.
MH-L NUC77-90068

Banjanin, Thomas George, 1942-
The administration of justice in the United States District Courts : an analysis of the impact of rule 50(b) of the Federal rules of criminal procedure / by Thomas G. Banjanin. -- Washington, D.C., 1975.
vii, 207 leaves.
Thesis--The George Washington University.
Bibliography: leaves 203-207.
Microfilm (positive) Ann Arbor, Mich. : University Microfilms, 1975. -- 1 reel ; 35 mm.
1. United States. District Courts. I. Title.
NNC-L NUC77-86579

Bañjar, Bagus
see
Yasadipura I, Radèn Ňabèhi, 1729-1803.

Banjar, Indonesia (Kabupaten)
For works by this jurisdiction issued before the change of orthography in 1972 see
Bandjar, Indonesia (Kabupaten)
74-215060

Banjarmasin, Indonesia (Kalimantan Selatan). Walikota.
Penulisan singkat tentang sasaran penggunaan tanah dalam Kotamadya Banjarmasin, partisipasi nyata warga kota Kotamadya Banjarmasin dalam Pelita I : kertas kerja Walikota Kepala Daerah Kotamadya Banjarmasin dalam Penataran Walikota Kepala Daerah Seluruh Indonesia, Februari-Maret 1974. — [Banjarmasin] : Pemerintah Daerah Kotamadya Banjarmasin, [1974]
[53] leaves : 33 cm.
1. Land—Indonesia—Banjarmasin (Kalimantan Selatan) 2. Banjarmasin, Indonesia (Kalimantan Selatan)—Economic conditions. 3. Banjarmasin, Indonesia (Kalimantan Selatan)—Social contitions. I. Title: Penulisan singkat tentang sasaran penggunaan tanah dalam Kotamadya Banjarmasin ...
HD899.B35B3 1974 74-940862

Banjermasin (Sultanate). Treaties, etc.
Surat-surat perdjandjian antara Kesultanan Bandjarmasin dengan pemerintahan[2] V. O. C., Bataafse Republik, Inggeris dan Hindia-Belanda 1635-1860. — Djakarta : Arsip Nasional Republik Indonesia, Kompartimen Perhubungan dengan Rakjat, 1965.
x, 271 p. : 23 cm.
Dutch and/or Malay.
1. Banjermasin (Sultanate)—Foreign relations—Treaties. I. Arsip Nasional Republik Indonesia. II. Title: Surat-surat perdjandjian antara Kesultanan Bandjarmasin dengan pemerintahan[2] V. O. C. ...
JX1574.A2B35 1965 75-949620

Banjević, Branko.
(Gavran hrani Crnu Goru)
Гавран храни Црну Гору. Титоград, "Графички завод," 1972.
80 p. 20 cm. (Библиотека "Антеј") 20.00Din Yu 72-8481
Poems.
I. Title.
PG1419.12.A5G3 73-970188

Banjević, Branko
see Pleme za oblakom. 1973.

Banjo, Adesegun Olufemi, 1939-
A morphometric study of the ultrastructural development of the chick embryo liver in ovo and in organ culture between the ages of 4 and 16 days : and, the Effect of sodium phenobarbital on the ultrastructural development during this period in ova and in culture / Adesegun Olufemi Banjo. -- [Philadelphia, Pa.] : Banjo, 1975.
xxxxi, 129 leaves : ill.
Thesis--University of Pennsylvania.
Bibliography: leaves xxiii-xxxvii.
Photocopy of typescript. Ann Arbor, Mich. : University Microfilms, 1975. 22 cm.
1. Chick embryo. 2. Liver. I. Title.
NIC NUC77-86578

Banjo, Bayo.
I was a "locum". [Ibadan, Nigeria] c1967.
25 p. 21 cm.
1. Negro physicians. 2. Physicians, Nigerian. I. Title.
MdU MiEM CtY NUC74-115154

Banjumas, Indonesia (Kabupaten)
Pedoman penjelenggaraan pemilihan kepala desa dalam Kabupaten Banjumas (Purwokerto) [Purwokerto] 1970.
25 l. 32 cm.
Cover title.
1. Elections—Banjumas, Indonesia (Kabupaten)
NIC NUC76-72883

Banjumas, Indonesia (Kabupaten)
Struktur organisasi pemerintahan desa di Daerah Kabupaten Banjumas. Purwokerto, 1970.
22 l. 32 cm.
Cover title.
1. Local government—Banjumas, Indonesia (Kabupaten) 2. Villages—Indonesia—Banjumas (Kabupaten) I. Title.
JS7205.D54B343 1970 73-940677

Banjumas, Indonesia (Kabupaten) Ordinances, local laws, etc.
Peraturan pengangkatan dan pemberhentian pamong desa (ketjuali kepala desa) didaerah Kabupaten Banjumas Purwokerto, 19 Nopember 1970. [Purwokerto, 1970]
18 l. 32 cm.
Cover title.
1. Banjumas, Indonesia (Kabupaten)—Officials and employees—Appointment, qualifications, tenure, etc.
NIC NUC76-93167

Bank, Aleksandr Samuilovich, joint author
see Askarov, M A (Khimicheskaia stabilizatsiia polimerov) 1974.

Bank, Barbara, ed.
see Readings in health care. 2d ed. Columbia, Human Ecology and Behavioral Science, Section of Health Care Studies, Dept. of Community Health and Medical Practice, School of Medicine, University of Missouri-Columbia, 1971-

Bank, Barbara, ed.
see Readings in health care. 3d ed. Columbia, Human Ecology and Behavioral Science, Section of Health Care Studies, Dept. of Community Health and Medical Practice, School of Medicine, University of Missouri-Columbia, 1972-

Bank, Barbara Julianne.
Social influence: an interactionist perspective. [Iowa City] 1974.
x, 374 l. 28 cm.
Thesis (Ph. D.)—University of Iowa.
1. Influence (Psychology) I. Title.
IaU NUC76-22130

Bank, Boris Vladimirovich, comp.
see Za boevuiu realizatsiiu ... 1934.

Bank, Gail Irvin, 1925-
see Association for Hospital Medicine Education. Role of community hospitals in continuing education of health professionals. Arlington, Va. [available from] National Technical Information Service, Springfield, Va., 1975.

Bank, Hans-Peter.
Rationale Sozialpolitik : ein Beitrag zum Begriff der Raionalität / von Hans-Peter Bank. — Berlin : Duncker & Humblot, [1975]
202 p. ; 24 cm. — (Beiträge zur politischen Wissenschaft ; Bd. 21) GFR***
Bibliography: p. [180]-194.
Includes indexes.
ISBN 3-428-03317-5
1. Political sociology. 2. Social systems. 3. Social problems. 4. Political psychology. I. Title. II. Series.
JA76.B28 301.5'92 75 75-507000 MARC

Bank, Hermann, 1928-
From the world of gemstones. [English translation by E. H. Rutland] Innsbruck, Pinguin-Verlag [1973]
178 p. illus. (part col.) maps, tables. 25 cm.
Translation of Aus der Welt der Edelsteine.
Bibliography: p. 175.
1. Precious stones. I. Title.
CLS NUC76-75844

Bank, Ira M 1942-
The effect of career word games on the vocational awareness of selected third and fifth grade students. Detroit, Mich., 1970.
166 p.
Thesis—Wayne State University.
Microfilm. Ann Arbor, Mich., University Microfilms. 1 reel. 35 mm.
CLSU NUC73-47555

Bank, J A
Tactus, tempo and notation in mensural music from the 13th to the 17th century [by] J. A. Bank. [Amsterdam, Annie Bank, Anna Vondelstraat 13, c1972]
260, xi p. facsims., music. 24 x 33 cm. Ne***
Bibliography: p. i-ix.
1. Measured music. 2. Tempo (Music) I. Title.
ML174.B3 781'.24 73-160422 MARC

Bank, Jan, 1940-
Kort Marcuse. Inleiding tot de denkwereld van Herbert Marcuse. [Odijk, Sjaloom, Studio Kosmopolitiek, 1969]
12 p. 22 cm. (Maandelijks kosmoschrift, 1969, nr. 1) 1.45 NeB 69-March
Cover title.
Bibliography: p. [3] of cover.
1. Marcuse, Herbert, 1898- I. Title.
B945.M2984B35 72-359930

Bank, Jan, 1940-
Rapport sur la démocratisation de l'enseignement aux Pays-Bas. [Amsterdam? 1971]
28 p. 30 x 10 cm.
1. Higher education and state—Netherlands. 2. Students—Netherlands—Political activity. I. Title.
MiU-L NUC73-34528

Bank, Mikhail Urovich.
(Élektricheskie i akusticheskie parametry radiopriemnykh ustroĭstv)
Электрические и акустические параметры радиоприемных устройств / М. У. Банк. — Москва : Связь, 1974.
286 p. : ill. ; 21 cm. USSR 74
Bibliography: p. 279-[281]
0.87rub
1. Radio—Receivers and reception. I. Title.
TK6563.B25 74-358637

Bank, Mort.
The North Dakota fishing guide / Mort Bank. — [s.l. : s.n.], c1977.
208 p. : ill. ; 23 cm.
1. Fishing—North Dakota. 2. Fishing—North Dakota—Maps. I. Title.
SH533.B36 799.1'1'09784 77 77-151477 MARC

Bank, Randolph Edwin.
Marching algorithms for elliptic boundary value problems / by Randolph Edwin Bank. -- [s.l. : s.n., 1975]
309, [7] leaves in various foliations ; 29 cm.
Thesis--Harvard.
Bibliography: leaves [310]-[316]
MH NUC77-86591

Bank, Rheta.
see **Safeguarding psychiatric privacy ... New York, Wiley, ₍1975₎**

Bank, Richard.
Public services under West Virginia law. Prepared by Richard Bank. Montgomery, West Virginia Institute of Technology, Community Service Center, 1971.
52 p. 36 cm.
1. Community development–West Virginia. 2. Municipal services–West Virginia. 3. Public utilities–West Virginia. I. Title.
WvU NUC76-75627

Bank, Rona King.
Formulation, application, and analysis of a method to study female underachievement. [Cambridge, Mass.] 1970 [c1972]
1 v.
Thesis (Ed. D.)–Harvard University.
Microfilm of typescript. Ann Arbor, Mich., University Microfilms, 1972. 1 reel. 35 mm.
1. Underachievers. 2. Education of women. I. Title.
FMU NUC73-113622

Bank, Rosemarie Katherine.
Rhetorical, dramatic, theatrical, and social contexts of selected American frontier plays, 1871 to 1960. ₍Iowa City₎ 1972.
iv, 242 l. 28 cm.
Thesis (Ph.D.)—University of Iowa.
1. America drama—19 cent.—Hist. & crit. 2. American drama—20th cent.—Hist. & crit. 3. The West in literature. I. Title.
IaU NUC73-114292

Bank, Śarah Erlikhman-
see
Erlichman, Sara, 1920-

Bank, Stephen Paul, 1941-
An investigation of the placebo effect. ₍n.p.₎ 1968.
152 l.
Microfilm.
Thesis—University of North Carolina.
1. Placebo (Medicine) I. Title.
OrU NUC73-126296

Bank, Ted.
People of the Bering Sea. ₍By₎ Ted Bank II. New York, MSS Educational Pub. Co. ₍c1971₎
101 p. (Readings in anthropology)
1. Anthropology—Bering Sea. 2. Aleutian Islands.
NcU MiEM CaBVaU NUC73-34522

Bank, Walter
see Schutz, L A Airborne asbestos fiber... [Washington] U.S. Dept. of the Interior, 1973.

Bank Abū Zaby al-Watanī. Annual report and balance sheet
see Bank Abū Ẓaby al-Watanī. al-Taqrīr al-sanawī wa-al-mizānīyah al-'āmmah. 1969-

Bank Abū Ẓaby al-Waṭanī.
التقرير السنوي والميزانية العامة. 1969–
₍ابو ظبي₎ بنك ابو ظبي الوطني.
v. 25 cm.
Added title, 1969– : Annual report and balance sheet.
Arabic and English.
1. Bank Abū Ẓaby al-Waṭanī. I. Bank Abū Ẓaby al-Waṭanī. Annual report and balance sheet.
Title romanized: al-Taqrīr al-sanawī wa-al-mīzānīyah al-'āmmah.
HG3266.A95B35 77-970480

Bank Administration Institute.
Audit questionnaire check list. 3d print. and revision. Park Ridge, Ill., 1970, c1954.
v, 22 p. 28 cm.
1. Bank examination. I. Title.
INS NUC75-47265

Bank Administration Institute.
The BAI index of bank performance. ₍Park Ridge, Ill., Bank Administration Institute₎
v. 22 x 28 cm.
Key title: The BAI index of bank performance, ISSN 0363-910X
1. Banks and banking—United States—States—Statistics—Periodicals. I. Bank Administration Institute. Index of bank performance. II. Title.
HG2493.B25a 332.1′0973 76-647571
MARC-S

Bank Administration Institute. Index of bank performance
see Bank Administration Institue. The BAI index of bank performance. [Park Ridge, Ill.]

Bank Administration Institute.
Job descriptions for bank personnel : a comprehensive guide. — Park Ridge, Ill. : Bank Administration Institute, c1975.
xvii, 308 p. ; 28 cm.
Includes index.
$20.00
1. Banks and banking—Job descriptions. 2. Banks and banking—United States. I. Title.
HG1615.7.J6B35 1975 331.7′02 75-26268
75 MARC

Bank Administration Institute.
Survey of the check collection system. Park Ridge, Ill., Bank Administration Institute.
v. ill. 28 cm.
1. Check collection systems—United States—Collected works. I. Title.
HG1692.B35a 332.1 76-14052
MARC-S

Bank Administration Institute
see DuMont, Desmond E Coding differences for Federal Reserve Wire... Park Ridge, Ill. [1973]

Bank Administration Institute
see Long, Robert H Bank by telephone... Park Ridge, Ill., c1973.

Bank Administration Institute
see Reich, Kenneth E Customer profitability analysis; a tool for improving bank profits. Park Ridge, Ill., Bank Administration Institute [c1972]

Bank Administration Institute.
see **Stafeil, Walter W. 1974 survey of the check collection system. Park Ridge, Ill., Bank Administration Institute, c1975.**

Bank Administration Institute.
see Stafeil, Walter W. 1975 survey of the check collection system. Park Ridge, Ill., Bank Administration Institute, c1976.

Bank Administration Institute. Audit Commission.
Audit organization and practice in banks over $50 million in deposits. Park Ridge, Ill., Bank Administration Institute ₍1973₎
iv, 27 p. 26 cm. $4.00
Cover title: Audit organization and practice in banks with more than $50 million in deposits.
"No. 213."
1. Bank examination. I. Title.
HG1707.5.B36 658.1′51 73-161309
MARC

Bank Administration Institute. Audit Commission
see Coen, Charles D Statistical sampling for bank auditors. Park Ridge, Ill. [1973]

Bank Administration Institute. Audit Commission.
see Kristofek, William A. A survey of bank operating losses ... Park Ridge, Ill., Bank Administration Institute, ₍1975₎

Bank Administration Institute. Bank Security Commission.
Your bank and armed robbery. Rev. by the Bank Security Commission. Assisted by BAI's Technical Division. ₍Rev. 3d ed.₎ Park Ridge, Ill., Bank Administration Institute ₍1973₎
vii, 40 p. illus. 24 cm. $2.00
1. Banks and banking — Security measures. 2. Bank robberies. I. Bank Administration Institute. Technical Division. II. Title.
HG1616.S37B3 1973 658.2′8 73-178304
MARC

Bank Administration Institute. Operations Commission.
"Due from banks" accounting and control standards. Park Ridge, Ill. ₍c1972₎
33 p. 23 cm. $4.00
1. Banks and banking—Accounting. I. Title.
HG1708.B28 1972 657′.833 72-84024
MARC

Bank Administration Institute. Operations Commission
see Coen, Charles D The Bank secrecy act and retention of bank records. Park Ridge, Ill. [1974]

Bank Administration Institute. Operations Commission
see Monroe, John S The Occupational safety and health act of 1970 as it applies to banks and bankers. ₍Rev. 2d ed.₎ Park Ridge, Ill., Bank Administration Institute ₍1973, c1972₎

Bank Administration Institute. Personnel Administration Commission.
A biennial survey of bank officer salaries. Park Ridge, Ill.
v. illus. 28 cm.
1. Wages—Bank employees—United States. I. Title.
HD4966.B262U43a 331.2′81′33210973 70-180921
ISSN 0525-4620 MARC-S

Bank Administration Institute. Personnel Administration Commission.
The biennial survey of bank personnel policies and practices. ₍Park Ridge, Ill., Bank Administration Institute₎
v. 28 cm.
1. Banks and banking—Personnel management. I. Title. II. Title: Bank personnel policies and practices.
HG1615.5.B3 658.3′7′3321 71-17658
rev

Bank Administration Institute. Personnel Administration Commission.
see McCurry, Charles M. Bank personnel administration ... Park Ridge, Ill., The Institute, c1975.

Bank Administration Institute. Personnel Administration Commission
see Monroe, John S The Occupational safety and health act of 1970 as it applies to banks and bankers. ₍Rev. 2d ed.₎ Park Ridge, Ill., Bank Administration Institute ₍1973, c1972₎

Bank Administration Institute. Research Commission
see Stafeil, Walter W The impact of exception items on the check collection system... Park Ridge, Ill., Bank Administration Institute [1974]

Bank Administration Institute. Research Commission
see Thompson, T C Lock box communications standards for banks ... Park Ridge, Ill., Bank Administration Institute [1972]

Bank Administration Institute. Research Commission.

For works by this body issued under its earlier name see

Bank Administration Institute. Research Committee on Communications Standards for Banks.

Bank Administration Institute. Research Committee on Communications Standards for Banks.
In 1968 when the name of NABAC, the Association for Bank Audit, Control and Operation changed to Bank Administration Institute, its Research Committee became the Research Committee on Communications Standards for Banks. About 1971 the name of the Committee was changed to Research Commission, and in 1975 to Research Council.
Works by this body are found under the following headings according to the name used at the time of publication:
NABAC, the Association for Bank Audit, Control and Operation. Research Committee.

Bank Administration Institute. Research Committee on Communications Standards for Banks.
Bank Administration Institute. Research Commission.
Bank Administration Institute. Research Council.

Bank Administration Institute. Research Council.
In 1968 when the name of NABAC, the Association for Bank Audit, Control and Operation changed to Bank Administration Institute, its Research Committee became the Research Committee on Communications Standards for Banks. About 1971 the name of the Committee was changed to Research Commission, and in 1975 to Research Council.
Works by this body are found under the following headings according to the name used at the time of publication:
NABAC, the Association for Bank Audit, Control and Operation. Research Committee.
Bank Administration Institute. Research Committee on Communications Standards for Banks.

Bank Administration Institute. Research Commission.
Bank Administration Institute. Research Council.

Bank Administration Institute. Research Council.
see Stafeil, Walter W. Guidelines for adjustment resolution ... Park Ridge, Ill., Bank Administration Institute, c1975.

Bank Administration Institute. Research Council.
see Stafeil, Walter W. Recommendations for exception item reduction ... Park Ridge, Ill., Bank Administration Institute, c1975.

Bank Administration Institute. Research Council.
see Steffen, George W. The bank message center ... Park Ridge, Ill., Bank Administration Institute, c1976.

Bank Administration Institute. Research Division
see Momjian, Dan. Securities depositories... Park Ridge, Ill., Bank Administration Institue [1972]

Bank Administration Institute. Smaller Bank Commission.
see Loynes, Anthony B. The community bank series on operations and automation ... Park Ridge, Ill., Bank Administration Institute, c1975-1976.

Bank Administration Institute. Technical Division.
Bank administration manual. [Golden anniversary ed.] Park Ridge, Ill. [1974]
2 v. 26 cm.
1. Banks and banking. 2. Banks and banking–Accounting. I. Title.
NmLcU NUC76-22101

Bank Administration Institute. Technical Division
see Bank Administration Institute. Bank Security Commission. Your bank and armed robbery. [Rev. ed ed.] Park Ridge, Ill., [1973]

Bank Administration Institute. Trust Commission.
Trust operations manual : prepared for the Bank trust series / by BAI's Trust Commission. — Park Ridge, Ill. : Bank Administration Institute, c1975.
xiii, 96 p. ; 28 cm. — (Bank trust series)
Includes bibliographical references.
$10.00
1. Trust companies. I. Title.
HG4315.B352 1975 658'.91'33226 75-32830
76 MARC

al-Bank al-Ahlī al-Miṣrī.
Annual report—National Bank of Egypt.
[Cairo, General Egyptian Book Organization]
v. ill. 24 cm.
1. al-Bank al-Ahlī al-Miṣrī.
HG3386.B332a 332.1'1'0962 76-648758
MARC-S

al-Bank al-'Arabī. al-Idārah al-'Āmmah.
(Khams wa-'ishrūn sanah fī khidmat al-iqtiṣād al-'Arabī, 1930-1955)
٢٥ سنة في خدمة الاقتصاد العربي ، ١٩٣٠ – ١٩٥٥ . —
عمان : البنك العربي ، الادارة العامة ، [1955?]
150 p. : ill. ; 27 cm.
1. al-Bank al-'Arabī. 2. Arab countries—Economic conditions. I. Title.
HC412.B323 1955 74-235943

al-Bank al-'Arabī. al-Idārah al-'Āmmah.
25 years of service to Arab economy, 1930–1955. Amman, 1956.
150 p. illus. 27 cm.
At head of title: Arab Bank ltd.
Translation of Khams wa-'ishrūn sanah fī khidmat al-iqtiṣād al-'Arabī, 1930–1955.
1. Arab countries—Economic conditions. I. Title.
HC412.B323 1956 N E 63-1075

al-Bank al-Dawlī lil-Inshā' wa-al-Ta'mīr
see
International Bank for Reconstruction and Development.

Bank al-Inmā' al-Ṣinā'ī.
Annual report and balance sheet — Industrial Development Bank.
Amman, Industrial Development Bank, Hashemite Kingdom of Jordan.
v. ill. 25–28 cm.
Added title page title : al-Taqrīr al-sanawī li-Majlis al-Idārah wa-al-mīzānīyah al-'umūmīyah wa-ḥisāb al-arbāḥ wa-al-khasā'ir.
Arabic or English.
1. Bank al-Inmā' al-Ṣinā'ī. I. Bank al-Inmā' al-Ṣinā'ī. al-Taqrīr al-sanawī li-Majlis al-Idārah wa-al-mīzānīyah al-'umūmīyah wa-ḥisāb al-arbāḥ wa-al-khasā'ir.
HG3361.J64B3a 332.1 76-646133
MARC-S

Bank al-Inmā' al-Ṣinā'ī. al-Taqrīr al-sanawī li-Majlis al-Idārah wa-al-mīzānīyah al-'umūmīyah wa-ḥisāb al-arbāḥ wa-al-khasā'ir see Bank al-Inmā' al-Ṣinā'ī. Annual report and balance sheet... Amman.

Bank al-Iskandarīyah. Idārat al-Buḥūth al-Iqtiṣādīyah.
(al-Nashrah al-iqtiṣādīyah—Bank al-Iskandarīyah)
النشرة الاقتصادية — بنك الاسكندرية .
[الاسكندرية] بنك الاسكندرية ،
v. 24 cm.
1. Commerce — Collected works. 2. Economics — Collected works. 3. Egypt—Commerce—Collected works.
HF46.B28a 77-648128
(MARC-S)

Bank al-Kuwayt al-Markazī.
Annual report. 1st- 1970-
Kuwait, Central Bank of Kuwait.
v. 29 cm.
Report year ends Mar. 31.
1. Kuwait (State)—Economic conditions—Periodicals.
HG3361.K83B34 330.9'53'67 76-615742

Bank al-Kuwayt al-Markazī.
Economic report—Central Bank of Kuwait. 1975-
[Kuwait] Central Bank of Kuwait.
v. ill. 28 cm. annual.
1. Kuwait—Economic conditions—Periodicals.
HC497.K8B36a 330.9'53'6705 77-648922
MARC-S

Bank al-Kuwayt al-Ṣinā'ī.
Annual report—Industrial Bank of Kuwait. 1975-
[Kuwait] Industrial Bank of Kuwait.
v. ill. 28 cm.
1. Bank al-Kuwayt al-Ṣinā'ī.
HG3361.K8B34a 332.3'7'095367 76-644507
MARC-S

al-Bank al-Markazī al-'Irāqī, Bagdad. Mudīrīyat al-Taḥwīl al-Khārijī.
ايضاح للجمهور [بموجب قانون مراقبة التحويل الخارجي رقم ١٩ لسنة ١٩٦١ والتعليمات الصادرة بموجبه. بغداد] البنك المركزي العراقي ، مديرية التحويل الخارجي [1961?]
12 p. 16 cm.
Cover title.
1. Foreign exchange—Law—Iraq. I. Title.
Title romanized: Īḍāḥ lil-jumhūr.
75-972344

(al-Bank al-Markazī al-'Irāqī, 1947–1972)
البنك المركزي العراقي ١٩٤٧ – ١٩٧٢ ، ذكرى اليوبيل الفضي لتأسيس البنك المركزي العراقي [اعداد محمد حسن سلمان وآخرين. بغداد ، مطابع ثنيان ، 1972]
193 p. port. 25 cm.
1. al-Bank al-Markazī al-'Irāqī, Bagdad. I. Ḥasan, Muḥammad Salmān.
HG3361.I 73B35 74-222994

al-Bank al-Markazī al-Miṣrī.
(al-Taṭawwurāt al-i'timānīyah wa-al-maṣrifīyah)
التطورات الائتمانية والمصرفية .
القاهرة ، البنك المركزى المصرى ، ادارة الرقابة على البنوك .
v. 25 cm.
Began with 1958 vol.
Vols. for issued by its Idārat al-Raqābah 'alá al-Bunūk.
1. Banks and banking—Egypt—Statistics—Periodicals.
2. Credit—Egypt—Statistics—Periodicals. I. Title.
HG3386.A5B36a 77-648686
(MARC-S)

al-Bank al-Markazī al-Miṣrī. Majlis al-Idārah.
(Lā'iḥat al-'āmilīn bi-al-Bank al-Markazī al-Miṣrī)
لائحة العاملين بالبنك المركزى المصرى. اعتمدها مجلس الادارة بجلسته المنعقدة بتاريخ ١٣ مايو سنة ١٩٦٨ ويعمل بها اعتبارا من أول يونيو سنة ١٩٦٨ . [القاهرة ، 1969]
74, 14 l. 24 cm.
Includes bibliographical references.
1. al-Bank al-Markazī al-Miṣrī. 2. Bank employees—Cairo. I. Title.
73-218754

al-Bank al-Markazī-al-Tūnisī.
Statistiques financières. no. 1-
sept. 1972-
[Tunis] Banque centrale de Tunisie.
no. 29 cm. monthly.
Earlier information included in: al-Bank al-Markazī-al-Tūnisī. Bulletin.
Vols. for Sept. 1972- issued by the bank under its French form of name: Banque centrale de Tunisie.
1. Finance—Tunisia—Statistics—Periodicals. 2. al-Bank al-Markazī-al-Tūnisī. 3. Tunisia—Statistics—Periodicals. I. Title.
HG188.T77B35a 332'.0961'1 75-644773
MARC-S

al-Bank al-Markazī al-Urdunī.
Monthly statistical bulletin.
[Amman] Dept. of Research and Studies.
v. 29 cm.
Continues: al-Bank al-Markazī al-Urdunī. Dā'irat al-Abḥāth wa-al-Iḥṣā'āt. Quarterly bulletin.
Other title : al-Nashrah al-iḥṣā'īyah al-shahrīyah.
English or Arabic.
1. Jordan—Economic conditions—Periodicals. 2. Jordan—Statistics—Periodicals. I. al-Bank al-Markazī al-Urdunī. al-Nashrah al-iḥṣā'īyah al-shahrīyah. II. Title.
HC497.J6B3 330.9'5695'04 76-644992
MARC-S

al-Bank al-Markazī al-Urdunī. al-Nashrah al-iḥṣā'īyah al-shahrīyah
see al-Bank al-Markazī al-Urdunī. Monthly statistical bulletin. [Amman] Dept. of Research and Studies.

al-Bank al-Markazī al-Yamanī. Idārat al-Buḥuth wa-al-Marāji'.
Financial statistical bulletin. v. 1-
July/Sept. 1973-
[Sana'a?]
v. 33 cm.
Includes comparative data for previous years.
Vols. for July/Sept. 1973- issued by the agency under its English form of name: Central Bank of Yemen, Research Dept.
1. Finance—Yemen—Statistics. I. Title.
HG188.Y4B35a 332.1'1'095332 74-644667
MARC-S

al-Bank al-Markazī al-Yamanī. Idārat al-Buḥūth wa-al-Marāji'
see Foreign trade statistics. 1970-
Sana'a, Central Bank of Yemen.

Bank al-Nīlayn.
Annual report—El Nilein Bank.
-10th; -1974.
[Khartum] El Nilein Bank.
v. ill. 21 cm.
Continued by: Bank al-Nīlayn. al-Taqrīr al-sanawī—Bank al-Nīlayn.
1. Bank al-Nīlayn—Yearbooks.
HG3387.A8B362 332.1'1'09624 77-640922
MARC-S

Bank al-Nilayn. Annual report
see Bank al-Nilayn. (al-Taqrir al-sanawi --Bank al-Nilayn) 11th- 1975-

Bank al-Nīlayn.
(al-Taqrīr al-sanawī—Bank al-Nīlayn)
التقرير السنوى — بنك النيلين .
11th- 1975-
[الخرطوم] بنك النيلين .
v. ill. 22 cm.
Continues: Bank al-Nīlayn. Annual report—El Nilein Bank.
Other title, 1975- : Annual report—El Nilein Bank.
Arabic and English.
1. Bank al-Nīlayn — Yearbooks. I. Bank al-Nīlayn. Annual report.
HG3387.A8B362 332.1'1'09624 77-640923
(MARC-S)

al-Bank al-Ṣinā'ī.
The development of industrial credit in Egypt : statute and complementary laws. — Cairo : Industrial Bank, 1956.
63 p. ; 24 cm.
Translation of Taṭawwur al-taslīf al-ṣinā'i fī Miṣr.
1. al-Bank al-Sinā'ī. I. Title.
HG3388.S5B23 1956 77-453245
77 MARC

al-Bank al-Ṣinā'ī.
(Taṭawwur al-taslīf al-ṣinā'ī fī Miṣr)
تطور التسليف الصناعى فى مصر : النظام الأساسى للبنك الصناعى والقوانين المكملة له / البنك الصناعى. — [القاهرة] : البنك ، 1955.
49 p. ; 24 cm.
1. al-Bank al-Ṣinā'ī. I. Title.
HG3388.S5B23 1955 75-549717

al-Bank al-Ṣināʻī al-Sūdānī.
(Taqrīr ʻan ziyārat wafd al-Bank al-Ṣināʻī al-Sūdānī lil-mudīrīyāt al-janūbīyah, 12–22 Dīsambar, 1970)
تقرير عن زيارة وفد البنك الصناعى السودانى المديريات الجنوبية، ١٢ – ٢٢ ديسمبر، ١٩٧٠. — [الخرطوم] : البنك الصناعى السودانى، [1971]
65 leaves in various foliations ; 33 cm.
1. Sudan—Economic conditions. 2. al Mudīrīyah al Istiwā'īyah, Sudan—Economic conditions. 3. Baḥr al-Ghazāl, Sudan (Mudīrīyah)—Economic conditions. 4. Aʻālī an Nīl, Sudan—Economic conditions. 5. al-Bank al-Ṣināʻī al-Sūdānī. 6. al-Bank al-Zirāʻī al-Sūdānī. I. Title: Taqrīr ʻan ziyārat wafd al-Bank al-Ṣināʻī al-Sūdānī ...
HC591.S8B25 1971 — 74–982507

al-Bank al-Ṣināʻī al-Sūdānī.
(Taqrīr ʻan ziyārat wafd al-Bank al-Ṣināʻi lil-mudīrīyāt al-janūbīyah, Ughusṭus/Sibtambar, 1972)
تقرير عن زيارة وفد البنك الصناعى للمديريات الجنوبية، اغسطس/سبتمبر، ١٩٧٢. — [الخرطوم : البنك الصناعى السودانى، 1972]
45 leaves ; 33 cm.
«أعضاء الوفد: فاروق يوسف مصطفى، اقتصادى. بشير حسن بشير، مهندس»
1. Sudan — Industries. 2. al Mudīrīyah al Istiwā'īyah, Sudan — Industries. 3. Baḥr al Ghazāl, Sudan (Mudīrīyah)—Industries. 4. Aʻālī an Nīl, Sudan—Industries. 5. al-Bank al-Ṣināʻī al-Sūdānī. I. Title: Taqrīr ʻan ziyārat wafd al-Bank al-Ṣināʻī al-Sūdānī lil-mudīrīyāt al-janūbīyah ...
HC591.S8B25 1972 — 74–982508

al-Bank al-Ṣināʻī al-Sūdānī. Majlis al-Idārah.
تقرير مجلس الادارة.
الخرطوم، البنك الصناعى السودانى.
v. 24 cm.
1. al-Bank al-Sināʻī al-Sūdānī.
Title romanized: Taqrīr Majlis al-Idārah.
HG3431.S84S53a — 70–968031

Bank al-Sudan.
The nationalisation of banks in the Sudan. Khartoum, Publication and Information Committee of the Bank of Sudan [1970 ?]
23 p. 23 cm.
1. Banks and banking–Sudan. 2. Banks and banking–Government ownership–Sudan. I. Title.
NNC — NUC74-115124

Bank al-Sūdān.
التقرير السنوى.
الخرطوم.
v. 24 cm.
1. Sudan—Economic conditions. 2. Bank al-Sūdān.
Title romanized: al-Taqrīr al-sanawī.
HC591.S8B27a — 77–981624

Bank al-Sūdān
see Green, Reginald Herbold. States in economic development... [Khartoum, 1965?]

Bank al-Sūdān. Idārat al-Buḥūth al-Iqtiṣādīyah.
Foreign trade statistical digest. v. [1]– 1968–
Khartoum, Research Dept., Bank of Sudan.
v. 24 cm. annual.
Title varies slightly.
1. Sudan—Commerce—Periodicals. I. Title.
HF273.S8B35a — 382'.09624 — 75–644736 MARC–S

Bank al-Sūdān. Idārat al-Buḥūth al-Iqtiṣādīyah.
الموجز الاحصائي للتجارة الخارجية.
الخرطوم، مصلحة البحوث الاقتصادية، بنك السودان.
v. 24 cm.
1. Sudan—Commerce—Statistics. I. Title.
Title romanized: al-Mujāz al-iḥṣā'ī lil-tijārah al-khārijīyah.
HF273.S8B35b — 76–981622

Bank al-Sūdān. Idārat al-Buḥūth al-Iqtiṣādīyah.
النشرة الاقتصادية والمالية.
الخرطوم، ادارة البحوث الاقتصادية، بنك السودان.
v. 24 cm. quarterly.
1. Sudan—Economic conditions. I. Title.
Title romanized: al-Nashrah al-iqtiṣādīyah wa-al-mālīyah.
HG3431.S83B35a — 70–981623

al-Bank al-Tijārī al-Sūdānī. Majlis al-Idārah.
(Taqrīr Majlis al-Idārah)
تقرير مجلس الادارة. 1970–
[الخرطوم] جمهورية السودان الديمقراطية، البنك التجارى السودانى.
v. 25 cm. annual.
1. al-Bank al-Tijārī al-Sudānī.
HG3387.A5B363 — 77–649233 (MARC–S)

al-Bank al-Waṭanī al-Lībī.
al-Bank al-Waṭanī al-Lībī was established in 1955. In 1963 the name was changed to Bank Lībiyā. In 1969 to Maṣrif Lībiyā, and in 1971, to Central Bank of Libya.
Works by this body are found under the name used at the time of publication.

al-Bank al-Waṭanī al-Lībī. Board of Directors.
Annual report. 1st–7th; 1956/57–1962/63. [Tripoli] Bank of Libya, Board of Directors.
7 v. 24–30 cm.
Report year ends Mar. 31.
Continued by: Bank Lībiyā. Board of Directors. Annual report.
1. al-Bank al-Waṭanī al-Lībī. 2. Libya—Economic conditions.
HG3417.L54C43a — 330.9'61'204 — 58–27641 MARC–S

al-Bank al-Waṭanī al-Lībī. Board of Directors
see also
Bank Lībiyā. Board of Directors.

al-Bank al-Waṭanī lil-Inmā' al-Iqtiṣādī.
L'économie marocaine en 1971 [i.e. mil neuf cent soixante et onze] / Banque nationale pour le développement économique. — [Rabat] : La Banque, [1971?]
99 p. : ill. ; 27 cm.
"Fascicule 2".
1. Morocco—Economic conditions. 2. Morocco—Statistics. I. Title.
HC591.M8B288 1971 — 330.9'64'05 76 — 76-464754 MARC

al-Bank al-Waṭanī lil-Inmā' al-Iqtiṣādī.
National Bank for Economic Development : [B.N.D.E.,- Banque Nationale pour le Développement Économique]. — 2d ed. — Rabat, Moroc. : B.N.D.E., 1974.
[42] p. : ill. (some col.), col. graphs ; 21 cm.
Cover title.
1. al-Bank al-Waṭanī lil-Inmā' al-Iqtiṣādī.
HG3431.M64W355 1974 — 332.1 76 — 76-367999 MARC

al-Bank al-Waṭanī lil-Inmā' al-Iqtiṣādī.
Rapport annuel—Banque nationale pour le développement économique.
[Rabat]
v. in ill. 29 cm.
Reports for issued in 3 fascicules.
1. al-Bank al-Waṭanī lil-Inmā'al. Iqtiṣādī. 2. Morocco—Economic conditions—Periodicals.
HG3431.M64W355a — 330.9'64'05 — 74–648578 MARC–S

al-Bank al-Zirā'ī al-'Arabī al-Sa'ūdī. Annual report
see al-Bank al-Zirā'i al-'Arabī al-Sa'ūdī. al-Taqrīr al-sanawī. 1384/85- [1964/65-

al-Bank al-Zirāʻī al-ʻArabī al-Saʻūdī.
التقرير السنوى. 1.– ؛ 1384/85.– [1964/65–
[جده ؟] البنك الزراعى العربى السعودى.
v. 25 cm.
In Arabic, 1964/65; Arabic and English, 1965/66–
Added t. p., 1965/66– : Annual report.
1. Mortgage banks—Saudi Arabia. I. al-Bank al-Zirāʻī al-ʻArabī al-Saʻūdī. Annual report.
Title romanized: al-Taqrīr al-sanawī.
HG2051.S25B38a — 74–204787

al-Bank al-Zirāʻī al-Sūdānī. Majlis al-Idārah.
(Taqrīr Majlis al-Idārah wa-al-mīzānīyah al-ʻumūmīyah)
تقرير مجلس الادارة والميزانية العمومية.
الخرطوم، البنك الزراعى السودانى، قسم التخطيط والتنميه.
v. 24 cm. annual.
Report year ends June 30.
Title varies slightly.
1. al-Bank al-Zirāʻī al-Sūdānī. Majlis al-Idārah. I. Title.
HG2051.S79B3a — 71–981653 (MARC–S)

al-Bank al-Zirāʻī al-Sūdānī. Qism al-Takhṭīṭ.
(al-Bank al-Zirāʻī al-Sūdānī)
البنك الزراعى السودانى : ماضيه وحاضره ومستقبله / قسم التخطيط والتنمية، البنك الزراعى السودانى. — [الخرطوم : المطبعة الحكومية، ؟1972]
49 p. : ill. ; 24 cm.
1. al-Bank al-Zirāʻī al-Sūdānī. I. Title.
HG3431.S84Z573 1972 — 74–982506

Bank Būr Saʻīd.
Vade-mecum. [Le Caire] Banque de Port-Said, 1965.
109 p. illus. 14 cm.
Cover title.
1. Bank Būr Saʻīd. I. Title.
HG3390.C34B318 — 73–165364 MARC

Bank by telephone... Park Ridge, Ill., c1973
see under Long, Robert H

Bank counsel 1976 / Harold E. Mortimer, chairman. — New York : Practising Law Institute, c1976.
312 p. : forms ; 22 cm. — (Corporate law and practice course handbook series ; no. 220)
"B4-4586."
"Prepared for distribution at the bank counsel workshop, July-August 1976."
Includes bibliographical references.
1. Banking law—United States. 2. Securities—United States. I. Mortimer, Harold E. II. New York (City). Practising Law Institute. III. Series.
KF975.B28 1976 — 346'.73'082 76 — 76-26816 MARC

Bank counsel 1977 / Harold E. Mortimer, chairman. — New York : Practising Law Institute, c1977.
680 p. ; 22 cm. — (Corporate law and practice course handbook series ; no. 240)
"B4-5535."
"Prepared for distribution at the bank counsel workshop, July-August 1977."
Includes bibliographical references.
1. Banking law—United States. I. Mortimer, Harold E. II. New York (City). Practising Law Institute. III. Series.
KF975.B28 1977 — 346'.73'082 77 — 77-82690 MARC

Bank counsel workshop 1974 / Harold E. Mortimer, chairman. — New York : Practising Law Institute, [1974]
216 p. (p. 214–216 blank) ; 22 cm. — (Corporate law and practice course handbook series ; no. 153)
"B4-3577."
"Prepared for distribution at the bank counsel workshop, July-September, 1974."
1. Banking law — United States. 2. Securities — United States. I. Mortimer, Harold E. II. New York (City). Practising Law Institute. III. Series.
KF975.B33 — 74–189826 MARC

Bank counsel workshop, 1975 / Harold E. Mortimer, chairman. — New York : Practising Law Institute, c1975.
320 p. ; 22 cm. — (Corporate law and practice course handbook series ; no. 187)
"B4-4546."
"Prepared for distribution at the bank counsel workshop, August-September 1975."
Bibliography: p. 19-22.
1. Banking law—United States. 2. Securities—United States. I. Mortimer, Harold E. II. New York (City). Practising Law Institute. III. Series.
KF975.B33 1975 — 346'.73'082 75 — 75-326560 MARC

The Bank dick
see Fields, W. C., 1879-1946. W. C. Fields in The Bank dick. London, Lorrimer Pub. [1973]

The Bank dick. [Motion picture]
see W. C. Fields in The Bank Dick. New York, Simon and Schuster [1973]

The Bank director, edited by Richard B. Johnson. Dallas, SMU Press [1974]
x, 205 p. 24 cm.
Papers presented at an assembly for bank directors or at a session of the Southwestern Graduate School of Banking.
Includes bibliographical references.
ISBN 0-87074-145-4
1. Bank management—Addresses, essays, lectures. 2. Business ethics—Addresses, essays, lectures. 3. Banks and banking—Addresses, essays, lectures. I. Johnson, Richard Buhmann, 1913– ed. II. Southwestern Graduate School of Banking.
HG1615.B33 — 658'.91'3321 — 74–14738 MARC

Bank directors and their selection, qualifications, evaluation, retirement. St. Louis, Mo., The Bank Board Letter [c1970]
22 p.
Cover title.
1. Bank directors. 2. Directors of corporations.
ScU NUC75-24026

Bank Ekspor Impor Indonesia.
In 1960 Bank Rakjat Indonesia and Bank Tani Nelajan merged to form Bank Koperasi, Tani dan Nelajan. In 1965 the name of the latter was changed to Bank Negara Indonesia Unit II, which in 1968 split into Bank Rakjat Indonesia and Bank Ekspor Impor Indonesia.
Works by Bank Rakjat Indonesia, including those by the related body, Algemeene Volkscredietbank, are found under the latest name:
Bank Rakjat Indonesia.
Works by the other bodies are found under the following headings according to the name used at the time of publication:

Bank Tani Nelajan, p. t.
Bank Koperasi, Tani dan Nelajan.
Bank Negara Indonesia Unit II.
Bank Ekspor Impor Indonesia.

Bank Ekspor Impor Indonesia.
Annual report—Bank Ekspor Impor Indonesia.
Jakarta.
v. illus. 26 cm.
Added t. p. Laporan tahunan.
English and Indonesian.
1. Bank Ekspor Impor Indonesia. I. Bank Ekspor Impor Indonesia. Laporan tahunan.
AG3310.J34E3522a 330.9'598'03 73-942228
MARC-S

Bank Ekspor Impor Indonesia.
The Indonesian economy in the wake of Repelita II (second five year development plan) [Jakarta, 1973]
46 p. illus. 26 cm.
1. Indonesia—Economic conditions—1945- I. Title.
HC447.B26 1973 330.9'598'03 73-942622
76 MARC

Bank Ekspor Impor Indonesia.
Indonesian fisheries / Bank Ekspor Impor Indonesia. — [Jakarta] : Directorate General for Fisheries, Dept. of Agriculture, 1974.
32 p. : ill. (some col.) ; 27 cm.
1. Fisheries—Indonesia. 2. Aquaculture—Indonesia. I. Title.
SH307.I64B37 1974 639'.2'09598 74-941646
76 MARC

Bank Ekspor Impor Indonesia. Laporan tahunan
see Bank Ekspor Impor Indonesia. Annual report— Bank Ekspor Impor Indonesia. Jakarta.

Bank Ekspor Impor Indonesia.
A look at economic conditions and opportunities / Bank Ekspor Impor Indonesia. — [Jakarta] : Bank, [between 1971 and 1975]
2 v. : ill. ; 28 cm. — (Window on Indonesia ; 1-2)
1. Indonesia—Economic conditions—1945- 2. Indonesia—Economic policy. 3. Investments, Foreign—Indonesia. I. Title. II. Series.
HC447.B26 1971 330.9'598'03 75-940181
76 MARC

Bank Ekspor Impor Indonesia.
Prospek pengusahaan udang di Indonesia = Prospects of shrimp fishery in Indonesia / Bank Ekspor Impor Indonesia. — [Jakarta] : Bank, [Between 1972 and 1975]
35 p. : ill. ; 26 cm.
English and Indonesian.
1. Shrimp fisheries—Indonesia. I. Title. II. Title: Prospects of shrimp fishery in Indonesia.
SH380.62.I5B36 1972 75-940234
75 MARC

Bank Ekspor Impor Indonesia.
Suatu penelitian mengenai berbagai aspek bidang perkayuan = A brief study on the timber industry / Bank Ekspor Impor Indonesia. — [Jakarta] : Bank, [1975]
46 p. : ill. ; 29 cm. — (Window on Indonesia ; 4)
Cover title.
English and Indonesian.
1. Lumber trade—Indonesia. 2. Timber—Indonesia. I. Title. II. Title: A brief study on the timber industry. III. Series.
HD9766.I72B3 1975 338.1'7'49809598 75-940314
75 MARC

Bank Ekspor Impor Indonesia.
Suatu tinjauan mengenai masalah kapas = A review on the cotton problem / Bank Ekspor Impor Indonesia. — [Jakarta] : Bank, [1975]
28 p. : ill. ; 29 cm. — (Window on Indonesia ; 6)
Cover title.
English and Indonesian.
1. Cotton trade—Indonesia. 2. Cotton—Indonesia. I. Title. II. Title: A review on the cotton problem. III. Series.
HD9086.I62B36 1975 338.1'7'35109598 76-940621
77 MARC

Bank Ekspor Impor Indonesia.
Timber in Indonesia. Singapore, Produced by Grant Public Relations [1971?]
20 p. col. illus. 28 cm.
1. Timber–Indonesia. I. Title.
NIC NUC73-70557

Bank Ekspor Impor Indonesia.
Warta eksim.
[Jakarta]
v. illus. 26 cm.
1. Indonesia—Commerce.
HF3806.5.B34a 74-645081
MARC-S

Bank Ekspor Impor Indonesia.
Window on Indonesia; a look at economic conditions and opportunities. [Singapore, Produced by Grant Public Relations, 1971?]
2 v. ([47] p. each in portfolio) illus. (part col.), map. 29 cm.
1. Indonesia–Econ. condit.–1945–
I. Title.
NIC NUC73-70558

Bank financing of the Southern agricultural revolution. [Atlanta] Research Dept., 1969
see under Federal Reserve Bank of Atlanta.

Bank for Agriculture and Agricultural Co-operatives
see
Thanākhān phū'a Kānkasēt læ Sahakōn Kānkasēt, Bangkok, Thailand.

Bank for International Settlements.
A collection of central bankers' speeches (1972-73) Basle, 1974.
iii, 156 l.
Cover title.
1. Banks and banking. 2. Finance. 3. International finance. I. Title.
MH-BA NUC76-22133

Bank for International Settlements. Monetary and Economic Dept.
United Kingdom monetary and economic situation, 1960–1969. Basle, 1970.
[40] p. illus. 30 cm. Sw***
Cover title.
1. Great Britain—Economic conditions—1945- 2. Finance—Great Britain—Statistics. I. Title.
HC256.5.B3 1970 330.9'42'085 74-155005
MARC

Bank für Gemeinwirtschaft.
see Aktiva ... Frankfurt/Main, Europäische Verlagsanstalt, [1975]

Bank für Gemeinwirtschaft
see Dali, Salvador, 1904- Salvador Dali: Alijah. (Frankfurt/M., Bank f. Gemeinwirtschaft, 1969.)

Bank für Gemeinwirtschaft.
see Loesch, Achim von. Die Bank für Gemeinwirtschaft ... Frankfurt am Main, Europäische Verlagsanstalt, 1975.

Bank für Handel und Industrie, Berlin
see Berlin (West Berlin). Laws, statutes, etc. Berlinförderungsgesetz 1970. [Hannover] Prisma-Verlag [1970].

Bank für Tirol und Vorarlberg Aktiengesellschaft
see Neue Graphik aus Tirol. (Innsbruck, Bank f. Tirol u. Vorarlberg, 1971.)

Bank Gapoalim b. m., Tel-Aviv
see
Workers' Bank, ltd., Tel-Aviv.

Bank ha-sapanut le-Yisrael.
דין וחשבון.
[תל-אביב]
v. in 25 cm. annual.
Added title, Report.
Hebrew and English.
I. Bank ha-sapanut le-Yisrael. Report.
Title romanized: Din ve-ḥeshbon.
HG3361.P24B33 HE 68-4373
PL 480: Is-S-851

Bank ha-sapanut le-Yisrael. Report. Bank ha-sapanut le-Yisrael.

The Bank holding company act amendments of 1970: a legislative history compiled by Carter H. Golembe Associates, inc. Washington, D.C., Financial Publications of Washington [c1971]
v, 853 p. 29 cm.
Bibliography: p. 849-853.
1. U.S. Laws, statutes, etc. 2. The bank holding company act. I. Carter H. Golembe Associates.
KyU NUC73-107197

Bank holding company marketing in transition. Chicago, 1973
see under Holding Company Marketing Workshop, 1st, Denver, 1972.

[Bank holiday] [Sound recording] American Forces Radio and Television Service RU 39-6, 5B [1976]
on side 2 of 1 disc. 33⅓ rpm. mono. 12 in. (Mystery theater, 306)
With: Ira Cook 4071 F.
Radio drama.
Recorded from a broadcast of the CBS program Suspense, July 19, 1945, starring Bonita Granville.
Duration: 25 min.
Recordings made for the use of the American Armed Forces only.
I. Granville, Bonita, 1923- II. Suspense (Radio program) III. Series: Mystery theater. [Sound recording] 306.
[PN1991.77] 76-742229

Bānk-i Īrān va Khāvar-i Miyānah. Annual report—Bānk-i Īrān va Khāvar-i Miyānah
see Iran economic review. Tehran.

Bānk-i Īrān va Khāvar-i Miyānah
see Iran economic review. Tehran.

Bānk-i I'tibārat-i Kishāvarzī va Umrān-i Rūstā'ī-i Īrān.
Activity of the Agricultural Credits and Rural Development Bank.
[Tehran] Agricultural Credits & Rural Development Bank.
v. ill. 24 cm.
1. Bānk-i I'tibārat-i Kishāvarzī va Umrān-i Rūstā'ī-i Īrān. 2. Agricultural credit.—Iran. I. Title.
HG3338.I 2b 332.7'1'0955 75-642067
MARC-S

Bānk-i I'-tibārāt-i Kishāvarzī va 'Umrān-i Rūstā'ī-i Īrān.
Annual report — Agricultural Credits & Rural Development Bank of Iran.
[Tehran] Agricultural Credits & Rural Development Bank of Iran.
v. ill. 24 cm.
Report year ends Mar. 20.
Arabic and English.
1. Bānk-i I'-tibārāt-i Kishāvarzī va 'Umrān-i Rūstā'ī-i Īrān.
2. Agricultural credit—Iran.
HG3338.I 2a 332 75-642348
MARC-S

Bānk-i I'tibārāt-i Kishāvarzī va 'Umran-i Rūstā'i-i Īrān.

For works by this body issued under its earlier name see

Bank-i Kishāvarzī-i Īrān.

Bank-i Kishāvarzi-ī Īrān.
The Agricultural Bank of Iran [report].
Tehran [Agricultural Bank of Iran]
v. 24 cm.
1. Bank-i Kishāvarzi-ī Īrān. 2. Agricultural Credit—Iran.
I. Title.
HG3338.K58a 332.3'1'0955 75-642347
MARC-S

Bank-i Kishāvarzī-i Īrān.
Annual report—Agricultural Bank of Iran.
[Teheran]
v. ill. 23 cm.
Report year ends Mar. 20.
1. Bank-i Kishāvarzi-i Īran.
HG3338.B284a 332.6 74-647556
MARC-S

Bank-i Kishāvarzī-i Īrān.

For works by this body issued under its later name see

Bānk-i I'tibārāt-i Kishāvarzī va 'Umrān-i Rūstā'i-i Īrān.

Bānk-i Markazī-i Īrān.
Annual report and balance sheet.
[Tehran]
v. illus. 27 cm.
Report year ends Mar. 20.
Vols. for issued under the English form of name: Bank Markazi Iran.
1. Bānk-i Markazī-i Īrān. 2. Iran—Economic conditions.
3. Iran—Economic policy.
HG3338.B29a 330.9'55'05 74-642881
MARC-S

Bānk-i Markazī-i Īrān.
Facts and figures about Iran. [Tehran, Printed by Offset Press, 1968?]
69 p. illus., map, ports. 16 cm.
1. Iran—Economic conditions—1945- I. Title.
HC475.B29 1968 330.9'55'05 78-286307
71[r75]rev MARC

Bānk-i Markazī-i Īrān.
Guzārish-i Hay'at-i 'Āmil-i Bānk-i Markazī-i Īrān bih panjumīn Majma -i 'Umūmī-i Sāliyānah-i Bānk. [Tihrān, 1970?]
213 l. tables (part fold.) 29 cm.
1. Iran. Economic conditions—1945-
NNC NUC75-76193

Bānk-i Markazī-Iran. Bureau of National Accounts.
National income of Iran, 1338-50 (1959-72). Bank Markazi Iran, Bureau of National Accounts. [Teheran] The Bureau, 1353 (1975)
[vi], 107 p. tables. 27 cm.
Earlier editions by the Economic Research Dept.
1. National income—Iran. I. Bānk-i Markazī Iran. Idarah-i Bar'rasīhā-yi Iqtisādī. II. Title.
CtY-E NUC76-76214

Bānk-i Markazī-i Īrān. Centre for the Attraction and Protection of Foreign Investments
see Iran. Laws, statutes, etc. Civil code of Iran... [Tehran? 19--]

Bānk-i Markazī-i Īrān. Idārah-i Āmār-i Iqtiṣādī.
Consumer price index in urban areas of Iran, annual report.
[Tehran]
v. illus. 34 cm.
Report year ends Mar. 20.
Vols. for issued under the English form of name: Bank Markazi Iran, Economic Statistics Dept.
1. Prices—Iran—Periodicals. I. Title.
HB235.I 7B32a 339.4'2'0955 74-642937
MARC-S

Bānk-i Markazī-i Īrān. Idārah-i Āmār-i Iqtiṣādī.
Survey of construction activities of the private sector in urban areas of Iran.
[Tehran]
v. illus. 34 cm. annual.
Report year ends Mar. 20.
Vols. for issued under the English form of name: Bank Markazi Iran, Economic Statistics Dept.
1. Construction industry—Iran—Statistics. 2. Construction industry—Finance—Statistics. I. Title.
HD9715.I 68B36a 338.4'7'6900955 74-642964
MARC-S

Bānk-i Markazī-i Īrān. Idārah-i Bar'rasīhā-yi Iqtiṣādī.
[Darāmad-i millī-i Īrān]
درآمد ملی ایران.
[تهران] اداره بررسیهای اقتصادی.
v. 27 cm.
1. National income—Iran—Periodicals. I. Title.
HC471.B318 72-225658

Bānk-i Markazī-i Īrān. Idārah-i Bar'rasīhā-yi Iqtiṣādī.
The revised cost of living index. Tehran, Bank Markazi Iran, Economic Research Dept. 1340 [1962]
ii, 149 l. 34 cm.
Cover title.
1. Prices—Iran. 2. Cost and standard of living—Iran. I. Title.
HB235.I 7B33 72-196271
MARC

Bank-i Markazī-i Irān. Idarah-i Bar'rasīhā-yi Iqtisādī
see Bānk-i Markazī-Iran. Bureau of National Accounts. National income of Iran, 1338-50 (1959-72). [Teheran] 1353 (1975)

Bānk-i Millī-i Īrān.
Balance-sheet.
[Tehran?]
v. 24 cm. annual.
1. Bānk-i Millī-i Īrān.
HG3340.T44M4219 54-36107 ‡
rev

Bānk-i Millī-i Īrān.
Bilan.
[Téhéran]
no. in v. diagrs. 26 cm. annual.
1. Bānk-i Millī-i Īrān.
HG3340.T44M422 332.11 51-18019
rev 2

Bānk-ī Millī-ī Īran.
Economic services of Bank Melli Iran, 1928-1971. [Teheran?, 1971]
28 p. illus. (part col.)
Cover title.
"In commemoration of the 2500th anniversary of the founding of the Iranian monarchy."
MH NUC73-41282

Bānk-i Millī-i Īrān.
Report.
[Teheran?]
v. 22 cm. annual.
Report year ends Mar. 21.
1. Bānk-i Millī-i Īrān.
HG3340.T44M4218 51-19910
rev

Bānk-i Rahnī-i Īrān.
Balance sheet and profit and loss account.
[Tehran] Bank Rahni Iran.
v. 24 cm. annual.
Report year ends Mar. 20.
1. Bānk-i Rahnī-i Īrān.
HG2040.5.I 7B36a 332.3'2'0955 76-640386
MARC-S

Bānk-i Rahnī-i Īran. Guzārish-i fa''ālīyathā-yi Bānk-i Rahnī-i Īran
see Bānk-i Rahnī-i Īrān. Idārah-'i Āmār va Bar'rasīhā. (Guzārish-i fa''ālīyathā-yi Bānk-i Rahnī-i Īran)

Bānk-i Rahnī-i Īrān.
نشریهٔ داخلی بانك رهنی ایران.
[تهران]
v. 24 cm.
Title romanized: Nashrīyah-'i dākhilī.
AP95.P3B36 77-970210

Bānk-i Rahnī-i Īrān.
Summary of the annual directors' report and balance sheet.
[Tehran] Bank Rahni Iran.
v. 24 cm.
Report year ends Mar. 20.
1. Bānk-i Rahnī-i Īrān.
HG2040.5.I 7B36b 332.3'2'0955 76-640387
MARC-S

Bānk-i Rahnī-i Īrān. Idārah-'i Āmār va Bar'rasīhā.
(Guzārish-i fa''ālīyathā-yi Bānk-i Rahnī-i Īrān)
گزارش فعالیتهای بانك رهنی ایران.
[تهران، بانك رهنی ایران، ادارهٔ آمار و بررسیها]
v. 27 cm.
Monthly,
bimonthly,
Title varies slightly.
Issue for Jan./Feb. 1970 issued by Bānk-i Rahnī-i Īrān.
1. Bānk-i Rahnī-i Īrān. I. Bānk-i Rahnī-i Īrān. Guzārish-i fa''ālīyathā-yi Bānk-i Rahnī-i Īrān.
HG2040.5.I 7A22 75-972621

Bānk-i Tawsi'ah-'i Ṣan'atī va Ma'danī-i Īrān. Board of Directors.
Annual report of the Board of Directors to the General Assembly of shareholders.
Tehran.
v. ill. 28 cm.
Report year ends Mar. 20.
1. Bānk-i Tawsi'ah-'i Ṣan'atī va Ma'danī-i Īrān.
HG3338.B327a 332.6 74-647768
MARC-S

Bānk-i 'Umrān.
نشریه نخستین عملیات ۱۸ ماهه بانك عمران. تهران
[pref. 1333 (1954)]
165 p. illus., ports. 27 cm.
1. Bānk-i Umrān. I. Title. II. Title: 'Amalīyāt-i hijdah māhah.
Title romanized: Nashrīyah-i nukhustīn-i 'amalīyāt-i hijdah māhah.
HG3338.B33 1954 74-225999

Bank Indonesia.
The name of Javasche Bank (established in 1827) was changed in 1953 to Bank Indonesia. In 1965 it became Bank Negara Indonesia Unit I and in 1968 the name was changed back to Bank Indonesia.
Works by this body are found under the name used at the time of publication.
73-218663

Bank Indonesia.
Data kredit perbankan. no. 1-
[Jakarta, 1972-
no. 33 cm. monthly.
1. Credit—Indonesia—Statistics. 2 Bank loans—Indonesia—Statistics. I. Title.
HG3304.B34a 73-940347
MARC-S

Bank Indonesia.
Himpunan ketentuan-ketentuan prosedur lalu lintas devisa (HKPLLD). Djakarta, Bank Indonesia, Urusan Luar Negeri [1971-
1 v. (loose-leaf) 23 cm.
1. Foreign exchange—Law—Indonesia. I. Title.
72-940771

Bank Indonesia.
Laporan tahun pembukuan,
[Djakarta] G. Kolff.
v. 27 cm.
Report year ends Mar. 31.
1. Indonesia—Economic conditions—1945- 2. Finance—Indonesia.
HG3306.A29 S A 68-19176
PL 480: Indo-S-904

Bank Indonesia.
Report of Bank Indonesia.
[Djakarta, Bank Indonesia]
v. 27 cm.
Report for 1969/70 covers period Jan. 1969-Mar. 1970.
1. Indonesia—Economic conditions—1945- 2. Finance—Indonesia.
HC446.B313a 330.9'598'03 76-641838
MARC-S

Bank Indonesia.
Saran-saran Bank Indonesia Surabaja tentang Bank Pembangunan Daerah Propinsi Djawa Timur. [Surabaja] Sekretariat D.P.R.D.—G.R. Propinsi Djawa Timur, 1969.
16 l. 32 cm.
1. Banks and banking—Indonesia—East Java (Province) 2. Malay literature—Economics.
NN NUC74-57807

Bank Indonesia.
Sistim perbankan Indonesia. [Djakarta, 1970]
28 p. 28 cm.
Cover title.
1. Banks and banking—Indonesia. I. Title.
HG3305.B35 1970 72-941256

Bank Indonesia. Urusan Ekonomi dan Statistik.
Statistik ekonomi-keuangan Indonesia. Indonesian financial statistics.
[Jakarta]
v. 21 x 30 cm. monthly.
English and Indonesian.
1. Finance—Indonesia—Statistics. I. Title. II. Title: Indonesian financial statistics.
HG188.I 7B34a 332'.09598 74-644229
MARC-S

Bank Indonesia. Urusan Pengawasan dan Pembinaan Bank-Bank.
Pedoman pelaksanaan peraturan-peraturan perbankan. [Djakarta] 1971-72.
3 v. 28 cm.
1. Banks and banking—Indonesia. I. Title.
HG3304.B35 72-941914

Bank Indonesia Surabaja.
Saran-saran Bank Indonesia Surabaja tentang Bank Pembangunan Daerah Propinsi Djawa Timur. [Surabaja] Diperbanjak oleh Sekretariat D. P. R. D.-G. R. Propinsi Djawa Timur, 1969.
16 l. 32 cm.
Cover title.
1. Bank Pembangunan Daerah Djawa Timur. I. Title.
HG3309.D57B36 1969 72-941351

Bank insurance news
see
Bankinsurance news.

(Bank' khratowts' nakhni imastasirats')
Բանք խրատուց նախնի իմաստասիրաց։ Ի Վէնէտիկ։ Ի Գործարանի Մխիթարեանց, 1853։
70 p. 12 cm. (Սոփերք հայկականք, 1)
«Հաւաքեալ ամփոփեցաք ի հինգ և աւելի գրչագիր մատենից։»
Bound with Պատմութիւն վասն Սրբոյն Սահակայ Հայրապետին և Մեսրովբայ Վարդապետին։ Վէնէտիկ, 1853; Hovhannēs Sarkawag, Vardapet. Յաղագս քահանայութեան և քահանայից և գլխոց նոցին։ Վէնէտիկ, 1853; and Գրիգոր Լուսաւորիչ։ Վէնէտիկ, 1853։
CONTENTS: Իմաստութիւն։—Ուսումն։—Բարեկամութիւն և բարեկամք։—Իշխանութիւն և իշխանք։—Արիութիւն։—Յաղագս ընչից։—Արծաթսիրութիւն։—Յաղագս փառաց։—Յաղագս մահուան և փոփոխելոյ ի կենաց։—Վասն լաւագգութեան։—Յաղագս լռութեան։—Բաղդ և անբաղդութիւն։—Գինի և արբեցութիւն։—Շողմոգք և շողմոգութիւն։—Վասն պատուոյ Հարց։—Յաղագս դաստիարակութեան որդւոց։—Յաղագս օրինաց։—Յաղագս անառակութեան։—Յաղագս խրատուց։—Յաղագս բժշկաց։—Յաղագս երգման։—Յաղագս մեղաց խոստովանութեան։—Յաղագս նախախնամութեան։—Յաղագս կնոջ չարաբարոյի։—Խօսք Սեկունդոսի իմաստասիրի առ Անդրիանոս կայսեր։
1. Conduct of life—Early works to 1900. 2. Philosophy, Ancient. I. Series: Sop'erk' haykakank', 1.
BX126.2.S66 vol. 1 75-972317
[BJ1550]

Bank Koperasi Propinsi Sumatera Utara.
Laporan tahun pembukuan—Bank Koperasi Propinsi Sumatera Utara.
Medan [Bank Koperasi Propinsi Sumatera Utara]
v. 28 cm.
1. Bank Koperasi Propinsi Sumatera Utara. 2. Banks and banking, Cooperative—Indonesia—Sumatera Utara.
HG3309.S85B36a 75-647268
MARC-S

Bank Koperasi, Tani dan Nelajan.
In 1960 Bank Rakjat Indonesia and Bank Tani Nelajan merged to form Bank Koperasi, Tani dan Nelajan. In 1965 the name of the latter was changed to Bank Negara Indonesia Unit II, which in 1968 split into Bank Rakjat Indonesia and Bank Ekspor Impor Indonesia.
Works by Bank Rakjat Indonesia, including those by the related body, Algemeene Volkscredietbank, are found under the latest name:
Bank Rakjat Indonesia.
Works by the other bodies are found under the following headings according to the name used at the time of publication:
Bank Tani Nelajan, p. t.
Bank Koperasi, Tani dan Nelajan.
Bank Negara Indonesia Unit II.
Bank Ekspor Impor Indonesia.

Bank Koperasi, Tani dan Nelajan
see Gemah ripah. [Djakarta] Bank Negara Indonesia Unit II.

Bank le-fituaḥ ha-ta'asiyah be-Yisrael
see Industrial Development Bank of Israel Limited.

Bank lending : some controversial issues / edited by Sampat P. Singh. — Bombay : National Institute of Bank Management, c1975.
ix, 209 p. ; 25 cm.
Bibliography: p. [189]-206.
Includes index.
CONTENTS: Singh, S. P. Ideas on bank credit.—Talwar, R. K. Banker and corporate customer.—Singh, S. P. Contextual world underlying lending policies.—Hingorani, N. L. Major issues in lending policy.—Singh, S. P. Planning for loans and advances.—Varde, S. D. Management of money position of a bank.—Singh, S. P. Credit appraisal, review and follow up.—Mishra, H. K. N. Some statistical evidence on basis of lending.—Bhukhanwala, H. S., Singh, S. P. Price rise and need for bank credit.—Naik, M. D. Profitability of borrowing customers.—Varde, V. S., Singh, S. P. Behaviour of borrowal accounts.
Rs2.00
1. Credit—India—Addresses, essays, lectures. 2. Banks and banking—India—Addresses, essays, lectures. I. Singh, Sampat Pal, 1929-
HG2069.I4B36 332.1'753'0954 76-900174
76 MARC

Bank Leu und Co.
For works by this body issued under its earlier name see
Leu und Compagnie, A. G., *Zürich*.

Bank Leu und Co. Numismatische Abteilung.
Antike Münzen; Kelten, Griechen, Römer, Byzantiner. Zürich [1973]
57 p. plates.
"Auktion 7 am 9. Mai 1973 in Zürich."
1. Coins—Ancient. I. Title.
InU NUC74-116645

Bank Leu und Co. Numismatische Abteilung.
Griechische Bronzemünzen Unteritaliens und Siziliens aus Sammlung Tom Virzi New York. Zürich [1973]
31 p. plates.
"Auktion 6 am 8. Mai 1973 in Zürich."
1. Coins—Greek. I. Title.
InU NUC74-116657

Bank Leu und Co. Numismatische Abteilung.
Münzen - Medaillen; Gold, silber, bronze. Auktion, Mittwoch und Donnerstag, den 11. und 12. Oktober 1961 vormittags 9.15 Uhr im Hotel Schweizerhof, Luzern. Bank Leu & Co. AG., numismatische Abteilung. Adolph Hess AG. [die Versteigerungsleitung. Luzern, C. J. Bucher, 1961]
48 p. 44 plates. 30 cm.
"Goldmünzen und Goldmedaillen von Europa und Übersee darunter bedeutende Serien von Deutschland, England, Frankreich, Italien, Römisch-Deutsches Reich, Nord- und Süd-Amerika aus einer Schweizer Privatsammlung. Löser von Braunschweig und Taler aus amerikanischem Besitz. Spezialsammlung von Chile, Sammlung Dr. H., Santiago. Medaillen der Renaissance aus einer new yorker Privatsammlung."
List of approximate valuations tipped in.
Bibliography: p. 47-48.
1. Coins, Modern. 2. Coins, Medieval. 3. Medals, Renaissance. 4. Gold coins. I. Hess (Adolph) A.G., Luzerne. II. Title.
PSt NUC74-135891

Bank Leu und Co. Numismatische Abteilung.
Münzen: Mittelalter, Neuzeit. ... Zürich, 1971.
63 p. 48 plates.
"Auktion 1 in Zürich."
1. Coins. I. Title.
InU NUC73-113629

Bank Leu und Co. Numismatische Abteilung.
Österreich. Kaiser Ferdinand I, 1835-1848. Münzen und Medaillen geprägt während seiner Regierungszeit. Zürich, 1972.
[27] p. illus.
Auction catalog.
1. Coins—Austrian. I. Title.
InU NUC73-113630

Bank Leu und Co. Numismatische Abteilung
see Griechische Münzen... Zürich: Bank Leu AG, [1974]

Bank Leu und Compagnie, A. G.
see Leu und Compagnie A. G., Zurich.

Bank Leumi Le-Israel, b. m.
Bank Leumi economic review.
[Tel Aviv] Bank Leumi Le-Israel B. M.
no. ill. 27 cm.
Continues: Economic review.
1. Israel—Economic conditions—Periodicals. I. Title.
HC497.P2R36 330.9'5694'05 76-649649
MARC-S

Bank Leumi Le-Israel, b.m.
Bank Leumi Le-Israel B.M., 1902-1968. [n.p., 196-?]
[27] p. illus.
Cover title.
1. Anglo-Palestine Bank, ltd.
MH NUC74-115141

Bank Leumi Le-Israel, b.m.
see Israel. ha-Hevrah ha-memshaltit le-tayarut. Touring map of Israel. [Tel Aviv, n. d.]

Bank Leumi Le-Israel, b. m.
see Ofek.

Bank Lībiyā.
al-Bank al-Waṭanī al-Lībī was established in 1955. In 1963 the name was changed to Bank Lībiyā. In 1969 to Maṣrif Lībiyā, and in 1971, to Central Bank of Libya.
Works by this body are found under the name used at the time of publication.

Bank Lībiyā. Board of Directors.
Annual report. 8th-13th; 1963/64-1968/69. [Tripoli] Bank of Libya. Board of Directors.
6 v. 25 cm.
Report year ends Mar. 31.
Continues: al-Bank al-Waṭanī al-Lībī. Board of Directors. Annual report.
Continued by: Maṣrif Lībiyā. Majlis al-Idārah. Annual report.
1. Bank Lībiyā. 2. Libya—Economic conditions.
HG3417.L54C43a 330.9'61'204 74-640772
MARC-S

Bank Libiya. Economic Research Dept.
see
Bank Lībiyā. Qism al-Buḥūth.

Bank Lībiyā. Idārat al-Buḥūth al-Iqtiṣādīyah.
Bank of Libya; a brief history of its first decade, 1956-1966. Prepared by Economic Research Division, Bank of Libya. [Tripoli, Printed at the Press of the Ministry of Information and Culture, 1967?]
149 p. illus. 27 cm.
1. Bank Lībiyā—History.
HG3417.L53B35 1967 332.1'1'09612 74-191672
MARC

Bank Lībiyā. Idārat al-Buḥūth al-Iqtiṣādīyah.
Economic bulletin. v. 6, no. 7/8-
July/Aug. 1966-
[Tripoli] Economic Research Division of the Bank of Libya.
v. 25 cm. bimonthly.
Continues Monthly economic bulletin issued by the division under its earlier name: Qism al-Buḥūth.
Title varies: July/Aug. 1966, Monthly economic bulletin.
Added title, July/Aug. 1966- :
النشرة الاقتصادية (varies slightly)
Arabic and English.
Continued by the publication with the same title issued by the division under the later name of the bank: Maṣrif Lībiyā.
Statistical supplements accompany some numbers.
1. Libya—Economic conditions—Periodicals. 2. Finance—Libya—Periodicals. 3. Libya—Commerce—Periodicals.
HC567.L5B28 74-645124
MARC-S

Bank Lībiyā. Idārat al-Buḥūth al-Iqtiṣādīyah.
(Tamwīl al-jam'īyāt al-ta'āwunīyah fī Lībiyā)
تمويل الجمعيات التعاونية في ليبيا ، اعداد ادارة البحوث الاقتصادية ببنك ليبيا. [طرابلس] 1969.
97 p. col. illus. 25 cm.
Includes bibliographical references.
1. Cooperative societies—Libya—Finance. I. Title.
HD3564.L5B36 1969 74-212842

Bank Lībiyā. Ministry of Information and Culture
see Bank Lībiyā. Idārat al-Buḥūth al-Iqtiṣādīyah.

Bank Lībiyā. Qism al-Buḥūth.
Monthly economic bulletin. v. -6, no. 5/6. -May/June 1966. [Tripoli] Research Dept. of the Bank of Libya.
v. 25 cm.
Added title, -May/June 1966:
النشرة الاقتصادية الشهرية.
Arabic and English.
Continued by Economic bulletin, issued by the dept, under its later name: Idārat al-Buḥūth al-Iqtiṣādīyah.
1. Libya—Economic conditions—Periodicals. 2. Finance—Libya—Periodicals. 3. Libya—Commerce—Periodicals. I. Title. II. Title: al-Nashrah al-iqtiṣādīyah al-shahrīyah.
HC567.L5B28 74-641123

Bank Markazi Iran
see Bank-i Markazi-i Iran.

Bank Marketing Association.
Analysis of 1972 bank marketing expenditures. Chicago [c1973]
29 p.
"1973 research report in cooperation with the American Bankers Association."
1. Bank marketing. I. American Bankers Association. II. Title.
AzTeS NUC76-75843

Bank Marketing Association.
Analysis of 1974 bank marketing expenditures : 1975 research report. Chicago : The Association, c1975.
18 p. ; 28 cm.
Cover title.
1. Bank marketing. 2. Banks and banking--United States. I. Title.
OU NUC77-87366

Bank Marketing Association.
The bank holding company: marketing in transition. Chicago, 1973.
139 p. 28 cm. (A Bank Marketing Association publication)
"Proceedings... First Holding Company Marketing Workshop sponsored by the Bank Marketing Association in Denver, August 1972."
1. Bank holding companies-United States. 2. Bank marketing. I. Title.
NRU NUC75-20194

Bank Marketing Association.
New perspectives in bank marketing research. Chicago, c1973.
271 p. illus. 28 cm. (A Bank marketing association research publication)
1. Marketing research-Addresses, essays, lectures. 2. Banks and banking. I. Title.
AU NUC75-20174

Bank Marketing Association
see Holding Company Marketing Workshop, 1st, Denver, 1972. Bank holding company marketing in transition. Chicago, 1973.

Bank Marketing Association
see Marketing Research Conference, Washington, D.C., 1973. New perspectives in bank marketing research. Chicago, c1973.

Bank Marketing Association
see Marketing Research Conference, 8th, Philadelphia, 1975. Relevant research in contemporary bank marketing. Chicago, 1975.

Bank Marketing Association
see Martindale, Robert M Public affairs and banking... [Chicago] c1971.

Bank Melli Iran
see Bānk-ī Millī-ī Īrān.

Bank Miṣr.
(Bank Miṣr: al-yūbīl al-dhahabī, 1920-1970)
بنك مصر : اليوبيل الذهبى ، ١٩٢٠ - ١٩٧٠. [اعداد الادارة العامة للتخطيط والبحوث والتدريب ، ادارة البحوث الاقتصادية ببنك مصر. القاهرة ، الشركة المصرية للطباعة والنشر ، 1971?]
12, 331 p. illus. 28 cm.
Includes bibliographical references.
1. Bank Miṣr. I. Title.
HG3390.C34B313 1971 73-210181

Bank Miṣr.
(Inshā' al-ṣinā'āt al-ahlīyah wa-tanẓīm al-taslīf al-ṣinā'ī)
انشاء الصناعات الأهلية وتنظيم التسليف الصناعى : مشروع بنك صناعى مصرى : تقرير مفصل مقدم لحضرة صاحب المعالى وزير المالية من بنك مصر. — مصر : البنك ، [1948?]
229 p. ; 28 cm.
1. Egypt—Industries. 2. Industrialization. 3. Industrial loan associations. I. Title.
HC535.B32 1948 76-970140

Bank Nasional.
P.T. Bank Nasional didirikan 1930. [Bukittinggi, 1961]
94, [26] p. illus. 32 cm.
Cover title: BN 30 tahun.
1. Banks and banking—Indonesia. 2. Malay literature—Economics.
NN NUC73-122989

Bank nationalization and the Supreme Court judgment. General editor: L. M. Singhvi. [Project personnel: Subhash C. Kashyap, Director; P. N. Bhatt, Deputy Director, and N. K. Jain, research assistant] Delhi, National [Pub. House, 1971]
viii, 274 p. 22 cm. Rs30.00
Papers presented at a symposium organized by the Institute of Constitutional and Parliamentary Studies in February 1970, and published under the auspices of the institute.
1. Banks and banking—Government ownership—India. I. Singhvi, Laxmi Mall, ed. II. Kashyap, Subhash C. III. Bhatt, P. N., 1922- IV. Jain, Narendra Kumar, 1937- V. Institute of Constitutional and Parliamentary Studies, Delhi.
346'.54'082 75-927409
MARC

Bank nationalization in India, a symposium. Bombay, Lalvani Pub. House [1969]
xxii, 272 p.
Compiled by Narendra Kumar.
1. Banks and banking—India—Government ownership. I. Narendra Kumar, 1922-
MoSW NUC73-33735

Bank Negara Indonesia.
Bank Negara Indonesia was established in 1946. In Aug. 1965 the name was changed to Bank Negara Indonesia Unit III and in 1968 to Bank Negara Indonesia 1946.
Works by this body are found under the name used at the time of publication.
75-589470

Bank Negara Indonesia.
Bank berdjoang tunggal: Bank Negera Indonesia. [Djakarta] Bagian Hubungan Masjarakat, Bank Negara Indonesia [1965]
52 p. illus. 24 cm.
1. Bank Negara Indonesia. 2. Banks and banking—Indonesia. I. Title.
HG3306.B34 1965 S A 68-20592
PL 480: Indo-3535

Bank Negara Indonesia.
Naskah kekeluargaan Bank Negara Indonesia. [Djakarta, 1960]
20 p. 15 cm.
1. Bank Negara Indonesia. 2. Bank employees—Indonesia. I. Title.
NIC NUC76-72876

Bank Negara Indonesia.
Report—Bank Negara Indonesia.
[Djakarta] Bank Negara Indonesia.
v. ill. 28 cm. annual.
Continued by: Bank Negara Indonesia Unit III. Report—Bank Negara Indonesia Unit III.
1. Bank Negara Indonesia. 2. Banks and banking, Central—Indonesia—Periodicals.
HG3306.B33 332.1'1'09598 76-641971
MARC-S

Bank Negara Indonesia 1946.
Bank Negara Indonesia was established in 1946. In Aug. 1965 the name was changed to Bank Negara Indonesia Unit III and in 1968 to Bank Negara Indonesia 1946.
Works by this body are found under the name used at the time of publication.
75-589468

Bank Negara Indonesia 1946.
Bank Berdjoang Tunggal: Bank Negara Indonesia. [Djakarta] Bagian Hubungan Masjarakat, Bank Negara Indonesia [1965]
52 p. illus. 24 cm.
1. Bank Negara Indonesia 1946. 2. Banks and banking—Indonesia. I. Title.
HG3306.B34 1965 S A 68-20592
PL 480: Indo-3535

Bank Negara Indonesia 1946.
Bank Negara Indonesia 1946: 25 years. [Djakarta, 1971]
138 p. illus. 28 cm.
1. Bank Negara Indonesia 1946.
HG3306.B34 1971a 72-942311
MARC

Bank Negara Indonesia 1946.
Bank Negara Indonesia 1946: 25 tahun. [Djakarta, 1971]
133 p. illus. 28 cm.
Issued also in English.
1. Bank Negara Indonesia 1946.
HG3306.B34 1971 72-941863

Bank Negara Indonesia 1946.
Laporan.
[Djakarta]
v. illus., ports. 27 cm. annual.
Issued also in English.
1. Bank Negara Indonesia 1946. 2. Indonesia—Commerce. I. Title.
HG3306.B32 S A 67-2679
rev PL 480: Indo-S-651

Bank Negara Indonesia 1946.
Laporan hasil survey di daerah Palangkaraya, Kalimantan Tengah / oleh team survey Bank Negara Indonesia 1946. — [Jakarta] : Bank, [1975?]
106 leaves in various foliations : maps ; 33 cm.
1. Palangkaraya, Indonesia—Economic conditions. I. Title.
HC448.P3B35 1946 76-941045
77 MARC

Bank Negara Indonesia 1946.
Majalah Bank Negara Indonesia 1946.
Jakarta, BNI 1946.
v. ill. 30 cm.
1. Banks and banking—Indonesia—Periodicals. 2. Indonesia—Periodicals.
HG3310.J34N432a 76-644703
MARC-S

Bank Negara Indonesia 1946.
Report—Bank Negara Indonesia 1946. 1969-
Djakarta, Bank Negara Indonesia 1946.
v. 26 cm. annual.
Continues: Bank Negara Indonesia Unit III. Report - Bank Negara Indonesia Unit III.
1. Bank Negara Indonesia 1946. 2. Indonesia—Commerce—Periodicals.
HG3306.B33 56-33178
MARC-S

Bank Negara Indonesia 1946. Bagian Hubungan Masjarakat

For informational publications of Bank Negara Indonesia 1946 issued by this body see

Bank Negara Indonesia 1946.

Bank Negara Indonesia Unit I.
The name of Javasche Bank (established in 1827) was changed in 1953 to Bank Indonesia. In 1965 it became Bank Negara Indonesia Unit I and in 1968 the name was changed back to Bank Indonesia.
Works by this body are found under the name used at the time of publication.
73-218662

Bank Negara Indonesia Unit I.
Economic data for investors in Indonesia. [Djakarta] Central Bank of Indonesia [1968]
xv, 220 p. 24 cm.
Errata slip inserted.
1. Investments, Foreign—Indonesia. 2. Indonesia—Economic conditions. I. Title.
HG5752.B36 1968 332.6'73'09598 73-940495
MARC

Bank Negara Indonesia Unit I.
Report of Bank Negara Indonesia Unit I.
[Djakarta, Bank Negara Indonesia Unit I]
v. 27 cm.
1. Indonesia—Economic conditions—1945- —Periodicals. 2. Finance—Indonesia—Periodicals. 3. Banks and banking—Indonesia—Periodicals.
HC446.B34a 330.9'598'03 76-644569
MARC-S

Bank Negara Indonesia Unit II.
In 1960 Bank Rakjat Indonesia and Bank Tani Nelajan merged to form Bank Koperasi, Tani dan Nelajan. In 1965 the name of the latter was changed to Bank Negara Indonesia Unit II, which in 1968 split into Bank Rakjat Indonesia and Bank Ekspor Impor Indonesia.
Works by Bank Rakjat Indonesia, including those by the related body, Algemeene Volkscredietbank, are found under the latest name: Bank Rakjat Indonesia.
Works by the other bodies are found under the following headings according to the name used at the time of publication:

Bank Tani Nelajan, p. t.
Bank Koperasi, Tani dan Nelajan.
Bank Negara Indonesia Unit II.
Bank Ekspor Impor Indonesia.

Bank Negara Indonesia Unit II
see Gemah ripah. [Djakarta] Bank Negara Indonesia Unit II.

Bank Negara Indonesia Unit III.
Bank Negara Indonesia was established in 1946. In Aug. 1965 the name was changed to Bank Negara Indonesia Unit III and in 1968 to Bank Negara Indonesia 1946.
Works by this body are found under the name used at the time of publication.
75-589469

Bank Negara Indonesia Unit III.
Ichtisar Rapat Kerdja Antar Pemimpin Kantor Wilajah Bank Negara Indonesia Unit III, Djakarta, 16 s/d 21 September 1968. — [Djakarta?] : B. N. I. Unit III, [1968?]
196 leaves in various foliations ; 33 cm.
English or Indonesian.
1. Banks and banking—Indonesia—Congresses. I. Title.
HG3306.B37 1968 72-940693

Bank Negara Indonesia Unit III.
Madjalah Bank Negara Indonesia.
[Djakarta, Bank Negara Indonesia Unit III]
v. ill. 22-24 cm. monthly.
Running title
Madjalah B. N. I.
Title varies slightly.
1. Bank Negara Indonesia Unit III—Periodicals. I. Bank Negara Indonesia Unit III. Madjalah B. N. I.
HG3306.B37a 75-643740
MARC-S

Bank Negara Indonesia Unit III.
Panel discussion BNI Unit III. [Djakarta, 1966?]
1 v. (various pagings) 33 cm.
1. Credit—Indonesia. 2. Malay literature—Economics.
NN NUC73-2952

Bank Negara Indonesia Unit III. Madjalah B. N. I.
see Bank Negara Indonesia Unit III. Madjalah Bank Negara Indonesia. [Djakarta]

Bank Negara Indonesia Unit III.
Report—Bank Negara Indonesia Unit III. 1965-68.
[Djakarta] Bank Negara Indonesia Unit III.
4 v. ill. 28 cm. annual.
Continues: Bank Negara Indonesia. Report—Bank Negara Indonesia.
Continued by: Bank Negara Indonesia 1946. Report—Bank Negara Indonesia 1946.
1. Bank Negara Indonesia. 2. Banks and banking, Central—Indonesia—Periodicals.
HG3306.B33 332.1'1'09598 76-641973
MARC-S

Bank Negara Indonesia Unit III
see Economic review. July/Aug. 1966- [Djakarta]

Bank Negara Malaysia. Annual report and statement of accounts
see Bank Negara Malaysia. Lapuran tahunan dan penyata kira-kira. [Kuala Lumpur]

Bank Negara Malaysia.
Annual report and statement of accounts—Bank Negara Malaysia.
[Kuala Lumpur] Bank Negara Malaysia.
v. 30 cm.
1. Malaysia—Economic conditions—Periodicals. 2. Bank Negara Malaysia. 3. Economic history—1945- —Periodicals.
HC445.5.A1B36a 330.9'595'05 75-648283
MARC-S

Bank Negara Malaysia.
Lapuran tahunan dan penyata kira-kira—Bank Negara Malaysia. Annual report and statement of accounts—Bank Negara Malaysia.
[Kuala Lumpur] Bank Negara Malaysia.
v. 30 cm.
English and Malay.
1. Bank Negara Malaysia. 2. Malaysia — Economic conditions — Periodicals. I. Bank Negara Malaysia. Annual report and statement of accounts.
HG3300.6.A7B36a 76-644726
MARC-S

Bank Negara Malaysia
see also Central Bank of Malaysia.

Bank Negara Malaysia. Pusat Latehan Kakitangan.
A guide to on the job training. Petaling Jaya, Bank Negara Malaysia Staff Training Centre [197-?]
12 l. 30 cm.
Cover title.
Includes bibliographical references.
1. Employees, Training of—Handbooks, manuals, etc. I. Title. II. Title: On the job training.
HF5549.5.T7B27 1970 658.31'243 73-940847
MARC

Bank Negara Malaysia. Pusat Latehan Kakitangan.
The practice of industrial relations in the banking industry : proceedings of a seminar. — Petaling Jaya : Bank Negara Malaysia Staff Training Centre, [1972]
19, 2 leaves ; 31 cm. — (Its Occasional paper series ; 5)
1. Collective bargaining—Banks and banking—Malaysia. 2. Industrial relations—Malaysia. I. Title. II. Series.
HD6820.6.Z7B262 1972 73-940942
331.89'041'332109595
75 MARC

Bank Negara Malaysia. Staff Training Centre
see
Bank Negara Malaysia. Pusat Latehan Kakitangan.

Bank of America.
Advertising. [San Francisco, c1969]
16 p. illus. 28 cm. (Small business reporter, v. 9, no. 1)
Cover title.
I. Title.
CLSU NUC75-24032

Bank of America.
Apparel manufacturing. [San Francisco, c1971]
24 p. illus. 28 cm. (Small business reporter, v. 10, no. 3)
Cover title.
Bibliography: p. 23.
I. Title.
CLSU NUC75-26588

Bank of America.
Apparel manufacturing in California. San Francisco, c1963.
12 p. illus. 28 cm. (Small business reporter, v. 5, no. 10)
Caption title.
Bibliography: p. 12.
I. Title.
CLSU NUC75-24029

Bank of America.
Apparel retailing. [San Francisco] c1968.
11 p. illus. 28 cm. (Small business reporter, v. 8, no. 3)
Caption title.
I. Title.
CLSU NUC75-24031

Bank of America.
Auto parts and accessory stores. [San Francisco, c1969]
12 p. illus. 28 cm. (Small business reporter, v. 8, no. 12)
Cover title.
I. Title.
CLSU NUC75-24028

Bank of America.
Avoiding management pitfalls. [San Francisco, c1973]
15 p. 28 cm. (Small business reporter, v. 11, no. 5)
Cover title.
Includes bibliography.
I. Title.
CLSU NUC75-17275

Bank of America.
Bars and cocktail lounges. [San Francisco, c1973]
16 p. 28 cm. (Small business reporter, v. 11, no. 9)
Cover title.
Bibliography: p. 16.
I. Title.
CLSU NUC75-16673

Bank of America.
Beauty salons. [San Francisco] c1964.
6 p. illus. 28 cm. (Small business reporter, v. 6, no. 2)
Caption title.
I. Title.
CLSU NUC75-24040

Bank of America.
Beauty salons. [San Francisco, c1969]
12 p. 28 cm. (Small business reporter, v. 9, no. 2)
Cover title.
I. Title.
CLSU NUC75-24033

Bank of America.
Bibliography: corporate responsiblity for social problems; budgets, costs, and expenditures. San Francisco, Bank of America NT & SA, 1973.
61 p.
1. Industry—Social aspects—Bibl. I. Title.
CLU NUC75-24041

Bank of America.
Bicycle stores. [San Francisco, c1974]
16 p. 28 cm. (Small business reporter, v. 12, no. 1)
Cover title.
I. Title.
CLSU NUC75-20235

Bank of America.
Bookstores. [San Francisco, c1973]
20 p. 28 cm. (Small business reporter, v. 11, no. 6)
Cover title.
Bibliography: p. 20.
I. Title.
CLSU NUC75-16663

Bank of America.
Bowling centers. [San Francisco] c1964.
8 p. illus. 28 cm. (Small business reporter, v. 6, no. 7)
Caption title.
Includes bibliographical references.
I. Title.
CLSU NUC75-24046

Bank of America.
Building contractors. [San Francisco, c1971]
16 p. illus. 28 cm. (Small business reporter, v. 10, no. 1)
Cover title.
Bibliography: p. 16.
I. Title.
CLSU NUC75-24044

Bank of America.
Business management: advice from consultants. [San Francisco, c1973]
16 p. illus. 28 cm. (Small business reporter, v. 11, no. 3)
Cover title.
I. Title.
CLSU NUC75-16664

Bank of America.
The California trend; facts about the State served by Bank of America, 1904–1954. [San Francisco? 1954]
[28] p. illus. (part col.) diagrs. 35 cm.
Cover title.
1. California—Economic conditions. I. Title.
HC107.C2B3 1954 330.9794 55-25882
rev

Bank of America.
Coin-operated drycleaning. [San Francisco, c1969]
8 p. illus. 28 cm. (Small business reporter, v. 8, no. 7)
Cover title.
I. Title.
CLSU NUC75-24037

Bank of America.
Coin-operated laundries. [San Francisco, c1969]
12 p. illus. 28 cm. (Small business reporter, v. 8, no. 6)
Cover title.
I. Title.
CLSU NUC75-24038

Bank of America.
Convenience food stores. [San Francisco, c1970]
20 p. illus. 28 cm. (Small business reporter, v. 9, no. 6)
Cover title.
I. Title.
CLSU NUC75-24057

Bank of America.
Day nurseries for preschoolers. [San Francisco, c1969]
8 p. 28 cm. (Small business reporter, v. 8, no. 10)
Cover title.
I. Title.
CLSU NUC75-24039

Bank of America.
Direct foreign investment in the United States; a special analysis. [San Francisco] 1973.
16 p. illus. (part col.)
Cover title.
1. Investments, Foreign—U.S. 2. Corporations.
MH-BA NUC74-116641

Bank of America.
Equipment rental business. San Francisco, c1963.
6 p. illus. 28 cm. (Small business reporter, v. 5, no. 9)
Caption title.
I. Title.
CLSU NUC75-24047

Bank of America.
Equipment rental business. [San Francisco, c1971]
18 p. 28 cm. (Small business reporter, v. 10, no. 6)
Cover title.
Bibliography: p. 18.
I. Title.
CLSU NUC75-24048

Bank of America.
Family billiard centers. [San Francisco] c1964.
6 p. illus. 28 cm. (Small business reporter, v. 6, no. 6)
Caption title.
Includes bibliographical references.
I. Title.
CLSU NUC75-24035

Bank of America.
Focus on Micronesia; an economic study of the U.S. Trust Territory of the Pacific Islands. [n.p., 1973]
20 p.
1. Micronesia—Econ. condit. 2. Trust Territory of the Pacific Islands—Econ. condit. I. Title.
HU NUC76-75626

Bank of America.
The foodservice business. [San Francisco] c1968.
33 p. illus. 28 cm. (Small business reporter, v. 8, no. 2)
Caption title.
I. Title.
CLSU NUC75-24034

Bank of America.
Foreign investment in Singapore / BA. — Singapore : BA, [1976]
24, 8 p. : ill. ; 25 cm.
Cover title.
1. Singapore—Commerce—Handbooks, manuals, etc. 2. Investments, Foreign—Singapore. I. Title.
HF3800.67.B35 1976 332.6'73'095952 76-941631
77 MARC

Bank of America.
The franchise business. [San Francisco] c1965.
7 p. illus. 28 cm. (Small business reporter, v. 6, no. 12)
Caption title.
Includes bibliography.
I. Title.
CLSU NUC75-24036

Bank of America.
Franchising. [San Francisco, c1970]
12 p. 28 cm. (Small business reporter, v. 9, no. 9)
Cover title.
Bibliography: p. 12.
I. Title.
CLSU NUC75-24049

Bank of America.
Gift stores. [San Francisco, c1970]
16 p. 28 cm. (Small business reporter, v. 9, no. 4)
Cover title.
I. Title.
CLSU NUC75-24030

Bank of America.
Golf in California. San Francisco, c1964.
12 p. illus. 28 cm. (Small business reporter, v. 6, no. 3)
Caption title.
Includes bibliographical references.
I. Title.
CLSU NUC75-24050

Bank of America.
The handcraft business. [San Francisco, c1972]
16 p. 28 cm. (Small business reporter, v. 10, no. 8)
Cover title.
Bibliography: p. 16.
I. Title.
CLSU NUC75-24051

Bank of America.
Health food stores. [San Francisco, c1973]
15 p. 28 cm. (Small business reporter, v. 11, no. 2)
Cover title.
Includes bibliography.
I. Title.
CLSU NUC75-16665

Bank of America.
Home furnishings stores. [San Francisco, c1972]
20 p. 28 cm. (Small business reporter, v. 11, no. 1)
Cover title.
Bibliography: p. 20.
I. Title.
CLSU NUC75-24043

Bank of America.
How to buy or sell a business. [San Francisco, c1969]
12 p. 28 cm. (Small business reporter, v. 8, no. 11)
Cover title.
I. Title.
CLSU NUC75-24042

Bank of America.
If you were trustee? In which the Trust Department of Bank of America National Trust & Savings Association briefly discusses trust investments and taxes; and what you expect of your trustee in the management of your estate. [San Francisco, The Kennedy-ten Bosch Company, c1938]
3 p. l., 5-36, [2] p. diagrs. 24 cm.
1. Trusts and trustees. I. Title.
HG4485.B23 1938 332.14 38-37565
rev

Bank of America.
Independent automotive services. [San Francisco] c1964.
8 p. illus. 28 cm. (Small business reporter, v. 6, no. 8)
Caption title.
I. Title.
CLSU NUC75-24045

Bank of America.
Independent drug stores. [San Francisco, c1970]
16 p. 28 cm. (Small business reporter, v. 9, no. 12)
Cover title.
Bibliography: p. 16.
I. Title.
CLSU NUC75-24054

Bank of America.
Independent grocery stores. [San Francisco] c1964.
10 p. illus. 28 cm. (Small business reporter, v. 6, no. 1)
Caption title.
Includes bibliographical references.
I. Title.
CLSU NUC75-24052

Bank of America.
Independent liquor stores. [San Francisco, c1973]
16 p. 28 cm. (Small business reporter, v. 11, no. 4)
Cover title.
Bibliography: p. 16.
I. Title.
CLSU NUC75-16667

Bank of America.
Independent pet shops. [San Francisco, c1971]
15 p. 28 cm. (Small business reporter, v. 10, no. 2)
Cover title.
Bibliography: p. 15.
I. Title.
CLSU NUC75-24053

Bank of America.
Independent sporting goods stores. [San Francisco, c1972]
15 p. 28 cm. (Small business reporter, v. 10, no. 11)
Cover title.
Bibliography: p. 15.
I. Title.
CLSU NUC75-24060

Bank of America.
Independent variety stores. [San Francisco] c1966.
11 p. 28 cm. (Small business reporter, v. 7, no. 8)
Caption title.
I. Title.
CLSU NUC75-24056

Bank of America.
Mail order enterprises. [San Francisco, c1973]
19 p. 28 cm. (Small business reporter, v. 11, no. 7)
Cover title.
Includes bibliography.
I. Title.
CLSU NUC75-16666

Bank of America.
Management succession. [San Francisco, c1972]
15 p. 28 cm. (Small business reporter, v. 10, no. 12)
Cover title.
Bibliography. p. 15.
I. Title.
CLSU NUC75-24061

Bank of America.
Manufacturing. [San Francisco, c1970]
12 p. illus. 28 cm. (Small business reporter, v. 9, no. 3)
Cover title.
I. Title.
CLSU NUC75-24059

Bank of America.
Marketing a new product. [San Francisco, c1971]
12 p. illus. 28 cm. (Small business reporter, v. 10, no. 5)
Cover title.
Bibliography: p. 11.
I. Title.
CLSU NUC75-24063

Bank of America.
Mobile home & recreational vehicle dealers. [San Francisco, c1970]
16 p. 28 cm. (Small business reporter, v. 9, no. 11)
Cover title.
I. Title.
CLSU NUC75-24058

Bank of America.
Mobile home parks. [San Francisco] c1966.
11 p. 28 cm. (Small business reporter, v. 7, no. 10)
Caption title.
I. Title.
CLSU NUC75-24062

Bank of America.
Model car racing centers. [San Francisco] c1965.
12 p. illus. 28 cm. (Small business reporter, v. 6, no. 9)
Caption title.
Includes bibliographical references.
I. Title.
CLSU NUC75-24064

Bank of America.
Money market investments and investment vocabulary. [San Francisco, 1969]
34 p.
"Statistical supplement" inserted in pocket.
Cover title.
1. Money market—Handbooks, manuals. I. Title.
MH-BA NUC73-2229

Bank of America.
Money-market investments and investment vocabulary. [3d ed. San Francisco] Bank of America, Bank Investment Securities Division [1974]
42 p.
1. Investments—U.S. 2. Finance—U.S. I. Title.
InU NUC76-22700

Bank of America.
Motels. San Francisco, c1962.
10 p. illus. 28 cm. (Small business reporter, v. 5, no. 3)
Caption title.
Bibliography: p. 10.
I. Title.
CLSU NUC75-24070

Bank of America.
Motels. [San Francisco] c1966.
11 p. 28 cm. (Small business reporter, v. 7, no. 6)
Caption title.
I. Title.
CLSU NUC75-24071

Bank of America.
Personnel for the small business. [San Francisco? 1970?]
12 p. 28 cm. (Small business reporter, v. 9, no. 8)
Cover title.
1. Personnel management. I. Title. II. Series.
CLSU NUC73-101653

Bank of America.
The printing business. [San Francisco] c1964.
10 p. illus. 28 cm. (Small business reporter, v. 6, no. 4)
Caption title.
Includes bibliographical references.
I. Title.
CLSU NUC75-24069

Bank of America.
Private vocational education. [San Francisco] c1965.
10 p. illus. 28 cm. (Small business reporter, v. 6, no. 11)
Caption title.
I. Title.
CLSU NUC75-24068

Bank of America.
Proprietary day care. [San Francisco, c1973]
15 p. 28 cm. (Small business reporter, v. 11, no. 8)
Cover title.
Includes bibliography.
I. Title.
CLSU NUC75-16668

Bank of America.
Recreational vehicle parks. [San Francisco] c1967.
11 p. illus. 28 cm. (Small business reporter, v. 7, no. 12)
Caption title.
I. Title.
CLSU NUC75-24067

Bank of America.
Repair services. [San Francisco, c1972]
19 p. illus. 28 cm. (Small business reporter, v. 10, no. 9)
Cover title.
Bibliography: p. 19.
I. Title.
CLSU NUC75-24055

Bank of America.
Report.
[San Francisco]
v. illus. 22 cm. annual.
1. Bank of America.
HG2613.S54B283 51-19901
rev MARC-S

Bank of America.
Retail financial records. [San Francisco, c1971]
14 p. 28 cm. (Small business reporter, v. 10, no. 4)
Cover title.
Bibliography: p. 14.
I. Title.
CLSU NUC75-24066

Bank of America.
Retail nurseries. [San Francisco, c1970]
12 p. illus. 28 cm. (Small business reporter, v. 9, no. 10)
Cover title.
I. Title.
CLSU NUC75-24074

Bank of America.
Retailing. [San Francisco] c1968.
19 p. illus. 28 cm. (Small business reporter, v. 8, no. 4)
Caption title.
I. Title.
CLSU NUC75-24072

Bank of America.
Service stations. [San Francisco, c1971]
15 p. 28 cm. (Small business reporter, v. 10, no. 7)
Cover title.
Bibliography: p. 15.
I. Title.
CLSU NUC75-24073

Bank of America.
Small business: a look ahead. [San Francisco] c1967.
7 p. 28 cm. (Small business reporter, v. 8, no. 1)
Caption title.
I. Title.
CLSU NUC75-24077

Bank of America.
Small job printing. [San Francisco, c1970]
16 p. 28 cm. (Small business reporter, v. 9, no. 5)
Cover title.
I. Title.
CLSU NUC75-24075

Bank of America.
Steps to starting a business. [San Francisco] 1972.
15 p. 28 cm. (Small business reporter, v. 10, no. 10.)
Cover title.
OCU CLSU NUC75-19121

Bank of America.
Timeplanned homes financed for Californians by Bank of America ... ⌈San Francisco, Independent Pressroom, inc., 1940⌉
⌈24⌉ p. illus. (part col., incl. plans) 30 cm.
1. Architecture, Domestic—Designs and plans. 2. Architecture, Domestic—California. 3. Housing—California—Finance. I. Title.
NA7235.C2B36 1940 728.6084 43-40722 rev

Bank of America.
Veterinary medicine: the small animal practice. ⌈San Francisco⌉ c1966.
9 p. illus. 28 cm. (Small business reporter, v. 7, no. 4)
Caption title.
I. Title.
CLSU NUC75-24076

Bank of America.
Women's apparel stores. ⌈San Francisco⌉ c1963.
10 p. illus. 28 cm. (Small business reporter, v. 5, no. 12)
Caption title.
Includes bibliographical references.
I. Title.
CLSU NUC75-24065

Bank of America
see The Andean Group; issued by Bank of America's Men-on-the-Spot. ⌈San Francisco?⌉ 1968.

Bank of America
see Corporate responsibility for social problems ... San Francisco.

Bank of America
see Memo from Bank of America's man-on-the-spot. San Francisco, 1972-

Bank of America. Economic Research Dept.
see Hopkin, John A. Commercial vegetable production in California ... ⌈San Francisco, Bank of America, Economics Dept.⌉ 1960.

Bank of America. Management Reference Service
see Foreign trade through the California customs districts. ⌈San Francisco?⌉

Bank of America. Management Reference Service
see Foreign trade through the Los Angeles and San Diego customs districts. [San Francisco?]

Bank of America. Mangement Reference Service
see Foreign trade through the San Francisco customs district. ⌈San Francisco?⌉

Bank of America. Mangement Reference Service
see Summary tables, foreign trade through the California customs districts. ⌈San Francisco?⌉

Bank of America; a second check [by an A. S. I. A. study group with a little help from my friends Fred Goff et al. Isla Vista, Calif., Dick Parker, Full Court Press, 1970]
54 p.
Cover title.
Primarily a work of Geoff Wallace-Associated Students UCSB.
I. Wallace, Geoff. II. A. S. I. A. Study Group.
CU-SB NUC74-91633

Bank of America National Trust and Savings Association.
Guide to foreign exchange regulations and investment in Pakistan; a report from Bank of America's man-on-the-spot in Karachi. ⌈San Francisco, 1963⌉
31 p. 28 cm.
1. Investments, Foreign—Pakistan. 2. Foreign exchange—Law—Pakistan. I. Title.
HG4538.B32 74-210380 MARC

Bank of America National Trust and Savings Association
see
Bank of America.

Bank of Bermuda, ltd.
see Pine, Sidney R Formation and operation... New York, Valicenti, Leighton, Reid & Pine ⌈1971⌉

Bank of Bhutan.
Annual report.
⌈Thimphu?⌉
v. 26 cm.
1. Banks and banking, Central—Bhutan.
HG3361.B53B35 354'.549'800825 73-214029

Bank of California, San Francisco.
Pacific Coast economic series, 1929-1965. ⌈San Francisco? 1966⌉
⌈49⌉ l.
Cover-title.
1. Pacific Coast—Economic conditions.
I. Title.
CLU NUC73-126327

Bank of Canada.
Annual report of the Governor to the Minister of Finance and statement of accounts for the year.
⌈Ottawa⌉
v. illus. 26 cm.
English and French, the latter inverted with title: Rapport annuel du Gouverneur au Ministre des Finances et relevé de comptes pour l'année.
1. Bank of Canada. 2. Canada—Economic conditions—1945- —Periodicals. I. Bank of Canada. Rapport annuel du Gouverneur au Ministre des Finances et relevés de comptes pour l'année.
HG2706.B35a 332.1'1'0971 74-645223 MARC-S

Bank of Canada. Emprunts du gouvernement du Canada
see Bank of Canada. Loans of Government of Canada and loans guaranteed by the Government of Canada. [Ottawa]

Bank of Canada.
Loans of Government of Canada and loans guaranteed by the Government of Canada.
⌈Ottawa⌉ Bank of Canada.
v. 23 cm. annual.
English and French.
Added title page title : Emprunts du gouvernement du Canada et emprunts garantis par le gouvernement du Canada.
1. Debts, Public—Canada—Periodicals. 2. Bonds—Canada—Periodicals. I. Bank of Canada. Emprunts du gouvernement du Canada. II. Title.
HJ8513.B32a 336.3'44'0971 75-645726 MARC-S

Bank of Canada. Rapport annuel du Gouverneur au Ministre des Finances et relevés de comptes pour l'année
see Bank of Canada. Annual report of the Governor to the Minister of Finance and statement of accounts for the year. [Ottawa]

Bank of Canada
see also
Bank of Canada, Ottawa.

Bank of Canada, Ottawa.
Evidence of the Governor of the Bank of Canada before the Royal Commission on Banking and Finance. ⌈Ottawa, 1964⌉
173 p. 28 cm.
I. Canada. Royal Commission on Banking and Finance. II. Title.
HG2706.B35 1964 74-204458

Bank of Canada, Ottawa
see Gorbet, Fred. The equations of RDX2... ⌈Ottawa⌉ 1973.

Bank of Canada, Ottawa
see Rasminsky. Louis. [Speeches of the Governor... Ottawa, 1961-1967]

Bank of Canada, Ottawa
see Rasminsky, Louis. Submission... [n.p.] 1971.

Bank of Canada, Ottawa
see also
Bank of Canada.

Bank of Canada, Ottawa. Research Dept.
see RDX 1. ⌈Ottawa?⌉ 1968.

Bank of Ceylon.
Annual report and accounts—Bank of Ceylon.
⌈Colombo⌉ Bank of Ceylon.
v. ill. 27 cm.
Continues: Bank of Ceylon. Annual report—Bank of Ceylon.
Cover title : Report & accounts.
1. Bank of Ceylon. 2. Ceylon—Economic conditions. I. Bank of Ceylon. Report & accounts.
HG3270.8.A7B36a 330.9'549'3 76-644533 MARC-S

Bank of Ceylon.
Annual report—Bank of Ceylon.
Colombo, Bank of Ceylon.
v. ill. 25 cm.
Report year for ends Sept. 30.
Continued by: Bank of Ceylon. Annual report and accounts—Bank of Ceylon.
1. Bank of Ceylon. 2. Ceylon—Economic conditions.
HG3270.8.A7B36a 330.9'549'303 76-644536 MARC-S

Bank of Ceylon. Report & accounts
see Bank of Ceylon. Annual report and accounts... [Colombo]

Bank of Clinton.
The name of the Deposit Guaranty Bank & Trust Co., Jackson, Miss., was changed to Deposit Guaranty National Bank in 1965. Works by this body are found under the name used at the time of publication.
Works by earlier related bodies are found under
Bank of Clinton.
Commercial Bank & Trust Co., Jackson, Miss.

Bank of Commerce, Sheridan, Wyo.
The story of our mural. [Written by R. E. McNally] Sheridan, Wyo. [19-]
[17] p. illus. 23 cm.
Pages [7]-[10] (printed on one side of sheet) 60 x 23 cm. folded to 23 x 15 cm.
Bernard Thomas, artist.
1. Wyoming-Hist. 2. Sheridan Co., Wyo.—Hist. 3. History in art. I. Thomas, Bernard. II. McNally, R. E.
OkU NUC75-29660

Bank of Cumming.
Navigational map of Lake Lanier: a community service project. ⌈Presented by⌉ the Bank of Cumming. ⌈Cumming? 1971?⌉
col. map 15 x 17 in.
Scale ca. 1:140,000.
Includes legend, points of interest and marinas/launching ramps.
1. Sidney Lanier, Lake, Ga.—Maps. 2. Sidney Lanier, Lake, Ga.—Navigation—Maps. I. Title.
GAT NUC74-85244

Bank of Delaware, Wilmington.
Progress in information systems. 5th ed., Wilmington, 1970.
76 p. 23 cm.
1. Electronic data processing-Banks and banking. I. Title.
NjR OU IaU NUC73-47931

Bank of England.
An introduction to flow funds accounting, 1952-70. London, Bank of England, Economic Intelligence Department, 1972.
98 p. 1 illus. 30 cm. £0.50 B 72-24603
Includes bibliographical references.
1. Flow of funds—Great Britain—Accounting. I. Title.
HC260.F55B36 339.2'6'0942 73-156458
ISBN 0-903312-01-8 MARC

Bank of England. **Statistical abstract**
see Bank of England. Economic Intelligence Dept. **Bank of England statistical abstract.** 1970- ⌈London⌉

Bank of England
see National Conference on Strategic Planning for Financial Institutions, 1972. Strategic planning for financial institutions. London : Bodley Head & HFL (Publishers), 1974.

Bank of England. Economic Intelligence Dept.
Bank of England statistical abstract. no. 1–
1970–
⌊London⌋
v. 30 cm.
1. Finance — Great Britain — Statistics. I. Bank of England. Statistical abstract. II. Title.
HG11.B3 332'.0942 72-624809

Bank of Finland
see Suomen Pankki.

Bank of Ghana.
Bye-laws. [Accra, 1957]
1 v.
Caption title.
CtY-L NUC75-100030

Bank of Greece
see Trapeza tēs Hellados.

Bank of Guyana.
Economic bulletin.
⌊Georgetown⌋
v. illus. 28 cm.
1. Guyana — Economic conditions — Periodicals. 2. Money — Guyana—Periodicals. I. Title.
HC206.B3 72-624541

Bank of Hawaii.
Gas utility industry projections to 1990. Arlington, Va., 1973.
15 p.
1. Gas utility. I. Title.
DHUD NUC74-116656

Bank of Hawaii.
Monthly review—Bank of Hawaii. v. 15–
Jan. 1970–
⌊Honolulu⌋ Bank of Hawaii.
v. ill. 29 cm.
Continues: Bank of Hawaii. Review of business and economic conditions.
ISSN 0005-5204
1. Hawaii—Economic conditions—Periodicals.
HC687.H3B26 330.9'969'04 75-644501
MARC-S

Bank of Hawaii. Dept. of Business Research.
Hawaii annual economic review.
⌊Honolulu⌋
v. illus. 28 cm.
1. Hawaii—Economic conditions. I. Title.
HC107.H3B34a 330.9'969'04 74-643340
MARC-S

Bank of Hawaii. Dept. of Business Research.
Hawaii '71 annual economic review. Honolulu, 1971.
48 p.
1. Economic conditions–Hawaii. I. Title.
DHUD NUC73-41290

Bank of Iran
see Sherkat, Kazem. A nation-wide survey on cotton-synthetic textile industry in Iran. Tehran, 1963.

Bank of Iran and the Middle East
see
Bānk-i Īrān va Khāvar-i Miyānah.

Bank of Israel.
see Israel. Miśrad ha-ḥaḳla'ut. The economy and agriculture of Israel. Jerusalem, The Ministry, 1959.

Bank of Israel
see Kindler, Arie. Coins of the land of Israel... Jerusalem, Keter Pub. House ⌊1974⌋

Bank of Israel
see Kindler, Arie. Matbe'ot Erets-Yisrael. 731 [1971]

Bank of Israel
see Ot u-ma'ot. 1967–

Bank of Israel
see Otot, b.m. Mahleket sekarim. Seker tokhniyot pensyah le-'atsma'iyim. 1967.

Bank of Israel. Examiner of Banks Dept.
(Ashrai banka'i le-fi 'anfe ha-meshek: nituaḥ statisti)
אשראי בנקאי לפי ענפי המשק: ניתוח סטטיסטי. –1969/70
⌊ירושלים⌋ בנק ישראל, המפקח על הבנקים.
v. 28 cm.
1. Credit—Israel—Statistics—Periodicals. I. Title.
HG3729.I 66B35a 73-955655
(MARC-S)

Bank of Israel. Examiner of Banks Dept.
(Hakhnasot ve-hotsa'ot shel ha-mosadot ha-banka'iyim be-Yisrael)
הכנסות והוצאות של המוסדות הבנקאיים בישראל.
–1970/71
⌊ירושלים⌋ בנק ישראל, המפקח על הבנקים.
v. 27 cm.
Data previous to 1970/71 included in the bank's דין וחשבון and סקר.
1. Banks and banking—Israel—Statistics. I. Title.
HG3361.P23B22a 73-955656
MARC-S

Bank of Israel. Examiner of Banks Dept.
(Yitronot le-godel ba-banka'ut ha-yisre'elit)
יתרונות לגודל בבנקאות הישראלית; עבודת מחקר. ⌊ירושלים⌋
בנק ישראל, המפקח על הבנקים ⌊1972 or 3⌋
55 p. 27 cm.
Study conducted by Ḥ. Dori.
Bibliography: p. 55.
1. Banks and banking—Israel. I. Dori, Ḥayim. II. Title.
HG3361.P22B345 1973 74-950859

Bank of Israel. Examiner of Banks Dept.
see Israel. Laws, statutes, etc. Hikukim ve-hora'ot. ⌊1972–

Bank of Israel. Examiner of Banks Dept.
see Israel. Laws, statutes, etc. ⌊Hok Bank Yisrael⌋ Ḥok va-ḥakikat mishneh be-vanka'ut. ⌊730 i. e. 1970⌋

Bank of Israel. Examiner of Banks Dept.
see Orgler, Yair E (ha-Sinuf ha-banka'i be-Yisrael) [1972]

Bank of Israel. Research Dept.
The economy of the administered areas.
Jerusalem.
v. illus. 21-24 cm.
Vols. for issued in two parts.
1. Israel-Arab War, 1967– —Occupied territories—Economic conditions.
HC497.P2B256a 330.9'5695 74-641309
MARC-S

Bank of Israel. Research Dept.
(Kalkalat ha-shetaḥim ha-muḥzakim)
כלכלת השטחים המוחזקים.
ירושלים, בנק ישראל, מחלקת המחקר.
v. 21-24 cm.
Semiannual, the second issue being the annual cumulation.
1. Israel-Arab War, 1967—Occupied territories—Economic conditions—Periodicals. I. Title.
HC497.P2B256b 73-952845
(MARC-S)

Bank of Israel. Research Dept.
A profitability study of Israel commercial banks 1956-1961. Jerusalem, 1963.
1 v. (various pagings) tables. 32 cm.
1. Banks and banking—Israel. I. Title.
NNC NUC75-53739

Bank of Israel. Research Dept.
(Taktsiv le'umi)
תקציב לאומי.
ירושלים, בנק ישראל, מחלקת המחקר.
v. 24-28 cm. annual.
Issues for issued with Misrad ha-otsar, ha-Lishkah le-yi'uts ule-meḥkar kalkali (with Agaf ha-taktsivim); with ha-Rashut le-tikhnun kalkali (-1965 with Misrad ha-otsar; 1966– with Misrad ha-otsar, Lishkat ha-yo'ets ha-kalkali); with Misrad ha-otsar.
1. Gross national product—Israel—Yearbooks. I. Israel. Misrad ha-otsar. ha-Lishkah le-yi'uts ule-meḥkar kalkali. II. Israel. Agaf ha-taktsivim. III. Israel. ha-Rashut le-tikhnun kalkali. IV. Israel. Misrad ha-otsar. V. Israel. Misrad ha-otsar. Lishkat ha-yo'ets ha-kalkali.
HC497.P23 I 513a 74-644933
MARC-S

Bank of Israel. Research Dept.
see Ben Basat, A (Melai ha-hon u-defuse ha-hashka'ah ba-haroshet) 1972.

Bank of Israel. Research Dept.
see Bregman, Arie. Economic growth in the administered areas, 1968-1973. Jerusalem, Bank of Israel, Research Dept., 1974 i.e. 1975.

Bank of Israel. Research Dept.
see Landsberger, Michael. Restitution receipts... Jerusalem, 1970.

Bank of Israel. Research Dept.
see Levy, Haim. (Hefreshe sakhar shel kevutsot sekhirim be-Yisrael) 1968.

Bank of Israel. State Loans Administration.
(Reshimat mispere igrot ḥov shel Medinat Yisrael)
רשימת מספרי איגרות חוב של מדינת ישראל.
תל-אביב, בנק ישראל, מינהל מילוות המדינה.
v. 22 cm. annual.
"שעלו בגורל ולא הוצגו לפדיון."
1. Loans—Israel. I. Title.
HG2069.I 7B32a HE 68-4235
PL 480 : Is-S-877

Bank of Italy
see
Banca d' Italia.

Bank of Jamaica.
Statistical digest.
⌊Kingston⌋
v. illus. 28 cm.
1. Finance—Jamaica—Statistics. 2. Jamaica—Statistics.
HG185.J3B35a 332'.097292 74-641161
MARC-S

Bank of Jamaica. Research Dept.
Balance of payments of Jamaica.
Kingston.
v. illus. 28 cm.
1. Balance of payments—Jamaica. I. Title.
HG3883.J2B34a 382.1'7'097292 74-644057
MARC-S

Bank of Jamaica. Research Dept.
Monthly review.
⌊Kingston⌋
v. ill. 28 cm.
1. Jamaica—Economic conditions—Periodicals.
HC157.J2B3a 330.9'7292'06 74-646979
MARC-S

Bank of Japan
see Nihon Ginkō.

Bank of Japan. Economic Research Dept.
see Nihon Ginkō. Chōsakyoku.

Bank of Korea
see Han'guk Unhaeng.

Bank of Leland
see Workman, Noel. 75 years in Leland. [Leland, c1974]

Bank of Libya
see
Bank Lībiyā.
Maṣrif Lībiyā.

Bank of London and South America Limited.
Bank of London and South America Limited; a short account of the bank's growth and formation. ⌊London, Blades, East & Blades, 1954⌋
15 p. 24 cm.
HG2998.B32L66 74-209565

Bank of London and South America Limited
see Venezuela now ... ⌈Sussex, Howe Print., 1975⌉

Bank of Monrovia.
Annual report.
Monrovia, Liberia.
v. illus. 41 x 31 cm.
1. Bank of Monrovia.
HG3431.L54M63a 332.1'1'09664 73-643969
MARC-S

Bank of Montreal.
Canada today. 12th ed. Montreal, 1965.
124 p. illus., map (fold.)
1. Canada—Description and travel—1951-
I. Title.
UU NUC75-53725

Bank of Montreal. Oil and Gas Dept.
A guide for oil and gas operators in Canada and those engaged in allied industries. ⌈Rev. ed. Calgary, Alta., 1972, c1969⌉
39 p. col. maps (2 fold. in pocket) 26 cm. C***
"Oil and gas highlights for the year 1972": 2 p. inserted.
1. Petroleum industry and trade—Canada. 2. Gas, Natural—Canada. 3. Petroleum—Taxation—Canada. I. Title.
HD9574.C22B35 1972 338.2'7'280971 74-176433
MARC

Bank of New Mexico.
Annual summary study: the economy of the State of New Mexico and the Albuquerque Standard Metropolitan Statistical Area.
Albuquerque, Bureau of Business & Economic Research, University of New Mexico.
v. ill. 28 cm.
Cover title : The New Mexico economy.
Key title: Annual summary study, the economy of the State of New Mexico and the Albuquerque Standard Metropolitan Statistical Area. ISSN 0363-3748
1. New Mexico—Economic conditions—Periodicals. 2. Albuquerque metropolitan area—Economic conditions—Periodicals. I. Title. II. Title: The New Mexico economy.
HC107.N6B35a 330.9'789'05 76-645446
MARC-S

Bank of New South Wales.
Australian commemorative stamps. ⌈9th ed. Sydney, 1967⌉
32 p. illus.
1. Postage stamps—Australia.
MH NUC73-101654

Bank of New South Wales.
Conserve your soil; a simple guide to soil erosion. Sydney, Australia, Issued by the Bank of New South Wales ⌈n. d.⌉
62, ⌈2⌉ p. illus. 24 cm.
1. Soil conservation—Australia. 2. Erosion.
I. Title.
TxU NUC75-28984

Bank of New South Wales.
Endeavour and achievement : highlights in the story of Australian development. — 13th ed. / prepared by Norman A. Little. — ⌈Sydney⌉ : Bank of New South Wales, 1973.
32 p. : ill. ; 25 cm. Aus***
Cover title.
1. Australia. I. Little, Norman A. II. Title.
DU96.B36 1973 994 75-308517
75 MARC

Bank of New South Wales.
Investing in Australia : a guide to Wales investment services. — ⌈Sydney : Bank of New South Wales, 1975⌉
16 p. : col. ill. ; 24 cm. Aus***
Cover title.
ISBN 0-909719-17-9
1. Bank of New South Wales. I. Title.
HG3460.S94B333 1975 332.1'223'09944 76-369925
76 MARC

Bank of New South Wales.
Sixteen explorers of Australia. ⌈5th ed. Sydney, 1967⌉
17 p. illus., maps, ports. 24 cm.
Cover title.
"First published as 'Fourteen explorers of Australia' in...1951." This ed. first published 1965.
1. Explorers, Australian. I. Title.
NcD NUC74-115142

Bank of New Zealand
see New Zealand economic statistics. [Wellington]

Bank of North America, Philadelphia.
In 1929 the Bank of North America (chartered in 1781) and the Pennsylvania Company for Insurances on Lives and Granting Annuities (chartered in 1812) merged and retained the latter name. In 1947 the name was changed to Pennsylvania Company for Banking and Trust. In 1955 the Pennsylvania Company for Banking and Trust and the First National Bank of Philadelphia (established in 1912) merged to form the First Pennsylvania Banking and Trust Company, which in 1974 changed its name to First Pennsylvania Bank N. A.
Works by these bodies are found under the following headings according to the name used at the time of publication:

Bank of North America, Philadelphia.
Pennsylvania Company for Insurances on Lives and Granting Annuities, Philadelphia.
Pennsylvania Company for Banking and Trust.
Philadelphia. First National Bank.
First Pennsylvania Banking and Trust Company.
First Pennsylvania Bank N. A.

Bank of Osaka
see
Ōsaka Ginkō.

Bank of Papua New Guinea.
Report and financial statements.
⌈Port Moresby⌉ Bank of Papua New Guinea.
v. ill. 24 cm. annual.
Report year ends June 30.
1. Papua—Economic conditions—Periodicals. 2. Bank of Papua New Guinea.
HC687.P3B325a 330.9'95'3 75-642957
MARC-S

Bank of Pensacola.
see Bank of Pensacola and Alabama, Georgia, and Florida Railroad Company charters. New-York, T. & C. Wood, 1835.

Bank of Pensacola and Alabama, Georgia, and Florida Railroad Company charters. — New-York : T. & C. Wood, 1835.
30, ⌈1⌉ p. : 2 fold. maps ; 25 cm.
1. Alabama, Florida and Georgia Railroad. 2. Bank of Pensacola. I. Bank of Pensacola. II. Alabama, Florida and Georgia Railroad Company.
HE2791.A326 1835 77-353264
77 MARC

Bank of St. John.
see Saint John the Baptist Parish on the corridor of history. Baton Rouge, La., N. C. Ferachi, c1974.

Bank of Sierra Leone.
Annual report and statement of accounts. 1964-
⌈Freetown⌉
v. 25 cm.
1. Bank of Sierra Leone.
HG3399.S52B33a 332.1'1'09664 73-643611
MARC-S

Bank of Sierra Leone.
Balance of payments.
⌈Freetown⌉
v. 19 x 30-26 cm.
Vols. for 19 -68 include figures from 1963; 1969- from 1965.
1. Balance of payments—Sierra Leone.
HG3883.S53B35a 382.1'7'09664 73-644047
MARC-S

FU

Bank of Sierra Leone.
Bank of Sierra Leone : the first 10 years. — ⌈Freetown⌉ : The Bank, 1974.
20 p. ; 21 cm.
"References": p. 19-20.
1. Bank of Sierra Leone.
HG3399.S52B33 1974 332.1'1'09664 76-370894
76 MARC

Bank of Sierra Leone.
Report of the Governors to the Board of Directors of the Bank of Sierra Leone.
⌈Freetown⌉ Bank of Sierra Leone.
v. 20 cm. annual.
Report year ends June 30.
1. Bank of Sierra Leone.
HG3399.S49A25 332.1'1'09664 75-643804
MARC-S

Bank of Sierra Leone.
Report of the working party on capital availability and Sierra Leonean entrepreneurship under the chairmanship of Dr. N.A. Cox-George. Freetown ⌈1969?⌉
38 p.
Cover title.
1. Economic development—Sierra Leone.
MBU NUC73-126323

Bank of Sierra Leone.
Symposium ; the impact of central banking on a developing economy : 10 years of central banking in Sierra Leone. -- ⌈Freetown⌉ 1975.
169 p.
1. Banks and banking--Sierra Leone.
MBU NUC77-86590

Bank of Sierra Leone. Research Dept.
Charts on the economy of Sierra Leone. -- ⌈Freetown⌉ : The Dept., 1975.
10 p., ⌈33⌉ leaves of plates : ill.
1. Sierra Leone--Economic conditions.
I. Title.
ViBlbV NUC77-86657

Bank of Sierra Leone. Research Dept.
West African economic co-operation-problems and possibilities. [Freetown] 1972.
104 p.
1. Economic development–West Africa, (Br)
2. Economic development–French West.
MBU NUC73-113624

Bank of Sudan
see Bank al-Sudan.

Bank of Taiwan (Founded 1946)
see T'ai-wan yin hang.

Bank of Tanzania.
Economic report.
Dar es Salaam.
v. 25 cm.
1. Bank of Tanzania.
HG3414.T3 332.1'1'09678 73-647297
MARC-S

Bank of Tanzania. Research and Statistics Dept.
Current report. no. 1-
⌈Dar es Salaam⌉ 1971-
no. 34 cm.
1. Bank of Tanzania. 2. Tanzania—Economic conditions.
HG3414.T33A3 354'.678'00825 72-620213

Bank of Thailand
see Thanākhān hāeng Prathēt Thai.

Bank of the Republic of Bogota.
see Banco de la República, Bogota.

Bank of the Ryukyus
see
Ryūkyū Ginkō.

Bank of the Southwest National Association. Industrial Development Dept.
Economic growth trends of Texas counties; past, present & future. Prepared by Industrial Development Dept., Banking Relations Division, Bank of the Southwest. Houston [1970]
1 v. (various pagings) map., chiefly tables. 28 cm.
On cover: Special report.
1. Texas–Econ. condit. I. Title.
TxU NUC76-32551

Bank of the Southwest National Association. Industrial Development Dept.
The Houston story '70. Houston, c1971.
200 p. illus., maps, facsims. 28 cm.
1. Houston, Tex.–Comm. 2. Houston, Tex.–Indus. I. Title.
TxU NUC76-32552

Bank of Tokyo, ltd.
see Tōkyō Ginkō.

Bank of Uganda.
Annual report.
[Kampala]
v. illus. 26 cm.
Report year ends June 30.
1. Bank of Uganda. 2. Uganda—Economic conditions—Yearbooks.
HG3399.U34B323 354'.676'100825 73-640034

Bank of Uganda.
Quarterly bulletin.
[Kampala]
v. 26 cm.
Began in 1969. Cf. New serial titles.
1. Uganda—Economic conditions—Periodicals.
HC517.U2B28 330.9'676'104 72-626861

Bank of Virginia (Chartered 1922)
The Morris Plan Bank of Richmond was incorporated in 1922. In 1928 the name was changed to Morris Plan Bank of Virginia; in 1945, to Bank of Virginia; and in 1972, to Bank of Virginia-Central.
Works by this body published before the change of name in 1972 are found under
Bank of Virginia (Chartered 1922)
Works published after that change of name are found under
Bank of Virginia-Central.
74-225886

Bank of Virginia-Central.
The Morris Plan Bank of Richmond was incorporated in 1922. In 1928 the name was changed to Morris Plan Bank of Virginia; in 1945, to Bank of Virginia; and in 1972, to Bank of Virginia-Central.
Works by this body published before the change of name in 1972 are found under
Bank of Virginia (Chartered 1922)
Works published after that change of name are found under
Bank of Virginia-Central.
74-225887

Bank of Washington
see National Bank of Washington.

Bank of Zambia.
Ten years of banking in Zambia : a publication / by Bank of Zambia. -- [Lusaka?] : The Bank, [1975?]
22 p. ; 14 x 22 cm.
1. Banks and banking, Central--Zambia. I. Title.
CtY-E DLC NUC77-86593

Bank Officials' Association, Australian
see Australian Bank Officials' Association.

Bank or no bank. [Washington, Published by Order of a Committee of the Democratic Members of Congress, 1844]
1 card (2 sides). 7.5 x 12.5 cm. (Slavery pamphlets)
Caption title.
At head of title: No. 9.
Micro-opaque. Louisville, Ky., Lost Cause Press, 1966.
Collation of the original: 8 p.
1. Independent treasury. I. Committee of the Democratic Members of Congress.
PSt NUC76-20636

Bank Pembangunan Daerah Djawa Timur.
Laporan.
[Surabaja] Sekretariat D. P. R. D. G. R. Propinsi Djawa Timur.
v. 33 cm.
1. Bank Pembangunan Doerah Djawa Timur.
HG4517.B257 71-941375

Bank Pembangunan Daerah Sulawesi Selatan Tenggara.
Laporan—Bank Pembangunan Daerah Sulawesi Selatan Tenggara.
Makassar.
v. 24 cm.
1. Bank Pembangunan Daerah Sulawesi Selatan Tenggara.
HG188.I 7B36a 74-645080 MARC-S

Bank Pembangunan Indonesia.
Berita Bank Pembangunan Indonesia. no 1-
Djakarta, 1962-
no. 27 cm.
Added title, Oct. 1962- : Press release.
1. Bank Pembangunan Indonesia. 2. Development banks—Indonesia—Periodicals. I. Bank Pembangunan Indonesia. Press release.
HG3304.B36a 74-648640 MARC-S

Bank Pembangunan Indonesia.
Operations of Bank Pembangunan Indonesia.
[Jakarta, Research Dept., Bank Pembangunan Indonesia]
v. 24 cm. semiannual.
1. Bank Pembangunan Indonesia. I. Bank Pembangunan Indonesia. Research Dept.
HG4517.B262a 75-645703 MARC-S

Bank Pembangunan Indonesia. Press release
see Bank Pembangunan Indonesia. Berita Bank Pembangunan Indonesia. Djakarta, 1962-

Bank Pembangunan Indonesia.
Statement of condition, December 31, 1972 and March 31, 1973. [Jakarta, Issued by Public Relations Division, Development Bank of Indonesia, 1973]
[10] p. 22 x 10 cm.
Cover title.
1. Bank Pembangunan Indonesia.
NIC NUC76-82962

Bank Pembangunan Indonesia. Research Dept.
see Bank Pembangunan Indonesia. Operations of Bank Pembangunan Indonesia. [Jakarta]

Bank Pertanian Malaysia.
Lapuran tahunan—Bank Pertanian Malaysia.
[Kuala Lampur]
v. illus. 24 cm.
English and Malay.
1. Bank Pertanian Malaysia. 2. Agricultural credit—Malaysia.
HG3300.6.A8B344a 74-644530 MARC-S

Bank protection bulletin.
Washington, American Bankers Association.
v. illus. 28 cm. monthly.
Continues Protective bulletin issued by the American Bankers Association.
1. Bank protection—United States—Periodicals. 2. Checks—United States—Periodicals. 3. Forgery—United States—Periodicals. I. American Bankers Association.
HG1698.B36 332.1'7 73-642672
ISSN 0091-0392 MARC-S

Bank Public Relations and Marketing Association. Research Committee.
A management guide to public relations. With a foreword by Herbert V. Prochnow and an introduction by John P. Anderson. Chicago, Financial Public Relations Association [1963]
xiv, 153 p. 24 cm.
1. Public relations—Banks and banking. I. Title.
CoU NUC73-2184

Bank Rakjat Indonesia.
In 1960 Bank Rakjat Indonesia and Bank Tani Nelajan merged to form Bank Koperasi, Tani dan Nelajan. In 1965 the name of the latter was changed to Bank Negara Indonesia Unit II, which in 1968 split into Bank Raqjat Indonesia and Bank Ekspor Impor Indonesia.
Works by Bank Rakjat Indonesia, including those by the related body, Algemeene Volkscredietbank, are found under the latest name: Bank Rakjat Indonesia.
Works by the other bodies are found under the following headings according to the name used at the time of publication:

Bank Tani Nelajan, p. t.
Bank Koperasi, Tami dan Nelajan.
Bank Negara Indonesia Unit II.
Bank Ekspor Impor Indonesia.

Bank Rakyat Indonesia.
Pedoman statistik perkreditan Bank Rakjat Indonesia. Djakarta, Kantor Besar Bank Rakjat Indonesia, 1969.
98 l. forms. 24 cm.
Includes bibliographical references.
1. Credit—Indonesia. 2. Banks and banking—Indonesia. I. Title.
HG3729.I 52B36 1969 74-941036

Bank secrecy act. — New York : Practising Law Institute, c1976.
144 p. (p. 142-144 blank) ; 22 cm. — (Corporate law and practice course handbook series ; no. 202)
"Prepared for distribution at the Bank secrecy act workshop."
"B4-4567."
Includes bibliographical references.
1. Banks and banking—Records and correspondence. 2. Confidential communications—Banking—United States. 3. Banking law—United States. I. New York (City). Practising Law Institute. II. Series.
KF1030.R3B3 346'.73'082 76-1521
76 MARC

Bank Sentral
see
Bank Indonesia.

Bank Simpanan Pejabat Pos Negeri[2] Tanah Melayu.
Laporan dan penyata tahunan. 1967-
[Kuala Lumpur]
v. in 25 cm.
Added t. p., 1967- Report and accounts.
In Malay and English.
HG1956.M4B314 72-623941
rev

Bank Sotsialisticheskoĭ Respubliki Rumynii
see
Banca Naţională a Republicii Socialiste România.

Bank Spółdzielczy w Pogorzeli.
Sto lat Banku Spółdzielczego w Pogorzeli, 1872-1972. [Jednińwke opracował Aleksander Jazdon] Pogorzela, 1972.
74 p. illus., ports. (Its Jednodniówka)
Includes bibliography.
1. Bank Spółdzielczy w Pogorzeli. 2. Banks and banking, Cooperative—Poland. I. Jazdon, Aleksander, ed. II. Title.
MiEM NUC76-93114

Bank Street College of Education, New York. Bulletin
see Winsor, Charlotte B comp. Experimental schools revisited... New York, Agathon Press [1973]

Bank Street College of Education, New York.
Uptown, downtown. Senior editor: Irma Simonton Black... Illustrated by Ron Becker [and others] New York, Macmillan, London, Collier-Macmillan [c1965]
191 p. col. illus. 24 cm. (Bank Street readers)
1. Readers—1950- I. Black, Irma (Simonton) 1906- ed. II. Title. III. Series.
MB NUC73-2182

Bank Street College of Education, New York
see Manual on organization... 2d ed. [New York, c1971]

Bank Street College of Education, New York
see Merrill, Jean. The toothpaste millionaire. Boston, Houghton Mifflin [c1972]

Bank Street College of Education Conference on Environment and Children, New York? 1971?
Children and the environment, Lucy Sprague Mitchell Memorial Conference. New York, 1971.
90 p. 22 cm.
1. Environmental policy–Study and teaching–U.S. I. Title.
ICD NUC76-93164

Bank Tani Nelajan, p. t.
In 1960 Bank Rakjat Indonesia and Bank Tani Nelajan merged to form Bank Koperasi, Tani dan Nelajan. In 1965 the name of the latter was changed to Bank Negara Indonesia Unit II, which in 1968 split into Bank Rakjat Indonesia and Bank Ekspor Impor Indonesia.
Works by Bank Rakjat Indonesia, including those by the related body, Algemeene Volkscredietbank, are found under the latest name: Bank Rakjat Indonesia.
Works by the other bodies are found under the following headings according to the name used at the time of publication:

Bank Tani Nelajan, p. t.
Bank Koperasi, Tani dan Nelajan.
Bank Negara Indonesia Unit II.
Bank Ekspor Impor Indonesia.

The bank torpedo... New-York, Printed by M'Carty & White, 1810 [1973]
see under [Davies, Benjamin]

Bank van Lening te Amsterdam.

For works by this body issued under its later name see

Stads-Kredietbank voor Roerende Zaken te Amsterdam.

Bank wage-hour and personnel report.
see Bank Wage-Hour and Personnel Service. Bank wage-hour and personnel service ... Washington, Bank Wage-Hour and Personnel Service, c1975 [i.e. 1950]-

Bank Wage-Hour and Personnel Service.
Bank wage-hour and personnel service : an up-to-date, loose-leaf compilation of all the Federal laws, regulations, rulings, relating to the Fair labor standards act, the Portal-to-portal act, the Federal equal pay law, the Age discrimination in employment act, the Federal fair employment practices act, executive orders on equal employment practices applicable to banks, plus separate sections concerning personnel relations and payroll taxes / edited for banks and similar institutions. — Washington : Bank Wage-Hour and Personnel Service, c1975 ₍i.e. 1950₎-
2 v. ; 25 cm.
Loose-leaf for updating.
Published in 1949 under title: Bank wage-hour labor service.
Includes Bank wage-hour and personnel report, v. 26, no. 7- Apr. 15, 1976-

1. Bank employees—United States. I. Bank wage-hour and personnel report.
KF3505.B25B32 1950 344'.73'012813321 77-364578
77 MARC

Bank wage-hour labor report
see also
Bank wage-hour and personnel report.

Bańka, Józef.
Technika a środowisko psychiczne człowieka; wprowadzenie do zagadnień eutyfroniki. ₍Wyd. 1.₎ Warszawa, Wydawnictwa Naukowo-Techniczne, 1973.
352 p. illus. 22 cm. zł55.00
Summary in English and Russian.
Bibliography: p. ₍341₎-347.
1. Technology—Social aspects. I. Title.
T14.5.B33 73-218942

Bańka, Józef, ed.
see Księga pamiątkowa ku czci księdza profesora doktora Alfonsa Schletza... Kraków ₍Instytut Wydawn. Nasza Przeszłość₎ 1971.

Bańka, Józef
see Polska myśl filozoficzna i spoleczna. Warszawa, Ksiazka i Wiedza, 1973-

Banka, Józef, ed.
see Technika á środowisko człowieka. Poznań [Wydawn. Naukowe Uniwersytetu im. Adama Mickiewicza] 1972.

Banka dat v informačních systémech : seminář poř. Čes. komitétem pro věd. řízení ve spolupráci s Federálním stat. úřadem ve dnech 20.-22. listopadu 1973 : ₍sborník přednášek₎. — Praha : Český komitét pro vědecké řízení, 1973.
345 p. : ill. ; 20 cm. Cz 73
Czech or Slovak.
Includes bibliographies.
1. Information storage and retrieval systems—Congresses. 2. Data base management—Congresses. I. Český komitét pro vědecké řízení.
Z699.A1B35 1973 75-403519

Banka ve ticaret hukuku dergisi.
₍Ankara₎ Banka ve Ticaret Hukuku Araştırma Enstitüsü.
v. 24 cm.
1. Commercial law—Turkey—Periodicals. 2. Banking law—Turkey—Periodicals. I. Ankara. Üniversite. Banka ve Ticaret Hukuku Araştırma Enstitüsü.
K2.A56 74-647492
MARC-S

Bankabehari Chakravorti
see
Chakravorti, Bankabehari, 1927-

Bankakademiet
see Melsom, Per, 1923- Pettslære. Bankakademiet, [1971-

Bankakademiet. Høyere Avdeling.
Banklaeren. Oslo, 1967-68. [v.1,3:1968]
4 v. 29 cm.
1. Banks and banking—Study and teaching.
I. Title.
OkU NUC75-96801

Baṅkaṭa Bihārī.
(Añjurī bhara pīṛā)
अंजुरी भर पीड़ा; ₍कविता संकलन. लेखक₎ बंकट बिहारी 'पागल.' ₍1.. संस्करण. जयपुर, हिन्दी प्रचार परिषद; वितरक आकाश दीप प्रकाशन, 1972₎
112 p. 22 cm. Rs6.00
In Hindi.

I. Title.

PK2098.13.A545A82 72-907224

Bankbetriebslehre. — Wiesbaden : Betriebswirtschaftlicher Verlag Gabler, 1975.
2 v. : ill. ; 25 cm. — (Bank-Enzyklopädie ; Bd. 2-3) GFR75-A (v. 1)
Includes bibliographical references and index.
CONTENTS: 1. Strukturlehre, Kapitalbeschaffung der Kreditinstitute, Aktivgeschäft und Dienstleistungsgeschäft.—2. Rechnungswesen, Bankpolitik, Spezialgebiete.
ISBN 3-409-46001-1 (v. 1) : DM150.00 (v. 1)
1. Banks and banking—Germany, West—Handbooks, manuals, etc. I. Series.
HG1605.B346 75-520829
76₍r77₎rev MARC

Banke, Lars.
Ulcussygdommens epidemiologi / Lars Banke. — København : F. A. D. L., 1975.
178 p. : ill. ; 25 cm. D 75-11
Thesis—Copenhagen.
Summary in English.
Bibliography: p. 161-172.
Includes index.
ISBN 87-7437-439-7 : kr34.50
1. Peptic ulcer—Statistics. 2. Denmark—Statistics, Medical. I. Title.
₍DNLM : 1. Peptic ulcer—Occurrence—Denmark. W4 C78 1975₎
[RC821.B28] 75-595085
Shared Cataloging with DNLM

Banke, Niels.
Socialismens historie : fra Babeuf til Mao Tse-tung / Niels Banke. — ₍København₎ : Gyldendal, 1974.
212 p. ; 22 cm. D 74-38
Bibliography: p. ₍201₎-₍202₎
Includes index.
ISBN 87-00-78181-9 : kr42.00
1. Socialism—History. I. Title.
HX21.B26 74-356084

(Bankei Zenji zenshū)
盤珪禪師全集 / 赤尾龍治編. — 東京：大蔵出版, 昭和51 ₍1976₎
xii, 945 p., ₍4₎ leaves of plates : ill. ; 22 cm. Ja ***
"盤珪法脈図" published as suppl. (1 leaf) and inserted at end.
CONTENTS: 法語集—伝記逸話集—詩歌及書翰集—資料集—資料解説—師伝·弟子伝·居士大姉伝—盤珪派寺院名簿—盤珪禅師遺跡案内記
¥1500

1. Eitaku, 1622-1693. 2. Priests, Zen—Japan—Biography. 3. Zen Buddhism—Sermons. I. Eitaku, 1622-1693. II. Akao, Ryūji.
BQ9399.E577B36 76-804469

Bankel, Stefan Rudolf.
The attitudes and time period predictions of public school administrators and teachers in Connecticut toward selected educational futures. ₍Storrs, Conn.₎ 1974.
3, xxvi, 418 l. tables.
Typescript.
Thesis (Ph.D.)—University of Connecticut.
Bibliography: leaves 304-309.
1. School superintendents and principals—Connecticut. 2. Teachers—Connecticut. 3. Educational innovations—Connecticut. I. Title.
CtU NUC75-20625

Die Banken im Spannungsfeld wirtschaftlicher Veränderungen : Beiträge aus der Bankpraxis / Josef Taus ... ₍et al.₎ ; ₍Hrsg., Adriano Passardi₎. — Bern ; Stuttgart : P. Haupt, c1975.
142 p. : ill. ; 23 cm. — (Bankwirtschaftliche Forschungen ; Bd. 28)
Sw75-A-4304
A revision in part of papers delivered at the 4th in a series of biennial lectures held at the Universität Zürich during the winter semester, 1974/75.
Includes bibliographical references.
28.00F
1. Banks and banking—Addresses, essays, lectures. 2. Banks and banking—Switzerland—Addresses, essays, lectures. I. Taus, Josef. II. Passardi, Adriano. III. Series.
HG1526.B27 Bd. 28 75-516551
₍HG1572₎ *75 MARC

Banker, James Roderick, 1938-
Giovanni di Bonandrea's ars dictaminis treatise and the doctrine of invention in the Italian rhetorical tradition of the thirteenth and early fourteenth centuries. ₍n.p.₎ 1971 ₍i.e. 1972₎
vi, 368 l. 29 cm.
Thesis (Ph.D.)—University of Rochester.
Vita.
"Selected bibliography": leaves 312-328.
1. Bonandrea, Giovanni di, 1250?-1290. 2. Rhetoric, Medieval. I. Title.
NRU NUC73-34512

Banker, James Roderick, 1938-
Giovanni di Bonandrea's Ars dictaminis treatise and the doctrine of invention in the Italian rhetorical tradition of the thirteenth and early fourteenth centuries. ₍n.p.₎ 1972.
vi, 368 l.
Thesis—University of Rochester.
Bibliography: leaves 312-328.
Microfilm (positive) Ann Arbor, Mich., University Microfilms, 1972. 1 reel. (Publication no. 18801)
NNC NUC74-116662

Banker, John
see Linguistic Circle of Saigon. Mon-Khmer studies. [Saigon] 1944-

Banker, John C
Personal finances for ministers, by John C. Banker. Rev. and updated ed. Philadelphia, Westminster Press ₍1973₎
125 p. forms. 19 cm. $1.65
1. Clergy—Finance, Personal. I. Title.
BV4397.B3 1973 332'.024 73-5394
ISBN 0-664-24972-8 MARC

Banker, Lynne.
Rain; poems. ₍New York, Theo Publication, c1967₎
₍34₎ p. 22 cm.
Cover title.
I. Title.
PS3552.A478R3 811'.5'4 74-190871
MARC

Banker, Marshall David.
Observability and controllability of two player discrete systems, and quadratic control and game problems, by Marshall D. Banker. ₍Stanford, Calif.₎ 1971.
iv, 172 l.
Thesis (Ph.D.)—Stanford University.
Bibliography: leaves 170-172.
1. Differential games. I. Title.
CSt NUC73-34519

Banker, Navin, 1941-
(Parāī ḍāḷanuṃ paṅkhī)
પરાઈ ડાળનું પંખી. ₍લેખક₎ નવીન બૅન્કર. અમદાવાદ, ભારતી સાહિત્ય સંઘ ₍1971₎
8, 215 p. 19 cm. Rs6.00
In Gujarati.
Short stories.

I. Title.

PK1859.B355P3 70-928209

Banker, Robert
see Grout, Roy A Beute und Biene. München, Ehrenwirth [1973, c1963]

The Banker.
₍Dar es Salaam₎ National Bank of Commerce, United Republic of Tanzania.
v. illus. 25 cm.
1. National Bank of Commerce (Tanzania) 2. Tanzania—Economic conditions. I. National Bank of Commerce (Tanzania)
HG3414.N384B35 330.9'678'04 73-644051
MARC-S

The Banker
see Financial centres of the world: Zurich. ₍London, 1970₎

The Banker
see Pigott, William, 1927- The monetarist controversy in the United States. ₍n.p.₎ Graduate School of Business Administration, University of Washington ₍1973?₎

Banker & businessman. v. 1-
Oct. 1971-
₍Karachi, National Publications Service₎
v. 29 cm. monthly
1. Banks and banking — Pakistan — Periodicals. 2. Banks and banking—Periodicals. 3. Business—Periodicals. 4. Pakistan—Economic conditions—Periodicals.
HG3290.6.A5B35 332.1'09549'1 72-930565
MARC-S

The Banker and hedging : ₍papers... presented at a Bankers Seminar sponsored by the Chicago Mercantile Exchange, May 29-30, 1975₎ / ₍Everette B. Harris... et al.]. -- Chicago : : Chicago Mercantile Exchange, 1975.
64 p. : ill. ; 21 cm.
1. Commodity exchanges - U.S. I. Harris, Everette B. II. Chicago. Mercantile Exchange.
MH-BA NUC77-96791

Banker Research Unit.
see An analysis of banking structures in the European Community. London, Banker Research Unit, 1973, 1974 printing.

Banker Research Unit.
see Who is where in world banking 1976-7 ... London, Banker Research Unit, [1976]

Bankern for Nørresundby og omegn
see Kristensen, Johannes Evald Tang, 1906- Nørresundbys historie i billeder. Nørresundby, 1973.

Bankers and beef. — New York : Arno Press, 1975.
86, 222 p., [5] leaves of plates : ill. ; 23 cm. — (American farmers and the rise of agribusiness)
Reprint of Financing the western cattle industry, by C. I. Bray, published by the Colorado Experiment Station, Colorado Agricultural College, Fort Collins, Colo., as Bulletin 338, 1928; and of The beef bonanza, by J. S. Brisbin, published by Lippincott, Philadelphia, 1881.
Includes index.
ISBN 0-405-06763-1
1. Cattle trade—United States. 2. Cattle trade—Colorado. 3. Agricultural credit—United States. 4. Agricultural credit—Colorado. I. Bray, Charles Iseard, 1882-1950. Financing the western cattle industry. 1975. II. Brisbin, James Sanks, 1837-1892. The beef bonanza. 1975. III. Series. IV. Series: Colorado. Agricultural Experiment Station, Fort Collins. Bulletin ; 338.
HD9433.U5C62 1975 338.1'7'6200973 74-30618
75 MARC

Bankers' Association for Foreign Trade.
Preparing a bank's written international lending policy / the Bankers' Association for Foreign Trade, Robert Morris Associates. — Washington, D.C. : the Association, c1977.
iv, 42 p. ; 23 cm.
Includes bibliographical references.
$6.00
1. Bank loans. 2. Loans, Foreign. I. Robert Morris Associates. II. Title.
HG1641.B36 1977 332.1'5 77-74628
77 MARC

Bankers' Association for Foreign Trade.
see Offshore lending by U.S. commercial banks. 1st ed. Washington, Bankers' Association for Foreign Trade, [1975]

Bankers handbook for Asia. 1976-
[Hongkong] Asian Finance Publications.
v. ill. 25 cm. annual.
"A total guide to banks and finance companies in Asia."
1. Banks and banking—Asia—Directories. 2. Banks and banking—Asia—Periodicals.
HG3251.B36 332.1'095 77-649440
MARC-S

Bankers' management handbook / editor-in-chief, Richard Handscombe. — London ; New York : McGraw-Hill, c1976.
xxii, 457 p. : ill. ; 26 cm.
Includes bibliographical references and index.
ISBN 0-07-084464-X : £12.95
1. Bank management—Handbooks, manuals, etc. I. Handscombe, Richard.
HG1615.B354 658'.91'3321 76-3632
76 MARC

Bankers National Investing Corp.
Beneficial Loan Society and Bankers National Investing Corp. were merged in 1929 to form the Beneficial Corporation. This was dissolved in 1968. In 1970, the Beneficial Finance Company (established in 1945 as a subsidiary of the Beneficial Corporation) changed its name to Beneficial Corporation, adopting the name of the former parent corporation.
Works by these bodies are found under the following headings according to the name used at the time of publication:
Beneficial Loan Society.
Bankers National Investing Corp.
Beneficial Finance Company.
Beneficial Corporation.

Bankers Research Institute
see Special study of unique private bankers ... Zurich [1971]

Bankers schools directory.
Washington, Bank Personnel Division, American Bankers Association.
v. 28 cm.
Key title: Bankers schools directory, ISSN 0145-5850
1. Banks and banking—United States—Directories. I. American Bankers Association. Bank Personnel Division.
HG1581.B34 332.1'07'1173 76-649212
MARC-S

Bankers' Training College
see
Reserve Bank of India. Bankers' Training College.

Bankers Trust Company, New York.
Bankers Trust 1972 study of employee savings and thrift plans. New York [c1972]
254 p. 28 cm.
1. Non-wage payments. 2. Incentives in industry. I. Title.
NNC PP NUC75-48083

Bankers Trust Company, New York.
Credit and capital markets, 1976. -- [New York : s.n., 1976]
13 p., 30 tables ; 25 cm.
1. Credit--United States. 2. Government lending--United States. 3. Finance--United States. I. Title.
NNU NUC77-88270

Bankers Trust Company, New York.
Federal, New York State and New York City individual income tax specimen returns; step by step explanations with filled-in forms for filing in 1973. Englewood Cliffs, N. J., [Prentice-Hall, 1973]
96 p. forms. 27 cm.
Cover title: Income tax guide.
1. Income tax—United States—Popular works. 2. Income tax—New York (State) — Popular works. 3. Income tax — New York (City)—Popular works. I. Title. II. Title: Income tax guide.
KF6369.6.B35 1973 343'.73'052 73-174875
MARC

Bankers Trust Company, New York.
Liberia. New York [196-?]
18 p. illus. 28 cm.
1. Liberia—Economic conditions. 2. Investments, foreign—Liberia. I. Title.
WU NUC75-48082

Bankers Trust Company, New York.
New York. [New York, 1961]
1 v. (chiefly illus.) 23 x 31 cm.
1. New York (City)—Description—Views.
NN NUC76-75699

Bankers Trust Company, New York.
New York [2d ed. New York, 1963]
1 v. (chiefly illus.) 23 x 31 cm.
1. New York (City)—Description—Views.
NN NUC76-75698

Bankers Trust Company, New York.
The private pension controversy. New York [1973]
72 p. col. illus.
Includes bibliographical references.
1. Pensions—U.S. 2. Pension trusts—U.S. I. Title.
MH-BA NNC-L OU NUC74-116644

Bankers Trust Company, New York.
Study of corporate pension plans. 10th-
[New York] Bankers Trust, 1975-
no. 28 cm.
Continues: Bankers Trust Company, New York. Study of industrial retirement plans.
ISSN 0360-2117
1. Old age pensions—United States. I. Title.
HD7106.U5B33 331.2'52'0973 75-647969
MARC-S

Bankers Trust Company, New York.
Study of employee savings and thrift plans. New York, 1972.
255 p. illus.
1. Non-wage payments—U. S.—Directories. I. Title.
MH-BA IU NUC73-113617

Bankers Trust Company, New York.
Washington agencies that help to finance foreign trade. 5th ed. [New York, 1967]
19 p. 28 cm.
1. Banks and banking, International. 2. Economic assistance, American. I. Title.
HG3881.B35 1967 332.1'5 74-184366
MARC

Bankers Trust Company of Detroit.
Suggested aids for drawing wills and trusts; a handbook for lawyers. Comments on perpetuities and suspension of powers, contributed by Lewis M. Simes. [Detroit, 1947]
iii, 112 p. 24 cm.
1. Wills—Michigan—Forms. 2. Trusts and trustees—Michigan—Forms. I. Title.
KFM4344.A65B3 346'.774'054 74-159760
MARC

The Banker's world directory.
[Bruxelles] Common Market Publications.
v. 18 cm.
English, French, German, and Spanish.
1. Banks and banking—Directories.
HG1536.B33 332.1'025 74-646360
MARC-S

Bankert, Peter J
An analysis of the operation of the Pediatric Outpatient Division of the New York Hospital, by Peter J. Bankert, Steven J. Baran [and] Jeffry M. Weberling. [Ithaca, N.Y.] 1973.
1 v. (various pagings) illus., maps. 29 cm.
"A project report presented to the Faculty of the Graduate School of Cornell University in partial fulfillment of the requirements for the degree of Master of Engineering (Industrial)".
1. New York Hospital. Pediatric Outpatient Division. 2. Hospitals—Cost of operation—Case studies. I. Baran, Steven J. II. Weberling, Jeffry M.
NIC NUC75-18549

Bankert, Stanley Fred.
Proton activation analysis of water samples. [Davis, Calif.] 1972.
107 l. illus.
Thesis (Ph.D.)—University of California, Davis.
CU-A NUC74-116661

Bankes, George.
Peru before Pizarro / George Bankes. — Oxford [Eng.] : Phaidon, 1977.
208 p. : ill. (some col.); 24 cm. GB***
Bibliography: p. 200.
Includes index.
ISBN 0-7148-1784-8. ISBN 0-7148-1785-6 pbk. : £4.95
1. Indians of South America—Peru—Antiquities. 2. Peru—Antiquities. I. Title.
F3429.B24 1977 985 77-75402
77 MARC

Bankes, Joyce.
The early records of the Bankes Family at Winstanley. Edited by Joyce Bankes and Eric Kerridge. Manchester, Printed for the Chetham Society, 1973.
viii, 113 p. ports. 22 cm. (Chetham Society, Manchester, Eng. Remains, historical and literary, connected with palatime counties and Lancaster and Chester, ser. 3, v. 21)
AAP CaOTP ICN InU NUC74-116643

Ein Bankgebäude heute : Hamburgische Landesbank u. Landesbank Galerie / Red. u. Hrsg., Fritz Rafeiner. — München : Callwey, 1975.
118 p. : 210 ill. ; 29 cm. GFR76-A
ISBN 3-7667-0335-8 : DM48.00
1. Hamburgische Landesbank, Girozentrale. I. Rafeiner, Fritz.
NA6243.H35H352 76-460777
76 MARC

Bankhaus Gebrüder Bethmann
see
Bethmann, Gebrüder, Frankfurt am Main.

Bankhead, Reid E., joint author.
see Pearson, Glenn Laurentz. Teaching with the Book of Mormon. Rev. and enl. ed. of the book formerly published under title Doctrinal approach to the Book of Mormon. Salt Lake City, Bookcraft, 1976.

Bankhead, Robert Crawford, 1933-
Liturgical formulae in the New Testament. Clinton, S.C., Jacobs Press, 1971.
205, [9] p. 24 cm.
Diss.—University of Basel, 1961.
Bibliography: p. [207]-[213]
1. Bible. N. T.—Criticism, interpretation, etc. 2. Liturgics—History. 3. Liturgies, Early Christian. I. Title.
NIC NUC76-75683

Bankhead, William H
Administrative policies and procedures for large multi-purpose arenas on university campuses... [n.p.] 1975.
xi, 121 l. 29 cm.
Thesis (Ed.D.)--Louisiana State University. Vita.
Bibliography: leaves 73-76.
Includes abstract.
1. Universities and colleges--Buildings. 2. College sports--Organization and administration. I. Title.
LU NUC77-89877

Bankhead, William H.
see Louisiana. State University and Agricultural and Mechanical College. Assembly Center. Self-study for Southern Association of Colleges and Schools. [Baton Rouge] 1972.

Bankhofer, Hademar.
Gespenster, Geister, Aberglaube; Okkultismus in unserer Zeit. ⌜Bayreuth⌝ Hestia ⌜c1974⌝
406 p. 22 cm. GFR***
1. Occult sciences. 2. Psychical research. I. Title.
BF1033.B34 74-336844
ISBN 3-7770-0122-9

Bankhofer, Hademar.
Gespenster, Geister, Aberglaube : Okkultismus in unserer Zeit / Hademar Bankhofer. — Rastatt : Zauberkreis-Verlag, 1976.
156 p. ; 18 cm. GFR76-A
DM2.80
1. Occult sciences. 2. Psychical research. I. Title.
BF1033.B34 1976 133'.09'04 77-454021
77 MARC

Bankhofer, Hademar.
Pepi und seine Prominenten : aus dem Leben des Star-Archivars Josef Treitl / Hademar Bankhofer. — Klosterneuburg ; Wien ; Bad Reichenhall ; Baden bei Zürich : Aktuell-Verl., ⌜1976⌝
69 p., ⌜4⌝ leaves of plates : ill., ports. ; 21 x 22 cm. Au76-5-199
S99.00
1. Treitl, Josef, 1921- I. Title.
PN1583.T68B3 76-461304
*76 MARC

Bankhofer, Hademar.
Tiere, Stars und Anekdoten. Geschichten um berühmte Tiere u. prominente Leute. (Photos: Ralph Hadley ⌜u. a.⌝) (Klosterneuburg / Wien) Aktuell-Verl. ⌜1972⌝.
186 p. illus. 21 cm. Au 73-1/2-140
S139.00
1. Pets. I. Title.
SF416.B36 75-582914

Banki, Ivan S
Dictionary of supervision and management; authoritative, comprehensive ⌜by⌝ Ivan S. Banki. ⌜Los Angeles, Calif.⌝ Systems Research ⌜1974⌝
208 p. 24 cm.
Bibliography: p. 203-208.
1. Management—Dictionaries. 2. Supervision of employees—Dictionaries. 3. Employees, Training of—Dictionaries. I. Title.
HD19.B33 658'.003 73-87439
ISBN 0-912352-02-7 MARC

Banki, Ivan S
Dictionary of supervision and management : authoritative, comprehensive / Ivan S. Banki. — Los Angeles : Systems Research, c1976.
276 p. ; 24 cm.
Bibliography: p. 270-276.
ISBN 0-912352-03-5
1. Management—Dictionaries. 2. Personnel management—Dictionaries. I. Title.
HD19.B33 1976 658'.003 74-12933
76 MARC

Banki, Judith.
Christian responses to the Yom Kippur War; implications for Christian-Jewish relations, by Judith Hershcopf Banki. New York, American Jewish Committee, Institute of Human Relations [1974]
122 p. 28 cm.
1. Israel-Arab War, 1973—Religious aspects. I. Title.
OCH NUC76-23707

Banki, Judith, comp.
Christian statements and documents bearing on Christian-Jewish relations; a compendium. New York, Interreligious Affairs Dept., American Jewish Committee ⌜1972⌝
45 p. 28 cm. $0.50
Cover title.
Bibliography: p. 45.
1. Judaism—Relations—Christianity. 2. Christianity and other religions—Judaism. 3. Israel—Foreign opinion. I. American Jewish Committee. Interreligious Affairs Dept. II. Title.
BM535.B26 74-151838
MARC

Banki, Judith.
Vatican Council II's statement on the Jews: five years later; a survey of progress and problems in implementing the Conciliar declaration in Europe, Israel, Latin America, the United States, and Canada. ⌜New York, American Jewish Committee, Institute of Human Relations, 1971⌝
31 p. 28 cm. $0.25
"⌜Data⌝ compiled by the Foreign Affairs and Interreligious Affairs Departments of the American Jewish Committee."
Includes bibliographical references.
1. Vatican Council. 2d, 1962-1965. Declaratio de Ecclesiae habitudine ad religiones non-Christianas. 2. Catholic Church — Relations—Judaism. 3. Judaism—Relations—Catholic Church. I. American Jewish Committee. Foreign Affairs Dept. II. American Jewish Committee. Interreligious Affairs Dept. III. Title.
BX830 1962.A45E27 261.2 73-170483
MARC

Bánki, Zsuzsanna.
Az István Király Múzeum gyüjteménye: római kori figurális bronz, ezüst es ólom tárgyak. La collection du Musée roi Saint Étienne: objets romains figurés en bronze, argent et plomb. Székesfehérvár, 1972.
69 p. illus. 23 cm. (Székesfehérvár, Hungary (City). István Király Múzeum. István Király Múzeum közlemenyei. B sorozat, 30 ⌜sz.⌝)
Hungarian and French.
1. Art metal-work, Roman—Székesfehérvár, Hungary (City) I. Székesfehérvár, Hungary (City). István Király Múzeum.
NN NUC76-74243

Banki-Horvath, Janos.
Vetesi szamitasok. Budapest, Mezogazdasagi Kiado, 1972.
214 p. illus.
Bibliography: p. 213.
1. Seeds. Hungary. 2. Seeds. Tables and ready reckoners. 3. Drill (Agricultural implements) I. Haffner, Andras. II. Title.
DNAL NUC74-119761

Banki-Horváth, Sandorné
see Blumauer, Aloys, 1755-1798. Blumauer Aeneis-travesztiájának Szalkay Antal-féle magyar átdolgozásához. Szeged, 1967-

(Banki i kredit razvivaiushchikhsia stran)
Банки и кредит развивающихся стран / под ред. Ю. М. Осипова. — Москва : Финансы, 1974.
223 p. ; 21 cm. USSR***
At head of title: Научно-исследовательский финансовый институт.
Includes bibliographical references.
1.05rub
1. Underdeveloped areas—Banks and banking. I. Osipov, Iurii Mikhaĭlovich, ed. II. Moscow. Nauchno-issledovatel'skiĭ finansovyĭ institut.
HG1607.R8B36 75-564069

Bankier, Joanna.
see The Other voice ... 1st ed. New York, Norton, c1976.

Bankiers, Künstler und Gelehrte : unveröffentlichte Briefe der Familie Mendelssohn aus dem 19. Jahrhundert / hrsg. und eingeleitet von Felix Gilbert. — Tübingen : J. C. B. Mohr, 1975.
lii, 328 p., ⌜12⌝ leaves of plates : 2 fold. geneal. tables (in pocket), ports ; 24 cm. — (Schriftenreihe wissenschaftlicher Abhandlungen des Leo Baeck Instituts ; 31) GFR***
Includes bibliographical references and index.
ISBN 3-16-836362-6 : DM87.00
1. Mendelssohn family. 2. Jews in Germany—Correspondence. 3. Converts from Judaism—Correspondence. 4. Germany—Politics and government—19th century—Addresses, essays, lectures. I. Gilbert, Felix, 1905- II. Series: Leo Baeck Institute of Jews from Germany. Schriftenreihe wissenchaftlicher Abhandlungen ; 31.
DS135.G5A12 74-78412
77 MARC

הבנקים ולקוחותיהם; קובץ הרצאות. ⌜תל־אביב⌝ המרכז הישראלי לניהול ⌜1965⌝
68, 3 p. 25 cm. (ניהול פיננסי, פ-23)
Cover title.
1. Banks and banking—Addresses, essays, lectures. I. Israel Management Center. II. Series: Nihul finansi, 23.
Title romanized: ha-Bankim ve-lakoḥotehem.
HG1591.B35 HE 68-4512
PL 480 : Is-5978

Bańkima Candra Sena
see
Sena, Bańkima Candra.

(Bankin no karyoku hatsudensho)
輓近の火力發電所　電氣學會編纂　⌜東京　電氣學會　昭和11 i.e. 1936⌝
608 p. illus. 23 cm.
本編は昭和七年十一月電氣學會東京支部に於て開催した第八回電氣工學專門講習會豫稿を蒐錄したものである
Includes bibliographical references.

1. Electric power-plants—Congresses. I. Denkigakkai. II. Denki Kōgaku Semmon Kōshūkai, 8th, Tokyo, 1932.
TK1041.B33 73-816029

The Banking & financial review. v. 1- Sept./Oct. 1975-
⌜Singapore, Times International (Media)⌝
v. ill. 30 cm.
"Journal for the banking, financial & industrial circles."
1. Finance — Asia — Periodicals. 2. Banks and banking — Asia — Periodicals. 3. Finance — Singapore — Periodicals. 4. Banks and banking—Singapore—Periodicals.
HG41.B38 332'.095 76-940395
MARC-S

Banking and insurance.
⌜Karachi, Sunrise Publications⌝
v. ports. 29 cm. annual.
1. Banks and banking—Yearbooks. 2. Insurance—Yearbooks.
HG1505.B335 72-939543

Banking and Securities Industry Committee.
BASIC, interindustry teamwork / ⌜compiled by Herman W. Bevis⌝. — ⌜New York⌝ : BASIC, 1974.
2 v. ; 28 cm.
Vol. 2 contains appendices.
Includes bibliographical references.
1. Clearing of securities—United States. 2. Stock transfer—United States. 3. Electronic data processing—Stocks. I. Bevis, Herman W., ed. II. Title.
HG4631.B35 1974 332'.028'54 74-82905
MARC

Banking and Securities Industry Committee.
Four uniform forms; transfer instruction, delivery ticket, comparison, reclamation form. Final report, Dec. 22, 1971. New York, 1971.
1 v. (various pagings) 28 cm.
Cover title.
1. Forms—United States. 2. Securities—United States. I. Title.
MH-L NUC73-68009

Banking and Trust Seminar, 2d, Mackinac Island, 1973
see 2nd annual Banking and Trust Seminar. Ann Arbor, Mich. [1973?]

Banking, corporation & business law newsletter.
⌜Albany, N. Y.⌝ New York State Bar Association.
v. 28 cm.
"Published for members of the New York State Bar Association's Banking, Corporation and Business Law Section."
Key title: Banking, corporation & business law newsletter, ISSN 0148-3684
1. Commercial law—New York (State)—Periodicals. 2. Commercial law—United States—Periodicals. I. New York State Bar Association. Banking, Corporation and Business Law Section.
KFN5225.A15B3 346'.73'066 77-641289
MARC-S

Banking developments in France, Belgium, Holland and Germany in the context of the evolution of the European Economic Community. A research paper by G. E. M.: Jonathan Davies [and others. London, Charter Consolidated] 1971.
36, [46] l. illus.
"Contains findings of a research project undertaken in the Spring of 1971 by four British participants at INSEAD, the European Institute of Business Adminsiatration, in Fontainebleau."
1. Banks and banking—European Economic Community countries. I. Davies, Jonathan. II. Insead.
MH-BA NUC76-17578

Banking Federation of the European Economic Community.
Report—Banking Federation of the European Economic Community.
Brussels, Banking Federation of the European Economic Community.
v. 27 cm.
1. Banking Federation of the European Economic Community. 2. Banks and banking—European Economic Community countries—Collected works. 3. Finance—European Economic Community countries—Collected works.
HG2980.5.A6B34a 332.1'5 76-642958
MARC-S

Banking for profit: the efficient use of resources: based on the seminar held at Christ's College, Cambridge, 10-16 September 1972. London, Institute of Bankers ⌜1972⌝
⌜5⌝, 131 p. 21 cm. £1.00 B 72-28358
Bibliography: p. 125-126.
1. Bank management—Addresses, essays, lectures. 2. Banks and banking—Great Britain—Addresses, essays, lectures. I. Institute of Bankers, London.
HG1615.B36 332.1'0942 73-150427
ISBN 0-85297-025-0 MARC

Banking in Australia. [Sydney, J. Sands, n.d.]
31 p. 21 cm.
The included articles appeared in "The Australian Banker", the official organ of the United Bank Officers Association and of the Bank Officials Association.
1. Banks and banking—Australia. I. The Australian banker.
TxU NUC75-29650

Banking industry.
⌜Carmel, International Computer Programs, inc.⌝
v. 28 cm. quarterly. (ICP software & data services publication) (Interface business series, v. 2)
Key title: Banking industry, ISSN 0364-3808
1. Banks and banking—Data processing—Periodicals. 2. Computer industry—Periodicals. I. International Computer Programs, Inc. II. Series: Interface business series, v. 2.
HG1709.B36 332.1'028'54 76-647973
MARC-S

The Banking law journal
see Banking law journal digest... Boston, 1971.

The Banking law journal.
see Clontz, Ralph C., 1922- Equal credit opportunity manual ... Boston, Warren, Gorham & Lamont, c1977.

Banking law journal.
see Clontz, Ralph C., 1922- Fair credit billing manual ... Boston, Warren, Gorham & Lamont, c1976.

Banking law journal
see Clontz, Ralph C 1922- Fair credit reporting manual... Boston: Warren, Gorham & Lamont, 1971.

Banking law journal
see Clontz, Ralph C 1922- Truth-in-lending manual. Boston, Warren, Gorham & Lamont [1972]

Banking law journal.
see Clontz, Ralph C. Truth-in-lending manual ... 4th ed. Boston, Warren, Gorham & Lamont, c1976.

The Banking law journal
see Modern banking forms. Annotated. Boston : Warren, Gorham & Lamont, [1974-

The Banking Law Journal
see Spolan, Harmon S Banker's handbook of federal aids to financing... Boston, Warren, Gorham & Lamont ₍c1971-

Banking law journal digest; 1971 cumulative supplement to 6th ed.; a classified digest of legal decisions published in the monthly issues of The Banking law journal during the years 1962-1970; vols. 79, 80, 81, 82, 83, 84, 85, 86, and 87, together with a digest of articles appearing in The Banking law journal since 1952 and digest of other cases on banking and commercial law since 1952. Editor: John R. Fonseca. Boston, 1971.
xviii, 580 p. 23 cm.
1. Banking law–United States. I. Fonseca, John R., ed. II. The Banking law journal
OU NUC73-120534

Banking, money and credit in Eastern Europe: main findings of Colloquium held 24th-26th January, 1973 in Brussels. Banque, monnaie et crédit en Europe orientale: conclusions du Colloque organise du 24 au 26 janvier 1973 à Bruxelles. Editor and chairman of colloquium: Yves Laulan. Brussels, NATO-Directorate of Economic Affairs, 1973.
166 p. 25 cm. Be***
English and/or French.
Includes bibliographical references.

1. Money—Europe, Eastern—Congresses. 2. Credit—Europe, Eastern—Congresses. 3. Banks and banking—Europe, Eastern—Congresses. 4. Finance—Europe, Eastern—Congresses. I. Laulan, Yves, ed. II. North Atlantic Treaty Organization. Directorate of Economic Affairs. III. Title: Banque, monnaie et crédit en Europe orientale.
HG925.B35 332'.0947 74-153343
MARC

Banking problems. New York, Kraus Reprint Co., 1968
see under American Academy of Political and Social Science, Philadelphia.

Banking Publicity Association of the United States
see Trusts & estates. Mar. 1904- [New York, Communication Channels, inc.]

Banking Research Fund. Trustees.
see Green, Donald S. The trust activities of the banking industry. ₍s.l., s.n., 1975?₎

Banking Research Fund. Trustees.
see Jacobs, Donald P. The financial structure of bank holding companies ... ₍Chicago, Association of Reserve City Bankers, 1975₎

Banking structures and sources of finance in the Far East: describing the banking systems of Japan, Korea, Hong Kong, China, Thailand, Malaysia, Singapore, Indonesia, Philippines, Australia and New Zealand / edited by Philip Thorn. — London : Banker Research Unit, ₍1975₎
₍5₎, 155 p. : ill. ; 30 cm. GB75-09467
ISBN 0-902998-01-3 : £14.00
1. Banks and banking—East (Far East)—Addresses, essays, lectures. 2. Banks and banking—Asia, South—Addresses, essays, lectures. 3. Banks and banking—Australia—Addresses, essays, lectures. I. Thorn, Philip.
HG3264.B35 332.1'095 75-317215
75 MARC

Banking structures and sources of finance in the Middle East : describing the banking systems of, and providing details of banks in Egypt, Jordan, Lebanon, Syria, Iraq, Iran, Kuwait, Gulf States, and Arabia / edited by Philip Thorn and Farida Mazhar. — London : Banker Research Unit, Financial Times, 1975.
259 p. ; 30 cm. GB***
1. Banks and banking—Near East. 2. Banks and banking—Near East—Directories. I. Philip Thorn. II. Farida Mazhar.
HG3260.8.A6B35 332.1'0956 76-362265
76 MARC

Bankinsurance news
see Pakistan insurance survey & who's who. 1975- ₍Karachi₎

Bankl, Hans.
Congenital malformations of heart and great vessels : synopsis of pathology, embryology, and natural history / Hans Bankl. — Baltimore : Urban & Schwarzenberg, 1977.
xii, 263 p. : ill. ; 23 cm.
Bibliography: p. 231-260.
Includes index.
ISBN 0-8067-0201-X : $24.50
1. Cardiovascular system—Abnormalities. 2. Embryology, Human. 3. Anatomy, Pathological. I. Title.
₍DNLM: 1. Heart defects, Congenital. WG220 B218c₎
RC669.B26 616.1'2'043 77-7354
77 MARC

Bankmann, Dorothea.
Ernst W. Middendorf: vida y obra [por] Dorothea Bankmann, Ulff Bankmann [y] Estuardo Núñez. [Lima, 1970?]
21 p. illus., port. 26 cm.
"Homenaje de la Biblioteca Nacional del Perú al XXXIX Congreso Internacional de Americanistas, Lima, 2-10 de agosto de 1970."
"Separata del Boletín de la Biblioteca Nacional, nos. 49-50, Lima, primer semestre de 1970."
TxU NUC75-47266

Banko, Daniel.
Very dry with a twist / Daniel Banko. — 1st ed. — New York : Saturday Review Press, ₍1975₎
184 p. ; 22 cm.
ISBN 0-8415-0365-6
I. Title.
PZ4.B2167 Ve 3 813'.5'4 74-23232
₍PS3552.A479₎ 74 MARC

Bankoff, Adrienne E.
see The Upper Saddle River Bicentennial cook book of fine old and new recipes. ₍s.l., s.n.₎ c1976.

Bankoff, George Alexis, 1903–
Cocaine for breakfast ₍by₎ George Sava. London, Hale, 1973.
256 p. 21 cm. £1.90 B 73-11878
I. Title.
PZ3.B22595Co 823'.9'12 73-165568
[PR6003.A543] MARC
ISBN 0-7091-3282-4

Bankoff, George Alexis, 1903–
Every sweet hath its sour ₍by₎ George Sava. London, Hale, 1974.
239 p. 21 cm. £2.10 GB 74-16312
I. Title.
PZ3.B22595Ev 3 823'.9'12 74-180652
[PR6003.A543] MARC
ISBN 0-7091-4108-4

Bankoff, George Alexis, 1903–
In quest of health ₍by₎ George Sava. ₍1st ed.₎ Madras, Little Flower Co. ₍1968₎
vi, 312 p. 19 cm.
5.00
1. Hygiene. I. Title.
[RA776.B225] 610 S A 68-20676
PL 480: I-E-10613

Bankoff, George Alexis, 1903-
Of men and medicine / George Sava ₍i.e. G. A. Bankoff₎. — London : Hale, 1976.
189 p. ; 21 cm. GB***
ISBN 0-7091-5229-9 : £3.10
I. Title.
PZ3.B22595 Oh 823'.9'12 76-373492
₍PR6003.A543₎ 76 MARC

Bankoff, George Alexis, 1903-
Pretty Polly / George Sava ₍i.e. G. A. Bankoff₎. — London : R. Hale, 1976.
190 p. ; 21 cm. GB***
ISBN 0-7091-5392-9 : £3.25
I. Title.
PZ3.B22595 Ps 823'.9'12 76-380620
₍PR6003.A543₎ 76 MARC

Bankoff, George Alexis, 1903–
Return from the valley ₍by₎ George Sava. London, Hale, 1973.
223 p. 21 cm. £1.80 GB 74-08151
I. Title.
PZ3.B22595Re 823'.9'12 74-174094
[PR6003.A543] MARC
ISBN 0-7091-3239-5

Bankoff, George Alexis, 1903–
Sheilah of Buckleigh Manor ₍by₎ George Sava. London Hale, 1974.
222 p. 21 cm. £1.90 GB 74-0421
I. Title.
PZ3.B22595Sh 823'.9'12 74-16899
[PR6003.A543] MAR
ISBN 0-7091-3851-2

Bankoff, George Alexis, 1903–
The sins of Andrea ₍by₎ George Sava. London, Hal 1972.
224 p. 21 cm. £1.80 B 72-3139
I. Title.
PZ3.B22595Si 823'.9'12 73-15378
[PR6003.A543] MAR
ISBN 0-7091-3109-7

Bankoff, George Alexis, 1903-
The years of the healing knife : a surgeon's autobiography / ₍by₎ George Sava. — London : Kimber, 1976.
191 p. ; 23 cm. GB76-17539
ISBN 0-7183-0334-2 : £2.95
1. Bankoff, George Alexis, 1903- 2. Surgeons—England—Biography. 3. Surgeons—United States—Biography. 4. Europe—Description and travel—1919- I. Title.
R489.B17A38 617'.092'4 77-367787
77 MARC

Bankoff, Herman Arthur.
The end of the Middle Bronze Age in the Bana Cambridge, Mass., 1974.
2 v. (xvi, 548 p.) plates, maps, plans, table (part fold.), photos. 29 cm.
Thesis (Ph. D.)–Harvard University.
MH-P NUC76-23702

Bankoku Hakurankai, Paris, 1900
see
Paris. Exposition universelle, 1900.

Bankoku Kahei Kenkyūkai.
(Kosen nyūmon hyakka)
古銭入門百科— コイン收集の手引— 万国貨幣研究会編著 ₍東京₎ 学習図書新社 ₍昭和 34 i. e. 1959₎
136 p. illus. 19 cm.

1. Numismatics—Collectors and collecting. 2. Coins as an investment. I. Title.

CJ89.B36 73-8198

Bankoku Shingōsho
see (Shaki to entō) [5 1. e. 1930]

(Bankoku zuan daijiten)
萬國圖案大辭典 = Thesaurus ornamentorum / [illegible] ; 和田三造 ; 編著者 大隅爲三 ; 圖案蒐集執筆擔當者 和田三造 ... [et al.]. — 復刻. — 東京 : 第一書房, 昭和51-52 [1976-1977]
7 v. (988, 66, 271, 33 p., [19] leaves of plates) : chiefly ill. (some col.) ; 38 cm. Ja 77-3506
Reprint of the 1928-1931 ed. published by Bankoku Zuan Daijiten Kankōkai.
Includes indexes.
¥12000 per vol.

1. Design, Decorative. 2. Decoration and ornament. I. Wada, Sanzō, 1883-1967. II. Ōsumi, Tamezō, 1881- III. Title: Thesaurus ornamentorum.
NK1530.B33 1976 77-810573

Bankokuhaku Kenkyūkai.
(Shichijūnen Bankokuhaku no kyozō)
'70年 万国博の虚像 そのねらいと都市住民の生活 万国博研究会 吹田市職労共編 東京 自治体研究社 1970.
296 p. 19 cm. ¥630 Ja 70-10921

1. Cities and towns—Planning—Suita, Japan. 2. Environmental policy—Suita, Japan. 3. Expo '70. I. Suita-shi Shokurō. II. Title.

HT169.J32S8 1970 74-808130

Bankole, E. Bejide, ed.
see Standing Conference of African University Librarians. Western Area. Western Area conference (SCAULWA)... Lagos, SCAULWA, 1972.

Bankov, Banko Petkov, 1936–
(Zagubata)
Загубата : повест / Банко П. Банков. — София : Нар. младеж, 1976.
118 p. ; 20 cm. Bu 76-1126
0.51 lv
I. Title.
PG1038.12.A46Z2 76-526198

Bankov, Liutso.
(Za nauchna organizatsiia i upravlenie na uchebniia protses po bŭlgarski ezik)
За научна организация и управление на учебния процес по български език. [Помагало за учителите от осн. у-ще]. София, Нар. просв. (В. Търново. печ. Д. Найденов) 1972.
227 p. with tables. 21 cm. 0.71 lv Bu 72-2954
Bibliography: p. 222-223.
1. Bulgarian language—Study and teaching. I. Title.
PG819.B3 74-303227

Bankov, Stefan, 1942–
(Kŭm svoia briag)
Към своя бряг. Стихотворения. София, Нар. младеж, 1973.
48 p. 17 cm. (Библиотека Смяна. Първи книги на млади автори. Лирика. № 107) 0.19 lv Bu 74-191
I. Title.
PG1038.12.A55K8 74-334061

Bankover, Joseph.
(Sipurim mi-derekh arukah)
סיפורים מדרך ארוכה / יוסף בנקובר ; המביא לדפוס, ישראל אבן־נור. — Tel Aviv : עם עובד־תרבות וחינוך, 1975.
178 p., [16] leaves of plates : ill. ; 22 cm.
On verso of t. p.: Stories from a long way.
I. Title.
PJ5054.B26S5 75-951182

Bankovska, Ana Vŭlkova.
(Estetika i muzika)
Естетика и музика. [2. прер. и доп. изд.] София, Наука и изкуство, 1973.
395 p. 20 cm. 2.66 lv Bu***
At head of title: Ана Банковска.
First ed. published under title: По някои проблеми на музикалната естетика.
Errata slip inserted.
Includes bibliographical references.
1. Music—Philosophy and aesthetics. I. Title.
ML3800.B217E8 73-365862

Bankovski, Khristo, 1937–
(Mŭzhki godini)
Мъжки години. Стихове. Пловдив, Хр. Г. Данов, 1974.
83 p. 20 cm. 0.64 lv Bu 74-513
I. Title.
PG1038.12.A48 74-334363

[Bankovskiĭ, Nikolaĭ Nikolaevich]
Skul'ptura Golubkinoĭ. Moskva, Reklama, 1970.
13 p. illus. (Gosudarstvennaia Tret'iakovskaia galereia pokazyvaet)
Sokrovishcha moskovskikh muzeev.
I. Title.
MH NUC74-21971

Bańkowicz, Ryszard.
Cyprysy na wietrze. [Wyd. 1. Warszawa] Kaiążka i Wiedza [1972]
253 p. illus. 18 cm. (Kontynenty)
1. Cyprus. I. Title.
NcD InU NUC74-116678

Bańkowska-Bober, Krystyna
see Ruch wydawniczy w liczbach, 1944-1973. [Warszawa] Biblioteka Narodowa, Instytut Bibliograficzny [1974]

Bańkowski, Jacek
see Encyklopedia techniki: Automatyka. Warszawa, Wydawnictwa Naukowo-Techniczne, 1972.

Bankowski, Z.
see Encyklopedia techniki, Chemia. Wyd. 3., przerob. i rozsz. Warszawa: Wydawnictwa Naukowo-Techniczne, 1972.

Bánkowski, Z., ed.
see Słownik chemiczny rosyjsko-polski. Warszawa, Państwowe Wydawn. Techniczne, 1955.

Bankowski, Zenon.
Images of law / Zenon Bankowski and Geoff Mungham. — London ; Boston : Routledge & Kegan Paul, 1976.
xiii, 178 p. ; 24 cm. — (Routledge direct editions) GB***
Bibliography: p. 166-174.
Includes index.
ISBN 0-7100-8339-4 : £2.50
1. Law and socialism. 2. Sociological jurisprudence. I. Mungham, Geoff, joint author. II. Title.
K357.B3 340.1'15 76-381001
77 MARC

Bankraub in der Bundesrepublik Deutschland, von Gerhard Gleissner [et al.] Mit einem Geleitwort von Thomas Würtenberger und Rüdiger Herren. Stuttgart, F. Enke, 1972.
2 v. 25 cm. (Kriminologie, Nr. 7-8) GDB***
Includes bibliographical references.
CONTENTS: Bd. 1. Phänomenologie des Bankraubes, von D. Schubert. Phänomenologies des Bankräubers, von V. May.—Bd. 2. Strafzumessung beim Bankraub, von W. Lorenz. Sicherungsverwahrung im Kampf gegen die Bankraubkriminalität, von G. Gleissner.
1. Bank robberies—Germany (Federal Republic, 1949–) I. Gleissner, Gerhard. II. Series.
HV6016.K7 Nr. 7-8 72-357885
[HV6665.G3]
ISBN 3-432-01746-4 (v. 1)

Bankrecht : Grundzüge d. bürgerl. Rechts, Grundzüge d. Handels- u. Gesellschaftsrechts, der Bankvertrag, Kreditsicherungsrecht, Recht d. Wertpapiere, Börsenrecht, Verfahrens- u. Insolvenzrecht, Arbeitsrecht, Rechtsfragen d. tägl. Bankpraxis, prakt. Rechtsfälle. — Wiesbaden : Betriebswirtschaftlicher Verlag Gabler, 1975.
1150 p. ; 25 cm. — (Bank-Enzyklopädie ; Bd. 1) GFR75-A
Includes the text of Gesetz über die Deutsche Bundesbank and Gesetz über das Kreditwesen.
Includes index.
ISBN 3-409-48012-9 : DM150.00
1. Banking law—Germany, West. 2. Law—Germany, West. I. Germany (Federal Republic, 1949-). Laws, statutes, etc. Bundesbankgesetz. 1975. II. Germany (Federal Republic, 1949-). Laws, statutes, etc. Gesetz über das Kreditwesen. 1975.
75-511241
75[r76]rev MARC

The Bankrupt real estate partnership : practice and procedure / Martin I. Klein, chairman. — New York : Practising Law Institute, c1977.
568 p. (p. 564-568 blank for "Notes") ; 22 cm. — (Tax law and practice course handbook series ; no. 110)
"Prepared for distribution at the bankrupt real estate partnership: practice and procedure workshop, July-August 1977."
"J4-3440."
Includes bibliographical references.
1. Bankruptcy—United States. 2. Real estate investment trusts—United States. 3. Limited partnership—United States. I. Klein, Martin I. II. New York (City). Practising Law Institute. III. Series.
KF1535.R43B3 346'.73'078 77-82679
77 MARC

Bankruptcy and the chapter proceedings / edited by Grace W. Holmes. — Ann Arbor, Mich. : Institute of Continuing Legal Education, c1976.
xviii, 352 p. ; 24 cm.
Includes bibliographical references and index.
1. Bankruptcy—United States. I. Holmes, Grace W. II. Institute of Continuing Legal Education, Ann Arbor, Mich.
KF1524.B33 346'.73'078 76-26835
77 MARC

Bankruptcy bar bulletin.
New York, Bankruptcy Lawyers Bar Association.
v. 29 cm.
1. Bankruptcy—United States—Periodicals. I. Bankruptcy Lawyers Association.
KF1524.A1B3 346'.73'07805 72-626691

Bankruptcy court decisions.
Washington, Corporate Reorganization Reporter, inc.
v. 28 cm. biweekly.
ISSN 0098-7336
1. Bankruptcy—United States—Cases. I. Corporate Reorganization Reporter, inc.
KF1519.B34 346'.73'07802643 75-643806
MARC-S

Bankruptcy practice / chapter authors, James A. Chatz ... [et al.]. — Springfield : Illinois Institute for Continuing Legal Education, c1975.
313 p. in various pagings ; 26 cm.
Includes index.
1. Bankruptcy—United States. I. Chatz, James A. II. Illinois Institute for Continuing Legal Education.
KF1527.B28 346'.73'078 75-32863
76 MARC

Bankruptcy: practice and procedure. Lewis Kruger, chairman. New York, Practising Law Institute [1974]
448 p. 22 cm. (Commercial law and practice course handbook series, no. 107)
"A4-2016."
"Prepared for distribution at the bankruptcy: practice and procedure seminar, March–May 1974."
Includes bibliographical references.
1. Bankruptcy—United States. I. Kruger, Lewis. II. New York (City). Practising Law Institute. III. Series.
KF1524.B35 346'.73'078 74-165317
MARC

Bankruptcy practice and procedure / Lewis Kruger, program chairman ; Henry W. Enberg II, staff editor. — New York : Practising Law Institute, [1975]
xix, 303 p. ; 24 cm. — (Commercial law transcript series ; no. 7)
"A2-1218."
Based on a series of programs held in spring 1974.
Includes index.
1. Bankruptcy—United States. I. Kruger, Lewis. II. Enberg, Henry W., 1940- III. New York (City). Practising Law Institute. IV. Series: Commercial law and practice transcript series ; no. 7.
KF1524.B35 1975 346'.73'078 74-31888
75 MARC

Bankruptcy, practice and procedure / Lewis Kruger, chairman. — New York : Practising Law Institute, 1977.
688 p. (p. 682-688 blank) ; 22 cm. — (Commercial law and practice course handbook series ; no. 165)
"A4-2089."
Prepared for distribution at the Bankruptcy practice and procedure 1977 program, July 1977."
Includes bibliographical references.
1. Bankruptcy—United States. I. Kruger, Lewis. II. New York (City). Pratising Law Institute. III. Series.
KF1524.B35 1977 346'.73'078 77-82237
77 MARC

Bankruptcy rules and practice in Florida. [Tallahassee] Continuing Legal Education, Florida Bar [1973]
vii, 255 p. 28 cm.
1. Bankruptcy—Florida. 2. Bankruptcy—United States. I. Florida Bar. Continuing Legal Education.
KFF221.B35 346'.759'078 73-89145
MARC

Bankruptcy Seminar, 2d, Detroit, 1970
see Second annual bankruptcy seminar... Ann Arbor, Mich., 1970.

Bankruptcy under the new rules of procedure / edited by Lawrence S. Lempert ; consulting editor, Frank R. Kennedy. — Ann Arbor, Mich. : Institute of Continuing Legal Education, 1974.
235 p. ; 23 cm.
Nine lectures delivered at a seminar held Dec. 14–15, 1973, sponsored by the Institute of Continuing Legal Education.
Includes bibliographical references.
1. Bankruptcy—United States. I. Lempert, Lawrence S., ed. II. Kennedy, Frank R., ed. III. Institute of Continuing Legal Education, Ann Arbor, Mich.
KF1527.B3 346'.73'078 74–81622
MARC

Banks, A
Handling sea-frozen fish. [Aberdeen, Scotland, n.d.]
7 p. (Torry advisory note no. 2)
1. Fish, Frozen. I. Title. II. Series.
DI NUC73-34518

Banks, A. Marion, ed.
see Hardy, Julius, 1763-1816. Diary of Julius Hardy, 1788-1793... [Torquay, Eng.] 1973.

Banks, Anna K., joint author
see Lewis, Dora S Teen horizons at home and school. [New York] Macmillan [1970]

Banks, Arnold S
A study of the mystical cube in Freemasonry. London, International Co-Freemasonry, Le Droit Humain [195-]
35 p. illus.
At head of title: The way, the truth, the life, the light.
1. Freemasons—Symbolism. 2. Cube. I. Title.
CLU NUC75-67069

Banks, Arthur.
A military atlas of the First World War / Arthur Banks ; commentary by Alan Palmer. — London : Heinemann Educational, 1975.
xii, 338 p. : of ill., maps, plans ; 26 cm. GB75-28847
Maps on lining papers.
Includes indexes.
ISBN 0-435-32008-4 : £8.50
1. European War, 1914-1918—Campaigns—Maps. 2. Geography, Historical—Maps. I. Palmer, Alan Warwick. II. Title.
G1037.B3 1975b 76-369232
76 MARC

Banks, Arthur.
A military atlas of the First World War / Arthur Banks ; commentary by Alan Palmer. — New York : Taplinger Pub. Co., 1975.
xii, 338 p. : ill., maps ; 26 cm.
Includes indexes.
ISBN 0-8008-5242-7 : $29.95
1. European War, 1914-1918—Campaigns—Maps. 2. Geography, Historical—Maps. I. Palmer, Alan Warwick. II. Title.
G1037.B3 1975 77-179660
76 MARC

Banks, Arthur.
A world atlas of military history; with an introduction by Lord Chalfont. London, Seeley Service, 1973–
v. maps. 26 cm. £3.95 (v. 1) GB***
CONTENTS: v. 1. To 1500.
1. Geography, Historical—Maps. 2. Military history—Maps. I. Title.
G1030.B27 1973 911 74–176337
ISBN 0–85422–078–X MARC

Banks, Arthur.
A world atlas of military history, with an introd. by Lord Chalfont. New York, Hippocrene Books [1973–
v. illus. maps. 26 cm. $12.95 (v. 1)
CONTENTS: v. 1. To 1500.
1. Geography, Historical—Maps. 2. Military history—Maps. I. Title.
G1030.B27 1973b 911 73–90857
ISBN 0–88254–177–3 MARC

Banks, Arthur
see Grant, Michael, 1914- Ancient history atlas. London, Weidenfeld and Nicolson, 1971.

Banks, Arthur, 1910-
An Africa book list. [Rev. ed.] London, Published for the Africa Committee of the Conference of British Missionary Societies by Edinburgh House Press, 1966.
38 p. 22 cm.
1. Africa—Bibliography. I. Conference of British Missionary Societies. Africa Committee. II. Title.
IEN NUC73-2073

Banks, Arthur A
Cross-polity time-series data, assembled by Arthur S. Banks and the staff of the Center for Comparative Political Research, State University of New York at Binghamton. Cambridge, Mass., MIT Press [1971]
xxiii, 299, [1] p. (chiefly figures) 29 cm.
"Principal serial publications consulted": p. [300]
1. Electronic data processing—Political science. 2. Comparative government. I. New York (State). State University at Binghamton. Center for Comparative Political Research. II. Title.
CLSU GAT NUC75-83625

Banks, Arthur S
Cross-national time-series data archive user's manual [by] Arthur S. Banks. Binghamton, Center for Comparative Political Research, State University of New York, 1975.
91 p. 26 cm.
Code books for data tapes.
A preliminary version appeared in 1971 by Arthur S. Banks entitled: Cross-polity time-series data; it was superceded in 1972 by the author's The Suny-Binghamton cross-national time series data archive.
This manual supercedes CCPR Technical Report no. 1-2.

1. Statistics. I. Title. II. Series: New York (State). State University at Binghamton. Center for Comparative Political Research. Technical report, no. 1-2.
CSt NUC77-89890

Banks, Arthur S
Domestic conflict behavior, 1919-1966. (Machine readable data file) [Ann Arbor, Interuniversity Consortium for Political Research, 1966]
magnetic tape.
1. Government, Resistance to. 2. Political statistics. I. Title.
CaBVaU NUC74-114354

Banks, Arthur S
Industrialization and development; a longitudinal analysis. Binghamton, 1971.
27 l. (New York (State). State University at Binghamton. Center for Comparative Political Research. Research paper no. 9)
"Prepared for delivery at the Conference on Comparative Analysis of Industrialized Societies, Bellagio, Italy, August 1-7, 1971."
1. Industrialization. 2. Comparative government. I. Title.
InU NUC73-34517

Banks, Arthur S
The SUNY-Binghamton Cross-National Time-Series Data Archive [by] Arthur S. Banks, Christian R. Grangor [and] Alfred G. Lynn. Binghamton, N.Y., 1972.
2 v. (New York (State). State University at Binghamton. Center for Comparative Political Research. Technical report, no. 1-2)
Contents: v. 1. Contents, file maintenance, data retrieval. v. 2. Variable definitions and resources.
InU NUC75-47264

Banks, Arthur S
Urbanization and modernization; a longitudinal analysis [by] Arthur S. Banks [and] David L. Carr. Binghamton, 1972.
27 l. (New York (State). State University at Binghamton. Center for Comparative Political Research. Research paper no. 18)
1. Urbanization—Mathematical models. I. Carr, David L. II. Title.
InU NUC73-115143

Banks, Arthur S.
see Hopkins, Terence K On the comparative study of historical sequences. Binghamton, N.Y. [1972]

Banks, Arthur S.
see Inter-university Consortium for Political Research. A cross-polity survey. Rev. ed. Ann Arbor, 1968.

Banks, C H
Kiln drying conditions; a development study [by] C.H. Banks. Submitted to the Timber Seasoning Research Steering Committee. Pretoria, South Africa [Timber Research Unit, Council for Scientific and Industrial Research] 1968.
vi, 80 p. 30 cm. (CSIR subject survey, O/Hout, 9)
At head of title: "Not for publication."
"Project no. 5131/4310."
Bibliography: p. 71-80.
1. Lumber-Drying. I. Timber Seasoning Research Steering Committee. II. Title. III. Series.
CoFS NUC76-93163

Banks, C. H.
see also
Banks, Cecil Henry.

Banks, Carl, 1933-
Perceptions of the secondary school held by higher and lower-income students and teachers in selected schools in eastern Kentucky. Lexington, Ky., 1974.
131 l.
Thesis—University of Kentucky.
Vita.
Bibliography: leaves [127]-131.
1. Kentucky—Education, Secondary. 2. Students—Attitudes. I. Title.
KyU NUC75-20173

Banks, Carl, 1933-
Perceptions of the secondary school held by higher- and lower-income students and teachers in selected schools in eastern Kentucky. [n. p.] 1974.
131, 4 l. illus.
Thesis—University of Kentucky.
Vita.
Bibliography: leaves 128-131.
Photocopy of typescript. Ann Arbor, Mich., University Microfilms, 1974. 21 cm.
1. Educational sociology. 2. Education—Kentucky. 3. Appalachian Region—Education. I. Title.
WvU NUC76-23708

Banks, Carl J 1945-
Banks' dictionary of the Black ghetto language / by Carl J. Banks, Jr. — [1st ed.]. — [Los Angeles : Saidi Publications, c1975]
[40] leaves ; 21 cm.
1. Black English—Glossaries, vocabularies, etc. I. Title. II. Title: Dictionary of the Black ghetto language.
PE3102.N46B3 1975 427'.9'73 75-24133
76 MARC

Banks, Carlie E
see Technical and economic study of an integrated single pass mining system... Dallas, Tex., 1975.

Banks, Cecil Henry, joint author
see Von Fraunhofer, J A Potentiostat and its applications. London, Butterworths [1972]

Banks, Charlotte.
Absconding from open prisons / by Charlotte Banks, Patricia Mayhew and R. J. Sapsford. — London : H.M.S.O., 1975.
viii, 87 p. ; 25 cm. — (Home Office research studies ; 26) GB75-16174
"A Home Office Research Unit report."
Bibliography: p. 54-56.
Includes index.
ISBN 0-11-340666-5 : £0.95
1. Open prisons—Great Britain. 2. Escapes. 3. Prisoners—Great Britain. I. Mayhew, Patricia, joint author. II. Sapsford, R. J., joint author. III. Great Britain. Home Dept. Research Unit. IV. Title. V. Series: Great Britain. Home Dept. Research Studies ; 26.
HV9647.B36 365'.641 75-327070
75 MARC

Banks, Charlotte.
The petty short-term prisoner / [by] Charlotte Banks, Suzan Fairhead ; foreword by Timothy Cook. — Chichester : Rose [for] the Howard League for Penal Reform, 1976.
iii, 23 p. ; 21 cm. GB76-21112
Bibliography: p. 23.
ISBN 0-85992-064-X : £.25
1. Prisoners—England. I. Fairhead, Suzan, joint author. II. Title.
HV9647.B37 365'.6 76-379221
76 MARC

Banks, Cherry A., joint author
see Banks, James A March toward freedom... 2d ed. Belmont, Calif., Lear Siegler, Inc./Fearon Publishers [c1974]

Banks, Danny, ed.
see Sheridan, Richard Brinsley Butler, 1751-1816. The rivals. [New York, 1971]

Banks, David.
Vocational agriculture in Liberia, 1952-1958 : a rural youth program / by David Banks. — [Monrovia? : s.n., 1958?]
iv, 23 leaves : ill. ; 27 cm.
1. Agriculture—Study and teaching—Liberia. I. Title.
S535.L4B36 77-357459
77 MARC

Banks, Dean, 1935-
Creating an "American dilemma" : the impact of Nazi racism upon American intergroup relations, 1933-1940, with special reference to Jewish Americans, German-Americans and the free-speech movement / Dean Banks. -- [Austin, Tex. : s.n.], 1975.
2 v. (xiii, 731 leaves) : map ; 29 cm.
Thesis (Ph. D.)--University of Texas at Austin.
Vita.
Bibliography: leaves 655-731.
1. Antisemitism--United States. 2. Germans in the United States. 3. Public opinion--United States. I. Title.
TxU NUC77-90423

Banks, Desmond, 1917 or 18-
The Liberal programme for Europe : a statement of Liberal Party policy / compiled by Desmond Banks. — London : Liberal Publication Department, [1975]
15 p. ; 22 cm. GB75-16207
ISBN 0-900520-42-6 : £0.30
1. European Economic Community—Great Britain. 2. Liberal Party (Gt. Brit.) I. Title.
HC241.25.G7B333 382'.9142 75-324624
75 MARC

Banks, Don C
Selected methods for analyzing the stability of crater slopes by D.C. Banks. Conducted by U.S. Army Engineer Waterways Experiment Station, Corps of Engineers. Vicksburg, Miss., 1968.
1 v. (various pagings) illus., diagrs., plates. (U.S. Waterways Experiment Station, Vicksburg, Miss. Miscellaneous paper, no. S-68-8)
Bibliography: p. 19-21.
"Sponsored by U.S. Army Engineer Nuclear Cratering Group under Engineering Properties of Nuclear Craters Project."
1. Slopes (Soil mechanics) 2. Soil stabilization. I. United States. Army Engineer Nuclear Cratering Group. II. Title. III. Series.
MsSM NUC75-51606

Banks, Donald.
Odd man out? : A 'rich' Christian in African / Donald Banks. — London : Inter-Varsity Press, 1974.
96 p. ; 18 cm. — (IVP way-in book) GB75-00412
ISBN 0-85110-453-3 : £0.40
1. Misssions—Africa. 2. Christian life—1960- I. Title.
BV3500.B25 266'.023'0924 76-358527
76 MARC

Banks, Donald Lee, 1938-
A comparative study of the reinforcing potential of verbal and nonverbal cues in a verbal conditioning paradigm. By Donald L. Banks. [Amherst] 1974.
viii, 109 l. illus. 28 cm.
Thesis (Ed. D.)—University of Massachusetts.
1. Reinforcement (Psychology) I. Title.
MU NUC76-23703

Banks, Edwin M.
see Vertebrate social organization. Stroudsburg, Pa., Dowden, Hutchinson & Ross, c1977.

Banks, Elbert Augustine, 1840-1902.
The genealogical record of the Banks family of Elbert County, Georgia, collected by the late Elbert Augustine Banks, with gleanings and character sketches compiled by Georgia Butt Young. Edited by Sarah Banks Franklin. 3d ed. Danielsville, Ga., Heritage Papers, 1972.
x, 379 p. illus. 24 cm. $16.00
Cover title: Banks of Elbert.
1. Banks family. I. Young, Georgia Butt, 1834-1911. II. Franklin, Sarah Banks (Walton) 1907- ed. III. Title. IV. Title: Banks of Elbert.
CS71.B2268 1972 929'.2'0973 72-82996
MARC

Banks, Elizabeth V H
see MacRury, Elizabeth Banks.

Banks, Ellen Cardone.
Infant activity patterns and maternal responses in the stages of increasing locomotion ability. Cambridge, 1974.
ii, 181 l.
Thesis—Harvard University.
1. Mother and child. 2. Human locomotion. 3. Child study. I. Title.
MH-Ed NUC76-23677

Banks, Elvalee.
A recruitment simulation game model for university administrators. [Minneapolis] 1975.
xii, 169 l. 29 cm.
Thesis (Ph. D.)--University of Minnesota.
Bibliography: leaves 160-169.
MnU NUC77-89433

Banks, Eugene Pendleton.
O metodologiji nauka koje proučavaju ponašanje. Zagreb, Institut za Društvena istraživanja Sveučilišta, 1971.
116 p. 29 cm. (Studija i izvjestaji)
Includes bibliography.
1. Sociology. I. Title.
NcWsW NUC73-34516

Banks, F. R.
see
Banks, Francis Richard.

Banks, Ferdinand E
The economics of natural resources / Ferdinand E. Banks. — New York : Plenum Press, c1976.
xiii, 267 p. : ill. ; 24 cm.
Bibliography: p. 255-260.
Includes index.
ISBN 0-306-30926-2 : $19.50
1. Natural resources. 2. Raw materials. 3. Economics. I. Title.
HC55.B25 333.7 76-25583
76 MARC

Banks, Ferdinand E
The world copper market: an economic analysis [by] Ferdinand E. Banks. Cambridge, Mass., Ballinger Pub. Co. [1974]
xvii, 151 p. illus. 24 cm.
Bibliography: p. 141-143.
1. Copper trade and industry. I. Title.
HD9539.C6B35 382'.42'43 73-16165
ISBN 0-88410-257-2 MARC

Banks, Florence.
Profile of labor in highway construction / by Florence Banks, Transportation Economics Division, Office of Program and Policy Planning, Federal Highway Administration. — [Washington] : U.S. Dept. of Transportation, Federal Highway Administration, 1976.
ii, 114 p. : graphs ; 27 cm.
Includes bibliographical references.
1. Road construction workers—United States—Statistics. I. United States. Federal Highway Administration. Transportation Economics Division. II. Title.
HD8039.R62U52 331.7'62'570973 76-602784
76 MARC

Banks, Francis Richard.
Kent / by F. R. Banks. — Harmondsworth, Eng. : Penguin Books, 1955.
319 p. : ill. ; 19 cm. — (The Penguin guides ; new ser., G14)
Includes index.
1. Kent, Eng.—Description and travel—Guide-books.
DA670.K3B3 914.22'3'0485 77-364550
77 MARC

Banks, Francis Richard.
The Lake District, the Pennines and Yorkshire Dales, by F. R. Banks; [maps by Jack Parker]. [1st ed., reprinted with corrections. London, Charles Letts and Co. Ltd, 1970.
66 p. illus., col. maps. 22 cm. (Letts motor tour guides) £0.35
B 72-07514
1. Yorkshire, Eng.—Description and travel—Tours. 2. Lake District, Eng.—Description and travel—Tours. I. Title.
DA670.Y6B19 1970 914.28 73-158477
ISBN 0-85097-036-9 MARC

Banks, Francis Richard.
The Peak District / F. R. Banks. — London : R. Hale, 1975.
226 p., [24] leaves of plates : ill. ; 23 cm. GB***
Includes index.
ISBN 0-7091-4913-1 : £3.50
1. The Peak, Eng.—Description and travel—Guide-books. I. Title.
DA670.D43B33 1975 914.25'11'04857 75-323478
75 MARC

Banks, Francis Richard.
The Penguin guide to London [by] F. R. Banks. 6th ed. Harmondsworth, Penguin, 1973.
554 p., fold. leaf. maps (1 col.) 18 cm. £0.75 GB 73-19729
Includes index.
1. London—Description—1951- —Guide-books. I. Title.
DA679.B26 1973 914.21'04'85 74-150428
ISBN 0-14-070417-5 MARC

Banks, Mrs. G Linnaeus
see Banks, Isabella (Verley) 1821-1897.

Banks, G N
Iron ore pelletizing; a literature survey [by] G. N. Banks, R. A. Campbell & G. E. Viens. [Ottawa, R. Duhamel, Queen's printer] 1963.
v, 23 p. 28 cm. (Canada. Dept. of Mines and Technical Surveys. Mines Branch. Information circular IC 152)
Cover title.
Résumé in French.
Bibliography: p. 11-13.
1. Pelletizing (Ore-dressing)—Bibliography. 2. Iron ores—Bibliography. I. Campbell, R. A., joint author. II. Viens, G. E., joint author. III. Title. IV. Series: Canada. Mines Branch (1950-) Information circular, 152.
Z6679.O7B35 74-229848

Banks, Gerald V
Camus, L'étranger / [by] G. V. Banks. — London : Edward Arnold, 1976.
64 p. ; 20 cm. — (Studies in French literature ; no. 30) GB76-24704
Bibliography: p. [63]-64.
ISBN 0-7131-5849-2 : £2.20. ISBN 0-7131-5850-6 pbk.
1. Camus, Albert, 1913-1960. L'étranger.
PQ2605.A3734E835 843'.9'14 77-361741
77 MARC

Banks, Gordon.
Intensity correlation spectroscopy of heme proteins and motile microorganisms. Albuquerque, N.M., 1973.
xv, 181 l. illus.
Thesis—University of New Mexico.
1. Hemoproteins. 2. Micro-organisms. 3. Spectrum analysis. I. Title.
ICU NUC75-20186

Banks, Gordon.
Teaching rugby to boys : a graduated programme for schools and clubs / by Gordon Banks ; [illustrations by Reg W. Hepple]. — London : Bell, 1976.
111 p. : ill. ; 20 cm. GB76-31138
ISBN 0-7135-1944-4 : £4.50
1. Rugby football coaching. I. Title.
GV945.75.B36 796.33'3'0712 77-360413
77 MARC

Banks, H. P.
see
Banks, Harlan Parker, 1913-

Banks, H T
Control of functional differential equations to target sets in function by H.T. Banks and G.A. Kent. Providence, R.I., Center for Dynamical Systems, Division of Applied Mathematics, Brown University [197-]
57 l. 29 cm.
Research supported in part by the National Aeronautics and Space Administration, Air Force Office of Scientific Research, U.S. Army, and U.S. Navy.
Photocopy of typescript.
Bibliography: leaves 54-57.
1. Control theory. 2. Differential equations. 3. Function spaces. I. Kent, George, Alan, 1943- II. Brown University. Applied Mathematics Division. III. Title.
KU NUC75-17346

Banks, H T
Convergence theorems for parameter estimation by quasilinearization, by H.T. Banks and G.M. Groome, Jr. Providence, R.I., Center for Dynamical Systems, Division of Applied Mathematics, Brown University [197-?]
32 l. illus. 29 cm.
Photocopy from typescript.
Bibliography: leaf 32.
1. Estimation theory. 2. Convergence. I. Groome, George Monroe, 1940- joint author. II. Brown University. Applied Mathematics Division. III. Title.
KU NUC75-18528

Banks, H T
Modeling of control and dynamical systems in the life sciences. [Providence, R.I., Center for Dynamical Systems, Brown University] 1973.
95 p. illus. (Brown University. Center for Dynamical Systems. Lecture notes, 73-1)
Includes bibliography.
1. Control theory. I. Title.
MiU NUC75-20187

Banks, H T
The synthesis of optimal controls for linear problems with retarded controls, by H. T. Banks, Marc Q. Jacobs [and] M. R. Latina. Providence, R.I., Center for Dynamical Systems, Division of Applied Mathematics, Brown University [197-?]
79 l. illus. 29 cm.
Research supported in part by the National Aeronautics and Space Administration, the Air Force Office of Scientific Research, and the National Science Foundation.
Photocopy of typescript.
Bibliography: leaves 77-79.
1. Automatic control. 2. Control theory. 3. Delay lines. I. Jacobs, Marc Q., joint author. II. Latina, M. R., joint author. III. Brown University. Applied Mathematics Division. IV. Title.
KU NUC75-17360

Banks, Harlan Parker, 1913-
Anatomy and morphology of Psilophyton dawsonnii, sp. n. from the late Lower Devonian of Quebec (Gaspé), and Ontario, Canada / by H. P. Banks, Suzanne Leclercq, and F. M. Hueber. — Ithaca, N.Y. : Paleontological Research Institution, 1975.
p. [77]-127, [4] leaves of plates : ill. ; 31 cm. — (Palaeontographica Americana ; v. 8, no. 48)
Bibliography: p. 115-116.
Includes index.
1. Psilophyton dawsonii. 2. Paleobotany—Devonian. 3. Paleobotany—Quebec (Province)—Gaspé Peninsula. 4. Paleobotany—Ontario. I. Leclercq, Suzanne, joint author. II. Hueber, F. M., joint author. III. Title: Anatomy and morphology of Psilophyton dawsonii ... IV. Series.
QE701.I82 vol. 8, no. 48 560'.973 s 75-8034
[QE960.5] 75 MARC

Banks, Harlan Parker, 1913-
Evolutions and plants of the past [by] Harlan P. Banks. [London] Macmillan [1972, c1970]
x, 170 p. illus. 24 cm. (Fundamentals of botany series)
Includes bibliographies.
1. Paleobotany. I. Title.
CLU NUC74-116647

Banks, Harvey O
The California Water Plan; a paper presented by Harvey O. Banks before the California Water Conference of the California State Chamber of Commerce, Thursday, February 23, 1956, Statler Hotel, Los Angeles. [Sacramento? 1956]
28 l.
1. Water resources development–California. I. California Water Conference, Los Angeles, 1956. II. California. State Water Resources Board.
CU NUC74-38772

Banks, Harvey O
Conceptual system design for an environmental information base for management of water and related resources by states, by Harvey O. Banks and Gerald T. Orlob. [Belmont, Calif.] 1973.
73 l. illus.
Final report of research supported by the U.S. Office of Water Resources Research under contract no. 14-31-0001-3424.
PB 221 124.
1. Information storage and retrieval systems—Natural resources. 2. Water—Information services. 3. State governments—Information services. I. Orlob, Gerald T. II. United States. Office of Water Resources Research. III. Title.
DI NUC74-120535

Banks, Harvey O
A plan for a comprehensive water resources research information exchange system; final report [by] Harvey O. Banks and Charles G. Wolfe. Springfield, Va., Clearinghouse for Federal Scientific and Technical Information, 1969.
1 v. 28 cm.
"PB 185801. Report 14-01-0001-1618."
In double columns.
"Prepared for Office of Water Resources Research, United States Dept. of the Interior."
1. Water resources development–Information services. I. Wolfe, Charles G. II. United States. Office of Water Resources Research. III. Title.
NjP NUC75-108892

Banks, Harvey O., joint author
see **Wendell, Mitchell.** Management of water... McLean, Va., Environments for Tomorrow, 1974.

Banks, Harvey Thomas, 1940-
Modeling and control in the biomedical sciences / H. T. Banks. — Berlin ; New York : Springer-Verlag, 1975.
iv, 114 p. : ill. ; 25 cm. — (Lecture notes in biomathematics ; v. 6)
Bibliography: p. [104]-114.
ISBN 0-387-07395-7
1. Biological models. 2. Medicine—Mathematical models. 3. Biological control systems. I. Title. II. Series.
[DNLM: 1. Models, Biological. 2. Enzymes. 3. Disease outbreaks. 4. Neoplasms. 5. Glucose—Metabolism. W1 LE334 v. 6 / QT34 B218m]
QH324.8.B36 610'.1'84 75-25771
75 MARC

Banks, Henry, fl. 1781-1826.
A review of political opinions. Published for the benefit of the people of Kentucky. By Henry Banks of Virginia. Frankfort, Ky., Printed by J. H. Holeman, 1822.
viii, 88 p. 23 cm.
1. Banks and banking—Kentucky. I. Title.
HG2611.K42B34 Toner Coll 77-364525
77 MARC

Banks, Henry, fl. 1781-1826.
Sketches & propositions, recommending the establishment of an independent system of banking; permanent public roads, a new mode for the recovery of interest on private loans, changes at the penitentiary, and a general system of defence, with some observations necessary to illustrate these several topics. Richmond, Manson, printer [1811?]
2 sheets. 8 x 13 cm. (The Library of Thomas Jefferson)
Sabin 3199.
Micro-transparency (positive). Washington, Microcard Editions, 1973.
Collation of the original: 65 p.
1. Bank of Virginia. 2. Banks and banking—Virginia. 3. Roads—Virginia. I. Title.
PSt NUC74-173319

Banks, Henry, 1921-
see Symposium on birth defects and the orthopedic surgeon. Philadelphia, Saunders, 1976.

Banks, Henry H., ed.
see Musculoskeletal disorders... Philadelphia, Saunders, 1967.

Banks, Henry Jonathan.
A revision of the genus Ptychandra (Lepidoptera, Nymphalidae) / by Henry Jonathan Banks, Jeremy Daniel Holloway and Henry Sackville Barlow. — London : British Museum (Natural History), 1976.
p. 218-252, 5 leaves of plates : ill. ; 25 cm. — (Bulletin of the British Museum (Natural History) : Entomology ; v. 32, no. 6) GB***
Bibliography: p. 251-252.
£4.25
1. Ptychandra. 2. Insects—Classification. I. Holloway, Jeremy Daniel, joint author. II. Barlow, Henry Sackville, joint author. III. Title. IV. Series: British Museum (Natural History). Bulletin : Entomology ; v. 32, no. 6.
QL461.B56 vol. 32, no. 6 76-381118
595.7'008 s
[QL561.S3] 76 MARC

Banks, Howard Michael, 1944-
British and Irish current affairs television in the crisis of civil war. [n. p.] 1975.
1 v.
Thesis (Ph. D.)--Northwestern University.
1. Television in politics--Northern Ireland. 2. Television audiences--Northern Ireland. 3. Northern Ireland--Politics and government. I. Title.
IEN NUC77-89432

Banks, Ian.
Nurse allocation. London, Heinemann Medical, 1972.
xix, 85 p. (2 fold.). col. illus. 29 cm. £3.50 R 72-29784
Bibliography: p. xv.
1. Nurses and nursing—Great Britain. I. Title.
[DNLM: 1. Nursing Supervisory. 2. Students, Nursing. WY 105 B218n 1972]
[RT11.B36] 658.31'2 73-594507
ISBN 0-433-01165-3 MARC
Shared Cataloging with DNLM

Banks, Isabella (Varley) 1821-1897.
God's providence house. By Mrs. G. Linnaeus Banks. London, Ward, Lock [19--]
iv, 446 p. 19 cm.
I. Title.
CSt NUC75-18551

Banks, J M Buchanan-
see
Buchanan-Banks, J M

Banks, James A
A content analysis of elementary American history textbooks: the treatment of the Negro and race relations. [East Lansing, Mich.] 1969 [1972]
viii, 150 l.
Thesis–Michigan State University.
Bibliography: leaves 143-150.
Photocopy. Ann Arbor, Mich., University Microfilms, 1972. 21 cm.
1. U. S.–Race question. 2. History–Textbooks. I. Title.
CtY NUC73-115228

Banks, James A
March toward freedom; a history of Black Americans [by] James A. Banks and Cherry A. Banks. 2d ed. Belmont, Calif., Lear Siegler, Inc./Fearon Publishers [c1974]
vi, 186 p. illus. 26 cm.
Traces the history of blacks in America from the early days of the slave trade to the present day.
1. Negroes–History–Juvenile literature. I. Banks, Cherry A., joint author. II. Title.
NjR NUC76-23694

Banks, James A
Teaching ethnic studies: concepts and strategies. James A. Banks, editor. Washington, National Council for the Social Studies, 1973.
xvii, 297 p. illus. 23 cm. (National Council for the Social Studies. Yearbook, 43d) $6.00 (pbk.)
Includes bibliographies.
1. Ethnic studies—United States—Addresses, essays, lectures. I. Title. II. Series.
H62.A1N3 no. 43 300'.7 s 74-169198
[E184.A1] [301.45'07'1073] MARC

Banks, James A
Teaching strategies for ethnic studies / James A. Banks. — Boston : Allyn and Bacon, [1975]
ix, 502 p. : ill. ; 22 cm.
Includes bibliographies and index.
ISBN 0-205-04674-6 : $12.50. ISBN 0-205-04673-8 pbk. : $5.95
1. Ethnic studies—United States. I. Title.
E184.A1B24 301.45'1'071073 74-31149
74 MARC

Banks, James A
Teaching strategies for the social studies: inquiry, valuing, and decision-making [by] James A. Banks, with contributions by Ambrose A. Clegg, Jr. Reading, Mass., Addison-Wesley Pub. Co. [1973]
xv, 590 p. illus. 24 cm.
Includes bibliographical references.
1. Social sciences—Study and teaching (Elementary) I. Clegg, Ambrose A. II. Title.
LB1584.B32 372.8'3'044 72-1935
MARC

Banks, James A
Teaching strategies for the social studies : inquiry, valuing, and decision-making / James A. Banks, with contributions by Ambrose A. Clegg, Jr. — 2d ed. — Reading, Mass. : Addison-Wesley Pub. Co., c1977.
xvi, 539 p. : ill. ; 25 cm.
Includes bibliographical references and indexes.
ISBN 0-201-00412-7
1. Social sciences—Study and teaching (Elementary) I. Clegg, Ambrose A., joint author. II. Title.
LB1584.B32 1977 372.8'3'044 76-5081
77 MARC

Banks, James E
Naming organic compounds : a programed introduction to organic chemistry / James E. Banks. — 2d ed. — Philadelphia : Saunders, 1976.
ix, 309, [22] p. : ill. ; 26 cm. — (Saunders golden sunburst series)
Bibliography: p. [14] (3d group)
Includes index.
ISBN 0-7216-1536-8
1. Chemistry, Organic—Nomenclature—Programmed instruction. I. Title.
QD291.B3 1976 547'.001'4 75-291
76 MARC

Banks, James G 1940-
Strom Thurmond and the revolt against modernity, by James Banks. [n.p.] 1970 [c1971]
vi, 399 l.
Thesis—Kent State University.
Bibliography: leaves 389-399.
Photocopy of typescript. Ann Arbor, Mich., University Microfilms, 1973. 22 cm.
1. Thurmond, James Strom, 1902-
I. Title.
ScCleU NUC74-116660

Banks, James G 1940-
Strom Thurmond and the revolt against modernity, by James G. Banks. [Kent, Ohio] 1971.
vi, 399 l.
Thesis—Kent State University.
Microfilm. Ann Arbor, Mich., University Microfilms, 1971. 1 reel. 35 mm.
1. Thurmond, Strom, 1902-
NIC NUC74-115165

Banks, James Huber
see Effects of continuous military operations on selected military tasks. Arlington, Va., Behavior and Systems Research Laboratory, 1970.

Banks, James Huber, joint author
see Farrell, John P Search effectiveness with the starlight scope... Arlington, Va., 1970.

Banks, Jane, joint author
see Dong, Collin H The arthritic's cookbook. New York, Crowell [1973]

Banks, Jane, joint author.
see Dong, Collin H. New hope for the arthritic. New York, Crowell, [1975]

Banks, Jane, joint author.
see Dong, Collin H. New Hope for the arthritic. London, Hart-Davis, MacGibbon, 1976.

Banks, Jason.
Notes on the works of John Donne. [Toronto] Forum House [c1970]
117 p. 22 cm. (Forum, 999) C***
Bibliography: p. 114-117.
1. Donne, John, 1572-1631. I. Title.
PR2248.B36 821'.3 73-153784
MARC

Banks, Jerry.
Hierarchy of procurement and inventory systems, by Jerry Banks. Ann Arbor, Mich., University Microfilms, 1967.
1 reel. 35 mm. (University Microfilms, 67-07183)
Microfilm copy.
Thesis (Ph. D.)—Oklahoma State University, 1966.
Collation of the original: xi, 181 l.
Bibliography: leaves 132-133.
1. Inventories. I. Title.
PSt NUC76-75697

Banks, Jimmy, 1925-
The Darrell Royal story. Austin, Tex., Shoal Creek Publishers [1973]
178 p. illus. 24 cm. $5.95
1. Royal, Darrell. I. Title.
GV939.R69B36 796.33'2'0924 [B] 73-86926
ISBN 0-88319-016-8 MARC

Banks, Joe L.
see Fowler, Laurie G Test of different components in the Abernathy salmon diet... Washington, U.S. Dept. of the Interior, Fish and Wildlife Service, Bureau of Sport Fisheries and Wildlife, 1967.

Banks, Joe L., joint author
see Fowler, Laurie G Tests of substitute ingredients... Washington, U.S. Dept. of the Interior, Fish and Wildlife Service, Bureau of Sport Fisheries and Wildlife, 1970.

Banks, Joe L., joint author
see Fowler, Laurie G Tests of vitamin supplements... Washington, U.S. Dept. of the Interior, Fish and Wildlife Service, Bureau of Sport Fisheries and Wildlife, 1969.

Banks, John.
Is there a word from the Lord? London, Epworth [1968]
130 p. 20 cm. (Sermons for today, nr. 3)
1. Methodist sermons. I. Title.
NjMD NUC73-47556

Banks, John Houston, 1911- Geometry, its elements and structure.
see Posamentier, Alfred S. Geometry, its elements and structure. 2d ed. New York, Webster Division, McGraw-Hill, c1977.

Banks, John Houston, 1911- joint author.
see Posamentier, Alfred S. Geometry, its elements and structure. 2d ed. New York, Webster Division, McGraw-Hill, c1977.

Banks, John Houston, 1911- joint author.
see Sobel, Max A. Algebra, its elements and structure. 3d ed. New York, Webster Division, McGraw-Hill, c1977-

Banks, Jon Steven, 1941-
A status assessment of educable mentally retarded adults' coping ability for the initial phase of a longitudinal follow-up study, by J. Steven Banks. [n.p.] c1972.
1 v. (various pagings) illus. 29 cm.
Thesis (Ph. D.)—University of Wisconsin.
Vita.
Includes bibliography.
1. Mentally handicapped—Rehabilitation.
I. Title.
WU NUC73-115146

[Banks, Joseph, Sir, bart.] 1743-1820.
The propriety of allowing a qualified exportation of wool discussed historically. To which is added an appendix: containing a table, which skews the value of the woolen goods of every kind that were entered for exportation at the custom-house, from 1697 to 1780 inclusive, as well as the prices of wool in England, during all that period. London, Printed for P. Elmsly, 1782. [Ann Arbor, Mich., Xerox University Microfilms, 1975]
88 p. 21 cm.
1. Wood trade and industry--Great Britain--History. I. Title.
NjP NUC77-96655

Banks, Joseph, Sir, bart., 1743-1820.
see Captain Cook's florilegium. London, Lion and Unicorn Press, 1973.

Banks, Sir Joseph, bart., 1743-1820
see Simcoe, John Graves, 1752-1806. Letter to Sir Joseph Banks ... [Toronto, Canadiana House, 1969]

Banks, Joseph Ambrose.
The sociology of social movements, [by] J. A. Banks. London, Macmillan [for the British Sociological Association], 1972.
62 p. illus. 21 cm. (Studies in sociology) £0.60 B 72-31549
Bibliography: p. 57-62.
1. Social movements. 2. Social change. I. Title.
HM101.B256 301.24'2 73-155533
ISBN 0-333-13433-8 MARC

Banks, Joseph Ambrose.
Trade unionism / J. A. Banks. — London : Collier-Macmillan, 1974.
vi, 138 p. ; 21 cm. — (Themes and issues in modern sociology) GB***
Bibliography: p. 125-134.
Includes index.
ISBN 0-02-972170-9. ISBN 0-02-972180-6 pbk. : £1.25
1. Trade-unions—Great Britain. 2. Trade-unions. 3. Collective bargaining—Great Britain. 4. Collective bargaining. I. Title.
HD6664.B25 331.88'0941 73-17755
75 MARC

Banks, Joyce
see Ottawa. National Library. Arthur S. Bourinot. Ottawa, 1971.

Banks, Kalani, 1938-
Octavia F. Rogan, Texas librarian. [Austin, Tex.] 1963.
ix, 151 l. 28 cm.
Report (M.L.S.)—University of Texas.
Vita.
Bibliography: leaves [148]-151.
1. Rogan, Octavia Fry, 1886-
TxU NUC73-2075

Banks, Kenneth.
Vanitas; poems to Lawrence Boyle. Guelph, 1972.
[32] p. illus.
I. Title.
CaOWtU NUC74-116659

Banks, Larry D
The Bentsen-Clark site, Red River County, Texas : a preliminary report / by Larry D. Banks and Joe Winters. -- San Antonio : Texas Archeological Society, 1975.
97 p. : ill. -- (Texas Archeological Society. Special publication ; no. 2)
1. Excavations (Archaeology)--Texas. 2. Bentsen-Clark site, Texas. I. Winters, Joe. II. Title. III. Series.
KMK NUC77-88500

Banks, Linda Jane, 1949-
Drama: what's really happening in the English classroom. [n.p.] 1975.
xi, 161 p. tables.
Thesis (Ed. D.)--Boston University.
Bibliography: p. 159-161.
1. Drama in education. I. Title.
MBU NUC77-89431

Banks, Louis Albert, 1855-1933.
[Twentieth century knighthood. Japanese]
二十世紀の武士道 = Twentieth century knighthood / バンクス原著. — 東京 : 内外出版協會, 明治40 [1907]
2, 148 p. ; 22 cm.

1. Young men—Conduct of life. I. Title.
Title romanized: Nijisseiki no bushidō.
BJ1671.B1516 75-794094

Banks, Lynne Reid.
The adventures of King Midas / story by Lynne Reid Banks ; pictures by George Him. — London : Dent, 1976.
95 p. : ill. (some col.) ; 23 cm. GB76-24671
ISBN 0-460-06752-4 : £2.75
1. Midas—Juvenile literature. I. Him, George, 1900- II. Title.
PZ8.1.B229 Ad 76-379385
76 MARC

Banks, Lynne Reid.
Dark quartet : the story of the Brontes / Lynne Reid Banks. — London : Weidenfeld & Nicolson, c1976.
x, 374 p. ; 23 cm. GB***
ISBN 0-297-77153-1 : £4.95
1. Brontë family—Fiction. I. Title.
PZ4.B2173 Dar 823'.9'12 76-381550
[PR6003.A528] 76 MARC

Banks, Lynne Reid.
Dark quartet : the story of the Brontës / by Lynne Reid Banks. — New York : Delacorte Press, c1976.
xi, 432 p. ; 24 cm.
ISBN 0-440-01657-6
1. Brontë family—Fiction. I. Title.
PZ4.B2173 Dar 3 823'.8'09 76-29727
[PR6003.A528] 76 MARC

Banks, Lynne Reid.
The farthest-away mountain / [by] Lynne Reid Banks ; illustrated by Victor Ambrus. — London : Abelard-Schuman, 1976.
[5], 140 p. : ill. ; 21 cm. GB76-36427
ISBN 0-200-72461-4 : £1.95
I. Title.
PZ7.B2262 Far 3 77-355295
77 MARC

Banks, Lynne Reid.
The kibbutz—some personal reflections: an address to the Anglo-Israel Association on Monday, January 24th, 1972. London, Anglo-Israel Association, 1972.
20 p. 23 cm. (Anglo-Israel Association. Pamphlet no. 35) £0.30
B 72-16486
1. Collective settlements—Israel. 2. Israel—Social life and customs. I. Title. II. Series.
DS126.5.A746 no. 35 73-152168
[HX765.P3] 301.29'42'05694 s MARC
ISBN 0-90063-34-3 [301.34'095694]

Banks, Lynne Reid.
The L-shaped room. [n.p.] 1971.
1 v.
OCl NUC74-115150

Banks, Lynne Reid.
My darling villain / Lynne Reid Banks. — 1st American ed. — New York : Harper & Row, c1977.
237 p. ; 21 cm.
SUMMARY: Fifteen-year-old Kate becomes aware of the class consciousness of her middle class family and friends when she falls in love with a boy from a working class family.
ISBN 0-06-020392-7 : $6.95. ISBN 0-06-020393-5 lib. bdg. : $5.79
[1. England—Fiction] I. Title.
PZ7.B2262 My 3 [Fic] 76-58718
77 MARC

Banks, Lynne Reid.
One more river. London, Vallentine, Mitchell [1973]
271 p. 23 cm. £2.10 B***
I. Title.
PZ7.B2262On 73-167519
ISBN 0-853-03149-5 MARC

Banks, Lynne Reid.
One more river. New York, Simon and Schuster [1973]
288 p. 22 cm. $5.95
SUMMARY: Resentful at being forced to leave Canada, Lesley's adjustment to life in the Israeli kibbutz is not easy.
[1. Collective settlements—Israel—Fiction. 2. Israel—Fiction] I. Title.
PZ7.B2262On 3 [Fic] 72-93971
ISBN 0-671-65205-2 MARC

Banks, Lynne Reid.
Sarah and after : five women who founded a nation / Lynne Reid Banks. — 1st ed. — Garden City, N.Y. : Doubleday, c1975.
183 p. ; 22 cm.
SUMMARY: Relates the lives of four generations of girls who became the matriarchs of the Hebrew nation.
ISBN 0-385-11456-7 : $6.95. ISBN 0-385-11455-9 lib. bdg.
1. Matriarchs (Bible)—Juvenile fiction. [1. Matriarchs (Bible)—Fiction. 2. Bible stories—O.T.] I. Title.
PZ7.B2262 Sar 3 823'.9'12 76-16250
77 MARC

Banks, Lynne Reid.
Sarah and after : the matriarchs / Lynne Reid Banks. — London : Bodley Head, 1975.
169 p. ; 23 cm. — (A Book for new adults) GB***
ISBN 0-370-10953-8 : £2.25
1. Matriarchs (Bible)—Juvenile fiction. I. Title.
PZ7.B2262 Sar 823'.9'12 75-318081
[PR6003.A528] 75[r77]rev MARC

Banks, Lynne Reid.
Two is lonely. London, Chatto & Windus, 1974.
280 p. 21 cm. £2.50 GB 74-06585
Final volume of the trilogy consisting also of The L-shaped room and The backward shadow.
I. Title.
PZ4.B2173Tw 823'.9'12 74-166715
[PR6003.A528] MARC
ISBN 0-7011-2011-8

Banks, Lynne Reid.
Two is lonely; a sequel to The L-shaped room and The backward shadow. New York, Simon and Schuster [1974]
318 p. 22 cm. $7.95
I. Title.
PZ4.B2173Tw 3 823'.9'12 73-20755
[PR6003.A528] MARC
ISBN 0-671-21732-1

Banks, M E
New chemical concepts for utilization of waste plastics. Prepared for the Federal solid waste management program by M.E. Banks, W.D. Lusk, and R.S. Ottinger, TRW Systems Group. Washington, U.S. Environmental Protection Agency, 1971.
129 p. illus.
1. Plastic scrap. 2. Refuse and refuse disposal. I. Lusk, W.D. II. Ottinger, Robert Stanley. III. United States. Environmental Protection Agency. IV. Title.
MiU NUC73-20091

Banks, Margaret A 1928–
Using a law library; a guide for students in the common law Provinces of Canada [by] Margaret A. Banks. London, Can., University of Western Ontario, School of Library and Information Science, 1971.
72 p. 23 cm. C***
Includes bibliographical references.
1. Legal research—Canada. I. Title.
340'.07'2071 73-181371
MARC

Banks, Margaret A 1928–
Using a law library : a guide for students and lawyers in the common law provinces of Canada / Margaret A. Banks. — 2d ed. — London [Ont.] : Carswell Co. Ltd., [1974]
ix, 171 p. ; 23 cm. C***
Includes bibliographical references.
ISBN 0-459-31350-9 : $20.00
1. Legal research—Canada. I. Title.
340'.07'2071 75-300121
MARC

Banks, Margaret A 1928-
Using a law library; a guide for students and lawyers in the common law provinces of Canada. 2d ed. [London, University of Western Ontario, School of Library and Information Science, c1974]
ix, 171 p. 23 cm.
Includes bibliographical references.
1. Legal research—Canada. I. Title.
NjR NUC76-23705

Banks, Margot Harper.
Out of the darkness. Collected by Margot Harper Banks. Illustrated by Randolph Adams. [Pittsburgh] Inner City Services, Carnegie Library of Pittsburgh [c1973]
56 p. illus. 22 cm.
1. American poetry—Negro authors. I. Title.
CtY NUC76-75696

Banks, Marie, 1903- joint author
see Lewis, Dora S Teen horizons at home and school. [New York] Macmillan [1970]

Banks, Marjorie Ann, 1905–
Missouri—the land where rivers meet, by Marjorie Ann Banks and Edith S. McCall. Pictures by James G. Teason. Additional art: Bill Jirkovski and Rudolph Magnani. Westchester, Ill., Benefic Press [c1973]
255 p. illus. 23 cm.
Editions for 1958 and 1962 published under title: Where rivers meet.
SUMMARY: An illustrated history of Missouri from early Indian settlements to the present day.
1. Missouri—History—Juvenile literature. [1. Missouri—History] I. McCall, Edith S., joint author. II. Teason, James G., illus. III. Jirkovski, Bill, illus. IV. Magnani, Rudolph, illus. V. Title.
F466.3.B34 1973 917.78 73-87506
MARC

Banks, Marshall Douglas, 1940-
Interactive effects of conceptual development of parents and teachers on enhancing creativity in children and conditions of home play by Marshall Douglas Banks. Urbana, University of Illinois, 1974. [Ann Arbor, Mich., University Microfilms, 1974]
viii, 97 l. illus. 21 cm.
Thesis (Ph. D.)—University of Illinois, 1973.
Vita.
Bibliography: leaves 59-61.
1. Creative ability. 2. Play. I. Title.
CoU NUC76-23704

Banks, Mary Macleod
see Alphabetum narrationum. An alphabet of tales. Millwood, N.Y., Kraus Reprint, 1972, 1904-05.

Banks, Mary Macleod, ed
see Morte Arthure. Morte Arthure; an alliterative poem of the 14th century, from the Lincoln ms. [New York, AMS Press, 1974]

Banks, Maxwell R.
see The Lake country of Tasmania ... Hobart, Royal Society of Tasmania, 1973.

Banks, Melvin James, 1903-
The pursuit of equality; the movement for first class citizenship among Negroes in Texas, 1920-1950. By Melvin James Banks. [Syracuse, N.Y.] 1962.
ix, 591 l.
Photocopy of typescript. Ann Arbor, Mich., University Microfilm, 1971. 22 cm.
Thesis—Syracuse University.
Vita.
1. Negroes—Civil rights. 2. Negroes—Texas. I. Title.
OU NUC75-48081

Banks, Midori Yamanouchi, 1928-
A study of the expression of traditional Japanese culture through selected social rituals as revealed in popular novels. [n.p., 1973]
[3], iv, 365, [i.e. 369] l.
Thesis (Ph.D.)—Michigan State University.
Bibliography: leaves 350-365.
1. Japan—Soc. life and cust. 2. Japan—Civilization. I. Title.
MiEM NUC75-20661

Banks, Mike, 1922-
Greenland / by Michael Banks. — Newton Abbot : David & Charles ; Totowa, N.J. : Rowman and Littlefield, 1975.
208 p. : ill. ; 23 cm.
Bibliography: p. 199-201.
Includes index.
ISBN 0-87471-722-1
1. Greenland.
G743.B32 1975 919.8'2 75-16443
75 MARC

Banks, Olive.
Sociology and education : some reflections on the sociologist's role : an inaugural lecture delivered in the University of Leicester, 5 February 1974 / by Olive Banks. — Leicester : Leicester University Press, 1974.
24 p. ; 23 cm. GB 74-17647
Bibliography: p. 23–24.
ISBN 0-7185-3054-3 : £0.40
1. Educational sociology. I. Title.
LC191.B256 301.5'6 74-195785
MARC

Banks, Olive.
The sociology of education / Olive Banks. — 3d ed. — London : Batsford, 1976.
294 p. ; 22 cm. GB***
Bibliography: p. 283-288.
Includes index.
ISBN 0-7134-3174-1 : £4.00. ISBN 0-7134-3173-3 pbk.
1. Educational sociology. I. Title.
LC189.B36 1976b 370.19'3 76-370332
76 MARC

Banks, Olive.
Success and failure in the secondary school; an interdisciplinary approach to school achievement [by] Olive Banks and Douglas Finlayson. London, Methuen [distributed by Harper & Row, Barnes & Noble Import Division, New York, 1973]
ix, 259 p. 21 cm. £3.50 GB***
1. Academic achievement. 2. Education, Secondary. 3. High school students' socioeconomic status. I. Finlayson, Douglas, joint author. II. Title.
LB1131.B3214 1973 373.1'2'7 74-155803
ISBN 0-416-76440-1; 0-416-76450-9 (pbk.) MARC

Banks, Paul Noble, 1934-
Lamination. Chicago, The Newberry Library [1971]
4 p. 22 cm.
1. Art objects—Conservation and restoration. 2. Laminated materials. I. Title.
AAP NUC75-48080

Banks, Peter.
The biochemistry of the tissues / P. Banks, W. Bartley, L. M. Birt. — 2d ed. — London ; New York : Wiley, c1976.
xv, 493 p. : ill. ; 24 cm.
First ed. by W. Bartley, L. M. Birt, and P. Banks.
Includes bibliographies and index.
ISBN 0-471-05471-2. ISBN 0-471-01923-2 pbk.
1. Biological chemistry. 2. Metabolism. 3. Human physiology. I. Bartley, Walter, joint author. II. Birt, Lindsay Michael, joint author. III. Title.
QP514.2.B35 1976 612'.015 75-26739
75 MARC

Banks, Peter M
Aeronomy [by] P. M. Banks [and] G. Kockarts. New York, Academic Press, 1973.
2 v. illus. 24 cm.
Includes bibliographical references.
1. Atmosphere, Upper. I. Kockarts, G., joint author. II. Title.
QC879.B27 551.5'14 72-88332
MARC

Banks, Peter M
Introduction to computer science / P. M. Banks, J. R. Doupnik. — New York : Wiley, c1976.
xiv, 362 p. : ill. ; 24 cm.
Includes bibliographies and index.
ISBN 0-471-04710-4
1. Electronic digital computers—Programming. I. Doupnik, J. R., 1938- joint author. II. Title.
QA76.6.B353 001.6'42 75-20407
75 MARC

Banks (R. L.) and Associates, inc., Washington, D. C.
An estimation of the distribution of the rail revenue contribution by commodity groups and type of rail car, 1969. An application of rail form A railroad costs to the one percent rail waybill sample. [Washington] U. S. Dept. of Transportation, 1973.
295 p.
"DOT-OS-00086/2."
Includes bibliographical references.
Photocopy. Springfield, Va., National Technical Information Service, 1973. 1 v.
"PB 220 076."
1. Railroads–Freight. 2. Railroads–Rates. 3. Freight and freightage–Classification. I. Title.
TxU NUC75-20184

Banks (R. L.) & Associates, inc., Washington, D.C.
Review of MBTA master plan; a report to the Special Commission Relative to the Finances and Operation of the Massachusetts Bay Transportation Authority. Washington, 1969.
ii, 42, A-3, B-2 l. illus., tables, maps.
WaU NUC74-115152

Banks (R. L.) & Associates, inc., Washington, D. C.
Study and evaluation of urban mass transportation regulation and regulatory bodies; final report [by] R. L. Banks & Associates, Stanford Research Institute [and] Real Estate Research Corporation. Washington, 1972.
2 v. in 1. illus., maps.
"Report UMTA TRD-65-72-1."
"Prepared for Office of Program Planning, Urban Mass Transportation Administration."
Bibliography: v. 2, p. 1-13.
Photocopy. Springfield, Va., National Technical Information Service, 1972? 28 cm.
"PB 211 077." "PB 211 078."
IU NUC73-115226

Banks, Richard C
Birds and mammals of La Laguna, Baja California. San Diego, 1967.
1 v.
MnU-B NUC75-30438

Banks, Richard C
The mammals of Cerralvo Island, Baja California. San Diego, 1964.
[397]-404 p. 26 cm. (San Diego Society of Natural History. Transactions. v. 13, no. 20)
Bibliography: p. 404.
1. Mammals. Cerralvo Island. I. Title.
MnU-B NUC76-75695

Banks, Richard C
Terrestrial vertebrates of Anacapa Island, California. San Diego, 1966.
[175]-188 p. illus. 26 cm. (San Diego Society of Natural History. Transactions. v. 14, no. 14)
Bibliography: p. 187-188.
1. Vertebrates. California. Anacapa Island. I. Title.
MnU-B NUC75-47269

Banks, Richard C
Wildlife importation into the United States, 1900-1972 / by Richard C. Banks. — Washington : U.S. Dept. of the Interior, Fish and Wildlife Service, 1976.
18 p. ; 26 cm. — (Special scientific report—wildlife ; no. 200)
Bibliography: p. 18.
Supt. of Docs. no.: I49.15/3:200
1. Wild animal trade—United States. 2. Wild animal trade. I. Title. II. Series.
SK361.A256 no. 200 639'.9'08 s 77-601822
[QL84.2] 77 MARC

Banks, Richard C., ed.
see Bird and Mammal Laboratories. Birds imported into the United States. Washington, Govt. Print. Off.

Banks, Richard C., joint author
see Clapp, Roger B Birds imported into the United States in 1971. Washington, 1973.

Banks, Richard C., joint author
see Short, Lester L Notes on birds of Northwestern Baja California. San Diego, 1965.

Banks, Richard Charles.
Isolation of certain toxic components of Kraft mill waste and attempts to determine their structure. Studies of the mechanism of the Cope rearrangement of 1, 2-divinyl-1, 2-cyclohexanediol. [Corvallis, Or.] 1969.
109 l. illus. 28 cm.
Thesis–Oregon State University.
Includes bibliographies.
Photocopy. Ann Arbor, Mich., University Microfilms, 1972. 21 cm.
1. Sulphate waste liquor. 2. Cope rearrangement. I. Title.
OrPS NUC76-75682

Banks, Robert F., 1936-
see Multinationals, unions, and labor relations in industrialized countries. Ithaca, New York State School of Industrial & Labor Relations, Cornell University, 1977.

Banks, Robert George.
A study of differential characteristics of freshmen music students in selected two-year and four-year colleges in Virginia / by Robert G. Banks. -- Greensboro : University of North Carolina at Greensboro, 1976.
vii, 73 leaves ; 28 cm. -- (North Carolina. University at Greensboro. [School of Music] Dissertation ; 76-1)
Thesis--University at Greensboro.
Bibliography: leaves 59-64.
I. Title. II. Series.
NcGU NUC77-88216

Banks, Robert J
Jesus and the law in the synoptic tradition / Robert Banks. — Cambridge, Eng. ; New York : Cambridge University Press, [1975]
x, 310 p. ; 22 cm. — (Monograph series - Society for New Testament Studies ; 28)
A revision of the author's thesis, Cambridge, 1969.
Bibliography: p. 264-280.
Includes indexes.
ISBN 0-521-20789-4
1. Jesus Christ—Attitude towards Jewish law. 2. Law (Theology)—Biblical teaching. 3. Jewish law. I. Title. II. Series: Studiorum Novi Testamenti Societas. Monograph series ; 28.
BT590.J34B36 1975 241'.2 75-7215
75 MARC

Banks, Robert J., ed.
see Reconciliation and hope : New Testament essays on atonement and eschatology. Exeter: Paternoster Press, 1974.

Banks, Robert J., ed.
see Reconciliation and hope... Grand Rapids, W. B. Eerdmans Pub. Co. [1975, c1974]

Banks, Robin K., joint comp.
see Walters, Richard H 1918-1967, comp. Punishment: selected readings... Harmondsworth, Penguin, 1972.

Banks, Roger Lee, 1941- joint author
see Davis, Charles A Some food habits of scaled quail... [Las Cruces] New Mexico State University, Agricultural Experiment Station [1973]

Banks, Ronald F comp.
A history of Maine; a collection of readings on the history of Maine, 1600–1974, by Ronald F. Banks. 3d ed. Dubuque, Iowa, Kendall/Hunt Pub. Co. [1974]
vii, 434 p. illus. 28 cm.
Includes bibliographical references.
1. Maine—History. I. Title.
F19.B3 1974 974.1 74-77124
ISBN 0-8403-0020-4 MARC

Banks, Ronald F comp.
A history of Maine : a collection of readings on the history of Maine, 1600-1976 / by Ronald F. Banks. — 4th ed. — Dubuque, Iowa : Kendall/Hunt Pub. Co., c1976.
ix, 460 p. : ill. ; 28 cm.
Maps on p. [2]-[3] of cover.
Includes bibliographical references.
ISBN 0-8403-0020-4
1. Maine—History—Addresses, essays, lectures. I. Title.
F19.5.B36 1976 974.1 76-150737
76 MARC

Banks, Ronald F
Maine becomes a State; the movement to separate Maine from Massachusetts, 1785–1820 [by] Ronald F. Banks. Somersworth, New Hampshire Pub. Co., 1973 [c1970]
xx, 266 p. illus. 23 cm. $6.95
"Second edition."
Bibliography: p. [246]-257.
1. Maine—History—1775-1865. I. Title.
[F24.B35 1973] 974.1'03 73-82845
ISBN 0-912274-35-2 MARC

Banks, Ronald F
Maine during the Federal and Jeffersonian period : a bibliographical guide / compiled by Ronald F. Banks. — Portland : Maine Historical Society, 1974.
49 p. ; 26 cm. — (Maine history bibliographical guide series)
Includes index.
1. Maine—History—1775-1865—Bibliography. 2. Maine—Politics and government—1775-1865—Bibliography. I. Title. II. Series.
Z1291.B83 016.9741'03 75-301735
MARC

Banks, Ronald F.
see The Maine bicentennial atlas... 1st ed. Portland, Maine Historical Society, 1976.

Banks, Rosa Maria Taylor, 1942-
A study of the supervisory services provided by southern state departments of education to selected high school business education programs / by Rosa Maria Taylor Banks. -- [s.l. : s.n.], 1974.
viii, 248 leaves.
Thesis--University of Pittsburgh.
Vita.
Bibliography: leaves [244]-247.
Photocopy of typescript. Ann Arbor, Mich.: University Microfilms, 1976. -- 21 cm.
MsU NUC77-88034

Banks, Russell, 1940-
Family life / by Russell Banks. — New York : Avon, 1975.
118 p. ; 21 cm. — (Equinox books)
ISBN 0-380-00258-2 : $2.95 ($3.45 Can.)
I. Title.
PZ4.B2175 Fam 813'.5'4 75-725
[PS3552.A49] 77 MARC

Banks, Russell, 1940-
Searching for survivors / Russell Banks. — 1st ed. — New York : Fiction Collective, 1975.
153 p. ; 23 cm.
CONTENTS: Searching for survivors (I).—With Ché in New Hampshire.—The investiture.—The blizzard.—The nap.—With Ché at Kitty Hawk.—The neighbor.—The lie.—With Ché at the Plaza.—The masquerade.—Impasse.—The drive home.—The defenseman.—Searching for survivors (II).
ISBN 0-914590-07-3 : $7.95. ISBN 0-914590-06-5 pbk. : $3.95
I. Title.
PZ4.B2175 Se 813'.5'4 74-24911
[PS3552.A49] 75 MARC

Banks, Russell Earl.
30/6. [New York, The Quest, 1969]
36 p. illus. 23 cm. (The Quest. Poetry pamphlet, no. 2)
Caption title.
Poems.
1. American poetry. 20th cent. I. Title.
OrU NUC74-115153

Banks, Sam A., 1928-
Limitation and self-worth in psychotherapy and salvation. [n. p.] 1971.
276 l.
Thesis (Ph. D.)–University of Chicago.
1. Tillich, Paul, 1886-1965. 2. Becker, Ernest. 3. Philosophical anthropology. 4. Psychotherapy. 5. Salvation. I. Title.
ICU NUC73-115241

Banks, Sam A., 1928-
see The Health of a rural county ... Gainesville, University Presses of Florida, 1976.

Banks, Samuel L
Stony the road; the Black American in the American experience [by] Samuel L. Banks. Northbrook, Ill., Whitehall Co. [c1972]
111 p. 21 cm.
Includes bibliographical references.
1. Negroes—Addresses, essays, lectures. 2. Negroes—Education—Addresses, essays, lectures. I. Title.
E185.B265 301.45'19'6073 73-163883
MARC

Banks, Steven.
The handicrafts of the sailor / Steven Banks. — New York : Arco Pub. Co., 1974.
96 p. : ill. ; 25 cm.
Bibliography: p. 93.
Includes index.
ISBN 0-668-03441-6 : $5.95
1. Handicraft. 2. Seamen. 3. Ship models. 4. Scrimshaws. 5. Knots and splices. I. Title.
TT149.B36 1974b 745.5 73-91687
MARC

Banks, Steven.
The handicrafts of the sailor. Newton Abbot, David & Charles [1974]
96 p. illus. 25 cm. £3.25 GB***
Bibliography: p. 93.
1. Handicraft. 2. Seamen. 3. Ship models. 4. Scrimshaws. 5. Knots and splices. I. Title.
TT149.B36 745.5 74-183244
ISBN 0-7153-6378-6 MARC

Banks, Thomas Israel.
The large order behavior of perturbation theory, by Thomas Banks. [n.p.] 1973.
[211] l. diagrs., tables. 30 cm.
Thesis (Ph. D.)—Massachusetts Institute of Technology.
Vita.
Includes bibliographical references.
1. Perturbation (Quantum dynamics) 2. Approximation theory. 3. Eigenvalues. I. Title.
MCM NUC75-21165

Banks, Thomas Royston.
A study of the imagery of Aristophanes' Wasps in its dramatic context. [Minneapolis] 1973.
iii, 272 l. 29 cm.
Thesis (Ph. D.)–University of Minnesota.
Bibliography: leaves 258-261.
MnU NUC76-75694

Banks, Thomas Wilson, 1938-
The dramatic career of Samuel Taylor Coleridge. [Atlanta] 1966.
392 p.
Thesis—Emory University.
"Works cited": p. [386]-392.
Microfilm copy.
1. Coleridge, Samuel Taylor, 1772-1834. I. Title.
NIC NUC75-58908

Banks, Vera J
Farm population by race, tenure, and economic scale of farming, 1966 and 1970 [by Vera J. Banks and Calvin L. Beale. Washington] U.S. Dept. of Agriculture, Economic Research Service [1972]
iv, 14 p. illus. (Agricultural economic report no. 228)
MH-BA NUC73-115221

Banks, Vera J
Farm population estimates, 1910-70 [by Vera J. Banks and Calvin L. Beale. Washington] Rural Development Service [1973]
ii, 47 p. illus. 27 cm. (U. S. Dept. of Agriculture. Statistical bulletin no. 523)
Cover title.
Bibliography: p. 13.
Supt. of Docs. no.: A 1.34: 523
1. United States—Population, Rural. I. Beale, Calvin Lunsford, 1923- joint author. II. Title. III. Series: United States. Dept. of Agriculture. Statistical bulletin no. 523.
HD1751.A5 no. 523 338.1'0973 s 73-602345
[HB2385] [312'.8] MARC

Banks, Vera J
Farm population estimates for 1974 / by Vera J. Banks. -- Washington : Economic Research Service, U.S. Dept. of Agriculture, 1975.
5 p. : ill. -- (U.S. Dept. of Agriculture. Agricultural economic report ; no. 319)
Includes bibliographical references.
1. Rural population. 2. Rural-urban migration. I. Title.
DNAL NUC77-94111

Banks, W
Starch and its components / by W. Banks and C. T. Greenwood. — Edinburgh : Edinburgh University Press, c1975.
xi, 342 p., [4] leaves of plates : ill. ; 24 cm. GB***
Bibliography: p. 309-325.
Includes indexes.
ISBN 0-85224-251-4
1. Starch. I. Greenwood, Charles Trevor, joint author. II. Title.
QD321.B23 1975b 547'.782 75-332841
76 MARC

Banks, W
Starch and its components / by W. Banks and C. T. Greenwood. — New York : Wiley, [1975]
xi, 342 p., [4] leaves of plates : ill. ; 24 cm.
"A Halsted Press book."
Bibliography: p. 309-325.
Includes indexes.
ISBN 0-470-04711-9
1. Starch. I. Greenwood, Charles Trevor, joint author. II. Title.
QD321.B23 1975 547'.782 75-19022
75 MARC

Banks, W B
The substitution of other materials for timber in the building industry implications for the import bill / W.B. Banks. -- Garston, Eng. : Building Research Establishment, 1975.
5 p. -- (Building Research Establishment current paper CP ; 50/75)
1. Building materials. 2. Timber. I. Building Research Establishment. II. Title.
DHUD NUC77-88246

Banks, William Curtis.
Variables affecting the choice of reward and punishment as strategies of interpersonal influence. [Stanford, Calif.] 1973.
vii, 139 l. forms.
Thesis (Ph. D.)—Stanford University.
Bibliography: leaves 136-139.
Copyright.
1. Interpersonal relations. 2. Reward (Psychology) 3. Punishment (Psychology) I. Title.
CSt NUC75-20666

Banks, William H.
see International Conference of Printing Research Institutes, 12th, Versailles, 1973. Proceedings of the twelfth International Conference of Printing Research Institutes, Versailles, France, June 1973. London, IPC Science and Technology Press, 1974.

Banks, William H.
see International Conference of Printing Research Institutes, 13th, Wildhaus, Switzerland, 1975. Advances in printing science and technology ... London, Pentech Press Ltd, 1977.

Banks, William J
Histology and comparative organology: a text-atlas [by] William J. Banks. Baltimore, Williams & Wilkins Co. [1973, c1974]
x, 285 p. illus. 29 cm.
Includes bibliographies.
1. Veterinary anatomy. 2. Veterinary histology. I. Title.
SF761.B33 636.089'1'018 73-8808
ISBN 0-683-00409-3 MARC

Banks, firm, law publishers, New York
see A Digest of decisions under the national bankruptcy act... [New York, Banks Law Pub. Co., 1899]

The Banks and industry : based on the seminar held at Christ's College, Cambridge, 5-10 September, 1976 / [organized by] the Institute of Bankers. — London : [The Institute], 1976.
[3], 106 p. ; 21 cm. GB77-00077
Bibliography: p. 100-101.
ISBN 0-85297-041-2
1. Banks and banking—Great Britain—Congresses. 2. Finance—Great Britain—Congresses. 3. Corporations—Great Britain—Finance—Congresses. I. Institute of Bankers, London.
HG2988.B26 332.1'7 77-357358
77 MARC

The Banks and society : based on the seminar held at Christ's College, Cambridge, 8-14 September 1974 / [organised by] the Institute of Bankers. — London : The Institute, [1974].
[7], 84 p. ; 21 cm. GB75-00175
Bibliography: p. 77-78.
ISBN 0-85297-035-8 : £1.50
1. Public relations—Banks and banking—Congresses. 2. Banks and banking—Congresses. I. Institute of Bankers, London.
HG1616.P8B36 658.4'08 75-309322
75 MARC

Banks and the securities laws. Alan B. Levenson, chairman; Manuel F. Cohen, co-chairman. New York, Practising Law Institute [1973]
232 p. forms. 22 cm. (Corporate law and practice course handbook series, no. 126)
"Prepared for distribution at the Banks and the Securities Laws Seminar, September-October 1973."
Pages 226-232 blank.
"B4-3567."
1. Securities — United States. 2. Banking law — United States. I. Levenson, Alan B., ed. II. Cohen, Manuel Frederick, 1912- ed. III. New York (City). Practising Law Institute. IV. Banks and the Securities Laws Seminar, New York and San Francisco, 1973. V. Series.
KF1070.Z9B3 346'.73'092 73-180883
MARC

Banks and the securities laws in 1974 / Alan B. Levenson, Richard B. Smith, co-chairmen. — New York : Practising Law Institute, [1974]
640 p. ; 22 cm. — (Corporate law and practice course handbook series ; no. 154)
"Prepared for use at the Banks and the Securities Laws in 1974 Program, September-October, 1974."
"B4-4505."
Includes bibliographical references.
1. Securities — United States. 2. Banking law — United States. I. Levenson, Alan B. II. Smith, Richard B., 1928- III. New York (City). Practising Law Institute. IV. Series.
KF1440.B36 346'.73'092 75-301336
MARC

Banks and the securities laws, 1975 / Alan B. Levenson, Richard B. Smith, cochairmen. — New York : Practising Law Institute, c1975.
256 p. ; 22 cm. — (Corporate law and practice course handbook series ; no. 188)
"B4-4554."
"Prepared for distribution at the banks and securities laws program, September-October, 1975."
1. Securities—United States. 2. Banking law—United States. I. Levenson, Alan B. II. Smith, Richard B., 1928- III. New York (City). Practising Law Institute. IV. Series.
KF1440.B36 1975 346'.73'0666 76-353367
76 MARC

Banks and the securities laws, 1976 / Alan B. Levenson, Richard B. Smith, chairmen. — New York : Practising Law Institute, c1976.
712 p. ; 22 cm. — (Corporate law and practice course handbook series ; no. 221)
"B4-4591."
"Prepared for distribution at the banks and the securities laws 1976 program, September-October, 1976."
Includes bibliography.
1. Securities—United States. 2. Banking law—United States. I. Levenson, Alan B. II. Smith, Richard, 1928- III. New York (City). Practising Law Institute. IV. Series.
KF1440.B36 1976 346'.73'0666 76-40757
76 MARC

Banks and the Securities Laws Seminar, New York and San Francisco, 1973
see Banks and the securities laws, Practising Law Institute [1972]

Banks Association of Turkey
see
Türkiye Bankalar Birliği.

Banks-Baldwin Law Publishing Company, Cleveland.
see Baldwin, William Edward, 1883-1966. Baldwin's Ohio township law ... 4th ed. Cleveland, Banks-Baldwin Law Pub. Co., c1977-

Banks-Baldwin Law Publishing Company, Cleveland
see Baldwin's Ohio legislative service. 1971- Cleveland.

Banks-Baldwin Law Publishing Company, Cleveland.
see Ohio. Laws, statutes, etc. Baldwin's Ohio revised code ... 4th (50th anniversary) ed. Cleveland, Banks-Baldwin Law Pub. Co., [1971-

Banks-Baldwin Law Publishing Company, Cleveland.
see Ohio. Laws, statutes, etc. Baldwin's Ohio school law ... 8th ed., complete to Jan. 1, 1973. Cleveland, Banks-Baldwin Law Pub. Co., c1973-

Banks-Baldwin Law Publishing Co., Cleveland
see Ohio. Laws, statutes, etc. Baldwin's Ohio tax law and rules. 3d ed., complete to Oct. 1, 1972. Cleveland [1973-

Banks-Baldwin Law Publishing Company, Cleveland
see Ohio. Laws, statutes, etc. 1971 laws issue, Baldwin's Ohio revised code and rules service ... Cleveland [1972]

Banks-Baldwin Law Publishing Co., Cleveland
see Ohio. Laws, statutes, etc. Ohio criminal justice 1974... Cleveland [Banks-Baldwin Law Pub. Co., 1973]

The Banks of Arkansas.
[s. l.] Sheshunoff & Co.
v. 23 x 29 cm.
ISSN 0360-232X
1. Banks and banking—Arkansas—Finance—Statistics. I. Sheshunoff & Company.
HG2611.A7B35 332.1'09767 75-648539 MARC-S

The Banks of Colorado.
[s. l.] Sheshunoff & Co.
v. 23 x 29 cm.
ISSN 0360-425X
1. Banks and banking—Colorado—Finance—Statistics. I. Sheshunoff & Company.
HG2611.C6B35 332.1'09788 75-648703 MARC-S

The Banks of Georgia.
[s. l.] Sheshunoff & Co.
v. 23 x 29 cm.
Key title: The Banks of Georgia, ISSN 0361-4808
1. Banks and banking—Georgia—Finance—Statistics. 2. Banks and banking—Georgia—Directories. I. Sheshunoff & Company.
HG2611.G42B35 332.1'09758 76-640894 MARC-S

The Banks of Illinois.
[s. l.] Sheshunoff & Co.
v. 23 x 29 cm.
ISSN 0360-4268
1. Banks and banking—Illinois—Finance—Statistics. I. Sheshunoff & Company.
HG2611.I 3B35 332.1'09773 75-647637 MARC-S

The Banks of Indiana.
[s. l.] Sheshunoff & Co.
v. 23 x 29 cm.
ISSN 0360-4276
1. Banks and banking—Indiana—Finance—Statistics. I. Sheshunoff & Company.
HG2611.I 4B35 332.1'09772 75-648704 MARC-S

The Banks of Iowa.
[s. l.] Sheshunoff & Co.
v. 23 x 29 cm.
ISSN 0360-4284
1. Banks and banking—Iowa—Finance—Statistics. I. Sheshunoff & Company.
HG2611.I 8B35 332.1'09777 75-647640 MARC-S

Banks of Kansas.
[s. l.] Sheshunoff & Co.
v. 23 x 29 cm.
Key title: Banks of Kansas, ISSN 0361-4816
1. Banks and banking—Kansas—Finance—Statistics. 2. Banks and banking—Kansas—Directories. I. Sheshunoff & Company.
HG2611.K22B35 332.1'09781 76-640886 MARC-S

The Banks of Kentucky.
[s. l.] Sheshunoff & Co.
v. 23 x 29 cm.
Key title: The Banks of Kentucky, ISSN 0361-4824
1. Banks and banking—Kentucky—Finance—Statistics. 2. Banks and banking—Kentucky—Directories. I. Sheshunoff & Company.
HG2611.K42B35 332.1'09769 76-640885 MARC-S

Banks of Louisiana.
[s. l.] Sheshunoff & Co.
v. 23 x 29 cm.
ISSN 0360-4292
1. Banks and banking—Louisiana—Finance—Statistics. I. Sheshunoff & Company.
HG2611.L6B35 332.1'09763 75-648701 MARC-S

The Banks of Michigan.
[s. l.] Sheshunoff & Co.
v. 23 x 29 cm.
ISSN 0360-2338
1. Banks and banking—Michigan—Finance—Statistics. I. Sheshunoff & Company.
HG2611.M5B35 332.1'09774 75-648538 MARC-S

Banks of Minnesota.
[s. l.] Sheshunoff & Co.
v. 23 x 29 cm.
ISSN 0360-4306
1. Banks and banking—Minnesota—Finance—Statistics. I. Sheshunoff & Company.
HG2611.M6B35 332.1'09776 75-648747 MARC-S

The Banks of Mississippi.
[s. l.] Sheshunoff & Co.
v. 23 x 29 cm.
Key title: The Banks of Mississippi, ISSN 0361-4832
1. Banks and banking—Mississippi—Finance—Statistics. 2. Banks and banking—Mississippi—Directories. I. Sheshunoff & Company.
HG2611.M72B35 332.1'09762 76-640890 MARC-S

The Banks of Missouri.
[s. l.] Sheshunoff & Co.
v. 23 x 29 cm.
ISSN 0360-4314
1. Banks and banking—Missouri—Finance—Statistics. I. Sheshunoff & Company.
HG2611.M8B35 332.1'09778 75-648746 MARC-S

Banks of Nebraska.
[s. l.] Sheshunoff & Co.
v. 23 x 29 cm.
Key title: Banks of Nebraska, ISSN 0361-4840
1. Banks and banking—Nebraska—Finance—Statistics. 2. Banks and banking—Nebraska—Directories. I. Sheshunoff & Company.
HG2611.N22B35 332.1'09782 76-640887 MARC-S

Banks of New England.
[s. l.] Sheshunoff & Co.
v. 23 x 29 cm.
Key title: Banks of New England, ISSN 0361-4859
1. Banks and banking—New England—Finance—Statistics. 2. Banks and banking—New England—Directories. I. Sheshunoff & Company.
HG2601.B35 332.1'0974 76-641844 MARC-S

The Banks of Ohio.
[s. l.] Sheshunoff & Co.
v. 23 x 29 cm.
ISSN 0360-2362
1. Banks and banking—Ohio—Finance—Statistics. I. Sheshunoff & Company.
HG2611.O3B35 332.1'09771 75-648535 MARC-S

Banks of Oklahoma.
[s. l.] Sheshunoff & Co.
v. 23 x 29 cm.
ISSN 0360-2354
1. Banks and banking—Oklahoma—Finance—Statistics. I. Sheshunoff & Company.
HG2611.O5B35 332.1'09766 75-648534 MARC-S

Banks of Pennsylvania.
[s. l.] Sheshunoff & Co.
v. 23 x 29 cm.
ISSN 0360-2346
1. Banks and banking—Pennsylvania—Finance—Statistics. I. Sheshunoff & Company.
HG2611.P4B35 332.1'09748 75-648537 MARC-S

Banks of Tennessee.
[s. l.] Sheshunoff & Co.
v. 23 x 29 cm.
Key title: Banks of Tennessee, ISSN 0361-4867
1. Banks and banking—Tennessee—Finance—Statistics. 2. Banks and banking—Tennessee—Directories. I. Sheshunoff & Company.
HG2611.T22B35 332.1'09768 76-640891 MARC-S

The Banks of Texas.
[s. l.] Sheshunoff & Company.
v. 15 x 28 cm.
At head of title : Sheshunoff.
ISSN 0096-3488
1. Banks and banking—Texas—Periodicals. I. Sheshunoff & Company.
HG2611.T4B28 332.1'09764 75-641650 MARC-S

The Banks of the Carolinas.
[s. l.] Sheshunoff & Co.
v. 23 x 29 cm.
Key title: The Banks of the Carolinas, ISSN 0361-4875
1. Banks and banking—North Carolina—Finance—Statistics. 2. Banks and banking—North Carolina—Directories. 3. Banks and banking—South Carolina—Finance—Statistics. 4. Banks and banking—South Carolina—Directories. I. Sheshunoff & Company.
HG2611.N82B35 332.1'09756 76-640889 MARC-S

Banks of the West.
[s. l.] Sheshunoff & Co.
v. 23 x 29 cm.
Key title: Banks of the West, ISSN 0361-4883
1. Banks and banking—The West—Finance—Statistics. 2. Banks and banking—The West—Directories. I. Sheshunoff & Company.
HG2609.B35 332.1'0978 76-640893 MARC-S

Banks of Wisconsin.
[s. l.] Sheshunoff & Co.
v. 23 x 29 cm.
ISSN 0360-4322
1. Banks and banking—Wisconsin—Finance—Statistics. I. Sheshunoff & Company.
HG2611.W6B35 332.1'09775 75-648748 MARC-S

Bankson, Douglas.
Lenore Nevermore; a play about Edgar Allan Poe. Vancouver, New Play Centre [1972]
64 l.
1. Poe, Edgar Allan, 1809-1849, in fiction, drama, poetry. 2. Canadian drama, English. I. Title.
CaOTP NUC75-47263

Bankson, Douglas.
Nature in the raw is seldom. A farce in one act. Vancouver, New Play Centre, c1972.
22 l.
1. Canadian drama, English. I. Title.
CaOTP NUC75-48065

Bankson, Douglas.
Rest home, or Many happy returns, Pratt; a play. Vancouver, B.C., 1967.
41, 21 p.
Mimeographed typescript.
1. Canadian drama, English. I. Title.
CaOTP NUC74-115169

Bankson, Douglas.
Shellgame. Vancouver, New Play Centre, 1968.
56 l.
1. Canadian drama, English. I. Title.
CaOTP NUC75-47260

Bankson, Douglas.
Shootup, a one-act farce. Vancouver, New Play Center, 1963.
25 l.
1. Canadian drama, English. I. Title.
CaOTP NUC75-47262

Bankson, Douglas.
Stonehenge or Many happy returns, Pratt. A play in two acts. Vancouver, New Play Centre [1969]
1 v. (various pagings)
1. Canadian drama, English. I. Title.
CaOTP NUC75-47259

Bankson, Douglas.
Vacation; a play. Vancouver, New Play Centre, 1972.
76 l.
1. Canadian drama, English. I. Title.
CaOTP NUC75-47261

Bankson, Nicholas W
Bankson language screening test / by Nicholas W. Bankson. — Baltimore : University Park Press, c1977.
73 p. : ill. ; 22 x 28 cm.
Bibliography: p. 5.
ISBN 0-8391-1126-6
1. Bankson language screening test. I. Title.
LB1139.L3B35 372.6'044 77-5575
77 MARC

Bankston, Benjamin Godfrey.
The Enthronement psalms: representative cult-functional interpretations. Fort Worth, Tex., 1971.
238 l.
Thesis (Th.D.)—Southwestern Baptist Theological Seminary.
Bibliography: leaves 218-238.
1. Bible. O.T. Psalms—Criticism, interpretation, etc. 2. Cultus, Jewish. 3. Weiser, Artur, 1893- 4. Mowinckel, Sigmund Olaf Plytt, 1884- 5. Johnson, Aubrey Rodway. I. Title.
TxFS NUC73-31300

Bankston, Benjamin H.
see Schretter, Howard An. An atlas of multi-county organizational units in Georgia. 2d revision. [Athens] Dept. of Geography, Institute of Community and Area Development, University of Georgia, 1974.

Bankston, Clyde Perry, 1949-
Determination of the physical characteristics of smoke particulates generated by burning polymers / by Clyde Perry Bankston. -- [s.l. : s.n.], 1976.
xiv, 189 leaves : ill. ; 28 cm.
Thesis (Ph. D.)--Georgia Institute of Technology.
Vita.
Bibliography: leaves 183-188.
1. Smoke. 2. Particles. I. Title.
GAT NUC77-87874

Bankston, Clyde Perry, 1949-
see Observations of fire behavior... Atlanta, Georgia Institute of Technology, School of Aerospace Engineering, 1973.

Bankston, Eddie Wilson, 1938-
An investigation into the nature of values and attitudes of labor arbitrators as influenced by education, age, and experience... [n.p.] 1975.
xv, 225 l. illus., map. 29 cm.
Thesis (D.B.A.)--Louisiana State University, Baton Rouge, La.
Vita.
Bibliography: leaves [191]-196.
Includes abstract.
1. Arbitration, Industrial--United States. I. Title.
LU NUC77-92259

Bankston, Gordon.
The oil patch : oil field cartoons / Gordon Bankston; introd. by James A. Clark. -- Kermit, Tex. : Bankston, [197-]
[64] p. : chiefly ill. ; 19 cm.
Cover title: Red in the oil patch.
1. Oil fields--Caricatures and cartoons. 2. Petroleum industry and trade--Caricatures and cartoons. I. Title.
TxU NUC77-88383

Bankston, Linda Verlene Cochran, 1943-
The effects of the readability of mathematical materials on achievement in remedial mathematics in a selected community college. [Austin, Tex.] 1975.
xii, 142 l. illus. 29 cm.
Thesis (Ph.D.)--University of Texas at Austin.
Vita.
Bibliography: leaves 137-142.
1. Mathematics--Study and teaching. 2. Textbooks--Readability. I. Title.
TxU NUC77-92256

Bankston, Nancy.
Economy recipes for Brannen homes, the menus you choose. Compiled by "Aunt Nancy" Bankston. [Flagstaff, Ariz., Brannen Homes] 1961.
62 p. 24 cm.
1. Cookery, American. I. Title.
IU NUC74-168010

Bankston, Patrick Walker, 1946-
The morphology, permeability, and phagocytic activity of the vascular lining of fetal rat liver and their relationship to hematopoietic activity. [n.p.] 1973.
232 l.
Thesis (Ph. D.)--University of Chicago.
1. Liver. 2. Hematopoietic system. 3. Embryology--Rats. I. Title.
ICU NUC75-18559

Bankston, Paul John, 1947-
Topological ultraproducts, by Paul Bankston. [n. p.] c1974.
68 l. 29 cm.
Thesis (Ph. D.)--University of Wisconsin.
Vita.
Includes bibliography.
I. Title.
WU NUC76-23676

Bankston, Thomas Arthur, 1942-
The relationship between market price and book value for regulated utilities / by Thomas Arthur Bankston. -- [n.p.] 1975.
ix, 191 leaves : diagrs. ; 28 cm.
Thesis--University of Florida.
Vita.
Bibliography: leaves 188-190.
1. Public utilities--Finance. I. Title.
FU NUC77-87727

Bankston, William Boleyn.
A structural level examination of forensic hospitalization : forensic commitment rates and social structural features of Louisiana Parishes / by William Boleyn Bankston. -- [s. l. : s. n.], 1976.
vi, 203 p. : ill. ; 28 cm.
Thesis (Ph. D.)--University of Tennessee, Knoxville.
Microfiche copy. Ann Arbor, Mich., University Microfilms, International, 1976. 3 sheets. 11 x 15 cm.
I. Title.
AAP NUC77-89178

Bankunga ya kintwadi. Revisé. [Kinshasa] Missions protestantes A. M. B. M. - B. M. M. [1969]
1 v. (unpaged) 16 cm.
On cover: Chants chvétiens en kituba.
1. Congo language--Texts. 2. Hymns, Congo.
NN NUC76-81919

Bankvall, Claes G
Guarded hot plate apparatus for the investigation of thermal insulations. Stockholm, The National Swedish Institute for Building Research, 1972.
75 p. illus. 30 cm. (Stockholm. Statens institut för byggnadsforskning. Document, 1972, no. 5)
Bibliography: p. 73-75.
AAP DHUD NUC73-31309

Bankvall, Claes G
Heat transfer in fibrous materials, by Claes G. Bankvall. Stockholm, National Swedish Institute for Building Research, 1972.
67 p. illus. (Document D4: 1972)
Bibliography: p. 64-67.
1. Materials--Thermal properties. 2. Heat--Transmission. I. Title. II. Series: Stockholm. Statens institut för byggnadsforskning. Document D4: 1972.
MCM NUC73-115251

Banmali, Bhooshan, 1938-
शब्दों का वृक्ष. [कवि] भूषण बनमाली. [1. संस्करण] New Delhi, Tomorrow Publication [1970]
110 p. 25 cm. Rs4.00
In Hindi.

I. Title.
Title romanized: Śabdoṃ kā vṛksha.
PK2098.13.A55S2 74-915963
Library of Congress 71 [3] SA

Bānmaw Tin Aung.
(Hsoshelit ạbḥdan)
ဆိုရှယ်လစ်အဘိဓာန် = A dictionary on socialism / ဗန်းမော်တင်အောင်....-- ရန်ကုန် : ပင်းယ ယတိုက်, 1964.
350 p. ; 22 cm.
In Burmese.
1. Communism--Dictionaries. I. Title. II. Title: A dictionary on socialism.
HX17.B32 1964 75-985371

Bānmaw Tin Aung.
(Myanma naing ngan taw thạmāing)
မြန်မာနိုင်ငံတော်သမိုင်း = History of Burma / ဗန်းမော်တင်အောင်ပြုစုသည်. -- ရန်ကုန် : ပြည်သူ့အလင်းစာပေ, 1963.
355 p. : ill. ; 19 cm.
In Burmese.
1. Burma--History. I. Title. II. Title: History of Burma.
DS528.5.B36 75-984796

Bānmaw Tin Aung.
[Ngạ Myat Htūn]
ဗန်းမော်တင်အောင်၏မြန်မာ့မျိုးချစ် ပြောက်ကျား ခေါင်း ဆောင်ကြီး ငမြတ်ထွန်း နှင့် ဝတ္ထုရှည်၂ပုဒ် : လှဥမ္မာ, မမမိနှင့်ကျွန်တော်.-- ရန်ကုန် : ပုဂံ, 1972.
247 p. ; 18 cm.
"ပုဂံစာအုပ်အမှတ် ၂၄၀."
In Burmese.
K3.00

1. Myat Htūn, fl. 1790-1851. I. Title: Ngạ Myat Htūn. II. Title: Hlạ Umma. III. Title: Mạ Mạ Mị hnị kyuntaw.
Title romanized: Bānmaw Tin Aung i myanmạ myō chit pyauk kyā hkāung hsaung kyị Ngạ Myat Htūn.
PL3988.B37A6 1972 75-985372

Banmeyer, Daniel.
Madagascar. [Johannesburg] South African Institute of International Affairs, 1971.
14 p. 31 cm. SANB***
1. Madagascar -- History. 2. Madagascar -- Relations (general) with South Africa. 3. Africa, South--Relations (general) with Madagascar.
DT469.M27B26 72-197798
MARC

Bann, Richard W.
see McCabe, John, 1920- Laurel & Hardy. London, W. H. Allen, 1975.

Bann, Richard W.
see McCabe, John, 1920- Laurel & Hardy. 1st ed. New York, Dutton, c1975.

Bann, Richard W., joint author.
see Maltin, Leonard. Our gang ... New York, Crown Publishers, c1977.

Bann, Robert F
Social research as applied to design determinants, by Robert F. Bann II. [Kent, Ohio, Kent State University School of Architecture and Environmental Design] 1973.
41 p. 29 cm.
1. Architectural design. 2. Public housing--Social aspects. I. Title.
OKentU NUC74-123744

Bann, Stephen.
Fleece [by] Stephen Bann, designer Alistair Cant. [Lanark, Scot.] Wild Hawthorn Press [n.d.]
1 l. 58.2 x 45.4 cm.
Poem.
InU NUC73-115106

Bann, Stephen, comp.
Russian formalism: a collection of articles and texts in translation, edited by Stephen Bann and John E. Bowlt. Edinburgh, Scottish Academic Press; London, distributed by Chatto and Windus, 1973.
[8], 178 p. 23 cm. (20th century studies) B 73-23409
Includes bibliographical references.
CONTENTS: Todorov, T. Some approaches to Russian formalism.--Jakobson, R. Letter to Haroldo de Campos on Martin Codax's poetic texture.--Sherwood, R. Viktor Shklovsky and the development of early formalist theory on prose literature.--Shklovsky, V. The resurrection of the word (1914).--Shklovsky, V. On the connection between devices of Syuzhet construction and general stylistic devices (1919).--Doležel, L. Narrative composition.--Reformatsky, A. A. An essay on the analysis of the composition of the novella (1922).--Kristeva, J. The ruin of a poetics.--Eikhenbaum, B. Literature and cinema (1926).--Shklovsky, V. Poetry and prose in cinematography (1927).--Bowlt, J. Russian formalism and the visual arts.--Bliznakov, M. The rationalist movement in Soviet architecture in the 1920's.--Eco, U. On the possibility of generating aesthetic messages in an Edenic language.
ISBN 0-7011-1938-1 : £2.50
1. Formalism (Russian literature) I. Bowlt, John E., joint comp. II. Title.
PG3026.F6B3 1973b 891.7'09'0042 75-315044
MARC

Bann, Stephen, comp.
Russian formalism; a collection of articles and texts in translation. Edited by Stephen Bann and John E. Bowlt. New York, Barnes & Noble [1973]
178 p. 23 cm. (20th century studies)
Includes bibliographical references.
CONTENTS: Todorov, T. Some approaches to Russian formalism.—Jakobson, R. Letter to Haroldo de Campos on Martin Codax's poetic texture.—Sherwood, R. Viktor Shklovsky and the development of early formalist theory on prose literature.—Shklovsky, V. The resurrection of the word (1914).—On the connection between devices of syuzhet construction and general stylistic devices (1919).—Doležel, L. Narrative composition—a link between German and Russian poetics.—Reformatsky, A. A. An essay on the analysis of the composition of the novella.—Kristeva, J. The ruin of a poetics.—Eikhenbaum, B. Literature and cinema (1926).—Shklovsky, V. Poetry and prose in cinematography (1927).—Bowlt, J. Russian formalism and the visual arts.—Bliznakov, M. The rationalist movement in Soviet architecture in 1920's.—Eco, U. On the possibility of generating aesthetic messages in an Edenic language.
1. Formalism (Russian literature) I. Bowlt, John E., joint comp. II. Title.
PG3026.F6B3 891.7'09 74-156762
ISBN 0-06-490298-6 MARC

Bann, Stephen, comp.
The tradition of constructivism / edited and with an introduction by Stephen Bann. — London : Thames and Hudson, 1974.
xlix, 334 p. : ill., facsims. ; 22 cm. — (The documents of 20th century art)
GB74-22139
Bibliography: p. 303-334.
ISBN 0-500-60010-4 : £3.75. ISBN 0-500-61010-X pbk.
1. Constructivism (Art)—Addresses, essays, lectures. 2. Art, Modern—20th century—Addresses, essays, lectures. I. Title. II. Series.
N6494.C64B36 1974b 709'.04 75-313552
75 MARC

Bann, Stephen
see East Kent and Folkestone Arts Centre. An exhibition of concrete poetry... [Folkestone, Eng., 1967]

Bann, Stephen.
see Finlay, Ian Hamilton. Ian Hamilton Finlay . . . [s.l., s.n., c1972 ([Hertford] : Shenval Press)

Bann, Steven, comp.
The tradition of constructivism. Edited and with an introd. by Steven Bann. New York, Viking Press [1974]
xlix, 334 p. illus. 22 cm. (The Documents of 20th-century art)
$16.50
Bibliography: p. 303-334.
1. Constructivism (Art)—Addresses, essays, lectures. 2. Art, Modern—20th century—Addresses, essays, lectures. I. Title. II. Series.
N6494.C64B36 1974 709'.04 72-75748
ISBN 0-670-72301-0 ; 0-670-01956-9 (pbk.) MARC

al-Bannā, 'Abd al-Raḥmān. Fī fann al-masraḥīyah. 1972?
see Ghazwat Badr al-kubrá. [1972?]

al-Bannā, Anwar al-Jindī.
(Qaḍāyā al-aqṭār al-Islāmīyah)
قضايا الأقطار الاسلامية : اول وثائق ومذكرات تاريخية عن يقظة الاسلام وزحفه الى قواعده فى قرن كامل ودراسة لقضايا الأقطار العربية الاسلامية / يقدمه انور الجندى البنــا. — القاهرة : شركة الاخوان المسلمين للصحافة والطباعة والنشر، [1946] 1365.
73 p. ; 22 cm.
1. Near East—History—20th century—Addresses, essays, lectures. I. Title.
DS62.4.B35 75-549798

al-Bannā, Ḥasan, 1906-1949.
(Allāh fī al-'aqīdah al-Islāmīyah)
الله في العقيدة الاسلامية [تأليف] حسن البنا. الطبعة 2. جدة، الدار السعودية للنشر، 1971.
55 p. 20 cm. (مجموعة آثار حسن البنا)
1. God (Islam) I. Title.
BP166.2.B35 1971 74-237420

al-Banna, Hasan, 1906-1949. al-Banna yutalibu bi-hukm al-Islam. 197-?
see al-Banna, Hasan, 1906-1949. (Nafahat Ramadan) [197-?]

al-Bannā, Ḥasan, 1906-1949.
[Bayna al-ams wa-al-yawm]
بين الامس واليوم. [دمشق، مطبعة الاتحاد الشرقي 196-؟]
53 p. 17 cm.
(His 8 (رسائل حسن البنا، رسالة 2) (His 2 (سلسلة آثار الامام حسن البنا، حلقة (رسائل الاخوان المسلمين، 2)
1. Islam and state—Addresses, essays, lectures. I. Title.
BP173.6.B37 1960z 73-200262

al-Bannā, Ḥasan, 1906-1949.
(Da'watunā fī ṭawr jadīd)
دعوتنا فى طور جديد [تأليف] حسن البنا. [الخرطوم] الدار السودانية للطباعة والنشر [196-؟]
31 p. 20 cm.
1. Jam'īyat al-Ikhwān al-Muslimīn (Egypt)—Addresses, essays, lectures. I. Title.
DT107.82.B277 1960z N E 68-4263

al-Bannā, Hasan, 1906-1949. Da'watunā fī tawr jadīd. 197-?
see al-Bannā, Hasan, 1906-1949. (Risālat al-ta'ālīm) [197-?]

al-Banna, Hasan, 1906-1949. Din wa-siyasah. 197-?
see al-Banna, Hasan, 1906-1949. (Nafahat Ramadan) [197-?]

al-Bannā, Ḥasan, 1906-1949.
(Fī al-da'wah)
فى الدعوة، وهى سلسلة من خطب ومقالات حسن البنا. [القاهرة] مطبعة التوكل [194-
v. 18 cm.
«سبق ان نشرت فى مجلة الاخوان المسلمين القديمة»
1. Islam—Addresses, essays, lectures. 2. Egypt—Politics and government—1919-1952—Addresses, essays, lectures. I. Title.
BP88.A2B36 74-220335

al-Bannā, Ḥasan, 1906-1949.
[Fī al-tafsīr]
رسالتان : في التفسير، وسورة الفاتحة [تأليف] حسن البنا. [الطبعة 1] بيروت، منشورات العصر الحديث [1972]
80 p. 20 cm.
Includes bibliographical references.
1. Koran. Sūrat al-fātiḥah—Addresses, essays, lectures. 2. Koran—Hermeneutics—Addresses, essays, lectures. I. al-Bannā, Ḥasan, 1906-1949. Koran. Sūrat al-fātiḥah. 1972. II. Title. III. Title: Sūrat al-fātiḥah.
Title romanized: Risālatān: fī al-tafsīr, wa-Sūrat al-fātiḥah.
BP128.16.B29 1972 74-218278

al-Bannā, Hasan, 1906-1949. al-Ikhwān al-Muslimūn tahta rāyat al-Qur'ān. 197-?
see al-Bannā, Hasan, 1906-1949. (Risālat al-ta'ālīm) [197-?]

al-Bannā, Ḥasan, 1906-1949.
(al-Imām al-shahīd Ḥasan al-Bannā yataḥaddathu ilá shabāb al-'ālam al-Islāmī)
الامام الشهيد حسن البنا يتحدث الى شباب العالم الاسلامي. — الطبعة 1. — دمشق : دار القلم، 1974.
276 p. ; 19 cm.
1. Islam—20th century—Addresses, essays, lectures. I. Title.
BP88.B24I45 1974 75-549134

al-Banna, Hasan, 1906-1949. Koran. Surat al-fatiḥah. 1972
see al-Banā, Hasan, 1906-1949. [Fī al-tafsīr] Risālatān: fī al-tafsīr, wa-Sūrat al-fātiḥah. [1972]

al-Bannā, Ḥasan, 1906-1949.
(Majmū'at rasā'il)
مجموعة رسائل الامام الشهيد حسن البنا. [بيروت] يطلب من مؤسسة الرسالة [197-؟]
624 p. 20 cm.
Includes bibliographical references.
1. Jam'īyat al-Ikhwān al-Muslimīn (Egypt)
DT107.82.B29 1970z 73-222308

al-Bannā, Ḥasan, 1906-1949.
(al-Ma'thūrāt)
المأثورات [تأليف] حسن البنا. الكويت، مكتبة المنار [195-؟]
103 p. 17 cm.
1. Islamic prayers. I. Title.
BP183.3.B35 1950z 74-211441

al-Bannā, Ḥasan, 1906-1949.
[Mudhakkirāt al-da'wah wa-al-dā'iyah. Urdu]
حسن البنا شهيد كى ڈائرى / مترجم خليل احمد حامدى. — اشاعت 1. — لاہور : اسلامى پبليكيشنز، -1974.
v. ; 18 cm.
Includes bibliographical references.
Rs13.00 (v. 1)
1. Jam'īyat al-Ikhwān al-Muslimīn (Egypt) I. Title.
Title romanized: Ḥasan al-Bannā Shahīd kī ḍā'irī.
DT107.82.B318 75-930250

al-Bannā, Ḥasan, 1906-1949.
(Muḥammad al-Nabī al-'aẓīm)
محمد النبي العظيم. كلمات خالدة. المرأة المسلمة. بقلم حسن البنا. [الطبعة 1] بيروت ؟ 1972]
71 p. 20 cm.
Essays.
1. Islam—Addresses, essays, lectures. I. Title.
BP88.B24M8 1972 74-236328

al-Bannā, Ḥasan, 1906-1949.
(Nafaḥāt Ramaḍān)
نفحات رمضان. دين وسياسة. البنا يطالب بحكم الاسلام، بقلم حسن البنا. [بيروت، مكتبة حطين ؟ 197-]
64 p. 20 cm. (من نور الاسلام، 3)
«الدين المعاملة» : p. 62-64.
1. Ramadan—Addresses, essays, lectures. 2. Islam and state—Addresses, essays, lectures. I. al-Bannā, Ḥasan, 1906-1949. Dīn wa-siyāsah. 197-? II. al-Bannā, Ḥasan, 1906-1949. al-Bannā yuṭālibu bi-ḥukm al-Islām. 197-? III. Title.
BP186.4.B36 1970z 74-215109

al-Bannā, Ḥasan, 1906-1949.
(al-Rasā'il al-thalāth)
الرسائل الثلاث. [بيروت] دار الكتاب العربى [195-؟]
120 p. 18 cm. (من رسائل الاخوان المسلمين)
Text signed: حسن البنا
CONTENTS: دعوتنا — الى اى شيء ندعو الناس — نحو النور
1. Jam'īyat al-Ikhwān al-Muslimīn (Egypt) I. Title.
DT107.82.B42 1950z 74-211729

al-Bannā, Ḥasan, 1906-1949.
(Risālat al-ta'ālīm)
رسالة التعاليم، لحسن البنا. [n. p., 197-?]
39, 24, 31 p. 17 cm.
CONTENTS: رسالة التعاليم. — الاخوان المسلمون تحت راية القرآن. — دعوتنا فى طور جديد.
1. Jam'īyat al-Ikhwān al-Muslimīn (Egypt) I. al-Bannā, Ḥasan, 1906-1949. al-Ikhwān al-Muslimūn taḥta rāyat al-Qur'ān. 197-? II. al-Bannā, Ḥasan, 1906-1949. Da'watunā fī ṭawr jadīd. 197-? III. Title. IV. Title: al-Ikhwān al-Muslimūn taḥta rāyat al-Qur'ān. V. Title: Da'watunā fī ṭawr jadīd.
BP10.J383B33 1970z 75-587693

al-Bannā, Ḥasan, 1906-1949.
(al-Salām fī al-Islām)
السلام في الاسلام [تأليف] حسن البنا. الطبعة 2. جدة، الدار السعودية للنشر، 1971.
82 p. 20 cm. (مجموعة آثار حسن البنا)
1. Islam—Addresses, essays, lectures. I. Title.
BP88.B24S24 1971 74-221040

al-Bannā, Ḥasan, 1906-1949.
(Ṣifāt al-muttaqīn wa-maqāṣid Sūrat al-baqarah)
صفات المتقين ومقاصد سورة البقرة [تأليف] حسن البنا. [بيروت] منشورات العصر الحديث، 1972.
63 p. 20 cm.
1. Koran. Sūrat al-baqarah—Criticism, interpretation, etc. I. Title.
BP128.17.B36 1972 74-219099

al-Bannā, Ḥasan, 1906-1949.
سيناء بين اطماع الاستعماريين والصهيونيين وتفريط الاشتراكيين الثوريين، مقالات تاريخية كتبها حسن البنا، سيد قطب [و] كامل الشريف. [الطبعة 1. القاهرة ؟ 1967]
66 p. 17 cm. (من رسائل الاخوان المسلمين)
1. Israel-Arab War, 1948-1949—Sinaitic Peninsula. 2. Jam'īyat al-Ikhwān al-Muslimīn (Egypt) 3. Sinaitic Peninsula—History—Addresses, essays, lectures. I. Quṭb, Sayyid, 1903-1966. II. al-Sharīf, Kāmil. III. Title.
Title romanized: Sīnā' bayna aṭmā' al-isti'mārīyīn wa-al-Ṣihyūnīyīn.
DS126.99.S6B36 1967 75-588480

al-Bannā, Ḥasan, 1906-1949.
(Tazkiyah-yi nafs)
تزكيۂ نفس؛ اوراد و وظائف كے ذريعے. [مصنف] حسن البنا. لاہور، المحراب؛ [ملنے كا پتہ: مكتبہ الخير، 1971]
114 p. 16 cm. Rs3.00
In Urdu.

1. Islamic prayers. I. Title.
BP183.3.B36 1971 79-933133

al-Bannā, Jamāl.
(Rūḥ al-Islām)
روح الاسلام، تأليف جمال البنا. [القاهرة] مطبعة حسان، المقدمة 1972]
198 p. 20 cm. £E0.15
Includes bibliographical references.
1. Islam—Appreciation. 2. Islam—Essence, genius, nature. I. Title.
BP88.B25R8 72-960795

al-Bannā, Jamāl.
(al-Thaqāfah al-'ummālīyah)
الثقافة العمالية بين حاضرها ومستقبلها ,تأليف, جمال البنا. ,القاهرة، المؤسسة الثقافية العمالية، 1970,
424 p. 24 cm. (المكتبة العمالية، مجموعة المراجع الاساسية، رقم 10)
Bibliography: p. 410–417.
1. Labor and laboring classes—Education—Egypt. 2. Labor and laboring classes—Education. I. Title.
LC5058.E3B36 75–972632

al-Bannā, Kamāl Ṣāliḥ.
(Tashrī'āt al-aḥwāl al-shakhṣīyah fī Miṣr, mu'allaqan 'alayhā bi-al-mudhakkirāt al-īḍāḥīyah wa-al-mabādi' al-qaḍā'īyah wa-ārā' al-shurrāḥ)
تشريعات الأحوال الشخصية فى مصر، معلقا عليها بالمذكرات الايضاحية والمبادئ القضائية وآراء الشراح / كمال صالح البنا. — الطبعة 1. — ,القاهرة, : الشركة المصرية للطباعة والنشر، 1976.
368 : ill. ; 24 cm.
Includes legislation.
Includes bibliographical references.
£E2.50
1. Persons (Law)—Egypt. 2. Domestic relations—Egypt. I. Title: Tashrī'āt al-aḥwāl al-shakhṣīyah fī Miṣr ...
77–960378

al-Bannā, Maḥmūd 'Alī
see Koran. ,Sound recording, al-Qur'ān al-karīm. ,1970,

el Banna, Mohamed, 1929- joint author.
see Hankinson, John. Pituitary and parapituitary tumours. London, Saunders, 1976.

al-Bannā, Muḥammad Ibrāhīm.
(Ibn Kaysān al-Naḥwī)
ابن كيسان النحوى : حياته، آثاره، آراؤه / محمد ابراهيم البنا. — الطبعة 1. — القاهرة : دار الاعتصام، 1975.
223 p. ; 24 cm.
Bibliography: p. 219–223.
£E1.20
1. Ibn Kaysān, Muḥammad ibn Aḥmad, d. 912? 2. Arabic philology—Biography.
PJ6064.I 185B3 76–960478

Banna, Muhammad Salim.
Gas-phase photoemission with soft (NaKa, MgDa) and ultrasoft (YM5) x-ray sources. -- ,Berkeley, 1975.
vii, 141 leaves : ill.
Thesis (Ph.D.)--University of California.
Bibliography: leaves 137-141.
CU NUC77-87873

Banna, S Al
see Al Banna, S.

al-Bannā, Salwá.
('Arūs khalfa al-nahr)
عروس خلف النهر، قصة ما روته «فلسطين» عن خطيبها في الزمن الممتد من عمر الثورة بين «الكرامة» والاستشهاد. ,تأليف, سلوى البنا. الطبعة 1. بيروت، دار الاتحاد، 1972.
72 p. 17 cm.
I. Title.
PJ7816.A6A9 74–205916

al-Bannā, Salwá.
(al-Wajh al-ākhar)
الوجه الآخر : مجموعة قصص / سلوى البنا. — الطبعة 1. — بيروت : المؤسسة العربية للدراسات والنشر، 1974.
176 p. ; 20 cm.
I. Title.
PJ7816.A6W3 75–587846

Banna Ventorino, Lia.
Il D'Artagnan di Nino Martoglio : un capitolo del giornalismo militante catanese (1889–1904) / Lia Banna Ventorino ; presentazione del prof. Carlo Muscetta. — Catania : N. Giannotta, ,1974,
559 p. ; 22 cm. — (Biblioteca siciliana di cultura ; 31) It 76–Jan
"Indice delle poesie di Nino Martoglio pubblicate sul D'Artagnan e non riportate nella Centona": p. ,315,–322.
"Indice generale del giornale": p. ,323,–551.
Bibliography: p. 555–559.
L10000
1. D'Artagnan. 2. Martoglio, Nino, 1870–1921. I. D'Artagnan. II. Title.
PN5250.D3B3 76–506661

Bannach, Horst.
Wunder beweisen garnichts. Probleme d. 20. Jahrhunderts im Spiegel d. Apostelgeschichte. (Übers. d. Apostelgeschichte: Horst Bannach.) Stuttgart, Quell-Verl. (1970).
200 p. with illus. 19 cm. GDB 70–A51–27
ISBN 3–7918–2048–6 : DM14.80
1. Bible. N. T. Acts—Criticism, interpretation, etc. I. Title. II. Title: Probleme des 20. ,zwanzigsten, Jahrhunderts im Spiegel der Apostelgeschichte. III. Bible. N. T. Acts. German. Bannach. 1970.
BS2625.2.B26 75–579708

Bannach, Klaus.
Die Lehre von der doppelten Macht Gottes bei Wilhelm von Ockham : problemgeschichtliche Voraussetzungen und Bedeutung / von Klaus Bannach. — Wiesbaden : F. Steiner, 1975.
424 p. ; 25 cm. — (Veröffentlichungen des Instituts für Europäische Geschichte Mainz ; Bd. 75 : Abteilung für Abendländische Religionsgeschichte) GFR76-A
A revision of the author's thesis, Munich, 1974.
Includes texts in Latin.
Bibliography: p. ,418,-423.
ISBN 3-515-02102-7
1. God—History of doctrines. 2. Creation—History of doctrines. 3. Ockham, William, d. ca. 1349. I. Title. II. Series: Institut für Europäische Geschichte, Mainz. Veröffentlichungen ; Bd. 75.
BT100.O25B36 1975 231 76-463631
76 MARC

Bannai, Tōru, 1923–
(Fuyu no Chichibu fudasho)
冬の秩父札所 / 坂内享. — 八王子 : ふだん記全国グループ, 1975.
71 p. : ill. ; 21 cm. — (ふだん記本 ; 44) Ja 75–16539
Cover title.
1. Buddhist pilgrims and pilgrimages—Japan—Chichibu region. I. Title. II. Series: Fudangibon ; 44.
BQ6450.J32C472 76–801766

Bannan, James F
The Thompson Submachinegun / by James F. Bannan ; ,photos. by Stephen Micklas,. — ,s.l., : Southwest Pub. Co., c1975-
v. : ill. ; 29 cm. — (Notes on auto ordnance)
Edition limited to 500 copies.
1. Thompson submachine gun. I. Title.
UF620.T5B36 623.4'424 75-30166
76 MARC

Bannan, John F
Law, morality, and Vietnam; the peace militants and the courts ,by, John F. and Rosemary S. Bannan. Bloomington, Indiana University Press ,1974,
vii, 241 p. 24 cm.
Includes bibliographical references.
1. Trials (Political crimes and offenses)—United States. 2. Vietnamese Conflict, 1961– —Protest movements—United States. I. Bannan, Rosemary S., 1925– joint author. II. Title.
KF221.P6B3 345'.73'0231 73–16522
ISBN 0–253–14732–8 MARC

Bannan, Rosemary S., 1925- joint author
see Bannan, John F Law, morality, and Vietnam; the peace militants and the courts. Bloomington, Indiana Univ. Press ,1974,

al-Bannānī, Fatḥ Allāh ibn Abī Bakr, b. 1864.
رسالة فتح الله في ذكر من سمي في الشقائق بلطف الله، لفتح الله البنانى. الرباط، المطبعة الوطنية، 1932.
12 p. 24 cm.
1. Sufism — Biography. 2. Ṭāshkubrīzādah, Aḥmad ibn Muṣṭafá, 1495–1561. al-Shaqā'iq al-Nu'mānīyah. I. Title.
Title romanized: Risālat Fatḥ Allāh.
BP189.4.B36 75–586756

al-Bannānī, Muhammad ibn al-Hasan, 18th cent.
al-Fath al-Rabbānī fī-mā dhahala 'anhu al-Zurqānī. 1890
see al-Zurqānī, 'Abd al-Bāqī ibn Yūsuf, 1611 or 12-1687 or 8. (Sharh 'Abd al-Bāqī al-Zurqānī 'alá Mukhtasar Abī al-Diyā' Khalīl) [1307 i. e. 1890]

Bannard, John.
Bibliography of electrochemical machining including electrochemical grinding / ,by, John Bannard and Lorna Bannard. — ,Nottingham, : ,The authors,, ,1975,
,13, p. ; 21 x 31 cm. GB76-01502
ISBN 0-905224-00-0 : £4.00
1. Electrochemical cutting—Bibliography. 2. Electrolytic grinding—Bibliography. I. Bannard, Lorna, joint author. II. Title.
Z7914.E36B35 016.6713'5 76-360999
,TJ1191, 76 MARC

Bannard, John, joint author.
see Bennett, Jim. Colour pigeons. Chilwell, The authors, ,1976,

Bannard, Lorna, joint author.
see Bannard, John. Bibliography of electrochemical machining including electrochemical grinding. ,Nottingham, ,The authors, ,1975,

Bannard, Walter Darby, 1934–
Walter Darby Bannard. Introd. and an interview with the artist by Jane Harrison Cone. ,Baltimore, Baltimore Museum of Art ,1973,
72 p. illus. (part col.) 27 cm.
Catalog of an exhibition held at the Baltimore Museum of Art, Oct. 2–Nov. 11, 1973; the High Museum of Art, Atlanta, Feb. 24–Mar. 31, 1974; and the Museum of Fine Arts, Houston, May 30–July 28, 1974.
Bibliography: p. 68–72.
1. Bannard, Walter Darby, 1934– I. Cone, Jane Harrison. II. Baltimore. Museum of Art. III. High Museum of Art. IV. Houston, Tex. Museum of Fine Arts.
ND237.B24A57 759.13 73–87987
MARC

Bannard, Walter Darby, 1934-
see Cleveland Museum of Art. Contemporary American artists. ,Cleveland, 1973,

Bannard, Walter Darby, 1934-
see Hofmann, Hans, 1880-1966. Hans Hofmann ... ,Houston, Museum of Fine Arts, c1976.

Bannasch, Hermann.
Das Bistum Paderborn unter den Bischöfen Rethar und Meinwerk (983–1036) Paderborn, Selbstverlag des Altertumsvereins, 1972.
xxxii, 365 p. geneal. table. 24 cm. (Studien und Quellen zur westfälischen Geschichte, Bd. 12) GDB***
Originally presented as the author's thesis, Marburg, 1968.
Bibliograpy: p. xiii–xxx.
1. Paderborn (Archdiocese) 2. Rethar, Bp. of Paderborn. 3. Meinwerk, Bp. of Paderborn, ca. 970–1036. I. Title. II. Series.
BX1538.P3B35 1972 72–359284

Bannat, Edward George.
An investigation of Lockheed's solvency by use of financial ratios by Edward George Bannat. Monterey, Calif., Naval Postgraduate School, 1974.
77 p.
"AD-782 314."
Bibliography: p. 76-77.
Microfiche (negative) Washington, D.C. United States National Technical Information Service, 1974. 1 sheet. 11 x 15 cm.
1. Lockheed Aircraft Corporation. 2. Ratio analysis. I. United States. Naval Postgraduate School, Monterey, Calif. II. Title.
NRU NUC76-24167

Bannatyne, Alexander.
How your children can learn to live a rewarding life; behavior modification for parents and teachers ,by, Alexander Bannatyne ,and, Maryl Bannatyne. Springfield, Ill., Thomas ,1973,
xiii, 119 p. 24 cm.
Bibliography: p. 109.
1. Behavior modification. 2. Children—Management. I. Bannatyne, Maryl, joint author. II. Title.
BF637.B4B36 649'.1'019 72–81669
ISBN 0–398–02572–X MARC

Bannatyne, Alexander.
Reading, an auditory vocal process / Alexander Bannatyne. — San Rafael, CA : Academic Therapy Publication, c1973.
96 p. ; 23 cm.
Bibliography: p. 95-96.
ISBN 0-87879-051-9
1. Reading. 2. Reading—Remedial teaching. I. Title.
LB1050.B35 372.4 72-95640
75 MARC

Bannatyne, Alexander, joint author
see Bannatyne, Maryl. Body-image/communication... Rantoul, Ill., Learning Systems Press [1973]

Bannatyne, Andrew.
Judicial statistics; speech of Andrew Bannatyne, at general meeting of the Faculty of Procurators in Glasgow, held on 4th May, 1863. Glasgow, Printed by J. Graham, 1863.
30 p. 21 cm.
1. Judicial statistics—Scotland. I. Glasgow. Faculty of Procurators. II. Title.
KDC161.B35 347'.41'013 74–185368
MARC

Bannatyne, Barry B
Cretaceous bentonite deposits of Manitoba, by Barry B. Bannatyne. Winnipeg, Man., Mines Branch, 1963.
44 p. 26 cm. (Manitoba. Mines Branch. Publication 62-5)
Bibliography: p. 44.
1. Bentonite deposits–Manitoba. I. Title. II. Series.
CaBVaU NUC76-75693

Bannatyne, Barry B
High-calcium limestone deposits of Manitoba / by B. B. Bannatyne. — Winnipeg : Dept. of Mines, Resources and Environmental Management, Mineral Resources Division, 1975.
103 p. : ill. ; 26 cm. — (Publication - Dept. of Mines, Resources and Environmental Management, Mineral Resources Division ; 75-1) C***
Part of illustrative matter in pocket.
Bibliography: p. 101-103.
1. Limestone—Manitoba. I. Title. II. Series: Manitoba. Mineral Resources Division. Publication - Dept. of Mines, Resources and Environmental Management, Mineral Resources Division ; 75-1.
TN967.B33 553'.5 76-370729
76 MARC

Bannatyne, Barry B
Potash deposits, rock salt, and brines in Manitoba. Winnipeg, Printed by R.S. Evans, Queen's printer, 1960.
30 p. illus. 25 cm. (Manitoba. Dept. of Mines and Natural Resources. Mines Branch. Publication 59-1)
1. Potassium–Manitoba. 2. Salt–Manitoba. 3. Brine–Manitoba. I. Title. II. Series.
TxBeaL NUC74-172187

Bannatyne, Barry B
Preliminary survey of bogs for peat moss in southeastern Manitoba by Barry B. Bannatyne. Winnipeg, Mines Branch, 1964.
iv, 43, A2-A16 p. illus., fold. map. (Manitoba. Dept. of Mines and Natural Resources. Mines Branch. Publication, 63-5)
Bibliography: p. 42.
1. Peat-bogs–Manitoba. I. Title.
CU NUC76-75681

Bannatyne, Barry B joint author
see McCabe, H R Lake St. Martin crypto-explosion crater... Winnipeg, Dept. of Mines and Natural Resources, 1970.

Bannatyne, Maryl.
Body-image/communication; a psycho-physical development program, by Maryl Bannatyne and Alexander Bannatyne. Rantoul, Ill., Learning Systems Press [1973]
358 p. illus. 26 cm.
1. Physically handicapped children–Education. 2. Perceptual-motor learning. 3. Motor ability. I. Bannatyne, Alexander, joint author. II. Title.
MsU NUC74-122903

Bannatyne, Maryl, joint author
see Bannatyne, Alexander. How your children can learn to live a rewarding life... Springfield, Ill., Thomas [1973]

The Bannatyne miscellany; containing original papers and tracts, chiefly relating to the history and literature of Scotland. New York, AMS Press [1973]
3 v. illus. 24 cm.
Edited by W. Scott, D. Laing, and T. Thomson.
Reprint of the 1827-55 ed. printed at Edinburgh, which was issued as no. 19 of Bannatyne Club Publications.
1. Scotland—History—To 1603—Sources. 2. Scotland—History—17th century—Sources. I. Scott, Sir Walter, Bart., 1771-1832, ed. II. Laing, David, 1793-1878, ed. III. Thomson, Thomas, 1773-1852, ed. IV. Bannatyne Club, Edinburgh. Publications, no. 19.
DA775.B35 941.06 71-144412
ISBN 0-404-52720-5 MARC

Banndorff, Traudlinde.
Die Frontalität in der griechischen Flachenkunst. [n.p.] 1969.
1 reel.
Negative made in 1970 by the Oesterreichischen Nationalbibliothek, Vienna.
Thesis (Ph.D.)—University of Vienna.
1. Human figure in art. 2. Vase–painting, Greek. 3. Bas-relief. 4. Art, Greek. I. Title.
ICU NUC74-118012

Banneker, Benjamin, 1731-1806.
The Virginia almanack, for the year of our Lord, 1794. Being the second after leap year. And the eighteenth of American independence. Calculated by the ingenious self taught astronomer, Benjamin Nanneker, a black man. Petersburg, Printed by William Prentis [1794]
1 reel. (Schomburg microfilm series no. 8)
Microfilm: New York, New York Public Library, 1969.
Collation of original: 1 v. (unpaged) illus.
1. Almanacs. I. Title. II. Series.
OKentU NUC76-47726

Banneker, Benjamin, 1731-1806.
see Tyson, Martha Ellicott, Mrs., 1795-1873. A sketch of the life of Benjamin Banneker... [Baltimore] Printed by J.D. Toy [1854]

Bannelier-Lavet, Marie Louise.
Brins d'herbe. Marseille, Leconte, 27, Bd Louis-Salvator, 1971.
67 p. 19 cm. F 72-12593
I. Title.
PQ2662.A54B7 73-323712

Bannemann, J J
Grain sorghum performance trials, 1972. Brookings, 1973.
19 p. (South Dakota. Agricultural Experiment Station. Circular 207)
I. Title.
DNAL NUC74-123745

Bannenberg, Theo.
Erhebung über den Schweinehandel in den Kreisen Arnsberg, Meschede und Brilon 1973 mit Berücksichtigung des Viehkaufsrechts in der Bundesrepublik Deutschland. Hannover, 1973.
115 p. (Hanover (City). Tierärztliche Hochschule. [Inaugural-Dissertation, 1973, no. 202])
English summary.
Bibliography: p. 113-115.
I. Title.
DNAL NUC76-72743

Banner, Albert H
The effects of urban pollution upon a coral reef system, a preliminary report by Albert H. Banner [and] Julie H. Bailey. [Honolulu] Hawaii Institute of Marine Biology [1970]
66 p. illus. (Hawaii Institute of Marine Biology. Technical report no. 25)
Bibliography: p. 53-55.
1. Marine pollution. 2. Coral reefs and islands. I. Baily, Julie H., joint author. II. Title. III. Series.
FTaSU NUC73-126237

Banner, Albert H
Thermal effects on eggs, larvae and juveniles of bluegill sunfish. [By] A. Banner and J.A. VanArman. Washington [Office of Research and Monitoring, U.S. Environmental Protection Agency] for sale by the Supt. of Docs., U.S. Govt. Print. Office, 1973.
vii, 111 p. illus. 26 cm. (Ecological research series EPA-R3, 73-041)
Project officer: Kenneth E.F. Hokanson.
NIC NUC75-18532

Banner, Albert H., joint author.
see Banner, Dora M. The alpheid shrimp of Australia. Sydney, [Australian Museum] 1973-

Banner, Angela.
Ant and bee go shopping, written and illustrated by Angela Banner. New York, F. Watts [c1972]
80 p. illus.
1. Buying, Domestic. I. Title.
OCl NUC74-123746

Banner, Arnold, 1942-
Thermal effects on eggs, larvae and juveniles of bluegill sunfish [by] A. Banner and J.A. Van Arman. Washington, U.S. Govt. Print. Off., 1972.
111 p. illus. (Ecological research series, 41)
Prepared for Office of Research and Monitoring, U.S. Environmental Protection Agency under contract 14-12-913, project 18050 GAB.
1. Bluegill. 2. Fishes—Reproduction. 3. Thermal pollution of rivers, lakes, etc. I. Van Arman, Joel A. II. United States. Environment Protection Agency. Office of Research and Monitoring. III. Title. IV. Series.
DI MiU DNAL NUC75-80106

Banner, David K
An analysis of the power and influence processes that affect organizational decision-making with regard to the evaluation of an experimentation/demonstration social action program: an empirical investigation of the Opportunity Funding Corporation (OFC) by David K. Banner. [Ann Arbor, Mich., University Microfilms, 1973]
1 reel. 35 mm.
Thesis–Northwestern University.
Collation of the original: 1 v. (various pagings) illus.
1. Decision-Making. I. Title.
ViBlbV NUC75-20189

Banner, David K
The politics of social program evaluation / David K. Banner, Samuel I. Doctors, Andrew C. Gordon ; foreword by David B. Hertz. — Cambridge, Mass. : Ballinger Pub. Co., c1975.
xx, 170 p. : ill. ; 24 cm.
Bibliography: p. 137-163.
Includes index.
ISBN 0-88410-009-X
1. Opportunity Funding Corporation. 2. Minority business enterprises—United States—Finance. 3. Evaluation research (Social action program)—United States—Case studies. I. Doctors, Samuel I., joint author. II. Gordon, Andrew C. III. Title.
HD2346.U5B25 362.5'0973 74-28452
74 MARC

Banner, David Lee, 1942-
Production of neutral kaons and lambdas from charged kaon interactions with complex nuclei. Ann Arbor, Mich., University Microfilms, 1972.
1 reel. 35 mm.
Thesis–University of Illinois at Urbana–Champaign.
Collation of the original: 86 leaves.
1. Mesons. 2. Nuclear physics–Experiments. I. Title.
ViBlbV NUC74-123747

Banner, Dora M
The alpheid shrimp of Australia, by Dora M. and Albert H. Banner. Sydney [Australian Museum] 1973-
v. illus. 24 cm. (Records of the Australian Museum, vol. 28, no. 15) $4.00 Aus***
Cover title.
Includes bibliographical references.
CONTENTS: pt. 1. The lower genera.
1. Snapping shrimps. 2. Crustacea—Australia. I. Banner, Albert H., joint author. II. Title. III. Series: Australian Museum, Sydney. Records of the Australian Museum, vol. 28, no. 15.
QH1.A985 vol. 28, no. 15 75-307658
500.9'08 s
[QL444.M33] 75 MARC

Banner, Gerald Paul, joint author
see Spence, Lee B Observations of synchronous satellite ATS-3... Lexington, Lincoln Laboratory, Massachusetts Institute of Technology, 1975.

Banner, Horace.
Voices in the rain forest. Illus. by Monica Young. London, Butterworth Press [1971]
84 p. illus., map. 19 cm.
1. Missions–Brazil. 2. Animal lore–Brazil. I. Title.
IEG NUC73-115145

Banner, James M 1935- comp.
Understanding the American experience: recent interpretations, edited by James M. Banner, Jr., Sheldon Hackney [and] Barton J. Bernstein. Under the general editorship of John Morton Blum. New York, Harcourt Brace Jovanovich [1973]
2 v. illus. 24 cm.
Includes bibliographical references.
1. United States—Historiography—Addresses, essays, lectures. 2. United States—History—Addresses, essays, lectures. I. Hackney, Sheldon, joint comp. II. Bernstein, Barton J., joint comp. III. Title.
E175.B36 917.3'03'072 73-75178
ISBN 0-15-592880-5 (v. 1) MARC
rev

Banner, János, 1888–
A Közep-Dunamedence régészeti bibliográfiája, 1960–1966 ₍írták₎ Banner ₍és₎ Jakabffy, összeállította Jakabffy Imre. Budapest, Akadémiai Kiadó, 1968.
242 p. 25 cm. 55.00
Title and introductory matter also in Russian, German, and French.
1. Hungary—Antiquities—Bibliography. 2. Hungary—Bibliography. 3. Transylvania—Bibliography. I. Jakabffy, Imre, joint author. II. Title.
Z2142.B32 74–210350

Banner, Lois W
The Protestant crusade; religious missions, benevolence, and reform in the United States, 1790–1840. [New York] 1970 [c1973]
403 l. 29 cm.
Thesis–Columbia University.
"Essay on sources": leaves 381–403.
1. Protestant churches–U. S. 2. U. S.–Church history–19th century. I. Title.
NNC NUC74-123748

Banner, Lois W
The Protestant crusade; religious missions, benevolence, and reform in the United States, 1790-1840. [New York] 1970 [c1973]
403 l. 29 cm.
Thesis–Columbia University.
"Essay on sources": leaves 381-403.
Xerox copy. Ann Arbor, University Microfilms, 1975.
InNd NUC76-30278

Banner, Lois W
The Protestant crusade; religious missions, benevolence, and reform in the United States, 1790-1840. [New York, c1973]
403 l.
Thesis–Columbia University.
Microfilm. Ann Arbor, Mich., University Microfilms, 1973. 1 reel.
1. Protestants in the U. S. 2. U. S.–Hist.–1783-1865. 3. U. S.–Pol. & govt.–1783-1865. I. Title.
IaU NUC74-123749

Banner, Lois W
Women in modern America; a brief history ₍by₎ Lois W. Banner. New York, Harcourt Brace Jovanovich ₍1974₎
xii, 276 p. illus. 21 cm. (The Harbrace history of the United States) $4.95
Bibliography: p. 252–254.
1. Women in the United States—History. 2. Women's rights—United States—History. I. Title.
HQ1419.B35 301.41'2'0973 73–20976
ISBN 0-15-596193-4 MARC

Banner, Lois W.
see Clio's consciousness raised ... New York, Octagon Books, 1976, c1974.

Banner, M L
On small scale breaking waves, by M. L. Banner and O. M. Phillips. ₍Baltimore?₎ Chesapeake Bay Institute, Johns Hopkins University, 1973.
23 p. illus. 28 cm. (Johns Hopkins University, Chesapeake Bay Institute. Technical report 82)
"... contains results of work carried out for the Office of Naval Research of the Department of the Navy under research project NR 083-016, NOOO 14-67-A-0163-0009 and the National Science Foundation under grant GA-35390 X."
Includes bibliographical references.
Wa NUC75-20624

Banner, Mae Guyer.
Black power and community decision making / Mae Guyer Banner. -- Knoxville : University of Tennessee, 1975.
xiii, 361 p. ; 28 cm.
Thesis (Ph.D.)--University of Tennessee, Knoxville.
I. Title.
TU NUC77-92792

Banner, Melvin E
The Black pioneer in Michigan ₍by₎ Melvin E. Banner. ₍Midland, Mich.₎ Pendell Pub. Co. ₍1973–
v. illus. 23 cm. $3.95
Includes bibliographical references.
CONTENTS: v. 1. Flint and Genesee County.—
1. Negroes—Michigan. 2. Frontier and pioneer life—Michigan. 3. Michigan—History. I. Title.
E185.93.M5B36 917.74'37 73–91313
ISBN 0-87812-053-X MARC

Banner, Selena Morrison Greer, 1915–
Strength for tomorrow; a story of Alexander Morrison and Selena Buck. ₍Bonneville, Idaho, 1974₎
xi, 165 p. illus. 22 cm.
1. Morrison family. 2. Buck family. I. Title.
CS71.M88 1974 929'.2'0973 74–178208
MARC

Banner, Stephen.
see How black? ... Wolverhampton, Wolverhampton Council for Community Relations, 1972.

Banner, Warren M plaintiff-appellant.
New York Supreme Court, appellate division - first department. Warren M. Banner, plaintiff-appellant, against National Urban League, Inc., defentant-respondent. Record on appeal. New York, Counsel Press ₍1970₎
121 l.
Cover title.
I. National Urban League, defendant-respondent. II. New York (State). Supreme Court. Appellate Division.
NN NUC74-118013

Banner, Zoltán.
Hans Mattis-Teutsch. Bukarest, Kriterion, 1974.
79 p., [20] leaves of plates. 57 illus. (some col.), port. 24 cm.
Translation of Mattis-Teutsch János.
Bibliography: p. 71-74.
1. Mattis-Teutsch, János, 1884-1960. I. Mattis-Teutsch, János, 1884-1960.
NjP NUC76-23721

Banner, Zoltán.
Mattis-Teutsch / Zoltán Banner. — București : Meridiane, 1970.
43 p., ₍16₎ leaves of plates : ill. (some col.) ; 22 cm.
Bibliography: p. ₍41₎
1. Mattis-Teutsch, János, 1884-1960.
N6822.5.M32B35 76–513485

Banner, Zoltán.
Mattis-Teutsch János. ₍Monográfia₎. Bukarest, „Kriterion," 1972.
75 p. with illus., 16 l. of illus. (part col.) 16 x 17 cm. lei 16.50
R 72–1347
Bibliography: p. 67–₍69₎
1. Mattis-Teutsch, János, 1884–1960.
N6822.5.M32B36 72–365089

Banner Elk, N.C. Ordinances, local laws, etc.
Zoning ordinance, Town of Banner Elk, North Carolina. Raleigh, Division of Community Services, N.C. Dept. of Natural and Economic Resources, 1973.
58 p. 28 cm.
Effective May 7, 1973.
1. Banner Elk, N.C.—Zoning. I. North Carolina. Division of Community Services.
NcU NUC75-46774

Banner of reform.
Mobile, Ala., Langdon.
v. 69 cm. weekly.
Began with May 4, 1840 issue. Cf. Ellison, R. Hist. and bibl. of Ala. newspapers in the nineteenth cent., 1954.
"Whig." Ellison, R. Hist. and bibl. of Ala. newspapers in the nineteenth cent., 1954.
₍I. United States—Alabama—Mobile₎
Newspaper 76–643886
MARC-S

Banner-Tribune
see St. Mary chapter, Louisiana Landmarks... Franklin, La., 1971.

Bannerman, A McK
Kippers. Aberdeen, Scot. ₍1970₎
15 p. (Torry Research Station, Aberdeen. Torry advisory note no. 48)
Includes bibliography.
1. Herring. I. Title. II. Series.
DI NUC73-40213

Bannerman, Charles J
A Ga grammar of function, by C. J. Bannerman. ₍2d ed.₎ Cape Coast. Methodist Book Depot, ₍1968, c1948₎
170 p. 22 cm.
Cover title: Ga wiemɔi komekomei anitsumɔ.

1. Ga language—Sentences. 2. Ga language—Composition and exercises. I. Title. II. Title: Ga wiemɔi komekomei anitsumɔ.
PL8191.2.B35 1968 496'.33 72–223605

Bannerman, Charles S
The Bannerman catalog, published on the occasion of the 100th anniversary of the founding by Francis Bannerman of his military goods business. Blue Point, N.Y., Francis Bannerman Sons ₍c1966₎
264 p. illus. 28 cm.
1. Firearms. 2. Ordinance. I. Title.
NBuHi NUC74-121766

Bannerman, David Armitage, 1886–
Handbook of the birds of Cyprus and migrants of the Middle East; by David Armitage Bannerman and W. Mary (Jane) Bannerman. Edinburgh, Oliver and Boyd, 1971.
xvi, 237, ₍28₎ p. (1 fold.). illus. (some col.), maps. 24 cm. index. £3.00 B 72–01442
1. Birds—Cyprus—Identification. 2. Birds—Near East—Identification. I. Bannerman, Jane Winifred Mary (Holland), joint author. II. Title.
QL691.C8B32 598.2'9564'5 73–165977
ISBN 0-05-002445-0 MARC

Bannerman (Francis) (Firm)
see
Francis Bannerman (Firm)

Bannerman, Gary.
Cruise ships : the inside story / Gary Bannerman. — Sidney, B.C. : Saltaire Pub., c1976.
270 p. : ill., ports. ; 19 cm. C76-3699-3
Distributed in the U.S.A. by Brooke House Publishers, Northridge, Calif.
$3.95
1. Ocean travel. I. Title.
G550.B3 910'.45 76-384029
77 MARC

Bannerman, Gary.
Gastown: the 107 years. North Vancouver, B. C., Printed by the Times of North and West Vancouver [1974]
40, 12 p. illus. 28 cm.
1. Gastown, Vancouver, B. C. I. Title.
CaBVaU NUC76-23675

Bannerman, Glenn Q
Guide for recreation leaders / Glenn Q. Bannerman, Robert E. Fakkema. — Atlanta : John Knox Press, c1975.
127 p. : ill. ; 23 cm.
Includes index.
ISBN 0-8042-2154-5 : $3.95
1. Recreation leadership. 2. Amusements. I. Fakkema, Robert E., 1920- joint author. II. Title.
GV14.5.B32 790 74-28523
77 MARC

Bannerman, Helen, 1862 or 3-1946.
The story of Little Black Mingo. London, Chatto & Windus ₍1972₎
72 p. illus.
I. Title.
InU NUC73-115108

Bannerman, Helen, 1862 or 3-1946.
The story of Little Black Sambo. New York, Frederick A. Stokes Co. ₍n.d.₎
56 p. illus. 14 cm.
I. Title.
NvU NUC75-20668

Bannerman, Helen, 1862 or 3-1946.
The story of Little Black Sambo. London, Chatto & Windus ₍1971₎
61 p. illus.
I. Title.
InU NUC73-115107

Bannerman, Helen, 1862 or 3-1946. The story of Little Black Sambo. 1976.
in Yuill, Phyllis J. Little Black Sambo ... New York, Racism and Sexism Resource Center for Educators, c1976.

Bannerman, James, 1807-1868.
The Church of Christ : a treatise on the nature, powers, ordinances, discipline, and government of the Christian Church / James Bannerman. — Edinburgh ; Carlisle, Pa. : Banner of Truth Trust, 1974.
2 v. : port. ; 23 cm. — (Students' reformed theological library)
GB75-09950
Reprint of the 1869 ed. published by T. and T. Clark, Edinburgh.
Includes bibliographical references and index.
ISBN 0-85151-186-4 : £4.00
1. Church. 2. Sacraments. 3. Church polity. I. Title.
BV600.B343 1974 260 75-322515
75 MARC

Bannerman, Jane Campbell.
Bermuda, as seen by Jane Campbell Bannerman. — [s.l. : s.n., 1976?]
[30] leaves of plates : all col. ill. ; 16 x 24 cm.
Cover title.
$11.50
1. Bannerman, Jane Campbell. 2. Bermuda Islands in art.
ND1839.B23A42 759.13 77-354153
77 MARC

Bannerman, Jane Winifred Mary Holland, joint author
see Bannerman, David Armitage, 1886-
Handbook of the birds of Cyprus... Edinburgh, Oliver and Boyd, 1971.

Bannerman, John.
Studies in the history of Dalriada / John Bannerman. — Edinburgh : Scottish Academic Press, 1974.
ix, 178 p. 22 cm. GB***
Includes bibliographical references and index.
ISBN 0-7011-2040-1 : £3.50 ($11.50U.S.)
1. Dalriada—History. 2. Senchus Fer nAlban. I. Title.
DA880.D34B36 941.01 75-301815
MARC

Bannerman, John MacDonald, Baron Bannerman of Kildonan
see
Bannerman of Kildonan, John MacDonald Bannerman, Baron, 1901-1969.

Bannerman, Kay
see Brooke, Harold, 1910- Better off dead. Acting ed. London, Evans Bros. [c1959]

Bannerman, M Graeme, 1945-
Unity and disunity in Oman, 1895-1920 / by M. Graeme Bannerman. -- Madison, Wis. : University of Wisconsin, c1976.
x, 336 leaves : 3 maps ; 29 cm.
Thesis--Wisconsin.
Thesis (Ph.D.)--University of Wisconsin.
Vita.
Bibliography: leaves 320-336.
1. Oman--History. 2. Oman--Politics and government. I. Title.
WU NUC77-87872

Bannerman, R.T.
see Phosphorus uptake and release... Corvallis, Or., 1975.

Bannerman, Robert Henry Obuabasa, joint author.
see Mace, David Robert. The teaching of human sexuality in schools for health professionals. Geneva, World Health Organization, 1974.

Bannerman, Ronald Moore, 1921-
Trade practices act 1974 : short summary / [by R. M. Bannerman]. — Canberra City : Trade Practices Commission Offices, [1974?]
[9] leaves ; 33 cm. Aus***
1. Restraint of trade—Australia. I. Title.
343'.94'0723 77-354663
77 MARC

Bannerman of Kildonan, John MacDonald Bannerman, Baron, 1901-1969.
Bannerman: the memoirs of Lord Bannerman of Kildonan; edited by John Fowler. Aberdeen, Impulse Books, 1972.
133, [9] p. illus., ports. 22 cm. £2.80 B 73-00075
1. Bannerman of Kildonan, John MacDonald Bannerman, Baron, 1901-1969. I. Fowler, John, ed.
DA822.B36A3 329.9'41 [B] 73-159777
ISBN 0-901311-19-7 MARC

Bannerman-Phillips, E Ivy A 1900-
Amulets and birthstones; their astrological significance. St. Paul, Llewellyn Publications [1969]
60 p. (p. 58-60 advertisements) 21 cm.
First printing 1950.
1. Astrology. 2. Amulets. I. Title.
IU NUC73-2074

Bannerman Son
see
Francis Bannerman Son.

Banners now... Montreal, Keylitho [197-?]
see under Wallace, Gwynneth.

Bannert, Dieter
see
Bannert, Dietrich N

Bannert, Dietrich N Das nördliche Afar-Dreieck: ein Mittelozeanischer Rücken auf Land? 1974
in Burek, Peter J Plattentektonische Probleme in der weiteren Umgebung Arabiens sowie der Danakil-Afar-Senke. Stuttgart: Schweizerbart, 1974.

Bannert, Dietrich N
Plate drift in the Afar and Issas territory (French Somalia) and eastern Ethiopia as seen on space photography. Washington, National Aeronautics and Space Administration, 1972.
26 p. illus. 27 cm. (NASA TN D-6277)
Cover title.
Includes bibliography.
1. Geology–Africa–Photographs from space. 2. Geology, Structural–Photographs from space. I. Title.
WU IEN NUC74-119254

Bannert, Dietrich N
Plate tectonics in the Red Sea region as inferred from space photography, by Dietrich N. Bannert and Ervin Y. Kedar. Washington, National Aeronautics and Space Administration; [for sale by the National Technical Information Service, Springfield, Va.] 1971.
16 p. illus. (part col.) 27 cm. (NASA technical note. NASA TN D-6261) $3.00
Cover title.
Includes bibliographical references.
1. Geology—Red Sea region. 2. Continental drift. 3. Earth—Photographs from space. 4. Geology, Structural. I. Kedar, Ervin Y., joint author. II. Title: III. Series: U. S. National Aeronautics and Space Administration. NASA technical note, NASA TN D-6261.
TL521.A3525 no. 6261 629.1'08 s 77-612029
[QE339.R] [551.4'1] MARC

Bannert, Dietrich N.
see Beiträge zur Geologie der Danakil-Senke (NE-Äthiopien). Hannover, Bundesanstalt für Bodenforschung, 1971.

Bannert, Herbert.
Die Fundmünzen vom Magdalensberg. Von Herbert Bannert u. Gernot Piccottini. Klagenfurt, Verl. des Landesmuseums f. Kärnten, 1972.
79 p. 7 plates (1 fold.) 26 cm. (Die Fundmünzen der römischen Zeit in Österreich. Kärnten, 1) (Archäologische Forschungen zu den Grabungen auf dem Magdalensberg, 2) (Kärntner Museumsschriften, 52) S180.00 Au 72-23-298
Errata slip inserted.
Includes bibliographical references.
1. Coins, Ancient. 2. Coin hoards — Magdalensberg, Austria. 3. Coins, Roman — Magdalensberg, Austria. 4. Coins, Greek — Magdalensberg, Austria. 5. Coins, Celtic—Magdalensberg, Austria. I. Piccottini, Gernot, joint author. II. Title. III. Series. IV. Series: Archäologische Forschungen zu den Grabungen auf dem Magdalensberg, 2. V. Series: Kärntner Museumsschriften, 52.
AM101.K246 no. 52 73-329775
[CJ277.M3]

Bannert, Robert.
Mittelbairische Phonologie auf akustischer und perzeptorischer Grundlage / von Robert Banner. — Lund : Liber-Läromedel/Gleerup, 1976.
172 p. : ill. ; 25 cm. — (Travaux de l'institut de linguistique de Lund ; 10) S76-49
Bibliography: p. 162-172.
ISBN 9140043487
1. German language—Dialects—Germany, West—Bavaria. 2. German language—Phonology. I. Title. II. Series: Lund. Universitet. Institutionen för lingvistik ; 10.
PF5314.B3 77-550614
77 MARC

Bannerth, Ernst, 1895-
Islamische Wallfahrtsstätten Kairos / von Ernst Bannerth. — Wiesbaden : Harrassowitz [in Komm.], 1973.
131 p. : ill. ; 31 cm. — (Schriften des Österreichischen Kulturinstituts Kairo ; Bd. 2) GFR 74-A16
Bibliography: p. 107-113.
Includes indexes.
ISBN 3-447-01504-7 : DM48.00
1. Islamic shrines—Cairo. I. Title. II. Series: Österreichisches Kulturinstitut Kairo. Schriften des Österreichischen Instituts Kairo, Bd. 2.
BP187.6.C3A16 74-353763

Bannerth, Ernst, 1895-
see Philosophische Anthropologie. Stuttgart, G. Thieme, 1975.

Bannester, E Michael.
Relevance and power: the elemental sociodynamics [by] E. Michael Bannester. London, Center of Sociodynamics, 1972.
xii, 236 p. 20 cm. GB73-16428
Bibliography: p. [223]-236.
1. Social interaction. I. Title.
HM291.B26 1972 301.11 74-157239
ISBN 0-9502687-0-5 74[r77]rev MARC

Banneux Notre Dame. Guide illustré. [n.p., 1964]
56 p. illus., plans. 21 cm.
ODaU-M NUC73-33698

Banni, Mallikarjun, 1947-
(Ārati)
ಆರತಿ; ಕವನ ಸಂಕಲನ. [ಲೇಖಕ] ಮಲ್ಲಿಕಾರ್ಜುನ ಬನ್ನಿ. ಗುಳೇದ ಗುಡ್ಡ, 1970.
56 p. 19 cm. Rs1.50
On verso of t. p.: ಪ್ರಕಾಶಕರು ಎಮ್. ವ್ಹಿ. ಬನ್ನಿ, ಹುಬ್ಬಳ್ಳಿ.
In Kannada.
Poems.
I. Title.
PL4659.B27A9 70-916935

Bannière, La
see
Tremblot, Jean Camille, 1893-1964.

Bannik, Grigoriĭ Ivanovich.
(Tekhnicheskaia melioratsiia gruntov)
Техническая мелиорация грунтов / Г. И. Банник. — Изд 2., перер. и доп. — Киев : Вища школа, 1976.
303 p. : ill. ; 22 cm. USSR***
"Допущено ... в качестве учебного пособия для студентов геологических специальностей вузов."
Bibliography: p. 299-300.
0.88rub
1. Soil stabilization. 2. Drainage. I. Title.
TA715.B3 1976 76-530756

Bannik, V. P.
see Osobennosti remonta sistem regulirovaniia turbin K-300-240 KhTGZ. 1975.

Bannik, V. P., ed.
see (Spravochnik montazhnika teplovykh elektrostantsii) 1971-72.

Bannikh, Mikhail P
see
Bannykh, Mikhail Petrovich.

Bannikov, A.G.
see Biologicheskie predposylki ratsional'nogo ispol'zovaniia nazemnykh pozvonochnykh. 1976.

Bannikov, Andreĭ Grigor'evich.
(Po zapovednikam Sovetskogo Soiuza)
По заповедникам Советского Союза / А. Г. Банников. — Изд. 2-е, доп. и перераб. — Москва : Мысль, 1974.
234 p., [1] fold. leaf. [16] leaves of plates : ill. (some col.) ; 21 cm. — (Рассказы о природе) USSR 75
1.04rub
1. National parks and reserves—Russia. 2. Game-preserves—Russia. I. Title.
SB484.R9B34 1974 75-589938

Bannikov, Andreĭ Grigor'evich.
Zemnovodyne i Presmykaiushchiesia SSSR. Moskva, Izdatel'stvo "Mysl", 1971.
303 p. illus.
At head of title: Spravochniki-opredeliteli geografa i puteshestvennika. A.G. Bannikov, I.S. Darevskiĭ, A.K. Rustamov.
MH-Z NUC74-21943

Bannikov, Iuriĭ Aleksandrovich, joint author
see Danilin, Nikolaĭ Semenovich. (Nerazrushaiushchiĭ kontrol' v radioėlektronike) 1974.

Bannikov, M.IA., comp.
see Srochno v nomer! Sverdlovsk, Sredne-Ural'skoe kn. izd-vo, 1968.

Bannikov, N., ed.
see Iz evropeĭskikh poetov XVI-XIX vv. Moskva, Gos. izd-vo khudozh. lit-ry, 1956.

Bannikov, N A
Puti snizheniia sebestoimosti produktsii zhivotnovodstva. Moskva, Izd-vo sel'skokhoziaĭstvennoĭ lit-ry, 1961.
390 p. 21 cm.
1. Animal industry—Russia. 2. Stock and stock-breeding—Economic aspects—Russia. I. Title.
PSt NUC74-45558

Bannikov, N A
(Spetsializatsiia i kontsentratsiia proizvodstva)
Специализация и концентрация производства. Москва, Россельхозиздат, 1973.
94 p. 20 cm. (Экономические знания—труженикам села)
0.20rub USSR 73
At head of title: Н. А. Банников.
1. Agriculture—Economic aspects—Russia (1917- R. S. F. S. R)
I. Title.
HD1992.B26 74-318091

Bannikov, N. A.
see Vygody kooperirovaniia. 1975.

Bannikov, N V
(Irkutskie gorizonty)
Иркутские горизонты / [Н. В. Банников, В. А. Румянцев, Л. И. Шинкарев]. — Иркутск : Вост.-Сиб. кн. изд-во, 1973.
76 p. ; 16 cm. USSR 73
0.09rub
1. Irkutsk, Siberia (Province)—Economic conditions. 2. Irkutsk, Siberia (Province)—Social conditions. I. Rumiantsev, V. A., joint author. II. Shinkarev, Leonid Iosifovich, joint author. III. Title.
HC487.I 7B25 74-353150

Bannikov, S. G., ed.
see Russia (1923- U.S.S.R.). Verkhovnyĭ Sud. Plenum. (Sbornik postanovleniĭ plenuma Verkhovnogo Suda SSSR) 1974.

Bannikov, Sergeĭ Petrovich
see Elektrooborudovanie i avtomatizirovannyĭ elektroprivod avtomobileĭ, elektromobilei i dorozhno-stroitel'nykh mashin. 1974.

Bannikov, V.
see Kuzbass. Kusbass; [fotoal'bom] Kemerovo, Kemerovskoe knizhnoe izd-vo, 1969.

Bannikov, V. G.
see Folosiria stylpilor de beton armat pentru spaliere yn viĭ. 1966.

Bannikova, Liudmila Aleksandrovna.
(Selektsiia molochnokislykh bakteriĭ i ikh primenenie v molochnoĭ promyshlennosti)
Селекция молочнокислых бактерий и их применение в молочной промышленности / Л. А. Банникова. — Москва : Пищевая пром-сть, 1975.
255 p. : ill. ; 21 cm. USSR 76
Bibliography: p. 242-255.
1.60rub
1. Lactic acid bacteria. 2. Dairy bacteriology. I. Title.
QR121.B33 76-518098

Bannikova, N. P.
see Vzaimosviazi vzaimodeĭstvie natsional'nykh literatur; bibliografiia (1945-1960) Moskva, 1962.

Bannikova, Viktoriia Pavlovna.
(TSitoembriologiia mezhvidovoĭ nesovmestimosti u rasteniĭ)
Цитоэмбриология межвидовой несовместимости у растений / В. П. Банникова. — Киев : Наук. думка, 1975.
283 p., [7] leaves of plates : ill. ; 23 cm. USSR 75
At head of title: Akademiia nauk Ukrainskoĭ SSR. Institut botaniki im. I. G. Kholodnogo.
Summary in English.
Bibliography: p. 241-[278]
Includes index.
2.38rub
1. Botany—Embryology. 2. Plant-breeding. I. Title.
QK665.B34 75-545434

Banning, Evelyn I
The enchanted circle. New Haven, Southern Connecticut State College, Division of Library Science, 1966.
8 l. 28 cm. (Connecticut. Southern Connecticut State College, New Haven. Library School. Papers in library and information science, no. 6)
On title page: Library science paper, no. 6.
1. Lyon, Mary, 1797-1849. I. Title. II. Series.
NNC NUC76-75685

Banning, Evelyn I
Helen Hunt Jackson, by Evelyn I. Banning. New York, Vanguard Press [1973]
xxi, 248 p. illus. 21 cm.
"Selected books by Helen Hunt Jackson": p. [237]-238.
"Selected list of Helen Hunt Jackson's publications in periodicals": p. [239]-240.
Bibliography: p. [233]-236.
1. Jackson, Helen Maria (Fiske) Hunt, 1831-1885—Biography.
PS2108.B3 818'.4'09 [B] 73-83038
ISBN 0-8149-0735-0 MARC

Banning, Johan Petrus Dorothée van.
Het huwelijk van Hare Koninklijke Hoogheid Prinses Christina / door J. P. D. van Banning. — Zaltbommel : Europese Bibliotheek, 1975.
91 p., [4] leaves of plates : ill., facsim. (in pocket) ; 28 cm. Ne 75-50
Bibliography: p. 79.
ISBN 90288-5035-X : fl 47.50
1. Maria Christiana, Princess of the Netherlands, 1947-
I. Title.
DJ289.A4M373 76-506898

Banning, John William, 1917-
A biographical approach to leadership identification. [College Park, Md.] 1971 [c1972]
124 l. 29 cm.
Typescript.
Thesis—University of Maryland.
Vita.
Includes bibliography.
1. Biography. 2. Questionnaires. 3. Leadership. I. Title.
MdU NUC73-31299

Banning, Kendall, 1879-1944, comp.
Songs for a wedding day : a cycle of XXIV poems of love triumphant / [selected and] edited by Kendall Banning. — New York : Triptych, 1907.
[48] p. : 1 ill. ; 27 cm.
"Printed for the Triptych at the Village Press, New York ... in an edition limited to one hundred two copies."
1. Epithalamia. I. Title.
PN6110.W4B27 821'.008'0352 75-311745
75 MARC

Banning, Knud.
Justus Lipsius / af Knud Banning. — København : Gad, 1975.
61 p. ; 21 cm. — (Studier fra sprog- og oldtidsforskning ; nr. 287) D 75-51
Includes bibliographical references.
ISBN 87-12-83837-3 : kr50.60
1. Lipsius, Justus, 1547-1606. I. Series.
B785.L44B36 76-506971

Banning, Lance Gilbert, 1942-
The quarrel with federalism: a study in the origins and character of Republican thought. [n.p.] 1971 [c1972]
446 l.
Thesis—Washington University.
Bibliography: leaves 425-446.
Microfilm (positive) Ann Arbor, Mich., University Microfilms, 1972. 1 reel. (Publication no. 17944)
NNC NUC73-115239

Banning, Lloyd H
Corrosion resistance of metals in hot brines: A literature review, by Lloyd H. Banning and Laurance L. Oden. [Washington] U. S. Bureau of Mines [1973]
39 p. tables. (U. S. Bureau of Mines. Information circular 8601)
Includes bibliography.
CaOTP NUC74-123750

Banning, Lloyd H
Fluosilicic acid acidulation of phosphate rock / by L.H. Banning. -- Pittsburgh, Pa. : U.S. Dept. of the Interior, Bureau of Mines, 1975.
13 p. : ill. ; 27 cm. -- (Report of investigations - Bureau of Mines ; 8061)
Tables.
Bibliography: p. 13.
1. Phosphate rock. 2. Fluosilicic acid. I. United States. Bureau of Mines. II. Title. III. Series: United States. Bureau of Mines. Report of investigations - Bureau of Mines ; 8061.
DI NUC77-87871

Banning Lloyd H
Fluosilicic acid acidulation of phosphate rock / by L. H. Banning. -- [Washington] : U. S. Dept. of the Interior, Bureau of Mines, [1975]
13 p. : ill. -- (Report of investigation--Bureau of Mines ; 8601)
"PB-244 373."
Bibliography: p. 13.
Microfiche (negative) Springfield, Va. : National Technical Information Services, 1975. -- 1 sheet ; 11 x 15 cm.
InU NUC77-89177

Banning, Margaret Culkin, 1891-
The splendid torments : a novel / Margaret Culkin Banning. — 1st ed. — New York : Harper & Row, c1976.
242 p. ; 21 cm. — (A Cass Canfield book)
ISBN 0-06-010207-1 : $7.95
I. Title.
PZ3.B2277 Sq 3 813'.5'2 76-5107
[PS3503.A55853] 76 MARC

Banning, Margaret Culkin, 1891-
The will of Magda Townsend. Boston, G. K. Hall, 1974.
543 p. 25 cm.
Large print ed.
1. Sight-saving books. I. Title.
[PZ3.B2277Wi 3] 813'.5'2 74-7295
[PS3503.A55853] MARC
ISBN 0-8161-6221-2

Banning, Margaret Culkin, 1891-
The will of Magda Townsend; a novel. [1st ed.] New York, Harper & Row [1974]
318 p. 21 cm. (A Cass Canfield book) $6.95
I. Title.
PZ3.B2277Wi 813'.5'2 73-14306
[PS3503.A55853] MARC
ISBN 0-06-010206-3

Banning, Thomas Allen, 1851-1927
see Pioneers ... Chicago, Lakeside Press, 1972.

Banning, Willem, 1888-1971.
Typen van zedeleer. Grepen uit de geschiedenis der niet in godsdienstig geloof gefundeerde ethiek. Een eerste inleiding. 5. d. herz. door A. van Biemen. Haarlem, Bohn, 1972, [1973].
225 p. 21 cm. fl 22.50 Ne 73-2
Includes bibliographies.
1. Ethics—History. I. Title.
BJ78.D8B35 1973 73-317421
ISBN 90-6051-445-9

Banning, Willem, 1888-1971
see Goed en kwaad... Utrecht, Het Spectrum, 1965.

Banning, Willem, 1888-
see Modern niet-godsdienstig humanisme. 3. ongewijzigde druk. Nijmegen, Dekker & Van de Vegt [1964]

Banning, Calif. Malki Museum
see
Malki Museum.

Bannink, J F
Vegetatie, groeiplaats en boniteit in Nederlandse naaldhoutbossen; vegetation, habitat and site class in Dutch conifer forests. Wageningen, 1973.
183 p. illus., maps. (Bodemkundige studies 9)
English summary.
Bibliography: p. 147-150.
I. Title.
DNAL NUC75-20663

Bannink, J. G., ed.
see Netherlands (Kingdom, 1815-) Laws, statutes, etc. Nijverheidsonderwijswet. 13. druk. Zwolle, W. E. J. Tjeenk Willink, 1967.

Bannink, R., joint author
see Somermeyer, W H A consumption-savings model and its applications. Amsterdam, North-Holland; New York, American Elsevier, 1973.

Bannister, Anthony.
see Russell, Franklin, 1922- Wild creatures ... New York, Simon and Schuster, [1975]

Bannister, Arthur.
Surveying, by A. Bannister and S. Raymond. 3rd ed. London, Pitman, 1972.
vii, 548 p., fold. leaf. illus., maps. 23 cm. index. £3.75
B 72-12529
1. Surveying. I. Raymond, Stanley, joint author. II. Title.
TA545.B25 1972 526.9 73-152758
ISBN 0-273-36149-X ; 0-273-36148-1 (pbk.) MARC

Bannister, Barbara.
see The United States patchwork pattern book ... New York, Dover Publications, 1976.

Bannister, Brian Roy.
Fundamentals of digital systems [by] B. R. Bannister [and] D. G. Whitehead. London, New York, McGraw-Hill [1973]
x, 325 p. 24 cm. $14.50(U.S.) GB***
Bibliography: p. 319.
1. Digital electronics. 2. Electronic digital computers—Circuits. I. Whitehead, Donald Gill, joint author. II. Title.
TK7868.D5B42 621.3815'3 73-165462
ISBN 0-07-084006-7 MARC

Bannister, Bryant.
Tree ring dates ... [by] Bryant Bannister [and others] Tucson, Laboratory of Tree-Ring Research, University of Arizona, 1966-
v.
Contents.—v.[1] Arizona K: Puerco-Wide Ruin-Ganado area.—v.[2] Arizona E: Chinle - de Chelly - Red Rock area.—v.[3] Arizona N-Q: Verde-Show Low-St. Johns area.—v.[8] New Mexico A, G-H: Shiprock-Zuni-Mt. Taylor area.
1. Dendrochronology—Southwest, New. I. Arizona. University. Laboratory of Tree-Ring Research. II. Title.
ICU NUC73-38295

Bannister, Donald.
Inquiring man: the theory of personal constructs [by] D. Bannister and Fay Fransella. Harmondsworth, Penguin, 1971.
221 p. 18 cm. index. (Penguin education) (Penguin modern psychology) £0.50 B 71-28951
Bibliography: p. [207]-216.
1. Personality. 2. Kelly, George Alexander, 1905-1967. I. Fransella, Fay, joint author. II. Title.
BF698.B3143 155.2 73-165637
ISBN 0-14-08617-2 MARC

Bannister, Donald.
Issues and approaches in the psychological therapies, edited by D. Bannister. London, New York, Wiley [1975]
xiv, 286 p. 24 cm.
Includes bibliographies.
1. Psychotherapy. I. Title.
[DNLM: 1. Psychotherapy. WM420 B2193i]
RC480.B25 616.8'914 74-6996
ISBN 0-471-04740-6 74 MARC

Bannister, Donald, joint author.
see Fransella, Fay. A manual for repertory grid technique. London, Academic Press, 1977.

Bannister, Eleanor Cunningham
see Adelphi University, Garden City, N.Y. Library. Paintings... [Garden City, N.Y., 1971]

Bannister, Frank T 1931-
Student teaching in urban schools. [Amherst] 1972.
v, 123 l. tables. 28 cm.
Thesis (Ed. D.)–University of Massachusetts.
1. Student teaching. 2. Urban schools. 3. Patterson, N. J.–Schools. I. Title.
MU NUC74-123730

Bannister, Geoffrey, 1945-
Modes of change in the Ontario economy by Geoffrey Bannister. [Toronto] 1974.
297, [8] l. diagrs.
Thesis–University of Toronto.
Vita.
Bibliography: leaves [208-305]
CaOTU NUC76-23714

Bannister, J. L.
see also
Bannister, John Lloyd.

Bannister, Jean.
From parish to metro : two centuries of local government in a Lancashire town / author, Jean Bannister. — Bury : Bury Times, 1974.
xi, 140 p., [8] p. of plates : ill., coat of arms, map, ports. ; 22 cm.
GB75-15384
Includes index.
ISBN 0-9504263-0-X : £1.35
1. Bury, Eng.—Politics and government. 2. Bury, Eng.—History. I. Title.
JS3325.L329B853 352.0427'38 77-359205
77 MARC

Bannister, Kathleen.
Shared phantasy in marital problems: therapy in a four-person relationship, by Kathleen Bannister and Lily Pincus. London, Institute of Marital Studies, Tavistock Institute of Human Relations; Distributed by Research Publications Services, 1971.
[2], 77 p. 22 cm. £1.00 B 72-17976
1. Marriage counseling—Great Britain—Case studies. I. Pincus, Lily, joint author. II. Institute of Marital Studies. III. Title.
HQ10.B35 362.8'2 73-156046
ISBN 0-901882-05-4 MARC

Bannister, Marcia L
An instrumental and judgmental analysis of voice samples from psychiatrically hospitalized and non-hospitalized adolescents. [Lawrence, 1973]
xii, 133 l. illus. 29 cm.
Thesis (Ph.D.)–University of Kansas.
1. Voice. 2. Adolescence. 3. Adolescent psychiatry. I. Title.
KU NUC75-20664

Bannister, Mary, joint author
see Thomas, Anne. Number work for infants. Oxford, Blackwell, 1974.

Bannister, Nathaniel Harrington, 1813-1847.
England's iron days; a tragedy in five acts. New Orleans, W. McKean, 1837 [1974]
57 p.
Microfilm (positive) Ann Arbor, Mich., University Microfilms, 1974. 5th title of 50. 35 mm. (American culture series, reel 552.5)
I. Title.
KEmT NUC75-20669

Bannister, Nathaniel Harrington, 1813-1847.
Gaulantus; a tragedy in five acts, by Nathaniel H. Bannister. Cincinnati, Flash, Ryder, 1836 [1974]
67 p.
Microfilm (positive) Ann Arbor, Mich., University Microfilms, 1974. 6th title of 50. 35 mm. (American culture series, reel 552.6)
I. Title.
KEmT NUC75-20667

Bannister, Nathaniel Harrington, 1813-1847.
The three brothers, or Crime its own avenger a play in one act. Buffalo, 1840 [1973]
1 reel. (On American culture series, reel 552, no. 7)
Microfilm (positive) 35 mm. Ann Arbor, Mich., University Microfilms, 1973.
Collation of the original: [4]-26 p.
I. Title.
PSt KEmT NUC75-18540

Bannister, Peter.
Introduction to physiological plant ecology / P. Bannister. — New York : Wiley : distributed in the United States of America by Halsted Press, 1976.
ix, 273 p. : ill. ; 23 cm.
Bibliography: p. 227-252.
Includes indexes.
ISBN 0-470-15161-7
1. Botany—Ecology. 2. Plant physiology. I. Title. II. Title: Physiological plant ecology.
[DNLM: 1. Plants—Physiology. 2. Ecology. QK901 B219i]
QK901.B34 581.5 76-16743
76 MARC

Bannister, Peter.
Introduction to physiological plant ecology / [by] P. Bannister. — Oxford : Blackwell Scientific, 1976.
ix, 273 p. : ill. ; 22 cm. GB77-03001
Distributed in the United States by Halsted Press, New York.
Bibliography: p. 227-252.
Includes index.
ISBN 0-632-08980-6 : £4.75
1. Botany—Ecology. 2. Plant physiology. I. Title.
QK901.B34 1976 581.5 77-358400
77 MARC

Bannister, Robert L., joint author.
see Posamentier, Alfred S. Geometry, its elements and structure. 2d ed. New York, Webster Division, McGraw-Hill, c1977.

Bannister, Roger
see Brain, Walter Russell Brain, Baron, 1895-1966. Brain's clinical neurology. 4th ed., London, New York, Oxford Univ. Press, 1973.

Bannister, Turpin C
An introduction to architecture [by] Turpin C. Bannister. A re-run ed. Troy, N.Y., Made by R.H. Prout [for the] Dept. of Architecture, Rensselaer Polytechnic Institute [195-?]
1 v. (various pagings) illus. 28 cm.
"This material distributed only for use in the course, 'Architecture'."
Includes bibliographical references.
1. Architecture–History. I. Rensselaer Polytechnic Institute, Troy, N.Y. School of Architecture. II. Title.
NTR NUC76-22808

Bannister, W.S., joint author
see Dugdale, Roger Houghton. Fluid mechanics. [2d ed.] London, Macdonald & Evans, 1971.

Bannius, Joannes Albertus, 1597 or 98-1644.
Kort Sangh-Bericht. 1969
in Bannius, Joannes Albertus, 1597 or 98-1644. Zangh-Bloemzel (theoretical part) ... [Amsterdam, Frits Knuf, 1969]

Bannius, Joannes Albertus, 1597 or 98-1644.
Zangh-Bloemzel (theoretical part) & Kort Sangh-Bericht. With an introduction by Frits Noske. [Vereniging voor Nederlandse muziekgeschiedenis. Amsterdam, Frits Knuf, 1969]
92 p. illus. 25 cm. (Early music theory in the low countries, v. 1) fl 30.00 Ne 69-34
"Reprint of the original editions, Amsterdam 1642/1643."
Includes bibliographical references.
1. Music—Theory—16th-17th centuries. I. Bannius, Joannes Albertus, 1597 or 98-1644. Kort Sangh-Bericht. 1969. II. Title. III. Series.
MT6.E232 vol. 1 72-169598
[ML194] MARC

CU NIC GU CtW CaBVaU WaU

Banno, Fumio, 1933-
(EC Yōroppa kokonotsu no kao)
EC＝ヨーロッパ九つの顔 / 伴野文夫. — 東京：日本放送出版協会, 昭和49 [1974]
251 p. : ill. ; 20 cm. Ja 75-1025
Bibliography: p. [245]
¥830

1. Europe—Economic integration. I. Title.

HC241.B35 75-804141

Banno, Kyōji, comp.
see Gotemba no komonjo. [1966]

Banno, Masataka, 1916–
(Kindai Chūgoku seiji gaikō shi)
近代中国政治外交史　ヴァスコ・ダ・ガマから五四運動まで　坂野正高著　東京　東京大学出版会 1973.
625 p. 22 cm. ¥2800 Ja 73-19301
Bibliography: p. 541-617.
1. China—History—Ching dynasty, 1644-1912. 2. China—Foreign relations. I. Title.
DS754.B32 74-800380

Banno, Masataka, 1916- ed.
see Kindai Chugoku kenkyu nyumon. [1974]

Bannock, Graham.
How to survive the slump : a guide to economic crisis / [by] Graham Bannock. — Harmondsworth ; Baltimore [etc.] : Penguin, 1975.
170 p. : ill. ; 19 cm. — (A Penguin special) GB75-30893
Bibliography: p. 153-[159]
Includes index.
ISBN 0-14-052315-4 : £0.60
1. Great Britain—Economic conditions—1945- 2. Finance, Personal. I. Title.
HC256.6.B35 330.9'41'0857 76-357271
76 MARC

Bannock, Graham.
The Penguin dictionary of economics [by] G. Bannock, R. E. Baxter and R. Rees. Harmondsworth, Penguin, 1972.
427 p. illus. 18 cm. (Penguin reference books) £0.50
GB 72-29738
1. Economics—Dictionaries. I. Baxter, Ron Eric, joint author. II. Rees, Raymond, joint author. III. Title.
HB61.B33 330'.03 73-176076
ISBN 0-14-051051-6 MARC

Bannock, Graham.
The smaller business in Britain and Germany / Graham Bannock. — London : Wilton House, 1976.
viii, 152 p. ; 29 cm. GB***
Bibliography: p. 151-152.
ISBN 0-904655-18-0 : £15.00
1. Small business—Great Britain. 2. Small business—Germany, West. I. Title.
HD2346.G7B36 338.6'42'0941 77-366175
77 MARC

Bannock, Graham.
see Economists Advisory Group. The larger private company in Britain ... London, Wilton House Publications, [1975]

Bannock (Ship)
see Trotti, L Crociera NATO... Trieste [La Editoriale Libraria] 1969.

Bannock Co., Idaho. Development Council.
Comprehensive plan, 1970-1990: Bannock County, Arimo, Chubbuck, Downey, Inkom, Lava Hot Springs, McCammon, Pocatello; maps; population and economic base study; neighborhood analysis. Boise, Environmental Planning Group, 1970.
3 v. maps. (HUD 701 report)
1. Master plan—Bannock Co., Idaho. I. Environmental Planning Group.
DHUD NUC75-108713

Bannock Co., Idaho. Development Council.
Comprehensive plan: 1, program organization and procedures; 2, goals and policies to guide future growth; 3, land use manual; 4, natural resources manual; 5, public utilities manual; 6, recreation and tourism manual; 7, social needs and community appearance manual; 8, transportation and circulation manual. Boise, Environmental Planning Group, 1970.
8 v. (HUD 701 report)
1. Master plan—Bannock Co., Idaho. I. Environmental Planning Group.
DHUD NUC76-11034

Bannock Co., Idaho. Development Council.
Zoning and subdivision proposals for 1, Bannock County; 2, Arimo; 3, Chubbuck; 4, Downey; 5, Inkom; 6, Lava Hot Springs; 7, McCammon; 8, Pocatello; 9, Maps. Boise, Environmental Planning Group, 1970.
8 v. maps. (HUD 701 report)
1. Master plan—Bannock Co., Idaho. I. Environmental Planning Group.
DHUD NUC76-11263

Bannockburn, Ill. Trinity Evangelical Divinity School
see
Trinity Evangelical Divinity School.

Bannon, Ann.
I am a woman / Ann Bannon. — New York : Arno Press, 1975, c1959.
224 p. ; 22 cm. — (Homosexuality)
Reprint of the ed. published by Fawcett Publications, Greenwich, Conn.
ISBN 0-405-07406-9
I. Title. II. Series.
PZ4.B2185 Iad 5 813'.5'4 75-13750
[PS3552.A495] 75 MARC

Bannon, Ann.
Journey to a woman / Ann Bannon. — New York : Arno Press, 1975, c1960.
222 p. ; 22 cm. — (Homosexuality)
Reprint of the ed. published by Fawcett Publications, Greenwich, Conn., in series: Gold medal books.
ISBN 0-405-07408-5
I. Title. II. Series.
PZ4.B2185 Jo 5 813'.5'4 75-13752
[PS3552.A495] 75[r76]rev MARC

Bannon, Ann.
Odd girl out / Ann Bannon. — New York : Arno Press, 1975, c1957.
192 p. ; 22 cm. — (Homosexuality)
Reprint of the ed. published by Fawcett, Greenwich, Conn., in series: Gold medal books.
ISBN 0-405-07405-0
I. Title. II. Series.
[PZ4.B2185 Od 5] 813'.5'4 75-13735
[PS3552.A495] 75[r76]rev MARC

Bannon, Ann.
Women in the shadows / by Ann Bannon. — New York : Arno Press, 1975, c1959.
175 p. ; 22 cm. — (Homosexuality)
Reprint of the ed. published by Fawcett Publications in series: Gold medal books.
ISBN 0-405-07407-7
I. Title. II. Series.
PZ4.B2185 Wo 5 813'.5'4 75-13751
[PS3552.A495] 75 MARC

Bannon, Edward
see
Herrick, Clyde N

Bannon, John Francis, 1905-
Latin America / John Francis Bannon, Robert Ryal Miller, Peter Masten Dunne. — 4th ed. — Encino, Calif. : Glencoe Press, 1977.
ix, 610 p. : ill. ; 27 cm.
Includes bibliographies and index.
ISBN 0-02-474350-X
1. Latin America—History. I. Miller, Robert Ryal, joint author. II. Dunne, Peter Masten, 1889-1957, joint author. III. Title.
F1410.B22 1977 980 76-4011
77 MARC

Bannon, John Francis, 1905-
The Spanish borderlands frontier, 1513-1821. Maps researched and drawn by Ronald L. Ives. Albuquerque, University of New Mexico Press [c1974]
x, 308 p. illus., maps, ports. 24 cm. (Histories of the American frontier)
Includes bibliographical references.
1. America—Discovery and exploration—Spanish. 2. Southwest New—History—To 1848. 3. Spain—Colonies—North America. I. Title.
NjR NUC76-23713

Bannon, John Thomas, 1939-
The regional accrediting associations and the courts: A study of the Marjorie Webster case. Syracuse, N.Y., 1973.
186 l.
Thesis—Syracuse University.
Vita.
Bibliography: leaves 179-185.
Microfilm of typescript. Ann Arbor, Mich., University Microfilms, 1974. 1 reel. (Doctoral dissertation series, 74-8224)
NSyU NUC76-23728

Bannon, Joseph J
The evaluation of the roving recreation leader training guide—an inservice training source for inner city youth service personnel. Urbana-Champaign, 1971.
119 l.
Thesis—University of Illinois.
Photocopy of typescript. Ann Arbor, Mich., University Microfilms, 1973.
1. Recreation leadership. 2. Youth—United States—Recreation. 3. Socially handicapped—United States—Recreation.
MoU NUC76-75691

Bannon, Joseph J
Leisure resources, its comprehensive planning / Joseph J. Bannon. — Englewood Cliffs, N.J. : Prentice-Hall, c1976.
xxii, 454 p. : ill. ; 24 cm.
Includes bibliographies and index.
ISBN 0-13-528208-X
1. Recreation—Administration. 2. Cities and towns—Planning—1945- I. Title.
GV182.15.B36 711'.4 75-30512
75 MARC

Bannon, Joseph J
Outreach: extending community service in urban areas [edited by] Joseph J. Bannon. Springfield, Ill., Thomas [1973]
xxi, 219 p. illus. 26 cm.
Includes bibliographies.
1. Recreation leadership. 2. Youth—United States—Recreation. 3. Socially handicapped—United States—Recreation. I. Title.
GV14.5.B33 301.5'7 73-7536
ISBN 0-398-02887-7 MARC

Bannon, Joseph J
Recreation handbook. [Rev.] Leonia, N.J., Leonia Recreation Commission [1963]
ii, 86 l. forms, col. map. 28 cm.
Title on cover: Operation manual.
Bibliography: leaf 86.
1. Recreation—Leonia, N.J. I. Leonia, N.J. Recreation Commission. II. Title.
IU NUC73-14802

Bannon, Joseph J
Survey of private campgraounds in Illinois, by Joseph J. Bannon and Paula Warwick. [Urbana] University of Illinois, Urbana-Champaign Campus, 1973.
35 l. 28 cm.
Survey conducted by Office of Recreation and Park Resources, University of Illinois at Urbana-Champaign, in cooperation with Association for Illinois Rural Recreation Enterprises.
IU NUC76-78143

Bannon, L. R.
see Towards a concept of environmental conservation—the Esk Valley. [Edinburgh] Heriot-Watt University [and] Edinburgh College of Art [1973]

Bannon, Laura.
Manuela's birthday. New ed. Chicago, A. Whitman [1972]
[32] p. col. illus. 24 cm.
Published in 1939 under title: Manuela's birthday in old Mexico.
SUMMARY: A little Mexican girl's fifth birthday turns out to be a very special occasion.
[1. Birthdays—Fiction. 2. Mexico—Fiction] I. Title.
PZ7.B229Man [E] 74-188426
ISBN 0-8075-4973-8 MARC

Bannon, Michael Joseph.
Office location in Ireland: the role of Central Dublin. [Dublin, An Foras Forbartha, 1973]
144 p. maps, plans. 30 cm.
Based on the author's thesis, entitled The structure and development of office activities in Central Dublin.
1. Central business districts—Dublin, Ireland. 2. Offices—Location—Dublin, Ireland. I. Title.
CaAEU NUC76-75680

Bannour, Wanda.
see Les Nihilistes russes ... Paris, Aubier-Montaigne, 1974.

Bannour, Wanda
see La Philosophie et l'histoire (1780-1880). [Paris] Hachette [1973]

Bannov, Boris Germanovich.
The Ulster tragedy / Boris Bannov. — Moscow : Novosti Press Agency Pub. House, 1973.
38 p. : ill. ; 17 cm. — (Current history) USSR***
0.09rub
1. Northern Ireland—History—1969- I. Title.
DA990.U46B224 941.6082′4 75-306564
MARC

Bannov, Semen Egorovich.
(Remont ėlektrooborudovanii͡a metallurgicheskikh zavodov)
Ремонт электрооборудования металлургических заводов / С. Е. Баннов. — Изд. 3., перер. и доп. — Москва : Металлургия, 1975.
421, [3] p. : ill. ; 23 cm. USSR***
Bibliography : p. [423]
1.56rub
1. Metallurgical plants—Electric equipment—Maintenance and repair. 2. Electric machinery—Maintenance and repair. I. Title.
TK4035.M4B36 1975 76-508567

Bannus, Joannes Albertus
see
Bannius, Joannes Albertus, 1597 or 98-1644.

Bannwart, Peter
see Archiv für die schweizerische reformationsgeschichte. Herausgegeben auf veranstaltung des Schweizerischen Piusvereins. Amsterdam, J. Benjamin, 1972.

Bannwart, Urs.
Die Stellung des Verteidigers im solothurnischen Strafprozessrecht / vorgelegt von Urs Bannwart. — Grenchen : Niederhäuser, 1974.
xx, 142 p. ; 21 cm. Sw 75-B-84
Thesis—Bern.
Bibliography : p. xvii-xviii.
1. Defense (Criminal procedure)—Solothurn (Canton) I. Title.
76-503242

Bannwart-Maurer, Elena.
Das Recht auf Bildung und das Elternrecht : Art. 2 des ersten Zusatzprotokolls zur Europäischen Menschenrechtskonvention / Elena Bannwart-Maurer. — Bern : Herbert Lang ; Frankfurt/M. : Peter Lang, 1975.
viii, 132 p. ; 23 cm. — (Europäische Hochschulschriften : Reihe 2, Rechtswissenschaft ; Bd. 132) Sw75-A-7431
Originally presented as the author's thesis, Zürich, 1974.
Bibliography: p. i-vii.
ISBN 3-261-01846-1 : 26.00F
1. Right to education—Europe. 2. Parent and child (Law)—Europe. I. Title. II. Series.
76-451708
•76 MARC

Bannwarth, Lutz, 1945-
Joseph Hellers Catch-22 : ein Paradigma des Grotesken / vorgelegt von Lutz Bannwarth. — [s. l. : s. n.], 1974.
196 p. ; 21 cm. GFR***
Thesis—Münster.
Vita.
Bibliography : p. [187]-196.
1. Heller, Joseph. Catch-22. 2. Grotesque in literature. 3. World War, 1939-1945—Fiction.
PS3558.E476C333 76-514238

Banny, Leo.
Gänseruf und Keilerfährte. Mit 32 Photographien auf 16 Taf. Wien, Österr. Jagd- u. Fischerei-Verl. des N.-Ö. Landesjagdverbandes (1972).
208 p., 16 plates 25 cm. S194.00 Au 73-3-133
1. Hunting—Austria. I. Title.
SK193.B36 73-316729

Bannyĭ, Nikolaĭ Pavlovich.
Основные проблемы экономики черной металлургии. (Учеб. пособие). Под ред. проф. д-ра экон. наук Н. П. Банного. Москва, 1969-
v. 20 cm. 0.27rub (v. 2) USSR 70-VKP (v. 2)
At head of title, v. : Министерство высшего и среднего специального образования СССР. Московский институт стали и сплавов. Факультет повышения квалификации преподавателей вузов страны по металлургическим специальностям. Н. П. Банный, А. А. Федотов.
1. Iron industry and trade—Russia. 2. Steel industry and trade—Russia. I. Fedotov, A. A., joint author. II. Title.
Title romanized : Osnovnye problemy ėkonomiki chernoĭ metallurgii.
HD9525.R9B25 74-343861

Bannykh, Mikhail Petrovich.
(Sessii raĭonnogo, gorodskogo Soveta)
Сессии районного, городского Совета / М. П. Банных. — Москва : Юрид. лит., 1974.
94 p. ; 20 cm. — (Библиотечка для работников районных, городских Советов) USSR 74
Includes bibliographical references.
0.15rub
1. Soviets. I. Title.
JS6058.B2556 75-578528

Bannykh, Mikhail Petrovich.
[Uchastie obshchestvennosti v deli͡atel′nosti ispolkomov mestnykh Sovetov. Bulgarian]
Участието на обществеността в дейността на изпълнителните комитети на местните съвети. (Прев. [от рус.] Иво Златанов). София (Наука и изкуство, Плевен, печ. Ал. Пъшев) 1974.
147 p. 20 cm. (Библиотека Народни съвети, 1973, 7/8) Bu 74-464
Cover title.
At head of title : М. П. Банних.
Includes bibliographical references.
1. Soviets. I. Title.
Title romanized : Uchastieto na obshchestvenostta v deĭnostta na izpŭlnitelnite komiteti na mestnite sŭveti.
JS6058.B2564 74-323165

Bannykh, Stepan Anisimovich.
(Boevye budni granit͡sy)
Боевые будни границы / С. А. Банных ; [лит. обраб. В. Лебединской]. — Минск : Беларусь, 1974.
253 p., [16] leaves of plates : ill. ; 21 cm. USSR 74
0.75rub
1. Russia (1923- U. S. S. R.). Pogranichnye voĭska. I. Lebedinskai͡a, V. II. Title.
UA776.P6B28 75-583544

Bannykh, Stepan Anisimovich.
[Gody i li͡udi granit͡sy]
Годы и люди границы. Москва, 1972.
110 p. with ports., 4 l. of illus. 16 cm. (Библиотечка журнала "Пограничник," № 1 (38)) 0.20rub USSR 72-VKP
At head of title: С. А. Банных.
1. Russia (1923- U. S. S. R.). Pogranichnye voĭska. I. Title.
UA776.P6B3 72-359856

Bano, Shah
see
Shah Bano, 1936-

Bañoch, Zdeněk
see Penka, Miroslav. Zavlažování rostlin. Praha, SZN, 1973.

Banocre, Tristan.
Des jours moissonnés / Tristan Banocre. — Paris : la Pensée universelle, 1974.
257 p. ; 18 cm. F74-15645
24.00F
1. World War, 1939-1945—Fiction. I. Title.
PQ2662.A554D4 843′.9′14 76-461726
76 MARC

Banoğlu, Niyazi Ahmet.
Atatürk'ün Istanbul'daki hayatı. Niyazi Ahmet Banoğlu. Istanbul, Millî Eğitim Basımevi, 1973-
v. ill. (Büyük Istanbul Derneği Yayını, 1.
Contents:—v. 1. 1899-1919-1927-1932. —v. 2
1. Atatürk, Kamal, pres. Turkey, 1880-1938.
I. Title.
CLU NUC76-72749

Banoğlu, Niyazi Ahmet.
Taksim Cumhuriyet Abidesi şeref defteri. Hazırlayan: Niyazi Ahmet Banoğlu. Istanbul [İtimat Kitabevi] 1973.
304 p. ill. (Büyük Istanbul Derneği Yayını, 4)
Chiefly facsims.
1. Istanbul—Monuments. I. Title.
CLU NUC76-72750

Banoğlu, Niyazi Ahmet.
Turkey, a sportsman's paradise / by Niyazi Ahmet Banoğlu ; Translated with annotations by Malcolm Burr. — Ankara : Press, Broadcasting & Tourism Dept., [1952?]
63 p., [24] leaves of plates : ill. ; 29 cm.
1. Hunting—Turkey. I. Title.
SK221.B3613 77-361371
77 MARC

Banoglu, Niyazi Ahmet, ed.
see Erkins, Ziya. The Topkapi Palace Museum ... Istanbul, Güzel Sanatlar Matbaasi, 196-?]

Banomyong, Pridi
see Pridi Banomyong.

Banorte
see
Banco Nacional do Norte
for publications by and about this body.
Titles and other entries beginning with this acronym are filed following this card.

Baños, Cipriano Muñoz
see Muñoz Baños, Cipriano.

Baños, Ignacio de la Cruz.
La devotion aux Sacrés Coeurs de Jésus et de Marie, dans la Congregation des Sacrés Coeurs, par le Ignace de la Croix Baños, SS.CC. Roma, Villa Senni, 1956.
543 p. 22 cm. (Etudes Picpuciennes, 4)
ODaU-M NUC73-57842

Banos, János, 1952-
see Ne mondj le semmiről ... Budapest, Szépirodalmi Könyvkiadó, 1974.

Baños, José Angel Fabre
see Fabre Baños, José Angel.

Baños, José de Oviedo y
see Oviedo y Baños, José de, 1671-1738

Bános, Mária.
Horgolás. Budapest, Minerva, 1971.
336 p. illus. 23 cm.
1. Crocheting–Patterns. I. Title.
MB NUC73-115217

Banos, R. Rodríguez
see Rodríguez Banos, R.

Banos, Roberto Martínez
see Martínez Banos, Roberto.

Bános, Tibor.
Regény a pesti színházakról. Budapest, Magvető Kiadó [1973]
507 p. illus. 19 cm.
Bibliography : p. 503-506.
32.00Ft
1. Theater—Budapest. I. Title.
PN2859.H83B83 75-565835

Banoub, Emile Farid.
Sandstorms and duststorms in U.A.R. Cairo, 1970.
35 p. 28 cm. (United Arab Republic. Maslahat al-Arsād al-Jawwiyah. Technical note, no. 1)
1. Dust storms–Egypt. I. Title. II. Series.
DAS NUC75-48075

Banov, Abel.
Book of successful painting / by Abel Banov, with Marie-Jeanne Lytle. — Farmington, Mich. : Structures Pub. Co., 1975.
114 p. : ill. (some col.) ; 29 cm.
Includes index.
ISBN 0-912336-36-6
1. House painting—Amateurs' manuals. 2. Interior decoration—Amateurs' manuals. I. Lytle, Marie-Jeanne, joint author. II. Title.
TT320.B28 698.1 74-21836
75 MARC

Banov, Abel.
Paints & coatings handbook for contractors, architects, builders and engineers. Farmington, Mich., Structures Pub. Co., 1973.
xii, 399 p. illus. 25 cm. $20.00
1. Protective coatings. 2. Paint. I. Title.
TA418.76.B36 667′.9 72-86397
ISBN 0-912336-04-8 MARC

Banov, Abel.
Wall coverings and decoration / Abel Banov, Jeanne Lytle, Douglas Rossig. — Farmington, Mich. : Structures Pub. Co., 1976.
132 p. : ill. (some col.) ; 29 cm.
Includes index.
ISBN 0-912336-24-2 : $12.00. ISBN 0-912336-25-0 pbk. : $4.95
1. Wall coverings. 2. Interior decoration. I. Lytle, Jeanne, joint author. II. Rossig, Douglas, joint author. III. Title.
NK2115.5.W3B36 747′.3 76-28710
76 MARC

Banov, Bancho, 1925-
(Basni)
Басни : избрано / Банчо Банов. — София : Бълг. писател, 1975.
151 p., [1] leaf of plates : port. ; 21 cm. Bu 76-440
1.32 lv
PG1038.12.A5B3 1975 76-524469

Banov, Bancho, 1925-
see Futbolistite na tridesetiletieto. 1976.

Banov, Bancho, 1925-
see Problemi na khumora i satirata. 1976.

Banov, Ivan N., joint author
see Terziiski, Ivan. (Otriad Anton Ivanov-brigada Georgi Dimitrov) 1970.

Báňová, Erika, ed.
see International Conference of the Technical Press, 11th, Brünn, 1972. Final report on the 11th International Conference of Technical Press, held on the occasion of the 14th International Engineering Fair, Brno, September 6-7, 1972. Brno, [Czechoslovak Scientific Technical Society, 1972?]

Banovec, Tomaž.
see Vodnik po slovenski planinski poti. 4., popr. in dop. izd. Ljubljana, Planinska založba pri Planinski zvezi Slovenije, 1974 (Ljubljana : "Ljubljana")

Banovetz, James M.
see Loyola University, Chicago. Center for Research in Urban Government. Leadership, localism, and urbanism. Chicago, 1968.

Banovski, Arpad.
["Gudit shar zemnoĭ"]
"Гудит шар земной." [Очерки]. Алма-Ата, "Казахстан," 1971.
84 p. 20 cm. 0.13rub USSR 71-VKP
At head of title: А. Бановски.
I. Title.
PG3479.N64G8 73-300601

Banowetz, Joseph
see Schumann, Robert Alexander, 1810-1856. [Album für die Jugend] Robert Schumann: an introduction to the composer and his music. Park Ridge, Ill.: General Words & Music Co.: c1975.

Banowsky, Lynn H. W.
see Stewart, Bruce H. Operative urology ... Baltimore, Williams and Wilkins, c1975.

Banowsky, William Slater
see Baxter, Batsell Barrett, 1916-
Making God's way our way... Nashville, Gospel Advocate Co., 1964.

Banphot Wirasai.
(Næo khambanyāi ratthasāt thūapai)
แนวคำบรรยาย รัฐศาสตร์ทั่วไป [โดย] บรรพต วีระสัย [และ] สุขุม นวลสกุล. [พระนคร, พิมพ์ที่โรงพิมพ์คุรุสภาลาดพร้าว, 2515 i.e. 1972]
4, 484 p. 22 cm. 25.00B
Cover title: รัฐศาสตร์ทั่วไป.
Bibliography: p. 473-484.
1. Political science—Study and teaching—Thailand. I. Sukhum Nūansakun, joint author. II. Title. III. Title: Ratthasāt thūapai.
74-226307

Banqaslī, Kāmil.
(Ābā' wa-abnā')
آباء وابناء / كامل بنقسلي، خالد قوطرش. — [دمشق : رابطة الأسرة والمدرسة، 1962؟]
319 p. : ill. ; 24 cm.
1. Father and child. 2. Child study. I. Qūṭrush, Khālid, 1912- joint author. II. Title.
BF723.P25B28 75-587051

Banque africaine de développement
see African Development Bank.

Banque belgo-congolaise
see
Belgolaise.

Banque canadienne nationale.
Annual statement—Bank Canadian National. [Montreal] BCN.
v. 21 cm.
1. Banque canadienne nationale.
HG2710.M8B2623 332.1'223'0971 76-645256
MARC-S

La Banque cantonale de Berne à Porrentruy
see Kantonalbank von Bern.

Banque centrale de Syrie
see Maṣrif Sūrīyah al-Markazī.

Banque Centrale de Tunisie
see Al-Bank Al-Markazī-Al Tūnisī.

Banque centrale des États de l'Afrique de l'Ouest.
West African Monetary Union; [treaty, agreements, conventions and statutes establishing the West African Monetary Union. [n.p., 196-?]
34 l.
I. Title.
MH NUC76-75686

Banque centrale des États de l'Afrique de l'Ouest
see Association of African Central Banks. Comité sous-régional de l'Afrique de l'Ouest. Rapport final de la deuxième réunion, Dakar, 3-4 mai 1972. [Paris] 1972.

Banque centrale des États de l'Afrique équatoriale et du Cameroun.
In 1955 the functions of the Caisse centrale de la France d'outre-mer (created in 1944) were transferred to the Institut d'émission de l'Afrique équatoriale francaise et du Cameroun. In 1959 the institute became the Banque centrale des États de l'Afrique équatoriale et du Cameroun. In 1972 the bank was reorganized and renamed the Banque des États de l'Afrique centrale.
Works by the Caisse centrale de la France d'outre-mer are found under
Caisse centrale de la France d'outre-mer, Paris.
Works by the Institut d'émission de l'Afrique équatoriale francaise et du Cameroun and the Banque centrale des États de l'Afrique équatoriale et du Cameroun are found under
Banque centrale des États de l'Afrique équatoriale et du Cameroun.
Works by the Banque des États de l'Afrique centrale are found under
Banque des États de l'Afrique centrale.

Banque centrale des États de l'Afrique équatoriale et du Cameroun.
The analytique des Études publiées dans le bulletin de la Banque Centrale des états de l'Afrique équatoriale et du Cameroun. (Avril 1956 - Avril 1971) [n.p., n.d.]
23 p. (It's Bulletin no. 163, Supplement)
Cover title.
1. Bibliography—Africa, French.
MBU NUC73-59757

Banque commerciale zaïroise.
The Banque du Congo belge was founded in 1909. In 1960 the name was changed to Banque du Congo and in 1971, to Banque commerciale zaïroise.
Works by this body are found under the name used at the time of publication.

Banque commerciale zaïroise. Bilan et compte de profits et pertes
see Banque commerciale zaïroise. Rapports présentés à l'assemblée générale des actionnaires. Kinshasa.

Banque commerciale zaïroise.
Rapports présentés à l'assemblée générale des actionnaires. Kinshasa, Banque commerciale zaïroise.
v. 22 cm.
Vols. for include Bilan et compte de profits et pertes.
1. Banque commerciale zaïroise. I. Banque commerciale zaïroise. Bilan et compte de profits et pertes.
HG3419.B28B35a 332.1'223'096751 76-642123
MARC-S

Banque commerciale zaïroise. Reports and balance sheet
see Banque commerciale zaïroise. Reports presented to the annual general meeting of shareholders ... 63- 1971- Kinshasa.

Banque commerciale zaïroise.
Reports presented to the annual general meeting of shareholders, balance sheet and profit and loss account. 63- 1971-
Kinshasa, Banque commerciale zaïroise.
v. 22 cm.
Continues: Banque du Congo. Reports presented to the shareholders at their annual general meeting, balance sheet and profit and loss account.
Title varies slightly.
Cover title, 1971- : Reports and balance sheet—Banque commerciale zaïroise.
1. Banque commerciale zaïroise. I. Banque commerciale zaïroise. Reports and balance sheet.
HG3419.B28B36a 332.1'223'096751 77-640472
MARC-S

La Banque dans le monde '75. — [Bruxelles] : L'Écho de la Bourse, [1975?]
80 p. : ill. ; 30 cm. Be***
Cover title.
1. Finance—Addresses, essays, lectures. 2. Finance—Belgium—Addresses, essays, lectures.
HG175.B35 332 76-461423
76 MARC

Banque de Bruxelles.
Belgium, land of investments. [Brussels] 1964.
1 v. (various pagings) illus. 21 cm.
Cover title.
1. Commercial law—Belgium. 2. Industrial laws and legislation—Belgium. I. Title.
MiU-L NUC73-14805

Banque de Bruxelles.
Belgium, land of investments. 2d. ed. [Brussels] 1965.
124 p. illus.
1. Belgium—Econ. condit. I. Title.
MiEM NUC73-14800

Banque de Bruxelles.
Belgium, land of investment. [3rd ed. Bruxelles, 1971].
vii, 86 p. tables, maps. 21 cm. Be 72-Nov
1. Investments—Belgium. 2. Belgium—Commercial policy. 3. Taxation—Belgium. I. Title.
HG5552.B36 1971 332.6'73'09493 74-150154
MARC

Banque de Bruxelles.
Belgium, land of investment. Essential background information for the prospective investor. (5th ed. completely reviewed and improved. Bruxelles, Rue de la Régence, 2, 1973).
100 p. col. illus., 3 col. maps (in pocket). 21 cm. Be***
1. Investments—Belgium. 2. Business enterprises—Belgium—Finance. 3. Taxation—Belgium. I. Title.
HG5552.B36 1973 332.6'73'09493 74-159633
MARC

Banque de développement du Laos.
Banque de développement du Laos, établissement publique de l'État. Vientiane [1968]
24 l. illus. 27 cm.
At head of title: Royaume du Laos.
Mimeographed typescript.
1. Banks and banking—Laos.
NIC NUC73-102879

Banque de développement du Tchad.
Rapport d'activité—Banque de développement du Tchad. N'Djamena (Fort-Lamy) Banque de développement du Tchad.
v. 30 cm.
1. Banque de développement du Tchad.
HG3409.C54B33a 332.2 75-642620
MARC-S

Banque de France, Paris.
La Banque de France et la monnaie. [Paris, 1972]
179 p. illus. 21 cm. 10.00F F***
1. Banque de France, Paris. 2. Money—France. 3. Monetary policy—France. I. Title.
HG3034.B36 1972 73-343833
MARC

Banque de France, Paris.
La Banque de France; son histoire, son organisation, ses opérations. [Paris] Cours Servais [1960]
96 p. 21 cm.
1. Banque de France, Paris.
HG3034.B36 1960 332.1'1'0944 74-184574
MARC

Banque de France, Paris.
Le négoce de la soie grège et les industries de la soierie. [Paris, 1971]
6 v. in 1. 30 cm. F***
Cover title.
Issued in portfolio.
CONTENTS: [0] Note de synthèse.—1. Aspects économiques.—2. Le financement du négoce de la soie grège.—3. Le financement de l'industrie de la manutention.—4. Le financement de l'industrie du moulinage.—5. Le financement de l'industrie du tissage des soieries et rubans.
1. Silk manufacture and trade—France. I. Title.
HD9922.5.B35 73-358037
MARC

Banque de France, Paris.
La situation économique et financière en région parisienne / Banque de France. — Paris : BF, 1974.
28 p. ; 30 cm. F***
Cover title.
1. Paris region—Economic conditions. 2. Finance—Paris region. I. Title.
HC277.P28B36 1974 330.9'44'36083 75-500946
MARC

Banque de France, Paris.
La situation économique et financière en région parisienne / Banque de France. — ₍Paris₎ : BF, 1976.
1 portfolio (105 p. in various pagings : ill.) ; 30 cm. F***
Title from portfolio.
"No 8."
CONTENTS: La situation économique et financière.—Annexe statistique.—Le logement en 1975.—Le département du Val-de-Marne.
1. Paris region—Economic conditions. 2. Finance—France—Paris region. I. Title.
HC277.P28B36 1976 77-453549
77 MARC

Banque de France, Paris.
Situation financière des régions en 1972; opérations des guichets bancaires. Paris ₍1973₎
23 p. illus. 30 cm. F***
1. Finance—France—Statistics. 2. Banks and banking—France. I. Title.
HG186.F8B25 1973 332'.0944 74-175189
MARC

Banque de France, Paris.
Stockage de céréales, 1974. — ₍Paris₎ : BF, ₍1975₎
₍97₎ leaves : ill. ; 30 cm. — (Étude sectorielle)
Added t.p.: Étude sur le stockage de céréales dans le département de la Somme.
1. Grain trade—Somme, France (Dept.) 2. Grain—Storage. I. Title. II. Title: Étude sur le stockage de céréales dans le département de la Somme.
HD9042.7.S64B35 1975 338.1'7'31094426 76-462786
76 MARC

Banque de France, Paris.
The tax on value added (TVA) and the tax reform of January 1, 1968. Drafted by D. J. McGrew. Washington, U. S. Dept. of Commerce, CID, 1968.
35 l. 27 cm.
At head of title: Department of State Airgram no. A-1995, unclassified.
Translation of a study prepared by the Research Department of the Bank of France.
1. Sales tax–France. 2. France–Sales tax. I. United States. Dept. of Commerce. II. Title.
NIC NUC76-75692

Banque de France, Paris.
see La Banque de France. Paris, Berger-Levrault, 1975.

Banque de France, Paris
see La Monnaie. 1970- [Paris] Banque de France.

Banque de France, Paris
see Monnaie et quasi-monnaie... [Paris, 1970]

Banque de France, Paris.
see Les Problèmes du financement des investissements ... ₍Paris₎ Banque de France, ₍1975?₎

Banque de France, Paris.
see Szramkiewicz, Romuald. Les régents et censeurs de la Banque de France nommés sous le Consulat et l'Empire. Genève, Droz, 1974.

Banque de France, Paris. Direction de la conjoncture.
Enquête mensuelle de conjoncture.
₍Paris₎
v. illus. 30 cm.
Vols. for issued in pts. in a folder.
1. France—Economic conditions—1945- I. Title.
HC276.2.B265 72-621828

Banque de France, Paris. Direction de la conjoncture.
Les principaux mécanismes de distribution du crédit. 4. éd. ₍Paris₎ 1971.
128 p. illus. 30 cm. F***
1. Credit—France. I. Title.
HG3729.F8B3 1971 72-373803

Banque de France, Paris. Direction de la conjoncture.
Les principaux mécanismes de distribution du crédit. 5 éd. ₍Paris₎ 1974.
134 p. 30 cm. 10.00F F***
Index inserted.
1. Credit—France. I. Title.
HG3729.F8B3 1974 332.7'0944 74-181396
MARC

Banque de France, Paris. Direction de la conjoncture.
Structure et évolution financière des régions de province: Opérations des résidents.
₍Paris₎
v. illus. 27 cm.
1. Finance—France—Statistics. 2. Banks and banking—France. I. Title.
HG186.F8B25a 332'.0944 74-644244
MARC-S

Banque de France, Paris. Direction de la conjoncture.
Structures et moyens de l'action régionale / Banque de France, Direction générale des études, Direction de la conjoncture. — 2. éd. — ₍Paris₎ : La Banque, 1976.
70 p. : maps ; 30 cm. F***
First ed. issued in 1964 by the Direction du crédit of the Banque de France.
Bibliography: p. 67.
Includes index.
1. Regional planning—France. I. Banque de France, Paris. Direction du crédit. Structures et moyens de l'action régionale. II. Title.
HT395.F7B34 1976 76-489887
77 MARC

Banque de France, Paris. Direction de la conjoncture
see Situation financière des régions de province: Opérations des résidents. [Paris]

Banque de France, Paris. Direction du crédit. Structures et moyens de l'action régionale.
see Banque de France, Paris. Direction de la conjoncture. Structures et moyens de l'action régionale. 2. éd. ₍Paris₎ La Banque, 1976.

Banque de France, Paris. Direction générale des études et du crédit. Direction du crédit
see
Banque de France, Paris. Direction du crédit.

Banque de France, Paris. Direction générale des service étrangers
see France. Direction du trésor. Balance des paiements entre la France et L'extérieur. [Paris]

Banque de France, Paris. Direction générale des services étrangers
see France. Direction du trésor. Règlements entre la France et l'extérieur. [Paris?, Ministère de l'economie et des finances[

Banque de France, Paris. Direction générale du crédit.
Le tableau des opérations financières de la comptabilité nationale française. ₍Paris, 1972₎
25 p. illus. 30 cm. F***
1. Finance—France. I. Title.
HG186.F8B25 1972 332'.0944 74-187015
MARC

Banque de France, Paris. Service d'études et statistiques des opérations financières.
see France. Ministère de l'économie et des finances. Système élargi de comptabilité nationale ... ₍Paris₎ Ministère de l'économie et des finances, Institut national de la statistique et des études économiques, 1976.

La Banque de France / travail collectif auquel ont participé des inspecteurs, directeurs-adjoints et adjoints de direction de la Banque de France, MM. Aubert ... ₍et al.₎. — Paris : Berger-Levrault, 1975.
254 p. ; 22 cm. — (L'Administration nouvelle) F***
ISBN 2-7013-0056-8 : 54.00F
1. Banque de France, Paris. I. Aubert, Félix. II. Banque de France, Paris.
HG3034.B34 76-451592
76 MARC

Banque de l'Indo-Chine, Paris.
Financial year - Banque de l' Indochine.
Paris.
v. 30 cm. annual.
1. Banque de l'Indo-Chine, Paris.
HG3040.P24B27a 332.1'509597 74-643027
MARC-S

Banque de l'union parisienne.
The Compagnie universelle du canal maritime de Suez was succeeded in 1958 by the Compagnie financière de Suez. In 1967, the company absorbed the Banque de l'union parisienne, and changed its name to Compagnie financière de Suez et de l'union parisienne, then in 1972, resumed the earlier name Compagnie financière de Suez.
Works by the Compagnie universelle du canal maritime de Suez, and the Compagnie financière de Suez, are found under
Compagnie financière de Suez.
Works by the other bodies are found under the following headings according to the name used at the time of publication:
Banque de l'union parisienne.

Compagnie financière de Suez et de l'union parisienne.

Banque de la République de Guinee
see Guinea. Banque de la République.

Banque de Madagascar et des Comptes. Conseil d'administration.
Rapports du Conseil d'administration, rapports des commissaires aux comptes, résolutions.
Paris.
v. 27-30 cm.
Title varies slightly.
1. Banque de Madagascar et des Comores.
HG3409.M34M33a 332.1'1'09691 74-648213
MARC-S

Banque de Paris et des Pays-Bas Belgique.
Un siècle de présence en Belgique. 1872-1972. Bruxelles, Banque de Paris et des Pays-Bas, Belgique, r. des Colonies, 31, ₍1972₎.
56 p. illus., map, tables. 30 cm. Be 73-524
1. Banque de Paris et des Pays-Bas Belgique. I. Title.
HG3040.P24B35 1972 73-336022

Banque de Syrie et du Liban
see Syria. Convention conclue en date 1 er septembre 1955... [Damas, 1956]

Banque des États de l'Afrique centrale.
In 1955 the functions of the Caisse centrale de la France d'outre-mer (created in 1944) were transferred to the Institut d'émission de l'Afrique équatoriale francaise et du Cameroun. In 1959 the institute became the Banque centrale des États de l'Afrique équatoriale et du Cameroun. In 1972 the bank was reorganized and renamed the Banque des États de l'Afrique centrale.
Works by the Caisse centrale de la France d'outre-mer are found under
Caisse centrale de la France d'outre-mer, Paris.
Works by the Institut d'émission de l'Afrique équatoriale francaise et du Cameroun and the Banque centrale des États de l'Afrique équatoriale et du Cameroun are found under

Banque centrale des États de l'Afrique équatoriale et du Cameroun.
Works by the Banque des États de l'Afrique centrale are found under
Banque des États de l'Afrique centrale.
73-220452

Banque des états de l'Afrique centrale.
Études et statistiques; bulletin mensuel. no 1- avril 1972-
₍Paris₎
no. 27 cm.
Continues the publication with the same title issued by the bank under its earlier name: Banque centrale des états de l'Afrique équatoriale et du Cameroun.
1. Banque des états de l'Afrique centrale. 2. Africa, French Equatorial—Economic conditions—Periodicals.
HG3409.E65B33 330.9'67 73-644698
MARC-S

Banque des états de l'Afrique centrale.
Rapport d'activité—Banque centrale des États de l'Afrique centrale. 1973/74-
₍Paris₎ BEAC.
v. ill. 27 cm.
Report year ends June 30.
1. Banque des états de l'Afrique centrale. 2. Africa, French Equatorial—Economic conditions.
HG3409.E65B332a 75-644523
MARC-S

La Banque des règlements internationaux. ₍Paris₎ La Documentation française, 1973
see under Pierot, Robert.

Banque du Canada
see
Bank of Canada.
Bank of Canada, Ottawa.

Banque du Congo.
The Banque du Congo belge was founded in 1909. In 1960 the name was changed to Banque du Congo and in 1971, to Banque commerciale zaïroise.
Works by this body are found under the name used at the time of publication.

Banque du Congo. Reports and balance sheet
see Banque du Congon. Reports presented to the shareholders at their annual general meeting... 52d-62d; 1960-70. Kinshasa.

Banque du Congo.
Reports presented to the shareholders at their annual general meeting, balance sheet and profit and loss account. 52d-62d; 1960-70. Kinshasa, Banque du Congo.
11 v. 22 cm.
Continues: Banque du Congo belge. Reports presented to the general meeting of shareholders.
Continued by: Banque commerciale zaïroise. Reports presented to the annual general meeting of shareholders, balance sheet and profit and loss account.
Cover title: Reports and balance sheet - Banque du Congo.
1. Banque du Congo. I. Banque du Congo. Reports and balance sheet.
HG3420.K55B35a 332.1'1'096751 77-640466
MARC-S

Banque du Congo belge.
The Banque du Congo belge was founded in 1909. In 1960 the name was changed to Banque du Congo and in 1971, to Banque commerciale zaïroise.
Works by this body are found under the name used at the time of publication.

Banque et capitalisme commercial : la lettre de change au XVIIIe siècle / Charles Carrière ... [et al.] ; préf. de Jacques Rueff. — [Marseille] : Institut historique de Provence, 1976.
220 p. : ill. ; 25 cm. — (Interrogations et recherches) F***
Includes bibliographical references.
60.00F
1. Bills of exchange—History. 2. Foreign exchange—History. I. Carrière, Charles.
HG3811.B3 77-458532
77 MARC

Banque europeenne d'investissement
see European Investment Bank.

Banque française du commerce extérieur, Paris.
Annual general meeting—Banque française du commerce extérieur.
[Paris] Banque française du commerce extérieur.
v. ill. 30 cm.
1. Banque française du commerce extérieur, Paris. 2. France—Commerce—Periodicals.
HG3040.P24C583a 382'.0944 75-642716
MARC-S

Banque française et italienne pour l'Amérique du Sud.
Études économiques—Banque française & italienne pour l'Amérique du Sud.
[Paris] Banque française & italienne pour l'Amérique du Sud.
v. in ill. 28 cm. bimonthly.
Issues for Jan./Feb.–Oct./Nov. 1972 called no. 2–6.
1. Latin America—Economic conditions—1945- —Periodicals.
HC121.B33a 330.9'8'003 76-643053
MARC-S

Banque française et italienne pour l'Amérique du Sud.
Problèmes et évolution de l'économie des pays sud-américains en 1970 et au cours des premiers mois de 1971. Paris, 1971.
223 p. maps.
1. Latin America–Economic conditions–1945- 2. Latin America–Commerce. I. Title.
InU NUC73-115555

Banque gabonaise de développement.
Rapport d'activité—Banque gabonaise de développement.
Libreville.
v. 30 cm.
Began in 1961. Cf. New serial titles.
1. Banque gabonaise de developpement. 2. Gabon—Economic conditions—Periodicals.
HG3409.G34B32a 332.3 74-646239
MARC-S

Banque internationale à Luxembourg.
[Luxembourg, Imprimerie Bourg-Bourger, 1956]
307 p. illus.
"Les cahiers luxembourgeois, 1956, XXVIIIe annee, no. 2."
1. Banque internationale à Luxembourg. I. Cahiers luxembourgeois.
CLU NUC73-59580

Banque internationale pour la réconstruction et la développement
see International Bank for Reconstruction and Development.

Banque marocaine du commerce extérieur.
Bulletin bimestriel d'informations — Banque marocaine du commerce extérieur.
نشرة اخبارية — البنك المغربي للتجارة الخارجية.
[Casablanca] BMCE.
no. 27 cm.
Continues: Banque marocaine du commerce extérieur. Bulletin mensuel d'information.
In French.
1. Morocco—Commerce—Periodicals. I. Banque marocaine du commerce extérieur. Nashrah ikhbārīyah—al-Bank al-Maghribī lil-Tijārah al-Khārijīyah.
HF46.B35b 76-640931
(MARC-S)

Banque marocaine du commerce extérieur.
Nashrah ikhbārīyah—al-Bank al-Maghribī lil -Tijārah al-Khārijīyah
see Banque marocaine du commerce extérieur. Bulletin bimestriel d'information. [Casablanca] BMCE.

Banque marocaine du commerce extérieur.
Revue bimensuelle de la Banque marocaine du commerce extérieur. no 1-
15 oct. 1972-
Casablanca, Département d'études et relations extérieures de la BMCE.
no. 30 cm.
1. Morocco—Commerce—Periodicals.
HF46.B35a 75-645230
MARC-S

Banque marocaine du commerce extérieur.
Zone franche de Tanger. Législation et réglementation. [Rabat, 19-
30 p.
1. Banks and banking–Morocco.
MBU NUC73-68087

Banque marocaine du commerce extérieur. Département d'études et des relations extérieures
see Le Maroc en chiffres. [Rabat] Direction de la statistique.

Banque nationale de Belgique, Brussels.
Belgische economische statistieken : 1960–1970 / Nationale Bank van België. — [Brussel, de Berlaimontlaan 5] : Nationale Bank van België, [1974?]
2 v. ; 30 cm. Be 74-1624
Fold. table in pocket of v. 2.
CONTENTS: deel 1. Toelichting.—deel 2. Tabellen.
1. Belgium—Statistics. I. Title.
HA1405.B35 76-510741

Banque nationale de Belgique, Brussels.
Statistiques économiques belges, 1960-1970 / Banque nationale de Belgique. — [Bruxelles] : La Banque, [1976?]
2 v. ; 30 cm. Be***
Text in French with tables in French and Dutch.
CONTENTS: t. 1. Notices.—t. 2. Tableaux.
1. Belgium—Statistics. 2. Belgium—Economic conditions—1945- I. Title.
HA1401.B36 1976 330.9'493'04 76-479253
76[r77]rev MARC

Banque nationale de développement.
Textes constitutifs et statuts. Ouagadougou [n.d.]
1 v. (unpaged) 30 cm.
1. Development banks–Upper Volta.
CtY-E NUC76-92321

Banque nationale de développement du Sénégal.
Rapport d'activité—Banque nationale de développement du Sénégal.
[s. l.] Banque nationale de développement du Sénégal.
v. 22 x 34 cm.
Report year ends Sept. 30.
1. Banque nationale de développement du Sénégal.
HG3409.S464B362 76-649235
MARC-S

Banque nationale de la République d'Haïti, Port-au-Prince. Département commercial.
Rapport [1935–1951] Port-au-Prince, 1955.
95 p. illus. 20 x 27 cm.
1. Banque nationale de la République d'Haiti, Port-au-Prince.
HG2813.B36 1955 332.1'1'097294 74-184175
MARC

Banque nationale de la République d'Haiti, Port-au-Prince. Département fiscal.
Importations & [i. e. et] exportations.
[Port-au-Prince] B. N. R. H., Département fiscal.
v. 36 cm.
1. Haiti—Commerce. I. Title.
HF151.B35a 382'.097294 75-640527
MARC-S

Banque nationale de la République socialiste de Roumanie
see
Banca Națională a Republicii Socialiste România.

Banque nationale du Congo.
Auszüge aus dem Zentralbankbericht 1968/1969. Köln, Schäuble, 1970.
63 p. 21 cm. (Schriftenreihe der Deutsch-Kongolesischen Gesellschaft, Heft 6)
1. Banks and banking—Congo (Democratic Republic)
NNC NUC74-121744

Banque nationale du Rwanda.
Rapport annuel.
[Kigali]
v. 27 cm.
1. Banque nationale de Rwanda. 2. Rwanda—Economic conditions—Yearbooks.
HG3414.R93B36a 73-645261
MARC-S

Banque nationale pour le développement économique
see
al-Bank al-Waṭanī lil-Inmā' al-Iqtiṣādī.

Banque régionale d'escompte et de dépôts.
Lexique de la bourse. — Paris : BRED, [1974]
[50] p. : col. ill. ; 19 cm. F***
1. Finance—Dictionaries—French. 2. Stock-exchange—Dictionaries—French. I. Title.
HG151.B3 1974 332.6'03 75-512589
75 MARC

Banques de données archéologiques. Marseille 12-14 juin 1972. — Paris : Éditions du Centre national de la recherche scientifique, 1974.
331 p. : ill. ; 28 cm. — (Colloques nationaux du Centre national de la recherche scientifique ; no 932) F***
"Colloque ... organisé ... par ... Mario Borillo ... et Jean-Claude Gardin."
Summaries in English.
Errata slip inserted.
Includes bibliographies.
ISBN 2-222-01661-4
1. Archaeology—Methodology—Data processing—Congresses. I. Borillo, Mario. II. Gardin, Jean Claude. III. Series: France. Centre national de la recherche scientifique. Colloques nationaux du Centre national de la recherche scientifique ; no 932.
CC80.4.B36 930'.1'0285 75-504612
75[r77]rev MARC

Banques de données pour le développement, Réunion internationale d'experts sur les
see
Réunion internationale d'experts sur les banques de données pour le développement, St. Maximin, France, 1971.

Banques étrangères en France, Colloque sur les
see
Colloque sur les banques étrangères en France, Paris, 1974.

Banquet of jests.
A banquet of jests; or, Change of cheare. Being a collection of moderne jests, witty jeeres, pleasant taunts, merry tales. The 5th impression, with many additions. London, printed for R. Royston, 1639 [1972]
Part 1 only.
"To the reader" signed: Anonymos.
Sometimes attributed to Archibald Armstrong.
Microfilm of original in the Huntington Library. Ann Arbor, Mich., University Microfilms, 1972. (Early English books, 1475-1640, reel 1265)
STC no. 1370.
1. English wit and humor. I. Armstrong, Archibald, d. 1672. II. Title.
CaBVaU NUC74-2608

Banri Toshokan.
(Hiji Chōritsu Banri Toshokan shozō kyōdō shiryō mokuroku)
日出町立萬里図書館所蔵郷土資料目録：昭和48年7月1日現在 / [編集　荒金錬次]. — 日出町(大分県)：万里図書館, 昭和48- [1973-
v. ; 26 cm. — (図書館叢書 ; 第8　集) Ja 74-1022 (v. 1)
Cover title.
Includes index.
1. Oita, Japan (Prefecture)—History—Sources—Bibliography—Catalogs. 2. Banri Toshokan. I. Arakane, Renji. II. Title. III. Series: Toshokan sōsho ; dai 8-shū [etc.]
Z3307.O4B35 76-811605
[DS5894.99.O36]

Banryoku
see (Banryoku kigo sen) 47 (1972)

(Banryoku kigo sen)
萬錄季語撰　中村草田男編　東京　刀江書院　昭和47(1972)
514 p.　20 cm.　¥2000　　Ja 72-6204

1. Haiku. 2. Seasons in literature. 3. Festivals in literature. I. Nakamura, Kusadao, 1901-　ed. II. Banryoku.
PL759.B35　　72-813457

Bansa, Helmut.
Die Register der Kanzlei Ludwigs des Bayern./ Bearb. von Helmut Bansa. — München : Beck 1971–74.
2 v. 25 cm. (Quellen und Erörterungen zur zayerischen Geschichte, n. F., Bd. 24)　GDB 72–A13 (v. 1)
Text in Latin or Middle High German; commentary and prefatory matter in German.
Includes bibliographical references.
CONTENTS: T. 1. Darstellung, und Edition des älteren Reichsregisters.—T. 2. Edition des jüngeren Reichsregisters.
DM35.00 (v. 1)
1. Ludwig IV, der Bayer, Emperor of Germany, 1287–1347. 2. Germany—History—Louis IV, 1314–1347—Sources. I. Title. II. Title: Kanzlei Ludwigs des Bayern. III. Series.
DD163.B35　　72–339445

Bánsághy, Milklos
see Hungary. Laws, statutes, etc. A fogyasztási, értékesito és beszerző szövetkezetekre vonatkozó jogszabályok. Budapest, Közgazdasági és Jogi Könyvkiadó, 1972.

Bánsági, Pál.
Gazdasági növekedés és a fejlődés intenzív periódusa / Bánsági Pál, Rácz Dezső, Szabó Béla. — Budapest : Közgazdasági és Jogi Könyvkiadó, 1975.
245 p. ; 21 cm.
Summary in English and Russian.
Includes bibliographical references.
ISBN 963220185X : 40.00Ft.
1. Technological innovations—Hungary. 2. Technological innovations. 3. Hungary — Economic conditions — 1945–　I. Rácz, Dezsö, joint author. II. Szabó, Béla, joint author. III. Title.
HC300.295.T4B35　　77–501102

Bansal, Bihari
see Thomas S. Clarkson Memorial College of Technology, Potsdam, N.Y. Analytical and experimental studies of reverse osmosis... [Washington] United States Department of the Interior, 1973.

Bansal, H　L　1908-
Magnetotherapy : the art of healing through magnets / H. L. Bansal. — 1st ed. — New Delhi : B. Jain Publishers : selling agents, Harjeet, 1976.
xv, 173 p., [7] leaves of plates : ill. ; 22 cm.
Bibliography: p. [171]-173.
Rs9.50
1. Magnetic healing. I. Title.
RZ422.B36　　615'.845　　76-903032
76　　MARC

Bansal, I.K., joint author
see Wiley, Averill J　Reverse osmosis concentration of dilute pulp & paper effluents. Washington [Environmental Protection Agency] 1972.

Bansal, Jagdish Prasad, 1938-
The lateral instability of continuous steel beams. [Austin, Tex.] 1971.
xv, 126 l. illus. 29 cm.
Thesis (Ph.D.)—University of Texas at Austin.
Vita.
Bibliography: leaves 122-126.
1. Steel, Structural—Testing.
TxU　　NUC73-115156

Bansal, Kamlesh.
Bases for rapid same-different judgments of letters. [Charlottesville, Va.] 1973.
ii, 101 l. illus. 29 cm.
Thesis—University of Virginia.
Bibliography: leaves 72-75.
1. Difference (Psychology) 2. Variability (Psychometrics) I. Title.
ViU　　NUC75-20665

Bansal, Prem Lata.
Administrative development in India / Prem Lata Bansal. — 1st ed. — New Delhi : Sterling Publishers, 1974.
viii, 196 p. ; 22 cm.
Originally presented as the author's thesis, University of Nebraska.
Bibliography: p. [142]-162.
Includes index.
Rs30.00
1. Civil service—India. 2. India—Politics and government—1947- I. Title.
JQ247.B34 1974　　354'.54　　75-905188
77　　MARC

Bansal, Prem Lata.
Administrative reorganization : an overview of the procedures and approaches in various states : a study prepared for State Office of Planning and Programming / by Prem Lata Bansal, under the direction of W. Don Nelson, director, Joseph S. Golden, social services coordinator. — Lincoln, Neb. : The Office, 1974.
42 leaves ; 29 cm.
Bibliography: leaves 27-42.
1. State governments. 2. Administrative agencies—United States—States. I. Nebraska. State Office of Planning and Programming. II. Title.
JK2443.B4　　353.9　　75-622419
76　　MARC

Bansal, Prem Lata.
General revenue sharing : promise, performance, and problems / research by Prem Lata Bansal. — Lincoln : State of Nebraska, Office of Planning and Programming, 1975.
i, 38 leaves ; 28 cm.
Cover title.
Includes bibliographical references.
1. Revenue sharing—United States. I. Nebraska. State Office of Planning and Programming. II. Title.
HJ275.B27　　336.1'85　　76-622412
76　　MARC

Bansal, Prem Lata.
Indian administrative service and development administration. Lincoln, Neb., 1973.
[4], ii, [6], 265 l. diagrs., tables.
Thesis (Ph. D.)—University of Nebraska.
Selected bibliography: leaves 220-240.
Appendices A–C: leaves 241-265.
I. Title.
NbU　　NUC 74-123731

Bansal, Prem Lata.
Patterns of State-regional cooperation in Nebraska : a study prepared for State Office of Planning and Programming / by Prem Lata Bansal ; under the direction of W. Don Nelson, director, Joseph S. Golden, social services coordinator. — [Lincoln : State of Nebraska, Office of Planning and Programming], 1974.
59, 7 leaves : map ; 28 cm.
Bibliography: leaves 55-59.
1. Nebraska—Politics and government. 2. Decentralization in government—Nebraska. 3. Regional planning—Nebraska. I. Nebraska. State Office of Planning and Programming. II. Title.
JK6638 1974.B35　　353.9'782'93　　75-620778
75　　MARC

Bansal, R　K　1920–
The intelligibility of Indian English; measurements of the intelligibility of connected speech, and sentence and word material, presented to listners of different nationalities, by R. K. Bansal. Hyderabad, India, Central Institute of English; [available from Orient Longmans, Madras] 1969.
xii, 174 p. illus. 25 cm. ([Central Institute of English] Monograph no. 4) Rs7.50
"An abridged version of the thesis approved by the University of London, for the award of Ph. D."
Includes bibliographical references.
1. English language—Dialects—India. I. Title. II. Series.
PE3501.B3 1969　　71–928448
MARC

Bansal, Romesh Chander, 1934-
Reductive amination and metal-amine reduction of polynuclear aromatic hydrocarbons. [Stillwater, Okla., 1966]
56 l. 29 cm.
Thesis (Ph.D.)—Oklahoma State University.
Includes bibliography.
Vita.
1. Hydrocarbons. 2. Amines. I. Title.
TxBeaL　　NUC74-117993

Bansal, Shyam Sunder, comp.
see Kṛshṇadatta, Brahmachari. Yogic wisdom of the ancient rishis... New Delhi, Vedic Anusandhan Samiti [1972]

Bansal, Suresh Chandra, 1942-
Town-country relationship in Saharanpur City-region : a study in rural-urban interdependence problems / by Suresh Chand Bansal. — Saharanpur : Sanjeev Prakashan ; Agra : authorized dealer, Vimal Prakashan Mandir, 1975.
171, xi, [1] p. : ill., maps ; 23 cm.
A revision of the author's thesis, Meerut University, 1973.
Bibliography: p. [i]-xi.
"Abbreviations & glossary": p. xii (2d group)
Rs30.00
1. Regional planning—India—Saharanpur. 2. Municipal services—India—Saharanpur. 3. Municipal powers and services beyond corporate limits—India—Saharanpur. I. Title.
HT395.I52S233 1975　　309.2'5'09542　　75-907104
76　　MARC

Bansat Ngoen Thun Qutsāhakam hāeng Prathēt Thai.
IFCT 1969. Bangkok, Industrial Finance Corporation of Thailand, 1969.
51 p. illus. 26 cm.
On cover: 10th annual report.
NIC　　NUC73-38293

Bansbach, Karen Renée, 1943-
The German opera libretto since 1945 / by Karen Renée Bansbach. -- [Madison, Wis.] University of Wisconsin, c1975.
303 l. ; 29 cm.
Thesis (Ph.D.)--University of Wisconsin.
Vita.
Bibliography: leaves 278-300.
1. Libretto. 2. Opera, German--History & criticism. I. Title.
WU　　NUC77-87870

Bansch, Frank, 1942–
Die Beleihung als verfassungsrechtliches Problem; zur Zulässigkeit einer Übertragung hoheitlicher Befugnisse auf Private nach dem Grundgesetz. [Frankfurt am Main] 1973.
157 p. 21 cm.　GFR***
Inaug.-Diss.—Frankfurt am Main.
Vita.
Bibliography: p. [9]–[22]
1. Concessions—Germany (Federal Republic, 1949–　) I. Title.
75–559765

Banschbach, Martin Way, 1946-
Evaluation of B-carotene binding to lamellar protein isolated from spinach (Spinacia oleracea) chloroplasts. [n.p.] 1972.
139 l. illus.
I. Title.
ViBlbV　　NUC73-115144

Bansdoc
see
Bangladesh National Scientific and Technical Documentation Centre.
for publications by and about this body.
Titles and other entries beginning with this acronym are filed following this card.

Banse, Karl.
Benthic errantiate polychaetes of British Columbia and Washington [by] Karl Banse [and] Katharine D. Hobson. Ottawa, Fisheries and Marine Service, 1974.
x, 111 p. illus. 25 cm. (Canada. Fisheries Research Board. Bulletin 185)
Bibliography: p. 99-103.
1. Polychaeta–British Columbia. 2. Polychaeta–Washington. 3. Worms–British Columbia. 4. Worms–Washington. I. Hobson, Katharine D., joint author. II. Title. III. Series.
AAP DI　　NUC75-18560

Banse, Manfred, joint author
see Schmidt, Günter, 1924-　Der Charakter der kapitalistischen Betriebswirtschaftslehre und der sozialen Betriebspolitik. Berlin, Verlag Die Wirtschaft, 1957.

(Bansei tokkō taiin no isho)
万世特攻隊員の遺書 / 苗村七郎編著. — 東京 : 現代評論社, 1976.
478 p. : ill. ; 20 cm.　　Ja 77-1688
Bibliography: p. 478.
¥2000

1. World War, 1939-1945—Personal narratives, Japanese. 2. Last letters before death. 3. Japan. Rikugun. Kōkūtai—Biography. I. Naemura, Shichirō, 1921-
D811.A2B36　　77-803777

Banser, Klaus-W
Modell eines Gesamt-Schulzentrums für behinderte und nichtbehinderte Kinder. Unter bes. Berücks. d. Anforderungen körperbehinderter Kinder. [Von] Klaus-W. Banser, Brigitte Eckert [u.] Ilke Uder. Weinheim, Berlin, Basel, Beltz, (1971).
154 p. illus., map. 30 cm. DM28.00 GDB 72-A13
Bibliography: p. [151]-154.
1. School buildings. I. Eckert, Brigitte, joint author. II. Uder, Ilke, joint author. III. Title.
LB3209.B28 72-367003
ISBN 3-407-18280-5

Banshchikov, Vasiliĭ Mikhaĭlovich, 1898–
(O temperamente cheloveka)
О темпераменте человека : очерки из истории вопроса в соврем. состоянии : материалы для симпозиума в февр. 1974 г. / В. М. Банщиков, Г. Д. Новинский, О. М. Эфендиев. — Москва : [s. n.], 1973.
276, [2] p. : ill. ; 21 cm. USSR 74
At head of title: Всероссийское научное медицинское общество невропатологов и психиатров.
Bibliography: p. 271-[277]
1.95rub
1. Temperament. I. Novinskiĭ, Georgiĭ Davydovich, joint author. II. Éfendiev, O. M., joint author. III. Title.
BF798.B36 74-352130

Banshchikov, Vasiliĭ Mikhaĭlovich, 1898–
(Problema alkogolizma)
Проблема алкоголизма. (Мед. и психол. анализ). Материалы для обсуждения на конф. Всерос. и Новосиб. науч. мед. о-в невропатологов и психиатров. Окт. 1973. [Москва], 1973.
112 p. 21 cm. 0.70rub USSR 73
At head of title: Всероссийское научное медицинское общество невропатологов и психиатров. Кафедра психиатрии Новосибирского медицинского института. Б. (sic) М. Банщиков, Ц. П. Короленко.
Bibliography: p. 109.
1. Alcoholism. I. Korolenko, TSezar' Petrovich, joint author. II. Title.
RC565.B26 74-307286

Banshchikov, Vasiliĭ Mikhaĭlovich, 1898- ed.
see Fedorovskiĭ, IU N Reoentsefalografiia pri nekotorykh psikhicheskikh zabolevaniiakh; metodicheskoe posobie dlia prepodavateleĭ i studentov starshikh kursov meditsinskikh institutov, Moskva, 1966.

Banshchikov, Vasiliĭ Mikhailovich, 1898- ed.
see Issledovanie funtsional'nogo sostoianiia kory nadpochechnikov i simpato-adrenalovoĭ sistmey. 1963.

Banshchikov, Vasiliĭ Mikhaĭlovich, 1898- ed.
see Izbiratel'nost' deĭstviia... Moskva, 1970.

Banshchikov, Vasilii Mikhaĭlovich, 1898- ed.
see Nauchno-prakticheskaia konferentsiia po ėlektrosnu vracheĭ Moskvy, Moskovskoĭ oblasti i Moskovskoĭ zheleznoĭ dorogi, Moscow, 1972. Ėlektroson v prakticheskoĭ meditsine. 1972.

Banshchikov, Vasiliĭ Mikhaĭlovich, 1898-
see Simpozium po probleme soznaniia, Moscow, 1966. Soznanie. Moskva, 1967.

Banshchikov, Vasiliĭ Mikhaĭlovich, 1898- ed.
see Son i ego narusheniia. 1972.

Banshchikov, Vasiliĭ Mikhaĭlovich, 1898-
see Sootnoshenie biologicheskogo i sotsial'nogo v cheloveke. 1975.

Ban'shchikov, Vasiliĭ Mikhaĭlovich, 1898- ed.
see Voprosy kliniki, patogeneza i terapii psikhicheskikh zabolevaniĭ. 1972.

Banshchikov, Vasiliĭ Mikhaĭlovich, 1898- ed.
see Vserossiĭskoe nauchnoe obshchestvo nevropatologov i psikhiatrov. Voprosy alkogolizma. 1973.

Banshchikov, Vasiliĭ Mikhailovich, 1898- ed.
see Vsesoiuznaia nauchno-prakticheskaia konferentsiia po psikhiatriĭ detskogo vozrasta, Moscow, 1957. Voprosy detskoĭ psikhonevrologii. Moskva, 1958.

Banshchikov, Vasiliĭ Mikhaĭlovich, 1898- ed.
see Vsesoiuznyĭ s''ezd nevropatologov i psikhiatrov, 4th, Moscow, 1963. Trudy. Moskva, 1965-

Banshō, Hikoji.
(Kubi no nai chūtai)
首のない中隊　第一中隊戦記　万正彦次著　金沢　北国出版社　昭和47(1972)
366 p. illus., port. 19 cm. ¥850 Ja 72-9425
LC copy: 2d impression: p. 367 wanting.
1. Sino-Japanese Conflict, 1937-1945—Personal narratives, Japanese. 2. Japan. Rikugun. Dokuritsu Konsei Dai 2 Rentai. Hohei Dai 1 Daitai. Dai 1 Chūtai. 3. Sino-Japanese Conflict, 1937-1945—Regimental histories—Japan—Dokuritsu Konsei Dai 2 Rentai. Hohei Dai 1 Daitai. Dai 1 Chūtai. I. Title.
DS777.53.B316 73-805896

Banshō Gyōshū Zenji
see
Hsing-hsiu, Shih, 1166-1246.

Banshtyk, Anatoliĭ Mironovich.
(Ėlektrogidravlicheskie servomekhanizmy s shirotno-impul'snym upravleniem)
Электрогидравлические сервомеханизмы с широтно-импульсным управлением. Под ред. д-ра техн. наук, проф. И. М. Крассова. Москва, "Машиностроение," 1972.
144 p. with diagrs. 21 cm. 0.90rub USSR 72-VKP
At head of title: A. M. Банштык.
Bibliography: p. 137-[142]
1. Hydraulic servomechanisms. I. Title.
TJ857.B28 73-330390

Banshū Ishikai Kaishi Hensan Iinkai.
(Banshū Ishikai shi)
磐周医師会史　磐周医師会会史編纂委員会編　袋井　磐周医師会　昭和48(1973)
629 p., 36 p. of ports. map. 22 cm. N.T. Ja 73-19805
Bibliography: p. 627-628.

1. Banshū Ishikai. I. Title.
R97.7.J3B323 74-801989

Bansi Lal
see Lal, Bansi.

Bansil, P C
Agricultural problems of India / P. C. Bansil. — 2d rev. and enl. ed. — Delhi : Vikas Pub. House, 1975.
xi, 608 p. ; 22 cm.
Includes bibliographical references.
Rs35.00
1. Agriculture—Economic aspects—India. 2. Agriculture and state—India. I. Title.
HD2072.B28 1975 338.1'0954 75-903617
76 MARC

Bansil, P C
Agricultural statistics in India / P. C. Bansil. — 2d. rev. ed. — New Delhi : Arnold Heinemann Publishers (India), 1974.
454 p. ; 23 cm.
Includes bibliographical references.
Rs19.00
1. Agricultural estimating and reporting—India. 2. Agriculture—India—Statistics. I. Title.
S494.5.E8B35 1974 338.1'0954 74-902562
MARC

Bansil, Rama Daga, 1947-
A general model of kinetics of cooperative ligand binding in proteins and its application to hemoglobin kinetics / by Rama Daga Bansil. -- [s.l. : s.n.], 1974 [i.e. 1975]
xii, 156 leaves : diagrs. ; 29 cm.
Thesis (Ph.D.)--University of Rochester.
Vita.
Includes bibliographies.
I. Title.
NRU NUC77-87869

Banská Bystrica, Czechoslovak Republic (City)
see also
Banská Bystrica, Czechoslovakia.

Banská Bystrica, Czechoslovak Republic (City). Oblastná galéria
see
Oblastná galéria v Banskej Bystrici.

Banská Bystrica, Czechoslovak Republic (City). Pedagogická fakulta.
Cudzie jazyky. 1-
[V Banskej Bystrici] 1972-
no. 21 cm. (Acta Facultatis Paedagogicae Banská Bystrica)
Cover title, 1- : Séria spoločenskovedná. Cudzie jazyky.
German or Slovak.
Some summaries in English or Slovak.
1. Philology — Collected works. 2. Languages, Modern — Study and teaching — Collected works. I. Banská Bystrica, Czechoslovak Republic (City). Pedagogická fakulta. Séria spoločenskovedná. Cudzie jazyky. II. Title. III. Title: Séria spoločenskovedná. Cudzie jazyky. IV. Series: Banská Bystrica, Czechoslovak Republic (City). Pedagogická fakulta. Acta.
P25.B25a 73-647816
MARC-S

Banská Bystrica, Czechoslovak Republic (City). Pedagogická fakulta.
Ruský jazyk a literatúra.
[V Banskej Bystrici]
no. ill. 21 cm. (Zborník Pedagogickej fakulty v Banskej Bystrici)
Cover title : Séria spoločenskovedná. Ruský jazyk a literatúra.
Russian or Slovak.
1. Russian philology—Collected works. I. Title: Ruský jazyk a literatúra. II. Title: Séria spoločenskovedná. Ruský jazyk a literatúra. III. Series: Banská Bystrica, Czechoslovak Republic (City). Pedagogická fakulta. Acta.
PG2013.B36a 75-640665
MARC-S

Banská Bystrica, Czechoslovak Republic (City). Pedagogická fakulta.
Séria prírodovedná. Fyzika. 1-
Bratislava, Slovenské pedagogické nakl., 1971-
no. illus. 20 cm. (Acta Facultatis Paedagogicae Banská Bystrica)
1. Physics—Collected works. I. Title. II. Series: Banská Bystrica, Czechoslovak Republic (City). Pedagogická fakulta. Acta.
QC1.B25 73-640048

Banská Bystrica, Czechoslovak Republic (City). Pedagogická fakulta. Séria spoločenskovedná. Cudzie jazyky
see Banská Bystrica, Czechoslovak Republic (City). Pedagogická fakulta. Cuzie jazyky. [V Banskej Bystrici] 1972-

Banská Bystrica, Czechoslovak Republic (City). Pedagogická fakulta.
Zborník.
Bratislava, Slovenské pedagogické nakl.
no. illus. 21 cm.
Continues: Banská Bystrica, Czechoslovak Republic (City). Pedagogický inštitút. Sborník.
No. issued in sections, e. g. no. 16: Geografia.
AS125.B3A3 72-626856

Banská Bystrica, Czechoslovak Republic (City). Pedagogická fakulta
see 10 [i.e. Desat] rokov Vysokoškolského učitel'ského štúdia v Banskej Bystrici, 1954-1964. [V Banskej Bystrici] Stredoslovenské vyd-vo [1966]

Banská Bystrica, Czechoslovak Republic (City). Pedagogická fakulta
see also
Pedagogická fakulta v Banskej Bystrici.

Banská Bystrica, Czechoslovak Republic (City). Pedagogický inštitút.

For works by this body issued under its later name see

Banská Bystrica, Czechoslovak Republic (City). Pedagogická fakulta.

Banská Bystrica, Czechoslovak Republic (City). Štátna vedecká knižnica
see
Štátna vedecká knižnica v Banskej Bystrici.

Banská Bystrica, Czechoslovak Republic (District). Štátny archív.
Slúžnovsky úrad v Banskej Bystrici, 1898-1922; katalog. [Autor] Alžbeta Nagyová. Bratislava, Slovenská archívna správa, 1970.
231 p. (Inventáre a katalógy fondov štátnych archívov na Slovensku, no. 24)
1. Slovakia—Politics and government—Sources. 2. Archives—Slovakia. I. Nagyová, Alžbeta. II. Title. III. Series.
WaU NUC76-106323

Banská Bystrica, Czechoslovak Republic (District). Štátny archív. Pobočka v Bytči.
Oravská župa; inventár [Compiled by] Jozef Kočiš. Bratislava, Slovenská archívna sprava, 1972-
v. (Inventáre a katalógy fondov štátnych archívov na Slovensku, 32)
At head of title: Státny archív v Bytci.
Limited edition, 200 copies.
Contents: -1. (1393) 1584-1849.
1. Orava, Czechslovak Republic (County)—Hist.—Bibl. I. Kociš, Jozef. II. Orava, Czechoslovak Republic (County) III. Title. IV. Series.
MH NUC76-40698

Banská Bystrica, Czechoslovak Republic (District). Štátny archiv. Pobočka v Bytci.
Zupa Považská 1923-1928; dejiny robotníckeho hnutia a KSČ [Compiled by] Františka Hrtánková & Kamila Chudá. Bratislava, Slovenská archívna sprava, 1971.
220 p. (Inventáre a katalógy fondov štátnych archívov na Slovensku, 30)
At head of title: Státny archív v Bytči.
One of a limited edition of 220 copies.
1. Považie, Chechoslovak Republic (County)—Hist.—Bibl. 2. Labor—Považie, Chechslovak Republic (County)—Bibl. 3. Komunistická strana Československa—Bibl. I. Hrtánková, Františka. II. Chudá, Kamila. III. Považie, Czechoslovak Republic (County) IV. Title. V. Series.
MH NUC76-40695

Banská Bystrica, Czechoslovak Republic (District). Štátny archív. Pobočka v Bytči.
Župa Turčianska; inventár. [Autor: Stanislav Palkovič] Bratislava, Slovenská archív na správa, 1970-
v. (Inventáre a katalógy fondov štátnych archívov na Slovensku, no. 26/1)
At head of title: Štátny archív v Bytči.
Contents.—v. 1. 1486-1849.
I. Palkovič, Stanislav.
WaU NUC76-106322

Banská Bystrica, Czechoslovakia
see also
Banská Bystrica, Czechoslovak Republic (City)

Banská Bystrica. Autori: Milan Gajdoš a kol. Vstupné básne nap. Štefan Žáry. Autori fot. Jozef Šťastný ... Texty pod obr. a resumé prel. Ruš. — Katarína Balanceková, nem. — Ján Lumtzer, angl. — Karol Haltmar, franc. — Miloslav Trnka. 1. vyd. Martin, Osveta, t. Tlač. SNP-Neografia, 1974.
[179] p. photos (part col.) 28 cm. CzS 74
Polyglot summary and list of illustrations (21 p.) laid in.
Kčs75.00
1. Banská Bystrica, Czechoslovak Republic (City)—Description—Views. I. Gajdoš, Milan.
DB879.B28B29 75-556005

Banska Stiavnica, Slovakia. Magyar Kiralyi Banyaszati és Erdeszeti Akadémia
see A Nehézipari Műszaki Egyetem... Miskolc, 1970]

Bansley, Charles.
A treatyse shewing and declaring the pryde and abuse of women now a dayes. London, Reprinted by T. Richards, for the executors of the late C. Richards, 1841. New York, Johnson Reprint Corp. [1965]
15 p. 19 cm. (Percy Society. Early English poetry...v. 30e)
"Reprinted from a unique copy."
1. Great Britain—Social life and customs. I. Title. II. Series.
ImacoW NUC74-135043

(Bansui Sensei to fujin)
晩翠先生と夫人 資料と思出 仙台 黒川 雄 昭和46(1971)
40, 226 p. ports. 22 cm. N.T. ...-15151
At head of title: 生誕百年記念
Errata slip inserted.

1. Doi, Bansui, 1871-1952. 2. Tsuchii, Yae (Hayashi) 1879-
PL804.O35Z6 73-805063

Banszerus, Georg, 1920-
Deutschland ruft Dich : eine Analyse über d. Probleme u. Spannungen d. Gegenwart u. Vorschläge zu ihrer Überwindung / Georg Banszerus. — 1. Aufl. — Höxter (Weser), [Grubestr. 9] : Selbstverl., c1972.
341 p. ; 22 cm. GFR 74-B15
Bibliography: p. 339-341.
DM18.00
1 Germany—Politics and government—20th century. 2. Germany (Federal Republic, 1949-)—Politics and government. 3. History—Philosophy. I. Title.
DD232.B33 320.9′43′08 75-565394

Bánszki, Pál
see Izlés és kultúra ... Budapest : Kossuth Könyvkiadó, 1974.

Banszky, Pal
see Budapest. Magyar Nemzeti Galéria. Magyar naiv muvészet a XX. században, Budapest, 1972. Budapest [1972]

Banta, Arthur W.
see Probate code—1975 reform ... [Indianapolis] Indiana Continuing Legal Education Forum, c1975.

Banta, Benjamin Harrison.
An annotated chronological bibliography of the herpetology of the State of Nevada. [San Francisco, University of San Francisco, 1965]
224 p. map. 23 cm. (Wasman journal of biology, v. 23, no. 1-2, Spring and Fall, 1965)
1. Reptiles—Nevada—Bibliography. 2. Amphibians—Nevada—Bibliography.
NIC NUC73-38294

[Banta (George) Company, inc.]
The Nightmare. [Menasha, Wis., 1961?]
[12] p. col. illus., port. 21 x 28 cm.
On cover: Behold a Child is Born.
1. Christmas poetry. I. Title.
RPB NUC75-58902

Banta, James E., 1927- joint author
see Doyle, Patrick J How to travel the world and stay healthy. New York, Arco Pub. Co. [1974, c1969]

Banta, John, joint author
see Bosselman, Fred P 1934-
The taking issue... [Washington, Govt. Print. Off., 1973]

Banta, John.
see Conservation Foundation. Groping through the maze ... Washington, Conservation Foundation, c1977.

Banta, John S., joint author
see Babcock, Richard F New zoning techniques... [Chicago, American Society of Planning Officials, 1973]

Banta, Martha.
Henry James and the occult; the great extension. Bloomington, Indiana University Press [1972]
273 p. 22 cm. $9.50
Originally presented as the author's thesis, Indiana University, 1964.
Bibliography: p. [213]-221.
1. James, Henry, 1843-1916. 2. Occultism in literature.
PS2127.O25B3 1972 813′.4 72-75386
ISBN 0-253-32732-6 MARC

Banta, Melissa Wickser, 1925-
Dream-vision and debate in the allegorical mode: a study of Wynnere and Wastoure, Parlement of the thre ages, and Death and liffe. [n.p.] 1966.
iv, 278 l.
Thesis—State University of New York, Buffalo.
Bibliography: leaves 266-278.
Microfilm (positive) Ann Arbor, Mich., University Microfilms, 1966. 1 reel. (Publication no. 7959)
NNC NUC75-48078

Banta, Michael E.
see Vacar, Thomas N A guide for establishing public interest... [Washington] 1971.

Banta, Paul R., joint author.
see Tremblay, Kenneth R. Effects of immigration in the community of Valdez. [Boulder, Colo.] Western Interstate Commission on Higher Education, 1974.

Banta, Richard Elwell, ed.
Hoosier caravan; a treasury of Indiana life and lore, selected with comment, by R. E. Banta. New & enl. ed. Bloomington, Indiana University Press [1975]
xx, 620 p. 24 cm.
ISBN 0-253-13861-2. ISBN 0-253-13862-0 deluxe ed.
1. American literature—Indiana. 2. Indiana—Literary collections. I. Title.
PS571.I6B3 1975 810′.8′09772 73-16521
74 MARC

Banta, Richard Elwell, comp. Indiana authors and their books, 1816-1916
see Thompson, Donald Eugene, 1913-
Indiana authors and their books, 1917-1966. Crawfordsville, Ind., Wabash College, 1974.

Banta, Richard L., 1934-
see Koehler, J H Water resources at Marine Corps Supply Center... Menlo Park, Calif., 1969-

Banta, Seth Emmet, 1877-
see Buckelew, F. M., 1852- Buckelew, the Indian captive. New York, Garland Pub., 1977.

Banta, Thomas J 1933-
Social attitudes and response style. Ann Arbor, Mich., University Microfilms [1965]
v, 91 l. illus. 22 cm.
"Authorized reprint... produced by microfilm-xerography."
Thesis—Columbia University, 1960.
Bibliography: leaves 89-91.
1. Attitude (Psychology) 2. Sociometry. I. Title.
NRU NUC76-75790

Banta, Trudy W
Bibliographical references from ERIC citations. Knoxville, University of Tennessee, Library, 1974.
26 p. illus.
1. Education Resources Information Center. Bibliography. 2. Educational research. Bibliography. I. Bowlby, Sylva M. II. Tennessee. University. Libraries. III. Educational Resources Information Center. IV. Title.
DNAL NUC76-23716

Banta, Trudy W
Description of school plant facilities in Tennessee, 1973 / by Trudy W. Banta. — [s.l. : s.n., 1973?]
xiv, 302 p. ; 28 cm.
Bibliography: p. 293-294.
1. School buildings—Tennessee—Statistics. I. Title.
LB3218.T35B36 371.6′2′09768 76-622451
76 MARC

Banta, Trudy W
Job-oriented education programs for the disadvantaged. By Trudy W. Banta, Douglas C. Towne and Linda G. Douglass. [Washington, U.S. Govt. Print. Off., 1972]
63 p. (PREP reports, no. 9)
1. Vocational education—U.S. 2. Industrial management—In-service training. 3. Socially handicapped—Education—U.S. I. Towne, Douglas C. II. Douglass, Linda G. III. Title. IV. Series.
MH-Ed NUC73-119411

Banta, Trudy W
Seminar on preparing the disadvantaged for jobs; a planning handbook. [Washington] National Center for Educational Communication, 1972.
42 p. (PREP report no. 10)
DHEW publication no. (OE) 72-9.
1. Hard-core unemployed–U. S. I. Title. II. Series.
MH-Ed NUC73-115216

Banta, Trudy W
see Work education... [Knoxville, Tenn., Bureau of Educational Research and Service, College of Education, University of Tennessee, 1973?]

Bantaş, Andrei.
Dicţionar de buzunar englez-român, [român-englez] / Andrei Bantaş. — Bucureşti : Editura Ştiinţifică, 1969.
671, 488 p. ; 17 cm.
In 2 parts, bound together back-to-back.
1. Romanian language—Dictionaries—English. 2. English language—Dictionaries—Romanian. I. Title.
PC779.B29 1969 77-467585
77 MARC

Bantaş, Andrei.
Dicţionar de buzunar englez-român, român-englez. Ediţia a 2-a. [De] Andrei Bantaş. Bucureşti, Editura ştiinţifică, 1973.
1133 p. 17 cm. lei 44.00 R 74-1071
1. Romanian language—Dictionaries—English. 2. English language—Dictionaries—Romanian. I. Title.
PC779.B29 1973 74-323481

Bantas, Andrei.
Dictionar roman-englez. Ediţia a II-a revăzută şi adăugită. Bucureşti, Editura Stiinifică, 1968.
294 p. 17 cm.
1. Romanian langugae–Dictionaries–English. I. Title.
NNC NUC75-47267

Bantaş, Andrei.
Mic dicţionar englez-român, de Andrei Bantaş. Bucureşti, Editura ştiinţifică, 1971.
735 p. 80 mm. lei 11.00 R 72-1663
1. English language—Dictionaries—Romanian. 2. Bibliography—Microscopic and miniature editions—Specimens. I. Title.
PC779.B3 1971 459′.3′21 73-311429

Bantas, Andrei
see Dictionar poliglot de mine, geologie si petrol-extractie ... Bucuresti, Editura tehnică, 1974.

Bantas, Andrei
see Leviţchi, Leon. Dicţionar român-englez. Editia a 3-a revizuită. Bucureşti, Editura ştiinţifică, 1973.

Bantaş, Ioana, 1937–
Scrisori către Orfeu. Versuri. [Coperta de Decebal Scriba]. [Bucureşti], „Cartea românească," 1972.
112 p. 19 cm. lei 6.75 R 73-2240
I. Title.
PC840.12.A587S3 74-340427

Bantas, Sōtērēs
see Vantas, Sōtērēs.

Banta's Greek exchange
see Zerman, William S "Fraternally yours"... [n.p., 1965?]

Banta's Greek exchange
see Zerman, William S "Fraternally yours". [Menasha, Wis., George Banta Co., 197-?]

Bantea, Eugen.
Insurecţia română în jurnalul de război al grupului de armate german "Ucraina de sud" / Eugen Bantea. — [Bucureşti] : Editura militară, 1974.
201 p. : ill. ; 20 cm. R 75-1906
Summary in English, French, and Russian.
Includes bibliographical references.
lei 7.50
1. World War, 1939-1945—Romania. 2. Romania—History—1914-1944. I. Title.
D766.4.B36 77-509443

Bantea, Eugen.
La Romania nella guerra antihitleriana, 23 agosto 1944 - 12 maggio 1945, a cura di Gheorghe Zaharia. [Roma] Editori Riuniti in collaborazione con l'Instituto di studi storici sociali e politici de Bucarest [1974]
261 p. illus., maps. 22 cm.
At head of title: E. Bantea, N. Constantin (!) G. Zaharia.
Translation of August 1944-Mai 1945.
Bibliography: p. 251-261.
1. World War, 1939-1945—Campaigns—Romania. I. Zaharia, Gheorghe.
CSt-H NUC76-24168

Bantea, Eugen.
La Roumanie dans la guerre antihitlérienne —août 1944-mai 1945 [par] Eugen Bantea, Constantin Nicolae [et] Gh. Zaharia. Bucarest, Éditions Meridiane, 1970.
309 p. illus., maps (part fold.)
Issued also in English.
Bibliography: p. [297]-305.
1. World War, 1939-1945—Campaigns—Romania. 2. Romania—Hist. —1914-1944. I. Nicolae, Constantin, joint author. II. Zaharia, Gheorghe, joint author. III. Title.
PPiU NUC73-126238

Bantea, Eugen.
La Roumanie dans la guerre antihitlérienne, 23 août 1944-12 mai 1945 / Eugen Bantea, Constantin Nicolae, Gheorghe Zaharia. — 2-e édition, revue et abrégée. — Bucarest : "Meridiane", 1975.
215 p., [3] leaves of plates (2 fold.) : ill., col. maps (2 fold.) ; 20 cm.
R77-223
Translation of August 1944-Mai 1945.
Bibliography: p. 207-[213]
lei19.73
1. World War, 1939-1945—Campaigns—Romania. 2. Romania—History—1914-1944. I. Nicolae, Constantin, joint author. II. Zaharia, Gheorghe, joint author. III. Title.
D766.4.B3414 1975 77-463832
•77 MARC

Bantea, Eugen, joint author
see Anescu, Vasile. Participarea armatei române la războiul antihitlerist. [Bucuresti] : Editura militară, 1966.

Bantel, Otto.
Alfred Andersch, Leopold Ahlsen, zwei Hörspiele: Interpretation/ von Otto Bantel. — München: Oldenbourg, 1973.
109 p.; 20 cm. — (Interpretationen zum Deutschunterricht) DM8.80 GFR 73-A
Bibliography: p. 108-109.
1. Andersch, Alfred, 1914– Fahrerflucht. 2. Ahlsen, Leopold. Philemon und Baukis.
PT2601.N353F333 73-349100
ISBN 3-486-09641-9

Bantel, Otto.
Grundbegriffe der Literatur. 9., erw. Aufl. Frankfurt a.M., Hirschgraben-Verl., 1972.
125 p. 22 cm.
1. Literature—Terminology. I. Title.
OOxM NUC75-48076

Bantelmann, Albert.
Die Landschaftsentwicklung an der schleswig-holsteinischen Westküste, dargestellt am Beispiel Nordfriesland; eine Funktionschronik durch fünf Jahrtausende. Mit Illustrationen von Fritz Fischer. [Heide/Holstein, Druck: Westholsteinische Verlagsdruckerei Boyens, 1966]
99 p. illus. (Schriften des Nissenhauses in Husum, 9)
Also published in Die Küste; Archiv für Forschung und Technik an der Nord- und Ostsee, v. 14, pt. 2, 1966.
MH NUC74-100188

Bantelmann, Albert.
Tofting; eine vorgeschichtliche Warft an der Eidermündung, von Albert Bantelmann. Mit Beiträgen von Udelgard Grohne [et al.] Neumünster, K. Wachholtz, 1955.
134 p. illus. 31 cm. (Offa-Bücher) (Vor- und frühgeschichtliche Untersuchungen aus dem Schleswig-Holsteinischen Landesmuseum für Vor- und Frühgeschichte in Schleswig und dem Institut für Ur- und Frühgeschichte der Universität Kiel, n. F., 12)
Includes bibliographies.
1. Tönning, Ger.—Antiquities. 2. Eider region—Antiquities. I. Körber-Grohne, Udelgard, joint author. II. Title. III. Series: Schleswig (City). Schleswig-Holsteinisches Landesmuseum für Vor- und Frühgeschichte in Schleswig. Vor- und frühgeschichtliche Untersuchungen, n. F., 12.
DD491.S6942B3 74-200804

Bantelmann, Niels.
Die Urgeschichte des Kreises Kusel; ein Beitrag zur Besiedlungsgeschichte des Nordpfälzer Berglandes. Speyer, Verlag der Pfälzischen Gesellschaft zur Förderung der Wissenschaften, 1972.
71 p. illus. (1 fold. col. in pocket) 30 cm. (Veröffentlichung der Pfälzischen Gesellschaft zur Förderung der Wissenschaften in Speyer, Bd. 62) GDB***
Bibliography: p. 68-70.
1. Man, Prehistoric—Germany—Kusel (Landkreis) 2. Kusel, Ger. (Landkreis)—Antiquities. I. Title. II. Series: Pfälzische Gesellschaft zur Förderung der Wissenschaften. Veröffentlichungen, Bd. 62.
GN814.K83B36 73-327378

Bantens, Robert James.
Eugène Carrière - his work and his influence. [n. p., 1975]
2 v.
Thesis (Ph. D.)--Pennsylvania State University.
1. Carrière, Eugène, 1849-1906. I. Title.
PSt NUC77-90815

Banterle, Renzo, ed.
see Scuola d'arte Paolo Brenzoni. I cento anni della Scuola d'arte Paolo Brenzoni... Verona, Cortella industria poligrafica, [1972?].

Bantey, William Anthony, 1928-
see Montreal. Museum of Fine Arts. Cultures du soleil et de la neige... [Montreal, 1973]

Bantey, William Anthony, 1928-
see Montreal. Museum of Fine Arts. Image... [Montreal, 1970]

Banthia, Mohanlal,
[Kriyā-kośa]
क्रिया-कोश; जैन दशमलव वर्गीकरण संख्या १२२२ तथा १३०१. Cyclopaedia of kriya. सम्पादक मोहनलाल बाँठिया [तथा] श्रीचंद चोरड़िया. वाचना प्रमुख आचार्य तुलसी. [1. आवृत्ति] कलकत्ता, जैन दर्शन समिति, 1969.
60, 364 p. (p. [363]-364 advertisements) 24 cm. (जैन आगम विषय-कोश ग्रंथमाला, पुष्प 2) Rs15.00
Prakrit or Sanskrit; introductory matter, translation, and notes in Hindi.
Bibliography: p. [358]-360.
1. Philosophy, Jaina. 2. Act (Philosophy). I. Choraria, Shrichand, joint author. II. Title. III. Title: Cyclopaedia of kriya.
B162.5.B35 72-913100

Banthia, Mohanlal, comp.
[Leśyā-kośa]
लेश्या-कोश. Cyclopaedia of leśyā. सम्पादक मोहनलाल बाँठिया [तथा] श्रीचन्द चोरड़िया. [1. आवृत्ति] कलकत्ता, मोहनलाल बाँठिया, 1966.
39, 296 p. 25 cm. (जैन विषय-कोश ग्रन्थमाला, पुष्प 1) Rs10.00
Hindi and Prakrit; foreword in English.
Bibliography: p. [284]-288.
1. Philosophy, Jaina. I. Choraria, Shrichand, joint comp. II. Title. III. Title: Cyclopaedia of lesya.
B162.5.B36 70-905240

Bān̆thiyā, Ghevaracandajī
see
Vīraputra, Maharaja.

Banthiya, Kastoor Mal, 1894-
see Desāi, Bālābhāī Vīracanda, 1908- Jāge tabhī saverā. 1968.

Banthiya, Kastoor Mal, 1894- ed.
see Doshi, Bechardas Jivraj, 1889- comp. [1966]

Banthorpe, Cyril Henry.
Television timebase circuits; principles and practice. [4th ed.] London, N. Price [1972]
104 p. illus. 22 cm.
1. Television—Receivers and reception. I. Title.
ScU NUC75-48077

Banti, Alberto.
Corpus nummorum romanorum ... Firenze, A. Banti, L. Simonetti, 1972–
v. illus. 26 cm. It 73-May (v. 1)
At head of title: A. Banti, L. Simonetti.
Italian and English.
Includes bibliographies.
CONTENTS: v. 1. Da Cneo Pompeo a Marco Antonio.—v. 2. Da Marco Antonio alla famiglia Licinia.—v. 3. Dalla famiglia Livineia alla famiglia Voconia. — v. 4. Augusto: Prospetto dei ritratti per l'identificazione delle zecche orientali. Monete d'oro e d'argento.
1. Coins, Roman. I. Simonetti, Luigi, joint author. II. Title.
CJ969.B3 73-327590
rev

Banti, Anna
see Longhi Lopresti, Lucia.

Banti, Luisa, 1894–
Etruscan cities and their culture. Translated by Erika Bizzarri. [1st English language ed.] Berkeley, University of California Press, 1973 [c1968]
vi, 322 p. illus., 96 plates. 23 cm. $14.50
Translation of Il mondo degli Etruschi.
Bibliography: p. 280–303.
1. Etruria—Antiquities. 2. Art, Etruscan. I. Title.
DG223.B313 1973b 913.37'5 74-145781
MARC

Banti, Luisa, 1894–
Etruscan cities and their culture, translated [from the Italian] by Erika Bizzarri. London, Batsford, 1973.
vi, 322 p. 96 p. of plates, illus., maps. 23 cm. £5.50
GB 74-06838
Translation of: Il mondo degli Etruschi.
Bibliography: p. 280–303.
Includes index.
1. Etruria—Antiquities. 2. Art, Etruscan. I. Title.
DG223.B313 913.37'5'03 74-176590
ISBN 0-7134-1130-9 MARC

Banti, Ottavio.
Iacopo d'Appiano : economia, società e politica del comune di Pisa al suo tramonto (1392–1399) / Ottavio Banti. — Pisa : Università degli studi di Pisa, Istituto di storia della Facoltà di lettere, 1971.
359 p. : map ; 24 cm. — (Pubblicazioni dell'Istituto di storia della Facoltà di lettere, Università degli studi di Pisa ; 4) It 75-Feb
"Appendice di documenti" (in Latin) : p. [317]–347.
Includes bibliographical references and index.
L6400
1. Pisa — Economic conditions. 2. Pisa — Social conditions. 3. Pisa — Politics and government. 4. Appiano, Iacopo d', 1325–1398. I. Series: Pisa. Università. Instituto di storia. Pubblicazioni ; 4.
HC308.P58B35 75-552868

Bantin, Colin Charles, 1944-
Antennas in a non-linear isotropic plasma. [Toronto] 1971.
xii, 223 l. illus.
Thesis—University of Toronto.
Bibliography: leaves 221-223.
1. Plasma (Ionized gases) 2. Plasma waves. 3. Satellites. 4. Radar—Antennas. I. Title.
CaOTU NUC73-31317

Banting, Daniel Richard.
Saxon England / by D. R. Banting and G. A. Embleton. — London : Almark, 1975.
80 p. : ill. (some col.) ; 24 cm. GB***
Bibliography: p. 80.
ISBN 0-85524-241-8 : £3.50. ISBN 0-85524-240-X pbk.
1. England—Civilization—To 1066—Juvenile literature. I. Embleton, G. A., joint author. II. Title.
DA152.2.B36 942.01 76-361166
76 MARC

Banting, Daniel Richard.
The Western Front, 1914-1918 / [by] D. R. Banting and G. A. Embleton. — London : Almark Publishing, 1974.
80 p. : ill. (some col.), maps, ports. ; 22 cm. — (Focus on history)
GB74-26865
Bibliography: p. 80.
ISBN 0-85524-172-1 : £2.00. ISBN 0-85524-173-X pbk.
1. European War, 1914-1918—Campaigns—Western. I. Embleton, Gerry, joint author. II. Title.
D530.B24 1974 940.4'144 75-307580
75 MARC

Banting, J D
Growth habit and control of wild oats / [J. D. Banting]. — Ottawa : Information Division, Canada Dept. of Agriculture, 1974.
33 p. : ill. ; 23 cm. — (Publication - Canada Department of Agriculture ; 1531)
C***
Cover title.
Bibliography: p. 33.
1. Avena fatua. 2. Avena fatua—Control. I. Title. II. Series: Canada. Dept. of Agriculture. Publication ; 1531.
S133.A346 no. 1531 630'.8 s 76-350858
[SB615.A9] 76 MARC

Banting, Meredith Black.
Banting banter. [Regina, Banting Publishers, 1967]
39 p. illus.
ISBN 0 9690064 5 4.
1. Canadian poetry, English. I. Title.
CaOTP NUC74-117991

Banting, Meredith Black.
Homespun stories and rhymes by Saskatchewan authors, compiled by Meredith B. Banting. Regina, Banting Publishers [1971?]
205 p. illus.
At head of title: Saskatchewan homecoming '71 anthology.
ISBN: 0969006470.
1. Canadian literature—Saskatchewan. I. Title.
CaOTU NUC73-31301

Banting, Meredith Black.
Prairie-tales: Saskatchewan, Alberta, Manitoba, by Meredith B. Banting. Regina, Banting Publishers [1971?]
1 v. (various pagings) illus.
ISBN: 096900066.
1. Frontier and pioneer life—Prairie Provinces. I. Title.
CaOTU CaOTY NUC73-115633

Banting, Meredith Black.
see Early history of Saskatchewan churches (grass roots). Regina, Sask., Banting, 1975.

Banting, Peter M
Marketing in Canada / Peter M. Banting ; with end-of-unit questions and activities by John F. Cloke. — Toronto : McGraw-Hill Ryerson, 1973.
221 p. : ill. ; 24 cm. — (McGraw-Hill Ryerson series in marketing) C 73-2904
Includes index.
ISBN 0-07-077555-9 : $4.95
1. Marketing—Canada. I. Cloke, John F., 1943– II. Title.
HF5415.12.C35B35 658.8'00971 75-300854
MARC

Bantle, Franz Xaver.
Unfehlbarkeit der Kirche in Aufklärung und Romantik : eine dogmengeschichtliche Untersuchung für die Zeit der Wende vom 18. zum 19. Jahrhundert / Franz Xaver Bantle. — Freiburg im Breisgau : Herder, 1976.
613 p. ; 23 cm. — (Freiburger theologische Studien ; Bd. 103) GFR***
Slightly rev. ed. of the author's Habilitationsschrift, Salzburg, 1975, presented under the title: Aspekte der Unfehlbarkeit der Kirche in Aufklärung und Romantik.
Bibliography: p. 574-604.
Includes index.
ISBN 3-451-17554-1
1. Church—Infallibility—History of doctrines. I. Title. II. Series.
BV601.6.I5B36 1976 262'.72 77-455134
77[r77]rev MARC

Bantle, John Albert, 1946-
The neurotrophic influence on RNA precursor incorporation into polyribosomes of regenerating adult newt forelimbs. [n. p.] 1973.
91 l.
Thesis–Ohio State University.
Bibliography: leaves 84–91.
1. Regeneration (Biology) 2. Neurology. 3. Ribonucleic acid. I. Title.
OU NUC74-123732

Bantleman, Lawrence.
The award; a satirical drama in two acts. Calcutta, A Writers Workshop publication c1972.
56 p. 23 cm. Rs50.00
"A Writers Workshop bluebird book."
I. Title.
PR6052.A5A9 822 72-900388
MARC

Bantleon, Werner.
Absatzwirtschaft : praxisorientierte Einf. in d. Marketing / Werner Bantleon, Eugen Wendler, Jürgen Wolff. — Opladen : Westdeutscher Verlag, 1976.
251 p. : ill. ; 23 cm. — (Moderne Wirtschaftsbücher : Betriebswirtschaftliche Funktionen und Institutionen ; 05) GFR77-A
Includes bibliographical references and index.
ISBN 3-531-11347-X : DM28.00
1. Marketing. 2. Marketing research. I. Wendler, Eugen, 1937- joint author. II. Wolff, Jürgen, 1927- joint author. III. Title.
HF5415.B285 658.8 77-459760
77 MARC

Bantli, Heinrich.
Electrophysiology of the turtle cerebellum. [Berkeley] 1973.
1 v. (various pagings) illus.
Thesis (Ph.D.)—University of California.
Includes bibliography.
CU NUC75-20662

Banto, Magdalena.
see Evaluarea sistemelor şi a proceselor educaţionale. Bucureşti, Editura Didactică şi Pedagogică, 1976.

Bantock, Gavin, 1939–
Anhaga. London, Anvil Press Poetry; Distributed by Routledge and Kegan Paul, 1972.
30 p. 22 cm. (Anvil Press poetry booklets, 1) £0.30 B 73-08546
"Six poems translated from the Anglo-Saxon."
I. Title.
PR6052.A53A8 829'.1 73-161622
ISBN 0-900977-35-3 ; (lim. ed.) ; 0-900977-34-5 MARC

Bantock, Gavin, 1939–
Eirenikon: a poem. London, Anvil Press Poetry; Distributed by Routledge and Kegan Paul, 1972.
31 p. 22 cm. £1.25 B 73-04693
I. Title.
PR6052.A53E5 821'.9'14 73-158226
MARC
ISBN 0-900977-87-6 ; 0-900977-88-4 (pbk.) ; 0-900977-89-2 (signed ed.)

Bantock, Gavin, 1939-
Gleeman. Cardiff, Second Aeon Publications [1972]
16 p.
I. Title.
ICU NUC74-123733

Bantock, Gavin, 1939-
Isles / Gavin Bantock ; illustrated by Paul Peter Piech. — Feltham : Quarto Press, 1974.
[28] p. : ill. ; 31 cm. — (The Quarto poets ; 4) GB75-00780
Limited ed. of 350 numbered copies. No. 170.
ISBN 0-901105-10-4 : £0.80
I. Title.
PR6052.A53I8 821'.9'14 76-360457
76 MARC

Bantock, Geoffrey Herman, 1914–
Education in an industrial society [by] G. H. Bantock. 2nd ed. London, Faber, 1973.
xiii, 238 p. 23 cm. £2.50 GB 73-16546
Includes bibliographical references and index.
1. Education—Philosophy. I. Title.
LB885.B25 1973 370.19'3 73-173064
ISBN 0-571-04791-2 MARC

Bantock, Geoffrey Herman, 1914-
see The Basic unity of education... London, National Council for Educational Standards [1972]

Bantoe Beleggingskorporasie van Suid-Afrika
see
Bantu Investment Corporation of South Africa.

Bantoemannekrag en -onderwys... Johannesburg, Suid-Afrikaanse Instituut vir Rasseverhoudings, 1969
see under Malherbe, Ernest Gideon, 1895-1969.

Banton, Michael P
The idea of race / Michael Banton. — London : Tavistock Publications, 1977.
190 p. ; 23 cm. GB***
Bibliography: p. [173]-181.
Includes index.
ISBN 0-422-76170-2 : £6.50
1. Race relations—History. I. Title.
HT1507.B36 1977 301.45'1'042 77-363157
77 MARC

Banton, Michael P
Police-community relations [by] Michael Banton; with foreword by Sir John McKay. London, Collins, 1973.
176 p. illus., maps. 20 cm. £1.95 GB 73-20743
Includes index.
Bibliography: p. 172–174.
1. Public relations—Police. 2. Police—Great Britain. I. Title.
HV7936.P8B3 659.2'9'36320942 73-177692
ISBN 0-00-460371-0 ; 0-00-460370-2 (pbk.) MARC

Banton, Michael P
The race concept / Michael Banton and Jonathan Harwood. — Newton Abbot [Eng.] : David & Charles, c1975.
160 p. ; 23 cm. GB***
Bibliography: p. 157-158.
Includes index.
ISBN 0-7153-6898-2 : £4.50
1. Race. I. Harwood, Jonathan, joint author. II. Title.
GN280.B36 1975b 572 75-319659
75 MARC

Banton, Michael P
The race concept / Michael Banton and Jonathan Harwood. — New York : Praeger, 1975.
160 p. ; 21 cm.
Bibliography: p. 157-158.
Includes index.
ISBN 0-275-33660-3 : $7.50. ISBN 0-275-85240-7 pbk. : $3.50
1. Race. I. Harwood, Jonathan, joint author. II. Title.
GN280.B36 1975 572 74-30995
75 MARC

Banton, Michael P
Racial minorities [by] Michael Banton. London, Fontana, 1972.
192 p. illus. 19 cm. index. £0 50 B 72-23870
Bibliography: p. [188]-190.
1. England—Race question. 2. Minorities—England. I. Title.
DA125.A1B34 301.45'1'0942 72-169504
ISBN 0-00-633047-9 MARC

Banton, Michael P
White and coloured : the behavior of British people towards coloured immigrants / by Michael Banton. — Westport, Conn. : Greenwood Press, 1976, c1959.
223 p. ; 23 cm.
Reprint of the 1960 ed. published by Rutgers University Press, New Brunswick, N.J.
Bibliography: p. 217-218.
Includes index.
ISBN 0-8371-9290-0
1. Blacks—Great Britain. 2. Great Britain—Race question. I. Title.
[DA125.N4B3 1976] 301.45'1'0420941 76-43335
76 MARC

Banton, O. T.
see History of Macon County, 1976. [Decatur, Ill.] Macon County Historical Society, c1976.

Bantova, Mariîa Aleksandrovna, joint author
see Moro, Mariîa Ignat'evna. Matematika; uchebnik dlîa pervogo klassa. Izd. 3. Moskva, "Prosveshchenie", 1970.

Bantova, Mariîa Aleksandrovna
see Moro, Mariîa Ignat'evna. Matematika; uchebnik dlîa vtorogo klassa. Izd. 2., ispravlennoe. Moskva, "Prosveshchenie", 1970.

Bantova, Mariîa Aleksandrovna, joint author
see Moro, Mariîa Ignat'evna. (Matematika v pervom klasse) 1972.

Bantt, Detlev, 1943–
Konsumgüter: prosaische Erfahrungen/ Detlev Bantt. — Frankfurt (am Main): Verlag Werkstätten Galerie tg Gierig, 1971.
53 p.; 20 cm. DM9.80 GDB 73-A10
I. Title.
PT2662.A57K6 73-323668
ISBN 3-921103-02-9

Bantu, Joseph Kasella, joint author
see Brauner, Siegmund. Lehrbuch des Swahili. [3., überarb. Aufl.] Leipzig, Verlag Enzyklopädie [1973]

Bantu education in the Republic of South Africa, 1971. Compiled by A. N. P. Lubbe. 2d ed. Johannesburg, Erudita Publications, 1971.
96 p. illus.
1. Bantus—Education. I. Lubbe, A. N. P.
MiEM NUC73-31311

Bantu Investment Corporation of South Africa.
Annual report — Bantu Investment Corporation of South Africa.
[Pretoria] Bantu Investment Corporation of South Africa.
v. in ill. 30 cm.
Report year ends Mar. 31.
Added title page title Jaarverslag—Bantoe Beleggingskorporasie van Suid-Afrika.
Title varies slightly.
Afrikaans and English.
1. Bantu Investment Corporation of South Africa. I. Bantu Investment Corporation of South Africa. Jaarverslag.
HG3729.S62B34a 338.7'61'3380968 76-644666
MARC-S

Bantu Investment Corporation of South Africa. Jaarverslag
see Bantu Investment Corporation of South Africa. Annual report. [Pretoria]

Bantu Mining Corporation.
Annual report—Bantu Mining Corporation.
[Pretoria] Bantu Mining Corporation.
v. 30 cm.
Added title page title: Jaarverslag - Bantoemynboukorporasie.
Report year ends Mar. 31.
Afrikaans and English.
1. Bantu Mining Corporation. 2. Mineral industries — Africa, South—Periodicals. I. Bantu Mining Corporation. Jaarverslag - Bantoemynboukorporasie.
HD9506.S74B33a 338.7'62'20968 75-641950
MARC-S

Bantu Mining Corporation. Jaarverslag-Bantoemynboukorporasie
see Bantu Mining Corporation. Annual report... [Pretoria]

Bantu? : Proverbes africains à l'usage de l'enseignement secondaire / C. M. Cornet, M. D. Vandenbulcke, Kalonji Mutambayi. — Bruxelles : A. De Boeck, [1976] c1975.
275 p. : ill., map ; 19 cm. Be76-4
Includes index.
210F
1. Proverbs, Bantu—Zaire. I. Cornet, C. M. II. Vandenbulcke, Marcel Désiré. III. Kalonji Mutambayi.
PN6519.B33B3 1976 77-470889
•77 MARC

Bantuelle, Jean Marie.
Boussu en cartes postales anciennes. Zaltbommel, Bibliothèque européenne, 1972.
[80] p. (chiefly illus.) 16 x 21 cm. Ne***
1. Boussu, Belgium—Description—Views. I. Title.
DH811.B63B35 73-327881

Bantul, Indonesia (Kabupaten)
Membangun masjarakat desa dengan unit desa dan badan usaha unit desa di Daerah Kabupaten Bantul. [Bantul, 1972?]
9 v. in 1. 30 cm.
Cover title.
1. Community development—Bantul, Indonesia (Kabupaten)
I. Title.
HN710.B36B35 1972 72-940943

Bantysh-Kamenskiĭ, Dmitriĭ Nikolaevich, 1788–1850.
(Dieíanīia znamenitykh polkovodtšev i ministrov, sluzhivshikh v tšarstvovanīe gosudarīa Imperatora Petra Velikago)
Дѣянія знаменитыхъ полководцевъ и министровъ, служувшухъ въ царствованіе государя Императора Петра Великаго. Изд. 2. Москва, Въ Тип. С. Селивановскаго, 1821.
2 v. in 1. ports. 23 cm.
1. Russia—History—Peter I, 1689-1725. 2. Generals—Russia. 3. Statesmen—Russia. I. Title.
DK130.A1B18 1821 74-236802

Bantysh-Kamenskiĭ, Dmitriĭ Nikolaevich, 1788–1850.
(Dieíanīia znamenitykh polkovodtšev i ministrov, sluzhivshikh v tšarstvovanīe Gosudarīa Imperatora Petra Velikago)
Дѣянія знаменитыхъ полководцевъ и министровъ, служившихъ въ царствованіе Государя Императора Петра Великаго / [Дмитрій Бантышъ-Каменскій]. — Изд. 2. — Москва : Въ Тип. С. Селивановскаго, 1821–
v. ; ill., ports. ; 22 cm.
1. Russia—History—Peter I, 1689-1725. 2. Generals—Russia. 3. Statesmen—Russia. I. Title.
DK130.A1B18 1821b 75-568665

Bantz, Charles Richard, 1949-
Organizing as communicating: a critique and experimental test of Weick's model of organizing [n. p.] 1975.
158 l.
Thesis--Ohio State University.
Bibliography: leaves 155-158.
1. Communication--Methodology. 2. Organization. I. Title.
OU NUC77-90814

Bantzinger, C. A. B.
see Groot, Jan Hendrik de, 1901- Heftsvacantie ... 's-Gravenhage : D. A. Daamen, 1940 [i. e. 1943]

Bānū, Akhtar
see
Akhtar Bānū.

Banu, Aurel, joint author
see Tufescu, Victor. Geografia Republicii Socialiste Romania... Bucareşti, Editura didactică si pedagogică, 1973.

Banu, C., joint author
see Baltac, Th Redresoare pentru material rulant electric. [Bucureşti] Centrul de documentare şi publicaţii tehnice, 1971.

Banu, C.
see Influenta proceselor tehnologice asupra calitatii produselor alimentare. Bucuresti: Editura tehnica, 1974-

Banu, Eugenia
see
Postelnicu, Ioana, 1910-

Banu, George
see Arta teatrului ... Bucureşti: Editura enciclopedică română, 1975.

Banu, George Maria.
Muntele alb. Schiţe şi nuvele. [Coperta şi portretul de Nicolae Apostol]. Bucureşti, Editura Eminescu, 1973.
148 p. 19 cm. lei 5.50 R 73-1838
CONTENTS: Cerc frînt.—Cum rămîne cu dragostea, Lici?—Sfînta tăcere din noi.—Timpul zăpezii.—Sînge în cristal.—Acompaniament la piculină.—Întîlnire cu mineri.—Mărul mereu tînăr.—Între două aşteptări.—Moina.—Dulcea mea aniversare.—Muntele alb.—Tîrziu.—Nedeia.—Moşteniri obscure.
I. Title.
PC840.12.A59M8 74-331517

Banu, Ion.
Platon Heracliticul ... Contribuţie la istoria dialecticii. Bucureşti, Editura Academiei Republicii Socialiste România, 1972.
243 p. 21 cm. lei 9.25 R 72-3328
Includes bibliographical references.
1. Plato. 2. Heraclitus, of Ephesus. 3. Dialectic. 4. Philosophy, Ancient. I. Title.
B187.D5B27 72-368936

Banu, Ion
see Mic dicţionar filozofic. Bucureşti: Editura politica, 1969.

Bānū, Jīlānī
see Jīlānī Bānū, 1936-

Bānū, Sayyidah Shahr
see Sayyidah Shahr Bānū.

Bānū, Zarīnah
see
Zarīnah Bānū.

Bānū Begam, Jahān
see Jahān Bānū Begam.

Bānū Qidvā'ī, Vasīm
see Vasīm Bānū Qidvā'ī, 1925-

Bănulescu, Ştefan, 1929-
Scrisori provinciale : [eseuri] / Stefan Bănulescu ; [coperta Ştefăniţă Sabin]. — [Bucureşti] : "Albatros", 1976.
178 p. ; 20 cm. R76-366
Includes bibliographical references.
lei5.50
I. Title.
PC840.12.A6S3 77-46048
•77 MAR

Banuls, André.
Heinrich Mann 1871/1971. Bonn-Bad Godesberg, Inter Nationes, 1971.
29 p. port. 24 cm. GFR***
Bibliography: p. 28-29.
CONTENTS: Banuls, A. Heinrich Mann, the Romantic.—Kantorowicz, A. Heinrich Mann as a champion of Franco-German understanding.—Chronology.
1. Mann, Heinrich, 1871-1950. I. Kantorowicz, Alfred, 1899-
PT2625.A43Z5913 838'.9'1209 [B] 73-173862
MARC

Bañuls, David Cervera
see Cervera Bañuls, David.

Bañuls, Jerónimo Cerdá
see Cerdá Bañuls, Jerónimo.

Bañuls, M V Dabrio
see
Dabrio Bañuls, M V

Banūnah, Khanātah.
(al-Ṣūrah wa-al-ṣawt)
الصورة والصوت : قصص / خناثة بنونة. ـــ الدار البيضاء : دار النشر المغربية ، c1975.
100 p. ; 22 cm.
CONTENTS: ـــ السلب والحتمية . ـــ الليل والنهار . ـــ لورق المقوى . ـــ لا يا سيد السادات . ـــ نهاية موكب . ـــ فى اليقظة فى الحلم . ـــ المنفى . ـــ البدء والتتمة . ـــ الحاضر والمنتظر . ـــ سقوط الانتظار . ـــ الوحل النقيض .
7.50MD
I. Title.
PJ7816.A63S9 76-96008

al-Banūrī, Muhammad Yūsuf. Yatīmat al-bayān li-Mushkilāt al-Qur'ān. 1974
in Shāh, Muhammad Anvar. (Mushkilāt al-Qur'ān) Dabhil [India]: Majlis-Ilmi, [19] 74.

al-Banūri, Muhammad Yūsuf
see Hammād Allāh al-Sindī, Muhammad. (al-Yāqūt wa-al-murjān fī sharh lughāt al-Qur'ān) 1393 [1973]

Banus, Eduardo R Agostini
see Agostini Banus, Eduardo R

Banús, Joaquim Ral i
see Ral i Banús, Joaquim.

Banuş, Maria, comp.
Din poezia de dragoste a lumii selecţie, tălmăcire şi prefaţă de Maria Banuş ; [ilustraţia copertei, Teodor Banuş].— Bucureşti : "Minerva," 1974.
2 v. ; 17 cm. — (Biblioteca pentru toti ; 785-786) R 74-2502
lei 10.00
1. Poetry—Collections. I. Title.
PN6109.R6B35 75-575918

Banus, Maria.
Nóru visătoru şi amicii sai. [Bucureşti] Edit. Ion Creanga [1971]
71 p. illus., col. plates.
I. Title.
OCl NUC74-117992

Bănuş, Maria.
Oricine şi ceva. [Versuri. Coperta de Done Stan]. Bucureşti, „Cartea românească," 1972.
184 p. 20 cm. lei 9.75 R 72-4544
I. Title.
PC839.B28O7 74-328207

Bănuş, Maria.
Poezii. [Bucureşti] Editura Minerva [1971]
2 v. illus. (Her Scrieri, 1-2)
Contents:—1. Ţara fetelor. —2. Absintos.
MH NUC76-72744

Banus Durán, José
see Coloquios sobre la Patentabilidad de las Inveciones Farmacéuticas y la Industria Farmacéutica Española, Salamanca, 1972. La protección jurídica ... Madrid: Montecorvo, 1974.

Banús y Aguirre, José Luis, 1914-
Glosas euskaras / José Luis Banús y Aguirre. — [s.l.] : Caja de Ahorros Provincial de Guipúzcoa, [1975?]
367 p. : ill. ; 20 cm. — (Colección Documento ; 7) Sp***
ISBN 8472312232
1. Basque Provinces—Collected works. I. Title.
DP302.B46B3 76-460887
76 MARC

Bānūsyān, Sumbāt
see
P'anosian, Smbat, 1909-

Bănuţ, Aurel P 1881-1970.
Scrieri : umor şi satiră / A. P. Bănuţ ; ediţie şi prefaţă de Petronela Negoşanu ; [coperta, Cristina Crinteanu]. — Bucureşti : "Minerva," 1974.
455 p., [1] leaf of plates : port. ; 20 cm. R 74-4241
CONTENTS: Curriculum vitae.—Tempi passati.—Piesă de teatru.—Evocări.
lei 13.00
PC839.B285S3 1974 75-565486

Bănuţ, Valeriu.
Stabilitatea structurilor elastice / Valeriu Bănuţ, Hristache Popescu. — Bucureşti : Editura Academiei Republicii Socialiste România, 1975.
190 p. : ill. ; 24 cm. R 75-2833
Summary in English.
Bibliography : p. [189]-190.
lei 13.00
1. Structural stability. I. Popescu, Hristache, joint author. II. Title.
TA656.B36 75-546482

Bănuţ, Valeriu, joint author
see Răutu, Sandu. Statica construcţiilor. Bucureşti, Editura didactică şi pedagogică, 1972.

Bănuţă, Ion, 1914-
Am rechemat iubirea. Ilustraţii de A. Stoicescu. [Bucureşti] Editura Tineretului [1962]
142 p. illus. 20 cm.
Poems.
I. Title.
PC840.12.A63A8 74-229986

Bănuţă, Ion, 1914-
Lacrima diavolului; poezii. [Ilustraţii: Petre Vulcanescu. Bucureşti] Editura Tineretului [1965]
159 p. illus., port. 18 cm.
I. Title.
LU NUC76-72745

Bănuţă, Ion, 1914-
Panorama focului albastru. (Olimpul diavolului). [Versuri. Ilustraţii: P. Vulcănescu]. [Bucureşti], „Albatros," 1972.
184 p., 4 l. of plates. 17 cm. R 72-4383
I. Title.
PC840.12.A63P3 74-328645

Bănuţă, Ion, 1914-
Panorama iubirii zugravului : olimpul diavolului : [versuri] / Ion Bănuţă ; [coperta şi ilustraţiile, Florin Rucă]. — [Bucureşti] : Editura Eminescu, 1974.
182 p. : ill. ; 17 cm. R 75-1272
lei 8.00
I. Title.
PC840.12.A63P34 75-543992

Banvard, Paul.
Méthode active d'orthographe; une exploration vivante et progressive du paysage orthographique [par] Paul Banvard [et] Marcel Didier. [Paris] Bordas [c1972]
160 p. 21 cm. 15.00F F***
1. French language—Orthography and spelling. I. Didier, Marcel, joint author. II. Title.
PC2145.B3 73-309663

Banville, Guy R.
see Industrial Marketing Conference, Atlanta, 1971. Industrial marketing '71; papers... Chicago [1971]

Banville, John.
Birchwood. London, Secker and Warburg, 1973.
[6], 171 p. 23 cm. £2.00 B 73-05896
I. Title.
PZ4.B223Bi 823'.9'14 73-163518
[PR6052.A57] MARC
ISBN 0-436-03262-7

Banville, John.
Birchwood. New York, Norton [1973]
170 p. 21 cm.
I. Title.
PZ4.B223Bi 3 823'.9'14 73-1699
[PR6052.A57] MARC
ISBN 0-393-08572-4

Banville, John.
Doctor Copernicus : a novel / by John Banville. — London : Secker and Warburg, 1976.
x, 242, [1] p. : map ; 23 cm. GB76-34844
Bibliography: p. vii-[viii]
ISBN 0-436-03263-5 : £3.90
1. Copernicus, Nicolaus, 1473-1543—Fiction. I. Title.
PZ4.B223 Do 823'.9'14 77-355057
[PR6052.A57] 77 MARC

Banville, John.
Doctor Copernicus : a novel / by John Banville. — 1st ed. — New York : Norton, c1976.
vii, 241 p. : map ; 22 cm.
ISBN 0-393-08757-3
1. Copernicus, Nicolaus, 1473-1543—Fiction. I. Title.
PZ4.B223 Do 3 823'.9'14 76-45754
[PR6052.A57] 76 MARC

Banville, Théodore Faullain de, 1823-1891.
Œuvres. Genève, Slatkine Reprints, 1972.
9 v. in 5. illus. 18 cm. Sw***
"Réimpression de l'édition de Paris, 1890-1909."
CONTENTS: 1. Odes funambulesques.—2. Les stalactites. Odelettes. Améthystes. Le forgeron. —3. Occidentales. Rimes dorées. Rondels. La perle.—4. Idylles prussiennes. Riquet à la Houppe.—5. Les Cariatides. Roses de Noël.—6. Le sang de la coupe. Trente-six ballades joyeuses. Le baiser.—7. Les exilés. Les princesses.—8. Petit traité de poésie française.—9. Comédies.
PQ2187.A1 1972 72-373813

Banville, Théodore Faullain de, 1823-1891.
Poésies de Théodore de Banville : Les cariatides (1839-1842). — New York : AMS Press, 1976.
ii, 296 p., [1] leaf of plates : port. ; 19 cm.
Reprint of the 1877 ed. published by A. Lemerre, Paris.
ISBN 0-404-14504-3
I. Title: Les cariatides.
PQ2187.C3 1976 841'.8 75-41015
76 MARC

Banville, Théodore Faullain de, 1823-1891.
Poésies de Théodore de Banville : Odes funambulesques, suivies d'un commentaire. — New York : AMS Press, 1976.
392 p. ; 18 cm.
Reprint of the 1880 ed. published by A. Lemerre, Paris.
ISBN 0-404-14505-1
I. Title: Odes funambulesques.
PQ2187.O4 1976 841'.8 75-41016
76 MARC

Banville, Théodore Faullain de, 1823-1891.
Rondels / Théodore de Banville ; texte présenté et annoté par Martin Sorrell. — Exeter : University of Exeter, 1973.
xvii, 37 p. : port. ; 21 cm. — (Textes littéraires ; 10) GB 74-07611
Bibliography : p. 35-36.
ISBN 0-900771-83-6 : £0.60
I. Sorrell, Martin, ed. II. Title. III. Series.
PQ2187.R6 1973 841'.8 74-196461
MARC

Banvir Singh, 1942-
see Seminar on Social Change in Contemporary India, Lucknow, 1971. Studies in social change... Lucknow, Ethnographic & Folk Culture Society, U. P. [1973]

Banwell, C N
Fundamentals of molecular spectroscopy [by] C. N. Banwell. 2nd ed. London, New York, McGraw-Hill, 1972.
xii, 348 p. illus. 22 cm. £2.90 B 73-00191
Bibliography : p. 334.
1. Molecular spectra. 2. Spectrum analysis. I. Title. II. Title: Molecular spectroscopy.
QD95.B33 1972 535'.84 73-159569
ISBN 0-07-084007-5 MARC

Banwell, L. G.
see Morrison, Arthur Cecil Lockwood, 1881-1960. Notes on juvenile court law ... 4th ed. Chichester, Sussex, Justice of the Peace and Local Government Review, 1962.

Banwell Commission on the Electoral System
see Mauritius. Commission on the Electoral System.

Bany, Bogdan.
Budownictwo z gliny w swietle badań i doświadczeń ITB. [Wyd. 1] Warszawa, Arkady, 1962.
93 p. illus. (Prace In-tu Techniki Budowlanej, nr. 261) (Materiały budowlane i ich zastosowanie, nr. 17)
At head of title: Bogdan Bany, Stalosław Choliński.
Summaries in English and Russian.
ICRL NUC74-121764.

Bany, Jean, 1938-
Auteuil première : [roman] / Jean Bany. — Paris : Éditions du Seuil, [1975]
157 p. ; 21 cm. F***
22.00F
I. Title.
PQ2662.A58A94 843'.9'14 75-510464
75 MARC

Bany, Jean, 1938-
Moi ma sœur / Jean Bany. — Paris : Éditions du Seuil, c1976.
155 p. ; 21 cm. F***
ISBN 2-02-004362-9 : 25.00F
I. Title.
PQ2662.A58M58 843'.9'14 76-469467
76 MARC

Bany, Mary A
Educational social psychology / Mary A. Bany, Lois V. Johnson. — New York : Macmillan, [1975]
xi, 451 p. : ill. ; 24 cm.
Includes bibliographies and index.
ISBN 0-02-305780-7
1. Educational psychology. 2. Social psychology. I. Johnson, Lois Vivian, 1913- joint author. II. Title.
LB1084.B36 301.5'6 74-3799
MARC

Bạnyā Dạlạ, ca. 1518-ca. 1572.
(Yaza Djyit ạyēi taw pon)
ရာဇာဓိရာဇ်အရေးတော်ပုံ / ဗညားဒလ ... [ရန်ကုန်] : မြဝင်း, 1969.
14, 360 p. ; 18 cm.
In Burmese.
1. Burma—History—To 1824—Fiction. I. Title.
PL3988.B38Y3 1969 76-985077

Bányai, Antal.
Sugárveszély, gázveszély, vegyi-, sugárfelderítés és mentesítés ₍írta₎ Bányai Antal, Kovács Ignác ₍és₎ Madaras Péter. Budapest, Zrínyi Katonai Kiadó, 1967.
189 p. illus. 21 cm. 17.00
1. Radiation—Toxicology. 2. Gases, Asphyxiating and poisonous—Toxicology. I. Kovács, Ignác, joint author. II. Madaras, Péter, joint author. III. Title.
RA1231.R2B25 74-215644

Bányai, László, 1907–
Destin commun, traditions fraternelles. ₍Traduit du roumain par Jean-Marie-Pierre Crainiceanu₎. Bucarest, Éditions de l'Académie de la République Socialiste de Roumanie, 1972.
211 p. 21 cm. (Bibliotheca hisorica Romaniae. Études, 42) R 73-709
Translation of Pe făgaşul tradiţiilor frăţeşti.
Includes bibliographical references.
lei 8.00
1. Romania—History. 2. Hungarians in Romania. 3. Minorities—Romania. I. Title. II. Series.
DR217.B2414 73-339032

Bányai, László.
Hosszú mezsgye: esszék, jegyzetek (1928-1968). Bukarest, Kriterion Könyvkiadó, 1970.
309 p.
I. Title.
MIEM NUC74-121765

Bányai, László, 1907–
Hosszú mezsgye / Bányai László. — 2. böv. kiad. — Bukarest : Kriterion, 1974.
350 p. : port. ; 21 cm. R 75-908
lei 19.50
I. Title.
AC95.H9B335 1974 75-540161

Bányai, László, 1907–
Pe făgaşul tradiţiilor frăţeşti. Bucureşti, 1971.
287 p. 19 cm. (Biblioteca de istorie) R 72-1419
At head of title: Institutul de Studii Istorice şi Social-Politice de pe lîngă C. C. al P. C. R. L. Bányai.
Includes bibliographical references.
lei 8.00
1. Romania—History. 2. Hungarians in Romania. 3. Minorities—Romania. I. Title.
DR217.B24 72-332391

Bányai, László, 1907-
see Studii de istorie a naţionalităţii germane şi a înfrăţirii ei cu naţiunea română. Bucureşti, Editura politică, 1976-

Bányai, László, 1907-
see Studii de istorie a naţionalităţii maghiare şi a înfrăţirii ei cu naţiunea română. Bucureşti, Editura politică, 1976-

Banyai, Richard A
Money and banking in China and Southeast Asia during the Japanese military occupation 1937-1945 / by Richard A. Banyai. — Taipei : Tai Wan Enterprises Co., ₍1974₎
150 p. : ill. ; 21 cm.
Bibliography: p. 140-150.
1. Money—Asia. 2. Banks and banking—Asia. 3. Occupation currency—China. 4. Occupation currency—Asia, Southeastern. 5. Occupation currency—Japan. I. Title.
HG1214.B35 332.1'0959 74-196070
MARC

Banyai, Richard A
Money and finance in Mexico during the constitutionalist revolution, 1913-1917 / by Richard A. Banyai. — Taipei : Tai Wan Enterprises Co., c1976.
126 p. : ill. ; 21 cm.
Bibliography: p. 121-126.
1. Money—Mexico—History. 2. Finance—Mexico—History. 3. Mexico—History—1910-1946. I. Title.
HG664.B25 332.4'972 76-150673
76 MARC

Banyard, Edmund.
One Friday in eternity; with songs by Edmund and Stephen Banyard and Peter Casey. London, Galliard Ltd, 1972.
12 p. music. 28 cm. £0.17 GB 72-10328
1. Easter—Drama. I. Banyard, Stephen. II. Casey, Peter. III. Title.
PR6052.A575O5 822'.9'14 73-165870
ISBN 0-85249-121-2 MARC

Banyard, Edmund.
Out of this world / ₍by₎ Edmund Banyard ; with music by Philip Banyard, arranged by Graham Bishop. — ₍London₎ : Galliard, 1976.
16 p. : music ; 27 cm. GB76-25268
Caption title.
ISBN 0-85249-386-X : £0.50
1. Jesus Christ—Drama. I. Title.
PR6052.A575O9 822'.9'14 76-381541
76 MARC

Banyard, Stephen
see Banyard, Edmund. One Friday in eternity. London, Galliard Ltd, 1972.

Bányászdalok Komárom megyéből / Pálinkás József. — Budapest : Komárom Megyei Múzeumok Igazgatósága, 1973.
135 p. ; 24 cm.
Unacc. melodies.
Bibliography: p. 134-135.
Includes index.
1. Miners—Songs and music. 2. Folk-songs, Hungarian—Komárom, Hungary (Comitat) I. Pálinkás, József.
M1977.M5B4 76-504426
[M1706]

Bányászélet versben és prózában. [Berde Mihály összeállításában. Komárom] A Magyar Dolgozók Pártja Komárom megyei Bizottsága és a Társadalom és Természettudományi Ismeretterjesztö Társulat, 1956.
42 p. ill. 21 cm.
1. Miners in literature. 2. Miners—Hungary. I. Berde, Mihály.
NNC NUC76-94565

Bányavizeink hasznosítása; ankét, Budapest, 1967. november 2–3. ₍Előadások. Budapest, 1968₎
241 p. illus., maps. 29 cm.
₍"A Magyar Hidrológiai Társaság 50 éves és az Országos Magyar Bányászati és Kohászati Egyesület 75 éves évfordulója alkalmából rendezte a Magyar Hidrológiai Társaság Vízkémiai és Víztechnológiai Szakosztálya, Vízellátási és Hidrológiai Szakosztálya, valamint az Országos Magyar Bányászati és Kohászati Egyesület Bányászati Szakosztálya."
1. Mine water—Congresses. I. Magyar Hidrológiai Társaság. II. Országos Magyar Bányászati és Kohászati Egyesület. III. Magyar Hidrológiai Társaság. Vízkémiai és Víztechnológiai Szakosztály.
TN318.B36 74-221458

Banykin, Viktor Ivanovich, 1916- Machekha. 1973
see Banykin, Viktor Ivanovich, 1916- (Vesnoĭ v polovod'e) 1973.

Banykin, Viktor Ivanovich, 1916–
(Neravnyĭ brak)
Неравный брак : повести / Виктор Баныкин. — Москва : Современник, 1976.
205 p. ; 21 cm. — (Новинки Современника) USSR***
Series romanized: Novinki Sovremennika.
CONTENTS: Неравный брак.—Старый кордон.
0.52rub
I. Banykin, Viktor Ivanovich, 1916– Staryĭ kordon. 1976. II. Title.
PG3476.B28695N4 76-527053

Banykin, Viktor Ivanovich, 1916–
(Rasskazy o Chapaeve)
Рассказы о Чапаеве. ₍Для мл. возраста₎. Рис. И. Година. Москва, "Дет. лит.," 1972.
144 p. with illus. 21 cm. 0.37rub USSR 72-VKP
At head of title: Виктор Баныкин.
1. Chapaev, Vasiliĭ Ivanovich, 1887–1919—Juvenile fiction. I. Title.
PZ65.B34 74-315953

Banykin, Viktor Ivanovich, 1916- Staryĭ kordon. 1976
in Banykin, Viktor Ivanovich, 1916- (Neravnyĭ brak) 1976.

Banykin, Viktor Ivanovich, 1916–
(Vesnoĭ v polovod'e)
Весной в половодье. Мачеха. Повести. Москва, Детская лит-ра, 1973.
140 p. illus. 21 cm. 0.37rub USSR***
At head of title: Виктор Баныкин.
I. Banykin, Viktor Ivanovich, 1916– Machekha. 1973. II. Title. III. Title: Machekha.
PZ63.B3299 74-316209

(Ban'yū hyakka daijiten)
万有百科大事典 東京 小学館 昭和47- (1972-
v. 30 cm. ¥3200 per vol. Ja 72-17151(v. 19)
Title also in Latin: Encyclopedia genre Japonica.
Text in Japanese.
CONTENTS:
19. 植物
1. Encyclopedias and dictionaries, Japanese.
AE35.2.B35 73-800622

Banz, George.
Computer uses in the construction industry / prepared for the Department of Industry, Trade and Commerce by George Banz. — ₍Ottawa : Dept. of Industry, Trade and Commerce : available from Information Canada, 1976₎
27 p. : ill. ; 28 cm. C***
1. Building—Data processing. I. Canada. Dept. of Industry, Trade and Commerce. II. Title.
TH153.B35 690'.028'5 77-366634
77 MARC

Banz, Hans.
Baukonstruktions-Details; Zeichnungen für die Praxis. Building construction details. Construction-details. ₍Übersetzung ins Englische: Hand, Bostwick & Associates. Übersetzung ins Französische: Heidrun Arnaud₎ Stuttgart, K. Krämer ₍c1973–
v. (chiefly plans) 31 cm. GDB***
English, French and German.
ISBN 3-7828-0440-6
1. Building—Details—Drawings. I. Title. II. Title: Building construction details.
TH2031.B36 729 79-188079

Banzai, Mayumi, 1923–
A pilgrimage to the 88 temples in Shikoku Island. Tokyo, Kodansha ₍1973₎
275 p. illus. 22 cm. ¥3000 ($12.00U.S.) Ja***
1. Temples, Buddhist—Japan—Shikoku. 2. Buddhist pilgrims and pilgrimages—Shikoku. 3. Shikoku—Description and travel. 4. Kūkai, 774–835. I. Title.
BQ6353.S56B36 915.2'3'044 74-166617
MARC

Banzai, Mayumi, 1923–
A visit to the old post town in Japan. Tokyo, Takeuchi Books ₍1972₎
131 p. 27 cm. ¥2000 ($8.00U.S.) Ja 73-15
1. Nagano, Japan (Prefecture)—Social life and customs. I. Title.
DS894.59.N334B36 915.2'16 74-182791
MARC

Banzai, Rihachirō, b. 1871.
(Rimpō no naimenkan)
隣邦の內面觀 坂西利八郎講述 東京 日支問題研究會 ₍昭和11 i. e. 1936₎
6, 7, 474 p. 19 cm.
1. China—Politics and government—1912-1949. 2. Japan—Relations (general) with China. 3. China—Relations (general) with Japan. I. Title.
DS774.B3 73-822177
rev

Banzai, Rihachirō, b. 1871.
(Rimpō o kataru)
隣邦を語る 坂西將軍講演集 ₍坂西利八郎述₎ 吉見正任編纂 東京 坂西將軍講演集刊行會 ₍1933₎
7, ₍7₎, 9, 520, 18 p. ports. 19 cm.
1. China—Politics and government—1912-1949. 2. China—Foreign relations—Japan. 3. Japan—Foreign relations—China. 4. Manchuria—History. I. Yoshimi, Masafumi, ed. II. Title.
DS775.B36 75-821650
rev

Banzer, Hugo
see
Banzer Suárez, Hugo, 1926-

Banzer Suárez, Hugo, 1926-
Bolivia : contexto internacional y perspectiva interna / ₍Hugo Banzer Suárez₎. — La Paz, Bolivia : Secretaría de Prensa e Informaciones, Presidencia de la República, 1976.
30 p. ; 17 cm.
1. Bolivia—Economic policy. 2. Bolivia—Politics and government—1938- 3. Bolivia—Foreign relations. I. Title.
HC182.B323 77-463483
77 MARC

Banzer Suárez, Hugo, 1926-
Mensaje a la nación : 6 de agosto 1975, año del sesquicentenario de la República / Hugo Banzer Suárez. — ₍La Paz : Secretaría de Prensa e Informaciones, Presidencia de la República, 1975?₎
62 p. : port. ; 18 cm.
1. Bolivia—Politics and government—1938- —Addresses, essays, lectures. 2. Bolivia—History—Addresses, essays, lectures. I. Title.
F3326.B263 77-4694[illegible]
77 MA[illegible]

Banzer Suárez, Hugo, 1926–
Mensaje de fin de año. ₍La Paz₎ Ministerio de Información y Deportes, 1971.
45 p. 19 cm.
Cover title.
1. Bolivia — Politics and government — 1938- — Addresses, essays, lectures. I. Title.
F3326.B264 73-221986

Banzer Suárez, Hugo, 1926–
Mensaje de fin de año a la Nación, 1973 : nuestro compromiso / Hugo Banzer Suárez. — [La Paz : MID, 1974?]
72 p. : ports. ; 22 cm.
Cover title.
1. Bolivia — Economic conditions — 1918– — Addresses, essays, lectures. 2. Bolivia—Social conditions—Addresses, essays, lectures. 3. Bolivia—Politics and government—1938– —Addresses, essays, lectures. I. Title.
HC182.B324 75-553892

Banzer Suárez, Hugo, 1926-
Mensaje-informe a la nación [por] Hugo Banzer Suárez. La Paz, 1972.
117 p. illus. 22 cm.
1. Bolivia–Economic policy. 2. Bolivia–Social policy. I. Title.
CtY NcU PPiU NUC74-119253

Banzer Suárez, Hugo, 1926–
Mensaje presidencial / Hugo Banzer Suárez. — [La Paz, Bolivia : MID], 1973.
72 p. : ill. ; 22 cm.
1. Bolivia—Economic policy. 2. Bolivia—Social policy. I. Title.
HC182.B3244 354'.84'035 75-566506

Banzer Suárez, Hugo, 1926–
1973 [i. e. Mil novecientos setenta y tres], año de la consolidación económica. [La Paz? 1973?]
63 p. ports. 21 x 22 cm.
Cover title.
1. Bolivia—Economic policy. 2. Bolivia—Social policy. I. Title.
HC182.B325 74-219635

Banzer Suárez, Hugo, 1926–
1973 [i. e. mil novecientos setenta y tres] año de la consolidación económica. [La Paz, MID, 1973]
78 p. ports. 20 x 22 cm.
CONTENTS: Mensaje del Excmo. Sr. Presidente de la República.—Política económica del gobierno nacionalista.
1. Bolivia — Economic conditions — 1918. 2. Bolivia — Economic policy. I. Title.
HC182.B325 1973b 74-228449

Banzer Suárez, Hugo, 1926–
El pensamiento del presidente Hugo Banzer Suárez. La Paz [Ministerio de Información y Deportes] 1971–72.
2 v. 19 cm. (v. 2 : 19 x 21 cm.)
LACAP 72-2075 (v. 1)
1. Bolivia—Addresses, essays, lectures. I. Title.
F3326.B265 72-335498
rev

Banzer Suárez, Hugo, 1926–
La política social del gobierno nacionalista; [la problemática social boliviana, por] Presidente Banzer. [La Paz] MID [1972 or 3]
70 p. illus. 20 x 21 cm.
Cover title.
1. Bolivia—Social policy. 2. Land reform—Bolivia. I. Title. II. Title: La problemática social boliviana.
HN273.5.B36 74-211953

Banzer Suárez, Hugo, 1926-
Programa y plan de emergencia del gobierno nacionalista; mensaje del Señor Presidente. [La Paz, Bolivia, Ministerio de Información y Deportes] 1971.
29 p. 19 cm. (Ministerio de Información y Deportes. [Publicación] 3)
Cover title: Esquema ideológico y de acción de la revolución nacionalista.
1. Bolivia–Economic policy. I. Title.
NIC NUC75-47272

Banzer Suárez, Hugo, 1926-
Retorno al mar. [La Paz, Ministerio de Información y Deportes, 1974]
16 p.
Cover title.
1. Bolivia–Boundaries–Addresses, essays, lectures. I. Adriázola Valda, Oscar. II. Title.
PPiU NUC76-23711

Banzer Suárez, Hugo, 1926-
see Documentos básicos. La Paz, [Secretaría General de Prensa e Informaciones de la Presidencia de la República] 1975.

Banzer Suárez, Hugo, 1926-
see Frente Popular Nacionalista. Comando Departamental (Cochabamba). Desarrollo de Cochabamba. Cochabamba, 1972.

Banzer Suárez, Hugo, 1926-
see Lanusse, Alejandro Agustin, 1918-
Entrevista de los presidentes de la Argentina y Bolivia. [Buenos Aires] Presidencia de la Nacion, 1971.

Banzer: presidente de los trabajadores. [n.p.] 1972.
48 p. ports. 19 cm.
At head of title: Política obrera del Gobierno Nacionalista.
1. Banzer Suárez, Hugo. 2. Bolivia—Politics and government—1938-
MB NUC75-58901

Banzhaf (George) & Company
see George Banzhaf & Company.

Banzhaf, Jane Corner, joint author.
see Greendyke, Robert M. Blood bank policies and procedures. Flushing, N.Y., Medical Examination Pub. Co., 1976.

Banzhaf, Jane Corner, joint author
see Greendyke, Robert M Introduction to blood banking. 2d ed. Flushing, N. Y., Medical Exaministion Pub. Co., [1974]

Banzhaf, Robert Arthur, 1937-
The technology of graphic arts: a curriculum resource stufy for industrial arts education. Raleigh, N.C., 1972.
275 l. tables. 29 cm.
Thesis (Ph.D.)–North Carolina State University at Raleigh.
Vita.
Bibliography: leaves [267]-272.
NcRS NUC74-119252

Banzi, Alex.
Titi la mkwe. Dar es Salaam, Tanzania Pub. House, 1972.
88 p. illus. 19 cm.
I. Title.
PL8704.B36T5 73-980202

Banziger, George J 1942-
Preference, training, and developmental trends in the classification behavior of Bukusu (Kenya) schoolchildren. Syracuse, N. Y., 1972.
247 l.
Thesis—Syracuse University.
Vita.
Bibliography: leaves 238-246.
Microfilm of typescript. Ann Arbor, Mich., University Microfilms, 1973. 1 reel. (Doctoral dissertation series, 73-19, 783)
NsyU NUC76-75770

Banziger, George J 1942-
Preference, training, and developmental trends in the classification behavior of Bukusu (Kenya) school children [n.p.] 1972 [1973]
x, 247 l.
Thesis–Syracuse University.
Vita.
Bibliography: leaves 238-246.
Photocopy of typescript. Ann Arbor, Mich., University Microfilms, 1973. 20 cm.
1. Child study. 2. Children in Kenya. 3. Bukusu (Bantu tribe) 4. Kenya–Bukusu (Bantu tribe) I. Title.
WvU NUC75-25469

Banzon, Feliciana C., joint author
see Casim, Consorcia Manalastas. Mga tala at patnubay sa pag-unawa sa Noli me tangere ni José Rizal. [Manila]: National Book Store, 1973.

Banzon, Genara F.
see Alabado, Ceres S. C. The rattan gatherer. Q[uezon] C[ity] Filipino Library, c1975.

Banzragch, Namsarain
see Namsarain, Banzragch, 1925-

Bao, Aleksandr Konstantinovich, 1863–1893.
Нравственныя воззрѣнія В. Вундта ("Этика," ч. 1 и 2, изд. "Русскаго богатства"); критическое изслѣдованіе. Воронежъ, Типо-лит. Губ. правленія, 1888–
v. 22 cm.
1. Wundt, Wilhelm Max, 1832–1920. Ethik. I. Title.
Title romanized: Nravstvennyi͡a vozzri͡enii͡a V. Vundta.
BJ1111.W73B36 73–216921

Bào, Bùi Xuân
see Bùi Xuân Bào.

Bao, Danny Chi-ding, 1946-
Protein synthesis in cerebral cortex during spreading depression. [Bloomington, Ind.] 1972.
131 p. illus.
Thesis (Ph.D.)–Indiana University.
Vita.
InU NUC73-115240

Bao, Francisco Flores
see Flores Bao, Francisco

Bao, Robert, joint author.
see Shingleton, John D. College to career, finding yourself in the job market. New York, McGraw-Hill, c1977.

Bao, Ruo-Wang.
Prisoner of Mao [by] Bao Ruo-Wang (Jean Pasqualini) & Rudolph Chelminski. New York, Coward, McCann & Geoghegan [1973]
318 p. 22 cm. $8.95
1. Forced labor—China (People's Republic of China, 1949–)—Personal narratives. I. Chelminski, Rudolph, joint author. II. Title.
HV8964.C5B3 365'.6'0924 [B] 73-78743
ISBN 0-698-10556-7 MARC

Bao, Ruo-Wang.
Prisoner of Mao / by Bao Ruo-Wang (Jean Pasqualini) & Rudolph Chelminski. — London : Deutsch, 1975.
319 p. : map ; 23 cm. GB75-14081
ISBN 0-233-96618-8 : £3.95
1. Bao, Ruo-Wang. 2. Political prisoners—China—Biography. 3. Forced labor—China. I. Chelminski, Rudloph, joint author. II. Title.
HV8964.C5B3 1975 365'.6'0924 76-383598
77 MARC

Bao, Ruo-Wang.
Prisoner of Mao / Bao Ruo-wang (Jean Pasqualini) and Rudolph Chelminski. — Harmondsworth, Eng. ; New York : Penguin Books, 1976, c1973.
325 p. : map ; 18 cm. GB***
ISBN 0-14-004112-5 : £0.90 ($2.50 U.S.)
1. Bao, Ruo-Wang. 2. Political prisoners—China—Biography. 3. Forced labor—China. I. Chelminski, Rudolph, joint author. II. Title.
HV8964.C5B3 1976 365'.6'0924 76-383599
77 MARC

Bao, Ruo-Wang.
[Prisoner of Mao. Japanese]
誰も書かなかった中国：毛沢東の"収容所群島" / 包若望；木庭謙二訳. — 東京：サンケイ新聞社出版局, 昭和49 [1974]
287 p. : ill., port. ; 19 cm. — (サンケイドラマブックス ; 43)
Ja 74-13822
¥800
1. Forced labor—China—Personal narratives. I. Title.
Title romanized: Dare mo kakanakatta Chūgoku.
HV8964.C5B316 74-808951

Bao, Sareng Orin
see Petu, Piet.

Báo Ảnh Việt-Nam, Hanoi.
Nước Việt-Nam dân chủ cộng hòa 15 tuổi, 1945–1960 / [Báo Ảnh Việt-Nam biên soạn]. — [s. l. : s. n., 1960] (Hà-nội : Nhà máy in Tiến Bộ)
1 v. : chiefly ill. ; 33 cm.
Cover title.
1. Vietnam (Democratic Republic, 1946–)—Description and travel—Views. I. Title.
DS560.4.B36 1960 75–984862

Báo chí tập san.
v. 25 cm. quarterly.
1. Journalism—Periodicals. I. Nguyễn Ngọc Linh.
PN4705.B35 73–642737
MARC-S

Bảo Đại, King of Vietnam, 1913–
Bài diễn-văn lịch-sử của Đức Quốc-trưởng Bão-Đại đọc tại Hà-Đông ngày 28–11–50 = Le discours de S. M. Bao -Dai à Hadong. — ⌜Saigon: Nha Tông Giám-dôc Thông-tin, 1950?⌝
⌜20⌝ p. : ill. ; 21 cm.
Cover title.
French and Vietnamese.
1. Vietnam—Politics and government—Addresses, essays, lectures. I. Title: Bài diễn-văn lịch-sử của Đức Quốc-trưởng Bao-Đại ... II. Title: Le discours de S. M. Bao-Dai à Hadong.
DS556.8.B34 75–985628

Bảo Đại, King of Vietnam, 1913–
Đức Quốc-trưởng Báo-Đại hiệu-triệu quốc-dân Tết Giáp-Ngọ, 3–2–1954. ⌜Saigon, Impr. française d'Outre-Mer, 1954⌝
10 p. illus. 24 cm.
Cover title.
Vietnamese and French.
1. Vietnam—Politics and government—Addresses, essays, lectures. I. Title.
DS556.8.B36 75–984095

Bảo Đại, King of Vietnam, 1913–
Đức Quốc-trưởng hiệu-triệu quốc-dân Việt-Nam, Tết nguyên-đán Quý-Tỵ. ⌜Saigon? 1953⌝
11 p. 24 cm.
Cover title: Lời hiệu-triệu của Đức Quốc-trưởng. Tết nguyên-đán Quý-Tỵ.
Vietnamese and French.
1. Vietnam—Politics and government—Addresses, essays, lectures. I. Title. II. Title: Lời hiệu-triệu của Đức Quốc-trưởng. Tết nguyên-đán Quý-Tỵ.
DS556.8.B364 76–985381

Bảo Đại, King of Vietnam, 1913–
Lời Đức Quốc-trưởng Báo-Đại. Hà-nội, Hồ Gươm ⌜1950⌝
55 p. 25 cm.
1. Vietnam—Collected works. I. Title.
DS556.3.B36 75–985414

Bao giờ chấm dứt chiến tranh tại Việt Nam? Nhóm chiến sĩ trẻ Việt Nam trình bày. ⌜Saigon, Quyết Thắng⌝ 1965.
59 p. 21 cm. (Tủ sách nghiên cứu chánh trị)
1. Vietnamese Conflict, 1961– —Addresses, essays, lectures. I. Nhóm chiến sĩ trẻ Việt Nam.
DS557.A6B335 74–218402

Bảo-Hạnh.
Thương yêu; thơ. ⌜Saigon?⌝ Thanh Hảo ⌜196-?⌝
v. 20 cm.
Contents.—tập 1. Điệp khúc ngày xưa.
I. Title.
NIC NUC73-2833

Bão lớn : tập truyện và ký. — Hà-nội : Phụ Nữ, 1975.
248 p. ; 19 cm.
1. Short stories, Vietnamese.
PL4378.8.B34 77-986458
77 MARC

Bao'Ma.
I berget ser barnet : dikter, bilder / Bao'Ma. — ⌜Sollefteå : Bao'ma förl., (box 243), 1975⌝
59 p. : ill. ; 21 cm. S 75-32/33
kr29.00
I. Title.
PT9876.12.A6 I 2 75–402176

Bảo-Sơn, tr.
Ngược giòng thời gian. ⌜Saigon?⌝ Đời Nay, 1962.
149 p. 19 cm.
1. Vietnamese literature—Translations from foreign literature. I. Title.
CtY NUC74-23498

Bảo-Sơn.
Phương thức kiến trúc ⌜của⌝ Bảo-Sơn ⌜và⌝ Nam-Anh. ⌜Saigon⌝ Đất Việt, 1971.
196 p. illus. 21 cm. (Tủ sách kỹ thuật)
1. House construction. I. Nam-Anh. II. Title.
NIC NUC73-115142

Bảo-So'n, trans.
see **Du Maurier**, Dame Daphne, 1907–
Ngư'ợ'c giòng thờ'i gian... [Saigon] Đờ'i Nay [1962]

Baoill, Colm O
see Ó Baoill, Colm.

Baon, Rogelio.
La cara humana de un caudillo : 401 anécdotas / Rogelio Baon. — Madrid : Librería Editorial San Martín, ⌜1975?⌝
256 p. : ill. ; 27 cm. Sp***
ISBN 8471401142
1. Franco Bahamonde, Francisco, 1892-1975. I. Title.
DP264.F7B3 76-455075
76 MARC

Baos, Zapheirios Antōniou.
Krētes agōnistai hidrytai tou Adamantos Melou [hypo] Zapheiriou Ant. Vaou. [Athēnai] Hetaireia Kykladikōn Meletōn, 1965.
[163]-272 p. illus. 24 cm.
1. Mēlos—History. 2. Adamas, Mēlos. I. Title.
OCU NUC74-118481

Baos, Zapheirios Antōniou.
(To magiko taxidi)
Τὸ μαγικὸ ταξίδι ⌜ὑπὸ⌝ Ζαφειρίου 'Αντ. Βάου. Σκίτσα, πρωτογράμματα ⌜ὑπὸ⌝ 'Εμμ. Α. Κόμη καὶ συγγραφέως. 'Αθῆναι, 1969.
173 p. illus. 25 cm.
I. Title.
PA5613.A55M3 77–511281

Baotić, Josip
see Mostarsko savjetovanje o književnom jeziku, 1973. Mostarsko savjetovanje o književnom jeziku : referati, diskusija, zaključci. Sarajevo : Institut za jezik i književnost : Oslobodenje, 1974.

Baouia, Mohamed Saleh
see
Bawiyah, Muhammad al-Salih.

Bapaev, Khalil.
Priroda kirgizskoi satiry. [By] Bapaev Kh. Frunze, "Kyrgyzstan", 1971.
142 p.
Title page and text in Kirghiz.
Russian title from colophon.
1. Satire–Kirghiz.
MH NUC75-129145

Bāpahaṇā, Sohanalāla, ed.
see Buddhamalla, Muni, 1920–1961. (Āvartta)

Bāpanā, Ushā.
(Santa kavi Ācārya Śrī Jayamalla)
संत कवि आचार्य श्री जयमल्ल : कृतित्व एवं व्यक्तित्व. लेखिका उषा बापना. निदेशक नरेन्द्र भानावत. जोधपुर, जयध्वज प्रकाशन समिति ⌜1973⌝
16, 170, 2 p. 23 cm. Rs10.00
"एम. ए. १९७०-७१ की परीक्षा (राजस्थान विश्वविद्यालय) के लिए प्रस्तुत शोध-प्रबन्ध."
In Hindi.
Bibliography: p. ⌜162⌝-163.
1. Jayamalla, 1708–1796. I. Title.
PK2096.J37Z58 73–905396

Bāpat, G.V., tr.
see Puranas. Bhāgavatapurāna. English. Bāpat. Parables of the sage. ⌜Poona, ⌜1969?⌝

Bapat, Lakshman Ganesh, 1872–1960.
श्रीसद्गुरु रामानंद बीडकर महाराज यांचे चरित्र. लेखक लक्ष्मण गणेश बापट. 4. आवृत्ति. ⌜पुणें, भालचंद्र लक्ष्मण बापट⌝ 1970.
38, 424 p. illus., geneal. table. port. 19 cm. Rs10.00
In Marathi.
1. Bidkar, Ramanand, 1839–1913. I. Title.
Title romanized: Śrīsadguru Rāmañanda Bīḍakara Mahārāja yañce caritra.
BL1175.B47B36 1970 74–920996

Bapat, Nilkanth Gangadher, 1936–
Economic development of Ahmednagar District, 1881–1960 / N. G. Bapat. — Bombay : Progressive Corp., 1973.
xiv, 492 p. : map ; 23 cm.
A revision of the author's thesis, Poona University.
Bibliography: p. 487–492.
Rs60.00 ($12.00U.S.)
1. Agriculture—Economic aspects—India—Ahmadnagar, (District) 2. Ahmadnagar, India (District)—Industries. I. Title.
HD880.A36B36 1973 330.9′54′792 74–901650
MARC

Bapat, Pandurang Mahadeo, 1880–1967.
(Senāpati Bāpaṭa samagra grantha)
सेनापती बापट समग्र ग्रंथ. संपादक जीवन किर्लोस्कर ⌜आणि इतर. प्रथमावृत्ति. मुंबई, वामन पांडुरंग बापट, 19
v. illus., ports. (part col.) 23 cm. Rs10.00 (v. 3)
English or Marathi.
I. Kirloskar, Jeewan Vasant, 1941– ed.
DS481.B36A3 S A 68–10789
PL 480: I-Mar-1677

Bapat, Purushottam Vishvanath, ed.
see Dhammasangani. (Abhidhammapiṭake Dhammasangaṇi) Dhammasangani: the first book of the Abhidhammapitaka of the Buddhists... Poona: R. N. Dandekar, 1940.

Bapat, S. R., joint author
see Sukhatme, Balkrishna V 1924–
Sample survey on vegetables... New Delhi, Institute of Agricultural Research Statistics [1973]

Bapat, Vasant Vaman, 1922–
(Sakīnā)
सकीना / वसंत बापट. — 1. आवृत्ती. — मुंबई : पॉप्युलर प्रकाशन, 1975.
111 p. ; 20 cm.
In Marathi.
Poems.
Rs9.00
I. Title.
PK2418.B327S2 75–904928

Bapat, Vijay.
⌜Prasādottara nāṭya-sāhitya⌝
प्रसादोत्तर नाट्य-साहित्य. ⌜लेखक⌝ विजय बापट. ⌜1. संस्करण⌝ भोपाल, मध्यप्रदेश हिन्दी ग्रन्थ अकादमी ⌜1971⌝
⌜7⌝, 246 p. 23 cm. Rs12.00
In Hindi.
Reviews of the author's works: p. 246.
Bibliography: p. 243–245.
1. Hindi drama—History and criticism. I. Title.
PK2041.B3 70–926893

Bāpaṭa, Divākara.
अण्णा; ... एका वृद्धाची काळीज हेलावणारी कहाणी. ⌜लेखक⌝ दिवाकर बापट. ⌜मुंबई⌝ आराधना प्रकाशन ⌜1970⌝
168 p. 19 cm. Rs5.00
In Marathi.
I. Title.
Title romanized: Aṇṇā
PK2418.B3272A8 77–92060[illegible]

Bāpaṭa, Divākara.
(Kheḷa)
खेळ; [कथासंग्रह. लेखक] दिवाकर बापट. [प्रथमावृत्ति] सोलापूर, सुरस ग्रंथमाला [1972]
96 p. 19 cm. Rs3.00
In Marathi.

I. Title.
PK2418.B3272K4 72-904354

Bāpaṭa, Divākara.
(Poshṭācī tikiṭē)
पोष्टाची तिकिटें : एक छंद. लेखक दिवाकर बापट. [मुंबई, आनंदवन प्रकाशन, 1968]
96 p. illus. 19 cm. Rs4.00
In Marathi.

1. Postage-stamps—Collectors and collecting—India. 2. Postage-stamps—India. I. Title.
HE6204.I 4B36 72-908567

Bāpaṭa, Divākara.
(Pūrṇimā)
पूर्णिमा; सामाजिक कादंबरी. लेखक दिवाकर बापट. [प्रथमावृत्ति] पुणें, रम्यकथा प्रकाशन [1971]
226 p. 19 cm. Rs9.00
In Marathi.

I. Title.
PK2418.B3272P8 72-908568

Bāpaṭa, Divākara.
उपेक्षित द्रष्टा : कै. र. धों. कर्वे. लेखक दिवाकर बापट. [प्रथमावृत्ती] मुंबई, अभिनव प्रकाशन [1971]
80 p. 18 cm. Rs3.00
In Marathi.

1. Karve, Raghunath Dhondo, 1882-1953. 2. Birth control—India. I. Title.
Title romanized: Upekshita drashṭā.
HQ766.5.I 5B29 79-923033

Bāpaṭa, Prabhākara Vāsudeva.
(Marāṭhī kādambarī)
मराठी कादंबरी : तंत्र आणि विकास / लेखक प्रभाकर वासुदेव बापट, नारायण वासुदेव गोडबोले. — 3. आवृत्ती, सुधारून वाढविलेली. — पुणे : व्हीनस प्रकाशन, 1973.
14, 447 p. ; 23 cm.
In Marathi.
Bibliography: p. [13]-14 (1st group)
Includes index.
Rs30.00
1. Marathi fiction—History and criticism. I. Godabole, Nārāyaṇa Vāsudeva. II. Title.
PK2412.B35 1973 76-905449

Bāpata, Vishnu Vāmana, 1871-1933
see Mahābhārata. Marathi. Śrīmanmahābhāratārtha. 1928-1937.

Bapco
see
Bahrain Petroleum Company, ltd.
Bahruny, P. T.
for publications by and about these bodies.
Titles and other entries beginning with this acronym are filed following this card.
73-220590

Bapeluma.
Abbreviation of Badan Pengendalian Lalu Lintas Muatan Antar Pulau. Publications by and about this body are found under its name written in full.
Titles and other entries beginning with this abbreviation are filed following this card.
73-217493

Bapenek
see
Badan Penyalur Buku² Ekonomi dan Keuangan
for publications by and about this body.
Titles and other entries beginning with this acronym are filed following this card.
75-589095

Bāphanā, Sohanalāla, ed.
see Mahendra Kumar I, Muni. (Jaina kahāniyām. 1961-

Bāphanā, Ushā
see
Bāpanā, Ushā.

Bapheiados, Marias
see Vapheiadē, Maria.

Bapheidēs, Philaretos
see
Vapheidēs, Philaretos.

Baphias, Grēgorēs
see Vaphias, Grēgorēs.

Baphopoulos, G Th
Epithanatia kai satires [tou] G.Th. Baphopoulou. Athenai, Bibliopoleion tes "Hestias" [1966]
43 p. 26 cm.
Poems.
I. Title.
MB NUC77-49860

Baphopoulos, G Th
(Ta poiētika tou G. Th. Baphopoulou)
Τὰ ποιητικὰ τοῦ Γ. Θ. Βαφοπούλου. ['Αθῆναι] Βιβλιοπωλεῖον τῆς Ἑστίας [1970]
371 p. 24 cm.
I. Title.
PA5610.B29T3 73-222364

Baphphata.
(Vaphphata kī śāyarī)
वफ्फत की शायरी; असली कजरी. लेखक बफ्फत. [20. संस्करण] कलकत्ता, श्री लोकनाथ पुस्तकालय, 1971.
120 p. 19 cm. Rs1.50
Cover title: कजरी बफ्फत की शायरी.
In Hindi.
Without the music.

1. Songs, Hindi—Texts. I. Title: Kajarī Baphphata kī śāyarī.
M1808.B365V4 76-925659

Bapiraju, Adivi, 1895-1952.
నరుడు. [రచన] అడివి బాపిరాజు. [1st ed.] మచిలీపట్నం, యం. శేషాచలం; [distributors: Andhra Pradesh Book Distributors, Secunderabad, 1971]
155 p. 18 cm. **(EMESCO pocket books, 170) Rs2.50**
In Telugu.
A novel.

I. Title.
Title romanized: Naruḍu.
PL4780.9.B33N3 1971 72-901380

Bapista da Silva Leitão de Almeida Garrett
Almeida Garrett, João
see Almeida Garrett, João Bapista da Silva Leitão de Almeida Garrett, 1. visconde de, 1799-1854.

Bappeda
Initials of Badan Perencanaan Pembangunan Daerah, the name of many Indonesian local development boards. Publications by or about any one of these boards are found under the name written in full and entered under the jurisdiction in which it is located, e. g.
Sumatera Barat, Indonesia. Badan Perencanaan Pembangunan Daerah.

Bappemda.
Initials of Badan Perencana Pembangunan Daerah, the name of many Indonesian local development boards. Publications by or about any of these boards are found under the name written in full and entered under the jurisdiction in which it is located, e. g.
Sumatera Barat, Indonesia. Badan Perencana Pembangunan Daerah.

Bappemka
Initials of Badan Perancang Pembangunan, the name of many Indonesian local development boards. Publications by or about any of these boards are found under the name written in full and entered under the jurisdiction in which it is located, e. g.
Cirebon, Indonesia (Kabupaten). Badan Perancang Pembangunan.

Bappenas
see
Indonesia. Badan Perencanaan Pembangunan Nasional
for publications by and about this body.
Titles and other entries beginning with this acronym are filed following this card.
74-228823

Bappenas.
List of project aid proposals.
[Jakarta]
v. 28 cm.
1. Indonesia—Economic policy. 2. Indonesia—Industries. 3. Technical assistance in Indonesia. I. Title.
HC447.B29b 338.9'1'598 73-940659
MARC-S

Bappenas.
List of technical assistance proposals.
[Djakarta?]
v. in 28 cm. annual.
Issued in parts.
1. Technical assistance in Indonesia. I. Title.
HC447.B29a 309.2'13'09598 74-643511
MARC-S

Bappenas.
Project aid review of proposals and commitments. [Jakarta] Republic of Indonesia, National Development Planning Agency, 1972.
ii, 53, ii, 41 l. 21 x 30 cm.
1. Economic assistance in Indonesia—Statistics. I. Title.
HC447.B29 1972 73-940979
MARC

Bappenas.
[Regional planning reports. Djakarta, Direktorat Tata Kota & Daerah, 196
v. (chiefly maps) 21 x 33 cm.
Cover title.
Includes bibliographical references.
CONTENTS: [1] Djawa Tengah, Jogjakarta.—[2] Lampung.—[3] Djambi.—[4] Sumatera Selatan.—[5] Sumatera Barat.—[6] Sumatera Utara.—[7] Atjeh.—[8] Kalimantan Barat.—[9] Kalimantan Selatan.—[10] Sulawesi Selatan.—[11] Nusatengg. Barat.—[12] Bali.
1. Regional planning—Indonesia—Collections. 2. Indonesia—Economic conditions—Collections. I. Title.
HT395.I 57B36 S A 68-15358
rev PL 480: Indo-7715

Bappenas
see Diskusi Panil Pembahasan Terbatas Regional Planning, Djakarta, 1972. Hasil. [Djakarta, 1972]

Bappenas
see Hasil konperensi kerdja Bappenas-Baperdep... Djakarta, Sekertariat Badan Perentjanaan Pembangunan Nasional [1964?]

Bappenas
see Hasil konperensi kerdja Bappenas/Baperdep-Bakopda, tangal 22 s/d 24 September 1964. Djakarta, Sekertariat Badan Perentjanaan Pembangunan Nasional [1965]

Bappenkar Jatim
see
Jawa Timur, Indonesia. Badan Pelaksana Penanggulangan Narkotika dan Kenakalan Anak-Anak Remaja
for publications by and about this body.
Titles and other entries beginning with this acronym are filed following this card.

Bappepda Kabupaten Kutai
see
Kutai, Indonesia. Badan Perencanaan dan Pengawas Pembangunan Daerah
for publications by and about this body.
Titles and other entries beginning with this acronym are filed following this card.
75-588615

Bappert, Günter, 1932-
Die Entwicklung der Finanzwirtschaft Ludwigshafen von 1853 bis zum Ende des Ersten Weltkrieges. [n. p.] **1964.**
iii, 137 p. illus. 21 cm.
Inaug.-Diss.—Wirtschaftshochschule Mannheim.
Vita.
Bibliography: p. 134-136.
1. Ludwigshafen—Economic conditions. 2. Finance—Ludwigshafen. I. Title.
HC289.L875B3 72-225131

Bappert (Joseph) and Associates
see Joseph Bappert and Associates.

Bappu, M. K. V., ed.
see Symposium on Wolf-Rayet and High-Temperature Stars, Buenos Aires, 1971. Wolf-Rayet and high-temperature stars. Dordrecht, Boston, D. Reidel Pub. Cp., 1973.

Bapst, Germain, 1853-1921.
Essai sur l'histoire du théâtre; la mise en scène, le décor, le costume, l'architecture, l'éclairage, l'hygiène. New York, B. Franklin [1971]
ii, 693 p. illus. 26 cm. (Burt Franklin research and source works series, 821. Theater and drama series, 23)
Reprint of the 1893 ed. published by Librairie Hachette, Paris.
Includes bibliographical references.
1. Theater—France—History. I. Title.
PN2621.B36 1971 792'.0944 71-168918
ISBN 0-8337-3965-4 MARC

Bapst, Jennis Joseph, 1933-
The effect of systematic student response upon teaching behavior. [Seattle] 1971.
98 l. illus.
Thesis (Ph.D.)—University of Washington.
Bibliography: leaves 68-70.
1. Feedback (Psychology) 2. Teacher-student relationships. 3. Interaction analysis in education. I. Title.
WaU NUC73-31318

Bapst, Valentin
see
Babst, Valentin, ca. 1530-1556.

Le baptême. Vevey, Editions Bibles et traités chrétiens, 1973.
see under Prod'hom, Frédéric.

Baptie, Robert.
Ackson / by R. Baptie. — Lusaka, Zambia : Neczam, 1974, c1971.
56 p. : ill. ; 19 cm. — (Eagle readers : Primary level)
I. Title.
PZ7.B2295 Ac 1974 823'.9'14 74-980265
77 MARC

Baptie, Robert.
The drummer of the west and other stories. [Lusaka, Zambia] Neczam [1970]
110 p. 22 cm.
I. Title.
PZ4.B225Dr 3 823'.9'14 73-981407
[PR6052.A58] MARC

Baptie, Robert.
Sakatoni, and other stories. [Lusaka] Neczam [1971, c1970]
93 p. 21 cm.
CONTENTS: Sakatoni.—The trousers of Jerry N'dbele.—No other than give.—The widow's husband.— Kaka and the vultures.—A child for Margaret.—Prince of the sun.—The fall of Nason Mutale.—Ibula Da wa Anzovu.—He never took advice.—A day of work.—Kilwa Island.—The obedient husband.—Through the skin of a lion.—Never laugh twice. Akasula women.—A family for Gilbert.—The monkey drums.—A woman called Sheeba.
I. Title.
PZ4.B225Sak 3 823'.9'14 79-981872
[PR6052.A58] MARC

Baptisit, A. G.
see Belgium. Groupe de travail pour l'étude des normes et standards de travail en agriculture. Arbeidsstudie in het zandleembedrijf nr. 132... [n. p.] 1961.

Baptism and marriage records of the Reformed Churches of Ghent, West Ghent, Mount Pleasant, and Stuyvesant Falls, 1775-1899. [Transcribed and indexed by Arthur C. M. Kelly. Rhinebeck, N. Y., 1972]
iv, 172 p. 28 cm.
1. Registers of births, etc.—New York (State) 2. New York (State)—Genealogy. I. Kelley, Arthur C. M.
F118.B36 929'.3747 73-160685
MARC

Baptism and marriage records of the Reformed Churches of Upper Red Hook, Tivoli, Melenville, and Linlithgo, 1766-1899. [Transcribed and indexed by Arthur C. M. Kelly. Rhinebeck, N. Y., 1973]
iv, 149 p. 30 cm.
1. Registers of births, etc.—New York (State) 2. New York (State)—Genealogy. I. Kelly, Arthur C. M.
F118.B37 929'.3747 73-179246
MARC

Baptism; how and by whom administered? [Salt Lake City, Utah, Church of Jesus Christ of Latter-day Saints, n.d.]
[4] p. 18 cm.
Caption title.
1. Baptism. 2. Mormons and Mormonism—Doctrinal and controversial works. I. Church of Jesus Christ of Latter-day Saints.
NjP NUC75-30595

Baptism: The family book; with notes by Peter Coughlan [and others] Published for St. Thomas More Centre for Pastoral Liturgy. London, G. Chapman, 1970.
32 p. illus. 22 cm.
1. Baptism (Liturgy) 2. Rituale Romanum. Ordo baptismi parvulorum. I. Coughlan, Peter. II. St. Thomas More Centre for Pastoral Liturgy.
MBtS NUC73-126262

Baptism; the sacramental rite for children. Staten Island, N.Y., Alba House, c1970.
26 p.
1. Baptism—Catholic Church. I. Catholic Church. Liturgy and ritual. Baptism for children. English.
OClJC NUC76-75792

Baptist, Albert Gerard.
Les exploitations cooperatives a vaches laitieres au Danemark. Gent, 1963.
30 l. (Belgium. Administration de la recherche agronomique. Publikatie no. 12A)
I. Title.
DNAL NUC75-32404

Baptist, Albert Gerard.
Normes de travail en agriculture / par A. G. Baptist, W. Coolen, et L. Verschraege, Groupe de travail pour l'étude des normes et standards de travail en agriculture. — [Bruxelles] : Ministère de l'agriculure, Administration de la recherche agronomique, Commission pour la rationalisation du travail à la ferme, 1963.
165 p. : ill. ; 21 cm.
Issued also under title: Arbeidsnormen in de landbouw.
Bibliography: p. 157-164.
1. Agriculture—Belgium—Production standards. I. Coolen, W. II. Verschraege, L. III. Belgium. Groupe de travail pour l'élude des normes et standards de travail en agriculture. IV. Title.
S564.5.B36 630'.9493 75-502811
75 MARC

Baptist, Edward Woodson.
Studies on the biosynthesis of thiamine in Neurospora crassa. [n.p.] 1973.
110 l. diagrs., tables. 30 cm.
Thesis (Ph.D.)—Massachusetts Institute of Technology.
Vita.
Includes bibliographical references.
1. Thiamine. 2. Biosynthesis. 3. Neurospora. I. Title.
MCM NUC75-21801

Baptist, Egerton C
Abhidhamma for the beginner; Buddhist metaphysics, by Egerton C. Baptist. With a foreword by Mirisse Gunasiri, Maha Thera. Colombo [1959?]
xix, 135 p. illus. 22 cm.
1. Abhidharma. I. Title.
BQ4195.B36 73-203686
rev

Baptist, Egerton C
The Buddhist doctrine of Kamma : the law of causation, of action and re-action / by Egerton C. Baptist ; with a foreword by Talalle Dhammananda. — [s.l. : s.n.], 1972 (Colombo : Felix Press)
xiii, 56 p. ; 20 cm.
1. Karma. I. Title.
BQ4435.B36 294.3'5 76-904015
77 MARC

Baptist, Eleanor, 1885-1973.
The Baptist and Harden families : with information on the Van Winkle, Salle, Phillips and Carter families / by Eleanor Baptist and Oren C. Baptist. — San Rafael, Calif. : O. C. Baptist, 1974.
102 leaves, [3] leaves of plates : genealogical tables ; 29 cm.
Bibliography: leaves 100-102.
1. Baptist family. 2. Harden family. I. Baptist, Oren C., 1912- joint author. II. Title.
CS71.B232 1974 929'.2'0973 76-360599
76 MARC

Baptist, Jo.
Fonctions et structures de la distribution. [Bruxelles, Comité belge de la distribution, 1973]
135 p. 30 cm. (Comité belge de la distribution. Information spécialisée, 1973, no 1) Be***
1. Retail trade. 2. Wholesale trade. 3. Marketing. I. Title.
HF5429.B2814 658.8 74-177452
MARC

Baptist, Oren C., 1912- joint author.
see Baptist, Eleanor, 1885-1973. The Baptist and Harden families ... San Rafael, Calif., O. C. Baptist, 1974.

Baptist-Catholic Regional Conference, Daytona Beach, Fla., 1971.
Issues and answers; [speeches] Sponsored by Home Mission Board, Dept. of Interfaith Witness and Bishops' Committee for Ecumenical and Interreligious Affairs for National Conference of Catholic Bishops. [Prepared by the Dept. of Interfaith Witness, Home Mission Board of the Southern Baptist Convention. Washington, United States Catholic Conference, 1972, c1971]
86 p. 22 cm.
Cover title.
1. Baptists. Relations. Catholic Church. 2. Catholic Church. Relations. Baptists. I. Southern Baptist Convention. Dept. of Interfaith Witness. II. Catholic Church. National Conference of Catholic Bishops. Bishops' Committee for Ecumenical and Interreligious Affairs. III. Title.
NcD NUC73-118690

Baptist-Catholic Regional Conference, Marriottsville, Md., 1974.
The church inside out. Sponsored by Home Mission Board, Dept. of Interfaith Witness [of the Southern Baptist Convention] and Bishops' Committee for Ecumenical and Interreligious Affairs for National Conference of Catholic Bishops. Washington, United States Catholic Conference, 1974.
v, 86 p. 22 cm.
1. Baptists—Relations—Catholic Church. 2. Catholic Church—Relations—Baptists. I. Southern Baptist Convention. Dept. of Interfaith Witness. II. Catholic Church. National Conference of Catholic Bishops. Bishops' Committee. for Ecumenical and Inter-religious Affairs. III. United States Catholic Conference. IV. Title.
DCU NUC76-76215

Baptist-Catholic Southwestern Regional Conference, Houston, Tex., 1972.
Living the faith in today's world; [speeches] sponsored by Home Mission Board, Dept. of Interfaith Witness and Bishops' Committee for Ecumenical and Interreligious Affairs for National Conference of Catholic Bishops. Atlanta, Ga., Home Mission Board, Southern Baptist Convention, 1972.
78 l. 28 cm.
Cover title.
I. Southern Baptist Convention. Dept. of Interfaith Witness.
NcWsW NUC76-93118

Baptist Church, Liberty, Mo. Amoma Bible Class.
The Amoma book of recipes. Liberty, Mo. [19--?]
1 v. (unpaged)
1. Cookery, American. I. Title.
KMK NUC74-15903

Baptist Church of Annapolis.
The Baptist Church of Annapolis was founded in 1899. In 1903 the name was changed to College Avenue Baptist Church and in 1972 to Heritage Baptist Church.
Works by this body are found under the name used at the time of publication.
74-224343

Baptist Convention of Ontario and Quebec
see Baptists. Canada. Baptist Convention of Ontario and Quebec.

Baptist Convention of the State of Georgia
see
Baptists. Georgia. Convention.

Baptist Education Society of Kentucky.
A booklet of information concerning the Baptist schools of Kentucky. [Louisville, n.d.]
44 p. illus. 24 cm.
1. Baptists—Kentucky. 2. Baptists—Education. I. Title.
KyLoS NUC73-78925

Baptist Federation of Canada.
Minutes of the council.
[Brantford, Ont.?]
v. 25 cm.
Continued by its Proceedings and minutes of the council.
1. Baptist Federation of Canada.
BX6251.B27a 286'.1'06271 74-642419
MARC-S

Baptist Federation of Canada. Proceedings and minutes of the assembly
see Baptist Federation of Canada. Proceedings and minutes on the council. Brantford, Ont.

Baptist Federation of Canada.
Proceedings and minutes on the council.
Brantford, Ont.
v. illus. 24 cm.
Continues its Minutes of the council.
Vols. for have title Proceedings and minutes of the assembly.
1. Baptist Federation of Canada. I. Baptist Federation of Canada. Proceedings and minutes of the assembly.
BX6251.B27a 286'.1'06271 74-642420
MARC-S

Baptist Federation of Canada.
The report volume.
Brantford.
v. illus. 23 cm.
1. Baptist Federation of Canada.
BX6251.B27b 286'.1'06271 74-642105
MARC-S

Baptist Federation of Canada. Committee on Missionary Education
see Langley, Thelma. Baptist family in global village. [Toronto] Canadian Baptist Overseas Mission Board, 1972.

Baptist Federation of Canada. Hymnal Committee.
The hymnal. [n.p., 1973]
632 p. 23 cm.
1. Baptist—Hymns. 2. Hymns, English. 3. Baptists—Canada—Hymns. I. Title.
KyLoS NUC75-75823

Baptist General Association of Virginia
see Baptists. Virginia. General Association.

Baptist General Convention of Oklahoma
see Baptists. Oklahoma. General Convention.

Baptist General Tract Society
see American Baptist Publication Society.

Baptist heritage... [Atlanta, Ga., Printed by Chatham Graphics, c1973]
see under [Gray, Sara Lois] 1901-

Baptist Historical Society
see Association records of the Particular Baptists of England, Wales and Ireland to 1660. London, Baptist Historical Society, 1971-

Baptist Hospital, Columbia, S.C.
see South Carolina Baptist Hospital.

Baptist hymnal.
see Reynolds, William Jensen. Companion to Baptist hymnal. Nashville, Broadman Press, c1976.

Baptist hymnal, 1975.
see Sing praise ... Nashville, Broadman Press, c1975.

Baptist Joint Committee on Public Affairs.
In the Supreme Court of the United States, October term, 1972, no. 72-694. Committee for Public Education and Religious Liberty, et al., appellants, against Ewald B. Nyquist, appellees, On appeal from the United States districk court for the Southern District of New York. Brief of the Baptist Joint Committee on Public Affairs as Amicus Curiae. Joseph B. Friedman, Attorney... Washington, D.C., Lucas, Selden, Friedman, & Mann, 1972.
1 v.
I. Friedman, Joseph B. II. Committee for Public Education and Religious Liberty, appellant. III. United States. Supreme Court.
KyLoS NUC75-7558

Baptist Joint Committee on Public Affairs
see Baptists. Oklahoma. General Convention. Report of future tax problems conference, February 24-26, 1969. [n.p.] 1969.

Baptist Joint Committee on Public Affairs
see Religious Liberty Conference, 9th, Washington, D.C., 1965. Study papers on church, state and public funds. Washington, 1965.

Baptist Joint Committee on Public Affairs
see Religious Liberty Conference, 12th, Washington, D.C., 1968. The role of the Christian through church and state. Washington [1968]

Baptist jubilee advance.
1961 SBC jubilee advance. 1961 emphasis: stewardship and enlistment. [n.p., 1960?]
[6] p. folder. 22 cm.
1. Stewardship, Christian. 2. Baptists—Missions. I. Title.
KyLoS NUC74-24712

Baptist jubilee advance
see Plan of organization, SBC jubilee advance... Rev. [n.p.] 1961.

Baptist Mid-Missions
see Field surveys. Cleveland, 1968.

Baptist Mission of Columbia
see Turnage, Loren C Evangelical work among the Indians of Colombia. Bogota, 1969.

Baptist Missionary and Education Convention
see Liberia Baptist Missionary and Educational Convention.

Baptist Missionary Association of America.
Directory and handbook. 1969/70–
Jacksonville, Tex., Baptist News Service Committee.
v. 22 cm.
1. Baptist Missionary Association of America—Directories.
BX6209.B37B36a 266'.6'102573 73-643086
ISSN 0091-2743 MARC-S

Baptist Missionary Association of America. Baptist News Service.

For informational publications of the Baptist Missionary Association of America issued by this body see

Baptist Missionary Association of America.

(Băpṭisṭ pravṛtti)
බැප්ටිස්ට ප්‍රවෘත්ති. The Baptist messenger.
Colombo.
v. 25 cm. quarterly.
In Sinhalese.

1. Baptists — Ceylon — Periodicals. I. Title: The Baptist messenger.

BX6316.C47B3 72-900361

Baptist Public Relations Association.
Years of achievement; a history of Baptist Public Relations Association, 1953-72. [Nashville, Tenn.] 1972.
40 p. 21 cm.
1. Public relations—Churches. I. Title.
KyLoS NUC74-6924

Baptist Sunday School Board
see Southern Baptist Convention. Sunday School Board.

Baptist Tabernacle, Raleigh, N.C.
Raleigh Baptist Tabernacle, Rev. Thomas Dixon, Jr., Pastor. [n.p., n.d.]
[4] p. 15 cm.
KyLoS NUC73-33742

Baptist Temple, Rochester, N.Y.
The Baptist Temple, Rochester, N.Y., 125th year souvenir [Glenn B. Ewell, Editor. [n.p., 1959?]
60 p. illus. 16 x 24 cm.
I. Ewell, Glenn Blackmer, ed.
KyLoS NUC73-113761

Baptist third jubilee celebration [Program] Convention Hall, Atlantic City, N.J., May 22-23, 1964. Theme: For liberty and light. [n.p.] 1964.
[15] p. 23 cm.
KyLoS NUC73-2831

The Baptist Union directory.
London, Council of the Baptist Union of Great Britain and Ireland.
v. 21 cm. annual.
1. Baptists—Great Britain—Directories. 2. Baptists—Ireland—Directories. I. Baptist Union of Great Britain and Ireland. Council.
BX6276.A1B43 286'.1'06242 74-644279
MARC-S

Baptist Union of Great Britain and Ireland.
Baptists and unity reviewed. London [1969]
15 p. 22 cm.
1. Baptist Union of Great Britain and Ireland. Baptists and unity. I. Title.
WU NUC73-38291

Baptist Union of Great Britain and Ireland
see Rowley, Harold Henry, 1890- Our resources and our task. London, Carey Kingsgate Press [1957]

Baptist Union of Great Britain and Ireland. Council
see The Baptist Union directory. London.

Baptist witness in Catholic Europe; addresses and reports from a conference of workers in traditionally Catholic areas. Edited by John Allen Moore. Rome, Baptist Pub. House [1973]
200 p. 21 cm. It***
1. Baptists—Europe—Congresses. I. Moore, John Allen, ed.
BX6275.B26 266'.6'132 73-179857
MARC

Baptist women's day of prayer, November 4, 1974. [n.p.] 1974.
19 p. 22 cm.
KyLoS NUC76-18039

Baptist World Alliance.
"...and the truth shall make you free"... study materials for the 11th Baptist World Congress, Miami Beach, USA, June 25-30, 1965. [Washington, Baptist World Alliance, 1965]
47 p.
1. Baptist World Congress, 11th, Miami Beach, Fla., 1965. I. Baptist World Congress, 11th, Miami Beach, Fla., 1965. II. Title.
CMIG NUC76-11271

Baptist World Alliance.
Study papers. [Washington, D.C.] 19-
Box. 8 x 32 cm.
A description of the contents precedes the papers for each year.
1. Baptists—Influence. 2. Church and the world.
MNtcA NUC76-9770

Baptist World Alliance. Commission on Baptist Doctrine.
Commission on Baptist Doctrine of the Baptist World Alliance; papers delivered during its annual meeting, Wolfville, Nova Scotia, August 4-5, 1971. [n.p.] 1971.
1 v. (various pagings) 28 cm.
KyLoS NUC74-7438

Baptist World Alliance. Commission on Christian Teaching and Training.
Commission on Christian Teaching and Training of the Baptist World Alliance; papers delivered during its annual meeting, Tokyo, Japan, July 7-10, 1970. [n.p.] 1970.
1 v. (various pagings) 28 cm.
KyLoS NUC74-7436

Baptist World Alliance. Commission on Christian Teaching and Training.
Commission on Christian Teaching and Training of the Baptist World Alliance; papers delivered during its annual meeting, Wolfville, Nova Scotia, August 2-6, 1971. [n.p.] 1971.
1 v. (various pagings) 28 cm.
KyLoS NUC74-7437

Baptist World Alliance. Commission on Cooperative Christianity.
Commission on Cooperative Christianity of the Baptist World Alliance; proceedings of and papers delivered during its first annual meeting Baden bei Wien, Austria, August 2-6, 1969, compiled by James Leo Garrett, Jr., Chairman. [n. p.] 1969.
1 v. (various pagings) 28 cm.
I. Garrett, James Leo.
KyLoS NUC76-11160

Baptist World Alliance. Commission on Cooperative Christianity.
Commission on Cooperative Christianity of the Baptist World Alliance; proceedings of and papers delivered during its second annual meeting, Tokyo, Japan, July 12-18, 1970, compiled by James Leo Garrett, Jr., chairman. [n. p.] 1970.
1 v. (various pagings) 31 cm.
I. Garrett, James Leo.
KyLoS NUC76-11159

Baptist World Alliance. Commission on Cooperative Christianity.
Commission on Cooperative Christianity of the Baptist World Alliance; proceedings of and papers delivered during its third annual meeting, Wolfville, Nova Scotia, August 2-6, 1971, compiled by James Leo Garrett, Jr., chairman. [n.p.] 1971.
1 v. (various pagings) 28 cm.
I. Garrett, James Leo.
KyLoS NUC74-12392

Baptist World Alliance. Commission on Cooperative Christianity.
Commission on Cooperative Christianity of the Baptist World Alliance; proceedings of and papers delivered during its fourth annual meeting, Kingston, Jamaica, July 27-29, 1972, compiled by James Leo Garrett, Jr., chairman. [n. p.] 1972.
1 v. (various pagings) 28 cm.
I. Garrett, James Leo.
KyLoS NUC74-6936

Baptist World Alliance. Commission on Evangelism and Missions.
Commission on Evangelism and Missions of the Baptist World Alliance; papers delivered during its annual meeting, Wolfville, Nova Scotia, August 2-6, 1971. [n.p.] 1971.
1 v. (various pagings) 28 cm.
KyLoS NUC74-7435

Baptist World Alliance. Commission on Evangelism and Missions.
[Papers delivered during the annual meeting, Louisville, Ky., August 5-7, 1974. n. p.] 1974.
[43] l. 28 cm.
KyLoS NUC76-23710

Baptist World Alliance. Commission on Religious Liberty and Human Rights.
[Papers delivered during the annual meeting, Louisville, Ky., August 5-7, 1974. n. p.] 1974.
[35] l. 28 cm.
KyLoS NUC76-76228

Baptist World Alliance. Executive Committee. Commission on Baptist Doctrine
see Baptist World Alliance. Commission on Baptist Doctrine.

Baptist World Alliance. Executive Committee. Commission on Christian Teaching and Training
see Baptist World Alliance. Commission on Christian Teaching and Training.

Baptist World Alliance. Executive Committee. Commission on Cooperative Christianity
see Baptist World Alliance. Commission on Cooperative Christianity.

Baptist World Alliance. Executive Committee. Commission on Evangelism and Missions
see Baptist World Alliance. Commission on Evangelism and Missions.

Baptist World Alliance. Theological Teachers Conference
see Hull, William Edward, 1930-
The theological task of Baptists today. [n.p., 1965?]

Baptist World Alliance. Youth Dept.
see Baptist Youth World Conference, 8th, Portland, Or., 1974. Christ - our challenge to live... [n. p.] 1974.

Baptist World Alliance. Youth Dept.
see Baptist Youth World Conference, 8th, Portland, Or., 1974. You count! [Philadelphia, Judson Press, 1974?]

Baptist World Congress, 11th, Miami Beach, Fla., 1965.
Program, 11th Baptist World Congress. [Miami Beach] Friday June 25, 1965-[Wednesday, June 30, 1965. Baptist World Alliance, 1965]
89 p. illus. 20 cm.
1. Baptists. Congresses. I. Title.
NcWsW NUC75-32403

Baptist World Congress, 11th, Miami Beach, Fla., 1965
see Baptist World Alliance. "...and the truth shall make you free." [Washington, 1965]

Baptist World Congress, 12th, Tokyo, 1970
see Tolbert, William Richard, 1913-
Message of Dr. William R. Tolbert, Jr... [n.p.] 1970.

Baptist Youth Fellowship.
Adventure guide. Philadelphia, Judson Press [n.d.]
5 pamphlets in packet. 23 cm.
1. Church work with youth. 2. Baptist youth fellowship. I. Title.
NRCR NUC73-68105

Baptist Youth World Conference, 8th, Portland, Or., 1974.
Christ - our challenge to live: 8th Baptist Youth World Conference, Portland, Oregon, U.S.A. [n. p.] 1974.
31 p. illus. 28 cm.
Title taken from cover.
Sponsored by Youth Department, Baptist World Alliance.
1. Baptists—Congresses. 2. Youth—Religious life. I. Baptist World Alliance. Youth Dept. II. Title.
KyLoS NUC76-23720

Baptist Youth World Conference, 8th, Portland, Or., 1974.
You count! 8th Baptist Youth World Conference, Portland, Oregon, U. S. A. [Philadelphia, Judson Press, 1974?]
50 p. illus. 28 cm.
Cover title.
1. Baptists—Congresses. 2. Youth—Religious life. I. Baptist World Alliance. Youth Dept. II. Title.
KyLoS NUC76-23719

Baptista Gariglio,
see
Gariglio, Baptista.

Baptista Mantuanus, 1448-1516. Apologeticon. ca. 1492
in Baptista Mantuanus, 1448-1516. Commendation Parthenices. [Deventer, Richardus Pafraet, ca. 1492]

Baptista Mantuanus, 1448–1516.
Aureū contra impudice scribentes opusculū, familiariter explicatū. [Parisiis, Labore R. Boucher, pro D. Roce, ca. 1505]
20 l. 20 cm.
Poem known as Contra poetas impudice loquentes; with prose commentary by Jodocus Badius Ascensius.
Cf. Goff. Third census, B–84.
I. Badius Ascensius, Jodocus, 1462–1535. II. Title: Aureum contra impudice scribentes opusculum.
PA8463.B7C65 76–528032

Baptista Mantuanus, 1448–1516.
Carmina de beata virgine Maria que et Parthenice dicuntur. [Daventriae, R. Paffraet, ca. 1506?]
[102] p. 21 cm.
Known as Parthenice prima sive Mariana.
Signatures: A–$D^{8.4}$, E^4, F–$I^{8.4}$ (I_4 blank)
Nijhoff-Kronenberg 193.
"Fratris Baptiste Mantuani Carmelite ad beatam virginem Votum": p. [100–102]
1. Mary, Virgin—Poetry. I. Title.
PA8463.B7P36 1506 76–528029

Baptista Mantuanus, 1448–1516.
Commendatio Parthenices. [Deventer, Richardus Pafraet, ca. 1492]
[12] l. 4°. 20.4 cm.
Leaf [1a] (t. p.): Fratris baptiste mātuani ad lodouicū fuscararium parthenices cōmendatio.
Copinger. Supplement, 831; Gesamtkat. d. Wiegendr., 3263; Goff. Third census, B–54.
CONTENTS: Commendatio Parthenices.—Apologeticon (leaves [4–12])
Rubricated.
I. Baptista Mantuanus, 1448–1516. Apologeticon. ca. 1492. II. Title. III. Title: Ad Lodovicum Fuscararium Parthenices commendatio.
Incun. X.B22 76–528014
[PA8463.B7]

Baptista Mantuanus, 1448-1516. Contra poetas impudice loquentes. 1489
in Baptista Mantuanus, 1448-1516. De suorum temporum calamitatibus. Bologna, Franciscus (Plato) de Benedictis, 1 Apr. (Kal. Apr.) 1489.

Baptista Mantuanus, 1448–1516.
Contra poetas impudice loquentes. [Paris] Thielman Kerver, for Jean Petit and Johann de Koblenz, 15 Oct. (ad Id. Oct.) 1499.
20 l. metal cuts: publisher's and printer's devices. 4°. 21.3 cm.
Leaf [1a] (t. p.): F. Baptistę Mātuani Carmelitę Theologi aureum contra impudice scribentes opusculum, familiariter explicatū ...
Poem, with prose commentary by Jodocus Badius Ascensius.
Hain. Repertorium, 2369 (III); Gesamtkat. d. Wiegendr., 3313 (naming as printers Georg Wolf and Thielman Kerver); Goff. Third census, B–82.
Rubricated.
I. Badius Ascensius, Jodocus, 1462–1535. II. Title. III. Title: Aureum contra impudice scribentes opusculum.
Incun. 1499.B35 76–528015
[PA8463.B7]

Baptista Mantuanus, 1448–1516.
Contra poetas impudice loquentes. [Paris] Gaspard Philippe, for Denis Roce [ca. 1500; not after 1502]
xxl. metal cuts: initials, publisher's device. 4°. 19.4 cm.
Leaf [1a] (t. p.): F. Baptistę Mantuani Carmelitę Theologi aureum contra impudice scribentes opusculum, familialiter explicatū.
Poem; with prose commentary by Jodocus Badius Ascensius.
Copinger. Supplement, 848 ([1499]); Brit. Mus. Cat. (XV cent.) VIII, p. 224 (IA. 41052); Gesamtkat. d. Wiegendr., III, column 356 ([between 1505 and 1511]); Goff. Third census, B–83.
Device and initials colored by hand.
I. Badius Ascensius, Jodocus, 1462–1535. II. Title. III. Title: Aureum contra impudice scribentes opusculum.
Incun. X.B224 76–528011
[PA8463.B7]

Baptista Mantuanus, 1448–1516.
De patientia. Brescia, Bernardinus de Misintis, 30 May (III Kal. Iun.) 1497.
[116] l. 20.6 cm.
Leaf [1^a] (t. p.): Reuerendi fratris Baptistae mantuani Carmelitae de patientia aurei libri tres.
With prefatory letter by Elia Cavriolo (Helias Capreolus) and, at end, a poem by Joannes Taberius.
Hain. Repertorium (with Copinger's Supplement) *2404; Gesamtkat. d. Wiegendr., 3304; Goff. Third census, B-76.
I. Title.
Incun. 1497.B36 76-528005
[PA8463.B7]
——— Copy 2. 20.9 cm. With the variant "his plagis includunt̄" on leaf [15^a] Thacher Coll.

Baptista Mantuanus, 1448–1516.
De patientia. Basel, Johann Bergmann, de Olpe, 17 Aug. (XVI Kal. Sept.) 1499.
[118] l. 4°. 20.9 cm.
Leaf [1^a] (t. p.): Baptiste Mantuani Carmelite de patientia aurei libri tres.
With prefatory matter by Johann Bergmann and, at end, a poem by Sebastian Brant.
Hain. Repertorium (with Copinger's Supplement) 2407; Brit. Mus. Cat. (XV cent.) III, p. 797 (IA. 37959) (L. C. copy has "Sebastinus Brant. salutem" on leaf [118^a]); Gesamtkat. d. Wiegendr., 3307; Goff. Third census, B-79.

I. Title.
Incun. 1499.B353 Thacher Coll. 76-528002
[PA8463.B7]
——— Copy 2. 22.2 cm. Contemporary blind-tooled calf, restored and rebacked; with remnants of metal clasps. Vellum ms. leaves (14th or 15th cent.) used as end papers: in front, one fold. leaf with fragment of a legal treatise (on marriage impediments); at end, 2 conjugate leaves from a commentary on Aristotle (Physics VI)
——— Copy 3. 21.9 cm. With the variant "Sebastinus salutem" on leaf [118^a] Thacher Coll.
——— Copy 4. 19.2 cm. With "Sebastinus salutem" on leaf [118^a]. First 3 leaves slightly damaged; headlines partly cropped. Inscription on t. p.: Reuerendo ... D burckardo monasterii uallis sanctj Gregorii Hieronimus Gebuilerus [= H. Gebweiler, d. 1545] dono mittit. Thacher Coll.

Baptista Mantuanus, 1448–1516.
De patientia. Venice, Jacobus Pentius, de Leuco, 6 Sept. 1499.
[136] l. 4°. 19.6 cm.
Leaf [1^a] (t. p.): Reuerendi fratris Baptistae mantuani Carmelitae de patientia aurei libri tres.
With prefatory letter by Elia Cavriolo (Helias Capreolus) and, at end, a poem by Joannes Taberius.
Hain. Repertorium (with Copinger's Supplement) *2408; Brit. Mus. Cat. (XV cent.) V, p. 565 (IA. 24529); Gesamtkat. d. Wiegendr., 3308; Goff. Third census, B-80.
Rubricated in red and blue. Some initials illuminated in gold and color.

Inscription on t. p.: Doctissimo viro D. M. Joanni Rabus' h[or]um φιλίασ ego sum sutor libr[oru]m. Titus Laurentius Frichtus [?] 1580.
I. Title.
Incun. 1499.B354 Thacher Coll. 76-528003
[PA8463.B7]
——— Copy 2. 20.3 cm. Without rubrication and initials. Thacher Coll.
——— Copy 3. 19.3 cm. Bound with the author's In Robertum Severinatem panegyricum carmen. Venice, 1499. Parthenice prima sive Mariana. Venice, 1[4]99. Parthenice secunda sive Catharinaria. Venice, 1499 and De suorum temporum calamitatibus. Venice, 1499. Seventeenth-century white leather, decorated in blind, with green ties.

Baptista Mantuanus, 1448–1516.
De suorum temporum calamitatibus. Bologna, Franciscus (Plato) de Benedictis, for himself and Benedictus Hectoris, 1 Apr. (Kal. Apr.) 1489.
[64] l. 4°. 20.9 cm.
Leaf [64^a]: Calamitatū nostri tp̄is opus diuinū Bon. ip̄ressū solerti animadiuersione Francisci Cereti Parmensis ...
In verse.
"Contra poetas ipudice loquentes Carmē": leaves [1^b]–[4^b]
"Francisci Cereti ... ad ... Iacobum mariā de Lino ... Carmen": leaves [63^b]–[64^a]

Hain. Repertorium, *2386; Brit. Mus. Cat. (XV cent.) VI, p. 823 (IA. 28875a); Gesamtkat. d. Wiegendr., 3246; Goff. Third census, B-89.
Initials supplied in red.
I. Cereti, Francesco. II. Baptista Mantuanus, 1448-1516. Contra poetas impudice loquentes. 1489. III. Title. IV. Title: Calamitatum nostri temporis opus.
Incun. 1489.B17 Thacher Coll. 76-528016
[PA8463.B7]

Baptista Mantuanus, 1448–1516.
De suorum temporum calamitatibus. [Paris] Thielman Kerver for Jean Petit and Johann de Koblenz, [not before] 30 Nov. (pridie Kal. Dec.) 1499.
[4], 151, [1] l. woodcuts: publisher's and printer's devices. 4°. 20.5 cm.
Leaf [1^a] (t. p.): De calamitatibus temporum seu contra peccatorum monstra Aureum Baptistę Mantuani Poema familiariter ac succincte declaratum.
With commentary by Jodocus Badius Ascensius.
Colophon has date 4 Sept. (pridie Nonas Sept.) 1499; dedicatory letter by Badius, 30 Nov. (pridie Kal. Dec.) 1499.
Hain. Repertorium, 2385; Brit. Mus. Cat. (XV cent.) VIII, p. 216 (IA. 40966); Gesamtkat. d. Wiegendr., 3255; Goff. Third census, B-95.

I. Badius Ascensius, Jodocus, 1462-1535. II. Title. III. Title: De calamitatibus temporum seu contra peccatorum monstra.
Incun. X.B23 60-373
[PA8463.B7]

Baptista Mantuanus, 1448–1516.
De suorum temporum calamitatibus. Venice, Jacobus Pentius, de Leuco, 10 Sept. 1499.
[60] l. 4°. 19.5 cm.
In verse.
With added poem Ad Jacobum Mariam de Lino carmen, by Franciscus Ceretus, reprinted from the Bologna 1489 edition prepared by him.
Hain. Repertorium (with Copinger's Supplement) *2384; Brit. Mus. Cat. (XV cent.) V, p. 566 (IA. 24533); Gesamtkat. d. Wiegendr., 3253; Goff. Third census, B-93.
I. Title.
Incun. 1499.B355 Thacher Coll. 76-528025
[PA8463.B7]
——— Copy 2. 19.3 cm. Bound with the author's De patientia. Venice, 1499.
Incun. 1499.B354

Baptista Mantuanus, 1448-1516. Epigrammata ad Falconem. 1489
in **Baptista Mantuanus, 1448-1516.** In Robertum Severinatem panegyricum carmen. Bologna, Franciscus (Plato) de Benedictis, 21 July (XII Kal. Aug.) 1489.

Baptista Mantuanus, 1448-1516. Fastorum libri duodecim. 1516
in Baptista Mantuanus, 1448-1516. Vltima pars operis. [In Lugdunensi ciuitate, Solertia Stephani de Basignana, in officina Bernardi Lescuyer, 1516]

Baptista Mantuanus, 1448–1516.
In funere Ferrandi regis oratio. Brescia, Bernardinus de Misintis, 8 Dec. 1496.
[6] l. 4°. 20.9 cm.
Hain. Repertorium (with Copinger's Supplement and Reichling's Appendices) 2415; Brit. Mus. Cat. (XV cent.) VII, p. 991 (IA. 31252); Gesamtkat. d. Wiegendr., 3275; Goff. Third census, B-56.
1. Ferdinando II, d'Aragona, King of Naples, 1467-1496. 2. Naples (Kingdom)—History—Spanish rule, 1442-1707. 3. Ferdinando I, King, of Naples, 1423-1494. 4. France—History—Charles VIII, 1483-1498. 5. Spain—History—Ferdinand and Isabella, 1479-1516. I. Title.
Incun. 1496.B23 76-528020
[DG848.112.F47]

Baptista Mantuanus, 1448–1516.
In Robertum Severinatem panegyricum carmen. Bologna, Franciscus (Plato) de Benedictis, for himself and Benedictus Hectoris, 21 July (XII Kal. Aug.) 1489.
[50] l. 4°. 19.9 cm.
CONTENTS: In Robertum Severinatem panegyricum carmen.—Somnium Romanum.—Epigrammata ad Falconem.
Hain. Repertorium, *2394; Gesamtkat. d. Wiegendr., 3256; Brit. Mus. Cat. (XV cent.) VI, p. 824 (IA. 28881); Goff. Third census, B-85.
Provenance: Georg Kloss (bookplate); Peter Force.
1. Sanseverino, Roberto da, conte di Caiazzo, 1418-1487—Poetry. I. Baptista Mantuanus, 1448-1516. Somnium Romanum. 1489. II. Baptista Mantuanus, 1448-1516. Epigrammata ad Falconem. 1489. III. Title.
Incun. 1489.B21 76-528009
[PA8463.B7]

Baptista Mantuanus, 1448–1516.
In Robertum Severinatem panegyricum carmen. Venice, Jacobus Pentius, de Leuco, 6 Aug. 1499.
[50] l. 4°. 20 cm.
Hain. Repertorium (with Copinger's Supplement) *2396; Brit. Mus. Cat. (XV cent.) V, p. 565 (IA. 24532); Gesamtkat. d. Wiegendr., 3260; Goff. Third census, B-87.
CONTENTS: In Robertum Severinatem panegyricum carmen.—Somnium Romanum.—Epigrammata ad Falconem.
1. Sanseverino, Roberto da, conte di Caiazzo, 1418-1487—Poetry. I. Baptista Mantuanus, 1448-1516. Somnium Romanum. 1499. II. Baptista Mantuanus, 1448-1516. Epigrammata ad Falconem. 1499. III. Title.
Incun. 1499.B36 Thacher Coll. 76-527979
[PA8463.B7]
——— Copy 2. 19.3 cm. Bound with the author's De patientia. Venice, 1499.
Incun. 1499.B354

Baptista Mantuanus, 1448–1516.
Omnia opera ... [Bononiae, Impressum per Benedictum Hectoris, 1502]
ccclxxxix l. 33 cm.
L. C. copy imperfect: leaves ccclxxxiii–ccclxxxix wanting.
CONTENTS: Eglogae X.—Syluarum libri VIII.—De calamitatibus libri III.—Prima Parthenicae Virgo Maria, libri III.—Secunda Parthenicae beata Chatherina, libri III.—Tertia Parthenicae Margarita & Agathae agon.—Luciae & Apolloniae agon.—Ludouici Morbioli uita.—Alfonsus; pro rege Hispaniae de uictoria Granate lib. VI.—Tropheum pro Gallis expul., pro Duce Mantuc lib. V.—Ad Falconem libellus in epigrammatis lib.
PA8463.B7 1502 76-528010

Baptista Mantuanus, 1448–1516.
Parthenice Catharinaria Fratris Baptistae Mantuani ab Ascensio familiariter exposita. Parisiis [J. Petit, ca. 1506]
[4], cv, [1] l. 22 cm.
Poem known as Parthenice secunda sive Catharinaria; with Badius' prose commentary and added poem by F. Cereti.
Signatures: a^4, B-S^6, T^4.
Device of Jean Petit on t. p.
Imprint date from Moreau. Inventaire chronologique des éditions parisiennes du XVI siècle.
1. Catharina, Saint, of Alexandria—Poetry. I. Badius Ascensius, Jodocus, 1462-1535. II. Title.
PA8463.B7P363 76-528031

Baptista Mantuanus, 1448–1516.
Parthenice Mariana Baptistę Mantuani ab Iodoco Badio Ascensio familiariter explanata. Parrhisiis, Venundatur sub leone argenteo in vico ac via publica sancti Iacobi ca. 1505]
viii, clvi l. 22 cm.
The main work, known as Parthenice prima sive Mariana, in verse; Badius' commentary in prose.
Device of Jean Petit on t. p.
Imprint from Moreau. Inventaire chronologique des éditions parisiennes.
Includes the author's Commendatio Parthenices and Apologeticon, in prose; and Ad beatam Virginem votum, in verse.
1. Mary, Virgin—Poetry. I. Badius Ascensius, Jodocus, 1462-1535. II. Title.
PA8463.B7P36 76-528030

Baptista Mantuanus, 1448–1516.
Parthenice prima sive Mariana. Bologna, Franciscus (Plato) de Benedictis, for Benedictus Hectoris, 17 Oct. (XVI Kal. Nov.) 1488.
[70] l. 4°. 19.7 cm.
Poem.
"Cura Caesaris de Nappis."
Includes the author's Commendatio Parthenices and Apologeticon, in prose; and Ad beatam Virginem votum, in verse.
Hain. Repertorium, *2364; Gesamtkat. d. Wiegendr., 3276 (L. C. copy: leaves [3^a] and [11^a] in the reset form); Brit. Mus. Cat. (XV cent.) VI, p. 823 (IA. 28869 (not 28869a)); Goff. Third census, B-58.
Provenance: Antonius Preys (inscription); Georg Kloss (bookplate); Peter Force.
1. Mary, Virgin—Poetry. I. Title.
Incun 1488.B36 CA 16-385
[PA8463.B7]

Baptista Mantuanus, 1448–1516.
Parthenice prima sive Mariana. Deventer [Richardus Pafraet] 10 Feb. 1492.
[50] l. 4°. 20.3 cm.
Leaf [1^a] (t. p.): Carmina de btā virgine Maria que : parthenice dicuntur.
Includes the author's Ad beatam Virginem votum.
Hain. Repertorium (with Copinger's Supplement) 2365; Gesamtkat. d. Wiegendr., 3278; Brit. Mus. Cat. (XV cent.) IX, p. 55 (IA. 47663); Goff. Third census, B-59.
Rubricated. Initial on leaf [2^a] supplied in red with ornamental work in black or brown.
1. Mary, Virgin—Poetry. I. Title. II. Title: Carmina de beata Virgine Maria quae et Parthenice dicuntur.
Incun. 1492.B36 76-528023
[PA8463.B7]

Baptista Mantuanus, 1448–1516.
Parthenice prima sive Mariana. Venice, Jacobus Pentius, de Leuco, 16 July 1[4]99.
[70] l. 4°. 20.6 cm.
Poem; preceded by the author's Commendatio Parthenices and Apologeticon, both in prose.
"Fratris baptistae Mantuani Carmelitae ad beatam uirginem uotum" (poem): leaf [69^a–70^b]
Hain. Repertorium (with Copinger's Supplement) *2368; Brit. Mus. Cat. (XV cent.) V, p. 565 (IA. 24534); Gesamtkat. d. Wiegendr., 3287; Goff. Third census, B-63.
1. Mary, Virgin—Poetry. I. Title.
Incun. 1499.B364 Thacher Coll. 76-528027
[PA8463.B7]
——— Copy 2. 19.3 cm. Bound with the author's De patientia. Venice, 1499.
Incun. 1499.B354

Baptista Mantuanus, 1448–1516.
Parthenice secunda sive Catharinaria. Bologna, Franciscus (Plato) de Benedictis, for himself and Benedictus Hectoris, 9 Feb. (5 Id. Feb.) 1489.
[44] l. 4°. 21.1 cm.
Leaf [2^a]: Fratris Bap. Mant. ... ad ... Bernardū bēbū ... secūda Parthenice īcipit.
In verse.
Edited, with added poem, by F. Cereti.
Hain. Repertorium, *2371; Gesamtkat. d. Wiegendr., 3290 (L. C. has the variant with īpenssis in colophon); Brit. Mus. Cat. (XV cent.) VI, p. 823 (IA. 28872 (not 28872a)); Goff. Third census, B-66.
1. Catharina, Saint, of Alexandria—Poetry. I. Cereti, Francesco. II. Title.
Incun. 1489.B24 76-528004
[PA8463.B7]

Baptista Mantuanus, 1448–1516.
Parthenice secunda sive Catharinaria. Paris, [Georg Wolf and] Thielman Kerver, for Jean Petit [and Johann de Koblenz, after 5 Aug. 1499]
[4], cv, [1] l. metal cuts: publisher's and printer's devices. 4° 19.8 cm.
Leaf [1^a] (t. p.): Parthenice Catharinaria Fratris Baptiste Mātuani: ab Ascensio familiariter exposita.
Poem; commentary in prose.
Includes In invidum lectorem carmen by Francesco Cereti.
Hain. Repertorium, 2369(II); Pellechet. Cat. gén., 1777; Copinger. Supplement, I, 2376; Gesamtkat. d. Wiegendr., 3303; Goff. Third census, B-72.
1. Catharina, Saint, of Alexandria—Poetry. I. Badius Ascensius, Jodocus, 1462-1535. II. Title. III. Title: Parthenice Catharinaria.
Incun. X.B24 76-528007
[PA8463.B7]

Baptista Mantuanus, 1448–1516.
Parthenice secunda sive Catharinaria. Venice, Jacobus Pentius, de Leuco, 14 July 1499.
[44] l. 4°. 20.2 cm.
Leaf [2^a]: Fratris Bap. Mant. ... ad ... Bernardū Bēbū ... secūda Parthenice īcipit.
Poem.
Includes In invidum lectorem carmen by F. Cereti, reprinted from the 1489 Bologna edition prepared by him.
Hain. Repertorium (with Copinger's Supplement) *2375; Brit. Mus. Cat. (XV cent.) V, p. 565 (IA. 24531); Gesamtkat. d. Wiegendr., 3302; Goff. Third census, B-71.
1. Catharina, Saint, of Alexandria—Poetry. I. Title.
Incun. 1499.B365 Thacher Coll. 76-528006
——— Copy 2. 19.3 cm. Bound with the author's De patientia. Venice, 1499. Incun. 1499.B354

Baptista Mantuanus, 1448-1516. Somnium Romanum. 1489
In Baptista Mantuanus, 1448-1516. In Robertum Severinatem panegyricum carmen. Bologna, Franciscus (Plato) de Benedictis, 21 July (XII Kal. Aug.) 1489.

Baptista Mantuanus, 1448-1516. Somnium Romanum. 1499
In Baptista Mantuanus, 1448-1516. In Robertum Severinatem panegyricum carmen. Venice, Jacobus Pentius, de Leuco, 6 Aug. 1499.

Baptista Mantuanus, 1448–1516.
Vltima pars operis. [In Lugdunensi ciuitate, Solertia Stephani de Basignana, in officina Bernardi Lescuyer, 1516]
[660] p. 17 cm.
Signatures: a–q^8 (q_7 blank), aa–cc^8, A–K^8 (K_7 blank), AA–KK^8, LL^4, a–b^8.
Portrait of the author on t. p. Printer's device. Coat of arms of Cardinal Sigismund Gonzaga.
Posthumous edition of selected poems; first of two volumes with same title printed by Basignana in 1516. Cf. Baudrier. Bibl. lyonnaise.
L. C. copy imperfect: t. p. mutilated, with loss of the title on recto and of last item of table of contents (Probae Centonae) on verso; p. [629–660] (with the Centones by Proba) wanting.
Slip pasted over 4 lines of verse on p. [251]

CONTENTS: Fastorum libri duodecim.—Vita sancti Blasii.—Nicolaus Tolentinus.—Bellum Venetum.—Interpretatio prodigii.—Exhortatio ad Insubres.—De Cupidine marmoreo ad Helisabellam.—Elegia de jejunio quadragesimali.—Ad Cornigerum carmen jocosum.—Varia epigrammata.—De morte et dedicatione poematum Nicolai Corregii.—Supplicatio ad Virginem.—Ad Herculem Cantelmum.—Ad Julium II.—Epitome vite autoris.—Chorus primus ex tragedia que dicitur Atila. Ex eadem tragedia alter chorus.—Agelariorum libri sex.—Probae Centonae.
I. Baptista Mantuanus, 1448–1516. Fastorum libri duodecim. 1516.
PA8463.B7A17 1516 76–528033

Baptista, Sister
see also
Rankin, Dorothy.

Baptista, Alfredo.
A vinha. Alfredo Baptista. [Lisboa?] Direcção-Geral do Ensino Primário, 1961.
120 p., 4 col. plates. ill. 17 cm. (Plano de educação popular. [Publicações] 92) (Colecção educativa. Serie N, no. 13)
1. Viticulture—Portugal. I. Title.
CU-A NUC76-72746

Baptista, António Alçada.
Conversas com Marcello Caetano. Lisboa, Moraes Editores, 1973.
274 p. 20 cm.
1. Portugal–Pol. & govt.–1945- 2. Caetano, Marcello, 1906- I. Caetano, Marcello, 1906- II. Title.
CSt-H NUC77-46841

Baptista, António Alçada.
Documentos políticos; precedidos de uma introdução onde se pretende contribuir para um diagnóstico da vida pública nacional. [Lisboa] Moraes [1970]
118 p. 18 cm. (Actualidade portuguesa)
1. Portugal—Pol. & govt.—1933- I. Title.
PPT NUC73-38292

Baptista, António Alçada.
Peregrinação interior; ou, Quadros da vida quotidiana numa sociedade em vias de desenvolvimento. Lisboa, Moraes, 1971-
v. 21 cm.
I. Title.
AC75.B2553 74–208289

Baptista, António da Silva.
Polítíca de emprego e classificações profissionais / António da Silva Baptista. — Lisboa : Ministério do Trabalho, Fundo de Desenvolvimento da Mão-de-Obra, 1974.
109 p. ; 23 cm.
"40."
Errata slip inserted.
Summary in Portuguese, French, English, and German.
1. Occupations—Classification. 2. Manpower policy. I. Fundo de Desenvolvimento da Mão-de-Obra. II. Title.
HD5707.B33 75–536391

Baptista, António Alçada.
Reflexões sobre Deus; ou, Fragmentos do memorial do combate que Jacob Alçada Baptista vem travando com o anjo que lhe foi atribuído. Lisboa, Moraes, 1971.
306 p. 21 cm. (His Peregrinação interior, v. 1)
1. God. 2. Theology. I. Title. II. Series.
AC75.B2553 vol. 1 74–208288
[BT102]

Baptista, António Alçada.
O tempo nas palavras, chronicas e outros escriptios de circunstância. [Braga] Moraes [1973]
224 p.
I. Title.
NcU NUC75-21624

Baptista, B Vinelli.
Musculus plantaris in Brazilian Negroes [by] B. Vinelli Baptista [and] J. Pereira Ramalho. [Rio de Janeiro, 1972?]
515-518 p. illus. 29 cm. (Trabalho do Instituto Anatômico Benjamin Baptista)
"Separata dos 'Arquivos do Instituto Benjamin Baptista', volume XV, ano XV, 1972."
1. Leg—Muscles. I. Ramalho, Jether Pereira, joint author. II. Title.
TxU NUC75-42616

Baptista, Ernesto de Mello.
Discurso sobre os filósofos gregos, pelo Almirante Ernesto de Mello Baptista, em 25 de maio de 1972, no Clube Positivista. Rio de Janeiro, 1972.
46 p. 23 cm.
"Comemoração do XXIV centenário da morte de Anaxágoras."
1. Philosophy, Ancient. I. Title.
B175.P65B36 73–213759

Baptista, Ernesto Pérez
see Pérez Baptista, Ernesto.

Baptista, Eusebio.
Una semilla en el aire; obra poética del Dr. Eusebio Baptista. Compilación y estudio biográfico de Lourdes Dubuc de Isea. [Boconó, 1970]
169 p. 24 cm. (Colección Temas y autores boconeses, 1)
Includes music.
I. Dubuc de Isea, Lourdes, ed. II. Title.
CSt NUC74-135025

Baptista, Fernando Paulo do Carmo.
A língua portuguesa como expressão literária de portugalidade. [Vizeu, Tip. Guerre, 1968]
56 p.
1. Portuguese language—Addresses, essays, lectures. I. Title.
ICU NUC74-135044

Baptista, Fernando Paulo Nunes.
O mar territorial brasileiro. Rio de Janeiro, Serviço de Documentação Geral da Marinha, 1971.
26 p. 24 cm.
"Artigo publicado na Revista maritima brasileira, 1. Trimestre, 1971."
Bibliography: p. 25-26.
1. Territorial waters—Brazil. I. Brazil. Serviço de Documentação da Marinha. II. Title.
CSt NUC75-86922

Baptista, J do Amparo.
Moçambique, província portuguesa de ontem e de hoje [por] J. do Amparo Baptista. Vila Nova de Famalicão, Centro Gráfico, 1962.
544 p. 24 cm.
1. Mozambique—Economic conditions. 2. Finance—Mozambique. 3. Agriculture—Economic aspects—Mozambique. I. Title.
HC578.M6B36 74–200540

Baptista, Jacinto, 1926-
Caminhos para uma revolução; sobre o fascismo em Portugal e a sua queda. [Lisboa] Livraria Bertrand [1975]
334 p. plates. 22 cm. (Documentos de todos os tempos)
1. Portugal--Hist.--Revolution, 1974. 2. Portugal--Pol. & govt.--1910-1974. I. Title.
CSt-H NUC77-92148

Baptista, José.
Pour un mouvement autonome des travailleurs étrangers, pour une sociologie politique des migrations internationales en Europe / par José Baptista. — Vienna : Vienna Institute for Development, [1974]
13 p. ; 30 cm. — (Occasional paper - Vienna Institute for Development ; 74/2)
Au76-16/17-132
"Version révisée de l'exposé 'Quelques problèmes et issues dans une sociologie politique de migrations internationales de travailleurs en Europe' présenté au séminaire 'La migration internationale dans ses relations avec les politiques d'adjustement industriel et agricole' ... Vienne, 13-15 mai 1974."
Not in trade.
1. Alien labor—Europe. 2. Political socialization. I. Title: Pour un mouvement autonome des travailleurs étrangers ... II. Series: Vienna Institute for Development. Occasional paper ; 74/2.
HD8378.5.B36 331.6′2′094 77-455845
•77 MARC

Baptista, José María.
Muestrario poético. [Trujillo, Venezuela] Ediciones del Ejecutivo del Estado Trujillo, 1974.
54 p. 23 cm.
I. Title.
TxU NUC76-23712

Baptista, Luis Felipe.
Song dialects and demes in sedentary populations of the white-crowned sparrow (Zonotrichia leucophrys nuttalli) / by Luis Felipe Baptista. — Berkeley : University of California Press, 1975, c1976.
52 p., [12] leaves of plates : ill. ; 26 cm. — (University of California publications in zoology ; v. 105)
Bibliography: p. 48-52.
ISBN 0-520-09522-7
1. White-crowned sparrow. 2. Bird-song. 3. Birds—California. 4. Bird populations. I. Title: Song dialects and demes in sedentary populations of the white-crowned sparrow... II. Series: California. University. University of California publications in zoology ; v. 105.
QL696.P246B36 598.8′83 74-620115
76 MARC

Baptista, Luiz Olavo.
Contrato de risco / Luiz Olavo Baptista. — São Paulo : J. Bushatsky, 1976.
156 p. ; 21 cm. — (Coleção jurídica JB ; 25)
Summary in French.
"Anexo, Lei sobre exploração do petróleo no Irã (Petroleum Act)," in English: p. 115-156.
Includes bibliographies.
1. Oil and gas leases—Brazil. 2. Contracts, Aleatory—Brazil. I. Title.
76-486382
76 MARC

Baptista, Maria Elisa
see
Fonseca, Maria Elisa Baptista.

Baptista, Mariano, Pres. Bolivia, 1832-1907.
Una página de política internacional : [la cuestión de límites entre Bolivia y Chile, desde sus orígenes hasta los tratados de 1874] / por Mariano Baptista. — Sucre : Impr. de la Capital, 1905.
131 p. ; 22 cm.
Includes bibliographical references.
1. Bolivia—Boundaries—Chile. 2. Chile—Boundaries—Bolivia. I. Title.
F3139.B27 77-469376
77 MARC

Baptista, Mariano, Pres. Bolivia, 1832-1907.
Páginas escogidas / Mariano Baptista ; selección, prólogo y notas de Mariano Baptista Gumucio. — 1. ed. — La Paz : Editorial Los Amigos del Libro, 1975.
388 p., [14] leaves of plates : ill. ; 20 cm.
1. Bolivia—History—Addresses, essays, lectures. 2. Bolivia—Biography. I. Title.
F3303.B34 1975 76-453661
76 MARC

Baptista, Mário.
Repensar Portugal para um futuro democrático. 1. ed. Lisboa, Arcádia, 1975.
274 p. tables. 21 cm.
1. Portugal--Economic conditions--1918- 2. Portugal--Economic policy. I. Title.
CSt-H NUC77-92158

Baptista, Myrian Veras.
Desenvolvimento de comunidade : estudo da integração do planejamento do desenvolvimento de comunidade no planejamento do desenvolvimento global / Myrian Veras Baptista. — São Paulo : Cortez & Moraes, 1976.
170 p. ; 21 cm.
Bibliography: p. 163-170.
Cr$55.00
1. Community development—Brazil. 2. Regional planning—Brazil. 3. Brazil—Economic policy. I. Title.
HN290.Z9C6155 76-487346
76 MARC

Baptista, N Doreste.
Do processo executivo no sistema do Código de 1973 / N. Doreste Baptista. — 1. ed. — Rio de Janeiro : Forense, 1975 [i. e. 1974]
194 p. ; 21 cm.
Bibliography: p. [157]-160.
Includes indexes.
Cr$40.00
1. Executions (Law)—Brazil. I. Title.
75-402873

Baptista, Olavo
see
Baptista Filho, Olavo.

Baptista, Patricia
see Lenguas de Panamá. [Panamá]: Instituto Nacional de Cultura, 1974-

Baptista, Raimundo Zito
see
Baptista, Zito, 1887-1926.

Baptista, Ranulpho Assis.
Prática de junta comercial : livro útil aos que se incumbem de fazer contratos mercantis, constituir firmas e sociedades, inclusive anônimas, alterá-las, reconstituí-las, extinguí-las ... / Ranulpho Assis Baptista. — [Ed. experimental]. — Salvador, Brasil : [Editora Beneditina], 1973.
270 p. : forms. ; 23 cm.
Includes index.
PARTIAL CONTENTS: Legislação federal: leis vigentes e portarias.—Junta Comercial do Estado da Bahia.—Formulários e minutas.
Cr$70.00
1. Recording and registration—Brazil. 2. Commercial law—Brazil. I. Title.
76-519113

Baptista, Robert Charles, 1922-
A history of intercollegiate soccer in the United States of America. [Bloomington, Ind.] 1962.
249 p.
Thesis (P.E.D.)–Indiana University.
Vita.
Microfilm copy.
1.Soccer–Hist. I.Title.
InU NUC73-57999

Baptista, Zito, 1887–1926.
Zito Baptista, o poeta e o prosador / [organização, estudos, notas e comentários de] A. Tito Filho. — [Teresina] : COMEPI, 1973.
324 p. ; 24 cm. — (Monografias do Piauí : Série literária)
Cover title.
PARTIAL CONTENTS: Harmonia dolorosa.—Chama extinta.—Pedaços do coração.—Poesias esparsas.—Prosa.
I. Title. II. Series.
PQ9697.B326A6 1973 75-563580

Baptista-Bastos, 1934–
Cidade diária. Lisboa, Editorial Futura, 1972.
139 p. 22 cm.
I. Title.
PQ9264.A6C5 74-206058

Baptista da Piedade, Voltaire Jorge
see
Piedade, Voltaire Jorge Baptista da.

Baptista de Mattos, João
see Mattos, João Baptista de.

Baptista de Oliveira, Fernando
see
Oliveira, Fernando Baptista de.

Baptista Dias da Fonseca, Manuel
see Fonseca, Manuel Baptista Dias da.

Baptista-Diniz, J Alexandre, 1952–
De passagem; [poemas, por] J. Alexandre Baptista-Diniz. [Coimbra, Depositário: Atlântida Editora] 1972.
93 p. 20 cm.
I. Title.
PQ9264.A63D4 74-215161

Baptista Filho, Olavo.
Avaliação de recursos humanos. [Rio de Janeiro, Centro Brasileiro de Estudos Demográficos, 1969]
16, [3] p. 25 cm. (Centro Brasileiro de Estudos Demográficos. Estudos e análises, no. 4)
Bibliography: p. [17].
1. Brazil—Population. I. Title. II. Series.
HB3563.C45 no. 4 72-225308

Baptista Filho, Olavo.
Economia da educação, planejamento e explosão demográfica / Olavo Baptista Filho. — São Paulo : Livraria Pioneira Editora, 1975.
88 p. ; 21 cm. — (Educação) (Biblioteca Pioneira de ciências sociais)
Bibliography: p. 87-88.
Cr$30.00
1. Brazil—Population. 2. Birth control—Brazil. 3. Education—Brazil. 4. Education—Economic aspects—Brazil. I. Title.
HB3563.B29 301.32'9'81 76-462802
76 MARC

Baptista Fonseca, Maria Elisa
see
Fonseca, Maria Elisa Baptista.

Baptista Gumucio, Mariano, comp.
Alfabetización; un programa para Bolivia. La Paz, Editorial Los Amigos del Libro, 1973.
243 p. illus. 22 cm.
"Documentos fundamentales y la estrategia que debía seguir el programa."
1. Illiteracy—Bolivia. 2. Educational law and legislation—Bolivia. I. Title.
LC155.B5B29 75-553592

Baptista Gumucio, Mariano. Cinco notas sobre el sistema educativo boliviano. 1974
see Analfabetos en dos culturas. La Paz : Los Amigos del Libro, 1974.

Baptista Gumucio, Mariano.
Cochabamba ; evocación y homenaje. Mariano Baptista Gumucio. La Paz, Universidad Mayor de San Andres, 1975.
31 p. port. 20 cm.
"Conferencia... en el acto de homenaje al Cuarto Centenario de fundación de la ciudad de Cochabamba..."
1.Cochabamba, Bolivia (Dept.) I.Title.
CtY NUC77-92149

Baptista Gumucio, Mariano.
La cultura que heredamos. La Paz [Bolivia] Ediciones Camarlinghi [1973]
213 p. 19 cm.
Essays previously published 1972–1973.
1. Bolivia—Civilization—Addresses, essays, lectures. I. Title.
F3310.B36 74-207087

Baptista Gumucio, Mariano.
La educación como forma de suicidio nacional. La Paz, Bolivia, Ediciones Camarlinghi [1973]
215 p. illus. 19 cm. (Colección popular. Serie XIV, v. 40)
Includes bibliographical references.
1. Education—Bolivia. I. Title.
LA551.B29 370'.984 74-217566

Baptista Gumucio, Mariano.
En lugar del desastre : Bolivia y el conflicto peruano-chileno / Mariano Baptista Gumucio. — 1. ed. — La Paz, Bolivia : Editorial Los Amigos del Libro, 1975.
105 p. : ill. ; 20 cm. — (Mini colección Un Siglo y medio)
Includes bibliographical references.
1. Bolivia—Foreign relations—Peru. 2. Peru—Foreign relations—Bolivia. 3. Bolivia—Foreign relations—Chile. 4. Chile—Foreign relations—Bolivia. 5. Bolivia—Relations (general) with foreign countries. I. Title.
F3321.3.P4B36 76-454814
76 MARC

Baptista Gumucio, Mariano.
Ensayos sobre la realidad boliviana / Mariano Baptista Gumucio. — 1. ed. — La Paz, Bolivia : Biblioteca del Sesquicentenario de la República, 1975.
273 p. ; 25 cm. — (Biblioteca del Sesquicentenario de la República ; v. no. 10)
"Una selección de ensayos que aparecieron originalmente en los libros La cultura que heredamos y Este país tan solo en su agonía, así como los folletos intitulados Analfabetos en dos culturas, Cochabamba, evocación y homenaje y En lugar del desastre."
1. Bolivia—Collected works. I. Title.
F3303.B357 77-458077
77 MARC

Baptista Gumucio, Mariano.
Una escuela para la vida. La Paz, Ministerio de Educación, Fundación "Rosa Agramonte," 1970.
51 p. group ports. 19 cm. (Colección Nuevos caminos, 3)
LACAP 70-1836
Speeches and other short writings.
1. Education—Addresses, essays, lectures. 2. Underdeveloped areas—Education—Addresses, essays, lectures. I. Title. II. Series.
LB41.B265 72-372029

Baptista Gumucio, Mariano.
Este país tan solo en su agonía. [1. ed.] La Paz, Editorial "Los Amigos del Libro," 1972.
282 p. illus. 19 cm.
LACAP 72-4012
A selection of articles written in 1971 for the author's column De la ciudad y del mundo in the daily Ultima hora and for the periodical Semana.
1. Bolivia—Addresses, essays, lectures. I. Title.
F3303.B36 72-375091

Baptista Gumucio, Mariano.
Historia gráfica de la guerra del Chaco / Mariano Baptista Gumucio ; [pinturas de Gil Coimbra ; fotografías de Luis Bazoberry]. — 2. ed. — La Paz, Bolivia : Ultima Hora, 1976.
254 p. : ill. ; 17 cm. — (Biblioteca popular boliviana de Ultima Hora)
$b.30.00
1. Chaco War, 1932-1935. I. Title.
F2688.5.B28 1976 77-468572
77 MARC

Baptista Gumucio, Mariano.
Pasajero en la aeronave tierra. [1. ed.] La Paz, Editorial "Los Amigos del Libro," 1972.
234 p. illus. 19 cm.
LACAP 73-0795
1. Europe—Description and travel—1945- 2. Chile—Description and travel—1951- 3. Human ecology. I. Title.
G470.B24 73-329786

Baptista Gumucio, Mariano.
see El País tranca ... La Paz, Editorial Los Amigos del Libro, 1976.

Baptista Gumucio, Mariano, joint author
see Ponce Sanginés, Carlos. Dependencia, historia y revolución tecnológica. La Paz, Bolivia : Ediciones Pumapunku, 1974.

Baptista Gumucio, Mariano.
see La Violencia en Bolivia. La Paz, Editorial Los Amigos del Libro, 1976.

Baptista Martins, Rodrigo
see
Martins, Rodrigo Baptista.

Baptista Morales, Javier.
Las campanas de Jerusalén (novela). [1. ed.] Cochabamba, Bolivia, Editorial Los Amigos del Libro [1973]
144 p. 20 cm.
I. Title.
PQ7820.B32C3 863 74-225237

Baptista Paino, João
see
Paino, João Baptista.

Baptista Pereira, Antonio, 1880-1960.
Figuras do Imperio e outros ensaios / Batista Pereira : pref. de Américo Jacobina Lacombe. — 3. ed. — São Paulo : Companhia Editora Nacional, 1975.
193 p. ; 21 cm. — (Brasiliana ; v. 1)
CONTENTS: Várias.—A queda de Zacarias.—Perfis do Império.—O idealismo da Constituição.—Rui na conferência de Haia.—Rudyard Kipling e o Rio de Janeiro.
Cr$25.00
1. Brazil—History—Addresses, essays, lectures. 2. Brazil—Biography. 3. Kipling, Rudyard, 1865-1936—Addresses, essays, lectures. I. Title.
F2503.B25 1975 76-471263
76 MARC

Baptista-Riquelme, Cécilia, joint author
see Maréchal, Jean François. Les salariés face à la formation... Paris, Editions d'Organisation, 1972.

Baptistae Armiti... Hamburg, Getruckt und verlegt durch Heinrich Werner, 1642
see under [Rist, Johannes] 1607-1667.

Baptiste, Ernst Jean.
Les heures hallucinées / Ernst Jean Baptiste ; préf. du Pradel Pompilus. — Port-au-Prince : Impr. Centrale, 1972.
83 p. ; 17 cm.
I. Title.
PQ3949.2.B36H4 841 75-507878
75 MARC

Baptiste, Gerard.
The vertical and horizontal division of whites and non-whites in employment in Washington State government / by Gerard Baptiste. — 1st ed. — Olympia, Wash. : Northern Publications, 1973.
127 leaves : graphs ; 28 cm.
Includes bibliographical references.
1. Discrimination in employment—Washington (State)—Statistics. 2. Washington (State)—Officials and employees. 3. Minorities—Employment—Washington (State)—Statistics. I. Title: The vertical and horizontal division of whites and non-whites ...
HD8011.W2B36 331.1'33'09797 75-622233
75 MARC

Baptiste, Gerard
Voice of black liberty. [n.p., 1971?]
25 l. illus. 29 cm.
1. Negroes. 2. Negroes—Politics and suffrage. I. Title.
Wa NUC73-31315

Baptiste, Victor N
La obra poética de Rosario Castellanos. [Santiago de Chile] Ediciones Exégesis [1972]
148 p. 23 cm.
DPU NUC75-21640

Baptiste le Mauvais.
Les Premières fadaises : poèmes / Baptiste le Mauvais ; traduites du patois par Candelustre, ... — Paris : les Paragraphes littéraires de Paris, 1973.
85 p. ; 19 cm. (Les Paragraphes littéraires de Paris) F 73-11400 10.00F
I. Title.
PQ2662.A59P7 841'.9'14 75-501281
MARC

Baptists. Alabama. Convention.
The work of Alabama Baptists; their organizations, their program. [n.p., Public Relations Office, Baptist State Executive Board, 1960]
[20] p. illus. 23 cm.
1. Baptists—Alabama. I. Title.
KyLoS NUC76-87340

Baptists. Canada. Baptist Convention of Ontario and Quebec. Home Mission Board
see Schutt, C H The call of our own land. Toronto, Canada [19--]

Baptists. Canadian Baptist Mission
see Canadian Baptist Mission.

Baptists. Colorado. General Convention.
Colorado Baptist General Convention. [Denver, 1972?]
[16] p. illus. 23 cm.
1. Baptists—The West.
KyLoS NUC76-75270

Baptists. Connecticut. Stonington Baptist Association.
Minutes of the Stonington Babtist [sic] Association, held at Montville, October 15 and 16, 1805. Together, with their circular & corresponding letters. Norwich: Printed by Sterry & Porter, 1805 [1973]
1 sheet. 7.5 x 12.5 cm. (The Library of Thomas Jefferson)
Copy owned by Thomas Jefferson.
Cf. Sabin 92164. Sowerby 1683.
Micro-transparency (positive) Washington, Microcard Editions, 1973.
Collation of the original: 8 p.
I. Title.
PSt NUC74-150675

Baptists. Florida. Convention.
The reaching people guide, Florida Baptist Convention, special emphasis, 1972-73. [Jacksonville, 1972?]
22 p. illus. 22 x 28 cm.
1. Evangelistic work. 2. Witness bearing (Christianity) I. Title.
KyLoS NUC75-26680

Baptists. Florida. Convention. Layman's Committee on Church Staff Salaries.
Florida church staff salaries; a study by a committee of laymen acting for the Florida Baptist State Convention. Rev. [n.p., 1972]
[40] p. illus. 22 x 28 cm.
Cover title.
1. Clergy—Salaries, pensions, etc. 2. Church finance. 3. Baptists—Clergy—Salaries, pensions, etc. I. Title.
KyLoS NUC75-26679

Baptists. Georgia. General Missionary Baptist Convention.
Souvenir program: state convention, Nov. 11-14, 1957. [Atlanta, 1957]
1 v. (unpaged) illus.
1. Baptist—Georgia. 2. Negroes—Religion.
WHi NUC75-75131

Baptists. Kentucky. Convention.
Kentucky Baptists and federal aid to education. [n.p., 1964?]
[4] p. 28 cm.
1. Baptists—Education. 2. Federal aid to higher education. I. Title.
KyLoS NUC73-1175

Baptists. Kentucky. Convention.
Missions in Kentucky. [n.p., 1967?]
[22] p. 28 cm.
1. Baptists—Kentucky. 2. Baptists—Missions. 3. Missions—Kentucky. I. Title.
KyLoS NUC73-1176

Baptists. Kentucky. Convention
see Mills, Robert Lee, 1916-
A matter of record. [n.p.] 1966.

Baptists. Kentucky. General Association. Brotherhood Dept.
New and enlarged royal ambassador program. [Prepared by Brotherhood Dept., Tennessee Baptist Convention. n.p., n.d.]
9 l. illus. 16 x 23 cm.
1. Royal Ambassadors. I. Baptists. Tennessee. Convention. Brotherhood Dept.
KyLoS NUC75-29658

Baptists. Kentucky. Long Run Association.
Christ, the hope of greater Louisville ... Season of prayer for associational missions, May 18-25, 1969 ... Louisville, Ky., 1969.
[40] p. 24 cm.
1. Missions—Louisville, Ky. 2. Baptists—Missions. I. Title.
KyLoS NUC73-47196

Baptists. Kentucky. Long Run Association.
Program material for season of prayer, associational missions, May 19-25, 1968. Louisville, Ky., Long Run Association of Baptists, 1968.
42 p. illus. 23 cm.
1. Baptists—Missions. 2. Missions—Kentucky. I. Title.
KyLoS NUC73-47195

Baptists. Kentucky. Long Run Association
see Boyd, J Leon. Program material for season of prayer... Louisville, Ky., 1967.

Baptists. Louisiana. Louisiana Baptist Convention.
see Greene, Glen Lee, 1915- Louisiana Baptist historical atlas. 1st ed. Alexandria, Executive Board of the Louisiana Baptist Convention, 1975.

Baptists. Maryland. Baptist Convention of Maryland. Historical Committee.
"...God gave the increase." [Lutherville, Md., 1971]
v, [ii], 65 p. illus. (ports.) 22 cm.
KyLoS NUC74-10539

Baptists. Maryland. State Association. State Mission Board
see Watts, Joseph T The rise and progress of Maryland Baptists, by Joseph T. Watts. [n.p.] Maryland Baptist Union Association, State Mission Board [195-?]

Baptists. Nebraska. Eastern Nebraska Association
see Eastern Nebraska Association.

Baptists. New Hampshire. New Hampshire Association.
Minutes of the New-Hampshire Association, held in the Baptist meeting-house in Epping, Wednesday and Thursday, June 12 and 13, 1805. Dover, N.H., Printed by S. Bragg, Jun., 1805.
11 p. 20 cm.
1. Baptists. New Hampshire. New Hampshire Association.
BX6248.N4B36 1805 77-351721
77 MARC

Baptists. New Hampshire. New Hampshire Association.
Minutes of the New-Hampshire Association, held in the parish of Gunstock, Gilmanton, Wednesday and Thursday, June 8 and 9, 1808. Portland, [Me.] Printed by W. Weeks and J. M'Kown, 1808.
12 p. 18 cm.
1. Baptists. New Hampshire. New Hampshire Association.
BX6248.N4B36 1808 77-351732
77 MARC

Baptists. New York. Hudson River Baptist Association
see Hudson River Baptist Association.

Baptists. North Carolina. Gaston Baptist Association
see
Gaston Baptist Association.

Baptists. Oklahoma. General Convention.
Report of future tax problems conference, February 24-26, 1969. Co-sponsored by Baptist General Convention of the State of Oklahoma and Baptist Joint Committee on Public Affairs. [n.p.] 1969.
7 p. 36 cm.
1. Church and state—Baptists. I. Baptist Joint Committee on Public Affairs. II. Title.
KyLoS NUC75-15432

Baptists. Oklahoma. General Convention.
see Raley, John Wesley, 1902-1968. Beyond survival. [Shawnee, Okla., Oklahoma Baptist University, 1960]

Baptists. Oklahoma. General Convention. Dept. of Child Care.
Hello! Why not see for yourself? [Oklahoma City, n.d.]
[4] p. illus. 22 cm.
I. Title.
KyLoS NUC73-78924

Baptists. Tennessee. Convention. Brotherhood Dept.
see Baptists. Kentucky. General Association. Brotherhood Dept. New and enlarged royal ambassador program. [n.p., n.d.]

Baptists. Tennessee. Convention. Executive Board.
Tennessee Baptists build to bring men to God through Jesus Christ. [Edited by Mrs. W. Alvis Strickland. Brentwood, Tenn., 1969?]
12 p. illus. 22 x 28 cm.
1. Baptists—Tennessee. I. Strickland, Mrs. W. Alvis, ed. II. Title.
KyLoS NUC74-29768

Baptists. Texas. General Convention. Association of Child Care Executives.
Messages from the challenge of Christian child care. First annual child care institute. [Dallas, Texas, 1958]
22 l.
Sponsored by the Association of Child Care Executives, Baptist General Convention of Texas, Highland Lakes Baptist Encampment, June 4-6, 1958.
1. Church work with children. I. Title.
TxFS NUC73-101641

Baptists. Virginia. General Association
see Moore, John S Meaningful moments... [Richmond, Va., Satterwhite Print.] 1973.

Baptists. Virginia. General Association. Woman's Missionary Union.
Circle devotional studies: laborers together with God, I Cor. 3:9. Richmond, Va. [n.d.]
61 p. 20 cm.
1. Bible—Study. 2. Devotional literature. I. Title.
KyLoS NUC76-76207

Baptists. Virginia. Woman's Missionary Union
see Baptists. Virginia. General Association. Woman's Missionary Union.

The Baptists [by Arthur D. Phelps. Latham, Kans., Kansas Baptist Convention, n. d.]
[14] p. illus. 16 cm.
1. Baptists—Doctrinal and controversial works. I. Phelps, Arthur D.
KyLoS NUC73-56268

Baptists and the American experience / James E. Wood, Jr., editor. — Valley Forge, Pa. : Judson Press, c1976.
384 p. ; 23 cm.
Bibliography: p. 361-376.
Includes index.
ISBN 0-8170-0721-0
1. Baptists—United States—Addresses, essays, lectures. I. Wood, James Edward.
BX6235.B36 286'.0973 76-22689
76 MARC

Baptists in Kentucky, 1776-1976 : a bicentennial volume / edited by Leo Taylor Crismon. — Middletown : Kentucky Baptist Convention, 1975.
vi, 330 p. ; 24 cm.
Includes bibliographical references.
1. Baptists—Kentucky. 2. Kentucky—Church history. I. Crismon, Leo T.
BX6248.K4B36 286'.1769 76-356672
76 MARC

Baptists of North America... Washington, D.C., 1972
see under North American Baptist Fellowship.

Baptists of the world, 1950 [i.e. 1905]-1970; recollections and reflections, by Josef Nordenhaug, J. D. Grey, Theodore F. Adams [and others] Fort Worth, Tex., Southern Baptists' Radio and Television Commission [1970]
103 p. ports. 23 cm.
1. Baptist World Alliance. I. Nordenhaug, Josef, 1903-1969. II. Adams, Theodore Floyd, 1898- III. Southern Baptists' Radio and Television Commission.
NcWfSB NUC76-24787

Baptists working together: laborers together with God for the advancement of his kingdom at home and abroad. [n.p., n.d.]
96 p. 20 cm.
Preface signed: M. A. Huggins.
Cover title.
1. Stewardship, Christian. I. Huggins, Maloy Alton, 1890-
KyLoS NUC74-6925

Baptizmanskiĭ, Vadim Ippolitovich.
(Teoriía kislorodno-konverternogo protsessa)
Теория кислородно-конвертерного процесса / В. И. Баптизманский. — Москва : Металлургия, 1975.
374, [2] p. : ill. ; 21 cm. USSR***
Bibliography : p. 366–[375]
2.24rub
1. Steel—Metallurgy—Oxygen processes. I. Title.
TN747.B36 75–584928

Bapty, Walter, 1884-
Memoirs. [Vancouver?] 1959.
1 v. (various pagings) 35 cm.
I. Title.
CaBVaU NUC74-168009

Bāpu, 1933- illus.
see Kandukuri Rudra Kavi, 16th cent. Kandukūri Rudrakavi Janārdanāstakam. [1968]

Bapu, Puthamkuzyihil Thomas.
Photoproduction of p⁺& p⁻ mesons in gamma deuterium interactions, by Puthamkuzhiyil Thomas Bapu. [Cincinnati] 1975.
62 l. ill. 29 cm.
Thesis (Ph.D.)--University of Cincinnati.
Includes abstract.
Bibliography.
OCU NUC77-92145

Bapu Deva Sastri, tr.
see The Súrya Siddhánta... Amsterdam, Philo Press [1974]

Bapu Reddy, J 1936–
In quest of harmony; [poetry, by] J. Bapu Reddy. [1st ed. Hyderabad, India, Sukhela Niketan, 1973]
[10], 66 p. 19 cm. Rs5.00 ($2.00U.S.)
I. Title.
PL4780.9.B34A24 73–906397
MARC

Bāpū Śāstrī Moghe
see
Moghe, Bāpū Śāstrī.

Bapurao Jagtap
see
Jagtap, Bapurao, 1944-

Bāpūrāva Jagatāpa
see
Jagtap, Bapurao, 1944-

Bāpūsāheba Kubade
see
Kubaḍe, K G

Bāpūśāstrī Moghe
see
Moghe, Bāpū Śāstrī.

Bapushree
see
Waghela, Jayendrasinhjee, 1904-

Bapuskopda
see
Indonesia. Badan Pusat Koordinasi Perusahaan Daerah
for publications by and about this body.
Titles and other entries beginning with this acronym are filed following this card.

Bapuśrī
see
Waghela, Jayendrasinhjee, 1904-

Baqā, Maẓhar, 1927–
(Uṣūl-i fiqh aur Shāh Valīullāh)
اصول فقہ اور شاہ ولی اللہ. [مصنف] مظہر بقا. [اشاعت 1.
اسلام آباد] ادارۂ تحقیقات اسلامی [1973]
13, 518 p. 25 cm. (سلسلہ مطبوعات ادارہ، نمبر 28) Rs22.00
In Urdu.
Bibliography: p. 504–518.
1. Waliullah, Shah, 1702 or 3–1762 or 3. 2. Islamic law. I. Title. II. Series: Islamic Research Centre. Silsilah-yi maṭbū'āt-i Idārah-yi Taḥqīqāt-i Islāmī, 28.
74–930117

Baqai, Mohammad Sabihuddin, 1914-
(Hamāre mu'āsharatī masā'il)
ہمارے معاشرتی مسائل : ایک عمرانیاتی جائزہ / صبیح الدین
بقائی. — اشاعت 1. — کراچی : شعبۂ تصنیف و تالیف و ترجمہ،
کراچی یونیورسٹی، 1974.
7, 212 p. ; 22 cm.
In Urdu.
Includes bibliographical references.
Rs8.50
1. Pakistan—Social conditions—Study and teaching. I. Title.
HN690.5.A8B35 74–930368

Baqai, Mohammad Sabihuddin, 1914-
Social order in Pakistani society / by M. Sabihuddin Baqai. — 1st ed. — Karachi : National Book Foundation, 1975.
xiii, 379 p. ; 22 cm.
Includes bibliographical references and index.
Rs50.00
1. Pakistan—Social conditions. I. Title.
HN690.5.A8B36 309.1'549'1 75-930375
76 MARC

Baqai, Moinuddin.
Development planning and policy in Pakistan, 1950–1970. Edited by Moin Baqai and Irving Brecher. Karachi, National Institute of Social & Economic Research [1973]
x, 186 p. illus. 23 cm. Rs20.00 ($5.00U.S.)
Bibliography : p. [175]–183.
1. Economic development. 2. Pakistan—Economic policy. I. Brecher, Irving, 1923– joint author. II. Title.
HC440.5.B28 338.9549 72–94636
MARC

Baqai, Moinuddin.
Pakistan's economic progress: possibilities of a take-off [by] Moin Baqai. [Montreal, McGill University, Centre for Developing-Area Studies, 1969]
v, 57 p. 22 cm. (McGill University, Montreal. Centre for Developing-Area Studies. Occasional paper series, no. 4) C***
Cover title.
Bibliography : p. 55–57.
1. Pakistan—Economic conditions. I. Title. II. Series.
HC440.5.B3 330.9'549'04 73–153157
MARC

Baqain, Hani Saleh.
Civil aviation law in Jordan, by Hani Saleh Baqain... Montréal, c1971.
[4], ii, [2], v, 166, [2] l.
Thesis (LL.M.)—McGill University.
Includes legislation.
Bibliography: p. [127]-137.
Microfilm. Ottawa, Central microfilm unit, Public archives of Canada, 1972. 1 reel. 35 mm. (National library of Canada. Canadian theses on microfilm, 9677)
1. Jordan. Laws, statutes, etc. Aviation law. 2. Aeronautics—Jordan. 3. Aeronautics, Commercial—Jordan. I. Title.
MH-L NUC76-93130

Baqal, Sabihuddin
see Latif, Muhammad. A dictionary of technical terms: sociology, English-Urdu. [Karachi] University of Karachi [1970]

al-Baqālī, Aḥmad 'Abd al-Salām, 1932–
(Yad al-maḥabbah)
يد المحبة : قصص / أحمد عبد السلام البقالي. —
الطبعة 1. — الرباط : وزارة الاوقاف والشؤون الاسلامية
والثقافة ، المديرية العامة للثقافة ، 1973.
158 p. ; 17 cm. — (سلسلة « والقلم » ; 4)
CONTENTS: يد المحبة. — لعبة الاعيان. — الياقوتة الزرقاء. — ولد الخادم. — الرقاص الاسود. — سلطان الطلبة.
I. Title. II. Series: Silsilat "Wa-al-qalam" ; 4.
PJ7816.A64Y3 76–960065

Bāqar, Āghā Muḥammad.
(Tārīkh-i naẓm o nas̱r-i Urdū)
تاریخ نظم و نثر اردو : یعنی زبان اردو کی مفصل تاریخ اور اس
کی عہد بعہد کی ترقیوں پر مفصل بحث . . . ریویو / مولف آغا محمد
باقر. — لاہور : شیخ مبارک علی, 1955.
8, 256 p. ; 24 cm.
In Urdu.
1. Urdu poetry—History and criticism. 2. Urdu prose literature—History and criticism. I. Title.
PK2167.B35 76–985969

Bāqar, Rashīd.
ہم کیوں روئے. [مصنف] رشید باقر. دہلی [1971]
158 p. 19 cm. Rs5.00
In Urdu.
A novel.
I. Title.
Title romanized: Ham kyūn ro'e.
PK2200.B3317H3 79–923774

Baqar, S. Ali, ed.
see Report on the performance of the industries taken-over by the Government of Pakistan on 2nd January 1972 under the Economic reforms order 1972. [Karachi] Pakistan Economist Research Unit [1972]

al-Baqarī, Aḥmad Māhir Maḥmūd.
(Laqaṭāt)
لقطات [تأليف] احمد ماهر محمود البقرى. الاسكندرية ، مؤسسة الثقافة الجامعية ، 1972.
113 p. 24 cm. £E0.30
Includes bibliographical references.
1. Aphorisms and apothegms. I. Title.
PN6277.A7B3 73-960822

al-Baqarī, Aḥmad Māhir Maḥmūd.
(Yūsuf fī al-Qur'ān)
يوسف فى القرآن ، تأليف احمد ماهر محمود البقرى. الاسكندرية ، مؤسسة الثقافة الجامعية [المقدمة 1971]
160 p. 24 cm. £E0.50
Includes bibliographical references.
1. Koran. Sūrat Yūsuf—Commentaries. 2. Joseph, the patriarch. I. Koran. Sūrat Yūsuf. II. Title.
BP128.4.B36 72-960717

Baqawī, Yūsuf Ibrāhīm.
(al-Asmā' al-Idrīsīyah al-sharīfah)
الأسماء الادريسية الشريفة / تأليف يوسف ابراهيم بقوى. — الطبعة 1. — [ام درمان : s. n., 1972]
64 p. ; 20 cm.
1. God (Islam)—Name. 2. Sufism. I. Title.
BP189.58.B36 76-971370

Baqbergenov, Săuīrbek.
(Dobrai͡a moi͡a mama)
Добрая моя мама; роман. Перевод В. Новикова. Агма-Ата, Жазушы, 1966.
298 p. illus. 21 cm.
I. Title.
PL65.K49R34 68-40243
rev

Baqbergenov, Săuīrbek.
(Kentau)
Кентау. Роман. Алматы, "Жазушы," 1973.
262 p. 21 cm. 0.59rub USSR 73-34511
I. Title.
PL65.K49B36 74-331896

Baqbergenov, Săuīrbek.
(Qargha tamghan qan)
Қарға тамған қан : роман-новелла / С. Бақбергенов. — Алматы : Жазушы, 1967.
169 p. ; 21 cm.
I. Title.
PL65.K49B364 75-972115

Baqbergenov, Săuīrbek.
(Qargha tamghan qan)
Қарға тамған қан : роман-новелла / С. Бақбергенов. — Алматы : Жазушы, 1967.
169 p. : port. ; 21 cm.
I. Title.
PL65.K49B364 1967b 75-972846

Baqī, Muhammad
see Muhammad Bāqī.

Baqi, Muhammad Fu'ād 'Abd al-
see 'Abd al-Baqi, Muhammad Fu'ād.

Bāqī, Samīr 'Abd al-
see 'Abd al-Bāqī, Samīr.

Bāqī Aḥmadpūrī.
(Bāqiyāt)
باقیات / باقی احمدپوری. — [لاہور] : پاکستان تھنکرز لیگ, [1974 or 1975]
128 p. ; 18 cm. — (پاکستان تھنکرز لیگ کی پیشکش ; 1)
In Urdu.
Poems.
Rs6.00
I. Title. II. Series: Pākistān Thinkarz Līg. Pākistān Thinkarz Līg kī peshkash ; 1.
PK2200.B3318B3 75-938794

Bāqī Billāh
see
Muhammad Bāqī.

Baqī'ī, Ghulām Ḥusayn.
اندیشه ، نگارش غلامحسین بقیعی. [تهران] کیهان ، 1342 [1963 or 4]
237, [2] p. illus. (part col.) 24 cm.
Bibliography: p. [239]
1. Senses and sensation. I. Title.
Title romanized: Andīshah.
QP431.B26 74-218470

al-Bāqillānī, Muḥammad ibn al-Ṭayyib, d. 1013.
[al-Intiṣār li-naql al-Qur'ān]
نكت الانتصار لنقل القرآن ، لأبى بكر الباقلانى. دراسة وتحقيق محمد زغلول سلام. الاسكندرية ، منشأة المعارف [1971?]
445 p. 24 cm. (كتب الدراسات القرآنية ، 1) £E1.25
Abridgment of the author's الانتصار لنقل القرآن by al-Ṣayrafī.
Includes bibliographical references.
1. Koran—History. 2. Koran—Criticism, Textual. I. al-Ṣayrafī, Muḥammad ibn 'Abd Allāh. II. Sallām, Muḥammad Zaghlūl, ed. III. Title.
Title romanized: Nukat al-Intiṣār li-naql al-Qur'ān.
BP131.B362 72-960377

al-Bāqillānī, Muḥammad ibn al-Ṭayyib, d. 1013.
[al-Tamhīd]
كتاب التمهيد ، تأليف ابي بكر محمد بن الطيب بن الباقلاني. عنى بتصحيحه ونشره رتشرد يوسف مكارثى. بيروت ، المكتبة الشرقية ، 1957.
46, 438, 13 p. facsims. 24 cm.
(منشورات جامعة الحكمة في بغداد. سلسلة علم الكلام ، 1)
Added t. p.: Kitāb at-tamhīd [by] Abū Bakr Muḥammad ibn aṭ-Ṭayyib al-Bāqillānī.
Introductory matter in Arabic and English.
Includes bibliographical references.
1. Islamic theology—Early works to 1800. I. McCarthy, Richard Joseph, ed. II. Title: al-Tamhīd. III. Series: Bagdad. al-Hikma University. Maṭbu'āt Jāmi'at al-Ḥikmah. IV. Series: Bagdad. al-Hikma University. Silsilat 'ilm al-kalām, 1.
Title romanized: Kitāb al-tamhīd.
BP166.B28 1957 74-214763

Baqir, Muhammad.
The Panjabi-English dictionary. Lahore, Panjabi Adabi Academy, 1970–
v. 24 cm. (Panjabi Adabi Academy publication no. 58–
Rs2.50 (v. 1)
Cover title.
Added back cover title in Punjabi: پنجابی - انگریزی لغت (romanized: Panjābī-Angrezī lughat)
Issued in parts.
1. Panjabi language—Dictionaries—English. I. Title. II. Title: Panjābī-Angrezī lughat.
PK2636.B34 491'.42'321 72-930267
MARC

Baqir, Muhammad.
(Urdū-yi qadīm Dakan aur Panjāb meṉ)
اردوے قدیم دکن اور پنجاب میں. از محمد باقر. لاہور، مجلس ترقی ادب [1972]
2, 376 p. 24 cm. Rs15.00
In Urdu.
Bibliography: p. 364-369.
1. Urdu language—History. I. Title.
PK1971.B3 72-931100

Baqir, Muhammad, ed.
see Allāhdād Fayẓī Sarhindī, d. 1595 or 6. Madār al-afāẓil. Panjab University Press, 1337-49 [1959-1970]

Baqir, Muhammad, ed.
see 'Awfī, Muhammad, fl. 1228. (Jami' al-hikāyāt-i Hindi) [1963]

Bāqir, Muḥammad
see also
Muḥammad Bāqir al-Mosavī al-Ṣafavī.

al-Bāqir, Muhammad, ṣāḥib Jarīdat al-balāgh
see al-Bi'thah al-'ilmīyah ilā Dār al-Khilāfah al-Islāmīyah. 1916.

al-Bāqir, Muhammad, sāhib Jarīdat al-Balāgh, ed.
see al-Khayyāt, Muhyī al-Dīn. (Durūs al-tārīkh al-Islāmī) 19

Bāqir, Muḥammad, 1923-
(Ā'imah arba'ah)
ائمہ اربعہ؛ جسمیں جمہور اہلسنت کے امام ابو حنیفہ، امام مالک، امام شافعیؒ، امام احمد بن حنبل کے تفصیلی حالات انتہائی تحقیق سے جمع کئے گئے ہیں ... مرتبہ محمد باقر النقوی. کجھوا، ضلع سارن، مطبوعہ اصلاح پریس، 1965.
400 p. 25 cm. Rs7.50
In Urdu.
1. Abu Hanīfah. d. 767 or 8. 2. Ibn Ḥanbal, Aḥmad ibn Muḥammad, 780-855. 3. Ja'far al-Ṣādiq, 702?-765 or 6. 4. Malik ibn Anas, d. 795. 5. al-Shāfi'ī, Muḥammad ibn Idrīs, 767 or 8-820. I. Ḥaydar, Asad. al-Imām al-ṣādiq wa-al-madhāhib al-arba'ah. II. Title.
BP70.B3 72-905130

Bāqir, Ṭāhā.
Aqar Quf, by Taha Baqir. 1st ed. Baghdad, Directorate General of Antiquities, 1959.
8 p. 15 plates. 24 cm.
At head of title: Title in cuneiform characters precedes title in Roman transcription: Dūr-ku-ri-gal-zu.
Translation of 'Aqarqūf.
Bibliography: p. 7.
1. Burj 'Aqarqūf, Iraq. I. Iraq. Mudīrīyat al-Āthār al-'Āmmah.
DS70.5.B8B3613 77-457324
77 MARC

Bāqir, Ṭāhā.
Babylon and Borsippa, by Taha Baqir. Baghdad, Govt. Press, 1959.
16 p. illus. 24 cm.
At head of title: Directorate General of Antiquities, Baghdad.
Title in cuneiform characters precedes title in English.
1. Babylon. 2. Borsippa. I. Iraq. Mudīrīyat al-Āthār al-'Āmmah. II. Title.
DS70.5.B3B36 913.35 74-210236

Bāqir, Ṭāhā.
تل حرمل ، شادوپوم القديمة. بقلم طه باقر. [الطبعة 1.] بغداد ، مطبعة الرابطة ، 1959.
8 p. facsims., fold. map., plans, plates. 25 cm.
Title in cuneiform, with romanization ša-du-pu-umki, precedes Arabic title.
At head of title: الجمهورية العراقية. مديرية الآثار العامة ، بغداد
Bibliography: p. 8.
1. Ḥarmal, Tall, Iraq. I. Iraq. Mudīrīyat al-Āthār al-Qadīmah al-'Āmmah. II. Title.
Title romanized: Tall Ḥarmal.
DS70.5.H27B36 77-970135

Bāqir, Taha, tr.
see Gilgamesh, Arabic. Malhamat Gilgāmish. [1971]

Bāqir al-Mosavī al-Ṣafavī, Muḥammad
see Muḥammad Bāqir al-Mosavī al-Ṣafavī.

Bāqir al-Shabībī
see
al-Shabībī, Muḥammad Bāqir, 1889-1960.

Bāqir Mahdī, 1932-
(Ṭūṭe shīshe kī ākhirī naẓmeṉ)
ٹوٹے شیشے کی آخری نظمیں. [شاعر باقر مہدی. بمبئی، گوشہ ادب، 1972]
135 p. 22 cm. Rs14.00
In Urdu.
I. Title.
PK2200.B332T8 72-908284

Bāqiriyān Humāyūnshahrī, Murtaẓá.
(Pīrāmūn-i Qur'ān va 'ahdayn)
پیرامون قرآن و عهدین (توراة و انجیل) نگارش مرتضی باقریان همایونشهری. [قم] چاپخانه حکمت ، 1350 [i. e. 1971]
232 p. 22 cm.
Includes bibliographical references.
1. Koran—Appreciation. 2. Koran—Relation to the Bible. I. Title.
BP130.7.B36 73-211167

al-Baqlī, Muḥammad Qandīl.
(al-Awzān al-mūsīqīyah fī azjāl Ibn Sūdūn)
الاوزان الموسيقية فى ازجال ابن سودون / محمد قنديل البقلى. — [القاهرة] : الهيئة المصرية العامة للكتاب ، 1976.
137 p. : ill. ; 28 cm.
ISBN 977-201-127-1 : £E0.80
1. Ibn Sūdūn al-Bashbughāwī, 'Alī, 1407 or 8-1464—Style. I. Title.
PJ7760.I 275Z6 77-960037

al-Baqlī, Muḥammad Qandīl
see al-Qalqashandī, Aḥmad ibn 'Alī, 1355 or 6-1418. Ṣubḥ al-a'shá. [1964]

Baqqādī, Aḥmad 'Alī.
('Alá al-sullam)
على السلم / احمد على بقادى. — [الخرطوم ؟ : s. n., 196-?]
56 p. ; 22 cm.
A novel.
I. Title.
PJ7816.A653A8 75-587882

al-Baqqāl, 'Abd al-Husayn Muhammad 'Alī, ed.
see Ibn al-Mutahhar al-Hillī, al-Hasan ibn Yūsuf, 1250-1325. Mabādi' al-wusūl ila ilm al-usūl. [1970]

Baqqūsh, 'Abd al-'Azīz
see Jāmī, 1414-1492. [Yūsuf va Zulaykhā. Arabic] Qiṣṣat Yūsuf wa-Zulaykhā. [1975]

Baqué, Françoise, 1946–
Le nouveau roman. Paris, Bordas [1972]
146 p. 17 cm. (Collection Bordas-connaissance. Série information, 34) 8.00F F***
Bibliography: p. 140–144.
1. French fiction—20th century—History and criticism. I. Title.
PQ671.B29 73–309529

Baqué, Gilbert.
Le Temps à perdre, poèmes. Honfleur, P. J. Oswald, 1970.
47 p. 18 cm.
Microfiche copy. 1 sheet. 11 x 15 cm. (NYPL FSN 15, 689)
I. Title.
NN NUC76-72747

Baqué, José-Carlos Mainer
see
Mainer, José-Carlos.

Baque, Lydie.
L'association andésitique cénozoïque de Logudoro et du Bosano (Sardaigne nord occidentale), au sein de l'ensemble du volcanisme andésitique calco-alcalin de l'île / par Lydie Baque. — Saint-Jérôme : Laboratoire de géologie dynamique, 1974.
193 p., [2] fold. leaves of plates : ill. ; 30 cm. — (Travaux des Laboratoires des sciences de la terre ; sér. B, 9) F***
Originally presented as the author's thesis, Aix-Marseille.
Bibliography: p. 187-193.
Free.
1. Andesite—Sardinia. 2. Volcanism—Sardinia. I. Title: L'association andésitique cénozoïque de Logudoro et du Bosano ...
QE462.A5B36 1974 552'.2 75-510988
75 MARC

Baqué, Monique
see Initiation aux arts plastiques. Paris, Bordas, 1966-

Baqué, Monique
see Initiation aux arts plastiques. [Paris] Bordas [1971-

Baqué, Monique
see Initiation aux arts plastiques. [Paris] Bordas [1972]

Baqué, Pierre.
Forgeage à chaud : transferts thermiques en frappe à chaud / P. Baqúe et P. Fernier. — [Senlis] : Centre technique des industries mécaniques, 1975.
71 p. : ill. ; 30 cm. — (Mémoires techniques du CETIM; 21) F***
Cover title.
Summary in English, French, German and Russian.
Bibliography: p. 70-71.
60.00F
1. Forging. 2. Heat—Transmission. I. Fernier, P., joint author. II. Title. III. Series: Centre technique des industries mécaniques. Mémoires techniques du CETIM ; 21.
TS225.B27 671.2 76-453678
76 MARC

Baqué, Pierre
see Mise en forme des métaux... Paris, Dunod [1973]

Baqueiro, Eloísa Ruíz Carvalho de.
Tradiciones, folklore, música y músicos de Campeche. Campeche, Publicaciones del Gobierno del Estado de Campeche, 1970.
141 p. illus., ports. (Campeche, Mexico (State) Publicaciones, 14)
Includes musical scores (1 fold.) and lyrics.
Includes bibliography.
1. Folk-lore—Mexico—Campeche. 2. Folk music—Mexico—Campeche. I. Title.
AzU NUC73-38296

Baqueiro Fóster, Gerónimo.
La canción popular de Yucatán, 1850-1950. México, Editorial del Magisterio, 1970.
319 p.
1. Mexican ballads and songs—Yucatan. I. Title.
InU NUC74-135045

Baquer, Lorenzo Martín-Retortillo
see Martín-Retortillo Baquer, Lorenzo.

Baquer, Sebastián Martín-Retortillo
see Martín-Retortillo Baquer, Sebastián.

Baquer Ferrer, Saturnino.
Comentarios sobre economía altoaragonesa / Saturnino Baquer Ferrer. — Huesca : Cámara Oficial de Comercio e Industria, 1974.
208 p. ; 22 cm. — (Publicaciones de la Cámara Oficial de Comercio e Industria, Huesca) Sp 74–Oct
Articles previously published in Economia altoaragonesa.
ISBN 84-500-6518-6
1. Aragón—Economic conditions—Addresses, essays, lectures. 2. Aragón—Economic policy—Addresses, essays, lectures. I. Title. II. Series: Huesca, Spain (Province). Cámara Oficial de Comercio e Industria. Publicaciones de la Cámara Oficial de Comercio e Industria, Huesca.
HC387.A68B365 75–401036

Baquerisse, Louis, 1874-1939
see Lourdes. Musée pyrénéen. Bibliothèque. Un fonds occitan de la Bibliothèque du Musée pyrénéen... Pau, Impr. Marrimpouey jeune, 1973.

Baquerizo, Jorge Enrique Zavala
see Zavala Baquerizo, Jorge Enrique, 1922-

Baquero, Fabián Núñez
see Núñez Baquero, Fabián.

Baquero, Francisco Ruiz-Jarabo y
see Ruiz-Jarabo y Baquero, Francisco.

Baquero, Gaston, joint author
see Bravo Villasante, Carmen. Gertrudis Gómez de Avellaneda ... Madrid : Fundacíon Universitaria Española, 1974.

Baquero, Jesus Bravo.
El movimiento Latinoamericano de reforma Universitaria en Michoacan; la Universidad Michoacana en su primer cincuentenario. Morelia, Universidad Michoacana de San Nicolas de Hidalgo, 1968.
281 p. 24 cm.
Apendice: Cuadernos Universitarios de la Sociedad de Profesores "Melchor Ocampo."
1. Morelia. Universidad Michoacana de San Nicolás de Hidalgo. I. Title.
MiA LbC NUC75-108919

Baquero Borda, Hernando.
La Policía Judicial : organización y funcionamiento / Hernando Baquero Borda. — Bogotá : Impr. Nacional, 1973.
249 p. ; 24 cm.
"Legislación": p. [225]-249.
1. Colombia. Policía Judicial. I. Title.
76-483727
76 MARC

Baquero de la Calle, José A
El derecho interamericano frente al comunismo internacional. [Disertación sustentada ante los micrófonos de la radio emisora Casa de la cultura ecuatoriana, el 14 de junio de 1957. Quito, Liga universitaria antimarxista, 1957?]
14 p. 15 cm.
Microfiche (neg.) 1 sheet, 11 x 15 cm.
1. Law and socialism.
NN NUC76-17669

Baquero de la Calle, José A
see Mississippi. State University. College of Business and Industry. A proposal for the improvement of the cooperative system in Ecuador. State College, Miss. [1962]

Baquero González, Antonio García-
see García-Baquero González, Antonio.

Baquero Goyanes, Mariano, 1923–
Estructuras de la novela actual. [1. ed.] Barcelona, Editorial Planeta [1970]
244 p. 22 cm. (Ensayos/Planeta)
Includes bibliographical references.
1. Fiction—Technique. I. Title.
PN3365.B3 1970 77–276220
rev

Baquero Goyanes, Mariano, 1923–
Estructuras de la novela actual. [2. ed.] Barcelona, Planeta [1972]
250 p. 22 cm. (Ensayos Planeta) 300ptas Sp 73–Mar
Includes bibliographical references.
1. Fiction—Technique. I. Title.
PN3365.B3 1972 73–366338

Baquero Goyanes, Mariano, 1923–
Temas, formas y tonos literarios. [Madrid] Prensa Española, 1972.
275 p. 18 cm. (El Soto, 16) 170ptas Sp 72–Apr
Includes bibliographical references.
1. Spanish literature—Addresses, essays, lectures. 2. Literature, Comparative—Addresses, essays, lectures. I. Title.
PQ6039.B3 72–363260

Baquero Goyanes, Mariano, 1923–
Visualidad y perspectivismo en las "empresas" de Saavedra Fajardo. Discurso leído el día 10 de Marzo de 1970 en su recepción pública por el Iltmo. Sr. Don Mariano Baquero Goyanes y contestación del Iltmo Sr. Don Manuel Muñoz Cortés. Murcia, 1969.
48 p. 24 cm. Sp 71–July/Aug/Sept
At head of title: Academia Alfonso X el Sabio.
1. Saavedra Fajardo, Diego de, 1584–1648. 2. Political science. 3. Kings and rulers—Duties. I. Muñoz Cortés, Manuel. II. Title.
JC160.S35B37 73–315411

Baquero Goyanes, Mariano, 1923-
see Alarcón, Pedro Antonio de, 1833-1891. El escándalo... Madrid, Espasa-Calpe, 1973.

Baquero Goyanes, Mariano, 1923-
see Cervantes Saavedra, Miguel de, 1547-1616. Novelas ejemplares. Madrid, Editora Nacional, D.L. 1976.

Baquero Goyanes, Mariano, 1923-
see Estudios literarios dedicados al profesor Mariano Baquero Goyanes. Murcia [s.n.] 1974.

Baquero Miguel, Godeardo.
Pesquisa psico-social; pontos básicos de estatística. [Brasília, Universidade de Brasília, Faculdade de Educação, 1968]
68 p. illus. 31 cm.
Bibliography: p. [67]–68.
1. Social sciences—Statistical methods. 2. Statistics. I. Title.
HA29.5.P6B3 72–224038

Baquero Morales, Lucrecia, joint author
see Bohorquez C , José Ignacio. Indice de los principales articulos de las revistas coleccionadas en la biblioteca de la ESAP hasta Julio de 1963. [n.p., n.d.]

al-Bāqūrī, Aḥmad Ḥasan.
(Fī 'ālam al-ṣayd)
في عالم الصيد ‹تأليف› احمد حسن الباقوري. الطبعة 1.
‹بيروت ؟› 1973.
254 p. 25 cm.
Bibliography: p. 247-249.
1. Hunting—Arab countries. I. Title.
SK247.A7B36 74-233662

Bar Hebraeus, 1226-1286. Ausar raze. English and Syriac. 1930
Walker, Henry Hammersley. The scholia of Bar Hebraeus on the book of Jeremiah. 1930.

Bar Hebraeus, 1226-1286.
Le candélabre du sanctuaire de Grégoire Abou'lfaradj dit Barhebræus. Dixième base: De la résurrection. Texte syriaque édité pour la première fois avec traduction française par Élise Zigmund-Cerbü. Turnhout, Brepols, 1969.
64 p. 27 cm. (Patrologia Orientalis, t. 35, fasc. 2) Be***
Syriac text and French translation of Menarat kudshe. Shet'esta 10.
Pages also numbered 222-280.
1. Resurrection—Early works to 1800. I. Zigmund-Cerbü, Élise, ed. II. Title: Le candélabre du sanctuaire. Dixième base: De la résurrection. III. Series.
BR60.P25 t. 35, fasc. 2 72-359253
[BT870]

NjPT InU IEG TxFTC

Bar Hebraeus, 1226-1286.
The Kĕthābhā dhē- Yaunā or Book of the Dove, an ascetic treatise for the use of monks, by Barhebraeus. [14th cent. n. p., n. d.]
[187] l.
Microfilm copy (positive)
Original in the Library of the University of Cambridge. Add. 2012.
1. Mysticism—Jacobite Church. I. Title.
CU NUC74-10396

Bar Hebraeus, 1226-1286.
The laughable stories / collected by Gregory John Bar-Hebraeus ; the Syriac text edited with an English translation by E. A. Wallis Budge. — New York : AMS Press, 1976.
xxvii, 204, 166 p. ; 23 cm.
Translation of Kĕthābhā dhĕ thunnāyē meghahĕkhānē.
Reprint of the 1897 ed. published by Luzac, London, which was issued as v. 1 of Luzac's Semitic text and translation series.
Includes index.
ISBN 0-404-11347-8
1. Wit and humor, Medieval. I. Title. II. Series: Luzac's Semitic text and translation series ; v. 1.
PJ5671.B35K513 1976 892'.3 73-18852
76 MARC

Bar Hebraeus, 1226-1286.
The scholia of Barhebraeus on the Book of the Twelve Prophets. [Edited] by Frank Garrett Ward. Chicago, 1933.
iii, 112 l. 32 cm.
The editor's thesis—University of Chicago.
An edited translation of a section of the Auṣar rāzē, or "Storehouse of mysteries."
Bibliographical footnotes.
Microfilm. Chicago, Dept. of Photoduplication, University of Chicago Library [1967?]
1 reel. 35 mm.
1. Bible. O. T. Minor prophets—Commentaries. I. Ward, Frank Garrett, 1893- ed. II. Title.
CBGTU NUC76-72748

Bar Hebraeus, 1226-1286.
(Tārīkh mukhtaṣar al-duwal)
تاريخ مختصر الدول، لغريغوريوس الملطي المعروف بابن العبري. وقف على طبعه ووضع حواشيه انطون صالحانى اليسوعي. بيروت، المطبعة الكاثوليكية، 1958.
6, 345 p. 25 cm.
Reprint of the 1890 ed.
Includes bibliographical references.
1. Islamic Empire—History. 2. Near East—History—To 622. I. Salhani, Antoine, ed. II. Title.
DS38.2.B37 1958 75-587495

Bar Hebraeus, 1226-1286
see Book of Hierotheus. The book which is called the Book of the holy Hierotheos. [Farnborough, Gregg International Publishers, 1969]

Bar, Adam.
Słownik pseudonimów i kryptonimów pisarzy polskich oraz Polski dotyczących. Opracował Adam Bar przy współudziale Wł. Tad. Wisłockiego i Tad. Godłowskiego. Kraków, 1936-38. Nendeln/Liechtenstein, Kraus Reprint, 1968.
3 v. in 1. 25 cm. (Prace bibljoteczne Krakowskiego Koła Zwiazku Bibliotekarzy Polskich, 7-9)
1. Anonyms and pseudonyms, Polish. 2. Anonyms and pseudonyms. I. Wisłocki, Władysław Tadeusz, 1887- II. Godłowski, Tadeusz. III. Title. IV. Series: Stowarzyszenie Bibliotekarzy Polskich. Krakowskie Koło. Prace biblioteczne, 7-9.
NIC NjP PPT NUC74-121533
TxU MiDW DGW LU

Bar, Christian von, 1952-
Territorialität des Warenzeichens und Erschöpfung des Verbreitungsrechts im Gemeinsamen Markt / von Christian von Bar. — 1. Aufl. — Frankfurt am Main : Metzner, 1977.
167 p. ; 24 cm. — (Arbeiten zur Rechtsvergleichung ; 86 ISSN 0066-5703)
GFR77-A
Bibliography: p. 158-167.
ISBN 3-7875-0186-X : DM42.00
1. Trade-marks—European Economic Community countries. 2. Trade-marks—Germany, West. I. Title: Territorialität des Warenzeichens ... II. Series.
77-472653
77 MARC

Bar, Decio.
No temporal. [São Paulo] Gráfica Editôra Hamburg [1965]
53 p. (Coleção maldoror, 3)
MH NUC75-21638

Bar, Elvire D
Dictionnaire des synonymes [par] Elvire D. Bar. Paris, Garnier frères [1972, c1967]
vi, 394 p. 19 cm.
1. French language—Synonyms and antonyms. I. Title.
IEdS NUC73-114747

Bar, Henry.
Les pierres levées; portes de la vie. Paris, Julliard [1973]
313 p. illus. 21 cm. 36.40F F***
Includes bibliographical references.
1. Megalithic monuments. 2. Tombs. I. Title.
GN792.E8B37 913.36 74-161549
MARC

Bar, Irena
see Lenartowicz, Teofil, 1822-1893. Katalog wystawy w Bibliotece Jagiellońskiej. Kraków [Wydawn. naukowe Wyzszej Szkoły Pedag. w Krakowie] 1972.

Bar, Joachim Roman, comp.
Polska bibliografia teologii i prawa kanonicznego za lata 1949-1968. Warszawa, Akademia Teologii Katolickiej, 1972.
455 p. 24 cm.
At head of title: Joachim Roman Bar, Remigiusz Sobański.
Table of contents also in French.
1. Religious literature, Polish—Bibliography. 2. Canon law—Bibliography. I. Sobański, Remigiusz, joint comp. II. Title.
Z7757.P6B32 74-209156

Bar, Joachim Roman.
Prawo zakonne po Soborze Watykańskim II. Warszawa, Akademia Teologii Katolickiej, 1971.
264 p. 25 cm.
Summary in Latin.
Bibliography: p. [253]-262.
1. Monasticism and religious orders (Canon law) I. Title.
75-565935

Bar, Joachim Roman.
O zakonach, o osobach świeckich. Warszawa, Akademia Teologii Katolickiej, 1968.
382 p. 25 cm. (Zarys prawa kanonicznego: t. 2. Prawo osobowe, zesz. 4)
Includes bibliographical references.
1. Monasticism and religious orders (Canon law) 2. Laity (Canon law) I. Title. II. Series.
75-575258

Bar, Joachim Roman
see Blogoslawiony Maksymilian Maria Kolbe ... Niepokalanów, OO. Franciszkanie, 1974.

Bar, Joachim Roman, ed.
see O. Maksymilian Kolbe... Warszawa, Akademia Teologii Katolickiej, 1971.

Bar, Joachim Roman, ed.
see Studia o ojcu Maksymilianie Kolbe. Warszawa, Akademia Teologii Katolickiej, 1971.

Bar, Joseph
see
Bar Yosef, Yosef, 1933-

Bar, Karl Ludwig von, 1836-1913.
Recht und Beweis im Civilprocesse, ein Beitrag zur Kritik und Reform des deutschen Civilprocesses von K. von Bar. Leipzig, B. Tauchnitz, 1867. [Leipzig, Zentral-Antiquariat der deutschen Demokratischen Republik, 1968]
xviii, 270 p.
1. Jury—Germany. 2. Evidence—Germany. 3. Criminal law—Germany. I. Title.
CSt-Law NUC76-74988

Bar, Leo, 1880-
Die illustrierten Historienbücher des 15. Jahrhunderts. Leo Baer. Osnabrück, O. Zeller, 1973.
213, xcvi p. ill. 28 cm.
The first part was presented as inaugural dissertation, Heidelberg, 1902.
"Verzeichnis der benutzten Litteratur": p. [13]-17.
"Anhang": p. [iii]-xcvi.
"Neudruck der Ausgabe von 1903."
ISBN: 3-535-01314-3.
1. Illustrated books—15th and 16th cent. 2. Printing—Hist. 3. Engraving—Hist. I. Title.
CU-SB NUC76-74987

Bar, Ludwik, ed.
see Grupowanie przedsiebiorstw panstwowych... Wrocław, Zakład Narodowy im. Ossolińskich, 1972.

Bar, Ludwik
see Instytucje prawa administracyjnego europejskich panstw socjalistycznych. Wroclaw, Zaklad Narodowy im. Ossolinskich, 1973.

Bar, Ludwik, ed.
see Poland. Laws, statutes, etc. Kodeks budowlany; przepisy i objaśnienia. Warszawa, Wydawn. Prawnicze, 1972.

Bar, Ludwik
see Polska Akademia Nauk. Instytut Nauk Prawnych. Studia z dziedziny prawa administracyjnego. Wrocław, Zakł. narodowy im. Ossolińskich, 1971.

Bar, Ludwik, ed.
see Studia z dziedziny prawa administracyjnego. Wroclaw, Zaklad Narodowy im. Ossolinskich, 1971.

Bar, Varda.
Solar seeing in Israel and Sinai; an investigation of seeing properties during daytime and climatological conditions of locations in Israel and surroundings that might provide the site for a solar observatory. Jerusalem, Israel Academy of Sciences and Humanities, 1972.
24, xviii p. illus. 27 cm. (Publications of the Israel Academy of Sciences and Humanities. Section of Sciences) IL6.00
Bibliography: p. 24.
1. Sun—Observations. 2. Israel—Climate. 3. Astronomical observatories—Israel. I. Title.
QB539.B3 523.7'07'23 72-950661
MARC

Bar, Varda
see Meteorological conditions at the Mizpe Ramon observatory site... Jerusalem, Israel Academy of Sciences and Humanities, 1972.

Bar, Yiśra'el.
(Bonim bayit)
בונים בית : סיפורים / ישראל בר. — תל־אביב : אל"ף - הוצאת ספרים, c1976.
177 p. ; 22 cm.
1. Bar, Yiśra'el. 2. Kefar Vitkin, Israel—Biography. I. Title.
HD1491.P32K432 77–951058

Bar, Yosef
see
Bar Yosef, Yosef, 1933-

Bar-Aba
see
Fleischer, Ezra.

Bar-Adon, Aaron.
Analogy and analogic change as reflected in contemporary Hebrew. [The Hague] Mouton, 1964.
[758]-763 p. 28 cm.
Offprint from Proceedings of the Ninth International Congress of Linguists, Cambridge, Mass., 1962.
1. Hebrew language—Analogy. I. Title.
OCH NUC74-122546

Bar-Adon, Aaron.
Child bilingualism in an immigrant society: implications of borrowing in the Hebrew 'language of games'. [n.p., 1973?]
264-317 p. 29 cm.
Photocopy of typescript.
1. Hebrew language. 2. Children—Language. 3. Bilingualism—Israel. I. Title.
OCH NUC74-126744

Bar-Adon, Aaron.
The evolution of modern Hebrew. New York, American Histadrut Cultural Exchange Institute, 1965.
65-95 p. 22 cm.
Reprint from Acculturation and integration.
1. Hebrew language. I. Title.
OCH NUC74-122537

Bar-Adon, Aaron.
Modern Israeli Hebrew. Austin, Jenkins Pub. Co., 1971-
v. 29 cm.
1. Hebrew language—Text-books for foreigners—English. I. Title.
OCH NUC75-21639

Bar-Adon, Aaron.
New imperative and jussive formations in contemporary Hebrew. [n.p., 1966]
410-413 p. 26 cm.
Offprint from Journal of the American Oriental Society, vol. 86, Oct/Dec. 1966.
1. Hebrew language—Imperative. I. Title.
OCH NUC74-122554

Bar-Adon, Aaron.
Primary syntactic structures in Hebrew child language. Englewood Cliffs, N.J., Prentice-Hall, 1971.
434-472 p. 28 cm.
Photocopy from Bar-Adon, A., and W.F. Leopold, eds., Child language.
1. Hebrew language—Syntax. 2. Children—Language. I. Title.
OCH NUC74-122536

Bar-Adon, Aaron.
The rise and decline of a dialect : a study in the revival of modern Hebrew / by Aaron Bar-Adon. — The Hague : Mouton, 1975.
116 p. : map ; 26 cm. — (Janua linguarum : Series practica ; 197)
Ne75-48
Bibliography: p. [91]-95.
Includes index.
fl 36.00
1. Hebrew language—Revival. 2. Hebrew language—Dialects—Galilee. I. Title. II. Series.
PJ4551.B3 492.4'7 74-80121
*76 MARC

Bar-Adon, Pessah, 1907–
(Telem ba-yam)
תלם בים; סיפור [מאת] פ. בר־אדון. מרחביה, הקיבוץ הארצי השומר הצעיר [1946]
264 p. 18 cm. (נעורים)
I. Title.
PJ5053.B22T4 73–212099

Bar-Adon, Pessah, 1907-
see (Yehudah, Shomron ve-Golan: seker ark-he'ologi bi-shenat tav-shin-kaf-het) [1972]

Bar-Adon, Shemu'el Binyamin.
[Ne'ume Shemu'el]
ספר נאומי שמואל : הגיונות ומחשבות על כל פרשיות התורה ... / מאתי שמואל בנימין בר־אדון. — חיפה : בר־אדון, [1936] 697.
223 p. ; 23 cm.
1. Bible. O. T. Pentateuch — Sermons. 2. Sermons, Jewish — Palestine. 3. Sermons, Hebrew—Palestine. I. Title: Ne'ume Shemu'el.
Title romanized: Sefer Ne'ume Shemu'el.
BS1225.B26 1936 76–951253

Bar-Am, Micha
see Situation: Israeli photographers '74. Jerusalem [1974]

Bar-Amon, A., joint author
see Ben-Hanan, Eli. Israel October 73, Yom Kippur War. Tel Aviv, Masad [1974?]

Bar-Avi, Israel.
Esseuri. Jerusalim, Cenaclul Literar "Menora," 1967.
53, 24 p. illus. (Pagini de istorie evreeasca) (Cenaclul Literar "Menora," Jerusalem. [Lucrari] 50)
Added t.p. in Hebrew.
Three essays in Romanian, one in Hebrew.
InU NUC73-33743

Bar-Avi, Israel.
Inseminări istorice şi literare (culegere). Jerusalim, 1959.
41, 10 p. 21 cm. (Pagini de istorie evreeasca, 2)
1. Jews in Romania—Addresses, essays, lectures. 2. Israel—Addresses, essays, lectures. I. Title. II. Series.
OCH NUC74-33079

Bar-Avi, Israel.
O istorie a Evreilor romani. Jerusalim, Cenaclul literar Menora [1964-
v. ports. 24 cm. (Scriitori din aliaua romana)
Microfiche (negative) 5 sheets. 11 x 15 cm. (NYPL FSN-2992)
Contents.—v.2. Evreii romani in lumina conferintelor si tratatelor de pace din 1918-1919.
1. Jews in Romania. 2. Romania—Hist. I. Series.
NN NUC73-38290

Bar-Avi, Israel.
Samson Lazar : (Lascar Şaraga) : retrospectivă (1872-1968) : volum comemorativ la doi ani de la moartea sa (5 iulie 1968-5 iulie 1970) ; / Israel Bar-Avi ; cu o evocare de Costică Motaş. — Ierusalim : [Cenaclul Literar Menora], 1970.
50 p. ; 22 cm. — (Cenaclul Literar "Menora" ; 90) (Scriitori ai generaţiei mele)
Cover title.
Includes bibliographical references.
1. Lazar, Samson—Biography. 2. Authors, Romanian—Biography. I. Series: Cenaclul Literar "Menora," Jerusalem. Lucrări ; 90.
PC839.L3Z59 77-460457
77 MARC

Bar-Avi, Israel
see Lieberman, Emanuel. Versuri... Jerusalim, Cenaclul Literar "Menora", 1971.

Bar Chaim, Dan, ed.
see Israel. Laws, statutes, etc. (Pekudat peshitat ha-regel 1936) c1973-

Bar-Dayan, Haim
see
Borodianski, Haim.

Bar-Dayan, Yehoshua.
Diary of a soldier, May-June 1967. Tr. from the Hebrew by E.A. Levenston. [Bombay, Indo-Israel Friendship League, 1967]
44 p. illus. 25 cm.
1. Israel-Arab War, 1967- -Personal narratives. I. Title.
PPT NUC73-2834

Bar-Droma, Joshua, 1900–1964.
המדיניות הפיננסית של מדינת־יהודה בימי הבית הראשון והשני [מאת] יהושע בר־דרומא. ירושלים, המוסיאון למסים, מינהל הכנסות המדינה, 1967.
65 p. port. 21 cm. IL3.00
Added t. p.: The finance policy of Judea during the period of the First and Second Temples.
"לביה"ס הגבוה למישפט ולכלכלה 'מכלל' בת"א ... בעבודת־סמיכה."
Bibliography: p. 62–65.
1. Finance, Public—Judea. 2. Bible. O. T.—Economics. I. Title.
Title romanized: ha-Mediniyut ha-finansit shel Medinat-Yehudah.
HJ214.B37 HE 68–4631
PL 480 : Is–5600

Bar-Haim, David
see The Tax system of Israel. Jerusalem, Museum of Taxes, State Revenue Administration, 1969.

Bar-Ḥayim, 'Imanu'el.
[Ba-derekh el Ramat Raḥel]
בדרך אל רמת רחל [מאת] עמנואל בר־חיים. [עריכה: שמשון מלצר] ירושלים, הספריה הציונית, 732 [1972]
352 p. illus. 22 cm. IL12.00
I. Title.
CT1919.P38B34 72–950602

Bar-Hillel, Yehoshua.
Argumentation in pragmatic languages. Jerusalem [Israel Academy of Sciences and Humanities] 1970.
15 p. 24 cm. (Israel Academy of Sciences and Humanities. Proceedings, v. 4, no. 8)
Cover title.
Translation of Ti'unim bi-sefot pragmatiyot.
Includes bibliographical references.
1. Languages—Philosophy. 2. Logic. I. Title. II. Series.
AS591.I 812 vol. 4, no. 8 74–151076
[P39] MARC

Bar-Hillel, Yehoshua, joint author
see Fraenkel, Abraham Adolf, 1891-1965. Foundations of set theory. 2d rev. ed. Amsterdam, Noord-Hollandsche U. M., 1973.

Bar-Hillel, Yehoshua
see Gracia, Francisco, comp. Presentación del lenguaje. [Madrid] Taurus (1972)

Bar-Hillel, Yehoshua, ed.
see International Colloquium on Mathematical Logic and Foundations of Set Theory, Jerusalem, 1968. Mathematical logic and foundations of set theory ... Amsterdam, North-Holland Pub. Co., 1970.

Bar-Hillel, Yehoshua, ed.
see International Congress for Logic, Methodology, and Philosophy of Science, 2d, Jerusalem, 1964. Logic, methodology, and philosophy of science ... Amsterdam, North-Holland Pub. Co., 1965.

Bar-Hillel, Yehoshua.
see Language in focus ... Dordrecht, Holland, D. Reidel Pub. Co., c1976.

Bar-Hillel, Yehoshua, ed.
see Pragmatics of natural languages. New York, Humanities Press, [1971]

Bar-Hillel, Yehoshua, ed.
see Pragmatics of natural languages. Dordrecht, Reidel, [1972].

Bar-Ilan, Meir, 1880–1949.
(Igrot)
אגרות / מאיר בר־אילן ; בעריכת נתנאל קצבורג. — רמת־גן :
אוניברסיטת בר־אילן, [ ]1976– [ ].736–
v. ; 23 cm.
Half title: Igrot ha-Rav Me'ir Bar-Ilan.
Added t. p.: Letters.
Includes bibliographical references and index.
CONTENTS: כרך 1 תרס"ג־תרפ"ח (1903–1928)
1. Mizrachi. 2. Bar-Ilan, Meir, 1880–1949. 3. Zionists—Correspondence. I. Katzburg, Nathaniel. II. Title: Igrot ha-Rav Me'ir Bar-Ilan.
DS150.R35B37 1976 76–952001

Bar-Ilan, Meir, 1880–1949, ed.
see Entsiklopedyah talmudit. [1947-

Bar-Joseph, M
(Bi'ografyot shel ḥakhme ha-Mishnah)
ביאוגרפיות של חכמי המשנה. מאת מ. בר יוסף. [תל־אביב,
מכון מרדכי, 1969 or 70]
48 p. 23 cm.
1. Tannaim. I. Title.
BM501.2.B37 75–953288

Bar-Joseph, M., ed.
see Mishnah. 1966- 727-

Bar-Joseph, M., ed.
see Moses ben Maimon, 1135-1204. Rabenu Mosheh ben Maimon. [1970

Bar-Kochba, Yoseph.
Rainfall and floods in northeastern Ohio, by Yoseph Bar-Kochba and Andrew L. Simon. [Akron] Dept. of Civil Engineering, University of Akron, 1971.
87 p. tables. 21 cm.
1. Floods–Ohio. 2. Meteorology–Ohio. I. Simon, Andrew L., joint author. II. Title.
OU NUC75-108460

Bar-Kochva, Bezalel.
The Seleucid army : organization and tactics in the great campaigns / Bezalel Bar Kochva. — Cambridge [Eng.] ; New York : Cambridge University Press, 1976.
xi, 306 p. : maps ; 23 cm. — (Cambridge classical studies) GB***
Bibliography: p. [277]–294.
Includes index.
ISBN 0-521-20667-7
1. Military art and science—History. 2. Military history, Ancient. 3. Seleucids. I. Title. II. Series.
U31.B37 355'.00935 76-365118
76 MARC

Bar-Kokhva, Betsal'el
see
Bar-Kochva, Bezalel.

Bar-Lev, Hayim
see 'Al ha-mefakdim ha-holkhim ba-rosh. 1968.

Bar-Lev, Moshe.
Initial flow over an impulsively started circular cylinder by Moshe Bar-Lev. [n. p.] 1974.
viii, 164 l. illus. 28 cm.
Thesis–University of Southern California.
1. Fluid mechanics. 2. Cylinders. I. Title.
CLSU NUC76-22875

Bar-Lev, Sha'ul, joint author
see Shem-Ur, Yonatan. (Sha'ul ve-Yonatan) [1974].

Bar-Lev, Zev.
Assertional structure. [Bloomington] Reproduced by the Indiana University Linguistics Club, 1972.
28 p. 30 cm.
Bibliography: p. 26-28.
1. English language–Semantics. 2. Semantics. I. Title.
CSt NUC75-21636

Bar-Mazal, Yeḥi'el
see
Yeḥi'el, Bar-Mazal.

Bar-Moshe, Benjamin.
Incidence, pathogenicity and classification of Mycoplasma in; final report. Bet Dagan, Kimron Veterinary Institute, 1973.
58, [4] l.
Grant no. FG-Is-283; project no. AIO-ADP-16.
Bibliography: leaves 59-62.
1. Mycoplasma diseases in animals. 2. Ruminantia. I. Kimron Veterinary Institute. II. Title.
DNAL NUC76-93126

Bar-Mosheh, Yitshak.
(Aswār al-Quds wa-qiṣaṣ ukhrá)
اسوار القدس وقصص اخرى / اسحق بار موشيه. —
القدس : اصدار الشرق ، 1976.
176 p. ; 24 cm.
Added t. p.: Ḥomot Yerushalayim.
CONTENTS: اللعنة الاولى. — الرسالة. — احمد والطبيب. — على جبل الطور. — انشودة لابي نايف. — الرشوة. — مكتب الاستاذ أنور. — يوم عمل بارد. — السدس. — أحلام الصخر. — اسوار القدس.
I. Title. II. Title: Ḥomot Yerushalayim.
PJ7816.A6537A9 77–970810

Bar-Mosheh, Yitsḥak.
(Warā'a al-sūr, wa-qiṣaṣ ukhrá)
وراء السور ، وقصص اخرى [تأليف] اسحق بار-موشيه.
[القدس] اصدار الشرق [1972]
199 p. 24 cm.
CONTENTS: — الجنازة. — معاناة قصة. — دار سعيد. — سهى. — الرابية الثالثة. — انفصام. — الحارس. — طريق الظلال. — عودة محبوب. — سجين وسجان. — الدار الميتة. — السرداب. — زواج. — وراء السور.
I. Title.
PJ7816.A6537W3 72–950656

Bār-Mūshīh, Isḥāq
see
Bar-Mosheh, Yitsḥak.

Bar-Ner, Joseph, 1906- ed.
see Tel-Aviv. Chamber of Commerce. Arba'im shanah le-yisud lishkat ha-mishar Tel-Aviv-Yafo. [1964]

Bar-Nir, Dov, 1911-
El sionismo y la izquierda; 4 ensayos. Montevideo, Ediciones M. Anilevich [197-]
74 p. 17 cm.
1. Zionism--Addresses, essays, lectures. 2. Jewish-Arab relations--Addresses, essays, lectures. I. Title.
TxU NUC77-92144

Bar-Ofir, David
see
Bar-Ophir, David, 1934-

Bar-On, Michael, ed.
see (Sefer zikaron shel kedoshe 'ayarotenu Samoshuivar–Iklod veha-sevivah) 1971.

Bar-On, Mordechay, 1928-
The process of integrating ethnic groups in Tsahal. [Tel Aviv] Israel Defence Forces [196-?]
12 p.
1. Israel. Defence Army.
MH NUC73-38289

Bar-On, Moshe Yehiel, 1896–
(Mevin ba-Mikra)
מבין במקרא : ילקוט פרשני הינוכי לפרשת השבוע, להפטרה, לחמש מגילות, למועדי השנה ולנושאים שבכל יום / ליקט והעתיק, הסביר והסדיר, משה יחיאל בר־און. — תל־אביב : הוצאת דון, 1974.
431 p. ; 23 cm.
Includes bibliographical references.
1. Bible. O. T. Pentateuch—Commentaries. 2. Jews. Liturgy and ritual. Haftaroth — Commentaries. 3. Bible. O. T. Five scrolls—Commentaries. I. Title.
BS1225.3.B37 75–950638

Bar-On, Moshe Yechiel, 1896– comp.
(Mivḥar perushe Rashi, Ra'av'a ve-Radak le-sefer Tehilim)
מבחר פירושי רש"י, ראב"ע ורד"ק לספר תהלים. נערך בלוית רשימות־באורים בידי יחיאל בן־נון. חיפה, בית הספר הריאלי העברי, 716 [1955 or 6]
180 p. 25 cm.
1. Bible. O. T. Psalms—Commentaries. I. Solomon ben Isaac, called RaSHI, 1040–1105. II. Ibn Ezra, Abraham ben Meïr, 1092–1167. III. Kimḥi, David, 1160?–1235? Perush Radak 'al Tehilim. Selections. 1955 or 6. IV. Title.
BS1429.B37 74–950231

Bar-On, N
see
Braun, Adam-Noah, 1892-1960.

Bar Oni, Bryna.
The vapor. Bryna Bar Oni. Chicago, Visual Impact, 1976.
x, 127 p. port. 23 cm.
1. Bar Oni, Bryna. 2. World War, 1939-1945--Personal narratives, Polish. I. Title.
OCH NUC77-92141

Bar-Ophir, David, 1934–
(Dine pinui- 'ilot ve-takdimim)
דיני פינוי־עילות ותקדימים / מאת דוד בר־אופיר. — תל־אביב :
[s. n.], 1974
139 p. : 25 cm.
Includes bibliographical references and index.
1. Eviction—Israel. I. Title.
74–951412

Bar-Ophir, David, 1934–
(Ḥoḳ ha-hotsa'ah le-fo'al)
הוק ההוצאה לפועל : הלכה למעשה / מאת דוד בר־אופיר, דב גרנדש, אברהם דיאמנט. — מהד' 2. מורחבת ומתוקנת. — תל־אביב : 1976 [s. n.]
247 p. ; 25 cm.
Includes bibliographical references and index.
1. Executions (Law)—Israel. I. Gerendas, Dov, 1923– joint author. II. Diamant, Avraham, 1928– joint author. III. Israel. Laws, statutes, etc. Ḥoḳ ha-hotsa'ah le-fo'al. 1976. IV. Title.
76–951963

Bar-Or, Marilyn, joint author
see Simri, Uriel, 1925- Practical English-Hebrew dictionary for terminology of physical education and sport. Provisional ed. [Netanya] Wingate Institute of Physical Education and Sport, 1970.

Bar-Or, 'O
see Simri, Uriel, 1925- Torat ha-kosher ha-gufani. [1971]

Bar-'Oz, Abraham.
(Be-etsba' geluyah)
באצבע גלויה; שירים [מאת] אברהם בר־עוז (תעיזי) ירושלים, אוגדן [1972]
iv, 48 p. illus. 24 cm. IL5.00
Vocalized.
I. Title.
PJ5054.B277B36 72–950702

Bar-Ratson, Matityahu
see Ner tamid. 1976.

Bar Sever, Reuven.
Aleph beth; an introduction to the Hebrew alphabet with reading exercises. New York, Ulpan Center of the Jewish Agency--American Section [197-?]
13 p. charts. 23 cm.
1. Hebrew language–Study and teaching. I. Title.
OCH NUC76-22866

Bar-Shalom, Dvora, tr.
see Keren, Yehezkel. [Sihon sefaradi-'ivri] [1972]

Bar Shushan, John
see
Yoḥannan X bar Shushan, Patriarch of the Jacobites.

Bar-Świech, Irena
see Bar, Irena.

Bar-Tal, Daniel.
Prosocial behavior : theory and research / Daniel Bar-Tal. — Washington : Hemisphere Pub. Corp. ; New York : distributed by Halsted Press, c1976.
x, 197 p. : ill. ; 24 cm.
Bibliography: p. 165-183.
Includes indexes.
ISBN 0-470-15223-0
1. Helping behavior. 2. Altruism. I. Title.
[DNLM: 1. Social behavior. HM276 B283p]
BF637.H4B37 155.2'32 75-43624
75 MARC

Bar-Tana, Asher.
[Kadmut ha-monote'izm ve-reshitah shel ha-mishpaḥah be-masoret Yiśrael uve-antropologyah)
קדמות המונותיאיזם וראשיתה של המשפחה במסורת ישראל ובאנתרופולוגיה / אשר בר־תנא. — [כפר־שמריהו] : בית האולפן ליהדות בכפר־שמריהו, 1976.
72 p. ; 22 cm.
Includes bibliographical references.
1. Religion, Primitive. 2. Anthropology. I. Title.
BL430.B37 77–951887

Bar-Tana, Asher.
(Pirke bereshit be-maḥashevet Yisrael)
פרקי בראשית במחשבת ישראל [מאת] אשר בר־תנא. [תל־אביב] אוצר המורה, [1973]
258 p. 24 cm.
On verso of t. p.: Genesis of Jewish thought.
Added title: פרקים במחשבת ישראל
1. Judaism—History of doctrines. 2. Creation—History of doctrines. 3. Man (Jewish theology) 4. Sabbath. 5. Cain. I. Title. II. Title: Perakim be-maḥashevet Yisrael.
BM601.B35 73–952704

Bar-Tsevi, G
['Ayaratenu Ternovkah]
• עיירתנו טרנובקה; פרקי זיכרון ומצבה [מאת] ג. בר־צבי. מהד׳ 2. מורחבת. תל־אביב, יוצאי טרנובקה; [ע״י הוצאת יזרעאל, 732 [1972]
103 p. illus. 23 cm. IL10.00
1. Jews in Ternovka, Ukraine (Vinnitsa) 2. Ternovka, Ukraine (Vinnitsa) I. Title.
DS135.R93T47 1972 72–950519

Bar-Yaacov, Nissim.
The handling of international disputes by means of inquiry / Nissim Bar-Yaacov. — London ; New York : Published for the Royal Institute of International Affairs by Oxford University Press, 1974.
xii, 370 p. ; 23 cm. GB***
Bibliography: p. [348]-355.
Includes indexes.
ISBN 0-19-218302-8 : £7.50
1. Pacific settlement of international disputes. I. Title.
JX4473.B37 341.5'2 75-308975
75 MARC

Bar Yeḥezkel, M
(Ba-ma'gal ha-satum).
במעגל הסתום / מאת מ. בר יחזקאל. — תל־אביב : הוצאת ברונפמן, c1973.
146 p. ; 23 cm.
1. Holocaust, Jewish (1939–1945) I. Title.
D810.J4B3145 75–950378

Bar-Yosef, Ofer.
The epi-palaeolithic cultures of Palestine. Jerusalem, 1970.
260, [13] p. illus.
Xerox copy.
Thesis (Ph.D.)–Hebrew University.
Includes bibliography.
1. Stone implements–Palestine. 2. Paleolithic period–Palestine. I. Title.
ICU NUC74-122545

Bar-Yosef, Ofer.
On the palaeo-ecological history of the site of 'Ubeidiya, by O. Bar-Yosef and E. Tchernov. Jerusalem, Israel Academy of Sciences and Humanities, 1972.
35 p. illus. 27 cm. (Publications of the Israel Academy of Sciences and Humanities) IL7.00 ($3.50 U.S.)
On cover: The Pleistocene of the Central Jordan Valley. The excavations at 'Ubeidiya.
Bibliography: p. 34-35.
1. Geology, Stratigraphic—Pleistocene. 2. Paleoecology—Israel—Galilee. 3. Glacial epoch—Israel—Galilee. I. Tchernov, Eitan, joint author. II. Title. III. Series: Israel Academy of Sciences and Humanities. Publications.
QE697.B28 560 72-950664
76 MARC

Bar-Yosef, Ofer, joint author
see Stekelis, Moshe, 1898-1967. Archaeological excavations at 'Ubeidiya. Jerusalem, Israel Academy of Sciences and Humanities, 1966-

Bar-Yosef, Rivkah.
(Histaglutam shel 'olim ḥadashim la-'avodah be-vet ḥaroshet)
הסתגלותם של עולים חדשים לעבודה בבית חרושת : חיבור / ע״י רבקה בר־יוסף. — [ירושלים? : s. n., 1962?]
191 leaves ; 32 cm.
Thesis—ha-Universiṭah ha-'Ivrit.
Bibliography: leaves 175–188.
1. Alien labor—Israel. 2. Israel—Emigration and immigration. I. Title.
HD8761.P33B37 77–951026

Bar-Yosef, Rivkah
see Mehkere 'avodah be-Yisrael. 1974.

Bar-Yosef, Rivkah
see Sistema politico, programmazione e amministrazione publica. [Milano] Edizioni di comunità [1973]

Bar-Yosef, Yehoshu'a, 1912–
[Ben Tsefat li-Yerushalayim]
בין צפת לירושלים; פרקי ילדות ובחרות [מאת] יהושע בר־יוסף. ירושלים, מוסד ביאליק [1972]
245 p. 19 cm. IL9.00
On verso of t. p.: From Safad to Jerusalem; memoirs [by] Yehoshua Bar-Yossef.
I. Title.
PJ5054.B3Z5 72–950714

Bar Yosef, Yosef, 1933– comp.
אחרי ..! שמואל גלינקא חייו ומותו. ״דבר.״
[Tel-Aviv, 1960]
194 p. illus., ports., map. 21 cm.
1. Glinka, Shmuel, 1927–1956. I. Title.
Title transliterated: Aḥarai.
CT1919.P38G582 A 62–454
Hebrew Union College. rev Library

Bar-Yosef, Yosef, 1933–
(Anashim kashim)
אנשים קשים; מין קומדיה בשתי מערכות [מאת] יוסף בר־יוסף. [תל־אביב] מפעלים אוניברסיטאיים להוצאה לאור [1973]
44 p. 21 cm. (ספרי סימן קריאה)
On verso of t. p.: Difficult people; a comedy of sorts.
I. Title.
PJ5054.B32A8 74–950998

Bar Yosef, Yosef, 1933-
Difficult people ; a comedy of sorts. Yosef Bar-Yosef; translated from the Hebrew. Tel-Aviv, Institute for the Translation of Hebrew Literature Ltd. in co-operation with the Cultural Division of the Department for Education and Culture in the Diaspora, W.Z.O., 1975.
xi, 56 p. 17 cm. (Modern Hebrew drama)
Translation of Anashim kashim.
I. Title.
NjR NUC77-92142

Bar-Yosef, Yosef, 1933– comp.
(Yorde ha-yam ba-oniyot)
יורדי הים באניות : ים, אניות ונמל בישראל / ליקט וערך יוסף בר יוסף ; עיצוב גרפי גד אולמן. — [חיפה?] : ביזמת שירותי רווחה לימאים ; חיפה : שקמונה, [1971]
144 p. : chiefly ill. ; 28 cm.
Added title: Israeli seafarers and shipping.
1. Shipping—Israel—Pictorial works. I. Title.
HE899.I 8B37 73–954456

Bar-Yossef, Yehoshua
see
Bar-Yosef, Yehoshu'a, 1912-

Bar-Zev, Asjer, 1932-
The effect of ecdysone on nucleic acid metabolism in tissues of Gromphadorhina. [Amherst] 1973.
xvii, 189 l. illus. 28 cm.
Thesis (Ph. D.)–University of Massachusetts.
1. Cockroaches. 2. Ecdysone. I. Title.
MU NUC74-128244

Bar-Zimra, S.
see Lewinski, Yom-Tow, 1899- Shabatot meyuhadot. [1969]

Bar-Zohar, Michel.
(Ben-Gurion)
בן־גוריון / מיכאל בר־זוהר. — תל־אביב : עם עובד, [1975–]
v. : ill. ; 22 cm.
On verso of t. p.: Ben Gurion, a political biography.
French ed. published in 1966 under title: Ben Gourion, le prophète armé.
Includes bibliographical references.
1. Ben-Gurion, David, 1886–1973.
DS125.3.B37B286 75–951189

Bar Zohar, Michel. Ben Gourion
in Gaxotte, Pierre. La France de Louis XIV au debut du regne... Paris, Le Cercle Historia, 1973.

Bar-Zohar, Michel.
Histoire secrète de la guerre d'Israël. Paris, Éditions J'ai lu, 1972.
384 p. 16 cm. (J'ai lu, A282. L'Aventure d'aujourd'hui) 4.10F
F 72-14213
1. Israel-Arab War, 1967– I. Title.
DS127.B35 1972 956'.046 73–338700
MARC

Bar-Zohar, Michel.
L'homme qui mourut deux fois / Michel Bar-Zohar ; traduit de l'hébreu par Raphaël Cidor et Jean Slavik. — Paris : Fayard, [1974]
xxiv, 265 p. ; 24 cm. F***
English translation has title: The London letter.
ISBN 2-213-000163-8 : 32.00F
I. Title.
PJ5054.B324H6 843'.9'14 74–190250
MARC

Bar-Zohar, Michel.
(ha-Ish she-met pa'amayim)
האיש שמת פעמיים [מאת] מיכאל בר־זוהר. ירושלים, ויידנפלר וניקולסון [1973]
195 p. 22 cm.
On verso of t. p.: The man who died twice (The London letter)
I. Title.
PJ5054.B324 I 8 74–951218

Bar-Zohar, Michel.
J'ai risqué ma vie; Isser Harel, le numéro 1 des services secrets israéliens [par] Michel Bar-Zohar. [Paris], Éditions J'ai lu, 1973.
434 p. 17 cm. (J'ai lu. Documents, 18) 5.80F F 74-696
Issued in Hebrew under title: ha-Memuneh.
1. Harel, Isser, 1912– 2. Israel. Sherut ha-bitaḥon ha-kelali. I. Title.
UB271.I 82H3214 1973 74–181273
355.3'432'0924 [B] MARC

Bar-Zohar, Michel.
The secret list of Heinrich Roehm / Michael Barak [i.e. M. Bar-Zohar]. — Boston : G. K. Hall, 1976.
415 p. ; 24 cm.
Large print ed.
ISBN 0-8161-6378-0
1. Sight-saving books. I. Title.
[PZ4.B2255 Se 4] 813'.5'4 76-11727
[PS3552.A58] 76 MARC

Bar-Zohar, Michel.
The secret list of Heinrich Roehm / by Michael Barak. — New York : Morrow, 1976.
228 p. ; 22 cm.
ISBN 0-688-02991-4
I. Title.
PZ4.B2266 Se 813'.5'4 75-28316
[PS3552.A58] 75 MARC

Bar-Zohar, Michel.
Spies in the Promised Land: Iser Harel and the Israeli Secret Service; translated from the French by Monroe Stearns. London, Davis-Poynter Ltd, 1972.
ix, 292 p. 22 cm. £3.00 B 72-20654
Translated from J'ai risqué ma vie.
First published in Hebrew, under title: ha-Memuneh.
1. Israel. Sherut ha-bitaḥon hakelali. 2. Intelligence service—Israel. 3. Harel, Isser, 1912– I. Title.
UB251.I 78B3713 1972b 327'.12'0615694 73–152670
ISBN 0-7067-0033-3 MARC

Bar-Zohar, Michel.
The spy who died twice / Michael Bar-Zohar ; translated from the French by June P. Wilson and Walter B. Michaels. — 1st American ed. — Boston : Houghton Mifflin, 1975.
212 p. ; 22 cm.
Translation of ha-Ish she-met pa'amayim.
ISBN 0-395-19417-2
I. Title.
PZ4.B2255Sp 3 843'.9'14 74–26598
[PJ5054.B324] MARC

Bar-Zohar, Michel.
The third truth [by] Michael Bar-Zohar. [Translated by June P. Wilson and Walter B. Michaels. 1st American ed.] Boston, Houghton Mifflin, 1973.
189 p. 22 cm. $5.95
Translation of La troisième vérité.
I. Title.
PZ4.B2255Th 843'.9'14 73-5833
[PQ2662.A75] MARC
ISBN 0-395-15458-8

Bar-Zohar, Michel.
The third truth [by] Michael Bar-Zohar. Translated by June P. Wilson and Walter B. Michaels. London, Hodder and Stoughton [1973]
189 p. 24 cm.
Translation of La troisième verité.
I. Title.
PZ4.B2974Th 843'.9'14 73-161938
[PQ2662.A75] MARC
ISBN 0-340-16411-5

Bar
see
Bay Area Review Course, inc.
Broadcast Advertiser's Reports, inc.
for publications by and about these bodies.
Titles and other entries beginning with this acronym are filed following this card.
74-233087

Bar.
Alpen, Martonair Druckluftsteuerungen GmbH.
v. illus. 30 cm.
Continues Zeitschrift für angewandte Drucklufttechnik.
1. Pneumatic control—Periodicals. 2. Pneumatic machinery—Periodicals.
TJ219.B36 629.8'04'505 73-641043
MARC-S

Bar.
[Austin] State Bar of Texas.
v. illus. 40 cm. monthly.
"Bar action report; news and information of immediate interest to Bar members."
1. Bar associations—Texas—Periodicals. I. State Bar of Texas.
KF200.B35 340'.06'2764 73-644576
ISSN 0092-3877 MARC-S

Bar Association of Alaska
see
Alaska Bar Association.

Bar Association of Arkansas.
Proceedings of the annual meeting of the Bar Association of Arkansas. 11th-49th, pt. 1; 1908-47. Little Rock [etc.]
38 v. in 36. ill. 22 cm.
Meeting for 1945 not held.
Continues Report of the proceedings of the Bar Association of Arkansas.
Proceedings of 40th-42d meetings issued together.
Proceedings of 49th meeting published in 2 pts.
Title varies slightly.
Proceedings of 29th meeting include the proceedings of the tri-state meeting of the bar associations of Arkansas, Louisiana, and Texas.
Part 2 of the proceedings of 49th meeting and proceedings of subsequent meetings are published each year as issues of Arkansas law review and bar association journal.
1. Bar associations—Arkansas—Addresses, essays, lectures.
I. Louisiana State Bar Association. II. Texas Bar Association.
KF332.A74B316 340'.06'2767 74-648850
MARC-S

Bar Association of Arkansas.
The proposed new constitution; modern proposals for increasing the efficiency of the various departments of government. Papers read before the meeting of the Bar association of Arkansas held May 31st and June 1st, 1917 at Hot Springs, Arkansas. [Little Rock?] Printed by the Bar association of Arkansas [1917?]
75 p. 23 cm.
1. Arkansas—Constitutional law. 2. Arkansas—Politics and government—To 1950.
KFA4002.B3 43-42055

Bar Association of Arkansas
see Arkansas law review and Bar Association journal. v. 1-21; winter 1946/47-winter 1968. Fayetteville, Arkansas Law Review and Bar Association Journal, inc.

Bar Association of Erie County
see Citizens Conference on Criminal Justice, New York, 1971. Final report... [Buffalo? 1971?]

Bar Association of Erie County
see Cockran, William Bourke, 1854-1923. John Marshall: an address. [Buffalo, Erie County bar association, 1901]

Bar Association of Greater Cleveland

For works by this body issued under its earlier name see

Cleveland Bar Association.

Bar Association of Greater Cleveland. Special Committee to Review Sentencing Procedures.
Report of the Special Committee to Review Sentencing Procedures. — [Cleveland : Bar Association of Greater Cleveland], 1975.
51 p. in various pagings : ill. ; 28 cm.
Cover title.
Includes a bibliography.
1. Sentences (Criminal procedure)—Ohio—Cleveland.
KFX1307.B3 345'.77132'077 77-366679
77 MARC

Bar Association of Hawaii.
The Bar Association of the Hawaiian Islands was founded in 1899. In 1914 its name was changed to the Bar Association of Hawaii. In 1974 the name was changed to the Hawaii State Bar Association.
Works by this body published before the change of name in 1974 are found under
Bar Association of Hawaii.
Works published after that change of name are found under
Hawaii State Bar Association.

Bar Association of Hawaii.
Annual directory.
[Honolulu, Crossroads Press]
v. illus. 28 cm.
1. Lawyers—Hawaii—Directories.
KF192.H3B37 340'.025'969 73-644125
MARC-S

Bar Association of India.
Parliament: emergency and personal freedom: opinion of jurists. M. C. Setalvad [and others] New Delhi, the Association [1963]
74 p. 22 cm.
1. War and emergency legislation—India.
I. Setalvad, Motilal Chimanlal. II. Title.
VtU NUC76-75721

Bar Association of Metropolitan St. Louis.

For works by this body issued under its earlier name see

Bar Association of St. Louis.

Bar Association of Metropolitan St. Louis. Consumer Affairs Committee.
Buyer beware : consumer rights handbook. — [St. Louis] : Bar Association of Metropolitan St. Louis, Young Lawyers' Section, Consumer Affairs Committee, c1976.
v, 28 p. ; 23 cm.
$1.00
1. Consumer protection—Law and legislation—Missouri. 2. Consumer protection—Law and legislation—United States. I. Title.
KFM8030.B3 343'.73'07 76-381514
76 MARC

Bar Association of Metropolitan St. Louis. Young Lawyers' Section. Consumer Affairs Committee
see
Bar Association of Metropolitan St. Louis. Consumer Affairs Committee.

Bar Association of Milwaukee
see
Milwaukee Bar Association.

Bar Association of Nassau County. Joint Medical-Legal Committee of the Nassau County Medical Society and the Nassau County Bar Association.
see Joint Medical-Legal Committee of the Nassau County Medical Society and the Nassau County Bar Association.

Bar Association of North Dakota
see State Bar Association of North Dakota.

Bar Association of St. Louis.
"John Marshall day"; proceedings of the bench and bar of St. Louis. Celebrating the centennial anniversary of the accession to the Supreme court of the United States of Chief Justice John Marshall. February 4, 1801-1901. [St. Louis] Bar association of St. Louis [1901]
3 p. l., [5]-91 p. front. (port.) 25 cm.
1. Marshall, John, 1755-1835. I. Title.
KF8745.M3B33 12-9044
—— Copy 2. (In Dillon, J. F., comp. Centenary and memorial addresses and proceedings ... on Marshall day, 1901. [New York, 190-] 27½ cm. v. 5) KF8745.M3D47 vol. 5

Bar Association of St. Louis.
see Missouri. Courts. Rules of court. [St. Louis, 1955?-

Bar Association of St. Louis.

For works by this body issued under its later name see

Bar Association of Metropolitan St. Louis.

Bar Association of San Francisco.
The Bar Association of San Francisco today. [San Francisco] The Association, 1975.
30 p. 26 cm.
Cover title.
Report prepaged by Richard B. Morris.
1. Bar Association of San Francisco. 2. Bar associations--San Francisco. I. Morris, Richard B., 1930- II. Title.
CLL NUC77-92143

Bar Association of San Francisco.
An exhibition of paintings, photographs and books on the occasion of the centennial of the Bar Association of San Francisco (1872-1972) and the ninety-fifth annual meeting of the American Bar Association in San Francisco, California, Hastings College of the Law, August 10-17, 1972. [San Francisco] 1972.
20 p. 23 cm.
Pages 18-20 blank for "Notes."
On cover: 100 years of law, an exhibition...
C NUC73-116565

Bar Association of San Francisco.
Youth & the law. San Francisco, 1972.
68 p.
1. Children—California. I. Title.
CSt-Law NUC74-126734

Bar Association of San Francisco
see Directory of San Francisco attorneys. San Francisco.

Bar Association of Sri Lanka.
News letter—Bar Association of Sri Lanka. no. 1- Aug. 1975-
Colombo, Bar Association of Sri Lanka.
no. 33 cm. monthly.
1. Bar associations—Ceylon—Periodicals.
340'.06'25493 76-913114
MARC-S

Bar Association of Thailand.
The administration of justice in Thailand. Bangkok, 1969.
101 p. 26 cm.
1. Justice, Administration of—Thailand.
I. Title.
CtY NUC74-10098

Bar Association of the City of Greensboro.
Greensboro Bar Association, 1956. [Greensboro, 1956]
96 p. ports. 23 cm.
1. Greensboro, N. C.—Biography. 2. N. C.—Lawyers.
NcU NUC74-9576

Bar Association of the City of Greensboro.
Greensboro Bar Association, 1968. Greensboro, N. C., 1968-
150 p. (loose-leaf) 25 cm.
Includes biographical sketches with running title: The Greensboro Bar.
1. Law—Biography. 2. Bar associations.
NcU NcD-D NUC74-7090

Bar Association of the City of New York
see
Association of the Bar of the City of New York.

Bar Association of the City of Richmond.
see Administration of decedents' estates. [Richmond?] Virginia State Bar, c1976.

Bar Association of the City of Richmond.
see What the lawyer in general practice should know about bankruptcy. [Richmond? Virginia State Bar] c1976.

Bar Association of the District of Columbia. Commission on Legal Aid.
Report. [Washington, 1958]
xi, 194 p. 23 cm.
1. Legal aid—District of Columbia.
KF337.D5B37 347'.753'01 74-157532
MARC

Bar Association of the District of Columbia. Committee on Legal Ethics and Grievance.
Report in the matter of advertising conducted by Monroe H. Freedman and the Stern Community Law Firm. Washington [1971]
[25] l.
1. Legal ethics—District of Columbia. 2. Stern Community Law Firm. I. Freedman, Monroe H.
CSt-Law NUC73-78974

Bar Association of the District of Columbia. Court of Claims Committee.
Manual for practice in the United States Court of Claims / Judith Ann Yannello ... [et al.]. — Washington : Court of Claims Committee, Bar Association of the District of Columbia, c1976.
1 v. ; 30 cm.
Loose-leaf for updating.
Includes bibliographical references and index.
1. United States. Court of Claims. 2. United States—Claims. I. Yannello, Judith Ann. II. Title.
KF9070.B37 347'.73'28 76-368132
76 MARC

Bar Association of the District of Columbia. Junior Bar Section.
Coroner's inquest; committee report 1966. [Washington, D.C., 1967]
20 l. 26 cm.
"Adopted by the Committee on Judicial Functions of the Coroner of the Judicial Conference of the D.C. Circuit in 1966, and then adopted by the Judicial Conference as a whole." Cover ltr.
1. Coroners—District of Columbia. I. Title.
WaU-L NUC75-58216

Bar Association of the District of Columbia. Juvenile Practice Committee.
see Areen, Judith C. Representing juveniles in neglect, pins, and delinquency cases in the District of Columbia ... Washington, [Bar Association of the District of Columbia] c1975.

Bar Association of the District of Columbia. Young Lawyers Section.
Lawyers reference to statutes of the Metropolitan area; a synopsis of the codes of the District of Columbia, Maryland, Virginia. [Washington, 1973]
1 v. (loose-leaf)
1. Statutes—Washington metropolitan area. I. Title.
DSI NUC76-75733

Bar Association of the District of Columbia. Young Lawyers Section.
Lawyers reference to statutes of the Metropolitan area; a synopsis of the codes of the District of Columbia, Maryland, Virginia. [Washington, 1974-
v. (loose-leaf)
1. District of Columbia law—Compends. 2. Maryland law—Compends. 3. Virginia law—Compends. I. Title.
CLL NUC75-30714

Bar Association of the District of Columbia. Young Lawyers' Section.
Will & testamentary trust forms / by the Young Lawyers Section of the Bar Association of the District of Columbia. — Washington : The Association, [1974-
1 v. ; 29 cm.
Loose-leaf for updating.
Includes bibliographical references.
1. Wills—United States—Forms. 2. Testamentary trusts—United States—Forms. 3. Wills—District of Columbia—Forms. 4. Testamentary trusts—District of Columbia—Forms. I. Title.
KF755.A65B37 346'.753'0540269 74-195253
MARC

Bar Association of the District of Columbia. Young Lawyers Section.
see Criminal Practice Institute, 13th, Washington, D.C., 1976. Trial manual. [Washington? The Institute, 1976]

Bar Association of the District of Columbia. Young Lawyers Section
see Juvenile Practice Institute, 2d, Washington, D.C., 1971. Second annual Juvenile Practice Institute. [Washington, 1971?]

Bar Association of the District of Columbia. Young Lawyers Section. Emergency Legal Assistance Project
see
Emergency Legal Assistance Project.

Bar Association of the District of Columbia. Young Lawyers Section. Juvenile Practice Committee
see
Bar Association of the District of Columbia. Juvenile Practice Committee.

Bar Association of the Seventh Federal Circuit.
Practitioner's handbook for appeals to the United States court of appeals for the seventh circuit, together with the rules of the seventh circuit and the federal rules of appellate procedure and the seventh circuit plan under the criminal justice act as of Apr. 1, 1973, sponsored by the Bar Association of the Seventh Federal Circuit. Chicago, Gunthorp-Warren [1973]
iii, 117 p. forms. 23 cm.
Cover title.
1. U.S. Circuit Court of Appeals (7th circuit) 2. Appellate procedure—United States. 3. Court rules—United States. I. Title.
MH-L NUC74-150690

Bar Association of the State of Kansas.
The journal of the Kansas Bar Association. v. 33-v. 36, no. 1; spring 1964-spring 1967. [Topeka]
4 v. illus. 29 cm. quarterly.
Continues its Journal of the Bar Association of the State of Kansas.
Continued by the Journal of the Kansas Bar Association issued by the association under its later name: Kansas Bar Association.
Key title: The Journal of the Kansas Bar Association.
ISSN 0022-8486
1. Law—Periodicals—Kansas. 2. Bar Associations—Kansas—Periodicals.
K2.A66 340'.09781 74-647947
MARC-S

Bar Association of the State of Kansas.

For works by this body issued under its later name see

Kansas Bar Association.

Bar Association of the State of New Hampshire.
Proceedings
v. 1-
(old ser., v. 6-
Concord, N. H., 1900-
v. plates, ports. 25 cm.
List of members in v. 1, 2.
Issued in parts, usually annually with general title-pages and indexes at intervals of several years.
Numbered "old ser., v. 6-9" in continuation of the numbering of the Proceedings of the Grafton and Coös bar association.
1. Law—Societies. 2. Lawyers—New Hampshire.
KF332.N38B3717 21-1564

Bar Association of the State of New Hampshire.
Proceedings of the Bar association of the state of New Hampshire at its celebration of John Marshall day held at Manchester, N. H., February 4, 1901. Concord, N. H., The Rumford press, 1901.
3 p. l., p. [275]-399. 2 ports. 25½ cm. (In its Proceedings, 1900-1903. Concord, 1900-03. v. 1; old ser., v. 6, no. 2)
Addresses by George B. French, Jeremiah Smith, Edgar Aldrich and Robert M. Wallace, with exercises at the annual banquet.
1. Marshall, John, 1755-1835. 2. John Marshall day.
KF332.N38B3717 vol. 1 15-18165
——— Copy 2. (In Dillon, J. F., comp. Centenary and memorial addresses and proceedings ... on Marshall day, 1901. [New York, 190-] 27½ cm. v. 1)
Extra portraits, mounted and ms. and typewritten letters inserted.
KF8745.M3D47 vol. 1

Bar Association of the State of New Hampshire
see New Hampshire. University. Cooperative Extension Service. Making a will in New Hampshire. Durham, University of New Hampshire [1972]

Bar Association of the State of New Hampshire
see New Hampshire law weekly. [Manchester]

Bar Association of the State of New Hampshire.
see New Hampshire tax law ... [Manchester] The Association, c1977.

Bar Association of the State of New York
see
New York State Bar Association.

Bar Council
see
General Council of the Bar of England and Wales.

Bar Council of India.
Journal of the Bar Council of India.
[New Delhi, Bar Council of India Trust]
v. 24 cm. quarterly.
1. Law—Periodicals—India. 2. Lawyers—India—Discipline—Cases.
K2.A67 340'.0954 77-912046
MARC-S

Bar Council of Maharashtra.
Maharashtra Bar Council journal.
Bombay, Bar Council of Maharashtra.
v. 25 cm. quarterly.
"A quarterly journal devoted to lawyers, law and law reforms."
1. Bar associations—Maharashtra, India (State)—Periodicals.
2. Law—Maharastra, India (State)—Periodicals. I. Title.
340'.0954792 75-907379
MARC-S

Bar Council of Victoria.
No fault liability [prepared by the Bar Sub-committee] Melbourne, Hawthorn Press [1972]
107 p. 25 cm. Aus***
Publication jointly sponsored by the Victorian Bar Council and the Council of the Law Institute.
1. Insurance, No-fault automobile. 2. Insurance, No-fault automobile—Victoria, Australia. I. Law Institute of Vitcoria. II. Title.
346'.945'086 74-160570
ISBN 0-7246-0085-3 MARC

Bar drinks and booze like granddad used to make / [compiled] by Kurt Saxon. — Eureka, Calif. : Atlan Formularies, c1976.
xii, 149 p. ; 28 cm.
Includes indexes.
CONTENTS: The mixicologist.—Dick's encyclopedia of practical receipts and processes.—Techno-chemical receipt book.—Scientific American cyclopedia.
1. Alcoholic beverages—Amateurs' manuals. 2. Cocktails. I. Saxon, Kurt.
TP506.B37 641.8'74 76-29814
77 MARC

Bar Harbor, Me. Jackson Laboratory
see
Jackson Laboratory, Bar Harbor, Me.

Bar-Ilan news.
[Ramat-Gan, Bar-Ilan University]
v. ports. 24 cm.
Continued by Bar Ilan University.
I. Ramat-Gan, Israel. Bar-Ilan University.
LG341.R33A33 HE 67-711
MARC-S
PL 480: Is-S-818

Bar-Ilan University
see Ramat-Gan, Israel. Bar-Ilan University.

Bar leader.
[Chicago, American Bar Association]
v. ill. 28 cm. bimonthly.
Began with March/April 1975 issue. Cf. New serial titles.
Formed by the union of: American Bar Association. Section of Bar Activities. Bar activities; Bar keys and: Communications co-ordinator.
ISSN 0099-1031
1. Bar associations—United States—Periodicals. 2. Practice of law—United States—Periodicals. I. American Bar Association.
KF200.B355 340'.06'273 75-645957
MARC-S

Bar of Lower Canada
see
Bar of the Province of Quebec.

Bar of the County of Clinton, N.Y.
see Proceedings of the Bar of the County of Clinton, New York, with other memorials, commemorative of the life and character of William Swetland. Albany, J. Munsell, 1865.

Bar of the Province of Quebec.
Colloque "Justice et Efficacité" sous la présidence de M. le Bâtonnier Marcel Cinq-Mars. [Montréal? 1970]
24 p. 28 cm.
Cover title: Justice et efficacité.
"Congrès du barreau, 1970."
Includes bibliographies.
1. Justice, Administration of—Quebec (Province) I. Cinq-Mars, Marcel. II. Title. III. Title: Justice et efficacité.
CaBVaU NUC76-25752

Bar of the Province of Quebec.
Colloque "l'administration d'une étude d'avocats" sous la présidence de Me Claude Vallerand. [Montréal? 1970]
16 l. 28 cm.
Photocopy.
Cover title: Administration d'une étude d'avocats.
"Congrès du barreau, 1970."
1. Practice of law—Quebec (Province) I. Vallerand, Claude. II. Title. III. Title: Administration d'une étude d'avocats.
CaBVaU NUC76-25753

Bar of the Province of Quebec.
Mémoire à la Commission conjointe de la justice et des affaires sociales sur la loi de la protection de la jeunesse (projet de loi 65) / Barreau du Québec. — [Montréal] : Le Barreau, 1973.
38 p. ; 28 cm. C***
1. Children—Law—Quebec (Province) I. Title: Mémoire à la Commission conjointe de la justice et des affaires sociales ...
75-521119
75 MARC

Bar of the Province of Quebec.
Mémoire du Barreau du Québec au Comité d'étude sur l'assurance-automobile. [Montréal?] 1971.
23 p. 28 cm. C***
Bibliography: p. 17.
1. Insurance, Automobile—Quebec (Province) I. Quebec (Province). Comité d'étude sur l'assurance-automobile. II. Title.
72-361557

Bar of the Province of Quebec.
• Procedure civile, session 1973-1974. [n. p., 1973]
1 v. (various pagings) 36 cm. (Its/Cours de formation professionnelle)
1. Civil procedure—Quebec (Province) I. Title. II. Series.
CaBVaU NUC76-75734

Bar of the Province of Quebec
see Barreau. [Montréal, Service d'information du Barreau du Québec]

Bar of the Province of Quebec. Service d'information.
For publications of the Bar of the Province of Quebec issued by this body see
Bar of the Province of Quebec.
72-226038

BAR quarterly. v. 73–
Jan. 1976–
[Folkestone, Eng., Wm. Dawson]
v. ill. 30 cm.
Continues: Book-auction records.
ISSN 0307-8647
1. Books—Prices—Periodicals. 2. Antiquarian booksellers—Periodicals.
Z1000.B65 017'.3 76-649174
MARC-S

Bar Review, inc.
Bar Review course materials. — [Chicago? : Bar Review, inc.], c1976.
2 v. ; 34 cm.
CONTENTS: v. 1. Agency, contracts, corporations, negotiable instruments, partnerships, torts, trusts, wills.—v. 2. Civil procedure, criminal law, credit transactions, evidence, equity, real property.
1. Law—North Carolina—Compends. 2. Law—United States—Compends. I. Title.
KFN7481.B37 1976 340'.09756 76-369398
76 MARC

Bar Review, inc.
Bar review course materials. — [Chicago : Bar Review, inc.], c1977.
3 v. ; 34 cm.
CONTENTS: v. 1. Criminal law, evidence, property.—v. 2. Agency, corporations, partnerships, torts, trusts, wills.—v. 3. Civil procedure, contracts, credit transactions, equity, negotiable instruments.
1. Law—North Carolina—Compends. 2. Law—United States—Compends. I. Title.
KFN7481.B37 1977 340'.09756 77-151801
77 MARC

Bar Review, inc.
Illinois. [Chicago, 1972]
3 v. 35 cm.
CONTENTS: v. 1. Commercial paper. Secured transactions. Wills. Corporations. Equity. Sales. Conflict of laws.—v. 2. Civil procedure. Personal property. Domestic relations. Suretyship. Trusts. Administrative law. Agency. Partnership. Federal jurisdiction & procedure. Taxation.—v. 3. Constitutional law. Contracts. Real property. Torts. Evidence. Criminal procedure. Criminal law.
1. Law—Illinois—Compends. 2. Law—United States—Compends. I. Title.
KFI 1281.B337 340'.09773 73-153195
MARC

Bar Review, inc.
Illinois. — [Chicago : Bar Review, inc., 1974]
399 p. in various pagings ; 35 cm.
1. Law—Illinois—Compends. 2. Law—United States—Compends.
KFI 1281.B339 340'.09773 74-195124
MARC

Bar Review, inc.
Illinois—questions and answers. [Chicago, 1972]
2 v. 35 cm.
CONTENTS: v. 1. Evidence. Criminal procedure. Constitutional law. Sales. Corporations. Trusts. Administrative law. Domestic relations. Commercial paper. Secured transactions. Conflicts. Agency. Partnership.—v. 2. Equity. Federal jurisdiction & procedure. Personal property. Suretyship. Criminal law. Torts. Contracts. Illinois civil practice. Wills. Real property. Future interests. Federal taxation.
1. Law—Illinois—Examinations, questions, etc. 2. Law—United States—Examinations, questions, etc. I. Title.
KFI 1281.B34 340'.09773 73-151858
MARC

Bar Review, inc.
Multistate outlines. [Chicago, 1972]
1 v. (various pagings) 35 cm.
CONTENTS: Contracts.—Evidence.—Constitutional law.—Criminal procedure.—Future interests.—Real property.—Criminal law.—Torts.
1. Law—United States—Compends. I. Title.
KF386.B32 340'.0973 73-152097
MARC

Bar Review, inc.
Multistate outlines. [Chicago] Bracton Press [1972]
1 v. (various pagings) 35 cm.
On cover: BRI, multistate.
1. Law—United States—Compends. I. Title.
KF388.B35 340'.0973 73-156596
MARC

Bar Review, inc.
see National bar examination digest. spring 1975- [Washington, D. C., BAR]

Bar Review, inc.

For works by this body issued under its later name see

BRI Bar Review Institute.

Bar Review Institute
see
BRI Bar Review Institute.

Bar room reveries. This book deals with the art of elbow-bending and with many cock-eyed tales concerning those who have excelled in this ancient pastime. Minneapolis, Coll-Webb Co., 1958.
1 v. (unpaged) 17 cm.
"Acknowledgements" signed E.A.W.: Edward A. Webster?
1. Drinking customs—Anecdotes, facetiae, satire, etc. I. Webster, Edward A.
MU NUC76-24034

Bar services directory. 1961/62–
New York, Bar Services Directory.
v. 21 cm. annual.
1. New York (City)—Commerce—Directories. 2. Law offices—New York (City)—Directories.
HF5068.N5B37 75-640970

Bar Sinister
see Cloke, Kenneth. Military counseling manual... Los Angeles [1970-

Bar-źi-ba Phun-tshogs-dbaṅ-rgyal.
Tibetan grammer [sic] book. བོད་ཀྱི་སྐད་ལ་ཉེ་བར་མཁོ་བའི་བསྡུན་བཙོས་སུམ་རྟགས་གཉིས་ཀྱི་རྣམ་བཤད་ཕྱོགས་བསྡེབས་ཀུན་ལས་མི་ལོང་ཞེས་བྱ་བ་བཞུགས་སོ. [གཙང་གངས་ལྗོངས་གར་བཤམ་, ལྷ་ས་པ་པ་ཞི་ཕུན་ཚོགས་དབང་རྒྱལ་གྱིས་སྒྲུར་བ་] Dharmsala Cantt., Togyal [1967?]
A-G, 193 p. 19 cm. 8.75
Cover title.
Contains Thon-mi Sambhoṭa's Sum cum pa and Rtags kyi 'jug pa.
In Tibetan.

"སུམ་ཅུ་པ་དང་, རྟགས་ཀྱི་འཇུག་པའི་དགོར་བརྗོད་རིགས་མིག་གསར་བུའི་ཅས [sic] ནོར་, བར་ཞི་པ་ཕུན་ཚོགས་དབང་རྒྱལ་ལམ་, མིང་གཞན་དབྱངས་ཅན་དགའ་བའི་བློ་གྲོས་ཀྱིས་སྒྲིག་པ": p. 142–188.

1. Thon-mi Sambhoṭa, fl. 632. Sum cum pa. 2. Thon-mi Sambhoṭa, fl. 632. Rtags kyi 'jug pa. I. Thon-mi Sambhoṭa, fl. 632. Sum cum pa. 1967? II. Thon-mi Sambhota, fl. 632. Rtags kyi 'jug pa. 1967? III. Title. IV. Title: Bod kyi skad la ñe bar.
PL3611.T53B3 S A 68-20007
PL 480: I-Tib-228

Bara, André.
L'expression par le corps; principes et méthodes. [Toulouse] Privat [1974]
254 p. 22 cm. (Époque) F***
Bibliography: p. [247]-250.
32.00F
1. Expression. 2. Exercise. I. Title.
GV463.B35 613.7'1 75-500282
MARC

Bara, J P
Controlling the expansion of desiccated clays during construction, by J. P. Bara. Denver, United States Bureau of Reclamation, Office of Chief Engineer [1969]
17, [10] l. illus. 28 cm.
Cover title.
"This paper is to be presented at the Second International Research and Engineering Conference on Expansive Clay Soils at Texas A & M University, College Station, Texas, August 17-19, 1969."
Bibliography: leaf 16.
1. Foundations. 2. Clay. 3. Soil mechanics. I. United States. Bureau of Reclamation.

II. Title.
DI NUC76-76841

Bara, Janine de.
The long long road / Janine de Bara. — London : Regency Press, 1974.
47 p. ; 22 cm. GB74-16773
ISBN 0-9503248-0-9 : £0.75
1. Bara, Janine de, in fiction, drama, poetry, etc. 2. France—History—German occupation, 1940-1945—Drama. I. Title.
PR6052.A588L6 822 75-320776
75 MARC

Bara, John P
see Bara, J P.

Bara, José Luis Raymond
see Raymond Bara, José Luis.

Barā, Padma.
(Manikā)
মণিকা. ₍লিখক₎ পদ্ম বৰা. গুৱাহাটী, গুৱাহাটী বুক ষ্টল ₍1973₎
146 p. 23 cm. Rs4.50
In Assamese.
A novel.

I. Title.
PK1569.B218M3 73-905930

Barā, Padma.
(Swarṇa swākshara)
স্বৰ্ণ স্বাক্ষৰ. ₍লিখক₎ পদ্ম বৰা. গুৱাহাটী, অলকা প্ৰকাশ ₍1971₎
79 p. 23 cm. Rs3.50
In Assamese.
A novel.

I. Title.
PK1569.B218S8 73-900037

Bara Temes, Francisco Javier, 1944-
Modes in the ferrite filled rectangular guide magnetized parallel to the direction of propagation. ₍Providence₎ 1972.
v, 66 l. diagrs., tables. 28 cm.
Thesis (Ph.D.)--Brown University.
Xerox.
Vita.
Bibliography: leaves 65-66.
RPB NUC73-114748

Bara Tankakai. Itami Shibu.
(Kusamomiji)
草紅葉：薔薇短歌会伊丹支部合同歌集 / ₍小原みつ子編₎. — 豊中：薔薇短歌会；₍京都₎：初音書房製作, 昭和49 ₍1974₎
173 p., ₍2₎ leaves of plates : ports. ; 19 cm. — (薔薇叢書；第16篇)
Ja 74-19834
Subtitle on cover: Bara Itami Shibu gōdō kashū.
¥1000
1. Waka. 2. Bara Tankakai. Itami Shibu. I. Title. II. Series: Bara sōsho ; dai 16-hen.
PL758.B3 76-801667

Barab, Seymour, arr
see Langstaff, John M comp. The season for singing... Garden City, N. Y., Doubleday ₍1974₎

Barabaner, Khanon Zelikovich
see Metodicheskie osobennosti optimizat͡sii sistem ėnergosnabzhenii͡a sel'skikh raĭonov. 1975.

Barabanov, Evgeniĭ Viktorovich, 1943-
Das Schicksal der christlichen Kultur / Evgenij V. Barabanow. — Einsiedeln : Benziger, c1977.
55 p. ; 20 cm. — (Theologische Meditationen ; Bd. 44) Sw77-4590
ISBN 3-545-27044-0 : 7.80F
1. Christianity and culture. I. Title. II. Series.
BX880.T47 Bd. 44 77-550465
₍BR115.C8₎ •77 MARC

Barabanov, Evgeniĭ Viktorovich, 1943-
see Samosoznanie. 1976.

Barabanov, Leonid Nikitovich.
Termal'nye vody Malogo Kavkaza. Moskva, Izd-vo Akademii nauk SSSR, 1961.
81 p. illus. (Akademii͡a nauk SSSR. Otd-nie geol.-geogr. nauk. Trudy Laboratorii gidrogeologicheskikh problem, t. 37)
ICRL NUC74-45559

Barabanov, Leonid Nikitovich
see Geodinamika vulkanizma i gidrotermal'nogo prot͡sessa. 1974.

Barabanov, Mikhail Vasil'evich.
(Izmenenie struktur konechnogo obshchestvennogo produkta glavnykh kapitalisticheskikh stran)
Изменение структур конечного общественного продукта главных капиталистических стран / М. В. Барабанов ; АН СССР, Ин-т мировой экономики и международ. отношений. — Москва : Наука, 1976.
268 p., ₍1₎ fold. leaf ; 22 cm. USSR 76
Bibliography: p. 259-₍266₎
1.36rub
1. Gross national product. I. Title.
HB601.B297 77-507843

Barabanov, V E
(Ėlektrooborudovanie traktorov i avtomobileĭ)
Электрооборудование тракторов и автомобилей / В. Е. Барабанов, В. И. Василевский, С. М. Левин. — 2-е изд., доп. и перераб. — Москва : Колос, 1974.
446 p. : ill. ; 20 cm. USSR 74
0.95rub
1. Motor vehicles—Electric equipment. 2. Tractors—Electric equipment. I. Vasilevskiĭ, Viktor Iosifovich, joint author. II. Levin, S. M., joint author. III. Title.
TL272.B27 1974 74-352927

Barabanov, Viktor Nikolaevich.
(Radiat͡sionnai͡a prochnost' konstrukt͡sionnogo grafita)
Радиационная прочность конструкционного графита / В. Н. Барабанов, Ю. С. Виргильев. — Москва : Атомиздат, 1976.
78, ₍2₎ p. : ill. ; 22 cm. USSR***
Bibliography: p. 76-₍79₎
0.51rub
1. Graphite, Effect of radiation on. I. Virgil'ev, I͡Uriĭ Sergeevich, joint author. II. Title.
TA455.G7B37 77-510940

Barabanov, Vladimir Fedorovich.
(Mineralogii͡a vol'framitovykh mestorozhdeniĭ Vostochnogo Zabaĭkal'i͡a)
Минералогия вольфрамитовых месторождений Восточного Забайкалья: Букука-Белуха. ₍Ленинград₎ 1961-
v. illus., profiles. 27 cm.
At head of title, v. 1- : Ленинградский государственный университет имени А. А. Жданова.
Vol. 2 has title: Mineralogii͡a vol'framitovykh mestorozhdeniĭ Zabaĭkal'i͡a.
Bibliography: v. 1, p. 345-₍358₎ ; v. 2, p. 347-358.
1. Wolframite. 2. Ore-deposits—Transbaikalia. I. Title.
QE391.W6B3 62-31068

Barabanov, Vladimir Fedorovich
see Voprosy geokhimii i tipomorfizm mineralov.

Barabanov, Vladimir Fedorovich
see Vsesoi͡uznoe soveshchanie po mineralogii, geokhimii, genezisu i vozmozhnosti kompleksnogo ispol'zovanii͡a vol'framitovykh mestorozhdenii SSSR, 3d, Leningrad, 1971. (Mineralogiia i geokhimiia vol'framovykh mestorozhdenii) 1975.

Barabanova, Galina Vasil'evna, joint author
see Toporova, Evdokii͡a Mikhaĭlovna. (V zagranichnom plavanii) 1976.

Barabanova, L. M., ed.
see Mogilev. 1971.

Barabanova, L.M., ed.
see Nauchno-teoreticheskai͡a konferent͡sii͡a "V.I. Lenin - velikiĭ teoretik, organizator i vozhd' Kommunisticheskoĭ partii i Sovetskogo gosudarstva", Mogilev, Russia, 1970. Sbornik materialov... Mogilev, 1970.

Barabanova, Nina Alekseevna, joint author
see Mochalov, Lev Vsevolodovich. The female portrait in Russian art ... Leningrad : Aurora Art Publishers, [1974]

Barabanova, Nina Alekseevna
see Pimenov, I͡Uriĭ Ivanovich, 1903-
I͡Uriĭ Pimenov. [1972]

Barabanow, Evgenij V
see Barabanov, Evgenii Viktorovich, 1943-

Barabanshchikov, Aleksandr Vasil'evich
see Militärisches Kollektiv. (Berlin) Militärverl. d. DDR (1972).

Barabanshchikov, Aleksandr Vasil'evich
see Problemy psikhologii voinskogo kollektiva. 1973.

Barabanshchikov, N. V.
see Kugenev, Petr Venediktovich. Praktikum po molochnomu delu. 1968.

Barabarua, Rādhānātha
see Kāśinātha Śarmma. (Asama buranji puthi) 1906.

Barabas, Alicia.
Hydraulic development and ethnocide : the Mazatec and Chinantec people of Oaxaca, Mexico / Alicia Barabas and Miguel Bartolomé. — Copenhagen : ₍International Work Group for Indigenous Affairs₎, 1973.
20 p. : map ; 21 cm. — (IWGIA document ; 15) D***
Bibliography: p. 20.
1. Mazatec Indians. 2. Chinantec Indians. 3. Papaloapan Valley I. Bartolomé, Miguel Alberto, 1945- joint author. II. Series: International Work Group for Indigenous Affairs. IWGIA document ; 15.
F1221.M35B37 323.1'19'70726 75-329688
75 MARC

Barabas, Andras, joint author
see Calnan, James. Speaking at medical meetings... London, Heinemann Medical, 1972.

Barabas, Andras, joint author
see Calnan, James. Writing medical papers; a practical guide. London, Heinemann Medical, 1973.

Barabás, Andrei.
A kémiai kód / Barabás A., Hodoşan F., Mantsch H. — Bukarest : Tudományos és Enciklopédiai Könyvkiadó, 1975.
77 p. : ill. ; 17 cm. — (Tudomány mindenkinek) R 75-4866
Translation of Mesagerii chimici.
lei 2.50
1. Biological chemistry. I. Hodoşan, F., joint author. II. Mantsch, H., joint author. III. Title.
QH345.B3716 76-508210

Barabas, Andrei.
Mesagerii chimici / A. Barabas, F. Hodoşan, H. Mantsch ; ₍coperta, Victor Wegemann₎. — Bucureşti : Editura ştiinţifică şi enciclopedică, 1975.
79 p. : ill. ; 17 cm. — (Ştiinţa pentru toţi) R 75-3255
lei 2.50
1. Biological chemistry. 2. Insecticides. I. Hodoşan, F., joint author. II. Mantsch, H., joint author. III. Title.
QH345.B38 76-511717

Barabás, Ladislao Holik-
see Holik-Barabás, Ladislao.

Barabas, Steven.
see Interpreting the word of God ... Chicago, Moody Press, c1976.

Barabás, Tibor.
Éjjeli őrjárat; Rembrandt életregénye. ₍3. változatlan kiad.₎ Budapest, Magvető Könyvkiadó, 1970.
284 p. 19 cm.
21.50
1. Rembrandt, Harmenszoon van Rijn, 1606-1669—Fiction. I. Title.
PH3213.B29E4 1970 73-495827

Barabás, Tibor.
Három portré : Mozart párizsi utazása, Beethoven, Chopin / Barabás, Tibor. — Budapest : Magvető Könyvkiadó, 1974, c1966.
486 p., ₍18₎ leaves of plates : ill. ; 19 cm.
30.00Ft
1. Mozart, Johann Chrysostom Wolfgang Amadeus, 1756-1791. 2. Beethoven, Ludwig van, 1770-1827. 3. Chopin, Fryderyk Franciszek, 1810-1849. I. Title.
ML390.B243H4 75-408075

Barabás, Tibor.
Kereszt a hegytetőn. Budapest, Szépirodalmi Könyvkiadó [c1972]
296 p.
I. Title.
MiEM DLC NUC76-74989

Barabás, Tibor.
Michelangelo élete; regény. Budapest, Szépirodalmi Könyvkiadó [1970]
399 p. illus., port. 23 cm.
38.00Ft
1. Buonarroti, Michel Angelo, 1475-1564—Fiction. I. Title.
PH3213.B29M5 79-285850

Barabás, Tibor.
Rákóczi hadnagya. Budapest, Magvető [1972]
198 p.
Hungarian.
I. Title.
OCl NUC74-128251

Barabash, ÎUriĭ ÎAkovlevych.
(Voprosy ėstetiki i poėtiki)
Вопросы эстетики и поэтики. Москва, Современник, 1973.
318 p. port. 21 cm. 1.00rub USSR***
At head of title: Юрий Барабаш.
Includes bibliographical references.
1. Literature—Aesthetics. 2. Aesthetics. 3. Poetics. I. Title.
PN45.B26 73-337787

Barabash, ÎUriĭ ÎAkovlevych.
(Voprosy ėstetiki i poėtiki)
Вопросы эстетики и поэтики / Юрий Барабаш. — Изд. 2., доп. — Москва : Современник, 1977.
398 p. ; 21 cm. USSR***
Includes bibliographical references.
1.23rub
1. Literature—Aesthetics. 2. Aesthetics. 3. Poetics. I. Title.
PN45.B26 1977 77-511512

Barabash, Ivan Ivanovych, 1912–
(P'ėsy)
П'єси / Іван Барабаш. — Київ : Дніпро, 1977.
205 p., [1] leaf of plates : port. ; 18 cm. USSR***
CONTENTS: Видно шляхи полтавські.—Три долі.—Закохані серця.
0.74rub
PG3949.12.A67P5 77-515090

Barabash, Sergeĭ.
(ÎA bolee vsego vesnu lûblû)
Я более всего весну люблю. [Фотоальбом о родине С. Есенина с. Константиново. Фото С. Барабаша и др. Стихи С. Есенина]. Москва, "Планета," [1971].
[184] p. with illus. 26 cm. (Памятные места СССР) 3.58rub USSR 72-VKP
By S. Barabash, E. Kassin and M. Red'kin.
1. Esenin, Sergeĭ Aleksandrovich, 1895-1925—Homes and haunts. 2. Konstantinovo, Russia (Ryazanskaya oblast')—Description—Views. I. Kassin, Evgeniĭ, joint author. II. Red'kin, Mark, joint author. III. Esenin, Sergeĭ Aleksandrovich, 1895-1925. IV. Title.
PG3476.E8Z558 73-325537

Barabash, Sergeĭ.
(V kraû velikikh vdokhnoveniĭ)
В краю великих вдохновений; времена года: Михайловское, Петровское, Тригорское, Святогорский монастырь. In the land of great inspiration. [Авторы фотоальбома: С. Барабаш, Е. Кассин, В. Савостьянов] Москва, Планета, 1972.
1 v. (chiefly illus., part col.) 27 cm. (Памятные места СССР) USSR***
4.30rub
Includes selections by A. S. Pushkin and others.
Preface and lists of illustrations also in English.

1. Pushkin, Aleksandr Sergeevich, 1799-1837—Homes and haunts. I. Pushkin, Aleksandr Sergeevich, 1799-1837. II. Kassin, Evgeniĭ, joint author. III. Savost'ânov, V., joint author. IV. Title. V. Title: In the land of great inspiration.
PG3351.5.B27 73-318253

Barabash, Vasyl' Iosypovych.
Poltavshchyna v dev'îatii p'îatyrichtsi. [By] V.I. Barabash. Kharkiv, Prapor, 1972.
124 p. illus. (Plany partiï - plany narodu)
1. Poltava, Ukraine (Province)—Econ. condit. 2. Russia (1917-)—Five year plans—Ninth, 1971-1975.
MH NUC75-129144

Barabash-Nikiforov, Il'îa Il'ich.
Die Desmane : Familie Desmanidae (Insectivora) / von I. I. Barabasch-Nikiforow ; [aus dem Russischen übers. von Günther Grempe]. — Wittenberg-Lutherstadt : A. Ziemsen, 1975.
99, [1] p. : ill. ; 21 cm. — (Die Neue Brehm-Bücherei ; 474) GDR***
Bibliography: p. 93-[100]
7.70M
1. Russian desman. 2. Pyrenean desman. I. Title.
QL737.I57B3715 77-469450
77 MARC

Barabashev, Georgiĭ Vasil'evich.
(Osnovy sovetskogo stroitel'stva)
Основы советского строительства : пособие для слушателей / Г. В. Барабашев, О. Е. Кутафин, К. Ф. Шеремет. — Москва : Знание, 1976.
189 p. ; 21 cm. — (Народный университет : Факультет правовых знаний) USSR***
Series romanized: Narodnyĭ universitet : Fakul'tet pravovykh znaniĭ.
Bibliography: p. 183-[185]
0.46rub
1. Soviets—Examinations, questions, etc. 2. Russia—Constitutional law—Examinations, questions, etc. I. Kutafin, Oleg Emel'îanovich, joint author. II. Sheremet, Konstantin Filippovich, joint author. III. Title.
77-501366

Barabashev, Georgiĭ Vasil'evich.
(Osnovy znaniĭ o Sovetskom gosudarstve i prave)
Основы знаний о Советском государстве и праве : учебное пособие / Г. В. Барабашев, О. Е. Кутафин ; под ред. Г. А. Кригера. — Москва : Изд-во Московского университета, 1977.
164 p. ; 22 cm. USSR***
Includes bibliographical references.
0.38rub
1. Russia—Constitutional law. 2. Law—Russia. 3. Law and socialism. I. Kutafin, Oleg Emel'îanovich, joint author. II. Title.
77-515464

Barabashev, Georgiĭ Vasil'evich.
(Raĭonnyĭ, gorodskoĭ Sovet na sovremennom ėtape)
Районный, городской Совет на современном этапе / Г. В. Барабашев. — Москва : Юрид. лит., 1975.
110 p. ; 20 cm. — (Библиотечка для работников районных, городских Советов) USSR 75
Series romanized: Bibliotechka dlîa rabotnikov raĭonnykh, gorodskikh Sovetov.
Includes bibliographical references.
0.17rub
1. Soviets. I. Title.
75-594024

Barabashev, Georgiĭ Vasil'evich
see Sovetskoe gosudarstvennoe pravo. 1975.

Barabashkin, Vladimir Pavlovich.
(Molotkovye i rotornye drobilki)
Молотковые и роторные дробилки. Изд. 2-е, перераб. и доп. Москва, "Наука," 1973.
143 p. with illus. 21 cm. 0.44rub USSR 73
At head of title: В. П. Барабашкин.
Bibliography: p. 140-[142]
1. Crushing machinery. I. Title.
TJ1345.B37 1973 74-303424

Barabashkin, Vladimir Pavlovich
see Otdelka prokata na potochnykh liniîakh 1972.

Barabasz, Arreed Franz, 1945-
Temporal orientation: a review of the literature. [Buffalo, Child Study Center, State University College at Buffalo, 1974]
43-49 p. (Child study journal monographs, no. 3)
Bibliography: p. 48-49.
1. Time perspective. 2. Time perception. I. Title.
MH-Ed IMacoW NUC75-41239

Barabé, Paul Henri, 1904-
Le mystère de Lourdes. Cap-de-la-Medeleine, Richesse Mariale, 1958.
23 p. 18 cm. (Richesse Mariale, 2)
Besuttti (1968) Y275.
ODaU-M NUC74-33078

Barabenec, Jiří.
Po stopach starých pověstí českých. [1. vyd.] Praha, Orbis, 1959.
271 p. illus., plates.
1. Tales, Czech—Hist. & crit. I. Title.
ICU NUC75-67073

Barabino, Angelo, 1883-1950
see Poggialini Tominetti, Mirella, 1936- Angelo Barabino. Torino: Teca, 1974.

Baraboĭ, Vilen Abramovich.
(ÎAdernye izluchenîa i zhizn')
Ядерные излучения и жизнь. Москва, "Наука," 1972.
232 p. with illus. 20 cm. (Серия: Проблемы современной науки и технического прогресса) 0.77rub USSR 72-VKP
At head of title: Академия наук СССР. В. А. Барабой, Б. Р. Киричинский.
Bibliography: p. 230-[231]
1. Radiobiology. I. Kirichinskiĭ, Boris Romanovich, joint author. II. Title.
QH652.B35 72-363355

Baraboĭ, Vilen Abramovich.
(Promenevi urazhennîa i mekhanizmy protypromenevoho zakhystu)
Променеві ураження і механізми протипроменевого захисту. Київ, "Здоров'я," 1971.
142 p. with illus. 21 cm. USSR 71-5053[illegible]
At head of title: В. А. Барабой.
Bibliography: p. 137-141.
1.10rub
1. Radiation—Toxicology. 2. Radiation-protective agents. I. Title.
[RA1231.R2B28] 75-59420[illegible]

Baraboĭ, Vilen Abramovich.
(Solnechnyĭ luch)
Солнечный луч / В. А. Барабой. — Москва : Наука, 1976.
239, [1] p., [2] leaves of plates : ill. ; 21 cm. — (Научно-популярная серия) USSR***
At head of title: Akademiîa nauk SSSR.
Series romanized: Nauchno-populîarnaîa seriîa.
Bibliography: p. 239-[240]
0.47rub
1. Photobiology. 2. Solar radiation—Physiological effect. 3. Photosynthesis. I. Title.
QH515.B37 77-515669

Baraboĭ, Vilen Abramovich.
(Spadkovist' i pryroda zhyvoho)
Спадковість і природа живого / В. А. Барабой. — Київ : Наук. думка, 1975.
207 p. : ill. ; 17 cm. — (Людина і природа) USSR***
Series romanized: Lîudyna i pryroda.
Bibliography: p. 204-[206]
0.31rub
1. Genetics. 2. Medical genetics. I. Title.
QH430.B37 75-591876

Baraboĭ, Vilen Abramovich, joint author
see Kirichinskiĭ, Boris Romanovich.
Lazernyĭ promin' i orhanizm. 1972.

Baraboliа, Marko, 1910–
(Tuteshnîats'ka hubernîa)
Тутешняцька губернія. Сатири. Це вид. виходить з нагоди шістдесятиріччя від дня нар. Марка Бараболі. Підготовка текстів упоряд. та післямова Михайла Мольнара. Вид. 1. Пряшів, Слов. педаг. вид., друк. Дуклянські друк., 1970.
179, [4] p. port., illus. on lining paper. 79 mm. (Перлини, № 2) Kčs6.50 CzS 70-MS
1. Bibliography—Microscopic and miniature editions—Specimens. I. Mol'nar, Mykhaĭlo. II. Title.
PG3948.B255T86 73-312619

Barabolîa, P. D.
see Okean, tekhnika, pravo. 1972.

Baraboo, Wis. Circus World Museum.
Circus World Museum Library; a guide to its holdings and services. [Baraboo, Wis? 1973]
22 p.
1. Circus World Museum, Baraboo, Wis. I. Title.
WHi NUC75-58264

Baraboo, Wis. Circus World Museum.
Circus World Museum [prospectus. Baraboo, Wis., 1970]
28 p. illus.
1. Museums—Circus. 2. Circus World Museum, Baraboo, Wis.
WHi NUC73-59554

Baraboshkin, Alekseĭ Nikolaevich, ed.
see Elektrokhimiîa rasplavlennykh solevykh i tverdykh elektrolitov. [1972]

Baraboshkin, Alekseĭ Nikolaevich, ed.
see Elektrokhimiîa rasplavlennykh solevykh i tverdykh elekrolitov. [1973]

Baraboshkin, Alekseĭ Nikolaevich, ed.
see Thermodynamics and kinetics of electrode processes. New York, Consultants Bureau, 1967.

Barac, Antun.
A history of Yugoslav literature. ⌈Translated by Petar Mijusković. Ann Arbor, Mich.⌋ Joint Committee on Eastern Europe of the American Council of Learned Societies and the Social Science Research Council ⌈1973 ?⌋
266 p. 24 cm. (Publication series, no. 1)
Translation of Jugoslavenska knjizevnost.
Reprint of the 1955 ed.
1. Yugoslav literature—Hist. & crit. I. Title.
IaU OU NUC74-127039

Barac, Antun.
A history of Yugoslav literature / Antun Barac ; ⌈translated by Petar Mijušković⌋. — Ann Arbor : Michigan Slavic Publications, Dept. of Slavic Languages and Literatures, University of Michigan, ⌈1976?⌋
266 p. ; 24 cm. — (⌈Publication series - Joint Committee on Eastern Europe ; no. 1⌋)
Translation of Jugoslavenska književnost.
Series covered by label mounted on t.p.
Includes index.
1. Yugoslav literature—History and criticism. I. Title. II. Series: Joint Committee on Eastern Europe. Publication series - Joint Committee on Eastern Europe ; no. 1.
PG561.B313 1976 891.8 76-623278
76 MARC

Barac, Olga Srdanovic-
see Srdanovic-Barac, Olga

Barac, Vladimir, 1931-
"Song of myself" as myth and reality: an American quest for epic. ⌈Austin, Tex.⌋ 1971.
xi, 422 l. 29 cm.
Thesis (Ph.D.)—University of Texas at Austin.
Vita.
Bibliography: leaves 418-422.
1. Whitman, Walt, 1819-1892. Song of myself.
TxU NUC73-114746

Baracca, Angelo.
Marxismo e scienze naturali : per una storia integrale delle scienze / Angelo Baracca, Arcangelo Rossi. — Bari : De Donato, c1976.
173 p. ; 18 cm. — (Dissensi ; 74) It76-Oct
Includes bibliographical references.
L2200
1. Science—Social aspects. 2. Science—Philosophy. 3. Communism and science. I. Rossi, Arcangelo, joint author. II. Title.
Q175.5.B35 76-483496
•76 MARC

Baracca, Angelo.
La spirale delle alte energie : aspetti politici e logica di sviluppo della fisica delle particelle elementari / Angelo Baracca, Silvio Bergia. — Milano : Bompiani, ⌈1975⌋
310 p. : ill. ; 22 cm. — (Studi Bompiani ; 11 : La Scienza critica) It 75-Aug
Includes bibliographical references and index.
L4000
1. Particles (Nuclear physics) 2. Atomic energy. 3. Science and state. I. Bergia, Silvio, joint author. II. Title.
QC793.29.B37 75-542777

Baracchi, Erio.
Erio Baracchi. [Mostra] dal 27 febbraio al 10 marso 1971, Istituti culturali del commune de Modena, Galleria dalla Salla di cultura. [Modena, Galleria della Salla di cultura, 1971]
[4] p. 9 plates. 21 cm.
Text signed: Franco Passoni.
1. Baracchi, Erio. I. Passoni, Franco. II. Modena. Galleria della sala di cultura.
TxU NUC76-74991

Baracchini, Clara.
Il Duomo di Lucca / Clara Baracchini, Antonino Caleca ; contributi di Anna Rosa Calderoni Masetti, Gigetta Dalli Regoli, Donata Devoti. — Lucca : Libreria editrice Baroni, 1973.
527 p. : ill. (some col.) ; 27 cm. It 74-Apr
Bibliography : p. 509-517.
Includes index.
1. Lucca. San Martino (Cathedral) I. Caleca, Antonino, joint author. II. Title.
NA5621.L78B37 75-552969

Baracchini, Hugo, joint author
see Altezor, Carlos. Historia urbana y social de Villa Colón. [Montevideo] Ediciones de la Banda Oriental [1973]

Baracchini, Hugo, joint author
see Altezor, Carlos. Historia urbanística y edilicia de la ciudad de Montevideo... Montevideo, Junta Departamental de Montevideo, 1971.

Baracchino, Nello
see Anderlini, Giuseppe F M Tecnica degli approvvigionamenti. Nuova ed. ampliata. Milano, F. Angeli, [1973].

Baracco, Lino.
see Gli Anziani come protagonisti ... Torino Leumann, Elle Di Ci, 1975.

Baracconi, Giuseppe.
Spettacoli nell'antica Roma. Roma, Edizioni del Gattopardo, 1972.
173 p. plates. 21 cm. (Roma confidenziale, 1) L2500 It 72-Nov
Includes bibliographical references.
1. Theater—Rome. I. Title.
PA6073.B3 72-373462

Barach, Arnold B
Famous American trademarks ⌈by⌋ Arnold B. Barach. Washington, Public Affairs Press ⌈1971⌋
viii, 192 p. illus. 23 cm. $5.00
1. Trade-marks—United States. I. Title.
T223.V2B37 602'.7'5 72-177402
71⌈r75⌋rev MARC

Barach, Jeffrey A., 1934-
see The Individual, business, and society. Englewood Cliffs, N.J., Prentice-Hall, c1977.

Barach, Jeffrey Truxton, 1948-
Recovery of heat injured Clostridium perfringens spores on selective media. Raleigh, N.C., 1973.
62 l. illus., tables. 29 cm.
Thesis—North Carolina State University at Raleigh.
Vita.
Bibliography: leaves 59-62.
NcRS NUC74-128243

Barach, Roland Israel.
Comparability of heart rate, electrodermal activity, and skin temperature during an anticipatory period prior to the presentation of aversive tones or test questions. ⌈Seattle⌋ 1976.
192 l. illus.
Thesis (Ph.D.)--University of Washington.
Bibliography: leaves 106-111.
WaU NUC77-91851

Barachevskiĭ, V. A.
see Registriruíushchie sredy dlía golografii. 1975.

Baracho, José Alfredo de Oliveira.
Participação nos lucros e integração social-PIS. ⌈Belo Horizonte⌋ Revista Brasileira de Estudos Políticos, 1972.
121 p. 24 cm. (Estudos sociais e políticos, 31) (Universidade Federal de Minas Gerais. Publicação no. 543)
Bibliography : p. ⌈113⌋-121.
1. Non-wage payments—Brazil. I. Title. II. Series: Revista Brasileira de Estudos Políticos. Estudos sociais e políticos, 31.
75-543213

Barack, Karl August, 1827-1900
see Fürstlich Fürstenbergische Hofbibliothek zu Donaueschingen. Die Handschriften... Hildesheim, G. Olms, 1974.

Barack, M
Wilhelm Tell. Mit Zugrundelegung von Schillers Schauspiel der Jugend erzählt. Stuttgart. K. Thienemanns Verlag ⌈n.d.⌋
158 p.
PPG NUC74-122585

Barack, Nathan A
The Jewish way to life, by Nathan A. Barack. Middle Village, N.Y., Jonathan David Publishers, c1975.
208 p., 22 cm.
1. Judaism. 2. Jewish way of life. I. Title.
BM565.B29 296 74-19272
ISBN 0-8246-0192-4 74 MARC

Barack, William Nicholas.
Stress analysis of prismatic shell structures / by William Nickolas Barrack. -- [Cincinnati: s.n.], 1975.
xiv, 170 leaves in various pagings ; ill. ; 29 cm.
Thesis (Ph.D.) -- University of Cincinnati.
Bibliography : leaf R-1.
OCU NUC77-83522

Barački, Stanimir
see Nakit Sarmata u Banatu sa pregledom sarmatskih nalazišta. 1975.

Barački, Stanimir
see Vršac, Yugoslavia. Narodni muzej. (Narodni muzej u Vršcu) [1974]

Baracs, Dénes.
A fal mögött, kína / Baracs Dénes. — Budapest : Gondolat, 1975.
558 p., ⌈50⌋ leaves of plates : ill. (some col.) ; 21 cm. — (Világjárók ; 98)
ISBN 963-280-230-6 : 59.00Ft
1. China—Description and travel—1949- 2. Baracs, Dénes. I. Title.
DS711.B35 77-502434

Barącz, Sadok, 1814-1892.
Żywoty sławnych Ormian w Polsce. We Lwowie, w Drukarni Zakładu im. Ossolińskich, 1856.
viii, 485 p.
Includes bibliographical references.
Microfilm. 1 reel. 35 mm.
1. Armenians in Poland—Biography. I. Title.
Microfilm 51408 DK 77-501226
[DK412.15]

Barad, Cary B
The disabled: means of meeting medical care charges. [Washington] U.S. Social Security Administration, Office of Research and Statistics, 1972.
43 p. (From the social security survey of the disabled, 1966. Report, no. 20) (DHEW publication no. (SSA) 72-11713)
1. Expenditures, Health. 2. Handicapped. 3. Insurance, Health—U.S. 4. Medical assistance. 5. Social security—U.S. I. Title. II. Series. III. Series: DHEW publication no. (SSA) 72-11713.
DNLM NUC74-126733

Barad, Cary B
Role conflict among vocational evaluators: sources, precursors, and adjustive correlates, by Cary B. Barad. ⌈College Park, Md.⌋ 1973.
138 l. 29 cm.
Typescript.
Thesis—University of Maryland.
Vita.
Includes bibliography.
1. Supervision of vocational rehabilitation. 2. Rehabilitation counseling. I. Title.
MdU NUC75-21631

Barad, Gerald, joint author
see Bing, Elisabeth D A birth in the family. Toronto, New York, Bantam Books [1973]

Barada, Bill
see World beneath the sea. [2d ed.] Washington [National Geographic Society, 1973]

Barada, William.
The relation of aquatic anomalies to marine pollution with special references ⌈sic⌋ to Florida, by William Barada, William M. Partington, Jr. Winter Park, Environmental Information Center of the Florida Conservation Foundation, inc., 1973.
84, 8 l. 28 cm.
"Prepared for the Florida Dept. of Natural Resources, Division of Marine Fisheries ⌈sic⌋ and the Florida Audubon Society."
Includes bibliography.

1. Marine pollution. 2. Fishes—Diseases and pests. I. Partington, William M., joint author. II. Florida. Division of Marine Resources. III. Florida Audubon Society. IV. Florida Conservation Foundation. Environmental Information Center. V. Title.
FU NUC76-102628

Baradalai, Nirmmalaprabhā
see
Bardoloi, Nirmal Probha.

Baradalai, Upendranatha
see
Bardoloi, U N

al-Baraddūnī, 'Abd Allāh.
(Madīnat al-ghad)
مدينة الغد / عبد الله البردونى. — عدن : وزارة الثقافة والسياحة : وكيل التوزيع فى جمهورية اليمن الديمقراطية الشعبية، مؤسسة ١٤ أوكتوبر، 1974.
172 p. ; 17 cm.
£L4.00
Poems.
I. Title.
PJ7816.A654M3 1974 — 75-960521

al-Baraddūnī, 'Abd Allāh.
(al-Safar ilá al-ayyām al-khuḍr)
السفر الى الأيام الخضر : شعر / عبد الله البردوني. — الطبعة 2. — دمشق : [s. n.], 1975
127 p. : ill. ; 17 cm.
£Syr3.00
I. Title.
PJ7816.A654S3 1975 — 76-960648

Baradel, P., joint author
see Stancher, B Sui molluschi dell'-alto Adriatico... [Udine] Del Bianco, 1968.

Baradi, Hasmukh, 1938–
(Kāḷo kāmaḷo)
કાળો કામળો : નાટક / હસમુખ બારાડી. — 1. આવૃત્તિ. — અમદાવાદ : રૂપાલી પ્રકાશન, 1974.
80 p. ; 19 cm.
In Gujarati.
Rs4.00
I. Title.
PK1859.B358K3 — 75-904978

Baradi, Subraman'ia
see Bharati, C Subrahmanya, 1882-1921.

al-Barādi'ī, Khālid Muḥī al-Dīn.
(al-Raḥīl naḥwa al-mustaqbal)
الرحيل نحو المستقبل، شعر خالد محي الدين البرادعي. دمشق، وزارة الثقافة، 1971.
148 p. 20 cm.
I. Title.
PJ7816.A655R3 — 74-227246

al-Barādi'ī, Khālid Muḥī al-Dīn.
(Ṣuwar 'alá ḥā'iṭ al-manfá)
صور على حائط المنفى، شعر خالد محي الدين البرادعي. [الطبعة 1. بيروت، توزيع دار الطليعة للطباعة والنشر، 1970]
159 p. illus. 23 cm.
Partially vocalized.
I. Title.
PJ7816.A655S8 — 72-218340
rev

Baradiīn, Badzar.
Statuia Maītrei v zolotom khrame v Lavrane. Neudruck der Ausgabe 1924. Osnabrück, Biblio Verlag, 1970.
011, 98 p. plan. (Bibliotheca Buddhica, v. 22)
1. Statues–Tibet. I. Title.
WaU — NUC75-40964

Baradja, Mohamad Farid, 1929-
A contrastive analysis of selected patterns of the noun phrases and verb phrases of English and Indonesian. Los Angeles, 1971.
x, 188 l. illus.
Thesis—University of California at Los Angeles.
Microfilm. Ann Arbor, Mich., University Microfilms, 1971. 1 reel. 35 mm.
1. English language—Noun. 2. Indonesian language—Noun. 3. English language—Verb. 4. Indonesian language—Verb. I. Title.
NIC — NUC74-122667

Bāradolīkara, Dīpaka
see
Bardolikar, Deepak, 1925-

Baradon, Eunice, joint author
see Kessler, Aharon. Teaching current affairs in the Jewish religious school. Pittsburgh, Council of Jewish Education, 1958.

Baradulin, Ryhor Ivanavich, 1935–
(Rum)
Рум : новая кніга лірыкі / Рыгор Барадулін. — Мінск : Мастацкая літ-ра, 1974.
189 p. ; 17 cm. — USSR***
0.64rub
I. Title.
PG2835.2.B3R8 — 75-526890

Baradulin, Ryhor Ivanavich, 1935-
Zhuravinka; humarystychnyia vershy, parod'ii, epihramy. [By] Ryhor Baradulin. Minsk, Mastatskaia lit-ra, 1973.
142 p. illus.
MH — NUC75-128325

Baraev, Aleksandr Ivanovich.
Борьба с ветровой эрозией почв. Алма-Ата, Казахское гос. изд-во сельхоз. лит-ры, 1963.
32, [4] p. illus., map. 20 cm.
At head of title: А. И. Бараев, А. А. Зайцева, Э. Ф. Госсен.
Bibliography: p. [34]
1. Soil erosion—Kazakhstan. I. Zaitseva, Aleksandra Alekseevna, joint author. II. Gossen, Ė. F., joint author. III. Title.
Title transliterated: Bor'ba s vetrovoĭ ėroziei pochv.
S625.R9B353 — 73-201993

Baraev, Aleksandr Ivanovich
see Iarovaia pshenitsa v Severnom Kazakhstane. 1976.

Baraev, Aleksandr Ivanovich
see Mekhanizatsiia i ėkonomika sel'skokhoziaistvennogo proizvodstva. 1974.

Baraev, Aleksandr Ivanovich
see Vetrovaia ėroziia i plodorodie pochv. 1976.

Baraf, Lupu.
Îmbunătățirea calității îmbinărilor sudate. București, Editura tehnică, 1973.
200 p. with figs. 21 cm. lei 8.00 — R 73-2432
At head of title: Lupu Baraf, Maria Sabac.
Summary in Romanian, English, French, German, and Russian.
Bibliography: p. 187–[193]
1. Welded joints—Defects. 2. Electric welding—Quality control. I. Sabac, Maria, joint author. II. Title.
TA492.W4B37 — 73-358638

Barag, Lev Grigor'evich
see Barah, Leŭ Ryhoravich.

Baraga, Friedrich, Bp., 1797–1868.
Geschichte, Character, Sitten und Gebräuche der nord-amerikanischen Indier. Theils aus zuverlässigen Quellen, theils aus eigener Erfahrung gesammelt und hrsg. von Friedrich Baraga. Laibach, Gedruckt bei J. Blasnik; verlegt und zu finden bei J. Klemens, bürgerl. Buchbinder, 1837.
193 p. front. 18 cm.
1. Indians of North America. I. Title.
E77.B2 — 74-203206

Baraga, Mich. Planning Commission
see Anderson (Max E.) Associates. Comprehensive plan. Madison, Wis., 1969.

Baraga Co., Mich. Planning Commission
see Vilican-Leman and Associates. Preliminary plan reports. Southfield, Mich., 1969.

Baraga County Historical Society.
100 years of history : L'Anse-Skanee centennial. --[s. l. : The Society], 1971.
76 p. : ill.
1. L'Anse, Mich.--History. 2. Skanee, Mich.--History. I. Title.
WHi — NUC77-94482

Baragan, J
Phonocardiologie dynamique : contribution des drogues vaso-actives au diagnostic des cardiopathies / J. Baragan, F. Fernandez, J.-M. Thiron ; préf. de A. Gerbaux. — Paris : J. B. Baillière, c1976.
343 p. : ill. ; 21 x 29 cm. — F***
Label on lining paper: Distributed in the U.S.A. by S.M.P.F. Corp., New York.
Bibliography: p. [325]-332.
Includes index.
ISBN 2-7008-0008-7
1. Phonocardiography. 2. Cardiovascular agents. I. Fernandez, F., joint author. II. Thiron, J. M., joint author. III. Title.
RC683.5.P5B37 — 616.1'2'0754 — 76-479706
76 — MARC

Baragaño, José Alvarez
see Alvarez Baragaño, José.

Baragar, Edith Anne, 1895–
Ripples from the creek, by Mrs. F. D. Baragar. Winnipeg, 1969.
vii, 247 p. illus., map (on lining papers) 23 cm. $8.00 — C 72-991
1. Elm Creek, Manitoba—History. 2. Elm Creek, Manitoba—Biography. I. Title.
F1064.5.E44B37 — 917.127'4 — 73-162848
MARC

Barager, Joseph R
Perón and the Argentine democratic parties, 1943-1946 [by] Joseph R. Baragar [sic] Buffalo, 1972.
21 l. (New York (State) State University, Buffalo. Council International Studies, no. 12)
1. Political parties—Argentina. 2. Argentina—Political parties. 3. Argentina—Politics and government 1943- 4. Perón, Juan Domingo, Pres. Argentina. I. Title. II. Series.
DS NBuU — NUC73-116626

Barager, W R A
Coppermine and Dismal lakes map-areas 86 O and 86 N [by] W. R. A. Barager and J. A. Donaldson. [Ottawa] Dept. of Energy, Mines and Resources [1973]
v, 20 p. 2 fold. col. maps (in pocket) 25 cm. (Geological Survey of Canada. Paper 71-39) $2.00 — C***
Summary in French.
Bibliography: p. 17-20.
1. Geology—Northwest Territories, Can.—Mackenzie District. I. Donaldson, J. A., joint author. II. Title. III. Series: Canada. Geological Survey. Paper 71-39.
QE185.A42 no. 71-39 — 557.1'08 s — 73-176976
[QE195] — [557.19'3] — MARC

Barager, W R A
The geochemistry of coppermine river basalts. With a contribution by R. N. Annells. [Ottawa] Dept. of Energy, Mines and Resources [1969]
43 p. (Geological Survey of Canada. Paper 69-44)
Includes bibliography.
1. Basalt. 2. Geochemistry. 3. Geology—Northwest Territories, Can. —Mackenzie District. I. Title.
MiU — NUC73-126145

Baraghini, Marcello, ed.
see Fare controinformazione. Roma: La nuova sinistra [1974]

Baragli, Enrico, comp.
Comunicazione, comunione e Chiesa / Enrico Baragli. — Roma : Studio romano della comunicazione sociale, 1973.
1447 p. ; 24 cm. — (Collana Magisterium ; 4) — It 74-Sept
English, French, German, Italian, or Latin.
"Questo volume raccoglie ottocentoquarantadue documenti, quasi tutti del magistero cattolico."
Bibliography: p. 49-50.
Includes index.
1. Catholic Church—Collected works. 2. Communication. I. Title.
BX850.B37 — 74-351774

Baragli, Enrico.
Gli strumenti della communicazione soziale nel Concilio Vaticano II. Roma, La Civiltà Cattolica [1963]
54 p. 21 cm.
1. Vatican Council, 2d., 1962-65. 2. Communication—Social aspects.
IMunS — NUC74-33081

Baragli, Enrico
see Pious Society of St. Paul. Catechesi e pastorale attraverso i mass-media. [Torino] Edizioni paoline [1973]

Baragli, Tina Gramigni
see Gramigni Baragli, Tina.

Baraguru Ramachandrappa
see
Ramachandrappa, Baraguru.

Barah, Leŭ Ryhoravich.
Беларуская казка. Пытанні вывучэння яе нац. самабытнасці параўнальна з іншымі ўсход.-славянскімі казкамі. Мінск, "Вышэйш. школа," 1969.
256 p. 21 x 12 cm. USSR 70-32351
At head of title: Л. Р. Барар.
Includes bibliographical references.
0.93rub
1. Tales, White Russian—History and criticism. I. Title.
Title romanized: Belaruskaia kazka.
GR203.W49B3 79-569056

Barah, Leŭ Ryhoravich
see Mezhvuzovskaia nauchnaia konferentsiia "Rastsvet i sblizhenie sotsialisticheskikh natsii v SSSR, Ufa? 1967. Rastsvet, sblizhenie i vzaimoobogashchenie kul'tur... Ufa, 1970-

Barah, Leŭ Ryhoravich
see Satsyial'na-bytavyia kazki. 1976.

Barah, Leŭ Ryhoravich
see Ufa, Russia. Bashkirskii gosudarstvennyi universitet. Slavianskii filologicheskii sbornik. Ufa, 1962.

Bārah Bankvī, Surūr
see
Surūr Bārah Bankvī.

(Bāraha Hindī kāvya)
बारह हिन्दी काव्य / सम्पादक यश गुलाटी. — दिल्ली : सूर्य-प्रकाशन, 1975.
296 p. (p. 294-296 advertisements) ; 22 cm.
In Hindi.
Includes bibliographical references.
Rs35.00

1. Hindi poetry—History and criticism—Addresses, essays, lectures. I. Gulāṭi, Yaśa.

PK2040.B35 75-905677

Barahal, Hyman S.
see Fears related to death and suicide. New York, MSS Information Corp., [1974]

Barāhanī, Riẓā
see
Baraheni, Reza, 1935-

Barahatta, Karni Dan, 1925-
(Ādami ro sīnga)
आदमी रो सींग; राजस्थानी रो मौलिक कथा-संग्रह. [लेखक] करणीदान बारहठ. [1. संस्करण] बीकानेर, राजस्थानी भाषा साहित्य संगम (अकादमी) [1974]
102 p. 22 cm. Rs6.00
In Rajasthani.
CONTENTS: सूवटी री बेटी.—ठिकाणो.—चूनकी री मां.—धरती रो रंग.—दोजख.—परलै.—पांड.—धन घड़ी धन भाग.—चिमनी रो च्यानणो.—पीळा हाथ, काळो मूंढो.—आपो.—मौतरी गोठ.—आदमी रो सींग.
I. Title.
PK2708.9.B37A67 74-902367
SA

Barahatta, Karni Dan, 1925-
कुहरा और किरणें. [लेखक] करणीदान बारहट[sic]. बीकानेर, सूर्य प्रकाशन मन्दिर [1971]
224 p. 19 cm. Rs8.25
In Hindi.
A novel.

I. Title.
Title romanized: Kuharā aura kiraṇeṃ.
PK2098.13.A78K8 72-925658

Barahatta, Karni Dan, 1925-
(Rāṇī satī)
राणी सती / करणीदान बारहठ. — फेफाना, श्रीगंगानगर : बारहठ प्रकाशन, 1975.
108 p. ; 18 cm.
In Rajasthani.
Poems.
Rs8.00

I. Title.
PK2708.9.B37R3 75-908699

Bārahbankvī, Abūlhasan
see
Abūlhasan Bārahbankvī.

Baraheni, Reza, 1935-
(Āhuvān-i bāgh)
آهوان باغ، منتخب اشعار رضا براهنی. [n. p., 196-]
181 p. 21 cm.
I. Title.
PK6561.B35A7 N E 68-3103

Baraheni, Reza, 1935-
The crowned cannibals : writings on repression in Iran / Reza Baraheni, with an introduction by E. L. Doctorow. — 1st ed. — New York : Vintage Books, 1977.
xv, 279 p. ; 21 cm.
Includes bibliographical references.
ISBN 0-394-72357-0 : $3.95
1. Iran—Politics and government—1945- 2. Baraheni, Reza, 1935- —Biography. 3. Poets, Persian—Biography. 4. Political prisoners—Iran—Biography. 5. Torture—Iran. I. Title.
DS318.B335 320.9'55'05 76-62496
77 MARC

Baraheni, Reza, 1935-
God's shadow : prison poems / Reza Baraheni. — Bloomington : Indiana University Press, c1976.
103 p. ; 24 cm.
ISBN 0-253-13218-5 : $6.95
1. Political prisoners—Iran—Poetry. I. Title.
PK6561.B35A22 891'.55'13 75-34731
76 MARC

Baraheni, Reza, 1935-
(Gul bar gustarah-'i māh)
گل بر گسترهٔ ماه، يك تذكرهٔ كوچك تغزل مربوط به سال ٤٨ [از] رضا براهنی. [چاپ 1. تهران، چاپ كاويان، 1349 i. e. 1970]
72 p. 25 cm.
I. Title.
PK6561.B35G8 78-282359

Baraheni, Reza, 1935-
(Jangal va shahr)
جنگل و شهر [از] رضا براهنی. [تهران، چاپخانه سرعت 1342? i. e. 1963?]
67 p. 21 cm.
Poems.
I. Title.
PK6561.B35J3 74-272850

Baraheni, Reza, 1935-
(Muṣībatī zīr-i āftāb)
مصيبتى زير آفتاب [از] رضا براهنی. تهران، مؤسسهٔ انتشارات امير كبير [1349 i. e. 1970 or 71]
150 p. 22 cm.
Poems.
I. Title.
PK6561.B35M8 73-200369

Baraheni, Reza, 1935-
(Qiṣṣah'navīsī)
قصه‌نويسى [از] رضا براهنی. چاپ 2، متن كامل [تهران] سازمان انتشارات اشرفى [1969] 1348.
713, [23] p. 23 cm.
Bibliography: p. [722]-[733]
CONTENTS: مقدمه‌ای بر قصه‌نويسى — قصه‌نويسى در عصر شب — ساختمان قصه — نظرى به قصهٔ روانى — مقدمه‌ای بر قصه‌نويسى معاصر ايران — نقدى بر آثار صادق چوبك.
1. Fiction. 2. Persian fiction—History and criticism. I. Title.
PN3353.B35 1969 71-248895

Baraheni, Reza, 1935-
(Ṭalā dar mis)
طلا در مس «در شعر و شاعرى» [از] رضا براهنی. [چاپ 2، با تجديد نظر كلى و اضافات. [تهران؟] زمان [1347 i. e. 1968 or 9]
16, 655, [20] p. 22 cm.
Bibliography: p. [665-675]
1. Poetry. I. Title.
PN1031.B23 1968 76-277990

Barāhim, 'Abd al-Wāḥid.
(Fī bilād Kisrá)
فى بلاد كسرى [تأليف] عبد الواحد براهم. [تونس] الشركة التونسية للتوزيع [1971?]
198 p. illus. 21 cm.
Includes bibliographical references.
1. Iran—Description and travel. I. Title.
DS259.B33 74-216809

Barāhim, 'Abd al-Wāḥid.
(Ẓilāl 'alá al-arḍ)
ظلال على الأرض : [مجموعة قصصية] / عبد الواحد براهم. — [تونس؟] : الشركة التونسية للتوزيع، c1973.
155 p. ; 20 cm.
CONTENTS: ثمن الحصير. — الكلاب الضالة. — رجل يستيقظ. — رجل لبى النداء. — عندما تصرخ الدماء. — المخاض. — فس. — آثار جرح. — مصير لكل يوم. — الرجل الاخر. — رجل حطم نفسه. — رجل غريب. — باب بحر. — كنز السعادة. — سفينة القمح. — جلد الثعبان. — مربعات البلاستيك.
I. Title.
PJ7816.A657Z3 77-971024

Barāhinī, Riẓā
see
Baraheni, Reza, 1935-

Barahona, Alejandro, fl. 1971-
see Mascaró, Jaime. Participación y convivencia. [Madrid] Doncel [1971]

Barahona, Amaru.
El problema agrario en Nicaragua. [Managua] CUNN, 1971.
45 p. 17 cm. (Coleccion CUUN, 2)
1. Land reform—Nicaragua. 2. Agriculture—Nicaragua. I. Title.
VtU NUC75-32407

Barahona, Heriberto Rodríguez
see
Rodríguez Barahona, Heriberto.

Barahona, Orlando.
De Nacional Financiera y el intervencionismo. México, Ediciones del BOI, 1959.
8 p. 17 cm.
1. Industry and state—Mexico. 2. Mexico—Economic policy. 3. Nacional Financiera, S. A., Mexico. I. Title.
CU-B NUC74-10576

Barahona da Fonseca, António
see Fonseca, António Barahona da.

Barahona Israel, Rodrigo, joint author
see Salas Marrero, Oscar A Derecho agrario. [San José, Impreso en el Departamento de Publicaciones de la Universidad de Costa Rica] 1973.

Barahona Jiménez, Luis.
El gran incognito / Luis Barahona J. -- San José : Editorial Costa Rica, 1975.
223 p. ; 21 cm.
First published in 1953.
Includes bibliographical references.
1. Costa Rica--Social life and customs. 2. Farmers--Costa Rica. 3. National characteristics, Costa Rican. I. Title.
ViU DLC NUC77-83523

Barahona Jiménez, Luis.
Ideas, ensayos y paisajes. [1. ed.] San José, Editorial Costa Rica, 1972.
227 p. 21 cm.
I. Title.
AC75.B2557 73-203569

Barahona Jiménez, Luis.
Juventud y politica. San Jose, C.R., Ministerio de Cultura, Juventud y Deportes, Departamento de Publicaciones, 1972.
203 p.
1. Youth—Costa Rica—Political activity. I. Title.
UU NcU NUC74-122584

Barahona Jimenez, Luis.
El pensamiento politico en Costa Rica [1. ed. San José] Editorial Fernandez-Arce [1971?]
180 p. 20 cm. (Serie renovación, no. 1)
1. Costa Rica—Politics and government—History. I. Title.
IEdS NUC73-31312

Barahona Jiménez, Luis.
La Universidad de Costa Rica, 1940-1973 / Luis Barahona Jiménez. — 1. ed. — San José : Editorial Universidad de Costa Rica, 1976.
408 p. ; 23 cm.
Includes bibliographical references and index.
1. Costa Rica. Universidad, San Pedro—History. I. Title.
LE11.C72B37 77-471426
77 MARC

Barahona S , José A
El desarrollo de la cartografia en Panama. [n.p.] Instituto Geografico Nacional [1972]
302 p. fold. maps.
Includes bibliography.
1. Panama—Maps. I. Title.
MiEM NUC74-126745

Barahona Streber, Oscar.
Una voz de alerta! El seguro y su imagen pública. [Versión de la plática dictada por el Presidente de la Conferencia Hemisférica de Seguros, Lic. Oscar Barahona Streber, ante el V. Congreso Brasileño de Seguros Privados y Capitalización, celebrado en Río de Janeiro, Brasil, del 20 al 23 de Septiembre de 1965. Guatemala: Conferencia Hemisférica de Seguros, 1965?]
30 p. 23 x 11 cm.
TxU NUC74-122692

Barahuna, Epaminondas.
Estórias amazônicas. [Rio de Janeiro] Edições "O Cruzeiro" [1974]
189 p. 21 cm. Cr$24.00
1. Amazon Valley—Description and travel. I. Title.
F2546.B24 918.1'1 74-225212

Barahura, Mariía
see Ukrainian National Women's League of America. (P'íat'desíat' lit—1925-1975) Fifty years—1925-1975... Clifton, N. J.: Computoprint Corp., 1975.

Baráibar y Zumárraga, Federico, 1851-1918, tr.
see Aristophanes. Comedias de Aristófanes. [2. ed.] Madrid, Libreria y Casa Editorial Hernando, 1962-1972 [v. 3, 1964]

Baraita of Rabbi Ishmael. 1897
see Saadiah ben Joseph, gaon, 892?-942. [Kitāb al-mawārith. Hebrew and Judeo-Arabic] Sefer ha-yerushot. [1897] 657

Baraita of Rabbi Ishmael. 1959
see Saadiah ben Joseph, gaon, 892?-942. [Perush] [1959] 620.

Baraita of Rabbi Ishmael. 1967 or 8
see Saadiah ben Joseph, gaon, 892?-942. Kitab al-mawarith. Hebrew and Judeo-Arabic. Sefer ha-yerushot. 728 [1967 or 8]

Baraita of Samuel. 1973
see Solomon ben Isaac, called RaSHI, 1040-1105. [Isur ve-heter le-Rashi] Shene sefarim niftahim. [1973]

Barajas V , Enrique
see Symposium on Cancer of the Penis, Mexico City, 1964. Symposium de cancer del pene. Mexico City, Instituto Nacional de Cancerología, 1964]

Baraji, A
La restauración española en el siglo XIX. [Madrid, Cráficas Coalla, 1968]
72 p. ports., illus. (Centro de Estudios Historicos, Cáceres. Circulo de Estudios Donoso Cortés, Badajoz. [Publicaciones] 4)
OCIW NUC74-122553

Barak, Aharon.
"עוולת הרשלנות"; הרצאותיו של א. ברק שניתנו בשנת תשכ"ו.
[תל-אביב, 1966?]
53 p. 24 cm. IL3.00
Cover title.
1. Negligence—Israel. I. Title.
Title romanized: 'Avlat ha-rashlanut.
HE 68-4431
PL 480: Is-7266

Barak, Aharon.
(Ḥok ha-sheliḥut)
חוק השליחות : תשכ"ה-1965 / אהרן ברק. — [ירושלים] : המכון למחקרי חקיקה ולמשפט השוואתי ע"ש הרי סאקר, הפקולטה למשפטים, האוניברסיטה העברית ירושלים, 1975.
xxix, 640 p. ; 25 cm. — (פירוש לחוקי החוזים)
Added t. p.: Agency law, 1965.
Includes bibliographical references and indexes.
1. Agency (Law)—Israel. I. Israel. Laws, statutes, etc. Ḥok ha-sheliḥut. 1975. II. Title. III. Title: Agency law, 1965. IV. Series: Perush le-ḥuke ha-ḥozim.
76-951188

Barak, Alan Vladimir, 1946-
Biological and behavioral studies with Attagenus elongatulus Casey (Coleoptera : Dermestidae) ; including notes on the trapping of dermestids with sex pheromones. 1975. -- [s. l. : s. n.], 1975.
115 l. ill. ; 29 cm.
Thesis (Ph. D.) -- University of Wisconsin.
Vita.
Includes bibliography.
I. Title.
WU NUC77-83517

Barak, Avner, 1936-1957.
(Avner Barak (Kimberg))
אבנר ברק (קימברג) [שער-הגולן] קיבוץ השומר הצעיר שער-הגולן, 717 [1957]
38, [2] p. illus. 23 cm.
"מדבריו": p. [19]-[40]
1. Barak, Avner, 1936-1957. I. Sha'ar ha-Golan, Israel.
CT1919.P38B32 74-950384

Barak, Gregg L
In defense of the poor, the emergence of the public defender system in the United States (1900-1920). [Berkeley] 1974.
vii, 199 l.
Thesis (Dr. of Criminology)—University of California.
Includes bibliographical references.
CU NUC76-22867

Barak, Jaroslav, ill.
see Galanda, Igor. Divadlo SNP: 30 [rokov, 1944-1974] Martin: Osveta, 1974.

Barak, Jim.
A guide to urban Saskatchewan / prepared by Jim Barak, Lynn Minja. [Regina : Urban Advisory Commission, 1976]
38 p. : ill. ; 23 cm. CP76-82285-9
Cover title.
Includes bibliographies.
1. Social service—Saskatchewan. 2. Municipal services—Saskatchewan. 3. Saskatchewan—Social conditions. I. Minja, Lynn, joint author. II. Title.
HV109.S34B37 361'.97124 77-369160
77 MARC

Barák, Josef, 1833-1883.
Vzpomínky Josefa Baráka. — V Praze : Nakladatelské družstvo Máje [1905]
160 p., [2] leaves of plates : ill., port. ; 20 cm.
1. Bohemia—History—1848-1918—Sources. 2. Barák, Josef, 1833-1883. I. Title.
DB214.8.B37A34 76-500890

Barak, R., comp.
see 25 [Fünfundzwanzig] Jahre Vertreibung. (Stuttgart-S, Bund d. Vertriebenen, 1970)

Barak, Robert J
Research in postsecondary education, 1974 : an inventory of research by professors and students in the field of higher education / by Robert J. Barak ; assisted by Gary Doberstyn. — Iowa City, Iowa : American College Testing Program for the Association of Professors of Higher Education, c1974.
v, 66 p. : forms ; 23 cm.
Includes indexes.
$3.00
1. Education, Higher—Bibliography. 2. Education, Higher—Research. I. Doberstyn, Gary. II. Association of Professors of Higher Education. III. Title.
Z5814.U7B33 016.378'0072 75-313226
[LB2322] 75 MARC

Barak, Ya'ir
see Be-tsel ha-tselav. c1976.

Barak, Ya'ir
see ha-Miḳra. c1974.

Barak, Ya'ir
see Yeme ha-Mishnah yeha-Talmud. c1975-c1976.

Barak, Ya'ir
see Yeme Hordos veha-mered ha-gadol. 1974.

Baraka, Imamu Amiri, 1934-
Afrikan revolution; a poem by Imamu Amiri Baraka. [1st ed. New Ark, N.J., Jihad Pub. Co., 1973]
6, [1] p. 14 cm.
Cover title.
I. Title.
RPB InU CtY ViBlbV NcU NUC75-72889

Baraka, Imamu Amiri, 1934-
Blues people; música negra en la América blanca. [Barcelona] Editorial Lumen [1969]
301 p. 19 cm. (Palabra en el tiempo, 48)
Translation of Blues people, translated by Carlos Ribalta.
1. Music—Negroes. 2. Jazz music. 3. Negroes. I. Title.
IU NUC73-76134

Baraka, Imamu Amiri, 1934-
El conferenciante muerto; poemas. [Traducción: Ninf Rivero y Martín Micharvegas. Buenos Aires] Ediciones de la Flor [1970]
80 p. 21 cm.
Translation of The dead lecturer.
I. Title.
MB NUC74-54931

Baraka, Imamu Amiri, 1934-
De vuelta a casa. [Traducción: Patricio Canto. Buenos Aires] Editorial Tiempo Contemporáneo [1969]
217 p. 20 cm. (Colección Mundo actual)
Translation of Home.
1. Negroes—Addresses, essays, lectures. 2. U. S.—Race question—Addresses, essays, lectures. I. Title.
MB NUC74-54930

Baraka, Imamu Amiri, 1934-
[Ideological papers] Newark, N. J., Congress of African People [1973?]
6 pts. illus. (ports.) 28 cm. (in case 29 cm.)
1. Black nationalism. I. Congress of African Peoples.
CtY NUC77-12440

Baraka, Imamu Amiri, 1934-
It's nation time, by Imamu Amiri Baraka (Leroi Jones) [1st ed.] Chicago, Third World Press [c1970]
24 p. 22 cm. $1.50
Poems.
I. Title.
PS3552.A583I8 811'.5'4 76-23141
71[r77]rev MARC

Baraka, Imamu Amiri, 1934-
Jello, by Imamu Amiri Baraka (LeRoi Jones) [1st ed.] Chicago, Third World Press [1970]
38 p. 22 cm. $1.50
I. Title.
PS3552.A583J4 812'.5'4 73-21043
71[r77]rev MARC

Baraka, Imamu Amiri, 1934-
Kawaida studies, the new nationalism [by] Imamu Amiri Baraka (LeRoi Jones) Chicago, Third World Press [1972]
55 p. port. 22 cm.
I. Title.
NcU NUC74-53786

Baraka, Imamu Amiri, 1934- Le métro fantôme
see Tabori, George, 1914- L'ami des nègres. Paris, 1973.

Baraka, Imamu Amiri, 1934-
New era in our politics : the revolutionary answer to neo-colonialism in Newark politics / Imamu Amiri Baraka. -- [s.l. : s.n., 197-]
18 leaves ; 28 cm.
Cover title.
1. Black nationalism--Addresses, essays, lectures. 2. Newark, N.J.--Politics and government. I. Title.
MiEM NUC77-100406

Baraka, Imamu Amiri, 1934-
Skuli Huru Afrikan ₍Afrikan Free School₎ 1973 kalenda 1973. ₍Newark, N.J., Afrikan Free School, 1973₎
1 v. (unpaged) 38 x 22 cm. (in case 44 cm.)
Poems signed: Imamu Amiri Baraka.
I. Afrikan Free School, inc. II. Title.
CtY NUC77-46292

Baraka, Imamu Amiri, 1934-
Spirit reach ₍by₎ Imamu Amiri Baraka (LeRoi Jones). ₍1st ed. Newark, N. J., Jihad Productions, 1972₎
25 p. 22 cm. $1.50
Poems.
I. Title.
PS3519.O4545S6 818'.5'407 72-171272
MARC

Baraka, Imamu Amiri, 1934-
Strategy and tactics of a Pan African Nationalist Party [by] Imamu Amiri Baraka. New Ark, N. J., National Involvement, CFUN [c1971]
[22] p. 22 cm.
1. Black nationalism. I. Title.
CtY NUC75-38410

Baraka, Imamu Amiri, 1934-
Tales. London, MacGibbon & Kee, 1969.
₍9₎, 132 p. 23 cm. 30/- B69-19742
Published under the author's earlier name: LeRoi Jones.
I. Title.
PZ4.B2267 Tal 1969 813'.5'4 78-456629
₍PS3552.A583₎ 70₍r77₎rev MARC
ISBN 0-261-01850-4

Baraka, Imamu Amiri, 1934-
Toward the creation of political institutions for all African peoples by Imamu Amiri Baraka. [n.p.] Black World, c1972.
24 p. illus.
"Reprinted from October, 1972 Black World."
1. Negroes—Politics and suffrage. I. Title.
NcU InU IU NUC74-180161

Baraka, Imamu Amiri, 1934-
see Congress of African Peoples, Atlanta, 1970. Political Liberation Council organizing manual. [Sausalito, Calif., Printed for Congress of African People by The Black World Foundation, c1971]

Baraka, Imamu Amiri, 1934-
see The Floating bear. La Jolla, Calif., L. McGilvery, 1973.

Baraka, Imamu Amiri, 1934-
see Focus on Imamu Amiri Baraka... Released by the Center for Cassette Studies 29217. c1973.

Baraka, Imamu Amiri, 1934-
see Trippin': a need for change. ₍New Ark, The Cricket? c1969₎

Barakaev, M B
(Opredelenie srokov poliva khlopchatnika i drugikh kul'tur po planiruemomu srednesutochnomu prirostu glavnogo stebli͡a)
Определение сроков полива хлопчатника и других культур по планируемому среднесуточному приросту главного стебля. Ташкент, "Фан," 1972.
197 p. 21 cm. 0.90rub USSR 73
At head of title: Министерство сельского хозяйства СССР. Всесоюзный научно-исследовательский институт хлопководства. М. Б. Баракаев, П. П. Языков.
Cover title: Полив хлопчатника и других культур по среднесуточному приросту главного стебля.
Bibliography: p. ₍181₎-195.
1. Cotton growing—Uzbekistan. 2. Cotton—Water requirements. 3. Forage plants—Water requirements. I. I͡Azykov, Petr Potapovich, joint author. II. Title. III. Title: Poliv khlopchatnika i drugikh kul'tur po srednesutochnomu prirostu glavnogo stebli͡a.
SB251.R9B1 74-353231

Barakaeva, G B
₍Lughati anglisī-tojikī₎
Луғати англисӣ-тоҷикӣ. (Барои студентҳои курси I, II шуъбаи филология). Тартибдиҳандагон: Баракаева Г. Б., Назирова Ҳ. А., Ҷалилова М. Н. Душанбе, 1970.
178 p. 21 cm. 0.50rub USSR 71-24878 Suppl.
At head of title: Вазорати Маорифи Халқи РСС. Тоҷикистон университети Давлатии Точикистон ба номи В. И. Ленин.
On cover: English-Tajik dictionary.
1. English language—Dictionaries—Tajik. I. Nazirova, Ḣ. A., joint author. II. Jalilova, M. N., joint author. III. Title. IV. Title: English-Tajik dictionary.
PK6976.B29 72-227937

Barakah, 'Abd al-Fattāḥ 'Abd Allāh
see al-Hakīm al-Tirmidhī, Muḥammad ibn 'Alī, fl. 898. [Ādāb al-murīdīn] Ādāb al-murīdīn wa-Bayān al-kasb. [1976]

Barakah, 'Abd al-Fattāḥ 'Abd Allāh, ed.
see al-Sanūsī, Muḥammad ibn Yūsuf, ca. 1427- ca. 1490. Umdat ahl al-tawfīq wa-al-tasdīd. [1972-

Barakah, al-Mahdi Bin
see Bin Barakah, al-Mahdi, 1920-

Barakat, Elie Georges.
A time that has gone. ₍n. p., c1973₎
223 p. 22 cm.
Poems.
I. Title.
PR6052.A59T5 821'.9'14 74-191343
MARC

Barakat, Fouad K., joint author
see Kronmüller, Heinz. Prozessmesstechnik. Berlin, Heidelberg, New York: Springer, 1974-

Barakat, Halim Isber.
Days of dust / Halim Barakat ; translated by Trevor Le Gassick ; introd., Edward Said. — Wilmette, Ill. : Medina University Press International, 1974.
xxxviii, 179 p. ; 21 cm.
Translation of 'Awdat al-ṭā' ir ilā al-baḥr.
ISBN 0-914456-08-3 : $7.00. ISBN 0-914456-09-1 pbk. : $4.00
1. Israel-Arab War, 1967—Fiction. I. Title.
PZ4.B227Day 3 892'.7'36 74-77250
[PJ7816.A67] MARC

Barakat, Halim Isber.
Lebanon in strife : student preludes to the civil war / by Halim Barakat. — Austin : University of Texas Press, c1977.
xiii, 242 p. ; 24 cm. — (Modern Middle East series ; no. 2)
Bibliography: p. ₍231₎-233.
Includes indexes.
ISBN 0-292-70322-8
1. Students—Lebanon—Political activity. 2. Lebanon—Politics and government. 3. Lebanon—Social conditions. 4. Lebanon—History—Civil War, 1975- I. Title. II. Series: Modern Middle East series (Austin, Tex.) ; no. 2.
LA1463.7.B37 378.1'98'1095692 76-50046
76 MARC

Barakat, Halim Isber
see Dodd, Peter. River without bridges. Beirut, Institute for Palestine Studies, 1969 ₍c1968₎

Barakat, Hisham A 1943-
Biosynthesis of triglycerides in Mycobacterium smegmatis. Amherst, 1971.
ix, 104 l. 28 cm.
Thesis (Ph.D.)—University of Massachusetts.
1. Triglycerides. I. Title.
MU NUC73-31313

Barakāt, Muḥammad Tawfīq.
(Sayyid Quṭb: khulāṣat ḥayātuh, manhajuhu fī al-ḥarakah, al-naqd al-muwajjah ilayh)
سيد قطب: خلاصة حياته، منهجه في الحركة، النقد الموجه اليه ₍تأليف₎ محمد توفيق بركات. بيروت، دار الدعوة ₍197-₎
254 p. 20 cm.
Includes bibliographical references.
1. Quṭb, Sayyid, 1903-1966. I. Title.
BP80.Q86B37 74-214969

Barakāt, Muḥammad Tawfīq.
(al-Taḥqīq)
التحقيق؛ مسرحية اسلامية ₍تأليف₎ محمد توفيق بركات. ₍دمشق ؟₎ دار الدعوة ₍197-؟₎
111 p. 20 cm.
I. Title.
PJ7816.A674T3 74-202780

Barakāt, Muṣṭafá.
(Ba'da al-nihāyah)
بعد النهاية. ظلال السحاب؛ مسرحيتان، تأليف مصطفى بركات. ₍القاهرة₎ الهيئة المصرية العامة للكتاب، 1973.
183 p. 20 cm. (مسرحيات مختارة، 4) £E0.10
I. Barakāt, Muṣṭafá. Ẓilāl al-saḥāb. 1973. II. Title. III. Title: Ẓilāl al-saḥāb. IV. Series: Masraḥīyāt mukhtārah, 4.
PJ7816.A675B3 73-960319

Barakāt, Mustafá. Zilāl al-sahāb. 1973
in Barakāt, Mustafá. Ba'da al-nihāyah. 1973. 1973.

Barakāt, Rajab.
(Min tārīkh ṣiḥāfat al-Khalīj al-'Arabī, 1889-1973 (ṣiḥāfat al-Baṣrah))
من تاريخ صحافة الخليج العربي، ١٨٨٩ - ١٩٧٣ (صحافة البصرة) / تأليف رجب بركات. — ₍بغداد₎ : ₍s. n.₎, 1977
253 p. : facsims. ; 24 cm. — (منشورات مركز دراسات الخليج العربي ؛ 8)
Cover title: Min ṣiḥāfat al-Khalīj al-'Arabī.
Title on p. ₍4₎ of cover: From Arab Gulf press, Basrah press.
Includes bibliographical references and index.
1. Iraqi newspapers—Iraq—Basra. I. Title. II. Title: Min ṣiḥāfat al-Khalīj al-'Arabī. III. Title: From Arab Gulf press, Basrah press. IV. Series: Basra. Jāmi'at al-Baṣrah. Markaz Dirāsāt al-Khalīj al-'Arabī. Manshūrāt Markaz Dirāsāt al-Khalīj al-'Arabī ; 8.
PN5449.I 7B3 77-970905

Barakat, Robert A
The Cistercian sign language : a study in non-verbal communication / Robert A. Barakat. — Kalamazoo, Mich. : Cistercian Publications, 1975.
220 p. : ill. ; 26 cm. — (Cistercian studies series ; no. 11)
Bibliography: p. 213-219.
ISBN 0-87907-811-1 : $14.95
1. Cistercians. 2. Sign language. I. Title. II. Series.
BX3403.B37 419 70-152476
76 MARC

Barakat, Robert A
Tāwula : a study in Arabic folklore / by Robert A. Barakat. — Helsinki : Suomalainen Tiedeakatemia, 1974.
32 p., ₍4₎ leaves of plates : ill. ; 24 cm. — (FF communication ; v. 90, no. 214)
Fi***
Bibliography: p. ₍31₎-32.
ISBN 9514101790 : Fmk10.00
1. Backgammon—History. 2. Arab countries—Social life and customs. I. Title. II. Series: Folklore Fellows. FF communications : no. 214.
GR1.F55 no.214 398 s 75-309348
₍GV1469.B2₎ 75 MARC

Barakāt, Salīm.
(Kull dākhil sa-yahtifu li-ajlī wa-kull khārij ayḍan ...)
كل داخل سيهتف لاجلى وكل خارج ايضا ... سليم بركات. — الطبعة 1. — بيروت : مواقف، 1973.
62 p. ; 20 cm.
I. Title.
PJ7816.A677K8 77-970756

Barakāt, 'Umar.
(Fayḍ al-Ilāh al-Mālik fī ḥall alfāẓ 'Umdat al-sālik wa-'uddat al-nāsik)
فيض الاله المالك فى حل الفاظ عمدة السالك وعدة الناسك، لعمر بركات ابن محمد بركات الشامى البقاعى المكى. وبهامشه متن عمدة السالك وعدة الناسك. وبأسفل الصلب والهامش تقريرات قيمة لمحمد على بن حسين المالكى. مصر، يطلب من **المكتبة التجارية الكبرى، 1955.**
2 v. 28 cm.
Reprint of the ed. published in 1358 (1939) by the same publisher.
1. Islamic law. 2. Shafiites. I. Ibn al-Naqīb, Shihāb al-Dīn Aḥmad ibn Lu'lu', d. 1368. 'Umdat al-sālik wa-'uddat al-nāsik. 1955. II. Title.
74-212744

Barakāt, Zayn al-'Ābidīn.
(Mabādi' fī al-qānūn al-idārī al-Sūrī wa-al-muqāran)
مبادئ في القانون الاداري السوري والمقارن ₍تأليف₎ زين العابدين بركات. ₍بيروت ؟₎ دار الفكر، 1972.
704 p. 24 cm.
Includes bibliographies.
1. Administrative law—Syria. 2. Administrative law. I. Title.
74-212926

Barakaṭakī, Polena.
(Ejana Dadhīcira anweshaṇata)
এজন দধীচিৰ অন্বেষণত. ₍লিখক₎ পোলেন বৰকটকী. গুৱাহাটী, ফ্ৰেণ্ডচ বুক এজেঞ্চি ₍1973₎
87 p. 23 cm. Rs4.00
In Assamese.
A novel.
I. Title.
PK1569.B25E5 73-907049

Barakaṭakī, Upendra
see
Barkatoky, Upendra.

al-Barakātī, Sharaf ibn 'Abd al-Muḥsin.
الرحلة اليمانية لصاحب الدولة والسيادة الأمير الأكبر الشريف حسين باشا أمير مكة المكرمة. بقلم شرف عبد المحسن البركاتي. مصر، مطبعة السعاده، 1912.
127 p. 20 cm.
1. al-Ḥusayn ibn 'Alī, King of Hejaz, 1853?-1931. I. Title.
Title romanized: al-Riḥlah al-Yamānīyah.
DS244.5.H87B37 1912 N E 68-3468

al-Barakātī, Sharaf ibn 'Abd al-Muḥsin.
الرحلة اليمانية لصاحب الدولة امير مكة المكرمة الشريف حسين باشا وأعماله فى محاربة الادريسى، مع جغرافية البلاد العربية واسماء قبائلها. تأليف شرف بن عبد المحسن البركاتي. الطبعة 2. ₍دمشق، المكتب الاسلامى للطباعة والنشر، المقدمة 1964₎
7, 173 p. 24 cm.
1. al-Ḥusayn ibn 'Alī, King of Hejaz, 1853?-1931. I. Title.
Title romanized: al-Riḥlah al-Yamānīyah.
DS244.5.H87B37 1964 N E 67-1542

Barakatoky, Upendra, comp.
see Beṇudhara Sarmmā. [1969]

Barakbah, Syed Agil
see Agil Barakbah, Syed, 1923-

Baraket, Mark.
Screen gems / Mark Baraket. — New York : Drake Publishers, 1977.
143 p. : ill. ; 18 cm.
ISBN 0-8473-1466-9 : $5.95
1. Horror films—History and criticism. I. Title.
PN1995.9.H6B3 791.43'0909'37 76-43414
77 MARC

(Barakhari)
बारखड़ी : राजस्थान रा सिरजणधरमी सिक्षकां री कलम / सम्पादक वेद व्यास. — 1. संस्करण. — जयपुर : शिक्षा विभाग, राजस्थान के लिए चिन्मय प्रकाशन, c1974.
iv, 106 p. ; 23 cm. —(शिक्षक दिवस ; 1974)
In Rajasthani.
Rs5.00

1. Rajasthani literature. I. Vyas, Ved, 1942–

PK2708.5.B3 75–901404

Barakhov, Vladimir Sergeevich.
(Iskusstvo literaturnogo portreta)
Искусство литературного портрета : Горький о В. И. Ленине, Л. Н. Толстом, А. П. Чехове / В. С. Барахов. — Москва : Наука, 1976.
184 p., ⌊8⌋ leaves of plates : ill. ; 20 cm. — (Серия Из истории мировой культуры) USSR 76
At head of title: Akademiia nauk SSSR.
Series romanized: Seriia Iz istorii mirovoĭ kul′tury.
Includes bibliographical references.
0.66rub
1. Gor′kiĭ, Maksim, 1868–1936—Criticism and interpretation. 2. Biography (as a literary form) 3. Lenin, Vladimir Il′ich, 1870–1924. 4. Tolstoĭ, Lev Nikolaevich, graf, 1828–1910. 5. Chekhov, Anton Pavlovich, 1860–1904. I. Title.
PG3465.Z8B28 76–525798

Barakhovskiĭ, Grigoriĭ IAkovlevich.
(Knizhnaia Moskva)
Книжная Москва. Справочник-путеводитель. Москва, "Реклама," 1973.
127 p. 16 cm. 0.20rub USSR 73
By G. IA. Barakhovskiĭ and B. A. Vial′tsev.
1. Booksellers and bookselling—Moscow—Directories. I. Vial′tsev, Boris Andreevich, joint author. II. Title.
Z373.6.M6B3 1973 74–300705

Barakhovskiĭ, Grigoriĭ IAkovlevich.
(Propaganda politicheskoĭ literatury v knizhnom magazine)
Пропаганда политической литературы в книжном магазине : методическое пособие / Г. Я. Бараховский. — Москва : Книга, 1975.
38 p. : ill. ; 22 cm. USSR***
At head of title: Gosudarstvennyĭ komitet Soveta Ministrov SSSR po delam izdatel′stv, poligrafii i knizhnoĭ torgovli. Vsesoiuznaia knizhnaia palata. TSentral′noe biuro nauchno-tekhnicheskoĭ informatsii i tekhniko-ėkonomicheskikh issledovaniĭ po poligraficheskoĭ promyshlennosti, izdatel′skomu delu i knizhnoĭ torgovle.
Bibliography: p. 32–⌊33⌋
0.14rub
1. Booksellers and bookselling—Russia. I. Title.
Z366.B253 76–509559

Barakhtian, V. O.
see Radians'ka demokratiia i svoboda osoby. 1972.

Barakhtin, V.N.
see Sinopticheskaia meteorologiia. 1975.

Baraković, Meho, 1945–
Azil. Sarajevo, "Veselin Masleša," 1972.
29, ⌊2⌋ p. 21 cm. Yu 73–2415
Poems.
I. Title.
PG1419.12.A65A97 75–970422

Barakovska, Emiliia.
(Georgi Karaslavov)
Георги Караславов : биобиблиографски очерк / Емилия Бараковска, Нина Николова. — София : Дом на лит-рата и изкуствата за деца и юноши, 1975.
41 p. : port. ; 20 cm. — (Библиотека Детски творци) Bu***
Series romanized: Biblioteka Detski tvortsi.
1. Karaslavov, Georgi—Bibliography. 2. Karaslavov, Georgi—Biography. 3. Authors, Bulgarian—20th century—Biography. I. Nikolova, Nina, joint author.
Z8460.26.B37 77–512640
[PG1037.K27]

Barakovskaia, Paraskov′ia Varlamovna.
Экономическое стимулирование работы предприятия. Москва, "Машиностроение," 1971.
40 p. 20 cm. (Библиотека рабочего машиностроителя: Основы экономики машиностроения, 16) 0.08rub USSR 72–VKP
At head of title: П. В. Бараковская, В. С. Вологжанин.
Bibliography: p. ⌊39⌋
1. Machinery—Trade and manufacture—Russia. 2. Incentives in industry. I. Vologzhanin, Valeriĭ Semenovich, joint author. II. Title.
Title romanized: Ėkonomicheskoe stimulirovanie raboty predpriiatiia.
HD9705.R92B37 73–319004

Barakovskaia, Paraskov'ia Varlamovna, joint author
see Voronkov, Ivan Ivanovich. (Opyt analiticheskoĭ raboty na Uralmashzavode) 1973.

Baraksanov, Gennadiĭ Grigor'evich, ed.
see Komi filologiia... Syktyvkar, 1972.

Baraksanov, Gennadiĭ Grigor'evich
see Komi filologiia. 1972, 1973 printing.

Baral, Abanikumar.
ଅପରାହ୍ନର ଛାୟା; ⌊ଉପନ୍ୟାସ. ଲେଖକ⌋ ଅବନୀକୁମାର ବରାଳ. ଖୋରଧା, କଢାବ ମହଲ ⌊1970⌋
183 p. 19 cm. Rs3.00
In Oriya.
I. Title.
Title romanized: Aparāhnara chāẏā.
PK2579.B27A8 77–921652

Baral, Abanikumar.
(Mañcakanyāra kāhāṇī)
ମଞ୍ଚକନ୍ୟାର କାହାଣୀ. ⌊ଲେଖକ⌋ ଅବନୀକୁମାର ବରାଳ. ⌊କଟକ⌋ ଓଡ଼ିଶା ବୁକ୍ ଷ୍ଟୋର ⌊1968⌋
171 p. 22 cm. Rs5.00
In Oriya.
A novel.

I. Title.

PK2579.B27M35 72–900909

Baral, Abanikumar.
(Uttara basanta)
ଉତ୍ତର ବସନ୍ତ; ଗଳ୍ପ-ସଂକଳନ. ଲେଖକ ଅବନୀକୁମାର ବରାଳ. କଟକ, ଜେ. ମହାପାତ୍ର ⌊1971⌋
2, 192 p. 21 cm. Rs7.00
In Oriya.
Short stories.

I. Title.

PK2579.B27U8 72–901931

Baral, Aleksandr Anatol'evich
see IUdovich, IUrii Borisovich. Exploratory fishing and scouting. [Springfield, Va.] 1970.

Baral, Basudev, 1951–
(Hindū saṃskṛti tathā dhārmika sampradāya)
हिन्दू संस्कृति तथा धार्मिक सम्प्रदाय / लेखक वासुदेव बराल. — 1. संस्करण. — काठमाडौं : पुस्तक-संसार, 2031 ⌊1975⌋
3, 51 p. ; 22 cm.
In Nepali.
Rs5.00

1. Nepal—Religion. I. Title.

BL2023.N35B37 75–904133

Baral, David Parsons.
Achievement levels among foreign-born and native-born Mexican American students / by David Parsons Baral. -- Tuscon, 1975.
x, 104 leaves ; 28 cm.
Thesis -- University of Arizona.
Bibliography : leaves 97-104.
Microfilm. Ann Arbor : University Microfilms, 1976. 1 reel.
1. Mexican-Americans--Education--Arizona. I. Title.
WU NUC77-83528

Baral, Isvar.
see National Education Plan as they see it. Kathmandu, National Education Committee Office, 1972.

Baral, Kamala Lochan, 1934–
ଦୁଇଟି ରେଖାର ବ୍ୟବଧାନ. ⌊ଲେଖକ କମଳ ଲୋଚନ ବରାଳ⌋ କଟକ, ଦାଶ ପବ୍ଲିକେସନ୍ସ ⌊1968⌋
130 p. 19 cm. Rs2.00
In Oriya.
A novel.

I. Title.
Title romanized: Duiṭi rekhāra byabadhāna.

PK2579.B28D8 77–921549

Baral, Laurie R
The evaluation of teachers : ERS annotated bibliography / ⌊compiled by Laurie R. Baral⌋. — Arlington, Va. : Educational Research Service, c1974.
18 p. ; 29 cm.
$5.00
1. Teachers, Rating of—Bibliography. I. Educational Research Service, inc., Arlington, Va. II. Title.
Z5814.T3B37 016.3711′44 75-320272
⌊LB2838⌋ 75 MARC

Baṛāla, Ramalā.
(Nishiddha darojā)
নিষিদ্ধ দরোজা. ⌊কবি⌋ রমলা বড়াল. কলিকাতা, গ্রন্থ-প্রচার ⌊1378, i.e. 1972⌋
41 p. 22 cm. Rs3.00
In Bengali.

I. Title.

PK1730.13.A63N5 72–902712

Barāla, Vāsudeva
see
Baral, Basudev, 1951-

Barald, Pamela Francesca, 1945-
Distribution and characterization of cholinesterases in cultured chicken embryo fibroblasts and in fibroblasts transformed by oncogenic RNA viruses. [n. p.] 1974.
265 l. illus. 29 cm.
Thesis (Ph. D.)—University of Wisconsin.
Vita.
Includes bibliography.
I. Title.
WU NUC76-22868

Baraldés, Maria Mercè Oromí i
see Oromí i Baraldes, Maria Mercè.

Baraldi, Egidio.
Ricordi di un partigiano : il contributo di Campagnola Emilia alla lotta di liberazione 1943-1945 / ⌊di⌋ Egidio Baraldi (Walter). — ⌊Reggio Emilia⌋ : Tecnostampa, 1975.
96 p., ⌊8⌋ leaves of plates : ill. ; 20 cm. It76-Nov
1. World War, 1939-1945—Underground movements—Italy—Campagnola Emilia. 2. Campagnola Emilia, Italy—History. I. Title.
D802.I82C323 77-479368
*77 MARC

Baraldi, Giuseppe.
Divenire e trascendenza : studio critico dal punto di vista dell'attualismo gentiliano / Giuseppe Baraldi. — ⌊s.l. : s.n.⌋, 1976. (Fribourg : Impr. St-Paul)
283 p. ; 21 cm. Sw76-8712
Thesis—Fribourg.
Bibliography: p. 276-281.
1. Gentile, Giovanni, 1875-1944. I. Title.
B3624.G54B27 77-464679
*77 MARC

Baraldi, S., illus.
see Abate, Rosario. Geschiedenis van het vliegen en van de luchtvaart. 2. druk. Den Haag, H. Meulenhoff [1972?]

Baraldi, Severino, ill.
see Perez, Francisco. Los medios de locomocion... Valencia: Mas-Ivars, ⌊1973?⌋

Baraldi, Severino, illus.
see Taylor, Susan, comp. A golden treasury of fairy stories from many lands... London, Ward Lock, 1972.

Barale, Massimo, 1941-
see Bodei, Remo, 1938- Hegel e l'economia politica. Milano : G. Mazzotta, [1975]

Barale, Vittorino.
La gente di Masserano. Famiglie antiche e persone illustri. Biella, Centro studi biellesi, 1972.
171 p. illus., plates. 24 cm. It 73–June
Three hundred numb. copies. L. C. copy no. 280.
Bibliography: p. 166–167.
1. Masserano, Italy—Biography. I. Title.
DG975.M454B37 74–307150

Barale, Washington H
El hombre cero / Washi⌊n⌋gton H. Barale. — 1. ed. — Montevideo : Editorial Girón, 1973.
163 p. ; 19 cm. — (Colección La Invención ; 5)
I. Title.
PQ8520.12.A67H6 75–578204

Baralis, Marta.
Ifigenia de Teresa de la Parra / Marta de las Mercedes Baralis. — Buenos Aires : Universidad de Buenos Aires, Facultad de Filosofía y Letras, Instituto de Literatura Iberoamericana, 1972.
158 p. ; 19 cm.
Includes bibliographical references.
1. Parra, Theresa de la, 1895-1936. Ifigenia. I. Title.
PQ8549.P35I433 863 77-457082
77 MARC

Baralt, Clara Eugenia López
see López Baralt, Clara Eugenia.

Bar'am, Bella.
(Tsemed gozalim le-yalde ha-gan)
צמד גוזלים לילדי הגן. לקט וספר בידי בלה ברעם. ציר בידי רות שלום. תל־אביב, מסדה ‎[1966]
207 p. col. illus. 25 cm.
Vocalized.
IL7.50
I. Title.
PZ90.H3B287 HE 68–795
PL 480: Is–4790

Baram, Bracha, joint author
see Globerson, Arye L Hasabah miktso'it la-akadema'im. 1971.

Baram, Giora, 1939-
The production-inventory control problem: a review and a new method of analysis. Toledo [Business Research Center, University of Toledo] 1971.
ix, 48 l. illus. 28 cm. (Papers in operations analysis. Working paper no. 7)
1. Production control. 2. Inventory control. 3. Critical path analysis. I. Title. II. Series.
NIC OrU NUC73-114765

Baram, Giora, 1939-
A state-variables systems approach to the production-inventory control problem. [Toledo] 1970.
xi, 160 l. illus.
Thesis—University of Toledo.
Bibliography: leaves 159-160.
Photocopy of typescript produced by microfilm-xerography. Ann Arbor, Mich., University Microfilms, 1972.
TxU NUC73-31314

Baram, Michael S
Environmental law and the siting of facilities : issues in land use and coastal zone management / Michael S. Baram, with contributions by Timothy Backstrom ... [et al.]. — Cambridge, Mass. : Ballinger Pub. Co., c1976.
x, 255 p. : ill. ; 24 cm.
Includes bibliographical references and index.
ISBN 0-88410-417-6
1. Regional planning—Law and legislation—United States. 2. Coastal zone management—Law and legislation—United States. 3. Environmental law—United States. I. Title.
KF5698.B337 346'.73'045 76-2664
76 MARC

Baram, Michael S
Environmental law and the siting of subsidized housing; conflicts and opportunities [by] Michael S. Baram. [Cambridge, Mass.] Joint Center for Urban Studies of M. I. T. and Harvard, 1974.
37 l. (Working paper no. 24)
Cover title.
I. Title. II. Series: Joint Center for Urban Studies. Working paper no. 24.
MCM NUC76-22869

Baram, Robert.
I search for peace. Boston, Branden Press [1972]
60 p. 23 cm. $4.25
Poems.
I. Title.
PS3552.A59 I 23 811'.5'4 78–175297
ISBN 0–8283–1330–X MARC

Baram, Robert.
Pot-claws & quince-tarts : poetry and pictures / by Robert Baram. — 1st ed. — [s. l. : s. n., 1974] (Hanover, N. H. : Dartmouth Print. Co.)
39 p. : ill. ; 23 cm.
At head of title: The Bicentennial.
$2.95
I. Title.
PS3552.A59P6 811'.5'4 74–18571
MARC

The Baram. Telang Usan. [Kuching? Baram Regatta Committee, 1965]
40 p. illus. 26 cm.
Cover title.
English or Malay.
1. Baram River, Sarawak. I. Baram Regatta Committee. II. Title: Telang Usan.
DS646.39.B37B37 72–171641
MARC

Baram Regatta Committee
see The Baram. Telang Usan. [Kuching? 1965]

Baramboĭm, Nikolaĭ Konstantinovich, joint author
see Koketkin, Petr Petrovich. Formovanie plastmassovykh detalei na izdelifakh legkoi promyshlennosti. 1972.

Baramidze, Aleksandr Georgievich, 1902-
see Kekelidze, Korneliĭ Samsonovich. Istorifa drevnegruzinskoĭ literatury V-XVIII vv. Tbilisi, Izd-vo Tbilisskogo univ., 1969.

Baramidze, Konstantin Moiseevich
see Nauka-proizvodstvu. 19

Baramidze, V
(V bitve s ognem)
В битве с огнем. Становление и развитие пожарной охраны Грузии. Тбилиси. "Сабчота Сакартвело," 1971.
186 p. with illus. 21 cm. 0.28rub USSR 71
At head of title: В. Барамидзе.
Bibliography: p. [185]
1. Fire prevention—Georgia (Transcaucasia) I. Title.
TH9565.G46B37 74–335675

Barāmij al-Atfāl fī al-Idhā'ah wa-al-Tilifizyūn, al-Ḥalqah al-Khāṣṣah bi-
see
al-Ḥalqah al-Khāṣṣah bi-Barāmij al-Atfāl fī al-Idhā'ah wa-al-Tilifizyūn.

Baramki, Dimitri Constantine, 1909–
The art and architecture of ancient Palestine; a survey of the archaeology of Palestine from the earliest times to the Ottoman conquest, by Dimitri C. Baramki. Beirut, Palestine Liberation Organization, Research Center, 1969.
iv, 258 p. illus. 24 cm. (Palestine books, no. 23)
Bibliography: p. [243]–245.
1. Palestine—Antiquities. I. Title. II. Series.
DS111.B26 913.33'03 73–172053
MARC

Baramki, Dimitri Constantine, 1909–
(Āthār al-Ḍaffah al-Sharqīyah min al-Mamlakah al-Urdunīyah al-Hāshimīyah)
آثار الضفة الشرقية من المملكة الاردنية الهاشميه؛ دليل موجز مصور، بقلم ديمتري برامكي. القدس، انطون نزال ‎[1951?]
84 p. illus. 23 cm.
1. Jordan—Description and travel—Guide-books. 2. Jordan—Antiquities. I. Title.
DS153.2.B33 74–221247

Baramki, Dimitri Constantine, 1909–
The coins exhibited in the Archaeological Museum of the American University of Beirut, by Dimitri Baramki. [Beirut] American University of Beirut, 1968.
186 p. illus. 25 cm. (American University of Beirut. Centennial publications)
1. Coins, Ancient—Exhibitions. I. American University of Beirut. Museum of Archaeology. II. Title.
CJ215.L42B433 737.4'074'095692 73–150628
CtY MARC

Baramki, Dimitri Constantine, 1909-
Guide to the Umayyad Palace at Khirbat al Mafjar. Amman, Hashemite Kingdom of Jordan, Dept. of Antiquities, 1956.
24 p. illus. 19 cm.
1. Khirbat al Mafjar.
KyLxCB NUC76-62414

Baramki, Dimitri Constance, 1909-
see American University of Beirut. Museum of Archacology. The coin collection of the American University of Beirut Museum ... [Beirut] American University of Beirut, 1974.

Baramzin, Sergeĭ Vasil'evich.
(Organizatsifa truda pri tekhnicheskom obsluzhivanii mashinno-traktornogo parka)
Организация труда при техническом обслуживании машинно-тракторного парка. Москва, Россельхозиздат, 1973.
103 p. with diagrs. 21 cm. 0.20rub USSR 73
At head of title: С. В. Барамзин, Г. И. Гуляев.
Bibliography: p. [102]
1. Agricultural machinery—Maintenance and repair. 2. Agricultural machinery—Russia. I. Gulfaev, Gennadiĭ Ivanovich, 1902– joint author. II. Title.
S675.5.B37 74–334026

Baramzin, Sergeĭ Vasil'evich.
(Spetsializirovannye zven'fa po tekhnicheskomu obsluzhivanifu mashin)
Специализированные звенья по техническому обслуживанию машин. Москва, "Моск. рабочий," 1973.
96 p. 20 cm. 0.15rub USSR 73
At head of title: С. Барамзин.
1. Agricultural machinery operators—Russia. I. Title.
S760.R9B27 74–344360

Baran, Alexander.
(Pytannfa ukraïns'koho patriſarkhatu v Shashkevychivs'kiĭ dobi)
Питання українського патріярхату в Шашкевичівській добі / Олександер Баран. — Вінніпеґ : Рада укр. організацій за патріярхат Української католицької церкви, 1974.
39 p. ; 23 cm. C***
Added t. p.: The question of Ukrainian patriarchate in the times of M. Shashkevych.
Includes bibliographical references.
1. Catholic Church. Byzantine rite (Ukrainian) 2. Ukraine—Church history. I. Title. II. Title: The question of Ukrainian patriarchate in the times of M. Shashkevych.
BX4711.633.B37 76–523882

Baran, Alexander.
(Tserkva na Zakarpatti)
Церква на Закарпатті в роках 1665–1691. The church in Subcarpathia from 1665–1691. Рим, 1968.
71 p. 24 cm. (Видання Богословії, ч. 36)
At head of title: Олександер Баран.
Summary in English.
"Extractum e Bohoslovia, t. XXXII (1968)."
Bibliography: p. 68–71.
1. Catholic Church. Byzantine rite (Ukrainian)—History. 2. Catholic Church in the Zakarpatshaya oblast'. I. Title. II. Title: The church in Subcarpathia.
BX4711.622.B37 73–202901

Baran, Alexander
see Sheptyts'kyi, Andrii, graf, Metropolitan, 1865-1944, comp. Monumenta Ucrainae historica. Romae, 1964-

Baran, Barbara, joint author
see Gabriner, Bob. The Wisconsin Draft Resistance Union. Boston, New England Free Press [1969?]

Baran, Dan.
see Frimu, Ioan C., 1871-1919. I. C. Frimu ... Bucureşti, Editura Politică, 1969.

Baran, Gregory.
Airport capacity analysis. [Seattle? Boeing Co.] Commercial Airplane Division [1968]
v, 119 p. 22 x 29 cm.
On cover: D6-23415.
1. Airports—Runways. 2. Airports—Traffic control. 3. Airports—Planning. I. Boeing Company. Commerical Airplane Division. II. Title.
CSt NUC73-126147

Baran, Henryk.
see Semiotics and structuralism ... White Plains, N.Y., International Arts and Sciences Press, c1976.

Baran, Ignacy.
Racjonalne oświetlenie pomieszczeń pracy. Warszawa, Instytut Wydawniczy CRZZ, 1972.
54 p. illus. 20 cm. (Fizjologia i higiena pracy) zł8.00
1. Factories—Lighting.
TK4399.F2B37 73–205932

Baran, Lîubomir Akimovich.
Kislorod i vitaminy v onkologicheskoĭ praktike. Kiev, Zdorov'ia, 1973.
150 p. illus. (Biblioteka prakticheskogo vracha)
1. Hyperbaric oxygenation. 2. Neoplasms—Therapy. 3. Vitamins—Therapeutic use. I. Title.
DNLM NUC75-128308

Baran, Lîubomir Akimovich.
Kompleksnoe lechenie zlokachestvennykh opukholeĭ kosteĭ. Kiev, Zdorov'ia, 1971.
153 p. illus. (Biblioteka prakticheskogo vracha)
1. Bone neoplasms—Therapy. I. Title.
DNLM NUC75-129129

Baran, Mary Rita, 1929-
The dependence of map reading skills on field articulation in sixth grade pupils. 1975.
-- [s. l. : s. n.], 1975.
xiii, 237 p. : ill., tables
Thesis -- Boston University.
Bibliography : p. 218-235.
1. Maps. 2. Field dependence (Psychology) 3. Sixth grade (Education) I. Title.
MBU NUC77-83518

Baran, Oleksander
see
Baran, Alexander.

Baran, Paul.
Communication policy issues for the coming computer utility. [Santa Monica, Calif., Rand Corp. 1968]
24 p. 28 cm. ([Rand Corporation. Paper] P-3685)
1. Computer industry—United States. 2. Trade regulation—United States. 3. Electronic data processing. I. Title. II. Series.
AS36.R28 no. 3685 081 s [384] 74–172649
[HD9696.C63]

Baran, Paul.
The future of newsprint, 1970-2000. Menlo Park, Calif., Institute for the Future, 1971.
vi, 49 p. chiefly illus. 29 cm. (A special industry report, report R-16)
1. Newsprint—Statistics. I. Title.
CtY NUC73-31319

Baran, Paul.
The future of the telephone industry, 1970-1985 [by] Paul Baran [and] Andrew J. Lipinski. Menlo Park, Calif., Institute for the Future, 1971.
171 p. illus. 28 cm. (A special industry report. Report R-20)
1. Telephone—U.S. I. Lipinski, Andrew J., joint author. II. Title.
CtY NUC73-31320

Baran, Paul.
The future of the telephone industry, 1970-1985 [by] Paul Baran [and] Andrew J. Lipinski. [2d ed.] Menlo Park, Calif., Institute for the Future, 1971.
vii, 172 p. illus. 28 cm. (A special industry report, R-20)
1. Telephone-United States. I. Lipinski, Andrew J. II. Title. III. Series: Institute for the Future. Report R-20.
NIC NUC76-75736

Baran, Paul.
Notes on a seminar on future broad-band communications. Middletown, Conn. [Institute for the Future] 1970.
21 p. 28 cm. (Institute for the Future. Working paper WP-1)
1. Television broadcasting. 2. Television advertising. 3. Communications. I. Title. II. Series.
NBuU NUC74-122550

Baran, Paul.
On the future computer era: modification of the American character and the role of the engineer; or, a little caution in the haste to number. Santa Monica, Rand Corporation [1968]
14 l. 28 cm. (Rand Corporation. [Paper] P-3780)
1. Electronic digital computers. 2. Electronic data processing—Psychology. I. Title. II. Series.
MB NUC73-126148

Baran, Paul.
Potential market demand for two-way informational services to the home, 1970-1990. Menlo Park, Calif., Institute for the Future, 1971.
vii, 131 p. illus. 28 cm. (Institute for the Future. Report R-26)
"IFF-R-71-26."
IU CtY NUC73-31302

Baran, Paul.
Some changes in information technology affecting marketing in the year 2000. [Santa Monica, Calif.] Rand Corp., 1968.
34 p. illus. 28 cm. (Rand Corporation. [Paper] P-3717)
Cover title.
Includes bibliographical references.
1. Marketing—Information services. 2. Market segmentation. 3. Marketing. I. Title. II. Series.
AS36.R28 no. 3717 081 s 74-191019
[HF5415] [381] MARC

Baran, Paul.
Some remarks on digital distributed communications networks. [Santa Monica, Calif., Rand Corporation] 1967.
23 p. illus. 28 cm. (Rand Corporation. Paper, P-3536)
Cover title.
Bibliography: p. 23.
1. System analysis. 2. Communication. I. Title. II. Series.
MB NUC73-40212

Baran, Paul, joint author
see Boehm, Sharla P On distributed communications: II. Digital simulation of hot-potato routing... Santa Monica, Rand Corporation, 1964.

Baran, Paul A
The absorption of surplus; the sales effort. [by] Paul Baran [and] Paul Sweezy. [Boston, New England Free Press, 196]
112-141 p. 21 cm.
Cover title.
1. Surplus commodities. 2. Advertising. I. Sweezy, Paul Marlor, 1910- joint author.
KU NUC74-10489

Baran, Paul A
La economía política del crecimiento [por] Paul A. Baran. [La Habana] Editorial de Ciencias Sociales [Instituto Cubano del Libro, 1971]
347 p. 23 cm. (Teoría económica)
Translation of The political economy of growth.
Bibliographical footnotes.
1. Economic development. I. Title.
FMU NUC73-114751

Baran, Paul A
Paul Baran on Marxism--crisis of Marxism?--on the nature of Marxism. Boston, New England Free Press [196-]
224-[234], 259-268 p. 22 cm.
Cover title.
Reprinted from Monthly review, Oct. and Nov. 1958.
1. Socialism. I. Title. II. Title: Marxism.
KU NUC74-29766

Baran, Paul A
The political economy of growth [by] Paul A. Baran. [1st Indian ed. New Delhi] People's Publishing House [1958]
xv, 364 p. 22 cm.
Bibliographical footnotes.
_ Economic development. I. Title.
IaU NUC75-67071

Baran, Paul A
Reflexiones sobre la Revolución Cubana [por] Paul Baran. Teorías y pensadores [por] Paul Sweezy. [Buenos Aires] Merayo Editor [1973]
129 p. 18 cm. (Colección Documentos)
Cover title.
Translation of Baran's Reflections on the Cuban Revolution.
TxU NUC76-80316

Baran, Paul A
El socialismo: única salida; ensayos. Con un prefacio de Paul M. Sweezy, y una introd. de John O'Neil. Traducción de Luis Felipe Salazar. [1. ed. en español. México] Ed. Nuestro Tiempo [1971]
356 p. (Colección Desarrolo económico)
1. Economics—Addresses, essays, lectures. 2. Comparative economics—Addresses, essays, lectures. I. Title.
NcU NUC74-122693

Baran, Peter
see Hermens, Ferdinand Aloys, 1906- Repräsentanz und Autorität in der Demokratie. Wien, Verein für Sozial- und Wirtschaftspolitik] 1972.

Baran, Richard T 1938-
Coaching football's polypotent offense [by] Richard T. Baran. West Nyack, N. Y., Parker Pub. Co. [1974]
207 p. illus. 24 cm.
1. Football—Offense. 2. Football coaching. I. Title.
GV951.8.B37 796.33'212 74-4074
ISBN 0-13-139055-4 MARC

Baran, Selçuk.
Bir solgun adam : roman / Selçuk Baran. 1. baskı. -- [İstanbul] : Milliyet Yayınları, 1975.
303 p. ; 20 cm. (Milliyet Yayın Ltd. Şti. yayınları : Türk yazarları dizisi ; no. 5)
I. Title.
ICU NUC77-83519

Baran, Selçuk.
Haziran : (hikâyeler) / Selçuk Baran. — İstanbul : [s. n.], 1972.
186 p. ; 19 cm.
CONTENTS: Odadaki.—İhtiyar adam ve küçük kız.—Konuklar odaları.—Kavak dölü.—Anne.—Işıklı pencereler.—Ceviz ağacına kar yağdı.—Kent kırgını.—Sokaklarda.—Zambaklı adam.—Islık.—Göç zamanı.—Oyun.—Tuba.—Analar ve oğullar.—Porto-Riko'lu.—Umut.—Leylâk dalları.—Saatler.—Haziran.—Bir yabancı.
I. Title.
PL248.B333H3 74-234358

Baran, Stanley J 1948-
The effects of prosocial and antisocial television content on the modeling behavior of children with varying degrees of self-esteem, by Stanley Baran. [Amherst] 1973.
vi, 97 l. illus. 28 cm.
Thesis (Ph.D.)—University of Massachusetts.
1. Television and children. 2. Self-respect. I. Title.
MU NUC74-126747

Baran, Stepan.
(Mytropolyt Andreĭ Sheptyts'kyĭ)
Митрополит Андрей Шептицький; життя і діяльність. Мюнхен, Вернигора, 1947.
151 p. illus. 22 cm.
1. Sheptyts'kyĭ, Andriĭ, graf, Metropolitan, 1865-1944. I. Title.
BX4711.695.S5B37 76-511226

Baran, Stepan.
(Vesna narodiv v avstro-uhors'kiĭ Ukraïni)
Весна народів в австро-угорській Україні. Мюнхен, Академія, 1948.
32 p. 21 cm.
Cover title.
"Відбитка з Народнього календаря на 1948 р."
1. Galicia — History. 2. Bukowina — History. 3. Ruthenia—History. 4. Ukrainians in Austria. 5. Austria—History—Revolution, 1848-1849. I. Title.
DB498.B37 73-317747

Baran, Stepan.
(Z moïkh spohadiv pro Ivana Franka)
З моїх спогадів про Івана Франка; в 36-ті роковини з дня смерти (28. 5. 1916-28. 5. 1952). [Neu Ulm, Donau, Вид. Укр. вістей] 1952.
58 p. 15 cm.
1. Franko, Ivan, 1856-1916. I. Title.
PG3948.F72B24 73-206062

Baran, Steven J.
see Bankert, Peter J An analysis of the operation of the Pediatric Outpatient Division... [Ithaca, N.Y.] 1973.

Baran, Sybil.
Development and validation of a TAT-type projective test for use among Bantu-speaking people. Johannesburg, National Institute for Personnel Research, Council for Scientific and Industrial Research, 1971.
ix, 178 l. illus. 30 cm. (CSIR special report, PERS 138)
Bibliography: leaves 169-178.
1. Picture interpretation tests. 2. Bantus. 3. Apperception—Testing. I. Title.
CtY NUC76-93129

Băran, Tudor.
Destine sentimentale. [Schiţe. Coperta: Const. Nicoleanu]. Iaşi, „Junimea," 1973.
256 p. 20 cm. lei 6.75 R 73-1839
I. Title.
PC840.12.A647D4 74-345890

Băran, Tudor.
Mîndra : roman / Tudor Băran ; [coperta, Teodor Bogoi]. — Craiova : "Scrisul românesc", 1976.
125 p. ; 20 cm. R76-2127
lei5.00
I. Title.
PC840.12.A647M5 76-482344
•76 MARC

Băran, Vasile.
Ambarcaţiunea eroică : roman / Vasile Băran ; [coperta, Eugen Palade]. — Bucureşti : Editura Ion Creangă, 1976.
234 p. ; 17 cm. — (Biblioteca contemporană) R76-3482
lei3.75
I. Title.
PZ90.R6B28 77-479455
•77 MARC

Băran, Vasile.
Călcîiul lui Ahile : microschiţe satirice / Vasile Băran. — Iaşi : "Junimea," 1974.
287 p. ; 15 cm. R 74-3263
lei 6.75
I. Title.
PC840.12.A65C25 75-576738

Băran, Vasile.
Cartea proverbelor. ⌈Povestiri. Coperta de Magda Bîrsan⌉. ⌈București⌉, „Albatros," 1973.
192 p. 20 cm. lei 5.00 R 73-2271
CONTENTS: Biruința șoferului.—Gîsca miraculoasă.—Soldatul și generalul. — Dincolo de geamandură. — Barba lui Gad. — Înalta statuie.—Eduard al II-lea. Cravata lui Sander.—O vizită misterioasă.—Vis de pădure.—Descoperirea grîului. Clopotul de sticlă.
I. Title.
PC840.12.A65C3 74-340852

Băran, Vasile.
Cascada : ⌈roman⌉ / Vasile Băran ; ⌈coperta de A. Perussi⌉. — ⌈București⌉ : "Cartea românească," 1974.
162 p. ; 21 cm. R 75-3099
lei 7.75
I. Title.
PC840.12.A65C67 75-404964

Băran, Vasile.
Insula manechinelor : roman fantastic / Vasile Băran ; ⌈coperta, Damian Petrescu⌉. — București : Editura Ion Creangă, 1975.
165 p. ; 20 cm. R 75-3611
lei 4.00
I. Title.
PC840.12.A65 I 5 75-410380

Băran, Vasile.
O.R.A. : (opinii, reportaje, anchete) / Vasile Băran ; ⌈coperta colecției, Done Stan⌉. — București : Editura Eminescu, 1976.
223 p. ; 20 cm. — (Reporter) R76-3707
On cover: Ora.
1. Romania—Description and travel—1945- 2. Baran, Vasile. I. Title. II. Title: Ora.
DR210.B35 77-452300
•77 MARC

Baran, Volodymyr Danylovych.
(Ranni slov'ïany mizh Dnistrom i Pryp'ïattïu)
Ранні слов'яни між Дністром і Прип'яттю. Київ, "Наук. думка," 1972.
244 p. with illus. and maps. 22 cm. 1.91rub USSR 72-39970
At head of title: Академія наук Української РСР. Інститут археології. В. Д. Баран.
Summary in Russian and German.
Bibliography: p. 235-⌈242⌉
1. Slavic antiquities. 2. Russia—Antiquities. 3. Slavs. I. Title.
GN549.S6B37 73-330448

Baran, Volodymyr Danylovych
see Noveĭshie otkrytiïa sovetskikh arkheologov. 1975.

Baran, William Lee, 1943-
Survival of selected pathogenic organisms during processing of a fermented turkey sausage product. [n.p.] 1973.
[2], x, 83, [i.e. 86] l. illus.
Thesis (Ph.D.)—Michigan State University.
Bibliography: leaves 61-70.
1. Food poisoning. 2. Sausages. 3. Turkeys. I. Title.
MiEM NUC74-126748

Baran, Władysław.
Związek bezimiennych. ⌈Wyd. 1.⌉. Katowice, Śląsk, 1973.
322 p. 20 cm. zł22.00
CONTENTS: Związek bezimiennych.—Kwarantanna.—Czarne diamenty.—Sam wśród swoich.
I. Title.
PG7161.A65Z47 74-207383

Baranangsiang.
⌈Bandung, Jajasan Kabudájaan Baranangsiang⌉
v. ill. 26 cm. monthly.
In Sundanese.
AP95.S8B37 74-648255
MARC-S

Barañano da Costa, M Sara.
Presencia del río Uruguay; panorama histórico, geográfico, económico, y jurisdiccional ⌈por⌉ M. Sara Barañano da Costa. 2. ed. Montevideo ⌈Tall. Gráf. de A. Monteverde y Cía⌉ 1968.
172 p. illus., maps (3 fold.) 19 cm.
Bibliography: p. 169.
1. Uruguay River. I. Title.
OrPS NUC74-57158

Baranauskas, Albinas.
Rudenys ir pavasariai; arba, Užplynių Pultinevičius namie ir svetur. Chicago, Lietuviškos Knygos Klubas, 1975-
v.
I. Title.
CaOTP NUC77-84136

Baranauskas, Antanas, Bp., 1835-1902.
The forest of Anykščiai. The original Lithuanian text with the English verse-translation by Nadas Rastenis. Introd. and editing by Juozas Tininis. 2d. ed. ⌈Los Angeles⌉ Lithuanian days, 1970.
61 p. illus. 25 cm. $4.00
A poem.
Added t. p.: Anykščių šilelis.
I. Rastenis, Nadas, tr. II. Title.
PG8721.B325A8 1970 891.9'2'12 72-196744
MARC

Baranauskas, M.
see Nauka. Spetsialisty. 1971.

Baranauskas, Marius.
Naujasis Vilnius. Vilnius ⌈Mintis⌉ 1972.
1 v. (chiefly illus.) 29 cm. 7.45rub USSR***
At head of title: Marius Baranauskas, Liudvikas Ruikas.
Legends in Lithuanian, Russian, and English.
1. Vilna—Description—Views. I. Ruikas, Liudvikas. II. Title.
DK651.V4B37 73-352127

Baranauskas, Vincentas.
Ekonominis gamybos efektyvumas ir jo didinimas. Vilnius, "Mintis," 1970.
190 p. with diagrs. 22 cm. 0.62rub USSR 71-21431
At head of title: V. Baranauskas.
Includes bibliographical references.
1. Labor productivity. 2. Labor productivity—Lithuania. I. Title.
HD57.B32 72-364017
DS

Baranavykh, Symon, 1900-1942.
⌈Mezhy. Russian⌉
Межи ; Новая дорога / Сымон Барановых ; ⌈перевел с белорусского Георгий Попов⌉. — Минск : Мастацкая літ-ра, 1976.
254 p. : ill. ; 21 cm. — (Библиотека белорусской повести) USSR***
Series romanized: Biblioteka belorusskoĭ povesti.
0.63rub
I. Baranavykh, Symon, 1900-1942. Novaïa daroha. Russian. 1976. II. Title.
Title romanized: Mezhi.
PG2835.B3M417 1976 77-504852

Baranavykh, Symon, 1900-1942. Novaïa daroha. Russian. 1976
see Baranavykh, Symon, 1900-1942. ⌈Mezhy. Russian⌉ Mezhi. 1976.

Baranchenko, Viktor Eremeevich.
Ïuriĭ Petrovych Haven. [By] V. Ė. Baranchenko. Simferopol', Tavriia, 1972.
86 p. illus. (Lenins'koï hvardiï biitsi)
1. Gaven, Ïuriĭ Petrovich, pseud., 1884-1936.
MH NUC75-129131

Baranchik, Alvin John.
Multiple regression and estimation of the mean of a multivariate normal distribution, by Alvin J. Baranchik. [Stanford, Calif., Dept. of Statistics, Stanford University] 1964.
39 p. (Stanford University. Technical report, no. 51)
"Prepared under contract Nonr-225(72) (NR-042-993) for Officc of Naval Research."
Bibliography: p. 39.
WaU NUC76-75719

Baranchikov, Vladimir Aleksandrovich.
(Oblastnoĭ Sovet deputatov trudïashchikhsïa)
Областной Совет депутатов трудящихся / Баранчиков В. А. — Москва : Юрид. лит-ра, 1976.
158 p. ; 20 cm. USSR***
Includes bibliographical references.
0.75rub
1. Soviets. I. Title.
JS6058.B27 76-527099

Baranchikov, Vladimir Aleksandrovich.
(Obrazovanie SSSR i razvitie sovetskoĭ formy sotsialisticheskogo gosudarstva)
Образование СССР и развитие советской формы социалистического государства. Москва, Изд-во Моск. ун-та, 1972.
78 p 21 cm. 0.31rub USSR 72-VKP
At head of title: В. А. Баранчиков, В. А. Масленников.
Includes bibliographical references.
1. Russia—Politics and government—1917- 2. Soviets. 3. Minorities—Russia. I. Maslennikov, Vïacheslav Andreevich, joint author. II. Title.
JN6515 1917.B37 73-334897

Baranchuk, Norberto S
Condiciones de eficiencia de los servicios de atención materno infantil; guías de evaluación y su adecuación a los niveles de complejidad hospitalaria. [2. ed.] Buenos Aires, Ediciones S.M.I., 1971.
206 p. tables.
1. Maternal health services—Argentina. 2. Maternal and infant welfare—Argentina. 3. Infants—Care and hygiene—Argentina. I. Title.
DPAHO NUC75-29248

Barancic, Frantisek.
Senazovani a silazovani ovsa / Frantisek Barancic. -- Praha : Ustav vedeckotechnickych informaci, 1975.
20 p. -- (Metodiky pro zavadeni vysledku vyzkumu do praxe, 1975 ; no. 9)
Bibliography : p. 19.
I. Title.
DNAL NUC77-83514

Barańczak, Stanisław, 1946-
Dziennik poranny; wiersze, 1967-1971. Opracował graficznie Wojciech Freudenreich. ⌈Wyd. 1. Poznań⌉ Wydawn. Poznańskie, 1972.
81 p. illus. 16 cm. zł12.00
I. Title.
PG7161.A67D9 73-205253

Barańczak, Stanisław, 1946-
Ironia i harmonia; szkice o najnowszej literaturze polskiej. ⌈Wyd. 1.⌉. Warszawa, Czytelnik, 1973.
217 p. 20 cm. zł20.00
Includes bibliographical references.
1. Polish literature—20th century—Addresses, essays, lectures. I. Title.
PG7051.B36 73-213396

Barańczak, Stanisław, 1946-
Język dziecięcy a poezja dla dzieci / Stanislaw Baranczak. -- [s. l. : s. n., 197-]
24 p. ; 29 cm.
Includes bibliographical references.
1. Children--Language. 2. Children's poetry--Polish.
MH NUC77-83515

Barańczak, Stanisław, 1946-
Jezyk poetycki Mirona Białoszewskiego. Wrocław, Zakład Narodowy im. Ossolińskich, 1974.
177 p. (Z dziejów form artystycznych w literaturze polskiej, t. 41)
Bibliographical footnotes.
1. Białoszewski, Miron—Style. I. Title.
InU NUC76-23089

Baranda, Julián García Sainz de
see García Sainz de Baranda, Julián, 1888-

Baranda, Ramiro Bañales
see Bañales Baranda, Ramiro.

Baranda de Carrión, Pedro.
El castillo de S. Alberto, drama en cinco actos, traducido del francés. Madrid, Yenes, 1839. [Louisville, Ky., Falls City Microcards, 1961]
102 p. 18 cm.
Microcard copy on 2 cards.
I. Title.
OrU NUC76-62491

Baranda de Carrión, Pedro.
Los padres de la novia, comedia en un acto, traducida del francés y arreglada. Madrid, Yenes, 1839. [Louisville, Ky., Falls City Microcards, 1961]
30 p. 18 cm.
Microcard copy on 1 card.
I. Title.
OrU NUC76-62490

Barande, Ilse.
Histoire de la psychanalyse en France / Ilse et Robert Barande. — Toulouse : Privat, [1975]
181 p. ; 21 cm. — (Regard) F***
Bibliography: p. [153]-177.
ISBN 2-7089-1324-7 : 24.50F
1. Psychoanalysis—France—History. I. Barande, Robert, joint author. II. Title.
BF173.B186 150'.19'50944 75-507117
75 MARC

Barande, Ilse.
Sandor Ferenczi. Paris, Payot [1972]
211 p. 18 cm. (Petite bibliothèque Payot, 204) (Collection Science de l'homme) F***
Bibliography: p. 193-209.
1. Ferenczi, Sándor, 1873-1933. 2. Psychoanalysis.
RC504.B27 72-356205

Barande, René, 1892-
see Madahil, Antonio Gomes da Rocha, 1893- Ex-libris... Porto [Portugal] Associaçao Portuense de Ex-Libris, 1960.

Barande, Robert.
La naissance exorcisée : ou, L'érotique anale de l'homme inachevé : essai psychanalytique sur l'origine et le destin de la pulsion et du fantasme / Robert Barande. — Paris : Denoël, [1975]
206 p. ; 23 cm. — (La Psychanalyse dans le monde contemporain) F***
Includes bibliographical references.
50.00F
1. Psychoanalysis. 2. Sex (Pscyhology) I. Title.
RC506.B3 150'.19'5 75-508927
75 MARC

Barande, Robert, joint author.
see Barande, Ilse. Histoire de la psychanalyse en France. Toulouse, Privat, [1975]

Barande, Robert
see Éducation et psychanalyse. [Paris, Hachette, 1973]

Barandiaran, Edgardo,
The control of money and bank credit in Argentina. [Minneapolis] 1973.
x, 163 l. illus. 29 cm.
Thesis (Ph.D.)—University of Minnesota.
Bibliography: leaves 161-163.
I. Title.
MnU-A NUC74-126749

Barandiarán, Edgardo.
The control of money and bank credit in Argentina. [n.p.] 1973.
x, 163 l.
Thesis—University of Minnesota.
Bibliography: leaves 161-163.
Microfilm. Ann Arbor, Mich., University Microfilms, 1973. 1 reel. 35 mm.
1. Banks and banking—Argentine Republic. 2. Credit—Argentine Republic. I. Title.
TxU NUC75-21629

Barandiarán, Edgardo.
The design of balance-of-payments policies for the Andean countries : a progress report / Edgardo Barandiarán, Fernando Ossa. — Santiago, Chile : Universidad Católica de Chile, Instituto de Economía, Oficina de Publicaciones, 1976.
62 p. ; 27 cm. — (Documento de trabajo - Instituto de Economía, Universidad Católica de Chile ; no. 50)
Bibliography: p. 59-62.
1. Balance of payments—Andes region. 2. Andes region—Foreign economic relations. 3. International finance. I. Eguiguren Ossa, Fernando, joint author. II. Title. III. Series: Santiago de Chile. Universidad Católica. Instituto de Economía. Documentos de trabajo ; no. 50.
HG3883.A5B37 382.1'7'098 77-553064
77 MARC

Barandiarán, Edgardo.
Teoría de los sistemas monetarios / Edgardo Barandiarán. — Santiago : Universidad Católica de Chile, Instituto de Economía, Oficina de Publicaciones, [1974]
134 p. in various pagings : ill. ; 27 cm. — (Documentos de trabajo — Universidad Católica de Chile, Instituto de Economía ; no. 28)
Includes bibliographical references.
1. Money. I. Title. II. Series: Santiago de Chile. Universidad Católica. Instituto de Economía. Documentos de trabajo ; no. 28.
HG221.B27 332.4'01 75-559719

Barandiarán, Ignacio
see
Barandiarán Maestu, Ignacio, 1937-

Barandiarán, José León
see León Barandiarán, José.

Barandiarán, José Miguel de.
Diccionario ilustrado de mitología vasca y algunas de sus fuentes. Bilbao, La Gran Enciclopedia Vasca, 1972.
452 p. illus. 24 cm. (His Obras completas, 1) (Biblioteca magna, 15) Sp***
Includes bibliographical references.
1. Mythology, Basque—Dictionaries—Spanish. I. Title.
BL975.B3B28 73-324258

Barandiarán, José Miguel de.
Estación prehistórica de Kurtzia, Barrica-Sopelana (1959) por José Miguel de Barandiarán, Antonio Aguirre y Mario Grande. Bilbao, Servicio de Investigaciones Arqueológicas de la Excma. Diputación Provincial de Vizcaya, 1960.
19 p. [29] p. of illus. 22 cm.
Cover title: Estación de Kurtzia.
IU NUC74-172182

Barandiarán, José Miguel de.
Estelas funerarias del país vasco (zona norte). Ed. bilingüe. San Sebastián, Txertoa [1970]
212 p. illus. 20 cm.
Spanish and Basque.
Includes bibliographical references.
1. Sepulchral monuments—Spain—Basque Provinces. 2. Design, Decorative—Basque Provinces. I. Title.
NB1624.B34B37 73-207370

Barandiarán, José Miguel de.
Eusko-folklore / José Miguel de Barandiarán. — Bilbao : Editorial La Gran Enciclopedia Vasca, 1973.
524 p., [1] fold. leaf of plates : ill. ; 24 cm. — (His Obras completas ; t. 2) Sp***
Basque or Spanish.
Includes bibliographical references and index.
ISBN 84-248-0192-X
1. Folk-lore, Basque. I. Title.
GR237.B3B36 75-545544

Barandiarán, José Miguel de.
Ikuska. Bilbao, Editorial La Gran Enciclopedia Vasca, 1973-74.
2 v. illus., maps. 24 cm. (His Obras completas, t. 3-4) Sp***
Includes bibliographical references.
CONTENTS: 1. Artículos y conferencias.—2. Monografías de la vida popular.
1. Folk-lore, Basque. I. Title.
GR237.B3B37 74-324582
ISBN 84-248-0190-3

Barandiarán, José Miguel de.
Lehen euskal gizona. Donostia, LUR, 1972.
120 p. illus. 19 cm. (Hastapenak, 13.)
1. Basque Provinces—Antiquities. 2. Ethnology—Basque provinces. 3. Man, Primitive. I. Title.
NIC NUC75-32410

Barandiaran, José Miguel de.
Obras completas. Bilbao, Editorial La Gran Enciclopedia Vasca, 1973-
v.
Contents: -2. Eusko-folklore.
MH NUC74-125059

Barandiarán, José Miguel de.
Vasconia antigua : trás las huellas del hombre / José Miguel de Barandiarán. — Bilbao : Editorial La Gran Enciclopedia Vasca, 1975-
v. : ill. ; 24 cm. — (His Obras completas ; t. 7) Sp76-Jan (v. 1)
Includes bibliographical references.
CONTENTS: 1. Ataún en la Edad Media. Monumentos del Aralar guipuzcoano. Prehistoria vasca y apuntes bibliográficos. Investigaciones prehistóricas en la diócesis de Vitoria. La prehistoria. Exploración de neuve dólmenes del Aralar guipuzcoano. Exploración de seis dólmenes de la sierra de Aizkorri. El arte rupestre en Alava. Exploración de siete dólmenes en la sierra de Ataún-Borunda. Fernando López de Cárdenas, naturalista.
1. Man, Prehistoric—Basque Provinces—Collected works. 2. Basque Provinces—Antiquities—Collected works. I. Title.
GN836.B3B32 936.6 76-465965
*76 MARC

Barandiaran, Joxemiel
see
Barandiarán, José Miguel de.

Barandiarán de Garland, Estela.
Problemática de la teleducación en América Latina / Estela Barandiarán de Garland. — [Piura, Perú] : Universidad de Piura : [distribuye A. Lulli, Lima], 1973.
52 p. ; 19 cm. — (Colección Algarrobo ; 15)
"Conferencia pronunciada en el Programa Académico de Artes Liberales de la Universidad de Piura el 13 de mayo de 1969. El texto ha sido posteriormente revisado y ampliado por la autora."
Includes bibliographical references.
1. Television in education—Latin America. I. Title.
LB1044.7.B27 75-559712

Barandiarán Irizar, Luis de.
Novios conscientes. [Vitoria, Editorial ESET, 1971]
216 p. plates. 19 cm. (Temas para la reflexión y el diálogo) Sp***
1. Marriage—Catholic Church. I. Title.
BX2250.B332 72-362265

Barandiarán Maestu, Ignacio, 1937-
Arte mueble del paleolítico cantábrico / Ignacio Barandiarán Maestu. — Zaragoza : Departamentos de Prehistoria y Arqueología e Historia de la Antigüedad de la Universidad de Zaragoza, 1972.
369 p., [67] leaves of plates (29 fold.) : ill. ; 23 cm. — (Monografías arqueológicas ; 14) Sp 73-Oct
Bibliography: p. 349-356.
Includes indexes.
1. Art, Prehistoric—Cantabria. 2. Cantabria—Antiquities. I. Title. II. Series.
N5310.5.C27B37 75-547322

Barandiarán Maestu, Ignacio, 1937-
La Cueva de los Casares, en Riba de Saelices, Guadalajara. Con la colaboración de Jesús Altuna [et al. Madrid, Ministerio de Educación y Ciencia, Dirección General de Bellas Artes, Comisaría General de Excavaciones Arqueológicas, 1973]
122 p. illus. 25 cm. (Excavaciones arqueológicas en España, 76) Sp***
Includes bibliographies.
ISBN 84-369-0281-5
1. Casares Cave, Spain. I. Title. II. Series.
DP44.E9 no. 76 76-528232
[GN836.G8]

Barandiarán Maestu, Ignacio, 1937-
Guipúzcoa en la edad antigua. Protohistoria y romanización. (San Sebastián) Caja de Ahorros Provincial de Guipúzcoa [1973]
102 p., illus., maps. 21 cm. (Colección Documento, no. 3) Sp 74-May
At head of title: Ignacio Barandiarán.
Includes bibliographical references.
1. Guipúzcoa, Spain—History. I. Title.
DP302.G89B37 914.6'61'03 74-350121
ISBN 84-7231-096-5

Barandica, Juanita Garavilla
see **Garavilla Barandica, Juanita.**

Barandun, Silvio, joint author.
see Morell, Andreas. IgG-Subklassen der menschlichen Immunglobuline ... Basel, S. Karger, 1975.

Baranek, Madge, joint author
see Meier, Walli. Recreative movement in further education. [London, Macdonald and Evans, 1973]

Baranelli, Domenico.
Baranelli, Siena, 18 maggio-20 giugno 1975. — Siena : a cura dell'Amministrazione comunale, Assessorato alla cultura [1975]
[44] leaves : ill. (some col.) ; 20 x 21 cm. It76-Ma
1. Baranelli, Domenico. I. Siena. Assessorato alla cultura.
NC257.B25S57 741.9'45 76-48198
*76 MARC

Baranenko, Valeriĭ Alekseevich, joint author
see Pochtman, IUriĭ Mikhaĭlovich. (Dinamicheskoe programmirovanie v zadachakh stroitel'noĭ mekhaniki) 1975.

Baranenkov, G. S.
see Demidovich, Boris Pavlovich. Zadachi i uprazhneniia po matematicheskomu analizu. Izd. 9., stereotip. Moskva, "Nauka", 1974.

Baranenkova, Antonina Sergeevna, joint author
see Lukmanov, Ėrnst Galimzīanovich. (Biologiia i promysel saĭdy v severoevropeiskikh moriakh) 1975.

Baranenkova, Antonina Sergeevna, ed.
see Sbornik, posviashchennyĭ nauchnoĭ deiatel'nosti Nikolaia Antonovicha Maslova. 1968.

Baranenkova, Taisiía Alekseevna.
(Vysvobozhdenie rabocheĭ sily i uluchshenie ee ispol'zovaniía pri sofsializme)
Высвобождение рабочей силы и улучшение ее использования при социализме / Т. А. Бараненкова. — Москва : Наука, 1974.
173 p. ; 20 cm. USSR 74
At head of title: Академия наук СССР. Институт экономики.
Includes bibliographical references.
0.61rub
1. Labor supply—Russia. 2. Incentives in industry—Russia. I. Title.
HD5796.B37 74-358087

Bărănescu, George.
Teoria echilibrajului motoarelor cu ardere internă în linie / George Bărănescu. — ₍București₎ : Editura Academiei Republicii Socialiste România, 1975.
302 p., ₍2₎ fold. leaves of plates : ill. ; 25 cm. R76-3064
Summary in English.
Table of contents in Romanian and English.
Bibliography: p. ₍283₎-284.
lei28.00
1. Internal combustion engines—Vibration. 2. Balancing of machinery. I. Title.
TJ759.B37 77-464315
•77 MARC

Bărănescu, Rodica.
Turism şi alimentaţie publică / Rodica Bărănescu. — Bucureşti : Editura didactică şi pedagogică, 1975.
247, ₍1₎ p. : ill. ; 21 cm. R 76-448
At head of title: Ministerul Educaţiei şi Învăţămîntului. Academia de Studii Economice Bucureşti.
Bibliography: p. 243-₍248₎
lei 9.75
1. Tourist trade. I. Title.
G155.A1B353 76-529491

Baranet, Nancy Neiman.
Bicycling. South Brunswick, A. S. Barnes ₍1973₎
152 p. illus. 29 cm.
Bibliography: p. ₍147₎
1. Cycling. 2. Bicycles and tricycles. I. Title.
GV1041.B33 796.6 77-37803
ISBN 0-498-01051-1 MARC

Baranga, Aurel, 1913-
Comedii. Bucuresti, Ed. Eminescu, 1971.
2 v.
I. Title.
OCl NUC76-78421

Baranga, Aurel, 1913-
Drame. [Bucuresti] Ed. Eminescu [1970]
341 p.
I. Title.
OCl NUC76-78422

Baranga, Aurel, 1913-
Les mois de la semaine. Introduction par Pierre Seghers. Traduction de Marica Beligan. ₍Paris₎ Seghers ₍c1968₎
75 p. 19 cm.
I. Title.
NcGU NUC73-40333

Baranga, Aurel, 1913–
(Obrazum'siâ, Khristofor')
Образумься Христофор! Водевиль в трех актах. Перевод с румынского и сценическая ред. Е. Азерниковой. Пьеса отредактирована и направлена для распространения Упр. театров Министерства культуры СССР. Отв. редактор А. Артемов. Москва, Отдел распространения драматических произведений ВУОАП, 1972.
8 l. 29 cm.
Translation of Fii cuminte, Cristofer.
1.50rub
I. Title.
PC839.B3F517 75-581665

Baranga, Aurel, 1913–
(Obshchestvennoe mnenie)
Общественное мнение; пьеса в двух частях. Перевод с румынского Е. Азерниковой. Пьеса отредактирована и направлена для распространения Упр. театров Министерства культуры СССР. Отв. редактор А. Артемов. Москва, Отдел распространения драматических произведений ВУОАП, 1972.
66 l. 29 cm.
Translation of Opinia publică.
1.30rub
I. Title.
PC839.B3A57 1972 75-581666

Baranga, Aurel, 1913–
Poezii. ₍Coperta: arh. Armand Crintea₎. Bucureşti, Editura Eminescu, 1973.
247 p. 20 cm. lei 16.50 R 73-4351
PC839.B3P6 74-340926

Baranga, Aurel, 1913–
Simfonia patetică : epopee dramatică în două părţi (10 tablouri) / Aurel Baranga ; ₍prezentarea grafică, Armand Crintea₎. — Bucureşti : Editura Eminescu, 1974.
158 p. : port. ; 19 cm. — (Colecţia Rampa ; 10) R 75-132
Includes bibliographical references.
lei 5.75
I. Title.
PC839.B3S5 75-577979

Baranga, Aurel, 1913–
Teatru. ₍Coperta: arh. Armand Crintea₎. Bucureşti, Editura Eminescu, 1973.
599 p. 20 cm. lei 24.50 R 73-4365
CONTENTS: Mielul turbat.—Siciliana.—Adam şi Eva.—Fii cuminte, Cristofor! ... — Sfîntul Mitică Blajinu. — Opinia publică. — Travesti.—Interesul general.
PC839.B3A19 1973 74-340470

Baranga, Aurel, 1913–
Teze şi paranteze : ₍articole din ziare şi publicaţii periodice din anii 1970 şi 1973₎ / Aurel Baranga. — Bucureşti : Editura Eminescu, 1974.
255 p. ; 22 cm. R 75-1461
lei 10.50
I. Title.
PC839.B3T4 75-540145

Baranga, Aurel, 1913–
₍Travesti. Russian₎
Травести; маска. Комедия в трех действиях. Перевод с румынского Вл. Павлова. Пьеса отредактирована и направлена для распространения Упр. театров Министерства культуры СССР. Отв. редактор В. Малашенко. Москва, Отдел распространения драматических произведений ВУОАП, 1972.
85 l. 29 cm. 1.50rub USSR***
I. Title.
Title romanized: Travesti.
PC839.B3T717 74-316279

Baranga, Aurel, 1913-
Viaţa unei femei : dramă în două părţi / Aurel Baranga ; ₍prezentarea grafică, Armand Crintea₎. — ₍Bucureşti₎ : Editura Eminescu, 1976.
86 p. ; 19 cm. — (Colecţia Rampa ; 25) R76-3906
Includes bibliographical references.
lei3.50
I. Title.
PC839.B3V5 77-462174
•77 MARC

Baranga, Aurel, 1913- joint author
see Moraru, Nicolae, 1912- For the happiness of the people; play in 3 acts... Bucharest, "The Book" Pub. House ₍1953₎

Baranga, Aurel, 1913-
see 3 ₍i.e. Trei₎ dramaturgi contemporani . . . ₍Bucureşti₎ "Albatros" 1976.

Baranger, Pierre.
Comment réussir votre gestion des stocks sur ordinateur. Préf. de G. Depallens. Paris, Éditions d'organisation, 1972.
223, ₍1₎ p. illus. 24 cm. (Collection Informatique et management) 49.00F F***
Bibliography: p. ₍224₎
1. Electronic data processing—Inventory control. I. Title.
HD55.B28 73-341149
MARC

Baranger, Pierre.
Le prix de revient : outil de décision et de rentabilité de l'entreprise / Pierre Baranger, Pierre Bonnassies. — Paris : Éditions d'organisation, 1976.
286 p. ; 24 cm. F***
Bibliography: p. ₍285₎-286.
ISBN 2-7081-0287-7 : 80.00F
1. Costs, Industrial. 2. Profit. 3. Management. I. Bonnassies, Pierre, joint author. II. Title.
HD47.B27 338.4'3 76-483578
76 MARC

Baranger, René.
Gardianage en Camargue: défendons la Camargue ₍par₎ René Baranger, lettre manuscrite et préface du marquis Folco de Baroncelli-Javon. Nouvelle éd. Clichy (12, bd Général-Leclerc, 92110), R. Baranger, 1973.
156 p. ill. 28 cm. 45.00F F 74-5577
1. Camargue, Île de la. 2. Cowboys—France—Camargue, Île de la. I. Title.
DC611.C2B294 1973 914.4'91 74-189778
MARC

Baranger, René.
Jouer au cow-boy; roman. Clichy, France, Baranger ₍1966₎
197 p. 19 cm.
I. Title.
PQ2662.A627J6 843'.9'14 74-161708
MARC

Baranger, Renée Martinage-
see Martinage-Baranger, Renée.

Baranger, Willy
see Entre théorie et technique. [1. éd.] Paris, Presses universitaires de France, 1970.

Barangolások a soproni erdőkben / ₍írta Csapody István ... et al. ; szerk. Gimes Endre₎. — ₍Budapest₎ : Panoráma, 1975.
136, ₍1₎ p., ₍12₎ leaves of plates : ill. (some col.), maps ; 17 cm.
Bibliography: p. 133-₍137₎
ISBN 963-243-406-4 : 20.50Ft
1. Parks—Hungary—Sopron region. 2. Sopron, Hungary—Parks. I. Gimes, Endre.
SB484.H8B37 77-505161

Baranguan, Vicente Correas
see Correas Baranguan, Vicente.

Barani, Eugenio.
Le frodi fiscali in materia di IVA. Montecchio E., A cura del CEDA, 1972.
158 p. 21 cm. (Collana di studi sulla riforma tributaria, 1)
L3500 It 72-Dec
Includes bibliographical references.
1. Value-added tax—Italy. 2. Tax evasion—Italy. I. Title.
HJ5715.I 8B3 73-329489

Baranick, Benzion Ḥayyim Ayalon-
see Ayalon-Baranick, Benzion Ḥayyim, 1901-

Baraniecki, M M
A market survey; techniques and potentialities [by] M. M. Baraniecki [and] D. M. Ellis. [Sheffield] Geographical Association, 1970.
9 p. illus. (Teaching geography, no. 12)
I. Ellis, D. M. II. Title.
InU NUC75-95697

Baranik, Muhammad Ahmad
see
Barāniq, Muḥammad Aḥmad.

Baranik, Rudolf,
Napalm elegy. Interview by Irving Sandler; preface by Lawrence Alloway. Edited by Daniel Newman. [New Brunswick, N. J., Livingston College, Rutgers University, 1973]
[39] p. illus.
1. Baranik, Rudolf, 1920- I. Sandler, Irving, 1925- II. Title.
InU NUC74-119807

Baranik, Rudolf.
see Artists Meeting for Cultural Change. Catalog Committee. An anti-catalog. New York, Catalog Committee of Artists Meeting for Cultural Change, 1977.

Baranin, Dušan, 1902–
(U oluji)
У олуји. Београд, "Вук Караџић," ⟨1972⟩.
2 v. 20 cm. 120.00Din Yu 72
I. Title.
PG1418.B276U2 72-971478

Barāniq, Muḥammad Aḥmad
see Arabian nights. Malay. Hikayat sa-ribu satu malam. Kuala Lumpur: Dewan Bahasa dan Pustaka, 19

Baranîuk, Valentin Aleksandrovich.
(Avtomatizirovannye sistemy upravleniîa shtabov i voennykh uchrezhdeniĭ)
Автоматизированные системы управления штабов и военных учреждений : (по материалам иностранной печати) / В. А. Баранюк, В. И. Воробьев. — Москва : Воениздат, 1974.
214 p. : ill. ; 21 cm. USSR***
Bibliography: p. 212.
0.69rub
1. Electronic data processing—Military art and science. 2. Management information systems. I. Vorob'ev, Vladimir Ivanovich, joint author. II. Title.
UG478.B37 75-558204

Baranji, Karlo
see
Baranyi, Károly, 1894-

Baranji Markov, Zlata
see
Baranyiné Markov, Zlata.

Baránková, Jarmila.
Jules Vallès, místo jeho Trilogie ve vývoji francouzské výpravné prózy. Praha, Universita Karlova [1972]
89 p. (Acta Universitatis Carolinae. Philologica. Monographica, 39)
Summary in French.
1. Vallès, Jules Louis Joseph, 1832-1885.
InU NUC74-127040

Barannik, Orest Viktorovich, joint author
see Markov, Nikolaĭ Andreevich. Ėkspluatatsionnyĭ kontrol' ėlektricheskikh parametrov dugovykh ėlektropecheĭ. 1973.

Barannikov, Alekseĭ Petrovich, 1890–1952.
Українські та південно-російські циганські діялекти. Ленинград, Изд-во Академии наук СССР, 1933.
72 p. 26 cm.
At head of title: О. Баранніков.
1. Gipsies—Language. 2. Gipsies—Ukraine. I. Title.
Title romanized: Ukraïns'ki ta pivdenno-rosiïs'ki tsyhans'ki dialekty.
DX161.B2 73-216428

Barannikov, Alekseĭ Petrovich, 1890–1952.
(Ukraïns'ki tsyhany)
Українські цигани. У Києві, 1931.
60 p. 26 cm. (Національні меншості Радянської України. Збірник нацменознавства, кн. 2)
60 p. illus. 26 cm.
At head of title: Всеукраїнська академія наук. Етнографічна комісія. Кабінет нацмен. О. П. Баранніков.
Summary in German.
Includes bibliographical references.
1. Gipsies—Ukraine. I. Title. II. Series: Natsional'ni menshosti Radians'koï Ukraïny. Zbirnyk natsmenoznavstva, kn. 2.
DX241.B37 73-215195

Barannikov, Oleg Vasil'evich.
(Spravochnik po kontroliu kachestva tekhnicheskikh kul'tur)
Справочник по контролю качества технических культур / [О. В. Баранников, В. В. Рощупкин, В. Ф. Селивончик]. — Алма-Ата : Кайнар, 1975.
256 p. ; 20 cm. USSR 76
0.68rub
1. Cotton — Russia. 2. Sugar beet — Russia. 3. Tobacco — Russia. I. Roshchupkin, Vasiliĭ Vasil'evich, joint author. II. Selivonchik, Valentina Fedorovna, joint author. III. Title.
SB251.R9B33 77-513628

Barannikov, P A
(Problemy khindi kak natsional'nogo iazyka)
Проблемы хинди как национального языка. Ленинград, "Наука," Ленингр. отд-ние, 1972.
187 p. with diagrs. and maps. 21 cm. 0.73rub USSR 72-VKP
At head of title: Академия наук СССР. Институт языкознания. П. А. Баранников.
Includes bibliographical references.
1. Hindi language. I. Title.
PK1931.B3 73-318987

Barannikova, Elizaveta Vasil'evna, ed.
see Buriatskie narodnye skazki. 1973.

Barannikova, Elizaveta Vasil'evna
see Buriatskie narodnye skazki, volshebno-fantasticheskie i o zhivotnykh. 1976.

Barannikova, Irina Alekseevna.
(Funktsional'nye osnovy migratsiĭ ryb)
Функциональные основы миграций рыб / И. А. Баранникова. — Ленинград : Наука, Ленингр. отд-ние, 1975.
209 p., [18] leaves of plates : ill. ; 23 cm. USSR 75
At head of title: Akademiia nauk SSSR. Nauchnyĭ sovet po kompleksnym problemam fiziologii cheloveka i zhivotnykh.
On verso of t. p.: Functional basis of fish migration.
Table of contents also in English.
Bibliography: p. 173-[206]
1.70rub
1. Fishes—Migration. 2. Fishes—Physiology. I. Title. II. Title: Functional basis of fish migration.
QL639.5.B37 75-533856

Barannikova, Irina Alekseevna
see Gormonal'naia reguliatsiia polovogo tsikla ryb v sviazi s zadachami vosproizvodstva rybnykh zapasov. 1975-

Barannikova, Margarita Vasil'evna, joint author
see Madera, Georgiĭ Il'ich. **Rekomendatsii po unifikatsii izdeliĭ.** 1967.

Barannyk, Dmytro Kharytonovych, ed.
see Issledovaniia po russkomu i ukrainskomu iazykam. Dnepropetrovsk, 1973.

Baranochnikova, L N
(Khlorella i ee ispol'zovanie v sel'skom khoziaĭstve)
Хлорелла и ее использование в сельском хозяйстве : указ. литературы за 1966–1973 гг., отеч.—425 названий, иностр.—123 названия / [составитель Л. Н. Бараночникова]. — Москва : ЦНСХБ ВАСХНИЛ, 1975.
100 p. ; 20 cm. USSR 75
At head of title: Vsesoiuznaia akademiia sel'skokhoziaĭstvennykh nauk imeni V. I. Lenina. TSentral'naia nauchnaia sel'skokhoziaĭstvennaia biblioteka.
0.32rub
1. Chlorella—Bibliography. I. Title.
Z5356.A6B37 76-513569
[QK569.C49]

Baranochnikova, L N
(Semenovodstvo odnoletnikh i mnogoletnikh trav)
Семеноводство однолетних и многолетних трав : библиогр. указ. литературы за 1969–1973 гг., отеч. и иностр. / [составитель Л. Н. Бараночникова]. — Москва : [s. n.], 1973.
111 p. ; 20 cm. USSR 73
At head of title: Vsesoiuznaia akademiia sel'skokhoziaĭstvennykh nauk imeni V. I. Lenina. TSentral'naia nauchnaia sel'skokhoziaĭstvennaia biblioteka.
0.48rub
1. Grass seed—Bibliography. I. Moscow. TSentral'naia nauchnaia sel'skokhoziaĭstvennaia biblioteka. II. Title.
Z5074.A8B37 75-544336

Baranoff, A von.
Eine Methode zur Berechnung der instationären Kräfte an Flügeln endlicher Spannweite in inkompressibler Strömung [von] A. von Baranoff. Braunscheweig, 1964.
40 p. illus. (Deutsche Forschungsanstalt für Luft-und Raumfahrt. Institut für Flugmechanik. Bericht Nr. 236)
ICRL NUC74-121999

Baranoff, A von.
Über einige Methoden der instationären Aerodynamik [von] A. von Baranoff. Braunschweig, 1963.
160 p. illus. (Deutsche Forschungsanstalt für Luft-und Raumfahrt. Institut für Flugmechanik. Bericht Nr. 213)
ICRL NUC74-121998

Baranoff, Nathalie.
Bibliographie des œuvres de Léon Chestov / établie par Nathalie Baranoff. — Paris : Institut d'études slaves, 1975.
xviii, 96 p. ; 25 cm. — (Bibliothèque russe de l'Institut d'études slaves ; 36 ISSN 0078-9976) (Série Écrivains russes en France) F75-10938
Title page also in Russian.
French and Russian.
Errata slip inserted.
Includes indexes.
ISBN 2-7204-0096-3 : 30.00F
1. Shestov, Lev, 1866-1938—Bibliography. I. Title. II. Series.
Z8816.62.B37 016.197'2 76-470597
[B4259.S54] 76 MARC

Baranoff-Rossiné, Vladimir, 1888–1942.
Vladimir Baranoff-Rossiné. [Paris] Éditions des musées nationaux [1972]
19 p. illus. 21 cm. F***
"Catalogue rédigé par Michel Hoog."
Catalog of an exhibition held at the Musée national d'art moderne, Dec. 12, 1972–Jan. 29, 1973.
Label on p. [2] of cover: Supplied by Worldwide Books, Boston.
1. Baranoff-Rossiné, Vladimir, 1888-1942. I. Hoog, Michel, ed. II. Paris. Musée national d'art moderne.
ND699.B35H66 73-329205

Baranoŭski, IAŭhen Ivanavich.
(Za druzhbu narodaŭ)
За дружбу народаў; дзейнасць Камуністычнай партыі Беларусі па ажыццяўленню ленінскай нацыянальнай палітыкі ў 1921–1925 гг. Мінск, Беларусь, 1972.
212 p. ports. facsims. 18 cm. 0.44rub USSR***
At head of title: Інстытут гісторыі партыі пры ЦК КПБ—філіял Інстытута марксізма-ленінізма пры ЦК КПСС. Я. Бараноўскі.
Includes bibliographical references.
1. White Russia—History. 2. Komunistychnaia partyia Belarusi. I. Title.
DK507.7.B37 74-348612

Baranoŭski, Vitaliĭ.
(Skaz pra Palesse)
Сказ пра Палессе. [Фотаальбом]. Фота Б. Бараноўскага. Тэкст Алеся Траяноўскага. [Мінск, "Беларусь," 1972.
[100] p. with illus. 20 x 24 cm. 2.42rub USSR 73-790
Title also in Russian and English; English title: The true story of Polesye.
White Russian, Russian, and English.
1. Polesie—Description and travel—Views. I. Traianoŭski, Ales'. II. Title. III. Title: The true story of Polesye.
DK511.P63B37 74-313449

Baranouski, Vitalii
see Sovetskaia Belorussiia. Soviet Byelorussia. 1976.

Baranouski, Vitalii
see Vitsebsk. 1974.

Baranov, A
(Oktiabr' i nachalo grazhdanskoĭ voĭny na Urale)
Октябрь и начало гражданской войны на Урале / А. Баранов. — Свердловск : Изд. Истпарта Уралобкома ВКП(б), 1928.
113 p. ; 18 cm.
Includes bibliographical references.
1. Ural Mountain region—History. I. Title.
DK265.8.U7B35 75-531774

Baranov, A.
see Barkley, Fred Alexander, 1908-
The sections of the Begoniaceae. Boston, 1972.

Baranov, A.
see also
Baranov, Andrei.

Baranov, A. I., ed.
see Fizika plenok. 1972-

Baranov, Aleksandr Abramovich
(IUnyĭ radiosportsmen)
Юный радиоспортсмен. Метод. пособие для внеклассной и внешкольной работы. Москва, Изд-во ДОСААФ, 1973.
97 p. 20 cm. 0.27rub USSR 73
At head of title: А. А. Баранов.
1. Radio—Competitions. I. Title.
TK6553.B255 74-307608

Baranov, Aleksandr Aleksandrovich.
(Fazovye prevrashchenia i termotsiklirovanie metallov)
Фазовые превращения и термоциклирование металлов / А. А. Баранов. — Киев : Наук. думка, 1974.
229, [3] p. : ill. ; 21 cm. USSR 7[illegible]
At head of title: Akademiia nauk Ukrainskoĭ SSR. Dnepropetrovskoe otdelenie Instituta mekhaniki.
Bibliography: p. 217-[230]
1.49rub
1. Physical metallurgy. 2. Metals—Thermal properties. I. Title
TN690.B29 75-53380[illegible]

Baranov, Aleksandr Alekseevich
see Osnovy ėkonomicheskikh znaniĭ. 1972.

Baranov, Aleksandr Alekseevich
see Osnovy ėkonomicheskikh znaniĭ. Azerbaijani. Igtisadi biliklärin äsaslary. 1972.

Baranov, Aleksandr Alekseevich
see Osnovy ėkonomicheskikh znaniĭ. Kirghiz. 1972.

Baranov, Aleksandr Alekseevich
see Osnovy ėkonomicheskikh znaniĭ. Turkoman Ykdysady bilimleriñ esaslary. 1973.

Baranov, Aleksandr Alekseevich
see Osnovy ekonomicheskikh znaniĭ dlia rabochikh. 1972.

Baranov, Aleksandr Alekseevich
see Osnovy ėkonomicheskikh znaniĭ dlia rabochikh. 1973.

Baranov, Aleksandr Alekseevich
see Osnovy ekonomicheskikh znaniĭ dli͡a rabochikh. 1974.

Baranov, Aleksandr Anatol'evich.
Обеспечение устойчивой работы объектов народного хозяйства в военное время. Москва, Атомиздат, 1970.
63 p. with diagrs. 20 cm. 0.10rub USSR 70–VKP
At head of title: А. А. Баранов.
Bibliography: p. [62]
1. Industry—Defense measures—Russia. 2. Atomic warfare. I. Title.
Title romanized: Obespechenie ustoĭchivoĭ raboty ob"ektov narodnogo khozi͡aĭstva v voennoe vremi͡a.
UA929.9.R9B37 73–348392

Baranov, Aleksandr Nikolaevich
see Staticheskie ispytanii͡a na prochnost' sverkhzvukovykh samoletov. 1974.

Baranov, Aleksandr Nikolaevich, 1864–
(V zashchitu neschastnykh zhenshchin)
Въ защиту несчастныхъ женщинъ. Изд. С. Даровatовскаго и А. Чарушникова. Москва, Типо-лит. В. Рихтеръ, 1902.
162 p. 19 cm.
At head of title: А. Барановъ.
Includes bibliographical references.
1. Prostitution—Russia. 2. Obshchestvo zashchity neschastnykh zhenshchin v gorode Kazani. I. Title.
HQ385.B37 74–201779

Baranov, Aleksandr Semenovich.
(Ėkonomicheskie osnovy realizat͡sii sel'skokhozi͡aĭstvennoĭ produkt͡sii)
Экономические основы реализации сельскохозяйственной продукции / А. С. Баранов. — Москва : Колос, 1976.
240 p. ; 20 cm. USSR***
Includes bibliographical references.
0.41rub
1. Farm management—Russia. 2. Agriculture and state—Russia. I. Title.
S562.R9B28 76–528468

Baranov, Alvin B
California legal secretarial procedures. 3d ed. Los Angeles, Legal Publications, 1973-
v. (loose-leaf) forms. 30 cm.
First-second eds. have title: Legal secretarial procedures.
Kept up to date by supplements.
1. Legal secretaries—California. I. Title.
C NUC74-126750

Baranov, Alvin B
California legal secretarial procedures, by Alvin B. Baranov. 4th ed. Los Angeles, Legal Publications, 1974-
1 v.
Loose-leaf for updating.
First ed. published in 1967 under title: Legal secretarial procedures.
1. Legal secretaries—Handbooks, manuals, etc. I. Title. II. Title: Legal secretarial procedures.
CLL NUC76-23088

Baranov, Alvin B
Incorporation made easy : form your own corporation with a minimum of expense, complete with forms / by Alvin B. Baranov. -- Los Angeles : Legal Publications, c1975.
v, 137 p. : ill. ; 29 cm.
1. Close corporations--California. 2. Corporations--California. I. Title.
CLSU NUC77-83520

Baranov, Anatoliĭ P., comp.
see Devi͡at' millionov. 1973.

Baranov, Anatoliĭ Petrovich.
(Ot Baĭkala do Amura)
От Байлака до Амура / А. П. Баранов. — Москва : Знание, 1975.
62 p. ; 20 cm. — (Новое в жизни, науке, технике : Серия Молодежная ; 12/1975) USSR 76
0.11rub
1. Baikal-Amur Railroad. 2. Youth—Employment—Russia. I. Title. II. Series: Novoe v zhizni, nauke, tekhnike : Serii͡a Molodezhnai͡a ; 1975, 12.
HQ768.N6 1975, no. 12 76–521308
[TF110.B34]

Baranov, Anatoliĭ Timofeevich, ed.
see I͡Acheistye betony s ponizhennoĭ ob"emnoĭ massoi. 1974.

Baranov, Anatoliĭ Timofeevich, ed.
see (Voprosy tekhnologii i͡acheistykh betonov i konstrukt͡sii iz nikh) 1972.

Baranov, Andrei.
The sections of the genus Begonia / A. Baranov & F. A. Barkley. — Boston : Northeastern University, 1974.
28 p. ; 28 cm.
Includes bibliographical references and index.
1. Begonias. I. Barkley, Fred Alexander, 1908- joint author. II. Title.
QK495.B4B37 583'.46 75-320822
75 MARC

Baranov, Artur Aleksandrovich.
(Reli͡ativistskai͡a termomekhanika sploshnykh sred)
Релятивистская термомеханика сплошных сред / А. А. Баранов, В. Л. Колпащиков ; под ред. акад. А. В. Лыкова. — Минск : Наука и техника, 1974.
149, [3] p. ; 20 cm. USSR 75
Bibliography: p. 95–[150]
0.82rub
1. Continuum mechanics. 2. Relativity (Physics) I. Kolpashchikov, Viktor Leonidovich, joint author. II. Title.
QA808.2.B35 76–528575

Baranov, B. I., ed.
see Posobie po obuchenii͡u molodykh soldat. 1973.

Baranov, Boris Fedorovich.
Штурм королевской крепости. Москва, "Физкультура и спорт," 1971.
63 p. with illus. 21 cm. (Библиотечка шахматиста) 0.14rub USSR 71–VKP
At head of title: Б. Ф. Баранов.
1. Chess—Collections of games. I. Title.
Title romanized: Shturm korolevskoĭ kreposti.
GV1452.B29 73–341539

Baranov, Boris Mikaĭlovich
see Posobie dli͡a izuchenii͡a pravil tekhnicheskoĭ ėkspluatat͡sii ėlektricheskikh stant͡siĭ i seteĭ. 1974.

Baranov, Boris Mikhaĭlovich
see Sooruzhenie i ekspluatat͡sii͡a kabel'nykh liniĭ. 1959.

Baranov, Boris Mikhailovich
see Sooruzhenie i ekspluatatsiia kabel'nykh linii. 1974.

Baranov, E. F.
see Voprosy issledovanii͡a bi͡udzheta... . Moskva, 1972.

Baranov, Evgeniĭ Adamovich.
(Tekhnika bezopasnosti pri ėkspluatat͡sii kontaktnoĭ seti ėlektrifit͡sirovannykh zheleznykh dorog i ustroĭstv ėlektrosnabzhenii͡a avtoblokirovki)
Техника безопасности при эксплуатации контактной сети электрифицированных железных дорог и устройств электроснабжения автоблокировки / Е. А. Баранов, Я. А. Зельвянский. — Москва : Транспорт, 1975.
121 p. : ill. ; 21 cm. USSR 76
Bibliography: p. 120.
0.39rub
1. Electric railroads—Safety measures. 2. Electric railroads—Current supply—Safety measures. I. Zel'vi͡anskiĭ, I͡Akov Aronovich, joint author. II. Title: Tekhnika bezopasnosti pri ėkspluatat͡sii kontaktnoĭ seti ...
TF962.B32 76–513081

Baranov, G. I.
see Treshnikov, Aleksei Fedorovich. Struktura t͡sirkuli͡at͡sii vod Arkticheskogo basseĭna. 1972.

Baranov, G. I.
see Treshnikov, Alekseĭ Fedorovich. Water circulation in the Arctic basin. Jerusalem, Israel Program for Scientific Translations, 1973.

Baranov, I. A., 1924-
see Overlie, George.

Baranov, Ippolit G
(Kraevedenie v kartinakh khudozhnika Sungurova)
Краеведение в картинах художника Сунгурова. Харбин, Тип. Кит. Вост. жел. дор., 1934.
5 p. plates (part col.) 27 cm.
At head of title: И. Г. Баранов.
"Каталог картин I-й Этнографической выставки художника Антонина Сунгурова": [6] p. laid in.
1. Sungurov, Antonin Ivanovich, 1894– 2. Figurative art—Russia. I. Title.
ND699.S75B37 74–222676

Baranov, I͡Uriĭ Aleksandrovich.
(Glubinnai͡a vakhta)
Глубинная вахта : повесть и рассказы / Юрий Баранов. — Москва : Молодая гвардия, 1974.
155 p. : ill., port. ; 17 cm. — (Молодые писатели) USSR***
0.23rub
I. Title.
PG3479.R25G6 74–355376

Baranov, I͡Uriĭ Ivanovich.
(Izmeritel'nye pribory na tranzistorakh)
Измерительные приборы на транзисторах. Москва, "Энергия," 1973.
96 p. with illus. 20 cm. (Массовая радиобиблиотека, вып. 836) 0.23rub USSR 73
At head of title: Ю. И. Баранов.
Bibliography: p. [95]
1. Electronic instruments. 2. Transistors. I. Title.
TK7878.4.B36 74–307473

Baranov, I͡Uriĭ Konstantinovich.
(Opredelenie mesta sudna s pomoshch'i͡u navigat͡sionnykh sputnikov)
Определение места судна с помощью навигационных спутников / Ю. К. Баранов. — Москва : Транспорт, 1976.
86 p. : ill. ; 20 cm. — (Библиотечка судоводителя) USSR***
Series romanized: Bibliotechka sudovoditeli͡a.
Bibliography: p. 85–86.
0.21rub
1. Artificial satellites in navigation. I. Title.
VK562.B37 77–500710

Baranov, I͡Uriĭ Konstantinovich.
Сборник задач по использованию радиолокатора для предупреждения столкновений судов. Утверждено в качестве учеб. пособия для высших инженерных морских училищ Министерства морстого флота. Изд. 2., доп. и перер. Москва, Транспорт, 1969.
80 p. illus. 22 cm. 0.17rub USSR***
At head of title: Ю. К. Баранов, М. М. Лесков.
1. Radar in navigation—Problems, exercises, etc. 2. Collisions at sea—Prevention—Problems, exercises, etc. I. Leskov, Mikhail Mikhaĭlovich, joint author. II. Title.
Title romanized: Sbornik zadach po ispol'zovanii͡u radiolokatora dli͡a preuprezhdenii͡a stolknoveniĭ sudov.
VK560.B36 74–344037

Baranov, I͡Uriĭ Petrovich
see Tekhnicheskai͡a ėkspluatat͡sii͡a avtomobileĭ. 1972.

Baranov, Ivan Georgievich, ed.
see Simpozium po soli͡anoĭ tektonike, 2d, Chernigov, 1966. Soli͡anokupol'nye regiony SSSR i ikh neftegazonosnost'. 1969.

Baranov, Ivan I͡Akovlevich, ed.
see Geokriologicheskie (merzlotnye) i gidrogeologicheskie issledovanii͡a pri inzhenernykh izyskanii͡akh. 1971.

Baranov, Ivan Vasil'evich, fl. 1962–
[Kompleksnai͡a mekhanizat͡sii͡a vozdelyvanii͡a i uborki l'na-dolgunt͡sa]
Комплексная механизация возделывания и уборки льна-долгунца. Ленинград, "Колос," [Ленингр. отд-ние], 1972.
207 p. with illus. 20 cm. 0.49rub USSR 72–VKP
At head of title: И. В. Баранов, Н. П. Новожилов.
Bibliography: p. [206]
1. Flax—Russia. 2. Agricultural machinery—Russia. I. Novozhilov, Nikolaĭ Pavlovich, joint author. II. Title.
SB253.B36 73–312728

Baranov, Ivan Vasil'evich, fl. 1962–
[Khimicheskie i biologicheskie metody povyshenii͡a bioproduktivnosti ozer]
Химические и биологические методы повышения биопродуктивности озер. Москва, "Пищевая пром-сть," 1969.
128 p. with illus. 21 cm. 0.77rub USSR 69–VKP
At head of title: И. В. Баранов, А. А. Салазкин.
Bibliography: p. 119–[128]
1. Fish-culture—Russia. 2. Lakes—Russia. 3. Biological productivity—Russia. I. Salazkin, Aleksandr Aleksandrovich. II. Title.
SH159.B36 71–484783
rev

Baranov, Ivan Vasil'evich, fl. 1962–
[Limnologicheskie tipy ozer SSSR]
Лимнологические типы озер СССР. Ленинград, Гидрометеорологическое изд-во, 1962.
275 p. illus., maps (1 fold.) 22 cm.
Bibliography: p. 266–[273]
1. Lakes—Russia. 2. Limnology. I. Title.
GB1707.B3 62–66047
rev

Baranov, Ivan Vasil'evich, fl. 1962- ed.
see Opyt povyshenii͡a bioproduktivnosti malykh ozer Severo-Zapada putem primeneniia mineral'nykh udobrenii. 1972.

Baranov, Kharlampiĭ Karpovich, 1892–
(Arabsko-russkiĭ slovar')
Арабско-русский словарь : около 42 000 слов / Х. К. Баранов. — Изд. 5., перер. и доп. — Москва : Русский язык, 1976.
942 p. ; 27 cm. USSR***
Added t. p.: Qāmūs 'Arabī-Rūsī.
Bibliography: p. [6]
4.51rub
1. Arabic language—Dictionaries—Russian. I. Title. II. Title: Qāmūs 'Arabī-Rūsī.
PJ6645.R9B3 1976 77–510537

Baranov, Konstantin Georgievich, joint author
see Tarasov, Vladimir Mikhaĭlovich. Posobie mekhaniku derevoobrabatyvai͡ushchego predpri͡atii͡a. 1972.

Baranov, Leonid Afanas'evich, joint author
see Prokhorov, Petr Konstantinovich. Elektromonter sel'skoĭ elektrifikat͡sii. 1973.

Baranov, Lev Aronovich
see Tekhnika bezopasnosti i proizvodstvennai͡a sanitarii͡a v stroitel'stve. 1974.

Baranov, Mikhail Grigor'evich.
Iz opyta organizat͡sii raboty mezhraĭonnykh prokuratur; pod red. gos. sovetnika i͡ustit͡sii 3-go klassa S. S. Nikiforova. Moskva, Gos. izd-vo i͡urid. lit-ry, 1959.
57, [3] p. 20 cm.
At head of title: Prokuratura SSSR. Metodicheskiĭ sovet. M. G. Baranov, G. R. Krylatykh.
1. Public prosecutors–Russia. I. Krylatykh, Gavrila Romanovich, joint author. II. Nikiforov, S. S., ed. III. Russia (1923- U. S. S. R.). Prokuratura. IV. Title.
MH-L NUC76-90413

Baranov, Mikheĭ Ėrastovich.
(Pereselenie i kollektivizat͡sii͡a)
Переселение и коллективизация / М. Э. Баранов. — Москва : Книгосоюз, 1929.
74 p. ; 22 cm.
At head of title: Vsesoi͡uznyĭ sovet kolkhozov.
1. Migration, Internal—Russia. 2. Collective farms—Russia. I. Title.
HB3607.B37 75–583519

Baranov, N. N., ed.
see Ėkonomika ispol'zovanii͡a udobreniĭ. 1974.

Baranov, Nikolaĭ Varfolomeevich.
(Glavnyĭ arkhitektor goroda)
Главный архитектор города. (Творч. и орг. деятельность). Москва, Стройиздат, 1973.
190 p. with illus. 27 cm. 2.42rub USSR 73
At head of title: Н. В. Баранов.
1. Cities and towns—Planning—Russia. 2. Urban renewal—Russia. I. Title.
NA9211.B37 74–303246

Baranov, Nikolaĭ Varfolomeevich, ed.
see Moscow. T͡Sentral'nyĭ nauchno-issledovatel'skiĭ i proektnyĭ institut tipovogo i ėksperimental'nogo proektirovanii͡a zhilishcha. Industrializat͡sii͡a zhilishchnogo stroitel'stva v SSSR. Moskva, 1965.

Baranov, Nikolaĭ Varfolomeevich
see Nauchno-tekhnicheskoe soveshchanie po planirovke i zastroĭke zhilykh raĭonov i mikroraĭonov, Moscow, 1964. Zhiloĭ raĭon i mikroraĭon. Moskva, Izd-vo lit-ry po stroitel'stvu, 1965.

Baranov, Nikolaĭ Varfolomeevich
see Staroe i novoe v arkhitekture Italii... [Moskva, 1969]

Baranov, O A
(Kinofakul'tativ v shkole)
Кинофакультатив в школе. (Метод. пособие для студентов). Калинин, 1973.
80 p. 20 cm. USSR 73
At head of title: Калининский государственный университет. О. А. Баранов.
Includes bibliographies.
0.70rub
1. Moving-pictures—Study and teaching. I. Title.
PN1993.7.B3 75–531737

Baranov, Petr Vasil'evich.
(Zvezdy rabocheĭ slavy)
Звезды рабочей славы. Герои Соц. Труда—хабаровчане. Хабаровск, Кн. изд-во, 1972.
174 p. with ports. 20 cm. 0.25rub USSR 72–VKP
At head of title: П. Баранов.
1. Labor and laboring classes—Khabarovskiy kray, Russia. I. Title.
HD8749.K42B37 73–325415

Baranov, Platon Ivanovich, 1827-1884, ed.
see Russia. Pravitel'stvui͡ushchiĭ Senat. Arkhiv. (Opis' vyoschaĭshim ukazam i povelenii͡am, Khranii͡ashchimsi͡a v S.-Peterburgskom Senatskom arkivi͡e za XVIII vi͡ek) 18

Baranov, S. S.
see Narodnai͡a Respublika Bangladesh. 1972.

Baranov, Samariĭ Iosifovich.
(Sintez mikroprogrammnykh avtomatov)
Синтез микропрограммных автоматов. Ленинград, "Энергия," Ленингр. отд-ние, 1974.
216 p. with diagrs. 22 cm. 0.87rub USSR 74
At head of title: С. И. Баранов.
Bibliography: p. 213–[214]
1. Sequential machine theory. 2. Graph theory. I. Title.
QA267.5.S4B38 74–329237

Baranov, Sergeĭ Ivanovich, joint author
see Lobko, Aleksandr Grigor'evich. (Radiobytovai͡a apparatura—proizvodstvo i rynok) 1976.

Baranov, Sergeĭ Kharlampievich.
(Zhuravli͡ata)
Журавлята : стихи / Сергей Баранов ; [рисунки Н. Чарушина]. — Москва : Детская лит-ра, 1975.
[32] p. : col. ill. ; 22 cm. USSR***
"Для дошкольного возраста."
0.17rub
I. Charushin, Nikita Evgen'evich. II. Title.
PZ64.3.B253 76–520739

Baranov, Sergeĭ Petrovich.
(Print͡sipy obuchenii͡a)
Принципы обучения : (Лекции по дидактике) / С. П. Баранов ; Моск. гос. пед. ин-т им. В. И. Ленина, Кафедра педагогики нач. обучения. — Москва : МГПИ, 1975.
94 p. ; 22 cm. USSR 75
At head of title: Ministerstvo prosveshchenii͡a RSFSR.
Includes bibliographical references.
0.60rub
1. Teaching. I. Title.
LB1025.2.B33 76–533151

Baranov, Sergeĭ Stepanovich.
(Vostochnai͡a Bengalii͡a)
Восточная Бенгалия : особенности экономического развития, 1947–1971 / С. С. Баранов ; АН СССР, Ин-т востоковедения. — Москва : Наука, 1976.
223 p. ; 21 cm. USSR 76
Bibliography: p. 215–[222]
1.19rub
1. Bangladesh—Economic conditions. I. Title.
HC440.8.B38 77–503464

Baranov, Vadim Il'ich, 1930-
Pravda obraza--pravda istorii. Ėsteticheskie problemy Leniniany. Russkai͡a sovetskai͡a proza. Gor'kiĭ, Volgo-Vi͡atskoe knizhnoe izd-vo, 1971.
152 p.
At head of title: V. I. Baranov.
1. Russian prose literature–Hist. & crit. 2. Russian literature–20th cent.–Hist. & crit. I. Title.
ICU NUC76-3973

Baranov, Vadim Il'ich, 1930–
(Si͡uzhetno-kompozit͡sionnye osobennosti sovetskogo romana 20-kh godov)
Сюжетно-композиционные особенности советского романа 20-х годов. (Вопросы худож. мышления писателя). Учеб. пособие. Горький, 1972.
98 p. 20 cm. 0.50rub USSR 72
At head of title: Министерство высшего и среднего специального образования РСФСР. Горьковский государственный университет им. Н. И. Лобачевского.
On cover: В. И. Баранов.
Includes bibliographical references.
1. Russian fiction—20th century—History and criticism. 2. Creation (Literary, artistic, etc.) I. Title.
PG3095.B3 73–363026

Baranov, Vasiliĭ Gavrilovich.
(Ozhirenie)
Ожирение. (Причины, проявления, заболевания, осложнения, предупреждение и лечение). Москва, "Знание," 1972.
32 p. 21 cm. (Новое в жизни, науке, технике. Серия: Медицина, 8) 0.06rub USSR 72–VKP
At head of title: В. Г. Баранов.
1. Corpulence. I. Title. II. Series: Novoe v zhizni, nauke, tekhnike. Serii͡a: Medit͡sina, 1972, 8.
R91.N62 1972, no. 8 72–375672
[RC628]

Baranov, Viktor Mikhaĭlovich.
(Ul'trazvukovye izmerenii͡a v atomnoĭ tekhnike)
Ультразвуковые измерения в атомной технике / В. М. Баранов. — Москва : Атомиздат, 1975.
262 p. : ill. ; 21 cm. USSR***
Bibliography: p. 248–[259]
Includes index.
1.61rub
1. Ultrasonics in nuclear engineering. 2. Nuclear reactors—Control. 3. Nuclear engineering—Materials—Testing. 4. Nuclear engineering—Instruments. I. Title.
TK9153.B37 76–51241

Baranov, Vladimir Filippovich.
(Dozimetrii͡a ėlektronnogo izluchenii͡a)
Дозиметрия электронного излучения / В. Ф. Баранов. — Москва : Атомиздат, 1974.
228 p. : ill. ; 21 cm. USSR***
Includes bibliographies.
1.30rub
1. Radiation dosimetry. I. Title.
QC795.32.R3B37 75–568551

Baranov, Vladimir Il'ich, 1892-
Potential fields and their transformations in applied geophysics / by Wladimir Baranov. -- Berlin : Gebrüder Borntraeger, 1975.
xv, 121 p. : ill. ; 25 cm. -- (Geoexploration monographs, series 1 ; no. 6)
Includes index.
Includes bibliographical references.
Errata slip inserted.
1. Geophysics. 2. Magnetism, Terrestrial. 3. Magnetic fields. I. Title. II. Series.
IU NUC77-83526

Baranov, Vladimir Il'ich, 1892–
(Radiogeologii͡a)
Радиогеология. [Учебник для геол. специальносте[й] ун-тов]. Москва, Изд-во Моск. ун-та, 1973.
242 p. with illus. 22 cm. 0.68rub USSR 7[3]
At head of title: В. И. Баранов, Н. А. Титаева.
Includes bibliographies.
1. Nuclear geophysics. I. Titaeva, Natal'i͡a Alekseevna, joint author. II. Title.
QE501.4.N9B37 74–33420

Baranov, Vladimir Kirillovich, joint author
see Budnikov, Vasiliĭ Ivanovich. Litologii͡a i fat͡sii verkhnego paleozoi͡a Tungusskoĭ sineklizy 1971.

Baranov, Vladimir Vasil'evich.
(Obrabotka i transportirovka ryby i moreproduktov)
Обработка и транспортировка рыбы и морепродук[тов] : [учеб. пособие для вузов МРХ СССР по специаль[ности] № 1606 "Судовождение на мор. путях"] / В. Б[.] Баранов. — Москва : Пищевая пром-сть, 1975.
143 p. : ill. ; 21 cm. USSR 7[5]
Bibliography: p. 141–[142]
0.34rub
1. Fishery products—Transportation. 2. Seafood processing. I. Title.
SH337.B37 75–53810

Baranov, Vladimir Vasil'evich
see Dary Atlantiki. 1973.

Baranov, Vladislav Vasil'evich
see Gidromekhanicheskai͡a peredacha avtobusa. 1977.

Baranov, Wladimir
see Baranov, Vladimir Il'ich, 1892-

Baranova, A.A.
see Moscow. Khimiko-tekhnologicheskiĭ institut. (Trudy sotrudnikov za 1946-1966 gg.) 1971.

Baranova, Alevtina Gavrilovna, joint author
see Taube, Petr Reingol'dovich. Praktikum po khimii vody. 1971.

Baranova, Antonina Ivanovna.
(Aėrometody v geologicheskikh issledovanii͡akh)
Аэрометоды в геологических исследованиях. Библиогр. указ. отеч. и иностр. литературы. Июль-декабрь 1970 г. Москва, ВИЭМС, ₍ОНТИ₎, 1971.
47 p. 20 cm. (Библиографическая информация) 0.21rub
USSR 71
Cover title.
At head of title: Министерство геологии СССР. Лаборатория аэрометодов.
By A. I. Baranova and N. N. Chizhova-Oreus.
1. Aerial photogrammetry—Bibliography. 2. Aerial photography in geology—Bibliography. I. Chizhova-Oreus, Natali͡a Nikolaevna, joint author. II. Laboratorii͡a aėrometodov Ministerstva geologii SSSR. III. Title.
Z7136.A3B37 74-319115

Baranova, G. I.
see Spravochnik lekarstveenykh preparatov. 1970.

Baranova, Galina Ivanovna, ed.
see Russkie romansy i pesni. Moskva, Sovetskai͡a Rossii͡a, 1959.

Baranova, Irina Vladimirovna.
(Zadachi na dokazatel'stvo po algebre)
Задачи на доказательство по алгебре; пособие для учителя. Ленинград, Гос. учебно-педагог. изд-во, Ленинградское отд-ние, 1954.
159 p. 23 cm.
At head of title: И. В. Баранова и С. Е. Ляпин.
1. Algebra—Problems, exercises, etc. I. Li͡apin, S. E., joint author. II. Title.
QA157.B22 55-36817
rev

Baranova, Irina Vladimirovna, ed.
see Obuchenie matematike po novym shkol'nym programmam. 1973.

Baranova, Irina Vladimirovna
see Obuchenie matematike v sredneĭ shkole po novym programmam. 1974.

Baranova, Irina Vladimirovna, ed.
see Prepodavanie matematiki v sredneĭ shkole. 1972.

Baranova, Irina Vladimirovna, ed.
see Voprosy ėlementarnoi matematiki i metodiki ee prepodavanii͡a. 1971.

Baranova, I͡Ulii͡a Pavlovna
see Cenozoic of the northeast of the USSR. [n. p.] 1968.

Baranova, I͡Ulii͡a Pavlovna
see Miot͡sen Mamontovoĭ Gory. 1976.

Baranova, K. V., joint author
see Borisenko, E I͡A (Praktikum po razvedenii͡u sel'skokhozi͡aĭstvennykh zhivotnykh) 1972

Baranova, Lidii͡a Fedorovna.
(Professor A. I. Razumov)
Профессор А. И. Разумов : библиография, 1925–1973 гг. / ₍Л. Ф. Баранова, Р. А. Галявин₎. — Казань : ₍s. n.₎, 1974.
34 p. ; 20 cm. USSR 74
Cover title: Aleksandr Ivanovich Razumov.
"Ученые института."
At head of title: Kazanskiĭ khimiko-tekhnologicheskiĭ institut imeni S. M. Kirova. Fundamental'nai͡a biblioteka.
Includes index.
0.14rub
1. Razumov, Aleksandr Ivanovich—Bibliography. I. Gali͡avin, Renat Abdulkhakovich, joint author. II. Title.
Z8735.37.B26 76-520414
[QD22.R39]

Baranova, Li͡udmila Emel'i͡anovna
see Problemy formirovanii͡a i ispol'zovanii͡a fonda razvitii͡a proizvodstva. 1973.

Baranova, Marta Petrovna.
நாய் சடைச்சியும், சிறுவன் போரியாவும், ராக்கெட்டும். ₍எழுதியவர்₎ ம. பரானவா ₍மற்றும்₎ யெ. வெல்தீஸ்தவ். ₍மொழிபெயர்ப்பாளர்: பூ. சோமசுன்தரம்₎. மாஸ்கோ, புரோகிரஸ் பதிப்பகம் ₍1965₎
184 p. illus. 22 cm.
In Tamil.
Translation of Тяпа, Борька и ракета (romanized: Tiapa, Bor'ka i raketa)
I. Veltistov, Evgeniĭ Serafimovich, joint author. II. Somasundaram, P., tr. III. Title
Title romanized: Nāy Caṭaicciyum, ciṟuvaṉ Pōriyāvum, rakkeṭṭum.
PZ90.T3B3 72-203575

Baranova, N. P.
see Raboty sovetskikh istorikov za 1970-1974 gg.. 1975.

Baranova, Natalii͡a Dmitrievna.
(M. Gor'kiĭ i sovetskie pisateli)
М. Горький и советские писатели : идейно-творч. взаимосвязи в 20-е гг. : ₍учеб. пособие для филол. специальностей ун-тов и пед. ин-тов₎ / Н. Д. Баранова. — Москва : Высш. школа, 1975.
214 p. ; 20 cm. USSR 75
Includes bibliographical references.
0.43rub
1. Gor'kiĭ, Maksim, 1868-1936—Criticism and interpretation. 2. Russian literature—20th century—History and criticism. I. Title.
PG3465.Z8B3 76-515871

Baranova, Nina Nikiforovna
see An Autumn tale. Moscow, Progress Publishers ₍1965₎

Baranova, T. I., ed.
see Stroitel'nai͡a mekhanika, prochnost' konstrukt͡siĭ i materialov, sot͡siologicheskie issledovanii͡a, fizika. 1970.

Baranova, Valentina Gordeevna.
(Metody analiza v proizvodstve monomerov dli͡a sinteticheskikh kauchukov)
Методы анализа в производстве мономеров для синтетических каучуков / В. Г. Баранова, А. Г. Панков, Н. К. Логинова ; под ред. канд. техн. наук А. М. Кутьина. — Ленинград : Химия, Ленингр. отд-ние, 1975.
212 p. : ill. ; 23 cm. USSR 75
At head of title: Nauchno-issledovatel'skiĭ institut monomerov dli͡a sinteticheskogo kauchuka.
Includes bibliographies.
0.90rub
1. Rubber, Artificial. 2. Monomers—Analysis. I. Pankov, Alekseĭ Gennad'evich, joint author. II. Loginova, Nina Konstantinovna, joint author. III. Title.
TS1925.B29 75-400425

Baranova, Z.I.
see Fauna moreĭ severo-zapadnoĭ chasti Tikhogo Okeana. Moskva, Nauka, 1965.

Baranova, Zinaida Efimovna.
(Stratigrafii͡a i flora i͡urskikh otlozheniĭ vostoka Prikaspiĭskoĭ vpadiny)
Стратиграфия и флора юрских отложений востока Прикаспийской впадины / З. Е. Баранова, А. И. Киричкова, В. В. Зауер. — Ленинград : Недра, 1975.
190 p. : ill. ; 27 cm. — (Труды - Всесоюзный нефтяной научно-исследовательский геологоразведочный институт ; вып. 332)
USSR***
At head of title: Ministerstvo geologii USSR.
Bibliography: p. 143-₍150₎
2.05rub
1. Paleobotany — Jurassic. 2. Paleobotany — Caspian Sea region. I. Kirichkova, Anna Ivanovna, joint author. II. Zauer, Veronika Vasil'evna, joint author. III. Title. IV. Series: Leningrad. Vsesoi͡uznyĭ nefti͡anoĭ nauchno-issledovatel'skiĭ geologorazvedochnyĭ institut. Trudy ; vyp. 332.
TN860.L372 vyp. 332 75-409800
[QE923]

Baranova, Zinaida Efimovna.
Stratigrafii͡a, litologii͡a i flora i͡urskikh otlozheniĭ Tuarkyra. Moskva, Gostoptekhizdat, 1963.
231, [1] p. illus., map, fold. diagrs., col. plates. (Trudy Vsesoi͡uznogo nauchno-issledovatel'skogo geologicheskogo instituta (VSEGEI) Novai͡a serii͡a, t. 88)
"Problema neftegazonosnosti Sredneĭ Azii, vyp. 13."
At head of title: Z. E. Baranova, A. T. Burakova, N. B. Bekasova.
MiU NUC76-4325

Baranova-Shestova, Natal'i͡a
see
Baranoff, Nathalie.

Baranovich, Anna Georgievna, 1908-
see [Bobernaga, S] Anna Baranovich. [Kishinev, Timpul, 1971]

Baranovskai͡a, Alla Nikolaevna, joint author
see Skripnik, Li͡udmila Zinov'evna. My govorim po-russki. Izd. 2. Kiev, Vyshcha shkola, 1972.

Baranovskai͡a, E. I., joint author
see Karpyshev, Evgeniĭ Sergeevich. Spravochno-bibliograficheskiĭ katalog po geologii osnovaniĭ plotin. 1967.

Baranovskai͡a, Rashel' Isaevna.
Aleksandr Kholminov; ocherk zhizni i tvorchestva. [By] R. Baranovskai͡a & B. Ionin. Moskva, Sovetskii kompozitor, 1971.
103 p. illus., ports.
MH NIC NUC75-129142

Baranovskai͡a, S. A., ed.
see Voprosy teoreticheskoĭ i prakticheskoĭ fonetiki. 1973.

Baranovskiĭ, Boris Konstantinovich, ed.
see Upravlenie i kontrol' v seti͡akh trekhprogrammnogo provodnogo veshchanii͡a. 1974.

Baranovskiĭ, Evgeniĭ Ivanovich
see
Baranoŭski, I͡Aŭhen Ivanavich.

Baranovskiĭ, Evgeniĭ Petrovich, 1924-
see Issledovanii͡a po geometriĭ polozhitel'nykh kvadratichnykh form. 1974.

Baranovskiĭ, Evgeniĭ Stepanovich, joint author
see Baranovskiĭ, Nikolai Timofeevich. (Sistema ekonomicheskoĭ informat͡sii v sel'skom khozi͡aĭstve) 1974.

Baranovskiĭ, Gavriil Vasil'evich, 1860–
(Zdanii͡a i sooruzhenii͡a Vserossiĭskoĭ khudozhestvenno-promyshlennoĭ vystavki)
Зданія и сооруженія Всероссійской художественн-промышленной выставки 1896 года въ Нижнемъ-Новгородѣ. Составилъ Г. В. Барановскій. Изд. ред. журнала "Строитель." С.-Петербургъ, Тип. Е. Евдокимова, 1897.
xiv, 145 p. illus. 35 cm.
Legends in Russian, French, German and English.
1. Gorki, Russia. Vserossiĭskai͡a promyshlennai͡a i khudozhestvennai͡a vystavka, 1896—Buildings. I. Title.
T618.5.C1B37 74-236781

Baranovskiĭ, Leonid Valentinovich.
5 ошибок в нашем питании. Москва, Знание, 1966.
30 p. 22 cm.
At head of title: Л. В. Барановский.
1. Nutrition. 2. Diet. I. Title.
Title romanized: Pi͡at' oshibok v nashem pitanii.
RA784.B27 75-564587

Baranovskiĭ, Mecheslav Evgen'evich.
(Obespechenie nesmeshchaemosti navalochnykh gruzov na sudakh)
Обеспечение несмещаемости навалочных грузов на судах / М. Е. Барановский. — Ленинград : Судостроение, 1976.
75 p. : ill. ; 22 cm. USSR***
Bibliography: p. 73-₍74₎
0.25rub
1. Bulk carrier cargo ships. 2. Stability of ships. I. Title.
VM393.B7B37 77-515447

Baranovskiĭ, Mikhail Adamovich
see Tekhnologii͡a metallov i drugikh konstrukt͡sionnykh materialov. 1973.

Baranovskii, Mikhail Ivanovich Tugan-
see Tugan-Baranovskii, Mikhail Ivanovich, 1865-1919.

Baranovskiĭ, Miroslav Iosifovich.
(Turistskie bazy)
Туристские базы / М. И. Барановский. — Москва : Стройиздат, 1976.
165, ₍3₎ p. : ill. ; 22 cm. — (Серия Архитектору-проектировщику)
USSR***
Series romanized: Serii͡a Arkhitektoru-proektirovshchiku.
Bibliography: p. ₍167₎
0.85rub
1. Tourist camps, hostels, etc. I. Title.
TX911.B34 77-501945

Baranovskiĭ, Nikolaĭ Timofeevich.
(Sistema ėkonomicheskoĭ informat͡sii v sel'skom khozi͡aĭstve)
Система экономической информации в сельском хозяйстве. [Учеб. пособие для с.-х. вузов по специальности "Экон. кибернетика"]. Москва, "Статистика," 1974.
207 p. with diagrs. 22 cm. 0.63rub USSR 74
At head of title: Н. Т. Барановский, Е. С. Барановский.
Includes bibliographical references.
1. Agriculture—Mathematical models. 2. Agriculture—Economic aspects—Mathematical models. 3. Information theory. I. Baranovskiĭ, Evgeniĭ Stepanovich, joint author. II. Title.
S494.5.M3B37 74-335588

Baranovskiĭ, Nikolaĭ Vasil'evich.
(Plastinchatye i spiral'nye teploobmenniki)
Пластинчатые и спиральные теплообменники. Москва, "Машиностроение," 1973.
288 p. with illus. 22 cm. 1.17rub USSR 73
At head of title: Н. В. Барановский, Л. М. Коваленко, А. Р. Ястребенецкий.
Bibliography: p. 285-[286]
1. Heat exchangers. 2. Chemical engineering—Apparatus and supplies. 3. Food industry and trade—Equipment and supplies. I. Kovalenko, Leonid Maksimovich. II. I͡Astrebenet͡skiĭ, Anisim Rudol'fovich. III. Title.
TJ263.B37 73-356041

Baranovskiĭ, Nikolaĭ Vasil'evich, ed.
see Chelyabinsk, Russia (City). Politekhnicheskiĭ institut. Kafedra filosofii. Dialektika prot͡sessa poznani͡a... Cheli͡abinsk, 1967.

Baranovskiĭ, V A
see
Baranoŭski, Vitaliĭ.

Baranovskiĭ, Valentin Viktorovich.
(Sloistye plastiki ėlektrotekhnicheskogo naznacheni͡a)
Слоистые пластики электротехнического назначения / В. В. Барановский, Г. М. Дулицкая. — Москва : Энергия, 1976.
285 p. : ill. ; 21 cm. USSR***
Bibliography: p. 283-284.
0.93rub
1. Laminated plastics. 2. Electric engineering—Materials. I. Dulit͡skai͡a, Galina Maksimovna, joint author. II. Title.
TK454.4.P55B37 77-506096

Baranovskiĭ, Vasiliĭ Alekseevich.
(Tekhnicheskoe razvitie lesnoĭ promyshlennosti)
Техническое развитие лесной промышленности / В. А. Барановский, М. И. Брик, Н. А. Бурдин. — Москва : Лесная промышл., 1976.
116, [4] p. : ill. ; 21 cm. USSR***
Bibliography: p. [118]
0.42rub
1. Logging—Russia. 2. Logging—Technological innovations. I. Brik, Mikhail Ivanovich, joint author. II. Burdin, Nikolaĭ Alekseevich, joint author. III. Title.
SD538.3.R9B37 77-514312

Baranovskii, Vladimir Aleksandrovich Tugan Mizra-
see Tugan-Mirza-Baranovskii, Vladimir Aleksandrovich, 1860-1887.

Baranovs'kyĭ, Mykhaĭlo Ivanovych Tuhan-
see
Tugan-Baranovskiĭ, Mikhail Ivanovich, 1865-1919.

Baranovych, Anna
see Baranovich, Anna Georgievna, 1908-

Baranowicz, Avigdor, 1937- joint author
see Eshel, Mosheh. Seker: yevu vi-yetsu yeda' be-Yisrael. 1968.

Baranowicz, Jan.
Fortel kota Myszopsota. Bajki. Ilustrował Mieczysław Piotrowski. [Warszawa] Czytelnik, 1956.
200 p. illus. 25 cm.
The trick of the cat Myszopsot.
I. Title.
IEdS NUC74-33080

Baranowicz, Jan.
Kolczyki Kalimury. Posł. opatrzył Andrzej Salamon. [Wyd. 1.] Katowice, "Śląsk", 1974.
247 p. illus.
1. Folklore—Gipsy.
MH NUC76-22903

Baranowicz, Jan.
Podwieczorek z Sylenem : satyry, fraszki, humoreski, bajki i dialogi heter / Jan Baranowicz ; [okładka i opracowanie graficzne, Krystyna Filipowska]. -- Wyd. 1. -- Katowice : Śląsk, 1976.
213 p. : ill.
ICRL NUC77-86977

Baranowicz, Jan.
Przyjaźń o zmierzchu. [Wrocław] Ludowa Spółdzielnia Wydawn. [1971]
261 p. 20 cm.
I. Title.
NjP NUC73-114749

Baranowicz, Jan.
Strzały na grobli; powieść. [Wyd. 1. Warszawa] Ludowa Spółdzielnia Wydawnicza [1974]
301 p. 20 cm. zł22.00
I. Title.
PG7161.A68S8 74-227588

Baranowicz, Jan.
Ucieczka przed cienim : powieść sensacyjna z pierwszych lat po wyzwoleniu / Jan Baranowícz. — Warszawa : Ludowa Spółdzielna wydawnicza, 1976.
373 p. ; 20 cm. P 76-3417
zł40.00
I. Title.
PG7161.A68U3 76-531642

Baranowicz, Zofia.
Polska awangarda artystyczna, 1918-1939 / Zofia Baranowicz. — Wyd. 1. — Warszawa : Wydawnictwa Artystyczne i Filmowe, 1975.
262 p. : ill. (some col.) ; 17 cm.
Bibliography: p. 252-[255]
zł38.00
1. Art, Polish. 2. Art, Modern—20th century—Poland. 3. Avant-garde (Aesthetics) I. Title.
N7255.P6B37 76-509152

Baranowska, Małgorzata, 1945-
Miasto / Małgorzata Baranowska. -- Wyd. 1. -- Warszawa : Czytelnik, 1975.
66 p. ; 20 cm.
Poems.
MH NUC77-83521

Baranowska, Maria.
Literatura a plastyka, muzyka, radio i film na lekcjach języka polskiego / Maria Baranowska, Felicja Blicharska, Barbara Kasprzak. ; pod red. Felicji Blicharskiej. -- Wyd. 1. -- Warszawa : Wydawn. Szkolne i Pedagogiczne, 1975.
188 p. ; 21 cm. -- (Z moich doświadczeń)
Bibliography : p. 183-[186]
1. Television in education--Poland. 2. Moving pictures in education. 3. Art and literature--Study and teaching--Poland.
MH NUC77-83529

Baranowska, Zofia
see Przedsiębiorstwo Państwowe Pracownie Konserwacji Zabytków. Oddział w Warszawie. Województwo warszawskie; katalog dokumentacji... Warszawa, Ośrodek Informacji Konserwatorskiej, 1973.

Baranowski, Anton
see
Baranauskas, Antanas, Bp., 1835-1902.

Baranowski, Bodgan.
Nichtgleichgewichts-Thermodynamik in der physikalischen Chemie / Bogdan Baranowski. — 1. Aufl. — Leipzig : Deutscher Verlag für Grundstoffindustrie, 1975.
211 p. ; 22 cm. GDR***
Includes bibliographical references and index.
36.00M
1. Thermodynamics. I. Title.
QD511.B35 76-456781
76 MARC

Baranowski, Bogdan.
Nierównowagowa termodynamika w chemii fizycznej / Bogdan Baranowski. — Wyd. 1. — Warszawa : Państwowe Wydawn. Naukowe, 1974.
vii, 175 p. : ill. ; 24 cm.
At head of title: Polska Akademia Nauk. Instytut Chemii Fizycznej.
Includes index.
zł42.00
1. Irreversible processes. 2. Thermodynamics. I. Title.
QD501.B29 75-580529

Baranowski, Bohdan.
O dawnej Łodzi / Bohdan Baranowski. — Wyd. 1. — Łódź : Wydaw. Łódzkie, 1976 (Łódź : ŁZG 1)
353, [3] p., [10] leaves of plates ; 21 cm. P77-666
Bibliography: p. 351-[354]
zł45.00
1. Łódź, Poland—History. I. Title.
DK4800.L6357B37 77-551446
77 MARC

Baranowski, Bohdan.
Organizacja wojska polskiego w latach trzydziestych i czterdziestych xvii wieku. [Warszawa] Wydawn. Ministerstwa Obrony Narodowej [1957]
283 p. illus., ports. 25 cm. (Prace Komisji Wojskowo-Historycznej Ministerstwa Obrony Narodowej. Seria A, nr. 10)
Summary in Russian, German, and French.
Bibliography: p. [215]-225.
1. Poland. Armia. Hist. I. Title. II. Series: Warsaw. Wojskowy Instytut Historyczny. Prace, Seria A., nr. 10.
KU NUC76-36314

Baranowski, Bohdan.
Położenie i walka klasowa chłopów w królewszczyznach woj. łęczyckiego w XVI-XVIII wieku. [Warszawa] Ludowa Spółdzielnia Wydawn., 1956.
139 p.
1. Peasantry—Łęczyca, Poland (Province) 2. Crown lands—Łęczyca, Poland (Province)
MH NUC76-63214

Baranowski, Bohdan.
Zanik tradycyjnego chowu krów oraz wierzén i zabobonów z nim związanych na terenie obecnego województwa łódzkiego. [Wyd. 1.] Łódź [Państwowe Wydawn. Naukowe; Oddz. w Łodzi] 1967.
114 p. 24 cm. (Łódzkie Towarzystwo Naukowe. Prace Wydziału II. Nauk Historycznych i Społecznych, nr. 66)
Bibliographical footnotes.
1. Cattle—Poland—Łódź (Voivodeship) I. Title. II. Series: Łódzkie Towarzystwo Naukowe. Wydział II. Nauk Historycznych i Społecznych. Prace, nr. 66.
SF196.P6B37 72-222791

Baranowski, Bohdan.
Życie codzienne małego miasteczka w XVII i XVIII wieku / Bohdan Baranowski. — Wyd. 1. — Warszawa : Państwowy Instytut Wydawniczy, 1975.
286 p., [20] leaves of plates : ill. (some col.) ; 25 cm. — (Seria Życie codzienne)
Includes bibliographical references and indexes.
zł45.00
1. Poland—Social life and customs—To 1795. 2. Cities and towns—Poland. I. Title.
DK4188.2.B37 75-546531

Baranowski, Bohdan
see Historia XIX [i.e. dziewietnastego] i XX [i.e. dwudziestego. Wyd. 1.] Łódź [Państwowe Wydawn. Naukowe, Oddział w Łodzi] 1972.

Baranowski, Bohdan
see Mikołaj Kopernik. Łódź : Państwowe Wydawn. Naukowe, 1974.

Baranowski, Frank P. The enriched uranium market. 1973
see Nuclear fuel resources and requirements... Washington, Atomic Energy Commission, 1973.

Baranowski, Gustav.
Ich bin der Fürst von Thoren; Erzählungen aus Masuren. München, Bogen-Verlag [1973]
276 p. 20 cm. GFR***
I. Title.
PT2662.A62 I 3 74-333369
ISBN 3-920119-14-2

Baranowski, Henryk.
Bibliografia Kopernikowska. [Wyd. 1.]. Warszawa, Państwowe Wydawn. Naukowe, 1958-
v. facsims. 25 cm.
At head of title, v. 1: Polska Akademia Nauk. Komitet Historii Nauki. v. : Polska Akademia Nauk. Zakład Historii Nauki i Techniki.
Preface also in French.
Includes bibliographical references.
CONTENTS: 1. 1509-1955.—2. 1956-1971.
1. Copernicus, Nicolaus, 1473-1543—Bibliography. I. Title.
Z8192.5.B3 58-49153
rev

Baranowski, Henryk.
Bibliografia miasta Torunia. ₍Wyd. 1.₎. Poznań ₍Państwowe Wydawn. Naukowe, Oddz. w Poznaniu, 1972₎
241 p. 24 cm. (Roczniki Towarzystwa Naukowego w Toruniu, rocz. 77, zesz. 1) zł60.00
1. Toruń, Poland—Bibliography. I. Title. II. Series: Towarzystwo Naukowe w Toruniu. Roczniki, rocz. 77, zesz. 1.
Z2527.T65B33 74-204632

Baranowski, Jerzy, 1931–
Bartłomiej Nataniel Wąsowski : teoretyk i architekt XVII w. / Jerzy Baranowski. — Wrocław ; Gdańsk : Zakład Narodowy im. Ossolińskich, 1975.
302 p., ₍27₎ leaves of plates (4 fold.) : ill., facsims. ; 26 cm. — (Studia z historii sztuki ; t. 20)
Includes Callitectonicorum seu de pulchro architecturae sacrae et civilis compendio collectorum liber unicus by B. N. Wąsowski in original Latin and parallel Polish translation.
Table of ill. also in English ; summary in English.
zł90.00
1. Wąsowski, Bartłomiej Nataniel, 1617-1687. 2. Architecture—Early works to 1800. I. Wąsowski, Bartłomiej Nataniel, 1617-1687. II. Callitectonicorum seu de pulchro architecturae sacrae et civilis compendio collectorum liber unicus. Polish and Latin. 1975.
NA1455.P63W372 76-513770

Baranowski, Jerzy, 1931-
Ekonomiczne aspekty budowy domów jednorodzinnych na terenach miast i osiedli w Polsce. Kraków, 1972.
116 p. 24 cm. (Architektura, z. 27) (Politechnika Krakowska. Zeszyt naukowy, nr. 6) zł9.00
Summary in French and Russian.
Bibliography: p. 106-111.
1. Housing—Poland. I. Title. II. Series: Krakow. Politechnika. Architektura, z. 27.
NA17.K7 zesz. 27 74-210857
[HD7345.7]

Baranowski, Karl-Heinz, joint author
see Runge, Berndt. Die Anwendung des Aussensteuergesetzes ... Heidelberg : Verlagsgesellschaft Recht u. Wirtschaft, 1974.

Baranowski, Krzysztof.
Wyścig do Newport / Krzysztof Baranowski. — Wyd. 1. — Warszawa : Iskry, 1976.
195 p., ₍8₎ leaves of plates : ill. ; 20 cm. — (Naokoło świata) P 76-4932
zł20.00
1. Yacht racing. I. Title.
GV826.5.B34 77-470658

Baranowski, Stanisław.
Thermic conditions of the periglacial tundra in SW Spitsbergen; Polish IGY and IGC Spitzbergen expeditions in 1957-1960. (Termika tundry peryglacjalnej SW Spitsbergen) ₍by₎ Stanisław Baranowski. Translated from Polish ₍by M. Radziwiłł₎ Warsaw, Translated and published for the U. S. Dept. of Commerce, Environmental Science Services Administration and the National Science Foundation, Washington, D. C. by the Scientific Publications Foreign Cooperation Center of the Central Institute for Scientific, Technical and Economic Information, 1971.
56 p. fold. charts. 24 cm.
Cover title.
"TT 70-55061."
1. Tundras—Svalbard. 2. Soil temperature—Svalbard. 3. Atmospheric temperature—Svalbard. I. Title.
GB648.99.B3713 551.5'232'09981 73-158270
MARC

Baranowski, Stanisław.
Wpływ niedoboru sodu w pokarmie na czynność nerek i gruczołu mlekowego. ₍Wyd. 1.₎. Szczecin ₍Wydawn. Uczelniane Wyższej Szkoły Rolniczej₎ 1972.
32 p. 24 cm. (Wyższa Szkoła Rolnicza w Szczecinie. Rozprawy, nr. 29) (Praca habilitacyjna) zł4.00
Praca habilitacyjna—Wyższa Szkoła Rolnicza w Szczecinie.
Summary in English and Russian.
Bibliography: p. 26-31.
1. Sodium—Physiological effect. 2. Kidneys. 3. Mammary glands. I. Title. II. Series: Stettin. Wyższa Szkoła Rolnicza. Rozprawy, nr. 20.
QP913.N2B37 73-207405

Baranowski, Tadeusz.
Archeologia po drodze : przewodnik / Tadeusz Baranowski, Wiesław Zajączkowski. — Wrocław : Zakład Narodowy im. Ossolińskich, 1976.
115 p. : ill., map (fold. in pocket) ; 20 cm. — (Popularnonaukowa biblioteka archeologiczna ; Nr. 19) P***
At head of title: Polskie Towarzystwo Archeologiczne i Numizmatyczne.
Includes index.
zł25.00
1. Poland—Antiquities. 2. Poland—Description and travel—1945- —Tours. I. Zajączkowski, Wiesław, joint author. II. Title.
DK4090.B37 77-554005
77 MARC

Baranowski, Tom.
Clinical judgment as a cognitive process: a comparison of linear regression and decision net models. [Lawrence, 1974]
159 l. 28 cm.
Thesis (Ph. D.)—University of Kansas.
Bibliography: leaves 116-122.
1. Judgment. 2. Cognition. Mathematical models. I. Title.
KU NUC76-22870

Baranowski, Zenon.
Chów zwierząt źródłem zwiekszania dochodu rolniczego : na przykładzie gospodarstwa Pawła Jurczyka z Gronowic, pow. Olesno / Zenon Baranowski. — Wyd. 1. — Opole : Wydawn. Instytutu Śląskiego, 1974.
41 p. : ill. ; 21 cm. — (Komunikaty - Instytut Śląski w Opolu ; Seria rolnicza ; nr. 7)
Includes bibliographical references.
zł6.00
1. Stock and stock-breeding—Poland. 2. Livestock housing—Poland. I. Title. II. Series: Oppeln. Instytut Śląski. Komunikaty. Seria rolnicza ; nr. 7.
S13.O65 nr. 7 75-571676
[SF55.P7]

Baranowsky, Wolfgang, 1929–
Mensch und Gesundheit. ₍Gütersloh₎ Bertelsmann Lexikon-Verlag ₍c1973₎
397 p. illus. (chiefly col.) 31 cm. GFR***
"Lexikothek."
Includes bibliographies.
1. Medicine, Popular. I. Title.
RC81.B234 610 73-339466
ISBN 3-570-08933-9

Barans, Charles Anthony, 1942-
Seasonal temperature selections of white bass, yellow perch, emerald shiners, and smallmouth bass from western Lake Erie. [n. p.] 1972 [c1973]
88 l.
Thesis—Ohio State University.
Bibliography: leaves 85-88.
1. Fishes—Behavior. 2. Fishes—Erie, Lake. I. Title.
OU NUC74-126751

Baranseli, Z. Mahir
see Kağizmanli Recep Hifzi, 1893-1918. Kağizmanli Recep Hifzi, 1893-1918. [Kars: Kars Halkevi, 1965?]

Barańska-Gachowska, Maria
see Zarys stomatologii zachowawczej... -- Wyd. 2. -- Warszawa : Państwowy Zakład Wydawn. Lekarskich, 1975.

Baranskaia, Natalia.
En ganske almindelig uge / N. Baranskaja ; ₍overs. fra russisk af Susanne Højlt ; ill. af Marianne Kibenich ; udg. af an kvindegruppe₎. — København, K. : Kvindehusets Bogcafé, : ₍eksp.₎, Åbenrå 26, ₍1972₎.
72 p. : ill. ; 21 cm. D 75
Cover title.
Translation of Nedelia kak nedelia.
kr5.00
I. Title.
PG3479.R27N412 75-409834

Baranskaia, Natalia.
Une semaine comme une autre. (Récit.) Trad. du russe, introd. et notes d'Hélène Sinany. (Lausanne, Éditions) l'Age d'homme, (1973).
125 p. 21 cm. (Slavica. Écrits contemporains, 2) 16.50F Sw 73-A-3282
Translation of Nedelia kak nedelia.
I. Title.
PG3479.R27N414 74-158106
MARC

Baranskaia, Natalia.
Une Semaine comme une autre : et quelques récits / Natalia Baranskaïa ; traduit du russe par Jeanne Rude et Hélène Sinany ; postface de Colette Audry. — Paris : Éditions des Femmes, 1976.
255 p. ; 18 cm. F76-11663
Translation of Nedelia kak nedelia.
ISBN 2-7210-0044-6 : 32.00F
I. Title.
PG3479.R27N414 1976 891.7'3'44 77-451945
77 MARC

Baranskaia, Natal'ia.
En uge som de andre / Natalja Baranskaja ; på dansk ved Allan Remouard. — ₍København₎ : Gyldendal, 1973.
86 p. ; 20 cm. D 75
Translation of Nedelia kak nedelia.
ISBN 87-00-67241-6 (F) : kr19.75
I. Title.
PG3479.R27N412 1973 76-504280

Baranski, Edmée Caseau-
see
Caseau-Baranski, Edmée.

Baranski, Heinz.
Die Taufregister der deutsch-reformierten Gemeinde Sadweitschen Kr. Gumbinnen 1714-1735 nach Abschriften von Arno de la Chaux. Hamburg, Im Selbstverlag des Vereins, 1974.
240 p. 21 cm. (Sonderschriften des Vereins für Familienforschung in Ost- und Westpreussen, Nr. 26) GFR***
1. Registers of births, etc.—Sadweitschen, Ger. 2. Sadweitschen, Ger.—Genealogy. I. La Chaux, Arno de. II. Title. III. Series: Verein für Familienforschung in Ost- und Westpreussen. Sonderschriften, Nr. 26.
CS670.V4 Nr. 26 74-334994
[CS627.S28]

Barański, Henryk.
O obliczeniu w maszynie programowanej. ₍Wyd. 1.₎. Warszawa, Państwowe Wydawn. Naukowe, 1972.
86 p. 24 cm. zł16.00
At head of title: Centrum Obliczeniowe Polskiej Akademii Nauk.
Praca doktorska—Warsaw.
Bibliography: p. ₍82₎
1. Programming (Electronic computers) I. Title.
QA76.6.B357 74-203435

Baranski, Johnny.
Lonesome journey. ₍Chicago₎ Sunburst Press ₍c1973₎
125 p. 22 cm. $2.00
Five hundred copies printed. L. C. copy unnumbered.
I. Title.
PS3552.A5915L6 811'.5'4 73-85734
MARC

Baranski, Michael Joseph, 1946-
An analysis of variation within white oak (Quercus alba L.) / by Michael Joseph Baranski. -- Raleigh : North Carolina State University, 1974.
241 leaves : ill. ; 29 cm.
Bibliography: leaves 238-241.
Vita.
Thesis (Ph.D.)--North Carolina State University.
NcRS NUC77-87604

Baranski, Michael Joseph, 1946-
An analysis of variation within white oak (Quercus alba L.) / Michael J. Baranski. -- Raleigh : North Carolina Agricultural Experiment Station, 1975.
iv, 176 p. ; ill. ; 23 cm. -- (Technical bulletin no. 236)
Bibliography : p. 171-176.
1. Fagaceae. 2. White oak. I. Title. II. Series : North Carolina Agricultural Experiment Station. Technical bulletin no. 236.
MH-A NUC77-83527

Barański, Rajmund.
Pediatria. Pod red. Rajmunda Barańskiego. ₍Autorzy: Irena Balukiewicz et al. Wyd. 2.₎ Warszawa, Państwowy Zakład Wydawn. Lekarskich, 1974.
811 p. illus.
1. Pediatrics. I. Balukiewicz, Irena. II. Title.
DNLM NUC76-23060

Barański, Stanisław, 1927-
Biological effects of microwaves / Stanisław Barański and Przemysław Czerski. — Stroudsburg, Pa. : Dowden, Hutchinson & Ross, c1976.
234 p. : ill. ; 25 cm.
Bibliography: p. ₍193₎-227.
Includes indexes.
ISBN 0-87933-145-3
1. Microwaves—Physiological effect. I. Czerski, Przemysław, 1928- joint author. II. Title.
QP82.2.M5B37 574.1'9151 74-7837
77 MARC

Barański, Władysław.
Vademecum przepisów prawa dla geodetów. Warszawa, Państwowe Przedsiębiorstwo Wydawnictw Kartograficznych, 1972.
323 p. 21 cm. zł31.00
Includes bibliographical references.
1. Surveying—Law and legislation—Poland. I. Title.
73-213688

Barański, Zbigniew, writer on history of literature.
Rosyjskie manifesty literackie / Zbigniew Barański, Jerzy Litwinow. — Wyd. 1. — Poznań : Wydawn. Naukowe Uniwersytetu im. Adama Mickiewicza, 1974–
v. ; 24 cm.
Text in Russian; table of contents also in Russian.
Includes bibliographical references.
CONTENTS: cz. 1. Przełom XIX i XX wieku.
zł50.00 (v. 1)
1. Russian literature—19th century—History and criticism—Addresses, essays, lectures. 2. Russian literature—20th century—History and criticism—Addresses, essays, lectures. 3. Russian literature—19th century. 4. Russian literature—20th century. I. Litwinow, J., joint author. II. Title.
PG3011.B36 76-531700

Barański, Zbigniew, writer on history of literature
see Literatura rosyjska w zarysie. Warszawa : Państwowe Wydawn. Naukowe, 1975.

Barański, Zbigniew, writer on history of literature
see Rosyjskie manifesty literackie. Poznań: Uniwersytet im. Adama Mickiewicza, 19

Baranskiĭ, Nikolaĭ Nikolaevich, 1881–1963, comp.
(Sot͡sialisticheskai͡a rekonstrukt͡sii͡a oblasteĭ, kraev i respublik SSSR)
Социалистическая реконструкция областей, краев, и республик СССР в постановлениях партийных и советских органов : пособие для проработки районного курса экономической географии СССР / составлено Н. Баранским и Б. Каминским ; под ред. Н. Баранского. — Москва : Гос. социально-экон. изд-во, 1932.
2 v. in 1 : maps ; 23 cm.
At head of title: Kafedra ėkonomicheskoĭ geografii Geograficheskogo otdelenii͡a MGU.
1. Russia—Economic policy—1928–1932. I. Kaminskiĭ, B., joint comp. II. Title.
HC335.4.B37 75–568752

Baranskiĭ, Nikolaĭ Nikolaevich, 1881-1963, ed.
see Ekonomicheskie svi͡azi i transport. Moskva, Gos. izd-vo geograficheskoĭ literatury, 1963.

Baranskiĭ, Nikolaĭ Nikolaevich, 1881-1963, ed.
see Ėkonomicheskoe raĭonirovanie SSSR. Moskva, Gos. izd-vo geogr. lit-ry, 1959.

Baranskiĭ, Nikolaĭ Nikolaevich, 1881-1963, ed.
see Geografii͡a gorodskikh i sel'skikh poseleniĭ. Moskva, Gos. izd-vo geogr. lit-ry, 1959.

Baranskiĭ, Petr Ivanovich.
(Poluprovodnikovai͡a ėlektronika)
Полупроводниковая электроника : свойства материалов : справочник / П. И. Баранский, В. П. Клочков, И. В. Потыкевич. — Киев : Наук. думка, 1975.
703 p. : ill. ; 21 cm. USSR***
Includes bibliographies and index.
2.83rub
1. Semiconductors—Handbooks, manuals, etc. I. Klochkov, Volodymyr Petrovych, joint author. II. Potykevich, Ivan Vasil'evich, joint author. III. Title.
QC611.45.B37 75–535702

Baranson, Jack.
The drive toward technological self-reliance in developing countries. [n.p., 1973]
[27] l. 28 cm.
1. Technology transfer. 2. Technology—Brazil. I. Title.
TxU NUC75-21627

Baranson, Jack.
International transfer of automotive technology to developing countries. [New York] UNITAR, 1971.
iv, 2, 95 p. 28 cm. (UNITAR research reports, no. 8)
Includes bibliographical references.
1. Underdeveloped areas—Automobile industry and trade. 2. Technology transfer. 3. Business enterprises, Foreign. I. Title. II. Series: United Nations Institute for Training and Research. UNITAR research report no. 8.
HD9710.A2B32 73–170482
338.4'7'629222091724 MARC

Baranson, Jack.
see Developing World Industry and Technology, inc. International transfers of industrial technology by U.S. firms and their implications for the U.S. economy. Washington, Developing World Industry and Technology, 1976-

(Baransu no hōkai wa itsu kuru ka)
バランスの崩壊はいつ来るか：人口と食糧の行方 / 第2回日本人口会議資料編集専門委員会編. — 第2版. — 東京：日本人口会議事務局：発売元 日本家族計画協会, 昭和51 [1976]
114 p. : graphs ; 26 cm. Ja ***
Title on spine: Jinkō to shokuryō no yukue.
"第2回日本人口会議 資料集 補遺"・
"資料：FAO, Production year book 1971年版より作成"
Includes bibliographical references.
¥1000

1. Population forecasting—Addresses, essays, lectures. 2. Japan—Population policy—Addresses, essays, lectures. 3. Food supply—Addresses, essays, lectures. 4. Food supply—Japan—Addresses, essays, lectures. I. Dainikai Nihon Jinkō Kaigi Shiryō Semmon Iinkai. II. Nihon Jinkō Kaigi, 2d, Tokyo, 1975. III. Title: Jinkō to shokuryō no yukue.

HB875.B27 76–805844

Barante, Amable Guillaume Prosper Brugière, baron de, 1782-1866.
Histoire de la convention nationale / [par M. de Barante]. — New York : AMS Press, 1976.
6 v. ; 18 cm.
Reprint of the 1851-1853 ed. published by Meline, Cans, Brussels.
ISBN 0-404-07780-3
1. France. Convention nationale, 1792-1795. 2. France—History—Revolution, 1792-1795. I. Title.
DC176.B22 1976 328.44'09 77-161739
75 MARC

Barante, **Amable Guillaume Prosper Brugière,** baron de, 1782-1866.
Histoire du directoire de la République française / par M. de Barante. — New York : AMS Press, 1977.
3 v. ; 23 cm.
Reprint of the 1855 ed. published by Didier, Paris.
ISBN 0-404-07770-6
1. France—History—Revolution, 1795-1799. I. Title.
DC186.B22 1977 944.04'5 71-161740
76 MARC

Barante, Amable Guillaume Prosper Brugière, baron de, 1782–1866.
Notes sur la Russie, 1835–1840 / par le baron de Barante ; revues et mises en ordre par le baron de Nervo. — Paris : M. Lévy frères, [1875]
464 p.
Microfiche. Paris : Microéditions Hachette, 1972?. — 8 sheets ; 11 x 15 cm.
"72 R.5."
1. Russia—Description and travel. 2. Russia—Politics and government—1825–1855. 3. Russia—Social life and customs. I. Title.
Microfiche DK25 75–553411

Barant͡sev, Aleksandr Pavlovich.
(Fonologicheskie sredstva li͡udikovskoĭ rechi)
Фонологические средства людиковской речи : дескриптивное описание / А. П. Баранцев. — Ленинград : Наука, Ленингр. отд-ние, 1975.
280 p. ; 22 cm. USSR 75
At head of title: Akademii͡a nauk SSSR. Karel'skiĭ filial. Institut i͡azyka, literatury i istorii.
Includes bibliographical references.
1.25rub
1. Ludic dialect—Phonology. I. Title.
PH532.B3 76–518399

Barant͡sev, Rėm Georgievich.
(Vzaimodeĭstvie razrezhennykh gazov s obtekaemymi poverkhnosti͡ami)
Взаимодействие разреженных газов с обтекаемыми поверхностями / Р. Г. Баранцев. — Москва : Наука, 1975.
343 p. : diagrs. ; 21 cm. USSR 75
Bibliography: p. [317]–343.
1.72rub
1. Rarefied gas dynamics. I. Title.
TA358.B37 77–513774

Barant͡sev, Vasiliĭ Ivanovich
see Stabnikov, Vsevolod Nikolaevich. (Prot͡sessy i apparaty pishchevykh proizvodstv) 1974.

Bárány, Ferenc.
A Csongrád Megyei forradalmi munkásmozgalom, 1925–1929, Szeged [MSZMP Csongrád Megyei Bizottsága Propaganda és Művelődési Osztálya] 1972.
60 p. 24 cm. (Csongrád Megye munkásmozgalmának története)
At head of title: Magyar Szocialista Munkáspart, Csongrád Megyei Bizottsága.
Bibliography: p. 59.
5.00Ft
1. Csongrád, Hungary (Comitat)—Politics and government. 2. Labor and laboring classes—Csongrád, Hungary (Comitat) I. Title.
DB975.C7B35 75–572926

Bárány, Ferenc.
A munkások és a szegényparasztok küzdelmei Csongrád megyében, 1919. aug. 1924. Szeged [MSZMP Csongrád Megyei Bizottsága Propaganda és Művelődési Osztálya] 1972.
79 p. 24 cm. (Csongrád Megye munkásmozgalmának története)
At head of title: Magyar Szocialista Munkáspárt, Csongrád Megyei Bizottsága.
Bibliography: p. 79.
5.00Ft
1. Csongrád, Hungary (Comitat)—Politics and government. 2. Labor and laboring classes—Csongrád, Hungary (Comitat) I. Title.
DB975.C7B37 75–572927

Bárány, Franz R.
see International Symposium on Gastrointestinal Emergencies, 1st, Stockholm, 1975. Gastrointestinal emergencies ... Oxford, Pergamon, 1977.

Bárány, László.
Adatok Magyarszecsőd helytörténetéhez (irodalom és forrásmunkák); a magyarszecsődi románkori templom és plébánia története. Körmend, 1972.
ii, 75 l. 30 cm.
"Kéziratként."
Errata slip inserted.
Bibliography: leaves 55–65.
1. Magyarszecsöd, Hungary. I. Title.
DB879.M15B37 74–229925

Bárány, Magda Oberschall, 1905–
Die Sankt Stephans-Krone und die Insignien des Königreiches Ungarn / Magda von Bárány-Oberschall. — 2., erw. Aufl. — Wien ; München : Herold, 1974.
173 p., [19] leaves of plates : ill. ; 21 cm. — (Die Kronen des Hauses österreich ; Bd. 3) Au 75–14–156
Bibliography: p. 161–[166]
ISBN 3–7008–0118–1 : S168.00
1. Regalia (Insignia)—Hungary. 2. Holy Crown of Hungary. I. Title.
NK7415.H8B3 1974 75–541384

Barany, Ronald.
Heat and free energy of formation data for crystalline cadmium and lead metasilicates. [Washington] U. S. Dept. of the Interior, Bureau of Mines, 1959.
7 p. tables. 27 cm. ([U. S.] Bureau of Mines. Report of investigations, 5466)
Bibliographical footnotes.
1. Cadmium—Silicates. 2. Lead silicates. I. Title. (Series)
TN23.U43 no. 5466 Int 59—29

Bárány, Tamás.
Emberi hang / Bárány Tamás. — Budapest : Szépirodalmi Könyvkiadó, 1975.
262 p. ; 20 cm.
CONTENTS: Vadászat.—Legendás barátság.—Ki, Budafokra.—Emberi hang.—Egy asszony meséli.—Itéletidő.—Az utolsó film.—Tizenkét amatőrkép.—Atmoszféra.—Másfél szoba összkomfort.—Két tekercs pillanatkép.
ISBN 963–15–0256–2 : 19.50Ft
I. Title.
PH3213.B292E5 76–526882

Bárány, Tamás.
Fényes rokonság; regény. Budapest, Szépirodalmi Könyvkiadó [1972]
261 p. illus. 21 cm. 19.00Ft
I. Title.
PH3213.B292F4 73–203260

Bárány, Tamás.
Kitagadottak : regény / Bárány Tamás. — Budapest : Kozmosz Könyvek, 1975.
197 p. ; 19 cm.
ISBN 9632111087 : 17.00Ft
I. Title.
PH3213.B292K5 77-474372
77 MARC

Bárány, Tamás.
Nagy idők tanúja / Bárány Tamás. — Budapest : Magvető Kiadó, 1974.
462 p. ; 19 cm.
28.00Ft
I. Title.
PH3213.B292N3 75–582603

Bárány, Tamás.
Város, esti fényben; regény. [2. kiad.] Budapest, Szépirodalmi Könyvkiadó [1972]
373 p. 21 cm. 26.00Ft
I. Title.
PH3213.B292V3 1972 73–203236

Bárány, Tamás.
Város, esti fényben : regény / Bárány Tamás. — 3. kiad. — Budapest : Szépirodalmi Könyvkiadó, 1974.
377 p. ; 20 cm.
ISBN 963–15–0127–2 : 26.00Ft
I. Title.
PH3213.B292V3 1974 77–502528

Baranya, Margit
see A Népi demokrácia kezdeti időszakának dokumentumai Baranyában. Pécs : Baranya Megyei Levéltár, 1971.

Baranya története az őskortól az Árpád-korig : (a Pécsi Janus Pannonius Múzeum állandó régészeti kiállításának vezetője) / Bándi Gábor ... [et al. ; szerk. Mándoki László]. — Pécs : [Janus Pannonius Múzeum], 1973.
63 p. : ill. ; 21 cm. — (A Janus Pannonius Múzeum füzetei ; 15. sz.)
Summary in English and German.
1. Baranya, Hungary—Antiquities—Exhibitions. I. Bándi, Gábor. II. Mándoki, László, ed. III. Pécs, Hungary. Janus Pannonius Múzeum. IV. Pécs, Hungary. Janus Pannonius Múzeum. A Janus Pannonius Múzeum füzetei ; 15. sz.
AM101.P295845 sz. 15 75–573733
[DB975.B3]

Baranyai, Gustav L. de, ed.
see Ludwig van Beethoven. [München, Beethoven-Gesellschaft] 1970.

Baranyai-Lörincz, Gustav von, 1886-
Ludwig van Beethoven. Hrsg. von der Beethoven-Gesellschaft. München, 1970.
215 p. illus.
1. Beethoven, Ludwig van, 1770-1827. I. Beethoven-Gesellschaft.
InU NUC74-12631

Baranyay, Eileen P
A lifetime of learning : a survey of further education facilities for mentally handicapped adolescents and adults / ⌜by⌝ Eileen Barahyay. — London : National Society for Mentally Handicapped Children : ⌜British Association for the Retarded⌝, 1976.
72 p. ; 21 cm. GB76-25022
Bibliography: p. 71.
ISBN 0-85537-033-5 : £1.30
1. Mentally handicapped—Education—Great Britain. I. Title.
LC4815.B37 371.9'28 76-381237
76 MARC

Baranyay, J A
Dwarf mistletoes in British Columbia and recommendations for their control. Victoria, 1972.
18 p. illus., maps. (Pacific Forest Research Centre. Information report BC-X no. 72)
Bibliography: p. 18.
I. Title.
DNAL NUC74-126766

Baranyay, J A
Glossary of dwarf mistletoe terms, by J.A. Baranyay, F.G. Hawksworth ⌜and⌝ R.B. Smith. Victoria, Pacific Forest Research Centre, Canadian Forestry Service, 1972.
42 p. illus. 26 cm.
Bibliography: p. 42.
1. Arceuthobium—Terminology. 2. Parasitic plants—Terminology. I. Hawksworth, Frank G., 1926- II. Smith, R.B. III. Title.
NNBG NUC74-119805

Baranyi, Ferenc, 1937–
Esőveréssel : válogatott és új versek / Baranyi, Ferenc. — Budapest : Magvető Kiadó, 1975.
159 p. ; 21 cm.
ISBN 963-270-006-6 : 20.00Ft
I. Title.
PH3213.B2926E8 76–503383

Baranyi, Ferenc, 1937–
Túl az éjszakán. Budapest, Magvető, 1969.
100 p. 20 cm.
Poems.
12.50Ft
I. Title.
PH3213.B2926T8 72–200834

Baranyi, Ferenc, 1937–
Változó szelek. Budapest, Magvető ⌜1972⌝
61 p. 21 cm.
Poems.
13.00Ft
I. Title.
PH3213.B2926V3 73–202293

Baranyi, Helmut A
A comparison of the effects of immediate presentation with delayed presentation of the written form on student proficiency in level I French classes. Pittsburgh, Pa., 1970.
80 p.
Thesis—University of Pittsburgh.
Microfilm. Ann Arbor, Mich., University Microfilms. 1 reel. 35 mm.
CLSU NUC73-42606

Baranyi, Judit
see I. [i.e. Első] Nemzetközi Kisplasztilai Biennálé, Mucsarnok—1971. [Budapest, I. Nemzetközi Kisplasztikai Biennálé Kiállítási Iroda] 1971.

Baranyi, Károly, 1894–
Karlo Baranji : 55 godina skulpture : Galerija Radničkog univerziteta Radivoj Ćirpanov Novi Sad, od. 15. maja do 7. juna 1974. godine / ⌜uvodni tekst Zlata Markov-Baranji ; prevodi sa mađarskog Andrija Stančić, Janoš Aladić ; fotografije Silvester More⌝. — Novi Sad : Radnički univerzitet Radivoj Ćirpanov, ⌜1974⌝
⌜40⌝ p. : ill. ; 33 cm. Yu 74–8063
Serbo-Croatian and Hungarian.
Bibliography: p. ⌜5⌝
1. Baranyi, Károly, 1894– I. Baranyiné Markov, Zlata. II. Radnički univerzitet Radivoj Ćirpanov. Galerija.
NB522.5.B3B37 75–971616

Baranyi, Sándor.
Utasítás a vízhozammérések végrehajtására a mérési eredmények számítása. ⌜Készült a Vizgazdálkodási Tudományos Kutató Intézet II. Felszíni Vizek Főosztályán⌝ Budapest, Vízügyi Műszaki Tájékoztató Iroda, 1966.
113 p. illus. 20 cm.
At head of title: Vízbgazdálkodási Tudományos Kutató Intézet.
Bibliography: p. 99.
1. Flow meters. I. Budapest. Vízgazdálkodási Tudományos Kutató Intézet. Második Felszini Vizek Főosztály. II. Title.
TC177.B36 74–207721

Baranyiné Markov, Zlata.
Vergödés (Farkas Béla napjai). A fedőlapon Farkas Béla. Szabadka, Munkásegyetem, 1971.
75 p. illus. 14 cm. (Életjel miniatűrök, 15) Yu 71
Edition limited to 300 copies, this is no. 214.
1. Farkas, Béla. I. Title.
ND522.5.F37B37 71–978676

Baranyiné Markov, Zlata.
Vergödés; Farkas Béla napjai. ⌜Szabadka⌝ Életjel, 1971.
75 p. illus. (Életjel miniatürök, 15)
1. Farkas, Béla, 1884- I. Title.
InU NUC73-114744

Baranyiné Markov, Zlata
see Baranyi Károly, 1894- Karlo Baranji : 55 godina skulpture... Novi Sad : Radnički univerzitet Radivoj Cirpanov [1974]

Baranzini, Mauro.
Un essai de modele monétaire de croissance; à deux classes et à taux d'intérèt différencié. ⌜Fribourg? 1971?⌝
xi, 129 p.
These—Fribourg.
1. Money—Mathematical models.
MH NIC NUC75-21784

Barão de Barnabé
see
Valente, Décio.

Baraoidan, Pedro Foronda.
On the numerical solution of a class or ordinary differential equations generalizing the restricted three-body problem equations. [Berkeley] 1972.
v, 104 l.
Thesis (Ph. D.)—University of California.
Bibliography: leaves 101-104.
CU NUC74-126752

Baraona, M Isabel Velasco
see Velasco Baraona, M Isabel.

Baraona Urzúa, Pablo
see Chile: a critical survey. Santiago, Institute of General Studies, 1972.

Baraona Urzúa, Pablo
see Fuerzas armadas y seguridad nacional. ⌜Santiago, Chile⌝ Ediciones Portad, 1973.

Baraona Urzua, Pablo
see Visión crítica de Chile. 1. ed. [Santiago] Ediciones Portada, 1972.

Baraona Urzua, Pablo
see Visión crítica de Chile. 3. ed. [Santiago] Ediciones Portada, 1972.

Baraona V , Carmen Gloria.
Homicidio en riña o pelea / Carmen Gloria Baraona V., María Antonieta Mendoza E. — Santiago de Chile : Editorial Jurídica de Chile, c1973.
92 p. ; 22 cm.
At head of title: Universidad Católica de Chile. Facultad de Ciencias Jurídicas, Políticas y Sociales. Escuela de Derecho de Santiago.
Bibliography: p. 92.
1. Homicide—Chile. I. Mendoza E., María Antonieta, joint author. II. Title.
74–232324

Baraqui W , Jaime.
Factibilidad técnico-económica de carretera oriental precordillerana San Fernando-Ñuble; elaborado por: Departamento de Obras Públicas, D.P. y P. ⌜y⌝ Consultores Plan-ing; a cargo del estudio: Jaime Baraqui W. con la colaboración de un equipo interdisciplinario... Estudio realizado por la Direccion de Planificación y Presupuesto M.O.P.T. ⌜Santiago, Chile⌝ 1970.
148 p. maps. 26 cm. (Publicacion, no. 46)
DPU NUC75-128428

Baraqui W , Jaime.
Identificación y evaluación de proyectos viales de desarrollo en la región Bio-Bio sur oriental; elaborado por: Departamento de Obras Públicas, D.P. y U. [y] Consultores Plan-ing. A cargo del estudio: Jaime Baraqui W. ; con la colaboración de un equipo interdisciplinario... [Santiago, Chile] 1971.
127 p. maps. 26 cm. (Publicación, no. 48)
DPU NUC74-21661

Baraqui Wasaff, Jorge.
Clasificaciones de los actos administrativos ⌜por⌝ Jorge Baraqui W. Santiago, Editorial Universitaria, 1964.
94 p. 21 cm.
Tesis (licenciatura en ciencias jurídicas y sociales)—Universidad de Chile.
Bibliography: p. 87-89.
1. Administrative acts. I. Title.
TxU NUC74-57159

Baraquin, Yves.
Les Français et la justice civile : enquête psycho-sociologique auprès des justiciables / par Yves Baraquin. — Paris : documentation française, c1975.
275, iii p. : ill. ; 24 cm. — (Collection Ministère de la justice) F***
At head of title: Centre de recherches et de documentation sur la consommation.
Errata slip inserted.
Bibliography: p. 231-234.
40.00F
1. Justice, Administration of—France—Public opinion. 2. Public opinion—France. I. Centre de recherches et de documentation sur la consommation. II. Title.
301.15'43'34744 76-459046
76 MARC

Barāṛa, H S
see
Brar, H S 1919-

Barāṛa, Jagajīta.
(Mādhiama)
ਮਾਧਿਅਮ. ⌜ਕਹਾਣੀਕਾਰ⌝ ਜਗਜੀਤ ਬਰਾੜ. ਮੁਕਤਸਰ, ਸੁਰਤਾਲ ਪ੍ਰਕਾਸ਼ਨ ⌜1972⌝
80 p. 19 cm. Rs4.00
In Panjabi.

I. Title.
PK2659.B34M3 72–905378

Barāṛa, Surindarajīta.
(Dāwānala)
ਦਾਵਾਨਲ. ⌜ਲੇਖਿਕਾ⌝ ਸੁਰਿੰਦਰਜੀਤ ਬਰਾੜ. ਲੁਧਿਆਣਾ, ਲਾਹੌਰ ਬੁਕ ਸ਼ਾਪ ⌜1963⌝
7-342 p. 19 cm. Rs5.00
In Panjabi.
A novel

I. Title.
PK2659.B35D3 S A 68–9085
PL 480: I-Pu-1273

Barari, Assad.
Ground-water investigation for the city of Baltic, South Dakota. Vermillion, Science Center, University of South Dakota, 1972.
i, 19 p. illus. 28 cm. (South Dakota. State Geological Survey. Special report 56)
1. Baltic, South Dakota–Water-supply. 2. Water, Underground–South Dakota–Baltic. I. Title. II. Series.
SdU NUC74-9901

Barari, Assad.
Ground-water investigation for the city of Hazel, South Dakota. Vermillion, Science Center, University of South Dakota, 1972.
ii, 26 p. illus. 28 cm. (South Dakota. State Geological Survey. Special report 53)
1. Hazel, South Dakota–Water-supply. 2. Water, Underground–South Dakota–Hazel. I. Title. II. Series.
SdU NUC73-77846

Barari, Assad.
Ground-water investigation for the city of Howard, South Dakota. Vermillion, Science Center, University of South Dakota, 1972.
ii, 45 p. illus. 28 cm. (South Dakota. State Geological Survey. Special report 47)
1. Howard, South Dakota–Water-supply. 2. Water, Underground–South Dakota–Howard. I. Title. II. Series.
SdU NUC73-77852

Barari, Assad.
Ground-water investigation for the city of Parkston, South Dakota. Vermillion, Science Center, University of South Dakota, 1972.
i, 26 p. illus. 28 cm. (South Dakota. State Geological Survey. Special report 55)
1. Parkston, South Dakota—Water supply. 2. Water, Underground–South Dakota—Parkston. I. Title. II. Series.
SdU NUC74-126732

Barari, Assad.
Ground-water investigation for the city of Spencer, South Dakota. Vermillion, Science Center, University of South Dakota, 1972.
i, 25 p. illus. 28 cm. (South Dakota. State Geological Survey. Special report 54)
1. Spencer, South Dakota–Water-supply. 2. Water, Underground–South Dakota–Spencer. I. Title. II. Series.
SdU NUC74-9902

Barari, Assad.
Ground-water investigation for the city of Volga, South Dakota. Vermillion, Science Center, University of South Dakota, 1971.
33 p. illus. (maps, tables) 29 cm. (South Dakota. State Geological Survey. Special report 51)
1. Volga, South Dakota–Water-supply. 2. Water, Underground–South Dakota–Volga. I. Title. II. Series.
SdSpeT NUC73-118715

Barari, Assad.
Hydrology of Lake Kampeska. ₍Prepared₎ for South Dakota Department of Game, Fish, and Parks. Vermillion, Science Center, University of South Dakota, 1971.
iv, 84 p. illus. 28 cm. (South Dakota Geological Survey. Report of investigations no. 103)
"Dingell-Johnson F–19–R completion report."
Part of illustrative matter in pocket.
Bibliography: p. 33.
1. Hydrology—South Dakota—Kampeska, Lake. I. South Dakota. Dept. of Game, Fish and Parks. II. Title. III. Series: South Dakota. State Geologist. Report of investigations no. 103.
GB1625.S6B29 551.4′8′0978323 72–611837
MARC

Barari, Assad.
Physical and geometrical approach to statistical concepts. -- Vermillion : University of South Dakota, 1975.
[10], 81 l. : ill. ; 29 cm.
Thesis (Ed. D.) -- University of South Dakota.
1. Statistics. I. Title.
SdU NUC77-83516

Bárarson, Hjálmar R
Ice and fire; contrasts of Icelandic nature, text and pictures by Hjálmar R. Bárarson. Reykjavík ₍c1971₎
171 p. illus. (part col.), maps. 26 cm.
Bibliography: p. 169-170.
1. Iceland–Description and travel. 2. Iceland–Physical geography. I. Title.
DI-GS NUC73-114769

Baras, Alexandros.
The hydra of birds; poems by Alexandros Baras, Andreas Embiricos ₍and₎ Nikos Engonopoulos. Translated from the Greek by Yannis Goumas. [Winchester, Green Horse, 1971]
₍23₎ p. 21 cm. (Platform/ Green Horse booklet no. 3)
Cover title.
I. Embiricos, Andreas, 1901- joint author. II. Engonopoulos, Nikos, 1910- joint author. III. Title.
NBuU NUC75-32398

Baras, Alexandros.
(Syntheseis)
Συνθέσεις / 'Αλεξάνδρου Μπάρα. – 'Αθήνα : 'Εκδόσεις τῶν Φίλων, 19
v. ; 19 cm.
I. Title.
PA5610.B296S9 75–409039

Báras, Aléxandros.
The yellow house and other poems (1933-1973) / Aléxandros Báras ; translated from the Greek by Yannis Goumas. — 1st ed. — Winchester ₍Eng.₎ : Green Horse, 1974.
80 p. ; 25 cm. GB***
Label mounted on t.p.: Distributed by Oasis Books, London.
£1.50
I. Title.
PA5610.B296A24 889′.1′32 76-360479
76 MARC

Baras, Basileios
see
Baras, Vasileios, 1887-1964.

Baras, Nehama, comp.
(Tekstim be-mada'e ha-ruaḥ)
טכסטים במדעי הרוח. לקטו וכתבו תרגילים נחמה ברס ₍ו₎מזל מוצרי. בעריכת שושנה בלום. ירושלים, אקדמון, 1970.
120 p. 24 cm. (סדרת חוברות טכסטים מדעיים) IL3.50
——— ——— מילון. ₍ירושלים, אקדמון, 1970 i. e. 730₎
83 p. 24 cm. IL3.25
Includes bibliographical references.
PJ4571.B28 Suppl.
1. Hebrew language—Readers. 2. Hebrew language—Glossaries, vocabularies, etc. I. Motsri, Mazal, joint comp. II. Title. III. Series: Sidrat ḥovrot tekstim mada'iyim.
PJ4571.B28 78–953294
rev

Baras, Nehama, comp.
(Tekstim be-mada'e ha-yahadut)
טכסטים במדעי היהדות. ליקטו וכתבו תרגילים נחמה ברס ₍ו₎מזל מוצרי, בעריכת שושנה בלום. ירושלים, אקדמון, 1970.
190 p. 24 cm. (סדרת חוברות טכסטים מדעיים) IL4.50
——— ——— מילון. ירושלים, אקדמון, 730 ₍1970₎
89 p. 24 cm.
BM43.B34 Suppl.
1. Judaism—Addresses, essays, lectures. 2. Hebrew language—Readers. 3. Hebrew language—Glossaries, vocabularies, etc. I. Motsri, Mazal, joint comp. II. Title. III. Series: Sidrat ḥovrot tekstim mada'iyim.
BM43.B34 74–953293
rev

Baras, Tsevi
see
Baras, Zvi.

Baras, Vasileios, 1887-1964.
To Delvino tēs Voreiou Ēpeirou kai hoi geitonikes tou perioches: Argyrokastrou, Cheimaras, Pōgōniou, Philiatōn, Paramythias klp. Prologos kai epimeleia L.I. Vranousē. Athēnai, 1966.
351 p. illus., plates, port. 26 cm.
1. Delvine, Albania. I. Branousēs, Leandros I., 1921-
NN MH DDO OCU NUC74-120061

Baras, Victor, 1945-
East Germany in Soviet foreign policy: the objectives of the new course and the impact of the uprising of June 17, 1953. ₍Ithaca, N.Y.₎ 1973.
viii, 232 l. 29 cm.
Thesis (Ph.D.)—Cornell University.
1. Russia—Foreign relations—Germany (Democratic Republic, 1949-) 2. Germany (Democratic Republic, 1949-)—Foreign relations—Russia. I. Title.
NIC NUC75-30712

Baras, Zvi.
see The Herodian period. ₍Tel-Aviv?₎ Jewish History Publications Ltd., 1975.

Barasain, Alberto, joint author
see Ribes, Francisco. Momentos historicos de España y America... [1. ed. Madrid] Santillana [c1969]

Barasch, Eugen A.
see Rudenia în dreptul Republicii Socialiste România. București, Editura Academiei Republicii Socialiste România, 1966.

Barasch, Eugen A.
see Tratat de drept civil. Bucuresti, 1967-

Barasch, Frances K
The "grotesque;" its history as a literary term, by Frances K. Barasch. ₍n.p.₎ 1964.
1 reel.
Thesis–New York University.
Microfilm. 35 mm.
1. Grotesque in literature. I. Title.
CaBVaU NUC77-15655

Barasch, Kenneth L
Marketing problem solver ₍by₎ Kenneth L. Barasch. 1st ed. Fullerton, Calif., Cochrane Chase ₍1973₎
2 v. (Loose-leaf) 30 cm.
1. Marketing research. 2. New products. 3. Advertising research. I. Cochrane Chase & Co. II. Title.
MeU NUC74-150669

Barasch, Kenneth L. Marketing problem solver.
see Chase, Cochrane. Marketing problem solver. 2d ed. Radnor, Pa., Chilton Book Co., c1977.

Barasch, Monique, 1929-
A study of synonomy and lexical statistics in Gothic. ₍n.p.₎ 1973.
192 p.
Thesis (Ph.D.)—New York University.
I. Title.
NNU NUC75-21628

Barasch, Norman.
Beginner's luck; a comedy in two acts, by Norman Barasch and Carroll Moore. ₍Rev. and rewritten₎ New York, French ₍1973₎
63 p. illus. 19 cm. $1.50
First published in 1967 under title: Best behavior.
I. Moore, Carroll, joint author. II. Title.
PS3503.A55863B4 1973 812′.5′4 73–159369
MARC

Barasch, Stephen, 1940-
Analytical and experimental studies on the transverse vibration of rotating disks. New Brunswick, N.J., 1972.
viii, 101 p. illus. 28 cm.
Typewritten.
Thesis (Ph.D.)—Rutgers University.
1. Vibration—Measurement. 2. Disks, Rotating—Testing. I. Title. II. Title: Transverse vibration of rotating disks.
NjR NUC73-31042

Barasch, Stephen B
Recreational planning for new communities ₍by₎ Stephen B. Barasch. ₍1st ed.₎ New York, Exposition Press ₍1974₎
54 p. illus. 24 cm. (An Exposition-university book) $5.00
Bibliography: p. 53–54.
1. Recreation — United States — Case studies. 2. New towns — United States—Case studies. I. Title.
GV53.B36 711′.4′0973 73–86541
ISBN 0–682–47775–3 MARC

Baraschi, Constantin, 1902-
Sculpture of the nude [by] Constantin Baraschi. London, Abbey Library, c1970.
370 p. illus. 31 cm.
On verso: "English edition published by Meridiane Publishing House, Bucharest."
Translation of Tratat de sculptura (v. 2): Nudul.
1. Nude in art. 2. Sculpture–Technique. I. Title.
INS NUC76-75708

Bărascu, Ion, joint author
see Cardalef, Stefan. Probleme de constucție și exploatare in fabricația de produse cărbunoase. [Bucuresti] Centrul de documentare și publicații tehnice al industriei matalurgice, 1974.

Barash, Asher, 1889–1952.
(Ish u-veto nimḥu, ve-ʻod shishah sipurim)
איש וביתו נמחו, ועוד ששה ספורים / אשר ברש. — רמת גן : מסדה, ₍1969₎
CONTENTS: — .איש וביתו נמחו. — אקמק. — ערביאים. — הניר הנשלם. — נכר. — "לוטה, הכנסי ... ". — באר לחי.
I. Title.
PJ5054.B273 I 8 1969 76–951775

Barash, Asher, 1889-1952. Mivḥar sipurim
see Barash, Asher, 1889-1952. Selected works.

Barash, Asher, 1889-1952.
Pictures from a brewery; a novel. Translated from the Hebrew by Katie Kaplan. Introduction by Israel Cohen. Indianapolis, Bobbs-Merrill [c1971]
xvi, 270 p. 22 cm.
Translation of Temunot mi-bet mivshal ha-shekhar.
I. Title.
IU IaU MiEM InU NUC75-21641

Barash, Asher, 1889-1952.
Pictures from a brewery; a novel. Translated from the Hebrew by Katie Kaplan. Introd. by Israel Cohen. [1st British Commonwealth ed.] London, P. Owen [1972]
270 p. (Unesco collection of representative works. Israel series)
Translation of Temunot mi-bet mivshal hashekhar.
I. Title.
MiU NjP NUC73-116598

Barash, Asher, 1889–1952.
[Selected works]
מבחר ספורים [מאת] אשר ברש. עריכה, מבוא, ביאורים ומילון: חיים ברנדוין. ניו-יורק, קרן התרבות [1969]
188, xv p. 18 cm.
Added t. p.: Selected stories of Asher Barash. Edited with introductions, notes, and vocabulary by Chaim Brandwein.
Introductions and notes in English.
Partially vocalized.
CONTENTS: — מספורי הארץ: מכתבים. זקנה ובחרות. באר לחי. ספורים הסטוריים: מול שער השמים. הנשאר בטולידה. במרבורג. — מספורי הגולה: בכפרים.
I. Brandwein, Chaim, 1921– ed.
Title romanized: Mivḥar sipurim.
PJ5053.B3A15 1969 73–204333

Barash, Asher, 1889-1952, ed.
see Hedim. 689-682 [1928-1922]

Barash, David P
The social biology of the Olympic marmot. London, Baillière Tindall, 1973.
[171]-245 p. illus. 25 cm. (Animal behaviour monographs. v. 6, pt. 3)
Bibliography: p. 245.
1. Marmots. I. Title. II. Series.
AAP NUC75-21630

Barash, David P
Sociobiology and behavior / David P. Barash ; foreword by Edward O. Wilson. — New York : Elsevier, c1977.
xv, 378 p. : ill. ; 24 cm.
Bibliography: p. 333-365
Includes index.
ISBN 0-444-99029-1. ISBN 0-444-99036-4 pbk.
1. Sociobiology. 2. Social psychology. 3. Social behavior in animals.
GN365.9.B37 301.1 76-54359
77 MARC

Barash, Moshe.
Gestures of despair in medieval and early Renaissance art / Moshe Barasch. — New York : New York University Press, 1976.
x, 162 p. : ill. ; 26 cm.
Includes bibliographical references and index.
ISBN 0-8147-1006-9 : $35.00
1. Gesture in art. 2. Despair in art. 3. Art, Medieval. 4. Art, Renaissance —Early Renaissance. I. Title.
N5975.B37 709'.45 76-4601
76 MARC

Barash, Moshe, ed.
see Studies in art. Jerusalem, Magnes Press, 1972.

Barash, Naomi Ellen, 1940-
Annihilations of antiprotons at rest in hydrogen VI: kaonic final states [by] N. Barash [and others] Irvington-on-Hudson, N.Y., Columbia University, Physics Dept., Nevis Laboratories, 1966.
25 p. illus. 28 cm. (Columbia University. Nevis Laboratories. [Report] 154)
Bibliography: p. 14-15.
I. Series.
NNC NUC73-40634

Barash, Zeev.
Histadrut: fifty years of building a nation. [New York, American Histadrut Cultural Exchange Institute, 1971]
14 p. 22 cm.
1. ha-Histadrut ha-kelalit shel ha-'ovdim be-Erets-Yisrael. I. American Histadrut Cultural Exchange Institute. II. Title.
OCH IH NUC73-116915

Barash, Zinoviĭ Davydovich.
(Opyt raboty ochistnykh sooruzheniĭ Leningradskogo Monetnogo dvora)
Опыт работы очистных сооружений Ленинградского Монетного двора. Ленинград, Ленингр. организация о-ва "Знание," РСФСР, ЛДНТП, 1973.
20 p. with illus. 21 cm. (Серия: Улучшение качества промышленной продукции (стандартизация, надежность, защитные покрытия, техническая эстетика)) 0.12rub USSR 73
At head of title: З. Д. Бараш, Ю. С. Гусев, Т. Н. Кожина.
1. Sewage—Purification. 2. Mints—Waste disposal. 3. Russia. Monetnyĭ dvor, Leningrad. I. Gusev, I͡Uriĭ Sergeevich, joint author. II. Kozhina, Tamara Nikolaevna, joint author. III. Title.
TD745.B28 74–349048

Barash-Schmidt, Naomi
see California. University. Lawrence Radiation Laboratory. Particle Data Group. Review of particle properties. Berkeley, 1968.

Barashenkov, Vladilen Sergeevich.
(Vzaimodeĭstvii͡a vysokoėnergeticheskikh chastit͡s i atomnykh i͡ader s i͡adrami)
Взаимодействия высокоэнергетических частиц и атомных ядер с ядрами. Москва, Атомиздат, 1972.
648 p. with diagrs. 26 cm. 6.38rub USSR 73–VKP
At head of title: В. С. Барашенков, В. Д. Тонеев.
Includes bibliographies.
1. Nuclear reactions. 2. Particles (Nuclear physics) I. Toneev, Vi͡acheslav Dmitrievich, joint author. II. Title.
QC794.8.H5B37 73–325128

Barashikov, Arnol'd I͡Akovlevich.
(Raschet zhelezobetonnykh konstrukt͡siĭ na deĭstvie dlitel'nykh peremennykh nagruzok)
Расчет железобетонных конструкций на действие длительных переменных нагрузок / А. Я. Барашиков. — 2-е изд., перераб. и доп. — Киев : Будівельник, 1977.
156 p. : ill. ; 21 cm. USSR 77
Bibliography: p. 151–[155]
0.51rub
1. Reinforced concrete construction. I. Title.
TA683.2.B37 1977 77–511728

Barashko, Anatoliĭ Sergeevich
see Bogomolov, Anatoliĭ Mikhaĭlovich. Ėksperimenty s avtomatami. 1973.

Barashkov, Georgiĭ Konstantinovich.
(Sravnitel'nai͡a biokhimii͡a vodorosleĭ)
Сравнительная биохимия водорослей. Москва, "Пищевая пром-сть," 1972.
336 p. with diagrs. 21 cm. 1.96rub USSR 72–VKP
At head of title: Г. К. Барашков.
Table of contents also in English.
Bibliography: p. 294–335.
1. Algae. 2. Botanical chemistry. I. Title.
QK565.B32 73–325165

Barashkov, German Timofeevich.
Sovetskai͡a sot͡sialisticheskai͡a demokratii͡a. [By] G.T. Barashkov. Moskva, Znanie, 1972.
63 p. (Novoe v zhizni, nauke, tekhnike. Serii͡a Gosudarstvo i pravo, 8)
1. Communist state. 2. Russia (1917-)—Govt.
MH NUC74-21556

Barashkov, N.M.
see Leningrad. Vsesoi͡uznyĭ geologicheskiĭ institut. Geologicheskai͡a karta SSSR, 1965. Moskva, Vsesoi͡uznyĭ aerogeologicheskiĭ trest, 1968.

Barashkov, Petr Petrovich.
(Sakha tylyn kylgas terminologicheckaĭ tyld'yta)
Саха тылын кылгас терминологическай тылдьыта / П. П. Барашков ; редактор Л. Н. Харитонов. — Якутскай : Саха сиринээҕи киниге издательствата, 1955.
299 p. ; 13 cm.
At head of title: ССРС наукаларын академията. Саха сиринээҕи филиал. Тыл, литература уонна история института.
Added t. p.: Краткий терминологический словарь якутского языка.
1. Russian language—Dictionaries—Yakut. I. Kharitonov, L. N., ed. II. Title. III. Title: Kratkiĭ terminologicheskiĭ slovar' i͡akutskogo i͡azyka.
PL363.Б3 74–237284

Barashkova, E A
Seasonal development of reindeer fodder lichens cladonia. New Delhi, Indian National Scientific Documentation Center, 1968.
6 p. (English translation of miscellaneous zoological literature no. 81)
Translated from: Moscow. Vsesoiuznyi nauchno-issledovatel'skii Institut sel'skogo khoziaistva Krainego-Severa. Trudy, no. 12, p. 141-144, 1963.
1. Reindeer–Food.
DI NUC75-108708

Barashkova, Elena Pavlovna, ed.
see Rukovodstvo gidrometeorologicheskim stant͡sii͡am po aktinometricheskim nabli͡udenii͡am. 1973.

Barashnev, I͡Uriĭ Ivanovich.
(Nasledstvennost' i zdorov'e)
Наследственность и здоровье / Ю. И. Барашнев. — Москва : Знание, 1976.
94 p. : ill. ; 21 cm. — (Наука и прогресс) USSR***
Series romanized: Nauka i progress.
0.18rub
1. Medical genetics. 2. Human genetics. I. Title.
RB155.B24 77–507875

Barasoain, Alberto.
Fray Luis de León. [Madrid] Ediciones Júcar [1973]
259 p. plates. 18 cm. (Colección Los Poetas, 5) Sp***
"Antología poética": p. [127]–237.
Bibliography: p. 253–254.
1. León, Luis Ponce de, 1528?–1591. I. León, Luis Ponce de, 1528?–1591. Poems. 1973.
PQ6410.L3B3 1973 74–304396
ISBN 84-334-0059-254

Barass, Reitzel & Associates.
A study of exemplary public library reading and reading-related programs for children, youth, and adults. Prepared for the Office of Education, U.S. Department of Health, Education and Welfare. Cambridge [Washington, Educational Resources Information Center] 1972.
v, 207 l. 28 cm. (ERIC reports)
1. Libraries and readers. 2. Public libraries. I. Title.
TU NUC75-100048

Barassin, A., joint author
see Barassin, Jacqueline. Problèmes, thermo-dynamique chimique et cinétique chimique. Paris, Centre de documentation universitaire, 1968.

Barassin, Jacqueline.
Problèmes, thermo-dynamique chimique et cinétique chimique, par J. Barassin, ... et A. Barassin, ... Paris, Centre de documentation universitaire, 1968.
179 p. illus. 27 cm. F 69-10186
At head of title: Certificat C 1 de la maîtrise de chimie. Chimie physique générale.
17.00F
1. Chemical reaction, Rate of—Problems, exercises, etc. 2. Thermodynamics—Problems, exercises, etc. I. Barassin, A., joint author. II. Title.
QD502.B36 74–356193

Barat, Antonio, joint author.
see Oliva, Horacio, fl. 1975- Patología del glomérulo renal ... Barcelona, Salvat, c1975.

Barát, Arnošt.
Boj proti alkoholizmu v právnej úprave / ₍zost. a úvod nap. Arnošt Barát₎. — 1. vyd. — Bratislava : Obzor, 1974.
71 p. ; 15 cm. — (Edícia Právo pre každého) CzS 74
Includes legislation.
Kčs7.00
1. Alcoholics—Law and legislation—Czechoslovak Republic. I. Title.
75-589776

Barát, Arnošt.
see Czechoslovakia. Laws, statutes, etc. Občanský soudní řád. Slovak. Občiansky súdny poriadok ; Notársky poriadok a súvisiace predpisy. 1. vyd. Bratislava, Obzor, 1976.

Barát, Arnošt
see Trestný zákon, trestný poriadok a s nimi súvisiace predpisy. Bratislava : Obzor, 1975.

Barát, Endre.
Alvó Vénusz : regény Lotz Károly életéről / Barát Endre. — ₍Budapest₎ : Corvina, 1974.
302 p., ₍8₎ leaves of plates : ill. (some col.) ; 21 cm.
ISBN 963-13-0721-2
1. Lotz, Károly, 1833-1904—Fiction. I. Title.
PH3213.B2927A8 75-585439

Barát, Endre.
Bátrak krónikája. ₍Budapest₎ Kossuth Könyvkiadó, 1962.
143 p. illus. 20 cm.
I. Title.
PH3213.B2927B3 67-117858

Barát, Endre.
Delfin követi a hajót / Barát Endre. — Budapest : Szépirodalmi Könyvkiadó, 1975.
304 p. ; 19 cm.
ISBN 963-15-0428-X : 23.00Ft
I. Title.
PH3213.B2927D4 76-526869

Barat, Endre.
Egy asszony vallomása / Barát Endre. — Budapest : Magvető Könyvkiadó, 1974.
231 p., ₍1₎ leaf of plates : port. ; 21 cm.
CONTENTS: Egy asszony vallomása.—Fájdalom.—Lidércnyomás.
20.00Ft
I. Title.
PH3213.B2927A9 75-528965

Barát, Endre.
Élt harminchárom évet : regény Paál László életéről / Barát Endre. — ₍Budapest₎ : Corvina, c1972.
255 p., ₍4₎ leaves of plates : col. ill. ; 21 cm.
1. Paál, László, 1846-1879—Fiction. I. Title.
PH3213.B2927E4 76-528248

Barát, Endre.
Hajnalban indultak el; regény. ₍Budapest₎ Athenaeum ₍1950?₎
358 p. 21 cm.
I. Title.
PH3213.B2927H3 55-25970

Barát, Endre.
Lidérc. Budapest, Magvető, 1965.
256 p. port. 20 cm.
I. Title.
PH3213.B2927L5 73-252867

Barat, George.
Age knows no sex; an integrative, metabolic aspect of aging. ₍New York, American Press Publications, c1969₎
xvi, 216 p. 21 cm.
Bibliography: p. 213-216.
1. Aging. I. Title.
CaBVaU NUC74-122549

Barat, George.
Rejuvenation; dietary and biochemical-therapeutical approaches to the prevention of premature aging. Beverly Hills, Calif., Neuroendocrine Research Center, c1970.
99 p.
Includes bibliography.
1. Rejuvenation. I. Neuroendocrine Research Center. II. Title.
MiEM OC NUC75-105475

Barat, Johann
see
Worath, Johann, 1609-1680.

Barat, Josef.
Estrutura metropolitana e sistema de transportes : estudo do caso do Rio de Janeiro / Josef Barat. — Rio de Janeiro : IPEA-/INPES, 1975.
xxiii, 292 p. : ill. ; 21 cm. — (Monografia - Instituto de Planejamento Econômico e Social, Instituto de Pesquisas ; no. 20)
Originally presented as the author's thesis, Universidade Federal do Rio de Janeiro, 1974.
Bibliography: p. 285-292.
1. Urban transportation—Brazil—Rio de Janeiro metropolitan area. 2. Traffic surveys—Brazil—Rio de Janeiro metropolitan area. 3. Urban transportation. I. Title. II. Series: Instituto de Planejamento Econômico e Social. Instituto de Pesquisas. Monografia ; no. 20.
HE311.B722R562 76-472635
76 MARC

Barat, Josef.
see Política de desenvolvimento urbano, aspectos metropolitanos e locais. Rio de Janeiro, IPEA/INPES, 1976.

Barat, S K
A fundamental study of the chemical and physical changes taking place in the rapid tannage of heavy leather to obtain information pertinent to the development of new rapid tanning processes; final technical report. Adyar, Madras, Central Leather Research Institute, [1971 ?]
115 p.
Grant no. FG-In-247, Project no. UR-A7-(60)-92.
Bibliography: p. 113-115.
1. Leather. Research. 2. Tanning. 3. Leather industry and trade. I. United States. Agricultural Research Service. Far Eastern Regional Research Office. II. Madras. Central Leather Research Institute. III. Title.
DNAL NUC73-105652

Barát, Tamás
see 25 [i.e. Huszonöt] éves a Chemolimpex, 1949-1974. Budapest : Chemolimpex, 1974.

Barata, Cipriano Nunes.
A indústria dos detergentes em Portugal : estudio histórico-económico / por Cipriano Nunes Barata. — Lisboa : Instituto do Azeite e Produtos Oleaginosos, 1974-
v. ; 21 cm.
1. Soap trade—History. 2. Synthetic detergents industry—History. 3. Soap trade—Portugal. 4. Synthetic detergents industry—Portugal. I. Title.
HD9999.S7B37 76-464917
76 MARC

Barata, Francesc Garriga i
see Garriga i Barata, Francesc.

Barata, Francisco José Rodrigues
see Rodrigues Barata, Francisco José.

Barata, Joaquim de Magalhães Cardoso, 1888-1957
see Estrada de Ferro de Bragança. Dados historicos... Pará [i.e. Belém] Tavares Cardoso, 1934.

Barata, José Bernardo
see Mozambique. Laws, statutes, etc. Educação e ensino... 2. ed. [Lourenço Marques, Minerva Central] 1973.

Barata, Júlio de Carvalho, 1905-
O trabalhador e a revolução. ₍Rio de Janeiro₎ Conselho Nacional do Serviço Social da Indústria, 1970.
30 p. port. 22 cm.
1. Labor policy — Brazil — Addresses, essays, lectures. 2. Trade-unions—Brazil—Addresses, essays, lectures. I. Title.
HD8286.5.B35 74-208356

Barata, Júlio de Carvalho, 1905-
A política social da revolução ₍por Júlio Barata₎ Brasília, Ministério do Trabalho e Previdência Social, 1972.
173 p. 22 cm.
Addresses.
1. Labor policy—Brazil—Addresses, essays, lectures. 2. Insurance, Social—Brazil—Addresses, essays, lectures. 3. Trade-unions—Brazil—Addresses, essays, lectures. I. Title.
HD8286.5.B34 74-203067

Barata, Julio de Carvalho, 1905-
see Brazil. Presidente, 1969- (Médici) Discursos de posse. [Rio de Janeiro, 1969]

Barata, Manuel.
Formação histórica do Pará; obras reunidas ₍por₎ Manoel Barata. ₍Belém₎ Universidade Federal do Pará, 1973.
376 p. port. 21 cm. (Coleção Amazônica. Série José Veríssimo)
"Edição comemorativa do sesquicentenário da adesão do Pará à independência política do Brasil."
Includes bibliographical references.
1. Pará, Brazil (State)—History—Addresses, essays, lectures. I. Title.
F2586.B22 73-221556

Barata, Maria do Rosario de Sampaio Themudo.
Rui Fernandes de Almada; diplomata portugûes do seculo XVI. Lisboa, 1971-73.
421 p. illus.
"Resumos e índice onomástico, toponímico e ideográfico" (p. 365-421) has imprint: Coimbra 1973.
Includes bibliography.
1. Almada, Rui Fernandes de.
MoSW NUC75-26693

Barata, Mário.
Escola Politécnica do Largo de São Francisco; berço da engenharia brasileira. Rio de Janeiro, Associação dos Antigos Alunos da Politécnica, Clube de Engenharia, 1973.
112 p. illus. 28 cm.
Includes bibliographical references.
1. Rio de Janeiro. Universidade Federal. Escola de Engenharia. I. Title.
T173.R647B37 73-221895

Barata, Mário.
Igreja da Ordem 3a. ₍i.e. Terceira₎ da Penitência do Rio de Janeiro / Mário Barata ; fotos de Marcel Gautherot. — Rio de Janeiro : AGIR, 1975.
76 p. : ill. (some col.) ; 23 cm. — (Arte no Brasil ; 3)
Bibliography: p. 76.
Cr$45.00
1. Convento de Santo Antonio. I. Title.
NA5357.R5B37 77-456532
77 MARC

Barata, Mário.
Poder e independência no Grão-Pará, 1820-1823 : gênese, estrutura e fatos de um conflito político / Mário Barata. — Belém : Conselho Estadual de Cultura, 1973-1974 i.e. 1975.
246 p. ; 24 cm. — (Série Arthur Vianna) (Coleção História do Pará)
Includes bibliographical references.
1. Pará, Brazil (State)—History. 2. Brazil—History—1822-1889. 3. Brazil—History—1763-1821. I. Title.
F2586.B225 77-469401
77 MARC

Barata, Oscar Soares.
Aspectos das condições demográficas de Angola. Lisboa, Universidade Técnica de Lisboa, 1964.
22 p. 24 cm.
Microfiche (neg.) 1 sheet. 11 x 15 cm. (NYPL FSN 16,457)
"Lição proferida no curso de extensão universitária sobre Angola, organizado pelo Instituto Superior de Ciências Sociais e Política Ultramarina da Universidade Técnica de Lisboa, no ano lectivo de 1963-64."
1. Angola—Population. I. Title.
NN NUC76-74969

Barata, Oscar Soares.
Introdução à demografia. Prefácio do Prof. Doutor Adriano Moreira. Lisboa, Instituto superior de ciências sociais e politica ultramarina, 1968.
xxiv, 486 p.
Bibliography: p. 477-486.
1. Demography. I. Title.
CLU NUC74-122552

Barata Salgueiro, Teresa
see
Salgueiro, Teresa Barata.

Baratakesawa, Faqier 'Abdu'l Haqq
see
Haqq, Faqier 'Abdu'l.

Baratashvili, Dmitriĭ Ivanovich.
(Sot͡sialisticheskie i molodye nat͡sional'nye gosudarstva)
Социалистические и молодые национальные государства. (Междунар.-правовые принципы сотрудничества). Москва, "Междунар. отношения," 1973.
165 p. 19 cm. 0.55rub — USSR 73
At head of title: Институт государства и права АН СССР. Д. И. Бараташвили.
Includes bibliographical references.
1. Russia—Foreign relations—1953– 2. Underdeveloped areas—Foreign relations. 3. Communist countries—Foreign relations. I. Title.
JX1395.B29 — 74–335559

Baratashvili, Nikolaĭ Melitonovich, kni͡az', 1816-1845.
Sochinenii͡a. Tbilisi, "Sabchota sakartvelo", 1968.
285 p.
Title in Russian from colophon; t.p. and text in Georgian.
InU — NUC76-3972

Baratashvili, Nikolaĭ Melitonovich, kni͡az', 1816-1845.
Stikhi. Perevod s gruzinskogo Borisa Pasternaka. Moskva, Gos izd-vo khudozh. lit-ry, 1957.
86 p. 15 cm.
At head of title: Nikolaĭ Baratashvili.
1. Georgian literature—Translations into Russian. 2. Russian literature—Translations from Georgian.
NBuU — NUC74-21966

Baratashvili, Nikolaĭ Melitonovich, kni͡az', 1816–1845.
(Stikhotvorenii͡a)
Стихотворения.—Поэма ["Судьба Грузии". Для старш. возраста]. Перевод с груз. М. Дудина. [Предисл. К. Кулиева . Примеч. Г. Цуриковой. Грав. А. Коковкина. Ленинград, "Дет. лит.," Ленингр. отд-ние, 1972].
95 p. with illus. 17 cm. 0.26rub — USSR 72–VKP
I. Dudin, Mikhail Aleksandrovich, 1916– tr.
PK9169.B33S8 1972 — 74–341714

Baratech, Carlos E Corona
see Corona Baratech, Carlos E 1917-

Baratelia, Nuri
see
Barathelia, Nuri.

Baratelii͡a, Nuri Takhut͡sovich
see
Barathelia, Nuri.

Baratella, Paolo, 1935–
Paolo Baratella. Galleria Toninelli, Milano 17. Januar bis 11. Februar 1973. Galerie Poll, Berlin 14. März bis 21. April 1973. Kunstverein München, München 25. April bis 20. Mai 1973. Palais des Beaux Arts, Bruxelles 23. Mai bis 25. Juni 1973. Mailand, Toninelli arte moderna [1973]
[91] p. (chiefly illus.) 22 cm. — It***
Stamped on t. p.: Supplied by World Wide Books, Boston.
1. Photography, Documentary—Exhibitions. I. Galleria Toninelli.
TR820.5.B37 — 74–356707

Baratelli, Franco Micali
see Micali Baratelli, Franco.

Barath, F.T., ed.
see Symposium on Radar and Radiometric Observations of Venus During the 1962 Conjunction. [Papers] Pasadena, Jet Propulsion Laboratory, California Institute of Technology, 1964.

Baráth, Kata Értavy
see Értavy Baráth, Kata.

Baráth, Lajos.
A félelem földje / Baráth Lajos. — Budapest : Magvető Könyvkiadó, 1975.
473 p. : ill. ; 19 cm.
ISBN 963–270–007–4 : 28.50Ft
1. Császár, Péter—Fiction. 2. Nagy, Ambrus—Fiction. I. Title.
PH3213.B2933F4 — 76–529379

Baráth, Lajos.
Örökség : regény / Baráth Lajos. — Budapest : Szépirodalmi Könyvkiadó, c1976.
369 p. ; 19 cm.
ISBN 963–15–0647–9 : 27.00Ft
I. Title.
PH3213.B2933O3 — 77–504963

Barath, Robert M
Interaction strategies of U.S. development agencies (state) and perceptions of selected reverse investors of U.S. investment attraction programs. Kent, 1974.
1 v.
Thesis—Kent State University.
1. Investments, Foreign. 2. International business enterprises. 3. Corporations, International. I. Title.
OKentU — NUC76-23061

Baráth, Tibor.
A külföldi magyarság ideológiája : történetpolitikai tanulmányok / Baráth Tibor. -- Montreal : Baráth Tibor, 1975.
242 p. : ill., maps, ports.
1. Hungarians in foreign countries. I. Title.
CaOTU — NUC77-88652

Baráth, Tibor.
Tájékoztató az újabb magyar östörténeti kutatásokról. Montreal [T. Baráth] 1973.
55 p. maps. 22 cm.
Cover title.
Bibliography: p. 53-54.
1. Hungary—History—to 894. 2. Hungary—History—Historiography. 3. Magyars. I. Title.
IEN — NUC76-74993

Baraṭhākura, Himendra Kumāra
see
Barthakur, Himendra Kumar.

Barathelia, Nuri.
(Ashẇaphsh' iaphylaz)
Ашәапшь иапылаз. Аҟуа, "Алашара," 1971.
116 p. 21 cm. 0.17rub — USSR 71–16195
I. Title.
PZ90.A2B3 — 73–366076

Barathová, Nora, 1944–
Muž, ktorý kráčal za smrťou / Nora Baráthová ; [ob. a väzbu navrhol Michal Lacko]. — 1. vyd. — Košice : Východoslovenské vydavateľstvo, 1975.
227 p. : ill. ; 21 cm. — (Pôvodná tvorba) — CzS 75
Kčs17.00
I. Title.
PG5439.12.A68M89 — 77–502572

Baratier, Édouard.
Histoire de Marseille, publiée sous la direction d'Édouard Baratier. [Toulouse] Privat [1973]
512 p. illus. 24 cm. (Univers de la France et des pays francophones. Série Histoire des villes) 80.00F — F***
Includes bibliographies.
1. Marseille—History. I. Title.
DC801.M36B35 — 944'.91 — 73–173125 MARC

Baratier, Édouard.
see Histoire de la Provence et civilisation médiévale ... [s.l., s.n., 1973] (Marseille : Impr. S.-Victor)

Baratier, Édouard
see Provence, Comtat Venaissin, principauté d'Orange, comté de Nice, principauté de Monaco. Paris, A. Colin, 1969.

Baratieri, Antonio
see European Organization for Research on Flourine and Dental Caries Prevention. Test de la carie dentaire... Pavia, Clinique dentaire de l'Université de Pavia, 1962.

Baraton, Danielle.
La Fâcheuse montagne : Sancerre, 1572-1573 : roman / Danielle Baraton. — Saint-Amand-Montrond (14, rue Guillon, 18200) : D. Baraton, 1976.
281 p. : maps ; 27 cm. — F76-13238
Two hundred copies printed. No. 171.
42.00F
1. Sancerre, France—Siege, 1573—Fiction. I. Title.
PQ2662.A63F3 — 843'.9'14 77 — 77-457253 MARC

Baratono, John R.
see Martin Marietta Corporation. Denver Division. Architectural/environmental handbook... Washington, Manned Spacecraft Center of the National Aeronautics and Space Administration, 1970.

Barátos, Endre, 1913–1943.
"A haza itt a vesztes" : Barátos Endre válogatott versei / az életrajzot írta és a verseket válogatta, Kellner Bernát. — Kaposvár : Palmiro Togliatti Megyei Könyvtár, 1975.
72 p., [1] leaf of plates : port. ; 25 cm.
Includes bibliographical references and index.
ISBN 963–7551–01–8
I. Title.
PH3213.B2934H3 1975 — 75–410416

Baratov, Anatoliĭ Nikolaevich
see Problems in combustion and extinguishment ... Amerind Pub. Co., 1974.

Baratov, K B
see
Barotov, K B

Baratov, Mubin B.
see Iz istorii progressivnoĭ obshchestvennoĭ i fibosofskoĭ mysli v Indii. 1976.

Baratov, P
Ўрта Осиёнинг табиий сув лабораторияси. Тошкент, "Фан," 1968.
50 p. with illus. and maps. 20 cm. 0.10rub — USSR 69–7224
At head of title: П. Баратов.
Bibliography: p. [49]
1. Glaciers—Soviet Central Asia. I. Title.
Title romanized: Ŭrta Osiëning tabiiĭ suv laboratorii͡asi.
GB2556.S6B3 — 72–340252

Baratov, P., ed.
see Ocherki geografii Sredneĭ Azii. Tashkent, Fan, 1966.

Baratov, Rauf Baratovich.
(Dat͡sit-liparitovai͡a format͡sii͡a I͡Uzhnogo Gissara)
Дацит-липаритовая формация Южного Гиссара. Под ред. акад. Р. Б. Баратова. Душанбе, "Дониш," 1973.
132 p. with illus. and maps. 25 cm. 1.60rub — USSR 73
At head of title: Академия наук Таджикской ССР. Институт геологии. Министерство геологии СССР. Всесоюзный научно-исследовательский геологический институт. Р. Б. Баратов, Е. Н. Горецкая, С. И. Шукин.
Bibliography: p. 127–[131]
1. Rocks, Igneous. 2. Petrology—Russia—Gissar Range. I. Goret͡skai͡a, Evgenii͡a Nikolaevna, joint author. II. Shchukin, Sergeĭ Ivanovich, joint author. III. Title.
QE461.B275 — 73–360282

Baratov, Rauf Baratovich, ed.
see Sredneaziatskoe regional'noe petrograficheskoe soveshchanie, 2d, Dushanbe, 1971.
Materialy Vtorogo sredneaziatskogo regional'nogo petrograficheskogo soveshchanii͡a. 1971.

Baratov, Sharif.
(Podkozhnye ovoda krupnogo rogatogo skota v Tadzhikistane)
Подкожные овода крупного рогатого скота в Таджикистане / Ш. Баратов. — Душанбе : Дониш, 1972.
137 p., 1 fold. leaf : ill. ; 26 cm. — USSR 72
At head of title: Академия наук Таджикской ССР. Институт зоологии и паразитологии им. акад. Е. Н. Павловского.
Added t. p. in Tajik.
Bibliography: p. 133–137.
0.72rub
1. Warble-flies—Control—Tajikistan. 2. Cattle—Tajikistan. I. Title.
SF967.W3B37 — 75–569711

Barafs, German Markovich, 1855-1922.
Sobranie trudov po voprosu o evreĭskom ėlementie v pamiatnikakh drevne-russkoĭ pis'mennosti. Parizh, 1924-27 [v. 1, 1927, 1972]
2 v. ports. 25 cm.
Photocopy. Ann Arbor, Mich., University Microfilms, 1972. 21 cm.
Vol. 1 in 2 pts., each with separate t.p.: v. 2, Berlin, 1924, has also special t.p.: O sostaviteliakh "Povfesti vremennykh lfet" i eia istochnikakh, preimushchestvenno evreĭskikh.
1. Literature, Comparative—Church Slavic and Hebrew. 2. Literature, Comparative—Hebrew and Church Slavic. 3. Church Slavic literature—Hist. & crit.
MdU NUC74-114668

Barafs, Isaak Seminovich, joint author
see Kulish, Grigoriĭ Prokof'evich. Khoziaĭstvennyĭ raschet v chernoĭ metallurgii. 1973.

Barats, Leon G
Tolstoĭ i evrei. Monte Carlo, 1961.
19 p.
Cover title also in French.
1. Tolstoĭ, Lev Nikolaevich, graf, 1828-1910. 2. Jewish question. I. Title.
NcU NUC74-45557

Barafs, Vladimir Aleksandrovich.
(Vodosnabzhenie sudov rechnogo flota)
Водоснабжение судов речного флота / В. А. Барац, М. В. Николаев, Л. И. Эльпинер ; под общей ред. В. А. Бараца. — Москва : Транспорт, 1974.
143 p. : ill. ; 22 cm. USSR***
0.50rub
1. Ships—Water-supply. 2. Inland waterway vessels. I. Nikolaev, Mikhail Vladimirovich. II. Ėl'piner, Leonid Itskovich. III. Title.
VM503.B37 75-558212

Barafs, Vladimir Isaakovich, joint author
see Isaev, Vasiliĭ Vasil'evich. (Za chistoe nebo) 1975.

Baratta, Alessandro.
Positivismo giuridico e scienza del diritto penale; aspetti teoretici e ideologici dello sviluppo della scienza penalistica tedesca dall'inizio del secolo al 1933. Milano, Giuffrè, 1966.
13 p. 25 cm. (Università degli studi di Camerino. Biblioteca degli Annali della Facoltà giuridica, 3)
Includes bibliographical references.
1. Law—Philosophy. 2. Criminal law—Germany. I. Title. II. Series: Camerino. Università. Facoltà giuridica. Annali. Biblioteca, 3.
75-543274

Baratta, Frank Salvador.
Normative and bargaining behaviors in married couples / by Frank Salvador Baratta. -- [s.l. : s.n.], 1976.
viii, 304 leaves ; 29 cm.
Thesis--Harvard.
Bibliography: leaves 213-221.
1. Interpersonal relations.
MH NUC77-85430

Baratta, José do Carmo.
Escola de heróis; o Colégio de N. S. das Graças, o Seminário de Olinda. Recife, Comissão Estadual das Comemorações do Sesquicentenário da Independência, 1972.
96 p. 23 cm.
Bibliography: p. [95]-96.
1. Colégio de Nossa Senhora das Graças. 2. Seminário de Olinda. I. Title.
BX920.O44B37 74-200282

Baratta, Mario, 1868-1935.
Piccolo atlante storico [di] M. Baratta, P. Fraccaro [e] L. Visintin. 62 tavole, 135 carte e cartine con testi descrittivi e indice dei nomi. Novara, Istituto geografico De Agostini [1973]
1 v. (various pagings) col. maps. 27 cm. L1800 It***
1. Geography, Historical—Maps. I. Fraccaro, Plinio, 1883- II. Visintin, Luigi. III. Title.
G1030.B35 1973 911 74-650114

Baratta, M'Lynn.
Love in freefall / M'Lynn Baratta ; photos. by Allen Silver. — Millbrae, Calif. : Celestial Arts, 1974.
[64] p. : ill. ; 22 cm.
Poems.
ISBN 0-912310-83-9 : $2.95
I. Title.
PS3552.A5917L6 811'.5'4 74-10122
MARC

Baratta, Vincenzo. La natura giuridica della funzione notarile
see Buttitta, Giacomo. Il notariato nella società moderna e le sue funzioni. Palermo, Edizioni giuridiche italiane [1966]

Baratta-Lorton, Mary.
Utilization of the Delphi technique to weight program evaluation criteria in vocational education. [n.p.] 1974.
314 l.
Thesis-Ohio State University.
Bibliography: leaves 308-314.
1. Vocational education-Curricula. I. Title.
OU NUC76-22871

Baratta-Lorton, Mary.
Workjobs; activity-centered learning for early childhood education [by] Mary Baratta-Lorton. Menlo Park, Calif., Addison-Wesley Pub. Co. [1972]
255 p. illus. 28 cm. (Addison-Wesley innovative series)
1. Activity programs in education—Handbooks, manuals, etc. 2. Handicraft—Handbooks, manuals, etc. 3. Education, Primary—1945- I. Title.
LB1027.B2549 372.1'3 78-185015
72[r76]rev MARC

Baratta-Lorton, Mary.
Workjobs ... for parents : activity-centered learning in the home / Mary Baratta-Lorton. — Menlo Park, Calif. : Addison-Wesley Pub. Co., c1975.
115 p. : ill. ; 28 cm. — (Addison-Wesley innovative series)
"A selection of activities from Workjobs : activity-centered learning for early childhood education."
1. Activity programs in education—Handbooks, manuals, etc. 2. Handicraft—Handbooks, manuals, etc. I. Title.
LB1027.B255 372.5'5 74-15526
76 MARC

Baratte, François.
Recherches archéologiques à Haïdra. Miscellanea I. Les mosaïques trouvées sous la Basilique I: Mosaïque d'Ulysse [et] Mosaïque fleurie. [Rome, Tip. s. Pio X, 1974]
61 p. 23 illus. 28 cm. (Collection de l'École française de Rome, 17)
At head of title: Recherches d'archéologie africaine publiées par L'Institut national d'archéologie et d'arts de Tunis et l'École française de Rome.
Bibliographical footnotes.
1. Mosaics—Tunisia. 2. Mosaics, Roman. I. Title. II. Series: École française de Rome. Collection, 17.
MdU NUC76-23343

Baratte, François.
see La Normandie souterraine ... Rouen, Musée départemental des antiquités, [1976?-

Baratte, Thérèse
see
Baratte-Eno Belinga, Thérèse.

Baratte-Eno Belinga, Thérèse.
Bibliographie: auteurs africains et malgaches de langue française. Paris, Office de coopération radiophonique, 1965.
50 p. 24 cm.
1. French literature—African authors—Bibliography. 2. French literature—Malagasy authors—Bibliography. I. Office de coopération radiophonique. II. Title.
Z3508.L5B35 72-222315
rev

Baratte-Eno Belinga, Thérèse.
Bibliographie: auteurs africains et malgaches de langue francaise. 2. ed., revue et mise à jour. Paris, Office de cooperation radiophonique (Ocora) 1968.
78 p. 23 cm.
1. French literature—African authors—Bibl. I. Title. II. Title: Auteurs africains et malgaches de langue francaise.
CaQMM NUC73-126144

Baratte-Eno Belinga, Thérèse.
Bibliographie, auteurs africains et malgaches de langue française [par] Thérèse Baratte-Eno Belinga; avec la collaboration du Service Études et documentation, O. R. T. F.-D. A. E. C., [Office de radiodiffusion télévision française -Direction des affaires extérieures et de la coopération]. 3e éd. revue et mise à jour. Paris, O. R. T. F.; Paris (38, rue Saint-Sulpice, 75006) 1972.
vi, 124 p. 23 cm. 10.00F F 73-3938
1. French literature—African authors—Bibliography. 2. French literature—Malagasy authors—Bibliography. I. Title.
Z3508.L5B35 1972 73-354595
MARC

Baratte-Eno Belinga, Thérèse
see Chateh, Peter. Catalogue des mémoires... [Yaoundé] 1974.

Baratte-Eno Belinga, Thérèsa, joint author.
see Chateh, Peter. Guide des bibliothèques et centres de documentation de Yaoundé. [Yaoundé] Université de Yaoundé, Service central des bibliothèques, 1973.

Baratti, Achille.
Il mito della V nera. A cura di: Achille Baratti, Renato Lemmi Gigli. Bologna, Poligrafici L. Parma, 1972.
574 p. illus. 29 cm. N. T. It 73-July
1. Società di educazione fisica Virtus. I. Lemmi Gigli, Renato, joint author. II. Title.
GV204.I 83S582 74-309455

Baratti, Carlo.
Figure e realtà: (parabole del vangelo) Carlo Baratti. Milano, Editrice Ancora, 1961.
183 p. 20 cm. (Collana "Pagina sacra")
1. Jesus Christ–Parables. 2. Bible–Parables. I. Title.
MCW NUC76-62500

Barattieri, Vittorio.
Le banche di sviluppo nei paesi emergenti. Milano, A. Giuffrè, 1972.
vii, 86 p. 25 cm. (Pubblicazioni dell'Istituto di politica economica e finanziaria della Facoltà di economica e commercio dell'Università di Roma, 15) L1500 It 72-Oct
Bibliography: p. [81]-86.
1. Development banks. 2. Underdeveloped areas—Finance. I. Title. II. Series: Rome (City). Università. Istituto di politica economica e finanziaria. Pubblicazioni, 15.
HG4517.B27 72-362693

Barattini, Luis P
Catalogo de las aves uruguayas por Luis P. Barattini & Rodolfo Escalante. Montevideo, Intendencia Municipal de Montevideo, Dirección de Divulgación Científica, 1958-
v. illus. (some col.) 24 cm. (Museo Damaso Antonio Larrañaga Publicaciones Cientificas: Serie, La fauna indígena)
Contents: pt. 1. Falconiformes.—pt. 2. Anseriformes.
1. Birds—Uruguay. I. Escalante, Rodolfo, 1911- joint author. II. Title.
NcU NUC76-62415

Baratto, Anna Fontes-
see Fontes-Baratto, Anna.

Baratto, Mario, 1920-
La commedia del Cinquecento : (aspetti e problemi) / Mario Baratto. — 2. ed. — Vicenza : N. Pozza, 1977.
157 p. ; 23 cm. — (Nuova biblioteca di cultura ; 36) It77-Mar
Includes index.
L3000
1. Italian drama (Comedy)—History and criticism. 2. Italian drama—To 1700—History and criticism. I. Title.
PQ4149.B35 1977 77-474995
*77 MARC

Baratto, Mario, 1920-
Teatro y luchas sociales (Ruzante, Aretino, Goldoni). Prefacio de Jaume Fuster. [Traducción de Jaume Fuster y M. A. Oliver] (Barcelona) Península [1971]
325 p., 1 l. 20 cm. (Historia, ciencia, sociedad, 74) 250ptas
Sp 71-July/Aug/Sept
Translation of Tre saggi sul teatro.
Includes bibliographical references.
1. Italian drama (Comedy)—History and criticism. 2. Aretino, Pietro, 1492-1556. 3. Beolco, Angelo, called Ruzzante, 1502?-1542. 4. Goldoni, Carlo, 1707-1793. I. Title.
PQ4135.B318 73-321881

Baratto, Mario, 1920-
Tre saggi sul teatro: Ruzante, Aretino, Goldoni. [2. edizione. Venezia] N. Pozza [1971]
239 p. 22 cm. (Collana di varia critica, v. 23)
First published in 1964, under title Tre studi sul teatro.
1. Beolco, Angelo, called Ruzzante, 1502?-1542. 2. Aretino, Pietro, 1492-1556. 3. Goldoni, Carlo, 1707-1793. I. Title.
FU NUC73-116627

Baratto, Mario, 1920-
see Un Teatro per una nuova società. [Venezia], Stamperia di Venezia, 1969.

Baratto, Sergio.
Problemi e metodi della educazione estetica / Sergio Baratto. — Padova : Liviana, 1974.
vi, 336 p., [4] leaves of plates : ill. ; 21 cm. — (Pubblicazioni dell'Istituto di pendagogie. Università di Padova) It 76–Jan
Bibliography : p. [325]–330.
Includes index.
L5000
1. Arts—Study and teaching. I. Title.
NX280.B37 76–510144

Baratynskiĭ, Evgeniĭ Abramovich, 1800–1844.
(E. A. Boratynskiĭ)
Е. А. Боратынскій; матеріалы къ его біографін. Изъ Татевскаго архива Рачинскихъ. Съ введеніемъ и примечаніями Ю. Верховскаго. Петроградъ, Тип. Имп. Академіи наукъ, 1916.
152 p. illus., facsims., ports. 27 cm.
Russian and French.
—— —— Microfilm. 1 reel. 35 mm.
Microfilm Slavic 8260 PG
1. Baratynskiĭ, Evgeniĭ Abramovich, 1800–1844. I. Verkhovskiĭ, ÎUriĭ Nikandrovich, 1878– ed.
PG3321.B3A6 1916 78–236619

Baratynskiĭ, Evgeniĭ Abramovich, 1800–1844.
Selected letters of Evgenij Baratynskij. [By] G. R. Barratt. The Hague, Mouton, 1973.
131 p. 25 cm. (Slavistic printings and reprintings, 280)
Ne 73–32
Includes bibliographical references.
I. Barratt, G. R., ed. II. Series.
PG3321.B3Z53 1973 891.7'13 [B] 73–78113
MARC

Baratynskiĭ, Evgeniĭ Abramovich, 1800–1844.
Стихотворения. Избр. лирика. [Для сред. и ст. возраста. Предисл. и примеч. С. Бонди. Москва, "Дет. лит.," 1972].
207 p. with illus. 15 cm. (Поэтическая библиотечка школьника)
0.30rub USSR 72–VKP
Title romanized : Stikhotvorenîa.
PG3321.B3S68 1972 74–332198

Baratynskiĭ, Evgeniĭ Abramovich, 1800–1844.
(Stikhotvorenîa)
Стихотворения / Е. А. Баратынский ; [предисл. К. В. Пигарева]. — Москва : Худож. лит., 1974.
127 p. ; 17 cm. — (Народная библиотека) USSR 74
Series romanized : Narodnaîa biblioteka.
0.18rub
PG3321.B3A6 1974b 76–520379

Baratynskiĭ, Evgeniĭ Abramovich, 1800–1844.
(Stikhotvorenîa i poėmy)
Стихотворения и поэмы / Е. А. Баратынский ; [сост., предисл. и примеч. К. В. Пигарева ; ил. Ю. Игнатьев]. — Москва : Дет. лит., 1974.
127 p. : ill. ; 21 cm. — (Школьная библиотека) (Для средней школы) USSR 74
0.28rub
PG3321.B3A6 1974 76–518122

Baratz, Bernard.
Water resource planning in urban redevelopment; final report for U.S. Office of Water Resources Research. Bernard Baratz, principal investigator; Bernard Wachter, project director. Washington, D.C., Wapora inc., 1971.
1 v. illus.
1. Water resources development. 2. Urban renewal. I. Wachter, Bernard. II. Title.
MoU NUC73-116562

Baratz, Bernard, joint author
see Boies, David B Technical and economic evaluations of cooling systems blowdown control techniques. Washington, U.S. Govt. Print. Off., 1973.

Baratz, Joan C
Language and cognitive assessment of Negro children; assumptions and research needs. [Washington, D.C., U.S. Dept. of Health, Education and Welfare, Office of Education, Educational Resources Information Center [1969]
[8] l. 23 x 31 cm. (ED-022-157)
Paper prepared for American Psychological Association, San Francisco, 1968.
Bibliography: leaves [7]-[8]
1. Sociolinguistics. 2. Children–Language. I. Title.
FU NUC75-108806

Baratz, Robert Sears, 1946-
Development of the rat dorsal lingual keratinizing epithelium : morphology and protein biochemistry. -- [s.l. : s.n.], 1975.
1 v.
Thesis (Ph.D.) -- Northwestern University.
1. Keratinization. 2. Epithelium. 3. Tongue. I. Title.
IEN NUC77-83513

Baraúna, Alberto Luiz, 1948-1971.
Quarenta quase sonetos e uma sextantina hexagonal para viola d'amore : obra dedicada ao geômetra do raro e ruivo isóceles perfeito entoada aos anjos de Jorge de Lima / Alberto Luiz Baraúna ; [capa e ilustração de Calasans Neto]. — [Salvador] : Edições Macunaima, 1975.
21 leaves : ill. ; 32 cm.
"Trezentos exemplares, dos quais cem numerados ... Exemplar no." 098.
Issued in portfolio.
Cr$50.00
I. Title.
PQ9698.12.A58Q3 1975 75-519066
75 MARC

Baraúna, Guilherme.
Ensaio crítico sôbre a teoria da co-redemçao receptiva. [n.p., n.d.]
627-45 p. 24 cm.
Offprint from Revista Fclesiástica Brasileira, v. 21, fasc. 3, Set., 1961.
ODaU-M NUC73-105139

Baraúna, Guilherme
see L'Église dans le monde de ce temps; études et commentaires... [Paris] Desclee de Brouwer [1967-

Barausova, Nina Sergeevna
see Kinooborudovanie—kino- i telestudiĭ. 1976.

Baraut, Cebrià.
Santa Maria del Miracle. [Montserrat] Publicaciones de l'Abadia de Montserrat [1972]
44 p. illus. 20 cm. Sp***
1. Santuari de la Mare de Déu del Miracle. I. Title.
NA5811.S67B37 74–326571

Baravāliyā, Gunjana
see
Barvalia, Gunjan.

Baravalle, Hermann von.
Geometric drawing and the Waldorf School plan. 2d. enl. ed. Englewood, N.J., Waldorf School Monographs [1967]
58 p. illus. 23 cm. (Waldorf School monographs)
1. Design. 2. Geometrical drawing. 3. Geometry. I. Series.
NBuC NUC73-2829

Baravalle, Hermann von.
Introduction to physics in the Waldorf Schools; the balance between art and science. 2d enl. ed. Englewood, N.J., Waldorf School Monographs, 1967.
44 p. illus. 23 cm. (Waldorf School monographs)
1. Physics–Study and teaching (Secondary) 2. Adelphi University, Garden City, N.Y. Waldorf School. I. Title. II. Series.
OU MB NUC73-126316

Baravalle, Hermann von.
Perspective drawing. Englewood, N.J., Waldorf School Monographs [c1968]
50 p. illus. 23 cm.
1. Perspective. I. Title.
OU NUC73-42438

Baravalle, Robert, 1891- Theater in Graz.
see Zitzenbacher, Walter. Ein Schauspielhaus für Graz ... Graz, Leykam, c1976.

Baravelli, Maurizio, joint author
see Alberici, Adalberto. Risparmio e casse di risparmio nei paesi africani. Milano, Cassa di risparmio delle provincie lombarde, 1973.

Baravikova, Raisa, 1947–
(Ramonkavy berah)
Рамонкавы бераг : вершы / Раіса Баравікова. — Мінск : Мастацкая, літ-ра, 1974.
79 p. ; 14 cm. — (Першая кніга паэта) USSR***
Series romanized : Pershaîa kniha paėta.
0.60rub
I. Title.
PG2835.2.B33R3 75–544555

Baravykas, Vaclovas.
Trumpas mokyklinis anglų-lietuvių ir lietuvių-anglų kalbų žodynas / sudarė V. Baravykas ir B. Piesarskas. — 3. leidimas. — Kaunas : Šviesa, 1973.
331 p. ; 21 cm. USSR***
0.68rub
1. English language — Dictionaries — Lithuanian. 2. Lithuanian language—Dictionaries—English. I. Piesarskas, Bronius, joint author. II. Title.
PG8679.B3 1973 76–511923

al-Barāwī, Rāshid
see al-Barrāwī, Rāshid.

Baraya, Felix José Lievano
see Lievano Baraya, Felix José.

al-Barāyirī, Ibrāhīm Muḥammad.
(Athar al-ḍarībah fī tawzī' al-dukhūl, wa-al-zakāh ka-badīl lil-ḍarībah)
أثر الضريبة فى توزيع الدخول، والزكاة كبديل للضريبة؛ دراسة مقارنة بالتشريع الاسلامى والقانون الوضعى. تأليف ابراهيم البرايرى. القاهرة، عالم الكتب، 1973.
291 p. 24 cm. £E1.25
Cover title: Tax effect on distribution of incomes, the zakat as substitute of taxes, by I. M. el-Brairy.
Bibliography : p. [279]–288.
1. Taxation. 2. Taxation—Egypt. 3. Zakat. I. Title. II. Title: Tax effect on distribution of incomes, the zakat as substitute of taxes.
HJ2315.B37 73–960249

Baraz, Ḥayim Joseph
see
Barras, Hyman J

Baraz, Vladimir Il'ich.
(Dobycha, podgotovka i transport neftîanogo gaza)
Добыча, подготовка и транспорт нефтяного газа / В. И. Бараз. — Москва : Недра, 1975.
150, [3] p. : ill. ; 22 cm. USSR***
Bibliography : p. [151]–[152]
0.53rub
1. Casinghead gas. I. Title.
TN880.B35 77–504531

Baraza la Taifa la Lugha ya Kiswahili.
Tafsiri za Kiswahili zitumiwazo ofisini na viwandani. — Dar es Salaam : Baraza la Taifa la Lugha ya Kiswahili, 1974.
20 p. ; 21 cm. — (Toleo - Baraza la Taifa la Lugha ya Kiswahili ; 1)
Cover title.
1. Public administration—Dictionaries—Swahili. 2. Swahili language—Dictionaries—English. I. Title. II. Series: Baraza la Taifa la Lugha ya Kiswahili. Toleo - Baraza la Taifa la Lugha ya Kiswahili ; 1.
JA64.S9B37 1974 76–983542

Baraza la Taifa la Lugha ya Kiswahili
see Semina ya Kiswahili, Dar es Salaam, 1970. Mapendekezo na maazimio ya Semina ya Kiswahili iliyofanywa tarehe 5-9 Juni, 1970, Dar ess Salaam, 1973.

Barazangi, Muawia, 1941-
Three studies of the structure and dynamics of the upper mantle adjacent to a descending lithospheric slab. [New York] 1971.
147 l. diagrs., maps. 29 cm.
Thesis—Columbia University.
Bibliography: leaves 44-52, 91-92, 135-142.
1. Seismic waves. 2. Earth—Mantle. 3. Earth movements.
NNC NUC75-21783

Barazar, Usman P
Paganadan, by Usman P. Barazar and Andrada Ditucalan. [Lanao del Sur?] 1961.
10 l. illus. 27 cm. (Philippine adult education series, project no. 1)
Cover title.
1. Primers, Maranao. 2. Maranao language. I. Ditucalan, Andrada. II. Title. III. Series.
NIC NUC75-66310

al-Barāzī, Muḥammad Muḥsin.
دروس في الفقه الروماني ، تأليف محمد محسن البرازى.
الطبعة 2. ‏[دمشق] مطبعة الجامعة السورية ‎-1939.
v. 23 cm.
Includes bibliographical references.
1. Roman law. I. Title.
Title romanized: Durūs fī al-fiqh al-Rūmānī.
76-971115

al-Barāzī, Muḥammad Muḥsin.
محاضرات في الحقوق الرومانية ، القاها على تلامذة الصف الاول من معهد الحقوق بدمشق محمد محسن البرازى. ‏[دمشق] مطبعة الجامعة السورية ‎19.
v. 24 cm.
Includes bibliographical references.
1. Roman law. I. Title.
Title romanized: Muḥāḍarāt fī al-ḥuqūq al-Rūmānīyah.
73-203761

Barazna, L.
see Skaryna, Prantsish, ca. 1490-ca. 1535. Hravîury Frantsyska Skaryny. [Minsk, Belarus', 1972]

Barb, Arthur Lee
see
Barb-Mingo, Arturo, 1944-

Barb, Charles E
Automated street address geocoding systems, their local adaptation and institutionalization, by Charles Elliott Barb, Jr. [Seattle, c1974]
182 l. illus.
Thesis (Ph. D.)—University of Washington.
Bibliography: leaves 181-182.
WaU NUC76-22863

Barb, Charles E
Directory of members; Urban and Regional Information Systems Association, Special Interest Group in Geographic Base File Systems [by Charles E. Barb. Seattle] Urban and Regional Information Systems Association, 1970.
23 p. 28 cm.
Photocopy by National Technical Information Service, Springfield, Va., 1970.
1. Information storage and retrieval systems—Cities and towns—Planning—Direct. 2. Information storage and retrieval systems—Direct. I. Urban and Regional Information Systems Association.

Special Interest Group in Geographic Base File Systems. II. Title.
CaBVaU NUC76-33389

Barb, Charles E
A guide to the 1970 census data and map products an evaluation of their utility in computer-assisted analysis, by Charles E. Barb, Jr. [Seattle] Urban Data Center, University of Washington [1970?]
69 l. maps. 28 cm. (Washington (State). University. Urban Data Center. Research report, no. 5)
Bibliography: leaves 64-69.
1. Census. 2. United States—Census. 3. United States—Statistics, Vital. I. Washington (State). University. Urban Data Center. II. Title. III. Series.
Wa NUC74-11282

Barb, Dănilă.
Efectul Mössbauer şi aplicaţiile sale. [Bucureşti], Editura Academiei Republicii Socialiste România, 1972.
403 p. with figs. 24 cm. lei 28.00 R 72-4146
Summary in English.
Includes bibliographies.
1. Mössbauer effect. 2. Mössbauer spectroscopy. I. Title.
QC490.B37 73-311932

Barb, Rosalba P de.
Propuesta sobre coordinacion entre el Centro Regional del Libro en America Latina y el Instituto Centroamericano de Libros de Texto; documento presentado por Rosalba de Barb. [n.p., 1970?]
15 l. 28 cm. (Unesco mineducacion, Documento, no. 7)
Cover title.
1. Publishers and publishing—Central America. 2. Book industries and trade—Central America. 3. Instituto Centroamericano de Libros de Texto. I. Title.
CSt NUC76-74970

Barb-Mingo, Arturo, 1944-
Poesías / por Arturo Barb-Mingo. — 1. ed. — Santa Ana, Calif. : Pioneer Press, 1972.
31 p. ; 22 cm.
PQ7079.2.B37P6 861 77-150200
77 MARC

Barba, A Tàpies-
see
Tàpies-Barba, A

Barba, Alma, ed.
see Regional Conference on Teacher Education for Mexican-Americans, New Mexico State University, 1969. Conference proceedings. Las Cruces, 1969.

Barba, Alvaro Alonso, b. 1569.
Arte de los metales en que se enseña el verdadero beneficio de los de oro, y plata por açogue. El modo de fundirlos todos, y como se han de refinar y apartar vnos de otros. Compuesto por el licenciado Albaro Alonso Barba, natural de la villa de Lepe, en la Andaluzia, cura en la Imperial de Potosi, de la Parroquia de S. Bernardo. Con privilegio. En Madrid, En la Imprenta del Reyno, 1640.
4 p.l., 120 l. diagrs. 20 cm.
Micro-opaque. New York, Readex Microprint, 1973. 3 cards. 23 x 15 cm. (Landmarks of science)

1. Metals. 2. Mines and mineral resources. 3. Metallurgy—Early works to 1800. 4. Mines and mineral resources—Spain.
IaAS NUC77-41906

Barba, Alvaro Alonso, b. 1569.
Arte de los metales, en que se enseña el verdadero beneficio de los de oro y plata por azogue: el modo de fundirlos todos, y como se han de refinar y apartar unos de otros. Nuevamente ahora añadido con el tratado de las antiguas minas de España, que escribió don Alonso Carrillo y Laso. Reimpreso por el Real Tribunal de Minería de esta capital de órden del Excmo. Sr. Virey. Lima, Impr. de los Huérfanos, 1817.
271 p. illus. 20 cm.
Ultra microfiche. Dayton, Ohio, National Cash Register, 1970. 3d title of 7. 10.5 x 14.8 cm. (PCMI library collection, 610-3)
1. Metals. 2. Metallurgy—Early works to 1800. I. Carrillo Laso de la Vega, Alonso, 1582-1647? De las antiguas minas de Espana.
KEmT NUC76-16261

Barba, Diego.
Calcolo elettronico nell'ingegneria chimica. Roma, Edizioni scientifiche Siderea, 1971.
439 p. illus., plate. 24 cm. L4500 It 72-Mar
Bibliography: p. [431]-434.
1. Electronic data processing—Chemical engineering. I. Title.
TP155.B375 74-333317

Barba, Diego.
Il problema dell'acqua. La dissalazione per lo sviluppo economico. Milano, F. Angeli, [1972].
165 p. illus. 21½ cm. (Collana scientifica, 22) L3500
It 72-Sept
At head of title: D. Barba, G. Liuzzo, G. Tagliaferri.
Bibliography: p. [163]-165.
1. Saline water conversion—Italy. 2. Saline water conversion. I. Liuzzo, Giuseppe, joint author. II. Tagliaferri, Giovanni, joint author. III. Title. IV. Title: La dissalazione per lo sviluppo economico.
TD478.6.I 8B37 72-361348

Barba, Enrique M 1909-
Quiroga y Rosas / Enrique M. Barba. — Buenos Aires : Editorial Pleamar, c1974.
253 p. ; 24 cm. — (Testimonios nacionales)
Includes bibliographical references.
CONTENTS: La misión Cavia a Bolivia.—La misión mediadora de Quiroga al Norte.—Los jefes federales ante la separación de Jujuy.—El Norte argentino y Bolivia en la época de Santa Cruz.—La lucha por el federalismo argentino.—Orígines y crisis del federalismo argentino.
1. Argentine Republic—Politics and government—1817-1860—Addresses, essays, lectures. 2. Quiroga, Juan Facundo, 1790-1835. 3. Rosas, Juan Manuel José Domingo Ortiz de, 1793-1877. I. Title.
F2846.3.Q572B37 75-536864

Barba, Enrique M 1909-
Unitarismo, federalismo, rosismo [por] Enrique M. Barba. Buenos Aires, Ediciones Pannedille, 1972.
101 p. 20 cm.
LACAP 73-1048
Includes bibliographical references.
1. Federal government—Argentine Republic. 2. Decentralization in government—Argentine Republic. 3. Argentine Republic—Politics and government. I. Title.
JL2020.S8B28 73-339468

Barba, Fernando E.
see Archivo Histórico de la Provincia de Buenos Aires Dr. Ricardo Levene. Indice de mapas, planos y fotografias... La Plata, 1968 [i. e. 1969]

Barba, Francisco Esteve
see Esteve Barba, Francisco, 1908-

Barba, Gregorio Peces- 1938-
see
Peces-Barba Martinez, Gregorio, 1938-

Barba, Harry.
One of a kind : the many faces & voices of America / by Harry Barba. — Ballston Spa, N.Y. : Harian Press, 1976.
x, 181 p. ; 18 cm.
ISBN 0-911906-12-6
I. Title.
PZ4.B228 On 813'.5'4 76-375102
[PS3552.A59177] 76 MARC

Barba, Jaime, 1910-
Más allá de la mies y del sonido (poemas). Miami, Fla., Ediciones Universal, 1973 [i. e. 1974]
80 p. 22 cm. (Colección Espejo de paciencia)
I. Title.
PQ7389.B29M3 1974 861 73-82303

Barba, Jaime, 1910-
Los mercaderes del alba : poemas / Jaime Barba. — [s.l. : s.n.], c1976 ([Miami, Fla.] : Ahora Printing)
48 p. ; 21 cm.
I. Title.
PQ7389.B29M4 1976 76-473112
76 MARC

Barba, Joseph.
The use of steel for constructive purposes; method of working, applying and testing plates and bars; By J. Barba, chief naval constructor at L'Orient.. New York, D. Van Nostrand, 1875 [1972]
ix, 110, 47 p. illus.
Micropublished as no. 50 on Reel 5, in "American Architectural Books," based on the Henry-Russell Hitchcock bibliography of the same title. New Haven: Research Publications, Inc., 1972.
Translated from the French; with a preface by Alex L. Holley. First appeared Paris, 1874.

Last unit of collation is publisher's list.
1. Steel, Structural. 2. Building, Iron and steel. I. Title.
UU NUC75-95699

Barba, Mario Hernández Sánchez-
see Hernández Sánchez-Barba, Mario.

Barba, Melitón.
Ortopedia y traumatología. [1. ed. San Salvador] Editorial Universitaria [1971]
171 p. 24 cm. (Colección Medicina, v. 2)
1. Orthopedia. 2. Wounds. I. Title. II. Series.
TxU NUC74-122000

Barba, Raffaele.
Strategia sindacale e Statuto dei lavoratori / Raffaele Barba. — [Napoli] : Liguori, [1974]
261 p. ; 24 cm. It 75-Apr
Bibliography: p. [257]-258.
L3500
1. Labor laws and legislation—Italy. 2. Trade-unions—Italy. I. Italy. Laws, statutes, etc. Legge 20 maggio 1970, n. 300. II. Title: Strategia sindacale ...
75-591205

Barba, Rose A
Elementary statistics for transportation planning. Rose A. Barba and Steven Rittvo. Albany, N.Y., New York State Dept. of Transportation, 1972.
iii, 145 l. ill. 28 cm.
At head of title: Research and Applied Systems Section, Preliminary report. Planning and Research Bureau. Planning Division.
"Report PRR 31."
Bibliography: leaves 143-144.
1. Statistics. 2. Statistics–Problems, exercises, etc. 3. Transportation–Research.
I. Rittvo, Steven, joint author. II. New York (State). Dept. of Transportation. Planning Division. III. Title.
NNC NUC76-80311

Barba, Salvatore.
Il contributo di miglioria specifica per la prima linea della metropolitana milanese. [Milano], Associazione milanese della proprietà edilizia, 1971.
166 p. illus. 24 cm. It 72-Apr
"Appendice" (legislative): p. [125]-153.
L2300
1. Metropolitana milanese. 2. Special assessments—Milan. 3. Taxation—Milan—Law. 4. Real property and taxation—Milan. I. Title.
75-563928

Barba, Sharon.
Willa Cather: a feminist study. Albuquerque, 1973.
vi, 151 l.
Thesis (Ph.D.)—University of New Mexico.
Bibliography: leaves 145-151.
1. Cather, Willa Sibert, 1873-1947. 2. Authors, Women. 3. Women in literature. I. Title.
NmU NUC74-126735

Barba, Sharon
see Chester, Laura. Rising tides... New York, Washington Square Press, Pocket Books [1973]

Barba, Vasile G
Economia întreprinderilor forestiere / Vasile G. Barba, Constantin V. Costea. — București : "Ceres," 1975.
354, [2] p. : ill. ; 25 cm. R 75-3778
Bibliography: p. 353-[355]
lei 25.00
1. Lumber trade—Romania. 2. Forests and forestry—Economic aspects—Romania. 3. Forest management—Romania. I. Costea, Constantin V., joint author. II. Title.
HD9765.R77B37 76-501712

Barba de Muñoz, Teresa.
Capacidad de la mujer casada en el derecho colombiano. [Bogotá] Pontificia Universidad Católica Javeriana, Facultad de Ciencias Jurídicas y Socioeconómicas, 1973.
84 p. 25 cm.
Tesis—Pontificia Universidad Católica Javeriana.
Bibliography: p. 83-84.
1. Married women—Colombia. I. Title.
75-592749

Barba del Brío, Gregorio Peces-
see Peces-Barba del Brío, Gregorio.

Barba Jordi, Jaime Eloy
see
Barba, Jaime, 1910-

Barba Martinez, Gregorio Peces-
see
Peces-Barba Martínez, Gregorio, 1938-

Barba Peyró, Eduardo.
Los valores mobiliarios y su mercado; temas de divulgación sobre los valores mobiliarios en la financiación, en la inversión y en la Bolsa. Madrid, Centro de Estudios Bancarios del Banco Popular Español, 1970.
176 p. illus. 21 cm.
Cover title: Valores mobiliarios.
1. Securities. 2. Stock-exchange. I. Title.
HG4661.B37 74-232448

Barbacciani Fedeli, Ranieri.
Saggio storico dell'antica e moderna Versilia / Ranieri Barbacciani Fedeli. — [Bologna] : A. Forni, 1975.
331, lxxxv p., [1] fold. leaf of plates : map ; 22 cm. It77-Jan
Reprint of the 1845 ed. published by Tip. Fabris, Florence.
1. Versilia. I. Title.
DG975.V57B37 1975 77-479161
•77 MARC

Barbacena, Felisberto Caldeira Brant Pontes, marquez de, 1772-1842.
Economia açucareira da Bahia em 1820. [Rio de Janeiro] Arquivo Nacional [1973]
[21] p. 21 cm.
A selection of letters from a recently acquired "copiador de cartas" in the Arquivo Nacional.
"Publicação destinada ao III Congresso de História da Bahia—Junho, 1973."
1. Sugar trade—Bahia, Brazil (State)—History. I. Brazil. Arquivo Nacional. II. Title.
HD9114.B23B72 1973 74-217699

Barbacena, Felisberto Caldeira Brant Pontes, marquez de, 1772-1842.
Economia açucareira do Brasil no séc. XIX : cartas de Felisberto Caldeira Brant Pontes, marquês de Barbacena / transcrição de Carmen Vargas. — Rio [de Janeiro] : M.I.C., Instituto do Açúcar e do Álcool, Departamento de Informática, Divisão de Informações, Documentação, 1976.
xi, 210 p. ; 21 cm. — (Coleção Canavieira ; no. 21)
1. Sugar trade—Brazil—Bahia (State)—History. 2. Barbacena, Felisberto Caldeira Brant Pontes, marquez de, 1772-1842—Correspondence. I. Title.
HD9114.B7B342 1976 77-555896
77 MARC

Barbach, Bob.
Understanding the prison environment: a selected interdisciplinary bibliography. [Monticello, Ill.] Council of Planning Librarians [1974]
13 p. 28 cm. (Council of Planning Librarians. Exchange bibliography, no. 632)
1. Prisons—Bibliography. 2. Social psychology—Bibliography. I. Title.
IaU NUC76-24380

Barbach, Lonnie Garfield, 1946–
For yourself : the fulfillment of female sexuality / Lonnie Garfield Barbach. — 1st ed. — Garden City, N. Y. : Doubleday, 1975.
xviii, 218 p. : ill. ; 22 cm.
Bibliography: p. [204]-211.
Includes index.
ISBN 0-385-05825-X : $7.95
1. Sex instruction for women. 2. Women—Sexual behavior. 3. Orgasm. 4. Masturbation. I. Title.
HQ46.B23 301.41'8'042 74-4873
MARC

Barbáchano, Carlos J
El cine, arte e industria [por Carlos Barbáchano. Barcelona] Salvat Editores [1973]
144 p. illus. 20 cm. (Biblioteca Salvat de grandes temas, 5) Sp***
Bibliography: p. 142.
1. Moving-pictures. I. Title.
PN1994.B278 74-304932
ISBN 84-345-7363-6

Barbáchano, Carlos J.
see Teoría de la novela. Madrid, Sociedad General Española de Librería, 1976 printing.

Barbachano, Fernando Cámara
see Cámara Barbachano, Fernando.

Barbachano Ponce, Manuel
see Art maya du Mexique. [Paris, 1974?]

Bărbăcioru, Constantin, joint author
see Bărbăcioru, Victoria. Eficiență-rentabilitate în economia socialistă ... Craiova : "Scrisul românesc," 1975.

Bărbăcioru, Victoria.
Eficiență-rentabilitate în economia socialistă : studiu teoretico-metodologic cu aplicații în industria chimică / Victoria Bărbăcioru, Constantin Bărbăcioru. — Craiova : "Scrisul românesc," 1975.
207 p. : ill. ; 20 cm. R 76-890
Table of contents in Romanian, English, and French.
Bibliography: p. 195-[201]
lei 9.25
1. Profit. 2. Efficiency, Industrial. 3. Chemical industries—Romania—Management. I. Bărbăcioru, Constantin, joint author. II. Title.
HB601.B298 76-519164

Barback, Joseph, 1937-
Contributions to the theory of isols. Ann Arbor, Mich., University Microfilms, 1965.
1 reel. 35 mm.
Microfilm copy of typescript.
Collation of the original: ii, 188 l. 29 cm.
Thesis–Rutgers University.
1. Recursive functions. 2. Logic, Symbolic and mathematical. I. Title.
NBuC NUC74-122548

Barbacki, A., joint author.
see Barbacki, R. Montreal air pollution, 1972. Montreal, STOP, 1972.

Barbacki, R
Montreal air pollution, 1972 / by R. Barbacki, E. Stein, A. Barbacki. — Montreal : STOP, 1972.
v. 94 p. ; 22 x 36 cm. C***
Bibliography: p. 92-94.
1. Air—Pollution—Montreal. I. Stein, Edward, joint author. II. Barbacki, A., joint author. III. Title.
TD883.7.C2B37 363.6 75-327891
76 MARC

Barbadillo, Alonso Jerónimo de Salas
see Salas Barbadillo, Alonso Jerónimo de, 1581-1635.

Barbadillo, Manuel
see Barbadillo Rodríguez, Manuel.

Barbadillo, Manuel, 1929–
Barbadillo : [exposición, Sala de Exposiciones del Palacio Provincial de Málaga del 2 al 19 de junio de 1973].— [Málaga : Diputación Provincial, 1973]
[17] p., [10] leaves of plates : ill. ; 22 cm. — (Cuadernos de arte del Instituto de Cultura de la Excma. Diputación Provincial de Málaga ; 19) Sp 74-Jan
Bibliography: p. [14]-[16].
1. Barbadillo, Manuel, 1929– I. Series: Málaga, Spain (Province). Instituto de Cultura. Cuadernos de arte del Instituto de Cultura de la Excma. Diputación Provincial de Málaga ; 19.
ND813.B24A42 75-578287

Barbadillo, María Teresa.
La prosa del s. XV. [Madrid] Editorial La Muralla [1973]
56 p. and 60 col. slides (film) 2 x 2 in. (in pockets) (Literatura española en imagenes, v. 8)
Includes bibliography.
1. Spanish prose literature–Hist. & crit. 2. Spanish literature–To 1500–Hist. & crit. I. Title.
MiU NUC76-74992

Barbadillo Rodríguez, Manuel.
Andalucía alegre [por] Manuel Barbadillo. Jerez [de la Frontera] Gráficas del Exportador [19
v. 19 cm. Sp***
I. Title.
PQ6603.A55A85 73-348581

Barbadillo Rodriguez, Manuel.
Antologia poetica. Jerez, Graficas del exportador [1969]
215 p. 20 cm.
I. Title.
TNJ NUC73-40699

Barbadillo Rodríguez, Manuel.
La baraja. (Novela corta). Jérez de la Frontera, Gráf. del Exportador (1971)
152 p., 1 l. 19 cm. Sp 72-Apr
At head of title: Manuel Barbadillo.
I. Title.
PQ6603.A55B27 72-362273

Barbadillo Rodríguez, Manuel.
Borradores : (últimas notes de mi recorrido) / [por] Manuel Barbadillo. — Jerez de la Frontera (Cádiz) : Gráficas del Exportador, 1976.
101 p. ; 18 cm. Sp76-Oct
ISBN 8485268091 : 150ptas
I. Title.
PQ6603.A55B67 868'.6'207 77-466138
77 MARC

Barbadillo Rodríguez, Manuel.
Cuidado con la gente / Manuel Barbadillo. — [s. l. : s. n., 1973?] (Jeréz : Gráf. del Exportador)
319 p. ; 19 cm. — (His Andalucía alegre ; 7) Sp***
ISBN 84-400-6815-8
I. Title. II. Series.
PQ6603.A55A85 vol. 7 75-560529

Barbadillo Rodríguez, Manuel.
La luz está dentro : [novela] / Manuel Barbadillo. — Jerez de la Frontera : Gráficas del Exportador, 1975.
269 p. ; 20 cm. Sp***
ISBN 8440082371
I. Title.
PQ6603.A55L8 863'.6'2 76-454062
76 MARC

Barbadillo Rodríguez, Manuel.
¡Me cachi ... en la gente! Jerez de la Frontera, Gráf. del Exportador (1972)
421 p., 2 l. 19 cm. (His Andalucía alegre, 6) 150 ptas Sp 72-Oct
At head of title: Manuel Barbadillo.
I. Title. II. Series.
PQ6603.A55A85 vol. 6 73-348583

Barbadillo Rodríguez, Manuel.
Mosaico (versos). Jérez, Gráf. del Exportador (1971)
128 p. 19 cm. 100ptas Sp 72-Apr
At head of title: Manuel Barbadillo.
I. Title.
PQ6603.A55M6 **72-362513**

Barbadillo Rodríguez, Manuel.
El pañuelo en los ojos : versos / Manuel Barbadillo. — Jerez de la Frontera : ₍Sexta, 1975?₎
147 p. ; 20 cm. Sp76-Feb
ISBN 8440094019 : 200ptas.
I. Title.
PQ6603.A55P3 861'.6'2 76-474500
*76 MARC

Barbadillo Rodríguez, Manuel.
!Qué de gente! !Qué barbaridad! / Manuel Barbadillo. — Jerez de la Frontera : Graf. del Exportador, ₍1975?₎
316 p. ; 19 cm. — (His Andalucía alegre ; 9) Sp76-Feb
ISBN 8440093225 : 250ptas.
I. Title. II. Series.
PQ6603.A55A85 vol. 9 76-476938
*76₍r77₎rev MARC

Barbadillo Rodríguez, Manuel.
¡Vaya gente! / Manuel Barbadillo. -- Jerez de la Frontera : Graf del Exportado, 1974.
369 p. ; 19 cm. -- (His Andalucía alegre ; 8)
ISBN 84-400-7913-3.
MH NUC77-101107

Barbadillo Rodríguez, Manuel.
see Alrededor del vino de Jerez. ₍s.l., s.n., 1975?₎ (Jerez : Gráficas del Exportador)

Barbadillo Rodríguez, Manuel.
see Otra vez la manzanilla. ₍s.l., s.n., 1975₎ (Jerez de la Frontera (Cádiz) : Gráficas del Exportador)

Barbadinho Neto, Raimundo.
Tendências e constâncias da língua do modernismo. Prefácio de Gladstone Chaves de Melo. Rio de Janeiro, Livraria Acadêmica, 1972.
148 p. 19 cm. Cr$12.00 LACAP 72-0652
Bibliography: p. 145-148.
1. Portuguese language in Brazil. 2. Brazilian literature—20th century—History and criticism. I. Title.
PC5443.B37 72-371483

Barbadoro, Idomeneo.
Storia del sindacalismo italiano dalla nascita al fascismo ... Firenze, La nuova Italia, 1973.
2 v. 21 cm. (Biblioteca di storia, 5) L4000 per vol. It 73-July
Includes bibliographical references.
CONTENTS: v. 1. La Federterra.—v. 2. La confederazione generale del lavoro.
1. Trade-unions—Italy—History. 2. Federazione nazionale dei lavoratori della terra—History. 3. Confederazione generale del lavoro—History. I. Title.
HD6709.B35 73-337223

Barbados.
Annual report on the local forces.
₍Bridgetown₎
v. 23 cm.
1. Barbados—Armed Forces—Periodicals. I. Title.
UA610.B3B37a 355'.009729'81 70-615309

Barbados.
A ten year development plan for Barbados; sketch plan of development, 1946-56. ₍Bridgetown, Advocate Co., printers to the Government of Barbados ₍1964?₎
63 p. 28 cm.
Cover title.
1. Barbados—Economic policy. 2. Barbados—Social policy. I. Title.
HC157.B35A4 1964 338.9729'81 74-190920
MARC

Barbados
see Caribbean Development Bank. [Miscellaneous pamphlets. Bridgetown, Barbados, 1970-

Barbados
see International Labor Office. Report to the Government of Barbados... Geneva, 1962.

Barbados
see International Labor Office. Report to the government of Barbados... Geneva, 1973.

Barbados
see The National food and nutrition survey of Barbados. Washington, Pan American Health Organization, 1972.

Barbados. Accountant General.
Detailed statement of the revenue for the financial year.
₍Bridgetown, Accountant General₎
v. 38 cm. annual.
Report year ends Mar. 31.
At head of title : House of Assembly.
1. Revenue—Barbados—Statistics—Periodicals. I. Barbados. Legislature. House of Assembly.
HJ27.B432a 336'.02'72981 75-647285
MARC-S

Barbados. Accountant General.
Report of the Accountant General.
₍Bridgetown₎
v. illus. 34 cm.
Report year ends Mar. 31.
1. Finance, Public—Barbados—Accounting.
HJ9923.B3A23a 354'.729'81007231 74-646106
MARC-S

Barbados. Audit Dept.
The name of the Barbados Audit Dept. was changed to Auditor General's Dept. Works by this body published under these names are found under the following headings according to the name used at the time of publication.
Barbados. Audit Dept.
Barbados. Auditor General's Dept.
Works by an earlier related body are found under the heading Barbados. Audit Office.

Barbados. Audit Dept.
Report on the audit of the accounts of the Housing Authority.
₍Bridgetown, Auditor General₎
v. 36 cm. annual.
Report year ends Mar. 31.
1. Barbados. Housing Authority. 2. Housing management—Accounting—Periodicals. I. Barbados. Housing Authority.
HD7319.B3B33a 354'.729'8100865 75-642954
MARC-S

Barbados. Auditor General's Dept.
The name of the Barbados Audit Dept. was changed to Auditor General's Dept. Works by this body published under these names are found under the following headings according to the name used at the time of publication.
Barbados. Audit Dept.
Barbados. Auditor General's Dept.
Works by an earlier related body are found under the heading Barbados. Audit Office.

Barbados. Auditor General's Dept.
Report on the audit of the accounts of the Auditor General's Department.
₍Bridgetown₎ Barbados Auditor General's Dept.
v. 37 cm. annual.
Report year ends Mar. 31.
Supersedes: Barbados. Audit Dept. Report of the Auditor General on the audit of the accounts of the colony.
1. Finance, Public—Barbados—Accounting—Periodicals.
I. Title.
HJ9923.B33B37a 354'.729'81007232 75-646498
MARC-S

Barbados. Auditor General's Dept.
Report on the audit of the accounts of the National insurance fund.
₍Bridgetown, Auditor General₎
v. 35 cm. annual.
1. Social security—Barbados—Accounting—Periodicals.
I. Title.
HD7145.Z8B33a 354'.729'810084 75-646530
MARC-S

Barbados. Commissioner of Police.
Annual report of the Commissioner of Police of Barbados.
₍Bridgetown₎ Commissioner of Police.
v. 35 cm.
Continues: Barbados. Commissioner of Police. Report on the organization and administration of the Barbados police force.
1. Police—Barbados—Periodicals.
HV7685.B3A3 354'.729'81007405 76-643042
MARC-S

Barbados. Dept. of Education.
The evaluation of education in Barbados : a first experiment : memorandum / by the Director of Education ; with a foreword by His Excellency the Governor. — ₍Bridgetown₎ : Dept. of Education, Barbados, ₍1945?₎
30 p., ₍2₎ fold. leaves of plates : graphs ; 25 cm.
Cover title.
"Appendix II: Standard score frequency distribution charts" (4 fold. leaves) in pocket.
1. Education—Barbados. I. Title.
LA505.B37B37 1945 379'.152'0972981 77-465091
77 MARC

Barbados. Director of Education
see
Barbados. Dept. of Education.

Barbados. Economic Planning Unit
see Barbados economic survey. ₍Bridgetown₎

Barbados. Education, Dept. of
see
Barbados. Dept. of Education.

Barbados. Health and Community Development, Ministry of
see
Barbados. Ministry of Health and Community Development.

Barbados. Health and Social Welfare, Ministry of
see
Barbados. Ministry of Health and Social Welfare.

Barbados. Health and Welfare, Ministry of
see
Barbados. Ministry of Health and Welfare.

Barbados. Housing Authority
see Barbados. Audit Dept. Report on the audit of the accounts of the Housing Authority. [Bridgetown, Auditor General]

Barbados. Industrial Development Corporation
see
Barbados Industrial Development Corporation.

Barbados. Laws, statutes, etc.
Commercial laws of the world : Barbados. -- Ormond Beach, Fla. : Foreign Tax Law Association, 1976-
v.
Loose-leaf for updating.
1. Commercial law--Barbados. I. Foreign Tax Law Association. II. Title.
CSt-Law NUC77-84586

Barbados. Laws, statutes, etc.
Financial instructions, 1957. ₍The public accounts rules, 1957. Bridgetown?₎ Advocate Co., Printers to the Government, 1957.
46 p. 22 cm.
Cover title.
1. Public administration. 2. Barbados—Pol. & govt. 3. Finance, Public—Barbados. I. Barbados. Laws, statutes, etc. The public accounts rules, 1957. II. Title.
FU NUC73-486

Barbados. Laws, statutes, etc.
The laws of Barbados in force on the 31st day of December, 1971. — Rev. ed. / prepared under the authority of the Law revision act 1967 (no. 1967-49) by Oshley Roy Marshall and Keith William Patchett. — Bridgetown, Barbados : Govt. Printer, 1974-
v. : diagrs. ; 26 cm.
Loose-leaf for updating.
Includes index.
B.D.S. $500.00
1. Law—Barbados. I. Marshall, Oshley Roy. II. Patchett, Keith.
348'.72981'022 76-351238
76 MARC

Barbados. Laws, statutes, etc. The public accounts rules, 1957
see Barbados. Laws, statutes, etc. Financial instructions, 1957.... ₍Bridgetown?₎ Advocate Co., Printers to the Government, 1957.

Barbados. Laws, statutes, etc.
see Barbados. Legislature. House of Assembly. A bill intituled an Act to amend the Town and Country Planning Act, 1965. ₍Bridgetown?₎ Govt. Print. Off. ₍1968?₎

Barbados. Legislature. House of Assembly.
Bill intituled an Act relating to the appointment and control of land surveyors and to the survey of lands of Barbados. [Bridgetown?] Govt. Print. Off. [1968?]
10 p. 22 cm.
"Short title: This Act may be cited as the Land Surveyors Act, 1968. Notice of this bill was given on the 18th June, 1968."
1. Surveyors—Barbados. I. Title.
FU NUC74-122700

Barbados. Legislature. House of Assembly.
A bill intituled an Act to amend the Barbados Harbours Act, 1960. [Bridgetown?] Govt. Print. Off. [1968?]
3 p. 21 cm.
"Short title: This Act may be cited as the Barbados Harbours (Amendment) (No. 2) Act, 1968. Notice of this bill was given on 18th June, 1968."
1. Habors—Barbados. I. Title.
FU NUC74-122689

Barbados. Legislature. House of Assembly.
A bill intituled an Act to amend the Exchange Control Act, 1967. [Bridgetown?] Govt. Print. Off. [1968?]
6 p. 22 cm.
"Short title: This Act may be cited as the Exchange Control (Amendment) Act, 1968. Notice of this Bill was given on the 18th June, 1968."
1. Banks and banking—Barbados. I. Title.
FU NUC74-122690

Barbados. Legislature. House of Assembly.
A bill intituled an Act to amend the Town and Country Planning Act, 1965. [Bridgetown?] Govt. Print. Off. [1968?]
19 p. 21 cm.
"Short title: This Act may be cited as the Town and Country Planning (Amendment) Act, 1968. Notice of this Bill was given on 18th June, 1968."
1. Cities and towns—Planning—Barbados. I. Barbados. Laws, statutes, etc. II. Title.
FU NUC75-32719

Barbados. Legislature. House of Assembly.
A bill intituled an Act to make provision for the grant to poor prisioners of legal aid in certain criminal cases. [Bridgetown] Govt. Print. Off. [1968?]
11 p. 22 cm.
"Short title: This Act may be cited as the Legal Aid in Criminal Cases Act, 1968. Notice of this Bill was given on 18th June, 1968."
1. Right to counsel—Barbados. 2. Legal aid—Barbados. I. Title.
FU NUC74-122691

Barbados. Legislature. House of Assembly.
Minutes of proceedings of the Honourable the House of Assembly.
[Bridgetown] House of Assembly.
v. 36 cm. weekly.
1. Barbados—Politics and government—Periodicals.
J137.K44a 328.729'81'01 75-644722
MARC-S

Barbados. Legislature. House of Assembly
see Barbados. Accountant General. Detailed statement of the revenue for the financial year. [Bridgetown]

Barbados. Legislature. House of Assembly
see Barbados. Registrar of Trade Unions. Report of the Registrar of Trade Unions for the year. [Bridgetown]

Barbados. Legislature. Legislative Council
see also the later heading
Barbados. Legislature. Senate.

Barbados. Legislature. Senate.
Minutes of proceedings of the Senate.
[Bridgetown] The Senate.
v. 36 cm. weekly.
1. Barbados—Politics and government—Periodicals.
J137.J455a 328.729'81'01 75-644899
MARC-S

Barbados. Legislature. Senate.
The Senate debates.
[Bridgetown] The Senate.
v. 36 cm. weekly.
"Official report."
Supersedes: Barbados. Legislature. Legislative Council. Debates.
1. Barbados—Politics and government—Periodicals.
J137.J24a 328.729'81'02 75-644785
MARC-S

Barbados. Legislature. Senate
see also the earlier heading
Barbados. Legislature. Legislative Council.

Barbados. Ministry of Education.
Barbados, an independent nation. [Nassau, Bahamas, Island Graphics, ltd., 1966]
1 v. (unpaged) illus. (part col.) 23 x 31 cm.
Cover title.
1. Barbados—Economic conditions. 2. Barbados—Description and travel—Views. I. Title.
FU NUC76-36383

Barbados. Ministry of External Affairs
see Barbados foreign affairs bulletin. Jan./June 1972- [Bridgetown]

Barbados. Ministry of Health and Community Development.
In 1969 the name of the Barbados Ministry of Health and Community Development was changed to Ministry of Health and Social Welfare and in 1971, to Ministry of Health and Welfare.
Works by this body are found under the following headings according to the name used at the time of publication:
Barbados. Ministry of Health and Community Development.
Barbados. Ministry of Health and Social Welfare.
Barbados. Ministry of Health and Welfare.

Barbados. Ministry of Health and Community Development.
Health services in Barbados. 19 -68. [Bridgetown]
v. illus. 23 cm.
Continued by the publication with the same title issued by the Ministry of Health and Social Welfare.
1. Hygiene, Public—Barbados—Periodicals. I. Title.
RA194.B35M56a 362.1'09729'81 72-624507

Barbados. Ministry of Health and Community Development
see also
Barbados. Ministry of Health and Social Welfare.

Barbados. Ministry of Health and Social Welfare.
In 1969 the name of the Barbados Ministry of Health and Community Development was changed to Ministry of Health and Social Welfare and in 1971, to Ministry of Health and Welfare.
Works by this body are found under the following headings according to the name used at the time of publication:
Barbados. Ministry of Health and Community Development.
Barbados. Ministry of Health and Social Welfare.
Barbados. Ministry of Health and Welfare.

Barbados. Ministry of Health and Social Welfare.
Health services in Barbados. 1969-
[Bridgetown]
v. illus. 23 cm. annual.
Continues the publication with the same title issued by the Ministry of Health and Community Development.
1. Hygiene, Public—Barbados—Periodicals. I. Title.
RA194.B35M56a 362.1'09729'81 72-624508

Barbados. Ministry of Health and Social Welfare
see also
Barbados. Ministry of Health and Community Development.

Barbados. Ministry of Health and Welfare.
In 1969 the name of the Barbados Ministry of Health and Community Development was changed to Ministry of Health and Social Welfare and in 1971, to Ministry of Health and Welfare.
Works by this body are found under the following headings according to the name used at the time of publication:
Barbados. Ministry of Health and Community Development.
Barbados. Ministry of Health and Social Welfare.
Barbados. Ministry of Health and Welfare.

Barbados. Ministry of Health and Welfare.
Annual report of Chief Medical Officer.
[Bridgetown] Ministry of Health & Welfare.
v. ill. 33 cm.
1. Public health—Barbados—Periodicals. 2. Barbados—Statistics, Medical—Periodicals. I. Title.
RA194.B35M57a 362.1'09729'81 76-647037
MARC-S

Barbabdos. National Insurance Board
see
National Insurance Board.

Barbados. National Nutrition Committee.
The national food and nutrition survey of Barbados. Undertaken by the Government of Barbados with the assistance of the Caribbean Food and Nutrition Institute, the Pan American Health Organization, and the Food and Agriculture Organization of the United Nations. Washington, Pan American Sanitary Bureau, 1972.
vii, 139 p. illus. (Scientific publication no. 237)
1. Food supply—Barbados. 2. Nutrition—Barbados. I. Caribbean Food and Nutrition Institute. II. Title. III. Series: Pan American Sanitary Bureau. Scientific publications, no. 237.
DPAHO NUC73-80694

Barbados. Parliament
see
Barbados. Legislature.

Barbados. Prime Minister.
Financial statement and budget proposals.
[Bridgetown] The Prime Minister.
v. 37 cm.
1. Finance, Public—Barbados—Periodicals. 2. Budget—Barbados.
HJ27.B456a 354'.729'8100722 75-641518
MARC-S

Barbados. Probation Service.
Report.
[Bridgetown] Govt. Print. Off.
v. illus. 22 cm.
1. Probation—Barbados. 2. Social work with delinquents and criminals—Barbados. 3. Juvenile delinquency—Barbados.
HV7329.B3B35a 362.6'3 74-642535
MARC-S

Barbados. Public Utilities Board.
Public Utilities Act 1951; report of the Public Utilities Board to the Cabinet under section 52 of the above act.
[Bridgetown] Govt. Print. Off.
v. 32 cm. annual.
1. Public utilities—Barbados.
HD2768.B37A3 354'.729'810087 73-641948
MARC-S

Barbados. Public Utilities Board.
Report and accounts of the Public Utilities Board.
[Bridgetown] Public Utilities Board.
v. 36 cm. annual.
1. Barbados. Public Utilities Board.
HD4075.7.Z8B372a 354'.729'810087 75-647250
MARC-S

Barbados. Registrar of Trade Unions.
Report of the Registrar of Trade Unions for the year.
[Bridgetown] Registrar of Trade Unions.
v. 36 cm. annual.
Report year ends Mar. 31.
At head of title : House of Assembly.
1. Trade-unions—Barbados—Periodicals. I. Barbados. Legislature. House of Assembly.
HD6595.7.Z8B372a 331.88'09729'81 75-647286
MARC-S

Barbados. Registration Office.
Report on vital statistics & registrations.
[Bridgetown] Govt. Print. Off.
v. 33 cm.
1. Barbados—Statistics, Vital.
HA865.A28 312'.09729'81 73-643545
MARC-S

Barbados. Standing Insurance Committee.
Report of the Standing Insurance Committee and statement of accounts of the General Insurance Fund.
[Bridgetown] Standing Insurance Committee.
v. 36 cm. annual.
Report year ends Mar. 31.
1. Barbados. Standing Insurance Committee. 2. Insurance, Government—Barbados—Periodicals. I. Title.
HG8220.B35B35a 368.4'009729'81 76-642368
MARC-S

Barbados. Statistical Service.
Barbados: housing. Garrison, 1972.
iii, 17 p. 34 cm. (Its Preliminary bulletin)
Cover title.
At head of title: Commonwealth Caribbean population census, 1970.
1. Housing—Barbados—Statistics. 2. Dwellings—Barbados—Statistics. I. Title. II. Title: Commonwealth Caribbean population census, 1970. III. Series: Barbados. Statistical Service. Preliminary bulletin—Barbados Statistical Service.
HD7319.B3B37 1972 301.5'4'0972981 74-170305 MARC

Barbados. Statistical Service.
Commonwealth Caribbean population census, 1970; Barbados preliminary bulletin: population. St. Michael, 1973.
iii, 12 p. 33 cm.
Cover title.
1. Barbados—Population—Statistics. 2. Barbados—Census, 1970. I. Title.
CSt NUC75-26650

Barbados. Statistical Service.
Monthly digest of statistics. Apr. 1974–
[Bridgetown] Barbados Statistical Service.
v. ill. 28 cm.
Continues: Barbados. Statistical Service. Quarterly digest of statistics.
1. Barbados—Statistics—Periodicals.
HA865.A312 317.29'81 75-643829 MARC-S

Barbados. Statistical Service.
A study of the national income of Barbados from 1956-59. Barbados, Government Printing Office [1959 ?]
50 p. tables.
1. Barbados—Econ. condit. 2. Income—Barbados. I. Title.
PPiU DLC NUC75-67065

Barbados. Sugar Workers' Provident Fund. Board.
Annual report of the Sugar Workers' Provident Fund Board.
[Bridgetown] Sugar Workers' Provident Fund Board.
v. 36 cm.
1. Barbados. Sugar Workers' Provident Fund.
HD7116.S852B372 354'.729'810083 76-643465 MARC-S

Barbados. Trade Unions, Registrar of
see
Barbados. Registrar of Trade Unions.

Barbados. Transport Board.
Annual report of the Transport Board.
[Bridgetown] Transport Board.
v. 36 cm.
Report year ends Sept. 30.
1. Barbados. Transport Board. 2. Transportation and state—Barbados—Periodicals.
HE43.5.B37T7a 354'.729'810087805 77-646775 MARC-S

Barbados Board of Tourism

For works by this body issued under its earlier name see

Barbados Tourist Board

Barbados Development Corporation.
Report and financial statements of the Barbados Development Corporation.
St. Michael, Barbados Development Corporation.
v. 36 cm. annual.
Report year ends June 30.
1. Barbados Development Corporation. I. Title.
HC167.B35B37a 338.7'61' 75-643659 MARC-S

Barbados economic survey.
[Bridgetown] Economic Planning Unit, Office of the Prime Minister.
v. ill. 25 cm. annual.
Cover title : Economic survey.
1. Barbados—Economic conditions—Periodicals. I. Barbados. Economic Planning Unit. II. Title: Economic survey.
HC157.B35B32 330.9'729'81 76-646449 MARC-S

Barbados Employers' Confederation
see Watson, Robert. Guide to conditions of service, rules and discipline... Bridgetown [1961]

Barbados foreign affairs bulletin. v. 1– Jan./June 1972–
[Bridgetown] Ministry of External Affairs.
v. 33 cm.
1. Barbados—Foreign relations—Collected works. I. Barbados. Ministry of External Affairs.
F2041.B215 327.729'81 74-641889 MARC-S

Barbados Industrial Development Corporation.
Annual report. 1969/70–
[Bridgetown]
v. illus. 31 cm.
Report year ends March 31.
1. Industrial promotion—Barbados.
HC157.B353 I 533a 354'.729'810082 73-646916 MARC-S

Barbados Industrial Development Corporation.
Barbados; a special survey for businessmen. [Rev. Bridgetown? 1973]
1 v. illus. 28 cm.
Cover title.
1. Barbados—Econ. condit. 2. Barbados—Indus. I. Title.
CtY NUC76-75720

Barbados, island in the sun. [5th impression, enl. Bridgetown? Barbados, Carib Publicity Co., 1969]
39 p. col. illus. 22 cm.
Cover title.
1. Barbados—Descr. & trav.—Guide-books.
FU NUC74-121979

Barbados Labour Party
see Labour Party (Barbados)

Barbados Light & Power Company.
Annual report—Barbados Light & Power Company Limited.
[Bridgetown] Barbados Light & Power Company Limited.
v. ill. 28 cm.
1. Barbados Light & Power Company.
HD9685.W43B33a 75-642949
338.7'61'363620972081 MARC-S

Barbados Oceanographic and Meteorological Analysis Project Office
see Environmental Research Laboratories. BOMAP Office.

Barbados Sugar and General Workers Union.
Rules and regulations of the Barbados Sugar and General Workers Union. [Bridgetown, Al Fresco Printery, 1967]
40 p. 17 cm.
I. Title.
FU NUC73-102881

Barbados Tourist Board.
Annual report.
[Bridgewater]
v. illus. 28 cm.
Report year ends Mar. 31.
1. Tourist trade—Barbados.
G155.B27B35a 72-624540

Barbag, Józef.
Geografia ekonomiczna Stanów Zjednoczonych i Kanady / Józef Barbag. — Wyd. 1. — Warszawa : Państwowe Wydawn. Ekonomiczne, 1974.
314 p., [12] leaves of plates : ill. ; 25 cm.
Bibliography: p. [299]-301.
Includes index.
zł47.00
1. United States—Economic conditions—1961– 2. Canada—Economic conditions—1945– I. Title.
HC106.6.B32 75-571560

Barbag, Józef.
Geografia polityczna ogólna. [Wyd. 2.] Warszawa, Państwowe Wydawn. Naukowe, 1974.
268 p. maps (1 fold. in pocket) 25 cm.
1. Geography, Political. I. Title.
CSt-H NUC76-32443

Barbag, Józef.
Iskier przewodnik panorama świata / Józef Barbag. — Wyd. 1. — Warszawa : Iskry, 1974.
353 p., [16] leaves of plates : ill. ; 17 cm.
Cover title: Panorama świata.
zł40.00
1. Geography—Dictionaries—Polish. I. Title. II. Title: Panorama świata.
G103.B32 76-510292

Barbag, Józef.
Zarys geografii politycznej. [Wyd. 1. Warszawa] Państwowe Wydawn. Naukowe [c1971]
253 p. illus. 24 cm. zł28.00
Bibliography: p. 246-[252]
1. Geography, Political. I. Title.
JC319.B35 74-206047

Barbag, Józef
see Encyklopedia powszechna PWN. Warszawa: Państ. Wydaw. Naukowe, 1973-

Barbag, Jozef
see Geografia Polski. Warszawa, Państwowe Zaklady Wydawnictw Szkolnych [1968-

Barbag, Józef, ed.
see Metodyka nauczania geografii. Wyd. 2., zmienione. Warszawa, Wydawnictwa Szkolne i Pedagogiczne [1974]

Barbag, Severin Eugen.
Die Lieder von Robert Franz. Wien, 1922 [1973]
145 l. music.
Dissertation—Universität Wien.
Microfilm (negative) Wien, Universität, 1973. 1 reel.
1. Franz, Robert, 1815-1892. I. Title.
IaU NUC74-126738

Barbagallo, Corrado, 1877-1952.
Il problema delle origini di Roma. Da Vico a noi ... Edizione anastatica. Roma, L'erma di Bretschneider, 1970.
vi, 149 p. 23 cm. (Studia historica, 73) It 73-Apr
Reproduction of the Milan 1926 ed.
Includes bibliographical references.
1. Rome—Historiography. I. Title.
DG205.B35 1970 913.37 73-327998

Barbagallo, Francesco, 1945–
Lavoro ed esodo nel Sud. 1861-1971. Napoli, Guida, 1973.
265 p. 21 cm. (Studio Sud., 4) L3000 It 73-Dec
Includes bibliographical references.
1. Italy, Southern—Population—History. 2. Italy, Southern—Economic conditions. 3. Migration, Internal—Italy—History. I. Title.
HB2059.B28 74-315498

Barbagallo, Ignazio.
Frosinone : lineamenti storici dalle origini ai nostri giorni : pubblicazione edita in occasione del III centenario del Santuario della Madonna della Neve e col patrocinio dell'Ente provinciale del turismo di Frosinone / Ignazio Barbagallo. — Frosinone : Editrice frusinate, 1975.
xv, 464 p. : ill. ; 25 cm. It76-Sept
Includes bibliographical references and index.
L5000
1. Frosinone, Italy—History. 2. Frosinone, Italy—Religious life and customs. I. Title.
DG975.F883B37 945'.622 77-451276
•77 MARC

Barbagallo, José F
Mejoramiento de campos bajos, por José F. Barbagallo, Luis J. Sabella y Jorge I. Bellati. [Buenos Aires? Instituto Nacional de Tecnología Agropecuaria, 1965]
[8] p. illus. 16 cm. (Serie Agriculturasuelos, no. 4603)
1. Soil conservation—Argentine Republic. 2. Terracing. 3. Soil conservation—Pictorial works. I. Sabella, Luis J., joint author. II. Bellati, Jorge I., joint author. III. Title. IV. Series.
TxU NUC73-126149

Barbagallo, Renato.
Lineamenti dell'ordinamento regionale valdostano. Aosta, Musumeci, 1973.
98 p. 21 cm. It 74-Mar
Includes bibliographical references.
1. Local government—Aosta, Valley of. I. Title.
74-349656

Barbagallo, Renato.
La regione : profili dell'ordinamento regionale in Italia / Renato Barbagallo. — 2. ed. — Aosta : Musumeci, 1976.
182 p. ; 24 cm. It76-Sept
Includes bibliographical references.
1. Regionalism—Italy. 2. Decentralization in government—Italy. I. Title.
JN5477.R35B35 1976 76-487424
•77 MARC

Barbagallo, Salvatore.
La lingua armena. Memoria presentata all'Accademi. Tiberina nel luglio 1972. San Lazzaro, Casa editrice armena dei Padri Mechitaristi, [1972].
16 p. 24 cm.
Includes bibliographical references.
1. Armenian language—Addresses, essays, lectures. I. Title.
PK8017.B28 75-559911

Barbagallo, Salvo, 1938-
Randazzo, 17 giugno 1945 : anatomia di una strage / Salvo Barbagallo. — [s.l.] : Associazione Nuovo mondo, Teatro Erwin Piscator, 1976.
43 p. ; 21 cm. It77-Mar
A play.
L1000
1. Italy—History—Allied occupation, 1943-1947—Drama. 2. Sicily—History—1870- —Drama. I. Title.
PQ4862.A6717R36 77-463174
•77 MARC

Barbagallo, Salvo, 1938-
Una rivoluzione mancata / Salvo Barbagallo. — [Catania] : Bonanno, [1974]
157 p., [2] leaves of plates : ill. ; 21 cm. It 75-Jan
Includes bibliographies.
L3500
1. World War, 1939-1945—Underground movements—Sicily. 2. Sicily—History—1870- I. Title.
D802.S55B37 940.53'458 75-553024

Barbagelata, Augustín Rolando.
Entre las grietas; versos. [Paraná, Argentina, 1971]
54 p. 19 cm. (Colección C.L.E.R., v. 1)
I. Title.
CtY NUC75-32400

Barbagelata, Héctor Hugo.
La leva de huelguistas ante el derecho uruguayo; estudio en memoria de Emilio Frugoni. Montevideo, 1969.
38 p. 25 cm.
LACAP 70-4706
"Apartado de la Revista de la Facultad de Derecho y Ciencias Sociales, año XX, nos 3-4, con un apéndice, que incluye el texto anotado del D. 402/968; la L. 13.657; el Conv. O. I. T. no. 105, y los DD. 380 y 515/969."
Includes bibliographical references.
1. Strikes and lockouts—Uruguay. I. Title.
74-318196

Barbagelata, Hugo David, 1886-
see Rodó, José Enrique, 1871-1917. ... Cinco ensayos ... Madrid, Sociedad Española de Librería [1915]

Barbagelata, Hugo David, 1886-
see Rodó, José Enrique, 1871-1917. ... Cinco ensayos ... Madrid, Editorial-América [1971?]

Barbagelata, Hugo David, 1886- ed.
see Rodó, José Enrique, 1871-1917. Epistolario... Paris, Agencia General de Librería [1921]

Barbagelata, Robert D.
see California Continuing Education of the Bar. New tort remedies in insurance cases... [Berkeley] 1974.

Barbagli, Marzio, 1938-
Disoccupazione intellettuale e sistema scolastico in Italia (1859-1973). Bologna, Il mulino, 1974.
481 p. 19 cm. (Universale paperbacks Il mulino, 4) L1900
It 74-July
Includes bibliographical references.
1. Education—Italy—History. I. Title.
LA791.B32 74-323318

Barbagli, Marzio, 1938-
Scuola, potere e ideologia / saggi di L. Althusser ... [et al.] ; a cura di Marzio Barbagli. — Bologna : Il mulino, 1975.
313 p. : ill. ; 22 cm. — (Serie di sociologia) (Problemi e prospettive)
It77-Feb
Essays previously published in various periodicals.
Bibliography: p. [303]-313.
L5000
1. Education and state—Addresses, essays, lectures. 2. Educational sociology—Addresses, essays, lectures. I. Althusser, Louis. II. Title.
LC71.B23 1975 77-467553
•77 MARC

Barbaglia Gai, Ester.
Una macchina per Claudio; romanzo per ragazzi. [Torino] Società Editrice Internazionale [1963]
168 p. illus. 22 cm. (Collana L'Aguilone, 18)
I. Title.
MB NUC76-71904

Barbaglio, Giuseppe.
see Nuovo dizionario di teologia. Alba, Edizioni paoline, 1977.

Barbaiani, Mihai, joint author.
see **Brînzan, Ion. Calculul şi alcătuirea structurilor etajate cu diafragme. Bucureşti, Editura tehnică, 1976.**

Barbaini, Piero, 1926-
La Chiesa sbagliata / Piero Barbaini. — Milano : Il formichiere, [1976]
294 p. ; 22 cm. It76-Oct
Includes index.
L4500
1. Catholic Church—Doctrinal and controversial works—Catholic authors. 2. Barbaini, Piero, 1926- 3. Ex-priests, Catholic—Italy—Biography. I. Title.
BX1779.5.B37 76-487799
•76 MARC

Barbakadze, Mark Shiovich, joint author
see Gulīamov, Saĭdakhrar Saĭdakhmedovich. (Modeli razvitiīa promyshlennykh uzlov) 1976.

Barbalace, Raúl R
Rostro de niebla / Raúl R. Barbalace. — Chivilcoy [Argentina] : Ediciones Figaro, [1975]
75 p. ; 18 cm.
I. Title.
PQ7798.12.A652R6 861 77-460760
77 MARC

Barbalace, Roberta Crowell.
An introduction to light horse management / by Roberta Crowell Barbalace ; with ill. by Rayona Hudson. — Fort Collins, Colo. : [Caballus Publishers, 1974]
302 p. : ill. ; 24 cm.
Includes bibliographies and index.
ISBN 0-912830-34-4
1. Horses. I. Title.
SF285.B29 636.1'08'0207 74-18651
75 MARC

Barbalarga, Carlos L.
see Difusión geográfica de cultivos índices en el Chaco argentino y sus causas. 2. ed. Buenos Aires : Instituto Nacional de Tecnología Agropecuaria, 1973.

Barbalarga, Carlos L
see Difusión geográfica de cultivos índices en la Provincia de Santiago del Estero y sus causas, [2. ed.] Buenos Aires, Centro de Investigaciones de Recursos Naturales, 1974.

Barbalas, Louis X
Great Lakes research project forecasts directory 1973 [by] Louis X. Barbalas. Detroit, Mich., Lake Survey Center, 1973.
xiv, 280 p. (United States. National Oceanic and Atmospheric Administration. NOAA technical memorandum NOS LSC D5)
On cover: Directory and project forecasts the Great Lakes-1973.
1. Great Lakes. 2. Great Lakes. Surveys. I. Lake Survey Center. II. Title. III. Title: Directory and project forecasts the Great Lakes-1973.
InLP NUC77-8651

Barbalato, Beatrice.
La controcultura tra radicalismo e integrazione : società di massa e fenomeni alternativi / Beatrice Barbalato. — Roma : Bulzoni, 1974.
178 p. ; 21 cm. — (L'Uomo e la società ; 34) It 74-Dec
Includes bibliographical references.
L3300
1. Social history—1945- 2. Mass society. 3. Popular culture. I. Title.
HN17.5.B32 75-407066

Bārbale, Marta, 1933-
Manas miglas. Rīgā, Liesma, 1969.
125 p. illus. 15 cm.
Poems.
I. Title.
NjP NUC75-21637

Bārbale, Marta, 1933-
Melni mani kumeliņi : dzejoļi / Marta Bārbale. -- Rīga : "Liesma", 1975.
138 p. ; 15 cm.
Russian title in colophon : Koni moi voronye.
Latvian text.
Bound in a pamphlet volume.
MH NUC77-83506

Bārbale, Marta, 1933-
Saules pirtī. [Māksliniece Māra Rikmane. Rīgā, "Liesma," 1971]
104 p. illus. 17 cm.
Poems.
I. Title.
MB NUC75-32405

Barbalho, Nelson, 1918-
Caruru, Caruaru (nótulas subsidiárias para a história do agreste de Pernambuco) Caruaru, 1972.
215 p. illus. 23 cm.
1. Caruaru, Brazil. 2. Pernambuco, Brazil (State)—History. I. Title.
F2651.C35B37 73-200116

Barbalho, Nelson, 1918-
Dicionário da aguardente / Nelson Barbalho. — Recife : [s. n.], 1974.
201 p. ; 23 cm.
Bibliography : p. 199-201.
Cr$25.00
1. Liquors—Dictionaries—Portuguese. I. Title.
TP503.B37 75-553490

Barbalho, Nelson, 1918-
Guerra dos mascates. [Caruaru? Brasil, 1972?-
v. 24 cm.
Cover title.
1. Pernambuco, Brazil (State)—History. 2. Olinda, Brazil—History. I. Title.
F2601.B29 73-213435

Barbalho, Nelson, 1918-
País de Caruaru : subsídios para a história do Agreste / Nelson Barbalho. — [s. l. : s. n.], 1974 (Recife : Companhia Editôra de Pernambuco)
211 p. ; 23 cm.
1. Caruaru, Brazil—History. I. Title.
F2651.C35B38 981'.3 75-577104

Barbalić, Radojica.
Oploviti Cape Horn ... Kronika. Rijeka, Vlastita naklada, 1972.
234, [1] p. with illus., ports. 20 cm. 45.00Din Yu 73
At head of title: Radojica F. Barbalić, Ivo Jurković.
Summary in English.
1. Seafaring life. 2. Merchant ships, Yugoslav. 3. Horn, Cape. I. Jurković, Ivo, 1933- joint author. II. Title.
G540.B24 73-970404

Barbalić, Radojica, joint author
see Kojić, Branko. Ilustrirana povijest jadranskog pomorstva. Zagreb: Stvarnost [1975]

Barbalić, Zoran.
Prilozi rješavanju problema pri izboru otvora mostova. Sarajevo, Zavod za hidrotehniku Građevinskog fakulteta, 1972.
[2], 41, [3] p., 9 l. with diagrs. (part fold.) 23 cm. (Zavod za hidrotehniku Građevinskog fakulteta u Sarajevu. Izdanja, br. 6)
Yu 72
Bibliography : p. [44]
1. Bridges—Design. I. Title. II. Series: Sarajevo. Univerzitet. Zavod za hidrotehniku. Izdanja, br. 6.
TG300.B37 72-970722

Barban, Arnold M
Advertising media sourcebook and workbook / Arnold M. Barban, Donald W. Jugenheimer, Lee F. Young. — Columbus, Ohio : Grid, inc., [1975]
186 p. : forms ; 28 cm. — (Grid series in journalism & advertising)
Includes bibliographies and index.
ISBN 0-88244-077-2 : $5.95
1. Advertising—United States. I. Jugenheimer, Donald W., joint author. II. Young, Lee F., joint author. III. Title.
HF5813.U6B327 659.1'0973 75-2912
75 MARC

Barban, Arnold M
Essentials of media planning : a marketing viewpoint / Arnold M. Barban, Stephen M. Cristol, Frank J. Kopek. — Chicago : Crain Books, c1976.
viii, 86 p. : ill. ; 22 cm.
Includes index.
ISBN 0-87251-019-0
1. Advertising media planning. 2. Marketing. I. Cristol, Stephen M., joint author. II. Kopek, Frank J., joint author. III. Title.
HF5826.5.B37 659.1'1 75-21743
76 MARC

Barban, Arnold M
Measurement of the differences in the perception of advertising by whites and Negroes through use of the semantic differential. Austin, Tex., 1964.
xv, 236 p. illus.
Thesis—University of Texas.
Photocopy. Ann Arbor, Mich., University Microfilms, 1972. 236 p. (on double leaves) 18 cm.
1. Advertising research. 2. Marketing research. I. Title.
CtY NUC73-31041

Barban, Arnold M., joint author
see Dunn, Samuel Watson, 1918-
Advertising: its role in modern marketing. 3d ed. Hinsdale, Ill., Dryden Press [1974]

Barbán, José H
Las huellas de un camino / José H. Barbán. -- 1. ed. -- La Habana : UNEAC, 1975.
57 p. : ill. ; 18 cm. (Colección David)
I. Title.
CtY NUC77-83509

Barbancho, Alfonso García
see García Barbancho, Alfonso.

Barbanel', Simon Rafailovich
see Kinoproektsionnaia tekhnika. 1973.

Barbanell, Maurice.
Philosophy of Silver Birch. Edited by Stella Storm. London, Spiritualist Press [1969]
158 p. illus. 19 cm.
Anthology of "Silver Birch's teachings," through Maurice Barbanell, medium. Cf. dust jacket.
1. Mediums. I. Silver Birch. II. Storm, Stella, ed. III. Title.
IU NUC74-23486

Barbanell, Maurice.
This is spiritualism. London, Spiritualist Press [1967, c1959]
223 p. illus. 23 cm.
Label covers imprint: Boston, Branden Press.
1. Spiritualism. I. Title.
MB NUC75-32406

Barbanis, B., ed.
see European Astronomical Meeting, 1st, Athens, 1972. Galaxies and relativistic astrophysics. Berlin, New York, Springer-Veralg, 1974.

Barbano, Enzo.
L'occupazione austriaca della Valsesia nel 1849. [Borgosesia], Società valsesiana di cultura, [1972?].
xv, 78 p. 24 cm. It 72-May
Includes bibliographical references.
1. Sesia Valley, Italy—History. 2. Austro-Sardinian War, 1848-1849. I. Title.
DG975.S43B27 73-305628

Barbano, Enzo
see Cronache poetiche della vecchia Borgosesia. [s.l.]: Società valsesiana di cultura, 1974.

Barbano, Filippo.
Classi e struttura sociale in Italia : studi e ricerche (1955-1975) / Filippo Barbano. — 1. ed. — Torino : Valentino, 1976.
397 p. ; 21 cm. — (Quaderni di ricerca del Progetto stratificazione e classi sociali in Italia della Fondazione Giovanni Agnelli ; 1) It76-Nov
Bibliography: p. 341-397.
L8500
1. Social classes—Italy. 2. Italy—Social conditions. I. Title. II. Series: Fondazione Giovanni Agnelli. Progetto stratificazione e classi sociali in Italia. Quaderni di ricerca del Progetto stratificazione e classi sociali in Italia della Fondazione Giovanni Agnelli ; 1.
HN490.S6B36 301.44'0945 77-454316
*77 MARC

Barbano, Filippo. Lineamenti di storia del pensiero sociologico
see Barbano, Filippo. Profilo critico di storia del pensiero sociòlogico. Torino, G. Giappichelli, 1971.

Barbano, Filippo.
Per una esposizione della sociologia. Critica delle istituzioni, paradigmi espositivi, immagini della società. Torino, G. Giappichelli, 1974.
xii, 208 p. 24 cm. L3800 It 74-Sept
At head of title: Università di Torino. Facoltà di scienze politiche. Indirizzo sociologico.
"Scheda bibliografica personale": p. [205]-208.
1. Sociology. I. Title.
HM59.B29 74-351199

Barbano, Filippo.
Profilo critico di storia del pensiero sociologico. Introduzione ai Lineamenti con una nota sulla storiografia sociologica in Italia. Torino, G. Giappichelli, 1971.
135 p. 25 cm. L2000 It Suppl-6
At head of title: Università di Torino. Facoltà di scienze politiche. Corsi di sociologia.
Bibliography: p. 129-132.
1. Sociology—Italy—History. 2. Sociology—Methodology. I. Barbano, Filippo. Lineamenti di storia del pensiero sociologico. II. Title.
HM22.I 55B37 74-330031

Barbano, Filippo.
Sociologia della politica : concetti, metodi e campo di ricerca : in appendice, Sociologia e contesto sociale / Filippo Barbano. — Milano : A. Giuffrè, 1961.
235 p. ; 25 cm.
Includes bibliographical references and index.
1. Political sociology. I. Title.
JA76.B29 76-524379

Barbano, Filippo.
Struttura e classi sociali in Italia : gli studi e le ricerche (1955-1975) / Filippo Barbano. — Torino : G. Giappichelli, 1975.
iv, 298 p. ; 25 cm. It 75-Sept
At head of title: Università di Torino, Facoltà di scienze politiche, indirizzo sociologico.
Includes bibliographical references.
L5000
1. Social classes—Italy. 2. Social mobility—Italy. I. Title.
HN490.S6B37 75-541402

Barbano, Filippo
see Estructuralismo y sociologia. Buenos Aires, Ediciones Nueva vision [1969]

Barbano, Joseph.
see United States. Bureau of Health Resources Development. Minorities and women in the health fields ... [Washington] U.S. Dept. of Health, Education, and Welfare, Public Health Service, Health Resources Administration, Bureau of Health Resources Development, 1974.

Barbanti, Luigi.
Indagini idrologiche e chimiche dei principali tributari piemontesi del Lago Maggiore in relazione alle sue modificazioni trofiche / Luigi Barbanti, Alcide Calderoni, Alfredo Carollo. — Verbania Pallanza : Edizioni dell'Istituto italiano di idrobiologia, 1974.
ii, 149 p. : ill. ; 29 cm. It***
Bibliography: p. 148-149.
1. Hydrology—Piedmont. 2. Water quality—Piedmont. 3. Limnology—Italy—Maggiore, Lago. I. Calderoni, Alcide, joint author. II. Carollo, Alfredo, joint author. III. Title.
GB738.P53B37 75-547968

Barbanti, Luigi
see Indagini ecologiche sul Lago d'Endine. Verbania Pallanza : Edizioni dell'Istituto italiano di idrobiologia, 1974.

Barbanti Grimaldi, Nefta.
Il Guercino, Gian Francesco Barbieri 1591-1666. [Rev. ed] Bologna, Edizioni GR [1968]
116 p. 252 plates (27 col.) 29 cm.
Bibliography: p. 81-84.
1. Barbieri, Giovanni Francesco, called Il Guercino, 1591-1666.
TxDaM CaBVaU NUC73-2827

Barbar, Aghil M
Ports of the Arab worlds [i.e. world] : an annotated bibliography / Aghil M. Barbar. — Monticello, Ill. : Council of Planning Librarians, 1977.
6 p. ; 29 cm. — (Exchange bibliography - Council of Planning Librarians ; 1243)
Cover title.
$1.50
1. Harbors—Arab countries—Bibliography. I. Title. II. Series: Council of Planning Librarians. Exchange bibliography ; 1243.
Z5942.C68 no. 1243 016.3092 s 77-364007
[Z7165.A67] 77 MARC
[HE559.A7]

Barbar, Aghil M
Urbanization in Libya / Aghil M. Barbar. — Monticello, Ill. : Council of Planning Librarians, 1977.
5 p. ; 28 cm. — (Exchange bibliography - Council of Planning Librarians ; 1241)
Cover title.
$1.50
1. Urbanization—Libya—Bibliography. 2. Libya—Population—Bibliography. I. Title. II. Series: Council of Planning Librarians. Exchange bibliography ; 1241.
Z5942.C68 no. 1241 016.3092 s 77-360179
[Z7164.U7] 77 MARC
[HT148.L5]

Barbar, Aghil M
Urbanization in the Arab world : a selected bibliography / by Aghil M. Barbar. — Monticello, Ill. : Council of Planning Librarians, 1977.
18 p. ; 28 cm. — (Exchange bibliography - Council of Planning Librarians ; no. 1198)
Cover title.
$2.00
1. Urbanization—Arab countries—Bibliography. 2. Arab countries—Social conditions—Bibliography. I. Title. II. Series: Council of Planning Librarians. Exchange bibliography ; no. 1198.
Z5942.C68 No. 1198 016.3092 s 77-357272
[Z7165.A65] 77 MARC
[HT147.5]

Barbar, James.
El Koura. [Dover, Del.] 1973.
70 p.
I. Title.
DeU NUC76-74990

Barbar, John
see Cycon Resource Management Ltd., Canada. A Cycon mini-information system... Richmond, B.C., c1971.

Barbara.
La partagée / Barbara ; [racontée à] Christine de Coninck. — Paris : Éditions de Minuit, c1977.
190 p. ; 22 cm. — (Autrement dites) F***
ISBN 2-7073-0173-6 : 25.00F
1. Barbara. 2. Prostitutes—France—Biography. I. Coninck, Christine de. II. Title.
HQ194.B3 301.41'54'0924 77-555470
77 MARC

Bárbara Virgínia.
A mulher na sociedade; manual prático e ilustrado de charme e etiquêta. [São Paulo] Edições Paulinas [1972]
148 p. illus. 20 cm. Cr$12.00
1. Entertaining. 2. Cookery, Brazilian. 3. Etiquette for women. I. Title.
TX731.B35 73-204571

Barbara, Dominick A
Loving and making love : a psychiatrist's guide to happiness and pleasure by Dominick A. Barbara. — Rockville Centre, N. Y. : Farnsworth Pub. Co., [1975]
169 p. ; 24 cm.
ISBN 0-87863-079-1 : $8.95
1. Sexual ethics. 2. Love. 3. Interpersonal relations. I. Title.
HQ31.B26 301.41 74-18439
MARC

Barbará, Esther, joint author
see Fretes, Hilda Gladys. Bibliografía anotada del modernismo. Mendoza, Argentina : Universidad Nacional de Cuyo, 1970.

Barbara, Frau
see
Frau Barbara.

Barbara, Leila.
Sintaxe transformacional do modo verbal / Leila Barbara. — São Paulo : Editora Ática, 1975.
184 p. ; 21 cm. — (Ensaios ; 11)
Bibliography: p. [178]-184.
Originally presented as the author's thesis, Pontifícia Universidade Católica de São Paulo, 1971 under the title: Um estudo da manifestação sintática da asserveração e da não-asseveração em português e em inglês.
1. Modality (Linguistics) 2. Grammar, Comparative and general—Syntax. 3. Generative grammar. 4. Portuguese language—Grammar, Comparative—English. 5. English language—Grammar, Comparative—Portuguese. I. Title.
P299.M6B3 1975 76-451351
76 MARC

Barbara, Luigi, ed.
see Simposio di fisiopatologia della nutrizione e di dietetica clinica, 1st, Bologna, 1972. La via metabolica dell'aterogenesi. Bologna, R. Patron, 1972.

Barbara, Michael A
Kansas criminal law handbook : a manual of criminal proceedings for judges and lawyers of the State of Kansas / by Michael A. Barbara. — Topeka : [Kansas Bar Association, 1974]
1 v. ; 26 cm.
Loose-leaf for updating.
Includes indexes.
1. Criminal procedure—Kansas. I. Title.
KFK575.B37 345.'781'05 75-303212
MARC

Barbará, Paulo Henrique.
Paralelo XX ⌈i. e. vinte⌉ : depoimentos, confissões, contos / Paulo Henrique Barbará. — ⌈Rio de Janeiro⌉ : Livraria São José ⌈1974⌉
121 p. ; 21 cm.
Cr$15.00
I. Title.
PQ9698.12.A59P3 74-235711

Barbará, Paulo Henrique.
O pijama, O jardineiro mau e outras histórias. Pref. de Nelson Rodrigues. Rio de Janeiro, Liv. São José, 1968.
100 p. 19 cm. NCr$6.00 BB 68-7
LACAP 68-0956
At head of title: Paulo Henrique Barbará Pinheiro.
I. Title. II. Title: O jardineiro mau.
PQ9698.12.A59P5 68-103445
rev

Barbará de Bittar, Esther
see
Barbará, Esther.

Barbará Pinheiro, Paulo Henrique
see
Barbará, Paulo Henrique.

Barbará, Spain
see also
Santa María de Barbará, Spain.

Barbaras, Judith Eleanor.
Quantitative studies on antigen inhalation. ⌈Cleveland⌉ 1973.
x, 166 l. illus., plates.
Thesis (Ph.D.)—Western Reserve University, Cleveland.
1. Antigens—Metabolism. 2. Antigen-antibody reactions—Analysis. 3. Lung—Immunology. 4. Models, Biological. 5. Pulmonary surfactant. I. Title.
OCIW-H NUC75-26649

Barbareschi Fino, Maria Antonietta.
Sogni d'infinito : poesie / Maria Barbareschi Fino. — Milano : La Prora, ⌈1973⌉
101 p. ; 21 cm. — (Poeti, narratori, saggisti contemporanei) It 74-Dec
CONTENTS: Dal tempo.—Ciottoli sul greto.—Sogni d'infinito.
L1000
I. Title.
PQ4862.A672S6 75-561201

Barbareschi Fino, Maria Antonietta.
L'urlo e altre novelle. Cosenza, Pellegrini, 1973.
225 p. 21 cm. L1600 It 74-Mar
At head of title: M. A. Barbareschi Fino.
I. Title.
PQ4862.A672U7 74-312935

Barbareschi Fino, Maria Antonietta.
Le valli di Lanzo tra storia e leggenda / ⌈di⌉ M. A. Barbareschi Fino ; illustrato da Edmondo Maneglia. — Torino : Piemonte in bancarella, 1975.
175 p. : ill. ; 26 cm. It76-Dec
1. Legends—Italy—Lanzo, Valley of. 2. Lanzo, Valley of—History. I. Title.
GR177.L33B37 77-456268
•77 MARC

Barbaresi, Patricia Nancy, 1937-
Towards a programmatic knowledge production system in educational administration: the research setting. ⌈Ithaca, N.Y.⌉ 1973.
3, x, 234 l. 28 cm.
Thesis (Ph.D.)—Cornell University.
Bibliography: leaves 227-234.
1. Education, Higher—1965- —Curricula. 2. Social science research—Methodology. I. Title.
NIC NUC75-30713

Barbaresi, Raffaello.
see Laureati e disoccupati. Firenze, Vallecchi, c1975.

Barbaresi, Sante.
Cavour, nocchiero del Risorgimento / Sante Barbaresi. — Bari : Edizioni del Levante, ⌈1962⌉
161 p. ; 22 cm.
1. Cavour, Camillo Benso, conte di, 1810-1861. 2. Italy—History—1849-1870. 3. Statesmen—Italy—Biography. I. Title.
DG552.8.C3B3 76-524288

Barbaretos, Geōrgios Achilleōs
see
Varvaretos, Geōrgios Achilleōs.

Barbargo-Galtieri, Angela
see **Herndon, David J** ⌈i.e. Pi⌉ **N partial-wave amplitudes... Berkeley, Calif., Lawrence Radiation Laboratory, University of California, 1970.**

al-Barbarī, Aḥmad Maḥmūd.
⌈al-Dīn bayna al-fard wa-al-mujtama'⌉
الدين بين الفرد والمجتمع ⌈تأليف⌉ احمد محمود البربرى.
⌈القاهرة، مكتبة مصر، 1972⌉
285 p. 20 cm. (فى رحاب الاسلام) £E0.30
Bibliography: p. 283-285.
1. Islam—Essence, genius, nature. I. Title.
BP88.B3D5 72-960466

al-Barbarī, Muhammad Yūsuf, joint author
see al-Subki, 'Abd al-Latif. Tarikh al-tashri' al-Islami. 1946.

Barbarī, Muslim.
('Āṣifah fī Marrākish)
عاصفة فى مراكش؛ او، اخطاء السياسة البربرية. الفه بالفرنسية مسلم بربرى. لخصته ونشرته بالعربية اللجنة الشرقية للدفاع عن المغرب. القاهرة، المطبعة السلفية ومكتبتها
.1350 ⌈1931 or 2⌉
48 p. illus. 20 cm.
1. Morocco—Politics and government—Addresses, essays, lectures. 2. Berbers—Addresses, essays, lectures. I. Title. II. Title: Akhṭā' al-siyāsah al-Barbarīyah.
DT324.B2212 74-217149

Barbari, Sophie.
Poèmes sans mesure. Paris (6e), Éditions de la Grisière, 184, Bd Saint-Germain, 1971.
61 p. 18 cm. 14.00F F 72-12273
I. Title.
PQ2662.A637P6 72-373247

Barbarić, Nera Karolina, 1955-
Jorbuli duše / Nera Karolina Barbarić. — Split : Marko Marulić, 1974.
51 p. ; 22 cm. — (Biblioteka MM) (Edicija Suvremeni pisci ; 3) Yu***
I. Title.
PG1619.12.A717J6 75-970814

Barbarič, Štefan
see **Kmečki uproi v slovenski umetnosti ... Ljubljana: Slovenska matica, 1974.**

Barbarič, Štefan
see Prijateljev zbornik: ob stoletnici rojstva. Ljubljana: Slovenska matica, 1975.

Barbarič, Štefan
see Študije o slovstvu in jeziku. Murska Sobota, "Pomurska založba," 1973.

La Barbarie hondureña y los derechos humanos (proceso de una agresión). San Salvador, Ministerio de Defensa, Prensa y Publicidad, 1969.
111 p. illus., maps. 25 cm.
"La Comisión Mixta de Investigación Histórica del Ministerio de Defensa ... determinó la publicación del presente folleto."
Includes bibliographical references.
1. Salvador—Foreign relations—Honduras. 2. Honduras—Foreign relations—Salvador. I. Salvador. Ministerio de Defensa Nacional.
JX1523.Z7H62 75-577500

Barbariga, Anton Antonovich.
Speak English. Govori po angliĭski. Izd. 2. Moskva, Prosveshchenie, 1970.
76 p. illus. 20 cm.
At head of title: A.A. Babariga.
"Kniga dli͡a razviti͡a navykov ustnoĭ rechi u uchashchikhsi͡a VI-VIII klassov sredneĭ shkoly."
1. English language—Conversation and phrase books—Russian. I. Title.
NIC NUC76-90400

Barbarigo, Girolamo, 1723-1782.
Principi di fisica generale. Padova, Nella Stamperia Corzatti, 1780.
xxxi, 318 p.
Microprint. New York, Readex Microprint, 1974. 4 cards. (Landmarks of science)
1. Physics—Early works to 1800. I. Title.
InU NUC76-23688

Barbarin, Georges.
Le Secret de la grande Pyramide ou la Fin du monde adamique. Paris, J'ai lu, 1969.
192 p. illus. 17 cm. (J'ai lu, A216. L'Aventure mystérieuse)
3.30F F 70-4
1. Pyramids—Curiosa and miscellany. 2. End of the world. I. Title.
DT63.5.B28 1969 73-343159
MARC

Barbarin, Oscar Anthony.
A comparison of overt and symbolic aversion in the self-management of chronic smoking behavior / by Oscar A. Barbarin, III. -- New Brunswick, N.J., 1975.
ix, 119 l. : ill. ; 29 cm.
Thesis (Ph.D.) -- Rutgers University.
Bibliography : leaves 90-95.
1. Smoking -- Psychological aspects. 2. Aversive stimuli. I. Title.
NjR NUC77-83510

Barbarin, V. V.
see Biologi͡a pitani͡a, razviti͡a i povedenie ptit͡s. 1976.

Barbarin, V. V.
see Khimicheskiĭ mutagenez. 1974.

Barbarin, V. V., ed.
see Pitanie, razmnozhenie i genetika zhivotnykh. 1972.

Barbarino, Joseph Louis, 1945-
A quantitative and comparative study of the B-V alternation in Latin inscriptions from Britain, the Balkans, Dalmatia, North Africa, Spain, Gaul and Italy. [New York] 1974.
v, 231 l. 29 cm.
Thesis—Columbia University.
Bibliography: leaves 220-231.
1. Inscriptions, Latin. 2. Latin language—Consonants. 3. Latin language—Phonetics. I. Title.
NNC NUC76-22865

Barbaro, Alfredo.
Esperienze di didattica ortofonica e riferimenti di attualità sulle strutture educative dei minorati dell'udito. Bari, Tip. Mare, 1973.
120 p. 24 cm. It 74-May
1. Deaf—Means of communication. 2. Deaf—Education. I. Title.
HV2483.B37 74-321570

Barbaro, Ermolao, 1410-1471.
Orationes contra poetas. Epistolae. Ed. critica a cura di Giorgio Ronconi. Firenze, Sansoni ⌈1972⌉
vii, 184 p. illus. (Pubblicazioni della Facoltà di magistero dell'Università di Padova, 14)
Text in Latin; critical matter in Italian.
I. Ronconi, Giorgio.
MH NUC74-136265

Barbaro, Ermolao, 1454-1493.
Castigationes Plinianae et Pomponii Melae. Rome, Eucharius Silber, 24 Nov. (VIII Kal. Dec.) 1492-13 Feb. (Id. Feb.) 1493.
⌈348⌉ l. f°. 32.8 cm.
Hain. Repertorium (with Copinger's Supplement) *2421; Brit. Mus. Cat. (XV ceut.) IV, p. 113 (IB. 18955); Gesamtkat. d. Wiegendr., 3340; Goff. Third census, B-100.
With editorial corrections. For similar corrections in other copies. cf. introd. to the Padova edition of 1973.
Contemporary half white leather over wooden boards.
Provenance: Wolfgang Moser (inscription); Domus probat. Soc. Jesu Viennae ad S. Annam, 1700 (inscription); J. B. Holzinger (bookplate)
1. Plinius Secundus, C. Naturalis historia. 2. Mela, Pomponius. De situ orbis libri tres. I. Title.
Incun. X.B246 76-528024
[PA6614.A2]
——— Copy 2. 31.1 cm. With editorial corrections. Thacher Coll.

Barbaro, Ermolao, 1454–1493.
Castigationes Plinianae et Pomponii Melae. [Venice, Eponymous press, 1493/94]
[160] l. (l. [126] blank) f°. 31.5 cm.
Leaf [1ª] (t. p.) : Castigationes Plinij Hermolai Barbari.
Printed at the instigation and expense of Daniel Barbaro.
Hain. Repertorium (with Copinger's Supplement) *2420; Brit. Mus. Cat. (XV cent.) V, p. 587 (IB. 25168) ; Gesamtkat. d. Wiegendr., 3341; Goff. Third census, B-101.
Stamp on t. p.: G. W. L. D. Bookplate of Edmund McClure.
1. Plinius Secundus, C. Naturalis historia. 2. Mela, Pomponius. De situ orbis libri tres. I. Title.
Incun. X.B247 76–528026
[PA6614.A2]

Barbaro, Ermolao, 1454–1493.
Castigationes Plinianae et Pomponii Melae. Cremona, Carolus de Darleriis, 3 Apr. (III Non. Apr.) 1495.
[160] l. (l. [126] blank) f°. 28.7 cm.
Leaf [1ª] (t. p.) : Castigationes Hermolai in Plinium castigatissimae ...
Reprint of the Venetian edition of 1493/94, with a laudatory poem by Augustinus Grandis and marginal contents-summaries added.
Hain. Repertorium (with Copinger's Supplement) *2423; Gesamtkat. d. Wiegendr., 3342; Brit. Mus. Cat. (XV cent.) VII, p. 959 (IB. 30843) ; Goff. Third census, B–102.
1. Plinius Secundus, C. Naturalis historia. 2. Mela, Pomponius. De situ orbis libri tres. I. Title.
Incun. 1495.B22 76–528008

Barbaro, Ermolao, 1454–1493.
Hermolai Barbari Castigationes Plinianse et in Pomponium Melam. Edidit Giovanni Pozzi. Patavii, In aedibus Antenoreis, 1973–
v. plate. 21 cm. (Thesaurus mundi, 11 It 74–Feb (v. 1)
Introd. in Italian.
Known as Castigationes Plinianae et Pomponii Melae.
1. Plinius Secundus, C. Naturalis historia. 2. Mela, Pomponius. De situ orbis libri tres. I. Pozzi, Giovanni, ed. II. Title: Castigationes Plinianae et in Pomponium Melam.
PA6614.A2B3 1973 75–556854

Barbaro, Ermolao, 1454-1493, ed.
see Mela, Pomponius. Cosmographia siue de situ orbis. Northridge, California State University, 1973.

Barbaro, Giosafat, d. 1494
see I Viaggi in Persia degli ambasciatori veneti Barbaro e Contarini. Roma, Istituto poligrafico dello Stato, Libreria, 1973.

Barbaro, Joseph S.
see Nassau Co., N.Y. Dept. of Social Services. Office for Legal Services. Legal services for welfare clients; three year report... [Nassau, N.Y., 1970?]

Barbaro, Paolo.
Le pietre, l'amore : romanzo / Paolo Barbaro. — 1. ed. — [Milano] : Mondadori, 1976.
192 p. ; 20 cm. — (Scrittori italiani e stranieri) It***
L3500
I. Title.
PQ4862.A6722P5 76-462038
76 MARC

Barbaro, Ronald.
Primer on environmental impact statements [by] Ronald Barbaro and Frank L. Cross, Jr. Westport, Conn., Technomic Pub. Co. [1973]
vii, 140 p. illus. 23 cm.
Includes bibliographical references.
1. Environmental impact statements. I. Cross, Frank L., joint author. II. Title.
TD194.5.B37 628.5 73–78925
ISBN 0–87762–112–8 MARC

Barbaro, Saverio, 1924–
Saverio Barbaro. [Exposition] Galerie internationale, Nice, du 5 au 30 mai 1964. [Nice, Galerie Internationale, 1964]
[26] p. illus. (part col.), port. 22 x 24 cm.
I. Galerie internationale.
MH NUC76-36635

Barbaro, Umberto, 1902–1959.
Il cinema tedesco. Prefazione di Mino Argentieri. Roma, Editori riuniti, 1973.
183 p. 19 cm. (Argomenti, 19) L1200 It 73–July
Bibliography: p. 183.
1. Moving-pictures—Germany—History. I. Title.
PN1993.5.G3B3 1973 73–336101

Barbaro, Umberto, 1902–1959.
Il film e il risarcimento marxista dell'arte. Con un profilo di Luigi Chiarini e una nota di Galvano della Volpe. Roma, Editori riuniti, 1974.
xxiii, 343 p. 18 cm. (Universale, 51) L1800 It 74–Apr
Bibliography: p. [327]–331.
1. Moving-pictures—Collected works. I. Title.
PN1994.B282 1974 74–312994

Barbaro, Umberto, 1902-1959.
Neorealismo e realismo / Umberto Barbaro ; a cura di Gian Piero Brunetta. — 1. ed. — Roma : Editori riuniti, 1976.
2 v. ; 19 cm. — (Universale ; 91-92) It76-Aug
Includes index.
CONTENTS: 1. Letteratura e arti figurative.—2. Cinema e teatro.
L5800
1. Realism in art. 2. Arts, Modern—19th century. 3. Arts, Modern—20th century. I. Title.
NX600.R4B28 1976 77-456450
*77 MARC

Barbaro, Umberto, 1902–1959.
Servitú e grandezza del cinema / Umberto Barbaro ; a cura di Lorenzo Quaglietti. — Roma : Editori riuniti, [1962]
599 p. ; 23 cm. — (Nuova biblioteca di cultura, 35)
"Raccoglie una gran parte degli scritti di Umberto Barbaro d'argomento cinematografico di carattere non strettamente teorico."
Includes bibliographical references and indexes.
1. Moving-pictures—Reviews. 2. Moving-pictures—Addresses, essays, lectures. I. Title.
PN1995.B26 1962 75–573378

Barbarossa London
see
Minshall, Merlin, 1906-

Barbarossa, Dhon.
Hantjurnja PKI-malam. Djakarta, Tri Dharma, 1968.
74 p. 18 cm.
Sequel: Pentjulikan seorang djendral.
I. Title.
PL5089.B35H3 S A 68–19954
PL 480 : Indo–8069

Barbaroux, Jean.
Images de Saint-Lo / Jean Barbaroux ... avec le concours de Jean-Pierre Dufrenne, André Dupont et Eugène Leseney ; illustration d'Olivier Barbaroux et Daniel Procope .... — Saint-Lô (8, rue du Maréchal-Leclerc, 50000) : P. Gobet, [1972]
73 p. : ill. ; 27 cm. F74-16129
"Il a été tiré de ce volume 30 exemplaires marqués H.C. et 200 exemplaires numérotés 1 à 200 ... constituant l'édition originale." No. 146.
Includes bibliographical references.
15.00F
1. Saint-Lô, France. I. Title.
DC801.S219B37 1972 914.4'21 75-508211
75 MARC

Barbaroux, Sophie.
Jardin d'enfant, comptines de Sophie Barbarous. Illustrations de Daniel Massonnet. Paris, L'ecole des loisirs [1972]
1 v. (unpaged) col. illus.
1. Poetry. 2. French language books.
I. Title.
RP NUC75-32401

Barbaroux, Sophie.
Pochette surprise, comptines de Sophie Barbaroux, illustrations de Daniel Massonnet. Paris, L'ecole des loisirs [1972]
1 v. (unpaged) col. illus.
1. Poetry. 2. French language books. I. Title.
RP NUC75-32402

Barbarua, Srinath Duara.
(Tuṃkhuṅgīẏā burañjī)
তুংখুঙ্গীয়া বুৰঞ্জী. Tungkhungia buranji; or, a chronicle of the Tungkhungia kings of Assam. শ্ৰীনাথ দুৱৰা বৰবৰুৱা সঙ্কলিত "শ্ৰীশ্ৰীতুংখুঙ্গীয়া ৺ৰ বংশাৱলী"ৰ পৰিবৰ্দ্ধিত সংস্কৰণ. Edited by S. K. Bhuyan. [Gauhati] Dept. of Historical and Antiquarian Studies, 1932.
188 p. col. ports. 22 cm.
In Assamese.
1. Assam—History. I. Bhuyan, Suryya Kumar, ed. II. Title. III. Title: Tungkhungia buranji. IV. Title: A chronicle of the Tungkhungia Kings of Assam.
DS485.A87B25 1932 76–985415
Library of Congress S A

Barbarua, Srinath Duara.
তুংখুঙ্গীয়া বুৰঞ্জী. Tungkhungia buranji, a chronicle of the Tungkhungia kings of Assam. শ্ৰীনাথ দুৱৰা বৰবৰুৱা সঙ্কলিত "শ্ৰীশ্ৰীতুংখুঙ্গীয়া ৺ৰ বংশাৱলী"ৰ পৰিবৰ্দ্ধিত সংস্কৰণ. Edited by Suryya Kumar Bhuyan. [2d ed.] Gauhati, Dept. of Historical and Antiquarian Studies, Assam, 1963.
45, 186 p. 22 cm.
In Assamese.
1. Assam—History—Chronology. I. Title. II. Title. Tungkhungia buranji.
Title transliterated: Tuṃkhuṅgīẏā burañjī.
DS485.A87B25 1964 S A 67–2118

Barbarus, Hermolous
see Barbaro, Ermolao, 1454-1493.

Barbarus, Iokhannes
see Barbarus, Johannes, 1890-1946.

Barbarus, Johannes, 1890–1946.
Relvastatud värsid. Tallinn, Eesti Raamat, 1970.
95 p. 17 cm. (Poeedilt sõjaveteranile) 0.51rub USSR 70–36399
I. Title.
PH665.B3R4 76–578666
rev

Barbarus, Johannes, 1890-1946.
Stikhi. [By] Iokhannes Barbarus. Per. s ėstonskogo. [Sost. Iokhannes Semper.] Moskva, Khudozhestvennaía lit-ra, 1971.
206 p. port.
MH NUC74-22002

Barbary, G. J.
see Debain, P Standards and specifications for the preparation of geological maps. [Ottawa] Dept. of Energy, Mines and Resources [1972]

Barbary, G. J., joint author.
see Debain, P. Standards and specifications for the preparation of geological maps. Rev. ed. Ottawa, Geological Survey of Canada, Dept. of Energy, Mines and Resources, 1975.

Barbary, J C
Swine erysipelas; a common pig disease. [Adelaide] 1973.
4 p. illus. (South Australia. Dept. of Agriculture. Extension bulletin no. 31)
I. Title.
DNAL NUC76-37801

Barbary, James.
The Crimean War / by James Barbary. — London : Gollancz, 1972.
159 p., [8] p. of plates : ill., 2 maps, ports. ; 21 cm. GB 72-23805
Bibliography: p. [153]-154.
Includes index.
ISBN 0-575-01457-1 : £1.80
1. Crimean War, 1853-1856—Juvenile literature. I. Title.
DK214.B3 1972 947'.07 75-325553
75 MARC

Barbary, James.
The Crimean War / James Barbary. — Harmondsworth : Puffin Books, 1975.
154 p., [8] p. of plates : ill., facsims., map, ports. ; 18 cm. — (Puffin books) GB75-06119
Bibliography: p. 147-148.
Includes index.
ISBN 0-14-030707-9 : £0.40
1. Crimean War, 1853-1856—Juvenile literature. I. Title.
DK214.B3 1975 947'.07 75-326933
75 MARC

Barbary, James.
The flight to Varennes. Illus. by Anne Mieke. London, MacDonald [c1968]
95 p. illus. 19 cm. (Famous events) (A Max Parrish book)
1. Louis XVI, King of France, 1754-1793. 2. France—History—Revolution, 1971. I. Title.
PSt NUC76-41342

Barbary, James.
Puritan & Cavalier : the English civil war / [by] James Barbary. — London : Gollancz, 1977.
192 p. : ill., facsims., maps, plans, ports. ; 23 cm. GB77-10679
Bibliography: p. [182]-183.
Includes index.
ISBN 0-575-02163-2 : £3.75
1. Great Britain—History—Civil War, 1642-1649. I. Title.
DA415.B27 1977b 942.6'2 77-367641
77 MARC

Barbary, James.
Puritan & cavalier : the English Civil War / James Barbary. — 1st ed. — Nashville : T. Nelson Inc., c1977.
192 p. : ill. ; 23 cm.
Bibliography: p. [182]-183.
Includes index.
ISBN 0-8407-6480-4 : $6.95
1. Great Britain—History—Civil War, 1642-1649. I. Title.
DA415.B27 941.06'2 76-44979
76 MARC

[Barbary Coast] [Sound recording] American Forces Radio and Television Service RU 10-4, 3B [1973]
on side 2 of 1 disc. 33⅓ rpm. mono. 12 in. (Playhouse 25, 74)
With: Ira Cook, 3289 W.
Radio drama starring Mary Astor and Charles Bickford.
Duration: 25 min.
Made for use by the American Armed Forces only.
SUMMARY: A story of early San Francisco and how Mary Rutlidge left her life of gambling.
I. Astor, Mary, 1906– II. Bickford, Charles, 1891–1967. III. Series: Playhouse 25. [Sound recording] 74.
[PN1991.77] 77–740484

Barbarych, Andrii Ivanovych.
(Zhyroolliini roslyny Ukrainy)
Жироолійні рослини України; довідник. Київ, Наук. думка, 1973.
131 p. illus., map. 20 cm. 0.52rub USSR***
At head of title: Академія наук Української РСР. Інститут ботаніки ім. М. Г. Холодного. А. І. Барбарич, О. М. Дубовик, Д. В. Стрелко.
Bibliography: p. 96–[102]
1. Oilseed plants—Ukraine. I. Dubovyk, Ol'ha Mykolaïvna. II. Strelko, Diana Vasylivna. III. Title.
SB298.B37 74–307837

Barbarych, Andreĭ Ivanovych
see Roslynnist' URSR. Kyïv, "Naukova dumka" [19–]

Barbarych, Andriĭ Ivanovich, ed.
see Stepy, kam'ı͡anysti vidslonennı͡a, pisky. 1973.

Barbaš, Jiří, comp.
see Anekdoty s krokodýlem. Ze sovět. časopisů text a il. vybral a uspoř. Jiří Barbaš. Praha, Lid. nakl., t. Tisk 4, Přerov, 1972.

Barbas, Lı͡udmila Grigor'evna.
(Pishu tebe)
Пишу тебе ... : [Стихи] / Людмила Барбас. — Ленинград : Сов. писатель, Ленингр. отд-ние, 1976.
111 p. : port. ; 16 cm. USSR 76
0.26rub
I. Title.
PG3479.R33P5 77–509023

Barbash, Gary.
see Sex Information and Education Council of the U. S. Film resources for sex education. 1976 ed. New York, Sex Information and Education Council of the U.S. : distributed by Human Sciences Press, c1976.

Barbash, Iosif Davidovich, joint author
see Polı͡akov, Vladimir Sergeevich. (Mufty) 1973.

Barbash, Iosif Davidovich, joint author
see Polı͡akov, Vladimir Sergeevich. (Spravochnik po muftam) 1974.

Barbash, Jack.
The industrial order and the tensions of work. Nitro, West Virginia University-Kanawha Valley Graduate Center, 1971.
20 p. 23 cm. (WVU-KVGC professional development lectures, v. 2, no. 6)
Cover title.
Includes bibliographical references.
1. Industrial relations—Addresses, essays, lectures. 2. Industry—Addresses, essays, lectures. I. Title II. Series: West Virginia University. Kanawha Valley Graduate Center. WVU-KVGC professional development lectures, v. 2, no. 6.
AS36.W33 vol. 2, no. 6 081 s 73–621775
[HD6961] [331] MARC

Barbash, Jack.
Job satisfaction attitudes surveys / by Jack Barbash. -- Paris : Organization for Economic Co-operation and Development, 1976.
36 p. ; 24 cm. --(OECD Industrials Relations Programme special studies)
Bibliography: p. 34-36.
I. Job satisfaction. I. Title. II. Series.
DC NUC77-86757

Barbash, Jack.
Labor's grass roots; a study of the local union. Westport, Conn., Greenwood Press [1974, c1961]
viii, 250 p. 22 cm.
Reprint of the ed. published by Harper, New York.
Includes bibliographical references.
1. Trade-unions—United States. I. Title.
[HD6508.B352 1974] 331.88'0973 73–11839
ISBN 0-8371-7064-8 MARC

Barbash, Jack.
Trade unionism and social justice. Madison, University of Wisconsin, 1971.
28, 4 p. 28 cm. (Wisconsin. University. Institute for Research on Poverty. Discussion paper, 89)
Includes bibliography.
1. Trade-unions—U.S. I. Title. II. Series.
CNoS NUC75-32399

Barbash, Jack.
Trade unions and national economic policy in Western Europe and the United States, by Jack Barbash with the assistance of Kate Barbash. Madison, Wis., 1970.
xiv, 206 p. 24 cm.
"Prepared under a grant from the Office of Manpower Policy, Evaluation, and Research, United States Dept. of Labor."
Includes bibliographical references.
1. Trade-unions—Europe, Western. 2. Europe, Western—Economic policy. 3. Trade-unions—United States. 4. United States—Economic policy. I. Barbash, Kate. II. United States. Dept. of Labor. Office of Manpower Policy, Evaluation, and Research. III. Title.
NIC NUC76-11278

Barbash, Kate
see Barbash, Jack. Trade unions and national economic policy in Western Europe... Madison, Wis., 1970.

Barbashev, Aleksandr Ippolitovich, 1858–
(Lietopisnye istochniki dli͡a istorii Litvy v srednie vi͡eka)
Лѣтописные источники для исторіи Литвы въ средніе вѣка / Составилъ А. И. Барбашевъ. — С.-Петербургъ : Изд. ред. журнала "Библіографъ," 1888.
29 p. ; 27 cm.
1. Lithuania—History—Bibliography. I. Title.
Z2537.B36 75–559066

Barbashev, Vladimir Maksimovich.
Istoricheskoe znachenie XXIV s"ezda KPSS. [By] V. M. Barbashev & N. V. Ruban. Moskva, Znanie; 1972.
55 p. (Serii͡a broshi͡ur "Vozrastanie rukovodi͡ashcheĭ roli KPSS v kommunisticheskom stroitel'stve") (V pomoshch' lektoru)
1. Kommunisticheskai͡a partii͡a Sovetskogo Soi͡uza. 24th Congress, Moscow, 1971. I. Ruban, Nikolaĭ Vasil'evich.
MH NUC75-129916

Barbashev, Vladimir Maksimovich, ed.
see Metodicheskie sovety po izucheniiu proizvedeniĭ V. I. Lenina... Izd. 2., dorab. Moskva, "Mysl'", 1974.

Barbashin, Anatoliĭ Ivanovich.
(Ėkonomicheskoe obosnovanie i organizat͡sionnye formy spet͡sializat͡sii sel'skogo khozi͡aĭstva)
Экономическое обоснование и организационные формы специализации сельского хозяйства. Москва, "Экономика," 1973.
199 p. 20 cm. 0.65rub USSR 73–VKP
At head of title: А. И. Барбашин.
Includes bibliographical references.
1. Agriculture—Russia—T͡Sentral'no-Chernozemnai͡a oblast'. 2. Farm management—Russia—T͡Sentral'no-Chernozemnai͡a oblast'. I. Title.
S469.R92T773 73–336416

Barbashin, Anatoliĭ Ivanovich
see Peredovoĭ opyt - v proizvodstvo. Voronezh, TSentral'no-Chernozemnoe knizhnoe izd-vo, 1973.

Barbashin, Mikhail Alekseevich.
(Sot͡sial'nye rezervy proizvodstva)
Социальные резервы производства / М. А. Барбашин, Н. С. Мансуров, К. А. Москаленко. — Москва : Московский рабочий, 1976.
84 p. ; 21 cm. USSR***
Includes bibliographical references.
0.13rub
1. Industrial sociology—Russia. 2. Personnel management—Russia. I. Mansurov, Nikolaĭ Sergeevich, joint author. II. Moskalenko, Kirill Alekseevich, joint author. III. Title.
HD6957.R9B37 77–500688

Barbashov, Fedor Alekseevich.
(Frezernoe delo)
Фрезерное дело. [Учеб. пособие для учеб. заведений проф.-техн. образования]. Москва, "Высш. школа," 1973.
279 p. with illus. 24 cm. (Профтехобразование: Обработка металлов резанием) 0.97rub USSR 73–VKP
At head of title: Ф. А. Барбашов.
Bibliography: p. [277]
1. Milling (Metal-work) 2. Milling-machines. I. Title.
TJ1225.B34 74–344132

Barbashov, Fedor Alekseevich.
(Frezernoe delo)
Фрезерное дело / Ф. А. Барбашов. — Изд. 2., перер. и доп. — Москва : Высшая школа, 1975.
213 p. : ill. ; 25 cm. — (Профтехобразование : Обработка резанием) (Библиотечная серия) USSR***
"Одобрено ... в качестве учебного по собия для средних профессионально-технических училищ."
Series 1 romanized: Proftekhobrazovanie : Obrabotka rezaniem. Series 2 romanized: Bibliotechnai͡a serii͡a.
Bibliography: p. [211]
0.74rub
1. Milling (Metal-work) 2. Milling-machines. I. Title.
TJ1225.B34 1975 76–507081

Barbashova, Z. I.
see Chelovek i sreda. 1975.

Barbasso, Salvatore.
Precalculus : a functional approach with applications / Salvatore Barbasso, John Impagliazzo. — New York : Harcourt Brace Jovanovich, c1977.
xiv, 413 p. : ill. ; 25 cm.
Includes index.
ISBN 0-15-571050-8
1. Functions. I. Impagliazzo, John, joint author. II. Title.
QA331.3.B37 515 77-70575
77 MARC

Barbastro, Francisco Antonio, 1734–1800.
Sonora hacia fines del siglo XVIII; un informe del misionero franciscano fray Francisco Antonio Barbastro, con otros documentos complementarios. Estudio preliminar, edición y notas por Lino Gómez Canedo. [1. ed.] Guadalajara [México] Librería Font, 1971.
133 p. map. 25 cm. (Documentación histórica mexicana, no. 3) LACAP 71–3042
"280 ejemplares." No. 196.
The report by Barbastro is a transcription of a manuscript in the Archivo General de la Nación.
1. Indians of Mexico—Missions. 2. Franciscans in Sonora, Mexico. 3. Sonora, Mexico—History. I. Gómez Canedo, Lino, ed. II. Title. III. Series.
F1219.3.M59B3 1971 72–337527

Barbastro, Spain (Diocese)
see also
Catholic Church. Diocese of Roda.

Bărbat, Al
Teoria statisticii sociale. Bucureşti, Editura didactică şi pedagogică, 1972.
344 p. with figs. 24 cm. lei 18.90 R 73–1895
At head of title: Ministerul Educaţiei şi Învăţămîntului. Universitatea „Al. I. Cuza" Iaşşi. Facultatea de Studii Economice. Al. Bărbat.
Bibliography: p. 335–[337]
1. Statistics. 2. Social sciences—Statistical methods. I. Title.
HA29.5.R6B37 73–353459

Barbat, Enric, 1943–
Cançons de la p . . . vida. [Barcelona, Lumen, 1973]
92 p. illus. 19 cm. (Paraula menor, 2) Sp***
Poems.
I. Title.
PC3942.12.A67C3 73–332408
ISBN 84-264-2852-5

Barbat, Ileana, ed.
see Die Entwicklung der rumänischen Wirtschaft, 1966-1970. Bukarest, Politischer Verlag, 1971.

Bărbat, Iuliu.
Paralele europene : note de călătorie / Iuliu Bărbat ; [coperta de Vasile Pop Silaghi]. — Cluj : "Dacia," 1974.
175 p., [10] leaves of plates : ill. ; 20 cm. — (Agora) R 75–1288
lei 8.00
1. Europe—Description and travel—1945–1970. 2. Bărbat, Iuliu. I. Title.
D922.B32 75–532128

Barbatenkova, V. P.
see Katalog demonstraťsionnykh, naglīādnykh i zvukovykh posobiĭ. [1972]

Barbatenkova, V. P.
see Spravochnik po ekrannym, zvukovym i pechatnym naglīādnym posobiīām. 1974.

Barbatenkova, V. P.
see Velikaia Otechestvennaia voina. [Phonodisc]. [1968] Matrix no. 033649-033658.

Barbati, Elia.
Nuovi orientamenti di psicologia dell'infanzia. [n. p.], La biblioteca dell'educatore, 1972.
116 p. 21 cm. L1500 It 73-Apr
Bibliography: p. 115-116.
1. Child study. I. Title.
BF721.B257 73-352637

Barbati, Fernando.
Il manuale dell'urbanista : i piani regolatori e gli altri strumenti urbanistici (schemi, norme, legislazione) / Fernando Barbati. — Roma : Rassegna I.V.A.-Informazioni parlamentari, 1975.
191 p. ; 24 cm. It76-Oct
"Legge urbanistica": p. [115]-135.
L6000
1. City planning and redevelopment law—Italy. I. Italy. Laws, statutes, etc. Legge 17 agosto 1942, n. 1150. II. Title.
77-464376
•77 MARC

Barbati, Vittorio, ed.
see La Pace fredda. Roma, Istituto affari internazionali, 1973.

Barbatia, Andreas, 1400 (ca.)-1479.
Repetitio legis: Cum acutissimi De fideicommissis. Bologna (Bononie), Ugo Rugerius, 8 Mar. 1492.
[34] l. woodcut: printer's device. f°. 42.1 cm.
Bound with Pontano, Ludovico. Singularia. [Rome, ca. 1475]
With addition, dated 22 Jan. 1493, by Ugo Rugerius.
Gesamtkat. d. Wiegendr., 3354; Indice generale degli incunaboli, 1225; Goff. Third census, B-110.
1. Legacies (Roman law) 2. Inheritance and succession (Roman law) I. Title.
Incun. X.P755 77-502715

Barbato, Gaetano.
Indagine idrobiologica sul lago d'Idro. Brescia, Tip. S. Eustacchio, [1972?].
30 p. illus. 21 x 31 cm. It 73-Feb
At head of title: Amministrazione provinciale di Brescia.
1. Hydrology—Italy—Idro Lake. I. Title.
GB1700.I 37B37 73-332876

Barbato, James Paul, 1943-
The sea breeze of the Boston area and its effect on the urban atmosphere. -- [s. l. : s. n.], 1975.
xvii, 232 p. : ill., maps, tables.
Thesis -- Boston University.
Bibliography : p. 224-231.
1. Sea breeze--United States--Boston. I. Title.
MBU NUC77-83511

Barbato, Nicolás Héctor, joint author.
see Meilij, Gustavo Raúl. Tratado de derecho de seguros ... Rosario, Zeus Editora, 1975.

Barbato de Silva, Celia
see Un Reajuste conservador... [Montevideo, Fundación de Cultura Universitaria, 1973]

Barbaud, Roger.
Dictionnaire des délais de procédure, de prescriptions et de formalités / Roger Barbaud. — Paris : Dalloz, 1974.
160 p. ; 21 cm. F***
Includes index.
ISBN 2-247-00545-4 : 32.00F
1. Time (Law)—France. I. Title.
347'.44'05 75-512349
75 MARC

Barbaud, Roger, fl. 1910-1935.
... Nouveau manuel de prestidigitation et de magie blanche, traité complet de tours de cartes à l'usage des gens du monde. 2. sér.: tours avec appareils, par Roger Barbaud ... ouvrage orné de 98 figures dans le texte. Paris, L. Mulo, 1912.
2 p. l., 320 p. illus. 15½ cm. (Half-title: Encyclopédie-Roret)
At head of title: Manuels-Roret.
1. Card tricks. I. Title.
GV1549.B3 1912 795.43 32-29116

Barbaud, Roger, fl. 1910-1935.
... Nouveau manuel de prestidigitation, traité complet de tours de cartes à l'usage des gens du monde, par Roger Barbaud ... ouvrage orné de 72 figures dans le texte. Paris, L. Mulo, 1910.
2 p. l., iv, 301 p. illus. 16 cm. (Half-title: Encyclopédie-Roret)
At head of title: Manuels-Roret.
1. Card tricks. I. Title.
GV1549.B3 1910 795.43 32-29117

Barbauld, Anna Letitia Aikin, 1743-1825.
Theodore Carleton, or, Perseverance against ill-fortune, by Mrs. Barbauld. New York, J.S. Redfield [n.d.]
24 p. illus. 15 cm. (Redfield's toy books, 4th series, no. 7)
I. Title.
MB NUC75-21613

Barbauld, Anna Letitia Aikin, 1743-1825
see Aikin, John, 1747-1822. Evening at home... 2d ed. Philadelphia, T. Dobson, 1797.

Barbault, André.
Analogies de la dialectique, Uranus, Neptune : leurs correspondances en mythologie, poésie, psychologie, sexualité, morphologie, sociologie, science, art, philosophie / André Barbault & Jean Carteret. — Braine-le-Comte : Éditions du Baucens, 1974.
50 p. ; 21 cm. — (Collection La Grande année ; 1) Be***
Includes bibliographical references.
ISBN 2-8019-0002-8
1. Astrology. 2. Uranus (Planet)—Miscellanea. 3. Neptune (Planet)—Miscellanea. I. Carteret, Jean, joint author. II. Title.
BF1724.B37 133.5'3 75-512309
75 MARC

Barbault, André.
Connaissance de l'astrologie / André Barbault. — Paris : Éditions du Seuil, [1975]
172 p. : ill. ; 21 cm. F***
Includes bibliographical references.
25.00F
1. Astrology. I. Title.
BF1708.2.B36 133.5 75-506558
75 MARC

Barbault, André.
Le pronostic expérimental en astrologie; essai de prévisions mondiales. Paris, Payot, 1973.
236 p. illus. 23 cm. (Aux confins de la science) 35.50F F***
1. Astrology. I. Title.
BF1708.2.B38 73-178967
ISBN 2-228-17150-6 MARC

Barbault, André.
Sagittaire. Avec le concours de Marilène Jauréguibéhère [et. al. Paris] Éditions du Seuil [1958]
xvi, 126 p. illus., ports. ("Le zodiaque", no. 9)
1. Sagittarius. I. Title.
NmU NUC76-62501

Barbault, Armand.
Gold of a thousand mornings / Arman Barbault ; translated from the French by Robin Campbell. — London : Spearman, 1975.
xvii, 130 p., [28] p. of plates : ill. ; 23 cm. GB75-14832
Translation of L'Or du millième matin.
ISBN 0-85435-052-7 : £2.50
1. Alchemy. I. Title.
QD26.B313 1975 540'.1 75-325540
75 MARC

Barbault, Jean, 1718-1762.
see Volle, Nathalie. Jean Barbault, 1718-1762 ... [s.l., s.n., 1975?] (Rouen : Impr. rouennaise)

Barbault, M C
Linguistique et mathématiques; recherches pédagogiques [par] Marie-Claire Barbault, Oswald Ducrot [et al.] Paris, Larousse, 1971.
127 p. (Langue française, 12)
1. Mathematical linguistics. I. Ducrot, Oswald. II. Title.
MH NUC75-32394

Barbault, M C
Transformations formelles et théories linguistiques, par M.-C. Barbault et J.-P. Desclés [Paris, Dunod] 1972.
iii, 110 p. illus. 25 cm. (Documents de linguistique quantitative, no 11) 32.00F F***
Bibliography: p. 105-108.
On t. p.: Association Jean-Favard pour le développement de la linguistique quantitative.
1. Linguistics. 2. Generative grammar. I. Desclés, J. P., joint author. II. Title. III. Series.
P25.D6 no. 11 72-364381
[P121]

Barbault, M. C., joint author
see Ducrot, Oswald. La preuve et le dire: langage et logique. [Paris] Mame [1974]

Barbay, Joseph Edgar.
Network optimization. [Columbia] 1971.
113 l. illus.
Thesis (Ph. D.)—University of Missouri.
Vita.
Includes bibliography.
MoU NUC73-31047

Barbay, Joseph Edgar.
Network optimization. [Columbia] 1971.
113 l. illus.
Thesis (Ph. D.)—University of Missouri.
Vita.
Microfilm copy.
Includes bibliography.
MoU NUC73-31055

Barbaza, Yvette.
see Journées de géographie du tourisme, 4th, Chalmazel, France, 1975. Tourisme en espace rural ... [n.p.] Comité national de géographie, 1976.

Barbazan, Étienne, 1696-1770.
Le chastoiement d'un père à son fils; a critical edition. Edited by Edward D. Montgomery. Chapel Hill [1971]
196 p. 23 cm. (University of North Carolina. Studies in the Romance languages and literatures, no. 101)
Bibliography: p. [195]-196.
I. Montgomery, Edward D., ed. II. Title.
CtY NUC73-123958

Barbazan, Étienne, 1696-1770, ed.
Fabliaux et contes des poètes françois des 11e, 12e, 13e, 14e et 15e siècles / [publ. par] Étienne Barbazan. — [Nouv. éd. augm. et rev. par M. Méon]. — Genève : Slatkine Reprints, 1976.
2 v. ; 23 cm. Sw76-8142
Reprint of the 1808 ed. published in 4 v. by B. Warée, Paris.
1. French poetry—To 1500. 2. Tales, French. I. Méon, Dominique Martin, 1748-1829. II. Title.
PQ1319.B3 1976 77-469582
•77 MARC

Barbe
see Auto défense de Paris. Paris, Editions ouvrières [1973]

Barbe, B B
"The Little Appalatian". [n.p., 1965?]
191 p. 21 cm.
Cover title.
I. Title.
WvU NUC74-122547

Barbé, Carlos.
Progresso e sviluppo : la formazione della teoria dello sviluppo e lo sviluppo come ideologia, (Auguste Comte -Herbert Spencer) / di Carlos Barbé ; prefazione di Filippo Barbano. — Torino : Giappichelli, 1974.
xxiv, 241 p. ; 23 cm. — (Pubblicazioni dell'Istituto di scienze politiche dell'Università di Torino ; v. 32) It 75-Apr
Includes bibliographical references and index.
L4500
1. Progress. 2. Social evolution. 3. Sociology—History. I. Title. II. Series: Turin. Università. Istituto di scienze politiche. Pubblicazioni ; v. 32.
HM101.B2593 75-569259

Barbe, Glenn Douglas
see Fuller, Thomas Charles, 1918-
List of California herbaria... Sacramento, Calif., Botany Laboratory, Division of Plant Industry, Dept. of Food and Agriculture [1972]

Barbe, J
Cours de chimie systématique des corps simples; initiation à l'étude de la chimie minérale [par] J. Barbe. Préf. de C. Luu Duc. Paris, Doin, 1973.
viii, 284 p. illus. 24 cm. 68.00F F***
Bibliography: p. [271]-273.
1. Chemistry, Inorganic. I. Title.
QD151.2.B34 546 73-166034
MARC

Barbé, María López de Victoria y
see López de Victoria y Barbé, María, 1893-

Barbe, Michel.
Adolescence et autres aventures. Michel Barbe ... [Paris, (6e),] Éditions de la Grisière, 184, Bd Saint-Germain-des -Prés, 1971.
30 p. 18 cm. (Collection Balises) 10.00F F 72-12858
Poems.
I. Title.
PQ2662.A648A7 1971 73-323681

Barbe, Richard
see John Dickinson School District. A new design for secondary educational excellence, 1968... [Wilmington, 1968]

Barbe, Walter Burke, 1926-
Individualized reading instruction [by] Walter B. Barbe, Roach Van Allen [and] Kenneth J. Smith. Tucson, University of Arizona [196-?]
14 p. (Arizona. University. College of Education. Monograph series, 3)
1. Individualized instruction. 2. Reading (Elementary) I. Allen, Roach Van 1917- II. Smith, Kenneth J. III. Title. IV. Series.
MH-Ed NUC73-39774

Barbe, Walter Burke, 1926-
Personalized reading instruction : new techniques that increase reading skill and comprehension / Walter B. Barbe and Jerry L. Abbott. — West Nyack, N.Y. : Parker Pub. Co., [1975]
216 p. ; 24 cm.
Includes bibliographical references and index.
ISBN 0-13-658104-8 : $8.95
1. Individualized reading instruction. I. Abbott, Jerry L., 1938- joint author. II. Title.
LB1050.38.B37 372.4'147 75-9861
75 MARC

Barbe, Walter Burke, 1926- ed.
Psychology and education of the gifted / edited by Walter B. Barbe and Joseph S. Renzulli. — 2d ed. — New York : Irvington Publishers : distributed by Halsted Press, [1975]
xii, 481 p. : ill. ; 24 cm.
Includes bibliographies and index.
ISBN 0-470-04775-5
1. Gifted children—Education—Addresses, essays, lectures. I. Renzulli, Joseph S., joint ed. II. Title.
[DNLM: 1. Education, special child, gifted—Education. LC3993 P974]
LC3993.B36 1975 371.9'5 75-14330
75 MARC

Barbe, Walter Burke, 1926- ed.
see Children around the world; facts and stories ... Columbus, Ohio, c1968.

Barbe, Walter Burke, 1926-
see Teacher guidepak for Creative growth... Columbus, Ohio, Zane-Bloser, c1975.

Barbe Duran, Luis, ed.
see Dinamica y perspectiva del Valles, 1969. [Sabadell, 1969-71, v. 0, 1971]

Barbé Durán, Luis, joint author
see Villazón Hervás, César. Estructura financiera y valoración... Madrid, Editorial Moneda y Crédito, 1971.

Barbé i Durán, Lluís
see
Barbé Durán, Luis.

Barbé Ilic, Mario E., joint author.
see Ovando Zeballos, Hugo. Corrección monetaria ... [s.l., s.n.] 1975 (Santiago : Impr. Editorial de la Universidad Católica de Chile)

Barbé-Marbois, François, marquis de, 1745-1837.
The history of Louisiana, particularly of the cession of that colony to the United States of America; with an introductory essay on the Constitution and government of the United States. By Barbé-Marbois... Tr. from the French by an American citizen. Philadelphia, Carey & Lea, 1830.
xviii p., 1 l., [17]-455, [1] p. 23 cm.
W. B. Lawrence, translator.
Ultra microfiche. Dayton, Ohio, National Cash Register, 1970. 10.5 x 14.8 cm. (PCMI library collection, 547-1)
1. Louisiana-Hist. 2. Louisana Purchase. I. Lawrence, William Beach, 1800-1881, tr.
KEmT NUC76-2107

Barbe Perez, Hector.
Estudios jurídicos sobre la administración publica que surge en el Uruguay. Montevideo, Oficina de Apuntes del Centro de Estudiantes de Notariado, 1970.
321 p. 24 cm.
At head of title: Cátedra de Derecho Administrativo (Notariado) de la Facultad de Derecho y Ciencias Sociales.
1. Public administration-Uruguay. I. Title.
MU NUC75-95693

Barbé Perez, Hector
see Uruguay. Laws, statutes, etc. Normas vigentes sobre la administración pública... Montevideo, Oficina de Apuntes del Centro de Estudiantes de Notariado [1971-

Barbeau, Alphonse, 1926-
Le droit constitutionnel canadien : lois, documents et jugements divers / par Alphonse Barbeau. — Montréal : Distribué par Wilson & Lafleur, 1974.
xviii, 440 p. ; 26 cm. C74-6715-X
Includes bibliographical references and indexes.
$25.00
1. Canada—Constitutional law. I. Title.
342'.71 75-503704
75 MARC

Barbeau, André, ed.
see Canadian-American Conference on Parkinson's Disease, 2d, Princeton, N.J., 1973. Second Canadian-American conference on Parkinson's Disease. New York, Raven Press [1974]

Barbeau, André.
see Dopaminergic mechanisms. New York, Raven Press, [1975]

Barbeau, André, joint author.
see Elliott, Jacques. Dossier mercure de Minamata à Matagami. Montréal, Plein-Air, [c1976]

Barbeau, André, ed.
see Huntington's chorea, 1872-1972. New York, Raven Press [1973]

Barbeau, André, ed.
see International Congress of Neuro-genetics and Neuro-ophthalmology, 2d, Montreal, 1967. Abstracts of papers presented. Amsterdam, Excerpta Medica Foundation, 1967.

Barbeau, André.
see International Symposium on Taurine, 1st, Tucson, Ariz., 1975. Taurine. New York, Raven Press, c1976.

Barbeau, Arthur E
The unknown soldiers; Black American troops in World War I [by] Arthur E. Barbeau and Florette Henri. Foreword by Burghardt Turner. Philadelphia, Temple University Press [1974]
xvii, 279 p. illus. 23 cm.
Bibliography: p. 249-270.
1. European War, 1914-1918—Negroes. 2. United States. Army—Negro troops. I. Henri, Florette, joint author. II. Title.
D639.N4B37 940.4'03 72-95880
ISBN 0-87722-063-8 MARC

Barbeau, Charles Marius, 1883-1969, comp.
Alouette! Nouveau recueil de chansons populaires avec mélodies, choisies dans le répertoire du Musée national du Canada. Montréal, Éditions Lumen [c1946]
216 p. 20 cm. (Collection humanitas)
Unacc. melodies.
Includes bibliographic notes.
1. Folk-songs, French-Canadian. I. Title.
M1678.B223 73-217292

Barbeau, Charles Marius, 1883-
Ceinture fléchée [par] Marius Barbeau. Nouv. préf. de Marcel Rioux. [Montréal] Editions l'Etincelle [1973]
110 p. illus.
First published in 1945, by Editions Paysana, Montreal.
ISBN 0-88515-034-1.
1. Sashes (Costume) 2. Design, Decorative—Quebec (Province) 3. Weaving—Quebec (Province) I. Title.
CaOTY NUC75-26676

Barbeau, Charles Marius, 1883-
The downfall of Temlaham. Illus. by A. Y. Jackson, Edwin H. Holgate, W. Langdon Kihn, Emily Carr and Annie D. Savage. Edmonton, Hurtig [1973]
253 p. col. plates.
Reprint of the 1928 edition.
ISBN 0-088830-070-0.
1. Indians of North America—Canada—Fiction. 2. Canadian fiction, English. I. Title.
CaOTP NUC75-26697

Barbeau, Charles Marius, 1883-
Le rêve de Kamalmouk [par] Marius Barbeau. [Dessins de Grace Melvin] Montréal, Fides [1962]
231 p. illus. 21 cm. (Collection du Nénuphar, 18)
Translation and revision of The downfall of Temlaham.
1. Tsimshian Indians—Legends. I. Title.
CFS NUC75-494

Barbeau, Clayton C
Creative marriage : the middle years / by Clayton C. Barbeau. — New York : Seabury Press, c1976.
121 p. ; 22 cm.
"A Crossroad book."
Bibliography: p. [119]-121.
ISBN 0-8164-0284-1 : $6.95
1. Marriage. 2. Middle age. 3. Middle age—Sexual behavior. I. Title.
HQ734.B24 301.42'7 75-38536
75 MARC

Barbeau, Clayton C
Dante & Gentucca : a love story / by Clayton Barbeau. — Santa Barbara, Calif. : Capra Press, 1974.
42 p. : ill. ; 18 cm. — (Yes! Capra chapbook series ; 19)
"From the [author's] novel The long journey."
ISBN 0-912264-95-0. ISBN 0-912264-94-2 : $1.95
1. Dante Alighieri, 1265-1321, in fiction, drama, poetry, etc. I. Title.
PZ4.B232 Dan 813'.5'4 75-318418
[PS3552.A5918] 75 MARC

Barbeau, Ernest, joint author
see Butler, Harry, 1933- Use of the adjudiciation process... [New York, National Association of Social Workers] 1973.

Barbeau, Gérard L
Épreuve individuelle d'intelligence générale; manuel abrégé [par] Gérard L. Barbeau et Adrien Pinard. Montréal, Institut de recherches psychologiques, 1969.
97 p. illus. 23 cm.
Bibliography: p. 59.
1. Mental tests. 2. Intellect. I. Pindard, Adrien, joint author. II. Montréal. Université. Institut de recherches psychologiques. III. Title.
PPT NUC76-2111

Barbeau, Jean, 1945-
Une brosse / Jean Barbeau. — [Montréal] : Leméac, c1975.
117 p. ; 20 cm. — (Théâtre/Leméac ; 42) C***
ISBN 0-7761-0041-6
I. Title.
PQ3919.2.B28B7 842 75-514398
75 MARC

Barbeau, Jean, 1945-
Le chant du sink. Préf. de Jean-Guy Sabourin. [Montréal] Leméac [1973]
82 p. illus. 18 cm. (Collection Répertoire québecois, 28) C***
A play.
I. Title.
PQ3919.2.B28C48 842 74-183738
MARC

Barbeau, Jean, 1945-
Citrouille / Jean Barbeau. — [Montréal] : Leméac, c1974.
105 p. ; 18 cm. — (Collection Répertoire québécois ; 53-54) C***
Play.
ISBN 0-7761-2048-4
I. Title.
PQ3919.2.B28C55 842 75-516817
76 MARC

Barbeau, Jean, 1945-
La coupe stainless ; Solange / Jean Barbeau. — [Montréal] : Leméac, [1974]
115 p. ; 18 cm. — (Collection Répertoire québécois ; 47-48) C***
Plays.
ISBN 0-7761-2044-1
I. Barbeau, Jean, 1945- Solange. 1974. II. Title: La coupe stainless.
PQ3919.2.B28C6 75-501034
MARC

Barbeau, Jean, 1945-
Dites-le avec des fleurs / Jean Barbeau, Marcel Dubé. — [Montréal] : Leméac, c1976.
130 p. ; 20 cm. — (Théâtre ; 55) C***
ISBN 0-7761-0054-8
I. Dubé, Marcel, 1930- joint author. II. Title.
PQ3919.2.B28D5 76-476962
76 MARC

Barbeau, Jean, 1945- Joualez-moi d'amour. 1972
in Barbeau, Jean, 1945- Manon Lastcall... [Montréal] Leméac [1972]

Barbeau, Jean, 1945-
Manon Lastcall et Joualez-moi d'amour. Introd. de Jacques Garneau. [Montréal] Leméac [1972]
98 p. 20 cm. (Collection Théâtre canadien, 25) C***
Bibliography: p. 97-98.
1. Barbeau, Jean, 1945- Joualez-moi d'amour. 1972. II. Title. III. Title: Joualez-moi d'amour.
PQ3919.2.B28M3 73-329062

Barbeau, Jean, 1945- Solange. 1974
in Barbeau, Jean, 1945- La coupe stainless... [Montréal] : Leméac, [1974]

Barbeau, Jean, 1945-
The way of Lacross. Translated by Laurence R. Berard and Philip W. London. [Toronto] Playwrights Co-op [1973]
28, 14 l.
Cover title.
Mimeographed typescript.
1. Canadian drama, French. I. Title.
CaOTP NUC73-114768

Barbeau, Joseph Ernest, 1933-
The historical development of cooperative education in American higher education. [n. p.] 1972.
ix, 220 p. maps, tables (1 fold.)
Thesis—Boston University.
Bibliography: p. 203-219.
Thesis submitted 1972; degree awarded 1973.
1. Education, Cooperative—United States—History. I. Title.
MBU NUC75-21625

Barbeau, Joseph Ernest, 1933-
The historical development of cooperative education in American higher education. [Boston] 1973.
ix, 220 p. illus.
Thesis (Ed. D.)—Boston University.
Microfilm edition (1 reel. positive) filmed by University Microfilms.
Period covered by this work is 1906-1971.
Vita: p. 220.
Bibliography: p. 203-219.
1. Education, Higher—United States. 2. Education, Cooperative—United States—History. I. Title.
OOxM NUC74-126736

Barbeau, Marcel, 1925-
see Canadian Cultural Centre. Marcel Barbeau: oeuvres postautomatistes... Paris, 1971.

Barbeau, Marius
see Barbeau, Charles Marius, 1883-

Barbeau, Victor, 1896-
Dictionnaire bibliographique du Canada français / Victor Barbeau et André Fortier. — Montréal : Académie canadienne-française, 1974.
246 p. ; 32 cm. C***
Bibliography: p. 245-246.
1. Canada—Imprints. I. Fortier, André, joint author. II. Title.
Z1365.B3 016.808 74-190062
MARC

Barbeau, Victor, 1896- ed.
see Académie canadienne-française. Contes et nouvelles. Montréal, 1959.

Barbeau, Victor, 1896- ed.
see Académie canadienne-française. Essais critiques. Montréal, 1958.

Barbeau, Victor, 1896- ed.
see Académie canadienne-française. Histoire. Montréal, 1957.

Barbeau, Victor, 1896- ed.
see Académie canadienne-française. Linguistique. Montreal, 1960.

Barbeau, Victor, 1896-
see Académie canadienne-française. Poésie. Québec, Éditions Garneau, [1974]

Barbeau, Victor, 1896-
see Histoire. Québec, Éditions Garneau, [1974]

Barbedette, Hippolyte, 1827-1901.
Stephen Heller : his life and works / by Hippolyte Barbedette ; translated by Robert Brown-Borthwick ; with new introd. by Ronald E. Booth. — Detroit : Detroit Reprints in Music, 1974.
xvi, 89, xii p. : ill. ; 19 cm.
Reprint of the 1877 ed. published by Ashdown & Parry, London.
Includes bibliographical references.
"Catalogue of pianoforte works by Stephen Heller": xii p. at end.
ISBN 0-911772-69-3
1. Heller, Stephen, 1813-1888.
ML410.H47B3 1974 786.1'092'4 [B] 74-75886
MARC

Barbedette, Loïc.
Quelques jalons pour préparer la régionalisation du plan gabonais : exploitation du Séminaire national de Franceville, Gabon (16 juillet 1973/3 août 1973) / Séminaires extérieurs/IPD, Loïc Barbedette. — Douala, R.U.C. : Institut panafricain pour le développement, Service de documentation et d'appui pédagogique, École de cadres de Douala, 1973.
107 p. : ill. ; 31 cm. — (Document - Institut panafricain pour le développement, École de cadres de Douala ; no 8)
On cover: Gabon, UNICEF, IPD.
Séminaire national sur la planification régionale, Franceville, Gabon, 1973.
1. Regional planning—Gabon—Congress. 2. Gabon—Economic policy—Congresses. 3. Gabon—Social policy—Congresses. I. Pan African Institute for Development. II. Gabon. III. United Nations. Children's Fund. IV. Title. V. Series: Pan African Institute for Development. École des cadres. Document - Institut panafricain pour le développement, École de cadres de Douala ; no 8.
HT395.G28B37 76-470363
76 MARC

Barbee, Alfred Clifton, 1929-
Relationships between organizational structures and job satisfaction among civil service managers. Ann Arbor, Mich., University Microfilms, c1973.
1 reel. 35 mm.
Thesis—American University, 1972.
Collation of the original: 104 leaves.
1. Job satisfaction. 2. Civil service.
I. Title.
ViBlbV NUC74-126737

Barbee, Daniel G., 1941- joint author.
see Foster, John L., 1945- National policy game ... New York, Wiley, [1975]

Barbee, David E
Accountability in education [by] David E. Barbee and Aubrey J. Bouck. 1st ed. New York, Petrocelli Books, 1974.
xvii, 142 p. illus. 24 cm.
Includes bibliographical references.
1. Educational accountability. I. Bouck, Aubrey J., 1914- joint author. II. Title.
LB2806.B29 379'.15 74-4481
ISBN 0-88405-065-3 MARC

Barbee, David E
A systems model for designing an instructional program for a comprehensive community college. [n. p.] 1970.
x, 419 l. illus. 28 cm.
Typescript.
Thesis (Ph. D.)—Catholic University of America.
Bibliography: leaves 400-419.
1. Curriculum planning—U. S. 2. Municipal junior colleges—U. S.—Curricula. 3. System analysis. I. Title.
DCU NUC73-126146

Barbee, Eva John
see History of Lovelady [Texas], 1872-1972. [Lovelady? Tex., 1972?]

Barbee, James Henry, 1942-
The flow of human blood through capillary tubes with inside diameters between 8.7 and 221 microns. Pasadena, 1971.
xvi, 271 l.
Thesis—California Institute of Technology.
Photocopy of typescript. Ann Arbor, Mich., University Microfilms, 1972.
1. Blood flow. 2. Blood flow. Measurement. I. Title.
InLP NUC76-37814

Barbée, Maurice Linÿer de La
see Linÿer de La Barbée, Maurice.

Barbee, Norman N.
see United States. Government Printing Office. An explanation of the Superintendent of Documents... [Rev. ed.] Washington, 1973.

Barbee, Robert.
100 masters; centennial collection from Wally F. Findlay Galleries International. [Kansas City, Mo., Smith-Grieves, 1970?]
47 p. illus. (part col.) ports. 28 cm.
On cover: Art for music's sake.
Catalog of an exhibition held Apr. 5-17, 1970, for the benefit of Kansas City Philharmonic Foundation.
1. Paintings, Modern—Catalogs. I. Wally Findlay Galleries International. II. Title. III. Title: Art for music's sake.
MoKU NUC76-48436

Barbee, Roy M
The budget motel: who stays there [by Roy M. Barbee and W. Earl Sasser of the Harvard Business School. Boston, Laventhol Krekstein Horwath & Horwath, 1974]
41 p. illus.
Cover title.
Study sponsored by Laventhol Krekstein Horwath & Horwath.
MH-BA NUC75-26692

Barbee, Ruth Elaine.
Personality variables related to the use of interaction analysis in a counseling practicum experience. Grand Forks, 1970.
149 p.
Thesis—University of North Dakota.
Microfilm. Ann Arbor, Mich., University Microfilms. 1 reel. 35 mm.
CLSU NUC73-44823

Barbee, Stanley N.
see Parke-Bernet Galleries, inc., New York. Impressionist & modern paintings and sculpture... [New York, 1969]

Barbee, Steve G.
see Energy for Austin. [Austin, Tex.] Energy Systems Laboratories, Univ. of Texas at Austin, Dept. of Mechanical Engineering 1972.

Barbee, William C
An inquiry into the relationship between market concentration and labor's share of value added. By William C. Barbee. [n. p.] 1974.
v, 78 l. 28 cm.
Thesis (Ph. D.)—Catholic University of America.
Bibliography: leaves 73-78.
I. Title.
DCU NUC76-24629

Barbehenn, Elizabeth Kern, 1933-
The explanation for the blockade of glycolysis in early mouse embryos. St. Louis, 1974.
x, 140 l. illus.
Thesis—Washington University.
Binding title: Mouse embryo metabolism.
Includes bibliography.
1. Glucose metabolism. 2. Embryology. 3. Mice. I. Title.
MoSW NUC76-24349

Barbeiro, Walter de Souza.
A rua dos meninos mortos / Walter de Souza Barbeiro ; ilustrações de Jeannette Antonios Maman. — São Paulo : A Gazeta Maçônica, 1975.
62 p. : ill. ; 21 cm.
Cr$15.00
I. Title.
PQ9698.12.A595R8 76-487810
76 MARC

Barbeito, Jose.
La violencia y la política. [Caracas, Centro de Informacion y Documentacion para America Latina] 1971.
22 p. (Centro de Informacion y Documentacion para America Latina. Documento: decima entrega)
1. Violence. 2. Insurgency. I. Title. II. Series.
MH-Ed NUC73-31040

Barbeito y Cerviño, María, 1880-1970.
Paises y escuelas / [por] María Barbeito y Cerviño. — La Coruña : Moret, 1975, cover 1976.
221 p. : port. ; 20 cm. Sp76-June
1. Education—Spain. I. Title.
LA921.B37 1975 77-450306
77 MARC

Barbeito y Morás, Carlos Martínez-
see Martínez-Barbeito y Morás, Carlos.

Barbelenet, D.
see Mélanges linguistiques offerts à M. Antoine Meillet. Genève, Slatkine Reprints, 1972.

Barbeler, Mary T
Supply response to price in the southern Queensland dairy industry. Brisbane, 1973-
v. (Queensland. Dept. of Primary Industries. Economic Services Branch. Research bulletin no. 24, etc.)
I. Title.
DNAL NUC75-21626

Barbelli, Gian Giacomo, 1604-1656.
Gian Giacomo Barbelli : dipinti e disegni : studio e catalogo / a cura di Ugo Ruggeri ; regesto di documenti a cura di Margherita Zanardi. Con 224 illustrazioni. — Bergamo : Monumenta Bergomensia, 1974.
142 p. : ill. (some col.) ; 32 cm. — (Monumenta Bergomensia ; 40) It 75-Oct
Bibliography : p. 5-[6]
1. Barbelli, Gian Giacomo, 1604-1656. I. Ruggeri, Ugo.
ND623.B228R83 75-407898

Barbellion, Catherine Finet-
see Finet-Barbellion, Catherine.

Barben, Arnold H
Cowing and Co.'s great fire engine and pump works, Seneca Falls, N.Y.; a story of their fire engines. [Seneca Falls, N.Y., Seneca Falls Historical Society, 1971]
42 p. illus.
1. Cowing and Co. 2. Fire extinction—Equipment. I. Title.
WHi NUC73-114771

Barbeque planet. fall 1975-
[Nashville, Tenn., Project House Publications]
v. 21 cm.
Key title: Barbeque planet, ISSN 0364-2194
1. American literature—20th century—Periodicals.
PS501.B35 810'.5 76-641984
MARC-S

Barber, Albert A., joint author.
see Grinnell, Alan, 1936- Laboratory experiments in physiology. 9th ed. Saint Louis, Mosby, 1976.

Barber, Alfred W 1906-
Practical guide to digital integrated circuits / Alfred W. Barber. — West Nyack, N.Y. : Parker Pub. Co., c1976.
240 p. : ill. ; 24 cm.
Bibliography: p. 212-213.
Includes index.
ISBN 0-13-690743-1
1. Digital integrated circuits. I. Title.
TK7874.B37 621.381'73 76-10138
76 MARC

Barber, Anthony, 1920- The tax credit income supplement. 1975
see Great Britain's tax credit income supplement. White Plains, N. Y.: Institute for Socioeconomic Studies [1975]

Barber, Anthony, 1920-
The United Kingdom and the European Communities; a statement on behalf of Her Majesty's Government made by Anthony Barber, Chancellor of the Duchy of Lancaster, at the meeting of the conference between the European Communities and the states which have applied for membership of these communities at Luxembourg on 30th June 1970. London, H. M. Stationery Off., 1970.
5 p. 24 cm. ([Gt. Brit. Foreign and Commonwealth Off. Papers] Miscellaneous, 1970, no. 12) ([Gt. Brit. Parliament. Papers by command] Cmnd. 4401)
I. Title. II. Series. III. Series: Great Britain. Foreign and Commonwealth Office. Papers by Command. Cmnd. 4401.
MiU-L NUC76-21342

Barber, Barrington.
How to find out about zoo animals [by] Barrington Barber and John Eason. London, Studio Vista; New York, Van Nostrand Reinhold Co. [1972]
68 p. illus. 22 cm. (A Studio Vista/Van Nostrand Reinhold how-to book) B***
SUMMARY: Puzzles, games, and things to make and do reveal the characteristics and habits of various animals found in zoos.
1. Zoo animals—Juvenile literature. 2. Handicraft—Juvenile literature. 3. Educational games—Juvenile literature. [1. Zoo animals. 2. Handicraft] I. Eason, John, joint author. II. Title.
QL77.5.B37 596'.0076 70-39849
ISBN 0-289-70244-5 rev MARC

Barber, Barry.
Computing and operational research at the London Hospital, [by] Barry Barber and W. Abbott. London, Butterworths, 1972.
x, 102 p., leaf. illus., form, port. 22 cm. (Computers in medicine series) £2.20 GB 73-09529
Includes index.
Bibliography: p. 94-97.
1. Electronic data processing—Medicine. I. Abbott, W., joint author. II. Title.
[DNLM: 1. Computers — Hospital adminstration. 2. Hospital equipment and supplies. 3. Hospital planning. 4. Operations research. WX 26.5 B234c 1972]
[RA971.B26] 658.5'3 73-595295
ISBN 0-407-51700-6 MARC
Library of Congress 73 [4]

Shared Cataloging with DNLM

Barber, Beckie.
The role of the public library in the community : what should it be and do : workshop report / by Beckie Barber and Frank Obljubek. — Thunder Bay, Ont. : Northwestern Ontario Library Action Group, [1972?]
iii, 50, [6] leaves. : form : 28 cm. C 73-2373
Bibliography: leaves [51]-[54]
1. Libraries and community. 2. Public libraries. I. Obljubek, Frank, joint author. II. Title.
Z716.4.B27 027.4 75-318336
75 MARC

Barber, Benjamin Aquila, 1876-1946.
Robert Louis Stevenson: an appreciation. [Folcroft, Pa.] Folcroft Library Editions, 1974.
66 p. 26 cm.
Reprint of the 1910 ed. published by W. H. Moss, Whitehaven, Eng.
1. Stevenson, Robert Louis, 1850-1894.
PR5496.B25 1974 828'.8'09 74-17085
ISBN 0-8414-3114-0 (lib. bdg.) 74 MARC

Barber, Benjamin R 1939-
The death of communal liberty; a history of freedom in a Swiss mountain canton [by] Benjamin R. Barber. Princeton, N. J., Princeton University Press [1974]
xii, 302 p. illus. 23 cm.
Bibliography: p. 275-291.
1. Grisons—History. I. Title.
DQ496.B37 309.1'494'7 72-14018
ISBN 0-691-07554-9 MARC

Barber, Benjamin R 1939-
Liberating feminism [by] Benjamin R. Barber. New York, Seabury Press [1975]
x, 153 p. 22 cm. (A Continuum book)
Bibliography: p. [149]-153.
ISBN 0-8164-9214-X : $6.95
1. Feminism. I. Title.
HQ1154.B29 301.41'2 74-13887
MARC

Barber, Bernard.
Songs along the way: poems, by Bernard Barber. Albion, Calif., Cloud Press, c1971.
64 p. ill. 17 cm.
I. Title.
CU-A NUC76-41341

Barber, Bernard
see Research on human subjects... New York, Russell Sage Foundation [1973]

Barber, Bernard, 1933-
Water : a view from Japan : text / by Bernard Barber ; photos. by Dana Levy. — 1st ed. — New York : Weatherhill, 1974.
207 p. : ill. (some col.) ; 31 cm.
ISBN 0-8348-0097-7 : $30.00
1. Water—Pictorial works. 2. Japan—Description and travel—Pictorial works. I. Levy, Dana, ill. II. Title.
GB665.B36 553'.7'0952 74-76103
MARC

Barber, Bernice More.
From beginnings to boom / by Bernice More Barber. — Haines City, Fla. : Barber, 1975.
viii, 428 p. : ill. ; 23 cm.
Includes bibliographical references and index.
1. Haines City, Fla. I. Title.
F319.H34B37 975.9'67 75-329317
75 MARC

Barber, Betty.
The original face : poems 1948-1959 and one poem from the seventies / by Betty Barber. -- 1st ed. -- Hicksville, N.Y. : Exposition Press, c1975.
48 p. ; 21 cm.
I. Title.
LU NUC77-83512

Barber, Brian Harold, 1948-
A nuclear magnetic resonance study of the protein concanavalin A. [Toronto] 1974.
xi, 220 l. illus.
Thesis—University of Toronto.
Includes bibliographies.
1. Molecular biology. 2. Concanavalin A. 3. Nuclear magnetic resonance. I. Title.
CaOTU NUC76-24630

Barber, C. L.
see
Barber, Charles Laurence.

Barber, C Renate.
Cost effectiveness of education [by] C. Renate Barber. [Headington, Eng.] Oxford College of Technology, Social Science Research Unit [1969?]
12 p. 21 cm. (Oxford College of Technology. Social Science Research Unit. Occasional papers, 1)
1. Education, Secondary—Great Britain. 2. Education—Great Britain—Finance. I. Title. II. Series.
LA635.B34 658.1'554 74-168849
MARC

Barber, Carolyn.
Animals at war. London, Macdonald and Co., 1971.
152 p. illus. (some col.), ports. 23 cm. (Animal life series [3]) (A Macdonald pictureback) GB 71-29058
1. Aggressive behavior in animals. I. Title. II. Series: Animal life series (London) 3.
QL758.5.B37 1971b 591.5 74-170340
ISBN 0-356-03901-3 MARC

Barber, Carroll G.
see Bilingualism in the Southwest. Tucson, Univ. of Arizona Press [1973]

Barber, Carroll Glenn.
Injuries to the lumbo-sacral plexus; a common cause of low-back pain and sciatica. Cleveland, 1965.
12 p. illus.
1. Lumbosacral Plexus. 2. Backache—Diagnosis. 3. Leg—Injuries. I. Title.
OClW-H NUC73-2830

Barber, Cecil Robert, ed.
see Temperature measurement at the National Physical Laboratory... London, H. M. Stationery Off., 1973.

Barber, Charles Bradford.
Origins. [n.p.] 1971.
1 v.
Honors thesis—Harvard.
1. Psychology—Mathematical models.
MH NUC73-114772

Barber, Chris.
The DH 104 Dove and DH 114 Heron / compiled by C. Barber, D. Shaw and J. Sykes ; edited by T. Sykes. — Saffon Waldon : Air-Britain, 1973.
63 p., [12] p. of plates : ill. ; 24 cm. GB 74-17734
Includes index.
ISBN 0-85130-033-2 : £1.00
1. Dove (Transport plane) 2. Heron (Transport plane) I. Shaw, Dave, joint author. II. Sykes, Terry, joint author. III. Title.
TL686.H33B37 387.7'33'43 74-188180
MARC

Barber, Chris.
The sharing of resources: problems of aid and development [prepared by Chris Barber and Olive Prescott for the Committee on Sharing World Resources of the Society of Friends] London, Friends Home Service Committee, 1970.
[2], 32 p. 19 cm. (Study in fellowship, 31) £0.10 B 71-01465
Cover title.
Bibliography: p. 31-32.
1. Economic assistance, British. 2. Underdeveloped areas. 3. Economic development. I. Prescott, Olive, joint author. II. Friends, Society of. Great Britain. Committee on Sharing World Resources. III. Title.
HC60.B285 309.2'232'1724 73-168705
ISBN 0-85245-025-7 MARC

Barber, Charles Laurence.
Early modern English / [by] Charles Barber. — London : Deutsch, 1976.
360 p. : ill. ; 23 cm. — (The Language library)
Bibliography: p. 339-349.
Includes index.
ISBN 0-233-96262-X : £7.50
1. English language—Early modern, 1500-1700—History. I. Title. II. Series.
PE1081.B3 420'.9'031 76-382522
76 MARC

Barber, Charles Laurence.
The story of language [by] C. L. Barber. Revised ed. London, Pan Books, 1972.
viii, 294 p. illus., maps. 18 cm. £0.45 B 72-24028
Bibliography: p. [291]-294.
1. Language and languages. 2. English language—History. I. Title.
P121.B32 1972 410 73-331115
ISBN 0-330-33048-9 MARC

Barber, Clarence L
Economic growth and development; notes for an address delivered to the Western Canada Liberal Policy Conference, Saskatoon, August 12, 13, 1966. [Ottawa, Liberal Federation of Canada, 1966]
3 p.
Caption title.
CaOTU NUC73-40332

Barber, Clarence L
Welfare policy in Manitoba; a report to the Planning and Priorities Committee of Cabinet Secretariat, Province of Manitoba, by Clarence L. Barber. Winnipeg, [Planning and Priorities Committee of Cabinet Secretariat] 1972.
74 p. illus. 23 cm. C**
Includes bibliographical references.
1. Public welfare—Manitoba. 2. Poor—Manitoba. 3. Economic assistance, Domestic—Manitoba. I. Manitoba. Planning and Priorities Committee of Cabinet. II. Title.
HV109.M44B37 362.5'097127 73-16734

Barber, Clarence L.
see Canada. Royal Commission on Farm Machinery. Technological changes in farm machinery. Ottawa, 1969.

Barber, Clifford L.
see Kester Solder Company. Solder, its fundamentals and usage. 3d ed. ⌈Chicago⌉ 1965.

Barber, Cyril J
The minister's library, by Cyril J. Barber. Foreword by Merrill F. Unger. Grand Rapids, Baker Book House ⌈1974⌉
xiii, 378 p. illus. 27 cm. $9.95
1. Theological libraries. I. Title.
Z675.T4B3 016.2 73-92977
ISBN 0-8010-0598-1 MARC

Barber, Cyril J
Nehemiah and the dynamics of effective leadership / by Cyril J. Barber. — Neptune, N.J. : Loizeaux Bros., 1976.
191 p. ; 20 cm.
Bibliography: p. 187-191.
ISBN 0-87212-021-5 : $2.75
1. Bible. O.T. Nehemiah—Criticism, interpretation, etc. 2. Nehemiah. 3. Leadership—Biblical teaching. I. Title.
BS1365.2.B37 222'.8'06 76-22567
76 MARC

Barber, D., joint author
see Mitchell, T F Introduction to Arabic. [London, c1972]

Barber, D. F.
see
Barber, Dulan Friar, 1940-

Barber, David.
Basic personnel procedures; guidance on setting up a personnel department. London, Institute of Personnel Management [1973]
52 p. forms. 30 cm.
1. Personnel management. I. Title.
IU NUC74-120272

Barber, David Arthur, 1944-
The production of available thunderstorm energy. ⌈n.p.⌉ 1974.
63 l. illus. 29 cm.
Thesis (Ph.D.)—University of Wisconsin.
Vita.
Includes bibliography.
I. Title.
WU NUC76-24631

Barber, David Williams.
Analytical study of displacements along faults with irregular fault-plane geometry / by David Williams Barber. -- ⌈College Station, Tex.⌉ : Barber, 1976.
viii, 57 leaves : ill. ; 28 cm.
Thesis--Texas A&M University.
Vita.
Bibliography: leaves 55-56.
1. Faults (Geology). I. Title.
TxCM NUC77-89938

Barber, Derek
see Donaldson, John George Stuart, Baron Donaldson of Kingsbridge, 1907- Farming in Britain today. Revised ed. Harmondsworth, Penguin, 1972.

Barber, Derek L. A.
see A Bibliography of computing. Maidenhead, Eng., Infotech Information, c1974.

Barber, Dick, illus.
see Knowles, Tillie M S Sue and Mindy find a new friend. Durham, N. C., Moore Pub. Co. ⌈1973⌉

Barber, Douglas Norman.
The problem of betterment in dental practice. ⌈n.p.⌉ 1969.
1 v.
CaBVAU NUC73-2802

Barber, Dulan Friar, 1940-
Concerning Thomas Hardy: a composite portrait from memory; edited by D. F. Barber and based on material researched & collected by J. Stevens Cox. London, Skilton, 1968.
xviii, 184 p. 20 plates, illus., table, ports. 26 cm. 42/- B68-20031
Maps on lining papers.
Includes bibliographies.
1. Hardy, Thomas, 1840-1920—Biography. I. Cox, James Stevens. II. Title.
PR4753.B3 823'.8 68-140008
⌈r76⌉rev MARC

Barber, Dulan Friar, 1940-
The horrific world of monsters / ⌈by⌉ Dulan Barber. — London : Marshall Cavendish, 1974.
⌈1⌉, 121 p. : chiefly ill. (some col.) ; 29 cm. — (A Golden hands book)
GB75-13920
Includes index.
ISBN 0-85685-070-5 : £1.95
1. Monsters in art. 2. Arts. I. Title.
NX650.M55B37 001.9'44'03 75-333208
76 MARC

Barber, Dulan Friar, 1940-
One parent families / edited by Dulan Barber. -- London : Davis Poynter, [1975]
167 p. ; 23 cm.
1. Single-parent family. I. Title.
TxU NUC77-83508

Barber, Dulan Friar, 1940-
Pornography and society, by D. F. Barber. London, Skilton, 1972.
192 p. 21 cm. £1.95 B72-22195
Bibliography: p. ⌈189⌉-192.
1. Pornography—Social aspects. I. Title.
HQ471.B27 364.1'74 72-195597
ISBN 0-284-98523-6 72⌈r76⌉rev MARC

Barber, Dulan Friar, 1940-
Unmarried fathers / Dulan Barber. — London : Hutchinson, 1975.
179 p. ; 23 cm. GB75-05512
ISBN 0-09-122130-7 : £3.25
1. Unmarried fathers—Great Britain—Case studies. 2. Father and child—Case studies. I. Title.
HQ756.B373 362.8'2 75-315949
75⌈r77⌉rev MARC

Barber, Dulan Friar, 1940- joint author.
see Kitchen, Paddy. The marriage ring. London, Allen, 1977.

Barber, Dulan Friar, 1940-
see "Members of the jury ...". London, Wildwood House, 1976.

Barber, E J W 1940-
Archaeological decipherment: a handbook ⌈by⌉ E. J. W. Barber. ⌈Princeton, N. J.⌉ Princeton University Press ⌈1974⌉
viii, 276 p. illus. 22 cm.
Includes bibliographical references.
1. Writing—History. I. Title.
P211.B28 1974 913'.031'0285 72-14019
ISBN 0-691-03544-X MARC

Barber, E.M.
see McQuitty, J B Feedlot pollution - a literature review. ⌈Edmonton, Alta., Dept. of Agricultural Engineering, University of Alberta, 1971⌉

Barber, Ed.
see Durham, N.C. Council on Human Relations. What's ahead for the Negro job seeker in Durham, N.C.? [Durham, N.C., 1964]

Barber, Eddice Belle.
Cotton Mather's literary reputation in America. ⌈Minneapolis⌉ 1972.
ii, 281 l. 29 cm.
Thesis (Ph.D.)—University of Minnesota.
Bibliography: leaves 267-281.
MnU NUC73-114745

Barber, Edward Gordon, 1908–
Win back the acres: the treatment and cultivation of PFA surfaces, by E. G. Barber. London, Central Electricity Generating Board, 1972.
⌈16⌉ p. col. illus. 30 cm. B 73-06509
1. Reclamation of land—Great Britain. 2. Fly ash. 3. Revegetation—Great Britain. I. Title.
[S663.B36] 631.6 73-166013
MARC

Barber, Edwin Atlee, 1851-1916. The ceramic collectors' glossary. 1976.
in The Ceramic, furniture, and silver collectors' glossary. New York, Da Capo Press, 1976.

Barber, Edwin Atlee, 1851-1916.
Marks of American potters / by Edwin Atlee Barber. — Ann Arbor : Ars Ceramica, 1976.
174 p. : ill. ; 24 cm.
Reprint of the 1904 ed. published by Patterson & White Co., Philadelphia.
ISBN 0-89344-001-9 : $11.50
1. Pottery—Marks. 2. Potters—United States. I. Title.
NK4215.B3 1976 738'.02'78 76-15310
76 MARC

Barber, Edwin Atlee, 1851-1916. Marks of American potters. 1976.
in Barber, Edwin Atlee, 1851-1916. The pottery and porcelain of the United States ... Combined ed. ⌈s.l.⌉ Feingold & Lewis, ⌈1976⌉

Barber, Edwin Atlee, 1851-1916.
The pottery and porcelain of the United States : an historical review of American ceramic art from the earliest times to the present day : to which is appended a chapter on the pottery of Mexico / by Edwin Atlee Barber combined with Marks of American potters / by Edwin Atlee Barber. — Combined ed. — ⌈s.l.⌉ : Feingold & Lewis ; New York : distributed thru J & J Pub., ⌈1976⌉
xxviii, 621, 174 p. : ill. ; 24 cm.
Reprint of 2 works each published separately: The pottery and porcelain of the United States, 3d ed., rev. and enl., published in 1909 by Putnam, New York and Marks of American potters, published in 1904 by Patterson & White, Philadelphia.
Includes bibliographical references and indexes.
$20.00
1. Pottery, American. 2. Pottery—Marks. 3. Porcelain, American. 4. Porcelain—Marks. 5. Pottery, Mexican. I. Barber, Edwin Atlee, 1851-1916. Marks of American potters. 1976. II. Title.
NK4005.B23 1976 738'.0973 77-361703
77 MARC

Barber, Elinore Louise.
Antonio de Cabezón's cantus-firmus compositions and transcriptions. ⌈Ann Arbor, Mich.⌉ 1959 ⌈1972⌉
3 v. illus., music, plates, ports. 28 cm.
Thesis—University of Michigan.
Contents.—v. 1. Historical and analytical study.—v. 2. Appendices, documents, treatise, and illustrations.—v. 3. Edition of selected works of Antonio de Cabezón.
Photocopy. Ann Arbor, Mich., University Microfilms, 1972. 3 v. 23 cm.
1. Cabezón, Antonio de, 1510-1566. I. Cabezón, Antonio de, 1510-1566.
IaU NUC76-29975

Barber, Elizabeth Jane Wayland, 1940-
The computer-aided analysis of undeciphered ancient texts. [n.p., 1968, c1969]
vii, 133 l.
Thesis—Yale.
Bibliography: leaves 111-113.
Microfilm. Ann Arbor, Mich., University Microfilms, 1972.
1. Linguistic analysis (Linguistics) 2. Mathematical linguistics. 3. Inscriptions, Linear A. 4. Inscriptions, Linear B. I. Title.
CSt NUC73-31033

Barber, Eric Arthur, 1888- joint ed.
see Powell, John Undershell, 1865- ed. New chapters in the history of Greek literature ... New York, Biblo & Tannen, 1974.

Barber, Eric Arthur, 1888- joint ed.
see Powell, John Undershell, 1865- New chapters in the history of Greek literature, second series ... New York, Biblo & Tannen, 1974.

Barber, Ernest M.
see McQuitty, J B An annotated bibliography of farm animal wastes. [Ottawa, Ont.] Water Pollution Control Directorate, Environmental Protection Service, 1972.

Barber, Estelle Blanton.
Comes the moment to decide; four dramas for play reading with questions for discussion. New York, Friendship Press [c1965]
47 p.
1. Christian life—Drama. 2. Conformity. 3. Prejudices and antipathies. 4. Juvenile delinquency. 5. Church work. I. Title.
MoSCS NUC74-122441

[Barber, Estelle Blanton]
25 memorable years, 1946-1971; one hundred twenty-fifth anniversay publication, First United Methodist Church, Dallas. Dallas, Printing by Saling Letter Service [1971]
1 v. (unpaged)
Cover-title.
1. Dallas, Texas. First United Methodist Church. 2. Dallas, Texas. First Methodist Church. 3. Methodist Church in Texas. I. Title.
TxDaM-P NUC73-31030

Barber, Eunice.
Narrative of the tragical death of Darius Barber / Eunice Barber. — New York : Garland Pub., 1977.
24 p. : ill. ;23 cm. 4. — (The Garland library of narratives of North American Indian captivities ; v. 36)
Reprint of the 1818 ed. printed for D. Hazen, Boston, under title: Narrative of the tragical death of Mr. Darius Barber.
Issued with the reprint of Shocking murder by the savages of Mr. Darius Barber's family. New York, 1977, the reprint of the 1817 ed. of Lewis, H. Narrative of captivity and sufferings. New York, 1977, the reprint of the 1833 ed. of Lewis, H. Narrative of the captivity of Jane Lewis. New York, 1977, the reprint of the 1957? ed. of Van Horne, J. A narrative of captivity and sufferings. New York, 1977, and the reprint of the 1818 ed. of Steele, Z. The Indian captive. New York, 1977.
ISBN 0-8240-1660-2 : $25.00
1. Barber, Eunice. 2. Seminole Indians—Captivities. 3. Seminole War, 1st, 1817-1818. 4. Indians of North America—Captivities. 5. Georgia—Biography. I. Title. II. Series.
E85.G2 vol. 36 973'.04'97 s 77-4089
[E83.817] 77 MARC

Barber, Everett M
Design criteria for solar-heated buildings / Everett M. Barber and Donald Watson. -- Guilford, Conn. : Sunworks, 1975.
1 v. (various pagings) : tables ; 28 cm. -- (Sunworks technical publication ; 1)
1. Environmental engineering (Buildings) I. Watson, Donald, 1937- joint author. II. Title.
WU NUC77-83507

Barber, F G
On the water of the Canadian Arctic archipelago; an atlas presentation of 1961 and 1962 data [by] F. G. Barber and A. Huyer. [Ottawa] Published for Environment Canada by Dept. of Energy, Mines and Resources, 1971.
i, 76 p. maps. 28 cm. (Manuscript report series, no. 21)
1. Hydrology—Arctic regions. 2. Arctic regions—Maps. 3. Water-supply—Canada. I. Huyer, A. II. Title. III. Series: Canada. Marine Sciences Branch. Manuscript report series no. 21.
NIC NUC75-95698

Barber, F G
A preliminary tidal exchange experiment in Masset Inlet / F.G. Barber, T.S. Murty and J. Taylor. -- Ottawa : Environment Canada, Fisheries and Marine Service, 1975.
41 p. : ill. ; 28 cm. -- (Manuscript report series - Marine Sciences Directorate ; no. 39)
Abstract also in French.
Bibliography: p. 37-40.
1. Tides—Canada--Masset Inlet--Mathematical models. 2. Ocean currents--Masset Inlet. I. Murty, T. S. II. Taylor, John David. III. Title. IV. Series : Canada. Marine Sciences Directorate. Manuscript report series ; no. 39.
NIC NUC77-83525

Barber, Geoffrey.
Builders' plant and equipment / G. Barber. — 2nd ed. — London : Newnes-Butterworths, 1973.
[8], 207 p. : ill. ; 22 cm. GB75-08974
Includes index.
ISBN 0-408-00092-9 : £4.40. ISBN 0-408-00093-7 pbk.
1. Construction equipment. I. Title.
TH900.B24 1973 690'.028 75-320100
75 MARC

Barber, Geoffrey, 1904-
Country doctor / Geoffrey Barber. — Ipswich : Boydell Press, 1974.
[2], x, 98 p., [4] p. of plates : ill., map, ports. ; 23 cm. — (The Essex library) GB75-00130
ISBN 0-85115-037-3 : £2.50
1. Barber, Geoffrey, 1904- 2. Physicians (General practice)—Correspondence, reminiscences, etc. 3. Essex, Eng.—Biography. I. Title. II. Series.
[DNLM: 1. History of medicine—Biography. WZ100 B233 1974]
[R489.B19A32] 610'.92'4 75-594692
Shared Cataloging with DNLM 75 MARC

Barber, George Bradford, 1906-
An analysis and evaluation of forensic contests as conducted in the secondary schools within the area of the North Central Association. Ann Arbor, Mich., University Microfilms [1958?]
1 reel. ([University Microfilms, Ann Arbor, Mich.] Publication no. 25,436)
Microfilm copy (positive) of typescript.
Collation of the original: xiv, 313 l. illus.
Dissertation (Ph. D.)—Ohio State University, 1953.
Vita.
Bibliography: leaves 242-250.
1. Debates and debating. I. Series.
LU NUC76-40385

Barber, George Max, 1930-
An analysis of the community services function in the North Carolina Community College System by George Max Barber. Raleigh, N.C., 1974.
158 l. ill. 29 cm.
Bibliography: leaves 137-141.
Vita.
Thesis (Ph. D.)—North Carolina State University.
NcRS NUC76-24351

Barber, George S
Gigas - Zeiss digital control unit. Fort Belvoir, Va., 1973.
47 p. illus. 26 cm. (United States. Army Engineer Topographic Laboratories. Report ETL-ETR-73-1)
1. Orthographic projection. I. Title. II. Series.
DME NUC75-21800

Barber, Gerald.
Occupational structure and population growth in the Ontario-Quebec urban system 1941-1966 [by] G. M. Barber and John N. H. Britton. [Toronto] Centre for Urban and Community Studies, University of Toronto [1971]
23, 2 p. 28 cm. (University of Toronto. Centre for Urban and Community Studies. Research paper no. 49)
Bibliography: p. 23.
1. Cities and towns—Ontario. 2. Cities and towns—Quebec (Province) 3. Ontario—Occupations. 4. Quebec (Province)—Occupations. I. Britton, John N. H. II. Title. III. Series: Toronto University Centre for Urban and Community Studies. Research paper no. 49.
CaBVaU NUC76-11142

Barber, Gerald.
An optimization approach to a node-network development problem by Gerald Maurice Barber. [Toronto] 1974.
x, 186 l. graphs.
Thesis—University of Toronto.
Vita.
Bibliography: leaves 177-186.
CaOTU NUC76-24352

Barber, Gerald, joint author
see MacKinnon, Ross Douglas, 1942- A new approach to network generation and map representation. [Toronto] University of Toronto - York University, 1971.

Barber, Gertrude Audrey.
Probate of wills, Kings County, New York, January 1, 1850 to December 31, 1890: index. Copied and alphabetically arr. by Gertrude A. Barber. New York, 1948.
3 v. in 1. 29 cm.
1. Wills—Kings County, N. Y.—Indexes. 2. Kings County, N. Y.—Genealogy. I. Title.
KFN5203.2.K55B37 929'.3747'23 74-160730
MARC

Barber, Giles.
Book making in Diderot's Encyclopédie; a facsimile reproduction of articles and plates with an introduction by G.G. Barber. [Hants, Eng.] Gregg International, 1973.
1 v. (unpaged) illus. 34 cm.
1. Printing—History—France. I. Diderot, Denis, 1713-1784. Encyclopédie. II. Title.
MdU NUC75-28937

Barber, Giles, ed.
see Encyclopédie; ou, Dictionnaire raisonné des sciences. Selections. Book making in Diderot's Encyclopedie... Farnborough, Gregg, 1973.

Barber, Hollis William.
An autecological study of salmonberry (Rubus spectabilis, Pursh) in western Washington, by Hollis William Barber, Jr. [Seattle] 1976.
152 [1] l. illus.
Thesis (Ph.D.)--University of Washington.
Bibliography: leaves [138]-148.
WaU NUC77-91850

Barber, Hugh O
Manual of electronystagmography / Hugh O. Barber, Charles W. Stockwell. — Saint Louis : Mosby, 1976.
ix, 207 p. : ill. ; 26 cm.
Bibliography: p. 202-203.
Includes index.
ISBN 0-8016-0446-X
1. Electronystagmography. I. Stockwell, Charles W., 1940- joint author. II. Title.
RE748.B35 617.7'62'0754 76-17897
76 MARC

Barber, Hugh O., ed.
see Current studies in otoneurologie; proceedings... Basel, New York, S. Karger, 1973.

Barber, Hugh R K 1918-
Immunobiology for the clinician / Hugh R. K. Barber ; foreword by Philip J. Disaia. — New York : Wiley, c1977.
ix, 310 p. : ill. ; 27 cm. — (A Wiley medical publication)
Includes bibliographies and index.
ISBN 0-471-04785-6
1. Immunologic diseases. 2. Immunology. I. Title.
RC582.B37 616.07'9 76-23386
76 MARC

Barber, Hugh R K 1918–
Surgical disease in pregnancy [edited by] Hugh R. K. Barber [and] Edward A. Graber. Philadelphia, Saunders, 1974.
xiv, 763 p. illus. 27 cm.
Includes bibliographies.
1. Pregnancy, Complications of. 2. Operations, Surgical. I. Graber, Edward A., joint author. II. Title.
[DNLM: 1. Pregnancy complications. 2. Surgery—In pregnancy. WQ 240 B234s]
RG572.B38 618.3 73-89171
ISBN 0-7216-1539-2 MARC

Barber, Irene Marshall.
Ancestors and descendants of Maj. Hezekiah Barber. [Tucson, Ariz.?] 1975.
v, 96 l. 29 cm.
1. Barber family. I. Title.
NN NUC77-84135

Barber, J. H.
see
Barber, James Hill.

Barber, James.
Ginger tea makes friends. Toronto, McClelland and Stewart [c1971]
45, (i.e. 90) p. illus.
ISBN 0 7710 1007 9.
1. Cookery. I. Title.
CaOTP CaBVaU NUC73-31046

Barber, James.
Once upon Anne elephant there was a time / [written by James Barber ; illustrated by Claudine Pommier]. — [Toronto] : McClelland and Stewart, [c1974]
[32] p. : col. ill. ; 16 x 24 cm. C***
ISBN 0-7710-1006-0 : $4.95
I. Pommier, Claudine. II. Title.
PZ7.B23316 On 75-325865
75 MARC

Barber, James
see Sibbison, Virginia Hayes. Pennsylvania day care consultants. [University Park] Pennsylvania State University, Center for Human Services Development, 1972.

Barber, James, Captain.
The overland guide-book; a complete vade-mecum for the overland traveller. By Captain James Barber ... London, W. H. Allen and co., 1845.
viii p., 1 l., 134, [2] p. front., illus., plates (partly fold.) fold. map. 22½ cm.
L. C. copy replaced by microfilm.
1. Voyages and travels—Guide-books.
[G153.B23] 5-37248
Microfilm 30279 G

Barber, James David.
The Presidential character : predicting performance in the White House / by James David Barber. — 2d ed. — Englewood Cliffs, N.J. : Prentice-Hall, c1977.
xi, 576 p. ; 24 cm.
Includes bibliographical references and index.
ISBN 0-13-697466-X. ISBN 0-13-697847-9
1. Presidents—United States—Case studies. 2. Prediction (Psychology) I. Title.
JK511.B37 1977 353.03'13 77-4094
77 MARC

Barber, James David.
The state of the states: what's their job? are they doing it? Rev. ed. [Washington, Conn., Center for Information on America, c1972]
21 p. illus. (Grass roots guides on democracy and practical politics, no. 47)
Includes bibliography.
1. State governments. I. Title. II. Series.
MiEM NUC73-31039

Barber, James David, ed.
see Choosing the President. Englewood Cliffs, N. J., Prentice-Hall [1974]

Barber, James Frederick.
The basis for a theological dialogue between the contemporary Disciples of Christ and the reformation thinker John Calvin on the subject of the Lord's Supper. Nashville [c1972]
125 l. 28 cm.
Thesis (D. Div.)–Vanderbilt University, 1971.
Bibliography: leaves 122-125.
1. Lord's Supper. I. Title.
TNJ-R NUC76-41854

Barber, James Hill.
see General practice medicine. Edinburgh, Churchill Livingstone, 1975.

Barber, James M
Gardening [Rev. Athens, Ga., 1973]
35 p. illus. (Georgia. University. Cooperative Extension Service. Bulletin 577)
I. Title.
DNAL NUC74-120273

Barber, James P
South Africa's foreign policy, 1945–1970 [by] James Barber. London, New York, Oxford University Press, 1973.
325 p. illus. 22 cm. £4.50 GB***
Bibliography: p. [309]–314.
1. Africa, South—Foreign relations. I. Title.
DT770.B3 327.68 73-172971
ISBN 0-19-215651-9 MARC

Barber, James P.
see European community... London, Croom Helm in association with Open University Press, c1973.

Barber, James P.
see External relations. [Bletchley, Bucks.] Open University Press [1972]

Barber, James P.
see Government and politics. [Bletchley, Bucks] Open University Press [1971]

Barber, James P
see Leftwich, Adrian. South Africa... London, Allison & Busby [1974]

Barber, James P.
see Leftwich, Adrian. South Africa... New York : St. Martin's Press, 1974.

Barber, James P.
see The Nature of foreign policy ... Edinburgh, Holmes McDougall for the Open University Press, 1974.

Barber, Janet.
Mexican machismo in novels by Lawrence, Sender, and Fuentes. [n.p.] 1972.
v, 415 l. 28 cm.
Thesis–Univ. of Southern California.
Typewritten.
1. Mexico–Social life and customs. 2. Lawrence, David Herbert, 1885-1930. 3. Sender, Ramón José, 1901- 4. Fuentes, Carlos. I. Title.
CLSU NUC74-120275

Barber, Janet.
Mexican machismo in novels by Lawrence, Sender, and Fuentes / by Janet Barber. -- [Ann Arbor, Mich. : University Microfilms, 1975.
v. 415 leaves ; 22 cm.
Photoreprint ed. of thesis, University of Southern California, 1972.
Bibliography: leaves 402-415.
1. Mexico--Social life and customs. 2. Lawrence, David Herbert, 1885-1930. 3. Sender, Ramón José. 1901- I. Title.
CLSU NUC77-85175

Barber, Janet.
Nature jewellery / Janet Barber ; illustrated by Elizabeth Haines ; photography by Gerald Hannibal. — London : Chatto & Windus, c1975.
48 p. : ill. ; 25 cm. — (A Chatto activity book) GB***
ISBN 0-7011-5072-6 : £1.95
1. Jewelry making—Juvenile literature. 2. Nature craft—Juvenile literature. I. Title.
TT212.B37 745.59'42 75-332979
76 MARC

Barber, Janet.
Pebbles as a hobby. New York, Hippocrene Books [1972]
160 p. illus. (part col.) 23 cm. $6.95
Bibliography: p. 152-153.
1. Pebbles—Collectors and collecting. 2. Grinding and polishing. I. Title.
QE432.B27 1972 552'.0075 72-86851
ISBN 0-88254-026-2 MARC

Barber, Janet.
Quiero aprender a coser. Barcelona, Molino, 1971.
61 p. col. illus.
1. Sewing. 2. Spanish language books. I. Title.
RP NUC76-72724

Barber, Janet.
The voyage of Jim. Illustrated by Fritz Wegner. Minneapolis, Carolrhoda Books [1973]
[32] p. col. illus. 22 x 28 cm.
SUMMARY: An English mouse goes to visit his friend, Eliza, in London, hazardously journeying by way of Africa.
[1. Mice—Stories] I. Wegner, Fritz, illus. II. Title.
PZ7.B2332Vo 3 [E] 72-7663
ISBN 0-87614-041-X MARC

Barber, Janet Miller.
Adult and child care; a client approach to nursing [by] Janet Miller Barber, Lillian Gatlin Stokes [and] Diane McGovern Billings. Saint Louis, C.V. Mosby Co., 1973.
xvi, 814 p. illus. 27 cm.
Includes bibliographies.
1. Nursing. 2. Pediatric nursing. I. Stokes, Lillian Gatlin, joint author. II. Billings, Diane McGovern, joint author. III. Title.
RT41.B272 610.73 72-92804
ISBN 0-8016-0443-5 73[r76]rev MARC

Barber, Janet Miller.
Adult and child care : a client approach to nursing / Janet Miller Barber, Lillian Gatlin Stokes, Diane McGovern Billings. — 2d ed. — St. Louis : C. V. Mosby Co., 1977.
xiv, 1036 p. : ill. ; 27 cm.
Includes bibliographies and index.
ISBN 0-8016-0444-3
1. Nursing. 2. Pediatric nursing. I. Stokes, Lillian Gatlin, joint author. II. Billings, Diane McGovern, joint author. III. Title.
[DNLM: 1. Nursing care. WY100 B234a]
RT41.B272 1977 610.73 76-26637
76 MARC

Barber, John.
A CYCON mini-information system on geology, geochemistry, geophysics, exploration, mining costs, & economics of porphyry and disseminated copper deposits, by John Barber in association with R. Ellison & G.L. Filippelli. Richmond, B.C., CYCON Resource Management, ltd., c1971.
1 v. (various pagings) 28 cm.
Cover title: Mini-information system: Porphyry & disseminated copper.
1. Information storage and retrieval systems. Copper mines and mining. 2. Copper mines and mining. Bibliography. 3. Porphyry. Bibliography. I. CYCON Resource Management, ltd. II. Title.
MnU NUC73-80695

Barber, John
see Cases & materials on family law. 1972 ed. [Toronto, 1972?]

Barber, John
see Cases & materials on family law. 1973 ed. [Toronto, 1973?]

Barber, John
see The Collective labour relations model applied to social welfare programmes. [Ottawa] 1970.

Barber, John A
Vandringsoverskud og lokale karakteristikker. Hvidovre, Eksp.: Gillesager 194, 1973.
vii, 136, [49] l. illus. 30 cm. kr25.00 D 73-32
Summary in English.
Includes bibliographies.
1. Migration, Internal—Denmark. I. Title.
HB2071.B36 73-364615
ISBN 87-980252-0-1

Barber, John R
Catalyzed outer-sphere reduction of cobalt (III) Kent, 1973.
ix, 87 l. illus. 29 cm.
Thesis—Kent State University.
1. Oxidation-reduction reaction. 2. Cobalt. 3. Chromium. I. Title.
OKentU NUC75-21632

Barber, John Warner, 1798-1885.
Early woodcut views of New York and New Jersey : 304 illustrations from the "Historical collections" / by John W. Barber and Henry Howe. — New York : Dover Publications, 1975.
118 p. : chiefly ill. ; 29 cm. — (Dover pictorial archive series)
Includes index.
ISBN 0-486-23196-8 : $3.50
1. Barber, John Warner, 1798-1885. 2. Howe, Henry, 1816-1893. 3. New York (State) in art. 4. New Jersey in art. I. Howe, Henry, 1816-1893, joint author. II. Barber, John Warner, 1798-1885. Historical collections of the State of New York. III. Barber, John Warner, 1798-1885. Historical collections of the State of New Jersey. IV. Title.
NE1112.B37H68 769'.92'4 75-3823
76 MARC

Barber, John Warner, 1798-1885. Historical collections of the State of New Jersey.
see Barber, John Warner, 1798-1885. Early woodcut views of New York and New Jersey ... New York, Dover Publications, 1975.

Barber, John Warner, 1798-1885.
United States book; or, Interesting events in the history of the United States; being a selection of the most important and interesting events which have transpired since the discovery of this country, to the present time; with biographical sketches of persons distinguished in American history. Compiled from the most approved authorities, by J. W. Barber. New Haven, L. H. Young, 1834.
404 p. front. (port.) plates, fold. map. 18 cm.
1. United States—History. I. Title.
E178.B252 2-1691
rev

Barber, Joseph E., joint author.
see Rapp, Marvin A. Career education ... Moravia, N.Y., Chronicle Guidance Publications, c1975.

Barber, Joseph E., joint author.
see Rapp, Marvin A. Career education ... Moravia, N.Y., Chronicle Guidance Publications, c1977.

Barber, Kenneth Frank.
Meinong's Hume studies: translation and commentary, by Kenneth Frank Barber. [Ann Arbor, University Microfilms, 1967]
Microfilm copy (positive)
Collation as determined from Diss. Abstracts: 237 p.
Translator's thesis—University of Iowa, 1966.
1. Hume, David, 1711-1776. 2. Meinong, Alexius, Ritter von Hanschuchsheim, 1853-1920. Hume Studien. I. Meinong, Alexius, Ritter von Hanschuschsheim, 1853-1920. II. Title.
NjR NUC74-173002

Barber, L Thomas.
Faculty perceptions of the institutional functioning of selected Illinois public multi-campus and single-campus community colleges, by Thomas L. Barber. [Carbondale, Ill.] 1973.
ix, 174 l., tables.
Thesis—Southern Illinois University.
Vita.
Bibliography: leaves 138-142.
Appendices: A-K (l. 145-173)
1. Municipal universities and colleges. 2. Municipal universities and colleges—Illinois. 3. College teachers. I. Title.
ICarbS NUC75-41240

Barber, Laura Martin, 1947-
see Hardman, Martha James. Aymar ar yatiqañataki. Gainesville, Fla. [1972?]

Barber, Leila Cook
see Vassar College. Art Gallery. The Italian Renaissance. [Poughkeepsie, 1968]

Barber, Leroy Edward.
Why some able high school graduates do not go to college. Pittsburgh, 1950.
75 l.
Thesis—University of Pittsburgh.
Bibliography: leaves 73-75.
Photocopy. Pittsburgh, University of Pittsburgh Library, 1974. 28 cm.
1. College attendance. 2. High school graduates. I. Title.
IU NUC76-24353

Barber, Lloyd Ingram, 1932-
The basis for native claims in Canada / by Lloyd Barber. -- [Saskatoon : Munk-ox Circle, University of Saskatchewan, 1975?]
14 leaves ; 29 cm. -- (Musk-ox Circle. / Paper ; 7)
1. Indians of North America--Canada--Government relations. 2. Indians of North America--Claims. I. Title. II. Series.
CaBVaU NUC77-85178

Barber, Lois M., joint author
see Wilson, Dorothy J Spinal cord injury... Thorofare, N. J., C. B. Slack [1974]

Barber, Louis M.
see Institute for the Study of Crime and Delinquency, Sacramento, Calif. Model Community Correctional Project. Model community correctional program, San Joaquin County, California. Rev. Sacramento? 1969

Barber, Lucie W
The relation of dogmatism to decision-making behavior in twelfth-grade high school students. [Albany] 1970.
Microfilm of transcript. Ann Arbor, Mich., University Microfilms, 1970.
Collation of original: 96 l. illus.
Thesis—State University of New York at Albany.
Includes bibliography.
1. High school students. Attitudes. 2. Decision-making. 3. Dogmatism. I. Title.
N NUC73-40331

Barber, Lucie W., joint author.
see Ligon, Ernest Mayfield, 1897- If you only knew what your baby is thinking. Burlingame, Calif., Panamedia. [1973]

Barber, Lucie W., joint author.
see Ligon, Ernest Mayfield, 1897- "Let me introduce mySelf"... Schenectady, N.Y., Character Research Press, c1976.

Barber, Lynn.
The single woman's sex book / [by] Lynn Barber. — London : Quartet Books, 1976.
[9], 156 p. : 1 ill. ; 23 cm. GB76-2739
Bibliography: p. 155-[156]
ISBN 0-7043-2102-5 : £3.95
1. Single women—Sexual behavior. I. Title.
HQ29.B33 1976 301.41'76'423 77-35421
77 MARC

Barber, Lynn Eileen, 1946-
Methane production in sediments of Lake Wingra. [n.p.] 1974.
145 l. illus. 29 cm.
Thesis (Ph.D.)—University of Wisconsin.
Vita.
Includes bibliography.
I. Title.
WU NUC76-24355

Barber, Margaret Fairless, 1869-1901.
The roadmender / by Michael Fairless [i.e. M. F. Barber]. — New York : Dutton, [1905?]
vii, 158 p. ; 18 cm.
"This series of papers appeared in the Pilot."
CONTENTS: The roadmender.—Out of the shadow.—At the white gate.
I. Title.
PR6003.A65R6 1905 824'.8 75-312633
75 MARC

Barber, Marjorie, joint author.
see Beall, James Lee. Laying the foundation. Plainfield, N.J., Logos International, c1976.

Barber, Martin.
A critical evaluation of the Indo-China ethnography of Georges Condominas. Hull [Eng.] 1971.
79 l. 28 cm.
Thesis (Ph.D.)—University of Hull.
Includes bibliography.
1. Ethnology—Asia, Southeastern. 2. Condominas, Georges. I. Title.
MU NUC74-122445

Barber, Mary, 1911-1965. Antibiotic and chemotherapy
see Garrod, Lawrence Paul, 1895- Antibiotic and chemotherapy. 4th ed. Edinburgh, Churchill Livingstone, 1973.

Barber, Mary Olivia
see Diabetes. Washington, R.J. Brady, 1972.

Barber, Melanie.
see Lambeth Palace. Library. Index to the letters and papers of Frederick Temple, Archbishop of Canterbury, 1896-1902 in Lambeth Palace Library. London, Mansell, 1975.

Barber, Michael Newton, 1947-
Critical phenomena in systems of finite thickness. [Ithaca, N.Y.] 1972.
vii, 194 l. illus. 29 cm.
Thesis (Ph. D.)—Cornell University.
1. Phase transformations (Statistical physics) I. Title.
NIC NUC74-125972

Barber, Michael P
Local government ⌊by⌋ Michael P. Barber. 2d ed. London, Macdonald & Evans, 1972.
x, 219 p. 19 cm. (M. & E. handbook series)
Bibliography: p. 207.
1. Local government—Great Britain. I. Title.
MB NUC75-32397

Barber, Michael P
Local government / Michael P. Barber. — 3rd ed. — London : Macdonald and Evans, 1974.
x, 221 p. ; 19 cm. — (The M. & E. handbook series) GB75-01509
Bibliography: p. 209.
Includes index.
ISBN 0-7121-1229-4 : £1.35
1. Local government—Great Britain. I. Title.
JS3113.B28 1974 352.042 75-331882
76 MARC

Barber, Michael P
Public administration. London, Macdonald & Evans, 1972.
x, 252 p. 19 cm. (M. & E. handbook series)
Bibliography: p. 243.
1. Gt. Brit.—Pol. & govt. 2. Public administration—Gt. Brit. 3. Civil service—Gt. Brit.
IU NUC75-41678

Barber, Nancy.
1975 graduate school vacancy survey / Nancy Barber, Denise Garcia. -- Boulder, Colo. : Western Interstate Commission for Higher Education, 1975.
30 p., chiefly tables ; 28 cm.
1. Universities and colleges--United States--Graduate work. 2. Universities and colleges--The West--Directories. I. Garcia, Denise. II. Title.
NmU NUC77-85287

Barber, Nancy
see Adams, Spike. Affirmative action recruitment directory... Boulder, Colorado, 1974.

Barber, Nancy.
see Schmatz, Linda M The management of innovation directory. Boulder, Colo., Western Interstate Commission for Higher Education, 1974.

Barber, Noël.
Let's visit the U. S. A. New ed. London, Burke, 1971.
96 p. illus. (some col.), map. 21 cm. £0.65 GB 71-30270
Includes index.
1. United States—Description and travel—Juvenile literature. I. Title.
E169.02.B33 1971 917.3'03'924 74-183990
ISBN 0-222-66844-X (lib. bdg.) ; 0-222-66856-3 MARC

Barber, Noël.
The lords of the Golden Horn; from Suleiman the Magnificent to Kamal Ataturk. ⌊London⌋ Macmillan ⌊1973⌋
304 p. illus. 24 cm. £3.50 GB***
Bibliography: p. 293-297.
1. Turkey—History. I. Title.
DR486.B37 949.6'00992 73-173815
ISBN 0-333-13861-9 MARC

Barber, Noël.
The lords of the Golden Horn; from Suleiman the Magnificent to Kamal Ataturk. London, Book Club Associates ⌊1974⌋
304 p. illus., maps, plans, ports. 25 cm.
Bibliography: p. 293-297.
OCU NUC76-24350

Barber, Noël.
La segreta di Calcutta. ⌊Traduzione di Paolo Serra. Milano⌋ Sugar ⌊1970⌋
267 p. illus. 22 cm. (Enigimi della storia, 7)
Translation of The Black Hole of Calcutta.
1. Calcutta, Black hole of. I. Title. II. Series.
IU NUC76-71903

Barber, Noël.
Seven days of freedom : the Hungarian uprising 1956 / Noël Barber. — London : Macmillan, 1973, c1974.
268 p., ⌊4⌋ leaves of plates : ill. ; 23 cm. GB***
Bibliography : p. ⌊250⌋-257.
Includes index.
ISBN 0-333-14943-2 : £3.95
1. Hungary—History—Revolution, 1956. I. Title.
DB957.B314 1973 943.9'05 74-195531
MARC

Barber, Noël.
Seven days of freedom : the Hungarian uprising 1956 / Noel Barber. — New York : Stein and Day, 1974.
266 p., ⌊4⌋ leaves of plates : ill. ; 24 cm.
Bibliography : p. 250-257.
Includes index.
ISBN 0-8128-1730-3 : $8.95
1. Hungary—History—Revolution, 1956. I. Title.
DB957.B314 943.9'05 74-78536
MARC

Barber, Noël.
The sultans ⌊by⌋ Noel Barber. New York, Simon and Schuster ⌊1973⌋
304 p. illus. 25 cm. $9.95
Bibliography : p. 293-296.
1. Turkey—History. I. Title.
DR486.B38 949.6'0992 73-7925
ISBN 0-671-21624-4 MARC

Barber, Noël.
The week France fell : June 1940 / Noel Barber. — London ⌊etc.⌋ : Macmillan, 1976.
320 p., ⌊8⌋ p. of plates : ill., facsim., map, plan, ports. ; 23 cm. GB76-25457
Ill. on lining papers.
Bibliography: p. ⌊308⌋-315.
Includes index.
ISBN 0-333-17801-7 : £4.95
1. World War, 1939-1945—France—Chronology. I. Title.
D761.B33 1976b 940.53'44 77-353227
77 MARC

Barber, Noël.
The week France fell / Noel Barber. — New York : Stein and Day, 1976.
321 p., ⌊4⌋ leaves of plates : ill. ; 24 cm.
Bibliography: p. ⌊308⌋-315.
Includes index.
ISBN 0-8128-1921-7
1. World War, 1939-1945—France—Chronology. 2. France—History—German occupation, 1940-1945—Chronology. I. Title.
D761.B33 1976 940.53'44 75-34398
75 MARC

Barber, Patricia G 1940-
Ralph Waldo Emerson's antislavery notebook, WO Liberty. [Amherst] 1975.
1, xi, 110 l. 28 cm.
Thesis (Ph. D.)-- University of Massachusetts.
1. Emerson, Ralph Waldo, 1830-1882. WO Liberty. 2. Slavery in the United States. I. Title.
MU NUC77-85055

Barber, Paul J
Perception and information / Paul J. Barber and David Legge. — London : Methuen, 1976.
144 p. ; 18 cm. — (Essential psychology ; A4) GB***
Bibliography: p. 135.
Includes indexes.
ISBN 0-416-82030-1. ISBN 0-416-82040-9 pbk. : £0.80
1. Perception. I. Legge, David, joint author. II. Title. III. Series.
BF311.B284 153.7 76-372775
76 MARC

Barber, Paul J., joint author.
see Legge, David. Information and skill. London, Methuen, 1976.

Barber, Peter N
The trees around us / Peter Barber and C. E. Lucas-Phillips ; drawings by Delia Delderfield : with an introd. by David G. Leach. — Chicago : Follett, c1975.
191 p. : ill. (some col.) ; 32 cm.
Includes index.
ISBN 0-695-80539-8 : $22.95
1. Ornamental trees. 2. Trees. I. Phillips, Cecil Ernest Lucas, 1898- joint author. II. Title.
SB435.B328 1975b 635.9'77'0912 74-18648
75 MARC

Barber, Peter N
The trees around us / Peter Barber and C. E. Lucas Phillips ; drawings by Delia Delderfield. — London : Weidenfeld and Nicolson in collaboration with The Royal Horticultural Society, c1975.
191 p. : ill. (some col.) ; 31 cm. GB***
ISBN 0-297-76932-4 : £8.50
1. Ornamental trees. 2. Trees. I. Phillips, Cecil Ernest Lucas, 1898- joint author. II. Title.
SB435.B328 635.9'77'0912 75-327081
75 MARC

Barber, Philip, 1946-
The road home : sketches of rural Canada / Philip Barber ; text by Brian Swarbrick. — Scarborough, Ont. : Prentice-Hall of Canada, c1976.
⌊32⌋ p., ⌊62⌋ leaves of plates : chiefly ill. ; 24 x 27 cm. C76-017072-X
ISBN 0-13-781559-X : $19.95
1. Barber, Philip, 1946- 2. Canada in art. I. Swarbrick, Brian, 1929- II. Title.
NC143.B37S93 741.9'71 77-357606
77 MARC

Barber, Philip Gellert.
Rock music, 1964-1970 : the limitations of youth protest as cultural revolution / by Philip Gellert Barber. -- [s.l. : s.n., 1975]
106 leaves ; 28 cm.
Honors thesis--Harvard.
Includes bibliography and discography.
1. Music and society. 2. Music--Popular (Songs, etc.)--United States.
MH NUC77-85456

Barber, R. W.
see
Barber, Richard W

Barber, Ralph W 1923-
The effects of open enrollment on anti-Negro and anti-white prejudices among junior high school students in Rochester, New York. Rochester, 1968.
xii, 131 p.
Thesis (Ed. D.)—University of Rochester.
Microfilm: Ann Arbor, University Microfilms, 1968. 1 reel.
1. Segregation in education. 2. Discrimination in education. I. Title.
MH-Ed NUC73-40697

Barber, Raymond W.
see Media services in open-education schools. [Philadelphia] 1973.

Barber, Raynal Bell, 1935-
The correspondence of Amy Lowell and John Gould Fletcher, by Raynal Bell Barber. Fort Worth, Tex., 1974.
898 p.
Thesis—Texas Christian University.
1. Lowell, Amy, 1874-1925. 2. Fletcher, John Gould, 1886-1950. 3. Imagist poetry. I. Title.
TxFTC NUC76-24354

Barber, Richard.
A dictionary of fabulous beasts ⌊by⌋ Richard Barber & Anne Riches. With illus. by Rosalind Dease. New York, Walker ⌊1972, c1971⌋
167 p. illus. 24 cm.
Bibliography : p. 159-167.
1. Animals, Mythical—Dictionaries. I. Riches, Anne, joint author. II. Title.
GR825.B28 1972 398'.469'03 70-188468
ISBN 0-8027-0385-2 MARC

Barber, Richard.
see The Director's guide to better offices. London, Director Publications Ltd for the Institute of Directors, 1975.

Barber, Richard, 1946-
Trade unions and the Tories / by Richard Barber. — London : Bow Publications ⌊for⌋ the Bow Group, 1976.
⌊2⌋, 13 p. ; 21 cm. GB76-34523
ISBN 0-900182-73-3 : £0.40
1. Labor policy—Great Britain. 2. Conservative Party (Gt. Brit.) 3. Trade-unions—Great Britain—Political activity. I. Bow Group. II. Title.
HD8391.B37 331.88'0941 77-355337
77 MARC

Barber, Richard J
Die Herrschaft der Manager; Amerikas business in der Welt von Morgen. München, Juncker [1970]
339 p. 25 cm.
Translation of the author's The American corporation; its power, its money; its politics.
1. Corporations—U. S.
CtY-L NUC73-124326

Barber, Richard J
Le Pouvoir américain; les grandes sociétés, leur organisation, leur puissance politique. Traduit de l'américain par Anne Laurens. [Paris] Stock [1972]
380 p. illus. 22 cm.
Titre original: The American corporation.
I. Title.
CaOOU NUC73-125649

Barber, Richard J
Survey of international relations of the University of Hawaii. Prepared for the Advisory Council on the International Relations of the University. [Honolulu, 1970.
iv, 223, [1] l.
1. Hawaii. University, Honolulu. 2. International relations. I. Hawaii. University, Honolulu. Advisory Council on the International Relations of the University. I. Title.
HU NUC73-119082

Barber (Richard J.) Associates
see Richard J. Barber Associates, inc.

Barber, Richard W
Arthur of Albion: an introduction to the Arthurian literature and legends of England [by] Richard Barber. London (60 Stanhope Gardens, S. W. 7), Boydell Press, 1971.
viii, 216 p., leaf. illus., geneal. tables, maps. 23 cm. index. £2.50
B 72-01369
Bibliography: p. 195-198.
1. Arthurian romances. 2. Arthurian romances—History and criticism. I. Title.
PR328.B3 1971 820'.9'351 73-151569
ISBN 0-85115-002-0 MARC

Barber, Richard W. Arthur of Albion
see Barber, Richard W King Arthur, in legend and history. Ipswich [Eng.] Boydell Press; Totowa, N. J., Rowman and Littlefield [1974, c1973]

Barber, Richard W
Cooking and recipes from Rome to the Renaissance [by] Richard Barber. [London] Allen Lane [1973]
vii, 160 p. illus. 23 cm. £2.50 GB***
Bibliography: p. 149.
1. Cookery, International—History. I. Title.
TX725.A1B34 641.5'09 74-155802
ISBN 0-7139-0489-5 MARC

Barber, Richard W
A dictionary of fabulous beasts, [by] Richard Barber & Anne Riches; with illustrations by Rosalind Dease. London, Macmillan, 1971.
168 p. illus. 24 cm. £2.95 B 71-26374
Bibliography: p. 159-167.
1. Animals, Mythical—Dictionaries. I. Riches, Anne, joint author. II. Title.
GR825.B28 1971 398'.469'03 72-175169
ISBN 0-333-10967-8 rev MARC

Barber, Richard W
A dictionary of fabulous beasts [by] Richard Barber & Anne Riches. With illus. by Rosalind Dease. New York, Walker [1972, c1971]
167 p. illus. 24 cm.
Bibliography: p. 159-167.
1. Animals, Mythical—Dictionaries. I. Riches, Anne, joint author. II. Title.
GR825.B28 1972 398'.469'03 70-188468
ISBN 0-8027-0385-2 rev MARC

Barber, Richard W
A dictionary of fabulous beasts / [by] Richard Barber & Anne Riches ; with illustrations by Rosalind Dease. — Ipswich : Boydell Press, 1975.
168 p. : ill. ; 24 cm. GB76-17457
Bibliography: p. 159-167.
ISBN 0-85115-061-6 : £2.50
1. Animals, Mythical—Dictionaries. I. Riches, Anne, joint author. II. Title.
GR825.B28 1975 398'.469'03 77-356076
77 MARC

Barber, Richard W
The figure of Arthur [by] Richard Barber. [London] Longman [1972]
160 p. map. 23 cm. £2.25 B***
Bibliography: p. 137-149.
1. Arthur, King. I. Title.
DA152.5.A7B37 398'.352 72-172109
ISBN 0-582-12583-9 MARC

Barber, Richard W
The figure of Arthur [by] Richard Barber. Totowa, N. J., Rowman and Littlefield [1973, c1972]
160 p. map. 23 cm. $7.50
Bibliography: p. 137-149.
1. Arthur, King. I. Title.
DA152.5.A7B37 1973 942.01'4 [B] 73-6957
ISBN 0-87471-129-0 MARC

Barber, Richard W
Henry Plantagenet [by] Richard Barber. [Ipswich, England, Boydell Press [1973]
278 p. illus. 23 cm.
Bibliography: p. [250]-260.
1. Henry II, King of England, 1133-1189. 2. Great Britain—History—Henry II, 1154-1189. I. Title.
NNC NUC75-21236

Barber, Richard W
King Arthur; in legend and history [by] Richard Barber. Ipswich, Boydell Press, 1973.
192 p., [32] p. of plates. illus. (some col.), facsims. (some col.) 21 cm. £2.50 GB 74-02264
Bibliography: p. 175-183.
Includes index.
1. Arthur, King. 2. Arthurian romances—History and criticism. I. Title.
PN57.A6B34 809'.933'51 74-164536
ISBN 0-85115-031-4 MARC

Barber, Richard W
King Arthur, in legend and history [by] Richard Barber. Ipswich [Eng.] Boydell Press; Totowa, N. J., Rowman and Littlefield [1974, c1973]
192 p. illus. 21 cm.
"Parts of this book were originally published under the title: Arthur of Albion, by Barrie and Rockliff with Pall Mall Press in 1961."
Includes bibliographical references.
1. Arthur, King. 2. Arthurian romances — History and criticism. I. Barber, Richard W. Arthur of Albion. II. Title.
PN57.A6B34 1974 809'.933'51 74-9502
ISBN 0-87471-565-2 MARC

Barber, Richard W
The knight and chivalry / Richard Barber. — Totowa, N.J. : Rowman and Littlefield, 1975, c1974.
399 p., [12] leaves of plates : ill. ; 21 cm.
Bibliography: p. 353-373.
Includes index.
ISBN 0-87471-653-5
1. Knights and knighthood. 2. Chivalry. I. Title.
CR4509.B37 1975 940.1'7 74-34075
75 MARC

Barber, Richard W
Samuel Pepys Esquire, Secretary of the Admiralty to King Charles & King James the Second. [Berkeley] University of California Press [c1970]
64 p. illus. (part col.), facsims., ports. (part col.) 22 cm. $3.95
Four essays which form a catalog of the exhibition held Nov., 1970, at the National Portrait Gallery, London.
1. Pepys, Samuel, 1633-1703—Exhibitions. I. London. National Portrait Gallery.
DA447.P4B3 828'.4'03 70-123622
ISBN 0-520-01763-3 rev MARC

Barber, Richard W
Samuel Pepys Esquire [essays which form a catalogue of the exhibition held at the National Portrait Gallery in 1970]. London, G. Bell, 1970.
[8], 64 p. illus. (some col.), facsims., ports. (some col.) 22 cm. 25/- B 70-29522
1. Pepys, Samuel, 1633-1703—Exhibitions. I. London. National Portrait Gallery.
DA447.P4B3 1970b 828'.4'03 75-578978
ISBN 0-7135-1782-4 rev MARC

Barber, Richard W
A strong land and a sturdy : England in the Middle Ages / Richard Barber. — 1st American ed. — New York : Seabury Press, 1976.
128 p., [4] leaves of plates : ill. ; 25 cm.
"A Clarion book."
Bibliography: p. [124]-125.
Includes index.
SUMMARY: Through a study of the political and social institutions, the rulers, artists, scientists and craftsmen of the Middle Ages, examines what everyday life in medieval times was like and what links with the era still survive.
ISBN 0-8164-3167-1
1. England—Civilization—Medieval period, 1066-1485—Juvenile literature. [1. England—Civilization—Medieval period, 1066-1485. 2. Civilization, Medieval] I. Title.
DA185.B23 1976 942 75-43895
75 MARC

Barber, Richard W
see Aubrey, John, 1626-1697. Brief lives... London, Folio Society, 1975.

Barber, Richard W.
see Camps, Francis E The investigation of murder. London, Joseph, 1966.

Barber, Richard W 1941-
The companion guide to south-west France : Bordeaux and the Dordogne / Richard Barber. — London : Collins, 1977.
288 p., [12] leaves of plates : ill. ; 23 cm. GB**
Bibliography: p. 280-281.
Includes index.
ISBN 0-00-211149-7 : £6.95. ISBN 0-00-216773-5 pbk.
1. Bordeaux region, France—Description and travel—Guide-books. 2. Dordogne Valley—Description and travel—Guide-books. I. Title.
DC611.B66B37 914.4'71 77-36833
77 MARC

Barber, Richard Walter, 1948-
Optimal control of the hospital inpatient census / by Richard Walter Barber. -- [s.l. : s.n., 1976]
295 leaves in various foliations : ill. ; 29 cm.
Thesis--Harvard.
Includes bibliography.
MH NUC77-85953

Barber, Ronald Jerry.
The importance of selected categories of employee benefits to public junior college teachers. Las Cruces, N. M., 1971.
xii, 127 l.
Thesis—New Mexico State University.
Includes bibliography.
1. College teachers—Salaries, pensions, etc. 2. Junior colleges—Faculty. I. Title.
CLU NUC74-123044

Barber, Rowland
see Graziano, Rocky 1921- Marcado por el odio. [Barcelona, Plaza, c1971]

Barber, Rowland
see Marx, Harpo, 1888-1964. Harpo speaks! [New York] B. Geis Asociates [1961]

Barber, Rowland
see Schulman, Arnold. The night they raided Minsky's. [Hollywood, Tandem Productions, Inc.] 1967.

Barber, Rupert T 1932-
An historical study of the theatre in Charlotte, North Carolina, from 1873-1902, by Rupert T. Barber, Jr. [n. p.] 1970.
viii, 356 l. illus.
Thesis—Louisiana State University.
Vita.
Bibliography: leaves 324-329.
Microfilm. Ann Arbor, Mich., Xerox University Microfilms. 1 reel. 35 mm.
1. Theater—Charlotte, N. C. I. Title.
TxU NUC76-41855

Barber, Sotirios A
The Constitution and the delegation of congressional power Sotirios A. Barber. — Chicago : University of Chicago Press 1975.
ix, 153 p. ; 21 cm.
Expanded and revised version of the author's thesis, University of Chicago.
Includes bibliographical references and index.
ISBN 0-226-03705-3 : $11.75
1. Delegation of powers—United States. 2. United States—Constitution law. I. Title.
KF4565.B3 342'.73'044 74-1668
74 MAR

Barber, Sotirios A
On the rule of non-delegation. [n. p.] 1972.
157 l.
Thesis (Ph. D.)—Univ. of Chicago.
1. Delegation of powers—U. S. 2. Constitutional law—U. S. I. Title.
ICU NUC74-120266

Barber, Theodore Xenophon, 1927–
Hypnosis; a scientific approach. New York, Van Nostrand Reinhold [c1969]
v, 282 p. 19 cm. (Van Nostrand insight series, 45) 2.95
An Insight book.
Bibliography: p. 255–278.
1. Hypnotism. I. Title.
BF1141.B27 154.7 79–9826
rev MARC

Barber, Theodore Xenophon, 1927–
Hypnosis, imagination, and human potentialities [by] Theodore X. Barber, Nicholas P. Spanos, and John F. Chaves. New York, Pergamon Press [1974]
ix, 189 p. 23 cm. (Pergamon general psychology series, 46)
Bibliography: p. 161–179.
1. Hypnotism—Therapeutic use. I. Spanos, Nicholas P., joint author. II. Chaves, John F., joint author. III. Title.
[DNLM: 1. Hypnosis. BF 1141 B234h 1974]
RC495.B34 1974 615'.8512 73–19539
ISBN 0–08–017932–0; 0–08–017931–2 (pbk.) MARC

Barber, Theodore Xenophon, 1927–
LSD, marihuana, yoga, and hypnosis. Chicago, Aldine Pub. Co. [1970]
xi, 337 p. 24 cm. (Modern applications of psychology)
Includes bibliographical references.
1. Hallucinogenic drugs. 2. Yoga. 3. Hypnotism. I. Title.
RM315.B35 615'.782 73–115935
ISBN 0–202–25004–1 rev MARC

Barber, Theodore Xenophon, 1927-
Pitfalls in human research : ten pivotal points / Theodore Xenophon Barber. — New York : Pergamon Press, c1976.
vi, 117 p. ; 24 cm. — (Pergamon general psychology series ; v. 67)
Bibliography: p. 92-111.
Includes indexes.
ISBN 0-08-020935-1. ISBN 0-08-020934-3 pbk.
1. Psychological research, Experiments effects in. I. Title.
[DNLM: 1. Behavioral sciences. 2. Research. BF76.5 B234p]
BF76.5.B37 1976 150'.7'2 76-13488
76 MARC

Barber, Theodore Xenophon, 1927-
Suggested ("hypnotic") behavior: the trance paradigm versus an alternative paradigm. Harding, Mass., Medfield Foundation, 1970.
79 l. (Medfield Foundation. Report no. 103)
Mimeographed copy.
Cover title.
Bibliography: p. 68-79.
1. Hypnotism. 2. Trance. 3. Mental suggestion. I. Title. II. Series.
CU-SB NUC74-123056

Barber, Theodore Xenophon, 1927-
A theory of hypnotic induction procedures, by T. X. Barber and W. De Moor. [n.p., 1971?]
29 l.
Cover title.
Mimeograph copy of an article taken from the American journal of clinical hypnosis.
Bibliography: p. 23-27.
1. Hypnotism. 2. Mental suggestion. 3. Hypnotic susceptibility. I. Moor, W. de, joint author. II. Title.
CU-SB NUC74-123057

Barber, Thomas.
Bradford, Bordell and Kinzua [by Thomas Barber and James Woods. Bradford, Pa., 1971]
vi, 140 p. illus., facsims., maps, ports. 28 cm.
1. Bradford, Bordell and Kinzua Railway Co. 2. Railroads, Narrow gauge—Pennsylvania. I. Woods, James, joint author. II. Title.
WHi NUC74-123050

Barber, Thomas Gerrard, 1875-1952.
Byron—and where he is buried. [Folcroft, Pa.] Folcroft Library Editions, 1974.
xxiv, 144 p. illus. 23 cm.
Reprint of the 1939 ed. published by H. Morley, Hucknall.
1. Byron, George Gordon Noël Byron, Baron, 1788-1824—Biography. 2. Poets, English—19th century—Biography. I. Title.
PR4381.B3 1974 821'.7 74-8562
ISBN 0-8414-3203-1 (lib. bdg.) 74[r77]rev MARC

Barber, Thomas Gerrard, 1875-1952.
Byron—and where he is buried / by Thomas Gerrard Barber. — Norwood, Pa. : Norwood Editions, 1976.
xxiv, 143 p., [30] leaves of plates : ill. : 23 cm.
Reprint of the 1939 ed. published by H. Morley, Hucknall.
ISBN 0-8482-0291-0 lib. bdg. : $27.50
1. Byron, George Gordon Noël Byron, Baron, 1788-1824—Biography. 2. Poets, English—19th century—Biography. I. Title.
PR4381.B3 1976 821'.7 76-48238
77 MARC

Barber, Victor C
Geometric design of military roads in the theater of operations (interim procedure) by V. C. Barber [and] D. N. Brown. Conducted by U. S. Army Engineer Waterways Experiment Station. Vicksburg, Miss., 1972.
ix, 13, [6], 6 p. illus., figures. (U. S. Waterways Experiment Station, Vicksburg, Miss. Instruction report no. 5-72-1)
"Sponsored by Office, Chief of Engineers, U. S. Army."
"Literature cited": p. 13.
1. Military roads. I. Title. II. Series.
MsSM NUC74-120252

Barber, Victor C., joint author
see Burns, Cecil Delisle, 1879-1942. Restoration of landing-mat-surfaced subgrades... Vicksburg, Miss., 1970.

Barber, Virginia, 1935-
The mother person / by Virginia Barber and Merrill Maguire Skaggs. — Indianapolis : Bobbs-Merrill, c1975.
220 p. ; 24 cm.
Bibliography: p. 219-220.
ISBN 0-672-51995-X
1. Mothers. 2. Children—Management. 3. Parent and child. I. Skaggs, Merrill Maguire, joint author. II. Title.
HQ759.B274 301.42'7 73-22679
76 MARC

Barber, Virginia, 1935-
The mother person / by Virginia Barber and Merrill Maguire Skaggs. — New York : Schocken Books, 1977, c1975.
220 p. ; 20 cm.
Reprint of the ed. published by Bobbs-Merrill, Indianapolis.
Bibliography: p. 219-220.
ISBN 0-8052-0565-9
1. Mothers. 2. Children—Management. 3. Parent and child. I. Skaggs, Merrill Maguire, joint author. II. Title.
[HQ759.B274 1977] 301.42'7 76-48850
76 MARC

Barber, W
Pressure water in the Chad formation of Bornu and Dikwa emirates, North-eastern Nigeria, with 12 plates and 34 text figures / by W. Barber. — [Lagos] : Federal Republic of Nigeria, Ministry of Mines and Power, 1965.
138 p., [8] leaves of plates : ill., maps ; 26 cm. — (Bulletin - Geological Survey of Nigeria ; no. 35)
Errata slip inserted.
1. Aquifers—Nigeria—Bornu. 2. Aquifers—Nigeria—Dikwa. I. Title. II. Series: Nigeria. Geological Survey. Bulletin ; no. 35.
GB1199.4.N6B37 556.69'08 s 77-367149
77 MARC

Barber, W., joint author.
see Du Preez, J. W. The distribution and chemical quality of groundwater in Northern Nigeria. [Lagos] Published by authority of the Federal Government of Nigeria, 1965.

Barber, William.
Some questions about labour force analysis in agrarian economies with particular reference to Kenya. Nairobi, University College, 1965.
24 p. (Its Discussion paper no. 13)
1. Labor supply—Kenya. I. Title.
MBU NUC75-29399

Barber, William Elmer, 1932-
A study to determine the nature and scope of police roll call training in cities with 25,000 to 100,000 population in the United States. [n. p.] 1972.
[5], viii, 140 [i. e. 147] l. illus.
Thesis (Ph. D.)—Michigan State University.
Bibliography: leaves 79-81.
1. Police training. I. Title.
MiEM NUC73-126100

Barber, William J
British economic thought and India, 1600-1858 : a study in the history of development economics / by William J. Barber. — Oxford : Clarendon Press, 1975.
viii, 243 p. : 23 cm. GB***
Bibliography: p. [235]-239.
Includes index.
ISBN 0-19-828265-6 : £6.00
1. East India Company (English) 2. Great Britain—Commercial policy—History. 3. India—Economic conditions. I. Title.
HF486.E6B37 330'.0941 75-309757
75 MARC

Barber, William J
A critique of aggregate accounting concepts in underdeveloped areas, by W. U. Barber. Dakar, United Nations, African Institute for Economic Development and Planning, 1967.
26 p. 17 cm.
At head of title: IDEP/ET/LXVII/978; Mr. M. F. Y. Afia.
Bibliographical footnotes.
1. Finance, Public—Africa—Accounting. I. African Institute for Economic Development and Planning. II. Title.
IEN NUC73-39920

Barber, William J
The economy of British Central Africa; a case study of economic development in a dualistic society. [London, Oxford University Press, 1961. Ann Arbor, Mich., University Microfilms, 1972]
271 p.
Includes bibliography.
Photocopy. 271 p. (on double leaves)
1. Rhodesia. I. Title.
MiU NUC73-58792

Barber and McMurry.
The architecture of Barber and McMurry, 1915-1940 : an exhibition of photographs and drawings, September 20-October 15, 1976, Dulin Gallery of Art, Knoxville, Tennessee / exhibition organization and catalog text, W. R. McNabb ; design by Ronald Childress. — Knoxville : Dulin Gallery of Art, c1976.
92 p. : ill. ; 19 x 27 cm.
Includes bibliographical references.
1. Barber and McMurry. 2. Architecture, Modern—20th century—United States—Exhibitions. I. McNabb, W. R. II. Dulin Gallery of Art. III. Title.
NA737.B25M32 720'.6'576885 76-150412
76 MARC

Barber-Ellis of Alberta, ltd.
see Fine papers and the printer... Calgary, Alta. [1962?]

Barber-Greene Company.
Bituminous construction handbook. [4th ed.] Aurora, Ill., Barber-Greene [c1963]
vii, 304 p. illus. 20 cm.
Published in 1943 under title: Construction data handbook for bituminous engineers and contractors.
1. Bituminous materials. 2. Road materials. 3. Mixing machinery. I. Title.
FU NUC73-102880

Barber Memorial Seminary.
In 1916 Scotia Seminary, Concord, N. C. (founded 1867) was renamed Scotia Women's College, which in 1930 merged with Barber Memorial Seminary to form Barber-Scotia College.
Works by these bodies are found under the name used at the time of publication.

Barber-Scotia College.
In 1916 Scotia Seminary, Concord, N. C. (founded 1867) was renamed Scotia Women's College, which in 1930 merged with Barber Memorial Seminary to form Barber-Scotia College.
Works by these bodies are found under the name used at the time of publication.

Barbera, Alberto.
Truffaut : François Truffaut / di Alberto Barbera. — Firenze : La nuova Italia, 1976.
157 p. ; 17 cm. — (Il Castoro cinema ; 27) It76-Oct
Cover title.
Filmography: p. 144-153. Bibliography: p. 154-157.
L1400
1. Truffaut, François.
PN1998.A3T729 76-484501
*76 MARC

Barbera, Augusto.
La regione come ente di governo / Augusto Barbera. — Bologna : Il mulino, 1974.
32 p. ; 22 cm. — (Interventi) It***
Cover title.
Includes bibliographical references.
L300
1. Local government—Italy. I. Title.
75–540447

Barbera, Augusto.
Regioni e interesse nazionale. Milano, A. Giuffrè, 1973.
xi, 370 p. 25 cm. (Università di Catania. Pubblicazioni della Facoltà di giurisprudenza, 69) L5000 It 73–Apr
Bibliography: p. [333]–365.
1. Federal government—Italy. 2. Local government—Italy. I. Title. II. Series: Catania. Università. Facoltà di giurisprudenza. Pubblicazioni, 69.
74–311448

Barberá, Carmen.
Tierras de luto : novela / Carmen Barberá. — 1. ed. — Barcelona : Editorial Planeta, 1976.
297 p. ; 19 cm. — (Autores españoles e hispanoamericanos) Sp***
ISBN 8432053538
I. Title.
PQ6603.A56T5 863'.6'4 76-476646
76 MARC

Barbera, Henry.
Rich nations and poor in peace and war.
[New York] 1971 [c1972]
ii, 288 l. 29 cm.
Thesis—Columbia University.
Bibliography: leaves 272-288.
1. Economic development. 2. War—Economic aspects. I. Title.
NNC NUC74-121146

Barbera, Henry.
Rich nations and poor in peace and war; continuity and change in the development hierarchy of seventy nations from 1913 through 1952. Lexington, Mass., Lexington Books [1973]
xiii, 213 p. 23 cm.
Bibliography: p. 195-208.
1. War—Economic aspects. 2. Economic development. 3. Economic history—20th century. I. Title.
HB195.B33 338.9 73-2003
ISBN 0-669-86900-7 MARC

Barbera, Jack Vincent, 1945-
"I have a sing to shay" : Berryman's Dream songs and Recovery / by Jack Vincent Barbera. -- [s.l. : s.n.], 1976.
v, 187 leaves ; 28 cm.
Thesis (Ph.D.)--University of Chicago.
Bibliography: leaves 181-187.
1. Berryman, John, 1914-1972. The dream songs. 2. Berryman, John, 1914-1972. Recovery. I. Title.
ICU NUC77-85949

Barbera, Juan Gil
see
Gil Barbera, Juan.

Barberá, Manuel.
Curiosidades numéricas ["2345", por M. Barberá. Buenos Aires, Editorial Albatros [1974]
78 p. 21 cm.
Running title: Curiosidades de los números.
1. Mathematical recreations. I. Title.
TxU NUC76-32236

Barberá, Martín Domínguez
see Domínguez Barberá, Martín.

Barberà, Pere Benavent de
see
Benavent, Pedro.

Barbera, Raymond E
Cervantes; a critical trajectory. Edited with an introd. by Raymond E. Barbera. Boston, Mirage Press [1971]
222 p.
1. Cervantes Saavedra, Miguel de, 1547-1616.
NhU NUC73-31872

Barbera, Renzo.
Mizzica. Introduzione di Ercole Patti. Palermo, S. F. Flaccovio, 1972.
119 p. 19 cm. L1600 It 73-Mar
Poems in Sicilian dialect with Italian translations.
I. Title.
PQ4862.A67243M5 74-326809

Barberá, Salvador, 1946-
Strategy and social choice. [n.p., 1975]
1 v.
Thesis (Ph. D.)—Northwestern University.
1. Games of strategy (Mathematics)
2. Econometrics. 3. Decision making—Mathematical models. I. Title.
IEN NUC77-84976

Barbera, Vicente Pelechano
see
Pelechano, Vicente, 1943-

Barberà i Abelló, Pere Benavent de
see
Benavent, Pedro.

Barberan, Manuel.
El hamster; cria y cuidados. 1. ed. Barcelona, Espana, Compania Editorial Continental, 1974.
103, [3] p. illus.
Bibliography: p. 106.
1. Hamsters. I. Title.
DNAL NUC76-32266

Barberán, Manuel Muñoz
see Muñoz Barberán, Manuel.

Barberán, Marcelo, 1935-
El desarrollismo de Arturo Frondizi; estudio de un proyecto político. Caracas, Centro de Información y Documentación para América Latina [1972?]
24 l. 29 cm. (Documentos; entrega no. 13)
First ed. published in 1970 by Fundación Argentina para la Promoción del Desarrollo Económico y Social.
DPU NUC73-125660

Barberán, Vicente González
see
González Barberán, Vicente.

Barbereau, Louis.
Manuel de la coexistence pacifique. [Tours? 1965]
270 p. 24 cm.
Microfiche (negative) 6 sheets. 11 x 15 cm. (NYPL FSN 14,455)
1. World politics, 1945- 2. Social policy.
3. Bolshevism and Christianity.
NN NUC73-124333

Barberena, Mário Costa.
Osteologia craniana de Tupinambis tequixin (Lacertilia teiidae) [por] Mário Costa Barberena, Norma Maria B. Gomes [e] Lucia Maria P. Sanchotene. Pôrto Alegre, 1970.
32 p. 9 plates. 27 cm. (Porto Alegre, Brazil. Universidade do Rio Grande do Sul. Escola de Geologia. Publicação especial no. 21)
1. Lizards, Fossil. I. Gomes, Norma II. Sanchotene, Lucia Maria P. III. Title.
NIC N DI-GS DLC NUC76-21047

Barberena Iraizoz, Fermín.
La parroquia diocesana regida por religiosos : problemas y orientaciones / Fermín Barberena Iraizoz. — Madrid : Confer, c1974.
582 p. ; 24 cm. Sp 74-Dec
Thesis—Universidad de Navarra, 1973.
Bibliography : p. [571]-578.
Includes index.
ISBN 84-400-7843-9
1. Parishes. 2. Monasticism and religious orders. I. Title.
BV700.B37 75-532289

Barberena Perez, Alejandro.
Granada, Nicaragua. [Managua, Nicaragua, Imprenta Nacional] 1971.
442 p. illus. 24 cm.
1. Granada, Nicaragua—History. 2. Granada, Nicaragua—Description and travel. I. Title.
OKentU NUC74-122439

Barberena Pérez, Alejandro.
El héroe nacional; biografía de José Dolores Estrada. [Managua, Nicaragua] Librería Cultural Nicaragüense [1971]
36 p. illus. 27 cm. (Biografías nicaragüenses (Colección Ediciones nicaragüenses de cultura general)
1. Estrada, José Dolores, 1792-1869. I. Title.
NIC NUC75-29398

Barberet, Joseph, 1837-
Les grèves et la loi sur les coalitions. Paris, Librairie de la Bibliothèque ouvrière, 1873. [Paris, Microéditions Hachette, 1971]
4 sheets: 189 p.
Microfiche copy.
Title from first frame.
"71-1104."
1. Trade unions—France.
MH NUC75-29394

Barberi, Andrea, joint author
see Fini, Marco. Valpreda. Milano, Feltrinelli, 1972.

Barberi, Benedetto.
Lineamenti di un programma di sviluppo economico della Puglia. Studio introduttivo a cura del prof. Benedetto Barberi. Roma, Unione Regionale delle Province Pugliesi, 1964.
136 p. map.
1. Apulia—Econ. condit. I. Unione regionale della province pugliesi. II. Title.
CLU NUC77-18729

Barberi, Benedetto.
Statistica. Teoria e applicazioni. Roma, Ceres, [1972].
331 p. illus. 23 cm. L6500 It 72-Apr
"2. edizione riveduta e ampliata."
Bibliography : p. 319-322.
1. Statistics. I. Title.
HA29.5.I 8B36 1972 72-357843

Barberi, Benedetto
see Camera di commercio, industria e agricoltura degli Abruzzi. Abruzzi. [Milano] Giuffrè [1966]

Barberi, Benedetto
see Campobasso, Italy (Province). Camera di commercio, industria e agricoltura. Molise. [Milano] Giuffre [1965]

Barberi, Giovanni, 1748-1821.
Compendio della vita e delle gesta di Giuseppe Balsamo denominato il conte Cagliostro. A cura di Giuseppe Quatriglio. Milano, U. Mursia, 1973.
197 p. plates. 21 cm. (Storia e documenti, 14) L3500 It 74-Jan
Bibliography : p. [30]-32.
1. Cagliostro, Alessandro, conte di, assumed name of Giuseppe Balsamo, 1743-1795. I. Title.
BF1598.C2B3 1973 74-301437

Barberi, Hernán Molina
see Molina Barberi, Hernán.

Barberi, Renato.
Le campane di Golasecca : poesie / Renato Barberi. — Milano : La prora, [1974]
86 p. ; 21 cm. — (Poeti, narratori e saggisti contemporanei) It 74-Sept
L2000
I. Title.
PQ4862.A67244C3 75-557566

Bàrberi Squarotti, Giorgio.
La cultura e la poesia italiana del dopoguerra. [Bologna] Cappelli [1968]
213 p. 19 cm. (Universale Cappelli, 112. Serie Storia della letteratura italiana)
At head of title: La letteratura italiana del Novecento.
1. Italian poetry—20th cent.—Hist. & crit.
2. Italy—Intellectual life. I. Title.
NBuU NUC74-19038

Bàrberi Squarotti, Giorgio.
Gli inferi e il labirinto: da Pascoli a Montale / Giorgio Bàrberi Squarotti. — Bologna : Cappelli, [1974]
269 p. ; 21 cm. — (Saggi Cappelli) It 75-May
L3500
1. Italian poetry—20th century—History and criticism—Addresses, essays, lectures. I. Title.
PQ4113.B32 75-585533

Bàrberi Squarotti, Giorgio.
Laberinto d'amore (1966–1971), di Giorgio Bàrberi Squarotti. Presentazione di Angelo Jacomuzzi. ₍Segue₎: L'onda, di Gianni Pisani. Napoli, Il centro, 1972.
₍37₎ l. illus. 17 x 17 cm. It 74–Feb
I. Pisani, Gianni, 1935– L'onda. 1972. II. Title.
PQ4862.A67246L3 75–575457

Bàrberi Squarotti, Giorgio, comp.
Letteratura e critica. Antologia della critica letteraria ... Messina-Firenze, G. D'Anna, 1970–
v. 22 cm. L2800 (v. 1) It 71–Feb (v. 1)
At head of title: Giorgio Bàrberi Squarotti, Angelo Jacomuzzi.
CONTENTS: ₍1₎ Dalle origini al Settecento.
1. Italian literature—History and criticism. I. Jacomuzzi, Angelo, joint comp. II. Title.
PQ4037.B28 1970 74–301764

Bàrberi Squarotti, Giorgio, comp.
Manzoni : testimonianze di critica e di polemica / Giorgio Bàrberi Squarotti, Marziano Guglielminetti. — 1. ed. — Messina ; Firenze : G. D'Anna, 1973.
542 p. : ill. ; 24 cm. It 75–Feb
Includes bibliographical references and index.
L3400
1. Manzoni, Alessandro, 1785–1873. 2. Manzoni, Alessandro, 1785–1873. I promessi sposi. I. Guglielminetti, Marziano, joint comp. II. Title.
PQ4715.B33 75–555884

Bàrberi Squarotti, Giorgio.
La narrativa italiana del dopoguerra / Giorgio Bàrberi Squarotti. — 3. ed. — Bologna : Cappelli, 1975, c1965.
250 p. ; 19 cm. — (Universale Cappelli ; 109) (Serie Storia della letteratura italiana) It***
Bibliography: p. ₍239₎
Includes index.
L1800
1. Italian prose literature—20th century—History and criticism. I. Title.
PQ4168.B3 1975 76–507618

Barberi Squarotti, Giorgio.
Natura e storia nella letteratura italiana fra Otto e Novecento. Torino, G. Giappichelli, 1973.
205 p. 25 cm. (Corsi universitari) L3000 It 73–Dec
1. Italian literature—19th century—History and criticism. 2. Italian literature—20th century—History and criticism. I. Title.
PQ4085.B3 73–363409

Bàrberi Squarotti, Giorgio.
Poesia e ideologia borghese / Giorgio Bàrberi Squarotti. — 1. ed. — Napoli : Liguori, 1976.
376 p. ; 21 cm. — (Le Forme del significato ; 18) It77-Mar
Includes index.
L6500
1. Italian poetry—19th century—History and criticism. 2. Italian poetry—20th century—History and criticism. 3. Modernism (Literature)—History and criticism. 4. Futurism—History and criticism. 5. Decadence (Literary movement)—History and criticism. 6. Literature and society. I. Title.
PQ4113.B323 851'.9'109 77-463609
•77 MARC

Bàrberi Squarotti, Giorgio.
Il tragico nel mondo borghese. Torino, G. Giappichelli, 1974.
69 p. 24 cm. (Corsi universitari) L1800 It 74–Sept
1. Italian drama—18th century—History and criticism. 2. Italian drama (Tragedy) I. Title.
PQ4147.B3 74–338764

Bárberi Squarotti, Giorgio, ed.
see Goldoni, Carlo, 1707-1793. La bottega del caffè. Torino, G. Petrini, 1967.

Barbería, María Emma
see Antología de la poesía lírica española. Buenos Aires, Editorial Kapelusz, 1973.

Barbería, María Emma.
see Bartolomé Hidalgo, Hilario Ascasubi ... Buenos Aires, Editorial Kapelusz, 1976, c1975.

Barberie, Michael Edmund.
Growth of muscle tissue during embryonic life ₍by₎ Michael E. Barberie. ₍Charlottesville, Va.₎ 1971.
139 l. illus., charts. 29 cm.
Thesis—University of Virginia.
"Literature cited": leaves 70-82.
1. Muscle. 2. Chick embryo. I. Title.
ViU NUC73-31034

Barberii, Efrain E
La industria petrolera y la economia del país ₍por₎ Efrain E. Barberii. ₍Caracas, Corporación Venezolana del Petroleo, 1969?₎
19 p. illus. 21 cm.
Cover title.
Bibliography: p. 19.
1. Petroleum industry and trade—Venezuela. I. Title.
CtY NUC73-124332

Barberini, Giovanni.
Stati socialisti e confessioni religiose. Milano, A. Giuffrè, 1973.
xvi, 537 p. 24 cm. (Università di Perugia. Pubblicazioni della Facoltà di giurisprudenza, 8. Istituto di diritto pubblico. ₍Pubblicazioni₎, 3) L7500 It 74–Aug
Includes bibliographical references.
1. Ecclesiastical law—Communist countries. I. Title. II. Series: Perugia. Università. Facoltà di giurisprudenza. Pubblicazioni, 8. III. Series: Perugia. Università. Istituto di diritto pubblico. Pubblicazioni, 3.
74–347105

Barberini, Urbano.
Ricordi romani. Roma, Fratelli Palombi, 1973.
122 p. 35 plates. 24 cm. L7000 It 73–July
1. Rome (City)—History—Miscellanea. 2. Rome (City)—Description. I. Title.
DG813.B3 73–357123

Barberino di Val d'Elsa.
La scultura Etrusca nelle urne di Barberino Val d'Elsa; mostra: 20 luglio-24 agosto 1968. ₍Edito a cura del Comune e dell'Associazione Turistica di Barberino Val d'Elsa del Chinati Fiorentino. Firenze, 1968₎
59 p. illus. 23 cm.
Introd. by Anna Talocchini.
Bibliography: p. 12.
1. Sculpture, Etruscan—Barberino di Val d'Elsa. 2. Tombs—Italy—Barberino di Val d'Elsa. I. Talocchina, Anna. II. Title.
NRU NUC73-14801

Barberio, Stephen John.
A detailed study of relict beach ridge and adjacent environments. Raleigh, N.C., 1971.
180 l. illus., tables. 29 cm.
Thesis—North Carolina State University at Raleigh.
Bibliography: leaves 74-76.
NcRS NUC73-31036

Barberis, Camillo, joint author
see Lagorio, Guido. Repertorio di giurisprudenza marittima. Genova, Stab. tip. e litografico P. Pellas, 1893.

Barberis, Carlo.
La valorizzazione agricola nei paesi in via di sviluppo : problemi, scelte e metodo della progettazione / Carlo Barberis. — Roma : REDA, c1974.
195 p. ; 24 cm. — (Saggi, memorie, documenti) It 75–May
Summary in English, French, Portuguese, and Spanish.
1. Underdeveloped areas—Agriculture. 2. Agricultural assistance. I. Title.
[HD1417.B37] 76–523779

Barberis, Corrado.
Produzione agricola e strati sociali / Corrado Barberis, Vincenzo Siesto ; prefazione di Giuseppe Medici. — Milano : F. Angeli, ₍1974₎
228 p. ; 22 cm. — (Collana dell'Istituto nazionale di sociologia rurale ; 1) It 75–Feb
"Appendice statistica": p. ₍103₎–228.
L4800
1. Agriculture — Economic aspects — Italy. 2. Farms, Size of — Italy. I. Siesto, Vincenzo. II. Series: Istituto nazionale di sociologia rurale. Collana dell'Istituto nazionale di sociologia rurale ; 1.
HD1970.B326 75–555833

Barberis, Corrado.
Sindaci, assessori e consiglieri nei municipi d'Italia. Prefazione di Giuseppe Medici. Roma, Cinque lune, 1973.
100 p. 21 cm. It 73–Oct
L1500
1. Municipal officials and employees—Italy. I. Title.
JS5727.B37 75–580662

Barberis, Corrado.
La società italiana : classi e caste nello sviluppo economico / Corrado Barberis. — Milano : F. Angeli, c1976.
355 p. ; 22 cm. — (La Società ; 37) It76-Aug
Includes bibliographical references.
L6000
1. Italy—Economic conditions—1945- 2. Italy—Social conditions. 3. Social classes—Italy. I. Title.
HC305.B365 76-473920
•76 MARC

Barberis, Corrado.
Sociologia del piano Mansholt. Pref. di Michele Bottalico. Bologna, Il mulino ₍1970₎
250 p. maps. (Osservatorio di economia agraria per l'Europa. Collana di studi e ricerche, 4)
1. Agriculture—Economic aspects—Italy. 2. Agricultural policies and programs—Italy. I. Title. II. Series.
ICU NUC73-44821

Barberis, Corrado.
Sociologia del piano Mansholt. Bologna, Societa editrice il Mulino, 1971.
250 p. illus., maps.
Includes bibliographical references.
1. European Economic Community countries. Economic policy. I. Istituto nazionale di sociologia rurale. II. Title.
DNAL NUC76-71935

Barberis, Corrado.
Sociologia rurale. Prefazione di Giuseppe Medici. 2. ed. interamente rinnovata. Bologna, Edagricole, 1973.
xiv, 377 p., incl. tables. 24 cm. It 73–Sept
Includes bibliographical references.
L6000
1. Sociology, Rural. I. Title.
HT421.B24 1973 73–363709

Barberis, Corrado.
Turismo e sviluppo rurale nella montagna abruzzese. A cura dell'Istituto nazionale di sociologia rurale. Relazione di Corrado Barberis ... ₍Roma₎, Ministero dell'agricoltura e delle foreste, Direzione generale della bonifica e della colonizzazione. ₍1973?₎.
49 p. 24 cm. (Studi e ricerche sulla bonifica e sullo sviluppo) It 73–Nov
Bibliography: p. 6.
1. Tourist trade—Abruzzi, Italy. 2. Abruzzi, Italy—Economic conditions. I. Title.
G155.I 8B36 73–367049

Barberis, Franco.
Wem gehört dieser Schwanz? ₍Von₎ Barberis. ₍Bilderbuch₎ Aarau, Frankfurt/M., Sauerländer, (1974).
₍35₎ p. ill. 23 x 27 cm. 16.80F Sw 74–A–2289
I. Title.
PZ36.3.B26 74–347433

Barberis, Franco, illus.
see Bondy, Fritz, 1888- Fabeln. Zürich, Stuttgart, Werner Classen, (1970)

Barberis, Gloria Evangelina. De mis contemporáneos. 1976.
in Cuentos y poemas para hacer con todos. Mar del Plata ₍Argentina, s.n., 1976₎

Barberis, Julio A
Fuentes del derecho internacional / Julio A. Barberis. — La Plata : Editora Platense, 1973.
368 p. ; 21 cm. — (Serie de ensayos jurídicos : 23)
Bibliography: p. ₍325₎–346.
Includes indexes.
1. International law. I. Title.
JX3651.B24F8 75–530839

Barberis, Marina, comp.
L'umorismo inglese. Milano, G. De Vecchi, 1971.
399 p. illus. 22½ cm. It 72–June
At head of title: Marina Barberis and Franca Feslikenian.
1. English literature—Translations into Italian. 2. American literature—Translations into Italian. 3. Italian literature—Translations from English. 4. English wit and humor. I. Feslikenian, Franca, joint comp. II. Title.
PR1115.B3 73–315296

Barberis, Mario Ricca-
see Ricca-Barberis, Mario, 1877-

Barbéris, Pierre.
Chateaubriand : une réaction au monde moderne / par Pierre Barbéris, ... — Paris : Larousse, 1976.
352 p. ; 17 cm. — (Collection Thèmes et textes) (Université) F76-18235
ISBN 2-03-035031-1 : 14.50F
1. Chateaubriand, François Auguste René, vicomte de, 1768-1848—Criticism and interpretation.
PQ2205.Z5B28 848'.6'09 77-470316
77 MARC

Barbéris, Pierre.
A la recherche d'une écriture : Chateaubriand / Pierre Barbéris. — Tours : Mame, [1976] c1974.
742 p., [4] leaves of plates : ill. ; 24 cm. F***
Bibliography: p. 735-737.
ISBN 2-250-00621-0 : 195F
1. Chateaubriand, François Auguste René, vicomte de, 1768-1848—Criticism and interpretation. I. Title.
PQ2205.Z5B27 1976 848'.6'09 77-468924
77 MARC

Barbéris, Pierre.
Lectures du réel. Paris, Éditions sociales [1973]
304 p. 18 cm. (Problèmes, 8) 15.00F F***
Includes bibliographical references.
1. French literature—Addresses, essays, lectures. I. Title.
PQ139.B3 840'.9 73-160933
MARC

Barbéris, Pierre.
Le monde de Balzac. [Paris] Arthaud [1973]
603 p. 24 cm. 60.00F F***
Bibliography: p. 595-[597]
1. Balzac, Honoré de, 1799-1850—Criticism and interpretation. I. Title.
PQ2181.B35 74-158270
MARC

Barbéris, Pierre.
Mythes balzaciens. Paris, A. Colin, 1972.
358 p. 24 cm. (Études romantiques) 43.00 F***
Includes bibliographical references.
1. Balzac, Honoré de, 1799-1850—Political and social views. I. Title.
PQ2184.S58B3 843'.7 73-309560

Barbéris, Pierre.
Le père Goriot de Balzac; écriture, structures, significations. Paris, Larousse [1972]
295 p. 17 cm. (Collection Thèmes et textes) (Larousse université) 9.90F F***
Includes bibliographical references.
1. Balzac, Honoré de, 1799-1850. Le père Goriot.
PQ2168.B35 843'.7 73-311532

Barbéris, Pierre.
René de Chateaubriand; un nouveau roman. Édition du texte intégral (avec la collaboration de Gérard Gengembre) et étude par Pierre Barbéris. Paris, Larousse [1973]
255, [1] p. illus. 17 cm. (Collection Thèmes et textes) (Larousse université) F***
Bibliography: p. 254-[256]
1. Chateaubriand, François Auguste René, vicomte de, 1768-1848. René. I. Title.
PQ2205.R43B3 74-158720
ISBN 2-03-035021-4 MARC

Barberis, Pierre
see Balzac, Honoré de, 1799-1850. César Birotteau. Paris, Livre de Poche, 1973.

Barbéris, Pierre, ed.
see Balzac, Honoré de, 1799-1850. La Cousine Bette. [Paris,] Gallimard, 1972.

Barbéris, Pierre.
see Balzac, Honoré de, 1799-1850. Le médecin de campagne. Paris, Garnier, c1976.

Barbéris, Pierre, ed.
see Balzac, Honoré de, 1799-1850. Splendeurs et misères des courtisanes. [Paris] Gallimard [1973]

Barbéris, Pierre.
see Beyle, Marie Henri, 1783-1842. Œuvres. Paris, Livre club Diderot, 1974.

Barberis, Pierre.
see La Lecture sociocritique du texte romanesque. Toronto, Samuel Stevens, Hakkert & Co., 1975.

Barberis, Pierre
see Literatura e ideologias. [Madrid, Talleres Gráficos Montaña, 1972]

Barberis, Robert, 1938-
De la clique des Simard à Paul Desrochers en passant par le joual : essai sur des parvenus du pouvoir / Robert Barberis ; [photos, M. Bergevin et revue Forces]. — [Montréal] : Éditions québécoises, 1973.
159 p. : ill. ; 20 cm. C74-2989-4
Includes bibliographical references.
$2.75
1. Sorel, Que.—Industries. 2. Simard family. 3. Barberis, Robert, 1938- 4. Renaud, Jacques, 1943- Le cassé. I. Title.
HC118.S6B37 338'.092'2 75-503923
75 MARC

Barberis, Robert, 1938-
Ils sont fous ces libéraux / Robert Barberis. — Longueuil : Éditions R. Antoine, [1974]
157 p. : ill. ; 20 cm. C***
1. Quebec (Province)—Politics and government—Anecdotes, facetiae, satire, etc. I. Title.
F1053.B24 320.9'714'04 74-190479
MARC

Barberis, Roberto.
Empresa social obligatoria / Roberto Barberis. — Florida [Argentina] : Ediciones Paulinas, [1973]
122 p. ; 18 cm. — (Colección Latinoamérica en marcha ; 7)
1. Employee ownership. I. Title. II. Series.
HD5650.B17 77-365459
77 MARC

Barbero, Abilio.
Sobre los orígenes sociales de la Reconquista [por] Abilio Barbero y Marcelo Vigil. Esplugues de Llobregat, Editorial Ariel [1974]
197 p. 18 cm. (Ariel quincenal, 91) Sp***
Includes bibliographical references.
1. Spain—Social conditions. 2. Feudalism—Spain. 3. Spain—History—Arab period, 711-1492. I. Vigil Pascual, Marcelo, joint author. II. Title.
HN583.B37 74-315617
ISBN 84-344-0741-8

Barbero, Angel Gallardo
see Gallardo Barbero, Angel.

Barbero, Edmundo.
Crónicas. [1. ed. San Salvador, El Salvador, Dirección de Cultura. Dirección de Publicaciones [1972]
169 p. 21 cm.
1. Performing arts—San Salvador—Addresses, essays, lectures.
PN2381.B3 74-235627

Barbero, Giorgio, comp.
Il pensiero politico cristiano. [Torino] Unione tipograficoeditrice torinese [1962-65]
2 v. facsims. 24 cm. (Classici politici, v. 13/1-2)
Includes bibliographical references.
1. Church and state—History. 2. Christianity and politics—History. I. Title.
CBGTU NUC74-172771

Barbero, Giovanni, avv., ed.
see Itlay. Laws, statutes, etc. Codice del vino. 3. ed. Roma, L. Scialpi, 1971.

Barbero, Giovanni Giacomo, 1590-1656.
Gian Giacomo Barbelli, di Crema (1656). Disegni inediti dell'Accademia Tadini di Lovere. [Bergamo, 1970]
[7] p. 51 col. plates. 43 cm. (Monumenta Bergomensia XXVIII)
"Pubblicazione promossa da Credito Bergamo."
I. Lovere, Italy. Accademia Tadini.
NIC NUC77-10095

Barbero, Giuseppe.
La Salette. Compendio storico. Nuova edizione completamente rifatta. [Catania] Edizioni Paoline [1960]
421, [2] p. 18 cm. (Stella Maris, 5)
Bibliography: p. 9-14.
ODaU-M NUC74-168013

Barbero, Giuseppe
see Food and Agriculture Organization of the United Nations. Evaluación del programa de concentración parcelaria y ordenación rural en España. Madrid : Ministerio de Agricultura, Instituto Nacionale de Refoma y Desarrollo Agrario, 1973.

Barbero, Jose Luis Jimenez
see Jimenez Barbero, Jose Luis.

Barbèro, Marcello, 1909-
Immagini e colori ... Firenze, B. I. E., 1971.
28 p. illus. 24 cm. L1500 It 72-Mar
On cover: Marcello Barbèro poeta-pittore presenta.
1. Barbèro, Marcello, 1909- I. Title.
NX552.Z9B37 74-345673

Barbèro, Marcello, 1909-
see 3 [Tre] voci nella città. Firenze, 1970.

Barbero, Raymond.
L'ombre des jours vécus. Préf. et final de Renée Rodriguez. Rodez, Subervie [1972, c1970]
103 p. 19 cm. F***
Poems.
I. Title.
PQ2662.A652O4 1972 74-330533
MARC

Barbero, Raymond
see Club des intellectuels français. Sélection 1970 de contes et nouvelles. Courbevoie, Haut-de-Seine, Editions L'Amitié par la plume [1970]

Barbero, Ruperto Núñez
see
Núñez Barbero, Ruperto.

Barbero, Teresa.
Gabriel Miró. [Madrid] Epesa (1974)
194 p., 2 l. 17 cm. (Colección Grandes escritores contemporáneos, 76) 60ptas Sp 74-Mar
Bibliography: p. 193-194.
1. Miró Ferrer, Gabriel, 1879-1930.
PQ6623.I 7Z584 863'.62 74-325607
ISBN 84-7067-209-6

Barbero, Teresa.
Un tiempo irremediablemente falso. Madrid, Organización Sala Editorial [1973]
341 p. 20 cm. Sp***
I. Title.
PQ6652.A66T5 863'.6'4 74-300217
ISBN 84-358-0032-6

Barbero B , Roberto.
Historia de un libro de texto. [1. ed.] México, Sectaría de Educación Pública, 1963.
165 p. illus. 17 cm. (Instituto Federal de Capacitación del Magisterio. Técnica y ciencia, 8)
1. Book industries and trade—Mexico. 2. Printing—Hist.—Mexico. I. Title. II. Series: Mexico. Instituto Federal de Capacitación del Magisterio. Técnica y ciencias, 8.
TxU NUC74-124828

Barbero Carmona Ovilo, Heliodoro.
Versos teatrales y escolares ... (Salamanca) [Imp. Núñez] (1972)
50 p., 1 l. 20 cm. 100ptas Sp 73
I. Title.
PQ6652.A6613V4 74-330616

Barbero Cruz, Livia Virginia.
Gitano / Livia Virginia Barbero Cruz ; [dibujos, Rob Show]. — [1. ed.]. — La Paz : [s. n.], 1972.
146 p. : ill. ; 19 cm.
Errata slip inserted.
I. Title.
PQ7820.B3217G5 75-533149

Barbero de Aguilera, Abilio
see
Barbero, Abilio.

Barbero Santos, Marino.
Estudios de criminología y derecho penal. Valladolid, Universidad, Secretariado de Publicaciones, 1972.
348 p., 2 l. 24 cm. (Studia iuris poenalis Vallisoletana, v. 1) Sp 72-Nov
Includes bibliographical references.
1. Crime and criminals—Addresses, essays, lectures. 2. Criminal law—Addresses, essays, lectures. I. Title. II. Series.
73-305035

Barbero Santos, Marino.
see La pena de muerte, 6 [i.e. seis] respuestas. Valladolid, Universidad, Departamento de Derecho Penal, 1975.

Barberot, Roger.
A bras le cœur. Paris, R. Laffont [1972]
466 p. plates. 24 cm. (Collection Vécu) 34.00F F***
I. Title.
DC373.B28A3 72-364080

Barberousse, Michel, fl. 196-?-
Cuisine basque et béarnaise. France [n.d.]
108 p.
MCR NUC77-84987

Barberousse, Michel, fl. 196-?-
Cuisine provençale. Paris, Seguret [n.d.]
131 p.
MCR NUC77-84986

Barberousse, Michel, fl. 196-?-
La Normandie, ses traditions, sa cuisine, son art de vivre / Michel Barberousse. — [Paris] : Hachette, 1974.
287 p. : ill. (some col.) ; 22 cm. — (H. L.) (Inventaire culinaire régional) F***
Bibliography: p. 282-283.
ISBN 2-01-001095-7 : 48.00F
1. Cookery, French. I. Title.
TX719.B34 641.5'944 74-183336
MARC

Barberoux, Gérard, joint author.
see Lambert, Guy, professeur. Cours de droit civil ... Sainte-Ruffine, Maisonneuve, [1974]

Barbers, Beauticians, and Allied Industries International Association.
The Journeymen Barbers' International Union of America was organized in 1887. In 1941 the name was changed to Journeymen Barbers, Hairdressers, and Cosmetologists' International Union of America and later, to Journeymen Barbers, Hairdressers, Cosmetologists, and Proprietors' International Union of America. In 1969 it became the Barbers, Beauticians, and Allied Industries International Association.
Works by this body published before the change of name in 1969 are found under
Journeymen Barbers, Hairdressers, Cosmetologists and Proprietors' International Union of America.
Works published after that change of name are found under
Barbers, Beauticians, and Allied Industries International Association.
73-210481

Barbers, Beauticians and Allied Industries International Association
see Journeyman barber and beauty cuture. [Huntington, Ind.]

Barbers, Beauticians, and Allied Industries International Association
see Plumb, Richard A Ancient and honorable barber profession. [2d ed. rev.] Indianapolis, Barbers, Beauticians, and Allied Industries International Association, AFL-CIO-CLC [1974]

Barbery, Hernán Molina
see
Molina Barberí, Hernán.

Barbesi, Luigi
see Scritti in onore di Caterina Vassalini. Verona: Fiorini, 1974.

Barbeski, Sergio.
see United Nations. Economic and Social Council. Transport and Communications Mission to Kenya. Report... [n.p.] 1964.

Barbet, Alix.
Recueil général des peintures murales de la Gaule / Alix Barbet. — Paris : Éditions du Centre national de la recherche scientifique, 1974-
v. : ill. ; 28 cm. — (Supplément à Gallia ; 27) F***
Includes bibliography and index.
CONTENTS: 1. Province de Narbonnaise. 1. Glanum. 2 v.
ISBN 2-222-01628-2 (v. 1)
1. Mural painting and decoration, Roman—France. 2. Mural painting and decoration—France. 3. France—Antiquities, Roman. I. Title. II. Series: Gallia : fouilles et monuments archéologiques en France métropolitaine. Supplément ; 27, etc.
ND2746.B37 759.9364 75-513118
75 MARC

Barbet, J fl. ca. 1635.
Livre d'architecture d'autels et de cheminees. Portland, Or., Collegium Graphicum [c1972]
2 v. (chiefly plates) facsim. 29 cm. (Printed sources of Western art, v. 12-13)
"Barbet's designs were engraved by Abraham Bosse."
1. Architecture—Details. 2. Decoration and ornament, Architectural. 3. Altars. 4. Mantels. I. Bosse, Abraham, 1602-1676. II. Title.
CSt NUC74-125024

Barbet, Jeanne, ed.
see Franciscus de Mayronis, ca. 1285-ca. 1328. François de Meyronnes-Pierre Roger disputatio... Paris, J. Vrin, 1961.

Barbet, Jeanne
see Joannes Scotus, Erigena. Expositiones in ierarchiam coelestem. Turnholti: Typographi Brepols, 1975.

Barbet, Jeanne
see Joannes Scotus, Erigena. Johannis Scoti Eriugenae Expositiones ... Turnholti: Typographi Brepols, 1975.

Barbet, Jeanne, ed.
see Kempf, Nikolaus, 1397-1497. Tractatus de mystica theologia. Salzburg : James Hogg, 1973.

Barbet, Jeanne, ed.
see Thomas Gallus, d. 1246. Le commentaire du cantique des cantiques "Deiformis animae gemitus Paris, Béatrice-Nauwelaerts, 1972.

Barbet, Pierre.
Baphomet's meteor. Translated by Bernard Kay. New York, Daw Books [1972]
144 p. 18 cm. (Daw books, no. 35)
Translation of L'empire du Baphomet.
First printing.
I. Title.
OU MB NUC75-29397

Barbet, Pierre.
The enchanted planet / translated by C.J. Richards. -- New York, Daw Books [1975]
159 p. ; 18 cm. -- (Daw books, no. 156)
Translation of La planète enchantée.
I. Title.
ViU NUC77-85286

Barbeta Antonès, Juan, joint author
see Gil Guasch, Miguel. Exposición de artes suntuarias del modernismo barcelonés ... [Barcelona] Museos de Arte [1965?]

Barbetta, Alessandro
see La Consultazione nelle biblioteche pubbliche... [Milano]: A. Mondadori, 1975.

Barbetta, Giulio Cesare, fl. 1569-1603
see Thomas, Benjamin William, 1937- The lute books of Giulio Cesare Barbetta... -- [s.l. : s.n.], 1973.

Barbey, Bruno.
see Maheu, René. L'Iran, pérennité et renaissance d'un empire. Paris, Éditions J.A., c1976.

Barbey, Bruno.
see Milley, Jacques. Ceylan... Paris (125, rue du Faubourg Saint-Honoré, 75008) A. Barret, 1974.

Barbey, Gilles.
Rapports entre l'environnement construit et le comportement humain: etude bibliographique et analytique—The relationship between the built environment and human behavior: a survey and analysis of the existing literature. Gilles Barbey & Cheryl Gelber. Lausanne, Institute for Research on the Built Environment, Federal Institute of Technology, 1973.
410 p. 30 cm.
1. Architecture—Psychological aspects—Bibl. I. Gelber, Cheryl. II. Title.
CaBVaU NUC76-71958

Barbey, Guy.
Un bonheur. Paris, Pensée universelle [1972]
186 p. 18 cm.
I. Title.
CaOOU NUC74-120253

Barbey d'Aurevilly, Jules Amédée, 1808-1889.
Amaïdée / Barbey d'Aurevilly. — Éd. critique / établie par John Greene, Andrée Hirschi, Jacques Petit. — Paris : Belles Lettres, 1976.
161 p. ; 24 cm. — (Annales littéraires de l'Université de Besançon ; 180) ([Publication] - Centre de recherches de littérature française (XIXe et XXe siècles) ; v. 17) F***
Includes bibliographical references.
45.00F
I. Greene, John. II. Hirschi, Andrée. III. Petit, Jacques, 1928- IV. Title. V. Series: Besançon, France. Université. Annales littéraires ; 180. VI. Series: Centre de recherches de littérature française (XIXe et XXe siècles). Publication ; v. 17.
AS161.B39 Vol. 180 76-488155
[PQ2189.B32] 77 MARC

Barbey d'Aurevilly, Jules Amédée, 1808-1889.
Articles inédits (1852-1884). Publiés par Andrée Hirschi et Jacques Petit. Paris, Les Belles lettres, 1972.
x, 306 p. 24 cm. (Centre de recherches de littérature française (XIXe et XXe siècles) [Publication] v. 7) (Annales littéraires de l'Université de Besançon, 138) 50.00F F***
Errata (leaf) inserted.
Includes bibliographical references.
I. Hirschi, Andrée, ed. II. Petit, Jacques, ed. III. Series. IV. Series: Besançon, France. Université. Annales littéraires, 138.
AS161.B39 vol. 138 73-317614
[PQ2189.B32]

Barbey d'Aurevilly, Jules Amédée, 1808-1889.
Les diaboliques. Texte présenté, établi et annoté par Jacques Petit. [Paris] Gallimard [1973]
378 p. 18 cm. (Folio, 342) F***
Bibliography: p. [375]-378.
I. Petit, Jacques, 1928- ed. II. Title.
PQ2189.B32D55 1973 843'.8 74-183439
MARC

Barbey d'Aurevilly, Jules Amédée, 1808-1889.
Les diaboliques. [Fribourg, Suisse] Editions du Lac [c1974]
317 p. 22 cm.
I. Title.
WU NUC76-31117

Barbey d'Aurevilly, Jules Amédée, 1808-1889.
Une histoire sans nom. Suivi de Une page d'histoire, Le cachet d'onyx, et de Léa. Texte présenté, établi et annoté par Jacques Petit. [Paris] Gallimard [1972]
280 p. 18 cm. (Collection Folio, 196) F***
I. Title.
PQ2189.B32H5 1972 843'.8 73-300855

Barbey d'Aurevilly, Jules Amédée, 1808-1889.
Premiers articles (1834-1852). Publiés par Andrée Hirschi et Jacques Petit. Paris, Les Belles lettres, 1973.
345 p. 24 cm. (Centre de recherches de littérature française (XIXe et XXe siècles) [Publication] v. 9) (Annales littéraires de l'Université de Besançon, 143) 60.00F F***
I. Hirschi, Andrée, ed. II. Petit, Jacques, 1928- ed. III. Series. IV. Series: Besançon, France. Université. Annales littéraires, 143.
PQ2189.B32A6 1973 73-173216
MARC

Barbey d'Aurevilly, Jules Amedée, 1808-1889.
La vengeance d'une femme. Utrecht, Stichting 'De Roos' [1973]
38, [2] p. illus. 31 cm.
At head of title: Barbey d'Aurevilly.
"Des illustrations à l'eau-forte par Roger Chailloux, a été réalisée au cours de l'année 1973 d'apres la maquette de Kees Nieuwenhuijzen sur les presses de l'imprimerie Hooiberg b.v. à Epe... Le tirage des eauxfortes a été exécuté sur la presse de P. Clement, Amsterdam. Les 175 exemplaires numerotés de 1 à 175 sont destinés exclusivement au membres de la société 'De Roos' à Utrecht."
1. Printing—Specimens—Netherlands, 20th cent., Epe, Hooiberg, 1973. I. Chailloux, Roger. II. Nieuwenhuijzen, Kees. III. Stichting 'De Roos'. IV. Title.
CtY NUC76-71961

Barbey d'Aurevilly, Jules Amédée, 1808-1889
see Création et critique. Paris, Lettres modernes, 1973.

Barbey d'Aurevilly, Jules Amédée, 1808-1889
see Jeanton Lamarche, Jean Marie. Itinéraires aurevillyens... Condé-sur-Noireau, Impr. Ch. Corlet, 1973.

Barbey d'Aurevilly, Jules Amédée, 1808-1889
see Petit, Jacques. Influences... Paris, Revue des lettres modernes, 1971.

Barbey d'Aurevilly, Jules Amédée, 1808-1889
see Petit, Jacques. Paysages romanesques. Lettres de Barbey à Hector de Saint-Maur. Textes réunis par Jacques Petit. [Paris] Revue des lettres modernes, 1966.

Barbey d'Aurevilly. 1- 1966-
[Paris]
v. 20 cm. annual. (La Revue des lettres modernes)
1. Barbey d'Aurevilly, Jules Amédée, 1808-1889—Societies, periodicals, etc. I. Series.
PN3.R4 subser. 72-491624
rev

Barbeyrac, Jean, 1674-1744
see Dumont, Jean, baron de Carlscroon, d. 1726. Corps universel diplomatique du droit des gens... Washington, Microcard Editions, 1964.

Barbeyrac, Michel de.
Léon, roi de Bayonne. [Biarritz, Imp. Ferrus, 1971]
144 p. 21 cm.
I. Title.
WU NUC74-120314

Barbezat, Gilbert O
Stimulation of intestinal secretion by polypeptide hormones. [Oslo] Universitetsforlaget, 1973.
21 p. illus. (Scandinavian journal of gastroenterology. Supplement, 22)
1. Intestinal secretions—Drug effects. 2. Peptides—Pharmacodynamics. I. Title. II. Series.
DNLM NUC76-73283

Barbhaiya, Bihari.
Batik [by] Bihari Barbhaiya. [1st ed.] Baroda [1968]
1 v. (chiefly illus.) 24 cm. Rs5.00
Cover title.
1. Batik.
NK9503.B34 746.6 72-918612
MARC

Barbi, Michele, 1867-1941.
Dante Alighieri: La vita nuova. Ed. M. Barbi. Bologna, Italy, Il Mulino, 1971.
ix, 191 p. 25 cm. (Spogli elettronici dell'italiano delle origini e del Duecento. II. Forme, 8)
1. Dante Alighieri, 1265-1321. Vita nuova. 2. Italian language—Word frequency. I. Title. II. Series.
CaQMM NUC74-123052

Barbi, Michele, 1867-1941.
Dante Alighieri: Rime. Edd. M. Barbi, F. Maggini [e] V. Pernicone. Bologna, Italy, Il Mulino, 1972.
x, 337 p. 25 cm. (Spogli elettronici dell'italiano delle origini e del Duecento. II. Forme, 11)
1. Dante Alighieri, 1265-1321. Rime. 2. Italian language—Word frequency. I. Maggini, Francesco. II. Pernicone, Vincenzo. III. Title. IV. Series.
CaQMM NUC74-121145

Barbi, Michele, 1867-1941.
La nuova filologia e l'edizione dei nostri scrittori da Dante al Manzoni. Firenze, Sansoni, 1973.
xii, 259 p. 20 cm. (Biblioteca Sansoni, 74) L2000 It 73-June
Includes bibliographical references.
1. Italian literature—History and criticism. I. Title.
PQ4037.B3 1973 73-333166

Barbi, Michele, 1867-1941.
Poesia popolare italiana : studi e proposte / Michele Barbi. — Firenze : Sansoni, 1974.
166 p. : music ; 20 cm. — (Biblioteca Sansoni ; 81) It 75-Jan
Reprint of the 1939 ed.
Includes index.
L1400
1. Folk-songs, Italian—History and criticism. I. Title.
PQ4119.B34 1974 75-559262

Barbi, Silvio Adrasto, ed.
see Dante, Alighieri, 1265-1321. La Divina Commedia... [Firenze] Sansoni [1972-

Barbian, Norbert M
A message from labor to management. Muskego, Wis., Hi-Way Press, c1966.
vii, 52 p.
1. Industrial relations. I. Title.
WHi NUC74-122438

Barbiana, Italy. Scuola
see Carta a una profesora. [2. ed. Montevideo] Biblioteca de Marcha [1970]

Barbiana, Italy. Scuola
see Carta a una profesora. [Buenos Aires] Marcha/Schapire [c1971]

Barbić, Jakša.
Ugovor o inžinjeringu / Jakša Barbić ; rukovodilac kursa Slavko Carić. — Novi Sad : Pravni fakultet, Institut privrednopravnih i ekonomskih nauka, 1976.
112 p. ; 29 cm. — (Poslediplomski magistarski kurs iz oblasti privrednopravnih nauka ; knj. 11) Yu***
1. Engineering—Contracts and specifications—Yugoslavia. I. Title. II. Series.
77-467632
77 MARC

Barbić, Jakša. Ugovor o ulaganju sredstava stranih osoba u domaće organizacije udruženog rada (joint venture). 1976.
in Mitrović, Dobrosav M. Zajedničko ulaganje domaćih i stranih sredstava. Novi Sad, Pravni fakultet, Institut privrednopravnih i ekonomskih nauka, 1976.

Barbić, Vesna
see Meštrović, Ivan, 1883-1962. Ivan Meštrović. Zagreb [Galerije grada Zagreba, 1967]

Barbić, Vesna
see Meštrović, Ivan, 1883-1962. Ivan Meštrović. [Katalog izložbe] Zagreb [1963]

Barbić, Vesna, ed.
see Meštrović, Ivan, 1883-1962. Ivan Meštrović : atelje Meštrović. Zagreb : Galerije grada, 1973.

Barbić, Vesna
see Paris. Musée Rodin. Ivan Mestrovic. [Paris] 1969.

Barbiche, Bernard.
see Beaune, Florimond de, 1601-1652. Doctrine de l'angle solide. Éd. première. Paris, J. Vrin, 1975.

Barbiche, Bernard.
see France. Archives nationales. Les actes pontificaux originaux des Archives nationales de Paris. Città del Vaticano, Biblioteca apostolica vaticana, 1975-

Barbie, Klaus
see
Altmann, Klaus, 1915-

Barbié du Bocage, Jean Denis, 1760-1825
see [Barthélemy, Jean Jacques] 1716-1795. Recueil de cartes géographiques, plans, vues et médailles... 3. éd. Paris, De Bure l'aîné, 1790.

Barbié du Bocage, Jean Denis, 1760-1825
see Philippidēs, Daniēl, b. ca. 1750. (Allēlographia, 1794-1819) 1966.

Barbié du Bocage, Jean Denis, 1760-1825
see Philippidēs, Daniēl, b. ca. 1750. Correspondance de Daniel Démétrius Philippidès ... Institute for Balkan Studies, 1965.

Barbiellini Amidei, Gaspare, 1934-
I labirinti della sociologia / [di] Gaspare Barbiellini Amidei, Ulderico Bernardi ; prefazione di Franco Ferrarotti. — 1. ed. — Roma ; Bari : Laterza, 1976.
ix, 273 p. ; 22 cm. — (Biblioteca di cultura moderna ; 794) It77-Apr
Includes bibliographical references and index.
L6500
1. Sociology—History. I. Bernardi, Ulderico, joint author. II. Title.
HM19.B264 77-481159
•77 MARC

Barbier, André, professeur.
La législation du travail aux C. A. P., B. E. I., B. P.; résumés, documents, questions. [Paris] Delagrave [1961]
79 p. 22 cm.
"Documents annexes": (7 forms) inserted in pocket.
1. Labor laws and legislation—France—Examinations, questions, etc. I. Title.
71-200028

Barbier, André, professeur.
La législation du travail aux C.A.P.-B.E.P.-B.T.-B.P. : résumés, documents, questions / A. Barbier. — Éd. mise à jour, mai 1975. — [Paris] : Delagrave, [1975], c1961.
79 p. : forms (7 fold. in pocket) ; 22 cm. F***
1. Labor laws and legislation—France—Examinations, questions, etc. I. Title.
344'.44'01076 77-450558
77 MARC

Barbier, Auguste, 1805-1882. **Iambes. 1973.**
in **Barbier, Auguste, 1805-1882. Il pianto suivi de Iambes ... Genève, Slatkine Reprints, 1973.**

Barbier, Auguste, 1805-1882.
Il pianto suivi de Iambes : [poèmes] / Auguste Barbier. — Genève : Slatkine Reprints, 1973.
126, xxx, 144 p. ; 22 cm. Sw73-A-3579
Reprint of the 1833 ed. (2d ed.) of Il pianto and of the 1832 ed. of Iambes, both published by U. Canel, Paris.
I. Barbier, Auguste, 1805-1882. Iambes. 1973. II. Title: Il pianto ...
PQ2189.B33A6 1973 75-512770
•75 MARC

Barbier, Auguste, 1805-1882.
Souvenirs personnels et silhouettes contemporaines. Genève, Slatkine Reprints, 1973.
iv, 379 p. 22 cm. 100F Sw 73-A-3389
"Réimpression de l'édition de Paris, 1883."
1. Barbier, Auguste, 1805-1882. 2. Authors, French—Correspondence, reminiscences, etc. I. Title.
PQ2189.B33Z52 1973 74-161263
MARC

Barbier, Bernard.
La Fréquentation des stations de sports d'hiver des Alpes du Sud ... B. Barbier. Aix-en-Provence, Université d'Aix-Marseille, 1969.
34 l. illus. 27 cm. (Les Cahiers du tourisme, sér. A, no 12)
9.00F F 71-1179
1. Winter sports—Alps, French. I. Title.
GV841.B318 74-339756

Barbier, Bernard, joint author.
see Préau, Pierre. Les Alpes. Paris, Larousse, 1974.

Barbier, Bernard.
see La Provence. Paris, Larousse, 1974.

Barbier, Carl Paul.
see Colloque Mallarmé, Glasgow, 1973. Colloque Mallarmé ... Paris, A.-G. Nizet, 1975.

Barbier, Charles.
Le Bienheureux François-Isidore Gagelin : missionnaire en Cochinchine, martyr, 1799-1833 / Charles Barbier ; ₍publié par les Missions étrangères de Paris₎. — Colmar : Éditions d'Alsace, 1976.
55 p. : ill. ; 21 cm. F77-1155
Bibliography: p. 54.
15.00F
1. Gagelin, François Isidore, 1799-1833. 2. Missionaires—Vietnam—Cochin China—Biography. 3. Missionaries—France—Biography. 4. Christian martyrs—Vietnam—Cochin China—Biography. I. Title.
BV3312.C633G342 77-481986
77 MARC

Barbier, Charles Henri.
D'homme à homme; l'aide coopérative suisse au Dahomey. ₍n.p., 1967?₎
44 p. illus. 19 x 24 cm.
1. Dahomey—Economic policy. 2. Economic assistance in Afric. I. Title.
MiEM NUC73-124331

Barbier, Charles Henri.
Wie weit sind wir in Dahomey? [n.p., 1966?]
39 p. illus., map.
"Der Text dieser Broschüre wurde in den Nummern 7-18 1965 der "Genossenschaft" publiziert."
1. Agriculture, Cooperative—Dahomey. 2. Technical assistance, Swiss. 3. Rehabilitation, Rural—Dahomey. I. Verband schweizerischer Konsumgenossenschaften. II. Title.
PPiU NUC74-133161

Barbier, Christian.
Les communes de la Loire : l'application du droit municipal dans un département / Christian Barbier. — ₍Saint-Étienne₎ : Centre interdisciplinaire d'études et de recherches sur les structures régionales, ₍1976₎
327 p. : ill. ; 22 cm. F***
At head of title: Université de Saint-Étienne.
Bibliography: p. 297-302.
1. Municipal government—France—Loire (Dept.) I. Title.
JS4991.L6B37 77-454403
77 MARC

Barbier, Dominique.
Les groupes scolaires : novembre 1975 : ₍dossier / réalisé par Dominique Barbier pour le compte du Plan construction₎. — Paris : Documentation française, c1976.
47 p. ; 30 cm. — (Fichier coûts des équipements collectifs) (Planification urbaine) F***
At head of title: Ministère de l'équipement, Direction de l'aménagement foncier et de l'urbanisme, Service des affaires économiques et internationales. Plan construction. Ministère de l'intérieur, Direction générale des collectivités locales.
Includes regulations.
Bibliography: p. 27-28.
12.00F
1. Education—France—Costs. I. France. Plan construction. II. Title. III. Series.
LB2909.B33 379.44 77-469800
77 MARC

Barbier, Élisabeth, 1911–
Dominique; roman. ₍Paris₎ Julliard. ₍Paris, Le Livre de poche, 1973, c1961₎
2 v. 17 cm. (Le Livre de poche, 3719-3720) (Her Les gens de Mogador, t. 5-6) F***
Earlier ed. published under title: Dominique Vernet.
I. Title.
PQ2603.A3145D6 1973 74-159304
MARC

Barbier, Élisabeth, 1911–
Julia Vernet. ₍Paris₎ Julliard. ₍Paris, Le Livre de poche, 1973, c1952₎
2 v. 17 cm. (Le Livre de poche, 3715-3716) (Her Les gens de Mogador, t. 1-2) F***
Earlier ed. published under title: Julia Vernet de Mogador.
I. Title.
PQ2603.A3145J8 1973 74-159303
MARC

Barbier, Élisabeth, 1911–
"Mon père, ce héros" ₍par₎ Elizabeth Barbier. Paris, le Livre de poche, 1972.
188 p. 17 cm. (Le Livre de poche, 3475) 3.30F F 73-3828
I. Title.
PQ2603.A3145M6 73-362735
MARC

Barbier, George.
The illustrations of George Barbier in full color / edited by François Meyer and Frederica T. Harlow. — New York : Dover Publications, 1977.
47 p. : col. ill. ; 29 cm.
ISBN 0-486-23476-2 : $5.00 ($5.75 Can)
1. Barbier, George. I. Title.
NC980.5.B37A46 759.4 76-42589
77 MARC

Barbier, George
see Galerie Annemarie Verna. The Roaring Twenties. [Zurich, 1971]

Barbier, J. P.
see Dictionnaire des maladies. Paris (30, rue des Saints-Pères, 75007) Éditions scientifiques internationales, 1973.

Barbier, Jacques.
Géographie de la Suisse, par J. Barbier, J.-L. Piveteau et M. Roten. ₍1. éd.₎ Paris, Presses universitaires de France, 1973.
126, ₍2₎ p. illus. 18 cm. (Que sais-je? No 1542) F***
Bibliography: p. ₍127₎
1. Switzerland—Description and travel. I. Piveteau, Jean Luc, joint author. II. Roten, M., joint author. III. Title.
DQ25.B34 914.94'03'7 74-179843
MARC

Barbier, Jacques Armand.
Imperial reform and colonial politics: a secret history of late Bourbon Chile. ₍Storrs, Conn.₎ 1972.
vii, 298 l. illus.
Typescript.
Thesis (Ph.D.)—University of Connecticut.
Bibliography: leaves 291-298.
1. Chile—Pol. & govt.—1565-1810. I. Title.
CtU NUC73-125165

Barbier, Jacques Armand.
Imperial reform and colonial politics: a secret history of late Bourbon Chile. ₍Storrs, Conn.₎ 1972.
vii, 298 p. illus.
Thesis (Ph.D.)—The University of Connecticut.
Microfilm edition (positive) by University Microfilms. 1 reel.
Bibliography: p. 291-298.
1. Chile—History. 2. Municipal government—Chile. 3. Spain—Colonies—America—Administration. 4. Bourbon, House of. I. Title.
OOxM NUC75-29374

Barbier, Jacques Armand.
Imperial reform and colonial politics: a secret history of late Bourbon Chile. [Storrs, Conn.] 1972 [c1973]
vii, 298 l. illus.
Thesis—University of Connecticut.
Bibliography: leaves 291-298.
Photocopy of typescript. Ann Arbor, Mich., University Microfilms, 1974. 21 cm.
1. Chile—Pol. & govt.—1565-1810. I. Title.
FMU NUC76-30300

Barbier, Jean, fl. 1940-
Pour vous qu'est-ce que Lourdes ? : 75 personnalités répondent : interviews / recueillies par Jean Barbier ; préf. et conclusion par A. Renard ; introd. par Bernard Billet. — Paris : P. Lethielleux, c1976.
255 p. ; 22 cm.
ISBN 2-249-60104-6 : 28.00F
1. Lourdes. I. Title.
BT653.B28 77-477354
77 MARC

Barbier, Jean, fl. 1940- joint author.
see Gorrée, Georges, 1908- For the love of God ... London, T. Shand Alba Publications, 1974.

Barbier, Jean, fl. 1940- joint author.
see Gorrée, Georges, 1908- Love without boundaries ... Huntington, Ind., Our Sunday Visitor, c1974.

Barbier, Jean Joel. Les eaux fourerées. 1975.
in **Barbier, Jean Joël.** Irradiante précédé de Ishtar ; Les eaux fourrées. Paris, Éditions Entente, ₍1975₎

Barbier, Jean Joël.
Irradiante précédé de Ishtar ; Les eaux fourrées / Jean-Joël Barbier. — Paris : Éditions Entente, ₍1975₎
319 p. ; 20 cm. — (Entente littérature) F***
ISBN 2-7266-0005-0 : 39.00F
I. Barbier, Jean Joel. Ishtar. 1975. II. Barbier, Jean Joel. Les eaux fourerées. 1975. III. Title: Irradiante ...
PQ2603.A3155I7 843'.9'14 75-508108
75 MARC

Barbier, Jean Joel. Ishtar. 1975.
in **Barbier, Jean Joël.** Irradiante précédé de Ishtar ; Les eaux fourrées. Paris, Éditions Entente, ₍1975₎

Barbier, Jean Paul.
Bronzes iraniens, IIe et Ier millénaires avant J.C. Genève, Barbier ₍c1970₎
143 p. incl. 106 plates. 27.5 cm.
Cover illustration.
1. Bronzes, Persian. 2. Luristan (prov. Pers.)—Bronzes.
NNMM NUC75-29383

Barbier, Jean Paul.
Ma bibliothèque poétique. Éditions des 15e et 16e siècles des principaux poètes français. Genève, Droz, 1973–
v. facsims. 32 cm. 78.00F (v. 1) Sw 74-A-801 (v. 1)
CONTENTS: 1. ptie. De Guillaume de Lorris à Louise Labé.
1. French poetry—To 1500—Bibliography—Catalogs. 2. French poetry—16th century—Bibliography—Catalogs. 3. Bibliography—Early printed books—16th century. 4. Incunabula. I. Title.
Z2174.P7B37 016.09 74-166834
MARC

Barbier, Jean Paul, fl. 1974-
Guide de la société anonyme immobilière / Jean Paul Barbier. — Genève : Société privée de gérance, ₍1975₎
344 p. ; 21 cm. Sw75-A-7812
Includes bibliographical references.
49.00F
1. Real estate business—Law and legislation—Switzerland. 2. Corporation law—Switzerland. I. Title.
346'.494'066 76-479153
•76 MARC

Barbier, Jean Paul, fl. 1974-
La Loi Furgler, son application. Arrêté fédéral du 21 mars 1973 et Ordonnance du Conseil fédéral du 21 décembre 1973 fixant la date d'entrée en vigueur de l'Arrêté au 1er février 1974. Genève, Société privée de gérance, (1974).
150 p. 21 cm. (Guide pratique) 18.80F Sw74-A-2452
1. Alien property—Switzerland. I. Switzerland. Laws, statutes, etc. II. Title.
342'.494'083 74-180183
74₍r77₎rev MARC

Barbier, Jean Philippe.
Les pancréatiques. Paris, Éditions "Heures de France," 1970.
63 p. illus. (Les monographies médicales et scientifiques, v. 22, no. 137)
ICRL NUC74-122437

Barbier, Juan de Aróstegui
see Aróstegui Barbier, Juan de.

Barbier, Jules, 1825-1901. Les contes d'Hoffmann
see Offenbach, Jacques, 1819-1880. [Les contes d'Hoffmann. Libretto. English & French] Les contes d'Hoffmann. New York, G. Schirmer [c1973]

Barbier, Jules, 1825-1901
see Gounod, Charles François, 1818-1893. Faust. Libretto. English & French. New York, Fred Rullman ₍n.d.₎

Barbier, Jules, 1825-1901
see Gounod, Charles François, 1818-1893. Romeo et Juliette. Libretto. English & French. [Los Angeles, Huber Pub., 196-?]

Barbier, Jules, 1825-1901
see Massé, Victor, 1822-1884. Paul et Virginie. Libretto. English & French. [New Orleans] J. Schweitzer [n. d.]

Barbier, Jules, 1825-1901
see Offenbach, Jacques, 1819-1880. [Les contes d'Hoffmann. Libretto. English & French] The tales of Hoffmann. Los Angeles, ABC Records, c1972.

Barbier, Jules, 1825-1901
see Thomas, Ambroise, 1811-1896. Mignon. Libretto. English & French. [New Orleans, n.d.]

Barbier, Marie.
Quand Dieu songe à Ville-Marie. [Montréal, 1962]
[16] p. 11 x 14 cm.
A poem.
1. French—Canadian poetry. I. Title.
RPB NUC74-122440

Barbier, Maurice.
Le Comité de décolonisation des Nations Unies. Paris, Librairies générale de droit et de jurisprudence, 1974.
757 p. tab. maps. (Bibliothèque africaine et malgache. Droit, sociologie, politique et économie, t. 22)
1. United Nations. General Assembly. Special Committee on the Situation with Regard to the Implementation of the Declaration on the Granting of Independence to Colonial Countries and Peoples. I. Title. II. Series.
CU-L NUC76-32100

Barbier, Maurice. Dictionnaire technique du bâtiment et des travaux publics
see Dictionnaire technique du bâtiment et des travaux publics. 4e édition mise à jour. Paris, Eyrolles, 1971.

Barbier, Maurice. Dictionnaire technique du bâtiment et des travaux publics
see Dictionnaire technique du bâtiment et des travaux publics, 5. éd. mise à jour. Paris, Eyrolles, 1973 [c1963]

Barbier, Maurice. Dictionnaire technique du bâtiment et des travaux publics.
see Dictionnaire technique du bâtiment et des travaux publics. 6. éd. revue et corr. Paris, Eyrolles, 1976.

Barbier, Maurice, O. P.
Le Comité de décolonisation des Nations Unies / par Maurice Barbier ; préf. de Pierre Gerbet. — Paris : Librairie générale de droit et de jurisprudence, 1974.
757 p. : ill. ; 25 cm. — (Bibliothèque africaine et malgache : Droit, sociologie politique, et économie ; t. 22) F***
Includes bibliographical references and index.
ISBN 2-275-01332-6
1. United Nations. General Assembly. Special Committee on the Situation with Regard to the Implementation of the Declaration on the Granting of Independence to Colonial Countries and Peoples. 2. Colonies. 3. Colonies in Africa. I. Title.
JX4021.B28 341.27 75-502289
MARC

Barbier, Michel.
Determination of elasticities of demand for the various means of urban passenger transport (postponement of trips by a given mode; cross-elasticity) [by] Michel Barbier and François Mellet. Paris, European Conference of Ministers of Transport [Economic Research Centre, 1971]
v, 69 p. illus.
"Report of the Thirteenth Round Table on Transport Economics, 28-30 April 1971."
Includes bibliographical footnotes.
MH-BA NUC73-31882

Barbier, Osvaldo.
Tempo e relatività : il significato del tempo nella concezione relativistica / Osvaldo Barbier. — Roma : Bizzarri, 1976.
151 p. : diagrams ; 24 cm. — (Scientific library ; 11) It77-Mar
Bibliography: p. [147]-148.
Includes index.
L3500
1. Space and time. 2. Relativity (Physics) I. Title.
QC173.59.S65B37 77-461049
*77 MARC

Barbier, Pierre.
Études sur notre ancienne poésie; le théâtre militant au XVIe siècle. La pastorale au XVIe et au XVIIe siècle. Un faiseur de pastorales au XVIIe siècle. Genève, Slatkine Reprints, 1970.
1 v. (various pagings) 22 cm.
1. French drama—16th cent.—Hist. & crit. I. Title.
TxU NUC74-124826

Barbier, Pierre, archaeologist.
Cinquante années d'archéologie; quelques souvenirs personnels. Saint-Brieuc, Presses bretonnes, 1973.
30 p. illus. 25 cm. F***
1. Barbier, Pierre, archaeologist. I. Title.
DC36.98.B32A33 913'.031'0924 74-178813
MARC

Barbier, Rainer.
Rechtsmittel des Gläubigers und Schutz des Verbrauchers bei Zahlungssäumnis und anderen Verletzungen von Ratenkreditverträgen im amerikanischen Recht / Rainer Barbier. — Bern : Herbert Lang ; Frankfurt/M. : Peter Lang, 1975.
xxiii, 139 p. ; 21 cm. — (Europäische Hochschulschriften : Reihe 2, Rechtswissenschaft ; Bd. 126) Sw75-A-5364
Originally presented as the author's thesis, Frankfurt am Main.
Bibliography: p. iii-xx.
ISBN 3-261-01648-5 : 27.60F
1. Sales, Conditional—United States. I. Title: Rechtsmittel des Gläubigers und Schutz des Verbrauchers bei Zahlungssäumnis ... II. Series.
KF1056.Z9B37 1975 346'.73'074 76-456237
*76 MARC

Barbier, René, 1890-
Golem. Illustrations de Jean Cuillerat. Préface de Serge Wellens. Paris, Jose Millas-Martin [1970]
137 p. illus., plates. 24 cm. (Collection "18")
I. Title.
MeU NUC73-124335

Barbier, Reynold.
Carrière et travaux scientifiques de Reynold Barbier, ... — [La Tronche] (7, route de Chartreuse, 38700) : [R. Barbier], 1974.
68 p. : maps ; 27 cm. F75-7223
"Liste des publications": p. [61]-66.
50.00F
1. Geological research. 2. Barbier, Reynold. I. Title.
QE40.B37 550'.92'4 76-472672
76 MARC

Barbier, Rina.
Van operaballet naar ballet van Vlaanderen. [Antwerpen, Sikkel, 1974].
235 p. with illus. 26 cm. F525 Ne 74-3
Summary in English, French, and German.
Bibliography: p. 228-229.
1. Ballet van Vlaanderen. 2. Ballet. I. Title.
GV1786.B33B37 74-311699

Barbier, Ruth Jean.
Racial awareness and preference of suburban Detroit white nursery school children. Detroit, 1972.
viii, 149 l. illus. 28 cm.
Thesis—Wayne State University.
Vita.
Bibliography: leaves 141-147.
1. Race awareness. I. Title.
MiDW NUC74-120274

Barbier d'Aucour, Jean, 1641-1694
see Observations sur Le festin de pierre. Genève, Slatkine Reprints, 1968.

Barbier de Meynard, Charles Adrien Casimir, 1826-1908.
Dictionnaire turc-français.
كتاب الدرر العمانية فى لغت العثمانية
Supplément au[x] dictionnaires publiés jusqu'à ce jour renfermant les mots d'origine turque et les mots arabes et persans employés en osmanli avec leur signification particulière, et aussi un grand nombre de proverbes et de locutions populaires, et un vocabulaire géographique de l'empire ottoman. Amsterdam, Philo Press, 1971.
2 v. 23 cm. (École des langues orientales, Paris. Publications, 2. sér., t. 4-5) Ne***
Reprint of the Paris, 1881-86 ed..
1. Turkish language—Dictionaries—French. 2. Turkish language—Foreign words and phrases. 3. Names, Geographical—Turkey. I. Title. II. Title: Kitap el-dürer el-ummaniyye fi lugat el-Osmaniyye. III. Title: el-Dürer el-ummaniyye fi lugat el-Osmaniyye. IV. Title: al-Durar al-'ummānīyah fī lughat al-'Uthmānīyah. V. Series: Paris: École des langues orientales vivantes. Publications, 2. sér., t. 4-5.
PL193.F8B3 1971 494'.35'341 73-312139
ISBN 90-6022-242-3

Barbier de Meynard, Charles Adrien Casimir, 1826-1908, ed.
see Ahund-zâde, Feth Ali, 1812-1878. L'ours et le voleur. Chicago, University of Chicago, 1972.

Barbier de Meynard, Charles Adrien Casimir, 1826-1908, ed.
see al-Mas'ūdī, d. 956? Les Prairies d'or. Paris, Société asiatique, 19

Barbier de Meynard, Charles Adrien Casimir, 1826-1908, ed.
see Yāqūt ibn 'Abd Allāh al-Hamawī, 1179?-1229. Dictionnaire géographique, historique et littéraire de la Perse et des contrées adjacentes. Amsterdam, Philo Press, 1970.

Barbier de Meynard, Charles Adrien Casimir, 1826-1908, ed. and tr.
see al-Zamakhsharī, Maḥmūd ibn 'Umar, 1075-1144. Kitāb aṭwāq al-dhahab. Paris, Imprimerie nationale, 1876.

Barbier de Montault, Xavier, 1830-1901.
Inventaires de la maison noble de La Levraudière au XVIIe siècle. Vannes, Impr. Lafolye, 1892.
12 p. 25 cm.
L. C. copy replaced by microfilm.
1. La Levraudière family—Archives.
[CD1219.5.L27B37] 74-213339
Microfilm 60103 CD

Barbiera, Lelio.
Disciplina dei casi di scioglimento del matrimonio. Art. 149. Supplemento Legge 1° dicembre 1970, n. 898. Bologna, N. Zanichelli; Roma, Soc. ed. del Foro italiano, 1971.
xvii, 419 p. 25½ cm. (Commentario del Codice civile. Libro 1: Delle persone e della famiglia. Art. 149) L5800 It 72-June
Bibliography: p. xv-xvii.
1. Divorce—Italy. I. Italy. Laws, statutes, etc. Legge 1 dicembre 1970, n. 898. II. Title. III. Series: Italy. Laws, statutes, etc. Codice civile. 19 Libro 1, Art. 149.
73-167126
MARC

Barbiera, Lelio.
Garanzia del credito e autonomia privata. Napoli, Jovene, 1971.
xii, 356 p. 24 cm. (Pubblicazioni della Facoltà giuridica dell'Università di Bari, 22) L4800 It 71-July
Bibliography: p. [334]-356.
1. Security (Law)—Italy. 2. Liberty of contract—Italy. 3. Security (Law) 4. Liberty of contract. I. Title. II. Series: Bari (City). Università. Facoltà di giurisprudenza. Pubblicazioni, 22.
73-343708

Barbieri, A. de
see Immunological Conference Pavia, 1974. Proceedings... Milano, Istituto Sieroterapico Milanese S. Belfanti, 1974.

Barbieri, Alain.
Etude pétrographique de la partie orientale du massif des Ecrins-Pelvoux. Les granites, appercu sur la geochronometrie du massif. [Grenoble] 1970.
[xii] 117, X p. illus., maps. 27 cm.
These—Grenoble.
Bibliography: p. I-X.
1. Geology—France—Ecrins—Pelvoux. 2. Petrology—France.
MH-GS NUC73-124336

Barbieri, Alberto.
L'antichissima terra di Sant'Agata Bolognese / Alberto Barbieri. — Bologna : Tamari, 1975.
303 p., [1] fold. leaf of plates : ill. ; 24 cm. It77-Jan
Bibliography: p. 271-272.
Includes index.
1. Sant'Agata Bolognese, Italy—History. I. Title.
DG975.S267B37 77-478202
*77 MARC

Barbieri, Alberto.
Modena dalle origini ai giorni nostri : profilo storico, fonti bibliografiche per lo studio della storia di Modena / Alberto Barbieri. — Modena : S. T. E. M., [1974?]
135 p. ; 17 cm. It 75-Mar
L1000
1. Modena—History. 2. Modena—Bibliography. I. Title.
DG975.M62B37 75-527504

Barbieri, Alberto.
Modenesi da ricordare. Modena, Societá tipografica editrice modenese, 1966.
160 p. illus., music, 48 plates (part col.), ports. 31 cm.
On spine: Musicisti, architetti, scultori, pittori.
Bibliography: p. 151-154.
1. Artists–Modena–Biography. 2. Musicians–Modena–Biography. I. Title.
ViU NUC73-47191

Barbieri, Alberto.
Modenesi da ricordare. Politici, diplomatici e militari. Modena, S. T. E. M., 1973.
2 v. illus., 18 plates. 31 cm. L5000 (v. 1); L10000 (v. 2) It 73–Sept (v. 1)
Cover title.
Includes bibliographies.
1. Modena—Biography. I. Title.
DG975.M63B36 73–356879
rev

Barbieri, Alexander F
Pennsylvania workmen's compensation and occupational disease: text, forms, case finder, by Alexander F. Barbieri. Philadelphia, G. T. Bisel Co. [1975-
v.
Loose-leaf for updating.
1. Workmen's compensation–Pennsylvania. I. Title.
CLL NUC77-84985

Barbieri, Antonio.
Latino delirante. Dai rustici di Roma a noi. Notazioni etimologiche per un riavvicinamento vivace alla madrelingua. Milano, Celuc, 1973.
237 p. 18 cm. (Ricerche. Nuova ser., 1) L2200 It 73–Sept
Bibliography: p. 231–236.
1. Italian language—Etymology. I. Title.
PC1582.L3B3 73–351648

Barbieri, Aroldo.
Cicerone e i neoattici / Aroldo Barbieri. — Roma : Edizioni dell'Ateneo, [1974]
63 p. ; 24 cm. — (Quaderni della Rivista di cultura classica e medioevale ; 14) It***
Bibliography: p. [61]–63.
L1500
1. Cicero, Marcus Tullius. 2. Oratory, Ancient. I. Title. II. Series: Rivista di cultura classica e medioevale. Quaderni ; 14.
PA6322.B3 75–534499

Barbieri, Arturo Enrique.
La moderna seguridad. Buenos Aires, Circulo Militar, c1967.
63 p. 18 cm. (Biblioteca de actualización militar, 3)
1. Economic development. 2. Security, International. I. Title.
IaU NUC73-47443

Barbieri, C.
see Società astronomica italiana. Atti delle celebrazioni... Padova, Tip. Antenore di B. Piazzon, 1974.

Barbieri, Carlo, joint author
see Lozia, Giorgio. Miagliano. Biella, Tip. Unione biellese, 1971.

Barbieri, Carlo, 1907-
Il giornalismo americano dalle origini a oggi. Roma, Edizioni Ricerche [1966?]
208 p. (Corsi universitari)
Bibliography: p. 200-208.
1. Journalism–U. S.–History. I. Title. II. Series.
CU NUC74-122454

Barbieri, Carlos E
see Santoro, Roberto Jorge. A ras del suelo .. [Buenos Aires] : Editorial Papeles de Buenos Aires, [between 1971 and 1975]

Barbieri, Colette Gillot.
Etude pétrographique de la partie orientale du massif des Ecrins-Pelvoux. Le complex intermediaire. [Grenoble] 1970.
[xii], 116, [X] p. illus., maps. 15 plates. 27 cm.
Thèse–Grenoble.
Bibliography: p. I-[X]
1. Geology–France–Ecrins-Pelvoux. 2. Petrology–France.
MH-GS NUC74-15786

Barbieri, Corrado.
Bombardieri 1939–45 [i. e. millenovecentotrentanove-quarantacinque] / Corrado Barbieri. — Parma : E. Albertelli, [1974]
227 p. : ill. ; 28 cm. — (Aerei di tutto il mondo ; 1) It 75–Jan
L12000
1. Bombers. I. Title.
TL685.3.B335 74–353433

Barbieri, Corrado.
Caccia e bombardieri, 1945–1955 [i. e. millenovecento-quarantacinque-millenovecentocinquantacinque] / Corrado Barbieri. — Parma : Delta, c1975.
267 p. : ill. ; 30 cm. It 75–Dec
L12000
1. Fighter planes. 2. Bombers. I. Title.
UG1242.F5B37 75–407287

Barbieri, Daniele, 1948-
Agenda nera : trent'anni di neofascismo in Italia / Daniele Barbieri. — 1. ed. — Roma : Coines, 1976.
338 p. ; 19 cm. — (Universale Coines ; 35) It76-Apr
Includes bibliographical references and indexes.
L3500
1. Italy—Politics and government—1945- 2. Fascism—Italy—1945- 3. Movimento sociale italiano. I. Title.
DG577.B27 76-457963
*76 MARC

Barbieri, Eugenio, 1927–
Made in Spain. Mutables. [Galería Juana Mordó del 11 de enero al 6 da febrero de 1971. Madrid, 1971]
[20] p. illus. 24 cm. Sp***
I. Galería Juana Mordó. II. Title.
N6923.B28G35 72–366022

Barbieri, Francesco.
Elementi di geologia marina. (Dalle lezioni tenute dal prof. F. Barbieri durante l'anno accademico 1970–'71). Parma, Studium Parmense, 1971.
282 p., incl. plates. illus., plates. 24 cm. L4000 It 72–Dec
At head of title: Università degli studi di Parma, Istituto di geologia. F. Barbieri, D. Rio.
Errata slip inserted.
Bibliography: p. 277–282.
1. Submarine geology. I. Rio, Domenico, joint author. II. Title.
QE39.B37 551.4′608 73–314198

Barbieri, Francesco, joint author
see Fasola, Mauro. Aspetti della biologia riproduttiva degli ardeidi gregari. Bologna: Laboratorio di zoologia applicata alla caccia, 1975.

Barbieri, Franco.
Illuministi e neoclassici a Vicenza. Con 222 illustrazioni in nero. Vicenza, Accademia olimpica, 1972.
xvi, 247 p. 99 plates. 24 cm. L10000 It 72–Dec
Bibliography: p. [193]–217.
1. Neoclassicism (Architecture)—Vicenza. I. Title.
NA1121.V72B37 72–374939

Barbieri, Franco.
L'Oratorio di San Nicola a Vicenza. 35 illustrazioni in nero e a colori. Vicenza, N. Pozza, 1973.
43, [32] p. illus., plate. 21 cm. It 74–Sept
Bibliography: p. 33–35.
1. Mural painting and decoration, Baroque — Vicenza. 2. Mural painting and decoration — Vicenza. 3. Oratorio di San Nicola a Vicenza.
ND2757.V54B37 74–335202

Barbieri, Franco.
La pianta prospettica di Vicenza del 1580 / a cura di Franco Barbieri. — Vicenza : N. Pozza, 1973.
48 p., 2 leaves of plates : ill. ; 34 cm. & portfolio (3 fold. leaves of plates : maps ; 47 cm.) It 74–May
Bibliography: p. [41]–48.
1. Vicenza—Maps—To 1800. 2. Vicenza—Description—Views. 3. Maps, Early—Facsimiles. I. Title.
G1989.V6B3 1973 912′.45′35 75–593218

Barbieri, Franco.
see Pigafetta, Filippo, 1533-1604. La descrizione del territorio e del contado di Vicenza (1602-1603). 1. ed. Vicenza, N. Pozza, 1974.

Barbieri, G Battista.
Lettera viva. [Brescia, Compagnia di S. Orsola, Istituto secolare delle figlie di S. Angela Merici, 1972]
95 p. illus. 20 cm. It***
"Supplemento al periodico bimestrale Responsabilità, n. 2."
1. Angela Merici, Saint, 1474–1540. I. Responsabilità. II. Title.
BX4700.A45B3 74–331235

Barbieri, Gino.
Il pensiero economico dall'antichità al Rinascimento / Gino Barbieri. — [Bari] : Istituto di storia economica, Università di Bari, [1963]
479 p. ; 22 cm.
Includes bibliographical references and index.
1. Economics—History. I. Title.
HB77.B37 75–408409

Barbieri, Giorgio.
Contributo alla conoscenza geologica della regione di Bolca (Monti Lessini). (Con 7 figure nel testo e 1 tavola fuori testo). Padova, Societa cooperativa tipografica, 1969.
36 p. illus., plate. 32 cm. (Memorie degli Istituti di geologia e mineralogia dell'Università di Padova, v. 27) It 70–Aug
At head of title: Consiglio nazionale delle ricerche. Centro di studio per la geologia e la petrografia. 1. sezione geologica. Giorgio Barbieri, Fabio Medizza.
Summary in English.
Bibliography: p. [34]–36.
1. Geology—Italy—Bolca region. I. Medizza, Fabio, joint author. II. Title. III. Series: Padua. Università. Istituto di geologia e paleontologia. Memorie degli Istituti di geologia e mineralogia dell'Università di Padova, v. 27.
QE272.P3 vol. 27, 1969 72–366023

Barbieri, Giovanna.
I Greci nell'età di Pericle. Torino, Loescher [1966-69]
2 v. illus., maps. 24 cm. (Enciclopedia monografica Loescher; la ricerca, serie storica, classe a, n. 1-2)
1. Civilization, Greek. I. Title.
NNC NUC74-122456

Barbieri, Giovanna.
Le strutture della nostra lingua; grammatica italiana per le scuole superiori. Firenze, La Nuova Italia [1971]
351 p. 24 cm.
1. Italian language–Grammar.
LNHT NUC73-124207

Barbieri, Giovanna.
Terza miscellanea greca e romana. Roma, 1971.
1 v. (Istituto italiano per la storia antica, Rome. Studi, fasc. 21)
I. Title. II. Series.
KU NUC74-122255

Barbieri, Giulio.
Il controllo dei contenitori metallici per conserve / a cura di Giulio Barbieri e Silvio Rosso. — 2. ed., 16 illustrazioni. — Parma : Stazione sperimentale per l'industria delle conserve alimentari, 1972.
111 p. : ill. ; 22 cm. — (Collana di monografie tecnologiche ; v. 6) It 74–Mar
"Supplemento della rivista Industria conserve."
Bibliography: p. 107–111.
1. Tin cans. I. Rosso, Silvio, joint author. II. Industria conserve. III. Title.
TS198.C3B36 1972 75–551708

Barbieri, Giulio.
Il controllo delle aggraffature delle scatole per conserve. A cura di Giulio Barbieri e Silvio Rosso. 99 illustrazioni. [3. ed.]. Parma, Stazione sperimentale per l'industria delle conserve alimentari, 1971.
90 p. illus. 22 cm. (Collana di monografie tecnologiche, v. 5) It Suppl–7
Supplement to Industria conserve.
1. Tin cans. 2. Sealing (Technology) I. Rosso, Silvio, joint author. II. Industria conserve. III. Title.
TS198.C3B37 1971 74–356938

Barbieri, Giuseppe, 1923–
Noi toscani. Aspetti e problemi regionali. Con un intervento del Presidente della Regione. Firenze, Sansoni, 1973.
140 p. illus. 24 cm. L1200 It 73–Nov
Bibliography: p. 140.
1. Tuscany. I. Title.
DG732.5.B37 73–361590

Barbieri, Giuseppe, 1923–
Toscana. 2. ed. riveduta e aggiornata. Con una carta geografica e 8 tavole a colori fuori testo, 289 figure e 21 cartine geografiche nel testo. Torino, Unione tipografico-editrice torinese, 1972.
xiv, 533 p. illus., map, 8 plates. (Le Regioni d'Italia, v. 8) L15000 It 73–Apr
Bibliography: p. 509–516.
1. Tuscany—Description and travel. I. Series.
DG734.2.B3 1972 73–333220

Barbieri, Giuseppe, 1923- joint author
see Almagià, Roberto, 1884-1962. L'Italia. Torino, Unione tipografico-editrice torinese [1971].

Barbieri, Guido
see Terza miscellanea greca e romana. Roma, 1971.

Barbieri, H J comp.
Cuentos del siglo XIX [i.e. diecinueve. Por] Alejandro Pushkin [et al. Selección y notas: H. J. Barbieri. Buenos Aires] Centro Editor de América Latina [1971]
158 p. 18 cm. (Biblioteca fundamental del hombre moderno, 34)
1. Short stories, Spanish–Translations from foreign literature. 2. Short stories–Translations into Spanish. 3. Short stories, Spanish. I. Pushkin, Aleksandr Sergeevich, 1799-1837. II. Title.
MB NUC73-125659

Barbieri, Ivo
see Castro Alves, Antônio de, 1847-1871. Espumas flutuantes. Rio de Janeiro : Editora Expressão e Cultura, [1974]

Barbieri, Juan de, joint author
see Calcagno, Alfredo Eric. Estilos políticos latinoamericanos... Santiago de Chile, Ediciones FLACSO [1972]

Barbieri, Lazaro
see Tucumán, Argentine Republic (Province) Obras para Tucumán; Lazaro Barbieri... [Tucumán, Dirección de Despacho de la Gobernación, 1964?]

Barbieri, Louis A
First and Second Peter / by Louis A. Barbieri. — Chicago : Moody Press, c1977.
126 p. ; 19 cm. — (Everyman's Bible commentary)
Bibliography: p. 126.
ISBN 0-8024-2061-3 : $1.95
1. Bible. N.T. Peter—Commentaries. I. Title. II. Series.
BS2795.3.B29 1977 226'.92'07 76-53760
76 MARC

Barbieri, Lucia Tumiati
see Tumiati Barbieri, Lucia.

Barbieri, Luciano.
In tuta di gennaio. [Padova], Rebellato, 1973.
82 p. 20 cm. (Quaderni di poesia 1973) L1800 It 73-Aug
I. Title.
PQ4862.A6726 I 5 74-330129

Barbieri, Luigi, 1827-1899
see Augustinus, Aurelius, Saint, Bp. of Hippo. Spurious and doubtful works. Il libro della vita contemplativa... Bologna, Commissione per i testi di lingua, 1967 [i.e. 1968]

Barbieri, Luigi, 1827-1899, ed.
see Petrarca, Francesco, 1304-1374. Le vite di Numa e T. Ostilio. Bologna, Commissione per i testi di lingua, 1968.

Barbieri, Luigi, 1827-1899, ed.
see Valerius Maximus. Saggio del volgarizzamento antico... Bologna, Commissione per i testi di lingua [1968] c1967.

Barbieri, Maria Silvia
see Beretta, Angelo. Il centauro e l'eroe: discussione interdisciplinare sul rapporto pedagogico. Bologna: Il mulino, [1974]

Barbieri, Matteo.
Notizie istoriche dei mattematici e filosofi del Regno di Napoli / Matteo Barbieri. — [Bologna] : A. Forni, [1975]
207 p., [1] fold. leaf of plates : ill. ; 22 cm. — (Italica gens ; n. 69) It 75-Nov
Reprint of the 1778 ed. published by V. Mazzola-Vocola, Naples.
Includes index.
1. Science—History—Italy. I. Title.
Q127.I 8B2 1975 75-404782

Barbieri, Orazio.
Ponti sull'Arno : la Resistenza a Firenze / Orazio Barbieri ; prefazione di Ferruccio Parri. — 3. ed. — Roma : Editori riuniti, 1975, c1958.
xix, 307 p. ; 22 cm. — (Biblioteca del movimento operaio italiano ; 48) It***
Includes index.
L2700
1. World War, 1939-1945—Underground movements—Florence. 2. Florence—History. I. Title.
D802.I 82F583 1975 75-531155

Barbieri, Renato
see Cella, Guido. Gli investimenti pubblici produttivi... Napoli : Istituto di studi per lo sviluppo economico, 1972.

Barbieri, Renzo.
I re Bamba : storia di una dinastia editoriale / Renzo Barbieri. — Firenze : Vallecchi, 1977.
285 p. ; 20 cm. — (Collana diversa) It77-June
L3300
I. Title.
PQ4862.A67263R4 77-477973
•77 MARC

Barbieri, Roberto.
Contabilita delle cantine sociali. [Bologna] Edagricole [1974]
63 p. tables. (Biblioteca pratica di cooperazione agricola, v. 8)
1. Wine and wine making Accounting. I. Title. II. Series.
DNAL NUC76-30460

Barbieri, Sante Uberto, Bp.
Chamarás o seu nome Jesus. São Paulo, Imprensa Metodista, 1971.
132 p.
1. Jesus Christ. I. Title.
TxDaM-P NUC76-74948

Barbieri, Sante Uberto, Bp.
Estranha Estirpe de Audazes, tradução de Luiz A. Caruso. São Bernardo, Imprensa Metodista [196-?]
183 p. 23 cm.
Translation of Una Extraña Estirpe de Audaces.
1. Wesley, John, 1703-1791. 2. Wesley, Charles, 1707-1788. 3. Methodism. I. Title.
NjMD NUC73-47189

Barbieri, Sante Uberto, Bp.
A exaltação do verbo feito carne: Meditações de Semana Santa Março, 1972. Sao Paulo, Imprensa Metodista [1972?]
46 p.
Poems.
I. Title.
TxDaM-P NUC76-74947

Barbieri, Sante Uberto, Bp.
Gotas de rocío. México, Casa Unida de Publicaciones [1956]
207 p.
Poems.
I. Title.
TxDaM-P NUC76-62502

Barbieri, Sante Uberto, Bp.
Llamarás su nombre Jesús. Traducido al espanol por Manuel V. Flores. Mexico, Casa Unida de Publicaciones [1973]
138 p.
Translation of Chamarás o seu nome Jesus.
1. Jesus Christ. I. Title.
TxDaM-P NUC74-120250

Barbieri, Sante Uberto, Bp.
El verdugo involuntario; cartas del centurión Marcos al centurión Coriolano [por] Sante U. Barbieri. Buenos Aires, Editorial La Aurora [1971]
76 p. 18 cm.
LACAP 72-3670
1. Jesus Christ—Fiction. I. Title.
PQ7797.B286V4 72-363607

Barbieri, Silvio.
5 [i. e. Cinque] giorni felici alla scoperta della Provincia granda. Bergamo, Edizioni orobiche, 1970.
194 p. illus. 21 cm. L2000 It 71-June
Cover title.
1. Cuneo (Province)—Description and travel. I. Title.
DG975.C87B37 73-340752

Barbieri, Torquato.
Opere anonime o pseudonime apparse fra il 1835 ed il 1907 conservate nella Biblioteca Carducci. Firenze, Edizioni Sansoni antiquariato, 1965.
75 p. facsims., port. 26 cm. (Biblioteca degli eruditi e dei bibliofili, 93)
"Trecentotrentatre esemplari." No. 31.
1. Anonyms and pseudonyms, Italian. 2. Bologna. Biblioteca Carducci. I. Title.
Z1070.B37 74-206387

Barbieri, Torquato.
Un plagio del primo Ottocento / Torquato Barbieri. — Firenze : Edizioni Sansoni antiquariato, 1962.
16 p. : ill. ; 26 cm. — (Biblioteca degli eruditi e dei bibliofili ; 74)
333 copies printed. No. 31.
1. Sestini, Bartolomeo, 1792-1825. La pia. 2. Sbrighi, Giorgio. La pia. 3. Plagiarism—Italy. I. Title.
PQ4732.S55P333 76-528139

Barbieri, Veljko, 1950-
Novčić Gordijana Pia i druge mediteranske priče / Veljko Barbieri. — Zagreb : Centar za kulturnu djelatnost Saveza socijalističke omladine, 1975.
103 p. ; 19 cm. — (Biblioteka Znaci : Kolo 1 ; sv. 4) Yu***
CONTENTS: Recipe Iuppiter quae commodasti.—More.—Ubojica i šuma.—Žena sa Naksosa.—Mušica.—Posljednji ribolov.—Novčić Gordijana Pia.
I. Title.
PG1619.12.A72N6 76-507794

Barbieri, Veljko, 1950-
Priča o gospodinu Zaku. Zagreb, Nakladni zavod Matice hrvatske; Centar za kulturu Narodnog sveučilišta grada, 1972.
55 p. 20 cm. (Biblioteka A. B. Šimić, br. 19) 25.00Din Yu 73
I. Title.
PG1619.12.A72P72 73-970957

Barbieri, Vicente.
Desenlace de Endimión / Vicente Barbieri. — Buenos Aires : Editorial Losada, c1974.
311 p. ; 22 cm. — (Novelistas de nuestra época)
I. Title.
PQ7797.B287D4 75-536403

Barbieri, Vicente.
Prosas dispersas de Vicente Barbieri; selección, advertencia preliminar. Cronología bio-bibliográfica, contribución a la bibliografía de Vicente Barbieri y notas de Aurelia C. Garat y Ana María Lorenzo. La Plata [Argentina] Universidad Nacional de La Plata, Facultad de Humanidades y Ciencias de la Educación [1970]
305 p. illus. 24 cm. (Textos, documentos y bibliografías, 4)
Bibliography: p. 221-284.
1. Barbieri, Vicente—Bibliography. I. Garat, Aurelia C., ed. II. Lorenzo, Ana María, ed. III. Title. IV. Series.
PQ7797.B287A6 1970b 73-200472

Barbieri de Santamarina, Estela.
Nueva bibliografía geográfica de Tucumán [por] Estela B. de Santamarina, Alicia I. García [y] Hilda M. Díaz. Tucumán, Universidad Nacional de Tucumán, Departamento de Geografía, 1972.
182 p. 27 cm. ([Universidad Nacional de Tucumán.] Publicación no. 1,092) (Universidad Nacional de Tucumán, Facultad de Filosofía y Letras, Departamento de Geografía. Serie monográfica, 20)
Cover title.
Based on Bibliografía geográfica de Tucumán, by W. Rohmeder and E. B. de Santamarina, published in 1946.
1. Tucumán, Argentine Republic (Province) — Description and travel—Bibliography. 2. Tucumán, Argentine Republic (Province)—Economic conditions—Bibliography. I. García, Alicia I., joint author. II. Díaz, Hilda M., joint author. III. Rohmeder, Wilhelm, 1902- Bibliografía geográfica de Tucumán. IV. Title. V. Series: Tucumán, Argentine Republic. Universidad. Departamento de Geografía. Serie monográfica, 20.
Z1634.T8B37 73-214906

Barbieri de Santamarina, Estela, joint author
see Santillán de Andrés, Selva E
La real distribución de la problación de la Provincia de Tucumán. Tucumán, Universidad Nacional de Tucumán, 1966.

Barbiero, Flavio.
Una civiltà sotto ghiaccio : alle soglie della scoperta del secolo / Flavio Barbiero. — Milano : Nord, [1974]
xiv, 179 p., [28] leaves of plates : ill. ; 24 cm. It 75-Mar
Half title has subtitle: Il più affascinante mistero archeologico di tutti i tempi.
Bibliography: p. 177-179.
L6500
1. Atlantis. 2. Man, Prehistoric. I. Title.
GN751.B295 75-570305

Barbiero, Maria Carmela.
Noi e gli altri : atteggiamenti e pregiudizi nel bambino / Maria Carmela Barbiero. — Napoli : Guida, [1974]
107 p. ; 18 cm. — (Psicologia e ricerca sociale ; 1) It 75-Aug
Summary in English.
Bibliography: p. [101]-107.
L2000
1. Prejudices and antipathies. 2. Child psychology. 3. Children in Italy. I. Title.
BF723.P75B37 75-541490

Barbilian, Dan, 1895-1961.
După melci [de] Ion Barbu. [Ilustraţii si copertă: Sabin Bălsa. Bucureşti] Editura Tineretului [1967]
26 p. illus., facsims. 20cm.
Includes a facsimile of the poem as originally published in Agora, with the author's revisions in manuscript added.
I. Title.
MB NUC 74-126118

Barbilian, Dan, 1895-1961.
Joc secund. Jeu second. [Versuri]. Traducere din limba română de Yvonne Stratt. Prefaţă de Dinu Pillat. [Ediţie bilingvă]. Bucureşti, Editura Eminescu, 1973.
239 p. 22 cm. lei 16.00 R 73-2489
At head of title: Ion Barbu.
Added t. p. in French.
I. Stratt, Yvonne, tr. II. Title. III. Title: Jeu second.
PC839.B33J6 1973 74-326100

Barbilian, Dan, 1895-1961.
Poezii. Ediţie îngrijita de Romulus Vulpescu. [Bucuresti] Editura Albatros, 1970.
xxiv, 549 p. illus., ports.
Bibliographical footnotes.
I. Vulpescu, Romulus, 1933- ed.
PPiU NUC74-149747

Barbilian, Dan, 1895-1961.
Poezii. Antologie, postfaţă şi bibliografie de Dinu Flămând. [Coperta de: Victor Feodorov]. Bucureşti, „Minerva," 1973.
199 p. 17 cm. (Arcade) lei 6.00 R 74-899
At head of title: Ion Barbu.
Bibliography: p. [191]-193.
PC839.B33P6 1973 74-340167

Barbilian, Dan, 1895-1961.
Poezii / Ion Barbu ; antologie, tabel cronologic, prefaţă şi comentarii de Marin Mincu ; [desenul copertei, Marcel Iancu]. — [Bucureşti] : "Albatros," 1975.
1, 164 p., [4] leaves of plates : ill., ports. ; 17 cm. — (Texte comentate) (Lyceum) R 75-4307
Bibliography: p. 149-[151]
lei 6.00
PC839.B33P63 1975 75-411247

Barbilian, Gerda.
Ion Barbu (Dan Barbilian) : amintiri / Gerda Barbilian ; cu un cuvînt înainte de Ov. S. Crohmălniceanu ; [coperta de Vasile Socoliuc]. — [Bucureşti] : "Cartea românească," 1975.
304 p., [8] leaves of plates : ill. ; 20 cm. R 75-3083
lei 10.50
1. Barbilian, Dan, 1895-1961. 2. Barbilian, Gerda.
PC839.B33Z6 75-408345

Barbin, Jacques.
Les pouvoirs des administrateurs dans les sociétés anonymes. Clermont-Ferrand, Imprimeries P. Vallier, 1933.
140 p. 25 cm.
Thèse—Poitiers.
Bibliography: p. 135.
1. Directors of corporations—France. I. Title.
74-216563

Barbin, Jean Yves.
see France. Conseil économique et social. Avis adopté par le Conseil économique et social au cours de sa séance du 9 juin 1976 sur la décentralisation qualitative. [Paris] Le Conseil, [1976?]

Barbin, Jean Yves.
see France. Conseil économique et social. La décentralisation qualitative ... Paris, Le Conseil, 1976.

Barbin, Madeleine, joint author
see Cornand, Monique. Colette: Paris, [10 mai-15 septembre] 1973... Paris, Bibliothèque nationale, 1973.

Barbin-Dajon, Martine.
Le Phénomène majoritaire en Irlande / Martine Barbin-Dajon. — [Paris] (62, rue Bayen, 75017) : M. Barbin-Dajon, 1975.
217 leaves : ill. ; 30 cm. — (Travaux du Séminaire de recherches sur les faits électoraux de Monsieur le Professeur Robert Villers ; no 1) F76-10417
At head of title: Université de droit, d'économie et de sciences sociales de Paris.
Errata slip inserted.
Bibliography: leaves 187-192.
1. Ireland—Politics and government—1922- 2. Elections—Ireland—History. I. Title.
JN1541.B37 329'.023'415082 76-486854
76 MARC

Barbina, Aldo, joint comp.
see Bongiorno, Arrigo, 1930- comp. Il pane degli altri... [Udine] Edizione La Situazione [1970]

Barbina, Alfredo.
see Alvaro, Corrado, 1895-1956. Cronache e scritti teatrali. Roma, ABETE, 1976.

Barbina, Alfredo
see Capuana, Luigi, 1839-1917. Capuana inedito. Bergamo: Minerva italica, 1974.

Barbina, Onorio, joint author
see Paroni, Igino. Arte organaria in Friul... [Udine] : Nuova base [1973]

Barbini, Bruno.
Svolgimenti letterari italiani : dal neoclassicismo al primo Novecento / Bruno Barbini. — 1. ed. — Roma : Gremese, 1974.
254 p. ; 21 cm. — (Collana L'Essenziale ; 5) It 76-Jan
Bibliography: p. 231-235.
L2200
1. Italian literature—19th century—History and criticism. 2. Italian literature—20th century—History and criticism. I. Title.
PQ4085.B34 76-501109

Barbiroli, Giancarlo.
Produzione di merci : criteri e metodi per una programmazione / Giancarlo Barbiroli. — Roma : Bulzoni, 1976.
x, 284 p. : graphs ; 21 cm. It77-Apr
Includes bibliographical references.
L7800
1. Industrial management. 2. Manufactures. 3. Production (Economic theory) I. Title.
HD37.I8B37 77-470531
•77 MARC

Barbisan, Giovanni, 1914-
Giovanni Barbisan. Opere di pittura 1950-1973. Mestre, Galleria San Giorgio, 1973.
[65] l. illus. 21 cm. It 74-Mar
Text by Paolo Rizzi, whose name appears at head of title.
1. Barbisan, Giovanni, 1914- I. Rizzi, Paolo.
ND623.B2382R59 74-309573

Barbisan, Giovanni, 1914-
Giovanni Barbisan : acqueforti 1933-1972 / [a cura di] Giuseppe Marchiori. — [Padova] : Rebellato, c1974.
236 p. : chiefly ill. ; 24 cm. — (Collana d'arte antica e contemporanea)
1. Barbisan, Giovanni, 1914- I. Marchiori, Giuseppe.
NE2052.5.B36M37 76-514480

Barbizon, France. Salle des fêtes.
see Barbizon au temps de J.-F. Millet, 1849-1875 ... [Barbizon] La Municipalité, [1975]

Barbizon, France.
see Barbizon au temps de J.-F. Millet, 1849-1875 ... [Barbizon] La Municipalité, [1975]

Barbizon au temps de J.-F. Millet, 1849-1875 : [exposition / organisée par la municipalité de Barbizon], Salle des fêtes de Barbizon, 3 mai-2 juin 1975. — [Barbizon] : La Municipalité, [1975]
326 p. : ill. (some col.) ; 20 x 21 cm. F***
Bibliography: p. 325-326.
1. Barbizon school. 2. Paintings, Modern—19th century—France—Exhibitions. 3. Barbizon, France—Exhibitions. 4. Millet, Jean François, 1814-1875. I. Barbizon, France. Salle des fêtes. II. Barbizon, France.
ND547.5.B3B37 76-454261
76 MARC

Barbizon House, London
see Peacock, Ralph, 1868- Profile portraits... [n.p., 19-]

Barblan, Andris.
L'image de l'Anglais en France pendant les querelles coloniales, 1882-1904 / Andris Barblan. — Berne : Herbert Lang ; Francfort/M : Peter Lang, 1974.
234 p. : ill. ; 23 cm. — (Publications universitaires européennes : Série 3, Sciences historiques et sciences auxiliaires de l'histoire ; v. 29) Sw74-A-6370
Bibliography: p. 221-232.
ISBN 3-261-01315-X : 41.00F
1. Great Britain—Foreign opinion, French. 2. Great Britain—Relations (general) with France. 3. France—Relations (general) with Great Britain. 4. Public opinion—France. I. Title. II. Series: Europäische Hochschulschriften : Reihe 3, Geschichte und ihre Hilfswissenschaften ; Bd. 29.
DA47.1.B18 301.29'41'044 75-515554
•75[r77]rev MARC

Barblan, Guglielmo.
Giorgio Federico Ghedini (Cuneo, 11 luglio 1892-Nervi, 25 marzo 1965); catalogo delle opere. Introd. di Guglielmo Barblan. [Milano] Ricordi [196-]
24 p. 21 cm.
In English, French, German, and Italian.
1. Ghedini, Giorgio Federico, 1892-1965—Bibliography.
NIC NUC73-47192

Barblan, Guglielmo.
Musiche e strumenti musicali dell'Africa orientale italiana. Napoli, Edizioni della Triennale d'oltremare, 1941 [1973]
147, [1] p. incl. illus. (music) plates, fold. map.
"Bibliografia": p. [139]-144.
Microfilm (neg.) Library of Congress, 1973.
InU NUC74-120251

Barblan, Guglielmo.
Toscanini e la Scala. Testimonianze e confessioni a cura di Eugenio Gara. Milano, Edizioni della Scala, 1972.
400 p. plates. 24 cm. L8000 It 72-Dec
Cover title.
Includes bibliographical references.
1. Toscanini, Arturo, 1867-1957. 2. Milan. La Scala. I. Gara, Eugenio. II. Title.
ML422.T67B4 782.1'092'4 [B] 73-301432

Barblan, Guglielmo
see Giorgio Federico Ghedini... Milano, Ricordi, 1965.

Barblan, Guglielmo, ed.
see Milan. Conservatorio di musica Giuseppe Verdi. Biblioteca. Catalogo della biblioteca. Firenze, L. S. Olschki, 1972-

Barblan, Marc A.
see Swiss Institute of Arms and Armour. Rapport d'activité pour les années 1972-1974. Grandson, Institut suisse d'armes anciennes, [1975]

Barbò, Francesca Rivetti
see Rivetti Barbò, Francesca.

Barbolani di Montauto, Lucrezia.
Il bobtail / Lucrezia Barbolani di Montauto. — [Firenze] : Olimpia, 1976.
113 p. : ill. ; 21 cm. — (Nuova cinofilia ; n. 8) It77-Apr
Bibliography: p. 112.
L3000
1. Old English sheepdog. I. Title.
SF429.O4B37 77-470774
•77 MARC

Barbolet, Roslyn H
Housing classes and the socio-ecological system. London, 1969.
47 p. 30 cm. (Centre for Environmental Studies. University working papers, 4)
Bibliography: p. 46-47.
1, Housing. 2. Home ownership. I. Title. II. Series.
NjP NUC73-124334

Barbolla García, Luz, joint author.
see Fernández Rodríguez, Manuel N. Manual de banco de sangre. Madrid, Ministerio de Trabajo, Instituto Nacional de Previsión, 1973.

Barbolla García, R.
see Introducción al análisis real. Madrid, AC, c1975.

Barbone, Guido.
Il libro completo del bridge di gara. Milano, U. Mursia, 1973.
537 p. illus. 20 cm. (Collana I Giochi. Serie Libri completi)
L6000 It 74-Apr
First ed.
1. Contract bridge. I. Title.
GV1282.3.B293 74-320065

Barboni, Renato, joint author
see Pascalino, S Flutter di pannelli continui... Roma, Università degli studi, 1969.

Barborica, Corneliu.
Prednášky o slovenskej literatúre : slovenská literatúra po roku 1918 = Prelegeri de literatură slovacă : literatura slovacă după 1918 / Corneliu Barborica. — București : Centrul de multiplicare al Universității, 1975.
198 p. ; 25 cm. R 75-4570
At head of title: Facultatea de limbi slave.
Text in Slovak.
Bibliography: p. 193-198.
lei 11.50
1. Slovak literature—20th century—History and criticism. I. Title. II. Title: Prelegeri de literatură slovacă.
PG5407.B3 76-517501

Barborică Elena.
Introducere în filologia română. Orientări în tehnica cercetării științifice a limbii române. București, Editura didactică și pedagogică, 1972.
144 p. with facsims. 20 cm. lei 6.50 R 72-3206
At head of title: Elena Barborică, Mirela Teodorescu, Liviu Onu.
Bibliography: p. 139-⌊141⌋
1. Romanian language — Study and teaching. 2. Romanian language—Bibliography. I. Teodorescu, Mirela. II. Onu, Liviu. III. Title.
PC619.B3 72-367590

Barborini, Bruno, 1924-
see Galleria Schneider. Barborini. ⌊Roma⌋ 1972.

Barborini. ⌊Roma⌋ 1972
see under Galleria Schneider.

Barborka, Geoffrey A
The divine plan, written in the form of a commentary on H. P. Blavatsky's Secret doctrine expressly for the purpose of those who wish to read and gain a deeper understanding of The secret doctrine, presenting an exposition of the doctrines of the esoteric philosophy, analysing and explaining all the terms used. [3d ed.] Adyar, India, Wheaton, Ill., Theosophical Pub. House, 1972.
xxvi, 564 p. diagrs. (1 fold.) 25 cm.
Includes bibliographical references.
IU NUC76-38178

Barborka, Geoffrey A
A glossary of Sanskrit terms; prepared as a key for pronunciation of Sanskrit, by Geoffrey A. Barborka. San Diego, California, Point Loma Publication [c1972]
76 p. 17 cm.
1. Sanskrit language—Terms and phrases. I. Title.
NBuU NUC73-124208

Barborka, Geoffrey A
The mahatmas and their letters, by Geoffrey A. Barborka. ⌊1st ed.⌋ Madras, Theosophical Pub. House, 1973.
xviii, 422 p. illus. 24 cm. Rs24.00
Bibliography: p. ⌊401⌋-404.
1. Theosophy. I. Title.
BP567.B35 212'.52 73-905645
MARC

Barborka, Geoffrey A
The peopling of the Earth : a commentary on archaic records in The secret doctrine / by Geoffrey Barborka. — Wheaton, Ill. : Theosophical Pub. House, 1975.
xiv, 233 p. : ill. ; 23 cm. — (Quest books)
Includes bibliographical references and index.
ISBN 0-8356-0221-4 : $10.00
1. Blavatsky, Helene Petrovna Hahn-Hahn, 1831-1891. The secret doctrine. 2. Theosophy. I. Title.
BP561.S43B37 212'.52 75-4243
76 MARC

Barborová, Eva.
Okresní archivy Jihočeského kraje; soupis archivních fondů. Zprac. Eva Barborová, Bedřich Nosek za spolupráce Jiřího Kadlece. Třeboň, Státní archív, Oddělení České Budějovice, 1966.
370 p.
1. Archives—Jihočeský kraj, Czechoslovakia. I. Statni archiv Trebon. Oddleni Ceske Budejouice. II. Title.
MH NUC74-130690

Barbosa, Adriano.
Mariel, um Ringo a sangue frio / escrito por Adriano Barbosa. — Rio ⌊de Janeiro⌋ : Lós Editora, c1971.
160 p. : ill. ; 21 cm.
Cr$18.00
1. Matos, Mariel Araújo Moryscotte de, 1940- —Fiction. I. Title.
PQ9698.12.A618M3 869'.3 75-553510

Barbosa, Adriano C
Folclore angolano : cinquenta contos quiocos : texto bilingue / por Adriano C. Barbosa. — Luanda : Instituto de Investigação Científica de Angola, 1973.
166 p. ; 25 cm. — (Memórias e trabalhos do Instituto de Investigação Científica de Angola ; 9)
Portuguese and Chokwe.
1. Tales, Chokwe. I. Title. II. Series: Luanda. Instituto de Investigação Científica de Angola. Memórias e trabalhos ; 9.
Q91.L823 vol. 9 76-527756
[GR358.32.C45]

Barbosa, Agostinho, Bp., 1590-1649.
Thesaurus locorum communium jurisprudentiae, ex axiomatibus Augustini Barbosae et analectis Joh. Ottonis Taboris aliorumqve concinnatus. Editio post Tobiae Ottonis Taboris secundam tertia, novis axiomatibus Samuelis Strykii aucta ... Lipsiae, Sumptu J. F. Gleditsch, 1691.
528, 436 p. 34 cm.
1. Roman law. 2. Canon law. I. Tabor, Johann Otto, 1604-1674. II. Tabor, Tobias Otto, fl. 1670, ed. III. Title.
74-228387

Barbosa, Alaor.
Campo e noite; contos. ⌊Goiânia⌋ Oriente ⌊1971⌋
172 p. 23 cm.
I. Title.
PQ9698.12.A62C3 73-200093

Barbosa, Alaor.
Monteiro Lobato das crianças / Alaor Barbosa. -- 3. ed., revista, aumentada e atualizada. -- Goiânia : Oriente, 1975.
148 p. : ill. ; 21 cm.
1. Lobato, José Bento Monteiro, 1883-1948. I. Title.
WU NUC77-85291

Barbosa, Alexandre.
Guinéus: contos, narrativas, crónicas. 3. ed. Lisboa, Livraria Progresso, 1968.
151 p. illus. 21 cm.
1. Guinea, Portuguese—Social life and customs. I. Title.
OU NUC76-74946

Barbosa, Alfeu, 1940-
Técnica de editoriais (para o curso de jornalismo). Belo Horizonte, Imprensa Oficial, 1970.
182 p. 23 cm.
Articles published in the periodical Minas Gerais during 1969.
1. Brazil—Addresses, essays, lectures. 2. Editorials. I. Title.
F2503.B27 75-565926

Barbosa, Almiro Rolmes
see Barbosa, José Almiro Rolmes.

Barbosa, Ana Mae Tavares Bastos.
Teoria e prática da educação artística / Ana Mae Tavares Bastos Barbosa. — São Paulo : Editora Cultrix, 1975.
115 p., ⌊5⌋ leaves of plates : 16 ill. ; 20 cm.
Includes bibliographical references.
CONTENTS: O artista no ensino da arte nos Estados Unidos.—Arte-educação: os casos brasileiro e norte-americano.—Um parêntese teórico: O "Método dos processos mentais" no ensino da arte.—Arte-educação: uma experiência programada.—Arte-educação: uma experiência para o futuro.
Cr$22.00
1. Arts—Study and teaching—Brazil. 2. Arts—Study and teaching—United States. I. Title.
LB1591.B28 76-483758
76 MARC

Barbosa, Ana Maria Naime.
see Associação Paulista de Bibliotecários. Comissão de Catalogação. Cabeçalhos uniformes para entidades coletivas. São Paulo, A Commisão, 1976.

Barbosa, Antônio Lemos, 1910-
Pequeno vocabulário português-tupi; com um apêndice: nomenclatura de parentescos [por] A. Lemos Barbosa. Rio de Janeiro, Livraria São José, 1970.
228 p. 18 cm.
1. Portuguese language—Dictionaries—Tupi. I. Title.
FU NUC76-74951

Barbosa, Arnoldo Parente Leite
see Superintendência do Desenvolvimento (Ceará, Brazil). Departamento de Recursos Sócio-Econômicos. Estudo da viabilidade econômica do porto de Camocim. Fortaleza, Serviço de Biblioteca e Documentação, 1972.

Barbosa, Beatriz Rodrigues.
Pássaros, tolos, peixes; novela em instantâneos. [Coimbra, Livraria Almedina, 1972]
88 p. 17 cm.
I. Title.
IU NUC74-125973

Barbosa, Beatriz Rodrigues.
Pássaros, tolos, peixes; novela em instantâneos. [Viseu, Portugal, Tip. Guerra, 1972]
88 p. 17 cm.
I. Title.
NIC NUC74-125974

Barbosa, Benedito.
Saúde mental e desenvolvimento : uma abordagem humanística / Benedito Barbosa. -- Manaus : Daou, 1975.
xiii, 204 p.
1. Civilization. 2. Psychiatry, Community. 3. Social Problems. I. Title.
DNLM DLC NUC77-85832

Barbosa, Cláudio Tavares.
As raízes / Cláudio Tavares Barbosa. — Rio de Janeiro : Editora Rio, 1976.
84 p. ; 20 cm.
Poems.
I. Title.
PQ9697.B333R3 869'.1 76-463622
76 MARC

Barbosa, Diogo Miranda, ed.
see Portugal. Laws, statutes, etc. Legislação dos mercados monetario... Coimbra, Livraria Almedina, 1972.

Barbosa, Eda Coutinho, 1939-
A study of the perceived and observed social-emotional climate in Brazilian secondary school classrooms. ⌊n.p., 1975⌋
126 l.
Thesis (D. Ed.)--Pennsylvania State University.
I. Title.
PSt NUC77-87283

Barbosa, Elias, joint author
see Xavier, Francisco Candido. Entre duas vidas... Sao Paulo, Edicao Calvario, 1974.

Barbosa, Fernando de Holanda, 1945-
Rational random behavior, extensions and applications / by Fernando de Holanda Barbosa. -- ⌊s.l., s.n.⌋, 1975.
iii, 50 leaves ; 28 cm.
Thesis (Ph. D.)--University of Chicago.
Bibliography: leaf 50.
1. Information theory in economics. 2. Economics, Mathematical. I. Title.
ICU NUC77-87442

Barbosa, Fidélis Dalcin.
Campo dos bugres : a vida nos primórdios da imigração italiana no Rio Grande do Sul : romance / Fidélis Dalcin Barbosa. — Porto Alegre : Escola Superior de Teologia S. Lourenço de Brindes : Distribuidora, Livraria Sulina, 1975.
99 p. ; 23 cm. — (Coleção Centenário da imigração italiana ; 6)
Cr$20.00
I. Title. II. Series.
PQ9698.12.A67C3 76-462424
76 MARC

Barbosa, Francisco de Assis, 1914–
Discursos na Academia de Francisco de Assis Barbosa e Marques Rebelo em sessão realizada a 13 de maio de 1971. Rio de Janeiro, J. Olympio, 1971.
x, 37 p. group ports. 22 cm. Cr$5.00
1. Meyer, Augusto, 1902– 2. Barbosa, Francisco de Assis, 1914– I. Cruz, Eddy Dias da, 1907–
PQ9697.M55Z57 73–203336

Barbosa, Francisco de Assis, 1914-
A vida de Lima Barreto, 1881-1922. 2. ed., rev. com 15 ilustrações. Rio de Janeiro, J. Olympio, 1959.
411 p. plates, ports., facsims. (Coleção Documentos brasileiros, 70)
"Inventario" (Catalog of Lima Barreto's library, from the manuscript in the Biblioteca Nacional, Rio de Janeiro): p. 360-382.
"Obras de Lima Barreto": p. 393-396.
"Obras consultadas": p. 396-400.
1. Lima Barreto, Afonso Henrique de, 1881-1922. I. Series.
ICIU NUC76-24197

Barbosa, Francisco de Assis, 1914-
A vida de Lima Barreto, 1881-1922 de Francisco de Assis Barbosa. — 5. ed. — Rio [de Janeiro] : Livraria J. Olympio Editora, 1975.
xiv, 412 p., [4] leaves of plates : ill., facsims., ports. ; 21 cm. — (Coleção Documentos brasileiros ; v. no. 70)
"Inventário" [catalog of Lima Barreto's library, from the manuscript in the Biblioteca Nacional, Rio de Janeiro]: p. 360-382.
Bibliography: p. 393-400.
Includes index.
Cr$28.00
1. Lima Barreto, Afonso Henrique de, 1881-1922—Biography. I. Title.
PQ9697.L544Z6 1975 75-508665
75 MARC

Barbosa, Francisco de Assis, 1914- ed.
see Lima Barreto, Afonso Henrique de, 1881-1922. Romance. 2. ed. Rio de Janeiro, AGIR, 1972.

Barbosa, Francisco Ignácio Quartim, ed.
see Brazil. Laws, statutes, etc. Lei no. 3.807, de 26 de agôsto de 1960. São Paulo, Instituto Paulista de Direito Tributário e Trabalhista [1967]

Barbosa, Francisco Ignácio Quartim.
see São Paulo, Brazil (State). Constitution, 1967. Constituição do Estado de São Paulo . . . São Paulo, J. Bushatsky, 1976.

Barbosa, Frederico Lopez Meira
see Brazil. Departamento Nacional da Produção Mineral. 4o. Distrito—Nordeste. Relatório preliminar sôbre as investigações as investigações geológicas na Mina Brejuí —RN. Recife, 1969.

Barbosa, Geraldo Alexandre.
Optical studies of the crystals KH_2PO_4 and $SrTiO_3$. [n.p.] 1973.
xi, 80 l. illus. 28 cm.
"Part I - Tunneling phenomenon in KH_2PO_4."
"Part II - Optical properties of $SrTiO_3$ at high temperatures."
Thesis—University of Southern California.
1. Raman spectroscopy. I. Title.
CLSU NUC76-38177

Barbosa, Geraldo de Morais.
Versos do meu outono / Geraldo de Morais Barbosa. — Natal : [s. n.], 1973.
45 p. ; 23 cm.
I. Title.
PQ9698.12.A673V4 75–585916

Barbosa, Geraldo Menezes.
As crônicas de Menezes Barbosa. Fortaleza, 1974.
211 p. 22 cm.
I. Title.
AC75.B2577 74–225267

Barbosa, Getúlio V
Geografi [i.e. Geografia] física; rebordos setentrionais da depressão de Belo Horizonte [por] Getulio V. Barbosa [e] David M. Santos Rodrigues. [Belo Horizonte, Instituto Central de Geo-Ciências, 1970]
12, [30] l. col. illus., col. maps. 33 cm.
Bibliography: l. [42]
1. Physical geography—Brazil—Belo Horizonte region. I. Rodrigues, David Márcio Santos. II. Title. III. Title: Rebordos setentrionais da depressão de Belo Horizonte.
GB155.B37 75-516808
76 MARC

Barbosa, Henry Chalu.
Primeiro semestre de direito processual civil / Henry B. Chalu Barbosa. — [1. ed.]. — Rio de Janeiro : Editora Artenova, 1975.
122 p. ; 21 cm.
Includes bibliographies.
Cr$35.00
1. Civil procedure—Brazil. 2. Civil procedure. I. Title.
347'.81'05 76-486503
77 MARC

Barbosa, Honório José.
Informações jurídicas para conhecimento da orgânica administrativa do Ultramar Português / Honório José Barbosa. — Lisboa : Agência-Geral do Ultramar, 1964.
97 p. ; 21 cm.
1. Portugal—Administrative and political divisions. 2. Portugal—Colonies — Constitutional law. 3. Portugal — Colonies — Administration. I. Title.
75–562429

Barbosa, João Alexandre.
Aa tradição do impasse ; linguagem da crítica & crítica da linguagem em José Veríssimo / João Alexandre Barbosa. — São Paulo : Ática, 1974.
255 p. ; 21 cm. — (Ensaios ; 8)
Bibliography: p. [215]–255.
1. Veríssimo de Mattos, José, 1857–1916. I. Title.
PQ9697.V3Z57 74–235496

Barbosa, João Alexandre.
A imitação da forma : uma leitura de João Cabral del Melo Neto / João Alexandre Barbosa. — São Paulo : Livraria Duas Cidades, 1975.
229 p. ; 21 cm. — (Série Universidade ; 4)
Includes bibliographical references.
Cr$45.00
1. Melo Neto, João Cabral de, 1920- —Criticism and interpretation. I. Title.
PQ9697.M463Z59 76-450206
76 MARC

Barbosa, João Alexandre.
A metáfore crítica / João Alexandre Barbosa. — São Paulo : Editôra Perspectiva, 1974.
163 p. ; 21 cm. — (Coleção Debates ; 105 : Crítica)
Includes bibliographical references.
Cr$30.00
1. Brazilian poetry—20th century—History and criticism—Addresses, essays, lectures. 2. Poetry, Modern—20th century—History and criticism—Addresses, essays, lectures. I. Title.
PQ9571.B33 75–553778

Barbosa, João Lucas Marques.
On minimal immersions of S^2 in S^{2m} [Berkeley] 1972.
1 v. (various pagings)
Thesis (Ph. D.)—Univ. of California.
Includes bibliography.
CU NUC74-120271

Barbosa, Jorge Emmanuel Ferreira.
Sôbre a lógica operacional dos juntores / Jorge Emmanuel Ferreira Barbosa. — Niteroi : Universidade Federal Fluminense, Faculdade de Filosofia, Departamento de Matemática, 1967.
ii, 287 p. ; 21 cm. — (Série Análise e lógica matemática) (Publicações de pesquisa - Universidade Federal Fluminense, Comissão Central de Pesquisas)
"Preprint."
1. Logic, Symbolic and mathematical. 2. Many valued logic. I. Title. II. Series.
BC135.B28 75–580447

Barbosa, Jorge Fairbanks.
Surgical treatment of head and neck tumors. Edited by Jorge Fairbanks Barbosa. Illus. by Jose Gonçalves. Translation by Rosemarie von Becker Froon. New York, Grune & Stratton [1974]
xiii, 311 p. illus. 28 cm.
1. Head—Tumors. 2. Neck—Tumors. 3. Tumors—Surgery. I. Title.
[DNLM: 1. Head—Surgery. 2. Neck neoplasms—Surgery. 3. Neoplasms—Surgery. WE 705 B238s 1974]
RD661.B38 616.9'92'91 74–3460
ISBN 0–8089–0811–1 MARC

Barbosa, Jorge Morais.
A língua portuguesa no mundo. Lisboa, Sociedade de Geografia de Lisboa, Semana do Ultramar, 1968.
191 p. 21 cm.
Bibliographical footnotes.
1. Portuguese language—Hist. I. Title.
PPT NUC73-46840

Barbosa, Jorge Morais, ed.
see Academia Internacional da Cultura Portuguesa. Estudios linguísticos crioulos. Lisboa, 1967.

Barbosa, José.
Laterna mágica; revista fantasia em 3 actos e 14 quadros. Ponta Delgada [Oficina Artes Gráficas] 1956.
104 p.
I. Title.
NcU NUC75-67064

Barbosa, José Almiro Rolmes, comp.
Obras-primas do conto moderno. Seleção, introdução e notas de Almiro Rolmes Barbosa e Edgard Cavalheiro. Retratos de Armando Pacheco. São Paolo, Martins [1962]
367 p. illus. 22 cm.
1. Short stories. I. Cavalheiro, Edgard, joint comp. II. Title.
KU NUC75-65969

Barbosa, José Celso, 1857-1921
see Barbosa de Rosario, Pilar. La Comision autonomista de 1896... San Juan de Puerto Rico, Imprenta Venezelena, 1957.

Barbosa, José Celso, 1857-1921
see La Obra de José Celso Barbosa. San Juan de Puerto Rico [Impr. Venezuela] 1937-

Barbosa, José Maria de Azevedo.
A polêmica de De Angelis com o Govêrno da Província do Pará. Belém, 1970.
7 p. illus. 23 cm.
1. De Angelis, Domenico. 2. Belém, Brazil. I. Title.
ND623.D3727B37 74–203699

Barbosa, José Maria de Azevedo.
Santa Maria de Belém do Grão-Pará, o nome da capital paraense / José Maria de Azevedo Barbosa. — Belém : [Impr. Oficial], 1977.
92 p., [1] leaf of plates : ill. ; 23 cm.
"Apêndice" (p. [33]-92) contains documents.
1. Belém, Brazil—Name. I. Title.
F2651.B4B37 77-556735
77 MARC

Barbosa, Júlio Martins.
Desidratação na clíncia pediatria cirurgia. 2. ed. Rio [de Janeiro] Editôra Cultura Médica, 1969.
256 p. illus.
1. Dehydration of infants. I. Title.
DPAHO NUC74-5089

Barbosa, L. A. Grandvaux
see
Barbosa, Luis Augusto Grandvaux.

Barbosa, Licínio Leal.
Direito procedimental [estudos, por] Licínio Barbosa. [Goiânia-Goiás, Brazil, Gráfica Oriente] 1970.
115 p. 19 cm. (Temas universitários)
Includes bibliographies.
1. Procedure (Law) Brazil. Addresses, essays, lectures. I. Title.
MnU-L DLC NUC73-47193

Barbosa, Luis Augusta Grandvaux
see Wild, Hiram. Vegetation map of the flora Zambesiaca area. Salisbury, M.O. Collins, 1967.

Barbosa, Luiz Carlos.
Cartas para o coração que ama. São Paulo, Nova Época [1973]
109 p.
1. Love—Literary collections. I. Title.
NmU NUC75-21197

Barbosa, Manoel.
Efemérides da Freguezia de N. Senhora de Conceição da Praia [por] Manoel de Aquino Barbosa. Salvador [Brasil] 1970.
617 p. 23 cm. (Coleção Conceição da Praia, v. 1)
1. Salvador, Brazil. Igreja de Nossa Senhora da Conceição da Praia—History—Sources. I. Title. II. Series.
BX4625.B6S243 73-212669

Barbosa, Manoel.
Retalhos de um arquivo; [artigos, por] Manoel de Aquino Barbosa. Salvador [Brasil] 1972.
405 p. 24 cm.
1. Salvador, Brazil—Addresses, essays, lectures. I. Title.
F2651.S13B37 73-213303

Barbosa, Marco Aurelio Caldas
see Caldas Barbosa, Marco Aurelio.

Barbosa, María del Consuelo Alcantara
see Alcantara Barbosa, María del Consuelo.

Barbosa, Menezes
see
Barbosa, Geraldo Menezes.

Barbosa, Miguel.
Irineu do Morro; [romance]. Rio de Janeiro, Editorial Nórdica [1972]
230 p. illus. 21 cm. Cr$20.00
Half title: As contraditórias reflexões de um pedaço de lama.
I. Title.
PQ9264.A72 I 7 74-206789

Barbosa, Miguel.
Mulher Macumba. Lisboa, Editorial Futura, 1973.
109 p. illus. 22 cm.
Short stories.
CONTENTS: Mulher-Macumba.—Um exercício de emigração: O velho e a secretaria. O velho e a galinha. O velho, a secretaria e a galinha. O velho, a secretaria e o diabo.
I. Title.
PQ9264.A72M8 75-580145

Barbosa, Miguel.
O palheiro / Miguel Barbosa. — Lisboa : [Distribuição da Editorial Organizações], 1963.
76 p. ; 19 cm. — (Colecção antológica Best-sellers ; v. extra D)
I. Title.
PQ9264.A72P27 76-482331
76 MARC

Barbosa, Miguel.
O paraíso reencontrado, de uma trilogia: "Os deuses e os homens"; peça em 3 actos. [Lisboa] Galeria Panorama [1969 or 70]
126 p. 21 cm.
"EP T 3."
I. Title.
PQ9264.A72P3 74-229869

Barbosa, Miguel.
Los profetas de la paja. O palheiro. Versión en castellano: José Luis Cerrato. [Barcelona, La Mano en el Cajón, 1973]
55 p. 21 cm. (La Mano en el cajón. Teatro, 5) Sp***
I. Title. II. Title: O palheiro.
PQ9264.A72P7 74-302680
ISBN 84-7300-013-7

Barbosa, Nélson.
Educação moral e cívica, organização social e política. 5. São Paulo, Editôra Itamaraty [1972]
328 p. illus. 21 cm.
"Hino nacional brasileiro" words and music: p. [207]-[208]
Bibliography: p. 328.
1. Civics, Brazilian—Study and teaching. 2. Brazil—Politics and government. I. Title.
LB1584.5.B7B37 73-200676

Barbosa, Octavian.
Dicționarul artiștilor români contemporani / Octavian Barbosa. — București : "Meridiane", 1976.
534 p. : ill., ports. ; 17 cm. R76-3653
lei40.00
1. Artists—Romania—Biography. 2. Art, Modern—20th century—Romania. I. Title.
N7228.B33 709'.2'2 77-451337
•77 MARC

Barbosa, Octavio
see Geologia da região do Triângulo Mineiro. Rio de Janeiro [Divisão de Fomento da Produção Mineral] 1970.

Barbosa, Osmar.
Dicionário auxiliar de gramática portuguêsa; com um apêndice contendo classes das palavras, coletivos, flexões dos substantivos e adjetivos, adjetivos pátrios. Supervisão de Dr. Francisco da Silva Ramos. São Paulo, Comérico e Importação de Livros Cil [1965]
2 v. (487 p.) 22 cm.
1. Portuguese language—Grammar—Dictionaries. I. Title.
TxU NUC74-124825

Barbosa, Osmar.
História da literatura da lingua portuguêsa, a mais atualizada. [Rio de Janiero] Ediçọes de Ouro [1969]
424 p. illus. 16 cm. (Biblioteca Mentor cultura, 239)
1. Portuguese literature—History and criticism. 2. Brazilian literature—History and criticism. I. Title.
MU NUC75-29390

Barbosa, Osmar.
Portuguêa fundamental. 5.ª e 6.ª series primárias admissão ao ginásio. [Rio de Janeiro] Edições de Ouro [1969]
234 p. 16 cm. (Biblioteca Linguas vivas) "1035, estrêla."
1. Portuguese language—Grammar—1950- I. Title.
MB NUC74-122444

Barbosa, Pedro.
Manual of basic techniques in insect histology / by Pedro Barbosa. — Amherst, Mass. : Autumn Publishers, [1974]
245 p. ; 23 cm.
Includes bibliographies and index.
1. Entomology — Laboratory manuals. 2. Histology — Laboratory manuals. I. Title.
QL464.B33 595.7'08'2028 74-84443
MARC

Barbosa, Pedro.
Some effects of overcrowding on the respiration of larval Aedes aegypti (L.) [Amherst] 1971 [1972]
109 l.
Thesis—University of Massachusetts.
Microfilm of typescript. Ann Arbor, Mich., University Microfilms, 1972. 1 reel. 35 mm.
1. Mosquitoes—Larvae. 2. Aedes aegyptic. I. Title.
INS NUC74-120254

Barbosa, Pedro.
Some effects of overcrowding on the respiration of larval Aedes aegypti (L.) Amherst, 1971.
[iii], 109 l. illus., appendix. 28 cm.
Thesis (Ph.D.)—University of Massachusetts. Microfilm no. 1451.
1. Theses—Entomology—Ph.D. 2. Aedes aegypti (L.) 3. Mosquitoes—Larvae. 4. Respiration. I. Title.
MU NUC73-32633

Barbosa, Pedro Franco.
see Brazil. Serviço do Patrimônio da União. Assessoria Jurídica. Pareceres. [Brasília] Ministério da Fazenda, Secretaria Geral, 1972-

Barbosa, Raul, joint author
see Abril, Eduardo R Cálculo de estructuras supuestamente fisuradas. Buenos Aires, Instituto Nacional de Tecnología Industrial, 1973.

Barbosa, Ricardo A
Las hachas de piedra y los núcleos de vidrio del rayo : nueva teoría comprobada / Ricardo A. Barbosa. — [Mendoza? Argentina : Barbosa, 1973?]
64 p., [27] leaves of plates : ill. ; 21 cm.
1. Man, Prehistoric—Tools. 2. Stone implements. I. Title.
GN799.T6B37 75-557527

Barbosa, Rita Alves, joint author
see Ramos, Jose Raymundo de Andrade. Roteiro geológico na Serra da Carioca... Rio de Janeiro, Ministério das Minas e Energia, Departamento Nacional da Produção Mineral, Divisão de Geologia e Mineralogia, 1965.

Barbosa, Rodrigo Ajace de Moreira
see
Ajace, Rodrigo, 1925-

Barbosa, Ruy, 1849-1923.
O Art.6°. [i.e. sexto] da Constituição e a intervenção de 1920 na Bahia / Rui Barbosa. — Rio de Janeiro : Ministério da Educação e Cultura, Fundação Casa de Rui Barbosa, 1975.
xvi, 328 p., [2] leaves of plates : facsims. ; 24 cm. — (His Obras completas ; v. 47, t. 3)
1. Federal government—Brazil. 2. Brazil. Constitution, 1891. 3. Intervention (Federal government)—Bahia, Brazil (State) I. Title.
F2537.B195 vol. 47, t. 3 76-450795
[JL2420.S8] 76 MARC

Barbosa, Ruy, 1849-1923.
Correspondência, primeiros tempos; curso jurídico, colegas e parentes. [Ruy Barbosa] Rio de Janeiro, Fundaçao Casa de Rui Barbosa, 1973.
172 p. 24 cm. (Arquivo da casa de Rui Barbosa, 3)
Bibliography: p. [11]
Includes indexes.
I. Title. II. Series.
CaBVaU NUC76-74936

Barbosa, Ruy, 1849-1923.
A imprensa / Rui Barbosa. — Rio de Janeiro : Ministério da Educação e Cultura, Fundação Casa de Rui Barbosa, 1975-
v. : facsims. ; 24 cm. — (His Obras completas ; v. 27, t. 4)
Includes bibliographical references.
1. Brazil—Collected works. I. Title.
F2537.B195 vol. 27, t. 4-5, etc. 76-452333
[F2503] 76 MARC

Barbosa, Ruy, 1849-1923.
Oração aos moços. 8. ed. Guanabara, Organização Simões, 1962.
67 p.
1. Baccalaureate addresses. I. Title.
UU NUC74-168014

Barbosa, Ruy, 1849-1923.
Oração aos moços [por] Rui Barbosa. Prefácio: Edgard Batista Pereira. Estabelecimento do texto e notas de Adriano da Gama Kury. [Rio de Janeiro] Edições de Ouro [1973]
127 p. illus. 16 cm. (Clássicos brasileiros) Cr$4.00
"Sêlo, 1425."
1. Barbosa, Ruy, 1849-1923. I. Title.
74-212495

Barbosa, Ruy, 1849-1923. Works
see Lacombe, Américo Jacobina, 1909- Roteiro das Obras completas de Rui Barbosa. Rio de Janeiro : Ministério da Educaçao e Cultura, 1974.

Barbosa, Ruy, 1849-1923
see Dantas, Manuel Pinto de Sousa. Correspondência do conselheiro Manuel P. de Souza Dantas. [Rio de Janeiro] Casa de Rui Barbosa, 1962.

Barbosa, Telma Conceição Carrilho.
Caracterização de um grupo de orientadores educacionais em formação e relação de algumas características com o desempenho no estágio supervisionado / por Telma Conceição Carrilho Barbosa. — Rio de Janeiro : Pontifícia Universidade Católica do Rio de Janeiro, [1975?]
x, 126 leaves ; 30 cm.
Originally presented as the author's thesis, Pontifícia Universidade Católica do Rio de Janeiro, 1974.
Summary in Portuguese and English.
Bibliography: leaves [119]-126.
1. Student counselors, Training of—Brazil. I. Title: Caracterização de um grupo de orientadores educacionais ...
LB1731.B237 1975 76-485592
76 MARC

Barbosa, Viriato.
Póvoa do mar. 2. ed., especial ampliada. Desenhos originais de Orlando Barbosa. [Porta] 1969.
178 p. illus.
"Edicao especial de 500 exemplares."
1. Povoa de Varzim, Portugal. I. Title.
MiU NUC75-29391

Barbosa, Waldemar de Almeida.
A Capitania de Minas Gerais. [Belo Horizonte, 1970]
35 p. 18 cm.
Microfiche copy. 1 sheet. 11 x 15 cm. (NYPL FSN 15, 943)
"Edição comemorativa dos dois séculos e meio da Capitania de Minas Gerais."
1. Minas Gerais, Brazil—History. I. Title.
NN NUC76-74945

Barbosa, Waldemar de Almeida.
Minas e a Independência. Belo Horizonte, 1972.
49 p. 17 cm.
"Colaboração das empresas mercantil de Minas para as comemorações do sesquicentenário da Independência Nacional."
Includes bibliographical references.
1. Minas Gerais, Brazil—History. 2. Brazil—History—1822-1889. 3. Pedro I, Emperor of Brazil, 1798-1834. I. Title.
F2581.B355 73-217609

Barbosa Borba, Oney
see
Borba, Oney Barbosa.

Barbosa da Silva, Raphael Chrysostome.
see Silva, Raphael Chrysostome Barbosa da.

Barbosa de Araújo, Alóisio
see
Araújo, Aloísio Barboza de.

Barbosa de Brito, Natal
see
Brito, Natal Barbosa de.

Barbosa de Deus, Pedro
see
Deus, Pedro Barbosa de.

Barbosa de Faria, Wander
see
Faria, Wander Barbosa de.

Barbosa de Oliveira, Rui
see
Barbosa, Ruy, 1849-1923.

Barbosa de Rosario, Pilar.
La Comision autonomista de 1896; 16 de septiembre de 1896 al 12 de febrero de 1897. San Juan de Puerto Rico, Imprenta Venezuela, 1957.
209 p. ports. 24 cm. (La obra de José Celso Barbosa, v. 6) (His Historia del autonomismo puertorriqueno, [2])
1. Puerto Rico—History—to 1898. I. Barbosa, José Celso, 1857-1921. II. Title.
NNF NUC76-63232

Barbosa de Rosario, Pilar.
De Baldorioty a Barbosa; historia del autonomismo puertorriqueño, 1887-1896. San Juan de Puerto Rico, Model Offset Printing, 1974.
xiii, 367 p. illus., ports. 24 cm. (His Historia del autonomismo puertorriqueño, 1887-1898) (La obra de José Celso Barbosa, v. 5)
"Segunda edición"; i.e. reprint of the 1957 ed.
Includes bibliographical references.
1. Puerto Rico—Pol. & govt.—To 1898. 2. Barbosa, José Celso, 1857-1921. 3. Baldorioty de Castro, Román, 1822-1898. I. Title. II. Series. III. Series: Barbosa, José Celso, 1857-1921. La obra de José Celso Barbosa, v. 5.
IaU NUC76-32320

Barbosa de Rosario, Pilar.
El ensayo de la autonomía en Puerto Rico, 1897-1898 / Pilar Barbosa de Rosario. — [s.l. : s.n.], 1975 (San Juan de Puerto Rico : Model Offset Printing)
221 p. : ill. ; 23 cm. — (La Obra de José Celso Barbosa ; v. 7)
Bibliography: p. 221.
1. Puerto Rico—Politics and government—To 1898. 2. Partido Autonomista Puerto-Riqueño. I. Title. II. Series.
F1975.B28O2 vol. 7 75-518440
[F1973] 75 MARC

Barbosa de Rosario, Pilar
see La Obra de José Celso Barbosa. San Juan de Puerto Rico [Impr. Venezuela] 1937-

Barbosa du Bocage, Manuel Maria de
see Bocage, Manuel Maria de Barbosa du, 1765-1805.

Barbosa Goulart, Ruth Maria
see
Bueno, Ruth.

Barbosa Guisard, Oswaldo
see
Guisard, Oswaldo Barbosa.

Barbosa Heldt, Antonio.
Cien años en la educación de México. [1. ed.] México, Editorial Pax [1972]
317 p. ports. 21 cm.
LACAP 72-3741
Bibliography: p. 317.
1. Education—Mexico—History. I. Title.
LA421.8.B37 72-361799

Barbosa Junior, José, 1875-
Um transe afflictivo ... monologo ... Lisboa, Liv. Pop. de F. Franco [n.d.]
8 p. (Collecção de peças theatraes para salas e theatros particulares, 479)
I. Title.
InU NUC75-30165

Barbosa Leão, Kosciuszko
see
Leão, Kosciuszko Barbosa.

Barbosa Lessa, Luis Carlos
see Lessa, Luis Carlos Barbosa.

Barbosa Lima, Cid
see
Lima, Cid Barbosa.

Barbosa Lima de Medeiros, Aldalita de Jesus
see Medeiros, Aldalita de Jesus Barbosa Lima de.

Barbosa Lima Sobrinho, Alexandre Jose
see Lima, Alexandre José Barbosa, 1897-

Barbosa Machado, Diego, 1682-1772.
Bibliotheca lusitana historica, critica, e cronologica. Na qual se comprehende e noticia dos aûthores portuguezes, e das obras, que compuseraõ desde o tempo da promulgaçaõ da ley da graça atè o tempo prezente. Lisboa, 1741-59. [New York, Readex Microprint, 1961]
36 cards. 16 x 23 cm.
Microprint copy.
Collation of the original: 4 v. 41 cm.
I. Title.
CaBVaU NUC75-108752

Barbosa Melo, José
see
Mello, José Barboza, 1903-

Barbosa Nunes da Cruz, Ubirajara
see
Cruz, Ubirajara.

Barbosa Ramirez, Rene.
El arrendamiento de tierras ejidales; en estudio en Tierra Caliente, Michoacán. [Por] A. René Barbosa [y] Sergio Maturana. México, Centro de Investigaciones Agrarias [1972]
99 p. map.
1. Agriculture—Economic aspects—Mexico—Michoacán (State) I. Maturana Medina, Sergio. II. Title.
InU NUC74-120249

Barbosa Ramírez, René.
La estructura económica de la Nueva España 1519-1810, por A. René Barbosa Ramírez. [1. ed. México, Siglo Veintiuno, 1971]
v, 259 p. illus. 18 cm. (Historia y arqueología)
Bibliography: p. 253-259.
1. Mexico—Econ. condit. 2. Spain—Colonies—Mexico—Economic policy. I. Title.
CtY AAP NjR OU NcU NUC73-126085
CaBVaU PPT CU-B MH KyLoU

Barbosa Ramos, Milton
see
Ramos, Milton.

Barbosa Ramos, Sonia Nadia de Carvalho
see
Ramos, Sonia.

Barbot, Jaime Ramirez-
see Ramirez-Barbot, Jaime, 1936-

Barbot-de-Marni, Evgeniĭ Nikolaevich, 1868–
(Dragirovanie rossypnykh mestorozhdeniĭ zolota i platiny)
Драгирование россыпных месторождений золота и платины. Москва, Гос. техн. изд-во, 1924.
112 p. illus. 26 cm. (Инженерно-промышленная библиотека, B. Серия, 4, № 4–7)
At head of title: Р. С. Ф. С. Р. Центр. комит. Всероссийского союза горнорабочих. Барбот де-Марни, Е. Н.
Bibliography: p. [111]–112.
1. Gold mines and mining. 2. Platinum mines and mining. 3. Hydraulic mining. I. Title.
TN421.B37 75–579311

Barbotin, Edmond.
Faith for today. Translated by Matthew J. O'Connell. Maryknoll, N. Y., Orbis Books [1974]
195 p. illus. 20 cm. $3.95
Translation of Croire.
Includes bibliographical references.
1. Apologetics—20th century. 2. Faith. I. Title.
BT1102.B2313 239 73–85155
ISBN 0–88344–125–X MARC

Barbotin, Edmond.
The humanity of God / Edmond Barbotin ; translated by Matthew J. O'Connell. — Maryknoll, N.Y. : Orbis Books, c1976.
vi, 310 p. ; 22 cm.
Translation of Humanité de Dieu.
Includes bibliographical references.
ISBN 0-88344-184-5
1. God—Biblical teaching. I. Title.
BS544.B3713 231 76-304
76 MARC

Barbotin, Edmond.
The humanity of man / Edmond Barbotin ; translated by Matthew J. O'Connell. — Maryknoll, N.Y. : Orbis Books, [1975].
vi, 345 p. ; 22 cm.
Translation of Humanité de l'homme.
Bibliography: p. 343-345.
ISBN 0-88344-183-7 : $12.95
1. Man. I. Title.
BD450.B2913 1975 128 74-21108
75 MARC

Barbotin, Edmond, tr.
see Aristoteles. De l'Ame. Paris, le Club francais du livre, 1969.

Barbotin, Edmond.
see Qu'est-ce qu'un texte? ... Paris, J. Corti, 1975.

Barbotin, Maurice.
Les communes et les bourgs de Marie-Galante. Maurice Barbotin. [n.p., 1968?]
19 p., [2] leaves of plates. ill., facsim. 24 cm.
Cover title.
"Extrait du Bulletin de la Société d'histoire de la Guadeloupe, no. 9-10, 1968."
Bibliography: p. 19.
1. Marie-Galante—History. 2. Marie-Galante—Historic houses, etc. I. Title.
FU NUC76-71989

Barbot'ko, Anatoliĭ Ivanovich, joint author
see IAshcherit͡syn, Petr Ivanovich. (Tonkie dovodochnye prot͡sessy obrabotki detaleĭ mashin i priborov) 1976.

Barbou, Alfred.
Dogs we love. Text by Alfred Barbou, followed by a "Portrait of the dog" by Buffon. Translated by Blanche Michaels. [Geneva] Minerva [c1972]
140 p. illus. (part col.)
"A Pierre Waleffe book."
1. Dogs. I. Buffon, Georges Louis Leclerc, comte de, 1707-1788. II. Title.
OCl NUC74-792

Barbour, Alan G
Cliffhanger : a pictorial history of the motion picture serial / Alan G. Barbour ; introd. by Linda Stirling. — New York : A & W Publishers, c1977.
248 p. : chiefly ill. ; 29 cm.
Includes index.
ISBN 0-89104-070-6 : $14.95
1. Moving-picture serials. I. Title.
PN1995.9.S3B24 791.43'5 76-49703
77 MARC

Barbour, Alan G
High roads to adventure; another collection of original serial ads. [Kew Gardens, N.Y., Screen Facts Press, 1971]
1 v. (unpaged) illus. 28 cm.
Cover title.
1. Moving-picture serials. 2. Playbills. 3. Posters. I. Title.
CLSU NUC74-122443

Barbour, Alan G
Humphrey Bogart, by Alan G. Barbour. New York, Pyramid Publications [1973]
160 p. illus. 20 cm. (A Pyramid illustrated history of the movies) $1.45
Bibliography: p. 140.
1. Bogart, Humphrey, 1899-1957.
PN2287.B48B3 791.43'028'0924 72-93667
ISBN 0-515-02930-0 MARC

Barbour, Alan G
Humphrey Bogart / by Alan G. Barbour. — London : W. H. Allen, 1974.
160 p. : ill., ports. ; 20 cm. — (Illustrated history of the movies) (A Star book) GB74-27256
"The films of Humphrey Bogart": p. 141-154.
Bibliography: p. 140.
Includes index.
ISBN 0-352-30004-3 : £0.60
1. Bogart, Humphrey, 1899-1957.
PN2287.B48B3 1974b 791.43'028'0924 75-328320
75 MARC

Barbour, Alan G
Humphrey Bogart / by Alan G. Barbour ; general editor, Ted Sennett. — New York : Galahad Books, [1974] c1973.
160 p. : ill. ; 22 cm. — (The pictorial treasury of film stars)
Originally published by Pyramid Publications, New York.
Bibliography: p. 140.
Includes index.
ISBN 0-88365-163-7 : $4.95
1. Bogart, Humphrey, 1899-1957.
PN2287.B48B3 1974 791.43'028'0924 73-90216
[B] MARC

Barbour, Alan G
John Wayne / by Alan G. Barbour ; general editor, Ted Sennett. — 1st ed. — New York : Pyramid Publications, 1974.
160 p. : ill. ; 20 cm. — (A Pyramid illustrated history of the movies)
"Films of John Wayne": p. 139-153.
Bibliography: p. 137.
Includes index.
ISBN 0-515-03481-9 : $1.75
1. Wayne, John, 1907-
PN2287.W36B37 74-1568
791.43'028'0924 [B] MARC

Barbour, Alan G
Lugosi. [Keu Gardens? N.Y., Screen Facts Press, 1971]
48 p. of illus.
Cover title.
1. Lugosi, Bela.
CaOTP NUC73-124210

Barbour, Alan G
The serials of Columbia, by Alan G. Barbour. [Kew Gardens, N. Y., Screen Facts Press, 1967]
[62] p. illus. 22 cm.
Cover title.
1. Moving-picture serials. 2. Columbia Pictures Corporation. I. Title.
PN1995.9.S3B297 791.43'05 73-151328
MARC

Barbour, Alan G
Thrill after thrill; another collection of original serial ads. [Kew Gardens, N.Y., Screen Facts Press, 1971]
1 v. (unpaged) illus. 28 cm.
Cover title.
1. Moving-picture serials. 2. Playbills. 3. Posters. I. Title.
CLSU NUC74-122093

Barbour, Alan G., joint author.
see Florescu, Radu R. N. In search of Frankenstein. Boston, New York Graphic Society, 1975.

Barbour, Alex V.
see Labor law for the general practitioner. Springfield, Illinois Institute for Continuing Legal Education, c1976.

Barbour, Alton.
Interpersonal communication: teaching strategies and resources [by] Alton Barbour [and] Alvin A. Goldberg. New York, Speech Communication Association, [1974]
ix, 85 p. illus. 23 cm.
"ERIC/RCS speech communication module."
"Prepared under the auspices of the ERIC Clearinghouse on Reading and Communication Skills."
Bibliography: p. 61-85.
1. Oral communication—Study and teaching. I. Goldberg, Alvin A., joint author. II. ERIC Clearinghouse on Reading and Communication Skills. III. Title.
P91.B3 301.14 73-91878
MARC

Barbour, Alton, joint author.
see Koneya, Mele. Louder than words ... . Columbus, Ohio, Merrill, c1976.

Barbour, Ambrose, 1822-1852. Antiquities at Idleberg. 1972
see Townsend, Dorothy Edwards, 1915-
The life and works of John Wilson Townsend... [1st ed.] Lexington, Keystone Printery, 1972.

Barbour, Anna Maynard.
Told in the Rockies; a pen picture of the West, by A. Maynard Barbour. Chicago, Rand, McNally [c1897, 1972]
335 p.
Microfilm (positive) Ann Arbor, Mich., University Microfilms, 1972. 7th title of 16. 35 mm. (American fiction series, reel 198.7)
I. Title.
KEmT NUC73-124212

Barbour, Arthur J 1926-
Painting buildings in watercolor, by Arthur J. Barbour. New York, Watson-Guptill Publications [1973]
143 p. illus. 29 cm. $15.95
Bibliography: p. 141.
1. Buildings in art. 2. Water-color painting—Technique. I. Title.
ND2310.B37 751.4'22 72-12765
ISBN 0-8230-3583-2 MARC

Barbour, Arthur J 1926-
Painting the seasons in watercolor / by Arthur J. Barbour. — New York : Watson-Guptill Publications, 1975.
159 p. : ill. (some col.) ; 29 cm.
Bibliography: p. 156.
Includes index.
ISBN 0-8320-3858-0 : $15.95
1. Water-color painting—Technique. 2. Seasons in art. I. Title.
ND2420.B35 1975 751.4'22 74-34136
74 MARC

Barbour, Beverly, 1927-
Cooking with spirits / by Beverly Barbour ; drawings by David Yeadon. — San Francisco : 101 Productions ; New York : distributed in the U.S. by Scribner, 1976.
168 p. : ill. ; 21 cm.
Includes indexes.
ISBN 0-912238-83-6 : $7.95. ISBN 0-912238-82-8 pbk. : $4.95
1. Cookery (Liquors) I. Title.
TX726.B33 641.6'2 76-6838
76 MARC

Barbour, Beverly, 1927-
see Private recipes from private clubs. Boston, Cahners Books International, c1976.

Barbour, Breese Fulton, 1921-
A comparison of two methods of teaching reading to culturally disadvantaged students, by Breese Fulton Barbour. [Syracuse, N.Y.] 1967.
xii, 172 l.
Thesis (Ed.D.)—Syracuse University.
Bibliography: leaves 165-172.
Photocopy.
1. Reading—Study and teaching (Secondary) 2. Socially handicapped children—Education (Secondary)—Onondaga County, New York. I. Title.
UU NUC73-47889

Barbour, Brian M 1943- comp.
American transcendentalism; an anthology of criticism, edited by Brian M. Barbour. Notre Dame [Ind.] University of Notre Dame Press [1973]
xiii, 302 p. 24 cm. $10.95
CONTENTS: Barbour, B. M. Introduction.—Bowers, D. Democratic vistas.—Carpenter, F. I. Transcendentalism.—Hochfield, G. An introduction to transcendentalism.—Tanner, T. Saints behold.—Miller, P. From Edwards to Emerson.—Thompson, C. John Locke and New England transcendentalism.—Wellek, R. The minor transcendentalists and German philosophy.—Joyaux, G. J. Victor Cousin and American transcendentalism.—Schlesinger, A. M., Jr. Transcendentalism and Jacksonian democracy.—Crowe, C. R. "This unnatural union of phalansteries and transcendentalists."—Goddard, H. C. Unitarianism and transcendentalism.—Hutchison, W. R. Ripley, Emerson, and the miracles question.—Albrecht, R. C. The theological response of the transcendentalists to the Civil War.—Smith, H. N. Emerson's problem of vocation.—Caponigri, A. R. Brownson and Emerson.—James, H. Emerson.—Winters, Y. The significance of The bridge, by Hart Crane.—Bibliography (p. 289-297)
1. American literature—19th century—History and criticism. 2. Transcendentalism (New England) I. Title.
PS217.T7B3 141'.3 72-12640
ISBN 0-268-00492-7; 0-268-00494-3 (pbk.) MARC

Barbour, Douglas, 1940-
He & she & / by Douglas Barbour. — Ottawa : Golden Dog Press, 1974.
28 p. ; 18 cm. C***
Poems.
ISBN 0-919614-09-4
I. Title.
PR9199.3.B37H4 811'.5'4 75-301126
MARC

Barbour, Douglas, 1940-
A poem as long as the highway. Kingston, Ont., Quarry Press [c1971]
[32] p. 23 cm. $2.00 C 71-5215
"Most of the sequence, A poem as long as the highway, appeared originally on CBC Anthology."
I. Title.
PR6052.A6P6 811'.5'4 72-197242
ICU RPB CaBVaU MARC
CaAEU NBuU CaOTU

Barbour, Douglas, 1940-
Songbook. Vancouver, Talonbooks, 1973.
100 p. 23 cm. $4.00 C 74-671-1
Poems.
I. Title.
PR9199.3.B37S6 811'.5'4 74-181319
MARC

Barbour, Douglas, 1940–
White. [Fredericton, N. B., Fiddlehead Poetry Books, 1972]
68 p. 22 cm. C***
Limited edition of 500 copies.
Poems.
I. Title.
PR9199.3.B37W5 811'.5'4 74-189313
ISBN 0-919197-1-9 MARC

Barbour, Floyd B
La revuelta del poder negro. Barcelona, Ed. Anagrama [1969?]
292 p. (Colección Documentos, 3)
Original title: The black power revolt.
1. Negroes—Civil rights—Addresses, essays, lectures. I. Title.
NcU NUC73-46841

Barbour, Frances M
A concordance to the sayings in Franklin's Poor Richard, by Frances M. Barbour. Detroit, Gale Research Co. [c1974]
vii, 245 p. 22 cm.
Bibliography: p. 245.
1. Franklin, Benjamin, 1706-1790. Poor Richard—Concordances. I. Franklin, Benjamin, 1706-1790. Poor Richard. II. Title.
PS749.B3 818'.1'07 73-20460
ISBN 0-8013-1009-0 73 MARC

Barbour, G Jeffrey, 1944-
American utility corporations: economic growth and change in the sector, 1896-1905, by G. Jeffrey Barbour. [Tallahassee, Fla.] c1973.
vii, 266 l. tables.
Thesis (Ph.D.)—Florida State University.
Bibliography: leaves 257-264.
Vita.
1. Dissertations, Academic—F.S.U.—Economics. 2. Public utilities—United States. I. Title.
FTaSU NUC75-21232

Barbour, G Jeffrey, 1944-
American utility corporations: economic growth and change in the sector, 1896-1905. [n.p., c1973]
1 reel. 35 mm.
Thesis (Ph.D.)—Florida State University.
Microfilm of typescript. Ann Arbor, Mich., University Microfilms [1973]
1. Public utilities—U.S.—Hist. I. Title.
WHi NUC76-37800

Barbour, George Brown, 1890-
In China when ... [by] George B. Barbour. Cincinnati, Ohio, University Publications, University of Cincinnati [1975]
254 p. illus., map. 22 cm.
I. Title.
NNUT NUC77-87313

Barbour, Henry Ogden
see Preparing teachers and instructional materials for the food service occupations. East Lansing, Michigan State University, 1966.

Barbour, Hugh, comp.
Early Quaker writings, 1650–1700. Edited by Hugh Barbour and Arthur O. Roberts. Grand Rapids, Eerdmans [1973]
622 p. 24 cm. $9.95
Includes bibliographical references.
1. Friends, Society of—Collected works. I. Roberts, Arthur O., joint comp. II. Title.
BX7615.B34 289.6'08 72-93617
ISBN 0-8028-3423-X MARC

Barbour, Hugh.
"The lamb's war;" the religious and social impact of early Quakerism. [n.p., 195-?]
129 l. maps. 29 cm.
"Much of the material in this book has appeared in a thesis completed in 1952, entitled 'The early Quaker outlook upon 'The World' & society, 1647-1672.' "
Typescript (carbon copy)
Bibliographical footnotes.
1. Friends, Society of. Gt. Brit. 2. Puritans—England. 3. Friends, Society of—Hist. 4. Church and social problems. I. Title.
CtY-D NUC75-110195

Barbour, Hugh.
Margaret Fell speaking / Hugh Barbour. — [Wallingford, Pa. : Pendle Hill Publications], 1976.
32 p. ; 20 cm. — (Pendle Hill pamphlet ; 206 ISSN 0031-4250)
Includes bibliographical references.
ISBN 0-87574-206-8 : $0.95
1. Fox, Margaret Askew Fell, 1614-1702. I. Fox, Margaret Askew Fell, 1614-1702. Margaret Fell speaking. 1976. II. Title.
BX7795.F75B37 289.6'092'4 76-4224
76 MARC

Barbour, Ian G
Issues in science and religion. New York, Harper and Row, 1971.
x, 470 p. 21 cm. (Harper torchbook)
"Originally published in 1966 by Prentice-Hall, Inc."
Includes bibliographical references.
OCU NUC76-37799

Barbour, Ian G
Myths, models and paradigms; the nature of scientific and religious language [by] Ian G. Barbour. London, S. C. M. Press, 1974.
vii, 198 p. 23 cm. £2.95 GB 74-10060
Includes index.
1. Religion and science—1946– I. Title.
BL240.2.B36 1974b 200'.1 74-180742
ISBN 0-334-01037-3 MARC

Barbour, Ian G
Myths, models, and paradigms; a comparative study in science and religion [by] Ian G. Barbour. [1st ed.] New York, Harper & Row [1974]
vi, 198 p. 21 cm. $6.95
Includes bibliographical references.
1. Religion and science—1946– I. Title.
BL240.2.B36 1974 200'.1 73-18698
MARC

Barbour, Ian G comp.
Western man and environmental ethics; attitudes toward nature and technology. Edited by Ian G. Barbour. Reading, Mass., Addison-Wesley Pub. Co. [1973]
276 p. 21 cm. (Addison-Wesley series in history)
Includes bibliographical references.
1. Human ecology—Moral and religious aspects. 2. Technology and civilization. I. Title.
GF80.B37 301.31'08 72-1936
MARC

Barbour, Ian G.
see Finite resources and the human future. Minneapolis, Augsburg Pub. House, c1976.

Barbour, James F
The chemical conversion of solid wastes to useful products by James F. Barbour, Robert R. Groner, and Virgil H. Freed. Cincinnati, National Environmental Research Center, Office of Research and Development, U.S. Environmental Protection Agency; Springfield, Va., distributed by National Technical Information Service, 1974.
167 p. ill.
1. Waste products. 2. Chemical processes. 3. Recycling (Waste, etc.) I. Groner, Robert R. II. Freed, Virgil H. III. Title.
ViBlbV NUC76-24392

Barbour, Jane.
Adire cloth in Nigeria; the preparation and dyeing of indigo patterned cloths among the Yoruba. By Nancy Stanfield [and others. Edited by Jane Barbour & Doig Simmonds. Ibadan] Institute of African Studies, University of Ibadan, 1971.
104 p. illus.
1. Adire cloth. 2. Indigo. 3. Textile industry and trade—Nigeria. I. Simmonds, Doig. II. Title.
InU NNC NUC73-32643

Barbour, Jane
see Nwanwene, Omorogbe. The progress of Nigerian public administration... 2d ed. [Ibadan] Institute of Administration, University of Ife, Nigeria, 1970.

Barbour, John, d. 1395.
Selections from Barbour's Bruce. Books I-IX, with the introd., notes and glossary, edited by Walter W. Skeat. Millwood, N.Y., Kraus Reprint Co., 1973.
ciii, 767 p. (Early English Text Society. Extra series [no.] 80a)
1. Robert I, King of Scotland, 1274-1329. 2. Scotland—Hist.—Robert I, 1306-1329—Sources. I. Skeat, Walter William, 1835-1912, ed. II. Title. III. Series.
CU-SB ViBlbV NUC74-127157

Barbour, Kenneth Michael, ed.
Essays on African population / edited by K. M. Barbour and R. M. Prothero. — Westport, Conn. : Greenwood Press, 1975, c1961.
x, 336 p. : ill. ; 22 cm.
Reprint of the ed. published by Routledge & K. Paul, London.
Includes bibliographies and index.
ISBN 0-8371-8399-5
1. Africa—Population. I. Prothero, R. Mansell, joint ed. II. Title.
[HB3661.B3 1975] 301.32'9'6 75-26210
75 MARC

Barbour, Kenneth Michael
see Prothero, R Mansell. A geography of Africa... [Rev. ed.] London, Boston, Routledge & Kegan Paul [1973]

Barbour, Lucius Barnes, 1878-1934.
Families of early Hartford, Connecticut / Lucius Barnes Barbour. — Baltimore : Genealogical Pub. Co., 1977.
736 p. ; 24 cm.
Includes index.
ISBN 0-8063-0764-1
1. Hartford—Genealogy. I. Title.
F104.H3B37 1977 929'.3746'3 77-71625
77 MARC

Barbour, Maureen
see The West Coast wolf study... [Vancouver, B.C., 1973]

Barbour, Michael G
Botany : a laboratory manual / Michael G. Barbour, Bruce A. Bonner, Gary J. Breckon. -- 5th ed. -- [New York] : Wiley, 1975.
viii, 263 p. : ill. ; 28 cm.
"A laboratory manual to accompany Botany, an introduction to plant biology, fifth edition [by] Weier, Stocking [and] Barbour."
Earlier ed. by T.E. Weier, R. Stocking and J.M. Tucker.
Includes index.
ISBN 0-471-04800-3.
1. Botany--Laboratory manuals. I. Bonner, Bruce Albert, 1929- II. Breckon, Gary J. III. Title.
CU-A NUC77-85279

Barbour, Michael G
see Coastal ecology: Bodega Head. Berkeley, Univ. of California Press [c1973]

Barbour, Michael G.
see Terrestrial vegetation of California. New York, Wiley, c1977.

Barbour, Michael G., joint author
see Weier, Thomas Elliot, 1903-
Botany, an introduction to plant biology. 5th ed. New York, Wiley [1974]

Barbour, Nevill, 1895- A survey of North West Africa (the Maghrib).
see Knapp, Wilfrid. North West Africa ... 3d ed. Oxford, Oxford University Press, 1977.

Barbour, Nita Hale, 1931-
Relationship of change in child language to nursery school climate as determined by teacher verbal behavior. [College Park, Md., c1974] 1973.
202 p. 29 cm.
Thesis—University of Maryland.
Vita.
Includes bibliography.
1. Children—Language. 2. Education of children. I. Title.
MdU NUC76-24628

Barbour, Robert Alfred
see Preliminary report on the development of a method for the solidification of process concentrates... Pelindaba, 1965.

Barbour, Robert D.
see Top of Alabama Regional Council of Governments. TARCOG housing study, phase II. [Huntsville, Alabama, 1971]

Barbour, Robert Stewart.
Traditio-historical criticism of the Gospels: some comments on current methods [by] R. S. Barbour. London, S. P. C. K., 1972.
[5], 54 p. 22 cm. (Studies in creative criticism, 4) B 72-28312
Includes bibliographical references.
1. Jesus Christ—Historicity. 2. Bible. N. T. Gospels—Criticism, interpretation, etc. I. Title. II. Series.
BT303.2.B24 226'.06 73-157117
ISBN 0-281-02676-9 MARC

Barbour, Robert Stewart.
What is the Church for? [By] R. S. Barbour. Aberdeen, R. S. Barbour, 1973.
76 p. 21 cm. £0.50 GB 74-05466
1. Mission of the church. I. Title.
BV601.8.B37 260 74-165753
ISBN 0-9503201-0-2 MARC

Barbour, Roger William, 1919–
Mammals of Kentucky / Roger W. Barbour & Wayne H. Davis. — Lexington : University Press of Kentucky, [1974]
x, 321 p., 16 leaves of plates : ill. (some col.) ; 23 cm. — (Kentucky nature studies ; 5)
Bibliography: p. 310-[318]
Includes index.
ISBN 0-8131-1314-8 : $14.95
1. Mammals—Kentucky. I. Davis, Wayne Harry, 1930– joint author. II. Title. III. Series.
QL719.K4B33 599'.09'769 74-7870
MARC

Barbour, Roger William, 1919- joint author
see Ernst, Carl H Turtles of the United States. [Lexington] The Univ. Press of Kentucky [c1972]

Barbour, Roger William, 1919-
see Kentucky birds... [Lexington, Ky.] Univ. Press of Kentucky [1973]

Barbour, Roger William, 1919- illus.
see Wharton, Mary E 1912- Trees & shrubs of Kentucky. [Lexington] Univ. Press of Kentucky [1973]

Barbour, Ruth P
Cruise of the Snap Dragon / by Ruth P. Barbour. — Winston-Salem, N.C. : J. F. Blair, c1976.
vii, 211 p. ; 22 cm.
Bibliography: p. 209-211.
ISBN 0-910244-88-X : $8.95
1. Burns, Otway, 1775-1850—Fiction. I. Title.
PZ4.B237 Cr 813'.5'4 76-40443
[PS3552.A596] 76 MARC

Barbour, Thomas DeForest.
The attitudes of teachers toward selected dimensions of educational administration relative to perceived rule structure. [Iowa City, c1972]
xxxi, 416 l. tables. 28 cm.
Thesis (Ph.D.)—University of Iowa.
1. School management and organization. 2. School personnel management. 3. Attitude (Psychology)—Testing. I. Title.
IaU NUC73-32637

Barbour, Wendell A.
see Illinois. University at Urbana-Champaign. Library. Newspaper Library microfilm holdings list. [2d ed. Urbana? 1970?]

Barbour, Willard Titus.
The history of contract in early English equity, by W. T. Barbour. The abbey of Saint-Bertin and its neighborhood, 900–1350, by G. W. Coopland. New York, Octagon Books, 1974.
vii, 237, 166 p. illus. 23 cm.
Reprint of the 1914 editions published by Clarendon Press, Oxford, which were issued as v. 4, no. 7-8, of Oxford studies in social and legal history.
Includes bibliographical references.
1. Contracts—Great Britain. 2. Equity—Great Britain. 3. Saint-Omer, France. Saint-Bertin (Benedictine abbey) 4. Land tenure—France—History. 5. Peasantry—France. I. Coopland, George William, 1896– The abbey of St. Bertin and its neighbourhood, 900–1350. 1974. II. Title. III. Title: The abbey of Saint-Bertin and its neighbourhood, 900–1350. IV. Series: Oxford studies in social and legal history, v. 4, no. 7-8.
KD1554.Z9B37 1974 346'.42'02 73-22303
ISBN 0-374-96163-8 MARC

Barbour-Cooper & Associates, Asheville, N. C.
Land use plan. Prepared by Barbour-Cooper and Associates. Spartanburg, City Planning Commission, 1968.
69 p. (HUD 701 report)
1. Land use—Spartanburg, S. C. I. Spartanburg, S. C. City Planning Commission.
DHUD NUC74-51907

Barbour-Cooper & Associates, Asheville, N. C.
Neighborhood analysis study. Prepared by Barbour-Cooper and Associates. Spartanburg, City Planning Commission, 1968.
130 p. (HUD 701 report)
1. City planning—Spartanburg, S. C. I. Spartanburg, S. C. City Planning Commission.
DHUD NUC74-51906

Barbour-Cooper & Associates, Asheville, N.C.
Statistical supplement to The population and economy of Sumter County, South Carolina. Prepared For: The Sumter County Planning Board. [n.p.] 1968.
44 l. 28 cm.
1. Sumter County, S.C.—Population—Statistics. 2. Sumter County, S.C.—Economic conditions. I. Sumter Co., S.C. Planning Board.
ScU NUC74-62398

Barbourville, Ky. City Planning Commission
see Booker (R. W.) & Associates. Planning, 1969. Barbourville, Ky., 1969.

Barbov, Toma Stefanov.
(Organizatsiia na upravlenieto na zhelezopŭtniia transport v NR Bŭlgariia)
Организация на управлението на железопътния транспорт в НР България : [ръководство] / Тома Ст. Барбов, Илия Д. Ламбев. — 1. изд. — София : Техника, 1976.
254 p. ; 22 cm. Bu 76-402
At head of title: Ministerstvo na transporta. DSO "Bŭlgarski dŭrzhavni zheleznitsi."
Bibliography: p. 254.
1.50 lv
1. Railroads—Bulgaria—Management. I. Lambev, Iliia Dimitrov, joint author. II. Title.
TF507.B37 76-528562

Barbov, Toma Stefanov.
(Transportniiat faktor i razpolozhenieto na proizvoditelnite sili v NR Bŭlgariia)
Транспортният фактор и разположението на производителните сили в НР България. (Отг. ред. Иван Захариев). [Изследване]. София, БАН, 1974.
176 p. with tables, 1 l. of tables. 19.5 cm. 1.22 lv Bu 74-356
At head of title: Българска академия на науките. Комисия по изучаване на производителните сили. Тома Барбов.
Added t. p.: Le facteur transport et l'aménagement du territoire en République Populaire de Bulgarie.
Summary in Russian and French.
Bibliography: p. 168-169.
1. Transportation — Bulgaria. 2. Industries, Location of — Bulgaria. I. Title. II. Title: Le facteur transport et l'aménagement du territoire en République Populaire de Bulgarie.
HE265.B38 74-321520

Barboza, Carlos.
Grabados de Carlos Barboza. San José, Editorial Costa Rica, 1972.
13 p. 24 plates. 28 cm.
I. Title.
TxU NUC75-29378

Barboza, Joe.
Barboza / Joe Barboza, with Hank Messick. -- New York : Dell Pub. Co., 1975.
204 p.
1. Barboza, Joe, 1932- . 2. Crime and criminals--Biography. I. Title.
WHi NUC77-85833

Barboza, Mário Gibson.
A cartografia política do Barão do Rio-Branco. [Brasília?, Ministério das Relações Exteriores, Seção de Publicações, 1970]
[33] p. maps. 31 cm.
"Conferência pronunciada na Sociedade Brasileira de Geografia, no Rio de Janeiro, em 4 de junho de 1970, por Sua Excelência o Senhor Ministro de Estado, Embaixador Mario Gibson Barboza."
1. Rio Branco, José Maria da Silva Paranhos, barão do, 1845–1912. 2. Brazil—Boundaries. I. Title.
F2537.R5733 74-208679

Barboza, Onédia Célia de Carvalho.
Byron no Brasil, traduções / Onédia Célia de Carvalho Barbosa. — S[ão] Paulo : Editora Ática, 1975.
284 p. ; 21 cm. — (Ensaios ; 12)
Bibliography: p. [277]-284.
1. Byron, George Gordon Noël Byron, Baron, 1788-1824—Translations, Portuguese. 2. Byron, George Gordon Noël Byron, Baron, 1788-1824—Influence. 3. Brazilian literature—19th century—History and criticism. I. Title.
PR4376.B28 75-512810
75 MARC

Barboza de Araújo, Aloísio
see
Araújo, Aloísio Barbosa de.

Barboza de la Torre, Pedro A
Trascendencia continental de la batalla de Ayacucho. Caracas, Sociedad Bolivariana de Venezuela, 1969.
30 p.
Cover title.
1. Ayacucho, Battle of, 1824—Addresses, essays, lectures. I. Title.
CLU NUC76-72716

Barboza de Oliveira, Tarquínio J
see
Oliveira, Tarquínio J B de.

Barbrack, Christopher R
Educational intervention in the home and paraprofessional career development: a first generation mother study. Nashville, John F. Kennedy Center for Research on Education and Human Development, 1970.
34 p. 28 cm. (Demonstration and Research Center for Early Education. DARCEE papers and reports, v. 4, no. 3)
I. Title.
TNJ-P NUC74-15781

Barbrack, Christopher R
The effect of three home visiting strategies upon measures of children's academic aptitude and maternal teaching behaviors. Nashville, John F. Kennedy Center for Research on Education and Human Development, 1970.
79 p. 28 cm. (Demonstration and Research Center for Early Education. DARCEE papers and reports, v. 4, no. 1)
TNJ-P NUC74-15780

Barbrack, Christopher R
A study of the developmental effect of rehearsal strategies upon various aspects of children's free recall ability. [Bloomington, Ind.] 1975.
240 p. illus.
Thesis (Ph. D.)--Indiana University.
Vita.
InU NUC77-87281

Barbree, Jay, joint author
see Caidin, Martin, 1927- Bicycles in war. New York: Hawthorn Books [1974]

Barbrook, Alec.
God save the Commonwealth; an electoral history of Massachusetts. Amherst, University of Massachusetts Press, 1973.
ix, 220 p. 23 cm. $12.50
Includes bibliographical references.
1. Elections—Massachusetts—History. I. Title.
JK3195.B37 329'.023'744 72-77572
MARC

Barbrook, Alec.
Patterns of political behaviour / Alec Barbrook. — London : Robertson, 1975.
vii, 209 p. ; 23 cm. GB75-13982
Includes bibliographical references and index.
ISBN 0-85520-051-0 : £4.50. ISBN 0-85520-050-2 pbk.
1. Political sociology. I. Title.
JA76.B33 301.5'92 75-324115
75 MARC

Barbrow, L E
What about metric. Washington, 1973.
16 p. illus. 26 cm. (U.S. National Bureau of Standards. NBS consumer information series, no. 7)
1. Metric system—United States. I. Title. II. Series.
AAP NUC74-151330

Barbrow, Louis E
see Barbrow, L E

Barbry, Francois Régis
see Sullerot, Evelyne. Temps libre, mille choses à faire. Paris, Éditions Fleurus, 1970.

Barbu, Ana.
Nisipuri. (Prologul, trei capitole și addenda). ₍Coperta: Micu Veniamin₎. București, Editura Eminescu, 1972.
156 p. 19 cm. lei 3.75 R 72-3673
I. Title.
PC840.12.A68N56 73-302688

Barbu, Constantin.
Delapidarea și furtul în paguba avutului obștesc, ₍de₎ Constantin Barbu. București, Editura științifică, 1973.
176 p. 20 cm. (Biblioteca juridică a cetățeanului) R 74-617
Includes bibliographical references.
lei 3.75
1. Embezzlement—Romania. 2. Larceny—Romania. I. Title.
75-542945

Barbu, Eugen, 1924–
Caietele Princepelui. Jurnal de creație. ₍Prezentare grafică de François Pamfil₎. Cluj, „Dacia," 1972–
v. with illus. 24 cm. lei 16.00 (v. 1) R 73-120 (v. 1)
I. Title.
PC840.12.A7C3 73-344100

Barbu, Eugen, 1924–
Cu o torță alergînd în fața nopții. ₍Reportaje₎. București, Editura Eminescu, 1972.
320 p. 20 cm. lei 9.25 R 73-1137
1. Romania—Description and travel—1945– I. Title.
DR210.B37 73-341016

Barbu, Eugen, 1924–
Facerea lumii; roman. ₍București₎ Editura pentru Literatură, 1964.
469 p. 20 cm.
I. Title.
PC840.12.A7F3 1964 74-232043

Barbu, Eugen, 1924-
Facerea lumii; roman. 2. ed. București, Editura Eminescu, 1971.
422 p. 20 cm.
I. Title.
NNC NUC76-38109

Barbu, Eugen, 1924–
Facerea lumii. Roman. Prefață și tabel cronologic de Liviu Călin. ₍Ilustrația copertei: Florica Petrache Cercel₎. București, „Minerva," 1973.
2 v. 17 cm. (Biblioteca pentru toți, 768–769) lei 10.00 R 74-718
I. Title.
PC840.12.A7F3 74-340128

Barbu, Eugen, 1924-
Foamea de spațiu; note de drum. ₍Coperta: A Perussi. București₎ Editura pentru Literatură, 1969.
293 p. 20 cm.
I. Title.
LU NUC73-124304

Barbu, Eugen, 1924–
Incognito : ciné-roman / Eugen Barbu ; ₍coperta de Cristina Maria Angelescu₎. — ₍București₎ : "Albatros," 1975–
v. ; 21 cm. R 76-341 (v. 1)
lei 13.00 (v. 1)
1. Romania—History—1914–1944—Fiction. I. Title.
PC840.12.A7 I 5 76-519523

Barbu, Eugen, 1924-
Jurnal in China / Eugen Barbu. — București : Editura Eminescu, 1970.
261 p. ; 20 cm.
1. Barbu, Eugen, 1924- —Journeys—China. 2. China—Description and travel—1949- 3. Authors, Romanian—Biography. I. Title.
PC840.12.A7Z52 76-477377
76 MARC

Barbu, Eugen, 1924–
Miresele : nuvele / Eugen Barbu ; ₍coperta, Damian Petrescu₎. — București : "Minerva," 1975.
487 p. ; 20 cm.
lei 16.00
I. Title.
PC840.12.A7M5 76-503151

Barbu, Eugen, 1924–
O istorie polemică și antologică a literaturii române de la origini pînă în prezent / Eugen Barbu. — ₍București₎ : Editura Eminescu, 1975–
v. ; 24 cm. R 76-1903 (v.1)
Bibliography: v. 1, p. ₍453₎-472.
CONTENTS: ₍1₎ Poezia română contemporană.
lei 32.00 (v. 1)
1. Romanian literature—History and criticism. I. Title.
PC801.B3 76-524847

Barbu, Eugen, 1924-
Princepele; roman. 2. ed. Cluj, Editura Dacia, 1971.
430 p. 17 cm.
I. Title.
NNC NUC75-29395

Barbu, Eugen, 1924–
Princepele. Roman. ₍din epoca fanarioților₎. Ediția a 3-a. ₍Ilustrația copertei: Ion Nedelcu₎. București, Editura Eminescu, 1972.
335 p. 20 cm. (Romane de ieri și de azi) lei 12.00 R 72-1591
1. Romania—History—To 1711—Fiction. I. Title.
PC840.12.A7P65 74-345282

Barbu, Eugen, 1924–
Principele : ₍roman₎ / Eugen Barbu ; ₍ilustrațiile, Mihu Vulcănescu₎. — București : Editura Eminescu, 1974.
338 p., ₍18₎ leaves of plates : col. ill. ; 27 cm. R 74-4063
lei 65.00
1. Romania—History—To 1711—Fiction. I. Title.
PC840.12.A7P65 1974 75-576720

Barbu, Eugen, 1924–
Prînzul de duminică. ₍București₎ Editura Pentru Literatură, 1962.
364 p. 21 cm.
CONTENTS: Prînzul de duminică.—Patru pești.—Bufet expres.—Intr-un loc de trecere.—Păunii.—Călătorie cu autocarul.—Oul.—Bătrînii.—Franzeluță.—Morcovii.—Înmormîntarea lui Dumitru Alexandru.—Domnișoara Aurica.—Pe ploaie.—Un pumn de caise.—Sfîrșitul vacanței.—O canistră cu apă.—De-a viața și de-a moartea.
I. Title.
PC840.12.A7P7 74-229210

Barbu, Eugen, 1924–
Războiul undelor : ciné-roman / Eugen Barbu, Nicolae Paul Mihail ; ₍ilustrația copertei, Ion Olaru₎. — București : "Albatros," 1974.
528 p. ; 20 cm. — (Cutezătorii) R 74-3414
lei 16.00
I. Mihail, Nicolae Paul, joint author. II. Title.
PC840.12.A7R3 75-576289

Barbu, Eugen, 1924–
Să nu-ți faci prăvălie cu scară : piesă în trei acte / Eugen Barbu ; ₍prezentare grafică, Armand Crintea₎. — ₍București₎ : Editura Eminescu, 1975.
118 p. : port. ; 19 cm. — (Colecția Rampa ; 19) R 75-4739
lei 5.50
I. Title.
PC840.12.A7S2 76-502956

Barbu, Filaret, 1903-
Partitura unei vieți : memorii / Filaret Barbu ; consemnate de Ladislau Füredi ; ₍coperta, Eugenia Dumitrașcu₎. — ₍Timișoara₎ : "Facla", 1976.
135 p., ₍8₎ leaves of plates : ill., ports. ; 22 cm. R76-3445
Autobiographical.
lei11.00
1. Barbu, Filaret, 1903- 2. Singers—Romania—Biography. I. Title.
ML420.B16A3 784'.092'4 76-485415
•76 MARC

Barbu, Gabriel.
Arta vindecării în Bucureștii de odinioară ₍de₎ G. Barbu. București, Editura Științifică, 1967.
301 p. illus., facsims., ports. 21 cm.
13.00
Bibliographical footnotes.
1. Medicine—Romania—Bucharest—History. 2. Bucharest—History. I. Title.
R575.R73B82 77-505232

Barbu, Ion.
Volumul, structura și eficiența investițiilor / Ion Barbu. — București : Editura politică, 1974.
62 p. ; 19 cm. — (Colecția Făurirea societății socialiste multilateral dezvoltate) (Seria Economie) R 75-3777
At head of title: Academia "Ștefan Gheorghiu" pentru Pregătirea Cadrelor de Conducere a Activității de Partid, Social-Politice, Economice, și Organizației de Stat.
Includes bibliographical references.
lei 1.75
1. Investments—Romania. I. Title.
HG5692.B3 75-408676

Barbu, Ion, 1895-1961
see
Barbilian, Dan, 1895-1961.

Barbu, Mia, comp.
150 ₍i.e. O suta cincizeci₎ romante. Culegere de Mia Barbu. Cu o prefata de Victor Eftimiu. Bucuresti, Editura Muzicala a Uniunii Compozitorilor, 1971.
252 p. music. 21 cm.
1. Rumanian poetry (Collections) I. Title.
CaQMM NUC75-29401

Barbu, N
M. Millo / ₍N. Barbu₎. — ₍București₎ : Meridiane, 1963.
27 p., ₍16₎ leaves of plates : ill., ports. ; 23 cm.
Includes bibliographical references.
1. Millo, Matei, 1814-1896. 2. Actors—Romania—Biography.
PN2848.M5B37 77-456375
77 MARC

Barbu, Nicolae.
Obcinele Bucovinei : ₍monografie₎ / Nicolae Barbu ; ₍coperta de Vasile Socoliuc₎. — București : Editura Științifică și Enciclopedică, 1976.
315, ₍4₎ p., ₍8₎ leaves of plates : ill., maps ; 21 cm. R76-4178
Bibliography: p. 303-₍316₎
lei15.00
1. Physical geography—Bukowina. 2. Bukowina—Description and travel. I. Title.
GB235.8.B8B37 77-456329
•77 MARC

Barbu, Nicolae I 1899–
Noi și clasicii : ₍studii literare₎ / N. Barbu ; ₍coperta, Petre Hagiu₎. — ₍București₎ : Editura Eminescu, 1975.
337 p. ; 19 cm. R 76-1904
Includes bibliographical references.
lei 8.00
1. Romanian literature—History and criticism. I. Title.
PC808.B298 76-525347

Barbu, Nicolae I 1899-
Les procédés de la peinture des caractères et la vérité historique dans les Biographies de Plutarque / Nicolae I. Barbu. — Ristampa anastatica. — Roma : L'Erma di Bretschneider, 1976.
v, 242 p. ; 22 cm. — (Studia philologica ; 19) It77-Jan
Reprint of the 1934 ed. published by Nizet & Bastard, Paris.
Bibliography: p. ₍iii₎-v.
1. Plutarchus. Vitae parallelae. I. Title. II. Series.
PA4385.B37 1976 77-482558
•77 MARC

Barbu, Nicolae I., 1899-
see Istoria literaturii latine. Ediția a 2-a. București, Editura didactică si pedagogică, 1972-

Barbu, Noel.
Revolucionarios de tres mundos [por] Noel Barbu, María Elena Vela, Carlos M. Gutiérrez. [Buenos Aires] Centro Editor de América Latina [c1971]
158 p. ports. 18 cm. (Biblioteca fundamental del hombre moderno, 35)
1. Ho-chi-Minh, Pres. Democratic Republic of Vietnam, 1894?-1969. 2. Lumumba, Patrice, 1925-1961. 3. Guevara, Ernesto, 1928-1967. I. Vela, María Elena, joint author. II. Gutiérrez, Carlos María, 1926- joint author. III. Title.
CtY NUC75-108361

Barbu, Vasile.
Tomis, orașul poetului exilat. [Monografie. Coperta: Teodor Bogoi]. București, „Albatros," 1972.
123 p., 14 l. of plates. 21 cm. lei 9.00 R 73-443
Bibliography: p. 119-[120]
1. Constanța, Romania (City)—History. 2. Constanța, Romania (City)—Antiquities. I. Title.
DR281.C6B38 73-319903

Barbu, Viorel.
Convexitate și optimizare în spații Banach / V. Barbu, Th. Precupanu. — București : Editura Academiei Republicii Socialiste România, 1975.
251 p. : ill. ; 24 cm. — (Analiză modernă și aplicații) R 75-4677
Summary in English.
Table of contents also in English.
Bibliography: p. [243]-251.
lei 14.00
1. Banach spaces. 2. Hilbert space. 3. Convex functions. 4. Convex programming. I. Precupanu, Theodor, joint author. II. Title.
QA322.2.B35 76-513714

Barbu, Viorel.
Nonlinear semigroups and differential equations in Banach spaces. -- București : Editura Academiei, 1976.
352 p. ; 25 cm.
1. Differential equations, Nonlinear. 2. Semigroups. 3. Banach spaces. I. Title.
NNF NUC77-85830

Barbu, Viorel.
Semigrupuri de contracții neliniare în spații Banach. București, Editura Academiei Republicii Socialiste România, 1974.
342 p. 24 cm. (Analiză modernă și aplicații) lei 16.50 R***
Summary in English.
Table of contents in Romanian and English.
Bibliography: p. [335]-342.
1. Banach spaces. 2. Semigroups. 3. Operator theory. I. Title.
QA322.2.B37 74-335509

Barbu, Zevedei.
Problems of historical psychology. New York, Grove Press [1960]
222 p. 21 cm. (Evergreen original, E-310)
1. Psychohistory. 2. National characteristics, English. I. Title.
D16.B15 1960 155 61-8013

Barbu, Zevedei.
Problems of historical psychology / by Zevedei Barbu. — Westport, Conn. : Greenwood Press, 1976, c1960.
x, 222 p. ; 22 cm.
Reprint of the ed. published by Grove Press, New York, which was issued as Evergreen original no. E-310.
Includes bibliographical references and index.
ISBN 0-8371-8476-2
1. Psychohistory. 2. National characteristics, English. I. Title.
[DNLM: 1. Civilization—History. 2. Psychology—History. BF57 B241p 1960a]
[D16.B15 1976] 301.24'7 75-28659
76 MARC

Barbu, Zevedei.
Psicología de la democracia y de la dictadura. [Versión castellana: Noemí Rosenblat] Buenos Aires, Editorial Paidós [1972]
278 p. 23 cm. (Biblioteca de psicología social y sociología, 19)
Translation of: Democracy and dictatorship, their psychology and patterns of life.
Includes bibliographical references.
1. Democracy. 2. Totalitarianism. 3. Communism. I. Title.
CSt-H NUC76-74231

Barbucci, Rolando.
see Summer School on Stability Constants, Bivigliano, Italy, 1974. Proceedings of the Summer School on Stability Constants ... Firenze, Scuola universitaria, 1977.

Bărbuceanu, Corneliu, 1923-
Ceața [de] C. Bărbuceanu. [București] Editura pentru Literatură, 1968.
348 p.
A novel.
MH NUC76-72853

Bărbuceanu, Corneliu, 1923-
Expresul de noapte : roman / C. Bărbuceanu ; [coperta de N. Claudiu]. — București : Editura Eminescu, 1974.
290 p. ; 20 cm. R 75-4080
"Ediție revăzută și adăugită a romanului 'Ceața,' 1968, E. P. L."
lei 10.75
I. Title.
PC840.12.A73E9 76-500257

Bărbuceanu, Corneliu, 1923-
Samsarul : roman / C. Bărbuceanu ; [coperta de Andrei Olsufiev]. — București : "Cartea Românească," 1975.
220 p. ; 20 cm. R 75-5169
lei 8.25
I. Title.
PC840.12.A73S3 76-519948

Barbudo, Antonio Sánchez
see Sánchez Barbudo, Antonio

Bărbuică, Nicolae.
Antiracheta. București, Editura militară, 1971.
112 p. with figs. 17 cm. (Noutăți tehnico-științifice) lei 5.50 R 71-1819
Bibliography: p. 110.
1. Antimissile missiles. I. Title.
UF880.B3 74-312014

Barbuk, Bernard.
Famous and fabulous dogs; text by Bernard Barbuk; illustrations by John Glover. London, Peter Lowe, 1973.
117 p. col. illus. 28 cm. £1.50 GB 73-16725
1. Dogs—Juvenile literature. I. Title.
QL795.D6B327 808.8'036 73-166735
ISBN 0-85654-004-8; 0-85654-008-0 (with picture boards) MARC

Bărbulescu, Aurelia.
Geologie cu elemente de pedologie. [Curs]. București, Centrul de multiplicare al Universității din București, 1973.
588 p. with figs. 24 cm. lei 18.00 R 74-1426
At head of title: Universitatea din București. Facultatea de Geologie-Geografie. Catedra de Geologie-Paleontologie.
Bibliography: p. [583]-588.
1. Geology. 2. Soil science. I. Title.
QE33.B3 74-343064

Bărbulescu, Aurelia.
Stratigrafia jurasicului din vestul Dobrogei centrale. București, Editura Academiei Republicii Socialiste România, 1974.
173 p. with figs. and maps, 4 l. of tables, 46 l. of plates. 24 cm. lei 21.00 R 74-1780
Summary in French.
Bibliography: p. [161]-173.
1. Geology, Stratigraphic—Jurassic. 2. Geology—Romania—Dobrudja. I. Title.
QE681.B35 74-337298

Bărbulescu, Aurelia.
see Roniewicz, Ewa. Les scléractiniaires du jurassique supérieur de la Dobrogea centrale, Roumanie. Warszawa, Państwowe Wydawnictwo Naukowe, 1976.

Bărbulescu, Constantin.
Știința organizării [economic aplicată]. București, Editura didactică și pedagogică, 1971.
133 p. with figs. and graphs, 6 l. of plates. 19 cm. lei 3.20 R 72-828
At head of title: C. Bărbulescu.
Part of illustrative matter in pocket.
Includes bibliographical references.
1. Production management. 2. Efficiency, Industrial. I. Title.
TS155.B266 72-356414

Bărbulescu, Constantin, joint author
see Drăgan, C M Metode noi de calcul și de urmărire... București, Consiliul National pentru Știință și Tehnologie, 1972.

Bărbulescu, Ilie, 1873-
Fonetica alfabetului cirilic în textele române din vécul XVI și XVII : în legătură cu monumentele paleo-, sîrbo-, bulgaro-, ruso- și romàno-slave, cu o introducere despre "Felurile de scriere" și "Alfabetul cirilic și ortografia slavă" la români / de Ilie Bărbulescu. — Bucuresci : Tipografia "Universitară", A. G. Brătănescu, 1904.
501 p. ; 25 cm.
Includes bibliographical references.
1. Cyrillic alphabet. 2. Church Slavic language—Writing. 3. Romanian language—Writing. I. Title.
PG92.B3 77-458433
77 MARC

Bărbulescu, Ilie, 1873-
Individualitatea limbii române și elementele slave vechi. București, Editura Casei Școalelor, 1929.
vii, 534 p. 24 cm.
Includes bibliographical references.
1. Romanian language—Foreign elements—Church Slavic. I. Title.
PC764.C5B3 76-506755

Bărbulescu, Marin, joint author
see Bartsch, Ferdinand. 100 [i. e. O sută] de ani de la inființarea Gării de Nord... [București], 1973.

Bărbulescu, Marta.
Dincolo de cercuri. [Versuri]. București, „Albatros," 1972.
104 p. 19 cm. lei 7.00 R 72-4203
I. Title.
PC840.12.A734D5 74-327947

Bărbulescu, Marta.
Ideea de înfrunzire : poeme / Marta Bărbulescu ; [coperta de Dumitru Verdeș]. — [București] : "Cartea românească", 1976.
119 p. ; 20 cm. R76-2660
lei7.25
I. Title.
PC840.12.A734I3 76-478395
*76 MARC

Bărbulescu, Mihai.
Măsură pentru o clipă : [versuri] / Mihai Bărbulescu ; [coperta de Anton Perussi]. — [București] : "Cartea Românească," 1975.
58 p. ; 20 cm. R 75-4940
lei 5.00
I. Title.
PC840.12.A7343M3 76-509038

Bărbulescu, Nicolae.
Chimie pentru muncitori [de] Bărbulescu N., Bănățeanu C. I. [și] Popescu A. București, Editura Tehnică, 1962.
554, [4] p. illus. 21 cm.
Bibliography: p. [557]
1. Chemistry. I. Bănățeanu, Ion Constantin, 1928- joint author. II. Popescu, A., joint author. III. Title.
QD33.B243 65-89434

Bărbulescu, Nicolae, profesor.
Bazele fizice ale relativității einsteiniene / Nicolae Bărbulescu. — București : Editura științifică și enciclopedică, 1975.
221 p. : ill., ports. ; 20 cm. — (Enciclopedia de buzunar) R 76-859
Includes bibliographical references and index.
lei 6.50
1. Relativity (Physics) 2. Einstein, Albert, 1879-1955. I. Title.
QC173.55.B37 76-516820

Bărbulescu, Nicolae, professor
see Fizica. București, Editura didactică și pedagogică, 1972-

Bărbulescu, Petre.
„Idee." Comedie într-un act. București, Consiliul Culturii și Educației Socialiste, Centrul de îndrumare a creatiei populare și a mișcării artistice de masă, 1972.
31 p. 17 cm. (Teatru) lei 3.10 R 72-2875
I. Title.
PC840.12.A735 I 3 72-369788

Barbulescu, Petre, prof. dr., ed.
see Colocviul Național de Pedagogie "Cercetarea Interdisciplinară a Invațamîntului," Bucharest, 1970. La recherche interdisciplinaire sur l'enseignement... Bucharest: Éditions didactiques et scientifiques, 1972.

Bărbulescu, Petre, prof. dr., ed.
see Simpozionul Pregătirea pentru Muncă, Obiect al Învățămîntului, Alexandria, Romania, 1971. Referate și comunicări prezentate la simpozionul organizat... București, 1972.

Bărbulescu, Petre, fl. 1971-
România la Societatea Națiunilor, 1929-1939 : momente și semnificații / Petre Bărbulescu ; cu un cuvînt înainte de prof. univ. dr. Aron Petric. — București : Editura politică, 1975.
442 p. ; 19 cm. R 75-4610
Summary in English, French, German, and Russian.
Includes bibliographical references and index.
lei 17.50
1. League of Nations—Romania. I. Title.
JX1975.5.R6B3 76-506123

Bărbulescu, Petre, fl. 1971- joint author
see Ionașcu, Ion. Tratatele internaționale ale României, 1345-1920 ... București : Editura științifică si enciclopedică, 1975.

Bărbulescu, Romulus, joint author
see Anania, George. Paralela-enigmă. Bucuresti, Albatros, 1973.

Barbusse, Henri, 1874-1935.
Auf zur Wahrheit! Nendeln/Liechtenstein, Kraus Reprint, 1973.
56 p. (Tribüne der Kunst und Zeit, Nr. 18/19-23)
Reprint of Berlin 1920 ed.
1. Truth. I. Title. II. Series.
CU-SB NUC76-71776

Barbusse, Henri, 1874-1935.
El fuego; diario de un pelotón [novela] La Habana, Instituto Cubano del Libro, 1973.
407 p. 18 cm. (Ediciones Huracán)
Translation of Le feu.
I. Title.
FMU NUC75-21235

Barbusse, Henri, 1874-1935.
150 [i. e. Hundertfünfzig] Millionen bauen eine neue Welt. Berlin, Neuer Deutscher Verlag, 1930.
369 p. 20 cm.
1. Russia—Description and travel—1917- I. Title.
DK27.B2715 1930 55-49025 ‡
rev

Barbusse, Henri, 1874-1935
see Henri Barbusse. [Paris, Editeurs Francais Réunis] 1969.

Barbusse, Henri, 1874-1935
see Hommage à Henri Barbusse... Choisy-le-Roi : Centre municipal d'activités culturelles, [1973]

Barbusse, Pierre.
Le port d'Anvers. Paris, La documentation francaise, 1971.
32 p. illus. 27 cm. (Notes et etudes documentaires, no. 3846)
1. Antwerp—Harbor. I. Title. II. Series: France. Direction de la documentation. Notes et etudes documentaires, no. 3846.
CSt NUC76-71990

Bărbut, Carmen, joint author
see Ionescu, Mircea, ing. Problema prevenirii și combaterii poluării în industria minieră și petrolieră. București, Ministerul Minelor, 1972.

Barbut, Jean
see L'Industrie des papiers, cartons et celluloses. Centre technique. Guide pratique pour l'application des méthodes statistiques dans l'industrie papetière. [2. éd.] Paris, 1964.

Barbut, Marc.
Mathématiques des sciences humaines ... / Marc Barbut .... — 4e éd. revue. — [Paris] : Presses universitaires de France, 1976-
v. : ill. ; 21 cm. — (Collection SUP) (Le Psychologue ; 30)
F76-16064 (v. 1)
Bibliography: v. 1, p. [13]-14.
Includes index.
CONTENTS: 1. Combinatoire et algèbre.
32.00F (v. 1)
1. Mathematics—1961- 2. Sociology—Methodology. I. Title.
QA37.2.B373 1976 510 77-550117
77 MARC

Barbut, Marc
see Bertin, Jacques, 1918- Sémiologie graphique. Paris, La Haye, Mouton [1968]

Barbut, Marc
see Bertin, Jacques, 1918- Sémiologie graphique... [2d éd.] Paris, Mouton, [1973, c1967]

Barbut, Marc
see Problemas del estructuralismo... [3. ed.] México, Siglo Veintiuno Editores [1969]

Bărbută, Margareta
see Dramaturgie românească, 1918-1944. [Bucuresti] Editura Tineretului [1969]

Barbuto, Antonio, 1936-
Le parole di Montale. Glossario del lessico poetico. Roma, Bulzoni, [1973].
154 p. 18 cm. (Bulzoni cultura paperbacks, 4) L1300 It 74-Jan
Bibliography: p. 13-15.
1. Montale, Eugenio, 1896- —Language—Glossaries, etc. I. Title.
PQ4829.O565Z49 1973 74-301554

Barbuto, Antonio, 1936-
La protesta, l'utopia, lo scacco : il Te Deum de'Calabresi di Gian Lorenzo Cardone / Antonio Baruto. — Roma : Bulzoni, [1975]
137 p. ; 21 cm. — (L'Analisi letteraria ; 13) It 75-Nov
Includes index.
L2500
1. Cardone, Gian Lorenzo, 1743-1813. Te Deum de' Calabresi. I. Cardone, Gian Lorenzo, 1743-1813. Te Deum de' Calabresi. [1975] II. Title.
PQ4684.C93T433 76-528109

Barby, Hanno von, 1942-
Verwaltungsgerichtliche Klagen auf Rechtsetzung? Unter Berücksichtigung der Allgemeinverbindlicherklärung von Tarifverträgen. Köln [1973?]
xxx, 171 p. 21 cm. GFR***
Inaug.-Diss.—Cologne.
Vita.
Bibliography: p. ix-xxvii.
1. Actions and defenses—Germany (Federal Republic, 1949-) 2. Administrative remedies—Germany (Federal Republic, 1949-) 3. Collective labor agreements—Germany (Federal Republic, 1949-) 4. Judicial review—Germany (Federal Republic, 1949-) I. Title.
73-361817

Barby, Henry, 1876-
Au pays de l'épouvante, l'Arménie martyre / Henry Barby ; avec une préf. par Georges Asmar. — Beyrouth : Édition Hamaskaïne, [1965?]
xv, 258, xxvi p., 7 leaves of plates : ill. ; 22 cm.
Bibliography: p. iii-xiii (3d group)
1. Armenian massacres, 1915-1923. 2. European War, 1914-1918—Armenia. I. Title.
DS195.5.B37 1965 947'.92 75-506302
75 MARC

Barby, Joachim von.
Der städtebauliche Bewertungsrahmen/ von Joachim v. Barby; Klaus Fischer. — Bonn: Dümmler, 1972.
36 p.: 8 ill.; 25 cm. — (Materialiensammlung Städtebau; Heft 4) DM5.00 GDB 73-A2
Bibliography: p. 33-36.
1. Cities and towns — Planning — Germany (Federal Republic, 1949-) 2. Real property—Valuation—Germany (Federal Republic, 1949-) I. Fischer, Klaus, Dr.-Ing., joint author. II. Title. III. Series.
HD1387.B375 73-310446
ISBN 3-427-77041-9

Barc-Ivan, Julius.
Železné ruky. [Vyd. 2. Bratislava] Slovenské Vydavatel'stvo krásnej literatúry, 1965.
188 p. 21 cm. (Hviezdoslavova knižnica, zv. 113) (71. zv. Slovenského radu)
I. Title.
PG5438.B32Z3 1965 72-227040

Barc
see
Bay Area Reference Center
United States. Agricultural Research Center, Beltsville, Md.
for publications by and about these bodies.
Titles and other entries beginning with this acronym are filed following this card.

Barca, Frances Erskine (Inglis) Calderón de la
see Calderón de la Barca, Frances Erskine (Inglis) 1804-1882.

Barca, Hamilcar.
America's Black dilemma / Hamilcar Barca. — 1st ed. — New York : Vantage Press, c1976.
xxxix, 220 p. : ill. ; 22 cm.
ISBN 0-533-01671-1 : $5.95
1. Afro-Americans—Social conditions—1964-1975. 2. United States—Race question. I. Title.
E185.86.B37 301.45'19'6073 76-14528
76 MARC

Barca, Luciano, 1920-
Dizionario di politica economica / Luciano Barca. — 1. ed. — Roma : Editori riuniti, 1974.
174 p. ; 19 cm. — (Universale ; 57) It 74-Dec
Bibliography: p. 173-174.
L1000
1. Economics—Dictionaries—Italian. I. Title.
HB61.B35 75-550475

Barca, Luciano, 1920-
L'Italia delle banche / Luciano Barca, Gianni Manghetti. — 1. ed. — Roma : Editori riuniti, 1976.
389 p. ; 19 cm. — (Argomenti ; 51) It76-May
Includes bibliographical references.
L2800
1. Banks and banking—Italy. 2. Banks and banking—Italy—State supervision. I. Manghetti, Gianni, joint author. II. Title.
HG3080.B37 332.1'0945 76-464591
*76 MARC

Barca, Luciano, 1920-
La lotta all'inflazione / [scritti di] Luciano Barca, Antonio Pedone, Eugenio Peggio ; introduzione di Giorgio Amendola. — Roma : Editori riuniti, 1977.
99 p. ; 19 cm. — (Il Punto ; 138) It77-May
Reports to a meeting held in Rome in 1977.
L900
1. Inflation (Finance)—Congresses. 2. Inflation (Finance)—Italy—Congresses. I. Pedone, Antonio, joint author. II. Peggio, Eugenio, joint author. III. Title.
HG229.B32 77-478199
*77 MARC

Barca, Luciano, 1920-
see I Comunisti e l'economia italiana 1944-1974... Bari: De Donato, c1975.

Barca, Luciano, 1920-
see I Problemi dell'energia in Italia. Milano, F. Angeli, [1977]

Barca, Pedro Calderón de la
see Calderón de la Barca, Pedro, 1600-1681.

Barcacel, Pedro Pablo.
Ensayos de cultivos rotativos para el control de nematodos del platano. Santiago de los Caballeros [1968]
7 p. (Instituto Superior de Agricultura. División de Investigaciones Agrícolas. Boletin, no. 11)
I. Title.
DNAL NUC73-124303

Barcalá, José Basabe
see
Basabe Barcalá, José.

Barcan, Alan.
see A Nation emerges ... South Melbourne, Vic., Macmillan, 1974.

Barcan, Alan
see Shaping our heritage... South Melbourne, Vic., Macmillan, 1973.

Barcan, Ruth Charlotte
see
Marcus, Ruth Barcan.

Barcárcel, Basilio Manuel Arrillaga y
see Arrillaga y Barcárcel, Basilio Manuel, 1791-1867.

Barcaski, Peter B., joint author
see Hill, Faith Fitch. Spaceship earth... Boston, Houghton Mifflin [1974]

Barcata, Louis, 1906-
China: la revolución cultural. [Traducción de J. Adsuar. 1. ed. Madrid] Ayma, 1968.
276 p.
1. China (People's Republic of China, 1949-)
I. Title.
ICU NUC74-126813

Barcata, Louis, 1906–
Qui Vienna. Testo di Louis Barcata, disegni di Erni Kniepert, vedute aeree di Fritz Olesko e di Alpine Luftbild, fotografie di Barbara Pflaum. Milano, Touring club italiano, [1972].
64 p. illus., plates. 27 cm. (Grandi città del mondo) It 73-Jan
1. Vienna—Description—Views. I. Touring club italiano. II. Title.
DB855.B36 914.36'13'035 73-340600

Barcella, Fausto.
L'Antike in Hegel e altri scritti marxisti / Fausto Barcella. — Urbino : Argalìa, 1975.
348 p. ; 22 cm. — (Studi filosofici) It76-Dec
Includes bibliographical references.
L4500
1. Hegel, Georg Wilhelm Friedrich, 1770-1831—Knowledge—Greece—Addresses, essays, lectures. 2. Marx, Karl, 1818-1883—Addresses, essays, lectures. I. Title.
B2949.G73B37 77-461333
•77 MARC

Barcelli S , Agustín.
Historia del sindicalismo peruano [por] Agustín Barcelli S. Lima, Editorial Hatunruna, 1971–
v. illus. 18 cm.
CONTENTS: t. 1. 1886–1932.
1. Trade-unions—Peru—History. 2. Syndicalism—Peru—History. I. Title.
HD6642.B37 74-207327

Barcellona, Francesco Scorza
see
Scorza Barcellona, Francesco.

Barcellona, Gemma Salvo
see Salvo Barcellona, Gemma.

Barcellona, Maria Donati
see Donati Barcellona, Maria.

Barcellona, Pietro.
Profili della teoria dell'errore nel negozio giuridico / Pietro Barcellona. — Milano : A. Giuffrè, 1962.
244 p. ; 26 cm. — (Pubblicazioni della Facoltà di giurisprudenza, Università di Catania ; 41)
Includes bibliographical references and index.
1. Mistake (Law)—Italy. 2. Juristic acts—Italy. I. Title. II. Series: Catania. Università. Facoltà di giurisprudenza. Pubblicazioni ; 41.
76-500619

Barcellona, Pietro.
Stato e giuristi : tra crisi e riforma / Pietro Barcellona, Giuseppe Cotturri. — Bari : De Donata, [1974]
241 p. ; 21 cm. — (Riforme e potere ; 2) It 75-Mar
Includes bibliographical references.
L2800
1. Lawyers—Italy. 2. Law and politics. I. Cotturri, Giuseppe, 1943– joint author. II. Title.
75-559225

Barcellona, Pietro.
Stato e mercato : fra monopolio e democrazia / Pietro Barcellona. — Bari : De Donato, c1976.
159 p. ; 21 cm. — (Riforme e potere ; 10) It76-Oct
Includes bibliographical references.
L2800
1. Industry and state—Italy. I. Title.
HD3616.I82B28 76-485229
•76 MARC

Barcellona, Pietro, ed.
see Scienza giuridica e analisi marxista...
[Roma] Laterza, 1973.

Barcellona, Pietro, ed.
see L'Uso alternativo del diritto.... Roma
-Bari, Laterza, 1973-

Barcellona, Roberto D
La primera muerte / Roberto D. Barcellona. — 1. ed. — Santa Fe, Argentina : Librería y Editorial Colmegna, [1975]
115 p. ; 20 cm.
Five hundred copies printed.
CONTENTS: ?Ladrón?—Dimensión.—Tosur.—Los buscadores del alma.—Cebollita.—El padre Estévez, de Laresipa.—La choza.—El accidente.—Casi la primera muerte.—La broma.—El bien y el mal.—A los cuerdos del 2.000.—El incendio.
I. Title.
PQ7798.12.A653P7 76-475466
76 MARC

Barcelloni Corte, Adriano.
La chiesa di S. [i. e. Santo] Stefano in Belluno. Notizie raccolte dall'ing. Adriano Barcelloni Corte. Belluno, Tip. Piave, 1972.
77 p., incl. plates. illus. 24 cm. It 73-June
Bibliography: p. 51.
1. Chiesa di Santo Stefano, Belluno, Italy.
NA5621.B39B37 74-329932

Barcelloni Corte, Adriano.
La famiglia Barcelloni: sua genealogia, suo palazzo del Cinquecento. Notizie raccolte dall'ing. Adriano Barcelloni-Corte ... Belluno, Tip. Piave, 1971.
61 p. illus. 24 cm. It 72-Apr
250 numb. copies. LC copy no. 115.
1. Barcelloni family. I. Title.
CS769.B33 1971 73-310440

Barcellos, Boaventura N
Informe geral sôbre a pesca no Rio Grande do Sul. Pôrto Alegre, Brasil, 1966.
120 p. illus. 24 cm.
"Editado com o patrocínio do Banco Regional do Desenvolvimento do Extremo Sul-BRDE-CODESUL."
"Tralaho... apresentado na 1.ª Reunião da Comissão Consultiva Regional de Pesca para o Atlântico Sul Ocidental (1962)"
IU NUC74-127562

Barcellos, Fernanda Augusta Vieira Ferreira.
A personalidade através do desenho : sóciodiagnósticos / Fernanda Barcellos. — [Rio de Janeiro? : s.n.], 1975.
200 p. : ill. ; 23 cm.
Cr$50.00
1. Personality assessment. 2. Drawing, Psychology of. 3. Draw-a-family test. 4. Draw-a-person test. I. Title.
BF698.4.B36 155.2'8 76-485212
76 MARC

Barcellos, Henrique de, ed.
see Centro de Ciências, Letras e Artes.
Revista do Centro de Sciencias ... Campinas, 1902-

Barcellos, Sandra Hervé Chaves.
Gôsto de vermelho; crônicas. Pôrto Alegre, Livraria do Globo, 1971.
97 p. 22 cm. Cr$10.00
I. Title.
PQ9698.12.A682G6 73-317001

Barcellos, Sandra Hervé Chaves.
Meio can.inho andado. Porto Alegre, Livraria do Globo, 1972.
106 p. 22 cm. Cr$10.00
Short stories.
I. Title.
PQ9698.12.A682M4 73-221562

Barcellos, Sandra Hervé Chaves.
[Poems]. — [Porto Alegre] : Livraria do Globo, [1974?]
[28] leaves : port. ; 27 cm.
Cr$100.00
I. Title.
PQ9698.12.A682P6 75-584034

Barcells, José María
see
Balcells, José María.

Barceló, Francisco
see
Barceló Gomila, Francisco.

Barceló, Gabriel.
El dirigente del futuro. [Madrid] Asociación para el Progreso de la Dirección (1972)
1 l., ii, 213 p. 23 cm. Sp 72-May
At head of title: Gabriel Barceló Matutano.
On spine: 101.
Includes bibliographical references.
1. Executives. 2. Management. 3. Executive ability. I. Title.
HF5500.2.B25 73-342271

Barcelo, J P
Experimental study of the hydraulic behaviour of groyne systems. Lisboa, Portugal, Laboratorio Nacional de Engenharia Civil, 1969.
26 p. (Memoria no. 350)
English, French, and Portuguese.
1. Flood control—Portugal. 2. Hydrology. I. Portugal. Laboratorio Nacional de Engenharia Civil.
DHUD NUC73-47190

Barceló, Javier Malagón
see Malagón Barceló, Javier.

Barceló, José R
Diccionario terminológico de química / José R. Barceló. — 2. ed. — Madrid : Alhambra, 1976.
xi, 774 p. : diagrs. ; 25 cm. Sp***
ISBN 8420505218
1. Chemistry—Dictionaries—Polyglot. 2. Dictionaries, Polyglot. I. Title.
QD5.B34 1976 574'.03 76-480438
76 MARC

Barceló, Julio Berenguer
see
Berenguer Barceló, Julio.

Barceló, Pau
see Junyent, Eduardo. Catalunya romànica : l'arquitectura del segle XI. [Barcelona] : Publicacions de l'Abadia de Montserrat, 1975.

Barceló, Pedro.
Diálogo de Dios con el hombre de hoy. Presentación de Ignacio Loring. Madrid, Acción Social Empresarial, 1971.
206 p. 19 cm. 70ptas Sp 71-Apr
Includes bibliographical references.
1. Christian life—Catholic authors. 2. Sociology, Christian. I. Title.
BX2350.2.B324 72-363465

Barceló, Pedro
see **El Medio sinovial.** Barcelona, 1970.

Barceló, Pedro, 1910–
... Reumatismos articulares crónicos ... 2. ed. Barcelona [etc.] Salvat, 1947.
189 p. illus. 23 cm. (Manuales de medicina práctica, 17)
1. Rheumatoid arthritis. I. Series.
[RC933.B34 1947] Med 47-2897

Barceló, Pedro, 1910–
... Reumatismos articulares crónicos (no vertebrales) [por el] dr. Pedro Barceló ... Barcelona-Buenos Aires, Salvat, 1941.
5 p. l., [13]-119 p. illus. 23 cm. (Manuales de medicina práctica. [17])
"Primera edición."
1. Rheumatism. 2. Arthritis deformans. 3. Joints—Diseases. I. Title.
RC292.B25 616.9'91 44-32524
rev

Barceló, Pedro, 1910–
... Tratamiento de los reumatismos, por Pedro Barceló ... Barcelona [Talleres gráficos de "Relieves Basa y Pagés, s. a."] 1942.
4 p. l., [5]-108 p. 21 cm. (Colección española de monografías médicas)
1. Rheumatism.
RC292.B26 616.9'91 45-29977
rev

Barceló, Pedro, 1910-
see **Rheumatologie in der täglichen Praxis. (München,) Aesopus- Verlag, (1972).**

Barceló, Ricardo Javier, joint author.
see Alcalde, Jesús. Celtiberia gay. Barcelona, Editorial Personas, 1976.

Barceló de Barasorda, María Antonia
see **Pedreira, Antonio Salvador, 1899-1939. Antonio S. Pedreira, antología de su obra. [San Juan] P. R., Editorial del Departamento de Instrucción Pública, 1967.**

Barceló Gomila, Francisco.
Estudio crítico sobre las miringoplastias / por Francisco Barceló Gomila. — Barcelona : Editorial Científico-Médica, 1975.
107 p. : ill. ; 24 cm. Sp76-Feb
Bibliography: p. 106-107.
Includes index.
ISBN 8422406454 : 480ptas
1. Myringoplasty. 2. Tympanic membrane—Wounds and injuries. I. Title.
[DNLM: 1. Ear, Middle—Injuries. 2. Ear, Middle—Physiopathology. 3. Myringoplasty—Methods. 4. Tympanoplasty. WV230 B242e 1975]
[RF126.B37] 617.8'5 76-675752
Shared Cataloging with 76 MARC
DNLM

Barceló i Fortuny, Francesc.
El paratge de l'aranya. [1. ed.] Barcelona, Nova Terra [1973]
250 p. 19 cm. (Col·lecció J. M., 14) 240ptas Sp***
I. Title.
PC3942.12.A68P3 74-306338
ISBN 84-280-0778-0

Barceló i Fortuny, Francesc.
La sabata de l'emperador Orfran i altres contes. Palma de Mallorca, Editorial Moll, 1974.
107 p. 16 cm. (Biblioteca Les Illes d'or, 111) Sp***
I. Title.
PC3942.12.A68S2 74-351289
ISBN 84-273-0361-0

Barceló i Tortella, Bartomeu, 1888-1973.
Obra poètica de Bartomeu Barceló i Tortella. Compilació, revisió i esbós biogràfic de Joan Roig i Montserrat. Amb Un poeta que no podem oblidar de Camil Geis. [1. ed.] Mallorca, 1974.
415 p. illus. 24 cm. Sp***
"Prosa": p. [349]-406.
Bibliography: p. 407-408.
ISBN 84-400-7368-2
I. Roig i Montserrat, Joan, ed.
PC3941.B343A17 1974 74-355647

Barceló Matutano, Gabriel
see
Barceló, Gabriel.

Barceló R , Víctor Manuel, 1936-
¿América Latina, integración o dependencia? / Víctor Manuel Barceló R. — Bogotá : [Universidad de Bogotá Jorge Tadeo Lozano], 1973.
178, [9] p. ; 24 cm.
Bibliography: p. [183]-[185]
1. Asociación Latinoamericana de Libre Comercio. 2. Latin America—Economic integration. 3. Latin America—Economic conditions—1945- I. Title.
HC125.B286 75-568975

Barceló R , Víctor Manuel, 1936-
La empresa multinacional en países del Tercer Mundo : apuntes para una empresa latinoamericana / Víctor Manuel Barceló R. — 1. ed. — Tlaltelolco, México : Secretaría de Relaciones Exteriores, 1975.
151 p. ; 23 cm. — (Cuestiones internacionales contemporáneas ; 6)
Includes bibliographical references.
1. Underdeveloped areas—International business enterprises. 2. Corporations, Foreign—Latin America. 3. Corporations—Latin America. I. Title. II. Series.
HD2755.5.B37 75-547900

Barcelo R., Victor Manuel, 1936-
see Panoramica del cuento mexicano ... [Bogota] : Ministerio de Educacion Nacional, [1974]

Barceló Rico-Avello, Gabriel.
Modelos de comportamiento directivo en la empresa española ... [Madrid, etc.] Asociación para el Progreso de la Dirección (1973)
178 p. 23 cm. (Asociación para el Progreso de la Dirección. [Publicaciones] 108) 400ptas Sp 74
1. Industrial management—Spain. I. Title.
HD70.S65B37 74-323522
ISBN 84-7019-149-7

Barceló Rubí, Bernardo.
El armamento portátil español (1764-1939), una labor artillera / B. Barceló Rubí. — Madrid : Librería Editorial San Martín, [1976?]
310 p. : ill. ; 27 cm. Sp***
Bibliography: p. 307-310.
ISBN 847140138X
1. Arms and armor—Spain—History. 2. Spain—Armed Forces—Firearms—History. I. Title.
U820.S7B37 77-470256
77 MARC

Barceló Salas, Antonio, ed.
see Consejo Económico Sindical Provincial (Gerona). Estructura y perspectivas de desarrollo económico de la provincia de Gerona. [Madrid] 1972.

Barceló Sifontes, Lyll.
Contribución a la bibliografía sobre el Congreso Anfictiónico de Panamá / Lyll Barceló Sifontes. — Caracas : [Oficina Central de Información, Dirección de Publicaciones], 1976.
72 p. ; 23 cm. — (Serie del Sesquicentenario del Congreso de Panamá)
Includes text of Decreto no. 1.295, 25 de noviembre de 1975.
1. Panama (City). Congress, 1826—Bibliography. I. Venezuela. Laws, statutes, etc. Decreto no 1.295, 25 de noviembre de 1975. 1976. II. Title. III. Series.
Z1609.I5B37 76-489331
[F1404] 77 MARC

Barceló Sifontes, Lyll.
Indice de la revista La Alborada (1909) / Lyll Barceló Sifontes. — Caracas : Universidad Católica Andrés Bello, Centro de Investigaciones Literarias, 1975.
44 p. : ill. ; 23 cm.
Bibliography: p. 44.
Includes index.
1. La Alborada—Indexes. I. Title.
AP63.A4322B37 77-462402
77 MARC

Barceló Sifontes, Lyll.
El Zulia, la ciudad y su mundo : catálogo bibliográfico : exposición homenaje al sesquicentenario de la batalla naval de Maracaibo, 1823-1973 / [por Lil Barceló Sifontes, con la colaboración del Lic. Camilo Balza Donatti]. — Caracas : [Instituto Zuliano de la Cultura], 1973.
79 p. ; 21 cm. — (Plan cultural Caracas)
1. Zulia, Venezuela—Bibliography—Catalogs. 2. Venezuela—Imprints—Catalogs. 3. Venezuela. Biblioteca Nacional, Caracas. I. Balza Donatti, Camilo, joint author. II. Title. III. Series.
Z1934.Z85B37 77-463620
[F2341.Z8] 77 MARC

Barceló Sifontes, Lyll.
see Caracas. Universidad Católica Andrés Bello. Escuela de Letras. Centro de Investigaciones Literarias. Bibliografía de Luis Manuel Urbaneja Achelpohl. [Caracas, Gobernación del Distrito Federal, 1971]

Barceló Torrent Pedro
see
Barceló, Pedro, 1910-

Barceló Valls, Carlos, 1929-
Nuevos productos, nuevos beneficios / C. Barceló. — Barcelona : Sagitario, [1974]
278 p. ; 22 cm. Sp76-July
ISBN 8471361728 : 425ptas
1. New products. 2. Marketing. I. Title.
HF5415.125.B36 76-487406
77 MARC

Barceló Valls, Carlos, 1929-
Lo que usted invierte en publicidad ... ¿es rentable? [guía práctica sobre la eficacia y la rentabilidad publicitaria, en España, por] C. Barceló. Prólogo de R. García Cairó. Barcelona, Sagitario [1967]
144 p. illus. 19 cm. (Colección "Empresa actual," no. 16)
Bibliography: p. 143-144.
1. Advertising—Spain. 2. Consumers—Spain. 3. Advertising research. I. Title.
HF5813.S8B35 74-206004

Barcélo Valls, Carlos, 1929-
7 [i. e. Siete] puntos básicos para la formación de vendedores [por] C. Barcelo. Barcelona, Sagitario [1968]
314 p. 22 cm.
1. Salesmen and salesmanship. I. Title.
HF5438.B24 72-223105

Barceló Valls, Carlos, 1929-
Ventas especiales [por] C. Barceló. [Barcelona] Sagitario [1966]
123 p. 19 cm. (Colección Empresa actual, no. 15)
1. Sales promotion. 2. New products. 3. Liquidation. 4. Salesmen and salesmanship. I. Title.
HF5438.B244 74-208654

Barceló Verdú, Joaquin.
El romancero español y las embajadas de sax; moros y cristianos. Sax [La victoria] 1965.
113 p.
1. Ballads, Spanish. I. Title.
WaU NUC74-149103

Barcelon Maicas, Emilio.
Naturaleza del derecho en el misterio de la Iglesia. Torrente (Valencia) 1973.
163 p. 24 cm.
Pars dissertationis—Pontificia Universitas S. Thomae, Rome.
Extractum e periodico Escritos del vedat, v. 3, p. 391-538.
Bibliography: p. [157]-160.
1. Canon Law—Philosophy. I. Title.
DCU NUC76-72729

Barcelona.
[Letter to Carlos II on abuses committed by the previous city government. Barcelona, 1682]
19 p. 29 cm.
Text begins: Señor. La Ciudad de Barcelona, representada en sus conselleres, y Consejo de Ciento, insiguiendo su deliberacion hecha a los 11. de março del corriente año de 1682. dize ...
1. Barcelona—Politics and government—History—Sources. I. Carlos II, King of Spain, 1661-1700. II. Title: La Ciudad de Barcelona, representada en sus conselleres ...
JS31.B282B37 1682 74-230211

Barcelona, plaintiff.
Demonstratio ivris accvrata: pro exemptione inclitae civitatis, et civivm Barcinonae a solvtione ivris mensuratici (vulgo de Cops) in qua, non minus solidis, quam legalibus rationibus, huc vsque nōdum excogitatis, ostenditur nusquam casum aliquem inveniri posse, in quo ex regia munificentia, & aliàs, non sint immunes a similis gabellae prestatione. Contra procuratorem fiscalem B. G. Cathaloniae, illvstrissimvm, ac reverendissimum Episcopum Barchinonen. & alios. In causa, quae in Tribunali Bajuliae Generalis ducitur, referente Nob. Raphaele de Moxò dictae Bajuliae Generalis meritissimo assessore. Scriba Cabanas. Barcin., Ex Typ. Cormellas, apud I. Cays, 1681.
44 (i. e. 56) p. coat of arms. 29 cm.
At head of title: Iesvs, Maria, Ioseph.
Pages after the first 48 numbered 37-44.
Arms of the city of Barcelona engraved on t. p.
Text signed: Ioffreu Aduocatus ordinarius Ciuitatis, Asprer Aduocatus ordinarius Ciuitatis, Molins Consulens, Rius, & Bruniquer Consulens.
1. Barcelona, plaintiff. 2. Privileges and immunities—Barcelona. I. Cabanes, 17th cent. II. Title. III. Title: Pro exemptione inclitae civitatis, et civium Barcinonae a solvtione ivris mensuraticí.
76-525516

Barcelona. Anti-Tuberculosis Institute Francisco Moragas
see
Instituto Antituberculoso Francisco Moragas.

Barcelona. Ayuntamiento.
Decretos de la Alcaldía y acuerdos municipales de carácter general. Barcelona, 1970.
xi, 669 p. 24 cm.
1. Law—Barcelona. I. Title.
74-200635

Barcelona. Ayuntamiento.
Plan general de acción municipal.
—— Apéndice: Cultura. [Barcelona] Secretaría General. Gabinete Técnico de Programación, 1971.
147 p. 24 cm. Sp***
HN590.B3B365 1971 Suppl.
—— Apéndice: Factores económicos. [Barcelona] Secretaría General. Gabinete Técnico de Programación, 1971.
74 p. 24 cm. Sp***
HN590.B3B365 1971 Suppl. 2
—— Apéndice: Sanidad. [Barcelona] Secretaría General. Gabinete Técnico de Programación, 1968.
127 p. plates. 24 cm. Sp***
HN590.B3B365 1971 Suppl. 3
1. Barcelona—Social policy. 2. Barcelona—Economic policy. 3. Cities and towns—Planning—Barcelona. I. Title.
74-337017

Barcelona. Ayuntamiento.
see Festival Internacional de Música, Barcelona, 1976. Festival Internacional de Música de Barcelona, 1976 ... Barcelona, Forum Musical, 1976.

Barcelona. Ayuntamiento
see Vilató Ruiz, José, 1916-1969. Exposición antológica J. Fin, 1916-1969... [Barcelona] 1971.

Barcelona. Ayuntamiento. Instituto Municipal de Educación
see
Instituto Municipal de Educación.

Barcelona. Ayuntamiento. Museo Picasso
see
Museo Picasso.

Barcelona. Ayuntamiento. Museos de Arte
see
Barcelona. Museos de Arte.

Barcelona. Ayuntamiento. Subdepartamento de Estadística.
Padrón municipal de habitantes en 31 Diciembre 1970 / Ayuntamiento de Barcelona, Subdepartamento de Estadística. — Barcelona : El Subdepartamento, [1973]
2 v. ; 24 cm. Sp 75-Sept
On cover: Tablas referentes a las características de la población barcelonesa deducidas del padrón municipal de habitantes de 1970.
Estadística municipal.
100ptas per vol.
1. Barcelona—Population—Statistics. I. Title.
HB3620.B35B37 1973 75-404904

Barcelona. Biblioteca Central.
Catálogo de la Exposición Bibliográfica Oriental. Galería de Exposiciones de la Biblioteca Central, Barcelona, mayo-junio de 1972. Organizada por la Asociación Española de Orientalistas con la colaboración de la Biblioteca Central de Cataluña, la Biblioteca y Seminario de Papirología de la Facultad Teológica de San Cugat del Vallés y el Museo Etnológico de Barcelona. Barcelona [1973]
45 p. 25 cm. Sp***
1. Asia—Bibliography—Catalogs. 2. Barcelona. Biblioteca Central. I. Asociación Española de Orientalistas. II. Title.
Z3001.B32 1973 74-342706

Barcelona. Biblioteca Central.
Inventario de publicaciones periódicas que se reciben en las bibliotecas de Barcelona. Barcelona, 1970 [c1971]
277 p. 28 cm. Sp***
At head of title: Biblioteca Central de la Diputación Provincial de Barcelona.
1. Periodicals—Bibliography—Union lists. 2. Catalogs, Union—Barcelona. I. Title.
Z6945.B35 73-351016

Barcelona. Biblioteca Central.
Inventario de publicaciones periódicas que se reciben en las bibliotecas de Barcelona. [Barcelona] Biblioteca Central de la Diputación Provincial de Barcelona, 1970.
277 p. 28 cm.
"Contiene las revistas que se recibían en las bibliotecas repertoriadas, entre los años 1966 a 1969."
1. Periodicals—Bibliography—Union lists. 2. Catalogs, Union—Barcelona. I. Title.
Z6945.B35 1970a 74-208155

Barcelona. Biblioteca Central.
La revista infantil en Barcelona; [antología histórica. Barcelona, 1964?]
[24] p. illus. (part col.) 22 cm.
Cover title.
Includes the catalog of an exhibition organized by the Biblioteca Central for the 4th Semana Nacional del Libro Infantil y Juvenil.
Includes bibliographical references.
1. Children's periodicals, Spanish—Barcelona. I. Title.
PN5317.J8B3 1964 75-573031

Barcelona. Biblioteca Central. Sección de Manuscritos
see Vilarrubias, Felio A Noticia de una colección de papeles de José Massanés y Mestres (1777-1857) ... Barcelona, 1966 [i. e. 1967]

Barcelona. Bolsa.
see Conmemoración de las "Ordinacions" de los mediadores mercantiles de Barcelona, de Jaime I, 1271 ... Barcelona, Bolsa Oficial de Comercio, 1974.

Barcelona. Centro de Estudios Interplanetarios
see
Centro de Estudios Interplanetarios.

Barcelona. Colegio Mayor Monterols
see
Colegio Mayor Monterols.

Barcelona. Consell de Cent Jurats.
Manual de novells ardits vulgarment apellat Dietari del antich consell barceloní ... Publicat per acort y á despesas del excm. Ajuntament constitucional é iniciat per los ilustres senyors regidors D. Frederich Schwartz y Luna y D. Francesch Carreras y Candi en comissió del mateix excelentíssim Ajuntament. Barcelona, Impr. de 'n Henrich y companyía, en comandita successors de 'n Arcís Ramírez y companyía, 1892-1975.
28 v. 24 cm. (Half-title: Colecció de documents históricchs inédits del Arxiu municipal de la ciutat de Barcelona)
At head of title of v. 18-28: Ayuntamiento de Barcelona, Instituto Municipal de Historia.
Vol. 18, 20-28: Dirección y prólogo del Dr. Pedro Voltes Bou; v. 19: Edición y prólogo de Jaime Sobrequés Callicó.
The first of a series of publications from the Barcelona archives, to be issued under the joint direction of the Ayuntamiento of Barcelona and of the Real Academia de Buenas Letras with the following announced plan: "1., los documents relatius al govern municipal de Barcelona fins al decret de Nova Planta; 2., los documents referents al exercici de les atribucions de la municipalitat; 3., los relatius á fets históricchs en los quals la nostra ciutat fou actor important; 4., aquells que demostran les costums de cada época, y 5., los que tractan de legislació y no venen enclosos en les series precedents." cf. Introduction, v. 1, p. vi.
L. C. copy imperfect: Half-title v. 1-3 wanting.
Vol. 18-28 without series statement.
ISBN 84-600-6633-9 (v. 28)
1. Barcelona—History—Sources. I. Schwartz y Luna, Federico, 1853-1929, ed. II. Carreras y Candi, Francisco, 1862-1937, ed. III. Voltes Bou, Pedro, 1926- ed. IV. Sobrequés i Callicó, Jaume, ed. V. Title.
DP402.B2B1825 1892 946.7 12-19987

Barcelona. Dau al Set, Galeria d'art
see
Dau al Set, Galeria D'Art.

Barcelona. Delegación de Servicios de Cultura.
Proyecto de fundación de un centro de educación general básica. Barcelona, Ayuntamiento. Delegación de servicios de cultura, 1971.
59 p., 1 l. fold. 20 cm. Sp 71-June
1. Education, Elementary—Spain—Curricula. I. Title.
LB1564.S7B37 73-303283

Barcelona. Delegación de Servicios de Cultura
see Cursillo de Técnicas de Expresión y Comunicación, 4th, Barcelona, 1972. IV [i.e. Cuarto] Cursillo de Técnicas de Expresión y Comunicación ... [Barcelona] [1973]

Barcelona. Delegación de Servicios de Cultura. Servicio de Publicaciones.
For publications of the Delegación de Servicios de Cultura issued by this body see:

Barcelona. Delegación de Servicios de Cultura.

Barcelona. Distrito XI. Junta Municipal.
I [i. e. Primer] Curso Oficial de Lengua Catalana. Barcelona, Junta Municipal del Dto. XI (1970)
20 l., plates. 29 cm. Sp 71-Nov
Catalan.
1. Fabra, Pompeu, 1868-1948. I. Title.
PC3809.F3B3 74-328171

Barcelona. Escola de l'Esplai
see
Escola de l'Esplai.

Barcelona. Escuela de Administración de Empresas. Departamento de Investigación
see Barquero Garcés, Celedonio. Inversiones extranjeras. La realidad española. Barcelona, Servicio de Publicaciones, 1971.

Barcelona. Escuela Técnica Superior de Ingenieros Industriales. Departament d'Activitats Culturals
see
Barcelona. Escuela Técnica Superior de Ingenieros Industriales. Departamento de Actividades Culturales.

Barcelona. Escuela Técnica Superior de Ingenieros Industriales. Departamento de Actividades Culturales.
A l'avantguarda de l'educació. Experiences pedagógiques 1900-1938. Barcelona (1972)
155 p., fold. organizational chart. 17 cm. 150ptas Sp 72-Nov
Bibliography: p. 140.
1. Education, Higher—Catalonia—History. I. Title.
LA919.C35B37 73-318176

Barcelona. Escuela Técnica y Superior de Arquitectura
see
Escuela Técnica y Superior de Arquitectura de Barcelona.

Barcelona. Feria Oficial e Internacional de Muestras
see Jornadas Técnicas del Medio Ambiente, 1st, Barcelona, 1971. Medio ambiente: jornadas técnicas. Barcelona: [1971]

Barcelona. Festival Internacional de Música
see
Festival Internacional de Música, Barcelona.

Barcelona. Galeria Adrià
see
Galeria Adrià.

Barcelona. Galería Arturo Ramón
see
Galería Arturo Ramón.

Barcelona. Galería Barbié
see
Galería Barbié.

Barcelona. Galeria Joan Prats
see
Galeria Joan Prats.

Barcelona. Galeria Maeght
see
Galeria Maeght.

Barcelona. Galería René Métras
see
Galería René Métras.

Barcelona. Hospital de Santa Cruz y de San Pablo
see
Hospital de Santa Cruz y de San Pablo.

Barcelona. Institución Milá y Fontanals
see
Institución Milá y Fontanals.

Barcelona. Instituto Antituberculoso.
For works by this body issued under its later name see

Instituto Antituberculoso Francisco Moragas.

Barcelona. Instituto Municipal de Ciencias Naturales
see also
Barcelona. Junta de Ciències Naturals.

Barcelona. Instituto Municipal de Ciencias Naturales. Museo de Zoología
see
Museo de Zoología.

Barcelona. Instituto Municipal de Educación
see
Instituto Municipal de Educación.

Barcelona. Instituto Municipal de Historia.
Barcelona, divulgación histórica, textos radiados desde la emisora de "Radio Barcelona." Barcelona, Ediciones Ayma, 1945–
v. illus. 22 cm.
Vols. 4–8, "Textos del Boletín semanal radiado desde la emisora Radio Barcelona."
Includes bibliographies.
Vol. 14 has title: Divulgación histórica de Barcelona; also special t. p.: Páginas de la historia económica de Barcelona.
1. Barcelona—Hist. I. Title. II. Title. Divulgación histórica de Barcelona.
DP402.B25B3 1945 946.7 51–16433

Barcelona. Instituto Municipal de Historia
see Cuadernos de historia económica de Cataluña. Barcelona, Universidad de Barcelona.

Barcelona. Museo de Arte Moderno
see
Museo de Arte Moderno, Barcelona.

Barcelona. Museo de Historia de la Ciudad
see Barcelona en la seva història ... [Barcelona] Ajuntament de Barcelona, 1970.

Barcelona. Museo de Historia de la Ciudad. Seminario de Arqueología e Historia de la Ciudad.
Estudios. 1–
[Barcelona] 1966–
no. 25 cm. (Its Publicaciones)
1. Barcelona—History—Collected works. I. Series.
DP402.B2B183a subser. 73–643600
MARC-S

Barcelona. Museo de Historia de la Ciudad. Seminario de Arqueología e Historia de la Ciudad.
Publicaciones.
Barcelona
no. in v. illus. 25 cm.
Catalan or Spanish.
1. Barcelona—History—Periodicals. 2. Barcelona—Antiquities—Periodicals.
DP402.B2B183a 73–647047
MARC-S

Barcelona. Museo de Historia de la Ciudad. Seminario de Arqueología e Historia de la Ciudad.
Series histórico-artística. 1–
Barcelona [1967–
no. illus. 32 cm. (Its Publicaciones)
1. Art—Barcelona—Collected works. I. Title. II. Series.
DP402.B2B183a subser. 73–647354
MARC-S

Barcelona. Museo de Historia de la Ciudad. Seminario de Investigación
see Cuadernos de arqueología e historia de la Ciudad. [Barcelona]

Barcelona. Museo de Zoología
see
Museo de Zoología.

Barcelona. Museo Picasso
see Museo Picasso.

Barcelona. Museos de Arte.
Exposición legado Isabel Escalada vda. Xavier Nogués; catálogo. Palacio de la Virreina, marzo 1972. [Barcelona, Sociedad Alianza de Artes Gráficas] 1972.
93 p. plates. 23 cm. Sp***
Exhibition of works by Xavier Nogués.
Bibliography: p. [89]
1. Nogués, Javier, 1874– 2. Escalada Nogués, Isabel—Art collections.
NC287.N58B37 1972 74–347804

Barcelona. Museos de Arte
see Gil Guasch, Miguel. Exposición de artes suntuarias del modernismo barcelonés ... [Barcelona] Museos de Arte [1965?]

Barcelona. Museu d'Història de la Ciutat
see
Barcelona. Museo de Historia de la Ciudad.

Barcelona. Ordinances, etc.
Ordenanza de circulacion ... : vigente desde el 2 de marzo, 1974. — Barcelona : Ayuntamiento, D.L. 1974.
94 p. ; 16 cm. Sp76-Oct
1. Traffic regulations—Spain—Barcelona. 2. Automobiles—Law and legislation—Spain—Barcelona. I. Title.
77-556683
77 MARC

Barcelona. Palacio de la Virreina
see Gil Guasch, Miguel. Exposición de artes suntuarias del modernismo barcelonés ... [Barcelona] Museos de Arte [1965?]

Barcelona. Palacio de la Virreina
see Junta de Museus de Barcelona. Exposición de dibujos para la illustración del "Voyage pittoresque et historique de l'Espagne". [Barcelona, 1960]

Barcelona. Palacio de la Virreina
see Klee, Paul, 1879-1940. Klee, 1879-1940. Madrid, 1972.

Barcelona. Patronato Municipal de la Vivienda.
La vivienda en Barcelona / Ayuntamiento de Barcelona, Patronato Municipal de la Vivienda. — Barcelona : El Patronato, 1973.
152 p. ; 24 cm. Sp 73
1. Housing—Barcelona metropolitan area, Spain. 2. Housing, Rural—Barcelona (Province) I. Title.
HD7351.B3B34 1973 301.5'4'094672 74–356552

Barcelona. Policía Municipal.
Estadística de accidentes de tránsito.
[Barcelona]
v. illus. 29 cm.
1. Traffic accidents—Barcelona—Statistics. I. Title.
HE5614.5.S63B37a 73–644008
MARC-S

Barcelona. Sala Gaspar
see Sala Gaspar.

Barcelona. Sala Gaudí
see
Sala Gaudí.

Barcelona. Sala Parés
see Sala Parés, Barcelona.

Barcelona. Universidad.
Ordinations e nou redreç de la Universitat de Barcelona, 1596. [Barcelona] Universitat de Barcelona, 1973.
152 p. 25 cm. Sp***
Reproduction of the Barcelona, 1596 ed.
1. Barcelona. Universidad. I. Title.
LF4612.A3A62 1973 74–311734
ISBN 84-600-5975-8

Barcelona. Universidad
see Jimeno, Emilio. Algunos problemas de la enseñanza. Barcelona, 1939.

Barcelona. Universidad
see Termes Ardévol, José. La Universidad de Barcelona. [Barcelona, Universidad] (1971)

Barcelona. Universidad. Biblioteca.
Obras existentes en la biblioteca de libre acceso de la sala de lectura de la Biblioteca General Universitaria de Barcelona. [Barcelona] (1970)
2 l., 30 l., 1 l. 32 cm. 2ptas Sp 71-Mar
1. Barcelona. Universidad. Biblioteca.
Z945.B376 1970 73–361431

Barcelona. Universidad. Biblioteca. MSS. (1)
see Jaime I, King of Aragon, 1208-1276. Libre dels feyts del rey en Jacme. Barcelona, 1972.

Barcelona. Universidad. Biblioteca. MSS. (78).
see Colegio de la Asuncion, Lerida, Spain. Statuta Domus Collegii Sanctae Mariae Civitatis Ilerdae ... Lerida : Instituto de Estudios Ilerdenses, [1973]

Barcelona. Universidad. Cátedra de Derecho Civil Catalán Durán y Bas
see Estudios jurídicos sobre la mujer catalana. Barcelona, Diputación Provincial (1971)

Barcelona. Universidad. Cátedra de Derecho Civil Catalán Durán y Bas
see Estudios sobre la legítima catalana. Barcelona (1973)

Barcelona. Universidad. Cátedra de Historia del Derecho Español.
see Apuntes de historia del derecho español ... Barcelona, Universidad de Barcelona, Facultad de Derecho, 1974.

Barcelona. Universidad. Cátedra de Historia Económica
see Cuadernos de historia económica de Cataluña. Barcelona. Universidad de Barcelona.

Barcelona. Universidad. Cátedra Durán y Bas
see
Barcelona. Universidad. Cátedra de Derecho Civil Catalán Durán y Bas.

Barcelona. Universidad. Departamento de Derecho Internacional.
[Las N. U. y el Tercer mundo] La cooperación internacional para el desarrollo. Departamento de Derecho Internacional de la Universidad de Barcelona ... Prólogo: Manuel Díez de Velasco. [Barcelona, Japizua, 1971]
1 l., 661 p. 22 cm. Sp 72-May
"Dirección: Victoria Abellán."
"Seminario sobre la cooperación internacional para el desarrollo ... octubre 1967–mayo 1968 ... octubre–mayo 1970."
Includes bibliographical references.
1. United Nations—Economic assistance. 2. United Nations—Technical assistance. 3. Commercial policy. 4. Industrial promotion. I. Abellán Honrubia, Victoria. II. Title. III. Title: La cooperación internacional para el desarrollo.
HC60.B287 1971 73–332561

Barcelona. Universidad. Departamento de Estadística Matemática
see Stochastica. [Barcelona, Universidad de Barcelona]

Barcelona. Universidad. Departamento de Filologia Catalana
see In memoriam Carles Riba, 1959-1969. [Barcelona] Editorial Ariel, 1973.

Barcelona. Universidad. Departamento de Hebreo y Arameo.
Catálogo de los libros del Departamento de Hebreo y Arameo y de la Sección de Hebreo de la Institución Milá y Fontanals del C.S.I.C. — Barcelona : Universidad de Barcelona, Facultad de Filología, Departamento de Hebreo y Arameo, 1974.
259 p. ; 32 cm. Sp***
Includes indexes.
ISBN 8460018113
1. Judaism—Bibliography—Catalogs. 2. Hebrew philology—Bibliography—Catalogs. 3. Jews—Bibliography—Catalogs. 4. Barcelona. Universidad. Departamento de Hebreo y Arameo. 5. Institución Milá y Fontanals. Sección de Hebreo. I. Institución Milá y Fontanals. Sección de Hebreo. II. Title.
Z6375.B27 1974 76-455292
[LB1745] 76 MARC

Barcelona. Universidad. Departamento de Historia de America
see Economía e integración hispanica. Barcelona, 1969.

Barcelona. Universidad. Departamento de Historia del Arte
see D'art. abr. 1972- [Barcelona]

Barcelona. Universidad. Departamento de Historia Económica
see Cuadernos de historia económica de Cataluña. Barcelona, Universidad de Barcelona.

Barcelona. Universidad. Departamento de Teoria Economica
see Cuadernos de economia. [Barcelona]

Barcelona. Universidad. Facultad de Derecho.
El derecho civil catalán en la jurisprudencia.
[Barcelona]
v. 23 cm. (Publicaciones de la Cátedra de Derecho Civil Durán i Bas)
1. Civil law—Catalonia. I. Title.
74-643016
MARC-S

Barcelona. Universidad. Facultad de Derecho. Cátedra de Derecho Civil Catalán Durán y Bas
see
Barcelona. Universidad. Cátedra de Derecho Civil Catalán Durán y Bas.

Barcelona. Universidad. Facultad de Derecho. Cátedra de Historia del Derecho Español
see
Barcelona. Universidad. Cátedra de Historia del Derecho Español.

Barcelona. Universidad. Facultad de Derecho. Departamento de Derecho Internacional
see
Barcelona. Universidad. Departamento de Derecho Internacional.

Barcelona. Universidad Facultad de Filología
see Anuario de filología. 1975-
Barcelona.

Barcelona. Universidad. Facultad de Filosofia y Letras
see González, Nazario. Contribución a la enseñanza de la Historia Contemporanea en la Universidad. Barcelona, Facultad de Filosofia y Letras, 1971.

Barcelona. Universidad. Facultad de Filosofía y Letras. Departamento de Historia del Arte
see
Barcelona. Universidad. Departamento de Historia del Arte.

Barcelona. Universidad. Facultad de Filosofía y Letras. Sección de Palma de Mallorca
see
Barcelona. Universidad. Facultad de Filosofía y Letras, Palma de Mallorca.

Barcelona. Universidad. Facultad de Filosofía y Letras, Palma de Mallorca
see Mayurqa. Palma de Mallorca, Estudio General Luliano.

Barcelona. Universidad. Instituto de Arqueología y Prehistoria.
Publicaciones eventuales.
Barcelona, 19
v. illus. 28 cm.
No. -6 issued by the institute under its earlier name: Instituto de Arqueología.
1. Man, Prehistoric — Collected works. 2. Man, Prehistoric — Spain—Collected works. 3. Spain—Antiquities—Collected works. I. Title.
GN700.B365 70-389484
MARC-S

Barcelona. Universidad. Instituto de Arqueología y Prehistoria
see Coloquio sobre Arquitectura Megalítica y Ciclópea Catalano-Balear, Bareclona, 1965. Arquitectura megalítica y ciclópea catalanobalear. Barcelona, Consejo Superior de Investigaciones Científicas, 1965.

Barcelona. Universidad. Instituto de Ciencias de la Educación.
see Seminario sobre Educación Bilingüe en Cataluña, 1st, 1974. Bilingüismo y educación en Cataluña ... 1. ed. Barcelona, Editorial Teide, 1975.

Barcelona. Universidad. Instituto de Estudios Helénicos
see In memoriam Carles Riba, 1959-1969. [Barcelona] Editorial Ariel, 1973.

Barcelona. Universidad. Instituto de Historia Medieval
see Miscelánea de textos medievales. 1972- Barcelona, Consejo Superior de Investigaciones Científicas.

Barcelona. Universidad Autónoma
see
Universidad Autónoma de Barcelona.

Barcelona (Province). Caja de Ahorros Provincial
see
Caja de Ahorros Provincial (Barcelona).

Barcelona (Province). Comisión de Turismo.
Museos de la Diputación Provincial de Barcelona. [Barcelona, 1972?]
98, [46] p. illus. 21 cm. (Arte, cultura, turismo, 2) 50ptas Sp***
English, French, German, and Spanish.
1. Museums—Spain—Barcelona (Province) 2. Barcelona (Province). Diputación Provincial. I. Title.
AM65.B3A44 73-332723

Barcelona (Province). Comisión de Urbanismo y Servicios Comunes de Barcelona y Otros Municipios
see
Comisión de Urbanismo y Servicios Comunes de Barcelona y Otros Municipios.

Barcelona (Province). Delegación Provincial de Cultura. Oficina de Información Cultural
see
Barcelona (Province). Oficina de Información Cultural.

Barcelona (Province). Diputación Provincial.
Aportación de la Diputación Provincial de Barcelona al XXX Congreso Mundial de Urbanismo y Vivienda. Barcelona, 1970.
38 l. illus., maps (part col.) 22 x 25 cm. Sp 71-Feb
1. Cities and towns—Planning—Barcelona (Province) 2. Parks—Spain—Barcelona (Province) 3. Architecture—Barcelona (Province)—Conservation and restoration.
HT169.S652B32 1970 73-335548

Barcelona (Province). Diputación Provincial.
Ceremonial; autoridades y altos cargos.
[Barcelona]
v. 21 cm.
1. Barcelona (Province). Diputación Provincial—Registers.
JN8399.B22A3 73-641736

Barcelona (Province). Diputación Provincial.
Cuía de las bibliotecas de la Diputación Provincial de Barcelona. [Barcelona?, 1972?]
38 p. illus. 21 cm. Sp***
1. Libraries—Spain—Barcelona (Province) I. Title.
Z831.B37A54 73-340185

Barcelona (Province). Diputación Provincial.
Diputación Provincial de Barcelona, 21 junio 1967–1972; un lustro de gestión corporativa. [Barcelona, 1972]
227 p. illus. 26 cm. Sp***
1. Barcelona (Province) — Economic conditions. 2. Barcelona (Province)—Politics and government. 3. Barcelona (Province)—Social conditions. I. Title: Un lustro de gestión corporativa.
HC387.B18B33 1972 74-300572

Barcelona (Province). Diputación Provincial.
Diputación Provincial de Barcelona, 21 junio 1967-1972 : un lustro de gestión corporativa. — [s.l. : s.n., 1972] (Barcelona : Imprenta-Escuela de la Casa Provincial de Caridad)
227 p., [2] fold. leaves of plates : ill. ; 26 cm. Sp***
1. Barcelona (Province)—Economic conditions. 2. Barcelona (Province)—Politics and government. 3. Barcelona (Province)—Social conditions. I. Title.
HC387.B18B33 1972a 77-452764
77 MARC

Barcelona (Province). Diputación Provincial.
La economía de la provincia de Barcelona. — [Barcelona] : Diputación Provincial de Barcelona, Gabinete Técnico, 1975.
59 leaves : graphs, maps ; 30 cm. Sp***
1. Barcelona (Province)—Economic conditions. I. Title.
HC387.B18B33 1975 330.9'46'72083 76-47767[illegible]
76 MARC

Barcelona (Province). Diputación Provincial.
Guía de las bibliotecas de la Diputación Provincial de Barcelona. [Barcelona?, 1972?]
38 p. illus. 21 cm. Sp***
1. Libraries—Spain—Barcelona (Province) I. Title.
Z831.B37B37 1972 73-340185
rev

Barcelona (Province). Diputación Provincial.
Presupuesto general ordinario de gastos e ingresos.
Barcelona.
v. 26 cm. annual.
On spine : Presupuestos ordinario y especiales.
1. Budget—Barcelona (Province) I. Barcelona (Province). Diputación Provincial. Presupuestos ordinario y especiales.
HJ60.B37A3 72-625795

Barcelona (Province). Diputación Provincial.
Presupuestos ordinario y especiales
see Barcelona (Province). Diputación Provincial. Presupuesto general ordinario de gastos e ingresos. Barcelona.

Barcelona (Province). Diputación Provincial.
I (Primera) exposición de miniaturas textiles celebrada durante la IV lonja textil de España. Barcelona, 1968.
viii, 33 p. 58 pl. 22 cm.
"Catalogo confeccionado bajo el asesoramiento del Dr. Francisco Torrella Niubó."
1. Textile industry—Spain. 2. Textiles, Spanish—Exhibition. 3. Barcelona—Lonja textil de España. I. Torrella Niubió, F.
NNMM NUC75-29400

Barcelona (Province). Diputación Provincial.
see Barcelona (Province). Laws, statutes, etc. Ordenanza provincial de prevención contra el fuego. Barcelona, Diputación Provincial de Barcelona, 1976.

Barcelona (Province). Diputación Provincial
see Cuadernos de información económica. Barcelona, Consejo Superior de Investigaciones Científicas.

Barcelona (Province). Diputación Provincial. Caja de Ahorros Provincial
see
Caja de Ahorros Provincial (Barcelona).

Barcelona (Province). Diputación Provincial. Comisión de Turismo
see
Barcelona (Province). Comisión de Turismo.

Barcelona (Province). Diputación Provincial. Instituto Provincial de Paleontología
see
Instituto Provincial de Paleontología.

Barcelona (Province). Diputación Provincial. Sección de Prensa

For publications of the Diputación Provincial issued by this body see

Barcelona (Province). Diputación Provincial.

Barcelona (Province). Diputación Provincial. Servicio Provincial de Prevención y Extinción de Incendios
see
Barcelona (Province). Servicio Provincial de Prevención y Extincion de Incendios.

Barcelona (Province). Instituto de Prehistoria y Arqueología
see Simposio Internacional de Arte Rupestre, Barcelona, 1966. Simposio Internacional de Arte Rupestre... Barcelona, 1968.

Barcelona (Province). Laws, statutes, etc.
Ordenanza provincial de prevención contra el fuego / ⌈aprobada por el pleno de la Corporación Provincial en 31 de mayo de 1974⌉. — Barcelona : Diputación Provincial de Barcelona, 1976.
120 p. : ill. ; 17 cm. Sp***
Includes index.
100ptas
1. Fire prevention—Barcelona (Province)—Laws and regulations. I. Barcelona (Province). Diputación Provincial. II. Title.
344'.4672'0537 76-472893
76 MARC

Barcelona (Province). Obra Sindical Educación y Descanso
see
Obra Sindical Educación y Descanso, Barcelona.

Barcelona (Province). Oficina de Información Cultural.
Indice de museos de la provincia de Barcelona. ⌈Barcelona, 1972⌉
46 p. illus. 17 cm. 50ptas Sp***
1. Museums—Spain—Barcelona (Province)—Directories. I. Title.
AM65.A3B37 1972 74-312672

Barcelona (Province). Oficina de Información Cultural.
Indice de museos de la provincia de Barcelona 1976 / Oficina de Información Cultural de la Delegación Provincial de Cultura. — 1. ed. — Barcelona : Ediciones de Nuevo Arte Thor, 1976.
⌈142⌉ p. : ill. ; 20 cm. Sp***
ISBN 8473270002
1. Museums—Spain—Barcelona (Province)—Directories. I. Title.
AM65.A3B373 1976 77-466937
77 MARC

Barcelona (Province). Servicio Provincial de Prevención y Extinción de Incendios.
see Folch i Guillén, Ramon. Los incendios forestales. Barcelona, Diputación Provincial, Servicio de Parques Naturales y Medio Ambiente, c1976.

Barcelona en la seva història : breu història de la ciutat / ⌈Frederic Udina ... et al.⌉ ; redactada sota la direcció del Museu d'Història. — ⌈Barcelona⌉ : Ajuntament de Barcelona, Delegació de Serveis de Cultura, 1970.
74 p., ⌈8⌉ leaves of plates : ill. ; 22 cm.
1. Barcelona—History. I. Udina Martorell, Federico. II. Barcelona. Museo de Historia de la Ciudad.
DP402.B27B33 75-540843

Barcelona: la ciudad, los museos, la vida. Con 252 ilustraciones en negro, 18 en color y 68 dibujor y planos. Barcelona, Editorial Labor, 1962.
338 p. illus. (part col.) 27 cm.
1. Barcelona—Descr.—Guidebooks. 2. Museums Spain—Barcelona.
VtU NUC74-126812

Barcelona : remodelación capitalista o desarrollo urbano en el sector de La Ribera oriental / M. Solà-Morales ... ⌈et al.⌉. — Barcelona : G. Gili, ⌈1974⌉
79 p., ⌈4⌉ leaves of plates (3 fold.) : ill. ; 25 cm. — (Colección Materiales de la ciudad) Sp***
Cover title.
Bibliography: p. 79.
ISBN 84-252-0819-X
1. Urban renewal—Barcelona. 2. Cities and towns—Planning—Barcelona. 3. Barcelona—History. I. Solà-Morales Rubió, Manuel de.
HT178.S62B372 75-583014

Barcelona Traction, Light and Power Co., ltd.
see El Caso de la "Barcelona Traction". [Madrid, 1970]

Barcelos, Frank.
A showing of scrimshaw. ⌈New Bedford? Mass., 1974⌉
55 p. col. illus. 26 cm.
1. Scrimshaws. I. Title.
NK6022.B36 736'.6 74-180369
MARC

Barcelos, Pedro Alfonso, conde de
see
Bragança, Afonso, duque de, 1377?-1461.

Barcelos, Ramiro Frota. Plácido de Castro. 1973
in Macedo, Sérgio D Teixeira de. Santos Dumont. [Porto Alegre] Bels, 1973.

Barcelos, Ramiro Frota
see Vida da morte. [Pôrto Alegre] Editôra BELS [1973]

Barcelos, Sergio.
Hitler. ⌈Texto: Sergio Barcelos e Mury Lydia. São Paulo, Editora Três, 1973⌉
235 p. ports. 21 cm. — (Biblioteca de historia, 5)
Bibliography: p. 221-222.
Cr$14.00
1. Hitler, Adolf, 1889-1945. I. Lydia, Mury, joint author.
DD247.H5B25 74-231186

Barcelos Massot, Ivete Simões Lopes
see
Massot, I Simões Lopes B

Barcelos, Portugal. Câmara Municipal
see Olaria. agosto 1968- [Barcelos] Museu de Cerâmica Popular Portuguesa.

Barcena, Alonso, 1528-1598. Vocabulario y phrasis en la lengua general de los indios del Peru, llamada quichua, y en la lengua española
see Vocabulario y phrasis en la lengua general de los indios del Peru... 5. ed. Lima, Universidad Nacional Mayor de San Marcos, 1951.

Bárcena, José María Roa
see Roa Bárcena, José María, 1827-1908.

Bárcena, Luis Pérez
see
Pérez Bárcena, Luis, 1905-

Bárcenas, Angel Silva-
see Silva-Bárcenas, Angel.

Bárcenas, María Luisa Poves
see Poves Bárcenas, María Luisa.

Barch, Ikhil' Zusevich.
(Vozvedenie prokatnykh tšekhov)
Возведение прокатных цехов / И. З. Барч, В. Б. Тойбис. — Москва : Стройиздат, 1974.
172, ⌈3⌉ p. : ill. ; 20 cm. USSR 74
Bibliography: p. 172-⌈173⌉
0.48rub
1. Rolling-mills—Design and construction. I. Toĭbis, Vladimir Borisovich, joint author. II. Title.
TS340.B316 75-526950

Barch, Joan Rubinstein.
Jewish egg farmers in New Jersey / by Joan Rubinstein Barch. — Columbia, Md. : Barch, c1977.
viii, 128 leaves, ⌈2⌉ fold. leaves of plates : ill. ; 29 cm.
Originally presented as the author's thesis (M.A.) Northeastern Illinois University, 1976.
Bibliography: p. 97-101.
1. Egg trade—New Jersey. 2. Poultry industry—New Jersey. 3. Farmers, Jewish—New Jersey. 4. Jews in New Jersey—Economic conditions. I. Title.
HD9284.U45N53 1977 77-24788
77 MARC

Barcha, Samir Felíco, joint author
see Arid, Fahad Moysés. Sedimentos neocenozóicos no Vale do Rio Grande... São Paulo, Universidade de São Paulo, 1971.

Barcham, William L
The imaginary view scenes of Antonio Canaletto / William L. Barcham. — New York : Garland Pub., 1977.
xxix, 345, xiv p. : ill. ; 21 cm. — (Outstanding dissertations in the fine arts)
Originally presented as the author's thesis, New York University, 1974.
Bibliography: p. i-xiv (3d group).
ISBN 0-8240-2677-2 : $45.00
1. Canal, Antonio, called Canaletto, 1697-1768. 2. Landscape in art. 3. Venice in art. I. Title. II. Series.
ND623.C2B37 1977 759.5 76-23603
76 MARC

Barchard, H., joint author
see Sutterlin, Arnold Martin, 1939- Effects of several experimental diets... St. Andrews, N.B., 1975.

Barchas, Jack D.
see Conference on Neuroregulators and Hypotheses of Psychiatric Disorders, Asilomar Conference Center, 1976. Neuroregulators and psychiatric disorders ... New York, Oxford University Press, 1977.

Barchas, Jack D.
see Psychopharmacology ... New York, Oxford University Press, 1977.

Barchas, Jack D., ed.
see Serotonin and behavior. New York, Academic Press, 1973.

Barchas, Kathryn U., joint author
see Fahs, Ivan J Nursing in the upper Midwest... Minneapolis, 1970.

Barchas, Sarah Elizabeth, 1938-
Expressed reading interests of children of differing ethnic groups. ₍Tucson₎ 1971.
1 v.
Thesis–University of Arizona.
Microfilm of typescript. Ann Arbor, Mich., University Microfilms, 1971. 1 reel. 35 mm.
1. Books and reading for children–Tucson. 2. Socially handicapped children, Books for. I. Title.
FMU NUC73-125182

Barchek, James.
A rationale and plan for improving written expression in the elementary schools / developed by Dr. James Barchek, Dr. Jack E. Kittell, Dr. Frank Love. -- [Olympia, Wash.] : Curriculum and Instruction Division, Superintendent of Public Instruction, 1975.
53 p. ; 22 cm.
1. Children--Writing. 2. Children as authors. I. Kittell, Jack E. II. Love, Frank. III. Washington (State). Dept. of Education. IV. Title.
Wa NUC77-88349

Barchenko, Svetozar Aleksandrovich, 1930–
(Zhit' by da zhit')
Жить бы да жить ... Рассказы. ₍Ил.: Э. Б. Аронов₎. Москва, "Сов. писатель," 1974.
254 p. with illus. 16 cm. 0.33rub USSR 74
At head of title: Светозар Барченко.
CONTENTS: На кордоне.—Еще один день.—Среди недели.—В гостях у тещи.—Возвращение.—Жить бы да жить ... —Шестой порог.—Долгие проводы.
I. Title.
PG3479.R36Z5 74–320811

Barchenkov, Aleksandr Grigor'evich.
(Dinamicheskiĭ raschet avtodorozhnykh mostov)
Динамический расчет автодорожных мостов / А. Г. Барченков. — Москва : Транспорт, 1976.
198 p. : ill. ; 22 cm. USSR***
Bibliography : p. 194–₍197₎
1.34rub
1. Bridges—Live loads. 2. Bridges—Design. I. Title.
TG153.B28 77–507041

Barchenkov, S A
(Chelovek razgovarivaet s mashinoĭ)
Человек разговаривает с машиной : автоматическое распознавание и воспроизводство речи / С. А. Барченков. — Москва : Воениздат, 1974.
133 p. : ill. ; 20 cm. USSR***
Bibliography : p. ₍132₎
0.20rub
1. Automatic speech recognition. 2. Speech synthesis. I. Title.
TK7895.S65B37 75–583496

Barchenkova, Valentina Ivanovna
see Orlova, Minna Zalmanovna. (Shveĭnye tovary, golovnye ubory i mekha). 1974.

Barchilon, Jacques.
Le Conte merveilleux français : de 1690 à 1790, cent ans de féerie et de poésie ignorées de l'histoire littéraire / Jacques Barchilon. — Paris : H. Champion, 1975.
xvii, 162 p. : ill. ; 25 cm. — (Bibliothèque de littérature comparée ; 114)
F75-6893
Bibliography: p. ₍151₎-154.
Includes index.
66.00F
1. Fantastic fiction, French—History and criticism. 2. Fairy tales—History and criticism. 3. French fiction—18th century—History and criticism. I. Title. II. Series.
PQ637.F3B3 843'.0872 75-516276
75 MARC

Barchilon, John.
Malpractice and you / John Barchilon. -- New York : Ace Books, c1975.
304 p. ; 18 cm.
"Ace 51663."
1. Malpractice--United States. I. Title.
CLSU NUC77-85307

Barchilón, José.
Gerchunoff, Bufano. ₍San Juan, Argentina₎ Editorial Sanjuanina, 1973.
60 p. 21 cm.
Cover title: Alberto Gerchunoff, Alfredo Bufano.
1. Gerchunoff, Alberto, 1883–1950. 2. Bufano, Alfredo Rodolfo, 1895–1950. I. Title.
PQ7797.G4Z6 74–219384

Barchilon, José.
Huckleberry Finn: a psychoanalytic study ₍by₎ Jose Barchilon and Joel S. Kovel. ₍New York, 1966₎
775–814 p. 23 cm.
Cover title.
Reprinted from Journal of the American Psychoanalytic Association, v. 14, no. 4, Oct. 1966.
IU NUC73-126202

Barchilón, José.
Prisa del canto / José Barchilón. — San Juan, República Argentina : Ediciones S. P. A. E., 1974.
92 p. : ill. ; 25 cm.
"500 ejemplares."
I. Title.
PQ7798.12.A655P7 75–544858

Barchugov, Pavel Vasil'evich, ed.
see Ocherki istorii partiĭnykh organizat͡siĭ Dona. 1973.

[Barchugova, E F]
Ukazatel' literatury po voprosam ėkonomiki i organizat͡sii narodnogo obrazovanii͡a. [Podgotovlen. E. F. Barchugovoĭ, V. P. Zelent͡sovoĭ & T. A. Kaverau] Moskva, 1969.
208 p.
At head of title: Moskovskiĭ ordena Trudovogo Krasnogo Znameni gosudarstvennyĭ pedagogicheskiĭ institut imeni V. I. Lenina. Problemnai͡a laboratorii͡a sot͡sial'no-ėkonomicheskikh issledovaniĭ v oblasti narodnogo obrazovanii͡a.
1. Education–Russia–Bibl. 2. Education–Bibl. I. Moscow. Moskovskiĭ gosudarstvennyĭ pedagogicheskiĭ institut. Problemnai͡a laboratorii͡a sot͡sial'no-ekonomicheskikh issledovaniĭ v oblasti narodnogo obrazovanii͡a. II. Title.
MH NUC76-21644

Barchuk, Ivan.
Al'kohol' i li͡udyna. Toronto, Doroha pravdy, 1957.
107, ₍3₎ p.
I. Title.
MiD NUC74-21965

Barchuk, Ivan.
(Radioblahovisti͡a "Holos I͡Evanhelii v Ukraïnu)
Радіоблаговістя "Голос Євангелії в Україну." Іван Барчук. Торонто, Чікаго, Накладом Християнського вид-ва "Дорога правди," 1971–
v. port. 21 cm. (Видавництво "Дорога правди," ч. 44)
$4.00 (v. 1) C 73–990 (v. 1)
Added t. p.: Gospel broadcast into Ukraine "The Ukrainian voice of the Gospel."
1. Radio in religion. 2. Sermons, Ukrainian. I. Title. II. Title: Gospel broadcast into Ukraine "the Ukrainian voice of the Gospel."
BV656.B35 73–365845

Barchuk, Ivan, comp.
see Rizdvi͡ana zirka. 1956.

Barchuk, Ivan, comp.
see Velykodnii ranok. 1957.

Barchuk, Ivan Danilovich
see Spravochnik zagotoviteli͡a potrebitel'skoĭ kooperat͡sii. 1976.

Barchus, Agnes, 1893–
Eliza R. Barchus, the Oregon artist, 1857–1959 / by Agnes Barchus. — 1st ed. — Portland, Or. : Binford & Mort, c1974.
ix, 166 p., ₍4₎ leaves of plates : ill. (some col.) ; 24 cm.
ISBN 0–8323–0245–7 : $8.95
1. Barchus, Eliza Rosanna, 1857–1959.
ND237.B2615A46 759.13 74–24495
MARC

Barcia, Dorothy R
Bibliography on insects destructive to flowers, cones, and seeds of North American conifers, by Dorothy R. Barcia ₍and₎ Edward P. Merkel. ₍Asheville, N. C., Southeastern Forest Experiment Station₎ 1972.
80 p. 27 cm. (USDA Forest Service research paper SE–92)
Cover title.
Supt. of Docs. no.: A 13.78 : SE–92
1. Coniferae—Diseases and pests—North America—Bibliography. 2. Insects, Injurious and beneficial—North America—Bibliography. 3. Conifer seed—Bibliography. I. Merkel, Edward P., joint author. II. Title. III. Series: United States. Southeastern Forest Experiment Station, Ashville, N. C. USDA Forest Service research paper SE–92.
SD11.A4576 no. 92 634.9'0975 s 72–603050
[Z5354.P3] [016.5349'75] MARC

Barcia, José.
El lunfardo de Buenos Aires / José Barcia. — Buenos Aires : Editorial Paidós, ₍1973₎
173 p. ; 19 cm. — (Biblioteca del hombre contemporáneo ; v. 241)
"Vocabulario" : p. 151–173.
1. Spanish language—Provincialisms—Argentine Republic. 2. Spanish language—Slang. I. Title.
PC4871.B3 467'.9'82 75–557343

Barcia, José
see Gobello, José, 1919- Tango y milonquita. Buenos Aires, Ediciones Republica de San Telmo, 1972.

Barcia, José Rubia
see Rubia Barcia, José.

Barcia y Zamhrana, José de, fl. 1678.
Despertador christiano quadragessimal de sermones doctrnales ₍sic₎, para todos los dias de la Quaresma, con remissiones copiosas al despertador christiano, de sermones enteros para los mismos dias. 3. impression. Madrid, En la Impr. de la Viuda de J. Garcia Infanzon, 1724–
v. front. 31 cm.
1. Lenten sermons. 2. Catholic Church — Sermons. 3. Sermons, Spanish. I. Title.
BV4277.B3 75–580323

Barciński, Florian.
Bogactwa kopalne Polski. Wyd. 2., zmienione. ₍Łódź₎ Czytelnik ₍1949₎
54 p. illus. 23 cm. (Wiedza Powszechna. Wydawnictwo popularno-naukowe, 70) (Bogactwa kopalne świata, zész. 1)
Cover title.
"Wszelkie prawa zastrzeżone."
Bibliography : p. 54.
1. Mines and mineral resources—Poland. I. Title. II. Series: Bogactwa kopalne świata, zesz. 1.
TN95.P7B37 1949 74–211989

Barck, Karlheinz.
Aspekte der Agrarreform in einigen lateinamerikanischen Ländern. ₍Rostock? 1962?₎
₍583₎–592 p. 30 cm.
Caption title.
Reprinted from Wissenschaftliche Zeitschrift der Universität Rostock, 11. jahr. 1962; gesellschafts- und sprachwissenschaftliche Reihe, heft 5.
Summaries in English, Russian and French.
Bibliographical footnotes.
TxU NUC73-126164

Barck, Karlheinz.
see Rimbaud, Jean Nicolas Arthur, 1854-1891. Gedichte ... Leipzig, P. Reclam jun., 1976.

Barck, Klaus.
Perspektiven des technischen Wandels und soziale Interessenlage / von Klaus Barck, Otfried Mickler, Michael Schumann, unter Mitarbeit von Frank Gerlach ... ₍et al.₎. — Göttingen : O. Schwartz, ₍1974₎
159 p. ; 23 cm. — (Schriften der Kommission für wirtschaftlichen und sozialen Wandel ; Bd. 12) GFR***
Bibliography : p. 158–159.
ISBN 3–509–00746–8
1. Industrial management—Germany (Federal Republic, 1949–) 2. Technological innovations—Germany (Federal Republic, 1949–) 3. Engineers—Germany (Federal Republic, 1949–) 4. Scientists—Germany (Federal Republic, 1949–) I. Mickler, Otfried, joint author. II. Schumann, Michael, joint author. III. Title. IV. Series: Kommission für Wirtschaftlichen und Sozialen Wandel. Schriften ; Bd. 12.
HD70.G2B37 75–556367

Barck, Oscar Theodore, 1902–
Since 1900; a history of the United States in our times ₍by₎ Oscar Theodore Barck, Jr. ₍and₎ Nelson Manfred Blake. 5th ed. New York, Macmillan ₍1974₎
xi, 821 p. illus. 24 cm.
Bibliography : p. 771–794.
1. United States—History—20th century. I. Blake, Nelson Manfred, 1908– joint author. II. Title.
E743.B343 1974 973.91 73–3894
ISBN 0–02–305930–3 MARC

Barck, Per Olov Fredrik, 1912–
Ansikten och möten. ₍Av₎ P. O. Barck. Borgå, Söderström & Co., 1972.
266 (2) p. 22 cm. Fmk36.00 HUL
1. Literature, Modern—Addresses, essays, lectures. I. Title.
PN710.B267 72–370978
ISBN 951–52–0022–9

Barck, Per Olov Fredrik, 1912–
Mina oroliga år. [Av] P[er] O[lov] Barck. [Helsingfors], Söderström & Co., 1973.
224 (2) p., 6 l. of plates. 22 cm. Fmk43.50 Fi 73
Autobiographical.
1. Barck, Per Olov Fredrik, 1912– I. Title.
PN5355.F5Z72 74-300531
ISBN 951-52-0112-8

Barckhausen, Henri Auguste, 1834–1914.
Montesquieu, ses idées et ses œuvres, d'après les papiers de La Brède. Genève, Slatkine Reprints, 1970.
vi, 346 p. 22 cm. 65.00F ($15.00U.S.) Sw 70–A–6126
"Réimpression de l'édition de Paris, 1907."
Includes bibliographical references.
1. Montesquieu, Charles Louis de Secondat, baron de La Brède et de, 1689–1755—Political science.
JC179.M8B3 1970 320'.092'4 74–180234
MARC

Barcklow, Brigitte, 1938-
Die Begriffe Barock und Manierismus in der heutigen Shakespeare-Forschung. Freiburg i. Br., 1972.
210 p.
Inaug.-Diss.-Freiburg i. Br.
1. Shakespeare, William—Criticism and interpretation.
MH NIC NUC75-29375

Barckow, Klaus.
see Bibliotheksverbund in Nordrhein-Westfalen ... 1. Aufl. München, Verlag Dokumentation, 1976.

Barclay, , capt.
see Allardice, Robert Barclay, 1779-1854.

Barclay, Alexander, 1810-1855.
see Hammond, George Peter, 1896- The adventures of Alexander Barclay, mountain man, from London corsetier to pioneer farmer in Canada, bookkeeper in St. Louis, superintendent of Bent's Fort, fur trader and mountain man in Colorado and New Mexico, builder of Barclay's Fort on the Santa Fe Trail, New Mexico, in 1848 ... Denver, Old West Pub. Co., 1976.

Barclay, Alexis.
Locura mambo. Barcelona, Euredit [1968]
191 p. 19 cm. (Colección Bringer advice nomenclatura Gemini. 6)
I. Title.
NN NUC73-124305

Barclay, Bertram Donald.
The origin and development of tissues in the stem of Selaginella Wildenowii Bak. 1928.
15 l. illus. 29 cm.
Typescript (carbon copy)
Thesis—University of Chicago.
Bibliography: l. 10.
1. Selaginella wildenowii. 2. Plant cells and tissues. 3. Stems (Botany) I. Title.
QK524.S46B37 74–152189
MARC

Barclay, Cornelia S
Mrs. Singleton. New York, The Authors' Publishing Company [c1880, 1972]
174 p. (Satchel series, no. 24)
Microfilm (positive) Ann Arbor, Mich., University Microfilms, 1972. 8th title of 16. 35 mm. (American fiction series, reel 198.8)
I. Title.
KEmT NUC73-125183

Barclay, David.
The barnhouse. [Eugene, Or., Toad Press, 1970]
[68] p., 1 l. illus. 25 cm.
Poems.
"Designed by Steve Gilbert with additional drawings by Art Hansen, Waldo Chase & Steve Gilbert."
"A Toad Press book."
I. Title.
RPB NUC76-37798

Barclay, David, d.1809.
An account of the emancipation of the slaves of Unity Valley Pen, in Jamaica. London, Printed and sold by W. Phillips [etc.] 1801.
1 card. 7.5 x 12.5 cm. (Slavery Pamphlets)
Micro-opaque. Louisville, Ky., Lost Cause Press, 1962.
Collation of the original: 20 p.
1. Slavery in Jamaica. I. Title.
PSt NUC73-58157

Barclay, David Edward.
Social politics and social reform in Germany, 1890-1933: Rudolf Wissell and the free trade union movement. [Stanford, Calif.] 1974 [c1975]
xii, 392 l.
Thesis (Ph.D.)--Stanford University.
Bibliography: leaves 348-392.
1. Trade unions--Germany--History. 2. Germany--Politics and government--1888-1918. 3. Germany--Politics and government--1918-1933. I. Title.
CSt NUC77-87280

Barclay, Donald A., joint author
see Myatt, DeWitt O Position paper on extra-library information Services... Washington, Science Communication, 1967.

Barclay, Doris L.
see Art education for the disadvantaged child. Kutztown, Pa., Eastern Arts Association [1969]

Barclay, Florence Louisa (Charlesworth) 1862-1921.
Le Rosaire. Roman traduit de l'anglais par E. de Saint-Segond. Paris, Payot, 1959.
287, [1] p. 19 cm.
ODaU-M NUC73-58132

Barclay, Florence Louisa (Charlesworth) 1862-1921.
El rosario. Buenos Aires, Editorial Difusion [1966, c1965]
350 p. 18 cm.
Translation of The rosary.
I. Title.
MB NUC73-124302

Barclay, G. St. J.
see
Barclay, Glen St. John, 1930-

Barclay, George, 1919-1942.
Fighter pilot : a self-portrait / by George Barclay ; edited by Humphrey Wynn ; with a foreword by Sir John Grandy. — London : Kimber, 1976.
224 p. : ill., facsims., maps, ports. ; 24 cm. GB76-23078
Includes index.
ISBN 0-7183-0294-X : £4.50
1. Barclay, George, 1919-1942. 2. World War, 1939-1945—Aerial operations, British. 3. Air pilots—Great Britain—Biography. 4. Great Britain. Royal Air Force—Biography. I. Wynn, Humphrey. II. Title.
D786.B258 1976 940.54'49'410924 77-353533
77 MARC

Barclay, Glen St. John, 1930-
The empire is marching : a study of the military effort of the British Empire 1800-1945 / Glen St. J. Barclay. — London : Weidenfeld & Nicolson, 1976.
276 p., [4] leaves of plates : ill. ; 23 cm. GB***
Bibliography: p. [247]-260.
Includes index.
ISBN 0-297-77125-6 : £6.00
1. Great Britain—History, Military—19th century. 2. Great Britain—History, Military—20th century. 3. Commonwealth of Nations—History, Military. 4. Great Britain—Armed Forces—History. 5. Commonwealth of Nations—Armed Forces—History. I. Title.
DA68.B35 355.03'3017'1241 77-356378
77 MARC

Barclay, Glen St. John, 1930-
Mind over matter: beyond the bounds of nature [by] Glen Barclay. Indianapolis, Bobbs-Merrill [c1973]
142 p. 22 cm.
Includes index.
Bibliography: p. 135-139.
1. Self-defense. 2. Hand-to-hand fighting, Oriental. 3. Spiritualism. I. Title.
IaU CtY NUC74-126396

Barclay, Glen St. John, 1930–
Mind over matter: beyond the bounds of nature [by] Glen Barclay. London, Barker, 1973.
142 p. 22 cm. £2.00 B 73-19807
Includes index.
Bibliography: p. 135-139.
1. Self-defense. 2. Hand-to-hand fighting, Oriental. 3. Spiritualism. I. Title.
GV1111.B26 133 73-174643
ISBN 0-213-16426-4 MARC

Barclay, Glen St. John, 1930–
The rise and fall of the new Roman empire: Italy's bid for world power, 1890–1943 [by] Glen St. J. Barclay. London, Sidgwick and Jackson, 1973.
210, [8] p. illus., ports. 23 cm. £3.95 GB 73-15113
Includes index.
Bibliography: p. 203–206.
1. Italy—History—1870–1915. 2. Italy—History—1914–1945. 3. Italy—Foreign relations—20th century. I. Title.
DG568.5.B37 327.45 73–169489
ISBN 0-283-97862-7 MARC

Barclay, Glen St. John, 1930–
The rise and fall of the new Roman Empire; Italy's bid for world power, 1890–1943 [by] Glen St. J. Barclay. New York, St. Martin's Press [1973]
210 p. illus. 23 cm. $8.95
Bibliography: p. [203]–206.
1. Italy—History—1870–1915. 2. Italy—History—1914–1945. 3. Italy—Foreign relations—20th century. I. Title.
DG568.5.B37 1973b 327.45 72–97412
MARC

Barclay, Glen St. John, 1930–
20th century nationalism [by] Glen St. J. Barclay. New York, Praeger [1972, c1971]
224 p. illus. 22 cm. (Revolutions of our time) $8.50
Bibliography: p. 215–216.
1. World politics—20th century. 2. Nationalism. I. Title.
D443.B343 1972 320.9'04 75–187271
rev MARC

Barclay, Glen St. John, 1930-
see Australian-American relations since 1945 ... Sydney, Holt, Rinehart and Winston, 1976.

Barclay, Glen St. John, 1930-
see The impact of the cold war ... Port Washington, N.Y., Kennikat Press, 1977.

Barclay, H. Douglas, 1932-
see New York (State). Legislature. Joint Committee on Housing and Urban Development. A public hearing... [On the Mitchell-Lama housing program] New York, December 13, 1972. [New York, 1972]

Barclay, H. Douglas, 1932-
see New York (State). Legislature. Select Committee on Housing and Urban Development. [Public hearing...] Albany, U.S. Court Reporters [1974]

Barclay, H. Douglas, 1932-
see New York (State). Legislature. Select Committee on Housing and Urban Development. Transcript of minutes of the Select Committee on Housing and Urban Development... White Plains, N.Y., O'Neill Reporting Co. [1974]

Barclay, Ian.
He is everything to me : an exposition of Psalm 23 / Ian Barclay. — New York : Scribner, c1972.
96 p. ; 21 cm. — (Lyceum editions) (The Scribner library)
Includes bibliographical references.
O.T. Psalms XXIII. English. 1972.
ISBN 0-684-14543-X : $1.95
1. Bible. O.T. Psalms XXIII—Meditations. I. Bible. O.T. Psalms XXIII. English. 1972. II. Title.
BS1450.23d.B36 242 75-29735
76 MARC

Barclay, Irene.
People need roots : the story of the St. Pancras Housing Association / Irene Barclay. — London : Bedford Square Press : distributed by Research Publications Services, c1976.
144 p. : ill. ; 23 cm. GB***
Includes bibliographical references.
ISBN 0-7199-0918-X : £2.50. ISBN 0-7199-0921-X pbk.
1. St. Pancras Housing Association—History. 2. Relocation (Housing)—England—St. Pancras. 3. Slums—England—St. Pancras. I. Title.
HD7334.S24B37 362.8 77-354569
77 MARC

Barclay, Isabel.
see Song of the forest ... [Ottawa] Oberon Press, c1977.

Barclay, J Richard.
The role of comprehension in remembering sentences. [Minneapolis] 1971.
v, 89 l. 29 cm.
Thesis (Ph.D)—University of Minnesota.
Bibliography: leaves 86-89.
MnU NUC73-32636

Barclay, J Richard.
The role of comprehension in remembering sentences. Minneapolis, Minn., 1971 [1972]
v, 89 l. illus.
Thesis—University of Minnesota.
Microfilm of typescript. Ann Arbor, Mich., University Microfilms, 1972. 1 reel.
Bibliography: leaves 86-89.
1. Educational psychology. 2. Psychology—Experiments. I. Title.
NSyU NUC74-124446

Barclay, James. An examination of Mr. Kenrick's review of Mr. Johnson's edition of Shakespeare. 1975.
in On Johnson's Shakespeare, 1765-1766. New York, Garland Pub., 1975.

[**Barclay, James**] fl. 1881.
Report of the expert on the test trials of automatic cut-off steam engines, at the first Millers' international exhibition. Cincinnati, June, 1880 ... [Cincinnati? c1881]
Cover-title, 84 p. 3 pl. 23 cm.
Plates printed on both sides.
1. Steam-engines—Testing. I. Cincinnati. Millers' international exhibition, 1880.
TJ475.B24 6-31862

Barclay, James Ralph, 1926-
The Barclay classroom climate inventory: a research manual and studies [by] James R. Barclay, with the assistance of Lisa K. Barclay [and] William E. Stilwell. Lexington, Ky., Educational Skills Development, 1972.
298 p.
Cover title.
Includes bibliography.
1. Interaction analysis in education. I. Title.
MoU NUC74-133469

Barclay, James Ralph, 1926-
Measuring the social change climate of the classroom. James R. Barclay. Englewood Cliffs, N.J., Educational Technology Publications, c1971.
20 p. 22 cm. (Educational technology research, 40)
Includes bibliographical references.
1. Education. I. Title. II. Series.
IMacoW NUC76-37797

Barclay, Janet M
Emily Brontë criticism, 1900–1968; an annotated check list [by] Janet M. Barclay. [New York] New York Public Library; [distributed by] Readex Books [1974]
76 p. 26 cm.
1. Brontë, Emily Jane, 1818–1848 —Bibliography. I. New York (City). Public Library. II. Title.
Z8121.98.B37 016.823'8 74-76459
ISBN 0-87104-227-4 MARC

Barclay, John, 1582–1621.
Euphormionis Lusinini Satyricon. (Euphormio's Satyricon) 1605–1607. Transl. from the Latin with introduction and notes by David A. Fleming. Nieuwkoop, B. de Graaf, 1973.
xxxvi, 383 p. 25 cm. (Bibliotheca humanistica & reformatorica, v. 6) fl 90.00 NeB 73-July-Sept
English and Latin.
Includes bibliographical references.
I. Title. II. Series.
PA8465.S3F5 873'.04 74-168727
ISBN 90-6004-299-9 MARC

Barclay, John, 1582-1621.
Ioan Barclai Argenis, Verdeutscht Durch Martin Opitzen. Amsterdam, Bey Iohan Iansson, 1644.
1 reel 35 mm. 23 plates. (German Baroque Literature, reel 50, no. 208a) Research Publications, New Haven, Conn., 1970.
Microfilm (positive)
Collation of the original: 750 p.
I. Opitz, Martin, 1597-1639. II. Title: Argenis.
PSt NUC74-151528

Barclay, John, 1582–1621.
Ioannis Barclaii Satyricon: cui accessit pars V. sive Alitophili Veritatis lachrymae. Cum clavi auctiore. Lvgdvni Batavorvm, Ex officina I. Marci, 1628.
470, 252, 244 p. 14 cm.
Parts 1–3 are paged continuously.
Parts 2–5 have special title pages. That of pt. 2 has imprint date 1627.
Author of the Veritatis lacrimae is C. B. Morisot. Cf. Dict. des lettres françaises.
CONTENTS: Euphormionis Lvsinini Satyricon (2 pts.)—Evphormionis Satyrici Apologia pro se.—Evphormionis Satyrici Icon animorum.—Alitophili Veritatis lacrymae.
I. Morisot, Claude Barthélemy, 1592–1661. Veritatis lacrimae. 1628. II. Title: Satyricon.
PA8465.S3 75-545221

Barclay, John, 1582-1621.
Iohn Barclay his Argenis, translated ovt of Latine into English; the prose vpon His Maiesties command, by Sir Robert Le Grys, and the verses by Thomas May. With a clauis annexed to it for the satisfaction of the reader, and helping him to vnderstand, what persons were by the author intended, vnder the fained names imposed by him vpon them. London, Printed by F. Kyngston for R. Meighen and H. Seile [1628 or 9]
489 (i. e. 499) p. 23 plates 22 cm.
This edition was issued in 1628 and also, with altered imprint date, in 1629. L.C. copy has a mutilated t.p. without a date.
STC 1393 or 1394.
L.C. copy is one of those containing plates engr. by L. Gaultier and C. Mellan.
I. Le Grys, Robert, Sir, d. 1635. II. May, Thomas, 1595-1650. III. Gaultier, Léonard, 1561-1641. IV. Mellan, Claude, 1598-1688. V. Title: Argenis.
PA8465.A72L4 1628 77-350320
77 MARC

Barclay, John Bruce.
A pot of paint : one hundred years of Rolland Decorators Limited / [text by J. B. Barclay]. — Edinburgh : Rolland Decorators Ltd, 1975.
48 p. : ill., ports. ; 21 cm. GB76-24208
ISBN 0-9504759-0-4
1. Rolland Decorators Limited. I. Title.
TT304.B37 338.7'69'809411 77-354599
77 MARC

Barclay, John Bruce.
The Tounis Scule : the Royal High School of Edinburgh / by J. B. Barclay. — Edinburgh [c/o University of Edinburgh, Department of Educational Studies, 11 Buccleuch Place, Edinburgh EH8 9JT]) : Royal High School Club, 1974.
vii, 152 p., [16] p. of plates : ill., coat of arms, music, ports. ; 20 cm. GB 74-17113
Includes index.
ISBN 0-9503433-0-7 : £2.50
1. Edinburgh. Royal High School. I. Title.
LF795.E34B37 373.414'45 74-188524
MARC

Barclay, John Bruce.
When work is done [by] J. B. Barclay. The Diamond Jubilee book of the Edinburgh University Extra-Mural Association. [Edinburgh] Edinburgh University Extra-Mural Association.
48 p. 12 cm. B***
1. Adult education—Great Britain. I. Title.
LC5256.G7B35 374.9'42 73-155117
MARC

Barclay, John Scribner
see Oklahoma. State University of Agriculture and Applied Science, Stillwater. Dept. of Zoology. The role of wildlife in the Stillwater Creek Greenbelt. Stillwater, John S. Barclay and Michael R. Dunbar, 1973.

Barclay, Katherine J
Brewerton, New York, U.S.A. / [by Katherine J. Barclay]. — [s.l. : Barclay, c1973]
96 p. : ill. ; 17 x 24 cm.
Includes index.
1. Brewerton, N.Y.
F129.B472B37 917.47'65 75-329072
76 MARC

Barclay, Kenneth B
The origins of the community college movement in Connecticut, 1946-1961 / Kenneth B. Barclay. -- Kent, Ohio 1975.
vi, 203 leaves ; 29 cm. -- Kent State University Graduate School Dissertations : Department of Education)
Bibliography: leaves 197-203.
Thesis (Ph.D.)--Kent State University.
1. Municipal junior colleges--Connecticut. I. Title. II. Series.
OKentU NUC77-86848

Barclay, Linda Louise, 1948-
Gospel writing in the later middle ages: three dramatic examples, Das St. Galler Passionsspiel, La Passion Nostre Seigneur (Ste. Genevieve) and the York plays. [Bloomington, Ind.] 1975.
233 p.
Thesis (Ph. D.)--Indiana University.
Vita.
InU NUC77-87282

Barclay, Lisa Frances Kurcz.
The comparative efficacies of Spanish, English and bilingual cognitive verbal instruction with Mexican-American head start children. [Stanford, Calif.] 1969.
xviii, 354 l.
Xerox copy.
Thesis–Stanford University.
Bibliography: leaves 343-354.
1. Socially handicapped children–Education–Union City, Calif. 2. Compensatory education. 3. Mexican Americans–Education–Union City, Calif. 4. Cognition (Child psychology) I. Title.
CU-SB NUC73-47888

Barclay, Lisa Frances Kurcz.
The comparative efficacies of Spanish, English and bilingual cognitive verbal instruction with Mexican-American Head Start children. [n.p.] 1969.
xviii, 354 l.
Thesis—Stanford University.
Bibliography: leaves 343-354.
Microfilm. Ann Arbor, Mich., University Microfilms. 1 reel. 35 mm.
TxU NUC74-126815

Barclay, Martha Thomson.
Major American emphases in theories of oral interpretation from 1890 to 1950. [Minneapolis] 1968.
v, 331 l. 29 cm.
Thesis—University of Minnesota.
Bibliography: leaves [301]-331.
Microfilm. Ann Arbor, Mich., University Microfilms. 1 reel. 35 mm.
1. Oral interpretation. I. Title.
TxU NUC73-124309

Barclay, Nancy A
Organizing of household activities by home managers. [n.p.] 1970 [1972]
83 l. tables.
Thesis–Ohio State University.
Vita.
Photocopy. Ann Arbor, University Microfilms, 1972. 21 cm.
1. Family. 2. Family research. I. Title.
GU NUC73-124209

Barclay, Nancy A.
see Adequacy of selected goods and services as evaluated b homemakers in a resource frontier community. Winnipeg Center for Settlement Studies, University of Manitoba, 1974

Barclay, Oliver R
Reasons for faith / Oliver R. Barclay. — Downers Grove Ill. : InterVarsity Press, 1974.
142, [1] p. ; 18 cm.
Bibliography: p. [143]
ISBN 0-87784-764-9 : $2.25
1. Apologetics—20th century. I. Title.
BT1102.B24 239 74-1430
MAR

Barclay, Oliver R
Reasons for faith / [by] Oliver R. Barclay. — London : Inter-Varsity Press, 1974.
143 p. ; 18 cm. — (Inter-varsity Press pocketbook) GB74-19827
Bibliography: p. [143]
ISBN 0-85110-376-6 : £0.50
1. Apologetics—20th century. I. Title.
BT1102.B24 1974b 239 75-307595
75 MARC

Barclay, Pamela.
Charley Pride. Illus.: Dick Brude. Mankato, Minn Creative Education; [distributed by Childrens Press, Chicago, 1974, c1975]
31 p. illus. (part col.) 25 cm. (Rock 'n pop stars)
SUMMARY: A biography of the black man who broke the col line in country music.
ISBN 0-87191-397-6
1. Pride, Charley — Juvenile literature. [1. Pride, Charley. Singers. 3. Negroes—Biography] I. Brude, Dick, illus. II. Tit
ML3930.P75B3 784'.092'4 [B] 74-146
[92] MAR

Barclay, Pamela.
Duke Ellington; ambassador of music. Illustrated b Harold Henriksen. Mankato, Minn., Creative Educatio [distributed by Childrens Press, Chicago, 1974]
29 p. col. illus. 25 cm. (Close-ups)
SUMMARY: A biography of the black musician who in fifty yea has composed 2000 songs and performed them all over the world.
ISBN 0-87191-367-4
1. Ellington, Duke, 1899- —Juvenile literature. [1. Ellingto Duke, 1899- 2. Musicians. 3. Negroes—Biography] Henriksen, Harold, illus. II. Title.
ML3930.E44B3 785.4'2'0924 [B] 74-82
MAR

Barclay, Pamela.
Secretariat. Illustrated by Harold Henriksen. Ma kato, Minn., Creative Education; [distributed by Childre Press, Chicago, 1974]
31 p. col. illus. 25 cm. (Superstars)
SUMMARY: A biography of the horse who in 1973 became t ninth horse in ninety-one years to win the Triple Crown.
ISBN 0-87191-377-1
1. Secretariat (Race horse)—Juvenile literature. [1. Secretar (Race horse) 2. Horses] I. Henriksen, Harold, illus. II. Tit
SF355.S42B37 798'.43 74-113
MAI

Barclay, Robert Edward, 1893-
The Copper Basin, 1890 to 1963 / by R. E. Barclay. — [Knoxville? Tenn.] : Barclay, c1975.
vii, 187 p. : ill. ; 29 cm.
1. Cooper industry and trade—Ducktown, Tenn.—History. 2. Copper mines and mining—Tennessee—History. 3. Ducktown, Tenn.—History. I. Title.
HD9539.C7U534 75-332106
338.2'7'4309768875
76 MARC

Barclay, Robert Edward, 1893–
The railroad comes to Ducktown, by R. E. Barclay. [Knoxville, Tenn., Printed by Cole Print. & Thesis Service, 1973]
x, 193 p. illus. 29 cm.
Bibliography: p. 186–187.
1. Railroads — Ducktown, Tenn. 2. Railroads — Polk Co., Tenn. 3. Ducktown, Tenn.—History. 4. Polk, Co., Tenn.—History. I. Title.
HE2781.D8B35 385'.09768'875 74–154287
MARC

Barclay, Roderick, Sir, 1909-
Ernest Bevin and the Foreign Office, 1932-1969 / [by] Sir Roderick Barclay. — London : Latimer : The author, 1975.
xii, 166 p., [8] p. of plates : 1 ill., facsim., ports. ; 23 cm. GB75-30270
Includes index.
ISBN 0-9504558-0-6 : £3.75
1. Barclay, Roderick, Sir, 1909- 2. Diplomats—Great Britain—Correspondence, reminiscences, etc. 3. Bevin, Ernest, 1881-1951. 4. Great Britain. Foreign Office. I. Title.
DA566.9.B48B37 354'.41'0610924 76-360828
76 MARC

Barclay, Rosalyn L 1943-
Modification of pregnancy anxieties; some comparisons between pregnant and non-pregnant women, by Rosalyn L. Barclay. [Detroit] 1972.
ix, 102 l. 29 cm.
Thesis—Wayne State University.
Vita.
Bibliography: leaves 81-85.
1. Pregnancy. 2. Anxiety. I. Title.
MiDW NUC74-124439

Barclay, Stephen Lorraine, 1945-
Mutations of helper phage P2 and E. coli which affect development of satellite phage P4. [n.p.] 1975.
165 l. illus. 29 cm.
Thesis (Ph.D.)--University of Wisconsin.
Vita.
Includes bibliography.
I. Title.
WU NUC77-88296

Barclay, Thomas Laird, ed.
see International Congress on Research in Burns, 3d, Prague, 1970. Research in burns. Bern, Hans Huber [1971]

Barclay, Thomas Laird, joint author
see Muir, Ian Fraser Kerr. Burns and their treatment. 2nd ed. London, Lloyd-Luke, 1974.

Barclay, W A
Taxation and the B.C. farmer : a layman's guide : a study / prepared for the British Columbia Department of Agriculture by Thorne Riddell & Co., W. A. Barclay is the author. — Victoria, B.C. : K. M. Macdonald, Queen's printer, [1975] C***
86 p. ; 28 cm.
1. Agriculture—Taxation—British Columbia. 2. Agriculture—Taxation—Canada. I. Thorne Riddell & Co. II. British Columbia. Dept. of Agriculture. III. Title.
343'.711'055 76-352534
76 MARC

Barclay, Wade Crawford, 1874–
History of Methodist missions. New York, Board of Missions and Church Extension of the Methodist Church, 1949–
v. maps. 24 cm.
Vol. 3 published by the Board of Missions of the Methodist Church, vol. 4 by the Board of Global Ministries of the United Methodist Church.
Includes bibliographical references.
CONTENTS: pt. 1. Early American Methodism, 1769–1844: v. 1. Missionary motivation and expansion. v. 2. To reform the nation.— pt. 2. The Methodist Episcopal Church, 1845–1939: v. 3. Widening horizons, 1845–95. v. 4. Copplestone, J. T. Twentieth-century perspectives, 1896–1939.
1. Methodist Church (United States)—Missions. I. Copplestone, J. Tremayne, 1907– II. Title.
BV2550.B33 266'.7'6 50–231
rev MARC

Barclay, William, lecturer in the University of Glasgow.
Ambassador for Christ; the life and teaching of Paul. Valley Forge [Pa.] Judson Press [1974, c1973]
183 p. 22 cm.
"Originally published in 1951 by the Church of Scotland Youth Committee."
1. Paul, Saint, apostle. I. Title.
BS2506.B34 1974 225.9'24 [B] 73–9762
ISBN 0–8170–0631–1 MARC

Barclay, William, lecturer in the University of Glasgow.
And he had compassion / William Barclay. — Revised ed. — Edinburgh : St. Andrew Press, 1975.
vii, 272 p. ; 19 cm. GB75-12906
Published in 1955 under title: And he had compassion on them.
Bibliography: p. [271]-272.
ISBN 0-7152-0247-2 : £0.90
1. Jesus Christ—Miracles. I. Title.
BT366.B36 1975 232.9'5 75-324380
75 MARC

Barclay, William, lecturer in the University of Glasgow.
Barclay introduces the Bible. [Phonotape] Nashville, Abingdon Audio-Graphics, 1973.
2 cassettes. 1 7/8 in. per sec.
Recorded 1973.
Contents.-Tape 1. The ancient book, The Old Testament, The New Testament.-Tape 2. The Apocrypha, A speciman demonstration, How to approach the Bible.
1. Bible—Introductions. I. Title.
NRCR IEG NUC74-131889

Barclay, William, lecturer in the University of Glasgow.
The Beatitudes and the Lord's prayer for everyman / William Barclay. — New York : Harper & Row, 1975, c1964.
256 p. ; 20 cm.
Combined ed. of the author's The plain man looks at the Beatitudes, and The plain man looks at the Lord's prayer.
ISBN 0-06-060393-3 : $2.95
1. Beatitudes. 2. Lord's prayer. I. Title.
[BT382.B369 1975] 226'.9'06 75-9309
75 MARC

Barclay, William, lecturer in the University of Glasgow.
By what authority? / William Barclay. — London : Darton, Longman & Todd, 1974.
221 p. ; 18 cm. GB75-02641
ISBN 0-232-51205-1 : £0.65
1. Authority (Religion)—History of doctrines. I. Title.
BT88.B35 1974 201.1 75-309676
75 MARC

Barclay, William, lecturer in the University of Glasgow.
By what authority? / William Barclay. — Valley Forge : Judson Press, [1975, c1974]
221 p. ; 22 cm.
ISBN 0-8170-0675-3 : $3.95
1. Authority (Religion)—History of doctrines. I. Title.
BT88.B35 1975 201.1 75-4532
75 MARC

Barclay, William, lecturer in the University of Glasgow.
Daily celebration; devotional readings for every day of the year. Edited by Denis Duncan. Waco, Tex., Word Books [1973, c1971]
316 p. 24 cm. $4.95
Readings originally appeared in British weekly, 1957–1970.
1. Devotional calendars. I. Title.
BV4811.B32 1973 242'.2 77–175724
ISBN 0–340–14990–6 MARC

Barclay, William, lecturer in the University of Glasgow.
Ethics in a permissive society. London, Collins, 1971.
223 p. 22 cm. (The Baird lecture)
"From the television series of Baird lectures, Jesus Today: the Christian ethic in the twentieth century."
Bibliography: p. 217-222.
1. Christian ethics. I. Title. II. Series.
IEN MU CaOTP NUC73-32646

Barclay, William, lecturer in the University of Glasgow.
Every day with William Barclay; devotional readings for every day. Edited by Denis Duncan. London, Hodder and Stoughton [1973]
285 p. 24 cm.
"A companion volume to Through the year with William Barclay, published in... 1971."
Articles originally appeared in British weekly.
1. Devotional calendars. 2. Meditations. I. Duncan, Denis, ed. II. Title.
GU NUC75-21196

Barclay, William, lecturer in the University of Glasgow.
The Gospels and Acts / William Barclay. -- London : SCM Press, 1976.
2 v. ; 23 cm.
"Volume one first published separately 1966," under title: The first three Gospels.
Published separately in Philadelphia, 1976, as: Introduction to the first three Gospels; and, Introduction to John and the Acts of the Apostles.
Bibliography: v. 1, p. [284]-288; v. 2, p. [320]-323.
Contents.--v. 1. The first three Gospels.--v. 2. The fourth Gospel. The Acts of the Apostles.
1. Bible. N. T. Gospels and Acts--Introductions. I. Title.
MSohG NUC77-91990

Barclay, William, lecturer in the University of Glasgow.
Introducing the Bible. Abingdon, 1972.
155 p.
1. Bible—Introductions. I. Title.
TxDaM-P PPiPT NjPT NUC74-125986
InAndC-T IEG NRCR MNtcA MBU-T MH-AH MChB-W

Barclay, William, lecturer in the University of Glasgow.
Introduction to John and the Acts of the apostles / by William Barclay. — Philadelphia : Westminster Press, c1976.
341 p. ; 22 cm.
Published in Great Britain as vol. 2 of The Gospels and Acts, entitled: The fourth Gospel and Acts of the apostles.
Bibliography: p. [320]-323.
Includes indexes.
ISBN 0-664-24771-7
1. Bible. N.T. John—Introductions. 2. Bible. N.T. Acts—Introductions. I. Title.
BS2615.2.B33 226'.5'077 75-38902
75 MARC

Barclay, William, lecturer in the University of Glasgow.
Introduction to the first three Gospels / by William Barclay. — A rev. ed. of The first three Gospels. — Philadelphia : Westminster Press, c1975.
303 p. ; 22 cm.
Bibliography: p. [284]-288.
Includes indexes.
ISBN 0-664-24798-9
1. Bible. N.T. Gospels—Introductions. I. Title.
BS2555.2.B27 1975 226 75-37545
75 MARC

Barclay, William, lecturer in the University of Glasgow.
Jesus Christ for today. Nashville, Tidings [1973]
86 p. 19 cm. $1.00
Page 86 blank for "Notes."
Bibliography: p. 5.
1. Bible. N. T. Luke—Criticism, interpretation, etc. 2. Evangelistic work. I. Title.
BS2595.2.B37 226'.4'06 73–86376
MARC

Barclay, William, lecturer in the University of Glasgow.
Jesus of Nazareth / William Barclay ; based on the film directed by Franco Zefirelli, from the script by Anthony Burgess, Suso Cecchi d'Amico and Franco Zefirelli ; photos. by Paul Ronald. — London ; Cleveland : Collins, 1977.
285 p. : col. ill. ; 26 cm. GB***
ISBN 0-00-250653-X : $14.95
1. Jesus Christ—Biography. 2. Christian biography—Palestine. I. Zefirelli, Franco. II. Burgess, Anthony, 1917- III. Cecchi d'Amico, Suso. IV. Jesus of Nazareth.
BT301.2.B25 232.9'01 77-365179
77 MARC

Barclay, William, lecturer in the University of Glasgow.
The making of the Bible. Nashville, Abingdon Press [1961]
94 p. 21 cm.
Includes bibliographical references.
1. Bible—Canon. I. Title.
IU NUC74-168004

Barclay, William, lecturer in the University of Glasgow.
Marching on : daily readings for younger people / William Barclay ; edited by Denis Duncan. — Philadelphia : Westminster Press, [1975] c1974.
223 p. ; 20 cm.
Companion volume to the author's Marching orders.
SUMMARY: Daily readings for six months, with suggested additional Bible readings, present the philosophies of Christian writer William Barclay.
ISBN 0-664-24827-6
1. Youth—Prayer-books and devotions—English. [1. Prayer books and devotions] I. Duncan, Denis, ed. II. Title.
BV4850.B28 1975 242'.2 74-30053
74 MARC

Barclay, William, lecturer in the University of Glasgow.
Marching orders : daily readings for younger people / William Barclay ; edited by Denis Duncan. — Philadelphia : Westminster Press, [1975] c1973.
192 p. ; 20 cm.
SUMMARY: Daily readings for six months, with suggested additional Bible readings, present the philosophies of Christian writer William Barclay.
ISBN 0-664-24826-8
1. Youth—Prayer-books and devotions—English. [1. Prayer books and devotions] I. Duncan, Denis, ed. II. Title.
BV4850.B29 1975 242'.2 74-26601
74 MARC

Barclay, William, lecturer in the University of Glasgow.
New Testament words. Philadelphia, Westminster Press [1974, c1964]
301 p. 18 cm. $3.95
"Keyed to specific passages in the Daily study Bible series ... includes all the words originally explained in Dr. Barclay's A New Testament wordbook and More New Testament words."
1. Greek language, Biblical—Dictionaries—English. I. The Daily study Bible series. II. Title.
PA881.B29 1974 487'.4 73-12737
ISBN 0-664-20994-7 MARC

Barclay, William, lecturer in the University of Glasgow.
The old law & the new law. Edinburgh, Saint Andrew Press, 1972.
vii, 121 p. 19 cm. £0.40 B 72-15770
1. Commandments, Ten. 2. Sermon on the Mount. I. Title.
BV4655.B377 1972b 241.5'2 73-155746
ISBN 0-7152-0197-2 MARC

Barclay, William, lecturer in the University of Glasgow.
The plain man's guide to ethics; thoughts on the Ten Commandments. [London] Collins Fontana Books [1973]
205 p. 18 cm. (Fontana religious) £0.40 GB***
1. Commandments, Ten. I. Title.
BV4655.B378 241.5'2 74-166199
ISBN 0-00-623010-5 MARC

Barclay, William, lecturer in the University of Glasgow.
A spiritual autobiography/William Barclay. -- Grand Rapids : Eerdmans, 1975.
122 p.
First published in 1975 by A.R. Mowbray under title: Testament of Faith.
ISBN 0-80280346-7.
1. Barclay, William, lecturer in the University of Glasgow. I. Title.
IObT NUC77-99173

Barclay, William, lecturer in the University of Glasgow.
The Ten Commandments for today. [1st U. S. ed.] New York, Harper & Row [c1973]
205 p. 21 cm. $5.95
1. Commandments, Ten. I. Title.
BV4655.B378 1973b 241.5'2 73-18673
ISBN 0-06-060416-6 MARC

Barclay, William, lecturer in the University of Glasgow.
Testament of faith / by William Barclay. — London : Mowbray, 1975.
xii, 124 p. ; 23 cm. GB75-09007
American ed. published under title: A spiritual autobiography.
Bibliography: p. 123-124.
ISBN 0-264-66137-0 : £2.75
1. Barclay, William, lecturer in the University of Glasgow. I. Title.
BS2351.B28A37 1975b 285'.2'0924 75-317650
75 MARC

Barclay, William, lecturer in the University of Glasgow.
Through the year with William Barclay. Devotional readings for every day. Edited by Denis Duncan. London, Hodder and Stoughton [1971]
316 p. 24 cm.
1. Devotional calendars. 2. Meditations. I. Duncan, Denis. II. Title.
IEG NUC73-32632

Barclay, William, lecturer in the University of Glasgow.
William Barclay : a spiritual autobiography. — [Grand Rapids] : Eerdmans, [1975]
122 p. ; 22 cm.
Bibliography: p. 122.
ISBN 0-8028-3464-7
1. Barclay, William, lecturer in the University of Glasgow. I. Title. II. Title: A spiritual autobiography.
BS2351.B28A37 1975 230'.092'4 73-76528
74 MARC

Barclay, William, lecturer in the University of Glasgow.
***see* Bible. N.T. Corinthians. English. Barclay. 1975. The Letters to the Corinthians. Rev. ed. Philadelphia, Westminster Press, c1975.**

Barclay, William, lecturer in the University of Glasgow.
see Bible. N.T. Epistles of John. English. Barclay. c1976. The letters of John and Jude. Rev. ed. Philadelphia, Westminster Press, c1976.

Barclay, William, lecturer in the University of Glasgow.
***see* Bible. N.T. Epistles of Paul. English. Barclay. 1975. The letters to the Philippians, Colossians, and Thessalonians. Rev. ed. Philadelphia, Westminster Press, c1975.**

Barclay, William, lecturer in the University of Glasgow.
see Bible. N.T. Galatians. English. Barclay. 1976. The letters to the Galatians and Ephesians. Rev. ed. Philadelphia, Westminster Press, c1976.

Barclay, William, lecturer in the University of Glasgow.
see Bible. N.T. Hebrews. English. Barclay. 1976. The Letter to the Hebrews. Rev. ed. Philadelphia, Westminster Press, c1976.

Barclay, William, lecturer in the University of Glasgow.
see Bible. N.T. James. English. Barclay. 1976. The letters of James and Peter. Rev. ed. Philadelphia, Westminster Press, c1976.

Barclay, William, lecturer in the University of Glasgow, ed.
see Bible. N.T. John. English. Barclay. 1975. The Gospel of John. Rev. ed. Philadelphia, Westminster Press, c1975.

Barclay, William, lecturer in the University of Glasgow, ed.
***see* Bible. N.T. Luke. English. Barclay. 1975. The Gospel of Luke. Philadelphia, Westminster Press, [1975]**

Barclay, William, lecturer in the University of Glasgow, ed.
see Bible. N.T. Mark. English. Barclay. 1975. The Gospel of Mark. Philadelphia, Westminster Press, [1975]

Barclay, William, lecturer in the University of Glasgow, ed.
see Bible. N.T. Matthew. English. Barclay. 1975. The Gospel of Matthew. Rev. ed. Philadelphia, Westminster Press, [1975]

Barclay, William, lecturer in the University of Glasgow.
***see* Bible. N.T. Pastoral epistles. English. Barclay. 1975. The letters to Timothy, Titus, and Philemon. Rev. ed. Philadelphia, Westminster Press, c1975.**

Barclay, William, lecturer in the University of Glasgow.
see Bible. N.T. Revelation. English. Barclay. 1976. The Revelation of John. Rev. ed. Philadelphia, Westminster Press, c1976.

Barclay, William, lecturer in the University of Glasgow.
see Bible. N.T. Romans. English. Barclay. 1975. The Letter to the Romans. Rev. ed. Philadelphia, Westminster Press, c1975.

Barclay, William, lecturer in the University of Glasgow.
see Biblical studies ... London, Collins, 1976.

Barclay, William, lecturer in the University of Glasgow.
see Biblical studies ... Philadelphia, Westminster Press, c1976.

Barclay, William, 1570?-1630?
De Potestate Papae. [Menston, Eng.] Scolar Press, 1973.
343 p. (English recusant literature, 1558-1640, v. 136)
Reprint of 1609 ed.
1. Papacy. I. Title.
UU ICN WMM NjMD NUC74-125985
KMK

Barclay, William, 1944-
see Racial conflict, discrimination, & power ... New York, AMS Press, c1976.

Barclay, William John, 1944-
The political economy of copper / by William John Barclay. -- [East Lansing] : Barclay, 1975.
[2], vii, 299, [i.e. 300] leaves : ill. ; 29 cm.
Thesis (Ph. D.)--Michigan State University.
Bibliography: leaves 279-299.
1. Copper industry and trade--Chile. I. Title.
MiEM NUC77-98947

Barclay, William L
By His Spirit [by] William L. Barclay. Washington, Review and Herald Pub. Association [1972]
375 p. 21 cm.
1. Devotional calendars. I. Title.
BV4811.B333 242'.2 70-190578
MARC

Barclay-Haft, Elisabeth.
Nonnie and her family: a canine autobiography for humans, recounted by Elisabeth Barclay-Haft. Illustrated by Ana-Lee. Los Angeles, 1956.
[68] p. illus.
I. Title.
CLU NUC76-62503

Barclay-Nitter, Johan.
Fløytelyd i moll. Dikt. Oslo, Lutherstiftelsen, 1971.
51 p. 21 cm. kr18.00 N 71-39
I. Title.
PT8951.12.A73F5 72-373482

Barclays Bank, ltd.
An eagle displayed. [London, 1964]
50 p. col. illus.
1. Banks and banking—Gt. Brit.—History. I. Title.
ICU NUC75-81132

Barclays Bank (Dominion, Colonial, and Overseas)
The Cayman Islands [an economic survey]. London, 1971.
23 p. illus., maps. 20 cm. GB***
1. Cayman Islands—Economic conditions.
HC157.C3B3 1971 330.9'7292'1 74-167365
MARC

Barclays Bank (Dominion, Colonial and Overseas).
Emigrating to South Africa: a guide to procedure and an introduction to life in the Republic; compiled and designed by Barclays Bank D. C. O. Johannesburg, the Bank, 1971.
83 p. illus. (some col.) 21 cm. free SANB Afl./B. 4
1. Africa, South—Emigration and immigration—Handbooks, manuals, etc. I. Title.
JV8819.A1 1971 325'.242'0968 73-152495
ISBN 0-620-00-190-9 MARC

Barclays Bank (Dominion, Colonial and Overseas)
Malawi. Blantyre, Malawi, 1970.
33 p. illus. 21 cm.
On cover: An economic survey.
1. Malawi—Economic conditions.
HC517.M3B37 330.9'689'704 73-171384
MARC

Barclays Bank (London and International) Limited
see
Barclays Bank International Limited.

Barclays Bank International Limited.
An economic survey of Bermuda. [London] 1972.
31 p. illus. 22 cm. (A Barclays international economic survey)
1. Bermuda Islands—Economic conditions. 2. Bermuda Islands—Social conditions. I. Title. II. Series.
HC157.B4B37 1972 330.9'7299 74-179951
MARC

Barclays Bank International Limited.
An economic survey of Cyprus.
London.
v. illus. 21 cm. (: A Barclays international economic survey)
Continues Cyprus, an economic survey issued by the bank under its earlier name: Barclays Bank (Dominion, Colonial and Overseas)
1. Cyprus—Economic conditions. I. Title. II. Title: Cyprus. III. Series.
HC497.C9B33 330.9'564'504 73-640240

Barclays Bank International Limited.
An economic survey of Israel. London, 1972.
27 p. illus. 21 cm. (A Barclays international economic survey) GB***
Cover title: Israel.
1. Israel—Economic conditions. I. Title. II. Series.
HC497.P2B262 1972 330.9'5694'05 74-167871 MARC

Barclays Bank International Limited.
An economic survey of Seychelles and British Indian Ocean territory. London, 1972.
31 p. illus. 21 cm. (A Barclays international economic survey) GB***
1. Seychelles Islands—Economic conditions. 2. British Indian Ocean Territory—Economic conditions. I. Title. II. Series.
HC517.S45B33 1972 330.9'69'6 74-167896 MARC

Barclays Bank International Limited.
An economic survey of Swaziland. London, 1972.
38 p. illus. 21 cm. (A Barclays international economic survey) GB***
1. Swaziland—Economic conditions. 2. Swaziland—Social conditions. I. Title. II. Series.
HC517.S9B37 1972 330.9'68'306 74-167385 MARC

Barclays Bank International Limited.
An economic survey of Trinidad and Tobago. London.
v. illus. 21 cm. (: A Barclays international economic survey)
Continues Trinidad and Tobago issued by the bank under its earlier name: Barclays Bank (Dominion, Colonial and Overseas)
1. Trinidad and Tobago—Economic conditions. I. Title. II. Title: Trinidad and Tobago. III. Series.
HC157.T8B33 330.9'729'8304 73-640239

Barclays Bank International Limited.
Report and accounts—Barclays Bank International Limited.
[London] Barclays Bank International Limited.
v. ill. 30 cm. annual.
Report year ends Sept. 30.
Continues: Barclays Bank (Dominion, Colonial and Overseas). Report and accounts.
1. Barclays Bank International Limited.
HG2998.B34A3 332.1'5'09421 75-649343 MARC-S

Barclays Bank Trust Co.
see Ruffels, Brian John. Barclaytrust guide to unified tax. London, Sweet & Maxwell, 1973.

Barclays National Bank
see Barclays national review. [Johannesburg]

Barclays National Bank. International Division.
Doing business in South Africa : investment, tax and corporate guidelines : the South African market-place / [International Division] Barclays National Bank Limited. — [3rd ed.]. — Johannesburg : The Bank, 1975.
136 p. : col. maps ; 30 cm. SA
Cover title.
Coloured end-paper maps, 1 folded.
Corrigenda slip inserted.
Bibliography: p. 112-113.
ISBN 0-620-01548-9 : free
1. Commercial law—South Africa. I. Title.
346'.68'07 77-351629
77 MARC

Barclays national review.
[Johannesburg, Barclays National Bank.
v. illus. 30 cm. quarterly.
1. Africa, South—Economic conditions—Periodicals. 2. Africa—Economic conditions—1945- —Periodicals. 3. Economic history—1945- —Periodicals. I. Barclays National Bank.
HC517.S7B33 330.9'68'06 74-643098 MARC-S

Barcley, Janet A
User analysis of the University of Kentucky Medical Library Health Sciences Information Service, by Janet A. Barcley. [Detroit] Kentucky, Ohio, Michigan Regional Medical Library, 1971.
ii, 10, [6] l. 28 cm. (Kentucky, Ohio, Michigan Regional Medical Library. Papers and reports, no. 10)
"Produced ... under contract no. NIH 71-4711, National Library of Medicine."
1. Kentucky. University. Health Sciences Information Service. I. Title. II. Series.
Z675.M4K45a no. 10 026'.61'08 s 76-380222
[R118.4.U5] 77 MARC

Barco, Aurelia.
Județul Argeș : [monografie] / Aurelia Barco, Eugen Nedelcu. — București : Editura Academiei Republicii Socialiste România, 1974.
167 p., [9] leaves of plates : ill., maps (some fold., 1 fold. col.) ; 21 cm. — (Județele patriei) R 74-3126
Bibliography: p. 164-[166]
lei 15.00
1. Argeș, Romania (Județ) I. Nedelcu, Eugen, joint author.
DR281.A69B37 74-352652

Barco, Eduardo Camacho
see Camacho Barco, Eduardo.

Barco, Miguel del, 1706-1790.
Historia natural y crónica de la antigua California; adiciones y correcciones a la noticia de Miguel Venegas. Edición, estudio preliminar, notas y apéndices: Miguel León-Portilla. [1. ed.] México, Universidad Nacional Autónoma de México, Instituto de Investigaciones Históricas, 1973.
lxxv, 464 p. illus. 24 cm. (Serie de historiadores y cronistas de Indias, 3)
Bibliography: p. lxvii-lxxv.
1. Baja California—History. 2. Baja California—Description and travel. 3. Natural history—Mexico—Baja California. I. Venegas, Miguel, 1680-1764? Noticia de la California. II. Title. III. Series.
F1246.B186 1973 917.2'2'042 74-217658

Barco, Oscar del.
Variaciones sobre un viejo tema / Oscar del Barco. — [Buenos Aires] : Ediciones Caldén, c1975.
88 p. ; 21 cm.
I. Title.
PQ7798.12.A657V3 76-459781
76 MARC

Barco Coone, Lucille
see Coone, Lucille Barco, 1916-

Barco López, J Alejandro.
Los tesoros de Pachacámac y Catalina Huanca [por] J. Alejandro Barco López. Lima, 1972.
484 p. illus. 22 cm.
Includes bibliographical references.
1. Incas. 2. Treasure-trove—Peru. I. Title.
F3429.B28 73-219516

Barco Teruel, Enrique.
Vosotros, los españoles. Ensayo de revisión. [2. ed.] Barcelona, Marte [1971]
305 p., 4 l. 17 cm. (Libros Satélite, 4) Sp 71-Oct
CONTENTS: Quienes son los españoles.—Como son los españoles.—El español hace y deshace.
1. National characteristics, Spanish. 2. Spaniards. 3. Spain—Civilization. I. Title.
DP52.B3 1971 73-353273

Barco-Vargas, Virgilio.
Estudio del desarrollo economico del valle del Magdalena y norte de Colombia. [Bogotá, Ministerio de Obras Públicas, 1961]
239-254 p. 29 cm.
Cover title.
"Separata de la memoria del Ministro de Obras Publicas de Colombia, a la legislatura ordinaria de 1960."
TNJ NUC73-29564

Barco-Vargas, Virgilio
see Bogotá. Presupuesto para la vigencia de 1967. Bogota, 1967.

Barco Vargas, Virgilio
see Estamos ante una revolución. 1. ed. Bogotá] Ediciones Tercer Mundo [1967]

Barcomb, Doris E
Road to independence; comprehensive evaluation and vocational rehabilitation services to disabled assistance clients in a residential rehabilitation center. Report prepared by Doris E. Barcomb, William M. Connelly [and] Caroline B. Herz. Greenfield, N.H., Crotched Mountain Rehabilitation Center, 1967.
ix, 58 p. map, tables.
Bibliography: p. 57-58.
1. Physically handicapped—Rehabilitation—New Hampshire. 2. Rehabilitation centers. I. Connelly, William M., joint author. II. Herz, Caroline B., joint author. III. Title.
MsSM NUC73-47892

Barcos, Maurice P 1935-
The effect of radiation on erythropoietin-induced erythroid differentiation in vitro / Maurice P. Barcos. -- [s.l. : s.n.], 1975.
viii, 94 leaves ; 28 cm.
Thesis (Ph.D.)--University of Chicago.
Bibliography: leaves 43-48.
1. Erythropoietin. 2. Radiation--Physiological effect. I. Title.
ICU NUC77-98951

Barcotsch, Nicolas
see
Warkotsch, Nicolaus.

Barcroft, Sir Joseph, 1872-1947.
The brain and its environment. Port Washington, N.Y., Kennikat Press [1973, c1938]
vii, 117 p. illus. 21 cm.
Original ed. issued in series: The Terry lectures.
Includes bibliographical references.
1. Brain. 2. Blood. I. Title. II. Series: The Terry lectures, Yale University.
QP376.B3 1973 612'.82 72-85306
ISBN 0-8046-1718-X MARC

Barcroft Centenary Symposium, Cambridge, Eng., 1972
see
Sir Joseph Barcroft Centenary Symposium, Cambridge, Eng., 1972.

Barcs, Vilmos.
Épülethatároló szerkezetek hőtechnikai méretezése párafelcsapódás szempontjából. [Budapest, 1964.
47 p. illus. 23 cm. (Építéstudományi Intézet. Tudományos közlemények, 35)
Summary in Russian, German, English, and French.
Bibliography: p. 40.
1. Dampness in buildings. 2. Building materials—Thermal properties. I. Title. II. Series: Budapest. Építéstudományi Intézet. Tudományos közlemények, 35.
TH7.B8 no. 35 74-200480
[TH9031]

Barcsay, Jenő.
Anatomy for the artist. [London] Octopus Books [1973, c1958]
320 p. illus. 33 cm. GB***
1. Anatomy, Artistic. I. Title.
NC760.B33 1973b 743'.4 73-171079
ISBN 0-7064-0243-X MARC

Barcsay, Jenő
see Petényi, Katalin. Barcsay. Budapest: Corvina, 1974.

Barcus, Francis Earle, 1927-
Children's television : an analysis of programming and advertising / F. Earle Barcus with Rachel Wolkin. — New York : Praeger, 1977.
xxvii, 218 p. ; 24 cm. — (Praeger special studies in U.S. economic, social, and political issues)
Includes bibliographical references.
ISBN 0-275-23210-7 : $15.00
1. Television and children. 2. Television programs for children—United States. 3. Television advertising—United States. I. Wolkin, Rachel, joint author. II. Title.
HQ782.T4B35 791.45'5 76-12843
77 MARC

Barcus, Francis Earle, 1927-
Concerned parents speak out on children's television, by F. Earle Barcus. Newtonville, Mass., Action for Children's Television, 1973.
vii, 95 l. 28 cm.
1. Television and children. 2. Television programs—U.S. I. Title.
CLSU InU NUC75-21223

Barcus, Francis Earle, 1927-
Network programming and advertising in the Saturday children's hours: a June and November comparison. Newtonville, Mass., Action for Children's Television, c1972.
ii, 32 l. 28 cm.
Imprint from label mounted on t.p.
IU InU NUC74-125979

Barcus, Francis Earle, 1927-
Role of agricultural extension in the suburban community [by] Francis E. Barcus. Amherst, Mass., 1962.
112 l.
Thesis—University of Massachusetts.
Microfilm of typescript. Syracuse, N.Y., Hall & McChesney, 1965. 1 reel.
1. Agricultural extension work. I. Title.
NSyU NUC75-29392

Barcus, Francis Earle, 1927-
Romper room: an analysis. Prepared for Action for Children's Television. [Newtonville, Mass., Action for Children's Television] 1971.
35, [12] p. 28 cm.
1. Romper room (Television program) I. Action for Children's Television.
IU NUC75-29376

Barcus, Francis Earle, 1927-
Saturday children's television; a report of TV programming and advertising on Boston commercial television. [Boston] Action for Children's Television, 1971.
1 v. (various pagings) tables. 29 cm.
1. Television and children. I. Action for Children's Television. II. Title.
OrU NUC73-116904

Barcus, Francis Earle, 1927-
Television in the after school hours : a study of programming and advertising for children on independent stations across the United States / F. Earle Barcus. -- Newtonville, Mass. : Action for Children's Television, 1975.
viii, 58, [20] p. ; 28 cm.
Cover title: Television in the afternoon hours.
1. Television and children. I. Action for Children's Television. II. Title.
IU NUC77-100333

Barcus, Francis Earle, 1927-
Weekend commercial children's television--1975 / by F. Earle Barcus. -- Newtonville, Mass. : Action for Children's Television, 1975.
viii, 59, [35] p. ; 28 cm.
1. Television and children. I. Action for Children's Television. II. Title.
AAP NUC77-99138

Barcus, James E 1938-
The homogenity of structure and idea in Coleridge's Biographia literaria, Philosophical lectures, and Aids to reflection. Philadelphia, 1968.
xxiii, 144 l.
Thesis—University of Pennsylvania.
Bibliography: leaves xiii-xix.
Microfilm. Ann Arbor, Mich., University Microfilms, 1969.
KyU NUC75-29293

Barcus, James E., 1938-
see Shelley ... London, Routledge & K. Paul, 1975.

Barcyńska, Hélène, pseud.
see Evans, Mrs. Marguerite Florence Hélène (Jervis) 1894-

Barcynski, Leon
see
Phillips, Osborne.

Barczak, Andrzej.
Ekonometryczne metody badania kosztów produkcji. [Wyd. 1.]. Warszawa, Państwowe Wydawn. Naukowe [1971]
190 p. illus. 20 cm. zł26.00
Summary in English and Russian.
Bibliography: p. 178-[187]
1. Costs, Industrial. 2. Econometrics. I. Title.
HD47.B28 74-209167

Barczak, Andrzej.
Makromodele ekonometryczne a planowanie gospodarki narodowej / Andrzej Barczak. — Wyd. 1. — Warszawa : Państwowe Wydawn. Naukowe, 1976.
150 p. : ill. ; 20 cm. — (Biblioteka ekonometryczna) P***
Summaries in English and Russian.
Bibliography: p. 135-[146]
Includes index.
zł26.00
1. Macroeconomics—Mathematical models. I. Title.
HB141.B37 76-527738

Barczak, Zbigniew, 1932-
Jak sen, jak zły sen. [Wyd. 1.] Kraków, Wydawn. Literackie [1971]
152 p.
Short stories.
MH NUC73-32625

Bárczay-Miller, Éva.
La Princesse de Clèves and the tragic dimension of classicism. New Brunswick, N.J., 1974.
vii, 167 l. 29 cm.
Thesis (Ph.D.)—Rutgers University.
Bibliography: leaves 163-166.
1. La Fayette, Marie Madeleine (Pioche de La Vergne) comtesse de, 1634-1693. La princesse de Clèves. 2. French literature—17th century—History and criticism. I. Title.
NjR NUC76-96141

Bárczi, Géza.
Nyelvművelesünk / Bárczi Géza. — Budapest : Gondolat, 1974.
136, [7] p. ; 21 cm.
Bibliography: p. [139]
ISBN 963-280-019-2 : 14.00Ft
1. Hungarian language—Idioms, corrections, errors. 2. Hungarian language—Style. I. Title.
PH2460.B3 75-566056

Barczyk, Augustyn.
Rekreacyjne ćwiczenia śródwarsztatowe / Augustyn Barczyk. — Wyd. 1. — Warszawa : Wydawnictwa Szkolne i Pedagogiczne, 1975.
293, [2] p. : ill. ; 21 cm. — (Biblioteka kształcenia zawodowego)
Bibliography: p. 283-[294]
zł33.00
1. Exercise. I. Title.
GV501.B37 76-505281

Barczyk, Augustyn
see Cwiczenia rekreacyjne w zakładzie pracy. Warszawa, Wydawn. Związkowe CRZZ, 1964.

Barczyk, Stefan.
Odwarcanie prądów powietrza pod wpływem działania innych prądów; teoria depresji kierunkowej. [Wyd. 1] Katowice, Śląsk, 1957.
16 p. illus. (Prace Głównego In-tu Górnictwa. Seria A. Komunikat nr. 199)
Summaries in English, French, and Russian.
ICRL NUC74-30730

Barczyński, Janusz.
Narracja i tendencja : o powieściach tendencyjnych Elizy Orzeszkowej / Janusz Barczyński. -- Wrocław : Zakł. Narod. im. Ossolińskich, 1976.
124 p. ; 21 cm. -- (Rozprawy literackie ; 14)
At head of title: Polska Akademia Nauk. Komitet Nauk o Literaturze Polskiej.
Includes bibliographical references and index.
1. Orzeszkowa, Eliza, 1842-1910. I. Series: Rozprawy literackie ; 14.
MH NUC77-99074

Bard, Allen J
Encyclopedia of electrochemistry of the elements. Editor: Allen J. Bard. New York, M. Dekker [1973-
v. illus. 26 cm.
1. Electrochemistry—Collected works. I. Title.
QD551.B37 541'.37 73-88796
ISBN 0-8247-6093-X MARC

Bard, Basil.
Peredacha tekhnologii. Doklad, predstavlennyĭ na II anglo-vengerskom ėkonomicheskom kollokvii, sostoi͡avshemsi͡a 11-13 sent. 1970 g. v g. Balatonfu͡urede, Vengrii͡a. Perevod s anglīĭskogo M. Sabo. Budapest, Vengerskiĭ nauchnyĭ sovet po mirovoĭ ėkonomike [1971]
15 p. (Napravlenii͡a razvitii͡a mirovoĭ ėkonomiki, No. 2)
MiU NUC76-90394

Bard, Basil.
see Applications and limitations of the patent system ... Guildford, IPC Science and Technology Press, 1975.

Bard, Chantal, 1943-
The effects of object flight variation and subject experience upon speed and accuracy of ball trajectory prediction in three-dimensional space. [n.p.] c1973.
182 l. illus. 29 cm.
Thesis (Ph.D.)—University of Wisconsin.
Vita.
Includes bibliography.
1. Movement, Psychology of. I. Title.
WU NUC74-124445

Bard, Chantal, 1943-
The effects of object flight variation and subject experience upon speed and accuracy of ball trajectory prediction in three-dimensional space. [Eugene, Ore., Microform Publications, College of Health, Physical Education and Recreation, University of Oregon, 1974]
2 sheets. 10.5 x 14.8 cm. [Oregon University. HPERMIC publications, PSY596f]
Microfiche (negative) of typescript.
Collation of the original: 182 l. illus. 29 cm.
Thesis (Ph.D.)—University of Wisconsin, 1973.
Vita.
Bibliography: leaves [98]-112.
1. Visual perception. I. Title.
PSt NUC76-96134

Bard, Diana L.
see Alcohol and opiates ... New York, Academic Press, 1977.

Bard, E. Ronald
see Connecticut. General Assembly. Committee on Legal Rights of Children. The legal rights of children in Connecticut... [Hartford: s.n.], 1974.

Bard, Harry.
Maryland State and Government, its new dynamics / by Harry Bard. — Cambridge, Md. : Tidewater Publishers, 1974.
xiii, 386 p. : ill. ; 24 cm.
Includes index.
ISBN 0-87033-198-1
1. Maryland—Politics and government. I. Title.
JK3825 1974.B37 320.4'752 74-22164
MARC

Bard, Harry.
Predicting pollution in the James River Estuary : a stochastic model / Harry Bard and Richard G. Krutchkoff. — Blacksburg : Virginia Water Resources Research Center, Virginia Polytechnic Institute and State University, [1974?]
ix, 144 p. ; 23 cm. — (Bulletin - Virginia Water Resources Research Center, Virginia Polytechnic Institute and State University ; 70)
Bibliography: p. 43-44.
1. Water quality—Virginia—James River estuary—Mathematical models. I. Krutchkoff, Richard G., 1933- II. Title. III. Series: Virginia Polytechnic Institute and State University. Water Resources Research Center. Bulletin ; 70.
TD201.V57 no. 70 551.4'8'08 s 75-621325
[TD224.V8] 75 MARC

Bard, Harry Elisha, 1948-
A stochastic model for the James, by Harry Bard and Richard G. Krutchkoff. [Blacksburg] Virginia Polytechnic Institute and State University, 1973.
84 l. illus. 28 cm.
Completion report. OWRR project no. A-048-VA, agreement no. 14-31-0001-38847. Funded by Office of Water Resources Research.
Bibliography: leaves 34-35.
1. James River estuary. 2. Water quality—Virginia—James River. I. Krutchkoff, Richard G., 1933- joint author. II. United States. Office of Water Resources Research. III. Virginia Polytechnic Institute and State University. IV. Title.
DI NUC77-14125

Bard, Harry Erwin, 1867-1955.
The city school district; statutory provisions for organization and fiscal affairs, by Harry Erwin Bard. New York, Teachers College, Columbia University, 1909. ⌜New York, AMS Press, 1972⌝
118 p. 22 cm.
Reprint of the 1909 ed., issued in series: Teachers College, Columbia University. Contributions to education, no. 28.
Bibliography: p. 114-118.
1. School districts—United States. 2. School management and organization—Law and legislation—United States. 3. Municipal corporations—United States. I. Title. II. Series: Columbia University. Teachers College. Contributions to education, no. 28.
KF4127.Z9B37 1972 344'.73'073 76-176536
ISBN 0-404-55028-2 MARC

Bard, Isaiah Sidney, 1919-
Section 315 of the Communications act of 1934 and the presidential election of 1952, by Isaiah S. Bard. [New York] 1957.
iv, 282 l.
Thesis–New York University
Bibliography: leaves [271]-282.
Microfilm of typescript. Ann Arbor, Mich., University Microfilms, 1957. 1 reel. 35 mm. (Doctoral dissertation series. Publication, no. 21695)
1. Radio–United States–Laws and regulations. 2. Presidents–United States–Election–1952. 3. Radio in politics. 4. Television in politics. I. Title.
OU NUC76-24196

Bard, J
Manual de piscicultura destinado a la America tropical, por J. Bard, J. Lemasson ⌜y⌝ P. Lessent. Nogent-sur-Marne, France, Centre Technique Forestier Tropical, France, 1970.
139 p. illus., tables.
1. Fish-culture–Latin America. I. Lemasson, J., joint author. II. Lessent, P., joint author. III. Title.
MiEM NUC74-23217

Bard, Jack. Le chant de nuit des sentinelles. 1976.
in Bard, Jack. Effilure suivi de Le chant de nuit des sentinelles. Paris, Éditions Saint-Germain-des-Prés, c1976.

Bard, Jack.
Effilure suivi de Le chant de nuit des sentinelles / Jack Bard. — Paris : Éditions Saint-Germain-des-Prés, c1976.
62 p. ; 21 cm. — (Collection La Poésie, la vie) F***
Poems.
ISBN 2-243-00411-9 : 25.00F
I. Bard, Jack. Le chant de nuit des sentinelles. 1976. II. Title: Effilure.
PQ2662.A675E34 841'.9'14 77-466839
77 MARC

Bard, Janina H
Anthelmintic index ⌜by⌝ Janina H. Bard. ⌜Farnham Royal, Bucks, Eng.⌝ Commonwealth Agricultural Bureaux ⌜1972⌝
ix, 71 p. 23 cm. (Commonwealth Institute of Helminthology. Technical communication no. 43) £2.00 ($5.20U.S.) B***
1. Anthelmintics—Indexes. I. Title. II. Series.
QL386.A1C65 595'.1'08 s 73-165116
[RM356] [616.9'6] MARC
ISBN 0-85198-257-3

Bard, Janina H
Nematicide index / Janina H. Bard. — Slough : Commonwealth Agricultural Bureaux, c1974.
vii, 98 p. ; 22 cm. — (Technical communication of the Commonwealth Institute of Helminthology ; no. 46) GB75-08380
ISBN 0-85198-309-X : £4.00
1. Helminthological abstracts. Series B: plant nematology—Indexes. 2. Helminthological abstracts—Indexes. 3. Nematocides—Indexes. I. Title. II. Series: Commonwealth Institute of Helminthology. Technical communication, no. 46.
QL386.A1C65 no. 46 75-327162
⌜SB998.N4⌝ 75 MARC

Bard, Jean, 1895-
Qui es-tu, Arlequin? Récit de ma vie. Neuchâtel, Victor Attinger, (1972).
208 p. 19 cm. 22.50F Sw 73-A-1023
1. Bard, Jean, 1895- I. Title.
PQ2603.A33Z515 73-326413

Bard, Jean Pierre
see Lumley Woodyear, Henry de. La grotte de l'Hortus (Valflaunès, Hérault). Marseille, Université de Provence [1972]

Bard, Jennie May, 1911- joint author.
see DuPriest, Maude Ward, 1896- Cherokee recollections ... Stillwater, OK, Thales Microuniversity Press, c1976.

Bard, Joseph
see Joint Task Force on Sexism in Education. Sexism in education; a report... ⌜Harrisburg⌝ 1972.

Bard, Maja
see Vogt, Hans, 1911- Neue Musik seit 1945. Stuttgart, Reclam [c1972]

Bard, Martin.
Biochemical and genetic aspects of nystatin resistance in Saccharomyces cerevisiae. ⌜Berkeley⌝ 1971.
v, 82 l. illus.
Thesis (Ph.D.)—University of California.
Bibliography: leaves 79-82.
CU NUC73-32639

Bard, Michael.
The bar: professional association or medieval guild? ⌜By⌝ Michael Bard ⌜and⌝ Barbara A. Bamford. ⌜Washington⌝ Catholic University of America Press, 1970.
393-458 p. 26 cm.
Cover title.
Reprinted from the Catholic University of America law review, v. 19, no. 4, summer 1970.
Bibliographical footnotes.
NIC NUC74-15750

Bard, Morton, 1924-
The function of the police in crisis intervention and conflict management ; a training guide / by Morton Bard, Project director ; with Stacy Braunstein... ⌜et al.⌝. -- ⌜Washington⌝ : Criminal Justice Associates, 1975.
359 p. in various pagings : ill. ; 28 cm.
This training guide was... awarded to Criminal Justice Associates by the National Institute of Law Enforcement and Criminal Justice.
1. Police--United States. I. National Institute of Law Enforcement and Criminal Justice. II. Title.
AU NUC77-100814

Bard, Morton, 1924-
An interview with Morton Bard. ⌜Sound recording⌝ New York, Harper & Row, p1976. 24-61267. 24-61481.
2 cassettes. (Audio colloquies)
Charles Harris, interviewer.
Descriptive notes on containers.
SUMMARY: In a two-part interview, Dr. Bard traces his career in crisis management. He discusses differences between crisis intervention and conflict management, changes that have been made towards the more human service aspects of the police function, authoritarian and authoritative police officers, and the real victims of crime.
1. Police. 2. Police social work. 3. Crisis intervention (Psychiatry) I. Harris, Charles William, 1945- II. Title.
[HV7921] 76-742225

Bard, Morton, 1924-
The police and interpersonal conflict : third-party intervention approaches / Morton Bard, Joseph Zacker. — ⌜Washington⌝ : Police Foundation, c1976.
xi, 59 p. ; 28 cm.
Bibliography: p. 59.
1. Norwalk, Conn.—Police. 2. Police social work—Connectict—Norwalk. 3. Interpersonal relations. 4. Social conflict. I. Zacker, Joseph, joint author. II. Title.
HV8148.N682B37 363.2'09746'9 76-29104
77 MARC

Bard, Morton, 1924-
Psychology and the police. ⌜Sound recording⌝ New York, Psychology Today, p1976.
1 cassette. (Psychology today library cassettes, 35)
Paul Chance, interviewer.
Biographical and descriptive notes in container.
SUMMARY: Dr. Bard discusses his studies on police intervention in family crises.
1. Police social work. 2. Crises intervention (Psychiatry) I. Chance, Paul. II. Title. III. Series: Psychology today library cassettes. ⌜Sound recording⌝ 35.
[HV8079.2] 77-740212

Bard, Morton, 1924-
see Issues in law enforcement ... Reston, Va., Reston Pub. Co., c1976.

Bard, Rachel, 1921-
Squash / Rachel Bard and Caroline Kellogg ; drawings by Rik Olson. — San Francisco : 101 Productions ; New York : distributed in the United States by Scribner, c1977.
96 p. : ill. ; 17 cm. — (Edible garden series)
Includes index.
ISBN 0-89286-113-4 : $2.50
1. Cookery (Squash) 2. Squash. I. Kellogg, Caroline, 1921- joint author. II. Title. III. Series.
TX803.S67B36 641.6'5'62 77-3917
77 MARC

Bard, Robert E
Finance: a function of corporate planning. [Urbana] Bureau of Business Management, College of Commerce and Business Administration, University of Illinois at Urbana-Champaign [1971]
12 p. tables. 23 cm. (Morris J. Weinstein, Groothuis and Company lectureship series, 1971) (University of Illinois bulletin, v. 69, no. 48)
IU NUC73-124539

Bard, Samuel W
Physical distribution of cement by railroads, by Samuel W. Bard. Louisville, Ky., 1961.
28 l. 28 cm.
Photocopy.
1. Cement—Transportation. I. Title.
CaBVaU NUC73-57835

Bard, Serge
see Mosset, Olivier. Catalogue no. 1. ⌜Paris, 1968⌝

Bard, Thérèse.
Informatique : ⌜bibliographie de base⌝ / par Thérèse Bard, avec la collaboration de Pierre Bard, Gérald Malenfant et Roland Perreault. — Montréal : Centre de bibliographie de la Centrale des bibliothèques, 1973.
147 leaves ; 28 cm. — (Cahiers de bibliographie : Collèges ; 1) C***
Includes bibliographical references.
ISBN 0-88523-002-7
1. Electronic data processing—Bibliography. I. Title. II. Series.
Z5640.B37 016.00164 75-521928
⌜QA76⌝ 76 MARC

Bard, Thérèse.
Techniques infirmières / par Thérèse Bard, avec la collaboration d'une équipe de professeurs du Collège de Rimouski et le Centre de bibliographie, avec la collaboration d'une équipe de professeurs du Collège de Maisonneuve. — Montréal : Le Centre, 1974.
202 p. ; 28 cm. — (Cahiers de bibliographie : Collèges ; 3) C***
Includes indexes.
ISBN 0-88523-005-1
1. Nursing—Bibliography. I. Centrale de bibliothèques. Centre de bibliographie. II. Title. III. Series.
Z6675.N7B3 016.61073 76-483032
⌜RT41⌝ 76 MARC

Bard, William Earl, 1892-
As a wild bird returning, by W. E. Bard. ⌜Quanah, Tex.⌝ Nortex Press ⌜c1973⌝
51 p. illus. 24 cm. $4.50
Poems.
I. Title.
PS3503.A5635A9 811'.5'2 73-84977
MARC

Bard, Yonathan.
Nonlinear parameter estimation. New York, Academic Press, 1974.
x, 341 p. illus. 24 cm.
Bibliography: p. 325–332.
1. Estimation theory. I. Title.
QA276.8.B37 519.5'4 72–13616
ISBN 0–12–078250–2 MARC

Bard College, Annandale-on-Hudson, N.Y.
see A Talk with Allen Ginsberg. Annandale-on-Hudson, c1970.

Barda, Any.
Bibliographie des œuvres de Zénaïde Hippius = Зинаида Гиппиус, библиография / établie par Any Barda ; [publié par le Laboratoire de slavistique de Paris I]. — Paris : Institut d'études slaves, 1975.
127 p. ; 25 cm. — (Bibliothèque russe de l'Institut d'études slaves ; t. 38 ISSN 0078–9976) (Série Écrivains russes en France)
F 76–6162
Text in Russian, introd. in French.
Includes indexes.
ISBN 2–7204–0106–4 : 30.00F
1. Gippius, Zinaida Nikolaevna, 1869–1945—Bibliography. I. Title. II. Series: Bibliothèque russe de l'Institut d'études slaves ; t. 38.
Z8343.47.B3 016.8917'1'3 76–475969
[PG3460.G5] (MARC)

Barda, Clive
see Wynne, David, 1926- The sculpture of David Wynne, 1968-1974. London: Phaidon Press, 1974.

Bārda, Fricis.
Bukurags; dzejoļu izlase bērniem. Džemmas Skulmes ilustrācijas. Rīgā, Latvijas Valsts izdevniecība, 1958.
23 p. col. illus.
Russian title from colophon: Boshibuzuk.
Latvian.
I. Skulme, Džemma, illus. II. Title: Boshibuzuk.
MH NUC74-140005

Bārda, Fricis.
Lietus vīrinš. [Māksliniece Ilona Ceipe] Rīgā, "Liesma", 1970.
38 p. col. illus. 29 cm.
I. Title.
MB NUC74-15749

Bārda, Fricis.
Zvaigznes un zeme. Lirikas izlase 1972. Sakārtojis Ernests Aistars. [Ann Arbor, Mich., Jaunatnes apgāds ceļinieks, 1972]
47 p. 17 cm. (Latviesu klasiku mazgramatiņu serija. Lirikas izlases)
Caption title.
I. Title.
MB NUC73-125016

Barda, L.
see Chirurgische Operationslehre ... 1. Aufl. Stuttgart, Schattauer, 1976.

Bārda, Paulīna.
Rudens putniņš. Daudzu gadu dzeja. [Sakārtojis I. Bērsons. Māksliniece K. Dāle]. Rīgā, "Liesma," 1973.
166 p. with illus. 17 cm. USSR 73–14872
0.55rub
I. Title.
PG9049.12.A76R8 75–403911

Bardabasso, Silvana Bonicelli
see Bonicelli Bardabasso, Silvana.

Bardach, Eugene.
The implementation game : what happens after a bill becomes a law / Eugene Bardach. — Cambridge, Mass. : MIT Press, c1977.
x, 323 p. ; 21 cm. — (MIT studies in American politics and public policy ; 1)
Includes bibliographical references and index.
ISBN 0-262-02125-0
1. Policy sciences. 2. Mental health laws—California. I. Title. II. Series.
H61.B25 309.2'12 76-52922
76 MARC

Bardach, Janusz.
Chirurgia plastyczna twarzy. Współautorzy Marian Górski [and] Kazimierz Ostrowski. Warszawa, Państwowy Zakład Wydawn. Lekarskich, 1972.
467 p. illus. 25 cm.
Includes bibliographical references.
1. Surgery, Plastic. 2. Face–Surgery. I. Górski, Marian, joint author. II. Ostrowski, Kazimierz, joint author. III. Title.
IaU NUC77-14077

Bardach, Juliusz.
Historia państwa i prawa Polski. Pod red. Juliusza Bardacha. Wyd. 4. Warszawa, Państwowe Wydawn. Naukowe, 19
v. 25 cm. zł75.00
Includes bibliographies.
CONTENTS:
t. 2. Od połowy XV wieku do r. 1795.
1. Poland—Constitutional history: 2. Law—Poland—History and criticism. I. Title.
73–201093

Bardach, Juliusz.
Historia państwa i prawa polskiego / Juliusz Bardach, Bogusław Leśnodorski, Michał Pietrzak. — Wyd. 1. — Warszawa : Państ. Wydaw. Naukowe, 1976 (Pozn. : PZGMK)
654, [1] p. : ill. ; 25 cm. P76-9470
Errata slip inserted.
Includes bibliographies.
zł90.00
1. Law—Poland—History and criticism. 2. Poland—Constitutional history. I. Leśnodorski, Bogusław, joint author. II. Pietrzak, Michał, joint author. III. Title.
77-468445
77 MARC

Bardach, Juliusz.
Wacław Aleksander Maciejowski i jego współcześni. Wrocław, Zakład Narodowy im. Ossolińskich, 1971.
330 p. ports, facsims. 24 cm. (Monografie z dziejów nauki i techniki, t. 71)
Summary in French.
Includes bibliographical references.
zł70.00
1. Maciejowski, Wacław Aleksander, 1793–1883. 2. Law, Slavic.
75–580752

Bardach, Sandorne.
A Balthes gyartmanyu dohanymuvelo gep novenyvedelmi berendezesenek fejlesztese. Godollo, 1974.
23 p. illus. (Budapest. Mezogazdasagi Gepkiserleti Intezet. Mezogazdasagi gepesitesi tanulmanyok, 1974 no. 10)
English summary.
I. Title.
DNAL NUC76-96133

Bardachd a Albainn Nuaidh / deasaichte le Calum Iain M. MacLeòid. — Glaschu : GAIRM, 1970.
108 p. ; 22 cm.
Includes bibliographical references.
1. Gaelic poetry—Nova Scotia. I. MacLeòid, Calum Iain M.
PB1646.N68B37 75–533614

Bardack, David.
Morphology and relationships of saurocephalid fishes [by] David Bardack and Gloria Sprinkle. [Chicago] Field Museum of Natural History, 1969.
297–340 p. illus. 24 cm. (Fieldiana: geology, v. 16, no. 11 [i. e. 12]) ([Field Museum of Natural History, Chicago. Publication] no. 1075)
Caption title.
Bibliography: p. 338–340.
1. Saurocephalidae. I. Sprinkle, Gloria, joint author. II. Title. III. Series. IV. Series: Field Museum of Natural History, Chicago. Publication no. 1075.
QE1.F4 vol. 16, no. 12 550'.8 s 79–86839
[567'.5] MARC
——— Copy 2. QE852.T2B32
rev

Bardack, David.
New agnathous fishes from the Pennsylvanian of Illinois / David Bardack and Eugene S. Richardson, Jr. — [Chicago] : Field Museum of Natural History, 1977.
p. 489-510 : ill. ; 24 cm. — (Fieldiana : Geology ; v. 33, no. 26) (Publication - Field Museum of Natural History ; 1261)
Caption title.
Bibliography: p. 509-510.
1. Pipiscius zangerli. 2. Gilpichthys greenei. 3. Paleontology—Pennsylvanian. 4. Paleontology—Illinois—Will Co. 5. Paleontology—Illinois—Kankakee Co. I. Richardson, Eugene Stanley, 1916- joint author. II. Title. III. Series. IV. Series: Field Museum of Natural History, Chicago. Publication ; 1261.
QE1.F4 vol. 33, no. 26 550'.8 s 77-76919
[QE852.A33] 77 MARC

Bardack, David.
Paracanthopterygian and acanthopterygian fishes from the Upper Cretaceous of Kansas / David Bardack. — [Chicago] : Field Museum of Natural History, 1976.
p. 355-374 : ill. ; 24 cm. — (Fieldiana : Geology ; v. 33, no. 20) (Publication Field Museum of Natural History ; 1235)
Caption title.
Bibliography: p. 373-374.
1. Teleostei, Fossil. 2. Paleontology—Cretaceous. 3. Paleontology—Kansas. I. Title: Paracanthopterygian and acanthopterygian fishes ... II. Series. III. Series: Field Museum of Natural History, Chicago. Publication ; 1235.
QE1.F4 vol. 33, no. 20 550'.8 s 76-23030
[QE852.T2] 76[r77]rev MARC

Bardack, Paul K
State constitutional prohibitions against the lending of state credit to municipal corporations / Paul K. Bardack. — [Washington?] : Bardack, 1977.
87 leaves ; 36 cm.
Includes bibliographical references.
1. Municipal finance—Law and legislation—United States—States. 2. Intergovernmental fiscal relations—United States—States. I. Title.
KF6794.B37 343'.73'037 77-150131
77 MARC

Bardadin, Tadeusz
see Zjazd Otolaryngologów Polskich, 27th, Katowice, Poland, 1968. Pamietnik... Warszawa, Państwowy Zakład Wydawn. Lekarskich, 1970.

Bardagjy, Joan C., joint author
see Diffrient, Niels. Humanscale 1/2/3... Cambridge, Mass., MIT Press, c1974.

Bardají, A
La restauración española en el siglo XIX. [Madrid, 1968]
72 p. illus., ports. (Centro de Estudios Históricos, Cáceres. Círculo de Estudios Donoso Cortés, Badajoz. 4)
1. Monarchy, Spanish. 2. Spain–Pol. & govt.–1868–1875. I. Title. II. Series: Centro de Estudios Históricos. Publicaciones, 4.
CU-SB OCU NUC74-15755

Bardají, Teodoro, 1882-1958.
El arte culinario práctico / [por] Teodoro Bardají. — Barcelona : Garriga, D.L. 1976.
771 p. : col. ill. ; 27 cm. Sp77-Feb
ISBN 8470790803 : 1900ptas
1. Cookery. I. Title.
TX651.B143 1976 641.5 77-484239
77 MARC

Bardají Giménez, Fernando, joint author
see Laraña Palacio, Manuel. Manual sistemático de seguridad social. Barcelona, Jims, 1970.

Bardakçı, Ayhan.
Yılmaz Güney olayı / Ayhan Bardakçı. — Çağaloğlu -İstanbul : Özgün Yayınları, 1974.
192 p. ; 20 cm.
15.00TL
1. Güney, Yılmaz, 1937- 2. Turkey—Politics and government—1960- I. Title.
PN1998.A3G942 76–971158

Bardakçı, İlhan.
Bir imparatorluğun yağması : [Balkan bozgunu ve I. Dünya Harbi] / İlhan Bardakçı. — [s. l. : s. n., 197–]
xii, 269 p., [1] leaf of plates : ill. ; 20 cm.
Bibliography: p. 241–243.
1. Turkey—History—Mohammed V, 1909–1918. 2. Balkan Peninsula—History—War of 1912–1913. 3. European War—Campaigns—Turkey and the Near East. I. Title.
DR584.B27 75–972881

Bardakdjian, Geneviève.
La Communauté arménienne de Décines : 1925-1971 ... / Geneviève Bardakdjian. — [s.l.] : [G. Bardakdjian], 1972.
127, [1] leaves : ill. ; 29 cm. F75-9544
1. Armenians in Décines-Charpieu, France. 2. Décines-Charpieu, France—Foreign population. I. Title.
DC801.D43B37 75-520586
76 MARC

Bardakhanova, S. S., comp.
see Buriatskie narodnye skazki. 1973.

Bardakhanova, S. S.
see Buri͡atskie narodnye skazki, volshebno -fantasticheskie i o zhivotnykh. 1976.

Bardakjian, Kevork B
A Textbook of modern western Armenian / by Kevork B. Bardakjian, and Robert W. Thomson. — 1st ed. — Delmar, N.Y. : Caravan Books, 1977.
viii, 319 p. ; 24 cm.
ISBN 0-88206-012-0
1. Armenian language, modern—West Armenian—Grammar. I. Thomson, Robert W., 1934- joint author. II. Title.
PK8373.B37 491'.992'82421 77-1774
77 MARC

Bardales Rodriguez, Armando
see Valladares Arriagada, Héctor. El traumatismo encéfalo craneano. [Santiago] Universidad de Chile [1970]

Bardallo, Julio R
Teoría de la técnica notarial / Julio R. Bardallo. -- [Montevideo] : Universidad de la República, División Publicaciones y Ediciones, 1975.
103 p. ; 23 cm.
Cover title.
At head of title: Facultad de Derecho y Ciencias Sociales.
Includes bibliographical references.
1. Notaries--Uruguay. I. Title.
TxU NUC77-100833

Bardaloi, U C
Health on the march 1948-1956 (Assam), corrected up to 31st December, 1956. Shillong, Printed at the Assam Govt. Press, 1958.
21 p. illus. fold. map. 34 cm.
Cover title.
At head of title: Directorate of Health Services, Assam.
1. Public health—India—Assam—Statistics. 2. Assam—Statistics, Medical. 3. Assam—Statistics, Vital. I. Assam. Directorate of Health Services. II. Title.
RA312.A85B37 76-360796
76 MARC

Bardanne, Jean, 1914-
Pourquoi la guerre est impossible / Jean Bardanne. — Paris : Baudinière, [1939]
253 p. ; 19 cm.
1. Europe—Politics and government—1918-1945. I. Title.
D727.B325 320.9'4'051 75-512566
75 MARC

Bardanne, Jean, 1914–
Stavisky, espion allemand. Paris, Éditions Baudinière [1935]
239 p. 19 cm. (La guerre secrète)
On cover: Histoires vécues.
1. Stavisky, Serge Alexandre, 1886–1934. 2. Spies—Biography. I. Title.
HV6248.S628B37 74–154059
MARC

Bardari, Giuseppe.
see Donizetti, Gaetano, 1797-1848. Maria Stuarda. Libretto. English & Italian. New York, Program Pub. Co., 1972.

Bárðarson, Hjálmar R
see
Hjálmar R Bárðarson.

Bardas, Doron.
A moderate resolution, wide band, astronomical Echelle spectrograph : a search for pulsations in the optical emission lines of HZ Herculis. -- [s.l. : s.n.], 1976.
181 leaves : ill. ; 28 cm. -- (Massachusetts Institute of Technology. Dept. of Physics. Thesis. 1976. Ph.D.).
Thesis (Ph.D.)--Massachusetts Institute of Technology.
Vita.
Bibliography: leaves 173-179.
1. Spectrograph. 2. X-ray astronomy. 3. Stars--Spectra. I. Title. II. Series.
MCM NUC77-99429

Bardash, Ivan Grigor'evich
see Rost i organizat͡sionnoe ukreplenie Kommunisticheskoĭ partii Moldavii, 1924-1974. 1976.

Bardaşu, Petre.
Brezoi, 100 [i. e. o sută] de ani de industrie forestieră, [1873–1973] / volum întocmit de Petre Bardaşu şi Gheorghe Simeanu. — Rîmnicu Vîlcea : [s. n.], 1973.
108 p. : ill. ; 21 cm. R 75–191
At head of title: Uniunea Generală a Sindicatelor din România. Consiliul Judeţean Vîlcea.
Includes bibliographical references.
lei 10.00
1. Lumbering—Romania—Brezoi—History. 2. Forests and forestry—Romania—Brezoi—History. 3. Brezoi, Romania—Industries. I. Simeanu, Gheorghe, joint author. II. Title.
SD538.3.R6B37 75–586015

Bardasz, Ewa Alice.
Adsorption at the mercury-hydrocarbon interface: I. benzene-cyclohexane, benzene-n-hexane, and cyclohexane-n-hexane, II. octadecanol from solution in cyclohexane, n-hexane, and benzene. [n. p., n. d.]
1 v.
Thesis.
OClW NUC75-21274

Bardavelidze, Vera Vardenovna.
Tradit͡sionnye obshchestvenno-kul'tovye pami͡atniki gornoĭ Vostochoĭ Gruzii. Tbilisi, Met͡sniereba [1974-
v. illus.
At head of title: Akademii͡a nauk Gruzinskoĭ SSR. Institut istorii, arkheologii i ėtnografii imeni I. A. Dzhavakhishvili.
Title page and text in Georgian.
Russian title from colophon.
Russian and English summaries.
Contents:–1. Pshavi.
1. Temples–Georgia (Transcaucasia) 2. Georgia (Transcaucasia)–Antiq.
MH NUC75-128309

Bardavio, Joaquin.
Biografia completa de Alfonso XIII. [Madrid, Iberico Europea de Ediciones, 1969]
32 p. illus. (part col.) (Los protagonistas de la historia)
Cover title.
1. Alfonso XIII, King of Spain, 1886-1941.
MH NUC73-46424

Bardavío, Joaquín.
La crisis : historia de quince días / por Joaquín Bardavío. — Madrid : Sedmay, 1974.
285 p., 1 leaf : ill. ; 21 cm. — (Historia viva) Sp 74 May
ISBN 84–400–7400–X : 375ptas
1. Carrero Blanco, Luis. I. Title.
DP271.C37B37 74–357412

Bardavío, Joaquín
see Dirigentes: España 1970. [Bilbao, Gráficas Ellacuria, 1970]

Bardavio, José María.
La versatilidad del signo / José M. Bardavio. — Madrid : A. Corazón, [1975]
205 p. : ill. ; 21 cm. — (Comunicación ; ser. B, no. 44) Sp***
Includes bibliographical references.
ISBN 8470531301
1. Semiotics. I. Title.
P99.B28 75-507788
75 MARC

Bardawil, Georges
see Hartmann, Erich. Au clair de la terre. (Bruxelles, Arcade, 1972).

Bardawil, Georges
see Hartmann, Erich. Space focus earth... [Bruxelles, Arcade, 1972]

Barday, Robert J
Free-air gravity anomalies south of Panama and Costa Rica (NOAA Ship Oceanographer - August 1969) Miami, Atlantic Oceanographic and Meteorological Laboratories, 1971.
51 p. illus., charts (1 fold. in pocket) 27 cm. (U.S. National Oceanic and Atmospheric Administration. NOAA technical memorandum ERL AOML-14)
1. Gravity anomalies—Panama Fracture Zone. I. Atlantic Oceanographic and Meteorological Laboratories. II. Title. III. Series.
DME NUC73-125734

Bardazzi, Silvestro.
La Chiesa di S. [i. e. Santa] Maria della Pietà in Prato / Silvestro Bardazzi, Eugenio Castellani, Aldo Petri. — Prato : Azienda autonoma di turismo, [1975]
52 p., [23] leaves of plates : ill. ; 25 cm. It 75–July
Includes bibliographical references.
1. Chiesa di Santa Maria della Pietà, Prato. I. Castellani, Eugenio, joint author. II. Petri, Aldo, joint author.
NA5621.P7888B37 75–531080

Barde, Jean Philippe, joint author
see Alexandre, Ariel. Le temps du bruit. Paris, Flammarion [1973]

Barde, Robert Elmer, 1925-
The Battle of Midway: a study in command. [College Park, Md.] 1971 [c1972]
2 v. (454 l.) 29 cm.
Typescript.
Thesis—University of Maryland.
Vita.
Includes bibliography.
1. Midway, Battle of, 1942. 2. U.S.—History, Naval. I. Title.
MdU NUC73-32624

Bardeau, Fabrice.
Les clefs secrètes de la chimie des anciens / Fabrice Bardeau. — Paris : R. Laffont, c1975.
204, [4] p., [4] leaves of plates : ill. ; 22 cm. — (Les Énigmes de l'univers) F***
Bibliography: p. 201-[205]
26.00F
1. Alchemy. I. Title.
QD26.B33 540'.1 75-516616
75 MARC

Bardèche, Maurice.
Nuremberg : ou, La terre promise / Maurice Bardèche. — Paris : Sept Couleurs, c1948.
270 p. ; 18 cm.
1. Nuremberg Trial of Major German War Criminals, 1945-1946. I. Title.
D804.G42B266 1948 76-374893
76 MARC

Bardèche, Maurice.
L'œuvre de Flaubert / Maurice Bardèche. — [Paris] : Sept couleurs, [1974]
424 p. ; 20 cm. F***
Includes bibliographical references and index.
1. Flaubert, Gustave, 1821-1880—Criticism and interpretation. I. Title.
PQ2249.B3 843'.8 75-502025
75 MARC

Bardeche, Maurice, ed.
see Balzac, Honoré de, 1799-1850. Eugénie Grandet. [Paris] Le Livre de poche [1974, c1972]

Bardèche, Maurice, joint author.
see Brasillach, Robert, 1909-1945. Historia de la guerra de España. Valencia, [s.n.] 1966.

Bardèche, Maurice.
see Études sur le fascisme. Paris, Sept couleurs, [1974]

Bardecki, Andrzej
Kościół epoki dialogu. [Wyd. 1. Kraków] Znak [19
v. 21 cm.
CONTENTS:
—t. 2. Przełom
zł48.00
1. Catholic Church—Doctrinal and controversial works—Catholic authors. I. Title.
BX1751.2.B26 75–573862

Bardeen, Charles William, 1847-1924.
Commissioner Hume; a story of New York schools, by C. W. Bardeen. Syracuse, N. Y., C. W. Bardeen, 1899.
210 p. 18 cm.
On cover: Standard teachers' library.
A sequel to Roderick Hume; the story of a New York teacher.
Published originally as a serial in the School bulletin.
Micro-transparency (negative) Louisville, Ky., Lost Cause Press, 1973. 4 sheets. 10.5 x 14.8 cm. (L. H. Wright. American fiction, 1876-1900, no. 293)
1. Education—New York (State)—Hist. I. Title.
PSt NUC75-21297

Bardeen, John, 1908-
see Kurşunoğlu, Behram, 1922- Impact on basic research on technology. New York, Plenum Press, 1973.

Bardehle, Peter.
see Niedersächsisches Hauptstaatsarchiv, Hanover. Quellen zur ländlichen Sozialgeschichte im Niedersächsischen Hauptstaatsarchiv in Hannover. Göttingen, Vandenhoeck & Ruprecht, [1975]

Bardejovské katechizmy z rokov 1581 a 1612. [Štúdiu napísal a s dvoma faksimiliami vydal Boris Bálent] Turčiansky sv. Martin [Nákladom P. Fábryho, 1947]
139 p. 21 cm.
Facsimile ed. of mss.; in portfolio.
Nr. 97 of an edition limited to 400 copies.
1. Lutheran Church—Catechisms and creeds—Slovak. I. Balent, Boris.
BX8070.L67B37 1947 74-221918

Bardeleben, Manfred.
The cooperative system in the Sudan; development, characteristics and importance in the socio-economic development process. München, Weltforum-Verlag [c1973]
126 p. 24 cm. (Afrika-Studien, Nr. 82) GFR***
At head of title: Ifo-Institut für Wirtschaftsforschung München, Afrika-Studienstelle.
Bibliography: p. 109-116.
1. Cooperation—Sudan. 2. Sudan—Economic conditions. I. IFO-Institut für Wirtschaftsforschung, Munich. Afrika-Studienstelle. II. Title. III. Series.
HD3566.S82B3 334'.09624 73-87503
ISBN 3-8039-0078-6 MARC

Bardeleben, Renate Schmidt-von
see Schmidt-von Bardeleben, Renate.

Bardeleben, Wolfdietrich von.
Methode zur Klassifizierung von Vorrichtungen: Fachbericht/ Wolfdietrich v. Bardeleben. — Berlin, Köln, Frankfurt (am Main): Beuth, 1973.
106 p.: ill.; 21 cm. — (Betriebstechnische Reihe) GFR 73-A
"... aus dem Laboratorium für Werkzeugmaschinen und Betriebslehre an der Rheinisch-Westfälischen Technischen Hochschule Aachen."
Bibliography: p. 105-106.
ISBN 3-410-37926-6 : DM18.00
1. Jigs and fixtures. I. Aachen. Technische Hochschule. Laboratorium für Werkzeugmaschinen. II. Title. III. Series.
TJ1187.B36 74-357944

Bardell, David.
Replication and cytopathic effect of human adenovirus types 5 and 12 in cell culture. [Durham, N. H., 1972]
x, 99 l. illus. 29 cm.
Thesis (Ph. D.)—University of New Hampshire.
1. Virus research. I. Title.
NhU NUC73-125018

Bardell, G S
Some aspects of national science policy in Poland / by G. S. Bardell. — [Birmingham, Eng.] : Centre for Russian and East European Studies, University of Birmingham, 1974.
19 p. ; 30 cm. — (CREES discussion papers : Series RC/C ; no. 10) GB***
Includes bibliographical references.
ISBN 0-7044-0094-4
1. Science and state—Poland. I. Title. II. Series: Birmingham, Eng. University. Centre for Russian and East European Studies. CREES discussion papers : Series RC/C ; no. 10.
Q127.P6B37 338.4'7'509438 75-326132
75 MARC

Bardella, Gilda.
A estrada de montanha. São Paulo [Martins] 1973.
90 p. 21 cm. Cr$35.00
I. Title.
PQ9698.12.A6825E8 74-212203

Bardella, Gilda.
Saiba escolher a porta, bata e entre. São Paulo, 1972.
xv, 111 p. 21 cm. Cr$25.00
1. Bardella, Gilda. I. Title.
CT688.B25A33 73-221705

Bardelli, Niccolo.
La giurisdizione in Atene studiata in rapporto allo spirito e all'evoluzione delle costituzione politica. Edizione anastatica. Roma, L'Erma di Bretschneider, 1972.
432 p. 23 cm. (Studia juridica, 69)
Reprint of Turin edition 1901.
OCU NUC77-14557

Bardelli, Sergio.
Chiamarsi per nome. Con disegni di Alfredo Fabbri. [Padova], Rebellato, 1973.
68 p. illus. 20 cm. (Collana poeti) L1500 It 74-Feb
Poems.
I. Title.
PQ4862.A6729C5 851'.9'14 74-322798

Bardelli, Sergio.
Un vestito per Giovannina / Sergio Bardelli. — Roma : Fratelli Palombi, [1975]
137 p. ; 22 cm. — (Sezione Fedro : Medici scrittori) It 75-Dec
L3000
I. Title.
PQ4862.A6729V4 75-407080

Bardelli, Umberto, 1903-
Manuale di radioestesia / Umberto Bardelli. — Torino : MEB, c1976.
162 p. : ill. ; 21 cm. — (Viaggi nel mistero ; 9) It76-June
L2500
1. Radiesthesia. I. Title.
BF1628.3.B37 76-466859
*76 MARC

Bardelli, Umberto, 1903-
I poteri ignoti dell'uomo. Torino, MEB, 1973.
245 p. illus. 21 cm. (Mondi sconosciuti, 11) L3200 It 74-Jan
Bibliography: p. 245.
1. Psychical research. 2. Occult sciences. I. Title.
BF1034.B35 73-366454

Bardem, Juan Antonio.
Arte, política, sociedad / J. Antonio Bardem, Ramón Tamames, Eugenio Triana. — Madrid : Editorial Ayuso, 1976.
80 p. ; 18 cm. — (Temas actuales ; 11 : Serie bolsillo) Sp***
ISBN 8433600028
1. Moving-pictures—Censorship—Addresses, essays, lectures. 2. Amnesty—Addresses, essays, lectures. 3. Professions—Addresses, essays, lectures. I. Tamames Gómez, Ramón, joint author. II. Triana, Eugenio, joint author. III. Title.
PN1994.B285 77-476253
77 MARC

Bardem, Juan Antonio.
El puente / J. A. Bardem, Javier Palmero, Daniel Sueiro. — [1. ed.]. — [Madrid] : Sedmay Ediciones : [distribuidora, Maydi, 1977]
190 p. : ill. ; 21 cm. — (Colección 7 arte ; 12) Sp***
Motion picture script.
ISBN 8473802527
I. Palmero, Javier, joint author. II. Sueiro, Daniel, joint author. III. El Puente. [Motion picture]
PN1997.P798 77-482657
77 MARC

Barden, Donald W.
see Suco Special Collections. Guide to the Marshall family papers (1762-1908) [Oswego, N.Y.] SUCO Special Collections, 1975.

Barden, Drew
see Starr, Philip C Economics: principles in action. Encino, Calif.: Dickenson Pub. Co. [1974] c1975.

Barden, Elaine Ann, 1933-
Object sorting and defining styles of emotionally disturbed and normal children. [New York] 1972 [c1973]
176 l. 29 cm.
Thesis—Columbia University.
Bibliography: leaves 174-176.
1. Mentally ill children. 2. Cognition (Child psychology). I. Title.
NNC NUC75-21298

Barden, Elizabeth Stavers, 1915-
see A Bibliography of avian mycosis. [3d ed.] Orono, Me. [1971]

Barden, Elizabeth Stavers, 1915-
see The Mycotoxic effects of fungi isolated from poultry feed ingredients ... Orono, Marine Agricultural Experiment Station, University of Maine, 1970.

Barden, Horace G
The accounting basis of inventories, by Horace G. Barden. New York, American Institute of Certified Public Accountants [1973]
xvi, 180 p. 23 cm. (American Institute of Certified Public Accountants. Accounting research study, no. 13)
Bibliography: p. 184-189.
1. Inventories—Accounting. 2. Inventories—Valuation. I. Title. II. Series.
HF5601.A775 no. 13 657'.08 s 73-166208
[HF5681.S8] [657'.72] MARC

Barden, Howard Stavers, 1945-
The association of vitamin A with health status and dental enamel abnormalities in Down's syndrome and other mentally retarded subjects. [n.p.] c1974.
240 l. 29 cm.
Thesis (Ph.D.)—University of Wisconsin.
Vita.
Includes bibliography.
1. Vitamin metabolism. I. Title.
WU NUC76-96137

Barden, John Glenn, 1900-
The student-teacher interface: differentiations in loads and class size to facilitate individual learning. John Barden. Englewood Cliffs, N. J., Educational Technology Publications, c1971.
40 p. 22 cm. (Educational technology research, 35)
Includes bibliographical references.
1. Class size. I. Title. II. Series.
IMacoW NUC77-13898

Barden, John Glenn, 1900-
A suggested program of teacher training for mission schools among the Batetela. New York, Bureau of Publications, Teachers College, Columbia University, 1941. [New York AMS Press, 1972]
xi, 181 p. 22 cm.
Reprint of the 1941 ed., issued in series: Teachers College, Columbia University. Contributions to education, no. 853.
Originally presented as the author's thesis, Columbia.
Bibliography: p. 177-181.
1. Teachers, Training of—Zaire. 2. Education—Zaire. 3. Batetela (African tribe) 4. Missions—Educational work. I. Title. II. Series: Columbia University. Teachers College. Contributions to education, no. 853.
LB1727.Z3B3 1972 370'.73'096751 75-176517
ISBN 0-404-55853-4 MARC

Barden, Leonard.
The Batsford guide to chess openings / Leonard Barden, Tim Harding. — London : Batsford, 1976.
168 p. : ill. ; 23 cm. — (Batsford chess books) GB***
Includes indexes.
ISBN 0-7134-3213-6 : £3.95. ISBN 0-7134-3214-4 pbk.
1. Chess—Openings. I. Harding, T. D., joint author. II. Title.
GV1450.B28 794.1'22 77-354726
77 MARC

Barden, Leonard.
How good is your chess? : Rate your skill and improve your strategy by participating in 35 master games / Leonard Barden. — New York : Dover Publications, 1976, c1957.
ix, 112 p. : ill. ; 22 cm.
ISBN 0-486-23294-8 : $2.00
1. Chess—Collections of games. I. Title.
[GV1452.B3 1976] 794.1'5 75-28848
76 MARC

Barden, Leonard.
How to play the endgame in chess / [by] Leonard Barden. — London : Collins, 1975.
128 p. : ill., plan ; 22 cm. GB75-17696
ISBN 0-00-410579-6 : £2.95
1. Chess—End games. I. Title.
GV1450.7.B37 794.1'24 76-352256
76 MARC

Barden, Leonard.
An introduction to chess. New York, Drake [1970]
viii, 96 p. illus. 19 cm. (Drake chess handbooks, 1)
1. Chess. I. Title.
Wa NUC73-46842

Barden, Leonard.
The King's Indian Defence ⌜by⌝ L. W. Barden, W. R. Hartston ⌜and⌝ R. D. Keene. 2nd ed. revised and enlarged. London, Batsford, 1973.
viii, 334 p. illus. 23 cm. (Contemporary chess openings) £3.30
B 73-12442
1. Chess—Openings. I. Hartston, William Roland, 1947– joint author. II. Keene, Raymond D., joint author. III. Title.
GV1450.B32 1973 794.1′22 73-164019
ISBN 0-7134-0367-5 MARC

Barden, Leonard.
The Ruy Lopez; winning chess with 1 P-K4. New York, MacMillan, 1964.
xv, 170 p. illus. 20 cm.
1. Chess problems. I. Title.
TU NUC73-46829

Barden, Leonard
see Fischer, Bobby, 1943- Chess games. [2d ed., rev. and enl.] Garden City, N. Y., Doubleday, 1973 [c1972]

Barden, Leonard
see Fischer, Bobby, 1943- The games of Robert J. Fischer. London, Batsford [1972]

Barden, Ned Thorson, 1946-
Quantitative estimation of factors affecting flagellar repolymerization. ⌜n.p.⌝ 1973.
119 l. illus. 29 cm.
Thesis (Ph. D.)—University of Wisconsin.
Vita.
Includes bibliography.
I. Title.
WU NUC74-124443

Barden, Robert.
The urban frontier. Syracuse, N. Y., Syracuse Univ., Urban Transportation Institute, 1971.
28 p. illus. 28 cm. (Syracuse University. Urban Transportation Institute. Metropolitan Program. Occasional papers, no. 4)
Reproduced by National Technical Information Service, Springfield, Va.
1. Real property—Valuation. 2. Urbanization. I. Title. II. Series.
OKentU NUC74-127587

Barden, Robert P.
see Chest disease syllabus. Chicago, American College of Radiology, 1972-

Barden, Ronald G.
see Sound pollution. St. Lucia, Q., University of Queensland Press, 1976.

Barden, Ronald Stephens, 1946-
The psychological impact of budget participation on performance. [Austin, Tex.] 1971 [c1972]
xvi, 269 l. illus. 29 cm.
Thesis (Ph. D.)–University of Texas at Austin.
Vita.
Bibliography: leaves 263-269.
1. Budget in business.
TxU NUC73-125017

Barden, Thomas E.
see Weevils in the wheat ... Charlottesville, University Press of Virginia, 1976.

Barden, Thomas Earl.
W.H. Auden : the poet's uses of drama / Thomas Earl Barden. --[s.l. : s.n.], 1975.
4, 224 leaves ; 29 cm.
Thesis--University of Virginia.
Bibliography: leaves 211-224.
1. Auden, Wystan Hugh, 1907-1973.
ViU NUC77-99185

Barden, William T
How to buy & use minicomputers & microcomputers / by William Barden, Jr. — 1st ed. — Indianapolis : H. W. Sams, 1976.
240 p. : ill. ; 28 cm.
Bibliography: p. 219.
Includes index.
ISBN 0-672-21351-6 : $9.95
1. Minicomputers. 2. Microcomputers. 3. Minicomputers—Catalogs. 4. Microcomputers—Catalogs. I. Title.
QA76.5.B28 001.6′4′04 76-19693
76 MARC

Barden, William T
How to program microcomputers / by William Barden, Jr. — 1st ed. — Indianapolis : H. W. Sams, 1977.
256 p. : ill. ; 22 cm.
Includes index.
ISBN 0-672-21459-8 : $8.95
1. Microcomputers—Programming. I. Title.
QA76.5.B283 001.6′42 77-77412
77 MARC

Bardens, Dennis.
The ladykiller: the life of Landru, the French Bluebeard. London, P. Davies, 1972.
⌜9⌝, 221, ⌜8⌝ p. illus., facsim., ports. 23 cm. index. £2.85
B 72-27765
1. Landru, Henri Désiré, 1869-1922. I. Title.
HV6248.L2B37 364.1′523′0924 73-150088
ISBN 0-432-01140-4 [B] MARC

Bardenwerper, Fred L
General liability insurance - 1973 revisions, edited by Fred L. Bardenwerper and Donald J. Hirsch. ⌜Milwaukee⌝ Defense Research Institute, 1974.
53 p. (Defense Research Institute. ⌜Monograph series⌝ v. 1974, no. 1)
At head of title: Insurance law.
Bibliography: p. 47-53.
1. Insurance, Liability—U. S. I. Hirsch, Donald J. II. Title. III. Title: Insurance law.
CSt-Law NUC75-21295

Barder, Richard Charles Remilly, 1937-
Dry-fly trouting for beginners / by Richard Barder. — Newton Abbot ; North Pomfret, Vt. : David & Charles, 1976.
132 p. : ill., ports. ; 23 cm. GB76-25280
Bibliography: p. 126-127.
Includes index.
ISBN 0-7153-7055-3 : £3.50 ($9.95 U.S.)
1. Trout fishing. 2. Fly fishing. I. Title.
SH687.B37 799.1′7′55 76-2887
77 MARC

Barder, Richard Charles Remilly, 1937-
Spinning for pike / ⌜by⌝ R. C. R. Barder ; with a foreword by Fred J. Taylor. — Newton Abbot : David and Charles, 1976.
144 p. : ill., ports. ; 23 cm. GB76-19271
Reprint of the 1970 ed. published by Arco, London; with new pref.
Bibliography: p. 141-142.
Includes index.
ISBN 0-7153-6881-0 : £3.50 ($8.95 U.S.)
1. Pike fishing. 2. Spin-fishing. I. Title.
SH691.P6B3 1976 799.1′7′53 76-376931
76 MARC

Bardes, Barbara Ann.
Senatorial realignment on foreign aid, 1953-1972 : a discriminant analysis of inter-party factions / by Barbara Ann Bardes. -- [Cincinnati : s.n.], 1975.
258 leaves ; 29 cm.
Thesis (Ph.D.)--University of Cincinnati.
Includes abstract.
Bibliography: leaves 251-258.
OCU NUC77-98950

Bardes, Barbara Ann.
Senatorial realignment on foreign aid, 1953-1972 : a discriminant analysis of inter-party factions / by Barbara Ann Bardes. -- [s.l. : s.n.], 1975.
258 leaves ; 29 cm.
Thesis--University of Cincinnati.
Bibliography: leaves 251-258.
Roll film. Ann Arbor, Mich. : University Microfilms, 1976. --1 reel ; 35 mm. --(76-05956)
1. Economic assistance, American. 2. United States--Foreign relations. 3. United States. Congress. Senate.--Voting. I. Title.
MCM NUC77-98949

Bardeschi, Marco Dezzi
see Dezzi Bardeschi, Marco.

Bardesio Vila, Orfila Celia, 1922-
La flor del llanto; viñeta de Augusto Torres [por] Orfila Bardesio. Montevideo, Editorial Letras, 1973.
77 p. 21 cm.
I. Title.
TxU NUC77-13814

Bardesio Vila, Orfila Celia, 1922-
Juego [por] Orfila Bardesio. Montevideo, Editorial Letras, 1972.
59 p.
Poems.
I. Title.
PPiU NUC77-13815

Bardet, Gaston.
Thiết-kế đô-thị. (L'urbanisme) Dich-gia: Đoàn-Thêm. ⌜Saigon?⌝ Ủy-Ban Dịch-Thuật Phủ Quốc-Vụ-Khanh Đặc-Trách Văn-Hóa ⌜1962?⌝
191 p. (Tu sách kim văn)
1. Cities and towns–Planning. I. Title. II. Title: L'urbanisme.
ICarbS NUC74-30725

Bardet, Jean Gaston.
Mystique et magies / Jean-Gaston Bardet. — Paris : La Pensée universelle, ⌜1974⌝
513 p., ⌜4⌝ leaves of plates : ill. ; 18 cm. F***
Includes bibliographical references.
1. Mysticism. 2. Magic. I. Title.
BL625.B37 291.3 75-504195
75 MARC

Bardet, M G
Géologie du diamant, par M. G. Bardet. Paris, Éditions B. R. G. M. ⌜1973–
v. illus. 28 cm. (Mémoires du B. R. G. M., no. 83
224.70F (v. 1) F***
Includes bibliographies.
CONTENTS: t. 1. Généralités.
1. Diamond deposits. 2. Geology, Economic. I. Title. II. Series: France. Bureau de recherches géologiques et minières. Mémoires, no 83
QE1.F7 no. 83, etc. 550′.8 s 74-169140
[TN990] [553′.82] MARC

Bardet, Vincent.
see Deshimaru, Taisen. Za-Zen ... Paris, Seghers, ⌜1974⌝

Bardet, Vincent, joint author.
see Smedt, Evelyn de. La pratique des arts divinatoires ... Paris, R. Laffont, ⌜c1976⌝

Bardet, Vincent, joint author.
see Smedt, Evelyn de. Techniques du bien-être ... Paris, R. Laffont, ⌜1975⌝

Bardez, Jean Michel.
Diderot et la musique : valeur de la contribution d'un mélomane / Jean-Michel Bardez. — Paris : H. Champion, 1975.
168 p. : ill., music ; 23 cm. — (Bibliothèque de littérature comparée ; 118)
F75-14330
Errata slip inserted.
Bibliography: p. ⌜1⌝-6.
50.00F
1. Diderot, Denis, 1713-1784. 2. Music—Theory—16th-17th centuries. I. Diderot, Denis, 1713-1784. Selections. 1975. II. Title. III. Series.
ML423.D556B4 75-521954
76 MARC

Bardhan, Amita, 1937- joint author.
see Dubey, Dinesh Chandra. Fertility behaviour of working and non-working women. New Delhi, National Institute of Family Planning, ⌜1975⌝

Bardhan, Amita, 1937- joint author
see Dubey, Dinesh Chandra. Status of women and fertility in India. New Delhi, National Institute of Family Planning [1972]

Bardhan, Ardhendu Bhushan, 1925–
Generalists, specialists, and the working class, by A. B. Bardhan. [New Delhi, Communist Party of India, 1974]
38 p. 23 cm. (Communist Party publication no. 1: January 1974 (C105)) Re1.00
Includes bibliographical references.
1. Industrial management—India. 2. Executives—India. 3. Technologists—India. 4. Labor and laboring classes—India. I. Title. II. Series: Communist Party of India. Publication no. 1, January 1974, C105.
JQ298.C6A23 1974, no. 1, C105 329.9'54 s 74–900703
[HF5500.3.I 5] [658.4'00954] MARC

Bardhan, Ardhendu Bhushan, 1925–
The unsolved tribal problem, by A. B. Bardhan. [New Delhi, Communist Party of India, 1973]
60 p. 22 cm. (Freedom jubilee series, no. 5) (Communist Party publication no. 13: June 1973 (C90)) Re1.00
1. India—Scheduled tribes. I. Title. II. Series. III. Series: Communist Party of India. Publication no. 13, June 1973 (C90).
JQ298.C6A23 1973, no. 13, C90 73–905044
[DS422.S3] 329.9'54 s [323.1'54] MARC

Bardhan, Kalpana.
Wage and employment of agricultural labourers in India; some cross-sectional analysis. [Delhi] Agricultural Economics Research Centre, University of Delhi, 1970.
1 v. (various pagings) 27 cm.
1. Agricultural laborers—India. 2. Agricultural wages—India. I. Title.
NIC NUC75-30846

Bardhan, Pranab K.
see Poverty and income distribution in India. Calcutta, Statistical Publishing Society [1974]

Bardhan, Pronob, 1945–
Atomic configurations in disordered Cu_3Au. [n.p., 1974]
1 v.
Thesis (Ph.D.)—Northwestern University.
1. Gold-copper alloys. 2. X-rays—Diffraction. 3. X-rays—Scattering. I. Title.
IEN NUC76-96143

Bardhan-Roy, B. K.
see Abeles, Paul William. Prestressed concrete designer's handbook. 2d ed. [Rev. and metricated] Flushing, N.Y., Scholium International Inc. [c1976]

Bardhan-Roy, B. K., joint author.
see Abeles, Paul William. Prestressed concrete designer's handbook. 2d ed. rev. and metricated. Slough, [Eng.] Cement and Concrete Association, 1976.

Bardhana, Adrīśa, 1932–
(Bishakanyā)
বিষকন্যা. [লেখক] অদ্রীশ বর্ধন. কলিকাতা, বেঙ্গল পাবলিশার্স [1377, i.e. 1970]
129 p. 23 cm. Rs5.00
In Bengali.
A novel.

I. Title.

PK1730.13.A66B5 72–921738

Bardhana, Adrīśa, 1932–
(Drāgana chorā)
ড্রাগন ছোরা. [লেখক] অদ্রীশ বর্ধন. কলিকাতা, রোমাঞ্চ [1378, i.e. 1972]
284 p. 23 cm. Rs9.00
In Bengali.
A novel.

I. Title.

PK1730.13.A66D7 72–903110

Bardhana, Adrīśa, 1932–
(Hirāmanera hāhākāra)
হীরামনের হাহাকার. [লেখক] অদ্রীশ বর্ধন. কলিকাতা, গ্রন্থ প্রকাশ [1378, i.e. 1971]
272 p. 23 cm. Rs10.00
In Bengali.
A novel.

I. Title.

PK1718.B35H5 72–902713

Bardhana, Adrīśa, 1932–
(Rupora ṭākā)
রুপোর টাকা. [লেখক] অদ্রীশ বর্ধন. কলিকাতা, রোমাঞ্চ [1963]
130 p. 23 cm.
In Bengali.
A novel.

I. Title.

PK1730.13.A66R8 SA 64–2815

Bardhana, Asīma.
বাঁচতে সবাই চায়. [লেখক] অসীম বর্দ্ধন. কলকাতা, আলফা-বিটা পাবলিকেশন্স্ [1961]
98 p. 19 cm.
In Bengali.

1. Conduct of life. I. Title.
Title romanized: Bāñcate sabāi cāẏa.

BJ1588.B4B37 72–220040

Bardhana, Haralāla.
(Deśe, deśe)
দেশে, দেশে. [লেখক] হরলাল বর্ধন. কলিকাতা, ক্লাসিক প্রেস [1969]
346 p. 23 cm. Rs10.00
In Bengali.

1. Europe—Description and travel—1945– I. Title.

D922.B35 70–910469

Bardhoshi, Besim.
The economic and social development of the People's Republic of Albania during thirty years of people's power / Besim Bardhoshi, Theodhor Kareco. — Tirana : 8 Nëntori Pub. House, 1974.
247 p. ; 17 cm.
At head of title: Tirana University, Faculty of Economics.
Includes bibliographical references.
1. Albania—Economic conditions. 2. Albania—Social conditions. 3. Albania—Politics and government—1944– I. Kareco, Theodhor, joint author. II. Title: The economic and social development of the People's Republic of Albania ...
HC402.B3 309.1'4965'03 76-357094
76 MARC

Bardi, Edward J 1943–
An analysis of noncost factors in the carrier selection decision: a study of household goods movement by industrial firms. [n.p.] 1971.
138 l.
Thesis (Ph.D.)—Pennsylvania State University.
I. Title.
PSt NUC73-32627

Bardi, Edward J., 1943– joint author.
see Coyle, John Joseph, 1935– The management of business logistics. St. Paul, West Pub. Co., c1976.

Bardi, Giuseppe, mons. Elisabetta Anna Seton.
see Daughters of St. Paul. Mother Seton ... Boston, St. Paul Editions, 1975.

Bardi, Giuseppe, mons.
S. [i. e. Santa] Margherita Maria Alacoque / Giuseppe Bardi. — 1. ed. — Alba : Pia società San Paolo, [1942?]
xiv, 424 p. ; 18 cm.
Bibliography: p. v–vi.
1. Alacoque, Marguerite Marie, Saint, 1647–1690.
BX4700.A37B3 75–533612

Bardi, Joseph
see
Bardi, Giuseppe, mons.

Bardi, Pietro Maria, 1900–
Architecture: the world we build, [by] P. M. Bardi. London, Collins; New York, Franklin Watts, 1972.
128 p. illus. (chiefly col.), plans. 26 cm. (International library) £1.75 GB 73–10150
Includes index.
Bibliography: p. 122.
1. Architecture—History. I. Title.
NA200.B18 720'.9 77–153826
ISBN 0–531–02104–1 (Watts) MARC

Bardi, Pietro Maria, 1900–
História da arte brasileira : pintura, escultura, arquitetura, outras artes / P. M. Bardi ; [desenhos, Dan Fialdini ; índice, Anna Carboncini]. — São Paulo : Edições Melhoramentos, c1975.
228 p. : ill. (some col.) ; 29 cm.
Includes index.
Cr$280.00
1. Art, Brazilian—History. I. Title.
N6650.B37 75-517770
75 MARC

Bardi, Pietro Maria, 1900–
Viaggio nell'architettura. Milano, Rizzoli, [1972?]
125 p. illus. 25 cm. (International library) L1500 It 72–July
At head of title: P. M. Bardi.
1. Architecture—History—Outlines, syllabi, etc. I. Title.
NA203.B24 72–373925

Bardi, Pietro Maria, 1900-
see Faruffini, Federico, 1831-1869. Federico Faruffini. Roma, Istituto nazionale L.U.C.E., [1934]

Bardi, Pietro Maria, 1900-
see Gola, Emilio, 1852-1925. Emilio Gola. Roma, Istituto nazionale L.U.C.E., [1930]

Bardi, Pietro Maria, 1900–
see São Paulo, Brazil (City). Museu de Arte. Museu de Arte de São Paulo "Assis Chateaubriand". São Paulo, Gráficos Brunner [c1973]

Bardi, Simonetta.
Parole fra noi. Roma, C. Bestetti, 1972.
[48] l. illus. 24 cm. It 72–Apr
500 numb. copies. LC copy no. 382.
Poems.
I. Title.
PQ4807.A726P28 73–306567

Bardi, Ubaldo.
La guerra civile in Spagna : saggio per una bibliografia italiana / Ubaldo Bardi. — Urbino : Argalia, [1974]
134 p. ; 21 cm. It 75–Jan
L2800
1. Spain—History—Civil War, 1936–1939—Bibliography.
I. Title.
Z2700.B37 75–550187

Bardi, Ubaldo, ed.
see Fanfani, Ugo, 1903–1971. La Certoas di Firenze nell'opera grafica di Ugo Fanfani. Firenze, Stabilimenti litografici La stampa, BO. BA. DO. MA., 1970.

Bardi, Ubaldo
see Premio nazionale di poesia Mugello-Resistenza, 1968. Poesia... [n.p.], I centauri, 1969.

Bardian, Antonina Markovna.
(Vospitanie deteĭ v sem'e)
Воспитание детей в семье. Психол.-пед. очерки. Москва, "Педагогика," 1972.
160 p. 20 cm. 0.23rub USSR 72
At head of title: А. М. Бардиан.
Bibliography: p. [159]
1. Domestic education—Russia. I. Title.
LC37.B16 74–310773

Bardian, Antonina Markovna.
(Vospitanie deteĭ v sem'e)
Воспитание детей в семье. Психол.-пед. очерки. Москва, "Педагогика," 1973.
208 p. 17 cm. (Воспитание в семье) 0.24rub USSR 73
At head of title: А. М. Бардиан.
Bibliography: p. [208]
1. Children—Management. 2. Parent and child. I. Title.
HQ769.B318 74-305413

Bardie, T.
see Suluh... -- Djogjakarta : Badan Penjebaran Pendidikan Kristen, [kata pengantar 1956]

Bardies, Bénédicte de Boysson-
see Boysson-Bardies, Bénédicte de.

Bardiier, Fedir Fedorovych.
Spetsializatsiia i kooperuvannia v sotsialistychnii promyslovosti. [By] F. Bardiier. Kyïv, Vyd-vo polit. lit-ry Ukraïny, 1970.
97 p.
1. Industrial management—Ukraine. 2. Ukraine—Indus.
MH NUC74-21964

Bardijewski, Henryk.
Jak zostać monarchistą, a właściwie królem / Henryk Bardijewski. — Wyd. 1. — Warszawa : Czytelnik, 1976.
222 p. ; 20 cm. — (Biblioteka satyry) P***
zł23.00
I. Title.
PG7161.A7J3 77-473993
77 MARC

Bardijewski, Henryk.
Lustra. [Wyd. 1] Warszawa, Iskry, 1971.
111 p. illus. 20 cm.
I. Title.
PCamA NjP NUC74-126794

Bardili, Christoph Gottlieb, 1761-1808.
Ursprung des Begriffes von der Willensfreiheit. Der, dabei unvermeidliche, dialektische Schein wird aufgedekt, und die Forbergerische Schrift über die Gründe und Gesezze freier Handlungen geprüft. Von C. G. Bardili. Stuttgart, Erhard und Löflund, 1796. [Bruxelles, Culture et Civilisation, 1974]
xxx, 96 p. (Aetas Kantiana, 16)
1. Free will and determinism. I. Title.
InNd NUC76-96147

Bardill, Donald R
The ego-ideal and clinical activity: an investigation of the effect of a formal explication of a client's ego-ideal elements on student workers' orientation to the client [by] Donald R. Bardill. [Northhampton, Mass.] 1967. [Ann Arbor, Mich., University Microfilms, 1973]
v, 142 l. 21 cm.
Thesis (D.S.W.)—Smith College.
1. Social case work. 2. Ego (Psychology) 3. Social work education. I. Title.
CLSU NUC74-133470

Bardill, Donald R
Family group casework; a casework approach to family therapy, by Donald R. Bardill [and] Francis J. Ryan. Rev. and enl. ed. Washington, Metropolitan Washington Chapter, National Association of Social Workers [1973]
vi, 70 p. 22 cm.
Bibliography: p. 66-70.
1. Family social work. I. Ryan, Francis John, 1919- joint author. II. Title.
HV43.B33 1973 362.8'2 72-97794
MARC

Bardill, Donald R., joint author.
see Mueller, Charles S. Thank God I'm a teenager. Minneapolis, Augsburg Pub. House, c1976.

Bardin, David J
How to survey Israeli law: a guide to preparation for the written bar examinations of the Israel Chamber of Advocates, by David J. Bardin and Richard E. Laster. Enl. 1972 ed. with guide to Hebrew language exam and translations of statutes, updated to 1 June 1972. Jerusalem [1972]
1-24, 101-121 p. 28 cm.
Cover title.
1. Law—Israel—Compends. I. Laster, Richard E., joint author. II. Title.
340'.095694 73-150146
MARC

Bardin, David J., ed.
see Israel. Courts. Consolidated rules of court of the State of Israel... [Jerusalem, 1972]

Bardin, David J.
see New Jersey. Dept. of Environmental Protection. An inventory of the New Jersey coastal area ... Trenton, State of New Jersey, Dept. of Environmental Protection, Coastal Zone Management Program, 1975.

Bardin, Desdémone, 1929-
Diphtongues et lutte de classes / Desdémone Bardin. — [Montréal] : Éditions québécoises, 1974.
63 p. : ill. ; 21 cm. C74-4453-2
Bibliography: p. 63.
$2.00
1. French-Canadian dialect—Pronuciation. I. Title.
PC3615.B3 447'.9'714 75-504650
75 MARC

Bardin, Dmitriĭ Mikhaĭlovich.
[Planomernoe razvitie sotsialisticheskoĭ ėkonomiki]
Планомерное развитие социалистической экономики. Экономическая роль социалистического государства. [Учеб. пособие по полит. экономии для сред. спец. учеб. заведений]. Москва, "Высш. школа," 1972.
64 p. 20 cm. (В помощь изучающим политическую экономию в средних специальных учебных заведениях) 0.07rub USSR 72-VKP
At head of title: Д. М. Бардин, А. В. Орлов.
Includes bibliographies.
1. Marxian economics—Study and teaching. 2. Russia—Economic policy—1966- I. Orlov, Aleksandr Vasil'evich, fl. 1958- joint author. II. Title.
HB97.5.B294 73-316929

Bardin, Etienne Alexandre, baron, 1774-1840
see Academie française, Paris. Complément du Dictionnaire de l'Academie francaise... Paris, Firmin Didot frères, 1842.

Bardin, Georgriĭ Sofronovich, 1895-
see Sofia. 1932.

Bardin, Igor' Alekseevich.
(Metodologicheskie voprosy sel'skokhoziaĭstvennoĭ nauki)
Методологические вопросы сельскохозяйственной науки / И. А. Бардин. — Москва : Высш. школа, 1975.
144 p. ; 20 cm. — (Философия : Учебное пособие для вузов) USSR 75
Series romanized: Filosofiia : Uchebnoe posobie dlia vuzov.
Bibliography: p. 139-143.
0.29rub
1. Agriculture—Study and teaching. I. Title.
S531.B34 77-508364

Bardin, Ivy H
One hundred words more or less. New York, Carlton Press [c1970]
31 p.
A Hearthstone book.
1. Children's writings. 2. School prose. I. Title.
LN NUC73-47442

Bardin, John Franklin.
The John Franklin Bardin Omnibus / John Franklin Bardin ; with an introduction by Julian Symons. -- Harmondsworth, Middlesex ; Baltimore : Penguin Books, 1976.
601, [1] p. ; 19 cm. -- (Penguin crime fiction)
I. Title.
MiEM NUC77-98990

Bardin, Kirill Vasil'evich.
Kak nauchit' deteĭ uchit'sia. Izd. 2, dop. Minsk, Narodnaia asveta, 1973.
141 p. 21 cm. (Roditeliam o detiakh)
1. Study, Method of. I. Title.
CoU NUC75-138733

Bardin, Kirill Vasil'evich.
(Problema porogov chuvstvitel'nosti i psikhofizicheskie metody)
Проблема порогов чувствительности и психофизические методы / К. В. Бардин ; АН СССР, Ин-т психологии. — Москва : Наука, 1976.
395 p. : ill. ; 22 cm. USSR 76
Bibliography: p. 379-[385]
Includes indexes.
1.82rub
1. Psychology, Physiological. 2. Threshold (Perception) I. Title.
QP360.B37 76-532281

Bardin, Laurence.
Les mécanismes idéologiques de la publicité / Laurence Bardin. — Paris : J.-P. Delarge, c1975.
304 p. : ill. ; 24 cm. — (Encyclopédie universitaire) (Section Sciences humaines) F***
Bibliography: p. 295-300.
69.95F
1. Advertising—Psychological aspects. I. Title.
HF5822.B248 75-519914
76 MARC

Bardin, Shlomo, 1898-
Pioneer youth in Palestine / by Shlomo Bardin. — [Westport, Conn. : Hyperion Press], 1976, c1932.
x, 182 p. ; 23 cm. — (The Rise of Jewish nationalism and the Middle East)
Reprint of the ed. published by Bloch Pub. Co., New York.
Originally presented as the author's thesis, Columbia University, 1932.
Bibliography: p. 174-180.
ISBN 0-88355-308-2 : $15.00
1. Labor Zionism—History. 2. Jews in Palestine—History. 3. Agricultural colonies—Palestine. 4. Collective settlements—Palestine. 5. Palestine—History. I. Title. II. Series.
DS150.L4B27 1976 334'.683'095694 75-6420
76 MARC

Bardin, Stepan Mikhaĭlovich.
[Ėtika vzaimnykh otnosheniĭ]
Этика взаимных отношений. [2-е доп. изд.] Москва, "Сов. Россия," 1972.
128 p. with illus. 16 cm. 0.18rub USSR 72-VKP
At head of title: С. М. Бардин.
1. Communist ethics. I. Title.
BJ1390.B283 1972 72-364511

Bardin, Stepan Mikhaĭlovich.
(... i shtatskie nadeli shineli)
... и штатские надели шинели / С. Бардин. — Москва : Сов. Россия, 1974.
285 p., [8] leaves of plates : ill., ports. ; 21 cm. USSR 74
0.92rub
1. Leningrad—Siege, 1941-1944—Personal narratives. 2. Bardin, Stepan Mikhaĭlovich. 3. Leningrad—Civilian defense. I. Title.
D764.3.L4B3 75-560970

Bardin, Stepan Mikhaĭlovich.
(Uchites' vlastvovat' soboĭ)
Учитесь властвовать собой / С. М. Бардин. — Москва : Сов. Россия, 1976.
192 p. ; 17 cm. USSR 76
0.39rub
1. Communist ethics. 2. Conduct of life. I. Title.
BJ1390.B32 76-529742

Bardin, Tsing Tchao, 1938-
The muonic x-rays of bismuth / Tsing Tchao Bardin. — [New York : s.n.], 1966.
iv, 80 leaves, [21] leaves of plates : ill. ; 29 cm.
Thesis—Columbia University.
Includes bibliographical references.
1. Bismuth—Isotopes—Spectra. 2. X-rays—Spectra. 3. Muons—Spectra. I. Title.
QC462.B5B37 76-358843
76 MARC

Bardin, Vladimir Igorevich.
(Zemlia Korolevy Mod)
Земля Королевы Мод / Владимир Бардин. — Москва : Молодая гвардия, 1974.
256 p., [16] leaves of plates : ill. ; 17 cm. — (Бригантина) USSR***
0.45rub
1. Queen Maud Land. 2. Antarctic regions. I. Title.
G890.Q4B37 75-567128

Bardina, Renata Arkad'evna.
(Tovarovedenie izdeliĭ narodnykh khudozhestvennykh promyslov i suvenirov i organizatsiia torgovli imi)
Товароведение изделий народных художественных промыслов и сувениров и организация торговли ими. [Учеб. пособие для проф.-техн. учеб. заведений и подгот. рабочих на производстве]. Москва, "Высш. школа," 1972.
247 p. with illus. 21 cm. (Профтехобразование: Ремесла) 0.43rub USSR 72-VKP
At head of title: Р. А. Бардина.
Bibliography: p. [244]
1. Folk art—Russia. 2. Art industries and trade, Russian. I. Title.
NK975.B37 73-323349

Bardinet, Anne Christine.
Monein : la principale église gothique du Béarn / Anne-Christine Bardinet et Louis Magendie ; photos, "Eldé" Mourenx. — Jurançon : Amis des églises anciennes du Béarn, [1975]
32 p., [4] leaves of plates : ill. ; 21 cm. F***
Includes bibliographical references.
1. Église Saint-Girons, Monein, France. 2. Architecture, Gothic—Monein, France. I. Magendie, Louis, joint author. II. Title.
NA5551.M617B37 944'.79 77-455358
77 MARC

Bardis, James Michael.
The design of a dynamic observer and feedback compensator, by James M. Bardis. [n. p.] 1972.
58 l. col. diagrs. 30 cm.
Thesis (Elec. E.)–Massachusetts Institute of Technology.
Includes bibliographical references.
1. Feedback control systems. 2. Eigenvalues. 3. Chemical process control. 4. Distillation. I. Title.
MCM NUC73-125019

Bardis, Panos Demetrios.
The future of the Greek language in the United States / by Panos D. Bardis. — San Francisco : R and E Research Associates, 1976.
v, 72 p. ; 28 cm.
Bibliography: p. 63-72.
ISBN 0-88247-396-4
1. Greek language, Modern, in the United States. 2. Greek Americans. I. Title.
PA1047.U5B3 301.2'1 75-36574
77 MARC

Bardissa, Jaume.
Cent ans de querre du vin / Jaume Bardissa. — Paris : Tema-éditions, c1976.
191 p. ; 22 cm. — (Tema action) F***
ISBN 2-7142-0042-7 : 30.00F
1. Wine and wine making—France. 2. Wine and wine making—European Economic Community countries. I. Title.
HD9382.5.B37 338.4'7'66320094 76-489679
77 MARC

Bardizh, Vsevolod Vianorovich.
(Magnitnye élementy tŝifrovykh vychislitel'nykh mashin)
Магнитные элементы цифровых вычислительных машин. Изд. 2-е, перераб. и доп. Москва, "Энергия," 1974.
488 p. with illus. 20 cm. 1.56rub USSR 74
At head of title: В. В. Бардиж.
Bibliography: p. 467–[485]
1. Electronic digital computers—Circuits. 2. Magnetic memory (Calculating-machines) I. Title.
TK7888.3.B27 1974 74–317930

Bardizian, A
see
Partizian, A

Bardo, Boris de.
Irido-nevraxologie : irido-diagnostic des états pathologiques : l'irido-diagnostic en acupuncture / B. de Bardo et M. Guillaume. — Rueil Malmaison : B. de Bardo, [1974]
71 p. : ill. ; 24 cm. F***
Bibliography: p. 71.
1. Acupuncture. 2. Iris (Eye) 3. Diagnosis. I. Guillaume, Michel, joint author. II. Title.
[DNLM: 1. Acupuncture. 2. Eye manifestations. 3. Iris. WW475 B247i 1974]
[RM184.B35] 616.07'54 75-594803
Shared Cataloging with DNLM 75 MARC

Bardo, Boris de.
L'iridonevraxologie dans la physiologie de l'acupuncture et du yoga / Boris de Bardo ; préf. du dr Guillaume. — Rueil-Malmaison : Bardo, [1974]
85 p., [5] leaves of plates : ill. ; 22 cm. F***
30.00F
1. Acupuncture. 2. Iris (Eye) 3. Yoga. I. Title.
[DNLM: 1. Acupuncture. 2. Eye manifestations. 3. Iris. 4. Yoga. WW475 B247i 1974]
[RM184.B36] 615'.892 74-595071
Shared Cataloging with DNLM 75 MARC

Bardo, John William, 1948-
An empirical analysis of an application of Lewis Mumford's theories of community planning. [n.p.] 1973.
93 l.
Thesis—Ohio State University.
Bibliography: leaves 87-93.
1. Mumford, Lewis, 1895- 2. Community. I. Title.
OU NUC75-21304

Bardo thödol.
Il libro tibetano dei morti. (Bardo tödöl). A cura di Giuseppe Tucci. [Torino], Unione tipografico-editrice torinese, 1972.
232 p. plates. 23 cm. (Classici delle religioni. Sezione 1: Le religioni orientali, [22]) It 72–Sept
Bibliography: p. 75–77.
I. Tucci, Giuseppe, 1894– ed. II. Title.
BQ1652.I 8T8 1972 72–375658

Bardo thödol.
The Tibetan book of the dead; or, The after-death experiences on the Bardo plane, according to Lama Kazi Dawa-Samdup's English rendering. By W. Y. Evans-Wentz; with foreword by Sir John Woodroffe. Introduction to the Causeway edition by Michael Lord. New York, Causeway Books [c1973]
xliv, 248 p. illus. 24 cm.
Translation of Bar-do thos-grol.
Bibliographical footnotes.
I. Wentz, Walter Yeeling Evans.
PPT NUC77-13959

Bardo thödol
see Karma-glin-pa, 14th cent. Zi khro dgons pa ran grol; a collection of rediscovered texts from the gter-ma... Kelang, 1969.

Bardo thödol. English.
The Tibetan book of the dead. Modern English translation by Frank J. MacHovec. Mount Vernon, N. Y., Peter Pauper Press [c1972]
61 p. 19 cm. $1.50
I. MacHovec, Frank J., tr. II. Title.
BQ1652.E5M32 1972 294.3'4'23 73–161229
MARC

Bardoel, Jo.
see Marges in de media . . . Baarn, Wereldvenster, [1976]

Bardolet, José Coll
see
Coll Bardolet, José.

Bardolikar, Deepak, 1925-
see Koran. Gujarati. Selections. (Ābe kavasara) 1973.

Bardollet, Louis.
see Aeschylus. Théâtre .... Paris, les Belles lettres : Denoël, 1975.

Bardoloi, Muktinath, 1910–
পাৰ্ব্বতী; নেফাৰ বিষয়ে লিখা দুকুৰি কৱিতাৰ পুথি. [লিখক] শ্ৰীমুক্তিনাথ বৰদলৈ. [2. সংস্কৰণ] কলিকতা, শ্ৰীভূমি পাবলিচিং কোম্পানী [1967?]
2, 112 p. illus. 23 cm. Rs3
In Assamese.
1. Poetry of places—India—North East Frontier Agency. 2. North East Frontier Agency, India—Descr. & trav.—Poetry. I. Title.
Title romanized: Pārbbatī.
PK1569.B263P3 S A 68–9109
PL 480 : I–As–421

Bardoloi, Nabinchandra, 1875–1936.
[Works]
বৰদলৈ ৰচনাৱলী : [নবীনচন্দ্ৰ বৰদলৈ স্মৃতি গ্ৰন্থ]. — গুৱাহাটী : অসম প্ৰকাশন পৰিষদ, 1975.
427 p., [1] leaf of plates : ill. ; 26 cm.
In Assamese.
Includes bibliographical references.
"বৰদলৈৰ জন্ম শতবাৰ্ষিকী উপলক্ষে অসম প্ৰকাশন পৰিষদৰ গ্ৰন্থ."
"নবীনচন্দ্ৰ বৰদলৈৰ চমু জীৱনী. [লিখক] নন্দ তালুকদাৰ": p. [403]–427.
Rs20.00
I. Talukdar, Nanda. Nabīnacandra Baradalaira camu jīwanī. 1975.
Title romanized: Baradalai racanāwalī.
PK1569.B264 1975 75–908572

Bardoloi, Nirmal Probha.
(Asamara loka-saṃskṛti)
অসমৰ লোক-সংস্কৃতি. [লিখিকা] নিৰ্ম্মলপ্ৰভা বৰদলৈ. [গুৱাহাটী]; পৰিবেশক লয়াৰ্ছ বুক ষ্টল [1972]
6, 267 p. illus. 23 cm. Rs8.00
In Assamese.
1. Folk-lore—India—Assam. 2. Assam—Social life and customs. I. Title.
GR305.5.A8B27 73–902358

Bardoloi, Prasanta.
(Manara pānacai)
মনৰ পানচৈ / প্ৰশান্ত বৰদলৈ. — ডিব্ৰুগড় : অভিযাত্ৰী : পৰিবেশক বনলতা, 1976.
9, 61 p. ; 22 cm.
In Assamese.
Poems.
Rs3.50
I. Title.
PK1569.B2645M3 76–905520

Bardoloi, U N
(Asamara arthanaitika paristhiti)
অসমৰ অৰ্থনৈতিক পৰিস্থিতি : ৰচনা সঙ্কলন / উপেন্দ্ৰনাথ বৰদলৈ. — 1. সংস্কৰণ. — গুৱাহাটী : দত্তবৰুৱা, 1974.
331 p. ; 22 cm.
In Assamese.
Rs10.00
1. Assam—Economic conditions—Addresses, essays, lectures. I. Title.
HC437.A8B36 76–900054

Bardoloi, U N
Local finance in Assam / U. N. Bardoloi. — 1st ed. — Gauhati : Dutta Baruah, 1972.
291, vii p. ; 23 cm.
Bibliography: p. [1]-vii.
Rs18.00
1. Local finance—Assam. I. Title.
HJ9553.A8B37 336.54'162 74-904015
75 MARC

Bardolph, Richard, 1915–
The Negro vanguard. Westport, Conn., Negro Universities Press [1971, c1959]
388 p. 24 cm.
"Essay on authorities": p. 343–369.
1. Negroes—Biography. 2. Negroes—History. I. Title.
E185.B267 1971 917.3'06'96073 77–135592
ISBN 0–8371–5183–X [B] MARC

Bardon, Colette, tr.
see La Pensée des lumières en Russie . . . Lille, Université de Lille III, [1973]

Bardon, Françoise.
Le portrait mythologique à la cour de France sous Henri IV et Louis XIII : mythologie et politique / Françoise Bardon. — Paris : A. et J. Picard, 1974.
326 p., [26] leaves of plates : ill. ; 27 cm. F***
Bibliography: p. [291]-313.
185F
1. Arts, French. 2. Mythology, Classical, in art. 3. Allegories. 4. Kings and rulers in art. 5. Henry IV, King of France, 1553-1610. 6. Louis XIII, King of France, 1601-1643. I. Title.
NX549.A1B37 700'.944 75-505456
75 MARC

Bardon, Franz.
The key to the true quabbalah: the quabbalist as a sovereign in the micro- and the macrocosm. Wuppertal, Western Germany, D. Rüggeberg, 1971.
270 p. port., col. diagr. 21 cm.
Translation of Der Schlüssel zur wahren Quabbalah by Peter A. Dimai.
1. Magic. 2. Cabala. 3. Alphabet (in religion, folk-lore, etc.) I. Title.
IU NUC74-126814

Bardon, Georges. L'insertion européenne. 1972
in EDF: ouverture sur le monde. [Paris? 1972?]

Bardon, Henry.
Explications latines de licence et d'agrégation [par] H. Bardon. Paris, Vuibert, 1946.
vii, 300 p. 22 cm.
French and/or Latin.
Includes bibliographical references.
1. Latin literature—Explication. I. Title.
PA2063.B3 870'.9 74–173398

Bardon, Henry.
Le vocabulaire de la critique littéraire chez Sénèque le rhéteur / par Henry Bardon. -- Paris : Société d'édition "Les Belles lettres," 1940.
114 p. : diagrs. ; 25 cm.
Thèse complémentaire--Univ. de Paris.
"Bibliographie": p. [5]-7.
Photocopy. Ann Arbor, Mich. : Xerox University Microfilms, 1975. -- 24 cm.
1. Seneca, Lucius Annaeus, "rhetor"--Dictionaries, indexes, etc. I. Title.
NRU NUC77-98948

Bardon, Henry, ed.
see Catullus, C. Valerius. Catulli Veronensis carmina. Stutgardiae Teubner, 1973.

Bardon, Jack I 1925-
School psychology ₍by₎ Jack I. Bardon ₍and₎ Virginia C. Bennett. Englewood Cliffs, N. J., Prentice-Hall ₍1974₎
xi, 195 p. illus. 23 cm. (Foundations of modern psychology series) $2.95 (pbk.)
Bibliography: p. 183-190.
1. Educational psychology. 2. School psychologists. I. Bennett, Virginia C., 1916- joint author. II. Title.
₍DNLM: 1. Psychology, Educational. LB 1051 B247s 1974₎
LB1051.B2472 1974 370.15 73-11419
ISBN 0-13-794420-9; 0-13-794412-8 (pbk.) MARC

Bardon, Jean.
Chasse, mon doux venin; ou, Les récits d'un chasseur au cœur tendre. Roman. Paris, Les Paragraphes littéraires de Paris ₍1970₎
253 p. plate. 19 cm. (Les Paragraphes littéraires de Paris) 14.00F F***
1. Hunting stories. I. Title.
PQ2662.A682C5 74-327583

Bardon, Jonathan.
The struggle for Ireland: 400-1450. [Belfast] Fallons [1970]
100 p. illus. 23 cm.
1. Ireland—History—To 1172—Text books. I. Title.
MB NUC77-14565

Bardon, Maurice.
"Don Quichotte" en France au XVIIe et au XVIIIe siècle, 1605-1815. New York, B. Franklin ₍1971₎
2 v. (932 p.) illus. 23 cm. (Burt Franklin research and source works series, 784. Essays in literature and criticism, 146)
Reprint of the 1931 ed., which was issued as no. 69 of Bibliothèque de la Revue de littérature comparée.
Bibliography: p. ₍845₎-897.
1. Cervantes Saavedra, Miguel de, 1547-1616. Don Quixote. 2. Cervantes Saavedra, Miguel de, 1547-1616—Influence. 3. French literature—History and criticism. I. Title. II. Series: Bibliothèque de la Revue de littérature comparée, no 69.
PQ6353.B33 1971 863'.3 79-166442
ISBN 0-8337-3966-2

Bardon, Michael J., joint comp.
see Brock, Fred R comp. The Biblical perspective of science... New York, MSS Information Corp. ₍1972₎

Bardon, Michel François Dandré-
see Dandré-Bardon, Michel François, 1700-1783.

Bardón, Salvador García
see García Bardón, Salvador.

Bardón M., Alvaro
see Itinerario de una crisis... 2. ed. [Santiago de Chile] Editorial del Pacífico [1972]

Bardone, Guy, 1927-
Bardone : ₍exposition₎ fevrier-mars 1975, Galerie Guiot, Paris. -- Paris : Galerie Guiot, 1975.
₍24₎ p. : chiefly ill. (some col.), port. ; 21 x 21 cm.
Includes essay by Jean Bouret.
List of works exhibited inserted.
Bibliography: p. ₍23₎
I. Galerie Guiot.
MH-FA NUC77-100997

Bardone... -- Paris : 1975
see under Bardone, Guy, 1927-

Bardorff, Wilhelm, writer on natural history.
Naturpark Bergstrasse-Odenwald. Karlsruhe, G. Braun ₍c1972₎
128 p. illus. 27 cm. GDB***
1. Naturpark Bergstrasse-Odenwald, Ger. I. Title.
SB484.G4B37 74-334520
ISBN 3-7650-8010-1

Bardorff, Wilhelm, writer on natural history
see Brehm, Alfred Edmund, 1829-1884. Brehms Tierleben in Farbe... Berlin, Safari-Verlag ₍1969₎

Bardorff, Wilhelm, writer on natural history, joint author
see Edschmid, Kasimir, 1890-1966. Weinheim: ₍Naturpark Bergstrasse-Odenwald₎. Karlsruhe: Braun, 1973.

Bárdoš, Augustín, 1921-
Žena-zdravie+krása : sprievodca modernej ženy / Augustín Bárdoš ; ₍ilustr. Mária Želibská ; väzbu a použ. ilustr. Márie Želibskej navrhol Robert Brož₎. — 1. vyd. — Martin : Osveta, 1976.
223 p. : ill. ; 13 cm. CzS 76
Kčs12.00
1. Women—Health and hygiene. 2. Beauty, Personal. I. Title.
RA778.B227 76-527952

Bárdoš, Augustín, 1921- ed.
see Gynekológia a pôrodníctvo. [Vyd. 1. Martin] Osveta, 1972-

Bárdos, Augustín, 1921-
see Zdravoveda pre rodinu. Martin: Osveta, 1975.

Bardos, Gertrude
see Romania. Arhivele Statului. Indrumator în Arhivele Statului Banat. Bucuresti, 1966-

Bárdos, György, ed.
see Hungray. Laws, statutes, etc. Hatályos pénzügyi jogszabályok gyüjteménye. Budapest, Közgazdasági és Jogi Könyvkiadó, 1972.

Bárdos, Józsefné
see Csoportos foglalkozások gyermekkönyvtárakban... Budapest, Könyvtártudományi és Módszertani Központ, 1971.

Bárdos, Kornél.
Pécs zenéje a 18. században / Bárdos Kornél. — Budapest : Akadémiai Kiadó, 1976.
167 p., ₍2₎ leaves of plates : ill. ; 25 cm.
Summary in German.
Bibliography: p. 159-161.
Includes music and index.
1. Music—Hungary—Pécs. 2. Music—History and criticism—18th century. I. Title.
ML248.8.P4B4 77-480214
77 MARC

Bárdos, Kornél.
Volksmusikartige Variierungstechnik in den Ungarischen Passionen (15. bis 18. Jahrhundert) / von Kornél Bárdos. -- Budapest : Akadémiai Kiadó, 1975.
240 p., [6] leaves of plates : facsims., music ; 25 cm. -- (Musicologia Hungarica : neue Folge ; 5)
Bibliography: p. 229-240.
1. Church music--Hungary--History and criticism. 2. Passion-music--History and criticism. I. Title. II. Series.
AzU NUC77-99172

Bárdos, Kornél.
Volksmusikartige Variierungstechnik in den Ungarischen Passionen (15. bis 18. Jahrhundert) / von Kornél Bárdos. -- Kassel : Bärenreiter, 1975.
240 p., ₍6₎ leaves of plates : facsims., music ; 25 cm. -- (Musicologia Hungarica : Neue Folge ; 5)
Bibliography: p. 229-240.
1. Church music--Hungary--History and criticism. 2. Passion music--History and criticism. I. Title. II. Series.
MoSW NUC77-98986

Bárdos, Lajos.
Liszt Ferenc, a jövő zenésze / Bárdos Lajos. — Budapest : Akadémiai Kiadó, 1976.
127 p. ; 25 cm.
Includes indexes.
Includes music.
ISBN 963-05-0739-0 : 32.00Ft
1. Liszt, Franz, 1811-1886—Harmonic system. I. Title.
ML410.L7B27 77-502347

Bárdos, Lajos.
Tíz újabb írás : 1969-1974 / Bárdos Lajos. — Budapest : Zeneműkiadó, 1974.
286 p. ; 25 cm.
Continuation of the author's Harminc írás ...
Includes music.
Includes index.
CONTENTS: A Bartók-zene stíluselemei.—Bartók dallamvilágából.—Kodály Gyermekkarairól.—Egy "kodályos" hangrendszer.—A szabadság kánonja.—Az új Kodály-kötetek kérdéséhez.—Stravinsky Zsoltárszimfóniájáról. — Organika. — A Magyar Kórus húsz éve. — Találkozásom a népdallal.
1. Music—Addresses, essays, lectures. 2. Harmony. 3. Music, Hungarian—History and criticism.
M160.B175T6 76-529133

Bárdos, László István.
Komárom megyei hírlapok és folyóiratok bibliográfiája. ₍Összeállította Bárdos László István ₍és₎ Horváth Géza. Tatabánya, "József Attila" Megyei Könyvtár, 1962.
82 p. illus. 21 cm.
1. Hungarian newspapers—Komárom (Comitat)—Bibliography. 2. Hungarian periodicals—Komárom (Comitat)—Bibliography. I. Horváth, Géza, joint author. II. Title.
Z6956.H8B37 74-232851

Bárdos, Pál, 1936-
Az első évtized : regény / Bárdos Pál. — Budapest : Szépirodalmi Könyvkiadó, 1975.
326 p. ; 19 cm.
ISBN 963-15-0530-8 : 23.50Ft
I. Title.
PH3213.B294E4 76-526945

Bárdosi Németh, János.
Fehér pille. Budapest, Magvető ₍1972₎
81 p. 20 cm. 12.50Ft.
Poems.
I. Title.
PH3213.B2944F4 73-201357

Bárdosi Németh, János.
A lélek lángjai / Bárdosi Németh János. — Budapest : Magvető, 1974.
235 p. ; 19 cm.
Poems.
18.50Ft
I. Title.
PH3213.B2944L4 77-556936
77 MARC

Bardossi, Fulvio.
La esclerosis múltiple: esperanzas para su curación. ₍New York, Public Affairs Committee, 1973, c1971₎
24 p. illus. 19 cm. (Folleto de asuntos públicos, no. 335A) $0.35
Cover title.
Translation of Multiple sclerosis: grounds for hope.
1. Multiple sclerosis. I. Title.
RC377.B3718 616.8'34 73-207346

Bardossy, György.
Bibliographie des travaux concernant les bauxites publiés en francais, anglais, russe et allemand. ⟨1965-1968⟩. Preparée par Gy. Bardossy. Zagreb, Académie yougoslave des sciences et des arts, 1971.
34 p. 24 cm. (Travaux du Comité international pour l'étude des bauxites, des oxydes et des hydroxydes d'aluminium, no 8) $4.00 Yu 72-2018
Cover title.
1. Bauxite—Bibliography. I. Jugoslavenska akademija znanosti i umjetnosti. II. Title. III. Series: International Committee for Studies of Bauxites, Oxides and Hydroxides of Aluminium. Travaux, no 8.
Z6033.B4B37 72-971201

Bardou, Paule.
Florilège [par] P. Bardou [et] Georges Vionnat. Illus. de Jean Reschovsky. Paris, F. Nathan [1966-67]
2 v. illus. 18 cm.
Contents.–1. Poèmes pour enfants de 5 à 8 ans.–2. Poèmes pour enfants de 9 à 13 ans.
1. Children's poetry, French. I. Vionnet, Georges. II. Title.
MB NUC74-19022

Bardou, Pierre, illus.
see Coyne, Gilles. L'Art roman dans les Pyrénées-Atlantiques. Bordeaux, Centre de recherche et de documentation pedagogiques, [75, cours d'Alsace-Lorraine,] 1971.

Bardouillet, Jean.
see Semaines de la pensée marxiste, Paris, 1975. Les Femmes aujourd'hui, demain. Paris, Éditions sociales, 1975.

[**Bardovskiĭ, Vasiliĭ Stepanovich**] 1804–1874.
[Vseobshchaía geografíía dlía nachal'nago prepodavaníía. Bulgarian]
Всеобща географія за дѣцата / преведи отъ русскій языкъ Иванъ А. Богоевъ. — Бѣлъградъ : Въ Княжеско -сжрбскжтж тип., 1843.
421, [16] p., [1] fold. leaf : ill. ; 22 cm.
1. Geography—Text-books—1800–1870. I. Bogorov, Ivan Andreev, 1818–1892. II. Title.
Title romanized : Vseobshta geografíía za díetsata.
G125.B3712 77–500829

Bardoz, C
On the pressure in the sea: a simple model, by C. Bardoz and E. Salusti. Roma, 1972.
16 p. 30 cm. (Istituto nazionale di fisica nucleare. Sezione di Roma. Nota interna, n. 377)
1. Pressure—Mathematical models. 2. Hydrodynamics—Mathematical models. I. Title. II. Series.
DME NUC75-30844

Bards, bohemians and bookmen : essays in Australian literature / edited by Leon Cantrell. — St. Lucia, Q. : University of Queensland Press, 1976.
xiii, 350 p. : port. ; 22 cm. Aus
Bibliography: p. 330-333.
ISBN 0-7022-1321-7
1. Australian literature—History and criticism—Addresses, essays, lectures. 2. Hadgraft, Cecil—Addresses, essays, lectures. I. Cantrell, Leon Nicolas, 1943-
PR9604.6.B3 820'.9 77-363841
77 MARC

Bardsley, Beverly Jean, 1945-
The soul as a self-moving motion: the synthesis of madness and sobriety in Plato's Phaedrus. [Austin, Tex.] 1975.
v, 176 l. 29 cm.
Thesis (Ph.D.)--University of Texas at Austin.
Vita.
Bibliography: leaves 171-176.
1. Plato. Phaedrus. I. Title.
TxU NUC77-99394

Bardsley, Frederick G 1928-
A comparative study of the role of the school superintendent and its influence on the items negotiated during the collective bargaining process in selected Massachusetts communities. [n. p.] 1973.
xv, 240 p. tables.
Thesis—Boston University.
Bibliography: p. 235-239.
1. School superintendents and principals—Massachusetts. 2. Collective bargaining—Teachers—Massachusetts. I. Title.
MBU NUC75-21303

Bardsley, J. Roy
see Bardsley & Haslacher, inc. Metropolitan Portland looks at governmental reorganization. [Portland, Or., 1965]

Bardsley, John Wareing, Bp. of Carlisle, 1835-1904.
Counsels to candidates for Confirmation. Founded upon "The Order of Confirmation" according to the use of the Church of England. London, Elliot Stock [n. d.]
78 p.
1. Church of England–Catechisms and creeds. 2. Confirmation–Instruction and study. I. Title.
CtHC NUC73-125020

Bardsley, Richard, joint author.
see Steffy, Wilbert. Production control for the small and medium-sized firms. Ann Arbor, Industrial Development Division, Institute of Science and Technology, University of Michigan, 1974.

Bardsley, Virginia O
James Rogan, hill country pioneer. State College, 1961.
vi, 235 p. illus. 28 cm.
Thesis—Mississippi State University.
Bibliography: p. [229]-235.
Reproduced by Xerox process.
1. Rogan, James, 1797-1885.
MsU NUC75-67082

Bardsley & Haslacher, inc.
Metropolitan Portland looks at governmental reorganization. Project director: J. Roy Bardsley. Consultant: Robert Agger. PMSC Research Committee: Estes (Pete) Snedecor, Jr., Ruth Hagenstein [and] Nina Aylsworth. [Portland, Or., 1965]
ix, 39, S-70, A-4 l. illus. 28 cm.
On cover: A public opinion study.
"Sponsored by [the] Portland Metropolitan Study Commission."
1. Local government–Portland metropolitan area, Or.–Public opinion. I. Bardsley, J. Roy. II. Portland, Or. Metropolitan Study Commission. III. Title.
OrPS NUC74-135896

Bardstown, Ky. Board of Trustees
see Thonen, Nellie Alwilda Brown. A summary of the "Minutes of the Board of Trustees, Bardstown, Ky."... Fresno, Calif., 1969.

Bardstown Chamber of Commerce.
Historic Bardstown and My old Kentucky Home. [Bardstown, Ky., 19--]
31 p. illus. 17 x 25 cm.
"Souvenir edition."
1. Bardstown, Ky. Description. Views. I. Title.
NcD NUC74-9883

Bardstown in retrospect. [n.p., 1965?]
see under [Muir, John W]

Bardtke, Hans.
Bibel, Spaten und Geschichte / Hans Bardtke. — 3., erw. Aufl. — Leipzig : Koehler & Amelang, 1974.
375 p. : ill. ; 25 cm. GDR 74-A
Bibliography : p. 347-355.
Includes indexes.
22.80M
1. Bible—Antiquities. I. Title.
BS621.B27 1974 75-407923

Bardtke, Hans
see Bible. O. T. Psalms. Hebrew. 1969. Liber Psalmorum. Stuttgart, Württembergische Bibelanstant Stuttgart, 1969.

Bardua, Heinz.
Stuttgarter Wappen; Wappenführung und heraldische Traditionen der Stadt und ihrer Vororte. Stuttgart, E. Klett, 1973.
91 p. col. coats of arms, 11 plates. 24 cm. (Veröffentlichungen des Archivs der Stadt Stuttgart, Bd. 18) GDB***
Includes bibliographies.
1. Heraldry—Germany—Stuttgart. I. Title. II. Series: Stuttgart. Archiv der Stadt Stuttgart. Veröffentlichungen, Bd. 18.
CR554.S78B3 73-335963

Bardua, Heinz, joint author
see Gönner, Eberhard. Wappenbuch des Landkreises Wangen. Stuttgart, W. Kohlhammer, 1972.

Barducci, Italo.
Appunti sulla trasmissione del calore. Roma, Sistema, 1971.
187 p. illus. 24 cm. L2000 It 72–Sept
At head of title: Università degli studi di Roma. Facoltà di ingegneria. Istituto di fisica tecnica. I. Barducci.
1. Heat—Transmission. I. Title.
QC320.B37 72–371776

Bardulet i Palau, Salvador.
Prègàries : individuals, en família, en grup / Salvador Bardulet i Palau. — [Montserrat] : Publicacions de l'Abadia de Montserrat, 1974.
300 p. ; 18 cm. — (El Gra de blat ; 9) Sp***
ISBN 84–7202–224–2
1. Prayers. 2. Family — Prayer-books and devotions — Catalan. I. Title: Pregàries : individuals, en família, en grup.
BV249.C37B37 1974 75–584559

Bardulla, Enver, 1944–
Ecologia e educazione / Enver Bardulla, Mario Valeri. — 1. ed. — Firenze : La nuova Italia, 1975.
vi, 224 p. ; 21 cm. — (Educatori antichi e moderni ; 320) It 75–Oct
Bibliography : p. [201]–219.
Includes index.
L2500
1. Human ecology—Study and teaching—Italy. I. Valeri, Mario, joint author. II. Title.
GF28.I 8B37 75–402761

al-Bardūnī, 'Abd Allāh, 1929 or 30–
(Li-'aynay Umm Balqīs)
لعيني ام بلقيس : شعر / عبد الله البردوني . — الطبعة 3. —
دمشق : [s. n.], 1975
109 p. ; 17 cm.
I. Title.
PJ7816.A68L5 1975 77–970819

al-Bardūnī, 'Abd Allāh, 1929 or 30–
رحلة فى الشعر اليمنى، قديمه وحديثه [تأليف] عبد الله
البردونى. [القاهرة] دار الهنا للطباعة، 1972.
354 p. 25 cm. £E0.70
Includes bibliographical references.
1. Arabic poetry—Yemen—History and criticism. I. Title.
Title romanized : Riḥlah fī al-shi'r al-Yamanī.
PJ8001.Y4B3 72–960132

Bardunov, Leonid Vladimirovich.
(Listostebel'nye mkhi Altaía i Saíàn)
Листостебельные мхи Алтая и Саян / Л. В. Бардунов ; отв. ред. д-р биол. наук А. В. Смирнов. — Новосибирск : Наука, Сиб. отд-ние, 1974.
167 p. : maps ; 21 cm. USSR 74
At head of title: Академия наук СССР. Сибирское отделение. Сибирский институт физиологии и биохимии растений.
Bibliography : p. 159–167.
0.79rub
1. Mosses—Russia—Altai Mountains. 2. Mosses—Russia—Sayan Mountains. I. Title.
QK537.B37 74–352980

Bardusco, Aldo.
La struttura dei contratti delle pubbliche amministrazioni : atti amministrativi e negozio di diritto privato / Aldo Bardusco. — Milano : A. Giuffrè, 1974.
404 p. ; 26 — (Pubblicazioni della Facoltà di giurisprudenza, Università di Milano : Studi di diritto pubblico ; ser. 2., n. 14) It 76–Jan
Includes bibliographical references.
L6400
1. Public contracts—Italy. I. Title. II. Series: Milan. Università. Facoltà di giurisprudenza. Studi di diritto pubblico ; ser. 2., n. 14)
76–510702

Bardusco, Aldo
see Italia, Vittorio. Commento allo statuto della Regione Lombardia. Milano, Giuffrè, 1973.

Bardwani, Muhammad Khalilur Rahman ibn Muhammad Ishaq.
نظام فقر؛ نظام اسلام کی صحیح جلوہ نمائی، مع تعلیم و لائحہ عمل،
کمیونزم کے اژدھا کو ہلاک کرنے کا عصائے موسٰی، اسلامی معاشرے
کی بنیادی باتیں. [مصنفہ] محمد خلیل الرحمٰن بن اسحاق بردوانی.
مع افتتاحیہ از حسن آرا عرف رئیسی بیگم. [ڈھاکہ؟ رئیسی بیگم و
فریدہ اسحٰق محبوبہ؛ ملنے کا پتہ: دارالسلم، ڈھاکہ، 1968]
2 v. 19 cm. (سلسلہ الفقر فخری کی کڑی، 1-2) Rs2.50 (v. 1); Rs0.50 (v. 2)
1. Islam. I. Title.
Title romanized: Niẓām-i faqr.
BP88.B33N5 78–931014

Bardwani, Muhammad Khalilur Rahman ibn Muhammad Ishaq.
صلٰوة و زکٰوة کی اصلیت اور مسئلہ عفو کا احیاء؛ مطابق اسوۂ رسول اکرم و خلفاء راشدین و صحابہ کرام و جملہ بزرگان دین و سلف صالحین. از محمد خلیل الرحمٰن بن محمد اسحاق بردوانی و حسن آرا عرف رئیسی بیگم. ڈھاکہ، مرکز نشریات نظام فقر ‏[1968]
32 p. 19 cm. Rs0.50
In Urdu.
1. Prayer (Islam)—Addresses, essays, lectures. 2. Zakat—Addresses, essays, lectures. 3. Forgiveness of sin (Islam)—Addresses, essays, lectures. I. Ḥasan Ārā, Ra'īsī Begam, joint author. II. Title.
Title romanized: Ṣalāt o zakāt kī aṣliyyat.
BP178.B37 74-931013

Bardwell, Ann Skinner, 1930-
Resource use of low-income families and its relationship to family patterns of adjustment to chronic maternal illness. [n.p.] 1968 [1972]
269 l. tables.
Thesis–Ohio State University.
Vita.
Photocopy. Ann Arbor, University Microfilms, 1972. 22 cm.
1. Family–United States. 2. Poor–United States. 3. Home economics research. I. Title.
GU NUC73-125015

Bardwell, Elizabeth.
More is less : the case study of a city that may be growing too big for its citizens' good / by Elizabeth Bardwell. — 2d ed. — Madison, Wis. : Capital Community Citizens, 1974.
105 p. : ill. ; 18 cm.
Bibliography: p. 103–105.
1. Madison, Wis.—Social conditions. 2. Madison, Wis.—Economic conditions. 3. Cities and towns—Growth. I. Title.
HN80.M18B37 1974 309.1'775'8404 74-194700
MARC

Bardwell, George E
Segregation; a social account, by George E. Bardwell. [Denver?] Colorado Civil Rights Commission [1971?]
94 l. illus.
1. Segregation in education—Denver, Colo. I. Title.
CU NUC74-126798

Bardwell, John D
Toward a New Hampshire information network; a study of the feasibility of establishing educational information links between Keene State College, Plymouth State College, and the University of New Hampshire [by] John D. Bardwell. [Durham] Audio Visual Center, University of New Hampshire at Durham, 1970.
40 p. 23 cm.
Bibliography: p. 39–40.
1. Education, Higher—New Hampshire. 2. Communication in education. I. Title.
LA328.5.B37 378.1'04'09742 73-172203
MARC

Bardwell, John D
The York Militia Company, 1642-1972, by John D. Bardwell. York, Me., 1972.
57 p. illus. 23 cm.
Bibliography: p. 49-50.
1. Maine–Militia. 2. York, Me.–Hist. I. Title.
MeU NUC77-13813

Bardwell, John D.
see Outreach Leadership Network. Leadership for change... Durham, N.H., Outreach Leadership Network, New England Center for Continuing Education, University of New Hampshire, 1972.

Bardwell, Leila Stone.
Vanished pioneer homes and families of Shelburne, Massachusetts. [Shelburne, Mass.] Shelburne Historical Society, 1974.
vi, 89, 44 p. ill., map. 26 cm.
Includes index.
1. Shelburne, Mass.–Hist. 2. Shelburne, Mass.–Geneal. I. Title.
WHi NUC76-96148

Bardwell, Wilma.
Early childhood education : personalities / Wilma Bardwell, Rose Spicola. — Dallas, Tex. : Bardwell, [1975]
iii, 125 p. ; 23 cm.
Includes index.
1. Education, American—Biography. I. Spicola, Rose, joint author. II. Title.
LA2311.B27 370'.92'2 75-7531
75 MARC

Bardwell Descendants American Ancestry Association
see
Robert Bardwell Descendants' American Ancestry Association.

Bardwick, Judith M 1933–
An interview with Judith Bardwick: self-esteem and changing roles. [Sound recording] New York, Harper & Row, p1975. [24-60970, 24-61010.
2 cassettes. (Audio colloquies)
Title from container.
Charles Harris, interviewer.
Descriptive notes on container.
SUMMARY: In part 1 Dr. Bardwick discusses the development of her ideas concerning the psychology of women and outlines the effects of psychoanalytic thinking and inherent beliefs and mystiques about women; in part 2 she talks about the development and results of the feminist movement and the changing roles of women and men.
1. Women—Psychology. 2. Feminism. 3. Sex role. 4. Self-respect. I. Harris, Charles William, 1945– II. Title.
[HQ1206] 76-740292

Bardwick, Judith M 1933- comp.
Readings on the psychology of women. Edited by Judith M. Bardwick. New York, Harper & Row [1972]
xiii, 335 p. 26 cm.
1. Women—Psychology—Addresses, essays, lectures. I. Title.
HQ1206.B24 301.41'2 71-188199
ISBN 0-06-040493-0 72[r76]rev MARC

Bardwick, Judith M., 1933-
see Feminine personality and conflict. Belmont, Calif., Brooks/Cole Pub. Co. [1970]

Bardy, Benjamin.
Mende, Lozère 48. Colmar-Ingersheim, S. A. E. P. [1973]
99 p. illus. (part col.) 20 x 22 cm. 29.50F F***
Bibliography: p. 96–97.
1. Mende, France.
DC801.M511B37 914.4'815 74-189742
MARC

Bardy, Benjamin.
Promenades dans Mende / Benjamin Bardy, ... illustrations de P. Commandré. — Mende (allée des Soupirs, 48000) : H. Chaptal, 1972.
52 p. : ill., [1] fold. map ; 21 cm. F 73-11156
Bibliography: p. 44–45.
Includes index.
1. Mende, France—Description. I. Title.
DC801.M511B38 914.4'815 75-500120
MARC

Bardy, Benjamin.
see Lozère. France (Dept.). Archives départementales. Direction des services. Répertoire numérique de la série O ... Mende, Les Archives, 1975.

Bardy, Gustave, 1881-1955
see Les Trophées de Damas... Turnhout, Belgique, Éditions Brepols, 1973.

Bardy, Roland.
1919 [i. e. Dix-neuf cent dix-neuf] La commune de Budapest. Paris, Éditions de la Tête de Feuilles [1972]
244 p. map, plates. 21 cm. 37 50F F***
"Documents": p. [179]-225.
"Textes publiés sous la direction de Max Chaleil."
Bibliography: p. 237–242.
1. Hungary—History—Revolution, 1918–1919. 2. Károlyi, Mihály, gráf, 1875–1955. 3. Kun, Béla, 1886–1939. I. Title. II. Chaleil, Max, ed.
DB955.B35 73-319659

Bardy, Roland.
Die Produktivität von Forschung und Entwicklung : eine ökonometr. Analyse d. Abhängigkeit industrieller Wertschöpfung von Forschungs- u. Entwicklungsausgaben aufgrund von Produktions funktionen, mit empir. Ergebnissen f. d. dt. Chemiewirtschaft / Roland Bardy. — Meisenheim (am Glan) : Hain, 1974.
286, [42] p. : ill. ; 23 cm. — (Schriften zur wirtschaftswissenschaftlichen Forschung ; Bd. 81) GFR 75-A
Bibliography: p. 258–286.
ISBN 3-445-01179-6 : DM45.00
1. Industrial productivity. 2. Production functions (Economic theory) 3. Research, Industrial. 4. Chemical industries — Germany (Federal Republic, 1949-) I. Title.
HD56.B37 75-527392

Bardyhola, ÎA K
Zhyttîa i tvorchist' Vladyslava Vanchury. [By] ÎA.K. Bardyhola. Kyïv, 1969.
26 p.
At head of title: Ministerstvo vyshchoĭ i seredn'oĭ spetsial'noĭ osvity URSR. Kyïvs'kyĭ ordena Lenina derzhavnyĭ universytet im. T.H. Shevchenka.
1. Vančura, Vladislav, 1891-1942.
MH NUC74-21962

Bardyshev, G. M.
see Nemet͡sko-russkiĭ politekhnicheskiĭ slovar'. 1973.

Bardyshev, Georgii Mikhaĭlovich
see Spravochnik mukomola, krupianshchika, kombikormshchika. Izd. 2., perer. i dop. Moskva, "Kolos", 1973.

Bardyshev, Oleg Andreevich.
(Ėkspluatat͡sii͡a stroitel'nykh mashin zimoĭ)
Эксплуатация строительных машин зимой / О. А. Бардышев. — Москва : Транспорт, 1976.
95 p. : ill. ; 16 cm. — (В помощь строителям БАМ) USSR***
Series romanized: V pomoshch' stroiteli͡am BAM.
0.17rub
1. Construction equipment—Cold weather operation. I. Title.
TH900.B25 77-502967

Bardzik, John Michael, 1945-
An investigation of the metabolic and physiological effects of alachlor on avena seedlings and coleoptile sections. [Amherst] 1974.
x, 87 l. illus. 28 cm.
Thesis (Ph.D.)—University of Massachusetts.
1. Alachlor. 2. Avena. I. Title.
MU NUC76-96139

Bare, B Bruce.
Computerized forest resource management games: an overview and assessment, by B. Bruce Bare. Seattle, Center for Quantitative Science in Forestry, Fisheries and Wildlife, University of Washington, 1971.
17 l. 28 cm. (Quantitative science paper, no. 30)
Cover title.
"Presented at Computer and Information Systems in Resources Management Decisions Workshop, SAF Annual Convention, September 30, 1971. Cleveland, Ohio."
"Literature cited": leaves 14-16.
1. Forest management–Mathematical models. 2. Digital computer simulation. 3. Management games. I. Title.
CtY NUC73-126078

Bare, B Bruce.
Selecting forest residue treatment alternatives using goal programing / B. Bruce Bare, Brian F. Anholt. -- Portland, Or. : U.S. Dept. of Agriculture, Forest Service, Pacific Northwest Forest and Range Experiment Station, 1976.
26 p. ; 27 cm. -- (USDA Forest Service general technical report PNW ; 43)
Cover title.
Bibliography: p. 24-25.
1. Electronic data processing--Forests and forestry. 2. Forests and forestry--United States. I. Anholt, Brian F., joint author.
II. Title. III. Series: United States. Pacific Northwest Forest and Range Experiment Station, Portland, Or. USDA Forest Service general technical report PNW ; 43.
MiU NUC77-99446

Bare, George Harlow, 1942-
Physical studies of heme proteins. [n.p.] 1973.
120 l.
Thesis—Ohio State University.
Includes bibliographical references.
1. Heme. I. Title.
OU NUC74-124451

Bare, John K
Psychology: where to begin. Washington, American Psychological Association; Boulder, Colo., ERIC Clearinghouse for Social Studies/ Social Science Education [1972?]
14 p. (ERIC/CHESS interpretive series no. 3)
Includes bibliography.
1. Psychology—Study and teaching. 2. Psychology—Bibliography. I. Title.
NbCrD NUC74-124444

Bare, Themi B
Në vitet e stuhishme / Themi (Thimo) B. Bare. — Tiranë : 8 Nëntori, 1976.
188, [1] p. : ill. ; 19 cm.
Bibliography: p. 186-[189]
L3.00
1. World War, 1939-1945—Underground movements—Albania. 2. Albania—History—1912-1944. I. Title.
D802.A38B37 77-502636

Bare, Viola Reed.
Adam - where art thou? and other poems, by Viola Reed Bare. [1st ed.] Detroit, Harlo Press [c1972]
117 p. 23 cm.
I. Title.
WvU NUC73-124572

Bare, William K
Fundamentals of fire prevention / William K. Bare. — New York : Wiley, c1977.
ix, 213 p. : ill. ; 24 cm. — (The Wiley series in fire science)
Includes bibliographies and index.
ISBN 0-471-04835-6
1. Fire prevention. I. Title.
TH9145.B38 628.9'22 76-23221
76 MARC

Bare breasts and bare bottoms : anatomy of film censorship in India / edited by C. K. Razdan ; contributors, Partap Sharma ... [et al.]. — Bombay : Jaico Pub. House, 1975.
158 p., [8] leaves of plates : ill. ; 18 cm.
"J-406."
Rs9.00
1. Moving-pictures—Censorship—India—Addresses, essays, lectures. I. Razdan, C. K. II. Sharma, Partap, 1939-
PN1994.A5I45 791.43'013 75-908414
76 MARC

Barea, Arturo, 1897-1957.
The forging of a rebel. Translated (from the Spanish mss.) by Ilsa Barea. London, Davis-Poynter, 1972.
14, 751 p. 23 cm. £5.00 GB 73-01598
Translation of La forja de unrebelde.
In 3 pts; each pt. also published separately under the titles: The forge, The track, and The clash.
1. Barea, Arturo, 1897-1957. 2. Spain—Social life and customs. 3. Rif Revolt, 1921-1926. 4. Spain—History—Civil War, 1936-1939—Personal narratives. I. Barea, Ilsa, tr. II. Title.
DP236.B3A213 1972 914.6'03'80924 74-170922
ISBN 0-7067-0044-9 [B] MARC

Barea, Arturo, 1897-1957.
The forging of a rebel. Translated by Ilsa Barea. New York, Viking Press [c1972]
xiv, 751 p. 25 cm. $15.00
"A Richard Seaver book."
CONTENTS: The forge.—The track.—The clash.
1. Barea, Arturo, 1897-1957. 2. Spain—Social life and customs. 3. Rif Revolt, 1921-1926. 4. Spain—History—Civil War, 1936-1939—Personal narratives. I. Title.
DP236.B3A213 1972b 914.6'03'80924 73-17675
[B] MARC

Barea, Arturo, 1897-1957.
Lorca, the poet and his people. Translated from the Spanish by Ilsa Barea. New York, Cooper Square Publishers, 1973.
xv, 176 p. 22 cm.
"Spanish text of quotations": p. [135]-176.
Reprint of the 1949 ed. published by Harcourt, Brace, New York.
1. García Lorca, Federico, 1898-1936.
[PQ6613.A763Z55 1973] 868'.6'209 72-92121
ISBN 0-8154-0447-6 MARC

Barea, Arturo, 1897-1957, joint author.
see Barea, Ilsa. Spain in the post-war world... [Nendeln/Liechtenstein, Kraus Reprint, 1972]

Barea, Calixto A Armas
see Armas Barea, Calixto A

Barea, Ilsa.
Spain in the post-war world, a report prepared by Ilsa and Arturo Barea for a committee of the Fabian International bureau. London, Fabian publications ltd. and V. Gollancz ltd. [1945. Nendeln/Liechtenstein, Kraus Reprint, 1972]
29 p. ([Fabian society, London] Research series, no. 97)
"Selected bibliography": p. 29.
1. Spain—Pol. & govt.—1939- 2. Spain—Econ. condit.—1918- I. Barea, Arturo, 1896- joint author. II. Fabian society, London. International bureau. III. Title. IV. Series.
INS NUC74-1665

Barea, Ilsa, tr.
see Barea, Arturo, 1897-1957. The forging of a rebel. London, Davis-Poynter, 1972.

Barea, José
see Sociedad de Estudios y Publicaciones. Seminario de Hacienda Pública. El gasto público en la agricultura (1958-1965) Madrid, Editorial Moneda y Crédito, 1969.

Barea-Kulcsar, Ilse
see Gewerkschaft der Eisenbahner. 80 [Achtzig] Jahre Gewerkschaft der Eisenbahner. (Wien, Osterr. Gewerkschaftsbund, Gewerkschaft d. Eisenbahner, 1972.)

Bareau, André.
Buddha: la vita, il pensiero, i testi esemplari. Traduzione di Lina Rossi Mazzucchetti. [Milano] Edizioni Accademia [1972]
252 p. illus. 19 cm. (I Memorabili, v. 32)
Bibliography: p. 243-246.
1. Buddha and Buddhism.
NN NUC77-13989

Bareau, André.
Recherches sur la biographie du Buddha dans les Sūtrapiṭaka et les Vinayapiṭaka anciens. Paris, École française d'Extrême-Orient, 1963-
v. in 28 cm. (Publications de l'École française d'Extrême-Orient, v. 53, 77
Bibliography: v. 1, p. [402]
CONTENTS: [1] De la quête de l'éveil à la conversion de Śāriputra et de Maudgalyāyana.—2. Les derniers mois, le Parinirvāṇa, et les funérailles. 2 v.
1. Gautama Buddha. I. Title. II. Series: École française d'Extrême-Orient. Publications, v. 53 [etc.]
BQ865.B37 66-44085
rev

Barecki, Józef
see O Zwiazku Razieckim zwięzle i ciekawie. Warszawa, Książka i Wiedza, 1972.

Baredhyo, Youan de
see
Youan de Baredhyo.

Barefield, Mary Nell
see Barefield, Sam S Nursery II storybook. Nashville, Graded Press, 1964.

Barefield, Russell M
Earnings variability as a risk surrogate, by Russell M. Barefield and Eugene E. Comiskey. West Lafayette, Ind., Institute for Research in the Behavioral, Economic, and Management Sciences, Purdue University, 1973.
17 l., 11 p. illus. 28 cm. (Institute for Research in the Behavioral, Economic, and Management Sciences. Paper no. 423)
Includes bibliographical references.
1. Corporations—United States—Valuation. 2. Stocks—United States. 3. Risk—United States. I. Comiskey, Eugene E., joint author. II. Title. III. Series: Purdue University, Lafayette, Ind. Institute for Research in the Behavioral, Economic, and Management Sciences. Paper no. 423.
HD6483.P8 no. 423 658'.001'9 s 74-620566
[HG4028.V3] [332.6'32'0973] MARC

Barefield, Russell M
Has line-of-business reportinghelped the investor-analyst? / By Russell M. Barefield and Eugene E. Comiskey. — West Lafayette, Ind. : Institute for Research in the Behavioral, Economic, and Management Sciences, Krannert Graduate School of Industrial Administration, Purdue University, 1976.
11, 8 p., [1] leaf of plates : ill. ; 28 cm. — (Paper - Institute for Research in the Behavioral, Economic, and Management Sciences, Purdue University ; no. 546)
Includes bibliographical references.
1. Line of business reporting. 2. Investment analysis. I. Comiskey, Eugene E., joint author. II. Title. III. Series: Purdue University, Lafayette, Ind. Institute for Research in the Behavioral, Economic, and Management Sciences. Paper ; no. 546.
HD6483.P8 no. 546 658'.001'9 s 76-622664
[HG4028.B2] 76 MARC

Barefield, Russell M
The smoothing hypothesis: an alternative test, by Russell M. Barefield and Eugene E. Comiskey. Lafayette, Ind., Herman C. Krannert Graduate School of Industrial Administration, Purdue University, 1971.
10 l. 28 cm. (Purdue University, Lafayette, Ind. Institute for Research in the Behavioral, Economic and Management Sciences. Paper no. 332)
Includes bibliographical references.
1. Income accounting. I. Comiskey, Eugene E., joint author. II. Title. III. Series.
IEdS NUC75-108774

Barefield, Sam S
Nursery II storybook [by] Sam and Mary Nell Barefield. Prepared by the General Board of Education of the Methodist Church through the Editorial Division. Nashville, Graded Press, 1964.
24 p. illus. 15 x 22 cm.
1. Methodist Church in the U.S.—Education. 2. Sunday schools, Methodist Church (U.S.) 3. Sunday schools—Curricula. I. Barefield, Mary Nell. II. Methodist Church (United States). Board of Education. Editorial Division.
IEG NUC74-83845

Barefoot, A D
Improvement of water application of self-propelled sprinkler irrigation systems : final technical completion report of OWRR project A-040-Oklahoma, agreement no. 14-31-0001-4036 : submitted to the Office of Water Resources Research / by A. D. Barefoot. -- [s.l.] : Oklahoma State University, 1975.
14, [3] leaves : ill. ; 28 cm.
Cover title.
Period covered by research investigation July 1, 1972 through June 30, 1975.
Bibliography: leaf [17]
1. Irrigation--Oklahoma. 2. Sprinkler irrigation. 3. Sprinklers. I. Oklahoma. State University of Agriculture and Applied Science, Stillwater. II. United States. Office of Water Resources Research. III. Title.
DI NUC77-99238

Barefoot, Aldos Cortez, 1927-
see Preliminary investigations on the effect of loblolly pine cell morphology on paper fibers... Raleigh, 1971.

Barefoot, J Kirk.
The polygraph story : dedicated to man's right to verify the truth / J. Kirk Barefoot, editor ; authors, Stanley Abrams ... [et al.] ; contributors, Richard O. Arther ... [et al.]. — Rev. 3d printing. — [Hollywood, Calif.] : American Polygraph Association, 1974.
34 p. ; 29 cm.
Published in 1973 under title: The polygraph technique.
Includes bibliographies.
1. Lie detectors and detection. 2. Privacy, Right of—United States. I. Abrams, Stanley. II. Title.
KF9666.Z9B3 1974 347'.73'62 75-316704
75 MARC

Barefoot, J Kirk.
The polygraph technique : dedicated to man's right to verify the truth / J. Kirk Barefoot, editor ; authors : Stanley Abrams ... [et al.] ; contributors : Richard O. Arthur ... [et al.]. — [Hollywood, Calif. : American Polygraph Association] c1972, 1973 printing.
55 p. ; 28 cm.
Includes bibliographies.
1. Lie detectors and detection. 2. Privacy, Right of—United States. I. Abrams, Stanley. II. Title.
KF9666.Z9B3 1973 347'.73'62 74-189454
MARC

Barefoot, J Kirk.
Undercover investigation / by J. Kirk Barefoot ; with a foreword by V. A. Leonard. — Springfield, Ill. : Thomas, [1975]
xii, 87 p. : ill. ; 24 cm.
Bibliography: p. 84.
Includes index.
ISBN 0-398-03345-5
1. Undercover operations. I. Title.
HV8080.U5B37 363.2'32 74-20662
74 MARC

Barefoot, Patience.
Community services : the health worker's A-Z / Patience Barefoot and P. Jean Cunningham. — London : Faber and Faber, 1977.
284 p. ; 20 cm. GB***
ISBN 0-571-11052-5 : £2.95
1. Community health services—Great Britain—Directories. 2. Social service—Great Britain—Directories. 3. Voluntary health agencies—Great Britain—Directories. 4. Public health—Great Britain—Dictionaries. 5. Social service—Great Britain—Dictionaries. I. Cunningham, Phyllis Jean, joint author. II. Title.
RA485.B34 362.1'0941 77-364369
77 MARC

Barefoot, R. R., joint author
see Foscolos, A E A buffering and standard addition technique as an aid in the comprehensive analysis of silicates by atomic absorption spectroscopy. [Ottawa] Dept. of Energy, Mines and Resources [1970]

A barefoot doctor's manual ... [Bethesda, Md.] National Institutes of Health, 1974
see under Hu-nan Chung i yao yen chiu so. Ko wei hui.

A barefoot doctor's manual ... Philadelphia: Running Press, c1977
see under Hu-nan Chung i yao yen chiu so. Ko wei hui.

Barefoot in the park... [n.p.] Paramount Pictures, 1967.
1 v. (various pagings) 28 cm.
From the play by Neil Simon.
Mimeographed film script: "Release dialogue script, March 27, 1967."
Stapled.
I. Simon, Neil.
InU NUC74-151587

Barèges, Jean de
see
Youan de Baredhyo.

Bareh, Hamlet.
Kohima, by H. Bareh. [Kohima, Copies available from the Nagaland District Gazetteers Unit] 1970.
xvi, 224 p. illus. 25 cm. (Nagaland district gazetteers, v. 1)
"No map has been included in the publication as the boundaries of Nagaland are subject to revision as provided for in the 1960 Delhi agreement."
Bibliography: p. 221-224.
1. Kohima, India (City)
NcD NUC75-31505

Bareh, Hamlet.
Meghalaya [by]. Shillong, North-Eastern India News & Feature Service [1974]
xi, 222 p. illus. 22 cm.
Bibliography: p. [221]-222.
Rs25.00
1. Meghalaya, India.
DS485.M58B37 915.4'164'035 74-902124
MARC

Bareh, Victor G
Ki poetry Khasi / da Victor G. Bareh. — [Enl. ed.] — [Shillong?] : Bareh, [1964], 1972 printing.
vii, ii, 97 p. ; 19 cm.
In Khasi.
Poems.
Rs3.50
I. Title.
PL4451.9.B3K5 1972 76-901295

Bareikis, Robert P
The transition to modern Germany : the eighteenth century : an exhibition / prepared and described by Robert P. Bareikis. — Bloomington : Lilly Library, Indiana University, 1975.
56 p. : ill. ; 28 cm. — (Lilly Library publication ; no. 23)
Errata slip inserted.
Includes index.
1. German literature—18th century—Exhibitions. 2. Germany—History—18th century—Exhibitions. 3. Germany—Intellectual life—Exhibitions. I. Title. II. Series: Indiana. University. Lilly Library. Publication ; no. 23.
Z881.I42P8 no. 23 081 s 76-357340
[PT2815] 76 MARC

Bareil, Eugène.
Lagrasse : 12 siècles d'histoire : l'abbaye bénédictine de Ste Marie d'Orbieu, le village et son terroir dans les Corbières / Eugène Bareil. — [Lagrasse] (12, rue de l'Hospice, 11220) : [Rivière Maussac], 1975.
188 p., [17] leaves of plates (1 fold.) : ill., fold. map ; 22 cm. F76-970
Bibliography: p. 185.
30.00F
1. Lagrasse, France. Notre-Dame de Lagrasse (Benedictine abbey) 2. Lagrasse, France—History. I. Title.
BX2615.L33B37 77-479028
77 MARC

Bareilvi, Maaya Khanna Rajey
see Rajey Bareilvi, Maaya Khanna, 1946-

Bareiro-Saguier, Rubén.
Le Paraguay. Traduit de l'espagnol par Jean-Paul Duviols. Paris, Bordas [1972]
128 p. illus. 24 cm. (Collection Études) (Bordas études, 201. Série rouge) F***
Bibliography: p. [120]-125.
1. Paraguay.
F2668.B25 73-352843

Bareither, Harlan Daniel
see Illinois. University. Small Homes Council—Building Research Council. Temperature and heat loss characteristics... [Urbana] 1958.

Bareja, Hanna Kotkowska-
see Kotkowska-Bareja, Hanna.

Bareje, René.
10 [i.e. Dixième] années de réalisations V.V.F.; anniversaire 1959-1969. [Paris, Villages vacances familles, 1970]
59 p.
1. Tourist trade—France. 2. Vacations. 3. France—Description and travel. 4. Family vacation villages.
NIC NUC75-4896

Bareket, M
Potassium nitrate in crop nutrition. Israel, Haifa Chemicals [1967]
50 p.
Bibliography: p. 37-50.
1. Fertilizers and manures. Israel.
I. Title.
DNAL NUC77-14564

Bareket, Re'uven, 1905–1972.
(Re'uven Bareket: sheloshim li-fetirato)
ראובן ברקת: שלושים לפטירתו. [תל־אביב] מפלגת העבודה הישראלית, מחלקת ההסברה, 1972.
32 p. illus. 24 cm.
Cover title.
"מדברין": p. 11–30.
1. Bareket, Reu'ven, 1905–1972. 2. Israel—Politics and government—Addresses, essays, lectures.
DS126.6.B28A33 74–950037

Barekman, June Beverly, 1915-
Barrickman-Barrackman of Crawford County, Pennsylvania / compiled and edited by June B. Barekman. — Chicago : Genealogical Services & Publications, 1974.
37, vi p. ; 28 cm.
Caption title: Records of the Barkman-Barrackman-Barrickman-Barackman family from Crawford County, Pennsylvania to Ohio-Kansas-Nebraska.
Includes indexes.
1. Barekman family. I. Title. II. Title: Records of the Barkman-Barrackman-Barrickman-Barackman family ...
CS71.B2553 1974 929'.2'0973 75-316427
75 MARC

Barekman, June Beverly, 1915-
Bible records on forty one (41) surnames and six (6) detailed family records...by Miss June B. Barekman... [and] Mrs. Edward Rickie. Chicago, 1974.
[4], 113 p. 28 cm.
ICN NUC76-96146

Barekman, June Beverly, 1915–
Francis Hannah, Revolutionary soldier of Greene County, Pennsylvania, and his children ... Compiled by June B. Barekman. Chicago [1971 or 2]
116 p., 117–137 l. 29 cm.
1. Hanna family. I. Title.
CS71.H242 1971 929'.2'0973 73–170484
MARC

Barekman, June Beverly, 1915–
Hunter's of early Rowan Co., N. C.; from records in the Mccubbins files and court house, Salisbury N. C. Abstracted by June B. Barekman. [Chicago] 1971.
21 l. 30 cm. $3.50
1. Hunter family. I. Title.
CS71.H944 1971 929'.2'0973 72–170491
MARC

Barekman, June Beverly, 1915–
John Barrickman and his children of Shelby County, Illinois, son of Jacob Barrickman, Revolutionary soldier of Maryland, Pennsylvania, Kentucky, Indiana. Grandson of George Peter Bergmann ... Rev. with new data. Chicago, Ill., 1972.
35, 6 l. 30 cm. $4.50
1. Barekman family. I. Title.
CS71.B2553 1972 929'.2'0973 74–151361
MARC

Barekman, June Beverly, 1915–
Kirk of Virginia [by] June B. Barekman. Chicago, Ill., 1972]
24 l. 29 cm. $4.00
Caption title.
1. Kirk family. I. Title.
CS71.K59 1972 929'.2'0973 72–197643
MARC

Barekman, June Beverly, 1915-
Knox County, Indiana; early land records and court indexes, 1783-1815. Chicago, Genalogical Services and Publications, 1973.
3 v. in 1. 29 cm.
ICN Mi NUC75-118939

Barekman, June Beverly, 1915-
Our Bowlby kin / compiled and edited by June B. Barekman. — Chicago : Genealogical Services & Publications, 1974-
v. ; 28 cm.
Includes index.
$12.50 (v. 1)
1. Bowlby family. I. Title.
CS71.B78715 1974 929'.2'0973 75-303720
75 MARC

Barekman, June Beverly, 1915-
Revolutionary war pensioners -- Post Falls, Idaho : Genealogical Reference Builders, 1976.
54 p.
1. Pensions, Military--Revolution, 1775-1783. I. Title.
WHi NUC77-100414

Barekman, June Beverly, 1915-
Some Dobbin(s)-Skiles lines from Pennsylvania to North Carolina and Tennessee, with additional lines of Coker, Cowan, Dailey, Graham, Hess, Palmer, Barekman, Lawrence, Newbill. 2d ed., rev. and enl. Chicago, [n.d.]
44 l.
1. Dobbin family. 2. Skiles family. I. Title.
WHi NUC73-67993

Barekman, June Beverly, 1915–
Who is William Hess? A sketch of the family of Apollos Hess who came from Shelby County, Kentucky, before 1819 to Floyd and Clark Counties, Indiana; being the lineage of, as far as possible of [sic] one son, William Hess, whose later kin are found in Washington and Knox Counties, Indiana. Researched and compiled by June B. Barekman, assisted by Elsie R. Swartz. Chicago, Hoosier Gals Press, 1971.
20 l. 30 cm. $3.00
Leaves 1–6, captioned "Hess families of early Indiana, v. 1," tabulate the Illinois Hess families listed in the censuses of 1830 & 1850.
1. Hess family. I. Title.
CS71.H586 1971 929'.2'0973 72–170490
MARC

Barekman, June Beverly, 1915-
see Butler, Jennie O. The Rodarmel family in Knox County Indiana ... Chicago, Genealogical Services & Publication, [1975?]

Bareksten, Tore G 1954-
Gnomen forteller / Tore G. Bareksten. — Oslo : Gyldendal, 1976.
92 p. ; 19 cm. — (Lanterne-bøkene ; L316) N76-Sept.
ISBN 8205088942 : kr34.50
I. Title.
PT8951.12.A74G58 839.8'2'374 77-466811
•77 MARC

Barel, C J A
Studies on dispersal of Adoxophyes orana F. v. R. in relation to the population sterilization technique. Wageningen, 1973.
107 p. illus. (Wageningen. Landbouwhogeschool. Mededelingen, 73-7)
Bibliography: p. 104-107.
I. Title.
DNAL NUC74-133473

Barel, Yves.
La reproduction sociale: systèmes vivants, invariance et changement. Paris, Éditions Anthropos [1973]
558 p. 21 cm. F***
Bibliography: p. [525]-537.
1. Social systems. 2. Reproduction. I. Title.
HM106.B265 301'.042 73-179947
MARC

Barela, D A
Supercritical flow in curved channels; hydraulic model investigation. [Vicksburg, Miss., U. S. Army Engineer Waterways Experiment Station] 1972.
1 v. (various pagings) illus. 27 cm.
"Report no. 1-109."
"Studies... conducted in the Hydraulic Laboratory of the U. S. Army Engineer District, Los Angeles."
IU MoU NUC74-124450

Barela, Dulce María Rojo de
see Rojo de Barela, Dulce María.

Barela, Fred.
The Puerto Rico Labor Relations Act: a state labor policy and its application. [n.p.] 1963 [c1965]
ix, 609 l.
Thesis—University of North Carolina.
Bibliography: leaves [574]-579.
Photocopy of typescript. Ann Arbor, Mich., Xerox University Microfilms, 1974. 22 cm.
1. Labor laws and legislation—Puerto Rico. I. Title.
NNCU-G NUC77-14573

Barela, Fred.
The Puerto Rico Labor Relations Act: a state labor policy and its application. Ann Arbor, Mich., University Microfilms, c1965.
1 reel. 35 mm.
Thesis (Ph.D.)—University of North Carolina, 1963.
Microfilm of typescript.
1. Labor laws and legislation—Puerto Rico. I. Title.
WHi NUC77-14572

Barella, Ana, joint author.
see Campos, Juana G. Diccionario de refranes. Madrid, [s.n.] 1975.

Barella, Carlos
see
Barella Iriarte, Carlos.

Barella, Giovanni.
Pierino in controluce; appunti sull'educazione del "pre-adolescente." Torino, Elle di ci [1965]
171 p. 20 cm. (Collana Famiglia e mondo d'oggi)
L700
1. Education of children. 2. Child study. I. Title.
LB1025.2.B35 75-566282

Barella, Richard V
A follow-up study of graduate service assistants who received a Master's degree in industrial education from Ball State University, 1953 to 1973. [n.p.] 1975.
297 l.
Thesis (Ph.D.)--Ohio State University.
Bibliography: leaves 289-297.
1. Technical education--Ohio. 2. Graduate teaching assistants. I. Title.
OU NUC77-99368

Barella, Richard V
Graduate service assistants : a research report / Richard V. Barella. — Muncie, Ind. : Ball State University, 1976.
v, 38 p. ; 23 cm.
Bibliography: p. 16-18.
1. Technical education—United States. 2. Graduate teaching assistants—United States. I. Title.
T73.B35 620'.07'1173 76-20168
76 MARC

Barella Iriarte, Carlos.
Lautaro guerrillero. [Santiago] Ediciones Nueva Universidad, Universidad Católica de Chile [c1971]
253 p. maps. 25 cm. (Colección Universidad y letras)
Bibliography: p. 251-253.
1. Lautaro, Araucanian chief, 1535?-1557. 2. Chile—History—To 1565. I. Title.
F3091.L3B37 73-205734

Barella Miró, Alberto
see Arrando Cot, Francisco. Estudios psicológicos sobre gerencia. Barcelona, A. I. T. A. [1968]

Barelli, Emma Spina
see Spina Barelli, Emma.

Barelli, Ettore, tr.
see Euripides. Tragedie. [Firenze], Club degli editori, 1972.

Barelli, Giuseppe, ed.
see Lesegno, Italy. Ordinances, local laws, etc. Statuti di Lesegno. Torino, Palazzo, 1966.

Barelli, Jacques.
L'Écriture de René Char [par] Jacques Barelii. Paris, la Pensée universelle, 1973.
60 p. 18 cm. 10.70F F 74-1646
1. Char, René, 1907- —Criticism and interpretation. I. Title.
PQ2605.H3345Z6 848'.9'1209 74-173732
MARC

Barello, Rudolph V 1938-
A propositional analysis of selected literature of two right wing organizations and their spokesmen, Billy James Hargis and Gerald L. K. Smith. [Carbondale] Southern Illinois University, 1970.
214 l.
Thesis (Ph. D.)—Southern Illinois University.
Vita.
Photocopy. Ann Arbor, University Microfilms, 1973. 21 cm.
1. Hargis, Billy James, 1925- 2. Smith, Gerald Lyman Kenneth, 1898- 3. Christian Crusade. 4. Christian Nationalist Crusade. 5. Right and left (Political Science). I. Title.
GU NUC75-21311

Barelopoulos, P., ed.
see United States. Constitution. To Syntagma tōn Hēnomenōn Politeiōn tēs Amerikēs. Nea Hyorkē, Ek tou Typogr. tōn Thermopylōn [19--]

Barelvī, Ḥasan Razā
see Ḥasan Razā Barelvī.

Barelvī, Nāz
see
Nāz Barelvī.

Barelvī, Shafīq
see Shafīq Barelvī.

Barelvī, Shafīq Bānū
see
Shafīq Bānū Barelvī.

Baren, F A van.
Environmental aspects of soil management and agricultural practices. Amsterdam, International Society of Soil Science [n.d.]
1 v.
Supplied: Miscellaneous basic paper for United Nations Conference on the Human Environment.
1. Agriculture—Environmental aspects. I. United Nations Conference on the Human Environ vironment, Stockholm, 1972. II. Title.
DWW NUC75-26639

Baren, F. A. van, joint author
see Mohr, Edward Carl Julius, 1873-1970. Tropical soils. 3rd, rev. and enl. ed. The Hague, Mouton-Ichtiar Baru-Van Hoeve, 1972 [1973]

Barėnas, Kazimieras.
Aštuntoji pradalgė; literatūros metraštis. London, Nida Press, 1972.
411 p. (Nidos Knygų Klubo leidinys, nr. 87)
1. Lithuanian literature. I. Title.
CLU NUC74-128269

Barėnas, Kazimieras, comp.
Primoji pradalgė literatūros metraštis. [London, Nida, 1964]
373 p.
Lithuanian.
1. Lithuanian lit. —Selections. I. Title.
OCl NUC74-127610

Barenbaum, Iosif Evseevich.
(Istoriíà zarubezhnoĭ knigi)
История зарубежной книги. Учеб. пособие. Ленинград, 1972–
v. 19 cm. USSR 73
At head of title, v. : Министерство культуры РСФСР. Ленинградский государственный институт культуры имени Н. К. Крупской. Кафедра библиографии. И. Е. Баренбаум.
Includes bibliographical references.
CONTENTS: т. 1. Франция.
0.30rub (v. 1)
1. Books—History. I. Title.
Z4.B38 75-568600

Barenbaum, Iosif Evseevich.
Полиграфическое и художественное оформление книги. Учеб.-метод. пособие по курсу "История книги." Ленинград, 1968.
51 p. with illus. 20 cm. USSR 69-VKP
At head of title: Министерство культуры РСФСР. Ленинградский государственный институт культуры им. Н. К. Крупской. И. Е. Баренбаум.
Bibliography: p. 29.
0.15rub
1. Book design. I. Title.
Title romanized: Poligraficheskoe i khudozhestvennoe oformlenie knigi.
Z116.A3B28 75-579013

Barenbaum, Iosif Evseevich
see Istoriíà russkogo chitateliíà. [s. n.], 1973-

Barenbaum, Sol Bruce.
A developmental study of Piagetian reasoning in mentally retarded persons [by] Sol B. Barenbaum. [Philadelphia] 1975.
xi, 199 leaves. tables. 28 cm.
Thesis (Ph.D.)--Temple University, 1976.
1. Cognition (Child psychology) 2. Piaget, Jean, 1896- 3. Mentally handicapped children--Testing. I. Title.
PPT NUC77-99366

Barenblatt, G I
Concerning the motion of suspended particles in turbulent flow occupying a half-space, or flat open channel of finite depth. Boston Spa, Yorkshire, National Lending Library for Science and Technology, 1970.
35 p. illus. 28 cm.
At head of title: National Lending Library for Science and Technology, Russian Translating Programme. RTS 6229.
Photocopy. Boston Spa, Yorkshire, National Lending Library for Science and Technology, 1970.
Translation of O dvizhenii vzveshennykh chastits v turbulentnom potoke, zaimaiushchem poluprostranstvo ili ploskiĭ otkrytyĭ kanal konechnoĭ glubiny.
1. Channels (Hydraulic engineering) 2. Turbulence. I. Title.
IaU NUC74-128706

Barenblatt, G I
(Teoriia nestatsionarnoĭ fil'tratsii zhidkosti i gaza)
Теория нестационарной фильтрации жидкости и газа. Г. И. Баренблатт, В. М. Ентов, В. М. Рыжик. Москва, "Недра," 1972.
288 p. with illus. 22 cm. 2.08rub USSR 73
Bibliography: p. 278-[286]
1. Seepage. 2. Permeability. I. Entov, Vladimir Mordukhovich, joint author. II. Ryzhik, Viktor Mikhaĭlovich, joint author. III. Title.
TC163.B37 73-341558

Barenboĭm, Abram Markovich.
Профилактика простудных заболеваний при строительно-монтажных работах. Москва, Изд-во лит-ры по строительству, 1967.
43, [1] p. illus. 22 cm.
At head of title: А. М. Баренбойм.
Bibliography: p. [44]
0.14rub
1. Construction workers—Diseases and hygiene. 2. Cold (Disease)—Prevention. I. Title.
Title romanized: Profilaktika prostudnykh zabolevaniĭ pri stroitel'no-montazhnykh rabotakh.
RC965.C75B37 75-570123

Barenboĭm, Aron Borisovich.
(Maloraskhodnye freonovye turbokompressory)
Малорасходные фреоновые турбокомпрессоры / А. Б. Баренбойм. — Москва : Машиностроение, 1974.
223 p. : ill. ; 22 cm. USSR 74
Bibliography: p. 216-[222]
0.80rub
1. Compressors. 2. Refrigeration and refrigerating machinery. I. Title.
TJ990.B37 74-353115

Barenboim, Carl Phillip, 1950-
An investigation of changes in the interpersonal cognitive system from middle childhood to adolescence / by Carl Phillip Barenboim. -- [s.l. : s.n.], 1975 [i.e. 1976]
x, 35 leaves ; 29 cm.
Thesis (Ph.D.)--University of Rochester. Vita.
Bibliography: leaves 33-35.
1. Social perception. 2. Developmental psychology. I. Title.
NRU NUC77-99258

Barenboim, Evseĭ L'vovich, 1922-
Pomniu ikh takimi; rasskazy. [By] E. Barenboim. Riga, Liesma, 1969.
245 p. illus.
MH NIC CaOTU NUC74-21975

Barenboĭm, Lev Aronovich.
(Muzykal'naia pedagogika i ispolnitel'stvo)
Музыкальная педагогика и исполнительство. [Статьи и очерки]. Ленинград, "Музыка," Ленингр. отд-ние, 1974.
336 p. with music. 22 cm. 1.63rub USSR 74
At head of title: Л. А. Баренбойм.
Includes bibliographical references.
1. Music—Instruction and study. 2. Music—Interpretation (Phrasing, dynamics, etc.) I. Title.
MT1.B314M9 74-343206

Barenboĭm, Lev Aronovich.
(Put' k muzitsirovaniiu)
Путь к музицированию. Ленинград-Москва, "Сов. композитор," [Ленингр. отд-ние], 1973.
270 p. with illus. and music. 20 cm. 1.25rub USSR 73
At head of title: Л. Баренбойм.
Includes bibliographical references.
1. Piano—Instruction and study—Juvenile. I. Title.
MT745.B223P9 74-307273

Barenboĭm, Lev Aronovich
see Rubinstein, Anton, 1829-1894. Etiudy dlia fortep'iano. Moskva, Gosudarstvennoe muzykal'noe izdatel'stvo, 1960.

Barenboĭm, Lev Aronovich
see Sistema detskogo muzykal'nogo vospitaniia Karla Orfa. Leningrad, Izd-vo "Muzyka," 1970.

Barenbrug, A W T
Psychrometry and psychrometric charts / A. W. T. Barenbrug. — 3d ed. — [Johannesburg] : Chamber of Mines of South Africa, [1974].
59 p., 31 leaves of plates : graphs ; 30 cm. SA***
ISBN 0-620-01586-1
1. Mine ventilation. 2. Hygrometry. I. Chamber of Mines of South Africa. II. Title.
TN301.B28 1974 622'.42 76-368251
76 MARC

Barenco, Manoel Rosa.
Versos sem A / Manoel Rosa Barenco ; prólogo de Aparício Fernandes. — [s. l. : s. n., 1974] ([Rio de Janeiro] : Gráfica Editora Fliper)
[62] p. ; 16 cm.
Cr$15.00
I. Title.
PQ9698.12.A683V4 75-563530

Het Barend Servet effect : teksten van en reflecties op vijf shows van de VPRO / door Wim T. Schippers ... [et al.]. — Amsterdam : Contact, 1974.
240 p. ; 21 cm. — (Contact/Tijdsdocument) Ne 74-41
"Dit ... boek bevat alle teksten van de vier ... Barend Servet Shows en de ... Kerstshow ..."
CONTENTS: Hofstede, P. O mijn lieve Augustijn of de gevaren der onttovering.—Schwarz, N. F. I. Politieke aspecten van het Barend-Serveteffect.—Hofland, H. J. A. Haché, Servet en Van Oekel.—Barend-Servetshow, deel 1, 23 november 1972: De huwelijksadvertentie.—Hoefnagels, G. P. Berispen heb nodig.—Barend-Servetshow, deel 2, 14 december 1972: Barend blijft aan de gang.—Rademakers, J. Waarom zo als het zo óók kan?—Barend Servetshow, deel 3, 25 januari 1973: Huldiging van onze held.—Barend Servetshow, deel 4, 29 maart 1973: Barend in België.—Haks, F. Over Fluxus en Wim T. Schippers.—Kerstshow, 27 december 1973: Waar heb dat nou voor noodig.
ISBN 90-254-2030-3 : fl 19.50
1. Dutch drama—20th century. 2. Barend Servet Show. I. Schippers, Wim T. II. Vrijzinnig Protestantse Omroep. III. Barend Servet Show.
PT5460.B34 74-357399

Barendrecht, Cor W
No man's land [by] Cor W. Barendrecht. [Grand Rapids, Mich., Being Publications, c1972]
[8] p. illus. 22 cm.
"This poem first appeared in Amaranthus."
I. Title.
RPB NUC77-14566

Barendrecht-Hoen, M
Leven in mijn tuin / M. Barendrecht-Hoen. — Amsterdam : Ploegsma, 1974.
160 p. : ill. ; 14 x 22 cm. Ne 74-44
Includes index.
ISBN 90-216-0056-0 : fl 15.90
1. Gardens. 2. Nature. 3. Flowers. I. Title.
SB455.B28 75-562679

Barendreght, Jerry Allen, 1939-
The effect of biaxial loading on the critical resolved shear stress of zinc single crystals. [n.p.] 1971.
[2], vii, 101, [i.e. 103] l. illus.
Thesis (Ph.D.)—Michigan State University.
Bibliography: leaves 91-93.
1. Zinc. 2. Strains and stresses. I. Title.
MiEM NUC73-32638

Barendregt, H J
Het Nederlands Joods geslacht Weijel (Weijl, Whyl) door H. J. Barendrecht. [n. p., 1972?]
33 p. illus. 25 cm. Ne***
1. Weijel family. I. Title.
CS829.W42 1972 73-315253

Barendregt, Hendrik Pieter.
On the interpretation of terms without a normal form. [By] H. P. Barendregt. (preliminary version). Utrecht, Electronisch Rekencentrum Rijksuniversiteit Utrecht (Budapestlaan 6), 1971.
ix, 18 l. 30 cm. (ERCU publikaties, no. 111) NeB 71-Juli-Sep
Supplementary part II to the author's thesis Some extensional term models for combinatory logics and λ-calculi.
Bibliography: p. 18.
1. Combinatory logic. I. Barendregt, Hendrik Pieter. Some extensional term models for combinatory logics and λ-calculi. II. Title. III. Series: Utrecht. Rijksuniversiteit. Electronisch Rekencentrum. ERCU publikaties, no. 111.
QA9.5.B37 511'.3 74-159205
MARC

Barendregt, Hendrik Pieter.
Some extensional term models for combinatory logics and λ-calculi. [Utrecht] 1971.
xxi, 140 p. 25 cm.
Proefschrift - Rijksuniversiteit te Utrecht.
CtY NUC73-124576

Barendregt, Hendrik Pieter. Some extensional term models for combinatory logics and λ-calculi
see Barendregt, Hendrik Pieter. On the interpretation of terms without a normal form. Utrecht, Electronisch Rekencentrum Rijksuniversiteit Utrecht, 1971.

Barendregt, J. T., ed.
see Cassee, A P Klinische psycholigie in Nederland. Deventer, Van Loghum Slaterus, 1973-

Barendse, Gerard.
Het groene hart van Nederland : Lopikerwaard, Krimpenerwaard, Alblasserwaard, Vijfherenlanden / Gerard Barendse, Piet Terlouw. — 's-Gravenhage : Boekencentrum, 1977.
88 p. : ill. ; 23 cm. — (Triangelreeks) Ne77-24
Bibliography: p. 82-83.
ISBN 9023927176 : fl 15.90
1. Netherlands—Description and travel—1945- I. Terlouw, Piet, 1923- joint author. II. Title.
DJ40.B37 77-555070
•77 MARC

Barendsen, Robert Dale, 1923-
The educational revolution in China [by] Robert D. Barendsen. [Washington] U. S. Office of Education, Institute of International Studies; [for sale by the Supt. of Docs., U. S. Govt. Print. Off., 1973]
v, 52 p. 24 cm. (DHEW Publication no. (OE) 73-19102) $0.65
Includes bibliographical references.
Supt. of Docs. no.: HE 5.2:C 44
1. Education—China (People's Republic of China, 1949-) I. Title. II. Series: United States. Dept. of Health, Education, and Welfare. DHEW publication no. (OE) 73-19102.
LA1131.B32 370'.951 74-601772
MARC

Barendsen, Robert Dale, 1923-
MAO's educational revolution. [Washington, U.S. Govt. Print. Off., 1972]
[10] p. (DHEW Publication no. OE 72-128)
Reprinted from American Education, May 1972.
1. Education—China (People's Republic of China, 1949-) I. Title.
MH-Ed NUC74-124441

Barendson, Maurizio.
Ivi per sempre / Maurizio Barendson. — Roma : Trevi editore, c1976.
147 p. ; 21 cm. — (La Girandola ; 30) It76-July
L3000
I. Title.
PQ4862.A673319 76-474170
•76 MARC

Barendson, Maurizio.
Il serpente ha tutti i colori ... Roma, Trevi editore, 1972.
106 p. 21 cm. (La Girandola, 16) L1000 It 73-Apr
I. Title.
PQ4862.A6733S4 73-328635

Bārene, Lucija.
Ardievas; romāns. [Grand Haven, Mich.] Aka, 1973.
285 p. 22 cm. $6.00
I. Title.
PG9119.B34A9 73-218861

Bārene, Lūcija.
Dzīves straume : romāns / Lūcija Bārene. — Grand Haven, Mich. : AKA, 1975.
322 p. ; 21 cm.
I. Title.
PG9119.B34D9 76-511573

Bārene, Lūcija.
Miera pēc / L. Bārene. -- [s.l. : s.n.], 1976.
336 p.
I. Title.
CaOTP NUC77-100415

Barenscheer, Friedrich.
Taufengel in Niedersachen./ Von Friedrich Barenscheer. — Celle: ⌈Bomann-Museum⌉ 1972.
67, ⌈8⌉ p.: ill.; 21 cm. — (Bomann-Archiv; Heft 9)
GDB 72-B13
1. Angels—Art. 2. Sculpture—Saxony, Lower. I. Title. II. Series.
N8090.B3 73-338253

Barenfs, Sergeĭ Kuz'mich.
(Radugi nad garnizonami)
Радуги над гарнизонами : стихотворения и поэмы / Сергей Баренц ; ⌈вступит. статья А. Софронова ; ил. Д. В. Орлов⌉. — Москва : Воениздат, 1975.
327 p. : ill. ; 18 cm. USSR 75
1.19rub
I. Title.
PG3479.R4R3 75-402563

Barenfs, Sergeĭ Kuz'mich.
(Za Naroĭ-rekoĭ)
За Нарой-рекой : Стихи и поэмы / Сергей Баренц ; ⌈Худож. Е. Скрытников⌉. — Москва : Моск. рабочий, 1976.
102 p. : ill. ; 16 cm. USSR 76
0.33rub
I. Title.
PG3479.R4Z22 77-503205

Barer, David, joint author
see Thurston, Rachel F A computer program for mixed hexagonal hierarchies. Cambridge, Mass., Laboratory for Computer Graphics and Spatial Analysis, Harvard University, 1975.

Barer, Sol Joseph.
The synthesis of macrocycles and topological isomers via the olefin metathesis reaction. New Brunswick, N.J., 1974.
xii, 123 l. illus. 29 cm.
Thesis (Ph.D.)—Rutgers University.
1. Isomers. 2. Olefines. I. Title.
NjR NUC76-96140

Barès,
Flooskes : fables et récits bruxellois / Barès ; préf. de Frans Fischer ; ill. de Jos. Tries et A. Brun. — Bruxelles : Labor, ⌈préf. 1944⌉
96 p. : ill. ; 18 cm.
1. Fables. I. Title.
PQ2603.A39F4 75-518667
76 MARC

Bareš, Jan, joint author
see Collins, Edward A Experiments in polymer science. New York, Wiley ⌈1973⌉

Bareš, Karel.
Afixace v anglickém odborném stylu. 1. vyd. Praha, SPN, rozmn. SCT 17, 1973.
185, ⌈1⌉ p. 24 cm. (Acta Universitatis 17. ⌈i. e. sedmnáctého⌉ listopadu) (Vědecký sborník Fakulty společenských věd. Řada monografická, sv. čís. 4) Kčs15.00 Cz 74
Summary in English.
Bibliography: p. 175-180.
1. English language—Suffixes and prefixes. 2. English language—Word formation. 3. English language—Technical English. I. Title. II. Series: Prague. Universita 17. ⌈i. e. sedmnáctého⌉ listopadu. Acta. III. Series: Prague. Universita 17. ⌈i. e. sedmnáctého⌉ listopadu. Fakulta společenskovědní. Vědecký sborník. Řada monografická, sv. čís. 4.
PE1175.B35 74-342575

Bareš, Richard.
Analysis of beam grids and orthotropic plates by the Guyon-Massonnet-Bareš method, by Richard Bareš and Charles Massonnet; translated ⌈from the French⌉ by J. Vaněk. London, Lockwood; Prague, SNTL, 1968.
459 p. plate, illus. 25 cm. 70/- B 68-07632
Translation of Výpočet roštů s uvažováním kroucení.
Bibliography: p. ⌈453⌉-459.
1. Bridges, Concrete—Floors. 2. Concrete slabs. 3. Plates (Engineering) 4. Grillages (Structural engineering) I. Massonnet, Charles Ernest, 1914- joint author. II. Title.
TG414.B3143 624.2'53 68-111115
rev MARC

Bares, Richard H.
see Preliminary land use, environmental and socio-economic assessment of the Roseau River... ⌈Grand Forks, N.D.⌉ 1973.

Bares, Richard H.
see Preliminary land use, environmental and socio-economic assessment of the Warroad River... Grand Forks, N.D., 1973.

Baresel, Alfred, 1893-
see Heym, Heinrich. Frankfurt und sein Theater. Frankfurt am Main, W. Kramer, 1971.

Baret, Eugène, 1816-1887.
De l'Amadis de Gaule et de son influence sur les mœurs et la littérature au 16ᵉ et au 17ᵉ siècle. Avec une notice biographique. 2e éd., revue, corrigée et augmentée. (Réimpr, de l'éd. de Paris, 1873.) Genève, Slatkine Reprints, 1970.
x, 236 p. 22 cm. 50.00F ($12.00U.S.) Sw 70-A-2191
1. Amadís de Gaula. I. Title.
PQ6277.B3 1970 73-304150

Baret, Eugène, 1816-1887.
Espagne et Provence : études sur la littérature du midi de l'Europe : accompagnées d'extraits et de pièces rares ou inédites pour faire suite aux travaux de Raynouard et de Fauriel / Eugène Baret. — Genève : Slatkine Reprints, 1970.
xi, 451 p. ; 23 cm. Sw 70-A-6494
"Réimpression de l'édition de Paris, 1857."
1. Romance literature—History and criticism. I. Title.
PN808.B3 1970 840'.09 74-195280
MARC

Baretje, René.
Aspects économiques du tourisme ⌈par⌉ René Baretje ⌈et⌉ Pierre P. Defert. Préf. de Lucien Mehl. Paris, Berger-Levrault, 1972.
355 p. illus. 22 cm. (L'Administration nouvelle) 40.00F F***
Bibliography: p. ⌈343⌉-346.
1. Tourist trade. I. Defert, Pierre, joint author. II. Title.
G155.A1B36 73-301699

Baretje, René.
Besoins de detente en tant que facteurs pour le developpement regional et agricole. ⌈Brussels ?⌉ 1973.
1 v. (various pagings) illus., maps. (European Economic Community. Informations internes sur l'agriculture, 116)
Includes bibliographies.
I. Title.
DNAL NUC75-30863

Baretje, René.
Bibliographie touristique ⌈par⌉ R. Baretje. Aix-en-Provence, Université d'Aix-Marseille, Centre d'études du tourisme, 19
v. 27 cm. (Université d'Aix-en-Provence, Centre d'études du tourisme. Études et mémoires, v. 9) 30.00F F 72-5492
1. Tourist trade—Bibliography. I. Title. II. Series: Aix-Marseille, Université d'. Centre d'études du tourisme. Études et mémoires, v. 9.
Z6004.T6B37 73-351585
MARC

Baretje, René.
La demande touristique. Aix-Marseille, 1968.
281 p.
Thesis (Ph.D.)—Universite d'Aix-Marseille.
1. Tourist trade.
NIC NUC74-15748

Baretje, René.
L'évaluation des recettes touristiques dans les Alpes du sud; une approche méthodologique regionale ⌈par⌉ R. Baretje. ⌈Aix-en-Provence, Université Aix- Marseille, 1963?⌉
29 l. 27 cm. (Aix-Marseille, Université d'. Centre d'études du tourisme. Cahiers du tourisme)
Communication presentée au congrès AIEST - 1963.
1. Tourist trade—Alps. I. Title. II. Series.
CaQMM NUC74-15739

Baretje, René.
Évaluation du chiffre d'affaires avion des agences de voyages françaises : 1968-1972 / R. Baretje, F. Senova. — Aix-en-Provence : Université de droit, d'économie et des sciences, Centre des hautes études touristiques, 1976.
18, ⌈39⌉ leaves : maps ; 30 cm. — (Les Cahiers du tourisme : Série C ; no 24)
F76-18892
25.00F
1. Travel agents—France. I. Senova, Fahrettin, joint author. II. Title. III. Series.
G154.B47 338.4'7'910944 77-554593
77 MARC

Baretje, René.
Évaluation du chiffre d'affaires 1971 des agences de voyages françaises / R. Baretje. — Aix-en-Provence : Université d'Aix-Marseille, Centre d'études du tourisme, 1973.
9, ⌈11⌉ leaves : maps ; 30 cm. — (Les Cahiers du tourisme : Série C ; no 22) F***
20.00F
1. Travel agents—France. I. Title. II. Series.
G155.F8B35 338.4'7'91 75-502462
75 MARC

Baretje, René.
Le Mouvement de concentration dans le tourisme moderne. Aix-en-Provence, Centre d'études du tourisme, ⌈3, Av. Robert Schuman,⌉ 1969.
58 l. 27 cm. (Les Cahiers du tourisme, série C, no 14) 15.00F
F 72-9200
1. Tourist trade. 2. Hotels, taverns, etc. I. Title. II. Series.
G155.A1B362 73-313303

Baretje, René.
Parcs nationaux, parcs régionaux et reserves analogues / R. Baretje. — Aix-en-Provence : Centre des hautes études touristiques, 1976.
98 leaves ; 21 cm. — (Essais - Centre des hautes études touristiques, Université de droit, d'économie, et des sciences ; no 3) F***
1. National parks and reserves—Bibliography. 2. Parks—Bibliography. I. Title. II. Series: Université d'Aix-Marseille III. Centre des hautes études touristiques. Essais - Centre des hautes études touristiques, Université de droit, d'économie, et des sciences ; no 3.
Z6905.B3 016.3337'8 76-483474
⌈SB481⌉ 76 MARC

Baretje, René.
Le tourisme en Afrique : essai bibliographique / R. Baretje. — Aix-en-Provence : Centre des hautes études touristiques, Faculté de droit, 1976.
153 leaves ; 21 cm. — (Essais - Centre des hautes études touristiques ; no 2) F***
1. Tourist trade—Africa—Bibliography. I. Title. II. Series: Université d'Aix-Marseille III. Centre des hautes études touristiques. Essais - Centre des hautes études touristiques, Université de droit, d'économie, et des sciences ; no. 2.
Z6004.T6B372 016.3384'7'916043 76-484748
⌈G155.A26⌉ 76 MARC

Baretje, René.
Tourisme et droit français : recueil des principaux textes législatifs, réglementaires et jurisprudentiels antérieurs au 31 décembre 1970 / R. Baretje. — Aix-en-Provence : Centre des hautes études touristiques, 1976.
137 leaves ; 30 cm. — (Études et mémoires - Université de droit, d'économie et des sciences, Centre des hautes études touristiques ; no 24) F***
Includes index.
1. Tourist trade—Law and legislation—France. I. Title. II. Series: Université d'Aix-Marseille III. Centre des hautes études touristiques. Études et mémoires - Université de droit, d'économie et des sciences, Centre des hautes études touristiques ; no 24.
343'.44'078 76-487727
77 MARC

Baretje, René.
Tourisme et forêt : bibliographie internationale / R. Baretje. — Aix-en-Provence : Centre des hautes études touristiques, 1976.
71 leaves ; 21 cm. — (Essais - Centre des hautes études touristiques, Université de droit, d'économie, et des sciences ; no 1) F***
1. Forest reserves—Recreational use—Bibliography. I. Title. II. Series: Université d'Aix-Marseille III. Centre des hautes études touristiques. Essais - Centre des hautes études touristiques, Université de droit, d'économie, et des sciences ; no 1.
Z7514.F75B35 76-489427
⌈GV191.67.F6⌉ 77 MARC

Baretski, Charles Allan.
The history of the American Council of Polish Cultural Clubs, 1948-1973; our quarter-century. Introd. by John A. Wojciechowicz. ⌈Newark? N.J.⌉ American Council of Polish Cultural Clubs, 1973.
xvi, 121 p. illus. 23 cm.
1. American Council of Polish Cultural Clubs. I. Title.
E184.P7B37 973'.004'9185 75-304194
75 MARC

Baretti, Giuseppe Marco Antonio, 1719-1789.
An account of the manners and customs of Italy; with observations on the mistakes of some travellers, with regard to that country. By Joseph Baretti. London, T. Davies, 1768.
2 v.
Microfilm (negative) Washington, Library of Congress, 1969. 1 reel.
On reel with Southerne, Thomas Plays. London, 1774.
IaU NUC77-14078

Baretti, Giuseppe Marco Antonio, 1719-1789.
An account of the manners and customs of Italy; with observations on the mistakes of some travellers, with regard to that country. By Joseph Baretti. London, T. Davies, 1768. [Ann Arbor, Michigan, University Microfilms, 1971.
2 v. illus. 22 cm.
Written in answer to Samuel Sharp's Letters from Italy, which was first published London, 1766.
1. Italy—Soc. life & cust. 2. National characteristics, Italian. 3. Sharp, Samuel, 1770?-1778. Letters from Italy. I. Title.
ViU NUC77-14199

Baretti, Giuseppe Marco Antonio, 1719-1789.
Discours sur Shakespeare et sur Monsieur de Voltaire, per la prima volta ristampato nel testo originale (1777) a cura di Francesco Biondolillo. Lanciano, R. Carabba, 1911.
133 p.
Contains also facsim. title-page.
Microfilm (negative) New York, Columbia University Libraries, 1966. 1 reel.
1. Shakespeare, William, 1564-1616. 2. Voltaire, François Marie Arouet de, 1694-1778.
NNC NUC75-37808

Baretti, Giuseppe Marco Antonio, 1719-1789. Epistolario.
see Baretti, Giuseppe Marco Antonio, 1719-1789. Lettere sparse ... Torino, Centro studi piemontesi, 1976.

Baretti, Giuseppe Marco Antonio, 1719–1789.
La frusta letteraria / ⌜Giuseppe Baretti⌝ ; a cura di Ferdinando Giannessi. — Treviso : Canova, 1974.
132 p., ⌜1⌝ leaf of plates : facsim. ; 22 cm. — (Le Riviste dell'Italia moderna e contemporanea ; 2) It 75–May
A periodical review of books published by Baretti under the pseudonym of Aristarco Scannabue. It was suppressed after the thirty-third number.
L2000
1. Italian literature—18th century—History and criticism. 2. Books—Reviews. I. Giannessi, Ferdinando. II. Title.
PQ4032.B3 1974 75–534314

Baretti, Giuseppe Marco Antonio, 1719-1789.
Lettere sparse : supplemento all'Epistolario / Giuseppe Baretti ; a cura di Franco Fido. — Torino : Centro studi piemontesi, 1976.
119 p. ; 25 cm. — (I Quaderni ; 9) It77-Mar
English or Italian.
Bibliography: p. 13-14.
1. Baretti, Giuseppe Marco Antonio, 1719-1789—Correspondence. 2. Italy—Intellectual life. 3. London—Intellectual life. 4. Baretti, Giuseppe Marco Antonio, 1719-1789—Homes and haunts—England—London. 5. Authors, Italian—18th century—Correspondence. I. Baretti, Giuseppe Marco Antonio, 1719-1789. Epistolario. II. Title.
PQ4683.B19A83 1976 77-463242
*77 MARC

Baretti, Giuseppe Marco Antonio, 1719–1789.
Opere scelte ... A cura di Bruno Maier. ⌜Torino⌝, Unione tipografico-editrice torinese, 1972.
2 v. plates. 23 cm. (Classici italiani, ⌜29⌝) (Classici UTET) L16000 It 73–Feb
Bibliography: v. 1, p. ⌜55⌝–60.
CONTENTS: v. 1. Da La Frusta letteraria.—v. 2. Dalle Prefazioni alle tragedie di Pier Cornelio tradotte in versi italiani (1747–8).—Primo cicalamento di Giuseppe Baretti sopra le Cinque lettere del signor Giuseppe Bartoli intorno al libro che avrà per titolo: La vera spiegazione del dittico quiriniano (1750).—De Le piacevoli poesie (1750).—Dalle Lettere familiari a'suoi tre fratelli: Filippo, Giovanni e Amedeo (1762–63).—Da Gl'Italiani o sia relazione degli usi e costumi d'Italia (1768).—Dal Viaggio da Londra a Genova passando per l'Inghilterra occidentale, il Portogallo, la Spagna e la Francia (1770).—Prefazione a tutte l'opere di Niccolò Machiavelli (1772).—Discours sur Shakespeare et sur monsieur de Voltaire (1777).—Da La scelta delle lettere familiari (1779).
I. Maier, Bruno, ed.
PQ4683.B19A6 1972 73–317189

Baretti, Giuseppe Marco Antonio, 1719-1789.
Scritti / Giuseppe Baretti ; a cura di Ettore Bonora. — Torino : G. Einaudi, c1976.
xv, 228 p. ; 20 cm. — (Classici Riccardi ; 12) It76-Aug
Reprint of the 1951 ed. published by R. Riccardi, Milan, from Letterati memorialisti e viaggiatori del Settecento, edited by E. Bonora, which was issued as v. 47 of La Letteratura italiana, storia e testi.
Includes bibliographical references.
L3000
I. Bonora, Ettore.
PQ4683.B19A6 1976 76-477326
*76 MARC

Barettini Fernández, Jesús.
Juan Carreño, pintor de cámara de Carlos II. (Madrid) ⌜Dirección General de Relaciones Culturales⌝ (1972)
212 p., 2 l. plates (part col.) 24 cm. Sp 73–Mar
Bibliography: p. 99–101.
1. Carreño de Miranda, Juan, 1614–1685. I. Carreño de Miranda, Juan, 1614–1685.
ND813.C3B37 73–354787

Barettini Fernández, Jesús.
N. Piñole. ⌜Madrid, Dirección General de Bellas Artes, 1973⌝
169 p. plates (part col.) 17 cm. (Artistas españoles contemporáneos, 71. Serie Pintores) 60ptas Sp***
Bibliography: p. 165–167.
1. Piñole, Nicanor, 1878–
ND813.P49B37 74–319530
ISBN 84–369–0310–2

Baretto, Felisa R
An analytical study of the "rice wage" formula / ⌜Felisa R. Baretto⌝. — Manila : Republic of the Philippines, Dept. of Trade, Bureau of the Census and Statistics, 1974⌝
vi, 31 p. : graphs ; 27 cm. — (Technical paper - Republic of the Philippines, Bureau of the Census and Statistics ; 4)
Includes bibliographical references.
1. Costs and standard of living—Philippine Islands—Statistics. I. Title. II. Title: "Rice Wage" formula. III. Series: Philippines (Republic). Bureau of the Census and Statistics. Technical paper - Republic of the Philippines, Bureau of the Census and Statistics ; 4.
HD7056.B37 339.4'7'09599 76-364855
76 MARC

Barety, Julio Edgardo, 1943-
Uniform convergence of lacunary Fourier series. Albuquerque, University of New Mexico, 1972.
vii, 83 l.
Thesis (Ph. D.)—University of New Mexico.
Bibliography: leaves 81-82.
1. Fourier series. 2. Convergence. I. Title.
NmU NUC74-124442

Barev
see Alda, Jan.

Barev, Dimitŭr Khristov.
(Mekhanizirano pribirane, sortirane i sŭkhrani͡avane na koreno-klubenoplodnite i lukovichnite kulturi)
Механизирано прибиране, сортиране и съхраняване на корено-клубеноплодните и луковичните култури. ⟨Обзор⟩. (Ред. Ив. Анастасова). София, ЦНТИИСГС, 1972.
125 p. with illus. 21 cm. 2.00 lv Bu 72–2405
At head of title: Център за научно-техническа и икономическа информация по селско и горско стопанство при ССА "Г. Димитров."
Summary also in Russian and German.
Bibliography: p. 115–⌜124⌝
1. Vegetables—Harvesting. 2. Harvesting machinery. I. Title.
SB129.B37 73–317353

Barev, Tsenko
see Bŭdeshte. L'Avenir.

Barey, André, 1936–
Grau-Garriga. Cumella. ⌜Paris, Éditions La Demeure, 1974⌝
100 p. illus. (part col.) 24 cm. F***
1. Cumella, Antoni. 2. Ceramic sculpture—Catalonia. 3. Grau-Garriga, Josep, 1929– 4. Tapestry—Catalonia. 5. Wall hangings—Catalonia.
NK4210.C79B37 738'.092'4 75–500289
MARC

Barey, André, 1936-
Réflexions sur l'artisanat / André Barey ; suivi d'une intervention de Claude Parent. — Mâcon (Hôtel de ville, 71000) : Action culturelle mâconnaise, 1973.
55 p. : ill. ; 21 cm. — (Cahier de l'Action culturelle mâconnaise ; no 1) F74-10252
Includes bibliographical references.
6.00F
1. Artisans—France. 2. Artists—France. I. Title. II. Series: Action culturelle mâconnaise. Cahier de l'Action culturelle mâconnaise ; no 1.
HD2346.F8B37 331.7'94'0944 75-505622
75 MARC

Barezzani, Andrea, 1934–
I peccati di un giovane povero ... Bologna, Club degli autori, 1973.
110 p. 21 cm. L2800 It 73–June
I. Title.
PQ4862.A6737P4 74–327915

Barfield, Billy J
Analysis of the sediment filtering action of grassed media / by Billy J. Barfield, David T. Y. Kao, principal investigators, E. W. Tollner, graduate student assistant. — Lexington : University of Kentucky, Water Resources Institute, 1975.
ix, 50 p. : ill. ; 28 cm. — (Research report - University of Kentucky Water Resources Institute ; no. 90)
"Project number: A-049-KY. Agreement numbers: 14-31-0001-4017 (FY 1974). 14-31-0001-5017 (FY 1975)."
"P.L. 88-379."
Bibliography: p. 44-45.
1. Sediment transport. 2. Grassed waterways. I. Kao, David T. Y., 1936- joint author. II. Tollner, E. W., joint author. III. Title. IV. Series: Kentucky. University. Water Resources Institute. Research report - University of Kentucky Water Resources Institute ; no. 90.
TC175.2.B37 627'.122 76-624551
77 MARC

Barfield, Billy J
Development of prediction relationships for water requirements with irrigation cooling ⌜by⌝ Billy J. Barfield, John N. Walker ⌜and⌝ F. A. Payne. Lexington, University of Kentucky, Water Resources Institute, 1974.
vi, 41 l. illus. 28 cm. (Kentucky. University. Water Resources Institute. Research report no. 70)
Completion report. Project no. A-028KY. Agreement nos. 14-31-0001-3217 (FY 1971), 14-31-0001-3517 (FY 1972) Partly funded by Office of Water Resources Research.
Bibliography: leaves 37-39.
1. Plant-water relationships. 2. Mist propagation. 3. Irrigation research. I. Walker, John N., joint author. II. Payne, F. A., joint author. III. United States. Office of Water Resources Research. IV. Title. V. Series.
DI NUC75-21277

Barfield, Billy J
Solar radiation on sloping surfaces in Kentucky. ⌜Lexington, 1973⌝
16 p. illus. (Kentucky. Agricultural Experiment Station, Lexington. Progress report 208)
Bibliography: p. 4.
I. Title.
DNAL NUC74-124440

Barfield, Dianne Chavers, joint author.
see Gibson, Dot Rees. Plains—Carter country, U.S.A. Waycross, Ga., Dot Gibson Publications, c1977.

Barfield, Jesse Tobias, 1938-
An inquiry into specialization for certified public accountants... ⌜n.p.⌝ 1971.
xi, 196 l. illus. 29 cm.
Thesis (Ph.D.)—Louisiana State University, Baton Rouge.
Vita.
Bibliography: leaves 187-195.
1. Accountants. I. Title.
LU NUC73-32634

Barfield, Jesse Tobias, 1938-
An inquiry into specialization for certified public accountants. Ann Arbor, University Microfilms, 1972.
1 reel. 35 mm.
Thesis—Louisiana State University and Agricultural and Mechanical College, 1971.
1. Accounting. I. Title.
MsU NUC77-14571

Barfield, John, B.A., joint author.
see Jeremy, David J. A century of grace. ⌜Southend-on-Sea⌝ Avenue Baptist Church, 1976.

Barfield, Joseph N., joint author
see Williams, Donald J Initial explorer 45 substorm observations... Boulder, Colo., 1973.

Barfield, Lawrence, 1935-
see Beiträge zur Archäologie des Mittelalters. Köln, Böhlau, 1968-

Barfield, Owen, 1898–
Poetic diction: a study in meaning. With afterword by the author. 3d ed. Middletown, Conn., Wesleyan University Press ⌜1973⌝
230 p. 21 cm. (Philosophy & literature, no. 626) $2.95
Includes bibliographical references.
1. Poetry. 2. Diction. I. Title.
PN1031.B3 1973 808.1 72–10631
ISBN 0–8195–6026–X MARC

Barfield, Owen, 1898-
The rediscovery of meaning, and other essays / by Owen Barfield. — 1st ed. — Middletown, Conn. : Wesleyan University Press, c1977.
260 p. ; 22 cm.
Includes bibliographical references.
ISBN 0-8195-5006-X : $15.00
1. Philosophy—Addresses, essays, lectures. 2. General semantics—Addresses, essays, lectures. 3. Philology—Addresses, essays, lectures. I. Title.
B1618.B281R4 121 76-41479
76 MARC

Barfield, Owen, 1898–
Speaker's meaning. London, Rudolf Steiner Press, 1967.
118 p. 18 cm. £0.55 B 72–03572
1. General semantics. I. Title.
B820.B3 1967b 149'.94 72–195598
ISBN 0–85440–249–7 MARC

Barfield, Owen, 1898–
What Coleridge thought. London, Oxford University Press, 1972.
xii, 285 p. illus. 24 cm. index. £3.70 B 72–11736
Includes bibliographical references.
1. Coleridge, Samuel Taylor, 1772–1834. I. Title.
PR4484.B3 1972 821'.7 73–162494
ISBN 0–19–212190–1 MARC

Barfield, Owen, 1898-
see Evolution of consciousness ... 1st ed. Middletown, Conn., Wesleyan University Press, c1976.

Barfield, Owen, 1898-
see Gibb, Jocelyn, ed. Light on C. S. Lewis. New York, Harcourt Brace Jovanovich, 1976, c1965.

Barfield, Owen, 1898-
see Imaginative expression in literature. [Folcroft, Pa.] Folcroft Library Editions, 1971.

Barfield, Owen, 1898- ed.
see Steiner, Rudolf, 1861-1925. The case for anthroposophy. [London] Rudolf Steiner Press [1970]

Barfield, Owen, 1898-
see Steiner, Rudolf, 1861-1925. Guidance in esoteric training... London, Rudolf Steiner Press, 1972.

Barfield, Rufus L
Relationships among innovation, organizational climate, and pupils academic achievement in selected elementary schools of Ohio. Oxford, Ohio, 1972.
184 l. illus. 28 cm.
Thesis (Ph. D.)–Miami University, Oxford. Typewritten.
1. Educational innovations. 2. Elementary schools–Ohio. 3. Academic achievement. 4. Motivation in education. I. Title.
OOxM NUC73-125528

Barfield, Terry
see Acadiana Health Planning Council. A consumer health needs survey... [Lafayette] The Council, 1974.

Barfield, Thomas J., joint author
see Mason, Jack, 1911- Last stage for Bolinas. Inverness, Calif., North Shore Books, 1973.

Barfield, Tony.
When there was steam : memories of a Western Region fireman / [by] Tony Barfield. — Truro : Barton, [1976]
116 p. : ill., map, plan ; 22 cm. GB76-16902
ISBN 0-85153-226-8 : £1.50
1. Barfield, Tony. 2. Locomotive firemen—Biography. 3. Great Western Railway (Great Britain) I. Title.
TF140.B37A34 385'.36'10922 76-375302
76 MARC

Barfield, Vivian Miller, 1930-
The pupil control ideology of teachers in selected schools. Albuquerque, 1972 [c1973]
[xiv], 105 l. illus.
Thesis (Ph. D.)–University of New Mexico.
Bibliography: leaves [82]-85.
1. School discipline. 2. Classroom management. I. Title.
NmU NUC73-124580

Barfivala, Chunilal Damodardas, 1889-
see The Directory of local self-government in Maharashtra state. Bombay, 1962.

Barfknecht, Thomas R
The effect of streptomycin resistance, caffeine and acriflavine on ultraviolet light-induced lethality and mutagenesis in strains of Escherichia coli. -- [Lawrence : s.n.], 1976.
ix, 154 leaves, [35] leaves of plates : graphs ; 29 cm.
Thesis (Ph.D.) - University of Kansas.
Bibliography: leaves 134-154.
1. Escherichia coli infections. 2. Streptomycin. 3. Caffeine. I. Title.
KU NUC77-99422

Barfod, Børge.
Konsumkreditten i Danmark; en foreløbig oversigt som bidrag til en belysning af konsumkredittens omfang, finansiering og udviklingsretning. København, Sekretariatet for Danmarks erhvervsfond, Handelsministeriets produktivitetsudvalg [I kommission hos A. F. Høst] 1960.
85 p. 24 cm.
1. Consumer credit—Denmark. I. Title.
HG3755.B35 74–205691

Barfod, Gustav.
Charles de Gaulle og hans republik. [1. opl., København, Haase] 1965.
167 p. 19 cm. (Haases facetbøger, F12)
Bibliography : p. [161]–163.
1. Gaulle, Charles de, Pres. France, 1890–1970. 2. France—Politics and government—1958– I. Title.
DC373.G3B28 74–207808

Barfod, Gustav.
Dollar och makt. [Utg. av] Utrikespolitiska institutet. Stockholm, Rabén & Sjögren, [1974.
32 p. 20 cm. (Världspolitikens dagsfrågor, 1974 : 2) kr4.50
S 74–16/17
"Översättning från danskt originalmanus."
Bibliography : p. 32.
1. Monetary policy—United States. 2. United States—Foreign economic relations. I. Title. II. Series.
[HG538.B194] 74–342131
ISBN 91–7182–039–6

Barfod, Hans Peter Gote Birkedal, 1843–1926.
Minder fra et langt liv. [Af] H. P. B. Barfod. København, August Bang, 1972.
189 p., 10 ports. 23 cm. (Memoirer og breve, 35) kr43.70
D 72–15
"Fotografisk optryk"
"... er et forkortet og bearbejdet Uddrag af Dr. med. H. P. B. Barfods Manuskript ..."
Includes bibliographical references.
I. Title. II. Series.
DL103.5.M52 bd. 35 72–364962
[DL249.B3]
ISBN 87–7226–030–0; 87–7226–031–9 (pbk.)

Barfod, Jørgen
see Denmark. Laws, statutes, etc. Vandløbsloven med kommentater. København : Juristforbundet, 1975.

Barfod, Jørgen Henrik Pagh, 1918-
Et centrum i periferien : modstandsbevægelsen på Bornholm / af Jørgen H. Barfod. — Rønne : Bornholms historiske Samfund : i kommission hos William Dams boghandel, [1976]
355 p. : ill. ; 25 cm. D76-21
Summary in English.
Bibliography: p. 343-[346]
Includes index.
ISBN 8787042061 : kr85.00
1. World War, 1939-1945—Underground movements—Denmark. 2. World War, 1939-1945—Denmark—Bornholm. 3. Bornholm—History. I. Title.
D802.D4B35 76-489083
77 MARC

Barfod, Jørgen Henrik Pagh, 1918-
The Museum of Denmark's Fight for Freedom 1940-1945 : a short guide / by Jørgen H. Barfod. — Copenhagen : The National Museum, 1975.
35 p. : ill. ; 21 cm. D***
ISBN 8748000884
1. Museet for Denmarks frihedskamp 1940-1945. I. Title.
D733.D4C653 940.53'489 76-372882
76 MARC

Barfod, Pie.
Grønlændere i Danmark 1971–72. kalâtdlit Danmarkime. [Af] Pie Barfod, Lone Nielsen [og] Johan Nielsen. Overs. Mâliâraq Vebæk med bistand af Carl Chr. Olsen. København, Nyt fra Samfundsvidenskaberne; Eksp. : DBK [1974].
589 p. 21 cm. (Nyt fra samfundsvidenskaberne, 34)
D 74–25–26
Danish and Eskimo.
Bibliography : p. 585–587.
ISBN 87–7034–078–1 : kr18.00
1. Greenlanders in Denmark. I. Nielsen, Lone, 1943– joint author. II. Nielsen, Johan, 1948– joint author. III. Title. IV. Title: kalâtdlit Danmarkime. V. Series.
DL142.G7B37 75–545046

Barfoed, Niels Aage, 1899–
Dres. Roman. København, Lohse, 1972.
137 p. 22 cm. kr20.25 (pbk.) D 72–43
I. Title.
PT8175.B353D74 72–372629
ISBN 87–564–0152–3 ; 87–564–0150–7 (pbk.)

Barfoed, Stig Krabbe, joint author
see Fuglsang, Mads, 1905- Bondedreng på valsen. [København] : Gyldendal, 1975.

Barfoot, Earl F
What does the Lord want / Earl F. Barfoot, editor. — Nashville : Tidings, [1974]
55 p. : 19 cm.
$1.25
1. Stewardship, Christian—Addresses, essays, lectures. 2. Laity—Addresses, essays, lectures. I. Title.
BV772.B27 248'.6 74–80892
MARC

Barfoot, Edith May. The joyful vocation to suffering. 1977.
in The witness of Edith Barfoot ... Oxford, Blackwell, 1977.

Barfoot, Edith May.
see The witness of Edith Barfoot ... Oxford, Blackwell, 1977.

Barfoot, Peter.
The universal British directory of trade and commerce. [Comp. by Peter Barfoot and John Wilkes] London, printed for the patentees, and sold by C. Stalker, 1790-97? [Ann Arbor, Mich., University Microfilm, 1972]
5 v. in 9. illus. 21 cm.
Vol. 2-5 have title: The universal British directory of trade, commerce, and manufacture; printed at the British Directory Office.
Pt. 2 of each vol. lacks t.p.
Vol. 5 of original ed. entered under title.
Photocopy.
1. London—Commerce—History. 2. Great Britain—History—George II, 1727-1760. 3. Great Britain—Commerce—History. I. Wilkes, John, fl. 1790. II. Title.
NjP NUC74-171269

Barford, Brian Dale, 1946-
The adsorption of ethylene and hydrogen on tungsten single crystal surfaces. [Ithaca, N.Y.] 1974.
ix, 163 l. illus. 29 cm.
Thesis (Ph.D.)—Cornell University.
Bibliography: leaves 131-136.
1. Chemisorption. 2. Tungsten. I. Title.
NIC NUC76-96142

Barford, Edward.
Reminiscences of a lance-corporal of industry. London, Elm Tree Books Ltd, 1972.
[71], 182, [8] p. illus., facsim., ports. 23 cm. £2.25 B 72–19986
1. Aveling-Barford ltd. I. Title.
HD9680.G74A92 338.4'7'62000924 72–193649
ISBN 0–241–02162–6 [B] MARC

Barford, Michael F. Feasibility report. 1965
in Bérend, Paul M A Tabac International; proposed World Tobacco Information Centre. London, New York, World tobacco [1965]

Barford, N C
Mechanics [by] N. C. Barford. London, New York, Wiley, 1973.
xv, 391 p. illus. 24 cm. £7.50 GB 73–31340
Includes index.
1. Mechanics.
QA805.B286 531 72–2639
ISBN 0–471–04840–2 ; 0–471–04841–0 (pbk.) MARC

Barfred, Troels.
Achilles tendon rupture; aetiology and pathogenesis of subcutaneous rupture assessed on the basis of the literature and rupture experiments on rats. Copenhagen, Munksgaard, 1973.
126 p. 23 cm. (Acta orthopaedica Scandinavica. Supplementum no. 152)
Bibliography: p. 105-124.
1. Tendon of Achilles. 2. Rats. I. Title. II. Series.
AAP NUC75-21302

Barfucci, Marino Bernardo, ed.
see Melani, Gaudenzio. Francescanesimo vivo. Sacro Monte della Verna, Edizioni La Verna, 1973.

Barfuel, Paul.
Vie et moeurs des oiseaux, avec trois cent dix photos et dessins dont quatre-vingt-quatorze en couleurs. Nouv. éd. entièrement refondue. Paris, Horizons de France [1971]
221 p. illus.
1. Birds. I. Title.
DNLM NUC73-32097

Barfus, Shimon Yaakov
see Aboth. 1966? Masekhet Avot. [727? i. e. 1966?]

Barfus, Shimon Yaakov
see Aboth. 1974. Masekhet Avot. 734 [1974]

Barfuss, H.
see Theorie und Praxis der Kreditkontrolle. Wien, Sparkassenverl., 1975.

Barfuss, Walter.
Aspekte einer Stromtarifreform / W. Barfuss, L. Scheiderer. — Wien : Jupiter-Verlag, 1975.
45 p. ; 21 cm. — (Schriftenreihe - Institut für Angewandte Sozial- und Wirtschaftsforschung ; Heft 25) GFR76-A
Papers presented at the third Energietag Ottenstein, March 6, 1975.
Includes bibliographical references.
1. Electric utilities—Rates. 2. Electric utilities—Law and legislation—Austria. I. Scheiderer, Lothar, joint author. II. Energietag Ottenstein, 3d, 1975. III. Title. IV. Series: Vienna. Institut für Angewandte Sozial- und Wirtschaftsforschung. Schriftenreihe ; Heft 25.
HN405.5.V53a Heft 25 76-457535
76[r77]rev MARC

Barfuss, Walter.
see Austria. Laws, statutes, etc. Lebensmittelrecht. Wien, Manz, 1975-

Barfuss, Werner, 1942–
Hausverträge und Hausgesetze fränkischer reichsgräflicher Familien (Castell, Löwenstein-Wertheim) [Würzburg] 1972.
xii, 224 p. geneal. tables. 21 cm. GFR***
Inaug.-Diss.—Würzburg.
Vita.
Bibliography: p. v–xii.
1. Castell, Counts of. 2. Löwenstein-Wertheim, Counts of. I. Title.
74–325225

Barg, ʻAbdurrashīd, 1891–
(Camanistān-i Barg)
چمنستان برگ / عبدالرشید برگ. — [s. l. : s. n.], 1974-.
(پشاور : شاہین پرنٹنگ پریس)
v., [1] leaf of plates : port. ; 21 cm.
Urdu or Persian.
Poems.
Rs10.00 (v. 1)

I. Title.

PK2200.B3323C3 75–930261

Barg, Leszek, ed.
see Polskie medale i odznaki medyczne... Wrocław, 1972.

Barg, Michele.
Cellular development in the gastrointestinal lymphoid tissue of the young rabbit. -- [Lawrence : s.n., 1975]
v, 119 leaves : ill. ; 28 cm.
Thesis (Ph.D.) - University of Kansas.
Bibliography: leaves 75-83.
1. Lymphoid tissue. 2. T cells. 3. Rabbits. Physiology. I. Title.
KU NUC77-99421

Barg, Mikhail Abramovich.
(Problemy sot͡sial'noĭ istorii v osveshchenii sovremennoĭ zapadnoĭ medievistiki)
Проблемы социальной истории в освещении современной западной медиевистики. Москва, "Наука," 1973.
230 p. 20 cm. 0.74rub USSR 73
At head of title: М. А. Барг.
On leaf preceding t. p.: Академия наук СССР. Институт всеобщей истории.
Bibliography: p. 217–[226]
1. Feudalism—Historiography. I. Title.
D131.B34 73–365668

Barg, Mikhail Abramovich.
(Shekspir i istorii͡a)
Шекспир и история / М. А. Барг. — Москва : Наука, 1976.
197 p., [2] leaves of plates : ill. ; 20 cm. — (Серия Из истории мировой культуры) USSR***
At head of title: Akademii͡a nauk SSSR.
Series romanized: Serii͡a Iz istorii mirovoĭ kul'tury.
Bibliography: p. 194–[195]
Includes index.
0.66rub
1. Shakespeare, William, 1564–1616—Knowledge—History. I. Title.
PR3014.B37 77–504861

Barga, Corpus
see García de la Barga y Gómez de la Serna, Andrés, 1887-

Barga, Rafael Rebollo García de la
see Rebollo García de la Barga, Rafael.

Barga Bensusan, Ramón.
El "afeitado" un fraude a la fiesta brava. [Madrid, Editora Nacional, 1972]
272 p. illus. 18 cm. (Libros directos, 9) 100ptas Sp***
1. Fighting bull. 2. Horns. I. Title.
SF199.F5B37 72–366985

Bargad, Warren, 1940-
Character, idea, and myth in the works of Hayim Hazaz. A dissertation presented to... Brandeis University, Department of Near Eastern and Judaic Studies, by Warren Bargad, December 1970. [Ann Arbor, Mich., University Microfilms, 1972, c1971]
340 p. 22 cm.
Thesis—Brandeis.
Bibliography: p. 313-340.
Photocopy.
1. Hazaz, Haim, 1898- I. Title.
OCH NUC73-124581

Bargad, Warren, 1940-
Exclamations, manifestoes, and other literary peripheries. [New York, American Jewish Congress, 1974]
[202]-211 p. 24 cm.
Reprint from Judaism, vol. 23, no. 2, Spring, 1974.
1. Siman keri'ah (Tel-Aviv) I. Title.
OCH NUC76-96145

Bargaehr, Lillie B.
see Scott, Hollis. William E. Gates... Provo, Utah, 1973.

Bargagli, Girolamo, 1537–1587.
La pellegrina. Edizione critica con introduzione e note di Florindo Cerreta. Firenze, L. S. Olschki, 1971.
225 p. plates. 25 cm. (Biblioteca dell'Archivum Romanicum, v. 111. Serie 1: Storia, letteratura, paleografia) It 71–Nov
At head of title: Girolamo Bragagli (1537–1587)
A play.
Bibliography: p. 209–211.
L5000
I. Cerreta, Florindo Vincent, 1921– ed. II. Title. III. Series: Biblioteca dell'Archivum Romanicum, v. 111.
PQ4607.B33P4 1971 76–889080

Bargagli, Piero.
Catagrafe / Piero Bargagli. — Pisa : Giardini, 1975.
91 p., [4] leaves of plates : ill. ; 23 cm. It 75–Sept
Poems.
L5000
I. Title.
PQ4862.A674C3 75–400271

Bargagli, Scipione, d. 1612.
Il Turamino : ovvero, Del parlare e dello scriver sanese / Scipione Bargagli ; a cura di Luca Serianni. — Roma : Salerno editrice, 1976.
xxxvi, 250 p. ; 22 cm. — (Testi e documenti di letteratura e di lingua ; 2) It77-Jan
Bibliography: p. xxx-xxxvi.
Includes indexes.
L15000
1. Italian language—Dialects—Italy—Siena. 2. Italian language—Grammar—1500-1800. 3. Italian language—History. I. Title. II. Title: Del parlare e dello scriver sanese.
PC1834.S5B37 1976 77-452911
*77 MARC

Bargaining & Marketing Cooperatives, National Conference of
see
National Conference of Bargaining & Marketing Cooperatives.

Bargaining Cooperatives, National Conference of
see
National Conference of Bargaining Cooperatives.

Bargaining : formal theories of negotiation / edited and with contributions by Oran R. Young. — Urbana : University of Illinois Press, [1975]
vi, 412 p. : ill. ; 26 cm.
Bibliography: p. [409]-412.
Includes index.
ISBN 0-252-00273-3 : $15.00
1. Negotiation—Addresses, essays, lectures. I. Young, Oran R.
BF637.N4B35 658.4'03 72-75493
75 MARC

Bargaining power. [Jackson, Miss., n.d.]
see under Trammell, David.

Bargaining under Economic Challenge, Conference on
see
Conference on Bargaining under Economic Challenge, University of Notre Dame, 1976.

Bargaining without boundaries : the multinational corporation and international labor relations / edited by Robert J. Flanagan and Arnold R. Weber. — Chicago : University of Chicago Press, 1974.
xxviii, 258 p. ; 24 cm. — (Studies in business and society)
"Proceedings of a conference sponsored by the Graduate School of Business, University of Chicago, the McKinsey Foundation, and the Johnson Foundation."
Includes bibliographical references and index.
ISBN 0-226-25312-0
1. Industrial relations—Congresses. 2. International business enterprises—Congresses. I. Flanagan, Robert J. II. Weber, Arnold Robert. III. Chicago. University. Graduate School of Business. IV. McKinsey Foundation for Management Research, New York. V. Johnson Foundation, Racine, Wis. VI. Series: Chicago. University. Graduate School of Business. Studies in business and society.
HD6971.B353 658.31'5 74-5724
75 MARC

Bargal, Haim, 1922–
(Ḥ. Bergel)
ח. ברגל : ציורים ורישומים / חיים ברגל ;
— .[English translation, Dov Vardi]
[שער הגולן] : קיבוץ שער הגולן, 1975.
[72] p. : chiefly ill. (some col.) ; 29 cm.
Added t. p.: Haim Bargal; paintings and drawings.
English and Hebrew.
1. Bargal, Haim, 1922– I. Title.
N7279.B28A47 77–951148

Bargalló, Salvador Rosas
see Rosas Bargalló, Salvador.

Bargalló Cervelló, Pedro.
Arturo Michelena; 14 estudios. Caracas, Banco Industrial de Venezuela [1967?]
72 p. illus. (part col.) 29 cm. (Publicaciones)
1. Michelena, Arturo, 1863-1898.
TxU NUC77-13812

Bargalló Cervelló, Pedro.
Lligam entre Catalunya i Egipte [por] Pere Bargallo i Cervelló. [Caracas?] Centre Català de Caracas, 1964.
29 p. illus. 23 cm. (Edicions del Centre Català de Caracas, quadern, no. 2)
1. Science—Hist.—Spain—Catalonia. I. Title.
TxU NUC74-125814

Bargar, Robert Roscoe.
Development of a national register of educational researchers [by] Rober Bargar, Egon Guba [and] Corahann Okorodudu. Columbus, Ohio, Ohio State University, 1965.
vi, 139 p. 28 cm.
"Cooperative Research Project No. E-014."
"The research... was supported by the Cooperative Research Program of the Office of Education, U.S. Department of Health, Education, and Welfare."
1. Educational research United States. I. Guba, Egon G., joint author. II. Okorodudu, Corahann, joint author. III. Title.
OU NUC76-29801

Bargar, Robert Roscoe.
Review of research related to training for research in education. Columbus, Ohio, Ohio State University Research Foundation, 1967.
1 v. (various pagings) illus. 30 cm. (Cooperative research project, no. 3191)
Principal investigators: Robert R. Bargar, Corahann Okorodudu; research asociates: Edward Dworkin and others.
"Supported by the Cooperative Research Program of the Office of Education, U.S. Dept. of Health, Education, and Welfare."
"Pre-publication draft."
1. Educational research. I. Okorodudu, Corahann, joint author. II. Title. III. Series: U.S. Office of Education. Cooperative research project, no. 3191.
OU NUC74-125817

Barge, Hermann, 1870–1941.
Florian Geyer: eine biograph. Studie/ Hermann Barge. — Nachdr. d. Ausg. Leipzig, Berlin, Teubner, 1920. — Hildesheim: Gerstenberg, 1972.
39 p.; 21 cm. — (Beiträge zur Kulturgeschichte des Mittelalters und der Renaissance; Bd. 26) DM8.40 GDB 73-A18
Includes bibliographical references.
1. Geyer, Florian, d. 1525. 2. Peasants' War, 1524–1525. I. Series.
DD183.B3 1972 73–350596
ISBN 3–8067–0124–5

Barge Canal Study Area Committee
see Erie and Niagara Counties Regional Planning Board. Barge Canal recreation and open space preservation plan. [Grand Island, N.Y.] 1973.

Barge, Waggoner and Sumner.
Comprehensive plan: 1. Economic base and population study; 2. Land use Plan; 3. Neighborhood analyses; 4. Zoning ordinance; 5. Subdivision regulations, by Barge, Waggoner and Sumner. Milan, Tenn., Regional Planning Commission, 1965-66.
5 v. (HUD 701 report)
1. Master plan—Milan, Tenn. I. Milan, Tenn. Regional Planning Commission.
DHUD NUC74-108267

Barge, Waggoner and Sumner.
For works by this body issued under its later name see
Barge, Waggoner, Sumner, and Cannon.

Barge, Waggoner, Sumner, and Cannon.
Comprehensive area-wide water and wastewater facilities plan for the mid-Cumberland region of Tennessee; a report to the Mid-Cumberland Council of Governments and Mid-Cumberland Development District. Nashville, 1972.
ii, 39 l. maps. 29 cm.
1. Water-supply—Tennessee—Mid-Cumberland region. 2. Sewerage—Tennessee—Mid-Cumberland region. I. Mid-Cumberland Council of Governments. II. Mid-Cumberland Development District. III. Title.
TD224.T2B37 1972 363.6'1'09768 73-170486
MARC

Barge, Waggoner, Sumner and Cannon.
Comprehensive area-wide water and wastewater facilities plan and program for the Mid-Cumberland Region of Tennessee. A report to the Mid-Cumberland Council of Governments and Mid-Cumberland Development District. Nashville, Tenn., 1973.
46 p.
Preparation of report financed in part through grant from Dept. of Housing and Urban Development and the Economic Development Administration. Contract no. CPA-TN-33-1002.
1. Water-supply—Tenn. 2. Sewerage and sewage disposal—Tenn. I. Mid-Cumberland Council of Governments. II. Title.
DHUD DLC NUC74-125929

Barge, Waggoner, Sumner, and Cannon.
For works by this body issued under its earlier name see
Barge, Waggoner and Sumner.

Bargebuhr, Frederick P 1904-
Salomo Ibn Gabirol: Wiedergeburt des Diesseits Judentum in Cordova und Granada. [Amsterdam, 1963]
5-36 p. 24 cm.
Offprint from Castrum peregrini, Heft 59, 1963.
1. Ibn Gabirol, Solomon ben Judah, ca. 1021-ca. 1058. I. Title.
OCH NUC74-125812

Bargel, Tino
see Bildungschancen und Umwelt. Braunschweig: Westermann, 1973-

Bargeliotes, Peter Constantine, 1939-
Numerical methods in electromagnetic field problems. [Tempe] 1974.
156 l. illus.
Thesis (Ph.D.)—Arizona State University.
Includes abstract and vita.
Bibliography: leaves 102-104.
1. Dissertations, Academic—ASU—Electrical engineering. 2. Electromagnetic fields. 3. Antennas (Electronics)—Computer programs. I. Title.
AzTeS NUC75-21294

Bargellini, Alberto.
La droga, questa epidemia moderna / [di] A. Bargellini, B. Macchia, I. Morelli. — Firenze : Libreria editrice fiorentina, 1977.
213 p., [4] leaves of plates : ill. ; 23 cm. — (Libri di Corea per la piena educazione ; 7) It77-July
Includes writings by S. Catalano et al.
Includes bibliographical references.
L2500
1. Drug abuse—Addresses, essays, lectures. 2. Narcotic habit—Addresses, essays, lectures. I. Macchia, Bruno, joint author. II. Morelli, Ivano, joint author. III. Title.
HV5801.B33 77-558490
*77 MARC

Bargellini, Alberto.
L'ecologia, una realtà per la scuola : attività sperimentali nella scuola media / di A. Bargellini, G. Lazzarini, M. A. Masini. — Firenze : Libreria editrice fiorentina, 1976.
116 p. : ill. ; 24 cm. — (Quaderni di Corea : 6. serie, Gruppo L'educazione ; 6) It76-Nov
Bibliography: p. 114-115.
L1500
1. Ecology. 2. Ecology—Experiments. I. Lazzarini, Giorgio, joint author. II. Masini, Maria Angela, joint author. III. Title.
QH541.B28 77-455770
*77 MARC

Bargellini, Alberto.
Nuove proposte per l'insegnamento scientifico : per il primo biennio della scuola secondaria superiore / Alberto Bargellini, Giancarlo Ghiselli. — Firenze : Libreria editrice fiorentina, 1976.
138 p. : ill. ; 23 cm. — (I Libri di Corea per la piena educazione ; 6) It76-Aug
Bibliography: p. 133-135.
L2500
1. Science—Study and teaching (Secondary)—Italy. I. Ghiselli, Giancarlo, joint author. II. Title.
Q183.4.I8B37 76-480842
*76 MARC

Bargellini, Alberto.
Problemi di chimica organica / di Alberto Bargellini. — Pisa : Giardini, 1976.
203 p. ; 25 cm. — (Quaderni di scienze ; 5) It77-Jan
Bibliography: p. 203.
1. Chemistry, Organic—Problems, exercises, etc. I. Title.
QD257.B29 547'.007'6 77-458251
77 MARC

Bargellini, Alberto.
see Voglia di scoprire... Firenze, Libreria editrice fiorentina, 1975-1976.

Bargellini, P. L., ed.
see AIAA Communications Satellite Systems Conference, 4th, Washington, D.C., 1972. Communications satellite systems. Cambridge, Mass., MIT Press [1974]

Bargellini, Piero, 1897–
L'Anno Santo. Nella storia, nella letteratura e nell'arte. Firenze, Vallecchi, 1974.
315 p. illus. 18 cm. L2500 It 74–Sept
1. Holy Year. I. Title.
BX961.H6B37 74–338531

Bargellini, Piero, 1897-
L'Arte del settecento. [Firenze] Vallecchi [1963]
330 p. illus., col. plates. 24 cm. (Belvedere: panorama storico dell' arte, v. 10)
I. Title. II. Series.
KU NUC77-14387

Bargellini, Piero, 1897–
Gli atti degli eretici. [Roma], De Luca, [1972].
173 p. 21 cm. (Rosso e azzurro, 2) L2200 It 72–June
1. Meditations. I. Title.
BX2185.B273 72–374111

Bargellini, Piero, 1897-
Bernardetta : l'umile messaggera dell'Immacolata / Piero Bargellini. — Milano : IPL, [1976]
63 p. : ill. ; 21 cm. It76-Aug
Cover title.
L600
1. Soubirous, Bernardette, Saint, 1844-1879. 2. Christian saints—France—Biography. I. Title.
BX4700.S65B37 282'.092'4 76-477464
*76 MARC

Bargellini, Piero, 1897–
Il bicentenario della Camera di commercio fiorentina. 1770–1970. Firenze, Camera di commercio, industria, artigianato e agricoltura, 1970.
162 p. illus., plates. 32 cm. It 71–Mar
"Documenti": p. 131–162.
1. Camera di commercio, industria, artigianato e agricoltura di Firenze—History. I. Title.
HF312.B318 73–339595

Bargellini, Piero, 1897–
Cento tabernacoli a Firenze. Firenze, Banca toscana, 1971.
42 p. 87 plates. 30 cm. It 72–Mar
Includes bibliography.
1. Florence—Chapels. 2. Art—Florence. I. Title.
N6921.F7B37 72–368568

Bargellini, Piero, 1897-
Dio nell'uomo. Testi di Piero Bargellini. Tavole di Francesco Messina... [Milano] Galleria D'arte Sacra dei contemporanei [1962]
119 p. illus., plates. 32 cm.
I. Messina, Francesco, 1900-
InStme NUC76-62504

Bargellini, Piero, 1897–
Firenze delle torri. Firenze, Bonechi, 1973.
229 p. illus. 27 cm. L7500 It 74–Feb
At head of title: Piero Bargellini, Ennio Guarnieri.
Bibliography: p. 227–228.
1. Florence—Biography. 2. Towers—Florence. I. Guarnieri, Ennio, 1928– joint author. II. Title.
DG731.7.B37 914.5'51 74–305973

Bargellini, Piero, 1897–
Fra Diavolo / Piero Bargellini. — 1. ed. per la Rusconi Libri. — Milano : Rusconi, c1975.
137 p. ; 20 cm. — (Biblioteca Rusconi ; 19) It 76–Feb
L1000
1. Fra Diavolo, 1771–1806—Fiction.
PQ4807.A733F7 76–505294

Bargellini, Piero, 1897–
Glimpses of Florence. [Firenze] Vallecci editore [c1972]
87, [64] p. illus. (part col.) 25 cm. It***
Translated from the Italian.
1. Florence—Description. I. Title.
DG734.2.B32513 914.5'51 73–178755
MARC

Bargellini, Piero, 1897-
La Madonna dell'arte. Roma, Centro Internationale di Comparazione e Sintesti [n.d.]
15, [1] p. 21 cm.
"Conferenze Mariane tenute nell'Aula Magna dell'Angelicum."
Besutti (1959) 4032.
ODaU-M NUC73-98713

Bargellini, Piero, 1897-
Le Palais Medicis et les fresques de Benozzo Gozzoli. Gladys Hutton, translator. Roma, Edizioni del Drago [1959]
44 p. illus. (part col.)
1. Florence. Palazzo Medici-Riccardi. 2. Mural painting and decoration—Florence. 3. Gozzoli, Benozzo, 1420-1497. I. Title.
DeU NUC74-30461

Bargellini, Piero, 1897-
Sie. Bild und Leben der Gottesmutter. [Übertragen aus dem Italienischen von Helene Moser] Würzburg, Augustinus-Verlag [n.d.]
111 p. illus. 25 cm.
ODaU-M NUC73-68104

Bargellini, Piero, 1897-
see Florence. Comitato del fondo internazionale per Firenze. Città di Firenze. [Firenze, 1966]

Bargellini, Piero, 1897-
see Signorini, Telemaco, 1835-1901. Disegni inediti. Firenze [1968]

Bargellini, Piero, 1897-
see Vita privata a Firenze nei secoli XIV e XV. Firenze, Leo S. Olschki, 1966.

Bargello: a Golden hands pattern book. [1st American ed.] New York, Random House [1973]
64 p. illus. (part col.) 30 cm. $4.95
First published in London under title: Zigzag stitchery.
1. Canvas embroidery—Patterns. I. Golden hands.
TT778.C3B34 746.4'4 73-5013
ISBN 0-394-48795-8 MARC

Bargeloh, John Frederick, 1941-
Effect of estrogen and progesterone on feed intake, calcium metabolism and interrelationships of calcium, phosphorus and magnesium in the bovine. [n.p.] 1973.
125 l.
Thesis—Ohio State University.
Bibliography: leaves 109-125.
1. Estrogen—Physiological effect. 2. Progesterone—Physiological effect. I. Title.
OU NUC74-125934

al-Bargeloni, Isaac ben Reuben
see
Al-Bargeloni, Isaac ben Reuben, b. 1043.

Bargemon, Christophe Villeneuve-
see Villeneuve-Bargemon, Christophe, comte de, 1771-1829.

Bargen, Ralph von, 1948–
Der finanzierte Ehemäklervertrag. [Köln, 1973?]
xx, 103 p. 21 cm. GFR***
Inaug.-Diss.—Cologne.
Vita.
Bibliography: p. ii-xii.
1. Marriage brokerage—Germany (Federal Republic, 1949–) I. Title.
74-306222

Bargen, Robert Burns.
An historical-rhetorical analysis of the critical parliamentary debates on the renewal of the charter of the British East India Company in 1793 and 1813. Lincoln, Neb., 1974.
vi, 486 l. maps.
Thesis (Ph.D.)—University of Nebraska.
Appendix I Photo reprint of "Resolutions proposed to the House of Commons by the Right Honourable Henry Dundas—April 23, 1793: l. 414-432.
Appendix II "Division lists on East India Company 1783-1813: l. 433-436.
Appendix III "The listing of the debates in the British Parliament on the British East India Company from 1773-1813: l. 437-451.
Appendix IV "Biographical Notes": l. 452-468.
Bibliography: leaves 469-486.
1. East India Company (English)—Charters. 2. Gt. Brit. Parliament—Hist. 3. Debates and debating. I. Title.
NbU NUC76-96136

Bargenda, Udo Wilhelm.
Pestalozzis Naturbegriff. Seine Entwicklung von der "Abendstunde" zu den "Nachfroschungen". [n.p.] 1972.
iv, 129 p.
Inaug.-Diss.—Muenster.
Bibliography: p. 127-129.
1. Pestalozzi, Johann Heinrich, 1746-1827.
CSt NUC77-14778

Bargenda, Udo Wilhelm, ed.
see Nicolaus Copernikus zum 500. [fünfhundertsten] Geburtstag. Köln, Wien: Böhlau, 1973.

Barger, Bill.
Human morals : an introduction to ethics / by Bill Barger. — [Manhattan Beach, Calif.] : Sheffield Press, c1975.
81 p. ; 28 cm.
Includes bibliographical references.
1. Ethics—History. I. Title.
BJ71.B24 170'.9 75-22998
75 MARC

Barger, Bob.
Keep it quiet, please. By Bob Barger. New York, Vantage Press [c1964]
58 p.
Teachers—Correspondence, reminiscences, etc.
(A) Keep it quiet, please!
MoU NUC77-13987

Barger, Bob, joint author.
see Nava, Julian, 1927- California . . . Beverly Hills, Calif., Glencoe Press, c1976.

Barger, George William, 1923-
Historical sociology: its nature and methods. [Columbia, Mo.] 1965.
iii, 136 l.
Thesis—University of Missouri.
Vita.
Bibliography: leaves [125]-136.
Microfilm (positive) Ann Arbor, University Microfilms [1965] 1 reel. 35 mm.
1. Historical sociology. 2. Historical sociology—Methodology. I. Title.
NRU NUC74-125811

Barger, Gerald L.
see Crutcher, Harold L A note on a gamma distribution computer program... Washington, U.S. Department of Commerce, National Oceanic and Atmospheric Administration, Environmental Data Service, 1973.

Barger, Harold.
American agriculture, 1899-1939 : a study of output, employment, and productivity / by Harold Barger and Hans H. Landsberg. — New York : Arno Press, 1975 [c1942]
xxii, 435 p. : ill. ; 23 cm. — (National Bureau of Economic Research publications in reprint)
Reprint of the ed. published by National Bureau of Economic Research, New York, which was issued as no. 42 of its Publications.
Includes bibliographical references and index.
ISBN 0-405-07574-X
1. Agriculture—United States. 2. Agriculture—Economic aspects—United States. I. Landsberg, Hans H., joint author. II. Title. III. Series. IV. Series: National Bureau of Economic Research. General series ; no. 42.
HD1761.B3 1975 338.1'0973 75-19693
75 MARC

Barger, Harold.
Distribution's place in the American economy since 1869 / by Harold Barger. — New York : Arno Press, 1976 [c1955]
xviii, 220 p. ; 24 cm. — (National Bureau of Economic Research publications in reprint)
Reprint of the ed. published by Princeton University Press, Princeton, which was issued as no. 58 of the General series of the National Bureau of Economic Research.
Bibliography: p. 198-215.
Includes index.
ISBN 0-405-07584-7
1. United States—Commerce—History. I. Title. II. Series. III. Series: National Bureau of Economic Research. General series ; 58.
[HF3021.B3 1976] 381'.0973 75-34957
75 MARC

Barger, Harold.
Foreign trade, by Harold Barger. London, V. Gollancz ltd., and the New Fabian research bureau [1936. Nendeln/Liechtenstein, Kraus Reprint, 1972]
39 p. (The New Fabian research bureau. [Publications] no. 30)
1. Gt. Brit.—Comm. 2. Socialism. 3. Currency question—Gt. Brit. I. Title. II. Series: Fabian Society, London. Research series, no. 30.
INS NUC73-125033

Barger, Harold.
Growth in developed nations. [New York, 1969]
143-148 p. tables. 28 cm. (Columbia University. European Institute. [Publications, no. 12)
Cover title.
Reprinted from the Review of economics and statistics, v. 51, no. 2, May 1969.
Bibliography: p. 147-148.
NNC NUC74-15734

Barger, Harold.
The mining industries, 1899–1939; a study of output, employment and productivity, by Harold Barger and Sam H. Schurr. New York, Arno Press, 1972 [c1944]
xxii, 452 p. illus. 24 cm. (Use and abuse of America's natural resources)
Original ed., which was issued as no. 43 of Publications of the National Bureau of Economic Research.
Includes bibliographical references.
1. Mining industry and finance—United States. 2. Mining engineering. I. Schurr, Sam H., joint author. II. Title. III. Series. IV. Series: National Bureau of Economic Research. General series, no. 43.
HD9506.U62B3 1972 338.2'0973 72-2833
ISBN 0-405-04502-6 MARC

Barger, Harold.
The mining industries, 1899-1939 : a study of output, employment, and productivity / by Harold Barger and Sam H. Schurr. — New York : Arno Press, 1975, c1944.
xxii, 447 p. : ill. ; 24 cm. — (National Bureau of Economic Research publications in reprint)
Reprint of the ed. published by the National Bureau of Economic Research, New York, which was issued as no. 43 of the Bureau's Publications.
Includes bibliographical references and index.
ISBN 0-405-07575-8
1. Mineral industries—United States. 2. Mining engineering. I. Schurr, Sam H., joint author. II. Title. III. Series. IV. Series: National Bureau of Economic Research. General series ; no. 43.
HD9506.U62B3 1975 338.2'0973 75-19694
75 MARC

Barger, Harold.
The transportation industries, 1889-1946 : a study of output, employment, and productivity / by Harold Barger. — New York : Arno Press, 1975, c1951.
xvi, 284 p. : ill. ; 24 cm. — (National Bureau of Economic Research publications in reprint)
Reprint of the ed. published by the National Bureau of Economic Research, New York, which was issued as no. 51 of the Bureau's Publications.
Includes bibliographical references and index.
ISBN 0-405-07573-1
1. Transportation—United States—History. I. Title. II. Series. III. Series: National Bureau of Economic Research. General series ; no. 51.
[HE203.B3 1975] 380.5'0973 75-19692
75 MARC

Barger, James.
Ernest Hemingway : American literary giant / by James Barger ; compiled with the assistance of the research staff of SamHar Press. — Charlotteville, N.Y. : SamHar Press, 1975.
28 p. ; 22 cm. — (Outstanding personalities ;no. 80)
Bibliography: p. 27-28.
1. Hemingway, Ernest, 1899-1961—Biography.
PS3515.E37Z5823 813'.5'2 75-33830
75 MARC

Barger, James.
James Joyce, modern Irish writer. D. Steve Rahmas, editor. Compiled with the assistance of the research staff of SamHar Press. Charlotteville, N.Y., SamHar Press, 1974.
30 p. 21 cm. (Outstanding personalities, no. 77)
Bibliography: p. 29-30.
1. Joyce, James, 1882-1941—Biography. I. SamHar Press. Research Staff. II. Title.
PR6019.O9Z52568 823'.9'12 74-14701
74 MARC

Barger, James D., joint author
see Young, Clara Gene. Introduction to medical science. 2d ed. Saint Louis, Mosby, 1973.

Barger, James D., joint author.
see Young, Clara Gene. Introduction to medical science. 3d ed. Saint Louis, Mosby, 1977.

Barger, James D., joint author.
see Young, Clara Gene. Learning medical terminology step by step. 3d ed. Saint Louis, C. V. Mosby Co., 1975.

Barger, James Willard, 1921-
A study of efforts toward uniformity in corporate financial statements. Ann Arbor, University Microfilms, 1963.
1 reel. 35 mm.
Thesis—University of Alabama.
1. Accounting. I. Title.
MsU NUC74-125810

Barger, Marlene
see United States. Bureau of Domestic Commerce. The acquisition and maintenance of medical equipment. [Washington] U.S. Domestic and International Business Administration, Bureau of Domestic Commerce, 1975.

Barger, Robert A
see Barger, Bob.

Barger, Robert Newton.
Amnesty: the history, the law, the people and the ethics. [Champaign, Ill., 1973]
13 p. 28 cm.
"End notes": p. 12-13.
1. Amnesty—U.S. 2. Vietnamese Conflict, 1961- —Conscientious objectors.
IU NUC74-125933

Barger, Robert Newton.
Amnesty: what does it really mean? [Champaign, Ill., Committee for a Healing Repatriation, 1974]
vii, 58 p. 22 cm. $1.00
Includes bibliographical references.
1. Amnesty—United States. 2. Vietnamese Conflict, 1961- —United States. I. Title.
DS557.A693B37 364.6 74-76366
MARC

Barger, Roland L
Effects of extractives on specific gravity of southwestern ponderosa pine. [Fort Collins, Colo.] 1971.
4 p. illus. (U.S. Rocky Mountain Forest and Range Experiment Station. U.S.D.A. Forest Service research note RM-205)
Bibliography: p. 4.
I. Title.
DNAL NUC73-32107

Barger, Roland L
Evaluating product potential in standing timber. By Roland L. Barger and Peter J. Ffolliott. Fort Collins, Colorado, Rocky Mountain Forest and Range Experiment Station, 1970.
20 p. illus. (U.S.D.A., Forest Ser. Res. Pap. RM-57)
MH-G NUC74-15733

Barger, Roland L
Physical characteristics and utilization of major woodland tree species in Arizona. Fort Collins, 1972.
80 p. illus. (U.S. Rocky Mountain Forest and Range Experiment Station. U.S.D.A. Forest Service research paper RM-83)
Bibliography: p. 50-55.
I. Title.
DNAL DHUD NUC73-32092

Barger, Thomas C
Arab States of the Persian Gulf / by Thomas C. Barger. — Newark : Center for the Study of Marine Policy, College of Marine Studies, University of Delaware, 1975.
93 p. : map ; 21 cm. — (Energy policies of the world)
Bibliography: p. 92-93.
$3.50
1. Petroleum industry and trade—Persian Gulf States. 2. Petroleum industry and trade—Arab countries. 3. Persian Gulf States—Politics and government. I. Title. II. Series.
HD9576.P47B37 333.8'2 75-13126
75 MARC

Barger, Thomas C
Oil and commerce in the Middle East. [Washington, 1969]
9 l. 27 cm.
Address presented at the Middle East Institute, Washington, D.C., January 1969.
Caption title.
1. Petroleum industry and trade—Near East. I. Title.
CSt-H NUC74-15732

Barger, Vernon D 1938-
Classical mechanics: a modern perspective [by] V. Barger [and] M. Olsson. New York, McGraw-Hill [1973]
xi, 305 p. illus. 24 cm. (McGraw-Hill series in fundamentals of physics) $11.95
1. Mechanics. I. Olsson, Martin, 1938- joint author. I. Title.
QA805.B287 531 72-5697
ISBN 0-07-003723-X MARC

Barger, Virginia A
Tombstones in St. Luke's Church cemetery, Isle of Wright County, Virginia. Newport News, Va., 1970.
54 p.
1. Churches—Virginia—Isle of Wright Co.—Genealogy—Sources. 2. Isle of Wright Co., Va.—Registers of births, etc. I. Title.
WHi NUC73-39365

Barger, William James.
The measurement of labor input: U.S. manufacturing industries, 1948-1966. [n.p.] 1972.
1 v.
Thesis—Harvard.
1. Labor productivity—United States.
MH NUC75-30862

Barges, John E
Photo cachet catalog, Fulton covers. -- 1st ed. -- Stewartsville, N.J. : First Day Covers Only, 1975.
[46] p. : ill.
1. Covers (Philately)--Catalogs. 2. Fulton (Robert) Stamp Co., Philadelphia. I. Finger, Marge. II. Title.
WHi NUC77-100407

Bargès, Louis.
Amis inconnus : impressions d'un prisonnier de guerre / Louis Barges. — Vienna : Panorama, [1947]
78 p. : 21 cm.
1. World War, 1939-1945—Personal narratives, French. 2. Bargès, Louis. 3. World War, 1939-1945—Prisoners and prisons, German. I. Title.
D811.B355 940.54'81'44 75-505770
75 MARC

Barghaus, Margot, 1943-
Versuchung und Verfuehrung im Werk Thomas Manns. Hamburg, 1971.
201 p.
Diss.—Hamburg.
1. Mann, Thomas, 1875-1955.
CSt NUC77-14555

Bargheer, Eduard, 1901-
Eduard Bargheer / Volker Detlef Heydorn ; mit e. Beitr. von Gretchen Wohlwill aus ihren Lebenserinnerungen. — Hamburg : Christians, [1976]
48, 86 p., [4] leaves of plates : chiefly ill. (some col.) ; 23 cm. — (Hamburger Künstler-Monographien des 20. [i.e. zwanzigsten] Jahrhunderts ; Bd. 5)
GFR77-A
Includes bibliographical references.
ISBN 3-7672-0459-2 : DM24.00
1. Bargheer, Eduard, 1901- 2. Painters—Germany, West—Biography. I. Heydorn, Volker Detlef. II. Wohlwill, Gretchen, 1878-1962. III. Series.
ND588.B1426H49 77-467352
77 MARC

Bargheer, Eduard, 1901-
Eduard Bargheer: Aquarelle. [Ausstellung] Galerie Welz Salzburg, 8. bis 30. September 1973. [Salzburg, Galerie Welz, 1973]
[48] p. illus. (part col.) 19 x 20 cm.
Foreword by Hans Platte.
I. Platte, Hans. II. Galerie Welz.
MH NUC75-21284

Bargheer, Eduard, 1901-
Eduard Bargheer : Werkverz. d. Druckgraphik 1930-bis 1974 / von Detlev Rosenbach ; [Fotografie, Erika Schmied]. — Hannover : Rosenbach, 1974.
[25] p., [88] leaves of plates : numerous ill. (some col.) ; 27 cm.
GFR 75-B3
DM60.00
1. Bargheer, Eduard, 1901- I. Rosenbach, Detlev.
NE654.B28R67 75-541660

Bargheer, Eduard, 1901-
Südliche Landschaft. [Stuttgart-Möhringen] Manus Presse, 1973.
[16] p. of col. illus. 41 cm. (Konzepte, 12) GDB***
Cover title.
1. Bargheer, Eduard, 1901- I. Title.
NC251.B32A57 73-333352

Bargheer, Friedrich W
Gebet und beten lernen: die theolog. anthropolog. Grundlagen u. d. lebensgeschichtl. Verarbeitung ihrer Krise/ Friedrich W. Bargheer. — Gütersloh: Gütersloher Verlagshaus Mohn, 1973.
250 p.; 23 cm. DM52.00 GFR 73-A
A revision of the author's thesis, Münster, 1970.
Bibliography: p. 237-250.
1. Prayer. I. Title.
BV210.2.B297 1973 73-363442
ISBN 3-579-04229-7

Bargheer, Friedrich W
Das Interesse des Jugendlichen und der Religionsunterricht. [Gütersloh] Gütersloher Verlagshaus Gerd Mohn [1972]
112 p. 23 cm. (Handbücherei für den Religionsunterricht, Heft 11)
Bibliography: p. 103-109.
1. Religious education. I. Title. II. Series.
NNG NUC73-32108

Bargheon, Jean.
Le bonheur d'être belle / Jean Bargheon. — Paris : A. Michel, c1977.
268 p. : ill. ; 25 cm. F***
Includes index.
ISBN 2-226-00475-0 : 39.00F
1. Beauty, Personal. 2. Women—Health and hygiene. I. Title.
RA778.B228 646.7 77-550620
77 MARC

Bargheon, Jean.
Le rôle du magnésium en pathologie humaine. 2. éd. Paris, Éditions Boissière [1973]
123 p. 24 cm. F***
Bibliography: p. 111-123.
1. Magnesium deficiency. 2. Magnesium metabolism. I. Title.
RC627.M3B37 1973 73-330893
MARC

Barghoorn, Adolf-Wilhelm.
Entwicklung und Stand der forst- und holzwirtschaftlichen akademischen Ausbildung und Forschung in Lateinamerika und Vorschläge zu deren künftiger Weiterentwicklung. (Development and actual state of professional education and research in forestry and the wood-based economy in Latin America and ideas and proposals concering their further development) (Análisis del desarrollo y de la situación actual de la preparación profesional y de la investigación en Latino-America, en los campos de la dasocracia y la economia basada en la madera e ideas y proposiciones relativas a la continuación de este-desarrollo)/ Adolf-Wilhelm Barghoorn. Hamburg, Wiedebusch [in Komm.] 1972.
v, 428 p.; 30 cm. (Mitteilungen der Bundesforschungsanstalt für Forst- und Holzwirtschaft, Reinbek bei Hamburg, Nr. 90)
GFR 73-A35
Summary and Table of contents in English and Spanish.
Bibliography: p. 339-350.
1. Forestry schools and education—Latin America. 2. Forestry research—Latin America. I. Title. II. Title: Development and actual state of professional education and research in forestry and the woodbased economy in Latin America. III. Series: Reinbek, Ger. Bundesforschungsanstalt für Forst- und Holzwirtschaft. Mitteilungen, Nr. 90.
SD1.R33 No. 90 634.9'08 s 74-306949
[SD263] [634.9'07'118]

Barghoorn, Elso S., joint author.
see Tiffney, Bruce H. The fossil record of the fungi. Cambridge, Mass., Harvard University, 1974.

Barghoorn, Frederick Charles, 1911-
Détente and the democratic movement in the USSR / Frederick C. Barghoorn. — New York : Free Press, c1976.
x, 229 p. ; 24 cm.
Includes bibliographical references and index.
ISBN 0-02-901850-1
1. Russia—Foreign relations—1953-1975. 2. Russia—Foreign relations—1975- 3. Russia—Politics and government—1953- 4. Dissenters—Russia. I. Title.
DK274.B28 327.47 76-4425
76 MARC

Barghoorn, Frederick Charles, 1911-
The general pattern of Soviet dissent. [New York, Research Institute of Communist Affairs, School of International Affairs, Columbia University] 1971.
14 p.
Prepared for Conference on Dissent in the Soviet Union, McMaster University, Hamilton, Ont., October 22 and 23, 1971.
1. Dissenters–Russia. 2. Russia–Pol. and Govt.–1953- I. Title.
InU NUC74-125842

Barghoorn, Frederick Charles, 1911-
Soviet Russian nationalism / Frederick C. Barghoorn. — Westport, Conn. : Greenwood Press, 1976, c1956.
ix, 330 p. ; 23 cm.
Reprint of the ed. published by the Oxford University Press, New York.
Includes bibliographical references and index.
ISBN 0-8371-8429-0
1. Nationalism—Russia. 2. Russia—Politics and government—1917- I. Title.
[DK268.3.B32 1976] 947.085 76-6861
76 MARC

Barghoorn, Steven F
New material of Vespertiliavus Schlosser (Mammalia, Chiroptera) and suggested relationships of emballonurid bats based on cranial morphology / Steven F. Barghoorn. — New York : American Museum of Natural History, 1977.
29 p. : ill. ; 26 cm. — (American Museum novitates ; no. 2618 ISSN 0003-0082)
Cover title.
Bibliography: p. 28-29.
$2.40
1. Vespertiliavus—Anatomy. 2. Emballonuridae—Anatomy. 3. Skull. 4. Mammals—Anatomy. I. Title: New material of Vespertiliavus Schlosser ... II. Series.
QL1.A436 no. 2618 500.9'08 s 77-151023
[QL737.C525] 77 MARC

Barghout, Saad Hassan, 1924-
Economic development and female participation in the labor force. [Minneapolis] 1970.
xiii, 385 l.
Thesis (Ph. D.)–University of Minnesota.
Bibliography: leaves 374-385.
Microfilm copy (positive) of typescript. Ann Arbor, Mich., University Microfilms, 1970. 1 reel. 35 mm.
1. Economic development. 2. Woman–Employment. 3. Labor supply. I. Title.
NIC NUC74-125809

Barghouti, Asem Nayef, 1935-
City planning in Syria-Palestine in Hellenistic and Roman times. [n.p.] 1974.
xxl, 466 l.
Thesis (Ph.D.)—University of Chicago.
1. Cities and towns—Planning—Palestine. 2. Cities and towns—Planning—Syria. 3. Cities and towns, Ancient. I. Title.
ICU NUC76-96135

Barghouti, Asem Nayef, 1935-
City planning in Syria-Palestine in Hellenistic and Roman times. [n.p.] 1974.
xxi, 446 l. ill.
Thesis--University of Chicago.
Microfilm of typescript. Chicago, University of Chicago Library, 1975. 1 reel. 35 mm.
1. Cities and towns--Planning--Syria. 2. Cities and towns--Planning--Palestine. I. Title.
OCH NUC77-99367

Barghouty, Azmi.
Die Entwicklungsprobleme Jordaniens. Wien, Notring, 1970.
222 p. diagrs., map. 21 cm. (Vienna. Hochschule für Welthandel. Dissertationen, 6)
Thesis–Hochschule für Welthandel in Wien.
1. Jordan–Economic conditions. 2. Jordan–Commerce. 3. Jordan–Economic policy. 4. Jordan–Social conditions. 5. Jordan–Population. I. Title. II. Series.
GU MdU NUC73-39281

al-Barghūthī, ʻAbd al-Laṭīf Maḥmūd.
(al-Tārīkh al-Lībī al-qadīm, min aqdam al-ʻuṣūr ḥattá al-fatḥ al-Islāmī)
التاريخ الليبي القديم ، من أقدم العصور حتى الفتح الاسلامي · تأليف عبد اللطيف محمود البرغوثي · [الطبعة 1. بنغازي ، 1971]
751 p. illus. (part col.) 25 cm. (منشورات الجامعة الليبية)
Includes bibliographies.
1. Libya—History. I. Title. II. Series: al-Jāmiʻah al-Lībīyah. Manshūrāt al-Jāmiʻah al-Lībīyah.
DT228.B37 73-206553

al-Barghūthī, ʻAbd al-Laṭīf Maḥmūd.
(Tārīkh Lībiyā al-Islāmī, min al-fatḥ al-Islāmī ḥattá bidāyat al-ʻaṣr al-ʻUthmānī)
تاريخ ليبيا الاسلامي ، من الفتح الاسلامي حتى بداية العصر العثماني / تأليف عبد اللطيف محمود البرغوثي · — [بنغازي] : الجامعة الليبية ، [1973]
699 p., [10] leaves of plates : ill. ; 25 cm. — (منشورات الجامعة الليبية)
Bibliography: p. 685-695.
Includes indexes.
1. Libya—History. I. Title. II. Series: al-Jāmiʻah al-Lībīyah. Manshūrāt al-Jāmiʻah al-Lībīyah.
DT229.B37 75-587421

al-Barghūthī, Murīd.
(al-Ṭūfān wa-iʻādat al-takwīn)
الطوفان واعادة التكوين [تأليف] مريد البرغوثي · بيروت ، دار العودة [1972]
95 p. 17 cm.
Poems.
I. Title.
PJ7816.A682T8 74-222261

Bargielski, Pat.
see Holl, Adelaide. Small Bear's name hunt. Champaign, Ill., Garrard Pub. Co., c1977.

Bargielski, Pat.
see Holl, Adelaide. Wake up, Small Bear. Champaign, Ill., Garrard Pub. Co., c1977.

Bargil, Marianne
see Chancengleichheit ... Wien: Dr.-Karl-Renner-Inst., 1974.

Bargioni, Giovanna, joint author
see Goby, Michelle. Florence. [Grenoble] Arthaud, 1972.

Barglăzan, Aurel
see Timisoara, Romania. Institutul Politehnic. Laboratorul de masini hidraulice. Timisoara, Rumania, 1964.

Barglow, Ray Charles.
Rationality in ethics and science. --[Berkeley : s.n.], 1975.
440 leaves.
Thesis (Ph.D.)--University of California.
Includes bibliographical references.
CU NUC77-99184

Bargman, Lyle Keith.
The role of the elementary school principal, an analysis of the literature and research since 1960. Lincoln, Neb., 1970.
[1], iv, 147 l. tables.
Thesis (Ed.D.)–University of Nebraska, 1970.
Bibliography: leaves [136]-147.
I. Title.
NbU NUC74-15729

Bargman, Robert D
Characterization of the activated sludge process, by Robert D. Bargman and Joseph Borgerding. Washington, D.C., U.S. Environmental Protection Agency [for sale by the Supt. of Docs., U.S. Government Printing Office] 1973.
63 p. 27 cm. (U.S. Environmental Protection Agency. Environmental protection technology series, no. 224)
I. Title. II. Series.
PSt NUC74-125932

Bargmann, Rolf.
Statistical distribution programs for a computer language, by Rolf E. Bargmann [and] Sakti P. Ghosh. Yorktown Heights, N.Y., IBM Watson Research Center, 1963.
56 l. (Research report, RC-1094)
"Supported in part by Air Force Research Contract AF19 (626)-10."
Photocopy of typescript.
1. Programming languages (Electronic computers) I. Ghosh, Sakti Pada, joint author. II. International Business Machines Corporation. Thomas J. Watson Research Center, Yorktown Heights, N.Y. III. Title.
ICU NUC73-9393

Bargmann, Theodore John, 1941-
An investigation of elementary school grade levels appropriate for teaching the metric system. Ann Arbor, Mich., University Microfilms, 1973.
1 reel. 35 mm.
Thesis—Northwestern University.
Collation of the original: 195 l.
1. Metric system—Study and teaching. I. Title.
ViBlbV NUC75-21301

Bargohain, Homen, comp.
বিংশ শতাব্দীৰ অসমীয়া সাহিত্য. সম্পাদক হোমেন বৰগোহাঞি. যোৰহাট, অসম সাহিত্য সভা [1967]
16, 196, 36, 51 p. illus., ports. 22 cm. Rs8
In Assamese.
1. Assamese literature—Addresses, essays, lectures. I. Title.
Title romanized: Biṃśa śatābdīra Asamīẏā sāhitya.
PK1560.5.B3 S A 68-9730
PL 480 : I-As-452

Bargohain, Homen.
(Hāladhīẏā carāẏe, bāo dhāna khāẏa)
হালধীয়া চৰায়ে বাও ধান খায়. [লিখক] হোমেন বৰগোহাঞি. গুৱাহাটী, ফ্রেণ্ড্‌চ বুক এজেন্সি [1973]
134 p. 22 cm. Rs5.00
In Assamese.
A novel.
I. Title.
PK1569.B265H3 73-907047
S A

Bargohain, Homen.
(Pitā, putra)
পিতা, পুত্ৰ / হোমেন বৰগোহাঞি. — কলিকতা : শ্ৰীভূমি পাবলিচিং কোম্পানী, 1975.
361 p. : 22 cm.
In Assamese.
A novel.
Rs15.00
I. Title.
PK1569.B265P5 75-906671
S A

Bargohain, Homen
see Asamīyā galpa saṅkalana. 1975-

Bargohain, Nirupama.
হৃদয় এটা নিৰ্জন দ্বীপ. [লিখিকা] নিৰুপমা বৰগোহাঞি. [গুৱাহাটী, গুৱাহাটী বুক ষ্টল, 1970]
80 p. 23 cm. Rs3.00
In Assamese.
A novel.
I. Title.
Title romanized: Hṛdaẏa eṭā nirjana dwīpa.
PK1569.B266H7 73-916306
S A

Bargohain, Nirupama.
(Kekṭācara phula)
কেক্‌টাচৰ ফুল. [লিখিকা] নিৰুপমা বৰগোহাঞি. গুৱাহাটী, ফ্রেণ্ড্‌চ বুক এজেন্সি [1973]
156 p. 22 cm. Rs5.00
In Assamese.
A novel.
I. Title.
PK1569.B266K4 73-907063

Bargon, Ernst.
Erläuterungen zur Bodenkarte von Hessen 1:25000, Blatt Nr. 5915, Wiesbaden. Mit Beiträgen von Willy Th. Stöhr und Heinrich Zimmermann. Wiesbaden, Hessisches Landesamt für Bodenforschung, 1967.
117 p. col. map (in pocket) 24 cm.
Includes bibliography.
1. Hesse. Maps. Topographic. I. Hesse. Landesamt für Bodenforschung. II. Title.
N NUC76-15781

Bargon, Ernst.
Erläuterungen zur Bodenkarte von Hessen 1:25000, Blatt nr. 6217, Zwingenberg. Mit einem Beitrag von Karl Asthalter. Wiesbaden, Hessisches Landesamt für Bodenforschung, 1969.
59 p. 21 cm.
Half title: Bodenkarte von Hessen.
Includes bibliography.
1. Hesse, Maps. Topographic. I. Hesse. Landesamt für Bodenforschung. II. Title. III. Title: Bodenkarte von Hessen.
N NUC74-4486

Bargon, Ernst
see Beiträge zur Bodenkunde ... Krefeld : Geolog. Landesamt Nordrhein-Westfalen, 1972.

Bargone, Charles
see Farrère, Claude, 1876-1957.

Bargoni, Augusto.
Lezioni di economia e finanza delle imprese assicuratrici. Torino, G. Giappichelli, 1973.
336 p. tables. 25 cm. (Corsi universitari) L5600 It 74-May
Includes bibliographical references.
1. Insurance—Italy. 2. Insurance—Italy—Finance. 3. Insurance companies—Italy. I. Title.
HG8628.B37 74-339816

Bargoni, Franco.
Corazzate ... Roma, Bizzarri, 1972–
v. illus., plates. 24 cm. (Orizzonte mare, 1– Navi italiane nella 2. guerra mondiale) L3000 (v. 1-2) It 73-May (v. 1-2)
Text by F. Bargoni and F. Gay.
CONTENTS: [1.] Classe conte di Cavour—[2.] Classe Caio Duilio.
1. Italy. Marina. 2. Armored vessels. I. Gay, Franco, joint author. II. Title.
VA543.B37 73-344564

Bargoni, María.
Kiu-Kiu [por] María Borgoni [sic. Traducción de Inés Matte Amunátegui. Madrid] Ediciones Paulinas [1960?]
95 p. illus. 19 cm. (Colección "universal")
On spine: M. Bargoni.
I. Title.
PZ73.B34 75-539364

Bargoot, Frederick George, 1945-
Visual pigments in solution: effect of preparation upon the intermediates of bleaching, by Frederick G. Bargoot. [Tallahassee] 1972.
xviii, 149 l.
Thesis (Ph. D.)—Florida State University.
Bibliography: leaves 141-148.
Vita.
1. Visual pigments. I. Title.
FTaSU NUC74-125920

Bargrave, John, 1610–1680.
Pope Alexander the Seventh and the College of Cardinals. With a catalogue of Dr. Bargrave's museum. Edited by James Craigie Robertson. [Westminster] Printed for the Camden Society, 1867. New York, AMS Press [1968]
xxviii, 144 p. 24 cm.
Original ed. issued as no. 92 of the Camden Society publications.
1. Alexander VII, Pope, 1599–1667. 2. Cardinals. 3. Bargrave, John, 1610–1680. I. Title. II. Series: Camden Society, London. Publications, no. 92.
BX4663.B37 1968 262'.13'0922 [B] 78-160001
MARC

Bargrave, John, 1610-1680.
Pope Alexander the seventh and the College of Cardinals. With a catalogue of Dr. Bargrave's museum. Edited by James Craigie Robertson. Reprinted with the permission of the Royal Historical Society. New York, Johnson Reprint Corp. [1968]
xxviii, 144 p. port. 24 cm. (Camden Society. Publications, no. 92)
Original printed for the Camden Society, 1867.
Bibliographical footnotes.
1. Alexander VII, Pope, 1599-1667. 2. Cardinals. I. Robertson, James Craigie, 1813-1882, ed. II. Series.
MB NUC73-17092

Bargum, Johan, 1943–
Tre skådespel / Johan Bargum. — [Helsingfors] : Söderström & Co., [1974]
212 p. ; 21 cm. Fi
CONTENTS: Som smort.—Bygga bastu.—Virke och verkan.
ISBN 951-52-0221-3 : Fmk34.70
I. Title.
PT9876.12.A7T66 75-569317

Bărġüshad, Jalal.
(Dărilmămish salkhym!ar)
Дәрилмәмиш салҹымлар / Чалал Бәркүшад. — [Бакы : Кәнчлик, 1973]
129 p. : port. ; 20 cm. USSR 74-12938
Short stories.
0.22rub
I. Title.
PL314.B34D3 74-237254

Barha Berrios, Gover.
La vicia villosa, el mejor forraje. La Paz, Ministerio de Agricultura, División de Investigación, 1961.
folder. 22 cm.
1. Vetch. I. Title.
TxU NUC75-66306

Barhadbeshabbā 'Arbāyā.
Cause de la fondation des écoles [par] Mar Barhadbšabba 'Arbaya, évêque de Halwan (VIe siecle) Texte syriaque publié et traduit par Addaï Scher. Turnhout, Belgique, Editions Brepols, 1971.
[319]-404 p. 28 cm. (Patrologia Orientalis, t. 4, fasc. 4, no. 18)
Syriac text with French translation on each page.
1. Religious thought—Ancient period. 2. Apologetic—Early church. I. Scher, Addai Ibrahin, Abp., 1867-1916, ed. II. Title.
NIC NUC75-37815

Barham, Fisher.
The creation of a cathedral : the story of St Mary's, Truro / [illustrations selected and text written] by Fisher Barham. — Falmouth : Glasney Press, 1976.
88 p. : chiefly ill. (some col.), plan, ports. ; 26 cm. GB76-28646
Plan and ill. on lining papers.
ISBN 0-9502825-2-9 : £3.95
1. Truro Cathedral. I. Title.
NA5471.T738B37 942.3'78 76-381807
76 MARC

Barham, Francis Frank Earl, 1937-
The educational ombudsman; a study of the ombudsman in American public schools, by Frank E. Barham. [Charlottesville, Va.] 1973.
ix, 250 l. forms. 29 cm.
Thesis (Ed. D.)—University of Virginia.
Bibliography: leaves 204-217.
1. Ombudsman. 2. Public schools—United States. 3. School management and organization. I. Title.
ViU NUC75-21299

Barham, Francis Frank Earl, 1937-
The educational ombudsman: a study of the ombudsman in American public schools, Frank E. Barham. [Charlottesville] 1973.
xiv, 250 p. illus.
Thesis (Ed. D.)—University of Virginia.
Microfilm edition (1 reel) Positive; filmed by University Microfilms.
Bibliography: p. 204-217.
1. Public schools—United States. 2. Ombudsman—United States. I. Title.
OOxM NUC74-125931

Barham, Henry, 1670?–1726.
Hortus americanus: containing an account of the trees, shrubs, and other vegetable productions, of South-America and the West-India islands, and particularly of the island of Jamaica; interspersed with many curious and useful observations, respecting their uses in medicine, diet, and mechanics, by the late Dr. Henry Barham. To which are added, a Linnaean index, &c, &c, &c. Kingston, Jamaica, A. Aikman, printer, 1794.
7, 212, [36] p. 22½ cm.
1. Botany—Jamaica. 2. Botany—South America. I. Title.
QK229.B37 1794 A 26-237

Barham, Henry Dudley, 1854- tr.
see Tales of Nasr-ed-Din Khoja. London, Nisbet [1923]

Barham, Jerry N
Anatomical kinesiology; a programmed text [by] Jerry N. Barham [and] William L. Thomas. London, Macmillan [1969]
148 p. illus.
1. Extremities (Anatomy). 2. Muscles. I. Thomas, William Leroy, 1920- II. Title.
NbU NUC77-13810

Barham, Jerry N
Structural kinesiology [by] Jerry N. Barham [and] Edna P. Wooten. New York, Macmillan [1973]
viii, 376 p. illus. 28 cm.
Bibliography: p. [371]-372.
1. Human mechanics. I. Wooten, Edna P., joint author. II. Title.
QP301.B33 612'.76 72-80072
MARC

Barham, Jerry N., joint author.
see Krause, Jerome V. The mechanical foundations of human motion ... Saint Louis, Mosby, 1975.

Barham, L Fisher.
Cornwalls electric tramcars: the history of the Camborne and Redruth system, by L. Fisher Barham. Penryn, Glasney Press, [1973].
84 p. illus. (some col.), ports. 26 cm. £2.50 GB 73-18562
Bibliography: p. 84.
1. Street-railroads—Camborne, Eng. 2. Street-railroads—Redruth, Eng. 3. Electric railroads—Cars. I. Title.
TF764.C33B37 388.4'6'094237 74-167688
ISBN 0-9502825-0-2 MARC

Barham, Patte, joint author.
see Rasputina, Mariia Grigor'evna. Rasputin, the man behind the myth, a personal memoir. Englewood Cliffs, N.J., Prentice-Hall, c1977.

Barham, R M
Orienting responses in a selection of cognitive tasks / R.M. Barham and F.J. Boersma. -- Rotterdam : Rotterdam University Press, 1975.
xiii, 154 p. : ill. ; 23 cm. -- (Studies in psycho-physiology ; 1)
Bibliography: p. 133-138.
ISBN 90-237-4122-6.
1. Orientation. 2. Reflexes. I. Boersma, F.J. II. Title. III. Series.
CaBVaU NUC77-100332

Barham, Rex.
The cancer of the earth. Cambridge, Cambridge Aids to Learning (Publishing) Ltd, 1973.
viii, 56 p. illus., maps. 21 cm. B 73-08082
Bibliography: p. 54.
1. Population. 2. Food supply. I. Title.
HB875.B3 301.3'2 73-165624
ISBN 0-902056-03-4 MARC

Barham, Richard Harris Dalton, 1815-1886.
see Hook, Theodore Edward, 1788-1841. The life and remains of Theodore Edward Hook. New York, AMS Press, 1975.

Barham, Tony.
Witchcraft in the Thames Valley; traditional witchcraft tales of the Thames Valley. Bourne End, Spurbooks, 1973.
63 p. illus. 19 cm. £0.60 GB 74-12663
1. Folk-lore—England—Thames Valley. 2. Witchcraft—Thames Valley. 3. Tales, English—Thames Valley. I. Title.
GR142.T48B37 133.4'09422 74-179903
ISBN 0-902875-37-X MARC

Barhebraeus, Johannes Gregorius Abulpharagius
see Bar Hebraeus, 1226-1286.

Barhnabas Gandzakets'i, Vardapet.
(Hajordowt'iwn patriark'ats'n Erowsaghemi)
Յաջորդութիւն պատրիարքացն Երուսաղեմի․ ի Յակոբայ Առաքելոյ Տեառնեղբօրէ մինչեւ ցմերս ժամանակ։ Կ. Պոլիս, Տպագրութիւն Յովհաննու Գավաֆեան, 1872։
106 p. 24 cm.
«Առաքելական յաջորդութիւն Հայաստանեայց Ս. Եկեղեցւոյ, սկսեալ յառաքելոց անտի Թադէոսէ եւ Բարթուղիմէոսէ մինչ ցՍուրբ Գրիգոր Լուսաւորիչ»։ p. [79]-96.
Includes bibliographical references.
1. Jerusalem (Patriarchate, Orthodox) 2. Armenian Church. Erowsaghēmi Hayots' Patriark'owt'iwn. 3. Armenian Church. Hayrapetowt'iwn Amenayn Hayots'. 4. Armenian Church—History. I. Title.
BX440.B37 73-215228

Bārī.
کمپنی کی حکومت؛ تاریخ. ⌐مصنف¬ باری. ⌐4. ایڈیشن¬ لاهور، نیا اداره ⌐1969¬
421 p. 23 cm. Rs15.00
In Urdu.
Includes bibliographical references.

1. India—History—British occupation, 1765–1947. 2. East India Company (English) I. Title.
Title romanized: Kampanī kī ḥukūmat.
DS465.B36 1969 71–931058

al-Barʻī, Aḥmad Ḥasan
see
al-Buraʻī, Aḥmad Ḥasan.

Bari, Fazlul.
Causes and effects of late operations of pumps and tubewells in Comilla Kotwali Thana, 1973-74 / Fazlul Bari. — Comilla : Bangladesh Academy for Rural Development, 1975.
12 p. ; 26 cm.
Tk3.00
1. Irrigation—Bangladesh—Comilla (Thana) I. Title.
HD1741.B35B37 333.9'13'0954923 75-906850
76 MARC

Bari, Fazlul.
An innovator in a traditional environment / Fazlul Bari. — 1st ed. — Comilla : Bangladesh Academy for Rural Development, 1974.
ii, 45 ⌐9¬ p. ; 24 cm.
Tk5.00
1. Agricultural innovations—Bangladesh—Joypur—Case studies. I. Title.
⌐S494.5.I5B37¬ 301.24'3 75-906764
76 MARC

Bari, Károly, 1952-
Elfelejtett tüzek. Budapest, Szépirodalmi Könyvkiadó, 1973.
43 p. ill.
I. Title.
CaOTP NUC77-14556

Bari, Lynn, 1917-
see [Second honeymoon] [Sound recording] American Forces Radio and Television Service RU 45-4, 3B [1974]

Bari, M A 1910–
বিষের পাহাড়. ⌐লেখক¬ এম. এ. বারি. ⌐ঢাকা, আলোছায়া¬ 1373–77 ⌐1966–70¬
4 v. port. 23 cm. (His ক্রন্দসী, 3) Rs21.00
Vol. 4 published by আহ্‌মেদ ব্রাদার্স.
In Bengali.
A novel.
Sequel to বাঁকা পথ (romanized: Bāṅkā patha)

I. Title.
Title romanized: Bishera pāhāṛa.
PK1718.B352B5 S A 68–16840
PL 480: EP-B-1269

Bārī, Nājamula, ed.
see Nināda. [1378 i. e. 1972]

Bari, Ruth A., 1917- ed.
see Capital Conference on Graph Theory and Combinatorics, George Washington University, 1973. Graphs and combinatorics; proceedings. Berlin, New York, Springer-Verlag, 1974.

Bari, S A 1924-
Universal foundation of Gandhi's religion. New Delhi, Sampradayikta Virodhi Committee [n.d.]
16 p.
Includes bibliographical references.
1. Gandhi, Mohandas Karamchand, 1869-1948. I. Title.
MoSW NUC73-124577

Bari, Shamsul
see Nicholas, Marta R Bangladesh: the birth of a nation... Madras, M. Seshachalam, 1972.

Bari (City)
Diamo le scuole ai nostri figli : estratto dal verbale delle sedute consiliari del 17-3, 1-4, 9-4 e 11-4 1960 / Città di Bari. — Bari : La Città, ⌐1960?¬
89 p. ; 25 cm.
1. Education—Italy—Bari (City). I. Title.
LA799.B37B37 1960 76-512203

Bari (City). Biblioteca nazionale
see
Biblioteca nazionale di Bari.

Bari (City). Scuola media Amedeo D'Aosta
see
Scuola media Amedeo D'Aosta.

Bari (City). Stazione agraria sperimentale
see Carrante, Vincenzo. Esperienze sui pascoli della murgia di Bari. Bari [1961]

Bari (City). Stazione agraria sperimentale
see Del Gaudio, Salvatore. Disciplina della produzione dell'uva da tavola per la conquista del mercati esteri. Bari, 1963 [i.e. 1952]

Bari (City). Università
see International Conference on Mechanisms in Bioenergetics, Pugnochuiso, Italy, 1972. Mechanisms in bioenergetics; proceedings. New York, Academic Press, 1973.

Bari (City). Università
see Simposio sulla magnetofluidodinamica, Università di Bari, 1961. Atti. Roma, Edizioni Cremonese, 1962.

Bari (City). Università. Facoltà di economia e commercio
see Campobasso, Gian Franco. Coobbligazione cambiaria e solidarietà disuguale. Napoli, Jovene, 1974.

Bari (City). Università. Facoltà di giurisprudenza.
see Les Clauses facultatives de la Convention européenne des droits de l'homme ... Bari, Edizioni Levante, 1974.

Bari (City). Università. Facoltà di medicina e chirurgia. Istituto di zoologia
see
Bari (City). Università. Istituto di zoologia.

Bari (City). Università. Istituto di geologia applicata e geotecnica
see Geologia applicata e idrogeologia. [Bari]

Bari (City). Università. Istituto di geologia e paleontologia
see Studi geologici e morfologici sulla regione lucana. Bari, Adriatica.

Bari (City). Università. Istituto di letteratura cristiana antica
see Puglia paleocristiana. Bari, Adriatica, 1970-

Bari (City). Università. Istituto di meccanica agraria
see Giornata della meccanica agraria, 18th, Bari, 1973. Atti della XVIII [i.e. diciottesima] Giornata della meccanica agraria, Bari, 11 dicembre 1973... Bari: A cura dell'Istituto di meccanica agraria dell'Università degli studi di Bari [1974]

Bari (City). Università. Istituto di zoologia
see Simposio nazionale sulla conservazione della natura, 1st, Bari, 1971. Atti del I Simposio nazionale sulla conservazione della natura. Bari, Cacucci, 1972.

Bari (Province)
Alle sorgenti del romanico Puglia XI secolo : Bari, Pinacoteca provinviale, giugno-dicembre 1975 : ⌐mostra / promossa e realizzata dalla Amministrazione provinciale di Bari¬ ; catalogo a cura di Pina Belli D'Elia ; schede di Clara Bargellini ... ⌐et al.¬ ; contributi di Corrado Bucci ... ⌐et al.¬ ; sintesi storica di Giosuè Musca. — Bari : Amministrazione provinciale, ⌐1975¬
343 p., ⌐7¬ leaves of plates : ill. (some col.) ; 28 cm. It 28–Nov
On spine: Puglia XI secolo.
Bibliography: p. 331–337.
Includes indexes.
1. Art—Puglia, Italy—Exhibitions. 2. Art, Romanesque—Puglia, Italy—Exhibitions. I. Belli D'Elia, Pina. II. Bari (Province). Pinacoteca provinciale. III. Title. IV. Title: Puglia XI ⌐i. e. undicesimo¬ secolo.
N6919.P84B37 1975 75–404146
Library of Congress *75

Bari (Province).
La provincia di Bari, 1960–64. ⌐Bari, 1964¬
281 p. illus. 31 cm.
1. Bari (Province)—Social policy. 2. Bari (Province)—Economic policy. 3. Bari (Province)—Politics and government. I. Title.
HN488.B37A5 74–205300

Bari (Province). Camera di commercio, industria e agricoltura.
Piano generale delle opere e della utilizzazione del porto di Bari; relazione della Commissione camerale. Bari, Grafiche Cressati ⌐1963?¬
40 p. maps. 25 cm.
1. Bari—Harbor. I. Title.
HE558.B32B37 1963 74–234494

Bari (Province). Ente provinciale per il turismo
see Aspetti dell'informale. [Bari, 1971]

Bari (Province). Pinacoteca provinciale.
Bari, Pinacoteca provinciale. ⌐A cura di¬ Pina Belli d'Elia. Bologna, Calderini, 1972.
viii, 65 p. illus. 27 cm. (Musei d'Italia. Meraviglie d'Italia, 4)
L2500 It 73–Feb
Bibliography: p. 64–65.
1. Bari (Province). Pinacoteca provinciale. I. Belli D'Elia, Pina.
N2515.4.A52 73–324370

Bari (Province). Pinacoteca provinciale
see Aspetti dell'informale. [Bari, 1971]

Bari (Province). Pinacoteca provinciale
see Bari (Province) Alle sorgenti del romanico Puglia XI secolo ... Bari: Amministrazione provinciale [1975]

Baria, Dorab N
Evaluation of gasification and liquefaction processes using North Dakota lignite / by Dorab N. Baria. — Grand Forks : Engineering Experiment Station, University of North Dakota, 1975.
ix, 130 p. : ill. ; 28 cm.
Includes bibliographical references.
1. Coal-gasification—North Dakota. 2. Coal liquefaction—North Dakota. 3. Lignite—North Dakota. I. Title.
TP343.B32 665'.772 76-621045
76 MARC

Baria, Dorab N
A survey of trace elements in North Dakota lignite and effluent streams from combustion and gasification facilities / by Dorab N. Baria. — Grand Forks : Engineering Experiment Station, University of North Dakota, 1975.
vii, 64 p. : map ; 28 cm.
Includes bibliographical references.
1. Pollution—North Dakota. 2. Lignite—North Dakota—Analysis. 3. Coal gasification—North Dakota. 4. Electric power-plants—North Dakota. 5. Trace elements. I. North Dakota. State University of Agriculture and Applied Science, Fargo. Engineering Experiment Station. II. Title.
TD181.N9B37 363 76-621026
76 MARC

Baribeau, Colette.
"Harry Dickson": une combinatoire narrative. Montreal, 1971.
89 l. 29 cm.
Thesis—McGill University.
Bibliography: leaves 84-88.
1. Ray, Jean. Harry Dickson. I. Title.
CaQMM NUC73-32109

Barić, Branko.
Osnove investicione izgradnje na Jugoslovenskim železnicama. Beograd, Zavod za novinsko-izdavačku i propagandnu delatnost JŽ, 1971.
154, ⌐2⌐ p. with diagrs. and illus. 24 cm. Yu 71-4372
1. Railroads—Yugoslavia—Finance. I. Title.
HE3243.B37 72-979980

Barić, Leo, ed.
see Behavioural sciences in health and disease. Geneva, International Journal of Health Education, 1972.

Barich, Dewey
see Michigan week county chairman's handbook. Lansing, 1969.

Barichard, Paulette.
Le temps d'une chanson / Paulette Barichard. — Sainte-Geneviève-des-Bois : Maison rhodanienne de poésie, ⌐1976⌐
35 p. ; 21 cm. F***
Poems.
I. Title.
PQ2662.A6837T4 841'.9'14 76-468616
76 MARC

Baricolo, Taína Dogo
see Dogo Baricolo, Taína.

Baridon, Michel.
Edward Gibbon et le mythe de Rome : histoire et idéologie au siècle des lumières / Michel Baridon. — Paris : H. Champion, 1977.
iv, 940 p. ; 22 cm. F***
Originally presented as the author's thesis.
Bibliography: p. 843-884.
Includes index.
120F
1. Gibbon, Edward, 1737-1794. 2. England—Intellectual life—18th century. 3. Enlightenment. 4. Rome—Historiography. I. Title.
DG206.G5B37 1977 77-477562
77 MARC

Baridon, Philip C
Addiction, crime, and social policy / Philip C. Baridon. — Lexington, Mass. : Lexington Books, c1976.
xxii, 126 p. : ill. ; 24 cm.
Bibliography: p. 115-122.
Includes index.
ISBN 0-669-00342-5
1. Drug abuse and crime. I. Title.
HV5801.B34 364.2'54 75-32221
75 MARC

Baridon, Silvio F.
see Notes et documents sur l'actualité française... ⌐Milano⌐ La Goliardica ⌐1968⌐

Barié, Manfred, 1944–
Das Vermögen als Gegenstand des Gleichheitssatzes und als geschütztes Rechtsgut der Europäischen Menschenrechtskonvention / vorgelegt von Manfred Barié. — ⌐s. l. : s. n.⌐, 1974.
146 p. ; 21 cm. GFR***
Thesis—Heidelberg.
Vita.
Bibliography: p. 134–146.
1. Right of property—Europe. 2. Equality before the law—Europe 3. Right of property—Germany, West. 4. Equality before the law—Germany, West. I. Title: Das Vermögen als Gegenstand des Gleichheitssatzes ...
75–545534

Barié, Ottavio.
Appunti di storia moderna e contemporanea. Dalle lezioni del ch.mo prof. O. Bariè. A cura di E. Bariè. (Pro munuscripto). Milano, C. E. L. U. C., 1970–
v. 21½ cm. It 71-Sept (v. 1)
Fasc. 2-3, 5-6 have title: Appunti di storia delle relazioni e delle istituzioni internazionali; fasc. 4 has title: Appunti di storia delle relazioni e istituzioni internazionali.
1. History, Modern—Addresses, essays, lectures. I. Title. II. Title: Appunti di storia delle relazioni e delle istituzioni internazionali.
D299.B27 909.8 74–339469

Barié, Ottavio.
L'Inghilterra e il problema italiano nel 1848–1849; dalle rivoluzioni alla seconda restaurazione. Milano, A. Giuffrè, 1965.
viii, 298 p. 25 cm. (Istituto di studi storico-politici. Università di Roma. Facoltà di scienze politiche. ⌐Pubblicazioni⌐ 13)
Bibliography: p. ⌐vii⌐–viii.
1. Great Britain—Foreign relations—Italy. 2. Italy—Foreign relations—Great Britain. I. Title. II. Series: Rome (City). Università. Istituto di studi storico-politici. Pubblicazioni, 13.
DA47.9.I 8B3 74–234644

Barié, Ottavio.
L'Italia, nascita di una nazione / Ottavio Barié. — Milano : Celuc, ⌐1974⌐
255 p. ; 20 cm. — (Ricerche ; nuova ser., 4) It 75–Jan
Bibliography: p. 231–251.
L3500
1. Italy—History. I. Title.
DG467.B28 945 75–555552

Barié, Ottavio.
Luigi Albertini. Con 26 tavole fuori testo. Torino, Unione tipografico-editrice torinese, 1972.
x, 569 p. 25 plates. 22½ cm. (La Vita sociale della nuova Italia, v. 21) L7000 It 72–July
Bibliography: p. ⌐537⌐–559.
1. Albertini, Luigi, 1871–1941.
PN5246.A7B3 72–360866

Barié, Ottavio.
Problemi storici della civiltà europea. Milano, Marzorati, 1972.
295 p. 19½ cm. (Clio) L2500 It 72–Dec
Bibliography: p. 277–289.
1. Europe—History. I. Title. II. Series.
D102.B3 73–300392

Barié, Paul.
Die mores maiorum in einer vaterlosen Gesellschaft. Ideologiekrit. Aspekte literar. Texte, aufgezeigt am Beisp. d. altsprachl. Unterrichts. Frankfurt a. M., Berlin ⌐West⌐, München, Diesterweg (1973).
128 p. 21 cm. DM14.80 GDR 73–A51
Includes bibliographical references.
1. Classical philology—Study and teaching—Germany. I. Title.
PA78.G4B3 74–315737
ISBN 3-425-04383-8

Barieau, Robert E., joint author
see Dalton, Beverly J Vapor-liquid equilibria data for the helium-nitrogen system... ⌐Washington⌐ U.S. Dept. of the Interior, Bureau of Mines ⌐1971⌐

Barieau, William G
The shooting of Sheriff Thomas Logan by Walter Barieau in Manhattan, Nevada, on April 6, 1906. [n.p.] 1971.
18 l. ports. 28 cm.
"A chapter taken from a book about the Barieau family."
1. Barieau, William Amphiloque, 1869–1953. 2. Logan, Thomas W. 3. Manhattan, Nev.—Hist. I. Title.
NvU NUC73-32106

Bariete
see Shimmura Takeshi Kyōju taikan kinen ron shū. 45(1970)

Bariety, Jacques.
Les relations franco-allemandes après la Première-Guerre mondiale : 10 novembre 1918-10 janvier 1925 : de l'exécution à la négociation / Jacques Bariety ; préf. de Jacques Droz. — Paris : Éditions Pedone, 1977.
xix, 797 p. : ill. ; 24 cm. — (Publications de la Sorbonne) (Série internationale ; 8) F***
Originally presented as the author's thesis, Panthéon-Sorbonne, 1975.
Includes bibliographical references and index.
ISBN 2-233-00034-X
1. France—Relations (general) with Germany. 2. Germany—Relations (general) with France. 3. France—Foreign relations—1914-1940. 4. France—Economic conditions—1918-1945. 5. European War, 1914-1918—Reparations. 6. Allied Powers (1919-) Reparation Commission. I. Title. II. Series: Université de Paris I : Panthéon-Sorbonne. Série internationale ; 8.
DC59.8.G3B423 1977 940.3'14 77-551411
77 MARC

Bariev, Nazim Vafinovich.
⌐Élektrooborudovanie ėkskavatora tipa E–2503⌐
Электрооборудование экскаватора типа Э–2503. Москва, "Энергия," 1972.
105 p. with diagrs. 20 cm. (Библиотека электромонтера, вып. 356) 0.22rub USSR 72–VKP
At head of title: Н. В. Бариев.
Bibliography: p. ⌐105⌐
1. Excavating machinery—Electric equipment. I. Title. II. Series: Biblioteka ėlektromontera, vyp. 356.
TK7.B5 vyp. 356 72–365194
[TA735]

Bariev, Nazim Vafinovich.
(Élektroprivod odnokovshovykh ėkskavatorov ĖKG–4 i ĖKG–4, 6)
Электропривод одноковшовых экскаваторов ЭКГ–4 и ЭКГ–4, 6 / Н. В. Бариев. — Изд. 3., перер. — Москва : Энергия, 1975.
160, ⌐1⌐ p. : ill. ; 20 cm. — (Библиотека электромонтера ; вып. 423) USSR***
Bibliography: p. ⌐3⌐ of cover.
0.32rub
1. Excavating machinery—Electric driving. I. Title. II. Series: Biblioteka ėlektromontera ; vyp. 423.
TK7.B5 vyp. 423 76–506536
[TA735]

Bariev, Nazim Vafinovich.
(Tiristornyĭ privod drag)
Тиристорный привод драг / Н. В. Бариев. — Москва : Недра, 1975.
78 p. : ill. ; 20 cm. — (Библиотека электрослесаря горных предприятий). USSR 75
0.11rub
1. Dredges—Electric driving. 2. Thyristors. I. Title.
TK4059.D73B37 76–524644

Barigazzi, Adelmo, comp.
Antologia virgiliana e oraziana. A cura di Adelmo Barigazzi e Angelo Casanova. Torino, Marietti, 1972.
461 p. 20 cm. (Collana di classici latini) L2500 It 73–Mar
Latin, with introductions and notes in Italian.
Includes bibliographies.
1. Latin literature (Selections: Extracts, etc.) 2. Latin literature—Translations into Italian. 3. Italian literature—Translations from Latin. I. Casanova, Angelo, joint comp. II. Vergilius Maro, Publius. III. Horatius Flaccus, Quintus. IV. Title.
PA6116.B3 74–328103

Barigazzi, Adelmo.
Catullo. Poeti elegiaci. Ovidio. Cesare. Antologia per il terzo anno del liceo scientifico ⌐di⌐ Adelmo Barigazzi ⌐e⌐ Benedetto Brugioni ⌐2. ed. Torino⌐ Società Editrice Internazionale ⌐1971⌐
447 p. 22 cm.
Texts in Latin.
1. Latin literature—Collections. I. Brugioni, Benedetto.
CtY NUC75-31494

Bariha, Gouranga, 1946–
(Sāgara Taraṅga)
ସାଗର ତରଙ୍ଗ. ଲେଖକ ଗୌରାଙ୍ଗ ବରିହା. ⌐ସମ୍ବଲପୁର, ମୁଦ୍ରଣ: ନ୍ୟାସନାଲ ପ୍ରିଣ୍ଟର୍ସ, 1971?⌐
81 p. 19 cm. Rs1.25
In Oriya.
A novel.

I. Title.

PK2579.B287S2 72–905171

Barik, Henri C
Bilingual education project: evaluation of the 1971-72 and 1972-73 French immersion program in Grades 8 and 9, Peel County Board of Education ⌐by⌐ Henri C. Barik & Merrill Swain. ⌐Toronto⌐ Ontario Institute for Studies in Education, 1974.
41 l.
1. Education, Bilingual—Peel County, Ont. I. Swain, Merill, joint author. II. Title.
CaOTY NUC75-21278

Barik, M A
ঝড়ে ভাংগা নীড়; সামাজিক নাটক. ⌐নাট্যকার⌐ এম. এ. বারিক. ⌐ঝা কাঠি, মন্‌জুরা বেগম; প্রাপ্তিস্থান: কহিনুর লাইব্রেরী, চট্টগ্রাম, 1968⌐
150 p. 19 cm. 2.00
In Bengali.

I. Title.
Title romanized: Jhaṛe bhāṃgā nīṛa.

PK1730.13.A685J5 70–930397

Baril, Denis.
Techniques de l'expression écrite et orale / Denis Baril et Jean Guillet. — 3. éd. / avec le concours de Sully Bernadie ... ⌐et al.⌐ ; avant-propos de Michel Dabène. — Paris : Sirey, 1975.
2 v. ; 27 cm. — (Uni-tech) F***
Includes bibliographical references and indexes.
Vol. 2: 2. éd.
ISBN 2-248-00260-2 : 34.00F (v. 1)
1. French language—Composition and exercises. 2. Oral communication. I. Guillet, Jean, joint author. II. Title.
PC2420.B3 1975 808'.0441 75-520640
76⌐r77⌐rev MARC

Baril, Marcel. Porte de bronze. 1974.
in Baril, Marcel. Rose-Fruide. Suivi de Porte de bronze. Marseille (118, la Grande Bastide Cazaulx) G.V., 1974.

Baril, Marcel.
Rose-Fruide. Suivi de Porte de bronze / Marcel Baril ; ₍publié par₎ G. V. ₍Groupe Voix₎. — Marseille (118, la Grande Bastide Cazaulx) : G.V., 1974.
63 p. ; 17 cm. F74-1/482
Poems.
8.00F
I. Baril, Marcel. Porte de bronze. 1974. II. Title.
PQ2662.A684R6 841'.9'14 75-504528
75 MARC

Barilari, André.
Organisation constitutionnelle et administrative de la France; enseignement général "B" ₍par₎ Barilari ₍et₎ Enjaume. ₍Paris, Ministère de l'économie et des finances, Centre de formation professionnelle et de perfectionnement₎ 1971.
152 p. illus. 27 cm. F***
1. France—Politics and government—1958– I. Enjaume, Michel, joint author. II. Title.
JN2594.2.B35 342'.44 74-177715
MARC

Barile, Angelo.
see Lagorio, Gina. Angelo Barile e la poesia dell'intima trasparenza ... Capua : Centro d'arte e di cultura L'airone, [1973]

Barile, Dolores P
Teaching vocational agriculture in the Philippines. Edited by Dolores P. Barile, Harold R. Cushman [and] Severino R. Santos. College, Laguna, Philippines, UPCA Textbook Board, 1973.
vii, 302 p. illus. 23 cm.
NIC NUC77-13988

Barile, George Conrad, 1948-
The photochemistry of 4-trichloromethyl-2, 5-cyclohexadienones : an interesting model system / George C. Barile. --[s.l. : s.n], 197 1975.
208 p. : ill. with charts.
Thesis (Ph.D.)--New York University.
I.Title.
NNU NUC77-99178

Barile, Giuseppe.
Diritto internazionale e diritto interno, rapporti fra sistemi omogenei ed eterogenei di norme giuridiche. Milano, Giuffrè, 1964.
140 p.
"Estratto dalla Rivista di Diritto Internazionale fasc. 4, 1956 e fasc. 1, 1957."
1. International and municipal law. I. Title.
CSt-Law NUC75-35125

Barile, Giuseppe.
Lezioni di diritto internazionale privato / Giuseppe Barile. — Padova : CEDAM, 1975.
xiii, 181 p. ; 25 cm. It 75-Sept
L4000
1. Conflict of laws. I. Title.
75-538812

Barile, John George, 1944-
A probabilistic model of water storage for reservoirs in series. [n.p., 1973?]
135 l. illus.
I. Title.
ViBlbV NUC74-125919

Barile, Paolo.
Istituzioni di diritto pubblico / Paolo Barile. — 2. ed. — Padova : CEDAM, 1975.
xxiv, 507 p. ; 25 cm. It 75-May
Includes index.
L9000
1. Public law—Italy. I. Title.
75-589512

Barile, Paolo.
Libertà di manifestazione del pensiero / Paolo Barile. — Milano : A Giuffrè, 1975.
151 p. ; 26 cm. It 75-Nov
Bibliography: p. ₍138₎-148.
L3000
1. Liberty of speech—Italy. 2. Liberty of the press—Italy. I. Title.
75-405418

Barile, Paolo
see Attenti al cavo! ... Rimini: Guaraldi, c1974.

Barile, Paolo.
see La Costituzione italiana ... Milano, F. Angeli, ₍1977₎

Barile, Paolo.
see La Stampa quotidiana tra crisi e riforma ... Bologna, Il mulino, c1976.

Barile, Pietro. Vicende delle popolazioni del Basso Uebi Scebeli secondo la tradizione locale. 1968.
in Grottanelli, Vinigi L. I bagiuni. Hamar, Ministero pubblica istruzione, Repubblica somala, Dipartimento culturale. 1968.

Barile, Ronald Gene.
Turbulent bed cooling tower / by Ronald G. Barile. -- Corvallis : National Environmental Research Center, Office of Research and Development, U.S. Environmental Protection Agency ; Springfield, Va. : For sale by National Technical Information Service, 1975.
iv, 28 p. : ill. ; 27 cm. -- (Environmental protection technology series ; EPA-660/2-75-027)
Bibliography: p. 23-25.
"Grant no. 801867. Program element 1BB392."
1. Thermal pollution of river, lakes, etc. 2. Cooling towers. 3. Packed towers. I. United States. Enviornmental Protection Agency. Office of Research and Development. II. Title.
IU NUC77-100813

Bariletti, Alessandro N
Il monte di Portofino. Genova, SAGEP, 1972.
139 p. illus. 22½ x 22½ cm. (La Quinta) L6000 It 72-Oct
At head of title: Alessandro N. Bariletti, Gianni Medri.
Bibliography: p. 113-139.
1. Portofino Promontory, Italy. I. Medri, Gianni, joint author. II. Title.
DG975.P85B37 72-368046

Barili, Carlo.
Italia Svizzera 1939 ₍i.e. millenovecentotrentanove₎ / Carlo Barili. — Milano : Tip. E. Padoan, 1939.
63 p. ; 21 cm. — (Collana di monografie alpine ; ser. 2., n. 2)
1. Ticino (Canton) 2. Nationalism—Switzerland—Ticino (Canton) I. Title.
DQ646.B37 77-454222
77 MARC

Barili, Lorenzo
see Antonelli, Giacomo, Cardinal, 1806-1876. Il carteggio Antonelli-Barili 1859-1861... Roma, Istituto per la storia del Risorgimento italiano, 1973.

Barili, Roberto T
Reducción de Nuestra Señora del Pilar; reseña histórica ₍por₎ Roberto T. Barili. Mar del Plata, Municipalidad del Partido de General Pueyrredón, 1968.
₍12₎ p. illus. 27 cm.
LACAP 68-2562
1. Reducción de Nuestra Señora del Pilar, Argentine Republic. 2. Indians of South America—Argentine Republic—Missions. I. Title.
F2821.3.M5B37 72-356366

Bariliak, Roman Aleksandrovich.
(Skleroma)
Склерома / Р. А. Бариляк, Н. А. Сахелашвили. — Киев : Здоров'я, 1974.
181, ₍3₎ p. : ill. ; 21 cm. USSR 74
Bibliography: p. 174-₍182₎
0.78rub
1. Rhinoscleroma. I. Sakhelashvili, Nina Andreevna, joint author. II. Title.
RF365.B37 75-568477

Barilier, Étienne, 1947–
L'incendie du château. ₍Roman.₎ (Lausanne, Éditions) L'Age d'homme, (1973).
160 p. 21 cm. (Collection Dédalus) 16.50F Sw 74-A-579
I. Title.
PQ2662.A685 I 5 74-161270
MARC

Barilier, Étienne, 1947–
Laura. ₍Roman.₎ (Lausanne, Éditions) L'Age d'homme, (1973).
107 p. 21 cm. (Collection Dédalus) 15.00F Sw 74-A-580
I. Title.
PQ2662.A685L3 74-161265
MARC

Barilier, Étienne, 1947–
Passion : ₍roman₎ / Étienne Barilier. — Lausanne : Éditions L'Age d'homme, ₍1974₎
210 p. ; 22 cm. — (Collection Dédalus) Sw 74-A-6981
22.00F
I. Title.
PQ2662.A685P3 843'.9'12 75-501220
MARC

Barilier, Étienne, 1947-
Une seule vie : roman réaliste / Étienne Barilier. — Lausanne : Éditions L'Age d'homme, ₍1975₎
183 p. ; 21 cm. — (Contemporains) Sw75-A-7524
23.00F
I. Title.
PQ2662.A685S4 76-450726
*76 MARC

Barilier, Roger.
La reine Berthe : ou, Mille ans sont comme un jour : jeu dramatique en six tableaux / Roger Barilier. — Lausanne : Cahiers de la renaissance vaudoise, c1976.
170 p. ; 19 cm. — (Cahiers de la renaissance vaudoise ; 89) Sw***
1. Berthe, consort of Rodolphe II, King of Burgundy, d. ca. 962—Drama. I. Title.
PQ2662.A687R4 842'.9'14 77-451187
77 MARC

Barillaro, Domenico. Dichiarazione di morte presunta, parentela e affinità. 1970
see Montuschi, Luigi. Domicilio e residenza. Bologna, N. Zanichelli, 1970.

Barillaro, Domenico.
Enfiteusi ecclesiastica e sua evoluzione nel Regno di Napoli. Padova, CEDAM, 1959.
111 p.
"Estratto dagli Studi economico-giuridici pubblicati per cura della Facoltà di Giurisprudenza della Università di Cagliari, v. 41."
Bibliographical footnotes.
1. Emphyteusis (Canon law). 2. Church property-Naples (Kingdom). I. Title.
CU-L NUC74-172183

Barillaro, Domenico.
Nozione giuridica di edificio destinato al culto. Modena, Società tipografoca Modenese, 1959.
134 p.
"Estratto dall'Archivio Giuridico, v. 157, fasc. 1-2, 1959."
1. Churches (Canon law) 2. Oratories (Canon law) 3. Sacred places (Canon law)
CU-L NUC74-30463

Barillaro, Emilio.
Calabria. Guida artistica e archeologica. (Dizionario corografico). Cosenza, L. Pellegrini, 1972.
612 p., incl. 113 plates. 29 cm. (Calabria) L27000 It 73-July
Bibliography: p. 359-363.
1. Calabria — Antiquities. 2. Castles — Calabria. 3. Churches — Calabria.
DG975.C15B35 73-351891

Barillaro, Emilio.
Giojosa Jonica : lineamenti di storia municipale / Emilio Barillaro. — Chiaravalle Centrale : Effe emme, 1976.
380 p., ₍90₎ leaves of plates (1 fold.) : ill. ; 24 cm. It77-May
1. Gioiosa Ionica, Italy. I. Title.
DG975.G442B37 77-476013
*77 MARC

Barillaro, Emilio.
Locri e la Locride; piccola guida turistica. Reggio Calabria, Editrice Nossis, 1970.
63 p. plans, plates.
1. Locri, Italy—Descr.—Guide-books. 2. Locri, Italy—Antiq. I. Title.
CU-SB NUC74-15754

Barillaro, Emilio.
Problemi archeologici: il porto di Locri Epizephyrii. Corigliano Calabro, Editrice MIT, 1959.
27, [1] p. 24 cm. (Quaderni di cultura, 2)
Bibliography: p. [28]
Includes bibliographical references.
1. Locri Epizephyrii, Italy. I. Title.
TxHR NUC74-30464

Barillaro, Francesco
see
Montalto, Saverio.

Barillaro, Raffaele.
Calabria agricola. Struttura e prospettive. Reggio Calabria, Libreria Ambrosiano, 1972.
66 p. 24 cm. It 73-Oct
Second rev. ed.
Bibliography: p. 66.
1. Agriculture—Economic aspects—Calabria. I. Title.
HD1975.C25B35 1972 73-357614

Barillatti, Rafael V Portela
see Portela Barillatti, Rafael V

Barillet, Pierre.
Cuatro historias de alquiler; de Barillet y Grédy, versión castellana de Felix Calderon. [Madrid] Escelicer [1970]
88 p. 16 cm. (Colección Teatro, no. 670)
I. Grédy, Jean Pierre, 1920- II. Title. III. Series.
PSt MnU NUC73-45305

Barillet, Pierre.
Fleur de cactus. [Paris, Théâtre des Bouffes-Parisiens, 23 septembre 1964.] Paris, le Livre de poche, 1970.
255 p. 17 cm. (Le Livre de poche, 2787) 3.50F F 72-917
At head of title: Barillet et Grédy.
I. Grédy, Jean Pierre, 1920- joint author. II. Title.
PQ2662.A688F5 842'.9'14 72-371255

Barillet, Pierre.
Flor de cactus; comedia en dos partes, original de Barrillet y Gredy; traduccion de Felix Calderon. [Madrid] Ediciones Alfil [1967]
112 p. illus. 16 cm. (Coleccion teatro, n. 535)
I. Gredy, Jean Pierre, 1920- II. Calderón, Félix, tr. III. Title. IV. Series.
MdBJ NUC73-2395

Barillet, Pierre.
4 [Quatre] pièces sur jardin, par P. Barillet et J.-P. Grédy. Paris, 1969.
46 p. illus. (Avant-scène, no. 425)
Microcard edition.
I. Grédy, Jean Pierre, 1920-
ICRL NUC74-19023

Barillet, Pierre.
Une rose au petit déjeuner; une comédie de Barillet et Gredy. [Paris, L'Avant-scène, 1974]
46 p. plates. 27 cm. (L'Avant-scène [du] théâtre, no 532) 5.00F F***
I. Grédy, Jean Pierre, 1920- joint author. II. Title. III. Series.
PN6113.A9 no. 532 790.2'09'04 s 74-183932
[PQ2662.A688] [842'.9'14] MARC

Barillet, Pierre
see Burrows, Adram S Four on a garden. New York, S. French [c1973]

Barilli, Calimero, joint author.
see Romani, Bruno. L'Italiano (1926-1942 [i.e. millenovecentoventisei-millenovecentoquarantadue]). Roma, Edizioni dell'Ateneo, c1976.

Barilli, Renato.
Dubuffet : oggetto e progetto, il ciclo dell'Hourloupe / Renato Barilli. — Milano : Fratelli Fabbri, 1976.
129 p. : ill. ; 33 cm. It77-Feb
L12000
1. Dubuffet, Jean, 1901-
ND553.D772B37 77-461931
*77 MARC

Barilli, Renato. Il liberty
see Scheidt, Bernd. Jugendstil. München: Schuler, c1973.

Barilli, Renato.
La linea Svevo-Pirandello. Milano, U. Mursia, 1972.
266 p. 20½ cm. (Civiltà letteraria del Novecento. Saggi, n. 18)
L3200 It 72-Dec
Includes bibliographical references.
1. Schmitz, Ettore, 1861-1928. 2. Pirandello, Luigi, 1867-1936. I. Title.
PQ4841.C482Z6 72-374818

Barilli, Renato.
Tra presenza e assenza : due modelli culturali in conflitto / Renato Barilli. — Milano : Bompiani, [1974]
303 p. ; 22 cm. — (Nuovi saggi italiani ; 13) It 75-Feb
Includes bibliographical references.
L4500
1. Aesthetics, Modern—20th century. I. Title.
BH204.B33 75-568862

Barilli, Renato
see Badaloni, Nicola. Cultura e vita civile tra Riforma e Controriforma ... Bari, Laterza, 1973.

Barilli, Renato.
see Estetica e società tecnologica. Bologna, Il mulino, 1976.

Barilli, Renato
see Ghiglia, Oscar, 1876-1945. Trenta dipinti di Oscar Ghiglia... Firenze : Galleria d'arte Spinetti, 1975.

Barilli, Renato
see Vaccari, Franco. Franco Vaccari. Pollenza, La nuova Foglio, 1973.

Barilli, Renato, ed.
see Zavattini, Cesare, 1902- Opere : romanzi, diari, poesie. Milano : V. Bompiani [1974]

Barilo, Tamara Sergeevna
see
Barylo, Tamara Serhiïvna.

Bariloni, Margherita Martelli
see Martelli Bariloni, Margherita.

Barin, Ihsan.
Thermochemical properties of inorganic substances [by] I. Barin [and] O. Knacke. With a pref. by O. Kubaschewski. Berlin, New York, Springer-Verlag, 1973.
lii, 921 p. illus. 28 cm. DM150.00 GDB***
Introd. also in French and German.
Bibliography: p. [l]-lii.
1. Thermochemistry—Tables, etc. 2. Chemistry, Inorganic—Tables. I. Knacke, Ottmar, 1920- joint author. II. Title.
QD511.8.B37 546 72-95058
ISBN 0-387-06053-7 (New York) MARC

Bārīṇa Biśvāsa
see
Biśvāsa, Bārīṇa.

Bařina, Miloslav.
Nová Paka / Miloslav Bařina. Z geologické minulosti Novopacka / Karel Tuček ; [fot. a barev fot. Otakar Hrdlička]. — 1. vyd. — Jičín : ONV, 1975.
79 p. : ill. (some col.) ; 20 cm. — (Edice českého ráje ; sv. 4) (Řada malých průvodců ; č. 2) Cz 75
Summaries and list of illustrations in various languages.
Includes bibliographies.
Kčs25.00
1. Geology—Czechoslovak Republic—Nová Paka. I. Tuček, Karel. Z geologické minulosti Novopacka. 1975. II. Title.
QE267.B37 76-503257

Barinaga Fernández, Augusto.
Movimientos literarios españoles en los siglos XIX y XX. [2. ed.] Madrid, Alhambra [1969]
311 p. illus.
1. Spanish literature—19th century—History and criticism. 2. Spanish literature—20th century—History and criticism. I. Title.
NbU ViU NbU NUC73-38833
MWiW TNJ KMK

Barinas, Fradique Lizardo
see Lizardo Barinas, Fradique.

Barinas Coiscou, Sócrates.
Renacer. [Santo Domingo? 1960?]
1 v. (unpaged) 21 cm.
Poems.
DPU NUC73-58158

Barinas, Venezuela (State). Asamblea Legislativa. Comision Delegada
see Acosta, César Romeo. Crónicas regionales. [Barquisimeto] 1973.

Barinavaja, W. Am Fluss. 1974.
in Ehm-Schulz, Rosemarie. Alte Polka ... Leipzig, Fachzeitschrift Der Tanz beim Zentralhaus für Kulturarbeit der DDR, 1974.

Barinbaum, Lea.
('Ezrah rishonah ba-ḥinukh)
עזרה ראשונה בחינוך; פסיכולוגיה למדריכי נוער [מאת] לאה ברינבאום. [עריכה: שלמה גרפונקל] חיפה, רנסנם [1971]
127 p. 22 cm. IL6.50
On verso of t. p.: First aid in education.
1. Educational psychology. I. Title.
LB1051.B2474 72-950999

Barinbaum, Lea.
הורים רוצים לדעת; על חינוך ילדים [מאת] לאה ברינבאום. [תל אביב] עם עובד [1971]
158 p. 22 cm. IL6.80
On verso of t. p.: Parents want to know.
1. Child study. I. Title.
Title romanized: Horim rotsim la-da'at.
LB1115.B265 72-953902

Barincou, Edmond.
Machiavelli / Edmond Barincou ; translated by Helen R. Lane. — Westport, Conn. : Greenwood Press, 1975.
192 p. : ill. ; 21 cm.
Translation of Machiavel, par lui-même.
Reprint of the 1961 ed. published by Grove Press, New York, which was issued as Evergreen profile book 23.
Bibliography: p. 191-192.
ISBN 0-8371-8185-2
1. Machiavelli, Niccolò, 1469-1527.
[DG738.14.M2B3713 1975] 945'.06'0924 75-11427
75 MARC

Barindra Basu
see
Basu, Barindra, 1930-

Baring, Alexander
see Ashburton, Alexander Baring, Baron, 1774-1848.

Baring, Arnulf.
Aussenpolitik in Adenauers Kanzlerdemokratie; Westdeutsche Innenpolitik im Zeichen der Europäischen Verteidigungsgemeinschaft. Mit einem Vorwort von Gilbert Ziebura. [Ungekürzte, vom Autor durchgesehene Ausg. München] Deutscher Taschenbuch Verlag [1971, c1969]
2 v. 18 cm. (DTV Wissenschaftliche Reihe, 4065-66)
Issued also as thesis, Freie Universität Berlin.
Originally published as Schriften des Forschungsinstituts der Deutschen Gesellschaft fur Auswärtige Politik e. V., Bd. 28.
Includes bibliographical references.
1. Adenauer, Konrad, 1876-1967. 2. European Defense Community (Proposed) 3. Germany (Federal Republic, 1949-)—Foreign relations. I. Title.
TxHR NUC73-34970

Baring, Arnulf.
Sehr verehrter Herr Bundeskanzler! : Heinrich von Brentano im Briefwechsel mit Konrad Adenauer, 1949-1964 / Arnulf Baring, unter Mitarb. von Bolko v. Oetinger u. Klaus Mayer. — 1.-5. Tsd. — Hamburg : Hoffmann und Campe, 1974.
511 p., [4] leaves of plates : ill. ; 23 cm. GFR 74-A
Includes the text of letters between H. von Brentano and K. Adenauer.
Includes bibliographical references and indexes.
ISBN 3-455-00305-2 : DM45.00
1. Brentano, Heinrich von, 1904-1964. 2. Adenauer, Konrad, 1876-1967. 3. Statesmen—Germany—Correspondence, reminiscences, etc. I. Brentano, Heinrich von, 1904-1964. II. Adenauer, Konrad, 1876-1967. III. Oetinger, Bolko von. IV. Mayer, Klaus. V. Title.
DD259.7.B75B37 943.087'092'2 75-551440
[B]

Baring, E
Despatch from the Governor of Kenya commenting on the East Africa Royal Commission 1953-55 report. [Nairobi, 1956]
106 p. 25 cm.
1. Africa, East—Economic conditions. I. Great Britain. East Africa Royal Commission. Report.
CtY-E NUC75-66309

Baring, Maurice, 1874-1945.
Diminutive dramas / by Maurice Baring. — Great Neck, N.Y. : Core Collection Books, 1977.
xii, 198 p. ; 20 cm. — (One-act plays in reprint)
Reprint of the 4th ed. published in 1938 by W. Heinemann, London.
ISBN 0-8486-2012-7
I. Title. II. Series.
PR6003.A67A19 1977 822'.9'12 77-70343
77 MARC

Baring, Maurice, 1874-1945, comp.
see The Oxford book of Russian verse. 2d ed. Oxford, Clarendon Press [1966, 1948]

Baring-Gould, Ceil
see Mother Goose. The annotated Mother Goose... [1st ed.] New York, Bramhall House [c1962]

Baring-Gould, Michael Darragh, 1937-
Agricultural and community development in Mexican ejidos : relatives in conflict / by Michael Darragh Baring-Gould. — [Ithaca, N.Y.] : Cornell University, 1974.
xiii, 240 p. : ill. ; 28 cm. — (Dissertation series - Cornell University, Latin American Studies Program ; no. 52)
Thesis—Cornell.
Vita.
Bibliography: p. 228-237.
1. Agriculture—Economic aspects—Mexico—Guanajuato (State) 2. Agriculture—Mexico—Guanajuato (State) 3. Community development—Guanajuato, Mexico (State) I. Title. II. Series: Cornell University. Latin American Studies Program. Dissertation series ; no. 52.
HD1792.B37 338.1'0972'4 75-321016
75 MARC

Baring-Gould, Sabine, 1834-1924, ed.
A book of nursery songs and rhymes / edited by S. Baring-Gould ; with ill. by members of the Birmingham Art School under the direction of A. J. Gaskin. — London : Methuen, 1895.
xvi, 159 p. : ill. ; 21 cm.
Includes bibliographical references.
1. Children's poetry. 2. Nursery rhymes. I. Title.
PN6110.C4B25 1895b 398.8 75-316270
75 MARC

Baring-Gould, Sabine, 1834–1924, ed.
A book of nursery songs and rhymes. With illus. by members of the Birmingham Art School under the direction of A. J. Gaskin. London, Methuen; Philadelphia, Lippincot, 1895.
xvi, 159 p. illus. 22 cm.
Includes bibliographical references.
1. Children's poetry. 2. Nursery rhymes. I. Title.
PN6110.C4B25 1895 398.8 74–163419
MARC

Baring-Gould, Sabine, 1834–1924.
The book of were-wolves : being an account of a terrible superstition / by Sabine Baring-Gould. — New York : Causeway Books, c1973.
xv, 266 p. ; 25 cm.
Originally published in 1865 by Smith, Elder, London.
Includes bibliographical references.
ISBN 0–88356–008–9 : $8.95
1. Werwolves. I. Title.
GR830.W4B3 1973 133.4'23 74–189409
MARC

Baring-Gould, Sabine, 1834-1924.
Legends of the patriarchs and prophets and other Old Testament characters from various sources. [Folcroft, Pa.] Folcroft Library Editions, 1974.
380 p. 24 cm.
Reprint of the 1872 ed. published by Holt & Williams, New York.
1. Bible. O.T.—Legends. I. Title.
BS1196.B37 1974 221.9'22 74-9741
ISBN 0-8414-3205-8 (lib. bdg.) 74[r77]rev MARC

Baring-Gould, Sabine, 1834-1924.
Legends of the patriarchs and prophets and other Old Testament characters, from various sources / by S. Baring-Gould. — Norwood, Pa. : Norwood Editions, 1976.
380 p. ; 23 cm.
Reprint of the 1872 ed. published by Holt & Williams, New York.
Includes bibliographical references.
ISBN 0-8482-0202-3 : $35.00
1. Bible. O.T.—Legends. I. Title.
[BS1196.B37 1976] 221.9'22 76-50074
76 MARC

Baring-Gould, Sabine, 1834-1924.
Noémi; a story of rock-dwellers, by S. Baring-Gould. London, Methuen & Co. [19--]
128 p. 23 cm. (Novels, no. 23)
I. Title.
WU NUC75-21275

Baring-Gould, Sabine, 1834-1924.
The story of Germany. With the collaboration of Arthur Gilman. New York, G. P. Putnam's Sons, 1887 [c1886, 1972]
xviii, 457 p. illus., fold maps. (The story of the nations)
Microfilm (negative) Emporia, Kan., William Allen White Library, 1972. 1 reel. 35 mm.
1. Germany—Hist. I. Gilman, Arthur, 1837-1909.
KEmT NUC73-125536

Baring-Gould, William Stuart, 1913-
see Mother Goose. The annotated Mother Goose... [1st ed.] New York, Bramhall House [c1962]

Baring-Gould, William Stuart, 1913-
see Mother Goose. The annotated Mother Goose. Cleveland, World Pub. Co. [c1967]

Baring Brothers and Company, London.
Merchant banking today. London [c1970]
34 p. port.
1. Banks and banking—Gt. Brit. I. Title.
MH-BA NUC73-112854

Baring Union Christian College, Batala, India. Christian Institute of Sikh Studies
see
Christian Institute of Sikh Studies.

Baringer, John.
Meetings. John Baringer. New Haven, New Quarto Editions, 1974.
80 p. 22 cm. (New Quarto editions, 6)
Cover title.
I. Title.
CtY NUC76-96138

Bařinka, Jaroslav
see Forman, Werner. El arte de la Corea antigua. México [c1963]

Barinka, Lawrence Louis.
A numerical and substructuring analysis for discontinuous thin shells of revolution. [Charlottesville, Va.] 1972.
1 v. (various pagings) illus. 29 cm.
Thesis—University of Virginia.
Includes bibliography.
1. Shells (Engineering) I. Title.
ViU NUC73-32104

Bařinka, Rudolf.
Černá hodinka. 1. vyd. Brno, Blok, t. Tisk 1, 1972.
55, [1] p. 19 cm. Kčs6.00 Cz 73–SKČ
Poems.
I. Title.
PG5439.12.A7C4 74–345866

Barinov, A.V., ed.
see Voprosy razvitiía sofsialisticheskoĭ promyshlennosti. Nizhniĭ Tagil, 1969.

Barinov, Aleksandr Lukich.
(Gorodskie, sel'skie, poselkovye Sovety deputatov trudiashchikhsia)
Городские, сельские, поселковые Советы депутатов трудящихся и самодеятельные организации трудящихся. Фрунзе, "Кыргызстан," 1969.
21 p. 16 cm. (В помощь депутату местного Совета) 0.40rub
USSR 69–VKP
At head of title: А. Л. Баринов.
1. Soviets—Kirghizistan. I. Title.
JS7267.2.B36 73–354035

Barinov, Konstantin Nikitovich.
(Dinamika i prinfsipy postroeniia orbital'nykh sistem kosmicheskikh apparatov)
Динамика и принципы построения орбитальных систем космических аппаратов / К. Н. Баринов, М. Н. Бурдаев, П. А. Мамон. — Москва : Машиностроение, 1975.
232 p. : ill. ; 22 cm. USSR 75
Bibliography: p. [230]
1.43rub
1. Artificial satellites—Orbits. I. Burdaev, Mikhail Nikolaevich, joint author. II. Mamon, Petr Andreevich, joint author. III. Title.
TL1080.B37 76–504598

Barinov, Mark Mikhaĭlovich.
(Soobshchaet Gidrometfsentr)
Сообщает Гидрометцентр / М. М. Баринов. — Ленинград : Гидрометеорологическое изд-во, 1971.
86 p., [8] leaves of plates : ill. (some col.) ; 20 cm. USSR***
0.30rub
1. Russia (1923- U. S. S. R.). Gidrometeorologicheskiĭ nauchno-issledovatel'skiĭ fsentr. I. Title.
GB746.B35 75–558867

Barinov, Nikolaĭ Aleksandrovich.
Metalurgia y metalografía [por] N. Barinov y A. Landa. Moscú, Editorial Mir [1966]
221 p. illus. 22 cm.
1. Metallurgy. 2. Metallography. I. Landa, Aleksandr Fedorovich, joint author. II. Title.
TN665.B3418 68–51096
rev

Barinov, Nikolaĭ Aleksandrovich.
(Proizvodstvo chugunnykh otopitel'nykh radiatorov)
Производство чугунных отопительных радиаторов. Под ред. М. А. Устинова. Москва, Гос. изд-во лит-ры по строит. материалам, 1952.
202 p. illus. 23 cm.
At head of title: Н. А. Баринов, В. И. Волков.
Errata slip inserted.
Bibliography: p. 200–[201]
1. Radiators. I. Volkov, V. I., joint author. II. Title.
TH7597.B37 56–27051
rev

Barinov, Nikolaĭ Aleksandrovich.
(Sanitarno-tekhnicheskie izdeliia i khoziaĭstvenno-pechnye pribory)
Санитарно-технические изделия и хозяйственно-печные приборы. Москва, Гос. изд-во по строит. материалам, 1957.
260 p. illus. 23 cm.
At head of title: Н. А. Баринов, М. А. Устинов.
Bibliography: p. 258–[259]
1. Iron-founding. 2. Plumbing—Equipment and supplies. 3. Boilers. I. Ustinov, M. A., joint author. II. Title.
TS230.B28 57–43380
rev

Barinov, Nikolaĭ Aleksandrovich.
(Tekhnologiia metallov)
Технология металлов. Под ред. Н. А. Баринова. Допущено в качестве учебника для немашиностроит. специальностей высших учеб. заведений. Москва, Гос. научно-техн. изд-во лит-ры по черной и цветной металлургии, 1963.
554 p. illus. 23 cm.
At head of title: Н. А. Баринов, А. Ф. Ланда, П. С. Паутынский.
1. Metals. 2. Metal-work. I. Landa, Aleksandr Fedorovich. II. Pautynskiĭ, Petr Stanislavovich. III. Title.
TN665.B35 65–53900
rev

Barinov, Nikolaĭ Aleksandrovich.
(Vodookhlazhdaemye vagranki i ikh metallurgicheskie vozmozhnosti)
Водоохлаждаемые вагранки и их металлургические возможности. Москва, Машиностроение, 1964.
225, [3] p. illus. 23 cm.
At head of title: Н. А. Баринов.
Bibliography: p. 223–[226]
1. Cupola-furnaces. I. Title.
TS231.B28 65–44070
rev

Barinov, Nikolai Aleksandrovich
see Pravo i kachestvo produktsii. 1972.

Barinov, Nikolaĭ Alekseevich.
(Prava grazhdan po dogovoru bytovogo zakaza i ikh zashchita)
Права граждан по договору бытового заказа и их защита. Саратов, Изд-во Сарат. ун-та, 1973.
161 p. 20 cm. 0.60rub USSR 73
At head of title: Н. А. Баринов.
Includes bibliographical references.
1. Service industries—Law and legislation—Russia. I. Title.
74–335942

Barinov, Nikolaĭ Georgievich.
(Optimizat͡sii͡a prot͡sessov i sistem upravlenii͡a)
Оптимизация процессов и систем управления в судовой автоматике / Н. Г. Баринов — Ленинград : Судостроение, 1976.
255 p. : ill. ; 22 cm. USSR 76
Bibliography: p. 251-253.
0.99rub
1. Ships—Automation. 2. Automatic pilot (Ships) 3. Mathematical optimization. I. Title.
VM480.B37 77-500638

Barinov, V A
(Vasiliĭ Vasil'evich Vitkovskiĭ)
Василий Васильевич Витковский. 1856–1924. Москва, "Наука," 1973.
65 p. with illus. 20 cm. (Академия наук СССР. Научно-биографическая серия) 0.20rub USSR 73-VKP
At head of title: В. А. Баринов.
Includes bibliographical references.
1. Vitkovskiĭ, Vasiliĭ Vasil'evich, 1856-1924. 2. Cartography—Russia—History.
GA407.V57B37 73-335129

Barinova, Elena Anatol'evna.
(Metodika russkogo i͡azyka)
Методика русского языка : ⌊учеб. пособие для фак. рус. яз. и литературы пед. ин-тов⌋ / Е. А. Баринова, Л. Ф. Боженкова, В. И. Лебедев ; под общ. ред. д-ра пед. наук, проф. Е. А. Бариновой. — Москва : Просвещение, 1974.
367 p. ; 23 cm. USSR 74
Includes bibliographies.
0.91rub
1. Russian language—Study and teaching. I. Bozhenkova, Lidii͡a Fedorovna, joint author. II. Lebedev, V. I., joint author. III. Title.
PG2065.B278 77-510425

Barinova, G. B.
see Analiz i sintez seteĭ svi͡azi s ispol'zovaniem ÉVM. 1974.

Barinova, G. I.
see Voprosy sovershenstvovanii͡a ucheta v otrasli͡akh narodnogo khozi͡aĭstva. 1972.

Barinova, Galina Ivanovna.
(Kak otzovetsi͡a slovo ...)
Как отзовется слово ... / Г. И. Баринова. — Ленинград : Лениздат, 1975.
43 p. ; 16 cm. — (Идеологическая работа, опыт, проблемы) USSR 75
Series romanized: Ideologicheskai͡a rabota, opyt, problemy.
0.11rub
1. Kommunisticheskai͡a partii͡a Sovetskogo Soi͡uza—Party work. I. Title.
JN6598.K7B333 76-533422

Barinova, Z. S.
see Leningrad. Vsesoi͡uznyi nauchno-issledovatel'skii institut gidrotekhniki. (Tipy i konstrukt͡sii vodosborsov vysokonapornykh gidrouzlov) 1975.

Barinque, Bertrand.
Pour un érotisme conjugal / Bertrand Barinque. — ⌊Paris⌋ : Balland, c1975.
230 p. ; 20 cm. F***
ISBN 2-7158-0035-5 : 39.50F
1. Sex in marriage. 2. Sex instruction. I. Title.
HQ31.B334 301.41'8 75-520808
76 MARC

Barinskai͡a, Al'dona Pavlovna.
(Sovetskoe zakonodatel'stvo o religioznykh kul'takh)
Советское законодательство о религиозных культах / А. П. Баринская, В. И. Савельев. — Йошкар-Ола : Марийск. кн. изд-во, 1973.
48 p. ; 20 cm. USSR 73
Includes bibliographical references.
0.08rub
1. Religious liberty—Russia. 2. Atheism—Russia. I. Savel'ev, Viktor Ivanovich, joint author. II. Title.
74-359376

Bario, Ruben, 1867-1916.
Poema del otoño, y otros poemas. 5. ed. Madrid, Espasa-Calpe ⌊1965⌋
4 p.l., ⌊11⌋-148 p. 18 cm. (Colección austral. ⌊282⌋)
I. Title.
CaQMM NUC73-39455

Barioli, Cesare.
Manual práctico de karate; la más terrible defensa personal ⌊por⌋ César Barioli. Barcelona, de Vecchi ⌊1970, c1964⌋
247 p. illus.
1. Karate. I. Title.
RP NUC75-30860

Barioli, Gino.
Miro Gasparello : catalogo della mostra a palazzo Chiericati, 5 giugno–31 ottobre 1974 / a cura di Gino Barioli. — Comune di Vicenza : Assessorato cultura, Museo civico, ⌊1974⌋
91 p. : ill. (some col.) ; 31 cm. It 75-Apr
Errata slip inserted.
1. Gasparello, Miro, 1891-1916. I. Vicenza. Museo civico.
N6923.G36B37 75-580340

Barioli, Gino.
Origini della ceramica in Vicenza / G. Barioli, F. Brunello. -- [Vicenza] : Ente Fiera Vicenza, 1976.
103 p. : ill. (some col.), plans ; 28 cm.
Bibliography: p. 82-83; 103.
1. Vicenza--Antiquities. 2. Pottery, Italian. I. Brunello, Franco.
MH-FA NUC77-100349

Barioli, Gino, ed.
see Il Restauro a Vicenza negli anni Sessanta. [n. p.] [1972]

Barioli, Gino
see Santuario di Monte Berico. Museo. Gli ex voto di Monte Berico. Monte Berico-Vicenza, Frati Servi di Maria, 1971.

Barion, Cathérine.
Les marques de bétail ches les Daza et les Azza du Niger. Niamey, Centre Nigérien de Recherches en Sciences Humaines, 1972.
296 p. illus., maps. (Études nigériennes, no. 29)
1. Cattle brands—Niger. 2. Ethnology—Niger. I. Title.
InU NUC74-139459

Barion, Jakob, 1898–
Was ist Ideologie? : Studie zu Begriff u. Problematik / Jakob Barion. — 3., erw. Aufl. — Bonn : Bouvier, 1974.
164 p. ; 20 cm.
Includes bibliographical references and index.
ISBN 3-416-00994-0 : DM19.80
1. Ideology. I. Title.
B823.3.B27 1974 75-567215

Bāriq Shafī'ī,
see
Shafī'ī, Bāriq.

Barīr, Maḥjūb.
⌊Nījiryā bayna al-ams wa-al-yawm⌋
نيجريا بين الامس واليوم ⌊تأليف⌋ محجوب برير. ⌊الخرطوم ،⌋
جامعة الخرطوم ، دار التأليف والترجمة والنشر ، 1971⌋
107 p. illus. 22 cm.
£S0.25 (His 1 ، سلسلة الكتب التعريفية بدول وشعوب القارة الافريقية)
1. Nigeria—Politics and government. I. Title.
DT515.75.B37 72-982518

Baris, D B
Opvolgingssituatie in de Zuidhollandse bollenstreek / D. B. Baris. — Den Haag : Landbouw-Economisch Instituut, Afd. Streekonderzoek, 1974.
34 p. : map ; 23 cm. — (⌊Publikatie⌋ - Landbouw-Economisch Instituut ; no. 2.61) Ne***
1. Bulb industry—Holland, South (Province) I. Title. II. Series: Hague. Landbouw-Economisch Instituut. Publikatie ; no. 2.61.
SB425.B29 75-565068

Baris, D B
Veranderingen in het aantal bedrijfshoofden en bedrijven in de Friese weidestreken en in de wouden in de periode 1966–1971 ⌊door⌋ D. B. Baris, A. J. Jacobs ⌊en⌋ B. H. Perdok. ⌊Den Haag⌋ Landbouw-Economisch Instituut, Afd. Streekonderzoek, 1973.
53 p. illus. 24 cm. (Landbouw-Economisch Instituut. ⌊Publikatie⌋ no. 2.46) fl 5.50 Ne***
1. Agriculture—Economic aspects—Netherlands—Friesland. I. Jacobs, A. J., joint author. II. Perdok, B. H., joint author. III. Title. IV. Series: Hague. Landbouw-Economisch Instituut. Publikatie no. 2.46.
HD1990.F7B37 74-324179

Baris, D B
Veranderingen in het aantal bedrijfshoofden en bedrijven op de Drentse zandgronden in de periode 1966–1971 ⌊door⌋ D. B. Baris, A. J. Jacobs ⌊en⌋ B. H. Perdok. Den Haag Landbouw-Economisch Instituut, Afdeling Streekonderzoek, 1973.
48 p. map. 24 cm. (⌊Hague⌋ Landbouw-Economisch Instituut ⌊Publikatie⌋ no. 2.45) fl 5.50 Ne***
1. Agriculture—Economic aspects—Drenthe, Netherlands. I. Jacobs, A. J., joint author. II. Perdok, B. H., joint author. III. Title. IV. Series.
HD1990.D7B32 74-347129

Barisaite, Laima, illus.
see Mieželaitis, Eduardas, 1919-
Dainos dienoraštis. Vilnius, "Vaga," 1973.

Barisan Rakyat
see
Peoples Front, Singapore.

Barisch, Hilde, comp.
Sportgeschichte aus erster Hand. Von d. Antike bis z. Olympiade 1972 in München. Berichte von Augenzeugen u. Zeitgenossen. Mit e. Geleitw. von Willi Daume. (Würzburg) Arena-Verl. (1971).
366 p. with illus. 24 cm. DM24.80 GDB 71-A44-517
1. Sports—History. I. Title.
GV571.B33 73-359169
ISBN 3-401-03593-2

Barisch, Klaus, 1938-
Istanbul / Klaus u. Lissi Barisch. — Köln : DuMont Schauberg, 1976.
257 p. : numerous ill. (some col.), maps ; 21 cm. — (Richtig reisen) GFR76-A
Many contributions by other authors, some of them translated from Turkish.
ISBN 3-7701-0761-8
1. Istanbul. I. Barisch, Lissi, 1940- joint author. II. Title.
DR719.B36 914.96'1 76-482706
77 MARC

Barisch, Lissi, 1940- joint author.
see Barisch, Klaus, 1938- Istanbul. Köln, DuMont Schauberg, 1976.

Barish, Herbert
see Main, Marjorie White, 1917- Curriculum project on drug abuse... New York ⌊1973⌋

Barish, J., joint author
see Alsmiller, R G NCDATA - nuclear collision data... Oak Ridge, Tenn., Oak Rdige National Laboratory; available from Clearinghouse for Federal Scientific and Technical Information, Springfield, Va., 1968.

Barish, Jonas A comp.
Jonson: 'Volpone'; a casebook edited by Jonas A. Barish. ⌊London⌋ Macmillan ⌊1972⌋
255 p. 20 cm. (Casebook series) £2.00 B***
Bibliography: p. ⌊241⌋
1. Jonson, Ben, 1573?-1637. Volpone.
PR2622.B3 822'.3 73-150745
ISBN 0-333-08896-4; 0-333-02615-2 (pbk.) MARC

Barish, Lawrence
see Wisconsin. Legislative Reference Bureau. An emerging trend: the nonfault concept of divorce... ⌊Madison, Wis.⌋ 1971.

Barish, Lawrence
see Wisconsin. Legislative Reference Bureau. The mortgage interest controversy. Madison, 1974.

Barish, Lawrence
see Wisconsin. Legislative Reference Bureau. Obscenity redefined: the search for a workable standard. Madison, Wis., 1974.

Barish, Lawrence
see Wisconsin. Legislative Reference Bureau. Privacy... Madison, 1972.

Barish, Lawrence
see Wisconsin. Legislative Reference Bureau. The use of the partial veto... Madison, the Bureau, 1975.

Barish, Louis.
Basic Jewish beliefs, by * and Rebecca Barish. [n.p.] Jonathan David, c1961, 1968.
222 p.
1. Jews–Religion. I. Title.
OEac NUC74-15756

Barish, Matthew.
The kid's book of cards and posters. Illustrated by Erika Wallace and others. Englewood Cliffs, N. J., Prentice-Hall [1973]
96 p. illus. (part col.) 22 cm. $5.95
SUMMARY: Lists appropriate holidays and occasions throughout the year for greeting cards and posters and discusses the necessary materials and techniques for creating them.
Bibliography: p. 93–94.
1. Greeting cards—Juvenile literature. 2. Posters—Juvenile literature. [1. Greeting cards. 2. Posters] I. Wallace, Erika, illus. II. Title.
TT872.B37 760 72–13859
ISBN 0-13-515114-7 MARC

Barish, Mort, 1927-
Mort's Guide to festivals, feasts, fairs & fiestas / by Mort Barish and Michaela M. Mole ; research and editorial staff, Deirdre Adams, Sally Kollmar, Abigail Houston. — International ed. — Princeton, N.J. : CMG Pub. Co., 1974.
192 p. ; 18 cm.
Pages 186-191, blank for "Notes."
Includes index.
ISBN 0-9600718-5-7 : $2.95
1. Festivals. 2. Fairs. I. Mole, Michaela M., joint author. II. Title. III. Title: Guide to festivals, feasts, fairs & fiestas.
GT3940.B37 394 74-82873
75[r77]rev MARC

Barish, Mort, 1927-
Mort's Guide to festivals, feasts, fairs & fiestas : U.S.A., Canada, Mexico / by Mort Barish and Michaela M. Mole ; research and editorial staff, Deirdre Adams, Sally Kollmar, Abigail Houston. — Princeton, N.J. : CMG Pub. Co., 1974.
176 p. (p. 172-175 blank for "Notes") : ill. ; 18 cm.
Includes index.
ISBN 0-9600718-4-9 : $2.95
1. Festivals—United States. 2. Festivals—Canada. 3. Festivals—Mexico. 4. Fairs. I. Mole, Michaela M., joint author. II. Title. III. Title: Guide to festivals, feasts, fairs & fiestas. IV. Title: Festivals, feasts, fairs & fiestas.
GT4802.M67 394.2'697 74-82875
75[r77]rev MARC

Barish, Mort, 1927-
Mort's Guide to low-cost vacations & lodgings on college campuses / by Mort Barish and Michaela M. Mole. — International ed. — Princeton, N.J. : CMG Pub. Co., 1974.
176 p. : ill. ; 18 cm.
ISBN 0-9600718-3-0 : $2.95
1. Hotels, taverns, etc.—Directories. 2. Dormitories—Directories. I. Mole, Michaela M., joint author. II. Title. III. Title: Guide to low-cost vacations & lodgings on college campuses.
TX907.B35 1974 647'.9473 74-82874
75[r77]rev MARC

Barish, Mort, 1927-
Mort's guide to 100,000 vacation jobs / by Mort Barish and Michaela M. Mole. -- Princeton, N.J. : CMG Pub. Co., 1975.
vi, 160 p. ; 18 cm.
1. Job descriptions. I. Mole, Michaela M., joint author. II. Title.
OkU NUC77-100330

Barish, Samoan.
The nature of clinical listening / by Samoan Barish. -- [s.l. : s.n.], 1975.
viii, 203 leaves ; 28 cm.
Thesis--University of Southern California.
Bibliography: leaves 185-203.
1. Listening. 2. Social workers. 3. Clinical psychology. I. Title.
CLSU NUC77-100897

Barishpolov, Viktor Fedorovich.
(Stroitel'stvo naruzhnykh teplovykh seteĭ)
Строительство наружных тепловых сетей. Москва, Стройиздат, 1974.
193 p. with illus. 20 cm. 0.54rub USSR 74
At head of title: В. Ф. Баришполов.
Bibliography: p. [192]
1. Heating-pipes. 2. Heating from central stations. I. Title.
TH7643.B37 74–325097

Barišić, Franjo, ed.
see Bogdanović, Dimitrije. Jovan Lestvičnik u vizantijskoj i staroj srpskoj književnosti. 1968.

Barišić, Franjo, ed.
see Spomenica Jorja Tadića. 1970.

Barišić, Franjo, ed.
see Spomenica Milana Budimira. 1967.

Barisone, Ermanno, ed.
see Chaucer, Geoffrey, d. 1400. I Racconti di Canterbury. Torino, Unione Tipografico-Editrice Torinese [1967]

Barisonzi, Judith Anne, 1945-
Black identity in the poetry of Langston Hughes. [Madison, Wis.] 1971 [1972]
iii, 203 l.
Thesis–University of Wisconsin.
Bibliography: leaves 198-203.
Photocopy. Ann Arbor, Mich., University Microfilms, 1972. 22 cm.
1. Hughes, Langston, 1902-1967. 2. Negroes in literature. I. Title.
CtY NUC73-125010

Barisov, Viktor Maksimovich
see Kniga druzeĭ. 1975.

Barit, Grigoriĭ I͡Ul'evich.
(Osnovy tekhnologii sudovogo mashinostroenii͡a)
Основы технологии судового машиностроения. [Для кораблестроит. специальностей вузов]. Ленинград, "Судостроение," 1972.
248 p. with diagrs. 22 cm. 0.77rub USSR 72–VKP
At head of title: Г. Ю. Барит.
Bibliography: p. 247–[248]
1. Marine engineering. 2. Machine-shop practice. I. Title.
VM605.B28 74–332081

Barit, William Philip, 1945-
Some properties of certain subsets of infinite dimensional spaces. [n.p.] 1971.
iv, 59 l. 29 cm.
Thesis (Ph.D.)—Louisiana State University, Baton Rouge, La.
Vita.
Bibliography: leaves 56-58.
1. Topology. 2. Hilbert space. I. Title.
LU NUC73-32105

Baritelle, J L
Long-run implications of alternative market allocation schemes for Washington's apple industry. [Pullman, 1973]
[1] 10 p. (Washington. Agricultural Experiment Station. Bulletin 785)
Bibliography: p. [11]
I. Title.
DNAL NUC75-21310

Bariţiu, Georgiu, 1812-1893
see Raţiu, Ioan, 1828-1902. Corespondenţa lui Ioan Raţiu cu George Bariţiu... Cluj, Editura Dacia, 1970.

Baritou, Jean Louis.
Maisons d'Auvergne / par Jean-Louis Baritou, avec la collaboration de Françoise Thinlot. — [Paris] : Hachette, c1975.
111 p. : ill. ; 29 cm. — (L'Inventaire régional) (Hachette littérature)
F***
Bibliography: p. 111.
ISBN 2-01-001200-3
1. Architecture, Domestic—Auvergne. 2. Decoration and ornament, Architectural—Auvergne. I. Thinlot, Françoise. II. Title.
NA7347.A95B37 728'.0944'59 75-514306
75 MARC

Barits, I I
see Baritz, Joseph.

Baritz, Joseph.
Sovetskai͡a voennai͡a doktrina i strategii͡a [by] I. I. Barit͡s. [Moskva] 1966.
1 v. (unpaged) diagrs., facsim., map (in pocket)
At head of title: Kurs peresmotren v sentiābre 1966 g. gospodinom Baritsem.
At head of title on cover label: Detachment "R" APO 09172 V.S. SSHA.
Typewritten copy (script)
Introd. also in English.
Bibliography: p. [6]-[8] and [11]-[12]
InNd NUC76-90453

Baritz, Loren, 1928-
The servants of power; a history of the use of social science in American industry. [1st ed.] Middletown, Conn., Wesleyan University Press [1960]
273 p.
Microfiche (positive) 3 cards.
1. Psychology, Industrial. 2. Industrial relations. 3. Industrial management–U.S. I. Title.
KMK NUC74-172184

Baritz, Loren, 1928–
The servants of power; a history of the use of social science in American industry. Westport, Conn., Greenwood Press [1974, c1960]
xii, 273 p. 22 cm.
Reprint of the ed. published by Wesleyan University Press, Middletown, Conn.
Includes bibliographical references.
1. Psychology, Industrial. 2. Industrial relations—United States—History. 3. Industrial management—United States—History. I. Title.
[HF5548.8.B244 1974] 658.4'00973 73–17924
ISBN 0–8371–7275–6 MARC

Bari͡utin, Lev Sergeevich.
(Osnovnye print͡sipy khozi͡aĭstvennogo rascheta v otraslevykh NII i KB)
Основные принципы хозяйственного расчета в отраслевых НИИ и КБ / Л. С. Барютин. — Ленинград : Судостроение, 1974.
39, [1] p. ; 22 cm. USSR 75
Bibliography: p. [40]
0.14rub
1. Research—Economic aspects. I. Title.
HC79.R4B36 75–531660

Barivelo, Jean Dossa.
La création d'une coopérative de pêche à Morondava. [Tananarive] École nationale des cadres [1970]
87 p. illus. 25 cm. (Série Mémoires - École national dés cadres, no 1) (Travaux et études de l'École nationale des cadres)
1. Fisheries, Cooperative—Madagascar—Morondava. I. Title. II. Series: École nationale des cadres. Série Mémoires - École nationale des cadres, no 1.
SH315.M24B37 334'.683'9209691 74–189808
MARC

Bāriyā, Sureśa.
[Candrakalaṅka]
ચંદ્રકલંક. [લેખક] સુરેશ બારિયા. [1. આવૃત્તિ. મુંબઈ, નંદિતા પ્રકાશન, પ્રદીપ પ્રકાશન વતી, 1972]
296 p. 19 cm. Rs8.75
In Gujarati.

I. Title.

PK1859.B36C34 72–901301

Bāriyā, Sureśa.
(Kuntala)
કુંતલ. [લેખક] સુરેશ બારિયા. [1. આવૃત્તિ. મુંબઈ, નંદિતા પ્રકાશન, પ્રદીપ પ્રકાશન વતી, 1972]
384 p. 19 cm. Rs11.00
In Gujarati.
A novel.

I. Title.

PK1859.B36K8 72–903038

Bāriyā, Sureśa.
વીખરાતા સૂર. [લેખક] સુરેશ બારિયા, જયંતિલાલ જોષી [અને] રવીન્દ્ર મોર-પરીઆ. [1. આવૃત્તિ. મુંબઈ, નગીન ગ્રંથાવલિ, 1970]
263 p. 19 cm. Rs8.50
In Gujarati.
A novel.

I. Jośī, Jayantīlāla, joint author. II. Moraparīā, Ravīndra, joint author. III. Title.
Title romanized: Vīkharātā sūra.

PK1859.B36V5 71–926679

Barizi, 1939-
An assessment and some applications of the empirical Bayes approach to random regression models. Raleigh, N.C., 1973.
85 l. tables. 29 cm.
Bibliography: leaves 77-79.
Vita.
Thesis (Ph.D.)—North Carolina State University at Raleigh.
NcRS NUC74-125930

Barja, J González-
see González-Barja, J

Barja Iglesias, Francisco.
Andadas do Xan Cativo. [Vigo] Galaxia [1972]
55 p. 16 cm. Sp***
I. Title.
PQ9469.2.B28A8 73-306553

Barja Iglesias, Francisco.
Viaxeiro da risa. Vigo, Castrelos, 1973.
51 p. 16 cm. (O Moucho, 34) Sp 73-Nov
ISBN 84-7041-059-8
I. Title.
PQ9469.2.B28V5 74-333575

Barjaktarević, Mirko.
Rugova; etnološka i antropogeografska proučavanja. [Beograd, Nauč. delo, 1960]
[163]-241 p. illus. 25 cm. (Srpska akademija nauka i umetnosti. Srpski etnografski zbornik, knj. 74. Odeljenje društvenih nauka. Naselja i poreklo stanovništva, knj. 36)
Summary in French.
1. Rugova, Yugoslavia—Population.
NIC NUC76-3984

Barjaktarevic, Mirko
see Smotra etnografskog i folklornog filma Balkanskih zemalja, 1st, Niš, Yugoslavia, 1964. Prva smotra etnografskog... [Beograd, Festival jugoslovenskog filma, 1964?]

Barjaktarević, Radomir.
(Vođen Kaliopom)
Вођен Калиопом. Сарајево, "Свјетлост," 1973.
78, [2] p. 19 cm. (Библиотека Хоризонти) Yu 74-1750
Poems.
I. Title.
PG1419.12.A7V6 75-970459

Barjaktarović, Miodrag Ž.
(Došaptavanja)
Дошаптавања. ⟨Ликовна опрема: Владислав Пешић. Београд, Издавач Миодраг-Миша Ж. Барјактаровић [Курсулина 4/I] 19- ⟩.
v. illus. 20 cm. (Ніз Дело 24, књ. 15) 85.00Din (v. 3)
Yu 73 (v. 3)
At head of title: Миодраг Ж. Барјактаровић.
I. Title.
PG1419.12.A75D6 73-970707

Barjau, Eustaquio, 1932-
Antonio Machado, teoría y práctica del apócrifo : tres ensayos de lectura / Eustaquio Barjau. — Esplugues de Llobregat : Editorial Ariel, 1975.
158 p. ; 18 cm. — (Letras e ideas : Minor ; 6) Sp***
Bibliography: p. 151-158.
ISBN 8434483181
1. Machado y Ruiz, Antonio, 1875-1939—Criticism and interpretation—Addresses, essays, lectures. 2. Idealism in literature—Addresses, essays, lectures. I. Title.
PQ6623.A3Z537 868'.6'209 76-460066
76 MARC

Barjau Riu, Eustaquio
see
Barjau, Eustaquio, 1932-

Barjavel, Josette.
Cris. [Roisel, Art et poésie, 1970?]
19 p. 19 cm.
I. Title.
IU NUC77-14563

Barjavel, René, 1911-
Les années de l'homme / René Barjavel. — Paris : Presses de la Cité, c1976.
312 p. ; 21 cm. F***
ISBN 2-258-00050-5 : 38.00F
I. Title.
PQ2603.A435A79 843'.9'12 76-474665
76 MARC

Barjavel, René, 1911-
Les Années de la liberté : 1972-1973 / René Barjavel. — Paris : Presses de la Cité, 1975.
305 p. ; 21 cm. F75-8400
32.10F
I. Title.
PQ2603.A435A8 76-460123
76 MARC

Barjavel, René, 1911–
Les années de la lune, 1969–1970–1971. Paris, Presses de la Cité [1972]
268 p. 21 cm. F***
21.50F
I. Title.
PQ2603.A435A84 909.82'7'08 72-350618

Barjavel, René, 1911-
Brigitte Bardot, amie des animaux / texte de René Barjavel ; [photos. de Miroslav Brozek]. — [Paris] : F. Nathan, c1976.
64 p. : col. ill. ; 29 cm. F***
42.00F
1. Animals—Pictorial works. 2. Bardot, Brigitte. I. Brozek, Miroslav. II. Title.
QL46.B19 599 77-463033
77 MARC

Barjavel, René, 1911-
Les dames à la licorne : roman / René Barjavel et Olenka de Veer. — Paris : Presses de la Cité, [1974]
338, [7] p. ; 21 cm. F***
Bibliography: p. [341]
34.90F
I. Veer, Olenka de, joint author. II. Title.
PQ2603.A435D3 843'.9'12 75-504381
75 MARC

Barjavel, René, 1911-
Future times three. Translated by Margaret Sansone Scouten. New York, Award Books [c1968]
185 p. 18 cm.
I. Title.
CNoS NUC75-30857

Barjavel, René, 1911–
Le grand secret; roman. Paris, Presses de la Cité [1973]
344 p. 21 cm. 30.00F F***
I. Title.
PQ2603.A435G7 843'.9'12 74-183938
MARC

Barjavel, René, 1911–
The immortals. Translated from the French by Eileen Finletter. New York, Morrow, 1974.
239 p. 21 cm.
Translation of Le grand secret.
I. Title.
PZ3.B23965 Im 843'.9'12 74-6234
[PQ2603.A435] MARC
ISBN 0-688-00269-2

Barjavel, René, 1911–
Jour de feu, roman. Paris, Denoël [1957]
201 p. 19 cm.
I. Title.
PQ2603.A435J58 58-16680

Barjavel, René, 1911-
Jour de feu : roman / René Barjavel. — Paris : Denoël, 1974.
200 p. ; 21 cm. F75-2485
29.00F
I. Title.
PQ2603.A435J58 1974 843'.9'12 75-513552
75 MARC

Barjavel, René, 1911-
La Nuit des temps / René Barjavel. — Paris : Éditions G. P., 1974.
316 p. : ill. ; 21 cm. — (Collection Super-bibliothèque ; 192) F75-6937
27.65F
I. Title.
PQ2603.A435N8 1974 843'.9'12 76-450975
76 MARC

Barjavel, René, 1911–
Le prince blessé. Avec Les enfants de l'ombre, La fée et le soldat et autres nouvelles. [Paris] Flammarion [1974]
245 p. 20 cm. 30.00F F***
I. Title.
PQ2603.A435A6 1974 843'.9'12 74-179730
MARC

Barjavel, René, 1911-
Ravage. [Paris] Denoël [1972, c1943]
311 p. 18 cm. (Collection folio)
I. Title.
ViU FU NUC74-125923

Barjavel, René, 1911-
Ravage / René Barjavel. — [Paris] : Rombaldi, 1974.
252 p. : ill. ; 19 cm. — (Bibliothèque du temps présent) F75-8047
Errata slip inserted.
ISBN 8439928025 : 16.00F
I. Title.
PQ2603.A435R3 1974 843'.9'12 75-519045
75 MARC

Barjavel, René, 1911–
Tarendol [par] René Barjavel. [Paris] Gallimard, 1972.
501 p. 18 cm. (Collection Folio, 169) 6.00F F 73-1161
Publisher on t. p.: Denoël.
I. Title.
PQ2603.A435T3 1972 73-332465

Barjavel, René, 1911–
Le Voyageur imprudent [par] René Barjavel. [Paris], [Gallimard], 1973.
244 p. 18 cm. (Collection Folio, 485) 4.00F F 74-6762
I. Title.
PQ2603.A435V6 1973 843'.9'12 74-179452
MARC

Barjavel, René, 1911-
see Le Futur en questions. Paris, J. C. Lattès, 1976.

Barjola, Juan.
Dibujos de Barjola, por Miguel Logroño. [1. ed.] Madrid, Ibérico Europea de Ediciones [1972]
[32] p. illus. 31 cm. (Colección Maestros contemporáneos del dibujo y la pintura, no. 20) Sp***
1. Barjola, Juan. I. Logroño, Miguel, ed. II. Title.
NC287.B37L63 73-300253

Barjola, Juan
see Castro Arines, José de. Juan Barjola. Madrid: Ibérico Europea de Ediciones, [1974]

Barjon, Louis.
Humanismo y teatro. [Buenos Aires, Ediciones Humanismo, 1960]
62 p. 17 cm. (Ediciones Humanismo, 23)
Includes bibliographical references.
1. Drama—20th cent.—Hist. & crit. I. Title.
TxHR NUC74-30462

Barjon, Louis.
Paul Claudel. Parid, Editions universitaires [c1958]
129 p. (Classiques du xxe siècle, 9)
Bibliography: p. 125-129.
1. Claudel, Paul, 1868-1955-Crit. & interp.
I. Title.
DAU NUC73-57841

Barjon, Robert.
Physique des réacteurs nucléaires de puissance / Robert Barjon ... ; [publié par l'] Institut des sciences nucléaires ... Grenoble. — Grenoble : Institut des sciences nucléaires, 1975.
[viii], 615 p. : ill. ; 25 cm. F75-11101
Errata slip inserted.
Includes bibliography.
ISBN 2-900020-06-9 : 80.00F
1. Nuclear reactors. I. Title.
TK9202.B32 76-451825
76 MARC

Barjonet, André.
Initiation au marxisme. Paris, Éditions universitaires [1973]
166 p. 20 cm. (Citoyens, 1) 15.00F F***
Includes bibliographies.
1. Communism. 2. Communism—Dictionaries—French. 3. Marxian economics—Dictionaries—French. I. Title.
HX56.B33 335.43 73-162838
MARC

Barjonet-Huraux, Marcelle
see Descartes, René, 1596-1650. Discours de la méthode. Paris, Éditions Sociales [1967, c1950]

Bark, Axel.
Terrestrische Navigation : Übungen u. Aufgaben / Axel Bark ; [graph. Gestaltung u. Zeichn., Françoise Pierzou]. — Bielefeld : Delius, Klasing u. Co., 1976.
100 p. : ill., map ; 21 cm. GFR77-A5
ISBN 3-7688-0229-9 : DM23.80
1. Navigation—Problems, exercises, etc. I. Title.
VK559.5.B37 77-554848
77 MARC

Bark, Conrad Voss
see Voss Bark, Conrad.

Bark, Dennis L
Agreement on Berlin : a study of the 1970–72 quadripartite negotiations / Dennis L. Bark. — Washington : American Enterprise Institute for Public Policy Research, 1974.
131 p. : map ; 23 cm. — (AEI-Hoover policy studies ; 10) (Hoover Institution studies ; 45)
Includes text of Quadripartite agreement on Berlin.
Includes bibliographical references.
ISBN 0-8447-3135-8 : $3.00
1. Quadripartite agreement on Berlin. I. Title. II. Series. III. Series: Hoover Institution studies ; 45.
JX4084.B38B27 341.2'9 74–83507
MARC

Bark, Dennis L
Die Berlin-Frage 1949–1955; Verhandlungsgrundlagen und Eindämmungspolitik. Mit einem Vorwort von Hans Herzfeld. Berlin, New York, de Gruyter, 1972.
xiv, 544 p. 24 cm. (Veröffentlichungen der Historischen Kommission zu Berlin, Bd. 36) GDB***
Enlarged translation of the author's thesis, originally in English, Freie Universität Berlin, 1969.
Bibliography: p. [527]–534.
1. Berlin question (1945–) I. Title. II. Series: Historische Kommission zu Berlin. Veröffentlichungen, Bd. 36.
DD881.B3515 73–329526
ISBN 3-11-003639-8

Bark, Gunnar, 1939–
Arbete med informationssystem. [Av] Gunnar Bark & Rune Brandinger. Lund, Studentlitteratur, 1973.
220 p. illus. 23 cm. kr40.00 S 73–17/18
Bibliography: p. 208–209.
1. Electronic data processing. 2. Management information systems. I. Brandinger, Rune, 1931– joint author. II. Title.
QA76.5.B2918 74–326624
ISBN 91-44-07871-4

Bark, H.
see Weeber und Partner, Büro für Stadtplanung und Sozialforschung. Mieter im Sanierungsgebiet ... Stuttgart, Die Gemeinschaft, 1976.

Bark, Hernfrid, 1895–
ABF [i. e. Arbetarnas bildningsförbund] i Västmanland 50 år. [Västerås, Tryckt hos Folkbladets civil, 1962]
253 p. illus. 23 cm.
Bibliography: p. 239–243.
1. Arbetarnas bildningsförbund—History. I. Title.
LC5001.A73B37 74–230978

Bark, Hernfrid, 1895–
Ur Skinnskattebergsbygdens historia / Hernfrid Bark. — [Skinnskatteberg] : Skinnskattebergs kommun, 1974.
339 p. : ill. ; 25 cm. S 75–10/11
Includes bibliographical references and indexes.
kr58.00
1. Skinnskatteberg, Sweden. I. Title.
DL991.S5923B38 75–527796

Bark, Joachim, comp.
Literatursoziologie / hrsg. von Joachim Bark. — Stuttgart, Berlin, Köln, Mainz : Kohlhammer, 1974.
2 v. 21 cm. GFR 74-A (v. 1)
Includes bibliographical references.
CONTENTS: 1. Begriff und Methodik.—2. Beiträge zur Praxis.
ISBN 3-17-001504-4 (v. 1) : DM20.00 (v. 1). ISBN 3-17-001505-2 (v. 2)
1. Literature and society—Addresses, essays, lectures. I. Title.
PN51.B3 74–346919

Bark, Julius.
Kobran : kriminalroman / Julius Bark. — [Göteborg] : Zinderman ; [Solna : Seelig], 1976.
215 p. ; 22 cm. S76-45
ISBN 915280173X : kr54.00
I. Title.
PT9876.12.A74K6 77-552855
•77 MARC

Bark, L. S., ed.
see United States. National Bureau of Standards. Computation Laboratory. Mnogoznachnye tablit͡sy elementarnykh funkt͡siĭ... Moskva, Vychislitel'nyĭ t͡sentr AN SSSR, 1960.

Bark, L. S.
see United States. National Bureau of Standards. Computation Laboratory. Tablit͡sy veroi͡atnostnykh funkt͡siĭ. Moskva, Vychislitel'nyĭ tsentr AN SSSR, 1958–59.

Bark, Laurence Dean, 1926–
Chances for precipitation in Kansas, by L. Dean Bark. [Manhattan, Agricultural Experiment Station, Kansas State University of Agriculture and Applied Science, 1963]
83 p. illus., maps. 28 cm. ([Agricultural Experiment Station, Kansas State University of Agriculture and Applied Science, Manhattan] Bulletin 461)
"Contribution no. 95, Department of Physics, KAES, KSU, Manhattan."
"Partially supported by U. S. Weather Bureau, Contract CWB. 9938."
Bibliography: p. 83.
1. Precipitation (Meteorology)—Kansas. I. Title. II. Series: Kansas. Agricultural Experiment Station, Manhattan. Bulletin 461.
QC925.1.U8K32 551.6'5'09781 63–64666
MARC

Bark, Laurence Dean, 1926-
A survey of the radar echo population over the western Kansas high plains / by L. Dean Bark, principal investigator ; data reduction by Geophysical Research and Development Corp. -- Manhattan : Department of Physics, Kansas Agricultural Experiment Station, Kansas State University, 1975.
2 v. : ill.
KMK NUC77-100991

Bark, Laurence Dean, 1926- joint author
see Brown, Merle J Drought in Kansas. Manhattan, 1971.

Bark, Laurence Dean, 1926-
see Feyerherm, A M Probabilities of sequences of wet and dry days... [Manhattan, Agricultural Experiment Station, Kansas State University of Agriculture and Applied Science] 1966.

Barka, Anne
see Barka, Norman F. Archaeology and the fur trade... -- Ottawa : Parks Canada, 1976.

Barka, el Mehdi ben
see Bin Barakah, al-Mahdī, 1920.

Barka, Norman F
Archaeology and the fur trade : the excavation of Sturgeon Fort, Saskatchewan / Norman F. and Anne Barka. -- Ottawa : Parks Canada, 1976.
191 p. : ill. ; 28 cm. -- (History and archaeology ; no. 7)
French summary: p. 5.
Bibliography: p. 93-113.
1. Sturgeon Fort, Sask. I. Barka, Anne. II. Title. III. Series.
CaBVaU NUC77-100334

Barka, Vasyl'.
Trojanden-Roman, 1949/50 [von] Wassyl Barka. Eine ukrainische Liebesdichtung ins Deutsche übertragen von Elisabeth Kottmeier. Mannheim, Kessler Verlag, 1956.
98 p. 21 cm.
German and Ukrainian on opposite pages.
Translation of Troi͡andnyĭ roman.
Printed in 500 copies.
I. Kottmeier, Elisabeth, 1902– tr. II. Title.
PG3948.B26T7 1956 74–200994

Barka, Vasyl'.
(Zemli͡a sadivnychykh)
Земля садівничих : есеї / Василь Барка. — [München] : Сучасність, 1977.
189 p. : ill. ; 19 cm. — (Бібліотека прологу і сучасности ; ч. 111) GFR***
Added t. p.: Earth of the gardeners.
Series romanized: Biblioteka prolohu i suchasnosty.
CONTENTS: Світло поезії старовинної і сучасної.—Речник обнови.—Багатство Франка.—Традиція і модернізм.—Відхід Тичини.—Відроджена лірика.—Поема—як відтворений вік.—Перехрестя кобзарів.—Апостолічний старчик.—Розповідь новоекспресіоністів.—Протилежні перемоги (поет і вождь).—Боржники святих.—Пророцтво поета.—Благословенний стиль.—Видіння художника.—"Фавст"—як доля людини.—Барокко в Україні.—Знахід Гоголя.—"Кобзар" і Біблія.—Загадка мистецькости.—Прикмета поетичного.—Живий спадок.
1. Ukrainian poetry—History and criticism—Addresses, essays, lectures. I. Title. II. Title: Earth of the gardeners.
PG3917.B3 76–50229

Barka, Vasyl'
see Shakespeare, William, 1564-1616. [King Lear. Ukrainian] Korol' Lir. 1969.

Barka, Vasyl'
see Shakespeare, William, 1564-1616. Korol' Lir. Shtutgart, "Na hori", 1969.

Barka z Dubé a Lipé, Zbyněk, 1551-1606
see Prague (Archdiocese). Synod, 1605. Synodus Archi-Dioecesana Pragensis, habita ab Sbigneo Berka ... [Pragae, Recusa per G. Czernoch, 1684]

Barkagan, Z. S.
see Altaĭskiĭ kraevoĭ s"ezd terapevtov, 3d, Barnaul, Siberia, 1966. Voprosy kardiologii i gematologii. Barnaul, 1967.

Barkai, Baruch.
(Entsiklopedyah le-nimusin)
אנציקלופדיה לנימוסין / ברוך ברקאי ; [עריכה, אליאונורה לב ; איורים, נורית יובל]. — [רמת-גן] : מסדה, c1976.
259 p. : ill. ; 25 cm.
Includes index.
1. Etiquette. I. Title.
BJ2007.H4B37 77–951408

Barkai, Haim, 1925-
Growth patterns of the kibbutz economy / Haim Barkai. — Amsterdam ; New York : North-Holland Pub. Co. ; New York : sole distributors for the U.S.A. and Canada, Elsevier North-Holland, c1977.
xix, 298 p. : ill. ; 23 cm. — (Contributions to economic analysis ; 108)
Bibliography: p. [293]-295.
Includes index.
ISBN 0-7204-0556-4
1. Collective settlements—Israel. I. Title. II. Series.
HX765.P3B249 1977 334'.683'095694 76-44024
76 MARC

Barkai, Haim, 1925–
The impact of experience on kibbutz farming, by Haim Barkai and David Levhari. Jerusalem, Hebrew University of Jerusalem, Dept. of Economics, 1971.
18 l. 28 cm. (Hebrew University of Jerusalem. Dept. of Economics. Research report, no. 35)
1. Agriculture, Cooperative—Israel. 2. Collective settlements—Israel. I. Levhari, David, joint author. II. Title. III. Series: Jerusalem. Hebrew University. Dept. of Economics. Research report, no. 35.
HD1491.I 7B37 72–959551
MARC

Barkai, Haim, 1925–
Industrialization and deflation: the monetary experience of tsarist Russia in the industrialization era. [Jerusalem] Hebrew University of Jerusalem, Dept. of Economics, 1969.
63, xiv l. 28 cm. (Hebrew University of Jerusalem. Dept. of Economics. Research report, no. 4)
Includes bibliographical references.
1. Money—Russia—History. 2. Monetary policy—Russia—History. 3. Russia—Economic conditions. 4. Deflation (Finance)—Russia—History. I. Title. II. Series: Jerusalem. Hebrew University. Dept. of Economics. Research report, no. 4.
HG1074.B33 332.4'947 72–959528
MARC

Barkai, Haim, 1925–
The kibbutz; an experiment in microsocialism. Jerusalem, Hebrew University of Jerusalem, Dept. of Economics, 1971.
59 l. 27 cm. (Hebrew University of Jerusalem. Dept. of Economics. Research report, no. 34)
1. Collective settlements—Israel. I. Title. II. Series: Jerusalem. Hebrew University. Dept. of Economics. Research report, no. 34.
HX765.P3B25 335'.9'5694 72–959550
MARC

Barkai, Haim, 1925-
The public, Histadrut, and private sectors in the Israel economy. [Jerusalem ?] Maruice Falk Institute for Economic Research in Israel, 1968.
87 p. illus. 24 cm.
Reprinted from the Sixth report 1961-1963 of the Falk Project for Economic Research in Israel.
1. Israel—Economic conditions. 2. General Federation of Jewish Labour in Israel. I. Title.
WU NUC75-31503

Barkai, Malachi, 1935-
Problems in the phonology of Israeli Hebrew. Urbana, Ill., 1973.
171 l.
Thesis–University of Illinois.
Vita.
1. Hebrew language–Phonology. 2. Hebrew language in Israel. I. Title.
InU NUC76-74068

Barkai, Malachi, 1935-
Problems in the phonology of Israeli Hebrew, by Malachi Barkai. Urbana, Ill., 1972.
171 l.
Vita.
Thesis—University of Illinois.
Bibliography: leaves 167-169.
Photocopy of typescript. Ann Arbor, Mich., University Microfilms, 1974. 22 cm.
1. Hebrew language—Phonology. I. Title.
OU NUC76-74069

Barkai, Meyer, tr.
see Zuckerman, Isaac. The fighting ghettos. [New York] Tower Publications [1962]

Barkai, Mordekhai
see Barkay, Mordechay, ed.

Barkai, Sarah.
Noar Oved Ve'lomed / [written by Sara Barkai, Meir Zarmi, and Asher Maniv ; drawings and graphics by Nini]. — [Tel Aviv] : Mapai—Israel Labour Party, [between 1962 and 1967]
[38] p. : ill. ; 16 x 17 cm.
Cover title.
1. Histadrut ha-no'ar ha-'oved veha-lomed. 2. Youth—Employment—Israel. I. Zarmi, Meir, joint author. II. Maniv, Asher, joint author. III. Title.
HD6276.I65B37 77-363739
77 MARC

Barkai, Yehuda, 1925–
(Yesodot ha-kalkalah)
יסודות הכלכלה [מאת] יהודה ברקאי. חיפה, שקמונה [1973]
171 p. illus. 23 cm.
On verso of t. p.: Basic economics.
"ראשיתו של הספר סידרת-הרצאות משודרת בקול ישראל."
1. Economics. I. Title.
HB180.H4B37 73-952692

(Barkai)
ברקאי.
יוהניסבורג, אגודת הסופרים העברים בדרום אפריקה.
no. in v. ill. 29 cm.
"לפנים "בסר"."
Monthly -Apr. 1962; biweekly, May 16, 1962–
Issues for called also ; May 16, 1962–
called also no. 1–
Afrikaans, English or Hebrew.
Supplements accompany some numbers.
ISSN 0005-5964
1. Jews—Periodicals. 2. Jews in South Africa—Periodicals. I. Agudat ha-sofrim ha-'ivrim bi-Derom Afrikah.
DS101.B29 75-644097
(MARC-S)

Barkaia, Valer'ian Fedorovich.
(Formoizmenenie listovogo metalla)
Формоизменение листового металла / В. Ф. Баркая, С. Е. Рокотян, Ф. И. Рузанов. — Москва : Металлургия, 1976.
263 p. : ill. ; 20 cm. USSR***
Bibliography: p. 257-[262]
1.39rub
1. Sheet-metal work. I. Rokotian, Sergeĭ Evgen'evich, joint author. II. Ruzanov, Feliks Ivanovich, joint author. III. Title.
TS250.B295 77-513338

Barkakati, Hari, 1927–
কোনোবা শীতৰ এটা বগা সন্ধিয়াত. [কবি] হৰি বৰকাকতি. তিনিচুকীয়া, অসম, মিত্ৰ এজেঞ্চি [1970]
51 p. 22 cm. Rs3.00
In Assamese.
I. Title. Title romanized: Konobā śītara eṭā bagā sandhiẏāta.
PK1569.B268K6 78-916298

Barkali, Saul. Hebraisch fur Jerdermann
see Barkali, Saul. Ivrit le-khoi ish.

Barkali, Saul.
['Ivrit le-khol ish]
עברית לכל איש. Hebräisch für Jedermann, von S. Barkali (Kaléko). Mit einem Vokabular der 1500 wichtigsten Wörter, Grammatik-Index und Anhang. Neue Aufl. Jerusalem, R. Mass [c1970]
88, xii p. 23 cm. IL2.80
1. Hebrew language—Text-books for foreigners—German. I. Title. II. Title: Hebräisch für Jerdermann.
PJ4575.G5B3 1970 75-954277

Barkalow, Frederick Schenck, 1914–
The world of the gray squirrel [by] Frederick S. Barkalow, Jr., and Monica Shorten. Illustrated with photos. [1st ed.] Philadelphia, Lippincott [1973]
160 p. illus. 26 cm. (Living world books) $5.95
Bibliography: p. 141-154.
1. Gray squirrel. I. Shorten, Monica, 1923– joint author. II. Title.
QL737.R68B37 599'.3233 72-2920
ISBN 0-397-00749-3 MARC

Barkaman, Lars
see Muhlethaler, Bruno. Conservation of waterlogged wood and wet leather. Paris, Eyrolles, 1973.

Barkan, Aleksandr Borisovich
see Maĭzel', IUriĭ Arkad'evich. Avtomatizatsiia proizvodstv fosfora i fosforsoderzhashchikh produktov. 1973.

Barkan, Barry.
Picking poverty's pocket [by] Barry Barkan [and] R. Baldwin Lloyd. [Huntington, W. Va., Appalachian Movement Press, 1972]
1 v. (unpaged) illus. 28 cm.
Cover title.
"Reprinted from Article one; a magazine for the new Virginia."
1. Coal miners—Appalachian region. 2. Coal mines and mining—Appalachian region. 3. United Mine Workers of America. I. Lloyd, R. Baldwin, joint author. II. Title.
CtY NUC75-31493

Barkan, D D
Сейсмовзрывные волны и действие их на сооружения. Москва, Гос. изд-во строит. лит-ры, 1945.
47, [1] p. diagrs. 19 cm.
At head of title: Наркомстрой СССР. ОСМЧ-5. Всесоюзная научно-исследовательская лаборатория по изучению оснований сооружений (б. ВИОС)
Bibliography: slip mounted on p. [48]
1. Blast effect. 2. Seismic waves. 3. Structural dynamics.
Title transliterated: Seĭsmovzryvnye volny i deĭstvie ikh na sooruzhniia.
TA654.7.B37 74-213829

Barkan, Glenn Mark, 1945-
The President and broadcasting: governing through the media, by Glen Barkan. Claremont, Calif., 1971.
170 l.
Thesis—Claremont Graduate School.
Includes abstract.
Bibliography: leaves 161-170.
1. Presidents—U. S. —Public opinion. 2. Mass media—U. S. —Political aspects. 3. Radio in politics. I. Title.
AzTeS NUC76-74144

Barkan, Glenn Mark, 1945-
The President and broadcasting: governing through the media, by Glenn Barkan. [n.p.] 1971.
iii, 170 l. illus.
Thesis—Claremont Graduate School.
Bibliography: leaves 161-170.
Microfilm (negative) of typescript. Ann Arbor, Mich., University Microfilms, 1972. 1 reel. 35 mm.
1. Presidents. U.S. 2. Government and the press. U.S. I. Title.
NcD NUC75-30858

Barkan, Glenn Mark, 1945-
The President and broadcasting; governing through the media, by Glenn Barkan. [Ann Arbor, Mich., University Microfilms, 1974]
iii, 170 p. 21 cm.
Thesis—Claremont Graduate School, 1971.
"Authorized facsimile...produced by microfilm xerography."
Bibliography: p. 161-170.
NcGU NUC76-29018

Barkan, IAkov Grigor'evich.
(Organicheskaia khimiia)
Органическая химия. [Учеб. пособие для с.-х. вузов]. Москва, "Высш. школа," 1973.
552 p. with illus. 22 cm. 1.06rub USSR 73-VKP
At head of title: Я. Г. Баркан.
Bibliography: p. [549]
1. Chemistry, Organic. I. Title.
QD251.2.B38 74-341521

Barkan, Irina Nikolaevna, joint author
see Stepanian, E P (Energetika operirovannogo serdtsa) 1971.

Barkan, Joel D
An African dilemma : university students, development, and politics in Ghana, Tanzania, and Uganda / Joel D. Barkan. — Nairobi ; New York : Oxford University Press, 1975 [i.e. 1976]
xvii, 259 p. ; 22 cm.
Bibliography: p. [247]-254.
Includes index.
ISBN 0-19-572374-0 : $15.75
1. College students—Ghana—Political activity. 2. College students—Tanzania—Political activity. 3. College students—Uganda—Political activity. I. Title.
LA1628.7.B37 378.1'98'109667 76-369164
76 MARC

Barkan, Joel D
African university students and social change: an analysis of student opinion in Ghana, Tanzania, and Uganda. Los Angeles, 1970.
xvi, 365 l.
Thesis—University of California.
Bibliography: leaves 295-303.
Microfilm. Ann Arbor, Mich., University Microfilms, 1971. 1 reel. 35 mm.
"71-16, 373."
1. Students—Africa. 2. Africa—Social conditions. I. Title.
NhD NUC73-38834

Barkan, Joel D
Elite perceptions and political involvement of university students in Ghana, Tanzania, and Uganda, by Joel D. Barkan. [New York, African Studies Association, 1968]
26 p. 28 cm. ([African Studies Association. Papers, no. 125])
Cover title.
"Prepared for the eleventh annual meeting of the African Studies Association, October 18, 1968."
Includes bibliographical references.
1. Students—Ghana—Political activity. 2. Students—Tanzania—Political activity. 3. Students—Uganda—Political activity.
CtY-L NUC75-31495

Barkan, Leonard.
Nature's work of art : the human body as image of the world / Leonard Barkan. — New Haven : Yale University Press, 1975.
x, 291 p. ; 24 cm.
Originally presented as the author's thesis, Yale University, 1971, under the title: Elementated man: studies in the metaphor of the human body.
Includes bibliographical references and index.
ISBN 0-300-01694-8 : $15.00
1. English literature—Early modern, 1500-1700—History and criticism. 2. Body, Human in literature. 3. Microcosm and macrocosm. I. Title.
PR429.B6B3 821'.009'353 74-77067
75 MARC

Barkan, Manuel.
Viktor Lowenfeld: his impact on art education. Washington, National Art Education Association, 1966.
iii, 24 p. 23 cm. (Research monograph 2)
"Delivered as a Viktor Lowenfeld memorial lecture at the 1965 National Art Education Association Conference."
"Response to Barkan's paper [by] W. Lambert Brittain": p. [20]-24.
Includes bibliographical references.
1. Lowenfeld, Viktor. 2. Art—Philosophy. I. Brittain, W. Lambert. II. Series: National Art Education Association. Research monograph 2.
N70.B24 707 79-265878
71[r75]rev MARC

Barkan, Ömer Lûtfi.
xv [i e. On beş] ve xvıncı [i. e. on altıncı] asırlarda Osmanlı imparatorluğunda ziraî ekonominin hukukî ve malî esasları. İstanbul, Bürhaneddin Matbaası, 1943 [cover 1945]–
v. facsims. 25 cm. (İstanbul Üniversitesi Edebiyat Fakültesi yayınlarından no. 256. Türkiyat Enstitüsü neşriyati)
CONTENTS: 1. cilt. Kanunlar.
1. Agricultural laws and legislation—Turkey. 2. Agriculture—Economic aspects—Turkey. I. Title.
56-28445
rev

Barkan, Ömer Lûtfi. On beş ve on altinci asirlarda Osmanli İmparatorluğunda ziraî ekonominin hukukî ve malî esaslari
see Safrastyan, Aram Khach'atowri, comp. Ōsmanyan ōrenk'nerĕ Arewmtyan Hayastanowm. 1964.

Barkan, Ömer Lûtfi.
Süleymaniye Cami ve imareti inşaatı (1550–1557) / Ömer Barkan. — Ankara : ⌜Türk Tarih Kurumu⌝ 1972–
v. : ill., facsims., graphs (some col.) ; 32 cm. — (Türk Tarih Kurumu yayınlarından ; 6. seri, sa. 10)
Includes bibliographical references.
1. Süleymaniye Cami, Istanbul. 2. Architecture, Islamic—Istanbul. I. Title. II. Series: Türk Tarih Kurumu. Türk Tarih Kurumu yayınlarından ; 6. seri, sa. 10
NA5870.S93B37 75–973117

Barkan, Raymond, 1912–
Un billet de deuxième classe pour Asnières. ⌜Paris, Balland, 1972⌝
254 p. 22 cm. 27.00F F***
I. Title.
PQ2662.A69B5 74–328538
MARC

Barkan, Stanley H.
see Americana anthology. Merrick, N.Y., Cross-Cultural Communications, 1976-

Barkan, Varlen Abramovich.
Sovershenstvovanie form ateisticheskoĭ propagandy v BSSR, 1954-1958 gg. [By] V. A. Barkan. Minsk, Izd-vo BGU im. V. I. Lenina, 1969.
71 p.
1. Communist education–White Russia. 2. Atheism–White Russia.
MH NUC75-129128

Barkana, Atila.
Application of signal perturbation theory to picture reconstruction / by Atila Barkana. -- ⌜s.l. : s.n.⌝, 1975.
xiv, 161 leaves : ill. ; 29 cm.
Thesis--University of Virginia.
Includes bibliographical references.
1. Perturbation (Mathematics) 2. Image converters. I. Title.
ViU NUC77-100992

Barkarakēs, Kōnstantinos I
see
Varkarakēs, Kōnstantinos I 1939-

Barkas, Janet.
Meatless cooking, celebrity style / by Janet Barkas ; photos. by the author ; ill. by Simms Taback. — New York : Grove Press : distributed by Random House, ⌜1975⌝
vii, 280 p. : ill. ; 24 cm.
Includes index.
ISBN 0-8021-0073-2 : $8.95
1. Vegetarianism. I. Title.
TX837.B29 641.5′636 74–7677
MARC

Barkas, Janet.
The vegetable passion. New York, Scribner ⌜1975⌝
xi, 224 p. illus. 24 cm.
Bibliography: p. 197–208.
ISBN 0-684-13925-1
1. Vegetarianism. I. Title.
TX392.B33 641.5′636 74–10983
MARC

Barkas, Janet.
The vegetable passion : a history of the vegetarian state of mind / Janet Barkas. — London : Routledge and Kegan Paul, 1975.
xi, 224 P. : ill., facsims., ports ; 22 cm. GB 75-14878
Bibliography: p. 197-208.
Includes index.
ISBN 0-7100-8180-0 : £3.95. ISBN 0-7100-8208-8 pbk.
1. Vegetarianism. 2. Vegetarians. I. Title.
TX392.B33 1975b 613.2′6 75-325548
75 MARC

Barkas, Pallister, 1889-
A critique of modern English prosody : (1880-1930) / von Pallister Barkas. — Walluf (bei Wiesbaden) : Sändig, 1973.
100 p. ; 21 cm. GFR 74-A
Reprint of the 1934 ed. published by Niemeyer, Halle, which was issued as Heft 82 of Studien zur Englischen Philologie.
Includes index.
ISBN 3-500-28690-9 : DM20.00
1. English language—Versification. I. Title. II. Series: Studien zur Englischen Philologie ; Heft 82.
PE1505.B24 1973 426 75-515958
75 MARC

Barkas, Walter H
Nuclear research emulsions. New York, Academic Press, 1963–73.
2 v. illus. 24 cm. (Pure and applied physics, v. 15)
Includes bibliographies.
CONTENTS: 1. Techniques and theory.—2. Particle behavior and emulsion applications.
1. Nuclear emulsions. 2. Particles (Nuclear physics) I. Title. II. Series.
QC787.N78B37 539.7′78 63–13639 ‡
ISBN 0-12-078301-0 (v. 1)
rev

Barkas, Walter H.
see Symposium on the Penetration of Charged Particles in Matter. Penetration of charged particles in matter. Washington, National Academy of Sciences, 1970.

Barkat, Anwar M
The Fellowship of Socialist Christians and its antecedents. [Chapel Hill, N. C.] 1965.
iv, 294 l. 21 cm.
Thesis–Duke University.
Photocopy of typescript.
Vita.
Bibliography: leaves 278-294.
1. Fellowship of Socialist Christians. 2. Niebuhr, Reinhold, 1892-1971. 3. Socialism, Christian. I. Title.
CBGTU NUC74-125808

Barkat, Anwar M., ed.
see Christian reflections on New Educational Policy. ⌜Lahore, Business Print. Press, 1972⌝

Barkat, Ella, joint author
see Rimovsky, Semion, 1911- (Ani Lovah Z'id) c1975.

Barkat, Re'uven, 1905-1972
see
Bareket, Re'uven, 1905-1972.

Barkat ʻAlī
see
ʻAlī, Barkat.

Barkataki, Annada Devi, comp.
বিয়ানাম. ⌜লিখিকা⌝ শ্ৰীঅন্নদা দেৱী বৰকটকী. সংশোধিত নতুন 7. সংস্কৰণ. ⌜যোৰহাট, বৰকটকী কোম্পানী⌝ 1886 শকাব্দ ⌜1964 or 5⌝
123 p. 19 cm. Rs1.50
In Assamese.
1. Assamese ballads and songs. I. Title.
Title romanized: Biẏānāma.
PK1568.B3 79–914880

Barkataki, Padma.
বিয়াৰ প্ৰথম নিশা. ⌜লিখক⌝ পদ্ম বৰকটকী. তিনিচুকীয়া, অসম, মিত্ৰ এজেঞ্চি ⌜1970⌝
67 p. 23 cm. Rs3.00
In Assamese.
Short stories.
I. Title.
Title romanized: Biẏāra prathama niśā.
PK1569.B27B5 70–916226

Barkataki, Padma.
পুতলাৰ নমস্কাৰ. ⌜লিখক⌝ পদ্ম বৰকটকী. তিনিচুকীয়া, অসম, মিত্ৰ এজেঞ্চি ⌜1968⌝
107 p. 23 cm. 3.50
In Assamese.
A novel.
I. Title.
Title romanized: Putalāra namaskāra.
PK1569.B27P8 72–905608

Barkataki, Padma.
ৰঙা, ৰঙা ৰং. ⌜লিখক⌝ পদ্ম বৰকটকী. ⌜গুৱাহাটী⌝ সাহিত্য-প্ৰকাশ ⌜1972⌝
197 p. 22 cm. Rs8.00
In Assamese.
I. Title. Title romanized: Raṅā, raṅā raṃ.
PK1569.B27R3 72–903443

Barkati, Mahmood Ahmad, 1926–
(Faẕl-i Ḥaq Khairābādī aur san sattāvan)
فضل حق خیرآبادی اور سن ستاون / محمود احمد برکاتی. —
اشاعت 1. — کراچی : برکات اکیڈمی, 1975.
128 p. ; 18 cm.
In Urdu.
Includes bibliographical references.
Rs5.00
1. Faẕl Ḥaq Khairābādī, 1797?-1859. 2. India—History—Sepoy Rebellion, 1857-1858. 3. Statesmen—India—Biography. I. Title.
DS475.2.F38B37 75–930564

Barkatoky, Upendra, comp.
see A' mora Asamī āi. [1973]

Barkatullah, 1891–
مسیحیت کی عالمگیری. ⌜مصنف⌝ برکت اللہ. 2. ایڈیشن. لکھنؤ،
ہنری مارٹن انسٹی ٹیوٹ ⌜1965?⌝
398 p. 19 cm. Rs4.00
In Urdu.
Includes bibliographical references.
1. Christianity—Essence, genius, nature. I. Title.
Title romanized: Masīḥiyat kī ʻālamgīrī.
BR121.2.B286 1965 77–917958

Barkatullah, Qazi Muhammad.
Islam, the religion for mankind. Jackson, Miss., 1972.
48 p.
Bibliography: p. 47–48.
1. Mohammedanism. I. Title.
MsSM NUC73-125053

Barkatullah, Qazi Muhammad.
Jesus, Son of Mary: fallacy and factuality. Philadelphia, Dorrance ⌜1973⌝
127 p. 22 cm. $4.95
Includes bibliographical references.
1. Jesus Christ—Historicity. 2. Jesus Christ—Biography—History and criticism. I. Title.
BT303.2.B276 232.9′08 73–77630
ISBN 0-8059-1857-4 MARC

Barkauskas, Antanas.
Kutūra ir visuomenė / A. Barkauskas. — Vilnius : Mokslas, 1975.
406 p. ; 21 cm. USSR 76-13330
Errata slip inserted.
Bibliography: p. 393–403.
2.04rub
1. Lithuania—Civilization. I. Title.
DK511.L212B37 76–532499

Barkauskas, Antanas.
The Lithuanian countryside : past, present, and future / A. Barkauskas. — Moscow : Novosti Press Agency Pub. House, 1976.
93 p., ⌜8⌝ leaves of plates : ill. ; 17 cm. USSR***
1. Lithuania. I. Title.
DK511.L2B25 947′.5 76-383155
76 MARC

Barkauskas, Mary Ellen.
Hiking and hiking trails; a trails and trail-based activities bibliography. Washington, U. S. Dept. of the Interior, Office of the Secretary, 1970.
ii l., 57 p. 27 cm. (Office of Library Services. Bibliography series, no. 20)
1. Hiking — United States — Bibliography. 2. Trails — United States—Bibliography. I. Title. II. Series: United States. Dept. of the Interior. Office of Library Services. Bibliography series, no. 20.
Z6016.H5B34 016.7965 72–602625
MARC

Barkay, Menahem Zvi, 1910- ed.
see Irgun safrane Yisrael. Duaḥ pe'ulot ha-irgun. [1969]

Barkay, Mordechay, ed.
see Ecrit au combat... Tel Aviv, Editions Ledory [1968?]

Barkdoll, Dorothy L
Relationship of patients' and spouses' preoperative anxiety and patients' postoperative pain / by Dorothy L. Barkdoll. -- [s. l. : s.n.], 1975.
xii, 93 leaves ; 28 cm.
Thesis (D.N.Sc.)--Catholic University of America.
Bibliography: leaves [87]-93.
1. Surgery--Psychological aspects. 2. Anxiety. 3. Pain. I. Title.
DCU NUC77-100893

Barke, Eckhard.
Beitrag zur Narkose des Geflugels; Literaturubersicht und Versuche. Hannover, 1970.
120 p. illus. (Hanover (City) Tierarztliche Hochschule. [Inaugural-Dissertation, 1970, no. 35])
Bibliography: p. 113-120.
I. Title.
DNAL NUC73-40554

Barke, Georg.
Fortschritte 1960–1964; Hannover—vier Jahre Ratsarbeit. [Zusammengestellt und bearb. von Georg Barke und Wilhelm Hatopp. Hrsg. von der Landeshauptstadt Hannover] Hannover, Steinbock Verlag [1964]
144 p. illus. 29 cm.
1. Hanover—History. I. Hatopp, Wilhelm, joint author. II. Title.
DD901.H48B37 72-223805

Barke, Georg
see Die Stadtbüchereien Hannover. Hanover, 1966.

Barke, James, 1905-1958.
The well of the silent harp : a novel of the life and loves of Robert Burns / James Barke. — London : Fontana, 1975.
288 p. : map ; 18 cm. — (His Immortal memory) GB75-06952
ISBN 0-00-613499-8 : £0.60
1. Burns, Robert, 1759-1796, in fiction, drama, poetry, etc. I. Title.
PZ3.B2397 We 6 823'.9'12 76-377980
[PR6003.A677] 76 MARC

Barke, James, 1905-1958.
The wonder of all the gay world : a novel of the life and loves of Robert Burns / James Barke. -- London : Collins, 1975.
2 v. (318, 250 p.) ; 18 cm. -- (Fontana Books)
GU NUC77-101010

Barke, Rudolf, illus.
see Meyer, Lothar. Einführung in die Geschichte der Bergstadt Clausthal-Zellerfeld/Lothar Meyer. Clausthal-Zellerfeld: Pieper, 1972.

Barke, V. N.
see Osnovy balansirovochnoĭ tekhniki. 1975.

Barke, V. N.
see Uravnoveshivanie gibkikh rotorov i balansirovochnoe oborudovanie. 1975.

Barke, V. N.
see Uravnoveshivanie zhestkikh rotorov i mekhanizmov. 1975.

Barkelees, Dad.
A l'aube des rivages perdus. Avec un poème-pref. de Jean-Paul Liégeois. [Honfleur] P. J. Oswald [1971]
107 p. 18 cm. 19.50F F***
Poems.
I. Title.
PQ2662.A692A62 73-321178

Barkelius, P.-G.
see Barks lilla bok om Köping. [Köping, Barkens förl., 1973]

Barkely, Theodore M 1934-
A manual of the flowering plants of Kansas by T. M. Barkley. Manhattan, Kan., Kansas State University Endowment Association, 1968.
402 p.
1. Botany—Kansas. I. Title.
FTaSU NUC74-15753

Barker, A. C.
see also
Barker, Alfred Charles, 1819-1873.

Barker, A J
Behind barbed wire [by] A. J. Barker. London, Batsford [1974]
xi, 242 p. illus. 22 cm. £3.30 GB***
Bibliography: p. [228]-235.
1. Prisoners of war. I. Title.
JX5141.B35 341.6'5 74-163780
ISBN 0-7134-1175-9 MARC

Barker, A J
Bloody Ulster [by] A. J. Barker. [New York, Ballantine Books, 1973]
159, [1] p. illus. 21 cm. (Ballantine's illustrated history of the violent century. Human conflict no. 5) $1.00
Bibliography: p. [160]
1. Northern Ireland—History. I. Title.
DA990.U46B226 941.6 73-165424
ISBN 0-345-03223-3 MARC

Barker, A J
British and American infantry weapons of World War II, by A. J. Barker. [New revised ed.]. London, Arms and Armour Press, [1973].
78 p. illus. 22 cm. (Illustrated studies in twentieth century arms) £0.75 B 73-11103
1. United States. Army—Firearms. 2. Great Britain. Army—Firearms. I. Title.
UF523.B36 1973 355.8'2 73-165888
ISBN 0-85368-489-8 MARC

Barker, A J
Famous military battles / [by] A. J. Barker. — London ; New York [etc.] : Hamlyn, 1974.
5-125 p. : ill. (some col.), maps, col. ports. ; 27 cm. GB75-03146
Includes index.
SUMMARY: Describes the events and strategy of ten decisive battles in history.
ISBN 0-600-33544-5 : £1.50
1. Battles. [1. Battles] I. Title.
D25.B34 904'.7 75-315974
75 MARC

Barker, A J
Fortune favours the brave—the Battle of the Hook, Korea, 1953 / by A. J. Barker. — London : Cooper, 1974.
xviii, 170 p., [8] p. of plates : ill., plans, ports. ; 23 cm. GB 74-24482
Bibliography: p. 164-165.
Includes index.
ISBN 0-85052-108-4 : £4.25
1. Korean War, 1950–1953—Campaigns. 2. Korean War, 1950–1953—Regimental histories—Great Britain—Duke of Wellington's Regiment. 3. Gt. Brit. Army. Duke of Wellington's Regiment. I. Title.
DS918.B3 1974 951.9'042 74-196313
MARC

Barker, A J
German infantry weapons of World War II / by A. J. Barker. — Rev. ed. — London : Arms and Armour Press; New York : Hippocrene Books, 1976, c1972.
78 p. : ill. ; 22 cm.
ISBN 0-88254-372-5 : $2.95
1. Germany. Heer—Firearms. I. Title.
UD385.G4B3 1976 356'.186 75-42353
75 MARC

Barker, A J
Principles of small arms. Aldershot [Eng.] Gale & Polden, 1952.
82 p. illus. 19 cm.
1. Firearms. I. Title.
UD380.B28 623.44 52-42408

Barker, A J
Prisoners of war / A. J. Barker. — New York : Universe Books, 1975.
249 p., [8] leaves of plates : ill. ; 22 cm.
Published in 1974 under title: Behind barbed wire.
Bibliography: p. [236]-242.
Includes index.
1. Prisoners of war.
JX5141.B35 1975 365'.6 74-27244
MARC

Barker, A J
Redcoats / A. J. Barker. — London : Gordon & Cremonesi, c1976.
156 p., [8] leaves of plates : ill. ; 22 cm. GB***
Bibliography: p. [149]-151.
Includes index.
ISBN 0-86033-007-9 : $14.95 (U.S.)
1. Great Britain. Army—History. 2. Canada—History—To 1763 (New France) 3. United States—History—Colonial period, ca. 1600-1775. I. Title.
UA649.B26 970.03 76-385035
76 MARC

Barker, A J
Redcoats : the British soldier in America / A. J. Barker ; illustrated by Andrew Farmer. — London : Dent, 1976.
[8], 85 p. : ill., maps, plan ; 24 cm. GB76-23113
Bibliography: p. 85.
ISBN 0-460-06674-9 : £2.45
1. United States—History—Revolution, 1775-1783—British forces. 2. Great Britain. Army—History. I. Title.
E267.B28 970'.03 77-363842
77 MARC

Barker, A J
Shotguns and shooting, by A. J. Barker. Edited by Robert K. Brown [and] Peder C. Lund. [Boulder, Colo., Paladin Press, 1973]
84 p. illus. 23 cm.
1. Shot-guns. 2. Shooting. I. Title.
TS536.8.B37 799.2'02834 74-172763
MARC

Barker, A J
Six day war / A. J. Barker. — New York : Ballantine Books, 1974.
159, [1] p. : ill. ; 21 cm. — (Ballantine's illustrated history of the violent century : Campaign book ; no. 27)
Bibliography: p. [160]
ISBN 0-345-24066-9 : $2.00
1. Israel-Arab War, 1967. I. Title.
DS127.B33 956'.046 74-196929
MARC

Barker, A J
The war against Russia, 1854-1856 [by] A. J. Barker. [U. S. ed.] New York, Holt, Rinehart and Winston [1971]
348 p. illus., maps, ports.
First published in 1970 under title: The vainglorious war.
Bibliography: p. [326]-338.
1. Crimean War, 1853-1856. I. Title.
FTaSU NUC73-124559

Barker, A J
The West Yorkshire Regiment: (the XIVth Regiment of Foot) by A. J. Barker. London, Cooper, 1974.
xii, 80 p., [12] p. of plates. illus., music, ports. 23 cm. (Famous regiments) £3.50 GB 74-15340
1. Great Britain. Army. Prince of Wales' Own (West Yorkshire Regiment)—History. I. Title.
UA652.P715B37 1974 356'.11'0942 74-179866
ISBN 0-85052-150-5 MARC

Barker, A J
Yamashita [by] A. J. Barker. [New York, Ballantine Books, 1973]
159 p. illus. 21 cm. (Ballantine's illustrated history of the violent century. War leader book, no. 24) $1.50
1. Yamashita, Tomoyuki, 1885–1946.
DS890.Y3B37 940.54'26'0924 74-156974
ISBN 0-345-23671-8 [B] MARC

Barker, A J
Yom Kippur War / A. J. Barker. — New York : Ballantine Books, 1974.
159 p. : ill. ; 21 cm. — (Campaign book ; no. 29) (Ballantine's illustrated history of the violent century)
ISBN 0-345-24295-5 : $2.00
1. Israel-Arab War, 1973. I. Title.
DS128.1.B37 956'.048 75-307177
MARC

Barker, A. J.
see Great Britain. War Office. Soviet Army uniforms & insignia, 1945- London, Arms & Armour Press, 1976.

Barker, A L 1919-
A source of embarrassment, by A. L. Barker. London, Hogarth Press, 1974.
3-208 p. 21 cm. £2.50 GB 74-06587
I. Title.
PZ4.B249So 823'.9'14 74-166764
[PR6052.A647] MARC
ISBN 0-7012-9387-0

Barker, A.N., ed.
see British Spore Group. Spore research 1973. London, New York, Academic Press, 1974.

Barker, A S
Bibliography of the helminth parasites of New Zealand (1879-1971). Bucks., Eng., Commonwealth Agricultural Bureaux [c1973]
79 p. (Commonwealth Bureau of Helminthology, St. Albans, Eng. Technical communication, no. 44)
1. Helminthology—Bibl. I. Title. II. Series.
MiEM IU NUC75-21292

Barker, Alan Vernon.
see Josling, J. F. Apportionments for executors and trustees. 4th ed. London, Oyez Pub., 1976.

Barker, Alfred Trevor, 1893-1941, ed.
see Blavatsky, Helene Petrovna Hahn-Hahn, 1831-1891. The complete works of H. P. Blavatsky. London, Rider [1933-36]

Barker, Alfred Trevor, 1893-1941, ed.
see Blavatsky, Helen Petrovna Hahn-Hahn, 1831-1891. The letters of H. P. Blavatsky to A. P. Sinnett... Pasadena, Calif., Theosophical Univ. Press [1973]

Barker, Alfred Trevor, 1893-1941.
see The Mahatma letters to A. P. Sinnett from the Mahatmas M. & K. H.. Facsim. ed., 2d ed. Pasadena, Calif., Theosophical University Press, 1926, 1975 printing.

Barker, Allen V 1937-
Nitrate determinations in soil, water and plants. Amherst, 1974.
35 p. (Massachusetts. Agricultural Experiment Station. Research bulletin no. 611)
Includes bibliographies.
I. Title.
DNAL NUC76-28345

Barker, Allen V., 1937-
see Maynard, Donald Nelson, 1932- Nutriculture... [Amherst, Massachusetts, Cooperative Extension Service, University of Massachusetts, 1970]

Barker, Anthony
see
Hayes, M Vincent.

Barker, Anthony, fl. 1902-1904.
An essay on the neck muscles and an article on how I trained Albert Treloar, by Prof. Anthony Barker. [New York, W. R. Robinson, printer, 1904]
31, [1] p. illus. (incl. port.) 12½ cm.
The article "How I trained Albert Treloar" has separate t.-p.
Advertising matter: p. 31.
1. Physical education and training. 2. Neck. I. Title.
GV508.B25 Ca 5-2276
rev

Barker, Anthony, fl. 1902-1904.
Physical culture simplified; a safe and rapid way to health and strength, by Professor Anthony Barker. New York, The author [1902]
111 p. incl. illus., port. 19½ cm.
A detachable measurement, blank inserted between p. 110 and 111.
1. Physical education and training. I. Title.
GV481.B24 2-17460
rev

Barker, Anthony, 1919 or 1920-
Physic and protocol among the Zulus. Johannesburg, Institute for the Study of Man in Africa [1972]
13 p. 21 cm. (ISMA paper no. 32) SA***
Cover title.
1. Zulus. I. Title. II. Series: Institute for the Study of Man in Africa. ISMA paper no. 32.
DT878.Z9B28 916'.06'963 73-173870
MARC

Barker, Anthony P.
see Civic Trust. The local amenity movement. London, The Trust, 1976.

Barker, Anthony P.
see Public policy and private interests ... London, Macmillan Press, 1975.

Barker, Anthony P.
see Runnymede Trust. Strategy and style in local community relations ... London, The Trust, 1975.

Barker, Arthur Edward, 1911-
Milton's schoolmasters, by Arthur Barker. [Folcroft, Pa.] Folcroft Library Editions, 1973.
20 p. 26 cm.
Reprinted from the Modern language review, vol. 32, no. 4, Oct. 1937, at the University Press, Cambridge, Eng.
Includes bibliographical references.
1. Milton, John, 1608-1674—Religion and ethics. 2. Young, Thomas, 1587-1655. 3. Gill, Alexander, 1565-1635. I. The Modern language review. II. Title.
PR3592.R4B3 1973 821'.4 73-16488
ISBN 0-8414-9887-3 MARC

Barker, Arthur Edward, 1911-
see Milton reconsidered ... Salzburg, Institut für Englische Sprache und Literatur, Universität Salzburg, 1976.

Barker, Ballard M
Platt National Park : environment and ecology / by Ballard M. Barker and William Carl Jameson. — 1st ed. — Norman : University of Oklahoma Press, [1975]
xii, 127 p. : ill. ; 19 cm.
Bibliography: p. 117-120.
Includes index.
ISBN 0-8061-1256-5
1. Platt National Park. I. Jameson, William Carl, joint author. II. Title.
F702.P7B37 917.66'57 74-15909
74 MARC

Barker, Barbara Underhill.
Houses of the Revolution in Hanover, Massachusetts / by Barbara Underhill Barker, Lucy Josselyn Bonney, Anne Bonney Henderson. — [Hanover, Mass.] : Hanover Historical Society, c1976.
vii, 151 p. : ill., fold. map (in pocket) ; 23 cm.
Bibliography: p. 151.
1. Historic buildings—Massachusetts—Hanover. 2. Hanover, Mass.—Dwellings. I. Bonney, Lucy Josselyn, joint author. II. Henderson, Anne Bonney, joint author. III. Hanover Historical Society. IV. Title.
F74.H2B19 974.4'82 77-355853
77 MARC

Barker, Benjamin Joseph.
An investigation of the impact of scheduling policy on airline operational efficiency. [Stanford, Calif.] 1974.
viii, 81 l. illus.
Thesis (Engineer)—Stanford University.
Bibliography: leaf 81.
1. Scheduling (Management) 2. Air lines—Management. I. Title.
CSt NUC76-28642

Barker, Bernard, ed.
see MacDonald, James Ramsay, 1866-1937. Ramsay MacDonald's political writings... London, Allen Lane, 1972.

Barker, Bernard, ed.
see MacDonald, James Ramsay, 1866-1937. Ramsay MacDonald's political writings. New York, St. Martin's Press [1972]

Barker, Brent G
Recycling : a research report / by the Long Range Planning Service, Stanford Research Institute ; [by Brent G. Barker]. — Menlo Park, Calif. : SRI, 1973.
36 p. : ill. ; 28 cm. — (Report - Long Range Planning Service, Stanford Research Institute ; no. 493)
Cover title.
"Report group: Global."
1. Recycling (Waste, etc.) I. Stanford Research Institute. Long Range Planning Service. II. Title. III. Series: Stanford Research Institute. Long Range Planning Service. Report ; no. 493.
HC101.S77 no. 493 330'.08 s 75-324662
[TD794.5] 75 MARC

Barker, Brent G., joint author
see Materials for autos. Menlo Park, Calif., 1969.

Barker, Brent G
see Nondestructive testing. Menlo Park, Calif., 1970.

Barker, Brian, O. B. E.
When the Queen was crowned / Brian Barker. — 1st American ed. — New York : D. McKay Co., 1976.
xiii, 224 p., [4] leaves of plates : ill. ; 25 cm.
Bibliography: p. [217]-218.
Includes index.
ISBN 0-679-50693-4 : $10.95
1. Elizabeth II, Queen of Great Britain, 1926- —Coronation. 2. Great Britain—Kings and rulers—Biography. I. Title.
DA590.B26 1976 394'.4'0941 76-17491
77 MARC

Barker, Brian Michael.
Antimicrobial agents in medicine [by] Brian M. Barker and Frederick Prescott. Oxford, Blackwell Scientific, 1973.
xi, 296 p. 24 cm. £4.50 GB 74-06327
Distributed in the U. S. A. by F. A. Davis Company, Philadelphia.
Bibliography: p. 280.
Includes index.
1. Anti-infective agents. I. Prescott, Frederick, 1904- joint author. II. Title.
RM262.B28 615'.329 74-170286
ISBN 0-632-09570-9 MARC

Barker, Bruce.
Little Wabash River basin study, a comprehensive plan for water resource development, by Bruce Barker, John B. Carlisle [and] Raymond Nyberg. [Springfield] Ill., Dept. of Public Works and Buildings, Division of Waterways, 1967.
78 p. illus., maps. 28 cm.
Bibliography: p. 76-78.
1. Water resources development—Illinois—Little Wabash River watershed. I. Carlisle, John B., joint author. II. Nyberg, Raymond, joint author. III. Illinois. Division of Waterways. IV. Title.
TC424.I3B37 333.9'102'0977379 73-650884
Illinois Univ. Library 71[r76]rev MARC

Barker, Carol.
King Midas and the golden touch. London, New York, F. Watts, 1972.
2-55 p. chiefly col. illus. 23 x 28 cm. £1.25 GB 72-19762
SUMMARY: King Midas enjoyed turning everything he touched to gold until he discovered that gold food was hard to eat and gold daughters cold to hug.
1. Midas—Juvenile literature. [1. Midas. 2. Mythology, Greek] I. Title.
PZ8.1.B25Ki [398.2] [E] 74-169355
ISBN 0-85166-114-9 MARC

Barker, Carol.
An oba of Benin / [written and illustrated by] Carol Barker. — London : Macdonald and Jane's, 1976.
[38] p. : ill. (some col.), maps ; 28 cm. — (Carol Barker's Worlds of yesterday) GB76-16151
ISBN 0-356-08179-6 : £2.50
1. Benin, Nigeria (Province)—History—Juvenile fiction. I. Title.
PZ7.B2504 Ob 3 76-371005
76 MARC

Barker, Carol.
An oba of Benin. — Reading, Mass. : Addison-Wesley, 1977.
[35] p. : ill. (some col.) ; 27 cm. — (Carol Barker's Worlds of yesterday)
SUMMARY: In West Africa in 1504, a young prince prepares to be the next ruler of his kingdom.
ISBN 0-201-00423-2
1. Benin, Nigeria (Province)—History—Juvenile fiction. [1. Benin, Nigeria (Province)—History—Fiction] I. Title.
PZ7.B2504 Ob 4 [E] 75-45370
75 MARC

Barker, Carol.
A prince of Islam / [written and illustrated by] Carol Barker. — London : Macdonald and Jane's, 1976.
[38] p. : ill. (some col.), map ; 28 cm. — (Carol Barker's Worlds of yesterday) GB76-16075
ISBN 0-356-08178-8 : £2.50
I. Title.
PZ7.B2504 Pr 3 76-373211
76 MARC

Barker, Carol.
A prince of Islam. — Reading, Mass. : Addison-Wesley, 1977, c1976.
[35] p. : ill. (some col.) ; 27 cm. — (Carol Barker's Worlds of yesterday)
SUMMARY: Simple text and illustrations describe the childhood and training of a young boy whose father is Caliph of the Muslim Empire in the ninth century.
ISBN 0-201-00424-0
[1. Civilization, Islamic—Fiction] I. Title.
PZ7.B2504 Pr 4 [E] 75-45479
75 MARC

Barker, Carol.
see Devils, devils, devils. New York, Watts, 1976.

Barker, Carol.
see If you should meet a crocodile ... London, Kaye & Ward, 1974.

Barker, Carol, illus.
see Mahy, Margaret. The princess and the clown. New York, Watts [1971]

Barker, Charles Albro, 1904–
Henry George. Westport, Conn., Greenwood Press [1974, c1955]
xvii, 696 p. 22 cm.
Reprint of the ed. published by Oxford University Press, New York.
Includes bibliographical references.
ISBN 0-8371-7775-8
1. George, Henry, 1839–1897.
[HB119.G4B3 1974] 330'.092'4 [B] 74-12949 MARC

Barker, Charles Edward, 1908-
The church's neurosis and twentieth century revelations / [by] C. Edward Barker. — London : Rider, 1975.
272 p. ; 23 cm. GB75-27000
Includes bibliographical references and indexes.
ISBN 0-09-123450-6 : £3.75. ISBN 0-09-123451-4 pbk.
1. Christianity—20th century. 2. Jesus Christ—Teachings. 3. Psychoanalysis and religion. I. Title.
BR121.2.B2865 230'.01'9 76 76-352239 MARC

Barker, Cheryl Faye.
The use of lateral thinking to facilitate openness to a broader range of teaching-learning situations. [n. p.] 1973.
1 v.
Thesis (Ph. D.)—Western Reserve University.
OClW NUC76-74143

Barker, Colin.
The power game. Illustrations by 'Rag.' London, Pluto Press Ltd for 'Advance,' 1972.
92 p. illus. 21 cm. GB 74-02186
Includes bibliographical references.
ISBN 0-902818-17-1 : £0.25
1. Electric industry workers—Great Britain. I. Title.
HD8039.E32G72 1972 331'.042'1310941 75-315075 MARC

Barker, Craig S
Starting a marine aquarium. [Neptune City, N.J., T.F.H. Publications, 1972]
93 p. illus. (part col.) 20 cm.
1. Marine aquariums. I. Title.
AAP NUC75-30861

Barker, D., joint author
see Addicott, John Leopold. The effect of reduction of gasoline lead content on road anti-knock performance. [London] British Petroleum Co. Ltd. [1971]

Barker, D.
see also
Barker, David.

Barker, D. E.
see
Barker, Douglas Edward.

Barker, D. J. P.
see
Barker, David James Purslove.

Barker, D.S.
see Stratigraphy of the Austin Chalk... Austin, Texas, Bureau of Economic Geology, the University of Texas at Austin, 1975.

Barker, Daisy King.
Echoes of the Old South. [n.p., n.d.]
168 p. port. 22 cm.
1. North Carolina. History. I. Title.
NcWsW NUC73-103115

Barker, Daniel Jackson.
Función temática de la técnica novelesca en el Quijote. Montreal, 1971.
84 l. 29 cm.
Thesis—McGill University.
Bibliography: leaves 83-84.
1. Cervantes, Saavedra, Miguel de, 1547-1616. Don Quixote. I. Title.
CaQMM NUC73-32110

Barker, Danny, joint author
see Buerkle, Jack Vincent, 1923- Bourbon Street Black... New York, Oxford Univ. Press, 1973.

Barker, David.
Muscle receptors, by D. Barker, C. C. Hunt [and] A. K. McIntyre. Edited by C. C. Hunt. Berlin, New York, Springer-Verlag, 1974.
310 p. illus. 25 cm. (Handbook of sensory physiology, v. III/2) GFR***
Includes bibliographies.
CONTENTS: Barker, D. The morphology of muscle receptors.—Hunt, C. C. The physiology of muscle receptors.—McIntyre, A. K. Central actions of impulses in muscle, afferent fibres.
ISBN 0-387-06891-0
1. Muscle receptors. 2. Neuromuscular transmission. I. Hunt, Carlton C., 1918- II. McIntyre, Archibald Keverall, 1913- III. Series.
[DNLM: 1. Mechanoreceptors. WL 700 H236 v. 3 pt. 2]
QP351.H34 vol. 3, no. 2 74-13983
[QP369] 591.1'82'08 s [596'.01'852] MARC

Barker, David Ernest, 1944-
Enlightenment politics: Voltaire, the infame, and the New Jerusalem. [Austin, Tex.] 1974.
vi, 218 l. 29 cm.
Thesis (Ph. D.)—University of Texas at Austin.
Vita.
Bibliography: leaves 213-218.
TxU NUC76-28354

Barker, David James Purslove.
Epidemiology in medical practice / D. J. P. Barker, G. Rose. — Edinburgh ; New York : Churchill Livingstone : [distributed in the U.S.A. by Longman], 1976.
viii, 140 p. : ill. ; 22 cm.
Bibliography: p. 133.
Includes index.
ISBN 0-443-01446-9 : £2.90
1. Epidemiology. 2. Medicine, Preventive. I. Rose, Geoffrey Arthur, joint author. II. Title.
[DNLM: 1. Epidemiology. WA100 B255e]
RA651.B36 614.4 75 75-43676 MARC

Barker, David James Purslove.
Practical epidemiology [by] D. J. P. Barker; with chapters by F. J. Bennett. Edinburgh, Churchill Livingstone, 1973 [i. e. 1972].
vii, 167 p. illus., map. 19 cm. £1.00 GB 73-08887
Includes index.
Bibliography: p. 161.
1. Epidemiology—Technique. I. Bennett, F. J. II. Title.
[DNLM: 1. Epidemiology. WA 100 B255p 1973]
[RA652.4.B37] 614.4'07'23 73-595297
ISBN 0-443-01003-X MARC
Shared Cataloging with DNLM

Barker, David James Purslove.
Practical epidemiology / D. J. P. Barker, with chapters by F. J. Bennett. — 1st ed. — Edinburgh ; New York : Churchill Livingstone, 1973, 1975 printing.
vii, 168 p. : ill. ; 18 cm. — (Medicine in the tropics) GB***
Bibliography: p. 161.
Includes index.
ISBN 0-443-01003-X : £1.50
1. Epidemiology—Technique. I. Bennett, F. J., joint author. II. Title.
[RA652.4.B37 1975] 614.4'07'23 76 76-675860 MARC

Barker, Dennis, 1929-
The scandalisers / Dennis Barker. — London : Weidenfeld and Nicolson, 1974.
247 p. ; 21 cm. GB74-16789
ISBN 0-297-76806-9 : £2.65
I. Title.
PZ4.B2515 Sc 823'.9'14 75-307627
[PR6052.A648] 75 MARC

Barker, Dennis Albert, 1927-
see Toronto. City Planning Board. Forest Hill area. [Toronto] 1972.

Barker, Dennis Albert, 1927-
see Toronto. City Planning Board. Yonge Street proposed deferred widening... [Toronto] 1975.

Barker, Diana Leonard
see Conference on Sexual Divisions and Society, Aberdeen University, 1974. Sexual divisions and society ... London, Tavistock Publications, 1976.

Barker, Diana Leonard.
see Dependence and exploitation in work and marriage. London, Longman, 1976.

Barker, Dianne.
Billy Graham in Big Orange country; the East Tennessee crusade 1970. Official document. [n.p., 1970?]
96 p. illus. (part col.) 23 cm.
1. Graham, William Franklin, 1918- 2. Revivals—Knoxvillle, Tenn. I. Title.
KyLoS NUC74-15728

Barker, Dorothy Erickson, 1919-
Growth studies on the early chick blastoderm. [Minneapolis] 1971 [1972]
iii, 140 l. illus.
Thesis—University of Minnesota.
Bibliography: leaves 77-85.
Photocopy of typescript. Ann Arbor, Mich., University Microfilms, 1972. 22 cm.
1. Chick embryo. I. Title.
NIC NUC73-124579

Barker, Douglas Edward.
The basic arts of buying / [by] D. E. Barker and B. Farrington. — London : Business Books, 1976.
xiv, 249 p. : ill. ; 23 cm. — (Basic arts series) GB76-29056
Bibliography: p. [239]
Includes index.
ISBN 0-220-66295-9 : £6.00
1. Purchasing. I. Farrington, Brian, joint author. II. Title.
HF5437.B358 1976 658.7'2 77 76-383719 MARC

Barker, Dudley.
Arafat is next! / Lionel Black [i.e. D. Barker]. — New York : Stein and Day, 1975.
206 p. ; 25 cm.905(d
ISBN 0-8128-1761-3 : $7.95
I. Title.
PZ3.B24234 Ar 3 823'.9'12 74 74-29318
[PR6003.A679] MARC

Barker, Dudley.
The bait, by Lionel Black. London, Cassell, 1966.
[4], 188 p. 19½ cm. (Cassell crime) B 66-11603
18/-
I. Title.
PZ3.B24234Bai 66-72193

Barker, Dudley.
Death by hoax / [by] Lionel Black [i. e. D. Barker]. — London : Colins [for] the Crime Club, 1974.
189 p. ; 21 cm. GB 74-20262
ISBN 0-00-231196-8 : £2.00
I. Title.
PZ3.B24234De 823'.9'12 75-301930
[PR6003.A679] MARC

Barker, Dudley.
Death has green fingers [by] Anthony Matthews. New York, Walker [1971]
192 p. 21 cm. $4.95
I. Title.
PZ3.B24234 Dh 3 823'.9'14 74-142842
[PR6003.A679] 71[r75]rev MARC
ISBN 0-8027-5222-5

Barker, Dudley.
Flood [by] Lionel Black. New York, Stein and Day [1971, c1970]
192 p. 22 cm. ([A Stein and Day mystery]) $4.95
I. Title.
PZ3.B24234 Fl 3 823'.9'14 74-122425
[PR6003.A679] 71[r75]rev MARC
ISBN 0-8128-1311-1

Barker, Dudley.
G. K. Chesterton: a biography. London, Constable, 1973.
304, [13] p. illus., ports. (some col.) 23 cm. £3.95 GB 73-18960
Includes index.
Bibliography: p. 289-295.
1. Chesterton, Gilbert Keith, 1874-1936—Biography.
PR4453.C4Z529 1973b 828'.9'1209 [B] 73-178640
ISBN 0-09-457830-3 MARC

Barker, Dudley.
G. K. Chesterton; a biography. New York, Stein and Day [1973]
304 p. illus. 25 cm. $8.95
Bibliography: p. 289-295.
1. Chesterton, Gilbert Keith, 1874-1936.
PR4453.C4Z529 828'.9'1209 [B] 72-95988
ISBN 0-8128-1544-0 MARC

Barker, Dudley.
The life and death of Peter Wade [by] Lionel Black. London, [published for] the Crime Club [by] Collins [1973]
192 p. 21 cm. (The Crime Club) £1.70 GB***
I. Title.
PZ3.B24234 Li 823'.9'14 74-170900
[PR6003.A679] 74[r75]rev MARC
ISBN 0-00-231462-2

Barker, Dudley.
The life and death of Peter Wade [by] Lionel Black. New York, Stein and Day [1974, c1973]
192 p. 22 cm. $5.95
I. Title.
PZ3.B24234 Li 3 823'.9'14 73-88398
[PR6003.A679] 74[r75]rev MARC
ISBN 0-8128-1649-8

Barker, Dudley.
Outbreak [by] Lionel Black. London, Cassell, 1968.
176 p. 19 cm. (Cassell crime) 16/- B68-07147
I. Title.
PZ3.B24234 Ou 823'.9'14 68-111430
ISBN 0-304-93029-6 [r75]rev MARC

Barker, Dudley.
Outbreak [by] Lionel Black. New York, Stein and Day [1968]
175 p. 22 cm.
I. Title.
[PZ3.P24234 Ou 4] 823'.9'14 68-16043
[r75]rev MARC

Barker, **Dudley.**
Ransom for a nude. London [Published for] the Crime Club [by] Collins [c1972]
190 p.
ISBN 0-00-231708-7.
I. Title.
CaOTP NUC73-118917

Barker, Dudley.
Ransom for a nude [by] Lionel Black. New York, Stein and Day [1972]
190 p. 22 cm. $5.95
I. Title.
PZ3.B24234 Ran 3 823'.9'14 72-81209
[PR6003.A679] 72[r75]rev MARC
ISBN 0-8128-1491-6

Barker, Dudley.
Swinging murder [by] Lionel Black. London, Cassell, 1969.
[4], 172 p. 19 cm. (Cassell crime) 21/- B69-05183
I. Title.
PZ3.B24234 Sw 823'.9'14 72-404712
[PR6003.H679] 69[r75]rev MARC
ISBN 0-304-93327-9

Barker, Dudley.
Swinging murder [by] Anthony Matthews. New York, Walker [1969]
171 p. 21 cm. 4.50
I. Title.
PZ3.B24234 Sw 3 823'.9'14 74-86965
[PR6003.A679] 69[r75]rev MARC

Barker, Dudley.
Two ladies in Verona [by] Lionel Black. London, Cassell, 1967.
223 p. 19.5 cm. B67-13967
I. Title.
PZ3.B24234 Tw 823'.9'14 67-95997
[r75]rev MARC

Barker, E. G.
see
Barker, Ernest Gail, 1939-

Barker, Ed.
Start living today : a natural and safe approach to health care / Ed Barker. — Montgomery, Ala. : Chiropractic Health Foundation, c1976.
144 p. : ill. ; 24 cm.
Bibliography: p. 133-135.
Includes index.
$7.95
1. Chiropractic—Popular works. 2. Hygiene. I. Title.
RZ244.B37 613 76-6307
76 MARC

Barker, Edward, joint author
see Farren, Mick. Watch out kids. London, Open Gate Books, 1972.

Barker, Edward Bruce Boughton, ed.
see Barker, John, 1771-1849. Syria and Egypt under the last five sultans of Turkey. New York, Arno Press, 1973.

Barker, Edward H
Oceanic fog, a numerical study. Monterey, Calif., 1973.
15 p. illus. 27 cm. (United States. Navy. Environmental Prediction Research Facility, Monterey, Calif. ENVPREDRSCHFAC technical paper no. 6-73)
1. Fog—Mathematical models. 2. Planetary boundary layer—Mathematical models. 3. Stratus—Mathematical models. I. Title. II. Series.
DAS NUC75-21279

Barker, Elisabeth.
Austria, 1918-1972. Coral Gables, Fla., University of Miami Press [1973]
xii, 306 p. illus. 23 cm. $12.50
Includes bibliographical references.
1. Austria—Politics and government—1918-1938. 2. Austria—Politics and government—1938-1945. 3. Austria—Politics and government—1945- I. Title.
DB96.B26 1973b 943.6'05 73-80034
ISBN 0-87024-262-8 MARC

Barker, Elisabeth.
Austria, 1918-1972. London, Macmillan, 1973.
xii, 306, [8] p. illus., ports. 23 cm. £4.95 GB 73-19058
Includes index.
Bibliography: p. [293]-295.
1. Austria—Politics and government—1918-1938. 2. Austria—Politics and government—1938-1945. 3. Austria—Politics and government—1945- I. Title.
DB96.B26 943.6'05 73-173765
ISBN 0-333-13369-2 MARC

Barker, Elisabeth.
British policy in south-east Europe in the Second World War / Elisabeth Barker. — London : Macmillan, 1976.
viii, 320 p. : ill. ; 22 cm. — (Studies in Russian and East European history) GB***
Bibliography: p. [307]-309.
Includes index.
ISBN 0-333-15994-2 : £10.00
1. World War, 1939-1945—Great Britain. 2. World War, 1939-1945—Diplomatic history. 3. World War, 1939-1945—Balkan Peninsula. 4. Balkan Peninsula—History—20th century. I. Title.
D750.B37 1976b 940.53'2 76-368608
76 MARC

Barker, Elisabeth.
British policy in South-East Europe in the Second World War / Elisabeth Barker. — New York : Barnes & Noble Books, 1976.
viii, 320 p. : maps ; 23 cm. — (Studies in Russian and East European history)
Bibliography: p. [307]-309.
Includes index.
ISBN 0-06-490301-X : $27.50
1. World War, 1939-1945—Great Britain. 2. World War, 1939-1945—Diplomatic history. 3. World War, 1939-1945—Balkan Peninsula. 4. Balkan Peninsula—History—20th century. I. Title.
D750.B37 1976 940.53'2 75-21102
76 MARC

Barker, Elisabeth.
The cold war. London, Wayland Publishers; New York, G. P. Putnam's Sons [1972]
128 p. illus. 32 cm. (The Wayland documentary history series) £1.70 B***
SUMMARY: An explanation of the causes and main events of the power struggle between the Soviet Union and the West since the end of World War II.
Bibliography: p. 125-126.
1. World politics—1945- [1. World politics—1945-]
I. Title.
D843.B32 320.9'04 72-79750
ISBN 0-399-11034-8 (U. S.) MARC

Barker, Elisabeth.
The Common Market. London, Wayland, New York, G. P. Putnam, 1973.
128 p. illus., maps, ports. 23 cm. ([The documentary history series]) £1.95 GB 73-19297
Includes index.
Bibliography: p. 119-120.
1. European Economic Community. I. Title.
HC241.2.B29 382'.9142'0904 73-174613
ISBN 0-85340-274-4 rev MARC

Barker, Elisabeth.
Macedonia, its place in Balkan power politics. London, New York, Royal Institute of International Affairs [1950]
129 p. maps. 21 cm.
Authorized facsimile produced by microfilm-xerography by University Microfilms, Ann Arbor, Michigan, 1973.
OCIU NUC75-21281

Barker, Elizabeth S., ed.
see Daughters of the American Revolution. Wisconsin. State History Committee. Wisconsin Society... [n. p., 1971]

Barker, Elliott Speer, 1886-
Ramblings in the field of conservation / by Elliott S. Barker. — [Santa Fe, N.M.] : Sunstone Press, c1976.
181 p., [6] leaves of plates : ill. ; 19 cm.
$4.95
1. Barker, Elliott Speer, 1886- 2. Conservationists—New Mexico—Biography. I. Title.
S926.B37A37 639'.9'0924 76-150808
77 MARC

Barker, Elliott Speer, 1886-
Western life & adventures in the great Southwest / by Elliott S. Barker ; illustrated by Dennis Anderson. — Kansas City, Mo. : Lowell Press, c1974.
xi, 313 p. : ill. ; 26 cm.
Published in 1970 under title: Western life and adventures, 1889 to 1970.
ISBN 0-913504-19-X : $9.95
1. Game protection—Personal narratives. 2. Barker, Elliott Speer, 1886- 3. Hunting—New Mexico. I. Title.
SK427.B37 1974 639'.9'0924 74-15149
75 MARC

Barker, Enno.
Die Rolle der Parteiorgane in der sowjetischen Wirtschaftslenkung: 1957–1965; zum Verhältnis von Partei u. Staat in d. Periode d. Chruščevschen Wirtschaftsreformen/ Enno Barker. — Berlin: Osteuropa-Inst. an d. Freien Univ.; Wiesbaden: Harrassowitz [in Komm.] 1973.
xi, 252 p.; 25 cm. — (Philosophische und soziologische Veröffentlichungen; Bd. 12) DM48.00 GFR 73-A
Originally presented the author's thesis, Freie Universität, Berlin.
Bibliography: p. [200]–218.
1. Russia — Economic policy — 1956–1958. 2. Russia — Economic policy — 1959–1965. 3. Kommunisticheskaia partiia Sovetskogo Soiuza.—Party work. I. Title. II. Series: Berlin. Freie Universität. Osteuropa-Institut. Philosophische und soziologische Veröffentlichungen, Bd. 12.
AS182.B63 Bd. 12 73-357816
[HC336]
ISBN 3-447-01518-7

Barker, Enno.
Russland, Sowjetunion: Landschaft, Geschichte, Kultur/ Enno Barker. — 2., verb. Aufl. — Stuttgart, Berlin, Köln, Mainz: Kohlhammer, 1973.
242 p.: ill., maps; 22 cm. DM25.00 GFR 73-A38
1. Russia—Description and travel—1970– I. Title.
DK29.B34 1973 914.7'03 74-338727
ISBN 3-17-001463-3

Barker, Eric E
A short history of Nyanza. Kampala, East African Literature Bureau [1973]
28 p. map.
1. Nyanza, Kenya—History.
InU NUC75-21285

Barker, Eric Ernest.
see York, Eng. (Diocese) Archbishop, 1480-1500 (Thomas Rotherham) The register of Thomas Rotherham, Archbishop of York, 1480-1500. [York, Eng.] Canterbury and York Society, 1976-

Barker, Eric J
Britain from the air, by Eric J. Barker and Lawrence H. Williams. London, Ginn [c1969]
63 p. (chiefly illus.) (Secondary geographies)
1. Physical geography—Gt. Brit. I. Williams, Lawrence Harding, joint author. II. Title.
MiEM NUC74-19015

Barker, Eric J
Design feasibility study for injecting an infill housing system into an older, residential district, by Eric Barker. [Winnipeg, Institute of Urban Studies, University of Winnipeg] 1972.
14 l. illus.
Cover title.
1. Architecture, Domestic—Winnipeg. 2. Unit construction. I. University of Winnipeg. Institute of Urban Studies. II. Title.
CaOTY NUC75-81155

Barker, Eric J
Europe from the air / by Eric J. Barker and Lawrence H. Williams. — London : Heinemann Educational, [1975]
64 p. : ill., maps ; 25 cm. GB75-13873
ISBN 0-435-34040-9 : £0.95
1. Europe—Description and travel—1971- I. Williams, Lawrence Harding, joint author. II. Title.
D923.B37 914 76-377209
76 MARC

Barker, Eric J
Geography and younger children; an outline of theory and practice [by] Eric J. Barker. London, University of London Press, 1974.
[7], 133 p. illus., maps. 23 cm. (Unibooks) £1.45 GB 74-14710
1. Geography—Study and teaching (Elementary)—Great Britain. I. Title.
G76.5.G7B37 372.8'91044'0942 74-182950
ISBN 0-340-15991-X; 0-340-15992-8 (pbk.) MARC

Barker, Eric J
The in-fill experimental housing project: phase I [by] Eric Barker. [Winnipeg, Institute of Urban Studies, University of Winnipeg, 1972?]
15 l.
Caption title.
1. Housing—Winnipeg. I. University of Winnipeg. Institute of Urban Studies. II. Title.
CaOTY NUC75-56272

Barker, Eric J
A report on the rehabilitation of older houses in a lower income, inner city district [by] Eric Barker. [Winnipeg, Institute of Urban Studies, University of Winnipeg, 1971]
43 l. illus.
Cover title.
1. Dwellings—Winnipeg—Remodeling. I. University of Winnipeg. Institute of Urban Studies. II. Title.
CaOTY NUC75-80002

Barker, Eric J
see The Citizen and neighborhood renewal : a collection of working papers .... [Winnipeg] University of Winnipeg, [1972]

Barker, Ernest, Sir, 1874-1960, ed.
The character of England / edited by Ernest Barker. — Westport, Conn. : Greenwood Press, 1976.
xii, 595 p., [52] leaves of plates : ill. ; 24 cm.
Reprint of the 1947 ed. published by Clarendon Press, Oxford.
Includes index.
ISBN 0-8371-9020-7
1. National characteristics, English—Addresses, essays, lectures. I. Title.
[DA118.B32 1976] 942 76-22422
76 MARC

Barker, Sir **Ernest,** 1874-1960.
Church, state, and study; essays. Westport, Conn., Greenwood Press [1974]
vii, 280 p. 22 cm.
Reprint of the 1930 ed. published by Methuen, London.
Includes bibliographical references.
1. Church and state—Addresses, essays, lectures. 2. Political science—Addresses, essays, lectures. 3. Education—Addresses, essays, lectures. I. Title.
JA41.B3 1974 320'.1 72-7829
ISBN 0-8371-6534-2 MARC

Barker, Sir Ernest, 1874-1960.
Essays on government. 2d ed. Oxford, Clarendon Press [1960, c1951]
vii, 304 p. 23 cm.
1. Constitutional law—Addresses, essays, lectures.
OU NUC73-57859

Barker, Sir Ernest, 1874-1960.
National character and the factors in its formation, by Ernest Barker ... London, Methuen & co., ltd. [1927]
vii, 288 p. 23 cm.
"List of books" at end of each chapter except the last.
Ultra microfiche. Dayton, Ohio, National Cash Register, 1970. 1st title of 6. 10.5 x 14.8 cm. (PCMI library collection, 136-1)
1. National characteristics. I. Title.
KEmT NUC74-15727

Barker, Sir Ernest, 1874-1960.
Political thought in England from Herbert Spencer to the present day, by Ernest Barker... New York, H. Holt and company; [etc., etc., 1915?]
v, 7-256 p. 18 cm. (Home university library of modern knowledge, no. 98)
Bibliography: p. 252-254.
Ultra microfiche. Dayton, Ohio, National Cash Register, 1970. 2d title of 7. 10.5 x 14.8 cm. (PCMI library collection, 454-2)
1. Political science—Hist.—Gt. Brit. I. Title.
KEmT NUC75-108875

Barker, Ernest, Sir, 1874-1960, comp.
Social contract, essays by Locke, Hume, and Rousseau. With an introduction by Sir Ernest Barker. London, New York, Oxford University Press [1973]
xliv, 307 p. 21 cm.
OU NUC76-75058

Barker, Sir Ernest, 1874-1960, tr.
see Aristoteles. The Politics. Oxford, Clarendon Press [1968]

Barker, Ernest Gail, 1939-
Diagnostic radiology continuing education review : 453 essay questions and referenced answers / by E. G. Barker, Jr. — Flushing, N.Y.: Medical Examination Pub. Co., 1976.
236 p. ; 22 cm.
Includes index.
ISBN 0-87488-372-5
1. Diagnosis, Radioscopic—Examinations, questions, etc. I. Title.
RC78.B335 616.07'57'076 75-43003
76 MARC

Barker, Esther T
Of the lineage of David : a sequel to The unused cradle / by Esther T. Barker ; [illustrated by Sally Moore]. — Chicago : Adams Press, c1976.
48 p. : ill. ; 17 cm.
Includes bibliographical references.
$1.25
1. Jesus Christ—Fiction. I. Title.
PZ4.B2523 Of 813'.5'4 77-354127
[PS3552.A617] 77 MARC

Barker, Esther T
Shooting Creek was our parish / by Esther T. Barker. — Chicago : Adams Press ; Maryville, TN : may be ordered from Barker, c1977.
209 p. : ill. ; 22 cm.
$3.95
1. Shooting Creek-Murphy Parish. 2. Barker, Paul A. 3. Barker, Esther T. I. Title.
BX6081.S53B37 287'.632'0922 77-353941
77 MARC

Barker, Eugene Campbell, 1874-
Stephen F. Austin and the independence of Texas. [n.p., n.d.]
[28] p.
Microfiche.
Reprinted from The Quarterly of Texas State Historical Association, v. 13, no. 4.
1. Texas—Hist. 2. Austin, Stephen Fuller, 1793-1836.
UU NUC76-28643

Barker, Felix, 1917- The first explorers. 1973
see The Glorious age of exploration. Garden City, N. Y., Doubleday [1973, c1971]

Barker, Felix, 1917-
London, 2000 years of a city and its people / Felix Barker & Peter Jackson. — London : Cassell, 1974.
[5], 379 p. : ill. (some col.), coats of arms, facsims., maps, plans, ports (some col.) ; 32 cm. GB75-03180
Includes index.
ISBN 0-304-29264-8 : £10.00
1. London—History. I. Jackson, Peter Charles Geoffrey, 1922- joint author. II. Title.
DA677.B36 1974b 942.1 75-319520
75 MARC

Barker, Felix, 1917-
London: 2,000 years of a city and its people [by] Felix Barker and Peter Jackson. [1st American ed.] New York, Macmillan [1974]
379 p. illus. 32 cm.
ISBN 0-02-507120-3 : $27.50
1. London—History. I. Jackson, Peter Charles Geoffrey, 1922- joint author. II. Title.
DA677.B36 1974 942.1'2 74-10884
MARC

Barker, Felix, 1917-
see Encyclopedia of discovery and exploration. London, Aldus Books [c1971]

Barker, Florence P., joint author
see Morgan, William Edward. Selected summary tables from demographic study of Wyoming population in transition... Laramie, Wyo., Division of Business and Economic Research, University of Wyoming, 1969.

Barker, Floyd V
Home heating in an emergency. Prepared by Floyd V. Barker, Francis E. Gilman [and] Dorothy A. Nickerson. Durham, Cooperative Extension Service, University of New Hampshire [1973?]
15 p. illus.
1. Heating. I. Gilman, Francis E., joint author. II. Nickerson, Dorothy A., joint author. III. New Hampshire. University. Cooperative Extension Service. IV. Title.
NhU NUC75-21290

Barker, Forrest L
Problems in technical mathematics for electricity/electronics / Forrest Barker. — Menlo Park, Calif. : Cummings Pub. Co., c1976.
xiv, 274 p. : ill. ; 24 cm.
Includes index.
ISBN 0-8465-0403-0
1. Electric engineering—Mathematics—Problems, exercises, etc. 2. Electronics—Mathematics—Problems, exercises, etc. I. Title.
TK168.B34 621.3'01'51 76-12728
77 MARC

Barker, Frank Granville, joint author
see Handley-Taylor, Geoffrey. John Gay and the ballad opera... New York, Hinrichsen Edition Limited [c1956]

Barker, G. M. A.
see
Barker, George M A

Barker, Gary L
A portable scale for cotton trailers. [New Orleans] 1973.
6 p. illus. (U. S. Agricultural Research Service. Southern Region. ARS-S-6)
I. Title.
DNAL NUC 75-21287

Barker, Geoffrey Russell.
Some problems of incentives and labour productivity in Soviet industry; a contribution to the study of the planning of labour in the U.S.S.R. [Oxford] Blackwell [1956]
2 sheets. 10.5 x 14.8 cm. (Dept. of Economics and Institutions of the USSR, University of Birmingham. Monograph on the Soviet economic system, no. 1)
Microfiche (negative) of typescript. p. diagr., tables. 22 cm.
Bibliographical footnotes.
1. Labor productivity—Russia. 2. Incentives in industry. I. Title. II. Series: Birmingham, Eng. University. Dept. of Economics and Institutions of the U.S.S.R. Monograph on the Soviet economic system, no. 1.
OOxM NUC75-71037

Barker, George, 1913-
The alphabetical zoo; illustrated by Krystyna Roland. London, Faber, 1972.
[65] p. illus. 21 cm. £1.30 B 72-23093
1. Animals—Juvenile poetry. I. Title.
PZ8.3.B243Al 821'.9'12 73-155350
ISBN 0-571-09892-4 MARC

Barker, George, 1913-
Dialogues etc / by George Barker. — London : Faber and Faber, 1976.
55 p. ; 20 cm. GB***
Poems.
ISBN 0-571-10834-2 : £1.95
I. Title.
PR6003.A68D5 821'.9'12 76-359920
76 MARC

Barker, George, 1913-
III Hallucination poems. [New York] Helikon Press, 1972.
[10] p. 24 cm.
110 copies numbered and signed by the poet.
I. Title.
NcU NUC73-32116

Barker, George, 1913–
In memory of David Archer. London, Faber ₍1973₎
77 p. 20 cm. £1.95 GB***
Poems.
I. Archer, David. II. Title.
PR6003.A68 I 5 821′.9′12 74–160365
ISBN 0–571–10398–7 MARC

Barker, George, 1913-
see Homage to George Barker on his sixtieth birthday. London, Martin Brian and O'Keefe, 1973.

Barker, George, 1913-
see Le Poète dans la société contemporaine. ₍Québec₎ Presses de l'Université Laval, 1968.

Barker, George Carpenter, 1912-1958. Pachuco, an American-Spanish argot and its social functions in Tucson, Arizona. 1976.
in The Mexican experience in Arizona. New York, Arno Press, 1976.

Barker, George Fisher Russell, 1848-1927, ed.
see Westminster School, Westminster, Eng. The record of old Westminsters ... London, Chiswick press, 1928.

Barker, George Fisher Russell, 1848-1927
see Westminster School, Westminster, Eng. The Westminster School register from 1764 to 1883. London, New York, Macmillan, 1892.

Barker, George Frederick, 1835-1910.
Memoir of John William Draper, 1811-1882. 197
see Draper, John William, 1811-1882. Thoughts on the future civil policy of America. New York, Garland Pub., 1974.

Barker, George Frederick, 1835-1910.
A text book of elementary chemistry, theoretical and inorganic. By George F. Barker. New Haven, C. C. Chatfield & Co., 1870, 1971.
(On American culture series, reel 474, no. 7)
Microfilm (positive) 35 mm. Ann Arbor, Mich., University Microfilms, 1971.
Collation of the original: 342 p.
1. Chemistry, Inorganic. I. Title.
PSt NUC73-32103

Barker, George M A
Wildlife conservation in the care of churches and churchyards, ₍by₎ G. M. A. Barker. London, Church Information Office, 1972.
19 p. illus. 19 cm. £0.25 B 72–14045
1. Nature conservation. 2. Church property. I. Title.
QH75.B28 639′.9 72–171581
ISBN 0–7151–6531–3 MARC

Barker, George Phillip, joint author
see Schneider, Hans, 1927 (Jan. 24)- Matrices and linear algebra. New York, Holt, Rinehart and Winston, c1967.

Barker, George Phillip, joint author
see Schneider, Hans, 1927 (Jan. 24)- Matrices and linear algebra. 2d ed. New York, Holt, Rinehart and Winston [c1973]

Barker, Gerard A
Henry Mackenzie / by Gerard A. Barker. — Boston : Twayne Publishers, c1975.
189 p. : port. ; 21 cm. — (Twayne's English authors series ; TEAS no. 184)
Bibliography: p. 185-186.
Includes index.
ISBN 0-8057-6651-0
1. Mackenzie, Henry, 1745-1831. 2. Authors, Scottish—18th century—Biography.
PR3543.M2Z63 823′.6 74-34318
75 MARC

Barker, Gordon H
A volunteer probation officer manual, by Gordon H. Barker and Ronald R. Matson in consultation with Horace B. Holmes ₍and others₎ Boulder, Colo., National Information Center on Volunteers in Courts, 1969.
64 p. illus. 28 cm.
Bibliography: p. 28.
1. Probation officers. 2. Social work with delinquents and criminals. I. Matson, Ronald R. II. Title.
CoU NUC75-31497

Barker, Graham Edward, 1951-
Highrise and superprofits; an analysis of the development industry in Canada, by Graham Barker, Jennifer Penney ₍and₎ Wally Seccombe. With an introd. by Leo Johnson. Kitchener, Ont., Dumont Press Graphix ₍1973₎
xii, 178 p. illus. 21 cm. $2.95 ($3.50 U.S.) C***
Bibliography: p. 171-178.
1. Housing—Canada. 2. Financial institutions—Canada. 3. Construction industry—Canada—Finance. I. Penney, Jennifer, joint author. II. Seccombe, Wally, joint author. III. Title.
HD7305.A3B37 338.4′7′6900971 75-300228
75₍r75₎rev MARC

Barker, Harley Granville Granville-
see Granville-Barker, Harley Granville, 1877-1946.

Barker, Harriett.
see **The One-burner gourmet. Chicago, Greatlakes Living Press, c1975.**

Barker, Herbert Luther.
The lachrymal sac and nasal duct in various mammals, by Herbert L. Barker. [Ithaca, N. Y.] 1890.
47 l. 13 plates. 27 cm.
Thesis (Ph. B.)—Cornell University.
Microfilm. Ithaca, N. Y., Photo Science, Cornell University, 1973. part of reel. 35 mm.
NIC NUC76-74072

Barker, Mrs. Herman H
see Barker, Elizabeth S

Barker, Horace.
Equal housing opportunities in the South: a challenge; report on Government and citizen action, ₍by Horace Barker and Robert E. Anderson, Jr.₎ Atlanta, Southern Regional Council, 1971.
27 p. illus. 23 cm. $0.50
"This report represents a cooperative effort between the Southern Regional Council's Urban Planning Project and the editorial section of Research and Information."
Includes bibliographical references.
1. Discrimination in housing—Southern States. I. Anderson, Robert Emmett, 1929- joint author. II. Southern Regional Council. Urban Planning Project. III. Southern Regional Council. Research and Information. IV. Title.
HD7296.B37 301.5′4 74–151363
MARC

Barker, Horace.
The Federal retreat in school desegregation. ₍Atlanta₎ Southern Regional Council, 1969.
iv, 70 p. 28 cm. (Southern Regional Council. Special report) 0.50
Includes bibliographical references.
1. Segregation in education—United States. I. Title. II. Series.
LA210.B34 370.19′342 74–191396
MARC

Barker, Howard. Claw. 1977.
in Barker, Howard. Stripwell ; Claw. London, Calder. 1977.

Barker, Howard.
Stripwell ; Claw / Howard Barker. — London : Calder, 1977.
230 p. ; 21 cm. — (Playscript ; 79) GB***
Plays.
ISBN 0-7145-3566-4 : £6.50. ISBN 0-7145-3572-9 pbk.
I. Barker, Howard. Claw. 1977. II. Title.
PR6052.A6485S8 822′.9′14 77-374220
77 MARC

Barker, Ian.
Paul Nash, 1889-1946. A Northern Arts exhibition organised by Ian Barker ₍and held at the₎ Northern Arts Gallery, Newcastel upon Tyne, September 20-October 16, 1971. Catalogue and research by Andrew Causey. ₍London? 1971₎
64 p. illus.
Includes bibliography
1. Nash, Paul, 1889-1946. I. Causey, Andrew. II. Nash, Paul, 1889-1946. III. Northern Arts Association.
CaOTP NUC74-10217

Barker, J.
see
Barker, James.
Barker, Jeremy.

Barker, J.A.
see The Structure and properties of water... Washington, U.S. Govt. Print. Off., 1972.

Barker, J. L.
see also
Barker, James L 1936-

Barker, Jack.
Arithmetic / Jack Barker, James Rogers, James Van Dyke. — Philadelphia : Saunders, 1975.
xi, 357 p. : ill. ; 27 cm.
Includes index.
ISBN 0–7216–1550–3
1. Arithmetic—1961– I. Rogers, James V., joint author. II. Van Dyke, James, joint author. III. Title.
[QA107.B36] 513 74–6678
MARC

Barker, James.
Yanomamö cajicö. Cartilla guaica. Caracas, Ministerio de Justicia, Comisión Indigenista [197-? -
v. illus.
Spanish and Guaica.
1. Guaica language. 2. Primers, Guaican. I. Title. II. Title: Cartilla guaica.
PPiU NUC74-3528

Barker, James Albert, 1942-
Location effects on heritability estimates and gain predictions for ten-year-old loblolly pine. Raleigh, N. C., 1973.
105 l. tables. 29 cm.
Bibliography: leaves 76-78.
Vita.
Thesis (Ph. D.)—North Carolina State University at Raleigh.
NcRS NUC74-125918

Barker, James C., joint author
see Sewell, John Ike, 1933- Effects on runoff, groundwater... Knoxville, University of Tennessee, 1973.

Barker, James K.
see Parry Sound District atlas ... Toronto, Ministry of Housing, 1976.

Barker, James L., 1936- joint author
see Ott, Arthur N 1934-
Physical, chemical, and biological characteristics of Conewago Lake drainage basin... Harrisburg : Dept. of Environmental Resources, 1973.

Barker, James M., joint author
see Beeton, Alfred Merle, 1927- Investigation of the influence of thermal discharge... Milwaukee, Wis., University of Wisconsin—Milwaukee, Center for Great Lakes Studies, 1974.

Barker, James Nelson, 1784-1858. The Indian Princess
in Bray, John, 1782-1822. The Indian princess. Piano-vocal score. English. New York, Da Capo Press, 1972.

Barker, James Nelson, 1784-1858.
Marmion; or, The battle of Flodden Field. A drama in five acts, by J. N. Barker. New York, D. Longworth, 1816.
79 p.
"First acted April, 1812."
Microfilm (positive) Ann Arbor, Mich., University Microfilms, 1974. 8th title of 50. 35 mm. (American culture series, reel 552.8)
I. Title.
KEmT NUC75-23077

Barker, Jane, fl. 1688.
Exilius; or, The banish'd Roman. With a new introd. for the Garland ed. by Josephine Grieder. New York, Garland Pub., 1973.
10, 142 p. 22 cm. (Foundations of the novel)
Reprint of the 1715 ed.
I. Title. II. Series.
PZ3.B2428Ex4 823'.4 70-170536
[PR3316.B28] MARC
ISBN 0-8240-0537-6

Barker, Jane, fl. 1688. Love intrigues. 1973
in Hearne, Mary. The lover's week... New York, Garland Pub., 1973.

Barker, Jane Valentine, 1930-
76 historic homes of Boulder, Colorado / by Jane Valentine Barker ; photography by Jerry Cleveland. — 1st ed. — Boulder, Colo. : Pruett Pub. Co., c1976.
vii, 200 p., [1] fold. leaf of plates : ill. ; 29 cm.
Includes index.
ISBN 0-87108-506-2 : $19.95
1. Historic buildings—Colorado—Boulder. 2. Boulder, Colo.—Buildings. 3. Boulder, Colo.—History. I. Cleveland, Jerry, 1946- II. Title.
F784.B66B37 978.8'63 76-17617
76 MARC

Barker, Jeremy, ed.
see Review and bibliography on aspects of fluid sealing... Bedford, British Hydromechanics Research Association, 1972.

Barker, Jeremy
see Second review and bibliography on aspects of fluid sealing. Bedford, c1975.

Barker, John.
The Meyrick Park Halt / by John Barker. — [Bournemouth] : [Dorset County Council, Education Committee], 1976.
[2], 5 [i.e. 6] p. : map ; 21 cm. — (Environmental studies leaflet ; no. 345) (Local studies) GB77-04722
£0.10
1. Railroads—England—Bournemouth. I. Title. II. Series. III. Series: Local studies.
TF64.B65B37 385'.314 77-362627
77 MARC

Barker, John, 1771-1849.
Syria and Egypt under the last five sultans of Turkey. Edited by Edward B. B. Barker. New York, Arno Press, 1973.
xi, 366, viii, 338 p. illus. 23 cm. (The Middle East collection)
Reprint of the 1876 ed. published by S. Tinsley, London.
1. Barker, John, 1771-1849. 2. Syria—Description and travel. 3. Egypt—Description and travel. I. Barker, Edward Bruce Boughton, ed. II. Title. III. Series.
DS94.B25 1973 915.691'04'3 [B] 73-6269
ISBN 0-405-05324-X MARC

Barker, John Alan. Control and co-ordination in organisms
in Teachers' guide to the laboratory guides... Harmondsworth, Penguin, 1971.

Barker, John C
Strange contrarieties : Pascal in England during the Age of Reason / John Barker. — Montreal : McGill-Queen's University Press, 1975.
xiv, 336 p. : ill. ; 24 cm. C***
Bibliography: p. 291-316.
Includes index.
ISBN 0-7735-0186-6 : $15.00
1. Pascal, Blaise, 1623-1662—Influence. 2. Philosophy, English. 3. Philosophy, American. I. Title.
B1903.B25 192 74-81661
76[r77]rev MARC

Barker, John Charles.
La Peur et la mort, une étude sur la peur, ses causes et ses effets [par] J. C. Barker. Traduit de l'anglais par Claude Elsen. [Paris,] Stock, 1969.
189 p. 21 cm. 16.00 F***
Translation of Sacred to death.
1. Death—Psychology. 2. Fear. I. Title.
[DNLM: 1. Death. 2. Fear. WM 178 B255s 1969]
BF789.D4B314 133 72-361608
Shared Cataloging with DNLM

Barker, John E
Biological removal of carbon and nitrogen compounds from coke plant wastes, by John E. Barker [and] R. J. Thompson. Washington, For sale by the Supt. of Docs., U.S. Govt. Print. Off., 1973.
178 p. illus. (Environmental protection technology series, 167)
Prepared for Office of Research and Monitoring, U.S. Environmental Protection Agency under project 12010 EDY.
1. Coke plants—Waste disposal. 2. Water—Purification—Biological treatment. I. Thompson, R. J. II. United States. Environmental Protection Agency. Office of Research and Monitoring. III. Title. IV. Series.
DI DNAL PSt NUC74-125921

Barker, John Elliot.
Patterns of water stress and stomatal behavior of Pinus ponderosa Laws. and Abies concolor (Gord. and Glend.) Lindl. in response to environment. [Berkeley] 1972.
xv, 201 l. illus.
Thesis (Ph. D.)—University of California.
Bibliography: leaves 136-146.
CU NUC74-3461

Barker, John Henry James, ed.
see Arthur, William, 1819-1901. The tongue of fire. Centenary ed. London, Epworth Press [1956]

Barker, John M.
see Read, Horace Emerson, 1898- The judicial systems of the common law... [Halifax, N.S. ? 1960?]

Barker, John R.
see Symposium on Chemical Kinetics Data for the Upper and Lower Atmosphere, Warrenton, Va., 1974. Proceedings of the Symposium on Chemical Kinetics Data for the Upper and Lower Atmosphere, held at Warrenton, Virginia, September 15-18, 1974. New York, Wiley, 1975.

Barker, John Sydney, 1910- joint author.
see Sobers, Garfield, Sir. Cricket in the sun ... London, Barker, [1967]

Barker, Jonathan Shedd.
Local politics and national development: the case of a rural district in the Saloum region of Senegal. [Berkeley, Calif.] 1967.
xiv, 271 l. maps.
Thesis—University of California, Berkeley.
Bibliography: leaves 266-271.
Microfilm. Ann Arbor, Mich., University Microfilms [n. d.] 1 reel. 35 mm.
1. Sine-Saloum, Senegal (Region)—Politics and government. 2. Senegal—Politics and government. I. Title.
IEN NUC75-21288

Barker, Jonathan Shedd.
Political integration and elite recruitment in the Saloum region of Senegal [by] Jonathan S. Barker. [n. p., 1966]
28 l. 28 cm. (African Studies Association. Papers, no. 72)
Caption title.
Prepared for the 9th annual meeting of the African Studies Association, Indiana University, 1966.
1. Saloum, Senegal—Politics and government. 2. Local government—Senegal.
CtY-L NUC75-108876

Barker, Joseph W.
see Schélandre, Jean de, 1585?-1635. Tyr et Sidon ... Paris, A. G. Nizet, 1974.

Barker, June.
Decorative braiding and weaving. [Newton Centre, Mass.] C. T. Branford Co. [1973]
112 p. illus. (part col.) 21 cm. $7.50
Bibliography: p. 111.
1. Braid. 2. Hand weaving. I. Title.
TT880.B3 746 72-10627
ISBN 1-8231-7031-4 MARC

Barker, Kathleen Mary Deborah.
Entertainment in the nineties, by Kathleen Barker. Bristol, Bristol Branch of the Historical Association, 1973.
20 p. illus. 22 cm. (Bristol Branch of the Historical Association. Local history pamphlets no. 33) £0.30 GB***
Cover title.
Includes bibliographical references.
1. Performing arts—Bristol, Eng.—History. I. Title. II. Series: Historical Association, London. Bristol Branch. Local history pamphlets, no. 33.
DA690.B8H5 no. 33 914.24'1 s 74-157410
[PN2596.B74] [790.2'09424'1] MARC

Barker, Kathleen Mary Deborah.
Report on diseases of cultivated plants in England and Wales for the years 1957-1968 [by] J. J. Baker. London, H. M. S. O., 1972.
x, 322, [16] p. illus., maps. 25 cm. (Ministry of Agriculture, Fisheries and Food. Technical bulletin 25) £3.00 GB 72-30641
Includes index.
1. Plant diseases—England. 2. Plant diseases—Wales. I. Title. II. Series: Great Britain. Ministry of Agriculture, Fisheries and Food. Technical bulletin 25.
S217.A6134 no. 25 630'.8 s 74-157408
[SB605.G7] [632] MARC
ISBN 0-11-240885-0

Barker, Kathleen Mary Deborah.
The Theatre Royal Bristol, 1766-1966; two centuries of stage history [by] Kathleen Barker. London, The Society for Theatre Research, 1974.
xii, 278 p. illus. 24 cm.
Bibliography: p. 231-233.
1. Bristol, Eng. Theatre Royal. I. Title.
CtY ViBlbV ICN InU NUC75-21293
CaOTP

Barker, Kathleen Mary Deborah.
Theatre Royal, Bristol; the first seventy years. 2d ed. Bristol, University, Historical Association, Bristol Branch, 1963.
20 p. facsims. (Historical Association. Bristol Branch. Local history pamphlets, 3)
Includes bibliography.
1. Bristol, Eng. Theatre Royal. I. Title. II. Series.
CLU NUC73-39278

Barker, Kenneth Dow.
see Nicholson, Norman, 1914- Stitch and stone ... Sunderland, Ceolfrith Press, 1975.

Barker, Kenneth L
Bibliography for Old Testament exegesis and exposition / compiled by Kenneth L. Barker, Bruce K. Waltke ; edited by Roy B. Zuck. — 3d ed., rev. — Dallas : Dallas Theological Seminary, 1975.
66 p. ; 23 cm.
1. Bible. O.T.—Bibliography. I. Waltke, Bruce K., joint author. II. Title.
Z7772.A1B37 016.2216'6 75-326988
[BS1140.2] 75 MARC

Barker, Kenneth Neil, 1937-
An analysis of the work and utilization of the pharmacist in small Mississippi hospitals to estimate some effects of the introduction of a pharmacy auxiliary worker. [University, Miss.] 1971 [1972]
ix, 239 l. plans.
Thesis—University of Mississippi.
Bibliography: leaves 227-239.
Photocopy of typescript. Ann Arbor, Mich., University Microfilms, 1972. 22 cm.
1. Hospital pharmacies. 2. Pharmacists—Mississippi. I. Title.
OU NUC74-125917

Barker, L.
see Moulam, Anthony John James. Snowdon east. 1st ed. [s.l.] Climbers' Club, 1970.

[Barker, L J Mrs.]
Influences of slavery upon the white population. By a former resident of slave states. [New York, American Anti-slavery Society, 1855. Westport, Conn., Negro Universities Press, 1970]
12 p. 22 cm. (Anti-slavery tracts, ser. 1, no. 9)
1. Slavery in the U.S.—Controversial literature—1855. 2. Southern states—Soc. life & cust. I. Title. II. Series.
NcD NUC75-31496

Barker, Larry Lee, 1941- comp.
Communication vibrations [by] Larry L. Barker. Englewood Cliffs, N.J., Prentice-Hall [1974]
x, 146 p. illus. 28 cm. (Prentice-Hall series in speech communication)
1. Communication. I. Title.
P90.B298 001.5 73-19516
ISBN 0-13-153007-0 MARC

Barker, Larry Lee, 1941-
see A Bibliography of required readings in speech communication research courses. [Tallahassee, Dept. of Communication, Florida State University, ca. 1971]

Barker, Larry Lee, 1941-
see United States. National Center for Educational Statistics. HEGIS IX requirements and specifications for the Survey of students enrolled for advanced degrees... -- Washington : The Center : for sale by the Supt. of Docs., U.S. Govt. Print. Off., 1974.

Barker, Larry Lee, 1941- joint author
see Wiseman, Gordon. Speech—interpersonal communication. 2d ed. New York, Chandler Pub. Co. [1974]

Barker, Laura Cooke.
Society silhouettes; collection of short stories by Laura Cooke Barker. Cleveland, The Helman-Taylor company, 1898.
271 p. 18 cm.
Micro-transparency (negative) Louisville, Ky., Lost Cause Press, 1973. 4 sheets. 10.5 x 14.8 cm. (L. H. Wright. American fiction, 1876-1900, no. 296)
I. Title.
PSt NUC75-21276

Barker, Lawrence K
Producing SNG by hydrogasifying in situ crude shale oil. ₍Washington₎ U.S. Bureau of Mines ₍1975₎
37 p. illus., tables. 26 cm. (United States. Bureau of Mines. Report of investigations 8011)
Includes bibliography.
Based on work done in cooperation with the University of Wyoming.
1. Shale-oils gasification. I. United States. Bureau of Mines. II. Wyoming. University. III. Title. IV. Series.
DI NUC76-28516

Barker, Lewis Marlin, 1942-
An investigation of radiation- and lithium chloride-induced conditioned taste aversions, by Lewis M. Barker. ₍Tallahassee₎ 1972.
viii, 156 l.
Thesis (Ph. D.)—Florida State University.
Bibliography: leaves 152-155.
Vita.
1. Conditioned response. 2. Taste. I. Title.
FTaSU NUC74-4061

Barker, Linda A
Preprimary enrollment, October 1971, by Linda A. Barker. [Washington, U. S.] National Center for Educational Statistics; [for sale by the Supt. of Docs., U. S. Govt. Print. Off., 1972]
vii, 30 p. illus. 26 cm. (United States. Dept. of Health, Education and Welfare. DHEW publication no. (OE) 72-197)
On cover: Elementary and secondary education. Supt. of Docs. no.: 5.220:20079-71.
1. Education, Preschool—United States—1945- —Statistics. 2. Compensatory education—United States—Statistics. I. Title. II. Series.
NTR NBuU NUC74-3518

Barker, Linda A.
see United States. National Center for Educational Statistics. Statistics of nonpublic elementary ... Washington, The Center, 1973.

Barker, Lonnie.
An assessment of the Miami University educational administration doctoral program. Oxford, Ohio, 1972.
128 l. 28 cm.
Typed.
Thesis (Ph. D.)—Miami University.
1. Doctoral of education degree. I. Title.
OOxM NUC74-4060

Barker, Lucius Jefferson, 1928-
Black Americans and the political system / Lucius J. Barker, Jesse J. McCorry, Jr. — Cambridge, Mass. : Winthrop Publishers, c1976.
ix, 383 p. : ill. ; 23 cm.
Includes bibliographies and index.
ISBN 0-87626-080-6. ISBN 0-87626-079-2 pbk.
1. Afro-Americans—Politics and suffrage. 2. United States—Politics and government—1945- I. McCorry, Jesse J., 1935- joint author.
E185.61.B23 323.1'19'6073 75-33043
75 MARC

Barker, Lucius Jefferson, 1928- comp.
Civil liberties and the Constitution : cases and commentaries / Lucius J. Barker, Twiley W. Barker, Jr. — ₍2d ed.₎ — Englewood Cliffs, N.J. : Prentice-Hall, ₍1975₎
vi, 474 p. ; 24 cm.
Includes bibliographies and index.
ISBN 0-13-134817-5. ISBN 0-13-134809-4 pbk.
1. Civil rights—United States. I. Barker, Twiley Wendell, 1926- joint comp. II. Title.
KF4748.B2 1975 342'.73'085 74-34364
75 MARC

Barker, Lucius Jefferson, 1928-
Offshore oil politics: a study in public policy making. Urbana, Ill., 1954 [1972]
243 l.
Thesis (Ph. D.)—University of Illinois.
Bibliography: leaves 237-242.
Photocopy of typescript. Ann Arbor, Mich., University Microfilms, 1972. 20 cm.
1. Petroleum in submerged lands—U. S. 2. U. S.—Pol. & govt.—1945- I. Title.
WaU-L NUC74-3533

Barker, Malcolm G
Yorkshire : the North Riding / Malcolm G. Barker. — London : Batsford, 1977.
198 p. : ill. ; 23 cm. GB***
Includes index.
ISBN 0-7134-3189-X : £3.95
1. Yorkshire, Eng. North Riding—History. I. Title.
DA670.Y6B26 942.8'4 77-365117
77 MARC

Barker, Marie Louise, 1890-1961.
The pocket Oxford German dictionary / German-English compiled by M. L. Barker and H. Homeyer ; English-German compiled by C. T. Carr. — Oxford : Clarendon Press, c1975.
xxii, 452, 224 p. ; 13 cm. GB***
Second pt. has t.p.: The pocket Oxford English-German dictionary, compiled by C. T. Carr.
ISBN 0-19-864121-4 : £3.25
1. German language—Dictionaries—English. 2. English language—Dictionaries—German. I. Homeyer, Helene, 1898- joint author. II. Carr, Charles Telford. III. Title.
PF3640.B32 1975 433'.21 76-351958
76 MARC

Barker, Mary.
see Pears encyclopaedia of myths and legends. London, Pelham, 1976-

Barker, Mary
see also Broome, Mary Anne (Stewart) Barker, Lady, 1831-1911.

Barker, Mary Constance.
The ancestry of Alfred Charles Barker, 1819-1873, of Christchurch, New Zealand / Mary Constance Barker. — ₍s. l. : s. n., 197-?₎ (Ashburton, N. Z. : Bruce Print Co.)
72 p. : ill., fold. geneal. table (in pocket) ; 23 cm. NZ***
1. Barker family. I. Title.
CS2179.B37 1970z 929'.2'09931 75-302302
MARC

Barker, Mary G
Early will records of Adams County, Mississippi / compiled by Mary G. Barker, Mavis Oliver Feltus, Diane A. Stockfelt. — ₍s.l. : Barker₎, c1975.
leaves A-I, 82, 38, ₍6₎ p. ; 28 cm.
1. Adams Co., Miss.—Genealogy. 2. Registers of births, etc.—Adams Co., Miss. I. Feltus, Mavis Oliver, joint author. II. Stockfelt, Diane A., joint author. III. Title.
F347.A2B37 929'.3762'26 76-358243
76 MARC

Barker, Mary L
The structure and content of environmental cognitions; an exploratory study of evaluations of air pollution among five professional and disciplinary student groups, by Mary L. Barker. [Toronto] c1972.
iii, 201 l. illus.
Thesis—University of Toronto.
Bibliography: leaves 133-139.
CaOTU NUC74-3532

Barker, Mary L
Water resources and related land uses : Strait of Georgia-Puget Sound Basin : report / by Mary L. Barker. — Ottawa : Lands Directorate, Dept. of the Environment, 1974.
viii, 55 p. : ill., maps (2 fold. col. in pocket) ; 28 cm. — (Geographical paper ; no. 56) C***
Summary in English and French.
Bibliography: p. 51-54.
$4.50
1. Water resources development—Puget Sound area. 2. Coastal resource management—Puget Sound area. I. Title. II. Series.
F1001.C145 no. 56 971 s 75-332452
₍TC227.B74₎ 76 MARC

Barker, Mary Lou.
Manual of routines for Cataloging Department, National Library of Nigeria, by Mary Lou Barker. Lagos, 1963.
103 l. 33 cm.
1. Cataloging. I. National Library of Nigeria.
CtY NUC76-25675

Barker, Michael K
Gladstone and radicalism : the reconstruction of liberal policy in Britain, 1885-94 / Michael Barker. — Hassocks ₍Eng.₎ : Harvester Press, 1975.
viii, 308 p. ; 23 cm. GB***
Includes bibliographical references and index.
ISBN 0-901759-27-9
1. Great Britain—Politics and government—1837-1901. 2. Gladstone, William Ewart, 1809-1898. I. Title.
DA560.B28 320.9'41'081 75-311907
75 MARC

Barker, Michael K
Gladstone and radicalism : the reconstruction of liberal policy in Britain, 1885-94 / Michael Barker. — New York : Barnes & Noble, 1975.
viii, 308 p. ; 23 cm.
Includes bibliographical references and index.
ISBN 0-06-490303-6 : $17.50
1. Great Britain—Politics and government—1837-1901. 2. Gladstone, William Ewart, 1809-1898. I. Title.
DA560.B28 1975b 320.9'41'081 75-311868
75 MARC

Barker, Muhammed Abd-Al-Rahman.
An Urdu newspaper reader / by Muhammad Abd-Al-Rahman Barker, Shafiqur Rahman, Hasan Jahamgir Hamdani. — Ithaca, N. Y. : Spoken Language Services, c1974.
xii, 453 p. : ill. ; 23 cm.
Added t. p. in Urdu: اردو اخباری زبان
ISBN 0-87590-337-8
1. Urdu language—Readers. I. Shafiqur Rahman, joint author. II. Hamdani, Hasan Jahangir, joint author. III. Title. IV Title: Urdū akhbārī zabān.
PK1975.B38 1974 75-590521

Barker, Muhammad Abd-al-Rahman
see A Course in Urdu. Ithaca, N. Y.: Spoken Language Services, c1975-

Barker, Nancy Nichols, comp.
The French Legation in Texas. Translated and edited with an introd. by Nancy Nichols Barker. With a foreword by John Connally. Austin, Texas State Historical Association ₍1971-73₎
2 v. (710 p.) illus., facsims., ports. 26 cm.
Vol. 1 contains chiefly the diplomatic and private correspondence, between 1839 and 1842, of A. Dubois de Saligny, Chargé d'affaires of the French Legation in Texas.
Includes bibliographical references.
CONTENTS: v. 1. Recognition, rupture, and reconciliation.—v. 2. Mission miscarried.
1. Texas—Foreign relations—France—Sources. 2. France—Foreign relations—Texas—Sources. 3. Texas—History—Republic, 1836-1846—Sources. I. Dubois de Saligny, A. II. France. Légation (Republic of Texas) III. Texas State Historical Association. IV. Title.
F390.B335 976.4'04 78-102766
ISBN 0-87611-026-X (v. 1)
rev

Barker, Nicholas, joint author.
see Bruce, Liza. Alternative cookery. London, Tandem, 1975.

Barker, Nicolas, comp.
In fair Verona; English travellers in Italy and their accounts of the city from the Middle Ages to modern times. ₍To Giovanni Mardersteig on his eightieth birthday from his friends. Cambridge, Eng.₎ 1972.
49, ₍1₎ p., ₍1₎ l. 31 cm.
"... set... at The Curwen Press, Plaistow. Reynolds Stone engraved the device on the title-page. One hundred copies were printed by Will and Sebastian Carter at the Rampant Lions Press... Cambridge ₍Eng.₎"
ICN NUC74-88819

Barker, Nicolas.
Italian writing books 1522-39; an attempted chronology. [n.p., 196-]
49, [5] l. 35 cm.
Xerox copy of typescript.
Caption title.
ICN NUC74-3687

Barker, Nicolas.
[Stanley Morison, by Nicolas Barker. n.p., 196-]-
v. 34 cm.
Xerox copy of draft.
ICN NUC74-3686

Barker, Nicolas.
Stanley Morison. London, Macmillan, [1972].
566, [16] p. illus., facsims., ports. 24 cm. index. £10.00 B 72-20284
Includes bibliographical references.
I. Morison, Stanley, 1889-1967.
Z250.A2B15 1972 686.2'092'4 73-163477
ISBN 0-333-13136-3 MARC

Barker, Nicolas.
see McBey, James, 1883-1959. The early life of James McBey ... Oxford [Eng.] Oxford University Press, 1977.

Barker, Ophelia.
Historical sketch of Connally United Methodist Church near Milton, North Carolina, Caswell County; organized 1821. Edited by Ophelia Barker. [Milton? N.C.] 1969.
23 p. 21 cm.
On cover: History of Connally United Methodist Church, Milton, North Carolina; organized 1821.
1. Milton, N.C. Connally United Methodist Church. Hist. I. Title.
NcD NUC73-38841

Barker, P H
RNZFA TUI oceanographic cruise - T 60, northeastern New Zealand waters, July to October 1964, by P.H. Barker and R.N. Denham. [Auckland, N.Z.] 1970.
1 v. (various pagings) maps, tables. 30 cm. (New Zealand. Defence Scientific Establishment. Report no. 73)
1. Oceanography—New Zealand. I. Title. II. Series.
DME NUC75-30859

Barker, Paul, comp.
A sociological portrait: a series from New Society. Harmondsworth, Penguin, 1972.
206 p. 18 cm. (Penguin education) £0.50 GB 72-25150
Bibliography: p. 186-203.
1. Social surveys—Addresses, essays, lectures. 2. Sociology—Addresses, essays, lectures. I. New society. II. Title.
HM51.B26 301'.08 73-179381
ISBN 0-14-080327-0 MARC

Barker, Paul, comp.
Waves, selected and edited by Paul Barker. Toronto, New York, McGraw-Hill Ryerson [1972]
80 p. illus. 28 cm. C***
1. Water sports. I. Title.
GV775.B34 1972 797 73-180166
ISBN 0-7700-3229-X MARC

Barker, Paul, comp.
Wings; selected and edited by Paul Barker. Toronto, New York, McGraw-Hill Ryerson [1972]
68 p. illus., ports. 28 cm. (Man in motion) C***
1. Aeronautics—Addresses, essays, lectures. I. Title.
TL559.B33 387.7'08 72-171469
ISBN 0-7700-3215-X MARC

Barker, Paul.
see The Social sciences today. London, Edward Arnold, 1975.

Barker, Paul.
see The Social sciences today. Totowa, N.J., Littlefield, Adams, 1977, c1975.

Barker, Paul, 1935- comp.
One for sorrow, two for joy; ten years of New society. London, Allen & Unwin 1972.
367 p. illus. 22 cm. £4.75 B***
1. Social history—1945 —Addresses, essays, lectures. I. New society. II. Title.
HN17.5.B33 301'.08 72-172023
ISBN 0-04-300040-1; 0-04-300041-x (pbk.) MARC

Barker, Peter J., joint author.
see Button, Kenneth John. Case studies in cost-benefit analysis. London, Heinemann Educational [for the Economics Association] 1975.

Barker, Philip, fl. 1971-
The armies and enemies of Imperial Rome: organization, tactics, dress and weapons, 150 BC to 600 AD by Phil Barker. [Goring by Sea], Wargames Research Group [1972]
[4], 90 p. illus. 26 cm. £1.75 B 72-13817
Cover title.
1. Military history, Ancient. 2. Armies—History. 3. Rome—History, Military. 4. Rome—Army. I. Title.
U29.B35 355'.00937 73-155246
ISBN 0-9500299-6-3 MARC

Barker, Philip, fl. 1971-
Armies of the Macedonian and Punic wars: organisation, tactics, dress and weapons, by Phil Barker. Goring by Sea (c/o B. O'Brien, 75 Ardingly Drive, Goring by Sea, Sussex), Wargames Research Group, 1971.
[3], 60 p. illus. (incl. 1 col.). 26 cm. £1.25 B 71-26976
Cover title.
1. Military history, Ancient. 2. Armies—History. I. Title.
U29.B37 355'.0093 72-188024
ISBN 0-9500290-4-7 rev MARC

Barker, Philip A
Techniques of archaeological excavation / Philip Barker. — New York : Universe Books, 1977.
279 p. : ill. ; 26 cm.
Bibliography: p. [264]-272.
Includes index.
ISBN 0-87663-291-6
1. Archaeology—Methodology. I. Title.
CC76.B37 930'.1'0283 77-24786
77 MARC

Barker, Philip Alan.
Basic child psychiatry / Philip Barker. — 2d ed. — Baltimore : University Park Press, 1976.
xiv, 274 p. : ill. ; 23 cm.
Includes bibliographies and index.
ISBN 0-8391-0899-0
1. Child psychiatry. I. Title.
[DNLM: 1. Child psychiatry. WS350 B255b]
RJ499.B27 1976 618.9'28'9 75-40278
75 MARC

Barker, Philip Alan.
Basic child psychiatry / Philip Barker. — 2d ed. — London : Crosby Lockwood Staples, 1976.
xiv, 274 p. : ill. ; 23 cm. GB***
Includes bibliographies and index.
ISBN 0-258-97024-3. ISBN 0-258-97039-1 pbk.
1. Child psychiatry. I. Title.
[DNLM: 1. Child psychiatry. WS350 B255b 1976]
[RJ499.B27 1976b] 618.9'28'9 76-675429
Shared Cataloging with 76 MARC
DNLM

Barker, Philip Alan.
Care can prevent; child care or child psychiatry. London [1973]
80 p. (National Children's Home convocation lecture, 1973)
1. Child behavior disorders—prevention & control. 2. Child care. 3. Child, Institutionalized. 4. Child psychiatry. I. Title. II. Series.
DNLM NUC75-21286

Barker, Philip Alan.
The residential psychiatric treatment of children / edited by Philip Barker. — London : Crosby Lockwood Staples, 1974.
xiii, 354 p., [4] leaves of plates : ill., plan ; 23 cm. GB 75-03380
Bibliography: p. [332]-346.
Includes index.
ISBN 0-258-96891-5 : £7.50
1. Child psychotherapy—Residential treatment. I. Title.
RJ504.5.B37 1974b 362.7'8'21 75-319000
75 MARC

Barker, Philip Alan.
The residential psychiatric treatment of children. Edited by Philip Barker. New York, Wiley [1974]
xiii, 354 p. illus. 23 cm.
"A Halsted Press book."
Bibliography: p. [332]-346.
ISBN 0-470-04910-3
1. Child psychotherapy—Residential treatment. I. Title.
[DNLM: 1. Mental disorders—In infancy and childhood. 2. Mental disorders—Therapy. 3. Residential treatment—In infancy and childhood. WS 350 B255r 1974]
RJ504.5.B37 1974 362.7'8'21 74-7208
MARC

Barker, Phyllis Ann Hollowell, 1924-
A study of errors by taxpayers on federal income tax returns with implications for instruction. DeKalb, Ill., 1966.
174 p.
Thesis (Ed. D.)-Northern Illinois University.
Includes bibliography.
1. Income tax-U.S. 2. Income tax-U.S.-Accounting. I. Title.
MiEM NUC74-125807

Barker, Phyllis Ann Hollowell, 1924-
A study of errors by taxpayers on Federal income tax returns with implications for instruction. By Phyllis Ann Barker. Dekalb, Ill., 1966.
vii, 174 l. 28 cm.
Thesis—Northern Illinois University.
Vita.
Bibliography: leaves 154-158.
Microfilm of typescript. Ann Arbor, Mich., University Microfilms, 1967. 1 reel. 35 mm.
1. Income tax—U.S. 2. Income tax—U.S.—Study and teaching. I. Title.
OrPS NUC73-45304

Barker, Pierce.
see Weiler, Daniel. A public school voucher demonstration, the first year at Alum Rock ... Santa Monica, Ca., Rand, 1974.

Barker, R A
Digital model of the gravel aquifer, Walla Walla River basin, Washington and Oregon / by R. A. Baker and R. D. MacNish ; prepared in cooperation with United States Geological Survey. — [Olympia] : State of Washington, Dept. of Ecology, 1976.
iv, 49 p. : ill. ; 28 cm. — (Water-supply bulletin ; 45)
Part of illustrative matter in pocket.
Bibliography: p. 47-49.
1. Aquifers—Walla Walla River watershed—Mathematical models. 2. Aquifers—Walla Walla River watershed—Data processing. I. MacNish, Robert D., joint author. II. United States. Geological Survey. III. Title. IV. Series.
GB1199.3.W2B37 551.4'9'0979748 76-622836
76 MARC

Barker, R. A., ed.
see MacNish, Robert D Appraisal of ground-water availability and management projections.. [Olympia] State of Washington, 1973.

Barker, R. A., joint author.
see MacNish, Robert D. Digital simulation of a basalt aquifer system, Walla Walla River basin, Washington and Oregon. [Olympia?] State of Washington, Dept. of Ecology, 1976.

Barker, R. G.
see
Barker, Richard G

Barker, Ralph, 1917-
Against the sea: true stories of disaster and survival. London, Chatto and Windus, 1972.
[6], 199, [8] p. illus., map, ports. 21 cm. £2.50 B 72-28846
1. Shipwrecks. 2. Survival (after aeroplane accidents, shipwrecks, etc.) I. Title.
G525.B263 1972 910'.453 73-150797
ISBN 0-7011-1696-X MARC

Barker, Ralph, 1917-
Against the sea; true stories of disaster and survival. New York, St. Martin's Press [1972]
199 p. illus. 21 cm. $6.95
1. Shipwrecks. 2. Survival (after aeroplane accidents, shipwrecks, etc.) I. Title.
G525.B263 1972b 910'.453 72-85511
MARC

Barker, Ralph, 1917-
The blockade busters / by Ralph Barker. — London : Chatto & Windus, 1976.
224 p., [6] leaves of plates : ill. ; 23 cm.
Bibliography: p. 213-215.
Includes index.
ISBN 0-7011-2198-0 : £5.00
1. World War, 1939-1945—Blockades. 2. World War, 1939-1945—North Sea. 3. World War, 1939-1945—Supplies. 4. Binney, George, Sir, 1900- I. Title.
D771.B28 1976b 940.54'52 76-382261
76 MARC

Barker, Ralph, 1917-
The blockade busters / Ralph Barker. — 1st American ed. — New York : Norton, 1977, c1976.
224 p., [6] leaves of plates : ill. ; 22 cm.
Bibliography: p. 213-215.
Includes index.
ISBN 0-393-05609-0
1. World War, 1939-1945—Blockades. 2. World War, 1939-1945—North Sea. 3. World War, 1939-1945—Supplies. 4. Binney, George, 1900- I. Title.
D771.B28 1977 940.54'52 76-49446
76 MARC

Barker, Ralph, 1917-
The cricketing family Edrich / [by] Ralph Barker ; with a statistical summary by Irving Rosenwater. — London : Pelham, 1976.
190 p., [18] p. of plates : ill., ports. ; 23 cm. GB76-20028
Bibliography: p. 7-8.
ISBN 0-7207-0909-1 : £4.50
1. Edrich family. 2. Cricket players—Biography. I. Title.
GV915.A1B26 1976 796.358'092'2 76-379119
76 MARC

Barker, Ralph, 1917-
One man's jungle : a biography of F. Spencer Chapman, DSO / by Ralph Barker. — London : Chatto & Windus, 1975.
x, 373 p., [6] leaves of plates : ill. ; 23 cm. GB***
Bibliography: p. vii-x.
Includes index.
ISBN 0-7011-2053-3 : £7.00
1. Chapman, Frederick Spencer, 1907-1971. I. Title.
CT788.C362B37 941.082'092'4 75-330660
75 MARC

Barker, Ralph, 1917–
The Schneider Trophy races. London, Chatto and Windus, 1971.
272 p. 31 plates, illus., maps, ports. 23 cm. index. £3.50
B 71-28707
Bibliography: p. [260]-262.
1. Aeroplane racing. 2. Seaplanes. I. Title.
TL721.6.S3B37 797.5'2'0904 72-195093
ISBN 0-7011-1663-3 MARC

Barker, Ralph, 1917-
Strike hard, strike sure : epics of the bombers / by Ralph Barker. — London ; New York : White Lion Publishers, 1975.
x, 210 p., [16] p. of plates : ill., maps. ports. ; 21 cm. GB75-29556
Includes index.
ISBN 0-7274-0089-4 : £3.25
1. World War, 1939-1945—Aerial operations, British. I. Title.
D786.B262 1975 940.54'49'41 76-365737
76 MARC

Barker, Randolph.
The changing pattern of rice production in Gapan, Nueva Ecija, 1965 to 1970 [by] Randolph Barker, Geronimo Dozina and Liu Fu-Shan. [Los Baños, Philippines, 1971]
[28] l. illus., maps. 28 cm.
"Saturday Seminar, Ag. Economics Dept., Dec. 11, 1971 [IRRI]"
Photocopy. New Haven, Yale University. Library, 1974.
1. Rice—Philippine Islands. 2. Gapan, Philippines (Nueva Ecija) I. Dozina, Geronimo, joint author. II. Liu, Fu-Shan, joint author. III. Title.
CtY NUC76-74046

Barker, Randolph.
The economics of rice production. New York, 1974.
[18] p. illus. (Agricultural Development Council. A/D/C teaching forum, no. 42)
I. Title.
DNAL NUC76-28355

Barker, Randolph.
The probable impact of the seed-fertilizer revolution on grain production and on farm labor requirements, by Randolph Barker, Mahar Mangahas & William H. Meyers. [Quezon City] 1972.
14, [13] p., [2] l. illus. 28 cm. (Institute of Economic Development and Research, School of Economics, University of the Philippines. Discussion paper no. 72-2)
Cover title.
1. Rice—Philippine Islands. 2. Rice—Varieties. 3. Agricultural laborers—Philippine Islands. I. Mangahas, Mahar. II. Meyers, William H. III. Title. IV. Series: Quezon, Philippines. University of the Philippines. Institute of Economic Development and Research. Discussion paper no. 72-2.
NIC NUC74-125922

Barker, Randolph, joint author
see Mangahas, Mahar. Labour absorption in Philippine agriculture. [Paris] Organisation for Economic Co-operation and Development [1972]

Barker, Raymond Charles.
You are invisible; no one has seen your consciousness. New York, Dodd, Mead [1973]
151 p. 22 cm. $4.95
1. New Thought. I. Title.
BF639.B233 131'.32 73-1654
ISBN 0-396-06784-0 MARC

Barker, Richard.
Netsuke : the miniature sculpture of Japan / Richard Barker & Lawrence Smith. — London : British Museum Publications for the Trustees of the British Museum, c1976.
184 p. : ill. (some col.) ; 26 cm. GB***
Bibliography: p. 174.
Includes index.
ISBN 0-7141-1409-X : £8.50
1. Netsukes—Catalogs. I. Smith, Lawrence R. H., joint author. II. Title.
NK6050.B34 736'.68'07402142 76-374796
76 MARC

Barker, Richard Clark, joint author
see Kmetz, Allan R Origin of threshold response delay... New Haven, Yale University, Dept. of Engineering and Applied Science [1968?]

Barker, Richard E.
see East Baton Rouge Parish, La. Community Renewal Program. Apartment feasibility study... [Baton Rouge] City-Parish Planning Commission, 1972.

Barker, Richard G.
see New horizons for the chemical engineer in pulp and paper technology. New York, American Institute of Chemical Engineers, 1976.

Barker, Richard Hindry, 1902–1968.
Thomas Middleton / Richard Hindry Barker. — Westport, Conn. : Greenwood Press, 1974, c1958.
viii, 216 p. ; 22 cm.
Reprint of the ed. published by Columbia University Press, New York.
Bibliography: p. [155]–209.
Includes index.
ISBN 0-8371-7767-7
1. Middleton, Thomas, d. 1627.
[PR2716.B3 1974] 822'.3 74-12880
MARC

Barker, Richard L
see New Hampshire. Dept. of Education. Vocational-Technical Division. Profile of vocational-technical education in New Hampshire, 1945-1970. Concord [between 1971 and 1973]

Barker, Richard McNeil
see Constituency and origins of cyclic growth layers... Berkeley, 1972.

Barker, Robert.
Love forty / Robert Barker. — 1st ed. — Philadelphia : Lippincott, [1975]
216 p. ; 22 cm.
ISBN 0-397-01069-9
I. Title.
PZ4.B2558 Lo 813'.5'4 75-2241
[PS3552.A65] 75 MARC

Barker, Robert E
The development of a method to determine recreation land-use alternatives by identifying and comparing environmental requirements for activities and resource characteristics for a recreation area. [Eugene, Ore., Microform Publications, College of Health, Physical Education and Recreation, University of Oregon, 1974]
2 sheets. 10.5 x 14.8 cm.
Folded maps accompanying this thesis were not reproduced.
KyU NUC76-28518

Barker, Robert H
Development of flame retardants for polyester/cotton blends : final report / Robert H. Barker and Michael J. Drews ; prepared for Experimental Technology Incentives Program. — Washington : U.S. Dept. of Commerce, National Bureau of Standards, 1976.
xvi, 452 p. : ill. ; 27 cm.
"NBS-GCR-ETIP 76-22."
"Contract 4-35963."
1. Fireproofing of fabrics. I. Drews, Michael J., joint author. II. United States. National Bureau of Standards. Environmental Technology Incentives Program. III. Title.
TP267.B37 677'.689 76-602979
76 MARC

Barker, Robert L
Educating the undergraduate for professional social work roles [by] Robert L. Barker, Thomas L. Briggs [and] Dorothy Bird Daly. [Syracuse, N.Y., Syracuse University Press, 1971]
iii, 11 p. (Syracuse University. School of Social Work. Division of Continuing Education and Manpower Development. Manpower monograph, no. 3)
1. Social work education. I. Briggs, Thomas L., joint author. II. Daly, Dorothy Bird, joint author. III. Title. IV. Series.
MoSW NUC74-34019

Barker, Robert W
Legislative history of the Indian Claims Commission act of 1946 / compiled by Robert W. Barker and Alice Ehrenfeld ; foreword by Omer C. Stewart ; introd. by Margaret H. Pierce. — New York : Clearwater Pub. Co., c1976.
12 sheets (xiii, 715 p.) ; 11 x 15 cm.
Microfiche.
Includes index.
ISBN 0-88354-004-5
1. United States. Laws, statutes, etc. Indian Claims Commission act. 2. United States. Indian Claims Commission. I. Ehrenfeld, Alice, joint author. II. Title.
Microfiche KF 8202 75-18934

Barker, Robert W.
see Allen, Preston, 1913- plaintiff. Preston Allen, suing for himself... [Salt Lake City? 1956?]

Barker, Robert Wadhams.
The formation of sulfides in the basal zone of the Stillwater intrusion, Montana. [Berkeley] 1971.
iii, 270 l. illus. (part col.), maps (part fold.)
Thesis (Ph. D.)—University of California.
Bibliography: leaves 159-179.
CU NUC73-32117

Barker, Rodney S
Studies in opposition; edited by Rodney Barker. [New York] St. Martin's Press [1971]
[5], 338 p. 1 illus. (Studies in comparative politics)
Originally published in Government and opposition, 1965-1970.
Includes bibliographical references.
1. Opposition (Political science)—Addresses, essays, lectures. I. Government and opposition. II. Title.
F NUC74-34014

Barker, Roger Garlock, 1903-
Frustration and regression : an experiment with young children / Roger Barker, Tamara Dembo, Kurt Lewin. — New York : Arno Press, 1976, c1941.
p. cm. — (Studies in play and games) (Reprint of the ed. published by University of Iowa Press, Iowa City, which was originally issued as v. 2 of Studies in topological and vector psychology, and also as v. 18, no. 1 of University of Iowa Studies in child welfare)
ISBN 0-405-07934-6
1. Frustration (Child psychology) 2. Regression (Psychology) 3. Play. I. Dembo, Tamara, joint author. II. Lewin, Kurt, 1890-1947, joint author. III. Title. IV. Series. V. Series: Studies in topological and vector psychology ; v. 2. VI. Series: Iowa. University. University of Iowa studies in child welfare ; v. 18, no. 1.
[DNLM: WS105 B255f 1941a]
BF723.F7B37 1971 155.4'18 75-34765
75 MARC

Barker, Roger Garlock, 1903–
Qualities of community life [by] Roger G. Barker [and] Phil Schoggen. [1st ed.] San Francisco, Jossey-Bass, 1973.
xii, 562 p. illus. 27 cm. (The Jossey-Bass behavioral science series)
Bibliography: p. 541-543.
1. Sociology, Urban—Case studies. 2. Cities and towns—United States—Case studies. 3. Cities and towns—Great Britain—Case studies. I. Schoggen, Phil, joint author. II. Title.
HT153.B34 301.36 72-13601
ISBN 0-87589-172-1 MARC

Barker, Ronald Ernest.
The book hunger, edited by Ronald Barker and Robert Escarpit. Paris, Unesco, 1973.
155 p. 21 cm. F***
1. Books and reading. I. Escarpit, Robert, 1918- joint author. II. United Nations Educational, Scientific and Cultural Organization. III. Title.
Z1003.B27 001.55'2 74-178347
ISBN 92-3-101085-9 MARC

Barker, Ronald Ernest.
La Faim de lire. Unesco; publié sous la direction de Ronald E. Barker et Robert Escarpit. Paris, Unesco, Presses universitaires de France, 1973.
169 p. 21 cm. F 74-1811
Issued also in English under title: The book hunger.
1. Books and reading. I. Escarpit, Robert, 1918- joint author. II. Title.
Z1003.B2714 028.5 74-183241
ISBN 92-3-201085-2 MARC

Barker, Ronald Ernest.
International copyright: the search for a formula for the 70s ₍by₎ Ronald E. Barker. London, Publishers Association, 1969.
22 p. 22 cm. £0.15 B 72-16571
1. Copyright, International.
341.7'58 73-161819
ISBN 0-85386-017-3 MARC

Barker, Ronald Ernest.
The revised Berne convention : the Stockholm act 1967 : a review with an article-by-article summary / Ronald E. Barker. — London : Publishers Association, 1967.
18 p. ; 22 cm.
ISBN 0-85386-002-5
1. Copyright, International. I. Title.
341.7'58 76-378838
76 MARC

Barker, Ronnie.
It's goodnight from him : the best of 'The two Ronnies' / ₍by₎ Ronnie Barker ; illustrated by John Painter ; designed by David Cox. — London : Hodder and Stoughton, 1976.
95 p. : ill. (chiefly col.) ; 29 cm. GB77-03706
ISBN 0-340-20525-3 : £2.95
1. English wit and humor. 2. Television plays—Great Britain. I. Title. II. Title: The two Ronnies.
PN6175.B26 791.45'7 77-361788
77 MARC

Barker, Ronnie.
Ronnie Barker's Book of bathing beauties. — London : Hodder & Stoughton, 1974.
97 ₍i.e.96₎ p. : ill. (some col.) ; 20 cm. GB75-02529
ISBN 0-340-19182-1 : £1.20
1. Bathing customs—Anecdotes, facetiae, satire, etc. I. Title. II. Title: Book of bathing beauties.
PN6231.B38B5 828'.9'1407 75-315960
75 MARC

Barker, Ronnie.
Ronnie Barker's Book of boudoir beauties. — London : Hodder and Stoughton, 1975.
96 p. : chiefly ill. (chiefly col.) ; 20 cm. GB76-16680
Bibliography: p. 2.
ISBN 0-340-19735-8 : £1.50
1. Sex customs—Anecdotes, facetiae, satire, etc. I. Title. II. Title: Book of boudoir beauties.
PN6231.S54B3 828'.9'1407 76-372763
76 MARC

Barker, Sebastian.
The dragon and the lion : poems for China and Africa / by Sebastian Barker and Robert Pollet. — ₍1st ed.₎ — ₍London₎ : Quill Books, ₍1976₎
56 p. : ill. ; 20 cm. — (Quill illustrated poetry series) GB***
ISBN 0-905034-03-1 : £1.25
1. Poetry of places—China. 2. Poetry of places—Africa. 3. China—Poetry. 4. Africa—Poetry. I. Pollet, Robert, joint author. II. Title.
PR6052.A6494D7 821'.9'1408 77-356277
77 MARC

Barker, Stephen Francis.
The elements of logic ₍by₎ Stephen F. Barker. 2d ed. New York, McGraw-Hill ₍1974₎
xii, 337 p. illus. 21 cm.
Includes bibliographical references.
1. Logic. I. Title.
BC108.B25 1974 160 73-14906
ISBN 0-07-003718-3 MARC

Barker, Stephen Francis.
see Thomas Reid ... Philadelphia, University City Science Center, 1976.

Barker, Sunny Lu, comp.
see Texas. University. Southwest Center for Law and the Behavioral Sciences. Readings in correctional change. Austin, Tex., 1970.

Barker, Ted Falcon-
see Falcon-Barker, Ted.

Barker, Terence S
Exploring 1972, with special reference to the balance of payments ₍by Terence S. Barker and Richard Lecomber. London₎ Chapman & Hall, 1970.
137 p. (Cambridge University. Dept. of Applied Economics. A programme for growth, 9)
1. Gt. Brit.—Economic conditions—1945- 2. Economic forecasting. I. Lecomber, J. R. C. II. Title.
InU NUC73-39702

Barker, Terence S.
see Economic structure and policy ... London, Chapman and Hall, 1976.

Barker, Theodore Cardwell.
Business history [by] T. C. Barker, R. H. Campbell [and] P. Mathias, with a section on business accounts by B. S. Yamey. Rev. 2d ed. London, Blackford, c1971.
39 p. (Helps for students of history, no. 59)
Includes bibliography.
1. Business. I. Title. II. Series.
WaU NUC73-32100

Barker, Theodore Cardwell.
The dietary surveys of Dr. Edward Smith, 1862-3; a new assessment ₍by₎ T. C. Barker, D. J. Oddy ₍and John Yudkin. ₍London₎ Staples Press ₍c1970₎
62 p. illus., ports. 22 cm. (Dept. of Nutrition. Queen Elizabeth College. University of London. Occasional paper no. 1)
1. Nutrition—History—England. 2. Nutrition surveys—England. 3. Smith, Edward, 1818?-1874. I. Oddy, D. J. II. Yudkin, John, 1910- III. Title. IV. Series: Queen Elizabeth College. Dept. of Nutrition. Occasional paper, no. 1.
WU-M NUC75-50933

Barker, Theodore Cardwell.
An economic history of transport in Britain / T. C. Barker, C. I. Savage. — 3rd ₍revised₎ ed. — London : Hutchinson, 1974.
280 p. ; 23 cm. GB75-04189
First-2d ed. published under title: An economic history of transport, by C. I. Savage.
Includes bibliographical references and index.
ISBN 0-09-121470-X : £5.50. ISBN 0-09-121471-8 pbk.
1. Transportation—Great Britain—History. I. Savage, Christopher Ivor, joint author. II. Savage, Christopher Ivor. An economic history of transport. III. Title.
HE243.A1S3 1974 380.5'0941 75-331368
75 MARC

Barker, Theodore Cardwell.
A history of London Transport; passenger travel and the development of the metropolis, by T. C. Barker and Michael Robbins. London, Allen & Unwin ₍1963-74₎
2 v. illus., ports., maps. 26 cm.
Includes bibliographical references.
CONTENTS: v. 1. The nineteenth century.—v. 2. The twentieth century to 1970.
1. London—Transit systems. 2. Great Britain. London Transport Executive. 3. London—Economic conditions. I. Robbins, Michael. II. Title.
HE4719.L78B3 64-121

Barker, Theodore Cardwell.
A history of London Transport : passenger travel and the development of the metropolis / by T. C. Barker and Michael Robbins. — Rev. ed. — London : Allen and Unwin for the London Transport Executive, 1975.
2 v. : ill., facsims., maps, ports. ; 24 cm. GB77-01341 (v. 1)
Includes bibliographical references and index.
CONTENTS: v. 1. The nineteenth century.—v. 2. The twentieth century to 1970.
ISBN 0-04-833002-2 (v. 1) : £5.50 (v. 1) : £7.50 (v. 2)
1. London—Transit systems—History. 2. Great Britain. London Transport Executive. 3. London—Economic conditions. I. Robbins, Michael, joint author. II. Title.
HE4719.L78B3 1975 388.4'09421 77-359609
77 MARC

Barker, Theodore Cardwell, joint author
see Hatcher, John. A history of British pewter. London : Longman, 1974.

Barker, Theodore Cardwell.
see The Long march of everyman. London, Deutsch, 1975.

Barker, Theodore T.
see Verdi, Giuseppe, 1813-1901. La traviata; opera in three acts. New York, E. F. Kalmus Orchestra Scores, Inc. ₍n.d.₎

Barker, Theodore T.
see Verdi, Giuseppe, 1813-1901. Il trovatore. Libretto. English & Italian... Hollywood, Huber ₍n.d.₎

Barker, Thomas.
An empirical typology of police corruption; a study in organizational deviance, by Thomas Barker and Julian Roebuck. Springfield, Ill., C. C. Thomas ₍1973₎
ix, 63 p. 24 cm.
Bibliography: p. 51-55.
1. Police corruption. I. Roebuck, Julian B., joint author. II. Title.
HV7935.B37 364.1'32 73-8525
ISBN 0-398-02896-6 MARC

Barker, Thomas Mack, comp.
Frederick the Great and the making of Prussia / edited by Thomas M. Barker. — Huntington, N.Y. : R. E. Krieger Pub. Co., 1976, c1972.
103 p. : map ; 23 cm.
Reprint of the ed. published by Holt, Rinehart and Winston, New York in series: European problem studies.
Bibliography: p. 101-103.
ISBN 0-88275-456-4 : $3.95
1. Friedrich II, der Grosse, King of Prussia, 1712-1786—Addresses, essays, lectures. 2. Prussia—History—Frederick II, the Great, 1740-1786—Addresses, essays, lectures. I. Title.
₍DD403.B37 1976₎ 943'.053'0924 76-23215
76 MARC

Barker, Thomas Mack.
The military intellectual and battle; Raimondo Montecuccoli and the Thirty Years' War ₍by₎ Thomas M. Barker. Albany, State University of New York Press, 1975.
xvii, 271 p. illus. 24 cm.
Includes a translated text of Montecuccoli's Concerning battle (Sulle battaglie)
Bibliography: p. 245-248.
Includes index.
ISBN 0-87395-205-2. ISBN 0-87395-251-0 (microfiche)
1. Military art and science—History. 2. Military art and science—Early works to 1800. 3. Montecuccoli, Raimondo, Conte, 1609-1680. 4. Thirty Years' War, 1618-1648. I. Montecuccoli, Raimondo, Prince, 1609-1680. Sulle battaglie. 1974. II. Title.
U39.B37 940.2'4'0924 74-837
74 MARC

Barker, Twiley Wendell, 1926- joint comp.
see Barker, Lucius Jefferson, 1928- comp. Civil liberties and the Constitution ... ₍2d ed.₎. Englewood Cliffs, N.J., Prentice-Hall, ₍1975₎

Barker, Vincent Allan, 1934-
see Course in Advanced Sparse Matrix Techniques, Technical University of Denmark, 1976. Sparse matrix techniques, Copenhagen 1976 ... Berlin, Springer-Verlag, 1977.

Barker, Virgil, 1890-
American painting, history and interpretation. New York, Macmillan, 1960.
717 p. illus.
1. Painting—United States—History. I. Title.
KMK NUC76-73003

Barker, W. R., joint author
see Burns, Cecil Delisle, 1879-1942. Comparative performance tests of AM2 mat from various extruders and fabricators. ₍n. p.₎ 1967.

Barker, Wayne G
Cryptanalysis of the simple substitution cipher with word divisions using non-pattern word lists / by Wayne G. Barker. — Laguna Hills, Calif. : Aegean Park Press, c1975.
20, ₍108₎ p. ; 28 cm. — (A Cryptographic series)
1. Cryptography. 2. Ciphers. I. Cryptanalysis of the simple substitution cipher ...
Z103.B3 793.7'3 75-18083
76 MARC

Barker, Wesley L
Soil survey of Morris County, Kansas / ₍by Wesley L. Barker₎ ; United States Department of Agriculture, Soil Conservation Service in cooperation with Kansas Agricultural Experiment Station. — Washington : For sale by the Supt. of Docs., U.S. Govt. Print. Off., 1974.
i, 53 p., ₍27₎ fold. leaves of plates : ill. ; 29 cm.
Cover title.
Bibliography: p. 52.
1. Soils—Kansas—Morris County—Maps. I. United States. Soil Conservation Service. II. Kansas. Agricultural Experiment Station, Manhattan. III. Title.
S599.K2B37 631.4'7'78158 74-603396
75 MARC

Barker, Wharton, 1846-1921, comp.
see Reports and correspondence, relating to projected coal and iron industries in Southern Russia. [n.p., 1881?]

Barker, Wiley F
Peripheral arterial disease / by Wiley F. Barker. — 2d ed. — Philadelphia : Saunders, 1975.
xvi, 503 p. : ill. ; 25 cm. — (Major problems in clinical surgery ; v. 4)
Includes bibliographies and index.
ISBN 0-7216-1546-5
1. Arteries—Surgery. 2. Arteries—Diseases. I. Title. [DNLM: 1. Arteries—Surgery. 2. Vascular diseases. W1 MA492R v. 4 / WG510 B155p]
RD598.B35 1975 616.1'31 72-78954
75 MARC

Barker, William.
The modern pâtissier : a complete guide to pastry cookery / by William Barker. — London : Northwood Publications Ltd, 1974.
viii, 247 p., [8] p. of plates : ill. (some col.) ; 26 cm. — (Catering Times book) GB75-25494
ISBN 0-7198-2603-9 : £6.50
1. Pastry. 2. Desserts. I. Title.
TX773.B35 641.8'65 76-366435
76 MARC

Barker, William G
The use of models in urban transportation planning. William G. Barker. Springfield, Va., National Technical Information Service, 1973.
74 p. ill.
1. Urban transportation—Mathematical models. 2. Urban transportation—Research. I. United States. Dept. of Transportation. II. Title.
KMK NUC76-74054

Barker, William G
The use of models in urban transportation planning final report [by] William G. Barker. [Cambridge, Mass., Transportation Systems Center] 1973.
viii, 74 p. 27 cm.
Cover title.
"Prepared for Department of Transportation."
Bibliography: p. 64-66.
1. Urban transportation—United States—Mathematical models. I. Title.
IU NUC76-74053

Barker, William H.
see ATPM/Fogarty Symposium on Preventive and Community Medicine in Primary Care, Bethesda, Md., 1973. Preventive and community medicine in primary care ... Bethesda, Md., The Institutes, 1976.

Barker, William Henry.
Positive definite distributions on semi-simple Lie groups, by William H. Barker. [n.p.] 1973.
124 l. 30 cm.
Thesis (Ph.D.)—Massachusetts Inst. of Technology.
Vita.
Bibliography: leaves 120-123.
1. Lie groups. 2. Harmonic analysis. 3. Spherical harmonics. I. Title.
MCM NUC75-26873

Barker, William L.
see Ohio. State University, Bowling Green. Library. Business student's guide to selected library sources. [Bowling Green] 1971.

Barker, William Pierson.
To pray is to live / William P. Barker. — Old Tappan, N.J. : F. H. Revel Co., c1977.
122 p. ; 21 cm.
ISBN 0-8007-0836-9
1. Prayer. I. Title.
BV210.2.B298 248'.3 76-54315
76 MARC

Barker, William Pierson.
When God says no [by] William P. Barker. Old Tappan, N. J., F. H. Revell Co. [1974]
160 p. 20 cm.
1. Bible—Biography. 2. Providence and government of God. I. Title.
BS571.B344 220.9'2 [B] 73-18148
ISBN 0-8007-0643-9 MARC

Barker-Benfield, G J
The horrors of the half-known life: aspects of the exploitation of women by men. Los Angeles, 1968.
ix, 849 l.
Thesis—University of California.
Vita.
Bibliography: leaves 835-844.
Microfilm of typescript. Ann Arbor, Mich., University Microfilms, 1968. 1 reel. 35 mm.
1. Woman—History and condition of women. 2. Women in the United States—History. 3. Todd, John, 1800-1873. 4. Gardner, Augustus Kinsley, 1821-1876. I. Title.
OU IaU NUC74-118545

Barker-Benfield, G J
The horrors of the half-known life : male attitudes toward women and sexuality in nineteenth-century America / G. J. Barker-Benfield. — 1st ed. — New York : Harper & Row, c1976.
xiv, 352 p. ; 24 cm.
Includes bibliographical references and index.
ISBN 0-06-010224-1
1. Sex role. 2. Masculinity (Psychology) 3. Sex customs—United States—History. 4. Gynecologists—United States. I. Title.
HQ18.U5B3 301.41'0973 75-6327
75 MARC

Barker Jørgensen, Julie.
Sig selv. København, Rhodos, 1972.
34 p. 22 cm. kr16.00 D 72-44
I. Title.
PT8176.12.A7S48 73-302435
ISBN 87-7496-327-9

Barker, N.Y.
see Somerset, N.Y. A comprehensive plan, town of Somerset and village of Barker. West Trenton, N.J., 1972-

Barker Texas History Center
see Eugene C. Barker Texas History Center.

Barkerville 1968. [Quesnel] 1968.
24 p. illus., ports. 42 cm.
Caption title.
I. Quesnel Cariboo observer.
CaBViPA NUC76-27983

Barket, Gary L
Effects of spindle-picker conveying and gin processing on cotton quality and seed damage. [New Orleans] 1973.
5 p. (U.S. Agricultural Research Service. Southern Region. ARS-S-5)
I. Title.
DNAL NUC75-26872

Barkey, Frederick Allan, 1933-
The Socialist Party in West Virginia from 1898 to 1920; a study in working class radicalism. [Pittsburgh] 1971.
269 l.
Thesis—University of Pittsburgh.
Microfilm. Ann Arbor, Mich., University Microfilms, 1971. 1 reel.
1. Socialist Party (U.S.) West Virginia. 2. West Virginia—Social conditions. 3. Socialism in the U.S. I. Title.
IaU NUC74-149264

Barkey, Peter.
Pädagogisch-psychologische Diagnostik am Beispiel von Lernschwierigkeiten / Peter Barkey, Hans-Peter Langfeldt, Gerda Neumann. — Bern : H. Huber, c1976.
175 p. : ill. ; 19 cm. — (Arbeiten zur Theorie und Praxis der Rehabilitation in Medizin, Psychologie und Sonderpädagogik ; Bd. 5) Sw***
Includes bibliographies and indexes.
ISBN 3-456-80253-6
1. Mentally handicapped children—Testing. 2. Educational tests and measurements. I. Langfeldt, Hans-Peter, joint author. II. Neumann, Gerda, joint author. III. Title. IV. Series.
LC4602.B27 76-465104
76 MARC

Barkhalov, Sh O
(Botanika terminläri lüghäti)
Ботаника терминләри луғәти. [Тәртиб едәнләр: Ш. Бархалов, З. Әзизбәјова, J. Исајев] Бакы, Азәрбајчан ССР Елмләр Академијасы Нәшријјаты, 1963.
220 p. 21 cm.
At head of title: Азәрбајчан ССР Елмләр Академијасынын Рәјасәт heј'әти јанында Терминолокија Комитәси.
Added t. p.: Словарь ботанических терминов.
1. Botany—Dictionaries—Russian. 2. Russian language—Dictionaries—Azerbaijani. 3. Botany—Dictionaries—Azerbaijani. 4. Azerbaijani language—Dictionaries—Russian. I. Azizbăĭova, Z., joint author. II. Isaev, I͡A. M., joint author. III. Akademii͡a nauk Azerbaĭdzhanskoĭ SSR, Baku. Terminologicheskiĭ komitet. IV. Title. V. Title: Slovar' botanicheskikh terminov.
QK9.B27 74-220798
Library of Congress 74 [2]

Barkhalov, Sh O
(Likhenoflora Talysha)
Лихенофлора Талыша : общая часть / Ш. О. Бархалов. — Баку : Элм, 1975.
151, [4] p. : ill. ; 22 cm. USSR 75
At head of title: Akademii͡a nauk Azerbaĭdzhanskoĭ SSR. Institut botaniki imeni V. L. Komarova.
Bibliography: p. 146-[152]
1.00rub
1. Lichens—Russia—Talysh Mountains. I. Title.
QK590.R9B36 76-502625

Barkham, Laurence Frederick.
The story of Townsend House, 1874-1974 : the South Australian Institution for Deaf and Blind Incorporated / [by] Laurence F. Barkham. — Adelaide : South Australian Institution for Deaf and Blind, 1974.
xi, 169 p. : ill., ports. ; 24 cm. Aus
ISBN 0-9598363-0-6
1. South Australian Schools for Deaf and Blind Children—History. 2. Deaf—Education—South Australia—History. 3. Blind—Education—South Australia—History. I. Title.
HV2968.B37 371.9'12'099423 76-369332
76 MARC

Barkhamsted heritage : culture and industry in a rural Connecticut town / edited by Richard G. Wheeler and George Hilton for the American Revolution Bicentennial Steering Committee of the Barkhamsted Historical Society, Inc. and the Town of Barkhamsted. — Barkhamsted, Conn. : Barkhamsted Historical Society, 1975.
xii, 345 p., [3] fold. leaves of plates : ill. ; 27 cm.
Bibliography: p. 238-243.
Includes indexes.
1. Barkhamsted, Conn.—History. I. Wheeler, Richard G. II. Hilton, George. III. Barkhamsted Historical Society. American Revolution Bicentennial Steering Committee.
F104.B2B37 974.6'1 75-28918
76 MARC

Barkhamsted Historical Society. American Revolution Bicentennial Steering Committee.
see Barkhamsted heritage ... Barkhamsted, Conn., Barkhamsted Historical Society, 1975.

Barkhatnyĭ, Viktor Dmitrievich.
(Vybor uchastkov i sposobov organizat͡sii raboty lokomotivnykh brigad)
Выбор участков и способов организации работы локомотивных бригад / В. Д. Бархатный, Н. Д. Крюков. — Москва : Транспорт, 1974.
33, [2] p. : diagrs. ; 22 cm. — (Достижения науки и техники—в производство) USSR 75
At head of title: Vsesoi͡uznyĭ nauchno-issledovatel'skiĭ institut zheleznodorozhnogo transporta.
Bibliography: p. [35]
0.12rub
1. Railroads—Russia—Management. I. Kri͡ukov, N. D., joint author. II. Title.
TF512.B34 75-536545

Barkhatnyi, Viktor Dmitrievich
see Nekrashevich, Vasilii Ivanovich. (Vybor granits uchastkov obrashcheniia lokomotivov i normirovanie kontingenta lokomotivnykh brigad) 1973.

Barkhatova, K. A.
see Geodezicheskie raboty na Urale. 1974.

Barkhatova, K.A., ed.
see Sbornik rabot po astronomii. [s.n.], 1970.

Barkhatova, N N
(Stratigrafii͡a i nummulitidy ėot͡senovykh otlozheniĭ Prikaspiĭskoĭ vpadiny)
Стратиграфия и нуммулитиды эоценовых отложений Прикаспийской впадины / Н. Н. Бархатова, С. С. Размыслова. — Ленинград : Наука, Ленингр. отд-ние, 1974.
91 p., [5] leaves (2 fold.) : ill. ; 22 cm. USSR 74
At head of title: Академия наук СССР. Институт геологии и геохронологии докембрия. Лаборатория континентальных образований.
Bibliography: p. 84-90.
0.70rub
1. Nummulites, Fossil. 2. Paleontology—Eocene. 3. Paleontology—Russia—Caspian Depression. I. Razmyslova, Sof'i͡a Svi͡atoslavovna. II. Title.
QE772.B33 75-558587

Barkhausen, Hans
see Mosaik-Film GmbH. Mossaik Handbuch...
[Berlin, Vorwort, 1970]

Barkhausen, Hans
see Österreichisches Filmmuseum. Propaganda und Gegenpropaganda im Film 1933-1945.
Wien, 1972.

Barkhausen, Werner Meyer-
see Meyer-Barkhausen, Werner, 1889-1959.

Barkhin, Mikhail Grigor'evich.
(Gorod)
Город : 1945–1970 : практика, проекты, теория / М. Г. Бархин. — Москва : Стройиздат, 1974.
206, ⌊1⌋ p. : ill. ; 22 cm. USSR 75
On leaf preceding t. p.: Institut istorii iskusstv Ministerstva kul'tury SSSR.
Bibliography : p. 206–⌊207⌋
1.94rub
1. Architecture—Russia. 2. Architecture, Modern—20th century—Russia. 3. Cities and towns—Planning—1945- I. Title.
NA1188.B37 75–583385

Barkhin, Mikhail Grigor'evich
see Mastera sovetskoĭ arkhitektury ob arkhitekture. 1975-

Barkhin, Mikhail Grigor'evich
see Problemy sovremennoĭ teorii arkhitektury. 1973.

Barkholt, Torben.
Jagthundens arbejde efter skuddet. København, J. Fr. Clausen, 1972.
101 p. illus. 19 cm. (En Clausen håndbog) D 72-41
ISBN 81-11-01755-4 : kr21.45
1. Hunting dogs. I. Title.
SF428.5.B33 74–354667

Barkhouse, Bob.
Engine repair : head assembly and valve gear / Bob Barkhouse. — 1st ed. — Bloomington, Ill. : McKnight, ⌊1975⌋
xiii, 459 p. : ill. ; 24 cm. — (A McKnight career publication)
Includes bibliographical references and index.
ISBN 0-87345-101-5
1. Automobiles—Motors—Maintenance and repair. I. Title.
TL210.B365 629.2'504 74–21562
MARC

Barkhouse, Joyce C
George Dawson, the little giant / Joyce C. Barkhouse. — Toronto : Clarke, Irwin, c1974.
138 p. : ill. ; 23 cm. C***
Bibliography: p. 135-137.
Includes index.
ISBN 0-7720-0734-9 : $7.50
1. Dawson, George Mercer, 1849-1901. I. Title.
QE22.D29B37 1974 551'.092'4 75-332926
76 MARC

Barkhovskiĭ, Grigoriĭ I͡Akovlevich.
Spravochnai͡a knizhka prodavt͡sa politicheskoĭ literatury. Moskva, "Sovetskai͡a Rossii͡a", 1969 ⌊1972⌋
76 p.
Microfilm (negative) Library of Congress, Photoduplication Service, 1972.
1. Booksellers and bookselling–Russia.
2. Book selection. I. Title.
InU NUC74-43212

Barkhowdaryan, Sedrak Geworgi, 1898–1970.
(Mijnadaryan hay chartarapetner ew k'argorts varpetner)
Միջնադարյան հայ ճարտարապետներ և քարգործ վարպետներ: Երևան, Հայկական ՍՍՌ ԳԱ Հրատարակչություն, 1963:
380 p. illus. 30 cm.
At head of title: Հայկական ՍՍՌ Գիտությունների Ակադեմիա: Հնագիտության և Ազգագրության Ինստիտուտ:
Added t. p.: С. Бархударян. Средневековые армянские архитекторы и мастера по камно.
Includes bibliographical references.
1. Architecture, Medieval—Armenia. 2. Church architecture—Armenia. 3. Sculpture, Medieval—Armenia. 4. Sculpture, Armenian. I. Title.
NA1492.6.B37 73–208866

Barkhudarov, Alekseĭ Stepanovich
see Khindi-russkiĭ slovar'. [1972]

Barkhudarov, Leonid Semenovich.
(Grammatika angliĭskogo i͡azyka)
Грамматика английского языка. Допущено в качестве учебника для ин-тов и факультетов иностранных языков. Москва, Изд-во лит-ры на иностранных языках, 1960.
422 p. illus. 21 cm.
At head of title: Л. С. Бархударов, Д. А. Штелинг.
1. English language—Text-books for foreigners—Russian. I. Shteling, Donat Al'bertovich, joint author.
PE1129.S4B3 61–27834 ‡
rev

Barkhudarov, Leonid Semenovich.
Grammatika angliĭskogo i͡azyka. Izd. 3 ⌊stereotypnoe⌋ Dopushcheno v kachestve uchebnika dli͡a in-tov i fakul'tetov inostrannykh i͡azykov. Moskva, Vysshai͡a shkola, 1965.
425 p. table (in pocket) 21 cm.
At head of title: L.S. Bakjidarov, D.A. Shteling.
1. English language–Grammar–1870-
2. English language–Textbooks for foreigners–Russian. I. Shteling, D.A., joint author.
NBuU NUC74-21999

Barkhudarov, Leonid Semenovich.
(Grammatika angliĭskogo i͡azyka)
Грамматика английского языка. ⌊Для ин-тов и фак. иностр. яз.⌋ Изд. 4-е, испр. Москва, "Высш. школа," 1973.
423 p., 1 l. of tables. 21 cm. 0.68rub USSR 73
At head of title: Л. С. Бархударов, Д. А. Штелинг.
1. English language—Grammar—1950- 2. English language—Text-books for foreigners—Russian. I. Shteling, Donat Al'bertovich, joint author. II. Title.
PE1129.S4B3 1973 74–344314

Barkhudarov, Leonid Semenovich.
(I͡Azyk i perevod)
Язык и перевод : вопросы общей и частной теории перевода / Л. С. Бархударов. — Москва : Международные отношения, 1975.
237, ⌊1⌋ p. : ill. ; 20 cm. USSR***
Bibliography : p. 237–⌊238⌋
0.80rub
1. Translating and interpreting. I. Title.
P306.B28 75–401450

Barkhudarov, Leonid Semenovich, ed.
see Voprosy romano-germanskoĭ filologii. 1973.

Barkhudarov, Rudol'f Mikhaĭlovich, joint author
see Mareĭ, Aleksandr Nikolaevich. (Global'nye vypadenii͡a t͡sezii͡a-137 i chelovek) 1974.

Barkhudarov, Stepan Grigor'evich.
Uchebnik russkogo i͡azyka. Moskva, Gos. uchebno-pedagog. izd-vo, 19-
v. 23 cm.
At head of t.p.: S.G. Barkhudarov i S.E. Kri͡uchkov.
Contents.–ch. 1. Fonetika i morfologii͡a, dli͡a 5-go i 6-go klassov sredneĭ shkoly. Izd. 7. 1960.–ch. 2. Sintaksis, dli͡a 6-go i 7-go klassov sredneĭ shkoly. Izd. 6. 1959.
TNJ NUC74-21557

Barkhudarov, Stepan Grigor'evich.
Uchebnik russkogo i͡azyka. Izd. 5. Moskva, Gos. ucheb.-pedagog. izd-vo, 195-
v. 23 cm.
At head of title: S. G. Barkhudarov i S. E. Kri͡uchkov.
Contents.–ch. 2. Sintaksis; dli͡a 6-go i 7-go klassov sredneĭ shkoly.
1. Russian language–Grammar. I. Kri͡uchkov, Sergeĭ Efimovich, joint author. II. Title.
MiDW NUC74-62923

Barkhudarov, Stepan Grigor'evich.
Uchebnik russkogo i͡azyka: dli͡a vos'miletneĭ shkoly. Utverzhden Ministerstvom prosveshchenii͡a RSFSR. Izd 17. Moskva, Prosveshchenie, 1970.
2 v. tables.
At head of title: S. G. Barkhudarov. S. E. Kri͡uchkov.
Contents.–ch. 1. Fonetika i morfologii͡a.–ch. 2. Sintaksis.
1. Russian language–Grammar. I. Kri͡uchkov, Sergeĭ Efimovich, joint author. II. Title.
MCM NUC74-62922

Barkhudarov, Stepan Grigor'evich, ed.
see Akademii͡a nauk SSSR. Institut russkogo i͡azyka. Orfograficheskiĭ slovar' russkogo i͡azyka. 1971.

Barkhudarov, Stepan Grigor'evich, ed.
see Akademii͡a nauk SSSR. Institut russkogo i͡azyka. (Orfograficheskiĭ slovar' russkogo i͡azyka) 1973.

Barkhudarov, Stepan Grigor'evich
see Akademii͡a nauk SSSR. Institut russkogo i͡azyka. (Orfograficheskiĭ slovar' russkogo i͡azyka) 1974.

Barkhudarov, Stepan Grigor'evich, ed.
see Obnorskiĭ, Sergeĭ Petrovich, 1888-1962, ed. Khrestomatii͡a po istorii russkogo i͡azyka... Izd. 2. Moskva, Gos. uchebno-pedagog. izd-vo, 1952-

Barkhudarov, Stepan Grigor'evich
see Problematika opredelenii terminov v slovariakh raznykh tipov. 1976.

Barkhudarov, Stepan Grigor'evich
see Slovar' russkogo i͡azyka odinnadt͡satogo-semnadt͡satogo vv. 1975-

Barkhudarov, Stepan Grigor'evich
see Voprosy istoricheskoĭ leksikologii i leksikografii vostochnoslavi͡anskikh i͡azykov. 1974.

Barkhuus, Arne, joint author
see Hilleboe, Herman Ertresvaag, 1906- Approaches to national health planning. Geneva, World Health Organization, 1972.

Barkiel, tr.
see Zohar. Hebrew & Aramaic. Sefer ha-Zohar ha-shalem. 706 ⌊1946- ⌋

Barkin, Barukh
see
Buki.

Barkin, Carol.
Are we still best friends? / Authors, Carol Barkin, Elizabeth James ; photographer, Heinz Kluetmeier. — Milwaukee : Raintree Editions ; Chicago : distributed by Childrens Press, ⌊1975⌋
30 p. : col. ill. ; 25 cm.
SUMMARY: Examines some of the conflicting feelings that can arise in friendships.
ISBN 0-8172-0032-0 : $4.95
1. Emotions—Juvenile literature. 2. Home and school—Juvenile literature. 3. Friendship—Juvenile literature. ⌊1. Friendship. 2. Emotions⌋ I. James, Elizabeth, joint author. II. Kluetmeier, Heinz. III. Title.
BF723.E6B28 158'.25 75-19482
75 MARC

Barkin, Carol.
Doing things together / authors, Carol Barkin, Elizabeth James ; photographer, Heinz Kluetmeier. — Milwaukee : Raintree Editions ; Chicago : distributed by Childrens Press, ⌊1975⌋
30 p. : col. ill. ; 25 cm.
SUMMARY: Discusses children's relationships with parents, peers, and teachers.
ISBN 0-8172-0036-3 : $4.95
1. Emotions—Juvenile literature. 2. Home and school—Juvenile literature. 3. Interpersonal relations—Juvenile literature. ⌊1. Interpersonal relations. 2. Parent and child. 3. Teacher-student relationships⌋ I. James, Elizabeth, joint author. II. Kluetmeier, Heinz. III. Title.
BF723.E6B29 158'.2 75-20083
75 MARC

Barkin, Carol.
I'd rather stay home / authors, Carol Barkin, Elizabeth James ; photographer, Heinz Kluetmeier. — Milwaukee : Raintree Editions ; Chicago : distributed by Childrens Press, ⌊1975⌋
31 p. : col. ill. ; 26 cm.
SUMMARY: Explores the fears and anxieties connected with leaving home and starting school.
ISBN 0-8172-0030-4 : $4.95
1. Emotions—Juvenile literature. 2. Home and school—Juvenile literature. 3. Fear—Juvenile literature. ⌊1. Emotions. 2. School⌋ I. James, Elizabeth, joint author. II. Kluetmeier, Heinz. III. Title.
BF723.E6B3 158'.24 75-19481
75 MARC

Barkin, Carol.
Slapdash alterations : how to recycle your wardrobe / Carol Barkin and Elizabeth James ; illustrated by Rita Flodén Leydon. — New York : Lothrop, Lee and Shepard Co., c1977.
92 p. : ill. ; 24 cm.
Includes index.
SUMMARY: Gives instructions for easy ways to remodel clothes, with diagrams and directions for adjusting length, fit, and style, and for transforming problem clothes into usable garments.
ISBN 0-688-41787-6. ISBN 0-688-51787-0 lib. bdg.
1. Clothing and dress—Alteration—Juvenile literature. 2. Clothing and dress—Remaking—Juvenile literature. [1. Clothing and dress—Alterations] I. James, Elizabeth, joint author. II. Leydon, Rita Flodén. III. Title.
TT550.B3 646.4'06 76-58365
77 MARC

Barkin, Carol.
Slapdash cooking / Carol Barkin and Elizabeth James ; illustrated by Rita Flodén Leydon. — New York : Lothrop, Lee & Shepard, c1976.
128 p. : ill. ; 24 cm.
Includes index.
SUMMARY: Recipes for quick, easy, economical meals without using complicated procedures or fancy equipment.
ISBN 0-688-41737-X. ISBN 0-688-51737-4 lib. bdg.
1. Cookery—Juvenile literature. [1. Cookery] I. James, Elizabeth, joint author. II. Laydon, Rita Flodén. III. Title.
TX652.5.B23 641.5'5 75-45183
75 MARC

Barkin, Carol.
Slapdash sewing / Carol Barkin and Elizabeth James ; illustrated by Rita Flodén Leydon. — New York : Lothrop, Lee & Shepard Co., [1975]
128 p. : ill. ; 24 cm.
Includes index.
SUMMARY: Simplified, step-by-step sewing instructions for creating a variety of "make it today, wear tonight" outfits.
ISBN 0-688-41714-0. ISBN 0-688-51714-5 lib. bdg.
1. Dressmaking. 2. Sewing. [1. Dressmaking. 2. Sewing] I. James, Elizabeth, joint author. II. Leydon, Rita Flodén. III. Title.
TT515.B35 646.4'3'04 75-16455
75 MARC

Barkin, Carol.
Sometimes I hate school / authors, Carol Barkin, Elizzbeth James ; photographer, Heinz Kluetmeier. — Milwaukee : Raintree Editions ; Chicago : distributed by Children's Press, [1975]
31 p. : col. ill. ; 25 cm.
SUMMARY: Discusses a child's feelings of anxiety and frustration caused by the disruption of a secure teacher-pupil relationship.
ISBN 0-8172-0034-7
1. Home and school. [1. Teacher-student relationships. 2. Emotions] I. James, Elizabeth, joint author. II. Kluetmeier, Heinz. III. Title.
LC225.B36 372.1'1'02 75-20143
75 MARC

Barkin, Carol, joint author.
see James, Elizabeth. Managing your money. Milwaukee, Raintree Editions, c1977.

Barkin, Carol, joint author.
see James, Elizabeth. The simple facts of simple machines. New York, Lothrop, Lee & Shepard, [1975]

Barkin, Carol, joint author.
see James, Elizabeth. Understanding money. Milwaukee, Raintree Editions, c1977.

Barkin, Carol, joint author.
see James, Elizabeth. What is money?. Milwaukee, Raintree Editions, c1977.

Barkin, David.
Los beneficiarios del desarrollo regional. Ensayos de Angel Palerm [et al. 1. ed. Mexico, Secretaría de Educación Pública, 1972]
189 p. (Sepsetentas, 52)
1. Mexico—Economic conditions—1918- —Addresses, essays, lectures. 2. Mexico—Economic policy—Addresses, essays, lectures. I. Palerm, Angel.
NcU InU NUC74-171327

Barkin, David.
Cuba: camino abierto. Compilación de David Barkin y Nita R. Manitzas. Traducción de Francisco González Aramburo (introducción y capítulos 1 as 6) [México] Siglo Veintiuno Editores [1973]
343 p. 18 cm. (Historia inmediata)
1. Cuba—Economic conditions—1959- 2. Cuba—Social conditions. I. Manitzas, Nita R. II. Title.
PPiU NUC74-171312

Barkin, David.
Cuba: the logic of the revolution. Edited with an introduction by David P. Barkin and Nita R. Manitzas. Andover, Mass., Warner Modular Pubs. [1973]
1 v. (various pagings) 28 cm. (Developmental economics series)
1. Cuba—Economic conditions. 2. Cuba—Social conditions. I. Manitzas, Nita R., joint editor. II. Title. III. Series.
PPiU InU NUC74-171330

Barkin, David.
Mexico's albatross: the United States economy. [Austin] University of Texas at Austin [Institute of Latin American Studies] 1973.
27 l. 28 cm.
"Paper presented at the Conference of Economic Relations between Mexico and the United States."
"Sponsored by U.S. Deptartment of State in cooperation with the Governmental Affairs Institute, Washington, D.C., and the Extension Teaching and Field Service Bureau of the University of Texas at Austin."
Includes bibliographical references.
1. Investments, American—Mexico. I. Conference on Economic Relations between Mexico and the United States, University of Texas at Austin, 1973. II. Title.
TxU NUC76-74071

Barkın, Rebii.
Şehirlere akın ve mesken dâvası; nüfus artışının doğurduğu bâzı sosyal ve ekonomik meseleler. [Yazanlar: Rebii Barkın, Osman Okyar ve Doğan Avcıoğlu] Ankara, Rüzgârlı Matbaa, 1959.
63 p. 18 cm. (Araştırma Bürosu, C. H. P. Yayın no. 8)
Cover title.
1. Rural-urban migration—Turkey. I. Okyar, Osman, joint author. II. Avcıoğlu, Doğan, joint author. III. Title.
HB2295.B37 73-219114

Barkin, Solomon, 1907-
Manpower policy: economic policy instrument and independent policy system; prospectus for a seminar. Solomon Barkin. Amherst, Labor Relations and Research Center, University of Massachusetts, 1973.
160 p. 28 cm.
Prepared for the Manpower Administration, U.S. Dept. of Labor.
Includes bibliographies.
1. Manpower policy—United States. 2. United States—Economic policy. I. Title.
CU NUC76-74070

Barkin, Solomon, 1907- ed.
see The Role of trade unionism in independent developing countries ... Paris, Crganisation for Economic Co-operation and Development. [1967]

Barkin, Solomon, 1907-
see Worker militancy and its consequences, 1965-75 ... New York, Praeger Publishers, 1975.

Barkin, Tom.
Legal implications of the Office [of] Education criteria for the self-supporting student / Thomas G. Barkin. — [Madison] : Institute for Research on Poverty, University of Wisconsin—Madison, 1974.
38 p. ; 28 cm. — (Discussion papers - Institute for Research on Poverty ; DP 222-74)
Includes bibliographical references.
1. Student aid—Law and legislation—United States. 2. United States. Office of Education. 3. Students—Legal status, laws, etc.—United States. I. Wisconsin. University—Madison. Institute for Research on Poverty. II. Title: Legal implications of the Office of Education criteria ... III. Series: Wisconsin. University—Madison. Institute for Research on Poverty. Discussion papers ; DP 222-74.
KF4235.B47 344'.73'079 77-621624
77 MARC

Barkin, Tom.
Mineral rights in Wisconsin : a mining information project / by Tom Barkin and John Preston. — Madison : University of Wisconsin—Extension, Geological and Natural History Survey, 1974.
[8], 11 p. ; 28 cm. — (Information circular - University of Wisconsin—Extension, Geological and Natural History Survey ; no. 25)
Includes bibliographical references.
1. Mining law—Wisconsin. I. Preston, John, 1947- joint author. II. Title. III. Series: Wisconsin. Geological and Natural History Survey. Information circular ; no. 25.
QE179.A33 no. 25 557.75'08 s 75-623624
[KFW2655] 76 MARC

Barkin, Tom.
see Wisconsin. Legislative Council. Narrative and statistical overview of post-secondary education in Wisconsin. Madison, The Council, 1976.

Barkin, Tom.
see Wisconsin. Legislative Council. School district wealth and school aid formulas in 5 selected states which include income as a factor. Madison, The Council, 1976.

Barking Sands Tactical Underwater Range
see Prince, J K Hawaiian Islands and the Barking Sands Tactical Underwater Range facilities: geographic background. Point Mugu, Calif., 1968.

Barkins, Evelyn Werner, 1918-
A grandparent's garden of verses, by Evelyn Barkins. New York, F. Fell Publishers [1973]
46 p. 20 cm.
I. Title.
PS3503.A5688G7 811'.5'4 72-96892
ISBN 0-8119-0218-8 MARC

Barkins, Evelyn Werner, 1918-
Love poems of a marriage / by Evelyn Barkins. — New York : F. Fell, c1975.
[64] p. ; 22 cm.
ISBN 0-8119-0249-8 : $1.95
I. Title.
PS3503.A5688L65 811'.5'4 74-20656
74 MARC

Barkley, Alben William, 1877-1956
see United States. Congress. Joint Committee on the Investigation of the Pearl Harbor Attack. Pear Harbor attack. Hearings, Seventy-ninth Congress, first [-second] session, pursuant to S. Con. Res. 27... New York, AMS Press [1972]

Barkley, Arlene Hoiland.
Sainte-Beuve and La Rochefoucauld. [Boulder] 1973.
vii, 242 l.
Thesis (Ph.D.)—Univ. of Colorado, 1972.
Bibliography: leaves [233]-242.
1. Sainte-Beuce, Charles Augustin, 1804-1869. 2. La Rochefoucauld, François, duc de, 1613-1680.
CoU NUC75-26889

Barkley, David S.
see Neurosciences Research Program. Genesis of neuronal patterns; a report... [Brookline, Mass., 1972]

Barkley, Fred Alexander, 1908-
A list of the orders and families of flowering plants. Boston, Northeastern University, 1971.
[28] p. 28 cm.
Caption title.
Mimeographed.
1. Botany—Nomenclators. 2. Spermatophyta—Classification. I. Title.
NNBG NUC74-157357

Barkley, Fred Alexander, 1908-
Outline classification of organisms [by] Fred A. Barkley. 5th ed. [n.p.] 1973.
iii. 48 l. 28 cm.
Bibliography: p. 26-29.
1. Biology—Classification. I. Title.
QH83.B37 1973 574'.01'2 76-379476
76 MARC

Barkley, Fred Alexander, 1908-
The sections of the Begoniaceae [by] Fred A. Barkley and A. Baranov. Boston, 1972.
8 p. 28 cm. (The Buxtonian, v. 1, suppl. 1)
Caption title.
Mimeographed.
1. Begoniaceae. I. Baranov, A. II. Title. III. Series.
NNBG NUC74-3530

Barkley, Fred Alexander, 1908-
The species of the Begoniaceae / Fred A. Barkley and Jack Golding. — Ed. 2. — Boston : Northeastern University, 1974.
iv, 144 p. : ill. ; 28 cm.
Cover title.
"An alphabetical list of the species (and varieties) which have been published for the Begoniaceae .... Place of publication, date of issue of the publication, geographical origin of the taxon, and the section of the genus to which it belongs is given."
1. Begoniaceae. 2. Begonias. I. Golding, Jack, joint author. II. Title.
QK495.B4B38 1974 583'.46 75-320823
75 MARC

Barkley, Fred Alexander, 1908- joint author.
see Baranov, Andrei. The sections of the genus Begonia. Boston, Northeastern University, 1974.

Barkley, Grace.
The differentiation of the vascular bundle of Trichosanthes anguina. 1926.
18 l. illus. 29 cm.
Typescript (carbon copy)
Thesis—University of Chicago.
1. Vascular system of plants. 2. Plant cell differentiation. 3. Trichosanthes anguina. I. Title.
QK725.B33 74-151675
MARC

Barkley, James, illus.
see Hieatt, Constance B The minstrel knight. New York, Crowell [1974]

Barkley, K.
see Brooke, W E Design your own craftwork. London, J. Murray, 1969.

Barkley, Lorne.
Electromagnetic diffraction by a planar array of dielectric cylinders. Montreal, 1971.
iv, 118 l. illus. 29 cm.
Thesis—McGill University.
Bibliography: leaves 114-117.
1. Electromagnetic theory. 2. Diffraction. 3. Dielectrics. 4. Cylinders. 5. Scattering (Physics) I. Title.
CaQMM NUC73-32098

Barkley, Murray Willis, 1948-
The Loyalist tradition in New Brunswick: a study in the growth and evolution of an historical myth, 1825-1914. [n.p., c1973]
vi, 271 l. (Canadian theses on microfilm, no. 14238)
Thesis (M.A.)—Queen's University, 1971.
Microfilm of typescript. Ottawa, National Library of Canada, 1973. 1 reel. 35 mm.
1. United Empire Loyalists. 2. New Brunswick—Hist. I. Title. II. Series.
WHi NUC75-26862

Barkley, Paul W
The economic effects of reservoir development on individual farms lying partially within the state, by Paul Weston Barkley. ⌜n.p., 1963⌝
175 l. (K.S.U. Doctor of Philosophy Dissertation; 1963)
Thesis (Ph.D.)—Kansas State University.
1. Flood dams and reservoirs—Kansas. 2. Farms—Kansas. I. Title.
KMK NUC76-74052

Barkley, Paul W
Economics : the way we choose / Paul W. Barkley ; under the general editorship of William J. Baumol ; ⌜ill. by Eric G. Heiber, cartoons by Sidney Harris⌝. — New York : Harcourt Brace Jovanovich, c1977.
xix, 652 p. : ill. ; 25 cm.
Includes index.
ISBN 0-15-518812-7
1. Economics. I. Title.
HB171.5.B27 330 76-52250
77 MARC

Barkley, Paul W
Introduction to macroeconomics / Paul W. Barkley ; under the general editorship of William J. Baumol. — New York : Harcourt Brace Jovanovich, c1977.
xiv, 418 p. : ill. ; 24 cm.
Includes index.
ISBN 0-15-518816-X
1. Macroeconomics. I. Title.
HB171.5.B273 339 77-72105
77 MARC

Barkley, Paul W
Introduction to microeconomics / Paul W. Barkley ; under the general editorship of William J. Baumol ; ⌜ill. by Eric G. Hieber⌝. — New York : Harcourt Brace Jovanovich, c1977.
xiii, 327 p. : ill. ; 24 cm.
Includes index.
ISBN 0-15-518817-8
1. Microeconomics. I. Title.
HB171.B249 330 77-72106
77 MARC

Barkley, Paul W., joint author
see Bills, Nelson L Public investments and population changes... [Washington, U.S. Dept. of Agriculture, 1973]

Barkley, Paul W., joint author
see Cordes, Sam M Physicians and physician services in rural Washington. ⌜Pullman, Washington State University, 1974⌝

Barkley, Paul W., joint author
see Rohdy, D D Secondary economic effects of irrigation on the Colorado High Plains. ⌜Fort Collins, Colo.⌝ 1971.

Barkley, Raymond Patrick.
Synthesis of some benzo ⌜f⌝-1, 7-naphthyridines. Lincoln, Neb., 1961.
⌜4⌝, 76 l. illus.
Thesis (Ph.D.)—University of Nebraska.
Bibliography: leaves 72-76.
I. Title.
NbU NUC74-30465

Barkley, Robert F
The new look in preventive dentistry. ⌜Macomb, Ill., 1973?⌝
1 v. (unpaged) forms. 30 cm.
Cover title.
1. Preventive dentistry. I. Title.
IU NUC74-147401

Barkley, Robert F
Successful preventive dental practices. Macomb, Ill., Preventive Dentistry Press, 1972.
256 p. illus. 28 cm.
1. Dentistry. 2. Pedodontia. 3. Dentists—Relation to patients. I. Title.
FU-HC IaU NUC73-32091

Barkley, Thomas Mitchell, 1934-
Manual of the Kansas flora. Compiled and edited by T. M. Barkley. Manhattan, Kan., Dept. of Botany, Kansas State University, 1963.
1 v. (various pagings) 29 cm.
Preliminary edition.
1. Botany—Kansas. I. Title.
DSI NUC76-74045

Barkley, William E
A message of hope : or, Difficult passages explained / by William E. Barkley. — ⌜s.l.⌝ : Barkley, c1926.
23 p. ; 17 cm.
1. Bible—Criticism, interpretation, etc. 2. Book of Mormon. I. Title.
BS530.B29 77-361227
77 MARC

Barkman, Émmanuil Moiseevich.
(Upravlenie bol'nitseĭ)
Управление больницей. (Пособие для гл. врача больницы). Москва, "Медицина," 1972.
247 p. 21 cm. 105rub USSR 72-VKP
At head of title: Э. М. Баркман, Я. И. Родов.
Bibliography: p. 242-⌜246⌝
1. Hospitals—Russia—Administration. I. Rodov, Íàkov Iosifovich, joint author. II. Title.
[RA989.R8B37] 73-336433

Barkman, Frieda.
Lad with summer eyes; a story of the Grace Children's Home, by Frieda and Paul Barkman. Chicago, Moody Press [c1958]
128 p.
KEmT NUC75-67063

Barkman, Lars.
Repliker av reliker. Repliktillverkningen vid Wasavarvets konserveringsavdelning. Replicas of relics. Replica production at the conservation department of the Wasa museum. Stockholm, Statens sjöhistoriska museum. 1969.
19, 19 p. illus. 25 cm. (Wasastudier, nr. 7) kr3.00 S 70-46
Swedish and English.
1. Modeling. 2. Models (Clay, plaster, etc.) 3. Epoxy resins. 4. Wasa (Warship) I. Title. II. Title: Replicas of relics. III. Series: Stockholm. Statens sjöhistoriska museum. Wasastudier, nr. 7.
NB1180.B26 74-323377

Barkman, Oscar Charles, 1929-
Perceptions of cognitive territories and boundary maintenance by teachers, board members, and administrators in Pennsylvania. [n.p.] 1971.
112 l.
Thesis (Ph.D.)—Pennsylvania State University.
I. Title.
PSt NUC73-32099

Barkman, Wilson A
Winos, dine-os and ding-bats, by Wilson A. Barkman. [2d ed. New York, Printed by the Graphicopy Press, 1972]
102 p. illus. 22 cm.
1. Alcoholics—Personal narratives. I. Title.
NN NUC75-46275

Barkóczi, László.
Die römischen Inschriften Ungarns (RIU). Von László Barkóczi und András Mócsy. Amsterdam, Hakkert, 1972, ⌜1973⌝-
v. illus. 25 cm. fl 92.00 (v. 1) Ne 73-10 (v. 1)
CONTENTS: 1. Lfg. Savaria, Scarbantia und die Limes-Strecke ad Flexum-Arrabona.
1. Inscriptions, Latin—Hungary. I. Mócsy, András. II. Title.
CN615.B37 73-327880

Barkov, Aleksandr Sergeevich. Letuchie koty. 1970
in Barkov, Aleksandr Sergeevich. (Ruslan i Tishka) 1970.

Barkov, Aleksandr Sergeevich. Na derevniu k babke. 1970
in Barkov, Aleksandr Sergeevich. (Ruslan i Tishka) 1970.

Barkov, Aleksandr Sergeevich.
(Ruslan i Tishka)
Руслан и Тишка.—⌜Летучие коты.—На деревню к бабке. Рассказы для дошкольного возраста. Илл.: Г. Козлов. Москва⌝, "Малыш," 1970.
18 p. with illus. 27 cm. 0.12rub USSR 70-VKP
Cover title.
At head of title: А. Барков.
I. Kozlov, G., illus. II. Barkov, Aleksandr Sergeevich. Letuchie koty. 1970. III. Barkov, Aleksandr Sergeevich. Na derevniu k babke. 1970. IV. Title. V. Title: Letuchie koty. VI. Title: Na derevniu k babke.
PZ68.B27 74-341496

Barkov, Alekseĭ Mikhaĭlovich.
(Planirovanie na mashinostroitel'nom predpriiatii)
Планирование на машиностроительном предприятии / А. М. Барков. — Ленинград : Машиностроение, 1975.
70 p. ; 20 cm. — (Экономическая библиотека инженера-машиностроителя : вып. 4) USSR***
Series romanized: Ėkonomicheskaia biblioteka inzhenera-mashinostroitela.
Includes bibliographical references.
0.19rub
1. Machinery—Trade and manufacture—Management. I. Title.
HD9705.A2B36 76-507408

Barkov, Evgeniĭ Vasil'evich, joint author
see Krushevskiĭ, Arkadiĭ Vladimirovich. (Ekonomiko-matematicheskie modeli v planirovanii i upravlenii narodnym khoziaĭstvom) 1973.

Barkov, Ivan Íàkovlevich, ed.
see Voprosy prepodavaniia matematiki v sredneĭ shkoleo. 1958-

Barkov, Ivan Semenovich, 1732-1768.
Luka Mudishchev. [By] Ivan Barkov. 2. izd. Moskva, Izd-vo TSK KPSS "Gospolitizdat", 1969.
80 p. ports. 11 cm.
"Posvíàshchaetsíà Mikhailu Aleksandrovichu Sholokhovu."
I. Sholokhov, Mikhail Aleksandrovich, 1905- II. Title.
CaBVaU NUC76-90398

Barkov, Ivan Semenovich, 1732-1768.
(Sochinenííà i perevody I. S. Barkova)
Сочиненія и переводы И. С. Баркова, 1762-1764 г., съ біографическимъ очеркомъ автора. — [s. l. : s. n.], 1872 (С.-Петербургъ : Тип. В. С. Эттингера)
v, 308 p. ; 22 cm.
PG3311.B3S6 1872 75-564788

Barkov, Leonid Ivanovich.
Abwehr Eestis / L. Barkov. — Tallinn : Eesti Raamat, 1974.
125 p., [4] leaves of plates : ill. ; 22 cm. USSR***
0.38rub
1. Espionage, German—Estonia. I. Title.
DK511.E6B34 75-548613

Barkov, Leonid Ivanovich.
(V debríàkh abvera)
В дебрях абвера. Таллин, "Ээсти раамат," 1971.
126 p., 8 l. of illus. 21 cm. 0.40rub USSR 72-VKP
At head of title: Леонид Барков.
Includes bibliographical references.
1. Espionage, German—Estonia. I. Title.
DK511.E6B37 73-306401

Barkov, N N
(Effektivnost' kapital'nykh vlozhenii v razvitie zheleznodorozhnogo transporta)
Эффективность капитальных вложений в развитие железнодорожного транспорта. Под общ. ред. канд. экон. наук Н. Н. Баркова. Москва, "Транспорт," 1972.
145 p. with diagrs. 21 cm. (Труды Всесоюзного научно-исследовательского института железнодорожного транспорта, вып. 472)
0.96rub USSR 72-VKP
At head of title: Н. Н. Барков, А. Л. Вольфсон, Н. А. Ядоловский.
Bibliography: p. 141-[144]
1. Railroads—Russia—Finance. 2. Capital investments—Russia. I. Vol'fson, Aleksandr L'vovich. II. Íàndolovskiĭ, N. A. III. Title. IV. Series: Moscow. Vsesoíùznyĭ nauchno-issledovatel'skiĭ institut zheleznodorozhnogo transporta. Trudy, vyp. 472.
TF4.M6 vyp. 472 73-333475
[HE3136]

Barkov, N N
(Effektivnost' stroitel'stva novykh zheleznodorozhnykh liniĭ)
Эффективность строительства новых железнодорожных линий / Н. Н. Барков, А. А. Пугачева. — Москва : Транспорт, 1976.
55 p. ; 21 cm. — (Труды Всесоюзного научно-исследовательского института железнодорожного транспорта ; вып. 555) USSR 77
Bibliography: p. [3] of cover.
0.41rub
1. Railroads—Russia. 2. Railroads—Economics of construction. 3. Capital productivity—Russia. I. Pugacheva, Alla Avramovna, joint author. II. Title. III. Series: Moscow. Vsesoíùznyĭ nauchno-issledovatel'skiĭ institut zheleznodorozhnogo transporta. Trudy ; vyp. 555.
TF4.M6 vyp. 555 77-512490
[HE3136]

Barkov, Sergeĭ Aleksandrovich.
(Galogeny i podgruppa margantsa)
Галогены и подгруппа марганца : элементы VII группы периодической системы Д. И. Менделеева : пособие для учащихся / С. А. Барков. — Москва : Просвещение, 1976.
112 p. : ill. ; 20 cm. USSR***
Includes bibliographical references.
0.14rub
1. Halogens. 2. Manganese group. I. Title.
QD165.B34 77-513460

[Barkova, Líùdmila Leonidovna]
Altaĭskie kurgany; vystavka "Kul'tura i iskusstvo drevnego naseleniíà Sibiri". Kratkiĭ putevoditel'. Leningrad, Avrora, 1973.
21 p. illus.
At head of title: Gosudarstvennyĭ ordena Lenina Ėrmitazh.
I. Leningrad. Ermitazh. II. Title.
MH NUC75-128943

Barkova, T. A.
see Kudríàtšev, Orest Konstantinovich. (Spravochnye tablitšy po tíàgovym raschetam gorodskogo transporta) 1956.

Barković, Josip.
Mala Jalta : novele / Josip Barković. — Zagreb : Prosvjeta, 1974.
147 p. ; 21 cm. Yu***
CONTENTS: Mala Jalta. — Najsretniji dan. — Crvena knjižica. — Pobjednici.—"Tricaš".—Talenti i obožavaoci.—Na rubu grada.—Fatamorgana.—Grin i Astra.—Grofica Ilonka.—Ljubav se prolomila rijekom.—Veliki obračun.—Devetka i psići.—Žigolo.
I. Title.
PG1618.B33M3 75-970684

Barković, Josip.
Sinovi slobode / Josip Barković. — Zagreb : Mladost, 1976.
205 p. ; 20 cm. — (Biblioteka Jelen) Yu***
1. World War, 1939-1945—Underground movements—Yugoslavia—Fiction. I. Title.
PG1418.B28S5 1976 76-525333

Barković, Vjekoslav.
Ekonomsko-geografski pregled socijalističkih republika SFRJ / Vjekoslav Barković. — U Osijeku : [Ekonomski fakultet], 1971.
140, [1] p. ; 29 cm. Yu***
Bibliography: p. [141]
1. Yugoslavia—Economic conditions—1945- I. Title.
HC407.B37 75-971346

Barković, Vjekoslav.
Pregled socijalističkih republika SFRJ / Vjekoslav Barković. — Osijek : Ekonomski fakultet, 1974.
59 p. ; 30 cm. — ([Publikacija] - Ekonomski fakultet u Osijeku ; knj. br. 36) Yu***
Bibliography: p. 59.
1. Yugoslavia. I. Title. II. Series: Zagreb. Univerzitet. Ekonomski fakultet u Osijeku. Publikacija - Ekonomski fakultet u Osijeku ; knj. br. 36.
DR305.B37 75-971478

Barkovskiĭ, Anatoliĭ Nikolaevich.
(Ėkonomika Pol'skoĭ Narodnoĭ Respubliki)
Экономика Польской Народной Республики / А. Н. Барковский. — Москва : Наука, 1976.
229 p. ; 20 cm. USSR***
At head of title: Akademiíà nauk SSSR. Institut ėkonomiki mirovoĭ sotšialisticheskoĭ sistemy.
Includes bibliographical references.
0.77rub
1. Poland—Economic conditions—1945- I. Title.
HC337.P7B33 77-501426

Barkovskiĭ, Igor' Valerianovich Dunin-
see Dunin-Barkovskiĭ, Igor' Valerianovich.

Barkovskiĭ, Lev Valerianovich Dunin-
see Dunin-Barkovskiĭ, Lev Valerianovich, ed.

Barkovskiĭ, Matveĭ Mikhaĭlovich.
(Russkoe slovesnoe udarenie)
Русское словесное ударение / М. М. Барковский. — Изд. 2-е, испр. и доп. — Минск : Вышэйш. школа, 1974.
143 p. ; 17 cm. USSR 74
0.17rub
1. Russian language—Accents and accentuation. I. Title.
PG2139.B3 1974 75-578515

Barkovskiĭ, Nikolaĭ Dmitrievich.
(Problemy kredita i denezhnogo oborota v usloviíàkh razvitogo sotšializma)
Проблемы кредита и денежного оборота в условиях развитого социализма / Н. Д. Барковский. — Москва : Финансы, 1976.
213 p. ; 23 cm. USSR***
Includes bibliographical references.
1.03rub
1. Credit—Russia. 2. Money—Russia. I. Title.
HG3729.R9B324 77-507003

Barkovskiĭ, Nikolaĭ Dmitrievich
see Mezhvuzovskaíà konferentsiíà nauchnykh rabotnikov finansovo-ėkonomicheskikh institutov i rabotnikov uchrezhdeniĭ Gosudarstvennogo banka SSSR, 3d, Moscow, 1960. Problemy kreditovaniíà narodnogo khozíàĭstva... Moskva, 1961.

Barkovskiĭ, Nikolaĭ Dmitrievich, ed.
see Organizatšiíà i planirovanie kredita. 1973.

Barkovskiĭ, Valerian Nikolaevich Dunin-
see Dunin-Barkovskiĭ, Valerian Nikolaevich, 1871-

Barkovskiĭ, Vladimir Filippovich.
(Fiziko-khimicheskie metody analiza)
Физико-химические методы анализа. [Учебник для хим. и хим.-технол. специальностей техникумов]. Москва, "Высш. школа," 1972.
344 p. with illus. 22 cm. 0.90rub USSR 73-VKP
At head of title: В. Ф. Барковский, С. М. Горелик, Т. Б. Городенцева.
Bibliography: p. 343-[344]
1. Chemistry, Analytic. I. Gorelik, Solomon Moiseevich. II. Gorodentševa, Tat'íàna Borisovna. III. Title.
QD75.2.B37 74-316054

Barkow, Al.
Golf's golden grind; the history of the tour. [1st ed.] New York, Harcourt Brace Jovanovich [1974]
viii, 310 p. illus. 22 cm.
1. Golf—Tournaments—History. I. Title.
GV970.B37 796.352'64'0973 74-13785
ISBN 0-15-190885-0 MARC

Barkow, Dietrich, joint author.
see Walther, Heinz, 1919- Dermatologie in der täglichen Praxis. München, Urban & Schwarzenberg, 1975.

Barkow, Jerome H.
see Canadian Ethnology Society. Proceedings of the first congress, Canadian Ethnology Society. Ottawa, National Museums of Canada, 1974.

Barkowsky, Gerd, illus.
see Hamilton-Merritt, Jane. Lahu wildfire. New York, Scribner [1973]

Barks, James H
Water-quality characteristics of six small lakes in Missouri / by James H. Barks ; prepared in cooperation with Missouri Department of Natural Resources, Division of Geology and Land Survey, Geological Survey. — [Rolla MO] : The Survey, 1976.
vi, 42 p. : ill. ; 28 cm. — (Water resources report ; no. 33)
Bibliography: p. 41-42.
1. Water quality—Missouri. 2. Lakes—Missouri. I. Title. II. Series: Water resources report (Rolla, Mo.) ; no. 33.
TD224.M8B37 553'.78'09778 76-620030
77 MARC

Barks, Robert A
Descriptive statistics and probability theory [by] Robert A. Barks. London, Hutchinson, 1972.
xv, 194 p. illus. 22 cm. £3.00 B 72-31710
1. Mathematical statistics. 2. Probabilities. I. Title.
QA276.B284 519.2 73-156124
ISBN 0-09-112510-3; 0-09-112511-1 (pbk.) MARC

Barks, Robert A
Distribution theory, [by] Robert A. Barks. London, Hutchinson, 1972.
vii, 207 p. illus. 22 cm. £2.75 GB 73-12901
1. Distribution (Probability theory) 2. Sampling (Statistics) I. Title.
QA273.6.B38 519.5'32 73-173886
ISBN 0-09-112810-2; 0-09-112811-0 (pbk.) MARC

Barks lilla bok om Köping. — [Köping : Barkens förl., 1973]
64 p. : ill. ; 22 cm. S73-53
Cover title.
Compiled by P.-G. Barkelius.
ISBN 9185244007 : kr13.00
1. Köping, Sweden. I. Barkelius, P.-G.
DL991.K652B37 76-481196
•76 MARC

Barksdale, Arvell Troy, 1940-
An evaluation of the elementary science study program in selected classrooms in East Baton Rouge, Parish, Louisiana... [n.p.] 1973.
xi, 73 l. illus. 29 cm.
Thesis (Ph. D.)–Louisiana State University, Baton Rouge.
Vita.
Bibliography: leaves 53-55.
1. Science–Study and teaching (Elementary) 2. Science–Study and teaching–East Baton Rouge Parish, La. I. Title.
LU NUC75-26878

Barksdale, E. C.
see also
Barksdale, Ethelbert Courtland, 1944-

Barksdale, Ethelbert Courtland, 1944–
The dacha and the duchess : an application of Lévi-Strauss's theory of myth in human creativity to works of nineteenth-century Russian novelists / E. C. Barksdale. — New York : Philosophical Library, [1974]
144 p. : ill. ; 22 cm.
Bibliography: p. 139–144.
ISBN 0-8022-2143-2 : $7.50
1. Russian fiction—19th century—History and criticism. 2. Lévi-Strauss, Claude. 3. Myth in literature. I. Title.
PG3096.M95B3 891.7'3'03 74-75086
MARC

Barksdale, Glen Edward, 1938-
The chorus in French baroque opera. Ann Arbor, University Microfilms, 1973.
Microfilm copy (positive) of typescript.
Collation of the original, as determined from the film: xi, 382 l. music.
Thesis (Ph.D.)—University of Utah, 1973.
Bibliography: leaves [363]-370.
1. Opera, French—History and criticism. 2. Choral music. I. Title.
OO NUC76-74043

Barksdale, Henry C
The Alabama water-resources spectrum; second progress report, by Henry C. Barksdale and L. B. Peirce. [Montgomery? Geological Survey of Alabama] 1972.
74 p. 28 cm.
Prepared by the Geological Survey of Alabama under contract WRP-71-3 with the Alabama Development Office... financially aided through a Federal grant from the Water Resources Council, under the State Planning Program authorized by Title III of the Water Resources Planning Act of 1965, as amended.
I. Alabama. Geological Survey.
AAP NUC74-3520

Barksdale, Henry C
An annotated outline of a water-resources development plan for Alabama. [Montgomery, Alabama Development Office?] 1971.
23 p. 28 cm.
Cover title: Water for Alabama: Plan of development–Annotated ouline.
"Prepared by the Geological Survey of Alabama under contract with the Alabama Development Office, February, 1971. Revised August 1971."
1. Water resources development–Alabama. I. Alabama. Geological Survey. II. Alabama. Development Office. III. Title. IV. Title: Water for Alabama.
AAP NUC76-7717

Barksdale, Henry C
Identification of objectives. Rev. ed. [Montgomery, Alabama Development Office?] 1970, 1969.
57 p. 28 cm.
Cover title: Water for Alabama; Identification of objectives.
"Prepared by the Geological Survey of Alabama under contract with the Alabama Development Office..."
I. Alabama. Geological Survey.
AAP NUC74-34020

Barksdale, Henry C.
see The Alabama water resources spectrum. Montgomery, Alabama Development Office, 1973.

Barksdale, Henry C., joint author
see Knowles, Doyle Blewer, 1924-
Elements of the water resources situation in Alabama. [Montgomery] 1970, 1969.

Barksdale, Jelks, 1901-
Doctor Bill / Jelks Barksdale. — Auburn, Ala. : Barksdale Books, c1976.
283 p. ; 23 cm.
I. Title.
PZ4.B2564 Do 813'.5'4 76-15776
[PS3552.A6723] 76 MARC

Barksdale, Julian Devreau, 1908-
Geology of the Methow Valley, Okanogan County, Washington / by Julian D. Barksdale. — Olympia : State of Washington, Dept. of Natural Resources, Division of Geology and Earth Resources, 1975.
ix, 72 p. : ill. ; 28 cm. — (Bulletin - Division of Geology and Earth Resources ; no. 68)
Part of illustrative matter in pocket.
Bibliography: p. 69-72.
$2.00
1. Geology—Washington (State)—Methow Valley. I. Title. II. Series: Washington (State). Division of Geology and Earth Resources. Bulletin - Division of Geology and Earth Resources ; no. 68.
QE176.M47B37 557.97'28 75-622914
76 MARC

Barksdale, Richard.
The Black college in a time of revolution, by Richard K. Barksdale. Atlanta, Atlanta University [1971]
11 l. 28 cm. (CAAS occasional paper, no. 2)
1. Negro universities and colleges. U.S. I. Title. II. Series: Atlanta University. Center for African and African-American Studies. CAAS occasional paper, no. 2.
NcD NUC73-32101

Barksdale, Richard D. Small-scale cratering tests
in Vesić, Aleksandar Sedmak, 1924-
Theoretical studies of cratering mechanisms... Atlanta, 1963.

Barksdale, Thomas Henry, 1932–
Tomato diseases and their control [by T. H. Barksdale, J. M. Good, and L. L. Danielson] Rev. Washington, Agricultural Research Service, U. S. Dept. of Agriculture; for sale by the Supt. of Docs., U. S. Govt. Print. Off., 1972.
vi, 109 p. illus. 24 cm. (Agriculture handbook no. 203) $0.70
1. Tomatoes—Diseases and pests. I. Good, Joseph Martin, 1927– joint author. II. Danielson, Loran Leroy, 1913– joint author. III. Title. IV. Series: United States. Dept. of Agriculture. Agriculture handbook no. 203.
S21.A37 no. 203 338.1'08 s 72-603366
[SB608.T75] [635'.642'9] MARC

Barksii, Lev Abramovich
see Ispol'zvoanie ekonomiko-matematicheskikh modelei v upravlenii i planirovanii v t͡svetnoi metallurgii. 1975.

Barksted, William, fl.1611.
Hiren; or, The faire Greeke ... London, Printed for R. Barnes, 1611 [1971]
In verse.
Microfilm of original in the Bodleian Library. Ann Arbor, Mich., University Microfilms, 1971. (Early English books, 1475-1640, reel 1226)
STC no. 1428.
I. Title.
CaBVaU MiU NUC73-68103

Barkstrom, Bruce Richard, 1944-
Energy transfer by fluctuations in a plasma. [n. p.] 1972.
1 v.
Thesis (Ph. D.)–Northwestern University.
1. Energy transfer. 2. Radiative transfer. 3. Astrophysics. 4. Plasma (Ionized gases) I. Title.
IEN NUC74-3529

Barkun, Michael.
Disaster and the millennium. New Haven, Yale University Press, 1974.
x, 246 p. 22 cm.
OClW InU TxU NUC75-26852

Barkun, Michael, comp.
Law and the social system. New York, Lieber-Atherton, 1973 [c1972]
128 p. 22 cm.
Bibliography: p. 119–125.
1. Sociological jurisprudence—Addresses, essays, lectures. I. Title.
340.1'15 77-169501
ISBN 0-88311-006-7; 0-88311-007-5 (pbk.) MARC

Barkun, Michael
see Gould, Wesley L Social science and international law in the United States. Tucson, Institute of Government Research, University of Arizona, 1970.

Barkun, Michael, joint author
see Gould, Wesley L Social science literature... Princeton, N. J., Princeton Univ. Press [1972]

Barkved, Martin, 1924-
Kystskogbruk; skogbrukslaere for Vestlandet og kyststrøk nordpå. Redaksjonsråd: Ragnar Aspenberg [et al. Oslo] Landbrukets brevskole og Norges skogeierforbund [1964]
352 p. illus.
1. Forestry schools and education–Norway. I. Title.
WaU NUC74-149295

Barkway, Michael.
A guide to the Canada business corporations act: Bill C-213, by Michael Barkway. [n.p.] Financial Times of Canada, 1973.
[11] p. 28 cm.
Cover title.
1. Canada. Parliament. House of Commons. Bill C-213. 2. Corporation law–Canada. I. Title.
CaBVaU NUC76-74075

Barla, Chainsingh, 1937-
An analysis of cooperative agricultural credit institutions in India: a case study of the primary credit societies in Rajasthan. [n.p.] 1973.
[3], xii, 232 [i.e. 234] l. illus.
Thesis (Ph. D.)–Michigan State University.
Bibliography: leaves 202-206.
1. Agricultural credit–India. I. Title.
MiEM NUC75-25988

Barla, Giovanni Battista, 1940-
On the distribution of stress around openings located in a rock mass. [New York] 1970.
201 l. illus., diagrs., tables. 29 cm.
Thesis–Columbia University.
Bibliography: leaves 198-200.
1. Rocks. 2. Strains and stresses. I. Title.
NNC NUC74-149294

Barla, Théodore Bougna-
see Bougna-Barla, Théodore.

Barla-Szabó, Ödön.
Az 1920-[i. e. ezerkilencszázhuszas] évek gazdasági vitái a Szovjetunióban. [Budapest] Kossuth Könyvkiadó, 1971.
398 p. 19 cm. 42.00Ft
Includes bibliographical references.
1. Russia — Economic policy — 1917–1928. 2. Economics — History—Russia. I. Title.
HC335.2.B35 74-205973

Barlaam, Alessandro.
see Italy. Laws, statutes, etc. Codice della ricerca scientifica e tecnologica ... Milano, A. Giuffrè, [1976]

Barlaam and Joasaph
see Kitāb Bilawhar wā-Budhāsaf. Russian. (Povest' e Varlaame pustynnike i Iosafe t͡sareviche indiiskom) 1947.

Barlaam and Joasaph. Arabic
see Kitāb Bilawhar wa-Būdhāsaf. Kitāb Bilawhar wa-Būdhāsaf. [1972]

Barlaam and Joasaph. English & Ethiopic.
Barlâm and Yĕwâsĕf, being the Ethiopic version of a Christianized rescension of the Buddhist legend of the Buddha and the Bodhisattva / the Ethiopic text edited for the first time with an English translation and introd., etc., by E. A. Wallis Budge. — New York : AMS Press, 1976.
2 v. : ill. ; 23 cm.
Reprint of the 1923 ed. published at the University Press, Cambridge, Eng.
Includes bibliographical references and index.
CONTENTS: v. 1. Ethiopic text.—v. 2. The introduction, English translation, etc.: Introduction. The Book of Baralâm and Yĕwâsĕf, English translation. The preaching of St. Thomas in India (p. [279]-297) The acts of St. Thomas in India (p. [298]-338)
ISBN 0-404-11300-1
I. Bible. N.T. Apocryphal books. Acts of Thomas. English. 1976. II. Budge, Ernest Alfred Thompson Wallis, Sir, 1857-1934. III. Title. IV. Title: Buddha and the Bodhisattva.
PJ9098.B313 1976 294.3'63 73-18832
76 MARC

Barlaam and Joasaph. French (Old French)
L'histoire de Barlaam et Josaphat. Version champenoise d'après le ms. Reg. lat. 660 de la Bibliothèque apostolique vaticane. Éd. avec une introd. par Leonard R. Mills. Genève, Droz, 1973.
189 p. 18 cm. (Textes littéraires français, 201) 28.00F
Sw 73-A-6626
Bibliography: p. [159]-160.
I. Mills, Leonard R., ed.
PQ1427.B4 1973 74-155643
MARC

Barlaam and Joasaph. Georgian.
Gruzinskie redaktsii povesti "Varlaam i Ioasaf". Izdal, issledovaniem i slovarem snabdil Il'ia Abuladze. Pod red. A. Shanidze. Tbilisi, Izd-vo Akademii nauk Gruzinskoĭ SSR, 1957.
216 p. (Akademiia nauk Gruzinskoĭ SSR. Pamiatniki drevnegruzinskogo iazyka, 10)
Title and text in Georgian.
Added introd. in Russian.
I. Shanidze, Akakiĭ Gavrilovich, ed. II. Abuladze, I. V.
InNd NUC76-90455

Barlaam and Joasaph. Russian.
(Balavariani)
Балавариани; мудрость Балавара. Предисл. и ред. И. В. Абуладзе. [Перевод с грузинского Бидзины Абуладзе] Тбилиси, Заря Востока, 1962.
xxxi, 159 p. illus. (part col.) 21 cm. (Академия наук Грузинской ССР. Институт рукописей имени К. С. Кекелидзе. Памятники древнегрузинской литературы)
Bibliography: p. xxxi.
I. Abuladze, I. V., ed.
PK9169.B35R8 1962 64-39709

Barlach, Ernst, 1870-1938.
Briefe. [Ausgewählt von Franz Fühmann. Nachwort: Kurt Batt. Anmerkungen auf der Grundlage der Ausg. "Ernst Barlach, Die Briefe, 1888-1938, in zwei Bänden"] Rostock, Hinstorff, 1972.
588 p. 21 cm.
I. Fühmann, Franz, ed.
CtW MH NUC74-150767

Barlach, Ernst, 1870-1938.
Ernst Barlach. Mit 27 einfarb. Taf. Hrsg. v. Jutta Schmidt. Wien, Die Buchgemeinde; Berlin, Henschelverl., 1971.
70, [2] p. illus. 28 cm. (Welt der Kunst) Au 72-11-170
Bibliography: p. [72]
S52.00
I. Schmidt, Jutta.
NB588.B35S33 1971b 72-359736

Barlach, Ernst, 1870-1938.
Ernst Barlach, das Wirkliche und Wahrhaftige; Briefe, Grafik, Plastik, Dokumente. Hrsg. von Franz Fühmann. Mit Fotos von Gisela Pätsch. [Rostok] Hinstorff [1970]
248 p. illus., front., plates, ports. 27 cm.
"Unter Mitarbeit von Friedrich Schult."
1. Barlach, Ernst, 1870-1938. 2. Drawings, German. 3. Sculpture, German. I. Fühmann, Franz. II. Title.
PPT NUC73-39708

Barlach, Ernst, 1870-1938.
Ernst Barlach, 1870/1890. Bonn-Bad Godesberg, Inter Nationes, 1971.
62 p. illus.
1. Barlach, Ernst. 1870-1938. I. Inter Nationes. II. Title.
OClSA NUC75-48528

Barlach, Ernst, 1870-1938.
Ernst Barlach Fragmente. [Hamburg, Ernst Barlach Gesellschaft, 1970]
13 p. 23 cm. (Jahresgabe der Ernst Barlach Gesellschaft zum 2. Januar 1970)
Cover title.
I. Ernst Barlach Gesellschaft. II. Title. III. Series: Ernst Barlach Gesellschaft . Jahresgabe, 1970.
CaQMM NUC75-46735

Barlach, Ernst, 1870-1938.
Ernst Barlach Gedenkstätte Güstrow, Gertrudenkapelle. ([Katalog.] Bearbeitung: Bernhard Blaschke.) Schwerin, Staatliches Museum (1971).
47 p. with illus. 24 cm. 2.00M GDNB 72-B10
1. Barlach, Ernst, 1870-1938. I. Blaschke, Bernhard. II. Ernst -Barlach-Gedenkstätte. III. Schwerin. Staatliches Museum.
NB588.B35B55 74-340340

Barlach, Ernst, 1870-1938.
Ernst Barlach Handzeichnungen; die Sammlung Niescher. Sonderausstellung im Ernst Barlach Haus. Hamburg, 1972.
[65] p. chiefly illus. 24 cm. GDB***
Text by Isa Lohmann-Siems.
Introduction also in English.
Bibliography: p. [65]
1. Barlach, Ernst, 1870-1938. 2. Niescher, Fritz—Art collections. I. Lohmann-Siems, Isa. II. Ernst Barlach Haus.
NC251.B33L63 73-198114

Barlach, Ernst, 1870-1938.
Ernst Barlach; Leben im Werk. Plastiken, Zeichnungen und Graphiken, Dramen, Prosawerke und Briefe [von] Naomi Jackson Groves. Königstein im Taunus, K. R. Langewiesche Nachfolger H. Köster [1972]
119 p. illus. 27 cm. (Die Blauen Bücher) GDB***
I. Groves, Naomi Jackson.
NX93.B35G76 72-369001
ISBN 3-7845-4150-X

Barlach, Ernst, 1870-1938.
Ernst Barlach : Plastik, Zeichnungen, Druckgraphik : [Ausstellung] Kunsthalle Köln 19. Dezember bis 5. Februar 1975 / [Katalog, Manfred Schneckenburger]. — 2. Aufl. — Köln : Kunsthalle, 1975.
164 p. : ill. ; 27 cm. GFR***
Bibliography: p. 161-162.
1. Barlach, Ernst, 1870-1938. I. Schneckenburger, Manfred. II. Cologne. Kunsthalle.
N6888.B35S36 1975 709'.2'4 75-508410
75 MARC

Barlach, Ernst, 1870-1938.
Das Wirkliche und Wahrhaftige; Briefe, Grafik, Plastik, Dokumente. Hrsg. von Franz Fühmann. Mit Fotos von Gisela Pätsch. [1. Aufl.] Wiesbaden, R. Löwit [1970]
248 p. illus.
I. Fühmann, Franz, ed.
MH NUC76-74058

Barlach, Ernst, 1870-1938
see Carus Gallery. Original prints, drawings and watercolors... [New York, 1971]

Barlach, Ernst, 1870-1938
see Ernst Barlach, 1870/1970. Bonn-Bad Godesberg, Inter Nationes, 1972.

Barlach, Ernst, 1870-1938
see Germany (Democratic Republic, 1949-). Ministerium für Kultur. Ernst Barlakh... Moskva, Sovetskiĭ khudozhnik, 1970.

Barlach, Ernst, 1870-1938
see Watzinger, Carl Hans, 1908- Erdseele. Ried im Innkreis, Oberösterr. Landesverl. [1973].

Barlage, Edith.
33 years of Christ in a religious community: St. Nazianz. [Compiled by Edith Barlage. Milwaukee, Wis., 1971?]
1 v. (unpaged) illus.
1. Oschwald, Ambrose, 1801-1873. 2. St. Naziana, Wis.—History. I. Title.
WHi NUC75-52192

Barlai, Zoltán.
Mérési adatok feldologozása és értelmezése a szénhidrogénkutatás és termelés mélyfurási geofizikai vizsgálatainál. Budapest, Tankönyvkiadó, 19
v. illus. 24 cm. (Mérnöki Továbbképző Intézet kiadványa, Nb. 13)
At head of title: Nehézipari Müszaki Egyetem, Miskolc, Bányamérnöki Kar, Szakmérnöki Tagozat.
1. Oil well logging, Electric. I. Title.
TN871.35.B38 74-221509

Barland, Gordon Herman, 1938-
Detection of deception in criminal suspects : a field validation study / by Gordon H. Barland. --[Salt Lake City] Barland, 1975.
xi, 61 leaves ; 28 cm.
Thesis (Ph.D.)--University of Utah.
Vita: leaves [59]-61.
Bibliography: leaves [56]-58.
1. Lie detectors and detection. I. Title.
UU NUC77-85810

Barland, Lois.
Barland and allied families. Compiled by Lois Barland. Assisted by Isabel Towne, George Barland [and] Betsy Barland Parker. [Stevens Point? Wis.] Worzalla Pub. Co. [1972]
432 p. illus. 29 cm.
Bibliography: p. 432.
1. Barland family. I. Title.
CS71.B268 1972 929'.2'0973 72-171890
MARC

Barland, Peter
see Greenwald, Edward S Cancer chemotherapy. 2d ed. [Flushing, N. Y., Medical Examination Pub. Co., 1973]

Barlaro, José P
Tránsito público [por] José P. Barlaro [y] Félix Carrasco. Buenos Aires, Editorial Policial [1971]
589 p. illus. 20 cm. (Editorial policial, 242/244)
LACAP 72-4583
"Apéndice: Leyes y decretos leyes. Ordenanzas y decretos municipales. Normas policiales y varios": p. [329]-550.
"Textos para insertar," ([15] p.) inserted.
Includes bibliographical references.
1. Traffic regulations—Argentine Republic. 2. Traffic safety—Argentine Republic. 3. Traffic signs and signals—Argentine Republic. I. Carrasco, Félix, joint author. II. Title.
HE373.A7B37 73-314115

Barlās, 'Alī Azhar.
(Tārīkhī shāh pāre)
تاریخی شه پارے. تصنیف: مرزا علی اظہر برلاس. تعارف: سید الطاف علی بریلوی. کراچی، اکیڈیمی آف ایجوکیشنل ریسرچ، آل پاکستان ایجوکیشنل کانفرنس، 1971.
352 p. (p. 349-352 advertisements) port. 19 cm. Rs10.00
In Urdu.
Includes bibliographical references.
1. Oudh—History. 2. East India Company (English) 3. India—History. I. Title.
DS485.O9B36 75-932884

Barlas, H Uğurol.
Anadolu düğünlerinde büyüsel inanmalar / Uğurol Barlas. — Karabük : Karabük Halk Eğitimi Derneği ; İstanbul : dağıtımı, Dilman Kitapevi, 1974.
191 p. : ill. ; 20 cm. — Halk eğitimi yayını ; 2 : Araştırma dizisi ; 1)
Bibliography: p. 165-170.
Includes index.
1. Marriage customs and rites—Turkey. I. Title. II. Series: Halk eğitimi yayını ; 2.
GT2773.B37 75-586606

Barlas, H Uğurol.
Gaziantep basın tarihi: 100. yıl [yazan] Uğurol Barlas. [Gaziantep, Genel Dağıtım: Gaziantep Kültür Derneği, 1972]
100 p. (p. 99-100 advertisements) illus. 20 cm. (Gaziantep Kültür Derneği. Yayın no. 60)
1. Press—Gaziantep, Turkey (Province)—History. I. Title.
PN5355.T8B34 72-225564

Barlas, H Uğurol.
Gaziantep Tıp Fakültesi tarihi ve azınlık okulları / Uğurol Barlas. — [Gaziantep : Gaziantep Kültür Derneği], 1971.
72 p. ; 20 cm. — (Gaziantep Kültür Derneği yayınları ; no. 57)
Includes bibliographical references.
1. Gaziantep Tıp Fakültesi—History. 2. Minorities—Education—Gaziantep, Turkey (City) 3. Gaziantep, Turkey (City) — Schools. I. Title. II. Series: Gaziantep Kültür Derneği. Gaziantep Kültür Derneği yayınları ; no. 57.
R802.G38B37 75-549459

Barlas, H Uğurol.
Hakkari evlenme töre ve törenleri. Yazan Uğurol Barlas. Karabük, Özer Basımevi, 1975.
80 p.
Cover title: Hakkari ili evlenme töre ve törenleri.
1. Marriage customs and rites--Turkey--Hakkari (Province). I. Title.
MiU DLC NUC77-85575

Barlas, H Uğurol.
Safranbolu masallari / Uğurol Barlas. -- Karabük : Özer Basimevi, 1975-
v. ; 20 cm.
1. Tales, Turkish. 2. Folk-lore -- Turkey -- Safranbolu. I. Title.
InU NUC77-85001

Barlas, Hayim, 1898-
(Hatsalah be-yeme sho'ah)
הצלה בימי שואה / חיים ברלס. — [לוחמי הגיטאות] : בית לוחמי הגיטאות, [1975] 735.
371 p. ; 25 cm.
Includes documents in English, French, and German.
Includes index.
1. World War, 1939-1945—Jews—Rescue. I. Title.
D810.J4B3146 75-951006

Barlas, Hayim, 1898-
see Eichmann, Adolf, 1906-1962, defendant (ha-Sho'ah veha-mishpat) [1961-63]

Barlas, Mehmet.
Türkiye üzerinde pazarlıklar. [İstanbul, Giray Yayınları, 1970]
116 p. 20 cm. (Giray yayınları, 2)
1. Turkey—Foreign relations. I. Title.
DR477.B28 72-218280
MH

Barlassina, Franco Arese Lucini, conte di
see
Arese, Franco.

Barlau, Stephen Bernhardt, 1941-
Germanic kinship / Stephen Bernhardt Barlau. -- [Austin, Tex. : s.n.], 1975.
ix, 246 leaves : diagrs. ; 29 cm.
Thesis (Ph.D.)--University of Texas at Austin.
Vita.
Bibliography: leaves 239-246.
1. German language--Etymology. 2. Kinship -- Germanic tribes. I. Title.
TxU NUC77-85166

Barlay, Stephen.
Blockbuster / Stephen Barlay. — New York : Morrow, 1977.
336 p. : map ; 22 cm.
ISBN 0-688-03127-7
I. Title.
PZ4.B2567 Bl 1977 823'.9'14 76-26909
[PR6052.A654] 76 MARC

Barlay, Stephen.
Double cross; encounters with industrial spies. London, Hamilton, 1973.
vii, 279 p. 23 cm. £3.00 GB 73-26128
Includes bibliographical references.
1. Business intelligence—Case studies. I. Title.
HD38.B244 658.4'7 74-154802
ISBN 0-241-02423-4 MARC

Barlay, Stephen.
Fire: an international report. [1st American ed.] Brattleboro, Vt., S. Greene Press [1973, c1972]
293 p. illus. 23 cm.
Bibliography: p. 281.
1. Fires. 2. Fire prevention. I. Title.
TH9448.B37 1973 614.8'4 72-85467
ISBN 0-8289-0176-7 MARC

Barlay, Stephen.
The secrets business. New York, Crowell [1974, c1973]
viii, 344 p. 21 cm. $7.95
First published under title: Double cross.
1. Business intelligence. I. Title.
HD38.B245 1974 658.4'7 73-18266
ISBN 0-690-00290-4 MARC

Barlay, Stephen.
Sex slavery / Stephen Barlay. — Revised [ed.]. — London : Coronet, 1975.
251 p. ; 18 cm. GB75-14079
American ed. published under title: Bondage; the slave traffic in women today.
ISBN 0-340-19679-3 : £0.45
1. Prostitution. I. Title.
HQ281.B32 1975 364.1'53 75-325153
75 MARC

Barlay, Stephen.
That thin red line : fire, the case for self-defence / [by] Stephen Barlay. — London : Hutchinson, 1976.
5-178 p., [16] p. of plates : ill. ; 23 cm. GB76-05804
Bibliography: p. 165.
Includes index.
ISBN 0-09-125710-7 : £4.50. ISBN 0-09-125711-5 pbk.
1. Fire prevention—Great Britain. 2. Fires—Great Britain. I. Title.
TH9537.B37 628.9'22'0941 76-361003
76 MARC

Barleben, Ilse.
Die Woestes vom Woestenhof im Kirchspiel Lüdenscheid: ein Beitr. z. Familien- u. Wirtschaftsgeschichte d. Märk. Sauerlandes/ Ilse Barleben. — Altena: Verlag Der Märker, 1971.
2 v.: ill.; 24 cm. — (Altenaer Beiträge: n. F.; Bd. 6) DM55.00
GFR 73-A22
Bibliography: v. 2, p. 158-168.
1. Lüdenscheid, Ger. (Kirchspiel) I. Title. II. Series.
DD491.J891M25 n. F., Bd. 6 73-350164
[DD901.L915]

Barlee, Neville Langrell, 1932-
The guide to gold panning / [N. L. Barlee]. — [Summerland, B.C. : Canada West Publications], 1972, 1973 printing.
192 p. : ill., maps, ports. ; 28 cm. C74-6958-6
Cover title: The guide to gold panning in British Columbia, gold regions, methods of mining and other data.
1. Gold mines and mining—British Columbia—History. I. Title. II. Title: The guide to gold panning in British Columbia.
TN424.B85B34 553'.41'09711 75-317780
75 MARC

Barler, Miles, 1833-1907.
Early days in Llano / by Miles Barler. — [s.l. : s.n., 1915?]
76 p. ; 14 cm.
Cover title.
Caption title: Personal reminiscences.
1. Barler, Miles, 1833-1907. 2. Llano, Tex.—Biography. 3. Pioneers—Texas—Llano—Biography. I. Title.
F394.L75B37 1915 77-363941
77 MARC

Barlet, J. B
see Physiologie comparée des échanges calciques... [Villeurbanne, Simep-éditions, 1974]

Barlett, Donald.
Oil: the created crisis [by] Donald Bartlett and James B. Steele. [Philadelphia, reprinted by the Philadelphia Inquirer, 1973]
[8] p. illus., maps. 39 cm.
Originally appeared as a three-part series in the Inquirer.
1. Oil industries--United States. 2. Petroleum industry and trade--United States. I. Steele, James B., joint author. II. Title.
Wa NUC75-26871

Barlett, Frank E
The Community Adaptation Schedule: a validational study on federal prisoners and vocational students [by] Frank E. Barlett, Patrick E. Cook [and] A. Cooper Price. [Tallahassee, Fla., Federal Correctional Institution, 1970]
iii, 7 p. illus. 23 cm. (FCI research reports, v. 2, no. 2)
Based on thesis, Florida State University.
Study supported by grant from Council on Training and Research, Florida Division of Mental Health.
Bibliography: p. 7.
1. Community Adaptation Schedule. 2. Social adjustment. I. Cook, Patrick E., joint author. II. Price, A. Cooper, joint author. III. Title. IV. Series.
Wa NUC75-56470

Barlett, Mary.
Gentians / Mary Barlett ; with line drawings by Rosemary Smith. -- Poole, Dorset : Blandford Press, 1975.
160 p. : ill. (some col.)
Bibliography: p. 157-158.
1. Gentians. I. Title.
KyU NUC77-85711

Barlett, Peggy Frederica, 1947-
Agricultural change in Paso; the structure of decision-making in a Costa Rican peasant community. [New York] 1975.
i, 250 l. illus. 29 cm.
Thesis--Columbia University.
Bibliography: leaves 245-250.
1. Peasantry--Costa Rica. 2. Costa Rica--Rural conditions. 3. Land--Costa Rica. 4. Agriculture--Social aspects--Costa Rica. 5. Agriculture--Economic aspects--Costa Rica. I. Title. II. Title: The structure of decision-making in a Costa Rican peasant community.
NNC NUC77-85056

Barletta, Andrea di
see
Bonello, Andrea.

Barletta, Edvige Aleandri
see Alendri Barletta, Edvige.

Barletta, Giuseppe, 1949-
Per una epistemologia materialista / Giuseppe Barletta. — Bari : Dedalo libri, 1976.
99 p. ; 21 cm. — (La Scienza nuova ; 41) It76-Nov
Includes bibliographical references.
L2500
1. Knowledge, Theory of. 2. Materialism. I. Title.
BD164.B33 77-454914
*77 MARC

Barletta, Leónidas, 1902-
Historia de perros. [Buenos Aires] Centro Editor de America Latina [1972]
143 p. 19 cm.
I. Title.
MU NUC74-3534

Barletta, Leónidas, 1902-
Un señor de levita; novela del barrio norte. Buenos Aires, Ediciones Metrópolis, 1972.
188 p. 20 cm.
LACAP 72-5055
I. Title.
PQ7797.B29S37 73-323171

Barletta, Riccardo, 1934-
see L'Arte moderna. [Milano] Fratelli Fabbri [1967-

Barletta, Riccardo, 1934- ed.
see Minervino, Primo. Vibrazioni oniriche di Primo Minervino. [Verona] Ghelfi, 1973.

Barletta, Riccardo, 1934-
see Mostra antologico di Galliano Mazzoni. Mostra antologico (1926-1969). [Milano, Quartiroli, 1969]

Barletta, Sergio, 1934-
see Simbari, Nicola. Nicola Simbari. Roma, Editoriale grafica, [1972?]

Barletti, Espartaco.
Jojutla mejorado, una nueva variedad de arroz para el Estado de Morelos obtenida en el Campo Agrícola Experimental de Zacatepec, Mor. [por] Espartaco Barletti T. [México] Secretaría de Agricultura y Ganadería, Instituto de Investigaciones Agrícolas, 1956.
41 p. illus. 23 cm. (Folleto de divulgación)
1. Rice—Mexico—Morelos. I. Title. II. Series: Instituto Nacional de Investigaciones Agrícolas. Folleto de divulgación.
CU-B NUC75-67062

Barlev, Benzion, 1936-
The effects of the property tax on investment in urban residential construction (a case study of Manhattan) ₍New York₎ 1969 ₍c1970.
Ann Arbor, Mich., University Microfilms, 1970₎
vii, 149 l. illus. 21 cm.
Thesis—New York University.
Facsim. produced by microfilm-xerography.
Includes bibliography.
1. Real property tax. New York (City)
2. Housing. New York (City) Finance. I. Title.
N NUC74-158048

Barley, Alfred H
The Drayson problem; in astronomical survey of the whole question, in the form of a reply to a recent article in the Journal of the British Astronomical Association entitled The Draysonian fallacy, by Alfred H. Barley. Exeter, W. Pollard, 1922.
xxiv, 48 p. illus. 22 cm.
Bibliography: p. 35-36.
1. Astronomy. 2. Glacial epoch. 3. Drayson, Alfred Wilks, 1827-1910. I. Title.
QB52.B37 75-590495

Barley, Delbert.
Grundzüge und Probleme der Soziologie: eine Einf. in d. Verständnis d. menschl. Zusammenlebens/ von Delbert Barley. — 6., überarb. Aufl. — Neuwied (am Rhein), Berlin: Luchterhand, 1973.
xii, 305 p.; 21 cm. — (Jugend im Blickpunkt) DM16.00
GFR 74-A
Bibliography: p. ₍291₎-297.
1. Sociology. I. Title.
HM57.B3 1973 74-324546
ISBN 3-7472-57020-2

Barley, Mary F 1888-1968.
Spears and related families / by Mary F. Barley. — ₍s.l. : s.n.₎, 1967.
115 leaves : ill. ; 36 cm.
Bibliography: leaves 2-4.
1. Spear family. 2. United States—Genealogy. I. Title.
CS71.S74 1967 929'.2'0973 76-374381
76 MARC

Barley, Maurice Willmore, 1909-
A guide to British topographical collections / by M. W. Barley ; with contributions by P. D. A. Harvey and Julia E. Poole. — ₍London₎ : Council for British Archaeology, 1974.
159 p. ; 22 cm. GB 74-19157
Includes index.
ISBN 0-900312-24-6 : £4.00
1. Art—Great Britain—Galleries and museums. 2. Art—Private collections—Great Britain. I. Title.
N1020.B37 016.7600942 74-189060
MARC

Barley, Maurice Willmore, 1909-
Lincolnshire and the Fens, ₍by₎ M. W. Barley; illustrated from photographs by the author and others. ₍1st ed.₎ re-published, with a new preface by the author. Wakefield, EP Publishing Ltd, 1972.
₍4₎, 192 p. illus., map. 22 cm. index. £2.50 B 72-19817
1. Lincolnshire, Eng. 2. Fens, Eng. I. Title.
DA670.L7B3 1972 914.25'3 73-154850
ISBN 0-85409-764-3 MARC

Barley, Maurice Willmore, 1909-
Nottingham now / by Maurice Barley and Robert Cullen. — Nottingham : Nottingham Civic Society, 1975.
49 p. : chiefly ill., maps (some col.), plans (1 col.) ; 30 cm. GB76-09655
ISBN 0-9504861-0-8 : £1.75
1. Historic buildings—England—Nottingham—Pictorial works. 2. Nottingham, Eng.—Buildings—Pictorial works. 3. Nottingham, Eng.—Description—Views. I. Cullen, Robert, joint author. II. Title.
DA690.N92B37 942.5'27 76-382919
77 MARC

Barley, Maurice Willmore, 1909-
see The Plans and topography of Medieval towns in England and Wales. ₍London₎ Council for British Archaeology, 1976.

Barley, Steven D
Photography and the visual arts ₍by₎ Steven D. Barley. ₍n.p., 1969?₎
14 l. 28 cm.
Cover title.
A paper presented at the Conference on Art Education, held in Elmira College, Oct., 1969.
Includes bibliographical references.
1. Visual education. 2. Photography in education.
3. Art—Study and teaching. I. Title.
CSt NUC74-6251

Barley, Steven D
Time : in school, and learning / by Steven D. Barley. -- ₍s.l. : s.n.₎, 1975.
xii, 125 leaves ; 29 cm.
Thesis (Ed.D.)--University of Rochester.
Vita.
Bibliography: leaves 123-125.
1. School attendance--New York (State)
2. Time allocation surveys--New York (State)
I. Title.
NIC NUC77-85292

Barley, Steven D
A visual literacy approach to developmental and remedial reading ₍by₎ Steven D. Barley. ₍n.p., 1969?₎
19 p. 28 cm.
Cover title.
A paper presented at the 4th annual Reading Conference of Wyoming, held in June, 1969.
Includes bibliographical references.
1. Visual education. 2. Reading—Remedial teaching. 3. Children—Reading. I. Title.
CSt NUC74-6250

Barley, Steven D
Why visual sequences come first ₍by₎ Steven D. Barley. ₍n.p.₎ 1969.
10 l. 28 cm.
Cover title.
Revision of the paper originally presented at the In-Service Teacher Training Workshop, held at Canandaigua, N.Y., 1969.
1. Visual education. 2. Children—Language.
3. Visual perception. I. Title.
CSt NUC74-6252

Barleycorn, Michael.
Moonshiners manual / by Michael Barleycorn ; ₍artist, Doug Moran₎. — Willits, Calif. : Oliver Press ; New York : distributed by Scribner, 1975.
x, 150 p. (p. 144 blank for notes, p. 145-149 advertisements) : ill. ; 22 cm.
ISBN 0-914400-12-6 : $3.95
1. Distilling—Amateurs' manuals. I. Title.
TP590.B24 641.8'74 75-7452
75 MARC

Barling, Thomas James.
The letter to the Colossians, five short studies followed by a commentary, by T. J. Barling. Birmingham, "The Christadelphian," 1972.
₍6₎, 189 p. 19 cm. £1.10 GB 73-19125
Includes bibliographical references.
1. Bible. N. T. Colossians—Commentaries. I. Bible. N. T. Colossians. English. Revised Standard. 1972. II. Title.
BS2715.3.B34 227'.7'077 74-169029
ISBN 0-85189-081-4 MARC

Barling, Thomas James.
see Palissot de Montenoy, Charles, 1730-1814. Les philosophes. Éd. critique avec introd. et notes. ₍Exeter₎ University of Exeter, 1975.

Barlmeyer, Werner.
see Russkaja mysl' 1905-1918. Giessen, W. Schmitz, 1977.

Barloco, Josefa Elizondo.
see The Wilton way of making gum paste flowers ... 1st ed. Chicago, Wilton Enterprises, 1975.

Barloewen, Constantin von.
see Talk Show ... München, C. Hanser, c1975.

Barłóg, Agnieszka, 1909-
Walkowa Pani. Angieszka Barłóg. Wyd. 1. Łódź, Wydawn. Łódzkie, 1974.
283 p. ill. 21 cm.
Memoirs.
1. Poland—Rural conditions.
MH DLC NUC76-28644

Barlog, Boleslaw
see Biografie eines Theaters... [Berlin] Rembrandt [c1972]

Barlott, P J
Fortran IV program to predict the thermal environment within total confinement livestock housing / by P. J. Barlott and J. B. McQuitty. — Edmonton ₍Alta.₎, : Dept. of Agricultural Engineering, University of Alberta, 1974.
v, 177 p. : ill. ; 28 cm. — (Research bulletin - Department of Agricultural Engineering, The University of Alberta ; 74-1) C***
Cover title.
Bibliography: p. 176-177.
1. Livestock housing—Heating and ventilation—Computer programs. 2. Swine—Housing—Heating and ventilation—Computer programs. 3. FORTRAN (Computer program language) I. McQuitty, J. B., joint author. II. Title. III. Series: University of Alberta. Dept. of Agricultural Engineering. Research bulletin - Department of Agricultural Engineering, The University of Alberta ; 74-1.
SF91.B25 636.08'31 76-372742
76 MARC

Barlotti, Adriano.
Alcuni procedimenti per la costruzione di piani grafici non desarguesiani. Bologna, Zanichelli, 1971.
17 p. 28 cm. (Conferenze del Seminario di matematica dell'Università di Bari, 127) It***
At head of title: III Gruppo dei seminari matematici delle università italiane.
"Conferenza tenuta nei giorni 19 e 20 novembre 1971."
Bibliography: p. 16-17.
L1000
1. Projective planes. I. Title. II. Series: Bari (City). Università. Seminario di matematica. Conferenze, 127.
QA3.B265 no. 127 75-556894
[QA471]

Barlotti, Adriano
see Centro internazionale matematico estivo. Finite geometric structures and their applications ... Roma, Edizioni Cremonese, 1973.

Barlou, Piter
see
Barlow, Peter, 1776-1862.

Barlough, J Ernest, 1953-
The archaicon; a collection of unusual, archaic English, selected, with an introd., by J. Ernest Barlough. Metuchen, N. J., Scarecrow Press, 1974.
viii, 312 p. 22 cm.
Bibliography: p. 310-312.
1. English language — Obsolete words — Dictionaries. 2. English language—Etymology. I. Title.
PE1667.B3 427'.09 73-14926
ISBN 0-8108-0683-5 MARC

Barlough, J Ernest, 1953- comp.
Minor British poetry: 1680-1800; an anthology. Selected, with an introd., by J. Ernest Barlough. Metuchen, N. J., Scarecrow Press, 1973.
xv, 367 p. 22 cm.
1. English poetry—18th century. I. Title.
PR1215.B3 821'.008 73-4878
ISBN 0-8108-0619-3 MARC

Barlow, A. Ruffell.
see English-Kikuyu dictionary. Oxford, Clarendon Press, 1975.

Barlow, Arthur, 1550 (ca.)-1620
see Federal Writers' Project. The ocean highway: New Brunswick, New Jersey to Jacksonville, Florida. St. Clair Shores, Mich., Somerset Publishers, 1972 [c1938]

Barlow, B A
Flora of New South Wales. No. 58A Viscaceae. [n.p.] 1971.
8 p.
MH-A NUC74-3694

Barlow, Benjamin W
Map of the city of Benicia. S₍an₎ F₍ran-cisco₎ Britton & Rey ₍1850₎; Ithaca, N.Y., Historic Urban Plans, 1969.
map. 51 x 75 cm.
Scale ca. 1:6,800.
Facsimile.
Date of situation: 1847.
Some streets named; blocks numbered.
1. Benicia, Calif.—Maps. I. Title.
KyU NUC76-74049

Barlow, Boris V
The astronomical telescope / Boris V. Barlow. — London : Wykeham Publications ; New York : Springer-Verlag, 1975.
viii, 213 p. : ill. ; 22 cm. — (The Wykeham science series ; 31) GB***
Includes bibliographical references and index.
ISBN 0-387-91119-7. ISBN 0-387-91118-9 pbk.
1. Telescope. I. Title.
QB88.B37 522'.2 74-78485 MARC

Barlow, Brent Alvin, 1941-
Mormon endogamy and exogamy in Northern Florida. [Tallahassee] c1971.
vi, 129 l.
Thesis (Ph.D.)—Florida State University.
Bibliography: leaves 121-128.
Vita.
1. Mormons and Mormonism in Florida. 2. Marriage, Mixed. 3. Endogamy and exogamy. I. Title.
FTaSU NUC74-6166

Barlow, Brent Alvin, 1941-
Mormon endogamy and exogamy in northern Florida. [Ann Arbor, Mich., University Microfilms, 1972]
vi, 130 p.
Thesis (Ph.D.)—Florida State University, 1971.
Photocopy of typescript.
Includes bibliography.
1. Mormon Church—Doctrine—Marriage. 2. Endogamy and exogamy. I. Title.
UU NUC74-150780

Barlow, Brigit.
The devil fish. London, Chatto & Windus, 1970.
221 p. 21 cm. £1.50 B 70-22607
I. Title.
PZ4.B2577De 823'.9'14 73-161862
[PR6052.A657] MARC
ISBN 0-7011-1623-4

Barlow, C
Robert Koch, by C. and P. Barlow. [Geneva] Distributed by Heron Books [1971]
x, 391 p. illus. 21 cm. (The Great Nobel prizes) Sw***
Bibliography: p. 379-[383]
1. Koch, Robert, 1843-1910. I. Barlow, P., joint author.
QR31.K6B37 616.01'4'0924 [B] 74-191801 MARC

Barlow, Claude W
Descendants of Reuben Micah Barlow (1819-1891) of Ashford, Conn., and of his wife Eunice Sophia Snow (1826-1900) Worchester, Mass., 1966.
20 l.
1. Barlow family. I. Title.
WHi NUC73-39371

Barlow, Claude W
John Steevens of Guilford, Connecticut : five generations of 17th & 18th century descendants with surnames Steevens, Stevens, Stephens, Kelsey ... / by Claude Willis Barlow. — Rochester, N.Y. : J. M. Stephens, c1976.
xv, 225 p. ; 23 cm.
Includes bibliographical references and index.
1. Stevens family. 2. United States—Genealogy. I. Title.
CS71.S844 1976 929'.2'0973 75-39127
77 MARC

Barlow, Claude W
Sources for genealogical searching in Connecticut and Massachusetts, by Claude W. Barlow. Cortland, N.Y. [Central New York Genealogical Society, 1973]
23 p.
1. Genealogy—Massachusetts—Sources—Bibl. 2. Genealogy—Connecticut—Sources—Bibl. I. Title.
WHi NUC75-26865

Barlow, Claude W., joint author.
see Hannibal, Edna Anne. John Briggs of Sandwich, Massachusetts and his descendants. [Palo Alto? Calif.] Hannibal, c1962.

Barlow, Clyde Howard, 1943-
Spectroscopic probes of the oxygen binding sites of hemes and hemeproteins. [Tempe] 1974.
155 l. illus.
Thesis (Ph. D.)—Arizona State University.
Includes abstract and vita.
Bibliography: leaves 148-155.
1. Dissertations, Academic—ASU—Chemistry. 2. Hemeproteins—Spectra. 3. Porphyrin and porphyrin compounds—Spectra. I. Title.
AzTeS NUC76-28998

Barlow, Colin, 1932-
The marketing of smallholders' rubber. Kuala Lumpur, Economics and Planning Division, Rubber Research Institute of Malaya [1967?]
[16] p. 24 cm.
1. Rubber industry and trade—Malaysia. I. Rubber Research Institute of Malaya. Economics and Planning Division. II. Title.
NIC NUC76-24200

Barlow, David Alan, 1941-
Kinematic and kinetic factors involved in pole vaulting. [Bloomington, Ind.] 1973.
212 p. illus.
Thesis (Ph.D.)—Indiana University.
Vita.
InU NUC74-150781

Barlow, David Alan, 1941-
Kinematic and kinetic factors involved in pole vaulting. [Bloomington, Ind., c1973]
xii, 212 l. illus.
Thesis—Indiana University.
Vita.
Microfilm. Ann Arbor, Mich., University Microfilms, 1974. 1 reel.
1. Vaulting. I. Title.
IaU NUC75-26877

Barlow, David H., joint author.
see Hersen, Michel. Single case experimental designs ... 1st ed. New York, Pergamon Press, 1976.

Barlow, David Thomas Chetwynd.
British general practice: a personal guide for students [by] D. T. C. Barlow; foreword by R. M. J. Harper; preface by Sir Edward Muir. London, H. K. Lewis, 1973.
xvi, 166 p. 23 cm. £2.25 GB 73-18516
Includes index.
1. Physicians (General practice)—Great Britain. I. Title.
[DNLM: 1. General practice—Great Britain. W89 B258b 1973]
[R729.5.G4B37] 362.1'04'25 73-595734
ISBN 0-7186-0392-3 MARC
Shared Cataloging with DNLM

Barlow, Derek.
Dick Turpin and the Gregory Gang. London, Phillimore [1973]
477 p. illus. 23 cm. £7.50 GB***
Includes bibliographical references.
1. Turpin, Richard, 1706-1739. 2. Brigands and robbers—England. I. Title.
HV6248.T85B37 364.1'55'0924 [B] 73-178641
ISBN 0-900592-64-8 MARC

Barlow, Diana Lynn.
A bibliography on program evaluation, compiled by Diana Lynn Barlow and Geoffrey Yates Cornog. Springfield, Ill., 1974.
78 p. (Sangamon State University, Springfield, Ill. Public Sector Program Evaluation Center. Public affairs paper no. 3)
1. Critical path analysis—Bibliography. I. Cornog, Geoffrey Yates, 1923- joint author. II. Title: Program evaluation.
InU NUC76-28517

Barlow, Dorothea, illus.
see Cox, Victoria. The laughing garbage disposal. New York, Golden Press [1974]

Barlow, E W R
Subsurface heating and irrigation of soils: its effect on temperature and water content and on plant growth. Prepared by E. W. R. Barlow, A. R. Sepaskhah, and L. Boersma. [Corvallis, Water Resources Research Institute, Oregon State University, 1974]
xii, 109 p. illus. 28 cm. (Oregon State University. Water Resources Research Institute. WRRI-23)
"Project completion report no. B-028-ORE."
Includes bibliographies.
1. Plants, Effect of temperature on. 2. Soil temperature. 3. Soil heating. 4. Irrigation. 5. Soil moisture. 6. Roots (Botany)—Temperature. I. Sepaskhah, A. R., joint author. II. Boersma, L., joint author. III. Title. IV. Series: Oregon. State University, Corvallis. Water Resources Research Institute. WRRI-23.
HD1694.O7A13 no. 23 74-622022
[QK755] 333.9'1'009795 s [581.3] MARC
Library of Congress 74 [4]

Barlow, E. W. R.
see Boersma, L Use of reactor cooling water... [Corvallis] Oregon State University [1972]

Barlow, Earl, comp.
see The Indian in the classroom... Helena, Mont., Office of the Superintendent of Public Instruction, 1972.

Barlow, Elizabeth, joint author.
see Epstein, Jason. East Hampton ... 1st ed. Sag Harbor, N.Y., Medway Press, [1975]

Barlow, Frank.
The feudal kingdom of England, 1042-1216. 3rd ed. London, Longman, 1972.
xii, 475 p. geneal. tables, maps. 22 cm. (A History of England in eleven volumes) £1.75 GB 73-22402
Bibliography: p. 442-444.
Includes index.
1. Great Britain—History—Medieval period, 1066-1485. 2. Great Britain—History—Edward, the Confessor, 1042-1066. I. Title. II. Series.
DA175.B26 1972 914.2'03'2 73-179670
ISBN 0-582-48237-2 MARC

Barlow, Frank.
William I and the Norman conquest. [1st ed.] New York, Collier Books [1967, c1965]
xiii, 210 p. illus. (Collier books, 03024)
1. William I, the Conqueror, King of England, 1027?-1087.
MH NUC74-3692

Barlow, Frank
see Leofric of Exeter: essays in commemoration of the foundation of Exeter Cathedral Library in A. D. 1072. Exeter, University of Exeter, 1972.

Barlow, Frank, joint author
see Sawyer, Peter. The Norman conquest. [Phonotape] Santa Monica, Calif., BFA Educational Media [1972]

Barlow, Gene Arlan, 1940-
An analysis of factors relating to federal funding in Florida school districts. [Gainesville] 1971.
vii, 78 l. illus. 28 cm.
Manuscript copy.
Thesis (Ed.D.)—University of Florida.
Vita.
Bibliography: leaves 76-77.
1. Federal aid to education—Florida. I. Title.
FU NUC73-34698

Barlow, Genevieve.
Leyendas latinoamericanas. Illustrated by Robert Borja. Skokie, Ill., National Textbook Co. [1973, c1970]
129 p. illus. 24 cm.
On cover: For intermediate students.
1. Spanish language—Readers—Legends. 2. Legends—Latin America. I. Borja, Robert, illus. II. Title.
PC4127.L4B3 1973 468'.6'421 74-220347

Barlow, Genevieve.
Leyendas latinoamericanas : [Argentina, Bolivia, Colombia, Guatemala, Honduras, México, Paraguay, Perú, Puerto Rico, Venezuela] / Genevieve Barlow ; illustrated by Robert Borja. — Skokie, Ill. : National Textbook Co., c1974.
129 p. : ill. ; 23 cm.
1. Spanish language—Readers—Legends. 2. Legends—Latin America. I. Borja, Roberto. II. Title.
PC4127.L4B3 1974 75-316903
75 MARC

Barlow, Genevieve.
Leyendas mexicanas : a collection of Mexican legends / Genevieve Barlow, William N. Stivers ; ill. by Phero Thomas. — Skokie, Ill. : National Textbook Co., [1974]
v, 119 p. : ill. ; 23 cm.
1. Spanish language—Readers. I. Stivers, William N., joint author. II. Title.
PC4117.B314 468'.6'421 73-94491
MARC

Barlow, George. History at the universities; a comparative and analytical guide to history syllabuses at universities in the United Kingdom.
see Blows, Roger Philip. History at the universities and polytechnics ... 4th ed. London, Historical Association, 1975.

Barlow, George, 1847-
The genius of Dickens / by George Barlow. — New York : Haskell House Publishers, 1975.
60 p. ; 22 cm.
Reprint of the 1909? ed. published by H. J. Glaisher, London.
ISBN 0-8383-2091-0
1. Dickens, Charles, 1812-1870—Criticism and interpretation. I. Title.
PR4588.B29 1975 823'.8 75-22401
75 MARC

Barlow, George, 1948- Flowers at the Jackson Funeral Home
see Boyd, Melba J 1965 (dedicate to all my Brothers and Sisters of southwest Detroit)... [Detroit, Broadside Press, 1972]

Barlow, George, 1948-
Gabriel / by George Barlow. — 1st ed. — Detroit : Broadside Press, [1974]
63 p. ; 22 cm. — (Broadside poets)
Poems.
ISBN 0-910296-92-8 : $5.25. ISBN 0-910296-84-7 pbk. : $2.00
I. Title.
PS3552.A6725G3 811'.5'4 74-186469
MARC

Barlow, George W
Animal behavior [by] George W. Barlow. [New York] McGraw-Hill [1974]
2 v. illus. 28 cm. (Biocore, unit 19-20)
Includes bibliographies.
ISBN 0-07-005350-2 (v. 19)
1. Animals, Habits and behavior of. I. Series.
[DNLM: 1. Behavior, Animal. QH 366.2 B615 v. 19-20 1974]
QH302.B57 unit 19-20 574'.08 s [591.5] 74-2207
[QL751] MARC

Barlow, Harold.
A dictionary of musical themes / by Harold Barlow and Sam Morgenstern ; introd. by John Erskine. — Rev. ed. — New York : Crown Publishers, c1975.
642 p. : music ; 23 cm.
Includes indexes.
ISBN 0-517-52446-5
1. Instrumental music—Thematic catalogs. I. Morgenstern, Sam, joint author. II. Title.
ML128.I65B3 1975 016.78 75-15687
75 MARC

Barlow, Harold.
A dictionary of opera and song themes : including cantatas, oratorios, lieder, and art songs = originally published as A dictionary of vocal themes / compiled by Harold Barlow and Sam Morgenstern. — Rev. ed. — New York : Crown Publishers, c1976.
547 p. : music ; 25 cm.
Includes indexes.
ISBN 0-517-52503-8
1. Vocal music—Thematic catalogs. I. Morgenstern, Sam, joint author. II. Title.
ML128.V7B3 1976 016.784 75-30751
75 MARC

Barlow, Henry M
Community power structure and decision making in an urban community. Ann Arbor, Mich., University Microfilms, 1969.
1 reel. 35 mm. (University Microfilms 69-4841)
Microfilm of typescript.
Thesis (Ph. D.)—Ohio State University, 1968.
Collation of the original: v, 216 l.
Bibliography: leaves 210-216.
1. Power (Social sciences) 2. Decision-making (ethics) I. Title.
PSt NUC74-158903

Barlow, Henry M., ed.
see Symposium on Higher Education and the Social Professions, Lexington, Ky., 1972. Higher education and the social professions... Lexington, University of Kentucky, 1973.

Barlow, Henry Sackville, joint author.
see Banks, Henry Jonathan. A revision of the genus Ptychandra (Lepidoptera, Nymphalidae). London, British Museum (Natural History) 1976.

Barlow, Hugh Denison, 1945-
A formal theory of crime and punishment. [Austin, Tex.] 1973.
viii, 187 l. illus. 29 cm.
Thesis (Ph. D.)—University of Texas at Austin.
Vita.
Bibliography: leaves 174-187.
1. Crime and criminals. 2. Punishment.
TxU NUC76-74044

Barlow, J
The story of the Uganda martyrs, by J. Barlow. [Kampala, Uganda Bookshop, 19—]
63 p. illus. 14 cm.
On cover: "Death hath no more dominion."
1. Martyrs—Uganda. I. Title.
BR1608.U45B37 272'.09676'1 74-153526
MARC

Barlow, J B
Some reflections of a cardiologist: inaugural lecture, delivered 29 March, 1971. Johannesburg, Witwatersrand University Press, 1971.
15 p.
1. Cardiology—Addresses, essays, lectures. I. Title.
MiEM NUC74-3693

Barlow, J. E.
see Sunderland, Eng. Planning Officer. Seaburn & Roker - a policy for coastal recreation. Sunderland, Eng., 1970.

Barlow, J Stanley, 1924-
The fall into consciousness, by J. Stanley Barlow. Philadelphia, Fortress Press [1973]
xi, 148 p. 21 cm. $3.75
Includes bibliographical references.
1. Consciousness. I. Title.
BF311.B287 150'.19'52 72-87059
ISBN 0-8006-0136-X MARC

Barlow, J. Stanley, 1924- ed.
see Greater Detroit Study Commission on Theological Education. Toward a center for theological studies; report... [Detroit? 1964?]

Barlow, James, 1921-
Liner; a novel. London, H. Hamilton [c1970]
456 p.
SBN 241 01918 4.
I. Title.
CaOTP NUC73-62893

Barlow, James A
Coal and coal mining in West Virginia, by James A. Barlow. Morgantown, West Virginia Geological and Economic Survey, 1974.
vi, 63 p. illus. 22 x 29 cm. (Coal-geology bulletin no. 2)
Rev., expanded, and updated version of O. Haught's Coal and coal mining in West Virginia.
Bibliography: p. 51.
1. Coal mines and mining—West Virginia. I. Haught, Oscar L. Coal and coal mining in West Virginia. II. West Virginia. Geological Survey. III. Title. IV. Series.
TN805.W4B28 1974 553'.24'09754 74-622497
MARC

Barlow, James A
Symposium abstracts and reference papers: I. C. White Memorial Symposium—The Age of the Dunkard, September 25-29, 1972. James A. Barlow, editor. Morgantown, West Virginia Geological Survey [1972?]
47 p. 27 cm.
1. Geology, Stratigraphic—Permian—Congresses. 2. Geology, Stratigraphic—Pennsylvanian—Congresses. 3. Geology—Appalachian Mountains—Congresses. I. I. C. White Memorial Symposium—The Age of the Dunkard, Morgantown, W. Va., 1972.
QE674.B36 551.7'5 75-326379
76 MARC

Barlow, James A.
see I. C. White Memorial Symposium—The Age of the Dunkard, 1st, Morgantown, W. Va., 1972. Proceedings of the first I. C. White Memorial Symposium "The Age of the Dunkard," September 25-29, 1972. Morgantown, West Virginia Geological and Economic Survey, 1975.

Barlow, James A., ed.
see Symposium on Tertiary Rocks of Wyoming, Casper, Wyo., 1969. Symposium on Tertiary Rocks of Wyoming. Casper, 1969.

Barlow, Jane, 1860-1917.
Maureen's fairing, and other stories. With illus. by Bertha Newcombe. Freeport, N. Y., Books for Libraries Press [1972]
191 p. illus. 22 cm. (Short story index reprint series)
CONTENTS: Maureen's fairing.—A cream-coloured cactus.—A formidable rival.—A year and a day.—Mac's luncheon.—Stopped by signal.—An escape.—The Murphys' supper.
I. Title.
PZ3.B248Mau 6 823'.8 72-4418
[PR4063.B3] MARC
ISBN 0-8369-4169-1

Barlow, Janelle Mary Schlimgen.
The images of the Chinese, Japanese and Koreans in American secondary school world history textbooks, 1900-1870. [Berkeley] 1973.
1 v. (various pagings)
Thesis (Ph. D.)—Univ. of California.
Includes bibliography.
CU NUC75-26876

Barlow, Jeffrey Garrigus.
Vietnam and the Chinese Revolution of 1911. [Berkeley] 1973.
x, 592 l. maps.
Thesis (Ph. D.)—Univ. of California.
Bibliography: leaves 578-592.
CU NUC75-26875

Barlow, Joel, 1754-1812.
Advice to the privileged orders, in the several states of Europe, resulting from the necessity and propriety of a general revolution in the principle of government / by Joel Barlow. -- London ; New York : Childs and Swaine, 1792-1794.
2 v. ; 19 cm.
Microfilm. [Philadelphia] : University of Pennsylvania, [19--]. -- 1 reel ; 35 mm.
1. Aristocracy. I. Title.
NmU NUC77-84997

Barlow, Joel, 1754-1812.
Oration delivered at Washington, July fourth, 1809; at the request of the Democratic citizens of the District of Columbia. Washington City: R. C. Weightman, 1809 [1973]
1 sheet. 7.5 x 12.5 cm. (The Library of Thomas Jefferson)
Sabin 3425. Sowerby 4686.
Micro-transparency (positive) Washington, Microcard Editions, 1973.
Collation of the original: 14 p.
1. U. S.—Pol. & govt.—Constitutional period, 1789-1809. 2. Fourth of July orations.
PSt NUC74-172400

Barlow, Joel, 1754-1812.
The political writings of Joel Barlow. New ed., with Joel Barlow: a bibliographical list prepared by Division of Bibliography, Library of Congress. New York, Burt Franklin [1971]
xlviii, 258 p. 21 cm. (Burt Franklin: Research & source works ser. 812. American classics in history and social science 205)
Originally published: 1796.
1. France—Hist.—Revolution—Causes and character. 2. Aristocracy.
FMU KyU NUC74-6167

Barlow, Joel, 1754-1812, ed.
see Bible. O. T. Psalms. English. Paraphrases. 1788. Psalms, carefully suited to the Christian worship in the United States of America... New York, H. Gaine, 1788.

Barlow, Joel, 1754-1812
see Todd, Charles Burr, 1849-
Life and letters of Joel Barlow ... New York, B. Franklin [1972]

Barlow, Joel, 1754-1812, ed.
see Watts, Isaac, 1674-1748. Imitation of the Psalms of David. New York: Samuel Campbell, M, DCC, XCV.

Barlow, Joel, 1754-1812, ed.
see Watts, Isaac, 1674-1748. Psalms... New York, Hodge & Campbell, 1792.

Barlow, Joel, 1754-1812, ed.
see Watts, Isaac, 1674-1748. Psalms... New York, White, Gallaher & White, 1831.

Barlow, Joel, 1754-1812, ed.
see Watts, Isaac, 1674-1748. Psalms, carefully suited to the Christian worship in the United States of America ... New-York, H. Gaine, 1788.

Barlow, John P
Eutrophication of water resources of New York state; observations on nutrient limitation on summer phytoplankton in Cayuga Lake, 1967 and 1968, by John P. Barlow, William Schaffner ₍and₎ Virginia B. Scarlet. ₍Ithaca, 1970₎
16 l. (Cornell University. Water Resources and Marine Sciences Center. Technical report no. 21)
Includes bibliography.
Work on report supported partially by funds provided by the U.S. Dept. of the Interior, Office of Water Resources Research.
1. Eutrophication. 2. Phytoplankton—Cayuga Lake. I. Schaffner, William, joint author. II. Scarlet, Virginia B., joint author. III. United States. Office of Water Resources Research. IV. Series.
DI NUC76-14956

Barlow, John P., joint author
see Peterson, Bruce J Experimental studies on phytoplankton succession... ₍Ithaca, N.Y., Cornell University₎ 1973.

Barlow, John S., 1925- ed.
see Complementary electrophysiological techniques... Amsterdam, Elsevier [c1973]

Barlow, Jon C., joint author.
see James, R. D. Annotated checklist of the birds of Ontario. Toronto, Royal Ontario Museum, 1976.

Barlow, Keith A
Massive retaliation, a monograph. Carlisle Barracks, Pa., U.S. Army War College [Distributed by NTIS, U.S. Dept. of Commerce] 1972.
75 l.
"AD764412."
At head of title: USAWC research paper.
Includes bibliography.
CaOTP NUC75-46389

Barlow, Marion A
Struggle : saga of a Colorado homesteader / by Marion A. Barlow ; edited by Thomas A. Barlow. — Boulder, Colo. : Hallmark, c1977.
ix, 63 p. : ill. ; 22 cm.
1. Barlow, Marion A. 2. Frontier and pioneer life—Colorado. 3. Pioneers—Colorado—Biography. 4. Colorado—History—1876-1950. I. Title.
F781.B277 978.8'03 77-80653
77 MARC

Barlow, Marjorie Dana.
Notes on woman printers in Colonial America and United States, 1639-1975 / compiled by Marjorie Dana Barlow. — New York : Hroswitha Club ; Charlottesville, Va. : distributed by the University Press of Virginia, 1976.
xi, 89 p. ; 26 cm.
Bibliography: p. 79-80.
Includes index.
1. Women printers—United States—Biography. I. Title.
Z231.B37 686.2'092'2 76-46686
77 MARC

Barlow, Matthew.
EMCAP-"earn and learn '75" / Matthew Barlow, Alex V. Delgado, Romie Tribble. -- Boulder, Colo. : Western Interstate Commission for Higher Education, 1975.
20, xxxxiv p. : ill., maps ; 28 cm.
Cover title: Earn and learn '75.
Bibliography: p. i-ii.
1. Education, Bilingual--Denver. 2. East Motivational Cooperative Program, Inc., Denver, Colo. I. Delgado, Alex V., joint author. II. Tribble, Romie, joint author. III. Title.
UU NUC77-86240

Barlow, Melvin L
EPDA leadership development program: graduate study, research, and internship in vocational education; second interim report, July 1970 - October 1972, submitted by Alan P. Wunsch, EPDA coordinator and awardee. Project Director: Melvin L. Barlow. [Los Angeles, Graduate School of Education, University of California] 1972.
47 p. ports.
1. Wunsch, Alan P.
CLU NUC75-93050

Barlow, Melvin L
Leadership development project in vocational and technical education, Sec. 552, Part F, Education Professions Development Act Graduate Fellowships; first interim report, July 1, 1970-June 30, 1971. Report submitted by Ralph D. Sylvester, Coordinator and fellow, EPDA Leadership Development Program. Project Director: Melvin L. Barlow. Los Angeles, Graduate School of Education, University of California [1971?]
19 p.
Grant no. OEG-0-70-1953 (721) Log -2560.
1. Vocational education—California. 2. Vocational teachers. 3. Leadership—Study and teaching. I. Sylvester, Ralph Kenneth, 1921- II. California, University. University at Los Angeles. Graduate School of Education. III. Title.
CLU NUC75-91091

Barlow, Melvin L
Profiles of trade and technical leaders: summary report 1969, by Melvin L. Barlow ₍and₎ Bruce Reinhart. Division of Vocational Education, University of California, Los Angeles, in cooperation with: Bureau of Industrial Education, California State Department of Education. ₍Sacramento, California Department of Education, 1969₎
vi, 62 p. illus. 28 cm.
1. Leadership. 2. Technical education—California. I. Reinhart, Bruce, 1926- joint author. II. Title.
OKentU NUC75-50599

Barlow, Melvin L
Profiles of trade and technical teachers: revised summary report 1968 by Melvin L. Barlow ₍and₎ Bruce Reinhart. Los Angeles, Division of Vocational Education, University of California in cooperation with Bureau of Industrial Education, California State Dept. of Education, 1968.
v, 35 p. illus. 28 cm.
1. Technical education—Teacher training. 2. Technical education—California. I. Reinhart, Bruce, joint author. II. California. University. University at Los Angeles. Division of Vocational Education. III. Title.
OKentU NUC73-33648

Barlow, Melvin L
The unconquerable Senator Page : the struggle to establish Federal legislation for vocational education / Melvin L. Barlow. — Washington : American Vocational Association, 1976.
138 p. ; 22 cm.
Includes bibliographical references.
1. Vocational education—Law and legislation—United States—History. 2. Federal aid to vocational education—United States—History. 3. Page, Carroll Smalley, 1843-1925. I. Title.
KF4205.B37 344'.73'077 76-54354
76 MARC

Barlow, Melvin L.
see The Philosophy for quality vocational education programs. Washington, American Vocational Association, 1974.

Barlow, Michel, 1940-
Mao Tsé-toung / Michel Barlow. — ₍Paris₎ : F. Nathan, 1975.
124 p., ₍8₎ p. of plates ; 22 cm. F76-13665
18.50F
1. Mao, Tse-tung, 1893-1976. 2. Heads of state—China—Biography.
DS778.M3B37 951.05'092'4 77-459214
77 MARC

Barlow, Nicholas.
Eton days / photos. by Nicholas Barlow ; text by Oliver Van Oss. — London : Lund Humphries, 1976.
112 p. : chiefly ill. ; 30 cm. GB***
ISBN 0-85331-395-4 : £5.95
1. Eton College. I. Van Oss, Oliver. II. Title.
LF795.E86B37 378.422'96 76-382878
76 MARC

Barlow, P., joint author
see Barlow, C Robert Koch. [Geneva] Heron Books [1971]

Barlow, P J
Comprehensive plan, Terry, Mississippi, by Paul J. Barlow. Jackson, Mississippi Research and Development Center, 1971.
ix, 89 p. illus., fold. col. maps. 29 cm.
"Subproject CA-528."
1. Cities and towns. Planning. Terry, Miss. I. Mississippi. Research and Development Center.
NcD NUC76-74056

Barlow, P.J., joint author
see Tyer, M C Soil survey of Marshall County, Mississippi. [Washington] Dept. of Agriculture, Soil Conservation Service and Forest Service, 1972.

Barlow, Peter.
The marine photography of Peter Barlow. New York, Motor Boating & Sailing Books ₍1973₎
173 p. illus. 26 cm. $12.50
1. Photography of ships. 2. Photography of sailing ships.
I. Title.
TR670.5.B36 779'.9'79710924 72-89439
ISBN 0-910990-14-X MARC

Barlow, Peter, 1776-1862.
₍Barlow's tables of squares, cubes, square roots, cube roots and reciprocals of all integers up to 12,500. Russian₎
Таблицы Барлоу квадратов, кубов, квадратных корней, кубических корней и обратных величин всех целых чисел до 15000 / ₍Перевод₎ ; Под ред. и с доп. Л. С. Хренова. — Москва : Наука, 1975.
376 p. ; 27 cm. USSR 76
Chiefly tables.
1.92rub
1. Mathematics — Tables, etc. I. Khrenov, Leonid Sergeevich. II. Title.
Title romanized: Tablit͡sy Barlou kvadratov, kubov, kvadratnykh korneĭ, kubicheskikh korneĭ i obratnykh velichin vsekh t͡selykh chisel do 15,000.
QA49.B3417 77-504229

Barlow, Philip Whidden, joint author
see Whidden, Helen H The Whidden family of Nova Scotia. [n.p., 1973?]

Barlow, Richard A
Here come the expandables : mobile homes of the future : an entirely new concept in mobile home design and park development meant to purposely change the thinking of mobile home manufacturers, developers, and municipalities / by Richard A. Barlow. — ₍Rockville, Md. : Mobilehome Designs by Barlow, 1974₎
₍56₎ p. : chiefly ill. ; 28 cm.
1. Mobile homes—Designs and plans. 2. Mobile home parks. I. Title.
NA8480.B37 728'.7 74-196863
MARC

Barlow, Richard E
Reliability growth during a development testing program ₍by₎ Richard E. Barlow and Ernest M. Scheuer. Santa Monica, Rand Corporation ₍1965₎
vii, 17 l. illus. 28 cm. (Rand Corporation. ₍Research₎ memorandum RM-4317-1-NASA)
"Prepared for National Aeronautics and Space Administration."
"References": p. 17.
1. Reliability (Engineering) I. Scheuer, E.M., joint author. II. Title. III. Series.
MB NUC74-10216

Barlow, Richard E
Statistical estimation procedures for the "burn-in" process [by] Richard E. Barlow, Frank Proschan [and] Ernest M. Scheuer, with and appendix by Albert Madansky. Santa Monica, Rand Corporation, 1966.
vii, 17 p. illus. 28 cm. (Rand Corporation. [Research] memorandum RM-5109-NASA)
Prepared for National Aeronautics and Space Administration.
1. Reliability (Engineering) I. Proschan, Frank, joint author. II. Scheuer, Ernest M., joint author. III. Madansky, Albert. IV. Title. V. Series.
MB NUC76-1787

Barlow, Richard E
Statistical theory of reliability and life testing: probability models [by] Richard E. Barlow [and] Frank Proschan. New York, Holt, Rinehart and Winston [1974, c1975]
xiii, 290 p. illus. 24 cm. (International series in decision processes) (Series in quantitative methods for decision-making)
Bibliography: p. 275-282.
ISBN 0-03-085853-4
1. Reliability (Engineering)—Statistical methods. I. Proschan, Frank, joint author. II. Title.
TS173.B37 620'.004'5 74-4480
MARC

Barlow, Richard E.
see Conference on Reliability and Fault Tree Analysis, University of California, Berkeley, 1974. Reliability and fault tree analysis ... Philadelphia, Society for Industrial and Applied Mathematics, 1975.

Barlow, Richard E.
see Statistical inference under order restrictions ... London, New York, J. Wiley [1972]

Barlow, Richard Francis Dudley.
see Williams, William James. Williams' Law relating to wills. 4th ed. London, Butterworths, 1974.

Barlow, Richard K
Comment on the Proposed regulations, dealing with 'Reconsiderations and appeals under hospital insurance program' in part A of title xviii (Health insurance for the aged (Medicare)) of the Social security act, published in the Federal register on October 27, 1970. Philadelphia, Health Law Project, University of Pennsylvania, Law School, 1970.
34 p. 28 cm.
In the form of a letter to Elliot L. Richardson, Secretary, Dept. of Health, Education & Welfare. Title from first paragraph.
"Errata and supplementary notes" (3 leaves) appended.
Photocopy. Chicago, National Clearinghouse for Legal Services, 1971.
1. Medical care—U.S. I. Pennsylvania. University. Law School. Health Law Project. II. Title.
MiU-L NUC76-17568

Barlow, Robert Hayward, 1918–
Diccionario de elementos fonéticos en escritura jeroglífica (Códice mendocino) por Roberto Barlow y Byron MacAfee. México, Universidad Nacional Autónoma de México, Instituto de Historia, 1949.
46 p. illus. 31 cm. (Publicaciones del Instituto de Historia. 1. ser., no. 9)
1. Codex Mendoza. 2. Mayas—Writing. 3. Names, Geographical—Mexico. I. MacAfee, Byron, joint author. II. Title. III. Series: Mexico (City). Universidad Nacional. Instituto de Investigaciones Históricas. Publicaciones, 1. ser., no. 9.
F1219.B268 74-212231

Barlow, Robin.
Planning public health expenditures, with special reference to Morocco. Ann Arbor, Center for Research on Economic Development, University of Michigan, 1972.
iv, 68 p. illus. 28 cm. (Discussion paper 27)
Includes bibliographical references.
1. Hygiene, Public—Morocco. I. Title. II. Series: Michigan. University. Center for Research on Economic Development. Discussion paper no. 27.
MiU-L NUC74-172392

Barlow, Roger
see Leckie, Robert

Barlow, Sarah W., joint author
see Ward, Martha. Your right to Indian welfare... [Washington] United States Commission on Civil Rights, 1973.

Barlow, Shirley Ann.
The imagery of Euripides : a study in the dramatic use of pictorial language / Shirley A. Barlow. — London : Methuen ; [New York] : distributed by Harper & Row, 1974.
xii, 169 p. ; 22 cm. — (University paperbacks) GB***
Based on the author's thesis, University of London, 1963.
Includes indexes.
ISBN 0-416-81310-0
1. Euripides—Style. I. Title.
PA3992.B3 1974 882'.01 75-307257
MARC

Barlow, Sumner.
In other words : a variety of verse, comment, environment, confession, whimsey / by Sumner Barlow ; ill. by Marietta Thomas Kust. — Doylestown, Pa. : Quixott Press, 1976.
[85] p. : ill. ; 23 cm.
I. Title.
PS3552.A672715 811'.5'4 76-151891
77 MARC

Barlow, T Ed, 1931–
Small group ministry in the contemporary church, by T. Ed Barlow. [Independence, Mo., Herald Pub. House, 1972]
190 p. 20 cm.
Bibliography: p. 187-190.
1. Church group work. I. Title.
BV652.2.B37 253.5 72-90357
ISBN 0-8309-0080-2 MARC

Barlow, T. Ed, 1931-
see Living saints witness at work. Independence, Mo., Herald Pub. House, c1976.

Barlow, Thomas A
Pestalozzi and American education / by Thomas A. Barlow ; with an introd. by Mehdi Nakosteen. — Boulder, Colo. : Este Es Press, 1977.
180 p. ; 23 cm.
Bibliography: p. 168-176.
Includes index.
1. Pestalozzi, Johann Heinrich, 1746-1827. 2. Education—Philosophy. 3. Education—United States—History. I. Title.
LB628.B28 370.1'092'4 77-80350
77 MARC

Barlow, Trafford Brereton, 1906–
President Brand and his times, by Trafford B. Barlow. Cape Town, Juta, 1972.
ix, 267 p. illus. 26 cm. R10.50 SANB***
Bibliography: p. 247-256.
1. Brand, Sir Johannes Henricus, Pres. Orange Free State, 1823–1888. I. Title.
DT905.B7B37 968'.5 [B] 73-167014
ISBN 0-7021-0368-3 MARC

Barlow, Vernon, 1899- joint author
see Etherton, Percy Thomas, 1879- Lundy... New ed. London, Lutterworth Press [1960]

Barlow, W Lewis.
A case study of the restoration of the Winedale Inn Properties, by W. Lewis Barlow, IV [College Station, Tex.] College of Architecture and Environmental Design, Texas A&M University, 1971.
73 p. 28 cm.
1. Winedale, Tex. 2. Texas—Historic houses, etc. 3. Architecture—Conservation and restoration. I. Texas. A&M University, College Station. College of Architecture and Environmental Design.
TxU NUC75-2527

Barlow, W Lewis.
John Brown's Fort, architectural data, Harpers Ferry National Historical Park, Maryland - W. Virginia / by W. Lewis Barlow IV. -- Denver : Denver Service Center, Historic Preservation Division, National Park Service, U.S. Dept. of the Interior, 1976.
viii, 87 p., 12 fold. leaves of plates : ill., maps ; 27 cm. -- (Historic structures report) (NPS ; 1030)
1. Brown, John, 1800-1859. 2. Harpers Ferry National Historical Park, Md. and W. Va. I. United States. National Park Service. Denver Service Center. Historic Preservation Team. II. Title. III. Series. IV. Series: United States. National Park Service. NPS ; 1030.
DI NUC77-86244

Barlow, Wilfred.
The Alexander Principle; illustrated by Gwyneth Cole. London, Gollancz, 1973.
223, [24] p. illus. 23 cm. £3.00 GB 73-16024
American ed. published under title: The Alexander Technique.
Includes bibliographical references and index.
1. Psychotherapy. 2. Physical therapy. 3. Alexander, Frederick Matthias, 1869-1955. I. Title.
[DNLM: 1. Posture—Stress. WE 103 B258a 1973]
[RC480.5.B34 1973b] 613.7 73-595633
ISBN 0-575-00563-7 MARC
Shared Cataloging with DNLM

Barlow, Wilfred.
The Alexander Technique. [1st American ed.] New York, Knopf; [distributed by Random House] 1973 [i. e. 1974]
221, vii p. illus. 22 cm. $7.95
"Originally published in Great Britain in a slightly different form under the title: The Alexander Principle."
Includes bibliographical references.
1. Psychotherapy. 2. Physical therapy. 3. Alexander, Frederick Matthias, 1869-1955. I. Title.
RC480.5.B34 1973 616.8'913 73-7285
ISBN 0-394-48686-2 MARC

Barlow, William, Bp. of Bath and Wells, d. 1568.
A dyaloge descrybyng the orygynall ground of these Lutheran saccyons [i.e. faccyons] / William Barlow. — Amsterdam : Theatrum Orbis Terrarum ; Norwood, N.J. : W. J. Johnson, 1974.
ca. 200 p. ; 16 cm. — (The English experience its record in early printed books published in facsimile ; no. 641)
Photoreprint of the 1531 ed., by W. Rastell, London.
"S.T.C. no. 1461."
ISBN 9022106411
1. Lutheran Church—Doctrinal and controversial works. 2. Luther, Martin, 1483-1546. I. Title. II. Series.
BX8064.B36 1974 284'.1 74-80161
75 MARC

Barlow, William, Bp. of Lincoln, d. 1613.
The conference at Hampton Court, January 14, 1603 / William Barlow. — Amsterdam : Theatrum Orbis Terrarum ; Norwood, N.J. : W. J. Johnson, 1975.
103 p. ; 22 cm. — (The English experience, its record in early printed books published in facsimile ; no. 711)
Photoreprint of the 1604 ed printed by I. Windet for M. Law, London, under title: The summe and substance of the conference which it pleased His Excellent Majestie to have with the lords, bishops, and other of his clergie, at which the most of the Lordes of the Council were present, in His Majesties privy chamber, at Hampton Court, January 14, 1603.
"S.T.C. no. 1456."
ISBN 9022107116
1. Hampton Court Conference, 1604. I. Title. II. Series.
BR757.B3 1975 274.1 74-28829
76 MARC

Barlow, William, Bp. of Lincoln, d. 1613.
see Fitzherbert, Thomas, 1552-1640. An adioynder to the supplement of Father Robert Persons, his discussion of M. Doctor Barlowe's answere. Ilkley, Scolar Press, 1975.

Barlow, William, Bp. of Lincoln, d. 1613.
see Parsons, Robert, 1546-1610. A discussion of the answers of M. William Barlow. Ilkley, Scolar Press, 1975.

Barlow, William, d. 1625.
The navigators supply : conteining many things of principall importance belonging to navigation : with the description and use of diverse instruments framed chiefly for that purpose, but serving also for sundry other of cosmography in generall / [William Barlowe]. — [Amsterdam : Theatrum Orbis Terrarum ; New York : Da Capo Press, 1972]
[116] p. : ill. (3 fold.) ; 24 cm. — (The English experience, its record in early printed books, published in facsimile ; no. 430)
Photoreprint of the 1597 ed. printed by G. Bishop, R. Newbery, and R. Barker, London.
"S.T.C. no. 1445."
ISBN 9022104303
1. Navigation—Early works to 1800. 2. Nautical instruments—Early works to 1800. I. Title. II. Series.
VK551.B35 1972 623.89'09 76-38150
75 MARC

Barlow, William J
Large closed-die forging on the hydraulic Press. Dearborn, Mich., Society of Manufacturing Engineers, c1970.
13 p. illus. (Technical paper MF70-594)
Cover title.
At head of title: Creative manufacturing seminars.
"For presentation at its Engineering Conferences."
1. Forging. 2. Forging machinery. 3. Hydraulic presses. I. Title. II. Series: Society of Manufacturing Engineers. Creative Manufacturing Engineering Programs. Technical paper, MF 70-594.
MiEM NUC75-10495

Barlow Road : bicentennial edition, 1974-1975. — 1st ed. — [The Dalles, Or. : Wasco County Historical Society, 1975]
viii, 90 p. : ill. ; 22 cm.
Includes bibliographical references.
1. Barlow Road, Or. 2. Wasco Co., Or.—History. 3. Clackamas Co., Or.—History. 4. Oregon—History—To 1859. I. Wasco County Historical Society.
F880.B26 979.5'62 75-322745
75 MARC

Barlowe, Dorothea, illus.
see Bruun, Bertel. Tiere: Wunder und Geheimnisse ihres Lebens. [Stuttgart] Delphin Verlag [1972]

Barlowe, Dorothea, illus.
see Cox, Victoria. Nature's smallest gravedigger. New York, Golden Press [1974]

Barlowe, Dorothea.
see Day, Jenifer W. What is a flower?. New York, Golden Press, [1975]

Barlowe, Dorothea.
see Pfadt, Robert E. Animals without backbones. Chicago, Follett Pub. Co., [1967]

Barlowe, Dorothea.
see Pringle, Laurence P. The minnow family—chubs, dace, minnows, and shiners. New York, Morrow, 1976.

Barlowe, Dorothea, illus.
see Shuttleworth, Floyd Stephen, 1913- Non-flowering plants. New York, Golden Press [1967]

Barlowe, Dorothea
see Zappler, Lisbeth. Then and now. New York, McGraw-Hill [1974?]

Barlowe, Dorothea.
see Zim, Herbert Spencer, 1909- The big cats. Newly rev. ed. New York, Morrow, 1976.

Barlowe, Raleigh.
Spanish land grants in Missouri. New York, Garland, 1974.
102, 347-381 p. 23 cm. (American Indian ethnohistory. North Central and Northeastern Indians) (Sac, Fox, and Iowa Indians, 1)
Report presented before the Indian Claims Commission, docket 83.
ICN NUC76-29016

Barlowe, Raleigh.
Trends in land and water use in Michigan [by] Raleigh Barlowe. [East Lansing, Michigan State University] Dept. of Resource Development, 1972.
15 p. 28 cm.
"Project '80 & 5."
Preliminary, for review only.
1. Land—Mich. 2. Water conservation—Mich. 3. Conservation of natural resources—Mich. I. Michigan. State University. Dept. of Resource Development.
Mi NUC76-74047

Barlowe, Russell G
Cotton situation. [Washington, U.S. Govt. Print. Off.] 1973.
34 p., illus. (U.S. Dept. of Agriculture. Economic Research Service. The cotton situation CS-263)
Bibliographical footnotes.
1. Cotton. United States. Statistics. I. Title.
DNAL NUC74-172393

Barlowe, Sy.
see Pringle, Laurence P. The minnow family—chubs, dace, minnows, and shiners. New York, Morrow, 1976.

Barlowe, Sy
see Zappler, Lisbeth. Then and now. New York, McGraw-Hill [1974?]

Barlowe, William
see
Barlow, William, Bp. of Lincoln, d. 1613.
Barlow, William, d. 1625.

Barloy, Jean Jacques.
Les Animaux domestiques : cent siècles de vie commune entre l'homme et l'animal / Jean-Jacques Barloy, ... — Paris : Éditions France-Empire, [1974]
264 p., [6] leaves of plates : ill. ; 20 cm. — (L'Homme face à la nature ; 14)
F75-302
Bibliography: p. [258]-261.
24.50F
1. Domestic animals. I. Title.
SF75.B37 636 75-503833
75 MARC

Barloy, Jean Jacques.
Le monde des ailes. Paris, A. Michel [1973]
213 p. illus. 20 cm. (Science parlante) 19.50F F***
1. Birds. I. Title.
QL676.B274 598.2 73-169889
MARC

Barloy, Jean Jacques.
Notre ami le dauphin / Jean-Jacques Barloy, Jean-Paul Ehrhardt. — Paris : France-Empire, [1974]
255 p., [4] leaves of plates : ill. ; 19 cm. — (L'Homme face à la nature)
F***
Bibliography: p. [247]-252.
1. Dolphins. I. Ehrhardt, Jean Paul, joint author. II. Title.
QL737.C432B37 599'.53 75-508926
75 MARC

Barloy, Jean Jacques.
see Le Bon, la bête et le chasseur. Paris, Stock, 1976.

Barlozzini, Guido, comp.
Le origini del romanticismo. A cura di Guido Barlozzini. Roma, Editori riuniti, 1974.
190 p. 19 cm. (Strumenti per la ricerca interdisciplinare, 1)
L1200 It 74-July
First ed.
Bibliography: p. 187-190.
1. Romanticism. I. Title.
PN755.B3 74-321817

Barlozzini, Guido.
I problemi della scuola nella letteratura del secondo dopoguerra / di Guido Barlozzini ; testi antologici da C. Marchesi ... [et al.]. — 1. ed. — Messina ; Firenze : G. D'Anna, 1974.
161 p. : ill. ; 21 cm. — (Secondo millennio ; 38) It***
"Testi antologici": p. [27]-157.
L1400
1. Education—Italy—1945- —History. I. Title.
LA791.82.B37 76-505770

Barltrop, Donald.
see Unigate Paediatric Workshop, 2d, London, 1974. Paediatrics and the environment ... London, Fellowship of Postgraduate Medicine, 1975.

Barltrop, J A
Excited states in organic chemistry / J. A. Barltrop and J. D. Coyle. — London ; New York : Wiley, [1975]
xii, 376 p. : ill. ; 24 cm.
Includes bibliographical references and index.
ISBN 0-471-04995-6
1. Photochemistry. 2. Chemistry, Physical organic. I. Coyle, John D., joint author. II. Title.
QD715.B37 547'.1'3 74-22400
74 MARC

Barltrop, Robert.
Jack London : the man, the writer, the rebel / Robert Barltrop. — London : Pluto Press ; [New York : available from Urizen Books], 1976.
206 p., [7] leaves of plates : ill. ; 23 cm. GB***
Includes bibliographical references and index.
ISBN 0-904383-18-0 : £4.50 ($10.00 U.S.)
1. London, Jack, 1876-1916—Biography. 2. Authors, American—20th century—Biography.
PS3523.O46Z6116 818'.5'209 77-357097
77 MARC

Barltrop, Robert.
The monument : the story of the Socialist Party of Great Britain / Robert Barltrop. — Short-run ed. — London : Pluto Press, 1975.
200 p. ; 20 cm.
Includes bibliographical references and index.
ISBN 0-904383-00-8 : £3.90
1. Socialist Party of Great Britain—History. I. Title.
JN1129.S62B37 1975 329.9'41 76-359860
76 MARC

Barlybaeva, Nagima Akhmetovna.
(Revmatizm u deteĭ na sovremennom ėtape)
Ревматизм у детей на современном этапе / Н. А. Барлыбаева. — Алма-Ата : Казахстан, 1974.
138 p. : ill. ; 21 cm. USSR 74
0.48rub
1. Rheumatic fever. 2. Children—Diseases. I. Title.
RJ520.R5B37 75-579159

Barm, Werner, 1926–
Totale Abgrenzung; zehn Jahre unter Ulbricht, Honecker und Stoph an der innerdeutschen Grenze. Ein authentischer Bericht. Stuttgart, Seewald [c1971]
253 p. 21 cm. GDB***
1. Germany (Democratic Republic, 1949-)—Politics and government. 2. Germany (Democratic Republic, 1949-)—Boundaries—Germany (Federal Republic, 1949-). 3. Germany (Federal Republic, 1949-) — Boundaries — Germany (Democratic Republic, 1949-) I. Title.
DD261.4.B39 72-359970

Barm, Werner, 1926–
Und Ulbricht kassiert. Ein authent. Bericht. (3., überarb. Aufl.) Stuttgart, Seewald (1971).
100 p. 21 cm. DM6.80 GDB 71-A41-193
1. Government ownership — Germany (Democratic Republic, 1949- —Popular works. I. Title.
74-315381

Barmā, Bhagabāna Nāýaka
see Nāýaka Barmā, Bhagabāna.

Barma, Bikram Keshari, 1941–
ଆମ ବାଲିବାବୁ. [ଲେଖକ] ବିକ୍ରମକେଶରୀ ବର୍ମା. [କଟକ, କଟକ ବୁକ୍ ଷ୍ଟଲ, 1964]
3, 56 p. 19 cm. Re1.00
A novel.
In Oriya.

I. Title.
Title romanized: Āma Bālibābu.
PK2579.B314A8 75-921472

Barma, Bikram Keshari, 1941–
ସାହିତ୍ୟ ଓ ରାଜନୀତି. ଲେଖକ ବିକ୍ରମକେଶରୀ ବର୍ମା. [1. ସଂସ୍କରଣ. କଟକ, 1969]
135 p. 19 cm. Rs2.00
In Oriya.

1. Oriya literature—Addresses, essays, lectures. I. Title.
Title romanized: Sāhitya o rājanīti.
PK2571.B35 71-921550

Barmā, Jagannātha Deba
see
Deva Varma, Jagannath, 1927-

Barmā, Jñānīndra
see
Verma, Jnanindra, 1916-

Barmā, Rājendra.
ନେତାଜୀ ସୁଭାଷଚନ୍ଦ୍ର. [ଲେଖକ] ରାଜେନ୍ଦ୍ର ବର୍ମା. କଟକ, ଓଡ଼ିଶା ବୁକ୍ଷ୍ଟୋର [1970]
214 p. 23 cm. Rs7.00
In Oriya.

1. Bose, Subhas Chandra, 1897-1945. I. Title.
Title romanized: Netāji Subhāshacandra.
DS481.B6B36 70-918527

Barmache, Nicolas.
(Mikhail Andreevich Osorgin)
Михаил Андреевич Осоргин, библиография. Составили Н. В. Бармаш, Д. М. Фини, Т. А. Осоргина. Bibliographie des œuvres de Michel Ossorguine, établie par N. Barmache, D. M. Fiene, T. Ossorguine. [Publié par l'U. E. R. de slavistique de l'Université de Paris IV et le Laboratoire de slavistique de l'Université de Paris I]. Paris, Institut d'études slaves, 1973.
xvi, 211 p. 26 cm. (Bibliothèque russe de l'Institut d'études slaves, t. 35. Série Écrivains russes en France) 40.00F F 73-8452
Russian text with French introd.
1. Osorgin, Mikhail Andreevich, 1878-1942—Bibliography. I. Osorgin, Mikhail Andreevich, 1878-1942. II. Fiene, Donald Mark, joint author. III. Bakunina, Tat'i͡ana A., joint author. IV. Title. V. Series: Bibliothèque russe de l'Institut d'études slaves, t. 35.
Z8647.82.B36 74-168925

Barmack, Joseph Ephraim, 1910-
Human factors problems in computer-generated graphic displays [by] Joseph E. Barmack [and] H. Wallace Sinaiko. [Arlington? Va.] Institute for Defense Analyses, Research and Engineering Support Division, 1966.
vii, 111 p. illus.
"Study S-234."
Bibliography: p. 103-110.
Photocopy reproduced 4 pages to the leaf. Springfield, Va., National Technical Information Service, 1974? 28 cm.
"AD 636 170."
IU NUC75-67137

Barmack, Joseph Ephraim, 1910-
see Recollections ... New York, Nyman, c1976.

Barmada, Riad, joint author.
see Ray, Robert D. Orthopedic surgery case studies ... Flushing, N.Y., Medical Examination Pub. Co., 1976.

Barmak, Sandra Lynn, 1946-
Altered cellular responses to interferon induction by poly I· poly C: hyporesponsiveness and priming. [n.p.] 1972.
101 p.
Thesis (Ph.D.)—New York University.
I. Title.
NNU NUC74-150776

Barmakian, Richard, 1931-
Hypoglycemia, your bondage? Or freedom! / by Richard Barmakian. — 1st ed. — Irvine, Calif. : Altura Health Publishers, c1976.
xxviii, 271 p. ; 23 cm.
Includes index.
$8.95
1. Hypoglycemia. I. Title.
RC662.2.B37 616.4'66 76-150689
76 MARC

Barmakov, I͡Uriĭ Nikolaevich, joint author
see Chakhmakhsazi͡an, Ekaterina Artem'evna. (Mashinnyĭ analiz integral'nykh skhem) 1974.

Barman, Alicerose S
Helping children face crises / by Alicerose Barman. — 1st ed. — [New York] : Public Affairs Committee, 1976.
24 p. : ill. ; 18 cm. — (Public affairs pamphlet ; no. 541)
$0.35
1. Emotional problems of children. I. Title.
BF723.E63B37 649'.1'019 76-151181
77 MARC

Barman, Alicerose S
Motivation and your child / by Alicerose Barman. — 1st ed. — [New York] : Public Affairs Committee, 1975.
20 p. : ill. ; 18 cm. — (Public affairs pamphlet ; no. 523)
Cover title.
$0.35
1. Motivation (Psychology) 2. Child psychology. I. Title.
BF723.M56B37 649'.1'019 75-320015
75 MARC

Barman, Everette Hayes.
The biology and immature stages of selected species of Dytiscidae (Coleoptera) of central New York State. [Ithaca, N.Y.] 1972.
[3], v, 207 l. illus. 28 cm.
Thesis (Ph.D.)—Cornell University.
Bibliography: leaves 179-184.
1. Dytiscidae. I. Title.
NIC NUC75-43454

Barman, John Farhad.
Well-posedness of feedback systems and singular perturbations. [Berkeley] 1973.
v, 90 l.
Thesis (Ph.D.)—Univ. of California.
Bibliography: leaves 87-90.
CU NUC75-26861

Barman, Thomas E
Enzyme handbook. [By] Thomas E. Barman. Berlin, Heidelberg, New York, Springer, 1969.
2 v. (xi, 927 p.) 23 cm. DM78.00 GDB***
Includes bibliographies.
——— Supplement. Berlin, New York, Springer, 1974-
v. 23 cm. DM51.80 (v. 1)
Includes bibliographical references.
QP601.B2435 Suppl.
1. Enzymes—Handbooks, manuals, etc. I. Title.
QP601.B2435 574.1'925 69-19293
ISBN 0-387-06761-2 (suppl. 1) MARC
rev

Il Barman e i suoi cocktails. Milano, Editoriale Selepress [1969]
see under Selepress libri.

Barmana, Bhubaneśwara, ed.
see Ekhani jīwanalekhya. [1970]

Barmana, Dīpti, joint author
see Kumar, Braj Bihari, 1941- (Hindī Dimāsā Kachāri kośa) Hindi Dimasa Kachari dictionary. 1975.

Barmash, A. I.
see Tekhnologii͡a mi͡asnykh i tekhnicheskikh produktov. 1973.

Barmash, Isadore.
For the good of the company : work and interplay in a major American corporation / by Isadore Barmash. — New York : Grosset & Dunlap, c1976.
x, 299 p. ; 22 cm.
ISBN 0-448-12245-6 : $10.00
1. McCrory Corporation. 2. Department stores—United States. 3. Conglomerate corporations—United States. I. Title.
HF5465.U6M223 658.8'71 74-5629
76 MARC

Barmash, Isadore, comp.
Great business disasters; swindlers, bunglers, and frauds in American industry. [Chicago] Playboy Press [1972]
viii, 309 p. 22 cm. $7.95
CONTENTS: Shaplen, R. The metamorphosis of Philip Musica.—Time magazine. The decline and fall of Billie Sol Estes.—The New York herald tribune. The great soybean scandal.—Brooks, J. The fate of the Edsel.—Bernstein, E. Real estate's Humpty-Dumpty: Bill Zeckendorf after the fall.—Barmash, I. The great electrical conspiracy.—Rossant, M. J. Atlantic acceptance: even the big ones got stung.—Communications problems at Texas Gulf Sulphur and Merrill Lynch.—Phillips, M. Gilbert wanted an empire of his own.—Robards, T. Fears fulfilled as big broker fails.—Hershey, R. D. The glamorous road to bankruptcy.—Gardner, W. D. Curtain act at RCA.—Tobias, A. The $3,754,103 footnote.—Newsweek magazine. What happened to the perpetual money-making machine?—Bedingfield, R. E. Pennsy: bad management or ailing industry debated.—Zimmerman, F. L. Penn Central officials sold stock as carrier was nearing disaster.—Pinkerton, W. S.—Penn Central faces lengthy legal snarls under bankruptcy laws.
1. Bankruptcy—United States—Case studies—Addresses, essays, lectures. 2. Commercial crimes—United States—Case studies—Addresses, essays, lectures. I. Title.
HG3766.B29 338.7'4'0973 72-85967
MARC

Barmash, Isadore.
The world is full of it; how we are oversold, overinfluenced, and overwhelmed by the communications manipulators. New York, Delacorte Press [1974]
xiv, 269 p. 21 cm.
1. Mass media—Social aspects—United States. 2. United States—Social conditions—1960- 3. Advertising—United States. I. Title.
HN90.M3B37 659.2 73-13632
ISBN 0-440-09726-6 MARC

Barmash, Vadim Nikolaevich, ed.
see Mekhanizirovannyĭ instrument i otdelochnye mashiny. 1967.

Barmash, Vadim Nikolaevich, ed.
see Mekhanizirovannyi instrument, otdelochnye mashiny i vibratory. 1972.

Barmbeck, Lord von
see
Petersen, Julius Adolf, 1882-1933.

Barmbek. Realschule.
Bericht.
Hamburg, Realschule in Barmbeck.
v. ill. 28 cm.
1. Barmbek. Realschule.
LF3195.H3R16 CA 9-4194
MARC-S

Barmby, John Glennon.
Indices of utilization of funds and personnel for naval research. Washington, 1956. [Ann Arbor, Mich., University Microfilms, 1970]
xi, 315 l. illus. 22 cm.
Thesis—American University.
Facsim. produced by microfilm-xerography.
Includes bibliography.
1. Naval research. U.S. I. Title.
N NUC74-161159

Barmeyer, Eike.
Science Fiction; Theorie und Geschichte, hrsg. von Eike Barmeyer. München, W. Fink [c1972]
383 p. 19 cm. (Uni-Taschenbücher, 132. Literaturwissenschaft)
DM16.80 GDB***
Bibliography: p. 365-374.
1. Science fiction—Addresses, essays, lectures. I. Title.
PN3448.S45B28 72-363898
ISBN 3-7705-0642-1

Barmeyer, J
Pathomorphologie, Pathophysiologie und Klinik bei ischämischer Herzerkrankung : ein Vergleich pathologisch-anatomischer und klinischer Befunde / J. Barmeyer und H. Reindell. — Bern : H. Huber, c1976.
90 p. : ill. ; 22 cm. — (Aktuelle Probleme in der Angiologie ; Bd. 32)
Sw***
Bibliography: p. 60-65.
Includes index.
ISBN 3-456-80287-0
1. Coronary heart disease. 2. Blood flow—Measurement. 3. Pathology. I. Reindell, Herbert, 1908- joint author. II. Title. III. Series.
RC685.C6B27 76-477856
76 MARC

Barmichev, Vitaliĭ Dmitrievich.
(V edinom soi͡uze)
В едином союзе. Ист.-публицист. очерк о развитии многонац. соц. культуры в СССР. Науч. ред. чл.-кор. АН БССР, д-р ист. наук, проф. И. М. Игнатенко. Минск, "Наука и техника," 1972.
247 p. 20 cm. 1.23rub USSR 72-VKP
At head of title: В. Бармичев.
Bibliography: p. 217-[235]
1. Russia—Intellectual life—1917- 2. Ethnology—Russia. 3. Cultural relations. I. Title.
DK276.B35 73-307713

Barmin, A
(Ruda)
Руда. Ист. роман. [Для сред. и ст. возраста. Ил.: В. Власов. Изд. 4-е]. Ленинград, "Дет. лит.," [Ленингр. отд-ние], 1973.
399 p. with illus. 20 cm. USSR 74
0.88rub
I. Title.
PZ63.B337 1973 75-581800

Barmin, I͡Uriĭ
see Pami͡atniki Sibiri. 1974.

Barmin, Sergeĭ Fedorovich, ed.
see Beskontaktnye sistemy i ustroĭstva upravlenii͡a na magistral'nykh gazoprovodakh. 1972.

Barmin, Sergeĭ Fedorovich, ed.
see Ėkspluatat͡sii͡a i remont gazovykh dvigateleĭ i gazomoto-kompressorov. 1973.

Barmin, Sergeĭ Fedorovich, ed.
see Spravochnik rabotnika magistral'nogo gazoprovoda. 1974.

Barmin, Viktor Vasil'evich.
(Analiz finansovo-khozi͡aĭstvennoĭ dei͡atel'nosti kommunal'nykh predprii͡atiĭ)
Анализ финансово-хозяйственной деятельности коммунальных предприятий / В. В. Бармин. — Москва : Финансы, 1976.
143 p. ; 21 cm. USSR 76
0.39rub
1. Public utilities — Russia — Auditing and inspection. 2. Public utilities—Russia—Finance. I. Title.
HD4676.B37 77-506050

Barmin, Viktor Vasil'evich.
(Analiz khozi͡aĭstvennoĭ dei͡atel'nosti kommunal'nykh predprii͡atiĭ)
Анализ хозяйственной деятельности коммунальных предприятий. Москва, Госфиниздат, 1963.
74 p. tables. 20 cm. (В помощь финансовому работнику)
1. Municipal government—Russia. 2. Public utilities—Russia. I. Title.
JS6058.B29 64-30431

Barmin, Viktor Vasil'evich.
(Analiz khozi͡aĭstvennoĭ dei͡atel'nosti predprii͡atiĭ po blagoustroĭstvu gorodov)
Анализ хозяйственной деятельности предприятий по благоустройству городов. Москва, Финансы, 1965.
83 p. 21 cm.
At head of title: В. Бармин.
1. Municipal government. 2. Public utilities—Management. I. Title.
JS91.B3 66-85411

Barmin, Viktor Vasil'evich.
(Finansovoe planirovanie i finansirovanie avtomobil'nogo transporta)
Финансовое планирование и финансирование автомобильного транспорта. Москва, Госфиниздат, 1951.
135 p. 23 cm.
Errata slip inserted.
1. Transportation, Automotive—Russia—Finance. I. Title.
HE5675.A6B3 52-23212

Barmine, Alexandre.
బ్రతికి బయటపడ్డవాడు. ₍రచన₎ అలెగ్జాండర్ బార్మైన్. ₍Madras? S. Narayanan, 195-?₎
251 p. 19 cm.
In Telugu.

1. Russia—Politics and government—1917-1936. 2. Communism—Russia. 3. Refugees, Russian—Personal narratives. I. Title.
Title romanized: Bratiki bayaṭapaḍḍevāḍu.

DK268.B3A4594 77-287529

Barmine, Alexandre.
Memoirs of a Soviet diplomat; twenty years in the service of the U. S. S. R. Translated by Gerard Hopkins. Westport, Conn., Hyperion Press ₍1973₎
xvi, 360 p. illus. 23 cm.
Reprint of the 1938 ed. published by L. Dickson, London.
1. Barmine, Alexandre. 2. Russia—Foreign relations—1917-1945. 3. Russia—Politics and government—1917-1936. I. Title.
DK268.B3A4 1973 327'.2'0924 [B] 73-3736
ISBN 0-88355-040-7 MARC

Barmine, Alexandre.
தப்பிப் பிழைத்தவர். ₍எழுதியவர்₎ அலெக்ஸாண்டர் பார்மைன். மொழி பெயர்த்தவர் ரா. அ. பத்மநாபன். ₍Madras? S. Narayanan, 195-?₎
₍228 p. maps (on lining papers) 19 cm.
"ஆசிரியரது மூல நூலிலிருந்து அவரது சொற்களைக்கொண்டே சுருக்கப் பெற்றது."
In Tamil.
Translation of One who survived.
1. Russia—Politics and government—1917- 2. Refugees, Russian—Personal narratives. 3. Communism—Russia. I. Padmanabhan, R. A., 1917- tr. II. Title.
Title romanized: Tappip pilaittavar.
DK268.B3A459 S A 68-13263

Barmint͡sev, I͡Uriĭ Nikolaevich.
Evoli͡ut͡sii͡a konskikh porod v Kazakhstane; opyt zootekhnicheskogo issledovanii͡a problemy porodoobrazovanii͡a. ₍Alma-Ata, Kazgosizdat, 1958₎
281, ₍3₎ p. illus.
Bibliography: p. 275-₍282₎
1. Horses. Breeds. 2. Horses. History. I. Kazakhskai͡a akademii͡a sel'skokhozi͡aĭstvennykh nauk. Institut zhivotnovodstva. II. Title.
DNAL NUC76-42789

Barmint͡sev, I͡Uriĭ Nikolaevich, ed.
see Konnozavodstvo i konnyĭ sport. 1972.

Barmore, Frank E
Davis-Chadwick family, miscellaneous information: grave stone inscriptions in the Mt. Vernon cemetery 1 mile north of Juda, Green Co., Wisconsin. Madison, Wis., 1969.
5 p.
1. Davis family. 2. Chadwick family. I. Title.
WHi NUC73-47510

Barmpagiannēs, Giannēs Grēgoriou.
Antilaloi tou vounou; poiēmata. ₍n.p.₎ 1957.
72 p. port. 23 cm.
I. Title.
OCU NUC74-120100

Barmpagiannēs, Giannēs Grēgoriou.
Ho tselinkas k'hē chōriatopoula. Prologos tou poiētē Koulē M. Kase. ₍n.p.₎ 1956.
29 p. 23 cm.
Poēm.
I. Title.
OCU NUC74-120003

Barn : rapport / från Barnmiljöutredningen. — Stockholm : ₍LiberFörlag/Allmänna förlaget₎, 1975-
v. : ill. ; 25 cm. — (Statens offentliga utredningar ; 1975 : 31-33, 35-38) S 75-53 (v. 1)
Cover title.
Includes bibliographies.
ISBN 91-38-02246-X (v. 1) :kr21.00 (v. 1) varies
1. Children in Sweden—Collected works. I. Sweden. Barnmiljöutredningen. II. Series: Sweden. Statens offentliga utredningar ; 1975 : 31-33 ₍etc.₎
J406.R15 1975 : 31, etc. 76-504439
[HQ792.S8]

A Barn well filled. ₍Lexington? Ky., Blood-horse magazine, 1971₎
96 p. illus.
"A collection of "how-to" articles which have appeared in the Blood-horse magazine during the past several years."
1. Barns. I. The Blood-horse.
DeU NUC73-34690

Barna, Alexander, ed.
see Za třídní a ideově politickou výchovu mladé generace. Praha, Kraj. pedagog. ústav, 1973.

Barna, Arpad.
₍High-speed pulse circuits. Chinese₎
高速脉冲电路 / A. 巴纳著 ; 杨树芬译. — 北京 : 科学出版社, 1974.
iv, 162 p. : ill. ; 19 cm.
Bibliography: p. 160-162.
$0.50

1. Pulse circuits. I. Title.
Title romanized: Kao su mo ch'ung tien lu.
TK7868.P8B2813 75-838206

Barna, Arpad.
Integrated circuits in digital electronics ₍by₎ Arpad Barna and Dan I. Porat. New York, Wiley ₍1973₎
xi, 483 p. illus. 23 cm.
"A Wiley-Interscience publication."
Includes bibliographical references.
1. Digital electronics. 2. Integrated circuits. I. Porat, Dan I., joint author. II. Title.
TK7868.D5B43 621.3819'58'35 73-6709
ISBN 0-471-05050-4 MARC

Barna, Arpad.
Introduction to microcomputers and microprocessors / Arpad Barna, Dan I. Porat. — New York : Wiley, c1976.
xi, 108 p. : ill. ; 24 cm.
"A Wiley-Interscience publication."
Bibliography: p. 98.
Includes index.
ISBN 0-471-05051-2
1. Miniature computers. 2. Microprocessors. I. Porat, Dan I., joint author. II. Title.
QA76.5.B293 001.6'4'04 75-31675
75 MARC

Barna, Béláné, ed.
see Biró, Ferenc, fl. 1963- Jövedelem és jövedelemrészesedés a termelőszövetkezetekben. Budapest, Károlyi Mihály országos Mezőgazdasági Könyvtár és Dokumentációs Központ, 1964.

Barna, Géza.
Fogyasztási cikkek minőségellenőrzése és minőségvédelme ₍írta₎ Barna, Bóc ₍és₎ Ormai. Budapest, Közgazdasági és Jogi Könyvkiadó, 1966.
302 p. illus. 21 cm.
Bibliography: p. 294-₍298₎
1. Quality control. 2. Consumer protection—Hungary. I. Bóc, Imre. II. Ormai Lajos. III. Title.
TS156.B38 74-208787

Barna, Ion.
Eisenstein, by Yon Barna. With a foreword by Jay Leyda. Bloomington, Indiana University Press ₍1973₎
287 p. illus. 23 cm. (Cinema two) $10.00
Translation of Serghei Eisenstein.
Includes bibliographical references.
1. Eisenstein, Sergeĭ Mikhaĭlovich, 1898-1948. I. Title.
PN1998.A3E53413 791.43'0233'0924 73-81159
ISBN 0-253-12135-3 [B] MARC

Barna, Ion.
Eisenstein / by Yon Barna ; with a foreword by Jan Leyda. — London : Secker & Warburg, 1973.
287 p. : ill. ; 22 cm. GB***
Translation of Serghei Eisenstein.
Includes bibliographical references and index.
ISBN 0-436-09702-8 : £4.00. ISBN 0-436-09703-6 pbk.
1. Eisenstein, Sergeĭ Mikhaĭlovich, 1898-1948. 2. Moving-picture producers and directors—Russia—Biography. I. Title.
PN1998.A3E53413 1973b 77-366446
791.43'0233'0924
77 MARC

Barna, Ion.
Eisenstein / by Yon Barna ; with a foreword by Jay Leyda ; ₍translated by Lise Hunter₎. — Boston : Little, Brown, ₍1975₎ c1973.
287 p. : ill. ; 22 cm
Translation of Serghei Eisenstein.
Reprint of the ed. published by Indiana University Press, Bloomington.
Bibliography: p. 279-281.
Includes index.
ISBN 0-316-08130-2
1. Eisenstein, Sergei Mikhailovich, 1898-1948.
₍PN1998.A3E53413 1975₎ 75-11632
791.43'0233'0924
75 MARC

Barna, Ion.
Erich von Stroheim. (Redaktion: Peter Konlechner und Peter Kubelka unter Mitarbeit von Reinhard Priessnitz. Übersetzung: Ilse Goldman) ₍Nach dem Manuskript₎ Wien, Österreichisches Filmmuseum, 1966.
108 p., 4 l. of illus. 19 cm. Au 66-24-138
Bibliography: p. ₍99₎-103.
S40.00
1. Von Stroheim, Erich, 1885-1957.
PN1998.A3V636 67-79890

Barna, Iosif, ed.
see Scoala fără ziduri. Resita, 1972.

Barna, József
see A Modern biológia címszavakban. [Budapest] : Natura, 1974.

Barna, Károly. Andrejszky, Géza
see Országos Munkaértekezlet a Csoportmegmunkálás Bevezetéséről, Budapest, 1963. Országos Munkaértekezlet a Csoportmegmunkálás Bevezetéséről. Budapest, 1963.

Barna, P. B., ed.
see Colloquium on Thin Films, 1st, Budapest, 1965. Proceedings. Budapest, 1967 [c1965]

Barna, P S
Investigations on the aerodynamic behavior of circular arc sheet metal airfoils in two-dimensional accelerating cascade for stagger angles 7 1/2 and 15 degrees and gap-chord ratios 0.5, 0.75 and 1.0, respectively. [Auburn, Ala.] Auburn University, Engineering Experiment Station, 1964.
vii, 16 p. 25 diagrs. (Auburn University. Engineering Experiment Station. Bulletin 46)
Bibliography: p. 16.
1. Aerofoils-Testing. 2. Aerodynamics. I. Title.
UU NUC73-47505

Barna, Tibor.
Monopoly and competition. ₍Phonotape. By T. Barna and Leslie Cook₎ New York, Holt Information ₍1972₎
1 cassette. 2½ x 4 in. (British and European economics series, E9) (Sussex tapes international)
Discussion.
Booklet containing notes on the discussion, study questions, and bibliography (6 p.) laid in container.
CONTENTS: Monopoly in the economy.—Two case studies: rayon and glass.
1. Monopolies. 2. Monopolies—Great Britain—Case studies. I. Cook, Leslie, joint author. II. Title. III. Series: British and European economics series, E9.
[HD2731] 74-760942

Barna, Tibor.
Profits during and after the war, by T. Barna. London, Fabian publications ltd., and V. Gollancz ltd. ₍1945, 1972₎
2 p.l., ₍3₎-25 p. (₍Fabian society, London₎ Research series, no. 105)
Bibliographical footnotes.
Reprinted by Kraus Reprint, Nendeln/Liechtenstein, 1972.
1. Profit. 2. Income-Gt. Brit. 3. Prices-Gt. Brit. I. Title.
INS NUC74-4059